Foremost Women in Communications

Foremost Women in Communications

A biographical reference work on accomplished women in broadcasting, publishing, advertising, public relations, and allied professions

FOREMOST AMERICANS PUBLISHING CORPORATION
in association with
R. R. BOWKER COMPANY

Copyright © 1970 by Foremost Americans Publishing Corporation
Published by Foremost Americans Publishing Corporation
Suite 628, Empire State Building, 350 Fifth Avenue, New York, New York 10001

International Standard Book Number: 08352-0414-6
Library of Congress Catalog Number: 79-125936

Manufactured by Edwards Bros., Ann Arbor, Michigan

Contents

Preface   vii

Acknowledgments   ix

Editorial Advisory Board   x

Editorial Staff   xiii

List of Abbreviations   xv

Foremost Women in Communications   1

Geographical and Subject Cross-index   695

Preface

The need for this reference work has become increasingly evident. Communications is the vehicle of ideas and the nucleus of progress and change. Women's full participation in this industry is important in itself, but represents a major step toward women's significant involvement in all aspects of American society. The link is **Foremost Women in Communications,** a first on reference works on women in the professions.

The book was conceived to recognize women's accomplishments and to promote increased awareness and utilization of their abilities.

The women in the directory were selected for their professional accomplishments, works of merit, contributions to communications and to the public, and recognition in their respective professions. The names of women were secured through the cooperation of professional organizations, response to direct mail requests to the presidents of companies and the media, recommendations made by industry leaders, and the publication of noteworthy promotions and accomplishments in the trade press.

The directory includes nearly 8,000 entries. Although we exhausted all the available sources for possible biographees, this directory does not include all the meritorious women in communications. We appreciate the cooperation of biographees, who filled out and returned questionnaires that made this compilation possible.

Information on women active in communications has not been readily available to the communications industry or the public. This directory was designed as a research tool for both. The index fulfills a primary reference function: it enables users to locate professionals by state and then by area of professional concentration.

Communications, as defined by this directory, includes publishing, broadcasting, advertising, public relations, and allied professions. Women are doing varied work in all the varied areas under the umbrella term; this naturally leads to a broad scope of activities covered in this volume. Communications as a field has always welcomed women. Only recently, however, have women been in high level positions. It is interesting that some biographees wrote notes to the editor indicating that they were the first women to be appointed or promoted to their current posts. These are important breakthroughs for all women in communications. Still, few women are city editors, newscasters of world events, political and editorial writers, library directors, officers in publishing firms or radio and TV stations.

Many women consider professional recognition the most important acknowledgment they could ever receive. This is a sign of our times, when women are seeking greater involvement and a greater voice in world activities.

Barbara J. Love
Editor and Publisher

Acknowledgments

Foremost Women in Communications required the time and dedication of many people—professionals, friends, and family. The company, the book, the staff, and the concept were all new.

The distinguished members of the Editorial Advisory Board had the foresight and the faith to back this directory from the beginning. They set the criteria for inclusion and frequently provided expertise in their specialized areas.

A number of women in the women's rights movement helped on the directory. One woman in particular encouraged me during all the trying phases of development and always found time to share her professional knowledge and personal wisdom. She is Muriel Fox Aronson, one of the Founders of the National Organization for Women and currently a national director.

Good public relations advice was contributed by James Abernathy, Florence Phillips, Jane Pinkerton, Marilyn Slauson, and David Williams, and legal counsel from Richard Prentiss, Jr.

I am grateful to my family—Egon Love, my father, Mrs. Lois (Love) Crane, my mother, and Dr. Douglas A. Love, my brother. They kept the faith, while, being practical people, they also prepared me for the realities.

Karen Gordon Greengard and Michael Greengard were involved in the early planning of the reference work before they moved to Illinois. Mike's knowledge of finance and Karen's writing ability were generously applied.

Judith Barry, the art director, faithfully and effectively rendered the spirit and purpose of the directory in graphic form, and Sidney Abbott, officially production editor, contributed talents beyond the scope of her title and related to all aspects of the book.

Friends were very willing to give time and talent to this effort, and many came on short notice and for long hours. I wish to formally thank Ramona Bechtos, Bill Carlin, Joe Casey, Dottie Cox, Lois Gaeta Crane, Sheila Dobrushin, Marguerite Eckart, Norma Edgar, Bill Icklan, Whitney LeCompte, and Kathleen McCahill.

Credit for printing the directory goes to Edwards Bros. and long-time publishing and distributing experience was brought into play by the R. R. Bowker Company.

B.J.L.

BESS MYERSON GRANT
Commissioner of Consumer Affairs
City of New York

DENNY GRISWOLD
Editor and Publisher
Public Relations News

MARK GOODSON
Partner, Goodson-Todman Productions

JAMES C. HAGERTY
Vice President, Corporation Relations
American Broadcasting Companies, Inc.

ANNE J. RICHTER
Former Editor-in-Chief, Book Division
R. R. Bowker Company

BARBARA WALTERS
Hostess, *Today Show*
National Broadcasting Company

Editorial Staff

List of Abbreviations

A

AAAA	American Association of Advertising Agencies
AA	Association of Arts
AAF	American Advertising Federation
AAIE	American Association of Industrial Editors
AAPOR	American Association of Public Opinion Research
AASL	American Association for School Librarians
AAUP	American Association of University Professors
AAUW	American Association of University Women
ABP	Associate Business Publications
acad	academy
acc	account
achiev	achievement
ACLU	American Civil Liberties Union
ACPRA	American College Public Relations Association
adm	administration, administrative
admr	administrator
adv	advertising, advertiser
AE	account executive
AEA	Actors Equity Association
AFA	Advertising Federation of America
AFTRA	American Federation of Television and Radio Artists
agcy	agency
agt	agent
AGVA	American Guild of Variety Artists
AID	American Institute of Interior Designers
AIGA	American Institute of Graphic Artists
AIM	American Institute of Management
ALA	American Library Association
Am	America, American
AMPAS	Academy of Motion Pictures Arts and Sciences
anncr	announcer
ANWC	American Newspaper Women's Club
AP	Associated Press
apptd	appointed
APRA	American Public Relations Association
apt	apartment
ARF	Advertising Research Foundation
ARTNA	Association of Radio and Television News Analysts
ASCAP	American Society of Composers, Artists and Performers
assigt	assignment
assn	association
assoc	associate, associated
asst	assistant
ATJ	Association of Teachers of Journalism
atty	attorney
auth	author
aux	auxillary
aw	award
AWNY	Advertising Women of New York
AWRT	American Women in Radio and Television

B

b	born
BA	Bachelor of Arts
BBA	Bachelor of Business Administration
Bd	Board
bdcst	broadcast, broadcasting
bdcstr	broadcaster
biog	biography
BJ	Bachelor Journalism
bk	book
BPW	Business and Professional Women's Club
br	branch
bul	bulletin
bur	bureau
bus	business
byr	buyer

C

c	children
cent	centennial
cert	certificate, certified
ch	channel, chapter
chmn	chairman
chptr	chapter
circ	circulation
cit	citation
cl	clerk
cnsl	counsel, counseling
cnslr	counselor
cnslt	consult, consulting, consultation, consultant
co	company
C of C	Chamber of Commerce
col	college
colm	column
colmst	columnist
comm	committee
comml	commercial
commn	commission, commissioned
commtns	communications
commty	community
conf	conference
cont	continuity, continue
contrb	contribute, contributing, contribution
contrbr	contributor
conv	convention
coop	cooperate, cooperating, cooperation
coord	coordinate, coordinating, coordination
coordr	coordinator
copywtr	copywriter
corp	corporation
corr	correspondent, corresponding
crtv	creative, creativity
ctr	center
CWPR	Committee on Women in Public Relations

D

DAR	Daughters of the American Revolution
DAVI	Division of Audio Visual Instruction
dec	deceased
deg	degree
Dem	Democrat
dept	department
dev	develop, developed, developing, development
dic	dictionary
dir	direct, directing, directed, director, directory
dist	district
distg	distinguished
distrb	distribute, distributing, distribution
div	division, divorced
doc	document, documentary
Dr	doctor

E

econ	economic, economy
econst	economist
ed	edit, edited, editing, editor
edtl	editorial
educ	educate, educated, educating, educational, education, educator
EFLA	Educational Films Library Association
ency	encyclopedia
Eng	England, English
EPAA	Education Press Association of America
EWA	Education Writers Association
exec	executive
exhbn	exhibition
exp	experience
expsn	exposition
expt	experiment
ext	extension, extend, extended, external

F

FAA	Financial Advertising Association
fac	faculty
fed	federal
fedn	federation
FPA	Foreign Press Association
fgn	foreign
fin	finance, financial
fndn	foundation
FRANY	Fashion Reporting Award of New York
frat	fraternity

G

GA	graphic arts
gen	general
geog	geography, geographic
govt	government
GPRA	Government Public Relations Association
grad	graduate, graduated
gtr	greater

H

h	husband
HEW	Health, Education and Welfare
hist	history, historic, historical
histrn	historian
HMI	House Magazine Institute
hon	honor, honorary, honorable
hosp	hospital
hq	headquarters
HS	high school
HUD	Housing and Urban Development

I

IAA	International Advertising Association
ICIE	International Council of Industrial Editors
IEA	Industrial Press Association
illus	illustrate, illustration, illustrator
IMBA	International Media Buyers Association
inc	incorporated
incl	include, including
indsl	industrial
info	information
ins	insurance
INS	International News Service
inst	institution, institute, institutional
instr	instruct, instruction, instructor
int	internal, interior
intl	international
intro	introduction
IPRA	International Public Relations Association
IRTS	International Radio and Television Society

J

jnl	journal
jnlsm	journalism
jnlst	journalist
Jr	Junior
juv	juvenile

L

lab	laboratory
lang	language
lect	lecture
lectr	lecturer
lib	library
librn	librarian
lit	literary
LPRC	Library Public Relations Council
Ltd	Limited
ltr	letter

M

MA	Master of Arts
mag	magazine
maj	major
mbr	member
mdse	merchandise
mdsng	merchandising
med	medicine, medical
met	metropolitan
mfg	manufacturing
mgr	manager
mgt	management
MJ	master of Journalism
mkt	market
mktng	marketing
ML	Master of Letters
mng	managing
modr	moderator
MPDA	Magazine Promotion Directors Association
MWA	Mystery Writers of America

N

NAACP	National Association for the Advancement of Colored People
NAB	National Association of Broadcasters
NAEA	National Art Education Association
NAEB	National Association of Educational Broadcasters
NAFB	National Association of Farm Broadcasters
NAMD	National Association of Market Developers
NAMP	National Association of Magazine Publishers
NAMW	National Association of Media Women

nat	national		reptr	reporter
NATAS	National Academy of Television Arts and Sciences		res	residence
			rev	review
NAVA	National Audio-Visual Association		revsd	revised
NEA	National Education Association		RNS	Religious News Service
NET	Newspaper Enterprise Association		RPRC	Religious Public Relations Council
NFAA	National Federation of Advertising Agencies		rsch	research
NFPA	National Federation of Press Women		rschr	researcher
NHFL	National Home Fashion League		RTCA	Radio-Television Correspondents Association
NIAA	National Industrial Advertisers Association		Rt Rev	Right Reverend
NLAPW	National League of American Pen Women			
NOW	National Organization for Women		**S**	
NPA	National Presentations Association			
NPC	National Press Club		SAA	Speech Association of America
NPWC	National Press Women's Club		SAG	Screen Actors Guild
NRPC	National Religious Publicity Council		SBME	Society for Business Magazine Editors
NSID	National Society of Interior Designers		sch	school
NSPRA	National School Public Relations Association		sci	science
NWC	Newspaper Women's Club		sec	section
nwsltr	newsletter		secy	secretary
nwsp	newspaper		SLA	Special Libraries Association
			sls	sales
O			soc	society
			sociol	sociology
occ	occupation, occupational		SPRC	Society of Public Relation Counselors
OEO	Office of Economic Opportunity		Sr	Senior
off	office		Sr	Sister
offcl	official		SRTCA	Senate Radio-Television Correspondents Association
offcr	officer			
OPC	Overseas Press Club of America		St	Saint
opn	operation		statis	statistics, statistical
opp	opportunity		supvsr	supervisor
org	organization		svc	service
ORSA	Operations Research Society of America		synd	syndicate, syndicated
P			**T**	
p	parent, parents		tchr	teacher
PEN	Poets, Playwrites, Editors, Essayists, and Novelists		tech	technical, technology, technician
pers	personnel		temp	temporary
pfsnl	professional		traf	traffic
pg	page		treas	treasurer
photog	photography		TV	television
photogr	photographer			
pic	picture		**U**	
polit	political			
PPA	Publishers Publicity Association		un	united, union
PR	public relations		UN	United Nations
prep	preparation		UNCA	United Nations Correspondents Association
pres	president		UNICEF	United Nations International Children's Emergency Fund
prin	principal			
prod	produce, produced, production		univ	university
prodr	producer		UP	United Press
prof	professor			
prom	promotion		**V**	
prop	proprietor		vol	volume
PRSA	Public Relations Society of America		VP	vice president
PSA	Poetry Society of America			
psych	psychology		**W**	
PTA	Parent-Teacher Association			
pubcty	publicity		WGA	Writers Guild of America
publ	publishing		WHCA	White House Correspondents Association
publr	publisher		wm	woman, women
pubn	publication		WNBA	Women's National Book Association
			WNPC	Women's National Press Club
R			WPA	Women's Press Association
			wtr	writer
rec	recording		WWA	Western Writers Association
reg	region, regional		WW II	World War II
rel	relation, religion			
rep	representative		**Y**	
Repl	Republican		yr	year
rept	report, reporting			

A

ABAZORIS, NANCY HODGES, Wms. Ed., The Commercial Appeal, 495 Union Ave., Memphis, Tenn. 38101, '67–; Wms. Ed., Reptr., Southern Illinoisan, '62–'67; Am. Press Inst. Seminar for Wms. Page Eds., Columbia Univ., '68; Chmn., Memphis Clubwms. Workshop ('69); Chi Omega, Memphis Better Bus. Bur.; Memphis Press Club; Who's Who of Am. Wm.; Merit Aw., Am. Cancer Soc., '69; Medill Sch. of Jnlsm., Northwestern Univ., BSJ, '62; Southern Ill. Univ., grad. study in jnlsm., '65–; b. Carbondale, Ill., 1940; p. Harlan and Helen Milburn Hodges; h. Gerald Abazoris; c. Eric E.; res: 5345 Haleville Rd., Memphis, Tenn. 38116.

ABBE, ELFRIEDE MARTHA, Scientific Illus., Div. of Biological Sciences, Cornell University, Ithaca, N.Y. 14850, '42–; Instr., Southern Vt. Art Center, summers, '66–; numerous works represented in public and private collections; Nat. Sculpture Soc. (Fellow), Nat. Arts Club (Bronze Medal, '66), Allied Artists of Am., Pen and Brush (Gold Medal, '64), Sigma Delta Epsilon; Tiffany Fellowship, '48; Roy A. Hunt Fndn. Grant, '61; Purchase Prize, Albany Print Club, '68; Col. of Architecture, Cornell Univ., BFA, '40 (Phi Kappa Phi); study under Ivan Mestrovic, Syracuse Univ., '47; b. Wash., D.C., 1919; p. Cleveland, Jr., and Frieda Dauer Abbe; res: 24 Woodcrest Ave., Ithaca, N.Y. 14850.

ABBEE, CATHERINE WALTERS, Pre-Doctoral Assoc., Univ. of Washington Speech Dept., Seattle, Wash. 98105; '68–; Grad. Asst. Instr., Univ. of Okla., Norman, Okla., '67–'68; Radio-TV Dir., Richard Roby Advertising, Okla. City, '67–'68; Comml. Mgr., Prom. Mgr., AE, various radio-TV stations, owner adv. agcy., '56–'65; World Affairs Cncl., AWRT, AAUW, Speech Assn., Quota Club, Zeta Phi Eta, Beta Sigma Phi, various civic orgs.; Faculty Wms. Club Aw.; educ: Univ. of Okla., BFA, '56 (Dean's Hon. Roll); MA, '70 (Grad. Scholarship); b. Webbers Falls, Okla. 1933; p. Elzie and Calla Mae Martin Walters; h. J.G. Abbee (div.); c. Twyla, James, Michelle; res: 7412 E. Green Lake Dr. N., Seattle, Wash. 98103.

ABBOTT, DOTTY, Radio-TV Dir., Cosmopolitan Agency for Holiday Inns, Inc., 3754 Lamar Ave., Memphis, Tenn. 38118, '68–; Prodr., radio show; Composer, Singer, on record album; formerly Gen. Mgr. of WHER (Memphis), WLIZ (Palm Beach, Fla.) and KNDI (Honolulu, Hi.); Lectr. in bdcst. adv., Memphis State Univ.; Actress (Show Stopper Aw., Phoenix Little Theatre, '55); Pres. and Exec. Prodr., Current Productions, Intl.; NARAS, AWRT, Memphis Adv. Club (Adv. Wm. of the Yr., '69), AFTRA; Univ. of Miss.; Memphis State Univ.; b. Memphis, Tenn., 1923; p. William and Lorena Yeates Abbott; res: 410 N. McLean Blvd., Memphis, Tenn. 38112.

ABBOTT, ELIZABETH, Translator, French, German, Italian lit. into English for publishers, 61 W. 9th St., N.Y., N.Y. 10011.

ABBOTT, KATHARINE NEFF, Dir. of PR, George Williams College, 555 31st St., Downers Grove, Ill. 60515; Assoc. Admr., PR, Ill. Nurses Anns., '64–'68; PR Asst., Ill. Soc. of CPA's, '62–'63; Wtr., Oh. Dept. of Highway Safety; Reptr., Garfieldian Pubns. (Chgo., Ill.); Reptr., Indpls. Star; Reptr., Louisville Courier-Journal; Theta Sigma Phi (Chgo. Chptr. VP), Pubcty. Club of Chgo., DuPage County Press Assn., Ill. Col. Relations Cncl (Dir.); Ind. Univ., AB (Jnlsm.), '56; Ohio State Univ., MA (Jnlsm.), '64.

ABBOTT, SIDNEY AFTON, Prod. Ed., Foremost Americans Publishing Company, 350 Fifth Ave., N.Y., N.Y. 10001, '70–; Asst. Ed., Architectural Record, McGraw-Hill, '65–'68; Chmn: Copy Editors Comm. (a co.-wide committee) '68; Asst. Ed., Co. Pubns., Metropolitan Life Ins. Co. (N.Y.C.), '64–'65; Ed., Wtr., Albuquerque (N.M.) Review, '60–'62; Home-Living Ed., Gen. Assigt. Reptr., Albuquerque Journal, '59–'60; PR, N.M. statewide oral polio vaccine campaign; Cnslt., Desert Review (Albq., N.M.); Mbr., Columbia Univ. Women's Liberation (Curriculum Committee, Contrbr., "Model Curriculum for Women's Studies," '70), Prof. Wms. Caucus (Steering Committee, '70), Assoc. Mbr., Amer. Institute of Planners, '70–; Tex. Christian Univ. Special Poetry Aw., '58; Smith Col., '55–'58; Univ. of N.M., BA, '62; Columbia Univ., MS (Urban Planning), '70; b. Wash., D.C., 1937; p. Ward Terry and Helen Lindsay Abbott; res: 43 Fifth Ave., N.Y., N.Y. 10003.

ABEL, BARBARA, Reptr., The Milwaukee Journal, 333 W. State St., Milw., Wis. 53201, '66–; Staff Wtr., Green Bay (Wis.) Press-Gazette, '65–'66; Copy Wtr., Marx Advertising Agcy., Milw., '65; Marquette Univ., BA (Jnlsm.), '64; b. Richmond, Ind. 1942; p. Burnell and Kathryn Barton Abel; res: 718 E. Wells St., Milw., Wis. 53202.

ABEL, JEANNE ALLGEIER, (pseud: Mrs. Yetta Bronstein), Auth., Spencer Productions, 507 Fifth Ave., N.Y., N.Y. 10017; Bks: "The President I Almost Was" (Hawthorn Books), "The Button Book" (Citadel Press); Rschr., League for Emotionally Disturbed Children, '58; Rschr., Police Athletic League, '58; Rschr., Yeshivah Univ., '59; Univ. of Cinn., '55–'58; b. Cinn., Oh., 1937; p. Mark and Mildred Feige Allgeier; h. Alan Abel; res: 736 West End Ave., N.Y., N.Y. 10025.

ABEL, JUANITA HAWK, Wms. Ed., Mansfield Journal Co., Times-Reporter, 172 N. Broadway, New Phila., Oh. 44663, '62–; Court Reptr., Feature Wtr.; b. Dover, Oh., 1917; p. Albert and Cora Munk Hawk; h. Ernest Abel; c. John F.; res: 314 Prospect St., Dover, Oh. 44622.

ABELS CYRILLY, Lit. Agt., 597 Fifth Ave., N.Y., N.Y. 10017, '62–; Assoc. Ed., The Reporter, '60–; 62; Mng. Ed., Mademoiselle, '44–'60; Ed., Pubn. Div. of Off. of

War Info., '43–'44; Ed., "Best Stories from Mademoiselle;" OPC, '61–'67; Radcliffe Col., BA (cum laude); h. Jerome Weinstein; res: 14 Fifth Ave., N.Y., N.Y. 10011.

ABERG, SIVI MARTA, Film and TV Actress, Ron Kaiser & Associates, 7771 Sunset Blvd., L.A., Cal. 90069; "Operation Entertainment" (TV series, '68–'69), "Killing of Sister George" ('68), numerous others; Beauty Specialist and Cnslt. (Sweden), '63; SAG, AFTRA; Hollywood Star of Tomorrow, '67; 3rd runner-up for Miss Universe, '64; 2nd runner-up for Miss Europe, '64; Miss Sweden, '64; Miss Stockholm, '63; Gavle Hogre Allmana Laroverk Col.; Swedish Special Sch. of Scientific and Biological Cosmetology, '62; b. Gavle, Sweden, 1942; p. Ragnar M. and Gertrud H. Martinelle Aberg; res: 1519 Schyler Rd., Beverly Hills, Cal. 90210.

ABERNATHY, JOAN KINDER, Wtr., definitive profiles of major companies; Portfolio Mgr., Kidder, Peabody & Co., Inc., 20 Exchange Pl., N.Y., N.Y. 10005, '66–; Rsch. Analyst, '64–'66; registered rep., N.Y. and Am. stock exchanges; Nat. Assn. of Securities Dealers; Pembroke Col., BA, '64; b. Fayetteville, N.C., 1942; p. Harold and Charlotte Halcro Kinder; h. James Abernathy; res: 685 West End Ave., N.Y., N.Y. 10025.

ABICHT, Sr. M. RITA JEANNE, FSPA, PR Dir., Franciscan Sisters of Perpetual Adoration, St. Rose Convent, 912 Market St., La Crosse, Wis. 54601, '64–; Tchr., Eng., Jnlsm., Bus. Educ., '33–'39, '41–'64; Nat. Bus. Educ. Assn., Wis. Bus. Educ. Assn., Catholic Bus. Educ. Assn., NEA, Nat. Cncl. of Tchrs. of Eng., Nat. Scholastic Press Assn., Catholic Scholastic Press Assn., Jnlsm. Educ. Assn. (Secy.–Treas., '55–), Quill and Scroll, Nat. PR Assn.; Who's Who of Am. Wm.; St. Ambrose-Marycrest Col., BS (Eng., Secretarial Sci.), '41; Univ. of N.D., MA (Bus. Educ.), '65; b. La Crosse, Wis. 1911; p. Frank and Emma Mosser Abicht; res: 912 Market St., La Crosse, Wis. 54601.

ABILEAH, MIRIAM M., Free-lance Translator, multi-lingual; Albert Einstein Col. of Med., '61–'68; British AF (WWII); Am. Translators Assn., Sierra Club; educated in Germany, England, and Israel; b. Berlin, Germany; p. Walter and Edith Gottlieb Kauders; h. (dec.); c. Ronald; res: P.O. Box 489, Forest Hills, N.Y. 11375.

ABOOD, FAY BARTON, Nat.-Reg. Sls. Mgr., Off. Mgr., KTRM, Incorporated, P.O. Box 5425, Beaumont, Tex. 78704, '67–; Traf. Mgr., '65–'67; AWRT (Bd., '68); Chenier's Bus. Col., Lamar State Col. of Tech; b. Hemphill, Tex., 1927; p. Robert Barton and Etta Brown; h. George Abood; c. Amy, George, Jr.; res: 5395 Rosemary Dr., Beaumont, Tex. 77708.

ABRAHAMS, SARAH C., AE, Adv. Copywtr., Waterman, Getz, Niedelman, 3 W. 57th St., N.Y., N.Y. 10019; Copywtr., Pubcty., Arndt, Preston, Chapin, Lamb & Keene; Asst. to Prodr., Warner Bros.-7 Arts; Sarah Lawrence Col., BA, '67; b. Tacoma, Wash. 1945; p. Meyer and Marguerite Pim Abrahams; res: 780 Madison Ave., N.Y., N.Y. 10021.

ABRAMOWITZ, SUSAN ISAACS, "You the Reader" Ed., Seventeen Magazine, 320 Park Ave., N.Y., N.Y. 10022; Queens Col.; b. N.Y.C. 1943; p. Morton and Helen Asher Isaacs; h. Elkan Abramowitz.

ABRAMSON, MARY FITZGERALD, Prod. Mgr., Gas Industries, 333 N. Michigan Ave., Chgo., Ill. 60611, 69–; Adv.-Prod. Mgr., Wisconsin Agriculturist, '66–'69; Dir., Photo Procurement, Compton's Encyclopedia, '64–'66; Ed., Spencer Publishing, '61–'64; Marquette Univ., BA, '54; b. Omaha, Neb.; p. Merle Fitzgerald and Eleanor; h. Rod Abramson; c. Michele, Denise, Heidi, Danielle, Tara; res: 7642 S. Kingston, Chgo. Ill. 60649.

ABRAVANEL, DIANE ROSENBERG, Dir. of PR, Montefiore Hospital, 3459 Fifth Ave., Pitt., Pa. 15213, '62–; AE, William H. Mazefsky Assocs., '57–'62; PR Asst. Un. Jewish Fedn. of Pitt., '55–'57; PR Asst., Susman & Adler, PR Cnslts., '46–'47; Free-lance PR and Adv. Cnslt; writing and prod of musical shows for commty. orgs. and clubs; PR Soc. of Western Pa. Hosps. (Pres., '67–'68), PRSA (Accredited Mbr.), Theta Sigma Phi, Am. Hosp. Assn. (PR Soc.), Hosp. Assn. of Pa. (aws: hosp. pubns., '65; nwspr. feature story coverage, '66; special event prom., '67, student nurse recruitment program, '68); Hospital Management Magazine Malcolm T. McEachern Aws. for int. hosp. bul., '65–'67; Bus. Training Col. of Pitt., '39; Univ. of Pitt.; b. Pitt., Pa., 1921; p. Nicholas and Etta Hazin Rosenberg; h. Ben Don Abravanel; c. Lynn, Nicki Ann; res: 2770 Fernwald Rd., Pitt., Pa. 15217.

ABRUZZO, MICHELE LINDA, Adv., Pubcty. Dir., David Cystal, Inc., 498 Seventh Ave., N.Y., N.Y. 10018, '68; Mdsng. Ed., Harper's Bazaar, '65–'68; AWNY; Nat. Outstanding Young Wm. of Achiev., '68; Col. Misericordia, BS; b. Englewood, N.J. 1942; p. Joseph and Emily Randon Abruzzo; h. Jules Berman; res: 6 Smithfield Terr., Waldwick, N.J. 07463.

ABSHIER, MARY ANNETTE, Ed., Columbia Gulf Transmission Company, P.O. Box 683, Houston, Tex. 77001, '65–; Edtl. Asst., '61–'65; Gen. Assigt. Reptr., Beaumont Jnl., '60–'61; Galveston Tribune, '57; Freelance, Omnis, Tex. Intl. Airways; Theta Sigma Phi (Pres., '65; VP, '67, '68), ICIE (Aws. of Excellence, Achiev., '65–'67; Dist. Five Aws. of Excellence, Merit, '65–'67); S.E. Tex. Indsl. Eds. (VP, '68; Aw. of Excellence, writing, photog., '67; Aw. of Excellence, photog., '68); Lamar State Col. of Tech., '53–'55, '60; Univ. of Tex., BJ, '57; Univ. of Houston, '58; b. Beaumont, Tex., 1935; p. John V. and Mary A. Cain Abshier; res: 4219 Bettis, #8, Houston, Tex. 77027.

ACHOR, JANE BACCUS, Crtv. Dir., W. W. Sherril Company, 3200 Maple Av., Dallas, Tex. 75201, '62–; Copy Dir., Grant Advertising, '58–'61; 7 yrs. Free-lance

Wtr./Prodr., Asst. Ed., Fashion Trade Journal, Advertising Trade Journal; Southern Methodist Univ., '42-'46; b. Dallas, Tex., 1925; p. Robert Baccus and Mary Crady; c. Jo Katherine, Christy; res: 3663 Ainsworth Dr., Dallas, Tex. 75229.

ACKERMAN, BETTYE LOUISE, Actress; Films: "Rascal" (W. Disney, '69), "Companions in Nightmare" (Universal, '68); TV: Co-star, "Ben Casey" (ABC, '61-'66), "Mannix" ('69), "Ironside" ('69), others; Theatre: numerous summer stock and off-broadway appearances; Instr., Lucy Feagin Sch. of Drama (N.Y.C.), '53; W. Coast Campaign Chmn., Muscular Dystrophy Assn., '63-'69; b. Cottageville, S.C., 1928; p. Clarence and Mary Baker Ackerman; h. Sam Jaffe; res: 302 N. Alpine Dr., Beverly Hills, Cal. 90210.

ACKLEY, BONNIE FRANZ, PR Dir., Juhl Associates, 529 Second St., Elkhart, Ind. 46514, '65-; Asst. Adv. Mgr., H. & A. Selmer, Inc.; State Ed., Elkhart Truth; Wms. Ed., Radio WDOW; Feature Wtr., Mich. nwsps.; PRSA, ICIE; b. Wayland, Mich., 1920; p. Albert and Marie Albert Franz; h. Richard T. Ackley; c. Roger S., Dana C.; res: 15 Manchester Lane, Elkhart, Ind. 46514.

ADAM, KARIN, Prod. Mgr., Design Counsel, 235 E. 57th St., N.Y., N.Y. 10022.

ADAMO, PATRICIA PRINCIPI, Wms. Ed., The Trentonian, Southard and Perry Streets, Trenton, N.J. 08602, '64-; b. Trenton, N.J., 1941; p. Oddino and Italia Principi; h. Leon Adamo; res: Plaza Park Apts., D-6, Plaza Blvd., Morrisville, Pa. 19067.

ADAMS, BARBARA E., Dir. of Subsidiary Rights, Wm. Morrow & Co., 105 Madison Ave., N.Y., N.Y. 10016; WNBA.

ADAMS, BEATRICE, Wtr.; Writing Bk. on Assigt.; (Retired), Bd. of Dirs., Exec VP, Crtv. Dir., Wtr. Gardner Adv. Co. (St. Louis, Mo.); Wtr. of fashion colm., St. Louis Star Times; Colmst. on TV Comml. Critique, Sponsor Magazine, Television Magazine; organization and teaching, writing courses (Adult Educ.); Lectr.; Wms. Adv. Club of St. Louis (Pres., '35; originated, wtr., dir., performed in Wms. Gridiron Show 35 yrs.), Theta Sigma Phi (St. Louis Chaptr. Pres., '62), Gamma Alpha Chi, ZONTA; Nat. Aw. for Best Copy by Wm., '41; Nat. Adv. Wm. of the Yr., '50; one of 27 Am. Wm. of Achiev. (story in Life Magazine, '51); St. Louis Globe Democrat Wm. of Achiev., '56; one of top 36 Am. Bus. Wm., Fortune, '56; Wash. Univ. of St. Louis (Founders Day Cit., '61); b. Belleville, Ill., 1902; p. William and Viola Cobb Adams; res: 530 North and South Rd., St. Louis, Mo. 63130.

ADAMS, DORIS A., Home Econst., Procter & Gamble, WHTC, Cinn., Oh. 45224; Better Homes & Gardens; Sears, Roebuck & Co.; Theta Sigma Phi, Home Econsts. in Bus., Electrical Wms. Round Table; Ia. State Univ., BS; b. Ames, Ia.; p. W. Neil and Frances French Adams; res: 1175 Hill Crest Rd., Cinn., Oh. 45224.

ADAMS, EDIE, Actress, Singer, 1735 N. Vine St., L.A., Cal. 90028; Comml. Spokeswm., Muriel Cigars (Comml. Spokeswm. of the Yr. aw., '61); Part-owner, Edie Adams Cut & Curl beauty salons; Broadway: "Wonderful Town" ('52-'54; two Donaldson aws.), "Lil Abner" ('56-'57; Tony aw.); regular on Ernie Kovacs radio, TV shows; "Here's Edie" (two Emmy nominations, '63); many guest appearances; 10 motion pics., incl. "The Apartment," "Mad, Mad, Mad World," "Under the Yum Yum Tree," "Love From a Proper Stranger;" SAG, AFTRA, AGVA, AFM, NATAS; Julliard Sch. of Music, five yrs.; Traphagen Sch. of Fashion Design; Lee Strassberg's Actors Studio; Columbia Sch. of Drama; b. Kingston, Pa.; p. Ada Adams Enke; h. 1. Ernie Kovacs (dec.) 2. Martin Mills; c. Betty Kovacs, Kippie Kovacs Lancaster, Mia Susan Kovacs, Joshua Dylan Mills.

ADAMS. ELEANOR, Soc. Ed., The Cincinnati Enquirer, 617 Vine St., Cinn., Oh. 45202, '69-; Asst. Soc. Ed., Colmst., '59-'69; Wms., Soc. Ed., The Indianapolis Times, '52-'56; Club Ed., '48-'52; Ohio Nwsp. Wms. Assn., Theta Sigma Phi (Cinn. Chptr. Pres., '63; Indianapolis Chptr. Pres., '46), Ohio Press Wm., NFPW, Wms. Press Club of Ind., Ind. Chptr. Arts & Letters; Butler Univ., '32-'34; Ind. Univ., AB (Jnlsm.), '36; Univ. of Mo., MA (Jnlsm.), '41; h. (div.); c. Mrs. William C. Pohlmann, Terence M.; res: 1071 Celestial St., Apt. 1103, Cinn., Oh. 45202.

ADAMS, ELEANOR FREEMAN, Ed., Forecast For Home Economics, Scholastic Magazines, Inc., 50 W. 44th St., N.Y., N.Y. 10036, '63-; Mng. Ed., Wms. Dept., New York Herald Tribune, '56-'63; Wms. Ed., Hartford (Conn.) Times, '51-'56; Colmst., Sales Management mag., '69-; NHFL, Electrical Wms. Round Table, Newspaper Women's Club of N.Y.; Assn. of Home Appliance Manufacturers Aw. "for excellence in communication of home appliance information to consumers," '68; Smith Col., BA; h. (div.); c. Mrs. John P. Fitzgibbons Jr., Mrs. John A. Yorker; res: 372 Central Park W., N.Y., N.Y. 10025.

ADAMS, ELIZABETH CALDER, Prodr.-Ed., WABC-TV, 77 W. 66th St., N.Y., N.Y. 10023, '67-; Reptr., '63-'65; Reptr., Prodr., Hostess for svc. programs, WBZ-TV (Boston, Mass.), Westinghouse Bdcst. Co., '59-'63; Prodr.-Hostess, "The World Around Us," WJAR-TV (Providence, R.I.), The Outlet Co., '56-'59; OPC, New England Wms. Press Club (VP), Nat. Cncl. of Wm. of the U.S., Radio-TV News Dirs. Assn., Jr. League of Boston; UPI's Best TV News Coverage of New England, '63; McCall's Golden Mike Aw., '61; U.S. Air Force Cert. of Distg. Svc., '59; Who's Who of Am. Wm., various aws., hons.; Smith Col., AB (Hist., Intl. Relations), (cum laude); h. David Adams (dec.); res: 620 The Pkwy., Mamaroneck, N.Y. 10543.

ADAMS, ELSIE DEE, Media Specialist, Utah State Board of Education, 1400 University Club, 136 E.S. Temple, Salt Lake City, Ut. 84111, '65-; Tchr., Brigham Young Univ., '68; Tchr., Univ. of Ut., '66-'68; Public

Librn., '53–'54; Tchr., Ut. Sch. System, '41–'65; conducted demonstrations on multi media approach to learning, '67–'69; Asst. Dir., Instructional Media Workshops, '66–'68; Ut. Lib. Assn., ALA, NEA; Brigham Young Univ., AB, '43; Univ. of Denver, MA, '53; Univ. of Ut.; b. Provo, Ut.; p. Samuel Conrad and Delilah Booth Adams; res: 445 N. Univ. Ave., Provo, Ut. 84601.

ADAMS, GRACE WOODWORTH, Publr., Sisseton Courier, Inc., 117 E. Oak, Sisseton, S.D. 57262, '44–; Reptr. and Farmer (Webster, S.D.); S.D. Press Assn. (Auxiliary); Am. Legion Auxiliary (Dist. Pres.), Order Eastern Star (Secy.); Masters Publrs. Aw., S.D. State Press, '69; b. Bristol, S.D., 1896; p. Judge L. H. and Marie Antoinette Woodworth; h. Albert J. Adams (dec.); c. Imogene, Grace (dec.), John A., Cynthia R.; Res; Sisseton, S.D. 57262.

ADAMS, HARRIET ARNOLD, Cnslt., Lib. Svcs., New Hampshire State Education Department, State House Annex, Concord, N.H. 03301, '66–; Instr., short course in basic lib. techniques, '67; Adult Svcs. Librn., Concord Public Lib., '62–'65; Young Peoples Librn., '55–'61; Circ. Librn., Leominster Public Lib., '50–'55; (Mass.); Army Librn. (Cal. and Wash. States) '43–'46; Children's Librn. '35–'43 (Wenatchee, Wash.); N.H. Lib. Assn. (Secy., '57–'59), ALA, New Eng. Lib. Assn., New Eng. Sch. Lib. Assn., NEA (Dept. of Audio-Visual Instr.), Appalachian Mountain Club, Commty. Players, ZONTA; Univ. of Ia., BA (Educ.), '26 (magna cum laude; Phi Beta Kappa); Univ. of Wash., BA (Lib. Sci.), '34; b. Garden Grove, Ia., 1905; p. Harry and Mabel Judd Arnold; h. Claude Adams (dec.); c. Ester (Mrs. Donn Kavanaugh), Charles S.; res: 25 Conant Dr., Concord, N.H. 03301.

ADAMS, JESSIE WELLS, Ed., Good Living, Westchester County Press, 61 Pinecrest Dr., Hastings-on-Hudson, N.Y. 10706, '50–; N.Y.C., Westchester Dept. of Welfare, '45–'50; Assoc. Ed., Fairfield County Press; h. Alger Adams.

ADAMS, JULIANNE McGRAW, Auth.; Tchr., Aiken County Board of Education, Augusta Rd., Aiken, S.C. 29801, '64–; Wms. Ed., Aiken Standard and Review, '68; Wtr., '60–'68; Tchr., Atlanta, Ga.; S.C. Press Assn. (Wms. Page Aw., '62), AAUW; Jr. Wms. Club First Pl. Art Aw., '66; Who's Who in Am. Cols. and Univs.; Brenau Col., BA; b. Smithfield, N.C. 1942; p. Annie Howell King; h. R. Thomas Adams; res: 908 Valley View Dr., Aiken, S.C. 29801.

ADAMS, LOUISE MEILY, TV-Radio Copy Dir., WHP, Inc., Telegraph Building, 216 Locust St., Harrisburg, Pa. 17108, '61–; Copywtr., Muscheno Agcy., Lebanon, Pa., '61; WHGB, Harrisburg, '58–'60; WCMB, '52–'58; AWRT; Smith Col., AB; b. Harrisburg, Pa.; p. George and Nelle Karper Meily; c. H. Ward; res: 327 N. 24th St., Camp Hill, Pa. 17011.

ADAMS, MERVYN W., Ed., Praeger Publishers, 111

Fourth Ave., N.Y., N.Y. 10003, '68–; Adm. Asst., E. Asian Inst., Columbia Univ., '64–'68; Ed., Exec. Secy., Conf. Group of U.S. Nat. Orgs. on the UN, '62–'64; Rsch. Asst., Cncl. on Religion & Intl. Affairs, '55–'62; Smith Col. '47–'50; Univ. of Chgo., BA, '51; Columbia Univ., MA (Polit. Sci.), '64; b. Chgo., Ill.; p. Robert and Janet Lawrence Adams.

ADAMS, PATRICIA SCOTT, Edtl. Asst., Dir. of Pubns., School of Veterinary Medicine, University of Missouri, 101 Connaway Hall, Columbia, Mo. 65201, '66–; Wtr., Office of Public Info., '66; Adv. Copywtr., C. B. Mosby Co., St. Louis, '65–'66; Several free-lance articles; Dir., Commtns., Info., Commercial Life Ins. Co., '64; Theta Sigma Phi (Columbia Club Chptr. VP, '67–'69; Secy-Treas., '66–'67); Univ. of Mo., BJ, '64; b. St. Louis, Mo., 1942; p. Virgil and Phyllis Baird Scott; h. John G. Adams; c. Cynthia Frances; res: Route 8, Columbia, Mo. 65201.

ADAMS, PHOEBE-LOU, Staff Ed., The Atlantic Monthly, 8 Arlington St., Boston, Mass. 02116; various positions since '44; Reptr., Hartford (Conn.) Courant, '42–'44; Auth., "A Rough Map of Greece;" Radcliffe Col., AB, '39 (cum laude); b. Hartford, Conn., 1918; p. Harold and Alice Burlingame Adams.

ADAMS, RUTH H., Decorating Ed., Brides Magazine, Conde Nast Publishing Co., 420 Lexington Ave., N.Y., N.Y. 10017, '69–; Assoc. Home Furnishings Ed., '67; Decorating Asst. Edtl., American Home, '59–'60, '63–'64; Free-lance Interior Designer; NHFL; res: 85 East End Ave., N.Y., N.Y. 10028.

ADAMS, SALLY PEPPER, Home Equipment Ed., The Family Circle, Inc., 488 Madison Ave., N.Y., N.Y. 10022, '55–; Assoc. Food Ed., '51–'55; Pic. Ed., Photog. Mgr., New York Star; Photog. Mgr., PM nwsp.; Photog. Ed., Friday mag.; Textbook Ed., John C. Winston Co.; Auth., four Cookbooks; Am. Home Econs. Assn., NHFL, Home Econsts. in Bus., Electrical Wms. Roundtable, Am. Inst. of Interior Decorators; Univ. of Pa., AB (Eng.), '35 (Phi Beta Kappa); Pratt Inst., BS (Home Econs.), '51 (honors); b. Phila., Pa.; p. H. Crowell and Elizabeth Hughes Pepper; h. Wayne Adams; c. Peter Wayne, Bruce Davidson; res: 230 Clinton St., Bklyn., N.Y. 11201.

ADAMSON, JUNE NEILSON, Wms. Ed., Church Ed., Reptr., The Oak Ridger, 101 E. Tyron Rd., Oak Ridge, Tenn. 37830, '59–'68; PR Dir., Oak Ridge Public Lib., '54–'59; Kappa Tau Alpha; Tenn. Press Assn. aws., '66–'68; McCune Sch. of Music, '39–'40; Brigham Young Univ., '40–'42; Univ. of Tenn., '59–'63 and Grad. work, '68–; b. Salt Lake City, Ut., 1922; p. Perry and Annie Livingston Neilson; h. George M. Adamson; c. Stanley, Neil; res: 382 East Dr., Oak Ridge, Tenn. 37830.

ADDIS, MARJORIE L., Ed., The Brewster Standard, 29 Main St., Brewster, N.Y. 10509, '22–; Smith Col., '11;

b. Brewster, N.Y., 1890; p. Emerson and Esther Lobdell Addis; res: 53 Prospect St., Brewster, N.Y. 10509.

ADES, KARIN ELIZABETH, Prom. Dir., WMVS/WMVT, 1015 N. 6th St., Milw., Wis. 53203, '68–; Ed., Wis. Edition, TV Guide, '65–'68; AWRT, Commty. Bdcst. Cncl.; 2,000 Wm. of Achiev.; Wis. State Univ., BS, '65; b. Chgo., Ill., 1943; p. Arthur and Donna Webster Ades; res: 1218 E. Kane Pl., Milw., Wis. 53202.

ADKINS, GRACIE, Assoc. Ed., children's mags., Am. Baptist Board of Education and Publication, Valley Forge, Pa. 19481, '66–; Ed., Curriculum Materials, '66–'68; Alderson Broaddus Col., BA, '64; Colgate Rochester Divinity Sch., MA, '66; res: Wm. Henry Apts., Dogwood 11, King and Frazer Roads, Malvern, Pa. 19355.

ADLER, SOPHIE, Free-lance Book Designer, 350 W. 31st St., N.Y., N.Y. 10001.

ADRIAN, MARY (Mary Venn Jorgensen), Auth., juv. bks: 14 Nature Mysteries, six Preserve Our Wildlife Series, four Easy Science Nature Books, two Balance of Nature Series; Am. Ornithologist Union, Nat. Audubon Soc., Nat. Wildlife Fedn.; N.Y.U., two yrs.; h. Henry Jorgensen; res: 209 E. Clackamas Circle, Woodburn, Ore. 97071.

ADWON, SAIDIE, AE, KTUL-TV, Leake TV Enterprises, P.O. Box 3204, Tulsa, Okla. 74107, '49–; Asst. Prom. Dir., KTUL Radio, '45–'49; Pubcty. Dir., Okla. State Symphony, '41–'45; AWRT (Nat. VP, '62–'64; Okla. State Chptr. Pres., '60–'62; Wm. of Yr., Southwestern Area, '64), Quota Club (Tulsa Chptr. Pres., '55), Tulsa Adv. Fedn. (Bd. of Dirs., '60–; Ad Man of the Yr. Aw., '68); three-time winner, Tulsa Sales Exec. Club Sammy Aw.; Okla. City Univ.; b. Wilson, Okla.; p. Addy and Rosa Mettry Adwon; res: 6828 E. 57th Pl., Tulsa, Okla. 74145.

AEIKER, CELIA SUE, Soc. Ed., Point Pleasant Register, 200 Main St., Point Pleasant, W. Va. 25550, '66–; Reptr.; Proofreader; Mason County Young Repls. Cl.; b. Henderson, W. Va., 1944; p. William and Dreama Carter Aeiker; res: Box 1, Rt. 17, Henderson, W. Va. 25106.

AGNEW, NANCY LONGLEY, Eng. Tchr., The Nightingale-Bamford School, New York, N.Y., '69–; Asst. Mgr., Bk. Div., American Heritage Publishing Co., '68–'69; PR Dir., '59–'68; Asst. to Pres., '56–'59; Prom. Mgr., Bk. Rev., New York Herald Tribune; Corr., Look Magazine; Articles, Glamour; Wellesley Col., BA, '50; N.Y.U., MBA, '68; b. Ia. City, Ia., 1928; p. Harry and Agnes Fulton Longley; h. Seth M. Agnew; c. Lydia, Rosanna; res: 145 E. 63rd St., N.Y., N.Y. 10021.

AGNEW, NANCY RUTLAND, Dir., Wheeler Basin Regional Library, 207 Church St., Decatur, Ala. 35601, '60–; Decatur Public Lib., '60–'64; Decatur HS, '56–'60; Ala. Public Lib. Svc. (Montgomery), '40–'42; Northside

HS '38–'40 (Fort Worth, Tex.); Handley HS, '36–'38 (Roanoke, Ala.); Ala. Lib. Assn. (Pres., Public Lib. Div., '66–'67), Southeastern Lib. Assn., DAR, C. of C., Wms. C. of C.; Ala. Col., BA, '35; Emory Univ. Lib. Sch., BA (Lib. Sci.); b. Cherokee, Ala., 1913; p. James and Effie Mahan Rutland; h. Robert Thurman Agnew; c. Nancy Lane, Robert Thurman, Jr.; res: 1612 Stratford Rd., Decatur, Ala. 35601.

AGNOR, EVELYN BARNES, Religion and Art Ed., The Alexandria Gazette, Inc., 717 N. St. Asaph St., Alexandria, Va. 22313, '63–; Colm., "Tips for Tots" and "Gold that Glitters"; Art Colmst.; Asst., recreational workshops; Conductor, wtrs. workshops; Lectr. to pfsnl. groups on news media; Tchr., Special Educ.; NLAPW, NFPA (Intl. Rels. Comm.), '68–'69; 3rd prize, best pages ed., '67), Va. Press Wm. (1st State Aw., juv. writing, '65; 1st State Aw., news story, '67; 2nd State Aw., page layout, '65; numerous other aws.); Wash. Nat. Symphony (Wm. Comm.), Anne Lee Memorial Home (Bd. of Dirs.), Alexandria Wm. Interfaith (Bd. of Advisors), Alexandria Wms. Club ('34–), numerous civic activities; Salem Col., BS (Math and Sci.), '30; AB (Elementary Educ.), '32; Duke Univ., MS (Psych., Special Educ.), '33; b. Nash County, N.C., 1913; p. Hayes and Mary Ida Odams Barnes; h. Earl Agnor; c. Joseph Pollard, Jocile Diann Pollard (Mrs. E. D. Johnson); res: 1105 Cross Dr., Alexandria, Va. 22302.

AHERN, ARLEEN FLEMING, Acquisitions Librn. and Archivist, Temple Buell College, 7055 E. 18th Ave., Denver, Colo. 80220, '43–; Asst. Prof. of Sociology, '59–; Lib. Asst., Army Air Force Lib. (Salt Lake City, Ut.); Asst. Prof. of Sociol.; ALA, Mountain Plains Assn., Colo. Lib. Assn. (VP-Pres., '69–'70), Adult Educ. Cncl. of Denver, Soc. of Am Archivists, Mountain Plains Adult Educ. Cncl., AAUP, Altrusa (Denver, 2nd VP, '69); Univ. of Ut., BA, '43; Univ. of Denver, MA, '62; Univ. of Colo. (grad. study in Sociol.); b. Mt. Harris, Colo., 1922; p. John Russell and Josephine Vidmar Fleming; h. George Irving Ahern; c. George, Jr.; res: 746 Monaco Pkwy., Denver, Colo. 80220.

AHLGREN, MILDRED CARLSON, PR Dir., General Federation of Women's Clubs, 1734 N. Street, N.W., Wash., D.C. 20036, '56–; Staff Wtr., Hammond (Ind.) Times; Theta Sigma Phi, NWPC, NFPW, ANWC, AWRT, NLAPW, Ind. Wms. Press Club, APRA; Aw. of Merit, U.S. Treasury Dept., '66; several other aws.; b. Chgo., Ill.; p. August and Hilda Peterson Carlson; h. Oscar A. Ahlgren (dec.); c. Mrs. Adrienne Haeuser; res: Dupont East, 1545 18th St., N.W., Wash., D.C. 20036.

AICHOLTZ, VIRGINIA LOUISE ZUMWALT, Pres., Exec. Dir., TV/RECORDERS, 6054 Sunset Blvd., Hollywood, Cal. 90028, family-owned corp.; VP, '55–'63; formerly, casting, legal, sound dept., Reader, Universal Studio; AMPAS (Assoc. Mbr.), NATAS; UCLA; b. Washington, Mo., 1920; p. James Clarence Zumwalt and Louise Duncan Quinn; h. Lawrence A. Aicholtz;

c. James Lawrence, Julie Louise; res: 3211 Oakdale Rd., Studio City, Cal. 91604.

AIELLO, ALICE BLACK, Deputy Dir., Research, Development Program & Resources, Cuyahoga County Public Library, 4510 Memphis Ave., Cleve., Oh. 44144; Coordr., Young Adult Svcs.; Br. Librn., Milw. Public Lib.; Young Adult Librn.; HS Librn. (Racine, Wis.); Lectr., Case-Western Reserve Univ. Lib. Sch.; Cnslt.; Cnslt., Kent State Univ. Lib. Sch.; weekly TV program (Milw., Wis.), '54–'59; ALA (Young Adult Svcs. Div., VP, '64–'65; Cnslt., "Richer by Asia" project), Oh. Lib. Assn.; Exec. Dir., State of Oh. Nat. Lib. Week Comm., '65; Univ. of Wis., BA (Jnlsm.), '50; MA (Lib. Sci.), '51; b. Madison, Wis., 1928; p. Bernard and Frances Holland Black; h. Albert Aiello; res: 11820 Edgewater Dr., Lakewood, Oh. 44107.

AIKEN, JOAN LAMBERT, Dir., Joan L. Aiken, Advertising and Public Relations, 120 Warwick Rd., Haddonfield, N.J. 08033, '65–; Adv. and PR Writer, Bauer-Tripp-Foley, '61–'65; PR Cnslr./Wtr., Gray & Rogers, '58–'60; PR Dir. and Dir. Crtv. Writing Svcs., Bauer & Tripp, '54–'58; PR Dir., McKee & Albright, '51–'54; Ed., Conventions and Trade Shows Magazine (now Sales Meetings), '46–'49; Adv. and PR Dir. Gold-Tex Fabrics Corp., '48–'51; Lectr., Adv. and PR, Annenberg Sch. of Commtns., Univ. of Pa.; Philadelphia Art Alliance, Hist. Soc. of Haddonfield, PRSA; Wildes Schl. of Jnlsm., Univ. of Pa.; Cleve. State Univ., BA; b. Phila., Pa., 1917; p. Isaac and Minerva Rodan Cherry; h. James G. Aiken.

AIMEE, Sr. M., O.S.U. (Carey) Auth., new series of bks. for parents, students, tchrs. (Wm. H. Sadlier, Inc., '67–); Lectr.; workshops for tchrs. Bk. Reviewer, Sisters Today mag. (Liturgical Press, 64–); Tchr., Adult Educ. Program, N.Y. Archdiocese, '68–; Schs., N.Y. and Wash., D.C., '54–'67; Head Start Coordr., N.Y.C., '65; Auth: "Bibliography for Christian Formation in the Family" (Paulist/Newman Press, '64); "Liturgical Celebrations for Home and School" (Abbey Press, '66); Four Tchrs. Manuals in "Our Life with God" series (Wm. H. Sadlier, Inc., '67–'68); numerous mag. and nwsp. articles; The Religious Educ. Assn., Nat. Catholic Educ. Assn., Westchester Wrtrs. Conf.; Contemporary Auths.; Nat. Winner, Primary Activities Contest, Scott Foresman & Co., '60; Catholic Sister (Order: Ursulines of the Roman Union); Col. of New Rochelle, BA, '54; Catholic Univ. of Am., MA, '63; Famous Wtrs. Sch., '67–; b. N.Y.C., 1931; p. Edward and Dorothy Makahon Carey; res: Ursuline Convent, 1338 N. Ave., New Rochelle, N.Y. 10804.

AINSWORTH, NORMA RUEDI, Ed., Manuscript Dept., Scholastic Magazines Inc., 50 W. 44th St., N.Y., N.Y. 10036, '67–; Fiction Ed., Scholastic Magazine and Bk. Svc., '62–'67; Asst. Ed., "Co-ed and Practical English" ('61–'62); Mng. Ed., MacFadden Pubns., '60–'61; Free-lance, '54–'60; Info. Chief, Bur. of Land Mgt., Dept. of Interior, '49–'54; Auth., "If Dreams Came True Inc." ('27), numerous poems, articles,

short stories; Ed. of numerous anthologies; MWA (Edgar Aw., 3 yrs.; juv. judge), WNPC, AWRT, ANWC, OPC, Auths. Guild, Chi Omega; Lindenwood Col., AB (Founder and Pres. of Latin Hon.; mbr. 5 hon. socs.); Southern Methodist Univ., MA (Comparative Literature and Eng.); Univ. of Mo., work on PhD; b. Clinton, Mo.; p. Paul and Minnie Lee Morris Ruedi; h. Freedom H. Ainsworth; res: 27 W. 10th St., N.Y., N.Y. 10011.

AKIN, LOIS QUINNETT, Asst. Ed., Nebraska State Education Association, '69–; Ed., Bankers Life Nebraska, '68–'69; Staff Reptr., The Wall Street Jnl. (Chgo., Ill.), '67; Copy Ed., The Lincoln Jnl., '67; Reptr., The Sioux City Jnl., '66; Cornhusker Eds. Assn. (Secy., '69–); Theta Sigma Phi; The Nwsp. Fund Aw., '66; Univ. of Neb., BA, '67; b. Shawnee, Okla., 1945; h. John F. Akin; res: 65 Trenridge Rd., Lincoln, Neb. 68505.

AKULLIAN, HELEN DOROTHY, Placement Mgr., Edtl. Specialist, Robert/Norman Agency, 366 Madison Ave., N.Y., N.Y. 10017, '65–; Macmillan Publ., '60–'64; Christian Dior, '57–'59; Harcum Jr. Col., '48; Tobe-Coburn, '49; b. Albany, N.Y., '28; p. Daniel Akullian; h. Monroe Bennett; res: 156 E. 79th St., N.Y., N.Y. 10017.

ALBERGHETTI, CARLA, Actress; Broadway: "Carnival" ('62–'63); Nat. Co.: "On a Clear Day You Can See Forever" ('68); U.C.L.A., '63; b. Rhodes, Greece, 1939; p. Daniele and Vittoria Ricci Alberghetti; h. (div.) c. Cosette Polena; res: 1424 Rising Glen Rd., L.A., Cal. 90069.

ALBERS, JO-ANN HUFF, Asst. Wms. Ed., The Cincinnati Enquirer, 617 Vine St., Cinn., Oh. 45201, '66–; Wms. Club Ed., '64; Wms. Features, Sunday Wms. Sec. Ed., '63; Asst. to TV Ed., '60–'63; Traf. Supvsr., WCPO Radio, '59–'60; Info. Specialist, General Electric; Oh. Nwspwms. Assn. (aws., '64–'66), Theta Sigma Phi (Region V Dir., '68–'69; Cinn. Chptr. Pres., '67–'68); Miami Univ., BA (Radio-TV), '59 (Alpha Epsilon Rho); Xavier Univ., MEd, '62; b. Cain's Store, Ky., 1938; p. Vertreese and Olowene Brown Huff; h. Henry H. Albers; c. Stephen, Henry; res: 241 Hunsford St., Cinn., Oh. 45216.

ALBERT, DORA, Free-lance Wtr., 13454 Chandler Blvd., Van Nuys, Cal. 91401, '32–; Asst. Ed., Movie Mirror, '31–'32; Asst. Ed., Silver Screen, '30; Auth: three non-fiction books; Hollywood Wms. Press Club (VP, '67–; Corr. Secy., '66), Cal. Press Wm., AWRT, NFPW (aw., "How to Cash in on Your Abilities" '61); Eight Ball Aw., L.A. Press Club, '57; Hunter Col., BA, '27 (cum laude); Columbia Univ., MA, '28; b. N.Y.C.; p. Isaac and Pauline Baker Albert; h. Samuel Heend; res: 13454 Chandler Blvd., Van Nuys, Cal. 91401.

ALBERT, IRENE HOLT, Feature Ed., Colmst., Clearwater Sun, 301 S. Myrtle Ave., Clearwater, Fla. 33515, '55–; art, music, drama critic, '63–; PR, Fla. Gulf Coast

Art Ctr., '58–'67; Stringer, Time Inc., '57–'58; short stories, poetry to nat. pubns., '40–; bk. revs., Wash. Post, '37–'39; Contrbr., Paris editions, N.Y. Herald Tribune, Paris Times, '27–'30; Fgn. Corr., '27–'30; Reptr., Moline (Ill.) Dispatch, '25–'26; Cnslt., Jr. Ballet Guild Fndn. of Fla., '67; Cnslt., Clearwater Opera Workshop, '69; WNPC, Fla. Wms. Press Club, (aw. in interviews, '64; state aw., colms., '66); NLAPW (Clearwater Br. Pres., '58–'60; 2nd nat. prize published short story; two biennial aws. in lyrics, '65), Theta Sigma Phi, Nat. Soc. of Arts and Ltrs.; first prize, McCall's Home of Tomorrow contest, '45; Fla. AP aw. in features, '64; Fla. State contest poetry aw., '65; educ: Tangier, Morocco; Starkey Seminary, '20–'22; Sorbonne, '27–'30; b. Moline, Ill., 1910; p. George E. and Jean B. Cox Holt; h. John Jacob Albert III; c. John J. IV (dec.).

ALBERT, MARCELLA, Free-lance Wtr., Publicist, '68–; Wtr.-Ed. and Yearbook Ed., Compton's Encyclopedia of Encyclopedia Britannica, Inc., '63–'68; Edtl. positions, Business Week magazine, '60–'63; Wtr., Publicist, Theta Sigma Phi, PRSA; Northwestern Univ., BS (Jnlsm.); L'Alliance Francaise; b. West Frankfort, Ill.; p. Dr. A.S. and Belle Radway Albert; res: 33 E. Cedar, Suite 11-A, Chgo., Ill. 60611.

ALBERT, MARGARET COOK, Free-lance Copywtr. and Ed. for publ. houses, '62–; Copy Chief, College Advertising, Houghton Mifflin Co. (Boston), '60–'62; Reptr., Daily Herald-Telephone (Bloomington, Ind.), '59–'60; Asst. Copy Ch., Cosmopolitan Magazine, '55–'57; Theta Sigma Phi (Pitt. Chptr. VP, '69; Boston Chptr. Treas., '65–'67), Ind. Univ., AB, '55 (cum laude, Phi Beta Kappa); Universite de Bordeaux, '57–'58 (Fulbright Scholarship); b. Madison, Wis., 1933; p. H. H. and Esther Marhoefer Cook; h. Walter Albert; c. Jennifer Ann, Bryan Walter; res: 7139 Meade St., Pitt., Pa. 15208.

ALBERTS, FRANCES JACOBS, Bk., "Gift for Genghis Khan" (McGraw Hill), others; Free-lance Wtr.; Cont. Wtr., KCRS (Midland, Tex.); Cont. Wtr. KHAS (Hastings, Neb.); Auth: juv. short stories, adult articles; Neb. Wtrs. Guild (Histrn.); Dakota State Col., Tchrs. Certificate; Purdue Univ. (Jnlsm.); Vanderbilt Univ., '69 (grant); h. Arnold Alberts; res: 1119 N. Elm St., Hastings, Neb. 68901.

ALBION, ELIZABETH, AE, Woody Kepner Associates, Inc., 3361 S.W. Third Ave., Miami, Fla. 33146, '65–; Dir., Adv., PR, Lauderhill Improvement Corp., '63–'65; Wtr., Publicist, City of Miami Beach, '53–'59; Wtr., Nat. Assn. of Manufacturers, '45–'53; Theta Sigma Phi; N.E. Mo. State Tchrs. Col., Columbia Univ., '41–'45; h. (dec.); c. Fred M.; res: 3639 S.W. LeJeune Rd., Miami, Fla. 33146.

ALBRECHT, RUTH E., Prof., The University of Florida, 312 Peabody Hall, Gainesville, Fla. 32601, '51–; Rsch. Prof., Auburn Univ. (Auburn, Ala.); Rsch. Assoc., The Univ. of Chgo.; Co-auth., "Older Peo-

ple" ('54); Ed: "Aging in a Changing Society" (The University of Fla. Press); chptrs. in six other scientific bks.; 22 articles in jnls.; Am. Sociological Assn. (Family Sec. Secy., '67–'70), Gerontological Soc. (Psychological, Social Scis. Sec. Secy., '61–'64; Chmn., '65–'66), Southern Sociological Soc. (Exec. Bd., '69–'72), Intl. Assn. on Mental Health, Nat. Cncl. on Family Relationships, others; The Univ. of Chgo., MA, '46; PhD, '51; b. Perry County, Mo., 1910; res: 1218 N.W. 6th St., Gainesville, Fla. 32601.

ALBRETHSEN, GWEN LANGDON, Ed., Itemizer-Observer, 521 Court St., Dallas, Ore. 97338, '69–; Wms. Ed., '65–'69; News Ed., Meridian (Idaho) News-Times, '65; Mng. Ed., The Ashton (Idaho) Herald, '57–'65; various nwsp. positions; Theta Sigma Phi, BPW (Chptr. Pres.), C. of C. (Local VP), various civic orgs.; numerous rept. aws., local civic aws.; Univ. of S.D., '34–'36; b. Bradley, S.D., 1917; p. Thomas and Mary Westover Langdon; h. Harvey Albrethsen (div.); c. Patricia (Mrs. David Kime); res: 704 Holman, Dallas, Ore. 97338.

ALDAN, DAISY, Tchr., Creative Writing, School of Art and Design, 1576 Second Ave., N.Y., N.Y. 10022, '48–; Founder, Ed., Publr., Folder Magazine, Am. Ed., Two Cities (bi-lingual mag. publ. in Paris), '62–'65; Auth: "Poems of India" (Thomas Crowell, '69), "Seven: Seven" (Folder Editions, '66), "The Masks Are Becoming Faces" (Goosetree Press, '65), numerous other works; Actress, WCBS, '38–'56; Acad. of Am. Poets, PSA (Bd. of Dirs.), Eng. Tchrs. Assn., on Faculte des Lettres, Co-operative Film Makers (Cinematheque); numerous poetry aws.; Irvine Sch. of the Theatre, '39–'41; Hunter Col., BA; Bklyn. Col., MA; N.Y.U., PhD; Sch. of Higher Studies, Goetheanum, Switzerland; b. N.Y.C., 1923; p. Louis and Ester Edelhelt Aldan; res: 325 E. 57th St., N.Y., N.Y. 10022.

AL-DOORY, SHIRLEY RAMSEY, Public Info. Specialist, San Antonio Air Materiel Area Information Office, Kelly Air Force Base, San Antonio, Tex. 78241, '67–; Edtl. Asst. in PR, Nat. Bank of Commerce, '65–'66; Med. Wtr., N.Y. Acad. of Med., '62–'64; Feature Wtr., Norman Transcript nwsp., '60–'61; Theta Sigma Phi; Univ. of Okla., BA (Jnlsm.), '62; b. Shawnee, Okla., 1936; p. A. R. and Adina Macon Ramsey; h. Dr. Yousef Al-Doory; c. Linda; res: 5335 N.W. Loop 410, Apt. 413, San Antonio, Tex. 78229.

ALDRICH, GEORGANNE, Pres., Animated I, 1407 Broadway, N.Y., N.Y. 10018, '68–; Publicist-Owner, Aldrich-Hoffman Assocs; Finch Col.; New Sch. for Social Rsch.; b. N.Y.C., 1931; p. Larry and Sydel Goldfarb Aldrich; h. Paul Heller; res: 59 Morton St., N.Y., N.Y. 10014.

ALDRICH, WILLIE LEE BANKS, Librn., Hood Theological Seminary/Livingstone College, 800 W. Thomas, Salisbury, N.C. 28144, '61–; Librn. W. J. Walls Gen., '60; Dunbar HS, E. Spencer, N.C., '57–'60; Tchr. Librn., Cleve. HS, Shelby, N.C., '57–'58; Asst. Librn., Rowan

County Br. Lib., '55–'58; AAUW, ALA, Rowan County for Better Libs., Tchr. Assn.; Livingstone Col., BA, '45, Hood Theological Seminary, C.R.E., Atlanta Univ. Sch. of Lib. Svc., MS (Lib. Sci.); b. Cleve., Oh.; p. Alfred and Hattie Ross Banks; h. Thomas N. Aldrich; res: 1337 W. Horah St., Salisbury, N.C. 28144.

ALDRIDGE, ANNE LANEY, Ed., Bull Ladle, Stockham Valves & Fittings, Inc., 4000 10th Ave., N., Birmingham, Ala. 35212; Birmingham Cncl. of Indsl. Eds., Theta Sigma Phi (Birmingham Chptr. Pres., '62–'63), AAUW; Who's Who of Am. Wm.; Birmingham-Southern Col., AB, '39; b. Elmore, Ala., 1918; p. Howard and Annye Owsley Laney; h. John T. Aldridge; res: 3905 40th Ave., N. Birmingham, Ala. 35217.

ALDRIDGE, CATHERINE LIGHTBOURNE, Wms. Ed., Amsterdam News, 2340 Eighth Ave., N.Y., N.Y. 10027, '64–; Tchr., '56–'64; Welfare Investigator, '55–'56; various edtl., prom. positions, Life, Look, Chgo. Defender, Ebony; NAMW; Who's Who of Am. Wm., '69, John B. Russwurm Aw., '67, L.I. Fashion Group Aw., Intl. Mannequins Fashions Wtrs. Aw.; W. Va. State Col., '46–'49; Ind. Univ., BS (Educ.), '52; b. Chgo., Ill.; p. Orrington and Mallie Levy Lightbourne; h. Ira Aldridge; c. Allison; res: 45 E. 135 St., N.Y., N.Y. 10037.

ALDRIDGE, HARRIETT KENNEDY, Food and Home Ed., Arkansas Gazette, Second and Louisiana Sts., Little Rock, Ark. 72203, '65–; Asst. Food and Home Ed., '61–'65; Phi Upsilon Omicron; Tex. Wms. Univ., BS (Home Econ. Educ.), '45; b. Plum Island, N.Y., 1923; p. Harry and Erna Loudon Kennedy; h. Herber J. Aldridge (dec.); c. Michael Edwin, Frederick James; res: 5143 Glenmore Rd., N. Little Rock, Ark. 72116.

ALEXANDER, ALICE LYNCH, PR Dir., Kroehler Mfg. Co., 666 N. Lake Shore Dr., Chgo., Ill. 60611, '64–; Acc. Supvsr., Public Relations Boards, '56–'64; Lib. Asst., Chicago Sun Times, '54–'56; Edtl. Asst., New York Times, '52–'54; Detroit News, '48–'49; NHFL (Ill. Chptr. Pres.); Western Mich. Col.; b. Decatur, Ill., 1925; p. Lawrence and Mary Finn Lynch; h. Howard Alexander; res: 1821 Lincoln Park W., Chgo., Ill. 60614.

ALEXANDER, BEA BERNICE, Prod. Mgr., MacManus, John & Adams, Inc., 8730 Wilshire Blvd., Beverly Hills, Cal. 90211, '67–; Prod. Mgr., Atherton-Privett; Prod. Mgr., Smith-Klitten; Prod. Mgr., Baus-Ross; Prod. Mgr., Boylhart, Lovett and Dean; b. Kan. City, Kan., 1937; p. Lloyd and Marie Kresin Alexander; c. Anita Alexander; res: 15744 Hartland St., Van Nuys, Cal. 91406.

ALEXANDER, DOLORES ANNE, Exec. Dir., National Organization for Women, 33 W. 93rd St., N.Y., N.Y. 10025, '69–; Reptr., Newsday, '65–'69; Gen. Assigt. Reptr., Copy Ed., '64; Newark Evening News, '61–'64; New York Times Corr., City Col. of N.Y., '60–'61; mag. articles: Glamour, Ladies Circle; NWCNY; Catherine

L. O'Brian Aw., '68; City Col. of N.Y., BA, '61; b. Newark, N.J.; res: 33 W. 93rd, N.Y., N.Y. 10025.

ALEXANDER, LINDA LEWANN, Auth., "A Job Well Done" ('67), story in "Read-The-Picture Stories" ('67), numerous children's stories; Mo. State Wtrs. Guild (Best Juv. Short Story, '64, '66, '67, '68); Intl. Correspondence Sch., '61 (mag. and bk. illus.); b. Carthage, Mo., 1935; p. John and Maxine Lewis Alexander; res: 3020 W. 24th, Joplin, Mo. 64801.

ALEXANDER, LOIS KINDLE, Dir.-Ed., Newsletter and Jnl., Harlem Institute of Fashion, National Association of Milliners, Dressmakers and Tailors, 157 W. 126th St., N.Y., N.Y. 10027, '66–; Dir., Neighborhood Facilities Program for U.S. Dept. of Housing and Urban Dev.; Ed., Fashion Cue, '51–'64; Tattler Magazine, '54–'56; former Wms. Ed., Pittsburgh Courier; Nat. Assn. of Fashion and Accessory Designers (Nat. Pres., '56–'64), NAMW (former N.Y.C. Chptr. VP), Nat. Cncl. of Wm. of U.S., Nat. Cncl. of Negro Wm. (former Bd. Mbr.), Capital Press Club (former VP); Hampton Inst., BS, '38; Univ. of Chgo.; American Univ.; N.Y.U., MS, '63; New Sch.; b. Little Rock, Ark.; p. Samuel and Leila Walker Kindle; c. Mrs. Joyce Henderson; res: 100 LaSalle St., Apt. 20H, N.Y., N.Y. 10027.

ALEXANDER, LUDMILLA (Ludmilla Jitkoff Bobroff), Free-lance Wtr., '67–; Reptr., Rahway (N.J.) News Record., '67; Travel Wtr., Parent's Magazine (N.Y.C.), '63–'66; PR Cnslt., Bd. of Educ., Clark, N.J.; Theta Sigma Phi; Columbia Univ., BS, '63; b. Manilla, Philippine Islands, 1941; p. Alexander and Eugenia Vitkovsky Jitkoff; h. Dimitry Bobroff; c. Michael Dimitry; res: 12865 Glen Brae Dr., Saratoga, Cal. 95070.

ALEXANDER, MILDRED JACKSON, Dir., Wms. News and Public Affairs, WTAR Radio & Television Corp., 720 Boush St., Norfolk, Va. 23510, '49–; AWRT (Bd. of Dirs.), Assoc. Press Bdcstrs. of Va. (Top Wm. in Bdcst., 12 yrs.), AFA (Dist. Governor), C. of C. (Pres., Wms. Div.), Norfolk Pilot Club (Pres.); Natl. Fashion Rept. Aw.; Tidewater Sls. Execs. Club "Sammy" Aw.; Norfolk Col., '27–'29; Col. of William and Mary, '29–'31; Salem Col., '31–'32; b. Norfolk, Va., 1909; p. Benjamin and Mozelle Harrison Jackson; h. Walter Raleigh Alexander; c. Jane (Mrs. William R. Hemingway, Jr.); res: 321 Susan Constant Dr., Virginia Beach, Va.

ALEXANDER, SHANA, Ed. McCall's Magazine, 230 Park Ave., N.Y., N.Y. 10017, '69–; first wm. ed. of McCall's for 48 yrs.; twice-monthly column "The Feminine Eye" for Life and now McCall's, '64–; Life's First Wm. Staffwtr., '61–'64; Life Reptr., '51; PM (old New York newspaper), Harper's Bazaar, and Flair, '42; Sigma Delta Chi; U.S.C. Nat. Jnlsm. Aw.; L.A. Times Wm. of the Yr., '67; Am. Newspwms. Club Golden Pen Aw. "for outstanding personal achievements in Jnlsm."; Vassar (Anthropology); b. N.Y.C., 1925; h. (div.); c. Katherine.

ALEXANDER, SUSANNA LAUN, Assoc. State Librn., Missouri State Library, 308 E. High St., Jefferson City, Mo. 65101, '66–; Dir. of Field Svcs., '65–'66; Dir., Columbia, Mo. libs., '55–'65; various positions, Stephens Col. Lib., '49–'55; ALA (J. W. Lippincott Aw. Jury), Mo. Lib. Assn. (Pres., '63; VP, '62; Treas. '57–'59); Stephens Col., AA, '36 (Alumnae Achiev. Aw., '59); Northwestern Univ., BS, '38; Univ. of Denver, MA (Lib. Sci.), '52; b. St. James, Mo. 1917; p. George and Violet Hubbard Laun; h. D. B. Alexander (dec.); c. Betty (Mrs. Dave Thomas); res: 408 Crystal View Terr., Jefferson City, Mo. 65101.

ALEXIS, ILA CHARLENE COFFEY, Librn., Metropolitan State College Library, 250 W. 14th Ave., Denver, Colo. 80204, '67–; Lib. Resources Selection Librn., '65–; Head, Young Adult Div., Denver Public Lib., '58–'62; Asst. Librn., Southwestern State Col. (Weatherford, Okla.), '55–'57; Wtr.-Cnslt., PR Planner; Tchr., Lib. Sci., Southwestern State Col.; Guest Lectr.; Cncl. of Librns. (Secy., '68–'70); Freedom Fndn. Aw., '64; Southwestern State Col., BA, '51; Univ. of Okla., MS (Lib. Sci.; magna cum laude); b. Mayfield, Okla., 1930; p. Thurston and Ruby Walker Coffey; h. Vincent A. Alexis; c. Lyndi, Cynthia Ann, Vincent A. III, Teresa Charlene; res: 1230 Peoria St., Aurora, Colo. 80010.

ALFONSI, MARIE RAIMONDI, Traf. Mgr., The Philadelphia Agency Inc., 275 S. 19th St., Phila., Pa. 19148, '60–; Radio, TV Opns., '60–; Traf. Mgr., Radio, TV Opns., Erwin Wasey, '60–; W. Chester State Tchrs. Col.; b. Phila., Pa., 1933; p. John and Vincenza Maimone Raimondi; h. Henry Alfonsi; res: 1311 Castle Ave., Phila., Pa. 19148.

ALFRIEND, RACHEL KAEBNICK, Food Ed., Virginian-Pilot, Norfolk-Portsmouth Newspapers, Inc., 150 W. Brambleton Ave., Norfolk, Va. 23501; Home Econst., Gen. Electric Co. (Louisville, Ky.), '62–'65; Home Econst., Colonial Stores Inc. (Atlanta, Ga.), '60–'62; Home Econst., Columbia Gas Co. (Pitt., Pa.), '56–'60; Tchr., Norfolk City Schs., '68; Am. Home Econs. Assn., Va. Home Econs. Assn. (Dist. VI, Pres., '69), Va. Home Econsts. in Bus., Jr. League of Norfolk, Who's Who of Am. Wm.; Albright Col., BS (Home Econs.), '56; b. Warren, Pa., 1934; p. Rev. Ernest A. and Gertrude Ristau Kaebnick; h. Richard Jeffery Alfriend III; res: 8225 Buffalo Ct., Norfolk, Va. 23518.

ALLEN, ALICE, Pubcty. and PR Cnslt.; Pubcty. Dir., J. B. Lippincott Company, 521 Fifth Ave., N.Y., N.Y. 10017, '66–'70; Hawthorn Bks., '63–'65; Walker & Co., '66; Publrs. Pubcty. Assn. (Pres., '69–'70; VP, '68–'69); Conn. Col. for Wm.; b. N.Y.C.; p. C. Edmonds and Helen McCreery Allen; res: 32 Gramercy Park S., N.Y., N.Y. 10003.

ALLEN, ANNE GILLESPIE, Dir., Anne Allen Associates, Educational Consultants, 2404 Wilshire Blvd., L.A., Cal. 90057; Cnslt., San Diego State Col., Univ. of Cal., and SW Reg. Lab. for Educ. Rsch. and Dev., educ. opp. pgms., speaker and participant in panel discussions at pfsnl. assns. and confs.; evaluator of compensatory educ. progs. at more than 75 cols., univs., educ. agcys., and nat. assn.; nwsp. and mag. Wtr. and Ed.; Nat. Assn. for Intergroup Rel. Offcls., PRSA, Am. Pers. and Guidance Assn., Am. Col. Pers. Assn., Nat. Educ. Assn., Cncl. for Exceptional Children, Cal. Pers. and Guidance Assn., NAACP, Nat. Assn. of Wm. Deans and Cnslrs., Commty. Svc. Org., Commty. Rel. Conf. of Southern Cal., EWA, Greater L.A. Press Club, AIGA; Mayor's and Distric Atty's Commty. Advisory Comm., L.A.; Who's Who of Am. Wm.; UCLA, BA, '43 (Distg. Californians); MS '51; PhD cand.; Tchrs. Col., Columbia Univ., MA, '46; h. Herb Allen; c. Carie, Anne, Laurel; res: 1636 San Onofre, Pacific Palisades, Cal. 90272.

ALLEN, BARBARA RAYBURN, Media Dir., H. H. Harney, Inc., 1600 M. St., Lincoln, Neb. 68508, '66–; Ed., USAID, Ankara, Turkey, '62–'63; Instr., Am. Sch., '56–'57; Asst. Med. Ed., Am. Osteopathic Assn., Chgo., '54–'56; Alpha Epsilon Rho, Turkish-Am. Wms. Cultural Soc. (Am. Pres., '61–'62); Cottey Jr. Col. for Wm., '46–'47; Univ. of Neb., BA, '50; b. Huron, S.D. 1929; p. Camden and Irene Deming Rayburn; h. Harold Allen; c. Carolyn Rae, Camden Whitney; res: 2320 Sheridan Blvd., Lincoln, Neb. 68502.

ALLEN, BELLE, Pres., Belle Allen, 900 N. Michigan Ave., Chgo., Ill. 60611, '52–; VP, Treas., William Karp Cnslt. Co., Inc., '60–; VP, Treas., Cultural Arts Surveys, Inc., '65–; special projects: Ill. Commn. on Technological Progress, '65–'67; Special Commtn. Program with The White House Press Off., '61; City Club of Chgo., Civic Assembly, '62–'65; Chgo. Press Club, Pubcty. Club of Chgo. (Distg. Svc. Aw., '68), Fashion Group, Indsl. Rels. Rsch. Assocs., Nat. Assn. of Intergroup Rels. Offcls., Welfare PR Forum; active in civic groups; Who's Who in PR; 2000 Wm. of Achiev.; Dic. of Intl. Biog.; Univ. of Chgo.; b. Chgo., Ill.; Isaac and Clara Allen.

ALLEN, CLARA VAN BUREN, Librn., Azusa Pacific College, Highway 66 at Citrus, Azusa, Cal. 91702, '67–; Lib. Cnslt., religious libs., '56–; Founder, Mgr., Librn's. Cooperative, '61–; Librn., L.A. County Public Lib., '64–'67; Librn., Fuller Theological Seminary, '48–'64; Librn., Psychology Prof., Nat. Bible Inst. (N.Y.C.), '43–'48; Sch. Librn., '33–'43; Auth., short story and one-act play; Lectr., theological rsch., '55–'64; Ed., Fuller Library Bul., '49–'60; Contrbr., articles to pfsnl. jnls.; San Gabriel Coord. Cncl., '64–; Cal. Lib. Assn., San Gabriel Wtrs. Assn. (Founder, Pres., '66–'67), Winner of Creative Writing Contest Southern Cal., '66; theological, cultural, pfsnl. assns.; N.Y. State Col. at Albany, BS (Lib. Sci.), '33; Nat. Bible Inst., BRE, '46; St. John's Univ., Bklyn., Grad. Work, '39; New Sch. of Social Rsch., '44–'47; Fuller Theological Seminary, '55–'60; b. Schenectady, N.Y., 1911; p. Edwin and Georgia Card Allen; res: 4809 N. Armel Dr., Covina, Cal. 91722.

ALLEN, DOROTHY JEAN, Colmst., Las Vegas Voice, P.O. Box 4038, Las Vegas, Nev. 89106, '69–; KTOO Radio; FaJah's Enterprises Public Relations; Wms. Dem. Club; res: 2108 Christina, N. Las Vegas, Nev. 89030.

ALLEN, EDITH BEAVERS, Wtr., non-fiction: "Bible Symbol Puzzles" ('70), "New Testament Bible Games" ('63), "Bridal Showers" ('69), others; Real Estate Broker, Herto, Inc., 2069 S. Druid Circle, Clearwater, Fla., '66–; Contrbr. to various mags.; Clearwater-Largo Bd. of Realtors; b. Berwind, W. Va., 1920; p. Charles Thomas and Bertha Belcher Beavers; h. Vivian (V.C.) Allen; c. Fred K., Dwight M.; res: 904 Sevard Ave., Clearwater, Fla. 33516.

ALLEN, GWENFREAD ELAINE, Free-lance Wtr.; Rsch. Assoc., Univ. of Hi., '47–'49; PR Dir., Honolulu Community Chest, '46–'47; Public Info. Specialist, U.S. War Manpower Commn., '44–'46; Ed., Hawaii Farm and Home, '39–'44; Edtl. Staff, Honolulu Star-Bulletin, '22–'44; Auth, "Hawaii's War Years 1941–'45" (Univ. of Hawaii Press, '50); Theta Sigma Phi (Honolulu Chptr. Past Pres.; Headliner Aw., '53), NLAPW (Honolulu Chptr. Past Pres.), ZONTA (Honolulu Club Past Pres.); Univ. of Hi., AB, '24 (Phi Beta Kappa, Alumni aw., '67); b. Denver, Colo., 1904; p. John and Gwenfread Morgan Allen; res: 3020 Kalakaua Ave., Honolulu, Hi. 96815.

ALLEN, HELENA GRONLUND, Auth.; Assoc. Prof. of Eng., Creative Writing, Cal. Baptist Col. and San Bernadino Valley Col.; Free-lance Wtr., Ed., and Auths. Rep. of five col. Eng. textbooks (Wm. C. Brown Company); Intl. Platform Assn., Cal. Wtrs. Guild; Who's Who of Am. Wm.; Univ. of Cal. at Berkeley, BA, '47; Grad. Work; p. Frederick and Helena Larson Gronlund; h. Paul F. Allen; c. Randall L.; res: 705 W. Highland Ave., Redlands, Cal. 92373.

ALLEN, MARYON PITTMAN, Weekly Colmst. for 14 daily Alabama newspapers, 363 N. St. S.W., Wash., D.C. 20024; Free-lance mag. wtr.; Wms. Ed., Sun Nwsps. (Birmingham, Ala.), '62–'64; Staff Wtr., The Birmingham News, '64; NLAPW, Ala. Wtrs. Conclave, Ala. Historical Commn., Ala. Art Commn., Congressional Club, 91st Congress Club, Birmingham Comm. of 100 for Wm. (charter mbr.), Ladies of the Senate Red Cross, numerous other charity and cultural orgs.; Who's Who of Am. Wm.; Who's Who in the South and Southwest; World's Who's Who of Commerce and Industry; Dic. of Intl. Biog.; 1st Pl. aw., Ala. Press Assn., '62–'64; numerous state and nat. aws. for fashion and food writing; Univ. of Ala. (Jnlsm. and Crtv. Writing); b. Meridian, Miss., 1925; p. John D. and Tellie C. Pittman; h. U.S. Sen. James Browning Allen; c. J. Sanford Mullins, III, John P. Mullins, James B., Jr., Maryon F.; res: 363 N. St. S.W., Wash., D.C. 20024 and 1321 Bellevue Dr., Gadsden, Ala. 35901.

ALLEN, PHYLLIS GENE, Public Svc. Dir., KOCO-TV, 3705 N.W. 63rd St. (P.O. Box 16538), Okla. City, Okla.

73116; AWRT; res: 4132 N.W. 62 Terr., Okla. City, Okla. 73112.

ALLEN, REGINA SOUDERS, Wms. Dir., Bdcstr., WAMD Radio, Harford County Broadcasting Company, P.O. Box 516, Aberdeen, Md. 21001, '57–; AWRT (Md. Chptr. Pres., '69–'70; VP, '68–'69; Secy., '67–'68; Harford Memorial Hosp. Ladies' Aux. (Pres. '67–'68); Soroptimist Fedn. of the Ams. (Harford-Cecil Counties Club Pres., '64–'66); aw., Md. TB Assn., '66; Inst. of Notre Dame; b. Balt., Md., 1913; p. Charles, Sr., and Sarah Eberling Souders; h. John Lawrence Allen; res: P.O. Box 516, Aberdeen, Md. 21001.

ALLEN, ROBERTA ETHRIDGE, Free-lance Wtr., Auth., Poet, '54–; Auth: "God With Us" ('67), "The Cammack Village Story" ('63); major feature articles: Arkansas Gazette, Arkansas Democrat, others, NEA Syndicate; PEN Women (Ark. Pioneer Br. Pres., '62–'64), WNBA, Poets Roundtable of Ark. (VP, '70–'71), Nat. Wtrs. Club; Who's Who of Am. Wm., Who's Who in the South and Southwest; Miss. Wms. Col., BA, '28; Columbia Univ., '37; b. Sandersville, Miss.; p. Mark D. and Mary Bostick Ethridge; h. Arthur A. Allen; c. Art M., Jim C.; res: 6604 Kenwood Rd., Little Rock, Ark. 72207.

ALLEN, RUTH FINNEY, Staff Mbr., Scripps-Howard Newspaper Alliance, 1013 13th St., N.W., Wash., D.C. 20005, '23–; Reptr. and City Ed., The Sacramento Star; Reptr., The San Francisco News; numerous mag. articles; WNPC, Theta Sigma Phi; San Jose State Col. (grad.); b. Chgo., Ill., 1898; p. John and Mary Morrison Finney; h. Robert S. Allen; res: 1525 28th St. N.W., Wash., D.C. 20007.

ALLEN, SARA ANN, Asst. Prof., Jnlsm., School of Journalism, University of Missouri, Jay H. Neff Hall, Columbia, Mo. 65201, '58–'69; Contrb. Wtr., Honolulu Advertiser, '56–'69; Wms. Pg. Ed., Feature Wtr., Douglas (Ariz.) Dispatch, '50–'56; Ed., WBA Fraternal Ins., '50–'56; WAC, WW II, '43–'46; Wms. Ed., Peekskill Star, Macy Nwsp. Chain, '28–'43; Reptr., Independence Examiner, '26–'27; Theta Sigma Phi, BPW (co-organizer, Independence, Mo. Chptr.), WAC Veterans; Univ. of Mo., BJ, '26, MA, '39; b. Deer Park, Mo. 1904; p. Emerson and Annie Hubbard Allen; res: 402 S. Ninth St., Columbia, Mo. 65201.

ALLEN, VICKI PACKER, Educ. Ed., Contra Costa Times, 1940 Mt. Diablo Blvd., Walnut Creek, Cal., 94596, '67–; News Reptr., Urbana (Ill.) News Gazette, '66–'67; Contra Costa Press Club aw., '68; Reader's Digest grants, '66, '65; Univ. of Ill., BS, (Jnlsm.), '66 (founding Ed., Oblique, Critique); b. Chgo., Ill., 1944; p. Paul and June Tarnopol Packer; h. Joseph Allen; res: 2516 Piedmont Ave., Berkeley, Cal. 94704.

ALLEN, VIRGINIA R., Ed., Co. Pubns., Lufkin Foundry & Machine Company, P.O. Box 849, Lufkin, Tex. 75901, '46–; Asst. Mgr., Lufkin C. of C., '46–; Area News Stringer, Houston Post, Houston Chronicle,

Beaumont Enterprise, '47–'50; numerous published trade articles; IEA (Dir., '55); ICIE (Aw. of Merit, '58), Tex. Press Wm., AAIE; Southern GA Assn. Aw., '65; Univ. of Tex., BJ, '46; b. Tyler, Tex. 1922; p. J. T. and Ruth Weeks Allen; res: 807 McGregor Dr., Lufkin, Tex. 75901.

ALLENDER, CORINNE HAYES, Head of Jnlsm. Employment Svc., Theta Sigma Phi, 6206 Castejon Dr., La Jolla, Cal. 92037, '68–; Employee Mags., Intl. Harvester,'46; Asst. Food Ed., Chgo. Daily News, '42; Food Ed., Rock Island Argus, '42; Cnslt., hosp. aux. nwsltrs.; Pubcty.; Free-lance Wtr.; Theta Sigma Phi, IEA; Univ. of Ia., BJ, '42; b. Owatonna, Minn., 1920; p. Donald and Mary Tulley Hayes; h. Dr. John S. Allender; c. Judy (Mrs. Richard W. Dierker), John, James, Jane; res: 6206 Castejon Dr., La Jolla, Cal. 92037.

ALLES, SYLVIA M., Media Byr./Planner, Smith/ Greenland Co., Inc., 1414 Avenue of the Americas, N.Y., N.Y. 10019, '65–; Media Mgr., Tatham-Laird (Chgo.), '64–'65; Bdcst. Supvsr., Post-Keyes-Gardner (Chgo.), '62–'64; Asst. Byr., North Adv. (Chgo.), '60–'62; b. Chgo., Ill., 1939; p. James and Stephanie Lech Alles; h. Peter Politis; c. Kristina.

ALLISON, ELSYE W., Soc. Ed., Kansas City Star, 18th and Grand Ave., Kan. City, Mo. 64108, '68–; Soc. Wtr., '66–'68; Wms. Ed., Independence Examiner, '62–'66; Nwsp. Reptr., Feature Wtr., Food Ed., Topeka (Kan.) State Jnl., '51–'57; Theta Sigma Phi; 1st Pl. aw., Mo. Press Assn., '66; Emba Mink Assn. Aw. for fur layout; b. Newton, Kan., 1927; h. (div.); c. Guy, John, Philip; res: 6441 Wornall Terr., Kan. City, Mo. 64113.

ALLISON, MARY L., Ed., Citation Press, Scholastic Magazines, Inc., 50 W. 44th St., N.Y., N.Y. 10036, '66–; PR, Pubns. Dir., Special Libs. Assn., '55–'66; Evaluations Ed., Educ. Film Lib. Assn., '50–'55; Auth., "The Mark Hopkins Controversy" ('50); Mt. Holyoke Col., BS, '47.

ALLOGGIAMENTO, NANCY THOMAS, Media Dir., Jameson Advertising Inc., 10 E. 44th St., N.Y., N.Y. 10017, '68–; Media Byr., '66–'68; Media Cnslt; Univ. of Ill., '55–'57 (Shi-Ai, '56); b. Palos Park, Ill., 1937; p. Warren and Ruth Martin Thomas; h. Alberto Alloggiamento; res: 60 Sutton Pl. S., N.Y., N.Y. 10022.

ALPERT, SYLVIE, Dir. of Pubcty. and Rights, Grossman Publishers, 125 A E. 19th St., N.Y., N.Y. 10003, '68–; Edtl., Farrar, Straus & Giroux; Doubleday; Prentice-Hall; Barnard Col., BA, '61; Tufts Univ., MA, '63; b. Brest, France; res: 320 E. 35th St., N.Y., N.Y. 10016.

ALSPAUGH, LILYAN M. Prof., Dept. of Mkt. and Commtns., Central Mich. Univ. of Mt. Pleasant, Mich., '64–; Exec. VP of PR and Commtns., Albros Engineering Company; Fac., Dept. of Commtns., Ferris State Col., Big Rapids, Mich., '60–'64; Dir., Commty. Rel. WKRC Radio-TV (Cinn., Oh.), '55–'58; numerous articles and European assigts.; AAUW

(past Branch Pres., State Pres., Nat. VP; Achiev. Aw., '52), SAA, AWRT, IPA, PRSA, AIA, Am. Mktng. Assn., Delta Kappa Gamma, Phi Mu (past Dist. Pres., Nat. Standards Chmn., Cent. Achiev. Aw., '52); Who's Who of Am. Wm., Outstanding Educators of Am., Crtv. and Successful Personalities of the World; Univ. of Chgo., PhB (Phi Beta Kappa, summa cum laude; Cit. Aw., '52); Oh. State Univ., MA (Econs., Mktng., Sociol.; outstanding alumnae, '47); PhD, Col. of Commtns. Arts, Mich. State Univ.; b. Chgo., Ill.; p. Frank R. Haas and Sarah E. Sanders; h. Ralph P. Alspaugh; res: Mt. Pleasant, Mich. 48858.

ALSTON, ELIZABETH, Food Ed., Look Magazine, Cowles Communications, Inc., 488 Madison Ave., N.Y., N.Y. 10022, '66–; Food Cnslt., offering PR, product dev. and mdsng. svcs. to food industry, '62–'66; Crtv. Food Svc., '60–'62; Tchr., French cooking, Cordon Bleu Cooking Sch. (London); Lectr. and Demonstrator, N.Y. State Expsn.; Silver Spoon Aw., Nat. Assn. for the Specialty Food Trade, '67; St. Felix Sch. (Southwold, Eng.); New Sch. for Social Rsch.; b. Lavenham, Suffolk, Eng., 1935; p. David and Bathia Davidson Alston; h. Richard Lansing.

ALTEPETER, Sr. MARY PAULINIA, O.S.F., Librn. (Lib. Admr.), University of Albuquerque, St. Josephs Pl., N.W., Albuquerque, N.M. 87120, '54–; Tchr., high schs., '45–'50 (Colo., N.M.); Elementary Schs., '25–'44 (Ind., Kan.); ALA, Catholic Lib. Assn., Gtr. Albuquerque Lib. Assn.; St. Francis Col., AB, '45; Our Lady of the Lake Col., MS (Lib. Sci.), '54; b. Dunnington, Ind., 1898; p. Theodore and Susan Leuck Altepeter; res: St. Josephs Pl., N.W., Albuquerque, N.M. 87120.

ALTER, PATRICIA ULRICH, Pubcty. Dir., WLBW-TV, L. B. Wilson, Inc., 3900 Biscayne Blvd., Miami, Fla. 33137, '60–; Pubcty., Mdsng., PR, WPST-TV, Public Svc. TV, Inc., '57–'60; articles, features, other works in local periodicals, papers, Bdcst. Trades; Theta Sigma Phi, Bdcst. Prom. Assn., Gtr. Adv. Club; Univ. of Miami, BBA, '60; b. Cinn., Oh., 1936; p. Emil and Ruth Wuelzer Ulrich; h. David B. Alter, III; c. David B., IV, Amie Patricia, Jennifer Leigh; res: 8721 S.W. 192 Terr., Miami, Fla. 33157.

ALTMAN, JULIE ANN, Reptr., Colmst., Pawtuxet Valley Daily Times, 1353 Main St., W. Warwick, R.I. 02893, '68–; Intern, CBS News (Wash., D.C.), '67; Colmst., R.I. Herald, '66, '67; Who's Who Among Students in Am. Univs.; Univ. of R.I., BA (Jnlsm.), '67; Wash. Jnlsm. Ctr., Cert., '67; b. Providence, R.I., 1946; p. Irving and Ruth Shaffrin Altman; res: 53 Holburn Ave., Cranston, R.I. 02910.

ALTMAN, MICHELLE KEVIN, Assoc. Cartoon Ed., Playboy, HMH Publishing Co., 919 N. Michigan Ave., Chgo., Ill. 60611, '66–; Girl Friday, Hugh M. Hefner, '65–'66; Corr., Playboy Clubs Intl., '64–'65; U.C.L.A., '59–'62; h. (div.); res: 3150 N. Sheridan Ave., Chgo., Ill. 60657.

ALTMAN, RUTH UNGER, Head of Radio/TV Dept., Farley Manning Associates, 342 Madison Ave., N.Y., N.Y. 10017, '67–; Acct. Coordr., Upjohn, '58–'66; Coordr. of Science Materials Ctr., '61–'62; Coordr. of 1st Educ. TV installation for Signal Corps (Camp Gordon, Ga.), '53–'54; Pubcty., The Lighthouse, '52; Free-lance Cnslt. and special projects, '62–'69; N.Y.U., BA; h. James Altman.

ALTOMARI, GRACE MARSLANO, AE, Doremus & Company, 120 Broadway, N.Y., N.Y. 10005, '65–; Asst. AE, '60–'65; Coordr., Wms. Div., Un. Cerebral Palsy of NYC, In., '55–'59; Secy.-Treas., Altomari Adv., '44–'54; Head Teller, Fiduciary Trust Co., '41–'43; N.Y. Fin. Advs., Kidney Fndn. of N.Y. (Offcr., Bd. of Govs.); b. Bklyn., N.Y.; p. Charles and Lucretia Petrulli Marslano; h. Michael Altomari; c. Grace L.; res: 1276 84th St., Bklyn., N.Y. 11228.

ALTSCHUL, ESTHER SAGER, Adm. VP, Journal Films, Inc., 909 W. Diversey Pkwy., Chgo., Ill. 60614, '66–; helped organize and build Journal Films for prod. and dist. of educ. films; directed co. mkt. and sls.; DAVI-NEA, EFLA, NAVA, Chgo. Film Cncl. (Bd. of Dirs., '66–'67); Univ. of Chgo., BA, '45; b. Chgo., Ill., 1924; p. Leon Sager and Hannah Shulman; h. Gilbert Altschul; c. David, Joel, Dan, Jeffrey; res: 1760 Clavey Rd., Highland Park, Ill. 60035.

ALWIN, SANDRA FRICKE, Bdcst. Traf. Mgr., N.W. Ayer & Son, Inc., 135 S. LaSalle St., Chicago, Ill. 60603, '68–; Assoc. Prodr., '67–'68; Prod. Coordr., '67; Traf. Coordr., '67; Traf. Coordr. other cos., '61–'67; Auth. of traf. manual; Northern Ill. Univ., '59–'60; b. Chicago, Ill., 1941; p. Walter G. and Daisy C. Williams Fricke; res: 1831 W. 107th St., Chgo., Ill. 60643.

AMATORA, Sr. MARY, O.S.F., Chmn., Dept. of Psych., Saint Francis College, 2701 Spring St., Ft. Wayne, Ind. 46808, '54–; Cnslt., Tchr., Rschr.; Dir., grad. cnslr. educ. program, '60–; Visiting Prof., Catholic Univ. of Am. (Wash., D.C.); Guest Lectr., Inst. on Mental Hygiene, Univ. of Detroit Grad. Sch.; Assoc. Ed., Education, '50–; Edtl. Bd., Catholic Psychological Record; Abstractor, Psych. Abstracts, '51–; Auth., four bks., incl. "The Queen's Portrait," extensive writings in jnls., nwsps., mags.; radio programs, child, adolescent cnsl., guidance, WOWO, two yrs.; Speaker, nat. pfsnl., reg., state convs.; Ind. Univ., BS (Hons. Student); Purdue Univ., MS, PhD (Hons. Student); res: 2705 Spring St., Ft. Wayne, Ind. 46808.

AMBROSE, LEE GALANT, Ed.-in-Chief, Columbia Forum, 605 W. 115th St., N.Y., N.Y. 10025, '68–; Co-ed., '66–'68; Mng. Ed., '65–'66; Ed., Wtr., UN, '63; Eng. Lang. Ed., ILO (Geneva), '61–'62; Sr. Ed., Harvard Univ. Press, '58–'61; Rsch. Asst., Inst. for Advanced Study (Princeton, N.J.), '49–'51; Sci. Writing Fellow, Rockefeller Inst., '64–'65; Auth., "People and Living" (U.N., '64); Univ. of Mich., BA, '46; b. Phila., Pa., 1923; p. Isaac and Sonia Galant; h. (div.); c. Adam, Ellen; res: 156 E. 79th St., N.Y., N.Y. 10021.

AMES, DOROTHY DEN, Dir. of PR, 92nd Street Young Men's and Young Women's Hebrew Assn., 1395 Lexington Ave., N.Y., N.Y. 10028, '62–; Dir. of PR, Jewish Family Svc., '60–'62; Free-lance Wtr., mag. articles; Colmst., True Story; Radio-TV Ed.; Contract Wtr., WCBS Columbia Sch. of the Air; Edtl. Wtr., CBJA News and Views; Cnslt., social worker recruitment comm.; Radio Wtrs. Guild, OPC, Wms. Strike for Peace, SANE; Hunter Col., BA, '41; Cornell Univ.; New Sch. for Social Rsch.; b. N.Y.C., 1923; p. Louis and Pauline Lipman Den; h. Allen Boretz; c. Jonathan Ames, Andrew Ames; res: 15 Vandam St., N.Y., N.Y. 10013.

AMES, ELINOR, Etiquette Ed., N.Y. News, 220 E. 42nd St., N.Y., N.Y. 10017; Asst. Child Guidance Ed.; Asst., Soc. Desk; gen. reptr.; Tchr. and Lectr., cols. and bus. groups; Auth: "Modern Etiquette," "Children's Table Manners," several articles on social protocol; Tchr: Columbia Univ., Fordham Univ., Pratt Inst., St. Joseph's Seminary; Modern teenage show, WPIX; participant, NBC's "Home Show;" appearances on TV shows; NWC (past Treas., past Rec. Secy.), Amateur Comedy Club, Nwsp. Guild, AFTRA; h. Walter Ranzini.

AMES, LOUISE BATES, Chief Psychologist and Assoc. Dir., Gesell Institute of Child Development, 310 Prospect St., New Haven, Conn. 06511, '67–; Dir. of Rsch., '50–'67; Asst. Prof., Rsch. Asst., Yale Univ. Med. Sch., '33–'50; Synd. Colmst., "Parents Ask"; TV show, "Child Behavior," WBZ (Boston, Mass.), '50–'53; "Guidelines: The Gesell Inst. Reports," syndicated radio show, '70; Auth. of 15 bks., 200 scientific articles and monographs; Univ. of Me., AB, '30; MA, '33; Yale Univ., PhD, '36; Univ. of Me., Hon. ScD, '57; Wheaton Col., Hon. ScD, '67; b. Portland, Me., 1908; p. Samuel and Annie Leach Bates; h. (div.); c. Joan (Mrs. Robert C. Chase); res: 283 Edwards St., New Haven, Conn. 06511.

AMON, RHODA SCHER, Reptr., Newsday, 550 Stewart Ave., Garden City, N.Y. 11530, '66–; L.I. Press; Newark (N.J.) Evening News; Nwsp. Wms. Assn. of N.Y., Newsp. Reptrs. Assn. of N.Y.; Upsala Col.; N.Y.U.; b. Newark, N.J., 1929; p. Harris Scher; h. Robert Amon; c. Robert Michael, Amelia Harriet; res: 56 Richards Rd., Port Washington, N.Y. 11050.

AMOURY, GLORIA, Wtr., short stories; Exec. Secy., Mystery writers of America, Hotel Seville, 29th St. and Madison Ave., N.Y., N.Y. 10016, '65–; Notre Dame Col. of S.I., BA; Columbia Univ., MS (Jnlsm.).

ANASTASI, ANNE, Prof. and Chmn. Dept. of Psych., Fordham University. N.Y., N.Y. 10458, '68–; Prof., '51–'68; Assoc. Prof., '47–'51; Asst. Prof., Queens Col., '30–'39; Cnslt., Ford Fndn., Rio de Janeiro, Brazil, '68; Visiting Prof., Univ. of Wis., summer '51; University of Minn., summer '58; Dir. of Rsch. Projects sponsored by U.S. Air Force, Nat. Inst. of Mental Health, and Ctr. for Urban Educ.; Ed., "Testing Problems In Perspective," ('66), "Individual Differences" ('65); Textbk. Auth., "Fields of Applied Psychology," ('64), "Psychological Testing" ('68), "Differential Psychology" ('58); more than 100 monographs and jnl. articles; Am. Psychological Assn. (Bd. of Dirs., '56–'59; '68–'71; Pres. Div. of Evaluation and Measurement, '65–'66; Pres. Div. of Gen. Psych., '56–'57; Rec. Secy., '52–'55), Am. Psychological Fndn. (Pres., '65–'67; Trustee, '65–'72), Eastern Psychological Assn. (Pres., '46–'47), Psychometric Soc., Psychonomic Soc., Sigma Xi; Barnard Col., BA, '28 (Phi Beta Kappa, Duror Memorial Fellowship); Columbia Univ., PhD, '31; Hon. LittD, Univ. of Windsor, Canada, '67; h. John Porter Foley, Jr.

ANDERS, NEDDA C., Ed.-in-Chief and Co-publr., Founder, Hearthside Press, 381 Park Ave. S., N.Y., N.Y. 10016.

ANDERSEN, ESTHER NYBY, Assoc. Media Dir., The Griswold-Eshleman Co., 1 E. Wacker Dr., Chgo., Ill. 60201, '68–; Media Supvsr., Earle Ludgin & Co., '61–'68; Sr. Timebyr., MacFarland, Aveyard, '58–'61; McCann-Erickson, '54–'57; AWRT, Chgo. Cncl. of Foreign Relations; Northwestern Univ.; b. Copenhagen, Denmark; res: 2201 Central, Evanston, Ill. 60201.

ANDERSON, ANNE SONOPOL, Free-lance Wtr., '60–; Assoc. Ed., Ed. of Kitchens and Equipment, Better Homes & Gardens, '52–'60; Am. Home Econs. Assn., Theta Sigma Phi (Des Moines Chptr. Jane Arden Aw., '60); Univ. of Ill., BS (Jnlsm.), '52; h. Curtiss Anderson; res: N.Y., N.Y.

ANDERSON, BARBARA JEANNEE, Actress, "Ironsides" TV Series, Universal Studio, Universal City, Cal.; SAG, AFTRA; Emmy, Best Supporting Actress in a Series, '68; Second Emmy nomination; Memphis State Univ.; b. Bklyn., N.Y.; p. George and Kathleen Jeter Anderson.

ANDERSON, BEATRICE PATE, Soc. Ed., Orange Coast Daily Pilot, PO. Box 1560, Costa Mesa, Cal. 92626, '62–; Reptr., Press-Courier (Oxnard, Cal.), '60–'62; Soc. Ed., Ojia Valley News, '58–'60; Soc. Ed., Desert Valley News Herald (Apple Valley, Cal.), '55–'58; Soc. Ed., Garden Grove News, '50–'55; Orange County Press Club, (Aws., '54, '68, '69), Ventura County Press Club (Secy., '60–'62), Theta Sigma Phi; special recognition aw., Orange County Heart Assn., '64, '65, '67 and Newport Harbor ZONTA Club, '67; Cal. Nwsp. Publrs. Assn., '64, '65; Long Beach City Col., '49–'50; b. Elysian, Minn., 1927; p. John and Alice Lawless Pate; h. Norman R. Anderson; res: 5116 Seashore Dr., Newport Beach, Cal. 92660.

ANDERSON, BEVERLY, Talent Agt., Pres., Beverly Anderson Agency, 1472 Broadway, N.Y., N.Y. 10036, '58–; h. Leonard Traube.

ANDERSON, BEVERLY STEIN, Mng. Partner, Atlanta Models & Talent, 67 Peachtree Park Dr., N.E., Atlanta, Ga. 30309, '63–; Bd. of Dirs., Anderson Enterprises; 1969–; free-lance retail copy, Rich's, Inc., '63; Retail Adv., Sears, Roebuck, '61–'62; Prod. Dept., Harris & Weinstein, '60; Adv. Dept., Stein Printing Co., '59–'60; Pfsnl. Model's Assn. (past Pres.), AWRT, Theta Sigma Phi, Atlanta Adv. Club, Atlanta C. of C., Atlanta Convention Bur., Greater Atlanta Arts Cncl.; Rollins Col., '54–'55; Univ. of Ga., AB (Jnlsm.), '58 (Dean's List; Who's Who Among Students in Am. Cols. and Univs.); b. Atlanta, Ga., 1937; p. Jack and Bess Segal Stein; h. John S. Anderson; c. five; res: 5905 Long Island Dr., N.W., Atlanta, Ga. 30328.

ANDERSON, ELIZABETH BROWNING, Fiction, TV-Screen Free-lance Wtr., '66–; Exec. Asst. to Prodr. of TV series; free-lance PR, prom., Ft. Lauderdale, Fla.; S. Cal. AWRT (Bd. of Dirs.), Hollywood Wms. Press Club, WGA (West), NATAS, Air Force Assn.; military Ltrs. of Commendation; Strayers Col.; Columbus Univ.; b. Md., 1916; p. J. Frank and May Williams Browning; c. Mrs. Wendy Anderson, Gayle, Nancy; res: 1067 Glenhaven Dr., Pacific Palisades, Cal. 90272.

ANDERSON, ERICA, Film Prodr., Wtr., Pres., Albert Schweitzer Friendship House, Hurlburt Rd., Great Barrington, Mass. 01230, '67–; Free-lance Dir., Cameraman, Doc. Films; Films, Bks. on Dr. Albert Schweitzer ("Oscar," AMPAS, '58); Hon. Deg., MacMurray Col., '58; b. Vienna, Austria; res: Hurlburt Rd., Great Barrington, Mass. 01230.

ANDERSON, EVA DABBS, Religious News Ed., State-Record, Box 1333 (Shop Rd.), Columbia, S.C. 29202; Asst. to City Ed., '53–; S.C. Press Wms. Assn.; Ed. of Newsprint house organ, three-time 2nd Place State winner, Second Place Nat. Aw., '68; Univ. of S.C.; b. Columbia, S.C.; p. Jesse and Ora Wall Dabbs; h. Julius Anderson; c. Eve Dabbs, Julius J., Jr.

ANDERSON, H. JEAN, Former Librn.; organized sch. libs. in Shaker Heights, Oh. and was first Coordr.; ALA, WNBA; Wellesley, BA, '18; Corlefreate Lib. Sch., BS, '23; b. West Hoboken, N.J.; res: 12700 Shaker Blvd., Cleve., Oh. 44120.

ANDERSON, HAZEL ANNETTE, Wms. Ed., Hastings & Sons Publishing Co., 38 Exchange St., Lynn, Mass. 01901, '40–; Radio Ed., Lynn Daily Evening Item, '31–'40; Quota Club (Lynn Pres., '54–'55); Bd. of Dirs: Pfsnl. Wms. Club of Boston ('48–'51), Lynn Home for Young Wm., Gregg Neighborhood House of Lynn, Wms. Bureau; Burdett Col.; b. Rockport, Mass. 1909; p. Carl and Annie Gustafson Anderson; res: 52 Broadway, Lynn, Mass. 01904.

ANDERSON, JEAN, Contrb. Ed., Venture, 488 Madison Ave., N.Y., N.Y. 10022, '67–; Sr. Ed., '63–'67; Mng. Ed., Ladies' Home Journal, '63; Edtl. Assoc., '62–'63; Asst. Ed., '59–'62; Edtl. Asst., '57–'59; Wms. Ed., The Raleigh Times, '56–'57; Wms. Ed., N.C. Agricultural

Ext. Svc., '52–'55; Auth., "Henry the Navigator—Prince of Portugal" ('69), "Food is more than Cooking" ('68), "Art of American Indian Cooking" ('65); Omicron Nu, Phi Kappa Phi, Am. Home Econs. Assn., Home Econsts. in Bus., Columbia Jnlsm. Alumnae; Southern Wms. Achiev. Aw. ('63); Miami Univ. (Oh.), '47–'49; Cornell Univ., BS, '51 (1st in class); Columbia Univ., MS (Jnlsm.), '57 (Pulitzer Traveling Scholarship, '57); b. Raleigh, N.C., 1930; p. Dr. Donald and Marian Johnson Anderson; res: 13 Bank St., N.Y., N.Y. 10014.

ANDERSON, KAY, VP, Pictorial Productions, Inc., 650 S. Columbus Ave., Mt. Vernon, N.Y. 10550, '50–; Pres., Vari-Vue Intl.; CBS, '42–'45; The Wings Club, '41–'42; The Sperry Corp., '37–'41; PPI Dir., Pension Trust Trustee, AWNY, Sls. Exec. Club; The Park Sch., Nutley, N.J., grad. '27; b. N.Y.C., 1912; p. James and Rose-Catherine Butler Griffin; h. S. Van Zandt Schreiber; c. Katherine Jean (Mrs. Alfons Wagner), Patricia Anne (Mrs. Thomas A. Reilling); res: 86 Wykagyl Terr., New Rochelle, N.Y. 10804.

ANDERSON, LAURA M., Media Dir.-Prod. Mgr., Cherry Enterprises, Inc., 614 Broad St., Beloit, Wis. 53511, '64; formerly Art Dir/Off. Mgr.; Corp. Secy., Cherry & Associates, Inc.; Rockford Adv. Club Chmn.; b. Rockford, Ill., 1935; p. Edward F. and Ruth A. Crandell Stucke; c. Dawn Carol, Mark Dana; res: 2270 Staborn Dr., Beloit, Wis. 53511.

ANDERSON, LILLIAN WALLIN, AE and Copywtr., Goodman & Associates, Inc., 1010 First Nat. Building, Ft. Worth, Tex. 76107; Retail Adv., Stripling's, The Fair, Titche's, Monning's '56–'66; Betty Crocker Kitchens, Gen. Mills, '48–'53; AWRT (Ft. Worth Chptr. Bd. Mbr., '68–'69), Theta Sigma Phi (Bd. Mbr., '68–'69), BPW, Press Club of Ft. Worth, Adv. Club of Ft. Worth, Eastern Star (past Matron); Univ. of Minn., BS (Home Econs. and Adv.); b. Mpls., Minn.; p. Axel and Ruth Englund Wallin; h. Raymond M. Anderson; res: 4821 Bryce, Ft. Worth, Tex. 76107.

ANDERSON, LOIS JANET, Dir., Prom.-Distrb., Broadcasting & Film Commission, National Council of Churches, 475 Riverside Dr., N.Y., N.Y. 10027, '65–; Asst. Dir., Radio-TV Dept., Am. Baptist Conv., '53–'65; worked on numerous commns.; Dir. of various commtns. workshops, seminars, U.S. & Europe; Ed., "How You Can Broadcast Religion"; Film consultant, N.Y. Worlds' Fair, St. Clement's Film Assoc.; RPRC (Nat. Secy., '64–'65; Bd. of Governors, '62–), Assn. for Pfsnl. Bdcst. Educ. of the NAB; Mary Washington Col., Univ. of Va., BS, '47; b. Evanston, Ill. 1924; p. Eugene and Margareta Nelson Anderson; res: 345 E. 19th St., N.Y., N.Y. 10003.

ANDERSON, MARIE WILLARD, Wms. Ed., The Miami Herald, 1 Herald Plaza, Miami, Fla. 33101, '59–; Wms. Dept., '50–'59; Miami News, '46–'50; Recept., Batten, Barton Durstine & Osborn, '46; Fla. Wms. Press Club (Gen. Excellence Wms. Pgs., '59–'68), Theta Sigma Phi (Nat. Headliner Aw., '64); J. C. Penney-Univ. of Mo. Aw. for Wms. Pgs., 1st, '60, '61, '64, 2nd., '63; Duke Univ., AB (Eng.), '37 (Phi Beta Kappa), Katharine Gibbs, '38–'39, Secy. Cert.; b. Pensacola, Fla. 1916; p. Robert H. and Marie Willard Anderson; res: 2840 S.W. 28 Terr., Miami, Fla. 33133.

ANDERSON, MARTHA, Free-lance Ed., Boxwood No. 12, Old Lyme, Conn. 06371; former Ed., Nat. Bureau of Econ. Rsch.

ANDERSON, MAXINE L., Owner, The Commercial Way, Comml. Prodr., Casting Dir., 9172 Sunset Blvd., L.A., Cal. 90069, '63–; Comml. Prodr. Radio-TV, North Advertising; Agcy. Prodr., Radio, Biow Co. Advertising.

ANDERSON, MARJORIE VALLEY (pseud: Mary Cullen), Fashion Ed., Dir., Mary Cullen's Cottage, The Oregon Journal, 1320 S.W. Broadway, Portland, Ore. 97201, '66–; Fashion Wtr., Food Wtr., '64–'65; Ore. Press Wm., Electrical Wms. Roundtable; 1st pl. aw., Fashion Writing, '68; 1st pl. aw., Food, Fashion writing, '69; Hon. mention, nat. home appliances writing, '68; Wash. State Univ., BA, '50; b. Shelton, Wash., 1928; p. William and Marjorie Swan Valley; h. A. Reinold Anderson; c. Robert Louis, John William; res: 1806 Laurel Dr., Newberg, Ore. 97132.

ANDERSON, NANCY LEONE, PR Dir., The Halle Brothers Company, 1228 Euclid Ave., Cleve., Oh. 44115, '68–; Training Rep., '66–'67; Eng. Tchr., Copley Bd. of Educ., '63–'66; Wms. Adv. Club of Cleve., AWRT, NEA, other educ. orgs., Copley Tchrs. Assn. (VP, '65–'66), Kent State, BS (Educ.), '63; b. Akron, Oh., 1941; p. Robert H. and Laura L. Bowman Anderson; res: 24455 Lake Shore Blvd., Americana E. #117, Euclid, Oh. 44123.

ANDERSON, PATRICIA LOUISE, Wms. Ed., WSB Radio, 1601 W. Peachtree St., Atlanta, Ga. 30309, '67–; Wtr., educ. TV, WGTV, Athens, Ga.; AWRT, Theta Sigma Phi; AP aws., '67–'68; Hood Col., '63–'65; Univ. of R.I., '65; Univ. of Ga., AB (Jnlsm.), '67; b. Highpoint, N.C. 1945; res: 1487 Druid Valley Dr., Apt. F N.E., Atlanta, Ga. 30329.

ANDERSON, PAULINE HARRIET, Dir., The Andrew Mellon Library, The Choate School, Wallingford, Conn. 06492, '50–; Pubns. incl. "The Library in the Independent School" ('68); Contrbr., pfsnl. jnls.; Independent Sch. Lib. Cnslt., '62–; Librn., Abbot Acad. (Andover, Mass.), '45–'50; Head, Eng. Dept., Ilion (N.Y.) Sr. HS, '43–'45; ALA, several state, reg. lib. assns.; Baritmayer Fellow, '66–'67; Keuka Col., '39; N.Y. State Univ., BLS, '43; b. Broadalbin, N.Y., 1918; p. Donald and Bertha Brooks Anderson; res: 71 N. Main St., Broadalbin, N.Y. 12025.

ANDERSON, PHYLLIS LORRAINE, Publr., New Glarus Post, 117 Fifth Ave., New Glarus, Wis. 53574, '64–; Ed., Proviso Herald (Maywood, Ill.); Asst. Ed.,

Oak Leaves (Oak Park); News Ed., The Journal (Franklin Park); Wis. Press Wm. (Past Pres.; several aws., '67–'69), Wis. Press Assn. (several aws., '65–'68), NFPW, numerous civic orgs.; b. Waupaca County, Wis.; p. John and Isabelle Hales Anderson; c. Brian C. Christenson; res: 318 Fifth Ave., New Glarus, Wis. 53574.

ANDERSON, RUTH IRENE, Prof., Bus. Adm., North Texas State University, Denton, Tex. 76203, '53–; Auth., Bus. Textbooks; Natl. Bus. Educ. Assn., Tex. Col. Tchrs. Assn., BPW (Denton Chptr. Pres.), Altrusa, Tex. Bus. Educ. Assn. Past VP, Un. Bus. Educ. Assn., Delta Pi Epsilon (Nat. Pres., '63–'65); Who's Who in Am. Educ.; Who's Who in the South and Southwest; Who's Who in Tex.; Who's Who of Am. Wm; Contemporary Auths.; Grove City Col., BS, '41; Ind. Univ., EdD, '46; b. Millerton, Pa., 1919; p. Ralph and Pearle Blakeslee Anderson; res: 810 Stanley St., Denton, Tex. 76201.

ANDERSON, RUTH WARREN, Wms. Ed., Shawnee News Star, Stauffer Publication, 215 N. Bell, Shawnee, Okla. 74801, '54–; Adv.; Adv., Seminole Producer; Altrusa (Shawnee Chptr. Pres., '58–'59; former Dir., Rec. Secy.; Ed., Dist. Eight Publn., '54–'55), BPW (Shawnee Chptr. Pres., '53–'54; Dist. Dir.; Ed., "Headband and Feather," '53–'54), DAR, First Christian Ch.; Okla. Baptist Univ., '55; b. Smithshire, Ill., 1905; p. Horace and Georgia Youmans Hodgson; h. 1. Charles W. Warren; 2. Frank Anderson; c. Charles Wayne Warren, Patricia Anne Home; res: 524 W. Kirk, Shawnee, Okla. 74801.

ANDERSON, SYLVIA FINLAY, Prof. Emeritus, University of Washington, Seattle, Wash. 98105, Retired Tchr., Eng., 46 yrs.; Co-auth., "Our Changing World" (Harpers, '39); Auth., "Westward to Oregon" (Heath, '58; revsd., '65); Ed., "Good Reading" Fine Arts Sec., '38–'56; Advisor, Nat. Cncl. of Tchrs. of Col. Eng., '60–'63; Theta Sigma Phi, Intl. Platform Assn., BPW; Univ. of Mont., '16–'18; Univ. of Wash., BA, '20; MA, '23 (Phi Beta Kappa, Alpha Chptr. VP); b. Killarney, Manitoba, Can., 1897; p. James and Sara Fisher Finlay; h. John E. Anderson (dec.); res: 5114 29th Ave. N.E., Seattle, Wash. 98105.

ANDERSON, VIOLET DEVOWE, Ed., Indian Valley Record, 222 Mill, Greenville, Cal. 95947, '62–; '60–'62; Greenville Soroptimist Club (Pres., '66–'67); Girl Scout aw. for pubcty., '69; Order of Eastern Star (Worthy Matron, '67), PTA (Pres., '55); b. Woodville, Mich., 1917; p. Carl E. and Emma Modrow Devowe; h. Travis O. Anderson; c. Raymond L., Janet Ruth Kyle, Judy Gail Brooks; res: E. Shore Lake Almanor, P.O. Box 125, Greenville, Cal. 95947.

ANDRE', MARJORIE COSTER, AE, Media Dir., Pacific National Advertising Agency, 310 Morgan Bldg., Portland, Ore. 97205, '66–; Prod. Mgr., '65; Media Dir., AE, Spokane Off., '60–'64; Adv. Mgr., King Bldg. Supply Stores, '65; Media Dir., Griffis/Smith

Assn., '64; Program Dir., Copywtr., KXLL Radio (Missoula, Mont.), '58–'60; Mont. State Univ., '51; b. Red Lodge, Mont.; p. Raymond A. and Marjorie H. Coster; h. Robert W. Andre', Jr.; c. Leslie Elaine, Lane C.; res: 23855 S.W. Boones Ferry Rd., Tualatin, Ore. 97062.

ANDRE, REBECCA A., Asst. to the Pres., Air Check Services Corp. of the World & Videochex, 1743 W. Nelson St., Chgo., Ill. 60657, '66–; b. Chicago, Ill., 1949; p. Louis A. and Mary B. Johnson Andre; res: Naked City, Roselawn, Ind. 46372.

ANDREEVA, TAMARA, Free-lance Wtr., Translator; formerly Fashion Ed., CBS, N.Y.C. and Hollywood, Cal.; Reptr., Chicago Times; Soc. Ed., Herald-Press Pubns.; Hollywood Corr., King Features; Assoc. Ed., Magazine Digest; articles in Sports Afield, True, Arizona Highways, American Home, numerous other nat. mags.; Wash. Nwsp. Wms. Club; Nev. State Publrs. Assn. Best Writing Aw., '61–'62; U.C.L.A., BA (Eng.); b. St. Petersburg, Russia, '17; p. Dimitri and Julia Andreeva; h. (div.); res: P.O. Box 644, Indio, Cal. 92201.

ANDREN, CAROL, Free-lance Wtr.; Translator of bks., films, articles (Swedish, German, Spanish, Danish, Norwegian, French); Auth., mag. articles; Am. Translators Assn.; b. Lund, Sweden; p. A. Severin and Maria Andren; res: 153 E. 57th St., N.Y., N.Y.10022.

ANDREWS, HELEN RILLING, Head Librn., Erie Public Library, South Perry Sq., Erie, Pa. 16501, '49–; Pa. Lib. Assn., ALA; Lake Erie Col., BA, '31; Columbia Univ., BS, '32; b. Erie, Pa., 1909; p. Emil L. and Henrietta Cameron Rilling; h. C. B. Andrews; res: 630 W. Ninth St., Erie, Pa. 16502.

ANDREWS, MARY EVANS, Auth: "When Jamestown Was Colonial Capital" (Garrard, '70), "Hostage to Alexander" (McKay, '61), three other juv. bks.; mag. articles; Soc. of Midland Auths., Ill. Wms. Press Assn. (VP, '62–'64), WNBA (Corr. Secy., '63–'64), Chgo. Children's Reading Round Table (Pres., '64–'65); Children's Reading Round Table Aw., '70; 8 vocational guidance paperbacks, Chgo. Inst. for Rsch., '62–'65; short stories & articles—in 6 elementary readers, Sci. Rsch. Assn., '65–'68; NFPW juv. bk. aw., '54; Friends of Am. Wtrs. children's bk. aw., '62; Boys' Clubs of Am. cit., '56; Randolph-Macon Wms. Col., BA, '30; b. Mobile, Ala.; p. Frank and Emma Childs Evans; h. A. Gregory Andrews; res: 108 Monticello Ave., Annapolis, Md. 21401.

ANDREWS, MILDRED GWIN, Asst. to Pres., American Textile Machinery Association, 1730 M Street, N.W., Wash., D.C. 20036, '52–; Cnslt. PR, Textile Industry Committee, Fieldcrest Mills and the Irving Trust Company of N.Y., '46–'50; Exec. Secy., Southern Combed Yarn Spinners Assn., '30–'46; War Production Bd.'s Comm. on Indsl. Salvage, World War II; Founder, ATMA Press Workshop, Am. Soc. of Assn.

Execs., Nat. Assn. of Expan. Mgrs.; b. Greenwood, Miss., 1903; p. Samuel L. and Sally Humphreys Gwin; h. Elmer F. Andrews (dec.); c. Gwin Barnwell Dalton; res: 6510 Sardis Rd., Charlotte, N.C. 28211.

ANDREWS, NAOMI FINE, Dir., Adv. Opns., Columbia Broadcasting System, 51 W. 52nd St., N.Y., N.Y. 10019, '68–; Dir. Adv., '62–'68; Copy Chief, '56–'61; Copywtr., '51–'56; Sponsor mag. Media Prom. Aw.; finalist, Andy Aw., '67; free-lance articles; Hunter Col., BA, '45; b. N.Y.C., 1925; p. Charles and Mary Frankfort Fine; res: 6 E. 65th St., N.Y., N.Y. 10021.

ANDREWS, VIRGINIA GARLAND, VP, Southeastern Services, 654 First St., Macon, Ga. 31202, '64–; VP, Southern Assn. Svcs.; Asst. Treas., Planned Services (Atlanta); Asst. Secy., Discount Centers of the South (Tifton); Dir., J & L Prod. (Macon); Mercer Univ., AB, '51; b. Screven County, Ga., 1930; p. Loyd and Mary Zeigler Garland; h. Joe W. Andrews, Jr.; c. Laura, Joe W. III; res: 720 Forest Ridge Dr. W., Macon, Ga. 31204.

ANDROS, ELEANOR ALBERT, Mgr. Employee Pubns., Daniel J. Edelman, Inc. 221 N. LaSalle St., Chgo., Ill. 60601, '57–; Ed., Toni Topics, The Toni Co., '51–'57; Ed. Asst., Kiwanis Magazine, '49–'51; Assoc. Ed., Chinese News Svc., '42–'49; IEA, ICIE, Theta Sigma Phi; Am. Heritage Fndn. aw.; Northwestern Univ., PhB (Jnlsm.); b. Chgo., Ill., 1922; p. Mary Albert; h. James H. Andros; c. Rebecca. res: 1720 S. Linden Ave., Park Ridge, Ill. 60068.

ANDRUSKEVITCH, BETTY AKERS, Partner, Corp. Secy., Baker Advertising, Inc., 200 S. Grand Ave., E. Springfield, Ill. 62704, '67–; Continuity Dir., WMAY Radio, '61–'67; Feature Corr., Ill. State Journal, '54–'64; Reptr., Feature Wtr., Pic. Ed., Ill. State Register, '44–'51; Sangamon County Hist. Soc. (Bd. of Dirs., '61–'63); first prize, continuity, Stuart Broadcasting Co., Lincoln, Neb., '66; b. Springfield, Ill., 1926; p. Jean H. and Ernestine Miller Akers; h. Edward Andruskevitch; c. Michael Edward, Paul Martin; res: RR 2, Pleasant Plains, Ill. 62677.

ANDRY, DONNA BILLARD, PR Dir., Leonard Rattner Co., Inc., 114 E. 32nd St., N.Y., N.Y. 10016, '67–; b. N.Y.C., 1937; p. William and Elsie Simmons Billard.

ANGEL, BEVERLY WOOD, Adm. Secy., Western Video Industries, Inc., 1541 N. Vine St., Hollywood, Cal. 90028, '68–; Mgr., Guest Rels. ABC, '58–'68; Asst. to Dir., Labor Rels. '49–'58; Off. Mgr., McCann-Erickson, '42–'46; Asst. to Art Dir., Cal. Bank, '41–'42; Off. Supvsr., KHJ-TV, '35–'37; Talent, KFAC, '32–'33; C. of C., Hollywood Visitors and Convention Bur. (Bd. of Dir.), Radio and TV Wm. of Southern Cal., AWRT, Pacific Pioneer Bdcstrs. (Charter Mbr.); Univ. of Southern Cal., '32–'35; b. L.A., Cal., 1915; p. Glen and Melva Kantz Wood; h. George Angel; c. Mrs. Glenna Becker; res: 4303 Irvine Ave., Studio City, Cal. 91604.

ANGLUND, SANDRA PHILLIPS, AE, PR, Barlow/Johnson Inc., 968 James St., Syracuse, N.Y. 13203, '68–; Asst. Dir. PR, State Univ. of N.Y. Upstate Med. Ctr., Syracuse, N.Y., '65–'68; AE, Robert D. Eckhouse & Assoc., N.Y., N.Y., '64–'65; Asst. AE, Lobenz Public Relations Co., N.Y., N.Y.; PRSA (Central N.Y. Chptr. Treas., '67–'69), Theta Sigma Phi; Syracuse Univ., AB, '63; b. Englewood, N.J., 1941; p. John and Janet Ryan Phillips; res: 210 Dickerson Dr., Camillus, N.Y. 13031.

ANN, DORIS, (SCHARFENBERG), Exec. Prod. Mgr., Religious Progs., National Broadcasting Company, 30 Rockefeller Plaza, N.Y., N.Y. 10020, '51–; formerly Placement Mgr.; BPW Professional Wm. of the Yr., '58; McCall's Golden Mike Aw., '62; Bucknell Univ., BA; N.Y.U., MA (educ.); Muhlenberg Col., LLD (hon.); p. Anna Scharfenberg; b. Newark, N.J.; res: 50 Sutton Pl., S., N.Y., N.Y. 10022.

ANNIXTER, JANE (Jane Comfort Sturtzel), Co-auth., nine fictional works for young people in collaboration with husband, Paul Annixter (Howard A. Sturtzel); two adult books published under maiden name; res: 2581 Bonita Way, Laguna Beach, Cal. 92651.

ANN-MARGRET, Actress: Motion Pictures and TV, Rogallan Productions, 9000 Sunset Blvd., L.A., Cal. 90069; Theatre Owners of Am. Outstanding Boxoffice Star of the Yr. Aw.; Pres. Johnson Special Cit. for outstanding performance throughout tour of Vietnam and Near East; Northwestern Univ.; b. Stockholm, Sweden, 1943; p. Gustave and Anna Ollson; h. Roger Smith.

ANSBERRY, LOUISE STEINMAN, VP, Bell & Stanton, 909 Third Ave., N.Y., N.Y. 10022; Intl. Acc. Supvsr., John Moynahan & Co., '66–'67; Intl. AE, Ruder & Finn Inc., '61–'66; Wash. Nwsp. Corr., Lancaster, Pa., Nwsps., '52–'61; Exec. Secy. to U.S. Senator James Duff, '50–'52; Wash. Corr., Bascom Timmons Bureau, '47–'50; Am. Wms. Press Club, 1925 F Street Club (Wash., D.C.), Sulgrave Club (Wash., D.C.); Finch Jr. Col.; Katharine Gibbs Secretarial Sch.; b. Baltimore, Md., 1930; p. Hale Steinman; c. Louise, Hale; res: 146 Central Park W., N.Y., N.Y. 10023.

ANSBRO, MARY CATHARINE, Ed., "Water in the News," Soap and Detergent Association, 485 Madison Ave., N.Y., N.Y. 10022, '65–; Asst. Ed., Publicist, Texaco; Wms. Ed., The Daily Argus (Mt. Vernon); Chemical PR Assn., Pubcty. Club of N.Y., Catholic Inst. of the Press, Nat. Pollution Control Fndn.; AAUW, Spanish Inst.; Col. of New Rochelle, BA (magna cum laude); b. Mt. Vernon, N.Y.; p. Walter and Anna Anderson Ansbro; res: 83 Maple Ave., Pelham, N.Y. 10803.

ANSCOMBE, DOROTHY IRELAND, Asst. to Program Dir., WGR-Radio, Taft Broadcasting Co., 184 Barton St., Buffalo, N.Y. 14213, '63–; Sls. Dept., Prod., Prom. Work, '60–'63; Radio-TV Dept., Comstock Adv. Agcy., '58–'59; PR Dir., Public Svc. Dir., Wms. Dir., WKBW-Radio, '50–'58; "Kay Cooke's Kitchen Party,"

'53–'58; Ernst and Ernst Accounting, '40–'46; Adv. Wm. of Buffalo (Treas., '57; VP, '58; Pres., '59–'61), AWRT (Western N.Y. Chptr. Pres., '60–'61, '67–'69; VP, '66); N. Park Bus. Col., '35–'38; b. Buffalo, N.Y., 1916; p. Joseph and Kathryn Boehm Ireland; h. Arthur Anscombe, Jr.; res: 246 Wallace Ave., Buffalo, N.Y. 14216.

ANTELL, JOAN BARKON, Asst. Ed., Current History, 12 Old Boston Rd., Wilton, Conn. 06880, '58–; Edtl. Asst., '56–'58; Auth., mag. articles; Co-ed., with others, "Current History Review of 1959"; Dir. Mail Copywtr.; articles selected among Ten Best Magazine Articles of Month; Who's Who of Am. Wm.; Conn. Col., BA, '55; b. Bridgeport, Conn., 1934; p. Paul and Beatrice Gordon Barkon; h. Herbert D. Antell; c. Andrew Gordon, Pamela Emily, Matthew Eric; res: 12 Greenwood Lane, Westport, Conn. 06880.

ANTES, EDNA DWINELL, VP, Corp. Secy., Wtr., Fairfield Echo Publishing Company, Inc., Fairfield, Oh., 05014, 60–; Corr., Cinn. Enquirer, Cinn. Post & Times-Star; Ed., Echo, '61–'66; Auth, History Textbooks; numerous civic orgs., aws.; Hamilton Bus. Col., '33; b. Hamilton, Oh., 1913; p. Harry and Georgianna Duncil Dwinell; h. Charles Antes; c. Ernest, Suzanne Antes Merkle; res: 270 Cole Dr., Fairfield, Oh. 45014.

ANTHONY, CAROLYN TAYLOR, Dir. Pubcty. and Prom., David McKay Co., Inc., 750 Third Ave., N.Y., N.Y. 10017, '57–; Pubcty. Wtr., Am. Express Co., '55–'57; Ed., Un. World Federalists, Inc., '53–'55; Wtr., Campus Mdsng. Bur., '52–'53; PPA (Secy., '61); Salem Col., AB, '49 (cum laude); Univ. of N.C., MA, '50; New Sch. for Social Rsch.; b. Moorhead City, N.C., 1928; p. Robert and Alethea Bracy Taylor; h. Robert Anthony; c. Robert, Katherine; res: 213 St. Johns Pl., Bklyn., N.Y. 11217.

ANTHONY, DOROTHY·SLOAN, Ed. of Religion, Warren Tribune Chronicle, Franklin S.E., Warren, Oh. 44482, '60–; Wtr., hist. features, '60–'69; Proof Reader, '52–'60; Prod. Control, Atlas Powder Co. (Ravenna Arsenal), '42–'45; Shenango Genealogical Assn.; b. Indiana, Pa., 1917; p. James and Sarah Monks Sloan; h. John Anthony; c. John Dennis, David Foster, Diane (Mrs. Jon Overly); res: 143 Main St., W. Farmington, Oh. 44491.

ANTOINETTE, Sr. MARY (Andalora), Librn. and Audio-visual Coordr., Mt. Mercy Acad., 88 Red Jacket Pkwy., Buffalo, N.Y. 14220; Instr., Trocaire Col.; NEA, N.Y. State Educ. Commtns. Assn., ALA, N.Y. Lib. Assn., Catholic Lib. Assn.; Who's Who of Am. Wm.; '68–'70; Fredonia State Tchrs. Col., BS (Educ.), '44; Marywood Col., MS (Lib. Sci.), '60; b. Jamestown, N.Y.; p. Michael and Ida Milioto Andalora.

APPEL, MARY CULLEN, Ed. Dir., Television Fact-book, Television Digest Inc., 2025 Eye St., N.W., Washington, D.C. 20006; Asst. Edtl. Dir., '66–'67; Edtl. Asst., '64–'65; Assoc. Doc. Examiner (with husband), '45–'64;

Doc. Examiner, FBI Lab., '42–'45; Trinity Col., BA; b. Scranton, Pa. 1922; p. Edward J. and Mary McDonough Cullen; h. Charles A. Appel Jr.; c. Edward J., Peter B., Margaret D., Paul C., Maryann Callaway; res: 3383 Stephenson Pl. N.W., Washington, D.C. 20015.

ARBUCKLE, DOROTHY FRY, Auth., fiction, non-fiction: "After-Harvest Festival," ('55), "Andy's Dan'l Boone Rifle" ('66); Composer: "The Church Wherein I Worship;" Pres., Arbuckle Oil Co., Inc., Lake Village, Ind. 46349, '68–; Librn., '45–'65; Tchr., '30–'32; h. Lloyd Arbuckle (dec.).

ARCHER, MARION FULLER, Auth.; Asst. Prof., Lib. Sci., Polk Library, Wisconsin State University, 800 Algoma Blvd., Oshkosh, Wis. 54901, '67–; Asst. Catalog Librn., '63–; various librn. positions, '41–'46; bks: "There Is a Happy Land" ('63; Cert. of Hon. Mention, Friends of Am. Wtrs.,' '64), "Keys for Signe" ('65), "Nine Lives of Moses on the Oregon Trail" ('68; Outstanding Juv. of Yr., Cncl. for Wis. Wtrs. Johnson Fndn., '69; Aw. of Merit for Outstanding Svc. to Hist., State Hist. Soc. of Wis., '69); Wis. Reg. Wtrs. Assn., Wis. Lib. Assn.; Univ. of Ore., BA, '38 (with hons., Phi Beta Kappa); Columbia Univ., MA (Lib. Sci.), '41; b. Eugene, Ore. 1917; p. Oscar and Erma Padden Fuller; h. Leonard B. Archer, Jr.; c. Marian Fuller (Mrs. Benjamin Timms), Ruth Fleming, Jane Erma, Benjamin LeRoy; res: 520 Mount Vernon, Oshkosh, Wis. 54901.

ARCHIBALD, ELIZABETH BUTCHER, County Librn., Warren Library Association, 205 Market St., Warren, Pa. 16365, '61–; Children's Librn., '32–'40; Carnegie Lib. Sch., BS (Lib. Sci.), '31; h. Gerry Archibald; c. Gerry, Jr., Mrs. Anne Acton; res: 403 Quaker Hill Rd., Warren, Pa. 16365.

ARDEN, SHERRY WARETNICK, PR Dir., Wm. Morrow & Co., 105 Madison Ave., N.Y., N.Y. 10016, '68–; Pubcty. Dir., G. P. Putnam's Sons, Coward-McCann, '64–'68; Asst. to Pres., University Book, Inc., '63–'64; Assoc. Prodr., TV docs; edtl., pubcty. positions: aws: Assoc. Prodr., "Of Men and Minds," film doc. receiving Am. Film Festival, Columbus Film Festival cits.; Univ. of Delaware, '45–'47; Columbia Univ., '47–'51; b. N.Y.C.; p. Abraham and Rose Bellak Waretnick; h. Hal Marc Arden; c. Mrs. Doren Berger, Cathy Lynn; res: 300 Central Park West, N.Y., N.Y. 10024.

ARDMORE, JANE KESNER, Wtr.; Auth: "A Portrait of Joan" (NFPW aw., '62), "To Love Is to Listen" (Cal. FPW aw., '67), others; Contrbr., numerous mags.; Theta Sigma Phi (Headliner Aw., '68), Cal. FPW, Hollywood Wms. Press Club; Univ. of Chgo., PhB; b. Chgo., Ill.; p. David and Florence Behrend Kesner; h. Albert Ardmore; c. Ellen; res: 10469 Dunleer Dr., L.A., Cal. 90064.

ARDOUREL, JEANINE, Prod. Mgr., Addison Wesley, Sandhill Rd., Menlo Park, Cal. 94025, '69–; Copyed. Dir., '64–'69; Copyed., '62–'64; Asst. Ed., '59–'61;

WNBA, Western Bkpublrs. Assn.; Univ. of Colo., BA, '58 (Phi Beta Kappa).

ARESTY, ESTHER BRADFORD, Auth: "The Grand Venture" (Bobbs-Merrill, '63), "The Delectable Past" (Simon & Schuster, '64), "The Best Behavior" (Simon & Schuster, '70); Free-lance Radio Script Wtr., '36–'45; Adv. Mgr., Mandel Bros. Dept. Store, Chgo., Ill., '33–'36; The Auths. Guild; De Paul Univ.; h. Julian Aresty; c. Robert J., Mrs. Jane Silverman; res: 32 Hilvista Blvd., Trenton, N.J. 08618.

ARGALL, GRACE ELIZABETH, Edtl. Adm. Asst., Society Press, State Historical Society, 816 State St., Madison, Wis. 53705, '59–; Univ. of Wis., BA, '30; b. La Crosse, Wis., 1908; p. John and Rose Wright Argall; res: 514 Shepard Terr., Madison, Wis. 53705.

ARKHURST, JOYCE COOPER, Librn., Chicago Public Library, Woodlawn Regional Branch, 6247 S. Kimbark Ave., Chgo., Ill. 60637, '68–; New Lincoln Sch. Lib., '58–'59; N.Y. Public Lib., '50–'57; Auth.: "The Adventures of Spider, a Collection of West African Folktales" (Little, Brown, '64); h. Frederick Arkhurst.

ARMER, ALBERTA ROLLER, Wtr.; Ed., Agricultural Pubns., Univ. of Cal., '53–'57; Rewrite Ed., WPA Wtrs. Project (Detroit, Mich.), '37; Reptr., Swanson Pubcty. Agcy. (S.F., Cal.), '28; Auth., Children's Bks.; Wms. Intl. League for Peace and Freedom, Am. Assn. for the UN; Univ. of Cal., BA, '26 (Phi Beta Kappa, summa cum laude); b. Huntingburg, Ind., 1904; p. Rev. Henry and Mary Katterhenry Roller; h. Austin Armer; c. Rollin, Elinor, Beret Armer Worsham; res: 725 Oak Ave., Davis, Cal. 95616.

ARMSTRONG, ALICE CATT, Ed., Publr., Auth., Pres., Who's Who Historical Society, 1331 Cordell Pl., L.A., Cal. 90069, '49–; Auth., Ed., Publr: "Who's Who in California," ('54–); "Who's Who Dining and Lodging on the North American Continent," ('68), "Executives' Who's Who—California," ('63), "Who's Who in Los Angeles County" ('50 '52); Tchr., dramatic arts, Hollywood, '47–'49; Auth., juv. bks., stories; Historic L.A. Assn. ('68), Wms. Press Club of Southern Cal. (past Pres.); Outstanding Citizen of Cal., Ariz. and Hi. Aw., Senior Citizens pubn., '66; Aw. of Hon., Wisdom Magazine, '65; Wm. of Achiev., "Cal. Wm. of the Golden West Aw., '51; Litt. D., St. Andrew's Univ. (England, '69); Jr. Col. Wichita Art Inst.; b. Fort Scott, Kan.; p. Charles and Elsie Pakenham Catt; res: 1331 Cordell Pl., L.A., Doheny Hills, Cal. 90069.

ARMSTRONG, BONNIE RAE, Pubcty. Dir., New Directions Publishing Corp., 333 Sixth Ave., N.Y., N.Y. 10014, '69–; Asst. to VP, '66–'69; Fgn. Rights Head; Head of Copyright Dept.; HS Tchr.; PPA ('69); Tchr. of the Yr. Aw., Hamburg, N.Y., '65; Houghton Col., BA (Eng.), '62; b. Titusville, Pa., 1940; p. Raymond and Donna Winans Armstrong; res: 410 W. 22nd St., N.Y., N.Y. 10014.

ARMSTRONG, CHERIE V., Press., Russell Birdwell & Assoc. Inc., 1 University Pl., N.Y., N.Y. 10003, '63–; Lectr. on PR and Cnsl.; Dir., Wms. Rsch. Guild; h. (dec.)

ARMSTRONG, ELIZABETH PHYLLIS, Chief Librn., California Institute of the Arts, 2404 W. Seventh, L.A., Cal. 90057, '68–; Cal. Western Univ. Lib., San Diego, Cal., '65–'68; Head Librn., '63–'65; librn. positions, '60–'63; Special Svcs. positions, '52–'59; ALA, numerous local, specialized lib. assns.; educ: Ithica Col., '45–'47; Tufts Univ. MA (Eng.), '51, (magna cum laude); Rutgers Univ., MS (Lib. Sci.), '60; b. Ridgefield, Conn. 1926; res: 1866 N. Rodney Dr., L.A., Cal. 90028.

ARMSTRONG, MELBA MAUNEY, Dir. of PR, Assoc., Department of Development, Geisinger Medical Center, Danville, Pa. 17821, '68–; West Pa. Hosp., Pittsburgh, '59–'68; Am. Red Cross, Charlotte, N.C., '46–'49; Asst. Dir., Fund Raising, Atlanta, Ga., '43–'46; PRSA (Pittsburgh Chptr. Bd., '66–'68), PR Soc. of Western Pa. Hosps. (Pres., '66–'67), Theta Sigma Phi, Hosp. Assn. of Pa.; several First Pl. Aws., Hon. Mention MacEachern Aws., special aw. for film, Pittsburgh Visual Aids and Commtns. Competition, '65; Kan. City Art Inst., '29–'30; Washburn Univ., '30–'33; b. Topeka, Kan. 1911; p. Clarence and Cora O'Dell Mauney; h. Thom Armstrong; c. Corlea, Laurea; res: 219 W. Market, Danville, Pa. 17821.

ARMSTRONG, PATRICIA CADIGAN, Infor. Specialist, National Academy of Sciences, Office of Public Information, 2101 Constitution Ave., Wash., D.C. 20418, '69–; Mgr. for Prom. and Distrb., '56–'59; Lib. Svc., various insts., '42–'56; Auth., "A Portrait of Bronson Cutting, Through His Papers, 1910–1917," (Univ. of N.M., '57); AAUW; Boston Univ., BS, '42; Am. Univ., MA, '57; b. Boston, Mass., 1921; p. Michael and Angelina MacFarlane Cadigan; h. George Armstrong; c. Michael F., Margaret L.; res: 1401 Dale Dr., Silver Spring, Md. 20910.

ARNDT, URSULA MARTHA H., Free-lance Illus., bks., mag. articles; Christmas card designer, H. G. Caspari, Inc., 208 Fifth Ave., N.Y., N.Y. 10010, '63–; Free-lance artist, Illus., '61–; Illus: "Trollweather," "All the Silverpennies" (Macmillan, '67), two other juv. bks.; Stipendiat in "Kulturkreis des Bundesverbandes der Deutschen Industrie," Aw., Germany, '54; Acad. of Arts, Duesseldorf, Germany, '42–'47; b. Duesseldorf, Germany; p. Ernst and Helene Plate Arndt; res: 224 Highland Blvd., Bklyn., N.Y. 11207.

ARNETT, VICKI LOTT, Mng. Ed., Co-Publr., Western Publications, P.O. Box 1107, Santa Monica, Calif. 90406, '65–; Mng. Ed., Lott Publ. Co., '65–; VP, Sissilla Development Corp., '65–; Nat. Confectioners Assn., Nat. Candy Wholesalers Assn., Nat. Assn. of Tobacco Distrbrs., Cal. Assn. of Candy and Tobacco Distrbrs., L.A. Tobacco and Candy Table; Jr. Charity League (Pres., '69); U.C.L.A., AB (Speech), '67; b. Seattle,

Wash., 1944; p. Davis and Arlene Peterson Lott; h. Jon D. Arnett; c. Kristen Arlene; res: 433 31st St., Manhattan Beach, Cal. 90266.

ARNOLD, BERNIE WYCKOFF, Food Ed., Nashville Tennessean, 1100 Broadway, Nashville, Tenn. 37202, '64–; volunteer civic worker; "Mrs. Nashville" Aw., '64; David Lipscomb Col., BA, '48; George Peabody Col., '49; b. Cambridge, Oh., 1927; p. Walter and Golda Pryor Wyckoff; h. Henry Arnold, Jr.; c. Henry III, Nancy, Cris, Timothy; res: 1110 Belvidere Dr., Nashville, Tenn. 37204.

ARNOLD, MARGARET JANE, Librn., Wellesley Free Library, 530 Washington St., Wellesley, Mass. 02181, '50–; Gen. Asst., Detroit Public Lib.; Asst. Dir., Simmons Col. Lib.; Mass. Lib. Assn., New England Lib. Assn., Met. Boston Lib. Planning Cncl.; b. N.Y.C., 1920; p. Glenn and Viola Schimpf Arnold; res: 606 A Washington St., Wellesley, Mass. 02181.

ARNOLD, MARIAN L., Exec. Dir., Nutrition Ed., Connecticut Dairy and Food Council, Inc., 95 Niles St., Hartford, Conn. 06105, '48–; Nutritionist in charge of br. off., '45–'48; Dir. of Jnlsm. Program; AWRT, offcr. in many orgs. in fields of nutrition and health; Dairy Rep., Intl. Trade Fair, '62; Hon. Recognition, Conn. State Grange, '62; Recognition for Outstanding Svc., Univ. of Conn. Dairy Club, '64; Cit. Aw., Hartford Dental Soc.; Barnard Col., '32; Pratt Inst., Cert. (Inst. Mgt.), '34; Columbia Univ.; Univ. of N.H., BS, '45; b. Mount Vernon, Oh., 1911; p. Edward O. and Carolyn MacFadden Arnold; res: 31 Woodland St., Apt. 11-B, Hartford, Conn. 06105.

ARNOLD, VIOLA SIEM, Media Dir., Winius Brandon Co., 1015 Locust, St. Louis, Mo. 63141, '62–; Media Buyer, Gardner Advertising, '56–'62; Univ. of Mo.; b. Augusta, Mo. 1924; p. Walter and Edna Osthoff Siem; h. John Arnold; c. Todd, Tim; res: 756 Gascogne Dr., Creve Coeur, Mo. 63141.

ARONFREED, EVA, Assoc. Prof. of Polit. Sci., Glassboro State College, Glassboro, N.J. 08028, '64–; Coordr. Public Info., '62–'64; Asst. Prof. Polit. Sci., Monmouth Col., '61–'62; Ed., PR Cnslt., '56–'61; Assoc. Ed., Nat. Off. Mgt. Assn., '55–'56; Pubns. Ed., Phila. City Planning Comm., '47–'55; Assoc. Ed., Nat. Org. Public Health Nurses, '45–'46; Ed., PR Cnslt., '33–'42; Am. Assoc. for Public Adm., Am. Acad. of Polit. Soc. Sci., NSPRA, others; Cert. of Merit, '61, World Congress of Intl. Union of Local Authorities; Univ. of Pa., BFA, '33, AM, '47, PhD, '58; b. Phila., Pa. 1911; p. Joseph and Johanna Scheindling Aronfreed; res: 403 S. Cummings Ave., Glassboro, N.J. 08028.

ARONSON, MURIEL FOX, VP, Carl Byoir & Associates, 800 Second Ave., N.Y., N.Y. 10017, '56–; Dir., TV-Radio Dept., Carl Byoir, '52–'55; Publicist, Carl Byoir, '50–'52; Political Campaigner, Fundraiser, Speechwtr., Radio-TV Wtr., Publicist, Tom Jefferson Assocs., '49–'50; Adv. Copywtr., nat. fashion off., Sears Roebuck, '48–'49; Reptr., UP, '46, '49; Art Critic and Bridal Ed., Miami Daily News, '46; Lectr. on PR to U.S. Army, Am. Med. Assn., U.S. Signal Corps., Am. Mgt. Assn., YMCA Dirs. Assn., adv., radio and TV organizations, civic organizations, state and county medical socs.; Edtl. Advisory Bd., Gambit mag., '70–; AWRT (Bd. of Dirs., '59–'61; PR Chmn., '57–'59; Pubns. Chmn., '55–'57; Prog. Chmn., N.Y. Chptr., '63–'64), NOW (VP, '68–; Bd. of Dirs., '66–'68), N.Y. Diabetes Assn. (PR Chmn., '56–'60; Advisory Comm., '61), VP Humphrey's Task Force on Wms. Goals (Co-chmn., '68), N.Y. Comm. for Young Audiences (Bd. of Dirs., '68–); twice winner, John Martin Essay Contest; Barnard Coll., BA, '48 (summa cum laude, Phi Beta Kappa; Mng. Ed., Barnard Bear; News Ed., WKCR); Rollins Coll., '44–'46 (Mng. Ed., Rollins Flamingo); b. Newark, N.J., 1928; p. M. Morris and Anne Rubenstein Fox; h. Dr. Shepard Gerard Aronson; c. Eric, Lisa; res: 40 E. 83rd St., N.Y., N.Y. 10017.

ARNOTT, ANN, Home Equipment Ed., Redbook Magazine, 230 Park Ave., N.Y., N.Y. 10017, '67–; Sr. Staff Home Econst., Maytag Co., '66–'67; Staff Home Econst., '64–'66; Home Econsts. in Bus., (Ia. Chptr: Chmn.-Elect, Secy.); Am. Home Econs. Assn., Electrical Wms. Round Table (Nat. Scholarship Comm.), NHFL, Theta Sigma Phi, Omicron Nu, Phi Upsilon Omricon, Phi Kappa Phi; ALMA Aw., '68; Kan. State Tchrs. Col., '60–'62; Kan. State Univ., BS (Home Econs., Jnlsm.), '64 (cum laude); b. Blue Rapids, Kan., 1943; p. Chester and Alice Britschge Arnott; res: 444 E. 75th St., N.Y., N.Y. 10021.

ARRINGTON, ALYNE ROGERS, Ed., Owner, The News-Commercial, P.O. Box 387, Collins, Miss. 39428, '57–; Asst. Ed., '31–'57; Ed., Owner, Mount Olive Tribune, Mount Olive, Miss. 39119, '60–; Miss. Press Assn., Miss. Press Wm. (VP, '56–'57), DAR (Treas.), '62–), NFPW, Nat. Edtl. Assn., Collins, Miss. C. of C., Covington County Democratic Exec. Comm., numerous philanthropic orgs.; Who's Who of Am. Wm., World Who's Who in Commerce and Industry; b. Collins, Miss., 1911; p. Thomas Carter and D. L. O. Buchanan Rogers; h. James Duncan Arrington, Sr. (dec.); c. Analyn (Mrs. James Rogers Goff), Carol Jeanne (Mrs. Albert Gooch, Jr.), James Duncan, Jr.; res: P.O. Box 387, Collins, Miss. 39429.

ARTERBURN, HELEN CLUTE, Ed., Marina News, 190 LaVerne Ave., Long Beach, Cal. 90803, '55–; Pacific News, '45–'55; War Corr., Trans Radio Press (Pearl Harbor, Hi.), '41–'45; Reptr., Long Beach Star-Progress, '34–'41; Theta Sigma Phi, Cal. Congress PTA (Hon. Life Mbr.); Univ. of Kan., AB; b. Bucklin, Kan.; p. Schuyler and Sadie Logsdon Clute; h. George Arterburn (dec.); res: 741 Temple Ave., Long Beach, Cal. 90804.

ARTHUR, HOPE RISSMAN, Chmn., Bd. of Dirs., Arthur Frommer Inc., 70 Fifth Ave., N.Y., N.Y. 10011, '60–; Chmn. Bd. of Dirs., Frommer/Pasmantier Publ. Corp., '62–; Co-auth., "Europe on $5 a Day," '60–;

Chmn. Bd. of Dirs., $5-A-Day Tours Inc., '61–; Drama Supvsr., The Lighthouse; actress in numerous Broadway and TV prods., AEA, AFTRA, SAG, ANTA, NATAS; Northwestern Univ., BS, '53 (Dramatic Interpretation Scholarship); Royal Acad. of Dramatic Art, '54–'55 (Best Dir. Aw.); b. Chgo., Ill.; p. Henry and Pauline Strassman Rissman; h. Arthur Frommer; c. Pauline; res: 50 Central Park W., N.Y., N.Y. 10023.

ARVEY, VERNA, Wtr.; Auth: book, articles on music and dance; libretti; ASCAP; b. L.A., Cal., 1910; p. David and Bessie Tark Arvey; h. William Grant Still; c. Duncan Allan, Judith Still Headlee; res: 1262 Victoria Ave., L.A., Cal., 90019.

ASCHER, MARY, Artist, Lectr.; 40 one-man traveling shows; represented in many museums, private collections; Huntington Hartford Fndn. Fellowship; many painting aws.; Nat. Assn. of Wm. Artists, ASCA, N.Y. Soc. of Wm. Painters, Fellow, Royal Soc. of Arts, London, Eng., FRSA, NLAPW, AAUW, Intl. Platform Assn., Art Students League; Who's Who in Am., Who's Who in Am. Art, Who's Who of Am. Wm., Dic. of Intl. Biog., Archives of Am. Art; City Col. of N.Y., grad.; N.Y.U., MA; b. Leeds, England; res: 336 Central Park W., N.Y., N.Y. 10025.

ASCHMANN, RUTH EMILY, Fashion Ed., Charlotte Observer, 600 S. Tryon St., Charlotte, N.C. 28201, '68–; Reptr., Montgomery Publ. Co.; Reptr., Niagara Falls Gazette; Theta Sigma Phi; Univ. of Mo., BJ, '65; b. Phila., Pa., 1943; p. Howard and Emily Fromm Aschmann; res: 1601 Eastcrest Dr., Charlotte, N.C. 28205.

ASH, AGNES McCARTY, Bur. Chief, Fairchild Publications, 595 N.E. 92nd St., Miami, Fla. 33138, '67–; Bus. Ed., Synd. Colmst., Miami News, '59–'67; Wms. Pg., '54–'59; Feature Wtr., N.Y. Times; Wms. Ed., Atlanta Constitution, '51–'54; Washington Times Herald, '51; Dayton Daily News, '49–'51; Free-lance mag. Wtr., travel wtr., former news stringer, N.Y. Times; N.Y. NWC (aw. for articles of special interest to wm., '57), Theta Sigma Phi, Fashion Group; Fla. Wms. Press Club aw. for colms., '51, Oh. Nwsp. Wms. Club aws., '51; Sinclair Col., Dayton, Oh.; b. N.Y.C., 1924; p. Mathew Paul and Olga Zacharias McCarty; h. Clarke B. Ash; c. David, Eric, Jim, Jennifer; res: 576 N.E. 97th St., Miami Shores, Fla. 33138.

ASH, MARIAN NEAL, Ed., Yale University Press, 149 York St., New Haven, Conn. 06511, '59–; Mng. Ed., '65–'69; Project Admin., Carnegie Endowment for Intl. Peace, '54–'59; Asst. Ed., '49–'54; Am. Polit. Sci. Assn., Am. Econ. Assn., Assn. for Asian Studies, Am. Soc. of Indexers (Bd. of Dirs., '69–'70); Wellesley Col., BA; Columbia Univ., MA; b. Englewood, N.J.; p. Kenneth and Jeannette Freudenvoll Neal; h. Lee Ash; res: 31 Alden Rd., Hew Haven, Conn. 06515.

ASH, MARIAN SHELDON, Publr.-Ed., Skirting the Capitol, legislative nwsltr. for wm., P.O. Box 4569, Sacramento, Cal. 95825, '67–; Exec. Dir., Advisory Commn. on the Status of Wm., State of Cal., '65–'67; Special Rep., State Dept. of Indsl. Relations, '65; Asst. Dir., Chile-Cal. Program, '63–'65; Cnslt., Cal. Legislature, '63; Pubcty. Wtr., PR Asst., Cal. State Fair, '61; Lectr.; Cal. Press Wm. (Bd. Mbr.; Third Place, Best Edtl., '68, Wm. of Yr. Nominee, '68), Cal. Fed. BPW, Wms. Equity Action League; (Nat. Adv. Bd., '68, '69, '70); Soroptimists Fedn. of the Ams. (S.W. Region, Status of Wm., Chmn., '69–'70); various reporting, special aws.; Incarnate Word Col.; b. Trenton, N.J. 1923; p. Grover C. and Elisabeth Godson Rippetoe; h. 1. Rand Sheldon (dec.) 2. Richard Ash (div.); c. Ridgley Elisabeth Sheldon; res: 2301 Parkwood Dr., Sacramento, Cal. 95825.

ASHBURN, MARY LOU, Media Dir., Couchman Advertising Agency, 3303 Lee Pkwy., Suite 306, Dallas, Tex. 75219, '62–; Asst. Dir. of financial operations, '55–'62.

ASHBY, NORMA BEATTY, Hostess and Prodr., "Today in Montana," KRTV, Box 1331, Great Falls, Mont. 59401, '62–; Rschr., MD (med. mag., N.Y.C.), '58–'61; Life Magazine, '57–'58; Reptr., Helena (Mont.) Independent Record., '53–'56; Wtr., Prodr., Dir. of doc. films; AWRT (Mont. Big Sky Chptr. Pres., '67–'69), BPW (Great Falls Wm. of the Yr., '66), L.A. Adv. Wm. (Outstanding Wm. in Adv. in the West aw., '63), Adv. Club of Great Falls (VP, '63–'64; Dir., '64–'67), Great Falls Press Club; Greater Montana Fndn. Aw. six times for Best TV Show in Mont.; Univ. of Mont., BA (Jrnlsm.); b. Helena, Mont., 1935; p. Raymond and Ella Lamb Beatty; h. Shirley Ashby; res: 3233 Third Ave. S., Great Falls, Mont. 59401.

ASHURST, BETTY BUCHANAN, City Ed., Advocate-Messenger, 326 W. Walnut St., Danville, Ky. 40422, '67–; Staff Wtr., Ashland Daily Independent, '66–'67; Prom. Dept., Lexington Herald-Leader, '61–'65; Pubcty., Nelson Air Corp. (Danville); Beta Sigma Phi (Lexington Chptr. Secy.), Lancaster Wms. Club, Danville Un. Commty. Fund (Chmn., '69); Fuggazi Bus. Col., '62; b. Hustonville, Ky., 1943; p. Ballard and Georgianna Wells Buchanan; h. Everett Ashurst; c. Scarlet René; res: 107 Pin Oak Dr., Lancaster, Ky. 40444.

ASSATOURIAN, ALICE HUSISIAN, Co-owner, Professional Editing & Typing Services, 410 E. 20th St., N.Y., N.Y. 10009, '50–; Boston Univ., 1940; Exec. Asst., Rsch. Cnslt., Clark Univ. (Worcester, Mass.), '43–'46; Guest Lectr., univs.; Modern Lang. Assn.; Girl Scout Cncl. aw., '67; Columbia Univ., BA (Eng., Writing), '64; N.Y.U., MA (Eng.), '66; b. Batoum, Russia, 1920; p. Dr. Leon and Arax Zorian Husisian; h. Haig G. Assatourian; c. Seta, Sona, Lora.

ATHANASIOU, BETTYE, Mgr.-PR, Geo Space Corporation, 5803 Glenmount Dr., Houston, Tex. 77036, '63–; Secy. and Ed., PR, Robert H. Ray Co., '52–'56; Am. Bus. Wms. Assn. (Houston Chapter Pres.), ICIE, Southeast Tex. IEA, Soc. of Exploration Geophysicists,

Geophysical Soc. of Houston (Service Aw.); active in numerous commty. hosp. groups; b. Dallas, Tex., 1923; p. J. L. and Edythe Stewart Raiden; c. Susan Saul, Mrs. F. J. MacKie, III; res: 3102 Suffolk Dr., Houston, Tex. 77027.

ATHAS, DAPHNE, Lectr., Crtv. Writing, University of North Carolina, Chapel Hill, N.C., 27514, '68–; Rsch. Asst., '67–'68; Coordr., Durham Tech. Inst., '65–'67; Tchr., Perkins Inst., '52–'58; Auth: three books, play; Auths. League, Dramatists Guild; Macdowell Fellowship, '61–'62; Nat. Fndn. on the Arts and Humanities aw., '67; Univ. of N.C., BA, '43; b. Cambridge, Mass., 1923; p. P. C. and Mildred Spencer Athas; res: Box 224, Chapel Hill, N.C. 27514.

ATHERTON, ELIZABETH MAE ANDERSON, Prod. Mgr., Iowa Plumbing, Heating, Cooling Contractor, Box 56, Boone, Ia. 50036, '62–; Sixth Dist. Secy. to Merwin Coad, U.S. Rep. to Congress from Ia., '56–'62; Life Mbr., Ia. Congress of Parents and Teachers; b. Boone, Ia., 1921; p. Edgar S. and Bessie W. Lamb Anderson; h. Robert H. Atherton; c. Robert John, Richard Cecil; res: 2009 Story St., Boone, Ia. 50036.

ATKIN, JERRIE, Horse Colmst. and Feature Wtr., The Roanoke Times, 201 Campbell Ave. S.W., Roanoke, Va. 24013, '68–; Ed., Gary Post-Tribune, '58–'65; Garden Ed.; TV Colmst.; Feature Wtr.; Gen. News Wtr.; Sports and Oil Ed., Lake Charles Am. Press, '43–'44; PR Dir., Un. Fund (Gary, Ind.), '47–'50; PR Dir., AIM, off-campus credit program at Univ. of Wis., '66–'69; Free-lance Wtr., mags. and nwsps.; AAUW, Chi Omega, Theta Sigma Phi, Va. Press Wm.; aws. for features and news series, Ind. Press Wm.; Stephens Jr. Col.; Ind. Univ., BA, '42; b. Gary, Ind., 1918; p. Herman and Myrtle Elser Werber; h. Robert Atkin; c. Bonnie, Scott, Rojer; res: 5119 Falcon Ridge Rd. S.W., Roanoke, Va. 24014.

ATKISS, ROBIN ALLAN, Art Dir., U.S. Office of Education, 400 Maryland Ave. S.W., Wash., D.C. 20202, '64–; Nat. Sci. Fndn., '62–'64; Staff Artist, Naval Propellant Plant, Indian Head, Md., '62; Creative Arts Studio, Wash., D.C., '61; Art Dir., Buchann Mfg. Co., Clifton Heights, Pa., '59–'60; Phila. Museum Col. of Art; res: 10613 Elmont Ct., Fairfax, Va. 22039.

ATTERBURY, ANNABEL LEE, Ed., Dodge County Independent-news, Inc., 350 Oak St., Juneau, Wis. 53039, '62–; Ed., Hustisford News, '58–'62, Asst. Librn., Fed. Reserve Bank of N.Y., '42–'48, Ref. Librn., N.J. State Teachers Col., '32–41; NFPW, Wis. Press Assn., Wis. Wms. Press Club; Best Local Colm.—Wis. Press Assn.; N.J. State Teachers Col. for Wm., '28; Columbia Univ. Lib. Sch., '35; b. W. Hoboken, N.J., 1910; p. George and Rose Blau Lee; h. Harold Atterbury; c. Lee, Bruce; res: 253 Oakwood Blvd., Hustisford, Wis. 53034.

ATTMORE, MARIE STEPHENSON, Home Living Ed., Albuquerque Journal, 701 Silver S.W., Albuquerque,

N.M. 87103, '64–; State Ed., Butte (Mont.) Standard, '62–'64; Summer News Ed., Cut Bank Pioneer Press (Mont.), '61; Kappa Tau Alpha, Theta Sigma Phi; Univ. of Mont., BA, '62 (Delta Delta Delta Scholarship, '59; Dean A. L. Stone Scholarship, '61; Mortar Bd.); Univ. of N.M., '68–'69; b. Bozeman, Mont., 1939; p. Alfred and Minnie Lohse Stephenson; h. John Attmore; res: 919 Silver S.W., Albuquerque, N.M. 87102.

ATWOOD, EVANGELINE RASMUSON, Feature Wtr., Anchorage Daily Times, 820 Fourth Ave., Anchorage, Alaska, 99501, '64–; Nwsp. Reprtr., '35–'38; Social Caseworker (Springfield, Ill.; Worcester, Mass.; N.O., La.), '30–'35; Auth., Alaskan hist.; Bks: "83 Years of Neglect" ('50), "Anchorage: All-America City" ('57), "We Shall Be Remembered" ('66); Alpha Kappa Delta; Univ. of Wash., BA, '27; Univ. of Chgo., MA, '30; Univ. of Alaska, LLD (Hon.), '67; h. Robert Atwood.

ATWOOD, MARGARET SMITH, Librn., York College of Pennsylvania, 321 Country Club Rd., York, Pa. 17405, '56–; Librn., York Hosp. Sch. of Nursing, '53–'56; Librn., Newburgh Free Lib., '41–'44; Delta Kappa Gamma (Beta Beta Chptr. Pres., '68–'70), York County Librns. Assn., Wms. Bur. of York Area C. of C. (Pres., '66–'67); Who's Who of Am. Wm., '68; N.Y. State Univ., AB, '39; N.Y. State Univ. BS (Lib. Sci.), '44; b. Newburgh, N.Y., 1919; p. Walter and Almeria Greaney Smith; c. Robin, Scott, Sarah; res: 1518 Fireside Rd., York, Pa. 17404.

ATWOOD, SARA ELAINE, Prom. Ed., Anchorage Daily Times, 820 Fourth Ave., Anchorage, Alaska, 99501, '68–; Wms. Ed., '65–'68; Reprtr., '64–'65; Wash., D.C. Corr., '63–'64; Dir., Info. Center, Boston World Affairs Cncl. '62–'63; Alaska Press Club (State VP, Anchorage Chptr. Chmn. of Bd.), Alaska Press Wm., NFPW; various nwsp. aws.; Mills Col., BA (Polit. Sci.); Univ. of Geneva; Am. Univ.; b. L.A., Cal.; p. Robert and Evangeline Rasmuson Atwood.

AUBLE, HELEN LOWE, Owner, Caribbean Publications, Drawer 1592, Lille Gronne Gade (3), Charlotte Amalie, St. Thomas, U.S. Virgin Islands 00801, '50–; Publr., "Caribbean Vacationlands," "Caribbean Panorama," '50–; Exec. Dir., St. Thomas-St. John Virgin Islands Tourist Dev. Bd., '47–'49; Pres., Printed Salesman, Inc. (PR), '43–'47; Wtr., Tech. Asst., Treasury Star Parade, U.S. Treasury Dept., '41–'43; established lib. of Caribbean-S. Am. color photos for pubn. reproduction, slide shows, '56–; established Caribbean Conservation Cnsl. for educ., tech. aid to Caribbean islands, '68–; act as unoffcl. emissary between area govts., '54–; Am. Soc. of Travel Agts., Caribbean Travel Assn. (Hon.; Caribbean Tourism, aws., '59, '69), OPC; The Clipper Club (Pan Am., for outstanding contrbs. to world transport and intl. understanding); Penn Hall Jr. Col., '32–'34; Cleve. Col. of Western Reserve Univ. (Jnlsm.), '36–'38; Columbia Univ. (Jnlsm.), '40–'41; b. W. Salem, Oh., 1915; p. Arthur L. and Fannie Camp

Lowe; h. John Auble (div.); res: Drawer 1592, Charlotte Amalie, U.S. Virgin Islands 00801.

AUCELLO, MAE D., Dir., Adv. and PR, Suburban Propane Gas Corporation, Rte. 10, Whippany, N.J. 07981, '53–; Adv. Mgr., '51–'53; Ed., co. pubn., '50–'57; Public Info. Subcomm. of Mkt. Dev. Cncl., Nat. LP-Gas Assn. (PR, Pubcty. and Pubns. comms.), Adv. Club of N.J. (Dir, '64–; Secy., '66–'68), PRSA. N.Y. League, Bus. and Professional Wm. (Pres., '66–'68), N.Y. Assn. of Indsl. Communicators (Gov., '63–'65), Intl. Cncl. Indsl. Eds. (Eastern Area Dir., '57–'58), ZONTA Intl. (Morristown, N.J. Club Dir., '67–), House Mag. Inst. (Pres., '56–'57), Nat. Conf. of Christians and Jews, Inc. (N.J. Reg.: Dir. '64; Chmn. of PR Comm., '64–'65; Cert. of Recognition, '60), Hon. Mbr., 4-H Clubs, Rutgers Univ. Ext. Svc., '62–; Bronze "Oscar" for Co. Annual Report to Stockholders, '53; N.Y.U., BS (Bus. Adm.), '51; Rutgers Univ. Urban Studies Ctr. under Ford Fndn. Fellowship, '61–'62; b. Pleasantville, N.Y.; p. Rosario and Marietta Tripolone Aucello; res: 280 Prospect Ave., Hackensack, N.J. 07601.

AUERBACH, ISABELLE, Exec. Asst. to the Publr. and Head of Educ. Dept., Intl. Pubs. Co., 381 Park Ave. S., N.Y., N.Y. 10016.

AUERBACH, SYLVIA SCHWARTZ, Free-lance Wtr., Ed.; Reader's Digest Books, 380 Madison Ave., N.Y., N.Y. 10017, '69–; Fac. New Sch. Wtrs. Workshop, '66–; Ed., Publrs. Wkly., '65–'68; Free-lance Wtr., '63–'65; Ed., Prentice-Hall, '61–'63; Rptr., Jnl.-Am., '60–'61; numerous mag. articles; U. of Pa., BA, '41; Columbia Grad. Sch. (Jnlsm.), '59–'60 (Helen Slade Sanders Scholarship, hons. in econs. and bus. writing seminar), b. Phila., Pa., 1921; p. Meyer and Edith Frankel Schwartz; h. Albert A. Auerbach; c. Carl, Steven; res: 2 Washington Square Village, N.Y., N.Y. 10012.

AUERBACH, VIVIAN, Dir., Retail Prom., McCall's Mag., 230 Park Ave., N.Y., N.Y. 10017, '69; VP, Dir., Adv. Prom., PR, Fashion and Design Dev., Regal Knitwear Co., Inc., '57–'69; Fashion Show Commentator and Coordr., '68; Guest Colmst., '66; AWNY (Pres. Cabinet), Fashion Group (Bd. of Govs.-Chmn., Career Course), Who's Who of Am. Wm., Who's Who in Adv.; h. Walter Rothschild; res: 490 Cumberland Ave., Teaneck, N.J. 07666.

AUGBURN, MARILYN KAY, Dir. of Pubcty. and Adv., WMCA, 415 Madison Ave., N.Y., N.Y. 10017, '70–; Publicist, Solters & Sabinson, '68–'70; Sr. Ed., Sponsor Magazine, '67–'68; AE, Phil Dean Assocs., '65–'67; Edtl. Asst., The New Yorker Magazine, '63–'65; Who's Who of Am. Wm., Outstanding Young Wm. of Am.; Burris Lab. Sch., Muncie, Ind., '46–'59; DePauw Univ., AB, '63; b. Muncie, Ind., 1941; p. Leslie and Mary Wells Augburn; res: 222 E. 75th St., N.Y., N.Y. 10021.

AUGELLO, DIANA ADAMS, Assoc. Ed., Pubn. Sec., Ruder & Finn Incorporated, 110 E. 59th St., N.Y., N.Y.

10022, '68–; Crtv. Dir., CMC & C, '62–'68; Copy Chief, Conti Adv., '56–'62; Kent State Univ., AB; res: 818 E. Ridgewood Ave. Ridgewood, N.J. 07450.

AUGUR, MARILYN HUSSMAN, Asst. Treas: Texarkana Newspapers, Inc., Texarkana, Tex., and Camden News Publishing Company, Camden, Ark, '69–; Bd. of Dirs., Treas., '66–'68; active in Dallas civic groups, DAR; Randolph Macon Col., '56–'58; Univ. of N.C., BA, '60; b. Texarkana, Ark., 1938; p. Walter and Betty Palmer Hussman; h. James Augur; c. Margaret M., Elizabeth H.; res: 4133 Shenandoah, Dallas, Tex. 75205

AUSTIN, LINDA FAYE, Teenage/youth Ed., Post Publishing Company, Inc., 131 W. Innes St., Salisbury, N.C. 28144, '67–; N.C. Press Wm.; Univ. of N.C., '66–'67; Catawba Col., '69–; b. Salisbury, N.C., 1948; p. Harle and Dorothy Eddleman Austin; res: Rte. 10, Box 549, Salisbury, N.C. 28144.

AUSTIN, NORMA KASSELHUT, Ed., Service Magazine, The Kansas Power and Light Company, 818 Kansas Ave., Topeka, Kan. 66601, '67–; Kan. Press Wm., NFPW, Greater Topeka C. of C., Kan. City IEA, ICIE; Aws: AAF, Adv. Club of Topeka; Washburn Univ.; b. St. Joseph, Mo., 1931; p. William and Gladys DeVore Kasselhut; h. Theodore R. Austin; res: 812 Monhollon Dr., Topeka, Kan. 66617.

AVERILL, ESTHER HOLDEN, Auth., Illus., juv. bks.; Reading Clinic, American Bk. Co., '48–'50; Children's Sec., N.Y.C. Public Lib., '44–'45; Publr., Domino Press, Paris, N.Y.C., '30's; Edtl. Dept., Women's Wear Daily, '23–'24; bks: "Cartier Sails the St. Lawrence" (Harper and Row, '56; ALA Notable Children's Bks., '40–'59), "Daniel Boone" (Harper and Row, '46), "King Philip, The Indian Chief" (Harper and Row, '50), 12 "Cat Club" bks. (Harper and Row, '44–'69; also illus.); "Eyes on the World" (Fund & Wagnalls, '69); Contrbr., "The Horn Book," "The Colophon"; WNBA; Vassar Col., '23; b. Bridgeport, Conn.; p. Charles and Helen H. Averill; res: 30 Joralemon St., Bklyn., N.Y. 11201.

AVERY, PATRICIA ANN, News Desk Ed., U.S. News & World Report, 2300 N St. N.W., Wash., D.C. 20037, '69–; Edtl. Asst., '59–'69; Copy Checker, Town & Country (N.Y.C.), '58–'59; Manhattanville Col. of the Sacred Heart, BA, '57; b. New Haven, Conn.; p. John and Vera Gallagher Avery; res: 2500 Q St. N.W., Wash., D.C. 20007.

AVERY, PATRICIA HETT, Hostess, "Miss Patsy's Playhouse," WTVM TV, (Columbus, Ga.), '59–; "Movietime," '58; "Free Babysitter," '58; "Romper Room," '58; "Adventure Time," '57–'58; AWRT (Pres., '64–'66), Columbus Arts Cncl., Columbus Little Theatre (Bd. Mbr., '63–'65), active in numerous civic groups; McCall's Gold Mike Aw. in the field of mental retardation, '63; Ga. Assn. for the Help of Retarded Children, Columbus Chptr. Gold Plaque Aw., '65; Sertoma Club Svc. to Mankind Aw., '67; Outstanding Young Wm. of Am., '66; Northwestern Univ., BA, '56;

b. Columbus, Ga., 1934; p. Charles and Evelyn Kyle Hett, Jr.; h. Lynn F. Avery; c. Lane Charles, Kyle Lynn, Lissa Anne, Lynn Francis; res: Edgewood Rd., Columbus, Ga. 31906.

AVERY, RUTH LORRAINE, Asst. to Pers. Dir., American Broadcasting Cos., Inc. 4151 Prospect Ave., Hollywood Cal. 90027, '51–; Co-auth; "Jest for Laughs" ('54); Actress, Summer Stock, N.Y. theatre, Radio; Dir. Home Talent Shows; AWRT, L.A. County Museum of Art; MacPhail Jr. Col., '38–'40; Chgo. Col. of Speech, '42–'43; L.A. City Col., '51–'61; b. St. Paul, Minn., 1919; res: 4433 Russell Ave., Hollywood, Cal. 90027.

AYER, MARGARET, Free-lance Wtr.; Artist; Illus.; Soc. of Illus., Artists Guild of N.Y. Inc., Asia Soc.; Phila. Museum Col. of Art; studied in private studios in Paris and Rome; b. N.Y.C.; p. Ira and Louise Foster Ayer; h. Alfred Smith; res: Westport Rd., Easton, Conn. 06880.

AYERS, EDEL YTTERBOE, Pres. and Publr., The Anniston Star, 216 W. Tenth St., Anniston, Ala. 36201, '64–; VP, Consolidated Publ. Co.; Tchr., Jacksonville State Univ., '21; Am. Scandinavian Fndn. (Ala. Chmn.), Intl. House, Jacksonville State Univ. (Bd. of Trustees); honored by Am. Scandinavian Fndn., '51; St. Olaf Col., BA, '20; Columbia Univ., '21; b. Northfield, Minn., 1897; p. Halvor and Elise Kittelsby Ytterboe; h. Harry Ayers; c. Harry, Mrs. Phillip A. Sanguinetti; res: 818 Glenwood Terr., Anniston, Ala. 36201.

AYLWARD, JUNE BOYLE, Wms. Dir., WMBD AM-FM-TV, 212 S.W. Jefferson Ave., Peoria, Ill. 61602, '65–; Radio Cont. Dir., '65–'67; Copywtr., Mace Adv. Agcy., Inc., '61–'65; Asst. Cont. Dir., WTVH-TV, '58–'61; Prodr.-Wtr.-Hostess, "Kaleidoscope" (TV Special); "June Aylward Show" (Radio); news features, docs., interviews; AWRT, Peoria Adv. & Selling Club (Wms. Dir., '68–; Aw. of Distinction, '69–;), Coronet (Bd. Dir., '66; Gen. Chmn., '67–'69), Assn. of Commerce Conv. Comm., MS Soc. (Central Ill. Chptr. Bd. Mbr., '67; Pubcty. Chmn., '69); Valley Forge Freedom Aw., '67; Am. Legion Aws., '67, '68; Mount Mary Col., '46; b. Peoria, Ill., 1927; p. Leonard, Sr., and Agnes Scurry Boyle; h. Frank Aylward; c. Frank, Jr., Guy, Nancy; res: 1417 W. Columbia Terr., Peoria, Ill. 61606.

AYRES, JACQUELYN MALANEY, Wms. Ed., Muncie Star, 125 S. High St., Muncie, Ind. 47302, '69–; Wms. News, '67–'69; Altrusa; Ball State Univ. (attending); b. Richmond, Ind., 1945; h. Don. C. Ayres; res: 204 Ellis Rd., Muncie, Ind. 47303.

AYRES, MARY ANDREWS, Exec. VP, Sullivan Stauffer Colwell & Bayles, Inc., 575 Lexington Ave., N.Y., N.Y. 10022, '68–; Mgt. Supvsr.-Sr. VP, '59–'68; Acc. Supvsr.-VP, '50–'59; AE, '48–'50; h. Charles Ayres; res: 45 Sutton Pl. S., N.Y., N.Y. 10022.

AYRES, PATRICIA MILLER, VP and Asst. to Pres., Parents' Magazine Enterprises, Inc., 52 Vanderbilt Ave., N.Y., N.Y. 10017, '69–; Asst. VP, '65; Asst. to Pres.,

'63; Sr. Dir. Mail Copywtr. and Dir., Group Svc. Bur., '53–'63; Circ. Mgr., Parents' Inst., '52–'53; Asst. Circ. Mgr., '51–'52; Copywtr., '50; Free-lance Dir. Mail Cnslt., '49–'50; Circ. Prom. Mgr., '48, Mag. of the Yr., '48–'49; Copywtr. and Asst. to Circ. Mgr., Time Inc., '44–'48; Copywtr., Scholastic Magazine, '44; Children's Bk. Cncl., Publrs. Lib. Prom. Group, Publr. Ad Club; Wms. Nat. Bk. Assn., Hundred Million Club, Theta Sigma Phi; Univ. of Tex., AB (cum laude), '44; Grad. Work, New Sch. for Social Rsch.; b. Tampico, Mexico, 1923; p. Joseph and Gladys O'Brien Miller; h. Warren D. Ayres; c. Page; res: 169 W. 88th St., N.Y., N.Y. 10024.

AZARIAN, IRENE, Ed., Intl. Univs. Press, 239 Park Ave. S., N.Y., N.Y. 10003, '56–.

AZORIN, ELLEN SCHWARTZ, VP, The Cadwell Davis Company, Inc., 437 Madison Ave., N.Y., N.Y. 10022; Adv. Wtrs. Assn. of N.Y. (Copy Club); City Col. of N.Y., '62 (cum laude; Phi Beta Kappa); b. N.Y.C., 1941; p. Frank and Sylvia Schwartz; res: 157 W. 79th St., N.Y., N.Y. 10024.

B

BAACK, BARBARA MARIE, Pubn. Ed., Asst. Public Affairs Offcr., Public Affairs Office, Room 129, Bldg. 1, Naval Air Station, Alameda, Cal. 95401, '66–; Public Info. Specialist, Naval Air Rework Facility, '61–'66; Wms. Ed., Watsonville Register-Pajaronian; Bay Area Soc. of Indsl. Communicators (First VP); Univ. of Cal., BA, '59; Free-lance Photojnlst., active in OEO, Oakland; b. Berkeley, Cal., 1937; p. Ernest C. and Frieda Baggley Baack; res: 16148 Via Sonora, San Lorenzo, Cal. 94580.

BABBAGE, JOAN D., Food Ed., Evening News, 215 Market St., Newark, N.J. 07101, '67–; Publicist, Paramount Intl. Films (N.Y.C.); Feature Wtr., Newark News; Mt. Holyoke Col., BA, '48; b. Glen Ridge, N.J.; p. Laurence and Dorothy Davenport Babbage; res: 412 Washington Ave., Montclair, N.J. 07042.

BABCOCK, LUCILLE HARRIS, Cons. Rels. Rep., The Sperry and Hutchinson Co., 2200 W. Alameda, Denver, Colo. 80223, '67–; Redemption Ctr. Mgr.; Owner-Mgr., Variety Store; Sect. to Purchasing Agt., Gen. Motors; Tchr., home econs.; ZONTA (Pres. '65–'66), BPW (Pres., '64–'65), Am. Bus. Wm., AWRT; Colo. Comm. on the Status of Wm. (apptd. by Gov. Love), '69; Black Hills State Col., '27; b. Lead, S.D., 1910; p. John and Blanche Mulholland Harris; h. Harold H. Babcock; c. Richard, Robert; res: 3720 S. Elati, Englewood, Colo. 80110.

BACH, ALICE HENDRICKS, Sr. Ed., bks. for young readers, The Dial Press, 750 Third Ave., N.Y., N.Y.

10017; Assoc. Ed., Harper and Row; Cnslt., Bedford-Stuyvesant Wtrs. Workshop; Barnard Col., BA, '63; b. N.Y.C., 1942; p. Henry and Irene Gibbs Bach; res: 222 E. 75th St., N.Y., N.Y. 10021.

BACH, JEAN ENZINGER, Prodr., WOR Radio 1440 Broadway, N.Y., N.Y. 10018, '60–; PR, Free-lance Wtr., '55–'60; TV Prod., '52–'55; Wtr., WNEW, '46–'52; Colmst., Reptr., Chicago Times, Chicago American, '39–'46; Vassar Col.; b. Chgo., Ill., 1918; p. George and Gertrude Enzinger (now Mrs. E. W. Passmore); h. Robert Bach; res: 60 Washington Mews, N.Y., N.Y. 10003.

BACH, MARGARET BAMBACH, Retired Wtr., Ed.; Reptr., Miami Beach, Miami (Fla.) Herald; Wms. Ed., Miami Tribune; First Pubcty. Wtr., Miami Beach; Ed., The Gondolier; Ed., Publr., The Soc. Pictorial (Miami Beach-Palm Beach); Jnlsm. Tchr., Miami Jackson HS; Auth., "The First Forty Years," hist. of Miami Beach Commty. Church ('61); Theta Sigma Phi (Miami Chptr., Headliner); Oh. State Univ. (Phi Beta Kappa; Mortar Bd.); Univ. of Miami; b. Ripley, Oh., 1896; p. George G. and Lina Ruckhaber Bambach; h. Wilbert Bach; res: 2200 N. W. 23rd Ave., Miami, Fla. 33142.

BACH, MARY CATHERINE, Wms. Ed., Scottsdale Daily Progress, 302 S. Ball Park Plaza, Scottsdale, Ariz. 85251, '67–; Educ. Wtr., '65–'66; PR, City of Scottsdale, '66–'67; Reptr., Suburban Life Nwsp. (La Grange, Ill.), '64–'65; Copy Reader, Wtr., Hi-Time Magazine, '64; Theta Sigma Phi, NPWC, Ariz. Press Wm. (State PR Offcr.; numerous writing aws.); Marquette Univ. Col. of Jnlsm., '64; b. Milw., Wis., 1942; p. Woodrow J. and Marcella M. Connelly Bach; res: 6040 N. 15th St. #27, Phoenix, Ariz. 85014.

BACH, Maj. SHIRLEY J., Instr., PR and Mass Commtns., Defense Information School, Ft. Benjamin Harrison, Ind. 46216, '66–; Chief, Int. Info., Public Info., Public Affairs Opn., Hq. 8th AF, Westover AFB, Mass., '63–'66; Info. Offcr. and Histrn., 1st Weather Wing, Fuchu AS, Japan, '59–'63; Sls., Instr., Asst. Dir., Educs. Assn., Pitt., Pa., '54–'59; Pa. Public Sch. System, '54–'59; Guest Lectr.; PR and Mass Commtn., Univ. of Mass., Amer. Int. Col., Springfield Col., '63–'66; Air Force Assn., NEA, Pa. State Tchrs. Assn., BPW; Freedoms Fndn. Aw., '60, '61; Who's Who in PR; Clarion Col., BS '54; Boston Univ., MS '63; b. Braddock, Pa., 1932: p. Mr. and Mrs. Mark Bach.

BACHARACH, FRANCES, Assoc. Ed., George Shumway, Publisher, R.D. 7, York, Pa. 17402, '65–; Free-lance Wtr., Photogr.; rsch. in Americana; Former Adv. Copywtr., Tech. Wtr.; Temple Univ.; b. Phila., Pa., 1914; p. Newton and Frieda Abrahams Bacharach; res: 6053 Ogontz Ave., Phila., Pa. 19141.

BACHNER, ANNETTE, Film & TV Dir., The TVA Group, Inc., 4 E. 46th St., N.Y., N.Y. 10017, '67–; Dir./Prodr.; Prod. Asst., 20th Century Fox Film Corp.; Prod. Asst., Stage Mgr., NBC TV; Dir., N. W. Ayer and

Son; Prodr., Benton and Bowles; Dir., WNYC Children's Classical Music Program; Wtr.; numerous articles on children's recordings; Dirs. Guild of Am., Screen Dirs. Intl. Guild, NATAS, AWRT; Am. TV Commls. Festival: Clio aw., Best in Product Category, '62; Certs. of Recognition, '64, '61, '62; 2nd in Product Category, '63; Cannes Film Festival Golden Lion aw., Best Comml., '69; res: 360 First Ave., N.Y., N.Y. 10010.

BACKSTER, NORMA VAN ALLEN, Dir. of PR, Employee Commtns., Monroe, Litton Industries, 550 Central Ave., Orange, N.J. 07051, '66–; Ed. of Pubns., '60–'66; Assoc. Ed. of Pubns., '49–'60; N.J. Assn. of Communicators (Secy.), AAIE (aws., '68–'69), BPW; Freedoms Fndns. Aws., '63, '67, Nat., County Un. Commty. Fund Aws., '69, '68, Printing Industries of Met. N.Y. aws.; Syracuse Univ., BA (Jnlsm.–Eng.), '49 (cum laude); Rutgers Univ., Seton Hall Univ.; b. Newark, N.J.; p. William and Marion Treadwell Van Allen; h. Frank Backster (dec.).

BACMEISTER, RHODA WARNER, Wtr., children's fiction, poems, adult non-fiction, bks: "Voices in the Night" (Bobbs Merrill, '65), "The People Downstairs" (Coward McCann, '64), "Growing Together" (Appleton Century, '47; Parents Inst. Aw. as best of yr.), several others; numerous articles, pamphlets, chptrs. for anthologies, in popular, pfsnl. media, on child care or parent, tchr. educ.; Cnslt., N.Y.C. Head Start Program, '66; Tchr., pre-sch. educ., Univ. of Chattanooga, '64; Instr., Early Childhood Educ., City Col. of N.Y., '56–'60; Pfsnlly. active in fields of teaching, writing, theater, since '16; Child Study Assn. of Am.; Nat. Assn. for Educ. Young Children; Vassar Col., AB, 14 (Phi Beta Kappa, Hons., Sutro Fellowship); Univ. of Chgo., AM, 15; Univ. of Ia; Nat. Col. of Educ.; Columbia Univ., Tchrs. Col.; Bank St. Col.; Univ. of Minn.; Columbia Univ.; b. Northampton, Mass., 1893; p. Charles and Mary Dawes Warner; h. Otto Bacmeister (dec.); c. Margaret E. (Mrs. F. R. Gruger, Jr.), Lucretia M. (Mrs. Paul F. Harrison), Theodore W.; res: 501 W. 123 St., 15 H, N.Y., N.Y. 10027.

BACON, UNA KEETER, News, Soc. Ed., Sayre Daily Headlight-Journal and Sun, 110 N. Fourth St., Sayre, Okla. 73662, '42–; Owner-Publr., '28–; Tchr., '30–'42; BPW (Sayre Chptr. Pres., '48), numerous study clubs, civic groups, holding many different offices; Okla. Presbyterian Col., Durant Jr. Col., '29; Southeastern State Col., Durant, AB (Eng.), '33; b. Boswell, Okla. 1911; p. Andrew and Emma Crump Keeter; h. William J. Bacon; c. Jennifer Sue (dec.), Charles Edward, Nancy Jane; res: 1304 N. Fourth St., Sayre, Okla. 73662.

BADE, ARVILLA WINIFRED, Supvsr., Employee Communications and Training, Economics Laboratory, Inc., Osborn Bldg., St. Paul, Minn. 55102, '66–; Pers. Admr., '60–'66; Pers. Tech., Midland Cooperatives, '55–'60; Dist. Dir., Girl Scouts, '50–'55; ICIE, Twin Cities Pers. Assn. (Secy., '60–'61; Dir. '63), NIEA (VP, '67; Pres., '68; Dir., '69), Am. Soc. of Training & Dev.,

Am. Soc. of Pers. Adm.; Edtl. Writing Aw., AAIE, '69; local writing aws.; Yankton Col., BA (Psych., Sociol.), '50 (magna cum laude); Univ. of Minn.; b. Yankton, S.D., 1928; p. Erich A. and Arvilla Heil Bade; res: 1771 Munster Ave., St. Paul, Minn. 55116.

BADENOCH, NENA WILSON, Free-lance Publicist, National Society for Crippled Children and Adults, 2023 W. Ogden Ave., Chgo., Ill. 60612, '58–'68; Wtr., Auth: articles, cookbooks; Bdcstr. and News Colmst., Peoples Gas Light and Coke Co., '27–'30; Corr. Tchr., Am. Sch. of Home Econs., '45–'58; Brain Rsch. Fndn., Status of Wm. Comm., President's Comm. on Employment of Handicapped, AWRT (Nat. Press., '58–'60; past Dir. of Nat. Bd.; Treas., Ill. Bd.), McCall's Golden Mike Aw., '53; Univ. of Chgo. Alumni Useful Citizen Aw., '52; Univ. of Chgo., PhB, '11; b. Washington, Ia., 1889; p. Frank L. and Harriet Williams Wilson; h. Ben H. Badenoch (div.); c. Harriet Kurtz, Benjamin W., Bruce R.; res: 544 Thatcher Ave., River Forest, Ill. 60305.

BADER, ELIZABETH SCHEIDEMANTEL, Wms. Ed., Colmst., Petoskey News-Review, Petoskey, Mich. 49770, '66–; BPW; b. Detroit, Mich. 1919; p. Karl Edward and Dorothy Mary Hebrank LaTulipe ScheideMantel; h. John J. Bader; c. John K., Fredric G., Dorothy E., Kathryn (dec.), triplets: Thomas E., Jeanne Marie, Robert A.; res: 1131 Emmet St., Petoskey, Mich. 49770.

BADGER, PRICILLA BOLGER, Ltrs. Ed., Time Inc., Rockefeller Ctr., N.Y., N.Y. 10020, '67–; Rschr., '59–; PR Asst., Pan Am. Un., '57–'59; Rschr. Wtr., Vision Magazine, '55–'57; Teaching Asst., Univ. of Wis., '53–'55; Eng. Tchr., Colegio Narino, Bogota, Columbia, '48–'49; Young Pres. Org. (conducted bus. and cultural tour through S.Am., '59), Sigma Delta Pi; Univ. of Wis., BA, '51; MA, '52; post MA, '53–'55; Colegio Mayor de Cundinamarca, Bogota, Columbia, '48–'49; b. Melrose, Wis., 1928; p. Arch and Grace Hutchins Bolger; h. (div.); res: 20 E. Ninth St., N.Y., N.Y. 10003.

BADHAM, MARY HEWITT, Motion Pic. and TV Actress, c/o Michael Selsman, 303 N. La Peer Dr., Beverly Hills, Cal. 90211; TV: "Dr. Kildare," "Twilight Zone," "Magic City"; SAG, AMPAS; Movies: "To Kill a Mockingbird" (Nomination for best supporting actress, '62), "Let's Kill Uncle," Golden Globe Aw., '62; Motion Pic. Critics of Am. Aw., Best Actress, "This Property is Condemned," '66; Birmingham C. of C. aw., gold key to city, '62; Hon. Ala. State Senator, '62; private tutoring in Hollywood; b. Birmingham, Ala., 1952; p. Henry Lee and Mary Hewitt Badham; res: 1223 S. 33rd St., Birmingham, Ala. 35205.

BAER, AVIS DAVIDSON, Drama Critic, The Hartford Times, Hartford, Conn., '65–; Colmst., The Bristol Press, Bristol, Conn., '58–; Colmst, drama reviewer, Farmington Valley Herald (Sunbury), '50–'58; Prof., French Dept., Central Conn. State Col.; Alliance Francaise, Faculty Assoc. Conn. State Cols.; Who's Who of Am. Wm.; Skidmore College, BA, '48; Temple Univ., MA, '49; Central Conn. State Col., Sixth Yr. Cert.; Several civic orgs.; b. Farmington, Conn. 1926; p. Arthur C. and Avis Cole Davidson; h. William Baer; c. William M. Jr., Carol Lee, Ronelle Grace; res: Washburn Rd., Canton, Conn. 06019.

BAER, BARBARA, Gen. Mgr., Aardvark, 526 W. 112th St., N.Y., N.Y. 10025, '66–; Columbia Univ., Bachelor's Degree, '70; b. N.Y.C., 1942; p. Rudolph and Else Thurnauer Baer.

BAER, BETTY LOUISE, Asst. Ed., Look Magazine, 488 Madison Ave., N.Y., N.Y. 10022, '67–.

BAER, ELEANORA A., Lib. Coordr., Clayton School District, 7530 Maryland St., Clayton, Mo. 63105, '66–; Librn., Clayton HS, '53–'66; Asst. Librn., St. Louis Univ., '46–'52; Librn., Fontbonne Col., '29–'46; ALA, Catholic Lib. Assn., NEA, Mo. State Tchrs. Assn., AAUW; Fontbonne Col., AB, '31; St. Louis Univ., MEd, '44; Univ. of Wis., MS (LS), '61; b. Springfield, Mo., 1907; p. Oliver and Agnes Robineau Baer; res: 1359 McCutcheon Rd., Brentwood, Mo. 63144.

BAER, IRENE R., Employee Pubns. Ed., Gimbels, 101 W, Wisconsin Ave., Milw., Wis. 53201, '52–; Wis. IEA (Bd. of Dirs., '63, '69–'70); Wis. Co. Pubns. Evaluations & Aws. Prog., 13 aws; Un. Fund Co. Pubns. Contest, six aws; Univ. of Chgo., PhB, '47; b. Berlin, Germany, 1928; p. Frank and Irmgard Lippmann Seckel; res: 4514 N. Woodburn St., Milw., Wis. 53211.

BAER, JEAN L., Sr. Ed., PR Dir., Seventeen Magazine, 320 Park Ave., N.Y., N.Y. 10022, '53–; Press Wtr., Mutual Broadcasting Co; Wtr., U.S.I.A.; bks: "Follow Me," "The Single Girl Goes To Town"; Contrbr., McCall's, Ladies' Home Journal and others; OPC, NYNWC, AWRT; Cornell Univ., BA; b. Chgo., Ill.; p. Fred E. and Helen Roth Baer; h. Dr. Herbert Fensterheim; res: 151 E. 37 St., N.Y., N.Y. 10016.

BAER, MARIANNE V., Group Head, Ogilvy & Mather Inc., 2 E. 48th St., N.Y., N.Y. 10017, '65–; Copywtr., '61–'63; Copy Training Groups, '65–; Grouphead, Needham Louis & Brorby, '64; Copywtr., '57–'60; Copywtr., N. W. Ayer & Son, '54–'57; Cnslt., '61–; Gran Prix aw., Venice, '66; numerous other aws. and hons.; b. Elizabeth, N.J., 1932; p. Werner and Anna Holzer Baer; h. Robert Chambers; res: 229 E. 79th St., N.Y., N.Y. 10021.

BAGBY, MARTHA GREEN, PR, Indsl. Ed., National Airlines, Inc., P.O. Box 2055, Miami, Fla. 33159, '65–; Jnslm. Lectr., Barry Col., '68–; Assoc. Ed., Alfred Hitchcock's Mystery Magazine, '65; City Ed., Palm Beach Daily News, '64–'65; Jnlsm. Instr., Pa. State Univ., '62–'64; Jnlsm. Tchr., Palm Beach County Schs., '59–'62; Theta Sigma Phi (Miami Chptr. VP, '69–'70; Corr. Secy., '68–'69; Nat. Fellowship, '64), Fla. PR Assn., ICIE; Pa. State Fellowship, '62, Wall St. Jnl. Fellowship '62; Univ. of Miami, BA (cum laude), '59; Columbia Univ.; Pa. State, MA, '64; b. W. Palm Beach, Fla., 1937; p. Hampton and Louise Lambert Green; h. Joseph R. Bagby; res: 2506 N. Greenway St., Coral Gables, Fla. 33134.

BAGGETT, LUCY ROGERS, Ed., National Business Woman, National Federation of Business & Professional Women's Clubs, Inc., 2012 Massachusetts Ave., N.W., Wash., D.C. 20036, '58–; Free-lance Wtr., Illus., '44–'56; Feature Wtr., Times Picayune (N.O., La.), '37–'44; pfsnl. activities in art field, portrait painting, teaching; Phila. Art Alliance (Pfsnl. Mbr., '45–'56), ANWC; Three Freedoms Fndn. aws. for Ed., '60, '61, '62; art shows aws.; painting, showing; represented by Veerhoff Gallery (Wash., D.C.); All Saints Col. (Vicksburg, Miss.); Gulf Park Col. (Gulfport, Miss.); b. Columbus, Miss.; p. Charles and Gertrude Hill Rogers; h. T. Burrage Baggett; res: 5117 Linnean Ave., N.E., Wash., D.C. 20008.

BAGLEY, GLADYS (Gladys Podratz Schaefer), Wms. Ed., The Phoenix Gazette, Box 1950, Phoenix, Ariz. 85001, '61–; Reptr., Entertainment Ed., Club Ed., Asst. Wms. Ed., '29–'61; Tchr., S.D., '20–'24; Ariz. Press Wm. (Pres., '64–'65; Ariz. Wm. of Yr., '68; BPW (Ariz. Fedn. Pres., '52–'53; Phoenix Club Wm. of Yr., '62 Club Pres., '48–'49), Phoenix Wtrs. Club (Pres., '67–'68), NLAPW (Phoenix Br. Pres., '66–'68), Theta Sigma Phi (Bd. Mbr., '64–'68); numerous writing aws.; Dakota Wesleyan Univ.; Black Hills Tchrs. Col.; b. Salem. S.D., 1902; p. Frank and Carrie Ostenberg Podratz; h. Richard H. Schaefer; c. Jesse F. Bagley, Jr.; res: 2202 N. Laurel Ave., Phoenix, Ariz. 85007.

BAHRINGER, ELSIE SMITH, Cnslt., Four County Library System, Club House Rd., Binghamton, N.Y. 13903, '63–; Librn., Bd. of Educ., Johnson City, N.Y., '56–'63; Your Home Public Lib., '50–'55; Binghamton Public Lib., '48–'50; NEA, ALA, N.Y. State Tchrs. Assn., N.Y. Lib. Assn., Beta Phi Mu; Syracuse Univ., AB, '32; Grad. Sch. of Lib. Sci., MS (Lib. Sci.), '61; b. Schenectady, N.Y. 1911; p. William and Minnie Faust Smith; h. Lee Bahringer; c. Sue (Mrs. E. E. Springmann), Nils, Nan (Mrs. David C. Hasler); res: 115 Thomas St., Johnson City, N.Y. 13790.

BAILES, EDNA SUE, Asst. Registrar, West Georgia College, 630 Burson Ave., Apt. 3, Carrollton, Ga. 30117; Eng. Tchr., Bd. of Educ., Richmond County (Augusta), '66–'67; Cnslt., Ed., The Med. Col. of Ga. (Augusta). '67; Wms. Ed., The Augusta Chronicle, '62–'67; Edtl. Assoc., Feature Wtr., The Methodist Publishing House (Nashville, Tenn.), '61–'62; Feature Wtr., The Florida (Jacksonville) Times-Union, '59–'61; Edtl. Assoc., Florida Business and Opportunity Magazine, '59; U.S. Navy (Wash., D.C.), '52–'56; B. F. Goodrich Co., (Albany, Ga.), '52; Fed. Bur. of Investigation (Wash., D.C.), '51; Theta Sigma Phi (co-founder, Nashville Alumni Chptr., '61); Univ. of Ga., AB (Jnlsm.), '58; Fla. State Univ., MA (Hist.), '69; b. 1932;

p. Mrs. Charles E. Bailes, Sr.; res: 1322 S. Mock Rd., Albany, Ga. 31705.

BAILEY, ALICE COOPER, Auth., Lectr.; nine juv. bks., one adult; short stories; articles; Boston Auths. Club (Dir., Past Pres.), NLAPW (Past Br. Pres., Honolulu, Hi.; Past State Pres., Hi. and Mass.), WNBA; Oahu Col., '07; Student, Univ. of Hawaii, '08; Teaching Diploma, '11; b. San Diego, Cal.; p. Henry Ernest and Mary Porter Cooper; h. George Bailey; c. Mary Alice (Mrs. Luke Hamilton Montgomery II), George William, Jr., Richard Briggs; res: 255 Lexington Rd., Concord, Mass. 01742.

BAILEY, BERNADINE FREEMAN, Free-lance Wtr., 253 E. Delaware Pl., Chgo., Ill. 60611; Ed., Laidlaw Brothers (educ. publrs.); Ed., Quarrie Co. (now Field Enterprises); Auth: "Famous Modern Explorers" ('63), "Denmark: Wonderland of Work and Play" ('66), "Austria and Switzerland: The Alpine Countries" ('69), "Jose" ('69), plus many other bks. for young people; Ill. WPA (Pres., '41–'45), Mystery Wtrs. of Amer. (Reg. VP, '66–'67), Soc. of Midland Auths., Arts Club of Chgo., Wms. Press Club of London; Wellesley Col., BA; Univ. of Chgo., MA; Sorbonne; b. Mattoon, Ill.; p. Dr. Thomas and Nellie Voigt Freeman; h. John H. Bailey (div.); res: 253 E. Delaware Pl., Chgo., Ill. 60611.

BAILEY, JANARA BROWN, Wms. Pg. Ed., Citizen's News, Chester Ave., Middlesboro, Ky. 40965, '67–'69; Beta Sigma Phi (Pres.); Personalities of the South; Outstanding Young Wm. of Am.; Lincoln Memorial Univ., '59–'63; b. Tarrant, Ala., 1940; p. James D. and Hazel Kile Brown; h. Rex L. Bailey; c. Erin LeAnn, Mary Elizabeth, Kristen Laine; res: 409 Dorchester Ave., Middlesboro, Ky. 40965.

BAILEY, MARGARET ELLEN, Asst. Ed., Nature and Science, American Museum of Natural History, 79th & Central Pk. W., N.Y., N.Y. 10024; '68–; Univ. of Ky., AB (Eng.), '66 (High distinction); Syracuse Univ., MA (Mag. Jnslm.), '68.

BAILEY, MARY GODBEY, Ed., Mansfield Advertiser, 46 N. Academy St., Mansfield, Pa. 16933, '62–; Assoc. Ed., '56–'62; Reptr., Williamsport Sun-Gazette, '53–; Reptr., Elmira (N.Y.) Star-Gazette, '53–'65; Feature-wtr., Petersburg (Va.) Progress-Index and other Va., Ky., nwsps., '40–'45; Tchr., Ky., '36–'40; BPW (Chptr. Pres.), Pa. Wms. Press (Dist. Dir., '63–'66); Kappa Delta Pi; First pl. edtl. aw., Nat. Edtl. Assn., '67; Univ. of Ky., AB, '38; b. Bristol, Tenn., 1915; p. S. B. and Zula Eads Godbey; h. Chester P. Bailey; c. C. Paul II, Barbara (Mrs. Robert W. McConnell); res: R.R. 1, Mansfield, Pa. 16933.

BAILEY, MARY POTTER, Pres., Bureau County Republican, Inc., 316–318 S. Main St., Princeton, Ill. 61356, '46–; Agt., Potter Insurance Agcy., Henry, Ill. '35–'37; Ill. Press Assn., BPW, C. of C. (Princeton Pres., '55); Stephen's Col., '33–'34; b. Henry, Ill.; p. Fredrick and Mary Harney Potter; h. John W. Bailey; res: 505 Park Ave. W., Princeton, Ill. 61356.

BAILEY, SUSAN MARGARET, PR AE, Fahlgren & Associates, 220 8th St., Parkersburg, W. Va. 26101, '68–; PR Asst., Ketchum, MacLeod & Grove, Pitt., Pa., '67–'68; Theta Sigma Phi; Oh. Univ., BS (Jnlsm.), '67; b. Alexandria, Va., 1945; p. Robert and Caroline Lohr Bailey; h. Gary Hess; res: 400 16th St., Parkersburg, W. Va. 26101.

BAILEY, VIRGINIA RUTH, Asst. to Mgr., WNAD radio, University of Oklahoma, 900 Asp Ave., Room 344, Norman, Okla. 73069; Prodr., Radio-TV Wtr., Lowe Runkle Co., Tulsa and Okla. City; Cont. Dir., Dir. of Sales Svc., KOTV, Tulsa, '60–'62; AWRT (Dir., '62–'63); S.F. State Col., BA, '59; b. Tulsa, Okla., 1936; p. Jesse and Marie Hill Bailey; res: 609 Wylie Rd., Norman, Okla. 73069.

BAIN, ELIZABETH ELLEN, Asst. VP of Audience Dev., Katz Television, 245 Park Ave., N.Y., N.Y. 10017, '69–; Asst. VP of Program and Engineering, CBS Inc., '61–'69; Exec. Dir. Participating Agreements, United Artists, '59–'61; Dir. of Film Programming, Metromedia, '58–'59; Mgr. Film Dept., WBBM-TV (Chicago), '57–'58; Film Dir., WGN-TV (Chicago), '48–'57; Public Sch. Tchr., '35–'41; Pres., Ware and Bain Inc., '61–'64; AWRT (Nat. Pres., '64–'65; Chmn., Educ. Fndn., '63–'64; N.Y.C. Chptr. VP); Clarke Col., BA (summa cum laude); Julliard Sch. of Music, '38; Northwestern Univ., '47; N.Y.U., '63; b. Dubuque, Ia., 1913; p. George and Elizabeth Behnke Bain; res: 5 Cat Rock Rd., Cos Cob, Conn. 06807.

BAIN, ROBERTA ANN, Gen. Sls. Coordr, Taft Broadcasting Company, WDAF-TV, Signal Hill, Kan. City, Mo. 64108, '67–; Sls. Secy., '62–'67; AWRT (Kan. City Chptr. Secy-Treas., '67–'68; VP, '68; Pres., '69); Kan. State Tchrs. Col., BS (Educ., Math., Bus.), '62; b. Kan. City, Kan. 1940; p. Horace and Jean Letellier Bain; res: 6624 Garnett Ct., Shawnee, Kan. 66203.

BAIRD, JEANNE, Actress, c/o Alper-Burch, 195 S. Beverly Dr., Beverly Hills, Cal.; Theatre, TV, Motion Pic.; "Anniversary Waltz," "Ironside," "Name of the Game," "The Medic," and many other appearances; panelist and personality on many game shows; active in children's causes and charities; AFTRA, SAG, AEA, NATAS; U.C.L.A.; L.A. City Col.; b. Meadville, Pa., 1937; p. Charles and Grace Billig Baird; c. Victoria Paige Meyerink; res: 7914 Hillside Ave., Hollywood, Cal. 90046.

BAIRD, VIRGINIA WILLITTS, Asst. News Ed., Information Services and Continuing Education Service, Room 7, Kellogg Center, Michigan State University, East Lansing, Mich. 48823, '63–; Wtr., Ed., Gtr. Mich. Fndn., '62–'63; Wms. Ed., Food Ed., Lansing State Journal, '52–'62; Info. Specialist, Mich. Dept. Civil Defense, '52; Ed., Michigan Public Health, Mich. Dept. of Health, '45–'52; PR, Edtl., Rsch., military schs.,

posts in Grand Rapids, Detroit, Dayton, Oh., '41–'45; owner-operator, News Bur. (Hastings, Mich.), '34–'41; numerous orgs., aws.; Western Mich. Univ., AB, '32; b. Eckford, Mich., 1911; p. William and Maude Gray Willitts; h. Thomas LeRoy Baird (div.); c. V. Johanna (Jodi) (dec.); res: 615 Glenmoor Rd., Apt. 90B, East Lansing, Mich. 48823.

BAKER, BETTY, Ed., Roundup, Western Writers of America, 6917 Bonnie Brae, Tucson, Ariz. 85710, '66–; Auth., 10 novels, '62–'69, incl. "Killer of Death" (Harper, '63; Western Heritage Aw.); Am. Press Wm. (mag. ed. aw., '66), WWA (Golden Spur aw., '68, for "The Dunderhead War"); b. Bloomsburg, Pa., 1920; p. Robert and Mary Wentling Baker; c. Christopher Venturo; res: 6917 Bonnie Brae, Tucson, Ariz. 87510.

BAKER, ELIZABETH FAULKNER, Auth. of textbks. and articles on econs.; Prof. (Emeritus), Barnard Col., Columbia Univ.; Cnslt.; Lectr.; Rsch. Worker; Columbia Univ. Faculty Club; educ: Univ. of Cal., AB, '14; Columbia Univ., MA, '19; PhD, '25; h. (dec.); res: 601 W. 113th St., N.Y., N.Y. 10025.

BAKER, ELIZABETH STEWART, PR Cnslt., Betty S. Baker, 3700 Pacific Ave., Marina del Rey, Cal. 90291; Wms. Ed., Seattle Times; Fashion Ed., Anncr. (pseud: Betty Goodwin), NBC (N.Y.C.); AE, Inst. of PR (N.Y.C.); Theta Sigma Phi, Fashion Group, Cal. Press Wm.; Univ. of Idaho; Univ. of Wash.; b. Boise, Idaho, 1914; p. Charles and Lillian Cahalan Stewart; h. William Ray Baker Jr.; c. C. Stewart Goodwin, Wendy M. Goodwin; res: 3700 Pacific Ave., Marina del Rey, Cal. 90291.

BAKER, JANET HOTSON, Free-lance Ed. for several Phila. Bk. Publrs., '62–; Discovery Dept., Ladies' Home Journal '61–'62; '54–'56; Assoc. Ed., Macrae Smith Co., '49–'54; PR Dept., Am. Friends Svc. Comm., '48–'49; Edtl. Asst., D. Van Nostrand Co., '47–'48; Swarthmore Col., BA, '47 (magna cum laude); b. N.Y.C., 1926; p. Ronald and Viola Williams Hotson; h. Norman W. Baker; c. Sally W., Joan K.; res: 115 Glen Riddle Rd., Media, Pa. 19063.

BAKER, LAURA NELSON, Free-lance Auth., bks. for children; Ed., Richfield (Minn.) News; NPWC Aws., '54, '55; Univ. of Minn.; b. Humboldt, Ia., 1911; p. Laurithz and Johanna Torkelson Nelson; c. Timothy; res: P.O. Box 291, Lagunitas, Cal. 94938.

BAKER, MARGARET VIRGINIA, Dir., South Georgia Regional Library, 300 Woodrow Wilson Dr., Valdosta, Ga., 31601, '48–; Librn., Emory Jr. Col., '46–'48; Reference Dept., Univ. of Fla., '46; Librn., Wash. Seminary, Atlanta, Ga., '43–'45; Gen. Lib., Univ. of Ga., Athens, '40–'43; Librn., Valdosta HS, '34–'40; Southeastern Lib. Assn., Ga. Lib. Assn., Phi Mu, AAUW, Delta Kappa Gamma, DAR, Lowndes County Hist. Soc., Valdosta Arts, Inc.; Randolph-Macon Wms. Col., '29–'31; Ga. State Wms. Col., AB, '33; Univ. of N.C., AB (Lib. Sci.), '39; b. Savannah, Ga., 1912; p. Clarence and Carrye

Keller Baker, Sr.; res: 1017 Slater St., Valdosta, Ga. 31601.

BAKER, MARY ANN HEDER, City Ed., Anchorage Times Publishing Co., 820 Fourth Ave., Anchorage, Alaska 99501, '67–; numerous edtl. positions, '58–'67; Wms. Ed., Anchorage Daily News, '52–'58; Asst. Soc. Ed., Grand Forks (N.D.) Herald, '51–'52; Alaska Corr. for N.Y. Times; Theta Sigma Phi; Alaska Press Club aws.; Univ. of N.D., BA (Jnlsm.), '51; b. Hoople, N.D.; p. Hjalmer and Emma Grand Heder; h. Donald R. Baker.

BAKER, NANCY BEARD, Reptr., Lafayette Journal and Courier, Sixth and Ferry Sts., Lafayette, Ind. 47901, '66–; Wms. Press Club of Ind., NFPW; Ball State Univ., BS (Educ.), '66; b. Portland, Ind., 1945; p. Merrill and June Maitlen Beard; h. Michael C. Baker; res: 805 S. Ninth St., Lafayette, Ind. 47905.

BAKER, NAOMI, Art Ed., Evening Tribune, Union-Tribune Publishing Co., 940 Third Ave., San Diego, Cal. 92112, '49–; numerous edtl. positions; Wtr., non-fiction.

BAKER, PATRICIA MARIE, Assoc. Bk. Ed., John Knox Press, 801 E. Main St., Richmond, Va. 23209, '69–; various edtl. positions, '62–'69; Maryville Col., BA, '62; Univ. of Fla., '68–'69; b. Ashland, Ky. 1940; p. Courtland and Dorothy Dalton Baker; res: 3412 Park Ave., Richmond, Va. 23221.

BAKER, PEARL BIDDLECOME, Auth: "The Wild Bunch at Robbers Roost," "Trail on the Water"; Cl.-Receptionist, Bureau Sport Fisheries & Wildlife, Bosque del Apache National Wildlife Refuge, P.O. Box 278, San Antonio, N.M. 87832, '63–; owned, operated trailer ct., rooming house (Green River, Ut.), '47–'63; operated White Canyon Trading Post on Colo. river, '55–'56; operated Robbers Roost ranch (Ut.); taught sch. (Hite, White Canyon, Ut.); WWA, Western Hist. Assn.; b. Ferron, Ut., 1907; p. Joe and Millie Scharf Biddlecome; h. (dec.); c. Joe, Jack, Capt. Noel; res: P.O. Box 278, San Antonio, N.M. 87832.

BAKER, PENNY (Mary Ellen Brummett), Pres., Penny Baker, Inc., 341 Madison Ave., N.Y., N.Y. 10017, '67–; Ed., Ojibway Press; Fashion Pubcty. Dir., Degnan Assoc.; Acc. Supvsr., Arndt, Preston, Chapin, Lamb & Keen; Fashion Group, Adv. Club of N.Y., NHFL, Nat. Soc. of Interior Designers; Univ. of Okla.; b. Chattanooga, Tenn.; p. Mike and Mary Vickers Brummett; h. (div.); c. James Arlen Baker; res: 132 East 35th St., N.Y., N.Y. 10016.

BAKER, SARA LANDERS, Wms. Ed., The Huntsville Times, 2317 S. Memorial Pkwy., Huntsville, Ala. 35807, '47–; The Press Club of Huntsville; Ala. Col., '39; b. Huntsville, Ala., 1918; p. Elroy and Henrietta Delp Landers; h. William Bradley Baker; res: 1213 Hermitage Ave., S.E., Huntsville, Ala. 35801.

BAKER, VIRGINIA MAY DAVIDSON, Wms. News Ed., Western Newspapers Inc., Evening Courier, 205 N. Cortez, Prescott, Ariz. 86301, '63–; Proof Reader, '60–'63; Ariz. Press Wm., NPWC, BPW; several nat. and state aws. for wms. pg.; Intl. DeMolay "Hat's Off" Aw., '69; Certs. of Recognition, Am. Cancer Soc., Am. Heart Assn., '63–'68; b. Richmond, Cal. 1925; p. Claude R. and Majorie Winebrenner Davidson; h. Archer Baker; c. Donald A., Mrs. Stephanie A. Eggen; res: 1141 Stetson Rd., P.O. Box 658, Prescott, Ariz. 86301.

BAKWIN, RUTH MORRIS, Auth., articles and bks. on child behavior; Prof., Clinical Pediatrics, New York University School of Medicine, 132 E. 71st St., N.Y., N.Y. 10021, '60–; Dir. Emeritus, Dept. of Pediatrics, N.Y. Infirmary (Aw. of Merit, '60); Assn. for Mentally Ill Children (Bd. of Dirs.), Nat. Assn. for Mental Health, Am. Acad. of Pediatrics (State Chmn., '65–'67; Elizabeth Blackwell Aw., '50, Alpha Phi Aw., '52; educ: Wellesley Col., BA, '19; Cornell Med. Col., MD, '23; Columbia Univ., MA, '29; b. Chgo., Ill.; p. Edward and Helen Swift Morris; h. Harry Bakwin; c. Patricia (Mrs. F. R. Selch), Barbara (Mrs. William Rosenthal), Edward, Michael; res: 132 E. 71st St., N.Y., N.Y. 10021.

BALAKIAN, NONA H., Asst. to Ed., Bk. Rev., The New York Times, 229 W. 43rd St., N.Y., N.Y. 10036, '43–; Contrbr., bk. revs., articles, to the Times and to literary pubns.; Co-ed., "The Creative Present: Notes on Contemporary American Fiction" (Doubleday, '63); PEN; Barnard Col., BA, '42; Columbia Univ., MS (Jnlsm.), '43; b. Constantinople, Turkey; p. Dr. Diran Balakian and K. (Panosyan) Balakian; res: 600 W. 116th St., N.Y., N.Y. 10027.

BALCIUS, HELEN, Prod. Mgr., Graceman Advertising, Inc. 999 Asylum Ave., Hartford, Conn. 06105, '65–; Traf. and Media Dept., '60–'65; Hartford Adv. Club; Northwestern Univ.; b. N.Y.C.; h. (div.); c. Roy Charles; res: 148B Sisson St., East Hartford, Conn. 06118.

BALD, MARGARET, Librn., Bob Jones University, Greenville, S.C. 29614, '48–; Head, Process Dept., Armed Forces Staff Col., '46–'48; Lib. Svcs., U.S. Navy, '44–'46; Reference Dept., Pasadena Public Lib. '40–'44; Asst. Librn., Carnegie Ill. Steel Corp. (Pitt., Pa.), '37–'40; Lib. Asst., Carnegie Public Lib., '35–'37; wrote chptrs. in "How I Found God's Will in My Life" and "Careers for Christian Youth" (auth: John W. Sigsworth); Adult Educ. Assn., S.C. Lib. Assn. Southeastern Lib. Assn., Asbury Col., BA, '34; Carnegie Inst. of Tech., BS (Lib. Sci.), '35; b. Pitt., Pa., 1913; p. Edmund and Margaret Sieman Bald; res: Bob Jones Univ., Greenville, S.C. 29614.

BALDRIGE, LETITIA K., PR, Burlington Industries, Inc., 1430 Broadway, N.Y., N.Y., 10018; Pres., Letitia Baldrige Enterprises, (Chgo., Ill.), '64–'69; Social Secy. to Mrs. John F. Kennedy, '61–'63; PR Dir., Tiffany &

Co., '56–'60; Social Secy. to Ambassador Clare Boothe Luce, '53–'56; Social Secy., Am. Embassy, Paris, '50–'53; Colmst., Chgo. Daily News; Auth: three non-fiction books; Am. Inst. of Interior Design, NHFL, Fashion Group; Vassar Col., BA; h. Robert Hollensteiner; c. Clare Louise, Malcom Baldrige.

BALDWIN, CLARA, Auth., juv. fiction; Phila. Corr. for several trade pubns., 2100 Walnut St., Phila., Pa. 19103; bks: "Cotton for Jim" (Abingdon, '54), "Timber from Terry Forks" (Abingdon, '56), "The Hermit of Crab Island" (Abingdon, '58), "Little Tuck" (Doubleday, '59); over 40 juv. short stories, two serials, numerous short items for Child Life, Jack and Jill, other pubns.; WNBA, Nat. Cncl. of Wm. of the U.S.; Northwestern Univ. (Eng., Fine Arts); b. Ironton, Mo.; p. John and Clara Delano Baldwin, Jr.

BALDWIN, FAITH, Auth., c/o Harold Ober Associates, 40 E. 49th St., N.Y., N.Y. 10017; novels, nonfiction, poetry and juv. bks. ('21–'66; Holt, Rinehart & Winston, Inc.; London: Robert Hale Ltd.) incl. "Take What You Want" ('70), "The Velvet Hammer" ('69), "Harvest of Hope" ('62), "Testament of Trust" ('60), "Many Windows: Seasons of the Heart" ('58); serials, short stories; verse; radio and motion pictures from bks. and stories; Contrbr., Woman's Day mag., '58–; TV appearances; Faith Baldwin collection begun by Boston Univ., '68–; Am. League of Pen Wm., Founding Faculty of Famous Wtrs. Sch., Westport, Conn., Save the Children Fedn. (Nat. Sponsor, Conn. Dir., Annual Aw., '59), Silver Hill Fndn. Bd., Wms. Nat. Bk. Assn.; Miss Fuller's, Briarcliff; b. New Rochelle, N.Y., 1893; p. Stephen and Edith Finch Baldwin; h. Hugh Cuthrell (dec.); c. Hugh (dec.), Hervey, Stephen, Ann; res: Rte. 2, Weed Ave., Norwalk, Conn. 06850.

BALDWIN, MARY KAY, Dir., Sales Prom., Pubcty., Waverly Fabrics, 58 W. 40th St., N.Y., N.Y. 10018, '65–; Asst. Byr., Allied Purchasing Corp., '63–'65; Interior Decorator, Lord & Taylor, '59–'62; NHFL; Syracuse Univ., BS (Int. Design), '59.

BALDY, MARIAN JACKSON, Dir. of Rsch., Metromedia Producers Corporation, 485 Lexington Ave., N.Y., N.Y. 10017, '69–; Dir. of TV Rsch., Metromedia, '66–'69; Rsch. Mgr., WNEW-TV, '60–'66; Media Rsch. Supvsr., Foote, Cone and Belding, '54–'60; Asst. Dir. of Rsch., Radio Adv. Bur., '52–'54; Presentation Analyst, A. C. Nielsen Co., '50–'52; Mathematics Tchr., High Sch. and adult level; Asst. Dir., two-yr. program, Sch. of Educ., N.Y.U.; NATAS, Radio and TV Rsch. Cncl. (VP, '61–'62; Secy., '58–'59, '60–'61); Pacific Univ., BA (Mathematics); Grad. Work, Univ. of Wash.; b. Cornelius, Ore.; p. Frank and Grace Elford Jackson; h. Jean M. Baldy; res: 333 E. 69th St., N.Y., N.Y. 10021.

BALES, CECILLE GRIFFITH, VP, Ackerman Advertising, Division of Lennen & Newell, Inc., 1600 Mid-Continent Bldg., 409 S. Boston, Tulsa, Okla. 74103, '67–; Whitney Advertising Agcy., '56–'67; Off. Mgr.,

Wilson Advertising Agcy., '54–'56; AAF (10th Dist. Bd. of Dirs., '66–'69), Tulsa Adv. Fedn. (Pres., '68–'69), Quota Club (Tulsa Chptr. Pres., '64), Tulsa C. of C.; Univ. of Okla. Col. of Continuing Educ., '65; b. Kechi, Kan. 1926; p. Walter and Ethel Cardner Griffith; h. Waldo Bales; c. Mrs. Steven Strong, Vaden; res: 5175 E. 27th Pl., Tulsa, Okla. 74114.

BALFOUR, BERNICE BRILE, Free-lance Wtr. and Copy Ed., 1219 Ralston St., Anaheim, Cal. 92801, '60–; Copy Ed., Harcourt, Brace & World, '56–'60; Wtrs. Club of Whittier; two aws. for essays on race rels.; Wooster Col., BA (Eng.), '44; b. Bklyn., N.Y. 1922; p. Lawrence and Fanny Rosenthal Brile; h. Leo Balfour; c. Laura Ruth; res: 1219 Ralston St., Anaheim, Cal. 92801.

BALFOUR, KATHARINE, Interviewer, WEVD, 1700 Broadway, N.Y., N.Y. 10019; Actress in motion pics.; voted one of 10 best supporting actresses for "America America"; b. N.Y.C.

BALL, LUCILLE, Actress; Pres., Lucille Ball Productions, Inc., 780 N. Gower St., Hollywood, Cal. 90038, '68–; Pres., Desilu Prods., '61–'68; VP, '51–'61; SAG, AGVA, AFTRA, AEA, AMPAS, NATAS (Emmy Aws. '52, '55, '67, '68), Jr. Achiev., Am. Heart Assn., Soroptomist Club, Nat. Soc. for Crippled Children and Adults; b. Jamestown, N.Y.; p. Henry and Desiree Hunt Ball; h. Gary Morton; c. Lucie Arnaz, Desi Arnaz, Jr.; res: 1000 N. Roxbury, Beverly Hills, Cal. 90210.

BALL, MILDRED PORTEOUS, Young People's Ed., The Times-Picayune Publishing Co., 3800 Howard Ave., New Orleans, La. 70140, '67–; Fla. State Univ., BA, '67; b. N.O. La., 1945; p. Harold and Mildred Porteous Ball; res: 1623 General Pershing St., N.O., La. 70115.

BALLANTINE, BETTY JONES, VP, Ballantine Books, Inc., 101 Fifth Ave., N.Y., N.Y. 10003, '52–; Ed., Bantam Bks., '45–'52; Penguin Bks., '39–'45; Jersey Ladies Col., '33–'37; b. Fyzabad, India, 1919; p. Hubert and Norah McNally Jones; h. Ian Ballantine; c. Richard.

BALLARD, SHIRLEY, Actress, Drama Tchr., Everywoman's Village, 5634 Sepulveda Blvd., Van Nuys, Cal. 91401, '70–; roles in five major Broadway plays; TV: "Bonanza," "Ben Casey," "Kraft Suspense Theatre," "GE Theatre," "Art Carney Revue" (Emmy and Sylvania Aws., Best Comedy Show, '60); Miss Cal., '44; currently teaching principles of acting to children and teenagers; b. Cal., 1925; p. Kenneth and Mildred Ballard; h. Jason Evers (div.); res: 11990 Laurelwood Dr., Apt. 24, Studio City, Cal. 91604.

BALSOM, MARY POINTNER, PR Dir., Dayton Art Institute, Forest and Riverview Aves., Dayton, Oh. 45409, '67–; News-Feature Wtr., Dayton (Oh.) Daily News; Fashion Ed.; Free-lance wtr:, Co-Auth., "History of Boy Scouting in Miami Valley;" ONWA (News, Feature writing aws., '63–'66), Am. Inst. of

Interior Designers; WLW-TV Aw., Wm. of the Day, '69; Oh. Wesleyan Univ., BA (Jnlsm.), '63; Univ. of Dayton; b. Sidney, Oh., 1941; p. Norbert and Mary Dustman Pointner; h. Michael J. Balsom, Jr.; res: 115 Forestview Dr., Dayton, Oh. 45459.

BAMBERGER, GAY GABRIELLE, Owner, Gay Bamberger Public Relations, 663 Fifth Ave., N.Y., N.Y. 10022, '68–; AE, Philip Lesly Co., '61–'68; Wtr., articles for consumer pubns.; Electrical Wms. Round Table, AWRT; Oberlin Col., BA, '60; b. Berlin, Germany, 1938; p. Fritz and Kate Schwabe Bamberger; res: 414 E. 65th St., N.Y., N.Y. 10021.

BANCROFT, ALICE WILLIAMS, Gen. Mgr., Alison-Biart Enterprises, P. O. Box 337, Lansing, Mich. 48902, '69–; Publicist, Mich. State Employees Assn., '59–'62; Assoc. Ed., Mich. State Univ. Bul., '59; Prom. Mgr., WJIM-TV, '49–'56; Cont. Dir., KSO (Des Moines, Ia.), '45–'49; Wtr., Bdcstr., WMIN (St. Paul, Minn.), '43–'44; MSEA NEWS, past Ed., Free-lance Wtr., Ed., Co-auth. of TV plays; ZONTA (Des Moines Chptr. Charter Mbr.; VP, '48), Altrusa (PR Dir., '64–'66), PR Assoc. of Mich., AWRT; Minn. Sch. of Music; Order of Eastern Star; b. Chicago, Ill., 1906; p. William R. and Esther Williams Williams; h. Lyle H. Bancroft; c. Mrs. E. C. Appleyard, Jr., Roger L. Buchanan, William G. Buchanan; res: 13420 Bancroft Dr., Grand Ledge, Mich., 48837.

BANCROFT, CAROL JANE, Art. Dir., McGraw-Hill Inc., 330 W. 42nd St., N.Y., N.Y. 10036, '62–; Asst. Art Dir., Ladies' Home Journal, '60–'62; Layout Desginer, McCall's Magazine, '56–'60; Layout Designer, Women's Day, '55–'56; N.Y. Assn. of Indsl. Communicators (Graphic Judge, '67–'69; Instr., evening course in edtl. layout, '69; Lectr., Bus. Communication Forum, '68); McGraw-Hill Art Dirs. (Instr., evening course on edtl. layout, '68; Chmn., '66), McGraw-Hill Art Dirs. Show (20 aw. plaques, '64, '65, '66), McGraw-Hill Photog. Show (1st prize black and white photog., '64, '65), Soc. of Pubn. Designers (Merit Aw. Plaque, '65); Lasell Jr. Col., AA, '49–'51; R.I. Sch. of Design, BFA, '54; b. Phila., Pa., 1930; p. Phineas and Mildred Provost Bancroft; res: 120 E. 83rd St., N.Y., N.Y. 10028.

BANDLER, RIVA LIPPA, Free-lance Copy Ed., '53–; Bklyn. Col., BA, '36; h. Arthur Bandler; res: 80–19 168 St., Jamaica, N.Y. 11432.

BANKS, ADE L., Aide to Lt. Gov. Ed Reinecke, Chmn., and California Bicentennial Celebration Commission, 1000 Wilshire, L.A., Cal. 90017, '69–; Press Secy., '66–'69; City Ed., San Fernando Valley Times, '56–'64; Free-lance Wtr.; Theta Sigma Phi; b. Hull, Ia; p. F. W. and Mary Weir Banks; res: 7740 Claybeck, Sun Valley, Cal. 91352.

BANKS, DOLLY, Stations Mgr., WHAT and WWDB, 3930–40 Conshohocken Ave., Phila., Pa. 19131, '44–; Ballerina, Phila. Ballet Co.; AWRT (Phila. Chptr. past Pres.), Phila. Club of Adv. Wm.; McCall's Golden

Mike Aw., '53; Temple Univ. Aw.; North City Congress Commty. Serv. Aw.; Christian Tabernacle Aw.; Scotty Prods. first Golden Merit Aw.; Park City West Club (Nwsp. Ed.); Univ. of Miami; b. Phila., Pa., 1919; p. Morris and Anna Fineman Banks; h. Shep Shapiro; res: Park City West Apts., 3900 Ford Rd., Phila., Pa. 19131.

BANNICK, NANCY MEREDITH, Hi. Ed., Sunset Magazine-Lane Magazine and Book Company of Menlo Park, Cal., 871 Kapiolani Blvd., Honolulu, Hi. 96813, '52–; Assoc. Ed., Hawaii Farm & Home Magazine, '50–'51 Ed., Honolulu Star-Bul. house organ, '50; Soc. Ed., Yakima (Wash.) Daily Republic, '48–'50; Auth., "Hawaii: A Guide to All the Islands" (Sunset) Theta Sigma Phi, Honolulu Press Club; Pacific Area Travel Assn. mag. aw., '66; Univ. of Hi. Travel Industry Mgt. Sch. cit., '67; Stanford Univ., BA (Jnlsm.), '48 (Phi Beta Kappa); b. Rochester, Minn. 1926; p. Dr. Edwin and Vesta Meredith Bannick; res: 2943 Kalakaua Ave., Honolulu, Hi. 96815.

BANNIGAN, BERNICE GATES, Head of Music, Art, Religion, Philosophy, Fgn. Depts., Utica Public Library, 303 Genesee St., Utica, N.Y. 13501, '48–; Info. Asst., '44–'48; Asst., Circ. Dept., '41–'44; ALA, N.Y. Lib. Assn., Catholic Lib. Assn., AAUW; Pro Dea et Juventute Aw. (Catholic Youth Org.), '68; Franciscan Laymen Pres., '68; N.Y. State Col. at Albany, BA, '41; BS (Lib. Sci.), '44; b. Utica, N.Y., 1915; p. Earl and Alice Whitton Gates; h. George E. Bannigan; res: 14 Watson Pl., Utica, N.Y. 13502.

BANNON, BARBARA A., Assoc. Ed., Publishers' Weekly, 1180 Ave. of the Ams., N.Y., N.Y. 10036; previously Asst. Ed., Edtl. Asst.; Colmst., Coronet, '65–; Publrs. Pubcty. Assn. (Co-founder), Publrs. Adv. Club, Eng. Speaking Union; Manhattanville Col., BA (Eng.); b. Auburn, N.Y.; p. Thomas and Rose MacCauley Bannon; res: 7 E. 14th St., N.Y., N.Y. 10003.

BANOCZI, JEANNETTE, Pres.-Owner, KNOB, 1700 S. Harbor Blvd., Anaheim, Cal. 92802, '66–; Pennino Music Co., L.A., '46–; Radio Station KGGK, Garden Grove, '61–'66; Musician; Sales & Mktng. Exec. of Orange County (Dir., '67), C. of C. (Orange County Dir., '68; Life Mbr.), Better Bus. Bur., Soroptimist Club (Pres., '63–'65); New Eng. Conservatory; b. Dracut, Mass. 1922; p. Albert and Rhea Venne Boulay; h. 1 H. R. Pennino (dec.), 2. John Banoczi; c. Mrs. Jeannette Rathbun, Madelaine Lynn Pennino, Naomi Gloria Pennino; res: 30151 Branding Iron Rd., San Juan Capistrano, Cal. 92675.

BANTA, THELMA DARRACOTT, Mgr., Customer Svc. Dept., Chilton Book Company, 401 Walnut St., Phila., Pa. 19106, '63–; with co. since '58; h. Joseph Bartlum.

BAPTISTA, MILDRED G., Dir. Club Svcs., American Advertising Federation, 1225 Connecticut Ave., N.W., Wash., D.C. 20036, '69–; Mgr., Radio-TV Adv., Woodward & Lothrop, Wash., D.C., '54–'68; Edtl. Asst., U.S.I.A., Wash., D. C.; '50–'53; YMCA Central Br., Wash., D.C. (only Wm. Bd. Mbr., '65–'70), Comm. on Status of Wm. (Labor Law Sub-Comm.), Wms. Adv. Club of Wash. (Pres., '65–'67), Am. Adv. Fedn. (Dist. Gov.), AWRT (Wash. Chptr. Corr. Secy., '68–'69), BPW (Cosmopolitan Chptr. Charter Mbr.); Boston Univ. Sch. of Jnlsm.; Bourdett Col.; b. Taunton, Mass., p. M. Perry and Anna Faria Baptista; res: 836 New Hampshire Ave., N.W., Wash., D.C. 20037.

BARAN, ELIZABETH T., Asst. to Adv. Mgr., House Organ Ed., Syntron Division, FMC Corporation, Homer City, Pa. 15748, '65–; Assn. of Indsl. Adv., Indsl. Mgt. Club; Indiana (Pa.) Bus. Col., '46–'48; Indiana Univ. of Pa., '69–; b. Homer City, Pa., 1928; p. Michael and Anna Barron Baran; res: 54 Center St., Homer City, Pa. 15748.

BARB, MARIAN L., Dir. Alumni Relations, The American University, Massachusetts and Nebraska Aves. N.W., Wash. D.C. 20016, '66–; PR Assoc. Dir., Un. Givers Fund of the Natl. Capital Area, '63–'66; Partner, Jeanne Viner Assoc., Wash. D.C., '60–'63; PRSA (Wash. Chptr. Bd. of Dirs., '69), Theta Sigma Phi, Phi Delta Gamma, AAUW, Am. Alumni Cnsl.; The Am. Univ., BA, '58; active in YWCA, Natl. Comm. on Household Employment, Health and Welfare Cncl.; b. L.A., Cal., 1925; p. Peter Keyes and Marian Chace; h. (div.); c. Jeannette Marie (Mrs. Robert Hurley); res: 4707 Connecticut Ave., N.W., Apt. 616, Wash., D.C. 20008.

BARBER, JEAN ELAINE, Ed., Locksmith Ledger, Inc., 1500 Cardinal Dr., Little Falls, N.J. 07424, '68–; Bus. Mgr., '63–'68; Asst. Ed., '60–'63; Asst. Gen. Mgr., Sls. Aids Publ. Co., '60–; Bus. Mgr., Auto & Flat Glass Jnl., Inc., '63–'68; Asst. Ed., '60–'63; Knox Col., '55–'57; b. Hackensack, N.J., 1936; p. George and Edna Ahrendt Barber; res: 5H Colonial Dr., Little Falls, N.J. 07424.

BARBER, JEAN Mc EVOY, Wms. Ed., The Evening Tribune, Gannett Florida Corporation, P.O. Box 1330, Cocoa, Fla. 32922, '67–; Staff Wtr., '64–'67; Dir., PR, Wood County Bank (Parkersburg, W. Va.), '61–'63; Cont. Dir., WTAP-TV, '57–'61; Kindergarten Dir., Tchr., '55–'57; Fla. Wms. Press Assn.; State Nwsltr. Ed., W. Va. Hosp. Auxiliaries; Pubcty. Dir., Am. Red Cross (Charleston, Parkersburg, W. Va.); Univ. of Ill., '34–'37; Oh. Univ.; W. Va. Univ.; b. Chgo., Ill.; p. Harry K. and Louise Cavey Mc Evoy; h. Timothy Barber; c. James, Daniel, Betsy, Andrew; res: P.O. Box 365, Merritt Is., Fla. 32952.

BARBER, MARGARET KILBOURNE, Free-lance Wtr.; Copywtr., McCann-Erickson (L.A., Cal.), '44–'48, '51–'68; Consumer Svcs. Wtr.; Wms. Svc. Dept. Wtr., Capper Pubns. (Topeka, Kan.), '30–'34, '39–'42; Theta Sigma Phi; Lulu Aw., L.A. Adv. Wm., '66; Don Belding Aw., Adv. Club of L.A., '67; Univ. of Kan., AB, '30; b. Minneapolis, Kan., 1909; p. Ernest and Sophie

Stelter Kilbourne; h. Wilbur A. Barber (div.); res: 3772 S. Van Ness, L.A., Cal. 90018.

BARBER, VIRGINIA FOSTER, Prom. Mgr., Smithsonian Institution Press, Wash., D.C. 20560, '66–'69; Dir., Kiplinger Bk. Svc., '64–'66; Asst. Dir., '63–'64; Mount Holyoke Col., BA, '62 (with distinction); b. Phila., Pa., 1940; p. Joseph and Theodora Maczis Foster; h. Everett Barber; res: 5015 42nd St., Wash., D.C. 20016.

BARBRE, ANITA TRUMAN, Pres. Barbre Productions, Inc., 2130 S. Bellaire St., Denver, Colo. 80222, '64–; founded co. with husband in '40; many aws. for motion pics. prod. by co.; b. Tipton, Okla., 1909; h. Thos. J. Barbre (dec.); c. Blakely F. Wilcox, Mrs. C. A. Latcham.

BARCKLAY, SUSAN SPERBER, Dir., Spokane County Library, 11811 E. First Ave., Spokane, Wash. 99206, '65; Base Librn., Geiger Field, Spokane, '59–'63; Asst. Librn., Kaiser Aluminum, '53–'58; Reference Librn., Mid-Columbia Lib. (Kennewick, Wash.), '48–'50; Asst. Librn., Linfield Col. (McMinnville, Ore.), '47–'48; Wash. Lib. Assn., Pacific Northwest Lib. Assn., ALA; Whitman Col., BA (Hist.), '44; Simmons Col., BS (Lib. Sci.), '47; b. Portland, Ore., 1922; p. William and Elva Wood Sperber; h. (div.); res: 24426 E. Third Ave., Liberty Lake, Wash. 99019.

BARDACKE, BEATRICE, Mgr., Mdsg. Dept., Doubleday and Company, Inc., 501 Franklin Ave., Garden City, N.Y. 11530, '66–; Supvsr., '61–'66; Trade Sls. Mdsg. Dept., '59–'61; WNBA; Univ. of Chgo., BA; h. Gregory J. Bardacke.

BARHAM, PATRICIA ANN. Pres., Guy B. Barham Co., 125 W. Fourth Street, L.A. Cal; Synd. Colmst., N.Y. and Tex. Chain; former Colmst., L.A. Herald Examiner; former W. Coast Ed., Diplomat; Theta Sigma Phi, Delta Gamma, Gtr. L.A. Press Club, Am. Nat. Theatre and Acad; Who's Who of Am. Wm., Intl. Biog., Who's Who of L.A. County; U.S. Olympic Comm.; Amateur Athletic Un. (Nat. VP for PR); Chivralous and Religious Order de San Luige de l'Ordie Souberain, Chebilaire et Religieux de la Couronne Epines, 67; Univ. of So. Cal.; Ariz. Univ.; b. L.A. Cal.; p. Dr. Frank F. and Princess Jessica Meskhi-Gleboff (Gorham) Barham; res. 165 S. Muirfield Road, L.A., Cal. 90004.

BARKAN, KAY KANER, Secy.-VP, Walter Kaner Associates, Inc., 274 Madison Ave., N.Y., N.Y. 10016, '58–; Partner, '50–'58; Pubcty. Club of N.Y.; C.C.N.Y.; b. West New York, N.J., 1916; h. Aaron Barkan; res: 53–01 32nd Ave., Woodside, N.Y. 11377.

BARKER, E. LOUISE, Agent in Food Mkt., Tennessee Agricultural and Extension Service, 701 Jefferson St., Nashville, Tenn. 37208, '58–; Weekly radio, TV bdcsts., press releases on food; Home Econst., '48–'51; Home Econst., Memphis Light Gas and Water, '51–'57;

AWRT (Nashville Chptr. Corr. Secy., '68-'69; Treas., '66-'67), Am. Home Econs. Assn., Home Econsts. in Bus. (Memphis Chptr. Chmn., '56-'57), Tenn. Home Econs. Assn. (Pres., '63-'65), Nashville Area Home Econs. Assn. (Pres., '59-'60), Nat. and Tenn. Assn. of Ext. Home Econsts.; Epsilon Sigma Phi, BPW, (Nashville Wm. of Year, '59), First Baptist Ch., Tenn. Future Homemakers of Am. (Hon. Mbr.); WLAC Radio Wm. of Day, '63, '64, '66, '68; Memphis State Univ., BS, '47; b. Camden, Tenn.

BARKER, JEAN MEEK, Fashion Ed., Redbook Magazine, 230 Park Ave., N.Y., N.Y. 10017, '66-; edtl. positions with Boot and Shoe Recorder, Harper's Bazaar, N.Y. Herald Tribune, Mademoiselle, '58-'66; Fashion Group, Shoe Wm. Execs. (Bd. Mbr., Secy.); L.A. City Col.; b. Monrovia, Cal.; h. Gilbert Wm. Barker.

BARKER, MILDRED JOY, Legislative Rep., Woman's Christian Temperance Union, 13 E St., N.W., Wash., D.C. 20004; Ed., Pen Wm. Magazine, '58-'62; Reprtr., Feature Wtr.: Md. News, Bethesda Tribune, The Record, Wash. Star, Wash. Post, Wash. Ltr.; Lectr. on phases of temperance work; various organizations; W. Va. Univ., AB, '21; b. Morgantown, W. Va., 1900; p. William Lawrence Barker and Evalena Brookover; h. Charles N. Harman; c. Alice Evalyn, Dr. Charles Morgan; res: 3908 Baltimore St., Kensington, Md. 20795.

BARKER, MYRTIE, Colmst., Indianapolis News, 307 N. Pennsylvania St., Indpls., Ind. 46206, '49-; Colmst., Sheridan (Ind.) News '38-'49; Lectr.; Non-fictional Auth: "Parade of Days" ('57), "I Am Only One" (Bobbs-Merrill, '63), "Where Is Everybody?" (Bobbs-Merrill, '68); Theta Sigma Phi, NLAPW, Ind. Wms. Press Club (Cits., '60-'68); DAR; numerous writing aws.; Ind. Univ.; b. Indpls., Ind., 1910; p. Harry and Mary Bush Barker; res: 699 E. 96th St., Indpls., Ind. 46240.

BARKER, RUTH J., Free-lance Cnslt. and Wtr: Mdsng., Prom., PR Edtl., Adv., '69-; Mdsng. Dir., Simplicity Pattern Co. Inc., N.Y.C., '63-'69; PR Dir., Fashion Coordr., Stanford Assocs., '58-'63; Adv. Rep., Mademoiselle, '54-'58; Asst. to Cosmetic Adv. Mgr., Harper's Bazaar, '47-'54; AWNY, Fashion Group; res: 35-36 76th St., Jackson Heights, N.Y. 11372.

BARKLEY, S. JOYCE LOWEN, Wms. Ed., Enterprise Publishing Co., 700 Broadway, Chico, Cal. 95926, '56-; Corr., Santa Rosa Press Dem.; Ed., Montgomery Village News; Wms. Ed., Reprtr., Photog., Ukiah Daily Jnl.; Speaker, Cnslt. on jnlsm.; Cal. Press Photogs. Assn.; Nat. AHLMA Aw., '61; active in civic affairs; Univ of Ore., '33-'38; Univ. of Cal., '39; b. Dalmany, Saskatchewan, Can., 1913; p. George and Marie Laubenstein Lowen; h. Edgar E. Barkley (div.); c. Karen, Michael, Eric; res: 1538 Sunset Ave., Chico, Cal. 95926.

BARLOW, ALICE TOWNSEND, Travel Ed., News

Gazette, 48 Main St., Champaign, Ill. 61820, '63-; Mng. Ed., Hoopeston Chronicle-Herald, '61; Feature Wtr., '50-'67; Sch.-Commty. Rels. Dir., Champaign Schs., '52-'63; Instr., Jnlsm.-Eng., Champaign HS, '47-'52; Gen. Reprtr., Mpls. Tribune, '20-'27; Ill. Advisor on teaching Econs. of Free Enterprise System; Mbr. and Cnslt. to Ill. Educ. Assn. on PR and teaching methods; PRSA, Intl. Platform Assn., Ill. Wms. Press Assn., Theta Sigma Phi (Ill. Dir., '55-'58), Ill. ATJ (Ill. Chptr. Pres., '49-'50; outstanding Tchr. of Jnslm., '51), Delta Kappa Gamma (State Radio Comm., '55-'57), Urbana-Champaign Br. of Pen Wm., NSPRA (Advisor, '62-'65), Nat. Educ. Assn. (Life Mbr.); outstanding achiev. aw., Champaign-Urbana Kiwanis Club, '61; Beloit Col., '18-'19; Univ. of Minn., '19-'21, AB, '50; b. Chgo., Ill., 1900; p. George and Mary Walls Townsend; h. (dec.); c. Richard, Townsend, Mary Alice (Mrs. Robert Persche), Charlotte (Mrs. W. G. Mathews); res: 1316 Grandview Dr., Champaign, Ill. 61820.

BARNES, DONNA MASTIN, Educ. Wtr., Citizen Patriot, 214 S. Jackson St., Jackson, Mich. 49204, '66-; Gen. Reprtr., '51-'66; Wms. Pg. Reprtr., '48-'51; EWA; Mich. Educ. Assn. aw., '68; Mich. Assn. of Airport Mgrs. aw., '62, '65; Mich. AP aw., '58; Jackson Commty Col., grad., '47; Mich. State Univ., '47-'48, '58; b. Jackson, Mich., 1927; p. Howard and Viva Wright Mastin; h. Francis Barnes; res: 3210 Ocean Beach Rd., Clark Lake, Mich. 49234.

BARNES, GEORGENE O'DONNELL, Radio-TV Special Events Dir., McFadden, Strauss, Eddy and Irwin, 509 Madison Ave., N.Y., N.Y. 10022, '65-; Prodr.-Wtr., NBC, Goodson-Todman Prods., '57-'65; Crtv. Supvsr., Wtr., Assoc. Prodr. film series, "It's Baby Time," with Am. Med. Assn., Chgo., Ill., '55-'57; AWRT (N.Y.C. Chptr. Pres., '70), NATAS (Aws. for Outstanding Children's and Teenage Program, Live Local Program, Program of Interest to Wm., '59, '61), Fashion Group; Northwestern Univ., '46-'49; Univ. of Chgo., '48; b. Chgo., Ill.; p. James and Mildred Schlundt O'Donnell; h. Wade Barnes; res: 20 Beekman Pl., N.Y., N.Y. 10022.

BARNES, JEANNE J., Home Ed., The Dallas Morning News, Commtns. Ctr., Dallas, Tex. 75222, '57-; The San Antonio Light, '56-'57; The San Antonio Express-News, '52-'56; The Houston Chronicle, '49-'52; The Ft. Worth Press, '45-'49; Theta Sigma Phi (Ft. Worth, Houston, San Antonio Chptr. Pres.), NHFL (Southwest Chptr. Treas.); aws: Dorothy Dawe, '54, '59, Dallas Mkt. Ctr., '61, '65, Nat. Soc. of Interior Designers, '65, Am. Inst. of Interior Designers, '60; Tex. Technological Col., BA (Jnlsm.), '41; b. Clarendon, Tex.; p. W. C. and Hazel Jefferies McDonald; res: 4138 Wycliff, Dallas, Tex. 75219.

BARNETT, HELEN CLEGG, Publr., Bedford County Press, 100 Masters Ave., Everett, Pa. 15537, '47-; Assoc. Ed., Ed.; Pa. Soc. Nwsp. Eds. (Bd. of Dirs., '64-'67), Pa. Wms. Press Assn. (VP); Pa. Nwsp. Publrs. aws.; Temple

Univ.; b. Everett, Pa., 1904; p. John and Gertrude Clegg; h. Milton L. Barnett; res: 311 E. Main St., Everett, Pa. 15537.

BARNETT, PHYLLIS SOULELES, Asst. Dir. of PR, The American Bankers Assn., 90 Park Ave., N.Y., N.Y. 10016, '62–; Exec. Asst., N.Y. Superintendent of Banks, '59–'62; Exec. Asst. to Exec. VP, American Bankers Assn., '58–'59; Exec. Secy. to Chief Exec. Ofcr., Universal Pictures, '53–'58; AWRT, IRTS; George Pepperdine Col., '49–'52; El Camino Col., '52–'53; Bank PR & Mkt. Sch., Northwestern Univ., '62–'64; b. L.A., Cal.; p. Nick and Florence Bon Souleles; h. Hal Barnett; res: 138–15 Franklin Ave., Flushing, N.Y. 11355.

BARNHART, LEEANNE SUE, Cont. Dir., Denison Broadcasting Co., KDSN AM-FM, Denison, Ia. 51442, '67–; News Asst., Anncr., Public Svc. Dir., '66–'67; Theta Sigma Phi, AAUW; Univ. of Ia., BA, '66; b. Cedar Rapids, Ia., 1944; p. Leland and Ethel Wieneke Barnhart; res: 910 Broadway, Denison, Ia. 51442.

BARNHART, MARGARET LOUISE, Ed., Accent on Youth, Methodist Publishing House, 201 Eighth Ave. S., Nashville, Tenn. 37215, '58–; Ed., Audio Visuals, '56–'58; Dir., Wesley Fndn., '49–'55; Dir., Christian Educ., local ch. '47–'49; Eds. of Ch. Magazines for Children and Youth, AAUW; Indiana (Pa.) State Tchrs. Col., BS, (Educ.) '41; Garrett Theological Seminary, Northwestern Univ., MA (Religion), '47; Syracuse Univ., MA (Religious Jnlsm.) '56.

BARON, SELMA ARLEEN, Group VP, Nelson Stern & Associates, Inc., 530 Hanna Bldg., Cleve., Oh. 44115, '60–; AWRT, Indsl. Mktng., Wms. Adv. Club, Zeta Phi Eta; Northwestern Univ., BS, '47.

BARONE, JULIA AUGUSTONI, Prod. Dir., St. John's University Press, Grand Central and Utopia Pkwys., N.Y., N.Y. 11432, '60–; Asst. Mgr., N.Y.U., '34–'60; GA Inst.; educ: N.Y.U.; b. N.Y.C., p. Stephen and Mary Keenan Augustoni; h. Daniel Barone; res: 340 E. 207th St., N.Y., N.Y. 10467.

BARR, GLADYS HUTCHISON, Ed., Wtr., David Hutchison Publishing Co., P.O. Box 706, Nashville, Tenn. 37215, '69–; Auth., novels (Holt, Abingdon Press), juv. bk. (Broadman Press); Ghosts Series (David Hutchinson Publishing Co.); Auths. Guild, Auths. League of Am., WNBA; Am. Legion Wm. of the Yr., '50; State Univ. of N.Y., Union Univ., Albany Law School, L.L.B.; b. Butte, Mont.; p. David and Laura Mooney Hutchison; h. Thomas Barr; c. Thomas, Jr., Ann B. Weems, Jane, William; res: 3201 Hillsboro Rd., Nashville, Tenn. 37253.

BARR, GLORIA DICKSON, Bdcst. Bus. Mgr., MacManus, John & Adams, Inc., 750 S. Mississippi River Blvd., St. Paul, Minn. 55116, '66–; AE, '60–; Radio-TV Dir., '64–'66; Wtr.-Prodr., '59–'64; Wtr.-Prodr., Zeuthen, Thomas & Hulbert, '57–'59;

Copywtr., John Forney, Inc., '54–'57; Copywtr., Al Colle Co., '52–'54; Mpls. Adv. Club, AWRT, Crtv. Club of Mpls.; Olaf Aw. (Cert. of Merit), '64; Univ. of Minn., BA (Jnlsm.) '45; b. Duluth, Minn., 1923; p. Frank G. and Kate Lindberg Dickson; h. Alan L. Barr; c. Peter, Martha, Kristine; res: 11435 Royzelle Lane, Minnetonka Village, Minn. 55343.

BARR, PHILOMENA GILL, The Center for Curriculum Development, Inc., 401 Walnut St., Phila., Pa. 19106, '55; b. Phila., Pa., 1913; p. Martin and Ella Denny Gill; h. Paul Barr; c. Mrs. Paul Wallin, Paul Jr.; res: 121 Shadeland Ave., Lansdowne, Pa. 19050.

BARRETT, GRACE A., Free-lance PR Cnslt., '58–; AE, Robinson-Hannagan Assoc., '54–'57; Gen. News Reptr., New York Times, '43–'53; PRSA, Atlanta Press Club, Adv. Club of Atlanta, Quota Club of Atlanta, Variety Club Wm. Tent 21 of Atlanta (Secy., '66–'67; Pres., '68); 2,000 Wm. of Achiev., '69; Who's Who of Am. Wm., '69; Barnard Col., Columbia Univ., BA, '42; Grad. Sch. of Jnlsm., Columbia, MS, '43; b. N.Y.C., 1920; p. George and Augusta Peters Barrett; res: 3648 Peachtree Rd. N.E., Atlanta, Ga. 30319.

BARRETT, HELEN LAZARUS, Publr., Bayonne Times, 579 Ave. C., Bayonne, N.J. 07002, '66–; VP, '55–'66; Secy., Carbon County Printing & Publ.; Intl. Press Inst., Nat. Cncl. of Christians and Jews (Dir., '68–'69; Medal, '68), Un. Fund (Dir., '67–'69); Smith Col., BA (cum laude), '32; b. Bayonne, N.J., 1911; p. Ernst and Anna Bose Thum; h. Lester J. Barrett; c. Herman Lazarus III, Mrs. Patti Lazarus Hoff; res: Milky Way Farm, Pittstown, N.J. 08867.

BARRETT, MARJORIE CHRISTINE, Wms. Ed., Rocky Mountain News, 400 W. Colfax Ave., Denver, Colo. 80201, '60–; Music Colmst.; Restaurant Colmst., '66; Music Critic, '56–'64; Food Ed., '57; Asst. Drama Ed., '56–'62; Feature Wtr., '56; Hist. and Architectural Wtr., '56; Drama, Dance and Music Reviewer, Denver Post, '48–'56; Ed., "Central City Festival Celebrity Cookbook" ('67); Theta Sigma Phi, Am. Inst. of Designers; FURN Club of Colo. Aw. for furniture coverage, '58; Loretto Heights Col., BA (Eng.; Wm. of the Yr. Aw., '67); Regis Col.; Univ. of Colo.; Denver Univ.; b. Denver, Colo.; p. William E. and Christine M. Rollman Barrett; res: 427 Downing St., Denver, Colo. 80218.

BARRETT, MARY ELIZABETH, Wms. Ed., Hartford Courant, 285 Broad St., Hartford, Conn. 06101, '57–; Soc. Ed., '42–'57; Asst. Librn., '35–'42; Conn. Cncl. Catholic Wm., Wadsworth Atheneum, Hartford Retail Trade Bd.; Col. of St. Elizabeth (Conn. Valley Alumnae Assn. Pres., '58–'59); St. Joseph Col., '35–'38; Univ. of Hartford, '57; b. Hartford, Conn. 1913; p. Robert and Helena Gaffey Barrett; res: 29 Linwood Dr., West Hartford, Conn. 06107.

BARRIE, BARBARA ANN, Actress, c/o Henry Guettel at Kaplan—Veidb Agency; Broadway: "The Wooden Dish;" Off-Broadway: "The Crucible," "Dr. Faustus," "The Beaux' Stratagem"; Tour: "The Miracle Worker;" TV: "The Virginian," "U.S. Steel Hour," "The Defenders," Others; Film: "The Caretakers," "One Potato, Two Potato" (Cannes Best Actress aw., '64); two yrs. with Am. Shakespeare Festival and N.Y. Shakespeare Festival; Univ. of Tex., BFA; b. Chgo., Ill.; p. Louis and Frances Boruszak Berman; h. Jay Harnick; c. Jane, Aaron.

BARROW, ELAINE QUINN, Family Living Ed., Suffolk Sun, 303 Marcus Blvd., Deer Park, L.I., N.Y. 11729, '68–; Feature Wtr., '66–'68; Reptr.-Wtr., AP, Newsday, Coronet; N.Y. NWC Front Page Aw., '67; h. John Barrow.

BARRY, AILEEN MARY, VP-Asst. Media Dir., Grey Advertising, Inc., 777 Third Ave., N.Y., N.Y. 10017; Col. of Mt. St. Vincent, AB (magna cum laude).

BARRY, ANNE MORSE, Wtr.; Mgr. Ed., Dial Press., '66–'68; articles in Esquire, Cosmopolitan; Radcliffe Col., BA, '62 (cum laude); b. Boston, Mass., 1940; p. Theodore and Helen Coleman Barry; res: 60 St. Mark's Pl., N.Y., N.Y. 10003.

BARRY, JANE POWELL, Novelist: "The Long March" ('55), "The Carolinians" ('59), "A Time in the Sun" ('62), "A Shadow of Eagles" ('64), "Maximilian's Gold" ('66), "Grass Roots" ('68); Ed., Greene County Examiner-Recorder, '50–'51; Reptr., Coxsackie Union News, '46–'48; N.Y. State Nwsp. Publr. Aw. for best single issue of weekly nwsp., '51; b. New Baltimore, N.Y., 1925; p. Levit and Ida Van der Poel Powell; h. John Barry; res: Lotus Point, Catskill, N.Y. 12414.

BARRY, JOAN, Merchandising Mgr., AE, Bdcstr. ("Bulletin" Show), WRCB-TV, 900 Whitehall Rd., Chattanooga, Tenn. 37405, '62–; in radio-TV since '54 as on-air-personality and time salesman; Copywtr., Prodr.; radio show on WDOD "At Home With Joan" until '61; actress in Chattanooga Little Theatre; creator of local charm sch.; AWRT (Chattanooga Chptr. Pres., '68–'69); Adv. Club of Chattanooga (Secy., '57–'59; Bd. of Dirs., '60–'62; Gold Aw., best TV color comml. over 30 seconds); Outstanding Commty. Svc. Aw., Catholic Commtns. Comm., Diocese of Nashville; Sullins Col., '43–'44; Univ. of Chattanooga, '44–'45; b. N.O., La.; p. Thomas and Madeline Pitot Barry; c. Madelina (Mrs. Michael Cody Jr.), Brian Cook, Stephanie Cook; res: 4111 Sunbury Ave., Chattanooga, Tenn. 37411.

BARRY, JUDITH WORACEK, Art Dir., Trade, Reference, Col. and El-Hi Bk. Divs., Thomas Y. Crowell Company, 201 Park Ave. S., N.Y., N.Y. 10003, '69–; Sr. Designer, '67–'69; Bk. Designer, '62–'67; Prod. Asst., '60–'62; Free-lance Graphic Artist; member, AIGA (bk. design, "Kennedy and the Press," selected for textbk. show. '66); Vassar Col., BA, '60; b. Brooklyn, N.Y., 1937; p. Anthony and Peggy Lee Woracek; h.

Thomas Barry; res: 215 W. 78th St., N.Y., N.Y. 10024; RFD Cornwall Bridge, Conn. 06754.

BARRY, LUCY BROWN, Librn., Charisma, 29 W. 57th St., N.Y., N.Y. 10019, '69–; Prod. Coordr., Charisma Films, '68; Asst., Leah Salisbury Lit. Agcy., '69; Prod. Asst., "How to Succeed in Business," '60–'61; Pubcty. Dir., Ogunquit (Me.) Playhouse, '66; Rschr., World Telegram & Sun, '61; Auth., "Stagestruck Secretary," ('66), "Emperor's New Clothes," ('62); Manhattan E. Republican Club, Am. Theater Wing; Radcliffe Col., BA, '55; N.Y.U. Sch. of Continuing Educ., '62, '63, '69; Middlebury Col. (Breadloaf Wtrs. Conf., '63); b. Boston, Mass., 1934; p. Herbert and Lucy Brown Barry; res: 350 E. 52nd St., N.Y., N.Y. 10022.

BARRY, PATRICIA WHITE, Actress, Motion Pics., TV, Broadway; four Emmy nominations, Ann Arbor Festival Most Promising Actress, '58, Sara Siddens Nominee, '59; Stephens Col. (Hon. Degree, '62; Advisory Bd.); Syracuse Univ.; Columbia Univ. Grad.; b. Davenport, Iowa; p. Paul and Alma Robbins White; h. Philip Barry; c. Miranda Robbins, Stephanie Ann T.; res: 144 N. Bristol Ave., L.A., Cal. 90049.

BART, CARROLL DeGRAFF, (dec.), Asst. Makeup Ed., Hollister Newspapers, 1232 Central Ave., Wilmette, Ill. 60091; '69–; Mng. Ed., Chgo. Fedn. of Musicians, '63–; Prom., PR Dir., Howard-Western Merchants Assn., '63–; Assoc., Robert T. Sanford & Assoc., '65–'69; Pubcty. Dir., Joseph L. Koach & Assoc., '63–'65; Edtl. Conslt., Cook County Sheriff's Juvenile Bur., '55–'62; Feature Wtr., Lerner Nwsps., '50–'56; Free-lance Wtr., '48–'53; Wms. Adv. Club of Chgo., Chgo. Nwsp. Guild; b. Spokane, Wash., 1911; p. George and Lua Butler DeGraff; h. Martin L. Bart; c. Bert A. F. Lindgren, Lawrence P. Lindgren; res: 7521 N. Winchester, Chgo., Ill. 60626.

BARTELSON, MARGUERITE, Media Supvsr., Clinton E. Frank, Inc., 120 S. Riverside Plaza, Chgo., Ill. 60606, '69–; Media Byr., '66–'69; Media Estimator, '64–'65; Radio-TV Dept., '63–'64; Jr. Wms. Adv. Club of Chgo., (VP, '66–'67; Program Chmn., '65–'66); DePauw Univ., BA, '63; b. Chgo., Ill., 1941; p. Raymond and Majorie Wilson Bartelson; res: 230 E. Ontario, Chgo., Ill. 60611.

BARTH, BETTY JANE, Exec. Prodr. and Chmn. of Bd., Cameo Productions, Inc., 1411-D W. Touhy Ave., Chgo., Ill. 60626, '62–; Dir. of Radio-TV, Nat. Lutheran Cncl., '58–'62; Dir. of Radio-TV, Indpls. (Ind.) Public Schs., '54–'58; Instr. Radio-TV, Butler Univ., '54–'58; Prodr.-Dir., WOI-TV (Ames, Ia.), '53–'54; Prodr., "Light Time," intl. children's TV series, and "Great Bible Stories," animated TV series; AWRT, NRPC; Luther Col., BA, '51; Columbia Col. (Chgo.), MA, '52; b. Chgo., Ill., 1928; p. Frank and Esther Pederson Barth; res: 7430 Foster St., Morton Grove, Ill. 60053.

BARTH, DIANA, Assoc. Ed., Simon & Schuster, 630 Fifth Ave., N.Y., N.Y. 10020; Contrb. Ed., After Dark magazine; Playbill; Equity; Standby; Free-lance Ed. and Wtr. specializing in theatre, the arts, medicine, travel; U.C.L.A., BA (Eng.), '50 (cum laude); b. L.A., Cal.; h. Leslie Barrett; res: 203 W. 81st St., N.Y., N.Y. 10024.

BARTH, EDNA SMITH, Ed.-in-Chief, Lothrop, Lee & Shepard Co., 105 Madison Ave., N.Y., N.Y. 10016, '69–; Assoc. Ed., Thomas Y. Crowell Co. Children's Bk. Dept., '63–'66; Assoc. Ed., McGraw-Hill Jr. Bks., '60–'63; Auth., four children's bks. ('56–'60); Children's Bk. Cncl.; Radcliffe, BA, '36 (Radcliffe Club of N.Y.); Simmons Col., BS, '37; b. Marblehead, Mass., 1914; p. Charlton and Elizabeth Bateman Smith; h. George Barth; c. Elizabeth, Peter and Paul Weiss; res: 85 Fourth Ave., N.Y., N.Y. 10003.

BARTH, PATRICIA LANE, Wms. Ed., Times-Leader, 200 S. Fourth St., Martins Ferry, Oh. 43935, '66–; Martins Ferry Lib., '65–'66; Pers. Asst., Stone & Thomas Dept. Store, (Wheeling, W. Va.), '46–'48; Oh. State Univ.; b. Martins Ferry, Oh., 1925; p. Eric and Gertrude Spence Lane; h. Charles Barth; c. Holly, Gary, Shannon, Brad, Spence; res: 430 Center St., Martins Ferry, Oh. 43935.

BARTLETT, BARBARA BURNELL, Program Dir., KRTR, 500 Arapahoe, Thermopolis, Wyo., 82443, '65–; Anncr., KWRB-TV; Univ. of Wyo., '54–'56; b. Gebo, Wyo., 1937; p. Francis and Margaret Stewart Burnell; h. Fred Bartlett (div.); c. Cynthia; res: 226 N. 5th, Thermopolis, Wyo. 82443.

BARTLETT, EDNA WELLINGHOFF, Wms. Dir., WELM Radio Elmira, Inc., 1705 Lake Rd., Elmira, N.Y. 14902, '47–; Radio Commentator and Wtr., Prodr. and Commentator for fashion shows; AWRT (Central N.Y. Chptr. Pres., '63, '64); Golden Slipper Aw., '65; FRANY Aw., '68; Northwestern Univ., BA, '28; b. Elgin, Ill., 1910; p. Edmund F. and Edna Allanson Wellinghoff; h. Loring Bartlett; res: 84 Greenridge Dr. W., Elmira, N.Y. 14902.

BARTLETT, ELIZABETH, Poetry Ed., International Society of General Semantics, 540 Powell St., S.F., Cal. 94108, '64–; Tchr., Eng. Dept.: Univ. of Cal., '62–'64; San Jose Col., '61; Dir., Crtv. Wtrs. Assn., New Sch. for Social Rsch., '55; Tchr., Speech Dept., Southern Methodist Univ., Dallas, '47–'49; Poet, Bk. Reviewer, Lectr., Wtrs. Cnslt.; Auth. of numerous books, poems in anthologies, and short stories; Intl. Soc. of Gen. Semantics; Writing Fellowships: Huntington Hartford Fdn. '59, '60; Montalvo Fdn. '60–'61 Nat. Inst. of Arts and Ltrs. Grant-in-aid, '68; Coord. Cncl. of Lit. Mags. Publ. Grant, '68; Tchrs. Col., BS, '31; Grad. Work., Columbia Univ., '34–'40; b. N.Y.C., 1911; h. Paul Bartlett; c. Steven; res: 5218 Mono Dr., Santa Barbara, Calif. 93105.

BARTLETT, VIRGINIA KOSTULSKI, Public Affairs Prodr., WQED, Metropolitan Pittsburgh Educational Television, 4337 Fifth Ave., Pitt., Pa. 15213, '66–; Free-lance Prodr., Wtr., WQED, WIIC (Pitt.), and WHDH-TV (Boston), '64–'66; Public Affairs Wtr., Prodr., WHDH-TV, '57–'63; Dir. of PR, Greater Boston Girl Scouts, '55–'57; Wms. Ed., WNET-TV (Providence, R.I.), '54–'55; Prodr. of films for UNICEF and Peace Corps; AWRT (Gateway Chptr. Pres., '66–'67); Bd. Mbr: Pitt. ACLU, Pitt. Cncl. for Public Educ., Shadyside Forum (civic assn.); Pa. Rep. for UNICEF: Nat. Educ. TV Public Affairs Aw., '68; Golden Quill, Sigma Delta Chi Public Affairs Aw., '68; McCall's Gold Mike Aw., '63, '61; Cit. as "Friend of UNICEF," '62; Fund for Adult Educ. travel and study grant, '60–'61; Ohio Wesleyan Univ., BA, '44; Ohio Wesleyan Univ., MA '51; b. Omaha, Neb., 1923; p. Adam and Idabelle Greathouse Kostulski; h. Irving H. Bartlett; res: 5816 Howe St., Pitt., Pa. 15232.

BARTON, CONSTANCE CORNICK, PR Dir., Barnes Hospital, Barnes Hospital Plaza, St. Louis, Mo. 63119, '65–; Press Rep., United Fund, '64–'65; Dist. Exec., Toledo (Oh.) Area Girl Scouts, '61–'64; Reptr. on various nwsps. in Ill., Ohio, Okla., '54–'61; PRSA, Indsl. Press Assn., Am. Hosp. PR Soc., Acad. Hosp. PR (Pres., '69–'70); ICIE Aw. of Merit for Employe Bul., '69, numerous aws. for hosp. and indsl. PR; Univ. of Mo., BJ; b. Quincy, Ill. 1932; p. Lester and Wilma Lohr Cornick; h. Robert Barton; c. Leslie Jane; res: 441 W. Jackson, Webster Groves, Mo. 63119.

BARTON, ELEANOR KEESE, Colmst. Feature Wtr., Greenville News-Piedmont Co., 305 S. Main St., Greenville, S.C. 29601, '51–; Wms. Ed., Greenville Piedmont, '21–'51; Radio News Commentator, '56–'62; Instr., Greenville Wms. Col., '21–'24; PR work '21–'29; Auth: "History of the Greenville Woman's Club" ('60), "History of Crescent Music Club" ('56), "History of Cresent Community Club" ('67), Nat. Fedn. of Music Clubs, Gen. Fedn. of Wms. Clubs; Nat. BPW Aw., '32; Boys Club of Amer. Cert. of Appreciation, '56; Nat. Recreation Assn. Cit., '61; Nat. Commty. Achiev. Cit., '56; USO cert. for distg. svc. to armed forces, '61; Nat. Red Cross cert. for work as Greenville County Chmn., '57; Furman Univ. Wms. Col., '21; Grad. Work, Cornell Univ., '23; active in civic and cultural affairs; b. Walhalla, S.C., 1901; p. John and Soula Reeder Keese; h. William P. Barton; c. Mrs. John O. Allen; res: 201 Broad St., Marion, N.C. 28752.

BARTON, JANE, Radio-TV Prog. Dir., State of New York, New York State Commerce Dept., 112 State St., Albany, N.Y. 12207, '48–; Stringer, Schenectady Union-Star, '68–; Public Affairs Ofcr., U.S. Naval Reserve, '42–'49; Jane Barton Pubcty.-Adv., '40–'42, '45–'48; Assoc. Ed., Cleaning & Laundry World, '39–'40; Colmst. and Script Wtr., Radio Guide, '37–'39; Cert. Tree Farmer; Tchr., PR on conservation; AWRT (N.E. area VP, '66–'69; Pres., Founder of N.Y. State Capital Dist. Chptr., '56–'58; Nat. Dir.-at-large, '53–'55), IRTS, Bdcst. Pioneers, BPW (N.Y. State Vice-Chmn., Radio-TV, '51–'53), ZONTA; Hunter Col., BA, '38; N.Y.U., Master of Public Adm., '54; b. N.Y.C.,

1918; p. Abraham and Matilda Gries Greenberg; res: Windy Hill Farm, Esperance, N.Y. 12066.

BARTON, MARGARET D., Free-lance Cnslt., Holt, Rinehart and Winston, Inc., 383 Madison Ave., N.Y., N.Y. 10017, '63–; Instr., French, Barrington (R.I.) Col., '65–'66; Coordr. of Fgn. Lang. Study, Tchr., Supvsr., of lang. lab., Barrington HS, '58–'63; Tchr., French, '26–'63; Tchr., French, Hist., Deep River (Conn.) HS, '23–'26; Textbk. Wtr: "Lire Parler et Ecrire" ('64); workbk. for "Parler et Lire" ('66), with Laura B. Gilmore; Collaborator, revision of workbk., "Ecouter et Parler"; Co-auth., work in Modern Lang. Assn. "News Ltr.", '62' New Eng. Modern Lang. Assn. (R.I. Chptr. Exec. Bd., '62–'63); Am. Assn. of Tchrs. of French (R.I. Chptr. Secy., Treas., '57–'58), AAUW (VP, Pres., '54–'60), R.I. State Advisory Comm. on Fgn. Lang. Study; Pembroke Col., AB (French), '23; R.I. Col., MEd (French), '40; Brown Univ; Ecole Francaise, Middlebury Col.; Tufts Univ; Columbia Univ; b. Fall River, Mass., 1902.

BARTOS, RENA ROSS, Dir. of Crtv. Rsch., J. Walter Thompson Company, 420 Lexington Ave., N.Y., N.Y. 10017, '68–; Group Head, Crtv. Rsch., '66–'67; Supvsr., Crtv. Dev., '66; Rsch. Dir., Fletcher Richards, '64–'65; Mgr., Adv. Rsch., Marplan, '62–'64; Motivational Rsch. Cnslt.; AWNY; Rutgers Univ., AB (cum laude), '39; h. Harold Bartos.

BARTZ, ALICE PUGH, Sch. Lib. Dev. Advisor, Pennsylvania Department of Education, Division of School Libraries, 6801 Ludlow St., Upper Darby, Pa. 19082, '68–; Librn., pub. libs., '36–'43; sch. libs., '54–'68; AAUW, ALA, various educ., lib. assns.; educ: Westhampton Col., Univ. of Richmond, BA, '36; Univ. of N.C., BS (Lib. Sci.), '38; grad. study at several other schs.; b. Vineland, Va. 1915; p. John and Camelia Brooks Pugh; h. Warren Bartz; c. Warren Frederick, Jr., John Davis; res: 646 Pine Tree Rd., Jenkintown, Pa. 19046.

BARZEL, ANN, Wtr., Dance Critic, Chicago Today, 445 N. Michigan Ave., Chgo., Ill. 60611, '51–; major contrbr. to "Dance Encyclopedia"; Lectr. on Dance, Univ. of Chgo., '52–'55; Edtl. Assoc., Dance Magazine, '36–'69; Chgo. Ed., Dance News, '42–; Chgo. Assn. of Dancing Masters (Hon. Mbr.); b. Mpls., Minn., 1913; p. Nahum and Freda Mirsky Barzel; res: 3950 Lake Shore Dr., Chgo., Ill. 60613.

BASCH, FRANCES SCOTT, Exec. VP, Gibraltar Advertising Agency, Inc., Basch Radio & TV Prods., 25 W. 45th St., N.Y., N.Y. 10036, '49–; Co-prodr., TV shows, '49–'53; Radio Reptr., '33–'49; 1st TV Aw. of Merit, '46, U.S. Army Aw. for shows during WW II; b. S.F., Cal.; h. Charles J. Basch; res: 771 West End Ave., N.Y., N.Y. 10025.

BASEMORE, JOYCE MARIE, Ed., New University Thought, P.O. Box 7431, Detroit, Mich. 48202, '68–; Exec. Secy., Monteith Col., '66–'68; Wayne State Univ., '67–'69; (Bd. of Governors Scholarship, Equal Opportunity Grant); b. St. Louis, Mo., 1941; p. Jerome and Victoria Harris Basemore; c. Regina; res: 253 Horton, Detroit, Mich. 48202.

BASINGER, JEANINE DEYLING, Cnslt., Weekly Reader Children's Book Club, 55 High St., Middletown, Conn. 06457, '69–; Visiting Lectr., Film History, Wesleyan Univ., '69–'71; Mktng. Dir., '68–'69; Adv. Dir., '62–'68; Copywtr., '60–'62; Tchr., S.D. State Univ., '58–'60; S.D. State Univ., MS (Commtns.), '58 (with high hons.); b. Ravenden, Ark. 1936; p. John and Sarah Pickett Deyling; h. John Basinger; c. Savannah Lee; res: 148 Church St., Middletown, Conn. 06457.

BASS, BEVERLY RUTENBERG, Prod. Mgr., Books for Libraries, Inc., 50 Liberty Ave., Freeport, N.Y. 11520, '68–; Asst. Adv. Mgr., Floyds Stores, '64–'68; b. Bklyn., N.Y.; p. Benjamin and Eva Breggin Rutenberg; h. Sidney Bass; c. Frederick, Barry; res: 1672 Francis Dr., East Meadow, N.Y. 11554.

BASS, DEE BURSTON, Partner, PR Cnslrs., Cotton & Bass, 667 Madison Ave., N.Y., N.Y. 10021, '63–; Treas., Exec. VP, Sound of Youth; Adv. and Sales Prom. Dir., Heirloom Needlework Guild; Adv. and Sales Prom. Dir., Jolles Studios; State Info. Dir., Wyo. War Manpower Comm.; Volunteer Bus. Cnslr., PR, Am. Progressing Together; many free-lance accs.; Tchr. of practical PR, Adams Sch.; PRSA; Dem. Party activity; b. N.Y.C., 1918; p. Gerson and Rebecca Zimmerman Burston; h. Sid Bass; c. Eric; res: 66–44 Selfridge St., Forest Hills, N.Y.

BASS, FLORA GARDNER, Lectr., Robert Armour National Artist & Lecture Service, 139 S. Beverly Dr., Beverly Hills, Cal. 90212, '66–; Lectr., Westbrook-Reeve & Assoc. Artists, '64–'65; Lectr., Mae Norton Hollywood Artist Bur., '52–'63; Assoc. Ed., Food Selling Digest (L.A., Cal.), '52–'54; Contrbr., Philippines Free Press (Manila, Philippines), '48–; Auth., "Philippine Women & Dolls" (Mermaid Bks., '55); Intl. Platform Assn., ZONTA, Catholic Press Cncl.; Philippine-Am. Relations Aw., Dic. of Intl. Biog., '67; 2,000 Wm. of Achiev., Philippine Col. of Commerce, '29–'31; b. Manila, Philippines, 1916; p. William and Ceferina de Castro Gardner; h. Henry C. Bass; c. Henry, James, David, Robert Richard (dec.); res: P.O. Box 803, Laguna Beach, Cal. 92652.

BASSETT, ANN KOBLITZ, VP, The Cuyahoga Savings Assn., One Erieview Plaza, Cleve. Oh. 44114, '65–; Owner, Ann Koblitz Adv. Agcy., '46–'62; AE, Ohio Adv. Agcy., '42–'46; Adv. Dept., The May Co. and B. R. Baker Co., '40–'42; Wms. Adv. Club of Cleve. (VP., '56–'58; Helping Heart Aw., '64), Fashion Group of Cleve. (Reg. Dir., '64), AWRT (Chptr. Pres., '59–'61), Salvation Army (Advisory Bd., '57–; Bronze Century of Service Aw., '65), Cleve. Welfare Fedn., Golden Age Ctrs. (Pres., Bd. of Trustees, '68–); First Prize, Mkt. Soc. of Am., '67; Silver Medal Aw., AFA, AAW and Printers' Ink, '67; Conn. Col. for Wm., '34–'36; b. Cleve., Oh.,

1917; p. Maurice J. and Bert Lederer Koblitz; h. Richard L. Bassett; res: 2620 Warrensville Center Rd., Cleve, Oh. 44118.

BASSETT, ELIZABETH EWING, Newsman, The Associated Press, 50 Rockefeller Plaza, N.Y., N.Y. 10020, '66–; Organizer and Stage Mgr. of Entertainment, N.Y. World's Fair, '64; Bradford Jr. Col., AA (honors); N.Y.U.; New Sch. for Social Rsch.; b. E. Cleve., Oh., 1937; p. Ben and Eileen Ewing Bassett; res: 345 W. 12th St., N.Y., N.Y. 10014.

BASSIMER, V. MARIE CLUCK, Soc. Ed., Carmi Times Publishing Company, 323 E. Main St., Carmi, Ill. 62821, '53–; Carmi PTA (Life Mbr.; Pres., '46–'47), Order of the Eastern Star (Carmi Chptr. Worthy Matron, '53), Order of the Amaranth (Charter Mbr., Jewel Court, Carmi), Order of the White Shrine of Jerusalem (Charter Mbr., McLeansboro Shrine); b. McLeansboro, Ill., 1914; p. Raymond and Edith Redfearn Cluck; h. Charles Bassimer; c. Louis Ray, Lyna May; res: 200 S. Eighth St., Carmi, Ill. 62821.

BASSIN, AMELIA KAUFMAN, Crtv. Dir.-Sr. VP, Fabergé, Inc., 5 W. 54th St., N.Y., N.Y. 10019, '57–; Art Dir., Prom., Pubcty. Dir., '50–'57; Art Dir., '49–'50; Adv., Pubcty. Dir., Parfums Charbert, '45–'49; Mag. Wtr., '40–'45; Fashion Group, AWNY (Bd. of Dirs., '69–'70), Cosmetics Career Wm.; N.Y. Film Festival for TV Commls. Gold Medal Aw., '65, The Hecht Co. Special Young Designers Aw. for Crtv. in Product Design, '69; Temple Univ.; b. Manhattan, Kan.; p. Charles and Manya Gale Kaufman; h. Sidney Bassin; res: 11 Fifth Ave., N.Y., N.Y. 10003.

BASTIEN, FAY, Controller, International Universities Press, Inc., 239 Park Ave. S., N.Y., N.Y. 10003, '68–; Controller, Basic Bks., '63–'67; Treas., Dial Press, '56–'62; Cnslt., automation conversions; Hunter Col., AB; b. N.Y.C.; res: 124 E. 84th St., N.Y., N.Y. 10028.

BATDORFF, NANCY STAMM, Photog. Ed., The Pioneer, Conine Publishing Co., 118 N. Michigan Ave., Big Rapids, Mich. 49307, '65–; Tchr., '61–; Stringer, UPI, '60–'69; numerous reporting, teaching positions, '55–'61; AAUW, BPW, Nat. and Mich. Press Photogrs. Assns.; Mich. Educ. Assn.; Univ. of Mich., BA; b. Boston, Mass. 1937; p. Thoburn and Madeleine Spafford Stamm; h. John Batdorff; c. Wendy Buckingham; res: 704 Cherry Ave., Big Rapids, Mich. 49307.

BATE, LUCY NEUMARK, Free-lance Wtr., '65–; Reptr., Ed., Hart Publ. Co. (N.Y.C.), '63–'65; Edtl., Am. Book Co., '61–'63; Edtl., Crown Publr., '61; Co-ed., The Bay State Citizen, Ams. for Dem. Action nwsltr., '67–; Playwright; OPC; Skidmore Col. "New Plays" aw. '69; Brandeis Univ., BA (cum laude), '60; b. Wash., D.C., 1939; p. Immanuel and Ruth Schmerler Neumark; h. Michael Bate; c. Gabrielle; res: 992 Memorial Dr., Cambridge, Mass. 02138.

BATES, ALICE ELIZABETH, Wms. Pg. Ed., Hour Publishing Company, Wall and Knight Sts., Norwalk, Conn. 06852, '67–; Asst. Wms. Pg. Ed., '46–'66; Soc. Ed., Evening Sentinel, '32–'45; Norwalk Cancer Soc. (Bd. of Trustees), Norwalk Symphony Assn. (Bd. of Dirs.); b. Norwalk, Conn., 1909; p. Dr. Harry and Alice Heath Bates; res: 21 Clinton Ave., Norwalk, Conn. 06854.

BATES, BARBARA SNEDEKER, Ed., Juvenile Trade Books, Westminster Press, 933 Witherspoon Bldg., Phila., Pa. 19107, '67–; Fiction Book Ed., '44–'46; Children's Mag. Ed., '41–'44; Free-lance Wtr., Tchr., '46–'67; Auth. Children's Bks.; Children's Bk. Cncl., Phila. Children's Reading Round Table, ALA, Auths. Guild; Wellesley Col., BA, '40; b. Phila., Pa., 1919; p. R. Cuyler and Dorothy Roberts Snedeker; h. Frederick H. Bates; c. Susan Penelope, Stephen Cuyler.

BATES, MARGARET JANE, Prof., Spanish Literature, Dir., Language Lab., Catholic University, Wash., D.C. 20017; Prodr., Voice of Am., Latin Am. Div., '59–'60; Prodr., Damascene Pic., '57; Lib. Cnslt., Lib. of Congress, Dept. of State, '40–'45; Bk., "Poesias completas de Gabriela Mistral" (Madrid, '66); Modern Language Assn., Am. Assn. Tchrs. of Spanish and Portuguese; Ford Faculty Fellowship, '53–'54; Hunter Col., BA, '38; Columbia Univ., MLS, '40; Catholic Univ., PhD, '45; b. N.Y.C., 1918; p. Herbert and Anne Flanagan Bates; res: 5914 Carlton Lane, Bethesda, Md. 20016.

BATES, MARY JOYCE RENN, Dir. of Public Info., Avco Broadcasting Corporation, 1600 Provident Tower, 1 E. Fourth St., Cinn., Oh. 45202, '67–; Asst. PR Dir., '65–'67; PR Dir., Indpls. Symphony Orchestra, '63–'65; AE, Bob Long Assocs., '61–'63; Program Admr., Crosley Bdcst. Corp.; PRSA (Cinn. Chptr.), Theta Sigma Phi, Beta Gamma Sigma; Univ. of Cinn., BBA, '42; b. New Albany, Ind.; p. Raymond W. and Joyce Austin Renn; h. Carl L. Bates; res: 1396 Teal Ct., Loveland, Oh. 45140.

BATES, NATALIE, Subsidiary Rights Mgr., Crown Publishers, Inc., 419 Park Ave. S., N.Y., N.Y. 10016; formerly Subsidiary Rights Mgr. with Crown Publishers Inc. and Clarkson N. Potter Inc.

BATIE, JEAN MUSSER, Art Reviewer, Seattle Times, Fairview N. and John St., Seattle, Wash. 98111, '67–; Eng. Tchr.; Wtr., poetry and plays; Seattle Matrix, Theatre Northwest; Inst. of Intl. Educ. scholarship to Oxford, '53; Am. Fedn. of Arts Fellowship, '68; Smith Col., BA, '50; Case Western Reserve, MA, '51; b. Akron, Oh., 1928; p. Dr. Harvey and Lucile Smart Musser; h. Robert Batie; res: 6505 225th Pl., S.W., Mountlake Terrace, Wash. 98043.

BATTELLE, PHYLLIS MARIE, Colmst., King Features Syndicate, 235 E. 45th St., N.Y., N.Y. 10017; column three days a week, Assignment: America, '55–; Wms. Ed., Fashion Ed., Intl. News Svc., '47–'54; began career as Police Reptr., Feature Wtr., Teenage

Colmst., The Dayton (Oh.) Herald, '45–'47; N.Y. Newspaperwomen's aw. for best domestic news coverage, '51; Oh. Newspaper Wms. Assn. prizes, '44–'47; Delta Gamma; N.Y. Newspaperwomen; Oh. Wesleyan Univ., BA, '44; b. Dayton, Oh., 1922; p. Gordon S. and Marie Sides Battelle; h. Arthur Van Horn; c. Jonathan Gordon; res: 310 E. 70th St., N.Y., N.Y. 10021.

BATTISTINE, RITA, PR & Adv. Dir., Scalamandre, 977 Third Ave., N.Y., N.Y. 10022, '64–; Dir., Scala-mandre Museum of Textiles, '68–; PR and Adv. Dir., The Felters Co., '58–'63; Guest Lectr., N.Y.U.; Resources Cncl., Inc. (VP, '64–; Secy., '58–;64) NHFL (Nat. Pres., '67–'68; N.Y. Chptr. Nat. Dir., '66–'67), Am. Inst. of Interior Design, Nat. Soc. of Interior Design-ers, Decorators Club, Fashion Group; Univ. of N.H., BA; Drexel Inst. of Textiles, '49–'50; b. Haverhill, Mass., 1921; p. Matthew and Clementine Bagni Battis-tine; res: 405 E. 63rd St., N.Y., N.Y. 10021.

BATTS, NATHALIE CHLAN, Cataloger, Columbia University Libraries, N.Y., N.Y. 10027, '62–; Ref. Librn., '55–'62; Asst., '51–'55; various librn. positions at Enoch Pratt Free Lib., Mt. Holyoke Col. Lib., '41–'51; Auth., Ed., lib. articles, bks.; Am. Econ. Assn. (Life Mbr.), ALA, (Life Mbr.), N.Y. Tech. Svcs. Librns. (Secy.-Treas., '68–'69), Beta Phi Mu (Nu Chptr. Pres., '69–'70; VP, '68–'69), various other orgs.; educ: Col. Notre Dame of Md.,., AB, '40; Columbia Univ. Sch. of Lib. Svc., BS, '46; MS '66 (with hons.); Mt. Holyoke Col., MA (Econ.), '51; b. Baltimore, Md. 1918; p. Frank and Bertha Prager Chlan; h. Walter Batts (dec.); res: 21 Claremont Ave., N.Y., N.Y. 10027.

BAUER, ELIZABETH HALLER, Prog. Dir., Transworld Broadcasting, Inc., 1303 Prospect Ave., Cleve., Oh., 44115, '63–; Free-lance German radio prog. Prodr. and Announcer, various Cleve. stations, '50–; AWRT, German Clubs, speaker for Un. Appeal, Repls.; b. Cologne, Germany, 1919; p. Theodor and Maria Hendricks Haller; h. Joseph F. Bauer; res: 4065 Diane Dr., Fairview Park, Oh. 44126.

BAUER, ETHEL M., Asst. Ed., Banking, The American Bankers Association, 90 Park Ave., N.Y., N.Y. 10016, '53–; Edtl. Asst., '50–'53; Adv., '40–'50; Circ., '30–'40; b. Haledon, N.J., 1908; p. John and Emily Smith Bauer; h. John Q. Pittman; c. Mrs. John Grigas; res: 39 74th St., N. Bergen, N.J. 07047.

BAUER, FLORENCE MARVYNE, Auth: "Behold Your King" ('45), "Abram, Son of Terah" ('48), "Daughter of Nazareth" ('55), "Lady Besieged" ('60); Co-auth. with husband: "Way to Womanhood" ('65), "To Enjoy Marriage" ('67); NLAPW, Soc. of Midland Auths.; Friends of Literature Aw., '47; Ch. Sch. of Art; Art Inst. of Chgo.; Layton Art Sch.; b. Elgin, Ill.; p. John and Mary Williams Chetwynd-Marvyne; h. Dr. William W. Bauer; c. John Robert, Ann Bauer Wetzel, Charles Marvyne; res: 400 E. Randolph St., Apt. 1624, Chgo., Ill. 60601.

BAUER, HELEN, Auth., non-fiction, c/o Doubleday & Co. Inc., 277 Park Ave., N.Y., N.Y. 10017; Supvsr., Lib. and Bindery, Instructional Aids and Svcs., L.A. City Schs., Lib. and Textbk. Sec., '38–'56; Tchr. (Dawson, N.M.), '21–'23; Tularosa, N.M., '20; L.A. Public Lib., '18; Auth: "California Mission Days," (Doubleday, '50), "Hawaii: the Aloha State," "Jap-anese Festivals," others; S. Cal. Cncl. of Lit. for Young People aw., '68; U.C.L.A., '18–'19; U.S.C., '31–'32; Cal. Inst. of Tech., '42; Columbia Univ., '34; b. De Queen, Ark.; h. Roy M. Bauer; c. Roberta Jean (Mrs. Calvin Logerman), Dr. Sherwin Carlquist; res: 4539 Via Huer-to, Hope Ranch Park, Santa Barbara, Cal. 93105.

BAUER, IONE ROSSMILLER, Asst. Mgr., Bauer Broadcasting Co., P.O. Box 640, Sandpoint, Idaho. 83864, '49–; Wms. News Ed., Bdcstr., '49–'68; Program Dir., '51–'67; Traf. Mgr., '49–'69; Univ. of Neb., BS, '43; b. Deshler, Neb., 1919; p. H. B. and Ann Harmes Rossmiller; h. Norman Bauer; c. Mardi; res: Ponder Point, Sandpoint, Idaho. 83864.

BAUER, RENA R., Adv. Mgr., Knoll Pharmaceutical Company, 377 Crane St., Orange, N.J. 07051, '69–; Copywtr., '67–'69; Adv. Mgr., Ivers-Lee Co., '65–'67; Adm. Asst., '57–'65; Univ. of Vienna, BA '38; Grad. Work, Univ. of Vienna; h. Erich Bauer; res: W. Orange, N.J. 07052.

BAUGHMAN, BARBARA ANN, Exec. Dir., Peach-tree Fashion Center, 635 Peachtree St., N.E., Atlanta, Ga. 30308, '67–; Exec. Dir., Peachtree Center Models, 240 Peachtree St. N.E., Suite 8C 8, 30303, '67–; Indsl. Rels. Dir., Fashion Inst. of Am., '66–'67; Dir., Apt. Acad. Sch. of Fashion, '65–'66; Tchr., Dekalb County Bd. of Educ., '63–'65; Asst. Fashion Coordr., Youth Dir., Davidson's Dept. Store, '61–'63; Fashion Cnslt., Dir., Fashion Group, BPW, AWRT; Oglethorpe Col., BA, '61; b. Atlanta, Ga.; p. Moses A. and Martha Sew-ell Baughman; res: 2469 Peachtree Rd., #203, Atlanta, Ga. 30305.

BAUM, HELEN SWARTENBERG, AE, Hank Meyer Associates, 407 Lincoln Rd., Miami Beach, Fla. 33139, '68–; Helen Baum & Assocs., '56–'68; AE, Robert S. Taplinger Assocs., '49–'54; Reprtr., Mt. Vernon (N.Y.) News; Lectr., groups, univs., others; Auth., "Instant Publicity"; many mag. articles; NHFL (Fla. Chptr. Pres.; aw.), Am. Inst. Interior Designers, Theta Sigma Phi, Children's Svc. Bur. (Bd. Mbr.); cit., Dade County Un. Fund; Who's Who of Am. Wm.; Who's Who in PR; Syracuse Univ.; Columbia Univ.; b. Perth Amboy, N.J., 1918; p. Bram and Rachel Zweigbaum Swarten-berg; h. Bernard Baum; c. Karen Baum Alexander, Gail Baum Reike; res: 4236 Alton Rd., Miami Beach, Fla. 33140.

BAUMANN, CHARLOTTE LOUISE, Media Dir., Lesseraux and Tandler, Inc., 275 S. 19th St., Phila., Pa. 19103. '68–; Media Byr., Lewis and Gilman, '66–'67; Bdcst. Media Byr., N.W. Ayer, '65–'66; Asst. Dir. Dev., PR, Presbyterian Hosp., '64–'65; Bdcst. Media Byr.,

Gray and Rodgers, '59–'63; Radio-TV Cont. Dir., Asst. Byr., '52–'59; AWRT (Phila. Chptr. Pres., '67–'68; Treas.; Secy.), TV and Radio Adv. Club of Phila. (Secy.; Bd. of Dirs., '64–'66); Drexel Inst. of Tech., Sch. of Bus. Adm., '44–'46; b. Warner, S.D., 1927; res: 716 Magill Avenue, W. Collingswood, N.J. 08107.

BAUSSAN, NANCY, Adv. and Prom. Dir., Charles Scribner's Sons, 597 Fifth Ave., N.Y., N.Y. 10017.

BAXT, SELMA ZASOFSKY, Copy Ed., Richmond Newspapers, Inc., 333 E. Grace St., Richmond, Va. 23213, '69–; Ed., Electric Storage Battery Co., '58–'60; Ed., Vertol Aircraft Corp., '56–'57; Asst. Ed., Am. Viscose Corp., '51–'56; Edtl. Asst., Bill Bros. Publ. Co., '49–'51; Free-lance Wtr., '60; Theta Sigma Phi, AAIE Secy., '57–'58; Exec. Secy., '58–'61); League of Wm. Voters, Nat. Cncl. of Jewish Wm. (V.P., '65–'66), Va. Cncl. on State Legislation (VP, '68–'69); Pa. State Univ., BA (Jnlsm.), '49; Temple Univ.; b. Johnstown, Pa., 1927; p. David and Helen Rosenberg Zasofsky; h. Dr. Lawrence Baxt; c. Joshua.

BAXTER, ELLA HOUSTON, Librn., Washington Elementary School, 1440 Superior Blvd., Wyandotte, Mich. 48192, '52–; Tchr., '48–'51, '30–'41; WNBA, Mich. Assn. of Sch. Librns., Mich. Educ. Assn., Wyandotte Educ. Assn., Wyandotte Bus & Profsnl. Assn.; Who's Who in Am. Educ.; Wayne State Univ., BS, '56; b. Wyandotte, Mich.; p. Justin and Della LaDue Houston; h. Lawson Baxter; c. Howard L.; res: 2322–21st, Wyandotte, Mich. 48192.

BAXTER, MERRY (Eula Lee Baxter), Wms., Ch. Pg. Ed., Imperial Valley Press, P.O. Box 251, El Centro, Cal. 92243, '66–; Social Worker, Kern County Welfare Dept., '65; Wms. Ed., Colmst., Delano Record, '63–'65; Wms., Sports, Church, Club Ed., Ojai Valley News, '62; Mgr., Ventura Col. News Bur., '57–'60; many poems, stories, juv. works; Cal. Press Wm., NFPW; Imperial Valley Wtrs. Workshop (Founder, '69); numerous state and local aws. and hons.; Ventura Col., '56–'60; p. William and Cannie Ridge Buchanan; c. two sons, two daughters.

BAYER, ANN, Asst. Ed., Life Magazine, Time-Life Bldg., Rockefeller Ctr., N.Y., N.Y. 10020, '68–; Contrb. Wtr., Saturday Evening Post, '67–'68; Assoc. Articles Ed., '65–'67; Asst. Fiction Ed., '64–'65; Sarah Lawrence Col., BA, '63; b. Cleve., Oh., 1941; p. Leo and Eleanor Rosenfeld Bayer; res: 3 E. 66th St., N.Y., N.Y. 10021.

BAYNE, EVE COMPTON, Head Librn., Dell Publishing Company, Inc., 750 Third Ave., N.Y., N.Y. 10017, '61–; Lib. Asst., Univ. of Mo.; Branch Librn., Johnson County Lib. (Shawnee-Mission, Kan.); Cnslt., Gracie Mansion Lib.; Southwestern Col., Univ. of Mo., Rutgers Univ.; h. Virgil A. Bayne.

BAYS, GWENDOLYN McKEE, Prof., French Literature, Clarion State College, Clarion, Pa. 16214, '64–; Assoc. Prof., '62–'64; Assoc. Prof., Antioch Col.,

'58–'62; Rsch. Assoc., Yale Univ., '56; Auth., "The Orphic Vision" ('64); numerous articles, pfsnl. jnls.; Modern Language Assn., Am. Assn. of Tchrs. of French, AAUP; Agnes Scott Col., BA (Phi Beta Kappa); Emory Univ., MA; Yale Univ., PhD, '56; b. Atlanta, Ga.; p. Oran and Mary Peek McKee; h. Robert A. Bays; c. Robert Jr.; Geoffrey Alan; res: 202 South St., Clarion, Pa. 16214.

BAZAR, JOAN WOOLLEY, Wms. Ed., Tri-City Herald, P.O. Box 2608, Pasco, Wash. 99302, '69–; Club Ed., Berkeley (Cal.) Daily Gazette '65–'68; Asst. Wms. Ed., Bethlehem (Pa.) Globe-Times, '56–'57; Reptr., Tucson Daily Citizen (Tucson, Ariz.); Who's Who of Am. Wm.; Univ. of Ariz., BA, '56 (cum laude); b. Phila., Pa., 1934; p. Ralph and Margaret McCoy Woolley; h. (div.); c. Annelise, Julia Beth; res: 920 W. Kennewick Ave., Kennewick, Wash. 99336.

BAZZINI, ROSILY, VP, Unisphere Motion Picture Corp., 663 Fifth Ave., N.Y., N.Y. 10022, '65–; Pres., Aquarian Productions Ltd.; VP, Harrington Film Dist. Corp.; Asst., film distrb. to theatres, Casting Dir. and Script. Supvsr., '68; Rsch. on hist. of maj. motion pic. studios, N.Y.U., '66; assisted in TV monitoring survey for SAG, '67; Variety Clubs Intl., B'nai B'rith-Cinema Lodge, The Troopers of the Friars Club; ltr. of tribute from Jt. Equality Comm., SAG, '67; Violionist, Drs. Orchestral Soc.; N.Y.U., BS, '63; b. N.Y.C., 1941; p. Emil and Molly Appel Bazzini; res: 224 W. 46th St., N.Y., N.Y. 10036.

BEAGLE, GAIL JOYCE, Adm. Press Asst., Rep. Henry B. Gonzalez, U.S. House of Representatives, 116 Cannon House Office Bldg., Wash., D.C. 20515, '63–; Off. Mgr., Press Aide, '61–'63; Adm. Asst., Tex. Methodist Student Movement, '60–'61; Asst., State Sen. Henry B. Gonzalez, '59; Asst., U.S. Sen. Ralph Yarborough, '59; Staff, Tex. Cncl. of Churches, '58; Reptr., San Antonio Light, '57; Theta Sigma Phi (San Antonio Chptr. Headliner aw., '68); Who's Who of Am. Wm., Who's Who in Am. Polits., 2,000 Wm. of Achiev.; Tex. Wms. Univ., BS (Jnlsm.), '58; b. Beaumont, Tex., 1935; p. Victor and Hazel Block Beagle; res: 220 Second St. SE, #204, Wash. D.C. 20003; 2943 W. Ashby Pl., San Antonio, Tex. 78228.

BEAIRD, BETTY JO, Actress, Marie Waggedorn on NBC's "Julia," 20th Century Fox, 10201 W. Pico, L.A., Cal., '68–; TV Prod: NBC, Arthur Murray Show, Edward H. Weiss Adv., Goodson-Todman Prods.; Univ. of Tex., BBA (Adv.), '56; b. El Paso, Tex.; p. Benjamin and George Rowell Beaird; res: 24942 Malibu Rd., Malibu, Cal. 90265.

BEAIRD, HELEN LEAKE, Soc. Ed. and Feature Wtr., Loveland Publishing Co., 450 Cleveland Ave., Loveland, Colo. 80537, '56–; Colmst., '67–; Reptr., '56–'67; X-ray Tech., Loveland Memorial Hosp.; X-ray Tech., Poudre Valley Memorial Hosp. (Ft. Collins, Colo.); BPW (cit., '68), Colo. DAR (cits. for civic work, '67), Colo. Mens Garden Club (cits. for civic work, '67),

Wm. of Achiev. aw. ('68); Tex. Wms. Univ., '35–'36; b. Abilene, Tex., 1917; p. Robert E. and Daisy C. Atkinson Leake; h. James E. Beaird; c. Mrs. Robert A. Zawacki; res: Star Rte., Box 92, Loveland, Colo. 80537.

BEALE, BETTY, Colmst., Evening Star, Second and Virginia Ave. S.E., Wash., D.C. 20003, '45–; Publishers-Hall Syndicate, '53–; Colmst., Wash. Post, '37–'40; Auth; mag. articles; WNPC, Wash. Jr. League; Assn. of Fed. Investigators Special Act Aw., '68; Freedom Fndn. Aw., '69; Smith Col., AB; b. Wash., D.C.; p. William and Edna Sims Beale; h. George Kenneth Graeber; res: 3200 Reservior Rd., Wash., D.C. 20007.

BEARD, ANTON MARIE, Ed., Lab Notes, General Motors Research Laboratories, 12 Mile and Mound Rd., Warren, Mich. 48090, '55–; Edtl. Asst., Engineering Journal; PR Staff; Supvsr., Pers. Control, Veterans Adm. (Detroit), '46–'48; Asst., Detroit Ordnance Dist., War Dept., '44–'46 (Aw. of Merit, '45); Engineering Soc. of Detroit, Intl. Platform Assn.; Wayne State Univ., BA, '48 (Phi Sigma Alpha); b. Ste. Agathe, Quebec, Can.

BEARD, MARGARET OVER, Assoc. Ed. of Pubns. (Nat. Pubcty.), TV Guide, Radnor, Pa. 19088, '69–; Assoc. Ed. of Pubns., Merck, Sharp & Dohme, Phila., '55–'57; Dir. of Pubcty., Pa. Hosp. Sch. of Nursing, '54–'55; Asst. to Reg. Mgr., Curtis Publishing, '52–'54; League of Wm. Voters (Radnor Bd. of Dirs., '65–'67, '69), Del. Valley Assn. of Communicators (Bd. of Dirs., Secy., '56–'57); St. Lawrence Univ., BA, '52; b. Phila., Pa. 1930; p. Stuart and Margaretta Tingley Over; h. Alexander Beard; c. Margaretta L., Alexander R., Jr., Mary-Stuart; res: Box 103, St. Davids, Pa. 19087.

BEARDMORE, J. FAITH SAUERS, VP, Radio-TV, Newhoff-Blumberg Advertising Agency Inc., 407 Court Square Bldg., Balt., Md. 21202, '67–; Copywtr., '54–; Balt. Sun, WMAR-TV, '50–'53; Wms. Adv. Club of Balt.; Strayer's Bus. Col.; b. Balt., Md., 1918; p. John and Josephine Kroupa Sauers; h. William J. Beardmore; c. William, John, Paul; res: 206 Fourth Ave., S.E., Glenburnie, Md. 21061.

BEARDSLEY, DAISY SANDERS, Ed., Herald News, Cayuga, Ind. 47928, '66–; weekly colm.; Delta Theta Tau; b. Newport, Ind., 1906; p. Fred and Maryetta Sanders; h. Joe Earl Beardsley; c. Joe II; res: Clinton, Ind. 47842.

BEARN, MARGARET SLOCUM, Dean, Laboratory Institute of Merchandising, 12 E. 53rd St., N.Y., N.Y. 10022, '56–; Field Rep.-PR, '53–'56; Atty., Lewinson, Lewinson & Fieland, '50–'53; Atty., Grossman & Grossman, '48–'50; Fashion Group (Bd. of Governors, '63–'65), AWNY, Inner Circle; Swarthmore Col., BA, '45 (honors); Yale Law Sch., LLB, '48; b. Fanwood, N.J., 1924; p. Clarence W. and Emma Elliot Slocum; h. Alexander G. Bearn; c. Helen, Gordon; res: 1225 Park Ave., N.Y., N.Y. 10028.

BEASLEY, MARGARET SIMPSON, Dir., PR, Ed., The Chuck Wagon, Exec. Asst. to VP, Tex. Restaurant Assn., '42–'66 (aws. for outstanding svc., Am. Soc. of Trade Assn. Execs., Nat. Restaurant Assn.); Labor Mkt. Analyst, Tex. Employment Commn., '41–'42; Ed., News & Views, Dr. Pepper Co., '39–'40; Adv. Mgr., Bowie News, '39; Edtl. Dept., Fort Worth Press, '38; Linotype Operator, Berger Daily Herald, '37–'38; Instr., Linotyping, Adv., Tex. Wms. Univ., '35–'37; Adv. Copywtr., Williams Dept. Store, '36–'37; Movie Critic, Interstate Theatres, '35–'37; Tex. Wms. Univ., BS (Jnlsm.), '37; b. Denton, Tex., 1917; p. Paul and Sallie Morris Simpson; h. Joseph Weldon Beasley; res: Box 373, 415 S. 16th St., Junction, Tex. 76849.

BEATTY, PATRICIA ROBBINS, Children's Auth., '60–; Bks: "Campion Towers" ('65; Bk. of Yr. Aw., Commonwealth Club of Cal.), "The Royal Dirk" ('66; aw.; Southern Cal. Cncl. on Children's Literature), "A Donkey for the King" ('66; "one of best bks. of yr.", Horn Book); many other bks.; Librn.; '53–'57; Eng. Tchr.; '47–'50; Southern Cal. Cncl. on Children's and Young People's Literature, Cal. Wtrs. Guild; Reed Col., BA, '44; b. Portland, Ore., 1922; p. Walter and Jessie Miller Robbins; h. Dr. John Louis Beatty; c. Ann Alexandra; res: 3113 Wendell Way, Riverside, Cal. 92507.

BEATTY, SARAH LOIS, Asst. Soc. Ed., The Denver Post, 650 15th St., Denver, Colo. 80202, '67–; Tchr., Aurora, Colo.; articles published in Grade Teacher, Western Skier, University Park News; Univ. of Ia., BA, '61; Stanford Univ., MA (Commtns.) '63; b. Iowa City, Ia.

BEATY, ELLYN BROOMELL, Wtr., "The Children's Book Sampler" program, KPFA-FM, Berkeley, Cal., '60–; Ref. Asst., Contra Costa County Lib. (Pleasant Hill); ALA, Cal. Wtrs. Club, Nat. Bk. Wms. Assn., Assn. of Children's Librns. of Northern Cal.; Univ. of Chgo., PhB, '13; N.Y. State Lib. Sch., '14; b. Chgo. Ill. 1890; Chester and Lena Johnson Broomell; h. (div.); c. Chester B. Beaty; res: 2325 McKinley Ave., Berkeley, Cal. 94703.

BEATY, JANICE JANOWSKI, Free-lance Wtr., '60–; Auth. of five non-fiction and children's bks., '64–'69, incl. "Nufu and the Turkeyfish" (Pantheon, '69); 100 mag. articles; weekly series features in Guam nwsprs., '65–'69; Tchr.; NEA (Life Mbr.), Nat. Audobon Soc., Cornell Ornithological Lab.; State Univ. Col., Geneseo, N.Y., BS, '52 (Who's Who Among Students in Am. Univs. and Cols., '51–'52); Cornell Univ.; Elmira Col., MS (Educ.); '69; b. Elmira, N.Y., 1930; p. Henry and Majorie Finch Janowski; h. James Beaty (dec.); c. William J., Bruce H., David C.; res: 546 Esty St., Elmira, N.Y. 14904.

BEAUCHAMP, B. GAIL ESTES, VP, Controller, Dodge & Delano Inc., 655 Madison Ave., N.Y., N.Y. 10022, '67–; Dir. of Budgetary Control, Northeast Airlines, '66–'67; Treas.-Controller, Storer TV Sales,

'61–'66; Asst. to Controller, Grey Adv., '58–'61; Am. Inst. of Cert. Public Accountants; Benjamin Franklin Univ., BCS, '54; CPA, '55; b. Dayton, Oh., 1931; p. Neil and Rae Salmon Estes; h. Jack Beauchamp; c. Dirk; res: 58 Pkwy. W., Mt. Vernon, N.Y.

BEAUCHAMP, CAROLYN DONNELLA, Pres., Beauchamp's Advertising and Public Relations, 4304 S. Park Rd., Louisville, Ky. 40219, '64–; PR Dir., Ky. Bankers Assn.; Radio-TV Dir., AE, Asst. Dir. of PR, Louisville Advertising Agcy., PRSA, Nat. Parliamentarians Assn.; Who's Who in Bus. Wm.; Univ. of Louisville; b. Louisville, Ky.; p. Raymond and Mary Armstrong Donnella; h. John W. Beauchamp, Jr.; c. Mary R., John W. III.

BEAUDRY, MARILYN PATRICIA, Pres., Comlab, Inc., 17 W. Grand Ave., Chgo., Ill. 60610, '69–; VP, Rsch. Opns., Audience Studies Inc., '63–'69; Mktng., Mgt. Conslt., several firms in L.A., '57–'63; Pers. Admr., State Farm Ins. (Cal.), '54–'57; Am. Sociological Assn., AAPOR, Am. Mktng. Assn.; Univ. Southern Cal., BS, '53 (Phi Kappa Phi, Beta Gamma Sigma, Mortar Bd.); MA (Sociol.), '62; b. L.A., Cal., 1932; p. Wilfrid and Josephine Billiet Beaudry; res: 6200 Rockcliff, L.A., Cal. 90028; 1255 N. State Pkwy., Chgo., Ill. 60610.

BEAUDRY, YVONNE ANGELINA, Free-lance Wtr. for nat. mags., nwsps., educ. and religious pubns., lit. quarterlies on numerous topics; contrbr., articles on France to 22 nwsps. in U.S.; "Jean Monnet—Europe's Hyphenator" ('68, Michigan Quarterly Review); Reader, Translator for motion pic. cos. in Hollywood; Tchr. of French; took part in econ. survey in Europe, '49–'50; Staff Rschr. and Wtr. on econ. development for U.S. Senate Appropriations Comm.; Auths. League of Am., OPC; Univ. of N.H.; Columbia Univ. Sch. of Jnlsm., B. Litt. degree; b. Claremont, N.H.; p. Alexis and Lillie Pratte Beaudry; res: 118 W. 79th St., Penthouse A, N.Y., N.Y. 10024.

BEAUMONT, LYNN, Pres., Lynn Beaumont, Inc., 4 W. 58th St., N.Y., N.Y. 10019, '68–; Dir., PR, U.S. Travel Svc., Dept. of Commerce, Wash., D.C., '61–'68; Am. Soc. of Travel Agts., N.Y.C., '55–'60; travel articles, N.Y. Times, World Ency., Doubleday Ency. of Travel, Saturday Review, trade pubns.; Soc. of Am. Travel Wtrs. (N.E. Chptr. Secy.); Spanish Govt. Orden del Merito Civil, '57; Wash., D.C. Ad Wm. of Yr., '64; Cornish Sch. of Drama, Music and Art, '36–'38; b. Seattle, Wash.; p. Alonzo and Evelyn Ormsby Taylor; h. (div.); c. Philip H. Warren, III; res: 125 E. 87th St., N.Y., N.Y. 10028.

BEAURET, MARGARET RECKERT, Pres.-Treas., The Carborid Company, Inc., 99 Hudson St., N.Y., N.Y. 10013, '48–; Asst. to Exec. Secy., Newsprint Svc. Bur., '47; Ed., monthly newsprint trade bul.; AWNY; Hunter Col., '32; b. N.Y.C., 1913; p. John and Rosa Wolff Reckert; h. Alfred Beauret (dec.); res: 511 W. 235th St., N.Y., N.Y. 10463.

BEAVER, MARTHA deBLASIIS, Wms. Ed., Daily Hampshire Gazette, 2 Armory St., Northampton, Mass. 01060; Music Critic, '52–; dance, theatre revs.; Piano Tchr., Stonleigh-Burnham, '52–'55; Pianist-Musician, Smith Col. Theatre-Dance Dept., '52–'60; civic activities, music progs. for youth; Curtis Inst. of Music (Phila., Pa.), '24–'27; Inst. of Musical Art (N.Y.C.), '27–'30; b. Glen Falls, N.Y.; p. David H. and Anna Moore deBlasiis; h. Donald E. Beaver; c. Donald deB., David E.; res: 61 Crescent St., Northampton, Mass. 01060.

BEAVERS, JESSIE BROWN, Wms. Ed., Los Angeles Sentinel, 1112 E. 43rd St., L.A., Cal. 90019, '49–; Soc. Ed., Colmst., California Eagle, '40–'49; NAMW (Nat. 2nd VP, '67–'68; Media Wm. of Yr., '68), Cal. Press Wm. Assn., Theta Sigma Phi (L.A. Chptr. Outstanding Wm. Jnlst., '69), Alpha Kappa Alpha, Iota Phi Lambda; Nat. Assn. of Col. Wm. Aw., '67, Outstanding Cal. Wm. of Yr., '66; U.C.L.A., '41–'46; b. L.A., Cal.; p. Albert and Arnetta Hoyt Brown; h. Leroy A. Beavers, Jr.; c. Deborah Elaine, LeRoy Albert, Kimberly Arnetta; res: 1809 Buckingham Rd., L.A., Cal. 90019.

BEBOUT, SHEILA RYAN, PR Dir., Copy Chief, Coit and Associates, Inc., 4004 S.W. Kelly Ave., Portland, Ore. 97201, '66–; Wtr., '63–'66; AE, Wtr., Bdcst. Dir., Ore. Citizens for Reagen, '68; Wtr., film for Ore. State Sch. for the Blind; PR, Founder, Pentacle Theatre, Salem, Ore., '54–'64; Portland PR Roundtable, Ore. Assn. of Communicators and Eds., ICIE, Ore. Press Wm.; Willamette Univ.; b. Wash., D.C. 1930; p. William and Madeleine Tenney Ryan; h. William Bebout; c. Alfred Christopher, Gretchen, Timothy, Gaelen, Matthew, Julia, Andrew Augustine; res: 785 Boxwood Lane S.E., Salem, Ore. 97302.

BECHTOLD, GRACE, Exec. Ed., Bantam Books, Inc., 666 Fifth Ave., N.Y., N.Y. 10019, '69–; Ed., '49–'69; Ed., Doubleday; Ed., Macmillan Co.; Univ. of Ill.; b. New Athens, Ill.; p. August and Mae Dake Bechtold; res: 95 Christopher St., N.Y., N.Y. 10014.

BECHTOS, RAMONA, Intl. Ed., Advertising Age, 630 Third Ave., N.Y., N.Y. 10021, '66–; Assoc. Ed., '59–'65; Assoc. Ed., Radio-TV Journal; Theta Sigma Phi (former Placement Chmn.); Syracuse Univ., BA; res: 160 E. 74th St., N.Y., N.Y. 10021.

BECK, MARILYN MOHR, Hollywood Colmst., North American Newspaper Alliance and Bell McClure Syndicate; West Coast Chief, Bell-McClure; West Coast Ed., Sterling Magazines; Colmst., Valley Times & Citizen News; Hollywood Wms. Press Club; Who's Who of Am. Wm.; Univ. of Southern Cal., AA, '48; b. Chgo., Ill., 1928; p. Maxwell and Rose Lieberman Mohr; h. Roger Beck; c. Mark Elliott, Andrea; res: 19653 Wells Dr., Tarzana, Cal. 91356.

BECK, ROSEMARY, Mng. Ed., Chronicle-Herald, 201 First Ave., Hoopeston, Ill. 60942, '66–; Wms. Ed., Reptr., '64–'66; Reptr., Kokomo (Ind.) Tribune,

'63–'64; Wms. Ed., Tipton (Ind.) Tribune, '51–'63; Theta Sigma Phi, Wms. Press Club of Ind. (Treas., '60–'61), BPW (Pres., '69); Ball State Univ., '64–'66; b. Tipton, Ind., 1930; p. Luther and Doris Dunn Beck; res: 117 N. West St., Tipton, Ind. 46072.

BECK, SARA A., Consumer Info. Specialist, U.S. Department of Agriculture, 14th and Independence Ave., S.W., Wash., D.C. 20250, '67–; Mgr. Trainee, Knott's Pentagon Cafeterias, The Pentagon, '61–'65; Home Svc. Advisor, Duke Power Co. (Winston-Salem, N.C.), '59–'61; Wtr., mag. articles; AWRT, NATAS, Am. Home Econs. Assn., Phi Delta Gamma; Catawba Col., BA (Home Econs., Gen. Sci.), '59; Univ. of N.C. Wms. Col. (Vocational Deg. in Home Econs.), '59; Univ. of Md., MS (Home Econs. and Commtns.), '67; b. Salisbury, N.C., 1936; p. Arthur and Zelma Weant Beck; res: 5535 Columbia Pike, Arlington, Va. 22204.

BECKER, ANGELA SIBELLA, Sub-Reg. Ed., TV Guide Magazine, 330 Stuart St., Boston, Mass. 02116, '56–; Copywtr., WPAX (Montgomery, Ala.), '55–'56; Pubcty. Dir., Manning Public Relations, '53–'55; Traf. Mgr., WOAI-TV (San Antonio, Tex.), '51–'53; Pubcty. Asst., WBZ (Boston), '49–'51; Copywtr., radio personality, WVOM '47–'49; Boston Pubcty. Club, AWRT, Boston Press Club; accredited Braillist; Boston Univ., '43–'45; Harvard Ext., '45–'48; Huntingdon Col., '55–'56; b. Bergamo, Italy, 1926; p. Giacomo and Giovanna Sibella; h. Daniel Becker; c. Michael; res: 140 Marlborough St., Boston, Mass. 02116.

BECKER, CALLIE DANIEL, Asst. Librn., California State College Long Beach, 6101 E. 7th St., Long Beach, Cal. 90801, '63–; San Diego State Col., '56–'61; Circulation Librn., '45–'56; teaching positions, Ariz. State Univ.; Cal. Lib. Assn., Special Libs. Assn., Assn. Cal. State Col. Profs. (Chptr. Secy.), Beta Phi Mu, active in civic orgs.; Who's Who of Am. Wm., '70–'71; educ: Shorter Col., BA, '43; Emory Univ., BA (Lib. Sci.), '45; Univ. of Southern Cal., MS (Lib. Sci.), '68 (Lib. Sch. Bd. of Dirs., '69–'71); b. Barnesville, Ga. 1922; p. Perry and Hattie Dunn Daniel; res: 1535 Termino, Long Beach, Cal. 90804.

BECKER, PAULA LEE, Dir. of PR, Southern Publishing Co., 2119 24th Ave. N., Nashville, Tenn. 37202, '68–; Adv. Dir., '67–'68; Asst. Bk. Ed., '64–'66; Asst. Dir. PR, Glendale Hosp., '63–'64; PR Cnslt., TEAM, special project in inner-city educ., George Peabody Col.; PRSA (accredited), Religious PR Cncl. (Nat. Bd. of Govs., '69; Chptr. Secy., '67–'68; Chptr. Pres., '70–'71; Crtv. Commtns. Aw. in Writing, Audio-Visual Prod., '69); Loma Linda Univ., BA, '60; grad. study, Vanderbilt Univ., George Peabody Col., '64–'65; b. Denver, Colo., '41; p. E. L. and Beauna Slater Becker; res: 2116 Hobbs Rd., Nashville, Tenn. 37215.

BECKERMAN, MARSHA R., Edtl. Rschr., Forbes Inc., 60 Fifth Ave., N.Y., N.Y. 10011, '66–; Redbook Magazine, '65–'66; Adelphi Univ., BA, 1966; b. N.Y.C.

1941; p. Irving and Esther Levine Beckerman; res: 562 West End Ave., PH-E, N.Y., N.Y. 10024.

BECKNER, MARY CANNON, Secy.-Treas: The Wayside Press, Inc., '41–; Kenneth B. Butler & Assoc., '44–; Butler Typo Design Research Center, '44–; all in Mendota, Ill. 61342; Mendota Wms. Club; b. Mendota, Ill., 1904; p. Edward and Emma Hoerner Cannon; h. L. W. Beckner; res: 1312 Burlington Rd., Mendota, Ill. 61342.

BECKWITH, ELINOR S., Free-lance Graphic Arts Designer, 81 Columbia Heights, Bklyn., N.Y. 11201; Cnslt., David McKay Publ., Look, Visual Panagraphics; Instr., Temple Univ., Pa. State Univ.; Educ: Yale Univ., Pratt Inst.; b. Holyoke, Mass.; res: 39 Towantic Hill, Oxford, Conn. 04683.

BECKWITH, YVONNE, Art Dir., Standard Educational Corp., 130 N. Wells, Chgo., Ill. 60606, '68–; Ed., Child's World; Asst. Art Dir., R. H. Donnelley Corp.; Co-auth., Ed., "Words to Know" ('69); Artists Guild, Bk. Clinic; Oh. State Univ., BFA, '58; b. Ashtabula, Oh., 1937; p. Clare and Isabelle Kaehler Beckwith; c. Anthony Beckwith Hobart; res: 7704 Kingston, Chgo., Ill. 60649.

BEDA, MARGARET CAPPS, Lib. Dir., Virginia Beach Library, 936 Independence Blvd., Virginia Beach, Va. 23455, '60–; Asst. to Registrar, McGill Univ. (Montreal, Can.), '59, '48–'51; Tchr., '51–'52; ALA, Va. Lib. Assn., AAUW; McGill Univ., BA (Eng.), '48 (Honors); MA, '50; BLS, '60; b. St. John, N.B., Can.; p. Talbot and Lottie Parlee Capps; h. Stephen W. Beda; res: 629 Cardiff Rd., Virginia Beach, Va. 23455.

BEDFORD, AMY ALDRICH, Mgr., Printing Dept., Corp. Secy., East Oregonian Publishing Company, P.O. Box 1089, Pendleton, Ore. 97801, '51–; Secy., Astorian-Budget Publ. Co. (Astoria, Ore.); Theta Sigma Phi, AAUW, Altrusa; Ore. State Univ., BS, '33; b. Pendleton, Ore.; p. Edwin and Elsie Conklin Aldrich; h. J.M. Bedford Jr. (dec.); c. Mrs. David M. Brown; res: P.O. Box 283, Pendleton, Ore. 97801.

BEEBE, BURDETTA FAYE, Auth, children's wildlife books: "Run, Light Buck, Run" ('62; Jr. Lit. Guild; Walt Disney TV prog.), "Ocelot" ('66; Jr. Lit. Guild), "Coyote, Come Home" ('63; Boys' Clubs of Am. aw.; Walt Disney TV prog.), many others; Am. Bus. Wms. Assn., Outdoor Wtrs. Assn.; Contemporary Auths.; Who's Who of Am. Wm.; b. Marshall, Okla., 1920; p. Alfred and Beulah Thurlow Beebe; h. James Ralph Johnson; res: 815 E. Alameda, Apt. 1, Santa Fe, N.M. 87501.

BEEBE, IDA ANN, Elementary Lib. Svcs. Cnslt., Bloomfield Public Schools, South Jr. High School, 177 Franklin St., Bloomfield, N.J. 07003, '60–; various cnslt., teaching positions; Intl. Platform Assn., NEA, ALA, N.J. Educ. and Sch. Lib. Assns.; Univ. of Wash., BA, '41; BA (Lib. Sci.), '42; Berkeley Baptist Divinity

Sch., MA, '47; Grad. work, Columbia Univ.; b. Yakima County, Wash. 1919; p. Hulbert and Jennie Folkerson Beebe; res: 186 Franklin St., Apt. 5E, Bloomfield, N.J. 07003.

BEEBE, KATHRYN, Free-lance Pubcty. and Non-fiction Wtr.; The Rowland Co., '66–'68; Selvage & Lee, '62–'65, '55–'57; Mastic Tile Co., '60–'62; N.Y. Daily News, '54; Wtr. for mags., synds., nwsps., radio and TV progs.; NHFL; Univ. of Kan. (Jnlsm.); Grad. Work, Wellesley (Eng.); b. Kan City, Mo., 1898; p. William and Laura Hunt Davis; res: 927 Madison Ave., N.Y., N.Y. 10021.

BEECH, LINDA MANGELSDORF, Dir., Linda Beech Enterprises, 4758 Aukai Ave., Honolulu, Hi. 96815, '68–; Cnslt., McCann Erickson Hakuhodo, '61–'65; TV Talent in several prods., '58–'65; Chgo. Daily News, '53–'58; Honolulu Advertiser, '51–'53; Wtr., TV dramas, articles; Doc. Prodr.; Theta Sigma Phi; Stephen Col., AA, '46; Univ. of Hi., BA, '48; grad. work, '65–'66; Univ. of Cal., '49; b. Honolulu, Hi.; p. Dr. Albert John and Celeste Ellis Mangelsdorf; h. Keyes Beech (div.); c. William Keyes Jr. and Barnaby Carden.

BEEMAN, ALICE L., Gen. Dir., American Association of University Women, 2401 Virginia Ave. N.W., Wash., D.C. 20037, '69–; Dir. of Info. Svcs., Univ. of Mich., '64–'69; Dir. of Pubns., '49–'60; Asst. Ed., News Svc., '46–'49; Asst. Dir., Special Svcs., Vanderbilt Univ., '43–'46; Reptr., Univ. of Tex. News Svc., '41–'43; ACPRA (Jnl. Ed., '50–'53), Theta Sigma Phi; Univ. of Tex., BJ, '41 (cum laude); b. Gainesville, Tex., 1919; p. William and Lucile Anderson Beeman; res: 6317 Poe Rd., Bethesda, Md. 20034.

BEER, LISL (Eloise Crowell Smith), Wtr., Painter; Auth: "Silver Series of Puppet Plays" (Branden Press, '62), "This, My Island" (Branden Press, '60), "Stones For Bread" (Branden Press, '50), Instr., Drama Dept., Univ. of Miami, '48–'50; NLAPW, Miami Puppet Guild (VP), Miami Art League, Fla. Artists Assn.; many painting aws.; Wellesley Col., BA, '26; b. Phila., Pa., 1903; p. Leonard and Eva Crowell Smith; h. Sanel Beer; res: 12300 Old Cutler Rd., Miami, Fla. 33156.

BEERSTECHER, FRANCES ADELE, Ed.—Publr., Malvern Daily Record, 133 S. Main, Malvern, Ark. 72104, '48–'68; Assoc. Ed., '36–'48; Corr., Arkansas Gazette, '38–'48; Supvsr., Printing Dept., The Col. of the Ozarks (Clarkville), '32–'36; Linotype Operator, Make-up Foreman, '24–'32; Reptr., '20; Ark. Press Wm. (charter mbr., Treas., '51; Second VP, '67; First VP, '68–'69), NFPW Ark. Press Assn. ('49–'68); Bus. Wm. of Yr., Hot Spring County, '67; The Col. of the Ozarks, BA (Eng.), '36; b. Searcy, Ark., 1902; p. Julian H. and Catherine Brice Beerstecher; res: 107 East Sullenberger, Malvern, Ark. 72104.

BEERY, LEE, Singer, Actress: Laurey, "Oklahoma," N.Y. State Theatre, Lincoln Ctr.; Maria, "West Side Story"; Dallas, Tex., summer musicals; "Julius Monk Revue," Plaza Nine; Plaza Hotel; "Tonight Show" (four appearances); Maid Marian, "Legend of Robin Hood," NBC Special; b. Mpls., Minn.; p. Lambert and May Briggel Beery; res: 300 W. 53rd St., N.Y., N.Y. 10019.

BEERY, MARY, French Instr., Ohio State University, Lima Campus, Lima, Oh. 45801, '60–; Tchr: Social Dev., Lima Memorial Hosp. Sch. of Nursing, '58–'60; South HS, '29–'53; St. Rita's Sch. of Nursing, '54–'67; Prodr. and Modr., "Teenpan Alley," WIMA, '52–'54; Auth., numerous bks. and articles for young teenagers; Speaker, educ. groups; Oh. Educ. Assn., NEA, AAUW, Lima Educ. Assn., Marquis Biographical Lib. Soc., Allen County Hist. Soc.; Contemporary Auths.; Who's Who of Am. Wm.; Who's Who in the Midwest; Dictionary of Intl. Biog.; Royal Blue Bk.; 2,000 Wm. of Achiev.; Col. of Wooster, BA, '28; special courses at accredited schs. in U.S., Can., Mexico and France; b. Phila., Pa.; p. Dr. William and Hattie Bowers Beery; res: 215 N. Woodlawn Ave., Lima, Oh. 45805.

BEETON, DIANA LA FAY, Dir., The Casting Couch, '70–; Dir. of TV, Jane Beaton Ltd., '69–'70; Sr. Casting Dir., Foote, Cone & Belding, '67–'69; Casting Dir., Papert, Koenig & Lois, '65–'67; Contract Negotiator, Talent Assocs., '62–'65; Asst. Casting Dir., Talent Payment Dept., BBDO, '57–'62; Asst. Traf. Mgr., Dancer-Fitzgerald-Sample, '56–'57; articles, Advertising Age; Col. of William and Mary, BA, '56 (Theatre Arts); b. Wash., D.C., 1934; p. John and Fay Gentry Beeton; res: 315 E. 68th St., N.Y., N.Y. 10021.

BEFAME, JEANETTE, Feature Wtr., Rptr., San Jose Mercury-News, 750 Ridder Park Dr., San Jose, Cal. 95131, '47–; Radio News, KGO (S.F.), '46–'47; Radio News, Off. of War Info., '44–'45; Reptr., Sacramento (Cal.) Union, '43–'44; Reptr., San Francisco (Cal.) News, '41–'42; Theta Sigma Phi (S.F. Peninsula Chptr. Charter Pres.; Matrix aw., '64); NFPW, AAUW, S.F. Press Club, Cal. Press Wm. (Peninsula Chptr. Charter Pres.); Edward McQuade jnlsm. aw., '55; Cal. State Fair rept. aw., '56; Stanford Univ., BA (Jnlsm.), '41; b. Wahpeton, N.D., 1919; p. Frederick and Sykea Ashton Befame; h. John Allen Sontheimer; res: 1615 Bel Air Ave., San Jose, Cal. 95126.

BEGNER, EDITH FRIEDMAN, Fiction Wtr: "A Dark and Lonely Hiding Place" ('68), "Red in the Morning" ('63), "Son and Heir" ('60), "Just Off Fifth" ('59); Auths. Guild; Wellesley Col.; Columbia Univ.; b. N.Y.C.; p. Herrman and Anna Dorfman Friedman; h. Dr. Jacob A. Begner; c. Thomas L.

BEHRENS, JUNE YORK, Tchr., Reading Specialist, L.A. City Schools, L.A., Cal., '65–; Tchr., '49–; Auth, four children's bks.; Reading Cncl. of L.A., NEA, AAUW, Cal. Tchrs. Assn., Delta Kappa Gamma; Univ. of Cal., BA; Univ. of Southern Cal., MA; h. Henry W. Behrens; c. two daughters; res: 1901 Laurel Ave., Manhattan Beach, Cal. 90266.

BEIGHLE, JANET ANNE, Home Econs. Ed., Plain Dealer, 1801 Superior Ave., Cleve., Oh. 44114, '63–; Cookbk. Ed., Meredith Publ. Co., '56–'63; Ed. Chmn., Food Eds. Conf., '69; Home Econsts. in Bus. (Cleve. Group Chmn., '65–'66), Oh. Home Econs. Assn. (Bd. Mbr.), Inst. of Food Tech.; Vesta Aw., Am. Meat Inst., '64 (Hon. Mention, '65, '67); Alma Aw., Assn. Home Appliance Manufacturers, '67; Ore. State Univ., BS (Home Econs.), '55; Univ. of Wis., MS (Home Econs. Jnlsm.), '56; b. Tacoma, Wash., 1933; p. Dan and Anne Murray Beighle.

BEIJER, LORETTA JANKE, George W. Wolpert Public Relations, 161 W. Wisconsin Ave., Milw., Wis. 53203, '57–; Ed., Milw. Gear Co. News, '50–'57; Wis. Indsl. Eds. Assn. (Bd. of Dirs., '52), ICIE, Beta Sigma Phi, Milw. City Cncl., '69; b. Milw., Wis. 1915; p. Robert and Augusta Steffen Janke; h. Albin Beijer; c. Mrs. Dorothy Koerner; res: 4125 N. 48th St., Milw., Wis. 53216.

BEILENSON, EDNA RUDOLPH , Pres., Peter Pauper Press, Inc. and Walpole Printing Office, Inc., 629 N. McQuesten Pkwy., Mt. Vernon, N.Y. 10552, '62–; Auth., Ed.; AIGA Dir., VP; Pres, '60–'61), The Goudy Soc. (Dir., Chmn. of Bd.); Bus. Wm. of Yr., '68, Who's Who of Am. Wm.; Hunter Col., BA, '28 (cum laude), Sorbonne Univ., Paris; b. N.Y.C. 1909; p. John and Anna Beilenson Rudolph; h. 1. Peter Beilenson (dec.) 2. Dr. Joseph E. Barmack; c. Anthony C., Roger N., Mrs. J. J. Schildkraut; res: 1035 Fifth Ave., N.Y., N.Y. 10028.

BEINEKE, VICTORIA ANDERSON, Co-ed., Nickerson Argosy, 6 N. Nickerson, Nickerson, Kan. 67561, '47–; b. Farmington, Kan., 1915; p. William and Maud Quinn Anderson; h. Hillis Beineke; c. Jan (Mrs. Herb Hilgers), Jerry, Randy, Kay; res: 607 N. Sill, Nickerson, Kan. 67561.

BEIRPONCH, DOLORES KEELING, Publr.-Ed., Wortham Journal, P.O. Box 246, Wortham, Tex. 76693, '63–; Secy. for City Mgr., '58–'59; Irving Public Schs., '57–'58; Sanger-Harris, '55–'57; Colmst., Dallas Morning News, '68; Tex. Press Assn., N. & E. Tex. Press Assn., Dallas Press Club; Tex. Fedn. of Wms. Clubs, Freestone County Hist. Soc., active in civic affairs; Westminster Jr. Col., '38; N. Tex. State Col., '61; Tex. Wms. Univ., '62; b. Wortham, Tex., 1920; p. Roy and Bess Calame Keeling; h. Michael Beirponch; c. Mrs. F. C. Justice, Jr., Mrs. James T. Modisette; res: Marlin, Tex. 76661.

BELAIR, M. PHYLLIS, Head City Librn., Willimantic Public Library, 905 Main St., Willimantic, Conn. 06226, '50–; WNBA; Eastern Conn. State Col., BS (Educ.), '48; Southern Conn. State Col., MS (Lib. Sci.), '68; b. Willimantic, Conn.; p. Henry and Loretta Labby Belair; res: 51 Jackson St., Willimantic, Conn. 06226.

BELK, ROSE KNOX, Librn., Colonial Williamsburg, Inc., Box C, Williamsburg, Va. 23185, '53–; Ref. Librn., Col. of William & Mary, '44–'53; AAUW (Williamsburg Br. Past Pres.), Va. Lib. Assn., League of Wm. Voters, Eng. Speaking Un.; Winthrop Col., AB; Univ. of N.C., BS (Lib. Sci.); b. Seneca, S.C., 1902; p. Fletcher and Betty Hudgens Knox; h. George W. Belk, Jr. (dec.); c. Betty (Mrs. Paul Moorhead), George III; res: Box 1173, Williamsburg, Va. 23185.

BELKNAP, ONA SWEET, Ed., Christian Woman mag., Sweet Publishing Company, 6721 N. Lamar, Austin, Tex. 78751, '67–; Wtr., Okla. City Safety Cncl., '46–'56; Okla. City Univ., '44–'45; b. Anadorko, Okla., 1911; p. Forest and Mary Fitts Sweet; h. Andrew T. Belknap; c. William E., F. Andy; res: 965 E.N. 10th St., Abilene, Tex. 79601.

BELL, ANNE W., Librn., English-Speaking Union, 16 E. 69th St., N.Y., N.Y. 10021, '68–; Librn., St. Margaret's Sch. (Waterbury, Conn.), '61–'68; Dir., New Brunswick (N.J.) Lib., '56–'61; Librn., Del. State Lib. Commn., '54–'56; Asst. Dir., New Brunswick Lib., '50–'54; Wilmington (Del.) Inst. Free Lib., '45–'50; N.J. Lib. Assn. (Secy.), '58–'60), Del. Lib. Assn. (Pres.), '49); Mt. Holyoke Col., '19–'20; Univ. of Del., BA, '34; Drexel Inst. of Tech., BS (Lib. Sci.), '47; b. Sayre, Pa.; p. Robert and Eleanor Wright Bell; res: 116 Livingston Ave., New Brunswick, N.J. 08902.

BELL, BARBARA SMITH, Staff Wtr., Ithaca Journal, 123 W. State St., Ithaca, N.Y. 14850, '62–; Free-lance Wtr., Photogr., '53–'62; Auth, four history books; cit., Historic Ithaca, '69; Schuyler County Hist. Soc.; b. Cortland, N.Y., 1920; p. Lloyd and Gladys Everett Smith; h. David Bell; c. Richard D., Judythe Bell Walters; res: Irelandville Rd., Watkins Glen, N.Y. 14891.

BELL, ELEANOR, Reptr., Seattle Post-Intelligencer, Seattle, Wash. 98111, '44–; also Ed., "What's Happening" colmn., entertainment guide; Prodr., "Quizdown," radio, TV, '48–'64; Ed., New Balt.-New Haven Star (Mich.), '30s; reptr., '24–; Wash. Educ. Assn. aw., '64, Wash. State Press Wm., Seattle-Tacoma Nwsp. Guild, N.W. Theater, Theta Sigma Phi; Detroit Tchrs. Col.; b. Detroit, Mich., 1906; p. Joseph and Adele Lang Engelman; h. 1. Charles C. Bell (dec.) 2. George E. McDermott (dec.); res: 2148 Fourth Ave. W., Seattle, Wash. 98119.

BELL, GERTRUDE WOOD, Free-lance Wtr.; Auth., numerous juv., ch. mag. stories; bk., "Posse of Two," (Criterion, '64); NLAPW (1st pl., nat. contest, "Posse of Two," '66), Mo. Wtrs. Guild (aw., "Posse of Two," '65); William Jewell Co., AB (Eng.), '33; b. Liberty, Mo., 1911; p. William and Myrtle Griffith Bell; res: 30 S. Fairview St., Liberty, Mo. 64068.

BELL, JOYCE DENEBRINK, Free-lance Wtr.; Rschr-Wtr., "The Generation Gap," Talent Assoc., '69; Asst. Ed., Cowles Family Circle Bks., '68; Auth: "Shopping for Women" in "The New York Spy," (David White), "Barbed Wires" (Simon & Schuster); Who's Who of Am. Wm.; Denison Univ., '54–'56; Stanford Univ., BA, '58; b. Long Beach, Cal., 1936; p. Francis and Fanny McCook Denebrink; h. Byron Bell; res: 136 W. 15th St., N.Y., N.Y. 10011.

BELL, LEE PHILLIP, Hostess, "The Lee Phillip Show," WBBM-TV, 630 N. McClurg Ct., Chgo., Ill. 60611; Acad. of TV Arts and Scis. (Bd. of Dirs; 12 Emmy aws.), Chgo. Unlimited, active in civic orgs.; Golden Mike Aw. for E. Central AWRT, TV Guide's Top TV Personality, McCall's Outstanding Wm. of Radio and TV three times, Chgo. Sun-Times' 10 Best Dressed Wm.; Northwestern Univ., BS; h. William Bell; c. William James, Bradley Phillip, Lauralee Kristen.

BELL, MARY HORSTMANN, Co-owner, Bell and Associates, 1000 Dallas Trade Mart, Dallas, Tex. 75207, '68; AE, Bloom Public Relations; PR Dir., Dallas Mkt. Ctr.; Bur. Chief, Corr., INS; PRSA, NHFL, (Secy.-Treas., '65–'66), Nat. Soc. of Interior Designers, Dallas Press Club; Wash. Univ., '37–'40; Western Ky. Univ., '40–'41; b. St. Louis, Mo., 1919; p. John B. and Edith Hermsen Horstmann; h. Carl Bell; c. John William, Carole Marie, Robert J., Mrs. Margaret Couch; res: 2928 Golfing Green, Dallas, Tex. 75234.

BELL, NELLE KEYS, Mag. Ed., Jack and Jill, Curtis Publishing Co., Independence Sq., Phila., Pa. 19106, '63–; Assoc. Ed., Ladies' Home Journal, '51–'63; Co-Auth., "The Chinese Ginger Jars"; E. Tenn. State Col., BS; b. Jonesboro, Tenn., 1910; p. William and Amy Taylor Keys; h. (div.); res: 2601 Pkwy., Apt. 847. Phila., Pa. 19130.

BELL, ROBERTA LINN, Singer-Actress, 3500 Eastern Ave., Las Vegas, Nev. 89109; TV, Radio, Night Clubs, motion pics., records, summer stock; song Wtr.; own ASCAP Publ. Firm "Robello Inc."; AGVA, AFTRA, SAG; Emmy Winner, outstanding female performer; Nominated, '52–'56; b. Gravity, Ia., 1930; p. Samuel and Madge Brisdow Dubin; h. Freddie Bell; c. Freddie Jr., Angela; res: 3500 Eastern Ave., Las Vegas, Nev. 89109.

BELL, SALLIE LEE RILEY, Auth, 38 novels; aws., "The Barrier" ('57), "Until the Day Break" ('50); Newcomb Col., '07; b. N.O., La.; p. Robert and Sallie O'Pry Riley; h. Thaddeus Bell; res: 3445 Vincennes Pl., N.O., La. 70125.

BELLAMY, JEANNE, Edtl. Wtr., Miami Herald Publishing Co., #1 Herald Plaza, Miami, Fla. 33101, '51–; Asst. City Ed., '49–'51; Reptr., '37–'49; City Hall, Courthouse Reptr., Miami Tribune, '35–'37; Mng. Ed., Coral Gables Riviera, '34–'35; Theta Sigma Phi (Gtr. Miami Pres.), Fla. Soc. of Eds. (Pres.); Fla. Bar aws. and Hon. Mention, Thomas L. Stokes Nat. Aws. for writing; Jane Natt Aw., outstanding commty. svc., Wms. Div.,

Miami-Dade C. of C.; Midtown Bank of Miami and Bank of Coral Gables (Dir.), Nat. Audubon Soc. (Dir.); Barnard Col., '28–'29; Rollins Col., AB, '33; b. Bklyn., N.Y., 1911; p. Donald L. and Ethel P. Houston Bellamy; h. John T. Bills; res: 2917 Seminole St., Miami, Fla. 33133.

BELLOWS, MARGARET CASE (Pseud: Maggie Savoy), Soc. Ed., Los Angeles Times, 145 S. Spring St., L.A., Cal. 90012; Urban Affairs Specialist, UPI; Feature Wtr., AP; Wms. Ed., Ariz. Republic (Phoenix); Wms. Ed., Phoenix Gazette; Theta Sigma Phi; Univ. of Southern Cal., '40 (Phi Beta Kappa, Phi Kappa Phi); b. Des Moines, Ia., 1917; p. Andrew and Alberta Williams Case; h. James G. Bellows; c. Clarke William Savoy; res: 2270 Betty Lane, Beverly Hills, Cal. 90210.

BELMAN, ISABELLE GINSBERG, Media Byr., Waring & LaRosa, Inc., 555 Madison Ave., N.Y., N.Y. 10022, '67–; Media Estimator, '65–'67; Media Asst., Webb Assoc., '64; b. Bklyn., N.Y., 1944; p. Sidney and Irene Chankin Ginsberg; h. Howard Belman; res: 68–30 Burns St., Forest Hills, N.Y. 11375.

BELYEA, DESA CUCUK, Wms. Ed., Fresno Bee, 1559 Van Ness, Fresno, Cal. 93721, '57–; h. George F. Belyea, Jr.

BENDEL, PEGGY RAFTIS, Sr. Public Info. Specialist, New York State Commerce Department, Woman's Program, 230 Park Ave., N.Y., N.Y. 10017, '68–; Public Info. Spec., Wms. Program, '67–'68; Public Info. Spec., Travel Bur., '65–'67; Tax Tech., Int. Revenue Svc., '65; AWNY; Georgian Court Col., '65; b. Yonkers, N.Y., 1943; p. J. Jerome and Dorothy Flanigan Raftis; h. Norman Bendel; res: 564 Willow Ave., Scotch Plains, N.J. 07076.

BENDER, MAY KAPLAN, Owner-Designer, May Bender Industrial Design, 301 E. 47th St., N.Y., N.Y. 10017; Free-lance Designer, Cnslt., '65–; Cnslt. Designer, Warner-Lambert, Cosmetics & Fragrances Div., '65–'68; Partner, Lane-Bender, Indsl. Design, '50–'65; Partner, Kavart Studios, '40–'49; Designer, '38–'40; Graphics Designer, Coordr., The Better Living Bldg., N.Y. World's Fair, '64–'65; Package Designers Cncl. (Secy., '62–'63), AWNY; Nat. Packaging Design aws., '56–'59, '66; Best of Yr. Aw., Ben Franklin Printing Week Exhibit, '59; Art Students League (N.Y.C.), '38–'45, '55–'69; Fairleigh Dickinson Univ.; Rutgers; N.Y.U.; b. Newark, N.J., 1921; p. Julius and Celia Brodsky Kaplan; h. Max Bender; c. Leslie, Sanford; res: 16 S. Woodland Ave., E. Brunswick, N.J. 08816.

BENDICK, JEANNE GARFUNKEL, Auth.-Illus., Bendick Associates, 360 Grace Church St., Rye. N.Y. 10580; Auth. of about 50 bks. and Illus. of about 100 for McGraw-Hill, Franklin Watts, Rand-McNally, Parents Press, Grosset; Wtr., NBC's "The First Look"; Auths. Guild, Auths. League, Wtrs. Guild E., Rye Cncl. for Human Rights (Exec. Bd.); Parsons Sch. of Design;

b. N.Y.C. 1919; p. Louis and Amelia Hess Garfunkel; h. Robert Bendick; c. Robert, Jr., Karen.

BENEDICT, SHIRLEY, Wtr., film, radio, print; Avon Products; Wtr., TV film for children, '67; Dancer Fitzgerald Sample, Lampert Advertising; Compton Advertising; AWNY; City Col. of N.Y., BBA, '58; Grad. Sch., '58–'59; N.Y.U., '68–'69; New Sch. for Social Rsch., '67; b. N.Y.C.; p. Jack and Beatrice Levy Benedict; h. David Yanover; res: 68–37 Yellowstone Blvd., Forest Hills, N.Y. 11375.

BENEDUCE, ANN KEAY, Ed.-in-Chief, Children's Bks., Thomas Y. Crowell Company, 201 Park Ave. S., N.Y., N.Y. 10003, '69–; VP, Ed., Children's Bks., World Publ. Co., '63–'69; Ed., Children's Bks., J. B. Lippincott Co., '60–'63; Ed., Doubleday & Company, '57–'60; Children's Bk. Cncl. (Bd. of Dirs., '69–); Bryn Mawr Col., '34–'36; Barnard Col., BA, '46; b. Maplewood, N.J.; p. Elmer and Winnifred Houghton Keay; h. Eugene Beneduce (div.); c. Wendy, Cynthia; res: 64 E. 94th St., N.Y., N.Y. 10028.

BENELL, JULIE, Food Ed., Dallas Morning News, Communications Center, Dallas, Tex. 75222, '52–; Wms. Dir., WFAA Radio, '48–; Free-lance food cnslt., TV comml. talent; Wms. Dir., WFAA TV, '50–'65; Program Dir., WKY, Okla. City, '40–'48; Fashion Coordr., Radio Dir., Kerrs Dept. Store, Okla. City, '40–'42; CBS, NBC daytime dramas, '35–'40; Dallas Fashion Group, Nat. Jewish Fndn. (Denver, Colo. VP), Two Pres. Cits. (radio, TV), GMA Aw. twice, Silver Spoon Aw. of Tex. Restaurant Assn., Freddy aw. of Nat. Ceramics Assn., Edgar Aw. of wine industry, City of Hope cit.; res: 6630 Walnut Hill Lane, Dallas, Texas, 75230.

BENENATI, VIOLA HOWISON, Asst. Bus. Mgr., The Times Herald Co., 907 Sixth St., Port Huron, Mich. 48060, '65; Exec. Secy., Dunn Paper Co., '52–'55; Nat. Purchasing Agts. Assn., Southeastern Purchasing Agts. Assn.; Spring Arbor Jr. Col., '38–'39; St. Clair County Commty. Col., '65–; b. Port Huron, Mich. 1921; p. Elton and Fannie Bowen Howison; h. Virgil Michael Benenati (dec.); c. Lou Ann, Charles Edward; res: 2476 Sharon Lane, Port Huron, Mich. 48060.

BENEZRA, BARBARA BEARDSLEY, Librn., Willowick-Eastlake School System, Eastlake, Oh.; Auth., "Gold Dust and Petticoats," "Nuggets in My Pocket"; AAUW; Univ. of Pacific; Univ. of Cal.; San Jose States Tchrs. Col.; b. Woodman, Colo., 1921; p. Earl and Alice Smith Beardsley; h. Leo L. Benezra; c. Heather (Mrs. Robert De Mare), Paul Louis, Judy Ann, David Allen; res: 7170 Hawthern Dr., Mentor, Oh. 44060.

BENFORD, JANE, Fashion Ed., Family Circle Magazine, 488 Madison Ave., N.Y., N.Y. 10022, '66–; Assoc. Fashion Ed., Good Housekeeping, '61–'66; Fashion Ed., Ingenue, '58–'61; Fashion Ed., Bride-to-Be, '52–'53; Assoc. Fashion Ed., Seventeen, '49–'52; Free-lance Wtr., Pageant; Fashion Group; Art Students League, '46–'48; N.Y.U., '52; b. Youngwood, Pa., 1927;

p. E. G. and Elsie Shakespeare Benford; c. Charles Schneider, John Schneider; res: 501 E. 87th St., N.Y., N.Y. 10028.

BENGE, CLAUDIA ELLIOTT, Exec. VP, Goodman & Associates, Inc., 1010 First Nat. Bldg., Fort Worth, Tex. 76102, '68–; VP, '54–'67; AE, Corp. Secy., '49–'54; Copywtr., '46–'49; Copywtr., KFJZ Radio, '44–'46; Edtl. Wtr., Wellington Leader, '43–'44; Lectr., Adv., Clubs, Adv. Classes, Tex. Christian Univ.; Theta Sigma Phi (Ft. Worth Chptr. Pres., '56–'57), BPW; Cocke Sch. of Drama, '34 (highest hons., crtv. writing aw.); b. Ft. Worth, Tex., 1914; p. Charles and Cora Derr Elliott; h. Lester Benge; c. William D.; res: 1805 Sixth Ave., Fort Worth, Tex. 76110.

BENGTSON, CARLA LABES, Ed.-Wtr., The Lind Lens, Lind, Wash. 99341, '52–; Article, American Press; b. Spokane, Wash., 1934; h. Einar C. Bengtson; c. Einar Lawrence, Sandra Jean; res: Lind, Wash. 99341.

BENGTSON, CAROLYN SEAY, Fashion, Beauty Ed., American-Statesman, 308 Guadalupe, Austin, Tex. 78767, '58–; Theta Sigma Phi; Nat. Shoe Inst. Aw., '66; cited as one of outstanding young wm. in beauty, Mademoiselle mag., '67; Alpha Delta Pi (Alumnae Pres.), Sci. Ctr. Guild; Univ. of Tex., BJ, '58; Law Sch., '59–'60; b. Austin, Tex., 1937; p. Henry A. and Minnie M. Leifeste Seay; h. Howard T. Bengtson; c. Avery, Bradley; res: 1904 Robin Hood Trail, Austin, Tex. 78703.

BENJAMIN, ANNA SHAW, Ed., Archaeological Institute of America, 260 W. Broadway, N.Y., N.Y., 10013, '67–; Prof. of Classics, Rutgers, The State University, New Brunswick, N.J. 08903, '64–; Acting Chmn., Dept. of Classics, Douglass Col., Rutgers Univ., '65–'66, '68–; Prof. of Classical Langs., Chmn., Dept. of Classics, Univ. of Mo., Prof., '53–'64; Chmn., '58–'64; Instr., Juniata Col., '51–'53; Am. Philological Assn., Archaeological Inst. of Am., Am. Oriental Soc.; Univ. of Pa., AB, '46; MA, '47; PhD, '55; Am. Sch. of Classical Studies, Athens (Thomas Day Seymour Fellow), '48–'50; b. Phila., Pa., 1925; p. Charles and Grace Shaw Benjamin; res: 208 Cedar Ave., Highland Park, N.J. 08904.

BENJAMIN, ANNETTE FRANCIS LEVY, Non-fiction Wtr.; Co-auth. (with husband): "New Facts of Life for Women" ('69), "In Case of Emergency" ('65); Colmst., "Health in the Home," American Home, '66–'69; Prom. Mgr., Drugs and Toiletries Dept., McCall's, '57–'59; Copy Supvsr., RKO Teleradio Pics., '55–'56; Free-lance Wtr., Audience Prom. Presentations, NBC, '54–'55; Asst. Prom. Mgr., WOR, WOR-TV (N.Y.C.), '53–'54; Copywtr., Frederic W. Ziv Productions (Cinn., Oh.), '51–'53; Wtr., Pianist, WSAI, WCPO-TV, WKRC-TV, '50–'51; ASCAP, Dramatists Guild; Sophie Newcomb Col. of Tulane Univ., '45–'47; Col. of Music of Cinn., BFA (Radio), '49; b. Waco, Tex., 1928; p. Abraham and Selma Saul Levy; h. Bry Benjamin, M.D.; c. Alan; res: 176 E. 71st St., N.Y., N.Y. 10021.

BENJAMIN, MARYE DURRUM, Radio-TV Special Programs Prodr., Communication Center, University of Texas, P.O. Box 7158, Austin, Tex. 78712, '67–; Freelance Wtr., numerous adv. agcys.; Supvsr., Special Student Projects, Sch. of Commtns., '66–; Dir., Special Programs, KLRN-TV, '64–; Special Lectr., Radio-TV and Film, Univ. of Tex., '43–'64; Prodr., Designer, Wtr., educ. films, TV progs.; Lectr., Cnslt., field of bdcst.; NAEB, AAUW, Alpha Epsilon Rho, Theta Sigma Phi; 14 nat. aws. for excellence in writing, rsch., prod. radio-TV programs; Presidential Cit. for radio series on returning veterans, WW II; active in numerous civic groups; Tex. State Col. for Wm., BS (Jnlsm.), '34; b. Hugo, Okla., 1913; p. William and Effie Lear Durrum; h. David G. Benjamin; c. Margaret Anne (Mrs. James A. Keys), David Gleason, Jr., William F.; res: 2305 Tower Dr., Austin, Tex. 78703.

BENKOVITZ, MIRIAM JEANETTE, Prof., Skidmore College, Saratoga Springs, N.Y. 12866, '60–; Instr., '46–'60; Auth: "Bibliography of Ronald Firbank" ('63) "Ronald Firbank a Biography" ('69); Ed., "Edwy" and "Elgiva" by Fanny Burney ('57); Non-fiction Wtr., Contrbr. of articles to bks. and periodicals; Visiting Prof., State Univ. of N.Y., '69; Nashville Tenn. Public Schs., '32–'43; Bibliographical Soc. of Am., AAUW; Vanderbilt Univ., BA, '32; George Peabody Col., MA, '42; Yale Univ., MA, '47; PhD, '51; b. Chattanooga, Tenn., 1911; p. Jake and Josephine Bloomstein Benkovitz; res: 17 Ten Springs Dr., Saratoga Springs, N.Y. 12866.

BENNETT, HAZEL TORMOHLEN, Exec. Dir., Airzona State Nurses' Association, 1130 E. McDowell Rd., Suite B-1, Phoenix, Ariz. 85006, '61–; Asst. Exec. Secy.; Am. Nurses' Assn., Nat. League for Nursing, Assn. Execs. Soc. of Ariz.; Ind. Univ., '42–'44; Univ. of Santa Clara, '63; b. Holland, Ind., 1920; p. Harry and Amelia Werremeyer Tormohlen; h. J. C. Bennett; c. John Eugene, Robert Lewis; res: 1401 E. Mulberry, Phoenix, Ariz. 85014.

BENNETT, HELEN BURKHART, Ref. Librn., University of Missouri, Kansas City Libraries, 5100 Rockhill Rd., Kan. City, Mo. 64110, '67–; Curator, Snyder Collection, '61–'67; Head of Reference, Public Lib. (Kan. City, Kan.), '54–'60; Readers' Advisor, Public Lib. (Kan. City, Mo.), '51–'52; Reference Librn., Public Lib. (Denver, Colo.), '53–'54; ALA, Mo. Lib. Assn., AAUP; Phillips Univ., '35–'37; Southwestern State Col., AB, '39; Univ. of Denver, MA (Librnship.), '53; b. Clinton, Ia.; p. Charles and Frances Roberts Burkhart; h. Calvin Bennett (div.); res: 1710 Brush Creek Blvd., Kan. City, Mo. 64110.

BENNETT, KATRINA NICOLLE, Prom. Offcr., International Wool Secretariat, Wool House, Carlton Gardens, London S.W. 1, England, '68–; Wtr., Sec. Ed., Home Furnishings Daily (N.Y.C.); Mgt., Fin. Ed., Drug News Weekly (N.Y.C.), Feature Wtr., Soap and Detergent Assn. (N.Y.C.); Pubns. Ed., State Hist. Soc. of Wis. (Madison, Wis.); Feature Wtr., Sun News Pictorial (Australia); Theta Sigma Phi; Univ. of Wis., JBA, '62 (Margaret Garner Winston Aw.); b. Houston, Tex., 1939; p. William and Verna Donelan Bennett.

BENNETT, KAY CURLY, Commissioner for Human Rights, State of New Mexico, Office of the Governor, Santa Fe, N.M. 85701, '69–; Tchr., Interpreter, Phoenix Indian Sch., '46–'52; Auth., non-fiction bks. on Navajo life: "Kaibah" (Westernlore Press, '64), "A Navajo Saga" (Naylor Co., '69); Prodr. and Publr. of Navajo songs; active in prom. of Indian Arts and Crafts; Western Wtrs. of Am., Intertribal Indian Ceremonial Assn.; N.M. Mother of the Yr., '68; Colonel-Aide-de-Camp on staff of Governor of N.M., '68; b. Sheepsprings, N.M.., 1922; p. Hosteen and Mary Chah Supaihi Chischillie; h. Russell Bennett; c. Rosalie Miglio, Alyce Rouwalk; res: 6 Aida Ct., Gallup, N.M. 87301.

BENNETT, WILLA MAE STEWART, Soc. Ed., The Mexia Daily News, 214 N. Railroad St., Mexia, Tex. 76667, '29–; La Belle Maison Club (Pres., three terms); b. Mexia, Tex., 1909; p. E. Joseph and Ida Aophin Stewart; h. John E. Bennett; c. John Elmo, Jr.; res: 209 S. Canton St., Mexia, Tex. 76667.

BENNETTS, CHAUCY HORSLEY, Assoc. Dir., Children's Bks., The World Publishing Co., 110 E. 59th St., N.Y., N.Y. 10022, '69–; Assoc. Ed., '64–'69; Free-lance Ed., '61–'64; Edtl. Dept., Doubleday & Co., '56–'61; Barnard Col. Grad., '46; h. Leslie S. Bennetts; c. Leslie, Bruce; res: 75 Lookout Circle, Larchmont, N.Y. 10538.

BENNS, IRALEE WHITAKER, Mgr., WVOK, Voice of Dixie, Inc., P.O. Box 2468, Bessemer Super Highway, Birmingham, Ala. 35201, '47–; Co-owner, Secy.-Treas., WFTM, Ft. Myers, Fla., '45; Prin., West Point, Ga. H.S., '09–'15; Midfield C. of C. (Pres., Bd. of Dirs.); Midfield Citizen of Yr., '62; Auburn Univ., BA (with hons.); b. West Point, Ga., 1889; p. Oroon and Dona H. Whitaker; h. William E. Benns; c. William E., Jr.; res: 225 Bessemer Super Highway, Birmingham, Ala. 35228.

BENSON, LENORE JOAN, Mdsng. Ed., Mademoiselle, 420 Lexington Ave., N.Y., N.Y. 10017, '60–; Assoc. Mdsng. Ed., '55–'60; Fashion Coordr., Publ. Dir., Franklin Simon, '47–'55; Fashion Coordr., Young-Quinlan (Mpls., Minn.), '45–'47; speaker at fashion groups, student career courses; Fashion Group (Bd. Mbr., '66–'67) Nat. Retail Merchants Assn. Aws., '63–'68; Wellesley Col., '42–'43; Univ. of Minn., '43–'44; b. Cleve., Oh.; p. Charles and Eleanor Hauck Benson; res: 430 E. 56th St., N.Y., N.Y. 10022.

BENSON, MILDRED WINIFRED, Special Edtl. Cnslt., Encyclopedia Britannica International, 425 N. Mich. Ave., Chgo., Ill. 60611, '69–; Head of Indexing, '49–'68; Edtl. Indexer, '43–'49; Buyer, Univ. of Chgo. Bookstore, '36–'43; educ: Drake Univ., BA, '29; Univ. of Chgo., MA, '31; b. Washington, Iowa 1903; p. David and Bess McKee Benson; res: 4980 Marine Dr., Apt. 633, Chgo., Ill. 60640.

BENSON, THELMA ATKINSON, Free-lance Wtr. (romance stories); Charlotte Wtrs. Club (Pres., '59–'60), Theta Sigma Phi; Nat. 2nd prize, True Experiences fiction contest, '62; Univ. of Alberta, BA, '32; Columbia Univ. Sch. of Jnlsm., '32–'33; b. Hillsdale, Ontario, Can., 1911; p. Dr. William A. and Edith Day Atkinson; h. Walter Clark Benson; c. 2nd Lieut. William A., Walter Clark, Jr.; res: 5701 Sardis Rd., Charlotte, N.C. 28211.

BENTLEY, HELEN DELICH, Chmn., Federal Maritime Commission, Wash., D.C., '69–; Maritime Ed., A. S. Abell, Baltimore Sunpapers (Balt., Md.), '52–; Gen. Assigt. Reptr., '45; Free-lance Film Prodr., WMAR-TV, '50; TV Prodr., "The Port That Built a City," '50–'64; Prodr., "Ports of Philadelphia, Gateway to the World," WFIL-TV, '59; Telegraph Ed., Lewiston (Idaho) Tribune, '45; Bur. Mgr., UP (Ft. Wayne, Ind.), '44–'45; Ed., "Seaport Histories, Ports of the World"; Auth., Ed., "The American Merchant Marine, Stepchild in Peace, Hero in War"; numerous mag. articles; Contrbr., Navy Magazine, Wash. Monthly, other pubns.; Theta Sigma Phi, Kappa Tau Alpha, WNPC, ANWC, Wms. Adv. Club of Balt. ("Wm. of the Yr.," '56), Propeller Club of U.S. (numerous writing aws.); numerous aws., hons., for work on port labor matters, TV shows on maritime activities, svc. to port commty.; Univ. of Nev., '41–'42; George Washington Univ., '43; Univ. of Mo., BJ, '44; b. Ruth, Nev., 1923; p. Michael and Mary Kovich Delich; h. William Roy Bentley; res: 408 Chapelwood Lane, Lutherville, Md. 21093.

BENZ, MARILYN ONDERDONK, Free-lance Wtr., PR Cnslt.; Ed., "Impressions", DYMO Industries, '64–; Edtl. Staff, Silver Burdett Co., '57–'58; bk: "Maestro Baton and His Musical Friends" ('68); Lincoln Child Ctr. Cabinet, Oakland Museum Assn., Oakland Symphony Guild, S.F. Opera Guild, Wms. Athletic Club of Alameda County, DAR (Outstanding Jr. Mbr. of Western Reg. Div., '68); Mt. Holyoke Col., BA, '56 (cum laude, Sarah Williston Scholar); Grad. Sch. of Bus. Adm., N.Y.U., '56–'57; Univ. of Cal., Berkeley, MJ, '65; b. Weehawken, N.J., 1934; p. Chester Douglas and Marion Ross Onderdonk; h. Bernard Benz; c. Mark Douglas, Dean Griffith; res: 35 Glen Alpine Rd., Piedmont, Cal. 94611.

BERCKMANN, EMILY JOAN, Dir. of Home Econs. and Acc. Supvsr., Rumrill-Hoyt, Inc., 380 Madison Ave., N.Y., N.Y. 10017, '66–; Dir. of PR, Charles W. Hoyt Co., '59–'65; AE, Theodore R. Sills & Co., '50–'59; Assoc. Ed., Good Housekeeping, '49–'50; Assoc. Ed., Everywoman's Magazine, '44–'48; Am. Home Econs. Assn., Home Econsts. in Bus., AWRT; Univ. of Wis., BS, '44; Grad. Work, Univ. of Wis., '48; b. N.Y.C.; p. Alexander and Elsie Pieper Berckmann; h. George J. Leroy.

BERG, DELLA FEAK, Ed., Bangor Independent, Box 55, Bangor, Wis. 54614, '65–; ins. firms, '43–'44, '40–'42; hist. articles; colm., "A-Line-O-Type"; recipe colm.; Wis. Press Assn.; active in ch., civic groups; b. LaCrosse, Wis., 1920; p. J. Blair and Geneva Jensen Feak; h. Oscar G. Berg; c. Carolyn (Mrs. Homer Armagost), Cristine, Syda; res: Box 55, Bangor, Wis. 54614.

BERG, FRANCES RUSSELL, District Supervisor of Libraries, Lawrence-Cedarhurst Public Schools, 195 Broadway, Lawrence, N.Y. 11559, '65–; Heraldic Rsch. Specialist, '48–; Head, Genealogy, Heraldry Sec., Am. Hist. Div., N.Y. Public Lib., '45–'52; HS Tchr., '38–'45; N.Y. Lib. Assn., ALA, Nassau-Suffolk Sch. Lib. Assn., Lawrence Public Sch. Assn. Admr. and Supvsrs. (Chief Negotiator; Corr. Secy., '67–); Who's Who of Am. Wm.; Who's Who in the East; Abernethy Lib. Prize, '37; Middlebury Col., BA, '38; State Univ. of N.Y., BS (Lib. Sci.), '42; b. Schenetady, N.Y., 1917; p. Nicholas and Harriet Perry Russell; h. Emanuel Berg (dec.); c. Riva Harriet, Merril Dorothy; res: 348 Mulry Lane, Lawrence, N.Y. 11559.

BERG, JEAN LUTZ, Auth, 22 Juv. Bks.; NLAPW (Chester County Branch Pres., '67–'68; Secy., '69–), Auths. Guild, Auths. League, ASCAP; City of Phila. Medallion '63; Follett Aw., '61; Univ. of Pa., BS (Educ.), '35; AM (Latin), '37 (Aw. of Merit, '69); b. Clairton, Pa.; p. Harry and Daisy Horton Lutz; h. Dr. John Berg; c. Jean H., Julie Joanne, John Joel; res: 207 Walnut Ave., Wayne, Pa. 19087.

BERGANE, VILMA, Media Dir., Doubleday Advertising Company, 277 Park Ave., N.Y., N.Y. 10017.

BERGEN, Sr. M. JEANELLE, Assoc. Prof., Chmn. Theatre Dept., Mundelein Col., Chgo., Ill. 60626, '62–; Co-Prodr., "Drama in the Church" (NBC, Chgo.), '62; Prodr., "American Nun in Intellectual World," CBS-TV; Auth.-Dir., "She Shall Be Called Woman," '56; AWRT, NAEB, Am. Educ. Theatre Assn.; Mundelein Col., AB, '44; State Univ. of Ia., MA, '48; b. Chgo., Ill. 1912; p. John and Helen Rafter Bergen; res: 6363 Sheridan Rd., Chgo., Ill. 60626.

BERGEN, POLLY, Pres. and Chief Exec., KAM Productions, Ltd., a Division of the Polly Bergen Company, 8899 Beverly Blvd., L.A., Cal. 90048, '57–; SAG, AFTRA, AGUA, AEA, Share Inc. (Dir.), Stephens Col. (Trustee), Presidents Club (N.Y., Wash., D.C.); Aws: Emmy (Best Actress), '57; Fame Aw. (Best Actress "Helen Morgan Story"), '57; Radio and TV Daily Best Actress '59; Congressional Cit. Wm. of the Yr., '68; Best Dressed Wm. Aw., '61, '62, '67, '68; b. Knoxville, Tenn. 1931; p. William and Lucy Lawhorne Bergen; h. Freddie Fields; c. Kathy, P. K., Peter; res: 8899 Beverly Blvd., L.A., Cal.

BERGENE, RUTH ANN, Owner, Gemini Creative Services, 4400 Minnetonka Blvd., Mpls., Minn. 55416, '69–; Prod. Mgr., Mktng. Svcs. Div., Premium Corp. of Am., '67–'69; Off. Mgr., Exec. Offs., Employers Overload Co., '64–'65; Adm. Asst. to Pres., Mike Fadell Adv. Agcy., '61–'64; Pinkerton Nat. Detective Agcy., '59–'61; Pubcty. Dir., Minn. Consumer Congress, '65; Colmst., Format Magazine, '63–'65; Adv. Club of Minn. (Dir., '62–'64; Ed., Tear Sheet, '64–'65); Who's Who of Am. Wm.; Sch. for Social Dev. of Mentally Retarded Adult (Dir., '62–'67; Pubcty. Cnslt.), Phi Beta; La Crosse State Col. (La Crosse, Wis.), '52–'54; Univ. of Minn., BA, '67 (Radio/TV); b. Rice Lake, Wis., 1935; p. Casper R. and Johanna E. Baldwin Bergene.

BERGER, ELIZABETH, Actress: Stage, TV, Commls.; Disease Simulator, Neurology Dept., Univ. of Southern Cal., '69–; Theatre West, L.A., Cal.; Skidmore Col., BS, '63; b. N.Y.C.; res: 6392 Bryn Mawr Dr., Hollywood, Cal. 90028.

BERGER, EVELYN ELSIE, Dir., The Lipton Kitchens, Thomas J. Lipton, Inc., 800 Sylvan Ave., Englewood Cliffs, N.J. 07632, '67–; Dir., Home Econs., AE, McCann-Erickson Adv., '64–'67; Dir. Home Econs., United Fruit and Food Corp., '61–'64; Dir. Home Econs., Wilson and Co., '55–'60; AWRT, AWNY , Am. Home Econs. Assn.; Univ. of Wis., BS (Home Econs. Educ.), '46.

BERGER, FRANCES SHAW, Ed.-Publr., The Farrell Press, 301–3 Roemer Blvd., Farrell, Pa. 16121, '64–; Off. Mgr., '39–'64; Who's Who of Am. Wm., '68; Hall's Bus. Col. Grad.; b. Boston, Mass.; p. Zelig and Jennie Sacks Shaw; h. Lewis H. Berger (dec.); c. Norman E., Joel S.; res: 1912 Paul St., Farrell, Pa. 16121.

BERGER, IDA EUGENIE, Contract Mgr., Nat. Sls., Columbia Broadcasting System, Inc., 51 W. 52 St., N.Y., N.Y. 10019; N.Y.U. Grad.

BERGER, KAY SINGER, Home Econst., AE, Harshe-Rotman & Druck, Inc., 3345 Wilshire Blvd., L.A., Cal. 90005, '69–; Mgr., Home Econs., Calavo Tropical Produce, '66–'69; Asst. Dir., Consumer Rel., Waste King Corp., '61–'66; Home Econsts. in Bus. (L.A. Group Chmn., '69), AWRT, Am. Home Econs. Assn., L.A. Adv. Wm., Intl. Fedn. for Home Econs., Cal. Home Econs. Assn., Electrical Wms. Round Table; 1st pl. aw., Nat. Cncl. of Farm Cooperatives; Who's Who of Am. Wm.; U.C.L.A., BS (Home Econs.), '61; b. Pitt., Pa., 1939; p. Alex and Eve Lando Singer; h. Alan M. Berger; res: 6748 Hillpark Dr., Apt. 405, L.A., Cal. 90028.

BERGER, MAJORIE SUE, Assoc. Dir., American Society of Planning Officials, 1313 E. 60th St., Chgo., Ill. 60637, '66–; Asst. Dir., '53–'65; Asst. to Dir., '47–'52; Nwsltr. Ed., '50–'68; Wtr., '47–' Pubns. Ed., '48–'55; Pubns., Pubcty. Dir., '47–'68; Econst., '42–'46; numerous articles on planning; Auth., "Opportunities in City Planning" (Vocational Guidance Manuals, Inc., '61); Co-auth., "Effect of the War on the British Retail Trade" (U.S. Senate Doc., '43); Cnslt., educ., careers in planning; Intl. Fedn. for Housing and Planning (U.S. Comm. Secy.-Treas., '57–'60), other groups;

Who's Who of Am. Wm.; Univ. of Chgo., BA (Polit. Sci.), '41; b. Chgo., Ill., 1916; p. Henry A. and Dorothy Cole Berger; res: 400 E. Randolph St., Chgo., Ill. 60601.

BERGER, MARCELLA, Mgr. of Rights and Permissions, John Day Co., 257 Park Ave., N.Y., N.Y. '69–; Rights and Permissions Dept., '67–'69; Edtl., '66–'67.

BERGEY, ALYCE MAE, Auth., juv. bks: "Rocky, the Rocket Mouse" ('61), "The First Rainbow" ('64; T. S. Denison), "The World God Made" ('65), "The Boy Who Saved His Family" ('66), "The Fishermen's Surprise" ('67), "The Great Promise" ('68), "The Beggar's Greatest Wish" ('69; Concordia); Outstanding Young Wm. of Am., '66; b. Lanesboro, Minn., 1934; p. Forest and Mabel Peterson Bergey; res: 705 Rochelle Ave., Lanesboro, Minn. 55949.

BERGIDA, HEDY, Sr. Ed., Hawthorn Books, 70 Fifth Ave., N.Y., N.Y. 10011, '67–; Assoc. Ed., Prentice-Hall, '66–'67; Asst. Ed., '65–'66; Skidmore Col., BA; b. N.Y.C.; p. Irving and Lillian Deutch Bergida; res: 200 E. 17th St., N.Y., N.Y. 10003.

BERGIN, G. MARIE WILHITE, Dir. of PR, Mobile College, Mobile, Ala., '69–; Dir. of PR, Sacred Heart Col. (Cullman), '64–'69; Jnlsm. Instr., '63–; Chmn., Dir. of Lang. and Lit., '66–'69; Reptr., Colmst., Feature Wtr., Photogr., The Cullman Times, '52–'64; Modernistic Printers, '52–'53; numerous orgs. and aws.; St. Bernard Col., Ala., AB (Eng.), '61 (cum laude); Univ. of Ala., MA (Jnlsm.), '69; b. Vinemont, Ala., 1922; p. Calvin and Zella Linton Wilhite; c. Mrs. John Oliver Nielsen; res: 764 Sullivan Ave., Mobile, Ala. 36606.

BERGMAN, ROSELYN J., Ed., Rand McNally & Company, P. O. Box 7600, Chgo., Ill. 60680, '66–; Assoc. Ed., '56–'65; WNBA, Children's Reading Round Table; Beloit Col., '46–'49; Drury Col., BA, '50; b. Chgo., Ill.; p. Edward and Anna Tichy Bergman; res: 7827 Niles Center Rd., Skokie, Ill. 60076.

BERGMAN, SLYVIA BERNSTEIN, Secy.-Treas., Lester V. Bergman & Assoc., Inc., Eigth E. 12th St., N.Y., N.Y. 10003, '40–; Adelphi Col., BA, '35 (magna cum laude) City Col. of N.Y., '38–'39; Bklyn. Col., '47–'49; b. Bklyn., N.Y., 1915; p. Harry and Pauline Storch Bernstein; h. Lester Bergman; c. George Mark, Alan R.; res: R.F.D. #1. E. Mountain Rd., Cold Spring, N.Y. 10516.

BERHEL, MARTHA MARIE, Head Librn., Bethune-Cookman College, Daytona Beach, Fla. 32015, '42–; Organizer, High Sch. Lib. (Sand Springs, Okla.), '42; Asst. Clerk, Ration Bd. (Jacksonville, Fla.), '41–'42; Librn., Edward Waters Col., '40–'42; Organizer, High Sch. Lib. (Meridian, Miss.), '40; Instr., Lib. Sci., Grambling Col., '38–'39; Asst. Librn., Southern Univ., '37–'40; Instr., Lib. Sci., '37–'39; numerous orgs., aws.; Southern Univ., BS, '36; Hampton Inst., MS (Lib. Sci.), '37; grad. work, N.Y.U., Univ. of Fla.; b. Baton Rouge,

La., 1917; p. Aby and Bettie Collins Berhel; res: 217 Garden St., Daytona Beach, Fla. 32015.

BERK, PHYLLIS LAVINE, Free-lance Auth., juv. fiction and non-fiction; Syracuse Univ., BA, '55 (Phi Beta Kappa, summa cum laude); b. Albany, N.Y.; p. Carl and Ester Weisburgh Lavine; h. Howard Berk; c. Celia, Brian; res: 23 Richmond Rd., Rockville Ctr., N.Y. 11570.

BERKE, ANITA DIAMANT, Lit. Agt., Anita Diamant, The Writers' Workshop, Inc., 51 E. 42nd St., N.Y., N.Y. 10017, '49–; Ed., Writers' Workshop, '42–'49; Edtl. Staff, McCall's, '38–'42; Forum, '36–'38; auth., numerous mag. articles; Adjunct Prof. of Jnlsm., L.I. Univ., '67–'68 (Judge, George Polk Aw.); OPC (Governor, '65–'71; svc. aw., '60), Theta Sigma Phi (Pres., '65–'67), Woman Pays Club (Bd. Mbr., '66–'68), ZONTA; N.Y.U., BS (Jnlsm.), '36; b. N.Y.C.; p. Sidney and Lea Lyons Diamant; h. Harold Berke; c. Allyson; res: Fanton Hill Rd., Weston, Conn.

BERKELEY, ELLEN PERRY, Sr. Ed., Architectural Forum, 111 W. 57th St., N.Y., N.Y. 10019, '67–; Asst. Tech. Ed., Assoc. Ed., Progressive Architecture, '59–'67; Rsch. Asst., Housing Rsch. Ctr., Cornell Univ., '58–'59; Environmental Rsch. Fnd. Hon. Mbr.; Smith Col., BA, '52; Harvard Univ. Grad Sch. of Design, '52–'55; b. New Rochelle, N.Y., p. Lee and Esther Fish Perry; h. Roy G. Berkeley; res: 241 Sixth Ave., N.Y., N.Y. 10014.

BERKOER, HARRIET, Prod. and Media Mgr., Curtis Advertising Agency, Inc., 1 Park Ave. S., N.Y., N.Y. 10016, '68–; Rsch. Dir., '67; Asst. Prod. Mgr., '67; Home Tenants Assn.; b. Manhattan, N.Y., 1949; p. William and Bernice Goldstein Berkoer; res: 1325 Edward L. Grant Highway, N.Y., N.Y. 10452.

BERLIN, LILLIAN TEECE, Nat. Adv. Dir., The Star-Courier, Div. of Lee Enterprises, 105 E. Central Blvd., Kewanee, Ill. 61443, '57–; Classified Dept., Retail Sls., '52–'57; Nwsp. Adv. Execs. Assn., C. of C.; Blackhawk East Jr. Col.; b. Kewanee, Ill., 1919; p. Norman and Mabelle Bain Teece; h. Robert Berlin; c. Robert; res: 1011 N. Main St., Kewanee, Ill. 61443.

BERLOWE, PHYLLIS H., VP, Edward Gottlieb & Associates, 485 Madison Ave., N.Y., N.Y. 10022, '68–; Dir. of Food PR Svcs., '65–'68; Sr. AE, Harshe-Rotman & Druck, Inc., '63–'65; AE, Theodore R. Sills & Co., '59–'63; Head, PR Dept., Toscany Fabrics, '55–'57; Pubcty. Club of N.Y. (Distg., Svc. Aw., '60, '61, '62; 11 yrs. Bd. of Dirs., two terms Rec. Secy., 1st and 2nd VP, Lectr. for Basic Pubcty. Course, '53–'62), PRSA, AWRT, Volunteers of the Shelters; Hunter Col., N.Y.U.; b. N.Y.C.; p. Louis and Rose Jatches Berlowe; res: 201 W. 77th St., N.Y., N.Y. 10024.

BERMAN, MIRA, Pres., Chief Exec. Offcr., Allerton Berman & Dean, 39 W. 55th St., N.Y., N.Y. 10019, '66–; Sr. VP, Lavenson Bureau of Advertising, '64–'66; PR

Dir., '59–'64; PR Fashion Dir., Snellenburgs (Phila., Pa.), '57–'59; Copy Dir., Gimbels, '56–'57; Copy Chief, Robert Hall Co., '55–'56; Adv. Dir., Bond Stores, '52–'55; Adv. Copywtr., Bamberger's (Newark, N.J.); Girl Scouts of America, '48–'50; Co-auth: "Marketing Through Retailers"; PRSA, Fashion Group (Bd. of Dirs., '62–'64); U.S. Indsl. Film Festival aw., '69; N.Y.U.; Columbia Univ.; res: 161 W. 54th St., N.Y., N.Y. 10019.

BERMAN, SELMA R., VP, Ruder & Finn Incorporated, 110 E. 59th St., N.Y., N.Y. 10022, '67–; Pubcty. Dir., Ingenue, '66–'67; Asst. Pubcty. Dir., Seventeen, '61–'66; Asst. PR Dir., Helena Rubinstein, '59–'61; Edtl. Asst., N.Y. Post, '51–'59; PRSA; Peggy Foldes Memorial Prize, NWC, most distg. writing of article in entertainment field, '58; Wash. Sq. Col. of N.Y.U., BA, '49; b. N.Y.C., 1929; p. Jack and Pearl Sann Berman; res: 150 E. 37th St., N.Y., N.Y. 10016.

BERN, PAULA RUTH, Dir., PR, Adv., Robert Morris College, 610 Fifth Ave., Pitt., Pa. 15219; Dir. of Pubcty., '67–'68; Instr., Joseph Horne Co., '67–; PR Cnslt., Dale Liken Agcy., '67–'68; Feature Interviewer, WJAS Radio, '67; Bk. Reviewer, Pitt. Press, '60–'66; Ed., Key Magazine, Guest Life (L.A., Cal.), '48–'50; News Ed., Allegheny Jnl., '46–'47; free-lance articles; Dir. of Pubcty., Pitt. Folk Festival, '68, '69; ACPRA, Theta Sigma Phi, AWRT, Fashion Group, Adv. Club of Pitt., Wms. Press Club of Pitt., PRSA, Pitt. C. of C., Pitt. Cncl. for Intl. Visitors; Golden Quill Aw., '66; Carnegie-Mellon Univ., '42–'44 (Civic Club scholarship); Pa. State Univ., BA, (magna cum laude, Phi Beta Kappa); Univ. of Pitt. Law Sch., '46–'48; Univ. of Pitt., '68 (Carnegie Fellow); h. Joseph Bern; c. five.

BERNABEI, OLIVIA DeP., Free-lance Wtr., 3721 Hamilton Ave., Fort Worth, Tex. 76107, '68–; Feature Wtr., Colmst., Trenton (N.J.) Times and Sunday Advertiser, '64–'68; Wtr., Long Lines Magazine, AT&T Co., N.Y.C., '52–'62; Col. of Wooster, BA; AAUW Scholarship, Delta Phi Alpha aw.; h. Anthony A. Bernabei.

BERNAY, BERYL, Free-lance Corr., Photogr., TV Hostess: U.N., S.E. Asia Corr., Group W Bdcst., '66–'69; Corr., ABC-TV News, '65–'66; Prodr., Wtr., Hostess, "All Join Hands" (WCBS-TV), '62–'65 (UNICEF Cit.); On-Air Talent, WNBC-TV, '64–'65; Creator, "Children's World" (WRVR, Oh. State Radio aw.), '64; Film Prodr., Talent, "Let's Be Friends" '66; Auth., Photogr., "Bali" (Angus and Robertson Ltd., '69); various mag. articles; Lectr., PR, Southern Christian Leadership Conf.; various prof. orgs., aws.; Pa. State Univ., Col. Univ.; res: 45 Univ. Pl., N.Y., N.Y. 10003.

BERNAYS, ANNE FLEISCHMAN, Auth: "Short Pleasures" ('62), "The New York Ride" ('65), "Prudence, Indeed" ('66); bk. revs., movie revs., poems, articles; Asst. Ed., Houghton Mifflin Co., '55–'57; Mng. Ed., Discovery, '53–'56; PEN; Wellesley Col., '48–'50; Barnard Col., BA, '52; b. N.Y.C., 1930; p. Edward L. and

Doris E. Fleischman Bernays; h. Justin Kaplan; c. Susanna Bernays, Hester Margaret, Polly Anne; res: 16 Francis Ave., Cambridge, Mass. 02138.

BERNAYS, DORIS FLEISCHMAN, PR Csnl., Partner, Edward L. Bernays, 7 Lowell St., Cambridge, Mass. 02138, '19–; Asst. Wms. Page Ed., Reptr., Feature Wtr., New York Tribune, '14–'17; Auth: "A Wife is Many Women"; Ed. and Contrbr., "An Outline of Careers for Women"; Contrbr., "An Outline of Careers and the Engineering of Consent ('28–'55), numerous articles in nat. and intl. mags, N.Y. Nwspwms. Club (Past Pres.), Wm. Pays Club, Wms. City Club (Boston), Wms. Col. Club (Boston); Trustee and Dir., numerous public svc. orgs.; Barnard Col., Grad., '13; b. N.Y.C., 1891; p. Samuel and Harriet Fleischman; h. Edward L. Bernays; c. Mrs. Richard Held, Mrs. Justin Kaplan.

BERNHARDT, TOBY CLIGMAN, Sr., Public Info. Asst., N.J. Dept. of Commty. Affairs, '67–'68; Assoc. Ed., Sales Meetings Magazine, '67; Reptr., Ed., Feature Wtr., Jewish Exponent, '64–'66; Publicist, Adephia Assocs. '62–'63; Theta Sigma Phi (Phila. Chptr. Treas. '63); Temple Univ., BS, '61 (Jnlsm.); b. Phila., Pa., 1939; p. Henry and Sophie Blaker Cligman; h. John H. Bernhardt; c. Shulamit Hannah; res: 141 W. Farrell Ave., Trenton, N.J. 08618.

BERNKOPF, JEANNE FRANK, Free-lance Ed.; Ed., Delacorte Press, '69–; Ed., Adult Bks., E. P. Dutton & Co., Inc., '56–'69; compiled "Boucher's Choicest," '69; Assoc. Ed. of Adult Bks., Macmillan Co., '49–'59; Reader, '48–'49; Asst. in Educ. Dept., '47–'48; Smith Col., BA, '47 (magna cum laude; Phi Beta Kappa); b. N.Y.C., 1926; p. Louis J. and Rayner Parver Frank; h. Michael Bernkopf; res: 242 E. 19th St., N.Y., N.Y. 10003.

BERNSTEIN, ADELE, Feature Wtr., Ed., Bd. of Dirs., The Sun-Bulletin, 60 Henry St., Binghamton, N.Y. 13902, '60–; David Bernstein Assoc., '43–'55; Reptr., Wash. Post; Wtr., Conslt., U.S. Dept. of State, U.S. Public Health Svc.; h. David Bernstein; res: 5 Vincent St., Binghamton, N.Y. 13905.

BERNSTEIN, ANITA KAHN, Asst. to Pres., Fred Bernstein & Associates, 24 Vendue Range, P.O. 275, Charleston, S.C. 29407, '65–; WSAI Radio (Cinn., Oh.), '56–'57; WTMA Radio (Trenton, N.J.), '51–'54; AWRT, Bdcst. Prom. Assn.; Syracuse Univ.; b. Trenton, N.J., 1928; p. Herbert and Fannie Warren Kahn; h. Fred L. Bernstein; c. Lynn Frances, Hal David, Teri Lee, Sandra Sue; res: 2 Morton Dr., Charleston, S.C. 29407.

BERNSTEIN, BEVERLY CHUCHIAN, Auth.-Tchr.; Reptr., Bakersfield Press, '52; various teaching positions; Theta Sigma Phi (Col. Chptr. Pres., '54); Bakersfield Col., '51 (Jr. Col. Feature Writing Contest winner); Univ. of Southern Cal., AB, '54 (Outstanding Wm. Grad. of Jnlsm., '54); MS, '58; b. L.A., Cal.; p. Melvin and Yevnike Sabonjian Chuchian; h. Robert Bernstein; c. Brenda Loren, Brigette Lynnelle; res: 3111 Linden Ave., Bakersfield, Cal. 93305.

BERNSTEIN, LAUREL CUTLER, Sr. VP, Crtv. Dir., McCann-Erickson, Inc., 485 Lexington Ave., N.Y., N.Y. 10017, '67–; VP, Assoc. Crtv. Dir., '65–'67; VP, Account Group Supvsr., Fletcher Richards, Calkins & Holden, '56–'64; Fashion Group; Wellesley Col., BA, '46; b. N.Y.C., 1926; p. A. Smith and Dorothy Glaser Cutler; h. Stanley Bernstein; c. Jonathan Cutler, Amy Sarah, Seth Perry; res: 378 West End Rd., South Orange, N.J. 07079.

BERNSTEIN, LEEMARIE BURROWS, Asst. to Dir. of Design, Cowles Communications, Inc., 488 Madison Ave., N.Y., N.Y. 10022, '68–'69; Asst. to Art Dir., Look Magazine, '53–'68; Free-lance Photogr., '49–'53; Rabinovich Sch. of Photogr. Grad.; Columbia Univ. Sch. of Social Work, '44; Labor Rels. Supvr., Fairchild Camera, '44–'45; Hunter Col.; h. Dr. Maurice H. Bernstein; res: 349 E. 49th St., N.Y., N.Y. 10017.

BERNSTEIN, SYLVIA, Dir. of Educ. Svcs., Globe Book Company, 175 Fifth Ave., N.Y., N.Y. 10010, '68–; Customer Rels., '64–'68; Adm. Asst., '63–'64; h. J. Alexander Bernstein.

BERRIEN, EDITH HEAL, Auth.; Asst. Prof., Fairleigh Dickinson Univ., Eng. Dept., Montross Ave., Rutherford, N.J. 07070; part-time copywtr., Vogue; Copy Chief, Conde Nast Pubns., '44–'53; educ: Univ. of Chgo., PhB, '25; Columbia Univ., MA, '57; b. Chgo., Ill. 1903; p. Charles and Eva Page Heal; h. Stephen Berrien; c. Leigh (Mrs. Procter Smith, Jr.); res: 130 Orient Way, Rutherford, N.J. 07070.

BERRY, ESTHER FEATHERER, TV News Wtr. and Net. Assigt. Desk Ed., WMAQ-TV, Merchandise Mart, Chgo., Ill. 60654, '66–; News Wtr. and Prodr., TV Newscaster, Acting News Dir., KXJB-TV (Fargo, N.D.), '65–'66; Doc. Rsch., WRCV-TV (Phila., Pa.) '65; News Wtr., KOMU-TV (Columbia, Mo.), '63–'64; Theta Sigma Phi, Alpha Epsilon Rho, Kappa Tau Alpha; Freedom of Info. Ctr., Univ. of Mo. prize for writing, '64; Am. Field Svc.; Dickinson Col., BA, '61; Univ. of Mo., MA (Jnlsm.) candidate; b. Phila., Pa., 1939; p. Norman P. and Esther White Featherer; h. Loren M. Berry, III; res: 2125 N. Clark, Chgo., Ill. 60614.

BERRY, EVALENA HOLLOWELL, Dir. of Pubns., Ark. Educ. Assn., 1500 W. Fourth St., Little Rock, Ark. 72201, '61–; Tchr., '42–'61; Ark. Educ. Assn., NEA, NLAPW, WNBA; Ark. Col., AB, '42; Univ. of Ark., MS, '54; b. Akron, Oh.; p. James and Theresa King Hollowell; h. Homer Berry; c. Albert A. Pool; res: 2724 Fair Park Blvd., Little Rock, Ark. 72204.

BERRY, MARILOU MADDOX, Soc. Ed., Sunday Courier & Press, 201 N.W. Second St., Evansville, Ind. 47701, '66–; Dir., wms. programs, Cont. Dir., WGBF Radio, '58–'66; Cont., Bdcstr., WJPS Radio, '51–'58;

Bdcstr., wms. programs, WIKY Radio, '47–'50; Sigma Alpha, Sinawik (Hon. Mbr.), Broadway Theatre League of Evansville (Bd. of Dirs.), Univ. of Evansville, Theatre Soc. (Hon. Mbr.); Ind. Univ., '44–'45; Univ. of Ia., '45–'47; Evansville Col., BA, '48; b. Evansville, Ind., 1926; p. Hobert Donald and Louise Marie Schultze Maddox; h. John W. Berry, Jr.; res: 1421 S.E. Second St., Evansville, Ind. 47713.

BERRY, OLIVE CATHERINE, Guest Lectr., Tobe-Coburn School For Fashion Careers, 851 Madison Ave., N.Y., N.Y. 10021, '66–; Home Econst., Allied Chemcial Corp., '61–'65; Educ. Dir., Conde Nast Pubns., '56–'57; Publicist, Bennington Mills, '57; Fashion Coordr., Simplicity Pattern Co., '32–'56; Lectr., Simmons Col., '61, Bklyn. Col., '58–'60; Auth., mag. articles, educ. material; TV appearances; Home Econsts. in Bus.; Home Econs. Assn., Electrical Wms. Round Table (N.Y. Chptr. Secy., '65–'66), Fashion Group; Tchrs. Col., Columbia Univ., BS, '32; N.Y.U., MA, '50; N.Y. Sch. of Interior Design, Cert., '62; b. Campbellton, New Brunswick, Can.; p. Arthur and Lulu Ramsay Berry; res: 2 Tudor City Pl., N.Y., N.Y. 10017.

BERRY, ROSE AUERSPERG, Prof. of Educ., University of Arkansas, 33rd and University Ave., Little Rock, Ark. 72204, '61–; Public Sch. Tchr.; Ark. Educ. Assn., NEA, Ark. Lib. Assn., WNBA, Assn. for Childhood Educ. Intl., Delta Kappa Gamma, Kappa Kappa Iota, Kappa Delta Pi, Altrusa; Who's Who of Am. Wm., Who's Who in Am. Educ., BPW Wm. Educ. of Yr., '69; Fedn. of Wms. Clubs Tchr. of Yr., '69; Peabody Col., Univ. of Maryland; Univ. of Ark., EdD, '65; h. Robert N. Berry; c. Charles W.; res: 146 Ridge Rd., Little Rock, Ark. 72207.

BERTIN, NADINE MICHELLE, Beauty Ed., Mademoiselle, Conde Nast Publications, 420 Lexington Ave., N.Y., N.Y. 10017, '69–; Fashion Prom. and Pubcty. positions at Vogue, Grey Advertising, Daniel & Charles, Milgrim's, Coulter's, L.A.; Finch Jr. Col., '50 (with distinction); b. N.Y.C. 1930; p. Michel and Mariamna Shreiber Bertin; h. Philip Olcott Stearns; res: 400 E. 57th St., N.Y., N.Y. 10022.

BERTINO, BELVINA WILLIAMSON, Ed., Mgr., The Searchlight, Culbertson, Mont. 59218, '63–; Bdcsts., KGCX Radio, '62–; Free-lance wtr., Photogr., Several Mont. nwsps., '57–'63; Rchr., '28–'32; Auth., numerous children's stories, '45–; Mont. Press Assn., Mont. Hist. Soc.; Mont. Inst. of the Arts; numerous aws: nwsp., bdcst., photog.; Western Mont. Col.; b. Ruthven, Ia., 1907; p. Christen and Jeanette Sandvig Williamson; h. Frank Bertino; c. Frank Christen; res: Culbertson, Mont. 59218.

BERTOLI, BARBARA KOONTZ, Art Dir., Avon Books, 959 Eighth Ave., N.Y., N.Y. 10019, '68–; Asst. Art Dir., '65–'68; Designer, Berkley Bks., '64; Designer, Pyramid Bks., '61–'64; William Woods Col., AFA, '53; Univ. of Mo., BA, '55 (Phi Beta Kappa, '55); b. Kan.

City, Mo., 1933; p. Theodore and Helen Schroeger Koontz; res: 142 E. 27th St., N.Y., N.Y. 10016.

BESS, SUSAN QUINN, Librn., American Chemical Society, 1155 16th St. N.W., Wash., D.C. 20036, '67–; Asst. Librn., Shipley Co. (Newton, Mass.), '67; Asst. Librn., Fisher Jr. Col. (Boston, Mass.), '65–'66; D.C. Lib. Assn.; Regis Col., AB, '64; b. Newton, Mass., 1942; p. Thomas and Eleanor Barry Quinn; h. David Bess; res: 6310 Wingate St., Alexandria, Va. 22312.

BESSER, MARIANNE, Free-lance Wtr., '57–; Mng. Ed., Writers' Digest, '54–'57; published articles in various magazines incl. Readers' Digest, Family Circle, Parents' Magazine, This Week, Goodhousekeeping; Auth., "Growing Up With Science" (McGraw-Hill, '60; Delta Kappa Gamma bi-annual aw. for best written book in educ. by a wm.), "The Cat Book" (Holiday House, '67); Oh. State Univ., BA, (Eng.), '52 (Phi Beta Kappa); res: 125 W. 12th St., N.Y., N.Y. 10011.

BESSEY, CAROL HOSSNER, Ed., The Ashton Herald, 512 Main St., Ashton, Idaho. 83420, '67–; Wms. Army Corps, '42–'45; two nwsp. aws., '69; b. Ashton, Idaho, 1919; p. Frederick and Luella Phillips Hossner; h. Grant Bessey; c. Helen, Herbert, Joyce, Jeanette; res: R.F.D. 1, Ashton, Idaho. 83420.

BEST, BARBARA, Partner, Freeman, Gordon & Best, 6565 Sunset Blvd., Hollywood, Cal. 90028, '68–; Exec. VP, Jay Bernstein PR; Owner, Barbara Best & Assoc., '53–'66; Stanley Kramer Co., '50–'53; 20th Century-Fox, '43–'49; Hollywood Wms. Press Club (Pres., '60, '61), Theta Sigma Phi; Univ. of Southern Cal., BA (Jnlsm.), '43; b. Coronado, Cal., 1921; p. Comdr. Charles and Leila Sanders Best; h. (div.); res: 4319 Rosario Rd., Woodland Hills, Cal. 91364.

BETHEA, MARY BELLE MANNING, Dillon County Librn., Latta Library, Marion and Main, Latta, S.C. 29565, '31–; Tchr., Latta Elementary Sch., '24–'30; New Hanover HS, '23; BPW (Wm. of the Yr., '55), Dames of the Magna Carta, DAR, DAC, ALA, Dillon County Hist. Soc., Am. Red Cross (Reg. Chmn., '41–'68), Columbia Col., BS; b. Latta, S.C., 1890; p. Holland and Clara Bethea Manning; h. Charles E. Bethea; c. Dr. Willaim S. (dec.), John M. (dec.); res: 315 Richardson, Latta, S.C. 29565.

BETTERTON, SARA BLANKENSHIP, Asst. Ed., Golden Triangle, Texas Gulf Sulphur Company, 811 Rusk, Houston, Tex. 77002, '61–; Contr., ICIE Stylebook, '62; Theta Sigma Phi, (Pres., '67–'68), Southeast Tex. IEA (Secy.-Treas., '62–'66; Bd. Mbr., '67–'68; Exec. VP, '69), San Jacinto Wms. Club; Tex. Wms. Univ., '55–'56; Tex. Acad. of Art, '56–'57; Univ. of Houston, '56–'61; Okla. State Univ., '67; b. Atlanta, Ga., 1938; p. John and Alva Allred Blankenship; h. Donald Betterton; c. Jeanmarie, Donald Ray, Jr.; res: 9825 Cedardale, Houston, Tex. 77055.

BETTS, DORIS WAUGH, Lectr., Crtv. Writing,

University of North Carolina, Bingham Hall, Chapel Hill, N.C. 27514, '66–; Jnlst., Chapel Hill Weekly, Statesville Record & Landmark, Sanford Daily Herald; Auth: "The Gentle Insurrection & Other Stories" (winner, Putnam prize, '54), others; Who's Who of Am. Wm.; Contemporary Auths., Mademoiselle fiction aw., '53; Univ. of N.C.; b. Iredell County, N.C., 1932; p. William and Mary Ellen Freeze Waugh; h. Lowry M. Betts; c. Doris LewEllyn, David Lowry, Erskine M., II; res: P.O. Box 142, Sanford, N.C. 27330.

BEVINGTON, HELEN, Assoc. Prof. of Eng., Duke University, Durham, N.C., 27706, '56–; Instr., Asst. Prof., '43–'56; Wtr: three vols. of verse, three of nonfiction; Contrbr. to numerous mags., '46–; Phi Beta Kappa, AAUP; Roanoke-Chowan Poetry Aw. ('56, '62); Univ. of Chgo., PhB, '26; Columbia Univ., MA, '28; b. Afton, N.Y., 1906; p. Charles Wesley and Elizabeth Raymond Smith; h. Merle Bevington (dec.); c. Philip R. and David M.; res: 4428 Guess Rd., Durham, N.C. 27705.

BEVLIN, MAJORIE ELLIOTT, Dir. of Art, Otero Community College, 18th at Colorado Ave., La Junta, Colo. 81050, '56–; Gibbs and Cox, Inc., '40–'43; retail sls., (N.Y.C.), '38–'40; Auth., "Design through Discovery" (col. textbk., Holt, Rinehart & Winston, '63); Delta Phi Delta, Nat. Assn. of Wm. Artists, Colo. Watercolor Soc., Colo. Art Educ. Assn.; exhibited paintings, France, '65; Eng., Scotland, '63; N.Y. World's Fair, '65; annually, Nat. Acad. of Design (N.Y.), '63–'69; Univ. of Colo., BFA, '38; N.Y.U., MS, '39 (Fellowship, '38–'39); Univ. of Wash., Col. of Architecture; b. The Dalles, Ore., 1917; p. John A. and Bess E. Cornelius Elliott; h. Ervin Bevlin; c. Kathleen Anne (Mrs. Dwight Gregory), Jennifer Jane (Mrs. David L. Cole); res: 12 Cactus Dr., La Junta, Colo. 81050.

BEYER, AUDREY WHITE, Auth. of juv. hist. fiction; Tchr., Northeastern Univ., Boston, Mass.; educ: Westbrook Jr. Col.; Univ. of Me.; b. Portland, Me. 1916; p. William and Hermie White; h. Walter A. Beyer; c. Henry G., II, Edmund Brand; res: 25 Sias Lane, Milton, Mass. 02186.

BEYER, BEE, Talent, Prodr., Auth., Originator, "Cooking Around the World," synd. TV show, 1154 Roberto Lane, L.A., Cal. 90024; started show, '67; Home Econst., Bridgford Foods Corp. (Anaheim, Cal.); Food Stylist, Cnslt., Dir. food photog., Paulsons Picture Foods (Chgo., Ill.); food photog., TV appearances, testing, dev. recipes, other work, Nat. Live Stock and Meat Bd., three yrs.; testing, dev. new packaging, Swift and Co.; Tchr., Home Econs., Art (Kan. City); AWRT, Mdsng. Execs. Club; Kan. State Tchrs. Col., BS (Educ. with Home Econs., Art); b. Gridley, Kan.; p. Frank and Elizabeth Luthi Beyer; c. Lisa Ann Wenger, Gemma Wenger.

BIALK, ELISA, Auth., children's bks., incl. "The Horse Called Pete" (Houghton-Mifflin), "Jill's Victo-

ry" (World Publ.), the "Tizz" Series (Children's Press), "Orville Mouse at the Opera House" (Albert Whitman), many others; Wtr., short stories, poems, one play, "Sainted Sisters"; Juv. workshop Tchr., Off-Campus Wtrs. workshop (Chgo., Ill.); Theta Sigma Phi (North Shore Chptr. Pres. '58–'60), Soc. of Midland Auths. (Secy., '64–); Northwestern Univ.; b. Chgo., Ill. 1912; p. John and Martha Holcher Bialk; h. Martin Krautter; c. Elena Krautter (Mrs. Joseph C. Lonsdorf), Elizabeth Krautter; res: 791 Bryant Ave., Winnetka, Ill. 60693.

BICKING, DOROTHY SCHAEFER, Publr., Bicking Publishing Co., 301 June St., Berlin, Wis. 54923, '64–; Publr., Green Lake County Reptr. (Wis. Press Assn. Best Edtl. Aw., '69); Publr., Princeton Time-Republic; Secy., Treas., Berlin Jnl. (Nat. Nwsp. Assn. Public Svc. Aw., '69; Wis. Press Assn. Govs. AAA Safety Aw., '69; Excellence in Commty. Svc. Aw., '69; Best Special Issue 2nd pl. aw., '69; Best Edtl. 3rd aw., '69); b. Marinette, Wis., 1928; p. Walter and Nina Skowlund Schaefer; h. Orvel Bicking; c. Steven, Scott; res: 106 N. Johnston St., Berlin, Wis. 54923.

BICKNELL, MARY PHELPS, Bus. Mgr., Courier Publishing Company, Inc., Box 331, Alva, Okla. 73717, '66–; VP; Mbr. of Bd.; Adv. Sls., '60–'66; Okla. Press Assn.; Univ. of Okla., BA (Eng.) '43; b. ElReno, Okla., 1921; p. Joseph and Helen Borden Phelps; h. Brooks Bicknell; c. Mary Kathryn, Barbara Brooks, Joseph Phelps; res: 1025 Fourth St., Alva, Okla. 73717.

BIDA, OLGA STOTZ, Asst. Lib. Dir., Hempstead Public Library, 115 Nichols Ct., Hempstead, N.Y. 11550, '54–; Cataloger, '48–'54; Cataloger, Great Neck Lib., '46–'47; Tchr., Librn., Wolf Jr. HS (Easton, Pa.), '35–'45; Nassau County Lib. Assn.; Mount Holyoke Col., AB (Archaeology), '31; Columbia Univ., BS (Lib. Sci.), '46; b. Easton, Pa., 1909; p. Clemens and Olga Judd Stotz; h. John Bida (dec.); res: 210 Cedar St., Hempstead, N.Y. 11550.

BIEMILLER, RUTH COBBETT, Free-lance Wtr., Fiction, Non-Fiction; Auth: "Dance: The Story of Katherine Dunham" (Doubleday, '69); Co-Auth: "Nat Fein's Animals" (Gilbert Press, '55); Crossword Puzzle Ed., Feature Wtr., New York Herald Tribune, '52–'66; Ed., The Shipworker, WWII; NWC (Educ. Chmn.), OPC; Col. of William and Mary, AB, '35 (Mortarboard; Pres., Chi Delta Phi; Flat Hat Club Soc. Key Aw.); New Sch.; N.Y.U.; b. Morristown, N.J., 1914; p. Frederick and Margaret Dickison Cobbett; h. Reynard F. Biemiller; c. Christopher; res: 3 Peter Cooper Rd., N.Y., N.Y. 10010.

BIENVENU, IRENE MARTIN, Free-lance Wtr.; Pres., B & B Publrs. Inc., '66–'67; Ed.-Publr., Jeanerette Times, '66–'67; Ed., Jeanerette Jnl., '64–'66; Asst. Ed., Ed., Feature Wtr., Daily Iberian-Jeanerette Enterprise, '58–'64; Wtr., poems, features, stories for mags., '41–'58; rsch., ed., "Historical & Progress Survey on City of Jeanerette La." ('65); Ed., "Creole Cajun

Cookery" ('62, '63); other pubn. rsch., ed.; various organizations and aws.; b. Jeanerette, La., 1917; p. Jack D. and Josephine Gulotta Martin; h. Edgar Bienvenu, Jr.; c. Michael Randolph; res: 522 S. Druilhet, Jeanerette, La. 70544.

BIERMAN, MILDRED THORNTON, Reptr., Feature Wtr., Marysville Globe, 1508 Fifth St., Marysville, Wash. 98270. '68–; Auth, "Ship A Heartbeat" (Macre Smith Co., Wash. Press Wms. aw., '64); Contrbr., several mags. and jnls.; b. North Bend, Ore., 1912; p. Ottie and Ethel Call Thornton; h. Charles Bierman; c. Dan C., Vicki Joan Senemar; res: 2905 71st Ave. N.E., Marysville, Wash. 98270.

BIESTERVELD, SARAH PARSONS, (pseud: Betty Biesterveld), Wtr: "Run Reddy Run" (Thomas Nelson & Sons, '62), other children's bks., articles, poems; Tchr., Navajo Gospel Mission (Oraibi, Ariz.); Tchr., Navajo Bible Acad.; Tchr., Akron Public Schs.; Mount Union Col., BA, '45; Akron Univ. (Elementary Cert.); b. Paducah, Ky., 1923; p. George and Elizabeth Dimmick Parsons; h. L. P. Biesterveld; c. Julia Elizabeth, Rebekah Jo; res: 980 Carlysle St., Akron, Oh. 44310.

BIGBEE, NELLE MORRIS, Corr: The Birmingham (Ala.) News; The Press-Scimitar (Memphis, Tenn), '47–; Fairchild Pubns., '55–'60; Wms. Ed., Colmst., Valley Voice (Tuscumbia, Ala.), '58–'60; Colmst., Colbert County Reptr., '49–'56; News Commentator, WOWL Radio-TV (Florence, Ala.), '48–'68; AWRT, NLAPW, Ala. Wtrs. Conclave (Past Pres.), Tenn. Valley Art Assn.; Superior Rating Aw. for news commentator, '54; Excellence Rating Aw., '55–'57; Who's Who of Am. Wm.; Florence State Col.; Freed-Hardeman Col.; Maren Elwood Col.; b. Haleyville, Ala.; p. John and Mattie Willingham Morris; h. J. Hatton Bigbee, Jr.; c. John Hatton III, Martha Nelle (Mrs. Jack Rainer), Perry Dean, Larry W., Stephen L.; res: 303 E. 6th St., Tuscumbia, Ala. 35674.

BIGELOW, MARTHA GASTON, Free-lance Bdcstr., Wtr.-Composer, '57–; Contributor, CBA News, '60–'61; AE, Radio Station KFOX, L.A., Cal. '38–'54; KFJB, Marshalltown, Iowa, '35–'37; L.A. Adv. Wm. (Pres., '43–'45), AAW (VP-at-large, '47–'48), AWRT, Western Radio and TV Assn., Bay Area Educ. TV Assn., numerous civic orgs.; Reed Dist. PTA Outstanding Svc. Aw., '69; Marshalltown Jr. Col., '34 Grad.; b. Marshalltown, Iowa 1914; p. William and Nelle Bassett Gaston; h. Charles Lowell Bigelow (dec.); c. William Gaston, John Lowell; res: 120 Stewart Dr., Tiburon, Cal. 94920.

BIGGERS, JANE RICHARDSON, Bd. of Dirs., Wms. Ed., Commonwealth Publishing Corp., 209 W. Market St., Greenwood, Miss. 38930, '57–; Fashion Ed., WLBT-TV, WJDX, '57–'67; Fashion Ed., Jackson State Times, '57–'58; NFPW, BPW (Greenwood Chptr. Pres., '66–'68), Fashion Group (Trea., '65–'67), NLAPW; PEN, "Wm. of the Yr.," '62; Who's Who of Am. Wm.; Who's Who in the South; Stephens Col., AA; Tobe-

Coburn Fashion Sch.; b. Johnson City, N.Y. 1926; p. William and Marion Yetter Richardson; h. William Biggers; c. William Michael, Jr., Robert Allen; res: 404 E. Park Ave., Greenwood, Miss. 38930.

BIGGS, GLORIA NEUSTADT, Wms. Ed., Gannett News Service, '68–; Exec. Wms. Ed., "Today," '66–; Gannett Newspapers, 308 Forrest Ave., Cocoa, Fla. 32922; Wms. Ed., Palm Beach Post-Times, '65–'66; Wms. Ed., St. Petersburg Times, '57–'63; Fla. Wms. Press Club; four time winner Penney-Mo. Aws. for best wms. pgs., '62, '66, '67, '69; b. N.Y.C.; p. Herbert and Helen McElhone Neustadt; h. Scott W. Biggs; res: 2150 Melaluca Dr., Merritt Island, Fla. 32952.

BIGGS, MARTHA LYDIA, Head Librn., Donnelley Library, Lake Forest College, Lake Forest, Ill. 60045, '43–; Assoc. Librn., '37–'43; Asst. Librn., Bradley Polytechnic Inst., '30–'37; AAUP (Local Chptr. Secy., '46–'47), Ill. Lib. Assn., ALA; Lake Forest Col., BA, '29; Univ. of Wis., Lib. Sch., '30; Univ. of Ill., MS (Lib. Sci.), '50; b. Dubuque, Ia., 1907; p. John A. and Lydia Eckhard Biggs; res: 754 Oak Ave., Lake Bluff, Ill. 60044.

BIGGS, MOLLY McCARTHY, Wtr.-Ed.; Teacher Corps Intern, Des Moines Independent School District, 1800 Grand, Des Moines, Ia. 50309, '68–; Edtl. Asst., Iowa Credit Union League, '65–'68; Theta Sigma Phi, Des Moines Pfsnl. Club; educ: Drake Univ., BA, '65; b. Des Moines, Iowa 1941; p. Frank and Eunice McKenzie McCarthy; h. Larry Biggs; c. Kimberly Claire; res: 2419 Cottage Grove, Des Moines, Ia. 50311.

BIGNER, BETTY PAUL, Wms. Ed., Shreveport Journal, 222 Lake St., Shreveport, La. 71101, '65–'69; Assoc. Wms. Ed., '57–'65; NPWC (aws., '67, '68), La. Press Wm. (various aws., '60–'69), Shreveport C. of C., Jr. League; Dallas Mkt. Ctr. Aw., '69, UPINAL Aw., '69; Randolph-Macon Wms. Col., '47–'48; Sophie Newcomb, BS (Chemistry), '51; b. Shreveport, La. 1931; p. Harry and Elizabeth Schaeffer Paul; h. Sterling Bigner; res: 472 Leo, Shreveport, La. 71105.

BILA, BONITA CATHERINE, Art Asst., Fortune Magazine, Time-Life Bldg., Rockefeller Center, N.Y., N.Y. 10020, '68–; Art Prod. Ed., Harper's Bazaar, '67–'68; Free-lance: Art Prod. Ed., Men's Bazaar Magazine, '68; Asst. Art Dir., Handman & Sklar Adv. Agency, '65; School of Visual Arts (N.Y.C.), '62–'65; b. Bklyn, N.Y., 1944; p. Vincent and Rose D'Angelo Bila, Jr.; res: 155 W. 68th St., N.Y., N.Y. 10023.

BILAS, BEVERLY ANN, Fashion Rep., Radio and TV, the Singer Co.; AWRT; Boston Univ., BS '58; Paterson State Col., MA, '62; Pa. State Univ., Doctoral Studies; res: 54 Notch Rd., Clifton, N.J. 07013.

BILINKAS, MARY LIVENGOOD, Mng. Ed., The Daily Advance, 87 E. Blackwell St., Dover, N.J. 07801, '68–; Copy Ed.; Reptr: Pittsburgh Post Gazette, Johnstown Tribune-Democrat, Greensboro Daily News,

Boise Statesman; numerous writing aws. from N.J. Press Assn. and N.J. Press Wms. Assn. ('66–'68); 1st pl., Nat. Aviation Writing Contest, '47; Juniata Col., BA, '43; b. Oxford, N.C., 1921; p. William S. and Martha Cupp Livengood; h. Edward W. Blinkas; c. Mary Lee Hobar, Barbara, William, Barry, Edward; res: Radtke Rd., Shongum Lake, R.D. 3, Dover, N.J. 07801.

BILL, DORA COX, Public Info. Specialist, U.S. Office of Economic Opportunity, S.E. Region, 730 Peachtree St., Atlanta, Ga. 30308, '67–; VP, Treas., Dora-Clayton Agency, '50–'67; Pres., Dora Dodson Agency, '48–'50; Forjoe Co., '49–'59; J. H. McGillvra Co., '48–'50; AWRT (Pres., '65–'66; Educ. Fndn. Bd. of Trustees, '67, '71; Atlanta Chptr. Pres., '57), Atlanta Adv. Club, Am. Fedn. of Adv. Clubs, Atlanta Bdcst. Execs. Club, Atlanta Press Club, Printer's Ink Aw., '68; IRTS, Platform Assn., Ga. Assn. of Bdcstrs., Ala. Assn. of Bdcstrs., S.C. Assn. of Bdcstrs.; WSB Radio Aw., '67; S.C. Bdcstrs. Aw., '68; LaGrange Col., '28–'29; Univ. of Ga., '50; b. Knoxville, Tenn. 1911; p. Charles and Imogene Cox; h. 1. Charles Ray Dodson (div.), 2. Clayton J. Cosse (div.), 3. Russell Welch Bill; c. Jeanie Dodson (Mrs. Albert Price); res: 6851 Roswell Rd. N.E., Atlanta, Ga. 30328.

BILLHEIMER, RUTH M., Soc., Fashion Ed., Pasadena Star-News, 525 E. Colorado Blvd., Pasadena, Cal. 91109, '38–; Reptr., Colmst., '30–.

BINDER, MYRNA G., VP, Lou Binder Creative Services, 263 Churchill Rd., Teaneck, N.J. 07666, '67–; Partner, "The Funny Farm," aw. winning prodrs. of humorous radio/TV commls.; Free-lance Publicist, Free-lance Model, '60–'62; three Intl. Bdcst. Aws.; Free-lance Comedy Wtr. for entertainers; Collegiate Inst., '57; Bklyn. Col., '57–'59; b. Bklyn, N.Y., 1940; p. Monroe and Rose Fein Glickman; h. Louis Binder; c. Jeffrey Ross, Stephanie Lynn; res: 263 Churchill Rd., Teaneck, N.J. 07666.

BING, BARBARA COHEN, VP, Ralph Bing Advertising Company, Park Bldg., Public Sq., Cleve., Oh. 44114, '54–; Dir., Viviane Woodard Cosmetics, '69–; Distbr., '68–; Cnslt., '67–; Cleve. Real Estate Bd.; Cleve. Adv. Club aws., '54; '61; Bowling Green State Univ., '49–'50; Univ. of Miami, '50–'52; Loyola Univ. '52–'53; b. N.O., La., 1931; p. Sam and Aleata Heid Cohen; h. Ralph Bing; c. Ralph, Aleta; res: 21500 Halworth Rd., Beachwood, Oh. 44122.

BINGHAM, JUNE ROSSBACH, Free-lance Non-fiction Wtr.; Edtl. Asst., The Washington Post, '45–'46; Wtr. Ed., War Bond Div., U.S. Dept. of Treasury, '43–'44; articles in N.Y. Times Magazine, Woman's Home Companion, Am. Jnl. of Psychiatry, Parents', Vogue, Glamour, Redbook, Mademoiselle, Am. Heritage and others; Bks: "The Inside Story: Psychiatry & Everyday Life" ('53), "Courage to Change: An Introduction to the Life and Thought of Reinhold Niebuhr" ('61), "U Thant: The Search for Peace" ('65); Auths. Guild; Vassar Col., '36–'38; Barnard Col., BA, '41; b. White Plains, N.Y., 1919; p. Max and Mabel Limburg Rossbach; h. Jonathan Bingham; c. Sherrell (Mrs. James Bland), June (Mrs. Erik Esselstyn), Timothy, Claudia (Mrs. Robert Hall); res: 5000 Independence Ave., N.Y., N.Y. 10471.

BINKOFF, KAREN BETH, Asst. Art Dir., Lewis & Gilman, Inc., 1700 Market St., Phila., Pa. 19012, '68–; Syracuse Univ., BFA (Design), '68; b. N.Y.C., 1946; p. Sanford and Miriam Sclar Binkoff; res: 116 Yew Rd., Cheltenham, Pa. 19012.

BINKOVITZ, FLORENCE, Asst. Media Dir. Media Planning, Needham, Harper & Steers, 909 Third Ave., N.Y., N.Y. 10022, '69–; Print Supvsr., '68–'69, Buyer, '66–'68; Buyer, Palmer, Willson and Worden, '60–'66; Claire Adv., '59–'60; Assn. of Indsl. Adv.; Ithaca Col. (Bus.), '55; Boston Univ. (Bus.), '55–'56; b. N.Y.C.; p. and Alice Breit Brody; res: 200 E. 78th St., N.Y., N.Y. 10021.

BINNS, BETTY, Free-lance Graphic Design, 16 Willow Pl., Bklyn., N.Y. 11201; formerly Art Dir., Col. Book Dept., McGraw-Hill; Am. Inst. of GA (VP, '69; Bd. of Dirs., '63–'68); h. David R. Esner; c. Racheal, Benjiman.

BIONDI, MARY HADLOCK, County Histrn., Ed., quarterly pubn., St. Lawrence County, P.O. Box 43, Canton, N.Y. 13617, '65–; Deputy County Histrn., '63–'65; Town Histrn., Hammond, '60–'64; Adm. Asst. to Publr., Northern N.Y. Publ. Co., '61–'65; Co-Auth: two bks; County Histrns. Assn., Am. Assn. for State and Local Hist., ZONTA, N.Y. Folklore Assn.; Bryant Col., Assoc. Deg., '38; b. Potsdam, N.Y., 1919; p. Perry and Doris Jones Hadlock; h. Edward Biondi; c. Laurie (Mrs. Bruce W. Smith), Scott Francis; res: P.O. Box 648, Ogdensburg, N.Y. 13669.

BIRD, CAROLINE, Free-lance Auth.; Staff Wtr., AE, Rsch. Dir., Dudley-Anderson-Yutzy, N.Y.C., '47–'68; Fortune, '44–'46; Edtl. Rschr., Newsweek, '43–'43; Desk Ed., N.Y. Jnl. of Commerce, '43–'44; Bks.: "Born Female: The High Cost of Keeping Women Down" ('68), "The Invisible Scar: The Great Depression and What it Did to American Life from Then to Now" ('66); numerous mag. articles; Soc. of Mag. Wtrs. (Secy., '53); b. N.Y.C., 1915; p. Hobart S. and Ida Brattrud Bird; h. Tom Mahoney; c. Carol (Mrs. John Barach), John T. Mahoney, Jr.; res: 31 Sunrise Lane, Poughkeepsie, N.Y. 12603, and 60 Gramercy Park, Apt. 4-A, N.Y., N.Y. 10010.

BIRDSALL, SHIRLEY ANNE, Librn., Harding College, Harding College Library, Searcy, Ark. 72143, '62–; Ref. Librn., La. State Univ. Law Sch., '59–'62; HS Tchr. (Ontario, Can.), '55–'57; ALA, Ark. Lib. Assn. (Past Col. Div. Chmn.), Am. Assn. Law Librns., Beta Phi Mu, AAUW; Harding Col., BA, '54; La. State Univ., MS, '59; b. Wichita Falls, Tex., 1932; p. Gilbert and Nova Graham Birdsall; res: 100 S. Turner St., Searcy, Ark. 72143.

BIRK, EILEEN PAWLOWSKI, Copy Ed., Antiques Magazine, 551 5th Ave., N.Y., N.Y. 10017, '69–; Asst. Ed., '67–'69; Edtl. Secy., '63–'67; several articles in "The International Antiques Yearbook,' '67–'68; Barnard Col., BA, '60; Fordham Univ., '61–'63; b. Glen Lyon, Pa., 1938; p. Theodore F. and Marcella Lipsky Pawlowski; h. Elliott Tucker Birk; res: 341 W. 87th St., N.Y., N.Y. 10024.

BIRKHEAD, EUGENIA McCHESNEY, Food and Family Ed., Colorado Springs Free Press, 103 W. Colorado Ave., Colorado Springs, Colo. 80901, '67–; Tchr., Librn.; Western Ky. State, AB, '36; b. Louisville, Ky., 1917; p. H. Field and Eugenia McCulloch McChesney; h. Herbert C. Birkhead; c. Roy F., H. Douglas, David L., John Andrew; res: 1324 Alexander Rd., Colorado Springs, Colo. 80909.

BIRMINGHAM, MARY LOUISE, Ed., Young Readers Dept., Praeger Publishers, 111 Fourth Ave., N.Y., N.Y. 07601, '68–; Free-lance Ed., Reviewer, '50–'68; Edtl. Archivist, UNESCO; '48–'49; Edtl. Asst., Newsweek, '45–'46; Barnard Col., AB, '45; b. N.Y.C., 1921; p. Thomas and Pauline Dawson Barrett; h. William Birmingham; c. Moira, John, Kate, Meg, Tom; res: 67 Willow Ave., Hackensack, N.J. 07601.

BIRMINGHAM, RUTH ATHERTON, Co-auth., "The Wedding Book" (Harper & Row, '64); Auth., TV scripts, plays incl: "Music for the Girls," "The News from a Woman's Point of View"; nat. lect. tour, W. Colston Leigh Agcy., '60–'61; Wms. Program Dir., WTVU-TV (Scranton, Pa.), '53–'55; civic groups; b. Scranton, Pa., 1915; p. Fred and Ruth Lansing Atherton; h. Frederic Birmingham; res: 801 Olive St., Scranton, Pa. 18510.

BIRNBAUM, AGNES BERENYI, Ed.-in-Chief, Award Books, 235 E. 45th St., N.Y., N.Y., 10017, '66–; Secy. HDB Publ. Co., '67–'68; Exec. Ed., TV-Radio Mirror, '65–'66; Ed., Macfadden Books, '64–'65; Ed.-in-Chief, One-Shot Dept., Dell Publ., '61–'63; Pres., Publ. Ventures; ACLU, NAACP; Who's Who of Am. Wm.; Dic. of Intl. Biog.; Intl. Blue Bk.; b. Budapest, Hungary; p. Emery and Barbara Weiss Berenyi; h. Herbert Birnbaum; res: 88 Bleecker St., N.Y., N.Y. 10012.

BIRSTEIN, ANN, Wtr.; Novels: "Star of Glass" ('50), "The Troublemaker" ('55), "The Sweet Birds of Gorham" ('66); Co-Ed., "The Works of Anne Frank" ('59); articles and short stories in Mademoiselle, McCall's, The New Yorker, The Reporter, Vogue; Tchr: Queens Col., New Sch. for Social Rsch.; PEN, Auths. Guild (Cncl. Mbr.); Intercollegiate Lit. Fellowship, '48; Fulbright Scholarship, '51–'52; Queens Col., BA, '48 (magna cum laude); b. N.Y.C., 1927; p. Bernard and Clara Gordon Birstein; h. Alfred Kazin; c. Cathrael; res: 440 West End Ave., N.Y., N.Y. 10024.

BISCHOFF, CAROL LOUISE, Plenum Journals Ed., Plenum Publishing Corp., 227 W. 17th St., N.Y., N.Y. 10011, '69–; Prod. Ed., '67–'69; Edtl. Asst., '64–'67;

Wagner Col., BS, '64; b. Flushing, N.Y., 1943; p. Charles and Louise Knaust Bischoff.

BISHOP, AUDREY J., PR Rep., E. I. du Pont de Nemours, 350 Fifth Ave., N.Y., N.Y. 10001, '59–; Feature Wtr., Baltimore (Md.) Sun, '48–'59; Script Wtr., WMAR-TV (Balt.), '47–'48; Theta Sigma Phi; Bucknell Univ., AB (Eng.), '45; b. Balt., Md.; p. Mark and Viola Kornmann Bishop; res: 41 Park Ave., N.Y., N.Y. 10016.

BISHOP, CAROLYN BENKERT, Ed., Budget Decorating, Maco Publishing Company, Inc., 1790 Broadway, N.Y., N.Y. 10019, '68–; Decorating Ed., '68; Copywtr., Woodward & Lothrop, '63–'65; Auth: "25 Decorating Ideas under $100" (Doubleday '68), "Make Room For Guest" (Doubleday '69); Script Wtr., In-Store Home Educ. Program, Nat. Retail Furniture Assn.; ghosting Decorating Newsletters, Doubleday; FHFL (VP Educ., '68–'69), Home Econsts. in Bus., Am. Home Econs. Assn., Univ. of Wis., BS (Home Econs.) '61 (hon. grad.); Tobe-Coburn Sch., N.Y.C., '62 (Gimbels Scholarship, hon. grad.); b. Monroe, Wis., 1939; p. Arthur C. and Delphine Heston Benkert; h. Floyd F. Bishop; res: 245 E. 25th St., Apt. 8B, N.Y., N.Y. 10010.

BISHOP, EDITH PARTRIDGE, Dir. of Brs., Los Angeles Public Library, 630 W. Fifth St., L.A., Cal. 90017, '61–; Children's Librn., Asst. Coordr., Children's Svcs., Br. Librn., Coordr. of Young Adult Svcs.; Asst. Children's Librn., King County (Wash.) Public Lib., '46–'49; Children's Librn., Missoula (Mont.) Public Lib., '30–'32; Children's Librn., Seattle Public Lib. '29–'30; Instr., Children's Lit., Immaculate Heart Col., '56–'57; ALA, CLA, Catholic Lib. Assn. (Southwest Unit Secy.), Soroptimist; Univ. of Wash. BS (Lib. Sci.), '29 (Phi Beta Kappa); b. Seattle, Wash., 1907; p. Alvin and Mary Potts Partridge; h. Emil Bishop; c. Rev. E. Louis, S.J., Lois Marie (Mrs. Robert E. Roberts), Alvin L.; res: 10318 Richlee Ave., South Gate, Cal. 90280.

BISHOP, INEZ S., Head Librn., White County and Searcy Library, Spring-Park, Searcy, Ark. 72143, '52–; Librn., Ark. Col., '46–'52; Asst. Librn., Muskogee Public Lib. '45–'46; Asst. Cataloguer, Okla. City Public Lib., '44–'45; Acting Librn., Ark. St. Tchrs. Col. (Conway), '43; Librn., Ark. Lib. Commn. (Little Rock), '39–'42; Librn., Pine Bluff and Jefferson County, '19–'39; Ark. Lib. Assn. (Pres., '27), Delta Kappa Gamma (Alpha Xi Chptr. Pres., '59–'61), BPW (Pres., '37–'38); Columbia Univ. (Lib. Sci.), La. Univ.; b. Parsons, Kan.; p. Rolf and Leonora Eistertz Shannon; h. Carroll Bishop (dec.); res: 204 S. Gum, Searcy, Ark. 72143.

BISHOP, MARY LEAGUE, Dir., Crawfordsville Public Library, 222 S. Washington St., Crawfordsville, Ind. 47933, '63–; Dev. Bk. Processing Ctr., serving state of Ind.; Head Librn., Marion (Ind.) Public Lib. '47–'62; Librn., Jonesboro (Ind.) Public Lib., '41–'45; Jonesboro HS '38–'40; Ind. Lib. Assn. (Secy., '56–'57, '68–); Butler Univ., AB; grad. work, '33–'39; Ind. Univ., '56; Western Mich. Univ., '65; b. Edinburg, Ind., 1915; p. Harry S. and Clara Smitha League; h. Chilson Bishop (dec.); c. Mrs. Carolyn Bujaki, Mrs. David McCuen, Chilson Marion II; res: 409 Hughes, Crawfordsville, Ind. 47933.

BISHOP, ROBBIE, Sr. Retail Mdsng. Coordr., Celanese Fibers Marketing Co., 522 Fifth Ave., N.Y., N.Y. 10036, '61–; Customer Info. Tech. and Fashion Dir., European Exchange System, '59–'61; Adv. Mgr., Sls. Prom., Pubcty., Mdsng. and Fashion Dir., Lanella Corp., '53–'58; Stylist, Burlington Mills, '50–'53; Auth., Fashion Dictionary ('54); Lectr. on fashion, home furnishing, fiber for bus. assns., wms. clubs, cols., press and bdcst. groups; AWNY, Fashion Group, NHFL; educ: Fashion Inst. of Tech. (Apparel Design); New Sch. for Social Rsch. (Pubcty. Writing); Traphagen (Fashion Sketching); N.Y.U. (oil painting); Progressive Sch. of Photog.; Charlotte Comml. Col. (Bus. Adm); res: 2 Tudor City Pl., N.Y., N.Y. 10017.

BISSELL, ELAINE McMAHON, Wms. Page Ed., The Standard-Star, 251 North Ave., New Rochelle, N.Y. 10802, '61–; Asst. Wms. Page Ed., Daily Times (Mamaroneck, N.Y.), '56–'61; free-lance radio and TV wtr., '51–'56; various organizations; N.Y.U., '69; b. Chgo., Ill., 1917; p. Harold and Edwinna Biederman Faulkner; h. Nicol Bissell; c. Mary Jane Christofferson, Kathleen Conroy, Susan McMahon, res: 828 The Parkway, Mamaroneck, N.Y. 10543.

BITENSKY, LORNA SILBERG, Network Program Atty., American Broadcasting Company, 1330 Ave. of the Americas, N.Y., N.Y. 10019, '68–; Assoc., Pryor, Braun, Cashman & Sherman, '68–'69; N.Y.U., BA, '57 (summa cum laude); Yale Law Sch., LLB, '60; b. Bklyn., N.Y., 1936; p. Sile and Elsie Weiss Silberg; h. Mark Bitensky; c. Harry, Susan; res: 300 E. 33rd St., N.Y., N.Y. 10016.

BITKER, MARJORIE MARKS, Free-lance Wtr.; Reviewer, Milwaukee Journal, Journal Sq., Milw., Wis. 53203; Ed., David McKay Co., '53–'56; Ed., G. P. Putnam, '47–'53; Ed., Farrar Straus, '46–'47; Instr., Hunter Col., '50–'55; Friends of Wis. Libs. (Founder, Pres., '64–'68), Bookfellows of Milw. (Founder), Wis. Lib. Assn. aw., '63; Barnard Col., AB (magna cum laude, Phi Beta Kappa), '21; Columbia Univ., MA, '22; b. N.Y.C., 1901; p. Cecil and Rachel Fox Marks; h. Bruno Y. Bitker; c. Mrs. F. A. Jacobi, Mrs. David T. Strange, Mrs. Frank J. Hahn; res: 2330 E. Back Bay, Milw., Wis. 53202.

BJORCK, MARGERET WOLFE, Assoc. Ed., Dir. AV Planning and Development, Language Arts, Encyclopaedia Britannica Education Corp., 425 N. Michigan Ave., Chgo., Ill. 60611, '68–; Asst. Ed., Wtr., '66–'68; Asst. Ed., Juv. Bks., Reilly & Lee Co., '65–'66; Elementary Tchr., '63–'65; '58–'62; cert. remedial reading tchr., cert. specialist in teaching disturbed children; Wms. Nat. Bk. Assn., Children's Reading Round Table; Univ. of Minn., BS, '37 (Mortar Bd., Rep. Minnesotan, '37); MA, '63.

BLACK, ANGELINE E., Mktng. Rsch. Project Dir., Dancer Fitzgerald Sample, Inc., 347 Madison Ave., N.Y., N.Y. 10017, '54–; Asst. Project Dir., '47–'54; Crtv. Rsch., Leo Burnet Adv., '45–'47; Econ. Anslyst, U.S. Dept. of Commerce, '43–'45; Auth., "Mortality of Retail and Wholesale Trade;" Am. Mktng. Assn., AWNY, Am. Statistical Assn.; Univ. of Ia., BA; Univ. of Chgo.; res: 37 W. 53rd St., N.Y., N.Y. 10019.

BLACK, ANITA BIESEMEYER, Men's Fashion Ed., Wms. News Reptr., The Sentinel, 918 N. Fourth St., Milw., Wis. 53201, '65–; Wms. News Ed., The Times-Dispatch (Richmond, Va.), '63–'65; Fashion Ed., Asst. to Wms. Ed., '62–'63; Wms. News Ed., The Daily Progress (Charlottesville, Va.), '49–'62; Soc. Ed., Herald-Times (Manitowoc, Wis.), '46–'47; NFPW (Va. affiliate charter VP, '58–'65), Theta Sigma Phi, Am. Inst. of Men's and Boys' Wear Lulu Aws., '65, '66–'67, Caswell-Massey men's fashion rept. aw., '68; Univ. of Wis., BA (Jnlsm.-Educ.), '45; b. Manitowoc, Wis.; p. Walter and Else Kaems Biesemeyer; h. (div.).

BLACK, CATHLEEN P., Mgr., Special Adv. Classifications, Travel & Camera Magazine, 200 Park Ave., Suite 2021, N.Y., N.Y. 10017, '69–; Dir., Special Adv. Secs., Holiday Magazine, '68–'69; Adv. Sls., '66–'68; Hotel Sls. Mgt. Assn., Am. Hotel & Motel Assn.; Trinity Col., BA (Eng. Literature), '66; b. Chgo., Ill., 1944; p. James and Margaret Harrington Black; res: 350 E. 52nd St., N.Y., N.Y. 10022.

BLACK, HELEN LOUISE, Soc., Wms. Ed., Martinsville Bulletin, 204 Broad St., Martinsville, Va. 24112, '49–; BPW (Past Pres.), Heart Fund (Past Chmn.), DAR (Good Citizens Aw., '44), Friends of Lib.; Col. of William and Mary, '48; b. Pulaski, Va., 1927; p. Malcolm and Annie Aust Black; res: 102 Broad St., Martinsville, Va. 24112.

BLACKBURN, IDA TURLEY, Talent-Prodr. of "Ida B. Show," KOCO-TV, 63rd and N. Portland, Okla. City, Okla. 73116, '60–; Adv. Dir., Dennis Donuts, '59; Tchr., Romper Room Sch., KOCO-TV, '58; Minister of Music, Methodist Ch. (El Reno, Okla.), '56; Elementary Tchr., '55; Public Sch. Music Tchr., '51–'53; Freelance PR Cnslt., Mkt. rsch. for nat. cos. on test products; After-dinner Speaker, "How to keep a Woman on Your Team," civic and social clubs; AWRT (Gen. Chmn., S.W. Area Conf., '69); Outstanding Local TV Show aw., Motion Pic. Magazine, '67; numerous aws. from Air Force, Army, commty., pfsnl. orgs.; worked with youth prog. for Mayor, '67; Gtr. Okla. Safety Cncl.; Okla. Col. for Wm., '48; Central State Col., BA (Music), '51 (Outstanding Sr. Girl); b. Ninekah, Okla., 1929; p. Jess and Effie Young Turley; h. (div.); c. Bob L., Betty Sue; res: 4129 N.W. 62nd Terr., Okla. City, Okla. 73112.

BLACKER, HARRIET, Pubcty. Dir., Coward-McCann, Inc., 200 Madison Ave., N.Y., N.Y. 10016, '69–; Pubcty. Dir., Hawthorn Books, '67–'69; Asst. to Exec. Dir., Nat. Bk. Comm., '66–'67; Admin. Asst. to

Pres., Feffer and Simons, '64–'66; Exec. Secy., Bernard Geis, '62–'64; Publrs. Pubcty. Assn.; Univ. of Mich., BA (Eng.), '62; b. N.Y.C., 1940; p. Louis and Rebecca Siegel Blacker; res: 225 W. 12th St., N.Y., N.Y. 10011.

BLACKMER, KATHLEEN CRISPELL, Wms. Ed., The Ann Arbor News, 340 E. Huron, Ann Arbor, Mich. 48106, '67–; Asst. Wms. Ed., '67; Univ. of Va. Info. Svcs.; Am. Press Inst. seminar for wms. eds., '68; 1st place aw., Wms. Div., Mich. AP writing contest, '69; Outstanding Young Wm. of Am.; Theta Sigma Phi; Univ. of Mich., BA (Jnlsm.), '67 (with hons.); b. Sayre, Pa., 1945; p. Dr. Kenneth R. and Marjorie Risk Crispell; h. Charles W. Blackmer; res: 1102 Prospect, Ann Arbor, Mich. 48104.

BLACKWELL, BETSY TALBOT, Ed.-in-Chief, Mademoiselle, Conde Nast Publications, Inc., 420 Lexington Ave., N.Y., N.Y. 10017, '37–; Fashion Ed., '35–'37; Adv. Mgr. Sisholz Bros., '31; Asst. to Fashion Ed., Beauty Ed., and Fashion Dir., Charm, '23–'31; Fashion Reptr., The Breath of the Ave., '23; Columbia Univ. Sch. of Gen. Studies Cncl., Fashion Group, (Chmn., Bd. of Governors, '60–'62), Girls Clubs of Am. (Bd. of Nat. Advisors), Am. Soc. of Mag. Eds. (Exec. Comm.), WNPC, Wms. Nat. Repl. Club., Inc.; Neiman-Marcus Aw. for Distg. Svc. in Fashion; Fed. of Jewish Charities Key Wm. of the Yr. Cit.; Jr. Achiev. Aw.; Am. Wms. Assn. Wm. of the Month Cit.; Lake Erie Col. Pres. Cit.; Dickinson Col. (hon. degree); b. N.Y.C.; p. Hayden and Benedict Bristow Talbot; h. James M. Blackwell; c. James M. IV; res: 1170 Fifth Ave., N.Y., N.Y. 10029.

BLACKWOOD, JEANNE OWENS, News Ed., Lomita News, 25332 Narbonne Ave., Lomita, Cal. 90260, '67–; Staff Wtr., Palos Verdes News, '67–; Adv. Press Nwsps., '65–'67; Lomita C. of C., L.A. County Deputy Sheriff (Reserve), L.A. County Dist. Attorney's Adv. Comm.; Fresno State Col., '49–'50; b. Joplin, Mo., 1932; p. William E. and Thelma Mix Owens; h. (div.); c. Janice Jean Halford, Forrest Dean Halford; res: 15617 Wharff Lane, Lawndale, Cal. 90260.

BLADEN, BARBARA C., Drama Ed., San Mateo Times, 1080 S. Bayshore, San Mateo, Cal. 94402, '55–; S.F. City Col. (Drama); b. S.F., Cal., 1930; p. John and Francis Gross; h. Rick Cluchey; res: 2 Fair Oaks #3, S.F., Cal. 94110.

BLAHA, MARIE STAUBLE, Edtl. Wtr., Suffolk Sun, 303 Marcus Blvd., Deer Park, N.Y., '67–; Founder, Pres., Ed. and Publisher, Syosset Tribune, '58–'69; Assoc. Ed., Litmor Pubns., '52–'57; Intl. Conf. of Weekly Nwsp. Eds., (Fellow, '64–'69); N.Y. State Press Assn. (Best Single Edtl. Aw., '63, 1st pl. aws. for edtl. excellence, '64, '65), Nassau County Press Assn., BPW, Syosset C. of C. (former Dir.); b. N.Y.C.; p. William and Corinne Clare Stauble; h. George Blaha; c. Steven, Michael, Thomas, Richard; res: 85 Sagamore Dr., Syosset, N.Y. 11791.

BLAIR, ANNE DENTON, Wash. Corr., Triangle Sta-

tions Inc. (Phila., Pa.), 3315 Dent Pl., N.W., Wash., D.C. 20007, '62–; Dir. of Radio-TV, Met. Area Red Cross Chptrs., '58–'62; Wms. Program Dir., Wash. Good Music Station, '48–'58; Commentator, programs incl. "Capital Shopping," "Music for Moderns," "Window on Wash."; covering maj. events, news; "Rhymes with Little Reason" (Mt. Vernon Press, '62); ANWC (Pres., '63–'65), AWRT, WNPC; Distg. Public Svc. Aw., 21 Jewel Sq. Club (Phila, Pa.), for integrity in bdcst., '64; Bryn Mawr Col.; b. Oakmont, Pa.; p. Hal P. and Eliza Russell Peachy Denton; h. Denton Blair (div.); c. Farnham Denton; res: 3315 Dent Pl., N.W., Wash., D.C. 20007.

BLAIR, KAY REYNOLDS, Music Dir., Weekday "All Girl Show," KBRR Radio, Box 968, Leadville, Colo. 80461, '69–; Staff, '66–'69; Copy Ed., Abingdon Press, '65–'66; WHER Radio, '64–'65; Career Mdsng. Bd., Mademoiselle Magazine; Co-Auth., "Fun With American Literature" (Abingdon Press, '68); Kappa Pi; Memphis State Univ., BS, '64; b. Franklin, Tenn., 1942; p. William and Louise Kimery Reynolds; h. Edward Blair; res: 511 East Eighth St., Leadville, Colo. 80461.

BLAISDELL, AMY, Pubcty., Adv. Cnslt., Amy Blaisdell, 264 Lexington Ave., N.Y., N.Y. 10016; PR Dir., Helena Rubinstein, '43–'63; Adv., Pubcty. Dir., Ogilvie Sisters Sales Corp, '33–'43; AWNY, Fashion Group, Cosmetic Career Wm., N.Y. Pubcty. Club (Founder; VP), AWRT, Assn. of Am. Wm.; Bates Col., BA, '23; b. York, Me., 1899; p. Samuel T. and Mary Abby Bragdon Blaisdell; h. Alex Maltz; res: 264 Lexington Ave., N.Y., N.Y. 10016; Redding, Conn. 06875.

BLAKE, BETTY, VP, Delta Queen, Greene Line Steamers, Inc., Public Landing, Foot of Broadway, Cincinnati, Oh. 45202, '67–; PR Dir., Mktng. Mgr.; Sls. Mgr., Avalon; Talent Prom. Coordr., WLW TV; PRSA (PR/Pubcty. Event Aw., for Steamboat Race, '66), Theta Sigma Phi, Soc. of Am. Travel Wtrs., Am. Soc. of Travel Agts., Mid-West Travel Wtrs., Kappa Alpha Theta; Outstanding Contrb. to Cinn. Aw., '67; Key to City of Louisville, '66; Key to City of Memphis, '68; Key to City of Covington, '68; Univ. of Ky., BS, '52; b. Lexington, Ky., 1930; p. H. Stanley and Ada Donnell Blake; h. John W. Simcox; res: 707 Dixmyth Ave., Cinn., Oh. 45220.

BLAKE, EILEEN, Sr. Media Byr., J. Walter Thompson Company, 420 Lexington Ave., N.Y., N.Y. 10017, '68–; Byr., '68; Sr. Byr., Hicks & Greist, '67; Byr., '65–'67; poem, "Life," '57; AWNY; Brigham Young Univ., '60; b. Murray, Ut., 1940; p. Ferron and Klea Tew Blake; res: 150 E. 27th St., N.Y., N.Y. 10016.

BLAKE, JEAN BEACHAM, Actress, TV Commls., William Cunningham Agency, 9000 Sunset Blvd., Hollywood, Cal. 90069, '57–; AFTRA, SAG; Miss Photoflash, Chgo. Photogrs., '58; Miss Ill., Miss Am. Pageant, '59; Lake Forest Col., '58; Monticello Wms.

Col., '59; h. Adam Roarke; c. Jordan Gerler; res: 12624 Martha St., North Hollywood, Cal. 91607.

BLAKE, SALLY MIRLISS (pseud: Sara) Asst. Ed., Jewish Community Bulletin, 40 First St., S.F., Cal., '66–, '53–'57; '48–'50; Adv. Copywtr., Promotion Programs, Inc., '57–'62; Ed., Miss America, Junior Miss (N.Y.C.), '48; Asst. Ed., Hillman Periodicals, '48; Publicist, Muriel Francis Agcy., '46–'48; Jnlst., UP, Boston Bur., '44–'46; Auth: "A House Divided" (McGraw-Hill, '68); "Where Mist Clothes Dream and Song Runs Naked" (McGraw-Hill, '65); O. Henry Aw., '64; Boston Univ., BS (Jnlsm.), '46 (magna cum laude); S.F. State Col., MA (Crtv. Writing), '62 (summa cum laude); b. Boston, Mass., 1925; p. Samuel and Eva Lansman Mirliss; h. Bernard P. Blake (div.); c. Andrew, Gail; res: 200 Julia Ave., Mill Valley, Cal. 94941.

BLAKELEY, NORMA WILLIAMS, Soc. Ed., Missouri Publications, The Daily St. Francois County Journal Inc., 22 E. Main St., Flat River, Mo. 63601, '65–; Proofreader, bkkeeper., '55–'65; Local news desk, '52; Flat River Jr. Col., '51; b. Flat River, Mo., 1931; p. Willard and Sarah Babb Williams; h. Floyd Blakeley; c. Sharon LuJean, Toni Lynne; res: 209 North State St., Desloge, Mo. 63601.

BLAKELY, JULIE BAUGHMAN, Wms. Ed., Tulsa Daily World, 315 S. Boulder Ave., Tulsa, Okla. 74102, '60–; Asst. to Ed., "Your World"; Wms. Ed., Tulsa Tribune; Staff, Oklahoma News; Ed., Tishomingo Herald; Theta Sigma Phi; Tulsa Press Club (Pres., '50–'51); Okla. Univ.; b. Davis, Okla., 1913; p. William and Deta Fagan Baughman; h. Merle Ferrin Blakely; c. Judith (Mrs. Neil Morgan), Betsy, Martha; res: 2303 N. Osage Dr., Tulsa, Okla. 74106.

BLAKELY, NELL R., Instructor, Dept. of Jnlsm. and Graphic Arts, East Texas State University, Commerce, Tex. 75428, '66–; PR Photogr., Miss. State Col. for Wm., '61–'65; N.E. Miss. Photog. Rep., Birmingham News, Memphis Press-Scimitar, Jackson Daily News; Owner, Photog. Studio, '45–'61; Tex. Assn. of Col. Tch., Theta Sigma Phi; Am. Radio Relay League, Pub. Svc. Aws.; Sophie Newcomb Col. (N.O., La.), '36–'38; La. State Univ., BA, '40; East Tex. State Univ., MA, '66; Univ. of Ia., '69; b. Greenville, Miss.; p. Frank N. and Hannah Aldridge Robertshaw; h. (div.); c. Mrs. Robert L. Erwin, Jan Uhler; Melanie, Mary Catherine, Hannah Paxton Blakely; res: 1605 Jackson St., Commerce, Tex. 95428.

BLAKEMORE, BARBARA, Asst. Mng. Ed., McCall's, 230 Park Ave., N.Y., N.Y. 10017, '70–; Bks., Fiction Ed.; Fiction Ed., Redbook; Assoc. Fiction Ed., Collier's; DePauw Univ., BA, '46 (Phi Beta Kappa); Columbia Univ., MS (Jnlsm.), '48.

BLAKEMORE, CAROLYN, Ed., J. B. Lippincott Co., 521 Fifth Ave., N.Y., N.Y. 10017.

BLAKESLEE, C. SANDRA, Sci. Reptr., The New York Times, 229 W. 43rd St., N.Y., N.Y. 10036, '68–; News Asst., UN Bur., City Desk, '67–'68; Peace Corps Volunteer, Borneo; Third Prize, AAGP Annual Competition, '69; Univ. of Cal. at Berkeley (Comparative Govt. of S.E. Asia), '65; b. Flushing, N.Y., 1943; p. Alton and Virginia Boulden Blakeslee; res: 114 W. 87th St., N.Y., N.Y. 10024.

BLANCH, ROSELIND DOLORES, Mgr., Adv. and Crtv. Svcs. Adm., CBS Records, Columbia Broadcasting System, Inc., 51 W. 52nd St., N.Y., N.Y. 10019, '69–; Mgr., Adm., Mktng., '66–'69; Supvsr., Crtv. Svcs. Costs, '61–'66; Supvsr., Sls. Audit, John G. Myers Co. (Albany) '52–'61; Am. Assn. of Accountants; Russell Sage Col., '55–'59; b. Watervliet, N.Y., 1934; p. Francis and Josephine Carmello Blanch; res: 52–40 39th Dr., Woodside, N.Y. 11377.

BLANCHFIELD, NINA MARCHESE, Edtl. Assoc., IBM Systems Manufacturing Division, South Rd., Poughkeepsie, N.Y. 12603, '60–; staff, '53–'60; Wtr., Beacon Light, Beacon News, '50–'53; active in polit., civic affairs; Who's Who, Wm. of Achiev., Who's Who in Polits.; b. Paterson, N.J.; p. Joseph and Maria Retiro Marchese; h. James Blanchfield; c. Thomas J., Joseph P.; res: 3 Deerfield Pl., Beacon, N.Y. 12508.

BLANCO, SUSANNE HALL, Ed., Wachovia Bank and Trust Company, N.A., P.O. Box 3099, Fourth St., Winston-Salem, N.C. 27102, '69–; bimonthly statewide banking mag.; Publr., biweekly mag. for Winston-Salem bank; copywriting, prom. depts., WBTW-TV (Florence, S.C.); AAIE, ICIE (Carolina Bus. Communicators), Am. Inst. of Banking; Univ. of S.C. Ext. at Florence, '64–'66; Univ. of S.C. (Columbia), '66–'68; b. Columbia, S.C., 1946; p. Edward Joseph and Mildred Chandler Hall; h. David Bennett Blanco.

BLANKENSHIP, CATHERINE, Eastern Story Ed., CBS Television Network, 524 W. 57 St., N.Y., N.Y. 10019, '59–; Assoc. Ed., '56–'59; Asst. to Ed., '53–'56; Visiting Lecturer in Television Writing, Yale Drama School; N.Y.U., Edtl. Rschr., play reviewer, dir. edtl. work, Eastern off., Universal Pictures, '46–'50; Story analyst, MGM; Radio Cont. Wtr., (Wins) (N.Y.C.), '44–'45; NATAS; Oh. Univ., AB; Columbia Univ., MA; Yale Drama Sch.; res: 149 W. Fourth St., N.Y., N.Y. 10012.

BLANKENSTEN, DEBORAH SCHUSSLER, Dir. of Lib. Svcs. and Genaeal Rsch, Tangley Oaks Educational Center, Lake Bluff, Ill. 60044, '63–; Rsch. Librn., World Book Encyclopedia, '53–'58; Bibliographic and Rsch. Specialist, Legislative Reference of the Library of Congress, '48–'50; Asst. Ed., Inst. of Inter-American Affairs, '44–'48; Rschr., Office of War Information. '42–'43; ALA, Ill. Lib. Assn., Political Science Assn.; Hunter Coll., BA, '39; Columbia Univ., '40–'42; Catholic Univ., '48–'49; Northwestern Univ., MA, '62; b. Bellinzona, Switzerland, 1920; p. Jack and Jane Gnderli Schussler; h. George Blanksten; res: 725 Lavergne Ave., Wilmette, Ill. 60091.

BLASKA, WANDA MACKO, Ed., Photogr., The Digester, Hercules, Inc., Parlin, N.J. 08859, '65–; N.J. Assn. of Communicators; Rider Col., '46; h. Henry Blaska.

BLATZ, Sr. IMOGENE, Joint Head Librn., St. John's University Library, Collegeville, Minn. 56321, College of St. Benedict, St. Joseph, Minn. 56374, '69–; Head Librn., Col. of St. Benedict, '60–'69; Asst. Librn., '55–'60; Tchr., Prin., '52–'55; Tchr., '32–'52; ALA, Catholic Lib. Assn., Minn. Lib. Assn., Am. Benedictine Acad.; Col. of St. Benedict; Seattle Univ.; Holy Names Col., Spokane, Wash., BA, '42, Col. of St. Catherine, St. Paul, Minn., BS (Lib. Sci.), '54; Marquette Univ.; b. Bloomington, Minn., 1911; p. Phillip and Clara Bungert Blatz; res: St. Benedict's College, St. Joseph, Minn. 56374.

BLAU, MELINDA TANTLEFF, Ed., Educ. Materials, Random House, 201 E. 50th St., N.Y., N.Y. 10022, '68–; Free-lance Wtr: educ. filmstrips, selections for a Skinner Reading Prog., adaptations of best sellers to lower reading level, '68–; Ed.-in-Chief, Educ. Pubn., '68; Program Supvsr., Mobilization for Youth, '65; Edtl. Asst., Portal Press, '65–'67; Asst. Ed., Adult Educ., Noble & Noble Publrs., '67–'68; Pi Lambda Theta; Who's Who of Am. Wm.; Syracuse Univ., BS (Special Educ.), '65 (N.Y. State Regents Scholarship, '61; Dean's List, '63–'65); b. S.I., N.Y., 1943; p. Julius and Henrietta Bass Tantleff; h. Mark Blau; res: 19 E. 80th St., N.Y., N.Y. 10021.

BLEAKLEY, HARRIET RICHARDSON, Ed., Publr., The News-Herald, 631 12th St., Franklin, Pa. 16323, '62–; Former Reptr., Soc. Ed., Secy.-Treas., VP; VP, Venango Nwsps. (Oil City, Pa.); Pa. Wms. Press Assn.; Clarion State Col., BS, '61; Pa. State Univ., MEd. '63; b. Franklin, Pa., 1921; p. Wayne and Margaret Amberson Bleakley; res: 410 15th St., Franklin, Pa. 16323.

BLEDSOE, ROBIN LELA, Art Ed., George Braziller, Inc., 1 Park Ave., N.Y., N.Y. 10016, '68–; Wellesley Col., BA, '67; Columbia Univ., MA (Art History), '68.

BLEDSOE, RUTH SHANNON, News Ed., Clinton Herald, 221 Sixth Ave. S., Clinton, Ia. 52732, '63–; Police-court Reptr., '53–'63; Feature Wtr., Movie Ed., Music Critic, '49–'53; State Ed., '49–'53; Asst. State Ed., '45–'48; NFPW (second pl. aw., news story, '59), Ia. Press Wm. (State Secy., '67–; first pl. writing aws., '58–'61), Ia. City Eds. Assn. (first wm. Pres., '67–'68); Northwestern Univ., '59; Columbia Univ., '64; b. Clinton, Ia., 1907; p. Thomas L. and Anne Farrell Shannon; h. Truman C. Bledsoe, Jr. (dec.); c. Truman C., III; res: 3525 Cleveland St., Clinton, Ia. 52732.

BLEEKER, SONIA, Auth., 17 bks. on Indians of N. and Central Am., six bks. on African peoples; many short stories and translations; Hunter Col., BA; Beloit Col., Hon. ScD (hon. life mbr., Delta Kappa Gamma),

'67; b. N.Y.C.; h. Herbert S. Zim; c. Aldwin, Roger; res: Florida.

BLEES, MARY CARLISLE, Home Econs. Dir., McCormick & Co., Inc., 444 Light St., Balt., Md. 21202, '56–; Dir. Homemakers Bur., Cal. & Hi. Sugar Refining Co., '54–'56; Home Econst. in charge of Special Proms. and Activities, Crosley Div., AVCO Mfg. Co., '49–'54; Home Econst., Moore, Handley Co., '47–'49; Home Econst., Birmingham Gas & Electric Co., '45–'47; Chemist, E. I. de Pont de Nemours & Co., Inc., '43–'45; McCormick Spices Of The World Cookbook; Who's Who of Am. Wm.; Miss. State Col. for Wm., BS, '39; b. Vossburg, Mass.; '17; p. William and May Arledge Carlisle; h. William Blees; res: 3811 Canterbury Rd., Balt., Md. 21218; 9550 Wilshire Blvd., L.A. Cal. 90024.

BLESCH, RUTH GERIKE, Prod. Mgr., Print Media Dir., Harwood Advertising, Inc., 1507 Tuscon Federal Savings Tower, Tuscon, Ariz. 85701, '64–; Prod. Mgr., Kossack Adv. Agency, '60–'64; Traffic Mgr., Adv. Agency (Kansas City, Mo.), '55–'60; h. Kurt P. Blesch.

BLEWETT, MARJORIE SMITH, Lectr., Placement Dir., Adm. Asst., Indiana University, Department of Journalism, Ernie Pyle Hall, Bloomington, Ind. 47401, '65–; Assoc. Ed., Ind. Alumni Magazine, '59–'65; News Ed., Bloomington Daily Herald-Telephone, '55–'57; Asst. News Ed., '48–'51; Asst. News Ed., Lafayette (Ind.) Jnl. and Courier, '51–'55; Theta Sigma Phi (Bloomington Pfsnl. Chptr. Pres., '60–'61, '61–'62), Assn. for Educ. in Jnlsm.; Ind. Univ., BA, '48; b. Bloomington, Ind., 1927; p. Elmer G. and Mary G. Riensch Smith; h. Harry Blewett; c. Daniel Keith, Barbara Jean; res: 1925 Viva Dr., Bloomington, Ind.

BLEWETT, NORMA VIRGINIA, Wms. Page Ed., Star-Courier, 105 E. Central Blvd., Kewanee, Ill. 61443, '54–; Ill. Press Assn., Wm's. Page Aw. (hon. mention); b. Prairie du Chien, Wis., 1923; p. William H. and Mertie Schroeder Blewett; res: 830 Columbus Ave., Kewanee, Ill. 61443.

BLOCH, MARIE HALUN, Auth.: "Tony of the Ghost Towns" (Coward-McCann, '56; N.Y. Herald-Tribune aw.); "Aunt America" (Atheneum, '63; ALA aw., Horn Bk. Hon. List), 15 other children's bks.; Econst., U.S. Dept. of Labor, '41–'43, '35–'38; Auths. League of Am., Free Ukrainian Acad. of Scis.; Univ. of Chgo., PhB, '35; b. Komarno, West Ukraine, 1910; p. Rudolf and Sofia Pelenska Halun; h. Donald Bloch; c. Hilary Flym; res: 654 Emerson St., Denver, Colo. 80218.

BLOCK, BARBARA ALEEN, VP, Radio-TV Dir., Winfield Advertising Agency, Inc., 500 Pierre Laclede Bldg., St. Louis, Mo. 63105, '63–; Radio-TV Prodr., Wtr., '62–'63; Radio-TV Prodr., Wtr., Horan Daugherty Adv. Agcy., '60–'62; Dir., Radio-TV, Prater Adv. Agcy., '53–'60; TV Prodr., Westheimer and Block Adv. Agcy., '44–'53; NATAS (St. Louis Chptr. Secy., '69), Wms. Adv. Club; Who's Who in Am. Cols. and Univs., '41–'42; Ky. Colonel, '68–'69; Fontbonne Col., BA

(Alumnae Hood aw.), '44; b. St. Louis, Mo., 1923; p. Alexander and Dorothy Burgard Block; res: 115 Lancaster Dr., St. Louis, Mo. 63105.

BLOCK, FLORENCE BODEN, PR Cnslt., 250 E. 73rd St., N.Y., N.Y. 10021, '66–; Free-lance Bdcstr., '66–; PR Dir., Consumer Div., Springs Mills, '60–'66; Cnslt., mktng., mdsng., PR, to Adv. Agcys., '58–'66; Exec. Dir., Co-publr., Fashion Pubns., Inc., Brides Bk. Publ. Co., '49–'58; AWRT (N.Y.C. Chptr. Dir., '69–'71), NHFL (N.Y.C. Chptr. VP, '69–'70); Brandeis Univ.-Wms. Comm. (Manhattan Chptr. Dir., '69–'70); Hunter Col.; N.Y.U.; b. N.Y.C.; p. Isadore M. and Rebecca Kommissaroff Boden; h. Herman B. Block; c. Ronald J.; res: 250 E. 73rd St., N.Y., N.Y. 10021.

BLOCK, JANET LEVEN, PR Dir., Shillito's Dept. Store, 7th and Race Sts., Cinn., Oh. 45202, '64–; Freelance Merchandising and PR Cnslt., '60–'64; AE, Abbot Kimbell Co., '46–'47; Asst. AE, Buchanan & Co., '44–'46; Dir. of PR and Stylist, Fashion Adv. Co., '42–'44; Reptr., Chicago-American; PRSA, Fashion Group of Cinn. (past Reg. Dir.), TV Soc. of Am. (Charter Mbr.), Adv. Club of Cinn. (Bd. Mbr.); Brenau Col. for Wm., Northwestern Univ.; b. Chgo., Ill.; h. Albert William Block; c. Mitchell William, Stephanie; res: 5300 Hamilton Ave., Cinn., Oh. 45224.

BLOCK, LILLIAN RACHEL, Mng. Ed.-Dir., Religious News Service, 43 W. 57th St., N.Y., N.Y. 10019, '57–; Asst. Mng. Ed., '43–'57; Jnlsm. Faculty, N.Y.U., '31–'42; Reptr., N.Y. and N.J. nwsprs.; Wtr., pfsnl. jnls.; Ed., bk. review synd.; VP, Nat. Conf. of Christian and Jews, '69–; Kappa Tau Alpha, Theta Sigma Phi, Religious Newswriters Assn., Beta Gamma Sigma; Editor and Publisher prize; James Fenimore Cooper Aw.; N.Y.U., BS (magna cum laude, Bradford Fellow), '31; Columbia Univ., MA, '41; b. Bklyn, N.Y.; p. Frank J. and Sarah Shapiro Block; res: 5 Roosevelt Pl., Montclair, N.J. 07042.

BLOCK, MAURINE, Owner, Maurine Block Advertising and Editorial Services, 203 Empire Bank Building, Dallas, Tex. 75201, '65–; Corr., numerous bus. and adv. mags.; Ed., Bankers Digest, '61–'65; Adv. Mgr., Dallas Iron and Wire Works, '52–'61; Free-lance Adv., '49–'52; Copywtr. and Adv. Mgr., Sears Roebuck Dallas Retail Group, '40–'49; Dallas Adv. League (Former Dir., Ed.; voted Adv. Wm. of the Yr., Most Valuable Mbr.), Adv. Club of Dallas (Charter Mbr.), Theta Sigma Phi (Dallas Chptr. Matrix Aw.), AAF (10th Dist. Dir., '57–'64), Press Club of Dallas; Who's Who of Am. Wm., Who's Who in Bus. and Industry, Who's Who in the South and Southwest, Dic. of Intl. Biog.; Royal Soc. of Arts, London (Benjamin Franklin Fellow); Univ. of Mo., BJ, '35; b. Ft. Worth, Tex., 1914; p. Louis and Rae Goldsmith Block; res: 4015 Stonebridge Dr., Dallas, Tex. 75204.

BLOCKI, PHYLLIS CRANE, Prom. Dir., Stackpole Books, Cameron and Kelker Sts., Harrisburg, Pa. 17105, '67–; Prom. Dir., WHP (AM, FM, TV), '64–'67;

Asst. to Sls. Mgr., adhesive mfg. (Stow, Oh.), '60–'63; ALA; Wilson Jr. Col., '48; b. Chgo., Ill., 1923; p. Merrell and Mabel Dedrick Crane; h. William Blocki (div.); c. Susan P., Mrs. A. J. Somerville, Barbara J., Mrs. Barry L. Thompson; res: R.D. #1, Rich Valley Rd., Mechanicsburg, Pa. 17055.

BLOCKLINGER, PEGGY O'MORE (pseuds: Jeanne Bowman, Betty Blocklinger, Peggy O'More, Juliet Mann), Auth., 166 bks., Crown Publishers, various paperback houses; bks. incl., "City Hospital Nurse" (paperback, top 10), many bks. with med. background; adult bks., polits., crime; series for teenagers; Ed., weekly; Librn.; Techr., crtv. writing; Nwsp. Reptr.; serials, AP; Colmst.; covered police courts, polit. beat (Cal., Ore., Tex.); many pfsnl. orgs.; complete set of bks., papers, lib., Univ. of Ore.; b. at sea; recorded, Tacoma, Wash., 1895; p. Wm. Harcourt and Iva Bowman O'More; h. Charles Blocklinger (dec.); res: P.O. Box 201, Amity, Ore. 97101.

BLONDELL, JOAN, Actress, currently appearing in TV series "Here Come The Brides"; Hollywood, Cal., motion pics., radio, stage, TV, '29–; stage plays, '27–'29; vaudeville, '15–'27; AEA, AGVA, AFTRA, SAG; Box Off. Aw. '30s; Acad. Aw. Nomination, '40s; Global Aw. Nomination, '60s; b. N.Y.C., 1912; p. Edward and Kathryn Cain Blondell; h. (ex:) 1) Georges Barnes, 2) Dick Powell, 3) Michael Todd; c. Norman Powell, Ellen Powell.

BLOOM, EVELYN DEUTSCH, Prom. Mgr., WTVN, 753 Harmon Ave., Columbus, Oh. 43223, '67–; Cont. Dir., WBNS Radio, '66–'67; Pubcty. Dir., WLW-C, '65–'66; Asst. Cont. Dir., WBNS Radio, '59–'63; Talent, WTMJ (Milw., Wis.), '37–'38; NATAS (Columbus Chptr. VP), Bdcstrs. Prom. Assn., Columbus Adv. Club. AWRT; Founders Aw., Columbus Jr. Theatre of the Arts, '63; Oh. State Univ., '58–'59, '63–'64, Univ. of Wis., '35–'36; b. Detroit, Mich., 1917; p. Simon and Cecilia Borg Deutsch; h. Howard Bloom; c. Gary S., Phillip J., Cecilia Dee; res: 184 S. Stanwood Rd., Columbus, Oh. 43209.

BLOOM, LILLIAN BLUMBERG, Prof. of Eng., Rhode Island Col., Providence, R.I., '64–; Asst. Prof., '56–'64; Asst. Prof., Univ. of R.I., '47–'50; Instr., Queens Col., '46–'47; Instr., Univ. of Ill., '45–'46; Wtr., Rschr.; AAUP, Phi Beta Kappa; Yale Univ., PhD, '46; b. N.Y.C., 1920; p. Benjamin and Frances Eisenberg Blumbery; h. Edward Bloom; res: 21 Creston Way, Providence, R.I. 02906.

BLOOMBERG, SYLVIA, Trade Sls. Prom. Mgr., Random House, 201 E. 50th St., N.Y., N.Y. 10022.

BLOSSOM, DAISY ANGELINE, Adv. Mgr., Brand and Puritz, 313 W. Eighth St., Kan. City, Mo. 64105, '58–; SP Mgr.; Owner, Daisy Blossom, Crtv. Adv. and Sls. Prom., '66–; Adv. Mgr., Tension Envelope Corp., '53–'58; Asst. to Southwestern Rep., Houston Port and Traf. Bur., '46–'53; Sls. Corr., A.P. Green Fire Brick Co.

(Mexico, Mo.), '42–'46; dist. off., Farm Security Adm. (Maryville, Mo.), '37–'42; Wtr., "Contribution of American Railroads to Financial and Industrial Growth of a City," series of radio programs, '48; Fgn. Trade Club of Kan. City (Bd., '48–'51), Kan. City Adv. Round Table (Bd., '55–'57); Who's Who of Am. Wm.; Northeast Mo. State Col. (Kirksville), '35–'36; b. Brookfield, Mo., 1917; p. George N. and Fannie Moore Blossom; res: 712 W. 48th St., Apt. 101, Kan. City, Mo. 64112.

BLOXOM, SANDA McQUERRY, Adv., Pubcty. Dir., Interstate Theatres, Palace Theatre Bldg., Ft. Worth, Tex. 76102, '65–; Adv., PR Dir., Ft. Worth Savings & Loan, '64–'65; Prom. Asst., Hostess, "Reveille," KTVT, '64; AWRT (Pres., '69–'70; VP, '68–'69), Theta Sigma Phi; Tex. Christian Univ., '62; (Best in TV Aw.); b. Ft. Worth, Tex., 1941; p. J. W. and Nell English McQuerry; h. Russ A. Bloxom; res: 3113 Santa Fe Trail, Ft. Worth, Tex. 76116.

BLUHM, ELSIE VALERIE, Assoc. Ed., Montee Publishing Co., 511 Oakland Ave., Balt., Md. 21212, '50–; Edtl., Rsch. Asst., "American Race Horses," '62–'63; b. Rutherfordton, N.C., 1926; p. Jacob and Ruth LaVallette Bluhm; res: 4904-G Crenshaw Ave., Balt., Md. 21206.

BLUM, ELEANOR, Librn., Assoc. Prof., College of Communications, University of Illinois, 122 Gregory Hall, Urbana, Ill. 61801; Tchr., Contemporary Bk. Publ., Grad Sch. of Lib. Sci., Univ. of Ill. '65–'69; Miss. State Col. for Wm., '33–'37; Columbia Univ., '37–'38; Univ. of Ill., '52–'58; b. Meridian, Miss.; res: 804 S. Lincoln, Urbana, Ill. 61801.

BLUM, REBECCA MULHOLLAND, AE, Public Relations Board, 75 E. Wacker, Chicago, Ill. 60601, '69–; Wtr., Assoc. Food Ed., Chgo. Sun-Times, '66–'68; Home Svc. Rep., Peoples Gas Light and Coke, '65–'66; Cnslt., adv. agcys.; Free-lance Adv. Copywtr.; Am. Home Econs. Assn., Ill. Home Econs. Assn., Home Econsts. in Bus. (Nwsltr. Ed., '68–'69); Nat. 4-H Alumni Aw., '68; Bradley Univ., B.S. (Home Econs.); b. Indpls., Ind., 1944; p. Ramon and Ruthe Felkins Mulholland; h. David Blum; res: 334 Ridge Ave., Evanston, Ill. 60202.

BLUMBERG, ANN M., Catalog Coordr., Premium Corporation of America, 12715-B State Highway 55, Mpls., Minn. 55427, '68; Coptwtr, '66–; Copywtr., Kerker Peterson Adv., '65–'66; Copywtr, KSTP, '64–'65; Copywtr., Ambro Adv.; Copywtr, Max Goldberg Adv.; AWRT (Northstar Chptr. Treas., '69); Theta Sigma Phi Aw., '58; 1000 Wm. in Communication, '69; Univ. of Minn., '58–'60; b. Lincoln, Neb.; p. Phil Blumberg and Charlotte Blumberg; res: 1551 E. 80th St., Mpls., Minn. 55420.

BLUMENTHAL, GERTRUDE, VP and Ed.-in-Chief, Simon & Schuster, 630 Fifth Ave., N.Y., N.Y.

BOARDMAN, EUNICE LOUISE, Co-Auth: "Musical Growth in the Elementary Schools" (Holt, Rinehart and Winston, '63), "Exploring Music" (Holt, Rinehart and Winston, '66); Prof. of Music Educ., Wichita State University, Wichita, Kan. 67208, '64–; Assoc. Prof., '61–'64; Asst. Prof., '57–'61; Instr., Music Educ., Northern Ill. Univ., '56–'57; Dir., Southwestern Inst. for Music in Contemporary Educ. (MENC and Ford Fndn.), '67–'68; Mu Phi Epsilon, Music Educs. Nat. Conf., Music Tchrs. Nat. Assn., Pi Kappa Lambda, ACLU, AAUP; Cornell Col., BME, '47; Columbia Univ., MME, '51; Univ. of Ill., EdD, '63; b. Cordova, Ill., 1926; p. G. Hollister and Anna Feaster Boardman; res: 3527 E. 15th St., Wichita, Kan. 67208.

BOAZ, MARTHA, Dean and Prof., School of Library Science, University of Southern California, L.A., Cal. 90044, '55–; Auth: "Fervent and Full of Gifts"; Ed. "A Living Library," "Modern Trends in Documentation"; Assoc. Prof., '53–'55; Instr., Univ. of Mich., '51–'52; Assoc. Prof., Univ. of Tenn., '50–'51; Asst. Librn., Madison Col. (Harrisonburg, Va.), '40–'49; Tchr., Librn., '35–'40; Assn. of Am. Lib. Schs. (Pres., '62–'63; Cal. Lib. Assn. (Pres., '62), ALA (Lib. Educ. Div. Pres., '68–'69), Beta Phi Mu (Nat. Chptr. Pres., '62); Madison Col., BS, '35; George Peabody Col., BS (Lib. Sci.), '37; Univ. of Mich., MA (Sesquicentennial Aw., '67), '50; PhD, '55; res: 1849 Campus Rd., L.A., Cal. 90041.

BOBULA, IDA, Auth. Histrn., Lectr.; Assoc. Prof., Limestone Col., Gaffney, S.C. 29340, '67–; Sociol., Anthropology Dept. Head, Ricker Col., Houlton, Me., '60–'67; Dir., Sarolta Col., '32–'47; Royal Hungarian Ministry of Public Instr., '26–'32; Assn. of Hungarian Histrns., Hungarian Sociological Soc., Hungarian Fedn. of Univ. Wm. (Pres., '46–'48); Pro Hungaria Gold Medal, '29, Pro Transylvania military medal, '42; Univ. Pazmany Peter (Budapest) PhD, '23 (summa cum laude); Bryn Mawr Col., '24–'25; b. Budapest, Hungary; p. John de Bobula and Ida Helcz; res: 212 Richardson, Gaffney, S.C. 29340.

BOCK, SADIE PATTERSON PADLEY, Colmst., The Lodi Enterprise, 146 Main St., Lodi, Wis. 53555, '58–; Ed.; Reptr., The Capitol Times and State Jnl. (Madison); Reptr., Colmst., Portage Daily Register; Wtr., fiction, non-fiction, nwsps., nat. pubns.; Free-lance Artist; Lake Wis. C. of C., Columbus Commty. Chest, Wms. Civic Club (Pres., '68–'69); Who's Who of Am. Wm.; Univ. of Wis., N.Y. Inst. (Jnlsm.); b. Dane, Wis., 1898; p. Frank and Elsie Mahaney Patterson; h. (1) Wayne Sidney Padley (dec.); (2) Walter B. Bock; c. Dorothy (Mrs. Ralph Ullring), Wayne, Carol (Mrs. Don Manke), Donovan, Howard, Ireta (Mrs. Delbert Ryan), Richard Padley; res: 236 W. James, Columbus, Wis. 53925.

BOCKMAN, PAULINE, Subsidiary Rights Contracts Mgr., Asst. to Sls. Mgr., Convention Mgr., Basic Books, Inc., 404 Park Ave. S., N.Y., N.Y. 10016, '68–; Info. Asst., Off. of the Mayor; Cnslr., N.Y.C. Human Resources Adm.; Hunter Col., BA; New Sch. for Social Rsch., Bank St. Col. of Educ.; b. N.Y.C.; p. Henry and Victoria Hoffman Berg; c. Peter, Claudia, Andrea; res: 208 W. 23rd St., N.Y., N.Y. 10011.

BODDY, ELLEN NEWBY, Reptr., Colmst., Wichita Daily Times, Wichita Falls, Tex.; Adv. Mgr., Perkins-Timberlake Co.; Adv. Copywtr., City Nat. Bank; Pres. Commn. on the Status of Wm., '61–'63, State Democratic Bd., '62–'64, Regent, Midwestern Univ.; educ: Wichita Falls Jr. Col., '32–'34; Univ. of Tex., BJ, '36; b. Palisades, Colo. 1916; p. Albert and Adaline Alexander Newby; h. Macon Boddy; c. Mrs. David Middleton, Macon Clark, Annie Coutant; res: Prairie Flower Commty., Henrietta, Tex. 76365.

BODEAU, VIVIENNE FITZSIMMONS-TRACEY, Ed.-Publr., Bodeau News Bureau, 6209 Lakeview Dr., Falls Church, Va. 22041, '63–; PR, '69–; Ed., Publr., Nat. Defense Byline, '63–; Military News Bdcstr., Wtr., WFAX radio, '63–'64; Military Ed., Colmst., Northern Va. Sun, '59–'63; European Corr., U.S. Lady, '54–'58; Ed., Serve Us, '54–'57; Military Wtr., Gazette Telegraph, '51–'53; Free-lance Military Wtr.; Lectr., TV Script Wtr., PR; various organizations and over 30 state and nat. writing aws.; Ohio Northern Univ., Boston Univ.; b. Indpls., Ind.

BODINE, PATT ROSS, Creative Supvsr., Foote, Cone & Belding, 200 Park Ave., N.Y., N.Y. 10017, '67–; Copywtr., Hockaday Associates, '64–'67; Free-lance Colmst., World Telegram & Sun, '65–'66; Copy Chief, S. Klein, '63–'64; Asst. Copy Chief, Franklin Simon, '62–'63; Asst. Prod. Mgr., Family Circle Magazine, '61–'62; Jr. Copywtr., W. T. Grant, '58–'60; Pubcty Mgr., Totem Pole Playhouse, '57; Juniata Col., '57; b. Richmond, Va., 1940; p. Wilson Srantz Ross and Grace Gulley Nickey; h. (div.); res: 425 E. 63 St., N.Y., N.Y. 10021.

BOE, SUE, Consumer Info. Specialist, Pharmaceutical Manufacturers Association, 1155 15th St. N.W., Wash., D.C. 20005, '68–; Field Rep., Am. Med. Assn., '65–'67; Free-lance Wtr., Prodr., Talent in Kan. City area and Ore., '44–'65; Wtr., Prog. Performer, KMBC-Radio (Kan. City. Mo.) '40–'43; Free-lance Wtr. and Radio Talent, '36–'39; Edtl. Bd., "MD's Wife," '64–'65; Vocal Performer; AWRT, Nat. Speakers Bur., Wms. Aux. to Ore. Med. Assn. (Pres., '65), Am. Med. Assn., PTA (former mbr., Kan. and Ore. State Bd. of Mgrs.), Lib. Bd. (Chmn., Josephine County, Ore., '64); Northeast Jr. Col., '35–'37; Univ. of Kan., '37–'38; Kan. State Univ., BS, '39 (cum laude); Univ. of Ia., MA, '40; b. St. Louis, Mo., 1920; p. Emil and Claire Roy Lohmeyer; h. (div.); c. Susan Marie, Christine; res: 1420 N. St. N.W., Wash., D.C. 20005.

BOECKER, BARBARA BYWATER (BOBI), Free-lance Talent, WTAR-TV, 721 Bousch St., Norfolk, Va. 23510; Motion Picture, Lead Actress, "To Labor As One"; KRNT-TV, summers '57–'58; Model, Ia., Md., Va., '55–'70; Substitute Secondary Sch. Tchr. of Eng. Dramatics; Wtr., Lectr., Singer, Swimming Tchr.; ESA (Treas.); active in commty., Navy wife orgs. (Prodr., Dir., Navy talent shows); winner, numerous beauty contests, '56–'60; State Univ. of Ia. (Radio-TV, Teaching), '58–'60; Drake Univ., Teaching Cert. (Eng., Dramatics), '61; b. Ia. Falls, Ia., 1939; p. Robert and Mildred Klopp Bywater; h. Donald Boecker; c. Michele Denise, Stephanie Valette, Barbara Danielle, Dione Noel; res: 1004 Abingdon Rd. (Bay Colony), Virginia Beach, Va. 23451.

BOGERT, ZEPHA SAMOILOFF, Travel Ed., Hollywood Reporter, 6715 Sunset Blvd., Hollywood, Cal. 90028, '69–; Co-owner, AE, The Bogerts, Inc., '48–'68; AE, Beaumont & Hohman, '45–'48; Western Family Preview & Magazine, '41–'45; Free-lance Wtr., Ed. PR Cnslt., '69–; Auth: "Handbook for Singers and Teachers" ('42); Cal. Press Wm. (Pres., '65–'67; L.A. dist. Pres., '63–'65), AWRT (Nat. Convention Chmn., '68), Hollywood Wms. Press Club, NFPW (Nat. Bd. Mbr.; 3 writing contest 1st place aws., '63), L.A. Adv. Wm., Frances Holmes aw., '47; Chouinard Art School, Otis Art Inst., Art Center School (L.A.); b. N.Y.C.; p. Dr. Lazar S. and Paulina Medvedyeva Samoiloff; h. Elliott vanden Bogert; res: 4446 Ledge Ave., N. Hollywood, Cal. 91602.

BOGGESS, LOUISE BRADFORD, Auth.; Tchr., College of San Mateo, 1600 Hillsdale, San Mateo, Cal. 94401, '56–; Kingsville (Tex.) Record, '48–'51; Tex. A. & I. Univ., '46–'47; Public Schs. of Tex., '41–'46; "Fiction Techniques That Sell," "Writing Articles That Sell" (Prentice-Hall); AAUW, Auths. Guild (Peninsula Br. of Cal. Wtrs. Pres., '67–'69); Who's Who of Contemporary Wtrs., Univ. of Tex., BA, '33 (Phi Beta Kappa, Phi Lambda Theta, Phi Sigma Alpha); MA, '34; Univ. of Okla., '47–'48; b. Sweetwater, Tex., 1912; p. Giles Edward and Hattie Maude Corbett Bradford; h. William F. Boggess; c. Patricia Anne (Mrs. H. G. Blair), William F., III; res: 4016 Martin Dr., San Mateo, Cal. 94403.

BOGLE, PATRICIA JONES, Dir., Rsch. and Dev., Fuller and Dees Marketing Group, Inc., 3734 Madison Ave., Montgomery, Ala. 36109, '67–; Bk. Prod. Dir., '64–'67; Art Dir., Paragon Press, '59–'64; Ed., several published titles for Fuller and Dees; Art Ed., "A Guide to the City of Montgomery"; Dir. Mail Adv. Assn (Coordr. of Showmanship Aw.-winning campaign, '67; active in commty. affairs; several Montgomery Adv. Assn. Aws. of Excellence, '59–'64; Mary Baldwin Col., '55–'56; Univ. of Ala., BFA, '59 (Kappa Pi); b. Talladega, Ala., 1937; p. George and Alice Dumas Jones; h. John Bogle; c. Allison M., Patricia E., Melissa K.; res: 1832 Galena Ave., Montgomery, Ala. 36106.

BOGUE, LUCILE MAXFIELD, Auth: "Typhoon! Typhoon!" ('69); "Blood Across the Bay" (S.F. Browning Soc. aw., '66); "Freedom Trail" (Colo. Govs. Aw., '59); Dean, Anna Head School, 4315 Lincoln Ave., Oakland, Cal. 94602, '68–; Dir. of Guidance, Am. Sch. (Tokyo, Japan), '66–'68; Founder, Pres., Colo. Alpine

Col., U.S. Intl. Univ., '62–'66; Tchr., Whiteman Sch., '57–'59; Tchr., Colo., '34–'57; NEA, Colo. Educ. Assn.; Colo. Wms. Club aw., '42; Who's Who of Am. Wm., '68; Dic. of Intl. Biog., '68; Colo. Col., AA, '32; Colo. State Col., BA, '34; b. Salt Lake City, Ut., 1911; p. Roy and Maude Callicotte Maxfield; h. Arthur Bogue; c. Sharon (Mrs. Robert Myers), Bonnie (Mrs. Frank Cebulski); res: 2611 Brooks St., El Cerrito, Cal. 94530.

BOHLMAN, EDNA McCAULL, Tchr., Bus., Mktng., Grandview Junior College, Ninth and Grandview, Des Moines, Ia., '65–; Co-auth: "Problems in Democracy; the United States in a Changing World" (Holt, Rinehart and Winston, '64), "Democracy and its Competitors" (Charles E. Merrill Bks., '62), "Our Economic Problems" (D. C. Heath & Co., '42); other bks., articles; Chmn., Social Studies Dept., Des Moines Tech. HS, '46–'65; adm., Wash., D.C. public schs., '42–'44; Tchr., '21–'34; Consumer Educ. Study, Nat. Assn. of Secondary Sch. Prins.; active in Des Moines educ., civic groups; Univ. of Ill., AB (Hist.), '20; Univ. of Wis., MA (Sociol.), '24; b. Joliet, Ill., 1897; p. William and Nora Hill McCaull; h. Herbert W. Bohlman; c. Mac; res: 1301 37th St., Des Moines, Ia. 50311.

BOLAND, IRENE OVIATT, Asst. to Pres., Arthur Brill Productions, Inc., 156 E. 52nd St., N.Y., N.Y. 10022, '62–; Space Buyer and AE, Campbell-Lampee, Inc.; Mag. Pubcty. Dept., CBS; Adv. Dept., Arts & Decoration Magazine, '35–'37; AWNY; Svc. Bureau, Girl Scout Cncl. of Gtr. N.Y.; Oh. Wesleyan Univ., '27–'28; Baldwin Wallace Col., '28–'29; Western Reserve Univ. (Cleveland Col.), '29–'31; b. Dayton, Oh., 1908; p. Elmo and Madeleine Platt Oviatt; h. Joseph Boland; c. Madeleine Jo, Bonnie Oviatt; res: 5101 39th Ave., Long Island City, N.Y. 11101.

BOLLING, TIFFANY ROYCE, Actress, ABC-TV, "New People"; Aaron Spelling-Danny Thomas Productions, Paramount Studios, 1242 N. Highland Ave., L.A., Cal. 90038, '69; 20th Century Talent School, '68; AFTRA, SAG; b. Santa Monica, Cal., 1949; p. William and Bettie Miller Bolling.

BOLSTER, JACQUELINE NEBEN, Dir., Mdsng., Prom., Harper's Bazaar, 717 Fifth Ave., N.Y., N.Y. 10022, '64–; Fashion, Beauty Prom. Mgr., Crtv. Mdsng. Mgr. All Classifications, McCall's '53–'64; Prom. Mgr., Photoplay, '47–'53; AWNY, Fashion Group; Andy Aw., '65; Aw., Soc. of Illus., '66; Aws., Art Dirs. Club, '61, '66; Aw., NRMA, '66; Pratt Inst., Columbia Univ.; b. N.Y.C.; p. Ernest W. B. and Emily Guck Neben; h. John Bolster; res: 8531-88th St., Woodhaven, N.Y. 11421; Halsey Neck Lane, Southampton, N.Y. 11968.

BOLTE, CAYE JAHRLING, Fashion, Wms. Ed., Hudson Dispatch, 400 38th St., Union City, N.J. 07087, '65–; Pubns. Cnslt., St. Peter's Col. (Jersey City), '69–; N.J. Daily Nwsp. Wms. Assn.; Caswell Massey aw., '65; N.J. Press Assn. aws., '63, '65; b. N.J.; p. Christian and Jennie Ackermann Jahrling; h. Henry Bolte; res: 8 Demarest Ave., Englewood Cliffs, N.J. 07632.

BOLTON, BARBARA WEEKS, Free-lance Wtr.; Exec. Dir., Western Pa. Nat. Cystic Fibrosis Rsch. Fndn., '67–'69; PR Dir., Asst. Exec. Dir., Western Pa. Heart Assn., '54–'67; Dir., Radio-TV, Films, Commty. Chest of Allegheny County, '51–'54; Colmst., Feature Wtr., Corr., Zanesville News, New Concord Enterprise, '48–'49; Assoc. Eds. Soc. of Pitt., ICIE, Pitt. Radio and TV Club, Soc. of Tech. Wtrs. and Publrs. Muskingum Col., BA (Eng.), '51, Columbia Univ., '63; b. Oil City, Pa.; p. Charles and Edna Baumbach Weeks; h. John Dickson Bolton, Jr.; res: 832 Graham Blvd., Pitt., Pa. 15221.

BOLTON, CAROLE ROBERTS, Assoc. Ed., Lothrop, Lee & Shepard Company, 105 Madison Ave., N.Y., N.Y. 10016, '67–; Morrow Jr. Bks.; Meredith Press; Auth: "The Dark Rosaleen" ('64), "The Stage is Set" ('63), "Reunion in December" ('62), others; Auths. Guild; b. Uniontown, Pa., 1926; p. Harry and Leone Shomo Roberts; h. John J. Bolton; c. Timothy Duke, John Christopher; res: 307 W. 71st St., N.Y., N.Y. 10023.

BOLTON, VIVIAN BROWN, Newsfeatures Wtr., Associated Press, 50 Rockefeller Plaza, N.Y., N.Y. 10020, '41–; NWC; Columbia Univ.; b. N.Y.C.; p. John and Cecile Reynolds Brown; h. Robert Bolton; c. Anthony; res: 102 Scribner Hill Rd., Wilton, Conn. 06897.

BOMBA, LINDA PICKERING, Sls. Prom. Assoc., Anchor Corporation, Elizabeth, N.J., '69–; Sls. Prom. Mgr., McDonell and Co. (N.Y.C.), '69–'69; Ed. and Sls. Prom. Cnslt., Prudential Insurance Co. of Am. (Newark, N.J.), '68; Asst. Ed., '67–'68; Staff Wtr., '65–'66; Who's Who Among Students in Am. Cols. and Univs.; Notre Dame Col. of S.I., AB (Hist.), '65 (cum laude; salutatorian; Alumnae Cncl.; Ed. "Dateline,"); Seton Hall Univ.; b. New Brunswick, N.J., 1944; h. Richard J. Bomba; res: 609 Britton St., Elizabeth, N.J. 07202.

BOMBECK, ERMA FISTE, Synd. Colmst., Newsday Specials, Garden City, L.I., N.Y., '65–; Staff Wtr., Dayton Jnl. Herald; Auth: "At Wit's End" (Doubleday, '67); Theta Sigma Phi (Headliner Aw., '69), Kappa Delta Epsilon; Univ. of Dayton, BA, '49; b. Dayton, Oh., 1927; p. Cassius and Erma Haines Fiste; h. William Bombeck; c. Betsy, Andrew, Matthew; res: 3875 Upper Bellbrook Rd., Bellbrook, Oh. 45305.

BOND, ALISON MARY, Ed., Gen. Bks., Holt, Rinehart & Winston, Inc., 383 Madison Ave., N.Y., N.Y. 10017, '68–; Trade Ed., Scribner's, '67–'68; Prep. Ed., Oxford Univ. Press, '60–'67; Univ. of London, BA, Hons. (Modern Langs.), '57; b. Surrey, England, 1935; p. Cyril and Dorothy Bond; res: 151 E. 81st St., N.Y., N.Y. 10028.

BOND, BEVERLY, Dir., Adv., Prom. and Pubcty., New American Library, 1301 Ave. of the Ams., N.Y., N.Y. 10019, '70–; Dir. of Mktg., Arno Press, '68–'70;

Dir. Lib. Mktg., Holt, Rinehart and Winston, '60–'68; Publrs. Pubcty. Assn., Publrs. Adv. Club; Univ. of Houston, '50; h. Laurence F. Reeves; res: 800 West End Ave., N.Y., N.Y. 10025.

BOND, BONNIE JEAN, Ed., Towse Publishing, 127 E. 31st St., N.Y., N.Y. 10016, '69–; Assoc. Ed., Irving Cloud Publishing; Reptr., Dowagiac Daily News; Pubns. Adv. Dir., Northwood Inst.; Cnslt., youth mkt.; Lecturer, creative writing and commty. rel.; Ghost Wtr., technical bks.; Mkt. Cnslt., housewares; Northwood Inst., '66; b. Dowagiac, Mich.; p. Charles W. and Agnes Hampel Sarabyn; res: 162 E. 88th St., N.Y., N.Y. 10028.

BOND, GLADYS BAKER, Auth. of 24 picture bks. and novels for young readers and 300 short stories; Lectr. at seminars and wtrs. confs.; Artist; Lewis-Clark Art Assn. (past Pres.), Lewis-Clark Wtrs., Friends of Lib. (Distg. Auth. Aw., '67), Idaho Wtr. of the Yr. ('68), Acad. of Fine Arts ('69), recipient of Edith Kempthorne Medal; Blairs Bus. Col., '33; Univ. of Mont.; Univ. of Idaho; Univ. of Wash.; b. Berryville, Ark., 1912; p. Coy Ernest and Clara Barton Clark Baker; h. Floyd James Bond; c. Nicholas Peter; res: 1425 Eighth St., Clarkston, Wash. 99403.

BONIME, FLORENCE LEVINE, Instr., The New School College, 66 W. 12th St., N.Y., N.Y. 10011, '65–; Lectr., Brooklyn Col., '64–'65; Assoc. Ed., Dodd Mead and Co., '50–'55; Auth: "The Good Mrs. Sheppard" ('50), "A Thousand Imitations" ('67); Auths. Guild, Modern Lang. Assn., Intl. Platform Assn., Alpha Sigma Lambda; Bklyn. Col., '64 (summa cum laude); N.Y.U., '64–'66; b. N.Y.C., 1907; p. Samuel and Lena Spieler Levine; h. Dr. Walter Bonime; c. Norma Cummings Lovins, Frank Cummings; res: 37 Washington Sq. W., N.Y., N.Y. 10011.

BONNELL, DOROTHY HAWORTH, Asst. Ed., Personnel Journal, 100 Park Ave., Swarthmore, Pa. 19081, '60–; Staff, '49–'60; Auth: five teenage bks.; Oberlin Col.; Wash. Univ.; b. Buffalo, N.Y., 1914; p. Lester and Ruby Peyton Haworth; h. Allen Bonnell; c. Anne (Mrs. Paul Vicinanza), Thomas Haworth, David Wellington, Daniel Churchill; res: 11 Single Lane, Wallingford, Pa. 19086.

BONNER, JUDY WHITSON, Partner, McClain, Fletcher & Bonner Public Relations, 1726 National Bankers Life Bldg., Dallas, Tex. 75201, '61–; Staff Wtr., The Dallas Times Herald, '53–'61; Auth., "Investigation of a Homicide"; articles; Dir., John F. Kennedy Living Ctr. of Dallas; Dir., Dallas Crtv. Learning Ctr; Theta Sigma Phi (Nat. Headliner Aw., '59; Dallas Alumnae Chptr: Pres., '59; Commtns. Aw., '66), Kappa Alpha Mu (Nat. Pres., '53), PRSA, Dallas Soc. of Indsl. Eds., Press Club of Dallas; Tex. Med. Assn. Anson Jones Aw., '58; Tex. Wms. Univ., BA, '53 (Who's Who in Am. Cols. and Univs).

BONNER, MARY GRAHAM, Auth., many bks., most

publ. by Knopf; revs.; synd. material, specializing in bks. connected with writing; WNBA (Constance Lindsay Skinner Aw., '43); Halifax Ladies Col.; b. Cooperstown, N.Y.; p. G. W. Graham and Margaret Bonner; h. (dec.); res: 706 Riverside Dr., N.Y., N.Y. 10031.

BONO, LILLIAN, Colmst., Post-Gazette, 5 Prince St., Boston, Mass. 02113, '54–; Treas., Near the Waterfront (PR), 6 Henchman St., Boston, Mass. 02113, '69–; Auth: "Profiles of the Builders of America"; Pfsnl. Astrologer, Wtr., Lectr.; Press Club of Boston, Am. Fedn. of Astrologers, Am. Guild of Astrologers, New England Astrological Assn.; Sorbonne Univ., Sch. of Linguistics, '52; Univ. of Bonn (Germany), '54; Portia Law Sch. (Boston, Mass.), '58; b. S. Attleboro, Mass., 1933; p. Charles H. and Madeleine A. Sauvage Bonneau; h. Philip Gioia; c. Melinda, Maryann, Joseph; res: 6 Henchman St., Boston, Mass. 02113.

BONTEMPI, FEDORA MORE, Dir. of Public Affairs, KLAS-TV, Hughes Tool Company, 250 E. Desert Inn Rd., Las Vegas, Nev. 89109, '68–; Bdcstr.: "Our Town" & "Recreation Directory" KLAS-TV, '68–; "Continental Cookery" WOR-TV (N.Y.C.), '59–'67; "Cinderella Weekend" WNHC-TV (New Haven, Conn.), '59; "Breakfast Time," "An Hour With Fedora Bontempi" (WNHC-TV), '52–'58; "Fashions, Food & Songs" WABC-TV (N.Y.C.), '57; "Continental Cookery" (WABC-TV), '51–'59; "Italian Cookery" WATV-TV (Newark, N.J.), '50–'51; WMCA, WINS Radio, '49–'58; Food Colmst. for Panorama Magazine (Las Vegas) '69–; AWRT, (Las Vegas Chptr. Pres., '69–'70), BPW, Las Vegas Press Club, Mesquite, Variety, AFTRA; numerous aws. including Star of Solidarity from Republic of Italy; b. N.Y.C.; p. August and Claudia Ghiselli More; h. Pino Bontempi; c. Diane Fugazy (Mrs. Walter E. Carson); res: 445 Desert Inn Rd., Las Vegas, Nev. 89109.

BOOK, IMOGENE CLARK, Librn., Rend Lake College, 315 S. Seventh, Mt. Vernon, Ill. 62864, '67–; Librn., Mt. Vernon Commty. Col., '56–'67; Librn., Mt. Vernon Township HS, '58–'62; Tch., secondary sch., '46–'48, '55–'57; Advisory Cncl., Univ. of Ill. Grad. Sch. of Lib. Sci., '62–'64; Cnslt., Student Ill. Educ. Assn., '64–; Advisory Cncl., Mt. Vernon Commty. Col., '61–'67; Ill. Tch. Advisory Cncl., Rend Lake Col. '67–'69 Educ. and Pfsnl. Standards Comm., '66–; Mt. Vernon Educ. Assn. (Pres., '59–'60), Jefferson County Educ. Assn. (Secy., '64–'65; Pres., '65–'66), Ill. Educ. Assn., NEA, Mt. Vernon Lib. Assn. (Secy., '61–'62; VP, '63–'64; Pres., '64–'65), Ill. Assn. of Sch. Librns. (Secy., '58–'59), Ill. Lib. Assn; Southern Ill. Univ., BS (Educ.), '46; Univ. of Ill., MS (Lib. Sci.), '65; Univ. of Ill., C.A.S. (Librarianship), '66; b. Mt. Vernon, Ill., 1924; p. Keith and Mona Hawkins Clark; h. Wiltz Book; c. Douglas Keith, Karen Lynn; res: 912 S. 21st St., Mt. Vernon, Ill. 62864.

BOOKER, HARRIET ANDERSON, Dir., Rsch. and Product Development, Winter Garden Co., 3039 Kingston Pike, Knoxville, Tenn. 37919, '55–; Dir., Home

Econ., American Can Co. (N.Y.C.), '53–'55; Dir. Home Inst., N.Y. Herald Tribune, '50–'53; Food Ed., This Week mag., '45–'50; Dir., Am. Red Cross, First General Hosp. (N.Y.C. Belleview Unit), '43–'45; State Extension Agent and Tch., '39–'43; articles, various pubns.; auth., "How to Eat Better and Save Money" ('53); Juvenile Court, Knox County Mental Health Clinic, Helen Ross McNabb Center, United Fund-Commty. Svc., Knox County Legal Aid; Who's Who of Am. Wm.; Univ. of Vt., BS, '39 (W. J. Stone Aw., Mortar Board, Omicron Nu); h. W. Edward Booker.

BOOKER, JANICE LEKOFF, Publr., Janice L. Booker Publications, P.O. Box 8861, Elkins Park, Pa. 19117, '63–; Med. Ed., Secre-phone Co., '53–'58; Indsl. Ed., H. L. Yoh Co., '51–'53; Free-lance Wtr. '50–; Dir. of Info., Oak Lane Day Sch., '65–; Colmst., Phila. Jewish Exponent; Theta Sigma Phi; Temple Univ., BS, '51; b. Phila., Pa., 1929; p. Max and Betty Cohen Lekoff; h. Alvin Booker; c. Ellis Carl, Susan Barbara; res: 530 Elkins Ave., Elkins Park, Pa. 19117.

BOOKHART, MARY ALICE WARREN, Wms. Ed., Mississippi Publishers (Clarion-Ledger), 311 E. Pearl, Jackson, Miss. 39205, '42–; Jackson Daily News, '37–'38; Pine Bluff (Ark.) Graphic, '33–'37; articles for Arkansas Gazette, other nwsps., '33–; Lecturer, PR Workshop, Miss. State Col. for Wm.; Symphony League of Jackson (Pubcty. Advisor, past Pres.), NLAPW (State Pres., '56–'58), Miss. Press Wm. (Pres, '62–'64; aw.); Miss. Arts Commn., Miss. State Cncl. on the Arts; NFPW aw.; b. Little Rock, Ark; p. Robert Chauncey and Alice Dodge Green Warren; h. John Bookhart; c. Robert C. Warren III, Mrs. Robert H. Patterson; res: 4546 Kings Highway, Jackson, Miss. 39206.

BOONE, GRACE BROWN, Wms. Ed., Bdcstr., WSMY Radio Station, P.O. Box 910, Roanoke Rapids, N.C. 27870, '68–; Wms. Program Dir., Bdcstr., "Woman's World," WCBT, '62–'69; AWRT; Mededith Col., '44–'47, Wake Forest Col., '45' '46; William & Mary, '60–'61; b. Murfreesboro, N.C., 1928; p. Bynum and Grace Pierce Brown; h. Dr. John Woodie Boone; c. John W. III, Laura L.; res: 822 W. Second St., Roanoke Rapids, N.C. 27870.

BOONE, JUDITH E., Edtl. Asst., Daedalus jnl., Am. Acad. of Arts and Sci., 7 Linden St., Cambridge, Mass. 02138, '68–'69; Cataloger, G. K. Hall & Co., '68; Univ. of Mass. (Amherst), BA, '68; b. Boston, Mass., 1945; res: 43 Langdon St., Cambridge, Mass. 02138.

BOONE, LOU SCHEPERS, Dir., Starved Rock Library System & Reddicks Library, 100 W. Lafayette, Ottawa, Ill. 61350, '67–; Head, Mich. State Lib. for the Blind; Asst. Dir., Grand Traverse Area Lib. Fedn.; Asst. Librn., Traverse City Public Lib.; Bookmobile Librn., Grand Traverse Area Lib. Project; ALA; Mich., Ill. Lib. Assns.; ZONTA; Western Michigan Univ., BS (Lib. Sci.); b. McBain, Mich., 1933; p. Percy and Geraldine Anderson Schepers; h. Wendell Boone; c. William G., Scott

M., Wendy L., Teresa S; res: R#1 Box 332A, Marseilles, Ill. 61341.

BOONE, WILLIE GODFREY, Librn., Durham High School, N. Duke, Durham, N.C. 27701, '60–; Audio-visual Coordr.; Asst. Prof., Lib. Sci. Dept., Applachian State Univ., '59–'64; Tchr., various high schs., '35–'59; NEA (Life Mbr.), N.C. Educ. Assn. (Sch. Lib. Div. Pres., '61), N.C. Lib. Assn., BPW (Pres., '67, '68), N.C. HS Lib. Assn. (Exec. Secy., '66–'72); Order Eastern Star (Past Matron); Wake Forest Col., AB, '35; Univ. N.C., M Ed, '58; b. Morganton, N.C., 1913; p. William and Fannie Quinn Godfrey; h. Robert S. Boone; c. Robert Sills, Jr., William Herbert; res: 2918 University Dr., Durham, N.C. 27707.

BOORMAN, ANNE SUTTON, Publr., The Lemmon Leader, 11 Third St., W., Lemmon, S.D. 57638, '64–; Printer; Tch.; Co. of St. Catherine (St. Paul, Minn.), BA; Univ. of Minn.; b. Stillwater, Minn., 1902; p. George Lyman and Jennie Stage Sutton; h. L. B. Boorman; c. Jane, Bruce, Catherine (Mrs. R. T. Becker); res: 311 Third Ave. W., Lemmon, S.D. 57638.

BOORSCH, SUZANNE RENEE, Cnslt., Metropolitan Museum Centennial; Asst. Ed., '62–'68; Free Lance Wtr., Ed., Translator; res: 332 E. 90 St., N.Y., N.Y. 10028.

BOOTH, ALEXANDRA PANOS, Asst. Soc. Ed., Wyoming Publishers, Casper Star-Tribune, P.O. Box 80, First and Jefferson Sts., Casper, Wyo. 82601, '65–; Ed., Wyoming Weekend, weekly supplement; Wtr., numerous features; Ed., "Women-1967" and "Women-1968," annual supplements (Special aws., Wyo. Press Assn); Soc. Ed., Casper Morning Star, '63–'65; Jefferson Sch. PTA (Pres., VP, Secy.), Wyo. Press.; Univ. of Ia., '41–'42; b. Ottumwa, Ia., 1917; p. Constantine and Angelica Polyzogopulos Panos; h. Marvin Booth; c. James Dean, Theodore Marvin, Edithe Angela, Marvin Floyd; res: 941 S. Melrose, Casper, Wyo. 82601.

BOQUIST, FAYE MARTIN, Wms. Ed., Community Publications, 155 S. Taaffe, Sunnyvale, Cal. 94086, '62–; Denver Post; Hon. Mbr: Beta Sigma Phi, Federated Wm's Club, Altrusa; Vesta Food Aw.; Who's Who of Am. Wm.; Holy Names Col. (Honor Roll), '41; b. Wilbur, Wash.; p. Henry and Lela Perkins Martin; h. Arthur Boquist; c. Barry Lynne, Scott Arthur, April Lori, Matt Henry; res: 909 Rose Blossom Dr., Cupertino, Cal. 95014.

BORAKS, JACQUELINE MIRKEN, Ed., Div. of Physical Scis., National Academy of Sciences, 2101 Constitution Ave., Wash., D.C. 20418, '69–; Chief Copy Ed., NAS Printing and Publishing Office, '67–'69; Prod. Ed., Copy Ed., '65–'67; Asst. to Mng. Ed., Applied Optics, Optical Soc. of Am., '62–'64; Edtl. Asst., The Physics of Fluids, Am. Inst. of Physics, '61–'62; Asst. Ed., Physics Today, '55–'61; Davis & Elins Col., '46–'48; b. Bklyn., N.Y., 1928; p. Burt and Ruth Ginzburg Mirken; h. (div.); res: 416 E. Capitol St., Wash., D.C. 20003.

BORDEN, FRANCES, Mgr., Consumer Products PR, Chas. Pfizer & Co., Inc., 235 E. 42nd St., N.Y., N.Y. 10017, '64–; AE, Edward Gottlieb & Assoc.; Acc. Supvsr., Roy Bernard Co.; VP, PR, Adv., Basic Books, Inc.; AWRT; Fashion Group; Who's Who of Am. Wm.; Who's Who in Commerce and Industry; Who's Who in the East; Radcliffe Col., BA (cum laude); b. Boston, Mass.; h. Daniel J. McConville; res: 137 E. 36th St., N.Y., N.Y. 10016.

BORDEN, MARY FRANCES, Asst. Dir., Tacoma Public Library, 1102 Tacoma Ave. S., Tacoma, Wash. 98402, '55–; PR Offcr.; Host, "Your Library and You," KTPS-TV; Moore Br. Librn., '50–'55; Mottet Br. Librn., '45–'49; Br. Asst., Children's Librn., '44–'45; ALA, Pacific N.W. Lib. Assn., Wash. Lib. Assn. (Exec. Bd., '57–'59), Quota Intl. (Tacoma Club Past Pres.), AAUW, Tacoma civic groups; Who's Who in Lib. Svc.; Who's Who of Am. Wm.; Dic. of Intl. Biog.; Univ. of Wash., BA, '43; BA (Librarianship), '44; b. Tacoma, Wash., 1919; p. Lindon A. and Mary C. Donnelly Borden; res: 3827 101st St., S.W., Tacoma, Wash. 98499.

BOREL, HELEN DEBRA, Sr. Wtr., Sudler & Hennessey, Inc., 130 E. 59th St., N.Y., N.Y. 10019, '68–; Med. Copywtr., '65–'67; Med. Copywtr., L. W. Frohlich, '67–'68; Med. Copywtr., BBDO; '67; Nurse, '56–'66; When Mother Must Work (nat. child care org.; Founder, Pres.); Mt. Sinai Hosp. Sch. of Nursing, R.N., '56; b. Passaic, N.J., 1933; h. (div.); c. Jonathan Reichbach; res: 46 W. 96th St., N.Y., N.Y. 10025.

BORLAND, BARBARA DODGE, Auth./Poet, Salisbury, Conn. 06068; Garden Colmst., Berkshire Eagle (Pittsfield, Mass.), '60; collaborated with husband on fiction, major mags, U.S. and abroad, '46–'58; Wtrs. Workshop (N.Y.C.), '34–'38; Edtl. Conslt., '23–'25; Auth, "The Greater Hunger" ('63), Auths. Guild, Hawthorne Club (Canaan, Conn.); Oberlin Col.; Columbia Univ. Sch. of Jnlsm.; b. Waterbury, Conn.; p. Harry G. and Grace Cross Dodge; h. Hal Borland; c. Diana (Mrs. James C. Thomson, Jr.); res: Weatogue Rd., Salisbury, Conn. 06068.

BORLAND, JILL STELLE, Acc. Mgr. and Dir. of Radio-TV, Arndt, Preston, Chapin, Lamb & Keen, Inc., 375 Park Ave., N.Y., N.Y. 10022, '69–; Dir. of Radio-TV, Sally Dickson Assocs.; guest appearances, radio-TV; AWRT; Northwestern Univ., BA, '64 (hons.); b. Phila., Pa., 1942; p. Joseph Stelle and Madeline Perlee Borland; h. John Edwin Flynn; res: 200 E. 15th St., N.Y., N.Y. 10003.

BORN, PATRICIA THORNTON, VP, Crtv. Dir., Dodson, Craddock & Born Advertising, Inc., 4711 Scenic Highwy., Pensacola, Fla. 32502, '62–; Art. Dir., '58–'62; Pres., Gaberonne Interiors and Displays, '64–; Pensacola Hist. Preservation Soc., Dorothy Walton Fndn. (Dir., '65–'69); AFA Pensacola Adv. Man of the Yr., '60; numerous nat., reg., and local adv. aws.; Fla. State Univ. (Fine Arts), '58 (Phi Beta Kappa); b. Pensa-

cola, Fla., 1938; p. Brooks and Carolyn Crosby Thornton; h. Thomas Born; c. Christine, Johnny, Rachel; res: 4345 Manolete, Gaberonne, Pensacola, Fla. 32504.

BORNE, RAY ZIPES, Free-lance Med. Wtr., Ed., Rsch., 107 S. Broadway, Nyack, N.Y. 10960; Assoc. Ed., Inst. of Contemporary Russian Studies Med. Reports, Fordham Univ., '59–; Contrbr., Medical Jnl. Abstracts, E. R. Squibb, '43–'44; Rsch. Asst., Laboratory of Experimental Biology, Am Museum of Natural History, '32–'41; Pfsn. Jnls.; N.Y. Acad. of Sci., '46–; (Bd. Mbr., Wms. Auxiliary), Am. Assoc. for the Advancement of Sci., Am. Med. Wtrs. Assn.; McGill Univ., BA; res: 107 S. Broadway, Nyack, N.Y. 10960.

BORTEN, HELEN JACOBSON, Auth., Illus., Children's Bks: "Do You See What I See" ('59), "A Picture Has a Special Look" ('61), "Copycat" ('62), "Halloween" ('66), "The Jungle," and many others; Auths. League of Am.; N.Y. Times Ten Best Illustrated Children's Bks. ("Little Big Feather"), '56; Am. Inst. of Graphic Arts Aw. ("Do You See What I See"), '60; Phila. Col. of Art, '48–'51; b. Phila., Pa.; p. Joseph and Fay Riser Jacobson; h. Marvin Borten; c. Laurence Drew, Peter Elliot; res: 225 W. 71st St., N.Y., N.Y. 10023.

BOSCH, PATRICIA CARROLL, VP, Richey-Bosch Associates, P.O. Box 5201, Beaumont, Tex. 77706; Free-lance Commls., '60–'69; Staff, "The Dorothy Richey Show;" "Bridging the Gap" (Spec. series on racial tensions), co-prdcr., "Half-Way House," "My Choice" (pilot); Co-auth., "How to Be Rich & Beautiful"; Co-auth., nwsp. colm., "Today's Woman in Today's World"; AWRT '65–, (Nat. PR comm. '67–'68, sec. proj. comm., '68–'69); Stephens Col., AA; Lamar State Col. of Tech.; b. Jackson, Miss.; p. William and Sue Pierce Ferguson; h. George A. Bosch; c. William Alexander; res: 1880 Karen Lane, Beaumont, Tex. 77706.

BOSL, FLORENCE BARRY, Publr., The Schulenburg Sticker, 405 N. Main St., Schulenburg, Tex. 78956, and 2016 Main St., Houston, Tex., 77002; Ed., '37–; Corr., The Houston Post, '37–'54; The Houston Chronicle, '37–'54; The San Antonio Express, '37–'54; Roving Reptr., AP, '37–; Contrbr., Life Magazine; Commtns. Cnslt. in oceanography; Crtv. Writing Seminar, Univ. of Houston; Tex. Press Wm. (Pres., '59; Dir., VP), NFPW (Dir., '58–'60), S. Tex. Press Assn. (Dir.), Tex. Indsl. Comm. (Charter Mbr., Dir.), Tex. Press Assn., Theta Sigma Phi (Headliner Aw., '58), Gulf Coast Press Assn. (Charter Mbr., Dir.), Tex. Navy (Admiral, '56–), Ambassador of Goodwill to Soviet Intl. Trade Exhbn. ('59), Am. Red Cross (Dir.), Travel Assigts. for Dept. of State; 150 state and nat. aws. in nwspr. writing and ed.; Tex. Wm. of Achiev. Aw., '59; Dic. of Intl. Biog.; Baylor Univ., '31–'32; Univ. of Tex., BBA, '37; b. Granger, Tex., 1913; p. David and Sudie Denson Barry; h. Charles Bosl; Res: 2016 Main St., Houston, Tex. 77002, and 702 West Ave., Schulenburg, Tex. 78956.

BOST, CECILE ROWE, Owner, Cecile Bost Productions, 503 E. Herman, Newton, N.C. 28658, '63–; Wtr., Prodr., Talent, radio programs, radio-TV comml s.; Talent, "Cecile Bost Reporting," WHKY (Hickory); Cont. Dir., Prom. Mgr., Talent, News Reptr., WIRC, '53–'63; Wms. Ed., Cont. Ed., Feature News Reptr., WNNC (Newton), '48–'53; Eng., drama tchr.; wtr., feature articles; commtns. cnslt.; AWRT (N.C. Chptr. Pres., '64–'66; VP, '62–'64), numerous aws. for radio programs, newscasting, commtns.; Newton's Wm. of Yr., '53; Catawba Col., AB (Eng. and Drama), '46 (cum laude); b. Newton, N.C., 1924; p. Marcus and Myrtle Gross Rowe; h. Robert Bost; c. W. Stephen.

BOSTWICK, JERI, Dir. of PR and Adv., Sheraton Hawaii Corporation, 2259 Kalakaua Ave., Honolulu, Hi. 96815; Sheraton Hawaii & Pacific, '61–; Dir. of PR and Adv., The Greenbrier (W. Va.), '59–'61; Dir. of Publicity, Matson Hotels (Honolulu), '54–'59; Nwsp. Colmst. and Adv. Copy Wtr.; Theta Sigma Phi (Pres., '42–'62), PRSA (Pres., '68), WAIF-ISS (Secy. and Bd. Mbr., '56–'69), Soc. of Am. Travel Wtrs., Honolulu Press Club; appointed to President's Defense Advisory Comm. on Wm. in the Svc., '68; Hon. Ky. Colonel, '65; Nat. Industrial Eds. Aw., '60; civic activities; Colo. Wms. Col., AA, '41; Univ. of Wash., BJ, '43; b. Portland, Ore., 1922; p. Jesse and Jennie Nell Benson Jacobs; c. Barik Michael O'Fiely; res: Royal Hawaiian Hotel, Honolulu, Hi. 96815.

BOSWELL, SADY (SARA J. BOSWELL), Assoc. Dir. Adv. and PR, Industrial Trust and Savings Bank, 117 E. Adams St., Muncie, Ind., 47305, '67–' VP, R. J. Poorman & Associates, '54–'66; Tchr., '37–'38; Nat. Fndn. for Infantile Paralysis (Dir., '55–'59), Family Cncl. Svc. (Dir., '63–'66), Am. Red Cross (Muncie Area Chptr. Dir., '68–'70), Commty Svcs. Cncl. ('68–), Altrusa Intl. (Ed., Dist. Six Svc. Bul., '67–'69; Muncie Club VP, '69–'70); Ball State Tchrs. Col., '36–'38; b. Rochester, Ind., 1918; p. Lon and Fern Bryant Zimmerman; h. William B. Boswell; c. Mrs. C. David Reece, Jeffrey W.; res: R.R. 1, Box 526, Muncie, Ind. 47302.

BOSWORTH, PHYLLIS RUTH, Wtr., Rschr., CBS News, 524 W. 57th St., N.Y., N.Y. 10018, '61–; Wtr., "A House Divided" (CBS Special, '69); AWRT, Cornell Univ., BS, '56; b. Long Beach, N.Y., 1934; p. Louis and Natalie Jacobs Bosworth; res: 150 West End Ave., N.Y., N.Y. 10023.

BOTTEL, HELEN BRIGDEN, Colmst., "Helen Help Us," "Youth Asked For It," King Features Syndicate, 235 East 45th St., N.Y., N.Y. 10017, '58–; Reptr., Ore.: Portland Oregonian, Medford Mail-Tribune, Grants Pass Daily Courier, '56–'58; Ed., Illinois Valley News, '54–'56; Reptr., I.V. News, '52–'54; Auth: "To Teens With Love" (Double-day, '68), numerous mag. articles; Lectr.; Soc. of Mag. Wtrs., Cal. Wtrs. Club, Intl. Platform Assn., Cal. Press Wm., Sacramento Area Mental Health Assn.; Dir., Childrens' Ctr. of Sacramento, Cal. Press Wm. Aw., '69, several nwsp. aws.; Riverside Col., A.A., '35; b. Beaumont, Cal., 1914; p. Alpheus and Mary Alexander Brigden; h. Robert E.

Bottel; c. Robert D., Rodger M., Roberta K., Suzanne V.; res: 2060 56th Ave., Sacramento, Cal. 95822.

BOTTINI, IVY GAFFNEY, Edtl. Feature Designer-Illus., Newsday, Inc., 550 Stewart Ave., Garden City, L.I., N.Y., '66–; Edtl. Staff Artist, '60–'66; Adv. Artist Designer, '47–'60; Free-lance Book Illus. (cookbooks) and Fashion Illus., Lectr. on advtg., art and production; NOW (N.Y. Chptr. Pres.); Pratt Inst., Adv. Art Sch., '47; b. Lynbrook, L.I., N.Y., 1926; p. Archibald and Ivy Fisher Gaffney; h. Edward Bottini; c. Laura, Lisa; res: 33 W. 93rd St., N.Y., N.Y. 10025.

BOUB, MARGUERITE HARVEY, Mgr., Direct Mail Promo., World Topics Div., United Educators, Inc., 801 Green Bay Rd., Lake Bluff, Ill. 60044, '64–; Mgr., Direct Mail Prom., F. E. Compton, '57–'64; Customer Rel. and Special Sales, Commerce Clearing House, '46–'52, '54–'57; Script Wtr., WJVB (Fla.), '53; Sales Rep., Bonnie I. Smith, '52–'53; b. Rockford, Ill., 1919; p. William and Marie Dugger Harvey; h. Kenneth Boub; res: 2121 Sunset Ridge Rd., Glenview, Ill. 60025.

BOUCHER, PEGI ESTELLE, Singer, Actress: TV Commls., musicals, dramas, records, night clubs, indsl. films; AFTRA, SAG; Bank of America aw., music, '66; Best Leading Lady Aw., Va. Country Theater, '64; Univ. of Southern Cal. (Drama); b. Long Beach, Cal., 1948; p. George and Margaret Ford Boucher; res: 4000 Chestnut Ave., Long Beach, Cal. 90807.

BOUGHTON, AMY PEDERSEN, Ed., Nashville Publications, Inc. (aws: Adv. Idea of the Year, Use of Pics., News Reporting), 110 Maple St., Nashville, Mich. 49073, '59–; varied duties, '56–; Mich. Press Assn., Mich. Acad. of Arts and Letters; b. Rawson, N.D., 1923; p. Martin Christian and Minnie Van Dyke Pedersen; h. John Boughton; c. Christopher, Alisande Fay, Anne; res: 440 Durkee St., Nashville, Mich. 49073.

BOUNDS, MARILYN JONES, Prods. Mgr., Mithoff Adv. Inc., '55–'68; Press Club of El Paso, Adv. Club of El Paso, AAUW; Univ. of Tex. (El Paso), BA, '55; b. Galesburg, Ill., 1933; p. Park P. and Vera Nelson Jones; h. Hal B. Bounds; c. Chana Lynn; res: 4204 Hampshire, El Paso, Tex. 79902.

BOUNDS, SARA MORGAN (Sandy Strand), Bdcst. Mgr., W. D. Alexander Company, 1225 Chattachoochee Ave. N.W., Atlanta, Ga. 30318, '65–; Talent, Asst. Prog. Dir., WCSC Radio, TV (Charleston, S.C.); Talent, WTAR-TV, WAVY-TV (Norfolk, Va.); AWRT, BPW; Univ. of Ky., BA; b. Tampa, Fla., 1928; p. Henry and Ruth Steele Morgan; h. Carroll J. Bounds (dec.); c. Carroll, Sandra, Stacey, Mark; res: 779 Windsor Pkwy. N.E., Atlanta, Ga. 30305.

BOURAS, ARLENE AKLIN, Copy Chief, Playboy Magazine, HMH Publishing Company, 919 N. Michigan Ave., Chgo., Ill. 60611, '57–; Continental Casualty Co., '56–'57; Proofreader, Scott, Foresman & Co., '55–'56; Univ. of Rochester; b. Rochester, N.Y., 1930;

p. George and Mary Shafer Aklin; h. Harry Bouras; c. Lorraine Ann; res: 850 Castlewood Terr., Chgo., Ill. 60640.

BOURDIER, LILLIAN JACOBS, City Wms. Ed., Daily World, 127 S. Market St., Opelousas, La. 70570, '50–; Corr., New Orleans Times Picayune, '39–; Former Ed., Clarion-News, Opelousas Herald; Theta Sigma Phi (Baton Rouge Chptr. aw., '59), La. Press Wm. (Past Treas.), Opelousas Wms. Club; numerous nwsp. writing aws., VFW Auxiliary aw., '66; La. State Univ., '24–'27; b. Opelousas, La., 1907; p. Aaron and Hannah Hirschman Jacobs; h. James M. Bourdier (dec.); c. James A.; res: 361 S. Main St., Box 828, Opelousas, La. 70570.

BOURGEOIS, MARY KATHLEEN, PR Dir., Southern Office, Institute of International Education, 1 A World Trade Ctr., 1520 Texas Ave., Houston, Tex. 77025, '61–; VP, Jacobs-Keeper-Newell (PR); AE, Max H. Jacobs Agcy.; Feature Ed., Staff Wtr., Tex. Industry Magazine, '47–'49; Theta Sigma Phi (Houston Chptr. Pres., '57–'58; Secy., '67–'68; Treas., '68–'69), SIENA; La. State Univ., BS, '39; Univ. of Mo., BJ, '47; b. Canton, Miss., 1919; p. Thomas E. and Louise Brunner Bourgeois; res: 2215 Shakespeare, Houston, Tex. 77025.

BOVAIRD, KATHRYN FIELDS, TV Wtr., Talent, Prodr., Dir., '47–; Radio Staff,; '43–'47; Cnsl. Tchr., Phila. Bd. of Educ., '36–'43; Tchr., Dramatics, Radio Script Writing, TV Prod.; Tchr., grade, Jr. HS (Eng.), '17–'29; Cnslt., Radio, TV; Auth., "Delaware River and Valley"; Lectr.; AWRT (Phila. Dir., '68), Sigmas of Sigma Chi (Pres., '65), three Freedom Fndn. aws.; Phila. Normal Sch., '15–'17 (Trustee, '20–'29); Temple Univ., Univ. Pa.; b. Phila., Pa.; p. Edgar and Eva Humphries Fields; h. James A. Bovaird; c. James Alexander III; res: 8307 Crittenden St., Phila., Pa. 19118.

BOWDEN, ANN, Asst. Dir., Austin Public Library, P.O. Box 2287, Austin, Tex. 78767, '67–; Coordr. of Adult Services '65–'67; Pubcty. Dir., '66–'67; Dir., Film and Recordings, '63–'65; Academic Center Librn, Univ. of Tex., '63; Humanities Rsch. Center Librn., '60–'63; Manuscript Cataloger, '58–'60; Reference Asst., Yale Univ. Lib., '51–'53; Descriptive Cataloger, '48–'49; Asst. Prof., Univ. of Tex. Grad. Sch. of Lib. Sci., '65–'68; Lecturer, '64–'65, '69–; auth: An Exhibition of Manuscripts and First Editions of T. S. Eliot (Univ. of Tex., '61), T. E. Lawrence/Fifty Letters (Univ. of Tex., '61); Asst. Ed., Papers of the Bibliographical Society of America, '67–'68; Assoc. Ed., '68–; ALA, Bibliographical Soc. of Am.; Tex. Lib. Assn. (Chmn., Pub. Comm., '65–'71), Southwestern Lib. Assn.; Radcliffe Col., BA, '48; Columbia Univ. M.S. (Lib. Sci.), '51; b. East Orange, N.J., 1924; p. William and Ann Herrstrom Haddon; h. William B. Todd; c. Lee, Susan, Eric Bowden; res: 2424 Wooldridge Dr., Austin, Tex. 78703.

BOWER, RUTH ANN, Dir. Prom.-PR, New York Magazine, 207 E. 32nd St., N.Y., N.Y. 10016, '67–; Dir. Prom.-Pr. World Journal Tribune, '66–'67; Assoc. Dir. Prom.-PR, N.Y. Herald Tribune, '61–'66; AE, Campbell-Ewald Co., '59–'61; N.Y.U.; b. Sparta, N.J., 1924; p. Lucas and Edna Bower; res: Marlboro House, Ridgefield Park, N.J.

BOWER, TRUE GEHMAN, Sch. Librn., Board of Education, Akron, Ohio, Goodrich Jr. High School, 700 LaFollette St., Akron, Oh. 44306, '54, '58–; Cataloger, Canal Fulton Pub. Lib., '57; Tchr., Eng., Hist., Sch. Librn., Green Twsp. Bd. of Educ., '47–'53; Co-auth., "Career Novel and Biography as a Source of Occupational Information in Junior High Schools" (Oh. State Dept. of Educ., Div. of Guidance, '68); Cnslt., Monitor Craft Bks., '64–; lib. assns. and selective directories; Otterbein Col., BA, '38; Kent State Univ., '37; Case Western Reserve Univ., MS (Lib. Sci.), '53; Western Mich. Univ., '68 (Higher Educ. Act for post Master's study in Librarianship); b. Canton, Oh., 1916; p. Edwin L. and Daisy Waltz Gehman; h. Aaron R. Bower; c. A. Howard, Miriam L. Poorman; res: 8205 Wales Ave. N.W., N. Canton, Oh. 44720.

BOWERS, JANET VOAKES, Ed., The Alton Democrat, 1020 Third Ave., Alton, Ia. 51003, '67–; Reptr., Copy Ed., Chicago Tribune, '65–'67; "The Worth, Strength and Endurance of Poetry" (Sigma Tau Delta Quarterly, '65); Pi Delta Epsilon (Sec., '64–'65); Sigma Tau Delta; Mabel Corbin Jnslm. Aw., '65; Western Ill. Univ., BS, '65; (Eds. Aw., '64); b. St. Thomas, Ontario, Can., 1944; p. Robert B. and Della R. Quick Voakes; h. Frank Bowers; res: Alton, Ia. 51003.

BOWERS, MARGARETTA KELLER, Auth., "Conflict of the Clergy" (Thomas Nelson, '63); Clinical Prof. of Psych. and Supvsr. of Psychotherapy, Adelphi Univ., Garden City, N.Y., '66–; Medical Practice (Tenn.), '33–'45; Clinical Prof. of Gynecology, Meharry Med. Col. (Nashville, Tenn.), '37–'41; Journal of Pastoral Psychology: Wm. of the Month Aw.; Am. Acad. of Psycotherapists; Fellow, Am. Psychiatric Assn.; Nat. Med. Assn.; Soc. for Clinical and Experimental Hypnosis: Shirley Schneck Aw.; Organizing Chairman of the Subcommittee of the Bishops' Committee on Pastoral Counselling of the House of Bishops of the Protestant Episcopal Church, 1960–63; La. Baptist Col., BA, '32; b. Russell, Pa., 1908; p. David Henry and Ella Phillips Keller; h. (div.); c. Marie Simpkins, Margarette Wagner; res: 4 Grove St., N.Y., N.Y. 10014.

BOWERS, VIRGINIA VAN DEUSEN, Nat. Adv. Mgr., The Huntsville Times, P.O. Box 1487 (W. Station), Memorial Pkwy., S., Huntsville, Ala. 35807, '61–; Ed., General co. nwsp. tor Huntsville plant, Gen. Shoe Corp., '48–'55; Pers. Secy., '48–'55; Intl. Nwsp. Adv. Execs., Pilot Intl. (Chptr. Pres., '52–'53, '65–'66); b. Chattanooga, Tenn., 1919; p. Dr. Dewitt C. and Marguerite Crawford Van Deusen; h. Thomas E. Bowers; res: 2733 Thornton Circle, S.W., Huntsville, Ala. 35801.

BOWLING, NORVELL PAYNE, Ed., The Mead Corporation, Lower Basin, Lynchburg, Va. 24503, '50–;

Southeastern Assn. of Indsl. Eds. (Va. Dir.), Adv. Club of Lynchburg (Secy.), Lynchburg Art Club; Randolph Macon Wms. Col., BA, '40; b. Lynchburg, Va., 1919; p. William and Winifred Hek Payne; h. William Bowling; res: 4010 Summit St., Lynchburg, Va. 24503.

BOWMAN, LEONA, Ed., Fashion Newsletter, 743 Fifth Ave., N.Y., N.Y. 10021; Exec. VP, Sterling Advertising Agcy.; Fashion Ed., Wms. Wear Daily; Ed., Harper's Bazaar Intl. Fashion Nwsltr.; h. Sidney Hill.

BOWMAN, SYLVIA E., Prof. of Eng., Indiana University, Ft. Wayne, Ind. 46805, '64–; Assoc. Prof., '64; Asst. Prof., '53–'59; Instr., '47–'53; Auth: "Edward Bellamy: An American Prophet's Influence" (Twayne, '62), "The Year 2000: A Critical Biography of Edward Bellamy" (Twayne, '58), articles, pamphlets; Ed., four series of bks. on literature; AAUP, Modern Lang. Assn., AAUW, Am. Acad. of Polit. and Social Sci.; Who's Who of Am. Wm., Dic. of Intl. Biog., 2,000 Wm. of Achiev., Dic. Eng. & Am. Auths.; other cits.; Central Normal Col., BS (Eng., Hist.), '39; Univ. of Chgo., MA (Eng.), '43; Univ. of Paris, PhD, '52 (summa cum laude); b. Boone County, Ind., 1914; p. Clarence and Alice Smith Bowman; res: P.O. Box 5205, Ft. Wayne, Ind. 46805.

BOWSER, BETTY ANN, Polit./Norfolk Corr., Radio-TV News, WTAR, 720 Boush St., Norfolk, Va. 23510 '69–; Night News Dir., News Anchorman, WAVT-TV (Portsmouth), '68–'69; Reptr., '67–'68; Reptr., Cleve., Ohio Press '67; Norfolk C. of C. (Outstanding Young Wm. of '68); Outstanding Young Wm. of Am.; Oh. Wesleyan Univ., BA (Eng.-Jnslm.), '66; b. Norfolk, Va., 1944; p. John and Elizabeth Martin Bowser; res: 530 Mowbray, Norfolk, Va. 23510.

BOYCE, DOROTHY MacAULAY, Feature Wtr., The Anderson Herald, P.O. Box 1090, 1133 Jackson St., Anderson, Ind. 46015, '69–; Wms. Ed., '53–'68; Ed., Indiana Civil Defender magazine, '69; Wms. Press Club (Pres., '56–'58; aws., '26, '65), NFPW, Theta Sigma Phi; Ind. Univ. photog. aws., '64, '69; b. Detroit, Mich., 1905; p. Murdock and Laura Klare MacAulay; h. Col. Lloyd L. Boyce; c. Beverly (Mrs. Donald Hamilton), Richard M. Buerger; res: 908 Longfellow Rd., Anderson, Ind. 46011.

BOYCE, MYRTLE BAGWELL, Instructional Coordr., KLRN-TV, P.O. Box 7158, University of Texas, Austin, Tex. 78712, '68–; Asst. Instructional Coordr., '65–'68; Classroom Tchr., 21 yrs.; Auth., "Sand in My Hand" ('65); Prodr., TV series, "Trends in Education," '67–'68; Exec. Prodr., "Science, a Process Approach," '69; AAUW, NAEB, several educ. orgs.; Theta Sigma Phi Wtrs. Roundup Aw., '66; Sam Houston State Tchrs. Col., BS, '47 (Alpha Chi scholarship); Univ. of Tex., MEd, '49; b. Trinity County, Tex., 1915; p. Levi W. and Evaline V. Fussell Bagwell; h. Floyd Boyce; c. Mrs. Janice Leah Palmer; res: 3316 Pecos, Austin, Tex. 78703.

BOYD, ALDA LEE, Pubcty. Dir., Seabury Press, 815 Second Ave., N.Y., N.Y. 10017, '66–; Juvenile Pubcty. Dir., David McKay Co., '63–'66; Pubcty. Dir., Abelard-Schuman, '61–'63; J. Walter Thompson, '60–'61; Fund Raiser, Church World Soc. and March of Dimes, '58–'60; On-air Prom. Wtr., WCBS-Radio, '54–'58; Prom. Wtr., WSIX-Radio (Nashville, Tenn.), '50–'54; Wms. Nat. Bk. Assn., Children's Bk. Cncl., Publr's. Lib. Prom. Group (Treas., '68; Advisory Comm., '67, '69), ALA; George Peabody Col. (Nashville), '48–'50; res: 71 Barrow St., N.Y., N.Y. 10014.

BOYD, ALICE FRAZIER, Wms. Ed., Sweetwater Reporter, 119 W. Third St., Sweetwater, Tex. 79556, '50–; Wms. Forum of Nolan County, BPW, Nolan County Hist. Soc.; Tex. State Tchrs. Assn. aw., '68–'69; b. Dunkirk, N.Y., 1918; p. Wesley and Birthal Hatley Frazier; h. G. Herschel Boyd; c. Charles Wesley Scott, Billy Roy Scott, Ivan M. Scott, Jr., Mrs. Barry Hendricks; res: 506 W. Arizona St., Sweetwater, Tex. 99556.

BOYD, BETTY CARMAN, On-Air Bdcstr., Public Svc. Dir., KTUL-TV, Box 9697, Tulsa, Okla. 74107, '65–; Wms. Dir.-Bdcstr., KOTV, '55–'65; Tchr., teen fashion and charm sch.; AWRT (Tulsa Chptr. Bd. Mbr.; Golden Mike Aw., '68), Pi Delta Epsilon; Hon. Air Force Recruiter; active in numerous civic groups; Univ. of Tulsa; Ia. State Univ.; b. Tulsa, Okla., 1924; p. Theodore and Marie Fairchild Carman; h. William Wray Boyd; c. Beverlie (Mrs. Barry L. Bryant), Barry Wray; res: 746 N. Xenophon, Tulsa, Okla. 74127.

BOYD, MAMIE, Assoc. Ed., Jewell County Record, 111 E. Main, Mankato, Kan. 66956; Reptr., Colmst., Co-publr., '45–; NFPW (Charter Mbr., Life Mbr., Rec. Secy.; Reg. VP; Emma Kinney Memorial Aw., '66), Kan. Press Assn. (past Pres., hon life Pres.), Kan. Edtl. Assn. (hon. Pres.), NW Press Assn. (hon. Pres.), Kan. Auths. Club (past Pres); past ed: First Flight, Kan. Clubwoman, Kansas Press Woman; BPW (past Pres., 6th Dist. Dir.), various state bds. and commns., civic orgs.; William Allen White Journalistic Merit Aw., '66; Kan. State Univ., (Manhattan, Kan.), BS, '02; b. Near Humboldt, Kan., 1876; p. Joseph McDill and Hester Scott Alexander; h. Frank W. Boyd; c. McDill George, Frank William; res: 409 S. Center, Mankato, Kan. 66956.

BOYD, JUDY, Home Econst., North Carolina Egg Marketing Assn., P.O. Box 6533, 2006 Fairview Rd., Raleigh, N.C. 27608, '64–; Am. Home Econ. Assn., Home Econsts. in Bus., AWRT (VP, N.C. Chptr.); E. Carolina Univ., BS; b. Charlotte, N.C., 1943; p. Ralph and Maxine Bobbitt Sikes; res: 805 Holt Dr., Raleigh, N.C. 27608.

BOYD, MILDRED WORTHY, Wtr. non-fiction; Designer, electronics, Hercules, Inc., '62–'68; Sperry Utah, '60–'62; Designer, Convair (Fort Worth Div.), '54–'60; Auth: "History in Harness," ('65), "Black Flags & Pieces of Eight," ('65), "The Silent Cities," ('67), two other bks.; holder: U.S. patent Electrical (coaxial) connector: Tex. Christian Univ., '54–'59; Univ. of Ut., Ext. Div., '60–'61; b. Ranger, Tex. 1921; p. James and Gladys Meek Worthy Sr.; h. C. W. Boyd (div.); c. Kathy Easley, Elizabeth Drummond, Judy Jenson; res: No. 33, 5199 Kearny Villa Rd., San Diego, Cal. 92123.

BOYD, SYDNEY WILSON, PR Cnslt.; PR Dir., The Leake and Watts Children's Home, Inc., '57–'67; PR Rep., PR News, 10th Anniversary Year, '53–'54; PR Dir., The Gunnery Centennial and Second Development Program, '50–'52; PR Dir., Memorial Cancer Ctr., '45–'50; PRSA, '50–; Comm. on Wm. in PR (Chmn., '62–'64); Mothers Comm. Inc. (Bd. Mbr., '68); Nat. Inst. Social Scis., '59–; Hon. Life Mbr. Bd. West Side Day Nursery, '62; Hon. Mem. Gunnery Alumni Assn. '65; Nat. Cncl. of Wm., U.S.; English Speaking Union; Who's Who of Am. Wm.; Who's Who in the East; b. Phila., Pa.; p. Joseph R. and Cora Shaw Wilson; h. Francis T. Boyd; res: 428 East 84th St., N.Y. 10028, and Washington, Conn. 06793.

BOYER, MARTHA M., Faculty Mgr., KCLC-AM, KCLC-FM, Lindenwood Col., St. Charles, Mo. 43301, '46–; developed commtns. program: bdcst., theater, film; Area Consortium of Cols. (Comm. on Multimedia), Mo. Speech Assn. (past Pres.), Assn. for Pfsnl. Bdcst. Educ., Nat. Assn. of Educ. Bdcstrs., AWRT; Maryville (Tenn.) Col., BA (cum laude) Univ. of Wis., MA, '37; study at BBC, London; res: 3339 Claxtonhill Dr., Bridgeton, Mo. 63042.

BOYES, ARDITH DUCKWORTH, Sls. Rep., KYOU and KGRE-FM Radio, 816 Ninth St., Greeley, Colo. 80631, '65–; Traf. Dir., KCOL Radio (Ft. Collins), '67–; Traf. Dir., KYOU, '58–'59; AWRT; b. Wray, Colo.; p. Lebearne and Ella Shively Duckworth; c. Valorie Christine, Stanley; res: 807 31st Ave., Greeley, Colo. 80631.

BOYKA, LOUISE JOHNSEN, Wtr., Ed., Publicist, Milady Publishing, 3839 White Plains Rd., Bronx, N.Y. 10467, '66–; Theatre Reviewer, Schenectady Gazette, 413 State St., Schenectady, N.Y., 12305; '56–; Wtr., Prodr., Hostess for wms. educ. TV series, fashion shows and beauty pageants; Wms. Press Club of N.Y. State; Am. Theater League; Skidmore Col., '39–'41; Union Col., '42–'43; b. Lake Luzerne, N.Y.; p. George and Zillah Ives Johnsen; h. Walter Boyka; c. Lawrence Michael, Christine Elaine, Stephen Walter; res: 148 Marriott Ave., Schenectady, N.Y. 12304.

BOYLE, KAY, (Baroness von und zu Franckenstein) Prof., San Francisco State College, 1600 Holloway Ave., S.F., Cal. 94117, '63–; Auth., 30 books; Nat. Inst. of Arts and Letters; O. Henry Aw., '34–'41; Guggenheim Fellowship, '34, '61; b. St. Paul , Minn., 1903; p. Howard and Katherine Evans Boyle; h. (dec.); c. Mrs. Sharon Brault, Mrs. Apple Goeser, Mrs. Faith Gude, Mrs. Kathe Kuhn, Mrs. Clover Rosenblum, Ian von Franckenstein; mail: c/o A. Watkins, 77 Park Ave., N.Y., N.Y. 10016.

BOYVEY, MARY O'NEILL, Media Program Dir., Tex. State Dept. of Educ., 11th and Brazos Sts., Austin, Tex. 78711, '65–; Lib. Cnslt., '63–'65; Media Ctr. Librn., '53–'63; HS Librn., '43–'53; Tex. Assn. of Sch. Librns. (Pres., '54), Tex. Lib. Assn., ALA, Tex. Assn. of Educ. Tech., DAVI, Assn. for Supervision and Curriculum Dev.; Tex. Wms. Univ., BA, '40; Univ. of Tex., MA, '45; PhD, '69; Univ. of Chgo., MA (Lib. Sci.), '56; b. Ft. Worth, Tex., 1920; p. James and Elizabeth Conway O'Neill; h. R. R. Boyvey; res: 505 W. Seventh St., Austin, Tex. 78701.

BRACHER, MARJORY SCHOLL, Free-lance Wtr., Auth: "SRO—Overpopulation and You" ('66), "Love is No Luxury"; four religious books; Wittenberg Univ., BA, '28; b. Connersville, Ind., 1906; p. J. Edgar and Grace Hill Scholl; h. Edwin Bracher; c. Peter S. Bracher, Alice E. Smith; res: 1998 Colony Dr., Toledo, Oh. 43614.

BRACKEN, HARRIET OELGOETZ, Dir. PR, The Huntington National Bank, 17 S. High St., Columbus, Oh. 43126, '66–; Free-lance, F & R Lazarus & Co., and The Huntington National Bank, '57–'65; Adv. Mgr., Ed. house organ, and various positions, F. & R. Lazarus & Co., '51–'57, '42–'47; PRSA, Columbus Adv. Club, Gamma Alpha Chi (Hon. Mbr., '56); Franklin County Child Welfare (PR Comm.), Central Oh. Heart Assn. (PR Comm.); named outstanding professional bus. wm. by Soroptimist, '66; Oh. State Univ., BS, '41; b. Columbus, Oh.; p. Joseph and Ida Kauderer Oelgoetz; h. George F. Bracken; c. Carol Lee, Drew J., res: 1430 Zollinger Rd., Columbus, Oh. 43221.

BRACKETT, LEIGH DOUGLAS, Free-lance Novelist, Short Story Wtr., '40–; approximately 20 novels, numerous short stories; Screen Wtr., '43–; screen credits incl: "The Big Sleep," "Rio Bravo," "El Dorado"; WGA, Auths. League, SFWA, WWA (Golden Spur, Best Western Novel, "Follow the Free Wind," '64); Jules Verne Fantasy Aw., '56; Nova Aw. for contrb. to sci. fantasy, '69; b. L.A., Cal., 1915; p. William and Margaret Douglass Brackett; h. Edmond Hamilton; res: R.D. 2, Kinsman, Oh. 44428.

BRACKMAN, HENRIETTA, Wtr., Photog. Agt., Owner, Henrietta Brackman Assoc., 415 E. 52nd St., N.Y., N.Y. 10022, '53–; Corr., Time-Life (Haiti, W.I.), '56–'57; Corr., Women's Wear Daily (Houston, Tex.), '40s; Ed., Retail Mdsng. Svc., New York Herald Tribune, '40–'43; OPC, Am. Soc. of Mag. Photogrs., Soc. of Photogrs. and Artists Reps.; Oh. State Univ.; b. N.Y.C., 1917; p. Jacob and Rosa Bernheimer Brackman; res: 415 E. 52nd St., N.Y., N.Y. 10022.

BRACKWINKLE, HILDA LOUISE, Secondary Sch. Librn., S. Newton Sch. Corp., R. R. 1, Kentland, Indiana 47951, '66–'70; HS Tch., various schs. (Ind., Ill.), '37–'53; Tch.-Librn., various Ind. schs., '54–'66; article, Builders mag.; Ind. State Tch. Assn., NEA, ALA, Ind. Sch. Librns. Assn. (Secy.), Univ. of Evansville, BA (Tau Kappa Alpha), '37; Ind. State Univ., MS, '61; b. Elberfield, Ind., 1915; p. John and Matilda Georges Brackwinkle; res: Box 216, Brook, Ind. 47922.

BRADBURY, BIANCA RYLEY, Auth: "The Curious Wine" ('48), 13 teenage novels, 10 juv. boys' bks.; Auths. League of Am.; Conn. Col. for Wm., BA, '30; b. Mystic, Conn., 1908; p. Thomas and Blanche Keigwin Ryley; h. Harry B. Bradbury; c. William Wyatt, Michael Ryley; res: Merryall Dist., New Milford, Conn. 06776.

BRADFORD, ALICE VIRGINIA, CDR, USN, Asst. for Wm., Fifth Naval District, United States Navy, Hq., Fifth Naval Dist., Norfolk, Va. 23511, '69–; Chief of Instr., Radio-TV Dept., Defense Info. Sch. (Ft. Harrison, Ind.), '65–'68; Offcr. in Charge, Armed Forces Radio, TV Stas. (Keflavik, Iceland), '64–'65; Projects Coordr., Defense Advisory Comm. on Wm. in the Svc. (Pentagon, Wash.), '60–'63; prepared radio-TV materials, prod. films; Wtr., bklets; AWRT (Hoosier Chptr. Rec. Secy., '67–'68), 2,000 Wm. of Achiev., numerous others; Georgia Col., BA (Eng.), '49; Boston Univ. Sch. of Public Commtn., MS (PR), '64; b. Atlanta, Ga., 1929; p. Lacy and Alice Young Bradford; res: 729 Stanwix Sq., Norfolk, Va. 23502.

BRADFORD, BARBARA TAYLOR, Ed.-in-Chief, Guide to Home Decorating Ideas, Synd. colmst., Newsday Specials (Garden City, L.I.), 415 E. 53rd St., N.Y., N.Y. 10022, '66–; Ed., Nat. Design Ctr., '64–'65; Features Ed., Woman Magazine, '62–'64; Exec. Ed., London Am., '59–'62; Colmst., London Evening News, '55–'57; Fashion Ed., Wms. Own, '53–'54; Wms. Ed., Yorkshire Evening Post, '51–'53; Reptr., '49–'51; synd. colmst. of "Designing Woman," '68; Auth: "How to be the Perfect Wife" (Simon & Schuster, '69), "A Garland of Children's Verse" (Lion Press, '68), "Complete Encyclopedia of Homemaking Ideas" (Meredith Press, '68), "Dictionary of 1001 Famous People" (Lion Press, '66), and numerous children's bks. NHFL, Auths. Guild, Nat. Soc. of Interior Designers, (Distg. Edtl. Aw., '69), Royal Soc. of Arts; b. Leeds, Eng., 1933; p. Winston and Freda Walker Taylor; h. Robert Bradford; res: 2 E. 86th St., N.Y., N.Y. 10028.

BRADLEY, DOROTHA HUTCHESON, Publr. and Ed., Brador Publications, Inc., 36 Main St., Livonia, N.Y. 14487, '62–; Coord. Ed., Empire State Architect Magazine, '58–'62; PR, Civic Music Assn. (Rochester, N.Y.), '55–'58; N.Y. Press Assn., Western N.Y. Press Assn. (Bd. of Dir., '67–'69), VP, '69); Syracuse (N.Y. Univ.; b. Newark, N.Y., 1905; p. Hermon and Myrta Eggleston Hutcheson; h. Frederic I. Bradley (dec.); c. Douglas, Richard, Barbara Bloomer; res: R.D. #2, Livonia, N.Y. 14487.

BRADLEY, JOY STEWART, Cnslr., Hillsborough Junior College, P.O. Box 1213, Tampa, Fla. 33601, '68–; Tchr., Drama, Eng., Jnlsm., '64–'67; Free-lance Wtr.; NEA, Fla. Educ. Assn., Hillsborough County Educ. Assn., Theta Sigma Phi; Pa. State Univ., BA (Jnlsm.), '50; Univ. of S. Fla., MA (Cnsl.), '68; b. Phila., Pa., 1929;

p. Samuel J. and Lillian Herbert Stewart; h. (div.); c. Thomas G., Randall S.; res: 7583 17th Ave. N., St. Petersburg, Fla. 33710.

BRADLEY, MARTHA NYE, Ed., Owner, Waterfront, 100 N. Main, Lake City, Mich. 49651, '57–; started nwsp. with husband, '57; Missaukee Repl., Marshall Evening Chronicle, Lake Odessa Wave; C. of C. (Pres., Secy., Treas.; Mbr. of Month Aw., '66), County C. of C. (Secy.), County Repl. Comm. (Secy.); Albion Col., '44–'46; b. Grand Rapids, Mich., 1926; p. Alton L. and Beulah Myers Nye; h. Ross Bradley; c. Richard Alton, Ross Jay; res: 100-1/2 N. Main, Lake City, Mich. 49651.

BRADLEY, VERDELLE VANDERHORST, Librn., Dir. of Audio-Visuals Dept., Virginia Union University, 1500 N. Lombardy St., Richmond, Va. 23220, '46–; Educ. Dept., Newark Public Lib., '44–'46; Barber-Scotia Jr. Col., '42–'44; Evaluation Team, Southern Assn. of Cols. and Schs.; Lib. Cnslt: Stillman Col., '68; Bethune Cookman Col., '69; ALA, Va. Lib. Assn.; Fla. A&M Univ., AB, '41; Atlanta Col., BS (Lib. Sci.), '42; Columbia Univ., MS, '60; b. Jacksonville, Fla.; p. Byron and Isolene Whittington Vanderhorst; h. Walter Bradley; c. Walter, Jr.; res: 1213 Corey Ave., Richmond, Va. 23220.

BRADY, ADELAIDE B., Dir., Public Affairs Div., Girl Scouts of the USA, 830 Third Ave., N.Y., N.Y. 10022, '68–; Dir., Relationships Div., '59–'68; Dir. Group Relations, Save the Children Fedn., '56–'59; Pres., Communication Cnslrs., Inc., '52–'65; PR Dir., Papagallo, Inc., '54–'56; Co-owner, Intl. PR Cnslrs., '65–'69; Wtr., Free-lance Photog., Contrbr. nat. pubns.; PRSA, NSPRA, Am. Mgt. Assn., RPRC, Assn. Exhibitors, NEA, BPW, Am. Legion Aux. (Cit., 38th Nat. Conv.); Boston Univ., BS, '46; b. N.Y.C., 1926; p. Earl Victor and Audrey Calvert Burks; c. James F. Brady, III; res: 52-40 39th Dr., Woodside, N.Y. 11377.

BRADY, BARBARA ROSEWATER, Jnlsm. Instr., Judson College, 1151 N. State St., Elgin, Ill. 60120, '69–; Reptr., Omaha World-Herald, '44; Fashion Ed., Chgo. Daily News, '41–'43; European Youth series, David C. Cook Publ. Co., '55; numerous mag. articles; Commentator, "Meet the Churches," WRMN (Elgin, Ill.), '50–'51; Theta Sigma Phi, AAUW, civic groups; Elgin Altrusa Woman of the Yr., '68; Who's Who of Am. Wm.; Who's Who in the Midwest; Dic. of Intl. Biog.; Univ. of Neb., BA, '39; b. Omaha, Neb., 1918; p. Stanley M. and Barbara H. McAlvay Rosewater; h. William Webb Brady; c. Barbara Leslie (Mrs. Richard Kent Karchmer), Nancy W., Katherine Anne, Margaret Louise; res: 332 Vincent Pl., Elgin, Ill. 60120.

BRADY, TONI ZIFF, Pres., WABY, Eastern New York Broadcasting Corp., 80 Braintree St., Albany, N.Y., 12205, '69–; Station Mgr., Gen. Mgr., '60–; Prog. Dir., '52–'60; Wms. Prog. Dir., '50–'52; Record Librn., '49–'50; Tri-City Adv. Club; George Wash. Univ., '43–'45; b. Beaufort, S.C., 1924; p. William and Amelia

Morton Ziff; h. Dirk Brady; res: Birch Hill Rd., Lou-donville, N.Y. 12211.

BRAINERD, DOROTHY MADGE, Food Ed., St. Louis Post-Dispatch, 1133 Franklin Ave., St. Louis, Mo. 63101, '52–; Homefurnishings Ed., '58–'69; Travel Ed., '52–'58; Feature Wtr., '49–'52; Secy. to Feature Ed., '44–'49; Theta Sigma Phi, Wms. Adv. Club of St. Louis (Wm. of the Yr., '64), Mo. Press Wm. (numerous aws., '64–), NFPW (several aws.); Vesta aws., Am. Meat Inst., '63, '64, '68; Univ. of Mo.; b. St. Louis, Mo.; p. Louis S. and Madge Kennett Brainerd; res: 7608 Carswold Dr., Clayton, Mo. 63105.

BRAMBLE, ANNABELLE FURMAN, Asst. Dir., Princeton Public Library, 65 Witherspoon, Princeton, N.Y. 08540, '65–; h. Geoffrey Bramble.

BRAMBLETT, LOUISE GINN, Mgr., Candy Dept., Wil-Kin Theatre Supply, Inc., 301 North Ave., N.E., Atlanta, Ga. 30308; Wm. of the Motion Pic. Industry (Atlanta Pres., '66–'67; Wm. of the Yr., '66), Quota Club of Atlanta (Pres., '63, '65; Quotarian of the Yr., '65), Variety Club Wm. (Tent 21 VP, '66); Southern Bus. Univ.; b. Greensboro, Ga., 1909; p. Zelic and Lula Porterfield Ginn; h. James Bramblett (dec.); c. James S., Jr. (dec.), Robin Louise; res: 2526 Fontaine Circle, Decatur, Ga. 30032.

BRANCHOR, RUTH, Crtv. Supvsr., The Griswold-Eshleman Company, 625 Madison Ave., N.Y., N.Y. 10022; Copy Supvsr., West, Weir, Bartel; Copy Group Head, Mogul, Baker, Bryne & Weiss; Auth., two chil-dren's bks.; AWNY, Fashion Group; Assoc. Bus. Pubns. aw., '60; Natl. Visual Presentation Assn. aw., '66; Columbia Univ., BA, '44; Queens Col. '69; b. N.Y.C., 1925; p. Samuel and Bertha Goldzweig-Bran-chor; h. Oscar Brotman; c. Elizabeth Ann, Barbara Louise; res: 15-78 212 St., Bayside, N.Y. 11360.

BRAND, EILEEN STRAWN, Ed., Lyle Stuart, Inc., 239 Park Ave. S., N.Y., N.Y. 10003, '59–; h. (div.).

BRAND, JEANNE L., Chief, Pubns., Translations Div., Extramural Programs, National Library of Medi-cine, 8600 Rockville Pike, Bethesda, Md. 20014; Scien-tist Admr., Nat. Inst. of Mental Health, '62–'67; Med. Rsch. Programs Specialist, '56–'60; Exec. Secy., Hist. of Med. Study Sec., NIH, '60–'62; Rsch. Asst. to Pres., Carnegie Corp. (N.Y.C.), '56; Assoc. Histrn., Nat. Fndn. for Infantile Paralysis, '53–'56; Docs. Offcr., U.S. Mission to UN, '46–'49; Hist. Offcr., Lt. (j.g.) U.S. Navy (Wash., D.C.), '45–'46; Offcr. Censor (Ensign), '43–'45; bks. incl. "Doctors and the State: The British Medical Profession and Government Action in Public Health, 1870–1912," (Johns Hopkins Press, '65) Co-ed "Psy-chiatry and Its History" (Charles Thomas, '69); Ful-bright Scholar; St. Lawrence Univ., BA, '41 (magna cum laude; hons. in hist.); Univ. of Rochester, MA, '42 (AAUW Fellow); Radcliffe Col., '42–'43 (Eugenie Emerson Fellow, Hist.); Univ. of London (Eng.), Ph.D.

(Modern Social, Econ. Hist.), '53 (Leverhulme Scholar).

BRAND, WINIFRED, Free-lance Wtr., pubcty. and house organs; Public Info. Dir., Mich. Cancer Fndn., '57–'68; PR, Great Lakes Steel Corp., '49–'57; reprtr., ed., Detroit nwsps., 15 yrs.; auth., two poetry collec-tions; Wayne State Univ., two yrs.; res: 6140 Horger, Dearborn, Mich. 48126.

BRANDENBERGER, JANE HARRIS, Info. Coordr., The University of Texas M.D. Anderson Hospital & Tumor Institute at Houston, Tex., Medical Center, Houston, Tex. 77025, '67–; PR Dir., YMCA of Houston, '63–'67; PR Assoc., Un. Fund, '60–'62; Ed., nat. indsl. mags.; R. L. Minns & Assoc., '59–'60; TV Prodr. Dir., Travis County Med. Soc., '55–'56; Continuity Dir., KONO-TV, '51–'55; Tchr., Tex. public schs., '50–'59; Lectr., Jnlsm. and PR, Univ. of Tex., Tex. Southern Univ.; Wtr.-Prodr. of numerous doc. films; PRSA, Theta Sigma Phi (Pres., '66–'67); Who's Who Of Am. Wm., '68; Rotary Intl. Fellow, '56–'57; Who's Who Among Am. Students, '50; Trinity Univ. of San Anto-nio, BA, '50; The Univ. of Tex. at Austin, MJ, '56 (hon grad); Inst. of Intl. Studies and Univ. of Geneva, Swit-zerland, '56–'57; b. San Antonio, Tex., 1931; p. William and Alda Mae Calhoun Harris; c. Joel Harris; res: 2418 Wordsworth, Houston, Tex. 77025.

BRANDON, FRANCES SWEENEY, Juv. Auth.; Instr., Middle Tennessee State University, Tennessee Blvd., Murfreesboro, Tenn. 37130, '69–; bks: "Raise the Rockhound" (Abingdon, '63), "Lonnie and the Flicker Family" (Macmillan, '68); Instr., Miss. State Col. for Wm., '64–'68; Tchr., Public Schs. (Nashville, Tenn.), '40–'62; Wtr., Educ. TV; NEA, AAUW; Tenn. Educ. Assn. aw., '65; Middle Tenn. State Univ., BS, '39; George Peabody Col., MA, '61; b. Nashville, Tenn., 1916; p. Howell and Eustacia Ellis Sweeney; h. Charles Morris Brandon; c. Stacia Ruth, Carl Morris; res: Muskrat Bend Farm, Christiana, Tenn. 37037.

BRANDT, DOROTHY MATTESON, Owner, Reviews on File, 46 Delaware St., Walton, N.Y. 13856, '46–; Staff, Literary Clipping Svc., '36–'46; b. N.Y.C., 1897; p. George and Estelle Conover Matteson; h. Neill Brandt (dec.); c. Neill M., George S., Dorothy M. Swanson.

BRANDVIG, MARY BURNS, Free-lance wtr., Jnlst.; Southern Cal. Corr., New Zealand Herald, Synd. World Trade Press; Wms. Ed., San Pedro News Pilot, '60–'69; Religion and Soc. Ed., South Bay Daily Breeze, '54–'59; Theta Sigma Phi., Cal. Press Wm. (1st place, pgs. regularly edited by wm., '63, '64); Am. Home Laundry Assn. Ahlma Aw., '59, '62, '66; Wm. of the Yr., San Pedro C. of C. Wms. Div., '64; Hon. PTA Life Mbrshp.; Copley Merit Aw., '67; Fresno State Col., '34–'35; b. Sanger, Cal., 1916; p. Archibald and Annie Overholt Burns; h. Erling Milton Brandvig (dec.); c. James M.; res: 853 Eighth St., Manhattan Beach, Cal. 90266.

BRANDWYNNE, JACQUELINE, Pres., Chief Exec. Offcr., Jacqueline Brandwynne Associates, Advertising Subsidiary of Benton & Bowles, 909 Third Avenue, N.Y., N.Y. 10022; '65–'69; VP, Crtv. Dir., Yardley of London, '63–'65: Beauty, Prom. Ed., Ingenue '62–'63: Free-lance Wtr., '59–'62; Dir., Intl. Prom., Helena Rubinstein, '56–'59; Reptr., Weltwoche (Zuerich, Switzerland); articles in Cosmopolitan, Harper's Bazaar, Vogue, Annabelle; pop music; Fashion Group; Cosmetics Fair aw., '68; hon. mention, TV commls., Univ. of Zuerich; New Sch. of Social Rsch.; b. Bienne, Switzerland, 1937; h. Jacqueline B. Brandwynne; res: 38 E. 63rd St., N.Y., N.Y. 10021.

BRANHAM, SALLY CRESWELL, Asst. Ed., The Tennessee Banker, Tennessee Bankers Asssociation, Life & Casualty Tower, Nashville, Tenn. 37219, '66–; Middle Tenn. Bus Press Club, ICIE; Washington Univ., St. Louis, '58–'60; Cumberland Col., Lebanon, Tenn., '64; b. Lebanon, Tenn., 1940; p. Robert and Nelda Graham Askew; h. John Branham; c. Lisa, Mark; res: 97 White Bridge Rd., Nashville, Tenn. 37205.

BRANIN, JEANNETTE WELLMAN, Club Ed., The San Diego Union, 940 Third Ave., San Diego, Cal. 92109, '68–; Wms. Ed., The San Diego Independent, '53–'68; Co-owner, The Branin Public Relations Agcy., '48–'53; Dir., Pubcty. Dept., San Diego C. of C. and San Diego Chptr., Am. Red Cross Blood Donor Ctr., '46–'48; TV Prodr., Hostess, "The Independent Woman," '55–'57; motion pic. scripts incl: "The Dream and the Reality" (San Diego YMCA, '50), "The Least of These" (San Diego Humane Soc., '51); Cal. Press Wm. (Wm. of the Yr., '64–'67), NFPW, Theta Sigma Phi, Alpha Iota; Univ. of Kan., BA, '29; b. Sterling, Kan., 1909; p. Edward C. and Jessie C. Coyle Wellman; h. Patrick Branin; c. Patrick C.; res: 4957 Pacifica Dr., San Diego, Cal. 92109.

BRANSTETTER, EVELYN HUESTIS, Command Librn., U.S. Air Force Systems Command, Hq. AFSC, Andrews Air Force Base, Wash., D.C. 20331, '67–; Librn., '64–'67; Command Librn., USAF Southern Command, '51–'64; Librn., Instr., Canal Zone Col., '44–'51; Instr., Univ. of Neb. Tchrs. Col., '42–'43; ALA, Special Libs. Assn., Intl. Platform Assn.; Univ. of Neb., BS (Educ.), '32; Univ. of Denver, MA (Librnship.), '57; b. Lincoln, Neb., 1911; p. William and Anne Darnell Huestis; h. Neil V. Branstetter; c. Margaret Anne; res: 7447 Gwynndale Dr., Clinton, Md. 20735.

BRANSTON, VIRGINIA MARDIS, Mgr., Swedenborg Foundation, Inc., 139 E. 23rd St., N.Y., N.Y. 10010, '62–; Accountant-Mgr., Marconi Instruments, '50–'62; Off. Mgr., Baumann Co., '44–'50; N.Y.C. Cncl. of Churches (Secy., Radio-TV Dept.), Swedenborg Publ. Assn. (Secy.), New Church Press (Treas.), WNBA; Hunter Col., BA, '48; grad. studies, Bernard Baruch Sch. of Bus. Admin.; b. Cleveland, Oh.; p. Andrew and Appolonnia Zelaska Grzanka; h. Arthur Branston (div.); four children; res: 330 E. 84th St., N.Y., N.Y. 10028.

BRASS, CHARLOTTE KNIAGER, Prom., PR Exec., Owner, Gemini Ind., 116 W. Broadway, Glendale, Cal., '68–; VP, Adm. Pubcty., Shelbar Industries, '66–'68; Contract Vinyl Cnslt., General Tire & Rubber Co., '62–'66; Gen. Mgr., Caliquilt Furn. Corp., '54–'62; Owner, Riviera Sofa Bed. Co. Sta. Monica, Culver City (franchise), '55–'59; Adv. Mgr., Secy. Bd. of Dir., Fedco, Inc., '51–'55; NHFL of S. Cal. (VP, '67); Boston Univ., Valley Col., San Fernando Valley State, U.C.L.A.; b. Manchester, N.H., 1924; p. Max and Frances Cream Kniager; h. Martin Brass; c. Robert Alan; res: 4229 Nogales Dr., Tarzana, Cal. 91356.

BRATEK, RUTH BRIGGS, Asst. Prof., University of Missouri, School of Journalism, Room 138A, Columbia, Mo. 65201, '56–; Asst. Adv. Mgr., Macon (Mo.) Chronicle-Herald '48–'49; Adv. Bus. Mgr., West Plains (Mo.) Daily Quill, '47; Display Adv. Rep., St. Joseph (Mo.) News, '45–'46; Mid-Mo. Press Club, Gamma Alpha Chi; Univ. of Mo., BJ, '45; MA, '64; b. Shawnee, Okla., 1923; p. Frank and Catherine Shull Briggs; h. (div.); c. Catherine Joanne; res: 401 Leslie Ct., Columbia, Mo. 65201.

BRATEL, BARBARA RIGGINS, Home Econ., Foods Ed., The Cleveland Press, 901 Lakeside Ave., Cleve., Oh. 44114, '67–; Asst. Food Ed., '65–'67; Home Svc. Rep., E. Ohio Gas Co.; Reg. Home Econst., E.I. Dupont; Reg. Home Econst., Honeywell; Am. Home Econ. Assn., Home Econ. in Bus., Oh. Nwsp. Wms. Assn.; Kent State Univ., BS, '56; b. Akron, Oh., 1934; p. Claude and Carrie Poling Riggins; res: 32 Trenton Sq., Euclid, Oh. 44143.

BRATTAIN, MARI, Media Dir., Kraft, Smith & Lowe, Inc., 1108 Tower Bldg., Seattle, Wash. 98101, '65–; AE, Beaumont & Hohman, '37–'64; Cont. Dir., KOL, '32–'37; Theta Sigma Phi (Seattle Chptr. Past Pres.); Univ. of Wash., BA (Jnlsm.); b. Spokane, Wash., 1909; p. Ross and Ottilie Houser Brattain; res: 4011 E. Mercer Way, Mercer Island, Wash. 98040.

BRAUDY, SUSAN ORR, Free-lance Wtr., '67–; Assoc. Ed., Contrb. Ed., The New Journal, Yale Univ.; articles in New York mag., McCall's, New York Times, American Home, others; Bryn Mawr Col., BA, '63; b. Phila., Pa., 1941; p. Bernard and Blanche Malin Orr; h. Leo Braudy; res: 350 Central Park W., N.Y., N.Y. 10025.

BRAUN, EUNICE ROCKSPEIER, Mng. Dir., Baha'i Publishing Trust, 110 Linden Ave., Wilmette, Ill. 60091, '55–; Bus. Mgr., '52–'55; Intl. Ed., Baha'i News, '52–; Free-lance Wtr., '47–'52; Auth: "Know Your Baha'i Literature," "Dawn of World Peace," "Call to the Nations;" Wms. Nat. Bk. Assn., Chgo. Bk. Clinic, NLAPW, Intl. Platform Assn.; Coe Col., '37–'39, Northwestern Univ., '44–'47; b. Alta Vista, Ia.; p. George and Lydia Reinhart Hockspeier; h. Leonard Braun; res: 1025 Forestview Lane, Glenview, Ill. 60025.

BRAUN, MARCELLA CARLSON, Dir. of Mktg. Svcs., Olsten's of Chicago, Inc., 22 W. Madison St., Chgo., Ill.

60602, '69–; Wms. Program Dir., Asst. Program Mgr., WFLD-TV (Field Commtns. Corp.), '65–'69; Wtr., Asst. Prod., Public Svc. Dir., Dir. of Bdcst. Standards and Practices, ABC, '46–'65; Exec. Planning Bd. Comm., '53–'65; NATAS (Treas.), '63–'65; Bd. Mbr., '60–'69), AWRT; b. Chgo., Ill., 1928; h. Clifford Braun; res: 168 Briarwood N., Oak Brook, Ill. 60521.

BRAXTON, MARGARET ELIZABETH, VP, Publr., Garrard Publishing Company, 2 Overhill Rd., Scarsdale, N.Y. 10583, '62–; Mng. Ed., '57–'62; Dir., Educ. Advisory Ctr. (Boston, Mass.), '52–'57; HS Tchr., '48–'52; Children's Bk. Cncl., Intl. Reading Assn., Am. Bk. Cncl.; Cap and Gown Aw., '47; Mary Wash. Col., Univ. of Va., AB, '48; Boston Univ., Harvard Univ., '52–'56; b. Roanoke, Va., 1926; p. Charles Corbin and Esther Waller Bryan Braxton; res: Hudson House, Ardsley-on-Hudson, N.Y. 10503.

BRAY, DORIS, Publr., Trona Argonaut, Box. 968, Trona, Cal. 93562, '64–; Staff Wtr., San Bernardino Sun; Corr., '57–; Adm. Cnslt., '38–'57; Co-Auth. "Ballarat—Facts & Folklore" ('65); Auth., "A Law Is Born" ('40); Instr., Polit. Sci., Occidental Col.; AAUW (Santa Monica Br., State Bd., Pres., '36–'37; Searles Lake Br., Pres., '58); Pi Sigma Kappa (Pres., '33); Trona BPW "Wm. of Yr."; org. plaques, aws.; Searles Valley Commty. Svcs. Cncl. (Secy., Past Pres.), San Bernardino County Mental Health Advisory Bd.; U.C.L.A., BA, '26; Grad. Work, '33–'34; b. Santa Monica, Cal., 1905; h. Emmett W. Bray; res: 84639 11th St., Trona, Cal. 93562.

BRAYCHAK, SANDRA J., Ed.-Photogr., Remington Arms Co., Inc., 939 Barnum Ave., Bridgeport, Conn. 06608, '64–; Asst. to Soc. Ed., Sunday Herald, '64; Free-lance Photogr.; Conn. IEA (Bd. of Dirs., '68–'69), ICIE; Notre Dame (Md.), BA, '60–'64; Intl. Univ. (Rome, Italy); Athens Col. (Greece); b. Bridgeport, Conn., 1942; p. George and A. Jeanne Potasky Braychak; res: 58 Cross Hill Rd., Monroe, Conn. 06468.

BRAYMER, MARGUERITE DODD, Pres-Treas., Questar Corp., New Hope, Pa. 18938, '65–; Secy., Bd. Mbr., '50–'65; Free-lance Wtr. and Decorator, '46–'65; Decorating Ed., Woman's Day Magazine, '44–'53; Auth: "America's Homemaking Book," "America's Cookbook" (Scribner's); Rutgers Univ.; b. Camden, N.J., 1911; p. Arthur and Annetta Sherman Adams; h. Lawrence Braymer (dec.); c. Peter Dodd; res: New Hope, Pa. 18938.

BRAZIER, DOROTHY BRANT, Free-lance Colmst., Seattle Times, Seattle, Wash., '67–; Wms. News Ed., Colmst., '47–'67; Reptr., '31–'47; Theta Sigma Phi (Seattle Pfsnl. Chptr. Pres., '47), WNPC (Wash., D.C.); 1st pl. for wms. colms., Wash. State Press Aws., '61; 1st pl. rept-writing aw. for series on alcoholic wm., J. C. Penney-Univ. of Mo. annual competition for wm. eds.; Wash. Athletic Club (Seattle, Wms. Advisory Bd.); Univ. of Wash.; b. Seattle, Wash., 1907; p. Edward Lee and Lucy Alexander Brant; h. Carl E. Brazier, Jr.; res: 1415 McGilvra Blvd. E., Seattle, Wash. 98102.

BREAKSTONE, ELAINE POLLOCK, Assoc. Crtv. Dir., Norman, Craig & Kummel Inc., 488 Madison Ave., N.Y., N.Y. 10022, '68–; McCann-Erickson, '68; Benton and Bowles, '61–'68; Young & Rubicam, '60–'61; Grey Adv., '59–'60; BBDO, '56–'59; N.Y. Sch. of Interior Design; Syracuse Univ., BA (Jnlsm.); b. Rochester, N.Y., 1932; p. Lester and Ethel Gruner Pollock; h. David Breakstone; c. Bart, Jill, Robert; res: 74 Locust Rd., Briarcliff Manor, N.Y. 10510.

BREARLEY, JOAN MC DONALD, Ed., Exec. VP, Popular Dogs Publishing Company, 2009 Ranstead St., Phila., Pa. 19103, Owner, Sahadi Kennels and Cattery; Assoc. Dir.-Prodr., Mutual Bdcst. Co. (N.Y.C.); Script Ed., Station WOR; Auth. of three bks.; Morris Animal Fndn. aw.; Columbia Univ., Am. Acad. of Dramatic Arts; p. Stephen and Lillian McDonald; res: Penthouse 3105, The Dorchester, Rittenhouse Sq., Phila., Pa. 19103.

BRECKENFELD, VIVIAN GURNEY (pseud: Vivian Breck), Wtr., of bks. for young adults, '45–; Reviewer of bks., plays for clubs, '31–'45; HS Tchr., '16–'30; Cal. Wtrs. Club; Sierra Club; Jr. Lit. Guild Aws: "High Trail," '48; "Hoofbeats on the Trail," '50; Vassar Col., AB, '15; Univ. of Cal., MA, '17; b. S.F., Cal., 1895; p Gilbert and Leonide Cook Gurney; h. Elmer Breckenfeld; c. Gurney, Robert R.; res: Box 6087, Carmel, Cal. 93921.

BREIG, JEAN MACKEY, Pres., Breig Associates, 2047 Locust St., Phila., Pa. 19103, '51–; Mgr., Wertheim Adv. Agcy., '48–'49; Adv., Prom. Mgr., John C. Winston Co., '41–'48; Adv. Mgr., Westminster Press, '40–'41; Asst., Adv., Presbyterian Bd., Christian Educ., '38–'40; Pubcty. Dir., Phila. Bk. Clinic, '63–; Auth., "One to Remember," '55; Phila. Bksellers Assn. (Pres., '63–'64); Charles Morris Price Soc. of Adv. Cit. of Merit, '68; Univ. of Pa., AB, '33; b. Pitt., Pa., 1913; p. William and Ethel Fleming Mackey; h. John Breig; c. Jean H.; res: 261 S. Van Pelt, Phila., Pa. 19103.

BREINING, EDITH L., Asst. Librn., Rockport Branch, 4421 W. 140th St., Cleve., Oh. 44135, '68–; Librn., West HS, '59–'68; Librn., Newton D. Baker Jr. HS, '55–'59; Asst. Librn., J. Marshall HS, '52–'55; Tchr., '34–'51; Oh. Lib. Assn.; Denison Univ., AB, '34; Western Reserve Univ., MS (Lib. Sci.), '52; b. Pitt., Pa.; p. Henry and Margaret Breining; res: 22400 Fairlawn Circle #6, Fairview Park, Oh. 44126.

BREITMEYER, ELEANOR AMELIA, Soc. Ed., The Detroit News, 615 Lafayette St., Detroit, Mich. 48231, '63–; Club Ed., '58–'63; Reptr., '52–'58; Northville Record, '48–'52; Theta Sigma Phi (Past Pres.; Headliner Aw., '64), Detroit Press Club; Mayor's aw., '60; Quota Club aw., '60; Univ. of Mich., BA, '48; b. Detroit, Mich., 1926; p. Martin and Elizabeth Goetz Breitmeyer; res: 9530 Faust St., Detroit, Mich. 48228.

BREMKAMP, GLORIA HOWE, VP, Dir. of PR, Lowe Runkle Co., 1313 Liberty Bank Bldg., Okla. City, Okla. 73102, '69–; Dir. of PR, '63–; Free-lance PR, '53–'63; House mag. Ed., AE, Radio-TV Dir., G. Knox Adv., '48–'53; AWRT (Okla. Sooner Chptr. Pres., '58–'60; Nat. VP, '60–'62), Okla. PR Assn., Theta Sigma Phi (Okla. City Chptr. VP, '63–'65), PRSA, Am. Soc. of Hosp. PR Dirs., PR Soc. of Okla.; Okla. Indsl. Eds. Assn. Ed. of Yr. aw., '59; Okla. City Adv. Club aw., '68; Art Dirs. Club of Denver aw., '66; Okla. City Univ., Univ. of Okla.; b. Hugo, Okla., 1924; p. Robert and Lucinda Sapaugh Howe; h. James K. Bremkamp; c. J. Patrick; res: 8012 W. Lakeshore Dr., Okla. City, Okla. 73132.

BRENNER, BARBARA JOHNES, Free-lance Wtr., Cnslt., Wtr., L. W. Singer & Co., '65–'67; Cnslt., Wtr., Bank St. Col. of Educ., '65–'66, '69–; Auth: "Barto Takes the Subway" (Alfred Knopf, '60; Nancy Bloch Aw.), 10 other children's bks.; Auths. Guild; Rutgers Univ., '43–'46; Seton Hall Col., '42; N.Y.U., '52; b. Bklyn., N.Y., 1925; p. Robert and Marguerite Furboter Johnes; h. Fred Brenner; c. Mark, Carl; res: 11 Richard Dr., W. Nyack, N.Y. 10994.

BRENNER, LEAH, Free-lance Wtr., fiction, non-fiction; Auth: "An Artist Grows Up in Mexico," "Boyhood of Diego Rivera"; articles in N.Y. Times, Town and Country, other nwsps. and mags.; OPC, Press Club of San Antonio; Lady of the Lake Univ., BA; Nat. Univ. of Mexico, MA, PhD; b. Aguascalientes, Mexico, 1915; p. Isidore and Paula Duchan Brenner; res: 805 W. Woodlawn, San Antonio, Tex. 78212.

BRENT, CATHERINE SCOTT, Ext. Commtns. Specialist, University of California, 2200 University Ave., Berkeley, Cal. 94720, '61–; TV, Radio Talent, Campbell-Mithun Adv. Co. (St. Louis, Mo.), '55–'61; Dir., Food Mktng. Program, Univ. of Mo. and U.S. Dept. of Agriculture, '50–'61; Home Econs. Field, various cos., '37–'50; Wtr., nwsp. articles; Publr., Mo. Home Econs. Nwsltr., ('59–'61), Food Mktng. Bul. ('50–'61); TV Prodr.; Cal. Agricultural Ext. Pubns. Comm.; N. Central Reg. Mktng. Comm., U.S. Dept. of Agriculture, '59; Am. Sch. Food Svc. Assn.; Advisory Comm. on Food Budgets; AWRT (S.F. Bay Area Chptr. Pres., '63–'64; Secy., '59–'60), Am. Home Econ. Assn. (Mo. Assn. Secy.-Treas., '58–'59; Secy., '62–'63), Am. Dietetics Assn. (St. Louis Chptr. Secy., '57–'58); Western Radio and TV Assn., Am. Assn. of Agricultural Col. Ed., AFTRA, Epsilon Sigma Phi; Am. Film Festival Hons. ('68), S.F. Intl. Film Festival Hons. ('67, '68), Mo. Turkey Fedn. Aw., outstanding educ. TV Commtr.; Baylor Col., BS, '37; Ia. State Univ., grad. studies, '38; b. Dallas, Tex., 1914; p. Daniel and Maude Paden Scott; h. James Brent (div.); c. Jeffrey Alexander, Chloe Eileen Baxter, Catherine Lynn Brendlen; res: 3664 Mosswood Dr., Lafayette, Cal. 94549.

BRENT, LISELLE, Mgr.-Ed., United Press Overseas, 663 Fifth Ave., N.Y., N.Y. 10022, '66–; Wms. Ed., '49–'66; Fashion Designer, '44–'49; OPC, Fgn. Press Assn., Fgn. Corr. Ctr.; Hon. Citizen, State of Tenn., '63; educ. in Eur.; h. Rudolph Brent (dec.); res: 12 E. 97th St., N.Y., N.Y. 10029.

BRENZ, ELIZABETH ANN, Employee Pubns. Ed., Kerr-McGee Corporation, Kerr-McGee Bldg., 133 Robert S. Kerr Ave., Okla. City, Okla. 73102, '48–; Coptwtr., El Reno Daily Tribune, '46–'47; Central Okla. IEA (Pres., '58; Ed. of the Yr., '56), ICIE; Freedoms Fndn. Aw., '66; Who's Who in Okla. City; Arkansas City Jr. Col., '39; Kan. State Col., '39–'41; Univ. of Okla., BA (Jnlsm.), '46; b. Arkansas City, Kan., 1919; p. Dr. Louis Sr., and Margaret McDonald Brenz; res: 1902 N. Robinson, Okla. City, Okla. 73103.

BRETON, LOIS RIVERS, Prod. Mgr., Allen and Dorward, Inc., 1660 Bush St., S.F., Cal. 94109, '66–; Prod. Mgr., Lennen & Newman, '64–'66; Prod. Mgr., L. C. Cole Co., '57–'64.

BRIAN, DORIS, Assoc. Crtv. Dir., Reader's Digest, Advertising Division, 200 Park Ave., N.Y., N.Y. 10017, '61–; Copy Group Head, J. Walter Thompson, '56–'61; Copy Dir., American Home, '51–'56; Feature Ed., House Beautiful, '47–'49; Ed., Art Digest, '49–'51; Mng. Ed., Art News; AWNY; Barnard Col., AB, '34; Inst. of Fine Arts, MA, '36; Univ. of Pa., '36 (Pepper Fellow); Univ. of Paris, '37 (Carnegie Fellow); Univ. of Brussels, '39 (CRB Fellow); b. Phila., Pa.; p. Alexander and Minna Schless Brian; h. Milton Hepner; res: 40 E. Ninth St., N.Y., N.Y. 10003.

BRICKELL, BONABETH GRUWELL, Garden Ed.-Rural Reptr., The Emporia Gazette, 517 Merchant St., Emporia, Kan. 66801, '28–; weekly garden colm., '50–; Reptr., features, '28–; Ed., iris bul.; Homemaker's colm., Kan. Stockman; features for farm, household mags.; Accredited Garden and Show Judge; talks on iris; Speaker, ch. socs., study clubs; Conducts 4-H mbrs. in reading, composition; Garden Wtrs. Assn. of Am.; Kan. Univ., '22–'24; Emporia State, '58; b. Agency, Ia., 1895; p. Issac and Rilla Baker Gruwell; h. Bert Brickell; c. Alberta (Mrs. T. A. Emch), Albert G.; res: Flowerhill Rte. 5, Emporia, Kan. 66801.

BRICKELL, MARGARET ANN WHITE, Dir., Production Agency of North Carolina; 608 W. Johnson, Raleigh, N.C. 27603, '68–; Free-lance Bdcstr., Radio, TV, '68–; Prodr., Narrator, "Your Man in the Legislature," '69–; Wms. Edm., WPTF Radio, Bdcstr. own daily show, "Time for Margaret," '63–'68; Kindergarten Tchr., Ravenscroft Sch., '62; TV Hostess, Tchr., "Romper Room Sch.," '58–'60; Reservationist, Pan Am., '54–'56; Stewardess, Delta Airline, '53; Tchr., etiquette course for children; Speaker, Radio TV Inst., Univ. of N.C.; Fashion Model, Narrator, major fashion shows, N.C.; TV, radio commls., S.E. states; AWRT; Special Aw., Wake County Mental Health Assn., for radio work, '65; '66 Radio Aw., N.C. Mental Health Assn.; Cert. of Appreciation, Distributive Educ. Clubs of Am.; Delta Delta Delta Alumni (Raleigh Chptr., Pres.), Raleigh Wms. Club; Univ. of Miss., BA (Speech, Eng.), '57; b.

Evanston, Ill., 1933; p. Howard Pete and Margaret Barry White; c. Kimberly, Jennifer, David, Kate; res: 4501 Keswick Dr., Raleigh, N.C. 27609.

BRIDE, ESTHER LEE, Free-lance Cnslt., TV home econs., photog., adv., '66–; Liaison, KETC, Electric Housewares Manufacturers, '55–; TV Cnslt. for Trade Coop., Un. Electric, '61–'66; Dir., Home Econs. Cnslt. Svcs., '49–'61; Dir. Home Econs., '34–'49; Script Wtr., TV-radio programs, '36–'69 Talent, TV Homemaking Show, KSD-TV, '50; High Sch. Tchr., '23–'34; Lectr., adv., Wash. Univ., '38; home econs., '39–'41; Contrbr., articles to pfsnl. jnls.; various orgs.; William Woods Col.; AA, '21; N.W. State Tchrs. Col., Maryville, Mo.; Mo. Univ., BS, '27; b. Hamilton, Ill.; p. Samuel and Lelah West Bride. res: 5361 Pershing Ave., St. Louis, Mo. 63112.

BRIDGES, DOROTHY MADDOX, PR Dir., Young Women's Christian Association, 72 Edgewood Ave., N.E., Atlanta, Ga. 30303, '59–'68, '42–'53; Theta Sigma Phi (VP, '67; Pres., '67–'68), Ga. State Co.. for Wm., BSHE, '34; b. Griffin, Ga., 1913; p. William and Irene Lindsey Maddox; h. John L. Bridges; c. James L.; res: 3609 Old Ivy Lane, N.E., Atlanta, Ga 30305.

BRIFFAULT, HERMA HOYT, Free-lance Wtr., Ed., Translator, 137 W. 12th St., N.Y., N.Y. 10011; Staff of Vilhjalmur Stefansson (Ed.-in-Chief, Ency. Arctica), '46–'50; Ghost Wtr., more than 12 books, incl. works on Arctic, gastronomy and soc. hist.; PEN, The Lucy Stone League, Assoc. member: Am. Museum of Natural Hist., Humane Soc. of the U.S., Columbus Normal Sch., Grad., 1918; b. Reedville, Meigs County, Oh., 1898; p. Ezra and Sarah Hetzer Hoyt; h. Robert Briffault (dec.); res: 137 W. 12th St., N.Y., N.Y. 10011.

BRIGGS, GRACE ALVA, Copyrights Mgr., Harvard University Press, 79 Garden St., Cambridge, Mass. 02138, '67–; Asst. Bus. Mgr., '62–'67; Asst. to Bus. Mgr., '43–'62; Asst. to Sls. Mgr., '37–'43; Subscription Mgr., Asst. Adv. Mgr., New England Publ. Co. (Boston), '26–'36; Secy. to Trustees, Loeb Classical Lib., Harvard, '43–; Burdett Col., '26; b. Bklyn., N.Y., 1906; p. Edwin and Harriet Briggs Briggs; res: 8 Vernon St., Newton, Mass. 02158.

BRIGGS, KATE HALLE, Corporation Secy., Holiday House, Inc., 18 E. 56th St., N.Y., N.Y. 10022; Trustee, Planned Parenthood, Eastern Westchester, '68; Briarcliff Col., '58; h. John Briggs, Jr.

BRIGGS, SHIRLEY ANN, Rachel Carson Trust for the Living Environment, Inc., 8940 Jones Mill Rd., Wash., D.C. 20015, '66–; Ed. and VP of Pubns., Audubon Naturalist Soc. of the Central Atlantic States, '48–'69; Tchr., Nat. Hist. Field Studies, U.S. Dept. of Agriculture Grad. Sch., '62–; Exhbns. Preparation, Smithsonian Inst., '54–'55; Nat. Park Svc., '56; Chief of Graphics Sec., Bur. Reclamation, U.S. Dept. of the Interior, '48–'54; Info. Specialist, Fish and Wildlife

Svc., '45–'48; Illus., Glenn L. Martin Co., '43–'48; Art. Instr., N.D. State Col., '41–'43; Ed. and Illus: "The Trumpeter Swan" ('60); Illus: "Insects and Plants" ('63), "The Wonders of Seeds" ('56), "The Pronghorn Antelope" ('48); Am. Ornithologists Un., Wilson Ornithological Soc., AAUW (Wash. D.C. Arts Chmn., '56–'57); Univ. of Ia., '39 (with highest distinction; Phi Beta Kappa, '38); MA (Art), '40; b. Iowa City, Ia., 1918; p. John Ely and Nellie Upham Briggs; res: 7605 Honeywell Lane, Bethesda, Md. 20014.

BRIGHT, SALLIE EVERSON, PR Dir., Community Service Society of New York, 105 E. 22nd St., N.Y., N.Y. 10010, '54–; Exec. Dir., Nat. PR Cncl. for Health and Welfare Svcs., '38–'54; PR Instr., Columbia Univ., '50–'53; Instr., N.Y.U., '51–'53; Auth., numerous manuals, articles on PR, Social Welfare; Nat. PR Cncl. for Health and Welfare Svcs. (Bd. Secy.), Family Svc. Assn. of Am., CWPR, PRSA; Pa. Col. for Wm., AB, '27 (magna cum laude); b. Cumberland, Md., 1905; p. George and Sallie Carpenter Everson; h. Robert Bright; c. Mrs. Edward Yates, Frank Fraysur; res: 171 W. 12th St., N.Y., N.Y. 10011.

BRIGHTWELL, JUANITA SUMNER, Dir. of Lib. Svcs., Lake Blackshear Regional Library, 111 S. Jackson St., Americus, Ga. 31709, '62–; Eng. Tchr., Lib. Asst., Americus HS, '56–'62; Tchr., New Era Elem. Sch., '55–'56; Asst. Librn., Americus Carnegie Lib., '52–'55; Tchr., Librn., since '37; ALA, AAUW, BPW (Pres., '68–'69), S.E. Lib. Assn., Ga. Lib. Assn., Ga. Assn. of Lib. Assts., NEA, Ga. Educ. Assn.; Who's Who of Am. Wm.; Who's Who in Am. Educ.; Who's Who in Lib. Svc.; Dict. of Intl. Biog.; Nat. Soc. Dir.; Personalities of the South, Who's Who Intl.; Ga. Col., BS, '38; Emory Univ., MLB, '65; b. Sylvester, Ga. 1918; p. Robert and Lottie Davis Sumner; h. Louie Brightwell; c. Claire (Mrs. Charlie Shaeffer, Jr.); res: 1307 Hancock Dr., Americus, Ga. 31709.

BRILLER, SARA WELLES, Free-lance Wtr., Ed.; Co-auth: "Diet Watchers Guide," "Diet Watchers Gourmet Cookbook" (Grosset and Dunlop), "Born Female" (David McKay); Project Ed., Rutledge Bks., '68–'69; Sr. Ed., Printer's Ink, '52–'64; Articles Ed., Woman's Home Companion, '53–'57; Mng. Ed., Family Magazine, '53; Sr. Ed., House and Garden, '51–'53; Assoc. Ed., Charm, Mademoiselle, '47–'51; Assoc. Art Dir., Parade, '41–'46; Soc. of Mag. Wtrs.; Hunter Col., BA, '41; b. Pitt., Pa.; h. Bert Briller; c. Robert, Joan; res: 12 Lyons Pl., Larchmont, N.Y.

BRINE, MARGARET M., Free-lance Wtr., non-fiction, travel and adventure; Auth., "Come Along to Taiwan"; World Traveler, '36–; Lectr., '46–'63; Lieutenant, U.S. Coast Guard Reserve '42–'46; NLAPW (Corr. Secy., '67–'69; Spanish Govt. Fellowship for rsch. on Spanish Art in Spain, '48–'49; Harvard Univ., AA, '36; Nat. Sch. of Art, Hungary, Czechoslovakia, Poland, summers '36–'37; Columbia Univ., MA, '37; b. Cambridge, Mass.; p. John and Mary Tracy Brine; res: Albee Ct., Larchmont, N.Y. 10538.

BRININSTOOL, JO ANN MITCHELL, Publr., Ed., The Jal Record, 113 N. Third St., Jal, N.M. 88252, '66–; Gen. Mgr., The Midland Flare, 218 N. Main St., Midland, Tex. 79701, '69–; Mgr., Jal C. of C., '59–'64; N.M. Press Assn., Tex. Press Assn., Natl. Nwsp. Assn., N.M. Press Wm., NFPW, W. Tex. Press Assn., BPW, Jal C. of C. (Citizenship Aw., '61), Repl. State Platform Comm., '68; Tex. Christian Univ., '68; b. Maud, Okla., 1929; p. Allen and Lucy Seawright Mitchell; h. William H. Brininstool; c. Lindsey, Mitchell; res: Highway 18, Jal, N.M. 88252.

BRINKER, JUNE STORY, Adv. AE, Lloyd Advertising, Inc., 336 Aquila Ct., Omaha, Neb. 68102, '62–; AE, Pleskach & Smith Adv., '50–'62; b. Butte, Neb.; p. Harvey and Blanche Staples Story; h. (div.); c. Patricia Jane; res: 1606 N. 72nd St., Omaha, Neb. 68114.

BRINKLEY, MARION BRADSHAW, Wms. Ed., Feature Wtr., Reptr., Suffolk News-Herald, 130–132 S. Saratoga St., Suffolk, Va. 23434, '64–; Wms. Ed., '44–'48; La Grange Col.; b. Suffolk, Va. 1915; p. Floyd and Mary Williams Bradshaw; h. Abram D. Brinkley; c. Marion Virginia; res: 219 Clay St., Suffolk, Va. 23434.

BRISTOW, GWEN, Auth. (Publr., Thomas Y. Crowell Co., N.Y.C.); Reptr., The New Orleans Times-Picayune, '25–'33; Bks: "The Invisible Host" (with Bruce Manning, '30, made into a play "The Ninth Guest" by Owen Davis, '30, and Motion Pic.), "Deep Summer" ('37), "The Handsome Road" ('38), "This Side of Glory" ('40); reissued as Gwen Bristow's "Plantation Trilogy," '62; "Tomorrow Is Forever" ('42; Motion Pic., '44), "Jubilee Trail" ('50; Motion Pic. '54); PEN (Secy., L.A. Ctr., '67–'69; Pres., '69–); Pen and Brush, Theta Sigma Phi, Auths. League of Am.; Judson Col., AB, '24; Columbia Univ. Sch. of Jnlsm., '24–'25; b. Marion, S.C., 1903; p. Louis and Caroline Winkler Bristow; h. Bruce Manning (dec.); res: Box 144, Encino, Calif. 91316.

BRITT, LORA SINKS, Ed., Palatka Daily News, 1801 St. Johns Ave., Palatka, Fla. 32077, '62–; Ed., Delray Beach News-Jnl., '59–'62; Ed. and Co-owner, Delray Beach Jnl., '48–'59; Fla. Wms. Press Club (Pres., '58–'59); Writing Aws., '56, '57, '59: Fla. Wms. Press Club, Fla. Press Assn.; b. Bloomington, Ill., 1914; p. Irwin and Mabel Van Winkle Sinks; h. Robert Lee Britt; c. Mathis I., Daniel D.; res: 1721 Carr St., Palatka, Fla. 32077.

BRITTON, BARBARA, Actress; 30 motion pics.; title role, "Mr. and Mrs. North" TV series; Revlon TV spokeswm., 12 yrs.; five Broadway plays, numerous stock appearances; Long Beach City Col.; b. Long Beach, Cal., 1926; p. Adna and Lillie Grim Brantingham; h. Dr. Eugene J. Czukor; c. Theodore Britton, Christopher Eugenia; res: 322 Central Park W., N.Y., N.Y. 10025.

BRITZ, ALVINA MARY, Gen. Mgr., KBIZ Radio, KTVO Television, 211 E. Second St., Ottumwa, Ia.

52501, '68–; Bus. Mgr., '54–'68; WLCX Radio, La Crosse, Wis., WBIZ Radio, Eau Claire, Wis., '50–'54; Sta. Mgr., WBIZ, '49–'50; Traffic Dir., '47–'49; AWRT (Chptr. Pres., '68–'69); b. Royalton, Minn., 1919; p. Henry and Theresa Zormeier Britz; res: 128 E. Fifth St., Ottumwa, Ia. 52501.

BROACH, JEANNE DuVAL, Librn., Meridian Public Library 2517 Seventh St., Meridian, Miss. 39301, '47–; Lt., U.S. Naval Reserve, Active Duty, '42–'45; Tchr., Pub. Sch., Meridian, Miss., '38–'42; Tchr., Pub. Sch., Newton, Miss., '36–'37; Tchr., Pub. Sch., Aliceville, Ala., '35–'36; Miss. Lib. Assn. (Pres., '57–'59; Exec. Bd., '55–'60), Southeastern Lib. Assn., ALA; Who's Who of Amer. Wm.; Miss. State Col. for Wm., BA, '34; Univ. of Ala., MA, '35; La. State Univ., BS (Lib. Sci.), '50; b. Meridian, Miss., 1913; p. Walker and Ella Bozeman Broach; res: 1827 23rd Ave. Meridian, Miss. 39301.

BROADCORENS, YVONNE RAMAUT, Dir. of Public Info., Simmons College, 300 The Fenway, Boston, Mass. 02115, '50–; Assoc. Ed., Modern Materials Handling, '47–'50; Ed., Along the Line, New Haven Railroad, '42–'44; ACPRA (Dist. Dir., '69), AWRT, Mass. IEA (aw., '45), Pubcty Club of Boston, New Eng. Wms. Press Assn., New Eng. Press Assn., Lambda Theta Pi; active in numerous civic groups; Boston Univ., BS (Jnlsm.), '29 (Outstanding Svc. Aw., '66); New Sch. of Rsch., N.Y.C., '52; Grad. Work, Harvard Univ.; b. Grammont, Belgium, 1905; p. Alfons and Clementine VanDamme Ramaut; h. Gustaf Broadcorens; c. Joan Nathalie; res: 9 Wolcott Park, W. Medford, Mass. 02155.

BROADLEY, HOPE LAPOF, Preliminary Interviewer/Employment Rep., National Broadcasting Company, 30 Rockefeller Plaza, N.Y., N.Y. 10019, '68–'69; Pers. Asst., '68; Pers. Dir., Bailey Employment System, '67–'68; Tchr., Speech Arts; Adelphi Univ., BA, '67; b. Bklyn., N.Y., 1945; p. Benjamin and Yvonne Weiner Lapof; h. Timothy S. Broadley; res: 810 Gehrig Ave., Franklin Sq., N.Y. 11010.

BROCARD, TULA SALPAS, Info. Offcr., National Institute of Dental Research, 9000 Rockville Pike, Bethesda, Md. 20014, '65–; Info. Offcr., Div. of Occ. Health, Public Health Svc., '47–'65; Off. of Price Adm., '43–'47; mag. articles, Indsl. Hygiene Nwsltr.; participant in numerous professional workshops and seminars; WNPC, PRSA, Am. Nat. Cncl. for Health Educ. of the Public, Am. Conf. of Govt. Indsl. Hygienists, 13th Intl. Congress on Occ. Health; Am. Conf. on Govt. Indsl. Hygienists (Chmn., Worker Health Educ.Comm. and various other offcs., '50–); Div. of Occup. Health, Superior Work Performance Aw., '64; Medill Sch. of Jnlsm., Northwestern Univ., '40–'46; b. Chgo., Ill., 1922; p. Dr. Spero and Mary Koursoumis Salpas; h. James Brocard; c. Mary Catharine, John Philip; res: 12112 Whippoorwill Lane, Rockville, Md. 20852.

BROCK, CAROL LANG, Food Ed., Parents' Magazine, 52 Vanderbilt Ave., N.Y., N.Y. 10017, '68–; Hostess Ed., Good Housekeeping, '49–'67; Asst. Food Ed., '44–'49; Co-ed: "Good Housekeeping Party Book"; Instr. in Adult Educ., '67; N.Y. Home Econsts. in Bus. (Chmn., '55–'56), N.Y. Home Econs. Assn. (V.P. '67–'68), N.Y. Home Econsts. in Bus., Omicron Nu (Chptr. Pres.), Queens Col. Home Econs. Assn. (Pres., '46–'47), Nat. Cncl. of Wm., Inter. Collegiate Alumni Assn.; Pi Lambda Theta, Who's Who of Am. Wm. ('58), Intl. Gold Bk., AWNY (aws. in PR and mdsng., '52); Queens Col., BA, '44; N.Y.U., MA, '63; b. Queens, N.Y., 1923; p. Charles and Helen Becker Lang; h. Emil Brock; c. Brian Stuart, Craig Winston, Keith (dec.); res: 303 Arleigh Rd., Douglaston Manor, N.Y. 11363.

BROCK, KATHI CONANT, AE, The Prescott Co., Inc., 601 Emerson, Denver, Colo. 80218, '66–; Gamma Alpha Chi, AWRT; Univ. of Colo., '59; b. Casper, Wyo., 1939; p. F. T. and Margaret Bigelow Kennelly; h. Jonathan Brock; res: No. 10 Emerson, Denver, Colo. 80218.

BROCKWAY, EDITH SWAIN, Assoc. Ed., Decatur Tribune, 1136 E. Wood St., Decatur, Ill. 62521, '68–; Adv. Layout Mgr., Montgomery Ward, '67–'68; Freelance Wtr.-Photog., '55–'67; Adv. Artist-Wtr., Cartlich Adv. Co., '37–'40; Auth., juv. bks: "Range Doctor" ('64), "Land Beyond The River" ('66), "The Golden Land" ('68); many articles and illus. in educ. and trade mags.; K. C. Art Inst., '34–'37; Akron Art Inst., '55; b. Dunlap, Okla., 1914; p. George and Emma Arnold Swain; h. Charles Brockway; c. Ann (Mrs. Neils Hansson), Joy, Katherine; res: 4070 Irving Dr., Decatur, Ill. 62521.

BROD, RUTH HAGY, Dir., Mayor's Volunteer Coordinating Council, City of New York, 250 Broadway, #1412, N.Y., N.Y. 10007; Dir. of Public Info., Job Orientation in Neighborhoods, City of New York, '63–'65; Foreign Corr., North American Newspaper Alliance, '62–'63; Prodr., "College News Conference" (ABC-TV, Radio, eight yrs.; NET, one yr.; over 50 aws., incl. Peabody); Ed., Wms. Activities, Phila. Bulletin, '48–'57 (Founder, Dir., Bulletin Forum); Wms. Ed., Pubcty. Dir., Un. War Chest, Commty. Chest, '42–'46; Feature Wtr., Evening Public Ledger, '39–'41; Ed., Macfadden mags., '36–'68; Reptr., Chgo: Daily Times, American, Daily News, '32–'36; AWRT, WNPC, ANWC, Adv. Club of N.Y., Nat. Cncl. of Wm.; many pfsnl., civic aws.; h. Albert Thomas Brod; c. Mrs. Sybil Buffman; res: 15 Park Ave., N.Y., N.Y. 10016.

BRODIE, FAWN McKAY, Sr. Lectr., Hist. Dept., University of California, Los Angeles, Cal. 90024, '68–; Biographer, Histrn.; Contrbr., nwsps., mags., encys.; Bks: "No Man Knows My History, The Life of Joseph Smith, The Mormon Prophet" (Knopf, '45), "Thaddeus Stevens" (Norton, '59), "The Devil Drives" (Norton, '67); Alfred A. Knopf Fellowship in Biog., '43; Commonwealth Club of Cal., Gold Medal, '59; Fellow of the Yr., Ut. Hist. Soc., '67; Univ. of Ut., BA, '34; Univ. of Chgo., MA, '36; h. Bernard Brodie; c.

Richard, Bruce, Pamela; res: 619 Resolano Dr., Pacific Palisades, Cal. 90272.

BRODSKY, ANNETTE, Exec. VP, Accredited Mailing Lists, Inc., 15 E. 40th St., N.Y., N.Y. 10016, '60–; AE, Dependable Mailing List, '58–'59; Prod. Mgr., Bert Garmise Assoc., '53–'58; Mailing List Brokers Pfsnl. Assn., Direct Mail Adv. Assn. (Hundred Million Club), Mail Ad Club of Wash., B'nai Brith, Direct Mail Industry Lodge; N.Y.U., BA, '50; b. N.Y.C.; p. Norman and Bella Gofsaof Brodsky; res: 225 E. 36th St., N.Y., N.Y. 10016.

BRODY, LESLIE G., Mkt. Rsch. Assoc., Time Magazine, Time and Life Bldg., N.Y., N.Y. 10020; AWNY, Am. Mktg. Assn.; Syracuse Univ., BS, '60; N.Y.U., MBA Candidate; h. Cal Brody.

BROKAW, EVELYN GLYDE, Ed., Co-publr., Founder, Minburn Booster, Minburn, Ia. 50167, '54–; Ed., Minburn sec., Dallas Ctr. Times; articles on camping, truckers; hostess, "Let's Go Camping," KDLS Radio (Perry, Ia.); NLAPW, Ia. Press Wm. (Wms. Grand Merit Aw., '57), Press Colmsts. of Ia., C & R Toastmistress Club (Perry, Ia., Organizing Pres.; aws.); numerous aws. for colm., "Counter Chatter"; Am. Inst. of Bus. (Des Moines, Ia.), '29; b. Big Timber, Mont., 1911; h. Bernard M. Brokaw; c. Rhea (Mrs. Bob Jackson), Judy (Mrs. Jon Luethje), Roger, Keith; res: Minburn, Ia. 50167.

BROKAW, ROBERTA MIRIAM, Assoc. Dir. and Ed., Princeton University Press, 41 William St., Princeton, N.J. 08540, '66–; Proofreader, Manuscript Ed., Mng. Ed., Assoc. Dir. and Ed., '46–'66; Edtl. Dept., Westminster Press, '37–'45; Am. Hist. Assn., Modern Language Assn.; Fulbright Fellowship, '65–'66; Wilson Col., DHL, '66; b. Kobe, Japan, 1917; p. Harvey and Olivia Forster Brokaw; res: The Red Barn, Box 249, Mt. Rose Rd., Pennington, N.J., 08534.

BROMAGE, MARY COGAN, Assoc. Prof., University of Michigan, Graduate School of Business Administration, Ann Arbor, Mich. 48104, '65–; Chief Adm. Off., UNRRA; Edtl., Wtr., for nwsps.; Cnslt., bus. corps. and govt. agcys.; Wms. Rsch. Club, Univ. of Mich., Am. Comm. for Irish Studies, Conf. on British Studies, Midwest Case Rsch. Assn., Am. Freedom Fndn. of Valley Forge. cert. of merit, '50; Radcliffe Col., BA, '28 (Phi Beta Kappa; summa cum laude); Univ. of Mich., MA, '32; b. Fall River, Mass.; p. James and Edith Ives Cogan; h. Arthur Bromage; c. Susanna (Mrs. John Paterson); res: 2300 Vinewood Blvd., Ann Arbor, Mich. 48104.

BROMAN, KATHRYN FLYNN, Asst. of Pres., WWLP (TV), Springfield TV Broadcasting Corporation, Box 2210, Springfield, Mass. 01101, '60–; Wms. Pgm. Dir., '55–; Bdcstr., Hostess, "At Home with Kitty," '54–; AWRT (New Eng. Chptr. Pres., '62–'63; Gold Mike Aw., '68), Valley Press Club (VP, '69), McCall's Golden Mike Aw. for svc. to the commty., '63; Beth El Brotherhood Aw. for svc. to youth, '67; Joint Civic Agcys. Wm. of the Yr. Aw., '68; Un. Comml. Travellers of Am. John F. Kennedy Aw., '68; active in numerous civic groups; Carnegie Inst. of Tech., '37–'38; b. Pitt., Pa.; p. F. A. and Florence Morgan Flynn; h. Paul Broman; c. Karen E., Paul Richard, Morgan Andrew, Erica Ann; res: 214 Converse St., Longmeadow, Mass. 01106.

BRONSON LILLIAN RUMSEY, Actress; 78 motion pictures, '43–; TV, N.Y.C., Hollywood, '49–; Stage Plays: "Five Star Final," "Camille," "The Druid's Circle," "Magnificent Yankee," others; AMPAS, L.A. Lib. Assn. (Dir.), Recs. for the Blind, Braille Inst.; Who's Who of Am. Wm.; Univ. of Mich., AB, '26; b. Lockport, N.Y., 1902; p. Sylvester and Emma Huber Bronson; res: 7358 Hollywood Blvd., Hollywood, Cal. 90046.

BROOKER, JOSEPHINE LUXFORD, Asst. Adv. Dir., Montana Highway Commission, Helena, Mont. 59601, '65–; Adv. Mgr., Buttrey Assocs. (Great Falls, Mont.), '53–'65; Copy Ed., Wms. Program Dir., KFBB Radio-TV, '44–'53; Great Falls Downtown Bus. Cncl. (VP, '63–'65), Great Falls Soroptimist Club (VP, '64), Helena Soroptimist Club (VP, '69), AWRT, Western Am. Conv. & Travel Inst., Mont. Press Wm. (1st pl., writing pubcty., '68, '69), NPWC (2nd pl., writing pubcty., '68), AAUW; LULU Aw., L.A. Adv. Wms. Club, '62; Col. of Great Falls, BA, '48 (summa cum laude, Kappa Pi Lambda); N.Y.U. Sch. of Retailing, '54; b. Great Falls, Mont., 1926; p. Charles W. and Mary Burk Brooker; res: Box 439, Helena, Mont. 59601.

BROOKMAN, DENISE CASS, Auth.; Copy Ed., Plant Engineering, Technical Publishing Co., 1301 S. Grove St., Barrington, Ill. 60010; bks: "The Tender Time," "The Look of Love," "The Young in Love" (Macrae-Smith); short stories; annual sch. writing workshops; Assoc. Judge of Poetry, Hospitalized Veterans Writing Project, '53–'69; HVWP Bd. Mbr., '62–'65; Who's Who of Am. Wm., Contemporary Auths.; Northwestern Univ., BS (Lib. Arts), '49; b. Chgo., Ill.; p. DeLysle and Norma Dorgan Cass; c. Geoffrey, Samantha; res: 462 Signal Hill Rd., Barrington, Ill. 60010.

BROOKOVER, SANDRA SUE, Consumer Meat Specialist, U.S. Department of Agriculture, Livestock Division, Consumer and Marketing Service, Wash., D.C. 20250, '67; Asst. Dir., News Svc. Dept., Nat. Live Stock and Meat Bd., Chgo., Ill., '64–'67; Staff Wtr., The Independent, K.C., Mo., '63; Info. Dir., Certified Livestock Mkts. Assn., '61–'62; AWRT, Nat. Assn. of Farm Bdcstrs; Stephens Col., '56–'57; Kan. State Univ., BS (Speech/Radio-TV), '61; b. Scott City, Kan.; p. Earl and E. Denelda Shafer Brookover; res: 2913 Q St. N.W., Wash., D.C. 20007.

BROOKS, ANITA HELEN, Pres., Anita Helen Brooks Associates, Public Relations, 155 E. 55th St., N.Y., N.Y. 10022, '65–; AE, Ted Howard Public Relations, '63–'65; AE, Marianne Strong Public Relations, '61–'63; Ted Deglin Public Relations, '59–'61; Dick Taplinger Public

Relations, '57–'59; PR Dir., WMCA Radio, '57; Dir. PR, N.Y. State Mental Health Fund Campaign, '56; PR, NBC, '56; PR, WOR, '55; Wtr., King Features "Here's How" by Peter Howe, '55–'59; PRSA, IRTS, Pubcty. Club of N.Y., MWA, AWRT, Assn. Motion Picture Advs., PPA; Hunter Col., BA; Columbia Univ., MA; b. N.Y.C.; p. Arthur and Bertha Stewart Sayle; h. Arnold Brooks (div.); res: 155 E. 55th St., N.Y., N.Y. 10022.

BROOKS, ELAINA PEARL, Pres., American Model Agency and American Artists Management, 625 Eighth Ave., N.Y., N.Y. 10018, '62–; Casting Dir., Grace del Marco Model Agcy., '61–'62; Fashion Model, '52–'58; Fashion Gommentator and Wtr.; AWRT, SAG, AFTRA, NAMD, Modelling Assn. of Am.; one of top ten models, '55; most outstanding, '56; Un. Negro Col. Fund Benefit Aw., '57; N.Y.U.; b. Mandeville, Jamaica, West Indies; c. Leslie, Lisa; res: 97 Boll St., Clifton, N.J. 07014.

BROOKS, FRANCES JONES, Wms. Ed., Key West Citizen, Manatee Publishing Co., Key West, Fla. 33040, '67–; Wms. Ed. and Colmst., Carlsbad (N.M.) Current Argus; Snyder (Tex.) Daily News; Beta Sigma Phi (plaque for outstanding off-campus writing, '41); Tex. Wms . Univ., BA, BS, '41; b. Yeso, N.M., 1921; p. William and Anna Hoag Jones; h. div.; c. Bruce, Annabel, Burke, Ernest, Jr.; res: 700 Waddell Ave., Key West, Fla. 33040.

BROOKS, GEORGINE LOCKWOOD-WHITE, Ed., Asst. Dir. Employee Rels., Stix, Baer and Fuller, 601 Washington Ave., St. Louis, Mo. 63101, '63–; Byr., '57–'63; Boyds, '53–'57; ICIE, Indusl. Press Assn. of Greater St. Louis (Ed., offcl. pubn., '64–'66; Secy., '66–'67); numerous aws., b. Ia.; p. Raymond and Jennie Hodges Lockwood; h. (div.); c. Patricia, Bradford, Mrs. Lee Sanguinette; res: 25 S. Maple Ave., Webster Groves, Mo. 63119.

BROOKS, GERALDINE, Actress, 760 N. La Cienega Blvd., L.A., 90069; Bdway. stage: Theatre Guild Repertory Co., "The Winter's Tale" "The Time of the Cuckoo," "Brightower"; touring cos. theatre: "Cat on a Hot Tin Roof" "The Voice of the Turtle" "The Petrified Forest"; motion pics: "Possessed" (Warner Bros.), "Volcano," "Streets of Sorrow," "The Green Glove" (Eur.), numerous others; appearances on leading dramatic TV shows; lects., poetry readings, RCA albums; assisted husband in establishing Watts Wtrs. Workshop and brs., '65–; two EMMY nominations; Am. Acad. of Dramatic Art, Neighborhood Playhouse, Actors Studio; studied mime with Etienne Decroux; b. N.Y.C., 1935; p. James and Bianca Stroock; h. Budd Schulberg.

BROOKS, LOIS, Prod., Wtr. Bdcstr.; two yrs. prod., moderator of "Our 2¢ Worth," WTTW and "Kumzitz," WLS-TV, Chgo., Ill.; Prod., Wtr., Talent, Boy Scouts of Am. synd. TV series, "The Den Mothers' Workshop"; AWRT, Chgo. Unlimited (Bd. Mbr., '69); Chgo. EMMY, '63–'64; McCall's Golden Mike Aw.,

'64; Northwestern Univ., BS, '68 (Zeta Phi Eta); Master's Program, '68–'69; b. Bklyn., N.Y., 1926; p. Reuben and Cecelia Essenfeld Shemitz; c. Abbey, Cara, Charles; res: 460 Lincoln Ave. W., Highland Park, Ill. 60035.

BROOKS, MARTHA, Bdcstr., WGY-WRGB Radio, TV, Balltown Rd., Schenectady, N.Y. 12309, '31–; Program Mgr., Jenkins TV (Jersey City, N.J.), '29–'30; AWRT (Capitol Dist. Chptr. Pres., '58–'62); many aws. for painting; Emerson Col., BLI, '29; b. Binghamton, N.Y., 1906; p. Gustav and Edna Smith Lemke; h. David B. Kroman; res: 811 Ashmore Ave., Schenectady, N.Y. 12309.

BROOKS, MARY ANN, Free Lance Publicist, Wtr., Prodr., Media Byr., '69–; Media Byr., Wtr., The Swigart Co., N.O., La., '67–'69; Prom. Dir., Oakwood Shopping Ctr., Gretna, '66–'67; Publicist, Prodr., Wtr., The Swigart Co., N.O. '65; Wtr., Prodr., Publicist, Media Byr., Weill-Carvin-Hebert-Mehaffey, '64–'65; Time Byr., Ted Liuzza Assoc., N.O., '61–'64; AWRT (Chptr. Pres., '62–'63); Famous Wtrs. Sch., '63–'66; b. Atlanta, Ga.; p. Jack L. and Helen Reid Brooks; res: 2825 St. Charles Ave., Apt. 209, N.O., La. 70115.

BROOKS, PEGGY JONES, Exec. Ed., E. P. Dutton & Company, Inc., 201 Park Ave. S., N.Y., N.Y. 10003, '68–; Ed., '57–'68; Adv. Dir., '53–'57; Adv., Pubcty. Dir., T. Y. Crowell Co., '47–'49; AE, Franklin Spier, '44–'47; h. John Benson Brooks.

BROOME, MARY ANN DeBRACY, Pres., Broome Agency, Inc., 415 A St., Box 848, Columbus, Mont. 59019, '69–; Partner, '63–'69; Proofreader, various pubns., '60–'62; Head Proofreader, Panama City (Fla.) News-Herald, '52–'60; Mont. Press Wm., NFPW; b. St. Augustine, Fla., 1910; p. William and Hannah Doyle DeBracy; h. Sherwood Broome; c. William F. Penrose, Jr.; res: 113 W. Fourth Ave. N., Columbus, Mont. 59019.

BROSAMER, VIRGINIA M., Employee Pubns. Ed., Staff Wtr., Field Enterprises Educational Corporation, 510 Merchandise Mart Plaza, Chgo., Ill. 60654, '53–; Exec. Secy., '48–'53; ICIE (Aw. of Merit, '69), AAIE; Lincoln Col., AA, '39; comml. course, '46; Northwestern Univ., '48–'52; b. Lincoln, Ill., 1920; p. Jacob and Mary Hickey Brosamer; res: 1200 N. Lake Shore Dr., Chgo., Ill. 60610.

BROSE, PAULA LYNN, Media Estimator, Campbell-Ewald Company, 3044 W. Grand Blvd., Detroit Mich. 48202, '69–; Adv. Copywtr., '68–'69; Prom. Asst. and Copywtr., WJBK-TV, '65–'68; Prog. Guide Subscription Handler, WDTM-FM, '65–'66; Tape Ed., Rec. Engineer and Student Asst., N.Y.U. Radio Dept., '61–'65; Asst. Gen Mgr., Program Dir. and Traf. Mgr., WCAG, N.Y.U.; AWRT, Pi Delta Phi, Sigma Delta Omicron, N.Y.U. Alumni Assn., (Detroit Chptr. 2nd VP), Mensa Soc., Stratford Shakespearean Festival Fndn. of Can.; N.Y.U., BA, '64 (cum laude); b.

Detroit, Mich., 1942; p. Max and Jean Miller Brose; res: 2260 Crooks Rd., Troy, Mich. 48084.

BROTHERS, BONNIE SNELL, Mng. Ed., Spencer Daily Reporter, Spencer Newspapers, 525 Grand Ave., Spencer, Ia. 51301, '64–; City Ed., '63–'64; Wms. Ed., '62–'63; Rptr., Perry Daily Chief, '48–'52; Ia. Press Wm., NFPW, Ia. Daily Press Assn.(numerous aws., incl. top aw., '64), Ia. Press Colmsts.; Jane Arden Aw., Des Moines Chptr., Theta Sigma Phi, '61; Northwestern Univ., '43; b. Perry, Ia., 1925; p. Silver and Wava Klingaman Snell; h. Philip C. Brothers; c. Cheryl (Mrs. Richard Agan); res: 303 W. Fifth, Spencer, Ia 51301.

BROTHERS, CASSIE CAMPBELL, Librn., Helena-West Helena School System, 225 S. Biscoe St., Helena, Ark. 72342, '52–; Phillips County Hist. Assn., Ark. Hist. Assn., Phillips County Lib. Assn., Ark. Lib. Assn., NEA, Ark. Educ. Assn., Assn. Childhood Educ. (Past Chptr. Pres.), Classroom Tchrs. Assn. (Past Chptr. Pres.), Sigma Alpha Iota, Delta Kappa Gamma; Who's Who of Am. Wm., Who's Who in Lib. Sci., Ark. Lives; Univ. of Ark., BSE; Univ. of Miss., MLS; b. Wabash, Ark., 1928; p. John and Marie Parker Campbell; h. William John Brothers, Jr.; c. William John, III, Brooke Ann; res: 123 Summit Dr., Helena, Ark. 72342.

BROTHERS, JOYCE BAUER, Psychologist; Colmst., Good Housekeeping, '62–; North Am. Nwsp. Alliance, '61–; Program Dir., Reading Dev. Ctr.; Lectr.: News Analyst, Metromedia TV; Hostess, "Dr. Joyce Brothers," "Consult Dr. Brothers," "Ask Dr. Joyce Brothers"; Instr., Hunter Col., '49–'52; Rsch. Project on Leadership, UNESCO, '49; Asst. Psychology, Columbia Univ., '48–'52; Auth: "Ten Days to a Successful Memory," "Woman"; Psychological Cnslt.; Am. Acad. of Achiev. Aw., '68; Mennen Baby Fndn. Aw., '59; Newhouse Nwsp. Aw., '59; Cornell Univ., BS, '47; Columbia Univ., MA, '50; PhD, '53; Franklin Pierce Col. (Dr., Humane Ltrs.), '69; b. N.Y.C.; p. Morris and Estelle Rapoport Bauer; h. (div.); c. Lisa Robin; res: 305 E. 86th St., N.Y., N.Y. 10028.

BROTMAN, MYRNA GLICK, Eng., Drama Tchr., N.Y.C., '66–; Asst. to Mgr., Dir. Mail Adv., Golden Press, '63–'66; Corr., Col. Textbook Dept., Harcourt, Brace and World, '62–'63; Wtr., direct mail brochures; N.Y.C. Tchrs. of Eng.; Queens Col., BA (Eng.), '61; N.Y.U., MA (Eng. Literature), '64; PhD candidate, Columbia Univ.; b. N.Y.C., 1941; p. Samuel and Pauline Rutkove Glick; h. Ronald Brotman (div.); res: 142-02 84th Dr., Briarwood, N.Y. 11435.

BROTMAN, PHYLLIS BLOCK, Pres., Image Dynamics., Inc., Public Relations, McDonogh Lane, Balt., Md. 21208; Coordr. of PR, Md. Cncl. for Educ. TV, '65–'67; Coordr. Special Events, Balt. Jr. Col., '65–'66; Reg. Legislative Agt., Md. Gen. Assembly, '66, '68; Ch. 13 TV, '53–'55; Auth., Your Voice In Annapolis; Md. Gen. Assembly; '68; Special Lectr. PR and Jnslm., Balt. County Schs., Coordr. of Wine Inst. Pgm., Calif. Cncl.

of Wines (Advisory Bd., diploma), Assoc. Mbr., PRSA (Balt. Chptr: Secy. '66; VP, '67); Balt. Cncl. of PR, Md.-Del. Press Assn.; Who's Who Of Am. Wm., Md. House of Delegates Resolution of Honor, '69; Cert. of Achiev., Assoc. Jewish Charities, '66; Outstanding Leadership Aw., B'nai B'rith Girls; Outstanding Commty. Achiev., B'nai B'rith Youth, '67; Aw. presented by Gov. of Md. at signing of Educ. TV Bill, '66; Offcr. and bd. mbr. numerous civic orgs.; Balt. Jr. Col., Mary Washington Col.; b. Baltimore, Md., 1934; p. Sol G. and Delma Herman Block; h. Dr. Don N. Brotman; c. Sol G., Barbara Gay; res: Box 554, RFD #7, Pikesville, Md. 21208.

BROUGH, JOANNE WALKER, Asst. West Coast Story Ed., CBS Television Network, 7800 Beverly Blvd., L.A., Calif. 90036, '68–; Sr. Reader, CBS-TV, '63–'68; Jerome S. Siegel Assocs. Lit. Agcy., '61–'63; Paramount TV Prods., '58–'61; Wilshire-Riviera Wms. Club (Pres., '56); AWRT; Univ. of Mo., '46; U.C.L.A., '44–'46; b. Joplin, Mo., 1927; p. James and Marion Tindall Walker; h. Charles H. Brough; c. Cheryl Chaves, Alice Chaves, Arthur Chaves; res: 3020 Club Dr., L.A., Calif. 90064.

BROWDE, HEDWIG, Edtl. Dir., Public Relations News, 127 E. 80th St., N.Y., N.Y. 10021, '43–; CWPR; b. N.Y.C.; p. Bernard William and Bertha N. Browde; res: 135 E. 39th St., N.Y., N.Y. 10016.

BROWER, BUNNY MORRISON, Copy Chief, Travel Ed., Seventeen Magazine, 320 Park Ave., N.Y., N.Y. 10022; Copy Chief, Shevlo Adv. Inc., '53–'55; Copy Chief, Oppenheim Collins, '52; Soc. of Am. Travel Wtrs., N.Y. Travel Wtrs. Assn.; William Smith Col., h. William S. Brower, Jr.

BROWER, SIDNA, Asst. Mgr. of Dev., Cresap, McCormick and Paget, 245 Park Ave., N.Y., N.Y. 10017, '69–; Offcr. in Charge, Citibank Magazine and Citibank News, First Nat. City Bank., '65–'69; Asst. Ed., Bay Area Bul., Pacific Telephone Co., '64–'65; Gen. News Deskman, UPI (London, Eng.), '64; Gen. Assigt. Reptr., World Telegram & Sun, '63–'64; N.Y. Assoc. of Indsl. Commtns., Theta Sigma Phi; Mademoiselle Magazine Merit Aw., '63; OPC Aw., dist. svc. in student jnlsm., '63; AAAA Aw. for edtls., '63; Nat. Headliner Aw., '63; Univ. of Miss., BA (Jnlsm.), '63; b. Memphis, Tenn., 1941; p. Rex and Sue Hopkins Brower; res: 117 Waverly Pl., N.Y., N.Y. 10011.

BROWN, ABBY, VP, Cassidy-Brown, Box 296, Scituate, Mass. 02066, '69–; Dir., Bdcst. Rel., '64–; Mgr., Radio-TV Rel., New American Lib., '60–'63; Edtl. Assoc., Broadcasting mag., '58–'60; Manhattanville Col., BA, '57; b. Utica, N.Y., 1936; h. Tom Cassidy; res: 16 Roberts Dr., Scituate, Mass. 02066.

BROWN, ANNE KINSOLVING, Auth., Lectr., Military, Hist. subjects; Co-auth: "The Anatomy of Glory: Napoleon and His Guard" (Brown Univ. Press, '61); Lectr., Univ. of Cal., '65; Music Critic, Feature Wtr.,

Colmst., Baltimore News, '25–'30; Co. of Military Collectors and Histrns. (Co-Founder, '49; Gov., '51–; Pres., '63–'65; VP, '53; Treas., '51–'63), Am. Military Inst., Soc. for Army Hist. Rsch., Musee de l'Armee (Paris) Societe de la Sabretache, Compagnie d'Elite de Gibernards, Gesellschaft fur Heereskunde; Brown Univ., LHD, '62 (Phi Alpha Theta); b. Bklyn., N.Y. 1906; p. Rev. Arthur and Sally Bruce Kinsolving; h. John Nicholas Brown; c. LCDR. Nicholas, U.S.N. John Carter, Mrs. Edwin G. Fischer; res: 357 Benefit St., Providence, R.I., 02903.

BROWN, BARBARA BUELL, AE, Franklin Spier, Inc., 270 Madison Ave., N.Y., N.Y. 10016, '53–; Asst. AE, '52; Farrar Straus, '51–'52; Beacon Press, '50–'51; WNBA; Smith Col., BA, '50; b. Fairmont, W. Va.; p. Harold and Frances H. Buell; h. M. Jay Brown; res: 44 W. 94th St., N.Y., N.Y. 10025.

BROWN, BARBARA RICHARDSON, Courthouse Reptr., Madera Daily Tribune, 200 E. Seventh St., Madera, Cal. 93637, '57–; City Reptr., '55–'57; San Jose State Col., AB (Jnlsm.), '55 (hons.); h. Alan Brown.

BROWN, BESSIE TAYLOR, Histrn., Private Rschr.; Co-auth: "Virginia, 1705–1786: Aristocracy or Democracy?" (Mich. State Univ. Press, '64); Auth. of numerous articles on Am. Hist.; Univ. of Wash., BA (Phi Beta Kappa); Mich. State Univ., MA, '52; b. Olympia, Wash., 1917; p. Guy and Agnes Giles Taylor; h. Robert E. Brown; res: 2070 Lagoon Dr., Okemos, Mich. 48864.

BROWN, BETH (Robert Elizabeth Brown), Staff Reptr., Evening Post Publishing Co., 134 Columbus St., Charleston, S.C. 29402, '67–; Summer Intern, Spartanburg Herald, '66; NFPW, S.C. Press Assn. Wms. Div. (Bd. of Dirs., '69–'70), Theta Sigma Phi (outstanding mbr., '66–'67); S.C. Press Assn. Aw. for best page make-up, '68; two photog. aws., '69; 2nd pl., Tad Quattlebaum Aw., '67; Who's Who in Amer. Cols. and Univs.; Univ. of S.C., AB (Jnlsm.), '67; b. Charleston, S.C., 1945; p. Joseph and Catherine Bouknight Brown; res: Cherry St., McCormick, S.C. 29835.

BROWN, BILLIE, AE, Cunningham and Walsh, 260 Madison Ave., N.Y., N.Y. 10016, '65–; Press and Customer Rels., Gen. Electric Co., '64–'65; Head of Music Dept., Miss Porter's Sch., Farmington, Conn., '59–'65; Yale Univ. Sch. of Music, BMus., '56; MMus., '57 (H. G. Fox Aw., highest acad. hons., Master Class); res: 520 E. 72nd St., N.Y., N.Y. 10021.

BROWN, BONNIE LOUISE, Bank Mktng. Offcr., Weld County Bank, 1000 Tenth St., Greeley, Colo. 80631, '68–; PR Dir., Geriatrics, Inc., '69–; Evening Faculty, Aims Col., '68; AWRT (Bd. Dir., '69), AAUW, Bank PR & Mktng. Assn., Altrusa Intl., C. of C.; Univ. of Wyo., BS, '63; b. Worland, Wyo., 1942; p. Wesley and Mildred Brown. res: 2439 W. 11th St., Greeley, Colo. 80631.

BROWN, BRENDA LAWSON, Dir. of Alumni Affairs, Alumni Ed., Howard University Magazine, Howard University, 2400 Sixth St., N.W., Wash. D.C. 20001; '67–; Asst. Dir., '66–'67; Program Asst., Media Rel., Commty. Rel. Svc., Dept. of Justice, '64–'66; Asst. to Dir., Planning, Evaluation & Rsch., Peace Corps, '64; Speech Tchr., Public Schs. (Wash., D.C.), '60–'64; Am. Alumni Cncl., ACPRA, Am. Speech & Hearing Assn.; Outstanding Young Wm. of Am., '65–'66; Who's Who in Am. Col. & Univ., '59–'60; ACLU, NAACP, Urban League; Howard Univ., BA, '60; b. Louisville, Ky., 1938; p. LaMont and Charlotte Hughes Lawson; h. John Scott Brown; c. Courtney Hughes; res: 4225 17th St., N.W., Wash., D.C. 20011.

BROWN, CAROL OSMAN, Free-lance Wtr., Photogr., 1445 N. 44th St., Phoenix, Ariz. 85008; PR AE, Ken Patton Agency, '66–'68; PR AE John S. Turner & Assoc. '64–'66; Reptr., Wms. Ed., Arizona Currents, '64–'66; Reptr., Photogr., The Phoenix Gazette, '60–'64; articles, photos in many mags., nwsps., wire svcs.; NFPW, (1st pl. photog. aw., '68), Ariz. Press Wm. (State Histrn., '67), Phoenix Press Club, Ariz, Press Club, Pi Delta Epsilon; Lulu Aws., L.A. Adv. Wm., '67, '68; several other writing, photog. aws.; Who's Who of Am. Wm.; Ariz. State Univ., BA (Mass Commtns), '63; b. Schenectady, N.Y., 1941; p. Sidney and Natale Charipper Osman; h. James Carrington Brown, III; c. James IV; res: 1445 N. 44th St., Phoenix, Ariz. 85008.

BROWN, DALLAS LINDSEY, Instr., Radio and TV, University of Texas at El Paso, El Paso, Tex. 79999, '68–; KINT Radio, '63; Alpha Epsilon Rho, Univ. of Tex., '64–'68; b. El Paso, Tex., 1945; p. Gale and Susanna Lindsey; h. Wilson L. Brown; res: 1929 St. Johns Dr., El Paso, Tex. 79903.

BROWN, DOROTHY DODD, Wms. Dir., KOLT Radio Station, Scottsbluff, Neb. 69361, '59; Asst. Mgr., C. of C.; Off. Mgr., W. Neb. Hosp.; Interviewer for on-the-spot bdcsts. of contests, tours, UN, World Fair; AWRT (Cornhusker Chptr. Treas.,) '65), AAUW, Soroptimist Club (Pres., '68–'69), Neb. State Alumni Aw., '65; Dorothy Carnegie Course (Grad.; Instr., '69), Dale Carnegie Courses (Grad.); Chadron State Col., BS, '63; Grad. Work, '66; b. Brush, Colo., 1913; p. W. W. and Ammie Royse Dodd; h. W. Kenneth Brown; c. Jeanne Ann (Mrs. Joe Nay), Lloyd Kenneth; res: R.R. 1, Mitchell, Neb. 69357.

BROWN, DOROTHY L., Dir., Bdcst. Standards and Practices, Western Division, American Broadcasting Company, 4151 Prospect Ave., Hollywood, Cal. 90027, '42–; NBC Radio, '31–'41; Bdcst. Pioneers, Pacific Pioneer Bdcstrs.; Col. of the Pacific, BA; b. Ia.

BROWN, EDDIE HOUSTON, Tchr., TV Prodr., Dallas Independent School District, 3010 Harry Hines Blvd., Dallas, Tex. 75201, '61–; Tchr., '54–'61; NHFL, Kappa Kappa Iota; Tex. Wms. Univ., BS, Southern Methodist Univ.; Univ. of Ut.; b. Mt. Pleasant, Tex., 1913; p. Clyde and Ruth Houston; h. Forris Brown; c.

Mrs. John W. Miller Jr.; res: Natchez House Apts., Houston, Tex.

BROWN, ELINOR BAADE, Auth., tchrs. pubns.; Pres., Treas., Midwest Publishing Company, Inc. Box 33, Ceresco, Neb. 68017, '69–; founded co. in '53; elementary tchr., '32–'39; State Hist. Soc., Nat. Trust for Hist. Preservation, Wilderness Soc., Lincoln-Lancaster Co. Hist. Soc. (Pres., '64–'68; Secy.,'68–'69); Who's Who of Am. Wm.; Neb. Wesleyan Univ., '32, '33, '37; Univ. of Neb., summers '34, '55; b. Bennett, Neb., 1915; p. Edward and Mary Zink Baade; h. James Lowell Brown; two children; res: 625 S. 56th St., Lincoln, Neb. 68510.

BROWN, ELIZABETH LEWIS, Mng. Ed., The Free Press, 103 W. Colorado Ave., P.O. Box 130, Colorado Springs, Colo. 80901, '66–; Reptr., '65; North Shores Sentinel, Independent (San Diego, Cal.), '58–'65; Asahi Evening News (Tokyo, Japan), '57; USNR WAVES, '42–'44; NPWC, Colo. Presswm.; numerous nwsp. aws.; b. Camp Grant, Ill.; p. James and Emma Reeder Lewis; h. Joseph Brown; c. Ross Piper, Jr., Ralph Piper; res: 2330 Twilight Dr., Colorado Springs, Colo. 80901.

BROWN, ELLEN HERRING, Wms. Ed., San Angelo Standard-Times, 34 W. Harris, San Angelo, Tex. 76901, '67–; Asst. Wms. Ed., '66–'67; Ft. Worth Press, '64–'66; Theta Sigma Phi; first place, AP Mng. Eds. competition in wms. news writing, '67, '68; Tex. Mental Health Assn. Aw., '68; Tex. Christian Univ., '60–'63; N. Tex. State Univ., '64; b. Ballinger, Tex., 1941; p. Loyd and Sue Gilliam Herring; h. Stephen Brown; c. Charles Stephen, II; res: 2113 St. Mary, San Angelo, Tex. 76901.

BROWN, EMMA GEISSINGER, Off. Mgr., Princeton University Press, 41 William St., Princeton, N.J. 08540, '69–; Adm. Asst., Robert W. Orr & Assoc., '52–'56; Southern Methodist Univ., '42; b. Richmond, Va., 1923; p. George and Elise Feys Geissinger; h. George F. Brown; c. Mary W.; res: 287 Edgerstoune Rd., Princeton, N.J. 08540.

BROWN, EVE, Dir. of Pubcty., The Plaza Hotel, Fifth Ave. and 59th St., N.Y., N.Y. 10022, '62–; Wms. Ed., Albany (N.Y.) Times Union, '56–'62; Chgo. (Ill.) American, '47–'56; Soc. Ed., N.Y. Journal American, '40–'45; Edtl. Staff, Paris Herald, '30–'33; Auth: "Champagne Cholly" ('47), "The Plaza" ('67); OPC, Auths. Guild; Columbia Univ. Sch. of Jnlsm.; b. N.Y.C.; h. (div.); res: 355 E. 72nd St., N.Y., N.Y. 10021.

BROWN, HAZEL DOELL, VP and Crtv. Dir., Halsey, Stakelum and Brown, Inc., 1820 St. Charles Ave., N.O., La., 70130, '69–; Copy Chief, Henderson Advertising Agency, '66–'69; Copywtr., Young & Rubicam, '61–'66; Copywtr., Fitzgerald Adv. Agcy., '51–'61; Copywtr., N.O. Public Svc., '43–'51; Instr. in Adv., Tulane Univ., '61; N.O. Adv. Club (Secy., '45–'51), L.A. Adv. Club, active in civic groups; Adv. aws. for campaigns for various cos.; Tulane Univ., Newcomb Col., BA, '43; b. N.O., La., 1921; p. Henry and Wilhelmina Diettel Doell; h. Beverly Brown; res: 5221 Meadowdale St., Metairie, La. 70002.

BROWN, HELEN GURLEY, Ed., Cosmopolitan, The Hearst Corporation, 1775 Broadway, N.Y., N.Y. 10019, '65–; Auth: "Sex and the Single Girl," "Sex and the Office," "Helen Gurley Brown's Single Girl's Cookbook" (all Bernard Geis Assocs.), "The Outrageous Opinions of Helen Gurley Brown" (Avon Books); Synd. TV Show," "Outrageous Opinions," '67–'68; Synd. Nwsp. Col., "Woman Alone," '63–'65; Copywtr., AE, Kenyon & Eckhardt, '58–'63; Copywtr., Foote, Cone & Belding, '48–'58; two record albums, "Helen Gurley Brown at Town Hall," "Lessons in Love," (Crescendo Records); Am. Soc. of Mag. Eds., Fashion Group, Auths. League, AFTRA; Frances Holmes Adv. Aws., '56–'58; Woodbury Col.; b. Green Forest, Ark., 1922; p. Ira M. and Cleo Sisco Gurley; h. David Brown; res: 605 Park Ave., N.Y., N.Y. 10021.

BROWN, HELEN MARIE, Asst. to the VP, Columbia Broadcasting System, Inc., 51 W. 52nd St., N.Y., N.Y. 10019, '68–; Assoc. Dir., Corp. Info., '67–'68; Rsch. Dir., Corp. Info., Corp. Affairs, '64–'67; free-lance edtl. and pic. rsch., '62–'63, '55–'57; AE, J. M. Hickerson, '61–'62; Asst. Ed., American Heritage, '57–'61; various positions, Time Inc., '46–'55; Special Libs. Assn., N.Y. Hist. Soc.; Hunter Col., BA, '50; b. N.Y.C. 1927; p. John and Margaret Wade Brown; res: 333 E. 46th St., N.Y., N.Y. 10017.

BROWN, INA CORINNE, Auth., Lectr., Cnslt., '66–; Prof. of Anthropology, Scarritt Col., Nashville, Tenn., '42–'66; Specialist and Sr. Specialist in Social Studies, U.S. Off. of Educ., Wash., D.C., '39–'42; Staff, Methodist Bd. of Educ., '26–'42; bks: "Understanding Other Cultures" ('63), "Race Relations in a Democracy" ('49), numerous others; chptrs., articles in pfsnl. jrnls.; AAUP, Auths. League, numerous anthropology orgs.; Univ. of Chgo., AB (Phi Beta Kappa, Sigma Xi; Rosenwald Fellow, '38–'39); PhD (Anthropology), '42; b. Gatesville, Tex.; p. John and Corinne Wells Brown; res: 1509 17th Ave. S., Nashville, Tenn. 37212.

BROWN, JUNE WILCOXON, Free-lance Wtr., '65–; Ed., Select Magazine (Madison, Wis.), '59–'65; Wtr., "Beverly Stark Radio Show," '63–'68; PR, Wilson Steamship Line and the Wash. Civic Theatre, '36–'41; auth. of numerous short stories, humor and travel articles for pubns. in U.S., Can., Eng.; NLAPW (Madison, Wis., Chptr. Pres., '54–'56), Theta Sigma Phi (Madison Chptr. Wtrs. Cup Aw., '51); Univ. of Md., BA, '35; b. W. Lafayette, Oh., 1914; p. Ralph and Almeda Marx Wilcoxon; h. Albert Brown; c. Peter; res: P.O. Box 2897, St. Thomas, Virgin Islands. 00801.

BROWN, KAY LOU, Program Prod. Coordr., Management TV Systems, 277 Park Ave., N.Y., N.Y. 10017, '69–; TV Prod. Dir., Univ. of Miami, '66–'69; TV Prodr.-

Dir., '63–'66; TV Prodr.-Dir.-Wtr., News Dept., WTHI-TV (Terre Haute, Ind.), '60–'61; AWRT, Theta Sigma Phi, Tri Delta, Alpha Epsilon Rho, Gamma Alpha Chi; Mich. State Univ., BS '59; Ind. Univ., MA, '63; b. Toledo, Oh., 1938; p. Louis and Helen Watts Brown; res: 170 West End Ave., N.Y., N.Y. 10023.

BROWN, LILLIAN BROOKS, Dir., The Broadcast Center, The American University, Massachusetts and Nebraska Aves. N.W., Wash., D.C. 20016; Dir., Radio-TV, George Wash. Univ.; Auth: "A Living Centennial," "Symbols of the Television Age: Let Us Preserve Them"; Cnslt., CBS Network (TV makeup); NATAS (VP, '64–'66; Presidential Emmy, '64–'66) AWRT, ANWC, NAEB, Intl. Bdcstrs. Soc.; Am. Univ. Fac. Wms. Club; McCall's Golden Mike Aw., '59; AAUW aw., ACPRA aw., '68; Who's Who of Am. Wm., Who's Who in Commerce and Industry, Nat. Gold Book, Distg. Wm. of the U.S., Gold Book of Wash.'s Most Distg. Wm., Royal Blue Book of Great Britain; Oh. State Univ., Bowling Green State Univ., George Wash. Univ.; b. Huntsville, Oh.; c. Carla (Mrs. Richard Gorrell), Kristi, Kimberley; res: 1200 N. Nash St., Arlington, Va. 22209.

BROWN, MABEL EDWARDS, Ed., Publr.-Owner, Bits and Pieces, Box 746, Newcastle, Wyo. 82701, '65–; Corr: Sheridan (Wyo.) Press and Rapid City (S.D.) Daily Jnl., '62–; Wyoming State Tribune (Cheyenne); '69–; Wyoming Eagle (Cheyenne); '69–; Denver (Colo.) Post, '69–; Wtr., Mont. Stockman Farmer, Wyo. Stockman Farmer, '62–'65; Co-Auth: " . . . And Then There Was One" ('62), "Coals of Newcastle" ('65), "Jubilee Memories" ('65); Hist. Cnslt.; various orgs. and aws.; b. Golden, Colo., 1914; p. R. O. and Jesse Fry Edwards; h. Charles Wesley Brown; c. Jean (Mrs. Richard J. Martin), Martha Marie (Mrs. John K. Allender); res: 10 W. Hill, Newcastle, Wyo. 82701.

BROWN, MABEL ESTLE, Dir. of Guidance, Lone Tree Community Schools, Lone Tree, Ia. 52755, '60–; Tchr., '30–'60; mag. contrbr.; Theta Sigma Phi; Ia. Acad. of Sci., Ia. State Educ. Asson., NEA, Am. and Ia. Pers. and Guidance Assns., Nat. Cncl. of Tchrs. of Eng.; Intl., State and Ia. City Reading Assns.; Lone Tree Educ. Assn (Secy., '62–); Univ. of Ia., BA, '32; Ia. State Univ., MS, '53; b. Letts, Ia., 1907; p. Chester and Mayme Bell Estle; h. Robert G. Brown; c. Patricia Jane (Mrs. Lester Hoback), Linnaeus E.; res: R.R. #1, Conesville, Ia. 52739.

BROWN, MARIE H., Pers. Off. Mgr., Treas., Edward Spilman and Associates, 1502 S. Boulder Ave., Tulsa, Okla. 74119, '64–; Media Exec., '63–; Exec. Secy., Gen. Controls Co., '56–'63; Okla. Accountancy Sch., '55; b. Skiatook, Okla., 1920; p. Emmert and Icie Rickey Turnbull; h. George Brown (div.); c. Roger Hurd, Mrs. Bill Hooker; res: 1204 S. Toledo Ave., Tulsa, Okla. 74112.

BROWN, MARION CLARE, Prod. Mgr., William H. Sadlier Inc., 11 Park Pl., N.Y., N.Y. 10007, '56–; in charge all Bookjacket & Endpaper Art, dies & prod. of dummies for sales conferences, The Macmillan Co., '36–'42; Plant Prod, The Conway Printing Co., one yr.; in charge composition, Kingsport Press, Inc. (N.Y.C.), '45–'52; Asst. to Off. Mgr., Westcott & Thomson, Inc. (N.Y.C.), '53–'56; all phases bk. typography, hot metal to computerized film, pioneer in use of photo composition; First book on Linotron; AIGA, Carnegie Medal for Heroism, '33; Northfield Seminary, '34; Ballard Sch., '35; N.Y.U., Columbia Univ., AIGA Workshop, Sch. of Printing, Julliard Sch., Guilmant Organ Sch.; b. Westwood, N.J., 1915; p. Harry and Ethel Hunting Brown; h. Paul J. Endres; res: 165 Park Row, 5C, N.Y., N.Y. 10038, and 8 E. Pelican St., Isles of Capri, Naples, Fla. 33940.

BROWN, MARION MUNRO, Colmst., Home Furnishings Daily, Fairchild Publications, Seven E. 12th St., N.Y., N.Y. 10003, '56–; Bedding Ed., '49–'55; Colmst., Bedding Magazine (Wash., D.C.) '59–; Furniture Bedding Mkt. Rd., Retailing Home Furnishings Weekly, '41–'49; Operator, The Furniture House (Concord, N.H.); Asst. Adv. Mgr., Edward Malley Co. (New Haven, Conn.); Asst. Adv. Mgr. and Copywtr., Denholm & McKay Co. (Worcester, Mass.); NHFL, Gamma Phi Beta; Boston Univ., BS (Liberal Arts), '29; b. Concord, N.H., 1910; p. Frank Guy and Laura Marion Munro Brown; h. John Meeker High (dec.); c. Peter Brown High; res: 269 Broadway, Dobbs Ferry, N.Y. 10522.

BROWN, MARTHA FRANCES, Ed., North DeKalb Record; Assoc. Ed., DeKalb New Era, New Era Publishing Company, 1833 Lawrenceville Highway, Decatur, Ga. 30031; free lance trade mag. wtr.; Theta Sigma Phi (Chptr. Pres., '68), Ga. Press Assn. (Bd. of Dirs., '57–'58, '58–'59); Ga. Conf. on Social Welfare Aw., '62; Salvation Army Aws., '58, '59, '60; Dixie Bus. Aw., '58; Univ. of Ga., AB (Jnlsm.), '43; b. Atlanta, Ga., 1921; p. Eugene and Frances Gaulding Smith; h. Hugh Mack Brown, Jr. (div.); c. Hugh A., William L.; res: 2308 Dellwood Dr., N.W., Atlanta, Ga. 30305.

BROWN, MARY FRIEL, Acquisitions Librn., Vanderbilt Medical Center Library, Nashville, Tenn. 37203, '67–; Librn., N. Nashville HS, '40–'67; Librn., Cohn HS, '38–'40; Tchr., '36–'38; WNBA (Bd. Mbr., six yrs.), Med. Lib. Assn., Tenn. Lib. Assn., Nashville Lib. Club, Mid Tenn. Lib. Assn.; Vanderbilt Univ., AB, '36; Peabody Col., BS (Lib. Sci.), '39; b. Birmingham, Ala.; p. Waldo and Theresa Regan Brown; res: 6112 Jocelyn Hollow Rd., Nashville, Tenn. 37205.

BROWN, MARY LORETTA THERESE, VP, Hill and Knowlton, Inc., 150 E. 42nd St., N.Y., N.Y. 10028, '66–; Dir., Wm. Activities, '60–; AE, Coca-Cola Co., '55–'60; Crtv. Coordr., Lux Products, Lever Brothers, '53–'54; Pubcty. Dir., Harriet Hubbard Ayer, '47–'53; Auth: "Angela in Public Relations" (Dodd, Mead & Co., '65); "The Gift" (Dimension Books, '68); Fashion Group, The Old York Club, AWRT, Eng. Speaking Un.; N.Y.C. Gold Key, '64; Columbia Univ.; b. N.Y.C.; p. John and Caecilia Reynolds Brown; res: 1025 Park Ave., N.Y., N.Y. 10028.

BROWN, CLEMENTINE MICHEL, Dir., Corporate Commtns., Stop & Shop Inc., 393 E St., Boston, Mass. 02210, '68–; Exec. VP, Hargood Assocs., '64–'69; Asst. Dir., PR, Wm. Filene's Sons; PR Rep., N.W. Ayer & Sons (N.Y.); Staff Colmst., Boston Post; PR Advisor to numerous orgs.; active in numerous civic affairs; res: 17 Front St., Marblehead, Mass. 01945.

BROWN, MYRA BERRY, Auth., 18 Children's bks.; PEN, Southern Cal. Cncl. on Literature for Children and Young People; U.C.L.A.; b. Mpls., Minn., 1918; p. Louis and Marion Hosenpud Berry; h. Ned Brown; c. Lorna Lou, Elizabeth Ann, Jonathan Martin; res: 21640 Pacific Coast Highway, Malibu, Cal. 90265.

BROWN, NETTIE CARDOZA, Publr., Ed., Imperial Valley Weekly, P.O. Box 908, El Centro, Cal. 92243, '52–; Corr., L.A. Times, '64–; News Ed., Tulelake Reptr., '50–'52; News Ed., Palo Alto News, '35–'36; Theta Sigma Phi (Matrix Aw.), '61; Jeane Hoffman Aw., '64), Bus. and Pfsnl. Dem. of Imperial County (Pres.), '69) Head of Col. of Bus., '33; b. Fresno, Cal.; p. Antone and Mary Perry Cardoza; h. George Brown (div.); c. James Philip, Mary Dolores (Mrs. Cecil Walker), George Edward, John Anthoney, Eleanor Anne, Jerry Noel, Philip Jean, Antone Joseph, Carl Lonnie Black; res: 1256 Brighton Ave., El Centro, Cal. 92243.

BROWN, PATRICIA SEWARD, Nightclub, Restaurant Ed., Gore Newspapers Co., 320 S.E. First Ave., Ft. Lauderdale, Fla. 33301, '64–; Nightclub Colmst., Miami Herald, '57–'64; Wms. Ed., N.Y. World-Telegram-Sun, '50–'56; Assoc. Fashion Ed., N.Y. Sun, '46–'50; Reptr., '43–'46; Free-lance Wtr.; Fla. Wms. Press Club, NWC of N.Y. (Pres., '55–'56), Theta Sigma Phi (Broward County Chptr. Treas., '66–); Charm Inst. aw., '51; Northwestern Univ. Medill Sch. of Jnlsm.; b. Columbus, Oh.; p. Alfred and Eva Haynes Seward; h. Elmore J. Brown (dec.); c. Jacqueline (Mrs. Jack. H. Nelson), Beverly (Mrs. William A. McGregor); res: 2436 Aqua Vista Blvd., Ft. Lauderdale, Fla. 33301.

BROWN, PATRICIA STRIBLING, PR Dir., Rockford Memorial Hospital, 2400 N. Rockton Ave., Rockford, Ill. 61101, '63–; previously PR Offcr., U.S. Army; Public Info. Offcr., Veterans Admin.; Ed., Wtr., Nat. Cncl. of the Episcopal Ch.; Theta Sigma Phi, ICIE, Am. Soc. for Hosp. PR Dirs. (Charter Mbr.); Drake Univ., AB (cum laude, Phi Beta Kappa); Columbia Univ. Grad. Sch. of Jnlsm., MS; h. Thomas J. Brown; c. Donald, William, Judy Lundstrom; res: 2210 Oaklawn Ave., Rockford, Ill. 61107.

BROWN, PATRICIA SUE, Ed., The Peace Corps Volunteers, Peace Corps, Wash., D.C. 20525, '65–; Theta Sigma Phi; Ind. Univ., AB, '63; b. East Chgo., Ind., 1941; p. James and Edna Fauser Brown; res: 541 Fourth St., S.E., Wash., D.C. 20003.

BROWN, REGINA SCHWENK, Mgr. Adv. and Sls. Prom., Davis & Geck, Div. of American Cyanamid Co., Middletown Rd., Pearl River, N.Y. 10965, '68–; Partner, Medrep Assoc.; Eastern Adv. Mgr., Gordon M. Marshall Co.; Media Dir., D. L. Burdick Assoc.; Adv., Sls. Mgr., Osteopathic Press; Copywtr., Fred Gardner & Co.; Pharmaceutical Adv. Club; Hunter Col., BA, '55; b. N.Y.C.; p. Gottlieb and Evelyn Unger Schwenk; h. John Callaghan; res: Waldwick, N.J. 07463.

BROWN, RITA MAE, Photo Ed., Sterling Publishing, 419 Park Ave. S., N.Y., N.Y. 10016, '69–; Edtl. Asst., '69; Adm. Coordr., Nat. NOW, '69; Ed., N.Y. NOW, '69–; Poetry published in APHRA, performed by New Feminist Theater; RAT Collective; NAMW; Univ. of Fla., '62–'63 (Hons. Program); N.Y.U., '65–'68; Grad Sch., '68; Sch. of Visual Arts (Cinematography), '68; b. Hanover, Pa., 1944; p. Ralph and Julia Buckingham Brown; res: 260 W. 15th St., N.Y., N.Y. 10011.

BROWN, STELLA RYDER, Radio-TV Bdcstr.-Wtr.-Prodr., WHLO, WAKR and Free-lance, '46–; TV, '52–; Radio-TV workshop tchr. and cnslt., many states; AWRT (Akron Chptr. Pres.), '55–'56; Western Reserve Chptr. Treas.), '63–'65), Wms. City Club Bus. and Pfsnl. Wm.; only wm. speaker, World Conf. Christian Bdcsting., Frankfurt, Germany, '57; Nat. Aw. for Christian Citizenship, '56; Nat. Chmn., Radio and TV for United Church Wm., '55; Secy., Nat. Bdcsting. and Film, '54; Bowling Green State Col., '25–'26; h. Hobart P. Brown; c. Thomas C.; res: 718 Chitty Ave., Akron, Oh. 44303.

BROWN, SUSAN ALICE, Ed., Statistical Laboratory, 102F Service Bldg., Iowa State University, Ames, Ia. 50010, '64–; Exec. Dir., Public Info. Chmn., West Story County Chptr., Am. Red Cross, '62–'63; Health Educ., Ia. State Dept. of Health, '59–'61; Grad. Asst., Ia. State Univ., '58–'59; Adv. Copywtr., Younkers Dept. Store, '55–'57; Theta Sigma Phi (Nat. VP, '61–'68; Treas., '68–), Phi Upsilon Omicron; Who's Who of Am. Wm.; Ia. State Univ., BS (Jnlsm.), '55 (Mortar Bd.); MS (Jnlsm.), '60; b. Champaign, Ill., 1934; p. W. Sterry and June Calahan Brown; res: 2015 Burnett St., Ames, Ia. 50010.

BROWN, VANESSA, Actress, Wtr.; Corr., Voice of America, Los Angeles Times Service, KTLA-TV, '62–; Co-star, "My Favorite Husband" (CBS-TV), '55; Co-Star, "The Seven Year Itch" (Broadway), '52–'54; Star, Motion Pics., "The Bad and The Beautiful," "The Late George Apley," "The Ghost and Mrs. Muir," "The Fighter," "Rosie," '45–'54; AMPAS, SAG, AFTRA, AEA, Alternate Delegate, Dem. Nat. Conv., '56; Citizenship aws., B'nai B'rith, Bonds for Israel, Hadassah; Radio/TV Comm. for political campaigns; U.C.L.A., BA (Eng.), '48; b. Vienna, Austria, 1928; p. Nah and Anna Butterman Brind; h. Mark R. Sandrich, Jr.; c. Cathy, Lisa, David; res: 1430 Mulholland Dr., L.A., Cal. 90024.

BROWN, VERNON KIMBALL, Dir. of PR, Passavant Memorial Hospital, 303 E. Superior St., Chgo., Ill.

60611, '57–; Wtr., Phila. Blue Cross, '56–'57; Educ. Dir., Nat. Arthritis and Rheumatism Fndn., N.Y.C., '53–'56; Dir. of Public Interest, Roosevelt Hosp., '50–'53; Campaign Wtr. and Pic. Ed., UN appeal for children, Red Cross, Un. Hosp. Fund, '47–'50; many articles on hosp. commtns.; Acad. of Hosp. PR (Pres., '69–), Soc. of Hosp. PR Dirs. of the Amer. Hosp. Assn., Am. Med. Wtrs. Assn., Chgo. Hosp. Cncl.; MacEachern Cit. for hosp. annual repts., '65; MacEachern Aws. for total PR program and special projects, '66–'68; 14 Helen Cody Baker Aws. for hosp. pubns., '57–'67; Duke Univ., '39; Univ. of Miami, '40; Fla. State Col. for Wm., '38–'41; b. Macon, Ga., 1921; p. Wilmer and Maude Deale Kimball; h. Madison B. Brown; res: 615 Chatham Rd., Glenview, Ill. 60025.

BROWN, VIRGINIA SUGGS, Dir., Early Childhood Educ., McGraw-Hill Book Company, Webster Div., Manchester Rd., Manchester, Mo. 63011, '66–; Dir., Head Start, St. Louis Human Dev. Corp., '65–'66; Supvsr., St. Louis Public Schs. System, '60–'65; Tchr.-in-charge, Banneker Reading Clinic, '56–'60; Tchr., '48–'56; TV Tchr., adult reading, CBS, summers '63–'67; Tchr., remedial reading, Harris Tchrs. Col., '61–'64; pfsnl. workshops, programs; cnslt.; Sr. Auth., "Skyline Series," four readers (McGraw-Hill, '65, '67), filmstrips and films ('67, '69); Co-auth., bk. on teaching art ('70); contrbr., mags. and pfsnl. jnls.; local offcr., numerous intl., nat., state and local educ. assns.; Hannah G. Solomon Aw., '66; active on bds. of children's and civic orgs.; Stowe Tchrs. Col., BA, '47; Wash. Univ., MA, '52; grad. work, '53–'56; b. St. Louis, Mo., 1924; p. Clarence and Viola Hampton Suggs; h. Charles F. Brown; res: 4106A San Francisco Ave., St. Louis, Mo. 63115.

BROWNE, FREDA, Owner, Freda Browne—Book Design-Production, 208 E. 28th St., N.Y., N.Y. 10016, '51–; VP, Ptnr., Visualart Assocs., '44–'50; Julian Messner, Publr., '35–'43; Claude Kendall, Publr., '29–'35; Am. Inst. of Graphic Arts; The Typophiles, WNBA (N.Y.C. Chptr. Treas., '61–'63; Exec. Secy., '64); Amy Loveman Nat. Aw. (Exec. Secy., '64–); b. Phila., Pa., 1910; p. Morris and Fannie Spivak Browne; res: 208 E. 28th St., N.Y., N.Y. 10016.

BROWNE, ROSALIND BENGELSDORF, Edtl. Assoc., Art Critic, Art News, 444 Madison Ave., N.Y., N.Y. 10022, '64–; Art Reviewer, '49; Tchr., art perception, New Sch., '66–; Contrbr. (art profiles), Ency. Judaica, '68–'69; Lectr., private groups and cols.; Auth.-Cnslt., U.S. Govt. rsch. project, Fed. Support for the Visual Arts; Art Ed., Critic, Colmst., N.Y. Star, '48–'49; Auth., articles in numerous mags.; Artists Equity Assn. of N.Y., Col. Art Assn. of Am., Am. Abstract Artists (Charter Member, '36), Am. Artists Congress, Artists Un.; educ: Art Students League, '30–'34; Annot Art Sch., '34–'35; Hans Hofmann Sch., '35–'36; N.Y.U.; b. N.Y.C., 1916; p. Isidore and Sadie Bengelsdorf; h. Bryon Browne (dec.); c. Stephen B.; res: 203 W. 86th St., N.Y., N.Y. 10024.

BROWNE-MAYERS, CHARLOTTE BROWNE, Ombudswm, Intl. Public Affairs, 45 W. 54th St., N.Y., N.Y. 10019; 1st wm. Assoc. Dir. Gen., World Council of Churches, also Exec. Dir., Inter-Church Aid, Refugees and World Service, Geneva, Switzerland, '68–'70; Dir., Adult Educ., Std. Oil Co., N.J. (N.Y.C.), '42–'70; Dir., Pubcty. and PR, Packard Bus. Sch. and Jr. Col., '39–'42; Dir., Adult Educ., YWCA (Bklyn.), '36–'39; Program Cnslr., Boston YWCA, '34–'36; PRSA, active in numerous nat. educ., ch., wms., econs., public svc. orgs., incl. bd. mbrships; Boston Univ., AB (Hist.), '32 (Nat. Alumni Cncl., '65–; Outstanding Public Svc. Aw., '64); Sch. Theology, '32–'33; Modern Sch. Applied Art, '34; Columbia Tchrs. Col., Columbia Sch. of Bus. Adm., grad. work, '64–'67; b. Lancaster, Mass., 1910; p. Benjamin and Lena Patterson Randall; h. 1. John T. Lochhead (div.) 2. Albert N. Browne-Mayers; c. Cecily Ann; res: Warren, Conn. 06754.

BROWNLOW, DIANE M., Cont. Dir., WIBX Radio, Box 950, Utica, N.Y. 13503, '64–; Copywtr., WINR Radio (Binghamton), '63–'64; Radio Adv. Bur. Aw., '65; b. Binghamton, N.Y., 1943; p. George and Anita Grambs Brownlow; res: Box 950, Utica, N.Y. 13503.

BROWNMILLER, SUSAN, Free-lance Wtr.; News Wtr., ABC Network, '65–'67; Reptr., NBC-TV (Phila., Pa.), '65; Auth., juv. bk. on Rep. Shirley Chisholm (Doubleday); Media Wm.; Cornell Univ., '52–'55; res: 61 Jane St., N.Y., N.Y. 10014.

BROYLES, MABEL GRUBBS, Assoc. Ed., The Mecklenburg Gazette, 108 S. Main, Davidson, N.C. 28036, '67–; Ed., '48–; Ed., Publr., '58–'67; Ed., Tar Heel Woman, '58–'59; BPW; b. Christian Co., Ky., 1916; p. Andrew and Georgia Burke Grubbs; h. Horace C. Broyles (dec.); c. Anne Elizabeth (Mrs. Harry Bagnal), Julia Faye (Mrs. James Chandler); res: 653 Concord Road, Davidson, N.C. 28036.

BRUBAKER, MARY CLARK, Wms. Dir., KRNT-TV, 9th and Pleasant Sts., Des Moines, Ia. 50309, '67–; Prodr., Talent, "The Mary Brubaker Show," '67–; Talent, '60–'67; Lib. Asst., Des Moines Register and Tribune, '50s; AWRT, Zeta Phi Eta (aw., '68), Drama Workshop of Des Moines (Acting, Dir. aws.), Ctr. for Crtv. Interchange (Bd. Mbr.), Ia. Commn. for Blind; Drake Univ., BFA, '57; b. Des Moines, Ia., 1935; p. John and Lora Goff Clark; h. Theodore Brubaker; c. Theodore John; res: 2725 Moyer St., Des Moines, Ia. 50310.

BRUCE, ELEANORE HILLEBRAND, PR Dir., Macy's New York, Herald Sq., N.Y., N.Y. 10001, '61–; Ed. in Chief, Charm Magazine; Fashion Mdse. Ed., Seventeen; Fashion Group, CWPR; Barnard Col., Columbia Univ., BS; b. N.Y.C., 1917; p. Henry and Eleanore Hillebrand; h. Frederic J. Bruce; c. Michael; res: 829 Park Ave., N.Y., N.Y. 10021.

BRUCE, JEANNETTE MAE, Auth., "The Wallflower

Season" ('62); Staff Wtr., Sports Illustrated, Time, Inc., Rockefeller Ctr., N.Y., N.Y. 10020, '69–; mag. short stories, articles; Univ. of Southern Cal., BA (Eng. Lit.), '51; b. Fargo, N.D., 1932; p. Maurice and Jennie Bruce Zelik; res: 50 W. Ninth St., N.Y., N.Y. 10011.

BRUECK, VIRGINIA L., PR Cnslt., Virginia L. Brueck, Public Relations, Rembrandt at 928 Rodin Dr., Baton Rouge, La. 70806, '56–; Dir. of PR, City Recreation Dept., '54–'55; Asst. Info. Dir. for govt. rsch. agy. and free-lance, '52–'54; Ed., three monthly church mags. for young people, '44–'46; Owner and Ed. weekly nwsp., '40–'44; Instr. of Jnlsm., NE State Col., '55–'56; Theta Sigma Phi (Baton Rouge Chptr., Pres., '66; Treas., '68–'69); La. Press Wm. (Pres., '60), NFPW, PRSA (Baton Rouge Chptr. Pres., '68); Baylor Univ., BA; Northwestern Univ.; La. State Univ., MA (Jnlsm., Sociol.).

BRUFF, NANCY, Auth: Novels "The Country Club" ('69), "The Fig Tree" ('64), "The Beloved Woman" ('49), "Cider From Eden" ('47), "The Manatee" ('45); Poems—"My Talon in Your Heart" ('46); PSA; The Sorbonne; b. Bridgeport, Conn., 1909; p. Austin and Alice Birdsall Bruff; h.Esmond Gardner; c. Thurston Bruff Clarke, Penelope Clarke; res: 168 E. 74th St., N.Y., N.Y. 10021.

BRUMETT, ROBIN ERIKSEN, AE, KIRO-TV (Bonneville Corporation), Third and Broad Sts., Broadcast House, Seattle, Wash. 98121, '67–; hostess, "Eye on Seattle," '67–'67; Dir. of Mchndsng., '64–'67; AWRT, NATAS, (Seattle Adv. Club (Bd. of Dirs.), Club, Theta Sigma Phi; Univ. of Wash., BA '64 (cum laude; Outstanding Dept. of Commtns. Jr., '63; Sr., '64); b. Seattle, Wash., 1942; p. Richard and Marguerite Eriksen; h. Bert Brumett, Jr.; res: 19335 22nd N.W., Seattle, Wash. 98177.

BRUMFIELD, BETTY DIAL, Wms. Pg. Ed., Enterprise-Journal, N. Broadway, McComb, Miss. 39648, '66–; Miss. Press Wm. Assn. (aws., '67, '68), NFPW; Memphis Acad. of Arts; Barbizon Sch. of Modeling; b. Wabash, Ark., 1927; p. David and Rosalie DeNio Dial; h. Robert L. Brumfield; c. Patricia Rosalie, E. Susan, William Allen; res: 315 Burke St., McComb, Miss. 39648.

BRUNER, LOUISE EISELE, Art Ed., Toledo Blade, Superior St., Toledo, Oh. 43604, '55–; Art Critic, Cleve. News, '38–'52; Contrbr. to Grolier Ency., Am. Artist, Art Voices, Arts, St. Louis Post-Dispatch; Lectr.: Univ. of Fla., '63–'64; Toledo Museum of Art, '64–'68; Midwest Corr., The Art Gallery; Cleve. Inst. of Art, '68; Nat. Cncl. of the Arts, AFA, Toledo Artists Club, Oh. Nwsp. Wms. Assn. (aw. for critical writing, '60–'68), Toledo Modern Art Group, Archaeological Inst. of Am.; Denison Univ., BA, '31; Grad. Work: Western Reserve Univ., Univ. of Fla., Univ. of Toledo, Mary Manse Col.; b. Cleve., Oh., 1910; p. Charles and Martha Bashold Eisele; h. Raymond A. Bruner; c.

Sylvia (Mrs. Charles Shapley), Madelin, Suzanne; res: 2244 Scottwood Ave., Toledo, Oh. 43620.

BRUNK, CHARLOTTE DICKSON, Travel Ed., Bk. Ed., Asst. Ed., Picture Magazine, Des Moines Register and Tribune, 715 Locust St., Des Moines, Ia. 50304.

BRUNNER, JOY, Radio Time Byr., Frank B. Sawdon, Inc., 555 Madison Ave., N.Y., N.Y. 10022; previously Media Byr., Recht and Co., Beverly Hills, Cal.; Publicist, Great Western Fin. Corp.; AWRT; UCLA, BA, '59; b. Columbus, Oh., 1937; p. Robert and Edna Vaught Brunner; res: 400 E. 55th St., Apt. 14D, N.Y., N.Y. 10022.

BRUNO, ANNE TURNER, Free-lance Wtr., c/o American Consulate Mail Room, Istanbul, Turkey, '63–; Dir., Nat. News Bur., Girl Scouts of U.S.A. PR, N.Y.C., '58–'62; Press and Info. Offcr., U.S.I.A., Germany and Italy, '47–'57; articles published in McCall's, Reader's Digest, Sports Illustrated; Univ. of Pa., BA, '43 (Phi Beta Kappa); b. Easton, Pa.; p. Col. William and Florentine Schneider Turner; res: 420 W. 51st St., N.Y., N.Y. 10019.

BRYAN, DOROTHY M., Advisory Ed., Exec., Dodd, Mead and Company, Inc., 79 Madison Ave., N.Y., N.Y. 10016, '39–; organized juv. dept.; Head, juv. dept., Doubleday; Auth., seven bks. for children, incl., "Just Tammie," "Michael and Patsy," "Johnny Penguin"; Nat. Girl Scouts (Pers. Div.), Glen Cove Visiting Nurse Assn. (Bd. of Dirs.); Packer Collegiate Inst.; Barnard Col.; Columbia Univ. Sch. of Jnlsm.; b. Wash., D.C.; p. Frank J. and Alice C. Bryan; res: 99 Walnut Rd., Glen Cove, N.Y. 11542.

BRYAN, MIRIAM MAY, Cnslt., Elementary and Secondary School Programs, Educational Testing Service, Princeton, N.J. 08540, '69–; Sr. Ed., Assoc. Dir., Coop. Test Div., '67–'68; Assoc. Dir., Test Dev., '61–'67; Senior Project Director, Test Dev., '60–'61; Educ. Testing Svc., Coadjutant Staff Mbr., '56–'58; Asst. Prof., Rutgers Univ., '58–'60; Test Specialist, Psy. Corp., '55–'56; Asst. Ed., Silver Burdett Co., '49–'55; Educ. Testing Svc., '48–'49; Coop. Test Svc., '43–'48; Tchr., '35–'43; AAUW, ACTFL, AAUP, AERA, ASCD, IRA, MLA, NCME, NCTE, NEA, Kappa Delta Pi, WNBA; Who's Who of Am. Wm.; Who's Who in the East, N. Tillinghast aw. from Bridgewater State Col., '70; Bridgewater State Col., BS (Educ.), '29; N.Y.U., MA, '40; b. Prince Edward Island, Can.; p. George and Emma Lawless May; h. James E. Bryan; res: 4978 Vernon Springs Dr., Atlanta, Ga. 30338.

BRYANT, BETH ELAINE, Free-lance Wtr., specializing in travel writing, '63–; travel articles, Cosmopolitan, Mademoiselle, Cara; "Ireland on $5 a Day" (Arthur Frommer Pubns., '67), "The Dollarwise Guide to Washington, D.C." (Frommer-Pasmentier Publ., '66), "The West Coast on $5 and $10 a Day" (Co-auth.; Arthur Frommer Pubns., '67), others; Ed., The Manhattan Shopper, trade nwsp., '64; Prod. Ed., Conde

Nast, '63; Soc. of Am. Travel Wtrs.; Barrington Col. (highest hons., '54–'56); Columbia Univ.; b. N.Y.C., 1936; p. Rev. Lloyd T. and Dorothy Richards Bryant; res: 647 W. 172nd St., N.Y., N.Y. 10032.

BRYANT, FRANCES JANE, Mng. Ed., The Norman Transcript, 215 E. Comanche St., Norman, Okla. 73069, '67–; City Ed., '59–'67; Wire Ed., '57–'59; Reptr., '55–'57; Guest Lectr., Univ. of Okla. Jnlsm. Sch.; Okla. Press Assn. (Instr., News Short Courses), Theta Sigma Phi (State Wm. of the Yr. in Commtns., '68); Best Heart Fund Story of the Yr. in Okla., '69; Altrusa Intl. (Norman Club 1st VP); Christian Col., AA, '53; Univ. of Mo., BJ, '55; b. Cushing, Okla., 1933; p. Edward and Dorothy McLean Bryant; res: 606 Sherwood Dr., Norman, Okla. 73069.

BRYANT, KATHERINE POTTER, Prof. of Govt., Woodbury College, 1027 Wilshire Blvd., L.A., Cal. 90017, '54–; former Dean of Wm.; Dir. of Rsch., Story Ed., Argosy Pictures; Bus. Commtns. Cnslt.; PR Lectr.; Auth. of bus. bks.; Adv. Club of L.A., Tau Kappa Alpha, Theta Alpha Phi, DAR (L.A. Chptr. Regent), Colonial Dames of 17th Century, Humane Soc. of the U.S.; Most Outstanding Tchr. of Woodbury Col., '59; Univ. of S.D., AB, '32 (cum laude; Phi Beta Kappa); Univ. of Southern Cal., MS (Educ.), '64; b. Blunt, S.D.; p. William S. and Mary Congdon Potter; h. W. C. Bryant; c. James Cliffton; res: 241 S. St. Andrews Pl., L.A., Cal. 90004.

BRYCE, MARTHA DOWELL, Wms. Ed., Waxahachie Daily Light, 215 S. College, Waxahachie, Tex. 75165, '67–; Wms. Ed.-Reptr., Current Argus (Carlsbad, N.M.), '35; Feature Wtr.-Reptr., Okla. City Times, '34–'35; Wms. Ed.-Colmst., Okla. Daily (Norman), '33–'34; News Reptr., El Reno (Okla.) Am., '30; Theta Sigma Phi (Okla. Chptr. Pres., '33–'34); Univ. of Okla., BA (Jnlsm.), '34 (Sigma Delta Chi. Aw., '34; Mortar Board, '33; Phi Beta Kappa, '34); active in numerous civic groups; b. El Reno, Okla., 1911; p. Clyde and Goldie Rockwell Dowell; h. John Bryce; c. James; res: 202 Overhill Dr., Waxahachie, Tex. 75165.

BRYDON, JEAN ARMSTRONG, Free-lance Wtr. and Colmst., Globe and Mail Ltd., 140 King St. W., Toronto, Ont., Canada, '63–; PR Wtr., Children's Aid, '67–; children's bk. critic, '66–'69; Encyclopedia Britannica Wtr., '60–'62; Reptr., '54–'56; Canadian Wms. Press Club ('52–'56); Univ. of Western Ontario, BA (Jnlsm.); b. Beamsville, Ont., Canada, 1930; p. Clarke and Ellen McLaren Armstrong; h. J. Arthur Brydon; c. Jo Ellen, Bill; res: 33 Kappele Ave., Toronto 319 Ont., Canada.

BRYSAC, SHAREEN BLAIR, Photo Ed., Random House, 201 Third Ave., N.Y., N.Y. 10003, '69–; Free-lance Photo Ed., Visual Cnslt., '66–'69; Wtr., filmstrips and articles on art, published in Art Annual, '69; Am. Soc. of Pic. Pfsnls., Am. Guild of Musical Artists; Who's Who in Dance, '65; Barnard Col., BA, '61; h. Peter Brysac; res: 50 W. 96th St., N.Y., N.Y. 10025.

BUCHAN, ELIZABETH LAWSON, Instr., Eng. and Jnlsm., Rockingham Community College, Wentworth, N.C. 27365, '66–; Pubcty. and PR, Ocean Spray Cranberries, '49–'64; Publicist/Pubn. Ed., Arlington Mills, Laurence, Mass., '47–'49; Assoc. Ed., Andover Townsman, '38–'47; Pubcty. Club of Boston, PRSA (accredited, '67), Mass. Indusl. Eds. Assn.; Jr. Col. Jnlsm. Assn., '70–; Tufts, BA (Eng.), '37; Univ. of Fla., MA (Commtns.), '65–'66; Univ. of Tex., Nwsp. Fund Fellow, summer '68; b. Andover, Mass., 1915; p. John and Anne Porter Buchan; res: Rte. 3, University Estates, Reidsville, N.C. 27320.

BUCHANAN, BONNIE FARLOW, Rschr., NBC News, 30 Rockefeller Plaza, N.Y., N.Y. 10020, '66–; Wtr.-Rschr., "FDR" NBC educ. film, '67; Prod. Asst., "Monitor," NBC Network Radio, '64–'66; Rschr. for "How To Steal An Election"; Rschr. for "Across The Top Of Russia"; Zeta Phi Eta, '63; Univ. of Mich., BA, '64; b. Detroit, Mich., 1942; p. Roger and Gwen Kriel Buchanan; res: 382 Central Park W., N.Y., N.Y. 10025.

BUCHANAN, CYNTHIA DEE, Pres., Sullivan Associates, Box 693, Los Altos, Cal. 94022, '69–; Dir. of Prog., VP, '61–'69; Lang. Instr., Dir. of Reading Lab., Hollins Col., '59–'61; Auth., reading textbks.; Nat. Soc. Prog. Instr. aw., '66–'67; Hollins Col., BA (French), '58; Radcliffe Col., MA (Linguistics), '59; b. Ft. Benning, Ga., 1937; p. David and Katherine Pritchett Buchanan.

BUCHANAN, GWEN DEW, Dir., Owner, World Adventure Series, 6021 N. 64th Pl., Scottsdale, Ariz. 85253, '56–; Travel Ed., Point West Magazine, '64–'65; Stringer for Newsweek, 18 nwsps.; Fgn. Corr., Far East, Detroit News, other pubns.; '33–'53; PR Dir., Florists' Telegraph Deliver, '25–'29; Auth: "Prisoner of the Japs," (Knopf's, '42), various mag. articles; OPC; Army and Navy E, '43; Order of the Rose, highest aw. of Delta Gamma, for outstanding svc. to the country, '63; Univ. of Mich., BA, '24; b. Albion, Mich. 1903; p. Arthur and Jettie Robinson Dew; h. Major James Tarbell Buchanan (dec.); res: 6021 N. 64 Pl., Scottsdale, Ariz. 85253.

BUCHANAN, JEANNE DE JARNATT, Owner, Mgr., KGST-Radio, Fresno, Cal., '50–'61; Wms. Commentator, '50–'61; Owner, Fresno Welcome Svc., '48–'61; AWRT (Western Area VP, Bd. of Dirs., '56–'60); ZONTA (Pres., '55); Fresno C. of C., (Pres., Wms. Sec., '58); Fresno State Col., '36–'37; b. Lodi, Cal., 1919; p. Benjamin and Hazel Bright De Jarnatt; h. Allen Buchanan; c. Larry Joseph Walters, James Bacher; res: 21 Windward Rd., Belvedere, Cal. 94920.

BUCHANAN, PEGASUS, VP, Federation of Chaparral Poets, P.O. Box 2124, Pomona, Cal. 91766; Auth., numerous bks., poems; Poetry Ed., L.A. Magazine, '59–'62; Cal. Wtrs. Guild, Pomona Valley Wtrs. Workshop (Club Aw.); Promenthian Lamp Aw., Col. Arts Aw., Pomona Valley Lib. Aw., Chaparral Poets Pres. Trophy; Mich. State Univ.; b. Lansing, Mich. 1920; p.

Milton and Gladys Bradshaw Perry; h. Barney Barnum; c. Daniel B., Samuel; res: 740 Washington Ave., Pomona, Cal. 91767.

BUCHER, MARY ALICE, Asst. Ed., Journal of Higher Education, Ohio State University Press, 2070 Neil Ave., Columbus, Oh. 43210, '68–; Edtl. Asst., '60–'68; Oh. State Univ., BA, '58 (cum laude, Phi Beta Kappa); b. Columbus, Oh., 1937; p. Paul and Florence Burington Bucher; res: 102 Glenmont Ave., Columbus, Oh. 43214.

BUCHMAN, MARION FRIEDMAN, Poet, Lectr. at Univs., Essex Col., Rider Col., others; poems widely published in nwsps., mags., poetry anthologies, incl: N.Y. Times, The N.Y. Herald Tribune, Poets of Today, many others; PSA, Acad. of Am. Poets, Poetry Soc. of Great Britain, London Wtr. Circle, Md. State Poetry Soc., Nat. Cncl. of Tchrs. of Eng. (Md. Cncl. of Eng. Tchrs. Br.); John Masefield Memorial Prize for poem, "Nancy Hanks Lincoln," '68; Stroud Poetry Festival Prize for six poems, '67; Ivan Franko Memorial Prize (Eng.); Kwill Klub Prize, Tex. Poetry Soc., for poem, "Writer"; Literature Intl. Prize for "Nehru's Rose"; Manifold Religious Festival Aw. for "Zoo Camel"; many aws. for poems in N. Am. Mentor Competitions; Theresa deFossett Memorial Aw., Am. Lit. Assn. Prize for "At Poe's Grave"; numerous other aws.; Md. Anti-Vivisection Soc., other Humane Socs.; b. Balt., Md.; p. Jacob and Winnifred Valinsky Friedman; h. Harold Buchman; c. Sara E., Sharon T.; res: 4578 Derby Manor Dr., Balt., Md. 21215.

BUCK, KATHRYN LOUISE, Assoc. Dir. of Lib., Doane College Library, Crete, Neb. 68333, '69–; Dir., '56–'69; Head Librn., Chadron State Col., '48–'56; Asst. Librn., '43–'48; Cataloger, Neb. Public Lib. Commn., '39–'43; ALA, Mt. Plains Lib. Assn., Neb. Lib. Assn., AAUP, Delta Kappa Gamma; Doane Col., '32–'34; Univ. of Neb., AB, '36; Univ. of Minn., BS (Lib. Sci.), '39; b. McCammon, Idaho; p. Ralph and Mabel Hoerger Buck; res: 1205 Forest Ave., Apt. 1, Crete, Neb. 68333.

BUCK, MARION ASHBY, Dept. Chmn., Prof. of Econs., California State College, 1000 E. Victoria St., Dominguez Hills, Cal. 90247, '67–; Sr. Econst., Federal Reserve Bank of Cleve., '65–'67; Assoc. Prof. of Bus. Adm., Syracuse Univ., '56–'65; Dir. of Studies, N.Y. State Joint Legislative Comm. on Commerce and Econ. Dev., '53–'64; Co-Auth: "What Price Progress" (Rand McNally, '63), "Economic Status of N.Y. State at Mid Century" (Syracuse Univ., '61); Am. Econ. Assn., Am. Acad. of Polit. and Social Sci., Polit. Sci. Assn., Econ. Hist. Assn., Bus. Hist. Assn., Soc. Hist. of Tech., Beta Gamma Sigma; Radcliffe Col., AB, '30 (magna cum laude, Phi Beta Kappa); PhD, '53; Syracuse Univ., MA, '31 (Grad. fellow); b. Watertown, N.Y., 1909; p. H. Duane and Carrie Dunbar Buck.

BUCK, SUSAN BROWN, Sr. Copywtr., Ogilvy & Mather, Inc., 2 E. 48th St., N.Y., N.Y. 10017, '62–;

Copywtr., '57–'62; Edtl. Asst., Univ. of Pitt. Press; Theta Sigma Phi; Intl. Festival of TV Commls. (Cert. of Merit, '62); Grove City Col., '52–'54; Pa. State Univ. (Jnlsm.), '52–'56 (summa cum laude); Radcliffe Col., '56; Univ. of Pitt.; New School for Social Rsch.; b. Rochester, Pa., 1934; p. Edward Thayer and Martha Morgan Brown; h. Ralph Dewees Buck; res: 79 W. 12th St., N.Y., N.Y. 10003.

BUCKINGHAM, BETTY JO, Lib. Cnslt., State of Iowa Department of Public Instruction, Grimes State Off. Bldg., E. 14th and Grand, Des Moines, Ia. 50319, '64–; Librn., Kurtz Jr. HS, '60–'64; Librn., Ft. Madison, Ia. Independent Schs., '54–'60; Tchr.–Librn. in several Ia. schs. '48–'54; ALA, NEA, DAVI, Ia. Lib. Assn., Ia. State Educ. Assn., Ia. Assn. of Sch. Librns., State Sch. Lib. Supvrs. Assn.; Kappa Delti Pi; Beta Phi Mu; Ia. State Tchrs. Col., BA (Eng.), '48; State Univ. of Ia. (Lib Sci.), '49; Univ. of Ill., MS, '53; b. Prairie City, Ia., 1927; p. Irvin and E. Dean Webb Buckingham; res: Box 83, RR2, Prairie City, Ia. 50228.

BUCKHINGHAM, LYNN ADELE, Arts Ed., The Albuquerque Tribune, Drawer T, Albuquerque, N.M. 87103; Econ. Rsch. Analyst, Republic Nat. Bank of Dallas (Tex.), '65–'66; Grad. Asst., Univ. of N.M., '64–'65; Theta Sigma Phi (Pres., '63), Pi Delta Phi, Pi Sigma Alpha, N.M. Press Wm., Albuquerque Goals Comm., Expt. in Intl. Living (N.M. Coordr.); Outstanding Young Wm. of Am., '66; Univ. of N.M., BA, MA; b. Albuquerque, N.M., 1941; p. J. H. and Selma Kouri Buckingham; h. Patrick S. Villella; res: 1020 Valencia S.E., Apt. A-3, Albuquerque, N.M. 87108.

BUCKLEY, HELEN E., Auth., juv. bks.; Prof. of Eng., State University College, Oswego, N.Y. 13126; bks: "The Wonderful Little Boy," "Grandfather and I," "Where Did Josie Go," nine others; articles, pfsnl. mags.; NLAPW, Auths. League, N.Y. State Eng. Cncl., Nat. Cncl. of Tchrs. of Eng.; Syracuse Univ., BS, MS; Columbia Univ. Tchrs. Col., EdD; res: 74 W. Cayuga St., Oswego, N.Y. 13126.

BUCKLEY, PRISCILLA LANGFORD, Mng. Ed., National Review Magazine, 150 E. 35th St., N.Y., N.Y. 10016, '59–; staff, '56–; Corr., UP, Paris, '53–'56; Repts. Offcr., CIA, '51–'53; News Ed., WACA-Radio (Camden, S.C.), '48–'49; Copy Girl, Sports Wtr., News Wtr., UP, Radio, '44–'48; OPC; Smith Col., '39–'43; b. N.Y.C., 1921; p. William F. and Aloise Steiner Buckley; res: Great Elm, Sharon, Conn. 06069.

BUCKNER, SALLY BEAVER, Grad. Tchr. Asst., North Carolina State University, 102 Winston Hall, Hillsborough St., Raleigh, N.C. 27607, '68–; Free-lance and assigt. wtr., The Methodist Publ. House, '59–; Freelance playwright, "Encounter at the Corner" (Westminster Press, '66); Entertainment Ed., The Raleigh Times, '67–'68; Wms. Page Wtr., '66–'67; Colmst., The Goldsboro News-Argus, '64–'65; organized crtv. writing competition, (Goldsboro, N.C.), '65; Wake County Mental Health Assn. (Educ. Chmn., '67–),

Commty. Arts Cncl. of Goldsboro, N.C. Press Wms. Assn. (Hon. Mention for feature series, '68); Outstanding Young Wm. of Am. ('65); Univ. of N.C., AB (Eng.), '53 (magna cum laude; Phi Beta Kappa); b. Statesville, N.C., 1931; p. Henry George and Foda Stack Beaver; h. Robert Buckner; c. Robert, Lynn, Ted; res: 3305 Ruffin St., Raleigh, N.C. 27607.

BUCKS, HELEN MORRISON, Dir. of Pubcty., Lancaster County Farmers National Bank, 23 East King St., Lancaster, Pa. 17604, '62–; Am. Inst. of Banking, Bank PR and Mktng. Assn., Lancaster County Bankers Assn., Lancaster C. of C.; Who's Who of Am. Wm.; b. Lancaster, Pa., 1912; p. Samuel and Lottie Sigman Morrison; h. Paul A. Bucks; res: 2184 W. Ridge Dr., Lancaster, Pa. 17603.

BUDDE, JEANNE FRANCES, Mgr., Adv., Sls. Prom., American Cyanamid Company, Fibers Div., 111 W. 40th St., N.Y., N.Y. 10018, '61–; Ed., Living For Young Homemakers, '53–'61; Secy., Charm Magazine, '51–'53; NHFL (N.Y. Chptr. VP, Program); Packard Jr. Col. '51; N.Y. Sch. of Interior Design, '56; b. Bklyn., N.Y., 1931; p. John and Amy Simonsen Budde; h. Joseph Malyniak, Jr.; c. Susan Jeanne, Jeffrey Budde; res: 6 Peter Cooper Rd., N.Y., N.Y. 10010.

BUDELL, ELIZABETH ERB, Dir., Madison Public Library, 39 Keep St., Madison, N.J. 07940, '62–; Asst. Dir., Berkeley Heights Public Lib., '60–'62; Librn., Passaic Township Public Lib., '57–'60; Cnslt.; N.J. Lib. Svcs. and Construction Act Advisory Bd., '68–'69; N.J. Public Lib. Survey Comm., '63–'64; Marquis Biographical Soc. (Advisory Mbr.), N.J. Lib. Dev. Comm., ALA, N.J. Lib. Assn. (Exec. Bd., '66–'69), LPRC, Wms. Nat. Bk. Assn., BPW; Nat. Lib. Week Cit., '66; Western Md. Col., BA, '38; Rutgers Univ., MLS, '60 (Grad. Sch. of Lib. Svc. Alumni Assn. Pres., '63–'64); b. Westminster, Md., 1917; p. Norman and Elda Byers Erb; h. William J. Budell; c. John; res: 110 Cross Hill Rd., Millington, N.J. 07946.

BUELL, BARBARA HAYES, Owner, Aristographia, 17 Bigelow St., Cambridge, Mass. 02139, '64–; Cambridge Civic Assn.; Brandeis Univ., BA, '64; b. Cambridge, Mass., 1942; p. James and Evelyn McMahon Hayes; h. Don Carlos Buell; res: 17 Bigelow St., Cambridge, Mass. 02139.

BUELL, ELLEN LEWIS, Free-lance Reviewer, Lectr.; New York Times Book Review, '31–'63; Lectr., Eng., Columbia Univ., '45–'61; WNBA (N.Y. Chptr. VP, '59); Marietta Col., AB, '26; b. Marietta, Oh.; p. Daniel and Ellen Buell; h. Harold Cash; res: Wildwood, Ga. 30757.

BUERGER, JANE THURMAN, Publr., The Child's World, Inc., P.O. Box 681, Elgin, Ill. 60120; Prod. Dir., David C. Cook Publ.; Dir., New Products Dept., Standard Publ. (Cinn., Oh.); Auth., bks., articles for church mags.; Cinn. Bible Seminary, BA.

BUERHAUS, KATHRYN WARNE, PR Dir., Lake Erie

Girl Scout Council, 1001 Huron Rd., Cleve., Oh. 44115, '53–; Field Dir., Zanesville and Area Girl Scouts, Tchr., public schls., Zanesville, Oh.; PRSA, Wms. Adv. Club of Cleve., Theta Sigma Phi; Oh. State Univ., BS (Educ.), '50, Muskingum Col. Tchr. Cert., '37; b. Carrothers, Oh. 1915; p. Harry Llewellyn and Hattie Stockdale Warne; h. Wilson Buerhaus (dec.); res: 2402 Overlook Rd., Cleve. Heights, Oh. 44106.

BUFF, DOROTHY DORCHESTER, Asst. Lib. Dir., Morris County Free Library, 30 E. Hanover Ave., Whippany, N.J. 07981, '62–; Sr. Librn., '56–'62; Asst. Librn., Pace Col., '37–'41; Tchr., Hist., Biology, Bernards HS, '55–'56; ALA, N.J. Lib. Assn.; Syracuse Univ., BA (Pi Gamma Mu), '35; Columbia Univ., BLS, '40; b. Bklyn., N.Y., 1914; p. Paul and Marion Alexander Dorchester; h. Ernest Buff; c. Ernest Dorchester, Paul Evans; res: 79 Mine Mount Rd., Bernardsville, N.J. 07954.

BUFFINGTON, HELEN TOLES, Ed. and Co-owner, Jackson Herald, 147 Lee St., Jefferson, Ga. 30549, '65–; Reptr., Summerville News '60–'65, '48–'50; Reptr., Rome News-Tribune, '50–'60, '46–'47; Theta Sigma Phi; Ga. Conf. on Social Welfare Aw., '57; AP aws. for feature writing and photog., Big Story TV Aw., '56; Young Harris Jr. Col., '44–'46; b. Menlo, Ga., 1927; p. Taylor and Minnie Sentell Toles; h. Herman Buffington; c. Michael, Scott; res: Roberts Rd., Jefferson, Ga. 30549.

BUGG, MARY COBB, AE, Burke Dowling Adams, Inc., Div. of BBDO, 1750 Peachtree St., Atlanta, Ga. 30309, '62–; Free-lance, '60–'62; PR, Southern Bell Telephone and Telegraph, '48–'60; Auth: "Top Dog," (Doubleday, '60; in Eng., Hammond, Hammond & Co., '60); Theta Sigma Phi (aw. for outstanding contrb. to jnlsm., '60), Atlanta Press Club; Glamour Magazine cit. for outstanding career wm., '54; Univ. of Ga., AB (Jnlsm.) '48; b. Temple, Ga., 1925; p. Paul and Loyal McColister Cobb; h. Owen T. Bugg; c. Owen, Paul; res: 30 Polo Dr., N.E., Atlanta, Ga. 30309.

BUHAGIAR, MARION, Dir., Story Dev., Fortune Magazine, Time Inc., Rockefeller Center, N.Y., N.Y. 10020, '69–; Wtr., Rschr., '60–'66; Asst. to Pres., Scott Co., '59; Rschr., Time, '57–'59; Econct., U.S. Govt., '54–'57; Hunter Col., BA, '53 (cum laude, Phi Beta Kappa); b. N.Y.C., 1932; p. George and Mary Pietrzak Buhagiar; h. Len Ragozin; c. Alexa; res: 433 W. 21st St., N.Y., N.Y. 10011.

BUHR, DOROTHY F., Plans Publicist, General Foods Corporation, 250 North St., White Plains, N.Y. 10605, '69–; J. Walter Thompson Co.; Dir. of Sch. Lunch Program: Pineapple Growers Assn., Cal. Raisin Advisory Bd.; Reg. Home Econst., Western Beet Sugar Prod.; Free-lance pubcty., Ruder and Finn Inc.; Special Cnslt. to Algerian Ministry of Educ., AID; Am. Home Econs. Assn., Home Econst. in Bus. (Denver Chptr. Chmn.), AWRT (Bd. of Trustees of Educ. Fndn.), '64; Nat. Membership Chmn., '62; Bay Area Chptr. Pres.); Mich.

State Univ., BS, '51; b. Buffalo, N.Y., 1923; p. Edward G. and Teresa Uebelhoer Buhr; res: 160 Theo. Fremd Ave. Rye, N.Y. 10580.

BULLARD, HELEN, Wtr., Artist; Auth: "The American Doll Artist" (Charles T. Branford Co., '64), "Doctor Woman of the Cumberlands" ('52), "Cumberland County's First 100 Years" (County Court, '56); Un. Fedn. of Doll Clubs (2nd VP, '67–'69), Southern Highland Handicraft Guild, Am. Craftsmen Cncl., Nat. Inst. of Am. Doll Artists (Founder; Pres., '63–'67, '69–'71), Intl. Platform Assn., E. Tenn. Hist. Soc., Tenn. Folklore Soc., Am. Fern Soc., Tenn. Citizens for Wilderness Planning; Univ. of Chgo., '20–'29; b. Elgin, Ill., 1902; p. Charles and Minnie Cook Bullard; h. Joseph Marshall Krechniak; c. Ann Louise Rohrke (Mrs. Ross Netherton), Barbara Jane Rohrke (Mrs. V. Emil Gudmundson), Mrs. Manya Krechniak Kavich; res: Ozone, Tenn. 37842.

BULLARD, MARY KIMBERLEY, Edtl. Asst., Iowa State University, Information Service, 109 Morrill Hall, Morrill Rd., Ames, Ia. 50010, '58–; Survey Interviewer, Wallaces' Farmer, Stewart Dougall Assoc., '47–'58; Free-lance Wtr., '45–; Info. Advisor, Farm Security Adm. (Indpls., Ind.), '42; Home Mgt. Supvsr., '39–'42; Theta Sigma Phi (Archivist, '67–'68, '64–'65); Ia. State Univ., BS, '38; b. Collins, Ia., 1914; p. Charles H. and Daisy Nowning Kimberley; h. Stanley C. Bullard; c. Charles S., Margaret S., Virginia L.; res: Maxwell, Ia. 50161.

BULLOCK, ALICE LOWE, Free-lance Wtr., Ed.; Bk. Ed., The New Mexican, 812 Gildersleeve, Santa Fe, N.M. 87501; Retired Educ.; articles publ. in 200 mags.; N.M. Press Assn., Western Wtrs. of Am.; Highlands Univ., Univ. of Southern Cal.; b. Buck, Indian Territory, 1904; p. Richard and Jeanette Nichols Lowe; h. Dale Bullock; c. Mrs. Tom Chumbley, Mrs. Walter Kiesov.

BUNCHEZ, GERTRUDE, Pres., Gert Bunchez and Associates, (Broadcast Representative) 7730 Carondelet, St. Louis, Mo. 63105, '68–; managerial positions, KCFM, KMOX, '60–'68; previously with St. Louis Star Times; Loew's Theatres, Balt., Md.; WITH; Balt. News Post; Press Club of Met. St. Louis, Intl. Platform Assn., AWRT; Bronze Aw., '42; several MGM Aws., '42–'47; Wm. of Wk., Balt., '43; Univ. of Balt.; b. Balt., Md., 1925; p. William and Goldie Yaniger Bunchez; res: 8227 Delmar Blvd., St. Louis, Mo. 63124.

BUNKER, NANCY LEE, Commtns. Supvsr., F. W. Means & Company, 35 E. Wacker Dr., Chgo., Ill. 60601, '68–; Copywtr., Montgomery Ward, '66–'68; Exec. Secy., Pers. & Training, Inland Steel Co.,''61–'66; Exec. Secy., Needham, Harper & Steers, '60–'61; Secy. to Special Asst. to Ambassador, Am. Embassy (Havana, Cuba), '60; IEA, ICIE: Northwestern Univ., b. Chgo., Ill., 1936; p. Warren and Nancy Parish Bunker; res: 3950 W. Lake Shore Dr., Chgo., Ill. 60613.

BUNTIN, MARY MOORE SCOTT, Dir., Consumer Service, Ball Brothers Co., Inc., Muncie, Ind. 47302, '63–; Dir., Home Econs., Mecklenburg Electric, Chase City, Va., '53–'63; Tchr., '45–'48; various organizations; North Ga. Col., BS (Home Econs.), '46; Univ. of Fla., '48, '50; Va. Polytechnic Inst., '57; b. Dahlonega, Ga. 1922; p. Charles and Callie Walden Moore; h. William W. Buntin; c. Mrs. Sandra M. Gregory; res: 518 Harvey Rd., Muncie, Ind. 47303.

BUR, JANET SKRIVSETH, Bur. Chief, Fairchild Publications, Milw., Wis., '60–'62; Educ. Ed., Reprtr., Green Bay Press-Gazette, '42–'60; Theta Sigma Phi; Univ. of Wis., BA, '42 (Hons.); b. Carleton, Minn., 1920; p. Clarence and Esther Tennstrom Skrivseth; h. Nicholas Bur; c. Catherine Margaret; res: 5663 N. Consaul Pl., Milw., Wis. 53217.

BURACK, SYLVIA KAMERMAN, Assoc. Ed., The Writer; Plays, The Drama Magazine for Young People, The Writer, Inc., Plays, Inc., 8 Arlington St., Boston, Mass. 02116; Ed: "50 Plays for Holidays" (Plays, Inc.), six other anthologies of plays; Smith Col., AB (Phi Beta Kappa), '38; b. Hartford, Conn., 1916; p. Abraham and Augusta Kamerman; h. Abraham S. Burack; c. Mrs. Alan D. Biller, Mrs. Chad A. Finer, Ellen J.; res: 72 Penniman Rd., Brookline, Mass. 02146.

BURAKOFF, SUZANNE WEINDLING, Ed., State University of New York Press, Thurlow Terr., Albany, N.Y. 12201, '68–; Edtl., Mktg. Mgr., Mgt. Ctr. Europe (Brussels), '68; Translator, FUAAV World Mag. (Brussels), '67; Proofreader, Translator, Presses Academiques Europeennes (Brussels), '65–'66; Asst. Copyrights Ed., Charles Scribner's (N.Y.C.); Hunter Col.; Am. Univ.; b. N.Y.C., 1943; p. Leon and Sonia Tarna Weindling; h. Steven Burakoff; res: 11 S. Lake Ave., Albany, N.Y. 12203.

BURCH, DIANE ROBERSON, Assoc. Ed., Northeast Utilities, P.O. Box 270, Hartford, Conn. 06101, '68–; Ed., Spotlight, Conn. Light & Power Co., '67–'68; Ed., Communicator, Conn. Bank & Trust Co., '63–'67; Copy Ed., Horticulture Magazine, '62–'63; Ed. Asst., The Packer Newspaper, '62; Am. Inst. of Banking; IEA (Conn. Chptr. Dir., Rec. Secy., '68–'69); Ia. State Univ., BS (Agricultural Jnlsm.), '61; b. New Hampton, Ia. 1939; b. Harvey and S. Elouise Walters Roberson; h. Donald Burch; res: 226 S. Whitney St., Hartford, Conn. 06105.

BURCK, MAHALA BARBARA, Asst. VP, Si Bon Imports, Brush Hill, Stowe, Vt.; in N.Y., c/o Connor, 125 E. 73rd St., N.Y., N.Y. 10021, '68–; Exec. Dir., Treas., Brush Hill Assocs., Inc. (Stowe, Vt.); prom., Am. Inst. for Fgn. Study (Greenwich, Conn.), '64–'66; teaching, cnsl., Bakersfield Col. (Bakersfield, Cal.), '65–'68; collaborated writing adaptation, Graham's "Wind in the Willows," prod., Lincoln Ctr. Forum Theatre, '69–'70; sls. aw., '64–'65; Vassar Col., BA (Eng.), '60; Univ. of Cal. (Berkeley), MA (Music), '65; b. L.A., Cal., 1938; p.

Gail J. and Barbara Douglas Burck; res: 206 E. 70th St., #2D, N.Y.C. 10021.

BURDEN, JEAN, Free-lance Wtr., '64–; Poetry Ed., Yankee Magazine, '54–; Own PR bus., Friskies Pet Foods Acc., Carnation Co. (PRSA Silver Anvil for best prod. pubcty., '68); Ed., Friskies Rsch. Digest; Edtl., Stanford Rsch. Inst.; PR, Adm., Meals for Millions Fndn., 10 yrs; Ed., house organ; adv.; poetry workshops, Pasadena City Col.; Wtr., more than 500 feature articles; poetry in many leading mags.; Lectr. on poetry, Auth: poetry bk., "Naked as the Glass" (October House), '63), essays, "Journey Toward Poetry" ('66); two pet bks. under pseud: Felicia Ames; 1st prize, Borestone Mountain Poetry Aws. Anthology, '62; Univ. of Chgo.; b. Waukegan, Ill., 1914; p. Harry and Miriam Biddlecom Prussing. res: 1129 Beverly Way, Altadena, Cal. 91001.

BURDICK, VIRGINIA, Publicist, Virginia Burdick Associates, 126 E. 19th St., N.Y., N.Y. 10003, owner '47–; Assis. Dir. PR, Helena Rubinstein, Inc., '47; AE, Fred Eldean Org., '45–'46.

BURGESS, ELEANOR S., Chief of Children's Dept., Grand Rapids Public Library, Lib. Plaza, Grand Rapids, Mich. 49502, '48–; Coordr., Work with Children, Scranton, Pa. Public Lib., '46–'48; Br. Children's Librn., Providence, R.I. Public Lib., '45–'46; Asst., Boys and Girls Rm., '31–'35; Local Exec. Secy., Girl Scouts, Kalamazoo, Mich. and Portland, Me., '41–'45; Children's Librn., Asst. Librn., Lyndhurst, N.J. Public Lib., '38–'40; Children's Librn., Glen Ellyn, Ill. Public Lib., '36–'38; Lectr., Lib. Sci., Univ. of Mich. Ext.; ALA (Secy., Children's Sec., '51–'52), Mich. Lib. Assn. (Secy., '52–'53; Children's Sec. Chmn., '64–'65), Grand Rapids Librns. Club, Audubon Club, WNBA, Nat. Story League, church groups; Beta Phi Mu, Delta Kappa Gamma; Wheaton Col., AB, '31; Univ. of Wis. Lib. Sch., '35–'36; Univ. of Mich. Sch. of Librnship., MA (Lib. Sci.), '59 (Phi Kappa Phi); b. Clinton, Mass., 1909; p. Stephen and Gertrude Saunders Burgess; res: 1244 Eastern Pl. N.E., Grand Rapids, Mich. 49505.

BURGESS, MARGARET ELAINE, Auth.; Prof., Univ. of North Carolina, Greensboro, N.C. 27412, '68–; teaching positions, various cols. and univ., '50–; bks: "Negro Leadership in a Southern City" (U.N.C. Press, '62), "An American Dependency Challenge" (APWA Press, '64), others; numerous articles and cntrbtns. to pfsnl. jnls.; Cnslt.; numerous rsch. grants; AAUP, Am. Assn. for Advancement of Sci., many other pfsnl. orgs; Phi Kappa Phi, Alpha Kappa Delta, Am. Men of Sci., Who's Who of Am. Wm.; Wash. State Univ., BA, '48 (cum laude; Mortar Bd.); MA, '49 (Teaching Fellow); Univ. of N.C., Chapel Hill, PhD, '60; b. Walla Walla, Wash., 1926; p. Halsey and Emma Layman Burgess; res: Box 144, Rte. #3, Greensboro, N.C. 27410.

BURKE, ELLEN COOLIDGE, Cnslt. Dir., Alexandria Library, 717 Queen St., Alexandria, Va. 22314, '69–;

Dir., '48–'69; Cataloguer, Ref., Asst. Dir.; Wash. D.C. Lib. Assn., Va. Lib. Assn., Alexandria Commty. Welfare Cncl., Wash., D.C. Urban League, League of Wm. Voters; Catholic Univ., BA, MA; b. Alexandria, Va., 1901; p. Henry and Rosella Trist Burke; res: 507 Virginia Ave., Alexandria, Va. 22302.

BURKE, R. MARIE, Wms. Ed., News Syndicate Company, Inc., 220 E. 42nd St., N.Y. N.Y. 10017, '69–; Asst. Wms. Ed., '52–'69; Wms. Dept. Asst., '42–'52; NWC; Albertus Magnus Col., BA (magna cum laude); b. Auburn, Pa.; p. Andrew and Dolores Thayne Burke; res: 42 Broad Ave., Ossining, N.Y. 10562.

BURKE, SHIRLEY, Lit. Rep., 370 E. 76th St., N.Y., N.Y. 10021, '48–; Assoc., Gale Mgt. Agency, '45–'48; Radio Supvsr. and Prodr., U.S. Treasury Dept. War Bond Program, '41–'45; Casting Dir., Theatre Guild, '30–'39; Asst. Casting Dir., Russell Janney, '23–'30; Am. Bksellers League, Wms. Nat. Bk. Assn.; Treasury Dept. Cit., '45; N.Y.U.; Columbia Univ.; b. Bklyn., N.Y., 1907; p. Sam and Anna Jacobs Burke; h. Harry J. Levine; c. one son; res: 370 E. 76th St., N.Y., N.Y. 10021.

BURKET, HARRIET, Ed.-in-Chief, House & Garden, Conde Nast Publications, Inc., 420 Lexington Ave., N.Y., N.Y. 10017, '58–; Exec. Ed., '55–'57; Home Furnishings, Mdse. Ed., '52–'55; Interior Design Ed., Woman's Home Companion, '44–'52; Assoc. Mdse. Ed., Mdse. Ed., Mng. Ed., House & Garden, '36–'44; Assoc. Ed., Crtv. Design, '34–'36; Assoc. Ed., Arts & Decoration, '32–'34; Lectr: Vassar Col., N.Y.U., Columbia Univ.; Intl. Fashion Group (VP, '58–'59; Bd. of Govs., '53–'55), NHFL (Founder, Trail Blazer aw.), Intl. Platform Assn., Am. Inst. of Interior Designers, Decorators Club, Nat. Soc. of Interior Designers, Cosmopolitan Club; Vassar Col., AB, '31; b. Findlay, Oh., 1908; p. John and Betty Hoege Burket; h. Francis Taussig; c. Rosalind (Mrs. David Connell); res: 14 Sutton Pl. S., N.Y., N.Y. 10022.

BURKS, SUSANNE MARTIN, Staff Reptr., Albuquerque News, Newspaper Printing Corp., 701 Second St., S.W., Albuquerque, N.M. 87102, '66–; Ed., The Messenger, First Presbyterian Ch., '65–; Rept., Ed., South Suburbia, Toledo, Oh., '62–'64; Reptr., Feature Wtr., Nevada Daily Mail, Nevada, Mo., '46–'52; Theta Sigma Phi (Albuquerque Chptr., Pres., '66–'68), New Mexico Press Wm.; Guy Rader Aw., N.M. Medical Soc. for medical rept., '67, Winner 1st pl., newswriting, Albuquerque Press Club, '66, hon. mentions, '67, '68; Univ. of Mo., Sch. of Jnlsm., BJ, '52; b. St. Louis, Mo. 1930; p. Forrest L. and Madalyn Ewing Martin; h. William F. Burks; c. William R., Julie Ann; res: 6901 Seminole Rd., N.E., Albuquerque, N.M. 87110.

BURLESON, KATIE SWAFFORD, Ed., Baird Star, Star Publishing Co., 211 Market, Baird, Tex. 79504, '67–; Colmst., "Kate's Korner," '67–'69; Circ. Mgr., '65–'67; Baird C. of C. (Dir.; Distg. Svc. Aw., given jointly by Shady Oaks Recreation Assn.); b. Rowden, Tex., 1933;

p. John and Lillie Brasher Swafford; h. Forrest Burleson; c. Leonna, Terri, Jeffrey; res: 4416 W. Dengar, Midland, Tex. 79701.

BURLEY, TERRY TOMOLILLO, Bus. Mgr., International Photographer, 7715 Sunset Blvd., Hollywood, Cal. 90046, '57–; Patterson Col.; b. Paris, France, 1925; p. Alexander and Nancy Soave Tomolillo; h. Fulton Burley; res: 4616 Fulton Ave., Sherman Oaks, Cal. 91403.

BURNETT, CAROL, Comedienne, Singer: "The Carol Burnett Show" (CBS-TV); "The Garry Moore Show" (CBS-TV, '58–'62); Broadway: "Fade Out-Fade In" ('64); "Once Upon a Mattress;" Film: "Who's Been Sleeping in My Bed?" ('63); numerous TV guest appearances; NATAS Emmy aws. (4); Golden Globe aw., L.A. Times Wm. of the Yr. aw., AGUA aw., '59; Daniel Blum Theatre World aw., '59; TV Guide aws.; U.C.L.A.; b. San Antonio, Tex.; h. Joe Hamilton; c. Carrie, Jody, Erin Kate; res: Beverly Hills, Cal.

BURNETT, HAZEL RAY, Exec. Dir., Dairy Council of St. Joseph Valley, Inc., 306 S. Notre Dame Ave., South Bend, Ind., 46222, '61–; TV Prodr. and talent, "Homemaker's Time," WSBT-TV and Radio, '54–'61; Freelance Home Econst., '40; Ext. Agt., Dept. of Agriculture, Purdue Univ., '38–'40; Vocational Home Econs. Tchr., St. Joseph County, Ind., '35–'38; AWRT (E. Central Area VP), Am. Home Econs. Assn. (Ind. Chptr. Newsltr. Ed., '66–'69), Am. Public Health Assn., Ind. Public Health Assn., Mental Health Assn. (Bd. and Exec. Comm. Mbr.; Gold Bell Aw., '58); Purdue Univ., BS, '35; grad. work at Ind. Univ., and Univ. of Notre Dame; b. Logansport, Ind., 1914; p. B. A. and Idella Burn Ray; h. Richard Burnett; c. Thomas, Robert Margaret (Mrs. Preston); res: 17833 Ponader Dr., South Bend. Ind. 46635.

BURNEY, VIRGINIA PICKETT, Prodr., Bdcstr., King Broadcasting Co., KGW- TV, 1501 S.W. Jefferson, Portland, Ore. 97201, '68–; Fashion Coordr., White Stag, '66–; Allan C. Edwards, '64–'68; Home Econs. Div., Oregonian Nwsp. (Hostess House), '63–'64; Home Econst., Fla. Power and Light, '59–'61; Tchr., Ind., Fla., '56–'59; AFTRA, Fashion Group; "Miss Cotton," Louisville, Ky., '52; Univ. of Louisville, BA, '56; Portland Art Museum, '65–'67; Northwest Arts and Crafts, '68; b. Owensboro, Ky., 1934; p. Charles and Virginia Thomas Pickett; c. Robert E., III, Charles T.; res: 2669 S.W. Vista Ave., Portland, Ore. 97201.

BURNHAM, LINDA EMILY, Wtr., K.L.M. Royal Dutch Airlines, North American Div., 609 Fifth Ave., N.Y., N.Y. 10017, '69–; Wtr., Ogilvy & Mather, '68–'69; Marschalk Co., '67–'68; Peter Rothholz Assoc., '66–'67; Vassar, AB (Drama and Eng.), '64; b. Chgo., Ill., 1942; p. James and Mabel Beach Burnham; res: 221 E. 66th St., N.Y., N.Y. 10021.

BURNLEY, ROSE BURKE, Home Econs. Cnslt.; Home Equipment Ed., Forecast, 50 W. 44th St., N.Y., N.Y. 10036, '68–; Home Equipment Ed., Redbook, '55–'59, '61–'67; Assoc. Ed. of Appliances and Home Care, Good Housekeeping, '60–'61; Reg. Home Econst., Crosley Div. of Avco Mfg., '54–'55; PR Rep., Nat. Dairy Cncl., '51–'53; Homemaking Tchr., '49–'51; Free-lance mag. wtr.; Home Econsts. in Bus., Am. Home Econs. Assn., Electrical Wms. Round Table, Omicron Nu, Pi Lambda Theta; Syracuse Univ., BS (magna cum laude); MS (Educ.); b. Syracuse, N.Y., 1927; p. Martin M. and Marie Cooney Burke; h. Richard N. Burnley; c. Christine, Susan; res: 26 Doris Dr., Scarsdale, N.Y. 10583.

BURNS, COLETTE WAGNER, Wtr.; Assoc. with Gwen Bristow, Hist. Novelist, '65–; Auth: "The Animal Fair" (Harcourt, Brace), "The Child and Nature" (Expression Co.); Copywtr., Hixson & Jorgensen Adv., '52–'65; Wtr., Asst. Ed., "The Richfield Reporter" news prog. (NBC Pacific Coast Network), '40–'52; h. (1) Robert Kolsbun (div.); (2) James W. Burns (dec.); res: Box 133, Encino, Cal. 91316.

BURNS, EVELYN LARGEN, Studio Tchr., (Sci. 4 and 5), WDCN-TV (Educational Television), P.O. Box 12555, Acklen Station, Nashville, Tenn. 37212, '68–'70; Tchr., Nashville Metro Elementary, '52–'68; Private expression and drama lessons, '38–'39; private kindergarten, '37–'38; MNEA, MTEA, TEA, NEA; George Peabody Col., BS, '52, MA, '60, grad. work, '67; b. Lincoln County, Tenn. 1917; p. William O. and Ora May Simms Largen; h. Walter Lewis Burns Jr.; c. Enola Gail, Mrs. Judith Ann Elliott; res: 1216 Littonwood Dr., Nashville, Tenn. 37216.

BURNS, JOAN SIMPSON, Free-lance Wtr., Ed.; Ed., "John Fitzgerald Kennedy as We Remember Him" (Atheneum, '65); Co-auth., "Dinosaur Hunt" (Harcourt, Brace & World '65); Auth., "Poetry and a Libretto" (Alan Swallow, '65); Trade Ed., Harcourt, Brace & World., '68; Bk. Ed., Special Projects, CBS Columbia Records, '64–'66; Univ. of Mich., BA; b. Boulder, Colo., 1927; p. George and Anne Roe Simpson; h. James M. Burns; c. Trina Anne Meyers, Peter Alexander Meyers; res: High Mowing; Bee Hill Rd., Williamstown, Mass. 01267.

BURNS, RUBY VERMILLION, Wms. Ed., El Paso Times, P.O. Drawer 20, El Paso, Tex. 79912, '48–; Asst. Ed., '47–'48; Tchr., '24–'29; Baylor Univ., BA; Juilliard Sch. of Music, '24; p. The Rev. H. F. and Ida Gray Vermillion; h. Earl S. Burns; c. Nancy; res: 6029 Bel Mar, El Paso, Tex. 79912.

BURNSIDE, RUTH ROBERTSON, Wms. Ed., Feature Wtr., Denison Newspapers, 1410 Broadway, Denison, Ia. 51442, '09–; Ia. Press Wm. (23 aws., '56–); numerous Charitable orgs.; aws.; b. Vail, Ia., 1892; p. Daniel and Alvena Holling Robertson; h. (dec.); c. Virginia (Mrs. Floyd Johnston), Willicence (Mrs. Peter Johnston); res: 1804 First Ave. N., Denison, Ia. 51442.

BURR, BARBARA, Copywtr., Gaynor and Ducas, 850 Third Ave., N.Y., N.Y. 10022, '67–; Copywtr., Ted Bates, '60–'67; Copywtr., J. W. Thompson, '56–'60; Hunter Col., BA, '56; b. N.Y., N.Y.

BURRELL, GERTRUDE CARPER, Assoc. Ed., Iowa State University Press, Press Bldg., Iowa State University, Ames, Ia. 50010, '65–; Univ. of Northern Ia., BA, '40; b. Olds, Ia., 1915; p. Arthur and Leona Morrison Carper; h. Harry Burrell; c. Steven K.; res: 402 Paulson Dr., Ames, Ia. 50010.

BURRELL, JAN, Actress, motion pics., TV, c/o Ivan Green Agency, 1800 Ave. of Stars, L.A., Cal. 90067; SAG, AFTRA, AEA; Wellesley Col., '47–'48; S.F. State Col., '48; Univ. of Cal., '48–'51; b. Oakland, Cal., 1930; p. Homer and Viola Hinchman Burrell; h. Len Lesser; c. David Charles Lesser, Michele Diane Lesser; res: 934 N. Evergreen St., Burbank, Cal. 91505.

BURROS, MARIAN FOX, Food Ed., Washington Evening Star-Sunday Star, 225 Virginia Ave. S.E., Wash., D.C. 20003, '68–; Washington Daily News, '64–'68; Maryland Monitor, '63–'64; Maryland News, '62–'63; Auth: "Elegant But Easy," "Second Helpings;" WNPC, ANWC; Wellesley Col., BA, '54; b. Waterbury, Conn.; p. Myron and Dorothy Derby Fox; h. Donald Burros; c. Michael, Ann; res: 7215 Helmsdale Rd., Bethesda, Md. 20034.

BURROWS, CHARLOTTE ANN, Special Assigt, Reptr., The Shreveport Times, 222 Lake St., Shreveport, La. 71101, '69–; City Hall Reptr., '65–'69; Educ. and Rel. Wtr., '62–'65; Gen. Assigt. Reptr., '61–'62; City Court Reptr. and Religion Wtr., '59–'61; Adv. Copywtr., Joske's of Houston, Tex., '58–'59; NFPW, Alpha Phi, Shreveport Press Club (Charter Mbr.; Bd. Mbr., '65–'67; VP, '65–'66), La. Press Wm. (Aws. for writing, '63–'69), UPI aws. ('63, '68); Univ. of Tex., BJ, '57; b. Nacogdoches, Tex., 1936; p. Jack and Mina Singleton Burrows; res: 2913 Weyman, Shreveport, La. 71104.

BURSTINER, ELAINE LEAH, Librn., Sales Management, The Marketing Magazine, 630 Third Ave., N.Y., N.Y. 10017, '62–; Ref. Librn., Arthur Young & Co., '59–'62; SLA.

BURT, DENISE MILLER, Ed., Omark Industries, 2100 S.E. Milport Rd., Portland, Ore., '64–; Ore. Assn. of Eds. and Communicators (Secy., '69–'70), Pacific Indsl. Communicators Assn. (aw., '67), ICIE; L.A. Adv. Wm. aw., '68; Portland State Univ., BA (Sociology), '63; b. Kalama, Wash., 1939; p. Morton and Rita LaRoy Miller; h. (div.); res: 1021 S.W. Stephenson Ct., Portland, Ore. 97219.

BURT, OLIVE WOOLLEY, Wtr., Bks. for Children, Adult Folk Lore, 34 Haxton Pl., Salt Lake City, Ut. 84102; Mag. Ed., Deseret News (Salt Lake City), '47–'57; Reptr., Salt Lake Tribune, '27–'45; Tchr., HS Eng., '18–'27; Auth: "American Murder Ballads and

Their Stories," '58; Auth of numerous bks. for children and poems, plays, articles and stories for adults and children, '35–'69; MWA (Edgar aw., '59), WWA, League of Ut. Wtrs., (Pres., '36–'38, '45–'47), NLAPW (Nat. Wm. of Achiev., '64; Chmn. Ltrs. Bd., '66–'68), NFPW (Reg. Dir., '65–'67; State Pres., '51–'53), Ut. Folklore Soc. (Bd. Mbr., '68–'70), Fellow, Ut. Hist. Assn., '64; Sigma Delta Chi Cit.; Delta Kappa Gamma Cit.; Univ. of Ut., BA, '18; Columbia Univ., '21; b. Ann Arbor, Mich., 1894; p. Jed and Agnes Forysth Woolley; h. Clinton R. Burt (dec.); c. Forsyth (Mrs. Winton R. Boyd), Beverly (Mrs. Burt E. Nichols), Robin; res: 34 Haxton Pl., Salt Lake City, Ut. 84102.

BURTSCHI, MARY PAULINE, Eng. Instr., Effingham Community Unit. No. 40, 1000 West Grove, Effingham, Ill. 62401, '39–; Rschr., Contrbr., bks. on Am. hist.; Vandalia Hist. Soc. (Pres., '62–'65; Dir., '65;), Ill. Assn. of Tchrs. of Eng., Ill. Educ. Assn., Ill. State Hist. Soc. (Dir., '65–'68; VP '68–); Webster Col. of St. Louis Univ., BA '33; Univ. of Ill., MA, '54; Grad. Work, Univ. of Ill., '61; b. Vandalia, Ill., 1911; p. Joseph and Olivia Yoos Burtschi; res: 307 N. Sixth, Vandalia, Ill. 62471.

BUSH, JENNIE RAY, A.D., Praeger Publishers, 111 Fourth Ave., N.Y., N.Y. 10003, '70–; Art Dir., George Braziller, Inc., 1 Park Ave., N.Y., N.Y. 10016, '65–'70; Random House, '64; Holt, Rinehart & Winston, '63–'64; AIGA (textbook design aw., '64); Ohio Univ., BFA, '63; b. Athens, Oh., 1942; p. Gordon and Izotta Ackerman Bush; res: 155 E. 37th St., N.Y., N.Y. 10016.

BUSH, LISSA MAYHUE, Wms. Ed., Seminole Daily Producer, 117 N. Main St., Seminole, Okla. 74868, '51–; Okla. Press Assn.; East Central State Col., BA; b. Seminole, Okla., 1911; p. Amos and Ida Luman Mayhue; h. Lester Bush; c. Bob, Elmer; res: 1007 North Park, Seminole, Okla. 74868.

BUSH, MIRIAM RONGA, Asst. to Mng. Ed., Asbury Park Press, Press Plaza, Asbury Park, N.J. 07712, '64–; Reptr., Photog. Ed., AP, '53–'64; PR Asst., N.Y. Univ., '52–'53; PR Asst., Univ. of Fla., '50–'52; Reptr., Jacksonville (Fla.) Times-Union, '50–'52; Reptr., The Trentonian, (Trenton, N.J.), '48–'50; Reptr., Bangor (Me.) Daily Comml., '47–'48; N.J. Daily Nwsp. Wm. (Founder; 1st. Pres., '57–'60), Gamma Alpha Chi (Hon. Mbr.); Georgian Court Col., AB '47 (magna cum laude); b. Trenton, N.J.,; p. Paul and Mary Moore Ronga; h. Eugene A. Bush; res: 419 Edgemont Dr., Loch Arbour, N.J. 07711.

BUSH, NAOMI SALVESON, Librn., Coordr., Kasson-Mantorville Schools, Kasson, Minn. 55944, '58–; Librn., Sr. HS (Winona), '56–'58; Asst. Librn., U.S. Navy, Camp Pendleton (Cal.), '51; Asst. Librn., Public Lib. (Austin, Minn.), '48–'50; Asst. Librn., U.S. Navy, Camp Lejeune (N.C.), '45–'46; Staff, U.S. Navy (Hastings, Neb.; Corpus Christi, Tex.), '44; Librn., HS (Viroqua, Wis.) '43–'44; Librn., Nashwauk Public Schs. (Minn.), '42–'43; Tchr., Librn., Clover HS (Va.), '40–'42;

Tchr., Librn., Public Schs. (Burtrum, Minn.), '38–'39; NEA, ALA, Minn. Educ. Assn.; Who's Who of Am. Wm.; Luther Col., BA, '38; Univ. of Minn., BLS, '40; b. Hesper, Ia., 1916; p. Gilbert and Minnie Ramlo Salveson; h. (div.); c. T. Langley; res: 108 N.W. First Ave., Kasson, Minn. 55944.

BUSHNELL, M. MARGARET, VP, Mbr., Bd. of Dirs., Pitman Publishing Corporation, 6 E. 43rd St., N.Y., N.Y. 10017, '64–; Initial Teaching, Alphabet Publications, Inc., Bd. of Dir., Abbott House; Mktng. Mgr., '62–'64; Adv. Mgr., Col. Dept., Holt, Rinehart & Winston, '59–'62; Pubns. Dir., Columbia Univ. Tchrs. Col., '51–'59; Adv. Copywtr., Prentice-Hall, '48–'51; Am. Educ. Publrs. Inst.; Univ. of Minn., BA, '46; b. Mpls., Minn., 1924; p. Charles Bradshaw and Muriel Robinson Bushnell; res: 80 Central Park W., N.Y., N.Y. 10023.

BUTCHER, FANNY, Reptr., Soc. Ed., Music Critic, Colmst., Chicago Tribune, '13–'63; Owner, Fanny Butcher Books (shop), '19–'27; PEN (Chgo. Chptr. Pres., '32), Friends of Am. Wtrs., Children's Reading Roundtable, Fortnightly, Chgo. Press Club, Soc. of Midland Auths., BPW, WNBA; C. L. Skinner aw., '55; Friends of Lit. aw., '52; Communicator of the Yr. Aw., '64; Lewis Inst., AA, '08; Univ. of Chgo., BA, '10; b. Fredonia, Kan.; p. L. Oliver and Hattie Young Butcher; h. Richard D. Bokum; res: 1209 Astor St., Chgo., Ill. 60610.

BUTLER, BEVERLY KATHLEEN, Crtv. Writing Instr., Mount Mary College, 2900 Menomonee Pkwy., Milw., Wis. 53222, '61–; Auth: Children's Bks., "Feather in the Wind" ('65; Cncl. for Wis. Wtrs. aw., '66), "Light a Single Candle" (Clara Ingram-Judson Aw., '63), "Song of the Voyageur" (17th Summer-Dodd Mead Prize, '55), others; Theta Sigma Phi, Allied Auths., Cncl. for Wis. Auths., Auths. Guild; Who's Who of Am. Wm.; Outstanding Young Wm. of Am.; Mt. Mary Col., BA, (cum laude); Marquette Univ., MA, '61; b. Fond du Lac, Wis., 1932; p. Leslie and Muriel Anderson Butler; res: 3019 N. 90th St., Milw., Wis. 53222.

BUTLER, FLORENCE WINIFRED, Dir. of Workshops, Sioux City Public Library, Sixth and Jackson Sts., Sioux City, Ia. 51105, '37–; Children's Librn., Winona (Minn.) Public Lib., '25–'35; Instr., Morningside Col., '49–; Instr., Western Reserve Grad. Lib. Sch., '65; WNBA, ALA, Ia. Lib. Assn. (Pres., '51–'52); Morningside Col. aw., '54, BPW aw., '53; Winona State Col., BE, '32; Colo. Univ., BS (Lib. Sci.), '42; b. Newry, Minn.; p. William and Mary Fitzgerald Butler; res: Bellevue Apts., D-3, Sioux City, Ia. 51104.

BUTLER, JILL, Adv. Dir., Vera, Inc., 1411 Broadway, N.Y., N.Y. 10018, '69–; Fashion Prom. Mgr., Puritan Fashions Corp., '69; Adm. Asst., Ketchum, MacLeod & Grove Adv., '68–'69; Prod. Asst., Burnaford Co., '66–'68; Stephens Col., AA, '64; b. Grand Rapids, Mich., 1944; p. LaVern and Virginia York Butler; h. Robin Lewis; res: 6713 Blvd. East, Guttenberg, N.J. 07093.

BUTLER, KATE ROBINSON, Pres., Buffalo Evening News, Station WBEN AM-FM-TV, 218 Main St., Buffalo, N.Y. 14240, '56–; WBEN, '67–; b. Atlanta, Ga.; h. Edward Butler; c. Kate (Mrs. James Righter).

BUTLER, MARY, Beauty Ed., Harper's Bazaar, 717 Fifth Ave., N.Y., N.Y. 10022, '69–; Asst. Beauty Ed., '65–'66; Ed., Bazaar Beauty Annual, '68; Beauty Ed., Bride's Magazine, '67; Beauty Tchr., Adult Educ.; Manhattanville Col., '54–'56; b. N.Y.C.; p. William and Martha Haskins Butler.

BUTLER, NANCY WALKER, Media Dir., AE, Schwab, Beatty & Porter, Inc., 660 Madison Ave., N.Y., N.Y. 10021, '67–; Adv. Mgr., Famous Artists Sch.; Ed., Carrier Corp.; Ed. Asst., Ladies Home Jnl.; Radcliffe Col., AB, '53; b. Richmond, Va. 1931; p. Bud and Mildred Holly Walker; h. Roger Butler; c. Kenneth B. and Julie H.; res: West Branch Rd., Weston, Conn. 06880.

BUTLER, ROBIN BOYER, Ed., Vogue, Conde Nast Publications, 420 Lexington Ave., N.Y., N.Y. 10017, '68–; PR, Christian Dior, '65–'67; Asst., Oleg Cassini; Vassar Col., Univ. of Florence; b. Phila., Pa.; p. Francis Boyer and Mary Holmes Jones; h. Michael Butler (div.); res: 7 Gracie Sq., N.Y., N.Y. 10028.

BUTTERFIELD, CAROL WILLEMSEN, Adv. Supvsr., Prod. Coordr., Wadsworth Publishing Company, Inc., 10 Davis Dr., Belmont, Cal. 94002, '68–; Copywtr., Designer, '66–'68; Asst. to VP of Adv., Prom., Holden-Day (S. F.); Univ. of Ore., '59–'62; Stanford Univ., BA, '64; b. Wilkesbarre, Pa., 1940; p. A. C. and Mildred Callister Willemsen; res: 439 Greenwich St., Apt. 3-A, S.F., Cal. 94133.

BUTTERS, DOROTHY GILMAN (Pseud: Dorothy Gilman in adult fiction), Auth.; Novels: "The Amazing Mrs. Pollifax" (Doubleday, due '70), "The Unexpected Mrs. Pollifax" (Doubleday, '66; motion pic.), "Uncertain Voyage" (Doubleday, '67); juv. fiction bks. (Alfred Knopf, '55; Macrae-Smith, '49–'63); adult short stories in leading mags.; Auths. Guild; Pa. Acad. of Fine Arts, '40–'45 (Cresson European Traveling Scholarship); Art Students League, '63–'64; h. (div.); c. Christopher, Jonathan; res: 33 Washington Ave., Westport, Conn. 06880.

BUTTS, BEULAH KIRBY, Lib. Dir., Melbourne Public Library, 730 Fee Ave., Melbourne, Fla. 32901, '63–; Reg. Librn., LaFayette, Ga., '58–'63; High Sch. Librn., LaFayette, Ga., '54–'58; Tchr., '54–'58; Gallatin, Tenn., '29–'54; Fla. Lib. Assn., BPW (Pres., '62–'63); Western Ky., '34; Middle Tenn. State Univ., BS, '41; MA, '54; Univ. of Ala., '41; Univ. of Chattanooga, '54–'55; Emory Univ. Lib. Sch., '61–'62; b. Smithville, Tenn., 1908; p. Harley and Olah Summers Kirby; h. (1) Ollie Tucker, (2) Charlie M. Butts; c. Ollie Shelby Tucker, Jr., James Kenneth Tucker; res: Wisteria Dr., Melbourne, Fla. 32901.

BYERS, EDNA HANLEY, Librn., Agnes Scott College, Decatur, Ga. 30030, '32–; Librn., Bluffton Col., '23–'27; Lectr., Univ. of Mich., summers, '52–'55, '57; ALA, Southeastern Lib. Assn., Ga. Lib. Assn., Phi Beta Mu; Bluffton Col., AB, '23; Univ. of Mich., AB (Lib. Sci.), '27; Am. (Lib. Sci.), '34; b. Trenton, Oh., 1900; p. James and Ida Augspurger Hanley; h. Noah E. Byers (dec.); res: 226 E. Hancock St., Decatur, Ga. 30030.

BYFORD, EUNICE MOHR, Bus. Mgr., North Idaho Press, 507 Cedar St., Wallace, Idaho 83873, '66–; McKim-Kiser Co., '64–'66; Ford Motor Accounting Aws.; b. Wallace, Idaho, 1927; p. James and Eunice D'Arcy Mohr; h. Harold Byford; c. William, Gary; res: Box 615, Wallace, Idaho 83873.

BYRD, ROBERTA, Modr., "Face to Face," King Broadcasting-Crown Network, 320 Aurora St., Seattle, Wash. 98109, '66–; KCTS Educ. TV (Univ. of Wash.), '64–'66; Modr., "Let's Imagine," KCTS TV, '62–'63, '60–'61; Vice Prin., Franklin HS, '68–; Librn., Seattle Elementary Sch., '65–'66; Tchr., '60–'65; Univ. of Wash., BA (Sociology, Educ.); b. Tacoma, Wash., 1920; p. Cora M. Spencer; h. Albert R. Barr; c. Robert King, Joseph Charles; res: 4224 W. Mercer Way, Mercer Island, Wash. 98040.

BYRNE, BOBBIE BECHTOLD, Ed., National Commercial Bank & Trust Company, 60 State St., Albany, N.Y. 12207, '67–; Free-lance Wtr.; Ed., "TripTips"; Gen. Electric Co., '50–'52; Wms. Press Club of N.Y. State (Assoc. Bd. Mbr., '68–'69), Pfsnl. PR Cncl., Jr. League (past Pres.); Several civic, ch. orgs.; Bryn Mawr Col., AB, '42; b. Coblenz, Germany, 1920; p. Jacob and Mary Louise Pero Bechtold; h. Jack D. Byrne; c. Darcey, John Jacob, Erin, Christopher; res: 1691 Van Antwerp Rd., Schenectady, N.Y. 12309.

BYRNE, RENETA SMITH, Fashion, Home Furnishings Ed., San Antonio Light, P.O. Box 161, San Antonio, Tex. 78206, '64–; Home and Garden Ed., San Antonio Express, San Antonio News, '59–'64; Theta Sigma Phi (Pres.), Am. Inst. of Interior Designers, San Antonio C. of C., San Antonio Conservation Soc; Who's Who of Am. Wm., Dorothy Dawe aws., '67, '62; b. Denison, Tex.; p. George and Iva Palmer Smith; h. Raymond Byrne Jr. (dec.); res: 3402 Stonehaven, San Antonio, Tex. 78230.

BYRNES, HAZEL WEBSTER, Asst. Dean and Lib. Organizer, of Institute of Lifetime Learning, 215 Long Beach Blvd., Long Beach, Cal. 90802, '65–; affiliate of Nat. Retired Tchrs. Assn. and Am. Assn. of Retired Persons, '65–'69; State Librn. and Ed., State Lib. Bul. (Bismarck, N.D.), '48–'65; Librn., State Tchrs. Col. (Mayville, N.D.), '25–'48; Auth., articles in mags., encys., pfsnl. jnls.; Adm. Wm. in Educ. (Pres. and Wm. of the Yr., '39), Adult Educ. Assn. of U.S., Wms. Nat. Bk. Assn., NLAPW (State Pres., '38; Nat. Histrn., '51–'53), AAUW, delegate to nat. and intl. confs., N.Y. Times 1st prize essay contest, '34; Northern Univ. of Ia., BA, '10; Univ. of Ia., '25; Am. Univ. of Wash., D.C., '31; Columbia Univ., MA, '35; b. Charles City,

Ia.; p. Abel and Susannah Haines Webster; h. Frank Byrnes; res: Petersburg, N.D. 58272.

BYRNES, SUZANNE HALBREN, Sr. AE, Ruder & Finn Incorporated, 1812 K. St., N.W., Wash., D.C. 20016, '67–; Public Info. Specialist, Nat. Capitol Transportation Agcy., '61–'64; Look Magazine, '55–'60; Centenary Col., AA, '54; b. N.Y.C.; p. Harry and Eleanor Finn Halbren; h. Leo Byrnes; c. Gregory; res: 4308 46th St., N.W., Wash., D.C. 20016.

BYRON, DORA L., Assoc. Dir., Commty. Educ. Svcs., Emory University, Atlanta, Ga. 30322, '59–; News Ed., '50–'59; Instr. in Jnlsm., Fla. State Univ., '47–'49; Special Writing Br., Wms. Army Corps, '45–'47; nwsp. work, HS teaching; Free-lance Wtr., articles for nwsps. and mags.; Theta Sigma Phi, Alpha Chi Alpha, Ga. Adult Educ. Cncl. (Bd. Mbr.), Ga. Gerontology Soc. (Bd. Mbr.; Educ. Aw., '67), Atlanta Comm. for Intl. Visitors (Bd. Mbr.), Ams. for Dem. Action; Fla. State Univ., BA; Emory Univ., MA (Jnlsm.), '50; MA (Librarianship), '67; b. Pomona Park, Fla.; res: 1766 N. Decatur Rd., N.E., Atlanta, Ga. 30307.

BYRUM, SUSAN SEALE, VP, Secy./Treas., John Byrum, Inc., 35 West Lane, Ridgefield, Conn. 06877, and John Byrum de Mexico, S.A., Ocampo 54, Ajijic, Jalisco, Mexico. '63–; Nat. Dir., WAIF, Hollywood, Cal.; Sls. and PR Rep., Gould & Assoc. Design, L.A. and N.Y.; PR and Sales, Lee Vitale Associates Design Firm, N.Y.; AWNY; Northwestern Univ., BM (Music), '42 (Phi Beta Kappa, Kappa Kappa Gamma); b. Cinn., Oh. 1919; p. Richard and Estelle Hood Seale; h. Jack Byrum; c. Kimberly Freshwater; res: 35 West Lane, Ridgefield, Conn. 06877.

C

CABLE, DOROTHY ANN, Educ. Ed., Reptr., The News-Herald, 301 Collett St., Morganton, N.C. 28655, '59–; Chief of Clemson Bur., Anderson (S.C.) Independent, '52–'59; Wire Ed., Spartanburg Herald, '52; Lake Wales (Fla.) News, Orlando (Fla.) Sentinel-Star, '50–'52; Teen Magazine, Houston, Tex., '48; N.C. Press Assn. runner-up aw. for commty. svc., '68; Christian Col., '42–'43; Mo. Valley Col., BA (Eng.), '47; Univ. of Mo. Sch. of Jnlsm., '49; b. St. Louis, Mo., 1924; p. Dr. John and Alma Steele Cable; res: Bellevue Farm, Rte. 5, Box 134, Morganton, N.C. 28655.

CADDEN, VIVIAN LIEBMAN, Sr. Ed., Wtr., McCall's magazine, 230 Park Ave., N.Y., N.Y. 10017; Articles Ed.; Sr. Ed., Redbook; Co-auth., "The Intelligent Man's Guide to Women;" Soc. of Mag. Wtrs.; Vassar Col., BA, '38; (Fellow); Columbia Univ., '38–'40 (Fellow); b. N.Y.C., 1917; p. Harry and Jennie Gus Liebman; h. Joseph E. Cadden; c. Joan, Wendy, Frank; res: 59 E. 73 St., N.Y., N.Y. 10021.

CADWELL, FRANCHELLIE M., Pres., Cadwell Davis Co., 437 Madison Ave., N.Y., N.Y. 10022, '64–; Auth., "The Un-Super Markets"; Art Dirs. Club and Copy Club aws.; Cornell Univ., BS, '55; N.Y.U. Bus. Sch., '59; b. Hamilton, Bermuda, 1934; res: 430 E. 86th St., N.Y., N.Y. 10028.

CAHN, PATRICIA LOVELADY, Ed.-in-Chief, American Education, and Chief of Periodicals Br., United States Office of Education, Department of Health, Education, Welfare, 400 Maryland Ave., S.W., Wash., D.C. 20202, '66–; Cnslt., Wtr.-Ed., '65–'66; Free-lance Wtr., '56–'65 (articles in Saturday Evening Post, McCalls, etc.); Pubcty. Dept., Samuel Goldwyn Prods., '54; EPAA (Exec. Comm., '67–); Fed. Eds. Assn. Aws. (best mag., '66, '67; best pubn. produced in govt., '66); George Washington Univ.; Am. Repertory Theatre Sch., L.A., Cal., '27; p. Merle and Bessie Turk Lovelady; h. Robert Cahn; res: 3416 O St., N.W., Wash., D.C. 20007.

CAIN, MARGO WENBERG, Acct. Exec., Tucker Wayne and Co., Advertising, 2700 Peachtree Ctr. Bldg., Atlanta, Ga. 30303, '67–; Wtr., Burke Dowling Adams/BBDO, '63–'64; Asst. VP, Citizens and Southern Nat. Bank, '54–'61; Univ. of Ga., AB, '48; Univ. of N.C., '50–'51; b. Wilmington, N.C.; p. J. E. and Fannie Russ Wenberg; h. Albert E. Cain; c. Alison E., Wiley E.; res: 5625 Glenridge Dr. N.E., Atlanta, Ga. 30305.

CAIN, MARY DAWSON, Ed.-Publr., The Summit Sun, 110 Chestnut, Summit, Miss. 39666, '36–; Ed.-Publr., The Woman Constitutionalist, '64–; Ed., Summit Sentinel '36–'37; Auth: "Clowns Remember," (bk. of lyric poetry), '37; "Keepers of the Flame," (publ. annually); frequent speaker on constitutional govt. and Americanism; Miss. Fedn. of Press Wm. (Founder and Past. Pres.), NFPW (Past Reg. Chmn.), Miss. Fedn. of BPW (Past Pres.), Miss. Wm. for Constitutional Govt. (Past Pres.), Nat. Wm. for Constitutional Govt. (Past Pres.), Congress of Freedom (Past Pres.); numerous aws. from wms. press clubs and civic orgs.; Miss. Col., '24; b. Burke, La., 1904; p. Charles Goodrich and Tulula Delagarza Dawson; h. John L. Cain; res: 110 Chestnut, Summit, Miss. 39666.

CAIN, MARY KAY, Media Supvsr., McCann-Erickson Inc., 3325 Wilshire Blvd., Cal. 90005, '50–; Space and Time Byr., '48–'50; Media Asst., Batton, Barton, Durstine and Osborn, '47; AWRT; active in amateur radio orgs.; Univ. of Southern Cal., AB (cum laude); b. Evansville, Ill.; p. Burt and Lida Weber Cain; h. Marlow Stewart; res: 1645 N. Lima St., Burbank, Cal. 91505.

CAIN, RACHEL KING, Soc. Ed., The Buffalo Evening News, 214–18 Main St., Buffalo, N.Y. 14240, '58–; Colmst., '52–'58; Reptr., '36–'52; Volta Review commendation, '31; b. Williamstown, W. Va., 1914; p. O'Dale and Gertrude Kennard King; h. Stephen P. Cain; res: 33 Winspear Ave., Buffalo, N.Y. 14214.

CALABRO, Dr. NATALIE, Opns. Rsch. and Mkt. Cnslt., Look, 488 Madison Ave., N.Y., N.Y. 10022, '63–; Asst. Prof. of Statis., St. John's Univ., Jamaica, N.Y.; Mkt. and Opns. Rsch. Mgr., Doubleday Publ. Co., '60–'63; Mkt. and Opns. Rsch. Statistician, Chesebrough-Pond's, '58–'60; Mkt. and Statis. Analyst, Allied Chemical and Dye Co., '52; Mkt. and Statis. Analyst, Chas. Pfizer and Co., '49–'52; Am. Statis. Assn. (Exec. Cncl.), Am. Mkt. Assn., ORSA, AWNY, Soc. Gen. Systems Rsch. (PR Chmn.), Cert. of Merit in Mkt. Commtns. '60; Who's Who Of Am. Wm.; Who's Who in East; Who's Who Intl. Commty. Leaders of Am.; Nat. Regis. Statisticians; numerous articles in mkt., adv. and statis.; N.Y.U., MBA, '57; PhD (Statis.), '66, (Founder's Aw., '66); b. Rhode Island; res: 102–30 66th Rd., Forest Hills, N.Y. 11375.

CALDERON, ELLA GEORGE, Art Dir., Scholastic Publications, 50 W. 44th St., N.Y., N.Y. 10036, '65–; Simplicity's food and fashion mag. for teenage group; Good Housekeeping; N.Y. Herald Tribune, Ideal Pubns., Ahlen and Akerleends (Sweden); Watercolor Aws., L. I., '65; Pratt Grad.; b. N.Y.C.; p. Harold and Angela George; h. Manuel Calderon; res: Pine Valley Rd., RFD 1251, Oyster Bay, N.Y. 11771.

CALDERWOOD, BETTY BOTT, Head Librn., Sterling College, Sterling, Kan. 67579, '67–; Supvsr. of Tchrs., Emotionally Disturbed Children, Univ. of Kan., '65; Tchr: Albuquerque (N.M.), '62–'63; Southard Sch., Menninger Fndn. (Topeka, Kan.), '61–'62; Topeka Public Schs., '59–'61, '63–'67; Assoc. Cols. of Central Kan. (Secy. of Librns., '67–); Curriculum Development Project, Retarded Children, Topeka, Kan., '66–'67; NEA, Local and Nat. Cncls. for Exceptional Children, Alpha Delta Kappa (Nat. Corr. Secy., '64–'67), AAUW, ALA; Outstanding Young Wm. of Am. '66; Sterling (Kan.) Col., BA, '59; Univ. of N.M., '62–'63; Univ. of Kan., ME, '64; Kan. State Tchrs. Col., MS. '68; Rennsaler Poly-technical Inst., '68; b. Grove City, Pa., 1937; p. Ernest and Bessie Gibson Bott; h. William Calderwood; res: R.D.#3, Sterling, Kan. 67579.

CALDWELL, BETTYE McDONALD, Ed., Child Development; Dir., Center for Early Development and Education, Society for Research in Child Development, 814 Sherman St., Little Rock, Ark. 72202, '68–; Prof. of Educ., Univ. of Ark.; previously Prof. of Child Dev. and Educ., Dir. of Children's Ctr., Syracuse Univ.; Soc. for Rsch. in Child Dev., Am. Psychological Assn., numerous other pfsnl. orgs.; Who's Who of Am. Wm., Men of Sci.; Phi Beta Kappa, '50; Baylor Univ., AB, '45 (cum laude); Univ. of Ia., MA, '46; Wash. Univ., PhD, '51; b. Smithville, Tex., 1924; p. Thomas and Juanita Mayes McDonald; h. Fred T. Caldwell, Jr.; c. Paul, Elizabeth; res: 187 Pleasant Valley Dr., Little Rock, Ark. 72207.

CALDWELL, DOROTHY JOHNSON, Assoc. Ed., State Historical Society of Missouri, Hitt and Lowry Sts., Columbia, Mo. 65201, '67–; Dir. of Hist. Sites Survey, '57–'63; Rsch. Assoc., '55; Ed., Mo. Hist. Sites

Catalogue, '63; Co-auth., "Rocheport, Romance Of A River Town," '68; numerous articles, incl. "Vignettes Of Famous Missourians" series published quarterly in the Missouri Historical Review; Mo. Wtrs. Guild (Pres., '65–'66), NFPW (three third-place aws., '57), Theta Sigma Phi (Columbia, Mo., Alumnae Club Pres., '58–'59), Friends Of Rocheport (Bd. of Dirs., '68–'69), Mo. Press Wm. (annual writing contest: first-place aw., '68; first-place aw., '63; three first-place aws., '57); N.E. Mo. State Col., BS, '26; Univ. of Mo., BFA, '30; BJ, '49; MA, '54; h. Joseph Caldwell (dec.); res: 1607 Ross St., Columbia, Mo. 65201.

CALDWELL, KATHERINE MURDOCH, Dir. of PR, Christ Hospital, 176 Palisade Ave., Jersey City, N.J. 07306, '51–; L. I. Fund, '64–'66; Un. Commty. Chest, '62–'64; Mich. Off. of Civil Defense, '57–'62; Mich. Div., Am. Cancer Soc., '51–'57; Un. Commty. Funds & Cncls. of Am., PR Advisory Cncl. (Mid East Reg. Secy., '65), Wms. Overseas Svc. League, Am. Overseas Assn.; Frances Shimer Col.; Armed Forces Inst., '67; b. Brookline, Mass., 1917; p. Louis R. and Elizabeth Hansen Murdoch; h. (div.); c. Christopher; res: 586 Van Emburgh Ave., Westwood P.O., N.J. 07675.

CALDWELL, LILY MAY, Entertainment, Fine Arts Ed. Emeritis, Birmingham News, Fourth Ave., N. 22nd St., Birmingham, Ala. 35202, '20–'67; one of the founders of Birmingham Civic Opera, Starlight Opera of Birmingham Festival of Arts (Past VP); mbr., Birmingham Music Club, and Birmingham Civic Ballet; Founder, Exec. Dir., Miss Ala. Scholarship Pageant, Ala. Jr. Miss Scholarship Pageants, Ala. Fedn. of Music Clubs cit., Birmingham Symphony cit., Motion Picture Industry cit., Miss Am. Pageant cit., Ams. Jr. Miss Pageant cit., Birmingham News cit.; Belhaven Col.; b. Houston, Tex., 1898; b. Houston, Tex., 1898; p. Arthur and Mamie Blue Caldwell; res: 4212 Clairmont Ave. S., Birmingham, Ala. 35222.

CALDWELL, ROSSIE BROWER, Asst. Prof., South Carolina State College, Library Service Department, Orangeburg, S.C. 29115, '57–; High Sch. Tchr., Librn., '45–'57, '37–'43; Rschr., Contrbr. to educ. jnls., dirs.; NEA, S.C. Educ. Assn., ALA, Southeastern Lib. Assn., S.C. Lib. Assn., Am. Assn. for Higher Educ., AAUP, Nat. Assn. of Col. Wm.; Who's Who in Lib. Svc.; Who's Who of Am. Wm.; active in numerous civic groups; Claflin Col., BA, '37 (magna cum laude); S.C. State Col., MS (educ.), '52; Univ. of Ill., MS (Lib. Sci.), '59; b. Columbia, S.C., 1917; p. Rev. Rossie and Henrietta Irby Brower; h. Harlowe Caldwell; c. Rossie Jenkins; res: 685 College Ave., Orangeburg, S.C. 29115.

CALDWELL, TAYLOR (pseud: Max Reiner), Auth., 29 best-seller novels, nat. and intl. (Doubleday & Co., Inc., 277 Park Ave., N.Y., N.Y. 10017), '38–, including "The Devil's Advocate" ('52), "Never Victorious, Never Defeated" (Grand Prix, Prix Chatrain, Paris, '56), "Tender Victory" ('56); Contrbr. to nat. mags.; Court reptr., '23–'24; Yeomanette, U.S.N., '18–'19;

public svc. aws. and orgs., Fellow Intl. Inst. Arts and Ltrs., Am. Acad. Polit. Sci.; Univ. of Buffalo, grad., '31; D'Youville Col., Buffalo, DHL; b. Prestwich, Manchester, Eng., 1900; p. Arthur F. and Ann Markham Caldwell; h. 1. William Fairfax Combs (div.) 2. Marcus Reback; c. Mary Margaret Combs (Mrs. Gerald Fried), Judith Ann (Mrs. Theodore Goodman); res: 34 Audley End, Buffalo, N.Y. 14226.

CALHOUN, MARY, Auth: 20 children's bks. incl. "House of Thirty Cats," "Witch of Hissing Hill," "The Thieving Dwarfs"; Trustee, Rangely (Colo.) Public Lib.; Univ. of Ia., BA, '48; b. Keokuk, Ia., 1926; p. William and Loubelle Waples Huiskamp; h. Rev. Leon Wilkins; c. Michael, Gregory; res: Box 363, Rangely, Colo. 81648.

CALHOUN, WANDA JUNE, Head Librn., Florida Presbyterian College, P.O. Box 12560, St. Petersburg, Fla. 33733, '63–; Head Librn., Heidelberg Col. (Tiffin, Ohio), '58–'63; Divisional Librn., Univ. of Mich. '55–'58; Visiting Specialist in Lib. Svcs., Un. Bd. of Christian Higher Educ. in Asia, '65–'66; Dir., Independent Study in Lib. Sci. at Fla. Presbyterian Col.; Am. Assn. of Univ. Profs., ALA, Fla. Lib. Assn.; Murray State Univ., (Ky.) BS, '53; Univ. of Mich., AMLS, '55 (Lib. Svc. Fellow, Lib. Svc. Scholar); b. Mayfield, Ky., 1932; p. Thomas and Lucile Hamlet Calhoun; res: 3215 Pinellas Point Dr. S., St. Petersburg, Fla. 33712.

CALIENDO, NICOLETTE ANNE, Asst. Art Dir. and Rschr., Forbes Magazine, 60 Fifth Ave., N.Y., N.Y. 10011; Edtl. Rschr., Reptr., Art Rschr., Ed. Prof. Model, Fashion Advisor, Time Magazine, '58–'68; Speech Writer; Auth., poems and stories; Am. Nwsp. Guild, Nwsp. Guild Press Club, N.Y. Knicks Basketball Team Press Club; St. John's Univ., BA, '58; b. Bklyn., N.Y., 1938; p. Leopold J. and Anna Verdeschi Caliendo; h. Kenneth Bastion Harlan, Jr., res: 145 E. 27th St., Apt. 7E, N.Y., N.Y. 10010.

CALLAHAN, ELSIE BARNHART, Edtl. Asst., Gulf Research and Development Company, P.O. Drawer 2038, Pitt., Pa. 15230, '64–; PR Admr., Pitt. Nat. Bank, '62–'64; Staff Asst., United Fund of Allegheny Co., '58–'61; PRSA; Assoc. Eds. Soc. of Pitt.; Smith Col., AB, '34; h. Albert B. Callahan; res: Royal York Apts., Pitt., Pa. 15213.

CALLAHAN, SIDNEY deSHAZO, Wtr., Lectr., University Speakers Bureau, 14 Pond View Rd., Canton, Mass. 02021; Auth: "The Illusion of Eve," ('65), "Beyond Birth Control" ('68); Bryn Mawr Col., AB, '55 (magna cum laude); Regis Col., hon. deg., '66; b. Wash., D.C., 1933; p. George and Lethama Jones deShazo; h. Daniel Callahan; c. Mark, Stephen, John, Peter, Sarah, David; res: 84 Summit Dr., Hastings-on-Hudson, N.Y. 10706.

CALLAN, MARY ANN, Dir. Dev.-PR, Pitzer College, 1150 Mills Ave., Claremont, Cal. 91711 (also Tutorial in Eng.) '68; Asst. to the Pres., '65–'68; Educ. Wtr., L.A.

Times, '57–'65; Wms. Ed., '52–'57; Feature Wtr., '48–'52; Instr. in Jnlsm., Univ. of Southern Cal.; Theta Sigma Phi (Achiev. Aw., '52; LA. Chptr. Pres., '52–'54), Ctr. for Continuing Educ. (Advisory Bd., '68–), Pilgrim Place, Claremont, Cal. (Bd. of Dirs., '67–); Conf. of Christians and Jews Aw.; Univ. of Southern Cal., BA, '44 (cum laude); MA (psych.); b. Fullerton, Cal., '22; p. Forest and Selma Salveson Callan; res: 466 W. Sixth St., Claremont, Cal. 91711.

CALLAWAY, ELIZABETH, Wms. Dir. and Hostess of "Charm Center," KTRE Radio, P.O. Box 729, Lufkin, Tex. 75901, '53–; AWRT, Zeta Phi Eta; Brenau Col., '32–'36; b. Mayfield, Ky., 1915; p. Houston and Marie S. Adams; h. John Callaway; c. Nancy (Mrs. Charles Hale), Johnny, Molly; res: 1301 Wildbriar, Lufkin, Tex. 75901.

CALLAWAY, MARY WEBB, Ed., The Southlander, Southland Life Insurance Company, 1524 Southland Ctr., Dallas, Tex. 75201, '54–; Ed., The Owl, '50–'54; Ed., Agency News, '49–'54; Mgr., Adv. and Pubcty Dept., '48–'49; Exec. Secy. to Pres., '44–'48; Asst. to Agcy. Dir., '42–'44; Jefferson Standard Life Ins. Co., '27–'42; ICIE, Dallas IEA (Pres., '55, VP, '54, Secy., '50); Theta Sigma Phi Matrix Aw., '64; Freedoms Fndn. aw.; Press Club of Dallas aw., '64; Tex. Med. Assn. aw., '69; Western Ky. State Col.; b. Smithland, Ky., 1906; p. David and Minnie Tolley Webb; h. John Marshall Callaway; res: 6122 Aberdeen Ave., Dallas, Tex. 75230.

CALLAWAY, RHEA HALL, Mgr., Brooklyn Amsterdam News, 1251 Bedford Ave., Bklyn. N.Y. 11216, '70–; Supvsr., Classified Adv., New York Amsterdam News, '63–'70; Owner, Rhea Callaway Assocs., Inc., '60–'62; Wms. Ed., New York Citizens' Call, '60–'61; Wms. Ed., New York Age, '58–'60; Owner-Dir., Peerless Adv. Agcy., '44–'50; On-Air Talent, WHBI; WWRL; Nat. Assn. of Negro Bus. & Prof. Wms. Clubs, (Nat. PR Chmn., '58–'60, '63–'64); Iota Phi Lambda; NAMW (Founder and 1st Nat. Pres.; Pres., N.Y. Chptr., Life mbr. aw. for devotion to org.); Nat. Assn. of Col. Wm. Community Svc. Aw., '59; b. Thomson, Ga., 1924; p. Nathan and Eva Hawes Hall; h. Ernest V. Callaway (dec.); c. Sharon Rhea; res: 10 W. 135th St., N.Y., N.Y. 10037.

CALLOMON, JANE L., VP-Crtv. Dir., Lando Inc., 725 Liberty Ave., Pitt., Pa. 15222, '59–; TV-Radio Dir., '53–'59; Copywtr., '51–'53; Co-Auth of musical revue, "Open Season" (Pitt. Playhouse), '60; Theta Sigma Phi, Pitt. Adv. Club (Dir., '67–; Adv. Wm. of the Yr. Aw., '66), N.Y. Intl. Bdcst. Festival Silver Medal aw. for TV comml., '67; Hollywood Intl. Bdcst. aws., '61, '63, '68; Brewers Assn. of Am. aw. for TV comml., '64, '68; Am. TV Festival CLIO, '69; Vassar Col., BA, '50 (cum laude); b. Pitt., Pa., 1929; p. Verner and Florence S. Callomon; res: 1227 Bennington Ave., Pitt., Pa. 15217.

CALVERT, NANCY ANN, PR Dir., School District of the City of St. Charles, 1916 Elm St., St. Charles, Mo. 63301, '68–; Time Byr., Batz Hodgson Neuwoehner

Adv. and Mkt. Svc., '65–'68; PR Dir., area schs. of Michigan City, Inc., '62–'65; Jnslm. Tchr., Michigan City HS, '62–'65; Co-host for wms. show, KWRE Radio (Warrenton, Mo.), '61; Speaker, Northern Ind. Jnlsm. Seminar, '65; AWRT (Secy., '68–'69), NSPRA, Wms. Adv. Club of St. Louis; Lindenwood Col., AB, '61; Univ. of Ariz., Grad. Work, '62–'64; b. Michigan City, Ind., '39; p. E. Preston and Eoise Worthington Calvert; res: 8415 Fresno Ct., St. Louis, Mo. 63121.

CALVERT, PATRICIA C., VP, Calvert-Stearns, Inc., 157 W. 57th St., N.Y., N.Y. 10019, '63–; N. Am. Corr., Le Repertoire Des Voyages, '63–; Reporter mag., '54–'58; Glamour, '52–'54; N.Y. Times, '48–'54; Alumnae Advisory Ctr. (Bd. of Dirs., '63–); Univ. of Cinn., '26–'28; Univ. of Pa.; N.Y.U.; b. Mason County, Ky.; p. Thomas and Maude Paynter Calvert; h. Torrey Stearns; res: 435 E. 57th St., N.Y., N.Y. 10022.

CAMACHO, MATHILDE, Asst. Ed., Life Magazine, Time and Life Bldg., Rockefeller Ctr., N.Y., N.Y. 10020, '57–; Rschr., Reptr., Fgn. Corr., '45–'57; Off. of War Info., '43–'45; Contrbr., Life Atlantic, Life en Espanol; translator, lectr.; Barnard Col., BA, '33; Columbia Univ., MA, '35; Sorbonne, Paris, Licence Lettres, '39; Doctorat Lettres, '39; b. Paris, France; p. Abel and Matilde Sarmiento Camacho; h. Alexander Solomon; res: 280 Riverside Dr., N.Y., N.Y. 10025.

CAMELLI, IMIE WATTS, Assoc. Prodr., "Beat the Clock," Goodson-Todman Productions, 375 Park Ave., N.Y., N.Y. 10022, '69–; Casting Dir., Assoc. Prodr., "To Tell the Truth," '66–'68; Copywtr., Fashion Coordr., "The Price is Right," '57–'66; Edtl. Adm., Esquire, '53–'57; Psy. Asst., Van Ophuijsen Center, '49–'53; AFTRA, AGVA; Southern Ill. Norman Univ., BA, b. Benton, Ill., 1923; p. Claude and Mayme Waller Watts; h. Allen Camelli; res: 751 E. Shore Rd., Hewitt, N.J. 07421.

CAMERON, JEAN, Faculty, Women's Feature Writing Division, School of Journalism, University of Missouri, Columbia, Mo.; Cnslt., J. C. Penney Co., Inc. (N.Y.C.) '67–; Fashion Cnslt., Acc. Work, Edward H. Weiss (Chgo., Ill.), '65–'67; Fashion and Beauty Ed., Chicago's American, '58–'65 (J. C. Penney-Univ. of Mo. Jnlsm. Aw. for Fashion Writing, Catherine L. O'Brien Aw. for Wm's. Feature Writing, Hadassah Aw. for Wm's. Feature Writing); free-lance prom. and adv., Bramson-Weathered, '56–'57; free-lance dress designer, '49–'57; Asst. Fashion Ed., Mademoiselle Magazine (N.Y.C.), '46–'49; Little Shop Accessory Byr., R. H. Macy, '44–'46; Fashion Show Prom. Dir., Marshall Field (Chgo.), '40–'44; (col.) Shop, Cotton Pirje Scott & Co., Chgo., '38–'40; Commentator, fashion shows, others; Regular Appearances, "Tie Line" show with Mal Bellairs, WBBM-CBS, two and one-half yrs.; Theta Sigma Phi, Gamma Phi Beta, Fashion Group of Chgo.; Northwestern Univ., BS (Rep. from Univ. to work on col. issue of Mademoiselle Magazine in N.Y.C.); b. Chgo., Ill.; h. (div.); c. son.

CAMERON, POLLY, Graphic Arts Dir., Guidance Associates, Harcourt Brace & World Publishers, Pleasantville, N.Y. 10570, '64–; Auth./Illus. of children's bks; "I Can't, Said the Ant" ('61), "The Two-Ton Canary and Other Nonsense Riddles" ('65) and others; Prom. Design, Time, '54–'64; Free-lance Illus. and Graphic Designer (Paris, France and N.Y., N.Y.); Display Designer, Goldwater Dept. Store (Phoenix, Ariz.), '49–'51; Am. Inst. of Graphic Arts Aw. for Outstanding Illus., '58–'60; Outstanding Design, '64; Univ. of Cal. at Santa Barbara, '46–'48; b. Walnut Creek, Cal., 1928; p. Donald and Dorothy Knox McQuiston; h. Richard Cameron (div.); res: Sneden's Landing, Palisades, N.Y. 10964.

CAMERON, SUE, Pres., Sue Cameron Enterprises, 9145 Sunset Blvd., L.A., Cal. 90069; Rptr., ABC-TV, '69–; Ed., Teen mag., '66–'68; TV Reptr., KHJ-TV, '67–'68; Pubcty. Dir., KFWB Radio, '65–'66; Crtv. Cnslt. to Cocoanut Grove, Ambassador Hotel; works published in L.A. Times; AWRT, AFTRA, Hollywood Wms. Press Club (Nwsltr. Ed.); Univ. of Southern Cal., BS, '65; b. L.A., Cal., 1945.

CAMP, CHARLOTTE CYRUS, Publr., Stockbridge Town Crier, 110-1/2 N. Clinton St., Stockbridge, Mich. 49285, '67–; Mng. Ed., '65–'67; Corr., Ingham County News, Jackson Citizen Patriot, '61–; Corr., Detroit News, '62–; Mich. Press Assn. (Gen. Excellence Aw., '66–'69), b. Gleiwitz, Germany, 1923; p. Joseph and Paula Tost Cyrus; h. Robert Camp; c. Ruth, Faye, Axel, David; res: 215 S. Center St., Stockbridge, Mich. 49285.

CAMP, NORMA COURNOW, Edtl. Supvsr., Dembar Educational Research Services, Inc., 2101 Sherman Ave., Madison, Wis. 53701, '67–; Project Asst., Univ. of Wis. Conservation Educ. Programs, '66–'67 (ed. "Conservation Centennial Symposium," '67); Wtr. Ed., Union Gospel Press, '63–'65; Asst. to Pubns. Ed., Miami Univ. (Oxford, Oh.), '65–'66; Edtl. Asst., Young Ambassador (Lincoln, Neb.), '61–'63; Auth.; numerous short stories; mbr. conservation orgs.; Outstanding Young Women of America, '68; The King's Col., Briarcliff Manor, AAS, '58; Piedmont Bible Col., BRE, '61; b. Petersburg, Va., 1939; p. Sherwood and Marguerite Price Cournow; h. Russell R. Camp; res: Rte. 1, Dowd Rd., Waunakee, Wis. 53597.

CAMPBELL, ALMIRA TAYLOR, Cataloguer, Deerfield Academy, Frank L. Boyden Library, Deerfield, Mass. 01342, '68–; Head Librn., Stoneleigh-Prospect Hill Sch., '60–'68; Tchr., French, '63–'67; Head Librn., Mount Hermon Sch., '48–'54; Asst., Order Dept., Mount Holyoke Col. Lib., '45–'48; Asst., Acquisitions Dept., Yale Law Sch. Lib., '43–'45; ALA, New Eng. Sch. Lib. Assn., Mass. Lib. Assn.; AAUW, Greenfield Public Lib. (Trustee); Colby Jr. Col., AA, '40; Mount Holyoke Col., AB, '42; Simmons Col., Sch. of Lib. Sci., BS, '43; b. Hyde Park, Mass., 1920; p. Arthur and Mildred Fuller Taylor; h. Vincent Campbell; c. Faith S.; res: 103 Burnham Rd., Greenfield, Mass. 01301.

CAMPBELL, ANNE J., Mgr., Commty. Rels. WCAU-TV, City Line and Monument Aves., Phila., Pa. 19131, '63–; Prodr., TV series "Capitol Hill To Philadelphia" and "Official Report;" Adm., CBS, '61–'63; Exec. Secy., '48–'61; Exec., Lichtman Theatres, Wash., D.C., '40–'46; AWRT, Fellowship Commn., Phila. Urban League, Phila.-Montgomery Tuberculosis and Health Assn. (PR Comm., '65–); U.S. Power Squadrons Aw., '67; E. Trenton Civic Ctr. Aw., '66; U.S. Army cit. for contrb. to recruiting mission, '65; Annenberg Sch. of Commtns. of Univ. of Pa., '62–'63; b. Phila., Pa., '20; p. Charles H. and Anna Schmidt Johnson; h. Charles E. Campbell; res: 16E Northgate Plaza, Camden, N.J. 08102.

CAMPBELL, BLANCHE FISH, Auth., "Gourmet's Gamble" (Naylor Co., '62); Free-lance wtr.; Home-making Colm., Dakota Farmer; Filler Wtr.; AP Newsfeature Synd.; articles, juv. and confession stories, in McCall's, American Home, House Beautiful, House and Garden, many other mags., U.S. and England; b. Blairstown, Ia., 1902; p. Thomas and Cordelia Edds Fish; h. Thomas Campbell; c. Lenore Royal, Helen Belnap; res: 1219 N. Lugo Ave., San Bernardino, Cal. 92404.

CAMPBELL, DELMA GIBSON, Ed.-Publr., The Campbell Company, 3339 W. Freeway, Ft. Worth, Tex. 76107, '64–; Ed., Publr., Key Magazine, '66–; Asst. Ed., The Bicycle Jnl., '60–; Circ. Mgr., '54–'64; Asst. Ed., Lawn Equipment Jnl., '60–; Ed., The Fort Worther, '58–'66; Ft. Worth C. of C., Adv. Club of Ft. Worth, Pan Am. Round Table #1, Wms. Club of Ft. Worth; E. Tex. State Tchrs. Col., '29–'32; b. Tyler, Tex., 1914; p. Robert and Beatrice Martin Gibson; h. Jack W. Campbell; c. Melinda, Melissa; res: 4020 White Settlement Rd., Ft. Worth, Tex. 76107.

CAMPBELL, ELIZABETH PFOHL, Pres., The Greater Washington Educational Television Association, WETA-TV, Channel 26, 2600 4th St., N.W., Wash., D.C. 20001, '57–; Tchr., Cathedral Sch. for Girls, '46–'51; Dean, Mary Baldwin Col. (Staunton, Va.), '29–'36; Dean of Wm., Moravian Col. for Wm., '28–'29; Arlington County Sch. Bd. (Chmn. '50–'51, '54–'55, '60–'61), Un. Ch. Wm. (Arlington Cncl. Pres. '59–'61; Comm. of 100, '62–), YWCA (Wash., D.C., Bd. of Dirs., '53–'59; Nat. Capital Area Bd. of Dirs., '64–), YMCA (Arlington Bd. of Dirs., '54–), Northern Va. Fine Arts Assn., (Bd. of Trustees, '65–), George Mason Col., (Advisory Comm.), Va. Mental Retardation Planning Cncl. (Reg. Chmn., Apptd. by Governor, '66), Nat. Citizen's Comm. for Public TV ('67), AWRT (Golden Mike Aw., '62), Am. Assn. of Educ. Bdcstrs. NATAS, PRSA (Aw. and Cit., '60), AAUW, Quota Club Intl. (Hon. Mbr.); Algernon Sydney Sullivan Aw. for Sch. and Commty. Svc., '56; Salem Col., AB; Columbia Univ., MA; b. Winston-Salem, N.C.; p. Rt. Rev. and Mrs. J. Kenneth Pfohl; h. Edmund Campbell; c. Rev. Edmund Campbell, Jr., Virginia (Mrs. Everett W. Holt), Rev. Benjamin Campbell, H. Donald; res: 2912 N. Glebe Rd., Arlington, Va. 22207.

CAMPBELL, FRANCES DENISE, Librn., Colorado Supreme Court Law Library, 220 State Capitol Building, Denver, Colo., '64–; Librn., Denver Public Lib., '62–'64; Am. Assn. of Law Libs., Special Libs. Assn., Kappa Beta Pi; Colo. Univ., BA, '60; Denver Univ., MS (Lib. Sci.), '62; b. Cape Girardeaux, Mo. 1937; p. Galen M. and Frances M. Campbell; res: 1390 Emerson, #501, Denver, Colo. 80203.

CAMPBELL, JOYCE BERNEY, Prodr./Dir., KQED (TV), 525 Fourth St., S.F., Cal. 94107, '67–; Assoc. Prodr., '66–'67; Exec. Secy., '61–'66; Asst. to Dir. of Sch. Bdcst., '59–'61; Stanford Univ., BA (Eng. Literature, '58 (honors); Harvard-Radcliffe, Cert. in Bus. Adm., '59; S.F. State Col., MA (Eng. Literature), '68; b. Walla Walla, Wash., 1936; p. Walter and Claire Torpey Berney; h. David Campbell; c. Allan; res: 327 Texas, S.F., Cal. 94107.

CAMPBELL, MARGUERITE DEXTER, Ed., Owner, Mariposa Gazette, Ninth and Jones St., Mariposa, Cal. 95338, '54–; weekly nwsps. 50 yrs., from age six with family, at 19 publr. of small weekly, LeGrand, Cal.; C. of C., OES, Soroptimist; Univ. of Redlands; b. Fourth Crossing, Cal., 1912; p. John and Katrina Bund Dexter; h. Dale K. Campbell (dec.); c. Dalmar John, Linda Kay, Dexter Joseph; res: Eighth and Jones St., Mariposa, Cal. 95338.

CAMPBELL, MARI KANDEL, Media Byr., Reach, McClinton & Co., Inc., 4390 Prudential Bldg., Boston, Mass. 02199, '69–; Estimater, BBDO, '68–'69; Asst. Claims Adjuster, Am. Intl. Underwtrs. (Frankfurt, Germany), '66–'67; New Eng. Media Evaluation Assn; Oh. Univ., BSJ, '66 (cum laude, hons.); Univ. of Ill., Grad. Sch. of Adv., '67–'68; b. Columbus, Oh., 1944; p. Herbert and Elizabeth Heiby Kandel; h. Gary Campbell; res: 12 Inman St., Cambridge, Mass. 02139.

CAMPBELL, MARIANNE B., Dir. of Commty. Affairs, AVCO Broadcasting Corp., 1600 Provident Tower, Cinn., Oh. 45202, '67–; Gen. Mgr., Oh. Valley on the Air, Inc., WJEH-AM-FM (Gallipolis), '50–'67; Public Affairs Comm., Nat. C. of C. ('68–'70); AWRT (Dir. at Large, '68–'70); Assn. for Pfsnl. Bdcst. Educ. (Pres., '69–'70; Bd. of Dirs. and only wm. to serve, '64–'70; first wm. apptd. to Radio Code Bd., '65–'66), Oh. Assn. of Bdcstrs. (Pres., '64), Oh. Fedn. of BPW (Pres., '68–'69), Daytime Bdcstrs. Assn. (Secy.-Treas., '63–'67), AAUW (past Pres.), Adv. Club of Huntington, W. Va., numerous other nat., state, and local offs. of civic and pfsnl. orgs.; Top Ten Women Of The Year, Am. Bus. Wms. Assn., '60; Who's Who Of Am. Wm.; Who's Who In Midwest; Who's Who In Commerce And Industry; Kentucky Colonel, '66; Pa. Col. for Wm., BA, '48; b. Pitts., Pa., 1926; p. William O. and Arista Harrington Boggs; h. Bill C. Campbell; res: Willowview Farm, Lower River Rd., Gallipolis, Oh. 45631.

CAMPBELL, PATRICIA PIATT, Auth: "Cedarhaven," "By Sun and Candlelight," "The Royal Anne Tree," four other novels; ZONTA, Pacific N.W. Wtrs. Conf. (Exec. Secy., Past Pres.); Univ. of Wash., Univ. of Ore.; b. Vashon, Wash., 1901; p. Jay and Margaretta Dilworth Piatt; h. William Campbell; c. Gordon R.; res: 1330 Boren Ave., Seattle, Wash. 98101.

CAMPBELL, PEARL CARLING, Auth., religious poems and essays; active in numerous religious orgs.; recs. for "Voice of America," "Sermonette"; Wm. of the Yr. in field of religion, Bergen Co. Br., from Nat. Cncl. of Negro Wm., '63; b. Newcastle, Pa.; p. The Rev. Alfred and Christiana von Staverfelt Carling; h. Neil A. Campbell; c. Neil C.; res: 715 Larch Ave., Teaneck, N.J. 07666.

CANARY, BETTY JANE, Colmst., Newspaper Enterprise Association, 230 Park Ave., N.Y., N.Y. 10017, '67; Reptr., Photogr., The Tribune (New Albany, Ind.), '66–'67; Wms. Press Club of Ind., NFPA, BPW; Columbia Univ.; Ind. Univ. Ext; b. E. St. Louis, Ill., 1929; p. Lyndon and Lenna Steele Canary; h. Robert Van Lare; c. Robert, Steven, Nancy, Theodore, Barbara; res: 815 Cedar Bough, New Albany, Ind. 47150.

CANN, ANN SIBOLD, Commtns. and Public Info. Offcr., Virginia Regional Medical Program, 700 E. Main St., Richmond, Va. 23219, '68–; Dir. of Public Info., Va. Heart Assn., '63–'68; Dir. of PR, Central YMCA, '61–'63; Asst. Dir. of PR, Un. Givers Fund, '60–'61; Mkt. Rsch., Southeastern Inst. of Rsch; Mgt. of Special Events (Celebrities); Richmond PR Assn. (Bd. of Dirs., '65–'66), Assoc. Bus. Eds. of Va. (Bd. of Dirs., '66); W. Va. Bus Col., '49–'50; Concord State Tchrs. Col., '51–'52; Va. Commonwealth Univ. Academic Div., '61–'63; b. Hinton, W. Va., 1932; p. John and Anna Sibold; h. Philip Cann; c. Donald G. Miller, Jr., John Miller; res: 9525 Beckham Dr., Richmond, Va. 23230.

CANNELL, KATHLEEN EATON, Dance Critic, The Christian Science Monitor, 398 Marlborough St., Boston, Mass. 02115, '64–; Wtr. of bk. revs., fashion roundups, wms. pg. features, edtl. pg. articles, '44–; Tchr., Bks. and Auths., Cambridge Ctr. for Adult Educ.; Reviewer, bks., The Providence Jnl., '58–; read French bks. for pubn., G. P. Putnam's Sons; Scriptwtr., Walter Winchell; Pubcty. Dir., Special Exhbns., Bklyn. Museum, '47–'48; covered German Press Confs., The N.Y. Times (Occupied Paris); Paris Fashion Ed., '30; Paris Fashion Corr., The New Yorker, '39; radio prog., "Women in France," Radio Diff. Nationale; Ed., three wms. mags., French, Am., Spanish; Fashion Cnslt.; Lectr.; OPC, French Ctr. in New Eng., Fashion Group, Academic Moderne Bd.; PEN grant for furthering cause of lit.; Univ. of Toronto; Sorbonne; b. Utica, N.Y.; p. Frederick and Mary Wilson Eaton; res: 398 Marlborough St., Boston, Mass. 02115.

CANNON, CHARLOTTE MARILYN, Librn., Auth.; Asst. Librn., Phillips Univ. (Enid, Okla.), '68; Circ. Librn., Tex. Wms. Univ. (Denton), '64–'67; Juv. Bookmobile Librn. (Portland, Ore.), '63–'64; Juv. Bookmo-

bile Librn., (Youngstown, Oh.), '58–'61; AAUW, ALA, Pi Lambda Theta, Sigma Alpha Iota, Alpha Beta Alpha, Intl. Platform Assn., Nat. Audubon Soc.; Royal Blue Bk.; Who's Who of Am. Wm.; Who's Who in Lib. Svc.; Dic. of Intl. Biog.; Two Thousand Wm. of Achiev.; Nat. Soc. Dir.; Warren Wilson Col., AA, '56; Tex. Wms. Univ., BS, '58; MLS, '63; b. Enid, Okla.; p. James and Eldora Wright Cannon; res: 440 Waringwood Rd., La Puente, Cal. 91744.

CANNON, POPPY, Roving Gourmet Ed., Colmst., Ladies' Home Journal; Sr. Food Ed., Los Angeles Times Syndicate; Colmst., Amsterdam News; Food Ed., Colmst., Town and Country, House Beautiful, Mademoiselle; Copywtr., Maxon, Inc.; Hilton-Riggio Consumer General Foods Service Dept.; Auth., 14 cookbooks; biography, "A Gentle Knight" of husband, Walter White; poetry, short stories; OPC, PEN, Auths. League; Vassar, Washington Square Col., BA; b. Cape Town, S. Africa; p. Robert and Marya Raskin; h. Walter White (dec.); c. Cynthia Cannon White, Claudia Philippe; res: 36 E. 38th St., N.Y., N.Y. 10016; Breakneck Hill, West Redding, Conn. 06896.

CANNON, SARAH COLLEY ("Minnie Pearl"), Comedienne; Hon. Chmn. of the Bd., Performance Systems, Inc., 2708 Franklin Rd., Nashville, Tenn. 37204, '67–; 29 yrs., "Grand Ole Opry"; numerous TV appearances; Country Wm. of the Yr., '66; Ward Belmont Jr. Col. grad.; h. Henry Cannon.

CANNON, VIVIAN, Ed., Wtr., and Photog., Alabama Sunday Magazine, Montgomery Advertiser-Journal, P.O. Box 950, Montgomery, Ala. 36102, '67–; Sun. Wtr., Aviation Ed., Movie Ed., Wms. Wtr., Mobile Press Register, '46–'67; Ed., Providence Hosp. Echo, '64–'66; PR Cnslt., Providence Hosp., '63–'64; Montgomery Cncl of Indsl. Eds. (1st and 2nd pl. aws., '68), Southern Cncl. of Indsl. Eds.; AP Newswriting Aw: 2nd pl., features, '57; 3rd pl., public svc., '64; aws. for sonic flight in F100 with U.S. Air Force and Navy F9F jet; Air Force Assn. and numerous civic orgs.; John McNeese Col.; b. Bogalusa, La.; p. Bruce M. and Sara Lee Bradley Cannon; res: Apt. 1, 3460 Gilmer Ct., Montgomery, Ala. 36105.

CANOVA, JUDY, Actress, Comedienne; Goldman & Kagon, 356 N. Cambden Dr., Beverly Hills, Cal. 90210; stage: "Calling All Stars," "Yokel Boy"; Films: "Huckleberry Finn," "WAC from Walla Walla," "Puddinhead," 14 others; radio: "Judy Canova Show," NBC, 13 yrs.; TV: "Alfred Hitchcock," "Pistols and Petticoats;" Motion Picture Cncl., Hon. Fire Chief (Boston, Mass.), Hon. Sheriff (Dallas, Tex.); b. Starke, Fla., 1919; p. Joseph and Henrietta Perry Canova; c. Julieta England Maurel, Diana Canova Rivero; res: 1558 N. Crescent Heights Blvd., L.A., Cal. 90046.

CANTWELL, MARY, Mng. Ed., Mademoiselle, Conde Nast, 420 Lexington Ave., N.Y., N.Y. 10017, '68–; Copy Chief; Feature Wtr., Vogue; Conn. Col., BA; h. Robert Lescher.

CAPERS, ELIZA VIRGINIA, Actress, Singer, c/o Lou Irwin, 9135 Sunset Blvd., L.A., Cal. 90069, '50–; 1st black Am. female to tour Israel with Israeli Musical Repertory Co.; TV: "Julia Show," "Judd for the Defense;" Film: "The Lost Man;" Theatre: "Sister Sadie and the Sons of Sam" (Mark Taper Forum); Volunteer Tchr., Broadway Elementary Sch. (Venice); AEA, AGVA, SAG, AFTRA, Family Svc. Org.; Howard Univ.; Juilliard Sch. of Music; b. Sumter, S.C., 1925; p. James and Jannie Montgomery Capers; c. Glenn Sylvester; res: 754 S. Spaulding Ave., L.A., Cal. 90036.

CAPREOL, EDYTHE ROBERTS, City Hall Reptr., Feature Wtr., Book Ed., Beaumont Journal, 380 Walnut St., Beaumont, Tex. 77704, '51–; Am. Press (Lake Charles, La.), '47–'50; Wtr., Indsl. Rel. articles, Sterling Research (Darien, Conn.), '45–'46; Recreation worker in New Guinea, Am. Red Cross, '43–'44; mag. articles, Gift and Art Shop, Ed. and Publr., Rice Journal and others; Lectr., S.W. Wtrs. Conf. five yrs. and at high schs.; BPW (Pres., '46–'47), Beaumont Art League, Beaumont Art Museum, ENABLE (Bd. Mbr.), Beaumont Mental Health Assn. (Bd. Mbr.), Christmas Bur. Advisory Bd.; Three state aws. and one nat. aw. from Texas and NPWC for nwsp. and feature writing, '53; b. Cambden, N.J., 1906; p. Mary Clark Roberts-Dineen and Raymond Victor Roberts; h. John Henry Dumble Capreol (div.); res: 1185 14th St., Apt. 4, Beaumont, Tex. 77702.

CAPRONI, JOANNA SLESINGER, Assoc. in Mkt. Rsch., Life Magazine, Time and Life Bldg., N.Y., N.Y. 10020, '62–; Rsch. Mgr., Space Byr., Luckie and Forney Adv., '60–'61; Rsch. Asst., Consumer Rsch., Batten, Barton, Durstine & Osborn, '55–'60; Am. Mkt. Assn., AAPOR, AWNY; Pembroke Col., BA, '54; b. Chicago, Ill., 1933; p. Donald and Dorothy E. Avery Slesinger; h. Leo F. Caproni, Jr.; res: 370 E. 76 St., N.Y., N.Y. 10021.

CARACCIOLI, KATHERINE FRANCES, Sr. Market Rsch. Analyst, Sudler & Hennessey, Inc., 130 E. 59th St., N.Y., N.Y. 10022, '67–; E. R. Squibb & Sons Intl., '60–'67; Alfred A. Knopf, Inc.; Hon. Richard C. Patterson, Jr. (public affairs); AWNY, League in Aid of Crippled Children, Inc. (past Pres., Bd. of Dirs.); N.Y.U., AB, '51; MA, '56; b. N.Y.C.; p. Louis N. and Catherine Gargan Caraccioli; res: 205 E. 66 St., N.Y., N.Y. 10021.

CARBINE, PATRICIA T., Exec. Ed., Look Magazine, 488 Madison Ave., N.Y., N.Y. 10022, '69–; Mng. Ed., '66–'69; Asst. Mng. Ed., '59–'66; Sr. Ed., '57–'59; Asst. Ed., '55–'57; Edtl. Rschr. '53–'55; Who's Who of Am. Wm.; b. Villanova, Pa.; p. James T. and Margaret J. Dee Carbine; res: 399 E. 72nd St., N.Y., N.Y. 10021.

CARLIN, ESTHER OSSER, Reptr., National Building News, Box 647, Ridgewood, N.J. 07450, '68–; Adv. Dept., Wms. Wear Daily (N.Y.C.); Press Sec., U.S. Dept. of Agriculture, (Wash., D.C.); Agricultural Adv. and Rsch. (Ithaca, N.Y.); Bev Barnett Pubcty. (Hollywood, Cal.); Theta Sigma Phi, Kappa Tau Alpha;

Univ. of Mich., AB, '41; Cal.-Western Univ.; b. Munising, Mich., 1920; p. Borah and Rose Zirlin Osser; h. Robert Carlin; c. Bruce, Martha; res: 3672 Liggett Dr., San Diego, Cal. 92106.

CARLIN, KATHRYN SCANLON, Dir. of Field Svcs., Tchr. Certification, Fordham University, Lincoln Center Campus, N.Y., N.Y. 10023; Prof., Assoc. Prof., Asst. Prof., Educ., '45–; Asst. Prof., Villanova Col., '44–'46; Head of Educ. Dept., Dir. of Placement, Asst. Prof., '36–'46; Wtr., bks., numerous articles on educ.; Nat. Soc. for Study of Educ., N.Y. Soc. for Experimental Study of Educ., AAUP, others; Who's Who of Am. Wm., Who's Who in Am. Educ., Dir., Special Educ. Program, Ford Fndn. Grant, '57; various pfsnl. honors; Fordham Univ., BS, '34; MA, '36; PhD, '56; b. Yonkers, N.Y., 1909; p. Edward J. and Ida Johnstone Scanlon; h. John J. Carlin (dec.); res: 1304 New York Ave., Bklyn., N.Y. 11203; and Cairo, N.Y. 12413.

CARLIN, SARAH STUDEBAKER, Pres., Ed., Publr., Alexandria Gazette Corporation, 717 N. St. Asaph St., Alexandria, Va. 22313, '66–; nwsp. work since '43; ZONTA, many other commty. charitable orgs.; Freedom Fndn. at Valley Forge Aw., '68; Who's Who of Am. Wm.; h. Charles Carlin, Jr. (dec.); c. Charles C., IV, Mrs. Sarah M. Roe.

CARLSON, BERNICE WELLS, Auth., children's bks., '39– incl. "Act It Out" (Abingdon, '56), "The Right Play for You" (Abingdon, '60), both on N.Y. Times "100 Outstanding Books for Children"; Reptr., Lansing (Mich.) State Jnl., '36–'43; Auth. Aw., N.J. Tchrs. of Eng., '63–'68; Ripon Col., AB, '32 (cum laude, Distg. Alumna Aw., '54); b. Clare, Mich. 1910; p. George and Bernice Cook Wells; h. Carl W. Carlson; c. Philip Wells, Marta Ann, Christine (Mrs. Paul J. Umberger); res: Rte. 3, Box 332 D Skillmans Lane, Somerset, N.J. 08873.

CARLSON, KAREN, Actress, Founder of Kara Soul Music Publishing Company with husband, David Soul; bus. c/o Irving Leonard & Assoc., 1900 Ave. of the Stars, suite #2270, L.A., Cal. 90067; first runner-up, Miss Am. Pageant (Miss Ark.), '64–'65; numerous TV programs, commls.; SAG, AFTRA; Univ. of Ark., '62–'65; b. Shreveport, La., 1944; p. Marvin and Margaret Stewart Carlson; h. David Soul.

CARLSON, MAUDE COOKE, Head Librn., Social Sci. and Gen Ref. Dept., California State Col., '59–'67; Ref. Librn. '52–'58; Bibliographer and Acquisitions Librn., Univ. of Redlands, '46–'52; Public Svcs., '43–'46; Circ. Librn., '31–'33; Asst. Librn., Rollins Col. (Winter Park, Fla.), '27–'30; Lib. Asst., Univ. of Mich., '26; hist. tchr., '23–'26; Assn. Cal. State Col. Profs., AAUP, Cal. Lib. Assn., Phi Mu, others; Univ. of Mich., AB, '23; MA, '29; b. Ithaca, Mich.; p. Nathaniel M. and Clara Smith Cooke; h. Glen E. Carlson (dec.); res: 3737 Atlantic Ave., #704, Long Beach, Cal. 90807.

CARLSON, NATALIE SAVAGE, Auth., 24 bks., children's fiction, incl: "The Talking Cat and Other Stories of French Canada" ('52), "Alphonse, That Bearded One" ('54), "Wings Against the Wind" ('55), "Hortense, The Cow for a Queen" ('57), all winners of N.Y. Herald Tribune aw.; bks. have also won Boys' Clubs of Am. and Child Study Assn. of Am. aws.; Reptr., Long Beach (Cal.) Sun, '26–'29; b. Winchester, Val, 1906; p. Joseph and Natalie Villeneuve Savage; h. Daniel Carlson; c. Stephanie (Mrs. Robert D. Sullivan), Dr. Julie Carlson; res: "Periwinkle," Perry St., Newport, R.I. 02840.

CARLTON, MARY ELLIS, Dir., Special Sections, Long Beach Independent, Press-Telegram, 604 Pine Ave., Long Beach, Cal. 90801, '69–; Dir., Wms. News, '64–'69; Fashion Ed., '60–'64; Wms. Ed., The Wichita (Kan.) Beacon, '56–'60; AE, Assoc. Adv., '50–'56; Info. Exec., Kan. State OPA, '43–'45; Nwsp. Publr., Pampa (Tex.) Army Air Base, '42–'43; NPWC (60 writing aw., '59-), Kan. Press Wm., Wichita Press Wm. (Past Pres.), Cal. Press Wm., Pacific Coast Press Club, Long Beach C. of C.; Univ. of Wichita, AB, '38; b. Okla. City, Okla., 1918; p. William and Hildreth Russell Brincefield; h. (div.); c. Dori (Mrs. Charles Schneider), Susan (Mrs. Frank Campanelli), Linda Ellis; res: 5215 E. Broadway, Long Beach, Cal. 90803.

CARMAN, CAROL MARLENE, Reptr., Cinn. Bur., Fairchild Publications, Inc., Carew Tower, Cinn., Oh. 45202, '66–; Wms. Ed., Western Hills Publ. Co., '63–'66; Copy Desk, Feature Wtr., Miami (Fla.) News, '62; Free-lance, Cincinnati Magazine, nwsp. shopping insert; Theta Sigma Phi (Cinn. Chptr. Secy., '64–'65; Pres. '66), Univ. of Miami, BA, '62; Sorbonne (Paris), '67–'68; b. Glendale, Oh.; p. Ralph and Carrie Reid Carman; res: 11512 Chester Rd., Cinn., Oh. 45246.

CARMICHAEL, EMIL BREWER, Info. Rep., Texas Tech University, Box 4640, Tech Sta., Lubbock, Tex. 79409, '65–; Educ. Ed., Lubbock Avalanche-Journal, '57–'65; formerly reptr., Amarillo, Pampa and Canyon, Tex., Portales, N.M.; Theta Sigma Phi (Chptr. Pres., '66–'67); Tex. Christian Univ., '28–'29; W. Tex. State Univ., '32–'34; Univ. of Mo., BJ, '35; h. Bernis Carmichael (dec.); c. Diane (Mrs. C. LeRoy Blank); res: 5305 43rd St., Lubbock, Tex. 79414.

CARMOSIN, MARJORIE RUTH, Dir., Pubcty./ Pubns., Hahnemann Medical College & Hospital, 230 N. Broad St., Phila., Pa. 19102, '60–; Chilton Pubns., '58–'60; Free-lance, '57–'58; Lavenson Bur. of Adv., '55–'57; Drexel Inst. of Tech., '46–'55; Guest Lectr.; Article, Jnl. of Am. Hosp. Assn.; Adv. Wm. of Phila. (Bd. Dir., '52–'54; Rec. Secy., '54–'56), Hahnemann Hosp. Assn. (Rec. Secy., '64–) Charles Morris Price Sch. of Adv. (Carrie May Price Aw.), '45; Distg. Alumna, '69); Barnes Fndn., '53; b. Phila., Pa., 1925; p. Julius and Isabelle Lam Carmosin; res: 6614 N. 13th St., Phila., Pa. 19126.

CARNAHAN, ALICE WHITTINGTON, Publr. and

Owner, The Eudora Enterprise, 135 S. Main, Eudora, Ark. 71640, '52–; Ark. Press Assn.; b. Eudora, Ark. 1924; p. James Andrew and Epsy McCullough Whittington; h. Francis Carnahan (dec.); c. Carolyn and Mrs. Willie Capers; res: 601 S. Archer, Eudora, Ark. 71640.

CARNES, FRANCES COX, Dir. Lib. Svcs., Pembroke State University, Pembroke, N.C. 28372, '68–; Staff, '59–; Central Col. (Fayette, Mo.) '56–'59; Mt. Pleasant (Ia.) Public Lib., '54–'56; McMurray Col. (Abilene, Tex.), '52–'54; Harvard Divinity Sch., '49–'52; Westminster Jr. Col., '47–'49; New Haven State Normal (Conn.) '29–'35; N. Tex. State Tchrs., '27–'28; S.F.A. State Tchrs., (Tex.), '27; ALA, N.C. Lib. Assn., Southeastern Lib. Assn.; educ: Univ. of Tex., BA, '25 (Mortar Board); Columbia Univ., BS (Lib. Sci.), '29; MS (Lib. Sci.) '35; b. Mexico City, Mexico, 1904; p. Jackson and Julia Barcus Cox; h. Otis Carnes; res: Box 745, Pembroke, N.C. 28372.

CARPENTER, FRANCES, Auth., 35 children's bks., geographical, folk tale; publrs. incl: Am. Bk. Co., Doubleday & Co., A. A. Knopf, others; Intl. Soc. of Wm. Geographers (Pres., '39–'42), Fellow Royal Geographical Soc. (London); Children's Hosp. (Bd. of Dirs., '47–'58; Bd. of Lady Visitors Pres., '44–'46), Children's Bk. Guild (Charter Mbr.); Smith Col., AB, '12 (Trustee, '36–'44; Alumnae Assn. Pres., '32–'35); b. Wash., D.C., 1890; p. Frank and Joanna Condict Carpenter; h. W. Chapin Huntington (dec.); c. Mrs. Huntington Noel, Mrs. David Benton Williams; res: 2101 Connecticut Ave., Wash., D.C. 20008.

CARPENTER, MARGARET HALEY, Wtr., Ed.; Poetry Reviewer, Chgo. Tribune, '62–'63. Ed., Va. Author's Yearbook, '56–'58; Guest Ed., The Lyric, '55; Auth: "Sara Teasdale: A Biography" ('60), "A Gift for the Princess of Springtime" ('64); Co-ed, "Anthology of Magazine Verse for 1958"; PSA (Co-winner, Arthur Davison Ficke Aw., '56), Poetry Soc. of Eng. (Greenwood Prize, '57), Vachel Lindsay Assn. (Advisory Bd., '68–'69), Poetry Soc. of Va. (Advisory Bd., '69); Westhampton Col., Univ. of Richmond, BA; res: 1032 Cambridge Crescent, Norfolk, Va. 23508.

CARPENTER, MARJ COLLIER, News Ed., Andrews News, 112 N.W. First St., Andrews, Tex, 79714, '65–; News Ed., Pecos Independent, '63–'65; Wms. Ed., '60–'62; Tchr., Ogden Sch. System, '47–'49; Tchr., Kingsville, HS, '46–'47; Reptr., Corpus Christi Caller, '46; Reptr., Mercedes Enterprise, '43–'44; Tex. Press Assn. (news writing aws., '66, '68; feature story aws., '62–'64), W. Tex. Press Assn., BPW (Andrews Club Pres., '67–'68), Who's Who in Am. Cols. and Univs.; AP Commty. Svc. Aw. (in Pecos), '63; Tex. Col. of Arts and Industries, BM, '46; b. Mercedes, Tex., 1926; p. Walter and Beatrice Diehl Collier; h. C. T. Carpenter, Jr. (dec.); c. Cathy, Carolyn, Jim; res: 507 N.W. 4th St., Andrews, Tex. 79714.

CARPENTER, NORMA LUCILLE, PR and Adv.,

Department Store; Proms. and PR, Miller & Paine, Lincoln, Neb., '35–'68; Adv., '31–'32; News Dept., Wayne Herald, '32–'35; Adv. Mgr., Weld County News (Greeley, Colo.), '30; Instr., Bus. Eng., Univ. of Neb., '46; USO Nat. Comm., AWRT, Altrusa Club (Pres., '68–'69), Gamma Alpha Chi (Nat. Pres.), Theta Sigma Phi, Neb. Press Wm., PEO, BPW, Lincoln Artists Guild, Neb. Art Assn., Lincoln Arts Cncl., Wms. Interclub Cncl. (Pres., '69–'70), Lincoln Better Bus. Bur. (Dir., '64–'69), Defense Advisory Comm. for Wm. in the Svcs., Govs. Comm. on Status of Wm., Neb. Comm. for Children and Youth; Lincoln Wm. of the Yr., '56; Lincoln Ad Club Adman of the Yr., '57; Alternate Delegate to Repl. Nat. Convs. ('52, '56); educ: Univ. of Neb., AB, '26; Univ. of Mo., BJ, '27; b. Lincoln, Neb., 1903; p. Harry and Etta Thompson Carpenter; res: 1616 G., Lincoln, Neb. 68508.

CARR, A. BEULAH MOTT, Head Librn., Fairhope Library Board, 10 N. Summit St., Fairhope, Ala. 36532, '57–; Librn., Sr. HS, Greeley, Colo., '37–'38; Mgr., Br., Farmer's Nat. Bank (Gaza, Ia.), '33–'35; ALA, Ala. Lib. Assn.; Who's Who of Am. Wm.; Kappa Delta Pi; Sigma Pi Lambda; Univ. of Denver, Sch. of Librarianship, BA, '36; Colo. State Col., MA (Educ.), '37; b. Viola, Ia.; p. James and Emma F. Waring Mott; h. Roland P. Carr; c. Jeffrey R.; res: Box 252, Fairhope, Ala. 36532; Summer: Ossipee, N.H. 03864.

CARR, ANNE ELIZABETH, Assoc. and Dir. of Adv., PR-New York, Inc., 342 Madison Ave., N.Y., N.Y. 10017, '67–; Asst. to the Feature Ed., Cahners Publ., '66–'67; Crtv. Dir., Takaro Adv. Agcy., '66; Am. Mgt. Assn.; Dormann & Auletta PR, '65; Asst. to the Pres., Communicorp PR, '64–'65; Dancer-Fitzgerald-Sample, '63–'64; WWCO Radio (Waterbury, Conn.), '62–'63; Pres., Kiddie Carr Prods.; free-lance anncr.-bdcstr. for sls. films, radio and TV commls.; Am. Bus. Press, Pubcty. Club of N.Y., PRSA, Mensa; Univ. of Rochester, '57–'60 (Dean's List); Univ. of Edinburgh, Scotland, MA (Eng. Lit.), '60–'62; b. Ithaca, N.Y., 1939; p. John, II, and Helen Ziegler Carr; res: 536 Madison Ave., N.Y., N.Y. 10022.

CARR, HARRIETT HELEN, Auth., young adults and biographies; Scholastic Magazines, '44–'63; Am. Vocational Assn. (Wash., D.C.), '43–'44; Educ. Dept., Mich. State, '39–'43; Ed., Ypsilanti (Mich.) Daily Press and Detroit News, '21–'39; St. Petersburg Wtrs. Club, Wms. Nat. Bk. Assn., BPW; Edgar Allan Poe Aw. for "The Mystery of Ghost Valley," (Macmillan '62); Literary Guild aws: "Borghild of Brooklyn" (Farrar, Strauss & Cudahy, '55), "Rod's Girl" (Hastings House, '63); Mich. State Normal Col.; Univ. of Mich.; N.Y.U.; b. Ann Arbor, Mich. 1899; p. Paul and Nellie Loomis Carr; res: 23 Third St. S., St. Petersburg, Fla. 33701.

CARR, LYNN HEYMAN, Sr. Ed., Popular Merchandise Company, Inc., 128 Dayton Ave., Passaic, N.J. 07055, '65–; Home Furnishings Ed., Fashion Ed., '63–'65; Ed., Freehold Transcript, '62–'63; Police, Polit. Reptr., Amboy Evening News, '60–'62; Publr., Madison (N.J.) Independent, '61–'63; PR Dir., Commty. Chest, Copy Ed., Damar Stores, '57; Adv., PR Dir., Frank H. Taylor & Sons, '50–'53; Nwsp. Guild of Am., NHFL, Fashion Group; Police Benevolent Assn. aw., '63; Nat. Ort Diary aw., '51–'52; Univ. of Ga.; b. Newark, N.J., 1925; p. Jerome and Ethel Lowenstein Heyman; h. George A. Carr; c. Theodore Pessin, Michele Pessin; res: 50 Hillcrest Ave., Ardsley, N.Y. 10502.

CARR, SYLVIA T., Ed., Co. Pubns., Gerber Products Co., 445 State St., Fremont, Mich. 49412; PR (Asheville, N.C.), '58–'67; ICIE, Mich. Communicators Assn., BPW (former Bd. Mbr.); Presidential Cit. for Meritorious Svc. in Promoting Employment of the Handicapped, '66; Flying Orchid Aw., Delta Airlines, '66; Army-Navy "E", '45; Cecil's Col., diploma, '37; Western Carolina Univ., '63–'66; b. Asheville, N.C., 1918; p. Lloyd and Lucy Vance Twiford; c. Mrs. Roger C. Sumner; res: Box 55, Fremont, Mich. 49412.

CARRIKER, WANDA GENE, Prom. Coordr., KCOP-TV, 915 N. La Brea Ave., Hollywood, Cal. 90038, '67–; Prom. Asst., '66–'67; On-Air Prom. Wtr., KTTV-TV (L.A., Cal.), '66; Cont. Dir., KLBK-TV (Lubbock, Tex.), '62–'65; Traf. Dir., KPAR-TV (Abilene), '60–'61; Bdcst. Prom. Assn., NATAS, AWRT, S. Plains Wtrs. Assn. (Past. Pres., Rec. Secy.); Mensa; b. Baird, Tex., 1940; p. William E. and Roberta Dickerson George; h. (div.); c. Conrad R.; res: 6037 Hazelhurst Pl., N. Hollywood, Cal. 91606.

CARROLL, ANDREA ZWEIFACH, Asst. Movie Ed., Parents' Magazine, 52 Vanderbilt Ave., N.Y., N.Y. 10017, '67–; N.Y.U., BS, '66; b. N.Y.C., 1945; p. Ira S. and Ellen Fuller Zweifach; h. Jerry Carroll; res: 321 W. 88th St., N.Y., N.Y. 10024.

CARROLL, GLADYS HASTY, Auth: "Christmas Through the Years" (Little, Brown, '68), "The Road Grows Strange" ('65), "To Remember Forever" ('63), "Only Fifty Years Ago" ('62), "Come with Me Home" ('60), several others; mag., TV stories; Bates Col., AB, '25; U. of Me., LittD; b. Rochester, N.H., 1904; p. Warren and Frances Dow Hasty; h. Herbert Carroll; c. Warren, Sarah (Mrs. Hazen L. Watson); res: Earl Rd., S. Berwick, Me. 03908.

CARROLL, KATHLEEN LEADER, Asst. Movie Critic, Wtr., The Daily News, 220 E. 42 St., N.Y., N.Y. 10017; NWC of N.Y. (Asst. Treas., '68–'69; Bd. Mbr., '69–'70), N.Y. Film Critics (Chmn., '69; Vice-Chmn., '68; Sec., '67; Col. of New Rochelle, AB; b. Lake Placid, N.Y., 1939; p. George and Lucille McDonald Carroll; res: 200 E. 36th St., N.Y., N.Y. 10016.

CARROLL, SHIRLEY (Shirley Horn O'Connor), Pres., The Carrolls Agency, Inc., 8432-1/2 Melrose Pl., L.A., Cal. 90069, '67; W. Coast PR, '48–; Theta Sigma Phi, L.A. Adv. Wm. (Cert. of Merit, '68), Cal. Assn. of Press Wm. (seven first place aws., '59), AWRT, L.A. Press Club, Assn. of Theatrical Press Agts. & Mgrs.,

Pacific Pioneer Bdcstrs., AAF; First place Aw., NFPW, '59; annual circus for handicapped children at Rancho Los Amigos Hosp., Downey; L.A.; City Col., '38–'40; b. Cleve., Oh., 1917; p. Max and Fannie Weisberger Horn; h. Norman O'Connor (dec.); c. Kevin; res: 2001 N. Curson Ave., L.A., Cal. 90046.

CARROLL, VICTORIA, Actress, c/o Hal Shafer, 1017 N. LaCienega Blvd., L.A., Cal. 90069, '62–; numerous Stage, Movie, TV Shows, night clubs, commls.; SAG, AFTRA, AEA; much charity work; b. L.A., Cal., 1942; p. O. K. and Lillian Ulirch Ford; res: 3430 Jasmine Ave., L.A., Cal. 90034.

CARROLL, VINNETTE JUSTINE, Actress, Wtr.; Dir., Ghetto Arts Program, New York State Council on the Arts, 250 W. 57th St., N.Y., N.Y. 10019, '68–; Assoc. Dir., Inner City Repertory Co. (L.A., Cal.); Dir., APA Repertory Co. (N.Y.C.); Dir., Urban Arts Corps; Obie aw., distg. performance in "Moon on a Rainbow Shawl" (N.Y.C., '61–'62); Emmy aw., creator, adapting of "Beyond the Blue" (CBS, '63–'64); L.I. Univ., BA, '44; MA, '45; N.Y.U.; Columbia Univ.; New Sch. for Soc. Rsch.; b. N.Y.C.; p. Edgar and Florence Morris Carroll; res: 864 Broadway, N.Y., N.Y. 10003.

CARSON, DORIS MILLER, Asst. Prof., Cataloger, Wichita State University, 1845 Fairmount, Wichita, Kan. 67208, '57–; Librn., McPherson (Kan.) HS, '50–'57; Kan. Wesleyan Univ., '48–'50; Asst. Librn., McPherson Public Lib., '47–'48; Tchr., Librn., Cheyenne County HS, '45–'46; Inspector, Goodyear Engineering Corp. (Charlestown, Ind.), '43–'44; Tchr., Lucas (Kan.) HS, '42–'43; Tchr., Norcatur (Kan.) Grade Sch., '37–'39; Tchr., Nortonville (Kan.) HS, '36–'37; Tchr., Healy (Kan.) HS, '34–'36; Instr., Kan. Wesleyan Univ., '33–'34; AAUP, Intl. Platform Assn., NEA, Mountain Plains Lib. Assn., Kan. Assn. of Sch. Librns., ALA, Kan. Lib. Assn. (Treas., '62–'63), Beta Phi Mu; Kan. Wesleyan Univ., AB, '33 (magna cum laude); Univ. of Kan., MA, '41; Univ. of Ill., MS, '54; b. Tescott, Kan., 1911; p. Wilbur and Christie Roy Miller; h. Andrew Carson; res: 1855 N. Lorraine St., Wichita, Kan. 67214.

CARSON, LORRAINE, Rsch. Assoc., Fortune Magazine, Time-Life Bldg., Rockefeller Ctr., N.Y., N.Y. 10020, '57–; Sr. Ed., "Dun's Review & Modern Industry," Dun & Bradstreet, '49–'57; Collaborator, "The Computer Age" (Harper & Row); Colby Col., BA.

CARSTENS, ETHEL SASKA, Co-publr., Eaton Rapids Journal, 156 S. Main St., Eaton Rapids, Mich. 48827, '54–'63, '67–; Pubcty. Agt., Tex. Southmost Col. (Brownsville), '66–'67; Pubcty. Wtr., Watts Public Relations, '64–'66; Rsch: 30-yr. hist. of Port of Brownsville, '65, and 75-yr. hist. of Brownsville Daily Herald, '66, both special editions of daily nwsp.; Mich. Press Assn., BPW; Owosso Bus. Col., '30, Hurley Hosp. Sch. of Nursing, '31; b. Chgo., Ill., 1915; h. Arthur Carstens; c. Mrs. Kay Diamond, Mrs. Carole Boulton; res: 1313 Hall St., Eaton Rapids, Mich. 48827.

CARSTENS, FRANCES ELLEN GIVEN, Adv. Prod.

Mgr., Prakken Publications, 416 Longshore Dr., Ann Arbor, Mich. 48107, '66–; Asst. Adv. Prod. Mgr., '66; Asst. to Librn., Northfield Sch. for Girls, '62; Audio-Visual Dir., '57–'59; b. Brattleboro, Vt., 1939; p. Sidney and Marion Gans Given; h. David Carstens; c. Scott Christian; res: 3072 Sunnywood, Ann Arbor, Mich. 48103.

CART, LILLIAN JOHANTGEN, Publr., The Rayne Independent, 104 W. Louisiana Ave., Rayne, La. 70578, '67–; Co-publr., Colmst., Crowley (La.) Daily Signal, '63–'68; Adv. Dir., '61–'68; Retail Adv. Mgr., '59–'61; Prom. Mgr., '57–'59; Classified Mgr., '55; Adv. Mgr., Kaplan Journal, '54; Weekly Acadian, '52–'53; Ed., Hadacol pubns., '50–'51; La. Press Wm. (State Pres., '70–'72), La. Press Assn., Intl. Nwsp. Adv. Execs., BPW (past state VP), La. News Photogrs. Assn.; Beta Sigma Phi, Rice Festival Bd. of Dirs., Retarded Children, "Cowbelles," numerous adv., nwsp. aws.; Acadia Parish Bus. Wm. of the Yr., '59; listed in many dirs.; b. Geary, Okla., 1926; p. Walter and Ruth Roberts Johantgen; h. Robert L. Cart; Sr.; c. Robert L., Jr., Walter T., John R.; res: 1309 Abbeville Highway, Rayne, La. 70578.

CARTER, ANDREA CARSWELL, Wms. Ed., Waycross Journal-Herald, 400 Isabella St., Waycross, Ga. 31501, '61–'69; Proofreader, one yr.; Who's Who Among Outstanding Young Wm. of Am.; Waycross Center Univ. of Ga.; b. Homerville, Ga., 1940; p. Roscoe N. and Wynelle Lance Carswell; h. Henry McCoy Carter, Sr.; c. Henry Jr., Andrea, Martha W., Kim O.; res: Rte. Two, Blackshear, Ga. 31516.

CARTER, GWENDOLEN MARGARET, Dir., Prog. of African Studies, and Prof., Polit. Sci., Northwestern University, 1813 Hinman Ave., Evanston, Ill. 60201, '64–; Prof. of Govt., Smith Col. (Northampton, Mass.), '51–'64; Assoc. Prof., '47–'51; Asst. Prof., '43–'47; Auth., Ed., many works on intl. polit. sci.; African-Am. Inst., Chgo. Cncl. on Fgn. Rels., Am. Polit. Sci. Assn., New Eng. Polit. Sci. Assn., African Studies Assn., AAUW (Achiev. Aw., '62), Advisory Comm. of the Africa Bur.; George V Medal for Public Svc., '35; Am. Acad. of Arts and Scis. Fellow, '65; Univ. of Toronto, BA, '29; Oxford Univ., BA, '31; MA, '35; Radcliffe Col., MA, '36; PhD, '38 (Distg. Achiev. Medal, '62); Hon. Degrees: Wheaton Col., DLitt, '62; Russell Sage Col., DHLitt, '63; Western Col. for Wm., LLD, '64; Goucher Col., DLitt, '64; Carleton Univ., Ottawa, Can. LLD, '65; Boston Univ., DLitt, '66; McMaster Univ., LLD, '66; b. Hamilton, Ontario, Can., 1906; p. Charles and Nora Ambrose Carter; res: 222 Lake, Evanston, Ill. 60201.

CARTER, HELEN HOUGHTON, Ed. and Publr., Conso Publishing Co., Div. of Consolidated Foods Corp., 27 W. 23 St., N.Y., N.Y. 10010, '66–; Co-auth., "1001 Decorating Ideas Homemakers Handbook," (Conso, '69); PR Dir. and Ed., Conso Products, '52–'66; Assoc. Ed., Ed., Fawcett Pubns., '47–'50; Rsch. Ed., Collier's, '46–'47; Copy girl, Cub Reptr., Bklyn. Eagle, '45–'46; Wms. Drapery & Curtain Club (Pres., '54–'56),

Am. Inst. of Interior Designers, NHFL; Cert. of Aw. from GA Aws., Competition for 1,001 Decorating Ideas; Allegheny Col., BA, '45; Columbia Univ., Jnlsm., '44; b. Bklyn, N.Y., 1924; p. Owen Edward and Helen Reeve Houghton; h. Richard Carter; c. Kimberly Ann, Tracey Alden; res: 121 Jennings Rd., Cold Spring Harbor, N.Y. 11724, and Reading, Vt.

CARTER, JODY (Judith Anne Carter), Actress, Theatre, TV, Motion Pic., c/o Armstrong-Deuser Agcy., 449 S. Beverly Dr., Beverly Hills, Cal. 90210; "Under the Weather," "Elektra," "Ghosts"; "Chrysler Theatre," "Hallmark Hall of Fame," "The Outsider;" "Wild in the Streets," others; Am. Repertory Theatre, Royal Poinciana Playhouse, other theatrical activity; AEA, SAG, AFTRA, ANTA, Actor's Studio; Seine Area Command Best Actress Aw., '58; French Govt. Theatre Fellowship and Fulbright Travel Grant, '56–'57; Pomona Col., BA, '56 (cum laude; Phi Beta Kappa); Sorbonne & Conservatoire National d'Art Dramatique; Middlebury Col., MA (French), '57; b. Madison, Wis., 1935; p. William and Anne Fairchild Carter; res: 457 N. Oakhurst Dr., Beverly Hills, Cal. 90210.

CARTER, LINDA MADDUX, Farm Ed., Feature Wtr., Waycross Journal-Herald, P.O. Box 685, Waycross, Ga. 31501, '67–; Ware County Forest Festival Comm., Tobacco Steering Comm., Ware County Commty. Action Comm. (Secy., '69–); Outstanding Young Wm. of Am.; Univ. of Ga.; b. Waycross, Ga., 1946; p. Samuel and Evelyn Booth Maddux Jr.; h. George M. Carter; res: 601 Owens St., Waycross, Ga. 31501.

CARTER, MARY ARKLEY, Visiting Lectr., Program in Creative Writing, University of Iowa, Iowa City, Ia. 52240, '68–; Auth: "The Minutes of the Night," ('65), "A Fortune in Dimes" ('63), numerous short stories; Free-lance Wtr., 10 yrs.; Univ. of Ore., '41–'43; Pitzer Col. for Wm., '65–'66; b. Coos Bay, Ore., 1923; p. Robert and Elizabeth Holzlin Arkley; h. (sep.); c. William, Robert, Victoria; res: 817 N. Gilbert, Iowa City, Ia. 52240.

CARTER, OMA B., Dir., Library Consultant Service, 1912 S. Blvd., Edmond, Okla., 73034; Librn., Edmond HS, '64–'67; Librn., Okla. Christian Col., '59–'64; Edmond Sch. Dist., '65–; Cnslt. to Sch., Col., Ch., Public Libs.; Auth: "What Is a Librarian?" (One-act Drama, '65), "How to Organize a Small Library" ('67); ALA, Southwest Libr. Assn., Okla. Libr. Assn., NEA, AAUW; Abilene Christian Col., BS, '52; Kan. State Tchrs. Col., MS (Lib. Sci.) '55.

CARTER, PATRICIA PATTERSON, Soc. Ed., Rocky Mountain News, 400 W. Colfax Ave., Denver, Colo. 80204, '67–; Dir., Wms. Activities, Am. Trucking Assns., '61–'65; Dir. of PR, Nat. Fedn. of Repl. Wm., '61–'62; Sls. Prom. Coordr., Woodward & Lothrop, '57–'61; PR Dir., Nat. Symphony Orchestra, '55–'57; Co-Owner, Carter's Trade Mark Rsch. Bur., '49–'55; Guest Lectr., PR, Univ. of Md., '57–'65; Univ. of Denver, '66; PRSA (Wash., D.C., Denver Chptrs. Bd. of

Dirs., '58–'66), Nat. Soc. of Arts and Letters, Colo. Press Wm.; Mt. Vernon Jr. Col., AA, '48; George Washington Univ., BS (Econs.), '50; b. Paterson, N.J., 1929; p. Robert and Ninotchka Zuk Patterson; h. J. Miles Carter (div.); c. Patricia M., Robert P.; res: 1040 Humboldt St., Denver, Colo. 80218.

CARTER, SHIRLEY THOMPSON, Founder, Exec. Dir., Texas Girls' Choir, Inc., 3341 Edith Lane, Fort Worth, Tex. 76117, '62–; Dir., YWCA, '63–'65; Teen Shows, local radio-TV, '41–'66; Tchr., Tex. Christian Univ., '61–'66; Music Tchr., public schs., '57–'59; Auth., "Voice and Musicianship," '68; various orgs., aws.; Tex. Christian Univ., BA (Music), '57; b. Fort Worth, Tex., 1935; p. Ewell and Elsie Cole Thompson; h. Jess W. Carter; res: 3133 Wabash, Fort Worth, Tex. 76109.

CARTER, VIRGINIA UNKOVIC, PR Dir., St. Mary's Hospital, 830 S. Jefferson St., Saginaw, Mich. 48601, '63–; Social Dir., St. Mary's Sch. of Nursing, '56–'63; Special Svcs. Dir., U.S. Army; Asst. to Bursar, Chatham Col., Pitt., Pa., '40s; Mich. Hosp. Assn., Am. Hosp. Assn., Am. Soc. for Hosp. PR Dirs., Acad. of Hosp. PR, Mich. Hosp. PR Assn., Acad. of Hosp. PR, Mich. Hosp. PR Assn. (Pres., '68–'69), Epsilon Eta Phi (Nat. Pres. '46–'50); Saginaw Symphony Comm., Saginaw Twp. Schs. Comm. of 100; Duquesne Univ., BS (Bus. Adm.) '41; Grad. Sch., '42; Univ. of Mich.; b. Pitt., Pa., 1919; p. Kosto and Josephine Polic Unkovic; h. Dean W. Carter; c. Dean W., II; res: 4333 Dirker Rd., Saginaw, Mich. 48603.

CARTUN, SUSAN HOROWITZ, Sr. Mkt. Rsch. Analyst, Columbia Broadcasting System, 51 W. 52 St., N.Y., N.Y. 10019, '67–; Labor Econst., U.S. Dept. of Labor, '64–'67 (Performance Aw., '67); Queens Col., BA (Econs.), '62; b. Rochester, N.Y. 1941; p. Hyman and Mary Weiss Horowitz; h. Joel Cartun; res: 4 Horizon Rd., Ft. Lee, N.J. 07024.

CARTWRIGHT, ANGELA MARGARET, Actress, 20th Century Fox Studios, 10201 W. Pico Blvd., W. L.A., Cal. 90015; Fashion Modeling; TV, "Lost in Space" series, '65–'68; Movie, "The Sound of Music," '64–'65; TV, "The Danny Thomas Show," '57–'64; Child Model; numerous other TV shows, movies; NATAS, SAG, AFTRA, AGVA; 7th Annual Teen Star, '68; Harlequin Aw.; Jr. Star Aw., '68; Outstanding Teenage Star of '67; Ambassador of People-to-People, '62; numerous certs. from orgs.; March of Dimes (San Fernando Valley Teen Chmn.); Wtr., Artist, Photogr.; Desilu Studio Sch., 20th Century Fox Studio Sch.; b. Altrincham, Cheshire, Eng., 1952; p. John and Margaret Bennett Cartwright.

CARTWRIGHT, MARGUERITE DORSEY, Free-lance Corr., United Nations, '55–; Tchr., Lectr.; Univ. of Nigeria (Founder, Trustee), UN Corrs. Assn., OPC, Theta Sigma Phi, Alpha Kappa Delta; Am. Assn. for the UN, Am. Comm. on Africa, Fndn. for African Educ., Harlem Hosp. Sch. of Nursing; numerous cits, aws. from govts., cities, civic orgs.; Boston Univ., BS

(Phi Beta Kappa); MA; N.Y.U., Doctorate, '48; b. Boston, Mass.; p. Joseph and Mary Ross Dorsey; h. Leonard C. Cartwright; res. 37 W. 12th St., N.Y., N.Y. 10011.

CARUSO, ELAINE FURNIER, Rsch. Assoc., Knowledge Availability Systems Center, Univ. of Pitt., 304 LIS Bldg., 135 N. Bellefield, Pitt., Pa. 15213, '67-; Asst. Prof., Grad. Sch. of Lib. and Info. Sci.; formerly Sci. Librn., California State Col., California, Pa.; Tech. Info. Specialist, Westinghouse Testing Reactor, Waltz Mills, Pa.; numerous pfsnl. activities; Am. Assn. for Info. Sci., ALA, Assn. for Computing Machinery, AAUP, Beta Phi Mu, Kappa Delta Pi; California State Col., BS, '47; Carnegie Inst. of Tech., MS (Lib. Sci.), '58; Univ. of Pitt., PhD, '69; b. Ronco, Pa., 1926; p. John and Anna Lint Furnier; h. Nicholas Caruso; c. Nicholas C.; res: 440 Second, California, Pa. 15419.

CARY, VERONICA F., Dir., Trenton Free Public Library, 120 Academy St., Trenton, N.J. 08608, '61-; Chief of Circ., '46-'57; Sr. Asst., '38-'46; Gen. Asst., '35-'38; Field Librn., '57-'61; ALA, N.J. Lib. Assn. (Pres., '65-'66); Douglass Col., AB, '33; Columbia Univ., BS (Lib. Sci.), '45; b. N.Y.C., 1911; p. James and Wanda Plawska Cary; res: 230 Garfield Ave., Trenton, N.J. 08629.

CARY, ZENJA E., Wtr., TV Talent, Cary Kitchens; Food Ed., My Baby; Food Pubcty., Dudley-Anderson-Yutzy, '56-'61; Asst. Food Ed., Parents Magazine, '54-'56; Am. Home Econ. Assn., Home Econsts. in Bus., AWRT, AFTRA, SAG, Electrical Wms. Round Table; Cornell Univ., BS (Home Econ.) '53; Columbia Univ., MA (Educ.), '58; b. N.Y.C.; c. Jane; res: 42 E. 64th St., N.Y., N.Y. 10021.

CASE, VIVIAN ELLS, Adv. Mgr., Davison's, 180 Peachtree St., Atlanta, Ga. 30303, '66-; Adv. Mgr., Bullock's (L.A., Cal.), PR Dir., Bloomingdale's (N.Y.C.); Sls. Prom. Mgr., Rhodes (Ore., Wash., Cal., Tex.); Tchr.; Gamma Alpha Chi, Fashion Group (Reg. Dir., '58-'60), Young Repls. of Ore. (Pres., '48-'50); two Lulu Aws. from L.A. Adv. Wm., '66; Nat. Retail Merchants' Assn. aws., '69; Univ. of Ore.; Univ. of Alberta, Tchr's. cert.; U.C.L.A.; b. Sovereign, Saskatchewan, Can., '25; p. Roy and Viola Burke Ells; h. Robert Ormond Case; res: 620 Peachtree St. N.E., Atlanta, Ga. 30308.

CASELLAS, ELIZABETH BRANNON, Dir., Graduate School of Business Administration Library, Assoc. Prof., Tulane University, N.O., La. 70118, '69; Head, Bus., Sci. and Tech. Dept., Orlando (Fla.) Public Lib., '66-'69; Asst. Prof., Grad. Sch. of Lib. Studies, Univ. of Hi., '65-'66; Head of Lib., Stewart, Dougall & Assocs. (N.Y.C.), '60-'65; Cresap, McCormick and Paget, '59-'60; Cmmtns. Cnslrs., Inc., '57-'59; tchr.; Rsch. Asst., Dean Clifford R. Lord, Gen. Studies, Columbia Univ., '64-'65; various orgs.; Chgo. Music Col., BM, '48; Columbia Univ., MA, '48; Pfsnl. Diploma, '49; MS (Lib. Sci.), '64; Sorbonne, '53-'54; b. N.O., La., 1925; p.

D. R. and Elizabeth Robinson Brannon; h. Joaquin Casellas; summer res: 1542 S. Shore Rd., Marmora, N.J.

CASEY, GENEVIEVE M., Assoc. Prof., Lib. Sci., Wayne State University, Detroit, Mich. 48202, '67-; Lib. Cnslt., several states, '67-; Mich. State Librn., '61-'67; Chief, Ext. Dept., Detroit Public Lib., '48-'61; Librn., U.S. Army, European Theatre, '46-'47; Bk. Reviewer, many pubns.; ALA (Cncl. Mbr., '68), Mich. Lib. Assn., Catholic Lib. Assn., Kappa Gamma Pi, Delta Phi Lambda; Col. of St. Catherine, BA, '37; Univ. of Mich., MA, '56; b. Mpls., Minn., 1916; p. Eugene and Cecilia Malerich Casey; res: 574 Goldengate W., Detroit, Mich. 48203.

CASEY, NANCY, Head Librn., Sherman Grinberg Film Libraries, Inc., 1040 N. McCadden Pl., L.A., Cal. 90046, '65-; Librn., Universal Studios, '63-'65; Librn., Grinberg Libs., '59-'63; New Sch. for Social Rsch., '51; Claremont Co., '53.

CASEY, ROSEMARY CHRISTMANN, Ed., Dodd, Mead & Company, Inc., 79 Madison Ave., N.Y., N.Y. 10016, '60-; Edtl. Asst., '55-'60; Secy., Girl Scout Cncl. of Gtr. N.Y., '44-'50; Auth., "The Cousinly Cousins" ('61); Co-auth., "Water Since the World Began" ('65); Who's Who of Am. Wm.; St. Joseph's Col. for Wm., BA (Eng.), '44 (hons.); b. Bklyn., N.Y., 1922; p. George and Lillian O'Haire Christmann; h. Michael T. Casey; c. Brigid, Maura; res: 625 E. 14th St., N.Y., N.Y. 10009.

CASEY, SUE (Suzanne Philips Eilen), Actress, theater, TV, motion pics.; b. L.A., Cal., 1926; p. Burke and Mildred Hansen Philips; h. Harold Eilen; c. Colleen (Mrs. Bernard O'Shaughnessy), John J. Durant, III, Christopher K. Durant, Diane M. Durant; res: 1230 Holmby Ave., L.A., Cal. 90024.

CASEY, TSUNEKO OGURE, Wtr., Ed. Sunday Mag., Honolulu Advertiser, 605 Kapiolani Blvd., Honolulu, Hi., 96813, '62-; TV Ed., '58-'60; Sp. Corr., Nat. Polit. Convs., '60; Feature Wtr.-Colmst., '60-'63; McCall's stringer, '67; Honolulu Press Club (Pres., '66-'68; Bd. Mbr., '68-'69; 1st VP, '65; 2nd VP, '64; Dir., '52-'55; '63-'64; Secy., '48-'51); Univ. of Hi., '41-'44; b. Honolulu, Hi., 1925; p. Kumaichi and Masako Ogure Hataoka; h. Brian L. Casey; c. Leo Brian, Sean Matsuo; res: 437 Hind Dr., Honolulu, Hi. 96821.

CASGRAIN, MILDRED DAVIS, Supervisory Librn., Patients Library, National Institutes of Health, Bldg. 10-7D37, Bethesda, Md. 20014; Lib. Asst., Walter Reed Army Med. Lib.; Librn. Tech., Geological Survey Lib; Lib. Cl.; Law Lib., Covington, Burling; Lib. Tech., Falls Church (Va.) Public Lib; Banshees—Irish Lit. Soc. (Secy.-Treas., '55-), Arts Club of Wash., Strawberrye Banke Restoration Assn. (Portsmouth, N.H.); dev. Deer Island (Me.) Handicrafts; Univ. of N.H.; Univ. of Wis; b. Winthrop, Mass., 1908; p. Harry and Lillian Harding Davis; h. Ardoin Casgrain; c. Charlotte,

Louise (Mrs. James H. Noyes, Jr.); res: 4000 Cathedral Ave., N.W., Washington, D.C. 20016.

CASPARY, VERA, Auth: "The Rosecrest Cell" ('68), "The Man Who Loved His Wife" ('66), "A Chosen Sparrow" ('64), "Evvie" ('60), "The Husband" ('57), "Thelma" ('52), "The Weeping and the Laughter" ('50) "Laura" ('42), and others; Screen wtr: "Les Girls" ('56), "Letter to Three Wives" (adaptation, '49), "Night of June 13th" ('32), and others; Auths. Guild, Dramatists Guild, Auths. League, Screenwtrs. Guild, PEN; b. Chgo., Ill., 1899; p. Paul and Julia Cohn Caspary; h. I. G. Goldsmith (dec.); res: 55 E. Ninth St., N.Y., N.Y. 10003.

CASSELL, Dr. SYLVIA ELIZABETH, Auth., "Nature Games & Activities" (Harper); game, activity, puppet bks., numerous mag., nwsp. articles; Instr., Northwestern Univ. Med. Sch., 303 E. Chicago, Chgo., Ill. 60610, '66–; Intern, Fellow, Children's Memorial Hosp.; '61–'64; Reptr., Feature Wtr., The Chgo. Tribune, '53–'57; The Arts Club of Chgo., Theta Sigma Phi, Am. Psychological Assn., Midwest, Ill. Psychological Assn.; U.S. Public Health Fellowship, '60–'61, '62–'63; Wellesley Col., BA (Fiske Prize for extemporaneous speech, '45); Univ. of Wis., MS; Northwestern Univ., MA, PhD (Fellowship, '61–'62); b. Evanston, Ill., 1924; p. Martin L. and Sylvia Schafer Cassell; res: 1350 Lake Shore Dr., Chgo., Ill. 60610.

CASSIDY, GERALDINE RUTH, Dir. of Public Info., City of Hawthorne, 4460 W. 126th St., Hawthorne, Cal. 90250, '63–; Pubcty., KTLA-TV (Hollywood); Off. Mgr., Ralph Edwards TV Enterprises; Bus. Mgr., Screen Wtrs. Guild; L.A. Adv. Wm. (Pres., '68–'69), AWRT (Southern Cal. Chptr. VP, '69–'70; Lulu Aw., '65, '68, three certs. of merit), NATAS, Hawthorne Quota Club (VP), Nat. Cncl. of Negro Wm.; L.A. City Col.; Univ. of Southern Cal.; U.C.L.A.; b. Woodbury, N.J., 1924; p. Terrence and Edna Hill Cassidy; res: 812 N. Sweetzer Ave., L.A., Cal. 90069.

CASSIDY, MARY FRANKOVICH, Feature Wtr., Colmst., Herald Democrat, 717 Harrison Ave., Leadville, Colo. 80461, '58–; Corr., DRGW railroad pubn., '43; Rsch. to establish museum, "House with the Eye," of Leadville; Lake County Arts and Humanities Cncl. (Secy., '69); La Salle Correspondence Univ. (Aw. in Bus. Writing and Stenotypy, '44); b. Leadville, Colo. 1914; p. Nicholas and Barbara Rogina Frankovich; h. George Cassidy; c. Barbara Bost, Joseph Bost; res: 129 W. Fourth St., Leadville, Colo. 80461.

CASTLEBERRY, VIVIAN ANDERSON, Wms. Ed., The Dallas Times Herald Publishing Co., 1101 Pacific Ave., Dallas, Tex. 75202, '58–; Home Ed., '56–'57; Petroleum Engineer Publ. Co., '54–'55, '44–'46; Wms. Ed., Texas A&M Battalion, '50–'51; Theta Sigma Phi (Aw. for Excellence in Commtn., '64), Zeta Phi Eta, Delta Kappa Gamma (Hon.), Dallas Press Club; UPI state aws.; Dallas Press Club first place aw., '68; J. C. Penney-Univ. of Mo. third place aws., '65, '67;

honored for outstanding contrb. to Wm., Mgt. Seminar for Wm. Execs., Southern Methodist Univ., '67; first place aws. for wms. pgs., '61, '63; Southern Methodist Univ., BS; b. Lindale, Tex., 1922; p. William and Jessie Henderson Anderson; h. Curtis Wales Castleberry; c. Carol, Chanda, Keeta, Kim, Catherine; res: 11311 Buchanan, Dallas, Tex. 75228.

CATES, ANNE KEITH, AE, Reach, McClinton & Co., 35 E. Wacker Dr., Chgo., Ill. 60601, '67–; McManus, John & Adams, BBDO, '64–'67; Bdcst. Bus. Mgr., Arthur Meyerhoff, Inc., '61–'63; Bdcst. Traf. Mgr., McCann Erickson, '60–'61; TV Traf. Mgr., D'Arcy Adv., '58–'60; Radio-TV Traf. Mgr., Asst. Prodr., Campbell-Mithun, Inc. (Mpls.), '52–'57; Cnslt., Talent & Residuals, Inc., '63; song, "Life With You" ('58); Chgo. Wms. Adv. Club, Bdcst. Adv. Club of Chgo.; Macalester Col., '46–'50; Univ. of Minn., '50–'51; MacPhail Col. of Music, BA, '51; b. Minot, N.D., 1929; p. John and Stelle Hoskins Keith; h. L. Cates; res: 9421 S. Wabash Ave., Chgo., Ill. 60619.

CATHON, LAURA ELIZABETH, Head, Central Boys & Girls Division, Carnegie Library of Pittsburgh, 4400 Forbes Ave., Pitt., Pa. 15213, '48–; First Asst., '34–'48; Instr., Ref. Work, Carnegie Lib. Sch. of Carneige Inst. of Tech., '44–'46; Tchr., HS (New Martinsville, W. Va.), '29–'30; Joint Compiler, "Treasured Tales," Stories of Courage and Faith," (Abingdon Press, '60), several other bks. and ref. works; Lectr. and Story-telling to adult groups; Bethany Col., BA, '29; Carnegie Lib. Sch. of Carnegie Inst. of Tech., BS (Lib. Sci.), '32; b. Pitt., Pa., 1908; p. Isaac and Elizabeth Scherer Cathon; res: 1219 Resaca Pl., Pitt., Pa. 15212.

CATON, HAZEL RITCH, PR Coordr., Belk Stores Services, Inc., P.O. Box 2727, 308 E. Fifth St., Charlotte, N.C. 28201, '63–; Ed., Store Mag., Training Inst., Lectr., '53–; Theta Sigma Phi; Charlotte Toastmistress Club (Pres., '69, VP, '68); Fashion Assoc. of the Carolinas (Exec. Dir., Organizer, '66); Queens Col., '34–'35, '53, '63–'64; b. Charlotte, N.C., 1916; p. Marvin and Hazel Robinson Ritch; h. (div.); c. Morris Lawing; res: 2204 Winter St., Charlotte, N.C. 28205.

CAUDILL, REBECCA, Auth: "Come Along!" ('69), "My Appalachia" ('66), "Did You Carry the Flag Today, Charley?" ('66), other (16) juv. bks.; Ed., Methodist Publ. House (Nashville, Tenn.), '24–'30; Theta Sigma Phi, Delta Kappa Gamma; Soc. of Midland Auths., '66; Nancy Bloch Memorial Aw., '56; Wesleyan Col., AB, '20; Vanderbilt Univ., MA, '22; b. Cumberland, Ky., 1899; p. George and Susan Smith Caudill; h. James S. Ayars; c. Rebecca Jean (Mrs. Carl J. Baker Jr.), James S. Ayars Jr. (dec.); res: 510 W. Iowa St., Urbana, Ill. 61801.

CAUDLE, VIOLET KATHLEEN, Asst. Dir., Iredell Public Library, 349 N. Center, Statesville, N.C. 28677, '67–; Librn., '59–'67; Greene Co. Public Lib., '55–'59; Gaston Co. Public Lib., '53–'55; W.A.C., '45–'49; ALA, Southeastern Lib. Assn., N.C. Lib. Assn., BPW; Appalachian State Tchrs. Col. grad.; Emory Univ., post-grad.; Lenoir Rhyne Col., '49–'52; b. Harmony, N.C., 1925; p. Nelson and Tracy Grose Caudle; res: 224-1/2 N. Center, Statesville, N.C. 28677.

CAVALLARO, JEANNE FISHER, Audio-Visual Cnslt., National Young Women's Christian Association, 600 Lexington Ave., N.Y., N.Y. 10022, '67–; Prodr.-Wtr., "Home Show," NBC-TV; PR, Robert Taplinger Co.; B. Lewis Inc; Mogul, Williams Adv.; Prodr.-Wtr., "Children of Earth" (doc. film), '69; AWRT; Oh. State Univ., BS; Cranbrook Art Sch. of Design; b. Dayton, Oh., 1921; p. Jacob and Wilhamina Simon Littwitz; h. Salvatore Cavallaro; res: 38 E. 75th St., N.Y., N.Y. 10021.

CAVALLO, DIANE, Auth., "A Bridge of Leaves" (Atheneum, '61); Auths. League; Fulbright Scholarship, '61–'63; MacDowell Fellowship, '60, '66; Univ. of Pa., BA, '53 (Phi Beta Kappa), W. Chester State Tchrs. Col., summers '55, '56; Sarah Lawrence Col., MA, '66; b. Philadelphia, Pa., 1931; p. Genuino and Josephine Petrarca Cavallo; h. Henry Weinberg.

CAVANAH, FRANCES, Auth.; 3000 39th St. N.W., Wash., D.C. 20016; Dir. of Biogs., Row, Peterson, '48–'52; Biog. Ed., World Bk. Ency., '43–'47; Contrb. Wtr., Ed., Western Printing Co., '39–'42; Assoc. Ed., Child Life, '30–'38; Auth., 14 hist., biog. bks. for young people; Theta Sigma Phi (Headliner aw., '41), Soc. of Midland Auths., ANWC, Wash., D.C. Children's Bk. Guild; Ind. Univ. Wtrs. Conf. aw., '60; several bks. selected by Weekly Reader Bk. Club, Jr. Lit. Guild, Cadmus; DePauw Univ., AB (cit.), '52); b. Princeton, Ind.; p. Rufus and Luella Neale Cavanah; res: 3000 39th St. N.W., Wash., D.C. 20016.

CAVANAUGH, JANE F., Soc. Ed., Greenwich Publishing Co., 20 E. Elm St., Greenwich, Conn. 06830, '60–; Soc. Reptr., Soc. Ed., Post Publishing Co.; Wtr., Radio; Fashion Wtr., Men's Apparel Forum; Adv., McCann-Erickson; N.Y.U.; b. Newtown, Conn.; p. Thomas and Susan Carroll Cavanaugh; h. (div.); res: Ituri Towers, Lafayette Ct., Greenwich, Conn. 06830.

CAVENDER, ELIZABETH PARKER, Lib. Svcs. Dir., Whitfield County Board of Education, 1306 S. Dixie Highway, Dalton, Ga. 30720, '65–; Librn., N. Whitfield HS; Asst. Librn., Dalton Reg. Lib.; Rsch. Inst., Univ. of Ga., '69; NEA, Ga. Lib. Assn. (Secy. '64–'65), Delta Kappa Gamma, Pilot Club of Dalton (Pres., '69–'70), Ga. Educ. Assn.; Ga. State Col. for Wm., BA, '52; George Peabody Tchrs. Col., MA, '57; b. Dalton, Ga., 1931; p. Eugene and Eva Lee Joyce Parker; h. William J. Cavender; c. William, Christopher; res: 109 Todd Ave., Dalton, Ga. 30720.

CAVIN, JANET KLIEBHAN, Ed., The Observer, 1806 Main St., Baker, La. 70714, '60–; News and Soc. Reptr., The Plainsman (Zachary), '57–'60; Commty. Corr., Morning Advocate (Baton Rouge), '61–; La. Press Assn., La. Press Wm., La. Pen Wm.; Deep South Wtrs.

Conf. aws. for hist. novel and feature article, '65; b. Milw., Wis., 1922; p. Anthony and Genevieve Gill Kliebhan; h. Glynn W. Cavin, Sr.; c. Mrs. Kathleen Cavin Bell, Martha (Mrs. Frank Morgan), Glynn, Jr.; res: Star Rte., Box 8, Zachary, La. 70791.

CAVIN, PATRICIA BURWELL, Mgr. of News and Info., Corp. Staff-Wash., RCA Corporation, RCA Bldg., 1725 K St., N.W., Wash., D.C. 20006, '62–; News Commentator, NBC, WRC, '54–'62; Fashion and Beauty Ed., Colmst., Wash. Times-Herald, Wash. Post, '49–'54; WNPC (Pres., '62–'63), ANWC (Bd. Mbr.), '65, '66, '68), AWRT (VP, '66; Nat. Bd., '67–'68), Theta Sigma Phi; Hamilton Time Aw. for public svc. bdcst., '56; Army Times Publ. Co. Individual Achiev. Aw. for NBC radio series, '56; McCall's Golden Mike Aw., '57; Univ. of Wash., '43–'45; Stanford Univ., BA (Jnlsm.), '47; b. Portland, Ore., 1925; p. L. Bernard and Lela Hatfield Burwell; h. F. Edward Cavin; c. Chandler, Brooks; res: 1628 21st St., S.W., Wash., D.C. 20009.

CAYER, SHIRLEY KAY, Supervising Ed., Calumet Publishing Co., 9120 Baltimore Ave., Chgo., Ill. 60617, '68–; Wms. Ed., '67–'68; Feature Ed., '66–'67; Gen. Assigt., '66–'67; Southeast Mental Health Clinic (Advisory Bd.); Ill. Press Assn. aws., '67, '68; Univ. of Wis., '56–'60; b. Chgo., Ill., 1937; h. Todd Cayer; c. Jennifer, Brett; res: 8158 Escanaba Ave., Chgo., Ill. 60617.

CAYLOR, MARIE L., PR Cnslr., Owner, Harry E. Caylor Organization, 3158 Des Plaines Ave., Des Plaines, Ill. 60018, '37–; Chgo. Nwsp. Guild (Past VP), Indsl. Rels. Rsch. Assn. (Past Secy.) Intl. Labor Press Assn. (Past VP), Chgo. Labor Eds. Round Table (Founder, Past. Pres.); St. Teresa Col., Univ. of Ill., Univ. of Berlin; b. Kan. City, Mo.; p. Joseph and Marie Weth Straub; h. Harry E. Caylor (dec.); c. Mrs. Mary L. Altmayer, Mrs. Sarah Jestadt; res: 318 Euclid Court E., Prospect Heights, Ill. 60070.

CEBALLOS, JACQUELINE, Coordr., New Feminist Talent Collective, '70–; PR for N.Y. Chptr., National Organization for Women, Theatre of Women's Liberation ("Mod Donna" prod. of Shakespeare Public Theatre), Career Workshop for Women, '70–; Formerly PR for New Feminist Theatre, Aphra lit. mag., Swedish Study Tours, Congress to Unite Women, National Academy of Ballet and Theatre Arts, Dimitri Mitropoulos Intl. Music Competitions, Founder, Prodr., Teatro de la Opera, Bogota, Colombia, '64–'65; participant, col. and secondary sch. seminars; Lectr.; TV, radio appearances; NOW (Bd of Dirs., '69–'70); University of Southwestern, BA (Music), '46; b. Mamou, La., 1925; p. Louis Michot and Adele Domas; h. Alvaro Ceballos Arboleda; c. Douglas, Denis, Michele, Janine; res: 148 W. 68th St., N.Y., N.Y. 10023.

CECIL, BERTA KELLY, Ed., Wolfe County News, Campton, Ky. 41301, '46–; Wtr., short stories, features for Lexington Herald; Bible Classes, Hazel Green

Acad. HS, '66–; Compiler: "Early and Modern History of Wolfe County" ('58); Wolfe County Wms. Club (Pres. '51–'52), Hazel Green Improvement Assn. (Mbr. Advisory Bd., '66–'68); Who's Who in South and Southwest; Who's Who of Am. Wm.; Nat. Gold Bk.; Intl. Who's Who; N. Tex. State Univ., '19–'21; Eastern Ky. State Univ., '55–'56; Lexington Theological Seminary, '68; b. Basin Springs, Tex., 1903; p. William and Mary Worthy Kelly; h. Roy M. Cecil; c. Mrs. Arthur Seesholtz, Charles.

CELENZA, REGINA GLORIA, Aide, Dean of New York Theological Seminary, 235 E. 49th St., N.Y., N.Y. 10017, '66–; Soc., Wms. News Ed., Hudson Dispatch (Union City, N.J.), '61–'65; Librn., '55–'61; Adm. Asst., World Literacy, Inc. (N.Y.C.), Un. Ch. Wm. '51–'54; Latin Am. Inst., '47–'50; Youth Cnslt. Svc., Episcopal Diocese, '44–'47; Hudson Trust Co., '41–'44; N.J. Oysterponds Hist. Soc., Bergen County Am. Legion Aux. cit., '61; N.J. Press Assn. aw., '62; Jersey City Am. Legion Aux. aw., '65, '64; b. Union City, N.J., 1919; p. Michael and Lillian Edwards Celenza; res: 4 Laird Pl., Cliffside Park, N.J. 07010.

CELLI, ANNE, Mgr. of Reader Rels., Look Magazine, Cowles Communications, Inc., 488 Madison Ave., N.Y., N.Y. 10022, '51–; Rsch. Librn., Am. Weekly, '46–'51; Asst. Librn., Indsl. Rels. Cnslrs., '41–'46; Cataloger, Engineering Socs. Lib; Special Libs. Assn. (Adv. Div., Publ. Div.); Hunter Col., BA, '41; Columbia Univ. Sch. of Lib. Sci., MLS, '44; b. N.Y.C., 1907; p. Joseph and Linda Sonsini Celli; h. S. Bizzano; res: 3511 Hull Ave., Bronx, N.Y. 10467.

CERF, PHYLLIS FRASER, Ed., VP-Beginner Books Division, Random House, Inc., 201 E. 50th St., N.Y., N.Y. 10022; Colmst., Newsday, '52–'60; Colmst., Good Housekeeping, '55–'59; Script Ed., McCann Erickson, '39–'40; Colmst., Fawcett Pubns., '32–'39; Auth: "Random House Reading Skilstarters" ('63); "The Complete Family Fun Book" ('57); "Puzzles, Quizzes & Games" ('47); Ed., "Great Tales of Terror and the Supernatural" ('44); Youth Cnsl. Bd., N.Y.C. (Bd. of Dirs.), Nat. Bk. Comm. (Nat. Bd.), Lib. Week Prog. Steering Comm., '67; Okla. Univ.; b. Kansas City, Mo., 1916; p. Albert and Virginia Brown Fraser; h. Bennett Cerf; c. Christopher, Jonathan; res: 132 E. 62nd St., N.Y., N.Y. 10021.

CERJANEC, RUTH WADE, Cnslt., Curriculum Svcs., Rhode Island Department of Education, Roger Williams Building, Hayes St., Providence, R.I. 02908, '69–; Coordr., '66–; Head Librn., Dighton-Rehoboth Reg. Sch. Dist. (Mass.), '60–'66; Cnslt., Univ. of R.I., '65–'66; Tchr., Barrington HS, '57–'59; Dir., Nursery Sch. (Central Falls), '52–'57; Substitute Tchr., '47–'52; Head Librn., U.S. Naval Air Facilities, '43–'47; Tchr. Librn., HS (Central Falls), '33–'43; Auth: "R.I. Title II ESEA Handbook" ('67); "Survey of Pre-College Reading Lists" ('60); Ed., "R.I. Media News" ('66); Contrbr., jnls., nwsps; ALA, NEA, many other lib. and educ. assns., incl. New Eng. Lib. Assn. (Exec. Bd., '67–'70);

Who's Who in Lib. Sci.; Who's Who of Am. Wm.; Pembroke, Brown Univ., AB, '33 (magna cum laude, hons., Phi Beta Kappa; Bd. of Dirs., Alumnae Assn., '62–'63, '65–'66); Brown Grad. Sch., '34–'35; R.I. Col., '32–'55; Providence Col., '41; Simmons Grad. Sch. of Lib. Sci., SM, '60 (hons.), '63; Univ. of R.I., '64; Univ. of Wash., '65; Univ. of Colo., '68; Western Mich., '69; b. Central Falls, R.I., 1913; p. John and Susanna McDowell Wade; h. Earl Cerjanec; c. Nicholas, Derek; res: 22 Binford St., Central Falls, R.I. 02963.

CERRATO, AJUANA JUNE ELMORE, Exec. Secy. and Adm. Asst. to Pres., Rives, Dyke and Company, Inc., 2503 Robinhood, Houston, Tex. 77005, '68; with co. since '57; Gamma Alpha Chi (Houston Chptr. Pres., '66–'69); affiliated: Houston Adv. Club. AAF (affiliate); U. of Houston; b. Lonoke, Ark., 1938; p. William and Martha LeMay Elmore; h. L. Douglas Cerrato; res: 5322 DeMile, Houston, Tex. 77018.

CESARIO, VIRGINIA NAILLE, Asst. Chief Librn. (Public Svc.), City College (City University of N.Y.), 135th St. and Convent Ave., N.Y., N.Y. 10031, '68–; Adm. Asst., '64–'68; Circ. Asst., '47–'64; City Univ. of N.Y. Lib. Assn., N.Y. Lib. Club, ALA, AAUP; Col. of William and Mary, BA, '45 (Phi Beta Kappa); Columbia Univ. Sch. of Lib. Svc., BS, '47 (Hons.); b. Balt., Md., 1923; p. Richard and Lucy Fitz Naille; h. Michael Cesario (div.); res: 3041 Edwin Ave., Ft. Lee, N.J. 07024.

CHADWICK, CATHERINE STRAHORN, Dir. of Lib. Svcs., Ventura County and City Library System, 651 E. Main St., Ventura, Cal. 93001, '60–; Adm. Librn., Black Gold Coop. Lib. System, '63–; Ext. Librn., Ariz. State Dept. Lib. and Archives, '57–'60; Dir. Lib. Svcs., Mont. State Lib., '55–'57; Tchr., Various high schs.; Contrbr., lib. pubns; ALA, Cal. Lib. Assn. (Pres., '68), several other lib. assns., AAUW, BPW, COMMUNITY Cncls. (offcr.), Soroptimist Club; Puget Sound Univ., BA, '28 (cum laude); Wash. State Col., '31; Univ. of Cal., Berkeley, BS (Lib. Sci.), '34; b. Spokane, Wash., 1907; p. Howard and Edna Prather Strahorn; h. Paul Chadwick; c. Mrs. Alan Ungar, Mrs. William L. Thiss, William; res: 454 Mariposa Dr., Ventura, Cal. 93001.

CHAFFIN, LILLIE D., Auth.; Librn., Kimper School, '68–; seven juv. bks., two adult poetry bks., numerous short stories and poems; Am. Poetry League Poetry Analyst; Ky. Poetry Soc.; Poet of the Yr., Alice Lloyd Col., '68; Intl. Poetry Prize, '67; NLAPW 1st prize for juv. bk., '65; Ky. Colonel, '67; Akron Univ., Pikeville Col., Eastern Ky. State Univ.; b. Varney, Ky.; p. Kenis R. Dorton and Fairy Bell Kelly; h. Thomas Chaffin; c. Tommy R.; res: Box 42, Meta, Ky. 41501.

CHAIKIN, MIRIAM, Ed., Bks. for Young Readers, Bobbs-Merrill Company, Inc., 3 W. 57th St., N.Y., N.Y. 10019, '68–; Ed., Walker Publ. Co., '67–'68; Dir. Subsidiary Rights, World Publ., three yrs.; Asst., Sen. Herbert H. Lehman, '53–'54; Asst., Sen. Guy M. Gillette, '48–'53; res: 107 Waverly Pl., N.Y., N.Y. 10011.

CHAISSON, DOROTHY KOCH, Art Ed., Flower and Garden Magazine, Mid-American Publishing Corp., 4251 Pennsylvania Ave., Kan. City, Mo. 64111, '62-; Art Dir., The Workbasket, Workbench Mags., '67-; Freelance artist, '58-'62; Artist, Modern Handcraft, '56-'58; Artist, Russell Stover Candies, '54-'56; Adv. Artists Guild of Kan. City (Pres., '63, VP, '62, Treas., '60, Secy., '58; aws., '65, '58-'62), Art Dirs. Club of Kan. City (Treas., '65-'67); b. Guilford, Conn., 1920; p. William and Elizabeth Fortner Koch; h. (dec.); c. Martin L., John W.; res: 12240 Holmes Rd., Kan. City, Mo. 64145.

CHAMBERLAIN, BEV, Assoc. Pic. Ed., Playboy Magazine, HMH Publishing Co., Inc., 919 N. Michigan Ave., Chgo., Ill. 60611, '61-; Asst. Pic. Ed., '58-'61; Crtv. Dir., Feldman Adv. Agcy., Evansville, Ind., '56-'58; Owner, Graphic Arts, Inc., '56-'58; res: 8457 Brier Dr., L.A., Cal. 10046.

CHAMBERLAIN, ELINOR LOUISE, Auth: "Appointment in Manila" ('45), "Manila Hemp" ('47), "Snare for Witches" ('48), "The Far Command" ('53), "Mystery of the Moving Island" ('65), "Mystery of the Jungle Airstrip" ('67); Instr. in Eng., Univ. of the Philippines, '23-'27; MWA; Avery Hopwood Major Aw. for fiction, '51; Univ. of Mich., BA, '22 (Phi Beta Kappa); MA, '51; Columbia Univ., MS (Lib. Svc.), '54; b. Muskegon, Mich., 1901; p. Charles and Marie Lambert Chamberlain; h. William Kuhns (div.); c. William, Mary (Mrs. Paul S. Fancher, Jr.); res: 308 N.E. 17th Ave., Ft. Lauderdale, Fla. 33301.

CHAMBERLIN, VIRGINIA SWIFT, Supervising Librn., City of Burbank, Buena Vista Branch Library, 401 N. Buena Vista St., Burbank, Cal. 91505, Librn., '49-'53; ALA, Cal. Lib. Assn., Burbank Altrusa Club, Burbank Coord. Cncl., Valley Univ. Wm., Alpha Omicron Pi, Repl. Wms. Club; Valley State Tchrs. Col.; Univ. of Minn., B.S.; b. Mpls., Minn., 1909; p. M. Vincent and Emma Holtz Swift; h. David Chamberlin; c. David Holmes, Jr.; res: 3315 W. Verdugo Ave., Burbank, Cal. 91505.

CHAMPAGNE, MARIAN MIRA, Wtr., fiction and non-fiction bks: "The Cauliflower Heart " (Dial, '44), "Quimby & Son" (Bobbs-Merrill, '62), "Facing Life Alone" (Bobbs-Merrill, '64); Lawyer, Schrade, Morris & Roche, 90 State St., Albany, N.Y. 12207, '55-; Smith Col., BA, '36; Albany Law Sch., LLB, '55; Juris Doctor, '68; b. Schenectady, N.Y., 1915; p. Joseph and Rae Grosberg; h. Herbert Champagne; c. Rev. Emily Champagne, Margot; res: 199 S. Allen St., Albany, N.Y. 12208.

CHANDLER, GLORIA, Cnslt., Children's and Commty. Svc. TV Programs, King Broadcasting Co., 320 Aurora Ave. N., Seattle, Wash. 98109, '48-; Founder, Gloria Chandler Recs., '47; Cnslt., Radio and Children's Theater Assn. of Jr. Leagues of Am., '33-'47, '31-'32; Dir., Children's Theater, Century of Progress, Chgo., Ill., '32; Tchr., '27-'32; Actress,

WMAQ Players, '23-'24; AWRT, Theta Sigma Phi, Zeta Phi Eta, Am. Educ. Theater Assn., Children's Theater Conf., ALA; Peabody Aws., '47, '57; many other aws. for extensive activities in children's theater, radio, TV; Smith Col., BA, '19; Hon. Dr. of Humane Ltrs., '68; special studies in commtns. Northwestern Univ., N.Y.U., Columbia Univ., '34-'41; b. Chgo., Ill., 1900; p. Homer and Mary Stryker Chandler; res: 906 E. Highland Dr., Seattle, Wash. 98102.

CHANDLER, LINDA, Actress, '65-; Films: "Ne'er Shall Invaders Trample The Sacred Shore" (Phillipines); TV: "Mannix," "Ironside," "Wild Wild West," "Bonanza," "Occasional Wife," "Red Skeleton," "Jonathon Winters;" Sigma Epsilon; Univ. of Ut., BS (Speech, Drama), '65 (Phi Kappa Phi); b. Hollywood, Cal.; p. LeGrand and Leola Hand Chandler; res: 11915 Burbank Blvd., N. Hollywood, Cal. 91607.

CHANDLER, MILDRED CONVERSE, Asst. Librn., Fiske Free Library, 110 Broad St., Claremont, N.H. 03743, '38-; Staff Asst., '29-'38; N.H. State Lib. Assn., Claremont Hist. Soc., Claremont SPCA; b. Newport, N.H., 1911; p. Sydney and Grace Spooner Converse; h. Earl C. Chandler; res: 17 Severance St., Claremont, N.H. 03743.

CHANEY, RUTH CARTY, Wms. Ed., The Daily Journal (Home News Enterprises), U.S. 31 (P.O. Box 366), Franklin, Ind. 46131, '63-; Publr., Whiteland Herald, '59-'63; Corr., Franklin Evening Star, '58-'63; Theta Sigma Phi, '66, BPW, '63; Cert. of Appreciation, Whiteland Jaycees, '60; Wabash-Brown Bus. Col., Terre Haute, '37; b. Libertyville, Ind. 1919; p. Claude B. and Gertrude Lewis Carty; h. Kenneth L. Chaney; c. Linda (Mrs. Stephen Oliver).

CHANEY, SARA, Asst. Ed., Sportfishing Magazine, Yachting Publishing Corp., 50 W. 44th St., N.Y., N.Y. 10036, '68-; Edtl. Asst., Yachting Magazine, '60-'68; Art and Prod. Dir., Forecast for Home Economics, '56-'57; Art Ed., offcl. organ of Nat. Fedn. of Bus. and Pfsnl. Wms. Clubs, '45-'56.

CHAPELLE, ETHEL H., Ed.-Publr., Alcona County Review, 111 Lake St., Harrisville, Mich. 48740, '66-; Staff, '32-'66; Tchr., '23-'29; Nat. Nwsp. Assoc., Mich. Press. Assn., Northern Mich. Publrs. Assn.; Central Mich. Col. of Educ., '23; Iosco County Normal, '28-'29; b. Oscoda, Mich., 1904; p. Henry and Elizabeth Pearson Holmes; h. Edward W. Chapelle (dec.); res: 220 State St., Harrisville, Mich. 48740.

CHAPMAN, JUNE RAMEY, Free-lance Wtr. for Christian Pubns., Am. Sunday Sch. Un., Southern Baptist Sunday Sch. Bd., Un. Gospel Press, Back to the Bible, Primary Worship Progs.; Berea Col.; b. Salt Lick, Ky.; 1918; p. Joseph and Colista Borders Ramey; h. Charles Chapman; c. Charles, Thomas; res: 1388 28th St., Huntington, W. Va. 25705.

CHAPMAN, LEE M., Assoc. Dir., Appliances and Home Care, Good Housekeeping Magazine, 959 Eighth Ave., N.Y., N.Y. 10019; Ed. "Emily Taylor," feature; mag. edtls., buying guides, bklets.; Home Econs. Wm. in Bus., Electrical Wms. Round Table, Am. Home Econs. Assn., Alpha Omicron Pi; Who's Who of Am. Wm., Univ. of Wash., BS (Home Econs.), '38; b. Portland, Ore., 1914; p. Alexander Kesterson and Margaret Terringer Chapman; h. William J. Nuss; res: 1575 Center Ave., Fort Lee, N.J. 07024.

CHAPMAN, LUCILLE MAY, Bus. Mgr., Sheep and Goat Raiser, 233 W. Twohig, San Angelo, Tex. 76901, 30 yrs.; recognized authority in above field of jnlsm; Secy. to law firm; b. Washington Co., Okla., 1897; p. Cleophas and Beatrice Hyder May; h. Frederick F. Chapman; c. Mrs. Loyd Norman; res; 2218 Waco, San Angelo, Tex. 76901.

CHAPMAN, MARY CATHERINE LONGFIELD, Wms. Ed., Enterprise-Sun Publications, 16 Liberty St., Marlboro, Mass. 01752, '64–; Auth., Prodr., Dir., children's plays, Little Theatre Groups; Emerson Col., Boston; b. Winchester, Mass., 1917; p. Henry and Ann Shinnick Longfield; h. Edward Chapman; c. Edward, Jr., Henry, Jeffrey; res: 136 Washington St., Hudson, Mass. 01749.

CHAPMAN, MARY LOU STOWELL, Home Econst., Colorado Wheat Administrative Committee, 1636 Welton St., Suite 300, Denver, Colo. 80202, '67–; Tchr., Paris (France) Am. Kindergarten, '65–'66; Asst. Ext. Home Agt., Cooperative Ext. Svc. (Colo.), '64; AWRT, Am. Home Econs. Assn., Colo. Home Econs. Assn., Am. and Colo. Home Econsts. in Bus. (Secy., '68–'69); Colo. State Univ., BS (Home Econs.), '65; b. Hodgeman County, Kan., 1942; p. Ralph and Vera Lilly Stowell; h. J. Kent Chapman; res: 7150 Lamar St., Arvada, Colo. 80002.

CHAPMAN, PATRICIA ANNE, Free-lance Wtr., Publicist, '67–; Home Furnishings Ed., Newark (N.J.) Star Ledger, '65–; Wms. Feature Ed., '65–'67; Home Accessories Ed., Home Furnishings Daily, '60–'65; Ed., Professional Florist, '59–'60; Special Svcs. Club Dir., Eur., '56–'58; Auth., "Celestial Scene" (Grosset and Dunlop, '68); Nwsp., Trade Pubn. Ed., '51–'56; OPC, NOW, Wms. Liberation, NHFL: Nat. Headliner Aw., '66; Svc. Club of the Yr., France, '58; Who's Who of Am. Wm.; Univ. of Mo., BJ, '51; b. Mpls., Minn., 1931; p. Andrew and Meta Schoening Chapman; res: 39 Jane St., N.Y., N.Y. 10014.

CHAR, SYLVIA RASNICK, Free-lance PR Wtr.; Coptwtr., Fischbein Adv., Mpls., Minn., '65–'67; Crtv. Dir., Jenkins Adv., '63–'65; VP, Star Garment Mfg., '57–'63; Adult Educ. Dir., St. Paul Jewish Commty. Ctr., '65–'67; Theta Sigma Phi; Univ. of Minn., BA (Jnlsm.); h. William Char; res: 2231 Scheffer, St. Paul, Minn. 55116.

CHARDIET, BERNICE KROLL, Ed., See-Saw Book Program, Scholastic Book Services, 50 W. 44th St.,

N.Y., N.Y. 10036, '67–; Prom. Copywtr., Dir. of Elem. Prom., '63–'67; Tchr., Speech and Eng., DeWitt Clinton HS, '54–'59; Free-Lance Wtr., script for aw.-winning jazz series for Radio Free Eur., mag. articles, lyrics and music for two Broadway revs.; jazz pianist and rec. artist; Children's Film Assocs. (VP, Bd. of Dirs.); Queens Col., BA, '49; studied music composition with Hall Overton; grad. courses, Juilliard Sch. of Music; Hunter Col. (Educ.), '54; Yale Drama Sch., '50–'51; Columbia Univ. (Educ., Comparative Lit.), '56; h. Oscar Chardiet, M.D.; c. two children.

CHARIF, JOAN, TV Prodr., Grey Advertising, Inc., 777 Third Ave., N.Y., N.Y., 10017, '66–; Asst. Prodr. Assoc., '65–'66; Asst. Casting Dir., '64–'65; Phonograph Record Prod., Sls. Prom., '59–'64; Bklyn Col. '58; b. Bklyn, N.Y., 1939; p. Samuel and Julia Charif; res: 411 E. 53rd St., N.Y., N.Y. 10022.

CHARLES, M. PATRICIA FINNEY, Co-publr., Wms. Ed., Staff Wtr., The Ketchikan Daily News, 501 Dock St., Ketchikan, Alaska 99901, '41–; Alaska Nwsp. Publrs. Assn; Tongass Hist. Soc., Ketchikan Commty. Col. Citizens Advisory Group; p. Charles and Ellin Strickland Finney; h. Paul Charles; c. Stuart, Donald, Douglas, Patrick; res: 308 Edmond St., Ketchikan, Alaska 99901.

CHARLESTON, GEORGIA HOLLOWAY, Chief, Schools Division, Detroit Public Library, 5201 Woodward Ave., Detroit, Mich. 48202, '69–; Children's Librn., '51–; Children's Librn., Mt. Vernon (N.Y.) Public Lib., '48–'51; Asst. Librn: Camp Lee, Va., '41–'43, Morgan State Col. (Balt., Md.), '39–'41, Prairie View (Tex.) State Col., '38–'39; ALA, Mich. Lib. Assn., Wms. Nat. Bk. Assn. (Detroit Br. Secy., '69–); Morgan State Col., BS, '32; Univ. of Mich., MA, '35; Hampton Inst., BS (Lib. Sci.), '38; h. Prince Charleston.

CHARLET, MARTHA C., Pers. Dir., Leaf Chronicle Co., Leaf Chronicle Bldg., 200 Commerce St., Clarksville, Tenn. 37040, '61–; Feature Stories Wtr.; Pan-Hellenic Cncl. (Past Pres.); Vanderbilt Univ. (Sociol., Psych.), '35; b. Union City, Tenn., 1914; p. D. J. and Ella Cloar Caldwell; h. James E. Charlet; c. James E., Jr., Mrs. Wm. Stacy; res: 13 Trahern Terr., Clarksville, Tenn. 37040.

CHARNÉE, NANCY O'CONNOR, Mng. Ed., 33 Magazine, Opec Inc., 24 Commerce St., Newark, N.Y. 07102, '67–; Staff Wtr., Record Nwsps. (Troy, N.Y.); News Ed., Adhesive Age; 2nd ed., Gordon Pubns.; Ed., Am. Indsl. Properties Rept. (Indprop Publ.); Metal Jnlsts. Soc.; Russell Sage Col., BA, '64; b. Troy, N.Y. 1942; p. Edward and Catherine Tholl O'Connor; h. Michael Charnée; res: 420 W. 24th St., N.Y., N.Y. 10011.

CHARNES, RUTH, Chanticleer Press, Inc., 424 Madison Ave., N.Y., N.Y. 10017, '69–; Assoc. Ed., Public Relations Journal, '68–'69; Prod. Ed., '67–'68; Assoc. Ed., Publishers' Weekly, '63–'67; Barnard Col., BA, '63.

CHASE, ALICE ELIZABETH, Docent, Yale Art Gallery; Asst. Prof., Hist. of Art, Yale University, Box 2006 Yale Sta., New Haven, Conn. 06520; Curator of Educ., Bklyn. (N.Y.) Museum, '46–'47; Tchr., Ware (Mass.) HS, '30–'31; Salem Acad., Winston-Salem, N.C., '27–'30; Col. Art Assn., Archeological Inst. of Am. (Pres., New Haven Soc., '66–'69), Soc. of Architectural Historians, New Haven Preservation Trust; Hon. Phi Beta Kappa, '61; Anniversary Cit., Wilson Col., '69; Radcliffe Col., BA, '27 (cum laude; Alumnae Recognition Aw., '69); Yale Univ., MA, '43; b. Ware, Mass., 1906; p. Arthur and Alice Rondthaler Chase; res: 324 Willow St., New Haven, Conn. 06511.

CHASE, LUCIE STODDARD, Reptr., Reporter-Time-Argus, S. Main, Barre, Vt. 05641, '66–; Pres., Vt. Wms. Christian Temperance Union; Ed.-in-Chief, State WCTU nwsp.; numerous other positions with WCTU; active in local govt., civic orgs.; Who's Who of Am. Wm.; Scholarship for Mission Study, '68–'69; Goddard Seminary, Univ. of Vt.; b. E. Montpelier, Vt., 1902; p. William and Flora Spafford Stoddard; h. Everett Chase; c. Francis S., Melvin W., Judith (Mrs. Dennis E. McGary); res: R.D. #1, Box 146, Plainfield, Vt. 05667.

CHASE, MARJORIE BINGHAM, Mng. Ed., Norwich Evening Sun, Norwich Publishing Company, 7 Lackawanna Ave., Norwich, N.Y. 13815, '66–; Gen. Assignment Reptr., City Ed., '41–'65; Proofreader, '37–'41; Soc. Reptr., '31–'37; Corr., '30; AP stringer, '50–'68; Corr., N.Y. Times, Utica, Syracuse, Binghamton nwsps.; auth., hist. of Chenango Co.; active in numerous civic orgs.; honored by C. of C.; Nwsp. Inst., N.Y.C., '31; b. Sherburne, N.Y., 1912; p. Albert and Jeannette Hayes Bingham; h. Edwin H. Chase; res: Bingham Rd., P.O. Box 297, Sherburne, N.Y. 13460.

CHAUVIN, LILYAN, Actress; Staff Dir., Film Industry Workshop, Columbia Studios, 1438 Gower, Hollywood, Cal., '63–; numerous TV, film roles; toured with Judith Anderson in "Macbeth" and "Medea"; Dir., "Windows of Heaven," CBS-TV; translator, tech. adv.; USO Aw.; Lycee de Sevres, BA; radio and movie sch.; b. Paris, France, 1931; p. P.P.P. and Emilia Speltiens Zemoz; h. Bernard Chauvin (div.); res: 3841 Eureka Dr., Studio City, Cal. 91604.

CHAVIS, VELERA SUE MODESITT, Soc. Ed., Feature Wtr., Brazil Daily Times, 119–121 E. National Ave., Brazil, Ind. 47834, '67–; Wabash Valley Auto Racing Fan Club (Membership Secy.); b. Spencer, Ind., 1936; p. William and Eunice Crosley Modesitt; h. Larry Chavis; c. John W. Metz, Robert A. Metz; res: Box 95, Harmony, Ind. 47853.

CHEATHAM, MARIE, Actress; commls., TV series, legitimate stage; "Days of Our Lives," NBC, four yrs.; Alley Theater, Houston, Tex.; Dallas Theater Ctr., Dallas; appearances on "Gunsmoke," "Ben Casey," "Outcasts," "CBS Repertory Workshop"; Tchr., Braille Inst., L.A., Cal.; SAG, AFTRA, AEA; Baylor Univ., BA (Theater Arts), '62; grad. work, Dallas Theater Ctr.; b. Okla. City, Okla, 1940; p. O. C. and Bettye Deer Cheatham; h. William M. Whitehead; res: 118 S. Detroit St., L.A., Cal. 90036.

CHEESEMAN, ELIZABETH MARGARET, Supvsr., Inst. Lib. Svc., and Coordr., Lib. Svc. to Blind and Physically Handicapped, Pennsylvania State Library, Box 1601, Harrisburg, Pa. 17126, '68–; Sch. Lib. Conslt., Mich. State Lib., '66–'68; Head Librn., Lakeview HS (Battle Creek), '60–'66; Bookmobile Librn., Grace A. Dow Memorial Lib. (Midland), '58–'60; Wtr., Pfsnl. jnls.; Mich. Chmn. Nat. Lib. Week, '61–'63 (Aw., Nat. Bks. Comm., '63); ALA, PLA, Am. Correctional Assn., NEA, Intl. Platform Assn., Dept. Audio-Visual Inst., Marquis Biographical Lib. Soc., Mich. Assn. Sch. Librns.; Northwestern Univ., BS, '53; Univ. of Chgo., MA (Lib. Sci.), '60; b. Muncie, Ind., 1931; p. Arthur and Eunice May Hollingsworth Cheeseman; res: 135 Williams Grove Mobile Homes, R. D. 2, Mechanicsburg, Pa. 17055.

CHEN, LYNN C. L., Cataloger, Hopkins Public Library, 22 11th Ave. N., Hopkins, Minn. 55343, '63–; Pfsnl. Asst., Mpls. Public Lib., '59–'60; Ref. Librn., Menlo Park Lib., Cal., '58–'59; Lib. Asst., Stanford Univ., '57–'58; ALA, Minn. Lib. Assn.; Nat. Taiwan Univ., BA, '55; Univ. of Minn. Lib. Sch., MA, '57; b. Peking, China, 1932; p. S. P. and S. C. Tao Wang; h. Di Chen; c. Andrew A. J., Daniel T. Y.; res: 5731 Woodland Rd., Minnetonka Village, Minn. 55343.

CHENERY, JANET DAI, Exec. Ed., Children's Bks., Simon & Schuster, Inc., 630 Fifth Ave., N.Y., N.Y. 10020, '67–; Sr. Ed., Juv. Dept., Harper & Row, '63–'67; Asst. Ed., Western Publ. Co., '57–'63; Prod. Mgr., Asst. Mng. Ed., Woman's Home Companion, '56–'57; Auth: "Wolfie" ('69), "The Toad Hunt" ('67); ALA, Children's Bk. Cncl.; Sweet Briar Col., h. French Conway (div.).

CHENEY, FRANCES NEEL, Assoc. Dir., Peabody Library School, Nashville, Tenn. 37203, '46–; Ed., Current Ref. Bks. Column, Wilson Library Bulletin; Vanderbilt Univ. Lib., '45–'46, '28–'42; Ref. Dept., Lib. of Congress, '44–'45; Asst. to Ch. of Poetry, '43–'44; Visiting Prof., Japan Lib. Sch. (Tokyo), '51–'52; Tenn. Lib. Assn. (Pres., '47–'48), ALA (Ref. Svcs. Div. Pres., '60–'61), Assn. of Am. Lib. Sch. (Pres. '56), SELA (Pres.), Tenn. Hist. Soc., Tenn. Folklore Soc.; Beta Phi Mu Good Teaching Aw., '59, Isadore Gilbert Mudge aw., '62; Vanderbilt Univ., BA, '28; Peabody Lib. Sch., BS (Lib. Sci.), '34; Columbia Univ., MS (Lib. Sci.), '40; Marquette Univ., Hon. DLitt., '66; b. Wash., D.C., 1906; p. Thomas and Carrie Tucker Neel; h. Brainard Cheney; res: 112 Oak St., Smyrna, Tenn. 37167.

CHENEY, HELEN BABCOOK, Wms. Pg. Ed., Salisbury Post, 131 W. Innes St., Salisbury, N.C. 28144, '59–; Reptr., Asst. to Wms. Ed.; Tchr., Eng., Gridley (Ill.) HS; N.C. Press Wms. Assn. (16 aws., '60–'68; incl. news, feature writing, make-up); Who's Who of Am. Wm.;

1st. features, N.C. Press Assn., '60; 1st. pl. aw. for excellence of wms. pgs., nat. contest sponsored by J.C. Penny Co., Mo. Sch. of Jnlsm., '65; Bradley Univ., AB; b. Carman, Ill., 1905; p. Alfred and Goldie Baxter Babcook; h. Teenus Cheney (dec.); c. Paul N.; res: 402 S. Ellis, Salisbury, N.C. 28144.

CHENEY, RUTH HELEN, Assoc. Ed., Progressive Architecture, Reinhold Publishing Corp., Div., Litton Industries, Inc., 600 Summer St., Stamford, Conn. 06851, '69–; Asst. Ed., '67–'68; Edtl. Asst., '65–'66; Columbia Univ., BS, '65; b. Wash., D.C., 1940; p. John and Ruth Cook Cheney; res: 49 W. 76th St., N.Y., N.Y. 10023.

CHENNAULT, ANNA CHAN, VP, The Flying Tiger Line, Inc., '68–; Pres., General Claire Lee Chennault Foundation, '61–; Pres., Chinese Refugee Relief, '62–; U.S. Corr., Hsin Shen Daily News, '58–; Special Corr. to Wash., D.C., Central News Agcy., '65–; Bdcstr., Voice of Am., '63–'66; Chief of Chinese Sec., Machine Translation Rsch., Georgetown Univ., '58–'63; Ed., Civil Air Transport Bulletin (Taipei, Taiwan), '46–'57; PR Offcr., Civil Air Transport, '47–'57; Feature Wtr., Bsin Ming Daily News (Shanghai), '44–'49; Central News Agcy. War Corr., '44–'48; Auth., "A Thousand Springs" (Paul S. Eriksson, '62), others, incl. 15 bks. in Chinese; Am. Acad. of Achiev. (Bd. of Govs., Golden Plate aw., '67), Tex. Technological Col. aw., '66; Order of Lafayette aw., '66; Free China Assn. aw., '66; Ling Nan Univ. (Hong Kong), BA, '44; Hon. Deg. Chung-ang Univ. (Seoul, Korea), DL, '67; b. Peiping, China, 1925; p. Y. W. and Bessie Joung Chan; h. Claire Lee Chennault; c. Claire Anna, Cynthia Louise; res: 2510 Virginia Ave. N.W., Wash., D.C. 20037.

CHENOWETH, PATIENCE GAUDET, Rsch. Acc. Supvsr., Ted Bates & Co., 666 Fifth Ave., N.Y., N.Y. 10019, '60–; Mgr., Special Rsch. Projects, McCall's, '53–'60; Asst. to Rsch. Dir., Marschalk & Pratt, '45–'53; AWNY, Am. Mkt. Assn.; Mt. Saint Mary Col., '44; b. Hartford, Conn, 1922; p. Maximilian J. and Clare Cavanagh Gaudet; h. Emory Roberts Chenoweth; res: 805-a Troy Towers, Bloomfield, N.J. 07003.

CHESNAR, LYNNE IRWIN, VP and Prod. Mgr., Lloyd Gregory and Associates Advertising and Public Relations, 1401 S. Post Oak Rd., Suite 200, Houston, Tex. 77027, '61–; VP, '62–; Asst. Prod. Mgr., '57–'61; Pers. Exec., Foley's, '52–'57; Asst. Ed., C. of C., '51; civilian pers. work, U.S. Govt., Yokohama, Japan, '46–'49; Cnslt., pers. admin.; mag. articles; active in civic orgs.; several aws. for art direction, prod.; Sam Houston State Col., BS, '45; b. Houston, Tex., 1924; p. James and Panola Qualls Irwin; h. (div.); c. James I.; res: Fountainview Plaza, Apt. 179, 6060 Skyline Dr., Houston, Tex. 77027.

CHESROWN, MELVA ANITA, Owner, Melva Chesrown Organization, 75 E. 55th St., N.Y., N.Y. 10022, '53–; VP, Fred Eldean Org., '44–'53; PR Dept., Gen. Motors Corp., '42–'44; PRSA (Treas., '61; Pres. Cit.),

CWPR (Chmn., '55), Fashion Group, Nat. Trust for Hist. Preservation, Soc. of Architectural Histrns.; Univ. of Mont.; Univ. of Minn.; b. Watauga, S.D., 1911; p. Joseph and Mathilda Mielke Chesrown; res: 433 E. 51st. St., N.Y., N.Y. 10022.

CHEVALIER, JANE GEISMAN, Dir. of Pubcty., Crown Publishers Inc., 419 Park Ave. S., N.Y., N.Y. 10016, '64–; Dir. of Prom., Pubcty., Adv., The World Publ. Co., '63–'64; Dir. of Prom., Pubcty., Adv., Funk & Wagnalls Inc., '60–'62; PPA, Publrs. Adv. Club (VP, '63); Swarthmore Col., BA, '56; N.Y.U., MA, '60; b. N.Y.C., 1934; p. Jess and Stella Meier Geisman; h. Gilbert Chevalier; c. Suzanne Jeanne, Gilbert Pierre; res: 460 E. 79th St., N.Y., N.Y. 10021.

CHILD, JULIA McWILLIAMS, TV Personality, "The French Chef," WGBH-TV, 125 Western Ave., Boston, Mass. 02134; Auth: "The French Chef Cookbook" (Alfred Knopf, '68); Co-auth: "Mastering the Art of French Cooking" (Alfred Knopf, '61); presently writing "Mastering the Art of French Cooking, Vol. 2, "Merite Agricole from French Govt. '68"; Emmy Aw.-Educ. TV, '66; NET Aw., '65; George Foster Peabody Aw. for distinguished achiev. in educ. TV, '65; Joint founder of l'Ecole des Trois Gourmandes; Smith Col., AB, '34; Cordon Bleu and private study, Paris; b. Pasadena, Cal., 1912; p. John and Julia Weston McWilliams; h. Paul Child.

CHILD, LOUISE AVERY, PR Cnslt.; United Bd. for Christian Higher Educ. in Asia, '59–'68; PR Dir., Berkshire Farm for Boys, '58–'59; Big Brothers, Inc., '41–'57; Youth Cnslt. Svc., N.Y.C.; '36–'41; Asst. Ed., Delineator and Fashions Art, '25–'35; Edtl. Staff, Time, '24; Religious PR Cncl (N.Y.C. Chptr. VP, '65), Nat. Soc. of Fund Raisers, UN Assn. USA, Andiron Club; numerous other civic, religious, pfsnl. orgs.; Wellesley Col., BA, '24; b. N.Y.C., 1901; p. William Bradford and Mary Sykes Child; res: 1 University Pl., N.Y., N.Y. 10003.

CHILDRESS, ANNE MATTHEWS, Motion Pic. Ed., The News American, Lombard and South Sts., Balt., Md., 21203, '65–; Reptr., Feature Wtr., Youth Ed., Asst. Music, Movie, Drama Critic, '60–'65; Washington Col., BA (Eng.), '60 (magna cum laude); b. Balt., Md., 1939; p. William, Jr., and Louisa Bowen Matthews; h. Richard W. Childress; res: Wetheredsville Rd., Balt., Md. 21207.

CHIN, RUTH, Free-lance Photogr., Ruth Chin Photography, 108 E. Jackson, Muncie, Ind. 47305, '54–; Colmst., Muncie Star, Weekly, '65–; Muncie Star-Press, '46–'54; Am. Soc. Magazine Photogrs., Press Wms. Club (six 1st pl. aws.), Pfsnl. Photogrs. of Am., Theta Sigma Phi; Ind. Univ. and AP News Photog. aws: First, '50; Second, '47, '49; Third, '48, '50; Bushemi Aw. '50; Graflex Aw.; Altrusa Club, Episcopal Ch., Muncie Art Assn., Ball Hosp. Auxilliary; John Herron Art Inst., '44; MacMurray Col., AB, '46; Chgo. Art Inst., '46; b. Chgo., Ill., 1924; p. Lloyd and Lee Shee Chin; res: 1803 Barcelona Dr., Muncie, Ind. 47304.

CHIOTES, HELEN KATINA, Coordr. of Program Info., Press Info. Dept., CBS Television Network, 51 W. 52nd St., N.Y., N.Y. 10019; various adm. and supervisory posts prior to present position; recognition for 20 yrs. outstanding suc. to CTN, '64; Barbizon and Harry Conover Fashion Model; Articles Wtr., Atlantis (nwsp.), National Herald, Atlantis monthly magazines and Greek Am. (Boston) Sunday News; AWRT (Educ. Fndn., '60–'69); Wms. Press Club of N.Y.C., 2000 Wm. of Achiev.; New Sch. for Social Rsch., N.Y.U., Henry George Sch. of Social Sci.; b. N.Y.C.; p. Constantine and Bess Demas Chiotes; res: 40 Park Ave., N.Y., N.Y. 10016.

CHISHOLM, GRACE HARTH, Adv. Dir., Thomas Kilpatrick and Co., 150 Central Park, Omaha, Neb. 68114, '48–; Asst. Adv. Dir., Guggenheimers, Lynchburg, Va., '47; Copywtr., '46; AAUW (Pres., Jr. Mbrs., '49), Omaha Adv. Club; Ia. State Univ., '42; Univ. of S.D., '43; Univ. of Mo., BJ, '45 (Kappa Tau Alpha); b. Sioux City, Ia; p. John and Grace Conlon Harth; h. Alexander G. Chisholm; res: 4001 Davenport, Omaha, Neb. 68131.

CHITWOOD, IONE DOWNS, Auth., fiction, nonfiction; Tchr., Lib., Physical Educ., J.L. Wagner Elementary School; Auth: "This Passing Night," (Zondervan Press), "Laughter in the House," (Zondervan Press), "After the Storm," (Zondervan Press); b. Boaz, Ala., 1918; p. Robert and Minnie Wills Downs; h. James William Chitwood; c. Mrs. Robert Corey, James W.; Jan; res: P.O. Box 2402, East Gadsden, Ala. 35903.

CHIVERS, JOYCE CLARICE, PR Mgr. for U.S. and Canada, QANTAS Airways, Ltd., 350 Post St., S.F., Cal. 94108, '68–; N.Y. Press Off., '57–; Australian Dept. of External Affairs, '47–'57; Tchr. of Classics (Australia), '44–'55; Jnlst. (Australia), '43; Registered Psychologist (Australia); BPW; Australian Jnlsts. Assn.; Sydney Univ. (Arts and Educ.).

CHOLAKIS, SARA DOLLEY, Free-lance Actress, '66–; Ford Model Agcy., '62–'66; b. Fairfield, Ia., 1936; p. John and Mary Eaton Dolley; h. John Cholakis; c. Elia; res: 309 E. 87th St., N.Y., N.Y. 10028.

CHOO, EDNA COFFIN, Dir. Industry Info., Point-of-Purchase Advertising Institute, Inc., 521 Fifth Ave., N.Y., N.Y. 10017, '61–; Eng. Instr., Sookmyung Wms. Univ. (Seoul, Korea), '59–'60; Town Librn. (Pembroke, Mass.), '53–'58; Adv. & Display Mgr., Fraser's Dept. Store (Brockton), '47–'52; Instr. Line & Design, Color, Display, Brockton HS Distributive Educ.; Educ. Therapy to Mental Patients, Veteran's Hosp. (Framingham), '52–'53; Asst. Mgr., Simon Adv. (Boston), '40–'45; AWNY, Nat. Visual Presentations Assn., '63– (Secy., '66–'67; Bd. Mbr. '64–); Cert. Librn., State of Mass., '55; Mass. Sch. of Art, '26; Univ. of N.H., '55–'57; Brandeis Univ., '54; Boston Univ., '58; b. Lynn, Mass., 1905; p. Vernon Eliphalet and Linda Sanborn Coffin; h. Wallace W. Choo (div.); c. Gwen-

dolyn (Mrs. Roger Sablone), Noel H. (Mrs. T. Robert Grieve, II), Bernardine (Mrs. Robert Mokrisky); res: 230 E. 58th St., N.Y., N.Y. 10022.

CHRISTENSEN, SYLVIA M., Mng. Ed., Overseas Press Bulletin, Overseas Press Club, Inc., 54 W. 40th St., N.Y., N.Y. 10018, '63–; Asst., Bell Labs News, Bell Telephone Labs., '62–'63; Adv., G. M. Basford Co., '59–'61; Pubcty., William Blakley Senate Campaign (Tex.), '58; Asst. Pubcty. Dir., Dallas Commty. Chest, '57–'58; Reptr., Port Arthur News, '56; Theta Sigma Phi (N.Y.C. Chptr. Treas., Nwsltr. Ed.); Tex. Wms. Univ., BS (Jnlsm.), '57.

CHRISTIAN, CAROL JOHNSON, Mgr. of Media Rsch., CBS Nat. Sales, Columbia Broadcasting System, Inc., 51 W. 52nd St., N.Y., N.Y. 10019, '68–; Supvsr. Media Rsch., '64–'68; Rsch. Asst., '58–'64; Circ. Mgr., Henry Publ. Co., '56–'58; Circ. Mgr., Management Magazine, Inc., '54–'56; Copy Chief, J. Grant Co., Inc., '52–'54; Grove City Col., BA, '51 (cum laude); b. Pitt., Pa., 1929; p. Roger and Allison Platts Johnson; h. Roger Christian; res: 264 Lexington Ave., N.Y., N.Y. 10016.

CHRISTIAN, SANDRA STAPLES, Wms. Ed., The Paris News, North Texas Publishing Co., 122 Lamar Ave., Paris, Tex. 75460, '63–; Staff Reptr., '50–'52; Tex. Press Wms. Assn. NPWC, BPW, Paris Commty Concert Assn., Paris Lamar County C. of C. (Royalty Cnslt., '64–), Beta Sigma Phi (Paris City Cncl. Pres., '67); Am. Cancer Soc., Outstanding Young Wm. in Am., '67; Paris Jr. Col., AA (Jnlsm.), '53; b. Paris, Tex., 1934; p. Robert and Esther Shannon Staples; h. Jim F. Christian; c. Jerian Gayle Spruell, Leslie Rene Spruell; res: 555 20th St. S.E., Paris, Tex. 75460.

CHRISTIANSEN, VIRGINIA, Owner, Virginia Christiansen Publicity, 2323 W. Third St., L.A., Cal., 90057, '54–; Crtv. Dir., Edward S. Kellogg Co., '48–'54; AE, Russell Birdwell Pubcty., '45–'48; W. Coast Dir., Al Paul Lefton Adv., '44–'45; Wms. Ed., Intl. Harvester Pubn., '40–'44; Conslt. on fund raising, adv. and pubcty., L.A. Travelers Aid Soc.; Un. Detector Technology (Bd. of Dir., '68); The Tidings nwsp. (Originator and 1st Ed., children's pg., '44–'45); short stories in Chgo. Daily News, Daily News Syndicate; Altrusa Intl.; Northwestern Univ., BA, '42 (cum laude); short story aw., '42); b. Chgo., Ill., 1923; p. Albert and Sophie Enbritt Christiansen.

CHRISTIE, AUDREY, Actress, theatre, vaudeville, night clubs, stock, radio, motion pics., TV; volunteer work for the blind; med. org., speech therapy; Donaldson Aw., "Voice of the Turtle," '44; several aws. for volunteer work; b. Chgo., Ill., 1910; p. Charles and Florence Ferguson Christie; h. Donald Briggs; c. Mrs. Richard Sear, Jeffrey Briggs; res: 1400 N. Sweetzer, L.A., Cal. 90069.

CHRISTIE, ISOBEL, Adv. PR Coordr., Ed., Schrafft's News, Frank G. Shattuck Co., 50 W. 23rd St., N.Y., N.Y.

10010, '67–; Asst. PR Mgr., Assoc. Ed., '65–'67; Adm. Asst., '60–'65; Pubcty. Club of N.Y. (Bd. of Dirs.), AWNY, IEA; N.Y.U.; New Sch. for Social Rsch.; b. Scotland, Great Britain, 1932; p. Alexander Chalmers and Isabella MacMillan Christie; h. Richard D. Tracy; c. Gillian Elizabeth.

CHRISTOFF, MARCELLA MARX, Ed./Adm. Asst., Indsl. Rels., J. W. Clement Co., 2750 Sand Hill Rd., Menlo Park, Cal. 94025, '66–; Pers. Asst., '62–'66; Grad. Asst., Univ. of Ore. Bus. Sch., '61–'62; Bay Area Soc. of Indsl. Communicators, ICIE; Univ. of Ore. BS, '61; Univ. of Ore. Grad. Sch. of Bus., '61–'62; b. Silverton, Ore., 1940; p. Theodore William and Thelma Hammond Marx; h. Carl Christoff; c. Diane Pearl; res: 1672 Hyde Dr., Los Gatos, Cal. 95030.

CHRISTOPHER, MAURINE BROOKS, Sr. Ed.-Bdcst., Advertising Age, 630 Third Ave., N.Y., N.Y. 10017, '54–; formerly Reptr., Kingsport (Tenn.) Times, Balt. (Md.) Sun; Contributor, the Nation; Author of America's Black Congressmen; AWRT; Tusculum Col., BA, '41; b. Three Springs, Tenn.; p. John and Zula Pangle Brooks; h. Milbourne Christopher; res: 333 Central Park W., N.Y., N.Y. 10025.

CHRISTOPHERSON, STEFANIANNA, Actress, Singer, Ricki Barr Agency, 8721 Sunset Blvd., Hollywood, Cal. 90039; TV appearances: "Mr. Deeds Goes To Town," "Stump the Stars," "Steve Allen Show," "That Girl," "Mayberry R.F.D.," "Here Come the Brides"; Stage, "Dumas & Son"; voice-over cartoons: "Scooby Doo, Where Are You?", "Here Comes the Grump"; Movie, "Grasshopper"; AEA, SAG, AFTRA; L.A. Civic Light Opera scholarship; Col. of San Mateo, S.F. State; b. S.F. Cal., 1946; p. Kjartan and Gudrun Snorradottir Christopherson; res: 6638 Leland Way, Hollywood, Cal. 90028.

CHRISTY, MARIAN, Fashion Ed., Boston Globe, Boston, Mass. 02107, '65–; WBZ-TV, United Feature Syndicate (N.Y.C.); formerly Mass. Dept. of Commerce, Women's Wear Daily; BPW Wm. of Achiev., '65, '66; J. C. Penney-Univ. of Mo. Jnlsm. Aw., '66, '68; Fashion Wtrs. Aw. of N.Y., '67; numerous other aws. for fashion writing; Boston Univ. Sch. of Jnlsm.; p. Peter and Anna Saba Christy; res: 27 Moreland Ave., Lexington, Mass. 02173.

CHU, DOREEN CHEN-YAN, Wtr., "Today" Show, National Broadcasting Company, 30 Rockefeller Plaza, N.Y., N.Y. 10020, '61–; Feature Ed., NBC Radio, "Nightline" and "Image" series, '53–'58; Rschr., "JFK Reports" 1, 2 & 3; Conn. Col. for Wm., BA; res: 320 Central Park W., N.Y., N.Y. 10025.

CHURCH, CORNELIA B., Reg. Admr., Western Massachusetts Regional Public Library System, 220 State St., Springfield, Mass. 01103, '67–; Asst. Dir., '62–'67; Reg. Librn., Reg. Lib. System (Greenfield), '56–'62; Reference Asst., Head of Bus., Sci., Tech. Div., Head of Adult Dept., Worcester Public Lib., '31–'56;

ALA, New Eng. Lib. Assn., Mass. Lib. Assn., Western Mass. Lib. Assn. (VP, 69–; Archivist, '58–'69); Univ. of Mass., BS, '28; Univ. of Wis. Lib. Sch., BLS, '41; b. New Paltz, N.Y., 1906; p. Frederick and Lucia Grover Church; res: 33 Pine St., N. Amherst, Mass. 01059.

CHURCH, HELEN SAEGESSER, Co-ed., Lebanon Advertiser, Lebanon, Ill., '45–; Asst. to Ed., '39–'45; Tchr., '56–'57, '34–'37; NLAPW, Lebanon Hist. Soc., Lebanon Public Lib. Bd.; Theta Sigma Phi svc. aw., '69; McKendree Col., AB, '34; b. Granite City, Ill., 1910; p. Walter and Emma Reimers Saegesser; h. Leon H. Church; c. Harrison L.; res: 313 W. St. Louis St., Lebanon, Ill. 62254.

CHURCH, MARGARET, Prof. of Eng., Department of English, Purdue University, Lafayette, Ind. 47907, '55–; Instr. of Eng., '53–'55; Instr. of Eng., Duke Univ., '46–'53; Instr. of Eng., Temple Univ., '44–'46; Auth., "Time and Reality: Studies in Contemporary Fiction," ('63) and modern lit. articles; Modern Lang. Assn., Midwest Modern Lang. Assn. (Secy., Comparative Lit. Sec., '69); Am. Comparative Lit. Assn., AAUP, James Joyce Fndn. (Paper, Dublin, '69); Mortar Bd. (Hon. Mbr., '67); Radcliffe College, BA, '41; (cum laude); Columbia Univ., MA, '42; Radcliffe Col., PhD., '44; b. Boston, Mass. 1920; p. Joseph W. and Sophy R. Phillips Church; res: Rt. 9, Box 302, Lafayette, Ind. 47906.

CHURCHILL, JOAN RUSSELL, Pres., The Churchill Company, 87 Wolfs Lane, Pelham, N.Y. 10803, '69–; PR Dir., Knudsen & Moore, Inc. (Stamford, Conn.), '60–'69; Exec. Ed., Builders Publ. Co.; House Organ Ed., Carrier Corp.; Reptr. on several dailies; Ed., weekly nwsp.; PR Group of Conn. Mgt. Assn.; Univ. of Vt., BA, '53; b. Greenfield, Mass., 1931; p. Dr. Rolfe S. and Hilda Belknap Russell; h. Frederick D. Churchill; c. Rolfe R., Lucius, Katherine D.; res: 131 Monterey Ave., Pelham, N.Y. 10803.

CLAASEN, CLARA, Edtl. Cnslt., '69–; with Doubleday & Co., Inc., '29–; Sr. Ed., '57–'59; Jr. Ed., '53–'57; Asst. Ed., '42–'53; Lectr., Mgr., Nat. TB Assn., '26–'27; Lab. Technician Dr. Frank G. Gephart, Chemist, '25–'26; Mem. Horticultural Soc., Garden Wtrs. Assn. Am., Soc. Am. Travel Wtrs.; OPC, Zonta; Goucher Col., AB, '25; b. Balt., Md.; p. Frank and Louise von Bungenberg Claasen; res: 20 Fifth Ave., N.Y., N.Y. 10011.

CLAFFORD, PATRICIA, Lectr. on "Personality Power"; Lit. Critic, 6158 N. Hamilton Ave., Chgo., Ill. 60645; Poetry Ed., Edtl. Wtr., Hinton (Okla.) Record; Prog. Cnslt., WBBM-FM Radio, '58–'60; Critique Staff, Northwestern Univ. (Chgo. Campus), Medill Sch. of Jnslm; Auth: "Even the Wind" (First Prize, NLAPW, '50); 1500 Modern Maxims in various pubns.; numerous features; Ill. Fedn. Wms. Clubs, Iota Sigma Epsilon, Nat. Soc. Arts and Ltrs. (Chgo. Chptr., VP, '55–'56), NLAPW (Chgo. Br. VP, '48–'49) Wms. Lit. Club of Chgo. (Hon. Mbr.), Co-founder, Pegasus Wtrs. Forum

('46); Northwestern Univ., '45–'48; b. Gridley, Ill.; p. R. Daniel and Mary-Constance Batemen Wise; h. Jean-Herbert Clafford; c. Kenneth W., Arthur H.; res: 6158 N. Hamilton Ave., Chgo., Ill. 60645.

CLAIBORNE, ADRIENNE AARON, VP, Assoc. Crtv. Dir., de Garmo, McCaffery Inc., 605 Third Ave., N.Y., N.Y. 10016, '68–; VP, Copy Chief, de Garmo, Inc., '63–'65; Free-lance Adv. Wtr., '65–'68; Copywtr., Sudler & Hennessey, '62–'63; Doyle, Dane, Bernbach, '59–'61; Cnslt., Leonard Sacks Adv., '65–'67; Tchr., with Bill McCaffery, ad. thinking, writing, Parson's, '64; private classes, '66, '67; various organizations and aws.; Wheaton Col., (Mass.), '41–'43; N.Y.U., '45; h. Robert Claiborne (div.); c. Amanda, Samuel.

CLAIR, VIRGINIA FLORENCE, Sch. Ed., The Standard-Star, Westchester-Rockland, 251 North Ave., New Rochelle, N.Y. 10801, '55–; Asst. Sch. Ed., '49–'55; Wms. Pg. Reptr., '47–'49; Music Reviewer, '49–; EWA, Nwsp. Week Aw., local, '59, Intl. Reading Assn. News Aw. '69; N.Y. Col. of Music, '40–'42; Hunter Col., AB, '47; N.Y.U., Grad. Sch., '49; b. Bklyn., N.Y.; p. Pierson and Kathryn Donovan Clair; res: 300 Pelham Rd., New Rochelle, N.Y. 10805.

CLAIRMONT, INGRID HULT, Fgn. Corr., Scandinavian Press, 1242 Aalappa Dr., Lanikai, Oahu, Hi., 96734; L.A. Staff Corr., Expressen, Sweden, '47–'60; Hi. Corr., '69; Feature Wtr. (Swedish mag.); Colmst., Norsk Ukeblad and Det Nye (Norwegian mags.); special assigts. in Central and S.A.; Hollywood Fgn. Press Assn. (Pres., '61–'62), Hollywood Wms. Press Club; Palmgrenska Samskolan, Stockholm, Sweden; Stockholms Journalistiskola; b. Gavle, Sweden, 1928; p. Oscar and Gerda Larsson Hult; h. Leonard Clairmont; c. Toby, Lenny; res: 1242 Aalapapa Dr., Lanikai, Oahu, Hi. 97634.

CLAIRMONTE, GLENN, Ed., Ms. Analyst, 8109 Third St., Downey, Cal. 90241, '34–; Auth., two biogs: "John Sutter of California" (Thos. Nelson, N.Y., '53), "Calamity Was the Name for Jane" (Swallow Press, '59), "Calamity Jane" (Neville Spearman Ltd., '61); numerous contrbs. to mags., fiction and non-fiction; two bks. of poems published (Univ. of Cal Press, '23; Columbia Univ. Press, '31); Lectr., Literature, Downey Adult Sch.; Tchr., Writing, N.Y.U.; Staff, N.Y. Mail, McClure's Magazine; Feature Wtr., S.F. Examiner, Carmel Pine Cone; Asst. Ed., Overland Monthly; U.S. Naval Aviation (French Sec., Paris and Brest), '17–'19; poems won: Emily Chamberlain Cook Poetry Prize, Univ. of Calif.; Kan. State Prize; hon. mention in Fugitive Poetry Prize; Strand Prize (London); Downey Wtrs. Guild; Univ. of Cal., AB, '23 (hons.); Columbia Univ.; b. S.I., N.Y., 1896; p. Herman and Nina Lambert Gerbaulet; c. Stephen (dec.); res: 8109 Third St., Downey, Cal. 90241.

CLAPPISON, K. GLADYS BONNER, Auth: "Vassar's Rainbow Division—1918"; Rsch., "Teaching Child Behavior to Student Nurses" (Master's thesis); Sch. Superintendent, '15–'18; Tchr., secondary, jr. col., schs. of nursing, WWII; Asst. Dir., Am. Red Cross classes; Public Health Nurse; Free-lance Wtr.; PTA, Wms. Clubs, AAUW, Cncl. of Family Rels., ZONTA, Phi Kappa Phi, Omicron Nu, Theta Sigma Phi; Ia. State, BS (Home Econs.), '13; Univ. of Ia., MA, '45; Ia. State Univ., Grad. Col., '60–'64; Univ. of Neb. at Omaha (Psych. of Commtns.), '68; b. Jewell, Ia., 1892; p. William and Louisa Anderson Bonner; h. Harry M. Clappison; c. Marian (Mrs. E. B. Meier), Gordon, Bonnie Louise (Mrs. J. B. Lynch); res: Masonic Manor, 801 S. 52nd St., Apt. 1705, Omaha, Neb. 68106.

CLARK, DEENA SPELIAKOS, Bdcstr., "Deena Clark's Moment With . . .," WRC-TV, 4001 Nebraska Ave., N.W., Wash., D.C. 20016; alternate moderator, "Meet the Press," NBC-TV; TV newscast, "Good News"; radio interviews, "Capital Bylines"; articles, numerous mags.; AWRT, Nat. Soc. of Arts and Ltrs. (Past Chptr. Pres.), Les Chevaliers du Tastevin; Wash., D.C. EMMY, '65; AAUW Aws., '65, '66; San Diego State Col., BA; Vanderbilt Univ., MA; b. La Jolla, Cal.; p. Christos and Charlotte Theade Speliakos; h. Blake Clark; c. Nikia S. (Mrs. Bruce Leopold); res: 2440 Kalorama Rd., N.W., Wash., D.C. 20008.

CLARK, DONA JEAN, Ed., Prom. Dir., Welfare Information Service, 729 S. Figueroa St., L.A., Cal. 90017, '68–; Ed., Donor Cnslt., '65–'69; Radio-TV Dir., L.A. County Heart Assn., '63–'65; Free-lance Writing and Prom., '61–'63; Cont. Wtr., Pubcty. Dir., Prod. Supvsr., Prod. Asst., Lux Radio Theatre, Lux Video Theatre, J. Walter Thompson Co., '45–'61; Prod., Dir., Wtr., little theatre workshop, '43–'53; Free-lance Wtr: TV, mag. fiction, one-act play, '61–'64; Radio-TV Wm. of Southern Cal. (Pres., '61–'62; VP, '59–'61; Secy., '57–'58), AWRT, Pacific Pioneer Bdcstrs; U.C.L.A.; b. San Diego, Cal., 1913; p. William and Ethel MacGillivray Barley; h. Irving Hardekopf; c. William Gary Hardekopf; res: 3750 Willow Crest Ave., N. Hollywood, Cal. 91604.

CLARK, EVELYN M., Assoc. Decorating Ed., House and Garden, Conde Nast Publications, 420 Lexington Ave., N.Y., N.Y. 10017, '61–; Furniture Fashion Ed., Home Furnishings Daily, '57–'60; PR, The Brooklyn Museum, '53–'57; NHFL, Am. Inst. of Interior Designers; Oberlin Col., BA, '50; b. Rochester, N.Y. 1928; p. Sidney and Gertrude Bolles Clark; h. Erik Norup; res: 450 E. 63rd St., N.Y., 10021.

CLARK, JEAN CARROLL, Staff Asst., Humble Oil & Refining Company, 1600 Woodlawn Rd., P.O. Box 420, Charlotte, N.C. 28209, '68–; Wms. Dir., Radio and TV, N.C. Petroleum Cncl., '56–; AWRT (N.C. Chptr. Pres., '60–'62; Southern Area VP, '62–'64), Children's Home Soc. of N.C.; Petroleum Industry Comm. aw., '61; Queens Col.; b. Charlotte, N.C., 1923; p. Lewis and Sally York Carroll; h. James Robert Clark; c. Carole, James, Jr.; res: 2334 Valencia Terr., Charlotte, N.C. 28211.

CLARK, LADY LOUISE, Librn., Franklin-Patrick Regional Library, Blue Ridge, Stuart, Va. 24171, '54–; Patrick Co. Lib., '40–'54; Tchr., '24–'40; ALA, Va. Lib. Assn.; Madison Col., BS, '32; William and Mary Col., AB (Lib. Sci.), '46; b. Stuart, Va., 1906; p. Thomas and Mary Dunkley Clark; res: Blue Ridge, Stuart, Va. 24171.

CLARK, LaVERNE HARRELL, Auth; currently doing rsch. in Spain on "Spanish Influence Upon Folklore of Southwestern U.S. Indians" (grant, Am. Philosophical Soc., '69); Folklore Prize, Univ. of Chicago, '67; Freelance Photogr: L.D. Clark's "Dark Night of the Body" (Univ. of Tex. Press, '64), various mags; Dir., Poetry Ctr., Univ. of Ariz., '62–'66; Asst. in Prom. and News Dept., Episcopal Diocese of N.Y., N.Y.C., '58–'59; Staff, Bulletin mag; Sls.-Adv. Dept., Columbia Univ. Press, '51–'53; Nwsp. Reptr., Librn., Ft. Worth Press, Ft. Worth, Tex., '50–'51; Theta Sigma Phi, Kappa Alpha Mu, NLAPW (2nd pl. non-fiction aw., '68), Western Wtrs. of Am., Western Am. Literature Assn., Southern Cal. Folklore Soc. (Hon. Mbr.); Chgo. Bk. Clinic, Top Hon. Aw. for excellence, GA and Prod., '67; Who's Who of Am. Wm.; Contemporary Auths.; Tex. Wms. Univ., BA, '50; Columbia Univ. '51–'54; Univ. of Ariz., MA, '62; b. Smithville, Tex., 1929; p. J. Boyce and Isabella Bunte Harrell; h. L. D. Clark; res: 4690 N. Campbell Ave., Tucson, Ariz. 85718.

CLARK, LOIS NABRIT, Head Librn., Knoxville College, 901 College St., Knoxville, Tenn. 37921; Lib. Cnslt., Nat. Baptist Sun. Sch. Publ. Bd. (Nashville, Tenn.); ALA, Tenn. Lib. Assn.; Sigma Upsilon Pi, Beta Phi Mu; Fisk Univ., BA, '40 (summa cum laude); George Peabody Col. for Tchrs., MLS, '60; Simmons Col., '64; b. Augusta, Ga., 1920; p. Dr. James M., Sr., and Augusta Gertrude West Nabrit; h. Dr. John H. Clark (dec.); c. Mrs. Claude Matthews, John H. Clark, Jr.; res: 1825 Brandau, Knoxville, Tenn. 37921.

CLARK, MARGARET GOFF, Auth., eight bks., '61–'69: "Mystery of Seneca Hill," "Mystery of the Buried Indian Mask" (Franklin Watts); "Mystery of the Marble Zoo," "Mystery at Star Lake," "Adirondack Mountain Mystery," "Mystery of the Missing Stamps," "Danger at Niagara," "Freedom Crossing," (Funk & Wagnalls); approx. 200 short stories, 25 one-act plays, poetry, numerous mags.; MWA, NLAPW, Assn. of Pfsnl. Wm. Wtrs. (Pres.), Delta Sigma Epsilon, Alpha Delta Kappa; adopted by Seneca Indians, Akron, N.Y., '62; Columbia Univ., '34; State Univ. Col., Buffalo, BS (Educ.), '36; b. Okla. City, Okla., 1913; p. Raymond and Fanny Church Goff; h. Charles Clark; c. Robert (M.D.), Marcia; res: 5621 Lockport Rd., Niagara Falls, N.Y. 14305.

CLARK, MARGUERITE SHERIDAN-, Dir. Pfsnl. Rels., Cybertek, Inc., 65 E. 55th St., N.Y., N.Y. 10021, '65–; Med. and Scientific Ed., Newsweek, 20 yrs.; Med. Wtr., Cornell Univ. Med. Col. four and a half yrs.; Auth.; med. bks.; over 100 sci. and med. articles, features; Nat. Assn. of Sci.

Wtrs., Ed. of World Scope Ency., Nat. Pr. Cncl. of Health and Welfare Svcs. (Bd. Mbr.), Med. Passport Fndn. (Bd. Mbr.), Am. Assn. for the Advancement of Sci. (Fellow), N.Y. Acad. of Scis., Am. Acad. of Polit. and Social Scis.; Headliner Aw. for Med. Features Series, '47; Southwestern Jnslm. Aw. for Leadership in Interpreting of Med. and Sci., '54; Columbia Univ., '26; Southern Methodist Univ., '28; b. Madison, Wis., 1907; p. Andrew and Louise Davis Sheridan; h. William Alexander Clark (dec.); res: 249 E. 48th St., N.Y., N.Y. 10017.

CLARK, MARIA GUIDISH, Rsch. Assoc., University of Pittsburgh, Learning Research and Development Center and School of Education, Pitt., Pa. 15213, '67–; Lectr., Univ. of Pitt., Johnstown; Tchr., Ligonier, '54–'66; Dir. of Rsch., Ill. Neuropsychiatric Inst., Chgo., Ill., '50–'51; Tchr., Ogontz Jr. Col., '49–'50; Sci. Educ. Cnst.; Auth., juv. bks. (Doubleday Aw., Best in Children's Bks., '64); Am. Assn. of Physics Tchrs., NEA, other pfsnl. orgs.; NSF Fellowship, '65; Univ. of Pitt., BS, '48; MS, '50; Carnegie-Mellon Univ., PhD, '70; b. Munhall, Pa., 1926; p. Frank and Mary Farkas Guidish; h. Daniel J. Clark; c. Sherry, Heather, Danny, Erin; res: 5564 Forbes Ave., Pitt., Pa. 15217.

CLARK, MAUREEN MORTON, Off. Mgr. and Local News Dir., Broadcast Service, Inc., P.O. Box E—Highway 570, McComb, Miss. 39648, '60–; Staff, '54–;b. McComb, Miss., 1936; p. Bayless E. and Mary Lewis Morton; h. Bruce G. Clark; c. Cynthia Ellen, Bill, Caryl Ann; res: 601 Hart Rd.—Box 476, McComb, Miss. 39648.

CLARK, PAULA, Prom. Mgr., The Hartford Courant, 285 Broad St., Hartford, Conn. 06790, '59–; own PR agcy., Miami, Fla., '57–'59; Sun. Ed., The Miami Herald, '47–'57; The Salt Lake Tribune; Reptr., AP; Fashion Group (Miami Rgnl. Dir., '58), Theta Sigma Phi; Univ. of Fla., BS (Jnlsm.); h. Hurlbut G. Clark; res: Burlington Rd., Harwinton, Conn. 06790.

CLARK, REBECCA TIMBRES, Free-lance Wtr: "We Didn't Ask Utopia" (Prentice Hall '39), poetry, mag. articles; Lectr.; Social Case Worker, Family Svc. of Chester County (Pa.), '60–'61; Friends Ctr., '58–'59; Cnslt. to Exec. Dir., Ha. Heart Assn., '58; Exec. Dir., '55–'58; Social Svc. Dept., Queen's Hosp., Med. Social Svc. Assn. of Ha., '47–'55; Supvsr., Am. Red Cross (Stratford, Conn.), '45–'47; Rsch. Asst., Tchrs. Col., Columbia Univ. (N.Y.C.), '45; Acting Dean and Dir. of Nursing Educ., Meharry Med. Col. (Nashville, Tenn. '43–'44); Assoc. Secy. and Case Worker, Am. Friends Svc. Comm. (Phila., Pa.), '41–'43; Public Health Nurse in Poland, Russia and India, '21–'37; Tchrs. Col., Columbia Univ., BS, '18; N.Y. Sch. of Social Work, MS, '41; b. Balt., Md., 1896; p. Dr. Oliver Edward and Anne B. Webb Janney; h. Edgar Sydenbaum Clark; c. Mrs. John Rosselli and Mrs. George C. Coleman; res: 28 E. Main St., Morrestown, N.J. 08057.

CLARK, RHETA ADELE, Sch. Media Cnslt., State

Department of Education, P.O. Box 2219, Hartford, Conn. 06115, '44–; Dean of Girls, Lyman Hall H.S., Wallingford, '30–'44; Librn., '26–'44; Tchr., Newington, '23–'26; Instr., New Haven State Tchrs. Col., summer '48; ext. course, '51; Univ. of Conn. ext. course, '56; ALA (Cnclr.-at-large, '66–), Am. Assn. of Sch. Librns. (Vice Chmn., Chmn., '45–'47), New Eng. Sch. Lib. Assn. (Pres., '40–'42), Conn. Sch. Lib. Assn. (Pres., '33–'34), NEA, Conn. Educs. Assn., AAUW, Delta Kappa Gamma; Rheta A. Clark Aw. for Excellence in Librnship. established by Southern Conn. State Col., '57; Conn. Col., AB, '23; Columbia Univ., MA, '31; BS (Lib. Sci.), '40; b. S. Glastonbury, Conn., 1902; p. Herbert and Alice House Clark; res: 131 Tryon St., S. Glastonbury, Conn. 06073.

CLARK, ROSETTA CROXTON, Bk. Dept. Mgr., University Book Center, Boulder, Colo. 80302, '60–; Textbk. Byr., '54–'60; Off. Mgr., '52–'54; Trade Bk. Byr., '47–'52; Nat. Assn. of Col. Stores, WNBA, Am. Bksellers. Assn.; Columbia Univ., BA, '47; b. Englewood, N.J.; p. Frederick and Rosetta R. Croxton; h. William Clark; c. David Michael, Rebecca Ann; res: 3050 15th St., Boulder, Colo. 80302.

CLARK, TOBY T., Pres., Toby Clark Agency, Inc., 18 E. 48th St., N.Y., N.Y. 10017, '56–; Adv. Mgr.; Fashion and Design Cnslt.; Publ. Cnslt.; Contrb. Ed./Wtr.; AWNY; The Fashion Group; Pers. Agcys. of N.Y. (Bd. of Dirs.); Equal Employment Opportunities Comm. (Co-chmn.); Guest Lectr., Fashion Inst. of Tech., Adv. Club of N.Y., Theta Sigma Phi, APANY (Chris Tobinson Aw., '66, '67); N.Y.U.; b. N.Y.C.; h. Harry Clark (dec.).

CLARKE, DOROTHY CLOTELLE, Asst. Dean, College of Letters and Science, University of California, Berkeley, Cal. 94720, '63–; Prof., Spanish, '61–; Assoc. Prof., '55–'61; Asst. Prof., '48–'55; Lectr., Spanish and Portuguese, '45–'48; Prof., Spanish, Dominican Col. of San Rafael, '35–'37; Wtr., numerous scholarly bks., monographs, articles in jnls.; Modern Lang. Assn. of Am., Philological Assn. of the Pacific Coast, AAUP, Am. Assn. of Tchrs. of Spanish and Portuguese, Modern Humanities Rsch. Assn., Inst. Intl. de Lit. Iberoamericana, Renaissance Soc. of Am., Hispanic Inst. in the U.S., Fgn. Lang. Assn. of Northern Cal., The Medieval Acad. of Am., Dante Soc. of Am., Am. Philological Assn., Am. Soc. for Aesthetics, Intl. Platform Assn., Marquis Biographical Lib. Soc.; U.C.L.A., AB, '29; Univ. of Cal., Berkeley, MA, '30; PhD, '34; b. L.A., Cal., 1908; p. Thomas and Zilpha Dever Clarke; h. Sundar S. Shadi; c. Zilpha Tedforda Shadi (Mrs. George Paganelli), Ramona Rhea Shadi (Mrs. William Miller), Verna Carol Shadi (Mrs. John Moir); res: 944 Arlington Ave., El Cerrito, Cal. 94530.

CLARKE, IRENE IRWIN, Pres., Clarke, Irwin & Company Ltd., 791 S. Clair Ave. W., Toronto 10, Ontario, Can., '55–; Assoc., '30–; Univ. Wms. Club, Heliconian Club; Represented Canadian Federation of University Women at Coronation of Queen Eliza-

beth II, '53; Ontario Classical Assn. (Hon. Pres., '54–'56); Victoria Univ., BA (Eng.), '24; Univ. of Toronto, MA (Greek Literature, Philosophy), '32; b. Toronto, Ontario, Can., 1903; p. John and Martha Fortune Irwin; h. William Henry Clarke (dec.); c. Garrick I., Martha (Mrs. George Leibbrandt), William Henry; res: 330 Spadina Rd., Apt. 1407, Toronto, Ontario, Can.

CLARKE, JOAN DORN, Librn., Girls' Latin School, Codman Sq., Boston, Mass. 02124, '60–; Harvard Col. Lib., '48–'54; Adv. Copywtr., Sears Roebuck & Co., '45–'48; Auth., "Your Future as a Librarian" ('63); ALA, Mass. Lib. Assn., Mass. Sch. Lib. Assn., Authors' League; Emmanuel Col., AB, '45 (cum laude); Simmons Col., MS (Lib. Sci.); b. N.Y.C., 1924; p. Hal and Evelyn Dornbach Clarke; res: 37 Concord Ave., Cambridge, Mass. 02138.

CLARKE, L. JEANNETTE, Vail-Ballou Press, Inc., 187 Clinton St., Binghamton, N.Y. 13902, '45–'54, '67–; Indsl. Ed., '60–'67; Wms. Nat. Bk. Assn. (Binghamton Chptr. Founder, First Pres., '62–'65; Ed., The Bookwoman, '64–'66; Nat. Mbrship. Chmn., '66–'68; Nat. Secy., '68–), ZONTA; Mt. Holyoke Col., AB, '31; b. Binghamton, N.Y.; p. Lyman and Theckla Klem Clark; res: 54 St. John Ave., Binghamton, N.Y. 13905.

CLARKE, LUCILLE V. Free-lance PR Cnslt., '67–; PR Dir., Children's Hosp. (Phila.), '63–'66; Assoc. PR Dir., Wms. Med. Col., '58–'63; Radio-TV Dir., Am. Cancer Soc., '53–'58; PR Dir., Christ Ch., '50–'53; PRSA (Secy., '59–'60), AWRT, Phila. Club Adv. Wm., Del. Valley Hosp. PR Assn. (Pres., '60–'62; Secy., '68); St. Lawrence Univ., BS, '29; Yale Drama Sch., '43; b. Chgo., Ill., 1907; p. Charles and Lucy Sima Clarke; res: 728 Clarendon Rd., Narberth, Pa. 19072.

CLARKE, MARTHA MARIANNE, Ed., Western Profile, Western Geophysical Company, 15300 Ventura Blvd., Suite 200-A, Sherman Oaks, Cal. 91403, '58–; formerly edtl. positions with Cal. Real Estate Assn., Blue Cross of Southern Cal., Soc. of Residential Appraisers, Am. Hosp. Assn., Cudahy Packing Co., U.S. Savings and Loan League, Marking Device Assn., Paris (Ill.) Beacon-News, Beatrice (Neb.) Daily News; Army PR, WW II; Tchr.; Theta Sigma Phi; five aws. for "Journalistic Standards" and "Graphic Excellence;" Doane Col., AB, '38 (cum laude, hons.); Northwestern Univ., MS (Jnlsm.), '44; b. Washington, Kan., 1916; p. Oscar and Zoe Nims Clarke, Sr.; res: 386 S. Burnside Ave., Apt. 7-F, L.A., Cal. 90036.

CLARKE, MARY WHATLEY, Auth: "The Palo Pinto Story" ('57), "Life in the Saddle" ('63), "David G. Burnet, First President of Texas" ('69); Feature Wtr., Cattleman Magazine, '40–; Ed.-Publr., Palo Pinto County Star, '33–'46; Ed.-Publr., Norwood Press (Manitoba, Can.), '25–'26; W. Tex. Press Assn. (Pres., '33); Theta Sigma Phi; active in numerous civic groups; N.M. State Col., '25; b. Palo Pinto, Tex., 1899; p. Cephas and Narcie Abernathy Whatley; h. Joe A.

Clarke; c. Mrs. Mary Harper; res: 3605 Bellaire Dr. S., Ft. Worth, Tex. 76109.

CLARKE, URANA, Free-lance Wtr., Radio Commentator, Log-A-Rhythm, Ninth St. Island, Livingston, Mont. 59047; Advisory Music Ed., Bk. of Knowledge; Own Radio Show, astronomy, "Skies Over the Big Sky Country," '64–; "New England Skies," WJAR-Radio (Providence, R.I.); Lectr: Roger Williams Planetarium (Star Identification and Nautical Astronomy), Hayden Planetarium (N.Y.C.), Hist. of Music (Mont. State Univ.); Big Sky Astronomical Soc. (Dir., '65–), Skyscrapers (R.I. Offcr.), AAAS, Royal Astronomical Soc. of Can., Intl. Musicological Soc., Am. Musicological Soc., Acad. of Polit. Sci., Marquis Biographical Lib. (Advisory Bd. Mbr.), Red Cross (Park County Chmn.); Mannes Music Col. (Artist's and Tchrs. Diploma), '25; Brown Univ.; Mont. State Univ., BS, '67; b. Wickliffe-on-the-Lake, Oh., 1902; p. Graham and Grace Olsaver Clarke; res: Log-A-Rhythm, Ninth St. Island, Livingston, Mont. 59047.

CLARKSON, JAN NAGEL, Rsch. Assoc., Fortune Magazine, Time-Life Bldg., Rockefeller Ctr., N.Y., N.Y. 10020, '66–; Conn. Col. for Wm., BA (cum laude), '65; Columbia Univ. (grad. sch. of Econs.), '65–'66.

CLAUDEL, ALICE MOSER, Eng. Instr., Salisbury State College, Salisbury, Md., '69–; Eng. Instr., W.Va. Wesleyan Col., '66–'69; Poetry Ed., Laurel Review, '66–; Tchr., St. Bernard Parish (La.) Elementary Schs., '56–'65; Past Asst. Ed., Pubcty Dir., Bus. Mgr., Experiment; poetry publ. in Prairie Schooner, N.M. Quarterly, Southern Poetry Review, others; Modern Language Assn. of Am., Nat. Cncl. of Tchrs. of Eng., Eng.-Speaking Union, LLAPW, S. Atlantic Modern Language Assn., Mark Twain Soc. (Pres., '58), Eugene Field Soc. (Hon. Mbr.), Who's Who of Am. Wm., Dic. of Intl. Biog., Dir. of Am. Scholars; Tulane Univ., BA (Eng.), '63; MA (Eng.), '68; b. New Orleans, La.; p. Herbert and Jeannette Hayes Moser; h. Calvin Andre Claudel; c. William McLeod Rivera; res: P.O. Box 1083, Chalmette, La. 70043.

CLAUDIA, Sr. (Carlen), IHM, VP, Corpus Instrumentorum, Inc., 1330 Massachusetts Ave., N.W., Wash., D.C. 20005, '68–; Index Ed., New Catholic Encyclopedia (McGraw-Hill), '63–'67; Librn., Marygrove Col. (Detroit, Mich.), '44–'69; Asst. Librn., '29–'44; articles for various prof. jnls. and bibliographer; monthly colm., Catholic Library World, '52–; ALA, Catholic Lib. Assn. (Pres., '65–'67, Mich. Unit Hon. Life Mbr.), Mich. Lib. Assn., Phi Beta Kappa, Beta Phi Mu, Marygrove Lib. Guild Cit., '59; Univ. of Mich., AB (Lib. Sci.), '28; AM (Lib. Sci.), '38; b. Detroit, Mich. 1906; p. Albert B. and Theresa M. Ternes Carlen; res: Marygrove Col., Detroit, Mich. 48221.

CLAYDON, DIANE SMITH, Colmst., The Tampa Tribune-Times, P.O. Box 191, Tampa, Fla. 33601, '69–; Reptr., '67–'69; Fla. Press Wms. Club ('69 Aws. in

Wms. Interest, Gen. Feature Writing, Reviews, Colms.), FPC; Univ. of S. Fla., grad. (Eng. Psychology), '67; b. Tampa, Fla., 1946; res: 2807 66th St., Tampa, Fla. 33619.

CLAYTON, MARGARET McCAULEY, Free-lance Wtr., Photo-jnlst., Contrbr., numerous mags., nwsps; Tchr., Writing to Sell course; Assoc. Bus. Wtrs. of Am., Theta Sigma Phi, Charlotte Wtrs. Club, Legal Auxiliary, PTA, AAUW; Goucher Col., '31–'33; Univ. of N.C., AB '35; (Phi Beta Kappa); b. Balt., Md., 1914; p. John and Pearl Piper McCauley; h. Overton W. Clayton; c. Virginia, Carol (Mrs. Marvin Eargle), Margaret (Mrs. Bruce Gebhart), Patricia (Mrs. Robert Giddings); res: 6500 Burlwood Rd., Charlotte, N.C. 28211.

CLEARY, FLORENCE DAMON, Prof. Emeritus, Wayne State University; Prof., Chmn., Lib. Sci. Dept., '50–'63; Detroit Citizenship Study, '45–'50; Lib. Sci. Instr., Col. of Educ., '32–'45; Librn., '19–'32; Asst. Librn., '17–'19; Auth: "Discovering Books and Libraries," "Blueprints for Better Learning," "Blueprints for Better Reading"; Fla. Lib. Assn., WNBA, N.A.A.P. Fla. Sch. Lib. Assn.; Univ. of N.Y., Columbia Univ.; Wayne State Univ., MA, '32 (Alumni svc. aw.); b. Livonia, N.Y.; p. Daniel and Jennie Disbrow Damon; h. Edmund Cleary; c. Elizabeth Fickes, Justine Johnston; res: 17 Spanish Main, Tampa, Fla. 33609.

CLEMENCE, JUDITH ARNOLD, Wms. Ed., The Flint Journal, 200 E. 1st St., Flint, Mich. 48502, '61–; Wms. Ed., The Pontiac Press, '62–'59; Dir., Northern Oakland County Girl Scout Camp, '50–'51; Cal. Fashion Aw., Flint Jr. Col.; Univ. of Mich.; Mich. State Univ.; b. Flint, Mich.; p. Roy and Iva Draper Arnold; h. Leland A. Clemence; c. Mrs. N. L. Rise; res: 2795 Silverhill Rd., Pontiac, Mich. 48055.

CLEMENS, IDA, Fashion and Beauty Ed., Med. Sci. Wtr., The Commercial Appeal, 495 Union Ave., Memphis, Tenn. 38101, '40–; Tenn. Med. Press Assn. Aw., '56; Tenn. Hosp. Assn. Aw., '62; Shelby Co. Tuberculosis and Health Assn. Aw., '62; b. New Bedford, Mass.; c. Hilliard Dawson Clemens, Jr.

CLEMENT, JANE TYSON, Auth., Asst. in Edtl. Work, Plough Publishing House, Society of Brothers, Rifton, N.Y. 12471; Bk., "The Sparrow," Short Story, "The Three Gifts," four lyrics in "Sing Through the Day," Intro. "The Shepherd's Pipe;" Soc. of Bros., (mbr. '55–, Tchr., '57–); Tchr., Shippen Sch., Lancaster, Pa. '40–'42; Germantown Friends Sch., '39–'40; Smith Col., BA, '39; b. N.Y.C., 1917; p. Levering and Reba Kittredge Tyson; h. Robert Clement; c. Jonathan, Timothy, Anne, Mark, Faith, Joel, Peter; res: Soc. of Bros., Woodcrest, Rifton, N.Y., 12471.

CLEMENTE, ELSIE HOFLING, Supvsr. Adm. Svcs., Ed. of Co. Nwsp., Carmet Co., Amcarb Division. 160 E. Union Ave., E. Rutherford, N.J. 07073, '67; Off. Mgr., '64–'67; Secy., '50–'64; Deborah Hosp. (N. Hudson Chptr. Pres., '68–'69); Fairleigh Dickinson Univ; b.

N.Y.C., 1920; p. Valentine and Anna Bauer Hofling; h. Patsy Clemente; c. Mrs. Carol Ann Cheringal, James; res: 310 37th St., Union City, N.J. 07087.

CLEMMEY, MARY, Lit. Agt., Julian Bach Literary Agency, 3 E. 48th St., N.Y., N.Y. 10017, '68–; Ed., Walker & Co., '66; Ed., Penguin Books (London), '65; Cnslt. to Crtv. Wrtng. Courses, Univ. of Cal. Ext., Berkeley, '67; Soc. of Auths. Reps.; London Univ., Eng., BSc (Part I), '65; Oxford Univ., Eng., BA, '64; MA, '68.

CLEMONS, CLARE FRANCIS, Music Librn., City College, Convent Ave. and 132nd St., N.Y., N.Y. 10036, '69–; Juilliard Sch., '69–; Media Specialist, Hunter Col., '67–'68; Bank St. Col. of Educ., '56–'67; Dalton Sch., '54–'56; Librn., Columbia Grammar Sch., '38–'54; Who's Who in Lib. Svc., Who's Who of Am. Wm.; Hunter Col., AB, '28; Columbia Univ., BS (Lib. Sci.), '42; Tchrs. Col., Columbia Univ., MS, '45; b. N.Y.C., 1899; p. John and Nettie Francis Clemons; res: 400 Central Park W., N.Y., N.Y. 10025.

CLEMONS, ELIZABETH (Elizabeth C. Nowell), Auth., juv. bks. Incl: "Waves, Tides and Currents" (Knopf, '67), "Here and There Stories" "Now and Then Stories" "Near & Far Stories," "A Source Book for the Teaching of Literature to Children" (Franklin Pubns., '67), 19 others; Wtr., Ed., General Mills, '47–'50; Eng. Dept., Univ. of Minn., '47; Ed., D.C. Heath and Co., '44–'46; Ed., Silver Burdett Co., '43–'44; Ed., John C. Winston Co., '42–'43; Univ. of Cal. Ext. Dept., '39–'42; San Jose State Col., Educ. Dept., '28–'39; NLSPW, Intl. Platform Assn., Auths. Guild, League of Wm. Voters; Who's Who of Am. Wm., Who's Who in the West, Contemporary Auths., Dic. of Intl. Biogs.; San Jose State Col., AB, '28; Stanford Univ., MA, '37; Oxford Univ., Columbia Univ., Univ. of Minn.; b. Berkeley, Cal.; p. Alfred and Edith Catton Cameron; h. 1. Arthur Granville Robinson (dec.) 2. Nelson T. Nowell; res: P.O. Box 686, Carmel, Cal. 93921.

CLEVEN, CATHRINE SEWARD, Auth., five bks. for young people; WNBA, Soc. of Midland Auths., Chgo. Children's Reading Round Table, MWA, NLAPW (Ft. Lauderdale Chptr. VP, '68–'70; Nat. Aw., juv., for "Black Hawk: Young Sauk Warrior"); Univ. of Ill., BA, '27; b. Dayton, Oh.; p. Edmund and Elizabeth Smith Seward; h. Edmund Cleven; c. Carol Cleven Engelking; res: 1545 S.E. 14th St., Deerfield Beach, Fla. 33441.

CLIFFORD, MARGARET CORT, Colmst., Aspen Times, Mountain States Communications, Box E, Aspen, Colo. 81611; Mng. Ed., '56–'59; Ed., Jr. Reviewers, '57–'59; Ed., Aspen Flyer, '54–'59; Reptr., Pitt. Sun-Telegraph, '49; Auth., "The Gnu and the Guru Go Behind the Beyond" ('69), "Aspen: Dreams & Dilemmas" ('69), "Elliott" ('67); Parkhurst Commty. Svc. Aw. (Co-winner, '58); Chatham Col., BA, '51; b. Cinn., Oh., 1929; p. George and Margaret Mackoy Clifford; res: Box 371, Aspen, Colo. 81611.

CLIFTON, JOE ANN CARTER, Mgr., Tech. Libs., Litton Industries, Inc. 5500 Canoga Ave., Woodland Hills, Cal. 91364, '54–; Hughes Aircraft Co., '52–'54; Pierce Col. Lib. Adv. Comm., '62–'66; Lectr., Beverly Hills School System, '60–'62; Adv., Colonial Sr. H.S. and Col. Youth Group, '49–'54; Am. Soc. for Info. Display, Am. Soc. Info. Sci., Special Libs. Assn. (John Cotton Dana Lectr., '68–'69), Assn. for Computing Machinery, Cal. Lib. Assn., Am. Mgt. Assn., Litton Mgt. Club; Santa Monica City Col., UCLA; b. Alton, Ill., 1929; p. Jesse and Lucille Wright Carter; h. Robert Clifton; c. Randy, Lucinda; res: 5359 Fallbrook, Woodland Hills, Cal. 91364.

CLIFTON, MARGUERITE ANN, Prof., Head, Department of Physical Education for Women, Purdue University, Lafayette, Ind., '64–; U.C.L.A., '56–'64; S.F. State Col., '51–'56; Tchr., '46–'51; Midwest Assn. for Health, Physical Educ. and Recreation (Pres., '69–'70; Am. Assn. for Health, Physical Educ. and Recreation (Bd. of Dirs., '67, '68 and '63, '64), Am. Acad. of Physical Educ.; Univ. of Redlands, BA; Univ. of Southern Cal., MS; Stanford Univ., EdD; b. Santa Monica, Cal., 1925; p. James and Bertha Flossman Clifton; res: 1630 Sheridan Rd., W. Lafayette, Ind. 47906.

CLINARD, DOROTHY LONG, Auth., children's short stories, '47–; Juv. bk., "The Hidey Hole" (Duell, Sloan & Pearce, '60); Pacific N.W. Wtrs. Conf. (Secy., '64); VP, '67; Pres., '68); Nat. Wtrs. Club, Whatcom Wtrs.; Tchr., Lectr. in writing; b. Belleville, N.J., 1909; p. Percy and Alice Southworth Long; h. Orville Clinard (div.); c. Mrs. Phyllis Pinkerton, Mrs. Marion Shelton; res: 2709 Lynn, Bellingham, Wash. 98225.

CLINE, CATHERINE ANN, Assoc. Prof. of Hist., Catholic University, Wash., D.C. 20017, '68–; Prof. of Hist., Notre Dame Col. of Staten Island, '54–'68; Instr., Hist., St. Mary's Col. (South Bend, Ind.), '53–'54; Asst., Dept. of Hist., Smith Col., '52–'53; Auth: "Recruits to Labour: The British Labour Party, 1914–31," numerous hist. articles; Am. Hist. Assn., Conf. on British Studies, Am. Catholic Hist. Assn., Soc. for Labour Hist., AAUP; Smith Col., AB, '48 (cum laude); Columbia Univ., MA, '50; Bryn Mawr Col., '50–'52 (Hist. Dept. Fellowship); PhD, '57; Am. Philosophical Soc. Grant, '60; b. W. Springfield, Mass., 1927; p. Daniel and Agnes Howard Cline; res: 3801 Connecticut Ave. N.W., Wash., D.C. 20008.

CLINE, DOROTHY HUNTSINGER, Wms. Ed., Spartanburg Herald-Journal, 177 W. Main St., Spartanburg, S.C. 29301; Soc. Ed. and Ch. Ed., The Herald and The Journal; S.C. Press Wms. Assn., NFPW; State Make-up Aw. for Daily Paper, '66; b. Spartanburg, S.C.; p. Edgar and Exey Tuck Huntsinger; h. William Cline; c. William, Jr.; res: 204 Briarwood Rd., Spartanburg, S.C. 29301.

CLINE, NORMA JEAN (Pseud: Norma Cline Klose), Auth., Fisher Body Div., General Motors Corporation, 4300 S. Saginaw St., Flint, Mich. 48507, '64–; Honolulu

(Hi.) Advertiser, '57–'58; Kaiser Steel Corp. (Oakland, Cal.), '58 –'64; Juv. Bk., "Benny, the Biography of a Horse" ('64); The Junior League of Flint; Univ. of Mich., '54–'55; Stephens Col., AA, '56; Miami (Oh.) Univ., '57; b. Flint, Mich., 1936; p. Howard and Ila Wood Cline; res: 9272 Hidden Valley Ct., Grand Blanc, Mich. 48439.

CLINTON, EDITH KING, Head of Tech. Svcs., East Cleveland Public Library, 14101 Euclid Ave., E. Cleve., Oh. 44112, '56–; Tech. Svcs., Cleve. Hts. Bd. of Educ., '50–'56; Tech. Svcs., E. Cleve. Public Lib., '33–'40; Tech. Svcs., Tulsa Public Lib., '30–'32; ALA, Oh. Lib. Assn., Wms. Nat. Book Assn.; Oh. Wesleyan Univ., BA, '29; Western Reserve, BLS, '30; b. Cleve., Oh., 1906; p. Harry and Mathilda Sharp King; h. Wills Clinton; c. Wills H. Jr., Stuart K.; res: 1830 Burnette St., E. Cleve., Oh. 44112.

CLINTON, MARY JANE, Society Ed., Amphlett Printing Company, Box 5400, San Mateo, Cal. 94402, '58–; Stanford Univ., BA, '55 (cum laude); b. San Mateo, Cal., 1934; p. J. Hart and Helen Amphlett Clinton.

CLIPPARD, JEAN FOX, Wms. Ed., Maryville-Alcoa Daily Times, 307 E. Harper St., Maryville, Tenn. 37803, '67–'70; Wms. Ed., Jackson, (Tenn.) Sun, '57–'63; Univ. of Wis.; b. Atlanta, Ga., 1927; p. Edward and Mildred Cress Fox; h. Bernard Cole Clippard; c. Bernard Cole, Jr., Richard Fox, Van Cress; res: 4405 Warner Pl., Nashville, Tenn. 37205.

CLISBY, ANNE DANIEL, Print Media Dir., Luckie & Forney, Inc., 11 Office Park, Birmingham, Ala. 35223, '63–; Asst. to Media Dir., '61–'62; Asst. to Bkkeeper, '60; Asst. to Off. Mgr., '59; Univ. of Ala., BA, '42; b. Birmingham, Ala., 1921; p. E. E. and AnnaBelle Huggins Daniel; c. Leslie, John; res: 4212 Overlook Rd., Birmingham, Ala. 35222.

CLOSE, ANNA KATHRYN, Ed., U.S. Department of Health, Education and Welfare, Wash., D.C. 20201, '54–; Assoc. Ed., The Survey and Survey Graphic, '48–'52; Instr., Carnegie Inst. of Tech., '47–'48; Asst. Ed., Survey Midmonthly, '38–42; Auth., "Transplanted Children," ('53), and numerous mag. articles.

CLOUD, BARBARA LOUISE, Fashion Ed., Pittsburgh Press, Blvd. of the Allies, Pitt., Pa. 15230, '63–; Theater Clmst.; Reptr., '57–'63; Soc. Ed., Uniontown Nwsps. Inc., '52–'57; Fashion Group, Wms. Press Club (Pres., '59–'62; numerous writing aws.); Pa. Nwsp. Publrs. Assn. Best Local Colm. Aw., '61; Golden Quill Aws. '64–'65; Best Dressed Career Wm. in Pitt., '65; Westminster Col., (Speech and Drama), '51 (Pres. of Qwens; Best Actress Aw.; Alumni Aw., '68); b. Uniontown, Pa., 1929; p. Milton and Elizabeth Miller Cloud; h. William A. Guerriero, Jr. (div.); res: 513 Shady Ave., Pitt., Pa. 15206.

CLOUGH, ROSA TRILLO, Head of Italian Dept.,

Finch Col., 52 E. 78th St., N.Y., N.Y. 10021, '56–; Prof. of Italian, Sarah Lawrence Col., summers '58–'61; Middlebury, summers '55–'58; Instr., Asst. Prof., Hunter Col., '28–'56; Auth., several art and lang. bks., articles in pfsnl. jnls.; AAUP, Columbia Univ. Seminar of Renaissance, Modern Lang. Assn., Am. Assn. of Tchrs. of Italian, various medieval and lang. orgs.; Hunter Col., BA, '26; Columbia Univ., MA, '34; PhD, '41; b. N.Y.C., 1906; p. Salvatore and Carmela Patrone Trillo; h. Shepard Clough; c. Shepard A., Peter N.; res: 460 Riverside Dr., N.Y., N.Y. 10027.

CLOUSE, RUTH GILBERT, Soc. Ed., New Haven Register, 367 Orange St., New Haven, Conn. 06503, '46–; Asst. Soc. Ed., '33– WW II; Lt. (j.g.), U.S. Coast Guard Wm.'s Reserve, WW II; AAUW (New Haven Br. Pres.), Mount Holyoke Club of New Haven (former Pres.); Wm. of Yr., New Haven BPW, '65; Americanism Aw. of Stanley Fishman Post Auxiliary, Jewish War Veterans; St. Thomas' Episcopal Ch. (vestry); Am. Legion Most Distg. Svc. cit., '69; Mount Holyoke Col., BA, '29 (cum laude); b. New Haven, Conn., 1909; p. Jacob F. and Augusta Schneider Clouse; res: 54 Woodlawn St., Hamden, Conn. 06517.

CLYMER, CATHERINE, Bdcst. Supvsr., Batten, Barton, Durstine & Osborn, Inc., 5670 Wilshire Blvd., L.A., Cal. 90036, '66–; Prod. Asst., '54–'66; free-lance TV-Radio prod., '52–'54; Radio Script Girl, Erwin Wasey, '49–'52; AWRT (Southern Cal. Chptr. Pres., '67–'68); USAF Defense Info. Sch. Distg. Svc. Aw., '69; Occidental Col., BA, '47 (Schumacher Aw.); b. El Dorado, Kan.; p. R. A. and Elizabeth Hoisington Clymer; res: 14836 Covello St., Van Nuys, Cal. 91405.

COACHMAN, DOROTHEA LOVE, Head Librn., Hanover Park High School, Mt. Pleasant Ave., Hanover, N.J. 07936, '66–; Sr. Librn., North Jr. HS, '61–'66; S. Orange Free Public Lib., '58–'61; Maplewood Free Public Lib., '52–'56; Asst. Field Dir., Am. Red Cross, European Theatre, '44–'46; Pers. Advisor, Prudential Ins. Co., '40–'44; Statistician and Special Cl., '36–'40; Instr., Lib. Sci., Newark State Tchrs. Col., '64–'66; ALA, N.J. Sch. Lib. Assn. (Pres., '67–'68; VP, '65–'66; Secy., '64–'65), Essex County Sch. Lib. Assn. (Pres., '65–'67), N.J. Lib. Assn., Beta Phi Mu; Mt. Holyoke Col., BA, '36; Rutgers Univ., MS (Lib. Sci.), '61 (Grolier Scholarship); Montclair State, Newark State Cols., Teaching Certs., '61; h. Joseph Coachman; c. Luanne; res: 8 Roosevelt Rd., Maplewood, N.J. 07040.

COAKLEY, ELEANOR M., Chief, Div. of Info. and Pubns., Women's Bureau, U.S. Department of Labor, Constitution Ave., at 14th St., Wash., D.C. 20024; Adm. Asst., Thomas L. Ashley, M.C., '55; Thomas H. Burke, M.C., '49–'52; Reptr., Toledo (Oh.) Blade, '39–'49; BPW (Membership, Program Dir., '56–'62), AWRT, WNPC; Univ. of Toledo, PhB., '34; Northwestern Univ., Medill Sch. of Jnlsm., '38; res: 1311 Delaware Ave., S.W., Wash., D.C. 20024.

COAKLEY, MARY LEWIS, Feature Wtr., The Philadelphia Bulletin, 30th and Market Sts., Phila., Pa. 19101, '68–; Auth., four bks.; Auths. Guild, Bucks County Wtrs. Guild (Treas., '67–'69), NLAPW (nat. feature story aw., '68); Dominican Col. of San Rafael, '25–'27; b. Balt., Md., 1907; p. Charles and Rose Kerchner Lewis; h. William Coakley; c. Joseph A.; res: 110 Hewett Rd., Wyncote, Pa. 19095.

COATES, BELLE, Auth., juv. fiction; Public Sch. Tchr., Mont., Wash., Cal., 20 yrs.; six bks., 70 short stories; Delta Kappa Gamma (Ed., Area XIII Newsltr., '66–'67); Who's Who of Am. Wm.; Wash. State Univ., '17–'18; Mont. Univ., '19; Success Bus. Col., '21; UCLA, '47; San Diego State Col., BA, '54; b. Victor, Ia., 1896; p. Louis and Belle Dyer Coates; res: 240-B Fredericka Parkway, Chula Vista, Cal. 92010.

COATES, GERENE BLANCHE, VP, Client Svcs. Mgr., Smith-Klitten, Inc., 11941 Wilshire Blvd., L.A., Cal. 90025; Adv. Mgr., Semi-conductor Div., The Bendix Corp; VP, AE, Thomas & White; Free-lance Wtr., Photogr; Am. Mktng. Assn., WGA, Pfsnl. Photogrs. of Am; Am. Bouvier des Flanders Club; Sweet Adelines; Brothers Col., Drew Univ., AB (Lit.); b. Bklyn., N.Y.; p. John and Dorothea Knorr Coates; res: 1453 Stanford St., Santa Monica, Cal. 90404.

COBB, ANNE De LISLE, Ed., Employee Nwsp., Shell Oil Co., 230 Peachtree St., N.W., Atlanta, Ga. 30303, '65–; Pubns. Ed., Federal Reserve Bank of Atlanta, '61–'65; Ga. IEA (1st VP, '68–'69) Atlanta Press Club, Southern Cncl. of Indsl. Eds. (Secy., '68–'69; Aws: '67, '68); Agnes Scott Col., BA (Eng.), '60; b. Asheville, N.C., 1938; p. Owen and Billie McChesney Cobb; res: 3501 Roswell Rd., B-6, Atlanta, Ga. 30305.

COBB, CONNIE CAROLYN MIDEY, Gen. Assigt. Reptr., Teen Ed., The Arizona Republic, 120 E. Van Buren, Phoenix, Ariz. 85004, '67–; Ariz. State Univ., BA (Eng.), '69; b. Cuba, N.Y., 1946; p. Vincent Midey and Eunice Boyd Lee; h. B. Clair Cobb; res: 511 E. Roanoke, Apt. A, Phoenix, Ariz. 85004.

COBB, JOSEPHINE, Iconography Specialist, National Archives, 7th and Constitution Aves., Wash., D.C. 20408, '60–; various titles since '40; Art Cnslt., Capitol Hist. Soc.; Wash. D.C. Landmarks Commn., D.C. Hist. Soc., Special Libs. Assn.; Abraham Lincoln Nat. Aw., '66; Abraham Lincoln Civil War Aw., '69; Abraham Lincoln Sesquicentennial Commn. Aw., '60; Simmons Col., BS, '31; Boston Univ., MA, '35; b. Portland, Me.; p. Allen and Nellie Cobb; res: 2393 N. Kenmore St., Arlington, Va. 22207.

COBLE, HELEN BROWN, Reptr., Colmst., DeLand Sun News, S. Blvd., DeLand, Fla. 32720, '47–'57, '59–; Fla. Wms. Press Club (Pres., '69–'71; VP, '67–'69; Treas., '59–'61; 1st pl. aws., '53, '56, '58), Volusia County Traffic & Safety Commn. (Chmn.), various civic aws.; b. Bridgeport, Conn. 1913; p. Albert and Anna Sachs Brown; h. Paul Coble; c. Mrs. Albert

Guenther, Mrs. Bruce Barker, Alicia; res: 922 N. Florida Ave., DeLand, Fla. 32720.

COCHRAN, JILL, Media Byr., Tucker Wayne & Co., 2700 Peachtree Ctr. Bldg., Atlanta, Ga. 30303, '67–; Burke Dowling Adams, '65–'67; AWRT, Media Planners; Univ. of Ga., AB (Jnlsm.), '64; b. Albany, Ga., 1942; p. John and Doris Gissendaner Cochran; res: 1416-B, Druid Valley Rd., N.E., Atlanta, Ga. 30329.

COCHRAN, KATRICIA RYLE, Feature Reptr., Wichita Falls Times, 13th and Lamar, Wichita Falls, Tex. 76307, '59–; Reptr., Record News, '57–'58; INS, '56–'57; Univ. of Okla., BA (Jnlsm.), '57; b. Norman, Okla., 1935; p. John and Eula Anderson Ryle; h. Jim Cochran; res: 4212 Prince Edward, Wichita Falls, Tex. 76308.

COCHRANE, PAULINE BORGET, Asst. to Secy., Standard Brands Inc., 625 Madison Ave., N.Y., N.Y. 10022, '61–; Exec. Secy., '49–'54; PR, Asst. AE, Philip Lesly Co., '60–'61; Admin. Asst., S. D. Leidesdorf and Co., '55–'60; Off. Mgr., Nat. Theatre Supply, '54–'55; Hunter Col. (Jnlsm.), '40–'50; N.Y.U. Bus. Sch., '56; N.Y. Inst. of Fin.; b. Niagara Falls, N.Y., 1922; p. Albert and Mary Dalton Borget; h. Malcolm J. Cochrane (div.); c. Julia B.; res: 411 E. 53rd St., N.Y., N.Y. 10022.

COCKING, GLADYS NEALY, Mng. Ed., The Review, 725 Eighth St., Erie, Ill. 61250, '57–; Sterling (Ill.) Daily Gazette, '44–'47; Erie Progressive Club, Erie Lioness Club (Pres., '68–'69), numerous org. aws. through The Review; civic proms; b. Tampico, Ill., 1915; p. Marshall and Zora Yarde Nealy; h. R. Gail Cocking; c. Janice (Mrs. Lowell A. Kelly), Melvin; res: 725 Eighth St., Erie, Ill. 61250.

CODY, SARAH ISABELLE, Dir., Cleveland Heights-University Heights Public Library, 2345 Lee Road, Cleve. Heights, Oh., 44118, '63–; Tchr., Polk County, Fla., '61–'62; Children's Librn., Cleve. Public Lib., '42–'61; Cnslt., Central Fla. Reg. Lib., '62; ALA, Oh. Lib. Assn. (Bd. of Dirs., '67–'70); Wms. Nat. Bk. Assn., Beta Phi Mu, League of Wm. Voters; Fla. State Col. for Wm., AB, '41; Emory Univ., AB (Lib. Sci.), '42; Western Reserve Univ., MS (Lib. Sci.), '58; b. Tampa, Fla.; res: Babson Park, Fla. 33827.

COEN, RENA NEUMANN, Asst. Prof., Art Hist., St. Cloud State College, St. Cloud, Minn., '69–; Auth. of numerous children's bks. and articles on art hist.; Rsch. Asst., Mpls. Inst. of Arts, '61–'66; Film Booker, Admiralty Shore Establishments Cinema Fund (London, Eng.), '50–'52; Docent, Jewish Museum (N.Y.C.), '47; Col. Art Assn. of Am., Twin Cities 7 Col. Conf. Comm., Minn. Hist. Soc., Mpls. Soc. of Fine Arts, Twin Cities Barnard Col. Alumnae Cl.; Barnard Col., B.A., '46; N.Y.U., '46–'47; Yale Univ., M.A., '48 (Jr. Sterling Fellowship); Univ. of Minn., Ph.D., '69 (Danforth Fndn. Grad. Fellowship for Wm.); b. N.Y.C., 1925; p. Joshua and Tamar Mohl Neumann; h. Edward

Coen; c. Deborah Ruth, Joel David, Ethan Jesse; res: 1425 Flag Ave. S., Mpls., Minn. 55426.

COFFEY, NANCY LOUISE, Mng. Ed., Avon Books, 959 Eighth Ave., N.Y., N.Y. 10019, '69–; Dir., Contracts, Rights and Permissions, '65–'69; Asst. Dir. of Rights, G. P. Putnam's Sons, Coward-McCann, '63–'65; Tchr., N.Y.C. Public Schs., '62; Hunter Col., BA, '62; b. N.Y.C., 1940; p. John and Alice Omark Coffey; res: 415 E. 72nd St., N.Y., N.Y. 10021.

COFFIN, ANNE GAGNEBIN, Asst. Ed., Look Magazine, Cowles Communications, 488 Madison Ave., N.Y., N.Y. 10022, '67–; various edtl. assignments, '61–'67; Smith Col., BA, '61; b. Neptune, N.J., 1939; h. John D. Coffin; res: 929 Park Ave., N.Y., N.Y. 10028.

COFFIN, BARBARA J., Ed., The Griffin Report, Griffin Publishing Corp., 462 Boylston St., Boston, Mass. 02116, '67–; Assoc. Ed.; Special Projects Dir.; Ed., Yankee Grocer, Shamie Publ. Corp.; Mktng. Dir., Rust Craft Greeting Cards; Sls. Prom., Wm. Filene's; Mkt. Study, New Eng. Food Industry, '69, '68, '67; Nat. Mgt. Assn., Grocery Manufacturers Assn., Super Mkt. Adv. Club, Pubcty. Club; aws. for edtl. achiev.; Tuft's Univ., '53–'54; Boston Univ., '55–'56; b. Brookline, Mass., 1934; p. Montique L. and Anne MacDonald Coffin; res: 677 Hammond St., Chestnut Hill, Mass. 02067.

COFFIN, PATRICIA, Modern Living Ed., Look Magazine, 488 Madison Ave., N.Y., N.Y. 10022, '55–; Staff Wtr. '42–'55; Colmst., Features Wtr., N.Y. World-Telegram, '38–'42; Pubcty., Waldorf-Astoria, '33–'38; Auth: "The Gruesome Green Witch" (Walker & Co., '69); numerous mag. articles and poetry; one-man show, water colors, Ward Eggleston Gallery, N.Y.C.; Fashion Group, PSA, Nantucket Hist. Assn; Charles Dana Gibson Art Scholarship, '31; Art Students' League; b. N.Y.C., 1912; p. William and Mabel Rees Coffin; h. Merrill K. Lindsay; c. Theodore Lee Gaillard, Jr., Tristram Coffin Gaillard, Dionis Coffin Lindsay, David M. K. Lindsay, Mrs. Richard Sutor; res: Branford Rd., N. Branford, Conn. 06471, and 50 E. 96th St., N.Y., N.Y. 10028.

COFFIN, WINIFRED DeFOREST, Actress, 7261 Hollywood Blvd., Hollywood, Cal. 90046; Assoc., Stage and Screen, '34–; Feature Roles: (Stage) Carousel, The Women, The Child Buyer; (Motion Pic.) Eight on the Lam, Hawaii Five-O, others; (TV) Bonanza, Red Skelton Hour, Death Valley Days; Tchr: Wayne Univ., '62; Oakland Univ., '63; SAG, AEA, AFTRA, St. Dunstans Guild, Theatre Arts (Detroit, Bd. of Dirs.); Conn. Col. for Wm., AB, '33; b. Chgo., Ill., 1911; p. Fred and Cella Goehring DeForest; h. Dean Coffin; c. Cella Alderson, Fred, William, Howard, Tristram; res: 7261 Hollywood Blvd., Hollywood, Cal. 90046.

COGGINS, CAROLYN, Auth.; Instr., Univ. of Cal.; New York Herald Tribune Books Review, '34–'51;

Auth: "Successful Entertaining at Home," "Fabulous Foods for People You Love" (Both, Prentice-Hall); "Lance and Cowboy Billy," "Lance and His First Horse" (both, Whittlesey House); three cooking paperbks.; PEN; b. Kan.; p. Aaron and Goldie Martin Simpson; h. (div.); res: 17191 Bernardo Center Dr., Rancho Bernardo, San Diego, Cal. 92128.

COGSWELL, CORALIE NORRIS HOWARD, Instr., Eng., Humanities, Pennsylvania State University, Worthington Scranton Campus, Dunmore, Pa., '68–; Sch. Librn. (Tunkhannock, Pa.), '66–'68; Serials Librn., Wilkes Col., '66; Sch. Librn., Reading Tchr. (Pinellas County, Fla.), '61–'64; Ed: "The First Book of Short Verse" ('64), "Lyric Poems" ('68); Auth, "What Do You Want to Know?" ('68); Contemporary Auths.; Univ. of Chgo., PhB, '48 (with hons.); N.D. State, BS (Social Sci.), '49; Univ. of Ark., MA (Eng.), '51; b. Cleve., Oh., 1930; p. Wendell and Mildred Winkler Norris; h. Theodore R. Cogswell; c. Madeleine Howard, Lucy Howard; res: 108 Robinson St., Chinchilla, Pa. 18410.

COHAN, CAROLE KRITZ, TV Commls., Prodr., McCann-Erickson, Inc., 485 Lexington Ave., N.Y., N.Y. 10017, '67–; Assoc. Prodr., Sammy Davis Show Enterprises, '65–'66; Asst. to Prodr., WABC-TV, '64–65; Kappa Gamma Chi (Pres.), '63–'64; Who's Who in Am. Cols. and Univs., '64; Outstanding Young Wm. of Am., '66; Emerson Col., BS (Speech, Eng. Educ.), '64; b. N.Y.C., 1942; p. Martin and Tulsa Rosenzweig Kritz; h. Ronald Cohan; c. Leslie; res: 1161 York Ave., N.Y., N.Y. 10021.

COHEN, BARBARA LEE, VP, Hank Meyer Associates, Inc., 919 N. Michigan, Chgo., Ill. 60657, '69–; Owner, Hatt and Assocs.; Bentley, Barnes & Lynn, Inc., Co-owner, "Up Tempo" TV show; Radio-TV, Commty. Discount Chain; Pubcty. Club of Chgo., Art Inst., Hemophilia Fndn., Young Adults for Leukemia Rsch.; Nat. paper mache sculpture aw., '52; active in numerous civic groups; Chgo. Conservatory; Roosevelt Univ.; Art Inst.; Col. of Jewish Studies; b. Chgo., Ill., 1937; p. Irving and Jean Schmetterer Cohen; res: 445 W. Melrose, Chgo., Ill. 60657.

COHEN, BETSY KAMERON, Exec. Prodr., Artists and Repertoire, CBS-Columbia Direct Marketing, 51 West 52nd St., N.Y., N.Y., '66–; Asst. Dir., '63–'66; Supvsr., '60–'63; Exec. Secy., '55–'60; N.Y.U., BA; Columbia Univ., MA; PhD; c. Nina, Nicholas; res: 2575 Palisade Ave., Riverdale, N.Y.

COHEN, DOROTHEA BEVILACQUA, Scientific Literature Analyst, The Council for Tobacco Research-U.S.A., 110 E. 59th St., N.Y., N.Y. 10022, '66–; Biochemistry Tech., Albert Einstein Med. Ctr. (Phila., Pa.), '65–'66; Rsch. Assoc., Jefferson Med. Col., '62–'64; Rsch. Asst., '61–'62; Bacteriology Tech., Hosp., '59–'61; Co-auth: "The Influence of Cigarette Smoke on Lung Clearance," ('66); "Synergistic Effect of Aerosols; III,'' ('63; IV, '64); N.Y. Acad. of Scis., Theta Sigma Phi; DePauw Univ., BA, '59 (cum laude); Univ. of Pa., MA, '64; b. Phila., Pa., 1938; p. Alfred and Mary Comly Bevilacqua; h. Jeffrey Cohen; res: 220 E. 26th St., Apt. 4K, N.Y., N.Y. 10010.

COHEN, JANE ELIZABETH, Prog. Dir., U.S. Communications of Philadelphia, WPHL-TV, 1230 E. Mermaid Lane, Phila., Pa. 19118, '68–; Adm. Asst., '67–'68; Prodr., Opns. Adm., Prog. Dir., WPBS, '63–'68; Rsch. Tech. Asst., Wms. Med. Col. of Pa., '58–'63; PR Comm., Phila. Area Girl Scouts; AWRT (Nat. VP, Mid-East Area, '69–'70); Phila. Chptr. Pres., '68–'69; Pres. Elect, '67–'68; Bd. of Dir., '66–'67); Voice of Democracy Aw., VFW, '66; George Washington Hon. Medals, Freedoms Fndn., '63–'64; b. Phila., Pa., 1938; p. Siebert and Ella Schultz Cohen; res: 472 W. Leverington Ave., Phila., Pa. 19128.

COHEN, MAXINE C., VP, Media, Redmond, Marcus & Shure, Inc., 32 E. 57th St., N.Y., N.Y. 10022, '66–; Media Dir., '64–'66; Media Supvsr., Clyne, Maxon, Inc., '63–'64; Media Byr., Ogilvy and Mather, Inc., '56–'63; Asst. Space Byr., Biow Co., Inc., '54–'56; Syracuse Univ., BS (Bus. Adm.), '53; b. Syracuse, N.Y., 1932; p. Simon and Rosalind Ruby Cohen; res: 340 E. 64th St., N.Y., N.Y. 10021.

COHEN, NANCY ODESSA, Sr. Copywtr., Haddon, Burns & Cohen Advertising, 188 W. Randolph, Chgo., Ill. 60601, '67–; previously with Maremont Corp., Marketing Catalysts; Bdcst. Adv. Club, Assn. of Indsl. Mktng.; Univ. of Ill., Univ. of Chgo.; b. Chgo., Ill., 1944; p. Walter and Olive Linklater Odessa; h. Joel Cohen; res: John Hancock Ctr., Chgo., Ill. 60614.

COHEN, SARA BARR, Pubcty. Dir., Commtns. Div., American College of Surgeons, 55 E. Erie St., Chgo., Ill. 60611, '57–; Asst. PR Dir., '52–'57; Asst. PR Dir., Chgo. Public Lib., '41–'51; PR Asst., Nat. Youth Adm., State of Ill., '38–'41; PRSA (Accredited Mbr.; Chgo. Chptr. Bd. of Dirs., '68–'70; Secy., '68–'69), Pubcty. Club of Chgo. (aw., '60; Second VP, '54, Bd. of Dirs., '53–'55, Secy., '53), Nat. Assn. of Sci. Wtrs., AWRT; Who's Who of Am. Wm.; Univ. of Chgo., BA, '38; Rosary Col., MA, '55; b. Chgo., Ill.; p. Joseph and Golde Barr Cohen; res: 777 N. Michigan Ave., Chgo., Ill. 60611.

COHEN, SELMA JEANNE, Ed., Dance Perspectives, Dance Perspectives Foundation, 29 E. Ninth St., N.Y., N.Y. 10003, '65–; Mng. Ed., '59–'65; New York Times, '55–'58; Instr., Dance Hist., Conn. Col. Sch. of Dance, '64–; Co-Auth., "Famed for Dance" ('60); Ed., "The Modern Dance: Seven Statements of Belief" (Wesleyan, '66); Am. Soc. for Theatre Rsch., Mod. Lang. Assn., Nat. Fndn. for the Arts; Univ. of Chgo., AB (Eng.), '41; AM, '42; PhD (Eng.), '46; b. Chgo., Ill., 1920.

COHLER, JANE S., Acc. Supvsr., Rogers, Cowan & Brenner, Inc., 598 Madison Ave., N.Y., N.Y. 10022,

'69–; AE, '68–'69; Asst. to Sr. VP, Sls. Prom., PR, Macy's, '68; Dir. of Pubcty., Special Events, May Co. (Cal.), '65–'68; Dir. of PR, Elgin Nat. Watch Co., '63–'65; Exec. Trainee, Grey Advertising, '62–'63; Theta Sigma Phi; Univ. of Minn., BA, '62 (cum laude); b. St. Paul, Minn., 1940; p. Arthur and Gertrude Metchnek Cohler; res: 166 E. 61st St., N.Y., N.Y. 10021.

COIT, MARGARET LOUISE, Assoc. Prof., Fairleigh Dickinson University, 140 Montross Ave., Rutherford, N.J. 07070, '65–; Instr., '55–'65; Reptr., Lawrence (Mass.) Daily Eagle, '41–'55; Auth: "John C. Calhoun: American Portrait," ('50; Pulitzer Prize, '51), "Mr. Baruch" ('57), "The Fight for Union" ('60), "The Growing Years and the Sweep Westward" (with the eds. of Life; '62), "Andrew Jackson" ('64), "Massachusetts" ('67), "Calhoun: Great Lives Observed" ('70); Soc. of Am. Histrn., Am. Hist. Assn., AAUP, Nat. Platform Assn., Auths. League, Theta Sigma Phi; Cncl. of Wm. of the U.S. Nat. Bk. Aw., '58; Thomas Edison Aw., '61; Univ. of N.C., AB, '41; DLitt, '59; b. Norwich, Conn., 1922; p. Arscha and Grace Trow Coit; res: 386 Park Ave., Rutherford, N.J. 07070.

COLBERT, JUNE, Pres., Partner, Crtv. Head, The Chicago Group, Inc.—The Interpublic Group of Companies, Inc., 10 S. Riverside Plaza, Chgo., Ill. 60606, '65–; Auth: articles, poems.

COLBURN, DONNA PELKEY, Wms. Dir., KAUZ-TV, Bass Bros. Telecasters, Inc., One Broadcast Ave., Wichita Falls, Tex. 76307, '61–; Interior Decorator, Bricktime Homes (Iowa Park, Tex.), '63; Dir., Commty. Club Aws. Campaign, '53; Vocalist, WKY-TV (Okla. City, Okla.), '51–'52; Copywtr., John A. Brown Co.; public appearances, speeches, TV guest for home econs.; AWRT; Aws: Mrs. Wichita Falls Home Owner, '63; Mrs. Texas, '65; Mrs. Congeniality in Mrs. Am. Contest, '65; Lion's Club Sweetheart; Pan. Am. Coffee Bur. Mrs. Coffee Queen of Southwest; b. Okla. City, Okla., 1934; p. Ralph and Mary Lou Sollars Pelkey; h. J. A. Colburn; c. Christie, Kellie; res: 4 Wrangler's Retreat, Rte. 3, Box 323C, Wichita Falls, Tex. 76308.

COLBY, ETHEL, Ed., Drama and Film Critic New York Journal of Commerce, 99 Wall St., N.Y., N.Y. 10005, '40–; Radio show, "Miss Hollywood," '48–'50; Star, TV shows, CBS, '44–'46; Star "Broadway Matinee," Dumont Network, '50–'51; Child Actress; Broadway Actress: Student Prince, Maytime, Blossom Time, others; Motion Pic. Actress, '27–'29; Wm. Bdcstrs. and Commentators Am. Club, N.Y. Drama Critics Circle (Treas.), Drama Desk; Columbia Univ., '25–'27; b. N.Y.C., 1908; p. Dr. M. Duckman and Scharlin Dallon; h. Julius J. Colby; c. Jeffrey; res: 44 W. 44th St., New York, N.Y. 10036.

COLBY, JEAN POINDEXTER, Ed.-Sports Pubns., Hastings House Publishing, Inc., 10 E. 40th St., N.Y., N.Y. 10016, '55–; Auth: "Mystic Seaport, The Age of Sail," "Writing, Illustrating and Editing," "Tear Down to Build Up," "Plimouth Plantation, Then and Now";

Lectr., Radcliffe Col., Wellesley Col., Boston Univ.; WNBA, ALA; Wellesley Col., BA, '28; b. Pine Orchard, Conn., 1909; p. Charles and Lena Von Steinhoff Poindexter; h. Dr. Fletcher H. Colby; c. Peter F., Antonia Colby Shoham, Jean Colby Bender.

COLCLOUGH, ELIZABETH SHEMPP, VP, Robert R. Mullen & Co., 1729 H St. N.W., Wash., D.C. 20006, '59–; Dir. of Orgs., Pubns., Radio-TV, Nat. Citizens Comm. for Educ. TV, '53–'56; Intl. Ed. for Special Events, Voice of Am., '52–'53; Prog. Dir., Am. Town Meeting of the Air, '48–'53; Asst. Prog. Dir., '42–'48; Radio Ed., N.Y. Herald Tribune, '41–'42; Sun. Dept., '37; AWRT, ANWC, WNPC; Univ. of Rochester, BA; Columbia Univ., grad. study; b. Hughesville, Pa.; p. William and Edith Hunt Shempp; h. Walter Raymond Colclough (dec.); res: 3130 Wisconsin Ave., N.W., Wash. D.C. 20016.

COLE, GEORGIA, Asst. Dir., Oregon State University Press, Oregon State University, P.O. Box 689, Corvallis, Ore. 97330, '69–; Asst. Dir. of Pubns., Ore. State Univ., '65–'69; Ed., '60–'65; Ed., Mont. State Univ., '45–'58; Instr., '42–'45; Rockford Col., AB, '30; b. Maxwell, Ia., 1907; p. George and Cora Dewel Cole; res: Box 863, Rte. 1, Bandon, Ore. 97411.

COLE, JEANNE, PR Group Head, J. Walter Thompson Company, 420 Lexington Ave., N.Y., N.Y. 10017, '66–; various positions at JWT as Acc. Rep., pubcty., '42–'66; Pubcty. Club of N.Y.; Bklyn. Col.; N.Y.C.

COLE, MARGARET PAYNE, Acquisitions Librn., Hofstra University Library, Hempstead, N.Y. 11550, '66–; Supt. of Bk. Selection, Queens Borough Public Lib., '48–'66; Children's Librn., Ref. Librn., Cataloguer, '32–'48; WNBA, ALA, N.Y. Lib. Assn., N.Y. Lib. Club, NCLA, Bksellers' League, LPRC; Beta Phi Mu; Mt. Holyoke Col., '27–'28; Barnard Col., AB, '31; Columbia Univ. Sch. of Lib. Svc., BS, '32; MS, '53; New Sch. for Social Rsch., '45–'47; N.Y.U., '56–'58; b. Astoria, N.Y.; p. George and Margaret Aitken Cole; res: 36–36 31st St., L.I. City, N.Y. 11106.

COLE, MARY ELIZABETH, Dir., Public Libraries Section, Tennessee State Library and Archives, Seventh Ave. N., Nashville, Tenn. 37219, '67–; Public Lib. Cnslt., Fla. State Lib., '60–'67; Dir., Blue Grass Reg. Lib. (Columbia, Tenn.), '54–'60; Bkmobile Librn., Upper Cumberland Reg. (Cookeville), '52–'54; High Sch. Librn. (Mt. Pleasant), '48–'52; Tchr., '42–'48; ALA, Tenn. Lib. Assn., Fla. Lib. Assn. (Secy., '63–'64), Southeastern Lib. Assn., Assn. of State Libs., AAUW, BPW, Tenn. Hist. Soc., Tallahassee Symphony Guild, Tallahassee Orchid Soc.; Tenn. Polytech. Inst., BS, '45; George Peabody Col. for Tchrs., MA (Lib. Sci.), '53; b. Huntland, Tenn., 1921; p. T. A. and Arie Mann Cole; res: 812 Capitol Towers Apts., 510 Gay St., Nashville, Tenn. 37219.

COLE, RUTH MARTIN, Geog. Ed., Encyclopaedia Britannica, Inc., 425 N. Michigan Ave., Chgo., Ill. 60611, '65–; Mng. Ed., Geog. Dept., '57–'65; Assn. of Am. Geographers; Univ. of Wash., BA, '56; b. Spokane, Wash., 1930; p. Roy A. and Freda Owen Martin; h. J. Paul Cole; res: 2052 Lincoln Park W., Chgo., Ill. 60614.

COLE, SUSAN, Media Byr., Marsteller Inc., 866 Third Ave., N.Y., N.Y. 10022, '66–; Assoc. Media Byr., '64–'66; Asst. Media Byr., '62–'64; Media Coord., '61–'62; Acct. Secy., '56–'61; free-lance media cnslt.; tchr., new employee training; AAAA, Nat. Agricultural Adv. and Mktng. Assn. (secy., '69–'70), Pharmaceutical Adv. Club; John Robert Powers Modeling Sch., '40; Paine Hall Med. Asst. Sch., '42; Aeronautical Sch., Naval Air Base, Fla., 44; b. Newtown, Conn.; p. Charles and Lois Hewitt Cole; h. (div.); res: 35 Davenport Ave., New Rochelle, N.Y. 10805.

COLLANDER, RUTH REISNER, Cont. Dir., Special Features, WRIE, Radio Erie, Inc., 2007 W. 32nd St., Erie, Pa. 16508, '60–; Free-lance feature programs, Erie radio-TV stations, '60–; Special Features, WICA Radio (Ashtabula, Oh.), '54–'60; Cont. Dir., KMO (Tacoma, Wash.), '41–'45; KFBB (Great Falls, Mont.), KTBI (Tacoma, Wash.), '40–'41; AWRT, AAUW, AFTRA, NABET, Erie Arts Cncl., Erie Civic Theatre; Who's Who of Am. Wm., Oh. State Wm. of Yr., '56; Am. Cancer cit.; Univ. of Puget Sound, BA, '39; b. Thiells, N.Y., 1918; p. Earl and Elizabeth Goodall Reisner; h. Ned Collander; c. Paul Josef, David Reisner; res: 1233 W. Ninth St., Erie, Pa. 16502.

COLLER, LEE, Copywtr., Avon Products, Inc., 30 Rockefeller Plaza, N.Y., N.Y. 10020, '68–; Sr. Copywtr., Cunningham & Walsh, '66–'68; Sr. Copywtr., West, Weir & Bartel, '65–'66; Copy Supvsr., Rayette House Agcy., '65; Sls. Prom. Mgr., Lehn & Fink Cosmetic Div., '63–'65; Copywtr., Revlon, '61–'63; AWNY, Fashion Group, Copy Club; 400 Best Read Ads, '68; N.Y.U., BA; b. N.Y.C.; p. Israel and Esther Litten Coller; h. (div.); res: 230 E. 88th St., N.Y., N.Y. 10028.

COLLETT, LOUISA BARRY, Ed., TRIMARK MAGAZINE, Cities Service Oil Company, 15th St. and Boulder Ave., Tulsa, Okla. 74102, '63–; Ed., Expanding Circle (Cities Svc. N.Y. Off.), '61–'63; Asst. Ed., Co. mag., Ark. Fuel Oil Corp. (Shreveport, La.), '54–'61; Cont. Dir., KTBS, '53–'54; Indsl. Eds. of Tulsa, ICIE, AAIE, Okla. Petroleum Cncl.; Tulsa Adv. Fedn. (First Place aw., '68; aws. and hons.); Southern Methodist Univ., '49–'50; La. State Univ., '50–'52; Centenary Col. of La., BA (Liberal Arts), '53; b. San Antonio, Tex., 1931; p. Charles Drew and Louise Burton Collett; res: 1422 E. 41st St., Tulsa, Okla. 74105.

COLLETT, NAOMI JEAN, Adv., Prom. Mgr., Col. Dept., Harper & Row, 49 E. 33rd St., N.Y., N.Y. 10016, '56–; Copywtr., Designer, '46–'56; Info. Bur. Cl., New York Daily News, '46; Colby Col., BA, '45; b. Cambridge, Mass., 1923; p. Charles and Edith Scamman Collett; h. Hugo R. Paganelli; res: 2 Horatio St., N.Y., N.Y. 10014.

COLLIER, SHIRLEY PALMER, Owner-Mgr., Shirley Collier Agency, 1127 Stradella Rd., L.A., Cal. 90024, '43–; actress, leading and supporting film roles, '27–'35; story analyst, 20th Century-Fox, Universal, '35–'36; h. John Collier (div.).

COLLIER, VIRGINIA ROLLWAGE, Wash., D.C. Corr., Associated Publications, Inc., 825 Van Brunt Blvd., Kan. City, Mo. 64124, '62–; Wtr., Econ. Analyst, U.S. Dept. of Commerce, U.S. Dept. of Agriculture, '34–'65; NLAPW (aw., '60), Am. Acad. of Polit. and Social Sci., Nat. Assn. for Am. Composers and Conductors (Wash., D.C. Chptr. Pres., '50–; aw., '53), Nat. Soc. of Arts and Letters (Nat. VP, '64–'66), Motion Picture and TV Cncl. of D.C. (Pres., '51–), D.C. Fedn. of Wms. Clubs aw., '58; Columbia Univ.; George Washington Univ.; Nat. Col. of Educ.; b. Forrest City, Ark.; p. Otto B. and Virginia Anderson Rollwage; h. John F. Collier (div.); res: 5112 Connecticut Ave. N.W., Wash., D.C. 20008.

COLLIER, VIRGINIA SPORE, Lib. Cnslt., Oklahoma Department of Libraries, 109 Capitol Bldg., Okla. City, Okla. 73105, '68–; Dist. Librn., Tulsa City-County Lib., '68; Br. Librn., Nathan Hale Br. Lib., '67; Dir of Bkmobiles, '61–'66; Librn., Okmulgee Public Lib., '53–'60; Asst. Br. Librn., Oakland (Cal.) Public Lib., '45; Asst. Librn., McCloskey Army Hosp. Lib. (Temple, Tex.), '43–'44; County Librn., Austin Public Lib., '40–'43; Tex. Lib. Assn., AAUW, ALA, Southwestern Lib. Assn., Okla. Lib. Assn. (Secy., '58–'59); Okmulgee County Mother of the Year Aw., '59; Univ. of Tex., BA, '40; Emory Univ., BS (Lib. Sci.), '41; b. Dallas, Tex., 1919; p. Leroy and Woodie Black Spore; h. James L. Collier (dec.); c. Dana, Douglas, Marilyn; res: 4316 N.W. 56 Terr., Okla. City, Okla. 73112.

COLLINGS, LOIS WIFFIN, Head Librn., Neb. Wesleyan Univ., 50th and St. Paul, Lincoln, Neb. 68504, '67–; Assoc. Dir., Lincoln City Libs., '64–'67; Children's Coordr., '61–'64; Librn., Christian Col. (Columbia, Mo.), '47–'50; Librn., Lakeview Jr. HS (Battle Creek, Mich.), '46–'47; Librn., Des Plaines Jr. HS (Des Plaines, Ill.), '42–'46; Tchr., '38–'42; ALA, Neb. Lib. Assn. (Pres., '64–'65, VP, '63–'64), Neb. Educ. Media Assn., Beta Phi Mu; Rockford Col., BA (cum laude), '38; Univ. of Chgo., BLS, '46; b. Des Plaines, Ill., 1916; p. Grant and Lillian Carrier Wiffin; h. Wayne Collings; c. Karen, Lawrence Grant, Abbie Jane; res: 2700 Van Dorn St., Lincoln, Neb. 68502.

COLLINS, CAROLE PATRICIA, Sr. Ed., R. R. Bowker Company, 1180 Ave. of the Americas, N.Y., N.Y. 10036, '69–; Ed., '66–'69; Edtl. Asst., New American Lib., '65–'66; Accessories Ed., Women's Wear Daily, '65; Wms. Nat. Bk. Assn., ALA; Manhattanville Col., BA (Eng.), '61; Columbia Univ. '69; b. Wash., D.C., 1939; p. Elmer and Mary Bowles Collins; res: 60 E. 83rd St., N.Y., N.Y. 10028.

COLLINS, DOROTHY, VP, Home & Fashions Div., Infoplan International, Inc., 1345 Ave. of Americas,

N.Y., N.Y. 10019, '66–; PR AE, Ellington & Co., '61–'64; Nat. Dir. Wms. Activities, Nat. Jewish Hosp., '57–'60; PR Mgr., Shwayder Bros., '51–'57; PR Dir., Woman's Home Companion, '49–'51; Fashion Ed., NBC, '47–'49; Wms. Page Ed., Rocky Mountain News, '44–'47; NHFL (VP, '69–'70), Denver Wms. Press Club, Asia House; Univ. of Denver, AB; b. Salt Lake City, Ut.; p. Joseph and Dorothy Frey Collings; h. Akiba Emanuel; c. Lynn Emanuel; res: Hollis Lane, Croton-on-Hudson, N.Y. 10520.

COLLINS, JANE MORIN, Copy Group Head, J. Walter Thompson Co., 420 Lexington Ave., N.Y., N.Y. 10017, '65–; Home Furnishings Ed., Popular Club Plan (N.J.), '60–'65; Partner, Crtv. Cell, crtv. commtns. corp.; Cinemark, art film distributing co: AWNY; b. Pitt., Pa. 1925; p. John and Dorothea Wilson Morin; h. Michael Snowday; c. Christopher Charles Collins, Catherine Victoria Collins; res: 500 W. 111th St., N.Y., N.Y. 10025.

COLLINS, KENALENE JENKINS, Vt. Corr., Colmst., Photogr., Reptr., North Adams Transcript, Bank St., North Adams, Mass., '61–; real estate broker currently; State Rep., '63–'66; Town Auditor, '62–'63; active in polit. and civic affairs; State Mgr., Beauty Cncler., '57–'60; Expediter-Cost Engineer, Free-lance Wtr.; State Pubcty. Dir., Vt., PTA, '64–'65, Citizen's Scholarship Fndn., Friends of Rehabilitation; b. Richford, Vt., 1919; p. H. Kenneth and Nina Colver Jenkins; h. James Foster Collins; c. Jill (Mrs. Harold White, Jr.), Bruce K., W. Scott; res: Readsboro, Vt. 05350.

COLLINS, MABEL L., Sports and Soc. Ed., Enterprise Publishing Company, 207 E. Central St., Harlan, Ky. 40831, '54–; numerous articles on hist. of Harlan County; res: 303 Mound St. Harlan, Ky. 40831.

COLLINS, MARION BRANDT, Publicist, local and nat. philanthrophic groups and commty. svcs., '35–'55, '61–; Staff Wtr., L.A. Times and L.A. Mirror-News, '56–'61; Staff Wtr., S.F. Bulletin, '20–'24; Theta Sigma Phi (Past Chptr. Secy., VP); Univ. of Cal., Berkeley, BA, '24; b. S.F., Cal.; p. Albert and Ruth Heck Brandt; h. Donald C. Collins, M.D. (dec.); c. Ruth (Mrs. Alin Peydad); res: Box 670, S. Lake Tahoe, Cal. 95705.

COLLINS, MAUREEN O'CONNOR, VP, Collins Associates, 225 E. 57th St., N.Y., N.Y. 10022, '66–; '64–; Art Dept., Holt, Rinehart & Winston, '63–'64; N.Y. Public Sch. System, '59–'63; Designer, Illus., Co-auth., five sets religious educ. materials, designed others; Univ. Nat. de San Marcos, '54–'55; Col. of New Rochelle, BA, '59; Pratt Inst., MA, '64; b. Ft. Jay, N.Y., 1936; p. Thomas and Maureen McAdam O'Connor; h. Thomas P. Collins; c. Bonnie Ann, Mark B.; res: 400 E. 56th St., N.Y., N.Y. 10022.

COLMAN, HILA CRAYDER, Auth., 26 bks, '57–, incl. "A Girl from Puerto Rico" (aw., Child Study Assn. of

Am., '62); numerous mag. stories, articles; Auths. Guild, Dem. Town Comm. (Bridgewater, Conn.); Radcliffe, Col.; b. N.Y.C.; p. Harris and Sarah Kinsberg Crayder; h. Louïs Colman; c. James, Jonathan; res: Hemlock Rd., Bridgewater, Conn. 06752; 177 Waverly Pl., N.Y., N.Y. 10014.

COLMAN, JOANNE ELKIN, Free-lance Graphic Designer; 15 bks. for Wayne State Univ.; Comml. Artist, Stone & Simons Adv., '67–'69; Asst. Art Dir., Wayne State Univ., '65–'67; Am. Soc. of Tool & Mfg. Engineers, '55–'56; Comml. Artist, Pictures Inc., '54–'55; Showings at: Bloomfield Art Assoc., Ann Arbor Art Festival, State Fair, Temple Israel, Oak Park Lib., Grand Rapids Art Museum; Wayne State Univ., BFA, '54; b. Detroit, Mich., 1932; p. Benjamin and Rebecca Hayman Elkin; h. (div.); c. Joel Matthew, Victor Jon; res: 21630 Cloverlawn, Oak Park, Mich. 48237.

COLON, CATHARINE RAMBEAU, PR Dir., Yaffe Stone August, Inc. 26711 Woodward Ave., Huntington Woods, Mich. 48070, Former Sportswtr., Soc. Ed., Colmst., weekly nwsp.; PR Dir., Detroit Chptr., CORE, '66; volunteer PR, Wtr., Eugene McCarthy campaign; Univ. of Mich. '54–'56; Wayne State Univ., '63–'65; b. Phila., Pa., 1935; p. Lawrence and Elizabeth Sheetz Rambeau; h. (div.); c. Lewis Lawrence.

COLONE, ANN L. M., Wms. Dir., WANE-TV, Indiana Broadcasting Corp., 2915 W. State Blvd., Ft. Wayne, Ind. 46808, '58–; Prodr., On-Air Hostess; Traf. Mgr. and disc jockey, '50–'58; Traf. Mgr., '47–'50; hostess and prodr., "Ann Colone Show," '58– (Radio TV Mirror Gold Medal, Best TV Wms. Interest Program, Midwest States, '60–'61); extensive personal appearances; leading roles in local theatrical prods.; Ft. Wayne Press Club (Charter Mbr., Bd. of Dirs., '61–'63); Who's Who of Am. Wm.; Bd. Mbr., many civic orgs.; several acting, civic aws.; b. Ft. Wayne, Ind., 1930; p. Joseph and Mary LaRosa Colone; res: 2114 E. Rudisill Blvd., Ft. Wayne, Ind. 46806.

COLSON, ELIZABETH F., Prof. of Anthropology, University of California, Berkeley, Cal. 94720, '64–; Prof., Brandeis Univ., '59–'63; Assoc. Prof., Boston Univ., '55–'59; Goucher Col., '54–'55; Sr. Lectr. Manchester Univ., '51–'53; Dir., Rhodes-Livingstone Inst., '48–'51; Auth: "The Makah, Marriage and the Family Among the Plateau Tonga," "Social Organization of the Gwembe Tonga," "The Plateau Tonga," numerous articles in anthropology field; numerous orgs.; Univ. of Minn., BA, '38; MA, '40; Radcliffe Col., MA, '41; PhD, '45; Manchester Univ. (Simon Sr. Fellowship), '51; Ctr. For Advanced Study in the Behavioral Scis. (Nat. Inst. of Health Special Fellowship), '67–'68; b. Hewitt, Minn., 1917; p. Louis and Metta Damon Colson.

COLSON, GERRY ANNETTE ANDERSON, Pubns. Project Coordr., Autonetics Division, North American Rockwell Corporation, 3370 Miraloma Ave., Anaheim, Cal. 92803, '64–; Sls. Prom. Supvsr., Autonetics

Indsl. Products, '59–'62; W. Coast Pubcty. Dir., Compton Advertising (L.A., Cal.), '55–'59; Asst. Adv. Mgr., Zellerbach Paper Co. (S.F., Cal.), '54–'55; Feature Prodr., NBC-TV "Today" Show (N.Y.C.), '52–'53; NBC, '50–'51; Pubcty.-Adv. Dir., Apollo Records, '47–'49; Copywtr., KJBS Radio (S.F., Cal.), '43–'45; Wtr., filmstrips; AWRT (Cal. State Pres., '55, '56), L.A. Adv. Wm., Adv. Assn. of the West; Univ. of Wash., '40–'42, '45; Columbia Univ., '47; Univ. of Cal., '61, '65; b. Seattle, Wash., 1921; p. Emil and Ida Vike Anderson; h. Harrison Colson (div.); res: 1143 Gleneagles Terr., Costa Mesa, Cal. 92627.

COLTMAN, NATALIE WALSH, Tech. Svcs. Librn., Bucks County Free Library, 50 N. Main St., Doylestown, Pa. 18901, '68–; staff, '64–'68; Head Librn., Del. Valley Col., '60–'63; Acting Librn., '58–'60; ALA, Pa. Lib. Assn.; Vassar Col., AB, '31; Drexel Univ., MS (Lib. Sci.), '60; b. Reading, Mass.; p. Richard and Ruby A. Walsh; h. Robert Coltman (dec.); c. Robert, Alan C.; res: R.R. 1, Box 165, Perkasie, Pa. 18944.

COLTOM, SCOTT B., Prod. Mgr., Excerpta Medica Foundation, 2 E. 103rd St., N.Y, N.Y. 10029, '68; Copywtr., Sears Roebuck; Asst. Sls. Prom., Lily Tulip Cup Corp.; Admr. Trade Sls., Hearst Magazines; Hunter Col., Sch. of Gen. Studies; b. N.Y.C., 1938; p. Irving and Sally Benard Colton; res: 242 E. 83rd St., N.Y., N.Y. 10028.

COLWIN, ESTELLE WOLFSON, Dir., Estelle W. Colwin Assn., Oak Lane Manor, Valley Rd., Melrose Park, Pa., '63–; Art Cnslt: WTTW (Chgo.), Vincent Price art exhibits for Sears Roebuck, Benjamin Franklin Hotel (Phila.), and others; Cheltenham Art Cntr. (VP, '59–'65), Artists Equity of Phila. (Bd. Mbr., '68–'69), NHFL (VP, '67–'69; Bd. Mbr.), Art Alliance of Phila.; Best Cook aw., Stokley Van Camp; Hon. Citizen of N.O., La.; Columbia Univ.; N.Y. Sch. of Interior Design; Phila. Fashion Group; b. N.Y.C., 1924; p. David and Fay Evelyn Stein Wolfson; h. Peter B. Colwin; c. Laurie Evelyn, Leslie Fay Friedman; res: Oak Lane Manor, Valley Rd., Melrose Park, Pa.

COMER, BETTY LOUISE, Textbk. Ed., Harper & Row, Publishers, 2500 Crawford Ave., Evanston, Ill. 60201, '68–; Textbk. Ed., Scott, Foresman and Co. (Glenview), '57–'68; Textbk. Ed., McGraw-Hill Book Co. (N.Y.C.), '52–'57; Instr. speech and drama, St. Louis Univ., '47–'49; Tchr., Wis. Public Schs., '43–'46; Lectr. in speech, Loyola Univ. (Chgo.), '59–'62; Marquette Univ., BA, '43 (cum laude); Northwestern Univ., MA, '47; b. Mauston, Wis.; p. M. M. and Helen Ely Comer; res: 1680 Landwehr Rd., Northbrook, Ill. 60062.

COMER, EVELYN F., Food Ed., Wtr., The Charleston Gazette, 1001 Virginia St. E., Charleston, W.Va. 25330, '56–; Movie, TV-Radio Ed., '55–'56; Wtr., WTIP Radio, '52–'55; Wtr., WKNA Radio, '49–'52; h. R. G. Comer.

COMPTON, SUSAN LaNELL, Auth., "Beauty Transient and Other Poems" (The Christopher Publ. House, '69); Head, Catalog Dept., Arkansas Library Commission, 506-1/2 Center St., Little Rock, Ark. 72201, '49–; Asst. Cataloger, Gen. Lib., Univ. of Ark., '48–'49; Jr. and Sr. Cl., Hygienic Lab., State Bd. of Health, '42–'47; Contrbr., Ark. state article for Crowell-Collier Encys., '57– (Special Ed. for Ark.), '62–'68; Cit. of Recognition, '67); ALA, Ark. Lib. Assn. (Life Mbr.), AAUW, Ark. Hist. Assn., Am. Acad. of Polit. and Soc. Sci., NLAPW; Dic. of Intl. Biog.; Who's Who, Lib. (Advisory Mbr.); Little Rock Jr. Col., '35–'36; Ark. State Tchrs. Col., BS (Educ.), '39; Peabody Lib. Sch., BS (Lib. Sci.), '48; b. Batesville, Ark., 1917; p. Thomas Smith and Susan Whitlow Compton, Jr.; res: 3615 W. 11th St., Little Rock, Ark. 72204.

COMSTOCK, NANINA EVELYN, Ed.-in-Chief, McCall Corporation, 230 Park Ave., N.Y., N.Y. 10017, '52–; Ed.-in-Chief: McCall's Summer Made-it Ideas, '66–; McCall's Christmas Made-it Ideas, '58–; McCall's Needlework & Crafts Magazine, '52–; Exec. Ed., '51–'52; Merchandising Ed., '48–'51; Prod. Mgr. '41–'48; Designer, McCall's Hot Iron Transfers, '41–'45; Needlework Designer, Wms. Educ. and Indsl. Un. (Boston, Mass.), '35–'40; Tchr., Home Industries and Handcrafts, '32–'34; NHFL, The Fashion Group, Pen and Brush Club, Am. Soc. of Dowsers, Assn. for Rsch. and Enlightenment; Museum Sch. of Fine Arts, Boston, Mass., '30; Cooper Un. Art Sch., '31; ext. courses, Boston Univ., N.Y.U. and private instr.; b. Vienna, Me.; p. Hiram A. and Ada Marr Comstock; res: 240 E. 52nd St., N.Y., N.Y. 10022.

CONARD, VIRGINIA POWELL, Co-publr., Co-ed., The Kiowa County Signal and The Haviland Journal, 112 N. Main, Greensburg, Kan. 67054, '56; Bus. Sch. Instr., Wash., D.C., Silver Spring, Md., '55–'56; Adm. Asst., Marshall Plan, Paris, France, '49–'54; Instr., Bus. Sch., Univ. of Kan., '48–'49; Kan. Press Wm. (Pres., '66–'68; several 1st place aws., writing contest, '56–'65), NFPW (2nd VP, '68); Theta Sigma Phi Outstanding Wm. Jnlst. of Kan., '64, '65; several 1st place writing, photog. aws., Kan. Press Assn. Better Nwsp. Contest, '56–'65; Univ. of Kan. grad., '48; b. Olathe, Kan., 1926; p. James and Maude Alfrey Powell; h. John J. Conard; c. James P., Spencer D., John J., Jr.

CONE, MOLLY LAMKEN, Auth, children's bks. incl. "Annie Annie" (Houghton Mifflin Co., '69), "Mishmash and Uncle Looey" (Houghton Mifflin Co., '68), 21 others; Auths. Guild of Auths. League of Am., Wash. State Press Wm., Free-lance Wtrs. of Seattle (Aw., '68), Hadassah (Seattle Chptr. lit. aw., '67); Univ. of Wash., '36–'38; b. Tacoma, Wash., 1918; p. Arthur and Frances Sussman Lamken; h. Gerald J. Cone; c. Susan (Mrs. Gary Dale), Gary, Ellen; res: 6500 50th St. N.E., Seattle, Wash. 98115.

CONFORTI, LORRAINE ROY, Rsch. Assoc., Lieberman Research, Inc., 633 Third Ave., N.Y., N.Y. 10017, '69–; Brand Group Rsch. Mgr., R. J. Reynolds Foods, '69; Rsch. Act. Mgr., Kenyon & Eckhardt, '67–'69;

Project Dir., '64–'67; Project Dir., Licensed Beverage Industries, '62–'64; Am. Mktng. Assn., Am. Psychological Assn.; Emmanuel Col., BA, '61 (with distinction); Université de Montréal, MA, '62 (Felicitas); b. Lewiston, Me., 1939; p. Victor and Stella Carignan Roy; h. Hashmonai Conforti; res: 101 W. 12th St., N.Y., N.Y. 10011.

CONGDON, JEANETTE LeBRECHT, Media Planning Cnslt. (Self Employed), Snow Hill Farm, Girdletree, Md. 21829, '68–; Media Dir., Johnstone, Inc., '66–'68; Media Dir./VP, Grant Adv., '60–'66; Asst. Media Dir., Cohen & Aleshire, '47–'60; AWNY (Treas., '60–'63), Media Planners Assn., (Dir., '60–'63), Media Byrs. Assn. (VP, '55–'56); Printers Ink Silver Medal, '66; N.Y.U., BS, '37; b. N.Y.C., 1917; p. Frank and Augusta Alexander LeBrecht; h. Robert S. Congdon; c. Robert S., Jr., Sidney B., II; res: Snow Hill Farm, Girdletree, Md. 21829.

CONKLIN, GLADYS PLEMON, Supvsr., Children's Work, Hayward (Cal.) Public Lib., '50–'65; Children's Librn., L.A. Public Lib., '34–'42; N.Y.C. Public Lib., '29–'31; Ventura, Cal., '26–'28; Auth: "Little Apes," "How Insects Grow," eight other juv. bks.; Cal. Lib. Assn. (Children's Sec. Pres., '64), ALA, WNBA, Assn. of Children's Librns.; Univ. of Wash., BS (Lib. Sci.), '26; b. Harpster, Idaho; p. L. O. and Hettie Myers Plemon; h. Irving Conklin; res: 16582 Kent Ave., San Lorenzo, Cal. 94580.

CONLEY, NELL HURLEY, Ed., Oregon Telephone News, Pacific Northwest Bell Telephone Co., 421 S.W. Oak St., Portland, Ore. 97204, '65–; Assoc. Ed., '64–'65; Special Asst., Adv., '57–'63; Wtr., '54–'56; Free-lance articles; ICIE (Aw. of Merit, '68), Ore. Assn. of Eds. and Communicators (Aw. of Merit, '68); Rodney Adair Award, 1969); b. Ellensburg, Wash., 1918; p. Thomas and Margaret Hunter Hurley; h. John Conley; c. Colleen Anne Peacock; res: 15005 S.E. Woodward St., Portland, Ore. 97236.

CONLEY, SUSANNE ENGLISH, Free-lance Drama and Gen. Trade Ed.-Wtr., '69–; Trade Bk. Ed., Bobbs-Merrill Co., '68–'69; Prod. Ed., Art Dir., '67–'68; Art Dir., '66–'67; Contrbr: The Village Voice, The Open Theatre, Theatre Genesis; HB Studio; Georgetown Jr. Col., AA, '57; The New Sch. for Social Rsch:, '64; b. Scranton, Pa. 1938; p. Joseph and Rosemary Sullivan English; h. John Conley (div.); c. Patrick, Michael; res: 237 W. 11 St., N.Y., N.Y. 10014.

CONNALLY, EUGENIA HORSTMAN, Ed.-in-Chief, National Parks Magazine, 1701 18th St., N.W., Wash., D.C. 20009, '69–; Mgr., Technipress, Inc., '63–'69; Univ. of Md., BA, '61 (First Hons., Phi Kappa Phi, Alpha Lambda Delta); b. Wash., D.C.; p. Emanuel E. and Maye Hemphill Horstman; c. Lara Kay.

CONNELL, ELEANOR BOYER, VP, Warwick & Legler, Inc., 375 Park Ave., N.Y., N.Y. 10022, '55–; Ogilvy & Mather Adv., '48–'55; Wtr., articles for Glamour,

Mademoiselle, Holiday; N.Y. Fashion Group, Fragrance Fndn.; adv. aws.; incl. Grand Aw., N.Y. Film Festival, TV Comml., '67; Univ. of Minn., BA; Reed Col., grad. work; b. Chatfield, Minn.; p. William and Eleanor Harrington Boyer; h. Howard Connell; c. Frederic Alan, Jane Andrea; res: 60 Sutton Pl., S., N.Y., N.Y., 10022.

CONNELL, LOUISE FOX, Free-lance Wtr., c/o Brandt & Brandt, 101 Park Ave., N.Y., N.Y. 10017; Contract Wtr., Conde Nast, '41–'43; Mng. Ed., Assoc. Ed., Charm (Newark), '23–'25; Assoc. Ed., Wtr., Delineator Magazine, Butterick, '20–'23; Adv. Wtr., J. Water Thompson, '15–'20; numerous articles on health, human rel., wms. problems; play: "The Queen Bee" (collaboration; Broadway, '29); Query Club, League of Wm. Voters, numerous ch. welfare, civic and peace orgs.; b. Bayonne, N.J.; p. Hugh and Virginia Herrick Fox; h. Richard Connell (dec.); res: 240 E. 82 St., N.Y., N.Y. 10028.

CONNELL, MARY ANN LOCASCIO, Asst. TV Prodr. TV Traf. Coordr., Perrin & Associates, Inc., 8 S. Michigan Ave., Chgo., Ill. 60603; Northern Ill. Univ., '60–'61; b. Chgo., Ill., 1942; p. Alphonso and Ann Sabas Locascio; h. John Connell.

CONNER, BERENICE GILLETTE, Chmn., Eng. Dept., Killian Senior High School, Dade County School Board, Lindsay Hopkins Bldg., Second Ave., Miami, Fla., 33146, '69; Tchr., Eng. Lit., '59–'69; Tchr., '55–'69; Girl Scout Exec. Dir., Overseas, '47–'55; Auth: Teaching Handbks., "Using Newspapers in Classroom," "Making Reading Fun," "Sequential Writing Units," "Comparative Religions": Delta Kappa Gamma (PR Chmn.), '68–'69), Theta Sigma Phi, NLAPW (Chmn. Writing Workshop, Opus Owls, '66–'69); Owner, Weaving Studio, fabrics created, articles, lectures on weaving; Univ. of Pitt., '30–'32; Univ. of Miami, BA, '55; MA, '57; Oxford Univ., England, '58; b. Balt., Md; p. N. Troy and Berenice Patterson Gillette; h. James Conner (dec.); c. Wm. W., Mrs. John Hooton, Mrs. Richard Tarbox; res: 8960 S.W. 192 Dr., Miami, Fla. 33157.

CONNER, SHIRLEY ROBERTS, Reptr., The News, Tonawanda Publishing Corp., 435 River Rd., N. Tonawanda, N.Y. 14121, '63–; News Corr., Feature Wtr; Buffalo News, Tonawanda News, Union Sun and Jnl., Niagara Falls Gazette; Am. Educ. Wtrs. Assn., Greater Buffalo Radio, Press and TV Assn., Buffalo Nwsp. Guild; Page one aw., '67; Sci. writing aw., Cornell Aeronautical Labs., '67 and '68; 1st Pl. aw., N.Y. State Publishers Assn., '69; State Univ. Col., Buffalo, BS (Educ.), '43; b. Lockport, N.Y., 1923; p. George and Marian Thompson Roberts; h. James Conner; c. Coleen, Janine; res: 4933 Mapleton Rd., Lockport, N.Y. 14094.

CONNOLLY, MARY JOE, Assoc. Ed., King Features Syndicate, 235 E. 25th St., N.Y., N.Y. 10017; Asst. Ed., Photogr.-Reptr.; Photogr.-Reptr., Hearst Predate

Svc.; Photogr., Intl. News Photos; OPC, NWC, N.Y. Press Photogrs. Assn., Ancient Order of Hibernians Ladies Aux.; Trinity Col., Univ. of Mo.; b. Mt. Vernon, N.Y., 1924; p. Joseph V. and Marguerite Stanford Connolly.

CONNOLLY, VIOLETTE MARTENS, Cnslt. PR, Radio-TV, Association of the Junior Leagues of America, 825 Third Ave., N.Y., N.Y. 10022, '64–; Partner, J. V. Connolly Co. (PR), '57–'64; Elser & Assoc. (PR), '54–'56; Analyst, The Payne Fund, '41–'53; Nat. Visual Commtns. Assn. (Treas., '67; PRSA (accredited mbr.), AWRT, Nat. PR Cncl. of Health & Welfare Svcs.; Hunter Col., BA, '40, Columbia Univ., MS, '41; b. N.Y.C., 1919; p. Gysbert and Marie DePont Martens; h. Joseph V. Connolly Jr.; res: 29 Fifth Ave., N.Y., N.Y. 10003.

CONNOR, MARION JONES, Colmst., News and Feature Wtr., Suburban and Wayne Times, and Daily Local News, '58–; Auth., short stories; hist. novel, "Norbert of Zanten" ('57); grad. nurse; h. C. Maurice Connor; res: Connemara, 111 Fennerton Rd., Paoli, Pa. 19301.

CONNORS, DORSEY, Synd. Colmst., "Hi I'm Dorsey Connors," Publishers-Hall Syndicate, 30 E. 42nd St., N.Y., N.Y. 10017; TV Commentator, NBC (Chgo., Ill.), '49–'64; Midwest Ed., "Home"; Auth, "Gadgets Galore" ('53); AFTRA, SAG, NATAS, Fashion Group, Guild of Chgo. Hist. Soc., Chgo. Beautiful Comm., Chi Omega, Ill. Epilepsy League (founder), Ill. Children's Home and Aid Soc. (Wms. Bd.); Univ. of Ill., BA; b. Chgo., Ill.; p. William J. and Sarah Maclean Connors; h. John E. Forbes; c. Stephanie (Mrs. Edward J. Lyng); res: 227 E. Delaware Pl., Chgo., Ill. 60611.

CONTE, ELIZABETH STUDIER, Art Dir., Campbell-Dickey Advertising, Inc., 2001 N.E. 48th St., Ft. Lauderdale, Fla. 33308, '68–; Asst. Art Dir., '62–'68; Free-lance Artist, '61–'62; Art Dir., J. Popovich Adv. (L.A., Cal.), '58–'62; Artist, Rochester (N.Y.) Poster, '58; NFAA (Aws. Competition, '67–'68); Haiku Design Contest Aw. ('67); Rochester Inst. of Tech. (Art and Design), '56–'58 (State Scholarship; Art Scholarship; Dean's List); b. Rochester, N.Y., 1939; p. Elmer and Mary Murphy Studier; h. Ralph Conte; c. Ralph, Rick, Robin; res: 2830 N.E. 59th St., Ft. Lauderdale, Fla. 33308.

CONWELL, CAROLYN MAIER, Actress: "Insight" (TV, '65); "Torn Curtain" (Alfred Hitchcock Prods., '65); "Boston Strangler" (20th Century Fox, '68), "The Big Valley" (TV, 4-Star Prod., '67–'68); "The World of Ray Bradbury" (Stage, '64); Peninsula Players (Fish Creek, Wis.); AEA, SAG, AFTRA; Lawrence Col. (Sunset Players); b. Chgo., Ill., 1938; p. Ernest and Sigrid Erickson Maier; h. Richard Conwell; c. Eric John, James Ernest, Virginia Jo; res: 907 Millmark Grove, San Pedro, Cal. 90731.

CONYERS, MARJORIE MILLER, Pres., Conyers

Agency, 749 W. Central Ave., Toledo, Oh. 43610; previously Toledo Assoc.; Toledo Bd. of Educ.; U.S. Adv. Agcy.; J. R. Flanagan Adv., N.Y.C.; Edelstein and Conyers; PRSA (Chptr. Secy., '65); Wms. Adv. Club of Toledo (VP, '61), Toledo Better Bus. Bur. (Bd. of Dirs., Secy., '69), Toledo Area C. of C., ZONTA; Toledo Adv. Wm. of the Yr., '59, '61; b. Defiance, Oh.; p. Frank and Edith Crandall Miller; h. Stark Conyers; c. Carole A., Charles W.; res: 3138 Scott-wood Ave., Toledo, Oh. 43610.

COOK, ELIZABETH RAPÉ, Pres., Metcalfe-Cook and Smith, Inc., 168 Fourth Ave. N., Nashville, Tenn. 37219, '69–; Crtv. Dir., '65–; Savage-Stanford-Hamil-ton and Kerr, '63–65; Sr. Copywtr., McCann-Erickson, Atlanta, Ga., '58–'62; Acct. Exec., Bearden-Thompson-Frankel, '55–'58; Prom. Wtr., Atlanta Journal-Consti-tution, '52–'55; PR, Trust Co. of Ga., '51; Cntrbr., Nashville Magazine; Nashville Adv. Fedn. (Bd. of Dirs.; Mbr. of the Yr., '67), AWRT (Chptr. VP); 2,000 Wm. of Achiev.; Diamond Aws. Winner, Outstanding TV Comml., '68; h. Joseph D. Cook (dec); res: 1204 Windsor Towers, Nashville, Tenn. 37205.

COOK, ESTHER HOWARD, Space Byr. and Media Dir., Gillham Advertising, Inc., Deseret Plaza, 15 E. First S., Salt Lake City, Ut. 84111, '52–; Univ. of Ut.; b. Salt Lake City, Ut., 1918; p. William and Ruth Hocking Howard; h. Joseph Cook; c. Linda Ann Gardner; res: 4700 Wander Lane, Holladay, Ut. 84117.

COOK, GLADYS EMERSON, Free-lance animal art-ist, 32 Union Sq., N.Y., N.Y. 10003; Illus., 22 bks.; Auth., 12 animals bks.; Soc. Am. Graphic Artists, Am. Artists Guild, AAUW, Fellow Royal Soc. of Arts of England; Skidmore Col., BS; Univ. of Wis., MS; b. Haverhill, Mass.; p. George and Hattie Emerson Cook; res: Hotel Wolcott, 4 W. 31st St., N.Y., N.Y. 10001.

COOK, MARY HAWKINS, High School Eng. Tchr. Text book Collaborator; Theta Sigma Phi (Chptr. Pres., '68–'69); Ind. Univ., BA, '22; Oh. State Univ. Col. of Educ., '30; Univ. of Chgo., '30–'31; b. Springfield, Ill.; p. Martin and Mary Devaney Hawkins; h. Dr. Kenneth W. Cook; c. Dr. William A., Thomas K.; res: 2140 Cambridge Blvd., Columbus, Oh. 43221.

COOKE, ANNA LEE, Librn., Lane College, 501 Lane Ave., Jackson, Tenn. 38301, '67–; Catalog Librn., '63–'67; Colmst., Defender Publ., '51–'63; Librn., Jack-son City Sch. System, '47–'51; Principal, Haywood Co. Sch. System, '44–'46; Ed., The Reporter (Lane Col. Alumni), '65–'69; Cnslt.; NEA, Tenn. Educ. Assn., ALA, Tenn. and W. Tenn. Lib. Assns.; Hon. Fellowship, Philosophical Soc. of Eng., '69; Delta Sigma Theta Aw., '68; Dic. of Intl Biog., Who's Who of Am. Wm.; Lane Col., BA, '44; Atlanta Univ., MS (Lib. Sci.), '55; b. Jack-son, Tenn., 1923; p. Thurston and Effie Cage Lee; h. James A. Cooke; c. Elsie Louise; res: 120 Hale St., Jack-son, Tenn. 38301.

COOKE, EILEEN D., Assoc. Dir., American Library Association, Washington Office, 200 C St., Wash., D.C. 20003, '68–; Asst. Dir., '64–'68; Co-ed., ALA Wash. Nwsltr.; Colmst., ALA Bul., Wilson Lib. Bul.; PR Spe-cialist, Mpls. Public Lib., '62–'63; Hosp. Librn., '59–'62; Br. Asst., '58–'59; Bookmobile Librn., '52–'57; Br. Asst., Queens Borough (N.Y.) Public Library, '57–'58; ALA, D.C. Lib. Assn.; Minn. Lib. Assn.; Col. of St. Catherine, BS (Lib. Sci.), '52.

COOKSON, BEATRICE STRAIGHT, Actress, Prodr., c/o Garfield-Brooks Associates, 527 Madison Ave., N.Y., N.Y. 10022; Broadway: "The Crucible" (Antoinette Perry Aw.), "Eastward in Eden," "The Innocents," many others; films: "The Nun's Story," "Patterns," "Phone Call From a Stranger," others; off-Broadway appearances incl: "Everything in the Garden," "Street Car Named Desire"; founder, Chekhov Studio, Eng., and Theatre, Inc., U.S.; b. Westbury, N.Y.; h. Peter Cookson.

COOLEY, ETHEL HALCROW, Pres., Minot Broad-casting Company, Inc., Box 10, Minot, N.D. 58701, '58–; Farm Ed., Grand Forks Herald and Watertown Public Opinion, '19–'60; Univ. of N.D., AB (Eng.), '14; Wesley Col. of Expression grad., '14; b. Norwesta, N.D., 1888; p. John and Elizabeth Manson Halcrow; h. John Booth Cooley; c. Mrs. W. O. S. Sutherland, Mrs. J. S. Massee; res: 710 S. Main, Minot, N.D. 58701.

COOLIDGE, MARGARET ENSOR, Auth., children's bks., "George Bernard Shaw" (Houghton Mifflin); "Tom Paine, Revolutionary" (Scribner); "The Maid of Artemis" (Houghton Mifflin), and numerous others; Tchr., Eng. Lit. (Boston, Mass.), '38–'46; Tchr., Latin and Greek (London, Eng.), '33–'37; Tchr., Eng. (Potsdam, Germany), '32–'33; Auths. Guild, Children's Bk. Guild of Wash., D.C.; Oxford Univ., Eng., BA, MA, '27–'31; b. London, Eng.; p. Sir Robert Charles Kirk-wood and Helen Fisher Ensor; h. Archibald C. Cool-idge; c. Archibald, Julian, Susan (Mrs. Barnes), Eliza-beth (Mrs. Miller); res: R.D. 3, Box 133, Cambridge, Md. 21613.

COOLIDGE, MARY RYAN, TV, Radio, Entertain-ment Ed., The Tampa Times, E. Kennedy Blvd., Tampa, Fla. 33601, '66–; Feature Wtr., Asst. Social Ed., The Patriot Ledger, Quincy, Mass., 20 yrs; b. Lincoln, Mass; h. Walter Coolidge; c. one son; res: 8404 Still-brook Ave., Bay Crest Park, Tampa, Fla. 33615.

COON, JACQUELINE MITCHELL, TV model, c/o Mary Webb Davis and William Cunningham, 8743 Sunset Blvd. and 9000 Sunset Blvd., Hollywood, Cal. 90060, '63–; formerly mag., film, TV work; charm sch. tchr.; pfsnl. radio sch.; b. Kan. City, Mo., 1930; p. Howard and Louise Klopf Owings; h. Gene Coon; c. Kathleen Kay Mitchell; res: 8015 Briar Summit Dr., L.A., Cal. 90046.

COONEY, BARBARA SCHENCK, Free-lance Illus., over 70 bks., mostly juv.; also Auth.-Illus.; Caldecott

Medal, '58; Smith Col., BA, '38; Art Students' League; b. Bklyn., N.Y., 1917; p. Russell S. and Mae Bossert Cooney; h. Charles Talbot Porter; c. Gretel Nandy, Barnaby Porter, Charles T. Porter, Jr., Phoebe Ann Porter; res: 1 Elm St., Pepperell, Mass. 01463.

COONEY, JOAN GANZ, Pres., Children's Television Workshop, 1865 Broadway, N.Y., N.Y. 10023, '68–; TV Cnslt., Carnegie Corp., '67–'68; Prodr., WNDT (Ch. 13), N.Y.C., '62–'67; Staff Asst., TV, U.S. Steel Corp., '55–'62; Wtr., Press Dept., National Broadcasting Company, '54–'55; study for Carnegie Corp., "The Potential Uses of Television in Preschool Education;" '66; AWRT, NOW; N.Y. Emmy for "Poverty, Anti-Poverty and the Poor," '65–'66; Oh. State Univ. Dirs. Aw. for "Sesame Street," '70; Univ. of Ariz., BA (Educ.), '51 (with distinction, senior honors, Baird scholar, '51; Pi Lamda Theta); DSc (hon.), Boston Col., '70; b. Phoenix, Ariz., 1929; p. Sylvan C. and Pauline Riordon Ganz; h. Timothy Cooney; res: 201 E. 21st St., N.Y., N.Y. 10010.

COOPER, BERNICE STEINBERG, Pres., Ani-Live Film Service, 45 W. 45th St., N.Y., N.Y. 10036, '54–; Film Ed., Academy Pics., '53–'54; Tempo Prod., '51–'53; Paramount Pics., '44–'51; TV commls. for adv. agencies; projects for Columbia Univ.; articles for wkly. TV nwsp.; NATAS aws., film festivals: Intl., Am., Cannes, '57–'69; numerous editing aws. for TV commls.; h. Sidney Cooper; c. Diane; res: Fairway Court, Roslyn Harbor, N.Y. 11576.

COOPER, CONSTANCE LEE, PR Wtr., Fund-raiser; Chmn., Jackson County Chptr., The Nat. Fndn., March of Dimes, '69–'70; Public Educ. Chmn., '68–'69; Mother's March Chmn., '67; AE, Barickman & Selders Adv. Agcy., '63–'66; Owner, Pres., Connie M. Skinner Gifts, '55–; AWRT (Kan. City Chptr. Pres., '65), Radio and TV Cncl. of Gtr. Kan. City (VP, '66), Planned Parenthood, Wms. C. of C.; 2,000 Wm. of Achiev.; b. Kan. City, Mo., 1923; p. Lester and Clara Broman Fisher; h. Thom R. Cooper; c. Thom Jr., Mrs. Jerry E. Druen, Jr.; res: 6542 Wenonga Rd., Shawnee Mission, Kan. 66208.

COOPER, EFFIE ANN, Wtr., Publicist, Jobson Associates, Inc., 9 Rockefeller Plaza, N.Y., N.Y. 10020, '67–; Station Mgr., KADS Radio (L.A., Cal.), '66–'67; Opns. Mgr., KPPC Radio (Pasadena), '64–'66; KHJ-TV (Hollywood), '64; KCOP-TV, '62–'63; AWRT (L.A. Chptr. Secy., '67); Ind. State Col., '55–'57; Adrian Col., '57–'58; b. Pitt., Pa., 1937; p. T. Stanley and Thelma Stell Cooper; res: 200 W. 54th St., N.Y., N.Y. 10019.

COOPER, ELEANOR A., Dir., Radio-TV Dept., Dudley-Anderson-Yutzy, 551 Fifth Ave., N.Y., N.Y. 10017; N.Y. Sch. of Interior Design; Hunter Col; b. Brooklyn, N.Y.; p. Isaac and Dora Sturman Cooper; res: 210 E. 58th St., N.Y., N.Y. 10022.

COOPER, GEORGIANA RICHARDSON, Wms. Pg. Ed., Portales News-Tribune, Box 848, Portales, N.M.

88130, '55–; Tchr., Roosevelt Co., N.M., Bailey Co., Tex., five yrs.; BPW (Corr. Secy.; Pres., '62–'63); Altrusa Club; Highlands Univ., '24; Tex. Tech, '25–'35; Eastern N.M. Univ., special courses, workshops, '52–'69; b. Floydada, Tex., 1906; p. Robert and Lillian Merrick Richardson; h. Marshall M. Cooper; c. Mrs. Laurie Wright, Mrs. Lillian Jones, Lewis L.; res: 1206 W. Fair, Portales, N.M. 88130.

COOPER, JEANNE, Actress, Suite 211, 315 S. Beverly Dr., Beverly Hills, Cal. 90212 SAG, AFTRA, AEA, AMPAS, ATAS; Emmy nomination, '63; Univ. of Pacific; b. Taft, Calif.; p. Troy and Sildeth Moore Cooper; h. Harry Bernsen; c. Corbin, Collin, Caren; res: 505 N. Hillcrest Rd., Beverly Hills, Cal. 90210.

COOPER, MARJORIE L., Illus. 50 children's bks.; Auth., one children's bk. (Rand McNally and Co.); Artist, Gibson Greeting Cards, Cincinnati, Oh. 45237, '58–; Rust Craft, Boston, Mass., '34–'58; WNBA; listed in "Romance of Greeting Cards" (U.S., '56), "History of Christmas Card" (Eng., '54); Student of W. F. Noyes, '25–'35; Sculpture Study, Copley Soc., '35–'40; Mass. Sch. of Art (Adv.); b. West Newton, Mass.; p. William and Edna Weeks Cooper; res: 6 Anchor Lane, E. Falmouth, Mass. 02536.

COOPER, RITA KELLER, VP, Review Publishing Company, Inc., 1100 Waterway Blvd., Indpls., Ind. 46202, '67–; Ed., Bus. Mgr., Child Life, Design, The Brownie Reader, Children's Playmate Mags., '67–; Ed., Bus. Mgr., Amateur Athlete, '69; Mng. Ed., Child Life and Design Mags., '66–'67; Assoc. Ed., Topics Newspapers, '65–'66; Asst. Dir. of Mktng., Stark and Wetzel Co., '64–'65; Purdue Univ., '58–'60; b. Indpls., Ind., 1940; p. Miller and Mary Lux Keller; h. V. K. Cooper, Sr.; c. Vernon Kelley, Jr., Catherine Marie; res: 4425 Berkshire Rd., Indpls., Ind. 46226.

COOTS, OLLIE BOYERS, Soc. Ed., Sun-Democrat, 408 Kentucky Ave., Paducah, Ky. 42001, '67–; Reptr., The Franklin Favorite, WFKN, Franklin, Ky.; Transylvania Col., Lexington, Ky.; Univ. of Ky.; b. Alexandria, Ky., 1915; p. Edward and Mary Truesdell Boyers; h. Woodrow Coots; c. Lou Anna, Mary Carol (Mrs. Joseph G. Katzel); res: 330 N. 38th St., Paducah, Ky. 42001.

COPE, SUSAN BOWEN, Dir., Sls. Svc., WCIV (TV), Highway 703, Charleston, S.C. 29464, '67–; Prom. Dir., Copywtr., Bdcstr., WQSN Radio, '62–'67; Prom. Dir., Copywtr., Bdcstr., WMRB Radio (Greenville); AWRT, Greenville Adv. Club; Furman Univ.; res: Zero South Battery, Charleston, S.C. 29401.

COPELAND, AMORITA SESINGER, Field Dir., Pennsylvania Department of Health, Timberhaven, R.D. 1, Lewisburg, Pa. 17837, '68–; PR, Fund Raising Cnslt., '67–; N.Y.U., '58–'67; Fairleigh Dickinson Univ., '57–'58; Girl Scouts of the U.S.A., '50–'57; N.Y. Infirmary, '49–'50; Columbia Univ., '48–'49; Planned Parenthood Fedn. of Am., '47–'48; Am. Wms. Voluntary

Svcs., '42–'44; PRSA (Accred., '65; Past Mbr., Bd. of Dirs.), Assn. of Fundraising Dirs. (Past Secy.), Nat. Soc. of Fund Raisers; DAR Citizenship aw., '43; War Prod. Bd. aw., '44; Bucknell Univ., AB, '22; b. Phila., Pa.; p. Charles and Pauline Beckler Sesinger; h. Charles E. Copeland (dec.); res: 1130 Washington Ave., Lewisburg, Pa. 17837.

COPELAND, HELEN J., Wms. Ed., Daily Times, 110 W. Jefferson St., Ottawa, Ill. 61350, '44–; BPW Career Wm. of the Yr., '67; UPI Aws.: two 1st Place aws., Ill. Wms. Page; 1st Place, Fashion Layout; 2nd Place, Feature Story, '69; 2nd Place, Wms. Pg., '67; three 2nd place aws. in state contests, '65; Who's Who in Am.; b. Kankakee, Ill.; p. John and Susie Crawford Copeland; res: 507 E. Main, Ottawa, Ill. 61350.

COPES, JOYCE McEOWN, Soc. Ed., Woodbury Daily Times, 309 S. Broad St., Woodbury, N.J. 08096, '65–'69; Marine Corps Colmst., Albany (Ga.) Herald, '64–'65; Feature Wtr., Merchants and Manufacturers, L.A., Cal., '52–'53; Claresholm (Alberta) Press, '50–'51; PR lectr.; judge: N.J. State Fedn. of Wms. Clubs press bks., beauty pageants, parades; active in commty., soc. orgs.; U.S. Army Cert. of Appreciation, '67; b. Saskatoon, Saskatchewan, 1928; p. Rosswell and Dorothy Powell McEown; h. William Copes; c. Warren E., Kenneth S.; res: 24 Cherry Lane, Woodbury, N.J. 08096.

COPLAN, KATE MILDRED, Wtr., Publicist, Display Cnslt.; Dir., Kate Coplan and Assoc., '64–'65; Chief, Exhibits and Pubcty., Enoch Pratt Free Lib., '34–'63; Pubcty Asst., '27–'34; Auth: "Poster Ideas and Bulletin Board Techniques" (Oceana Pubns., '62), "Effective Library Exhibits" (Oceana Pubns., '58); ALA, Md., Lib. Assns., Balt. PR Cncl. (Secy., '51); Balt. Wm. of Achiev., '50; Display World mag. aw., '50; Balt. Bpw Wm. of the Yr. aw., '63; Hadassah aw., '67; b. Balt., Md., 1901; p. Max and Sarah Hermon Coplan; res: 8 Korado Ct., 2B, Balt., Md. 21207.

CORAM, HELEN F., Layout-Prod. Dir., Wms. Dept., The Miami Herald Publ. Co., 1 Herald Plaza, Miami, Fla. 33101, '68–; Copy Ed., '64–'68; Reptr., '61–'64; Theta Sigma Phi, Fla. Wms. Press Club; Miss. State Col. for Wms., BS, '59; State Univ. of Ia., MA, '61; Post-Grad. Work, Univ. of Miami; b. Starkville, Miss., 1938; p. Thomas and Earlene Simmons Ferguson; h. Richard L. Coram; res: 2343 Tigertail Ave., Coconut Grove, Fla. 33133.

CORBEN, BEVERLY BALKUM, Art-Wtr., non-fiction, poetry, '50–; Owner-Dir., Studio 244, '66–'67; Edtl. Assoc., Tech. PR, TRW, Inc., '54–'57; Tech. Wtr., Art Coordr., Hughes Aircraft Co., '50–'54; art exhibits in various galleries; tchr. of painting, drawing, mixed media, '66; Tech. Publ. Soc. (Secy., '55); Theta Sigma Phi; Santa Monica City Col., AA, '50; Art Ctr. Sch., '55–'57, Univ. of Cal., L.A., BA, '60 (with hons.); Case Western Reserve Univ.; b. L.A., Cal. 1926; p. James and Alice Wardwell Balkum; h. Her-

bert C. Corben; c. (step-children) Deirdre (Mrs. John W. DeGroote), Sharon (Mrs. Allen Golden), Gregory B.; res: 2925 Broxton Rd., Shaker Heights, Oh. 44120.

CORBETT, DOROTHY OSBORN, Traf. Dir., Post-Keyes-Gardner Inc., 875 N. Michigan Ave., Chgo., Ill. 60611, '66–; Svc. Mgr., '65–'66; Traf. Mgr., Grant Advertising, '49–'65; Exec. Secy., '46–'48; Secy., WHO Radio, '39–'45; Traf. Mgr., '35–'38; Drake Univ., '30–'33; h. James Corbett.

CORBETT, ELIZABETH, Auth: "Ladies Day" ('68), "Harry Nartin's Wife" ('67), "The Old Callahan Place" ('66), 53 other books; res: 20 Commerce St., N.Y., N.Y. 10014.

CORBETT, JANICE M., Ed., Action Magazine, American Baptist Convention, Valley Forge, Pa. 19481, '64–; PR Asst., Jack T. Holmes and Assoc. (Ft. Worth, Tex.), '62–'64; Ed., Contact, '59–'62; Auth: "Running the Race," "Decisions, Decisions," and many articles in religious mags.; Conf. of Eds. of Church Mags. (Secy., '68–'69), Nat. Cncl. of Churches Commn. on Public Schs.; Nat. Comm. for Support of the Public Schs.; Eastern Baptist Col., BA, '57; Eastern Baptist Seminary, MRE, '59; res: 500 Wayne Dr., King of Prussia, Pa. 19406.

CORBETT, LINDA STALTER, Reptr., Feature Wtr., Irvington Herald, 22 Union Ave., Irvington, N.J. 07111, '69–; Asst. Ed., Today's Secretary, '65–'68; Edtl. Dept., Look, '63–'65; Info. Wtr., Kan. Highway Commn., '61–'62; Tchr., Cranford Public Schs.; Theta Sigma Phi; Who's Who of Am. Wm.; Medill Sch. of Jnlsm., Northwestern Univ., BSJ, '62; MSJ, '63; b. Council Grove, Kan., 1941; p. Stanley and Ellen Burns Stalter; h. David Corbett; res: 128 Makatom Dr., Cranford, N.J. 07016.

CORBIN, CLAIRE ROTHENBERG, Assoc. Prof., Mktng.-Mgt. Dept. Chmn., Fordham University, Col. of Bus. Adm., Bronx, N.Y. 10458, '57–; Partner, Counseling Lab., '57–; Assoc. Prof., Hofstra Univ., '49–'57; Partner, Corbin Assoc., '48–; Ed., Today's Woman, '47–'48; Pers.-Training, Loft Candy Co., '45–'46; Co-owner, The Guildery, '44–'47; Asst. Prof., L.I. Univ., '39–'44; Co. Ed., Haire Publ. Co., '33–'39; Co-auth: "Implementing the Marketing Concept," "New Trends in American Marketing," "Decision Exercises in Marketing," "Principles of Advertising," "Principles of Retailing;" AAUP (Fordham Chptr. Secy., '58–), Am. Mktng. Assn., NHFL, Fashion Group, AWNY, Pubcty. Club of N.Y., Am. Inst. of Interior Designers; Gamma Alpha Chi, Kappa Delta Pi, Pi Lambda Theta, Eta Mu Pi; N.Y.U., Washington Sq. Col., BS, '33; Sch. of Retailing, MS, '41; Sch. of Educ., PhD, '56; Post-Grad. Work, N.Y.U., Yeshiva Univ., '56–'59; b. N.Y.C., 1913; p. Herman and Anna Kessler Rothenberg; h. Arnold Corbin; c. Karen Sue, Lee H.; res: 330 Harvard Ave., Rockville Centre, N.Y. 11570.

CORBITT, HELEN L., Dir. of Restaurants, Neiman-

Marcus, 1620 Main St., Dallas, Tex. 75201, '55–; Dir., Catering Dept., Driskill Hotel (Austin), '51–'55; Mgr., Houston Country Club, '42–'51; Instr., Univ. of Tex., '40–'42; Adm. Dietician, Cornell Med. Ctr. (N.Y.C.), '36–'40; Auth., three cookbooks; Cnslt., cooking schs.; Lectr.; Nat. Restaurant Assn., Tex. Restaurant Assn., Confrerie de la Chaine des Rotisseurs, Confrerie des Chevaliers du Tastevin (Hon. Mbr.); Gold Plate aw., '61; Food Service mag. aw., '65; Escoffier aw., '68; Skidmore Col., BS, '28 (Alumnae Trustee, '59–'62); b. Benson Mines, N.Y., 1906; p. Henry and Eva Corbitt; res: 4430 University Blvd., Dallas, Tex. 75205.

CORCELLI, DIANE MARIE, Dir. of PR, Euclid General Hospital, E. 185th St. and Lake Erie, Euclid, Oh. 44119, '62–; PR, Ernest Wittenberg, '60–'62; Adv., PR, Natl. City Bank, '57–'60; Theta Sigma Phi (Past Treas., Secy.), Northern Oh. Hosp. PR Assn.; Outstanding Young Wm. of Am., '65; Northern Oh. IEA aw., '64, '65; Oh. Univ., BS (Jrnlsm.), '57; b. Cleve., Oh., 1935; p. Dominic and Anna Corcelli; res: 855 Rondel Rd., Cleve., Oh. 44110.

CORCORAN, JEAN KENNEDY, Fin. Wtr., AE, Employers-Commercial Union Companies, 110 Milk St., Boston, Mass. 02109, '69–; Asst. Prod. Mgr., S. Gunnar Myrbeck Adv., '66–'69; Ed., D.C. Heath & Co., '64–'66; Ed.-Publr., Program Guide, WTCX-FM (St. Petersburg, Fla.), '63–'64; AE, E. D. Mossman Adv., '61–'64; Fashion Copywtr., Ed., Gilchrist, Inc. (Boston, Mass.), '60–'61; Auth., three bks. (Bobbs-Merrill), numerous mag. articles; Auths. League of Am., Intl. Platform Assn., Direct Mail Adv. Assn.; Who's Who of Am. Wm., Contemporary Auths.; b. L.I., N.Y., 1926; p. John and Iris Moore Kennedy; h. William Corcoran; c. Kathleen Ann, Colleen Maire; res: 1193 Furnace Brook Pkwy., Quincy, Mass. 02125.

CORCORAN, KATHRYN SORENSEN, Asst. to the Gen. Mgr., WETA-TV, 2600 Fourth St., N.W., Wash., D.C. 20001, '64–; Secy. to the Pres., '61–'64; NATAS, Potomac BPW (VP, '65–'66); active in numerous civic groups; b. North Troy, N.Y., 1913; p. Hans and Cecelia Williamsen Sorensen; h. Charles Corcoran; c. Thomas John, Judith Ellen, Peter Sandem; res: 1600 S. Eades St., Arlington, Va. 22202.

CORDELL, FRANCES WRIGHT, Wms. Ed., News-Times Publishing Co., 111 N. Madison Ave., El Dorado, Ark. 71730, '30–; Corr., Arkansas Gazette; Freelance Reprtr., Feature Wtr.; Ark. Press Wm., NFPW; Goucher Col., AB, '30; b. Savannah, Ga.; p. Robert and Anna Harmon Cordell; res: 2001 N. Madison Ave., El Dorado, Ark. 71730.

CORDTS, NELDA FRYE, Assoc. Ed., Better Homes & Gardens, 1716 Locust St., Des Moines, Ia. 50303, '65–; Home Furnishings, Garden Ed., San Antonio (Tex.) Express/News, '64–'65; PR Dir., Symphony Soc. of San Antonio, '63–'64; Wtr., Prodr., Talent, WOAI-TV, '60–'63; Theta Sigma Phi (San Antonio Chptr. Pres., '55), Nat. Home Furnishings League, Am. Inst. of Decorators, Des Moines Art Ctr., Civic Music Assn.; Sigma Delta Chi aw., '61; San Antonio Bar Assn. aw., '63; San Antonio Conservation Soc. aw., '63; Northwestern Univ., '40–'42; b. Armstrong, Ill., 1922; p. Alan and Mary Thomas Frye; h. Hugo J. Cordts Jr.; res: 3500 48th Pl., Des Moines, Ia. 50310.

COREA, GERTRUDE VAN PELT, Ed., Info. Coordr., Instructional Materials Center for Handicapped Children and Youth, State of Illinois Public Instruction, 1020 S. Spring St., Springfield, Ill. 62706, '67–; Ed., Wtr., PR, Ill. Dept. of Public Health, '59–'67; Feature Wtr., Colmst., Soc. Ed., Illinois State Journal, '55–'59; Wtr., short stories, '39–'55; NLAPW (Past Br. Secy., Treas., Pres.; State Secy., '68–'70); b. Springfield, Ill; p. Leon and Gertrude Jesberg Van Pelt; h. Harry F. Corea (dec.); c. Lisa A. (Mrs. William Maslauski), Shirley D. (Mrs. H. A. Schrenk); res: 1620 S. Lincoln Ave., Springfield, Ill. 62704.

COREY, JANET CURTIS, Mng. Ed., Co. Mag., Off. Mgr., International Flying Farmers, Inc., Municipal Airport, Wichita, Kan. 67209, '60–; PR Dir., '56–'60; Registrar, Wichita HS East, '53–'56; Tchr., Winona (Minn.) Jr. HS, '25–'26; Kan. IEA (Secy.-Treas., '65–'66), ZONTA; Winona State Col., '25; Wichita State Univ., '51–'52; b. Winona, Minn., 1906; p. Julius and Harriet Townsend Curtis; h. Bruce Corey (dec.); c. Barbara (Mrs. Robert Mallonee); res: 19 Laurel Dr., Wichita, Kan. 67206.

CORMAN, JUDY LISHINSKY, Mgr., Press and Public Info., Popular Music, RCA Records, 1133 Ave. of the Americas, N.Y., N.Y. 10036, '68–; Pubcty. and Adv. Mgr., Vanguard Recs., '68; Pubcty. Mgr., Epic Recs., '63–'68; free-lance photogr.; Adult Educ. courses, New Sch., Bklyn. Col., C.C.N.Y.; b. Bklyn., N.Y., 1938; p. Ben and Roslyn Krystal Lishinsky; h. Avery Corman.

CORNSWEET, SANDRA D., Harold Cornsweet Productions, 7461 Beverly Blvd., Suite 306, L.A., Cal. 90036, '67–; Rsch.; Santa Monica Playhouse; Santa Monica Jr. Col.; b. L.A., Cal., 1945; p. Harold and Adele Bowman Cornsweet; res: 125 N. Barnington Ave., W. L.A., Cal. 90049.

CORNWELL, BERTHA TERRY, Assoc. Ed. and Typographer, The Oil City Visitor, 330 W. Seventh St., Sour Lake, Tex. 77659, '60–; Librn., Sour Lake Sch. Dist.; Librn., French Sch. Dist. (Beaumont); Curator, Armstrong Robert Browning Lib., '33–'39; Pres., Sour Lake Bank's Exec. Secy., '27–'32; Tex. Lib. Assn. (Secy.), '45), Tex. Lib. Trustee Assn. (Chmn., '63–'68; Reg. Dir., '64; Trustee of the Year Aw., '63), Sour Lake Wms. Club (Pres., '68–'70), active in numerous civic groups; Baylor Univ., '33–'39; N. Tex. State, BS, '41; MS (Lib. Sci.), '46; Univ. of Houston, '50–'54; b. Marshall, Tex., 1898; p. Henry and Bertha Fraley Terry; h. B. L. Cornwell; c. Paul, David, Mrs. Fredrick LaDuke; res: 326 W. Seventh St., Sour Lake, Tex. 77659.

CORREA, CARMEN TRISTAO, Chancellory Offcr., Brazilian Consulate General, 630 Fifth Ave., N.Y., N.Y. 10020, '63–; Admr. Offcr., '61–'63; Brazilian Govt., '52–; creation of "Brazilian Column," '65; staff, A Luta nwsp., '64–'68; Corr., Natal mag., '60–'63; numerous mag. articles; Art. Mgr., Brazilian painter, Victor Correa, '57–; Lectr., Pan-Am. Wms. Assn., '68; OPC, Brazilian Press Assn., Pan-Am. Wms. Assn; Notre Dame de Sion (Brazil), '28; New Sch. for Social Rsch., '57; b. Juiz de Fora, M. G., Brazil, 1911; p. Prof. Ottoni and Ignez de Aquino Tristao; c. Manoel, Victor, Celia; res: 167 E. 67th St., N.Y., N.Y. 10021.

CORSON, GRACE, Fashion Ed., Illus., King Features Syndicate, '32–'68; formerly Ladies' Home Journal, Paris; fashion bdcstr., NBC Radio; Harper's Bazaar, '21–'24; Best Comml. Artist, Metropolitan Museum, N.Y.C., '20's; b. Hyde Park, Mass.; p. Orrin and Charlotte Fuller Corson; h. Frederick Stevens Rockwell; res: Vineyard Haven, R.F.D. Martha's Vineyard, Mass. 02568.

COSGROVE, GRACE R., Adv. Mgr., Barnes and Noble, Inc., 105 Fifth Ave., N.Y., N.Y. 10003, '50–; various edtl., adv., sls. positions with The Baker and Taylor Co., '39–'50; Booksellers' League of N.Y. (Rec. Secy.); Hunter Col., BA, '38; b. N.Y.C., 1915; p. John and Margaret Corrigan Cosgrove; res: 2315 University Ave., Bronx, N.Y. 10468.

COSGRAVE, MARY SILVA, Ed., Outlook Tower, The Horn Book, Inc., 585 Boylston St., Boston, Mass. 02116, '69–; Children's Bk. Reviewer, '63–'68; Children's Bk. Ed., Pantheon Books, '59–'62; Juv. Ed., Houghton Mifflin Co., '51–'59; Lectr., Sch. of Lib. Sci., Simmons Col., '50; Cnslt., Children's Schl. Lib. Supvsr., Commonwealth of Mass., '49–'51; Jr. Librn., Mt. Vernon (N.Y.) Public Lib., '47–'49; Children's Librn., '49–'47; Asst., Children's Depts., N.Y. Public Lib., '36–'40; Auth., "The Life and Times of Thomas Bailey Aldrich" ('66); ALA, AIGA, Simmons Col. Lib. Sch. Advisory Bd., '58–'60; Simmons Col., BS, '36; Columbia Univ.; b. Taunton, Mass., 1914; p. Manuel and Mary Frates-Pimental Silva; h. John O'Hara Cosgrave (dec.); res: 597 Circuit Ave., Pocasset, Mass. 02559.

COSGROVE, VICTORIA SHAMAS, Adv. Mgr., McCall Pattern Co., 230 Park Ave., N.Y., N.Y. 10017; '68–; Adv. Mgr., '68–'69; Mdsng. Mgr., '62–'68; Edtl. Cnslt., '62–'67; b. Bklyn., N.Y. 1915; p. Charles and Julia Kaydouh Shamas; h. Edward F. Cosgrove; res: 22 Sherwood Rd., Colonia, N.J. 07067.

COSTA, JOAN KOKKINS, Designer, Adv. and Sls. Prom., Columbia Broadcasting System, 51 W. 52nd St., N.Y., N.Y. 10019, '66–; Designer, Adv., Sls. Prom., Delahanty, Kurnit & Geller, '66; R.I. Sch. of Design, BFA, '64; b. N.Y.C., 1943; p. John and Esther Posselt Kokkins; h. Neil Costa; res: 201 E. 79th St., N.Y., N.Y. 10021.

COSTANTINO, JOSEPHINE M., Asst. Ed., Elementary School Journal, University of Chicago Press, 5835 Kimbark Ave., Judd Hall, Chgo., Ill. 60637, '57–; Asst. Ed., PTA Magazine, '51–'56; Edtl. Asst., Field Enterprises, '50–'51; Ctr. for Intergroup Educ., Univ. of Chgo., '49–'50; Wtr., Rschr., Am. Cncl. on Educ., Wash., D.C., '47–'49; Cornell Univ., MA, '40; b. Dunkirk, N.Y.; p. Charles Costantino and Margaret Gerage Costantino; res: 5716 Kimbark Ave., Chgo., Ill. 60637.

COTELLESSA, HELEN DODDS, Trustee, Hugo Public Library, Seventh St., Hugo, Colo. 80821, '65–; Ed., Annual Bul., Willimantic (Conn.) State Tchrs. Col., '51–'54; Librn., Tchr., Hugo Public Schs. (Hugo, Colo.), '60–'65; Tchr., various schs., '17–'60; ALA, several lib. and educ. assns.; fed., state sponsored fellowship, summer workshop, Home Life, Sex Educ., '53; civic groups, aws.; Park Col., '13–'15; Randolph-Macon Wms. Col., BA, '17 (full tuition scholarship); Colo. A & M Col., '49–'50; Columbia Univ., MA (Student Pers. Adm.), '50; Pfsnl. Diploma (Guidance), '54; Univ. of Denver, MA (Librarianship), '55; b. Bklyn., N.Y., 1896; p. Robert and Mary Jane Bissland Dodds; h. Joseph Cornelius Cotellessa; c. Dr. Robert F., Alice E. (Mrs. Carl Beverly Bledsoe); res: 717 Fourth Ave., Hugo, Colo. 80821.

COSTELLO, JOAN MACDONALD, Sr. Ed., J. G. Ferguson Publishing Co., Ed. Off: 277 Park Ave., N.Y., N.Y. 10017, '68–; Ed., '66–'68; Free-lance Ed., '63–'66; Copywtr., Doubleday & Co., '60–'61; Art Ed., C. L. Barnhart, '60; Edtl. Asst., Field Enterprises, '56–'59; WNBA; St. Mary-of-the-Woods Col., BA, '56; b. Chgo., Ill.; p. Edward K. and Genevieve Murphy MacDonald; h. James F. Costello; c. Genevieve, Edward; res: 63 Seventh Ave., Bklyn., N.Y. 11217.

COSTELLO, MARICLARE CATHERINE, Actress; Broadway: "Harvey," "A Patriot for Me," "Lovers and Other Strangers," "After the Fall" (Lincoln Ctr.); off-Broadway: "The Hostage," "The Private Eye and The Public Ear;" TV: "NYPD," "The Choice," St. Joan on "Once Upon a World;" movies: "The Tiger Makes Out;" Clarke Col., BA; Catholic Univ., MA; Univ. of Vienna (Philosophy), '57; b. Peoria, Ill.; p. Dallas and Margaret Feeney Costello; res: 55 W. 68th St., N.Y., N.Y. 10023.

COTÉ, CAROL KOUNTZ, Assoc. Ed., The Writer, Inc., 8 Arlington St., Boston, Mass. 02116, '67–; Pa. State Univ., '61–'62; Univ. of Mich., AB (Greek, Latin), '64 (hons.); b. San Jose, Cal., 1944; p. R. Rupert and Alice Stong Kountz; h. Laurie H. Cote; res: 236 Rawson Rd., #3, Brookline, Mass.

COTHERN, FAYLY HARDCASTLE, Jnlsm. Instr., Grand Canyon College, 330 W. Camelback Rd., Phoenix, Ariz. 85031; Dean of Wm.; Auth: "I've Been Wondering" (Broadman), "So You Want to Be Popular" (Zondervan), "Where Do We Go From Here" (Zondervan), many articles in religious pubns.; active in numerous civic youth groups; Royal Academic Lit. Soc., Alpha Psi Omega; Who's Who of Am. Wm.; Who's Who in the West; Mary Hardin Baylor Col., BA, '47; Southwestern Theological Seminary, MA (Religious Educ.), '50; Grad. Work, Arizona State Univ., Phoenix Col.; b. Andice, Tex.; p. L. W. and Katheryn Hardcastle; h. Gaylon Cothern; c. Kathy, Clark.

COTREAU, JEANNE ELLISON, Sr. AE, WBOS Radio, 275 Tremont St., Boston, Mass. 02158; Movie Actress: "The Out of Towners," "Tell Me That You Love Me, Junie Moon;" AE, '65–'69; AE, WORL, '65; Talent-TV Comml. Work, '68–'69; Talent and Wtr., Radio Cmml. Work, '66–'69; Adv. Club of Boston, Bdcst. Exec. Club of Boston, AFTRA, AWRT; various beauty contest aws; Malden (Mass.) Bus. Sch., '50; b. Melrose, Mass., 1928; p. Irwin and Mabel Meller Ellison; h. Andrew Cotreau (div.); c. Gregory, Douglas; res: 58 Debbie Rd., Brocton, Mass. 02402.

COTT, BETTY, Sr. VP, Ruder & Finn Incorporated, 110 E. 59 St., N.Y., N.Y. 10017, '69–; VP, Sr. Assoc., AE; Tchr., Guest Lectr., N.Y.U., L.I. Univ.; PRSA, N.Y.U. BA, '49; b. N.Y.C. 1928; p. Albert and Etta Cohen; h. Ted Cott; c. Jennifer; res: 680 West End Ave., N.Y., N.Y. 10025.

COTTON, DOROTHY WHYTE, Ed.-in-Chief, VP, Parents' Magazine Enterprises Inc., 52 Vanderbilt Ave., N.Y., N.Y. 10017, '65; h. Dr. John M. Cotton.

COTTONE, MARYLIN, AE, Conahay & Lyon Inc. 485 Madison Ave., N.Y., N.Y. 10022, '68–; Mktng. Mgr., Revlon, '65–'67; Brand Mgr., Warner Lambert, '63–'65; Asst. Dir., Adv., Pubcty., Charles of the Ritz, '58–'63; Prom. Mgr., Yardley of London, '53–'54; Asst. Prom. Mgr., Cannon Mills, '47–'53; b. New Jersey, 1925; p. Phillip and Mildred Royer McCormick; c. Marc; res: Summit Dr., Denville, N.J. 07834.

COTTRELL, GRACE GRIGGS, Dir. of Pubns., Wesley-Jessen, The Plastic Contact Lens Co., 37 S. Wabash, National Eye Research Foundation, 18 S. Michigan Ave., Chgo., Ill. 60603; Asst. Ed., Journal of Cryosurgery; Asst. Ed., Annals of Ophthalmology; Ed., The Covenant Club News; ICIE, Soc. of Tech. Wtrs., Iota Sigma Epsilon (Northwestern Univ. Chptr. Pres., '69–'70), Beta Sigma Phi, Lyric Guild, Cncl. on Fgn. Rels., Art Inst.; Northwestern Univ.; b. Gadsden, Ala.; p. Rhodum and Maude Turner Griggs; res: 630 Prairie Ave., Wilmette, Ill. 60091.

COUCH, HILDA JUANITA, Reptr., Wms. Dept., The Jersey Journal, 30 Journal Sq., Jersey City, N.J. 07306, '24–; Ed., The Woman Republican, six yrs.; Wms. Press Club of N.Y.C. (Pres., eight yrs.; Ed., monthly bul.; Dir.), Nwsp. Wms. Club of N.Y. (past Dir.); Pulitzer Travelling Scholarship Alternate, '24; Smith Col., '22; Columbia Univ. Sch. of Jnlsm. (Alumni Treas.); b. Nyack, N.Y.; p. Dr. Louis and Natalie Kreuder Couch; res: Apt. 11D, 102 E. 22nd St., N.Y., N.Y. 10010.

COUCH, SUZAN KULP, Adv. Mgr., WCBS-TV, 51 W. 52nd St., N.Y., N.Y. 10019, '67–; Sls. Prom. Dir., WPIX-TV, '65–'67; Mdsng. Coordr., WCAU-TV, '62–'65; Bdcst. Prom. Assn., Cncl. of Wm's Col. Clubs of Westchester, AAUW; Who's Who of Am. Wm.; Wilson Col., BA, '60 (Westchester County Alumnae Pres.); b. Pottstown, Pa., 1938; p. Harry M. and Bessie Weaver Kulp; h. Andrew G. Couch; res: 89 W. Brookside Dr., Larchmont, N.Y. 10538.

COUDERT, JO, Auth: "The I Never Cooked Before Cookbook" ('63), "Advice from a Failure" ('65); Smith Col.; b. Williamsport, Pa., 1923; p. John and Jane Krouse Coudert; res: 372 Bleecker St., N.Y., N.Y. 10014.

COULBOURN, LUCILLE CHEATHAM, Wms. Ed., The Raleigh Times, P.O. Box 191, Raleigh, N.C. 27602; Retail Adv. Salesman, '64–'66; Adv. and Sls. Prom. Asst., Occidental Life Ins. Co. of N.C., '62–'64; Adv. Mgr., Boylan-Pearce Dept. Store, '61–'62; N.C. Press Wm. (first and second pl. aws.), '67; hon. mention, '68); Penney-Mo. Jnlsm. Aw., second pl., '67; Who's Who of Am. Wm.; Raleigh Spinsters Club (Pres.); Greensboro Col., '57–'58; E. Carolina Univ., AB (Fine Arts), '61; b. Windsor, N.C., 1939; p. Fenton and Eleanor Cheatham Coulbourn; res: 2452 Wade Ave., Raleigh, N.C. 27607.

COUNIHAN, MAUREEN CORNELIA, Free-lance Wtr., Ed., '67–; writing and visuals for radio and TV public svc. announcements, '69; Ed., Reptr., ships' nwsps., Home Lines Steamship Co., '68; Ed., Colmst., Feature Wtr., N.Y. Daily News, '55–'67; Nwsp. Wms. Club of N.Y. (Governing Bd., four yrs.), Nwsp. Reptrs. Assn.; OPC; N.Y. Nwsp. Guild (Rep. Assembly Delegate, six yrs.); Hunter Col.; Ind. Univ., BA; Columbia Univ. Grad. Sch. of Jnlsm. courses; Herbert Berghof Studio of Theater; b. N.Y.C.; p. Timothy and Charlotte Foley Counihan; res: 274 E. Tenth St., N.Y., N.Y. 10009.

COUPE, IRENE DRIPS, Ed., General Publications, Ltd., 3923 W. Sixth St., L.A., Cal. 90005, '64–; Ed., The Statesman Newspapers, '61–'64; Tchr., '46–'50; Western Soc. of Bus. Pubns. Aw. for news presentation, '65, '66; Col. of Idaho; b. Rapid City, S.D., 1928; p. John and Dorothy Barr Drips; c. Cecil John, Larry Douglas; res: 923 N. Vendome, L.A., Cal. 90026.

COURTNEY, WINIFRED FISK, Ed., Reader's Adviser, R. R. Bowker Co., 1180 Ave. of the Americas, N.Y., N.Y. 10036, '66–; Copy Ed., Special Bks. Dept., Reader's Digest '62–'66; Free-lance ed., Copy Ed., '59–'62; Wms. Nat. Bk. Assn.; Radcliffe Col., '36–'39; Barnard Col., BA, '41; State Univ. Tchrs. Col., New Paltz, MS (Elementary Educ.), '59; b. Flushing, N.Y., 1918; p. Charles and Cara Lane Fisk; h. Denis Courtney; c. Jennifer L., Stephen D.; res: 197 Cleveland Dr., Croton-on-Hudson, N.Y. 10520.

COUSIN, MICHELLE, Wtr., Capital Cities Broadcasting, 12 W. 40th St., N.Y., N.Y. 10018, '69–; Wtr. for Betsy Palmer, Robert Jennings, Inc., 15 E. 55th St.; Staff Wtr., CBS (Wash., D.C.); Wtr., Betty Furness "Dimension" show, CBS; Wtr., synd. radio progs. for Betsy Palmer and Bill Cullen; Auth., TV original dramas: Kraft Theatre, Matinee Theatre, Lux Video, Armstrong, others; Adjunct Asst. Prof., TV and Film Writing, N.Y.U.; Head, Lit. Dept., Richard/Allan Prods; Special Workshop, Johannesburg, S. Africa; WGA; City Col. of L.A., Drama (Prodr. of first original musical for campus radio); b. U.S.S.R., 1921; p. Morris and Esther Polay Cousin; h. (dec.); res: Fifth Ave. Hotel, 24 Fifth Ave., N.Y., N.Y. 10011.

COUSINS, MARGARET, Sr. Ed., Doubleday & Company, Inc., 277 Park Ave., N.Y., N.Y. 10017, '61–; Mng. Ed., McCall's, '58–'61; Mng. Ed., Good Housekeeping, '45–'58; Assoc. Ed., '42–'45; Assoc. Ed., Pictorial Rev., '37–'38; Advisory Bd., Univ. of Tex. Sch. of Jnlsm.; Bd. Dir., Episcopalian Magazine; Auth., over 200 short stories; Contrbr., short stories, articles, essays to mag. press in U.S., Europe; Auths. Guild, Auths. League (Secy., '65–'69), Fashion Group (Bd. of Govs., '57), Am. Inst. of Int. Designers, Decorators Club, Eds. Lunch Club, Theta Sigma Phi (Headliner Aw., '48), Alpha Chi Omega (Achiev. Aw., '55); Penney-Univ. of Mo. Jnlsm. Aw. for mag. writing, '69; Univ. of Tex., BA, '26 (Aws. of Achiev.); b. Munday, Tex., 1905; p. Walter and Sue Reeves Cousins; res: 125 E. 63rd St., N.Y., N.Y. 10021.

COVET, SYLVIA S., Exec. Ed., Postgraduate Medicine, McGraw-Hill, Inc., 4015 W. 65th St., Mpls., Minn. 55435, '47–; Nat. Assn. of Sci. Wtrs., Am. Med. Wtrs. Assn. (Fellow), Soc. of Tech. Wtrs. and Publrs. (Sr. Mbr.), Minn. Press Club; American Business Press Neal Aw., '69; Univ. of Wis., BA.

COVINGTON, GERALDINE, Ed., co. field mag., Great Southern Life Insurance Co., 3121 Buffalo Speedway, Houston, Tex. 77006, '56–; Assoc. Ed., '53–'56; Edtl. Asst., The Progressive Farmer, '47–'53; Tchr., Dudley (Ga.) Consolidated Sch., '40–'42; S.E. Tex. IEA (Bd. of Dirs., '56, '66), Secy.-Treas., '54), Life Advs. Assn. (Aws. of Excellence for co. mag., '54, '55, '57, '61, '62); Ga. State Col., Normal Diploma, '40; b. Moultrie, Ga.; p. Dr. James F. and Annis Hawkins Covington; res: 3803 Audley, Apt. D, Houston, Tex. 77006.

COWAN, FAY GALLAHER, City Ed., News-Tribune, Tribune Printing Company, 715 13th St., Beaver Falls, Pa. 15010, '65–; New Castle News; Ellwood City Ledger; Pa. Wms. Press Assn. (Treas., '52–'54; Pres., '54 '56); Pa. News Wm. of Yr., '54; State writing aws., '54–'69; Duff's Iron City Col., '30; b. Ellwood City, Pa., 1913; p. James and Emma Mecklem Gallaher; h. Wilbert S. Cowan (dec.); c. Jerome; res: 23 Portersville Rd., Ellwood City, Pa. 16117.

COWAN, GENEVIEVE C., Fashion Dir., Duplan Corporation, 1440 Broadway, N.Y., N.Y. 10018, '68–;

Fashion Mdsng.-Prom. Dir., Good Housekeeping, '63–'68 Mktng. Rep., Textile Fibers, DuPont Co., '55–'63; AWNY, Fashion Group.

COWELL, RUTH FRANCES, Lib. Dir., Manhasset Public Library, 30 Onderdonk Ave., Manhasset, N.Y., 11030, '45–; Reference Asst., Newark (N.J.) Public Lib., '42–'45; Reference Asst., Carnegie Lib., Pitt., '39–'42; Lectr., State Univ. of N.Y., Geneseo, '55–'59; Lecturer, St. John's Univ., '59–'62; Adjunct Asst. Prof., Grad. Lib. Sch., C. W. Post Col., L.I. Univ., '62–; Nassau County Lib. Assn. (past VP), N.Y. Lib. Assn., ALA, AAUW; Mt. Holyoke Col., AB, '32; St. Bonaventure Univ., MA, '33; N.Y. State Col. for Tchrs., Albany, BS (Lib. Sci.), '39; b. Olean, N.Y., 1909; p. Walter Allen and Violet Parrish Cowell; res: 4 Bayview Ct., Manhasset, N.Y. 11030.

COWEN, SANDRA BRANDY, Media Dir., Owens & Associates Advertising, Inc., 3424 N. Central Ave., Phoenix, Ariz. 85012, '68–; Time Byr., Curran-Morton Adv., '65; Traf., KHJ Radio (L.A., Cal.), '63; Ed. Asst., Phoenix Tucson Editions, TV Guide, '63; Traf. Mgr., KOOL Radio (Phoenix), '62; Tchr., Ariz. State Univ., Adv. Forum, Phoenix Ad Club, "Buying Radio," '68, '69; Various lects. to col., civic, pfsnl. groups; Phoenix Adv. Club, AAW (Ayres Speaking Contest Winner, Dist. Seven and Finalist, '66), AAF, Phoenix Jr. Adv. Club (Bd. of Dirs., '66–'67), NATAS (Phoenix Chptr. Bd. of Govs.); Phoenix Col.; Ariz. State Univ.; b. Mpls., Minn., 1944; p. Edward and Marie Swank Brandy; h. Robert Cowen; res: 11239 N. 33rd St., Phoenix, Ariz. 85028.

COWING, JEAN LAURENCE, Wms. Ed. and Colmst., Daily Democrat, 702 Court St., Woodland, Cal. 95695, '66–; Cal. Press Wm.; Sacramento City Col., '31; b. Woodland, Cal., 1912; p. Jesse and Estelle Packer Laurence; h. Ralph Cowing (dec.); c. Mrs. Donald Bruce Geer, Ralph Jeffrey, Eric Cavell, Robert Devlin; res: 901 College St., Woodland, Cal. 95695.

COX, BETTY JANE, Pres., Pacific Colorfilm, Inc., 574 N. Larchmont Blvd., L.A., Cal. 90004, '53–; Mgr., Dunningcolor Corp., '45–'52; Soc. of Motion Pic. and TV Engineers; indsl. Photog. Certs. of Merit, '62, '64, '65, '69; Asst. Prodr., 3 films for Union Pacific Railroad, '69; b. L.A., Cal., 1923; p. Ted and Cordelia Dawson Cox; res: 2693 Carmar Dr., L.A., Cal. 90046.

COX, CLAIRE, Pres., Claire Cox Associates, Inc., 301 E. 48th St., N.Y., N.Y. 10017, '69; Eastern PR Rep., Combined Ins. Co. of Am., '62–'69; Rptr., Rewrite, Feature Wtr., Clmst., UPI (Chgo.), '44–'47; N.Y.C., '47–'62); Rptr., Balt. Sun, '42–'44; Rptr., Ft. Lauderdale Daily News, '42; Auth: numerous mag. articles, bks., '61–'69; Religious News Wtrs. Assn., OPC, Nat. Cncl. on Illegitimacy; Writing aw., N.Y. Nwsp. Wms. Club '56; Citizens Scholarship Fndn. of Am. (Bd. Mbr.), Laymen's Nat. Bible Comm. (Bd. Mbr.), Armadillo Breeders Assn; U.C.L.A., AB, '41; Columbia Grad. Sch. of Jnlsm., MS, '42; b. St. Louis, Mo., 1919; p. Klaire

Hasgall Cox; h. M. L. Lowenthal, Jr.; res: R.D. 3, Brewster, N.Y. 10509.

COX, JANET TRASK, Ed., McCall's Piece Goods, Yarn & Notions Merchandiser, McCall Corp., 230 Park Ave., N.Y., N.Y. 10017, '64–; Soc. Ed., Billings Gazette (Billings, Mont.); Partner, PR, Adv., Publ., '69–; NFPW, Wms. Fashion Fabrics, Assn., Theta Sigma Phi; Univ. of Ore., '59–'60; Univ. of Mont., BA (Jnlsm., European Hist.), '63; b. Billings, Mont., 1941; p. Willard and Margaret Johnston Trask; h. Leslie C. Cox; c. Adam Richard; res: 223 Clark, Billings, Mont. 59102.

COX, JEAN VANDEVEER, Commtns. Specialist, University of Washington, 400 Lewis Hall, Seattle, Wash. 98105, '60–; Tchr., Feature Wtr., Drama Critic, News Ed.; Hostess-Prodr., "University News and Views"; AWRT, NATAS, Seattle Adv. Club, Campus Bus. and Pfsnl. Club, NFPW Aw.; ACPRA Aw.; Offcl. Histrn., Western Radio and TV Assn.; b. Evansville, Ind., 1923; p. H. A. and Regina Harl Vandeveer; h. James W. Cox; c. James W., Jr., Jerry Lee, Jon Randolph; res: Rte. 4, Box 4756, Bainbridge Island, Wash. 98110.

COX, JENNIE H., Publr. of Arapahoe Public Mirror and Holbrook Observer, Cox Printing Co., 402 Nebraska Ave., Arapahoe, Neb. 68922, '61–; Co-ed. for 45 yrs.; Neb. Press Assn. (Gen. Excellence Aw. to Holbrook Observer, '57), Nat. Edtl. Assn., Alpha Phi Gamma, Govs. Comm. on the Status of Wm. ('69); Neb. Fed. of Wms. Clubs, OES, PEO; Ak-Sar-Ben Aw. for outstanding commty. svc. to Arapahoe Public Mirror ('62); b. Arapahoe, Neb., 1903; p. Dominicus S. and Sarah Sadonia Otter Hasty; h. Ralph L. Cox (dec.); c. Rodney T., Cathlenn Cox Weber; res: 1216 4th St., Arapahoe, Neb. 68922.

COX, MARTHA McCORMICK, Dir. of Learning Aids, Malone College, 515 25th St. N.W., Canton, Oh. 44709, '64–; Kent State Univ., '63; Carnegie Inst. of Tech., '48–'50; Wooster Col., '46–'48; Stark County Librns. Assn. (Pres., '68), AAUW (1st VP), Oh. Lib. Assn., ALA; Carnegie Inst. of Tech., BA, '51; Kent State Univ., MA, '64; b. Lisbon, Oh., 1928; p. Alvy and Mary Crawford McCormick; h. J. Morgan Cox; c. Ariel Sibylla, Shannon Elise, Claudia Renee; res: 151 33rd St. N.W., Canton, Oh. 44709.

COX, MARTHA WILLIAMS, Prodr., WRC-TV, 4001 Nebraska Ave., Wash., D.C. 20016, '64–; Asst. Prodr., '60–'64; Model, Prodr., Film Ed., WBTM-TV, '54–'55; AWRT; nominated for local Emmy, '66, '68; Univ. of Va., '54–'55; b. Charlottesville, Va., 1928; p. John and Louise Anderson Williams; h. Richard Cox; c. Mrs. Ralph A. Dowell; res: 6800 Lupine Lane, McLean, Va. 22101.

COX, PATRICIA, Owner, Patricia Cox Public Relations, Inc. Publicist, Mike Goldstein, Inc., Youth Concepts, Ltd., The Rascals; Feature Wtr., Eye, Pace, '66–

'69; Columbia Univ., BA, MA (Phi Beta Kappa); b. New Britain, Conn., 1942; p. Arthur and Hellen Ruble Cox; res: 654 Broadway, N.Y., N.Y. 10012.

COX, RUTH CROW, Traf. Mgr., Simon & Gwynn, Inc., 3329 Poplar Ave., Memphis, Tenn. 38111, '68–; Acc. Supvsr., Pepper Sound Studios, '66–'68; Exec. Asst. to VP Radio, Eastern Div., Avco Radio Sls., '64–'66; KOB-AM (Albuquerque, N.M.), '62–'64; ABC-TV Network Programming, '58; IRTS, Phila. Ad Club; Katharine Gibbs Sch., '58; Univ. of N.M., '62–'64; b. N.Y.C., 1939; p. Max and Rose Zeitlin Winstin; h. James Cox; c. Michael D. Crow, Amanda L. Crow; res: 1632 Ellsworth St., Memphis, Tenn. 38111.

COX, VIVIEN BOGGS, Pers. Mgr., Lansing B. Warner, Inc., 4210 W. Peterson Ave., Chgo., Ill. 60646, '61–; Pers. Coordr., Pure Milk Assn., '58–'61; Pers. Cnslr., Tops, '57–'58; Horders, Inc., '55–'57; Speed-O-Print, '53–'55; Co-owner, Breco, Inc., '50–'53; Tchr., Morton Sch. of Music, '38–'42; Wm. of Pers., Soroptimist Club (VP, '67–'68), Adm. Mgt., Hist. Soc. of Colo., Intl. Platform Assn., Nat. Social Dir., Bus. Rsch., AAIE; Morton Sch. of Music, '36–'41; Chgo. Bus. Sch., '52; Northwestern Univ., '65; b. Raymondville, Mo., 1918; p. Lilburn and Blanche Hemphill Boggs; h. William A. Cox (dec.); res: 6225 N. Kenmore Ave., Chgo., Ill. 60626.

CRAFT, EVA ROSSMAN, Sr. Tech. Wtr., EG&G, P.O. Box 1912, Las Vegas, Nev. 89101, '67–; Ed., EG&G Desert Scope, '61–'65; Tech. Wtr., '63–'67; Jr. Tech. Wtr., '62–'63; Jr. Engineering Asst., '56–'62; Ed., Las Vegas Bird Dog Club Nwsltr., '68–; Health Physics Soc.; Nev. Wildlife Fedn., (Bd. of Dirs., Ed., Nwsltr., '69–); Flint Jr. Col. (Flint, Mich.), AA, '38; Wayne State Univ. (Detroit, Mich.), BA, '40; b. Armada, Mich.; p. Herbert E. and Gunhilda Bjorndal Rossman; h. Lewis F. Craft (dec.); res: 3701 Kell Lane, Las Vegas, Nev. 89110.

CRAIG, ELOISE BURNER, Ed., Publr., The Normalite, 106 Broadway, Normal, Ill. 61761, '45–; Publr., '60–; Mng. Ed., '35–'45; Reptr., '28–'35; Founder, Pres., Normal Reforestation Rsch; Colmst., American Kennel Gazette; NLAPW, Alpha Gamma Delta (Conv. Asst. Ed., Arc of Epsilon, '32); Ill. Wesleyan Univ., '25–'28; b. Normal, Ill., 1906; p. Clarence and Florence Curtis Burner; h. Robert H. Craig; res: 301 Dewey Ave., Normal, Ill. 61761.

CRAM, ELSIE McKAY, Staff Wtr., Toledo Blade, 541 Superior St., Toledo, Oh. 43604, '43–; Reptr., Fremont (Oh.) News-Messenger, '42–'43; Theta Sigma Phi, Oh. Nwsp. Wms. Assn. (numerous aws.), Am. Nwsp. Guild, Toledo Nwsp. Guild (past Pres.); Oh. State Univ., BA, '42; b. Vickery, Oh., 1920; p. Grover and Glenna Hughes McKay; h. W. Winston Cram (dec.); res: 2640 Overbrook Dr., Toledo, Oh. 43614.

CRAM, MARGARET CREIGHTON (PEG), Colmst., Librn., Syracuse Herald-Journal American, 220 Herald Pl., Syracuse, N.Y. 13201, '48–; formerly sports reptr., wms. sports colmst., city desk news wtr., col. corr., soc. colmst., theatrical critic Herald-Journal American (Syracuse, N.Y.); Ed., Horse Colmst.; NLPW (past Chptr. Treas.), Theta Sigma Phi (past Ed., Chptr. Bul.), Altrusa Intl. (past Pres., charter mbr.); Syracuse Wms. Dist. Golf Assn. Aw. for 20 yrs. of golf writing, '67; Syracuse Univ. Col. of Liberal Arts, Sch. of Educ.; b. Millville, N.J., 1915; p. Jacob and Katherine Harman Cram; res: 4990 Fayetteville Rd., Manlius, N.Y. 13104.

CRAMER, ANNE, Head Librn., Southwestern State College, Weatherford, Okla. 73096, '62–'69; Cataloger, '61–'62; Hq. Librn., Johnson County (Kan.) Lib., '59–'61; Kan. City Public Lib., '51–'58; Weatherford Lib. Advisory Bd., Okla. Lib. Assn. (Secy., '65–'66), Okla. Cncl. on Libs., Okla. Reg. Med. Program (Advisory Comm. on Biomedical Info. Svcs., '67–), Southwestern Lib. Assn. (Secy., Col. and Univ. Lib. Div., '69–'70), ALA, Beta Phi Mu; Stephens Col. '47–'48; Univ. of Okla., BA (Lib. Sci.), '51; MLS, '68, Florida State Univ., '69– (doc. prog.) b. Norman, Okla., 1929; res: Osceola Hall-Box 163, 500 Chapel Drive, Tallahassee, Fla. 32304.

CRAMER, POLLY, Colmst., "Polly's Pointers," Newspaper Enterprise Association; Decorating Wtr., Cinn. Post and Times-Star; bk., "Polly's Homemaking Pointers" (Doubleday); Am. Inst. of Interior Designers (Corporate Mbr.), NHFL; b. Garfield, Ky., 1903; p. Paul and Elizabeth Macy Compton; h. Douglas S. Cramer (dec.); c. Douglas, Jr., Paul, Peyton; res: 1110 Delta Ave., Cinn., Oh. 45208.

CRANDALL, DOROTHY, Food Ed., Boston Globe, Boston, Mass. 02107, '51–; Instr., Home Econs., Boston Univ.; Garland Jr. Col.; Cnslt., Brides Cookbook; Am. Home Econs. Assn.; Univ. of Vt., BS (Home Econs.), '28; MA, '62; b. Burlington, Vt., 1907; p. Arthur and Nellie Crandall; res: 8 Norway Rd., Milton, Mass. 02187.

CRANDALL, ELLA JOHNSON, Cnslt. Ed., Cumulative Index to Nursing Literature (originator, first Ed.); Chief Med. Librn., L.A. Co. Gen. Hosp., '50–'67; Med. Librn., Loma Linda Univ., '35–'50; Librn., Southwestern Jr. Col., '30–'34; med. lib. cnslt.; articles in pfsnl. jnls.; Special Libs. Assn. (Southern Cal. VP, Secy., '42; Pres., '44), Med. Lib. Assn., Med. Lib. Group of Southern Cal. (organizer, first Pres., '49), BPW (Wilmington Wm. of the Yr., '55); Union Col., BA, '30; Univ. of Southern Cal., BS (Lib. Sci.), '40; b. Elm Creek, Neb.; p. Gabriel and Sarah Jacobsen Johnson; h. Judge Howard E. Crandall; res: 357 S. Curson Ave., L.A., Cal. 90036.

CRANDALL, NORMA, Wtr., Ed., bk. revs., The New Republic, The Nation, The N.Y. Times, other pubns.; essays in Trace, other pubns.; biog., "Emily Bronte" ('57; reprint,'70); dramatic reading based on biog., Melodrama in the Bronte Parsonage," performed by the Travelling Lib. Players, N.Y. Public Lib. brs., The Livingston, Lib. Theatre (N.J.), other locations; articles in mags: Collier's, Pageant; Free-lance Ed., to wtrs.; Translator, French to Eng.; Cnslt., French Bks., publrs.; former Edtl. Advisor, Harcourt Brace Co., other N.Y.C. publrs.; PSA, Auths. Guild, Bronte Soc. of Eng. (Haworth, Yks., Eng.); Who's Who in Intl. Poetry; Lycee (Paris, France), '24–'25; Barnard Col., '26–'27; b. Bklyn. Heights, N.Y., 1907; p. Edward Crandall and Marie Vanderveer Hall; h. Wilson Chamberlain McCarty (dec.); res: Apt. 3B, 149 E. 61st St., N.Y., N.Y. 10021.

CRANDALL, OPAL MARGARET, Asst. Wms. Ed., Food Ed., The San Diego Union and Copley News Service, 940 Third Ave., San Diego, Cal. 92112, '52–; Wms. News Dept., San Diego Union, '50–'52; La Mesa Scout, '48–'50; El Cajon Valley News, '46–'48; Theta Sigma Phi, NFPW; Wms. State Writing Contest: 1st and 2nd place, '62; 2nd place, '63; 1st place, '65; 1st and 3rd place, '66; San Diego State Col.; b. Phoenix, Ariz., 1908; p. Thomas and Ella Carter Levy; h. (div.); c. Thomas A., Sidney (Mrs. Edson Johnson), Mary (Mrs. Harold Wilson); res: 4484 Illinois St., Apt. 3, San Diego, Cal. 92116.

CRANE, CAROL LINDER, Contrb. Ed., House Beautiful Special Publications, 717 Fifth Ave., N.Y., N.Y. 10022, '61–; Ladies Home Journal, '53–'57; Designer, Virginia Harlow Interiors, '52–'53; Design Rsch., Dorothy Liebes Textiles, '50–'52; House & Garden, '47–'49; NHFL; Who's Who of Am. Wm.; Beaver Col., BFA, '46; Columbia Univ., MA (Fine, Indsl. Arts), '47; b. Yonkers, N.Y., 1924; p. Israel and Sara Lazarus Linder; h. David Crane; c. Susan, Andrea, Nancy; res: 11 Douglas Circle, Rye, N.Y. 10580.

CRANE, CAROLINE, Free-lance Wtr., 317 W. 93rd St., N.Y., N.Y. 10025; Staff Wtr., U.S. Comm. for UNICEF, '57–'60; Auth: "Pink Sky at Night" (Doubleday, '63), "Wedding Song" (David McKay, '67), "A Girl Like Tracy" (David McKay, '66), "Lights Down The River" (Doubleday, '64); Auths. League of Am.; Bennington Col., AB, '52; b. Chgo., Ill., 1930; p. Roger and Jessie Taft Crane; h. Yoshio Kiyabu; c. Ryo, Laurel; res: 317 W. 93rd St., N.Y., N.Y. 10025.

CRANE, FRANCES KIRKWOOD, Free-lance Wtr., c/o Robert E. Mills, 156 E. 52 St., N.Y., N.Y. 10022; Auth: 26 mystery novels (Lippincott, Random House); satirical novel (Rinehart); numerous articles; MWA; Univ. of Ill. (Phi Beta Kappa); b. Lawrenceville, Ill.; p. Robert and Leonora Gatterton Kirkwood; h. Ned Crane (dec.); c. Mrs. Marshall Smith; res: Taos and Santa Fe, New Mexico.

CRANE, LOIS GAETA, Ed. Scoreboard Magazine, Ayerst Laboratories, Division of American Home Products Corporation, 685 Third Ave., N.Y., N.Y. 10017, '69–; Asst. Ed., '67–'69; Free-lance Copywtr., Marshall Field and Carson, Pirie and Scott (Chgo., Ill.), '61–'64; TV-Radio Copywtr., J. Walter Thompson,

'55–'61; Mount Holyoke Col., AB, '55; b. Hackensack, N.J., 1934; p. Sebastian and Katherine Aversa Gaeta; h. (div.); res: 640 Maple Ave., Wyckoff, N.J. 07481.

CRANE, MARGERY HALE, Assoc. Ed., Changing Times, Kiplinger Magazine, 1729 H St., N.W., Wash., D.C. 20006, '65–; Rsch. Ed., '55–'64; Edtl. Asst., '46–'55; Asst. Bk. Rev. Ed., Am. Statis. Assn., '44–'46; WNPC (Treas., '57–'58), ANWC (Pres., '65–'66; Bd. Mbr., '66–'68), Intl. Club of Wash.; American Univ., BA, '42; b. Akron, Oh.; p. Laurence and Hilda Schmidt Hale; h. Robert Crane (div.); res: 4706 Windom Pl., N.W., Wash., D.C. 20016.

CRANE, TINA LOUISE, Actress, Mot. Pic., "The Happy Ending" ('69), "Kismet" ('55), others; Theatre Roles: "Fade Out—Fade In" ('64), "Lil Abner" ('56), others, '52–; TV role of Ginger, "Gilligan Island," CBS ('63–'64), "Johnny August," Studio One ('56); Actors Studio, AEA, SAG, AFTRA; Scarborough Prep Sch., Miami Univ., Neighborhood Playhouse Sch. of Theatre, N.Y.C.; b. N.Y.C., 1937; p. Joseph and Betty Blacker; h. Les Crane.

CRANK, NELLIE MAE, Commtns. Svc. Coordr., Farmland Industries, Inc. 3315 N. Oak Trafficway, P.O. Box 7305, Kan. City, Mo. 64116, '69–; Circ. Mgr., '47–; Dir., Coop. Health Assn., '51–'56; Kan. City Direct Mail Club; Kan. City Jr. Col.; Kan. City Univ.; b. Carrollton, Mo., 1917; p. Eugene O. and Marguerite Keys Crank; res: 2612 Amie Ct., Kansas City, Mo. 64124.

CRARY, MARGARET COLEMAN, Free-lance Wtr., 3213 Viking Dr., Sioux City, Ia. 51104; Auth., eight bks., young people's fiction; NLAPW, Sioux Wtrs.; Morningside Col., BA, '26; LittD (hon.), '65; b. Carthage, S.D., 1906; p. James and Ella Brown Coleman; h. Ralph W. Crary; c. Bruce, David, Nancy Crary Veglahn; res: 3213 Viking Dr., Sioux City, Ia. 51104.

CRAVEN, KIP MURPHY, PR Dir., American National Red Cross, 848 Peachtree St., Atlanta, Ga. 30308, '62–; Gtr. Boston Chptr. '54–'56; Rocky Mountain News, '52–'54; U.S. Dept. of Army (Tokyo, Japan), '50–'52; Honolulu Advertiser, '49–'50; Lectr., Emory Univ., Ga. State Col.; PRSA (Ga. Chptr. Secy., '67; Cert. of Achiev., '67); Ga. IEA, Theta Sigma Phi, Atlanta Press Club (Charter Mbr.); Univ. of Southern Cal., '44–'46; State Univ. of Ia., ABJ, '47; Sophia Univ., (Tokyo) grad. study; b. L.A., Cal., 1929; p. Charles and Lillian Myrick Murphy; h. Eugene Paul Craven; c. Michellin Ann, Kimberly Cynthia, Maile Jean; res: 145 Copeland Rd., Atlanta, Ga. 30305.

CRAWFORD, BARBARA, Dir. of Art, Chestnut Hill Academy, 500 W. Willow Grove Ave., Phila., Pa. 19118, '42–; Founder-Dir., Summer in the Arts (Sch. for Crtv. Children), '60–'64; Tchr., Phila. Col. of Art, '43–'45; Wtr: "Day of the Circus" (New Ventures, '50), part I of Trilogy incl. "Cat's Cradle," II, "Lost & Found," III; "Billy the Kid" (musical, '61), "Express with All Stops" (play, '63), "Yes No" (cantata, '64), "Relax, the

Chances Are . . ."; Painter: mural for post off. (Bangor, Pa.); costume design, Phila. Dance Assn.; stage design, Acad. of Music, Co-Opera, Dell Concerts, New Theatre, others; paintings, drawings, prints shown: Print Club, Moore Col. of Art, Acad. of Fine Arts, N.Y. World's Fair, Dubin Gallery, Gallery 55, Art Alliance, Phila. Museum of Art, others; work incl: "Best American Illustration" (by Henry Pitz), bks., mags., collection Phila. Museum of Art, private collections; Analytical Psych. Club of Phila., C. G. Jung Fndn. of N.Y., Mental Health Assn. of S.E. Pa., Phila. Art Alliance (Bd. of Dirs., '40–'45); educ: Phila. Col. of Art, '32–'36; b. New Castle, Pa., 1914; p. Frank H. and Anna Beal Crawford; h. Samuel L. Feinstein (div.); res: 2008 Chancellor St., Phila., Pa. 19103.

CRAWFORD, CAROLYN, Visiting Lectr., Graduate School of Librarianship, Univ. of Denver, Denver, Colo. '69–; Dir., Sch. Libs. and Instructional Materials, Hawaii Dept. of Education (Honolulu), '64–'69; Program Specialist, '59–'64; Asst. Prof., Univ. of Hi., '47–'59; Instr., Oh. Univ (Athens), '42–'47; Children's Librn., Akron, Oh. Public Lib., '37–'42; Lansing, Mich., '36–'37; ALA (Children's Div., Secy., '46), Hi. Lib. Assn. (Pres., '59), Hi. Audio Visual Assn. (Dir., '63–'65), Assn. for Supervision, Curriculum Dev., Nat. Cncl. of Tchrs. of Eng.; Univ. of Mich., AB, '34; AB (Lib. Sci.), '34; Case-Western Reserve, MS (Lib. Sci.), '36; N.Y.U., MS (Lib. Sci.), '53; b. Grant, Mich. 1911; p. David and Agnes Houlding Crawford; res: 1020 15th St. Denver, Colo. 80202.

CRAWFORD, GAY JOHNSTON, Pubcty. Chmn., Junior League of San Jose, Inc., 1990 The Alameda, San Jose, Cal. 95126, '69–; Wtr., Public Affairs, Univ. of Cal., '66–'68; Prod. Asst., San Diego Magazine, '65–'66; Fashion Ed.-Reptr., Berkeley Daily Gazette, '65; Ed.-Reptr., special assigt., Oakland Tribune; Theta Sigma Phi (San Diego Chptr. Founding Mbr., '66), PR Club of San Diego; Bradford Jr. Col., AA, '63; Univ. of Cal., Berkeley, BA, '65 (Outstanding Wm. Jnlst.); Univ. of Salzburg, Austria; active in numerous civic groups; b. N.Y.C., 1943; p. W. D. and J. L. Holmes Johnston; h. Roy Crawford; res: 14711 Aloha St., Saratoga, Cal. 95070.

CRAWFORD, GRACE CREAGER, Wms. Program Dir.-Bdcstr., KQTV, Box 268 Farleigh Station, St. Joseph, Mo. 64506, '61–; Sls., Gen. Diaper Svc., '60–'61; Sls., Avon Cosmetics, '58–'60; Sls., "Better Light for Better Sight" Prog., St. Joseph Light & Power Co., '40–'41; City of St. Joseph, Mo., '36–'40; S. S. Kresge Co., '33–'36; TV Prog. aw., Nat. Assn. for Mental Health, '65, '67; TV Prog. aw., Un. Cerebral Palsy, '63; UNICEF aws., '62–'65; March of Dimes svc. aw., '63; TV Prog. aw., U.S. Air Force, aw., U.S. Navy Recruiting Svc., '69; Public Svc., civic, ch. groups; Platt-Gard Bus. Univ., '33, '34; St. Joseph Jr. Col., '34–'40; b. St. Joseph, Mo., 1915; p. Vernon and Christena Yauchzy Creager; h. James Oren Crawford (dec.); c. Capt. James Jay, U.S.A.F., Stephen C., Robert O., Kay M.; res: 620 N. 23rd St., St. Joseph, Mo. 64506.

CRAWFORD, IRENE SEAGAL, Controller, Secy.-Treas., Chiat/Day Inc., Advertising, 1300 W. Olympic Blvd., L.A., Cal. 90015, '67–; Accountant; Am. Wm. Accountants Soc.; U.C.L.A.; b. Cal., 1927; p. Roy and Jessie McMakin Malicoat; c. Rod; res: 645 Westbridge Pl., Pasadena, Cal. 91105.

CRAWFORD, JOAN, Dir., Pepsi-Cola Co., 500 Park Ave., N.Y., N.Y. 10022, '60–; Dir., Frito-Lay, Inc.; Actress, '25–; Auth: "A Portrait of Joan," (Doubleday, '62); Am. Mktng. Assn. aw. for distinguished achievement in the science of mktng., '70; USO of N.Y.C. (VP and Dir.; Wm. of the Year Aw., '65), Muscular Dystrophy Assn. of Am. (Dir.), Childville, N.Y.C. (Dir.), Nat. Bd. of City of Hope (Wm. of the Year Aw., '67), People to People, Inc. (K.C. Bd. of Trustees), World Rehabilitation Fund, ANTA (Bd. Chmn.), Who's Who in America, CARE, Inc. (Ambassador at Large), N.Y. Tuberculosis and Health Assn. (Christmas Seal Campaign Sponsor), Sls. Exec. Cl. of N.Y.C. (1st wm. mbr., '68), Brandeis Univ. (Fellow, '68); AMPAS (OSCAR for "Mildred Pierce," '45); b. San Antonio, Tex., 1908; p. Thomas and Anna Johnson LeSueur; h. Alfred N. Steele (dec.); c. Christopher, Christina, Cynthia (Mrs. John Jordan), Cathy (Mrs. Jerome LaLonde); res: 150 E. 69th St., N.Y., N.Y. 10021.

CREAGH, AGNES ELIZABETH, Assoc. Dir. of Pubns., College Entrance Examination Board, 475 Riverside Dr., N.Y., N.Y. 10027, '68–; Asst. Dir., '64–'68; Geological Soc. of Am: Ed., Exec. Dir., '62–'64; Mng. Ed., '52–'62; also, Bd. of Dirs., '64–'68; Secy., '64–'67; Fellow, '48–; Geological Soc. of Wash.; Barnard College, BA, '35; Northwestern Univ. Grad. Sch., '35–'36; b. Ridgefield, Conn., 1914; p. William and Mary Brady Creagh; res: 51 Jane's Lane, Stamford, Conn. 06903.

CREASY, KATHRYN SHAFFER, Wms. News Ed., Daily Gazette Company, 332 State St., Schenectady, N.Y. 12301, '67; McGraw-Hill Co., '43–'44; U.S. Naval Reserve Aw.; b. Schenectady, N.Y., 1924; p. Ernest and Lillian Minckler Shaffer; h. Douglas Creasy; c. John, Bruce, Judson, Kathleen, Marueen, Barbara (Mrs. Martin Jacobson); res: 1088 Waverly Pl., Schenectady, N.Y., 12308.

CREE, DOLORES A., PR Cnslt., Rogers, Cowan and Brenner, Inc., 598 Madison Ave., N.Y., N.Y. 10022, '67–; PR Cnslt., Arndt, Preston, Chapin, Lamb & Keen; PR Cnslt., The Rowland Co.; PR Dir., Hawthorn Bks.; Prodr., "Barry Farber Show," WOR Radio; Prod. Asst., Goodson-Todman TV; Free-lance Wtr., nat. mags.; Douglass Col., BS (Polit. Sci.); New School for Social Rsch.; b. Elizabeth, N.J.; p. Theodore and Ann Cree; res: 59 E. 92nd St., N.Y., N.Y. 10028.

CREECY, AUDREY BENNEWITZ, Prodr., Hostess, "Its a Woman's World," KFBB-TV, Harriscope Broadcasting Co., Box 1139, Great Falls, Mont. 59401, '66–; Commty. Club Aws. Dir., KFBB Radio, '65–'66; AWRT (Mont. Big Sky Chptr. VP, '67–'68), Adv. Club of Great Falls, AWRT (Mont. Big Sky Chptr. Pres., '69–'70),

Great Falls Press Club, Theatre Guild; Am. Music Assn. aw., '68; Assn. Inventors Congress aw., '68; Two Thousand Wm. of Achiev., '69; b. St. Cloud, Minn., 1935; p. Leo and Anna Mathiasen Bennewitz; c. Bruce James, Rebecca Sue; res: 421 Riverview Dr. N.E., Great Falls, Mont. 59401.

CREEL, JANE ESTELLA, Dir. of Home Econs., Lever Brothers Company, 390 Park Ave., N.Y., N.Y. 10022, '60–; Mgr., Home Econs., '57–'60; Mgr., Home Econs., Monsanto Co. (St. Louis, Mo.), '55–'57; Svc. Mgr., Macy's (S.F., Cal.), '47–'51; Sr. Staff Asst., Am. Red Cross (S. Pacific Area), '45–'47; AWNY (1st VP), ZONTA, Am. Home Econs. Assn., Home Econsts. in Bus. (Former mbr., Nat. Exec. Comm.; Past Chmn., N.Y. Chptr.), N.Y. Wms. Cncl. of N.Y. State Dept. of Commerce, Nat. Cncl. of Wm. of the U.S., CWPR, Am. Home Econs. Assn., Am. Nat. Standards Inst., Grocery Mfrs. of Am., Electrical Wms. Round Table (former Nat. Bd. Mbr.), Assn. of Home Appliance Manufacturers (Consumer Ed. Comm.), Advisory Cncl. of N.Y. State Col. of Human Ecology (Cornell Univ.); Univ. of Nev., BS (Home Econs.), '45; b. Reno, Nev., 1923; p. Cecil and Laura Stevens Creel; Res: 201 E. 66th St., N.Y., N.Y. 10021.

CRENSHAW, WANDA L., Dir., Univ. Libs., Central State University, Hallie Q. Brown Memorial Library, Wilberforce, Oh. 45384, '66–; U.S. Army Librn., European Command, '60–'66; Delta Sigma Theta, Inter-Univ. Lib. Cncl. (Chmn.), Oh. Lib. Assn.; Paine Col., BA (Sociol.), '55; Carnegie Inst. of Tech., MS (Lib. Sci.), '60; b. Cinn., Oh., 1936; p. Walter and Anna Williams Crenshaw; res: P.O. Box 183, Wilberforce, Oh. 45384.

CRIDLAND, NANCY A., Off. Mgr., Radio Station WCLV, Penthouse East, Terminal Tower, Cleve., Oh. 44113, '68–; Fyffe's Bus. Col., Kirkcaldy, Scotland, 3rd Class Engineer's License with Bdcst. Endorsement; b. Kirkcaldy, Fife, Scotland, 1931; p. Alex and Margaret Grieve; res: 4432 Norma Dr., Cleve., Oh. 44121.

CRISAFULLI, MARY ALICE, Media Supvsr., Clinton E. Frank, Inc., 120 S. Riverside Plaza, Chgo., Ill. 60606, '65–; Time Byr. of the Yr., '67; p. Samuel J. Crisafulli.

CRISPO, DOROTHY HUMMEL, Pres., Dorex Features International, 235 E. 57th St., N.Y., N.Y. 10022, '68; Free-lance Wtr., special surveys, assigts; Cnslt., Spanish-Eng., Portuguese Texts; Reader, Doubleday, Spanish, French, Portuguese, Italian; Translator; Rsch; Co-auth: "Speak Everyday Spanish," (Dell, '67); Auth: "Tell Me, Dorothy . . ." (synd. nwsp. colm.); Wtr., gags, material for performing artists; educ: Schs. in Latin American and Europe; b. Chgo., Ill; p. Ragnar and Eleanor Boyle Hummel; h. Paul Crispo; res: 420 E. 52st St., N.Y., N.Y. 10022.

CRISS, CHERYL, Staff Wtr., Dayton Daily News, Fourth and Ludlow, Dayton, Oh. 45401, '67; 1st pl. aw., Oh. State Heart Assn. Public Info. Contest, '69;

Oh. Wesleyan Univ., BA, '67; b. Rahway, N.J., 1944; p. Richard and Miriam Bigelow Criss; res: 14 McDaniel St., Dayton, Oh. 45405.

CRIST, JUDITH, Film Critic, New York mag., '68–; TV Guide, '66–; Film, Theatre Critic, "Today Show," NBC-TV, '63–; Film Critic, N.Y. World Journal Tribune, '66–'67; Film Critic, New York Herald-Tribune, '63–'66; Assoc. Drama Critic, '57–'66; Ed. for the Arts, '60–'63; Reptr., '45–'60; Adjunct. Prof. of Jnlsm., Columbia Univ. Grad. Sch. of Jnlsm., '58–; Auth., "The Private Eye, The Cowboy & The Very Naked Girl," ('68); Columbia Grad. Sch. of Jnlsm. Alumni (Pres., '67, '69) N.Y. NWC (VP, '64–'65; aws., '67, '65, '63, '59, '55), N.Y. Nwsp. Guild aw., '55; George Polk aw., '51; Educ. Wtrs. Assn. aw., '52; Hunter Col., BA, '41; Columbia Grad. School of Jnlsm., MS, '45 (alumni aw., '61, medal, '63); b. N.Y.C., 1922; p. Solomon and Helen Schoenberg Klein; h. William B. Crist; c. Steven Gordon; res: 180 Riverside Dr., N.Y., N.Y. 10024.

CRITTENDEN, LOUISE, Free-lance Wtr. and Ed.; Ed., Rutgers Univ. Press, '64–'66; Head of Pubcty. for children's bks., Viking Press, '55–'63; Adv., Sls. Prom., and Pubcty., Pocket Bks., '41–'44; Bk. Byr., Stern Bros., '35–'40; Asst. Bk. Byr., R. H. Macy, '30–'35; ALA, Wms. Nat. Bk. Assn.; Rutgers Univ., AB, '30 (with hons.); b. N.Y.C., 1909; p. Holt Wilson and Lizzielee Mahon Crittenden; h. Joseph Reiner (div.); c. Carolyn (Mrs. David Kinsley); res: Newton, Va. 23126.

CROCKETT, FRANCES WOOD, Librn., Walter Cecil Rawls Library & Museum, Courtland, Va. 23837, '62–; U.S. Naval Reserve WAVE Offcr., '43–'47; Dist. Lib. Supvsr. (Gainesville, Ga.), '40–'43; County Librn., Lunenburg (Va.) Public Lib., '39–'40; High Sch. Tchr., '32–'38; Va. Lib. Assn., John Tyler Commty. Col. Lib. Advisory Comm.; Madison Col., BS, '32; Col. of William and Mary, '35; George Washington Univ., '37–'38; Emory Univ. Lib. Sch., AB '39; b. Chesterfield County, Va., 1912; p. Clarence and Lillie Cole Wood; h. David Crockett; c. David, Jr., Joseph, Harold; res: 522 Butler Ave., Suffolk, Va. 23434.

CROCKETT, OPAL, Fashion Ed., Indianapolis Star, Indianapolis Newspapers, Inc., 307 N. Pennsylvania St., Indpls. Ind. 46206, '65–; Reptr., Fashion, Beauty, Homes Ed., Indianapolis Times, '49–'65; Reptr., Soc. Ed., Logansport (Ind.) Pharos-Tribune, '33–'46; Reptr., Bloomington (Ind.) '31–'33; Theta Sigma Phi; h. Robert Surendorf (div.); res: 1638 N. Pennsylvania St., Indpls., Ind. 46202.

CROFFORD, LENA HENRICHSON, Auth., Tchr., Wichita Falls Public Schs., 1912 11th, Wichita Falls, Tex. 76302, '57–; Agua Dulce Public Schs., '41–'56; Novice Public Schs., '56–'57; Auth., "Pioneers on the Nueces" (Naylor Co., '63); Poems publ. in "Verses" ('66); AAUW, Delta Kappa Gamma, Wichita Falls Poetry Soc. (Pres., '63–'66); Tex. A. and I. Col., BA, MA; Univ. of Tex., '49–'50; Univ. of Colo., '59–'61; Univ. of Wyo., '62–'63; b. San Patricio, Tex., 1908; p. Horace and

Jurdena Poole Henrichson; h. Verner R. Crofford; c. Mrs. Clara Vernelle Whitson; res: 3703 Sheridan, Wichita Falls, Tex. 76302.

CRONE, RUTH BEVERLY, Asst. Prof. of Eng., Wtr., Mankato State College, Box 53, Box 209, MSC, Mankato, Minn. 56001, '65–; Tchr., various cols., '58–'64; Reptr., Edtl., Beatrice (Neb.) Daily Sun, '54–'58; News, Circ., Edtl., N.Y. Times, '51–'53; U.S. Dept. of State (Shanghi, Seoul), and Army Intelligence (Tokyo), '49–'50; Repts. Ed., Port of N.Y. Authority, '44–'49; Proof-reader, Rschr., Wtr., U.S. Dept. of Commerce (Wash., D.C.), '40–'44; numerous articles, short stories, revs.; Modern Lang. Assn., AAUW; 12 aws., Neb. Press Wm.; short story aw. for "Deep, Down Under," NPWC, '59; Jr. Lit. Guild Selection, "The Silent Storm;" Peru (Neb.) State Col., AB, '42; George Washington Univ., MA, '45; N.Y.U., PhD, '61; b. Lincoln, Neb., 1919; p. Burley R. and Willie Ethel Jones Crone; res: Apt 53, 418 S. 38th Ave., Omaha, Neb. 68131.

CROOK, CLARA BROSSELL, Asst. Dean, Student and Industry Relations, University of Wisconsin, Milw., Wis. 53201, '69–; Asst. to Dean, '66–'69; Dir. PR, Bostrom Corp., '63–'66; PR Dir., Fairlea Farms, '58–'63; PR Dir., Gen. Mdse. Co., '55–'58; Cnslt., pfsnl. socs.; Coordr., Bus. Dynamics; PRSA, APRA, Wms. Adv. Club, Intl. Platform Assn.; Downer Col., BA, '33; grad. work, Keene State Tchrs. Col.; b. Newcastle, New Brunswick, Can., 1913; p. I. V. and Celia Grossman Brossell; c. David B. Zenoff, Victoria B. Zenoff; res: 803 E. Glen Ave., Milw., Wis. 53217.

CROOKSTON, MARY EVALYN, Rsch. Librn., House Organ Ed., Meldrum and Fewsmith, Inc., 1220 Huron Rd., Cleve., Oh. 44115, '46–; Ref. Asst., Cleve. Public Lib., '44–'46; Svc. Command Librn., '42–'44 (Army Aw. for outstanding and meritorious svc., '44); Camp Librn., Ft. Eustis, Va., '41–'42; ALA Fellow, U.S. Off. of Educ., '40–'41; Chief, Circ. Dept., Lincoln Lib., Springfield, Ill., '37–'39; Guest Lectr., Case Western Reserve Univ., '47–'68; Special Libs. Assn. (Nat. Adv. Div. Chmn., '51, '52; Chptr. Pres., '48–'49); Eureka Col., AB, '40 (magna cum laude); Western Reserve Univ., Cert. in Lib. Sci., '31; b. Thayer, Ill.; p. James and Bertha Jackson Crookston; res: 312 Cornell Ave., Elyria, Oh. 44035.

CROSBY, CATHY LEE, Actress, Singer, model, c/o Jack Wormser Agency, Hollywood, Cal.; active in films, TV for 17 yrs.; numerous TV commls.; appearances at Univ. of Southern Cal. summer stock theater; regular on "Dean Martin Summer Show," '68; SAG, AFTRA; Univ. of Southern Cal., BA (Sociol.), '67; b. L.A., Cal.; p. Lou and Linda Hayes Crosby; h. Alexander W. Ingle; res: 222 N. Ave. 66, L.A., Cal. 90042.

CROSBY, JOAN CAREW, Entertainment Ed., Newspaper Enterprise Association, 230 Park Ave., N.Y., N.Y. 10017, '67–; TV Ed., '60; Free-lance Wtr., Pubcty. Dir., Sports Wtr., Bklyn Eagle; Lectr., Radio, TV; Nwsp. Wms. Club of N.Y. (3rd VP, '69), Catholic Inst. of the

Press (Charter Mbr.), SAG, AFTRA; b. Balt., Md., 1933; p. Thomas and Mary O'Rourke Crosby.

CROSLAND, DOROTHY MURRAY, Dir. of Libs., Georgia Institute of Technology, Atlanta, Ga. 30332, '53–; Librn., '27–'53; Asst. Librn., '25–'27; Cataloger, Br. Librn., Atlanta Public Lib., '23–'25; Cnslt., Libs. and Bldgs; Special Investigator, NSF Study on Training Sci. Info. Specialists, '61–'62; ALA, active in many other lib. orgs., incl. Intl. Assn. of Tech. Univ. Libs.; Atlanta Art Assn., Atlanta Hist. Soc.; Atlanta's Wm. of the Yr. in Educ., '45; Ga. Inst. of Tech., Hon. Alumnus, '61; educ: Atlanta Lib. Sch., Cert., Lib. Sci; b. Stone Mountain, Ga., 1903; p. Robert and Lena Jones Murray; h. J. Henry Crosland; c. Dorothy (Mrs. Ben Daugherty); res: 125 Lakeview Ave., N.E., Atlanta, Ga. 30305.

CROWDER, CAROLYN ALEXANDER, Free-lance PR, '69–; Asst. Info. Coordr., Univ. of Tex., Anderson Hosp. and Tumor Inst. (Houston), '68–'69; Asst. Ed., '64–'65; PR Supvsr., Associated Credit Burs., '65–'68; Theta Sigma Phi (Houston Pfsnl. Chptr. Pres., '68–'69; Univ. of Ala. Chptr. Pres., '63–'64), Wms. PR Cncl. of St. Joseph's Hosp. (Hon. Mbr.), Delta Zeta; Outstanding Young Wm. of Am.; Univ. of Ala., BA (Jnlsm.), '62; b. Greenville, S.C., 1941; p. Claude and Blanche Byars Alexander; h. Henry Johnston Crowder; res: 3700 Mountain Ave., Apt. 5-B, San Bernardino, Cal. 92404.

CROWE, LOIS RAY, Ed., Holiday Inn Magazine, 3779 Lamar Ave., Memphis, Tenn. 38118; '61–; Staff Wtr., Memphis Press-Scimitar, '44–'61; Mng. Ed., Continental Trailways Magazine, '68–; Mag. Publrs. Assn., Intl. Platform Assn.; Am. Soc. of Magazine Eds.; George Washington Honor Medal, '65; Murray State Col., Murray, Ky., '39–'40; b. Jackson, Tenn., 1920; p. John and Mary Lee Smith Ray; h. Charles Crowe (div.); c. Charles David, Jr., John Hunter; res: 1836 Cherry Rd., Memphis, Tenn. 38117.

CROWE, MARY BENNETT, Co-publr., Co-ed., Dos Palos Star and Firebaugh-Mendota Journal, 1527 Center Ave., Dos Palos, Cal. 93620; '40–; active in local poverty pgm., '64–'70; Cal. Press Wm. (VP, '64–'65; state aws.: second place, ed., '65; second place, feature, '65), ADAPT (Central Valley Commtns. Task Force Chmn., '68–'69); Cal. Elem. Sch. Adm. Assn. Golden Apple Aw., '67; Univ. of Cal., Berkeley, '37–'40; b. Trinidad, Colo., 1918; p. Harlo and Mary Marty Bennett; h. William M. Crowe; c. Maradeane Adler; res: P.O. Box 157, Pebble Beach, Cal. 93953.

CROWE, ROSALIND ROBLES, Free-lance Hist. Rschr.-Wtr.; Yuma County Hist. Soc., '69–; Corr., Ariz. Republic, '64–'69; Reptr., Wms. Features, Tucson Daily Citizen, '60–'63; Reptr., Ariz. Daily Star, '58–'59; Theta Sigma Phi; Univ. of Ariz., BA, '58; b. Jerome, Ariz., 1936; p. Robert and Amparo Mayagoitia Robles; h. Tommy Keith Crowe; c. Kathleen, David; res: 3095 Del Mar Ave., Yuma, Ariz. 85364.

CROWELL, NANI LEWIS, Edtl. Adm. Asst. and Secy.

to Ed., The Honolulu Advertiser, P.O. Box 3110, Honolulu, Hi. 96802, '68–; Honolulu Press Club (Secy., '69); h. Richard L. Crowell.

CROWLEY, JUDITH ANNE, Traf. Mgr., Ingalls Associates, Inc., 137 Newbury St., Boston, Mass. 02116, '66–; Prod. Mgr., Boston mag., '64–'66; Traf. Mgr., Harold Cabot & Co., '58–'64; Artist, Shattuck Clifford McMillan, '56–'58; Cnslt: set up traf. dept. for Boston agcy.; organized art studio (Boston, Mass.); Boston Univ. (Ga., Adv.), '57–'64; b. Boston, Mass.; p. Joseph F. and Alice Cherbuy Crowley; res: 57 Gallivan Blvd., Dorchester, Mass. 02124.

CRUICKSHANK, HELEN GERE, Wtr., Photogr., specializing in wildlife; Auth: "Thoreau on Birds" (McGraw-Hill, '65), "A Paradise of Birds" (Dodd, Mead, '68), nine other bks.; Soc. of Wm. Geographers, Fla. Fedn. of Garden Clubs, Nat. Audubon Soc., Nat. Parks Assn., Nature Conservancy, Fla. Govs. Natural Resources Comm.; John Burroughs medal, '49; Oppenheimer nature bk. aw., '68; Pa. State Univ., BS, '27; Syracuse Univ. Lib. Sch., '35; b. Bklyn., Pa., 1907; p. Charles and Hilda Alworth Gere; h. Allan Cruickshank; res: 1925 Indian River Dr., Rockledge, Fla. 32955.

CRUMBAKER, MARGE, Feature Wtr., Tempo Sunday Magazine, The Houston Post, 2410 Polk, Houston, Tex. 77001, '63–; Pres., Charter Properties, Inc. '69–; Houston Press, '56–'63; Dir., Wms. Prog., KHOU-TV, '53–'56; Pres., Highland Village Music Agcy., '46–'53; Crumbaker Music Agcy., '46; AWRT, Tex. Cattleman's Assn., Nwsp. Guild of Am., Am. Press Club, C. of C., Tau Beta Sigma; Tex. Headliner's Club Aw. '62; UPI Edtl. Writing Aw., '63; Tex. Tech. Col., '44–'46; b. Sand Springs, Okla. 1924; p. Howard and Katherine Lucas Simpson; res: 2620 Crocker, Houston, Tex. 77006.

CRUMPACKER, BETTE, VP, Bauer Tripp Heninc & Bressler, 211 E. 43rd St., N.Y., N.Y. 10017, '67–; VP, Crtv. Dir., Vernon Pope Co.; Acc. Supvsr., Grey Adv.; Acc. Supvsr., Harshe, Rotman & Druck; Mgr., Daniel J. Edelman Assoc.; Edtl. Chief, Toni Co.; Prom. Features, Chicago Tribune; Cnslt., The Brides' Inst., Urban Renewal Projects; Pres., Sound of Youth rehabilitation program; PRSA (Accredited Mbr.), NHFL; Univ. of Pitt., BA, '48; b. Northfield, N.J., 1924; p. Charles and Margaret Meyer Allardice; h. Norman Seigerman; c. Catherine Diane; res: 375 West End Ave., N.Y., N.Y. 10024.

CRUSE, HELOISE, Auth., Colmst., Bdcstr., "Hints from Heloise," King Features Syndicate, 235 E. 45 St., N.Y., N.Y. 10017, '61–; Colmst., The Honolulu Advertiser, '59–'69; Synd. Radio Prog., "Here's Heloise," '65–; Auth: Heloise's "Housekeeping Hints," "Kitchen Hints," "All Around the House," "Work and Money Savers;" Bklet: "Heloise's Hints on Rug and Carpet Care;" "Silver Lady" aw., Banshees, '64.

CRUSE, IRMA RUSSELL, PR Supvsr. and Ed., BAMA

Bulletin, South Central Bell Telephone Co., 1710 Building, Birmingham, Ala. 35202, '66–; Comml. Engineering Dept., '54–'56; Free-lance Wtr. (numerous non-fiction articles), '58–; Birmingham Assn. of Indsl. Eds. (Pres., '68–'69; 2nd VP, '66–'67; Dir of Nat. Affairs, '68–'69), Southern Cncl. of Indsl. Eds., Theta Sigma Phi (Corr. Secy.), BPW (Birmingham Met. Chptr.) Wm. of Achiev., '68–'69; Birmingham Southern Col.; b. Hackneyville, Ala., 1911; p. Charles Henry and Nellie Ledbetter Russell; h. J. Clyde Cruse (dec.); c. Alan B., Howard R.; res: 136 Memory Ct., Birmingham, Ala. 35213.

CRUTCHER, MARY E., Asst. City Ed., The Fort Worth Press, Fifth at Jones, Fort Worth, Tex. 76109, '50s–; formerly reptr.; Theta Sigma Phi (aw. for excellence in jnlsm., '60), Press Club of Ft. Worth; Fort Worth Sigma Delta Chi Aw., '54, '50, '47; Tex. Wms. Univ., BS; res: 2909 South Hills Ave., Ft. Worth, Tex. 76109.

CUDDY, C. VICKI, FORSTER-CLARKE, Dir. PR, Riverside Methodist Hospital, 3535 Olentangy River Rd., Columbus, Oh. 43214, '62–; Asst. Dir., Volunteer Svcs., '61–'62; Cnslt., Photographic Audio-Visuals, '59–'61; Owner, Comml. Photog. Studio, '52–'59; Co-owner, Columbus Light Opera Co., '46–'51; bklets., mag. articles; PR Soc. Columbus, Oh. Hosp. Assn., Intl. Platform Assn., Soc. of Hosp. PR Dirs., Theta Sigma Phi, ZONTA; N.Y. Bus. and Law Sch., '32–'34; Oh. State Univ., '64–'65; b. N.Y.C., 1914; p. Alvanley and Irene Dossor Forster-Clarke; h. William T. Cuddy; c. William H., John C.; res: 642 Beautyview Ct., Columbus, Oh. 43214.

CULLEN, BONNIE MAUREEN, Bdcst. Mgr., Scali, McCabe, Sloves, Inc. 345 Park Ave., N.Y., N.Y. 10022, '67–; Traf. Mgr., Carl Ally, '66–'67; Traf., Grey Adv., '64–'66; Bucknell Univ., BA, '64; N.Y. Inst. of Adv.; N.Y. Sch. of Interior Design; b. Mineola, N.Y., 1942; p. William and Sylvia Tuomola Cullen; res: 1558 Second Ave., N.Y., N.Y. 10028.

CULLIGAN, GLENDY, Free-lance Wtr.; Instr. in Eng., Montgomery College, Rockville, Md., '69–; Bk. Ed., Washington Post, '56–'65; Features Ed., '52–'56; Asst. to Wms. Ed., '49–'52; Wms. Ed., New Orleans (La.) Item, '45–'49; Asst. News and Telegraph Ed., '44–'47; Chief Copy Ed., '43–'44; Reptr., Feature Wtr., '42–'43, '37–'40; h. William R. Pabst, Jr.

CULLMAN, MARGUERITE WAGNER, Auth: non-fiction, "Occupation Angel" (W. W. Norton, '65), "Ninety Dozen Glasses" ('60); Wtr., contrbr., N.Y. Times Magazine, '44–'50; Assoc. Ed., Stage Magazine, '35–'36; PR Head, Bonwit Teller, '34–'35; PR Cnsl., Marguerite Wagner, '31–'34; Ed., Vincent Lit. Agcy., '31; Ed. Asst., McNaught Synd., '27–'29; Lectr.; Commentator, drama radio and TV; Free-lance Wtr., mags., nwsps., ency.; Belgian Order of Leopold, '59; Cross Pro Ecclesia et Pontifica (Pope Pius XII, '60); Spence Chapin Home for Adoption (Bd. of Dir.),

Lighthouse (Bd. of Dir.), N.Y. Assn. for Blind, Sch. of Performing Arts (Chmn. Adv.); Columbia Col.; b. N.Y.C., 1908; p. Albert and Marguerite Henry Sanders; h. Howard S. Cullman; c. Marguerite (Mrs. John Andrew Hesse, III), Brian; res: 480 Park Ave., N.Y., N.Y.; Woodbrook Farm, Purchase, N.Y. 10577.

CULVER, KATHERINE B., Cnslt., Educational Media Utilization, Dade County Public Schools, 1410 N.E. Second Ave., Miami, Fla. 33132, '69–; tchr., Dade County and Ga. Schs.; Cnslt., Educ. TV, Ford Fndn. and FSU, '60–'61; Coordr., ETV Utilization, '61–'69; contrb., pfsnl. jnls.; NEA, Fla. Educ. Assn., Dade County Educ. Assn. (Charter Mbr.), ACEI (Dade County Br. Pres., '69–'70; 1st VP, Corr. Secy., Rec. Secy.), Delta Kappa Gamma (Chptr. Pres.), Fla. Assn. for ETV (Area Dir., Pres., '69–'70), ASCD, FASCD, FAVA (Fla. AV Assn.), DAVI; Shorter Col., Rome, Ga. (Special Art Aw., '37–'38), Univ. of Ga., BFA, '47 (cum laude), Univ. of Miami, MEd., '64; b. Girard, Ala., 1920; p. Lewis and Marie Dudley Culver; res: 12895 N.W. Sixth Ave., Miami, Fla. 33168.

CULVERHOUSE, RUTH JULIA, Radio and TV Prod. Dir., Parker and Associates, Inc., 1515 City Federal Bldg., Birmingham, Ala. 35203, '67–; Traffic Asst., Cont. Dir., WBRC-TV, '61–'67; Blue Cross-Blue Shield of Ala., '59–'61.

CUMBER, LILLIAN JOHNSON, Owner, Lil Cumber Attractions, 6515 Sunset, Hollywood, Cal. 90028, '56–; Agt. for religious groups, Herald Attractions, '49–'55; Nwsp. Colmst.; Magazine Publr.; NAACP (Hollywood Beverly Hills Br. Secy.); Pioneer in Bus., Nat. Assn. Negro Bus. and Pfsnl. League, '67; b. San Antonio, Tex., 1920; p. David and Lora L. Johnson; res: 6478 Ivarene Ave., Hollywood, Cal. 90028.

CUMMING, PATRICIA ARENS, Edtl. Assoc., Daedalus, American Academy of Arts and Sciences, 7 Linden St., Cambridge, Mass. 02138, '66–; Eng. Instr., Univ. of Mass. Boston Campus, '69–; Co.-Prodr., Theatre Co. of Boston, '64–'65; Eng. Instr., Mass. Inst. of Tech., '69–; Radcliffe Col., BA, '54 (magna cum laude, Phi Beta Kappa); Middlebury Grad. Sch., MA; b. N.Y.C., 1932; p. Egmont and Camille Davied Arens; h. Edward Cumming; c. Julie Emelyn, Susanna Arens; res: 83 Phillips St., Boston, Mass. 02114.

CUMMINGS, DAWN CALHOUN, Wms. News Ed., Arlington Daily News, 208 S. East St., Arlington, Tex. 76010, '63–; Tchr., Gordon, Annona Schs., '42–'45; Wtr., Ed., Tex. nwsps., '41–'42; Theta Sigma Phi, Tex. State Tchrs. Assn. (Secy., Palo Pinto County Unit), Arlington C. of C., Soroptimist Intl.; Tex. State Col. for Wm., BJ, '41; b. Gordon, Tex., 1919; p. Beal and Claudia Harrison Calhoun; h. John R. Cummings; c. Joe; res: 841 Roosevelt St., Arlington, Tex. 76010.

CUMMINS, LINDA LEEDS, Asst. Ed., Modern Manufacturing, McGraw-Hill Publications, 330 W. 42nd St., N.Y., N.Y. 10036, '67–; Asst. Ed., Product

Engineering, '65–'67; Edtl. Asst., Am. Cncl. of Voluntary Agcys. for Fgn. Svc., '64–'65; William & Mary Col., '54–'56; Toutorsky Acad. of Music, '56–'63; b. Norfolk, Va., 1936; p. William and Newell Lacy Cummins; res: 319 W. 18th St., N.Y., N.Y. 10011.

CUNNINGHAM, EVELYN, Dir., Women's Unit, Office of the Governor, Special Assistant to the Governor, New York State Executive Chamber, 22 W. 55th St., N.Y., N.Y. 10019, '69–; Assoc. Dir., '67–'69; Special Asst. to Jackie Robinson, '66–'67; Commentator, WLIB, '61–'66; City Ed., N.Y. Courier, '55–'63; Reptr., '45–'55; CWPR, Media Wm., Interracial Cncl. for Bus. Opportunities, N.Y. State Wms. Cncl., Harlem Cultural Cncl; Long Island Univ., BS, '43; h. (div.); res: 725 Riverside Dr., Apt. 8B, N.Y., N.Y. 10031.

CUNNINGHAM, JEAN A., Graphic Designer, Columbia Records, 51 W. 52nd St., N.Y., N.Y. 10019, '64–; Designer, Pavey, Jones & Lewis, '62–'64; Designer, James Valkus, '61–'62; Designer, Doubleday Publ., '60–'61; NARAS, Nat. Arts Club; Cooper Union, '60 (Graphic Design Aw., '60); b. Norwalk, Conn., 1938; p. Arthur and Pauline Troiano Cunningham; res: 546 Third Ave., N.Y., N.Y. 10016.

CUNNINGHAM, ROSEMARY ANDERSON, PR Rep., Unevangelized Fields Mission, 4200 W. 67th Terr., Prairie Village, Kan. 66208, '64–; Missionary to Brazil in Evangelism, Educ., Lit., '39–'64; Auth: "Under a Thatched Roof," "Harvest Moon on the Amazon," "When the Arrow Flies"; Wms. Radio Progs., '65–'69; St. Paul Bible Col., '36; Nyack Missionary Col., '37; Missionary Med. Sch., '38; b. Chgo., Ill., 1916; p. Harry and Mable Anderson; h. Angus Cunningham; c. Maryellen, John, Mark, Donald, Laurel, Carol Smuland; res: 4200 W. 67th Terr., Prairie Village, Kan. 66208.

CUNNINGHAM, SARAH MARTHA, Ed., Concern Magazine, United Presbyterian Women, 475 Riverside Dr., N.Y., N.Y. 10027, '63–; Assoc. Ed., '62; Assoc. Ed., youth pubns., Friendship Press, Nat. Cncl. of Churches, '60–'62; Ed., church sch. pubns., Cumberland Presbyterian Church (Memphis, Tenn.), '53–'59; AAUW; Who's Who of Am. Wm.; Southeast Mo. State Col., BA, '47; Syracuse Univ., MA, '53; b. Girard, Ala., 1925; p. Moses and Zula Easterwood Cunningham; res: 606 W. 116th St., Apt. 84, N.Y., N.Y. 10027.

CUNNINGHAM, VIRGINIA MEEKS, Head, Music Sec., Descriptive Cataloging Div., Library of Congress, Wash., D.C. 20540, '57–; Head, Copyright Cataloging Div., '46–'57; Music Lib. Assn. (Pres., '56–'58), Intl. Assn. of Music Libs., ALA, D.C. Lib. Assn., League of Wm. Voters (Prince George's County Pres., '69–'71); Stephens Col., AA, '30; Univ. of Wis., AB, '32; b. Bridgeport, Ill., 1910; p. William and Lora Madding Meeks; h. Charles Howard Cunningham; c. William Howard, David Martin, Lora Comfort; res: 3649 Greenway Dr., Suitland, Md. 20023.

CURLEY, DOROTHY NYREN, Coordr. of Adult Svcs., Brooklyn Public Library, Grand Army Plaza, Bklyn., N.Y. 11238, '68–; Chief Librn., Northbrook Public Lib. (Ill.), '66–'67; Publ. Dept., ALA, '65; Town Librn. (Concord, Mass.) '59–'64; Br. Librn., Newton Public Lib., '58; Dir., Young Lib. (Daytona Beach, Fla.), '55–'57; Head, Svc. Dept., Ginn and Co., '53–'54; Auth: "Modern Romance Literature" (Ungar, '67), "Modern American Literature (Ungar, '60, '61, '63); ALA, active in lib orgs.; Boston Univ., BA, '52 (Phi Beta Kappa); MA, '54; Simmons Col., MS (Lib. Sci.), '62; h. Arthur Curley.

CURRIE, HAZEL SHORE, Publicist, Chris Dundee Enterprises, Inc., Miami Beach Auditorium, Miami Beach, Fla.; Dir., Hazel Shore PR (Wash., D.C.); News Ed., Pacific Edition, Stars and Stripes (Tokyo, Japan); Publicist, Peekskill Enterprises ("Jackie Gleason Show"); Dir. PR, D.C. Soc. for Crippled Children; Wash., D.C. Heart Assn.; Am. Red Cross, Mediterranean, WW II; Montagu Beach Hotel, Nassau, Bahamas; Reptr: Miami Beach Reptr., Greensboro Daily News, Winston Salem Jnl.; Feature Wtr., Miami Herald; Fgn. Corr., UN, Korea War; Contrbr., Holiday, Town and Country, Diplomat, AMA Jnl.; OPC, Am. Overseas Assn. (Wash., D.C. Chptr. Pres.); Univ. of N.C., (Jnlsm.); h. (div.); res: 6972 Carlyle Ave., Miami Beach, Fla. 33141.

CURRIER, BETTY YATER, Mng. Ed., California Farm Bureau Federation, 2855 Telegraph Ave., Berkeley, Cal. 94705, '64–; Asst. Ed., '61–'64; Agricultural Feature Wtr., '55–'61; Wms. Ed., Classified Adv. Dept., '51–'55; Bay Area Soc. of Indsl. Communicators (Secy.-Treas., '66–'67); Coop. Farm Eds. Assn.; Univ. of Cal., AB, '51; b. Oakland, Cal., 1928; p. Roscoe and Ruth Crawford Yater; h. Philip Currier; res: 4066 Harding Way, Oakland, Cal. 94602.

CURRO, EVELYN MALONE, Free-lance Artist, Art Publr., Wtr., Illus.; res: 255 W. 18th St., N.Y., N.Y. 10011.

CURRY, JEAN, Corp. Asst. Sec., Pers. Dir., Cunningham & Walsh, Inc., 260 Madison Ave., N.Y., N.Y. 10016, '61–; Asst. Secy., '57–; Adm. Asst. to Opns. Comm., '55–'57; Adm. Asst. to Pres., Convair Div. of Gen. Dynamics Corp., '48–'55; Secy. to Pres., TWA, '43–'48; AWNY; Baker Univ., AB, '39; N.Y.U., '62; b. Cherokee, Kan.; p. Olin and Sadie T. Curry; res: 201 E. 19th St., N.Y., N.Y. 10003.

CURTIS, ALICE PARTLOW, PR Offcr., The Merrill-Palmer Institute, 71 E. Ferry Ave., Detroit, Mich. 48202, '66–; PR Dir., YWCA of Met. Detroit, '50–'66; Asst. PR Dir., Mich. Blue Cross, '44–'50; Nwsp. Ed., Ft. Wayne Army Post, '43–'44; Wtr., Jam Handy Org., '41–'43; Auth., "Is Your Publicity Showing?" (D. Van Nostrand Co., '49); Cit., Jnlsm. Dept., Mich. State Univ., '50; Wms. Adv. Club of Detroit aw., '50); Free-lance Photgr., "Pet Portraits by Alice Curtis;" Contrbr., nwsps., prof. jnls.; PRSA (accredited mbr.), Theta

Sigma Phi, Detroit Press Club; Marshall Col., AB, '28; King's Col., Univ. of London, '32; Columbia Univ., '33; b. Keystone, W.Va.; p. Ira and Andrea Martin Partlow; h. Hal Curtis (dec.); res: 16826 Cranford Lane, Grosse Pointe, Mich. 48230.

CURTIS, CHARLOTTE MURRAY, Wms. News Ed., The New York Times, 229 W. 43rd St., N.Y., N.Y. 10036, '65–; Feature Wtr., '61–'65; Feature Wtr., The Columbus (Oh.) Citizen Journal, '50–'61; Radio Commentator, WMNI, '60–'61; Auth: "First Lady" ('63); Contrbr: "The Soviet Union: The Fifty Years," ('67); Freelance Wtr., various mags.; Oh. Nwsp. Wms. Assn. (numerous rept. and writing aws., '50–'61), N.Y. Nwsp. Wms. Club (aws. for news stories, features, '63, '65, '68), ANWC (Gold Pen Aw., '69); Vassar Col., BA; b. Chgo., Ill.; p. Dr. George and Lucile Atcherson Curtis.

CURTIS, EDITH ROELKER, Auth: "Mexican Romance," "A Season in Utopia, the Story of Brook Farm" ('61; NLAPW non-fiction aw., '62), "Love's Random Dart" ('60); Biographer: "Lady Sarah Lennox, An Irrepressible Stuart" ('46), "Anne Hutchinson, A Biography" ('30); Poet; Instr., several wtrs. confs.; NLAPW (State Pres., '56; Boston Br. Pres., '54–'55; aws., '61, '62), Boston Auths. Club (Pres., '67–'69; 2nd VP, '66–'67), Marquis Biographical Soc. (Advisory Mbr., '69); Who's Who in the East; Who's Who of Am. Wm.; Radcliffe Col., '20–'22; b. E. Greenwich, R.I. 1893; p. William G. and Eleanor Jenckes Roelker; h. (dec.); c. Sally (Mrs. Lewis Iselin, Jr.), Anita Curtis McClellan, Dr. Charles P., William R., Richard C. (dec.); res: Two Apple Trees, Main St., Dublin, N.H. 03444.

CURTIS, LISA, VP in Charge of Fashion and PR, Fur and Sport, Inc., Suite 808, 276 Fifth Ave., N.Y., N.Y., '69–; Fashion and Pubcty. Dir., '62–'69; formerly freelance pubcty, prom.; Fashion Chmn., Botticelli Ball, four yrs.; Coordr., parties, fashion shows; Fashion Group, Pubcty. Club of N.Y., AWNY; Institution des Essarts, Switzerland; Goring Hall, Eng.; b. Munich, Germany; p. Norbert and Olga Enoch Fischman; h. Kurt Curtis; c. Thomas Michael, Linda Ann; res: 117-03 Curzon Rd., Kew Gardens, N.Y. 11418.

CURTIS, OLGA, Feature Wtr., The Denver Post, 650 15th St., Denver, Colo. 80201, '61–; Wms. Ed., Parade, '59–'61; Wms. Ed., INS, '55–'58; Feature Wtr., N.Y.C. and Denver Burs., '52–'55; Theta Sigma Phi (Pfsnl. Aw., '66; Colo. Press Wm. (1st Aw., '63–'68); NWC of NY (1st Aw., '56, '60); NFPW aws. '65–'67; Outstanding Jnlst. of Colo. Aw., Univ. of Colo., '69; Hunter Col., BA; b. Crimea, Russia; h. (dec.); res: 669 Washington St., Denver, Colo. 80203.

CUSACK, BETTY BUGBEE, Auth.-Publr., '67–; Bks: "Collectors Luck—Giants Steps Into Prehistory" ('68), "Collectors Luck—A Thousand Years at Lewis Bay, Cape Cod" ('67); Cnslt., U.S. State Dept. for UNICEF, '55–'58; Am. Red Cross (Winchester Mass. Chptr. Exec. Dir., '57–'60), Mass. Wms. Repl. Club (Pres.,

'49–'50); Nat. Park Col., '22; b. Hanover, N.H.; p. Perley and Elizabeth Campbell Bugbee; h. William C. Cusack; c. William C., Jr., James C.; res: 35 West Rd., West Yarmouth, Mass. 02673.

CUSHMAN, KATHERINE MOORE, Legislative Info. Chmn., Michigan Council of Churches, '64–'68; Corr., Mich. State Constitutional Conv., '61–'63; Auth., "A Christian Heritage, the Centennial History of Christ Episcopal Church, Dearborn" ('67); Theta Sigma Phi; Univ. of Mich., AB, '38; b. Detroit, Mich., 1916; p. George Edwin and Gertrude Snow Moore; h. Edward L. Cushman; c. Robert M., Elizabeth (Mrs. Milton Rohwer); res: 23633 Elmwood Ct., Dearborn, Mich. 48124.

CUSTIN, JOAN V., PR AE, Ross Roy of New York, Inc., 555 Fifth Ave., N.Y.C., N.Y. 10017, '69–; PR Cnslt., Intl. Basic Economy Corp., '68–'69; PR Dir., Puerto Rico Br., '65–'68; Rptr., Dorvillier News Agcy., '63–'65; Corr., McGraw-Hill World News, '63–'65; PRSA; Simmons Col., BS, '52; Boston Univ., Sch. of Public Commtns., MS, '54; b. Boston, Mass., 1931; p. Harold and Anna Shanker Custin; res: 185 West End Ave., N.Y., N.Y. 10023.

CUTHBERT, EVELYN RACHEL, Librn., Lincoln High School, 29 Council St., Sumter, S.C. 29150, '43–; Librn., Lincoln Public Lib., '43–'66; Tchr., Lincoln HS, '34–'43; Whittemore HS (Conway), '31–'34; ALA, Southeastern Lib. Assn., S.C. Lib. Assn., S.C. Educ. Assn., Sumter County Tchrs. Assn., Palmetto Lib. Assn. (State Pres., '44); Sumter Bd. of Educ. aw., '66; Who's Who of Am. Wm., Dic. of Intl. Biog., Royal Blue Bk., Who's Who in the South and Southwest, Who's Who in Lib. Svc.; Allen Univ., AB, '31; b. Sumter, S.C.; p. Edgar and Dollie Sanders Cuthbert; res: 502 N. Main St., Sumter, S.C. 29150.

CUTLER, CAROL RATAIC, Art Critic, International Herald Tribune, 21 Rue de Berri, Paris 8, France, '61–; Paris Corr., Art in America, 635 Madison Ave., N.Y., N.Y. 10022, '64–; Adv. Copywtr., Joseph Horne Co., Pitt., '47–'51; Assn. Internationale des Critique's d'Art; Univ. of Pitt., Carnegie Tech., Hunter Col., Ecole du Louvre; b. Rankin, Pa., 1926; p. John and Stella Rataic; h. Bernard Cutler; res: 4, rue de la Renaissance, Paris 8, France.

CYHEL, FLORENCE VIRGINIA, Copy Dir., Mo.-Kan. Div., Macy's, 1034 Main St., Kan. City, Mo. 64105, '67–; AE, Wtr., Prodr., Potts-Woodbury Advertising, '54–'67; Cont. Ed., Bdcstr., KCKN Radio, '49–'54; Nwsp. Adv., The Jones Store Co., '48–'49; Adv., Sears Roebuck & Co., '47–'48; House Organ, Phillips Petroleum Co., '45–'47; AWRT (Kan. City Chptr. Pres., '60–'61; W. Central Area Treas., '60, '62), Gamma Alphi Chi (Kan. City Chptr. Pres., '62–'63), Mo. Press Wm. (aw., '62), NFPW, Radio & TV Cncl. of Kan. City, Am. Bus. Wms. Assn., Wms. C. of C., People-to-People Cncl. of Gtr. Kan. City; Kan. City Adv. Wm. of the Yr., '66; Kan. State Univ., BA (Jnlsm.), '47; b. Kan. City,

Kan., 1926; p. Joseph and Olga Borosiewic Cyhel; res: 242 S. 10th St., Kan. City, Kan. 66102.

CYR, HELEN WHEELER, Dir. of Instructional Media, Oakland Public Schools, 1025 Second Ave., Oakland, Cal. 94606, '67–; Coordr., Lib. Svcs., '63–'67; Librn., '54–'63; Tchr., '49–'53; Contrbr., pfsnl. jnls.; Guest Lectr.; Cal. Assn. of Sch. Librns. (State Pres., '71–'72; VP, '70–'71), ALA, WNBA; Who's Who of Am. Wm.; Univ. of Cal., AB, '47, BLS, '54; b. Oakland, Cal.; p. Edward and Lilly Zimmer Wheeler; h. Gordon Cyr; res: 1736 Sonoma Ave., Berkeley, Cal. 94707.

D

DABBS, ELIZABETH OHLROGGE, TV and Pubcty. Art Conslt., Binney and Smith, Inc., 4439 Trierwood Park Dr., Ft. Wayne, Ind. 46805, '46–; Art Tchr. in Public Schs. and Univ., '33–'46; Artist, Auth., Narrator, Collaborator-Prodr. of Educ. Films; AWRT, Intl. Platform Assn., NAEA, Art Educ. Assn. of Ind. (Cncl. Mbr., '67–'68), Oh. Art Educ. Assn., Mich. Art Educ. Assn.; Who's Who of Am. Wm.; Who's Who In Am. Educ.; Exhibitor and Judge in numerous midwest art exhibts. and painting exhbns., '35–; John Herron Art Sch. (Emma Harter Sweetser Scholarship Aw., '32–'33); Sioux Falls Col., '39–'40; Ind. Univ., MS, '49; Mich. State Univ., '56; b. Franklin, Ind., 1911; p. Grover C. and Jesse Barnett Ohlrogge; h. Le Moyne Dabbs; c. James Ohlrogge, Lisa Ann; res: 4439 Trierwood Park Dr., Ft. Wayne, Ind. 46805.

DABNEY, KATHLEEN JOHNSON, Actress, Singer, Composer; Lavinia, "Androcles and the Lion"; Karin, Motion Pic. "Alice's Restaurant"; prods. of Cafe La Mama, Lincoln Ctr., Shakespeare Festival, Broadway, TV; AEA, SPCA, Black Hat Aw.; Stephens Col., AA; Univ. of Miss., BA (Speech); MA (Theatre); b. Brownwood, Tex., 1942; p. J. Edward and Blanche Daleney Johnson; res: 47 Jane St., New York, N.Y. 10014.

DaCOSTA, JACQUELINE, VP, Dir. of Media, Info. and Analysis Div., Ted Bates & Company, Inc., 666 Fifth Ave., N.Y., N.Y. 10019, '65–; Media Coordr., Intl., '65–; Asst. VP, '63–'65; Media Rsch. Analyst, '55–'63; Media Rsch. Supvsr., Biow, Beirn, Toigo, '52–'55; Asst. Export Mgr., Morse Intl., '46–'52; Speaker, reg. adv. clubs; Cnslt., bdcst.; Auth., articles in trade press; AWNY (Bd., '65–'69), IRTS, Radio-TV Rsch. Cncl. (Secy.-Treas., '66–'67), Agcy. Media Rsch. Cncl.; Hunter Col., BA (Bus. Adm.) '50; b. N.Y.C., 1927; p. Joachin and Tirsa Olmeda DaCosta; res: 97–07 63rd Rd., Rego Park, N.Y. 11374.

DAEHLER, POLLY NEWMAN, Dir. of Wms. Activities, WPAY, 1009 Gallia St., Portsmouth, Oh. 45662, '53–; Bdcstr., "The Polly Daehler Show"; AWRT Alumna (Chptr. Treas., '58); numerous civic activities;

Delta Kappa Gamma; Am. Cancer Soc. Aw., '58; Oh. Rep. to White House Conf. on Children and Youth, '60; Miami Univ., '33–'34; Portsmouth Intl. and Interstate Bus. Col., '36; b. Portsmouth, Oh., 1915; p. Phillip and Effie Easter Newman; h. Frederick Carl Daehler; c. Carl, Jr., Mrs. Bruce Kulp, Mrs. Larry Katz, Mrs. Jeffory Born; res: Star Route, Stout, Oh. 45684.

DAHL, ARLENE, Actress and Auth., P.O. Box 911, Beverly Hills, Cal. 94713; Pres., Woman's World (N.Y.C.); VP, Kenyon & Eckhardt, Inc. (Adv.), '67; Actress "The Way to Kathamandu," many films; Broadway plays; Auth: "Always Ask a Man" (Prentice Hall, '65), 12 "Beauty Scope" bks. (Simon & Schuster); Beauty Colmst., Chgo. Tribune, N.Y. News Synd., '50–; Designer, A. N. Saab & Co., '52–'57; AMPAS, Auths. League; Box Off. Magazine's Laural Aw.; voted one of best-hatted wm., Millinery Inst. of Am., '60–'61; Helene Curtis Guild of Pfsnl. Beauticians Aw. for Best Coiffed, '62–'63; L.A. County Hollywood Museum (Bd. of Dirs., Founder), Father Flanagan's Boys Town (Hon. Citizen); Univ. of Minn.; b. Mpls., Minn., 1928; p. Rudolph S. and Idelle Swan Dahl; h. Rounsevelle W. Schaum; c. Lorenzo, Carole Christine.

DAHLHAMER, GLORIA MOSER, Ed., Family Sec., The Herald-Mail Company, 25–31 Summit Ave., Hagerstown, Md. 21740, '53–; Reptr., '47–'53; BPW; Md.-Del. Press Assn. News Writing Aws. annually since '62; Pa. Nwsp. Assn. Aws., '66, '69; b. Hagerstown, Md., 1929; p. Lionel and Golden Bussard Moser; h. Charles Dahlhamer; c. Loren W., James M.; res: R.F.D. #3, Box 148A, Hagerstown, Md. 21740.

DAHLHAUS, ELEANOR VAN BUREN, Adv. Mgr., Rosenbaum's Inc. of Elmira, 110–112 W. Water St., Elmira, N.Y. 14901, '52–; Cont. Dir., WELM, '48–'52; Fashion Adv. Mgr., McLean's (Binghamton), '47–'48; Asst. Adv. Mgr., S. F. Isward Co. (Elmira), '39–'47; Elmira-Corning Adv. Club (Charter Mbr., Bd. of Dirs., Treas., Secy., VP, '66–'65; Adv. Man of the Yr., '64–'65), AFA (Printer's Ink Silver Medal Aw., '64–'65); Reader's Digest Aw. for Commty. Svc. Ads, '64; NRMA First Place Aw. for best campaign of yr., '64; Who's Who of Am. Wm.; Am. Cancer Soc. (Bd. of Dirs., Secy., VP, Pres.), active in civic groups; Elmira Col., '34–'37; b. Lowman, N.Y., 1915; p. Fred M. and Ada Lowman Van Buren; h. Roy M. Dahlhaus; c. Fredrick W. (dec.); res: 1108 Hoffman St., Elmira, N.Y. 14905.

DAILY, LAURA CHRISTENSEN, Ed., The Iowa State Alumnus, Iowa State University Alumni Assn., Room 226, Memorial Union, Ames, Ia. 50010, '53–; Ed., '53–'68; Copy Ed., Ia. State Univ. Press, '51–'53; Freelance Wtr., '40–'51; Instr., Household Equipment, Ia. State Univ., '37–'40; Theta Sigma Phi (Ames Club Pres., '61), Phi Kappa Phi, Omicron Nu, Phi Upsilon Omicron; Ia. State Univ., BS, '35; b. Urbana, Ill., 1913; p. Nels A. and Verna Johnson Christensen; h. William M. Dailey, Sr.; c. Susan, William M., Jr., Christie; res: 1605 Burnett, Ames, Ia. 50010.

DAITCH, PEGGY FRIEDMAN, Cont. Dir. Prodr., "Our Town," Dir. of Public Affairs, WTAK-Radio, P.O. Box 2069, Livonia, Mich. 48151, '67–; PR, Steiner Proms.; AWRT; Univ. of Mich., '63–'67; Univ. de Grenoble, France, '66; b. Detroit, Mich., 1946; p. Stanley and Miriam Levin Friedman; h. Marvin C. Daitch; res: 1611 Lafayette Towers E., Detroit, Mich. 48207.

DALE, GERTRUDE R., Free-lance Publicist, 165 E. 83rd St., N.Y., N.Y. 10028; PR Exec., Young & Rubicam, '53–'63; Mdse. Pubcty. Mgr., Fieldcrest Mills, '51–'53; Pubcty., E. I. du Pont, '47–'49; Edt;. Asst., Town & Country; Wms. Ed., Trenton Sunday Times Advertiser; Fashion Group, Am. Inst. of Designers, Nat. Soc. of Interior Designers; Smith Col., AB, '36; b. Trenton, N.J. 1914; p. G. Ernest and Gertrude Reynaud Dale; res: 165 E. 83rd St., N.Y., N.Y. 10028.

DALE, MAGDALENE LARSEN, Wtr., D. C. Heath & Co. Division of Raytheon Education Company, 1008 S. Gulph Rd., Gulph Mills, Conshohocken, Pa. 19428, '35–; Auth., collaboration with husband, numerous French textbks.; Fac., French: Univ. of Del., Upper Darby Sr. HS, Germantown Friends Sch.; Am. Cncl. on the Teaching of Fgn. Langs., Am. Assn. of Tchrs. of French, Modern Lang. Assn.; Who's Who of Am. Wm., Who's Who in the East, Dic. of Intl. Biog.; Univ. of Mont., AB, '26; Univ. of Paris (The Sorbonne), '25–'26; Univ. of Nancy (France), '25; Grad. Study: Johns Hopkins (Balt., Md.), Univ. of Pa. (Phila.); Columbia Univ., MA, '31; Institut de Phonetique (Paris), Institut du Pantheon (Paris), Centre International Pedagogique (Sèvres, France); b. Mohall, N.D., 1904; p. Biger and Hilda Larsen; h. John Dale; res: (Oct. 15 to May 1) 1008 S. Gulph Rd., Gulph Mills, Conshohocken, Pa. 19428; (May 1 to Oct. 15) Parc Vigier A 4, 23 Blvd. Franck-Pilatte, Nice, 06, France.

DALEY, NANCY OLDFIELD, Guidance Cnslr., Miami Coral Park HS, Miami, Fla., '68–'69; Reading Instr., Miami-Dade Jr. Col., '65–'68; Tchr., Coral Gables, '52–'65; Bookkeeper, Regaline Mfg. Co., '50–'52); Adv. Sls. and Svc., Miami Daily News, '47–'48; Elyria (Oh.) Chronicle-Telegram, '43–'47; Ironwood (Mich.) Daily Globe, '42–'43; Ed., Skokie (Ill.) News, '42; Theta Sigma Phi (Miami Pres., '55–'56; Headliner, '67); Oh. Wesleyan Univ., AB, '41 (cum laude; Phi Beta Kappa); Northwestern Univ., MS, '43; b. Elyria, Oh.; p. Robert and Ellen Roberts Oldfield; h. Thomas Daley (dec.); c. Mary Ann (Mrs. Ronald Harris), Patricia Ellen; res: Apt. 104, 1409 S.E. Eighth Ave., Deerfield Beach, Fla. 33441.

DALKA, SANDRA SUE, Commty. Rels., Asst. Coor., Oakland Community College, 2480 Opdyke St., Bloomfield Hills, Mich. 48013, '69–; Educ. Wtr., Daily Tribune, '67–'69; Theta Sigma Phi, Detroit Hist. Soc. Guild; Wayne State Univ., BA (Mass Commtns.), '69; b. Detroit, Mich., 1944; p. Gerald and Anna Pauli Dalka; res: 703 Lafayette Towers E., Detroit, Mich. 48207.

DALLAS, DOROTHY CONKLIN, Mng. Ed. and Bus. Mgr., Daily Court Reporter, 124 E. 3rd St., Dayton, Oh., 45402, '21–; VP, Beringer Printing Co.; Secy.; Mgr., '21–; Advisory Comm., Sinclair Commty. Col., '69; Assoc. Court and Comml. Nwsps. (Pres., '53, VP, Secy.-Treas., Ed.), Altrusa Club (Dayton Treas.), Nat. Secys. Assn. (Dayton Pres.), Dayton Legal Secys. Assn. (VP, Treas., charge of educ. workshop, '66–); b. Dayton, Oh., 1901; p. Harry and Elizabeth Connaroe Conklin; h. Robert J. Dallas (dec.); res: 454 E. Schantz Ave., Dayton, Oh. 45409.

DALTON, PHYLLIS BULL, Asst. State Librn., California State Library, P.O. Box 2037 (Library and Courts Building), Sacramento, Cal. 95809, '57–; Cnslt., Alaska State Dept. of Educ., '68–'69; Chief of Reader Svcs., California State Lib., '52–'57; Cnslt. to State Agencies and Employees, California State Lib., '48–'52; Div. Librn. in the Humanities, '42–'48; Asst. Ref. Librn., Univ. of Neb., '42–'45; Asst., Circ., Lincoln Public Lib., '42; Lib. Cataloging, Holy Family HS, Denver, '41–'42; Reader's Advisor, Lincoln Public Lib., '40–'41; Tchr., high sch. and grade sch., '28–'40; Lectr.; Cnslt. for survey of statewide lib. svc. Alaska with published report "Library Service for all Alaskans"; California Lib. Assn. (Pres., '69; Golden Empire District Pres., '57), Am. Assn. of State Libs., (Pres., '60; Chmn., Survey and Standards Comm.), ALA (Chmn., Survey and Standards Comm.), Am. Assn. of Hospitals and Institutions (Chmn., Special projects Comm.; Univ. of Nebraska, BS, '31; Univ. of Neb., MA, '41; Univ. of Denver, BS in LS, '42; b. Marietta, Kan., 1909; p. Benjiman R. and Pearl Travelute; h. Jack M. Dalton; res: 2589 Garden Highway, Sacramento, Cal. 95833.

DALY, Sr. EMILY JOSEPH, C.S.J., Scholar in Res., The College of Saint Rose, 432 Western Ave., Albany, N.Y. 12203, '68–; on leave for study, Tokyo, Japan, '66–'67; VP, '65–'66; Prof. of Classics, Dept. Chmn., '40–'66; translator and ed. of religious books; numerous articles pfsnl. and lit. jnls.; Am. Classical League, Classical Assoc. of Empire State, Clasical Assoc. of Middle Atlantic States, Vergilian Soc.; D'Youville Col., BA, '33; Catholic Univ. of Am., MA, '41; Fordham Univ., PhD, '46; Fulbright Grant, Am. Sch. of Classical Studies, Rome, Italy, '55; b. Utica, N.Y., 1913; p. George and Marie Hurley Daly; res: The College of Saint Rose, 432 Western Ave., Albany, N.Y. 12203.

DALY, MARGARET VENNUM, Assoc. Ed., Shopping Ed., Better Homes and Gardens, Meredith Corporation, 750 Third Ave., N.Y., N.Y. 10017, '65–; Asst. Ed., '63–'65; Vassar Col., BA, '59, (Phi Beta Kappa); b. Mpls., Minn., 1937; p. Thomas and Margaret Newhall Vennum; h. Derry Daly; res: 63 E. Ninth St. Apt. 3H, N.Y., N.Y. 10003.

DAMRON, REBECCA JANE, Prom. Dir., Indianapolis Capitols Professional Football Team, 901 N. Pennsylvania, Indianapolis, Ind. 46204, '68–; Marion County Residential Coordr., Am. Cancer Soc., '67–'68; Wms. News Dir., "Telescope," WLW, '66–'67; TV

Hostess-Girl Friday for "Easy Money," WFBM-TV, '64-'66; Tchr., John Robert Powers Sch.; AWRT (Hoosier Chptr. Pres., '68-'69; VP, '67); AFTRA, Press Club of Indianapolis; Miami Univ., BA, '64; b. Wabash, Ind., 1942; p. Dr. W. K. and Florence Nagel Damron; res: 3470 N. Meridian #312, Indianapolis, Ind. 46208.

DANA, BARBARA, Auth., Actress, 200 W. 57th St., N.Y., N.Y. 10019; Novels: "Spencer and his Friends" (Atheneum), "Rutgers and the Water-Snouts" (Harper & Row); Roles: "Enter Laughing," "Who's Afraid of Virginia Wolf?", "Wher's Daddy?"; Films: "P.J.," "Popi"; b. N.Y.C.; p. Richard and Mildred Dana; h. Alan Arkin; c. Anthony; res: 30 Bank St., N.Y., N.Y. 10014.

DANA, MARGARET, Synd. Colmst., "Before You Buy," "Consumer's Question Box"; Cnslt. on consumer attitudes to govt., industry; Auth., "Behind the Label" ('38), many articles on consumer affairs; Consumer Cncl., Am. Nat. Standards Inst., Nat. Retail Merchants Consumer Coord. Comm., other pfsnl. groups; Nat. Alliance of TV and Electronic Svc. Assns. aw., '65; Am. Apparel Manufacturers Assn. aw., '68; Oberlin Col.; h. H. Trumbull Dana; c. Margaret, Cynthia; res: R.D. 3, Doylestown, Pa. 18901.

DANBOM, ROWENE BYERS, Public Info. Offcr., Colorado Department of Health, 4210 E. 11th Ave., Denver, Colo. 80203, '64-; Conslt. on PR to Training Div., Colo. State Civil Svc. Commn., '63-'64; Asst. Dir., PR, Colo. Dept. of Highways, '59-'64; Night Ed., UPI (Denver), '58; Statehouse Reptr., AP (Des Moines, Ia.), '44-'46; Bur. Mgr., Ins, '44; Reptr., UP, '42-44; Reptr., Evening Sentinel (Shenandoah, Ia.), '41-'42 and '37-'38; ICIE (designated "Editor-in-Focus", '65), Colo. State Civil Svc. Employees Assn. (Edtl. Bd., '65; Chmn., PR Comm., '68), Colo. Press Assn., PRSA; Am. Inst. of Bus., '39; Univ. of Denver, '63; Univ. of Colo., '60-'67; b. Shenandoah, Ia., 1920; p. Seth William and Emma Townsend Byers; h. Raymond Carl Danbom; c. David Byers, Daniel Raymond; res: 1250 Willow St., Denver, Colo. 80220.

DANDIGNAC, PATRICIA, Mng. Ed., Craft Horizons, 16 E. 52nd St., N.Y., N.Y. 10022, '67-; Asst. Ed., Edtl. Asst., '57-'67; Beaver Col.; b. Astoria, N.Y., 1938; p. Charles and Mathilda Sesselmann Dandignac; h. Salvatore Scarpitta; res: 240 E. 94th St., N.Y., N.Y. 10028.

DANENHOWER, ELOISE GARTON, Dir., PR, The Pennsylvania Society for the Prevention of Cruelty to Animals, 350 E. Erie Ave., Phila., Pa. 19134, '55-; Wms. Dir., WCOJ, West Chester and Coatsville, Pa., '51-'55; Pres., Chester County SPCA, '52-'53; Exec. Secy. for Educ. and PR, '53-'55; Free-lance Wtr., children's songs and stories; Ed., Animaldom; AWRT (Phila. Chptr: Corr. Secy., '61; Pres., '66; Nat. Educ. Fndn. Trustee, '67-'69), PRSA (Phila., Chptr. Pepper Pot Aw., '66-'67), Human-Aminal Relationship Aw.,

'66; Lassie Gold Aw.; b. N.Y.C., 1916; p. Cyril S. and Elsie Stapleton Garton; h. William H. Danenhower; c. Diane (Mrs. John Paul Bonfiglio); res: 620 W. Ellet St., Phila., Pa. 19119.

DANFIELD, BETTY EVERS, Wms. Ed., Press Enterprise Company, 14th and Orange Grove, Riverside, Cal. 92501, '69-; formerly Wms. Ed., The Paper (Oshkosh, Wis.); Wms. Daily Pages Ed., Des Moines (Ia.) Register and Tribune; Asst. Wms. Ed., The Capitol Times (Madison); Edtl. Asst., Journal of the American Oil Chemists Society (Chgo., Ill.); Theta Sigma Phi, Altrusa Intl.; Penney-Mo. Aw., 1st place, '68 and '69; Dorothy Dawe Home Furnishings Trophy, '68; Emba Mink Fashion Aw., '68; three 1st place Wis. Press Wm. writing aws., '68; Univ. of Wis., BA; h. Dr. Richard Danfield; res: 22855 Arliss Dr., Grand Terrace, Cal. 92324.

DANFORTH, MARY A., Ed., Schlage Lock Co., P.O. Box 3324, S.F., Cal. 94119, '55-; Ed., H. S. Crocker Co., Inc., San Bruno, Cal. '51-'66; Ed., Nordstrom Valve Div. of Rockwell Mfg. Co., Oakland, Cal., '48-'53; Free-lance Wtr.-Photog., '50-; Bay Area Soc. of Indsl. Communicators, Soc. of Am. Archivists; Northwestern Univ., BS (Jnlsm.), '47 (Sigma Delta Chi Scholarship Aw., '47); b. Chgo., Ill., res: 2200 Hillside Dr., Burlingame, Cal. 94010.

DANIEL, ANITA, N.Y. Corr., Nationalzeitung (Basil, Switzerland), other Swiss Pubns.; Auth., Colmst. (pseud: "Anita"), for European pubns.; travel bks. on Europe; Bk., "The Story of Albert Schweitzer"; numerous mag. articles in U.S.A.; b. Iassy, Rumania (now Am. citizen); res: 120 E. 62nd St., N.Y., N.Y. 10021.

DANIEL, ELNA WORRELL (Elna Stone), Auth: "Speak Up!" (Zondervan, '64), "How to Choose Your Work" (McMillan, '69), "How to Get a Job" (McMillan, '69); mag. fiction, articles; Cnslr., Fla. State Employment Svc., '61-'66; Tchr., Pensacola Jr. Col., '69-; Alpha Lambda Delta, Alpha Beta Alpha, Kappa Delta Pi; Univ. of Ala., BS; Fla. State Univ; Univ. of W. Fla.; h. Donald S. Stone; c. Thalia Jane Daniel, Jeffrey Daniel, Robert Stone, Richard Stone; res: 6714 Chelsea St., Pensacola, Fla. 32506.

DANIELL, CONSTANCE, Soc. Ed., The Milwaukee Journal, Journal Sq., Milw., Wis. 53201, '67-; Part Time Reptr., Wms. Dept., '62-'67; Cont. Wtr. and Commentator, Wms. TV prog., WTMJ, '47-'52; PR, Bernie Milligan Agency (Hollywood, Cal.), '46-'47; Soc. Reptr., Milw. Jnl., '45-'46; Univ. of Wis., BA (Jnlsm.), '45; b. Hamburg, N.Y.; p. Arthur and Edith Knubbe Lamy; h. (div.); c. Tina, Laurie, Wendy; res: 301 Glenview Ave., Wauwatosa, Wis. 53213.

DANIELL, EDITH F., Pubns. Ed., Pitney-Bowes, Inc., Stamford, Conn. 06904, '63-; Ed., PR, '61-'63; Asst. to VP, Pers. Rels., '50-'61; Pers. Dept., '43-; ICIE, N.Y. Assn. of Indsl. Communicators; House Organ Ed. Aw.,

Bus. Equipment Expsn., '63; 1st Prize, Recruitment Adv., Fairfield County Adv. Club, '66; Columbia Univ. (Sch. of Gen. Studies); N.Y.U.; b. Stamford, Conn., 1921; p. William and Hazel Thurston Daniell; res: 44 Mohawk Trail, Stamford, Conn. 06903.

DANIELS, ANITA, Sr. Wtr., McCann-Erickson Advertising Agency, 485 Lexington Avenue, N.Y., N.Y., '69–; Sr. Wtr., Daniel & Charles Adv. Agcy., '67–'69; Copywtr., McCann-Erickson Adv. Agcy., '66–'67; Prodr., indsl. films, TV commls., VPI (Video Pictures, Inc.), '65–'66; actress; Copy Club; b. N.Y.C.; p. Samuel and Bess Mednick Yager; h. (div.); c. Julie Samantha; res: 145 W. 96th St., N.Y., N.Y. 10025.

DANIELS, ANNA KLEEGMAN, Auth: "The Mature Woman, Her Richest Years," "It is Never Too Late to Love"; physician, marriage cnslr.; lectr., N.Y.C. Dept. of Health; first wm. house physician, Bellevue Hosp.; first woman Military Surgeon, U.S. Army; numerous other med. posts, '16–; N.Y. Wms. Med. Soc., Am. Med. Assn., N.Y.C. and N.Y. State Med. Socs., many other pfsnl. orgs.; "My Mother the Doctor," by Joy Daniels Singer (E. P. Dutton, '70); Cornell Univ., BA, '13; M.D., '16; post-grad., Vienna, Switzerland, Paris; b. Kiev, U.S.S.R.; p. Israel and Ekla Siergutz Kleegman; h. (dec.); c. Dorothea Daniels Glass, M.D., Joy Daniels Singer; res: 322 W. 72nd St., N.Y., N.Y. 10023.

DANIELS, MARLENE SCHULER, Wms. Ed., Panax Corporation, The Mining Journal, 249 W. Washington St., Marquette, Mich. 49855, '69–; Theta Sigma Phi; Univ. of N.D., BA, '69 (Radio-TV, Jnlsm.); b. Balt., Md., 1947; p. Alfred and Ione V. Schuler; h. Louis P. Daniels; res: 500 Baraga Ave., Marquette, Mich. 49855.

DANIELS, MURIEL GRIFFIN, Asst. Prof. of Jnlsm., University of Texas, School of Communications, Austin, Tex. 78712, '69–; Ed., University Extension and Agriculture Extension, Univ. of Wis., '66–'69; Univ. Rels., Univ. of Mich., '66; Prof., Okla. City Univ.; Jnlsm. Tchr., San Antonio, Tex., Okla. City, '56–'64; Theta Sigma Phi (VP, '54–'55; Secy., '68–'69), Assn. for Educ. in Jnlsm.; Wall St. Journal Nwsp. Fund Fellow, '63; E. B. Fred Scholarship, '68; sponsor of state, nat. aw-winning sch. nwsps. and yrbks., '58–'65; Univ. of Mont., BA (Jnlsm.), '55 (Mortar Board); Univ. of Okla., MA (Jnlsm.), '64; Univ. of Wis., Soviet Area Studies Cert., '69; b. Missoula, Mont., 1933; p. William and Frances Ferguson Griffin; h. Jack Daniels; res: 4104 Paint Rock Dr., Austin, Tex. 78731.

DANIELS, MYRA JANCO, Pres., Draper Daniels, Inc., 520 N. Michigan Ave., Chgo., Ill. 60611, '65–; Exec. VP, Roche, Rickerd, Henri, Hurst, Inc., '62–'65; Acc. Supvsr., Kuttner and Kuttner, '61–'62; Assoc. Prof. of Adv., Ind. Univ., '54–'61; Pres., Wabash Advertising, '50–'54; Ford Fndn. Study, '60; numerous articles on mktng. and adv.; AFA (Bd. of Dirs., '65–'67), Am. Mktng. Assn. (Ind. Chptr. Bd. of Dirs., VP, '58–'60), Wms. Adv. Club of Chgo. (Bd. of Dirs., VP, '66–'67), AAUP, Gamma Alpha Chi (Nat. VP, '60–'64);

Kappa Delta Pi, Pi Omega Pi, Pi Lambda Theta, Delta Pi Epsilon, Tau Kappa Alpha; Nat. Adv. Wm. of the Yr. ('65); Ind. State Univ., BS, '48; MA, '54; PhD, '61 (all with hons.; Distg. Alumnae Aw., '66); b. Gary, Ind., 1925; p. Elias and Cecelia Remstein Janco; h. Draper Daniels; res: 910 Lake Shore Dr., Chgo., Ill. 60611; Franklin Grove, Ill., R.F.D. 61031.

DANIELS, PERRY HAY, Copy Ed., P.O. Box 1026, Wall St. Station, N.Y., N.Y. 10005; Hartford Col. for Wm., AA, '67; Feminist Movement, N.Y.C.; b. Middletown, Conn., 1947; p. William and Dorothy Cornwall Hay.

DANIELS, RUTH (Shapiro), Owner, Pres., Associated Advertising Agency, 330 Congress St., Boston, Mass. 02110, '63–; fashion adv. and PR for Coppercraft Guild of Taunton; Free-lance adv.; Golden Advs. Assocs., Dickerman Adv. (N.Y.C.); Fashion Illus., Grover Cronin, Dept. Store; Tchr., Mass. Sch. of Art, '56–'58; Boston Ad Club; Boston Univ., BS, '54; b. Boston, Mass., 1933; p. Bernard and Rose Davis Dokton; h. Daniel Shapiro; c. Susan, Jeff.; res: 4 Harwick Rd., Chestnut Hill, Mass. 02167.

DANIELSON, DORIS ANDRESEN, Asst. Mgr., Adv. and PR Dept., The Northern Trust Company, 50 S. LaSalle St., Chgo., Ill. 60690, '68–; Supvsr., PR, '66–'68; Ed., '62–'66; Edtl. Cl., Argonne Nat. Lab., '61–'62; PRSA, Pubcty. Club of Chgo. (Best Employee Rels. Prog., '65; Best Special Commtns. Project, '68), Chgo. Fin. Advs., Wms. Adv. Club of Chgo., IEA (Aw. of Merit); Ill. Wesleyan Univ., BA, '61 (Dean's List, Gamma Upsilon, Green Medallion); Roosevelt Univ., Grad. work; b. Chgo., Ill., 1940; p. A. Arnold and Lillian Rice Andresen; h. Philip Danielson; res: 4900 Forest, Downers Grove, Ill. 60515.

DAPPER, GLORIA, Pres., Free Lance Associates, Inc., 8 Garmany Pl., Yonkers, N.Y. 10710, '62–; VP, Glick & Lorwin, '60–'62; PR Dir., Nat. Citizens Commn. for The Public Schs., '50–'60; Cont. Dir., Am. Forces Network, '46–'50; News Wtr., WCCO (Mpls., Minn.), '44–'46; Auth., "Public Relations for Educators" (MacMillan, '64); Co-auth., "A Guide for School Board Members" (Follett, '66); EWA, OPC; Univ. of Minn., BA, '44; b. Faribault, Minn., 1922; p. George and Ethyl Shields Dapper; res: 8 Garmany Pl., Yonkers, N.Y. 10710.

DARC, KATHERINE, Actress, c/o Screen Actors Guild, 7750 Sunset Blvd., Hollywood, Cal. 90046, '67–; 13 motion pictures; TV shows, TV Commls., radio; Univ. of Cal.; b. Wash., D.C., 1948; p. Paul and Catherine Kane Peruzzi; res: 2575 Beachwood Dr., Hollywood, Cal. 90028.

DARCY, KATHLEEN MARY, Young Adult Librn., Lakewood Public Library, 15425 Detroit Ave., Lakewood, Oh. 44107, '67–; ALA, Oh. Lib. Assn., Young Librns. Assn., WNBA (Cleve. Chptr. Secy., '69–'71), Catholic Lib. Assn.; Col. of Mt. St. Joseph-on-the-

Oh., BA, '66; Western Reserve Univ., MS (Lib. Sci.), '67; b. Chgo., Ill.; p. William and Patricia Darcy; res: 12530 Lake Ave., #213, Lakewood, Oh. 44107.

DARCY, MARY DOLAN, Wtr., Off. of Exec. Dir., St. Vincent Hospital, 25 Winthrop St., Worcester, Mass. 01610, '68–; PR Dr., '60–'68; Contrbr., Hosp. House Organ; Am. Hosp. Assn., Mass. Hosp. Assn., Catholic Hosp. Assn.; Col. of Our Lady of the Elms, AB, '40; b. Worcester, Mass., 1918; p. Francis and Mary Honney Dolan; h. Bernard Darcy; c. Mary Ellen, Bernardette, Bernard; res: 127 Providence St., Worcester, Mass. 01604.

D'ARCY, RUTH CUNOV, Wms. Ed., The Detroit News, 615 Lafayette Blvd., Detroit, Mich. 48211, '68–; Ed., Experience colm., Teen News and Views pg., Teen Guideposts colm., '58–'68; Theta Sigma Phi (Headliner of the Yr., '60); Interpfsnl. Org. on Marriage, Divorce and the Family; b. Detroit, Mich., 1921; p. Charles and Hilda Otto Cunov; res: 25102 Annapolis, Dearborn Heights, Mich. 48125.

DARDEN, NANCY WHITFIELD, Fashion Designer, Fashion Galore, Ltd., 1400 Roosevelt Blvd., Box 892, Monroe, N.C. 28110, '65–; Fashion Cnslt., Athol Mfg. Co. (Butner, N.C.); Design Cnslt., York Mills (York, S.C.); Design Cnslt., After the Fox (Rutherfordton, N.C.); Public Schs. Tchr. (Clothing, Textile), nine yrs.; private students in Fashion Art classes; rsch. with textile mfg.; Alpha Delta Kappa, N.C. Educ. Assn., Am. and N.C. Home Econs. Assn., N.C. Vocational Assn., Am. Vocational Assn.; E. Carolina Col., BS (Home Econs.), '56; Univ. of N.C.; b. Creedmoor, N.C., 1934; p. Wilbur and Marjorie Lyon Whitfield; h. Donald Darden; res: 109 Sunnybrook Dr., Monroe, N.C. 28110.

DARER, SUSAN SILVERSTONE, VP, The Darer Corporation, 1 E. 57th St., N.Y., N.Y. 10022; Wellesley Col., BA, '60; b. N.Y.C., 1938; p. Murray and Dorothy Littman Silverstone; h. Stanley Darer; c. John D., Sarah E., Anne M.; res: Highline Trail S., Stamford, Conn. 06902.

DARROW, DOROTHY, Librn., The Academy of the Assumption, 1517 Brickell Ave., Miami, Fla. 33129, '69–; Head, Central Cataloging Dept., Dade County Schs., '55–'68; Head Librn., Ft. Lauderdale Public Lib., '34–'48; Tchr., Librn., Broward County and Dade County Schs., '24–'34, '48–'68; Instr. in Lib. Sci., Univ. of Miami, '55–'57, '68; ALA, Rec. for the Blind (Vice-Chmn.), Fla. Educ. Assn., NEA, Fla. Lib. Assn., Dade County Lib. Assn. (Pres., '52), Kappa Kappa Gamma, ZONTA Club of Greater Miami (Pres., '65–'66); Rollins Col., AB, '24; Columbia Univ., BS (Lib. Sci.), '35; Univ. of Chgo., '28; Univ. of Wis., '53; Univ. of Miami, '55–'68; b. Kirksville, Mo., 1903; p. Charles and Anna Lindstedt Darrow; res: 511 Santander Ave., Coral Gables, Fla. 33134.

DARROW, ESTHER LOUISE SWANSON, Treas.,

American Association of University Women, 1802 Keeaumoku St., Honolulu, Hi. 96822; Dir., Waikiki Imp. Assoc., '49–'51; Dir., Taniong Olak Rubber Co., '27–'29 Jnlsm. Tchr. and Advisor, McKinley HS (Honolulu), '24–'31; Tchr., Redlands, Cal., '23–'24; Reptr., Mpls. Journal, '15–'18; Theta Sigma Phi (Bd. Mbr., Honolulu, '26–'51; Pres., Honolulu, '26); Hi. Educ. Assn., Honolulu Artist Assn '66–'69; AAUW (Exec. Bd.), '38–'51; Univ. of Minn., BA, '18; Univ. of Hi., MA, '30; b. Mpls., Minn., 1892; p. Theo Pluteau and Mathilda Seppingbol Berntsen Swanson; h. Donald Francis Darrow; c. Vano., Mrs. Wiley F. Cairns, Mrs. Glenn L. Derr, Wm. P. Head, II, Mrs. Janice Breithaupt; res: 268 Wailupe Circle, Honolulu, Hi. 96821.

d'ASSISI, Sr. CLARE, S.C., Librn., John F. Kennedy Youth Library, 294 Bowdoin St., Dorchester, Mass. 02122, '65–; ALA, New England Lib. Assn., Catholic Lib. Assn. (New England Unit Chmn., '65–'67); Fordham Univ., BA, '29; Mt. St. Vincent, BLS, '49; b. Boston, Mass.; p. Timothy and Ellen Sullivan McCarthy; res: Boston, Mass.

DATCHÉ, RUTH, Pres., Datché Advertising Company, 3615 Olive St., St. Louis, Mo. 63108, '44–; Owner, art studio, '35–'44; Adv. Art Dir., '34–'35; Apprentice Fashion Artist, Stix, Baer and Fuller, '33; Fashion Group; Wms. Adv. of St. Louis, AFA, AWRT; active in civic, bus. orgs.; Washington Univ. Fine Arts Sch.; p. John and Letha Ditch; h. Maurcie Falchero (div.); c. Mary R., Ruth A.; res: 5125 Lindell Blvd., St. Louis, Mo. 63108.

DAUGHERTY, JEAN SANDERS, Public Info. Off., U.S. Army, Information/Orientation Office, Fort Huachuca Support Command, Fort Huachuca, Ariz. 85613, '69–; Asst. Ed., Children's Convalescent Hosp. nwsp. (Bethany, Okla.), '59–'66; PR Asst., World Neighbors, Inc. (Okla. City, Okla.), '64–'65; Theta Sigma Phi, Ariz. Press Wm., numerous others; Who's Who of Am. Wm., Who's Who in South and Southwest; Univ. of Neb., BA, '40; b. Superior, Neb., 1919; p. Morton and Nellie Head Sanders; h. William M. Daugherty; c. Patricia Ann (Mrs. Thomas E. Hampton); res: P.O. Box 1332, Sierra Vista, Ariz. 85635.

DAULTON, SUSAN M., AE, Leber Katz Paccione Inc., 767 Fifth Ave., N.Y., N.Y. 10022, '65–; William Smith Col., BA, '62; b. Abington, Pa., 1940; p. Vincent Daulton and Alicia Everitt Lavelle; res: 49 East 74th St., N.Y., N.Y. 10021.

DAUM, RHODA, Copywtr., J. Walter Thompson, 420 Lexington Ave., N.Y., N.Y. 10017, '69–; Crtv. Dir., H.J. Siesel Co., '67–'68; Copy Chief, Markland Adv., '66; A/R/M, '65; Sr. Copywtr., Ted Bates, '63–'64; Copywtr., Chirurg and Cairns, '61–'63; Kastor, Hilton, '59–'61; Copy Club of N.Y. (Charter Mbr.); Wellesley Col., BA; b. N.Y.C.; p. Paul and Sarah Markowitz Daum; c. Jonathan Wechsler, Jill Wechsler, Winifred Wechsler; res: 1015 Old Post Rd., Mamaroneck, N.Y. 10543.

DAUME, MARY ROSSITER, Dir., Monroe County Library System, 3700 S. Custer Rd., Monroe, Mich. 48161, '63–; Librn., '47–'62; Asst. Librn., '46–'47; Dorsch Memorial Lib., '43–'46; Librn., St. Mary's Oh. Public Lib., '35–'37; Prof., Wayne State Univ. Sch. of Lib. Sci., '66–'67; Univ. of Mich., '68–; ALA, Mich. Lib. Assn.; Monroe Co. Rotary Club Wm. of the Yr., '54; Lib. Binding Inst. Silver Bk. Aw., '63; Mich. Minuteman Governor's Aw., '67; Col. of Wooster, AB, '34; b. Detroit, Mich., 1913; p. Frederick and Anna Etta Rossiter; h. Karl Daume; c. Kurt F., John E.; res: 102 E. Grove St., Monroe, Mich. 48161.

DAUTRICH, ELISABETH C., Dir., Hazleton Area Public Library, Church and Green Sts., Hazleton, Pa. 18201, '63–; Reading Public Lib., '57–'63; Tchr., Pa. State Univ. Ext. courses, '64–'66; ALA, Pa. Lib. Assn., AAUW, Hazleton Commty. Workers, Hazleton Art League; Ithaca Col., BS, '38; Drexel Inst. of Tech., MS (Lib. Sci.), '63; b. Reading, Pa., 1916; p. Robert P. and Harriet V. Heath Kerling; h. (dec.); c. Mrs. Marilyn L. Cockley; res: 417 W. Diamond Ave., Hazleton, Pa. 18201.

DAVENPORT, DONA LEE, Station Mgr., WTVI, Charlotte-Mecklenburg Board of Education, 42 Coliseum Dr., Charlotte, N.C. 28205, '61–; Tchr., Dir. of Radio-TV, '55–'60; Chmn., FCC Instructional TV Fixed Svc. Comm.; State of N.C.; Southern Educ. Commtns. Assn., NAEB, AWRT, AAUW, BPW, Delta Kappa Gamma; Commths. aw., '67; Bdcst. Industry Conf. Precepter Aw., '69; Univ. of Mich., BA, (Bdcst., Speech, Secondary Educ.); Univ. of N.C.; N.C. State; Queens Col.; Winthrop Col.; b. Toledo, Oh.; p. Juston and Opal Davenport.

DAVERN, JEANNE MARGUERITE, Mng. Ed., Architectural Record, 330 W. 42nd St., N.Y., N.Y. 10036, '63–'70; Staff, '48–'63; Staff, Plattsburgh (N.Y.) Press-Repl., '44–'48; Architectural League of N.Y. (past Secy., and Program Chmn.), Am. Inst. of Architects, Public Affairs Comm., Student Affairs Comm.

DAVIAU, IRENE MARTINIK, Pubns. Ed., Thom McAn Shoe Co., 67 Milbrook St., Worcester, Mass. 01606, '66–; Ed., Asst. to Adv. Mgr., Worcester County Nat. Bank, '62–'66; Indsl. Ed., Am. Optical Co., '52–'62; Free-lance Wtr., Ed., Radio Personality; Chmn., Intl. Center of Worcester, '70; Intl. Cncl. of Indsl. Eds., Am. Assn. of Indsl. Eds., Worcester County Eds. Cncl. (Pres., '69–'70), Worcester Area C. of C., Adv. Club Worcester (Secy., '66–'69; Ed., '69–'70); Bryant Coll., Clark Coll.; b. Webster, Mass.; p. August Michael and Catherine Kalvinek Martinik; h. Roger E. Daviau (div.); c. Julie Ann, Valerie Jean; res: Point Breeze, Webster, Mass. 01519.

DAVID, IRIS RAHN, Soc. Ed., Arkansas City Daily Traveler, Fifth Ave. and A St., Arkansas City, Kan. 67005, '67–; News, Feature Wtr.; Instr., 4-H reptrs.; County Homemakers unit reptrs., County Ext. Advisory Cncl. (past Chmn.); Cowley County Commty. Jr. Col., '46–'47; Kan. State Univ., BS, '49–; b. Arkansas City, Kan., 1927; p. George and Lucy Klinginsmith Rahn; h. Walter E. David; c. Jody Mae, Karen Kay, Ruth Ann; res: Rural Rte. 1, Dexter, Kan. 67038.

DAVID, MADELON BETH, Head of Pubcty. Dept., Zale Corporation, 512 S. Akard, Dallas, Tex. 75201, '69–; Pubcty., Bloom Adv. Agcy., '69; Theta Sigma Phi, PR Student Soc. of Am.; Sophie Newcomb Col., '65–'66; Univ. of Tex. at Austin, BJ, '69; b. Dallas, Tex., 1947; p. Stanley and Pauline Brand David; res: 4506 Isabella Lane, Dallas, Tex. 75229.

DAVID, MARTHA LOUISE, Supvsr., Consumer Rels. Div., Burson-Marsteller, 1 E. Wacker Dr., Chgo., Ill. 60601, '69–; Sr. VP, Daniel J. Edelman, '59–'68; Assoc., Commty. Programs Cnslrs., '57–'59; Asst. PR Dir., Adlai Stevenson Presidential Campaign, '56; Dir., Midwest Off., CARE, Inc., '51–'57; Asst. to Dir. of Radio-TV, Commty. Fund of Chgo., '50–'51; PRSA, Pubcty. Club of Chgo. (Bd. of Dirs., '63–'66; Supvsr. of five aw. winning progs. in annual Golden Trumpet Aws.); Who's Who of Am. Wm.; World Understanding Aw., Chgo. Cncl. on Fgn. Rels., '55; Menomonee Club for Boys & Girls (VP, Bd. of Dirs.), Old Town Triangle Assn. (Bd. of Dirs.); Mac Murray Col., BA, '47; Univ. of Southern Cal.; b. Evanston, Ill., 1926; p. Sigmund and Louise Lippett David; res: 208 W. Eugenie St., Chgo., Ill. 60614.

DAVID, TERRY, Media/Traf. Dir., Chace Co. Advertising, 114 E. de la Guerra, Santa Barbara, Cal. 93101, '68–; Asst. Adv. Dir., Rayne Soft Water Svc., '66–'68; Asst. Gen. Mgr., Rockett-Lauritzen Adv., '56–'62; Pubcty.-Prom. Dir., Sta. WROC-TV, WHAM Radio, '52–'56; Am. Bus. Wms. Assn.; U.C.L.A., Univ. of Rochester, Columbia Univ., Univ. of Wis.; b. Cleve., Oh., 1928; p. Carl and Alice Zeitz David; res: 1022 Garden, Santa Barbara, Cal. 93101.

DAVIDSON, DIANA GOHLINGHORST, Media Dir., Martin-Williams Advertising, Inc., Midwest Plaza, 801 Nicollet Mall, Mpls., Minn. 55402, '66–; Asst. Media Supvsr., Knox-Reeves Adv. Agcy., '65–'66; Media Byr., Clyne Maxon Adv., Inc., '60–'65; Secy. to Adv. and Sales Prom. Mgr., McCulloch Corp., '55–'60; Adv. Club of Minn. (Bd. of Dirs.), AWRT (North Star Chptr. VP), C. of C. Wms. Div., William Woods Col.; Mpls. Bus. Col.; Twin Cities Adv. Inst.; b. Councill Bluffs, Ia., 1934; p. Donald W. and Maxine Aney Gohlinghorst; h. J. Robert Davidson; c. Douglas Lee; res: 3412 Skycroft Dr., Mpls. Minn. 55418.

DAVIDSON, L. AGNES DEVINE, Free-lance Wtr., poetry in nat. mags., '66–; travel features in nwsps., '62–'63; '48–'51; Free-lance edtl., proofreading, manuscript and thesis prep., W. Lafayette, Ind., '55–'61, Balt., Md., '51–'54; Asst. Ed., MacPherson County Herald (Leola, S.D.), '42; News Reptr., Reporter and Farmer (Webster), '40–'41, '43–'46; Purdue Wms. Club (Pubcty., '56–'58; compiled pubcty. handbk.; Crtv. Writing Sec.), Theta Sigma Phi, Un. Cncl. of Wm. of U.S.A., Haiku Soc. of Am. (Charter Mbr.), numerous past orgs.; Winona Col., '36–'38 (Purple Key; Scholarship, '37; edtl. positions; Co-colmst., news for Col., Winona Republican Herald, city nwsp., '37–'38); Univ. of Minn., BA (Jnlsm.), '40 (magna cum laude; Sigma Delta Chi Aw.; Edtl. Writing Staff, Minn. Daily, '39–'40; pubns.); b. Roy, Mont., 1917; p. Everett and Eva Hassinger Devine; h. Ralph Kirby Davidson; c. Karen, Laura; res: 2 Wash. Sq. Village, Apt. 8-O, N.Y., N.Y. 10012.

DAVIDSON, MARGARET ELIZABETH, Home Mgt. Ed., Ladies' Home Journal, 641 Lexington Ave., N.Y., N.Y. 10022, '47–; Home Econs. Dir., Hotpoint, '43–'47; Home Svc. Dir., Cleve. Electric Illuminating Co., '39–'43; Cnslt., nwsp. colmst.; Dean's Adv. Cncl., Cornell Univ., Ia. State Univ.; Am. Home Econs. Assn., Home Econsts. in Bus. (Treas.), Electrical Wms. Round Table (Dir.), AWNY (Dir.), Nat. Cncl. for Homemaker Svcs. (Dir.); Ia. State Univ., BS (Home Econs.); b. Ames, Ia.; p. Jay and Jennie Baldridge Davidson; res: N. Midland Ave., Upper Nyack, N.Y. 10960.

DAVIDSON, MARY BETH, PR Asst., National Cotton Council, 1918 N. Parkway, P.O. Box 12285, Memphis, Tenn. 38112, '62–; Copywtr., Lake-Spiro-Shurman Adv. Agcy., '60–'62; Assoc. Ed., TV Star Parade Mag., (N.Y.C.), '59; Copywtr., WMC Radio (Memphis), '56–'59; Tchr., St. Mary's Episcopal Sch. (Memphis), '55–'56; Soc. Reptr., The Memphis Commercial Appeal, '54–'55; AWRT, Tenn. Poetry Soc.; Volunteer of Yr. aw., Boys Club of Memphis, '69; Southwestern at Memphis, BA, '54 (Peter Pauper Press Essay Aw., '50–'51); b. Dyer, Tenn., 1932; p. Asa and Ellen Glisson Davidson; res: 2429 Union Ext., Apt. 4, Memphis, Tenn. 38112.

DAVIDSON, RUTH BRADBURY, Contrb. Ed., Antiques Magazine, 551 Fifth Ave., N.Y., N.Y. 10017, '68–; Rsch. Ed., Features Ed., '45–'68; Free-lance Wtr. on art subjects; Mills Co., Cal., BA, '33; MA, '34; b. Ray, Ariz., 1911; p. Walter and Georgia Irwin Bradbury; h. Marshall B. Davidson; res: 140 E. 83rd St., N.Y., N.Y. 10028.

DAVIED, CAMILLE, Lectr. on writing for publication, Hunter College, '67–; Lectr., N.Y.U., '63–'67; Exec. Ed., McCall's Magazine, '33–'62; Ed., Arts & Decoration, '32–'33; Ed., Charm, '30–'32; Asst. Ed., Vogue, '29–'30; free-lance wtr. and ed. for Amerika, '62–'65; Reader, Conslt., Family Bk. Club, Meredith Press, '62–'65; Auth., "How to Write Successful Magazine Articles," The Writer, '67; Barnard Col. Pubns. Comm. Chmn., '61–'64; OPC (Judge for articles on fgn. affairs), Nat. Arts Club (Chmn., Lit. Aws. Comm.), WNPC (Wash., D.C.); Univ. of Ky., one yr., Barnard Col., one yr.; b. Chattanooga, Tenn.; p. John Felix and Elizabeth Williams Davied; h. Marc A. Rose; c. Patricia (Mrs. Edward Cumming); res: 115 E. 82nd St., N.Y., N.Y. 10028.

DAVIS, ALICE COBURN, Crtv. Dir., Michelin Tire Corporation, 2500 Marcus Ave., Lake Success, N.Y. 11040, '69–; Adv. Mgr., Osrow Products Co., Glen Cove, '64–'69; PR Mgr., '61–'64; Copywtr., Gamut Adv., Hempstead, '59–'61; Prod. Asst., Newsday, Garden City, '58–'59; AWNY, L.I. Adv. Club (Dir., '60), Electrical Wms. Round Table; Hunter Col., BA; h. (div.); c. Ellen, Allison, Robert; res: 26 Lincrest St., Syosset, N.Y. 11791.

DAVIS, ANNA KING, Free-lance Wtr., '52–; Tchr., '18–'30; Colmst., North Little Rock Times, '58–'59; NLAPW, AAUW, WNBA; Who's Who of Am. Wm.; Drury Col., AB, '28; b. Houston, Mo.; p. William and Lydia Covert King; h. Henry O. Davis; c. Jack William, James Henry; res: P.O. Box 125, Salem, Ark. 72576.

DAVIS, ELISA SAVILLA, Wtr., IBM Corporation, Office Products Div., 590 Madison Ave., N.Y., N.Y. 10022, '68–; Asst. to Pubcty. Dir., Trade Book Dept., Holt, Rinehart and Winston, '64–'68; Theta Sigma Phi (N.Y.C. Chptr. VP-Special Projects, '67–; Corr. Secy., '65–'67); AAF, Gamma Alpha Chi; Univ. of Tex., BJ, '64 (Marjorie Darilek Memorial Scholarship Aw.); b. Detroit, Mich., 1941; p. Jarrell and Elizabeth Johnson Davis; res: 220 E. 57 St., N.Y., N.Y. 10022.

DAVIS, EMILY LOUISE, Asst. Ed., The Book Review, Library Journal, Bowker Co., 1180 Ave. of the Ams., N.Y., N.Y. 10036, '68–; Ed., The Book Review, School Library Journal, '46–'68; Tchr., '36–'45; Wms. Nat. Bk. Assn.; Bryn Mawr Col., BA, '34; Columbia Univ. (Tchrs. Col.), MA, '36; b. Bronx, N.Y., 1911; p. Royal J. and Louise Stanton Davis; res: 3615 Greystone Ave., Bronx, N.Y. 10463.

DAVIS, GLORIA SCHACHTER, Publr., Free-lance Wtr., Distributor of Contemporary Art, PR, 733 Middle Neck Rd., Great Neck, N.Y. 11024; Publr., Great Neck Tribune, '58–; Publr., Manhasset Tribune, '60–; Gloria Davis Public Relations; PR, 10 yrs.; Free-lance Wtr., 15 yrs.; Wholesale Art Distributor, Gloria Davis Gallery; organized or participated in many art shows for benefit of orgs.; Wtr., colm., Nat. Hearing Aid Jnl.; hearing aid work; Nat. Edtl. Assn., N.Y. Press Assn., Nassau County Press Assn.; certs. of merit, 11 yrs., Am. Cancer Soc.; Nassau Tuberculosis, Heart and Public Health Assn., UF, Kidney Disease Fndn.; b. N.Y.C.; p. Herman and Toby Connor Schachter; h. Sidney Davis (dec.); c. Roger Craig, Pamela Stephanie; res: 50 Sunset Rd., Kings Point, N.Y. 11024.

DAVIS, HELEN FULLER, Gen. Mgr., Greater Toledo Educational Television Foundation, Manhattan Blvd. at Elm St., Toledo, Oh. 43608, '66–; Coordr., Prodr.-Dir., instructional programming, Toledo Public Schs., '62–'66; Elementary, Jr. HS Tchr., '48–'62; Toledo Educ. Assn., Oh. Educ. Assn., Nat. Educ. Assn., NAEB, Central Educ. Network (Bd. of Dirs.); Univ. of Toledo, BEd, '35; MED (Audio-Visual Aids), '65; b. Toledo, Oh.; p. Lawrence J. and Ella B. Atkinson Fuller; h.

Keith A. Davis; c. Lawrence, James, Thomas; res: 11123 Lakeway Dr., Curtice, Oh. 43412.

DAVIS, HELEN RODGERS, Home Econst., Foods & Nutrition, University of Missouri Extension, 1216 N. 13th St., St. Louis, Mo. 63106, '61–; same position, Univ. of Mo., Jefferson City, '60–'61; in Home Econs. field as Tchr., Advisor, since '31; Ed., bi-weekly Marketing Bulletin; AWRT (Pubcty. Chmn., '68–'69), Am. Home Econs. Assn. (VP, '66–'68), Nat. Assn. of Ext. Home Econsts.; Christian Col.; Univ. of Mo.; Grad. Work: Univ. of Wis., Univ. of Mo.; b. Belleflower, Mo., 1909; p. John and Anna Clare Rogers; res: 8841 Eager Rd., St. Louis, Mo. 63144.

DAVIS, JEAN WALTON, Librn., Eastern Montana College, Billings, Mont. 59101, '62–; Asst. Librn., '59–'62; Reference Librn., Univ. of Mont., '56–'59; Librn., Anchorage Commty. Col., '55–'56; Reference Librn., Univ. of Denver, '51–'54; Tchr., Wash. State Univ., '29–'51; Auth., "Shallow Diggin's; Tales From Montana's Ghost Towns" (Caxton, '63); Mont. Lib. Assn. (Pres., '67–'68), Pacific Northwest Bibliographic Ctr. (Exec. Bd., '65–), Pacific Northwest Lib. Assn.; Wash. State Univ., BA, '29; MA, '34; Univ. of Denver MA (Lib. Sci.), '51; b. St. Thomas, N.D., 1909; p. Albert and Martha Romfo Walton; h. George Davis; c. Erwin; res: 2012 Virginia Lane, Billings, Mont. 59101.

DAVIS, JEANNE LOUISE, Mgr., Audio-Visual Dept., New York Times, 229 W. 43rd St., N.Y., N.Y. 10036, '68–; Assoc. in Educ. TV, N.Y. State Educ. Dept., '67–'68; Dir. of Educ. Commtns., Yorktown Sch., '65–'67; Fulbright Exchange Tchr. (Great Britain), '64; Tchr., '57–'63; Media Cnslt., various orgs.; NEA, NAEB, Am. Assn. of Sch. Adm., Educ. Commtns. Assn.; NDEA Media Inst. grant; Delta Kappa Gamma; State Univ. of N.Y., BS, '57; N.Y.U., MA (Educ. Commtns.), '63; grad. work, Univ. of Colo.; b. N.Y.C., 1936; p. John and Mabel Reed Davis; res: 465 W. 23rd St., N.Y., N.Y. 10011.

DAVIS, JEANNE WEST, Ed., The Seymour Herald, 116 N. 4th St., Seymour, Ia. 52590, '47–; News Ed., Clarinda (Ia.) Herald-Jnl., '44; Theta Sigma Phi; Drake Univ., BA, '44; b. Chariton, Ia., 1922; p. Thomas and Maude Baxter West; h. Wayne P. Davis; c. Kenneth Wayne, Polly Jeanne; res: 300 E. Lee St., Seymour, Ia. 52590.

DAVIS, LELA RUPP, Amusements Ed., Beaumont Enterprise & Beaumont Journal, 380 Walnut, Beaumont, Tex. 77701; Daily Colmst., gen.; Features Ed.; h. Charles Davis.

DAVIS, M. MARGARET, Wtr.-Ed., Economic Development Administration, U.S. Dept. of Commerce, 14th St. and Constitution Ave. N.W., Wash., D.C. 20230, '69; Public Info. Specialist, '68–'69; Assoc. Dir. of PR, Asst. Dir. of PR, Wtr., George Wash. Univ., '46–'68; Reptr., Edtl. Asst., Wash. Post; Auth., "A University in the Nation's Capital" ('47); ANWC (Pres.,

'62–'63), WNPC (Treas., '49–'50), ACPRA (Dist. Dir., '55–'56), Theta Sigma Phi, Phi Delta Gamma, Pi Delta Epsilon, Soc. of Wm. Geographers (Exec. Cncl., '69–), ZONTA, Wash. Forum, AAUW (Wash. Chptr. Scy., '44); George Wash. Univ., BA, '37; MA, '41 b. Wichita, Kan., 1916; p. Dale and Elanora Burch Davis; res: 1657 31st St. N.W., Wash., D.C. 20007.

DAVIS, MARILYN KORNREICH, Auth., educ. bks. on music, '50–; "Music Dictionary" (Doubleday & Co., N.Y.C.; four fgn. editions); Composer: music bks., "Group Activities at the Keyboard" series (Bourne Co., N.Y.C., '58, '60, '61); numerous articles in pfsnl. music pubns.; Piano Tchr., private studio, '43–; Class Piano Instr., W. Hempstead, Garden City, Freeport High Schs., '56–'58; Grad. Fac., Hofstra Univ., '60; Seminar, Queens Col., '62; Nat. Guild of Piano Tchrs. (Adjudicator), Piano Tchrs. Forum (Founder), N.Y. State Sch. Music Assn., N.Y. State Music Tchrs., Assn., Music Educs. Nat. Assn., Assoc. Music Tchrs., Assn., Music Tchrs. Nat. Assn., Juilliard Alumni Assn.; Inst. of Musical Art, Diploma, '46; Juilliard Sch. of Music, BS (Piano), '50; grad. study in music pedagogy, Columbia Univ., '56–'58; Queens Col., MA (Musicology), '68; p. Max and Rae Keit Kornreich; h. Joel Davis; c. Marcie Cheryl; res: 3442 Bertha Dr., Baldwin, N.Y. 11510.

DAVIS, MARJORIE FRIEND, Head Librn., Montgomery County Community College, 612 Fayette St., Conshohocken, Pa. 19428; '66–; Adm. Asst., Quaker Col., Haverford Col. Lib., '64–'66; Asst. to Curator, '60–'64; Librn., Lower Merion Senior HS, Ardmore, Pa., '56–'60; Univ. of Pa. Lib., '35–'43; ALA, Pa. Lib. Assn.; Delta Kappa Gamma; Juniata Col., AB, '32 (summa cum laude); Drexel Inst. of Tech., MS (Lib. Sci.), '61 (highest hons., Phi Kappa Phi, Beta Phi Mu); b. Phila., Pa., 1910; p. George C. and Elsie Horn Friend; h. James B. Davis (dec.); c. Martha Emily; res: 135 Winchester Rd., Merion Station, Pa. 19066.

DAVIS, MARY BALDWIN, Free-lance Wtr., '69–; Media and Prod. Dir., Robert L. Stevenson (Pitt., Pa.), '67–'69, Prod. and Traf. Control, '64–'67; Media Dir., AE, Louis J. Sautel, '60–'64; Media and Prod. Mgr., Copy Wtr., Dan A. Sullivan, '47–'59; Prod. Dept., Ketchum, MacLeod & Grove, '42–'47; Traf. Mgr., WCAE Radio, '36–'41; Pitt. Radio and TV Club, Intl. Beta Sigma Phi (Life Mbr.), OES; Univ. of Pitt., BA, '34; Duquesne Univ., '46–'47; b. Carnegie, Pa., 1911; p. Gilmore and Blanche Adams Davis; res: 1053 Greenlawn Dr., Pitt., Pa. 15220.

DAVIS, NANCY ANN CLINE, Assoc. Wms. Ed., Glendale News-Press, '57–'60; Reptr., South County Publishing Co. of Arroyo Grande, Cal., '62–'63; Reptr., Post-Advocate, Alhambra, '52–'56; Theta Sigma Phi; Pasadena City Col., AA, '54; Univ. of Southern Cal., BA, '57; b. Indianola, Ia., 1933; p. Ralph Cline and Irene Summy Cline Horridge; h. Lewis Lee Davis II; c. Douglas, Paula; res: 1431 Newport Ave., Arroyo Grande, Cal. 93420.

DAVIS, SARAH MARIE, Rsch. and Dev. Librn., Northern Illinois University, Swen Franklin Parson Library (De Kalb, Ill.), '68–; Reserve Librn., '52–'67; Lib. Ref. Asst., Pub. Lib. (Detroit, Mich.), '49–'52; High Sch. Tchr. (Neb., Ia., Ill., Mich.), '40–'47; works published; journal hist. pubns.; ALA, Am. Assn. of Higher Educ., AAUW, NEA, Ill. Educ. Assn.; Coe Col., BA (Hist.), '38 (magna cum laude, Phi Kappa Phi, Phi Sigma Iota Essay Aw., Alpha Gamma Delta Rose Bowl Aw.); Univ. of Ia., MA (Am. Hist.), '39 (Pi Gamma Mu); Univ. of Mich., MA (Lib. Sci.), '50 (Fellowship: '47–'49); Am. Univ., Cert. (Archives), '52; b. Washington, Is., 1916; p. Don and Rose Springman Davis; res: 143-1/2 John St., DeKalb, Ill. 60115.

DAVIS, ZONA BUCHHOLZ, News Dir., WCRA, Effingham Broadcasting Company, Washington and Banker, Effingham, Ill. 62401, '49–; Ed., County Rev., '34–'38; Daily Record, '28–'33; Wtr., UPI, AP, WCIA TV (Champaign, Ill.); prod. two radio programs daily; Co-auth., "Effingham County Illinois-Past and Present"; write 500 servicemen in Vietnam, sent every two weeks, '66– (Golden Mike aw., Am. Legion Aux.; same aw., for outstanding programs in interest of youth, '61); Intl. Platform Assn., Ill. News Bdcstrs. Assn. (Bd. Dirs.), UPI Bdcstrs. of Ill. (Pres., '67); Lake Land Col.; b. Effingham, Ill., 1911; p. George and Mollie Westfall Buchholz; h. Plaford Davis; c. Paul M.; res: 701 S. First St., Effingham, Ill. 62401.

DAVITT, JOSEPHINE, Sls. Commtns. Coordr., Ayerst Laboratories, Division of American Home Products, 685 Third Ave., N.Y., N.Y. 10017, '69–; Head, Policy and Procedure Manuals, Monroe Div., Litton Industries, '65–'69; Asst. Ed., PR Dept., '62–'65; Douglass Col., BA (Eng.), '62; b. Framingham, Mass., 1940; p. John and Josephine Golomb Davitt; res: 1033 Grandview Ave., Westfield, N.J. 07090.

DAWES, NANCY ROSS, Dir. of PR, Memorial Hospital, Northern Blvd., Albany, N.Y. 12204, '61–; Area Rep., The Merchandising Group (N.Y.C.), '55–'61; PRSA (Albany Chptr., Secy., Bd. Mbr., '66–), Professional PR Cncl. (Capital Dist. VP, '65–), Am. Soc. for Hosp. PR Dirs., Am. Hosp. Assn. (Area Rep.), ZONTA (Pbcty. Chmn.); b. Elmira, N.Y., 1918; p. Francis and Marjorie Nimbs Ross; h. Robert Dawes (dec.); c. Thomas, Mrs. Robin Ducey; res: 7 Bacon Lane, Loudonville, N.Y. 12211.

DAWKINS, CECIL, Wtr., Fiction, Drama: "The Quiet Enemy," collection of stories ('63); "The Displaced Person," adaptation of stories by Flannery O'Connor, prod. at the Am. Place Theatre (N.Y.C.); Wtr.-in-res., Stephens Col. (Columbia, Mo.), '61–'62; Tchr., Eng., '54–'58; Stanford Univ. Writing Fellow, '52–'53; Guggenheim Fellow, '66–'67; Harper Saxton Fellowship, '68; Univ. of Ala., BA, '50; Stanford Univ., MA, '53; b. Birmingham, Ala., 1927; p. Dr. James T. and Lucile H. Thiemonge Dawkins; res: 2727 Palisade Ave., Riverdale, N.Y. 10463.

DAWKINS, MARY SAUNDERS, Reg. Librn., State of Kentucky, Dept. of Libraries, Buffalo Trace Regional Library, Carlisle, Ky. 40311, '64; County Librn. (Flemingsburg, Ky.), '62–'63; Sec. Ed., Times Dem., '61–'62; Youth Dir., Flemingsburg Christian Ch., '66–'69; BPW, Ky. Lib. Assn., Southeastern Lib. Assn., Friends of Ky. Libs., Kappa Delta Alumnae; Univ. of Ky., BS (Home Econs.), '64; b. Flemingsburg, Ky., 1922; p. Noel and Lela Estill Saunders; h. Joseph Dawkins (dec.); c. James; res: 120 Pumphrey Ave., Flemingsburg, Ky. 41041.

DAWSON, HELEN A., Cnslt., Kitchens and Equipment, 2219–53rd St., DesMoines, Ia., 50310 '70–; Appliances, Housewares and Mgt. Ed., Meredith Corporation, '64–'70; Dir., Home Econs. Inst., Westinghouse, '61–'64; Home Svc. Dir., Travelling Home Econst., West Bend Co., '53–'59; Registrar and Cnslr., Zinser Pers., '50–'53; Mdsg. Specialist, J. R. Ozanne, '48–'50; Harry S. Manchester, '46–'48; WAC, '43–'46; Vocational Home Econs. Tchr., Thorp, Wis., '39–'42; Am. Home Econs. Assn. (VP, Housing and Equipment, '62–'63), Home Econsts. in Bus. (Milwaukee Group Chmn., '59–'60), Electrical Wms. Round Table (VP, Newsletter Ed., '68–'70; Newsletter Ed., '66–'67; Ia. Chptr. Chmn., '67–'69); Assn. of Home Laundry Manufacturers Aws., '64, '65, '66; Assn. of Home Appliance Manufacturers Aws., '67, '68; Stout State Univ., BS, '39; Oh. State Univ., MS, '60; b. Wis., 1917; p. Joseph and Alice Pedley Dawson; res: 2219–53rd St., Des Moines, Ia. 50310.

DAWSON, SUE-MAR SHOEMAKER, Exec. Dir., Honolulu Chapter, National Foundation-March of Dimes, 245 N. Kukui St., Honolulu, Hi. 96817, '64–; Adm. Asst., Hi. Congress of Parents and Tchrs., '58–'64; In-svc. tchr. training, Hi. Dept. of Educ., '55–'57; PR, Citizenship Day, '64–'66; PRSA, ICIE (Hi. Chptr. Treas., Bd. of Dirs.), PR Wm. of Honolulu, Honolulu Press Club, Hi. Public Health Assn., Altrusa (Honolulu Club: Pres., '68–'70; VP, '67; Treas., '66); St. Helen's Hall Jr. Col., '32–'34; Univ. of Hi., '54–'55, '64; b. Roseburg, Ore., 1915; p. Carl D. and Loa Turney Shoemaker; c. Mrs. Nga Anderson, Peter, David, Michael; res: 2257 Noah St., Honolulu, Hi. 96816.

DAY, BETH (Beth Feagles), Free-lance Wtr., non-fiction articles and bks., c/o Paul Reynolds Inc., 599 Fifth Ave., N.Y., N.Y. 10009, Auth., 18 bks.; mag. articles; Soc. of Mag. Wtrs.; Univ. of Okla., BA, '45; b. Ft. Wayne, Ind., 1924; p. Ralph and Mary Anna West Feagles; h. (dec.); res: 427 W. 21st St., N.Y., N.Y. 10011.

DAY, BILLEE MASDEN, Dir., Chickasaw Library System, 22 Broadlawn Village, Ardmore, Okla. 73401, '64–; Ext. Librn., '63; Bookmobile Librn., '60–'62; Reference Librn., Okla. State Univ., '47–'48; Asst. to Librn., '46; Librn., Okmulgee Br., '46–'47; Cnslt., Okla. Dept of Libs.; Tchr., Lib. Sci., Southeastern State Col.; ALA, S.W. Lib. Assn., Okla. Lib. Assn. (Ed., Okla. Librn.), Chickasaw Hist. Soc. (Trustee, Pres.); Hon. Princess, Chickasaw Indians; p. Harold and Ruth Tyer

Masden; h. John P. Day; c. Paul L., Philip C., Priscilla R., Peter M.; res: 1615 W. Broadway Place, Ardmore, Okla. 73401.

DAY, GERRY, Free-lance Wtr., Ed., for radio, TV, motion pictures, 8102 W. Norton Ave., Hollywood, Cal. 90046; TV scripts for "University Medical Center," "Judd For The Defense," "The Outcasts," "Here Come The Brides," "Lancer," "The Virginian," "Wagon Train," numerous others; Staff Wtr., "Peyton Place," '65; Script Ed., Les Mitchel Prods., '46–'49; Reptr., Feature Wtr., Hollywood Citizen-News, '44–'46; novel, "The Bitter Wind," in the Toronto Star; short stories in Canadian Home Journal and Ten Story Western; NFPW (L.A. Dist. Pres.), '65–'66; aws. for best TV scripts, '63, '65–'68), AWRT, ATAS, WGA, WWA, Zeta Phi Eta; selected by Univ. of Ore. to contrb. all scripts, notes, rsch. material to lib.; U.C.L.A., '40–'44; b. Hollywood, Cal.; p. Lenox and Ruth Lallande Day; res: 1546 N. Fairfax Ave., Hollywood, Cal. 90046.

DAY, HELEN, Wms. Bdcst. and Public Svc. Dir., WKHM, 1700 Glenshire Dr., Jackson, Mich. 49201, '63–; Wms. Telecaster, WBAY-TV (Green Bay, Wis.), '53–'60; Wms. Bdcstr., WMAW (Milw.), '48–'51; Wms. Bdcstr., WQUA (Moline, Ill.), '46–'48; Wms. Bdcstr. (WHBY, Appleton, Wis.), '43–'46; Tchr., Radio, Lawrence Col., '45–'46; AWRT, Wms. Adv. Club of Milw., '49–'62 (Bd. of Dirs. '52); Ill. Wesleyan Univ., AB, '27; Grad. Work, Sch. of Speech, Northwestern Univ.

DAY, KATHLEEN MARY, Asst. Ed. Straus Editors Report; Radio Corr., Straus Broadcasting Group, Inc., 1211 Connecticut Ave. N.W., Suite 501, Wash., D.C.; Radio News Corr., Metromedia News; Wtr., Voice of Am.; AWRT, WNPC, Wash. (D.C.) Nat. Symphony; Univ. of San Diego, BA (Polit. Sci.), '63 (Dean's List); p. John and Mary Hurley Day; res: 3040 Idaho Ave. N.W. Apt. 530, Wash. D.C. 20016.

DAY, LYNDA L., Actress; Broadway, "The Devils"; Phoenix Little Theater, Sombrero Playhouse, Arizona, '60–'64; Ford Models Agcy. (N.Y.C.); summer stock theaters; numerous TV shows; commls.; SAG, AEA, AFTRA; b. San Marcos, Tex., 1944; p. Lt. Col. Claude and Betty Avey Day; c. Nickos; res: 119 N. Oakhurst, Beverly Hills, Cal. 90201.

DAY, PATRICIA JEAN, VP, Stein and Day, Inc., 7 E. 48th St., N.Y., N.Y. 10017, '62–; VP, Mid-Century Book Soc., '59–'62; b. Villisca, Ia.; p. Russell and Brenice King Day; h. Sol Stein; c. Robert Bruce, David Day, Elizabeth Day; res: Linden Circle, Scarborough, N.Y. 10510.

DEAL, BABS HODGES, Auth., fiction; novels, short stories (various mags.); Auths. Guild, PEN; Edgar Scroll Aw., '67 ("Fancy's Knell," '66, Doubleday); Ala. Lib. Assn. Aw., '69 ("The Walls Came Tumbling Down," '68 (Doubleday); Univ. of Ala., BA, '52; b. Scottsboro, Ala., 1929; p. Hilburn and Evelyn Coffey Hodges; h. Borden Deal; c. Ashley, Brett,

Shane; res: 4740 Ocean Blvd., Sarasota, Fla. 33581.

DEAN, RUTH ALDEN, Assoc. Publr., Inglewood Daily News, Inc., 121 N. LaBrea Ave., Inglewood, Cal. 90301, '46–; Corp. Secy-Treas., Modern Housing, Inc., and Pen & Sword, Inc.; Assoc. Publr., Marengo (Ill.) Republican-News, '34–'46; Assoc. Publr., Seymour (Ia.) Herald, '32–'34; Inglewood Wms. Club (Past Pres.), Inglewood Lib. Study Comm., Inglewood Philharmonic Assn.; Am. Legion Post 188 Wm. of Yr. Aw., '62; Ia. State Univ., BS, '30; b. Elburn, Ill., 1909; p. Harry and Eva Riplets Dean; h. Edwin Wendell Dean; c. Edwin, Jr., Dennis; res: 806 S. Myrtle Ave., Inglewood, Cal. 90301.

DEAN, STEPHANIE, Media Supvsr., Siteman/Brodhead, Inc., 8665 Wilshire Blvd., Beverly Hills, Cal. 90211, '64–; Media Dir., Prod. Mgr., Ross/Kauffman Co. (L.A.); Media Dir., Adams & Keyes, Edward S. Kellogg Co., '61–'63; Univ. of Ill., BS; U.C.L.A., MS; b. Wood River, Ill.; p. Joseph and Sophia Sara Slinsky; res: 9015 Burton Way, L.A., Cal. 90048.

DEAN, VERA MICHELES, Prof. of Intl. Adm., Graduate School of Public Administration, New York University, N.Y., N.Y. 10003, '62–; Visiting Prof. and Dir. of Non-Western Studies, Univ. of Rochester (N.Y.), '62; Auth., bks. on world affairs; Conslt., UN. Relief and Rehabilitation Adm., '45–'46; Asia Soc., Fgn. Policy Assn., French Legion of Hon. Aw. for contrb. to world understanding; hon. degrees from numerous cols. and univs.; Radcliffe Col., AB, '25 (summa cum laude; Alumna Assn. Medal); Ph.D. (Intl. Law and Intl. Rels.), '28; Yale Univ., AM, '26; b. St. Petersburg, Russia, 1903; p. Alexander George and Nadine Micheles; h. William Johnson Dean (dec.); c. Elinor Gardner (Mrs. Charles W. Wilder), William J.; res: 70 E. 96th St., N.Y., N.Y. 10028.

DEANE, BARBARA ALLISON, Wms. News Ed., Chanute Tribune, 15 S. Highland, Chanute, Kan. 66720, '67–; Photogr., Reptr., '59–'61; Ed., employee nwsp., Lear Jet Industries (Wichita), '66–'67; BPW; Chanute Jr. Col., '57; Kan. State Univ., '57–'58; b. Chanute, Kan., 1938; p. Marion J. and Nola Webb Allison; c. Daniel David, Lorie Allison; res: 17 S. Kansas, Chanute, Kan. 66720.

DEANE, RONNIE, Copy Dir., Stephan & Brady Advertising, Inc., 2 E. Gilman St., Madison, Wis. 53701, '66–; Talent, radio and TV with own programs, '39–'65; Reptr., Duluth (Minn.) Herald, '42–'43; Copy Dir., KATE, Albert (Lea, Minn.), '39–'41; Pfsnl. Actress (summer stock and repertory); Zeta Phi Eta, Wis. Reg. Wtrs. Assn. (Jade Ring winner, '63); MGM Talent Search winner, '37; numerous writing aws.; Col. of St. Catherine; b. Blue Earth, Minn., 1918; p. John and Gertrude Small Spencer; h. Jerry Deane; c. David, Robert, Sara, Kathleen (Mrs. Frederick Kruger); res: 5822 Suffolk, Madison, Wis. 53711.

DEARCOPP, JOANNE, Dir., Lib. Svcs., The McCall

Publishing Company, Bk. Div., 230 Park Ave., N.Y., N.Y. 10017, '69–; Prom. Mgr., Educ. and Lib. Dept., Simon & Schuster, Inc., '68–'69; Prom. Coordr., New Products Coordr., Grolier Educ. Corp., '66–'68; Cnslt., Preventive Med. Inst./Strang Clinic, currently; Wm's Nat. Bk. Assn., ALA, Publrs.' Lib. Prom. Group; Gettysburg Col., AB, '62 (Phi Psi).

DEARMIN, JENNIE TARASCOU, Project Dir., Title I ESEA, Santa Barbara School District, 720 Santa Barbara St., Santa Barbara, Cal. 93101, '66–; Asst. Prin., girls jr. high, '65–'66; Supvsr. of Tchr. Educ., Univ. of Cal. (Santa Barbara), '60–'65; Tchr.-Ext. Class, '62; Tchr., '46–'60; Spanish Cnslt., State Dept. of Educ.-Cal., '61–'64; CTA, CASCD (Bd.), Delta Kappa Gamma (Pres., Treas.), S.B. Tchrs. Assn. (Bd., Treas.); Contemporary Auths., other dirs.; Univ. of Cal. (Santa Barbara), BA, '46; Stanford (Palo Alto, Cal.), MA, '57; b. Upland, Cal., 1924; p. John B. and Trini Gallardo Tarascou; h. George Dearmin; res: 2705 Clinton Ter. Santa Barbara, Calif. 93105.

DE ARMOND, CHARLOTTE SNYDER, Statewide Dir. of PR, Children's Home Society of California, 3100 W. Adams Blvd., L.A., Cal. 90018, '66–; Owner, Charlotte De Armond Public Relations, '56–'65; Cnslt., Children's Home Soc., '56–'65; PR Dir., Hoffman Electronics Corp., '55–'56; PR Dir., Pacific Airmotive Corp., '52–'55; PR Dir. and Adv. Mgr., Gladding, McBean & Co., '50–'52; PR Dir. and Adv. Mgr., Am. Wine Co., '47–'50; PR Staff, Douglas Aircraft Corp., '44–'47; Mgt. Control Staff, Lockheed Aircraft Corp., '41–'44; Theta Sigma Phi, PRSA, L.A. Adv. Wm. (Pres., '53–'54), The Fashion Group, Aviation/Space Wtrs. Assn.; Frances Holmes Achiev. Aws: PR, '59; Dir. Mail, '47; Univ. of Neb., AB, '40; Grad. Study, Polit. Sci., U.C.L.A., '47–'48; b. Chgo., Ill., 1919; p. M. J. and Edna Brenner Snyder; h. Henry W. De Armond; c. Peggy Anne; res: 5200 Los Caballeros Way, L.A., Cal. 90027.

DeBORD, SHARON L., Actress, "General Hospital," American Broadcasting Co., 4151 Prospect Ave., L.A., Cal. 90028, '65–; TV Shows, "Bewitched," "No Time for Sergeants," "Flying Nun," "Rosie Grier Show," "Blackwell Show"; motion pics., plays, recordings; Columbia Workshop; b. Baker, Ore., 1939; p. Everett and Merle De La Mater DeBord; res: 942 Hammond, L.A., Cal. 90069.

De BORHEGYI, SUZANNE SIMS, Wtr., fiction, non-fiction; Tchr., World Hist., Anthropology, University School, 2100 W. Fairy Chasm Dr., Milw., Wis. 53211, '66–; Rschr., ethno-hist., Spanish colonial hist., Maya archaeology; Soc. of Midland Auths. (Clara Ingram Judson Memorial Aw., '62), Children's Reading Roundtable of Chgo.; Auth: "The Secret of the Sacred Lake" (Holt, Rinehart & Winston, '68), "Ships, Shoals and Amphoras" (Holt, Rinehart & Winston, '61), "Museums: A Book to Begin On" Holt, Rinehart & Winston, '62); Ohioana Bk. Aw., '62; Oh. State Univ., BA, '48; Univ. of Ariz., '48–'49; San Carlos Univ. (Guatamala), '50–'53; Univ. of Okla. (Tch.

Cert.), '64; Univ. of Wis., '66–; b. Pitt., Pa.; p. Clarence and Corinne Landgraf Sims; h. Stephan F. de Borhegyi (dec.); c. Ilona, Stephan, Carl, Christopher; res: 2709 E. Bradford, Milw., Wis. 53211.

DEBRODT, BARBARA JO REAM, PR Cnslt., Barbara Jo Ream Debrodt, 515 Soule Blvd., Ann Arbor, Mich. 48103, '58–; Dir. of Pubns., Nat. Educ. TV, '56–'58; Asst. VP, PR, Detroit Trust Co., '54–'55; Asst. to PR Cnslts., H. H. Shuart, Frank Webb (Detroit), '54; Dir. PR, Methods Engineering Cncl. (Pitt., Pa.), '51–'53; Asst. Dir., Public Info., Pitt. Red Cross, '51; Adv. Colm. Wtr., Modern Bride Magazine, '49–'50; Free-lance Prod.-Wtr., Educ. TV progs., Univ. of Mich. TV Ctr., '66–'67; PRSA; Intl. Neighbors (Bd. Mbr. 5 yrs.), Ann Arbor, Mich., Volunteer Sch. posts, '53; Univ. of Mich., BA, '49; Boston Univ., MA (PR) '53; b. Summit, N.J. 1928; p. Merrill Jay and Catherine Ada Terrill Ream; h. Robert Earl Debrodt; c. Donna Catherine, Carol Jeanne; res: 515 Soule Blvd., Ann Arbor, Mich. 48103.

DECKER, MARJORIE REESE, Ed., Okmulgee County News, 105–7 E. Fifth, Okmulgee, Okla. 74447, '55–; Soc. Ed., '53; Okla. Press Assn., Okla. Wtrs. Assn., BPW, Okmulgee Public Lib. Bd.; Muskogee Jr. Col., '36–'37; b. Ft. Smith, Ark., 1919; p. John and Hazel Shults Reese; h. Howard C. Decker; c. David, Laura (Mrs. Don R. Lehman); res: 812 S. Alabama, Okmulgee, Okla. 74447.

DEEMS, BONNIE, Part Owner, Exec. VP, Stallion Productions, 7 W. 28th St., N.Y., N.Y. 10001, '64–; Co.-dir., ABC "Discovery," '63–'64; Assoc. in Prod., "Roosevelt Years," "The Valiant Years," Winston Churchill Series, ABC, '60–'63; prod., co-dir., "Out of the Shadows," Lighting Industry; wrote, dir., prod., "Outskirts of Hope," Nat. Urban League; Intl. Bdcst. Aw., '67; Clio, Am. TV Film Festival, '68; Aw. of Excellence, CA Magazine, '68; City Col. of N.Y., BA, '52; b. N.Y.C., 1934; p. Moe and Mary Beck Abrams.

DEEN, EDITH ALDERMAN, Auth., Lectr.; Bks: "The Bible's Legacy For Womanhood" ('70), "All of the Women of the Bible" ('55), "Great Women of the Christian Faith" ('59), "Family Living in the Bible" ('63); Radio Commentator, '49–'55; Wms. Ed., Daily Colmst., Fort Worth Press, '25–'54; Tex. Inst. of Ltrs., Auths. Guild, Theta Sigma Phi (Nat. Headliner Aw., '63); First Lady Altrusa Aw., '49; Nat. Conf. of Christians and Jews cit., '60; Fort Worth City Cncl. ('65–'67); Univ. of Tex., '22–'23; Tex. Wms. Univ., BA, '53; MA, '60; Hon. DLett, '59; b. Weatherford, Tex., 1905; p. James and Sara Scheuber Alderman; h. Edgar Deen (dec.); res: 2420 Refugio, Fort Worth, Tex. 76106.

DEERE, GRETCHEN ROBERTA CLARK, Classified Adv. Mgr., The Daily Democrat, Ed. E. Leake Publishing Co., Inc., 702 Court St., Woodland, Cal. 95695, '62–; Teletype Dept. Mgr., '60–'62; Bk. Rev. Ed., Religion Ed., Edtl. Staff, '57–'60; Artist, exhibited; Assn. of Nwsp. Classified Adv. Mgrs.

(First Place Aw., world-wide, '65); Beta Sigma Phi (Chptr. Pres., '42–'43); Aw. of Excellence, Western Classified Adv. Assn., '64; active in numerous civic and ch. svcs.; Univ. of Cal. at Davis, '62–'68; b. Grants Pass, Ore., 1916; p. Ira and Mabel Mahan Clark; h. Harley Deere (dec.); c. Dr. Harley, Jr., Robert; res: 1305 Colette Way, Woodland, Cal. 95695.

DEES, BETTY JANE, Wms. Dir., TV and radio Hostess, WLOX-TV, Radio, Buena Vista Hotel, Biloxi, Miss. 29530, '62–; Biloxi/Ocean Springs Jr. Auxiliary (Charter Mbr.; past Pres., '61), Altrusa, Biloxi C. of C., AWRT; Wm. of Achiev.; Special Aw. for commtn. coverage, U.S. Army Recruiting Svc. Station, Montgomery, Ala., '66; Whitworth Col., '48–'59; Univ. of Miss., '51–'52; b. Biloxi, Miss.; p. Clifton L. and Ionia Mills Dees; res: Apt. E-5, Le Chateau Apts., Biloxi, Miss. 39530.

DE FRANCO, RUTH DECATUR, Radio Bdcstr., Wms. Prog. Dir., WWSC Radio Normandy Broadcasting Co., 217 Dix Ave., Glens Falls, N.Y. 12801, '67; Radio TV Chmn., League of Wm. Voters (Cuyahoga County, Oh.), '62–'64; Public Svc. Prog. Dir. and permanent Panelist of Project '66 and '67; LWV and Radio Sta. WBZA, '65–'67; Sch. Music Instr. private Piano and Theory Tchr., '56–'64; AWRT; Peter Bent Brigham Sch. of Nursing, RN, '38–'41; John Carroll Univ.; b. Natick, Mass. 1919; p. Joseph and Agnes Noel Decatur; h. Carl A. DeFranco; c. Carl, Jr., Paul, Philip; res: Gurney Lane, R.D. #2, Glens Falls, N.Y. 12801.

DEFTY, SARAH BIXBY, Reptr., St. Louis Post-Dispatch, 1133 Franklin Ave., St. Louis, Mo. 63101, '68–; Wms. Ed., '66–'68; Wms. Dept. Reptr., '65–'66; Prog. Analysis Div., CBS (N.Y.C.); Vassar Col., BA, '53; b. St. Louis, Mo., 1932; p. Ralph and Lucy Butler Bixby; h. Eric Defty (div.); c. Stephen, Matthew, Sarah; res: 7386 Kingsbury Blvd., St. Louis, Mo. 63130.

DEGENHARD, HELEN NISSEL, Staff Asst., The C. & P. Telephone Co. of Maryland, Sun Life Bldg., Charles Ctr., Balt., Md. 21201, '66–'67; Asst. Ed., Employee Nwsp., Message Register; Adm. Supvsr., '62; Adm. Asst., '56; Staff, '46–'56; Ed., The Guilder, ch. nwsp., '62; Compiled MAAIE Mbrship. Kit, accepted by ICIE, '60; Middle Atlantic AIE (Pres., '62–'63; VP, '62; Treas., '61; Ed. of the Yr., '62), Wms. 1st Fri. Club of Balt. (Pres., '63–'64); Notre Dame Col. (Md.), '46–'47; Loyola Col., BS (Social Sci.), '58; Am. Univ.; b. Balt., Md., 1928; p. John and Helen Sullivan Nissel; h. Richard Degenhard; c. Joseph, Robert; res: 729 Charing Cross Rd., Balt., Md. 21229.

DeGERING, ETTA FOWLER, Auth., four biogs. for juvs.; picture books; "Seeing Fingers, The Story of Louis Braille" (David McKay), '62; Thomas Alva Edison Fndn. Annual Children's Aw.; Lit. Guild Selection); Tchr., 32 yrs., Can.; Edtl. work, Braille mags., Christian Record Braille Fndn. (Lincoln, Neb.), '47–'52; Ed.,

Braille mag., The Children's Friend, '52–'60; Cert. Braille transcriber; Colo. Auths. League Tophand Aw. for teenage non-fiction ('65); Walla Walla Col.; Univ. of Colo.; b. Arcadia, Neb., 1898; p. Charles and Beryl Brown Fowler; h. Claud DeGering; c. Mrs. Trudy Anne Johnson, Harvey; res: 2945 16th St., Boulder, Colo. 80302.

DeGRÉ, MURIEL HARRIS, Info. Offcr., University of Waterloo, Waterloo, Ontario, Can., '68; Alumni Ed., Bard Col., '61–'68; Ed., Dutchess Country Journal, '57–'59; "Muriel DeGré Show": WKNY, '52–'57; WEOK, '49–'52; Pres., Fashion Prom. Cnslts., '39–'41; Auth., "Jack Sprat Cook Book" (Doubleday, '67); Who's Who of Am. Wm.; two Dartnell Ltr. Aws., '39; Columbia Univ.; N.Y.U.; b. N.Y.C.; p. Charles and Frances Pelcyger Harris; h. Gerard DeGré; c. Erica Ducornet; res: 230 Shakespeare Dr., Waterloo, Ontario, Can.

DE HAVEN, KATHRYN, Asst. Media Dir., Hoefer, Dieterich & Brown, Inc., 414 Jackson Sq., S.F., Cal. 94111, '69–; Sr. Media Byr. '66–'69; Sr. Media Byr., Dancer-Fitzgerald-Sample, '65–'66; Media Byr., Guild, Bascom & Bonfigli, '59–'65; Asst. Tchr. in Bdcst. Commtns., S.F. State Col.; Dir. of Teenage Musical Theater, Peninsula Conservatory (Burlingame, Cal.).

de HELLERMAN, MONICA C., VP, Bass and Company, Inc., 111 Broadway, N.Y., N.Y. 10006, '69–; Corporate Accs. Admr.; Specialist in financial PR for publicly-held firms; PR Mgr., Trans Caribbean Airways; NOW; Instr., N.Y. Univ., Columbia Univ.; Yale Univ., MA; b. 1940; c. Brett; res: 401 E. 86th St., N.Y., N.Y. 10028.

DEININGER, DIANE, Poet, Free-lance Actress: TV, motion pictures, commls.; Drama Tchr., Portals House; Rschr., mental illness; Fedn. of Chapparal Poets of Cal. (Ocotillo Chptr. Secy.), Phi Beta, SAG, AEA, AFTRA; Univ. of Ore., BA, '31 (Psych., Outstanding Wm. of the Yr.); b. near Denver, Colo.; p. John and Joanna Deininger; res: 416-1/2 S. Kenmore Ave., L.A., Cal. 90005.

DeJONG, LINDA CLARK, Exec. Prodr., Time-Life 8 Productions, 120 College S.E., Grand Rapids, Mich. 49502, '63–; PR Secy., '61–'62; Copywtr., Prod. Asst., Axelband & Brown & Assoc., '60; Alpha Epsilon Rho; Mich. State Univ., BA, '60 (cum laude); b. Cleve., Oh., 1938; p. Kenneth C. and Elizabeth Basler Clark; h. W. Frank DeJong; res: 505 College S.E., Grand Rapids, Mich. 49503.

DeJONG, MARILYN, Asst. Ed., Marketing/Communications, 501 Madison Ave., N.Y., N.Y. 10022, '69–; Tchr. (Farmingdale, N.Y.), '64–'68; Asst. Ed., Dun's Bulletin, Dun & Bradstreet, '62–'63; Copywtr., Montgomery Ward, '59–'60; N.Y. State Univ., '56–'58; Adelphi Univ., BA (Eng. Literature), '62; Bank St. Col. of Educ., MS; b. Bklyn., N.Y.; p. Thomas and Mary Scobie Burns; res: 207 E. 15th St., N.Y., N.Y.

DELAMATER, GERMAINE GONZALEZ, Actress, '68–; Model, '59–'68; U.C.L.A. (Lee Strasberg Drama), '68; b. N.Y.C., 1945; p. Augustine and Rosario Ordonez Gonzalez; h. Neil Delamater; res: 16155 High Valley Pl., Encino, Cal. 91316.

DeLAN, STEPHANIE LORD, Copy Chief, Richard Solay Advertising, 342 Madison Ave., N.Y., N.Y. 10017; Copy Supvsr., Warwick & Legler; Crtv. Supvsr., Reach McClinton; Copy Chief, Taplinger Millstein; Copy Supvsr., Clairol, Inc.; Sr. Wtr., Grey Adv.; Copy Supvsr., Al Paul Lefton; AWNY, Adv. Wtrs. of N.Y., Cosmetic Wm. of N.Y., Natl. Soc. of Interior Designers, Psi Chi; Sculptress (three aws.); N.Y.U., BA; Columbia Sch. of Jnlsm., MS; b. N.Y.C.; h. Daniel DeLan; c. Douglas, Dalton; res: 130 E. 94th St., N.Y., N.Y. 10028.

DELANEY, M. CONSTANCE MOORE, Publr., Lake Placid Journal, 230 N. Main St., Lake Placid, Fla. 33852, '68–; Ed., '63–'68; Soc. Ed., Okeechobee News, '60–'63; b. Wabash, Ind., 1928; p. Lamonte and Emmalene Carson Moore; c. Mrs. Warren B. Maples, Lamonte, Mathew, Mark, Mary Margaret; res: P.O. Box 785, Lake Placid, Fla. 33852.

DELANEY, MARGARET AGNES, Free-lance Wtr., News Corr., Syndicated World Trade Press, '70–; Wms. Ed., Times-Standard, '53–'70; News Reptr., Humboldt Standard, '50–'53; News Reptr., Farm Ed., Watertown (S.D.) Daily Public Opinion, '44–'50; News Corr., many pubns. (S.D., Ia.), before '44; Reptr., Clark County (S.D.) Courier and Marshfield (Wis.) Jnl.; free-lance work, mags., anthologies; NFPW (press aws., nat. and state, incl: wms. dept., edtl., others, '46–'68), Cal. Press Wm., Theta Sigma Phi, Pi Kappa Delta, BPW, AAUW, civic groups; Quotarian of Yr., '57; numerous aws., literature dept., S.D. state fair; Univ. of Ill., BA (Jnlsm.), '24; Univ. of Mo., MA (Jnlsm.), '33; b. Clark, S.D., 1898; p. Barney and Alice Lynch Delaney; res: 1140 E St., Eureka, Cal. 95501.

De LANEY, MARIE BOWERY, Comptroller-Adv. Dir., Morris Katz & Sons, Inc., 200 S. Peyton St., Alexandria, Va. 22314; Chief, Mortgage Servicing Dept., Thomas J. Fisher & Co. (Wash., D.C.), '66–'68; Adv. Dir.-Rental Property Mgr., Dorfmann Bros., '63–'66; Media Dir.-Corp. Offcr.-Comptroller, Earle Palmer Brown & Assoc., '62–'63; Co-auth., "17th Va. Inf. Reg. CSA," '61; numerous organizations and aws.; Smithdeal-Massey Col., BS (Bus. Adm.), '40; b. Petersburg, Va., 1922; p. John and Anne England Bowery; h. Wayne R. De Laney; c. Jan R.; res: 2122 Decatur Place, N.W., Wash., D.C. 20008.

de la SALLE, CHINA MACHADO, Crtv. Fashion Dir., Harper's Bazaar, 717 Fifth Ave., N.Y., N.Y. 10022, '69–; Sr. Fashion Ed., '62–'69; Prodr., fashion films, '66; previously model, Givenchy (Paris), Ford Agcy. (N.Y.C.); stylist to fashion photogrs., TV commls.; La Plata Univ., Argentina, '54–'56; b. Shanghai, China; p.

Frederico and Maria Thu-Sami Machado; h. Martin de la Salle; c. Blanche, Manuela, Anne; res: 41 Central Park W., N.Y., N.Y. 10023.

DELATINER, BARBARA ANN, TV Critic, Newsday, 550 Stewart Ave., Garden City, N.Y. 11530, '57–; Feature Wtr., Long Branch Daily Record, '54–'55; NWC of N.Y.C. (Front Page Aw., '64, '66, '68), Kappa Tau Alpha; N.Y.U., BA (Phi Beta Kappa), '54; b. N.Y.C., 1932; p. William and Rae Miller Delatiner; h. David Davidson; c. Beth, Wendy; res: 30 E. 9th St., N.Y., N.Y. 10003.

DeLAURENTIS, LOUISE BUDDE, Free-lance Wtr., 983 Cayuga Heights Rd., Ithaca, N.Y. 14850; Auth., "Etta Chipmunk" ('62); numerous poetry; Nat. Wtrs. Club, Wtrs. Assn. of Ithaca (Pres. '63–'64); Ottawa Univ., BA, '42 (hons.); b. Stafford, Kan., 1920; p. Louis and Mary Lichte Budde; h. M. A. DeLaurentis; c. Delbert Louis; res: 983 Cayuga Heights Rd., Ithaca, N.Y. 14850.

DE LAY, MARGARET B., Film Ed., The Film-Makers, Inc., 615 N. Wabash, Chgo., Ill. 60611, '68–; Prod. Ed. and Asst. Film Ed., Walter Schwimmer, Inc., '65–'66; TV Feature Re-Ed., WBBM-TV; AWRT; Univ. of Ill., BA, '65; Northwestern Univ., '53–'56; res: 4180 N. Marine Dr., Chgo., Ill. 60613.

De LEEUW, CATEAU WILHELMINA, Auth., 43 bks. (pseuds: Kay Hamilton, Jessica Lyon), others in collaboration with Adele De Leeuw; Artist; Plainfield Art Assn. (Founder, '27; Hon. Mbr.), Pen and Brush, Am. Artists Pfsnl. League; Cit., Martha Kinney Cooper Ohioana Lib. Assn., '58; Met. Art Sch., '21; Art Students' League, '23–'24; Acad. de la Grande Chaumiere, Paris, '30; b. Hamilton, Oh., 1903; p. A. Lodewyk and Katherine Bender De Leeuw; res: 1763 Sleepy Hollow Lane, Plainfield, N.J. 07060.

De LEON, SHIRLEY FELTMANN, Free-lance Wtr., '60–; numerous mag., nwsp. articles on educ., social problems, family, Latin Am.; Assoc. Ed., Children's House mag. (Caldwell, N.J.), '68–; rsch., mag., nwsp. articles (Santiago, Chile and Latin Am.), '61–'62; Staff Wtr., Jubilee Magazine (N.Y.C.), '59–'60; Wms. Pg. Reptr., Feature Wtr., music pg. colm., revs., Kalamazoo (Mich.) Gazette, '58–'59; news, features, Wash. (Mo.) Missourian; KWRE radio sta.; grant, rsch. for series of mag. articles, The Philip M. Stern Family Fund; Theta Sigma Phi (N.Y.C. Chptr.; Col. Chptr. Secy.); Marquette Univ., Col. of Jnlsm. (Milw., Wis.), AB, '57 (Gamma Pi Epsilon VP; Eta Sigma Phi); b. Washington, Mo., 1935; p. John and Josephine Patke Feltmann; h. Candido de Leon; c. Mark, Sarah, Paul; res: 434 W. 260th, N.Y., N.Y. 10471.

della CHIESA, ANN, Ed., Contact, National Life Insurance Co., Nat. Life Dr., Montpelier, Vt. 05602, '62–; Soc. Ed., Wms. Pg. Ed., Burlington Free Press; Mass. IEA; ICIE aws., '64, '67; Univ. of Vt., BA, '52; b. Montpelier, Vt., 1931; p. Joseph and Antonietta della

Chiesa; res: 10 Baldwin St., Montpelier, Vt. 05602.

DELMAN, ALICE, Pic. Rschr., Audio Productions, 630 Ninth Ave., N.Y., N.Y. 10036, '69; Pic. Rschr., Current Affairs Filmstrips, New York Times, '67; Dir. of Rsch., Mills-Widener indsl. films, '64–'65; Rschr., ABC-TV, '64; Pic. Rschr., CBS News, '64; Mkt. Dev. Mgr., John Sutherland Prods., '62–'63; Wtr., Louisville Courier-Jnl., '62–'63; Contrbr., "Readings in Health Education" (Wm. C. Brown Co., '64); Free-lance Wtr., '61–'63; Feature Ed., Globe Photos, '52–'53; Colmst., N.Y. Rev., '51; NATAS; Who's Who of Am. Wm.; City Col. of N.Y., BS (Educ., magna cum laude); Columbia Univ., MA; b. N.Y.C.; p. David and Kate Eleston Delman; res: 140 E. 63rd St., N.Y., N.Y. 10021.

DeLON, FRANCES GOOCH, Special Asst. to Pres., Photo-Art Commercial Studios, 420 S.W. Washington St., Portland, Ore. 97204, '63–; Portrait Photogr., '60–'63; Design of mural exhibits for: Pfsnl. Photogrs. of Am. '68; Hall of Fame, '68; U.S. Travel Fair for Tokyo, Japan, '64; Seattle World Fair, Ore. Exhibit, '62; U.S.I.A. photo exhibit for Europe, Asia, '57, and others; Ore. Adv. Club (Bd. of Dirs., '65, '68), Portland C. of C., Ore. Assn. of Eds. and Communicators, Prof. Photogrs. of Ore. (Blue Ribbon Aws., '64–'66, '68), Adv. Assn. of the West Aws., '65–'67; Berea Col., '27–'29; b. Terre Haute, Ind., 1909; p. Evin and Goldie Fagg Gooch; h. James Thurman De Lon (dec.); c. Joy (Mrs. C. M. Barnette, Jr.), Thomas T.; res: 1717 S.E. Hazel St., Portland, Ore. 97214.

DeLONG, ALVHILD WIMAN, Ed., The Portal, Fortnightly Club of Summit, '68–'70; Ed., Sheets and Cases, hospital quarterly, '56–'60; Wtr., Bdcstr., WABF, '42–'47; Pubcty., YWCA (Bklyn., N.Y.), '34–'40; Theta Norwalk, Conn., 1906; p. Gustaf and Anna Dahl Wiman; h. Charles Eugene DeLong; c. Mrs. Frederick Mandeville, Mrs. Robert F. Bernhard; res: 45 Woodland Ave., Summit, N.J. 17901.

DeLONG, TERESA GILSON, Soc. Ed., The Emporia Gazette, Emporia, Kan. 66801, '60–; Kan. State Tchrs. Col., BS, '33 (cum laude); b. Winfield, Kan., 1911; p. Franklin and Lulu Purdy Gilson; h. John DeLong; c. David Gilson, Richard Gareth; res: 628 Exchange St., Emporia, Kan. 66801.

DEL REY, PILAR, Actress, TV, Motion Pictures; Jack Wormser Agency; "And Now Migell" (Lead), "Black Horse Canyon" (2nd Lead), "Seige at Red River" (2nd Lead); Screen Actors Guild; AFTRA, b. Ft. Worth, Tex.; p. Earl and Junita Barrera Bouzas; res: 841 Sayre Lane, L.A., Cal. 90026.

De LUDE, MARGARET BOWLES, Dir. of Wms. Programming, Radio Claremont WTSV, AM, FM, 221 Washington St., Claremont, N.H. 03743, '65–; N.H. State Rep., '53–'57 (Chmn., House Apportionment Comm.); N.H. State Senate, '57–'67 (Chmn. Senate Ways and Means Comm., '63); Sch. Bd. (Trustee Trust Fund), N.H. Employment Svc., Sullivan County Easter Seal Fund, Repl. Comm., N.H. Commn. on Interstate Coop. (Ranking Mbr.), Order of Wm. Legislators (Nat. Parliamentarian, '68–'70; N.H. State Pres., '67–'69); BPW (State Legislative Chmn., Status of Wm. Chmn., currently; Claremont Pres., '67–'69; Wm. of the Yr. Aw., '59), AWRT; numerous civic orgs.; Polit. Who's Who; N.H. Tchrs. Assn. Distg. Svc. Aw., '55; Am. Cancer Soc. Crusade Cit., '68; N.H. Marine Corps League Aw. and Cit for Meritorious Svc., '66; Cazenovia Seminary, Jr. Col.; Columbia Univ.; Nat. Acad. of Design; b. Lynchburg, Va., 1918; h. Floyd De Lude; c. one; res: Star Route, N. Charlestown, N.H. 03603.

deLUISE, EUGENIE STEINHAUER, "Romper Room" Tchr., KWGN, 550 Lincoln, Denver, Colo. 80203, '61–; "Romper Room" Tchr., KTAR (Phoenix, Ariz.), '57; AWRT, Colo. Heart Assn., Med. Soc. Aux.; Univ. of Colo.; b. Denver, Colo., 1930; p. George and Lucy Scott Steinhauer; h. Dr. Rudolph L. deLuise; c. R. Scott, Holly, Lucy Marie; res: 2023 Goldenvue Dr., Golden, Colo. 80401.

De LUISE, HELEN MARGUERITE, VP, PR, East River Savings Bank, 26 Cortlandt St., N.Y., N.Y. 10007, '66–; Asst. VP, PR, '63–'66; Dir., PR & Adv., '59–'63; Asst. to PR Dir., '57–'59; PR Asst., '50–'57; Nat. Assn. of Bank Wm., FAA, Mktng. Soc. of Am., Bank PR and Mktng. Assn., AWNY, PRSA (Gold Key Aw., '67), CWPR (Treas., '68); St. Johns Univ., AB, '55; Sch. of Fin. PR, Northwestern Univ., '58; b. N.Y.C.; p. Michele and Immacolate Martinetti De Luise; res: 8801 Shore Rd., Fort Hamilton, N.Y. 11209.

DEMARAY, BARBARA L., Crtv. Supvsr., The Children's Television Workshop, 1865 Broadway, N.Y., N.Y. 10023, '69–; Crtv. Supvsr., Young & Rubicam, '52–'68; Copywtr., '44–'51; TV Mktng. Cnslt., General Foods; Wtr., "What Color is a Doorbell?"; Aws: Art Dirs. TV aw., '48, '52–'54; Adv. Age 10 Best TV, '52, '53; Am. TV Festival, '63; Am. TV Festival Classics aw.; b. Somerville, N.J.; p. Howard Hopping and Idabelle Collings Demaray; res: 166 W. Cliff St., Somerville, N.J. 08876.

DE MARIO, J. JOAN, Dir., Prod. and Design, Association Press, 291 Broadway, N.Y., N.Y. 10011, '61–; Prod. & Design Dir., Gernsback Lib., '61; Prod. Mgr., Guinn Co., '47–'60; Galaxy Publ., '52–'60; Mail Order Dept. Mgr., Wallace Brown, Inc., '41–'47; Productioneers (Pres., '65–; Treas., '52–'53), Club of Printing Wm. of N.Y. (Treas., '53–'56; Secy., '52–'54); Exhibn. of Printing Cert. of Special Merit, '63, '66, '69; freelance prod. and design; conducts edtl. and design workshops; Cnslt. on design, printing, publ.; Lectr. on wm. in the graphic arts; N.Y.U. Sch. of Publ. and Printing, N.Y. Employing Printers Sch., New Sch.; b. Ernest, Pa.; p. Francisco and Bonita Victoria Galletti De Mario; res: 16 W. 16th St., N.Y., N.Y. 10011.

DeMARS, ALICE BECK, Publr., Miltonvale Record, Miltonvale, Kan. 67466, '58–; Adv. Sales, Soc. Wtr., Glasco Sun, '36–'39; b. Glasco, Kan., 1916; p. Henry and Alice McClellan Beck; h. Albert DeMars; c. Jim, Armond, Carole, Fred; res: Miltonvale, Kan. 67466.

DEMING, ANN HOLYWELL, Co-owner, Pictures for Business, Box 2309, Hollywood, Cal. 90028, '55–: Wtr., Prod. of factual films; Estate Mgr.; Free-lance PR (N.Y.C.); L.A. Adv. Wm. (Pres., '69–'70; First VP, '68–'69; Second VP, '67–'68; Lulu, Annual Achiev. Aw., film, '67; Certs. of Merit, films, '65–'66), AAF, WGA, Assistance League of Southern Cal., Nat. Assistance League; b. Bklyn., N.Y., 1921; p. Effingham and Florence MacKeever Holywell; h. Wilford E. Deming; res: 4321 Kling St., Toluca Lake, Burbank, Cal. 91505.

DEMING, BARBARA, Free-lance Wtr., Edtl. Bd., Liberation magazine, 339 Lafayette St., N.Y., N.Y. 10012; active in nonviolent movement, '60–; Peace Aw., War Resisters League; Bennington Col., BA, '38; Western Reserve Univ., MA, '40; b. N.Y.C., 1917; p. Harold S. and Katherine Burritt Deming; res: RFD 1, Box 98A, Monticello, N.Y. 12701.

DEMING, EVELYN JARRETT, PR, volunteer, civic and ch. orgs.; bk. and play reviewer for orgs.; pfsnl. actress (Chgo., Ill., and Can.); Regent Daughters Am. Colonists (Ill. and Middle-West PR Chmn., '67–'69), WCTU (Winnetka-Wilmette PR Chmn., '69–; Pres., '48–'55), Hospitalized Veterans Writing Program Nat. PR Chmn., '61–'62, DAR (PR Chmn., chptr. and state confs., '58–'60), Theta Sigma Phi; Lawrence Col., BA (Philosophy), '24; b. Chgo., Ill., 1903; p. Delta and Maud Vinton Jarrett; h. James Deming; c. James H., Jr. (dec.), Vinton, Evelyn J. (Mrs. Jacques Reymond); res: 959 Spruce St., Winnetka, Ill. 60093.

DEMPSEY, IVY LINDSAY, Poetry Ed., Nimrod, University of Tulsa, Tulsa, Okla. 74104, '67–; Fiction Ed., '65–'66; Wtr., poetry, critical essays; Modern Lang. Assn; Univ. of Tulsa, BA, '63 (hons.); MA, '67; PhD Candidate; h. Joseph Dempsey.

DEMPSEY, MARY JO, Gen. Adv. Mgr., Greeley Daily Tribune, 714 Eighth St., Greeley, Colo. 80631, '45–; adv. dept., '41–'45; Adv., Display Mgr., Home Light and Power Co., '53–; Gamma Alpha Chi; Altrusa; Univ. of Mo., BJ, '41; b. Greeley, Colo., 1919; p. Richard and Berdenia Kightlinger Dempsey; res: 1207 Tenth St., Greeley, Colo. 80631.

DeMUTH, AUDREY HARRIS, Ed., Crete Record, Russell Printing Co., 111 N. First St., Peotone, Ill. 60468, '63–; Asst. Ed., Home Life Magazine (Chgo., Ill.), '52–'53; Mng. Ed., Sun Colony Magazine, (Ft. Lauderdale, Fla.), '51–'52; Univ. of Dubuque, BA, '50; h. Winston DeMuth; c. Joan, James, Donna; res: 616 First St., Crete, Ill. 60417.

DEMY, CAROLINE STELLA, Assoc. Media Dir. Intl., J. Walter Thompson Company, 420 Lexington Ave., N.Y., N.Y. 10017, '53–; Asst. Media Mgr.-Intl.; Off. of Cert. Circ. (Bd. Mbr., '55–), IAA (N.Y. Chptr: VP, Bd. Mbr., '60–), IMBA (Pres., '61); Hunter Col.; b. N.Y.C.;

p. Amerigo and Rose Rossi Stella; h. Basil Demy; res: 35–25 78 St., Jackson Heights, N.Y. 11372.

De NAVE, CONNIE M., Pres., Connie De Nave & Associates, Inc. (PR), 200 W. 57th St., N.Y., N.Y. 10019; Dir. of PR, Dick Clark & Cos.; Asst. Mag. Info. Mgr., ABC-TV; OPC; Hunter Col., BA; h. Paul Jonali.

DENKO, GLORIA SANDALIS, Amusements Ed., Amarillo Globe-News Publishing Company, P.O. Box 2091, Amarillo, Tex. 79105, '66–; Univ. of Chgo., PhB, '48; b. Gibbon, Neb., 1925; p. Samuel and Fanchion Scott Sandalis; h. Dr. John Denko; c. Madeleine, John Scott, Kathryn; res: 2507 Harmony, Amarillo, Tex. 79106.

DENMAN, MARY WILLIAMS, Talent and Prod., "Our Town Show" KENS-TV, Box 2171, San Antonio, Tex. 78206; Talent, Free-lance 10 yrs., KVDO (Corpus Christi); AWRT (Southwest area Nat. VP; San Antonio Chptr. Pres., '67–'68); San Antonio Cystic Fibrosis Chptr. (Campaign Chmn., '67–'68; Nat. Rsch. Fndn. Svc. Aw., '67); San Antonio C. of C. Amigo de Turista Aw., '66; Christmas Seal Aw., '67; Miami Univ., BS, '43; b. Power, W.Va., 1922; p. Thomas and Rose Care Williams; h. Richard Denman; c. Daryl Ann (Mrs. Monty Retallack), Deborah Lee, Richard Thomas; res: 705 Strings, San Antonio, Tex. 78216.

DENNIS, BARBARA DUNHAM, Edtl. Assoc., University of Wisconsin—Industrial Relations Research Institute, 1180 Observatory Dr., Madison, Wis. 53706, '67–; Ed., Inst. of Labor and Indsl. Rels., Univ. of Ill., '52–'67; Theta Sigma Phi; Univ. of Ill., BS, '40; MS (Jnlsm.), '58; b. Oak Park, Ill., 1918; p. Walter E. and Belle Shellabarger Dunham; h. William W. Dennis (dec.); c. William W., Jr., Jane Ann; res: 2051 Allen Blvd., Middleton, Wis. 53562.

DENNIS, KATHRYN SEXSMITH, Publr., Bus. Mgr., Bk. Reviewer, Hightstown Gazette, 114 Rogers Ave., Hightstown, N.J. 08520; Partner in publn., '68–; full-time, '55–; Bk. Reviewer, '44–; High Sch. Librn. (N.J.), '44–'55; Bk. Reviewer, Cranbury Press, several yrs.; Hightstown Memorial Lib. Bd. of Trustees, 10 yrs.; Douglass Col., AB (Educ.), '38; grad. study (lib. field, educ.); b. George P. and May Belle Sexsmith Dennis; res: 248 Stockton St., Hightstown, N.J. 08520.

DENNIS, MARIAN B., VP-Media, Provandie Eastwood & Lombardi, Inc., 4620 Prudential Tower, Boston, Mass. 02199; Media Dir., '66; AE, '62; Off. Mgr., '57; Exec. Secy. to Pres., '55; Bdcst. Execs. Club of New England; Endicott Jr. Col., '42; b. Nahant, Mass., 1921; p. George and Pearl Strout Dennis; res: 103 Broad St., Lynn, Mass. 01902.

DENNIS, SHIRLEY RAE, Pubcty.-PR Dir., Seattle Repertory Theatre, 225 Mercer, Seattle, Wash. 98109, '65–; Prom. Asst., KOMO-TV; Traf. Mgr., KIRO Radio; Cont. Dir., KTNT Radio; Wms. Dir., KRKO Radio; Wash. Press Wms. Assn.; AWRT; Stanford Univ.; b.

Portland, Ore., 1924; p. Dolph and Irene Sutton Rae; h. Lee Dennis (dec.); res: 11057—40th N.E., Seattle, Wash. 98125.

DENSON, MARY GILSTRAP, Free-lance Ed.; Bus. Mgr., R. O. Hunter, M.D., 1512-1/2 S. Congress Ave., P.O. Box 3506, Austin, Tex. 78704, '57–; Med. Secy., '57–; Ed., S. Austin News, '53–'57; Reptr., '52–'53; Free-lance Sportstr., Ft. Worth Star Telegram, Temple Telegram, Taylor Daily Press, Houston Chronicle, '47–'52; Ed., Granger (Tex.) News, '46–'52; Asst. City Secy., '44–'49; various organizations; b. Granger, Tex., 1914; p. Clarence F. and Mary Ann Denson Gilstrap; h. Fred P. Denson Sr.; c. Fred P. Jr., Molly Ann; res: 1405 Newning Ave., Austin, Tex. 78704.

DENTON, GISELE PEZZETTA, Media and Rsch. Dir., Henderson, Bucknum & Co., 909 Sherman St., Denver, Colo. 80203, '69–; Media Rsch. Analyst, '67–'69; Mdsng. Asst., McMurtry Mfg., '61–'66; Am. Statis. Assn., AAUW (Bul. Ed.), Pfsnl. Panhellenic Assn. of Denver, Phi Gamma Nu (Alumni Chptr. Pres., '67, '69); Univ. of Denver, BS (Statistics), '61; Univ. of Colo., '68–'69; b. 1937; p. Erasmus and Amelia C. Finamour Pezzetta; h. L. Karl Denton; c. Lewis Karl II; res: 2036 E. Mineral Ave., Littleton, Colo. 80120.

DERDARIAN, MAE MIKJIAN, Dir. of PR and Educ., United Community Services of Metropolitan Detroit, 51 West Warren, Detroit, Mich. 48201, '65–; Pubcty., '55–'60; PR Dir., '60–'65; Cont. Dir. for WJKB and WJLB (Detroit); Copywtr., Simons-Michelson Advertising Co.; Wms. Adv. Club of Detroit (Pres., '60–'61), Detroit Press Club, PRSA (Mich. Chptr. Public Svc. Chmn., '66–'67), Theta Sigma Phi, Inter-Am. Commtns. Conf. (Prog. Chmn., '68), Mid-Am. Conf. of Un. Commty. Funds and Cncls. of Am. (Vice-chmn.); Top Ten Working Wm. in Detroit, '67; Detroit Adv. Wm. of the Yr., '65; Cited by Gov. George Romney as one of Mich.'s 50 most important wm., '54; Wayne State Univ.; b. Detroit, Mich., 1921; p. Paul and Serpouhi Kalayjian Mikjian; c. Christine Anne; res: 2676 Heathfield Rd., Birmingham, Mich. 48010.

de RIVER, JESSIE ROSS, Free-lance Playwright, 500 Leavenworth St., S.F., Cal. 94109; three-act plays; "Greater Love," and "Blood Will Tell," also one-act plays; radio plays, poetry readings; tchr. of play writing; 1st prize for 3-act drama and one-act radio play, "Way of a Man With a Maid"; Asst. Ed., WASP and Nwsltr.; NLAPW (S.F. Br. Past Pres.), Cal. Wtrs. Club, Armed Forces Wtrs. League, Canadian Auths. (Life Mbr.), Reginald Travers Sch. of Theatre (Exec. Secy.); Humberside Collegiate, Toronto, Can., N.Y. Post Grad. Med. Sch., Univ. of Cal. (Alumni Life Mbr.), special drama and art courses; b. Mississauga, Ontario, Can.; p. Samuel and Annie McPhee Ross; h. Dr. Paul de River (dec.).

DERRICK, ARLYS ALLARD, Wms. Ed., News-Palladium Publishing Co., Michigan and Oak, Benton Harbor, Mich. 49022, '69–; Wms. Ed., St. Joseph Herald-Press; with papers, six yrs.; Ludington (Mich.) Daily News; NFPW (Bd.), Mich. Wms. Press Club (Pres., '67–'70; 1st VP, '65–'67); Western Mich. Univ.; h. Richard V. Derrick; c. Richard V. II, Mary Therese, Deborah Ann (Mrs. R. A. Brightbill), Peter, Joan; res: 1614 Forres Ave., St. Joseph, Mich. 49085.

DE SANTILLANA, DOROTHY TILTON, Exec. Ed., Houghton Mifflin Company, 2 Park, Boston, Mass. 02107, '69–; Ed., Mng. Ed., Sr. Ed., '41–'69; Bradford Jr. Col.; Goucher Col., AB; Grad. work, Radcliffe Col.; b. Haverhill, Mass.; p. John and Elizabeth Seeley Tilton; h. Giorgio de Santillana; c. Stanley H. Hillyer; res: Curtis Point, Beverly, Mass. 01915.

DeSANTIS, FLORENCE STEVENSON, Ed., Beauty, Fashion, Wms. Interests, Bell-McClure Syndicate and North American Newspaper Alliance, Inc., 1501 Broadway, N.Y., N.Y. 10036, '56–; Assoc. Beauty Ed., Charm, '52–'55; Adv. Asst., Mademoiselle, '50–'52; Tchr., '41–'50; Hunter Col., BA, '40 (Phi Beta Kappa); Columbia Univ., MA, '50; b. N.Y.C., 1918; p. George and Florence Paddock Stevenson; h. Arthur DeSantis; c. Solange Alba, Arthur Louis; res: 61–32 228th St., Bayside, N.Y. 11364.

DESKIN, RUTHE GOLDSWORTHY, Asst. to Publr., Las Vegas Sun, 121 S. Highland, Las Vegas, Nev. 89106, '54–; Corp. Secy., '64–; Pubcty. Dir., Last Frontier Hotel, '53; Asst. Program Dir., KLAS Radio, '50–'53; Cont. Wtr., KENO Radio, '48; Wms. Ed., Reno Evening Gazette, '46–'47; Dir., PR, Ordnance Depot, '43–'46; Bd. of Dirs: CATV, N. Las Vegas News, Las Vegas Television, Inc. ('54–'68, also Secy.); Secy., Nev. State Press Assn. (Pres., '66; Wms. Aw., '59; Best Colm. in State, '62, '63, '68); Las Vegas Press Club (Pres., '54); Clark County Juvenile Welfare Advisory Bd., Governor's Comm. on Housing, Governor's Comm. on Status of Wm.; Univ. of Nev., BA, (Jnlsm.), '37; b. Yerington, Nev., 1916; p. James and Viola West Goldsworthy; h. James Deskin; c. Mrs. Michael Cummings, Terri Woodbury; res: 4417 Hillcrest, Las Vegas, Nev. 89102.

DeSPAIN, DAYSIE SPENCER, Publr., Histrn., Anchorage Press, Inc., Cloverlot, Anchorage, Ky. 40223, '45–; Who's Who of Am. Wm., '68–'69; Ky. Lives; Western State Col.; b. Ft. Spring, Ky., 1894; p. Joseph and Julia Vaughan Spencer; h. Charles R. DeSpain; c. Charles Jr.; res: 11402 Ridge Rd., Anchorage, Ky. 40223.

D'ESSEN, LORRAIN DeROY, Pres., Dir., Animal Talent Scouts, Inc., 331 W. 18th Street, N.Y., N.Y. 10011, '52–; Cnslt., Films, TV Cmmls., Met. Opera, RCMH Fashion Magazine & Adv. Agcy; AE, Roy Durstine Adv., '50–; PR, Coty; Model, Saks Fifth Ave.; Lectr. on animal behavior; Tchr., training animals; Auth., "Kangaroos in the Kitchen" (David McKay, '59); AWNY, N.Y. Adv. Club, AFTRA, SAG, Am. Museum of Nat. Hist., Am. Assn. of Zoological Pks. and Aquariums, Nat. Recreation and Park Assoc.,

Great Dane Club of Am., Hudson Guild; Boy Scout Merit Aws; Wellesley Col., '37–'40; b. Sawersworth, N.H., 1921; p. Adolph and Athela Labissonier DeRoy; h. D'Essen Berne; res: 331 W. 18th St., N.Y., N.Y. 10011.

DeSZEKELY, EILEEN BENNETT, Graphic Artist, Newsweek, 444 Madison Ave., N.Y., N.Y. 10022, '65–; Art Dir., McCartin Advertising, '62–'65; Package Designer, Paul Sherry Associates, '61; Asst. Art Dir., N. W. Ayer (Honolulu, Hi), '61; Asst. to Art Dir., MacFadden Pubns., '60; Art Dirs. Club of N.Y.; Pratt Inst., BFA, '60; b. Red Bank, N.J., 1938; p. Raymond and Flossie England Bennett; h. Alexander DeSzekely; res: 333 E. 75th St., N.Y., N.Y. 10021.

DeTHOMAS, RUTH NORBY, Ed., Minidoka County News, 625 Fremont Ave., Rupert, Idaho 83350, '65–; Assoc. Ed., '64–'65; Soc. Ed., '57–'64; Off. Mgr., Burson Auto Co.; Head of Academic Records, Santa Ana AFB; Rupert C. of C. (Secy., '68–'70), Idaho Youth Ranch (Area Trustee, '65–), PTA (Pershing PTA Pres., two yrs.), Idaho Press Assn. Better Nwsps. Contest (Seven aws., '65–'69) Aw. for Svc. to Grassman Contest ('68); Boise Bus. Col., '36; Santa Ana Jr. Col., '39; b. Rupert, Idaho, 1918; p. John and Fannie Heyerdahl Norby; h. Condido DeThomas; c. Lt. John Victor, Christine, Deborah, Dennis, Edward, Anna; res: Rte. 1, Rupert, Idaho 83350.

de TREVINO, ELIZABETH BORTON, Free-lance Wtr., fiction and non-fiction adult and juv., Apartado 827, Cuernavaca, Mexico; Reptr., Boston Herald; Stringer, Life, Time, Christian Science Monitor and Laredo Times from Monterrey, Mexico; Eng. Pubcty. Nat. Symphony Orchestra of Mexico, Mexican Tourist Dept. and Nat. Railways of Mexico; At Present: Mexican Corr. for Religious News Service, and Staff Wtr., Camihos del Aire (Mexican aviation mag.); Theta Sigma Phi, Altrusa Club, Nat. Hispanic Soc. (Order of Don Quijote), Pan-American Round Table of Cuernavaca, Auths. Guild; Newbery Medal for "most ditg. contrb. to literature for children," '66; Stanford Univ., '25 (cum laude, Phi Beta Kappa); b. Bakersfield, Cal. 1904; p. Fred E. and Carrie Christensen Borton; h. Luis Trevino-Gomez; c. Luis, Enrique.

DETROI, JEAN BARANY, Wms. Dir., KILO Radio, 211 S. Fourth St., Grand Forks, N.D. 58201, '67–; KNOX Radio, '65–'67; AWRT, BPW, Grand Forks C. of C.; N.Y. Bus. Col., '48; b. Bound Brook, N.J., 1928; p. Alexander and Lillian Davis Barany; h. Andrew Detroi; c. Frank Jay, Jeff Alexander, Jan Margaret, Joe Allen; res: 621 S. Fifth Street, Grand Forks, N.D. 58201.

DEUVALL, JANE A. Mgr., Compensation Projects, Columbia Broadcasting System, Inc., 51 W. 52nd St., N.Y., N.Y. 10019, '69–; Sr. Compensation Analyst, Preliminary Interviewer, Exec. Placement; Tchr., Eng., Jnlsm.; AAUW; Univ. of Mich., BA (Eng.), '55; b. Steubenville, Oh., 1933; p. Charles and Lavinia McQuillan Deuvall; res: 165 West End Ave., N.Y., N.Y. 10023.

DEVINE, JANICE, Wtr., Edtl. PR, The Devin Adair Co., 23 E. 26th St., N.Y., N.Y. 10010, '57–; Radio, TV Asst., Mary Margaret McBride, '40–'57; Feature Wtr., N.Y. World Telegram, '38–'40; Co.-Auth.: "Bali to Bahrein" (Devin-Adair, '69), "How to Sleep Well 2920 Hours a Year" ('66), "Fare Thee Well" ('65); Pa. State Univ., AB, '38; b. Lemoyne, Pa.; p. Augustus and Estella Hartzler Steinmetz; h. Frank Devine (dec.); c. Michael.

DEVINE, LAUREEN ANN, News Ed., University Times, University of Pittsburgh, 601 Bruce Hall, Pitt., Pa. 15213, '69–; News Prod., KDKA-TV, current; Reptr., The Pitt. Point, '68–'69; Mng. Ed., The Sharpsburg Herald, '67–'68; Reptr., Butler Eagle; Reptr., Hagerstown (Md.) Morning Herald; Theta Sigma Phi (Jo Caldwell Memorial Fellowship); Hearst Nat. Writing Aw., '66; Pa. State Univ., BA (Polit. Sci. and Jnlsm.), '67; Univ. of Pitt., grad. work on MA (Polit. Sci.), '67–; b. Pitt., Pa. 1946; p. Thomas and Mildred Palmer Devine; res: 912 Limestone Dr., Allison Pk., Pa. 15101.

DE VIVIER, JEANNE FRANCES, Talent Coordr., Albets, Inc., 1356 N. Van Ness, Hollywood, Calif. 90028, '69–; Talent Coordr., VTP Enterprises, '60–'69; Talent Coordr., "Woody Woodbury Show," "Everybody's Talking," "Chain Letter;" AWRT, Radio and TV Wm. of Southern Calif. (Pres., '65–'66); Univ. of Denver, BA, '49; b. Prescott, Ariz., 1928; p. John and Grace Taylor De Vivier; res: 3809 Blue Canyon Dr., Studio City, Calif. 91604.

DEVLIN, POLLY, Feature Assoc., Contrb. Ed., Vogue, Condé Nast Publications, 420 Lexington Ave., N.Y., N.Y. 10017, '67–; Colmst., Evening Standard (London, England), '66–'67; Colmst., New Statesman, '66; Features Ed., British Vogue, '64–'66; b. Newry, N. Ireland, 1943; p. Thomas and Eileen O'Hare Devlin; h. Adrian J. F. Garnett; res: 5 East 88th St., N.Y., N.Y. 10028; (abroad: 2 Halkin Str., London S.W. 1, Eng.; 191 Rue St. Honore, Paris, France).

De VRIES, MARY ANN, Owner, Mng. Ed., Editorial Services, 55 Palmer Square W., Princeton, N.J. 08540, '68–; Partner, Pubns. Cnslt., De Vries & De Vries, '66–'68; Ed., Numerical Control Soc., '65–; Free-lance Wtr., '61–; Ed., four bks.; "NC Scene," nat. nwsltr., '65–; Auth., Ed., numerous articles, repts., bklets; Cnslt., '66–; Tchr., '60; AAIE, Am. Bus. Commtns. Assn., Soc. of Tch. Wtrs. and Publrs., Nat. Soc. for the Study of Commtns.; Who's Who of Am. Wm.; Grad. Teaching Aw., '60; George Washington Univ., BA, '59; Univ. of Colo. (grad. sch.), '60; b. Pella, Ia., 1937; p. John and Anna Kool De Vries.

DEVRY, ELAINE (Elaine Davis), Actress, TV and movies, c/o Lou Irwin Agency, 9165 Sunset Blvd., Hollywood, Cal. 90069, Movies: "Cheyenne Social Club" ('69), "With Six You Get Egg Roll" ('68), several others; numerous TV shows, commls; Songwtr., Composer, '65–, incl. "Yellow Haired Woman," others; Photogr. Model.

DEWEY, MARGARET W., Educ. Cnslt., Visual Education Consultants, Inc., P.O. Box 52, Madison, Wis. 53701, '68–; Nwsp. Colmst., "Your News Quiz," '53–'67; Ed.-in-Chief, "News Filmstrip Program," '51–'67; Ed., Auth., numerous filmstrips on news and world affairs for U.S. Comm. for UNICEF, schs., '57–'67; Theta Sigma Phi (Madison Chptr. VP, '66), Who's Who of Am. Wm., various others; Univ. of Wis., '33–'36; b. Milw., Wis., 1914; p. Frank and Frances Harbeck Whiting; h. (div.); c. Jeanne (Mrs. Richard Pflug), Michael Dewey; res: 10163 W. Forest Home Ave., Milw., Wis. 53130.

de WINTER, JO (Juanita Maria-Johanna Daussat), Free-lance Actress, TV drama, '64–; motion pics., '52–; Leading Lady, Theatre Guild of Rome, Italy; TV Commentator, '63–'64; Fashion Dir., Shamis (Gulfport, Miss.); Fashion Dir., Scott's (Ventura, Cal.); Tchr., '62–'63; '60; SAG; Hon. Italian Air Force Wings, '51; Dominican Col. (San Rafael, Cal.), (outstanding drama aw.); Univ. of Pacific (Cal.); b. Sacramento, Cal.; p. Arthur and Blanche Rodgers Daussat; h. Robert Adamina; c. Robert, Jr., Mrs. Robert Schott; res: 2090 Pacific Ave., S.F., Cal. 94109.

DeWITT, CAROLYN KERR, Ed.-in-Chief, Notions & Home Sewing Magazine, Haire Publishing Corp., 111 Fourth Ave., N.Y., N.Y. 10003, '69–; Fashion Copy Ed., Wms. Wear Daily, '67–'69; Ed.-in-Chief, Children's World, '65–'67; Assoc. Ed., McGraw-Hill, '59–'65; Wtr., children's stories; Univ. of Minn., BA (Jnlsm.), '59; b. Kingston, N.Y., 1938; p. John and Mildred Goodnow Dewitt; res: 327 W. 76th St., N.Y., N.Y. 10023.

DIAL, ANNE BROWN, Commtns. Specialist, Deposit Guaranty National Bank, P.O. Box 1200, Jackson, Miss. 39205, '67–; IEA of Miss., ICIE, Southern Cncl. of Indsl. Eds.; Miss. Col., BS, '65; b. Greenwood, Miss., 1943; p. Kimbriel and Louise Campbell Brown; h. John F. Dial, III; res: P.O. Box 654, Clinton, Miss. 39056.

DIBELKA, SUSAN SHAFFER, Staff Wtr., The Institute For Research, 537 S. Dearborn St., Chgo., Ill. 60605, '51–; Mng. Ed., The United Signal (Evanston, Ill.), '42–'49; Edtl., World Bk. Ency. (Chgo., Ill.), '40–'41; Pubcty., house organ, Thrift, Inc., '30–'40; Chgo. Evening Post, '29–'31; Edtl. Asst., Redbook, '21–'22; Free-lance Wtr.; Christian Science Monitor; Tchr., crtv. writing, Whittier Sch. of Adult Educ., '60–'69; numerous orgs., aws.; Univ. of Ill. AB (Jnlsm.), '19; grad. work, Northwestern Univ., Cal. State Col. at L.A., Whittier Col.; b. Harrisburg, Pa., 1895; p. George and Gertrude Kurzenknabe Shaffer; h. James C. Dibelka; c. James C., Jr., Allison (Mrs. Donald T. Eggen), George Shaffer, Susanne (Mrs. Lewis W. Walker); res: 13427 E. Russell St., Whittier, Cal. 90602.

DICKENS, MONICA ENID, Auth., fiction; 20 novels; Lectr.; St. Paul's Sch. (London); D. Ltt., SEMU; b. London, England, 1915; p. Henry and Fanny Runge Dickens; h. Roy Stratton; c. Pamela, Prudence; res: Box 386, N. Falmouth, Mass. 02556.

DICKERMAN, MICHELE PHYLIS, Prod. Mgr., Marketing & Advertising Associates, 1405 Locust St., Phila., Pa. 19102, '66–' Prod. Mgr., S.E. Zubrow Adv.; Charles Morris Price School (Adv.); Temple Univ.; b. Phila., Pa., 1938; p. Jacob and Ann Zevin Dickerman; res: 1928 Lombard St., Phila., Pa. 19146.

DICKERSON, NANCY HANSCHMAN, Wash. Corr., NBC News, National Broadcasting Company, 4001 Nebraska Ave. N.W., Wash., D.C. 20016; "Nancy Dickerson With the News" (network) and "Column Of The Air" (syndication); formerly CBS News Prodr., "The Leading Question" and "Capital Cloakroom"; Assoc. Prodr., "Face The Nation;" Staff Mbr., Senate Fgn. Rels. Comm., '51–'53; Magazine Colmst.; Sch. Tchr., Model; Radio-TV Daily Wm. of the Yr., '64; Harper's Bazaar 100 Am. Wm. of Accomplishment; WNPC (former Bd. Mbr.), RTCA, AWRT; Univ. of Wis.; Am. Intl. Col., Doctorate; Grad. Work: Harvard, Am. Univ.; b. Wauwtosa, Wis.; p. Florence and Frederick Hanschman; h. C. Wyatt Dickerson; c. Elizabeth, Ann, Jane, Michael, John; res: Merrywood, McLean, Va. 22101.

DICKES, MIRIAM JOY, Copy Chief, Scope Advertising, Inc., 12 E. 41st St., N.Y., N.Y. 10017, '66–; Staff Wtr., '61–'66; Contract Wtr., Warner Bros.-7 Arts, '56–'61; Jr. PR Wtr., Jewelry Industry Cncl., '55–'56; Co-auth., Prodr., "Look Listen Learn" (pre-sch. audio-visual series) '66; Hunter Col., '55 (Phi Beta Kappa); h. Herman Zuckerman; res: 52 Meadow View Rd., Westport, Conn. 06880.

DICKINSON, JULIE MAY, Info. Specialist, Dept. of Health, Educ., and Welfare, 5454 Wisconsin Ave. N.W., Chevy Chase, Md. 20015, '63–; Travel Ed., Nat. and Intl., Am. Automobile Assn., '59–'63; Cnslt. in Public Affairs, Intl. Trade Fairs, Greece and Turkey, '56–'59; Wash. Rep., J. Walter Thompson Co., '46–'56; War-time Chief of Radio, Am. Nat. Red Cross, '42–'46; AWRT (Wash. Chptr. Past VP), ANWC (Corr. Secy.; past-VP); Columbia Univ., '41–'42; b. N.Y.C.; p. Edward and Jeannette Guelpa Dickinson; res: 2800 Woodley Rd. N.W., Wash., D.C. 20008.

DICKSON, SALLY, Pres., Sally Dickson Associates, Inc., 1345 Ave. of the Americas, N.Y., N.Y. 10019; formerly Partner; '43–; Pres., Nat. Needlecraft Bur., '40–'43; AE, Roger William Riis Assocs.-Public Relations, '38–'40; Co-auth., "A Woman's Guide to Financial Security" ('53); Contrbr., pfsnl. pubns., PR bks. incl. "Building the Corporate Image," by Lee H. Bristol, Jr. ('60); PRSA (first agcy. to receive Silver Anvil Aw. for meritorious performance in PR, '45), AWNY, CWPR; Katherine Gibbs Sch. (N.Y.C.); b. Westport, Conn.; p. William D. and Lulu B. Taylor Dickson; res: 60 Sutton Pl. S., N.Y., N.Y. 10022.

DIEGEL, JOY M., Ed., Business News, General Telephone of California, 2020 Santa Monica Blvd., Santa Monica, Cal. 90404, '68–; PR Dir., Ameco, Inc., '65–'68; PR Wtr., Mountain States Tel., '57–'65; Night News Ed., KOY Radio, '49–'50; Southern Cal. IEA (Intl. Aws. Steering Comm., '69), Ariz. Indsl. Eds. (Bd. of Dirs., '62–'68; Ed. Aw., '64 and numerous other aws., '63–'68), Phoenix Press Club (Bul. Ed., '67–'68); Univ. of Ill., BS, '49; b. Chgo., Ill., 1927; p. David and Wanda Williams; h. (div.); c. Kerry, Dulcy, Linda; res: 555 S. Barrington #12, L.A., Cal. 90049.

DIEKEN, GERTRUDE, Crtv. Dir., Consumer Enterprises Div., Edtl. Dir., The Farmer's Wife, Farm Journal, West Washington Sq., Phila., Pa. 19105, '69–; Ed., '45–'69; PR Dept., DuPont Co., '42–'45; Home Econs. Ed., Ia. State Univ., '35–'42; WNPC, Am. Home Econs. Assn., Am. Assn. Agriculture Col. Eds. (Reuben Brigham Aw., '56), Farm Home Eds. Assn. (Pres., '62), Theta Sigma Phi (Headliner Aw., '49); Coe Col., Cedar Rapids, Ia., BA, '32 (magna cum laude; Phi Beta Kappa, '69, hon. to alumna); b. Ia.; p. J. D. and Louise Theerman Dieken; res: 2031 Locust St., Phila., Pa. 19103.

DIERKING, SHARON LEE, Actress, Singer, c/o Dorothy Day Otis Agency, 511 N. La Cienega Blvd., L.A., Cal. 90048; Lincoln Ctr. (N.Y.C.), Broadway; TV; Music Ctr. (L.A., Cal.); Tchr., music educ., music therapy at mental hosps.; AEA, SAG, AFTRA; Univ. of Mich., B Mus Ed, '63; b. Joliet, Ill.; h. Albert Lantieri.

DIETZ, MARILYN J., Commty. Rels., Assoc., WCNY-TV, Old Liverpool Rd., Liverpool, N.Y. 13088, '66–; Public Affairs Wtr., Syracuse and Onondaga County, '66; Commty. Rels. Asst., Un. Commty. Chest and Cncl., Onondaga County, '56–'66; Colmnst., "Silver and Gold,": The Post Standard (Syracuse); Exec. Ed., Syracuse Prestige mag.; Free-lance Copywtr. of TV commls., Spitz Adv., Osborn-Propst. Adv.; AWRT, Theta Sigma Phi, ICIE (Upstate N.Y. Chptr. Secy. '63–'68), Pfsnl. Wms. League, Syracuse Univ.; b. Syracuse, N.Y.; p. Robert and Irene Wakeless Dietz; res: 123 Annetta St., Syracuse, N.Y. 13207.

DIETZ, MARJORIE JOHNSON, Free-lance Garden Wtr., Ed.; Ed., Plants & Gardens, Brooklyn Botanic Garden, 1000 Washington Ave., Bklyn., N.Y. 11225, '68–; Ed., Home Garden Magazine, 15 yrs.; Auth.: various books, articles on gardening; b. New Haven, Conn., 1918; p. George and Marjorie Thatcher Johnson; h. William Dietz; res: 240 W. 98th St., N.Y., N.Y. 10025.

DIEZ, SYLVIA HOWARD, Free-lance Wtr., non-fiction, light verse, '40–; Edtl. Bd., "Select" mag.; Special Corr., The Milw. Jnl., '52–'64; Theta Sigma Phi (Secy., '57; Current Treas.); Boehm Poetry Aw.; Marquette Univ., '38; Univ. of Wis. Ext. Div., '34–'36, Marquette Univ., PhB (Jnlsm.), '40; b. Milw., Wis., 1917; p. Harold and Lillian Hutchings Howard; h. Fernando Diez; c. Mark, Glen; res: 449 Toepfer Ave., Madison, Wis. 53711.

DIKEMAN, HELEN GRACE, Rsch. Dept. Librn., Monsanto Company, 730 Worcester St., Indian Orchard, Mass. 01051, '44–; Asst. Librn. Rsch. Dept., Plastics Div., '43–'44; Jr. Lib. Asst., Tech. Dept., Bridgeport Public Lib. '39–'43; Cl., McKesson & Robbins (Fairfield, Conn.) '34–'39; Special Libs. Assn. (Conn. Valley Chptr. Pres., '48–'49; Nat. Chmn., Chemistry Sec., '52–'53). Am. Chemical Soc., Soc. of Plastics Engineers, Amer. Documentation Inst.; Who's Who of Am. Wm.; Duke Univ., BA, '34; b. Bridgeport, Conn. 1913; p. Harry and Grace Boyles Dikeman; res: 83 Lincoln Rd., Longmeadow, Mass. 01106.

DILLARD, KATHERINE RAWLINGS, Wms. News Ed., Dallas Morning News, Communications Ctr., Dallas, Tex. 75222, '47–; Feature Wtr., Asst. to City Ed., San Antonio Light, '42–'45; Feature Wtr., Amusements Ed., Soc. Ed., Fort Worth Star-Telegram, '37–'42; Theta Sigma Phi (Matrix Aw., '69), Delta Kappa Gamma, Fashion Group (VP, Dir., '54–'56), NHFL (VP, '66–'68), commty. svc. aws., cits.; Jr. League, YWCA; Tex. Christian Univ., '38–'39; Columbia Univ.; Univ. of Tex.; Southern Methodist Univ.; b. Sulphur, Okla.; p. Frank and Floy Dickinsheets Rawlings; h. Tom Dillard; c. Shannon (Mrs. Shyam H. Gurbaxani); res: 7022 Merrilee Lane, Dallas, Tex. 75214.

DILWORTH, CATHY LEWIS, Sponsoring Ed., Audiovisual Media, McGraw-Hill Book Co., Blakiston Division, 330 W. 42nd St., N.Y., N.Y. 10036, '69–; Assoc. Ed., '68–'69; Ed. Supvsr., '67–'68; Ed. Asst., '66–'67; Wtr., Today's Secy.; Ed., Word Teasers; Free-lance copy ed.; Volunteer, Mayor Lindsay's off.; Duke Univ., AB, '65; Radcliffe Col., '65; b. Hinsdale, Ill., 1943; p. Thomas and Elizabeth Walker Dilworth; res: 14 E. 37th St., Apt. 3C, N.Y., N.Y. 10016.

DIMOS, HELEN ALEXANDRA, Cont. Wtr., CBS, WCBS Radio, 51 W. 52 St., N.Y., N.Y. 10019, '69–; Press Rep., WCBS Radio; Ed., Jnl. of Intl. Affairs, Columbia Univ. '67–'68; Rschr., Fgn. Affairs Div., Legislative Ref. Svc., Lib. of Congress, '67; Bryn Mawr Col., BA (Hist.), '64; Columbia Univ., Sch. of Intl. Affairs, '66–'68; b. Wash., D.C., 1942; res: 808 West End Ave., N.Y., N.Y. 10025.

DINEEN, TRUDY ELIZABETH, Media Negotiator., J. Walter Thompson, 420 Lexington Ave., N.Y., N.Y. 10017, '69–; Media Byr., Ted Bates, '58–'67; Media Byr., Dancer-Fitzgerald-Sample, '52–'57; PR, Girl Scouts; AWNY; Univ. of N.C., BA (Sociol.), '49.

DINERMAN, BEATRICE, Rsch. Assoc., University of Southern California, School of Public Administration, L.A., Cal., '69–; Cnslt., Health Planning Assn. of Southern Cal., '68–'69; Rsch. Assoc., Sch. of Public Health, U.C.L.A., '66–'67; Social Sci. Rsch. Analyst, Econ. and Youth Opps. Agcy., '65–'66; Dir., Ford Fndn. Project on Priority Planning, Welfare Planning Cncl. of L.A., '62–'65; Public Adm. Analyst, Bur. of Governmental Rsch., U.C.L.A., '56–'62; Auth., numerous pubns. in public adm.; Co-auth: "Southern California Metropolis" (Univ. of Cal. Press, '63), "Structure and Organization of Local Government in the United States"; Cnslt., L.A. County Dept. of Commmty. Svcs., '59; Am. Soc. for Public Adm. (L.A. Met. Chptr. Secy., '57–'60), active in many polit. sci. orgs.; Am. Men in Sci., Contemporary Auths.; Hunter Col., '50–'52; Bklyn. Col., BA (Polit. Sic.), '54 (cum laude); U.C.L.A., MPA (Public Adm.), '57; b. Bklyn., N.Y., 1933; h. Norman Wartell; res: 15097 Encanto Dr., Sherman Oaks, Cal. 91403.

DINERMAN, HELEN SCHNEIDER, Chmn. Exec. Comm., International Research Associates, Inc., 1270 Ave. of Americas, N.Y., N.Y. 10020, '68–; VP, '52–'58; Project Dir., '48–'52; Project Dir., Scientific Dept., Am. Jewish Comm., '47–'48; Rsch. Analyst, Rsch. Dept., Bur. of Applied Social Sci., Columbia Univ., '44–'47; Rsch. Analyst, Off. of War Info., '42–'44; Rsch. Asst., Off. of Radio Rsch., Columbia Univ., '40–'42; Dir., Intl. Rsch. Assocs., C.A., Caracas, Venezuela; numerous articles, prof. jnls.; Who's Who in Am.; World Assn. for Public Opinion Rsch. (VP, Pres.-Elect), AAPOR (Secy.-Treas. Exec. Cncl.); Hunter Col., BA, '40 (magna cum laude, Phi Beta Kappa); Columbia Univ., MA, '48; b. N.Y.C., 1920; p. Maurice and Lillian Blau Schneider; h. James Dinerman; c. Robert David, Alice Eve; res: 179 E. 70 St., N.Y., N.Y. 10021.

DINSMORE, NANCY REYNOLDS, W. Coast Ed., Harper's Bazaar, 1777 N. Vine St., Hollywood, Cal. 90028, '58–; AE, Abbott Kimball, '48–'54; Jr. Exec. Training Prog., Carson Pirie Scott, '41–'43; Fashion Group, Inc., Fashion Circle W., Hollywood Wms. Press Cl., U.C.L.A. Art Cncl. (Mbr. of Bd.), L.A. County Museum of Art (Art Cncl.; Costume Cncl.), L.A. Jr. Philharmonic Comm., Nat. Art Assn.; Ia. State Col., BA (Jnlsm.; Textile and Design); h. Wayne Dinsmore, Jr.

DINWIDDIE, AINSLIE, Contributing Ed., Business Week Magazine, 330 West 42, N.Y., N.Y. 10036, '69–; Asst. Ed., Newsweek Magazine, '65–'69; Edtl. Asst., '63–'65; Edtl. Copy Girl, '62; KNOE Radio-TV (La.), '58; Smith Col., '56–'57; Tulane Univ. Col., '58; La. State Univ., '58–'62; b. N.O., La., 1938; p. George and Augusta Benners Dinwiddie; h. (div.); c. Wilcox Snellings; res: 59 E. 79th St., N.Y., N.Y. 10021.

di SERNIA, PATRICIA RHINEHEARDT, Ed.-in-Chief, American Girl, Girl Scouts of the U.S.A., 830 Third Ave., N.Y., N.Y. 10022; '67–; Asst. to Publr., Mktng., '57–'67; Fashion and Mdsng. Dir., '56–'57; Fashion Dir., '52–'56; Fashion Ed., '50–'52; dev. youth mktng. program, Formfit Rogers Div, Genesco, '67; Cnslt., Jantzen, Portland, Ore., '61; launched first nation-wide prom. for pre-teens, '53; dev. Charm Sch. Program for Young Teens, Thalhimen, Richmond, Va., '52; Polit. Speech Wtr.; various organizations; b. Richmond, Va., 1929; p. John and Margaret Ballard Rhineheardt; h. Eugene A. di Sernia; c. David Rudolf; res: 656 Westbury Ave., Westbury, L.I., N.Y. 11590.

DISSINGER, JOYCE ANN, Wms. Ed., Lebanon News Publishing Company, S. Eighth and Poplar Sts., Lebanon, Pa. 17042, '59–; Gen. Rept., Copy Ed., '54–; news, feature, adv., copy writing depts., Lebanon radio and TV stations; Pa. Wms. Press Assn. (Secy., '68–'70), Fresh Air Fund Plaque, '69, VFW Dept. of Pa. Ladies Auxiliary Cit., '67–'68; b. Lebanon, Pa., 1935; p. Russel and Bernice Bainbridge Dissinger; res: 991 Lilac Lane, Lebanon, Pa. 17042.

di VALENTIN, MARIA AMELIA MESSURI, Auth: fiction and nonfiction bks., '42–; Inter-Am. Bar. Assn., Am. Soc. of Intl. Law, Wash. Foreign Law Soc., Societe de Legislation Compare; UN. Art Exhibit Chmn., '63; Who's Who of Am. Wm.; Who's Who Intl.; Dic. of Intl. Biog.; 2,000 Wm. of Achiev.; Col. of New Rochelle, BA, '33; Columbus Law Sch., JD, '39, Catholic Univ., grad. sch., '40–'42; b. N.Y.C., N.Y. 1911; p. Philip and Anna Castaldi Messuri; h. Louis di Valentin; c. Val Philip; res: 121 Inwood Rd., Scarsdale, N.Y. 10583.

Di VECCHIO, JERRY ROTHA, Assoc. Home Econs. Ed., Sunset Magazine, Lane Magazine & Book Co., Menlo Park, Cal. 94025, '68–; Asst. Ed., '66–'68; Home Econst., '59–'66; Home Econs. Dir., San Mateo County Fair and Floral Assn., '53–'57; Adult Educ., '69; Ed., Sunset bks.; AHEA (S.F. Home Econsts. in Bus. Secy., '61–'62); Phi Upsilon Omicron, Phi Kappa Phi, Conservation groups; San Jose State Col., BS (Home Econs.), '57 (magna cum laude); b. Burden, Kan., 1935; p. Max and Ethel Gibson Rotha; c. Angela Anne; res: 1200 Woodland Ave., Menlo Park, Cal. 94025.

DIXON, ELIZABETH COMPTON, Head Librn., Chester County Free Public Library, Main and Wylie Sts., Chester, S.C. 29706, '67–; Public Sch. Tchr. '28–'44; (N.C.), '44–'46; Ga., '27–'28; Col. Lib. Sci. Tchr. (Newberry, S.C.), '40; Furman Univ. (S.C.), AB, '27 (summa cum laude); Peabody Col. (Nashville, Tenn.), BS (Lib. Sci.), '38; b. Campobello, S.C.; p. John Gill L. and Francis C. Dorman Compton; h. William Howard Dixon, Jr.; res: Rt. 1. Box 60, Blackstock, S.C. 29014.

DIXON, EVA JOHNSON, Dir. of Lib. Svcs., Chipola Junior College, College St., Marianna, Fla. 32446, '58–; Librn., '55–'58; Librn., Meigs HS, '54–'55; Librn., Eng. Tchr., Visual Aids Dir., Jefferson County Schs., '45–'50; NEA, ALA, Jefferson County Educ. Assn. (Pres. '48–'50), Fla. Educ. Assn. (Pres., '50–'51), Fla. Lib. Assn., Kappa Delta Pi, Fla. Assn. of Sch. Librns., Fla. Assn. of Jr. Cols., Fla. BPW Cits., '63, '64, '68; Marianna Chptr. Pres., '58–'59, '62–'63); Who's Who of Am. Wm.; Who's Who in Am. Educ.; Who's Who in Fla. Lives; Who's Who in Lib. Svcs.; Univ. of Fla., AB (Educ.), '37 (hons.); MA (Educ.), '48; Fla. State Univ., '50; Appalachian Tchrs. Col., '53; b. Evinston, Fla., 1909; p. William A. and Willie Crawford Johnson; h. Thomas Gordon Dixon (div.); res: 506 Kelson Ave., Marianna, Fla. 32446.

DIXON, MARTHA (Madeline Fern Bricker), Dir. of Wms. Programs, Talent, Gross Telecasting, Inc., 2320 E. Saginaw St., Lansing, Mich. 48904, '55–; Mgr., Pear & Pardritge Restaurant, '63–'68; Food Supvsr., Kellogg Ctr., Mich. State Univ. '53–'55; Mgr., Food Svcs., Cat Cay Yacht Club (Bahamas), '51–'53; Chief Dietitian, "The Homestead," (Lake Mich.), '49–'51; compiled "Copper Kettle Cook Book" ('63); Talent for "Kitchen Karnival-1967," film; AWRT (Mich. Chptr. Treas., '67), numerous others; Humaness Aw., Ingham County Humane Soc., '69; Central Dist. Dental Soc. Cit. for Significant Contrbs.; Commty. Col., Oh. Univ.; b. Adrian, Mich., 1921; p. Roy and Etta Potts Bricker; c. Robert Ver Planck, Thomas Ver Planck; res: 418 Cypress Lane, E. Lansing, Mich. 48823.

DIXON, RUTH HURT, Women's Travel Adviser, Holland America Line (West Coast) '69–; Dir., Wms. Commty. Affairs, KRON-TV; On-camera TV performer, commentator; Wtr., Prodr., Radio stas.: KNBR, KFRC, (KLX) KCBS, Colmst., "East of the Bay," S.F. Examiner; Wms. World and Travel features, S.F. Chronicle; Soc. Ed., Wms. Features, Berkeley Gazette; Free-lance fashion commentator and coordr., PR, Fashion Ed., Colmst., "San Francisco Today" mag.; Theta Sigma Phi (Past Pres., Oakland-Berkeley Chptr.), AWRT (Past Pres., S.F. Chptr.), S.F. Press Club, E. Bay Press Wms. Club; Univ. of Cal., Berkeley, AB; b. Memphis, Tenn.; p. James and Clara Crutchfield Hurt; h. Harvey Dixon; c. Pamela Franklin; res: 9 Cresta Blanca, Orinda, Cal. 94563.

DIXON, SHIRLEY SANTEE, AE, Hogan & Vecchio Advertising, 4333 Orange St., Riverside, Cal., 92501, '65–; AE, Ewing & Upp Adv. '60–'64; Adv. Mgr., Schweitzers Dept. Store, '59–'60; Guest Lectr. on Mktng., San Bernardino Valley Col.; Cnslt., Mktng. students at UCR; Dir. of Adv. and Pubcty., Padua Inst.; Colmst., Wtr., for H.B.A. of San Bernardino and River Counties; Colmst., "House of the Week," San Bernardino Sun; BPW, Exec. Secys. Inc., ZONTA, PTA (Pres.; Hon. Life Mbr.), Santa Claus, Inc. of San Bernardino (Pres., Hon. Life Mbr.); Peabody Inst. of Music, '42–'44; b. Fresno, Cal., 1925; p. Lester and Gracia Markle Santee; h. Frederick Dixon; c. Shirley (Mrs. Walter E. Brim), Frederick, Jr., Lester, Dean, Bradley; res: P.O. Box 3221, San Bernardino, Cal. 92404.

DOBELL, MERCY, Ed.-in-Chief, Corset & Underwear Review and Intimate Apparel magazines, Harcourt Brace & World publications, 757 Third Ave., N.Y., N.Y. 10017, '59–; Sls. Training, Mdsng. Ed., 12 Haire Publ. Trade mags.; Adv. Mgr., Prom. Dir., Genung Stores of N.Y. and Conn.; Am. Photograph Studios; Divisional Adv., Prom. Dir., The May Co. (L.A., Cal.); Prom., Copywtr., Grey Advertising Agcy. (N.Y.C.); reprints of studies on mdsng. sold to stores, agcys., used in more than 60 countries; Guest Speaker, panels (London, Paris, Japan); Fashion Group, NHFL (VP, '58), AWNY, Underfashions Club (Pres., '68–'70, '61–'63), Pen and Brush Club; 12 Indsl. Mktng.

Aws.; four Jesse H. Neal Aws., edtl. excellence; Oh. State Univ., BA, MA (cum laude); b. Columbus, Oh.; p. Edwin B. and Eleanor F. Monroe Dobell; h. George Wolfe; res: 20 W. Tenth St., N.Y., N.Y. 10011.

DOBIE, WILMA, Free-lance Wtr., Publicist, Rschr., '65–; AE, Pubcty. Cnslts. Inc., '50–'65; Assoc. Ed., Colmst., Am. Legion Magazine, Paris Edition, '48–'50; Ed.-in-Chief, Radiodiffusion Francaise, Service Amerique du Nord (French Govt. Radio, Paris), '46–'48; Radio, J. Walter Thompson, '45; Rsch., Newsweek, '43–'44; wtr., commentator, WWSW Radio (Pitt., Pa.), '42; Pittsburgh Bulletin Index, Sun-Telegraph, '31–'41; Houston (Tex.) Press, '39; OPC, AWRT; Univ. of Pitt., BA (Xylon, Hons.); N.Y.U. '45; p. Charles and Laura Loughner Dobie; h. Dr. John Dougherty; c. William, Michael, Anne; res: 15 Autenrieth Rd., Scarsdale, N.Y. 10583.

DOBLER, LAVINIA GRACE, Head Librn., Scholastic Magazines and Book Services, 50 W. 44th St., N.Y., N.Y. 10036, '44–; Auth: "National Holidays Around the World" (Fleet, '68), "A Business of Their Own" (Dodd, '58; Nat. Librn. Aw. by Dodd, Mead & Co., '57), "Black Gold at Titusville" (Dodd, '59; Pitt. Hon. Bk. Aw., '60); Compiler, "The Dobler International List of Periodicals for Boys and Girls, 1960," revsd. edition, "The Dobler World Directory of Youth Publications", ('65; third edition, Criterian Press '70); Tchr., '40–'44, '33–'35; Supvsr. of Eng. (Puerto Rico), '35–'40; Reptr., Long Beach (Cal.) Press-Telegram-Sun, '28–'35; Wms. Nat. Bk. Assn. (Secy.), AAUW, Auths. Guild; Univ. of Cal. (Berkeley), AB, '33; b. Riverton, Wyo., 1910; p. George F. and Grace L. Sessions Dobler; res: 347 E. 50th St., N.Y., N.Y. 10022.

DOBRUSHIN, SHEILA, Commtns. Coodr., Am. Inst. of Mining, Metallurgical and Petroleum Engineers, '70–; PR, Pubns. Asst., '70; Publicity Coordr., Reuben H. Donnelley, Inc., Magazine Publ. Div. (N.Y.C.), '68–'69; Asst. to Mgr., PR, Holland-Am. Line, '65–'68; Asst. Sls. Prom. Mgr., H-R TV, Inc., '62–'65; Univ. of Pitt., BA (Jnlsm.), '60 (Senatorial Scholarships, '56–'60); b. Pa.; res: 300 E. 33rd St., #4H, N.Y., N.Y. 10016.

DOBSON, GWEN ARMSTRONG, Wms. Ed., The Washington Star, 225 Virginia Ave. S.E., Wash., D.C. 20003, '64–; Sunday Ed., '61; News Reptr., Wms. Ed., Alexandria Gazette, '47–'50; '56–'61; Inst. PR; Fashion Show Coord.; Prom., PR, Wash.-Intl. Horse Show; WNPC, ANWC (Bd., '67–'68, Second VP, '68–'69); b. Fairfax County, VA., 1930; p. John S. and Helen V. Dove Armstrong; h. Robert V. Dobson; c. Michael C., Robyn L., John L.; res: 5515 Calhoun Ave., Alexandria, Va. 22311.

DOCKING, VIRGINIA BLACKWELL, Colmst., Kan. nwsps.; Lectr.; former Math Tchr.; Beta Sigma Phi (Hon. Mbr.), ZONTA, Kan. State Univ. Art Bd., Kan. Cultural Art Advisory Bd., NLAPW, Kan. Auths. Club, Intl. Platform Assn., Topeka Civic Theatre Bd., Valley

Hope (Bd.), Sulgrave Club, Wash., D.C., Wms. Nat. Democratic Club; Southeast Mo. State Col.; Wichita State Univ.; Kan. Univ., BS; b. Columbus, Miss.; p. Thomas and Annie Duncan Blackwell; h. Ex. Gov. George Docking; c. Gov. Robert B. Docking, George R. Docking; res: 1444 Westover Rd., Topeka, Kan. 66604.

DODD, DIXIE LEE, Secy. to Kan. Congressman Keith Sebelius, Suite 206, Hays Nat. Bank, Hays, Kan. 67601, '69–; Wmns. Ed., Great Bend Daily Tribune, '65–'69; Copywtr., KAYS Radio, '63–'64; Copywtr., Blackhawk Bdcstr. (Waterloo and Cedar Rapids, Ia.), '62–'64; Kan. Nwsp. Wm. (Pres., '69, Secy., '68), Kan. Press Wm., (Writing Aws.) Kan. Press Assn., NPWC, Great Bend Civic Theatre, '65–'69, Great Bend City Band; Kan. Assn. for Retarded Children Public Educ. Aw., '67; Univ. of Kan., '57–'59; Ft. Hays Kan. State Col., BA (Eng.) '62; b. Hill City, Kan., 1939; p. Raymond and Marie Montgomery Dodd; res: Apt. 14, 2712 Canal Blvd., Hays, Kan. 67601.

DODD, EVELYN CLEAVER, Off. Mgr., Asst. to Prodr., Kayro Enterprises, Inc., 100 Universal Plaza, Universal City, Cal. 91608, '59–; AWRT; Keuka Col.; b. Odessa, N.Y.; p. Robert and Mary Louise Catlin Cleaver; h. Howard Dodd.

DODD, JoANN CAMILLE, Special Events Mgr., Media Buying and Commtns. Coordr., Macy's Missouri-Kansas, 1034 Main St., Kan. City, Mo. 64105, '69–; Special Events Mgr., '67–; res: 4445 Terrace St., Apt. 207, Kan. City, Mo. 64111.

DODDS, LEE WILLIAMS, Gen. Mgr., Anthony Wayne Standard, 217 S. St., Waterville, Oh. 43566, '64–; Asst. Ed., '63–'64; Soc. Ed., Kenton Times, '60–'62; Teletypesetter, '55–'59; b. Auglaize County, Oh., 1937; p. Luther and Cleta Campbell Williams; h. Gary L. Dodds; c. Cheri Lee, Tracy; res: 160 Concord Ave., Waterville, Oh. 43566.

DOEPKEN, KATHERINE JEFFERSON, Wms. Ed., News Publishing Co., 1500 Main St., Wheeling, W. Va. 26003, '67–; Reptr., Feature Wtr., Photogr., Colmst., Ed., '59–; Lectr.; wms. radio "talk" show, 14 mos.; Jr. League of Wheeling, Inc., Am. Pen Wm.; Catherine O'Brien Feature Story Aw. ('64); Jr. Col.; Va. Polytech.; Columbia Univ.; b. Wheeling, W. Va., 1920; p. George and Katherine Ebbert Jefferson; h. Louis F. Doepken; c. James Jefferson McLain, David Louis Doepken; res: One Vista Ave., Wheeling, W. Va. 26003.

DOERING, DOROTHY DOLORES, Acting Lib. Dir., Drury College, Benton at Central, Springfield, Mo. 65802, '67–; Ref. Librn., '53–'67; Tchr., Children's Lit. '54–'59; Colmst., '40s–'50s; ALA, Mo. Lib. Assn; Springfield Librns. Assn., AAUP, Renaissance Soc. of Am.; Audubon Soc.; Wilderness Soc.; S.W. Mo. State Col., BS; Univ. of Ill., MS (Lib. Sci.); b. St. Louis, Mo.,

1912; p. Wilhelm and Edna Burgener Doering; res: RFD, Nixa, Mo. 67514.

DOERING, PATRICIA F., Pres., PR Associates, P.O. Box 7487, San Diego, Cal. 92110, '69–; Adv. Rep., Palm Springs Life, '69–; Adv. Rep., San Diego Magazine, '66–'69; Adv. Coordr., '65; Exec. Secy. PR, Del Webb's Ocean House Hotel, '64–'65; Exec. Secy. and Media Coordr., Barnes-Champ Adv., '60–'64; Adv. Liaison between Agcy. and Manning's Coffee Co., San Francisco, '58–'60; Adv. Cnslt., resort and restaurant accs; Articles: "Guided Tour of San Diego" (Phoenix Magazine, '69), "San Diego—Southern California's Outdoor Wonderland" ('68); Wtr: mag. articles, '68–'69; res: 1119 Barcelona Dr., San Diego, Cal. 92107.

DOHERTY, ANNA MARIE, Food Ed., Suffolk Sun, 303 Marcus Blvd., Deer Park, N.Y. 11729, '67–; Acting Food Ed., World Jnl. Tribune, '66–'67; Assoc. Food Ed., N.Y. Herald Tribune, '52–'66; Asst. Food Ed., This Week Magazine, '52–'66; NWC of N.Y.C. (Asst. Rec. Secy., '68–'70); Wine and Food Soc. of N.Y.; Immaculata Col., AA, '49; b. Baldwin, N.Y.; p. Dennis and Helen Koch Doherty; res: 154 E. 61st St., N.Y., N.Y. 10021.

DOHERTY, PHYLLIS ROSE, Dir. of PR, WNAC-TV General, Inc., RKO General Bldg., Govt. Ctr., Boston, Mass. 02114, '43–; Pubcty. Dir., WNAC Radio and the Yankee Network; Asst. to the Ed., New England Purchaser, '40–'43; Ed. of Nwsltr. and TV mag.; PR Cnslt.: March of Dimes, Dem. State Comm. (Wm. of Achievement, '63), Marist Sisters; numerous aws. for promos.; Pubcty. Club, PRSA (N.E. Chptr. Secy., '68; 2nd VP, '69), Bdcst. Execs. Club (Secy., '65; Treas., '66), Adv. Club of Gtr. Boston (Dir., '66–'68); Simmons Col., BS, '40 (Bd. Mbr. for 12 yrs.; Advisor on Adv. and PR); b. Boston, Mass., 1918; p. John Joseph Francis and Christine Marie Smith Doherty; res: 23 Thetford Ave., Dorchester, Mass. 02124.

DOLAN, JACQUELYN WARREN, Pubcty. Rep., Mng. Ed., "Sunshine Service News," Florida Power & Light Company, P.O. Box 3100, Miami, Fla. 33101, (Pubcty. Rep.), '63–; (Mng. Ed.) '66–; Pubcty. Asst. '60–'62; Sls. Rep., Prod. Asst., McMurray Printing Co., '58–'59; Theta Sigma Phi (Miami, Chptr. Pres., '67–'68), Delta Delta Delta, Alpha Sigma Epsilon, ICIE; Fla. Mag. Assn. aws: Best Feature Story, '62; Best Pic. Story, '67; Gen. Excellence for an Int. Employee Mag., '66, '67; Univ. of Miami, BA, '58; b. Gettysburg, Pa., 1937; p. E. W. and Gladys Palmer Warren; h. Dr. William W. Dolan.

DOLAN, MARY I., Mktng. Commtns. Assoc., The Philadelphia Agency Inc., 275 S. 19th St., Phila., Pa. 19103, '67–; Adv. Copywtr., Pubcty. Wtr., Greenfield-Ullman, '64–'67; articles in trade, consumer pubns.; PRSA, Phila. PR Assn.; Univ. of Pa.; b. Phila., Pa., 1935; p. William J. and Mary Kendra Dolan; res: 530 Spruce St., Phila., Pa. 19106.

DOLEZAL, WILMA HRABANEK, Prof., St. Mary's University, 2700 Cincinnati Ave., San Antonio, Tex. 78228, '68–; Prof., Univ. of Tex., '66–'68; Instructional Supvsr., San Antonio Public Schs., '53–'66; Ed., San Antonio weekly, '46–'64; Aircraft Design Engineer, various aircraft firms (Cleve., Oh.), WW II; Curriculum Cnslt., schs., cols.; work in aerospace educ.; Tex. Press Wm. (Reg. II Pres., '68–'70), Theta Sigma Phi (Secy., '67–'68), AAUP (St. Mary's Univ. Secy., '69–'70), Am. Inst. of Aeronautics and Astronautics, Civil Air Patrol; Oh. State Univ., BA, '37; B. Engr., '42; S.W. Tex. State Univ., MA, '51; Univ. of Tex., PhD, '68; b. Cleve., Oh.; p. Joseph and Antionette Dietrich Hrabanek; h. Edward S. Dolezal; c. Wilma (Mrs. Roy Alcala), Antoinette (Mrs. Jesse Galaviz), Edward J.; res: 402 Faith Dr., San Antonio, Tex. 78228.

DOLIN, EVA FISHER, Chief Copywtr., RHC-Spacemaster, 1400 N. 25th Ave., Melrose Park, Ill. 60160, '68–; Feature Ed., Leener/Life Nwsps., '68; Pres., Newsmakers PR, '65–'68; Nat. PR Dir., Mercury Record Corp., '60–'65; Colmst., Feature Wtr., various mats.; Pubcty. Club Chgo. (Hall of Fame, '68; achiev. aw., '64), PRSA, Chgo. Press Club, Am. Camp & Hosp. Svc.; Music Business Mag. aw., '63, '62; Northwestern Univ., BS (Jnlsm.), '58; b. Chgo., Ill., 1926; p. Ben and Bertha Edison Fisher; h. (div.); c. Denny, Edwin; res: 3950 N. Lake Shore Dr., Chgo., Ill. 60613.

DOLINAR, JOANNE M., Sr. Ed., Laurel Editions, Delta Books, Dell Publishing Co., Inc., 750 Third Ave., N.Y., N.Y. 10017, '67–; Assoc. Ed., '63–'66; Univ. of Pitt., BA, '61 (magna cum laude; Phi Beta Kappa); b. Washington, Pa., 1940; p. Louis and Helen Dermotta Dolinar; res: 588 West End Ave., N.Y., N.Y. 10026.

DOLLAGHAN, HELEN FRANCES, Food Ed., The Denver Post, 650 15th St., Denver, Colo. 80201, '58–; Nwsp. Reptr., Wms. Dept.; Univ. of Denver, BA (Jnlsm.).

DOLSON, HILDEGARDE, Auth: "Open the Door" (Lippincott '66), "We Shook the Family Tree" (Random House '46), and others including juvs., '38–; numerous mag. pieces for New Yorker, Ladies' Home Journal, McCall's, Harpers, Woman's Day, Reader's Digest, others; Adv. Copywtr., dept. and specialty stores, '33–'38; Auths. Guild, Civil Liberties Un., NAACP, Kappa Kappa Gamma; Allegheny Col., '26–'29 (Hon. Dr. Lit., '58); b. Franklin, Pa., 1908; p. Clifford and Katherine Brown Dolson; h. Richard Lockridge; res: R.F.D. #1, S. Salem, N.Y. 10590.

DONAHUE, KATHRYN IDSO, Librn., Sunnyvale Public Library, 665 W. Olive Ave., Sunnyvale, Cal. 94086, '69–; Free-lance Publicist, '50–'60; Dir., Public Info., Honolulu Army Port Command, '48–'49; Special Svcs. Rep., U.S. Coast Guard Pacific Loran Stas., '47; PR Rep., Pan Am. World Airways (L.A., Honolulu), '43–'48; Copy Ed., Cal. Publisher, Cal. NPA, '42–'43; Univ. of S. Cal., AB (Jnlsm.), '41; San Jose State Col., MA (Lib. Sci.), '69; b. Morristown, S.D., 1919; p. Bern-

hard and Golda Lambert Idso; h. Mark Donahue; c. Mary Kathleen, Janice Patricia; res: 7545 Rainbow Dr., San Jose, Cal. 95129.

DONALDSON, MARGARET F., Dir. of commty. rels., United Hospital, 406 Boston Post Rd., Port Chester, N.Y. 10573, '64–; Dir. of Prom. and PR, N.Y. Area of Methodist Ch., '53–'64; Sports Ed., News Ed., City Ed., Daily Times (Mamaroneck, N.Y.), '43–'53; contrb. staffs, N.Y. Times Sunday Bk. Rev., Herald Tribune Bks., '30s; synd. bk. colm., "The Book Mark," '30s; Dir., fund pubcty., Westchester Chptr., Am. Red Cross; Auth: "Giving and Growing" (Fleming H. Revell and Co., '46), "How to Put Church Members to Work" (Fleming H. Revell and Co., '48); NRPC (N.Y. Chptr. Past Pres.), Am. Soc. of Hosp. PR Dirs., Am. Hosp. Assn., Gtr. N.Y. Hosp. Assn., Hosp. PR Assn. of Westchester County (Secy.); aws. for svc. and publishing; Goucher Col., AB, '30 (Westchester Alumnae Club Past Pres.); Met. Col. of Music (N.Y.C.); h. Lewis H. Donaldson (dec.).

DonDERO, GERTRUDE, Nat. Exec. Dir., Girls Clubs of America, 133 E. 62nd St., N.Y., N.Y. 10021, '63–; PR and Fund Raising Cnslt., '45–'63; Commty. Drama, U.S.O. Overseas, '32–'45; OPC, Old Kimmul Club (London); cits: Caribbean Defense Command for meritorious achiev., War Dept. Special Svcs. Div., N.Y. Comm. of Nat. War Fund; Boston Univ., BS, '32; Grad. Work: Columbia, N.Y.U., New Sch. Drama Workshop; b. Willimantic, Conn., res: "Donnybrook," 275-Rockrimmon Rd., Stamford, Conn. 06903.

DONDI, DOLORES A., VP Client Svcs., Jules L. Klein Advertising, Inc., Kimball Towers Penthouse, Springfield, Mass. 01103, '68–; Asst. to Pres., '65–'68; Asst. AE, '62–'65; Med. Dir., '57–'62; Secy., '52–'57; Lectr. at local high sch. and col.; Adv. Club of Springfield (Dir., '64–'68), Joint Civic Agcys. of Springfield, Photographic Soc. of Springfield (aws. for color slides); Berkshire Bus. Col., '40–'42; Davenport Inst. of Bus., '50–'51; b. Pittsfield, Mass.; p. Didimo and Rose Vanotti Dondi; res: 109 School St., Springfield, Mass. 01105.

DONEGAN, Sr. M. DENIS, I.H.M., Assoc. Dir. (Acquisitions), Marywood College Library, Scranton, Pa.; '24–; Bklyn. Botanic Garden Lib., '21–'25; Fed. Reserve Bank of N.Y., '18–'21; Jr. Asst., Bklyn. Public Lib., '15–'18; ALA (Life Mbr., '28–), Catholic Lib. Assn. (Scranton Diocesan Unit Pres., '50s; Secy., several terms, '40s, '50s), Pa. Lib. Assn.; Marywood Col., BA, MA; Columbia Univ. Sch. of Lib. Svc., MLSD; Catholic Univ.; Carnegie Lib. Sch.; b. Bklyn., N.Y.; p. Denis P. and Bride Whalen Donegan; res: Marywood Col., Scranton, Pa. 18509.

DONER, MARY FRANCES, Free-lance Wtr., Auth: 22 novels, '30–'63; other bks., '58, '68; articles; bk. revs.; Staff Wtr., Dell, '26–'34; Crtv. writing tchr. (Ludington, Mich.), '64–'69; Boston Ctr. for Adult Educ., '42–'44; private tutoring; Lectr.; work transcribed into Braille; Boston Auths. Club, Pen and Brush Club, Wms. City Club of Boston, Wms. Nat. Bk. Assn., Intl. Inst. Arts and Ltrs., Marquis Biographical Lib. Soc. (Advisory Mbr.), Mark Twain Soc. (Hon. Mbr.), League of Catholic Wm., Ladies' Lib. Assn., St. Clair Wms. Club, Lioness Club, Lib. Bd., Ludington Lit. Club; Cathedral Conservatory of Music; Columbia Univ.; N.Y.U.; b. Port Huron, Mich., 1893; p. James and Mary O'Rourke Doner; res: 210 N. Lewis St., Ludington. Mich. 49431.

DONNA, NATALIE, Auth., "Boy of the Masai" ('64); Game Designer: "Snakes in the Grass," "The West Point Story Game," "Betsy Ross and the Flag Game," "The F.B.I. Story Game"; Copywtr., Grey Adv., '65–'67; Intl. Platform Assn.; b. N.Y.C., 1934; res: 320 E. 73rd St., N.Y., N.Y. 10021.

DONNELLY, Sr. DOROTHY, CSJ, Dir., Leadership Training Institute, Roman Catholic Diocese of Oakland, Cal., 2918 Lakeshore Ave., Oakland, Cal. 94610, '67–; Asst. Dir., Adult Educ., '69–; Dir., Cmmtns. Workshops, St. Joseph Col. (Orange), St. Mary's Col. (Oakland); Auth: "Sister—Apostle" ('64); Young Christian Students, Christian Family Movement; Dominican Col., San Rafael, BA, '50; Catholic Univ., MA, PhD, '62 (Pius X Pace Scholarship, '61); Am. Acad. Rome (Post-Doctoral Study, Fulbright Grant, '62); Theological Union, Berkeley, ThD, '70; b. S.F., Cal., 1920; p. Joseph and Julia O'Sullivan Donnelly; res: 380 S. Batavia St., Orange, Cal. 92666.

DONNELLY, DOROTHY BOILLOTAT, Auth. and Poet: "Trio in a Mirror" (poetry; Univ. of Ariz. Press, '60), "The Golden Well" (Sheed & Ward, '50); Longview Fndn. Aw. for poem, "People," '59; Harriet Monroe Memorial Aw. (Poetry), '57; Union League Aw. (Poetry), '54; Univ. of Mich., BA, '31 (high distinction; Phi Beta Kappa, Phi Kappa Phi); MA, '32; b. Detroit, Mich., 1903; p. Alexander and Theresa Ferstl Boillotat; h. Walter Donnelly; c. Stephen, Jerome, Denis; res: 612 Lawrence St., Ann Arbor, Mich. 48104.

DONOVAN, BARBARA STARKEY MARCO, Ed.-in-Chief, The Bride's Magazine, Condé Nast Publications, Inc., 420 Lexington, Ave., N.Y., N.Y. 10017, '66–; Dir. of Wms. Svcs., Bartell Media Corp.; Beauty Ed., Vogue; Copy Ed., Vogue Pattern Book; Food Ed., Look; Staff, two adv. agcys.; Auth: "ABC's of Beauty" (MacFadden-Bartell Corp., '63), sls. bklets; Beauty Cnslt., Fashion Group, Cosmetic Career Wm., NHFL, Nat. Cncl. of Wm., Nat. Cncl. on Family Rels., Am. Soc. of Mag. Eds., Nat. Soc. of Interior Designers; Am. Inst. of Interior Designers; Pan Pacific Southeast Asia Wms. Assn.; ALMA aw., '68; numerous civic orgs.; N.Y. Sch. of Interior Design; Traphagen Sch. of Fashion; Fashion Inst. of Tech.; b. Summit, N.J., 1934; p. Rodney and Maude Grebbin Starkey; h. Cornelius Peter Donovan.

DONOVAN, MARY CAYE, Ed., Mktng. Asst., Bud-

get Cnslt., Society National Bank of Cleveland, 127 Public Sq., Cleveland, Oh. 44114, '58–; Ed. and PR Asst., '51–; Budget Dir., The Cleveland Press, '58–; Free-lance Wtr. for nwsps., mags., TV, radio, '49–'51; Dir. of PR, Oh. State Nurses Assn., '48–'49; Dir. of PR and Instr. of Jnlsm., Eng., Notre Dame Col. (South Euclid), '44–'48; Adv. Asst., Cleveland Plain Dealer, '43–'44; Wms. Adv. Club of Cleveland (Chmn., 50th Anniversary; Bd. Mbr.; Past Pres.), Jennings Home for the Aged (Dir.), AFA (Fifth Dist. Secy.; First Aw. Ed. of Club Nwsp., '56), Catholic Fedn. of Wms. Clubs (Dir.), Press Club of Cleveland (Trustee), Theta Sigma Phi (Cleveland Chptr. VP), IEA of N.E. Oh. (First Aw. Ed. in Field, '59), Am. Inst. of Banking, "Invest in America" (hon., '63); Notre Dame Col., '43 (Alumnae Assn. Past Pres.); John Carroll Univ., post grad., '44–'45; b. Cleveland, Oh.; p. David and Katherine Kruse Donovan; res: 20000 Lorain Rd., Fairview Park, Oh. 44126.

DONOVAN, ROBERTA MESSIER, News Ed., Lewistown Daily News, 521 W. Main, Lewistown, Mont. 59457, '64–; Mont. Press Wm. (State Pres.); NFPW (First Place in nation for special edition ed. by wm., '68); Mont. Press Assn., Mont. Press Wm. of the Yr. ('68), numerous writing aws.; First Methodist Ch. (Offcl. Bd.); b. Lewistown, Mont. 1921; p. Isaac and Ruth Covert Messier; h. Bert A. Donovan; c. James, Robert, Patricia Wilbur, Mary Murchie, Joyce, Jeanne; res: 135 14th Ave., S. Lewistown, Mont. 59457.

DOOLEN, DOROTHY HELEN, Rsch. Dir., Earle Ludgin & Company, 410 N. Mich., Chgo., Ill. 60611, '67–; Rsch. Project Dir., Compton Advertising; Rsch. Supvsr., John W. Shaw Advertising; Am. Mktng. Assn.; Univ. of Ill., BA; p. C. D. and Laurine Wilson Doolen; res: 30 E. Elm St., Chgo., Ill. 60611.

DOOLEY, MARY LUCETTA, Atty. at Law, private practice, 224 Hayes Bldg., 20 E. Milwaukee St., Janesville, Wis. 53545, '51–; Bus. Cnslt., '53–; Rsch. Assoc., State of Wis., Off. of Atty. Gen., '52–'53; Tchr., various colls., univs., '54–'69; Rsch., Ford Fellow, Univ. of Minn., '57–'58; Dept. of Wis.-Judge Advocate, '54–'57; Auth., tech. articles, Labor Law Jnl., Wis. Bar Bull.; St. John's Law Rev., '70; bk. (Univ. of Mich. Press, '57); ZONTA, Nat. Assn. of Wm. Lawyers, numerous other orgs.; Wis. Wildlife & Conservation Award '64; Univ. of Wis., BA (Econs.), '47; LL.B. (Law), '51; MA (Econs.), '53; PhD (Econs.), '57; D.L. (Law), '67; Indian Studies Fellow, '62; b. Sp. Valley Twp., 1924; p. Francis and Lucetta Dickey Dooley; res: Rte. 1, Brodhead, Wis. 53520.

DOORLEY, LARREEN MARY, Adv. Copywtr., Ogilvy & Mather Inc., 2 East 48th St., N.Y., N.Y. 10017, '65–; Copywtr., Compton Adv., '63–'65; Pa. State Univ., BA, '62; b. Steubenville, Oh., 1941; p. Lawrence and Emmalou Sage Doorley; res: 153 E. 57th St., N.Y., N.Y. 10022.

DORAN, CLARE E., PR Dir., Columbia Hospital,

Penn Ave. and West St., Pitt., Pa. 15221, '68–; Wtr., Calgon Corp., '65–'68; PR Dir., Martin Anthony School of Beauty Culture, '64–'65; Theta Sigma Phi (Pitt. Chptr. Secy., '67–'68); Duquesne Univ., BA (Jnlsm.), '64; b. Pitt., Pa., 1942; p. Stanley and Frances Diges Paulukonis; h. Richard Doran (dec.); res: 5631 Phillips Ave., Apt. 10, Pitt., Pa. 15217.

DORAN, MARGARET CAMERON, Librn., Palms Junior High School, 10860 Woodbine St., L.A., Cal. 90034, '57–; Head Librn., Saugus (Mass.) Public Lib., '36–'41; Librn., Framingham Town Lib., '35–'36; Visiting Lectr., Loyola Univ., '67–; Contrbr., pfsnl. jnls.; Friends of the Lib., New England Jr. Mbrs. Lib. Assn. (Secy. '43), ALA, Cal. Assn. of Schl. Librns.; Simmons Col., BS (Lib. Sci.), '35; Loyola Univ. (L.A.), MA, '62; b. Cranston, R.I., 1913; p. Walter and Alice Hager Cameron; h. Harold Doran; c. Walter C.; res: 8026 Loyola Blvd., L.A., Cal. 90045.

DORAN, PATRICIA ANN, Fashion Ed., Ski Magazine, 235 E. 45th St., N.Y., N.Y. 10017, '68–; Free-lance, '66–; Fashion Ed., McCall's Fashionews, '66–'68; Ed., McCall's Sportswear Merchandiser, McCall's Loungewear, '64–'66; Mkt. Ed., Wms. Wear Daily, '61–'64; Owner, Byr., Boutique "Le Weekend," N.Y.C.; Tobe Coburn, '54; Oglethorpe Univ., '50; b. Atlanta, Ga., 1934; p. James and Mary Doran; c. Michael, Patrick; res: 27 Washington Sq. N., N.Y., N.Y. 10011.

DORCY, Sr. MARY JEAN, O.P., Wtr., Tchr., Missionary to Mexico, '64–'69; Auth.-Illus. 18 Children's bks., '39–'62; Contrbr. many periodicals, synds.; Delta Phi Delta; Gonzago Univ., BA, '41; Cal. Col. of Arts and Crafts, MFA, '45; b. Anacortes, Wash., 1914; p. William and Emma Knapp Dorcy; res: Nuestros Pequenos Hermanos, 1851 136th Ave., San Leandro, Cal. 94578.

DOREN, MERHL NORTON, Gen. Reptr., Northern N.Y. Publishing Co., Inc., 308 Isabella St., Ogdensburg, N.Y. 13669, '56–; Adv. Mgr., Empsall-Clark Dept. Store, '46–'56; Reptr., Ogdensburg Journal, Sunday Advance-News, '44–'46; Onondaga Bus. Sch., Syracuse, N.Y., '25; b. Syracuse, N.Y., 1904; p. Charles and Alida Walrath Norton; h. (div.); c. David, Rodger B.; res: 410 Knox, Ogdensburg, N.Y. 13669.

DORESE, EVELYN BELL, Corr., Mutual Broadcasting Company, Nat. Press Bldg., Wash., D.C. 20004, '60; Comm., ABC Network; Television MC, WMAL-TV, WTOP-TV; AWRT (Pres., '67–'68), Un. Clipped Wings (Pres., '64), WHCA, SRTCA, WNPC; Radio-TV Daily aw. for outstanding bdcst., '63; Hecht Co. Aw., '66; Arlington Hall Col., '42; Am. Acad. of Dramatic Arts, '43–'44; Univ. of Rochester, '45; b. Decatur, Ala.; p. Clyde and Esterlene Rogers Bell.

DORFMAN, COLLEEN KINNEY FRIES, Publicist, AE, Barkin, Herman & Associates, 565 Fifth Ave., N.Y., N.Y. 10017, '67–; Publicist, Fred Rosen & Assocs., '64–'67; The Mdsng. Group, '62–'64; Harshe-Rotman

and Drucke, '56–'60; AWRT, N.Y. Adv. Club, active in church and civic groups; Syracuse Univ., '47–'49; b. Bethlehem, Pa.; p. Joseph and Isabelle Yost Kinney; h. Richard Dorfman; c. Isabelle Scott Fries; res: 75 Argyle Pl., Rockville Centre, N.Y. 11570.

DORIAN, EDITH McEWEN, Auth., juv. bks.: "Animals that Made U.S. History" ('64), "No Moon on Graveyard Head" ('53), "Ask Dr. Chistmas" ('51), "The Twisted Shadow" ('56), "Hokahey!" ('57), "Trails West" ('55), "High-Water Cargo" ('50); many bk. aws.; Lectr., Douglass Col., '60–'62; Eng. Prof., '22–'32; Lit. Advisor, Macmillan Co., '38–'48; Eng. Prof., Douglass Col., Rutgers Univ., '22–'32; Auths. Guild; Cncl. of Christians and Jews Cit., '53; Boys Club of Am. Jr. Bk. Aw., '58; civic orgs.; Smith Col., BA (Eng.), '21 (Phi Beta Kappa); Harvard Univ., '22; Columbia Univ., AM, '28; b. Newark, N.J., 1900; p. Dr. Floy and Antoinette Currier McEwen; h. Donald Dorian; c. Donald M. (dec.), Nancy; res: 39 Elm St., Topsham, Me. 04086

DORKEN, DIANA B., Adv. Prod. Mgr., Scott Paper Company, Phila., Pa. 19113, '67–; Procter & Gamble of Canada, '59–'67; Klenman-Davidson Prodns., '58–'59; Canadian Bdcst. Corp., '54–'58; AWRT (Bd. Mbr., '69–'70), Little Theatre Stage Lighting; Ryerson Inst., '50–'54; b. St. Lambert, Quebec, Can.; p. H. R. and Effie Jones Dorken; res: 220 Locust St., Apt. 4-H, Phila., Pa. 19106.

DORMAN, RUTH GAMMAGE, Tchr., Milton Hershey School, Catherine Hall, Hershey, Pa. 17033, '68–; Bk. Reviewer, Lib. Jnl., '59–; Librn., (N.Y., N.H.), '55–'66, '51–'53; Lib. Cl. (Oh.), '47–'50; Cnslt., sch. lib. org., adm.; N.H. Sch. Lib. Assn. (Pres.), High Sch. Lib. Bk. Club (Exec. Bd.), AAUW; Phi Chi Theta; Oh. State Univ., BS, '50 (Mortar Bd.); Columbia Univ., MS, '52; b. Malden, Mass.; p. Earle C. and H. Agnes Horton Gammage; h. David Dorman; c. D. Douglas, William G.; res: 71 Brownstone Dr., Hershey, Pa. 17033.

DORR, MARY WRIGHT, Dir. Wms. Activities, Western and Pacific Region, U.S.A., American Bible Society, 1662 Wilshire Blvd., L.A., Cal. 90017; Free-lance talent; lectr., current commentary; tchr., air media techniques; free-lance commls., film narration, '59–'69; Public Svc. Coordr., KRE (Berkeley, Cal.), '56–; WFIL-TV (Phila., Pa.), '54–'55; WFAS (White Plains, N.Y.), '52–'53; various orgs., aws.; Univ. of Cal., BA, '39, grad. study, '41–'42; b. Megargel, Tex. 1918; p. William and Harper Ethel Dennis Wright; h. John Dorr (dec.); c. Diane Jeanne, John, Jr., Robert D., Donald James, Kenneth William; res: 920 Euclid St., Apt. 315, Santa Monica, Cal. 90403.

DORSETT, CORA MATHENY, Dir., Public Library of Pine Bluff and Jefferson County, 200 E. Eighth St., Pine Bluff, Ark. 71601, '65–; Tchr.; ALA, WNBA, Ark. Lib. Assn. (Public Lib. Div. Chmn.), Southwestern Lib. Assn.; Centenary Col., BS, '63; Univ. of Miss., MS (Lib. Sci.), '65; b. Camden, Ark; p. Walter and Cora

Smith Matheny; h. George Dorsett; c. Ann, Edward; res: 1305 W. 35th St., Pine Bluff, Ark. 71601.

DORSEY, DONNA, PR Dir., Children's Home Society of California, 530 N. First St., San Jose, Cal. 95112, '68; PR Cnslt., Volunteer Bur. of Santa Clara County, PR Dir., Santa Clara County Un. Fund, '66–'68; PRSA, San Jose Adv. Club (Bd. of Dir., '67–'69); San Jose State Col., BA, '62–'64 (Alumni Assn. Bd. of Dirs.).

DORWORTH, ALICE GREY, Assoc. Prof., Hofstra University, Hempstead, L.I., N.Y. 10003, '56–; Special Lectr., N.Y.U., '53–'56; Assoc. Prof., Marshall Univ., '46–'53; City Supvsr., Erie Sch. System, '41–'45; Tchr., Rschr., Indsl. Systems Cnslt.; Auth: "Channels of Distribution" ('55), "Change-over of Credit & Accounts Receivable Depts. to Computers" ('65), "Economic Abstracts" ('56, '57); ORSA, Am. Statis. Assn.; Who's Who of Am. Wm., Who's Who in Am., Who's Who in Educ., Am. Men of Sci.; Edinboro State Col., BS, '39; Univ. of Pitt., MS, '43; N.Y.U., PhD, '56 (Fellowship); b. Oil City, Pa.; p. Hugh and Margaret Dougherty Dorworth; res: 54 E. Eighth St., N.Y., N.Y. 10003.

DOSCHER, VIRGINIA BECKER, Staff Assoc., American Public Welfare Assn., 1313 E. 60th St., Chgo., Ill. 60637, '65–; PR Cnslt., Pubns. Dir., '56–'65; Exec. Dir., Nat. PR Cncl. of Health and Welfare Svcs., '54–'56; PR Dir., Welfare Cncl. of Milw. County, '44–'54; Pubcty. Secy., Duluth Minn. Commty. Chest, '42–'44; County Ed., Pontiac Press, '41–'42; Caseworker, Oakland County Bur. of Social Aid, '38–'42; PRSA, Nat. Conf. on Social Welfare, Intl. Cncl. on Social Welfare; Mich. State Normal Col., '32–'34; Univ. of Mich., AB, '34–'36; Grad. Work, Univ. of Mich. Sch. of Social Work; b. Pontiac, Mich.; p. Frank and Ruth Johnston Becker; h. William Doscher; res: Apt. 2130, 400 E. Randolph St., Chgo., Ill. 60601.

DOTY, JUDITH GREENE, Wms. Ed., The Evening News, Dickson St., Newburgh, N.Y. 12550, '65–; Dir., Home Econs., Lloyds Shopping Ctrs., '62–'64; Wms. Ed., Middletown (N.Y.) Times-Herald Record, '58–'62; Dir., children's division volunteers, Mt. Sinai Hosp. (N.Y.C.), '51–'54; Club Dir. PR, Am. Red Cross overseas, '45–'49; Soc. Ed., Middletown Times-Herald, '42–'45, '49–'50; Compilation, Writing Hist. of Am. Red Cross in Far East; Two N.W. Ayer Aws. (to paper, while Wms. Ed.); J. C. Penney-Mo. Aw. for Wms. Pgs.; Marot Col.; Syracuse Univ.; b. Middletown, N.Y., 1920; p. Lawrence and Mytra Gibbs Greene; h. Wallace A. Doty (div.); res: Rt. 208, Box 414, Walden, N.Y. 12586.

DOUCETTE, GAIL IRENE, Ed., Employee Commtns., Connecticut Bank and Trust Company, One Constitution Plaza, Hartford, Conn. 06115, '67–; Asst. Ed., Merit Students Ency., Crowell Collier Educ. Corp., '64–'67; Am. Inst. of Banking, ICIE; Fairleigh Dickinson Univ., BA, '63; b. N.Y.C., 1940; p. George and Lillian Beck Doucette; res: 21 Willard Street, Hartford, Conn. 06105.

DOUGAN, DIANA LADY, CATV Mktng. Cnslt., Dougan & Tunks (Investments), 901 American Oil Bldg., Salt Lake City, Ut.; CATV Prom. Mgr., Time-Life Bdcst., '66–'68; Free-lance Cnslt., Phil Dean Assoc. (Wash., D.C.), '66; Free-lance Cnslt., Larry Hogan Assoc. (N.Y.), '66; Asst. to Chief Clk., Md. House of Delegates, '65, '66; Asst. Pubcty. Dir., Artists Repertory Theatre (Wash., D.C.), '62; other work incl: TV comml's, writing; presently Prodr., MC, "Way of Art," TV show, KUED (Salt Lake City, Ut.); AWRT, AAUW; "Distg. Citizen of Md.," Governor's Aw., svc. to Md. Gen. Assembly, '65–'66; "Key to the City," Hon. Citizenship (Seoul, Korea), '66; Pi Eta Delta; Univ. of Md., BA, '64 (Jr. C. of C. scholarship, Pepsi Cola scholarship, various col. hons., aws.); grad. work; b. Dayton, Oh., 1943; p. Harold W. and Hon. Elaine Staggers Lady; h. John Lynn Dougan II; res: 4300 Parkview Dr., Salt Lake City, Ut. 84117.

DOUGHERTY, ANNA ELIZABETH, Asst. Librn., National Institutes of Health Library, Bethesda, Md. 20008, '59–; Nat. Lib. of Med., '51–'59; Bklyn. Col. Lib., '49–'51; Univ. of Mich., Law Lib., '48–'49; Bryn Mawr Col. Lib., '44–'48; Bucknell Univ. Lib., '38–'44; DuPont Jackson Lab. Patent Lib., '35–'38; Contrbr., "A Guide to Comparative Literature," '68–; Joint Ed., Proceedings 2nd Intl. Congress on Med. Librnship, '63; ALA, Assn. of Col. and Rsch. Libs., Cncl. of Nat. Lib. Assns. (Joint Comm. on Lib. Educ. Secy./Treas., '67–'69), Med. Lib. Assn. (Assoc. Ed., Bul., '52–'56), Special Libs. Assn. (Wash., D.C. Chptr. Assoc. Ed., '58–'59; Corr. Secy., '57–'58; Advisory Cncl., '57–'59); Am. Soc. of Info. Scis., D.C. Lib. Assn.; Beta Phi Mu; Univ. of Del., AB, '32; Drexel Inst., Lib. Sch., BS in LS, '33; Columbia Univ., Sch. of Lib. Svc., MS, '48. b. Wilmington, Del., 1910; res: 3001 Veazey Terr. N.W., Wash., D.C. 20008.

DOUGHERTY, CATHARINE ANN, Ed., Planette, Maryland Hospital Service, Inc., 7800 York Rd., Balt., Md. 21204, '69–; Wtr., Ed., Bon Secours Quarterly and Fac. Mbr., Bon Secours Hosp. Sch. of Nursing, '64–'68; Supvsr., Nursing Unit, '59–'61; Md. State Nurses' Assn., ICIE, Am. Nurses' Assn., Sigma Theta Tau (Kappa Chptr.); Bon Secours Hosp. Sc. of Nursing, Grad., '59; The Catholic Univ., BS (Nursing), '64; Manhattanville Col., grad. student; b. Chester, Pa., 1936; p. George Sr. and Catherine McCarron Dougherty; res: 102 S. Collins Ave., Balt. Md. 21223.

DOUGHERTY, MARY BETH WAGNER, Placement Mgr., Columbia Broadcasting System, Inc., 51 W. 52nd St., N.Y., N.Y. 10019, '65–; Tester, Preliminary Interviewer, '62–'65; Col. of New Rochelle (New Rochelle, N.Y.), BA (Psych.), '62; b. Elmira, N.Y., 1940; p. Harold M. and Rita E. O'Leary Wagner; h. Francis Dougherty; res: 780 Greenwich St., N.Y., N.Y. 10014.

DOUGLAS, AURIEL MACFIE, Ed.-PR Dir., The Ward

Ritchie Press, 3044 Riverside Dr., L.A., Cal. 90039, '68–; Edtl. Dir., Price/Stern/Sloan Publrs., '64–'68; AE, Furman Assocs., '62–'64; AE, The Sloan Co., '60–'62; Free-lance Writing, '55–'59; Mag. Ed., Press Dept., NBC, '49–'55; Bk. Publrs. Assn. of Southern Cal. (PR Dir., '66, '69; Rec. Secy., '67; VP, '68); L.A. City Col.; Columbia Univ.; b. N.Y.C.; p. Robert F. and Edith G. Snelling Macfie; c. Russell B., III, Heather D.; res: 390 S. Hauser Blvd., L.A., Cal. 90036.

DOUGLAS, MARJORY STONEMAN, Auth: "Florida, The Long Frontier" ('67), "The Everglades: River of Grass" (Rivers of Am. Series, '47), "The Gallows Gate," play ('28) 2nd Prize O. Henry Memorial Collection '28), other adult, jr. bks.; Lectr., Fla. hist., Miami-Dade Jr. Col., '64–; Pres., Hurricane House Pubns., Inc., '64–; Pres., Friends of the Everglades, '70–; Dir., winter lit. insts., museum, civic confs., currently; Col. Lectr., '25–'29; Ed., Univ. of Miami Press, '60–'63; Dir. Emeritus, '63–; Wtr., edtl. colm., N.Y. Times, '50; bk. revs., N.Y. Herald-Tribune, '49; short stories, articles in nat. mags., '24–'40; Bk. Ed., Miami (Fla.) Herald, '42–'49; Asst. Ed., Colmst., '20–'23; Reptr., '15–'18; Overseas Dept. Pubcty., Am. Red Cross in Europe, '18–'20; Wm. Geographers of Wash.; Wellesley Col., AB, '12; Univ. of Miami, LittD (hon.), '52; b. Mpls., Minn., 1890; p. Frank and Lillian Trefethen Stoneman; h. (div.); res: 3744 Stewart Ave., Coconut Grove, Fla. 33133.

DOUGLAS, MARTHA LESLIE, TV Colmst., Ed., Arkansas Gazette, P.O. Box 1821, Little Rock, Ark. 72203, '55–; Reptr., Feature Wtr., '50–'55; Edtl. Staff, '50–; Reptr., Denton (Tex.) Record-Chronicle, '48–'49; PR Dept., Tex. Wms. Univ., '47–'48; EWA; Tex. State Col. for Wm., BA (Jnlsm.), '47 (Alpha Chi; Ed., Col. paper); b. Warren, Ark., 1922; p. Luther and Bessie Thompson Leslie; h. Robert R. Douglas; c. Bruce, Alan, Leslie; res: #5 Fair Hill Circle, Little Rock, Ark. 72205.

DOUGLAS, MARY STAHLMAN, Bk. Pg. Ed., Nashville Banner, 1100 Broadway, Nashville, Tenn. 37202, '35–; Reptr., Features Ed., '32–'35; Reptr., Drama Critic, '16–'21; WNBA (Nashville Chptr. Charter Mbr.); Cumberland Col. aw., '70; Randolph-Macon Wms. Col., AB, '16; b. Nashville, Tenn.; p. Edward and Mary Geddes Stahlman; h. Byrd Douglas (dec.); c. Mary Byrd (Mrs. George M. King); res: 2215 Abbott-Martin Rd., Nashville, Tenn. 37215.

DOUGLASS, PAULA, Ed., Exec. Secy., Better Bellevue Assn., Bellevue Hospital, First Ave. at 28th St., N.Y., N.Y. 10016; N.Y. Assn. of Indsl. Communicators (Bd. Dirs.), Commty. Agcys. PR Assn., Twenty Third St. Assn.; Tulane Univ., BA, '60; Univ. of Paris, MA, '62; b. Atlanta, Ga.

DOWD, GERI HACKER, Auth. and Ed. of Science and Special Publications, World Arts and Science Publishing Company, 7922 Oakleaf Ave., Elmwood Park, Ill. 60635, '50–; Free-lance Wtr: scientific papers, short stories, poems, plays; supplied to National Aeronautics & Space Administration "Lunar Glass, A Possible Key to a New Selenology" ('69); "Discussion on the Etiology and Chemotherapy of Cancer and Other Virus Diseases" ('52), "The Visual Educators: Bonny and Barry Busy Scientists" (educational toy books, '51), "Circus Parade" (satirical poems, self-illustrated, '50); Colmst. and Founder of wms. page, MontClare-Leyden Herald Newspapers, Oak Park and West Suburban towns, Chicago, '40–'44; First Elmwood Park Chief of Staff, '41; Credit Mgr., Binks Mfg. Co., '29–'39; Midwestern Writers' Conference of Northwestern Univ., Children's Reading Roundtable, WNBA, Federation Chaparral Writers of America, Poetry Workshop Leader; North Shore Creative Writers, PEN, Astronomical Society of the Pacific, Am. Assn. for the Advancement of Science, Am. Academy of Political and Social Science, Am. Sociological Assn., NEA; Wright Jr. Col., AA, '58; Roosevelt Univ., BA, '61; b. Chgo., Ill.; p. Frederick and Selma Peterson Hacker; h. Lawrence Bernard Dowd; res: 7922 Oakleaf Ave., Elmwood Park, Ill. 60635.

DOWDELL, DOROTHY KARNS, Auth., non-fiction for young people; six bks: "The Japanese Helped Build America," "Careers in Horticultural Sciences," "Sierra Nevada," "Your Career in Teaching," "Secret of the ABC's," "Tree Farms"; Tchr., Sacramento, Cal., '48–'61; Auths. Guild, Cal. Wtrs. Club (Sacramento Br. Pres., '53–'54, '63–'64), Cal. Congress PTA (Hon. Life Mbrship., '61), AAUW, PEO; Univ. of Cal. (Berkeley), AB, '31; Sacramento State Col., '50; b. Reno, Nevada, 1910; p. Albert and Florence Lusk Karns; h. Joseph Dowdell; c. Joan Eva (Mrs. William R. Moore), John Lawrence; res: 21549 Old Mine Rd., Los Gatos, Cal. 95030.

DOWLING, SYLVIA, Dir. of Wms. Svcs., Jack Byrne Advertising, 770 Lexington Ave., '70–; formerly Polit. Colmst., Connecticut Sunday Herald, 1150 Post Rd., Fairfield, Conn. 06430; VP Crtv. Group Head, Benton & Bowles', Assoc. Crtv. Dir., John Murray; TV Copy Supvsr., Sullivan, Stauffer, Colwell & Bayles; Film, TV Dir., Copywtr., Young & Rubicam; Speech Wtr. for Gen. Dwight Eisenhower, Eleanor Roosevelt, and others in WW II; Campaign Adv: Pres. Dwight Eisenhower, Cong. Lowell Weicker, state senators, rep., mayors, judges in Conn.; TV Dir., Arthur Godfrey, Repl. and Dem. convs.; Gag Wtr., Jack Parr, Steve Allen, others; Cnslt., Conn. food chain; Bus. Wm. of Yr., '62; aws. for film commls: Cannes Film Festival, N.Y. TV Film Festival, Art Dirs. Club; Who's Who of Am. Wm.; World's Who's Who in Commerce and Industry; h. John B. Dowling; c. John B., III, Susan Dowling Coes; res: Southfield Point, Stamford, Conn. 06902.

DOWNE, LOUISE, Exec. Dir., Prodr. of Talent, On Camera Unlimited, Inc./Creative Communications, Inc., 226 E. Ontario St., Chgo., Ill. 60611, '59–; PRSA, Adv. Wtrs. Club, Wms. Variety Club, Wm. of the Motion Picture Industry; Beeline Fashion Aw., '69;

Dade County C. of C. aw., '63; Univ. of Miami, BS (Psych.), '59; b. Miami, Fla., 1939; p. Hector and Alma Hamby Downe.

DOWNIE, JEAN B., Wms. Ed., Trenton Times, 500 Perry St., Trenton, N.J. 08605, '68–; Food Ed., '48–; Reptr., '48–'68; Travel Cnslr., Pubn. Ed., Auto Club of Central N.J.; '45–'48; N.J. Daily Nwsp. Wm. (Charter Mbr.), Soroptimist Club; Rider Col.; b. Holyoke, Mass.; p. James and Janet Simpson Downie; res: 1 Mallow Lane, Levittown, Pa. 19054.

DOWNING, MARILYN HUBBARD, Ed., Wtr., Photogr., Northwest Tribune, Danker Corporation, Hamilton, Mont. 59840, '66–; St. Luke's Hosp. Sch. of Nursing (Denver, Colo.); b. Blue Island, Ill., 1926; p. Max and Hannah Bender Hubbard; h. Claude Downing; c. Max, Claudia Downing Puschmann; res: Rt. 2, Box 54, Stevensville, Mont. 59870.

DOWNS, JO ALYS, Bk. Designer, University of Texas Press, 102 W. 20th, Austin, Tex. 78712, '63–; Artist II, '58–'63; Prod. Asst., '55–'58; Biologist, USPHS Rsch. Lab., '51–'53; 25 aws., Southern Bks., '60–'68; 18 aws., Chgo. Bk. Clinic; two aws., AAUP; three aws., Tex. Inst. of Ltrs., '62, '63, '66; two aws., Western Bks., '66, '68; Mary Washington Col. of Univ. of Va., BA, '51; Univ. of Tex., '53–'55 (Art; Student Asst., '53–'55); b. Waco, Tex., 1930; p. F. Latham and Lillian Etchison Downs; res: 3717 Windsor Rd., Austin, Tex. 78703.

DOWNS, ROSALIND GERSON, Free-lance Wtr., Ed., Rschr., '68–; Wtr., Ed., U.S.I.A., Voice of Am., '66–'68; Rsch. Ed., TV Doc. Unit, Nat. Geog. Soc., '64–'65; Rsch. Ed., '62, '63; work for husband, CBS Corr. (Italy, Middle East, Germany, '53–'56; '48–'50); Program Wtr., news, CBS, '44–'47; AWRT, Intl. Bdcstrs. Soc.; Queens Col., '42–'44; U.S. Cadet Nurse, Mt. Sinai Hosp., '44; b. N.Y.C., 1926; p. Ephraim and Clara Millman Gerson; h. William Downs; c. William R. III, Karen Louise, Adam Michael; res: 5535 Warwick Pl., Chevy Chase, Md. 20015.

DOWNUM, EVELYN BENSON, Librn., University Elementary School of Northern Arizona University, Box 5712, Flagstaff, Ariz. 86001, '67–; '58–'66; Asst. Librn., '56–'59; Librn., Flagstaff Public Schs., '66–'67; Instr., Northern Ariz. Univ., '45, '65–, ALA, Ariz. State Lib. Assn., Kappa Delta Pi, Delta Kappa Gamma, Pi Lambda Theta, AAUW (Local Pres., State Treas., VP), Beta Sigma Phi (Pres.), Flagstaff Commty. Concert Assn. (Bd. of Dirs.), Northern Ariz. Soc. of Sci. and Art; Who's Who of Am. Wm., Who's Who in the West, Who's Who in Lib. Sci., Dic. of Intl. Biog.; Univ. of Ill., BA, '37 (cum laude); Univ. of Tex., MA, '41; b. Chgo., Ill., 1916; p. Arthur and Rose Anderson Benson; h. Garland Downum; c. Philip, Carolyn (Mrs. Larry White), Janice E.; res: 1609 N. Aztec St., Flagstaff, Ariz. 86001.

DOYLE, IRENE MAY, Emeritus Prof., University of

Wisconsin, 227 Langdon St., Madison, Wis. 53703, '67–; Dir., In-svc. Training, Univ. of Wis. Lib., '65–'67; Head, Catalog Dept., '41–'65; Visiting Instr., Univ. of Minn., '43; Univ. of Ill., '42; Univ. of N.C., '36; Head, Catalog Dept., Joint Univ. Libs., '37–'41; Assoc. Prof., Peabody Lib. Sch. (Nashville, Tenn.), '36–'41; Asst. Prof., '31–'36; lib. work, '29–'30; Tchr., '19–'29; Bibliographical Soc. of Am., ALA (VP, div. of cat., '42), AAUP; civic groups; Univ. of Ill., AB, '19 (Phi Beta Kappa, Kappa Delta Pi, Pi Gamma Mu, Beta Phi Mu, Theta Phi Alpha); MA, '24; BS (Lib. Sci.), '30; MS, '31 (Carnegie Fellow, '30–'31); b. Monticello, Ill., 1898; p. Martin and Anne Walsh Doyle.

DOYLE, PATRICIA JANSEN (Patricia Jansen), Educ. Ed., The Kansas City Star, 1729 Grand Ave., Kan. City, Mo. 64108, '62–; City Desk Reptr., Kan. City Times, '51–'62; articles, Saturday Rev.; Cnslt., appraisal of health, educ. and welfare in Pitt. for Health and Welfare Assn. of Allegheny County by Inst. for Commty. Studies, Inc., '68; Theta Sigma Phi (Col. Chptr. Pres., '51), Educ. Wtrs. Assn. (Secy.-Treas., '68; exec. comm.; top aw., news coverage, '66; European travel grant from assn. and Carnegie Corp., '66); AAUW (State Div. Bd., '67–'68; Kan. City Br. Pres., '63–'65); Avila Col. (Kan. City, Mo.), '47–'49; Univ. of Kan., BS (Jnlsm.), '51; Stanford Univ., Pfsnl. Jnlsm. Fellow, '68–'69; b. Kan. City, Mo., 1929; p. Dr. Robert and Marie Alexander Jansen; res: 410 E. 66th St., Kan. City, Mo. 64131.

DOZIER, KATHLEEN COWDREY, Wms. Ed., Springdale News, 133 W. Emma Ave., Springdale, Ark., 72764, '66–; Pine Bluff Commercial, '63–'66; Herald (Big Spring, Tex.), '60–'63; Northwest Ark. Times (Fayetteville), '50–'58; Alpha Delta Pi, Ark. Press Wm., NPWC; Penney-Univ. of Mo. Jnlsm. Aw., '63–'64; Ark. State Press Jnlsm. Aws., '68; 13 in '69; Springdale Fine Arts Assn. (Bd. Mbr.), United Cerebral Palsy (Bd. Mbr.), Hosp. Aux., Episcopal Wms. Guild; Lee Acad.; b. Yellville, Ark., 1918; p. Thurman and Alsey Berry Cowdrey; h. Edgar Dozier; c. Edgar W., Jr., Phillip C. Dozier, Mrs. Larry Giles, Mrs. Scottie Vibrock; res: 1012 Mayes Ave., Springdale, Ark. 72764.

DRAKE, DOROTHY M., Chief Librn., Prof., Scripps College, 10th & Columbia, Claremont, Cal. 91711, '38–; Head Librn., L.A. Sch. System, '25–'38; Acting Librn., Knox Col., '30–'31; organized Social Affairs Lib., UN, '49; Lib. Sch., U.C.L.A., Berkeley (Adv. Cncl., '58–'61); Univ. of Southern Cal. (Adv. Cncl., '61–'64); Cal. Lib. Assn. (Pres., '52), ALA (Cncl., '53–'56; '60–'64, '69–'72), Am. Col. Rsch. Librns., (Dir., '69–'72; Exec. Ed., '60–'64), AAUP, Delta Sigma Rho; Who's Who in Am.; Who's Who of Am. Wm.; Knox Col., BA, '25 (Phi Beta Kappa; Alumni Achiev. Aw., '50); Claremont Grad. Sch., MA, '47; b. Canton, Ill., 1904; p. Carl and Amanda Erickson Drake; res: 1030 N. College Ave., Claremont, Cal. 91711.

DRAKE, SARA ELIZABETH, Asst. Mgr. for Sch. Svcs., South Central Educational Broadcasting Council,

WITF-TV, Box Z, Hershey, Pa. 17033, '64–; Tchr., Teaching Prin., Elementary Supvsr., Camp Hill Sch. Dist., '46–'64; Off. Assigts., U.S. Air Force, '43–'46; Tchr: West Fairview, '41–'43; Halifax, '31–'41; Wiconisco, '28–'31; NEA, Pa. Educ. Assn., Delta Kappa Gamma (Kappa Chptr. Intl's. Pioneer Wm. of the Yr., '65), AWRT (Harrisburg Chptr. VP, '67–'69; Robert E. Eastman Aw. for Outstanding Wm. in Bdcst., Mid-East Area, '65), NAEB; NET Aw. for Individual Contrb. to Outstanding TV Programming, TV Series "Sons and Daughters," '68; Educ. Depts., Lutheran Ch; Shippensburg State Col., BS, '36; Pa. State; Lebanon Valley Col.; Univ. of Denver, '58; b. Harrisburg, Pa., 1908; p. William F. and Daisy Jury Drake; res: 214 W. Caracas Ave., Hershey, Pa. 17033.

DRAKE, VIVIAN LOUISE, Head, Regional Film Center, Carnegie Library of Pittsburgh, 4724 Baum Blvd., Pitt., Pa. 15213, '66–; Asst. Head, Catalogue Dept., '64–'66; Librn., Monessen (Pa.) Public Library, '57–'64; Head, Adult Svcs., Lucas County Library (Ohio), '52–'57; Head, Order Dept., Univ. of S. Ill., '50–'51; Acquisition Librn., Univ. of Cinn., '46–'50; Acquisitions Librn., Vassar Col., '43–'46; Asst. Librn., Bard Col., '42–'43; Asst., Periodicals, Serials Div., Cinn. Public Lib., '36–'40; ALA, Pa. Lib. Assn.; Miami (Oh.) Univ., BS (Educ.), '30; Columbia Univ., BS (Lib. Sci.), '42; Univ. of Mich., AMLS, '52; b. Hamersville, Oh., 1910; p. Albert and Lillie Boehm Drake; res: 5440 Fifth Ave., Apt. 11, Pitt., Pa. 15232.

DRALLE, ELIZABETH M., Free-lance Wtr.; Cnslt., Tchr., Hunter College; Designer, numerous cos.; Auth., "Angel in the Tower" (Ferrar, Straus); Indsl. Designers Inst. (former Nat. Secy.); educ: Pratt Inst.; Univ. of Colo.; N.Y.U.; N.Y. State Cols., Buffalo, Albany; b. Schenectady, N.Y., 1920; p. William and Elizabeth Brennan Dralle; res: 413 W. 21st St., N.Y., N.Y. 10011.

DREBERT, ELLEN CHRISTENSON, Prin. Librn., Ext. Div., San Diego Public Library, 820 E. St., San Diego, Cal. 92101, '52–; Head of Brs., '49–'52; Br. Librn., Logan Heights, '43–'48; Children's Librn., E. San Diego Br., '41–'43; Cal. Lib. Assn., ALA, Altrusa Club of the Heartland (Charter Mbr.; Past Treas., Rec. Secy., Corr. Secy.), Beta Phi Mu, Phi Kappa Phi, Pi Gamma Mu, Kappa Delta Pi, Alpha Sigma Alpha; b. Vancouver, B.C., Can. 1913; p. Lars and Kerstin Nilsson Christenson; h. Lynn C. Drebert; res: 425 Aldwych Rd., El Cajon, Cal. 92020.

DREIFUS, CLAUDIA, News Ed., East Village Other, 105 Second Ave., N.Y., N.Y. 10011, '69–; formerly Mng. Ed., Furniture Workers Press; Wtr., Organizer, Local 1199-Drug and Hosp. Union; Publicist, Nat. Comm. for a SANE Nuclear Policy; Prodr., bdcsts., news specials, WBAI; Contrbr., The Nation, Cavalier, New York Scenes, Esquire; Intl. Labor Press Svc. Best Feature Story Aw., '68; N.Y.U., BS, '66; b. N.Y.C., 1944; p. Henry and Mariannya Willdorff Dreifus; h.

Dr. Sidney Weinheimer; res: 158 Ninth Ave., N.Y., N.Y. 10011.

DRESBACH, BEVERLEY GITHENS, Lit. Critic, Eureka Springs Times-Echo, Eureka Springs, Ark; Auth./ Jnlst: "Novitiate" ('38), "No Splendor Perishes" (winner: Dierkes Press Aw., '45); Contrbr. numerous feature stories and poetry to Christian Science Monitor, N.Y. Times, St. Louis Post Dispatch, Arkansas Gazette, Christian Home, Ave Maria and others; Nat. Fedn. State Poetry Socs., Panama Canal Soc.; Numerous aws., incl. Rosa Zagnoni Marinoni Natl. Poetry Aw., '53; Poet of the Yr. Aw., Ark. Poetry Day, '68; Boyesen Sch., Chgo., '20; Univ. of Chgo., '27–'28; Sherwood Music Sch., '29–'30; b. Chgo., Ill., 1903; p. John and Elizabeth Barr Githens; h. Glenn Ward Dresbach (dec.); res: Bon Repos, Eureka Springs, Ark. 72632.

DRESSER, HELEN McCLOY, Auth: fiction, nonfiction, '38–; Pres., Torquil & Co., Publrs., '55–'65; London Corr., N.Y. Times, '30–'31; Paris Corr., Intl. Studio, '30–'31; OPC, MWA (Treas., '46–'47; Pres., '53–'54; Edgar Aw., '53); Sorbonne Univ. (Paris), '23–'24; b. Bklyn., N.Y., 1904; p. William and Helen Clarkson McCloy; h. Davis Dresser; c. Chloe (Mrs. Robert Johnson); res: 130 Bowdoin St., Boston, Mass. 02108.

DREW, DORIS GRUEN, Spokeswm., Ralph's Markets, L.A., Cal., '66–; Commls., on and off camera, '54–; Actress, Singer, Announcer; Radio, "Jack Carson Show," "Ernie Ford Show," "Johnnie Desmond-Doris Drew Show"; TV, "Ernie Ford," "Music Is My Beat," "Music for Fun"; AFTRA, SAG, AGUA, active in Dem. party; b. San Antonio, Tex., 1930; p. Henry and Elenora Donaldson Gruen; h. Larry Allen; c. Daniel, Gregory; res: 7059 Atoll Ave., N. Hollywood, Cal. 91605.

DREW, ELIZABETH B., Wash. Ed., The Atlantic Monthly, Room 722-A, 1028 Connecticut Ave. N.W., Wash., D.C. 20036, '68–; Wtr., non-fiction; Wellesley Col., '57 (Phi Beta Kappa); b. Cinn., Oh., 1935; p. William and Estelle Jacobs Brenner; h. J. Patterson Drew.

DREWELOW, GLADYS K., PR and Commcns. Admr., Compressor and Engine Div., Worthington Corp., P.O. Box 69, Clinton St. and Roberts Ave., Buffalo, N.Y. 14240; Employee and Commty. Rels. Dept., '49; PR Assn. of Western N.Y., Frontier Press Cl., Am. AIE, Niagara Frontier IEA (Pres., '66–'67), other orgs.; Who's Who of Am. Wm.; Jr. Achiev. Grand Aw.; numerous other aws.; Central Bus. Col.; b. Buffalo, N.Y.; p. Ernest and Orpha Stressinger Drewelow; res: 43 Lisbon Ave., Buffalo, N.Y. 14214.

DRIGGS, LOUISE RUST, Home Econs. Ed. and Cnslt., Harvest Years Magazine, 440 Gravatt Dr., Berkeley, Cal. 94705, '66–; Cnslt. to adv. agcys. and food co's. for recipes and pubcty., '49–; Cnslt., Spice Islands Co., '55–'62; Staff Ed., Homemakers' Bur.,

Safeway Stores, '44–'47; Lectr., Mills Col., '50–'51; articles in Rudder Magazine, Sunset Magazine, home econs. pubns., Spice Islands Cookbk. ('61); Home Econst. in Bus. (S.F. Chptr. Pres., '48–'49), Cal. Home Econs. Assn. (Bay Dist. Pres., '51–'52), Inst. Food Technologists, Cal. Wtrs. Club, Theta Sigma Phi; Univ. of Mo., BJ, '32; Kan. State Univ., BS, '33 (Home Econs.); N.Y.U., MS, '34 (Retail Mdsng.; Phi Kappa Phi, Omicron Nu); b. Many, La., 1912; p. Milburn and Lucile Osborn Rust; h. E. Ogden Driggs; c. James Ogden; res: 440 Gravatt Dr., Berkeley, Cal. 94705.

DRING, R. JOANNE SPONSLER, Sr. Assoc., The Public Relations Board, Inc., 75 E. Wacker Dr., Chgo., Ill. 60601, '66–; Asst. Dir. of Public Info., Am. Hosp. Assoc., '63–'66; Edtl. Asst., Business Week, '59–'63; Pubcty. Club of Chgo. (Golden Trumpet Aw., '68); Ill. Wesleyan Univ., BA, '59; h. Douglas E. Dring; res: 4112 W. 98th St., Oak Lawn, Ill. 60453.

DRISCOLL, LUCY VILLAROSA, Acc. Supvsr., Consumer Products, Zigman-Joseph Associates in Public Relations, 18 E. 41st St., N.Y., N.Y. 10017, '69–; AE-PR, MacManus, John & Adams, '64–'69; AE-PR, Hicks & Greist, '61–'64; Off./Adv. Prod. Mgr., Nat. Geographic, '57–'61; Dir. Wms. Activities for Dodge Div., Chrysler, Grant Advertising, '55–'57; Writer, monthly colm. for Sylvania Electric, '53; Press Mbr. Nat. Soc. of Interior Designers, NHFL, Electrical Wms. Round Table, AWNY, AWRT; N.Y.U., '46–'48; b. Montclair, N.J.; p. Nicholas and Angela Cudone Villarosa; res: 250 E. 39th St., N.Y., N.Y. 10017.

DROSSEL, MARGARET RALSTON, Mgr., News Bur., McGraw-Hill Publishing Co., 255 California St., S.F., Cal. 94111, '46–; Reptr., UP (Sacramento), '45–'46; Ia. State Univ., BS, '44 (Mortar Bd.; Phi Kappa Phi).

DROST, EDE HANSEN, VP, Air Check/Videochex, Naked City, Roselawn, Ind. 46372, '60–; Wtr., Poet; Pres., various charitable orgs.; b. Kotka, Finland, 1911; p. Frithjof and Sofia Nybom Hansen; h. Albin Drost; c. Dick; res: Naked City, Roselawn, Ind. 46372.

DROTAR, EVELYN BAILEY, Prod. Mgr., Wendt Advertising Agency, 747 Spitzer Bldg., Madison Ave., Toledo, Oh. 43604; Staff, '49–; Comml. Artist and Wtr., Radio, TV Commls.; nwsp., mag. adv.; b. Ann Arbor, Mich; p. Vern and Marie Smith Bailey; h. Stephen Drotar; res: 202 Kevin Pl., Toledo, Oh. 43610.

DRUCKER, TERRY, Admr., Sls. Dev. and Rsch., National Broadcasting Company, 30 Rockefeller Plaza, N.Y., N.Y. 10020, '67–; Dir. of Media Analysis, Gumbinner-North, '64–'67; Dir. of Radio Rsch., Adam Young Inc., '63–'64; Sr. Rsch. Analyst, Foote, Cone & Belding, Inc., '61–'63; Hunter Col., BA, (Deans List; Alumni Assn. Bd. Dirs., Asst. Treas., '69–'72); b. Phila., Pa.; p. Hyman and Fannie Rosen Drucker; res: 235 E. 22nd St., N.Y., N.Y. 10010.

DRUMMOND, ELLEN LANE, Auth., "Swallow Cliff"

('61); Co-Auth: "Chinaman's Chance" ('56), "Queen of the Dark Chamber" ('53); Missionary to China, Reformed Presbyterian Church, '46–'51; Un. Presbyterian Ch., '25–'46; Univ. of Mich., BA, '23; N.Y. Theological Seminary, '25; Merrill Palmer Sch. (Detroit), '43; Moore Art Inst., '53; b. Asbury Park, N.J., 1897; p. William James and Emma Lane Drummond; res: Presbyterian Home, Quarryville, Pa. 17566.

DRURY, MAXINE COLE, Wtr., children's bks.; Auth: "Danger Afloat" ('51), "Rosemont Riddle" ('53), "Marty and the Major" ('55), "George and the Long Rifle" ('57), "A Career for Carol" ('58), "Half a Team" ('60), "Glory for Gil" ('64), "To Dance, to Dream" ('65), "Liberty Boy" ('67); Auths. Guild; Ohio State Univ., '31–'35; b. Mt. Auburn, Ia., 1914; p. Spencer and Fern Kieffer Cole; h. John Drury; c. Donna Larson, Creighton; res: 24 Ridgeley St., Darien, Conn. 06820.

DRYER, ELLEN HUSER, Media Dir., W. B. Doner and Company, 1060 First National Bldg., Detroit, Mich. 48226, '52–; Media Dir., Century Advertising Agcy., '50–'52; Controller, '47–'50; Accountant, Monarch Mfg. Co., '45–'47; Intl., Sls. Dept., Micromatic Hone Corp., '41–'45; Wms. Adv. Club (Detroit, Mich.), AWRT; U.S.O. Jr. Hostesses (Dir.); Wayne State Univ., '39–'40; Valparaiso Univ., '40–'41; b. Detroit, Mich., 1916; p. Victor E. and Pearl E. Kaps Huser; h. Edward Thomas Dryer; res: 4714 Bedford Rd., Detroit, Mich. 48224.

DUBE, MARIANNE, Pres., Marianne Dube Assoc., '66–; Prom., Mdsng. Dir., MacManus, John & Adams, '51–'66; Fashion Group, NHFL; b. N. Anson, Me., 1914; p. Joseph and Thurza Williams Dube; h. (dec.); c. son; res: 123 E. 26th St., N.Y., N.Y. 10010.

Du BOIS, ISABEL C., Home Econs. Ed., Chicago Daily News, 401 N. Wabash Ave., Chgo., Ill. 60611, '50–; Dir. of Home Econs., Red Star Yeast and Products Co., '45–'50; cookbk., "Invitation to Cooking" ('58); Home Econs. in Bus. (Chgo. Group Pres., '58–'59), Am. Home Econs. Assn., Ill. Home Econs. Assn.; numerous aws. incl: Distg. Svc. Aw., Am. Dairy Assn., '53, '54, '55, '56; Top Aws., Vesta Aws. competition; other aws.; Milw.-Downer Col. (Milw., Wis.), BS (Foods, Nutrition); res: 5916 W. Wisconsin Ave., Wauwatosa, Wis. 53213.

DuBOSE, DOROTHY, Edtl. Dir., CCM Threshold Learning, Inc. and Teachers Publishing Corporation, 260 Heights Rd., Darien, Conn. 06820, '70–; Project Ed., Macmillan, '69–'70; Sr. Ed., New Dimensions in Education, '67–'69; Assoc. Ed., Macmillan, '65–'67; developed Elementary Edition of Scholastic Teacher, '63–'65; formerly Ed of The N.J. Education Journal and Tennessee Teacher; Outstanding Young Women of America, Contemporary Authors; Berry Col., BA (Eng. and Educ.); Columbia Univ., MA (Eng.); res: 44 Spicer Rd., Westport, Conn. 06880.

DuBROFF, PAULA COHEN, Asst. Ed., Newsweek Magazine, 444 Madison Ave., N.Y., N.Y. 10022, '66–; Rschr., Reptr., '61–'66; Douglas Col., AB, '61; b. N.Y.C., 1939; p. Louis and Selma Goldberg Cohen; h. Kenneth DuBroff; c. Cara Elizabeth; res: 240 W. 98th St., N.Y., N.Y. 10025.

DUCAS, DOROTHY, PR Cnslt., Communications, 240 E. 46th St., N.Y., N.Y. 10017, '60–; Dir. of PR, Nat. Cystic Fibrosis Fndn., '69–; Special Mag. Cnslt., Am. Museum of Natural History, '68–'69; Special Cnslt. to Surgeon Gen., U.S. Public Health Svc., '60–'68; Public Svc. Dir., Lobsenz Public Relations Co., '60–'68; PR Dir., The Nat. Fndn. for Infantile Paralysis, '49–'60; Chief, Mag. Bur., Off. of War Info., '42–'44; Free-lance Mag. Wtr., Non fiction Ed., McCall's Mag., Reptr., N.Y. Evening Post, N.Y. Herald Tribune, Intl. News Svc. and London Sun. Express; Auth., Modern Nursing; Co-auth., More House For Your Money; Dir., Nat. PR Cncl. for Health and Welfare Svcs.; PR Instr., N.Y.U.; Nat. League for Nursing, PRSA, OPC, WNPC, N.Y. Press Wms. Club, Theta Sigma Phi (Headliner Aw., '43); Columbia Sch. of Jnlsm., BL, '26, (Pulitzer Traveling Scholarship, '26); London Univ.; N.Y.U.; Columbia Univ.; b. N.Y.C., 1905; p. Charles and Doris Pottlitzer Ducas; h. James B. Herzog (dec.); c. John, Thomas; res: Spring St., S. Salem, N.Y. 10590.

DUCHEIN, ANNETTE OGDEN, VP, Dir. of Indsl. and PR, Spartan Mills and Southern Powell Corporation, Howard St., Spartanburg, S.C. 29301, '48–; Exec. Asst. to Pres., '43–'48; Indsl. Rels. Mgr., '39–'43; Lectr., La. State Univ., '35–'39; Asst. to Grad. Dean, '33–'35; Reptr., Feature Wtr., N.O. Times-Picayune, '29–'32; Feature Wtr., N.Y. Herald Tribune, '28; Am. Soc. for Pers. Adm. (Nat. Secy., '67; Nat PR Comm., '69–; Bd. Mbr., '69–'71), PRSA Am. Assoc. of Indsl. Nurses (Advisory Bd.), S.C. Indsl. Nurses Assn. (Advisory Bd.), S.C. Textile Mfrs. Assn. (Advisory Bd.), numerous other indsl. and commty. orgs.; Boss of the Yr., '63; La. State Univ., BA, '27; Columbia Univ., BJ, '29; La. State Univ., MJA, '33; b. Baton Rouge, La., 1907; p. Charles and Louisa Ogden Duchein; res: 2470 Old Knox Rd., Spartanburg, S.C. 29302.

DUCKWORTH, SARA ALLEN, Asst. Secy.-Treas. and Comptroller, Winter Haven Publishing Co., Inc., P.O. Box 1440, Winter Haven, Fla. 33880; nwsp. work, '57–; positions in citrus industry, '43–'57; Fla. Dept. of State Welfare, '41–'43; Intl. Inst. of Nwsp. Controllers and Fin. Offcrs., Special Aw. for assisting U.S. Savings Bonds program ('68); Winter Haven Bus. Col.; b. Hilton, Ga., 1916; p. Robert and Lollie Kennedy Allen; h. Fred Duckworth; c. James Allen Daniels, Clifford Lamar Daniels; res: 448 Ave. B, N.E., Winter Haven, Fla. 33880.

DUDLEY, TERRI CRAWFORD, Prom. Dir. and Asst. Ad Mgr., Valley News, Box #877, White River Jct., Vt. 05001, '65–; Asst. Ad Mgr., '64–; Ad Salesman, '59–'63; Classified Mgr., '57–'59; Draftsman, State Highway Off., '50–'52; active in civic groups, Dems.;

b. Lebanon, N.H., 1929; h. Roger Dudley; c. Sharon Lee Smardon, Michael, JoAnn; res: 89 South Main St., West Lebanon, N.H. 03784.

DUFFIELD, PAULINE, Librn., Texas Medical Association Memorial Library, 1801 N. Lamar Blvd., Austin, Tex. 78701, '52–; Med. and Chirurgical Fac. Med. Librn. (Balt., Md.), '45–'52; Asst. Librn., Vanderbilt Univ. Med. Sch. (Nashville, Tenn.), '44–'45; HS Librn., Parker Dist. (Greenville, S.C.), '41–'43; HS Librn. (Richwood, W. Va.), '36–'41; Cnslt., Austin State Hosp. Lib.; Med. Lib. Assn. (Treas., '54–'58), SLA, Tex. Med. Asst. Assn. (Hon. Mbr.), ZONTA (Austin); Chgo. Normal Sch. of Physical Educ., Dip., '29; George Peabody Col., BS (Physical Educ.), '36; BS (Lib. Sci.), '40; b. Sutton, W. Va., 1910; p. John and Mary Marlow Duffield; res: 1219 Castle Hill, Austin, Tex. 78703.

DUFFY, BEVERLEY HUDSON, Staff Wtr., Religious Ed., Cedar Rapids Gazette, 500 Third Ave. S.E., Cedar Rapids, Ia. 52406, '63–; Wms. Staff Wtr., Waterloo Daily Courier, '59–'63; Ia. AP Mng. Eds. Competition (3rd Place, Feature Div., '67), Alpha Lambda Delta; Univ. of Ia., '59–'60; Univ. of Northern Ia., '60–'62; b. Mt. Ayr, Ia., 1940; p. Robert and Ruth Busby Hudson; h. William Duffy; c. Mark Christopher; res: 400 Jacolyn Dr. N.W., Cedar Rapids, Ia. 52405.

DUFFY, CAROL CULLEN, Dir. of Pubcty., Dell Publishing Co. Inc., 750 Third Ave., N.Y., N.Y. 10017, '69–; Pubcty. Mgr., Harcourt, Brace & World, '66–'69; Pubcty. Assoc., Random House, '63–'66; Briarcliff Col., Assoc. in Sci., '58; b. Paterson, N.J., 1937; p. Vincent and Ruth Cullen Duffy; res: 140 E. 46th St., N.Y., N.Y. 10017.

DUFFY, DOROTHY BOTTOM, Free-lance Ed., Reviewer, 120 W. 70th St., N.Y., N.Y. 10023; Non-fiction Trade Ed., Charles Scribner's Sons; Edtl. Asst., R. R. Bowker; Sweet Briar Col., BA, '49; grad. study; b. Newport News, Va., 1928; p. Raymond B. and Dorothy Rouse Bottom; h. John Charles Duffy; c. Mark Whitney Gilkey.

DUFFY, FRANCES H., Off. Mgr., X-TRA/KOST Radio, 5670 Wilshire Blvd., Suite 940, L.A., Cal. 90036, '67–; X-TRA News, '66–'67; Asst. Dir., U.S.O., '42–'43; AWRT; Valley Col. (Music), '63–'65; b. Wood Ridge, N.J., 1921; p. Arthur and Frances Rapp Heinrichs; h. Matthew Duffy; c. Michael, Patrick, Terrence, Daniel; res: 16452 Moorpark St., Encino, Cal. 91316.

DUFFY, HELENE K., VP, Carter H. Golembe Associates, Inc., 270 Madison Ave., N.Y., N.Y. 10016, '68–; Secy., Banking Educ. Comm., '61–'68; Am. Bankers Assn., '55–'59; Econst., N.Y. Stock Exchange, '59–'61; N.Y.C. Tax Fndn., '52–'55; Colmst., Banking Magazine, '59–'68; Lectr., Queens Col.; Co-auth., "Forecasting Business Conditions;" N.Y. Reg. Cncl./Industry Educ. Coop. (Secy., '67; VP, '68); Univ. of Ill., BA, '48; b. Chgo., Ill., 1926; h. Robert Duffy; c. Robert Franklin; res: 321 Ave. C., N.Y., N.Y. 10009.

DUFOUR, JEANNE HANKINS, VP, Dufour Editions, Inc., Chester Springs, Pa. 19425, '65–; Secy., Publicist, '54–'64; Copywtr., J. F. Arndt Adv. Agcy., '53; Retail Copywtr., John Wanamaker's (Phila.), '51–'52; Nat. Bk. League, Wms. Nat. Bk. Assn., Children's Bk. Cncl., PPA; Gettysburg Col., BA, '50; b. Princess Anne, Md., 1929; p. James and Helen Beahler Hankins; h. Paul Dufour; c. Jeanne Louise, Kristin Elizabeth, David E., Jonathan P., Anthony P.; res: Conestoga Rd., Chester Springs, Pa. 19425.

DUGAN, GRETTA CHEATHAM, Tchr., Broken Arrow Public Schools, 117 W. Commercial, Broken Arrow, Okla. 74012, '55–; Broken Arrow BPW (Pres., '64–'65; VP, '63), Theta Sigma Phi, Phi Upsilon Omicron, Kappa Phi, Pi Zeta Kappa; Okla. State Univ., BS, '55; b. Mt. Judea, Ark., 1934; p. Archie and Velma Pruitt Cheatham; h. Kenneth Dugan; c. Constance Denise, Karen Lynn, Katherine Kellie; res: 9901 S. Lynn Lane Rd., Broken Arrow, Okla. 74012.

DUHAMEL, HELEN SEIDELL, Press., Gen. Mgr., Duhamel Broadcasting Enterprises, Duhamel Bldg., Sixth and St. Joe Sts., Rapid City, S.D. 57701, '54–; Mgr., Duhamel Co. Bldg., '37–; Owner, Duhamel's store, '37–; Mgr., '37–'57; Pres., Dir., Black Hills Bdcst. of Neb., '56–; Dir., Radio Station, '44–'54; Dir., Treas., Rushmore Ins. Co. (Rapid City, S.D.), '48–'60; ZONTA (Charter Mbr.), Bdcst. Pioneers, Radio & TV Industry (N.Y.C.), AWRT; Herbert Hoover Aw., Nat. Boy's Club, '66; Boss of Yr. Aw., first time given to wm., Jr. C. of C., "Boss of the Year Aw." '65; aw., person doing most for Big Brothers, '67; NAB Ambassador, to S.A., '62; Bus. Col. (Rapid City, S.D.); b. Windsor, Mo., 1914; p. Wm. F. and Mae F. Reilly Seidell; h. Francis Duhamel; c. Mrs. John N. Heffron, Mrs. Ted Tarrant, Dr. Wm. F., Dr. Peter A.; res: 307 St. Charles St., Rapid City, S.D. 57701.

DUHON, HELEN BLOEDORN, Wtr., The Colorado Alumnus, University of Colorado, Koenig Alumni Ctr., Boulder, Colo. 80302, '68–; Nwsltr. Ed., '66–'68; Nwsltr. Ed., Am. Alumni Cncl. Dist. VII, '67–'69; Theta Sigma Phi, Delta Delta Delta (VP, '57–'58); Sigma Delta Chi Scholarship Cit., '38; Univ. of Colo., BA, '38; b. Franklin, Neb., 1915; p. Charles and Zoe Schrock Bloedorn; h. S. C. Duhon (div.); c. Joan (Mrs. Richard Dana), Annette (Mrs. Robert Fenner), Sam C., Jr.; res: 675 Cascade Ave., Boulder, Colo. 80302.

Du JEAN, RENEE, Asst. Dir., Black Executive Exchange Program, Ed. of BEEP, National Urban League, Inc., 55 E. 52nd, N.Y., N.Y. 10022, '69; Asst. to Pres., Chester Burger & Co., Inc., 275 Madison Ave., N.Y., N.Y. 10016, '68–'69; Exec. Secy., '66–'68; Wtr., Press Rep., Elegant mag., Elegant Publ. Co., '66–'68; Edtl. Asst., Ebony, also Jet, Johnson Publ. Co., '63–'64; NAMW (N.Y. Chptr. PR Chmn., '68–), NATAS, Nat. Assn. of Negro Bus. and Pfsnl. Wm., Home for the Aged Svc. Aw. ('57), St. Augustine's P.E. Ch. (Pubcty.-Prom. Commn.; Ed., Involved, nwsltr.,), Pubcty. Club of N.Y. (Cert., '68), Bklyn. Urban League (Wms. Div.);

City Col. of N.Y., '63–'65; Manhattan Commty. Col. (NUL Secretarial Scholarship Program); b. Vidalia, Ga., 1935; p. Hosea and Eva McLendon Johnson; res: 456 Bklyn. Ave., Bklyn, N.Y. 11225.

DUKE, JUDITH SILVERMAN, Asst. to Dir. of Mkt. Dev., Life Magazine, Time, Inc., Rockefeller Ctr., N.Y., N.Y. 10020, '67–; Rsch. Analyst, Life mag., '60–'67; Rsch. Analyst, Statistician; Nat. Assn. of Footwear Manufacturers, '56–'59; Rsch. Analyst, Boni, Watkins & Jason, '55; Am. Mktng. Assn., AWNY; Univ. of Mich., '51–'53; Cornell Univ., BA (Econs.), '55 (Phi Beta Kappa; Phi Kappa Phi); b. Portchester, N.Y., 1934; p. Herbert and Fannye Cohen Silverman; h. Alan Duke; res: 9727 Mt. Pisgah Rd., Silver Spring, Md. 20903.

DUKERT, BETTY COLE, Assoc. Prodr., "Meet the Press," NBC News, H-228, Sheraton Park Hotel, Washington, D.C. 20008, '57–; Prod. Asst., WRC/WRC-TV, '52–'56; Adm. Asst., Greene County (Mo.) Juv. Ct., '50–'52; Traf. Mgr., KICK (Springfield, Mo.), '49–'50; AWRT, ANWC, WNPC, RTCA; Univ. of Mo., BJ, '49 (Alumnae Aw., '68); b. Muskogee, Okla.; p. Irvan and Ione Bowman Cole; h. Joseph M. Dukert; res: 4709 Crescent St., Washington, D.C. 20016.

DUKES, EVA ALTMAN, Exec. Ed., Encyclopedia of Food and Food Science, Interscience Div., John Wiley & Sons, Inc., 605 Third Ave., N.Y., N.Y. 10016, '69–; Assoc. Ed., Kirk-Othmer Ency. of Chemical Tech., second edition, '59–'69; Tech. Wtr., Gen. Aniline & Film Corp., '51–'59; Asst. Perfumer, de Laire div. Dodge & Olcott, '49–'51; Henri Robert, Inc., '46–'49; Lab. Asst., Columbia Col. of Physicians and Surgeons, '45–'46; wtr., article and translations, Am. Dyestuff Reptr.; Soc. of Tech. Wtrs. and Publrs., Nat. Assn. of Bk. Eds., Nat. Assn. of Sci. Wtrs., Inc., scientific orgs.; Hunter Col., BA (Chemistry), '45; grad. work, Columbia Univ., '46; b. Vienna, Austria, 1923; p. Heinrich and Theresa Braun Altmann; h. Paul Dukes; c. Gary; res: 330 E. 33rd St., N.Y., N.Y. 10016.

DULEY, PAT, VP, Off. Opns., Benton & Bowles, Inc., 909 Third Ave., N.Y., N.Y. 10022, '59–; Purchasing Mgr., Adm. Asst.; AWNY, Adm. Mgt. Soc., Adv. Agcy. Off. Mgt. Assn. (Past Pres.); N.Y.U.; b. Bklyn., N.Y., 1924; p. Paul and Ethel Duley; h. Robert Masterson; res: 10 Kingsbury Rd., Garden City, N.Y. 11530.

DULLES, ELEANOR LANSING, Prof., Georgetown Univ., Wash., D.C., '63–; Stanford, '67–'68; Ctr. for Strategic Studies, '64–'67; Duke Univ., '62–'63; Dept. of State, '42–'62; Chief, Fin. Div., Social Security Bd., '36–'42; Rsch. Assoc., Tchr: Univ. of Pa., Wharton Sch., '32–'36; Bryn Mawr Col., '28–'30, '32–'36; Simmons Col., '24–'25; Rsch. Assoc., Harvard and Radcliffe Bur. of Rsch: Paris, '25–'27; Basle, Switzerland, '30–'32; Indsl. Mgt., '20–'21; relief work, Am. Friends Svc., France, '17–'19; Auth: "One Germany or Two? the Struggle at the Heart of Europe" (The Hoover Inst., forthcoming), bks. on econ. and intl. affairs;

Cosmopolitan Club (N.Y.C.), The Intl. Club (Wash., D.C.), PEN, Am. Econ. Assn., Polit. Sci. Assn., Fed. Republic of Germany (Grand Cross of Merit, '60), World Affairs Cncl. (Cal.), City of Berlin (Carl Schurz Plaque, '58; Ernst Reuter Plaque, '59); Bryn Mawr, AB, '12; MA, '20; Radcliffe, MA, '24; PhD, '26; London Sch. of Econs.; Fac. de Droit, Univ. of Paris; Hon. Degrees: Wilson Col., Western Col., Mt. Holyoke, Free Univ. of Berlin; b. Watertown, N.Y., 1895; p. Allen and Edith Foster Dulles; h. (dec.); c. David Dulles, Ann Dulles Joor; res: 1114 Spring Hill Rd., McLean, Va. 22101.

DUMBAULD, BETTY E., Head Librn., J. Walter Thompson Company, 875 N. Michigan Ave., Chgo., Ill. 60611, '68–; Needham, Harper & Steers, '55–'68; Meredith Publ. Co., '46–'55; Denison Univ., '40–'45; Special Libs. Assn., Ill. Lib. Assn., Alpha Omicron Pi; Simmons Col., BS, '39; b. Bklyn, Ia.; p. James and Vada Beery Dumbauld; res: 1255 N. Sandburg Terr., Chgo., Ill. 60610.

DUNCAN, ARDINELLE BEAN, Free-lance Wtr., Lectr., bk. revs.; Auth., children's bk., "Twirly Hurly, The Helicopter Rabbit" (Wake-Brook House), '62); Radio Talent, "The Talk of the Town," WFIN AM-FM (Findlay, Oh.), '69–; Ed., Fla. Keys News (Homestead, Fla.), '57–'58; edtl. staff, Broadcasting Magazine (Wash., D.C.), '47–'50; TV Digest FM Reports, '46–'47; FBI, '43–'46; Rsch. Librn., Abitibi Power and Paper Co., '30–'32; NLAPW (Coral Gables Br. Secy.), '62–'63; Nwsltr. Ed., '59), Intl. Platform Assn.; The 2,000 Wm. of Achiev.; Iroquois Falls Collegiate (Iroquois Falls, Ontario); b. Berlin, N.H.; p. Sylvester J. and Mary Ellen Connors Bean; h. Robert Duncan; c. Carole (Mrs. D. B. Weimer), Robert Leon Jr., Jamie B.; res: RD# 3, Bloomsburg, Pa. 17815.

DUNCAN, PAMELA RITA, Actress, c/o Leon O. Lance, 8961 Sunset Blvd., L.A., Cal. 90069; AMPAS, NATAS, AWRT, Adv. Club of N.Y.; Hollywood Deb Star, '59–'60; Who's Who of Am. Wm.

DUNCAN, VIRGINIA BAUER, Prodr.-Dir., KQED-TV, 525 Fourth St., S.F., Cal. 94107, '61–; Reader's Digest Fndn. Educ. TV aw., '69; Assn. of Catholic Newsmen Edward V. McQuade Aw.; NET Aw., '66; Univ. of Mich., BA, '51; b. Lansing, Mich., 1929; p. Theodore and Maureen Foote Bauer; h. Bruce Duncan; c. John C., Michael G., Timothy B.; res: 3864 Jackson St., S.F., Cal. 94118.

DUNHAM, PHYLLIS LORENA, Dir. of Lib., Adams State College, Alamosa, Colo. 81101, '54–; Asst. Librn., '49–'54; docs. div., Univ. of Colo., '48–'49; docs., acquisitions, Univ. of Mo., '44–'48; Ia. State Univ. (Ames, Ia.), '40–'41; Translator (San Antonio, Tex.), '42–'43; ALA, Colo. Lib. Assn. (Treas.), AAUW, AAUP; Alpha Zeta Pi, Kappa Delta Pi, Sigma Epsilon Sigma, Delta Kappa Gamma, P.E.O.; Univ. of Colo. (Boulder), BA, '31 (Phi Beta Kappa); MA, '32; Univ. of Denver, BS (Lib. Sci.), '41; b. Boulder, Colo., 1909; p. Clifford and Lillian Shackelton Dunham; res: 1424 Second St., Alamosa, Colo. 81101.

DUNKELBURG, BARBARA ROBERTS, Educ. Wtr., Walla Walla Union-Bulletin, First and Poplar, Walla Walla, Wash. 99362, '65–; Asst. Wm's Ed., '58–'64; Ed., Rose City Herald (Portland, Ore.), '48; Miller-Freeman Pubns. (Portland), '47; Wm.'s Dept., Yakima Republic, '46; News Ed., Baker (Ore.) Dem.-Herald, '44–'46; City Ed., '42–'44; Theta Sigma Phi, EWA; Univ. of Ore., BA, '42; b. Walla Walla, Wash., 1921; p. George Roberts and Thelma Lasater Roberts Hahn; h. Gail Dunkelburg; c. David, Barbara, Christy, Steven, Mrs. Carl Banks, Mrs. John Blom; res: Route 3, Box 235A, Walla Walla, Wash. 99362.

DUNLAP, MARTHA, PR Cnslt., '67–; Exec. Dir., Nat. Truck Leasing System, '44–'67; Ed., Furniture Warehouseman, '34–'44; Asst. Dir. of PR, Pure Milk Assn., '32–'34; Wms. Adv. Club of Chgo. (Past Dir.), PRSA, Theta Sigma Phi, Am. Trucking Assn., Nat. Safety Cncl., Art Inst. of Chgo., Alpha Chi Omega, Chgo. Cncl. of Fgn. Rels., Japan-Am. Soc. of Chgo., numerous other orgs.; Bobit Publ. Co. Aw. for Outstanding Svc. in Leasing, '68; Who's Who of Am. Wm., Who's Who in Bus. and Industry; Univ. of Mont., BA (Jnlsm.); b. Hankinson, N.D., 1911; p. Willis and Ida Gordon Dunlap; h. (div.); c. Martha Moore (Mrs. Joseph A. Day); res: 2317 Geneva Terr., Apt. D, Chgo., Ill. 60614.

DUNLEVY, PATRICIA CASEY, Exec. VP, Gen. Mgr., Howard Parish Asso., Inc., 1345 E. 10th Ave., Hialeah, Fla. 33010, '67–; Exec. VP, '62–'67; Dir.; VP, '61–'62; Asst. to Exec. VP, '60–'61; Classified Adv. Sls. Mgr., automotive adv., Waterloo (Ia.) Daily Courier, '58–'60; Classified Acc. Rep., '50–'58; Cnslt.; Speaker; AFA, Nat. Nwsp. Prom. Assn., Assn. Nwsp. Classified Adv. Mgrs., other pfsnl. groups; named one of S. Fla.'s top 10 bus. wm., '66; State Col. Ia., '45–'48; b. Iowa City, Ia., 1927; p. Lawrence E. and Lucretia Faber Casey; h. Bill Winslow Dunlevy (div.); c. Casey James, Riley Patrick, Bill Michael, Matthew Lawrence; res: 8360 S.W. 184th Lane, Miami, Fla. 33157.

DUNN, HELEN EULALIA, Dir., PR, Greater Toledo Area Chapter, American Red Cross, 2205 Collingwood Blvd., Toledo, Oh. 43620, '57–; Soc. and Wms. Pg. Ed., Toledo Blade, '42–'57; Dir., PR, Lucas County Civilian Defense, '41–'42; Wtr., Fund Campaign Publicist, Toledo Commty. Chest, '38–'41; Owner, PR firm; Instr. in jnlsm., PR, feature writing, Univ. of Toledo, '56–'58; several short stories and features published; Wms. Adv. Club of Toledo (Pres. '49–'50, '58–'59; First VP, '48–'49; Second VP, '47–'48; Public Svc. Aw. for news coverage, '60; scholarship, '36), PRSA (NW Oh. Chptr. Secy., '63–'64); Oh. Nwsp. Wms. Aws: Best Sun. Sec., Best Feature Stories, Best Makeup, '51–'56; Univ. of Toledo, BA, '30; b. Holland, Oh., 1908; p. Patrick and Philomena Champion Dunn; res: 208 Maumee St., Holland, Oh. 43528.

DUNNAM, INA McCLELLAND, Pubns. Dir., Ed., TRACE Magazine, Teledyne Exploration Company, P.O. Box 36269, Houston, Tex. 77036, '68–; Interior Decorator, Mak's Designs (own Co.); Auth. of children's bks.; Designer, children's dresses; Artist; Exec. Secy., KHTV, 2 yrs.; AWRT, ICIE, Southwest Tex. Cncl. Indsl. Eds.; Detroit Conservatory of Music; Univ. of Mich.; Chgo. Inst. of Interior Design; b. Detroit, Mich., 1932; p. William and Ina Koski McClelland; c. Sherry Lynn, Sandra Liane, Edwin Earl II; res: 12326 Woodthorpe Lane, Houston, Tex. 77024.

DUNNE, ELIZABETH KELLOGG, Chief, Cataloging Div., U.S. Copyright Office, Library of Congress, Wash., D.C. 20540, '68–; Asst. Chief, '66–'67; Sec. Head, '61–'66, '51–'57; Rsch. Analyst, '57–'61; Cataloger, '46–'51; Cataloger, Hunter Col., '42–'46; Mng. Ed., Educ. Index, '39–'42; Auth: "Deposit of Copyrighted Works" ('60); with J. W. Rogers, "Catalog of Copyright Entries"; ALA, D.C. Lib. Assn.; Conn. Col. for Wm., '27–'29; N.Y.U., BA, '39 (cum laude); Columbia Univ. Sch. of Lib. Svc., BLS, '42 (with hons.); b. Orange, Mass., 1910; p. Nathaniel P. and Nellie Lewis Kellogg; h. James Dunne; res: 1734 P St. N.W., Wash., D.C. 20036.

DUNNE, FAITH RUBINOW, Exec. VP, Dunne and Associates, Inc., 2975 Wilshire Blvd., L.A., Cal. 90005, '59–; Pres., Idea Mart, '57–'59; Asst. to Pres., Aseptic-Thermo Indicator, '56–'57; Mgr., Special Svc. Dept., Heli-Coil, '53–'56; Adv. Asst., '51–'56; NIAA (L.A. Chptr. Exec Secy., '62–'68; Distg. Svc. Aws., '65–'68), Adv. Club of L.A.; Who's Who of Am. Wm., Who's Who in the West, Dic. of Intl. Biog.; Booth and Bayliss Bus. Sch., BA, '53; b. N.Y.C., 1933; p. Howard and Ruth Brown Rubinow; h. Fred J. Dunne; c. John Bruce, Robert Frederick, Laurie Ann, Bonnie Jean; res: 3541 N. Chaparro Rd., Covina, Cal. 91722.

DUNNIGAN, ALICE ALLISON, Edtl. Asst., President's Council on Youth Opportunity, 801 19th St. N.W., Wash., D.C. 20006, '67–; Info. Specialist, U.S. Dept. of Labor, '66–'67; Educ. Cnslt., President's Committee on Equal Employment Opportunity, '61–'65; Chief, Wash. Bur., Assoc. Negro Press, '47–'61; Econst., Off. of Price Adm., '44–'47; Statistician, War Labor Bd., '42–'44; Public Sch. Tchr.; Colmst., Ky. nwsprs.; Contrb. Ed., Sepia Magazine; WNPC ('54), Capital Press Club ('47), Intl. Platform Assn. ('65), Tongue and Quill Soc. ('68); Honneur et Merit Aw. (Republic of Haiti, '59), "Ky. Colonel" Commn., '62; Gtr. L.A. Press Club, '62 Negro Press Aw.; Capital Press Club, Newsmen's Newsman Trophy '51; Ky. State Col., Frankfort; W. Ky. Indsl. Col., Paducah; Tenn. A. & I. State Univ., Nashville; Howard Univ.; b. Russellville, Ky. 1906; p. Willie and Lena Pittman Allison; h. Charles Dunnigan; c. Robert William; res: 1462 Ogden St. N.W., Wash., D.C. 20010.

DUNNING, VIRGINIA TEIGELER, Ed., Laurentis Publishing Corp., 6123 Vineland, N. Hollywood, Cal.

91606; Assoc. Program Dir., KSFO, '41–'45; Wtr. non-fiction, MGM, '38–; NBC, '40–; Fashion Coordr.-wtr., '50s–'60s; b. S.F., Cal., 1919; p. Herman and Julia Hardwick Teigeler; h. Harlan Dunning (div.); c. Gene H.; res: 4221 Longridge Ave., Apt. 2, Studio City, Cal. 91604.

DUNPHY, LEILA HANSSON, Owner, Northwest Advertising Agency, 419 Wheeler St., Seattle, Wash. 98109, '59–; AE, Media Mgr., Prod. Mgr., Office Mgr., Taskett Agency, Copywtr., Cole & Weber; Public Info. Asst., Seattle Transit System; Free-lance Wtr: "Success Story" TV program, Sunset Magazine, Seattle Times, Seattle Post-Intelligencer, trade pubns.; Pacific N.W. Indsl. Ed. Assn. (Pres., '61; Edtl. Orchids, '58, '59, '61, '63, '64, '66, '67), AWRT, NATAS, Wash. Press Wm. (Aw., '61, '68), NFPW, ICIE (Aw. of Excellence, '57, '58, '59, '60, '61, '65), Pacific Intermountain Communicators Assn. (Aw. of Excellence, '61), Seattle Copy Club (Radio Writing and TV Adv. Aws., '63), L.A. Adv. Wm. (PR Cert. of Merit, '65; Campaign Aw., '66); Univ. of Wash., '54–'56; b. Seattle, Wash., 1920; p. Captain Rudolph and Lilly Miller Hansson; h. (dec.); c. Kurtis, Lawrence; res: 419 Wheeler St., Seattle, Wash. 98109.

DUNWIDDIE, CHARLOTTE, Sculptor, 35 E. Ninth St., N.Y., N.Y. 10003; three one-wm. shows; numerous exhbns., '40–'66; work in public places in Argentina, Peru, Bolivia, Italy, Wash., D.C., N.Y., Conn., and many private cols.; numerous orgs. and aws.; Bus. Col., Duesseldorf, Germany; Acad. of Art, Berlin; private art studies in Spain and Argentina; b. Strasbourg, France, 1907.

DURAN, JUNE CLARK, Asst. VP, CTB, Division of McGraw-Hill Book Company, Del Monte Research Park, Monterey, Cal. 93940, '65–; Adm. VP, '59–'65; Dir. of Opns., '55–'59; Secy.-Treas., Clark Dev. Corp., '60–'65; Off. Mgr., Cal. Test Bur., '49–'55; Am. Pers. & Guidance Assn., Cal. Educ. Rsch. Assn., Soc. for Advancement of Mgt. (Dir., '56–'59; VP, '59–'60); U.C.L.A., '37–'39; Univ. of Southern Cal., BA, '49; Grad. Work, '53; b. L.A., Cal., 1919; p. Willis and Ethel King Clark; h. Frank M. Duran; c. Timothy Clark, Patricia Ellen; res: 6 Cielo Vista Pl., Monterey, Cal. 93940.

DURBIN, MARY VAN HORN, Ed.-Co-publr., The Brockway Record, 516-20 Main St., Brockway, Pa. 15824, '46–; Brockwayville Publ., Inc.; Bookkeeper-Reptr., '26; Pa. Nwsp. Publrs. Assn., Pa. Soc. of Nwsp. Eds. (1st wm. elected Dir. of Soc.; 1st wm. State Treas., Secy., '57–'58), Pa. WPA; DuBois Bus. Col., '26; Pa. State Col., '44; b. Punxsutawney, Pa., 1907; p. Harry E. and Edna Leola McMinn Van Horn; h. Ralph E. Durbin; c. Keith E. Edward; res: 1108 Pershing Ave., Brockway, Pa. 15824.

DURHAM, DOROTHY MAY, Wms. Ed., Elwood Call-Leader, 317 S. Anderson St., Elwood, Ind., 46036, '44–; City News Desk; Area News; Circ., Classified Adv. Mgr.; Wms. Press Club of Ind. (Treas., past

Pres.), Theta Sigma Phi (past Pres.), Indpls. Press Club, Elwood C. of C., Kappa Delta Phi (past Pres., Secy.), Ind. Fed. of Clubs, numerous civic orgs.; b. Elwood, Ind., 1908; p. David and Lenora Gavin Durham; res: 1635-1/2 South A. St., Elwood, Ind. 46036.

DURHAM, MAGI COMPTON, Exec. Prodr., Telpac Management Inc., 777 Third Ave., N.Y., N.Y. 10017, '69–; Prodr., Jack Tinker & Partners, '66–'69; Assoc. Prodr., Grey Adv., '64–'66; film making, England; Aws: TV Comml. Festival Recognition Overall Campaign, '68; CA Magazine Aw. of Merit and Aw. of Excellence, '67; Southend Municipal Col. (Eng.); b. London, Eng., 1937; p. John and Amelia Dorras Compton; h. Guy Durham; res: 25 Bethune St., N.Y., N.Y. 10014.

DURHAM, MARY JOINES, Acquisitions Librn., Valdosta State College Library, Valdosta, Ga. 31601, '68–; Librn., Norman Col., '56–'68; Instr., Children's Literature, '60–'65; Visiting Tchr. (Camilla, Ga.), '45–'46; Instr., Lib. Sci., Tift Col., '42–'46; Asst. Librn., '42–'44; ALA, Southeastern Lib. Assn., Ga. Lib. Assn., Delta Kappa Gamma, Beta Phi Mu, Who's Who of Am. Wm., Who's Who in Am. Educ.; Tift Col., BA, '38; Fla. State Univ. MALS, '59; b. Sale City, Ga., 1921; p. James and Dita Saunders Joines; c. Beth, James Samuel; res: 2207 Park Lane, Valdosta, Ga. 31601.

DURKIN, MARY LUCILE, Chief Librn., United States Army, U.S. Army Aviation Sch., Bldgs. 5906 & 5907, Ft. Rucker, Ala. 36360, '59–; Dir., U.S.I.A. Libs. (Egypt, Morocco, Greece), '48–'58; lib. work; Red Cross (Europe), '44–'45; Supvsr., Sch. Libs., Chattanooga (Tenn.) City Sch. System, and city, county Negro Br. libs., '42–'44; Dist. Supvsr., U.S. Govt. Program, '41–'42; Sch. Librn., County Field Librn., '36–'41; writing program, U.S.I.A., '58–'63; Adult Educ. Assn., Special Lib. Assn., Pi Lambda Theta, Sigma Delta Pi, AAUW; Simmons Col. (Boston), BS, '36; Univ. Chattanooga, BA, '44; Columbia Univ. (N.Y.C.), MA, '55; Univ. of Mich., '67, '68; b. Battle Creek, Mich.; p. James H. and Ella M. Durkin; res: 207 Westview Dr., Enterprise, Ala. 36330.

DURKIN, MOLLIE ROCHE, Dir. of Commty. Involvement, WPHL-TV, 1529 Walnut St., Phila., Pa. 19103; Prom. Dir., '68–'69; Dir. of Radio, TV, Gann-Dawson Advertising (Scranton, Pa.), '57–'68; Cont. Dir., WNEP-TV, '55–'57; AWRT (Chptr. Pres.), '66; Phila. Chptr. Bd. Dirs., '69); Am. TV Commls. Festival Aw., '66; Marywood Col., BA (Eng.), '54 (Guest Lectr.); Univ. of Scranton (Guest Lectr.), Wilkes Col.; b. Scranton, Pa., 1932; p. Frank J. and Marian Miller Roche; h. Thomas Durkin; c. Colleen, Michael, Meg; res: 112 W. College Ave., Flourtown, Pa. 19031.

DURR, JOAN, Assoc. Prodr., Muller, Jordan, Herrick Inc., 666 Fifth Ave., N.Y., N.Y. 10019, '69–; Casting Dir., Daniel & Charles, '67–'69; Prod. Asst., McCann-Erickson, '67; Dir., "The Room Upstairs" (Golden Age Group), '68; Instr., Weist-Barron TV Comml. Classes,

'68; actress, singer, dancer; AEA, SAG, AFTRA, AGVA, NATAS, Theta Alpha Phi, Phi Sigma Iota; Otterbein Col., BA (Psych., Sociol.), '58; Stella Adler, '59–'62; b. Wash., D.C., 1936; p. Frank and Margaret Gottman Durr; res: 155 E. 38th St., N.Y., N.Y. 10016.

DUSAY, MARJ MAHONEY, Actress (Agt: Abrams-Rubglott & Assoc.); Nat. TV Commls., guest leads, TV Series Shows, movies; L.A. County Art Museum, Synonan; Univ. of Kan.; b. Hays, Kan., 1940; p. Joe and Marie Pivonka Mahoney; h. (div.); c. Debra, Randall, res: 1315 Malcolm Ave., L.A., Cal. 90024.

DUTCHER, VIRGINIA BOYD, Wtr., The Pitluk Group, 100 Richmond by the River, San Antonio, Tex. 78205, '68–; Prom. Mgr., KENS-TV, '65–'68; Radio-TV Dir., Aylin Adv., '62–'65; Owner, Publr., Alamo Heights News, '60–'62; PR, Rsch. Wtg., Assn. for Retarded Children; Wtr., audio-visual presentation for C. of C. Tourism; Theta Sigma Phi (VP, '68–'69), AWRT, San Antonio Adv. Club; Univ. of Tex., BA, '52; b. Berryville, Ark., 1930; p. Bennett and Hettye McGee Boyd; h. Harold W. Dutcher, Jr.; c. Derek Boyd, Harold W. III, Debbie L.; res: 118 Covina, San Antonio, Tex. 78218.

DUTHIE, (DECKER) HERMINE J., Chmn., Drama and Speech, Clark College, 1800 McLaughlin Blvd., Vancouver, Wash. 98660, '50–; Tchr., Syracuse Univ., '30–'32; Free-lance Wtr., '30–; Playwright, plays published, on radio, prod., '30–; Wtr., Prod., KVOS, '32; Old Slocum House Theatre Co. (Pres., '65–), Soroptomists, Theta Sigma Phi, Assoc. Collegiate Players (Nat. Pres., '62–'68), aws: Dramatists Alliance ('46), Kanawaha Playwriting ('64), Portland Civic ('56), N. W. Wtrs. ('68), Sacramento State Col. Playwriting ('68); b. Pullman, Wash., 1908; p. John and Ida Gibson Duthie; c. Aletha Hermine Carlton, Tamara Maureen Noble; res: 801 W. 45th St., Vancouver, Wash. 98660.

DUTOIT, AUDREY L., VP, Crtv. Svcs., PR Associates, Inc., 575 Madison Ave., N.Y., N.Y. 10022, '66–; Dir. of Commtns., '65–'66; Pubcty. Mgr., The Magnavox Co., '62–'65; PRSA; Duke Univ., BA, '54 (magna cum laude, Phi Beta Kappa).

DUVALL, CAROL REIHMER, Program Hostess/Wtr., WWJ-TV, 622 Lafayette, Detroit, Mich. 48231, '62–; Dir., Public Affairs Dept., WOOD-TV, '60–'62; Talent, Wtr., Prodr., Radio and TV, '51–'60; Auth, "Carol Duvall's Idea Book," based on "Here's Carol Duvall" program of craft projects; Peabody Aw. (for station); Mich. State Univ., '43; N.Y.U., '44; b. Milw., Wis., 1926; p. Leo L. and Alice J. Davies Reihmer; h. Carol Duvall; c. Jack R., Michael D.; res: 15125 Grandville, Detroit, Mich. 48223.

DUVALL, EVELYN MILLIS, Cnslt.-Wtr., 700 John Ringling Blvd., Suite 804–805, Sarasota, Fla. 33577, '46–; Authority on sex and family life educ.; Exec. Dir., Nat. Cncl. on Family Rels., '41–'46; Founding Dir., Assn. for Family Living, '34–'41; Auth. of text and reference bks.; Visiting Prof: George Williams Col., Kent State Univ., Fla. State Univ., Univ. of Chgo., Univ. of Southern Ill., Univ. of Tenn.; Am. Assn. of Marriage Cnslrs. (Fellow), Am. Sociological Assn. (Fellow), Nat. Cncl. on Family Rels. (Life Mbr., exec. comm.), Intl. Un. of Family Orgs. (Gen. Cncl.); Partner in 4-H, Fed. Ext. Svc., '69; Syracuse Univ., BS, '27 (summa cum laude; George Arents Pioneer Medal, '52); Vanderbilt Univ., MS, '29; Univ. of Chgo., PhD, '46; b. Oswego, N.Y., 1906; p. Charles L. and Bertha Palmer Millis; h. Sylvanus Duvall; c. Joy Duvall Johnson, Jean Duvall Walther.

DUVALL, MARY GRAVES, AE, Roy Duffus Associates, 605 Third Ave., N.Y., N.Y. 10016, '69–; AE, Padilla, Sarjeant, Sullivan & Speer, '67–'69; Asst. to PR Dir., Reynolds Metals Co., '66–'67; Green Mountain Col., AA, '62; New Sch. for Social Rsch.; b. Utica, N.Y., 1943; p. Robert Lee and Janet Graves; res: 512 E. 79th St., N.Y., N.Y. 10021.

DWORCZAK, HELEN ROZAJESKI, Bdcastr., Scranton Radio Corporation, WICK, 116 Adams Ave., Scranton, Pa. 18503, '45–; Secy., Chmn. of Workmen's Compensation Bd., '40–'45; AWRT (Northeastern Pa. Chptr. Secy., '63–'64; Pres.-elect, '69–'70); Lackawanna Jr. Col., Scranton, Assoc. Degree (Bus. Adm.), '29, b. Throop, Pa., 1909; p. Frank and Maryann Grabowski Rozajeski; h. Joseph Dworczak; res: 604 Dundaff St., Dickson City, Pa. 18519.

DYAR, JEAN JOHNSTON, Pres., Jean Dyar Associates, 3420 S.W. 31st St., Des Moines, Ia. 50321, '63–; (own PR firm, Denver, '63–'65; Des Moines, '67–); Ed., Healthways Magazine, '66–'67; currently PR Cnslt., Dir. of Public Svc. Progs., Nat. Springwall Assocs.; Theta Sigma Phi, PRSA (Ia. Chptr. Secy.-Treas., '68–'69); Univ. of Colo., BA, '47; b. Fort Morgan, Colo., 1925; p. Fred and Dorothy Curruth Johnston; h. Joe Dyar; c. Barry, Todd; res: 3420 S.W. 31st St., Des Moines, Ia. 50321.

DYAR, JULIA TRAYLOR, Asst. Exec. Mgr., Georgia Press Association, 1075 Spring St., N.W., Atlanta, Ga., 30309, '62–; Asst. Mgr., '58–'62; Ed., Editor's Forum, offcl. pubn. Ga. Press Assn., '62–; Mng. Ed., '58–'62; Assoc. Ed., Royston Record, '48–'58; Theta Sigma Phi (Corr. Secy., '66; Second VP, '67; First VP, '68); LaGrange Col., AB, '46 (Who's Who in Am. Cols. and Univs., '46); b. LaGrange, Ga., 1925; p. James Edward and Gladys Marchman Traylor; h. Hubert L. Dyar; res: 1944 Ardmore Rd. N.W., Atlanta, Ga. 30309.

DYBIEC, MARGARET CATANZARO, PR Dir., The Children's Hospital, Inc., 311 Pleasant Ave., St. Paul, Minn. 55102, '69–; Braddock General Hospital, '66–'69; Home Econs. Rep., The Calgon Co., '56–'57; Pers. Training Supvsr., Shillito's (Cinn., Oh.), '55–'56; Theta Sigma Phi (Pitt. Chptr. Pres., '65–'66; Nat. VP for Dev., '67–), Am. Hosp. Assn., Hosp. Assn. of Pa., PR Soc. of W. Pa. Hosps.; Who's Who of Am. Wm.; Mt. Mercy Col., Pitt., BS (Home Econ.), '58; Oh. Univ., BS

(Jnlsm.), with hons.; b. Pitt., Pa., 1933; p. Patrick and Essie Campisi Cantanzaro; h. Alfred Dybiec; c. Catherine Ann, David A., Paul Alfred; res: 922 Fairmount Ave., St. Paul, Minn. 55105.

DYER, MARJORIE C., VP, Dir., American Heritage Publishing Company, Inc., 551 Fifth Ave., N.Y., N.Y. 10017, '61–; Dir., FCA (Computer Svc. Co.), Marion, Oh., '67–; Circ. Dir., Fortune, Architectural Forum, Time Inc., '51–'61; Chestnut Hill Col., BA, '38; N.Y.U., MBA, '52; b. Newark, N.J., 1918; p. Val R. and Clare Kessner Dyer; res: 235 E. 22nd St., N.Y., N.Y. 10010.

DYKE, JUNE SAXTON, Dir., Sul Ross State College Library, Sul Ross State College, S.R. Box 6019, Alpine, Tex. 79830, '68–; Asst. Librn., '67–'68; Am. Sch. Librn. (Karachi, Pakistan), '59–'61, '66–'67; Alpine HS Librn., '52–'59, '61–'63; HS Tchr.; AAUW (Pres., '55–'56), Delta Kappa Gamma (Pres., '56–'58), Cncl. of Tex. Col. Librns., ALA, Tex. Lib. Assn., Am. Wms. Club (Karachi, Pakistan, Pres., '66–'67), Zeta Tau Alpha; Personalities of the South, '69; Okla. State Univ., BS, '35; Middle Tenn. State Col., MA, '62; Sul Ross State Col., Lib. Cert., '62; E. Tex. State Univ., MS (Lib. Sci.), '69; b. Lansing, Mich., 1914; p. Ren and Gladys Smith Saxton; h. Dr. Delbert A. Dyke; c. Dee, Dennis; res: 604 E. Ave. B, Alpine, Tex. 79830.

DYKEMAN, ALICE JANSEN, PR Dir., Methodist Hospital of Dallas, P.O. Box 5999, Dallas, Tex. 75222, '61–; Supvsr. of Media, Prod., Pubcty., Contact Corp., '60–'61; PR, Fashion Coordr., A Harris & Co., '57–'60; Wms. Ed., Fremont (Neb.) Guide and Tribune, '50–'52 and '53–'54; Feature Wtr., Biloxi (Miss.) Daily Herald, '52; Guest Lectr., Southern Methodist Univ. and El Centro Jr. Col., Dallas, '62–'68; Wtr. of numerous playlets and training progs. for hosps.; articles for mags., journals and nwsps.; PRSA (N. Tex. Chptr. Pres., '69: formerly Treas., VP), Press Club of Dallas, Dallas Hosp. Cncl. PR Comm. (Chmn., '63, '68), numerous other orgs.; Un. Fund Edtl. Aw., '63, '66, '67; Matrix Aw., Theta Sigma Phi, '69; Hosp. Mgt. MacEachern Aws. for Hosp. Pubns., '63, '64, '66–'68; PULSE on Patient Rels. Aw., '66; Tex. Hosp. Assn. Aws. for PR Progs. and Pubns., '62–'68; Neb. Wesleyan Univ.; Dallas Col. of Southern Methodist Univ.; b. Fremont, Neb.; p. Cecil and Dorothy Sillik Jansen; c. Cinda, David; res: 736 Stevens Hills, #102, Dallas, Tex. 75208.

DYKEMAN, WILMA, Free-lance Wtr., Lectr., Colmst., Knoxville News-Sentinel; Auth: numerous novels, non-fiction bks., articles, bk. revs.; PEN, Authors League; Southern Hist. Assn., Tenn. Hist. Commn.; Guggenheim Fellowship, '56; Hillman Aw., '58; Chgo. Friends of Am. Wtrs. aw., '62; Thomas Wolfe Memorial Trophy, '55; Colonial Dames Aw., '56; Northwestern Univ., BS (Speech), '40; b. Asheville, N.C., 1920; p. Willard and Bonnie Cole Dykeman; h. James R. Stokely; c. Dykeman Cole, James Rorex III; res: 405 Clifton Heights, Newport Tenn. 37821.

E

EAGER, BEVERLY TAYLOR, Ed., The American Soroptimist, The Soroptimist Federation of the Americas, Inc., 1616 Walnut St., Phila., Pa. 19103, '68–; Asst. Ed., The Spectator mag., Chilton Publ. Co., '66–'67; Wms. Ed., Kings Lynn Advertiser & News, (Norfolk, Eng.), '63–'64; Colmst., Free-lance Wtr.; Theta Sigma Phi; S.F. Jr. Col., S.F. State Col.; b. S.F., Cal., 1922; p. Harold and Ann Elizabeth Lawler Taylor; h. Lloyd Eager; c. Mrs. Pamela Sodaski, Sean, Christian, Jason; res: 408 Minden Way, Wynnewood, Pa. 19096.

EAKIN, MARY KATHERINE, Assoc. Prof. of Educ., University of Northern Iowa, Cedar Falls, Ia. 50613, '68–; Librn., Youth Collection, '58–'68; Librn., Ed., Ctr. for Children's Bks., Univ. of Chgo., '46–'58; Auth: "Good Books for Children" (Univ. of Chgo. Press, 3rd Edition, '66), numerous bibliographies, articles in pfsnl. jnls.; AAUP, AAUW, ALA, NEA, Ia. Lib. Assn., Cedar Falls C. of C., Black Hawk County "Freedom to Read" Org. (Chmn.), Black Hawk County Mental Health Assn. (Bd. Mbr.); Drake Univ., BA, '43; Univ. of Chgo., BLS, '46; MA, '54; b. Nashville, Tenn., 1917; p. Joseph and Hela Blakely Eakin; res: 3104 McClain Dr., Cedar Falls, Ia. 50613.

EAST, SHIRLEY RONNQUIST, Asst. Mgr., Continental Divide Broadcasting Co., Inc., Box 968, Leadville, Colo. 80461, '66–; Wms. Program Dir., KBRR-Radio; Comml., Anncr., KGHF-Radio, KKTV-TV; Tchr., 10 yrs.; Univ. of Colo., BA (Educ.), '53; b. Moline, Ill., 1930; p. Herman and Ann Forsberg Ronnquist; h. John H. East; res: Mount Elbert Plamore Subdiv., Leadville, Colo. 80461.

EASTERLING, SYBIL WILLIAMS, Soc. Ed. and Pres., Richmond County Daily Journal, 105 E. Washington St., Rockingham, N.C. 28379; BPW (Past Pres., Rockingham); E. Carolina Univ.; b. Jones County, N.C.; p. Ebb H. and Beulah Buck Williams; h. Col. Robert Q. Easterling; c. J. Neal Cadieu Jr., Anne (Mrs. William Boyd); res: 1310 Ann St., Rockingham, N.C. 28379.

EASTERLY, LUCILE WALKER, Assoc. Publr., The La Follette Press and The Jellico Advance-Sentinel, 139 N. Tennessee Ave., P.O. Box 1454, La Follette, Tenn. 37766, '68–; Publr., '63–'68; VP, Assoc. Publr., '33–'63; Pres., The La Follette Publ. Co., Inc., '63–'68; Cnslt. to Pres. of Lincoln Memorial Univ., '63–'64; Librn., HS, '31–'33; Tchr., Art, '42–'43; Illus., bk., '33; Bus. Leaders of Am. ('67), Tenn. Press Assn. (Dir., '66–'67), Nat. Nwsp. Assn., La Follette C. of C. (Dir., '64–'65), Bus. and Pfnl. Wms. Club, Commty. Hosp. (Mbr. Advisory Bd., '66–'68); aws. for rept: State Depts. of N.Y., La., Md., '52, '53, '54; cits: Am. Legion, '67; Am. Heart Assn., '64; plaques: FFA, '63; 4-H Clubs of Am., '67; La Follette Bk. Club (Pres., '35), E. Tenn. Hist. Soc., Campbell County Hist. Soc.; Maryville Col., '24–'28 (Hons.); Univ. of Tenn., BA, '31 (Phi Kappa Phi); b. La Follette, Tenn., 1907; p. Silas and Virginia St. John

Walker; h. Guy Easterly (dec.); c. Mrs. Ralph Walter Tucker, Elenora; res: Loop Rd., La Follette, Tenn. 37766.

EASTHAM, GENEVIEVE REYNOLDS, Asst. PR Dr. in Charge of Press, District of Columbia Chapter, American Red Cross, 2025 E. St. N.W., Wash., D.C. 20006; Congressional Colmst., Wash. Magazine, '53–'55; Free-lance pubns., '53–'54; Press Offcr., U.S. Embassy (Rio de Janeiro), '50–'53; Reptr., Feature Wtr., Colmst., Club Ed., Wash. Post, '39–'53; WNPC, ANWC (Pres., '45–'46; VP, '44); U.S. Treasury Aw.; U.S. Navy PR Dept. Commendation; Columbia Col., '29–'31; Univ. of S.C., BA; Fgn. Svc. Inst., '50; b. Lamar, S.C.; p. William and Ada Spears Reynolds; h. Rosser Jackson Eastham; res: 2122 Massachusetts Ave. N.W., Wash., D.C. 20008.

EASTLAND, DOROTHY PAGE, Edtl. Wtr., Hartford Courant, 285 Broad St., Hartford, Conn. 06101, '67–; Asst. News Dir., Conn. Col., '65–'67; Reptr., New London Day, '62–'65; Conn. Col.; Univ. of Hartford; b. Waterbury, Conn., 1921; p. Charles and Gertrude Anderson Page; h. George Eastland; c. Jane E.; res: 35 Virginia Rd. RD 2, Oakdale, Conn. 06370.

EATON, MARJORIE MORLEY, Actress: 40 stage plays; 30 TV films, including Cynthia Pitts, "My Three Sons"; 40 motion pics., including Mme. Romanovitch, "Night Tide" (Spoleto Film Festival), Mrs. Larkin in aw.-winning "Bullitt," Miss Persimmon in "Mary Poppins"; assoc. with Ojai Repertory; toured in aw.-winning "In the Summer House"; Artist: One-man exhbn., Legion of Honor, S.F., Cal.; SAG, AEA; Katharine Delmar Burke's Sch., S.F., '20; Sch. of Fine Arts, Art Student's League of N.Y.C. (Scholarship); Howard Walker's School of Design (Boston); studied painting in France, Italy, N. Mex., Mex.; trained as actress with Hans von Twardowski, Andrius Jawalinsky, Michael Chekhov; b. Oakland, Cal., 1906; p. George and Helen Morley Eaton; res: 950 Old Trace Rd., Palo Alto, Cal. 94306.

EAVES, CAROLYN VIRGINIA, Head Librn., Howard Payne Col., Brownwood, Tex. 76801, '67–; Assoc. Librn., Univ. of Tex. M.D. Anderson Hosp. (Houston), '65–'67; Acquisition Librn., Trinity Univ. (San Antonio), '63–'65; Librn., Amon Carter Museum of Western Art (Ft. Worth), '61–'63; Librn., Tex. Christian Univ. Harris Col. of Nursing, '59–'61; Asst. Circ. Librn., Stephen F. Austin State Col. (Nacogdoches), '57–'59; ALA, Tex. Lib. Assn., Med. Lib. Assn.; Baylor Univ., '53–'55; Tex. Wms. Univ., BA, '56; MLS, '57; b. Marlin, Tex., 1935; p. Lloyd and Sybial Odneal Eaves; res: Wayside Plaza 210, Eight St., Brownwood, Tex. 76801.

EBBE, DOROTHY WILSON, Bk. Publ. Exec., Franklin Watts, Inc., 575 Lexington Ave., N.Y., N.Y. 10022, '64–; Asst. Sls. Mgr., Thomas Nelson & Sons, '60–'64; Secy. of Corp., Am. Sports Publ. Co., '57–'60; NBC, '42–'45; A. S. Barnes & Co; '38–'42; N.Y. Publrs. Rights and

Permissions Group; b. N. Bergen, N.J., 1921; p. John E. and Mabel W. Wilson; h. George W. Ebbe; c. Donna Jane, Deborah Joy; res: 110 Spring St., Harrington Park, N.J. 07640.

EBERHART, SYLVIA ROTHMAN, Bk. Rev. Ed., Science, American Association for the Advancement of Science, 1515 Massachusetts Ave. N.W., Wash., D.C. 20005, '65–; h. John Carol Eberhart.

EBERLE, ANNE RINEHART, Free-lance Artist, Instr., Jewelry Making, People's Art Ctr., St. Louis, Mo.; '56–'59; Finish Artist, Hallmark Cards (Kan. City, Mo.), '54–'56; Monroe Art Assn. (Secy., '68–'70), Theta Sigma Phi, La. Crafts Cncl.; Purdue Univ., BS, '54 (with distinction); b. St. Louis, Mo., 1932; p. Chandler and Elizabeth Milbank Rinehart; h. Robert Todd Eberle; c. Sarah C.; res: 2009 Lexington Ave., Monroe, La. 71201.

EBERLY, CAROL PHILLIPPI, Wtr., Radio Station KYMS, Santa Ana, Cal., '67–; Wtr., Anncr., Saleswm., Radio Sta. KAFM (Salina, Kan.), '64; TV Sta. Rels. Dept., ABC, Hollywood, '63; Theta Sigma Phi, Alpha Epsilon Rho; Stephens Col., '59–'60; Univ. of Kan., BS (Radio-TV), '63 (outstanding sr. wm. in radio-TV); Don Martin Sch. of Radio-TV, Hollywood, '61; b. Salina, Kan., 1941; p. Peter and Hazel Brenizer Phillippi; h. Robert D. Eberly; c. Brian; res: 436 W. Southgate Ave., Fullerton, Cal. 92632.

EBERT, IDA CLAIRE, Commty. Rels., Adm. Secy., Township of Jackson, Commerce St., Jackson, N.J. 08527, '69–; Ed., Publr., Jackson Bul., '54–'69; Fed. Profile Grants (Rural Student Svcs., '66; Home orientation to motivate educ., '67), Bd. of Educ. ('65–'68), Nat. Cncl. on Youth (Apptd. by Governor R. Meyner, '58), Educ. Wtrs., N.J. League of Weekly Nwsps. (VP, '58–'60), active in numerous civic and health orgs.; b. N.Y.C., 1914; p. Philip and Esther Miller Scheiner; h. B. Lee Ebert; c. Barbara S., Jason S.; res: P.O. Box D, Jackson, N.J. 08527.

EBKEN, RUTH MARJORIE, Dir. of Art, Pittsburgh Board of Public Education, 341 S. Bellefield Ave., Pitt., Pa. 15213; Art Tchr., Supvsr. of Art; Tour Dir., NEA Educ. Travel Svc., '66–'67; Eastern Arts Assn. (Ed., Prospect and Retrospect), '60; Art Educ. Bul., '62; VP, '58–'60; Pres., '60–'62), Nat. Art Educ. Assn. (Pres.-Elect, '65–'67; Pres., '67–'69; Cncl. Mbr., '58–), Eastern Arts Cncl. ('56–'66), Nat. Cncl. of Adm. Wm. in Educ. (VP, '63–'65), Pa. Art Educ. Assn., Intl. Soc. for Educ. through Art, Who's Who in Am. Educ., Altrusa, Delta Kappa Gamma, Assoc. Artists of Pitt.; Col. of Fine Arts, Carnegie-Mellon Univ., BFA, '33 (hons.); MFA, '47; Intl. Sch. of Art (Travel progs: Mexico, Guatemala, Europe, N. Africa, S. America., Scandinavia, Egypt); b. Pitt., Pa.; p. William and Edith Poerstel Ebken; res: 3210 Niagara St., Pitt., Pa. 15213.

EBLE, JEANNE SHARPE, Media Specialist, Fraser High School Media Center, Garfield St., Fraser, Mich., '67–; Head Librn., Highland Park Col.; Lib. Cnslt., Mich. Lutheran Col.; NEA, Mich. Lib. Assn. (Secy.-Treas., '64–'65); Univ. of Rochester, AB, '43; Western Reserve Univ., BS (Lib. Sci.), '43; Wayne State Univ., MEd, '51; Univ. of Mich., AM (Lib. Sci.), '66; b. Syracuse, N.Y.; p. Clarence and Florence Sharpe; h. Louis Eble, Sr.; c. Louis B., Jr.; res: 12490 E. Outer Dr., Detroit, Mich. 48224.

ECKBLAD, EDITH BERVEN, Auth: "A Smile Is To Give" (Rand McNally, '69), "Danny's Orange Camel" (Augsburg Publ. House), four other children's bks.; poetry, assigts. for David C. Cook; NLAPW (Lake Shore Br. Pres., '66–'68), Cncl. for Wis. Wtrs., Wis. Reg. Wtrs. Assn. (Bd. Mbr.), Soc. of Lit. Designates, Racine Wms. Club, Contemporary Auths.; Wheaton Col., '42; Univ. of Wis. Ext. Br., '63–'66; b. Baltic, S.D., 1923; p. Leander and Louise Simonson Berven; h. Marshall Eckblad; c. Peter, Nancy, James, Jonathan, Mark; res: 5224 Spring St., Racine, Wis. 53406.

ECKERT, MARGUERITE, AE, Reuben H. Donnelley Corporation, 466 Lexington Ave., N.Y., N.Y., '58–; Acc. Rep., '49–'58; Distg. Sls. Performance Club, '68; Hunter Col., BA, '45; b. Phila., Pa.; p. Emiland and Lillie Evans Eckert; res: 370 E. 76th St., N.Y., N.Y. 10021.

EDDY, ELIZABETH SCHLAMM, VP and Assoc. Crtv. Dir., Benton & Bowles, Inc., 666 Fifth Ave., N.Y., N.Y. 10019, '68–; (formerly VP and Crtv. Supvr., Copy Group Head, Copywtr.); Judge, Am. TV Commls. Festival, '66–'68; Lectr. on adv. at cols. and high schs., '64–; AWNY; Cornell Univ., BA (Mortar Bd.; mbr. at large Adm. Bd., Cornell Univ. Cncl.); b. N.Y.C.; p. Nathaniel and Josephine O'Neill Schlamm; h. Scott Eddy; res: 215 E. 31 St., N.Y., N.Y. 10016.

EDELL, CELESTE LOEB, Auth: "A Present From Rosita" (J. Messner, Wash. Sq. Press), "Lynn Pamet—Caterer" (J. Messner), "Here Come the Clowns" (Putnam); Auths. Guild, WNBA; Hunter Col., BA; N.Y.U.; b. N.Y.C.; p. Julius and Irma Rothschild Loeb; h. Harold Edell; res: 9472 Bay Dr., Surfside, Fla. 33154.

EDEN, DOROTHY F., Prodr., Wtr., On-Air Hostess of "A Woman's World," WKTV, Smith Hill, Utica, N.Y. 13503, '66–; Prop. and Dir., Dottie Eden's World of Beauty and Finishing School (New Hartford, N.Y.), '67–; Gen. Mgr., Brooks Fashion Stores (Utica), '64–'66; Univ. of Cal., Berkeley, '42–'45; Powers Modeling Sch., '43; h. (dec.); res: 1610—Oneida St., Utica, N.Y. 13501.

EDGINGTON, DOROTHEA B., Free-lance Wtr.; educ. Pr; Pubns. Asst., Rapid City Public Schs., '67–'68; '65–'66; Edtl. Asst., News Bur., S.D. State Univ., '66–'67; PR Dir., Douglas Sch. System (Ellsworth Air Force Base, S.D.), '62–'65; Jnlsm. Tchr.; numerous articles in educ. pubns.; Kappa Tau Alpha; S.D. State Univ., BS, '60; MEd (Commtns.), '67; Univ. of Tex., '65; b. Sioux Falls, S.D., 1938; p. J.R. Edgington; res: Box 406, Hill City, S.D. 57745.

EDGREN, MARY LOUISE, Dir. of Commtns., The Pick-Congress Hotel, 520 South Michigan Ave., Chgo., Ill. 60605, '63–; Dir. PR, Edgewater Beach Hotel, '61–'63; Asst. Pubcty. Dir., Palmer House, '59–'61; Pubcty. Dir., Trade Bk. Div., Rand McNally, '55–'58; Adm. Asst., Intl. Mineral & Chemical Corp., '53–'55; Pubcty. Wtr., Campbell-Mithun, '50–'53; Edtl. Asst., Indsl. Marketing Magazine, '47–'49; Pubcty. Club of Chgo., PRSA; Who's Who in PR; Who's Who of Am. Wm.; Who's Who of Am. Wm. in the Midwest; Drake Univ., '46; Northwestern Univ. evening sch.; b. Chgo., Ill., 1926; p. Paul and Louise Wilson Edgren; res: 4950 Marine Dr., Chgo., Ill. 60640.

EDINGER, DORA M., Librn., Soc. Advancement of Judaism, 32 W. 86th St., N.Y., N.Y. 10024; Wtr., biogs.; numerous biographical studies in German and Eng.; Librn., Adult Educ., Solel (Highland Park, Ill.); Rschr. Ency. Britannica; Biog. Wtr., Appleton Century; Army Librn., '45–'47; AAUW; Ill. Lib. Assn.; Heidelberg Univ. (Germany), MA, PhD (Magna cum laude); h. Dr. Friedr. Edinger (dec.); c. Wolfgang (dec.), Martin J. (dec.), Lewis J.; res: 21 W. 86th St., N.Y., N.Y. 10024.

EDMAN, MARION LOUISE, Prof. of Educ., Wayne State University, 231 Education Bldg., WSU, Detroit, Mich. 48203; Gustavus Adolphus Franklin Lectr.; Auth.; Lectr., numerous univs: Chgo., Cal., Minn., Mich., W. Va., Western; Cnslt., AID (Germany, Lebanon, Vietnam); Fulbright Rsch. Scholar (Korea); Comparative Educ. Soc. (VP, '64–'65), Nat. Cncl. of Tchrs. of Eng., Assn. Childhood Educ. Intl.; Univ. of Minn., PhD, '38 (Distg. Alumni Aw.); Gustavus Adolphus Col., DHL (hon.), '54; res: 50 Moss, Highland Park, Mich. 48203.

EDSALL, SHIRLEY ANN, Librn., Corning Community College, Corning, N.Y. 14830, '61–; Sch. Librn., Campbell (N.Y.) Central Sch., '55–'61; Instr., Lib. Sch., Mansfield (Pa.) State Col., summer, '62; Ref. Librn., Lib.-U.S.A., World's Fair (N.Y.C.), '64; ALA, N.Y. Lib. Assn., Am. Assn. of Jr. Col. Assn., AAUW; Beta Phi Mu; State Univ. at Albany, AB, '64 (cum laude; Signum Laudus); MS (Lib. Sci.), '65; b. Bath, N.Y., 1933; p. Otis and Marjorie Phillips Edsall; res: R.D. #1, Campbell, N.Y. 14821.

EDSTROM, EVE MARK, Reptr., Washington Post, 1515 L St., Wash., D.C. 20005, '51–; Reptr., Louisville (Ky.) Courier-Jnl., '45–'51; Reptr., Columbia (Mo.) Daily Tribune, '43–'45; Reptr., New Bedford (Mass.) Standard-Times, '42–'43; WNPC (Pres., '66–'67; Bd. of Governors, '63–'66); 14 nwsp. aws., incl: Wash. Nwsp. Guild Memorial Grand Prize, '55, '56; first prizes: Guild public svc., '57; Guild gen. news, '60; Guild feature writing, '62; Catherine O'Brien First Prize, '62; Univ. of Mo., BJ, '45 (Sigma Delta Chi hon. aw.); b. Fall River, Mass., 1923; p. Abbott and Elsie Krises Mark; h. Ed Edstrom; res: 4201 Cathedral Ave. N.W., Wash., D.C. 20016.

EDWARDS, BEVERLY SCROGGS, Wms. Staff Wtr., Ed., Van Nuys Publishing Co., 14539 Sylvan St., Van Nuys, Cal. 91407, '64–; Indsl. Ed., Packard-Bell Electronics, '57–'59; Indsl. Ed., Consolidated Electrodynamics, '57; Wms. News, Glendale News-Press, '56–'57; San Fernando Valley Press Club (Bd. Mbr., '69–'70; aw. for headline, '68; aw. for feature story, '65), Theta Sigma Phi, Cal. Press Wm. (aw. for pg. make-up, '67); Occidental Col., '51–'53; Univ. of Southern Cal., BA (Jnlsm.), '56; b. Carthage, Mo., 1933; p. Paul J. and Elma Mae Corum Scroggs; h. Sam Edwards; c. William Motley III, Deborah Motley, Linda Motley; res: 11043 Canby Ave., Northridge, Cal. 91324.

EDWARDS, FRANCES, Pers. Librn., Ohio University Library, Ohio University, Athens, Oh. 45701, '68–; Radio Commentator, bks., events, occasions; Nwsp. Colmst.; Dir., Wash. County Public Lib. (Marietta), '63–'68; Br. Coordr., Public Lib. (Toledo), '62–'63; Dir., Public Lib. (Norwalk), '48–'62; Gen. and Med. Librn., VA, '46–'48; U.S. Army, '42–'46; Tchr.-Librn., '32–'41; Cnslt., Interior Decorator for Lib. bldgs.; Cnslt., Lib. reg. reorg.; ALA (First Radio Aw., '67), Oh. Lib. Assn. (Exec. Bd., '66–'68), AAUW, BPW, League of Wm. Voters; Longwood Col., BS (Educ.), '32; Geo. Peabody Col. (Lib. Sci.), '40–'41; b. Chatham, Va., 1912; p. Bruce and Kate Reynolds Edwards; res: 10-202 Monticello Dr., Athens, Oh. 45701.

EDWARDS, JANE CAMPBELL, Cnslt., Santa Clara County Office of Education, 45 Santa Teresa St., San Jose, Cal. 95110, '68–; Auth., mysteries, career novels for teenage girls, other works; bks. incl. "Island Interlude" (Avalon, '69), "Believe no Evil" (Avalon, '69), "What Happened to Amy?" (Lothrop, '61), "The Houseboat Mystery," "Lab Secretary," "Carol Stevens, Newspaper Girl"; work on educ. TV series; b. Miles City, Mont., 1932; p. Christopher M. and Josephine Cecilia Gast Campbell; h. Richard Edwards; c. Linda, Richard, Andrew, Sheila, Patrick; res: 1531 Queenstown Ct., Sunnyvale, Cal. 94087.

EDWARDS, JOSEPHINE CUNNINGTON, Tchr. of Hist., Spanish, South Bay Academy, Torrance, Cal., '68–; Tchr., Special Educ. (Idaho), '63–'68; HS Tchr. (Ellijay, Ga.), '57–'63; TV Script Wtr., "Faith for Today," '53–'57; Missionary (Malawi, Africa), '45–'52; Auth, bks; Andrews Univ. (Berrien Springs, Mich.), BA; Peabody Col. for Tchrs., MA; b. Muncie, Ind., 1904; p. David and Elizabeth Gray Cunnington, Jr.; h. Lowell A. Edwards (dec.); c. Robert E., Charles G.; res: 5326 Norton St., Torrance, Cal. 90503.

EDWARDS, JUDITH, Mng. Ed., Psychotherapy: Theory, Research & Practice, c/o Department of Psychology, University of Chicago, Chgo., Ill. 60637, '66–.

EDWARDS, JULIA SPALDING, Free-lance Wtr., Ed., '63–; Reptr., Balt. Sun.; Wash. Corr., Indpls. Star; Mng. Ed., Worldwide Press Svc.; Ed., U.S. Info. Svc.

(Tokyo); War Corr., 100 countries, Nwsp. Enterprise Assn., Overseas News Agcy., Worldwide Press Svc., NANA; Auth., "The Occupiers" (Fleet Press, '67); OPC (Fndn. Bd. Mbr., '64–'67), ANWC, WNPC; Who's Who of Am. Wm.; Barnard Col., AB; Columbia Univ., MS (Jnlsm.); b. Louisville, Ky.; p. James and Margaret Wathen Edwards; res: 2440 Virginia Ave. N.W., Wash., D.C. 20037.

EDWARDS, JUNE DE WEES, Ed., Better Homes and Gardens, Meredith Publishing Co., Des Moines, Ia. 50303, '57–; DAR, Theatre Arts League, NHFL; Univ. of Miami, '40–'41, Univ. of Ala., '41–'43; b. Guatemala, Central Am., 1925; p. Ledyard and Sara Barnett DeWees; h. Robert Edwards; c. Dianne O., David K., Gail June; res: 1240 San Remo Ave., Coral Gables, Fla. 33146.

EDWARDS, KATHLEEN BRIDGES, Ed. and Publr., The Luling Signal, 629 Davis, Luling, Tex. 78648, '58–; S. Tex. Press Assn.; b. Luling, Tex., 1917; p. Hal and Lois King Bridges; h. Robert L. Edwards; c. R. Dennis, Richard Lewis; res: Old Lockhart Rd., Luling, Tex. 78648.

EDWARDS, VIRGINIA LEE, Assoc. Ed., Americas, Pan American Union, 19th and Constitution, N.W., Wash., D.C. 20006, '68–; pen and ink illus.; Mgt. Analyst, Small Bus. Adm. (rsch., speech wtr: "The Problems of Small Business in the Transportation Industry"), '67–'68; Indexer, Nat. Geog. Soc., '65–'66; Freelance translating: Spanish to Eng., Portuguese to Eng.; Vassar Col., BA (Eng. Lit.); b. St. Louis, Mo., 1942; p. Dr. Joseph Castro and Virginia Moser Edwards; res: 1732 21st St. N.W., Wash., D.C. 20009.

EERDE, ELLEN EPPS, Public Affairs Dir., Biafra Relief Services Foundation, 28 E. Jackson Blvd., Chgo., Ill. 60604, '69–; Pubcty. Dir., Mount Sinai (Chgo.) Hosp. Med. Ctr., '68–'69; PR (N.Y.C.), '64–'67; Dir., Educ. Dept., Cosmopolitan Magazine, '62–'63; Public Info. Offcr., S.C. Civil Defense Agcy., '59–'61; Legislative Reptr., Charlotte Observer, '58–'59; Tchr: Univ. of the Ams. (Mexico City), Columbia Col., Univ. of Neb., '54–'59; Wtr., articles for nat. mags.; Pubcty. Club of N.Y. (Distg. Svc. Aw., '65); Winthrop Col., BA; Univ. of S.C., MA, '52; c. Mical R., Hugh B.

EFRON, EDITH CAROL, Staff Wtr., TV Guide, 1290 Ave. of the Americas, N.Y., N.Y. 10019, '61–; Wtr., Mike Wallace Show, '58–'60; PR, Farley-Manning Co., '56–'58; Mng. Ed., Special Edtl. Depts., LOOK, '54–'56; Central Am. Reptr., Time-Life, '48–'54; Mag. Sec., N.Y. Times, '44–'47; AWRT; Barnard Col., BA, '42; Columbia Univ., BS (Jnlsm.), '43; b. N.Y.C., 1922; p. Alexander and Rose Kunitz Efron; h. (div.); c. Fortune Leonard Bogat; res: 77 W. 55th St., N.Y., N.Y. 10036.

EGAN, MARTHA MYERS, Bdcst. Time Byr., Grubb Advertising, Inc., 111 N. Market St., Champaign, Ill. 61820, '63–; Sales-Traf. Coordr. and Traf. Mgr., Ch. 3

TV, Champaign, '53–'61; AAF (6th Dist., Treas., '65–'66), AWRT, Champaign-Urbana Adv. and Sales Club Bd. Mbr., '66; Treas., '55; Secy., '54); Champaign-Urbana Dir. Mail Day Nat. Blue Ribbon Aw., '64 and '63; Ill. Comml. Col., '36–'37; b. Mansfield, Ill., 1918; p. John and Phebe James Myers; h. (div.); res: 1504 W. University Ave., Champaign, Ill. 61820.

EGGER, ELLEN, Assoc. Dir., Mktng./Rsch., Young & Rubicam, Inc., 285 Madison Ave., N.Y., N.Y. 10017, '65–; Mktng./Rsch., 19 yrs.; Am. Rsch. Fndn.; Denison Univ., BA; Univ. of Cal.; b. Toledo, Oh., 1924; p. Chester and Lucille Egger; res: 250 E. 39th St., N.Y., N.Y. 10016.

EHLERS, SABINE BARDACK, Owner-Mgr., E & E Associates, P.O. Box 3602, Tallahassee, Fla. 32303, '63–; PR Asst., Polaroid Corp. (Cambridge, Mass.), '59–'63; Ed., Pearl Harbor Naval Shipyard, '53–'59; Agricultural Ext. Ed., Univ. of Hi., '53; Ed., Family News, Honolulu Star-Bulletin, '52–'53; Kauai Corr., '50–'52; Owner, Ideas Promoted (Lihuo, Hi.), '50–'52; Mill Valley Record, '48–'50; Co-auth., Ed., "Kauai Guide Book," '51; Ed., Revsd. Edition, '57; Auth., "Hawaiian Stories for Boys and Girls" (Watkins and Sturgis, '58), "The Big Hawaiian Moon" (Mtro Printing) ICIE (Area Dir., '58–'59), IEA (Pres., '57–'59); N.Y.U., BS (Educ.), '35; (Child Psych.), '37; Univ. of Hi., '57; b. Harbin, Manchuria, 1910; h. Walter H. Ehlers; c. Rhea Judith Maxwell, Joyce Reed, Carol Joan McMahon; res: 2006 Lee Ave., Tallahassee, Fla. 32303.

EHRLICH, RUTH GRETA, Exec. VP, Brother International Corp., 680 Fifth Ave., N.Y., N.Y. 10019, '60– (previously Adv. Mgr.); Nat. Sales Prom. Mgr., Knit King Corp; appeared in radio and TV commls.; numerous articles for wms. svc. mags. and trade pubns.; AWNY, AFA, Nat. Sch. Supply and Educ. Assn., Nat. Off. Products Assn., Independent Housewares Assn.; VASPA Sales Prom. Aw. of Distinction, '68, '64–'66; Nat. Installment Assn., Best Packaging Aw., '67, '65; City Col. of NY.; New Sch.; Leonardo da Vinci Sch. of Arts; b. N.Y.C.; h. Manuel Ehrlich.

EICHELBERGER, ROSA KOHLER, Auth., Ed., Book Industry Representative; WNBA Representative to the UN Non-Governmental Organizations and to the Non-Governmental Organizations accredited to the U.S. Mission to the UN and to the Conference of UN Representatives of the UN Assn of the U.S.A., Democratic Committeeman, '68; published Bronko (Wm. Morrow & Company); Auth., stories and articles for young people, '48–'55; Book Review Ed., League of Nations Chronicle (later Publication of the Am. Assn. for the UN), '30–'55; Volunteer, Citizens Welfare Corps, Emergency Welfare Div., City of N.Y., '42–'45; Leader, Freedom Forums, League of Wm. Voters, N.Y.U., '41–'45; Story Lady, Radcliffe Chautauqua, Hull House, Greenwich House, '20–'40; Playground Dir., Baltimore, Md., '16–'20; Training Sch. for Recreation Leaders, Baltimore, Md.; French courses, Sorbonne and other French Univs.; b. Baltimore, Md.; p. Jacob G. and Mary Elizabeth Condon Kohler; h. Clark M. Eichelberger; res: 139 E. 33rd St., N.Y., N.Y. 10016.

EICHELSDOERFER, MARGARET, Copy Group Head, Needham, Harper & Steers, Inc., 909 Third Ave., N.Y., N.Y. 10022; Fashion Ed., Wms. Wear Daily; Pubcty. Dir., Hope Skillman Fabrics; Copywtr., Donahue & Coe; Copy Group Head, West, Weir & Bartel; AWNY,Theta Sigma Phi; Effie Aw. for TV, Household Prods. Category, '69; Univ. of Mo., BJ.

EINIK, EILEEN, PR Exec., Greater Miami C. of C., 303 Biscayne Blvd. Miami, Fla 33132 '70–; Asst. to Dir. of PR and Adv., Roberts Realty of the Bahamas, Ltd., (Coral Gables, Fla.), '69–'70; Pubcty. Copywtr., PR Asst., KTTV-TV, (L.A., Cal.), '68–'69; ad prod., on air prom. and prod., WTVJ-TV (Miami, Fla.), '67–'68;Theta Sigma Phi (Student Chptr. Pres., '66–'67); Univ. of Fla., BS (Adv.), '67 (Dean's List); b. Naples, Italy, 1946; p. Issac and Minna Einik; res: 1002 N.E. 176 Terr., N. Miami Beach, Fla. 33162.

EINSELEN, ANNE F. (pseud: Anne Paterson), Freelance Ed. and Wtr., Cnslt., 2 E. Newfield Way, Bala-Cynwyd, Pa. 19004, '63–; Edtl. Cnslt., Fortress Press and Chilton Books, Phila.; Sr. Ed., Chilton Book Co., '62–'63; Assoc. Ed. and Head of Discovery Dept., Ladies' Home Journal, '53–'62; Asst. Ed., '47–'53; Edtl. Asst., '46–'47; Novels incl: "Take These Hands," "Sleepless Candle," "Queen Street Story," all published under pseudonym Anne Paterson; Theta Sigma Phi, Phila. Art Alliance, Phila. Booksellers, Phila. Athenaeum, Phila. Museum of Art; Breadloaf Fellowship, '39; Who's Who of Am. Wm. since first edition; b. Phila., Pa., 1900; p. Harry and Jennie Gamon Einselen; res: 2 E. Newfield Way, Phila., Pa. 19004.

EISNOR, ANNA LYON, Mng. Ed., The Balfour Craftsman, L. G. Balfour Company, 25 County St., Attleboro, Mass. 02703, '66–; Exec. Secy., '65–'66; Store Mgr., Kitchen Specialists, '48–'58; Cl., Tex. Instruments, '43–'48; Bryant Bus. Col., Providence (R.I.), '43; h. (div.).

EITEL, CAROLYN HOLLOWAY, Prod. Mgr., Carlton Advertising, Inc., 925 Penn Ave., Pitts., Pa. 15222, '67–; Prod. Asst., The Hansen Company, Chgo., Ill., '65–'66; External Traf., Compton Advterising, Chgo., Ill., '64; Phi Beta; Northwestern Univ., BS, '64; b. Pitts., Pa., 1943; p. Clark and Dorothy Bain Holloway; h. John A. Eitel Jr., res: 235 Edgewood Ave., Pitts., Pa. 15218.

EITZMAN, ARDATH McGREGOR, GA Mgr., The Arizona Bank, 44 W. Monroe, Phoenix, Ariz. 85003, '66–; Asst. Dir., PR, '64–'66; Ed., '63–'64; Employees Svcs. Admr., Sperry Phoenix, '63; Ed., Roadway Express Inc., '62–'63; Reptr., Kent (Oh.) Record Courier, '61; Reptr., Columbus (Oh.) Dispatch, '59; ICIE (Ariz. Pres., '66; Dist. Five VP, '66; Dist. Five Pres. Aw. for Leadership, '66–'67), Nat. Assn. Bank Wm.,

Ariz. Press Wm.; AAIE Aw. for publicizing traf. safety '63; Oh. State Univ., '61; b. Coshocton, Oh., 1938; p. Arthur L. and Jean A. Blind Dickerson; h. Walter M. Eitzman, Jr.; c. JoJene; res: 3636 W. Hayward Ave., Phoenix, Ariz. 85021.

ELAM, BARBARA ANN, Ed., Republic National Life Insurance Co., 3988 N. Central Exprwy., Dallas, Tex. 75204, '59–; Wms. Newscaster, WFAA (Dallas), '58–'59; Ed., '56–'58; Cont. Dir., '55–'59; Edtl. Asst., Christian Youth mag., '51–'52; Adv. Asst., Shelby (N.C.) Daily Star, '44–'51; SMU Dallas Col. and Art schs.; b. Shelby, N.C., 1926; p. Roland B. and Mary Annie Brackett Elam; res: 2310 Cedar Way Dr., Dallas, Tex. 75241.

ELDRIDGE, HAZEL LEWIS, Ed., Junior Review, Civic Education Service, 1733 K St. N.W., Wash., D.C. 20006, '62–; News Wtr., '48–'61; Rsch. Librn., '44–'48; Tchr., '37–'41; EPAA; Eleanor Fishburn Aw. for Intl. Understanding, '68; Who's Who of Am. Wm.; Keene State Col., BE, '41; b. Windsor, Vt., 1914; p. Hiram and Lena Ashton Lewis; h. (div.); c. Alice; res: 914 N. Irving St., Arlington, Va. 22201.

ELDRIDGE, VERA HAWORTH, Ed., McCleary Memorial Hospital, Excelsior Springs, Mo. 64024, '69–; Modern Theatre Ed., Boxoffice Pubn., '69–; Ed., PR, Nat. Bellas Hess (Kan. City); Rschr., Wtr. of Hist. articles, Lectr.; active in civic projects and volunteer work; Kan. City IEA (Placement Dir., '65–'69), Mo. Hist. Soc.; Mo. Press Wm. State Contest Aws., '69; NFPW Aw., '69; Heart of Am. Un. Campaign Cit. for Leadership, '65; Kan. City Art Inst.; b. Kan. City, Mo., 1910; p. Vincent and Grace Taylor Haworth; h. William E. Eldridge; c. Margaret Ann, Richard Haworth; res: 832 Hillside Ave., Liberty, Mo. 64068.

ELFWING, MARGARETA RUTH, Rsch. Dir., Hoefer, Dietrich & Brown Inc., 414 Jackson Sq., S.F., Cal. 94111, '69–; Project Supvsr., CMCR, Inc., '66–'67; Asst. to the Mgr., Swedish C. of C., '65–'66; Adv. Cnslt., AB Zander & Igestrom (Stockholm, Sweden), '60–'65; PR Asst., The Ins. Info. Ctr., '58–'59; Am. Mktng. Assn., S.F. Adv. Club; Swedish Export Assn., "%000 scholarship for U.S. studies in mktng., '65; Bar-Lock-Institutet, '58; Konstfackskolan (art sch.), '60; Inst. of Adv., BA, '63; b. Ostersund, Sweden, 1936; p. John and Henny Olsson Elfwing; res: 520 Liberty St., El Cerrito, Cal. 94530.

ELIAS, MARIANNE, Media Planner, Crestwood Advertising, Inc., 909 Third Ave., N.Y., N.Y. 10022; Media Buyer; N.Y. Inst. of Adv.; b. N.Y.C., 1943; p. Edward and Millie Mann Elias; c. Laura Beth; res: 668 Mace Ave., Bronx, N.Y. 10467.

ELKON, DOROTHEA McKENNA, Fashion Ed., Vogue Magazine, Condé Nast Publications, Inc., 420 Lexington Ave., N.Y., N.Y. 10017, '64–; h. Robert Elkon.

ELKS, HAZEL HULBERT, Dir., Free Public Library, 11

S. Broad St., Elizabeth, N.J. 07202, '61–; Pers. Dir., '50–'61; Br. Librn., '44–'50; Children's Librn., '41–'44; ALA, N.J. Lib. Assn.; Cuban Tchrs. Assn. aw.; Rutgers Univ., N.J. State Lib. Sch. (Trenton); b. Franklin, N.J.; p. Harry C. and Hazel Ball Hulbert; h. David Elks; res: 1389 Vauxhall Rd., Union, N.J. 07083.

ELKUS, LEONORE ROSENBAUM, Exec. Prodr., Public and Commty. Affairs, WQED-TV, 4337 Fifth Ave., Pitts., Pa. 15213, '63–; Bd. of Dirs., '68–; Prodr., "Key To The City" and "Womens Window"; Weekly nwsp. colm.; Co-auth., "A Treasure Of Art Songs"; AWRT (VP), Mass Media Comm. of Pa., AAUW, NAEB, Who's Who Of Am. Wm.; active in various civic groups; Sarah Lawrence Col., BA; h. James H. (dec.); c. two boys and a girl.

ELLER, GIZELLA CZEKMANY, Asst. Ed./Prod. Mgr., American Helicopter Society, Inc., 30 E. 42nd St., N.Y., N.Y. 10017, '57–; City Col. of N.Y., '32; p. Frank and Suzanna Breitenbach Czekmany; h. John Andre; c. John Andre, Jr., Kathleen Sue Cunningham; res: 94-41 218th St., Queens Village, N.Y. 11428.

ELLINGTON, BETH, Ed., Mgr., Sls. Pubns., Luzier Incorporated, P.O. Box 496, Kan. City, Mo. 64141, '64–; Wtr.; ICIE (Secy., '68), Wms. C. of C.; Univ. of Mo.; b. Pittsburg, Kan., 1919; p. Dr. W. H. and Genelle Selecman Graves; res: 609 W. 46th, Kan. City, Mo. 64112.

ELLIOTT, JEAN ANN, Asst. Librn., Asst. Prof. of Lib. Sci., Shepherd College, Library, Shepherdstown, W. Va. 25443, '66–; Asst. Librn., '61–; Ref. Asst., Univ. of Pitt. (Pitt., Pa.), '60–'61; Asst. Librn., Fairmont State Col. (Fairmont, W.Va.), '57–'60; Alpha Beta Alpha (Nat. Exec. Secy., '68–), ALA, W. Va. Lib. Assn., Tri-State ACRL (Secy.-Treas., '68–'69); Shepherd Col., AB, '54; Syracuse Univ., MS (Lib. Sci.), '57; Shippensburg State Col. (Shippensburg, Pa.), '66–'69; b. Martinsburg, W. Va., 1933; p. Howard and Dorothy Horn Elliott; res: 414 S. Rosemont Ave., Martinsburg, W. Va. 25401.

ELLIOTT, KATHLEEN DAUM, Nwsp. Reptr., Lafayette, Ind.; Corr. Fairchild Pubns. '59; Purdue Ed., Lafayette Journal-Courier '56; Society Reptr., '58; Wms. News Ed.-Photog., Oskaloosa (Ia.) Daily Herald, '53–'54; Theta Sigma Phi, (Cinn. chptr: Pres., '69; VP '68; Secy., '66–'68); Ohio Univ., BS, '53; p. Carl H. and Edna Ray Daum; h. Richard L.; c. Philip, Suzanne, Carl; res: 3519 Monteith Ave., Cinn. Oh. 45208.

ELLIS, AMANDA MAE (dec.), Auth: "Elizabeth, the Woman," "Literature of England," "Rebels and Conservatives" numerous others: popular small bks., incl. "Pioneers," others; Wtr. in Res., Colo. Col., '62–; Retired Prof., '67–; teaching, Ill. Univ., Ia. Univ.; Colo. Auths. League; Phi Beta Kappa, Theta Sigma Phi, AAUW (Colo. Pres., '40–'41), Nat. Cncl. of

Tchrs. of Eng. (Nat. VP, '42); "Order of Rose Hon.", Delta Gamma; Colo. Who's Who; Colo. Col., AB, '20; Ia. Univ., MA, '22; b. Jefferson City, Mo.

ELLIS, BILLIE BRITTON, Wms. Ed., Winter Haven Publishing Company, 124 3rd St. N.W., Winter Haven, Fla. 33880, '49–; Fla. Wms. Press Club; Columbia Univ.; Univ. of Mo.; b. Winter Haven, Fla., 1927; p. William and Ann Barnes Britton; h. David Ellis; res: 805 22nd St. N.W., Winter Haven, Fla. 33880.

ELLIS, HARRIET WILSON, AE, John Van Zant & Associates, 11 S. LaSalle St., Chgo., Ill. 60603, '69–; PR AE, Griswold-Eshleman Co., '66–'69; PR Dir., Bradley & Vrooman Co., '60–'66; PR Tchr., Central YMCA Commty. Col. (Chgo., Ill.); Pubcty. Club of Chgo. (Bd. of Dirs., '66–; Secy., '67–'68; Treas., '68–'69; "Pub-Clubber," Aw. Winner, Outstanding Svc., '68), Wms. Adv. Club of Chgo. (Bd. of Dirs., '69–'70), PRSA; Roosevelt Univ.; Northwestern Univ.; Univ. of Chgo., '56–'59; b. Chgo., Ill., 1938; p. Herman and Bertha Buffen Wilson; h. Robert E. Ellis; res: 2242 N. Fremont St., Chgo., Ill. 60614.

ELLIS, JERI WISBROD, Wtr., Prodr., Narrator, "On Campus With Jeri Ellis," KUDO-TV, 760 Harrison St., S.F., Cal., 94107, '68–; Commty. Rel. Dir., KPIX-TV (S.F.), '68; Bdcstr., Interviewer, Theatre Revs., KFOG (S.F.) '66–'67; "The Jeri Ellis Show," KMPX (S.F.), '65–'66; PR Cnslt., '62–'68; AWRT (S.F. Chptr. Treas., '67–'68), NATAS, PRSA (Peninsula Chptr. Secy., '64–'66; Bd. Mbr., '66–'67); Northwestern Univ.; Univ. of S.F.; Pasadena City Col.; Univ. of Cal. at S.F.; b. Chgo., Ill., 1928; p. Elliott and Sophia Dick Wisbrod; h. Bernard Ellis; c. Gregory Scott, Geoffrey Neil; res: 515 Jefferson Dr., Palo Alto, Cal. 94303.

ELLIS, LINDA A., Ed., house organ mag. for National Bellas Hess, Inc., 715 Armour Rd., N. Kan. City, Mo. 64116, '68–; Adv. Asst., Adv. Dept., Interstate Securities Co.; Free-lance poetry, stories; Kan. City IEA, ICIE, Theta Sigma Phi, Gamma Alpha Chi, Kan. City Numismatic Soc. (Secy.), others in area; Univ. of Kan., BS (Jnlsm.); b. Kan. City, Mo., 1943; p. Albert and Esther Joseph Ellis; res: 1008 E. 44th St., Kan. City, Mo. 64111.

ELLIS, MARY JACKSON, Tchr., Minneapolis Public Schools, 4548 Oakland Ave., S., Mpls., Minn. 55407, '39–; Auth: "Spaghetti Eddiw" (Denison, '57), "Gobble, Gobble, Gobble" (Denison, '56), other children's bks., tchrs. aids; NEA, Minn. Educ. Assn., Wm. in Educ., ZONTA; Opportunity Mag. aw., '47; Who's Who of Am. Wm., Who's Who in the Midwest, Contemporary Auths.; W. Va. State Col., AB, '39; Univ. of Minn.; b. Wheeling, W. Va., 1916; p. James and Bessie Kennedy Jackson; h. Carter Ellis; c. Susan (Mrs. Charles Crutchfield), Joy (Mrs. Jeffrey Bartlett), Carter III; res: 4548 Oakland Ave. S., Mpls., Minn. 55407.

ELLIS, PEARL MAY, Librn., Southwestern Assemblies of God College, 1200 Sycamore, Waxahachie, Tex. 75165, '43–; Tchr., three yrs.; child evangelism work, Sunday Sch. Superintendent; ALA, Tex. Lib. Assn.; Tex. Jr. Col. Tchr. Assn.; N. Tex. Univ. at Denton, BA; Southwestern Assemblies of God Col., BA; b. Paden, Okla.; p. C. H. and Tela Nicholson Ellis.

ELLIS, REVA JEAN, Asst. Lib. Dir., Greensboro Public Library, 201 N. Greene St., Drawer X-4, Greensboro, N.C. 27402, '59–; Circ. Librn., '57–'59; Librn. (Leesburg, Fla.), '54–'57; Asst. Librn., Spartanburg (S.C.) Public Lib., '47–'54; Asst. Ext. Librn., Durham (N.C.) Public Lib., '46–'47; Mathematician, Nat. Advisory Comm. for Aeronautics (Langley Field, Va.), '41–'45; ALA, Southeastern Lib. Assn., N.C. Lib. Assn., Greensboro Lib. Club, Kappa Nu Sigma, BPW; Meredith Col., AB, '41; Univ. of N.C., BS (Lib. Sci.), '42; b. Marion, N.C., 1920; p. Virgil and Chloe Price Ellis; res: 802 N. Eugene St., Greensboro, N.C. 27401.

ELLIS, RUTH J., Dir. of PR, Georgia Easter Seal Society for Crippled Children and Adults, Inc., 1211 Spring St., N.W., Atlanta, Ga. 30309, '59–; Med. Rec. Librn., Ga. Warm Springs Fndn., '55–'59; Public Speaker, Greater N.Y. March of Dimes, '52–'54; Maxon Adv. Agcy., '46, terminated at onset of poliomyelitis; PRSA (Ga. Chptr.), AWRT (Ed., Tower Talk, Atlantia Chptr. nwsltr.); San Diego State Col. (Mdsng.), '36–'38; Fla. Southern Col. (Speech), '49–'50; Univ. of Fla. at Gainesville, BA (Speech and Radio Writing), '52 (cum laude; Phi Kappa Phi); grad. study; b. San Diego, Cal., 1918; res: 1394 Harvard Rd., N.E., Atlanta, Ga. 30306.

ELLISON, JUNE DARBY, PR Offcr., Mercantile Trust Company, 721 Locust, St. Louis, Mo. 63130, '67–; Staff Wtr., Commentator, KHMO (Hannibal), WMBA (Joplin), KSD and KXLW (St. Louis); Conducted radio progs. for children, "June Darby's Musical Story Book," two years; helped org. Downtown Activities Unlimited, '62–; Wms. Adv. Club of St. Louis (Pres., '64–'65), Nat. Assn. of Bank Wm., E. Oscar Thalinger Aw. for one-act verse drama (performed at Poetry Ctr., '65); Kan. State Univ., BS (Jnlsm.), '40; b. Topaka, Kan., 1917; p. Harry and Alberta Sellers Darby; h. Jay Ellison; c. Jodi, David Scott, John Michael; res: 7615 Stanford, St. Louis, Mo. 63130.

ELPERN, BETH SCHACHTER, Wtr., Prod., WHA Radio and Wisconsin State Broadcasting Service, Radio Hall, University of Wisconsin, Madison, Wis. 53706, '67–; Cont. Wtr., Traf. Mgr., '66–'67; Special Radio projects; Asst. Dir., Commty. Action Commn., Dane County, '66; Free-lance Ed., Tutor, Israel, '64–'66; Corr., Israel, '67; Major Armstrong Aws: Public Affairs, co-prod., "Black Christmas in Milwaukee," '67; News Wtr., co-prod., "The Anatomy of a Gyp," '68); Oh. State Univ. Aw., Wtr., Co-prod., "Pride and Prejudice: An American Heritage," '69; Univ. of Chgo., BA, '64 (Ill. State Scholar); Ulpan Beit Ziona America (Israel), '64–'66; Univ. of Wis., '66–'67; b.

Chgo., Ill., 1942; p. Abraham and Resea Kutok Schachter; h. Israel Elpern.

ELSE, CAROLYN WAHLBERG, Dir., Pierce County Library, 2356 Tacoma Ave. S., Tacoma, Wash. 98402, '65–; Br. Librn., '63–'65; Lincoln City (Neb.) Libs. '62–'63; U.S. Army Lib. Svcs. (France, Germany), '59–'62; Queensborough (N.Y.) Public Lib., '57–'59; ALA, Pacific N.W. Lib. Assn. (Secy., '69–'71); Wash. Lib. Assn. (Second VP, '69–'71); Stanford, BA, '56; Univ. of Wash., MS (Lib. Sci.), '57; b. Mpls., Minn., 1934; p. Elmer W. and Irma Seibert Wahlberg; h. (div.); c. Stephen, Catherine; res: 1414 N. Alder, Tacoma, Wash. 98406.

ELSON, RUTH MILLER, Prof. of Hist., Finch College, 52 E. 78th St., N.Y., N.Y. 10027, '62–; Auth., "Guardians of Tradition: American Schoolbooks of the 19th Century" ('64); teaching: Hunter Col., '60–'62, '46–'49; Vassar Col., '51–'60, '43–'45; Rockford Col., '49–'51; Am. Hist. Assn., Am. Studies Assn.; AAUW Fellowship, '57–'58; Vassar Col., BA, '39 (Phi Beta Kappa; Vassar Col. Fellowships, '39–'41; Vassar Fac. Fellowship, '57–'58); Columbia, MA, '40 (Columbia Univ. Fellowship, '45–'46; Fellow of Univ. Seminar in Am. Civilization); PhD, '52; b. Scranton, Pa., 1917; p. William C. and Margaret R. Smithson Miller; h. Robert Elson; c. Elizabeth; res: 100 La Salle St.-Apt. 12 D, N.Y., N.Y. 10027.

ELSTON, LORRAINE HIND, Free-lance Wtr., '69–; Ed., Wtr., colm., Albuquerque Tribune, '68; Gen. Assigt. Reptr., Feature Wtr., Lubbock Avalanche-Jnl., '55–'57; Info. Specialist, News Wtr., U.S. Army, '54–'55; Publicist, Feature Wtr., The Wool Bur., Inc., '54; Asst. Ed., Publrs. Auxiliary, '53; Asst. Ed., Current Biog., '52; Reptr., Chgo. Lerner and Peacock Nwsps., '49–'51; Theta Sigma Phi (Albuquerque Chptr. Treas., '68–'69), Ill. WPA; Medill Sch. of Jnlsm., Northwestern Univ., BS, '51 (with distinction); Grad. Sch. of Jnlsm., Columbia Univ., MS, '52 (Phillips Scholarship); b. Chgo., Ill.; p. Joseph and Dorothy Burmester Hind; h. Wolfgang Elston; c. Stephen F., Richard J.; res: 1023 Columbia Dr., N.E., Albuquerque, N.M. 87106.

ELTING, MARY LETHA, Auth: children's books; Auths. Guild of the Auths. League of Am., Archeological Soc. of N.J.; Univ. of Colorado, BA (Magna Cum Laude, Phi Beta Kappa) '27, One yr. grad. study, Univ. of Strasbourg, France; b. Creede, Colo. 1906; p. Charles and Clara Shawhan Elting; h. Franklin Folsom; c. Michael Brewster, Rachel Alice; res: Roosevelt, N.J. 08555.

ELVIN, ELLA ISABEL, Food Ed., New York Daily News, 220 E. 42nd St., N.Y., N.Y. 10017, '53–; Writing Asst., '53; Home Demonstration Agt., Mich. State Univ., '48–'53; Home Svc. Rep., L.I. Lighting Co., '46–'48; Am. Home Econs. Assn., Home Econsts. in Bus. (N.Y.C. Treas., Nwsltr. Ed.), N.Y. State Home Econs. Assn. (Treas., Nwsltr. Ed.), Adelphi Univ., BS (Home Econs.), '45; Columbia

Univ., Tchrs. Col., MA, '57; b. Ambler, Pa.; p. Clarence and Agnes Dickson Elvin; res: 160 S. Middle Neck Rd., Great Neck, N.Y. 11021.

ELY, VIRGINIA SHACKELFORD, Auth., 12 published books; AAUW, Theta Sigma Phi (Chaplain, '68); Tex. Wesleyan Col., AB, '37; Southwestern Baptist Theological Seminary, MRE, '37; Tex. Wms. Univ., MS, '51; p. Franklin Pierce and Susan Goldman Ely; res: 2700 Sixth Ave., Ft. Worth, Tex. 76110.

EMBREE, MARTHA LOUISE, Adv. Supvsr., Glidden Organic Chemicals, SCM Corp., P.O. Box 389, Jacksonville, Fla. 32201, '69–; Mktng. Asst., '68–'69; Freelance Copywtr., '66–'68; Adv. Asst., Chemagro Corp., '64–'66; Copy Chief, R. S. Townsend Adv. '62–'64; Prod. Asst., Opns. Secy., Film Mgr., KPRC-TV, '60–'62; AWRT, AAF, Fla. PR Assn., N.E. Fla. IEA; Univ. of Houston, BFA (Radio-TV), '58 (Alpha Epsilon Rho); b. Houston, Tex., 1936; p. Dr. Elisha D. and Alma B. Embree; res: 14660 Stacey Rd., Jacksonville, Fla. 32250.

EMBRY, MARGARET JACOB, Wtr., children's bks: "Blue Nosed Witch" ('53), "Kid Sister" ('56), "Mr. Blue" ('59), "Peg-Leg Willy" ('63); Tchr., Albuquerque Indian School, 920 Indian School Rd., Albuquerque, N.M. 87106, '69–; Tchr., Magdalena Public Sch. System; Lib. Asst., Mesa Public Lib.; Rschr., Bilingual Program, Univ. of N.M.; AAUW, Nat. Wtrs. Club, NEA; Univ. of Ut., BA, '40; Univ. of N.M., Grad. Sch.; b. Salt Lake City, Ut., 1919; p. Clarence C. and Florence C. Johnson Jacob; h. Alvin Leon Embry (dec.); c. Kristin Litchman, Susan Lee, Patricia Claire, Alan Laird, Meredith Gael, Jonathan Derek; res: 1352 Sage Loop, Los Alamos, N.M. 87544.

EMCH, LUCILLE BERTHA, Assoc. Librn., Assoc. Prof., University of Toledo Library, 2801 W. Bancroft St., Toledo, Oh. 43606, '53–; Assoc. Librn., '40–; Lib. Staff, '29–'40; WNBA, ALA, Oh. Lib. Assn., ZONTA, Phi Kappa Phi (Pres., '60–'61), Delta Kappa Gamma; Univ. of Toledo, BA, '30, MA, '39; Univ. of Mich., BA (Lib. Sci.), '41; b. Toledo, Oh.; p. Albert and Martha Welke Emch; res: 752 Alvison Rd., Toledo, Oh. 43612.

EMERSON, LAURA S., Assoc. Prof. of Speech, Marion College, Marion, Ind. 46952, '50–; Assoc., '35–'50; Miltonvale Wesleyan Col., '31–'35; Auth: "Aunt Laura's Storyhour Record" (Nat. Evangelical Film Fndn. Aw., '69), "Storytelling, the Art and Purpose ('59); Speech Assn. of Am., Intl. Platform Assn., NLAPW, Delta Kappa Gamma; Marion Col., AB, BS (Educ.), '30 (magna cum laude); Univ. of Wis., MA, '39; res: 223 E. 42nd, Marion, Ind. 46952.

EMERSON, LUCY GODFREY, Ed., Angola Herald, Angola, Ind. 46703, '61–; Colmst., '37–; Special Asst. to the Pres., Tri-State Col. '68–; Dir. of News Svcs., '50–'68; Wms. Press Club of Ind., Ft. Wayne Press Club, NFPW, Steuben Tuberculosis Assn. (Bd. of Dirs., Pubcty. Chmn., '41–); b. Allen, Mich., 1902; p. Roy

and Augusta Schultz Godfrey; h. Kenton C. Emerson (dec.); c. David F., Andrew C.; res: 309 E. Broad St., Angola, Ind. 46703.

EMERY, ANNE McGUIGAN, Wtr. for young people, 16 bks. (The Westminster Press, '49–), ten bks. (Macrae Smith, '52–'65), eight bks. (Vanguard, Putnam, Rand McNally); Visiting Lectr., Northwestern Univ., Medill Sch. of Jnlsm., '60; Wtrs. Workshop, '64–'65; Tchr., '29–'40; Theta Sigma Phi, Midland Auths; Friends of Literature Cit., '69; ZONTA Aw. of Merit; Northwestern Univ., BA, '28 (Alumni Merit Aw., '62); b. Fargo, N.D., 1907; p. Hugh and Mabel Leininger McGuigan; h. John Douglas Emery; c. Mary Elizabeth (Mrs. Gustav Bittrich, Jr.), Katherine (Mrs. Bill Pogue), Joan (Mrs. Harry Hagey), Martha (Mrs. Michael Galbreath), Robert H.; res: Orcas, Wash. 98280.

EMMONS, DELIA GOULD, Auth: hist. novels incl. "Nothing in Life is Free" (Wash. State's offcl. cent. novel), pageants, plays, symphonic drama, motion pic. based on novel; Script Wtr., Paramount Pics. (Hollywood, Cal.), '53; Wtr. for Wash. State Hist. celebrations, '47, '53, '55; Curator, Wash. State Hist. Soc., '50 (Distg. Svc., '53; Life Mbr.); Histrn., Old Fort Nisqually Restoration Cncl., '46; numerous aws. for hist. writing on Wash. and Northwest; Who's Who of Am. Wm.; Who's Who in the West; Dic. of Intl. Biog.; Personalities of the West and Midwest; Royal Blue Bk.; The 2000 Wm. of Achiev.; educ: Seminary (Glencoe, Minn.); Univ. of Minn., BA, '12; Univ. of Wash.; work under Arthur Sullivant Hoffman, Crtv. Writing; b. Glencoe, Minn.; p. William and Katherine Wadel Gould; h. Allen Burdette Emmons; c. Allen G., Kathryn Nettelblad; res: 814 N. Lawrence, Tacoma, Wash. 98406.

EMMONS, FRANCES MARCIA, Ed., GM Engineering Staff, GM Technical Center, Warren, Mich. 48090, '56–; Ed., Publicist, S. S. Kresge Co., '49–'56; Asst. to Ed., Children's Fund of Mich. Lab., '42–'49; IEA of Detroit (Pres., '58–'59; Secy., VP; Distg. Svc. Plaque, '62), GM Girls' Club (Secy., '58–'59), ICIE (VP); Wayne State Univ., AB; b. Detroit, Mich., 1915; p. Frank and Bernice C. Green Emmons; res: 22580 Visnaw, St. Clair Shores, Mich. 48081.

ENERSEN, GABRIELLA BECVAR, Ed., Weekly Nwsp., McFarland Community Life, Community Publications, Inc., 6002 Exchange St., McFarland, Wis. 53558, '66–; Secy.-Treas.; Ed., Verona (Wis.) Press, '65–'66; Ed.-Owner, Fox Lake (Wis.) Rep. '62–'65; Wis. Press Wm., Wis. Press Assn., Nat. Nwsp. Assn., Madison Press Club; numerous aws. for nwsp. writing, photog.; Wis. Educ. Assn. Sch. Bell Aw. to the McFarland Commty. Life; Northwestern Univ., '56–'57; Univ. of Wis. Ext.; b. Chgo., Ill, 1938; p. Dr. L. E. and Sonja Kosner Becvar; h. David Enersen; res: 4908 Burma Rd., McFarland, Wis. 53558.

ENFIELD, GERTRUDE DIXON, Auth: "Verse Choir Technique," "Poetic Plays", "Holiday Book for Verse

Choirs," "The Courageous Houston"; assembled, ed. "The Life and Letters of Christopher Houston"; bk. of verse "Cups of Destiny"; Prof. of Speech, Univ. of Southern Cal.; Elementary Sch. Prin., 20 yrs.; Intl. Platform Assn., PEN Wm. (Laguna Beach Pres., '63–'64), Cal. Retired Tchrs., Assn. (Life Mbr.); U.C.L.A., BA (Educ.), '30; summer study in Verse Choir work (Oxford, Stratford, London), '34; Univ. of Southern Sal., MA. (Speech), '40; b. Hume, Mo., 1883; p. Thomas and Frances Norfleet Dixon; h. John Broughton Enfield (dec.); c. Dorothy (Mrs. Roy Thoroughman), Virginia, John; res: 201 Cypress Dr., Laguna Beach, Cal. 92651.

ENGELMYER, ROSE LERMAN, Commty. Club Aws. Dir., WSCR Radio, Rice Communications Inc., 1520 N. Keyser Ave., Scranton, Pa. 18503, '50–; Coordr., Elks Club; Secy., Head Bookkeeper, Penn Plumbing Supply Co., '46–'53; AWRT; active in Jewish groups; p. Hyman and Sadie Lerman; h. Earl Engelmyer; c. Steven, Deby; res: 840 Quincy Ave., Scranton, Pa. 18510.

ENGELS, LAONE GAGNON, Artist, Muralist, Tchr., Exhibitor; Green Bay (Wis.) Art Colony (Pres., '55–'60), Palettables (Pres., '65–); many blue ribbon, other aws. at private, public, traveling exhibits of art; Univ. of Wis., '64–'66; b. Marinette, Wis., 1909; p. Joseph A. and Gertrude Gordon Gagnon; h. Norbert Engels; res: Half Moon Lake, Pound, Wis. 54161.

ENGELSON, JOYCE, Sr. Ed., The Dial Press, 750 Third Ave., N.Y., N.Y. 10017, '62–; Ed.-in-chief, Abelard-Schuman Ltd., '57–'59; Ed., '55–'57; Edtl. Asst., The Viking Press, '52–'53; Wtr., novel, "Mountain of Villainy"; Co-Auth., "Silent Slain"; short fiction, Playboy, Atlantic Monthly, Quarterly Rev. of Lit., others; Wms. Nat. Bk. Assn.; Chmn., Nancy Bloch Aw., The Downtown Commty. Sch. (best bk. for yr. in intergroup rels.); Smith Col., '46–'48; Barnard Col., BA, '50 (Phi Beta Kappa; cum laude; distinction in maj. field-hist.); Columbia Univ., '50–'52; b. N.Y.C.; p. David and Marion Muriel Abrams Engelson; h. Norman Keifetz; c. Brom Daniel, Amanda Sara; res: 250 W. 24th St., N.Y., N.Y. 10011.

ENGINTUNCA, LOIS HUGHES, Assoc. Ed., World Publishing Co., Encyclopedia Division, 2080 W. 117 St., Cleve., Oh. 44111, '69–; Univ. of Mich., BA (with hons.); MA; b. Detroit, Mich.; p. Francis and Gertrude Otto Hughes; h. Mehmet Engintunca; res: 4605 Telhurst Rd., S. Euclid, Oh. 44121.

ENGLE, ELOISE KATHERINE, Free-lance Wtr.; Bks: "Dawn Mission" ('62), "Princess of Paradise" ('62), "Countdown for Cindy" ('62), "Sea Challenge" ('62), "Escape" ('63), "Pararescue" ('64), "Sea of the Bear" ('64), "Sky Rangers" ('65), "Earthquake" ('66), "Medic" ('67); Wash. Rep., D. Van Nostrand, '67–'68; PR, Robert Fulton Co., '67–'68; PR, Visiting Nurse Assn., '66–'68; Aviation/Space Wtrs. Assn., Combat Corrs. Assn., Auths. Guild, Wm.'s Adv. Club of Wash.,

Soc. of Wm. Geographers; George Washington Univ., '44–'47; b. Seattle, Wash., 1923; p. Floyd and Lois Best Hopper; c. Paula, David, Margaret; res: 6348 Cross Woods Dr., Falls Church, Va. 22044.

ENGLES, MARGARET LOUISE, News Ed., Drumright Derrick and Journal, 205 S. Ohio, Drumright, Okla. 74030, '53–; Mng. Ed., Lake Keystone News, '69–; Soc. Ed., '52–'53; Ed., Okla. PTA mag., '52; Soc. Ed., Lovington Press (N.M.), '51–'52; Drumright BPW Club (Pres., '67–'69; Secy., '65–'67); Beta Sigma Phi; headed commtys. Heart Fund and Cancer Fund Drs.; Univ. of Okla., BA (Jnlsm.), '51 (Sigma Delta Chi Aw. for Scholarship, '51); Okla. State Univ.; b. Sapulpa, Okla., 1928; p. Everett W. and Grace M. Heisten Engles; res: 324 W. Broadway, Drumright, Okla. 74030.

ENGLISH, ELIZABETH LOIS, Auth., poetry, 15 bks. published; Pres., Macksville State Bank, Macksville, Kan. 67557; Kan. Auths. Club; Intl. Dic. of Biog.; The 2,000 Wm. of Achiev.; Kan. Univ.; b. Macksville, Kan.; p. Alexander and Florence McMarran English; res: Macksville, Kan. 67557.

ENGLISH, SANDAL DAILEY, Food Ed., Arizona Daily Star, Tucson, Ariz., '69–; with husband, weekly synd. colm., "Gourmet On a Budget;" Staff Wtr., Tucson Daily Citizen, '65–'69; Wms. Ed., KTUC, '60–'65; Asst. Wms. Ed., Food Ed., Dallas News, '44–'52; Theta Sigma Phi, NPW (nat. radio Aws., '63–'65), Ariz. Press Wm. (aws., '63–'68); Hockaday Jr. Col. grad.; SMU; Univ. of Ark.; b. Dallas, Tex., 1916; p. Lawson and Madge Roberts Dailey; h. S. Pritchard English, Jr.; c. Tres, Lawson; res: 624 Texas Circle, Tucson, Ariz. 85711.

ENGLUND, SHIRLEY SIBERT, Ed., The Secretary, The National Secretaries Association, 1103 Grand Ave., Kan. City, Mo. 64106, '57–; Secy., Superior Distrb. Co., '60; A. F. Parmelee Cos., U.S. Safety Svc. Co., '58; Asst. Assn. Secy., Am. Hereford Assn., '56; Secy., Employers Reinsurance Corp., '51; Adv. and Sales Exec. Club of Kan. City, Adv. Wms. Round Table of Kan. City, Am. Soc. of Bus. Pubn. Eds. (Dir.), Nat. Secys. Assn.; Kan. City Jr. Col., '50; Univ. of Mo., '54; b. Kan. City, Mo., 1932; p. Durwood and Helen Darr Sibert; h. Curt England; c. Eda Darla, Eric Darr; res: 10214 Belmont, Kan. City, Mo. 64136.

ENID, HAMELIN, Copy Chief, Salit & Garlanda Advertising Inc., 275 Madison Ave., N.Y., N.Y. 10016, '67–; Copywtr.; Free-lance Comedy Wtr.; Film Wtr., Hilary Harris Films; N.Y. Univ. Heights, BA; b. N.Y.C.; p. Samuel and Michelle Holman.

ENNIS, LEE, Fashion Dir., Donahue Sales Corp., 41 E. 51st St., N.Y., N.Y. 10022, '50–; Fashion Coordr. Nachman's Dept. Store (Newport News, Va.), '49; Prom. Stylist, Butterick Pattern Co., '46–'48; Asst. Byr., Fashion Coordr., Bonwit Teller, '44–'46; Fashion Group, Inc., AWNY, AWRT, Wms. Fashion Fabric Assn., Who's Who of Am. Wm.; Muskingum Col., BS, '44;

N.Y.U., MS, '47; b. Floral Park, N.Y.; p. Arthur James and Lillian Kammerer Ennis; h. Daniel Rosenblath; res: 136 Roosevelt St., Garden City, N.Y. 11530.

ENSIGN, ALICE THROOP, Free-lance Artist, Art Dir., Negro History Bulletin, Graphic Arts Press, 1110 Oki St. N.E., Wash., D.C. 20002, '67–; Art Dir., Negro Hist. Bul., Designer of Prom. Material, F-I Artist, Books Inc., '67, Designer of Prom. Material, Jand's Inc., '66–'67; Mechanical, Layout Artist, Kaufmann Printing, '64–'66; Nat. Assn. of Indsl. Artists; Western Reserve Univ., '61–'64; Dept. Agriculture Grad. Sch., '64–'67; b. Portland, Ore., 1943; p. Vincent M. and Beatrice Terry Throop; h. Frederic Ensign; c. Marikka Elinor, Jordan Lorinda; res: 3050 Emerson St., Palo Alto, Cal. 94306.

ENSLEY, BERNIECE (TONI) ELLISON, Ed., Publr., Otero County Star, 922 New York, Alamogordo, N.M. 88310, '67–; Salesman, Waddell and Reed Mutual Fund, '66–'67; Exec., Aaronson Brs., '61–'66; Base Exchange Mgr., Army & Air Force Exchange Svc.; Byr. (Fort Carson, Colo.); Free-lance Wtr. (Seattle, Wash.); Free-lance poetry, humorous fiction; N.M. Press Assn., NLAPW, Altrusa, Alamogordo C. of C.; Univ. of Ore., '31–'33; Univ. of Wash. (Jnlsm.); b. Mansville, Alberta, Can. 1912; p. Emmett M. and Ella M. Johnson Ellison; h. Burt De Witt Ensley, Sr.; c. Enid (Mrs. Glenn Spruell), Lesli (Mrs. Richard Anderson), Burt De Witt, Jr., Janine; res: 1506 Mountain View, Alamogordo, N.M. 88310.

ENTRINGER, ROSEMARY, Ed., Railroad Bks., '65–; Mng. Ed., Trains Magazine, Kalmbach Publishing Co., 1027 N. Seventh St., Milw., Wis. 53233, '54–; Assoc. Ed., '48–'54; Edtl. Secy., '48; Theta Sigma Phi (VP-Membership, '69–'70), Assn. of Railway Eds., Railroad PR Assn.; Mundelein Col., BA, '47 (Crtv. Writing Aw.); b. Madison, Wis., 1925; p. Col. Joseph B. and Geraldine M. Hickey Entringer; res: 1129 N. Jackson St., Apt. 509, Milw., Wis. 53202.

EPSTEIN, BEVERLY, News Prodr., Westinghouse Broadcasting Co., WJZ-TV, 3725 Malden Ave., Balt., Md. 21211, '68–; Rschr.-Prod. Asst., ABC News, '65–'68; Prod. Asst., NBC News, '65; AWRT, Theta Sigma Phi; Am. Univ., BA (Jnlsm.), '65; b. Wash. D.C., 1943; p. Julius and Shirley Zinkow Epstein; res: 500 West University Pkwy., Apt. 14-U, Balt., Md. 21210.

EPSTEIN, ELENI SAKES, Fashion, Beauty Ed., Washington Evening Star, 225 Virginia Ave., S.E., Wash., D.C. 20008; Free-lance Fashion Wtr.; Lectr.; Adv. Club of Wash., Fashion Group (Reg. Dir., '53–'55), ANWC (VP, '52–'54), WNPC (Secy., '49–'50); First Fashion Writing Aw., J. C. Penney-Univ. of Mo., '61; Fashion Cits: fur industry, shoe industry; Cal. Fashion Aw.; George Washington Univ.; Columbia Univ. (Jnlsm.); b. Wash., D.C., 1925; p. Constantine D. and Aspasia Econonon Sakes; h. Sidney Epstein.

EPSTEIN, KATHRYN, Radio-TV Info. Offcr.,

Health Services & Mental Health Administration, United States Public Health Service, Health, Education and Welfare, Parklawn Bldg. Rockville, Md. 20852, '67– (High Quality Performance aw., '68); Pres., Owner, Kathryn Epstein Asso., '65–'67; Sls. Mgr., Radio Stations WDON, WASH-FM, '57–'65; Assoc. Ed., TV Digest, '57; Adv. Mgr., Leo M. Bernstein Co., '56–'57; Partner, Jay-Kay Assocs., '53–'56; Acting Head, Distilled Spirits and Wines Sec., OPS, '51–'53; Sls. Off. Mgr., Frankfort Distillers Corp., '48–'51; adm. work, U.S. Dept. of Agriculture, '37–'48 (svc. aw., '47); AWRT; President's Comm. for Employing Handicapped, John F. Kennedy Ctr. for Performing Arts; March of Dimes (Campaign Mgr., '55–'56; Coordr., '53–'55), active in Am. Cancer Soc., Nat. Fndn. Infantile Paralysis (aw., '54); b. Milw., Wis.; p. Benjamin and Rose Margolis Epstein; res: 2107 Belvedere Blvd., Silver Spring, Md. 20902.

ERDMAN, LOULA GRACE, Wtr. in Residence, West Texas State University, Canyon, Tex.; Assoc. Prof. of Eng., '45–; Auth: short stories, articles, novels, collections, non-fiction bks., incl. "The Years Of The Locust" (Dodd, Mead-Redbook prize novel, '47), "The Edge Of Time" ('50), "The Wind Blows Free" (Dodd, Mead-American Girl prize, '52), "Many A Voyage" ('60), "Room To Grow" (Tex. Inst. of Letters Aw., '62), "Life Was Simpler Then" ('63), "Another Spring" ('66), "A Time To Write" ('69); Theta Sigma Phi, Kappa Delta Pi, NEA; Central Mo. State Col., BS, '31; Tchrs. Col., Columbia Univ., MA, '41; Univ. of Wis.; Univ. of Southern Cal.; b. Alma, Mo.; p. August F. and Mollie Maddox Erdman; res: 2208 Lipscomb, Amarillo, Tex. 79109.

ERDMANN, VIRGINIA MAE, Free-lance PR Cnslt.; Wtr., Publicist, Manpower, Inc., World Hq. (Milw.), '65–'68; Wms. Ed., Green Bay Press-Gazette, '56–'65; Wms. Program Dir., WJPG, '56; Adv.-Sls. Prom. Wtr., Hardware Mutuals Ins. Cos., '53–'55; numerous nat. aws.; Univ. of Wis., BSJ; St. Norbert Col., Marquette Univ.; b. Green Bay, Wis., 1931; p. Dr. Winford and Clara Shalhoub Erdmann; res: 3231 S. Webster Ave., Green Bay, Wis. 54301.

ERICKSON, CATHERINE LINDHSTROM, Radio Copywtr., Radio Station WJTN, Hotel Jamestown Bldg., Jamestown, N.Y. 14701, '67–; Prom. Dir., '40–'45; Prom. Dir., Copywtr., WJOC, '50–'60; Adv. Mgr., Bigelow's (Dept. Store), '45–'48; Dir. of Local Adv., Augustana Synodical Convs., '56, '58, '61; Music Tchr., Piano, '61–'67; BPW, Music Study Club (Treas., '66–'67), Mozart Club, Order of Eastern Star (Mt. Sinai Chptr. Musician, '65–'69); Alfred Univ.; private piano instr. under supervision of Julliard Sch. of Music; b. Jamestown, N.Y., 1920; p. Alex and Sarah Anderson Lindhstrom; h. Sherwood Erickson; c. Rachel Ann, Robert Alex; res: 345 Price St., Jamestown, N.Y. 14701.

ERICKSON, GLADYS A. (Finston), Staff Wtr., Reptr., Chicago Today, 441 N. Mich. Ave., Chgo., Ill. 60611; Reptr., Wtr., Colmst., nwsps. and radio (Joliet); Prod.-

Commentator, radio; Pfsnl. Drama, '39–'46; Auth: "Warden Ragen of Joliet" (Dutton, '57), mag. articles, bk. revs.; Theta Sigma Phi (Headliner Aw., '66; Chgo. Chptr. VP, '68–'69), Chgo. Alliance of BPW (Past Pres.), Friends of Literature (Bd. Mbr., '65–'69), NFPW (Wm. of Achiev., '67), IWPA (first mbr. to be Wm. of Yr. twice, '63, '67); John Howard Assn. Aw., '65; Golden Cross Royal Order of Ephoiia from King Paul of Greece; Distg. Svc. Medal, City of Athens, Greece, '69; Joliet Jr. Col.; Joliet Musical Col.; b. Joliet, Ill.; p. George and E. Kittie McBride Arbeiter; h. Charles Finston; c. Carl Richard Erickson; res: 1400 Lake Shore Dr., Chgo., Ill. 60610.

ERICKSON, JACQUELINE L., Features Ed., Armed Forces Journal, 1710 Connecticut Ave., N.W., Wash., D.C. 20009, '69–; Prom. Mgr., '68; Mng. Ed., Nat. Defense Transportation Jnl., '60–'67; Mng. Ed., Export Trade (N.Y.C.), '55–'59; OPC, ZONTA; Northwestern Univ., BS, '53; b. Chgo., Ill., 1931; p. John W. and Margaret Lemerle Nolan Erickson; res: 560 "N" St. S.W., Wash., D.C. 200024.

ERICKSON, LOIS DARLENE, Engraver-Reptr., Chanute Publishing Co., 15 S. Highland, Chanute, Kan. 66720, '60–; Proofreader, four yrs.; Chanute Jr. Col., '50; b. Chanute, Kan., 1930; p. Knoke D. and Esther L. Erickson; res: 215 N. Lafayette, Chanute, Kan. 66720.

ERICKSON, MARION IHRIG, Special Educ. Tchr. Cnslt., Ypsilanti Public Schs., 125 N. Huron, Ypsilanti, Mich. 48197, '60–; Supvsr., Follow Through Project, Dept. of Rsch. and Dev., '68–'69; Elementary Tchr. (Wis., Ore., Ill., Mich.), '35–; incl. six yrs. in special educ.; Visiting Lectr., Eastern Mich. Univ., '61; Smith-Mundt Grantee to Nepal as Educ. Advisor, '58–'59; Auth., educ. materials, bks. incl. "The Mentally Retarded Child in the Classroom" (The Macmillan Co., '65), "We Speak, Read and Write," Bks. 1, 2 (pubn. in Nepal); NEA, state and local educ. assns., Cncl. of Exceptional Children; Wis. State Col., BA, '35; Eastern Ore. Col., '48, '49; Eastern Mich. Univ., MA, '58; Univ. of Mich., '58; b. Centuria, Wis., 1913; p. William and Mabel TenEyck Ihrig; h. E. Walfred Erickson; c. Karen (Mrs. James Spaulding), Susan, David; res: 1209 Whittier Blvd., Ypsilanti, Mich. 48197.

ERICSSON, MARY KENTRA, PR Rep., Pittsburg Unified School District, 2000 Railroad Ave., Pittsburg, Cal. 94565, '59–; PR, Pittsburg Commty. Hosp., '57–'59; Nwsp. Reptr., Pittsburg Post-Dispatch; Free-lance Wtr., Nwsp. Reptr.; Auth., children's factual bk., "Glasses for Gladys"; educ. articles in Grade Tchr., Instr., numerous trade pubns., '52–'69; Cal. Wtrs. Club, Pittsburg BPW (Wm. of Yr., '57; Charter Mbr., Past Pres., Secy.), NSPRA, Cal. Sch. Employees Assn. #44; excerpt of work in "Effective Public Relations"; Scholarship, Nat. Sch. PR (Portland, Ore.), '64; Univ. of Cal.; Kennedy Univ.; Diablo Valley Col.; b. S.F., Cal., 1910; p. Tony and Pere Kentra; h. (div.);

c. Kent, Keith, Victor; res: 1903 Railroad Ave., Pittsburg, Cal. 94565.

ERIKSEN, VIVIAN LUND, Ed., Pers. & Commty. Rel., Haveg Industries, Inc., Super Temp Wire Div., P.O. Box 7, Winooski, Vt. 05404, '66–; City Ed., Vt. Publ. Co. (Burlington), '65–'66; Ed., Publr., Surburban Observer (Sandy, Ut.), '62–'63; Adv., Provo (Ut.) Daily Herald, '58–'59; AAIE; Vivian Eriksen Survival Aw., '69; b. Mpls., Minn., 1937; p. Norman and Josiephine Thornburg Lund; c. G. Keith, Dennis Donn, Kathryn Janeth, Steven Scott, Susan Elizabeth; res: 236 S. Winooski Ave., Burlington, Vt. 05404.

ERIKSSON, MARGUERITE ANNE, Chmn., Elementary French Dept., York City School District, 329 S. Lindbergh Ave., York, Pa. 17405, '52–; Tchr., '31–'53; Co-auth., "Foreign Languages in the Elementary School" (Prentice-Hall, '64); NEA, Pa. Modern Lang. Assn. (VP, '64–'66), Pa. Educ. Assn.; Valley Forge Freedom Fndn. aw., '59; Pa. State Univ., BA, '38; Western Reserve Univ., MA, '60; b. Rochester, N.Y., 1911; p. August and Margaret Kunkel Eriksson; res: 170 E. Springettsbury Ave., York, Pa. 17403.

ERLANDSON, CHARLOTTE RATHMANN, Wtr., Leader Printing Company, Box 176, Lake Mills, Wis. 53551; Ed., Co-publr., Lake Mills Leader, '39–'65; Tchr., Elmhurst (Ill.) Public Schs., '30–'39; Wis. Reg. Wtrs. Assn., Lake Mills Wms. Club; active in civic orgs.; Sigma Delta Chi Jnlsm. aw., '40; Marquette Univ., '24–'25; Univ. of Wis., BA (Jnlsm) '27; b. Milw., Wis., 1904; p. Otto and Charlotte Ludovici Rathmann; h. Willis Erlandson; c. Mrs. John J. Schroeder; res: 365 W. Prospect St., Box 176, Lake Mills, Wis. 53551.

ERLICH, LILLIAN, Dir. of Pubns., Child Study Association of America, 9 E. 89th St., N.Y., N.Y. 10028, '68–; Assoc. Ed., Jr. Lit. Guild, '63–'68; Auth., "What Jazz Is All About" (Julian Messner, '62); Co-auth., "Modern American Career Women" (Dodd, Mead, '59); Auths. League of Am.; Cornell Univ.; Columbia Univ.; b. Johnstown, Pa.; p. Abraham and Bessie Ginsberg Feldman; h. John J. Erlich; c. John L., Nina E. Singer; res: 145 E. 16th St., N.Y., N.Y. 10003.

ERNSTES, MARY ANN, Publr., Ed., The Brookshire Times, 806 Ave. C, Katy, Tex. 77450, '47–; News Wtr.; Gulf Coast Press Assn., Tex. Press Wm., Tex. Vocational Agriculture Assn. (Distg. Svc. Aw., '58), active in civic and ch. groups; Burroughs Bus. Course, '41; Univ. of Houston; b. Houston, Tex., 1917; p. John and Rose Bischof Ernstes; res: Rte. 1, Katy, Tex. 77450.

ERSOFF, MARCIE FEINGOLD, Info. Specialist, Dade County Public Schools, 1410 N.E. Second Ave., Miami, Fla. 33132, '69–; Journalistic Cnslt., Dept. of Public Info., '68–'69; Dade County Coordr., Project Public Info., Elementary and Secondary Educ. Act of '65 Title V grant, '67–'68; Cnslt.; PR staff, Fla. Gubernatorial Campaign, Governor Haydon Burns, '66; Staff Reptr., Miami (Fla.) Herald, '58–'64; Fla. Wms.

Press Club (First Prize Aws., '60, '61, '62), Theta Sigma Phi, Phi Kappa Phi, Kappa Tau Alpha, Alpha Kappa Delta; Jewish Family and Childrens Svc. Bur. (Bd. Dirs., '64–'70), City of Miami Lib. System (Bd. Trustees, '69–'70), civic, polit. groups; Syracuse Univ., '54–'55; Univ. of Fla., BS, '58 (summa cum laude); b. Monticello, N.Y., 1937; p. Moe and Natalie Barer Feingold; h. Stanley Ersoff; c. Brett, Seth; res: 149 Shore Dr. W., Miami, Fla. 33133.

ERVIN, JANET HALLIDAY, Free-lance Wtr.; The White House Cook Book ('64); Reptr., Muncie Evening Press, '41–'44; Guest Ed.-in-Chief, Mademoiselle Col. Issue, '45; Winner, Vogue Prix de Paris, '46; Theta Sigma Phi; Univ. Chgo., PhB, '46; b. Muncie, Ind., 1923; p. Everett and Lois Kidnocker Halliday; h. Howard Ervin; c. Howard, Dennis, David; res: 2450 N. 97th St., Milw., Wis. 53226.

ESALA, LILLIAN DUNBAR, Head Librn., Virginia Public Library, 215 Fifth Ave. S., Virginia, Minn. 55792, '61–; County Librn., '45–'46; Hoyt Lakes Public Lib., '59–'60; Social Worker, St. Louis County, '55; Lib. Asst., N.Y. Public Lib., '44–'45; ALA, Arrowhead Lib. Assn., Minn. Lib. Assn. (Cert. of Merit, '66); Univ. of Toledo, BA, '44; Columbia Univ. Sch. of Lib. Svc., BS, '45; b. Toledo, Oh., 1923; p. Walter and Helen Roth Dunbar; h. Sulo Esala; c. Duane B., Lanette; res: Rte. 1, Box 180, Embarrass, Minn. 55732.

ESCH, KAREN EILEEN, AE, Fourth Allegheny Corporation, 2020 Investment Bldg., Pitt., Pa. 15222, '67–; Feature Wtr., Staff Wtr., two free Wash. County Nwsps: The Advertiser, The Almanac; Theta Sigma Phi; Duquesne Univ., BA (Eng.), '65; Univ. of Pitt., MEd, '66; b. Pitt., Pa., 1943; p. William and Veronica Heffernan Esch; res: 1556 Tolma Ave., Pitt., Pa. 15216.

ESCHMANN, CLARA HOOKS, Ed., Food Sec., Macon Telegraph and News, P.O. Box 4167, Macon, Ga. 31208, '68–; Free-lance wtr., 13 yrs.; Wms. Ed., Griffin News, 4 yrs.; Dir. of Pubcty., Wesleyan Col., 7 yrs.; Tchr. of Jnlsm.; Macon Wtrs. Club (Offcr.); Georgia Southwestern Col., '34–'36; Univ. of Ga., ABJ, '38 (Theta Sigma Phi; Phi Mu); b. Americus, Ga., 1917; p. William Glenn and Clara Belle Davenport Hooks; h. Edgar A. Eschmann, Jr.; c. Edgar A., III, Clare B., Mrs. John D. Spear; res: 1180 S. Jackson Springs Rd., Macon, Ga. 31201.

ESHELMAN, MIRIAM JEAN, Prodr., Earle Ludgin & Co., 410 N. Michigan Ave., Chgo., Ill. 60611, '60–'69; Reservation Supvsr., Eastern Airlines, '55–'58; Sales Rep., George A. Hormel & Co., '52–'55; Soprano Soloist and Concert Artist; Cinn. Conservatory of Music (Scholarship); b. Pitt., Pa.; p. Paul and Jane Thompson Eshelman; res: 3200 N. Lake Shore Dr., Chgo., Ill. 60657.

ESPEDAHL, MARTHA ELIZABETH, Fashion Ed., News-Journal, 831 Orange St., Wilmington, Del. 19899, '64–; Home Furnishings Ed., Post-Courier (Charleston, S.C.), '63–'66; Wilmington Press Club, Fashion Group of Philadelphia; Dorothy Dawe Home Furnishings Aw., '63; NPWC aw., '64; S.C. Press Assn. aws., '63–'67; Univ. of S.C., BA, '63; b. Columbia, S.C., 1941; p. Kaare and Elizabeth Stark Espedahl; res: 223 Greenbank Rd., Wilmington, Del. 19808.

ESSIG, NANCY CLAIRE, Pubcty. Dir., Columbia University Press, 440 W. 110th St., N.Y., N.Y. 10025, '66–; Pubcty. Assoc., Dell Publ. Co., '65–'66; Asst., Pubcty. Dir., Charles Scribner's Sons, '62–'64; PPA, Wms. Fac. Club, Columbia Univ.; Ohio Univ., BA, '62; b. Canton, Oh., 1939; p. Atlee and Bernice Bowen Essig; res: 336 West End Ave., N.Y., N.Y. 10023.

ESTERGREEN, MARION MORGAN, Auth., "Kit Carson: A Portrait in Courage" (Univ. of Okla. Press), others; Kit Carson Memorial Park Advisory Bd. (Chmn.), C. of C. (Exec. Secy.); Am. Post Lauretate Search aw.; NLAPW aw.; Univ. of N.M., Univ. of Wis.; h. (dec.); res: P.O. Box 343, Taos, N.M. 87571.

ESTES, RITA ZENZEN, VP, PR, S. L. Brown & Associates, 3231 Audley, Houston, Tex. 77006, '67–; Dir. of PR, Weekley & Valenti, '63–'67; Dir. of PR, Richard L. Minns, '59–'63; Special Ed., Made in Europe, Frankfurt, Germany; Houston C. of C., PRSA (Accreditation, '68; Dir., Treas.), Tex. PR Assn. (former Dir.); Univ. of Ill.; Northwestern Univ.; b. Chgo., Ill., 1929; p. Nicholas and Marie Reiser Zenzen; h. Leland Estes; c. Victoria, Lorilei, Erik; res: 5503 Lymbar, Houston, Tex. 77035.

ESTES, THELMA JONES, Dir. of Lib. Svcs., Fort Knox Dependent Schools, Building 7474, Fort Knox, Ky. 40121, '60–; Librn., '54–'60; Tchr., '53–'54; Librn., Crab Orchard, Ky. HS, '51–'53; Tchr., '50–'51; Pulaski County (Ky.) Schs., '37–'40; ALA, Fourth Dist. Lib. Assn. (Pres., '60), Ky. Assn. of Sch. Librns. (Treas., '59), Ky. Audio Visual Assn., Ky. Lib. Assn., Ky. Educ. Assn., NEA, Southeastern Lib. Assn., Fort Knox Educ. Assn.; Univ. of Ky., AB, '54; Nazareth Col., MS (Lib. Sci.), '62; b. Mt. Victory, Ky., 1915; p. James and Polly Garrison Jones; h. James L. Estes; c. Betty Deane (Mrs. David Youmans), James B.; res: 414 East Spring Rd., Radcliff, Ky. 40160.

ESTIN, LIBBYADA STRAVER, Med. Wtr., Kallir, Philips, Ross, Inc., 866 Third Ave., N.Y., N.Y. 10022, '69–; Med. Wtr., L. W. Frohlich and Company/Intercon International Inc., '68–'69; AE, Dir. PR, J. S. Fullerton, Inc., '67–'68; VP Adv., PR, Behrman/Estin Inc., '65–'67; Pres., Design Cnslt., PR Cnslt., Libbyada Estin Interiors, '62–'65; med. rsch., tech. wtr., med. PR, '60–'62; RN; PRSA, AWNY, AAF; Sigma Theta Tau; Who's Who in PR; Syracuse Univ., '55–'57; Columbia Univ., BS, '60; N.Y. Sch. of Interior Design, '62; b. Newark, N.J., 1937; p. Barney and Florence Tenkin Straver; h. Leonard A. Estin; res: 33 E. 22nd St., N.Y., N.Y. 10010.

ETS, MARIE HALL, Artist, Auth., Children's Bks., incl: "Automobiles for Mice" (Jr. Lit. Guild Selection,

'64), "Cow's Party" (Viking Press; '58), "Nine Days to Christmas" (Caldecott Medal, '60), "Play With Me" (Intl. Jury Hon. Bk., '56), "Mr. Penny's Circus" (Weekly Reader's Bk. Club, '61), numerous others; Auth., (adult biog.), "Rosa, the Life of an Italian Immigrant" (Univ. of Minn. Press, '70); Auths. Guild; New York Herald Tribune's Spring Bk. Festival Aw., '47; Lawrence Col., '11–'12 (Latin Aw.); N.Y. Sch., Fine & Applied Art, '12–'13; Univ. of Chgo., PhB; grad. work, Chgo. Sch. of Civics and Philanthropy; Art Inst. of Chgo.; Columbia Univ.; b. N. Greenfield, Wis.; p. Walter and Mathilda Carhart Hall; h. Harold Ets (dec.); res: 501 W. 123rd St., N.Y., N.Y. 10027.

EVANS, EDNA HOFFMAN, Tchr., English Department, Phoenix College, 1202 W. Thomas Rd., Phoenix, Ariz. 85013, '48–; Auth: "Written with Fire" (Holt, Rinehart, '62), "Bob Vincent, Veterinarian" (Dutton, '49), other juv. bks.; Photog. Ed., Nature Magazine, '46–'54; Corr., Tampa Tribune, '43–'46; Reptr., Feature Wtr., Lakeland Ledger, '42–'46; Tchr., St. Petersburg HS, '38–'42; Reptr., Feature Wtr., St. Petersburg Times, '36–'38; AAUP, Delta Kappa Gamma, Nat. Humane Soc., Nat. Wildlife Fedn., Westerners; Fla. State Col. for Wm., AB, '34; MA, '35; Duke Univ., Fla. Southern Col., Ariz. State Univ., Northern Arizona Univ.; b. Fairport Harbor, Oh., 1913; p. George and Veda Biery Hoffman; h. William J. Evans (div.); res: 1607 W. Orangewood Ave., Phoenix, Ariz. 85021.

EVANS, ELIZABETH GAUDELLI, Mgr., Co-owner, Radio Station WSUX, Dual Highway 13, Seaford, Del. 19973, '55–; Former owner, WMRA (WMYB), '50–'54; Radio WDOV, '48–'50; Secy., Radio Corp. of America, '30–'48; Moore Inst. of Art, Phila., '39; b. Camden, N.J., 1911; p. Nicholas and Clara Iacovelli Gaudelli; h. William Courtney Evans; res: 723 Hurley Park Dr., Seaford, Del. 19973.

EVANS, ELIZABETH WRIGHT, Educ. Dir., KING-TV, King Broadcasting, 320 Aurora, Seattle, Wash. 98109, '51–; Colmst. and Wtr., Seattle Times, '46–; PR Dir., Seattle Public Lib., '51–; Owner, PR agcy., '46–; AWRT (Nat. Bd., '62–'63; Evergreen Chptr. Pres., '68–'69), Theta Sigma Phi (Nat. Headliner Aw., '57; Alpha Chptr., Univ. of Wash., Wm. of Achiev., '55), Wms. Univ. Club of Seattle, UN Bd.; Alpha Gamma Delta Distg. Svc. Aw., '63; B'nai B'rith Svc. Aw., '54; Univ. of Wash., BA, '29; b. Seattle, Wash., 1909; p. Elias Allen and Mary Bailey Wright; h. Alfred Goldblatt; c. John Rhys Evans Jr., Wayne Evans, Gwyneth Evans (Mrs. Theodore Gamble); res: 5414 N.E. 44th St., Seattle, Wash. 98105.

EVANS, JUDY LEE, Ed., First Family, First National Bank in Dallas, 1401 Elm St., Dallas, Tex. 75222, '65–; Reptr., Photogr.; Titche-Goettinger Career Advisory Bd., '68–'69; Am. Inst. of Banking (Dallas Chptr. Dir., '69–'72), Secy., '67–'68), ICIE, Dallas IEA (3rd VP, '68–'69; three Eddy aws.); Aw. of Excellence, S.W. Conf. of Indsl. Eds., '67; numerous other photog. aws.; Harding Col. (Searcy, Ark.), BA (Bus. Educ.), '65;

b. Martinez, Cal., 1944; p. Everett and Beulah Rogers Evans; res: 3525 Travis, #101, Dallas, Tex. 75204.

EVANS, MARY ELLEN, Editor, Writer, Librn., Pacem in Terris Library, 323 E. 47th St., N.Y., N.Y. 10017, '69–; Ed., P. J. Kenedy & Sons, '65–'68, '51–'54; Staff Ed., New Catholic Encyclopedia, '61–'65; Asst. Ed., Regnery, '49; Asst. Ed., Books on Trial, '45–'49; WNBA; Clarke Col., AB, '34; State Univ. of Ia., AM, '39; b. Dubuque, Ia.; p. John David and Nell Early Evans; res: 410 W. 24th St., N.Y., N.Y. 10011.

EVANS, NELL WOMACK, Free-lance Wtr., Artist, articles and colms. in numerous nwsps. and mags. plus several bks.; two one-man art shows in '68; Denver Post, '47–'50; Seattle Times, '46–'47; Spokane (Wash.) Chronicle, '43–'46; Utah, '41–'43; Pueblo (Colo.) Star-Journal-Chieftain, '39–'41; Fountain (Colo.) Herald and Knob Hill Journal, '37–'39; Colo. Springs Art Guild, Colo. Springs Fine Arts Ctr., Theta Sigma Phi (Colo. Springs Pres., '66–'68), Colo. Press Wm. (Pres., '62; Wm. of Achiev., '62), Colo. Auths. League (Tophand Aw., '57, '62, '65, '67), Typographical Un., NLAPW (Nat. Ed., Panorama section of The Pen Wm., '64–'66; Nat. Letters Bd., The Pen Wm.; biennial aw. for features, '56, '60, '66; first place for bk. manuscript, '66; Pikes Peak VP and Mbrship. Chmn.); Ark. A & M., '28–'29; Ark. Tchrs. Col., '29–'31; b. Kirby, Ark., 1910; p. Henry M. and Minnie Taylor Womack; h. Rex M. Evans; res: 3311 Pennsylvania Ave., Colorado Springs, Colo. 80907.

EVANS, ROSA BARTELL, Bdcst. Corp. Conslt., Bartell Broadcasters, Inc., 3500 N. Sherman Blvd., Milw., Wis. 53216, Pres. four yrs.; VP (adm.) Bartell Media-Publishing and Adm. TV sta., Netherlands Antilles; Gen. Mgr., WOKY (Milw.), seven yrs.; AWRT, Milw. Adv. Club; Who's Who Of Am. Wm.; Univ. Wis., '41 grad.; b. Milw. Wis., 1918; p. Benjamin and Lena Tarkowski Beznor; h. Ralph E. Evans; c. Ralph, III, Lawrence, Bruce, Benjamin; res: 3657 North Point Dr., Milw., Wis., 53217.

EVANS, VERDA BACH, Dir. Supvsr. of Eng., Cleveland Public Schools, 1380 E. Sixth St., Cleve., Oh. 44114, '63–; Supvsr. of Eng., East HS, '46–'54; Eng. Jnlsm. Tchr., John Adams HS, '34–'46; Book Review Staff, Cleveland Plain Dealer, '49–; Auth: "Types of Literature" (Ginn & Co., '70), "Using Your Language" (McGraw-Hill Bk. Co., '57); WNBA, Cleve. Cncl. of Tchrs. of Eng. (Pres., '64–'66), Delta Kappa Gamma (Upsilon Chptr. Pres., '50–'52), Trustee, Otterbein Col., '62–; Great Lakes Shakespeare Assn. (Bd. Mbr., '56–); Otterbein Col., AB, '28; Radcliffe Col., MA, '40; Otterbein Col., LHD (hon.), '57; b. Navarre, Oh.; p. Benjamin and Alice Shetler Evans; c. four.

EVARTS, DRU RILEY, free-lance non-fiction wtr. and bk. ed., 39 Strouds Run Rd., Athens, Oh. 45701; currently teaching asst. pursuing PhD in mass commtns.; Ed. or Ghost Wtr., 10 bks., 15 dissertations; Free-lance Ed. or Indexer, publrs. Harper & Row,

McGraw-Hill, D. C. Heath, John Wiley and Sons, Follett Corp., and auths.; Asst. to Ed. for Jnl. of Mktng., five yrs.; Pers. and PR Dir., Trumbull Memorial Hosp. (Warren), '52–'56; Wtr., News Bur., Oh. Univ. (Athens), '51–'52; Theta Sigma Phi (Oh. Univ. Student Chptr. Pres., '50–'51; N. Shore Chgo. Alumni Chptr. past offcr.), Kappa Tau Alpha, Sigma Delta Chi, AWRT; Oh. Univ., Athens, BSJ, '51 (cum laude; Fund Aw., '51); MS, '70 (magna cum laude); b. Summit County, Oh., 1929; p. Alfred Ervin and Etna Twyman Riley; h. (dec.); c. Dale Irene, Leslie Alan, Valerie Dru, Jill Ann.

EVATT, HARRIET TORREY, Auth., Illus. juv. bks., "The Secret of Solitary Cove" ('64), "An Army in Pigtails" ('62), "The Mystery of Lonesome Manor" ('62), many others; numerous mag. stories, illus.; NLAPW, Theta Sigma Phi, Columbus Art League (Don Casto portrait aw., '45), Worthington Hist. Soc.; Ohioana aw., best juv. bk., '45; Who's Who of Am. Wm.; Columbus Art Sch., '27–'28; b. Knoxville, Tenn.; p. John McCullough and Lenna Richardson Torrey; h. William S. Evatt; res: 74 E. Kanawha Ave., Columbus, Oh. 43214.

EVERETT, FRIEDA WYANDT, Dir. of Info., Dairy Society International, 1145 19th St. N.W., Wash., D.C. 20036, '52–; PR Cnslt. Dairy Industries Supply Assn., Dairy Industries Soc., Intl., '47–'51; Press Info. Unit, OIC, Dept. of State, '47; Chief of Doc. Articles Sec., Intl. Info. Svc., '46–'47; Chief of Pubns., Asst. Chief, Off. of Inter-Am. Affairs, '42–'46; mag. writing, '25–'42; PR, campaigns for Westchester County Dept. of Welfare, other groups, '25–'42; ed., Club Mbrs. of N.Y., '40; staff, Liberty Magazine (N.Y.), '36; Part Owner, Westchester County (N.Y.) nwsps.; Ed., Westchester County Times, Tuckahoe Record, '30–'37; Edtl. Staff, N.Y. Daily Investment News, N.Y. Evening Graphic, N.Y. Daily News Sunday Magazine; WNPC, ANWC (Treas., '67–'69), Soc. of Wm. Geographers, NWC (N.Y.), Theta Sigma Phi (Nat. Headliner, '47); Hiram Col. (Hiram, Oh.), AB (Eng.), '21; Columbia Univ. Sch. of Jnlsm., BLitt., '24; b. Angola, Ind.; p. J. W. and Martha E. Purinton Wyandt; h. Roberts Everett; res: 12602 Eldrid Ct., Silver Spring, Md. 20904.

EVERETT, SARAH JOHNSON, Librn., East Rome High School, 1401 McCall Blvd., Rome, Ga. 30161, '60–; Librn., '33–'60; ALA, Southeastern Lib. Assn., Ga. Lib. Assn., Rome Educ. Assn.; Who's Who of Am. Wm., '68–'69; b. Cornelia, Ga., 1910; p. Allison and Minnie Glover Johnson; h. Alvin Everett; c. Mrs. Marvin Smith; res: 301 E. Fifth Ave., Rome, Ga. 30161.

EVERHART, JANE MARCIN, Pubns. Ed., Mt. Sinai Hospital, '69–; Asst. Fiction Ed., Cosmopolitan Magazine, '68–'69; PR Wtr., L.I. Jewish Hosp., '68; Reptr., L.I. Press, '67; Reptr., Newsday, '66–'67; Reptr., Bergen Record, '65–'66; Edtl. Asst., The Doctor's Wife mag., '60–'61; NOW (Ed., Nwsltr.; Pubcty. Co-chmn.); State Univ. of Ia., BA, '56 (magna cum laude, Phi Beta Kappa, merit scholarships), b. Springfield, Mass., 1935; p. Stanley and Aniela Traks Marcin; h. Dean Everhart, M.D. (div.); c. April, Brook, Dean Allen Jr.; res: 125 E. 87th St., N.Y., N.Y. 10028.

EVERNDEN, MARGERY ELIZABETH, Asst. Instr., Department of English, Fifth Floor, Cathedral of Learning, University of Pittsburgh, Pitt., Pa. 15213; Wtr., children's bks.: "Secret of the Porcelain Fish" (N.Y. Herald Tribune Bk. Fair Hon. Mention), "Sword with the Golden Hilt," "The Runaway Apprentice," "Knight of Florence," "Wilderness Boy," "The Golden Trail," "Simon's Way"; published plays incl.: "The Secret of Han Ho," "Davy Crockett and His Coonskin Cap," "The Frog Princess and The Witch"; pubn. for adults; Theta Sigma Phi; Playwriting Aws.: Seattle Jr. Programs, Kan. City Children's Theatre, others; Williams Jr. Col., '33–'35; Univ. of Cal. at Berkeley, AB, '38 (Phi Beta Kappa, Mortar Bd.); Univ. of Pitt., MA, '66; b. Okeechobee, Fla., 1916; p. Hans and Rose Wagner Everden; h. Earl Gulbransen; c. Karen (Mrs. Steven Cohn), Kristin, David; res: 63 Hathaway Ct., Pitt., Pa. 15235.

EVERS, JEAN GRAF, Cnslt., PR, Wtr., 109 E. 36th St., N.Y., N.Y. 10016, '67–; Dir. Interior Furnishings, PR, The Mohair Council, Co-owner, Graf & Graf (PR), '47–'63; Dir., PR, Galbraith-Hoffman Adv. Agcy., '57–'59; PR, Am. Carpet Inst., '55–'57; Housing Dept., Life, '45–'47; Assoc. Ed., Prom. Mgr., House & Garden, '41–'45; Auth., "Practical Houses for Contemporary Living" (F. W. Dodge, '53); Contributor of design articles to nat. pubns., '47–; NHFL (VP, Pubns., '60–'61), PR Assoc., AID, NSID, Press Assoc.; N.Y. Architectural League; Who's Who of Am. Wm; Who's Who in the East; Dir. Mail Adv. Assn. Aw., '47; Vogue Prix de Paris, '40; Northwestern Univ., BA, '40 (summa cum laude; Phi Beta Kappa); b. Columbus, Oh., 1917; p. Ray and Marie Dooley Arms; h. Carl G. Evers; res: Grant's Lane, Ossining, N.Y. 10562.

EVERSON, MURIEL WELLS, Ed., The Belington News, Crim Ave., Belington, W.Va. 26250, '58–; Corr., Clarksburg Publ. Co., '56–'58; W.Va. Gov. cit., '67; Who's Who of Am. Wm., Dic. of Intl. Biog.; Barlow Ch. of Eng. Sch. (Barlow, Eng.); Chesterfield Inst. of Tech. (Chesterfield, Eng.), '40–'43; b. Barlow, Eng., 1926; p. Harold and Jessie Yeates Wells; h. Joe Everson; c. Harold W.; res: Dayton Blvd., Belington, W. Va. 26250.

EVERY, MARY PATRICIA, Wms. Ed., News-Press Publishing Co., Inc., Santa Barbara, Cal., 93102, '63–; Reptr., '60–'63; Rschr. Asst., Consolidated Freightways; Sanford, BA, '59; (magna cum laude; Phi Beta Kappa;) b. N.Y.C., 1937; p. Paul and Ellen Lacy Every; res: 1370 School House Rd., Santa Barbara, Cal. 93103.

EVETT, ALICE CALKINS, Dir. of Pubns., American Hospital & Life Insurance Company, P.O. Box 2341, San Antonio, Tex. 78206, '69–; Ed. of Pubns., '61–'69;

Sigma Tau Delta, ICIE, San Antonio Press Club, Alamo IEA (Pres., '63; VP, '62; Secy.-Treas., '67–'68; Pres., '69–'70); Aw. of Merit, S.W. Conf. of Indsl. Eds., '65; George Wash. Univ., '42–'44; Baylor Univ., BA, '46; Univ. of Tex., MA, '51; San Antonio Art Inst.; St. Mary's Univ.; Trinity Univ.; San Antonio Col.; b. Waco, Tex., 1925; p. Col. Harry R. and Maribelle Chamberlin Calkins; h. (div.); res: 111 Grotto Blvd., San Antonio, Tex. 78216.

EVETTS, ANNA HEIL, Ventura County Assessor's Office, 2055 N. Ventura Ave., Ventura, Cal. 93001, '68–; Reptr., Woman's Review, '67; Head, Ventura Col. News Bur., '63; Theta Sigma Phi; Ventura Col., AA, '64; Univ. of Cal., BA, '66; b. Visalia, Cal., 1944; p. Grant and Marion Youngborg Heil; h. John Evetts; res: 3765 Paloma Dr., Ventura, Cal. 93003.

EWOLSKI, DARLENE SUE, Traf. Mgr., WGAR, Statler-Hilton Hotel, Cleve., Oh., '64–; PR Comm., Parma Sch. Bd. Wm.'s Adv. Club of Cleve. (Rec. Secy. '68–'70), Serious Exec. Action Comm.; Dyke Bus. Col. '60–'62; b. Cleve., Oh., 1942; p. Joseph and Virginia Odorizzi Ewolski; res: 6364 Tanglewood Lane, Seven Hills, Oh. 44131.

EYERLY, JEANNETTE HYDE, Auth: "Escape from Nowhere" ('69), "Gretchen's Hill" (Susan Glaspell Aw., '65), six others ('61–'68); Pubcty. Dir., Des Moines Public Lib., '30–'33; Contrbr. to numerous mags.; Lectr., convs., univs., assns.; Des Moines Child Guidance Ctr. (Pres., '52–'54), St. Joseph Acad. Guild (Pres. '56–'57), Des Moines Art Ctr., Polk County Mental Health Ctr. (Bd., '66–'69; Secy., '69); Auths. League of Am.; Drake Univ.; State Univ. of Ia., BA, '30; b. Topeka, Kan., 1908; p. Robert and Mabel Young Hyde; h. Frank Eyerly; c. Jane (Mrs. Larry Kozuszek), Susan (Mrs. Joseph Pichler); res: 231 42nd St., Des Moines, Ia. 50312.

F

FABER, DORIS GREENBERG, Wtr: 15 bks. for children; for adults, "The Mothers of American Presidents" (New Am. Lib., '68); Reptr., N.Y. Times, '43–'51; Goucher Col.; N.Y.U., BA, '43; b. N.Y.C., 1924; p. Harry and Florence Greenberg; h. Harold Faber; c. Alice, Marjorie; res: 50 High Ridge Ct., Pleasantville, N.Y. 10570.

FABER, JUDITH ANN, KWHL-FM, Opns. Mgr., Black Hawk Broadcasting Co., KWWL Bldg., E. 4th & Franklin St., Waterloo, Ia. 50703, '68–; Coordr. of Crtv. Sls. Svcs., KWWL-TV, '67; Dir. of Opns., WBOO AM Radio (Baraboo, Wis.), '67; Cont. Dir., Asst. to Gen. Mgr., KWWL AM Radio (Cedar Rapids, Ia.), '66; Cont. Dir., KWWL AM Radio (Waterloo, Ia.), '65; Cont. Wtr., '64; Cont. Trainee, '63; Guest Lectr.,

Speech, Communicative Arts, Univ. of Northern Ia., '68–'69; Guest Lectr., Visual Arts Dept., Hawkeye Tech. Inst., '68–'69; Prom., Adv. Cnslt., Country Cobbler Shoes, '66–'67; Prom. Cnslt., Lohnes Photo., '65; b. Dubuque, Ia., 1945; p. Evlon and Helen Werner Faber; res: 1021 Burton Ave., Waterloo, Ia. 50703.

FABER, NANCY JOAN, Dir. of Adv. and Prom., Cowles Book Company, Inc., 488 Madison Ave., N.Y., N.Y. 10022, '68–; Asst. Adv. and Sales Prom. Mgr., Indian Head Hosiery Co., '67–'68; Media-Mktg. Dir., HMA/Norman, Craig & Kummel, '66–'67; Free-lance Mktg. Cnslt., Copywtr., Designer of sales prom. materials; AWNY, AAF, Publrs. Adv. Club; Columbia Univ., '61; N.Y.U., '61–'62; City Col. of N.Y. (Dean's List, Nat. Hon. Soc.), '62–'67; b. Reading, Pa., 1938; res: 25 W. 13th St., N.Y., N.Y. 10011.

FABIAN, JOSEPHINE CUNNINGHAM, Auth., fiction, non-fiction; Bks: "The Jackson's Hole Story" (novel), "Jackson Hole, How to Discover and Enjoy It," (guide bk., 11 editions); Play prod., "Night Operator" (musical, '65); songs: "The Utah Song," "Stand Up and Cheer for the Flag;" NLAPW (Salt Lake Chptr. former VP); Univ. of Ut., Columbia Univ., Univ. of Chgo.; b. Sheridan, Wyo., 1903; p. Joseph and Mary Elizabeth Landrigan Cunningham; h. Harold Pegram Fabian; res: 29 South State St., The Belvedere, Apt. 415, Salt Lake City, Ut. 84111.

FAGAN, BARBARA, Fashion Group Head, Rumrill-Hoyt, Inc., 380 Madison Ave., N.Y., N.Y. 10017, '66–; Crtv. Group Head, West, Weir, Bartel, '66; Copy Group Head, Benton & Bowles, '64; Copywtr., Grey Advertising, '62; Copywtr., J. Walter Thompson, '60; Univ. of Pitt., BA, MA; b. Pitt., Pa.; p. Leo and Sarah Madden Fagan; h. Truett Evans Allen; c. Jefferson Madden Allen; res: 33 E. 30th St., N.Y., N.Y. 10016.

FAGAN, BETH VIRGINIA (pseud: Jane Allen), Fashion Ed., Art Ed., Oregonian Publishing Company, 1320 S.W. Broadway, Portland, Ore. 97201, '62–; Fashion Ed., '47–; '45–; Fashion Group, Theta Sigma Phi (Hon. Mbr.); Clark Col. (Dubuque, Ia.), '37–'38; Univ. of Ia., BS, '41; res: 2636 S.W. Davenport Ct., Portland, Ore. 97201.

FAGERSTROM, DOROTHY I., Rsch. Ed., Copp Organization, 72 W. 45 St., N.Y., N.Y. 10036, '66–; Asst. Ed., '59–'66; Edtl. Asst., '58–'59; Secy., Bookkeeper, '56–'58; Cargo Claim Adjuster, Isthmiam Steamship Co., '46–'51; Cargo Claim Adjuster, Alcoa Steamship Co., '43–'46; Intl. Assn. Chiefs of Police, Intl. Juv. Offcrs. Assn. (cit., '68); Intl. Assn. of Wm. Police (cit., '62), other police groups, police hons.; res: 9 Melrose Ave., E. Norwalk, Conn. 06855.

FAGG, DOROTHY PORTER, Home Furnishings Ed., Dallas Times Herald, Herald Sq., Dallas, Tex., '65–; City Zone Ed.; Wms. Ed., Oak Cliff Tribune; Free-lance Wtr., poetry, short stories, C. of C. mags.; NHFL,

Theta Sigma Phi; Who's Who of Am. Wm.; Dallas Trade Mart Aw., outstanding work in the field, '67; aw., Dallas Retail Furniture Merchants Assn., '67; E. Tex. State Univ., BA; MA; b. Ladonia, Tex.; p. William Roy and Addie Crowson Porter; h. Max Weldon Fagg; c. Karen Faith, Marilyn; res: 1905 Old Orchard, Dallas, Tex. 75208.

FAGG, ELIZABETH, Free-lance Wtr.; AE, Dudley-Anderson-Yutzy; Reptr., Reader's Digest (Europe); Bur. Chief, Time-Life (Mexico); Fashion Ed., Women's Wear Daily; Asst. Prof., Tex. Wms. Univ.; OPC, Pen & Brush Club, Soc. of Wm. Geographers, N.Y. Zoological Soc.; Pat Davis short sty. aw., '69; Univ. of Tex., BA (summa cum laude, Phi Beta Kappa); La. State Univ., MA; Columbia Univ., N.Y.U., New Sch. for Social Rsch.; b. Greenville, Tex.; p. Carey and Edna Rouse Fagg; h. Lawrence B. Olds; c. Cynthia C.; res: 315 E. 72nd St., N.Y., N.Y. 10021.

FAHL, CECI SOULIERE, Sales Mgr., Exec. Secy. to Gen. Mgr., Bdcstr., WWSR Radio, 75 N. Main St., St. Albans, Vt. 05478, '59–; Hostess, "Take Five", "Sound Off", "Woman of the Week"; Off. Mgr., Comml. Traf., disc jockey, cl., '40–'59; AWRT (State Rep. and Dir., '67–'68); BPW (Chptr. Treas., '68–'69); Cert. of Appreciation, Kerbs Memorial Hosp., '66; b. St. Albans, Vt., 1922; p. Alfred A. and Evelyn L'Ecuyer Souliere; h. Earl Fahl; c. David; res: 24 N. Elm, St. Albans, Vt. 05478.

FAIN, HELLEN McCOMBS, Ed., Ideal Women's Group, 295 Madison Ave., N.Y., N.Y. 10017, '64–; Ed., KMR Publ. Co., '62–'64; Dir. of Special Pubns., Nat. Recreation Assn., '60–'62; Wtr., PR; Columbia Univ., BS, '49; b. Seattle, Wash., 1919; p. Leo and Evelyn McCombs; h. Yonia Fain; c. Ephraim; res: 202 Carroll St., Bklyn., N.Y. 11231.

FAIN, LUCILLE HAMMACK, Asst. Publr., Herald Publishing Co., Box 68, Nacogdoches, Tex. 75961, '46–; City Ed., The Redland Herald, '37–'43; City Ed., The Daily Sentinel, '36–'37; AAUW (Pres.), Theta Sigma Phi, E. Tex. Tourist Cncl. (Dir.), Hist. Soc. (Dir.), Good Govt. Assn. (Secy.-Treas.); Univ. of Tex., '36 (hon. grad., Daily Texan Night Ed.); b. Ennis, Tex., 1914; p. Nathaniel A. and Louella Hammack; h. Victor B. Fain; c. Robert Nathan, Ferris H., Luellen; res: 1315 Garner, Nacogdoches, Tex. 75961.

FAIRFIELD, VIRGINIA ANN, Owner, Operator, Kenton-Fairfield, 911 21st St., Santa Monica, Cal. 90403, '66–; PR, Campaign Dir., Girl Scout Cncl. of Gtr. N.Y., Inc. (Bklyn., N.Y.), '65–'66; PR, Adv., Dev. Dir., St. Margaret's Sch., '62–'64; Asst. to Dir. of Adv., U.S. Rubber Co. (N.Y.C.), '50–'61; PR, Adv., Sls. Prom. Mgr., Elof Hansson, Inc., '48–'49; Copywtr., Contact Person, Biow Co. (S.F., Cal.), '46–'47; Wms. Ed., Phila. (Pa.) Daily News, '44–'46; Tchr., Woodbury Col. (L.A., Cal.), '68; S.F. Adv. Club, Am. Inst. of Interior Designers (Press Assoc.), NHFL (VP), Fashion Group, AWNY, Nat. Assn. of Fund Raising Dirs.;

Univ. of Ill., AB, '44 (Pi Delta Phi); N.Y.U., MBA, '51; b. Phila., Pa.; p. Earl S. and Virginia F. Kenton Fairfield; res: Santa Monica, Cal. 90403.

FAIRHURST, MILLICENT, Prod. Mgr., Holiday House Inc., 18 E. 56th St., N.Y., N.Y. 10022, '67–; Prod. Mgr., Morrow Jr. Bks., William Morrow & Co., '65–'67; Prod. Asst. to Mgr., Children's Bks., Thos. Y. Crowell, '62–'65; Little Brown & Co. (Boston, Mass.), '59–'61; Wms. Nat. Bk. Assn., AIGA; cultural, polit. orgs.; Middlebury Col., BA (Music), '59; b. Syracuse, N.Y., 1938; p. Harold E. and Janet Perry Fairhurst; res: 341 E. 19th St., N.Y., N.Y. 10003.

FALCO, JUDITH ANDERSON, Free-lance Statistician, R. R. Bowker Co., 1180 Ave. of Americas, N.Y., N.Y. 10036; Secy. to VP; Mensa; Reed Col.; b. Mt. Vernon, N.Y., 1937; p. Howard and Ruth Megrath Anderson; h. Frank Falco; c. Joseph, Edith, Paul, Ruth; res: 115 Haynes Ave., W. Islip, N.Y. 11795.

FALCON, ELEANOR D., PR, Arts Cnslt., Dublin Rd., Hancock, N.H. 03449, '69–; PR Dir., The Met. Museum of Art (N.Y.C.), '64–'69; Tchr., PR for Nonprofit Insts., Museum In-Training Program of N.Y. State Cncl. on the Arts, '67–'69; Pubcty. Dir., Ed., Calendar of Events, The Boston Museum of Fine Arts (Boston, Mass.), '57–'63; Promotional Wtr., Cnslt., '54–'57; Cnslt., N.Y. State Cncl. on the Arts, '66–; Cnslt., PR, Commty Rels., Albany Inst. of Hist. & Art; PR Cnslt., CRIA; PR Cnslt., Nat. Trust; Lectr., PR to pfssnl., lay groups; Am. Assn. of Museums, Monadnock Cncl. on the Arts, hist. socs.; Simmons Col., BS, '54; b. Jaffrey, N.H., 1932; p. Gilborn and Evonne Blanchette Duval; h. William Dyche Falcon; c. Adam D.

FALES, JERRY LYNN, Asst. Ed., Science Digest Magazine, 224 W. 57th St., N.Y., N.Y. 10019, '67–; Copy Ed., The Dallas Morning News, '65–'67; Wtrs. Aide, Hospitalized Veterans Writing Project, '68; Theta Sigma Phi; Outstanding Young Wm. of Am., '68; Hon. Mention, Headline Writing, Dallas Press Club Aws., '66; Outstanding Daily Texas Worker, '65; Univ. of Texas, BA (Jnlsm.), '65; b. New Orleans, La., 1943; p. Earnest and Dorothy Raines Greer; res: 400 E. 55th St., N.Y., N.Y. 10022.

FALKENBERRY, ELEANOR RENNIE, Wms. Pg. Ed., Selma Times-Journal, 1018 Water Ave., Selma, Ala. 36701, '65–; Instr., Eng., Speech, Auburn Univ. Ext., '68–; Univ. of Ala. Ext., '45–'68; Speech Instr., Ala. Col. (Montevallo), '36–'39; Ala. Col., BA, '34 (with hons.), Northwestern Univ., MA (Speech), '40; b. Selma, Ala., 1914; p. John and Nell Foster Rennie; h. Roswell Falkenberry; c. John C., George Alan, Florence Anne, N. Rennie; res: 319 Cedar Dr., Selma, Ala. 36701.

FANCHER, PAULINE M., Librn., Chautauqua Institution, Box 1093, Chautauqua, N.Y. 14722; Winter Program Dir., '66–; Summer Librn., '61–; N. Palm

Beach (Fla.) Lib., Winters, '64–'65; Dir., James Prendergast Free Lib., (Jamestown, N.Y.), '56–'63; Librn., PR, Air Force, '43–'50; weekly bk. rev. program, Kissin Radio, '56–'63; Contrbr., lib. periodicals, Wilson Bul., N.Y. State Bookmark; Ed., lib. nwsltrs. incl., Smith Memorial Lib. Nwsltr. (Chautauqua, N.Y.), '66–; N.Y. Lib. Assn., Pi Kappa Phi, AAUW, Fortnightly Club of Jamestown (Bd. Chmn.); active in lib. work; Air Force aw.; Univ. of Buffalo, BA, '34; BS (Lib. Sci.), '36; b. Jamestown, N.Y.; p. Leon L. and Kate Eleanor Waters Fancher.

FANNING, MARILYN HERMANT, Free-lance Talent, Prodr., Wtr.; Radio Hostess, "Moment With Marilyn," TV News Features, WLVA Radio and TV, 2320 Langhorne Rd., Lynchburg, Va. 24505, '68–; Hostess and Prodr., "Partyline" TV prog., '66–'68; Wtr. and Prodr., radio and TV comml.; Fashion Coordr., Miller and Rhoads; Continuity and Bdcstr., WIBX, Uitca, N.Y., '45–'47; Copywtr., Leighton and Nelson, Schenectady, N.Y., '44; Bdsctr., WSNY, '44; AWRT; Lynchburg Fine Arts Center (Former mbr., Bd. of Dirs.); Leland Powers Sch. of Radio, Theatre and TV, '44; b. Utica, N.Y., 1925; p. William and Mildred Canfield Hermant; h. William Fanning; c. Wayne, Lesley, Claire; res: 2005 Indian Hill Rd., Lynchburg, Va. 24503.

FAORO, MADGE MacFARLAND, Coordr. of Adult Svcs., Davenport Public Library, 312 Main St., Davenport, Ia. 52801; Head, '66–'68; Head, Ext. Dept., '60–'68; Head, Young Adult Dept., '57–'60; Circ. Asst., '56–'57; Free-lance Consumer Rschr., '47–'56; Eng. Tchr., Davenport High Sch., '44–'45; Cl.-Ed., Rock Island Arsenal, '42–'43; Proofreader, Davenport Dem., '41–'42; Ia. Lib. Assn. (Bd. Dirs., '68–'70), ALA, Beta Phi Mu; Milw. State Tchrs. Col., BS, '34; Marycrest Col., '56; Univ. of Ill., MS (Lib. Sci.), '65; b. Buffalo, N.Y., 1916; p. Allison M. and Florence Bromley MacFarland; h. Victor J. Faoro; c. Vicki Jo (Mrs. Wm. Fleischman); res: 2328 W. High, Davenport, Ia. 52804.

FAOUR, ANNA ROSE, Free-lance PR Wtr.; Eng. Tchr., Cypress-Fairbanks Independent School District, P.O. Box 40040, Houston, Tex., 77040, '65–; Tchr., Houston Independent Sch. Dist., '64–'65 and '57–'61; Proofreader, McCann-Erickson (Houston), '62–'64; Pubcty., Eisenhower-Nixon Campaign, '56; Wms. Dept. Reptr., Houston Post, '53–'54; Reptr., Houston Chronicle, '58–'59 and '52–'53; Corr., The Heritage, nwsp.; Theta Sigma Phi (Chptr. Historian, '68–'69), Tex. State Tchrs. Assn., Greater Houston Area Reading Cnsl., Intl. Reading Assn.; Univ. of Houston, BS, '52; b. Houston, Tex., 1929; p. Jack F. and Alice Emmett Faour; res: Rte. Ten, Box 800, Houston, Tex. 77040.

FARFEL, LOIS, Rschr., Network Doc. Films, NBC News, 4001 Nebraska Ave. N.W., Wash., D.C. 20016, '67–; Co-prodr., "Operation Awareness", WRC-TV, Wash., D.C. '67; Asst. to Pres., Intl. Commtns. Assocs., '66; Analyst and Interviewer, Harvard Student Agcys., Survey of Educ. Film Industry, '66; Rsch. and Prod.

Asst., Pubcty. Dept., KTRK-TV (Houston, Tex.), '65; WRC-TV Prod. Internship, '67; Sarah Lawrence Col., BA, '65; Boston Univ., MEd (Adult Educ., Pi Lambda Theta; '66; Am. Univ., grad. studies; b. Houston, Tex., 1943; p. Aaron J. and Esther Susholtz Farfel; res: 2913 Q. St. N.W., Wash., D.C. 20007.

FARISH, MARGARET KENNEDY, Rsch. Assoc., Univ. of Ill., Urbana, Ill.; Auth: "String Music in Print" (R. R. Bowker Co., N. Y., '65), "Supplement to String Music in Print" (R. R. Bowker Co., N.Y., '68); Violinist, Tchr: Univ. of Okla., Northwestern Univ., Indpls. Public Schs., Boys Town, Neb.; Prin. Investigator, music instruction project supported by Off. of Educ., HEW; Am. String Tchrs. Assn., Music Educs. Nat. Conf.; Eastman Sch. of Music (Rochester, N.Y.), Bachelor of Music, '39; Master of Music, '46; b. Omaha, Neb., 1918; p. Alfred C. and Lois Logan Kennedy; h. Philip Farish; res: 925 Elmwood Ave., Evanston, Ill. 60202.

FARISS, HELEN BRAMWELL (dec.), Exec. Dir., Middle Tennessee Heart Association, 209 23rd Ave. North, Nashville, Tenn. 37203, '50–'69; Methods Engineer, Remington Rand, Inc., '43–'49; Tchr., Issac Litton HS, '34–'43; Case worker, Davidson Co. Welfare Comm., '33; AWRT: BPW Outstanding Wm. of the Yr., '69; b. Nashville, Tenn., 1911; p. Harry L. and Lillie Robinson Bramwell; h. George C. Fariss; res: Glendale Apts., Apt. 5, Nashville, Tenn. 37204.

FARLEY, JEAN, Assoc. Poetry Ed., Kenyon Review, Gambier, Oh. 43022, '68–; Instr. in Eng., Hollins Col. (Roanoke, Va.), '66–'67; Instr. in Eng., Richmond Pfsnl. Inst. (Richmond, Va.), '54–'56; Jr. Instr. in Eng. writing, Johns Hopkins Univ., '52–'54; Assoc. Ed., The Hopkins Review, '52–'54; Contrbr. of poems, revs. to mags.; Univ. of N.C., BA, '50 (magna cum laude, with hons. in Eng.); Johns Hopkins Univ., MA, '53; b. Phila., Pa., 1928; p. Dr. David Labauve and Jean Clark Farley; h. Ellington White; c. David, Nancy, Susan.

FARLEY, LEONA BEYER, Mng. Ed., Milford Advertiser, Four Main St., Milford, Oh. 45150, '66–; Adv. Mgr., '63–'66; Asst. Soc. Ed., The Democrat (Davenport, Ia.), '44–'47; Reptr., '43–'44; Tri-City Wms. Press Club (Pres., '47); Am. Inst. of Commerce, '42 (bus. scholarship); b. Mount Carroll, Ill., 1925; p. Lewis and Lena Walthers Beyer; h. John E. Farley; c. John E., Jr., Michael J.; res: 1564 Vera Cruz Pike, Milford, Oh. 45150.

FARLEY, MARGUERITE MARY, Radio-TV Asst., School District of Philadelphia, Bd. of Educ. Bldg., 21st and Pkwy., Phila., Pa. 19103, '56–; Originator, Hostess, "Seed of a Nation," WHYY-TV, '69–; Prodr., Hostess, "TV Bookshelf," '58–; Wtr., Originator, Prodr., Narrator, "Americana" WFIL, '55–'68 (George Washington Hon. Medal, Freedoms Fndn., '60, '62, '63, '66; Hon. Cert., '65); Wtr., Prodr., Narrator, "Radioland Express," "Storyland," '55–'60; Wtr., Prodr., Narrator, "Magic of Books," '55–'59; Coordr., "Junior Town Meeting of Air," KYW, '55–'58; Tchr., Phila. schs.,

'52–'55; Prodr., Phila. Segments, "Crisis: Congo," TV simulation, WHYY-TV and E.E.N., '69; Chestnut Hill Col., AB, '52; Temple Univ., M.Ed., '66; b. Phila., Pa., 1930; p. David F. and Marguerite Dorsey Farley; res: 4614 Disston St., Phila., Pa. 19135.

FARMER, HELENE MOORE, Former PR Dir., Pubcty., Prom. Dir., 10-100 N.E., Bellevue, Wash. 98004; two Repl. gubernatorial campaigns; two annual Parade of Homes, Seattle Master Builders (first won Nat. Aw., Nat. Home Builders Assn.); nwsp. contests; theatre proms; Conventions; 7 yrs. Special Events, Pubcty. Dir., Bon Marché, Seattle, Allied Stores; Pubcty., PR Dir., Northgate, four and one-half yrs.; only wm. State Dir. of Pubcty for U.S. War Bond Sls., two yrs., WW II; Free-lance Publicist, PR for events incl. Intl Trade Fair, others; work for Film Daily, Wid's, trade pubns.; Script Wtr., Universal Film Co. (Hollywood); feature writing, Post-Intelligencer (Seattle); Theat Sigma Phi; '54 Governors Conference; Gamma Alpha Chi, Seattle Adv. & Sls. Club (Bd., three yrs.), Kappa Kappa Gamma; currently Christian Science practitioner; aws. for work incl., Paul Bunyan Aw., Seattle C. of C., three times; Univ. of Wash. Sch. of Commtns. (Seattle, Wash.), BA (Mortar Bd.); b. Pocatello, Idaho; p. I. H. and Emma Hart Moore; h. (dec.); c. Sunny Sue (Mrs. Kirk Kaynor) Bellevue.

FARMER, VIRGINIA GODDARD, Coordr., Akron Public Library, 55 S. Main St., Akron, Oh. 44308, '58–; Head, Main Children's Room, '50–'57; Children's Librn., Cleve. Heights Public Lib., '44–'50; Asst., Children's Dept., Lima Public Lib., '42–'44; Oh. Lib. Assn. (Exec. Bd., '56–'57, '49–'50), WNBA, Quota Club Intl. (Akron Club Pres., '58–'59); Mt. Union Col., AB, '41; Carnegie Inst. of Tech., BS (Lib. Sci.), '42; b. Alliance, Oh.; p. Ralph and Helen Goddard; h. Jack Farmer; res: 5256 S. Arlington Rd., N. Canton, Oh. 44720.

FARRAR, MARGARET MARSHALL, Dir. of PR, New York State Department of Mental Hygiene, 44 Holland Ave., Albany, N.Y. 12208, '48–; Ed., Mental Hygiene News, '48–; Visiting Lectr. and Chief Cnslt., Grad. Prog. in Mental Health Info., Sch. of Jnlsm., Syracuse Univ., '64–; Ad hoc Cnslt. on PR to many health orgs.; Auth. of many pamphlets; PR, N.Y. State Div. of Housing, '46–'48; Statistician and Rsch. Ed., N.Y. State Educ. Dept., '38–'46; PRSA (Accredited Mbr.; Chptr. VP, '67; Bd. of Dirs., '66–), Nat. Assn. of Psychiatric Info. Specialists (Founder; Pres., '63–'64; Bd. of Dirs., '64–'67), N.Y. State Govt. PR Assn.; Hunter Col., BA (Ritchter Aw. in Jnlsm.; Sigma Tau Delta; Sigma Alpha Gamma); b. N.Y.C.; h. Joseph Winthrop Musial; res: 30 Van Buren Ave., E. Greenbush, N.Y. 12061 and 152 Colonial Pkwy., Manhasset, N.Y. 11030.

FARRAR, SALLY HOLMES, Sunday Ed., Rapid City Journal, 507 Main St., Rapid City, S.D. 57701, '69–; Ch. Ed., Educ. Ed., Gen. Assigt. Reptr.; Deputy Sheriff, Pennington County (S.D.); NFPW (annual aws.); S.D. Press Wm. (annual aws.); Am. Polit. Sci. Assn. ("Distg.

Rept. of Public Affairs" Aw., '67); active in civic groups; Black Hills State Col. (Spearfish, S.D.), '53–'56; Fresno State Col. (Fresno, Cal.), '54–'55; b. Rapid City, S.D., 1934; p. Oliver G. and Anne Smith Rose; h. Don Roderick Farrar (div.); c. Leslie Anne; res: 202 E. St. Charles St., Rapid City, S.D. 57702.

FARRAR, SUSAN GONTARD, Kan. City Program Ed., TV Guide Magazine, 800 W. 47 St., Kan. City, Mo. 64112, '66–; AWRT; Kan. City Jr. Col., Univ. of Mo. at Kan. City; b. Kan. City, Mo., 1944; p. Herbert and Ellen Brown Gontard; res: 2014 W. 74 St., Prairie Village, Kan. 66208.

FARRELL, BRIONI, Actress, Paul Kohner, Inc., 9169 Sunset Blvd., L.A., Cal. 90069; Pfsnl. Stage Work, L.A., S.F.; TV, Hollywood; SAG; Northwestern Univ.; b. Athens, Greece, 1943; p. Panos Gratsos and Danae Martin; c. Alexis, Stefan; res: 1340 Roscomare Rd., L.A., Cal. 90024.

FARRELL, LOIS FEGAN, Wms. and Travel Ed., The Jersey Journal, 30 Journal Sq., Jersey City, N.J. 07306, '52–; Wms. Ed., Patriot and Evening News (Harrisburg, Pa.), '48–'52; Reptr., Harrisburg Telegraph, '41–'48; Reptr., Daily Local News (Mechanicsburg, Pa.), '37; N.Y. Nwsp. Wms. Club, N.J. Daily Nwsp. Wm., N.J. Press Assn., Soc. of Am. Travel Wtrs.; b. Mechanicsburg, Pa., 1916; p. Milton and Mabel Shoap Fegan; h. Eugene Farrell; res: 644 Jersey Ave., Jersey City, N.J. 07302.

FARRELL, SHARON, Actress, c/o Kurt Frings Agency, 242 N. Canon Dr., Beverly Hills, Cal. 90210; Films: co-star, "Marlowe," "The Reivers."

FARSACE, DUVERNE KONRICK, Sr. Advance Reader, Lawyer's Co-operative Publishing Company, Aqueduct St., Rochester, N.Y. 14614, '67–; Poet, Short Story Wtr., poetry, stories in numerous mags.; incl: Rotarian, Wings, Blue Moon; Little Magazine Publr., Golden Atom Pubns.; Co-chmn., Rochester World (and Nat., Inc.) Poetry Day, '58–; Co-chmn., Western N.Y.; Chmn., La. State Poetry Day; Contrb. Ed., Nat. Poetry Soc. (Wash., D.C.), '50–'51; Librn., Sully Bookmobile, Rochester Public Lib., '56–'62; Librn., Bookmobile, N.O. Public Lib., '45–'56; NLAPW; Composers, Auths. & Artists; Avalon World Arts Assn. (Sidney Lanier Chptr. Poetry Workshop Dir., '51–'56); bk., cash prizes, medals, diplomas for poetry incl: James C. Doty Memorial Aw., '48; Allison Nichols prize, best poem of Yr., Chromotones, '52; Sigma Medal, to Poet Laureate, for Poetry Day in N.Y., '68, from Pres. F. Marcos, Philippines; Assistant New York State Chairman, National Poetry Day, Inc., '70; others; St. Mary's Dominican Col. (N.O., La.), BA, '45; b. Jasper, Tex., 1923; p. Rudolph and Vera Bishop Konrick; h. Larry Farsace; res: 187 N. Union St., Rochester, N.Y. 14605.

FASEL, IDA, Asst. Prof. of Eng., University of Colorado, Denver Center, 1100 14th St., Denver, Colo. 80202, '62–; Univ. of Conn.; Midwestern Univ.; poetry widely published; articles in pfsnl. mags.; translations, poems in anthologies; Modern Language Assn., Milton Soc. of Am., PSA; educ: Boston Univ., BA, '31 (Phi Beta Kappa); MA, '45; Univ. of Denver, Ph.D., '63; b. Portland, Me., 1909; p. I. E. and Lilian Harwich Drapkin; h. Oscar Fasel; res: 165 Ivy St., Denver, Colo. 80220.

FAST, ELIZABETH TRYGSTAD, Dir. of Educ. Media, Groton Public Schools, Box K, Groton, Conn. 06340, '68–; Dir. of Lib. Svcs., '65–'68; Elementary Sch. Librn., '62–'65; Auth: articles in pfsnl. jnls.; Educ. Bk. Revs.; Cnslt., publrs., sch. systems; Cnslt., N.D.E.A. Lib. Inst., Columbia Univ., '67; Tchr., courses, workshops, Univ. of Conn., Univ. of N.H., Southern Conn. State Col.; ALA, Several state and reg. lib. assns., NEA, D.A.V.I., A.S.C.D., Conn. Educ. Assn., Groton Educ. Assn., Film Lib. Info. Cncl.; S.E. Conn. Mental Health Cncl. (VP), White House Fellows Prog. (Alternate, '65), PTA of Conn. (State Bd., '62–'64), Groton LWV (Past Pres.); John Cotton Dana Lib. Aw. for Groton Public Lib., '61; Alpha Delta Kappa, '67; Radcliffe Col., AB, '52 (cum laude, Phi Beta Kappa); Univ. of R.I., MLS, '68; b. Bklyn., N.Y., 1931; p. Dr. Reidar and Dr. Ethel Hirsch Trygstad; h. Nicholas Fast; c. Stephen R., James W., Carl D., Kenneth R.; res: 2 Chestnut Hill Sq., Groton, Conn. 06340.

FAULKNER, ANNE I. (Nancy Faulkner), Auth: 20 fiction bks., incl: "Second Son" ('70), "Mystery of the Limping Stranger" ('67), "Journey To Danger" ('66); Cnslt. on jr. bks., Walker & Co., '61–'62; VP, Chandler Records, '46–'56; Ed., Recreation Mag., '44–'46; Dir., Bur. Sch. and Commty. Drama, Univ. of Va., '39–'44; Auths. Guild; MWA aw., '65; Wellesley Col., AB, '28; Cornell Univ., MA, '33; b. Lynchburg, Va., 1906; p. John and Tucker Clark Faulkner; res: 942 Rosser Lane, Charlottesville, Va. 22903.

FAULKNER, VIRGINIA LOUISE, Ed. in Chief, University of Nebraska Press, 901 N. 17th St., Lincoln, Neb. 68508, '59–; Asst. Ed., '56–'59; Assoc. Ed., Prairie Schooner, '59–; Free-lance Wtr., '38–'56; Scenarist, Metro-Goldwyn-Mayer, '35–'38; Assoc. Ed., Town and Country, '34–'35; Special Wtr., Wash. Post, '33–'34; Pubns. incl: "Willa Cather's Collected Short Fiction, 1892–1912" (Ed., '65), "Hostiles and Friendlies: Selected Short Writings of Mari Sandoz" (Ed., '59); novels: "Friends and Romans" ('34), "The Barbarians" ('35), stories, articles in numerous nat. mags.; Broadway prods., incl. "It Takes Two" (Co-auth., '46); Univ. of Neb., '32; Radcliffe Col., '35; b. Lincoln, Neb., 1913; p. Edwin J. and Leah Meyer Faulkner; res: 721 S. Fourteenth St., Lincoln, Neb. 68508.

FAWCETT, EUGENIA, Mng. Ed., Follett Publishing Company, 201 N. Wells, Chgo., Ill. 60606, '65; Prod. Mgr., '63–'66; Prod. Mgr., Henry Regnery Co., '56–'61; Prom. Mgr., '49–'56; Adv. and Sls. Asst., Univ. of Chgo. Press, '46–'49; Owner, The Coach House Print

Shop; Publr.; Lectr., bk. publ., Univ. of Chgo., pfsnl. seminars; Chgo. Bk. Clinic (Past Pres.; bk. show aw. for private pubn. of bks.), Wms. Nat. Bk. Assn., Soc. of Typographic Arts, Chgo. Heritage Comm.; San Diego State Col., BA, '44 (hons.); Univ. of Chgo., MA, '46; b. Colo. Springs, Colo., 1923; p. Harwood Hoyt and Ida Price Fawcett; res: 4935-1/2 Greenwood, Chgo., Ill. 60615.

FAY, JOHANNA, Free-lance Bdcstr., Radio, TV, 3030 Lombardy Dr., Port Arthur, Tex. 77640; Public Svc. Dir., KPAC-TV, '55; Prodr., Wtr., Master Ceremonies, Johanna Fay Show, TV (Beaumont, Tex.), '53–'55; Wms. Dir., radio show, "This Is Your Civil Defense," Fed. Civil Defense Adm. (Battle Creek, Mich.), '50–'53; Wms. Dir., radio shows incl. "Theatre of the Air," "Book Review Time"; Coordr., Wms. Activities of Civil Defense and Disaster Relief for Jefferson County; Am. Red Cross, (S. Jefferson County Chptr., Dir., '47–), Tex. Assn. Hosp. Auxs. (Third VP, PR Dir., '53–; State Bd., Second VP), Tex. Fedn. Wms. Clubs, AWRT, Thalians (Pres.), Wtrs. Club, Port Arthur Choral Club (Pres., '66), active in civic groups; numerous nat., local cits., aw.; Univ. of Tex., '50–'52; Univ. of Houston, '52–'54; Lamar State Col. Tech., BS (Speech), '56; b. Port Arthur, Tex., 1919; p. Edmund and Sophie Szafir; h. Hugh Fay; c. Coleman Ed, Ralph; res: 3030 Lombardy Dr., Port Arthur, Tex. 77640.

FAY, MARY S., Free-lance Wtr.; Shell Development Co., Houston, Tx. '48–'69; Asst. Supt., Monmouth Memorial Hospital, (Long Branch, N.J.), '46–'48; Pers. Offcr., Univ. of Mich. Hospital, '41–'45; part-time instr. Coll. Bus., U. Houston, '50–'60; S.E. Tex. Industrial Eds., '51–'60, (Sec.-Treas., '58–'59); U. of Illinois BS '36; MS '37; DAR (Regent, Ann Poage Chpt., '61–'63), Houston Genealogical Forum (Pres., '67–'69); b. Burnt Prairie, Ill., 1915; p. William Logan and Myrtle Hunsinger Smith; h. Dr. Charles Hemphill Fay; res: 5403 Beverly Hill Lane, Houston, Tex. 77027.

FAYE, DORIS R., Exec. Prodr., Britten-Faye Productions, Inc., 325 W. 45th St., N.Y., N.Y. 10036, '59–; TV Program Developer, WABC-TV, '56; WNEW, '57; WPIX, '58–'64; Prodr., Wtr., Rschr., Performer on children's, game, interview, comedy-variety shows.

FAYE, LINDA (Linda Watson Ford), Weather Girl, Reptr., WQXI-TV, 1611 W. Peachtree St., Atlanta, Ga. 30309, '64–; "Emphasis Women," '66–'67; interview show, "People on the Go," '64–'66; Wtr., Prodr., prom. dept., WAGA-TV, '63–'64; Free-lance Model, Anncr., Ivey Talent Agcy., '60–'63; AFTRA, AWRT, Pfsnl. Models Assn. (Bd. Dirs., '66–; Pres., '66), Atlanta Press Club, Wms. C. of C.; Hon. Col., U.S. Navy, '68; Red Cross Aw., svc. to men in Vietnam, '68; W. Ga. Jr. Col. (Carrollton, Ga.); Mercer Univ. (Macon, Ga.), AB (Psych., Eng.), '60; b. Atlanta, Ga., 1938; p. Calvin and Mary Moore Watson; h. Donald Ford; c. Donald Gary; res: 862 Rowland Rd., Stone Mtn., Ga. 30083.

FEAGANS, ELIZABETH W., VP, Copy Dir., Provandie Eastwood & Lombardi Inc., 4620 Prudential Tower, Boston, Mass. 02199, '68–; Copy Chief, '67–'68; Copywtr., Cargill, Wilson & Acree (Richmond, Va.), '62–'67; Copywtr., Thalhimer's, '62; Crtv. Chief, Nelly Don Dresses, Georgia Bullock of Cal., '50–'54; Adv. of Club of Boston; Andy Aw. '67 from Adv. Club of N.Y. and numerous other awards in adv. since '63; Univ. of Kan., William Allen White Sch. of Jnlsm., BS, '50; b. Atlanta, Ga., 1929; p. Roy W. and Iola Elizabeth Harwood Webb; h. William M. Feagans; c. William Christopher, Kevin Winfield and Timothy Laurance; res: 220 Ridgeway Rd., Weston, Mass. 02193.

FEAGLES, ANITA MacRAE, Auth: 10 children's bks., one young adult novel; Co-auth: three mystery novels; bk. revs., N.Y. Times; Guest Lectr.; MWA; numerous best bk. cits.; Knox Col., BS, '47; C.C.N.Y., MS (Educ. Psych.), '51; b. 1926; p. Cuyler and Anita Foley MacRae; h. Robert Feagles; c. Wendy, Cuyler, Priscilla, Patrick; res: 8 Annandale Rd., Chappaqua, N.Y. 10514.

FEARON, DEE (Harriet Dean Hathaway Fearon), Feature Wtr., Bangor Daily News, Bangor Publishing Co., 491 Main St., Bangor, Me. 04402, '65–; Fashion copy, Filene's of Boston, '33; Adv. Copy, Cont., WBZ, '32; Radio Copy, J. Walter Thompson Co. (Chgo., Ill.), '31; Reptr., Chgo. Sunday Tribune, '30; Me. Press, Radio-TV Wm. (Pres., '66–'67), New Eng. WPA feature writing aw., '67); League of Wm. Voters (Vt. Pres., '41); Univ. of Chgo., PhB, '30; b. Taunton, Mass., 1908; p. Clarence and Addie Vanderwarker Hathaway; h. W. Ross Fearon; c. Robert Ross, John Rogers; res: 19 Chapel Rd., Orono, Me. 04473.

FEDDER, FELICE R., Bus. Mgr., Atlas Magazine, The World Press Company, 1180 Ave. of the Americas, N.Y., N.Y. 10036, '65–; Chief Accountant, Show Magazine, '63–'65; Staff Accountant, Scientific Am., '62–'63; Comml. Fin. industry; Oriental Art, Felice Fedder, Inc.; Prom. Roundtable; Univ. of Md., BA, '51; b. Balt., Md., 1929; p. Earl M. and Pearl C. Fedder; res: 200 East End Ave., N.Y., N.Y. 10028.

FEDOSIUK, POLLY CURREN, Free-lance Wtr., children's fiction and non-fiction; conducted Children's Sch. of Expression; pfsnl. reader, radio; Russell Sch. of Expression and Literature, '36; b. Boston, Mass.; p. Frank and Mary Dolan Curren; h. George Fedosiuk; c. Donald; res: 52 Southbourne Rd., Boston, Mass. 02130.

FEEZOR, BETTY DANIELS, Home Econst., WBTV, 1 Julian Price Pl., Charlotte, N.C. 28208, '53–; Home Demonstration Agt., Tenn. and N.C., '46–'52; Auth., bks: "Betty Feezor's Best", "Betty Feezor's Carolina Recipes", AWRT (Chptr. Pres., '65–'67), Home Econs. Assn., Home Econsts. in Bus.; First Lady in Food Aw., '59; Jr. Wms. Club Commty. Achiev. Aw., '57; Tex. State Col. for Wm., '42–'43; Univ. of Tenn., BS, '46; b. Texarkana, Tex., 1925; p. John Buford and Florence Owen Daniels; h. Turner Feezor; c. Robert Milton, John Daniels, Betty Cole; res: 6209 Glenridge Rd., Charlotte, N.C. 28211.

FEHL, ANNA ELIZABETH, Specialist in Radio and TV, Baltimore City Public Schools, Annex 562, Smith and Greely Rd., Balt., Md. 21209, '68–; TV Tchr.-Librn., '65–'68; Talent, Wtr., Prodr., ITV, '65–'67; Librn.-Tchr., '52–'65; Librn., Harford County Public Lib. (Belair, Md.); Librn., Milw. (Wis.) Public Lib.; Cnslt.-Prodr., Balt. Archdiocese Radio-TV Off., '67–; Talent, Wtr., "Poetry on Parade"; NAEB, ALA, Nat. Educ. Assn. Div. of Audio-Visual Instr., AWRT (Chptr. VP, '69; Chptr. Treas., '68), Md. Sch. Tchrs. Assn., Phi Delta Gamma; St. Joseph Col., AB, '48; Carnegie Inst. of Tech., MLS, '50; Johns Hopkins Univ., '53; Univ. of Wis., MA (Radio-TV, Speech), '64; b. Balt., Md., 1926; p. William A. and Anna Eberhardt Fehl; res: 6801 Everall Ave., Balt., Md. 21206.

FEIL, NAOMI WEIL, Script Wtr., Edward Feil Productions, 1514 Prospect Ave., Cleve., Oh. 44115, '63–; Doc. film Actress, '63–'68; Group Worker, Montefiore Home, '63–'68; Actress, Off-Broadway, '60–'63; Physical Educ. Coordr., N.Y.C. Sch., '59–'60; Tchr., Field Work; Sch. of Applied Social Sci., Case Western Reserve Univ.; Rschr. and Auth., "Group Therapy In A Home For The Aged," Gerontologist, '67; Nat. Assn. of Social Workers, Cleve. Film Assn., Music Therapy Assn.; Chris Aw., scripting film, "Step A Little Higher", '67; U.S. Indsl. Film Festival Aws., scripting and acting, "The Inner World Of Aphasia"; CINE aw., film "Where Life Still Means Living"; Oberlin Col.; Western Reserve Univ.; Columbia Univ., BS, '65 (magna cum laude); N.Y. Sch. of Social Work, Columbia Univ., MS, '58; b. Munich, Germany, 1932; p. Julian and Helen Kahn Weil; h. Edward Feil; c. Edward, Kenneth, Victoria, Beth; res: 21987 Byron Rd., Shaker Heights, Oh. 44122.

FEIL, NELLIE ELGUTTER, (pseud: Florence Field), free-lance wtr., food articles, 2343 Ardleigh Dr., Cleve., Oh. 44106; Auth., "Gourmet Cooking for Cardiac Diets" (World Publ. Co., '53; rev., '62, paperback, Collier Bks.; 4th ed. hard-cover, '65); Smith Col., BA, '14; b. Omaha, Neb.; p. Charles and Nellie Rosewater Elgutter; h. Harold Feil; c. George H., Mary F. Hellersten, Edward R.

FEINSILVER, LILLIAN MERMIN, Free-lance Copyed., Wtr.; Rsch. Asst., John Wiley & Sons (N.Y.), '44–'46; Asst. Secy. (ed., rsch), Comm. on the Hygiene of Housing, Am. Public Health Assn., Yale Sch. of Med. (New Haven, Conn.), '39–'44; Asst. (Secy.-Wtr.), Univ. Secys.,Yale Univ., '37–'39; Auth., bk. ('70), articles, features; Edtl. Cnslt., Lit. Agt.; Hon. Mention, Ellery Queen Mystery Magazine Contest, '46–'47; Silver Badge, St. Nicholas Magazine; Univ. of Chgo., '41; New Sch. for Social Rsch., '45; b. New Haven, Conn. 1917; p. Charles and Nechame Rosen Mermin; h. Alexander Feinsilver; c. David, Ruth; res: 510 McCartney St., Easton, Pa. 18042.

FEINSTEIN, NICOLETTE CAREY, Ed., New University Thought, P.O. Box 7431, Detroit, Mich. 48202, '60–; Asst. Ed., Bul. of Atomic Scientists, '58–'60; Edtl. Asst., Scott Foresman, '56–'58; Univ. of Chgo., BA, '55; b. Chgo., Ill., 1938; p. Thomas and Tonia Anderson Carey; h. Otto Feinstein; res: 667 W. Hancock, Detroit, Mich. 48201.

FELDKAMP, PHYLLIS, Fashion Ed., Evening and Sunday Bulletin, 30th and Market Sts., Phila., Pa. 19101, '68–; Free-lance Wtr., Paris, France, '61–'68; Reptr., Life, '44–'51; Reptr., Phila. Record, '42–'44; Contrbr. various nat. mags.; Bryn Mawr Col.; b. Chgo., Ill.; p. Charles and Anna Martony Dubsky; h. Fred Feldkamp; c. Phoebe Ann.

FELDMAN, ELANE GLICK, Pubcty. Dir., Schocken Books, 67 Park Ave., N.Y., N.Y. 10016, '66–; Asst. Pubcty. Dir., Frederick A. Praeger, '63–'65; juv. bks.; work published, mags.; numerous poetry jnls., mags.; fashion article with original designs, Disc-o-Scene, '68; Wtr., jacket copy, various publrs.; h. Daniel Feldman.

FELDMAN, GERALDINE S., Publr., Long Island Herald, 185–26 Union Tpke., Flushing, N.Y. 11366, '65–; Cunningham Wms. League; U.S. Army Recruiting aw., '67; March of Dimes aw., '68; Queensboro TB & Health Assn. Aws., '54, '62, '63, '64; Pedestrian Safety Aw., '58; Treasury Dept. Aw., '66; Boys Scouts Aw.; Indsl. Home for the Blind Friendship Aw., '66; b. Amsterdam, N.Y.; p. Benjamin C. and Jane Belloff Schaffer; h. Dr. George Furst; res: 75–44 199 St., Flushing, N.Y. 11366.

FELDMAN, JOAN MARCIA, Ed., American Aviation Publications, 1156 15th St. N.W., Wash., D.C. 20005, '68–; Assoc. Ed., Armed Forces Management; Asst. Ed., American Aviation Magazine; ANWC; Univ. of Mich., BA, '62; Am. Univ. (Intl. Rels.), '62–'63; b. Toledo, Oh., 1940; p. David J. and Min Goldberg Feldman; res: 1884 Columbia Rd. N.W., Wash., D.C. 20009.

FELLOWS, ANN RINGO, PR Dir., KVOO-TV, 3701 S. Peoria, Tulsa, Okla., 74101, '55–; AE, Ferguson Adv., '54–'55; Asst. Ed., D-X House Organ, '53–'54; Prom. Dir., KRMG, '52–'53; Guest Lectr. (TV writing) Univ. of Tulsa, '54; AWRT (Chptr. Pres., '66–'68; VP, '64–'66); Secy., Pubcty. Chmn., nat. conv., '64); Theta Sigma Phi (Chptr. Pres., '68–'69), Delta Delta Delta, Quota Club; Who's Who of Am. Wm.; Who's Who Of Am. Wm. Of The Southwest; Univ. of Oklahoma, BA, '44; b. Bartlesville, Okla., 1922; p. Dr. William Preston and Alberta Hand Ringo; c. Cheryl Ann, Caryl Lynn; res: 462 S. 78th East Ave., Tulsa, Okla. 74112.

FELT, LEE CRAIG, AE, Wtr., Radio and TV Dir., Circuit & Eddington Advertising, 10 S. Main, Salt Lake City, Ut. 84108, '68–; Free-lance talent, '60–'68; Bdcstr.-Wtr., KWIC, '60–'67; Continuity Dir.-Prodr., KLUB, '58–'60; Continuity Dir., KFEL-TV (Denver, Colo.), '54–'56; Continuity Dir., KUTA (Salt Lake City),

'50–'52; Auth., "History Of Radio In Utah To 1950"; Tchr., Eng. Composition and Rhetoric, Colo. Wms. Col., '52–'53; AWRT (Chptr. past Pres.); Univ. of Ut., BA, '49; MA , '50 (with hons.); b. Tooele, Ut., 1927; p. Samuel E. and Ruby Baldwin Craig; h. div.; Res: 900 Donner Way, Salt Lake City, Ut. 84108.

FELT, MARGARET ELLEY, Public Info. Offcr., Washington State Department of Natural Resources, P.O. Box 168, Olympia, Wash. 98501, '61–; Ed., Totem; Auth., "Gyppo Logger" ('64); Free-lance Wtr., Publicist, '55–'59; logging business with husband, '45–'60; Wash. State Presswm. (aw., '67), Wash. State Info. Cncl. (Dir., '69), numerous others; Univ. of Wash., '47, '49, '50–'53 (Crtv. Writing); b. Payette, Idaho, 1917; p. Walter and Lavina Schwabauer Elley; h. Horace W. Felt; c. Vicki Anne Davis, Kimberley Jane; res: P.O. Box 81, Olympia, Wash. 98501.

FENMORE, SYLVIA TANENBAUM, Dir. of PR, 52 Association, 147 E. 50th St., N.Y., N.Y. 10022, '68–'70; Ed.-Pres., City Desk Features, '67–'70; Reptr., Wtr., L.I. Press, '66–'67; Asst. to Ed., Feature Wtr., N. Am. Nwsp. Alliance, '63–'66; Asst. to Synd. Broadway Colmst. Louis Sobol, N.Y. Jnl. Am., '56–'62; Pratt Inst., BFA (Interiors, Liberal Arts), '63; b. N.Y.C., 1932; p. Abe and Ida Fishbein Tanenbaum; h. George Fenmore (div.); res: 310 E. 75th St., N.Y., N.Y. 10021.

FENN, DOLORES, Assoc. Ed., Art News, 444 Madison Ave., N.Y., N.Y. 10022, '67–; Edtl. Assoc.; George Washington Univ., AA (Art Hist.), '49; Columbia Univ., BS (Art Hist.), '64; res: 15 E. 76, N.Y., N.Y. 10021.

FENNELL, MARY THÉRÈSE, AE, PR, Mktng., Lubar Associates, 15 W. 38th St., N.Y., N.Y. 10018, '67–; Fashion Dir., AE, Lester Harrison, Inc., Advertising, '65–'66; AE, Johnstone, Inc., '63–'65; Asst. AE, Hockaday Assocs., '60–'63; Fashion Group, NHFL; Centenary Col. for Wms., AA, '54 (Crtv. Writing Aw.); Columbia Sch. of Gen. Studies, BA (Govt.), '70; b. Mt. Vernon, N.Y.; p. Joseph and Helen Grace Fennell; h. Andrew Gerber; c. Carol Jean; res: 118 E. 93rd St., N.Y., N.Y. 10028.

FENNER, MILDRED LEE SANDISON, Ed., Today's Education, NEA Journal, National Education Association, 1201 16th St. N.W., Wash., D.C. 20036, '55–; Mag. Ed., '49–'55; Asst. Ed., '43–'49; Staff Mbr., '31–'43; Auth., "NEA History" ('45); Co-auth., "Pioneer American Educators" ('47); numerous articles in educ. periodicals; Prof., Lectr., Univ. of Wyo., Am. Univ., Southern Ill. Univ.; conducted edtl. courses, Intl. Educ. Eds. Workshops in Canada, Philippines, Netherlands, U.S.; conducted TV program, Am. Assn. of Sch. Admrs. convs., many yrs.; educ: N.W. Mo. State (Tchrs.) Col., BS, '31; George Wash. Univ., MA, '38; Ed.D, '41; Glassboro State Col., Litt.D., '60; Huntsville, Mo., 1910; p. John Forte and Minnielee Holliday Sandison; h. Wolcott Fenner; res: 530 "N" St. S.W., Apt. S-205, Wash., D.C. 20024.

FENNER, PHYLLIS REID, Wtr., Anthologist; Librn., Plandome Road Sch., Manhasset, N.Y. 11030, '23–'54; Instr., Lib. Sci., St. John's Univ., Bklyn., N.Y., '38–'45; Published 46 anthologies for young people; Bk. Reviewer: N.Y. Times, The Instructor, Children's Digest, '40–'55; Cadmus Bks. (Ed. Mbr., '45–'69); Wms. Nat. Bk. Assoc., Weekly Reader Bk. Club (Edtl. Bd., '62–), The Pen and Brush Club, Wm. Geographers, Auths. Guild; Who's Who of Am. Wm.; Mount Holyoke Col., BA, '21; Columbia Univ. Lib. Sch., '34; b. Almond, N.Y., 1899; p. William and Viola Van Orman Fenner; res: Box 653, Manchester, Vt. 05254.

FENNER, THEODOSIA HICKMAN, Ed., Field Pubns, and Sls. Incentive Brochures, Mid-Continent Life Insurance Company, 1400 Classen Dr., Okla. City, Okla. 73122, '59–; Free-lance Wtr., '59–; articles in trade jnls., ins. co. pubns., poetry; ICIE (Aw. of Merit, '66), Central Okla. Indsl. Ed. Assn. (Bd. of Dirs.; Outstanding Svc. Aw., '67), Okla. State Wtrs. (Pres., '40s), Okla. Poetry Soc., NLAPW; Homemaker of Week Aw., Okla. Publ. Co., '56; Who's Who in Okla. City; Univ. of Okla.; b. Lebanon, Mo., 1908; p. K. Ross and Edith Bryan Hickman; h. Robert P. Fenner; c. Mrs. Robbie Jane Deaton; res: 4641 N.W. 60th St., Okla. City, Okla. 73122.

FENTON, ELSIE, Ed., Alpha Iota Notebook, Alpha Iota Executive Offices, 1002 Grand Ave., Des Moines, Ia. 50309, '31–'70; Secy. and PR, Am. Inst. of Bus., '25–'60; Ed., house organ and Adv. Copywtr., Harris-Emery Co., '21; Reptr., Times Jnl. (Dubuque, Ia.), '17–'18; NFPW (VP, '50–'51; aws.), Soroptimist (Intl. Assn. Governing Body, '52–'58; Fedn. of the Am. Pres., '52–'54; Edtl. Bd., The Am. Soroptimist; special study, rept., "The Handicapped Child," given intl. conv., '52), White House Conf. Highway Safety (Advisory Comm., '54), Alpha Iota (Founder, Grand Pres.), AAUW, Wms. Med. Col. of Pa. (Nat. Bd.); Ia. Mother of Yr., '55; Nat. Aws. Jury, Freedoms Fndn. at Valley Forge, '53; Guest, German Govt., '58; State Univ. of Ia., BA, '21 (Theta Sigma Phi, Beta Gamma Sigma); b. Dubuque, Ia., 1899; h. Everett O. Fenton; c. Marilyn Fenton Munson, Ronald E., Keith D., Janice Fenton Harris; res: 1224 E. Escondido Dr., Phoenix, Ariz. 85014.

FERGUSON, ANN CHRISTENSEN, Actress, c/o Kenneth Daniels Agency, 7188 Sunset Blvd., L.A., Cal. 90046; or c/o Serenella Rossi Agency, 96 Via Veneto, Rome, Italy; Currently in "Togetherness"; TV commls.; stock, repertory cos. throughout U.S.; AEA, SAG, AFTRA; Univ. of Wash., BA (Drama); Independent Study Tour incl: Moscow Art Theatre, Leningrad's Maly Mime Theatre, Warsaw Drama Theatre, Bayreuth Festival Master Classes (Stage Direction, Coaching); h. Gary Gene Ferguson; res: 325 Bay St., Santa Monica, Cal. 90405.

FERGUSON, ELIZABETH (BESS) STORM, Newsltr. Ed., National Association for Student Affairs, 3425 Woodland St., Ames, Ia. 50010, '68–; Contrbr., Ency.

Britannica Jr., '38–; Free-lance Wtr., '21–; Jnlsm. Instr., Ia. State Univ., '63–; Mng. Ed., Jnl. of Nursery Educ., '58–'64; Wms. Ed., Intl. Harvester Farm Magazine, '56–'68; Wms. Ed., Ia. Rural Eelctric News, '58–'66; Theta Sigma Phi (Alumni Club Pres., '60–'61; Matrix Aw., '61), NFPW (First Pl. Nat. Aw. for Mag. Sec. Ed. by a Wm., '63; many state aws.), NLAPW, Am. Home Econs. Assn.; Ia. State Univ., BS, '21; b. Nevada, Ia., 1897; p. Jeremiah Velasco and Anna Lynch Storm; h. Fred E. Ferguson; c. Frank Elmo, John Frederick, Alice (Mrs. Harold Holmes), Elizabeth (Mrs. A. A. Lockhart); res: 3425 Woodland St., Ames, Ia. 50010.

FERRANTE, CAROLYN FRANCES, Edtl. Assoc., Esquire Magazine, 488 Madison Ave., N.Y., N.Y. 10022, '67; Secy., Adv. Dept., '66–'67; Holiday Magazine, '64–'66; Taylor Bus. Inst., '63; Hunter Col., AA; res: 9019 Grand Ave., N. Bergen, N.J. 07047.

FERRANTE, GENEVIEVE SHIRLEY, Dir., Pubcty., PR, Van Nostrand Reinhold Company, 450 W. 33rd St., N.Y., N.Y. 10001, '69–; Pubcty. Assoc., McGraw-Hill, '69; Pubcty. Asst., '63–'69; Pubcty. Mgr., Kendall Co., '61–'63; PPA, Children's Bk. Cncl.; Univ. of R.I., BA, '61 (Phi Kappa Phi); b. Providence, R.I., 1929; p. Pasquale and Marietta Fornaro Ferrante; res: 43-23 Colden St., Apt. 5-H, Flushing, N.Y. 11355.

FERRAR, CATHERINE ANN, Actress, Stage Society Theater, Melrose Ave., L.A., Cal.; many TV shows, incl. "Man from UNCLE," "Batman," "Days of our Lives," others; SAG, AFTRA, AEA; Best Actress, Fall Festival of Dramatic Arts, '60; U.C.L.A.; b. Waterbury, Conn., 1946; p. Rocco A. and Gertrude Truncale Ferraro; res: 3360 Manning Ct., L.A., Cal. 90064.

FERRARA, PATRICIA DWYER, Wms. Ed., The Daily Home News, Home News Publishing Co., 123 How Lane, New Brunswick, N.J. 08903, '66–; Reptr., '60–'66; Reptr., The News Tribune; Johnson & Johnson; N.J. Press Assn., N.J. Daily Nwsp. Wm., Inc. (Bd. of Dirs.; Rec. Secy.); Rutgers Univ.; b. Perth Amboy, N.J., 1927; p. Patrick L. and Josephine Schultz Dwyer; h. Carmine A. Ferrara; c. Patricia, Janice May, Carol Jo; res: 204 Ward St., New Brunswick, N.J. 08920.

FERRING, GERALDINE, Supvsr., Libs., Textbks., San Francisco Unified School District, 135 Van Ness Ave., S.F., Cal. 94102, '58–; Librn.-in-charge, Order, Catalog Dept., '50–'58; Librn., Mission HS, '49–'50; Librn., Napa Jr. Col., '47–'49; Librn., Long Beach, '46–'47; Librn., Lectr., Univ. HS, Univ. of Mich., '45–'46; Librn., Northern Mich. Univ., '43–'46, '40–'42; Cal. Assn. of Sch. Librns. (Pres., '61–'62), Cal. Lib. Assn., ALA, WNBA; Drake Univ., BA, '34; Univ. of Mich., MA (Lib. Sci.), '40; b. Dubuque, Ia.; p. Nicholas and Catherine Banfield Ferring; res: 405 Serrano Dr., S.F., Cal. 94132.

FERRY, NANCY LEE (Nancy Terry), Bdcstr.; Program Dir., KITY-FM, Mission Broadcasting Co., 317 Arden Grove, San Antonio, Tex. 78206, '66–; varied adm., crtv., on-air positions, radio and TV stations in Cleve., Chgo., White Plains, N.Y., San Antonio, since '45; AWRT, AFTRA, SAG; The Play House, Cleve., '42-'43; Cleve. Col., co-op student, '43-'44; b. Cleve., Oh., 1924; p. James and Garnett Russell Ferry; h. Bert H. Crockford (div.); res: 420 E. Dewey Pl., San Antonio, Tex. 78212.

FETTO, EDITH PISELLI, Exec. Prodrs. Asst., Johnny Seven Productions, 11213 McLennan Ave., Granada Hills, Cal. 91344, '66-; Secy.-Treas., Wrajon Prods., '63-'66; p. John H. Piselli; h. John Fetto.

FEUERSTEIN, BARBARA, Fashion Ed., Ingenue Magazine, 750 Third Ave., N.Y., N.Y. 10017, '68; PR Cnlst., Clairol, '67-'68; Smith Col., BA, '68; b. Bay Shore, N.Y., 1944; p. Dr. Benjamin and Lucille Feuerstein; res: 220 E. 57th St., N.Y., N.Y. 10022.

FEY, TERESA KRIZEK, Radio-TV Dir., Wyatt Advertising Inc., 427 Ninth St., San Antonio, Tex. 78206, '68-; Off. Mgr., Fraser-Wiggins, Collins & Lewis Advertising, '67-'68; Asst. Film Dir., Copywtr., Asst. Prog. Dir., Nat. Traf. Mgr., KONO-TV (now KSAT-TV), '57-'67; AWRT; Catholic Archdiocese of Seguin, Tex. (Dir. of Commty. Affairs Comms.); b. San Antonio, Tex. 1939; p. Bartholomew and Mary Ellen Routzen Krizek; h. Curtis Fey; c. Curtis A. Jr., Melissa Marie; res: P.O. Box 13, Converse, Tex. 78109.

FICHTNER, MARGARET CAUFIELD, Asst. Prod. Mgr., WAPI Television, P.O. Box 1310, Birmingham, Ala. 35205, '59-; Copywtr., WEZB Radio, '57-'59; AWRT (VP, '62), Secy., '67), Birmingham Press Club, Jefferson County Radio & TV Cncl., Birmingham Children's Theatre; John Brown Univ., BS, '37; b. Birmingham, Ala., 1916; p. George and Maggie White Caufield; h. John J. Fichtner; c. Victor, George, Kip; res: 1300 20th St., S., Birmingham, Ala. 35205.

FICKERT, PHOEBE SUTHERLAND, Area Dir., PR, National Cystic Fibrosis Research Foundation, 1111 E. 54th St., Indpls., Ind., 46220, '69-; N.Y. Off., '68; Exec. Dir., Chgo., Cinn., Indpls., '63-'68; Exec. Dir. Nat. Fndn.-March of Dimes, '61-'63; Free-lance PR, Radio-TV talent, '43-'68; Colmst., Indianapolis News, '63-'64; Instr., Patricia Stevens, John Robert Powers, Loretta Young Finishing Schs., '54-'65; AWRT (Chptr. VP, '67), NLAPW, PRSA, Am. Bus. Wms. Assn., Mutual Svc. Assn., Nat. Soc. of Fund Raisers; b. Lake City, Minn., 1923; p. George and Genevieve McMillan Sutherland; h. Alan Fickert; c. Stephen Sutherland; res: 4119 Commonwealth Dr., Indpls., Ind. 46220.

FIEDLER, JEAN FELDMAN, Auth: "In Any Spring" ('69), "Jill's Story" ('65), "A Yardstick for Jessica" ('64), numerous bks.; stories in collections, mags.; Librn., The Highland School, 172-79 Highland Ave., Jamaica, N.Y. 11432, '67-; Substitute HS Eng. Tchr., '62-'65; Librn., Bklyn. Public Lib., '48-'49; Copywtr., Gimbel's Dept. Store (Pitt., Pa.), '47; HS Eng. Tchr., '46; Social Worker, Children's Aid Soc., '45; Auths. League of Am. (Auths. Guild), Nat. Wms. Bk. Assn.; Univ. of Pitt., BA, '45 (with hon.); N.Y.U.; Banks St. Col. of Educ.; The New Sch. for Social Rsch.; b. Pitt., Pa., 1923; p. Harry and Dina Diness Feldman; h. Harold Fiedler; c. Judith Laurel, Joan Barbara; res: 69-23 Bell Blvd., Bayside, N.Y. 11364.

FIELD, BARBARA, Free-lance Wtr., Jnlst.; free-lance TV script adv. copy, fashion shows; Sls. Prom. Mgr., Helena Rubinstein, '43-'47; Soc. Ed., Herald Tribune Paris Edition, '30-'39; Soc. Pubcty., '28-'30; shopping, Park Ave. Rev., '24-'28; soc. dept., Jnl. Am., '20-'24; Fashion Group, OPC; b. N.Y.C.; h. Daniel Crohn; c. Burrill L.; res: 251 W. 71st St., N.Y., N.Y. 10023.

FIELD, CAROLYN WICKER, Coordr., Off. of Work with Children, The Free Library of Philadelphia, Logan Sq., 19th and Vine Sts., Phila., Pa. 19103, '53-; Instr., Univ. of N.C., '52; County Librn., New Castle County Free Lib. (Wilmington, Del.), '50-'53; Head of Children's Work, Wilmington Inst. Free Lib., '46-'50; Field Worker, Cuyahoga County Lib. (Cleve., Oh.), '43-'44; Instr., Simmons Col. (Boston, Mass.), '42-'43; Children's Librn., N.Y. Public Lib., '38-'40; ALA-CSD (Pres., '59-'60); Bksellers' Assn. of Phila (Pres., '67-'70), numerous others; Simmons Col., BS, '38; b. Melrose, Mass., 1916; p. Charles Currie and Barbara Miller Wicker; h. Richard Atherton Field; res: 1 A Manheim Gardens, Phila., Pa. 19144.

FIELD, CHARLOTTE, Dir. of Nat. Food Pubcty., Washington State Apple Commission, 511 Second Ave. W., Seattle, Wash. 98119, '57-; AE, Abbott Kimball (S.F. Cal.), '51-'54; Merchandising Coordr., Design Cnslt., Asst. to Pres., Gump's, '49-'50; Asst. Dir. Pubcty., Lord and Taylor, '46-'47; Resident Rep., N.Y. Off., Bon Marche (Seattle), '45-'46; Asst. Merchandising Mgr., '44-'45; Display Coordr., '41-'44; AWRT (Western Reg. Educ. Fndn., Rep.; Evergreen Chptr. Pres.), NFPW, Adv. and Sales Club; Univ. of Wash., BA, '36; b. Seattle, Wash., 1915; p. Charles and Evelyn Westcott Field; res: 348 W. Olympic Pl., Seattle, Wash. 98119.

FIELD, ELEANORE WAGNER, Staff Wtr., Casper Star-Tribune, Box 80, Casper, Wyo. 82601, '67-; Wtr., Dixie mag., New Orleans (La.) Times Picayune, '66-'67; News Ed., Queen Anne News (Seattle, Wash.), '65-'66; Wms. pg. Reptr., Staten Island (N.Y.) Advance, '63-'64; Wms. pg. Reptr., Denver Post; Pi Delta Epsilon; Univ. of Wyo., '58-'60; Univ. of Wash., '65-'66; b. Chgo., Ill., 1940; p. Richard and Louise Ehlers Wagner; h. John C. Field; res: 2919 E. Fourth St., Casper, Wyo. 82601.

FIELD, Sr. MARY, Chief Librn., Rosary College, 7900 W. Division St., River Forest, Ill. 60305, '64-; Ref. Librn., '60-'64; Tchr., Librn., Sinsinawa Dominican High Schs., '46-'60; Tchr.-Librn., Medford and Reedsburg (Wis.) Public High Schs., '42-'44; Secy. to Treas., Employers Mutuals Ins. Co. (Wausau), '40-'41; ALA,

Ill. Lib. Assn., Catholic Lib. Assn. (Northern Ill. Unit., Secy. '62–'64); Kappa Delta Pi; Rosary Col., BA, '39; MA (Lib. Sci.) '60; Univ. of Wis., MA, '40; b. Wis. Dells, Wis., 1918; p. Henry A. and Georgia Coakley Field; res: 7900 W. Division St., River Forest, Ill. 60305.

FIELDER, MILDRED CRAIG, Free-lance Wtr., 618 Ridgeroad, Lead, S.D. 57754, '50–; Auth: hist. bks., articles, juv. stories, poems; NLAPW (Natl. Chmn., '58, '62, '64, '66), Soc. of Am. Histrns., S.D. Press Wm., S.D. Hist. Soc., S.D. Poetry Soc. (Reg. VP, '55–); Huron Col., '29–'31; Univ. of Colo., '46; b. Quinn, S.D., 1913; p. William and Verna Edzards Craig; h. Ronald Fielder; c. Robert, John; res: 618 Ridgeroad, Lead, S.D. 57754.

FIELDING, ELIZABETH M., Special Asst. to the Asst. Postmaster General, U.S. Post Office Dept., 12th and Pennsylvania Ave., Wash., D.C. 20260; Fin. Coordr., Inaugural Comm., '68–'69; PR Dir., Nat. Fedn. of Repl. Wm., '61–'68 (Svc. Aws., '62, '67); Legislative Analyst, News Ed., Nat. Assn. of Electric Cos., '57–'60; Pubcty., Assoc. Rsch. Dir., Repl. Nat. Comm., '44–'57; Legislative Aide to U.S. Senator, '53–'54; Cnslt. to two U.S. Congressmen, '44–'52; Am. Polit. Sci. Assn., Am. Assn. for the Advancement of Sci., Am. Acad. of Polit. and Social Sci., Am. Soc. for Public Adm., Am. Mgt. Assn., Am. Soc. for Training & Development, Capitol Hill Club, Columbia Hist. Soc.; Who's Who in America; Conn. Col. for Wm., BA (Polit. Sci.), '38 (Phi Beta Kappa); Am. Univ. Sch. of Public Affairs, MA (Public Adm.), '44; b. New London, Conn., 1917; p. Frederick J. and Elizabeth Martin Fielding; res: 3 D.C. Village Lane, S.W., Wash., D.C. 20032.

FIELDING, JANE PADDOCK, Sch. Librn., Williams Air Force Base Elementary School, 11th and Coolidge Sts., Chandler, Ariz. 85224, '69–; Librn., Warrensville Hgts. (Oh.) Jr. HS, '66–'69; Librn., Middle Sch. (Independence, Oh.), '65–'66; Asst. Prof., Ariz. State Univ., '61–'64; Instr., '57–'61; Pi Lambda Theta, NEA, Ariz. Educ. Assn., WNBA; Western Reserve Univ., BS, '42; Univ. of Wis., MS, '57; b. Zanesville, Oh.; p. Arthur and Helen Fielding; res: 743-B W. Ray Rd., Chandler, Ariz. 85224.

FIELDING, VERA VICTOREEN, PR Dir., Berkshire Medical Center, 725 North St., Pittsfield, Mass. 01201, '60–; Pubcty. Dir., Un. Commty. Svcs.; Photo Ed., Yankee Magazine (Dublin, N.H.); Reptr., Feature Wtr., The Berkshire Eagle (Pittsfield, Mass.); Kappa Tau Alpha, various others; MacEachern aw. for hosp. PR project, '61; Boston Univ., BS (Jnlsm), '34; b. Pittsfield, Mass., 1911; p. Walfrid and Mary Benson Victoreen; h. Wendell S. Fielding; c. Mrs. Frank P. Maxant, Mrs. Alce L. Bergh (married Aug. 2, 1969); res: 121 Fort Hill, Pittsfield, Mass. 01201.

FIELDS, HARRIET BEERY, Wms. Ed., Adrian Daily Telegram, 133 N. Winter St., Adrian, Mich. 49221, '66–; Asst. Wms. Ed., Ch. Ed., '57–'66; ZONTA, Adrian Dramatic Club; Principia Col., '34–'35; b. Davenport, Ia., 1916; p. Harrison and Antoinette Hoenes Beery; h.

Clyde G. Fields; c. Douglas, Diana; res: 537 Dennis St., Adrian, Mich. 49221.

FILLEY, BETTE RILEY, Free-lance Wtr., Ed., Bette Filley Communications Service, 2431 S. 115th Pl., Seattle, Wash. 98168, '66–; Ed., Smyth, Totes & Quotes (house organ); Ed., Pacific Marketer, trade jnl. for Home Furnishings Industry in N.W.; Ed., Puget Sound Cooperative League Cooperator; Ed., Legend, Pacific N.W. IEA; PR Dir., Sicks' Rainier Brewing Co., '60–'66; Wms. Ed., Johnstown (Oh.) Independent, '58–'60; Illus., Indoor Gardening Colm. synd. by Chgo. Sun-Times, '58–'60; Lectr., Burnley Sch. of Pfsnl. Art; Temple Univ.; Famous Artists Schs., '57–'58; b. Phila., Pa., 1933; p. Russell S. and Martha S. Spayd Riley; h. Laurence D. Filley; c. Richard D., Barbara Nan, Patricia Lynn, Kathryn Owyn, Thomas John; res: 2431 S. 115th Pl., Seattle, Wash. 98168.

FINCHER, BARBARA CARLTON, Dir. of Public Info., Alabama Educational Television Commission, 2101 Magnolia Ave., Suite 512, Birmingham, Ala. 35205, '68–; Asst. to PR Dir., Jnlsm. Instr., Samford Univ. '67–'68; Theta Sigma Phi (Prof. Chptr. Birmingham, VP) NAEB, Birmingham Press Club, Ala. Press Assn.; Univ. of Ala., BA (Jnlsm.), '63 (Phi Beta Kappa); MA (Jnlsm.), '67; b. Wash., D.C., 1942; p. Clayton C. and Ann Sherrod Carlton; res: 665 Idlewild Circle, Apt. B-3, Birmingham, Ala. 35205.

FINCHER, MISTY, Station Mgr., McAlister Broadcasting Corp.-KSEL-FM, P.O. Box 2805, Lubbock, Tex. 79408, '66–; Anncr., KSEL-AM and FM, '66–; Anncr., Program Dir., KBFM-FM Radio, '59–'66; Anncr., KDUB Radio, On Camera Anncr., KDUB-TV, '56–'59; Anncr., KXOL Radio (Ft. Worth, Tex.), '55–'56; Music Librn., '54–'55; Free-lance Voice Talent, various nat. ad agcys., '52–'54; AWRT; b. Ft. Chadbourne, Tex., 1924; p. William A. and Moda M. Fincher; res: 2838 65th St., Lubbock, Tex. 79413.

FINELL, ALYCE SUZANNE, Assoc. Prodr., "A.M. New York," ABC-TV, 1130 Ave. of the Americas, N.Y., N.Y. 10019, '70–; Prize Coodr., "Dream House," Don Reid Productions, '68–'70; Bob Stewart Prods., '67; Griffin Prods., '66; Talent Assocs., '66; Goodson-Todman Prods., '62; NBC, '61; Free-lance Talent, '58–'60; Osborn Propst Adv. Agcy. (Syracuse, N.Y.) Pres., Founder, L'Etoile Prods., Free-lance PR, '67–; Staff, Radio WAER, WOLF, WFBL, WBIC, WGLI, WTFM; Wtr., CARE, '59; Lyric Wtr., "Ivanov," '58; Falmouth (Mass.) Playhouse, '58; AWRT, NATAS, Alpha Epsilon Rho (Chptr. Pres.), Zeta Phi Eta (Chptr. Pres.); Syracuse Univ., BS (Radio-TV), '61; N.Y.U. (Commtns.); b. Bay Shore, L.I., N.Y., 1940; p. Dr. Philip and Miriam Ross Finell; res: 225 E. 79th St., N.Y., N.Y. 10021; 280 E. Main St., Bay Shore, L.I., N.Y. 11706.

FINK, JOYCE ERLEEN, Dir. of Pubns., State University College at Buffalo, 1300 Elmwood Ave., Buffalo, N.Y. 14222, '67–; Asst. to Dir. of Public Info., '65–'67; PR Cnslt. (self-employed), '64–'65; Asst. to Pres.,

Rosary Hill Col., Buffalo, '59–'64; Dir. of Dev., '57–'59; Dir. of PR, '54–'57; Curriculum Cnslt. in Art Educ., Dept. of Educ., Diocese of Buffalo, '52–'54; Auth: Rosary Hill College Alumnae Follow-Up Study, '59; Public Relations Problems In Higher Education (Univ. of Buffalo, '58); Co-ed., Art In The Elementary School ('54); PRSA (Niagara Frontier Chptr. Secy., '67–'68), AAUW (Bd. of Dirs.), other orgs.; numerous aws. for graphics and pubns. from ACPRA, Buffalo Art Dirs. Club, Mead Paper Co.; semi-finalist, White House Fellowship, '65; Rosary Hill Col., AB, '52 (outstanding alumna, '65); Univ. of Buffalo, Master of Educ., '59; b. Buffalo, N.Y., 1930; p. Frank and Florence Honeck Fink; res: 408 Ruskin Rd., Buffalo, N.Y. 14226.

FINKE, BLYTHE FOOTE, News-Feature Wtr., United States Information Agency, Room 1609, 250 W. 57th St., N.Y., N.Y. 10019, '63–; Info. Offcr., Turkey and Germany, '51–'58; Asst. to Gen. Mgr., Intl. Cultural Exchange Prog. of Am. Nat. Theatre and Acad., '61–'62; Radio News Wtr., Voice of UN Command (Japan), '60–'61; PR Dir., Bklyn. Public Lib. System, '59–'60; Ed., House Organ, Shell Oil Co. (Wilmington, Cal.), '49–'50; OPC, PRSA; Univ. of Cal., Berkeley, BA; b. Pasadena, Cal., 1922; p. Robert and Blythe Mendenhall Foote; h. John Finke; res: Woods Rd., Palisades, N.Y. 10964.

FINKELSTEIN, AUDREY ROTHENBERG, Hostess, "Woman's View," WTHS-TV, Community Television, 1410 N.E. Second Ave., Miami, Fla. 33132, '68–; AWRT, Theta Sigma Phi (Headliner Aw., '64), Cncl. for Continuing Educ. of Wm. (Chmn.); active in numerous civic groups; Outstanding Citizen of Dade County, '64; Urban League Equal Opportunity Aw., '65; Miami News Permanent Hall of Fame, '65; Who's Who of Am. Wm.; Alpha Epsilon Phi Outstanding Alumnae, '69; Univ. of Miami, AB, '38 (cum laude; Mortar Board); b. Chgo., Ill., 1916; h. Charles H. Finkelstein; c. Jay N., Evelyn Hirschhorn; res: 815 Catalonia Ave., Coral Gables, Fla. 33134.

FINLAY, DOLORES MARILYN, Pres., Dolores Finlay & Associates, 2608 N. Beachwood Dr., Hollywood, Cal. 90028, '68–; Partner, Dee-Lin Assocs., pubcty. and prom. co., '67; Asst. PR Dir., KTTV (L.A.), '64–'67; Pubcty. Dir., KNBC, '57–'63; Asst. PR Dir., '55–'57; guest speaker for orgs.; AWRT (Southern Cal. Chptr., Bd. of Dirs., '67), Radio-TV Wm. of Southern Cal. (Bd. of Dirs., Treas., other offs.; group merged with AWRT in '67), Hollywood Wms. Press Club (Pubcty. Chmn., '67–'68), Pacific Pioneer Bdcstrs., NATAS (Hollywood Chptr., Co-chmn. Hospitality Comm., '67–'69), Hollywood Radio & TV Soc., AAF, Cal. Press Wm., NFPW (numerous honors and aws.), Several civic orgs.; El Camino Col., Assoc. of Arts., '51; Univ. of Southern Cal., '51; L.A. City Col., '51, '55 b. Torrance, Cal.; p. Hubert and Lolita Mahn Finlay; res: 2608 N. Beachwood Dr., Hollywood, Cal. 90028.

FINLEY, GLENNA, Wtr., bks: "Death Strikes Out"

('57), "Career Wife" ('64), "Nurse Pro Tem" ('67); Free-lance Radio Wtr., '50–'53; Publicist, '50–'53; March of Time, '49–'50; Life, '48; Prodr., Intl. Div., NBC, '45–'47; Stanford Univ., BA, '45 (cum laude); Univ. of Wash., Educ. Certification, '60; b. Puyallup, Wash., 1925; p. John Ford and Gladys Winters Finley; h. Donald MacLeod Witte; c. Duncan MacLeod; res: 2645-34 Ave. W., Seattle, Wash. 98199.

FINN, JOAN LOCKWOOD, Dir. of Press Rels., Motion Picture Association of America Inc., 522 Fifth Ave., N.Y., N.Y. 10017, '69–; Auth., fiction, "Heritage of Evil" (Belmont Press, '68); Acc. Supvsr., Henderson & Roll, '67–'69; AE, Ted Bates, '63–'67; AE, Ted Sills, '61–'63; Jr. AE, Dudley-Anderson-Yutzy, '58–'61; Copywtr., J. C. Penney, '57–'58; PRSA; Radcliffe Col., BA (Am. Hist.); b. Plainfield, N.J., 1929; p. William and Ada Dayton Finn; res: 285 Riverside Dr., N.Y., N.Y. 10025.

FINNEGAN, HELEN M., Eastern Rep., Crowell Collier & Macmillan Professional Magazines, 866 Third Ave., N.Y., N.Y. 10022; Rep., Catholic Sch. Jnl., '68–; Rep., Grade Tchr. Magazine, '62–'68; special project, WOR Childrens Fund; AWNY (Offcr., Dir.), Catholic Press Assn., Nat. Assn. Industry-Educ., Mag. Publrs. Assn.; Aw., Fordham Univ., for outstanding special svc., '57; Columbia Univ.; b. N.Y.C.; p. Peter J. and Mary Shields Finnegan; res: 175 Ramsey Ave., Yonkers, N.Y. 10701.

FINNEY, GERTRUDE BRIDGEMAN, Auth., nine published bks., '51–'66; two pubns. in Eng., one pubn. in Braille; Publr: David McKay Co., Inc.; Panel Instr., Pacific N.W. Wtrs. Conf., '59–'67; Speaker, Idaho Wtrs. League, '67; Speaker, Jr. high schs. for past 10 yrs.; Spokane Wtrs. (Pres., '50), N.W. Hist. Soc., Theta Sigma Phi (Hon. Mbr.), Delta Kappa Gamma (Hon. Mbr.); Aw. for Most Distg. Writing, Univ. of Ind., '66; Magazine Inst. Correspondence Courses, '49; Wash. State Univ., '50–'51; b. Morocco, Ind., 1892; p. George E. and Lillian G. Rolls Bridgeman; h. John M. Finney; c. John M., Jr., Joseph Bertrand, Ruth M. (Mrs. William Laughlin), David Stanley; res: 2946 Grandview Ave., Spokane, Wash. 99204.

FINNEY, MARION COLEMAN, AE, Gutman Advertising Agency, Peoples Federal Bldg., Wheeling, W. Va. 26003, '68–; Asst. Dir. of Pers., Sls. Prom., Adv., The Hub Dept. Store, '58–'67; Nat. Adv. Dept., Wheeling Intelligencer and Wheeling News-Register, '48–'53; Dir., Teenqueen Oh. Valley, '66; Fifth Dist. Adv. Achiev. Aws., '69; Col. of Commerce (Wheeling, W. Va.); b. Martins Ferry, Oh., 1925; p. Harry and Marion Rentsch Coleman; h. Bruce Finney; c. Leigh Ann, Melissa D., Robert Bruce; res: 415 Clinton, Martins Ferry, Oh. 43935.

FINNICUM, BETTY JO, Adv. Mgr., Lewistown Daily News, 521 W. Main, Lewistown, Mont. 59456, '69–; Soc. Ed., Sports Ed.; Mont. State Press Wm. Aw., '69; Eastern Mont. Col., '48; b. Culbertson, Mont., 1930; p.

Thedore and Leota Hall Wix; h. Curtis Finnicum; c. Linda, Curtis, Peggy, Boyd, Michael, Mark; res: 208 S.W. Cedar, Lewistown, Mont. 59456.

FIORA, CATHERINE ONORINA, Edtl. Asst., International Brotherhood of Electrical Workers, 1200 15th St. N.W., Wash., D.C. 20005, '62–; Ed., Industrial Atomic Energy Uses, Hazards and Controls, '60–'61; Pubcty. and Prog. Asst., Meet The Professor, Nat. Educ. Assn., '61–'62; Continuity Dir., Wms. Dir., WCUM AM and FM (Cumberland, Md.) '52–'55; Theta Sigma Phi, ILPA, Off. and Professional Employees Intl. Un.; W. Va. Univ., BS, '52; b. Clarksburg, W. Va., 1931; p. Anthony and Angioletta Olmo Fiora; res: 3312 Senator Ave., District Heights, Md. 20028.

FIORANI, ROSE FLOREY, Co-owner, Treas., PR Dir., WPTS Radio, Midway Broadcasting Co., Inc., 83 Foote Ave., Duryea Boro, Greater Pittston, Pa. 18642, '53–; Co-founder, Fiorani Radio Products, '32; AWRT (NE Pa. Chptr., Founder and first Pres., '59), Scranton Adv. and Sales Club (Offcr. and Dir., '47; Aw. for 30 Yrs. of Outstanding Svc. in the Field of Commtns., '60); Mother of the Yr. Aw., Un. Mothers of Am., '67; Lady of the Holy Sepulchre of Jerusalem, honor bestowed by Pope John XXIII, '60; Amita Aw., '61; Who's Who Of Am. Wm.; Who's Who In The East; Nat. Social Directory (N.Y.); Dic. of Intl. Biog.; Royal Blue Book; numerous other aws., honors, cultural and civic orgs.; b. Scranton, Pa., 1903; p. Francis and Maria Valverde Florey; h. Angelo Fiorani; c. Eleanor (Mrs. Al Castelli), Rosemary (Mrs. Terrence Gallagher Jr.); res: 1000 Clay Ave., Scranton, Pa. 18510.

FIRESTONE, LILLIAN, Pres., Lillian Firestone Associates, 43 Fifth Ave., N.Y., N.Y. 10003, '64–; Acct. Exec., Robert S. Taplinger, '62–'64; Auth., Fawcett bks. on decorating, beauty, child care; Contrbg. Ed., Children's Day; Cosmetic Career Wm. (Bd. of Govs., '66–'67), Fashion Group (Ed., The Fashion Group Bulletin, '69); Barnard Col., BA (Hons., Putnam Publ. Co. Aw. for Crtv. Writing); b. Harbin, Manchuria, 1936; p. Michael and Celia Firestone; h. Robert Greco (dec.); c. Risa Catherine.

FIRESTONE, SHULAMITH, Auth., Ed., Artist, Radical Feminist Activist; Ed., "Notes on Radical Feminism"; Auth., "The Dialectic of Sex: The Case for Feminist Revolution (William Morrow, '70), second book for Random House in process; A Founder of N.Y. Radical Women, Redstockings, N.Y. Radical Feminists; Washington Univ., Art Inst. of Chgo, BFA (painting); res: 230 E. 2nd St., Apt. 3A, N.Y., N.Y. 10009.

FISCH, JANET JAFFE, City Ed., The Journal-News, 51 Hudson Ave., Nyack, N.Y. 10960, '69–; Reptr., '66–'69; News Dir., Radio Sta. WRRC, Spring Valley, '65–'66; Ed., Rockland County Citizen, Rockland Independent, '63–'65; Reptr., '60–'63; b. Utica, N.Y., 1927; p. Morris and Sophia Ellis Jaffe; h. Howard Fisch; c. David, Judy, Robert; res: 37 Park Ave., Nanuet, N.Y. 10954.

FISCHER, JOSEPHINE HAMILTON, Edtl. Rschr., The Reader's Digest Association, Inc., 200 Park Ave., N.Y., N.Y. 10017, '66–; Edtl. Asst., Crown Publrs., '64–'66; Jr. League of N.Y.; Univ. of Pa., BA, '64; b. Phila., Pa., 1942; p. Henry and Maryallis Morgan Hamilton; h. George Fischer; res: Eastborne Apts. Alger Ct. Bronxville, N.Y. 10708.

FISCHER, LORETTA O'CONNELL, Wms. News Ed., Council Bluffs Nonpareil, 117 Pearl St., Council Bluffs, Ia. 51501, '67–; Asst. Wms. Ed., '60–'67; b. Griswold, Ia., 1912; p. John and Frances Casey O'Connell; h. Donald E. Fischer; c. Donald E., Erin Sheila (Mrs. Michael D. Boylan), Nan Colleen (Mrs. Donald A. Dew); res: Rte. 2, Box 190, Council Bluffs, Ia. 51501.

FISCHL, IRENE PACHANIK, Youth Ed., Look Magazine, 488 Madison Ave., N.Y., N.Y. 10021, '68–; Asst. to the Eds., '67–'68; Secy. to Ed., '57–'67; bk: "Love Is When You Meet a Man Who Doesn't Live with His Mother" (Price-Stern-Sloan, '66); light verse published; Bklyn. Col., BA, '51 (cum laude, Dean's List, Alpha Kappa Delta); b. Bklyn., N.Y.; p. Isadore and Clare Pachanik; h. Dr. Robert A. Fischl; res: 177 E. 75th St., N.Y., N.Y. 10021.

FISHER, AILEEN LUCIA, Free-lance Wtr. for children: verse, plays, fiction, biog., natural hist.; Theta Sigma Phi (Dir., Wms. Nat. Journalistic Regis., Chgo., '28–'31); U.S. Treasury Dept. Silver Medal for Distg. Svc., WW II, for Contrbs. to Sch. Savings Prog.; Auth, "Valley Of The Smallest," selected as U.S. title for Intl. Honors List by Intl. Bd. on Bks. for Young People, '68; Univ. of Chgo., '23–'25; Univ. of Mo., BJ, '27; b. Iron River, Mich., 1906; p. Nelson and Lucia Milker Fisher; res: 505 College Ave., Boulder, Colo. 80302.

FISHER, ELIZABETH ANDREWS, Ed.-Publr., The Toy Trader, 2112 Middlefield, Middletown, Conn. 06457, '48–; Tchr. (Falmouth, Mass.), '26–'38; Wtr., compiled, published: "The Japanese Doll" ('52), "Doll Stuff" ('59), "Doll Stuff Again"; educ: Tchrs. Col., Hyannis, Columbia, Clark; h. Harold Fisher.

FISHER, GWENDYNE McCULLEY, Wms. Ed., Lawton Publishing Company, Box 648, Third and A St., Lawton, Okla. 73501, '67–; Ed., Woodward (Okla.) County Jnl., '67; Wms. Ed., Arkansas City (Kan.) Daily Traveler, '60–'67; Wms. Ed., Blackwell (Okla.) Jnl.-Tribune, '44; Composer, words, music, approximately 400 musical numbers copyrighted, many used on TV; various organizations; Okla. State Univ. (Stillwater), '45–'50; Northern Okla. Col. (Tonkawa), '56–'60; b. Wichita, Kan., 1928; p. Hardie M. and Mabel L. Welsh McCulley; h. Robert Fisher (dec.); c. Kenneth W., Robert W.; res: 4 N.W. 60th, Lawton, Okla. 73501.

FISHER, HELEN STEVENS, Asst. Public Info. Dir., American Cancer Soc. (Chgo.), '59–'67; PR Dir., Chgo. Heart Assn., '55–'59; Wms. Commentator, NBC, '26–'38; Auth: bks. on party games; mag. articles;

Free-lance pubcty; Ill. WPA (Past Pres.), Chgo. Pubcty. Assn.; Univ. of Ill., BA, '21; b. La Salle, Ill., 1899; p. Fayette and Jessie Patterson Stevens; h. Robert McCold Fisher; c. Barbara Fisher Kohler; res: 561 Surf St., Chgo., Ill. 60657.

FISHER, LAURA HARRISON, Auth.; short stories: "The Mysterious Key," (Kindergartner, '69), "Carrie's Chance" (Five/Six, '68); novels: "Never Try Nathaniel" (Holt, '68), "You Were Princess Last Time" (Holt, '65), "Amy and the Sorrel Summer" (Holt, '64); Laramie Wtrs. Group; Brigham Young Univ., BA, '56 (cum laude); b. Malad, Idaho, 1934; p. Parry and Laura Wells Harrison; h. Roger D. Fisher; c. Paul, Eric, Scott, Cari; res: 168 Carthell, Laramie, Wyo. 82070.

FISHER, MARGARET BARROW, Dean of Women, Prof., Behavioral Sciences, University of South Florida, Tampa, Fla., 33620, '60–; Asst. to Pres., Hampton Inst., '58–'60; Dean of Students, Mills Col., '55–'58; Dir. of Student Affairs, Univ. of Buffalo, '53–'55; Reg. Dir., Nat. Student YWCA, '47–'50; Dir., YWCAs: Univ. of Okla. '45–'47; Beaumont, Tex., '44–'45; S.F., Cal., '41–'44; Co-auth: "College Education as Personal Development" ('60), "Companion of Standard and Programmed Textbooks" ('64), "Leadership and Intelligence" ('54); Nat. Assn. of Wm. Deans and Cnslrs., Am. Pers. and Guidance Assn., Nat. Vocational Guidance Assn., Am. Assn. for the Advancement of Sci., Assn. for Higher Educ., NLAPW (Tampa Chptr. Pres., '68–'70), AAUW, ZONTA, Kappa Delta Pi, Delta Gamma, Pi Lambda Theta; Univ. of Tex., BA, '39 (Phi Beta Kappa); Columbia Univ., MA, '41; PhD, '53; b. Lockhart, Tex., 1918; p. Thomas and Lula Barrow Fisher; res: 6703 32nd St., Tampa, Fla. 33610.

FISHER, WELTHY HONSINGER, Pres., World Education, Inc., 667 Madison Ave., N.Y., N.Y. 10021, '58–; Hon. Pres., World Literacy of Can.; Founder, Literacy House (Lucknow, India); Free-lance Lectr., student, world affairs, '18–'24; YWCA War Work Cncl., '18–'20; Head Mistress, Baolin Sch. (Nanching, China), '07–'18; Auth.; Boston Auths. Club, Pen & Brush Club, Beta Sigma Phi (Hon. Intl. Mbr.), Delta Kappa Gamma (Hon. Intl. Mbr.); Cit., Merrill Palmer Inst., '42; Founder, Literacy House (Allahabad, India), '53; Syracuse Univ., MA (hon.), '21 (George Arents Medal, '48); L.H.D., '65; Fla. Southern Col., Litt. D., '37; Western Col. for Wm. (Oxford, Oh.), L.H.D., '60; b. Rome, N.Y., 1879; p. Abraham W. and Welthy B. Sanford Housinger; h. Bishop Frederick Bohn Fisher; res: New Delhi, India.

FISHLER, ESTHER BAKER, Dir., The Ridgewood Library, 125 N. Maple Ave., Ridgewood, N.J. 07450, '40–; Ref. Librn., '36–'40; Field Worker, State of Mass., '35; Gen. Asst., Albany (N.Y.) Public Lib., '31–'34; ALA, N.J. Lib. Assn. (Pres., '50–'51), Bergen and Passaic County Lib. Assn. (Pres., '41–'42), Ridgewood Adult Sch. (Pres., '53–'58); Wellesley Col., BA, '29; Columbia Univ., M.L.S., '34; b. Boston, Mass., 1906; p. Alfred

and Martha Nichols Baker; h. Bennett H. Fishler; res: 335 Bedford Rd., Ridgewood, N.J. 07450.

FISHLER, MARY SHIVERICK, Wtr.; Co-auth. with Lois Hamilton Fuller, "Mystery of the Old Fisk House" (Abingdon Press, '60); adv. dept., Ridgewood nwsps., '43–'45; Discussion Leader, Liberal Arts in Ext. program, N.Y.U., '66–'67; volunteer work as Pubcty. Chmn. or Bul. Ed. for civic, other groups; Mount Holyoke Col., AB, '42; Yale Univ. Sch. of Nursing, '42–'43; b. Chgo., Ill., 1920; p. Arthur and Mary Brown Shiverick; h. Bennett Hill Fishler, Jr.; c. Bennett H. 3rd, Mary S., Sally; res: 357 Prospect St., Ridgewood, N.J. 07450.

FISHMAN, SHIRLEY G., Owner, Shirley Fishman Agency, Chester Twelfth Building, Cleve., Oh., 44414, '54–; Nat. Pubcty. Dir., Horace Heidt Enterprises, N.Y.; Adv.-Pubcty. Dir., RKO N. Oh. Theatres; Publicist, Cleve. YMCA and Fenn Col.; Adv. Copywtr., The Higbee Co., Cleve.; Story Analyst, Warner Bros. Studios (Burbank, Cal.); Ann Arbor (Mich.) Corr., The Toledo Blade and Cleveland Plain Dealer; PRSA; Univ. of Mich., BA; b. Detroit, Mich.; p. Jess and Jean Charnas Fishman; res: 3270 Warrensville Ctr. Rd., Shaker Heights, Oh. 44122.

FISK, MARGARET DeVIEW, Mng. Ed., Gale Research Company, 1400 Book Tower, Detroit, Mich. 48226, '65–; Ed., '63–'65; Mktng. Asst., Abitibi Corp., '62–'63; Copywtr., Florez, Inc., '45–'47; ALA, Wms. City Club of Detroit; Wayne State Univ., BA, '42; b. Flint, Mich., 1921; p. Elmer and Lucille Springsteen DeView; h. Robert S. Fisk; c. Kathleen (Mrs. Daniel Turner); res: 190 Riverside Dr., Detroit, Mich. 48215.

FITCH, GERALDINE TOWNSEND, Contrbr., stories about Chinese, Korean personalities for bilingual editions of Guideposts International; Colmst. for The Korea Times (Seoul); Auth., "Formosa Beachhead" (Regnery, '53); Free-lance Wtr.; Cnslt. Ed., Govt. Info., Republic of China (Taiwan), '57–'61; Colmst., The China Post (Taipei); Lectr.; RNS, Nwsp. Enterprises Associated, The New Leader (Korea), '47–'49; Bk. Reviewer, China Weekly; Feature Wtr., N. China Daily News (Shanghai met. nwsp.); Sr. HS Tchr.; AAUW (Shanghai Br. Pres.; Claremont, Cal., Br. Founding Mbr.), OPC, Phi Beta Kappa, Delta Sigma Rho, Who's Who of Am. Wm., Who's Who in the East; Govt. decoration: Order of Brilliant Star, Republic of China; DLitt., Chung-Ang Univ. (Korea), '68; Albion Col., BA (Distg. Alumni Aw., '66); b. Forester, Mich.; h. Dr. George A. Fitch; c. Marion (Mrs. John Exter), George K., Albert C., Edith (Mrs. F. H. Stephens), John T., Robert M.; res: 937 W. Bonita Ave., Claremont, Cal. 91711.

FITZ, CAROLINE M., Lib. Dir., Amityville Free Library, 166 Broadway, Amityville, N.Y. 11701, '67–; Head Librn., '45–'49; Lib. Dir., Public Lib. (Valley Stream, N.Y.), '50–'67; Lib. Dir., Receiving Station Lib., Norfolk Naval Base, '49–'50; Librn., lib. work (Oh.,

Pa.), '42–'45; articles, pfsnl. periodicals; ALA, state, local lib. assns.; Wilson Col., AB; Drexel Inst. of Tech., MS; b. Hanover, Pa.; p. Earl and Virginia W. Lewis Fitz; res: 12 Ballard Ave., Apt. A 1, Valley Stream, N.Y. 11580.

FITZGERALD, CATHLEEN MONA, Mng. Ed., The New Book of Knowledge, Grolier Inc., 575 Lexington Ave., N.Y., N.Y. 10022, '64–; Tchr., Ireland, Eng., U.S., '54–'62; Auth., "Let's Find Out About Words" (Franklin Watts, Inc., '70); Assn. for Supervision and Curriculum Dev., Nat. Cncl. Tchrs. of Eng., Org. Mondiale d'Educ. Primaire; fellowship to Salzburg Seminar in Am. Studies; Nat. Univ. of Ireland, BA, '53 (Hons.); Higher Diploma in Educ., '54; b. Dublin, Ireland, 1932; p. Thomas and Mona Hardiman Fitz-Gerald; res: 240 W. 71st St., N.Y., N.Y. 10023.

FITZGERALD, KATHRYN SULLIVAN, Head of Children's Bk. Dept., Prentice-Hall, Inc., Englewood Cliffs, N.Y. 07632, '69–; Assoc. Ed., Adult Trade, '68–'69; Asst. Ed., Dept. of Econs., '63–'65; Portfolio Assoc., Donaldson, Lufkin and Jenrette, '66–'68; Confidential Asst. to Admin. for Public Affairs, Small Bus. Admin., Wash., D.C., '65–'66; Wells Col., BA (Econs.), '63; grad work in econs., N.Y.U., '64; b. N.Y.C., 1942; p. Joseph and Helen Dougherty Fitzgerald; res: 502 E. 89th St., N.Y., N.Y. 10028.

FITZGERALD, MARY L., Asst. Dir., Loyola University Press, 3441 N. Ashland, Chgo., Ill. 60657, '69–; Sales Svc. Mgr., '59–'69; Sales Cnslt., '51–'59; Ed., Commerce Clearing House, '50–'51; Am. Assn. of Univ. Presses, Nat. Catholic Educ. Assn., Nat. Catholic Exhibitors Assn., Chgo. Bk. Clinic (Treas., '60–'61); Rosary Col., BA, '49; b. Chgo., Ill., 1927; p. Edmund and Mary Cunneen Fitzgerald; res: 1127 Bonnie Brae, River Forest, Ill. 60305.

FITZGERALD, PEGEEN SWEENEY-WORRALL, Artist-Performer, 40 Central Park S., N.Y., N.Y. 10019; Originator, with husband, of first husband-and-wife conversation program for radio, TV, "The Fitzgeralds," WOR; prod., own program; Pres., Bakon-Yeast, Inc.; Adv. Dir., James McCreery & Co.; Adv. Mgr., O'Connor Moffatt & Co. (S.F., Cal.); Adv. Mgr., Meier & Frank Co. (Portland, Ore.); Millennium Guild (Pres.), Vivisection Investigation League (Pres.); Catholic Actors Guild (Secy.); Seton Hall Univ., LLD (hon.), '60; b. Norcatur, Kan.; p. Fred C. and Jane Sweeney Worrall; h. Edward Lee Fitzgerald; res: Log Cabin Rte. #1, Kent, Conn. 06757.

FITZPATRICK, ANN FEUERBACH, Pres., The Parker Advertising Company, 333 W. First St., Dayton, Oh. 45402, '59–; Exec. VP, '49–'59; Secy., '46–'49; Reg. Cnslt., Better Homes & Gardens, '51–'57; AAAA (Dayton Cncl. Bd. of Dirs., '63–'68), Pilot Club (Intl. Pubcty. Dir., '46–'47), NLAPW, Who's Who of Am. Wm., Who's Who in Adv., Distg. Achiev. Aw., '62; Distg. Svc. Medal, '66; numerous other orgs., aws.; b. St. Louis, Mo., 1913; p. John and Marie Von Hundred-

mark Feuerbach; h. John C. FitzPatrick; c. Carole Ann; res: 1119 Oakwood Ave., Dayton, Oh. 45419.

FITZSIMMONS, Dr. CLEO, Prof. Emeritus, School of Home Economists, Purdue University, W. Lafayette, Ind. 47907, '68–; Prof. and Head, Dept. of Home Mgt. and Family Econs., '46–'68; Tchr., Rschr., Admr., Univ. of Ill., '44 '46; Asst. Prof., Asst. Chief, Agricultural Experiment Sta., '42–'44; Assoc. in Home Econs. '36–'42; Rural Youth Specialist, '31 '26; Auth. and Joint Auth., many works in prof. jnls. and buls. for Purdue Experiment Sta.; bks: "Management of Family Resources" (W. H. Freeman, '50), "Management For You" (J. B. Lippincott, '58), "Consumer Buying" (John Wiley & Sons, '61); Theta Sigma Phi, Am. Econ. Assn., Am. Home Econs. Assn., Ill. Home Econs. Assn., Ind. Home Econs. Assn. (Distg. Svc. cert., '69), Omicron Nu, Phi Upsilon Omicron; Drake Univ., '23–'24; Ia. State Univ., BS, '28 (Phi Kappa Phi; Mortar Bd.; Pi Gamma Mu; Alumni Merit Aw., '53); Univ. of Ill., MS (Econs.), '36; PhD (Econs.), '44; Univ. of Chgo., '36; b. St. Paul, Kan., 1900; p. Edward and Jennie Parker Fitzsimmons; res: 900 Elm Drive, W. Lafayette, Ind. 47906.

FitzSIMONS, ELEANOR, Exec. VP, Weintraub & FitzSimmons, Inc., 635 Madison Ave., N.Y., N.Y. 10022; Exec. Secy., Morris Morgenstern Fndn., '60–'61; Asst. to Pres., Heublein, Inc., '57–'60; Asst. to Gen. Mgr., Steve Hannagan Assocs., '49–'52; Assoc. Ed., U.S. Trust Co. of N.Y., '43–'49; VP, Photo Commtns. Co. N.Y.C.); PR Advisor to N.Y. Citizens Budget Comm.; FPA, PRSA, AWNY; Cit. for Meritorious Svc., The President's Comm. on Employment of the Handicapped, '64; N.Y.U.; The New Sch.; b. N.Y.C.; p. Ludwig and Helene Wolf Brandt; c. Leslie; res: 35 Pierrepont St., Bklyn., N.Y., 11201.

FLAGG, FANNIE, Free-lance TV Actress, Comedienne, '66–; c/o William Morris Agency, 1350 Ave. of The Americas, N.Y., N.Y. 10019; numerous appearances: "Tonight" Show; "Jackie Gleason," "Mike Douglas," "David Frost," Columbia Pictures, '70; Actress, Wtr., Upstairs at the Downstairs (N.Y.C.), '65–'66; Actress, Wtr., CBS-TV, "Candid Camera," '65–'66; Actress, WBRC-TV (Birmingham, Ala.), '64–'65; Prodr., "Morning Show"; nwsp., mag. articles published; AFTRA, SAG, AEA, AGVA, AWRT; scholarship, Pasadena Playhouse, '62; Fashion Aw., Ad. Club, '65; Outstanding Young Wm. of Am., '66; Pitt. Playhouse, '62 (scholarship, '62); Univ. of Ala., '63; b. Birmingham, Ala.; p. William H. and Marion LeGore Neal.

FLAHAVE, PEARL ANDERSON, Wms. Ed., Times Publishing Co., 20 N. 6th St., St. Cloud, Minn. 56301, '64–; BPW; Minn. Presss Wm. (Journalistic aw., '69); Univ. of Minn., '27; h. Harold Flahave; c. Harold, Jr., Dennis; res: 1121 3rd Ave. S., Sauk Rapids, Minn. 56379.

FLANAGAN, BARBARA, Colmst., Minneapolis Star and Tribune, 425 Portland Ave., Mpls., Minn. 53415,

'65–; Wms. Ed., '58–'65; Reptr., '48–'57; numerous writing aws.; Minn. Arts Forum of Mpls. Inst. of Arts (founder, '60), Eng. Speaking Un., Mpls. Soc. of Fine Arts; Drake Univ.; b. Des Moines, Ia.; p. John M. Flanagan and Marie Barnes Flanagan Forney; h. Earl S. Sanford; res: 17 S. First St., Mpls., Minn. 55401.

FLANARY, MILDRED KATHLEEN, Home Econs. Ed., Independent, Press-Telegram, 604 Pine Ave., Long Beach, Cal. 90801, '46–; colm., "Chefs of the Week"; radio shows; NFPW (numerous aws.), Cal. Press Wm. (numerous aws.), Gtr. L.A. Press Club (first pl., foods, '62); Who's Who of Am. Wm., Who's Who in Food and Lodging; Kan. City Art Inst., Univ. of Mo. Sch. of Jnlsm.; b. Kan. City, Mo., 1915; p. Edward W. and Anne E. Davidson Flanary; res: 1366 St. Louis Ave., Long Beach, Cal. 90804.

FLANDERS, FRANCES VIVIAN, Head Librn., Ouachita Parish Public Library, 1800 Stubbs Ave., Monroe, La. 71201, '46–; Librn., Nevelle HS, '36–'46; Bldg. Cnslt., Fayetteville, Ark. Public Lib.; Bldg. Cnslt., La. State Lib., '67–; ALA, La. Lib. Assn. (Pres., '51; Treas., '37; VP, '50), Delta Kappa Gamma; Phi Mu, DAR, Daughters of Founders and Patriots, Colonial Dames of the 17th Century; Mansfield Female Col., '27; Northwestern State Col., BA, '29; La. State Univ., B.S. (Lib. Sci.), '36; b. Howe, Okla., 1908; p. Frank and Vivian Fair Flanders; res: 1703 N. Third, Monroe, La. 71201.

FLANDERS, LEATHA HARRIS, Ed., Commty. Living Sec., Longmont Daily Times-Call, 717 Fourth Ave., Longmont, Colo. 80501, '60–; Colmst., Reptr., '57–; Group Head, Pers. Dept., Lockheed Aircraft Corp., '42–'44; Pubelo Air Force Base (Colo.), '42; part-time, Placement Bur., Univ. of Colo., '38–'41; Beautician (Colo. Springs, Colo.), '34–'37; numerous adult educ. workshops on PR; volunteer PR, pubcty. work for civic groups; Ed., Offcrs. Wives' newsp., Chanute Air Force Base; Free-lance Wtr., PR Dir., numerous projects; Feature Wtr.; various organizations; Travel Tour Dir.; Marinello Beauty Col., '35; Univ. of Colo., BA, '41; Am. Press Insts. Wm. Eds. Seminar, Columbia Univ., '68; b. Hugo, Colo., 1916; p. Benjamin and Hazel V. Moore Harris; h. Franklin Flanders; c. Francea (Mrs. Howard Phillips Jr.), F. Fred, David H. (dec.); res: 430 Pratt St., Longmont, Colo. 80501.

FLANNERY, NAOMI FELTON, Acc. Dir., Myers-Infoplan International, 1414 Ave. of the Americas, N.Y., N.Y. 10019, '69–; Asst., '67–'69; Co-owner, Manufacturing Dress Firm, '63–'66; PR, McGuire Sisters, four yrs.; Auth., "101 Great Storage Ideas," "101 Great Window Decorating Ideas" (Bantam Press); New Sch.; res: 44 W. Tenth St., N.Y., N.Y. 10011.

FLEISCHBEIN, Sr. M. CATHERINE FREDERIC, FMSC., Head Librn., Ladycliff College, Highland Falls, N.Y. 10928, '62–; Auth., five bks., incl: "A Handbook of Catholic Practices" (Hawthorn Bks., '64), "Beneath the Lamp's Rays" (Pageant Press, '61), ". . . And

Spare Me Not in the Making" (Bruce Publ. Co., '52); Contrbr., articles, bk. revs.; Tchr., '27–; ALA, Catholic Lib. Assn., Southeastern N.Y. Resource and Ref. Librns. Assn., Franciscan Srs. Educ. Conf. (Treas., '63–'65), Who's Who of Am. Wm., Who's Who in Lib. Sci., others; Manhattan Col., BA, '42; Villanova Univ., MA, '50; St. John's Univ., MS (Lib. Sci), '57; b. N.Y.C., 1902; p. Frederick and Katherine Mourlet Fleischbein; res: Ladycliff Col., Highland Falls, N.Y. 10928.

FLEMING, ALICE MULCAHEY, Free-lance Wtr., 315 E. 72nd St., N.Y., N.Y. 10021, '58–; articles, Redbk., Ladies Home Jnl., McCall's; Auth., seven bks. for young people, incl: "The Senator from Maine" (Thomas Y. Crowell, '69), Auths. Guild, Soc. of Magazine Wtrs.; Who's Who in the East; Who's Who of Am. Wm.; Trinity Col., AB, '50; Columbia Univ., MA, '51; b. New Haven; Conn., 1928; p. Albert and Agnes Foley Mulcahey; h. Thomas J. Fleming; c. Alice, Thomas, David, Richard; res: 315 E. 72nd St., N.Y., N.Y. 10021.

FLEMING, JUNE DWELLINGHAM, Dir. of Libs., City of Palo Alto, 1213 Newell Rd., Palo Alto, Cal. 94303, '68–; Librn. I, Mt. View (Cal.) Public Lib.; Chief, Librn., Philander Smith Col. Lib. (Little Rock, Ark.); Librn., Horace Mann HS; Asst. Br. Librn., Bklyn. (N.Y.) Public Lib.; Comm. to dev. model sch. project for ESEA Title III grant, '66; Ark. Lib. Assn., S.W. Lib. Assn., ALA, Cal. Lib. Assn.,; Who's Who in the Methodist Ch.; Who's Who in Lib. Svc.; Who's Who in Am. Educ.; Who's Who in the Southwest; Who's Who of Am. Wm.; Talladega (Ala.) Col., BA, '53; Drexel Inst. of Tech., MLS, '54; b. Little Rock, Ark., 1931; p. Herman and Ethel Thompson Dwellingham; h. Roscoe Fleming; c. Ethel L.; res: 4167 Donald Dr., Palo Alto, Cal. 94306.

FLEMING, MILLICENT CLOW, Mgr., Bdcst. Prod., Earle Ludgin and Company, 410 N. Michigan Ave., Chgo., Ill. 60611, '68–; Assoc. Radio, TV Prodr., '66–'68; Fred Niles films; Dean of Wm., Adm. Asst. to Pres., Patricia Stevens Career Col. and Finishing Schs., '62–'65; Lectr., Tchr.; Lyric Opera Guild, Art Inst. of Chgo., Chgo. Cncl. of Fgn. Rels.; Chgo. Musical Col.; De Paul Univ.; Univ. of Ill. (Navy Pier Div.); Roosevelt Univ.; Northwestern Univ. Summer Inst. (Scholarship Student), '53; b. Chgo., Ill., 1935; p. William and Pearl Touhy Clow; h. (div.); res: 2930 N. Sheridan, Apt. 203, Chgo., Ill. 60657.

FLEMING, SANDRA GIBSON, Ed., Schlumberger, 5000 Gulf Freeway, Houston, Tex., '69–; Gulf & Western Industries, '68–'69; asst. Ed., Univ. of Tex. M.D. Anderson Hospital and Tumor Inst., '66–'68; Bus. Pg. Ed., Tuscaloosa (Ala.) News, '65–'66; Theta Sigma Phi (Houston Prof. Chptr., VP, '68–'69; Secy., '69–'70), S.E. Tex. IEA; Univ. of Ala., AB, '64; MA, '68; h. Randall Fleming; res: 8915 Hazen, Houston, Tex. 77036.

FLETCHER, ADELE WHITELY, Free-lance Wtr., mag. articles and wms. bks., '61–; Wms. Feature Ed., The American Weekly, '52–'61; Ed., Photoplay Magazine,

'43–'52; N.Y. Nwsp. Wms. Aw. with Bette Davis for "Our Adopted Daughter," '60; b. N.Y.C., 1897; p. William and Helen Clarke Fletcher; h. Robert Ormiston (dec.); c. Susan Bridson; res: 83-09 Talbot St., Kew Gardens, N.Y. 11415.

FLETCHER, GRACE NIES, Auth., articles, stories, nine bks. incl. "In Quest of the Least Coin" (William Morrow Co., '68); Lectr. in English, Oh. Wesleyan; Memorial Collection of manuscripts established at Boston Univ.; New Eng. Wms. Press Cl. (mag. story aw., '46); Who's Who of Am. Wm.; Boston Univ., BA, '17 (Phi Beta Kappa); Columbia Univ.; Oh. Wesleyan; b. Townsend, Mass.; p. Leopold and Myrtle Rouse Nies; h. Vivian A. Fletcher (dec.); c. Richard Nies; res: 434 Concord Rd., Sudbury, Mass. 01176.

FLETCHER, HELEN JILL, Free-lance Wtr.; Substitute Sch. Tchr., Bd. of Educ.; 122 bks. published, '49–'69; own radio program, "School Can Be Fun," ABC; Artist; numerous aws., incl., best 50 of yr., '66; N.Y.U., and Columbia; b. N.Y.C.; p. Charles Morey and Celia Sperling Siegel; h. Jack Fletcher; c. Carol; res: Hotel Buckingham, 101 W. 57th St., N.Y., N.Y. 10019; and Woodstock, N.Y. 12498.

FLETCHER, KATHLEEN, Asst. Prof., I.M. Dept. Southern Illinois University, 321 Pulliam Hall, Carbondale, Ill. 62901, '57–; Supvsr., High Point City Sch. Libs. (N.C.), '52–'55; Librn., Froebel Sch. (Gary, Ind.), '48–'52; Librn., MacDill Army Air Base (Tampa, Fla.), '41–'46; Librn., Fla. H.S. FSCW (Tallahassee, Fla.); Tchr. (summer sessions); Univ. of N.C., Emory Univ., Portland State Col., San Jose State Col., Arizona State Univ.; ALA, Ill. Lib. Assn., DAVI, AAUW (Carbondale Br. Secy.); Beta Phi Mu; La. Polytechnic Inst., BA, '32; La. State Univ., BS, '33; Univ. of Ill., MS (Lib. Sci.), '47; b. Ruston, La.; res: 606 Glen View Dr., Carbondale, Ill. 62901.

FLINCHUM, MARJORIE DRUMMOND, Credit Mgr., Capital-Gazette Press, Inc., 213-33 West St., Annapolis, Md. 21401, '67–; Annapolis Bus. Credit Assn., (Secy., '68), Soroptimist (Treas., '69, Secy., '67); b. Dolphin, Va., 1925; p. Clarence and Marion Spiers Drummond; h. Allen J. Flinchum (div.); c. Marion Elain House, Allen Jones Flinchum, III; res: Oak Grove Circle, Severna Park, Md. 21146.

FLINN, NINA M., VP and Media Dir., The Bruns Advertising Agency, Inc., 605 Third Ave., N.Y., N.Y. 10016, '63–. '61; Rsch. Dir., Bolling Radio-TV Rep., '59–'61; Fuller & Smith & Ross, '58–'59; Robert W. Orr & Assocs., '56–'58; Doyle Dane Bernbach, Inc., '54–'56; Duane Jones/S. Beck & Werner, Inc., '49–'54; Pembroke Col.; b. Yonkers, N.Y., 1929; p. Harry and Marion Flinn; res: 32 E. 61st St., N.Y., N.Y. 10021.

FLINT, EMILY PAULINE, Mag. Ed., The Atlantic Monthly Co., 8 Arlington St., Boston, Mass. 02116, '51–; Rsch. Ed., '48–'51; Edtl. Asst., '45–'47; Instr., Jnlsm., Boston Univ., '48–'51; Humanities Librn., Mass.

Inst. of Tech., '35–'44; Co-ed., "Jubilee: 100 Years of the Atlantic" ('57); Ed., "Atlantic Supplement on Mexico" ('64) New Eng. WPA (Bd. of Dirs., '58, '61–'69; Pres., '67–'69); L.H.D. (hon.), New Eng. Col., '67; various others; Barnard Col., AB, '30; Tufts Univ., MA, '32; Columbia Univ., Sch. of Lib. Svc., BS, '35; b. N.Y.C., 1909; p. Louis and Emma Schaufele Riedinger; h. Paul H. Flint; c. Paul H., Jr.; res: 26 Edison Ave., Medford, Mass. 02155.

FLIRT, JO ANN, Pres., Public Relations Counsel Inc., 108 Claiborne St., Mobile, Ala. 36602, '61–; Publr.-Owner, Colbert County Reporter, Tuscumbia, Ala.; State Ed., Staff Wtr., Montgomery Advertiser, '56–'68; News Ed., Foley Onlooker, '54–'56; Asst. Mgr., Ala. Press Assn.; Jnlsm. Dept. Secy., Ext. Div. Staff Mbr., Univ. of Ala.; Auth. of Chptr., "Rivers Of Alabama" (Strode Publrs., '68); Theta Sigma Phi, PRSA (Ala.-Miss. Chptr., Charter Mbr. of Bd.), Ala. Press Assn.; Outstanding Young Wm. Of Am.; Huntington Col., '49–'50; Univ. of Ala., BA, '53; MS (Jnlsm.), '60; b. Loxley, Ala., 1932; p. Aubrey and Rose Epperson Flirt; res: 1921 Clearmont St., Mobile, Ala. 36606.

FLOETHE, LOUISE LEE, Auth. of 19 children's bks. including: "Floating Market" ('68) and "A Thousand and One Buddhas" ('67); Auths. Guild, Friends of the Libs. (Sarasota County Pres.), Sarasota City Bi-racial Cncl. (Chmn.); Who's Who of Am. Wm.; Columbia Univ. of Drama Sch. '31–'32; Neighborhood Playhouse Studios, '32–'33; b. N.Y.C., 1913; p. Louis and Selma Van Praag Lee; h. Richard Floethe; c. Stephen Lee, Ronald K.; res: 1391 Harbor Dr., Sarasota, Fla. 33579.

FLOOD, ELIZABETH GAUCAS, Legislative Corr., Cuyler News Service, State Capitol, Rm. 358, Albany, N.Y. 12203, '56–; Owner, '60–; Bus. Partner, '58–'60; Dir., PR. Wms. Unit. of State Exec. Chamber, '67; News Reptr., WRGB-TV, '67; guest, radio, TV panel shows; Wms. Press Club of N.Y. State (Founder, 1st Pres. '66; Dir., '67, '68); Legislative Corr. Assn., OPC; Sigma Delta Sigma; Russell Sage Col., '52–'55; b. Albany, N.Y. 1933; p. B. Relf and Mary Ann Reid Gaucas; h. John J. Flood; res: Game Farm Rd., Delmar, N.Y. 12054.

FLOOD, JUDY ANN, Prod. and Traf. Mgr., Behr, Otto, Abbs & Austin Advertising, 1650 Guardian Bldg., Detroit, Mich. 48226, '63–; b. Monroe, Mich., 1942; p. Claude and Marguerite Rahn Flood; res: 17731 Quarry, Riverview, Mich. 48192.

FLORIANI, ELSIE WIGNALL, Employee Commtns. Specialist, Philco-Ford Corporation, WDL Division, 3939 Fabian Way, Palo Alto, Cal. 94303, '68–; Sr. Pers. Svcs. Rep. and Ed. of Reflector, '65; Opns. Planner, '65; Group Supvr., Engineering Svcs., '64; Pers. Adm., '63; Engineering Coordr., '61; Tchr: Adult Educ., Los Altos HS, '65–'67; Typing and Bus. Eng., '61–'63; ICIE (Achiev. for Mgt. Aw., '66; hon. mention, int. newsltr. '67), BPW, Bay Area Soc. for Indsl. Communicators

(Secy.-Treas., '69); Top aw., indsl. rept./coverage of Un. Fund, Santa Clara County, Cal., '67; Chaffey Jr. Col., Assoc. of Arts, '57; San Jose State Col, BS, '59, Secondary Teaching Credential, '61; b. Wash., D.C., 1937; p. Coleman and Elizabeth Connely Kinne; h. Roberto Floriani; res: 1461 Nome Ct., Sunnyvale, Cal. 94087.

FLOTRON, MARGE M., Media Supvsr., Fuller Smith & Ross, 410 N. Michigan Ave., Chgo., Ill. 60611, '69–; Free-lance Media Cnslt.; Media Mgr., Earle Ludgen & Co., '60–'62; Media Byr., Leo Burnett, '57–'60; Contract Mgr., CBS-TV Spot Sls., '50–'57; Media Cnslt., mktng. and media rsch.; Bdcst. Adv. Club, Wms. Adv. Club; b. Chgo., Ill., 1923; p. Harry J. and Margaret Berni Flotron; res: 4514 N. Paulena St., Chgo., Ill. 60640.

FLYNN, BETTY K., U.N./N.Y. Corr., Chicago Daily News, Room 448, United Nations, N.Y. 10017 (Main office, 401 N. Wabash Ave., Chgo., Ill.), '66–; Fgn. svc., Wash. D.C. Bur., '68; Cityside Reptr., '62–'65; Cityside Reptr., Mpls. (Minn.) Tribune, '61–'62; U.N. Corrs. Assn. (Exec. Bd.), WNPC, Chgo. Nwsp. Guild; Sigma Delta Chi nat. aw., team investigative rept. '63; Ill. AP aw., Public Svc. team investigative rept., '63; Ill. Tchrs. Fedn. Sch. Bell Aw., '65; Monmouth Col., '57–'59; Univ. of Wisc., BA, '61 (Phi Beta Kappa; Russell Sage Fellowship, '65); b. Chgo., Ill., 1939; p. Timothy C. Flynn and Mrs. Elizabeth Scanlon; res: 350 E. 51st St., 2A, N.Y., N.Y. 10022.

FLYNN, SUZANNE KENNEDY, Dir. of Crtv. and Fashion Activities, Yardley of London, '69–; Sr. Ed., Beauty, Seventeen Magazine, '67–'69; Assoc. Beauty Ed., Redbook, '67; Beauty Ed., McCall's Fashionews, '67; Asst. Beauty and Health Ed., Family Circle, '59–'66; Lectr.; Fashion Group, Cosmetic Career Wm., Cosmetic Club of N.Y. (Co-founder); Misericordia Col. (Dallas, Pa.), BA, '60; New Sch. for Social Rsch.; b. N.Y.C., 1937; p. Patrick and Anne Sullivan Kennedy; h. Arthur E. Flynn; c. Kerry K., Tracy K.; res: 1160 Fifth Ave., N.Y., N.Y. 10029.

FLYNN, TRISHA, Dir. of PR, Hospital of the University of Pennsylvania, 34th and Spruce Sts., Phila., Pa. 19104, '67–; Asst. Dir. of PR, '66–'67; Communications advisory comm., Un. Fund Torch Dr., '69; Del. Valley Assn. of Communicators (Bd. Dirs., five yrs.; Exec. Offcr., '68–'69, '69–'70; VP, '67–'68); OVAC two top aws., nwsltr., '68; Del. Valley Hosp. PR Dirs. Assn. (Bd. Dirs., '68), Academy of Hospital PR, Am. Soc. of Hosp. PR Dirs.; first prizes, Hosp. Assn. of Pa. PR Dirs., '66; medals, hon., Del. Valley Printers Week, '66, '67, '68; Malcolm T. Maceachren Aws. hon. mentions, '67, '68; top design prize, AAIE, '69; Syracuse Univ., BFA, '63; Univ. of Pa. Annenberg Sch. of Commtns.; b. Wilkes-Barre, Pa., 1942; p. Henry J. and Mary H. McDermott Flynn; res: 1612 Pine St., Phila., Pa. 19103.

FOERTSCH, KATHRYN ANN, Buyer, Asst. Planner,

Tatham-Laird & Kudner, Inc., 64 E. Jackson Blvd., Chgo., Ill. 60604, '69–; Media Analysis, '67–'69; Media Estimator, '65–'67; Marquette Univ., BS, '65; b. Chgo., Ill., 1943; p. Edward L. and Elizabeth Sahn Foertsch; res: 6531 Eldorado Dr., Morton Grove, Ill. 60053.

FOGEL, RUBY, Poet, "Of Apes and Angels" (Swallow Press, '66); poems in lit. jnls., incl: Southern Poetry Rev., The Lyric, Voices; other pubns. incl: Ladies Home Jnl., N.Y. Times, Chgo. Tribune Sunday Magazine; Tchr., Leader, discussion course, "Discovering Modern Poetry," '64–'65; Readings of own poetry: Miami-Dade Jr. Col., '68; Fla. Presbyterian Col., '68; Lib. of Congress Rec., '69; nat. revs. of works; Chi Delta Phi; James Joyce Aw., PSA, '68; The Lyric Cummins Memorial Aw., '65; one of three Am. poets honored at Stroud Intl. Festival of the Arts (Eng.; poems published in "Festival Poems"); Duke Univ., AB; b. Georgetown, S.C.; p. Harry and Clara M. Hepler Fogel; h. J. I. Levkoff; c. Lizabeth, Mary; res: 6020 Pine Tree Dr., Miami Beach, Fla. 33140.

FOGELMAN, PHYLLIS GENSBURG, Ed.-in-Chief, Bks. for Young Readers, The Dial Press, 750 Third Ave., N.Y., N.Y. 10021, '66–; Sr. Ed., Jr. Bks., Harper & Row, '61–'66; Children's Bk. Cncl., Publrs. Lib. Prom. Group, AIGA; Barnard Col., '51–'52; N.Y.U., BA, '61; b. Phila., Pa., 1933; p. Emanuel and Tillie Resch Gensburg; h. Sheldon Fogelman; c. David Howard; res: 420 E. 72nd St., N.Y., N.Y. 10021.

FOGLE, CORNELIA MAUDE, Prod. Ed., Lane Magazine & Book Co., Menlo Park, Cal. 94025, '63–; Asst. Prod. Ed., '62–'63; Edtl. Asst., '61–'62; Asst. Prom. Coordr., Ampex Intl., '60; Sales Prom. Asst., West Coast Life Ins. Co., '58–'60; Theta Sigma Phi (Peninsula Chptr. Pres., '66–'67); Univ. of Ore., BA, '58; b. Eugene, Ore., 1936; p. Victor and Crystal Bryan Fogle; res: 1300 Mills St., Menlo Park, Cal. 94025.

FOLEY, BERNICE WILLIAMS, Ed., Quarterly Magazine & Ohio Year Book, and Dir., The Martha Kinney Cooper Ohioana Library, 1109 Ohio Depts. Bldg., Columbus, Oh. 43215, '66–; Fashion Commentator: WKRC, WSAI, WCPO-TV (all, Cinn.); PR, Mabley & Carew Dept. Store; Tchr., Crtv. Writing; AAUW; Bk. Reviewer, Sunday Columbus Dispatch; Former lectr., Univ. of Cinn; Oh. Arts Cncl., Literary Adv. Panel; Theta Sigma Phi, AWRT, Oh. Press Wm., NLAPW, MacDowell Soc. of Am., Oh. Historical Soc., English Speaking Un. (Columbus Br. Pres., '67); Who's Who in the Midwest; Univ. of Cinn., '20–'24; Nanking Univ., China, '25; Columbia Univ.; Jesus Col., Oxford, Eng. '68; b. Wigginsville, Oh., 1902; p. Karl and Bertye Young Williams; h. Warren Massey Foley; c. Williams M., Karlanne Foley Hauer; res: The Canterbury Apts., 3440 Olentangy River Rd., Columbus, Oh. 43202.

FOLEY, HARRIET ELIZABETH, Librn., Carlisle Local School, Fairview Dr., Carlisle, Oh. 45005, '61–; ALA, Oh. Lib. Assn.; Who's Who in Lib. Sci., Who's

Who of Am. Wm.; Col. of Mt. St. Joseph, AB (Educ.), '57 (magna cum laude); Univ. of Ky., MS (Lib. Sci.), '61; b. Franklin, Oh., 1935; p. Milo and Lucile Babb Fealy; res: 22 E. Fifth St. (P.O. Box 225), Franklin, Oh. 45005.

FOLEY, HELEN MARIE, Ed., Abraham & Straus, 420 Fulton St., Bklyn., N.Y. 11201, '54–; Asst. to Dir. of Pers. Activities, Employees' Activities Off., '41–'54; Tchr., N.Y.C. Public, Parochial Schs., '39–'41; ICIE, N.Y. Assn. Indsl. Eds. (Fin. Secy.), N.Y. Assn. Indsl. Communicators; Communicator of the Yr., '65; Misericordia Col., '39; Grad. Work: Columbia Univ., N.Y.U., Bklyn. Col.; res: 600 E. 18th St., Bklyn., N.Y. 11226.

FOLEY, JOAN COLEMAN, Lit. Agt., Co-owner-Partner, The Foley Agency, 34 E. 38th St., N.Y., N.Y. 10016, '56–; Videocast Prods., and Eastern Bdcst. System, Inc., '51–'54; Writing and Pubcty., Burl Ives, '50–'51; Co-auth. (pseuds., Jack and Jill Smedley), "The Hangover Cookbook" (Simon & Schuster, '68); Barry Col., BA, '50; b. Stafford Springs, Conn., 1930; p. Francis and Kathryn Cummiskey Coleman; h. Joseph Foley; res: N.Y., N.Y., and Madison, Md.

FOLEY, JOAN L., Librn., Broome Tech. Commty. Col., Binghamton, N.Y., '47–; N.Y. Lib. Assn., WNBA, Altrusa, Intl. (Triple Cities Club VP, '62, Secy., '65), N.Y. State Assn. Jr. Cols.; State Univ. of N.Y., BS (Lib. Educ.), '54; b. N.Y.C.; p. George and Alice Coyle Foley; res: 16 Arthur St., Binghamton, N.Y. 13905.

FOLEY, LOUISE KIRBY, VP, PR, Lippincott & Margulies, Inc., 277 Park Ave., N.Y., N.Y. 10017, '69–; Dir. of PR, '67–'69; Publicist, Wolcott Carlson & Assoc., '66; VP, Ray Josephs Assocs., '61–'65; Wtr., The Economist (London, England), '59–'60; U.S. Embassy (Brussels, Belgium), '52–'57; Foreign Service Officer, U.S. Consulate General (Antwerp, Belgium), '49–'52; Northwestern Univ., BS, '44 (cum laude); b. Gillette, Wyo., 1924; p. Jesse and Roxa Simpson Kirby; h. Armund E. Foley; c. Barbara; res: Hemlock Farms, Lords Valley, Hawley, Pa. 18428.

FOLEY, PATRICIA M., Asst. Mgr., Commtns. Programs, The Quaker Oats Company, 354 Merchandise Mart, Chgo., Ill. 60654, '69–; Philip Lesly Co., '68–'69; Harshe-Rotman & Druck, '60–'68; Mayer & O'Brien, '56–'60; Drake Hotel; Toni Co.; Chicago American; PRSA, Pubcty. Club of Chgo. (Secy., '66), Fashion Group (Secy., '69–'70); Lawrence Col., BA; Cornell Univ., Northwestern Univ.; b. Oak Park, Ill.; p. Frank and Meryl Graessle Foley; res: 201 E. Walton Pl., Chgo., Ill. 60611.

FOLLMER, MARJORIE, Mktng. Asst. Dir., CCM Professional Magazines, Crowell Collier & Macmillan, Inc., 22 Putnam Ave., Greenwich, Conn. 06830, '64–; Ed., Publr., N.Y.C. Nwsltr., '63–'64; prom., pubcty., free-lance, '57–'63; Copy Rsch. Dir., Ruthrauff & Ryan, '43–'57; AWNY (Pres. Cabinet), Alpha Xi Delta (Nat. Trustee); Univ. of Mich., AB, '30 (Phi Beta Kappa); Stanford Univ., AM, '36; b. Kalamazoo County, Mich.; p. J. Frank and Mary D. Follmer; res: 100 Blachley Rd., Stamford, Conn. 06902.

FOLTZ, FLORENCE PICKETT, Librn., South High School, 1700 E. Louisiana Ave., Denver, Colo. 80210, '46–; Instr., Lib. Sci: Univ. of Colo., summers, '61–; Univ. of Wash., '58; Univ. of Denver, '56; Librn., West HS, '35–'46; ALA, Colo. Lib. Assn. (Pres., '47, VP, '46; Secy., '45), Mt. Plains Lib. Assn. (VP, '49), Colo. Assn. for Sch. Librns. (Pres., '61–'62; VP, '60–'61); Colo. Col., AB, '30; Univ. of Ill., BS, '31; b. Las Animas, Colo., 1907; p. Hugh and Minta St. Clair Pickett; h. Everett F. Foltz; res: 1886 S. Federal Blvd., Denver, Colo. 80219.

FONG, FRANCES CHUNG, Actress, '45–; Activities Dir., R &.B Development, South Bay Club, Mid-Wilshire, 209 S. Westmoreland, L.A., Cal. 90004, '69–; Free-lance Actress, TV, motion pics., '45–; legit. stage, '62–'66; nite-club act, '57–'60; SAG, AGVA, AEA, S.F. Chinatown Optimists (VP); Who's Who of Am. Wm.; Who's Who in the West; Dic. of Intl. Biog.; Long Beach City Col., '45; Dorothy Farrady Sch. of Charm, '52; Univ. of Cal. Ext., '58; Elizabeth Halloway Sch. of Drama, '58; Valley City Col., '65; b. Honolulu, Hi.; p. Francis H. and Emma H. Leong Chung; h. George K. Fong (div.); c. Leslie H., Brian F., Geoffrey W.; res: 6257 Saloma Ave., Van Nuys, Cal. 91401.

FONSTEIN, EVELYN, Librn., James Ward Thorne School of Nursing, Passavant Memorial Hospital, 244 E. Pearson, Chgo., Ill. 60611, '66–; Librn., Sch. of Nursing, Grant Hosp., '62–'66; Asst. Librn., Serials Librn., Chgo. Med. Sch., '61–'62; File Cl., Exchange Nat. Bank, '59–'61; Librn., Ill. Commn. for Handicapped Children, '52–'59; File Cl., Proofreader, Social Security Adm., '52; Librn., Children's Memorial Hosp., '48–'51; ALA, Special Libs. Assn., Med. Lib. Assn.; Roosevelt Col., BA, '46; Rosary Col., BS (Lib. Sci.), '47; b. Chgo., Ill., 1923; p. George and Molly Vaslow Fonstein; res: 5124 Dorchester Ave., Chgo., Ill. 60615.

FONTAINE, ELIZABETH LEITZBACH, PR Cnslt., Rm. 201, Empire State Bldg., N.Y., N.Y. 10001; Nat. Chmn., Hospitalized Veterans Writing Project, Inc. non-profit, nat. rehabilitation service for hospitalized veterans, also publishing Veterans Voices Magazine; formerly Asst. Ed., Prairie Farmer; Ed., McClurg's Monthly Bulletin of New Bks.; pubcty. for AMA Journals, Metropolitan Life Ins. Co., Chgo. YWCA, Nat. Dairy Cncl. daily column Bell Syndicate; Am. Wtrs. Conf. of Middle West, Northwestern Univ.; WNBA, Armed Forces Wtrs. League, Theta Sigma Phi (Distg. Svc. Aw., '57), Alpha Chi Omega, Wm. of Achiev. Aw., '70; Query Club, VA Vol. Study Commn.; VA Cert. of Merit, '51; Ward-Belmont Col., Univ. of Ill.; b. Fairmount, Ill.; p. Augustus and Clara Dougherty Leitzbach; h. Everett Orren Fontaine; c. Martha Anne (Mrs. William H. Anderes); res: 116 Pinehurst Ave., N.Y., N.Y. 10033.

FONTAINE, JOAN (de Havilland), Actress, Lectr.,

Panelist; AFTRA, Hollywood Acad. of Arts, Scis. and Pfsnls., AMPAS (Acad. Aw., '41), SAG, AFTRA, Actors Equity E. Roosevelt Aw., '66; N.Y. Film Critics Aw., '41; Max Rheinhardt Sch. of Acting; p. Tokyo, Japan; p. Walter and Lilian Ruse de Havilland; c. Deborah Dozier; res: 160 E. 72nd St., N.Y., N.Y. 10021.

FONTENOT, MARY ALICE, Colmst., Feature Wtr., The Daily World, 127 S. Market St., Opelousas, La. 70570, '68–; Area Ed., '62–'68; Ed., Iberville South (Plaquemine, La.), '62; Acadian-Tribune, Ch. Point News, '59–'62; Edtl. Staff, Lafayette Advertiser, Eunice News, '46–'59; Auth., "Ghost of Bayou Tigre," '65; five other juv. bks.; Asst. Rschr., "Blue Camellia," "Victorine"; various procs., aws.; Univ. of Southwestern La.; b. Eunice, La., 1910; p. Valrie and Kate King Barras; h. Vincent L. Riehl, Sr.; c. Mrs. Burton Ziegler, Mrs. Michael Landry; res: 1309 Choctaw Dr., Opelousas, La. 70570.

FOONER, HELEN GREENBLATT, Exec. Dir., N.Y.C. Chptr., Nat. Assn. of Social Workers, 79 Madison Ave., N.Y., N.Y. 10016, '69–, Dir., PR Jamaica Water & Utilities, Inc., '53–'69; Ed., bus. nwsltr., and Reptr., Wash., D.C. '45–'47; Info. Offcr., U.S. Fed. agcys. and Presidential Comm., '34–'44; previously Wtr.-Rschr., Child Psychologist, Social Worker; PRSA, CWPR, Wm.'s City Clyb of N.Y.; Barnard Col., BA, '28 (Phi Beta Kappa); Columbia Univ. Grad. Sch. of Psych. formerly Dir., Queensboro Tuberculosis and Health Assn., Queensboro Cncl. for Social Welfare; Wash., D.C., Mothers Cncl. (Pres., '49–'53); b. N.Y., N.Y., 1907; p. Max and Pauline Kasdam Greenblatt; h. Michael Fooner; c. Andrea, Laura (Mrs. Steven Wexler); res: 131 Riverside Dr., N.Y., N.Y. 10024.

FORBES, DELORIS STANTON, (Tobias Wells, Stanton Forbes), Assoc. Ed., Wellesley Townsman, 1 Crest Rd., Wellesley, Mass. 02181, '58–; Auth.: "Die Quickly, Dear Mother" (Doubleday, '69), "Dead by the Light of the Moon" ('67), "Go to Thy Deathbed" ('68), numerous other mystery novels; MWA, Boston Auths. League, Quota Club Intl.; b. Kans. City, Mo., 1923; p. Lawrence and Florence Ellis Stanton; h. William J. Forbes, Jr.; c. Daniel, Anne, Andrew; res: 20 Howe St., Wellesley, Mass. 02181.

FORBES, MARY LOU WERNER, State Ed., The Evening Star, 224 Virginia Ave. S.E., Wash., D.C. 20003, '69–; Asst. State Ed., '60–'63; Reptr., '47–'59; Copy Girl, '44–'47; WNPC (VP, '67–'68), ANWC (VP, '65–'66); Pulitzer Prize, '59; Wash. Nwsp. Guild aw., '59; Univ. of Md., '42–'44; b. Alexandria, Va., 1927; p. William and Anne Wall Werner; h. James Dexter Forbes; c. James W.; res: 312 Cloverway, Alexandria, Va. 22314.

FORBUS, INA B., Auth., bks. published by Viking Press, N.Y: "The Magic Pin," "The Secret Circle" (AAUW aw. for best juv. bk. published in N.C., '58), "Melissa," "Tawny's Trick"; N.C. Wtrs. Conf.; Univ. of Rochester; Univ. of N.C.; b. Crieff, Perthshire,

Scotland; p. William Duncan and Margaret Drummond Syme Bell; h. Sample Bouvard Forbus; res: Apt. 1, 1919 Southwood Dr., Yorktown Village, Durham, N.C. 27707.

FORD, AGNES GIBBS, Interim PR Dir., Belmont College, Belmont Blvd. at Belcourt Ave., Nashville, Tenn. 37203, '69–; Adv., PR, for Baptist Sunday Sch. Bd., '50–'67, '27–'49; Baptist PR Assn. (Treas., Past Secy.), Religious PR Cncl (Pres., '64–'65), AAUW, WNBA; Bus. Wm. of the Yr., BPW, '66; G. Peabody Col., BA, '55, MA, '64; b. Carthage, Tenn.; p. Calvin and Lucy Warren Gibbs; h. Arthur T. Ford; res: 325 Gun Club Rd., Nashville, Tenn. 37205.

FORD, ALICE E., Wtr., Ed., Histrn., Biographer; Auth: "Audubon's Animals" (Crowell-Studio, '51; Lit. Guild bonus bk., '51), "Audubon's Butterflies and Other Sketches" (Crowell-Studio, '52; Natural Hist. Bk. Club bonus bk., '52), "Edward Hicks, Painter of the Peaceable Kingdom" (Univ. of Pa. Press, '52, "50 Best Bks.," Brentano, '52); "John James Audubon" (Univ. of Okla. Press, '64; aw., Am. Inst. of GA, '64), Who's Who of Am. Wm., Gayler Dir.; Univ. of Mich., BA, '29; MA, '31 (Eng. Lit.); Sorbonne, N.Y.U.; b. Fort Dodge, Ia., 1906; p. John Francis and Ellen Howard Ford; res: Wash. D.C.

FORD, BARBARA O'CONNELL, Asst. Ed., Science Digest, 575 Lexington Ave., N.Y., N.Y. 10022, '67–; PR, Am. Museum of Natural Hist., '65–'67; Wtr.-Ed., Wash. Univ. (St. Louis, Mo.), '63–'64; Theta Sigma Phi; St. Louis Univ., BS, '56; N.Y.U., MA, '67; b. St. Louis, Mo., 1934; p. Daniel R. and Marie Lawlor O'Connell; h. Douglas Ford; res: 231 E. 76th St., N.Y., N.Y. 10021.

FORD, BARBARA SANDERS, Soc. Ed., The Courier-Times, 201 S. 14th St., New Castle, Ind. 47632, '67–; Altrusa, Sigma Phi Gamma (Past Pres.); Ball State Univ.; b. New Castle, Ind., 1932; p. Robison and Thelma Poulson Sanders; h. Kenneth C. Ford; res: 400 Bundy Ave., New Castle, Ind. 47362.

FORD, LINDA WATSON, News and Weather Reptr., WQXI-TV, 1611 W. Peachtree St. NE, Atlanta, Ga. 30309, '64–; weekly interview show, "People On The Go"; Wtr. and Reptr. for daily wms. feature, "Emphasis Women"; On-air Wtr., Prodr., Prom. Dept., WAGA-TV, '63–'64; AWRT (Educ. Fndn. Chmn.; Wtr., Prodr., Ed., Narrator of hour video-tape show for Ga. servicemen in Viet Nam which received aw. from Red Cross), Atlanta Press Club, Atlanta Wms. C. of C., Atlanta Variety Club, Pfsnl. Models' Assn. (Pres.); W. Ga. Col., '56–'58; Mercer Univ., Macon, Ga., AB, '60; b. Atlanta, Ga., 1938; p. Calvin and Mary Moore Watson; h. Donald Ford; c. Donald; res: 862 Rowland Rd., Stone Mountain, Ga. 30083.

FORD, MARY FORKER, Auth: "Murder, Country Style" ('64), "Dude Ranch Murders" ('65), others; Lincoln Nat. Life Ins. Co., '24–'32; MWA, Intl. Platform Assn., Un. Methodist Ch., Alpha Gamma; Nwsp. Inst.

of Am., '66; b. Noble County, Ind., 1905; p. Edward and Mina Bowen Forker; h. Harland Ford (dec.); c. Jane Leigh (Mrs. I. C. Crandall); res: 2949 Holton Ave., Ft. Wayne, Ind. 46806.

FORD, VELMA HILDEGARDE, Chief Exec., Morrison Book Co., Princeton, Ill. 61356, '53–; Auth: 15 bks. for children; Tchr., reading skills, handicapped children; Wms. Nat. Bk. Assn., Am. Booksellers Assn., Nat. Story Tellers' League; Am. Cancer Soc. (Ill. Div. State Bd., 10 yrs.); Drake Univ., '29 (Elementary Educ.); b. Madrid, Ia., 1909; p. William and Hildegarde Berg Ford; h. Hugh Morrison; c. Hugh, Jr., Sarah (Mrs. Douglas Criner), Mary (Mrs. James Anderson), John; res: R.F.D. 5, Princeton, Ill. 61356.

FORDYCE, JOYCE LOUISE, Adv. Copywtr., Broadman Press, 127 Ninth Ave. N., Nashville, Tenn. 37203, '58–; Dictaphone Corp., '57–'58; Armco Steel Corp., '46–'52; WNBA (Corr. Secy., '66–'67, Treas., '69–'71), Religious PR Cncl., Baptist PR Cncl.; Tenn. Temple Col., BA, '57; b. Middletown, Oh.; p. Harold and Iva Pieratt Fordyce; res: 2406 Blair Blvd., Nashville, Tenn. 37212.

FORENBACH, RITA, (pseud: R. F. Wright), Juv. Ed., Funk & Wagnalls, 380 Madison Ave., N.Y. N.Y. 10017 '56–; William Sloane Assoc., '52–'54; Reynal & Hitchcock, '45–'51; Childrens Book Cncl.; Hunter Col.; b. Richmond Hill, N.Y.; p. Joseph and Elizabeth Raas Foehrenbach; h. George Wright.

FORGANG, ISABEL FRIEDMAN, Shopping Ed., New York Daily News, 220 E. 42nd St., N.Y., N.Y. 10017, '68–; Secy. to Shopping, Fashion Eds., '65–'67; NWC; Cedar Crest Col., '60–'62; Bklyn. Col., BA, '64; b. Bklyn., N.Y., 1943; p. Jack and Estelle Shenker Friedman; h. Richard M. Braun.

FORMAN, BRENDA, Polit. Analyst, The Mitre Corporation, Dolley Madison Blvd., McLean, Va. 22101, '69–; Auth., educ. bks. for teenage readers, incl: "America's Place in the World Economy" (Harcourt, Brace & World, '69), "The Story of Thailand" (McCormick-Mathers, '65), "The Land & People of Nigeria" (Lippincott, '64); Fellow of European Inst., Columbia Univ., '64–'65; Barnard Col., BA, '56 (Phi Beta Kappa); City Univ. of N.Y., PhD (Polit. Sci.), '69 (Fellow, '65–'66; Herbert H. Lehman Fellow, '66–'68); b. Hollywood, Cal., 1936; p. Harrison and Sandra Carlyle Forman.

FORMAN, PENELOPE PENNIMAN, AE, Kalish, Spiro, Walpert & Ringold, 22 Central Park S., N.Y., N.Y. 10036, '68–; Fashion Ed., Am. Girl, '64–'68; Assoc. Ed., McCall's Piece Goods Merchandiser, '63–'64; Newhouse Sch. of Jnlsm., Syracuse Univ. (Jnlsm., Fashion Mdsng.), '63; h. Maurice Forman; res: 188 Columbia Heights, Bklyn. Heights, N.Y.

FORNERO, JANE ELIZABETH, PR Asst., Young Men's Christian Association of Detroit, 2020 Wither-

ell, Detroit, Mich. 48226, '67–; PR Staff-Radio-TV, Un. Fndn.; Prom. Wtr., WWJ-AM-FM; Theta Sigma Phi, AWRT (Treas., '68; Bd. Mbr., '67–'69), Wms. Ad. Club; Wayne State Univ., BA (Mass Commtns.; Alpha Epsilon Rho, hon mbr., '64); b. Detroit, Mich., 1944; p. Joseph and Isabel Fornero.

FORREST, JEAN E., Ed., Tinnerman Products, Inc., 8700 Brookpark Rd., Cleve., Oh. 44129, '63–; Pers. Asst., '54–'63; AAUW, N. Oh. Indsl. Eds. Assn.; Cleve. Health Fund aw., '64; Oh. Univ., AB (Arts and Sci.), '54; b. Cleve., Oh., 1932; p. David and Edna Kilmer Forrest; res: 5253 Hauserman Rd., Parma, Oh. 44130.

FORSEE, FRANCES AYLESA, Free-lance Wtr., 1845 Bluebell Ave., Boulder, Colo. 80302, '56–; Auth., children's books; Nat. Wtrs. Club, Colo. Auths. League (Top Hand Aw., '66); Helen Dean Fish Aw., '56; Am. Ambassador Bk. Aw., '59; S.D. State Univ., BS; Univ. of Colo., MA; MacPhail Col. of Music, BMus.; b. Kirksville, Mo.; p. Dr. Edward and Lena Moore Forsee; res: 1845 Bluebell Ave., Boulder, Colo. 80302.

FORSYTH, HEATHER DAY, Adm. Asst., Sterling Movies U.S.A., 6290 W. Sunset Blvd., Hollywood, Cal. 90028, '67–; TV Programming, Sales, '65–'67; AWRT; b. Santa Barbara, Cal.; p. Ralph and Mary Wells Forsyth; res: 1521 N. Wilton Pl., #2; Hollywood, Cal. 90028.

FORSYTH, ROBERTA, Tchr., Librn., Chgo. Elementary Schs., 21 yrs.; Tchr., 37 yrs.; Cnslt., Britannica Bk. of the Yr.; Houghton, Mifflin Co.; Contrbr., pfsnl. jnls.; Bk. Reviewer, Chicago Tribune; ALA, Ill. Lib. Assn., WNBA, Children's Reading Roundtable (Pres., '57–'58, VP, '56–'57), Chgo. Tchr.-Librn. Club (Pres., '46–'47, VP, '45–'46); Chgo. Bd. of Educ. Speakers Bureau—Subject, "Children, Authors & Books," '45, '46, '47; b. N.Y.C.; h. John R. Forsyth; c. son; res: 233 E. Fig St., Fallbrook, Cal. 92028.

FORTIER, LILLIAN S., Dir., Dept. of Public Info., Hunters Point-Bayview Community Health Service, 5815 Third St., S.F., Cal. 94124, '68–; Wms. Ed., Cal. Voice, '59–; Assoc. Dir., Pubcty./Prom. Dept., KQED-TV (public TV), '66–'68; Public Svc. Dir., KPIX-TV, '64–'66; Exec. Dir., Fortier Assocs. PR Firm, '59–'64; Dir., W. Coast Speakers Bur., '59–'62; NATAS (S.F. Chptr. Bd. of Govs.) '67–), AWRT, Adv. Club of Oakland, NAMD, Govs. Comm. on Status of Wm. in Cal. ('62–'64); numerous aws.; private educ.; Univ. of Cal., L.A. City Col.; res: P.O. Box 2151—Station A, Berkeley, Cal.

FORTIS, GENEVIEVE SCOTT, Assoc. Ed., La Jolla Light-Journal, 7580 Fay Ave., La Jolla, Cal. 92307, '65–; Edtl., '60–; Ed., Rancho Santa Fe Times, '57–'60; PR, '55–'57; City Desk, Chicago Tribune, '44–'48; Reptr., UP (Des Moines, Ia., Chgo., Ill., Detroit, Mich.), '41–'44; Reptr., Omaha (Neb.) World Herald, '40–'41; Free-lance reptr., colmst.; numerous orgs., aws.; Ia. State Col.; b. Omaha, Neb., 1921; p. William and Hazel Hamilton Scott; h. (div.); c. Joyce D.,

Deborah A.; res: 2630 Torrey Pines Rd., Apt. E. 25, La Jolla, Cal., 92307.

FORTUNE, BEVERLY PEDIGO, Staff Wtr., Louisville Courier-Journal, Lexington Bureau, 161 Walnut St., Lexington, Ky. 40507, '67–; Educ. Ed. and Feature Wtr., Lexington Leader, '65–'67; Theta Sigma Phi, Bluegrass Press Club (Treas.); Univ. of Ky., BA, '64; Grad. work: Univ. of Wis., '64; Univ. of Ky., '67; b. Akron, Oh., 1941; p. Martin and Elaine Dicks Pedigo; h. William Fortune; c. Sarah Merrit; res: 434 Fayette Park, Lexington, Ky. 40508.

FOSSCECO, ROSALIE ANN, VP, Recht & Co., Inc., Advertising, 177 S. Beverly Dr., Beverly Hills, Cal. 90212, '69–; VP, Holzer/McTighe Adv., '64–'69; Media Dir., Brangham/Brewer Adv., '61–'64; L.A. Adv. Wm. (Treas.), AAF; Pueblo Col., '57–'59; b. Alamosa, Colo., 1939; p. Charles and Anna Bartalussi Fossceco; res: 1617 N. Fuller, L.A., Cal. 90046

FOSTER, BETTY KELLEY, Asst. to Pres., Dir. of PR, Adm., Memorial Medical Center & Nueces County Hospital District, 2606 Hospital Blvd., Corpus Christi, Tex. 78405, '68–; VP, Inst. of Applied Psycho-Cybernetics; Asst. to Adm., Dir. Rsch. and Dev., Spohn Hosp., '66–'68; Dir. PR, Memorial Med. Ctr., '64–'66; Adm., Okla. State Univ. Hosp. (Stillwater), '61–'64; Mgr. and Dir., Fund Raising Campaign, Ponca City (Okla.) Hosp., '59–'61; Asst. Adm., Dir. Pers. and PR, '58–'59; Hosp. in-svc. educ. and employee dev., '66–'68; PR Cnslt. to various civic and social orgs., '60–'68; PRSA, PR Dirs. of Am. Hosp. Assn., Am. Hosp. Assn., Several other hosp. assns., Corpus Christi Press Club (Bd. of Dirs.), AWRT (past mbr.); Who's Who In Public Relations, '67–'68; numerous aws. and cits. for hosp. work; Ardmore Bus. Col., Cert. in Bus. Adm., '39; b. Waurika, Okla., 1920; p. Elijah and Mamie Gay Kelley; h. J. E. Foster; c. June (Mrs. Maurice Weddle), Joann (Mrs. Lester Cramton), Charlotte, Justin, Mark; res: 402 University Pl., Corpus Christi, Tex. 78412.

FOSTER, BLANCHE ANDREWS, Adv. Mgr., Hounds & Hunting, 146 W. Washington St., Bradford, Pa. 16701; b. Bradford, Pa., 1918; p. James and Ida Carson Andrews; h. Francis E. Foster (dec.); c. Stephen A.; res: 1128 E. Main St., Bradford, Pa. 16701.

FOSTER, CLAIBORNE BANKS PERROW, Tech. Cnslt., Snelling & Snelling, Inc., '67–; Ed., J. H. Hudson & Assoc., '66–'67; Adv. Dir., Ivey's, '61–'64; Adv. Mgr., '59–'61; Adv. Mgr., Leggett's Dept. Store (Roanoke, Va.), '57–'59; Studio Mgr., Am. Photographic Corp., '55–'57; Adv. Mgr., Baldwin's, '53–'55; Adv. Mgr., Leggett's (Lynchburg, Va.), '52–'53; Adv. Club of Greenville (Treas.), '60–'61; ZONTA, C. of C., D.A.R., Am. Field Svc. (Greenville Chptr. Pres., '61); Readers' Digest/Nat. Retail Merchants aw., '63; b. Lynchburg, Va., 1921; p. J. Archer and Ellen Smith Perrow; h. Wm. Urquhart Foster Jr.; c. Cay Alexandra Urquhart (Mrs.

N. Stavrakas); res: 211 Cleveland St., Greenville, S.C. 29601.

FOSTER, EDITH LENORE, Dir., West Georgia Regional Library, Rome St. at Spring, Carrollton, Ga. 30117, '44–; Asst. Prof. of Lib. Educ., W. Ga. Col., '58–'63; Experimenter in dev. of Rural, Reg. Libs.; Auth: "Beside the Wishing Well" ('37), "To Wind a Chain" (Exposition Press, '52), "Silver Arabesques" in "First 500 Poems from Ga. Magazine" ('64); mag. jnl. articles; published in bks.; Cnslt.; numerous offices and aws. for lib. svc. and educ; LaGrange Col., '26; Emory Univ., Grad. Deg. in Librarianship; b. Carrollton, Ga., 1906; p. Robert and Margaret Byrom Foster; res: 219 E. Sims St., Carrollton, Ga. 30117.

FOSTER, ETHYL, Political Rsch., News Dept., American Broadcasting Company, 1330 Ave. of the Americas, N.Y., N.Y. 10009, '69–; Paul Miner Adv., '65–'67; Talent Coordr., WOR-TV, (Editorial Page Conference), '63–'65; Asst. to Prodr., "Hundred Grand," ABC-TV, '62–'63; Prodr., Wtr., Narrator, "Showbusiness" (WCAU-TV), "Around the World" (WFIL-TV), Phila., Pa., '51–'61; AWRT, NATAS, Theta Sigma Phi, League of Wm. Voters, United Nations Assn., Nat. Cncl. of Jewish Wm.; Temple Univ., BS (Jnlsm.); Univ. of Pa., MA (Mass Commtns.); Ford Foundation Fellowship, Columbia Univ., MFA (Film and Television), '67–'69; b. Phila., Pa.; p. Fred Donner and Jennie Felt; h. Ted Rosenberg; c. Fred Donner Rosenberg; res: 353 W. 56th St., N.Y., N.Y. 10019.

FOSTER, EUNICE SWAEBLY, Wms. Ed., The Bellevue Gazette, Sandusky St., Bellevue, Oh. 44811, '66–, '39–'50; Lib. Asst., Bellevue Public Lib., '63–'66; Capital Univ., '40; b. Monroeville, Oh., 1916; p. Charles and Emma Blake Swaebly; h. William T. Foster; c. Dixie Ann; res: 136 Euclid Ave., Bellevue, Oh. 44811.

FOSTER, JOANNA, VP, Connecticut Films, Inc., 6 Cobble Hill Rd., Westport, Conn. 06880, '66–; Bk. Review Ed., Scholastic Teacher, '63–'65; VP, Weston Woods Studios, '63–'64; Children's Bk. Review Ed., Publishers Weekly, '61–'63; Dir., Children's Bk. Cncl., '58–'61; Assoc. Children's Bk. Ed., Harcourt Brace & Javanovich, '53–'57; Asst. Children's Bk. Ed., Charles Scribner's & Sons, '50–'52; Auth.-Illus: "Pete's Puddle" ('50), "Pages, Pictures, & Print" ('58); Co-prodr., "There's Something About a Story," "Lively Art of Picture Books," other films; Instr., S. Conn. State Col.; Vassar Col., BA; Art Inst. of Chgo.

FOSTER, OLIVE OLMSTEAD, Dir. of PR, Fairleigh Dickinson University, Rutherford, N.J. 07070, '52–; Eng. Tchr., '50–'51; Rsch. Asst., '28–'36; "Fine Arts, Including Folly" ('66); ACPRA (pubn., Techniques, '67); Syracuse Univ., AB, '26; Fairleigh Dickinson Univ., MA, '60; h. Newton Foster; c. Newton S., Jr., James A.; res: 15 E. Pierrepont Ave., Rutherford, N.J. 07070.

FOSTER, PEGGY BONSACK, Head of Adult Svcs.,

Oakland Public Library, 125 14th St., Oakland, Cal. 94612, '70–; Chief Ref. Librn., '67–'70; Chief Circ. Librn., '60–'67; Sr. Librn., '58–'60; Jr. Librn., '51–'58; ALA, Cal. Lib. Assn.; Univ. of Ut., AB, '33 (Phi Kappa Phi); Univ. of Cal., Cert. of Librnship., '34; b. Bonsack, Va., 1912; p. John and Lela Saunders Bonsack; h. Richard H. Foster; c. Richard Jr., Mercedes F. McDiarmid; res: 1693 Grand Ave., Piedmont, Cal. 94611.

FOSTER, POLLY CONROY, Dir. of PR, Girl Scout Council of Greater New York, Inc., 335 E. 46th St., N.Y., N.Y. 10017, '68–; St. Joseph Col., BS, '45; h. John Foster; c. J. Hunton Foster, Jr., James T.; res: 355 Short Dr., Mountainside, N.J. 07092.

FOURTON, ROSE MARIE DeMAUPASSANT, Scheduling Specialist, Traf. & Sls., Pan American World Airways, 200 Park Ave., N.Y., N.Y. 10017, '67–; Asst. to Sls. Prom. Mgr., Supvsr. of Displays, '51–'67; Staff Asst. to Sls. Prom. Mgr., '49–'51; Secy. to Sls. Prom. Mgr., '48–'49; Am. Airlines, '41–'48; AWNY; b. N.Y.C., 1922; p. Frank and Elizabeth Shields Fourton; res: 65–84 Booth St., Rego Park, N.Y. 11374.

FOWLE, MARGUERITE STARK, PR Wtr., Howard B. Stark Co., Pewaukee, Wis., '58–; "Exclusively Yours," Magazine & others, Conn. Col. for Wm., BS (Psych.), '50; b. Milw., Wis., 1928; p. Howard and Hulda Hayssen Stark; h. Alonzo Fowle; c. Mark Charles, Suzanne, Alonzo Michael, Amy; res: 9736 N. Lake Dr., Milw., Wis. 53217.

FOWLER, ELLEN MARGARET, Asst. Dir., PR, American Nurses' Association, 10 Columbus Circle, N.Y., N.Y. 10019, '64–; Ed., Insider Magazine, A. C. Nielsen Co. (Chgo., Ill.), '55–'64; Ed., Sls. Magazine, Employee Nwsp., The Trane Co. (La Crosse, Wis.), '51–'55; Nwsp. Reptr., The La Crosse Tribune, '46–'51; ICIE (aw., placing among best pubns., '61), Theta Sigma Phi (Chgo. Chptr. Pres., '63–'64); Crusade of Mercy Aw., Chgo. Commty. Fund., '60; Mead Papers aw., Nat. GA Competition, '60; Drake Univ., BA, '46.

FOWLER, FERN WRIGHT, Wms. Dir., Forward Television, Inc., Box 4269, 615 Forward Dr., Madison, Wis. 53711; Wtr., Prodr., Bdcstr., Fern Fowler Show, WMTV, '59; WKOW-TV, '54–'59; started show, '53; Regular Participant, "The Beverly Stark Show," synd. radio show, '66–'67; work on nwsps. (Monticello, Ind.; Danville, Ill.); Tchr., Home Econs., Hist., Eng.; colm., "Fern Fowler Suggests," monthly mag.; freelance craft articles; Cnslt., Lectr., arts, crafts; AWRT, NLAPW, Home Econsts. in Bus., Madison Art Assn., Madison Art Guild, Wis. Acad. of Arts & Scis., Zeta Tau Alpha, Theta Sigma Phi; Who's Who of Am. Wm.; Dic. of Intl. Biog.; The 2000 Wm. of Achiev.; Purdue Univ., BS, '30; Wis. Sch. of Art; b. Assumption, Ill.; p. Rawley E. and Martha R. Price Wright; h. Russell Winslow Fowler; res: 3315 Blackhawk Dr., Madison, Wis. 53705.

FOWLER, FLORENCE HADLEN, VP, Exec. Prodr., Vista Productions, Inc., 371 Fifth, S.F., Cal. 94107, '60–; Prodr.-Dir., W. A. Palmer Films, Inc., '45–'59; Cnslt.; Bus. Mgr., Ginger Rogers, '42–'45; Guest Lectr., Stanford Univ. Radio & TV Dept., Golden Gate Col., Sch. of Adv.; AWRT (Golden Gate Chptr. Pres., '68–'69; Western Area Dir., '69–'70), S.F. Adv. Club (Bd. Dirs., '62–'65; Secy., '60); Adv. Wm. of Yr., '59; winner of three "LULU's" for film direction, L.A. Adv. Wms. Club, '64, '68, '69; Univ. of Cal. (Berkeley), '38; b. Berkeley, Cal., 1917; p. Edward and Rose McGlinchey Hadlen; h. Richard Fowler; res: 960 Union, S.F., Cal. 94133.

FOX, BETTY D., Dir. of Rsch., Corinthian Broadcasting Corporation, 280 Park Ave., 38th floor, W. Wing, N.Y., N.Y. 10017, '66–; Mgr., TV Rsch., Metromedia, '63–'66; Mgr., Special Analysis, A. C. Nielsen Co., '56–'63; Hunter Col., AB (Sociol.), '54 (Alumni Assn. Pres., '66–'69); N.Y.U., MA (Sociological Rsch.), '56; b. Bklyn., N.Y., 1933; p. Philip and Fanny Joseph Fox; res: 3 Sheridan Sq., N.Y., N.Y. 10014.

FOX, CHRISTY, Colmst., Los Angeles Times, Times Mirror Sq., L.A., Cal. 90053, '51–; Soc. Ed.; own radio show, KNX; numerous TV Emcee appearances; h. Ludlow Shonnard Jr.

FOX, FRANCES PIERCE, Publr., Sodus Record Corporation, 14–18 W. Main St., Sodus, N.Y. 14551, '60–; Assoc. Ed., Moravia Republican-Register '59–'60; Ed., Candor Courier, '52–'59; Jamestown Post Journal, '48–'49; Ed., Port Byron Chronicle, '46–'48; Adv. Copywtr., Fowler's Dept. Store (Binghamton), '41–'46; N.Y. Press Assn., Nat. Nwsp. Assn.; Who's Who of Am. Wm; Houghton Col., BA, '41; b. Owego, N.Y., 1920; p. Daniel and Hazel Pierce Pierce; h. Robert Fox (div.); c. Roberta, Daniel; res: 17 Orchard Terr., Sodus, N.Y. 14551.

FOX, JANE STARKES, Ed., Employee Pubns., Kemper Insurance Group, 4750 Sheridan Rd., Chgo., Ill. 60640, '66–; Assoc. Ed.; Copywtr., Warner Slimwear-Lingerie (Bridgeport, Conn.), '64–'66; Wtr., Assoc. Ed., Charlton Publ. Co. (Derby, Conn.), '63–'64; IEA of Chgo.; Lasell Jr. Col., AA, '63; b. Hartford, Conn., 1943; p. John and Verna Peterson Starkes; h. Larry Fox; res: 2220 Scott Rd., Northbrook, Ill. 60062.

FOX, MAUREEN THERESA, Ed., The East Wind, The Federal Reserve Bank of Boston, 30 Pearl St., Boston, Mass. 02106, '67–; Tchr., '62–'67; ICIE, Mass. IEA, Am. Inst. of Banking, Nat. Tchrs. Assn.; Ladycliff Col., BA, '62, Seton Hall Univ., MA, '65; b. Jersey City, N.J., 1941; p. John and Mary Ellen O'Brien Fox; res: Village on the Hill, 80 Queens Way, Apt. 4, Framingham, Mass. 01701.

FOX, PATRICIA COOMBS, Auth., Illus., children's bks., incl: "Dorrie's Magic," (Lothrop, Lee & Shepard Co., Inc., '62; N.Y. Times Top 10), "The Lost Playground," (Lothrop, Lee & Shepard Co., '63; N.Y.

Times Top 100), "Dorrie and the Blue Witch," (Lothrop, Lee & Shepard Co., '64; Jr. Lit. Guild), "Dorrie and the Weather-Box" (Lothrop, Lee & Shepard Co., '66; Jr. Lit. Guild); Illus: "P.J. My Friend," (Doubleday, '69), adult bk., other children's bks.; Univ. of Wash. (Seattle), BA, '49; MA (Eng. Lit.), '51; b. L.A., Cal., 1926; p. Donald and Katherine Goodro Coombs; h. C. James Fox; c. Ann Claire, Patricia; res: 178 Oswegatchie Rd., Waterford, Conn. 06385.

FOX, PATRICIA MAY, Assoc. Ed., American Historical Review, American Historical Association, 400 A St. S.E., Wash., D.C. 20003, '69–; Asst. Ed., '59–'69; Edtl. Asst., '56–'59; Am. Hist. Assn., Phi Alpha Theta; Am. Univ., BA '56; MA, '61; res: 2814 30th St. N.E., Wash., D.C. 20018.

FOX, RUTH, M.D., Pres., The American Medical Society on Alcoholism, 150 E. 52nd St., N.Y., N.Y. 10022; Head, Dept. of Labs., Neurological Inst., Columbia-Presbyterian Med. Ctr.; Biochemical Rsch. Fellow, Fifth Ave. Hosp.; Lectr.; Auth: "Alcoholism, Its Scope, Cause and Treatment" (Random House, '55); "The Effect of Alcoholism on Children," ('63); "Is LSD of Value in Treating Alcoholics?" (Bobbs-Merrill, '67); "Treating the Alcoholic's Family," ('68), and numerous articles on psychiatric and alcoholic studies; Sorbonne; Rush Med. Col.; Peking Un. Med. Col.; Colo. Psychopathic Hosp.; post-grad. work, Germany and Vienna.

FOXWORTH, JO, Pres., Jo Foxworth, Ind., 75 E. 55th St., New York, N.Y. 10028, '68–; formerly Exec. VP, Calkins & Holden; VP, Johnstone Inc.; Crtv. Supvsr., McCann-Erickson; Adv., PR Dir., Nan Duskin (Phila., Pa.); AAF (Governor, '66–'67; '67–'68); Nat. Adv. Wm. of Yr., '66–'67; AWNY, '65, '66; numerous adv. aws.; Wtr. of fiction, non-fiction, light verse, lyrics.

FRADIN, ELLEN HARRIET, Admr., Bdcst. Standards, WNBC Radio, National Broadcasting Company, 30 Rockefeller Plaza, N.Y., N.Y. 10020, '68–; Sales Svc. Coordr., '66–'68; Script Routing Cl., '66; Scheduling Cl., '65–'66; Queens Col., '63–'65; Candy Jones Charm and Modeling Sch., '65–'66; b. Bklyn., N.Y., 1947; p. Sidney and Theresa Wolf Fradin; res: 79-25 150 St., Flushing, N.Y. 11367.

FRAESDORF, MARIE STEINMETZ, Prog. Asst., ETV, Tucson Public School System, 1010 E. 10th St., Tucson, Ariz. 85717, '69–; Tchr., TV Prod., '66–'69; Bdcstr., KVOA-TV, '58–'65; Talent Coordr., KOLD-TV, '56–'58; Free-lance Bdcstr., '47–'56; AAUW (VP, '47–'49), AWRT, Tucson Press Club, Pi Lambda Theta; McCall's Golden Mike aw., '60; Mrs. Ariz., '66; Tucson Industry Assn. aw., '62; Hunter Col., BA, '43; Univ. of Ariz., MEd, '67; b. N.Y.C., 1922; p. Winfred and Bertha Steinbeck Steinmetz; h. William O. Fraesdorf Jr.; c. William III, Lori; res: 4801 Camino Antonio, Tucson, Ariz. 85718.

FRAKES, FLORENCE MARGARET, Assoc. Ed., The Christian Century, 407 S. Dearborn St., Chgo., Il. 60605, '51–; News Ed., '44–'51; Asst. Ed., The Epworth Herald, '34–'40; Tchr., '26–'31; Free-lance Wtr., '40–'44; Conducted motion pic. reviewing svc., Independent Filmscores, '40–'53; Auth., "Bridges to Understanding" (Fortress Press, '60); Ed., bk., "The Christian Century Reader" (Assn. Press, '62); NRPC (Chgo. Chptr. Pres., '59–'60); Baker Univ., AB, '26 (magna cum laude); Northwestern Univ., MS (Jnlsm.), '32; res: 3001 Martin Luther King, Jr. Dr., Chgo., Ill. 60616.

FRAKES, MARGARET HINDS, Dir., Field Opns., Educational Communication Assoc., Faith Media, Inc., Suite 612-615, 143 N. Meridian St., Indpls., Ind. 64204, '63–; Ind. Commty. Coordr. of Programs, '62–'63; RPRC (Treas., '68–'69), AWRT, Fellowship of Christians in the Arts, Media & Entertainment; Delta Delta Delta "Mother of the Year," DePauw Univ. Chptr., '62; Ind. Univ. ext., '33–'34; New Albany Bus. Col., '35; b. Salem, Ind., 1916; p. Roy and Monta Thompson Hinds; h. Fred Frakes; c. Karleen, Sandra (Mrs. Warren Parsons, Jr.); res: 1625 Forrest Dr., Plainfield, Ind. 46168.

FRAME, HELEN DUNN, Free-lance Wtr.; Private Secy. to Pres., Whitaker & Baxter Intl., '65; Wtr., employee mag., Adv., Public Info. Bur., Cadet Analyst, Mgt. Trainee Program, Consolidated Edison of N.Y., Inc., '60–'64; Theta Sigma Phi (N.Y. Corr. Secy.; S.F. Pres.), Wms. Engineering Soc. (London, Assoc. Mbr.), The Electrical Wms. Round Table, Edison Engineering Soc. of N.Y.C., Alpha Kappa Delta; German-Am. Club (Nurnberg-Furth, Germany), Eng.-Speaking Un. (London), Zeta Tau Alpha; Syracuse Univ., BA, '60 (scholarship, Grant-in-aid, '58, '59); N.Y.U., MA, '67; b. N.Y.C., '39; p. Edward and Eunice Elizabeth Harvey Dunn; h. David W. Frame; c. Dana Edward; res: Pers. Pol. & Proc. Br., Personnel Div. Headquarters, AAFES Dallas, Tex. 75222.

FRANCE, MARGARET BELL, Ed., The East Canton Printing Co., The Press-News, 200 Church St. S.W., East Canton, Oh. 44730, '58–; b. McDonald, Pa., 1916; p. John and Carolyn Oliver Bell; h. George France; c. James A.; res: 4912 Ridge Ave. S.E., North Industry, Oh. 44707.

FRANCES, EVAN BARBARA, Special Projects Ed., Ladies Home Journal, 641 Lexington Ave., N.Y., N.Y. 10022, '69–; Free-lance Cnslt., '67–'69; Tchr., St. John's Univ., '68; Home Furnishings, Architectural Ed., Family Circle, '55–'67; Housing Ed., Today's Woman, '54; Feature Ed., House Beautiful's Guide for the Bride, '50–'53; Feature, Mng. Ed., Pic., '46–'50; Assoc. Ed., Look, '45–'46; Esquire's Apparel Arts, '42–'46; Lectr.; Am. Inst. of Interior Design, NHFL (VP), Architectural League of N.Y.; Dorothy Dawe Aw., '62, '64, '68; Scandinavian Design Aw., '58; Dallas Mkt. Aw., '63; Univ. of Chgo., AB (Eng., Lit.), '37; N.Y.U., MA, '40; grad. study: American Univ., Hunter Col., Architectural Inst.; p. Charles and Mary Cohan Reese; h. Alexander Frances; c. Andrew, James, Scott.

FRANCIS, ANNETT, Wtr., Ed.; Exec. Ed., House & Garden, '69–; Merchandising Ed., '65–; Copy Ed., '60–; Merchandising Wtr., Vogue, '55–; b. Pitt., Pa.; p. Harold Van Pelt and Helen Watson Francis; res: 1142 Madison Ave., N.Y., N.Y. 10028.

FRANCIS, ARLENE, Actress; "What's My Line?" CBS-TV; "Arlene Francis Show," WOR; previously appeared in plays: Orson Welles' Mercury Theatre prod. of "Horse Eats Hat" and "Danton's Death," "All That Glitters," "Journey to Jerusalum," "The Doughgirls," "The Overtons," "The French Touch," "The Cup of Trembling," "The Little Blue Light", "Dinner at Eight," "Tchin-Tchin", "Mrs. Dally", "Beekman Place"; TV: "What's My Line?," "Home," "Soldier Parade"; radio: Mistress of Ceremonies on "What's My Name?", "Blind Date," "Arlene Francis at Sardi's," "Family Living"; movies: "All My Sons"; bk., "That Certain Something" (Messner, '60); AFTRA, AEA, SAG, Bonwit Teller Bd. of Dirs.; Univ. of Utah Nat. Advisory Cncl.; Mount St. Vincent Academy, Finch Coll.; Honorary Dr. of Humanities, Springfield Intl. Coll., '65, and Keuka Coll., '67; U.S. Hall of Fame, '68; b. Boston, Mass.; p. Aram and Leah Davis Kazanjian; c. Peter Joseph Gabel; Bus. Res: 465 Park Ave., N.Y., N.Y. 10022.

FRANCIS, HELEN ALSBURY, Sr. HS Librn., Pendleton School District 16R, 1207 S.W. Frazer Ave., Pendleton, Ore. 97801, '60–; Tchr., Librn. (Osceola, Mo.), '42–'59; Tchr., '34–'37; '31–'32; various organizations; Harris Tchrs. Col., AB, '30; Univ. of Denver, MA (Lib. Sci.), '57; Univ. of Mo. (Nat. Defense Educ. Act Scholarship), '60; Univ. of Hi. (Asian Studies Scholarship), '64; b. Springfield, Ill., 1908; p. Edward and Kathryn Looby Alsbury; h. Joseph Francis; c. Joseph Lee; res: 319 N.W. Baileg, Pendleton, Ore. 97801.

FRANCIS, HELEN DANNEFER, Free-Lance Wtr.; Auth., several teenage, young adult bks.; Jnlsm. Instr., Dir. of News Svc., Ft. Hays (Kan.) State Col., '53–'60; Kan. Cultural Arts Comm., Hays Arts Cncl.; Contemporary Auths.; Ind. Univ. Wtrs. Conf. aw., '60; Fort Hays Kan. State Col., AB, BS, '35 (Phi Kappa Phi); b. Cuba, Kan., 1915; p. Edward and Lily Nutter Dannefer; h. Alex Francis; c. Michael Jackson, John Alexander; res: 401 Walnut, Hays, Kan. 67601.

FRANCIS, JAN (Mary Frances Janovetz), Acc. Supvsr., The Rowland Company, 415 Madison Ave., N.Y., N.Y. 10017, '68–; Dir. Wms. Affairs, The Schaefer Corp., '67–'68; AWRT, PRSA; Western Ill. Univ., BA, '65; b. St. Louis, Mo., 1943; p. Francis and Goldia Jones Janovetz; res: 301 E. 47th St., N.Y., N.Y. 10017.

FRANCIS, JEAN O'BANION, Pres., The Tipton Daily Tribune Publishing Co., Inc., 221-223 E. Jefferson St., Tipton, Ind. 46072, '63–; City Ed., Adv. Mgr., Soc. Ed.; worked on Bloomington Daily Herald; Gamma Alpha Chi; Kappa Kappa Kappa (Beta Omicron Chptr. Pres., Secy.), AAUW (VP), Delta Gamma; Ind. Univ., AB, '50; b. Indpls., Ind., 1928; p. Clayton L. and Mary Newsom O'Banion; h. James Craig Francis; c. Mary Ann, Martha Ellen; res: 216 N. Independence St., Tipton, Ind. 46072.

FRANCIS, JOANN, Wtr., Ed., JoAnn Francis, Jamestown, N.C., '60–; Edtl. Advisor, '60; VP, Idea Books, Inc., '69; Edtl. Advisor, Maco Publ., '68–; Ed., Budget Decorating Magazine, '60–'68; Copywtr., Alderman Studios, '60–; Pubcty. Acc. Supvsr., Arndt Advertising, '55–'60; Radio-TV Pubcty. Wtr., J. Walter Thompson, '50–'55; Ed., The Bronxville Reprtr., '49–'50; Auth., "The World of Budget Decorating" (Simon & Schuster, '67); b. Pitt., Pa.; p. Harold Van Pelt and Helen Watson Francis; h. Gilbert A. Gray; res: 213 Knollwood Dr., Jamestown, N.C. 27282.

FRANCIS, MARILYN A., Dir., Winged Arts, Inc., P.O. Box 1187, Sedona, Ariz. 86336, '69–; Sedona Off. Mgr., The Verde Independent nwsp., '68–; Freelance poet, '55–; Investigator, The Retail Credit Co., '45–'51; Interviewer, Western Electric Co., '41–'45; Poetry Ed., Scottsdale Arizonian, '58–'62; works published: "Thunder in the Superstitions" ('59), "Tangents at Noon" ('61), "Space for Sound" ('62), "Mirror Without Glass" ('64), "Symbols for Instants" ('65); "Rivers of Remembrance" (Prod. '67, '68, '69); reading recitals, "Symbols for Instants"; PSA, NLAPW (Phoenix Br. Pres., '59–'61), Nat. Wtrs. Club (Psnl. Mbr.; Cert. of Merit for significant contrbs. to poetry via radio, '58), Soroptimist Club of Sedona (Pres., '65–'66); Cert. of Appreciation for significant contrb. to Arts Festival, Phoenix Arts Cncl., '68; Sedona Arts Ctr., Sedona Public Lib. Trustees (Past Pres.); Oh. Univ., B.S.C., '41 (Cert. of Merit for "distg. attainments in literature," '61); b. Columbus, Oh., 1920; p. Roy and Ruth Needles Francis; res: P.O. Box 196, Sedona, Ariz. 86336.

FRANK, EDITH SINAIKO, Free-lance Wtr.; AAUW, Madison Press Club (Secy., '69), Univ. Club, Arts Club of Chgo., Theta Sigma Phi (Madison Chptr. Pres., '67–'68); Who's Who of Am. Wm.; Who's Who in the Mid-West; Nwsp. Guild (Toledo, Oh.) Outstanding Citizen Aw., '51; Univ. of Wis., BA (Jnlsm.), '24 (Beta's Own Aw.); b. Madison, Wis., 1902; p. Issac and Sarah Goldberg Sinaiko; h. David S. Frank (dec.); c. Suzanne (Mrs. Roberto Freund); res: 1515 Vilas Ave. Circle, Madison, Wis. 53711.

FRANK, ELIZABETH POPE, Articles Ed., Good Housekeeping, 959 Eight Ave., N.Y., N.Y. 10019, '59–; Free-lance Wtr., several mags., '51–'58; Edtl. Staff, Look; Edtl. Cnslt., Tobe Assocs.; Soc. of Mag. Wtrs.; Vassar Col., BA, '36; b. Detroit, Mich., 1914; p. Melville and Belle Oberfelder Welt; h. Morton Frank; c. John Pope, Anne Pope, Barbara Pope; res: 25 W. 11th St., N.Y., N.Y. 10011.

FRANK, GOLDALIE, Pres., Contempo Advertising

Agency, 475 Fifth Ave., N.Y., N.Y. 10017, '46–; Art Dir., Cramer-Tobias-Meyer, '37–'46; men's trade pubn., '36–'37; Lee Barnett Adv., '31–'36; Lester Harrison Adv., '30–'31; Auth., "Mother, I'd Rather Buy It Myself" (Macfadden Bartell, '65); articles in trade pubns.; Colmst., Department Store Economist, '48–'50; OPC, Wms. City Club; active in civic affairs; Dallas Art Inst., N.Y. Art Schs., '28–'29; b. Jacksonville, Tex., 1908; p. Louis and Tillie Mandelstam Frank; h. Solomon Balsam; res: 914 Crestwood Dr., Jacksonville, Tex. 75766.

FRANK, HELEN SOPHIA, Free-lance Painter, Costume Designer, Illus.; illus. for six juv. music bks. (Belwin), five juv. textbks. (Barnes and Noble), "The Life of Mozart" (Holt); spots, illus. for The N.Y. Times, Saturday Rev., Harper's; many one-man exhbns., group exhbns., U.S. and abroad; costumes for dancers in S.F., Cal., and N.Y.C.; Cal. Col. of Arts & Crafts, '44; private study: Painting, Glenn Wessels, Morris Kantor; Costume Design, Joseph Paget-Fredericks; Art Students League (Scholarship, '52); b. Berkeley, Cal.; p. Oskar and Ada S. Matson Frank; res: 241 Lexington Ave., N.Y., N.Y. 10016.

FRANK, JO ANN, Wms. Dir., Piedmont Television Corporation, Glenburnie Gardens, P.O. Box 2325, New Bern, N.C. 28560, '63–; Asst. Mgr., Twin City Bdcst. (Weldon, N.C.), '59–'63; Asst. Media Dir., Liller, Neal, Battle, Lindsey Adv. (Richmond, Va.), '53–'59; Asst. Byr. Thalhimers, '51–'53; AWRT, numerous civic orgs.; Wms. Col., '48–'49, Va. Commonwealth Univ., '49–'51; b. New Bern, N.C., 1930; p. Nathan and Margaret Hurtt Frank; res: 1408 Phillips Ave., New Bern, N.C. 28560.

FRANKE, DOROTHY McCRABB, Colmst., Urbana Citizen, 220 E. Court St., Urbana, Oh. 43078, '56–; Polit. Colmst., Farm Colmst., Reptr.; Free-lance Wtr., Dayton Daily News (Sunday Leisure Magazine Section); League of Wm. Voters; b. Dayton, Oh., 1917; p. Maris and Grace Wogaman McCrabb; h. Arthur Franke; c. Maris, Michael, Marc; res: R. R. #1, St. Paris, Oh. 43072.

FRANKEL, CAROLE SKOLNICK, Home Fashions Coordr., Wool Bureau, Inc., 360 Lexington Ave., N.Y., N.Y. 10017, '67–; Staff, '63–'67; AE, Christopher Cross Assoc., '61–'63; Home Furnishings, Equipment Ed., Redbk. Magazine, '59–'61; NHFL (VP, '64), Home Econsts. in Bus., Am. Home Econs. Assn., Am. Inst. of Interior Designers; Cornell Univ., BS (Home Econs.), '50; h. Marvin D. Frankel.

FRANKENFIELD, PEARL DENNIS, Exec. Dir., Montgomery County-Norristown Public Library, 542 De Kalb St., Norristown, Pa. 19401, '68–; Lib. Cnslt.; Contrbr. to pfsnl. jnls.; Head Librn., Norristown Public Lib., '54–'68; Pa. Lib. Assn. (Aw. of Merit; Pres. '65–'66), ALA, Adult Educ. Assn., Pa. Citizens Cncl., Pa. Comm. for 1970 White House Conf. on Children and Youth, Lib. PR Assn. of Greater Phila., Phila. Booksell-

ers Assn.; John Cotton Dana Nat. Lib. Pubcty. Aw. (3 times); Presidential Cit. for Youth Opportunity Work, '67; b. Phila., Pa., p. Lazarus and Fanny Valiensky Dennis; h. Herbert Frankenfield (dec.); c. David, Joan F. Sinclair; res: 94 E. Germantown Pike, Plymouth Meeting, Pa. 19462.

FRANKLIN, LOTTIE MAE, Ed., Adult Curriculum, and Mng. Ed., Vital Christianity, Warner Press, 1200 E. Fifth St., Anderson, Ind. 46012; Auth., "So You Work With Young Adults" ('60); articles in various mags.; curriculum materials; Tchr., Pacific Bible Col., '40–'42; Pastor (Bandon, Ore.), '35–'37; Tchr., '24–'34; Nat. Bd. of Christian Educ. of Church of God (Bd. of Dirs.); Anderson Altrusa Club (Pres. '59–'60); Southern Oregon Normal Sch. Cert., '31; Anderson Col., BA, '39, BTh, '40; Oberlin Col., MA, '45; b. Chgo., Ill., 1906; p. Benjamin J. and Ella Mountford Franklin; res: 607 Walnut, Anderson, Ind. 46012.

FRANKLIN, MELVINA HEAVENRIDGE, Free-lance PR, 154 Wood St., S.F., Cal. 94118, '68–; PR, Barbara Dorn Assoc., '66–'68; Screen Gems TV Prod. '60–'66; E. Williams, '55–'60; Arthur P. Jacobs Co., '54–'56; Oriental Intl. Films, '49–'54; Metro Goldwyn Mayer Studios, '41–'49; Am. Airlines, '36–'41; Theta Sigma Phi (L.A. Alumni Pres., '39–'40), Hollywood Wms. Press Club (VP, '66 and '67), Screen Publicists Guild, Nat. Home Furnishings League; Assoc. Prodr. film, "The River", made in India, '50, won 26 aws.; Univ. of Ky., BA, '29; b. Spencer, Ind.; p. Lyman D. and Gertrude Griffin Heavenridge; h. Clare Franklin; c. Melvina Gay (Mrs. Patrick Williams); res: 154 Wood St., S.F., Cal. 94118.

FRANKMAN, BETTY SKELTON, VP, Dir. Wms. Adv. and Mktng. Dept., Campbell-Ewald Company, 3044 W. Grand Blvd., Detroit, Mich. 48216, '69–; AE; Dir. selection, training, Chevrolet Teen Team, '64; with husband wrote, dir., co-prod., "Challenge" (N.Y. Intl. TV and Film Festival Aw.); Wms. Adv. Club of Detroit ("Top 10 Career Wm." '64), Parachute Club of Am., Experimental Aircraft Assn., Aircraft Owners and Pilots Assn., Mich. Aeronautics and Space Assn.; b. Pensacola, Fla., 1926; p. David and Myrtle Lowry Skelton; h. Donald A. Frankman; res: 9421 Macey Rd., Willis, Mich. 48191.

FRANZBLAU, ROSE NADLER, Psychologist; Nwsp. Colmst., "Human Relations," N.Y. Post, '51–; colm., N.Y. Daily Compass, The Star, '48–'51; Radio Commentator, "The World of Children," WCBS, '65–; Magazine, Feature Wtr., '67–; feature articles, Cosmopolitan, other pubns.; Auth: "The Way It Is Under Twenty" (Avon Bks., '64), monograph, chptr. in bk.; nwsp. article series; Lectr., psych., human rels. problems; Cnslt., industry, U.S. govt., others; TV guest appearances; Assoc. Dir., Intl. Tensions Rsch. Project, UNESCO, '47–'51; Reg. Training Offcr., Off. of Price Adm. (N.Y.C.), '46–'47; Dir. of Placement, Training Overseas Pers., UNNRA (Wash., D.C.), '44–'46; Dir., Training of Girls, Nat. Youth Adm., '43–'44; Dir. of Pers. (Columbus, Cinn., Oh.), '40–'43; Pers.

Worker, '37–'40; Cinn. Commty. Cncl. Worker, '35–'37; Tchr., Prin., '17–'43; travel, rsch: youth guidance survey (Europe), '58; juv. delinquents court study (Europe, Tel Aviv), '60; public svc., many groups incl., Univ. of Jerusalem (Israel) Psych. Dept. (Advisory Bd.); Hunter Col., BA, '26; Columbia Univ., MA, '31; PhD, '35 (Sigma Xi); b. Vienna, Austria; h. Dr. Abraham N. Franzblau; c. Dr. Michael, Jane (Mrs. Richard A. Isay); res: 1 Gracie Terr., N.Y., N.Y. 10028.

FRANZEN, JANICE GOSNELL, Wms. Ed., Christian Life, Gundersen Dr. and Schmale Rd., Wheaton, Ill. 60187, '65–; Dir. of Studies, Christian Wtrs. Inst.; Assoc. Ed., Christian Bookseller; Former Ed., Choice, Christian Writer & Editor; LaCrosse Univ., BS; Northern Baptist Seminary, MRE; h. Ralph Franzen.

FRARY, GRACE L., Edtl. Asst., McKinsey & Company, Inc., 245 Park Ave., N.Y., N.Y. 10017, '70–; Prom. Asst., Metro TV Sales, '66–'69; Syracuse Univ., BA (Jnlsm.), '68 (cum laude; Secy., Commtns. Alumni Society, '65–'68); b. Bklyn., N.Y.; p. Charles C. and Dorothy Diveny Frary.

FRASER, GRACE C., Secy.-Treas., David McKay Company, Inc., 750 Third Ave., N.Y., N.Y. 10017, '50–; formerly Asst. to Treas. and VP, G.P. Putnam's Sons; WNBA; b. New Rochelle, N.Y.; p. Thomas and Lillian Fraser; res: 123 E. 37th St., N.Y., N.Y. 10016.

FRASER, JOAN LEWIS, Ed., Family News, Niagara Falls Gazette, 310 Niagara St., Niagara Falls, N.Y. 14302, '66–; Reptr., Feature Wtr., '64–'66; Ed., Robert Simpson Co., (Toronto, Ont.), '44–'46; Reptr., Port Hope (Ont.) Guide, '43–'44; Globe and Mail, Toronto, '42–'43; ZONTA; Univ. of British Columbia; b. Vancouver, B.C., 1925; p. Burton and Barbara Wolfe Lewis; h. Edward Tryon Fraser; c. Mrs. Glen Meyers, Margo, Hugh H., Bruce T., Jeffrey B.; res: 6600 Grauer Rd., Niagara Falls, N.Y. 14305.

FRASER, VIRGINIA MARIE, Dir., Public Info. Svcs., Ball State University, Muncie, Ind. 47306, '61–; Jnlsm. Instr., Butler Univ. (Indpls.), '60–'61; Mng. Ed., The Indiana Teacher, Indiana State Teachers Assn., '52–'61; Overseas special wtr., Indpls. News, '53, '55; Copy desk, '51–'52; Jnlsm., photog. tchr., Southport HS, '45–'52; Theta Sigma Phi (Indpls. Chptr. VP, '52), Wms. Press Club of Ind. (Pres., '58–'60), NFPW, ACPRA, Ind. Col. PR Assn.; Alumni Distg. Svc. Aw., '61; 15 nat. writing aws.; NFPW, '56–'66; Ball State Univ., BS, '45; grad. work, Univ. of Wis., '48; Ind. Univ., '58–'60; b. Detroit, Mich., 1923; p. James and Faye Clouser Fraser; res: R. R. 9, Box 47, Muncie, Ind. 47302.

FRAZER, WINIFRED DUSENBURY, Assoc. Prof. of Eng., University of Florida, 207 Anderson Hall, Gainesville, Fla. 32601, '65–; Eng. Fac., '55–'65; Auth: "The Theme of Loneliness in Modern American Drama" ('60), "Love as Death in the Iceman Cometh" ('67); Fla. Cncl. of Tchrs. of Eng. (Secy., '60), Zeta Phi Eta; Univ. of Wis., BA, '37; Univ. of Me., MA, '40; Univ. of Minn., '42–'46; Univ. of Fla., PhD, '56; b. Chgo., Ill., 1916; p. Richards and Margaret Johnson Loesch; h. Percy Warner Frazer; c. John Dusenbury, Richard Dusenbury, David Dusenbury; res: 1007 N.W. 14th Ave., Gainesville, Fla. 32601.

FRAZIER, NETA LOHNES, Wtr., bks. for young people, '42–; Ed., Spokane Valley Herald, '28–'42; HS Tchr., Waitsburg, Wash., '12–'14; AAUW (Spokane Br. Pres., '51–'53), Spokane Wtrs. (Pres., '68–'69), Theta Sigma Phi; Jr. Lit. Guild aws: "By-Line Dennie," '47; "My Love is a Gypsy," '52; "Young Bill Fargo," '56; "The Magic Ring," '58; Kappa Kappa Gamma Achiev. Aw., '60; Fort Wright Col. Hist. Aw., '67; State of Wash. Governor's Aw., '68; Whitman Col., Walla Walla, Wash., AB, '12 (Phi Beta Kappa); b. Owosso, Mich.; p. Emory and Jennie Osborn Lohnes: h. Earl C. Frazier; c. Lesley Frazier Thompson, Philip E., Richard B.; res: W. 2340 First Ave., Spokane, Wash. 99204.

FREDE, HELENE SPOONER, AE, Copywtr., Sussman & Sugar, Inc. 24 W. 40 St., N.Y., N.Y. 10018, '62–; Copywtr., Franklin Spier, '61–'62; AE, Copywtr., Irving Berk Co., '51–'56; Pubcty., Adv., Steralon Products, (Chattanooga, Tenn.); Phila., Pa.), '47–'52; Secy.-Treas., Pubcty. Dir., Henry H. Frede & Co. (Chattanooga, Tenn.), '41–'51; Fashion Group, Publrs. Adv. Club; Smith Col.; Columbia Sch. of Jnlsm., B. Lit., '30; b. N.Y.C.; p. Louis and May Joachim Spooner; h. Henry Frede; c. Richard, Karen Frede Nangle; res: 26 E. 93 St., N.Y., N.Y. 10028.

FREDERICK, CHRISTINE, Tchr., Wtr., Orange Coast College, Newport, Cal., '49–; Wms. Ed., Hearst Am. Weekly, 27 yrs.; Ladies' Home Jnl.; Suburban Life; McCall's Magazine; Auth. of bks. on adv., housekeeping; Auth., adv. bklets., many cos.; U.S. Rep. and Lectr. on wms. work in many fgn. cities; AWNY (Founder); Northwestern Univ., '06 (Phi Beta Kappa); Columbia Univ.; Ballard Sch.; b. Boston, Mass., 1883; p. William Rogers Campbell; c. David M., Phyllis F., Jean Joyce; res: 320 Los Olivos at Glenneyre, Laguna Beach, Cal. 92651.

FREDERICK, JANE DOANE, Tech. Wtr., Texaco, Inc., 6400 Southwest Freeway, Houston, Tex. 77036, '67–; Southwestern Indsl. Electronics, '66; NASA Industries, '64–'66; McGraw-Hill Publ. Co., '63–'64; Tex. Instruments Inc., '56–'63; Theta Sigma Phi; Soc. Tech. Wtrs. and Publrs.; Gamma Alpha Chi; Univ. of Houston, BS (Jnlsm.), '63; b. Watertown, N.Y., 1922; p. Earl and Clara Jones Doane; h. (div.); res: 7225 Beechnut Ave., Houston, Tex. 77036.

FREDERICK, PAULINE, NBC News United Nations Corr., National Broadcasting Company, 30 Rockefeller Plaza, N.Y., N.Y. 10020; previously ABC Radio-TV News Corr.; Lectr.; Auth., "Ten First Ladies of the World" (Meredith Press, '67); UN Corrs. Assn. (Pres., '59); currently a mbr. of Wms. Nat. Press Club,

AWRT, Assn. of Radio and Television News Analysts; numerous aws. incl. George Foster Peabody, DuPont, McCall's Golden Mike (twice), Univ. of Mo. Sch. of Jnlsm., Univ. of Southern Cal. Sch. of Jnlsm., East-West Center (Honolulu), First Pa. Achievement Aw. in Jnlsm., Theta Sigma Phi Headliner Aw.; American Univ., AB, AM; 15 honorary doctorate degrees; b. Gallitzin, Pa.; p. Matthew Phillip and Susan Stanley Frederick; h. Charles Robbins.

FREDERICK, THEO JOAN, Pers. Dir., HMH Publishing Company, Inc., Playboy Clubs International, Inc., 919 N. Michigan Ave., Chgo., Ill. 60611, '56–; Radio-TV Ed., Doubleday (N.Y.C.), '52–'56; Edtl. Asst., Park East, '51–'52; Exec. Secy., Michael Saphier Assocs., '50–'51; Am. Mgt. Assn., Am. Soc. for Pers. Adm., Mgt. Soc.; b. N.Y.C., 1925; p. Edwin and Flora Russ Feigenspan; h. A. C. Spectorsky; c. Brooke E., Lance D; res: 900 N. Michigan Ave., Chgo., Ill. 60611.

FREED, LAURA E., Prog. Mgr., Keep America Beautiful, Inc., 99 Park Ave., N.Y., N.Y. 10016, '59–; Asst. Exec. Dir., '54–'59; Assoc. Ed., Public Relations Journal, and Asst. to Exec. VP, PRSA, '49–'53; PR Staff, Nat. Assn. of Ins. Agts., '47–'49; Field Rep., Am. Red Cross, European Theater, '44–'46; PRSA, Trade Assn. Execs. in N.Y.C., League of Wm. Voters; N.Y.U.; b. Goodlettsville, Tenn., 1919; p. Walter and Ella DeBow Freed; res: 211 E. 53rd St., N.Y., N.Y. 10022.

FREED, LINDA WEAVER, Wms. Ed., The Bryan Times, P.O. Box 268, Bryan, Oh. 43506, '68–; Adv. Dept., '66–'68; Miami Univ., '55–'56; b. Bryan, Oh., 1936; p. Robert and Mildred Stevens Weaver; h. Lyle Freed; c. David William, Douglas Hobart; res: Rte. 3, Bryan, Oh. 43506.

FREED, NANCY WURZBURGER, Dir. of PR, Art Center College of Design, 5353 W. Third, L.A., Cal. 90005, '69–; AE, Harshe-Rotman and Druck, '64–'69; Colmst., Brentwood Independent, '63–'64; Free-lance PR, '60–'63; AE, Carl Ruff Assocs., '56–'60; Asst. Prodr., NBC, '50–'51; Owner, Nancy Lee Waring, '48–'50; active in numerous civic groups; AWRT, 2000 Wm. of Achiev., '69; Columbia Univ., '40–'43; b. N.Y.C., 1923; p. Sigfried and Dorothy Kahn Wurzburger; h. Bert Freed; c. Andrew, Carl, Gigi; res: 418 N. Bowling Green Way, L.A., Cal. 90049.

FREEDMAN, BETTY L., Crtv. Dir., Grey Advertising, 777 Third Ave., N.Y., N.Y. 10017, '70–; Copy Group Head, Kenyon & Eckhardt, '69–'70; Copy Supvsr., Foote, Cone & Belding, '67–'69; h. Barson Albert.

FREEDMAN, NANCY MARS, Co-auth. with husband of seven novels incl. "Mrs. Mike" (Coward McCann, '47), "Cyclone of Silence" (Simon and Schuster, '69); articles in numerous mags.; Who's Who of Am. Wm., Who's Who; Benedict and Nancy Freedman Collection established at Boston Univ.; L.A. City Col., U.C.L.A., '37–'40; b. Evanston, Ill., 1920; p.

Dr. Hartley and Brillie Hintermeister Mars; h. Benedict Freedman; c. Johanna, Michael Hartley, Deborah; res: 315 Via de la Paz, Pacific Palisades, Cal. 90272.

FREELAND, MARY MAUDE, Ext. Ed. in Jnlsm., University of Missouri, 19 Walter Williams Hall, Columbia, Mo. 65201, '65–; Ext. Instr., Jnlsm., '57–'65, '48–'54; Ed. Emeritus, Taney County Repl., White River Leader; Ed., Publr.; Jnlsm. Rschr: Schs., nwsps., radio corrs.; Publr., The Listening Post; work with schs. in jnlsm.; Kappa Tau Alpha, Theta Sigma Phi, Mo. Press Wm. (Treas.) '40s), Nat. Assn. for Educ. in Jnlsm., Nat. Edtl. Assn., Mo. Press Assn. (Secy., '34), Ozark Press Assn. (Secy.), Mo. Newswtrs. Assn. (Secy., '48–'54), Repl. Edtl. Assn. (Past Pres.) AAUW, BPW, Fortnightly; Univ. of Mo., BS (Educ.), '30; AM (Jnlsm.), '65; b. Wichita, Kan., 1908; p. William E. and Minnie Freeland Freeland; res: 1215 Frances Dr., Columbia, Mo. 65201.

FREEMAN, ANNE HUETHER, Free-lance Artist; Auth: "Glass and Man" (J.B. Lippincott Co., '63); Asst. to Mgr., Cmmtns. and Employee Rels., Crouse-Hinds Co., Syracuse, N.Y., '64–'65; Curator of Educ., Corning Museum of Glass, '61–'63; Coordr. Ed. Svcs., '59–'61; Rsch. Asst., '57–'59; Wtr., articles on glassmaking, mags., '59–'63; Art Tchr., '59–'63; PR, Corning Museum, '59–'61; Am. Assn. of Museums, '59–'63; "Auth. of the Yr.," Ind. Univ., '63; John Herron Art Sch., '54–'57; Elmira Col., BA, '64; b. Milw., Wis., 1936; p. Edward and Agatha Mihm Huether; h. John Freeman; c. Robert, John; res: 8 Ilex Lane, Liverpool, N.Y. 13088.

FREEMAN, CARMENA MITCHELL, Free-lance Wtr., '68–; Ed.-in-Chief, Front Page Detective, Inside Detective, Dell Pubns., '48–'68; Ed.-in-Chief, Buse Pubns., '45–'47; Assoc. Ed., Fawcett Pubns., '42–'44; Ed., Pontaic (Mich.) News, '40–'42; Lectr., Jnlsm., Univ. of Mich.; Theta Sigma Phi; Univ. of Mich., BA (Jnlsm.), '39; b. Goshen, Ind., 1914; p. Dr. Floyd and Elizabeth Miller Freeman; res: 236 Nevada City, Cal. 95959.

FREEMAN, DORIS BRANCH, ("Cousin Tuny") Radio AE, TV Bdcstr., WDXI, Williams Bldg., Jackson, Tenn. 38301, '55–; Free-lance Bdcstr., PR, '50–'55; Bdcstr., Program Secy., Music Librn., WDXI, '47–'50; Prom. Dir., Old Hickory Mall, '67–; BPW, AWRT (Golden Mike Aw., '67), West. Tenn. Heart Assn. (Secy.-Treas.), '60); Hon. Dr. of Aerospaceology, USAF Systems Command, '67; b. Jackson, Tenn., 1925; p. Felix and Mattie Weakes Branch; h. (div.); c. Mrs. Patricia Freeman Little; Cynthia, James, Constance; res: 218 Fairmont, Jackson, Tenn. 38301.

FREEMAN, ELSA, Dir., Lib., U.S. Department of Housing and Urban Development, 451 7th St. S.W., Wash., D.C. 20410, '66–; Head Librn., Housing & Home Fin. Agcy., '56–'66; Head Librn., Off. of Geog., Dept. of Interior, '51–'56; Asst. Librn., Bur. of Ordnance, Dept. of the Navy, '49–'51; Jr. Librn.-Asst. Chief, Circ. Sec., Dept. Agriculture, '42–'44; Ref., Sch. Asst., N.Y. Public Lib., '41–'42; Contrbr., pfsnl. jnls.; ALA, Special Libs. Assn. (Wash. Chptr. Pres., '54–'55) D.C. Lib. Assn.; Beta Phi Mu; Who's Who of Am. Wm., Dic. of Intl. Biog.; Columbia Univ., BA, '39 (cum laude, Phi Beta Kappa); BS, '40 (cum laude); h. Stuart Irvington Freeman; res: 3519 Fort Hill Dr., Wilton Woods, Alexandria, Va. 22310.

FREEMAN, GRACE BEACHAM, Ed., Winthrop College Alumnae Magazine, '62–; Ed., Converse Alumnae Mag., '64–'68; Wtr., educ. materials, scripts; numerous articles, plays for children; Colmst., King Features, '54–'64; Auth: "Children Are Poetry" (Tulane Univ. Press, '51); AAUW, Charlotte Wtrs. Club (Numerous aws.), Who's Who of Am. Wm.; Converse Col., AB, '37; b. Spartanburg, S.C., 1916; p. Henry and Grace Bailey Beacham; h. John Freeman; c. John Jr., Katharine (Mrs. D. Parker), Henry B., David B.; res: Box 5097, W.C. Station, Rock Hill, S.C. 29730.

FREEMAN, LUCY, Free-lance Wtr., 28 bks., most about psychoanalysis; mag. articles; Reprtr., N.Y. Times, '41–'53; PEN, Nat. Assn. of Sci. Wtrs., MWA, Soc. of Magazine Wtrs.; N.Y. NWC aw., '49; Theta Sigma Phi, N.Y. Chptr. aw., '50; Bennington Col., BA, '38; b. N.Y.C., 1916; p. Lawrence S. and Sylvia Sobel Greenbaum; h. (div.); res: 120 Central Park S., N.Y., N.Y. 10019.

FREEMAN, MARGARET NADGWICK, Free-lance Wtr., Auth: "Thank You, God" "Twelve Devotionals for Women's Meetings"; b. Essex. Ia., 1915; p. Joseph and Vilma Hart Nadgwick; h. Stanley Freeman; c. Dennis, Douglas; res: 1203 S. Maple St., Shenandoah, Ia. 51601.

FREEMAN, RUTH SUNDERLIN, Pres., Century House, Inc., Old Irelandville, P.O. Watkins Glen, N.Y. 14891, '69–; Auth: "Children's Picture Books Yesterday & Today" ('67); D.A.B.A. Aw., '67), "How to Repair & Dress Old Dolls" ('60), "Ency. of American Dolls" ('52), other bks.; Educ. Dir., Yorker Yankee Village Preservation, '60–'68; Co-founder, Century House Americana Publ. Co., '42; Arethusa (State Treas., '27; VP, '27 '28), Yale and Northwestern Univ. Fac. Club, ZONTA (Watkins Glen-Montour Falls, N.Y., Pres., Bd. of Dirs.); Cortland State Tchrs. Col., '29; Columbia Univ.; Tchrs. Col., Chgo. Univ., '31–'34; b. Penn Yan, N.Y., 1907; p. George Lazear and Edith May Crosby Sunderlin; h. Dr. G. L. Freeman; c. James Lazear, John Crosby, Peter Sunderlin; res: Old Irelandville, P.O. Watkins Glen, N.Y. 14891.

FREESE, WINIFRED ANDERSON, Asst. Ed., Huntington Library Quarterly, Henry E. Huntington Library and Art Gallery, 1151 Oxford Rd., San Marino, Cal. 91108, '62–; Edtl. Asst., '61–'62; Scripps Col., BA, '34; Radcliffe Col., MA, '35; b. San Diego, Cal., 1913; p. Arthur and Alice Cattle Anderson; h. Ernest

Freese; c. William Arthur; res: 6247 Pine Crest Dr., L.A., Cal. 90042.

FREIBURGER, ROSEMARY McDANIEL, Ed., Photogr., Waupaca County Post, 717 10th St., Waupaca, Wis. 54981, '66–; Circ. Mgr., Appleton (Wis.) Post Crescent; Wtr., news off.; Corr.; "Lioness of the Yr.", Lions Club, '67; "Hon. Chptr. Farmer," Future Farmers of Am., Waupaca HS Chptr., '69; Cert. of Appreciation, Jaycettes, '69; b. New London, Wis., 1922; p. Henry and Nia Schneider McDaniel; h. Maurice Freiburger; c. Laurie Lee, Julie Ann; res: Route 1, Waupaca, Wis. 54981.

FRENCH, DOROTHY KAYSER, Free-lance Wtr.; Auth: "The Mystery of the Old Oil Well" ('63), "Swim to Victory" ('69); stories, articles, in Teen mag., Jack and Jill, Oklahoma Today, others; Theta Sigma Phi; Bartlesville Intl. Club; Univ. of Wis., BA (Jnlsm.), '48 (Mortar Bd.); b. Milw., Wis., 1926; p. Paul and Gertrude Ament Kaysar; h. Louis N. French; c. Nancy, Laura; res: 2136 Starlight Ct., Bartlesville, Okla. 74003.

FRENCH, MARION FLOOD, Edtl. Asst., Bangor Publ. Co., 491 Main St., Bangor, Me. 04401, '65–; Auth., children's bks.; articles, various mags., religious educ., bus., sch. pubns.; Me. Wtrs. of Fiction for Juvs.; Jr. Book of Auths.; Bangor Theological Seminary.

FRENZ, FAITH, Gen. Prog. Exec., Columbia Broadcasting System Television Network, 51 W. 52nd St., N.Y., N.Y. 10019; Prod. Asst., Cartoon Coordr.; Queens Col.

FRESCHET, BERNIECE SPECK, Auth., children's bks: "The Owl and the Prairie Dog" (Scribners, '69), "The Old Bullfrog" (Scribners, '68), "The Little Woodcock" (Scribners, '67), other bks.; Burlingame's Wtrs. Club, Sierra Club; Mont. State Univ., '46–'48; b. Miles City, Mont., 1927; p. Paul and Rose Zeigle Speck; h. Ferruccio Freschet; c. Leslie Ann, Gina Marie, Dinah Sue, Maria Teresa, Frankie Paul; res: 2228 Cobblehill Pl., San Mateo, Cal. 94402.

FRESE, ANNE HORVATH, Head Librn., Niles Public Library, 620 E. Main St., Niles, Mich. 49120, '66–; Librn., '58–'66; U.S. Steel Corp., '40–'47; Mich. Lib. Assn., Public Lib. Div. (Secy., '69–'70), Mich. Lib. Film Circuit '69–'70; Berrien Coop. Lib. Assn. (Secy., '68–'69); ALA; Western Mich. Univ. (Lib. Sci.); Univ. of Budapest; b. Chgo, Ill., 1921; p. F. L. and J. Talaber Horvath; h. Henry C. Frese; c. Annemarie (Mrs. T. Pierce), Henry; res: 3105 Creek Rd., Niles, Mich. 49120.

FREUDEMANN, TONI DeCESARE, Wtr., Publicist, Wms. News Dept., Carl Byoir & Associates, Inc., 800 Second Ave., N.Y., N.Y. 10017, '63–; formerly Pubcty. Agt. for husband portrait artist; NHFL; educ: ballet acads.; Univ. of Southern Cal. (Eng. Literature); b.

N.Y.C.; p. John and Alice DeCesare; h. (dec.); res: 300 E. 40th St., N.Y., N.Y. 10016.

FREY, HELEN LeBLOND, PR, Ind. School District 274, 1001 Highway 7, Hopkins, Minn. 55343, '65–; Edtl. Asst., Lakewood Publications, 731 Hennepin, Mpls., Minn., '68–; Ed., Wtr., Finney Co., '61–'64; Theta Sigma Phi; Univ. of Minn., '38–'41; Sch. of Jnlsm., BA (Adv.), '64; b. Butte, Mont., 1921; p. Charles and Rachel Hill LeBlond; h. Robert Frey; c. Robert, Jr., Barbara, Constance; res: 5517 Doncaster Way, Edina, Minn. 55436.

FREYMAN, EVELYN GALL, Exec. Secy., American Federation of Television and Radio Artists, Washington-Baltimore Local, 4706 Wisconsin Ave., N.W., Wash., D.C. 20016, '54–; Pres., '46–'54; AFTRA Nat. VP, seven terms; Radio, TV Performer, '34–'63; Prodr., Owner, Olney Theatre, nine-yrs.; AWRT, NATAS (Trustee), Am. Guild of Musical Artists (Rep., '63–); AFTRA, highest hon., '69; civic, philanthropic, ch. work; Univ. of Ky., AB, '33; b. Lexington, Ky., 1912; p. Phillip and Rose Scher Gall; h. Myer Freyman; c. David, Jeffrey; res: 2500 Virginia Ave. N.W., Wash., D.C. 20037.

FRIEBUS, FLORIDA, Actress, "Peyton Place," 20th Century Fox, 10201 Pico Blvd., L.A., Cal. 90064; Creator, Wtr., Star, "Look and Listen," KNXT, '60–'62; "Let's Listen to a Story," WMCA, '47–'57; Broadway Theatre Personality for 30 yrs.; Radio, 25 yrs.; TV, "Dobie Gillis," '59–'63; TV roles, 17 yrs.; Co-adaptor, "Alice in Wonderland," prod. on Broadway, and by Hallmark, NBC, '55; AEA (Cnslr., '49–'65), AFTRA (Bd. Mbr.); John Golden Aw., "Why the United States Needs the United Nations," '54; NATAS nomination for Emmy Aw., '61; Pine Manor Music Sch., '25–'26; Theatre Guild Sch., '26–'27; b. Auburndale, Mass., 1909; p. Theodore and Beatrice Mosier Friebus; res: 7711-1/2 Lexington Ave., L.A., Cal. 90046.

FRIEDAN, BETTY, Auth., "The Feminine Mystique" (W. W. Norton and Co., '63; excerpted by Ladies Home Journal and McCall's); articles on psych., sociol., educ. for Harper's, Good Housekeeping, Redbook, Parents Magazine, Mademoiselle, McCall's, Reader's Digest, other leading nat. mags.; Lectr. on status and problems of wm.; Founder and former Pres., NOW; five yrs. of rsch. for "The Feminine Mystique," including interviews with doctors, psychoanalysts, marriage cnslrs., child guidance authorities, motivational rschrs., (in depth) 80 wm. throughout U.S.; student of Gestalt psychologist Kurt Koffka; assisted in early experiments in group dynamics at Univ. of Ia. under direction of Kurt Lewin; Smith Col., BA, '42 (summa cum laude); Rsch. Fellowship, Univ. of Cal., Berkeley; b. Peoria, Ill., 1921; p. Harry and Miriam Goldstein; h. Carl Friedan (div.); c. Daniel, Jonathan, Emily; res: N.Y., N.Y.

FRIEDEL, MARILYN L., Commtns. Cnslt., Marilyn L. Friedel & Associates, 162 E. Superior St., Chgo., Ill. 60611, '63–; Exec. Dir., Un. Commtns. Corp., '66–'68; Nat. Dir., PR, Sls. Prom., Un. Film & Rec. Studios, '54–'66; Nat. Dir., Sls., Svc., Universal Studios. '51–'54; Exec. VP, Jack London Prods., '50–'51; Asst. Mgr., Un. Bdcst. Co., '47–'51; Exec. Sls. Div., World Bdcst. System, '46–'47; Cnslt., Nat. Assn. of Real Estate Bds.; AFTRA, Chgo., Unlimited, ACTAS, Film Cncl.; active in civic, charitable orgs.; b. Cohoes, N.Y., 1926; p. Robert and Norma Gordon Friedle; h. William Klein; c. Leopold, Julius, Regina; res: 451 Barry Ave., Chgo., Ill. 60657.

FRIEDERICHS, MARION ACKROYD, Family Living Ed., Port Huron Times Herald, 915 Sixth St., Port Huron, Mich. 48060, '68–; Copy Dir., WPHM; ZONTA, Lioness Club; Marygrove Col., BA (Eng.), '47; b. Detroit, Mich., 1925; p. Charles and Marie Small Ackroyd; h. Donald C. Friederichs; res: 515 Brown St., St. Clair, Mich. 48079.

FRIEDERICHSEN, KATHLEEN HOCKMAN, Religious Wtr., Missionary, Association of Baptists for World Evangelism, Phila., Pa.; Missionary in Philippines, '39–'56; Auth: "God's Word Made Plain" ('59), "God's Will Made Clear" ('62), "God's Truth Made Simple" ('65), "God's Way Made Easy" ('69); b. Szechwen, China, 1910; p. Rev. William and Katie Rogers Hockman; h. Paul Friederichsen; c. Douglas, Robert; res: 1114 N. President St., Wheaton, Ill. 60187.

FRIEDMAN, ESTELLE EHRENWALD, Auth., G. P. Putnam's Sons, Madison Ave., N.Y., N.Y. 10010; bks: "Ben Franklin" ('61), "Boy Who Lived in a Cave" ('60), "Digging into Yesterday" ('58; Cadmus Edition, '64), "Man in the Making" ('60); Tchr., Remedial Reading, disadvantaged children; Wms. Nat. Bk. Assn. (Bd. Mbr.); Jr. Bk. Aw., Boys Clubs of Am., '59; Vanderbilt Univ., BA (Mortar Bd., Phi Beta Kappa); b. Nashville, Tenn., 1920; p. Alfred and Marie Weil Ehrenwald; h. Jack E. Friedman; c. Mrs. Michael Hall, Katherine; res: 4633 Tara Dr., Nashville, Tenn. 37215.

FRIEDMAN, GERRY GEWIRTZ, Fashion, China, Glass Ed., Chilton Publications, 100 E. 42nd St., N.Y., N.Y. 10017, '56–; Ed., Jewelry; Exec. Ed., Package Store Management; Fashion Group, NHFL, Vassar Col., '41; b. N.Y.C., 1920; p. Max and Min Weiss Gewirtz; h. Dr. Eugene Friedman; c. John Henry, Robert James; res: 55 E. 86th St., N.Y., N.Y. 10028.

FRIEDMAN, LILLIAN, VP, Brentano's, Inc., 586 Fifth Ave., N.Y., N.Y. 10036, '60–; Book Byr., '50–'60; Book Byr., Stix, Baer & Fuller Dept. Store (St. Louis, Mo.), '40–'50; Co-Ed: "Europe Looks at the Civil War;" weekly prog., "The World in Books," WEVD Radio; b. St. Louis, Mo. 1909; p. Jacob and Rose Zalman Friedman; c. Toby (Mrs. R. Sanchez); res: 86 W. 12th St., N.Y., N.Y. 10014.

FRIEDMAN, MARCIA MANSON, Dir. of PR, The Griswold-Eshleman Company, 625 Madison Ave.,

N.Y., N.Y. 10022; Dir. of PR, Recht & Company, Inc., '68–'70; AE, '65–'70; Copy Chief, Spencer/Benveniste Adv.; Copywtr., Curtis Adv.; Jr. Copywtr., Biow Adv.; Wtr.-Prod. of TV and radio commls.; conducts audio visual studies for industry; Hollywood Radio and TV Soc., Am. Adv. Assn. of the West (Cert. of Merit, '63), Adv. Wtrs. of L.A. (Secy., '64), L.A. Adv. Wm. ('58–'59); Hunter Col., BA, '48 (Dean's List); b. N.Y.C., 1927; p. S. E. and Rose Farber Manson; h. Irving Friedman; res: 225 E. 47th St., N.Y., N.Y. 10022.

FRIEDRICH, DORA THOMPSON, Colmst., Wms. Ed., Concord Daily Transcript, 1741 Clayton Rd., Concord, Cal. 94520, '55–; Colmst., Weekly Transcript, '49; Contra Costa Times, Walnut Creek Suns, '50–'53; Assoc. Ed., Pleasant Hill News, '54; Fashion Show Coordr., Commentator; various orgs.; Diablo Valley Col.; b. Afton, Wyo., 1917; h. Reuben Friedrich; c. Louis L. Christensen, Jr., Robert J. Christensen, Patricia Lynn (Mrs. Gary Foster), DiaAne (Mrs. Daniel T. Juarez III), Margo Del (Mrs. Craig Schirato); res: 1040 Pleasant Valley Dr., Pleasant Hill, Cal. 94523.

FRIEL, CHARLOTTE, Mgr., Rsch. and Adm., Corporate Affairs, Columbia Broadcasting System, Inc., 51 W. 52nd St., N.Y., N.Y. 10019, '66–; Adm. Asst. to the VP, Corporate Info., '58–'66; Mgr., Audience Mail, '56–'58; Rschr., '55–'56; Secy., '54–'55; Dir., Dept. of Bdcst. and Drama, Olympia (Wash.) HS, '51–'54; Theta Sigma Phi (N.Y.C. Chptr. Pres., '62–'64), AWRT, NATAS, IRTS; Wash. State Univ., BA, '51; (Mortar Bd., Phi Kappa Phi, Pi Lambda Theta, Pi Kappa Delta); Columbia Univ., MA, '60; N.Y.U., PhD, '68; b. Colfax, Wash., 1929; p. John B. and Catherine Mathews Friel; res: 15 Sheridan Square, N.Y., N.Y. 10014.

FRIERMOOD, ELISABETH HAMILTON, Wtr., Doubleday & Company, 277 Park Ave., N.Y., N.Y. 10017; Bks. incl: "Head High, Ellen Brody" ('58; Ind. Univ. Wtrs. Conf. aw. as most distg. bk. in juv. fiction by an Ind. auth., '59), "Focus the Bright Land" ('67; The Ohioana Bk. Aw., best juv. fiction by an Ohioan, '68), "Peppers' Paradise" ('69), numerous bks.; Children's Librn. (Marion, Ind.; Dayton, Oh.), '25–'42; ALA; Northwestern Univ., '23–'25; Univ. of Wis. summer schs., '34–'39; b. Marion, Ind., 1903; p. Burr and Etta Hale Hamilton; h. Harold T. Friermood; c. Mrs. Herbert H. Franck; res: 51 Clifford Ave., Pelham, N.Y. 10803.

FRIES, MYRA LANGE, Comptroller, The New Yorker, 25 W. 43rd St., N.Y., N.Y. 10036, '51–; Secy., '46–; b. N.Y.C., 1909; p. Alfred and Mary Hruza Lange; h. Ralph Fries; c. Donald Arthur and Ronald Andrew; res: 5 Foxboro Lane, Old Brookville, N.Y. 11545.

FRISBIE, REGINA GABRIEL, Dir. of Dept. of Home Econs. Svcs., Kellogg Company, 235 Porter St., Battle Creek, Mich. 49016, '49–; Asst. Dir., '42–'48; Staff Home Econst., '35–'37; Wtr., bks., articles, on educ., home econs; Am. Dietetic Assn., AWRT, active in dietetic, home ec. orgs.; Omicron Nu; Mich. State

Univ., BS (Foods, Nutrition), '35; b. Battle Creek, Mich., 1911; p. Edward and Catherine Martin Gabriel; h. Walter Rees Frisbie; c. Walter, Jr., Elizabeth (Mrs. Donald R. Disbrow), Alice (Mrs. William Hill Wright); res: 53 Garrison, Battle Creek, Mich. 49017.

FRISKEY, MARGARET RICHARDS, Ed.-in-Chief, Childrens Press, 1224 W. Van Buren St., Chgo., Ill. 60607, '45–; Auth., 35 children's bks.; Arts Club of Chgo.; Northwestern Univ., BA, '22 (Alumni Assn. Merit Aw., '56); res: 1708 Harrison St., Evanston, Ill. 60201.

FRITZ, JEAN GUTTERY, Auth., numerous children's bks., mag. fiction; Dir., Jean Fritz Writing Workshop (Katonah, N.Y.), '60–'69; Free-lance Bk. Reviewer, New York Times, Chicago Tribune, '64–'69; Children's Librn., Dobbs Ferry Lib., '53–'56; Rschr., Silver Burdett Co., '37–'41; Authors Guild; Wheaton Col., AB, '37; Columbia Univ. Tchrs. Col., '40–'41; b. Hankow, China, 1915; p. Arthur and Myrtle Chaney Guttery; h. Michael Fritz; c. David Minton, Andrea Scott; res: 50 Bellewood Ave., Dobbs Ferry, N.Y. 10522.

FROOKS, DOROTHY, Lawyer, Publr., The Murray Hill News, 237 Madison Ave., N.Y., N.Y. 10016, '50–; Lawyer, '21–; Auth: "All In Love," "The Olympic Torch" ('46), "Wills and Estates" ('29), other pubns.; Colmst., N.Y. World, '27–'33; Judge Advocate's off., U.S. Army, WWII (commn. Lt. Col., '41); Chief Yeoman, in charge wm. enrollments, 3rd Naval Dist. recruiting, U.S. Navy, WWI (highest off. held by wm.; medal, patriotic svc., Woodrow Wilson); First Wm. Atty., Salvation Army, '20–'21; created Poor Man's Court (now Small Claims Court), '21; Owner, Ed., Public Svc. Record (N.Y.C.), '20–'21; Publr., Oyster Bay News weekly, '16–'19; Dir., Round the World Corp., House of Ideas Publ. Co.; Wm. Lawyers (organized; First Pres., '21), Wm. World War Veterans (Nat. Commander, '20, '50, '60), Wm. Veterans Am. Legion (Pitt., Pa., Commander, '46), Veterans of WWI of U.S.A., Inc., (Nat. Judge Advocate), Westchester County Bar, N.Y. State Bar, Inter-Am. Bar, American Bar Assn., Iota Tau Tau, Epsilon Eta Phi; Hamilton Col., LL.B., '18; LL.M., '19; Nat. Inst. Psych., '46; N.Y.U., PhD, Lulane Univ., Univ. of N.C.; Admitted to U.S. Supreme Court, N.Y., Cal., Alaska, Puerto Rico; b. Ulster County, N.Y., 1899; p. Reginald L. and Rosita Siberez Frooks; res: 237 Madison Ave., N.Y., N.Y. 10016; and Lake Mohegan, N.Y.

FROST, ALICE, Actress, c/o William Barnes, 23 S. Beverly Dr., Beverly Hills, Cal. 90212, '33–; Broadway: "The Bad Seed," "Roomful of Roses," Orson Welles Mercury Theatre; TV: "Mama," "Farmer's Daughter," other motion pics.; radio: "Mr. and Mrs. North"; AFTRA (Bd. Mbr., '53–'58), Am. Nat. Theatre and Acad. (West Coast Bd. of Dirs.), SAG, AEA, NATAS, Pacific Pioneer Bdcstrs.; b. Mpls., Minn.; p. John and Hilma Lager Frost; h. Willson Tuttle (dec.).

FRUECHTENIGHT, BARBARA GOETTE, Wms. Ed.,

Journal Gazette, 600 W. Main St., Ft. Wayne, Ind. 46802, '66–; Mental Health Assn. (Bd. of Dirs.), American Cancer Soc. (Bd. of Dirs.), Press Club; Degs. in Math, Nursing, MS (psyc.); b. Ft. Wayne, Ind., 1926; p. Fred and Beulah Baker Goette; c. Kip, Carla Marie, Brent; res: 2136 Springfield Ave., Ft. Wayne, Ind., 46805.

FRUITS, BETTIE ANN STICKLER, Feature Wtr., The Indianapolis News, 307 N. Pennsylvania, Indpls., Ind. 46206, '66–; Edtl. Wtr., The N. Side Topics, '65; Photogr., Indpls. Weekly, '64; psychiatric rsch., Larue Carter Hosp., '62–'64; psychiatric rsch., Camarillo State Hosp. (Cal.), '59–'62; Theta Sigma Phi, Ind. Press Wm.; numerous writing aws.; Ind. Univ., '57–'59; b. Bainbridge, Ind., 1936; p. Earl M. and Ruthanna Doherty Keesee Stickler; h. (div.); c. Catherine Ann, Laura Elise, Tad W.; res: 4232 Rue Biscay, 2B, Indpls., Ind. 46226.

FRUMKIN, EVALYN, TV Prodr., Grey Advertising, 777 Third Ave., N.Y., N.Y. 10017, '67–; Film Prodr., Mercurio Films, Savage Friedman, Elektra Films, '65–'67; Dirs. Guild of Am.; Bklyn. Col., BA, '61; b. Bklyn., N.Y.; p. Henry and Dorothy Handelman Frumkin; res: 2 Beekman Place, N.Y., N.Y. 10022.

FRUTH, ZENITH FUNK, Soc. Ed., Review Times, 113 E. Center, Fostoria, Oh. 44830, '68–; owned bus., mew talent; Colmst.; photog.; BPW, OES, Am. Cancer Soc. (Bd.), active in civic groups; Tiffin Univ., '25; b. McCutchenville, Oh., 1906; p. Oliver M. and Mercy Cypher Funk; h. Roscoe Fruth; res: 1134 W. Tiffin St., Fostoria, Oh. 44830.

FRY, HELEN GEIB, Nwsp. Reprtr., Feature Wtr., Religion Ed., The Medina County Gazette, Medina, Oh. 44256, '64–; Corr., Cleveland Plain Dealer, '52, '69–; Tchr., Eng., Norton HS (Oh.), '62–'64; Club Reprtr., Akron Beacon Journal, '47–'52; PR Dir., Summit County Chptr. Am. Red Cross, '50–'52; Rep., UPI, '50–'52; Ed., Summit County Dem., '45–'50; Oh. Nwsp. Wms. Assn. (Exec. Secy., '52–'68); Nat. Assn. of Press Wm., writing aws. for news, features, drama revs., headlines, layout; Univ. of Akron, BA; b. Akron, Oh.; p. Edward and Nellie Burgess Geib; h. John Alfred; res: 8150 River Styx Rd., R.D. 2, Wadsworth, Oh. 44281.

FUHRMAN, LAUREL KISSINGER, Wms. Prog. Dir., C and H Broadcasting Co., 201 S. Fifth St., Cherokee, Ia. 51012, '60–; Wtrs. Workshop Prog. Chmn., '69; contrbr. of articles to farm pubns.; Wtrs. Club (VP, '69), BPW (Ed., Monthly Nwsp., '65, '66, '68, '69); Cherokee County Homemaker of the Yr. Aw., '57; b. Washta, Ia., 1914; p. Wallace and Hazel Strickling Kissinger; h. Walter Fuhrman; c. Douglas, Daniel, Keith; res: 310 S. Tenth St., Cherokee, Ia. 51012.

FUJARSKI, SONYA WILDPRETT, Ed., Federal Reserve Bank of New York, 33 Liberty St., N.Y., N.Y. 10045, '66–; Ed., Manufacturers Hanover Trust Co.,

'60–'63; Theta Sigma Phi, ICIE, AAIE; Printing Industries of Met. N.Y. cert., '67; Univ. of Mich., BA, '60; Cert., Jnlsm., '60; b. N.Y.C., 1938; p. Alwin and Martha Mettler Wildprett; c. Jennifer Anne Janssen; res: 84-42 151 St., Jamaica, N.Y. 11432.

FULCHER, NORMA JEANNE, Acc. Supvsr., Carson/Roberts, Inc., 8322 Beverly Blvd., L.A., Cal. 90048, '66–; AE, '59–'66; Copy Chief, Crtv. Dir., Jantzen, Inc., '57–'59; Adv. Mgr., Neiman-Marcus, '55–'57; Copy Chief, '49–'55; The Fashion Group (Portland Chptr. Secy., '59; Dallas Chptr. Treas., '56), Theta Sigma Phi; 16 LULU, Merit Aws. for LAAW, '61–'68; AAW Aw., '66; various others; Texas Wms., BA (Jnlsm.) (hon. list), Univ. of Cal., L.A. Ext.; b. Newport, Tex.; p. R. B. and Ruth Scott Fulcher; res: 958 Hilgard Ave., L.A., Cal. 90024.

FULKERSON, BETTY FULK, Wms. Ed., Arkansas Gazette, Third and Louisiana, Little Rock, Ark. 72201, '52–; Mgr., Club Travel Agcy.; Contrb. Ed., The Delta Review (Memphis, Tenn.); Cal. Fashion Creators (Eds. Bd.); Fur Fashion Excellence Aw., The Fur Cncl. of the Nat. Retail Merchants Assn. and Emba Mink Breeders Assn.; Pulaksi County Health and Welfare Bd. (Family Life Div., Bd.), others; Little Rock Jr. Col., '35; Vassar Col., AB, '38; b. Little Rock, Ark., 1916; p. Augustus Marion and Elizabeth Keane Fulk; h. Baucum Fulkerson; c. Catherine Embry (Mrs. Joseph Young Smreker), Josephine Bond (dec.); res: #1 Beverly Pl., Little Rock, Ark. 72207.

FULLER, CHRISTA LANG, Actress; plays, TV show on poet Heinrich Heine in Paris, two films with Chabrol, one with Godard (appearing in Alphaville), mot. pic. in Rome; Realschule (Essen, Germany), Alliance Francaise diplomas; Univ. of Nancy, '62; Theater Sch. in Paris; b. Winterberg, Germany, 1943; p. Herman and Edith Langewiesche; h. Samuel Fuller; res: L.A., Cal.

FULLER, IOLA, Auth: "All the Golden Gifts" ('67), "The Gilded Torch" ('57), "The Shining Trail" ('43), "The Loon Feather ('40); Assoc. Prof. of Lib. Sci., Clarion State Col., '69–; Assoc. Prof. of Eng., Ferris State Col.; Avery Hopwood Aw. for Crtv. Writing, '39; Univ. of Mich., AB, '35 (Phi Beta Kappa); Am. (Eng.), '40; AM (Lib. Sci.), '62 (Alumni Aw., '67); b. Marcellus, Mich.; p. Henry and Clara Reynolds Fuller; h. Raymond McCoy (dec.); c. Paul Goodspeed; res: 163 Westwood Dr., Applewood Valley, Clarion, Pa. 16214.

FULLER, MARY STIEHM, Ed., Clark Publishing Co., 500 Hyacinth Pl., Highland Park, Ill 60035, '56–; Exec. Ed., '54–'56; Asst. Ed. FATE Magazine, '52–'54; Freelance Wtr; Ill. Soc. for Psychic Rsch. (Pres., '66–'68; Bd. Mbr., '68–), Theta Sigma Phi; Univ. of Wisc., BA, '38 (cum laude); b. Lincoln, Neb., 1914; p. Ewald and Marie Douglass Stiehm; h. Curtis Fuller; c. Michael Curtis, Mrs. Nancy Abraham; res: 301 S. Ridge Rd., Lake Forest, Ill. 60045.

FULLERTON, GAY, Pres., Computer Field Express, Inc., 1790 Broadway, N.Y., N.Y. 10019, '68–; Founder, Pres., Chief Exec., Data Decisions Corp., '63–'67; Dir., Mkt. Rsch., Computech, Inc.; J. Walter Thompson; McCann-Erickson; AWNY, ART, Am. Mktng. Assn.; Bryn Mawr Col.; George Washington Univ., MA (Social Psych.); Columbia Univ. (Psych.); b. N.Y.C., 1930; p. Bradford and Dorothy Gay Fullerton; res: 15 W. 72nd St., N.Y., N.Y. 10023.

FULLING, KAY PAINTER, PR Dir., Welcome Aboard Travel Center, 425 N. Frederick St., Gaithersburg, Md. 20760, '67–; Lectr., Mag. Corr., '53–'56; Tchr., '53–'55; Auth: "Jottings Round the World" ('62), "Mantilles and Silver Spurs" ('52); AAUW, NLAPW, BPW, League of Wm. Voters, WPA, Wash. Drama Soc.; Northwestern Univ., BA, '45; Columbia Univ., MA, '47; b. Dodge City, Kan.; p. William and Carrie Lopp Painter; h. Virgil Fulling; res: S-515, Capitol Park, 800 Fourth St., S.W., Wash., D.C. 20024.

FULTZ, MARIANNE L. M., VP, Media Dir., Reach McClinton & Co., Inc., 3 Center Plaza, Boston, Mass. 02108, '66–; Media Dir., '59–'66; Media Buyer, Humphrey Alley & Richards, '53–'59; New England Media Evaluators, Broadcasting Execs. Club; Katharine Gibbs '49–'51; Boston Univ., '52–'53; h. L. C. Kenneth Howard Fultz, USAF (Ret).

FUNDIS, DONA L., Dir., Home Service Institute, Calgon Corp., Box 1346, Pitt., Pa. 15230, '64–; Acting Dir., '62–'64; Eastern Reg. Home Econst., '60–'62; Am. Home Econs. Assn., Home Econs. in Bus. (Pitt. Chptr. Chmn., '66–'67), Grocery Manufacturers Assoc., Soap and Detergent Assoc., Am. Home Appliance Manufacturers, AWRT, Pa. Home Econs. Assn., Electrical Wms. Round Table; Kent State Univ., BS, '60; b. Pitt., Pa., 1938; p. Donald and Ruth Knode Fundis; res: 326 Emerson St., Pitt., Pa. 15206.

FUNK, ELINOR McCLURE, Pres., Santa Monica Evening Outlook, 1540 Third St., Santa Monica, Cal. 90406, '62–; Smith Col.; b. Columbus, Oh.; p. Samuel and Louise Truesdell McClure; h. Jacob D. Funk; c. Deane, Ron, Mrs. C.J. Urstadt; res: 833 San Vicente Blvd., Santa Monica, Cal. 90402.

FUNSTON, ELIZABETH THOMPSON, Bus. Mgr., Arabian Horse News, P.O. Box 1009, Boulder, Colo. 80302, '59–; Wells Col., BA, '39 (cum laude, Phi Beta Kappa); h. Thomas Young Funston; res: 3365 Fourth St., Boulder, Colo. 80302.

FURLOW, BARBARA BLAIR, White House Corr., U.S. News & World Report, 2300 N. St. N.W., Wash., D.C. 20037, '65–; Feature Wtr., '54–'64; Chief Caption Wtr., Ed. Asst., Rschr. '54–'64; WNPC, WHCA; Middlebury Col., BA, '45; b. Balt., Md., 1924; p. Bryce and Marian Davenport Blair; h. Walter S. Furlow, Jr.; res: 7925 Orchid St., N.W., Wash., D.C. 20012.

FURNESS, BETTY, Lectr.; Colmst., McCall's, c/o W. Colston Leigh, Inc., 521 Fifth Ave., N.Y., N.Y. 10017. Special Asst. for Consumer Affairs to President Lyndon B. Johnson, '67–'69; Prom., VISTA, Head Start progs., '64–'67; CBS-Radio, Dimension '60–'67; Commls., Westinghouse, '49–'60; Actress (Hollywood, Cal.), six yrs.; Films: "Swing Time," "The Magnificient Obsession," others; NATAS (Past Pres.), Acad. of Dram. Arts, Consumers Un. (Bd. of Dirs.); Bennett Jr. Col.; b. N.Y.C.; h. Leslie Midgley.

FURNESS, EDNA LUE, Auth: "Spelling for the Millions" (Appleton-Century, '64); Co-auth., "New Dimensions in the Teaching of English" (Pruett Press, '67), numerous monographs, bk. revs., articles; Prof. of Lang., Lit., Kearney (Neb.) State Col.; Visiting Prof: Neb. State Col., Univ. of Chattanooga, Central Mich. Univ., Univ. of Denver, Adams State Col., Univ. of Wyo., Casper Col., Southern Colo. State Col.; HS Lang. Tchr., '28–'39; Translator of Spanish-Am. works; educ: Univ. of Colo., BA, BE, '28; MA, '40; PhD, '51 (Comparative Lit.); Nat. Univ. of Mexico; p. Frank and Nellie Swanson Furness.

FURNISS, MARGARET YOUNG, Rschr., Reader's Digest, 200 Park Ave., N.Y., N.Y. 10017, '64–; Wheaton Col., BA; b. Phila., Pa.; p. H. Russell and Margaret Cornbrooks Young; h. Richard A. Furniss, Jr.; res: 110 East End Ave., N.Y., N.Y. 10028.

FURROW, JUNE DAVIS, Colmst., Beckley Newspaper Corp., 341 Prince St., Beckley, W. Va. 25918, '69–; City Ed., '67–'69; Teen Ed., Reprt., '62–'67; Shady Spring Dist. Wms. Club (Secy.); Beckley Col.; b. Big Stick, W. Va., 1944; p. Roy and Ruth Martin Davis; h. Charles Furrow; c. Mark W.; res: Box 237, Shady Spring, W. Va. 25918.

FUTH, SARA M. BARBAREST, Free-lance Wtr., Ed.; Auth., series of bks. on how to raise, train dogs; Assoc. Ed., Newtown Bee, '65; Colmst., '65–; Asst. to Dir., Gaines Dog Rsch. Ctr., Gen. Foods Corp., '55–'62; Dog Wtrs. Assn. of Am.; Collie Club of Am. (Secy., '59–'64); horse, dog show judge; Vassar Col.; Univ. of Conn., AB, '55; b. N.Y.C., 1933; p. Alfred and Margaret McBurney Barbaresi; h. Robert H. Futh, Jr.; c. Stephen Barry; res: Kinney Hill Rd., Washington Depot, Conn. 06794.

FUTTERMAN, ENID SUSAN, Copywtr., Grey Advertising, Inc., 777 Third Ave., N.Y., N.Y. 10017, '65–; Copy Trainee, '64–'65; Cannes Film Festival Silver Lion Aw., '69; Art Dirs. Club of N.Y. aw., '68, '69; Am. TV Commls. Festival Recognition, '67; Am. Radio Commls. Festival Recognition, '69; Andy Aws. hon. mention, '68; Intl. Bdcst. Aw., '68; Moral Tone in Adv. Aw., '68; Rutgers Univ., BA (Jnlsm.), '64; b. Bklyn., N.Y., 1943; p. Samuel and Mimi Gutman Futterman; res: 230 E. 48th St., N.Y., N.Y. 10017.

G

GABBARD, ROBERTA JOHNSON, Media Dir., Ackerman Associates, Inc., 5708 Mosteller Dr., Okla. City, Okla. 73112, '64–; Traf. Mgr., '64–; Media Byr., Bookkeeper, Ken Juergens Assocs., Okla. City, '61–'64; Nat. Sales Secy., Radio Sta. KTOK (Okla. City), '56–'61; Secy. to Sta. Mgr., Radio Sta. KFDA (Amarillo), '49–'51; AWRT (Dir., '66–'67; Okla. City Chptr.; VP, '68–'69; Chmn., Educ. Fndn., '68); Draughon's Jr. Col., '41–'42; b. Wellington, Tex., 1924; p. Kenneth and Ruth Howard Johnson; h. (div.); c. Daniel, Rebecca; res: 4505 N. MacArthur Blvd., Okla. City, Okla. 73122.

GABLE, MARTHA ANNE, Ed., American Association School Administrators, 1201 16th St. N.W., Wash., D.C. 20036, '68–; Dir., Instructional Materials, Phila. Public Schs., '66–'68; Dir., Radio-TV, '55–'66; Asst. Dir., Sch. Commty, Rels., '48–'55; Tchr., Health, Eng., Elementary, Secondary Schs.; Contrbr., bks. on instructional TV; U.S. Off. of Educ. Advisory Comm. on TV Facilities, '69; Chmn., Pa. State Advisory Comm. on Educ. Bdcst., '60–'68; pioneered ETV in Phila. on comml. stations, '47; on educ. stations, '57; Delegate, bdcst. confs.; John B. Kelly Aw., '61; Ind. Univ., BEd, '27; Temple Univ., MEd, '35 (Distg. Alumni Aw., '64); b. Phila., Pa., 1905; p. James and Stella Gingrich Gable; res: 1315 16th St., N.W., Wash. D.C. 20036.

GABRIEL, ETHEL NAGY, Artist and Repertoire Prodr., RCA Records Division, 1133 Ave. of the Ams., N.Y., N.Y. 10036, '57–; RCA Staff, '40–; Co-owner and Tchr., Nagy Ceramic and Liberal Arts Sch., '48–'52; Trombonist, Phila. Wms. Symphony Orchestra, '39–'40; Own danceband, '34–'40; AWNY, NARAS, Country Music Assn.; Co-prodr., Grammy Aw. album "Beautiful Isle of Somewhere," '68; Grammy nominations, '67, '63; Temple Univ. (Music Supervision), '43; Columbia Univ., '45–'48; b. Milmont Pk., Pa., 1921; p. Karoly and Margaret Horvath de Nagy; h. Gustave Gabriel; res: 425 Weaver St., Larchmont, N.Y. 10538.

GAFFNEY, BETTY JANE, Public Affairs and Prom. Dir., WCWA "Seaway" Radio, Reams Broadcasting Corporation, 604 Jackson St., Toledo, Oh. 43604; Exec. Asst. to Frazier Reams, Jr., Titular Head of Oh. Democratic Party; Democratic Nat. Comm. Wm. (Elected, '68), active in Democratic politics, holding positions in all org. work on local, state, nat. levels, '48–; State Coordr. for Ohio Gubernatorial campaign, '66, League of Wm. Voters, Wms. Adv. Club of Toledo, Dept. of Cmmtns. of Catholic Conf. of Oh., ZONTA, NAB, Oh. Assn. of Bdcstrs., AWRT, Commty. and World Svc. Assn., numerous other religious and civic orgs.; St. Louis Univ.; Mary Manse Col., Grad.; b. Toledo, Oh., 1928; p. John and Helen Quinn Gaffney; res: 2848 Rockwood Pl., Toledo, Oh. 43610.

GAGLEARD, ADELINE WOLIN, Off. Mgr., Corporate Secy., Fred Yaffe and Company, 917 Fox Building, 2211 Woodward Ave., Detroit, Mich. 48201, '59–; Minn. Mining & Mfg. Co., '46–'48; Cook Coffe Co., '44–'46; b. Detroit, Mich., 1926; p. Abraham and Frances Berkowitz Wolin; h. Sam Gagleard; c. Michael, Alan; res: 16950 New Jersey, Southfield, Mich. 48075.

GAINES, EDITH QUINN, Sr. Assoc. Ed., Antiques Magazine, Straight Enterprises, 551 Fifth Ave., N.Y., N.Y. 10017, '66–; Assoc. Ed., '59–'66; Copy Ed., '54–'59; compiled five dics. for Wms. Day: "American Glass," "Pottery and Porcelain," "Furniture," others, '60–'64; Lectr., antiques, glass; Nwsp. Guild; City Col. (N.Y.C.), New Sch. for Social Rsch., N.Y.U., Columbia Univ.; b. Bklyn., N.Y., 1907; p. Dean and Bertha Hulse Quinn; h. David I. Gaines; c. Judith K., Laura L.; res: 41 W. 96 St., N.Y., N.Y. 10025.

GAINEY, LOUISE HAUT, Media Byr., Kenyon & Echkardt, 200 Park Ave., N.Y., N.Y. 10017, '62–; Space Byr., '56–'61; Asst. Media Byr., '56; Asst. Space Byr., Biow Co., '53–'56; Print Media Asst., Morey, Humm & Johnstone, '49–'53; AWNY (Annual Survey Course, first prize and scholarship, '51), IMBA (Secy., '68; Treas., '62–'64); Cert. of Merit in Mkt. Rsch., Mkt. Rsch. Cncl. of N.Y.C. '55; Hunter Col., '49–'50; N.Y.U., BS, '54; Master of Bus. Adm., '56; b. N.Y.C., 1930; p. Gustav and Bertha Kempa Haut; h. Jack Gainey; c. Patricia; res: 10 Stonewall Circle, White Plains, N.Y. 10607.

GALANOPLOS, RUTH, Magazine Specialist, Carl Byoir & Associates, Inc., 800 Second Ave., N.Y., N.Y. 10017, '47–; NHFL; N.Y.U., '44; b. Pitt., Pa., 1922; p. Christ and Catherine Theofilakis Galanoplos; res: 741 Parker St., Newark, N.J. 07104.

GALEN, HELEN, AE, Burton Sohigian Advertising, 1400 Penobscot Bldg., Detroit, Mich. 48226, '69–; Benton & Bowles (N.Y.C.), '64–'67; Deutsch & Shea Adv., '53–'63; b. Newark, N.J.; p. Chris and Catherine Theofilakis Galanoplos; res: One Lafayette Plaisance, Detroit, Mich. 48207.

GALEN, HETTY, Free-lance Voice-over Talent, 35 W. 57th St., N.Y., N.Y. 10019; 165 local, nat., and intl. aws.; Best Actress, ASIFA East, '69; AFTRA, SAG, AEA, AWRT, IRTS, NATAS; Script Development Workshop; Friends Select Sch., Univ. of Pennsylvania, Am. Academy of Dramatic Arts, Dramatic Workshop, Am. Theatre Wing; b. N.Y.C., 1938; res: Sunset Ave., East Quogue, L.I., N.Y. 11942.

GALICK, V. GENEVIEVE BOISCLAIR, Dir., Massachusetts Bureau of Library Extension, 648 Beacon St., Boston, Mass. 02215, '49–; Asst. Dir., '46–'49; Librn., U.S. Army, '42–'45; Special Instr., Simmons Col. Sch. of Lib. Sci., '40–'42; Head, Young Adults Dept., Lynn, Mass. Public Lib., '34–'42; Cnslt., state educ., lib. agcys. in N.Y., Conn., Tex., Mass.; ALA (Cnclr.-at-

Large, '66–'70; Exec. Bd., Assn. of State Libs., '66–'70), New Eng. Lib. Assn. (VP, '67–'68; Pres., '68–'69), Mass. Lib. Assn. (Secy., '47–'49); Who's Who of Am. Wm., Who's Who in Lib. Svc.; Simmons Col., BS, '34; b. Lynn, Mass.; p. Arthur and Veronica Kuhns Boisclair; h. George J. Galick; res: 28 Travis Rd., Natick, Mass. 01760.

GALLAGHER, DOROTHY HINKLE, Soc. Ed., Ashland Publishing Co., 224 17th St., Ashland, Ky. 41101, '69–; Asst. Soc. Ed., '51–'69; Ashland Jr. Col.; h. Thomas Gallagher; res: 1313 Montgomery Ave., Ashland, Ky. 41101.

GALLAGHER, RACHEL, Assoc. Ed., Workman Publishing Co., Inc., 231 E. 51 St., N.Y., N.Y. 10022, '69–; Edtl. Assoc., Esquire Magazine, '65–'69; Assoc. Ed., rsch., articles, Good Grooming Guide, '67–'68; Co-auth: "The New York In/Out Quiz Book (or The Book That Tells You How In You Really Are)" (Random House, '66; pseud: Kimbal Drake); Roanoke Col., '61–'64; b. N.Y.C., 1942; p. John and Ethelyn Gallagher; res: 65 Bank St., N.Y., N.Y. 10014.

GALLAHER, MARJORIE MARY, Dir., Public Info., State Home & Training School, 10285 Ridge Rd., Wheat Ridge, Colo. 80033, '62–; Dir., Public Info., Wallace Village for Children, '60–'62; Dir., Commty. Svcs., Met. Cncl. Commty. Svc., '42–'69; AAUW (VP, '35–'36), League of Wm. Voters, Denver Wms. Press Club, Acad. of Cert. Social Workers; Who's Who of Am. Wm., Who's Who in the West; Univ. of Colo., '24–'27; Breneau Col., AB, '30; Univ. of Denver, MS, '56; b. Denver, Colo.; p. John and Marjorie Dooner Gallaher; res: 1443 Monroe St., Denver, Colo. 80206.

GALLIN, MAJORIE STROM, Prod. Coordr., Movie-record Inc./Estudios More S.A., 437 Madison Ave., N.Y., N.Y. 10022, '66–; Founder, Pres., Staymar Industries, '64–'66; Prod. Asst., Ted Lloyd Inc., '61; Adelphi Col., '61 (grad. with hons.; full scholarship); b. Far Rockaway, N.Y., 1939; p. Arthur and Evelyn Gluckman Strom; h. Samuel Gallin; c. Stacy; res: 630 W. 246th St., Riverdale, N.Y. 10471.

GALLOWAY, LINDA BENNETT, Librn., Goldsboro City Schools, P.O. Drawer 1179, Goldsboro, N.C. 27530, '67–; Coordr. Sch. Libs., Webster County Schs., '61–'67; Librn., Dixon (Ky.) Pub. Lib., '48–'54; Histrn., Ed. Bd., 15th Army, (Bad Nauheim, Germany), '45–'46; Librn., U.S. FET (Rheims, France), '44; Librn. Camp Breckinridge (Ky.) '41–'44; Librn., Evansville, Ind., '39–'41; Auth., "Andrew Jackson, Jr., Son of a President"; Wtr., articles in Library Jnls., children's mag. stories, hist. articles; NEA, Ky. Ed. Assn., Ky. Assn. of Sch. Libs. (Pres. Elect; Secy., '64–'66); ALA, Ky. Lib. Assn., N.C. Ed. Assn., N.C. Lib. Assn., Goldsboro N.C. Ed. Assn. (Treas., '69), LEADS, numerous civic orgs.; Wm. of the Yr., Evansville, Ind., Press, Tri-State, '52; Tri-Delt Nat. Fellowship, '44; Ky. Colonel, '63; Stephens Col., AA, '36; Univ. of Ill., AB, '38; BS (Lib. Sci.), '39; b. Dixon, Ky.; p. Charles and Bonnie Fugate

Bennett; h. E. Agnew Galloway; c. Lisa; res: Walnut Creek Estates, Rte. 3, Goldsboro, N.C. 27530.

GALT, ALFREDA SILL, AE, VP, Jobson Associates, Inc., 9 Rockefeller Plaza, N.Y., N.Y. 10020, '60–; AE, '50–'60; Comm. Organizer, '41–'50; Dir., Wms. Div., British War Relief Fund Soc.; Pubcty. Dept., Comm. to Defend Am. by Aiding the Allies; Dir., Wms. Div., Polish Relief Fund; Pubcty. Dept., YMCA Cent. Campaign Comm., '39–'41; The Lifwynn Fndn. Inc. (Secy. and Bd. Mbr., '55–); Chmn. Fndn. Edtl. Comm. (prepared various papers and bks. relative to human exp. and sanity); PRSA (Cnslrs. Sec.), Am. Assn. of Humanistic Psych., Inst. of Gen. Semantics, Am. Geographical Soc.; b. Ithaca, N.Y.; p. Henry A. and Alfreda Payson Sill; h. William E. Galt, PhD (dec.); c. George E., John P., Elizabeth Anne; res: 108 Hillandale Rd., Westport, Conn. 06880.

GALYARDT, CYNTHIA CARSWELL, Ed., Kansas Business Review, Center for Regional Studies, 210 Summerfield Hall, Lawrence, Kan. 66044, '66–; Theta Sigma Phi (Lawrence Club, Pres., '65–'67), NFPW, Kan. Press Wm. (Bd. Mbr., '68–'69); Kan. State Univ., BS, '55 (Sigma Delta Chi Aw. for Excellence, '55); b. Emporia, Kan., 1934; p. J. H. and Lena Anderson Carswell; h. M. A. Galyardt; c. Susan, Thomas, Mark; res: 3046 Steven Dr., Lawrence, Kan. 66044.

GAM, RITA E., Actress: 15 motion pics., seven Broadway plays, TV dramatic shows; Auth: "The Beautiful Woman"; lectured for Nat. Repertory Co. at univs.; Actors Studio, Tyrone Guthrie Theatre; Berlin "Best Actress" Aw. for "No Exit"; Columbia Univ.; b. Pitt., Pa., 1928; p. Ben and Belle Gam; h. (div.); c. Kate Guinzburg, Mike Guinzberg; res: 1095 Park Ave., N.Y., N.Y. 10028.

GAMEL, PEGGY MOORE, Ed., Monthly Bulletin, Fort Worth Women's Club; Vice-chmn., Bk. Rev. Dept., '66–'68; St. Mary's Guild (Pres., '67; Wms. Bd., '66–'67); Trinity Episcopal Ch.; Southern Methodist Univ., '30–'32; Tex. Univ., BJ, '34; b. Okla. City, Okla., 1913; p. Walter and Pearl Atwood Moore; h. Don Gamel; c. Cynthia (dec.), Don; res: 3500 Autumn Dr., Fort Worth, Tex. 76109.

GAMMILL, NOREEN, Actress, TV commls. at present; Actress, Wtr., Prod., radio, '27–'50; also stage and motion pics.; one-act plays and five bks. of sketches published; Featured Wtr., leading western story mkt., '48–'51; short stories and articles in nat. mags.; more than 4,000 radio, TV shows, incl. 14 featured roles on Lux Radio Theatre, Aunt Hattie in "Great Gildersleeve," wife of sch. principal in "Our Miss Brooks," Ma Simpson in "Sunny Valley," others; SAG, AFTRA, AEA; Univ. of Okla.; Univ. of Ia.; b. St. Louis, Mo.; p. Carl and Bertha Bedford Ellers; c. Gloria Ann (Mrs. Harold Wilkins), William E.; res: 15124 Del Gado Dr., Sherman Oaks, Cal. 91403.

GAMORAN, MAMIE GOLDSMITH, Free-lance

Wtr., pubns. incl: "Hillel's Happy Holidays" ('39), "Hillel's Calendar" ('60), "The Story of Samson Benderly" ('63), others; Auth: stories, poems, articles, religious, secular mags.; Supvsr., Religious Sch., Adath Israel Synagogue (Cinn., Oh.), '48–'49; Educ. field, '20–'41; Hadassah (Nat. Bd.), Hebrew Culture Fedn. of Am., Hadoar, Hebrew Weekly (N.Y.), Religious Educ. Assn. (Bd. Mbr.), Am. Comm. for Israel White House Libs. for Children (secy.); educ: Columbia Univ.; Univ. of Cinn.; Jewish Theological Seminary ext. courses; b. L.I. City, N.Y., 1900; p. Nathan I. and Mamie Aronson Goldsmith; h. Dr. Emanuel Gamoran; c. Abraham C., Rabbi Hillel N., Judith R. (Mrs. Eli Chernin); res: 229 W. 78th St., N.Y., N.Y. 10024.

GANZ, IRMA, Mng. Ed., Soccer News, P.O. Box 634, New Rochelle, N.Y., '68–; Dir. and Secy.-Treas., Wide World Bk. Ctr., Ltd., '66–; Bus. Mgr., Jeffrey Lee Synd., '53–; Pres., Sport Shelf, '53–; Dir., Soccer Assocs., '48–; Sports Cnslt.; Sports News Reptr.; only wm. accredited to cover soccer Intl. World Cup; Soccer Wtrs. Assn., Nat. Recreation Assn., Am. Assn. of Health, Physical Educ. and Recreation, Am. Booksellers Assn., Nat. Park and Recreation Assn.; Pa. State Univ., BA, '38; b. Scranton, Pa., 1916; p. Jacob and Dora Weinburger Ganz; h. Milton Miller; c. Jeffrey Harold Miller, Lee James Miller; res: 2 Holly Dr., New Rochelle, N.Y. 10801.

GARCIA, SHERRILL LEIST, Free-lance Wtr.; Theta Sigma Phi, Kappa Tau Alpha; Univ. of Fla., BS (Jnlsm.), '67; h. John Garcia; c. John Todd, Robert Troy; res: 8026 Hummingbird Lane, San Diego, Cal. 92123.

GARCIA, STELLA ELIZABETH, Actress, Stage, Radio, TV, Motion Pics.; Warner Bros., 20th Century Fox, Desilu, M.G.M., Universal Studios; Prods. incl: "West Side Story," "Comancheros," "Baby Jane"; SAG, AFTRA; Am. Sch. of Ballet, '62; b. Colombia, S. Am., 1939; p. Alberto and Aura Guevara Garcia; h. Donald Como; c. Brenda Como; res: 702 E. San Jose, Burbank, Cal. 91501.

GARDELLA, KAY (GENEVIEVE), Radio-TV Ed., Daily News, 220 E. 42, N.Y., N.Y. 10017, '64–; Radio-TV Dept. Wtr., '46; Copy Girl, '45; "Ladies of the Press" TV, other TV panel shows; NWC, Nwsp. Reptrs. Assn.; AMITA Jnlsm. Aw., '61; Upsala Col., BA, '44; N.Y.U.; b. Belleville, N.J., 1923; p. Charles and Genevieve H. Harrington Gardella; h. Anthony Marino; res: 300 E. 40th St., N.Y., N.Y. 10016.

GARDINER, NANCY TUCK, Beauty Ed., Bride's Magazine, Condé-Nast Publications, 420 Lexington Ave., N.Y., N.Y. 10021, '67–; Sls. Prom. Asst., Yardley of London, '65–'67; Majorie Webster Jr. Col. (Eng.), '64; Tobe-Coburn (N.Y.C.), '65; b. N.Y.C., 1944; p. Frederick and Merle Fisk Tuck; h. Sylvester B. Gardiner; res: Bayville Rd., Locust Valley, L.I., N.Y. 11560.

GARDNER, JEANNE Le MONNIER, Auth: "Mary Jemison: Seneca Captive" (Harcourt, Brace & World, '66; nominated for Dorothy Canfield Fisher Aw., '66), "Sky Pioneers: The Story of Wilbur and Orville Wright" (Harcourt, Brace & World, '63; Weekly Reader Bk. Club Slection, '64); Rschr., Edtl. Asst. to Pfsnl. Auth. Carl Carmer, '58–; Nwsp. Reptr., The Daily Register-Mail (Galesburg, Ill.), '48–'51; Airline Stewardess, Pan Am. World Airways (Latin Am. Div.), '46–'48; Passenger Agt., Trans World Airlines (Chgo., Ill.), '45–'46; Dension Univ.; b. Chgo., Ill.; h. Richard Gardner; c. Susan, Jamie; res: Harriman Rd., Irvington, N.Y. 10533.

GARDNER, MARILYN JANE, Wms. Ed., The Milwaukee Journal, 333 W. State St., Milw., Wis. 53201, '67–; Asst. Wms. Ed., '65–'67; Soc. Ed., '63–'65; Wms. Dept. Reptr., '53–'63; Ed., Barrington Courier-Review (Ill.), '50–'53; J. C. Penney-Univ. of Mo. aws. for wms. pages (1st Place in Circ. class); Univ. of Ill., BA (Jnlsm.), '49; b. Barrington, Ill., 1927; p. Anthony and Elizabeth Jurs Gardner.

GARDNER, MARJORIE HYER, Prof., Sci. Educ., University of Maryland, Room 009, Science Teaching Center, College Park, Md. 20742, '64–; Dir., Vistas Sci. Prog., Nat. Sci. Tchrs. Assn. (Wash., D.C.), '60–'64; Instr., Chemistry and Sci. Educ. Depts., Oh. State Univ., '58–'60; Mbr., Nat. Sci. Fndn. Academic Yr., Oh. State Univ., '57–'58; Tchr. of sci. and jnlsm., Ut., Nev. and Oh., '47–'56; Cnslt., Wash. (D.C.) Planetarium and Space Ctr., '60–; Edtl. Planning Dir. of Pfsnl. Growth For Sci. Tchrs., '68–'69; Dir. of Tchr. Preparation, Earth Sci. Curriculum Project, '67–'69; Dir. of Nat. Sci. Fndn. Leadership Confs. and Insts., '67–'69; Cnslt., Columbia Univ. AID Prog., 3 summers in India, '64–'67; Co-auth: "Chemistry In The Space Age" ('65); Ut. State Univ., BA, '47; Oh. State Univ., MA, '58; PhD, '60; b. Logan, Ut., 1923; p. Saul and Gladys Christiansen Hyer; h. Paul Gardner; c. Pamela, Mary; res: 6908 Nashville Rd., Lanham, Md. 20742.

GARFF, GEORGIA, Field Reptr., KRON-TV, 1001 Van Ness Ave., S.F., Cal. 84111, '68–; Field Reptr., News Show On Air, KSL-TV (Salt Lake City, Ut.); Univ. of Ut., Theatre Dept.; h. David R. Owens.

GARFUNKEL, BARBARA, Assoc. Prof. of Jnlsm., Miami-Dade Junior College North, 11380 N.W. 27th Ave., Miami, Fla. 33167, '60–; Jnlsm. Tchr., Miami Sr. HS, '36–'60; Theta Sigma Phi, Delta Kappa Gamma (Scholarship Chmn., '67–'69); Columbia Gold Key Aw., '55; Fla. State Col. for Wm., AB (Phi Beta Kappa), '35; Univ. of Miami, ME, '48; res: 9175 S.W. 77th Ave., Miami, Fla. 33156.

GARLAND, AVIS PITTS, PR Cnslt., P.O. Box 7429, Phoenix, Ariz. 85011, '64–; VP, Garland Agcy., '55–'64; Public Info. Dir., Maricopa Chptr., Am. Red Cross, '46–'50, Adm. Asst., '43–'46; Theta Sigma Phi, PRSA, Phoenix Adv. Club (Pres., '61–'62), PR Soc. of Phoenix (VP, '62); Phoenix Jr. Adv. Club aw., '63; Oberlin Col., '29–'31; Univ. of Mich., BA, '34; b.

Cleve., Oh., 1911; p. Walter and Marjorie Alexander Pitts; h. Charles Garland; res: 1448 E. Maryland Ave., Phoenix, Ariz. 85014.

GARNER, CHARLOTTE JOAN, Assoc. Ed., Home Furnishings Division, Better Homes & Gardens, Meredith Corporation, 1716 Locust St., Des Moines, Ia. 50303, '65–; Copywtr., Adv., Sls. Prom., '64–'65; Copywtr., Mabley & Carew (Cinn., Oh.); PR Dir., Copywtr., H. & S. Pogue Co.; decorating talks throughout U.S., for store openings, home shows, C. of C. meetings, convs., other groups; Phi Beta, NHFL, A.I.D. (Press Assoc.); Wesleyan Univ., '46–'48; Univ. of Cinn., '52–'53; b. Dayton, Oh., 1928; p. Glen and Cora Cassiday Garner; res: 2600 Kingman Blvd., Des Moines, Ia. 50311.

GARNER, PEGGY ANN, Free-lance Actress, all studios and networks, '36–; Child Model, age four, John Roberts Powers; under contract to 20th Century Fox, '43, "A Tree Grows In Brooklyn" (Acad. Aw. from Motion Pic. Arts and Scis., '45; LOOK Aw., '45); other motion pics., Hollywood, seven yrs.; four Broadway shows; toured in "Bus Stop"; own live TV wkly. show. "Two Girls Named Smith," '51; live TV, N.Y.C., 10 yrs.; summer stock; SAG, AFTRA, AEA, 20th Century Fox Studio Sch.; New Sch. for Soc. Rsch.; b. Canton, Oh., 1932; p. Wm. George and Virginia Craig Garner; h. (div.); c. Catherine Ann (Cas) Salmi; res: 16534-1/2 Sunset Blvd., Pacific Palisades, Cal. 90272.

GARRARD, JEANNE SUE, Cnslt. Exec. Ed., Visitor Publishing Co., P.O. Box 1248, Sixth and Washington Ave., Miami Beach, Fla. 33139, '69–; Exec. Ed., '64–'69; Ed., '56–'58; Mng. Ed., '55–'56; Feature Ed., '52–'55; Tchr., Adult Educ., '56–; PR, '56–; Free-lance Wtr., numerous mags.; Pubcty. for Victor Borge, musical shows, convs.; Auth: "Growing Orchids for Pleasure" ('66; Nat. Lit. Horticulture Aw. of Nat. Cncl. of Garden Clubs, '67), "Potted," ('67; Co-Auth., "Flowers of the Caribbean" ('69); Miami Beach Garden Ctr. and Conservatory (Bd. Mbr., '66–'68); Miami Beach Garden Club (Pres., '66–'68; 3rd VP, '68–'70), Theta Sigma Phi (Chptr. Pres., '66–'67; Treas., '65; Commty. Headliner aw.), S. Fla. Orchid Soc., Naples Orchid Soc. (Hon. Life mbr.), Gold Coast. Unlimited Orchid Soc. (Hon. Life mbr.), Pi Beta Phi; Stetson Univ., '40–'43; Lindsey Hopkins Hotel Sch.; Fla. State Univ.; b. Birmingham, Ala., 1923; p. Oscar and Jeanne Holomon Garrard; h. Huber Ebersole (div.); res: 5768 Pine Tree Dr., Miami Beach, Fla. 33140.

GARRETT, ADELE J., Free-lance Ed.; Ed., Univ. of Tex. Press, '57–'61; Mng. Ed., Falcon's Wing Press, '55–'56; Educ. Specialist, USAF, Maxwell & Gunter AFB, Ala., '50–'53; Edtl. Cnslt., "Nat. Nuclear Energy Series," Oak Ridge, '49–'50; Assoc. Ed., Ziff-Davis Publ. Co., '42–'44; Textbk. Ed., Houghton Mifflin, '39–'40; Auth: "Early American Trade Cards" ('27); Wms. Nat. Bk. Assn., Nat. Assn. of Bk. Eds., Am. Soc. of Indexers; Univ. of Wis., BA; h. Edmund A. Garrett (div.); res: 425 E. 79th St., N.Y., N.Y. 10021.

GARRETT, PAULINE E., Pres., Tempo Advertising, Inc., 555 Fifth Ave., N.Y., N.Y. 10017, '66–(pers. recruitment adv.); Adv., '61–'66; Pers., several large corps.; Univ. of Ia., BA, '54 (cum laude); b. Muscatine, Ia.

GARST, DORIS SHANNON, Auth: "A Horse and a Hero for Blyth" ('62), "The Burro Who Sat Down" ('61), more than 40 other juv. bks.; teaching, rsch.; Univ. of Colo.; b. Ironwood, Mich., 1894; p. Julius and Cinta von Diltz Jensen; h. Joseph Garst; c. Joseph, Warren, Mrs. Barbara Spurlock; res: 500 Cedar, Douglas, Wyo. 82633.

GARTNER, DIANA, VP, Dir. of Mkt. Rsch., Daniel and Charles, 261 Madison Ave., N.Y., N.Y. 10016, '70–; Asst. Dir., '69; Mkt. Rsch. Mgr., Lever Bros., '67–'69; Project Dir., Marplan, '66–'67; Grey Adv., '65–'66; Teaching Fellow, Grad. Seminar in Experimental Psych., New Sch. for Social Rsch., '64; Rsch. Asst.-Experimental Psych., '62; Am. Mktg. Assn., NOW; Radcliffe Col., BA, '56 (cum laude); New Sch. for Social Rsch., MA, '64; currently PhD Candidate; b. New London, Conn., 1934; p. Gerald and Irene Hoffman Goldfaden; h. (div.); c. John; res: 220 E. 60th St., N.Y., N.Y. 10022.

GARTON, MALINDA DEAN, Auth: "Teaching the Educable Mentally Retarded—Practical Methods" (Thomas Publ., '64), "Making Friends" (Stanwix House, '65); Tchr., Asst. Prof.; NEA, NLAPW, Intl. Platform Assn., (Cncl. for Exceptional Children; Finneytown Sch. Bd. of Educ. aw., '69; Univ. of Okla., BA, '18; Colo. State Col., MA (Educ.), '46; Bradley Univ., Univ. of Ill., Cinn. Univ., Pacific Univ.; b. Gallatin, Mo.; p. David and Mary Wier Dean; h. Fay Lester Garton (dec.); c. Norman L., Martin W; res: P.O. Box 277, Danvers, Ill. 61732.

GASKILL, MYRTLE ESTES, Wms. Ed., Michigan Chronicle, 479 Ledyard, Detroit, Mich. 48201, '48–; Contrb. Ed., Jet mag., '52–'54; Tchr., Exceptional children (Atlanta, Ga.), '30–'37; Colmst., Pittsburgh (Pa.) courier, '30–'37; League of Wm. Voters; Un. Fndn. aw., '60; March of Dimes cit., '61; Atlanta Univ., '25–'30; Wayne State Univ., '39–'41; b. Atlanta, Ga., 1907; p. William and Euchee Hutchins Estes; h. Alfred Gaskill; c. Alfred Jr., Nicole (Mrs. Ronald Smith), Joyce (Mrs. Julius Haynie); res: 290 Woodland St., Detroit, Mich. 48202.

GASPAROTTI, ELIZABETH SEIFERT, Free-lance Wtr.; Auth., 58 novels; Auths. Guild; Dodd, Mead-Redbook 1st Novel aw., '38; Washington Univ. (St. Louis, Mo.), AB, '18; b. Washington, Mo., 1897; p. Richard and Anna Sanford Seifert; h. John J. Gasparotti (dec.); c. John, Richard, Paul, Anna (Mrs. William Felter); res: 511 Fort, Moberly, Mo. 65270.

GASSER, BERNYCE BEAN, Telegraph Ed., Owensboro Publishing Co., 1400 Frederica St., Owensboro, Ky. 42301, '42–; b. Ch. County, Ky.; p. James Bean; h.

Lawrence D. Gasser; c. Mrs. Frederick Carroll Park Jr.; res: 2224 St. James Ct., Owensboro, Ky. 42301.

GASSERT, SALLY ANNE, Dir. of PR, Bill Publications, Inc., 630 Third Ave., N.Y., N.Y. 10017, '68–; Prom. Mgr., '66–'68; Ed., Simmons-Boardman Publ. Co., '56–'65; Ed., The Advocate (N.J.), '51–'55; Copywtr., Montgomery Ward, '48–'51; Am. Bus. Press, Publrs. Employment Program, Inc. (Pres.); Manhattanville Col., BA; b. Newark, N.J., 1927; p. Frederick and Sara Hayes Gassert; res: Saddle Ridge Farm, RR #1, Colts Neck, N.J. 07722.

GATES, CONSTANCE CLEMENS, Ed., Copywtr., Prodr., Ross Jurney Associates, Inc. (Salt Lake City), '56–'64; Cont. Dir., Wms. Ed., KFJB Radio (Marshalltown, Ia.), '53–'56; Auth., non-fiction articles; Theta Sigma Phi (Tucson Chptr: VP, '69–'70; Secy., '68–'69); Indsl. Eds. of Ut. (past Secy., VP); Marshalltown Jr. Col., '51 (Valedictorian); Grinnell Col., BA, '53 (Outstanding Jnlsm. Student); Univ. of Utah, '56–'58; h. Joseph Gates; res: 5050 E. Hawthorne, Tucson, Ariz. 85711.

GATES, GENEVA ARTHUR, Wms. Ed., Hillsdale Daily News, 33 McCollum St., Hillsdale, Mich. 49242, '64–; Asst. to Publr., Litchfield Gazette, '59–'64; Colmst., Livestock Market Digest; Am. Legion Commty. Svc. Aw., '69; b. Litchfield, Mich., 1931; p. James and Elsie Weese Arthur; h. Frank Gates; c. Molly, Tony, Sally; res: 207 W. St. Joe St., Litchfield, Mich. 49252.

GATES, PATRICIA LAWRENCE, Prodr.-Bdcstr., The Breakfast Show, Voice of America, 330 Independence Ave., Wash., D.C. 20003, Wtr.-Narrator, Gateway To Science, weekly prog. to the Far East; Hostess, Soundstage 1220, WFAX (Falls Church, Va.); appears on TV progs., WETA (Wash., D.C.); has bdcst. from Europe and Middle East for NBC Monitor and Am. Forces Network; AWRT (Intl. and Nat. Advisory Comms.; Wash., D.C. Chptr. Pres., '66–'67); Intl. Red Cross Comm., ANWC, Northern Va. Commty. Col. Radio-TV Advisory Comm.; Public Svc. Aw., Dept. of the Army, '60; Intl. Red Cross Comm.; b. U.S.A., 1926; p. William Charles and Mary McNamee Lawrence; h. Brig. Gen. Mahlon E. Gates; c. Pamela, Lawrence; res: Prospect House, 1200 N. Nash St., Arlington, Va. 22209.

GAUDET, CORAL KUKUK, Contrb. Ed., Latin American Reports, 1027 International Trade Mart, N.O., La. 70130, '64–; Literacy Tchr. to Maya Indians (Nacahuil, Guatemala), '63–'64; Docs. Librn., Transportation Corps Lib. (Fort Eustis, Va.), '52–'58; articles on Central and S. Am. Indians; N.O. Press Club, Ft. Eustis Little Theatre (Secy., '57), Program Dir. of Neighborhood Ctr. ('68–'69); Westhampton Col., Univ. of Richmond, BA, '63; Univ. of N.D., '63, grad work; b. Brookings, S.D., 1924; p. S. P. and Margaret Dallenbach Kukuk; h. William Gaudet; c. H. Michael Mears; res: 1142 Harrison Ave., N.O., La. 70122.

GAUSS, CECELIA SNEYD, VP, Gerity Broadcasting Company, 121 W. Maumee St., Adrian, Mich. 49221, '69–; Station Mgr., WABJ, '68–; WNEM-TV-FM, WABJ, '63–'68; Gerity Products; Asst. to Pres., Lee Travel Burs.; Asst. Purchasing Agt., Gerity Mich. Corp., '54–'58; Class, Adv., Adrian Col.; Career Day Participant, Hillsdale Col.; AWRT (Nat. Membership Chmn., '68–'69), Wms. Adv. Club of Detroit, Detroit Press Club, Bdcstrs. Prom. Assn., Mich. Assn. of Bdcstrs., Adrian Area C. of C., Tecumseh C. of C.; Goodwill Industries of Southeastern Mich. (Dir., Secy.; Recognition); Adv. Wm. of the Yr., Detroit Adv. Club, '69; Gerity Bdcst. Co., Gerity Products (Bd. of Dirs.); Adrian Col., '44–'45; b. Adrian, Mich., 1923; p. Seth and Anna Dart Sneyd; h. Duane Gauss; c. Gordon Dale; res: 445 College Park Dr., Adrian, Mich. 49221.

GAUT, BETTY SCREWS, Wms. Dir., Prom. Dir., WTVY-TV, Box 1089, Dothan, Ala. 36301, '58–; Tchr., '54–'55, '50–'51; AWRT; Ala. Fedn. Garden Clubs TV aw., '69; Ala. State Pubcty. Dept. aw., '68; Montevallo Univ., AB (Eng., Music); h. George P. Gaut III; res: 408 Azalea Circle, Dothan, Ala. 36301.

GAUTHIER, LOIS, Mgr., PR and Commtns., The Pantasote Company, 277 Park Ave., N.Y., N.Y. 10017, '68–; AE, PR, Vic Maitland, '68; Asst. Mkt. Planning Dept. Film Div., Olin Mathieson Chemical Corp., '53–'68; Copywtr., Warner Lambert, '49–'53; Asst. to Dir., Advisory Svc., Johnson & Johnson, Chicopee Div., '47–'49; AWNY, Sls. Prom. Execs. Assn.; Smith Col., BA, '46; N.Y. Sch. of Interior Design, Cert., '53; b. Pittsfield, Mass., 1923; p. Marcel and Helen Burgess Gauthier; res: 15 W. 84th St., Apt. 10A, N.Y., N.Y. 10024.

GAUVREAU, WINIFRED ROLLINS, Bk. Review Colmst., Nevada State Journal, Reno, Nev. 89504, '58–; Wms. Pg. Ed., Colmst., Register-Pajaronian (Watsonville, Cal.), '64–'69; Pubcty. Wtr., Ed., First Nat. Bank of Nev. (Reno), '58–'64; County Ed., Feature Wtr., Suffolk (Va.) News Herald, '55–'57; Asst. to Roto Ed., Philadelphia (Pa.) Inquirer, '36–'39; Cal. Press Wm., NFPW, Reno Press Club; Elmira Col., '26–'29; b. N.Y.C.; p. Maxwell and Winifred Glaser Rollins; h. Farren B. Jensen; res: 6 Morehouse Dr., Watsonville, Cal. 95076.

GAVER, MARY VIRGINIA, Prof., Graduate School of Library Service, Rutgers University, New Brunswick, N.Y., 08903, '54–; Prof., '60–; Librn., Assoc. Prof., Trenton State Col., '42–'54; Librn., Scarsdale, N.Y. HS, '39–'42; Tech. Dir., State Lib. Project, WPA of Va., '38–'39; High Sch. Librn., Danville, '28–'37; Leader-Specialist, Univ. of Tehran, Iran, '53–'54; N.J. Sch. Librns. Assn. (Pres.), N.J. Librns. Assn. (Pres.); Am. Assn. of Sch. Librns. (Pres.), ALA (Pres.), N.J. Sch. Media Assn., Dept. of Audio-Visual Instr., AAUP; Herbert Putnam Hon. Fund Aw., Rutgers Rsch. Cncl. Aw.; R-MWC, AB, '27 (Phi Beta Kappa); Columbia Univ., BS (Lib. Sci.), '32; MS (Lib. Sci.), '38 (Carnegie Fellowship); hon. degrees from C.W. Post Col., Mt. Holyoke; b.

Wash., D.C.; p. Clayton and Ruth Clendening Gaver; res: 29 Baldwin St., New Brunswick, N.J. 08901.

GAYLOR, ANNE NICOL, Ed., Middleton Times Tribune, 7621 Terrace Ave., Middleton, Wis. 53562, '67–; Organizer, Girl Friday Inc., '57–'66; Organizer, Placements of Madison, '59–'66; Wis. Citizens for Family Planning (Bd. of Dirs.); Wis. Educ. Assn. Sch. Bell Aw. for Educ. Feature Series, '68; three Wis. Press Assn. hon. mention aws., '67, '68; Univ. of Wis., BA (Eng.); b. Tomah, Wis. 1926; p. Jason and Lucie Sowle Nicol; h. Paul Gaylor; c. Andrew, Ian Stuart, Annie Laurie, Jamie; res: 726 Miami Pass, Madison, Wis. 53711.

GAYLORD, JOANE, Artist, Actress, Wtr., 2375 Prosser Ave., L.A., Cal.; Wtr., Dir., Prodr., "To G.I. With Love" ('45); AWRT, Radio and TV Wm. of S. Cal., Hollywood Studio Club Alumni Assn. (Pres., '61–'62); U.S. Treasury Dept. aws., '42–'44; Whittier Col., San Jose State Col., U.C.L.A.; h. Frank J. Gillis (dec.); c. Ronald Blair Gillis; res: 10524 Selkirk Lane, L.A., Cal. 90024.

GAYNES, CORAL, Artist, Designer, Lectr.; media: water color, casein, collage, polymers, "Encaustique" (her own discovery, in which 27 subjects have been reproduced for nat. distribution); current theme: Undersea Life, using mixed media, Encaustique for abstract version; nine one-man shows; Designer, Stylist of printed textiles, printed papers, dinnerware, soft goods, gift wares, sculpture maquettes; Lectr. on art and design with demonstrations, exhibits; private students prepared for pfsnl. work in art and design; Artists Equity Assn. of N.Y., NLAPW (Art Div.); five aws. for paintings, two aws. for design; studied Pratt Inst., New Sch., China Inst., Rudolf Steiner Sch.; private studies with Prof. Salvatore Lascari, Prix de Rome, N.A.; b. Austria; p. Samuel and Sarah Warter; res: Apt. 5-D, 200 W. 54th St., N.Y., N.Y. 10019.

GAYNOR, HELEN INEZ, Adv. Prod. Dir., Gutman Advertising Agency, Peoples Federal Bldg., Wheeling, W. Va. 26003, '53–; Prom. Dir., WTRF Radio-TV, '50–'53; Cont. Wtr., WTRF Radio, '48–'50; Ed., co. nwsp., Imperial Glass, '41–'48; Wtr. for touring show prods., "The Word," Marine Corps Wms. Reserve, '43–'46; Pilot Intl., Oh. Valley Adv. Club; AFA Dist. adv. aw., '61; Best Medium Campaign to Advs., '61; b. Bellaire, Oh., 1922; p. Ralph and Elvira Gentile Gianangeli; res: 207 Bennett St., Bridgeport, Oh. 43912.

GEARIN, LOUVAN ANITA (Brabham), Librn., Steger Junior High School, 425 Brownbert Lane, Webster Groves, Mo. 63119, '53–; Instr., Atlanta Univ. Sch. of Lib. Sci., '66; Ref. Lib., Tuskegee Inst., '51, '56; Librns. Lincoln Inst. of Ky., '50–'53; Reviewer, Sch. Lib. Jnl., '66–'67; ALA, Mo. Lib. Assn., Mo. Assn. of Sch. Librns. (Pres., '60–'62); Who's Who of Am. Wm.; Fisk Univ., AB, '37; Atlanta Univ., BS (Lib. Sci.), '49; Univ. of Mich., MA (Lib. Sci.), '54; b. St. Louis, Mo., 1917; p.

William and Ira Haskell Brabham; h. (div.); res: 11999 Villa Dorado Dr., Apt. C., St. Louis, Mo. 63141.

GEARY, KATHLEEN ANNE, Librn., Fletcher Free Library, 227 College St., Burlington, Vt. 05401, '63–; Asst. Librn., '63; Desk Asst., Simmons Col., '62–'63; Circ. Asst., St. Michael's Col., '58–'61; New England Lib. Assn., ALA, Vt. Lib. Assn. (VP, '65; Pres., '65–'67; Pres. Pro-Temp. Public Lib. Sec., '68), ZONTA, League of Wm. Voters, Chittenden County Hist. Soc., Vt. Archaeological Soc.; Trinity Col., BA (Eng.), '61; Simmons Col., MLS, '63; b. Pittsfield, Mass., 1939; p. William and Catherine Geary; res: 361 Pearl St., Burlington, Vt. 05401.

GEARY, MAUREEN LOGAN, Asst. to Pubcty. Dir., Cosmetics Div., Lehn & Fink Products Co., 680 Fifth Ave., N.Y., N.Y. 10019, '68–; Asst. Ed., Nat. Design Ctr., '66–'68; Asst. to Adv. and Prom. Mgr., '64–'66; NHFL; Hunter Col., BA; b. N.Y.C., 1942; p. Thomas and Elizabeth Duggan Logan; h. Neil Geary; res: 521A E. 85th St., N.Y., N.Y. 10028.

GEASTNER, EDNA SUCKAV, Auth, Fiction: "Song By The River," (Zordervan and Oliphants, London, '60), "Joelette," (Zondervan Pub. Co. '63); Wheaton Col., BA, '34, Univ. of Penn., MA, '36; b. Champa C. P. India, 1916; p. Cornelius H. and Lulu O. Johnston Suckav; h. John Geastner; c. Judy Black, Rachel Gwen, Jonathan N.; res: Journey's End, R.D. 1, Ligonier, Pa. 15658.

GEFFERT, ELEANOR RUTH, Actress, Singer, Dorothy Day Otis Agency, 511 N. LaCienega Blvd., L.A., Cal. 90048; Theatre: "To Broadway With Love" (N.Y. World's Fair, '64), Jones Beach ('62–'63), summer stock, '61–'64; Soundtracks: "Hello Dolly," "Star," ('68); "Finian's Rainbow" ('67); "On a Clear Day" ('69); Tchr., '57–'59; Copywtr., WSBT (South Bend, Ind.), '55–'57; Thornton Jr. Col., '50–'52; Depauw Univ., BA (Music), BMus. (Education), '55; b. Harvey, Ill., 1932; p. Rudolf and Meta Hackbarth Geffert; res: 2020-1/2 N. Argyle Ave., L.A., Cal. 90028.

GEIGER, JEAN ROBERTS, Dir. of PR, New Jersey College of Medicine and Dentistry, 36 Commerce St., Newark, N.J. 07102, '67–; PR Dir., Un. Hosps. of Newark, '58–'67; AE, Williams & London, '57–'58; Reptr., Feature Wtr., Edtl. Off. Mgr., Newark News, '47–'58; PRSA, Am. Hosp. Assn., Am. Soc. for Hosp. PR Dirs., N.J. Hosp. Assn., N.J. Hosp. PR Assn. (Exec. Comm., '60–'64; Secy., '59–'60); MacEachern Aws: '67, 2 in '62, '61; APRA, N.J. Chptr. Aw., '59; Colby Jr. Col., '37–'38; b. Orange, N.J., 1919; p. E. Weston and Anna DuBois Roberts Johnson; h. Robert L. Geiger; c. Merritt Budd 3rd, David Budd, Pamela Budd (Mrs. Robert Lawrence), Stephen, Mark, Lauren; res: 23 Old Forge Rd., Millington, N.J. 07946.

GEISER, ELIZABETH ABLE, VP, R. R. Bowker, 1180 Ave. of the Americas, N.Y., N.Y. 10036, '70–; Dir. of

Marketing, '68–'70; Sls. Mgr., '60–'67; Bd. of Dirs., '65–'68; Dir., Bowker Publ. Co., Ltd., London, '65–; Prom. Mgr., R. R. Bowker, '54–'60; Adv. and Prom. Mgr., Col. Dept., Macmillan Company, '47–'54; Lectr., Radcliffe Publ. Procedures Course; Chmn., Exhibits Round Table of ALA, '67–'69; Publrs. Lib. Prom. Group, Publrs. Adv. Club; Hood Col., AB (magna cum laude and Dept. Honor; Mortar Bd.; Who's Who Among Am. Cols. and Univs.); b. Phillipsburg, N.J., 1925; p. George W. and Margaret Ross Geiser; res: Village Green, 495 Main St., Orange, N.J. 07050.

GEISLER, MARTHABEL, Adm. Asst. to Sta. Mgr., WFBM-TV, 1330 N. Meridian St., Indpls., Ind. 46202, '66–; Traf. Mgr., WFBM Radio, '42–'66; Secy. to Prog. Dir., '30–'42; AWRT (Hoosier Chptr.; Pres.-elect, Secy., '65–'66; Wm. of the Yr., '61); b. Louisville, Ky., 1911; p. Edward and Isabel Wetzelberger Geisler; res: 529 N. Colorado Ave., Indpls., Ind. 46201.

GELB, CAROL PATRICIA, Quality Control Supvsr., Corporate Market Research, General Foods Corporation, 250 North St., White Plains, N.Y. 10605; Pres., Trend Finders, Inc., '57–'67; AWNY (Chmn., Career Conf., '65–'66).

GELLER, EVELYN GOTTESFELD, Ed.-in-Chief, School Library Journal, R. R. Bowker Co., 1180 Ave. of the Americas, N.Y., N.Y. 10036; Asst. Dir. of Rsch., D. H. Blair, '63–'64; Asst. Ed., Wilson Lib. Bulletin, '61–'63; Asst. Ed., Ref. Bks. Dept., H. W. Wilson, '60–'61; Contrbr., "European Authors" (H. W. Wilson), "Book Selection and Censorship in the Sixties" (R. R. Bowker, '69); Bowker Annual, '69; ALA, Wms. Nat. Bk. Assn., NEA, Cncl. on Interracial Bks. for Children; Bklyn. Col., BA, '54 (magna cum laude), Catholic Univ., Columbia Univ.; h. (div.).

GELLIS, ROBERTA JACOBS, Auth: "Knight's Honor," "Bond of Blood" (both, Doubleday), "The Psychiatrist's Wife" (Signet); Auths. Guild, Pen and Brush; Hunter Col., BA, '47; Bklyn. Polytech., MS, '52; N.Y.U., MA; b. Bklyn., N.Y., 1927; p. Morris and Margaret Segall Jacobs; h. Charles Gellis; c. Mark; res: 119 Princeton St., Rosyln Heights, N.Y. 11577.

GENETT, ADRIENNE GAYE, Pubns. Ed., North Central Airlines, Inc., 6201 34th Ave. S., Mpls., Minn. 55450, '68–; Ed., PR Rep., Trans.-Tex. Airways (Houston, Tex.), '67–'68; Wtr., Rschr., Features Dept., The Houston Chronicle Publ. Co., '65–'67; ICIE, Northwestern IEA, Theta Sigma Phi, Gamma Alpha Chi, Airline Eds. Conf. of the Air Transport Assn. of Am.; aws. for Trans.-Tex. Airways pubn. The Starliner (Aw. of Merit, ICIE, '69; S.W. Conf. of Indsl. Eds. Merit Aw., '67; S.E. Tex. Indsl. Eds. Aw. of Excellence for Photog., '68; Dallas Indsl. Eds. Crtv. Commtns. Aw., '68), Univ. of Houston, BA (Jnlsm.), '67 (cum laude); b. Glendale, Cal., 1945; p. James and Gladys Miller Genett; res: 9045 Cedar Ave. S., Apt. #104, Bloomington, Minn. 55420.

GENN, LILLIAN G., Free-lance Wtr., non-fiction mag. articles; Colmst., Newhouse nwsps., King Features, North Am. Nwsp. Alliance, '52–'58; Edtl. staff, Voice of Am., '51; Non-fiction Ed., Argosy, '42–'49; Feature Wtr., Fgn. Corr., Ledger Synd., '34–'41; OPC; Hunter Col., New Sch. for Social Rsch.; b. N.Y.C., 1910; p. Abraham and Golde Marrow Genn; h. Edward T. Wilkes; c. Dan Wilkes; res: 2 Sutton Pl. S., N.Y., N.Y. 10022.

GENTHNER, ANN DEICH, Asst. Mgr., WIGS, FM & AM, 40 Church St., Gouverneur, N.Y. 13642, '64; Wms. Dir., Program Dir.; AWRT, NAB, N.Y. State Bdcstrs. Assn.; N.Y. State AP Bdcstrs. Assn. (First Wm. Dir.); Univ. of N.H., BS, '55; Univ. of Zurich, Switzerland, '55–'56; b. Bklyn., N.Y., 1934; p. Herman and Rose Leicht Deich; h. Morris Genthner; c. Wayne Richard, Diana Mercedes; res: 226 Clinton St., Gouverneur, N.Y. 13642.

GENTRY, DOROTHY FREE, Ed., The Ohio County News, 125 Center St., Hartford, Ky. 42347, '61–; Assoc. Ed., '56–'61; Feature Wtr., Reptr., '43; Colmst., weekly, Rough River Ripples, '63–; Auth., "Life and Legend of Lawrence County, Alabama," ('62); Ky. Press Assn. (Best Hometown Colm., '66), Western Ky. Press Assn., Intl. Conf. of Weekly Nwsp. Eds., Nat. Nwsp. Assn.; res: 517 Mulberry St., Hartford, Ky. 42347.

GENTRY, HELEN, Free-lance Bk. Designer, Art Dir.; Partner, Art Dir., Holiday House Publ. (N.Y.C.), '35–'63; Gentry Press, '25–'34; Co-auth., "Chronology of Books and Printing" ('36); Univ. of Cal., BA, '22; b. Temecula, Cal., 1897; p. Irvin and Elizabeth Hind Gentry; h. David Greenhood; res: 1170 Camino Delora, Santa Fe, N.M. 87501.

GEORGE, ELIZABETH WEBB, Art. Dir., The Michener Co., 6 Penn Center Plaza, Phila., Pa. 19103, '62–; Artist, H. L. Yoh Co., '52–'62; h. Robert F. George; res: 2309 Chestnut Ave., Ardmore, Pa. 19003.

GEORGE, VIVIENNE L., Pubns. Mgr., The California State Colleges, Chico State College, Chico, Cal. 95926, '67–; Pubns. Mgr., Humboldt State Col. (Arcata), '57–'67; PR Dir., Bethany Col. (Lindsborg, Kan.), '55–'57; Free-lance Wtr., Photogr. of mag. features; Lectr., on hist. of Cal. Mother Lode; Cal. Press Wm. (Reg. Dir., '65–'67; three State aws: Best Promotional Brochure, '65, '67; Best Mag. Photo., '65); NFPW, Assoc. Bus. Wtrs. of Am.; First annual "Life on the Desert" feature writing aw., Desert mag., '50; three Ore. Presswm. state aws: Best Feature in Nat. Mag., Best Hist. Feature in Ore. Nwsp., Best Wms. Page in Weekly Nwsp., '56; sole scholarship aw. for writing competition in U.S.A., Mexico, Can., Inst. Allende, San Miguel, Mexico, '58; ACPRA reg. Cit. for excellence in educ. writing, '67; Ore. State Univ., BS, '41; b. Howard, Kan.; p. Donald and Sue Painter Lockhart; h. W. S. George; res: 641 W. Sixth Ave., Chico, Cal. 95926.

GEORGES, JUSTINE FLINT, Pubns. Ed., Walsh Publishing Corp., 3 Sheafe St., Portsmouth, N.H. 03801, '66–; Currently Ed: N.H. Profiles Magazine; Bay State Architect Magazine; Maine, N.H., Vermont Beverage Jnl.; Exec. Ed: New Englander Magazine, Granite State Architect Magazine (Am. Inst. of Architects top aw. for consistency of edtl. excellence, '66); formerly Wms. Page Ed., Portsmouth Herald; Assoc. Ed., New England Home Magazine (Boston, Mass.); Feature Wtr., several Sunday nwsps. in N.E.; Auth. of numerous brochures and bklets. on New England Hist.; b. Worcester, Mass., 1920; p. George and Helena Troeltzsch Flint; h. Herbert Georges; c. Mrs. Christopher MacLeod, Melissa; res: 39 Pine Rd., North Hampton, N.H. 03862.

GERACI, LOIS R., Crtv. Dir., F. Wm. Free & Co., 730 Fifth Ave., N.Y., N.Y. 10019, '69–; Crtv. Dir., Marchalk Adv., '68; Exec. Crtv. Dir., New Product Workshop, Interpublic, '65–'68; Assoc. Crtv. Dir., West Weir Bartel, '62–'65; Elmira Col. for Wm., BA; (Phi Beta Kappa); Duke Univ., MA (Eng. Literature).

GERARDIA, HELEN, Artist; 2231 Broadway, N.Y., N.Y. 10024, '51–; represented in 45 museum, col. collections incl. Met. Museum of Art (N.Y.C.), Bklyn. Museum, Cinn. (Oh.) Museum, Ga. Museum; 19 one-man shows, '53–; numerous aws., fellowships; Am. Soc. of Contemporary Artists (Past Pres.), Artists Equity, Nat. Assn. of Wm. Artists; Who's Who in Am., Who's Who of Am. Wm., Who's Who in the East, Who's Who of Am. Artists; N.Y. Training Sch., BS; b. Ekalerenslov, Russia, 1913; p. Jacob and Sophie Lipshitz Goldberg; res: 490 West End Ave., Apt. 4-C, N.Y., N.Y. 10024.

GERGELY, SHAR SOUTHALL, Wms. Ed., The Desert Sun, 611 S. Palm Canyon Dr., Palm Springs, Cal. 92262, '68–; Colmst., Riverside (Cal.) Daily Enterprise, '58–'63; Colmst., Diplomat mag., '59–'62; Soc. Ed., Palm Springs Life mag., '58–'61; Feature Wtr., Reptr., Wheeling (W.Va.) News-Register, '49–'56; NLAPW (Wheeling Br. VP, '56), Am. Press Wms. Assn.; Bethany Col.; b. Weirton, W.Va., 1930; p. Edgar and Freda Kay Southall; h. Alfred J. Gergely; c. Stuart M.; res: 222 Chino Dr., Palm Springs, Cal. 92262.

GERHARDT, LILLIAN N., Exec. Ed., School Library Journal Book Review and R. R. Bowker Juvenile Projects, R. R. Bowker Co., 1180 Ave. of Americas, N.Y., N.Y. 10036, '66–; articles, revs.; Assoc. Ed., Kirkus Svc., '62–'66; Ref. Librn., Curtis Memorial Lib. (Meriden, Conn.), '57–'60; Asst. Librn., '55–'57; Jr. Asst., New Haven (Conn.) Public Lib., '54–'55; Tchr., Columbia Univ., Sch. of Lib. Svc., '69; ALA, Wms. Nat. Bk. Assn., lib. orgs.; Southern Conn. State Col., BS, '54; Univ. of Chgo., Grad. Lib. Sch., '61; b₈ New Haven, Conn., 1932; p. Victor and Lillian Beecher Gerhardt.

GERICH, CAROL KNECHT, Cultural Arts and Teen Ed., Livermore Herald and News, P.O. Box 31, Livermore, Cal. 94550, '68–; Wms. Page Feature Ed., '68; Tchr., Bryant Jr. HS (Livonia, Mich.); Open Door, advice svc. for troubled teens (Bd. of Dirs.); Teen Employment Svc.; AAUW, Theta Sigma Phi Jnlsm. Aw. ('60); Univ. of Mich., BA (Eng.), '64; Univ. of Colo., '61; Cal. State, grad. work; b. Evanston, Ill., 1942; p. William and Jean Bonisteel Knecht; h. Jerry Gerich; res: 723 Hazel St., Livermore, Cal. 94550.

GERMAIN, ANGELA MIDDLEMAS, Asst. to Publr., Monterey Peninsula Herald, Pacific and Jefferson Sts., Monterey, Cal. 93940, '65–; Feature Wtr., News Photogr., KSBW-TV (Salinas of Cal.), '63–'64; Feature Wtr., News Reptr., San Jose Mercury-News, '62; Ed., Photogr., Reptr., Colmst., Los Gatos Times-Observer, '58–'61; Publicist for State Senator Fred Farr, Cal. Legislator, '65; Publicist for World Affairs Cncl., Monterey Peninsula, '66–'67; Theta Sigma Phi; Best Wms. Pages Aw., '58; Colo. Wms. Col., '45–'47; Univ. of Cal., '49–'51; b. Helena, Mont., 1928; p. George and Alice Blaisdell Middlemas; h. Richard Germain; c. Laren (Mrs. Jesse Brill), Wendy Croft; res: 282 Mar Vista Dr., Monterey, Cal. 93940.

GERNGROSS, FRANCES BANZHAF, Corp. Treas., AE, H. O. Gerngross & Co., Inc., 200 W. 57th St., N.Y., N.Y. 10019, '63–; New York Times, '49–'62; AWNY, Friends of the Whitney Museum, Friends of the Guggenheim; Col. of Mt. St. Vincent, AB, '49; b. N.Y.C., 1927; p. John and Margery Banzhaf; h. Hans Gerngross; c. Thomas James, Andrew B., Julie Ann; res: 115 Central Park W., N.Y., N.Y. 10023.

GERRY, ROBERTA, Pubcty. Mgr., Marsteller Inc., 866 Third Ave., N.Y., N.Y. 10022, '67–; Edtl., PR Dir., AIA; Acc. Dir., PR Dept., Benton & Bowles; Assoc. Ed., Marketing/Communications; N.Y.U., BA; b. N.Y.C.

GERSON, JEANNE, Actress, c/o Herman Zimmerman Agency, 12007 Ventura Pl., Studio City, Cal. 91604; SAG, AEA, AFTRA (Life Mbr.); Boston Univ., Vassar, Boston Conservatory of Music.

GERSTNER, EDNA SUCKAU, Auth: "Song By The River," "Idelette;" Wheaton Col., AB, '34; Univ. of Pa., MA, '36; b. Champa, India, 1914; p. C. H. and Lulu Johnston Suckau; h. John Gerstner; c. Judy Black, Rachel Gwen, Jonathan Neil; res: R.D. #1, Ligonier, Pa. 15658.

GERVAIS, PATRICIA JEAN JOY, Film Ed., King Broadcasting Co., KGW-TV, 1501 S.W. Jefferson St., Portland, Ore. 97201, '68–; Cont. Dir., Public Svc. Dir., KGW Radio, '67–'68; Reptr., Photogr., Lake Oswego Rev., '67; Entertainment Ed., Portland State Univ., Vanguard, '66–'67; Prod. Mgr., Madison-West Adv., '65–'66; Actress, Sound Tech., Portland Actor's Co., '68–'69; AWRT; Glendale Col., AA (Art-Theatre Arts), '59; Portland State Univ., '66–'67; b. Glendale, Cal., 1939; p. Richard Joy and Jean Wessa Harber; h. Kenneth R. Gervais (div.); c. William Walker McDonald, Lise Catherine Gervais.

GESNER, ELSIE MILLER, Auth: about 200 published short stories, articles, biographical sketches; bks: "The Lumber Camp Kids" ('57), "In the Stillness of the Storm" (Zondervan, '63); Free-lance Wtr. for religious periodicals; personality sketches; Baptist Ch. Work; children's work; Barrington Col.; b. Guilford, Conn., 1919; p. William and Katherine F. Hart Miller; h. Rev. Lewis G. Gesner, Jr.; c. Joy, Lewis Grant, III; res: Rte. 35, Box 339A, Tenants Harbor, Me. 04860.

GETMAN, LOLA WOODCOCK, Chief, Technical Library, U.S. Air Force, Rome Air Development Center, Griffiss Air Force Base, N.Y. 13440, '56–; Ref. Librn., '51–'56; Librn., Jervis Lib. (Rome, N.Y.), '46–'51; Tchr., Waterville (N.Y.) Central Sch., '35–'41; ZONTA, Special Libs. Assn.; St. Lawrence Univ., BS, '31; Syracuse Univ., MS, '39; BS (Lib. Sci.), '50; b. Rome, N.Y.; p. James and Edith Thayer Woodcock; h. Ernest Getman (div.); c. James Jeffrey; res: 405 Elm St., Rome, N.Y. 13440.

GETTEMY, GRETCHEN HARRISON, Free-lance Wtr., 3431 S.W. 20th St., Ft. Lauderdale, Fla. 33312; Feature Wtr., Broward Times, '69; Educ. Wtr., Williamsport (Pa.) Grit, '59–'60; Ft. Lauderdale News, '61–'67; Gen. Assigt. Reptr., Valley Daily News (Tarentum, Pa.), '60–'61; various orgs., incl. Theta Sigma Phi, Fla. Wms. Press Club; Pa. State Univ. '58–'61; Fla. Atlantic Univ., BA, '66; b. Tarentum, Pa., 1940; p. Hal H. Harrison; h. Scott C. Gettemy; res: 3431 S.W. 20th St., Ft. Lauderdale, Fla. 33312.

GEYER, GEORGIE ANNE, Fgn. Corr., Chicago Daily News, 401 N. Wabash Ave., Chgo., Ill., '64–; Roving World Corr., Latin Am. Corr., Reptr., Southtown Econst.; articles, Look, The Nation, The Atlantic Monthly, others; Theta Sigma Phi (nat. merit aw., '67); Chgo. 1st pl., human interest aw., Am. Nwsp. Guild, '62; Latin Am. Aw., OPC, '66; Northwestern Univ., BS (Jnlsm.), '56 (alumnae merit aw., '66); Univ. of Vienna, Fulbright Scholarship, '56–'57; b. Chgo., Ill., 1935; p. Robert G. and Georgie H. Gervens Geyer; res: 339 W. Barry Ave., Chgo., Ill. 60657.

GIBBONS, CELIA TOWNSEND, Founder, Pres.-Publr., Bulletin Board Pictures, Inc., Box 16222, Elmwood Sta., Mpls., Minn. 55416, '54–; Founder, Pres., Periodical Litho Art Co., '62; Partner, Mines and Escholier mags., '54–'69; Partner, Youth Assocs. Co., '42–'69; Contrb. Ed., Children's Magazines, '35–; Adv. Mgr., Hotel Nicollet, '33–'37; Univ. of Minn., '30–'33; b. Fargo, N.D., 1911; p. Harry and Helen Haag Townsend; h. John Gibbons; c. Mrs. Mary Vee Ellenberg, John Townsend; res: 1416 Alpine Pass, Tyrol Hills, Mpls., Minn. 55416.

GIBBONS, HELEN BAY, Free-lance Wtr.; Auth.: "On Your Way," "Saint and Savage"; Clinical Psych. Secy., VA Psychiatric Hosp. (Palo Alto, Cal.), '48–'50; Secy., Children's Svc. Soc. (Salt Lake City, Ut.), '47–'48; Secy. to Dean, Univ. of Ut. Sch. of Law, '46–'47; Missionary, Church of Jesus Christ of Latter-Day Saints,

'43–'45; NLAPW (Salt Lake City Br. Mbr., '66–'68; Owl Aw., '67), League of Ut. Wtrs. (Salt Lake City Br. VP, '68–'70); b. Junction, Ut., 1921; p. Horace and Elizabeth Maxwell Bay; h. Francis Gibbons; c. Suzanne, Mark, Ruth, Daniel; res: 1784 Yale Ave., Salt Lake City, Ut. 84108.

GIBBS, ILA MAE, Asst. Secy. and Ed., Mutual Reinsurance Bureau, 1550 Pearl St., P.O. Box 188, Belvidere, Ill. 61008, '49–; Asst. Secy., Ill. Assn. of Mutual Ins. Cos., '41–'47; Mutual Ins. Communicators, IEA, ICIE, BPW (former Treas.); b. DeKalb County, Ill., 1907; p. Charles Willard and Emma Theresa Brandt Gibbs; res: 415 Julien St., Belvidere, Ill. 61008.

GIBBS, MAJORIE GOOD, Free-lance PR and Consumer Info. Rep., Talent, daily radio show, weekly TV show, to '68; Mkt. Info. Agt., Mich. State Univ., '54–'68; Home Svc. Advisor, Consumer Power Co., '48–'54; Nutrition Advisor, Sealtest Foods, '45–'48; Lab. Tech., Chrysler Corp., '43–'45; Homemaking Tchr., Dearborn Public Sch., '42–'43; Esther Peterson's Comm., Info. for Families with Limited Incomes, '64–'65; Theta Sigma Phi, AWRT (Detroit Chptr. VP, '60–'62), Mich. Home Econs. Assn. (VP, '50–'51), Home Econsts. in Bus. (Detroit Chptr. Pres., '51–'53), Wms. Adv. Club of Detroit (Pres., '63–'65), Adult Educ. of Met. Detroit (Pres., '60–'62), Highland Park Jr. Col., '37–'39; Wayne State Univ., BS, '42 (Headliner of the Yr. Aw., '68); b. Highland Park, Mich., 1920; p. Chester and Iva Clemens Good; h. James R. Gibbs; res: 9186 Arnold, Detroit, Mich. 48239.

GIBERSON, DOROTHY DODDS, Auth., "The Echoing Wave" (Coward McCann; John Gresham), mag. articles, short stories; bk. revs. for local nwsps.; Auths. League, Cal. Wtrs. Club, Burlingame Wtrs. Club (past Pres.), Peninsula Art Assn. (past VP); Univ. of Wash., AB; b. Seattle, Wash.; p. John and Elizabeth Knowles Dodds; h. Woods Giberson; c. William, Michael; res: 2714 Easton Dr., Burlingame, Cal. 94010.

GIBONEY, BETTY O'NEAL, Farm Ed., The Courier-Times, 201 S. 14th St., New Castle, Ind. 47362, '52–; Staff Feature Wtr., '47–; County Ed., '51–'60; Prod., wms. progs., WCTW, '47–'51; Mng. Ed., Compass Points, Gibbs & Cox (N.Y.C.), '44–'45; Freelance Wtr., '39–'41; Dancer, Roxy Theatre, '32–'38; Columbia Univ.; N.Y.U.; Traphagen Sch. of Fashion; b. Cincinnati, Oh., 1913; p. Corwin and Norma Collas O'Neal; h. David Giboney; res: 778 N. Fair Oaks Dr., New Castle, Ind. 46362.

GIBSON, AUDREY WILLIAMS, Mgr., Public Commtns., WCBS-TV, 51 W. 52 St., N.Y., N.Y., 10019, '65–; Secy., Dir. of Info Svcs., three yrs. Interviewer, Asst. to Dir., Adoption, Placement Svcs., N.Y.C. Dept. of Welfare; Lectr., bdcst., career aims; Hunter Col., BS (Bus. Adm.); b. Elizabeth City, N.C.; p. Oscar and Mae Coggins Williams; h. Arnett Gibson (div.); c. Rhonda; res: 2332 Tiebout Ave., Bronx, N.Y. 10458.

GIBSON, ELEANOR BEATRICE, Tech. Supvsr., Union Catalog, Connecticut State Library, 231 Capitol Ave., Hartford, Conn. 06115, '68–; Logan Lewis Lib., Carrier Corp., '47–'70; U.S. Army WAC, '50–'52, '42–'46; Aetna Life & Casualty Safety Engineering Lib., '33–'42; WNBA, Col. Art Assn. of Am., Am. Soc. for Info. Sci., Special Libs. Assn.; (Hall of Fame, aw., '68); Cornell Univ., AB, '28; Syracuse Univ., MS (Lib. Sci.), '57; b. London, England; p. Harry and Anne White Gibson; res: 23 Fernridge Rd., W. Hartford, Conn. 06107.

GIBSON, EVA GALLAHAR, Wms. Program Dir., WGAD, 2500 Forrest Ave., Gadsden, Ala. 35902, '61–; Copywtr., Adm. Asst., Sls. Exec., Nwsp. By-line; AWRT, Birmingham Press Club, BPW; b. Piedmont, Ala., 1936; p. J. C. and Nina Coleman Gallahar; h. (div.); c. Adrianne Elizabeth, Jonathan Douglas; res: 115 Carol Ave., Gadsden, Ala. 35901.

GIBSON, FRANCES M., Educ., Ch., Aviation Ed., The Daily Ardmoreite, Ardmore, Okla. 73401; HS Jnlsm. Tchr., '57–'67; Adv. Copywtr., '53–'56; Stewardess, TWA, '44–'45; Theta Sigma Phi, Ninety-Nines, Lost Angels; Pilot; Nwsp. Fund Fellow, Univ. of Tex., '61; h. Henry Murray Gibson.

GIBSON, GWEN, Free-lance Wtr., '65–; Staff Wtr., New York Herald Tribune, '61–'65; Colmst., Wash. Corr., New York Daily News, '56–'61; Reptr., UP, '51–'56; Co-auth., "The Jewish Wife"; WNPC (past VP), ASCAP; h. Sidney Schwartz.

GIBSON, JEWEL HENSON, Asst. Prof., Sam Houston University, Huntsville, Tex. 77340, '60–; Auth: "Black Gold" ('50), "Joshua Beene and God" ('46); AAUW (Huntsville Br. Pres., '61–'63), Tex. Tchrs. Assn., Tex. Inst. Letters; Sam Houston State Tchrs. Col., BS, '32; MA, '50; b. Bald Prairie, Tex., 1904; p. Jasper and Mary Davis Henson; h. Felix A. Gibson; res: Rte. 3, Box 111, Huntsville, Tex. 77340.

GIBSON, MARY BASS, Associate Director, MacDowell Colony for Creative Artists, 1083 Fifth Ave., N.Y., N.Y. 10022, '67–; Roving Ed., Family Circle, '69–; Home Career Series, currently; Special Projects Ed., Seventeen, '63–'65; Exec. Ed., Ladies' Home Journal, '44–'62; "How America Lives"; Feature Pubcty. Dir., Abraham & Straus (Bklyn.), '35–'40; WNPC (Wash., D.C.), OPC, Cosmopolitan; Barnard Col., AB; b. Chgo., Ill.; p. James and May Emerson Carson; h. 1. Basil N. Bass (dec.) 2. George Rollings Gibson; c. Richardson C. Bass; res: 850 Park Ave., N.Y., N.Y. 10021.

GIBSON, MARY SUE, Mgr. of Wms. Sls. Dev., American Airlines, 633 Third Ave., N.Y., N.Y. 10017, '68–; Dir. of Adv. and PR, Haggar Co. (Dallas, Tex.), '63–'67; VP of Mktng., Paragon Industries, '60–'63; Free-lance Wtr., covered Olympics, Grenoble, France, '68; Adv. League of Dallas, Adv. Club of N.Y., Pi Beta Phi, Old Merchants House Assn.; Who's Who of Am. Bus. Wm.; Univ. of Okla., '56–'57; Southern

Methodist Univ., BBA, '60; b. Wichita Falls, Tex., 1938; p. William and Ruth Maxey Gibson; res: 1160 Fifth Ave., N.Y., N.Y. 10028.

GIBSON, ROSSIE ANN, Mgr., Home Economists Institute, Hotpoint-General Electric Company, 5600 W. Taylor St., Chgo., Ill. 60644, '63–; Sales Prom. and PR, O. M. Scott & Co., '61–'63; Reg. Home Econst., Western Beet Sugar Prodrs., '56–'61; Home Econst., Harvey & Howe, '56; Home Makers Svc. Dept., Nat. Livestock and Meat Bd., '51–'55; Home Econst., A. J. Lindeman & Hoverson Appliance Manufacturers, '50–'51; Home Econst., Rural Gravure, '49; Am. Home Econs. Assn. (Nat. Conv. Delegate, '67), Ill. Home Econs. Assn. (Exec. Bd., '67–'68), Home Econsts. In Bus., Electrical Wms. Round Table (Chgo. Chptr. Chmn., '65–'66), Home Appliance Assn., AWRT, Clarke Col.; Mundelein Col., AB, '49; b. Mpls., Minn.; p. E. Stuart and Mary Cosgrove Gibson; res: 2450 W. Greenleaf, Chgo., Ill. 60645.

GIBSON, THEODORA ROXANNA, Home Mag. Ed., Cleveland Press, 901 Lakeside Ave., Cleve., Oh. 44114, '67–; Reptr., '62–'67; Oh. Nwsp. Wms. Assn. (aw., '65), NHFL, Design Wtrs. Intl. (Co-Founder, Secy.), Nat. Soc. of Interior Designers (aw., '66); Oh. Wesleyan Univ., BA, '62; b. Cleve., Oh.; p. Theodore and Virginia Cook Gibson; res: 15234 Clifton Blvd., Lakewood, Oh. 44107.

GIDDENS, NANCY BRYANT, Wms. Ed., Philadelphia Tribune, 524 S. 16th St., Phila., Pa. 19146, '57–; Owner, N. L. Giddens Fashion Clinic; Gtr. Phila. Press Wms. Club (Pres.; Founder), Theta Sigma Phi; many civic aws.; h. Earl W. Giddens; res: 5611 Gainor Rd., Phila., Pa. 19131.

GIDNEY, MARGARET D., Head Librn., D'Youville College Library, 320 Porter Ave., Buffalo, N.Y. 14201, '68–; Asst. Librn., Librn., '62–'68; Librn., Western Reserve Hist. Soc. (Cleve., Oh.), '39–'47; ALA, N.Y. Lib. Assn., AAUP; Sioux Falls Col., AB, '38; Western Reserve Univ., BS (Lib. Sci.), '39.

GIEHLL, JEANNINE CATHERINE, Traf. Mgr., Sykes Advertising, Inc., 411 Seventh Ave., Pitt., Pa. 15219, '66–; Finalist in Miss Torch Contest ('67), volunteer hosp. work; Univ. of Pitt., '61–; b. Canonsburg, Pa., 1943; p. Beatrice Bushmire Giehll; res: 400 Cochran Rd., Pitt., Pa. 15228.

GIESECKE, MILDRED WHITTEMORE, Auth: "Hymn Writers of the Christian Church" (Publ. under maiden name; Whittemore Assoc., U. S.; Hodder & Stroughton, Eng.); Beloit Col. (Wis.); Univ. of Me.; b. Boston, Mass., 1946; p. Carroll and Roberta Cooper Whittemore; h. Rainer Giesecke; res: E. Grand Ave., R.F.D. #4, Scarborough, Me. 04074.

GIESEN, EDNA JOHANNA, Pres., Giesen Management Inc., Columbia Lecture Bureau Inc., P.O. Box 287, Brookfield, Conn. 06804, '53–; Dir., Exec. VP, '46–

'53; rep. of artists and lectrs. as Clare Booth Luce, Adolphe Menjou, Trygve Lie, Tallulah Bankhead, Rudolph Bing, Salvador Dali, Burl Ives, James Reston, Anna Russell, Arthur Schlesinger, Jr.; M. W. Rep., Columbia Artists Management, '42–'46; E. Rep., Columbia Lect. Bur., CBS, '40–'42; Prom. Mgr., Berlitz Schs. of Langs., '38–'40; Wms. Nat. Repl. Club; Columbia Univ.; b. Lafayette, Ind., 1906; p. Hermann and Mary Schaal Giesen; res: Ironworks Hill Rd., Brookfield, Conn. 06804.

GIFFIN, F. MARIE RITCHIE, Publr., The New England Homestad, '69–; Gen. Mgr., The Inquirer and Mirror, Inc., Milestone, Nantucket, Mass. 02554, '66–; VP, '65; Adv. Mgr., '64; Asst. Treas., '63; Cl., '62; numerous adv. aws., New Eng. Press Assn.; Straight Wharf Theatre (Summer Stock), Am. Cancer Soc., Am. Red Cross; MacMurray Col. for Wm. (Jacksonville, Ill.), '49–'51; b. Hillview, Ill., 1931; p. Kenneth L. and Wilmeth Murray Ritchie; h. Thomas H. C. Giffin; c. Marianne Riddell, James Ritchie; res: Somerset Rd., Nantucket, Mass. 02554.

GIFFORD, DIANE SAMPANES, PR Asst., Munsingwear, Inc. 718 Glenwood Ave., Mpls., Minn. 55405, '62–; Prom. Asst., WTCN Radio and TV, '60–'61; Prom. Dept., Grand Rapids Press, '59–'60; Purchasing John Widdicomb Co., '54–'59; ICIE (Dir. Nat. Affairs), N.W. IEA, Fashion Group, Press Club, PRSA, Mpls. C. of C., Minn. Ad. Club, various offs. and chmnships; Grand Rapids Jr. Col.; Univ. of Minn.; Univ. of Mich.

GIFFORD, ELEANOR R., Publicist, Field Ed., Meredith Press, 1716 Locust St., Des Moines, Ia. 50303, '68–; Consumer Svc. Dir., Oscar Mayer & Co., '58–'67; Consumer Mkt. Agt., Cooperative Ext. Svc., Mich. State Univ., '56–'58; AWRT (Educ. Fndn. Trustee, '66–'67; Badger Chptr. Pres., '61–'63), HEIB, AHEA, Madison Adv. Club, Madison Press Club; Mich. State Univ. BS (Sch. of Home Econs.), '45; b. Jackson, Mich. 1923; p. Clinton D. and Majorie F. Dake Bacon; h. (div.); c. Charles J., John C., Mary Evalyn, Sarah Lee; res: 3909 Monona Dr., Madison, Wisc. 53716.

GIFFORD, MARIE BATTEY, Pres., KEEL, Inc., 710 Spring, Shreveport, La. 71102, '69–; VP, '63; Gen. Mgr., '62; Comml. Mgr., '57–'62; VP, LIN Bdcst., '65; La. Bdcstrs. Assn. (Bd. of Dirs., '67–'68), AAF (10th Dist. Dir., '64–'67); Adv. Club of Shreveport (Pres., '64–'65); Univ. of Okla., BFA, '37; b. Cordell, Okla., 1917; p. John and Mary Yoder Battey; h. Joseph Gifford (dec.); res: 3818 Akard, Shreveport, La. 71105.

GILBERT, ALMA MAGGIORE, Dir., VP, Secy., Aircasters, Incorporated, P.O. Box 182, Scottsdale, Ariz. 85252, '60–; Dir., VP, Corp. Secy., Glendale (Ariz.) Bdcst. Corp.; Program Dir., KYND (Tempe) 1960–1966; Dir., Secy., Ariz. Aircasters; Dir., Secy., Scottsdale Bdcst. Co.; Prog. Dir., KPOK (Scottsdale) 1956–1958; Dir., VP, Secy., Northern Ariz. Aircasters; Bdcst. Cnslt.; numerous aws., hons.; b. Canton, Oh.;

p. Vincent D. and Florence Manack Maggiore; h. Richard B. Gilbert; c. Gary Richard; res: P.O. Box 182, Scottsdale, Ariz. 85252.

GILBERT, ANNE WIELAND, PR Dir., Grant Advertising, Inc., 10 S. Riverside Plaza, Chgo., Ill. 60606, '67–; Free-lance Wtr., motion pictures, film strips, '65–'67; AE, Herbert Rozoff PR, '68; PR Dir., Lobsenz Co., '64–'65; PR Dir., Wms. Architectural League of Chgo., '64; PR Dir., Ac'cent Intl., '52; Chgo. Commty. Music Fndn., Ch. Fedn. Chgo., Pubcty. Club of Chgo.; Wms. Adv. Club Chgo.; Northwestern Univ., BSS, '49; b. Chgo., Ill., 1927; p. David and Joy Arnold Wieland; h. George Gale Gilbert, III; c. Douglas, Christopher; res: 932 15th St., Wilmett, Ill. 60091.

GILBERT, EDITH PORTER, Special Asst. to the Secy., United States Department of Housing and Urban Development, 451-7th Street S.W., Wash., D.C. 20410, '65–; Special Asst. to Admr., HHFA, '60–'65; Info. Specialist, '50–'60; Ed., Federal Housing Adm., '48–'50; Wtr., '40–'48; WNPC (Bd. Mbr., '57–'60; Treas., '54), ANWC (VP, '60–'62; Secy., '55; Bd. Mbr., '56–'58), Theta Sigma Phi; Univ. of Wis., BA (Jnlsm.); b. Glen Carlyn, Va.; p. Herbert and Augusta Brindley Porter; h. J. Hite Gilbert; res: 3336 O St. N.W., Wash., D.C. 20007.

GILBERT, MARY JORDAN, Adm. Dir., Off. of PR, Vassar College, Poughkeepsie, N.Y. 12601, '59–; Staff, Elmo Roper and Assocs. (N.Y.C.), '58–'59; Tchr., '46–'50; ACPRA, Met. Col. PR Cncl., Jr. League of New Haven (Bd. Mbr.), Jr. League of Poughkeepsie; Vassar Col., AB, '45; Wesleyan Univ., MA, '47; Yale Univ. Grad. Sch., Dept. of Educ.; b. New Haven, Conn., 1924; p. William and Marion Porter Jordan; h. N. Charlton Gilbert (div.); c. Charlton; res: Vassar Garden Apts., Poughkeepsie, N.Y. 12601.

GILBERT, MILDRED TAYLOR, Intl. Exec. Ed., Vogue, 420 Lexington Ave., N.Y., N.Y. 10017, '66–; Exec. Ed.; Fashion, Product Dir., Adv. Mgr., Charles of the Ritz; Vassar Col.; b. Romney, Ind.; p. Bennett and Gertrude Simison Taylor; h. Gar K. Gilbert; res: 815 Park Ave., N.Y., N.Y. 10021.

GILBERT, PATTI, Actress, c/o Herb Tannen & Assoc., 6640 Sunset Blvd., L.A., Cal., and c/o George Morris, 1801 Ave. of The Stars, Century City, L.A., Cal., '45–; Leading Lady, Stagelight and Candlelight Theaters, '64–'69; Chgo. Theater, Drury Lane, '58–'64; Narrator, voice on radio, TV, films; Wtr., TV presentations, Films, '69; Dir., The Prisoner, Stagelight Theater, '64; Artist (pseud: Pagi): One-wm. show (L.A.), '68; Tchr., art; AEA, AFTRA, SAG; Hermes Trophy (Radio, '64), Venice Film Festival aw., Comml. TV, '68; N.Y.U.; b. N.Y.C., 1931; p. Edwin H. and Dorothy Wolfe Friedman; h. Henry G. Saperstein; c. Laurel, Gilbert, Gina Gilbert; res: 624 N. Alpine Dr., Beverly Hills, Cal. 90210.

GILBERT, RUTH HELEN, Ed., "In And Around

Town," New York Magazine, 207 E. 32 St., N.Y., N.Y. 10016, '68–; TV Ed., '68 (innovated theme continuity for TV sec. illustrations); TV Ed., N.Y. Herald Tribune, '42– folding; N.Y. Nwsp. Wms. Assn.; b. N.Y.C., 1916; p. Joseph and Anne Reimer Gilbert; c. Mrs. Gwynne Denson; res: 9601 Shore Rd., Bklyn., N.Y. 11209.

GILBERT, VIRGINIA BAKER, Cnslt.; Adv. Dir., Nash Phillips-Capus Real Estate; Dir. PR, Tex. Educ. Fndn., Inc. (San Marcos); Dir. PR, Northern Systems Company (Lincoln, Neb.); Dir. of Adv., Capital Plaza Shopping Ctr. (Austin); Feature Wtr: Air Force Times, '48–'49; San Marcos Record, '65–'66; Austin States-man, '63–; Home Life Magazine, '64–'65; This Day Magazine, '64–; Austin Adv. Club, BPW; Univ. of Md., Ext. Br., Munich, Germany; Univ. of Tex.; b. Karnes City, Tex., 1925; p. Joseph and Minnie Lee Baker; c. Kathleen Sears, Don; res: 2011 Cheshire, Austin, Tex. 78723.

GILBERTSON, MILDRED GEIGER, Auth: "Academy Summer," "The Unchosen," "Champions Don't Cry," others; 500 stories; Univ. of Tex.; b. Galena, Ill.; h. Philip Gilbertson; c. Bruce, Gay; res: 950 Park Ave., Eugene, Ore. 97402.

GILBORNE, JEAN ELIZABETH, Unit Librn., Geneseo Community Unit, Dist. 228, 115 W. Pearl St., Geneseo, Ill. 61254, '51–; Asst. Librn., Univ. HS (Urbana), '50–'51; HS Tchr., '38–'50; Ill. Educ. Assn., NEA, Ill. Lib. Assn., ALA, Geneseo BPW (past Pres.), Ill. Fed. BPW (Dist. Chmn., '62–'64); Ill. State Univ., BE, '37; Univ. of Ill., MA, '44; MS (Lib. Sci.), '51; b. Bonfield, Ill., 1910; p. John and Anna Stroud Gilborne; res: 607-1/2 S. Center, Geneseo, Ill. 61254.

GILCHREST, MARJORIE SPRIGGS, Dir. of Nat. Orgs., Schools and Women's Activities, U.S. Savings Bonds Division, Department of the Treasury, Wash., D.C. 20226, '65–; Asst. to Dir., Adv. Prom. Bur., Wash., D.C., '51–'65; Dir. of Adv. and Prom., Mass. State Off. '43–'46; Chief, Radio Sec., '42–'43; Dir. of Wms. and Children's Radio Progs., '40–'42; Partner, Gilchrest-Spriggs & Co., Boston, '46–'51; Pubcty. Dir. and Copywtr., WORL Radio, '38–'40; Theatrical Pubcty. Dir., '36–'38; Tchr., Boston Univ. Sch. of PR, '48–'50; AWRT (Vice Chmn., Educ. Fndn., '67–; Wash., D.C., Chptr. Pres., '65–'66), Zeta Phi Eta (Advisory Bd. Chmn.; Fndn. Chmn.; Nat. Pres., '57–'64), ZONTA; Emerson Col., BLI, '36; N.Y.U.; Boston Univ.; b. Rome, N.Y., 1913; p. Charles J. and Sadie Payne Spriggs; h. Charles J. Gilchrest; res: 2000 S. Eads St., Arlington, Va. 22202.

GILCHRIST, E. BRENDA, Sr. Ed., Art Book Division, Praeger Publishers, 111 Fourth Ave., N.Y., N.Y. 10003, '65–; Staff Wtr., Am. Heritage Publ. Co., '64; Reptr., Show Magazine, '62–'64; Museum of Modern Art, '59–'62; U.S. Fine Arts Program, Brussels World's Fair, '57–'58; Durlacher Bros. Art Gallery, '54–'57; Translat-ed, French into Eng., "Marc Chagall: The Ceiling of the Paris Opera" by Jacques Lassaigne, '66; The Draw-

ing Soc., Soc. of Architectural Hists.; Smith Col., BA; b. Coulsdon, Surrey, Eng.; p. Huntington and Eliza-beth Brace Gilchrist; res: 175 W. 93rd St., N.Y., N.Y. 10025.

GILDER, ROSAMOND, Pres., International Theatre Institute of the United States, 245 W. 52nd St., N.Y., N.Y. 10019, '48–; Founder, Hon. Pres.; Ed./Drama Critic, Theatre Arts, '24–'48; Am. Nat. Theatre and Acad. (Bd. Mbr., Secy.); Auth: "Enter the Actress," "John Gielgud's Hamlet," "Theatre Collection in Libraries and Museums" (with George Freedley), "A Theatre Library," Ed., Theatre Arts Anthology (Theatre Arts Books, '50); Nat. Comm. for UNESCO (Chmn., Panel on Dramatic Art, '48–'54); N.Y. Drama Critics Circle (Secy., '46–'50; Hon. Mbr., '50–); Chmn., U.S. Delegations to Intl. Theatre Congresses; Ful-bright Fellowship, '55–'56; Guggenheim Fellowship, '50; b. Marion, Mass.; p. Richard Watson and Helena deKay Gilder; res: 24 Gramercy Park, N.Y., N.Y. 10003.

GILGREEN, MINA MARTINEZ, Actress: Margarita in Motion Pic. "One-Eyed Jacks,"; Pacific Telephone film for schs.; TV role of Linda Martinez in series "Redigo," role in "Troubleshooters," others; Clairol, Inc., 907 Flower St., Glendale, Cal. 91201, '64–; SAG; b. Laredo, Tex., 1935; p. Estanislao and Micaela Villarreal Martinez; h. John Gilgreen; c. Tina Marie; res: 337 Hollywood Way, Burbank, Cal. 91505.

GILL, HELEN GILLIS, Pres., Gill-Perna, Inc., 575 Lex-ington Ave., N.Y., N.Y. 10022, '52–; Dir., New Tools For Learning; AWNY, NAB, Pa. Assn. of Bdcstrs.; Am. Acad. of Dramatic Arts; b. N.Y.C.; p. Thomas and Margaret Gill; h. John J. Perna, Jr.; res: 201 E. 77th St., N.Y., N.Y. 10022.

GILLESPIE, JANET WICKS, Auth: "Peacock Manure and Marigolds" (Viking, '64); "The Joy of a Small Garden" (Dodd-Mead, '63), "Bedlam in the Back Seat" (Crowell, '56); Copy Ed., MacMillan and Har-vard Presses; Tchr., Miss Fine's Sch. (Princeton, N.J.), '37–'38; Shady Hill Sch. (Cambridge, Mass.), '36–'37; Mt. Holyoke, BA, '36 (magna cum laude); b. E. Orange, N.J., 1913; p. Robert and Eleanor Hall Wicks; h. 1—William Gillespie (dec.); 2—Robert F. Grindley; c. Helen (Mrs. Hendrik van Loon), Christopher, Margaret, Timothy; res: Westport Point, Mass. 02791.

GILLESPIE, Sr. MARGARET JANE, Librn., St. John Cathedral High School, 830 N. Jackson, Milw., Wis. 53202, '62–; Librn., Trinity HS (River Forest, Ill., '47–'62); ALA, Am. Assn. of Sch. Librns., Catholic Lib. Assn., Wis. Lib. Assn., Wis. Catholic Lib. Assn., North-ern Ill. Unit Catholic Lib. Assn., Nat. Cncl. of Tchrs. of Eng., NDEA Fellow (Univ. of Denver, '65); Marylhurst Col., '41–'44; Rosary Col., BA, '45; MA, '61; b. Port-land, Ore., 1922; p. Emmett and Marguerite Dillon Gillespie; res: 845 N. Van Buren, Milw., Wis. 53202.

GILLEY, EVANGELINE CHATMAS, Tchr. Placement Supvsr., University of Houston, Cullen Blvd., Houston, Tex. 77004, '65–; Tchr., '64–'65, '57–'59, '35–'39; Librn., '34–'35; Theta Sigma Phi, Houston Pers. and Guidance Assn., Assn. For Sch. Col. and Univ. Staffing; Univ. of Tex., BA (Eng., Jnlsm.), '32 (magna cum laude); b. Marlin, Tex.; p. James and Mary Xydias Chatmas; h. L. Ray Gilley (dec.); c. Mary Alice, James F.; res: 1527 Milford, Houston, Tex. 77006.

GILLHAM, MARY MEWBORN, Univ. Librn., University of Toledo, 2801 W. Bancroft St., Toledo, Oh. 43606, '21–; Prof., '50–; Assoc. Prof., '45–'50; ALA, Oh. Col. Assn. (Lib. Div. Pres., '58–'59), Oh. Lib. Assn. (1st VP, '37–'38; Col.—Univ. Div. Chmn., '57–'59), Toledo Municipal League (Treas., '57–; Bd. Mbr., '54–;) AAUW, ZONTA; Who's Who in Am.; Who's Who in Lib. Sci.; Who's Who in Educ.; Who's Who of Am. Wm.; Who's Who in the Mid-West; Dir. of Am. Scholars; Dic. of Intl. Biog.; Univ. of Toledo, AB, '27; MA, '31; Univ. of Mich., AB (Lib. Sci.), '41; b. Atlanta, Ga., 1899; p. Clarence and Sally Matthew Mewborn; h. Dr. Richard Gillham; res: 618 Sylvania Ave., Toledo, Oh. 43612.

GILLHAM, OTHA WADE, Librn., Supvsr., Hardin County Schools, 616 Harlem St., Savannah, Tenn. 38372, '69–; Librn., Central HS, '57–'69; NEA, AAUW, Tenn. Lib. Assn., BPW, Delta Kappa Gamma, Who's Who of Am. Wm., Who's Who in Lib Sci.; Union Univ., BS, '49; Univ. of Tenn., MS, '54; b. Adamsville, Tenn., 1919; p. M. B. and Bertha Johnson Wade; h. Phil Gillham; res: Crump, Tenn. 38327.

GILLIAM, DOROTHY BUTLER, Bdcstr., Channel Five, Metromedia, 5151 Wisconsin Ave., Wash., D.C. 20016, '68–; Reptr., Washington Post, '61–'66; Assoc. Ed., Jet, '57–'59; AFTRA, WNPC; Capitol Press Club aw., '69; '67; N.Y. Nwsp. Wms. aw., '61; Lincoln Univ., BA, '57 (cum laude); Columbia Univ., MS (Jnlsm.), '61; b. Memphis, Tenn., 1936; p. Adee and Jessie Norment Butler; h. Sam Gilliam; c. Stephanie, Melissa, Leah; res: 1752 Lamont St. N.W., Wash., D.C. 20010.

GILLIES, JEAN E., Home Mgt.-Equipment Ed., Farm Journal, Inc., 230 W. Washington Sq., Phila., Pa. 19105, '61–; Ed., Consumer Mktng. Agent, Mich. State Univ. Ext. Svc.; Am. Home Econs. Assn., Home Econsts. in Bus., Electrical Wms. Round Table; Mich. State Univ., BS (Home Econs.); Univ. of Wis., MS (Home Econs. Jnlsm.).

GILLIES, MARY DAVIS, Free-lance Wtr., Interior Design Cnslt.; Interior Design Ed., McCall's, '29–'65; AE, Gardner Adv., '28–'29; Textile Specialist, Bur. of Home Econs., U.S. Dept. of Agriculture, '26–'27; Instr., Applied Design, Univ. of Ore., '24–'25; Auth: "McCall's Decorating Book" (Random House, '64); "How to Keep House" (Harper & Row, '49; revsd., '68); others; NHFL (Pres., '56), Fashion Group, Nat. Soc. of Interior Designers, Design Wtrs. Intl.; Freedom Fndn. Gold Medal aw., '49; Dorothy Dawes aw., '61, '54; Univ. of Wash., BS, '23; MA, '24; b. Partridge, Kan., 1900; p. Robert and Harriet Rehm

Davis; h. 1. Robert C. Gillies (div.); 2. Joseph E. Johnston; res: 5 Ridge Rd., Sparta, N.J. 07871.

GILLILAND, MARY-ELLEN BARBER, PR Cnslr., Milici Advertising Agency, Inc., 1100 Ward Ave., Honolulu, Hi. 96814, '66–; Free-lance Wtr.; Mag. Articles, PR, Assoc. Ed., Family Circle Magazine, '66; Sr. Supervising Ed., News Front Magazine (N.Y.C.), '64–'66; Theta Sigma Phi (Honolulu Chptr. Secy., '68–'69); Marquette Univ., BA (Jnlsm., John W. Thomas Co. Scholarship; Kappa Tau Alpha; Gamma Pi Epsilon); b. Mpls., Minn., 1942; p. Joseph P. and Frances B. Barber; h. Lawrence Gilliland; res: 1504 Alexander St., Honolulu, Hi. 96822.

GILLMOR, FRANCES, Auth: three novels, three biogs.; numerous univ. bulls., short stories, articles, revs. on Mexico, Am. Southwest, Aztec hist., folklore; Prof. of Eng., Univ. of Ariz., '52–; various teaching posts since '31; Nwsp. Reptr., Fla., '23–'25; Lectr.; Am. Folklore Soc. (VP, '58, '64; Fellow), Am. Anthropological Assn., Wtrs. Guild of Auths. League of Am., Modern Lang. Assn.; Fellow, John Simon Guggenheim Mem. Fndn., '59–'60; Univ. of Ariz., BA, '28; MA, '31; Universidad Nacional Autonoma de Mexico, '57; Univ. of Chgo., '21–'23; b. Buffalo, N.Y., 1903; p. Churchill and Annie McVicar Gillmor; res: P.O. Box 4605, University Sta., Tucson, Ariz. 85717.

GILMORE, ARABY ALLEN, Mgr., Sls. Aids, Prom., Look Magazine, Cowles Communications, Inc., 488 Madison Ave., N.Y., N.Y. 10022, '67–; Copy Chief, Look Prom., '57–'67; Sr. Copywtr., Asst. Prom. Mgr., '55–'57; Sr. Copywtr., Ed., Radio Adv. Bur., '52–'55; Sr. Copywtr., Asst. Mgr., CBS Radio Adv. & TV Sls., '49–'52; AWNY (Dir., '69); Nat. Cncl. of Wm., AFA; Mag. Prom. Group; Smith Col., AB; b. Summit, N.J.; p. Robert and Arabella Allen Gilmore; res: 145 E. 92nd St., N.Y., N.Y. 10028.

GILMORE, JANE O., Graphic Designer, Department of Medical-Dental Communication, Georgetown University, 3800 Reservoir Rd. N.W., Wash., D.C. 20007, '68–; Artist with adv. agcy. (Miami Beach, Fla.), '67–'68; Fla. State Univ., BA (Adv. Design), '67; b. Phila., Pa., 1945; res: 10201 Grosvenor Pl., Apt. 1111, Rockville, Md. 20852.

GILROY, GLORIA ANDERSON, Gloria Anderson Public Relations, 1435 N. Fairfax Ave., Hollywood, Cal. 90046, '59–; Fashion Coordr., "Queen For A Day," TV, '54–'58; Raymond R. Morgan Adv., '53–'54; Hoffeld Estates, Buffalo, N.Y. '51–'52; Universal Film Exchange, Buffalo, '47–'50; AWRT; Cert. of Merit, special event prom. L.A. Adv. Wm.'s LuLu Aw; Univ. of Buffalo; b. Buffalo, N.Y.; p. Orval E. and Maryellen Anderson; res: 3780 Willow Crest Ave., Studio City, Cal. 91604.

GIMBEL, ELINOR STEINER, Chmn. of the Bd., S. S. Steiner Inc., 655 Madison Ave., N.Y., N.Y. 10021; Staff, PM Nwsp.; Dir., Liebmann Breweries; Dir., Electronized Chemical Co.; OPC, Wms. City Club, U.S. Brewer's Fndn.; b. West End, N.J.; p. Sam S. and Sadie Liebmann Steiner; h. Louis S. Gimbel Jr.; c. Dr. Nicholas S., Louis S., 3rd, S. Stinor; res: 163 E. 78 St., N.Y., N.Y. 10021.

GIMPLE, JUDITH HELENE, Prod. Mgr., Sneed & Ward, 64 University Pl., N.Y., N.Y. 10003, '69–; Prod. Mgr., Morrow Jr. Bks., '67–'69; Prod. Mgr., N.Y.U. Press, '64–'67; Free-lance bk. design; Wtr., article on bk. prod. for Special Lib. Assn. N.Y. Nwsltr.; Prod. "Eighteenth Century Architecture in Piedmont" (AAUP Aw., '67); Univ. of Ill., '56–'57; Barnard Col., BA (Hist.), '58–'60; London Sch. of Econs., '61–'62, grad. rsch.; b. Omaha, Neb., 1938; p. Nathan and Rose Ricks Gimple; res: 14 Willow Pl., Bklyn., N.Y. 11201.

GINIGER, CAROL WILKINS, VP, The K. S. Giniger Company, Inc., 1140 Broadway, N.Y., N.Y. 10001, '68–; Am. Edtl. Rep., George G. Harrap & Co., Ltd. (London), '62–'67; Ed., "The Little Book of Proverbs" (Golden Press, '68); Sarah Lawrence Col., BA, '52; b. Boston, Mass.; p. G. Edward and Leona Rio Wilkins; h. Kenneth Seeman Giniger; res: 1065 Lexington Ave., N.Y., N.Y. 10021.

GINSBERG, BARBARA HAGEN, PR Dir., Akron General Hospital, 400 Wabash Ave., Akron, Oh. 44307, '67–; PR Dir., Am. Soc. of Agronomy, '66–'67; Commtns. Asst., Univ. of Wis., '63–'66; NE Oh. Hosp. PR Assn., ICIE (Treas., '68–'69), Planned Parenthood Assn. (PR Chmn., '69), Multiple Sclerosis Soc. (Akron Chptr. PR Comm., '67–'69); Un. Fund aws.; Univ. of Wis., BS (Jnlsm.), '62; b. LaFarge, Wis., 1940; p. Robert and Betty Hatter Hagen; h. Allan Ginsberg; res: 557 Long Lake Blvd., Akron, Oh. 44319.

GIPPLE, JOAN ELAINE, PR Dir., Tri-County United Fund, 201 South St., Harrisburg, Pa. 17101, '62–; Continuity Wtr., WTPA, '53–'62; Continuity and News Wtr., WKBO, '51–'53; "An Experiment In Community Understanding," Community Magazine, '68; AWRT (Harrisburg Chptr. Pres., '65, '67–'69), PRSA (Central Pa. Chptr. Secy., '68–'69), Pa. PR Soc., Adv. Club of Harrisburg, Quota Club of Harrisburg (Pubcty. Chmn.), AAUW (Harrisburg Chptr. Pres., '66; Pubcty. Chmn., Bd. Mbr., '68–), Harrisburg YWCA (Life Mbr.; former Bd. Mbr.), Harrisburg Symphony Assn.; Harrisburg BPW Wm. of Yr., '68; Harrisburg Am. Bus. Wms. Assn. Wm. of Yr., '62; Dickinson Col., AB, '51; b. Harrisburg, Pa., 1928; p. Frank L. and Floy Gelbach Gipple; res: 333 15th St., New Cumberland, Pa. 17070.

GIRARD, JUDITH ANN, Retail Adv. Dir., WFIL-TV, 4100 City Line Ave., Phila., Pa. 19131, '68–; Mgt. Training Program, Triangle Bdcst., '68; NATAS; Ithaca Col., BS (Radio, TV, Film), '68 (Dean's List; Outstanding Achiev. in TV Prod., '68; Dept. Hons., '68); b. Newark, N.J., 1946; p. Charles and Marian Davis Girard; res: 5023 Erringer Pl., Apt. C, Phila., Pa. 19144.

GIRSON, ROCHELLE, Bk. Review Ed., Saturday

Review, 380 Madison Ave., N.Y., N.Y. 10017, '58–; Auth., "Maiden Voyages: A Lively Guide for the Woman Traveler"; PEN; State Univ. of Mont.; b. Spokane, Wash.; p. David and Minnie Parson Girson; res: 60 Sutton Pl. S., N.Y., N.Y. 10022.

GITTELSON, NATALIE, Special Projects Ed., Harper's Bazaar, Hearst Publishing Corp., 717 Fifth Ave., N.Y., N.Y. 10022, '59–; Copy Ed.; Assoc. Ed., Seventeen; Asst. Ed., Glamour; Jr. Ed., Vogue (special writing aw., Prix de Paris); articles in McCall's, N.Y. Times Magazine, others; h. Mark R. Gittelson.

GLADISH, MARY LOUISE, Med. Rsch. Librn., Vanderbilt Medical Center Library, Nashville, Tenn. 37203, '64–; Assoc. Prof., E. Tenn. State Univ., '59–'63; Public Health Educ., Lee County Health Dept. (Tupelo, Miss.), '45–'47; Camp Forrest Dist. Health Dept. (Shelbyville, Tenn.), '44–'45; Co-auth., "Classification of Medical Literature;" WNBA, Med. Lib. Assn., Tenn. Lib. Assn., Am. Public Health Assn.; Swift Fellowship (Harvard), '48–'49; Univ. of Tenn., '37–'41; MSPH, Univ. of N.C.; MA, Univ. of N.C.; MS (Lib. Sci.), Peabody; b. Prospect, Tenn.; p. William and Cleo Potts Gladish; res: 3210 Orleans Dr., Apt. #2, Nashville, Tenn. 37212.

GLAETTLI, HEDY, Owner, Hedy Glaettli Advertising, 134 W. University Dr., Rochester, Mich. 48063, '67–; Mng. Ed., The Woman's National Magazine, '66–'68; Rsch. Analyst, Campbell-Ewald Co.; educ: SKV, Aurich (Adv.), '57; Institut Oesch, Zurich (Adv.), '58; Univ. of Zurich (Psych.), '58; b. Bonstetten, Switz., 1938; p. Rudolf H. and Hedwig Wuest Glaettli; res: 2375 Walton Blvd., Rochester, Mich. 48063.

GLANTZ, GINA STRITZLER, AE, Nadler & Larimer, Inc., 595 Madison Ave., N.Y., N.Y. 10022, '69–; AE, Daniel & Charles, Inc., '67–'69; Asst. AE, Tobey & Crothers, '65–'67; Univ. of Cal. (Berkeley), BA, '65; b. Jamaica, N.Y., 1943; p. Nathan and Lillian Rosenbaum Stritzler; h. Ronald Glantz; res: 884 Carroll St., Bklyn., N.Y. 11215.

GLASER, ALICE C., Assoc. Ed., Esquire Magazine, 488 Madison Ave., N.Y., N.Y. 10022, '65–; '59–; UN Security Cncl., '58–'59; Am. Govt. agcys. (Paris, France), '52–'58; short story, "Science Fiction Anthology" ('63); monthly colm., Bk. World, '68–'69; Radcliffe Col., BA, '50; b. N.Y.C., 1929; p. Lewis and Hilda Wallace Glaser; h. Jean-Paul Surmain (div.); res: 961 Lexington Ave., N.Y., N.Y. 10021.

GLASER, RENEE, Prod., "Urban Affairs Report," WRVR-FM, 490 Riverside Dr., N.Y., N.Y. 10027, '69–; Info. Offcr., Human Resources Admin., '65–'68; Wtr.-Prod., WNDT, '62–'64; Wtr., Special Projects, WABC-TV, '61; Prod., WOR Radio-TV, '59–'60; Nwsp. Reptr., Ed., '51–'59; N.Y. Wms. Press Club Aw., '54; Freedoms Fndn. George Washington Hon. Medal, '59; George Polk Aw., '63; Wilson Col., BA, '50; Columbia Univ.

Grad. Sch. of Jnlsm., MS, '54; b. Germany, 1929; p. Dr. Kurt Glaser; res: 332 W. 83rd St., N.Y., N.Y. 10024.

GLASER, VERA ROMANS, Colmst., Corr., Knight Newspapers, Inc., '69–; Wash. Bur. Chief, North American Newspaper Alliance, '66–'69; Wash. Corr., '63–'66; Press Secy., Sen. Kenneth B. Keating of N.Y., '62–'63; Dir. of PR, Wms. Div., Repl. Nat. Comm., '59–'62; Reptr. Wash. Bur., N.Y. Herald Tribune; Reptr., Wash. Times-Herald; Contrb. Ed., "Capital Newsmakers," The Washingtonian, '66–; Panelist, Lectr., WNPC (Treas., Bd., '68–'69), Theta Sigma Phi, OPC, ANWC, Wms. Equity Action League (Cleve., Oh.); Vigilant Patriot Aw., '66; Wash. Univ. (St. Louis, Mo.); George Washington Univ.; Am. Univ.; b. St. Louis, Mo.; p. Aaron and Mollie G. Romans; h. Herbert R. Glaser; c. Carol (Mrs. R. Michael LeVesque); res: 5000 Cathedral Ave. N.W., Wash., D.C. 20016.

GLASSCOCK, ANNE BONNER (pseud: Michael Bonner), Wtr.; novels incl: "Kennedy's Gold" ('60), "The Iron Noose" ('61), "Disturbing Death of Jenkin Delaney" ('66); hist. novel on Mexico ('70); Lectr., civic groups, schs.; Cal. Wtrs. Club (Sacramento Br.), WWA (VP, '64–'65), NLAPW, People-to-People (Bd. of Dirs., '69–'72); Stephens Col., '40–'41; Univ. of Tex., BA, '44 (Phi Beta Kappa); Univ. of Mexico, '44; b. Dallas, Tex., 1924; p. Thomas S. and Anna Belle Newman Bonner; h. R. Kerns Glasscock (dec.); c. Margaret Anne, David Thomas; res: 3115 Sierra Oaks Dr., Sacramento, Cal. 95825.

GLAZENER, MARY UNDERWOOD, Asheville School for Boys, Asheville, N.C. 28806, '68–; Am. Red Cross, '68; Wtr., Prod., Performer, "Tot Town," WLOS-TV, '56–'57 (nominated for Sylvania Aw.); Cnslr., Rockbrook Camp for Girls (Brevard), '67; Auth., religious plays, produced (Broadman Press, Nashville, Tenn., '61 '66); Mars Hill Col., '38–'40; Brevard Col., '40–'41; Univ. of N.C. (UNC at Asheville); b. Atlanta, Ga., 1921; p. John and Eunice Underwood; h. O. W. Glazener; c. Janet, Charles, Joy; res: Rte. 2, Box 349, Candler, N.C. 28715.

GLAZER, SUZANNE M., Dir. of Lib. Svcs., Atheneum Publishers, 122 E. 42nd St., N.Y., N.Y. 10017, '69–; formerly Asst. Coordr. of Work with Children, Bklyn. Public Lib.; ALA, N.Y. Lib. Assn., Children's Bk. Cncl.; Hunter Col., BA; Columbia Univ., MLS; b. N.Y.C.; p. Lewis and Dorothy Glazer; res: 96 Fifth Ave., N.Y., N.Y. 10011.

GLENN, ROBIN DAY, Assoc. Ed., Media Decisions, 10 E. 44th St., N.Y., N.Y. 10017, '70–; Rsch. Ed., '69–'70; Edtl. Secy., Library Journal, '68–'69; Rschr., Corr., Ladies' Home Journal, '68; Am. Bus. Press; New Col., '65–'67; Am. Acad. of Dram. Arts, '67; b. Bronxville, N.Y., 1947; p. Norman and Elaine Couper Glenn; res: 16 W. 16th St., N.Y., N.Y. 10011.

GLIDDON, STELLA KLAERNER, Assoc. Ed., Colmst., Co-owner, The Record-Courier, Box 185, Johnson City, Tex. 78636; Owner, Publr., '40–'67; Soc. Ed., Fredericksburg Standard, '17–'20; Postmaster (Johnson City, Tex.), '43–'67; various orgs., aws.; St. Anthony's Bus. Col.; b. Fredericksburg, Tex., 1897; p. Charles and Mary Kuenemann Klaerner; h. (dec.); c. Reverdy, Roselyn Bustin, James F., Merrill Holquin, Charles, Martha Ann Schulze, Inez Johnson, Iofie Marie Odiorné; res: Johnson City, Tex. 78636.

GLUBOK, SHIRLEY, Auth., Lectr., Metropolitan Museum of Art, Fifth Ave. and 82nd St., N.Y., N.Y., '58–; Auth: "Knights in Armor" ('68), "The Art of India" ('69); "The Art of Ancient Egypt" ('62), 16 other bks.; Lewis Carroll aw., ALA aws.; Wash. Univ., AB; Columbia Univ., MA, '58; b. St. Louis, Mo., 1933; p. Yale and Ann Astor Glubok; h. Alfred Tamarin; res: 50 E. 72nd St., N.Y., N.Y. 10021.

GOAN, FAVA ELOISE, Librn., Northwestern University-Deering Library, Evanston, Ill. 60201, '54–'66; Dir., Children's Work, Halsted St. Inst. Ch., '46–'54; Librn., Ind. Univ. Lib., '28–'44; Librn., Marinette HS, '26–'27; Tchr., Librn., Cuba City HS, '22–'23; Ed., list of serials in Ind. libs., '40; rsch. on family hists., Washburn, Horsfall, Goan; ALA, ILA; Platteville State Tchrs. Col., '19–'21; Lawrence Col., BA, '24; Simmons Col., BLS, '28; Garrett Theological Seminary, '45; b. Millville, Wis., 1898; p. Frank and Martha Patience Horsfall Goan; res: 1940 Sherman Ave., Evanston, Ill. 60201.

GODDARD, MARY ELLEN, Ed., The Nestle Company, Inc., 100 Bloomingdale Rd., White Plains, N.Y. 10605, '67–; Ed., Fed. Reserve Bank (Chgo., Ill.), '64–'67; Reptr., State Journal-Register (Springfield), '62–'64; N.Y. Assn. of Indsl. Communicators (Treas. 1st VP); Copley Aw., '63; Univ. of Ill., BS (Commtns.), '62; b. Streator, Ill., 1940; p. Wilbur and Phyllis Crowl Goddard; res: 11 Lake, White Plains, N.Y. 10603.

GODFREY, JEAN ORTH, Chief Librn., The Branch Library System, The New York Public Library, 8 E. 40th St., N.Y., N.Y. 10016, '63–; Asst. Chief, '57–'63; Coordr., Manhattan Br. Libs., '54–'57; Superintendent, Ext. Div., '52–'54; Asst. Superintendent, '45–'52, '42–'43; Librn., Welch Convalescent Hosp., U.S. Army, '44; ALA, Am. Assn. of Museums, N.Y. Lib. Club, N.Y. Lib. Assn., several other libr., educ. assns.; St Lawrence Univ., AB, '36; Columbia Univ., BS (Lib. Svc.), '37; b. N.Y.C., 1915; p. Dr. Frederick C. and Estelle J. Potts Orth; h. George Godfrey; res: Cedar St., Stony Brook, N.Y. 11790; 278 First Ave., N.Y., N.Y. 10009.

GOEDECKE, SALLY ANN, Mgr., Pubcty., Chemicals and Plastics, Union Carbide Corporation, 270 Park Ave., N.Y., N.Y. 10017, '67–; Sr. Copywtr., Mgt. Asst. Admr.; Analytical Chemist, Lederle Lab.; AWNY, Am. Chemical Soc., Am. Mktng. Assn., Chemical PR Assn.; Smith Col.

GOERTZEN, DORINE DIMOND, Info. Specialist, Idaho Department of Commerce & Development,

Room 108, Capitol Bldg., Boise, Idaho. 83707, '69–; PR Cnslt., Idaho Heart Assn., '59–'66; Ed., Scenic Idaho, '53–'65; Ed., State Peace Officer Magazine, '54–'67; Wtr., Cnslt., Gem Sparks, Idaho Acad. of Gen. Practice, '57–'59; Ed., Idaho Parent Teacher Magazine, '43–'48; Auth: "Boise Basin Brocade" ('62), "Idaho—the 43rd State" ('69); Idaho Wtrs. League (Pres., '47–'48), Idaho Press Wm. (Pres., '52–'53, Treas., '46–'47, '62–'66, Secy., '48–'50), Theta Sigma Phi; NFPW aws., '60–'66; Univ. of Idaho; b. Twin Falls, Idaho; p. John and Clara Walton Dimond; c. Dolly Rose, Charles D., John W., Suzann F.; res: 1429 E. Washington, Boise, Idaho. 83702.

GOETZ, MARY A., Reptr.-Photogr., Newport News Daily Press, Inc., 521 Prince George St., Williamsburg, Va. 23185, '68–; Daily Democrat (Woodland, Cal.), '58–'67; Va. Press Wm. (photog. aws., '69), NFPW (photog. aw., '69), Theta Sigma Phi, Kappa Alpha Mu; San Jose State Col., AB (Jnlsm.); b. Sacramento, Cal., 1937; p. Adam and Mary O'Brien Goetz; res: 1900 Richmond Rd., Williamsburg, Va. 23185.

GOLD, SHERYL F., Press Info. Mgr., WTVJ, Wometco Enterprises, Inc., 316 N. Miami Ave., Miami, Fla. 33128, '68–; Prom. Asst., '67; PR Cnslt., Adv. Club of Gtr. Miami; PR Cnslt., Mental Health Assn. of Dade County; Theta Sigma Phi, Fla. PR Assn.; Oh. State Univ., '66; Univ. of Fla., BS (Adv.), '67 (Dean's List); b. Phila., Pa., 1946; p. Mrs. Ethel Gold; res: 7388 S.W. 80th St. Plaza, #251, Miami, Fla. 33145.

GOLD, SIS LEVINE, Actress, TV., c/o Bernyce Cronin, '67–; numerous TV commls.; nat. mag. advertisments; Litton Industries annual rept., '68', SAG, Thalians (Bd. of Dirs.); Wash. Sch. for Secys., '54 (Scholarship); b. Newark, N.J., 1935; p. Samuel and Minnie Lehner Levine; h. (div.); c. Jill, Jami, Jeffrey; res: 1133 S. Hayworth Ave., L.A., Cal. 90035.

GOLDBERG, BARBARA FEIT, Collaborative Rsch. Dir., McCann-Erickson, Inc., 485 Lexington Ave., N.Y., N.Y. 10017, '68–; Rsch. Dir., Prod. Dev. Workshop, '66–'68; Econ. Analyst, Kenyon & Eckhardt Adv., '64–'66; Am. Mktg. Assn.; Pa. State Univ., BS (Bus. Adm.); b. N.Y.C., 1941; p. Nat and Rose Miller Feit; h. Barry Goldberg; res: 1230 Park Ave., N.Y., N.Y. 10028.

GOLDBERG, LUCIANNE CUMMINGS, News Ed., Women's News Service, 1501 Broadway, N.Y., N.Y. 10036, '66–; Pres., Cummings and Assoc. (Wash., D.C.), '63–'66; Staff, Dem. Nat. Comm.; Reptr., Washington Post; George Washington Univ., BA (Jnlsm.), '57; b. Boston, Mass., 1935; p. Raymond and Jane Moseley Steinberger; h. Sidney Goldberg; c. Joshua, Jonah; res: 255 W. 84th St., Apt. 6-A, N.Y., N.Y. 10024.

GOLDBERG, MARILYN ADLER, Pres., Goldberg Market Research, '53–; Exec. Dir., Lancaster C. Unit, American Cancer Society, 1231 "F" St., Lincoln, Neb. 68508, '67–; Sigma Delta Tau (Nat. Treas.; White-Gold

Torch Aw., '68), AAUW (Past Dir.), Cncl. of Jewish Wm. (Past Pres.); Univ. of Neb., BSC, '46 (Past Pres., Panhellenic Advisory Bd.; Past Pres., Home Econs. Alumnae Assn.); Grad. Sch., '54; b. Omaha, Neb.; p. Leo and Nellie Moskovitz Adler; h. A. Stuart Goldberg; c. Linda Lu; res: 2731 Van Dorn, Lincoln, Neb. 68502.

GOLDBERG, PHYLIS, Adv., Sls. Prom. Dir., Harry Camp Co., 48 W. 38th St., N.Y., N.Y. 10018, '67–; Mdsng. Dir., Modern Bride, '66–'67; Ed., McCall's Children's Wear Merchandiser, '64–'66; Ed., Infant's & Children's Review, '61–'64; Assoc. Ed., Corset & Underwear Review, '58–'61; AWNY, Fashion Group, Copy Club of N.Y.; Fla. Fashion Guild aw., '65; Julliard Sch. of Music; b. N.Y.C.; p. Abraham and Tilly Goldberg.

GOLDEN, RUTH ISBELL, Dept. Head in Secondary Eng., Detroit Public Schools, 5057 Woodward Ave., Detroit, Mich. 48203, '53–; Tchr., HS, '43–'53; Tchr., Lincoln HS (Van Dyke, Mich.), '35–'41, '42–'43; Auth: "Improving Patterns of Language Usage"; Speaker on lang. for the disadvantaged; Ford Fndn. Grant ('55–'56), USOE Rsch. Grants; Alpha Delta Kappa (Past Grand Pres; Mich. Chptr. Past Pres.), Mich. Jaycee Aux. (Past Pres.), Wayne State Univ. Col. of Educ. Alumni Assn. (Bd. of Govs.), NEA, Mich. Educ. Assn.; Detroit Educ. Assn.; Central Mich. Univ., AB, '31; Wayne State Univ., MA, '42; EdD, '63; b. Mt. Pleasant, Mich., 1910; p. Elbert and Rosanna Burns Isbell; h. Judge David L. Golden; c. Dr. Patricia Gayle (Mrs. William Steinhoff); res: 40 Colorado Ave., Highland Park, Mich. 48203.

GOLDEN, SOMA SUZANNE, Contrb. Ed., Business Week, McGraw-Hill, Inc., 330 W. 42nd St., N.Y., N.Y. 10036, '69–; Asst. Econs. Ed., '62–'69; Adjunct Prof., Columbia Univ. Grad. Sch. of Jnlsm., '69; chptrs., textbk., "Economics for Our Times" ('65); study, Joint Cncl. on Econ. Educ., '65; rept. (Yugoslovia, Israel), '68; Pfsnl. Jnlsm. Fellowship, Stanford Univ., '66–'67; Radcliffe Col., BA (with hons. in econs.), '61; Columbia Univ. Grad. Sch. of Jnlsm., MS (with hons.), '62; b. Wash., D.C., 1939; p. Dr. Benjamin E. and Mrs. Dita E. Seiden Golden; res: 201 E. 66th St., (10D), N.Y., N.Y. 10021.

GOLDFARB, LOIS BLOCK, Assoc. Prodr., The Zlowe Company, Inc., 770 Lexington Ave., N.Y., N.Y. 10021, '69–; Casting Dir., Warwick & Legler Advertising, '67–'69; Prod. Asst., Filmex, '66–'67; Prod. Asst., WPIX-TV, '65–'66; Free-lance Artist Apprentice, Golden Bks.; Auth., Illus., children's bk.; interior design bus.; N.Y. Sch. of Interior Design, '66–'68; Queens Col., BA, '63; b. N.Y.C., 1942; p. Herbert and Ruth Epstein Block; h. Ralph Goldfarb; res: 699 W. 239 St., Riverdale, N.Y. 10463.

GOLDFARB, MICKIE B., Adv. Dir., S. Augstein & Co., Inc., 1407 Broadway, N.Y., N.Y. 10018, '68–; Adv.-Prom. Dir., Garland Corp., '67–'68; Adv.-Prom. Dir.,

Trimfit (Kramer Bros.), '65–'66; Adv., Sls. Prom. Dir., Country Tweeds, '62–'65; Retail Prom. Mgr., Glamour Magazine, '56–'61; Prom. Chief, Copy, Ellington & Co., '53–'55; Adv. Mgr., Majestic Specialities; USESCO Public Info., '46–'47; Lt., WAVES, '43–'46; Fashion Group of N.Y.; Univ. of Miami, BA, '42; City Col. of N.Y., Sp. Diploma (Adv.), '50; b. Bklyn., N.Y., 1920; p. Dr. Barnett and May Steinbert Goldfarb; res: 221 E. 78th St., N.Y., N.Y. 10022.

GOLDFRANK, HELEN COLODNY (pseud: Helen Kay), Auth., juv. fiction, non-fiction; bks: "A Lion for a Sitter" (Abelard, '69), "A Name for Little No Name" (Abelard, '68), many others; Wms. City Club N.Y., PEN, Auths. League, Am. Bk. Wm., Am. Nwsp. Guild; b. N.Y.C. 1912; p. Hyman and Tessie Herman Colodny; h. Herbert J. Goldfrank; c. Lewis, Deborah, Joan; res: 435 E. 87th St., N.Y., N.Y. 10028.

GOLDIN, AMY MENDELSON, Assoc. Ed., Art News, 444 Madison Ave., N.Y., N.Y. 10022; Cnslt., Helena Rubenstein Fndn., '69; Visiting Lectr., Univ. of Cal. (San Diego), '69; Wayne Univ. (Detroit, Mich.), '45–'46; Univ. of Chgo., '46–'48; h. Morton Goldin (div.).

GOLDIN, AUGUSTA, Auth: "How to Release the Learning Power in Children" (Parker Publ. Co., '70); Principal, Public School 39 R., New York City Board of Education, S.I., N.Y. 10305, '44–; Tchr: Elementary, Junior High Schs.; Wtr., Children's bks. incl: "Lets-Read-and-Find-Out Science Series" (T. Y. Crowell) incl: "Spider Silk," "Ducks Don't Get Wet," "Salt," "Straight Hair, Curly Hair," "Where Does Your Garden Grow?", "The Bottom of the Sea," "The Sunlit Sea"; educ. articles: The Grade Tchr., The Instructor Magazine; fiction: short stories, confession and romance Magazines; Ed., "Classroom Films," Film News Magazine; Assoc. Ed., "The N.Y. Supervisor"; Nat. Cncl. of Adm. Wm. in Educ. N.Y.C. (1st VP; Ed.-in-chief, Newsltr.), Doctorate Assn. of N.Y. Educs. (1st VP), Nat. Audubon Soc. (scholarships '65, '67), Cncl. of Supervisory Assns.; Hunter Col., BA, '27; Col. of the City of N.Y., MS, '29; Teachers Col., Columbia, EdD, '47; b. N.Y.C., 1906; p. Jacob and Fanny Harris Reider; h. Oscar Goldin; c. Kenneth, Valerie; res: 590 Bard Ave., S.I., N.Y. 10310.

GOLDINA, MIRIAM, Translator (from Russian): "The Brilliant Heir of Stanislavsky—Eugene Vakhtangor" (Drama Bk., forthcoming), "Stanislavsky Directs" (Funk & Wagnals, '54); Assoc. Prof. of Drama, Tampa Univ., '66; Dir. of Workshop, Circle in the Sq., '50; Drama Guest Dir., Bryn Mawr, '49; Nat. Day Cit., WLCV (Tampa, St. Petersburg, Fla., '66); Univ. of Leningrad, Juristic Fac., student of Stanislavsky and Vakhtangor; b. Stalingrad, U.S.S.R., 1899; p. Joseph and Betty Brudno Goldin; h. Nahum Zermach; c. Charles.

GOLDMAN, CAREN SUSAN, Gen. Assigt. Reptr., Cleveland Plain Dealer, 1801 Superior Ave., Cleve., Oh. 44114, '67–; PR Offcr., Jnlsm. and Humanities

Instr. in OEO, Oh. Wesleyan Univ., '67; Wtr., mag. articles; pfsnl. art agt.; Pi Delta Epsilon; Ohio Wesleyan Univ., BA, '67; N.Y.U.; Fairleigh Dickinson Univ.; Ohio State Univ.; b. Bklyn., N.Y., 1947; p. Bernard and Muriel Stock Goldman; h. John Clark; c. Jamie Beth; res: 21050 Southbend Circle, Rocky River, Oh. 44116.

GOLDSHOLL, MILDRED MONAT, Prodr., Dir., Goldsholl & Associates, 420 Frontage Rd., Northfield, Ill. 60093, '38–; N. Shore Film Soc., Dirs. Guild, Film Cncl., Film Forum; numerous aws. for doc., indsl. films incl. Intl. Film & TV Festival Gold Medal, '69; Info. Film Prodrs. of Am. aw., '69; b. N.Y.C., 1920; p. Joseph and Yetta Frederick Monat; h. Morton Goldsholl; c. Gleda, Harry; res: 800 Kimballwood Lane, Highland Park, Ill. 60035.

GOLDSMITH, BARBARA, Contrb. Ed., New York Magazine, 207 E. 32nd St., N.Y., N.Y. 10016; Harper's Bazaar, Town & Country, 717 Fifth Ave., N.Y., N.Y.; Ed., Comment on Culture U.S.A., '69; profiles, articles, TV scripts, '53–'69; Ed., special projects, pubns.; Museum of Modern Art, Cncl. for Parks and Playgrounds; Park Assn. Dir.; Wellesley Col., BA, '53; h. C. Gerald Goldsmith; c. John, Alice, Andrew; res: 655 Park Ave., N.Y., N.Y. 10021.

GOLDSMITH, JANE INNES, Assoc. Ed., Ebel-Doctorow Publications, Inc., 23 E. 26th St., N.Y., N.Y. 10010, '64–; Asst. Ed., The New York Graphic, '66–'67; Asst. Ed., Stamps, '63–'64; Asst. Ed., Travel Trade, '63; Theater Reviewer, Labor Chronicle, '63; Restaurant Reviewer, '61–'62; Ed., National Buyers Guide; Asst. Ed., Curtain and Drapery Department mag., '59–'62; Baby Products Mdsng. Ed., Parents' Magazine, '57; Fashion and Prom. Copywtr., Harper's Bazaar, '56–'57; TV-Radio Wtr., WOR-MBS, '55–'56; Edtl. Staff Verse Wtr., Norcross, '52–'55; Theater Reviewer, Intl. News Svc., '53; Auth., "Fire Men and Fire Engines" (Simon & Schuster, '58); Wheaton Col., BA, '52; b. N.Y.C., 1931; p. Joseph Miller and Helen Innes Goldsmith; res: 208 E. 21 Street, N.Y., N.Y. 10010.

GOLDSON, RAE LILIAN, Auth. and Tchr. on flower arrangements; N.Y. Horticultural Soc. (Life Mbr.), N.Y. State Fedn. of Garden Clubs (Life Mbr.), Nat. Cncl. of State Garden Clubs (Life Mbr.), Ikebana Intl. (Charter Mbr.), Five Towns Garden Club (Hon. Pres.), Belle Harbor Garden Club (Hon. Mbr.); Silver Trophies at Horticultural Soc. Flower Shows; Bronze Medal, Intl. Flower Show, '54; Silver Trophy at Jackson & Perkins Rose Festival; N.Y. School of Interior Design, '35; b. N.Y.C., 1893; p. Israel and Jainie Yessof Segalowitz; h. George Goldson; c. Henry, Arlene M.; res: 374 Forest Ave., Woodmere, N.Y. 11598.

GOLDSTEIN, DORIS, PR AE, Chirurg & Cairns, Inc., 641 Lexington Ave., N.Y., N.Y. 10022, '67–; AE, Mogul Baker Byrne Weiss, '63–'67; Fashion Group, NHFL; Smith Col., BA.

GOLDSTEIN, MARILYN SILVERSTEIN, Reptr., Family Page, Newsday, 550 Stewart Ave., Garden City, N.Y. 11530, '66–; Free-lance Adv. Copywtr., Feature Story Wtr., '60–'66; Copywtr., McCann-Erickson Advertising, '58–'60; Syracuse Univ., BS (Home Econs.), '58; b. Bklyn., N.Y., 1937; p. Morris and Emma Wolinsky Silverstein; h. Robert J. Goldstein; c. Karen, Susan; res: 66 Davis Rd., Port Washington, N.Y. 11050.

GOLDSTEIN, NAOMI (NICKI), Nat. Exec. Admr., The National Academy of Television Arts and Sciences, 54 W. 40th St., N.Y., N.Y. 10018, '69–; Asst. to Exec. Dir., '63–'69; Mktng., Sls., various cos., '55–'63; AWRT, The Theatre Arm Players (Co-Founder); Baruch Col., N.Y.U.; b. N.Y.C., 1937; p. Morris and Alfreda Bertin Goldstein; res: 1230 Croes Ave., Bronx, N.Y. 10472.

GOLDSTEIN, ROBERTA BUTTERFIELD, Speech Therapist, Burlington School System, Old Champlain Bldg., Pine St., Burlington, Vt. 05401, '66–; Bus. partner with husband, restauranteur, '54–'66; Lectr. on poetry, speech and voice, Jewish heritage, etc. '48–; former Narrator, radio program, "Your Literary Heritage"; Auth., poetry bks: "The Searching Season" (Queen City Press, '61), "The Wood Burns Red" (The Golden Quill Press '66); "Fling Jeweled Pebbles" (The Golden Quill Press, '63); Poetry Soc. of Vt. (VP, Corinna Eastman Davis Aw., '67), Intl. Platform Assn., '68–; Centro Studi E. Scambi Internazionali, Accademia Leonardo da Vinci of Rome (Fellow, '64–'67), Avalon Intl. Contest aw., '64; various others; Univ. of Vt., PhD, '39 (cum laude, Phi Beta Kappa), MS (Speech Pathology), '69; b. North Troy, Vt., 1917; p. Dr. Alfred and Anne Huckins Butterfield; h. Frank Goldstein; c. Harold, Mark, Jan Mordecai, Ethel Faith; res: 30 Adsit Ct., Burlington, Vt. 05401.

GOMEZ, RUTH PALACIOS, Tchr., Brownsville Independent School District, 1108 W. Madison, Brownsville, Tex. 78520, '66–; Copywtr., KTBC, '65–'66; Traf. Mgr.; Suburban Star (San Antonio), '64–'65; part-time Reptr., dist. paper and orgs.; Theta Sigma Phi (Alpha Phi Chptr. Treas., '64–'65; delegate, Nat. Conv., '63); Tex. Wms. Univ., BS, '64; b. San Antonio, Tex., 1942; p. Leonardo and Joaquina Rohan Palacios; h. Charles Gomez; c. Charles Paul; res: 801 Gentleman, Apt. 206, San Antonio, Tex. 78201.

GONDECK, ELLEN WOZNIAK, Soc. Ed., Star Publishing Company, 217 N. Fourth St., Niles, Mich., 49120, '59–; NPWC; Mich. Wms. Press Club (Ed. of Bannerlines); Ind. Univ. Ext. (South Bend, Ind.), Jnlsm. Sch.; b. Chgo. Heights, Ill., 1915; p. Edward J. and Maud R. Iden Wozniak; h. Frederick V. Gondeck; c. Sr. Mary Ellen, Marcia (Mrs. John W. Williams, Jr.), David F.; res: 431 Mead Rd., Niles, Mich. 49120.

GONZALEZ, MARTA, Asst. Mgr. Ratings, CBS TV Network, Columbia Broadcasting System, 51 W. 52 St., N.Y., N.Y. 10019, '66–; Supvsr. Ratings, '64–'66; Supvsr. Ratings, CBS Stations, '68–'69.

GOODE, CAROL BARKER, Wms. Ed., The Times News, 125 6th Ave., E., Hendersonville, N.C. 28739, '59–; NPWC; St. Petersburg, Fla. Jr. Col.; Fla. State Univ.; b. Springfield, Mass.; p. John and Estelle Grow Barker; h. Clarence Goode; c. Linda (Mrs. Herbert C. Quarles), Joan Jenkins; res: 903 Thornton Pl., Hendersonville, N.C. 28739.

GOODMAN, DENISE WINTER, Urban Affairs Reptr., Dayton Journal Herald, 37 S. Ludlow St., Dayton, Oh. 45402, '65–, '61–'64; Asst. News Ed., Nat. Cncl. of Churches, '64–'65; Theta Sigma Phi; Oh. State Univ., BA (Jnlsm.), '61; N.Y.U., '64–'65; b. Akron, Oh., 1939; p. Adolph and Denise Winter Goodman; res: 1909 Haverhill Dr., Dayton, Oh. 45406.

GORDON, DOROTHY, Founder and Prodr., Dorothy Gordon Youth Forums, National Broadcasting Company, 30 Rockefeller Plaza, N.Y., N.Y. 10020, '45–; prog. bdcst. over WNBC-TV and NBC Radio Network; Cnslt. on youth activities for N.Y. Times; formerly Music Prog. Dir. of the Am. Sch. of the Air, CBS; Song and Story Lady for "The Children's Corner"; Cnslt. on children's progs. for NBC and conducted "Yesterday's Children"; Auth. of numerous bks. for youth; 3 Peabody aws.; numerous aws. and cits.; Fairleigh Dickinson Univ., Hon. Doctor of Laws; Fellow, Wroxton Col., Oxford, Eng.; b. Russia (father in diplomatic svc.); c. Frank H., Lincoln; res: Chetwood, George's Mills, N.H. 03751.

GORDON, ELAINE TAYLOR, Acc. Supvsr., Bell and Stanton, 909 Third Ave., N.Y., N.Y. 10022, '66–; Mgr., Prod. Svcs., Monroe Scharff & Co., '64–'66; Fashion Dir., Saul Krieg Assoc., '62–'64; PR Dir., Carole Stupell Ltd., '61–'62; Sls. Prom. Mgr., Renault, '59–'60; Sls. Prom. Mgr., Elle mag.; Coty Aws. Jury; Colmst., "The Male Bag," Chicago Tribune/New York News Synd.; Fashion Group, AWRT; Univ. of Vt., BA (Speech, Psy.), '59; b. N.Y.C., 1939; p. Harry and Gertrude Milchan Schneider; h. Mort Gordon; c. Jennifer B.; res: 180 E. 79th St., N.Y., N.Y. 10021.

GORDON, JOAN HONKALA, County and Radio-TV Ed., The Daily Sentinel-Tribune, 117 E. Wooster St., Bowling Green, Oh. 43402, '66–; Jnlsm. Instr., Bowling Green State Univ., '69; Edtl. Asst., Pubns. Off., '61–'62; Tchr., Eng., Jnlsm., Bowling Green HS, '59–'61; Asst. Cataloguer, Elyria Public Lib., '58–'59; various orgs., aws.; Bowling Green State Univ., BA, '57 (cum laude); Oh. State Univ., BS (Educ.), '59; b. Painesville, Oh., 1935; h. James Gordon; c. Keven James, Melissa Lynn; res: 1446 Conneaut Ave., Bowling Green, Oh. 43402.

GORDON, LEAH SHANKS, Head Rschr., Time Magazine, Time Inc., Rockefeller Ctr., 50th and Sixth Ave., N.Y., N.Y. 10020, '69–; Art Rschr.-Reptr., '64–'69; Press Rschr., '63–'64; Gen. Rschr., '62–'63; Religion Rschr., '61–'62; Bus. Rschr., '60–'61; Gen. Edtl. Rschr., Engineering News Record, McGraw Hill, '58–'60; Text Rschr., Funk & Wagnalls Dic., '58; Bryn Mawr Col., BA, '56; b. Sharon Pa., 1934; p. Martin and Mildred

Freedman Shanks; h. John Gordon; res: 313 W. 57th St., N.Y., N.Y. 10019.

GORDON, MARIANNE YARBROUGH, 20th Century-Fox Film Corp., Suite 1010, 100 N. Main Bldg., Memphis, Tenn. 38103, '56–; Wm. of the Motion Pic. Industry (Pres., '65–'66; 1st VP, '64–'65; Secy., '68–'69); b. Memphis, Tenn., 1930; p. Thomas Curtis and Minta Baker Yarbrough; h. Jack Gordon; c. Patricia Kay McDaniel; res: 180 Pontotoc St. N.E., Hernando, Miss. 38632.

GORDON, PATRICIA NEALE, Edtl. Rschr., TV, TIME, Inc., Time & Life Bldg., Rockefeller Ctr., N.Y., N.Y. 10020, '65–; Humble Oil & Refg. Co. (Houston, Tex.); Theta Sigma Phi, AWRT; Univ. of Ariz., BA; Univ. of Houston; b. Houston, Tex.; p. Robert and Patricia Hamilton Gordon; res: 221 E. 48th St., N.Y., N.Y. 10017.

GORDON, ROSANNE, VP, Media Dir., Chalek and Dreyer, Inc., 485 Madison Ave., N.Y., N.Y. 10022, '68–; Media Dir., '67–; Emerson Foote, '58–'67; Doyle, Dane, Bernbach; Street & Finney; b. Bronx, N.Y., 1929; h. Charles Leighton; res: 152 W. 58 St., N.Y., N.Y. 10019.

GOREAU, LAURRAINE ROBERTA, Colmst., New Orleans States-Item, 3800 Howard Ave., New Orleans, La. 70140, '57–; Wms. Ed., '56–'58; Wtr., Dir., Moderator, "Top News," KDAL-TV (Duluth, Minn.), '54–'55, Prodr., Moderator, "Press Conf.," "Good News," Arrowhead TV Network, '53–'54; Mng. Ed., Chief Edtl. Wtr., Superior (Wis.) Evening Telegram, '53–'56; Wtr., CBS (Hollywood, Cal.), '52–'53; Mng. Ed., Chief Edtl. Wtr., Lafayette (La.) Daily Advertiser, '45–'52; Telegraph Ed., '44–'45; Wtr., Pubcty., Navy Dept., '43–'44; Supvsr., Instr., Ed., Off. of Censorship, '41–'43; Composer, 49 folk, jazz, rock, blues, gospel songs; Auth., bks., plays; ASCAP, Am. Guild of Auths. & Composers, New Orleans Press Club; numerous writing aws.; La. State Univ., '38–'39; Univ. of N.C., '40; b. New Orleans, La., 1918; p. Nelson and Anna Wilson Goreau; res: Upper Pontalba, 538 St. Peter St., New Orleans, La. 70116.

GORHAM, THELMA THURSTON, Exec. Dir., Twin Cities Opportunities Industrialization Center, Inc., 834 N. Seventh St., Mpls., Minn. 55411, '68–; Inst., Communication, Univ. of Minn., '68; Assoc. Prof., Fla. A&M Univ., '63–'68; Tchr., '62–'63; '56–'60; Asst. Prof., Southern Univ., '60–'62; Exec. Ed., The Black Dispatch (Okla. City, Okla.), '55–'56; Mng. Ed., The Oklahoma Eagle (Tulsa), '54–'55; Exec. Ed., Step-Up (St. Louis, Mo.), '53–'54; Asst. Prof., Jnlsm., Lincoln Univ., '47–'51; various edtl. positions, '31–'47; Minn. Press Wm., APRA, Assn. for Educ. in Jnlsm., Theta Sigma Phi; Who's Who in Am., Who's Who in the Midwest, Who's Who in the South and Southwest, Dic. of Intl. Biog.; Who's Who of Am. Wm.; Univ. of Minn., BA (Jnlsm.), '35; MA (Jnlsm.), '51; b. Kan. City, Mo., 1913; p. Frank Thurston and Bertha Smith Thurston

Lee; h. Richard Gorham (div.); c. Darryl Theodore; res: 3835 Fifth Ave. S., Mpls., Minn. 55409.

GORIN, ELEANOR CARLSON, Publr., Greensburg Record-Herald, 102 W. Court St., Greensburg, Ky. 42743, '63–; Mng. Ed., '60–'63; News Ed., '58–'60; Soc. Ed., '52–'58; Reptr., '45–'52; Greensburg C. of C., Ky. Press Assn., Green County Lib. Bd.; numerous nwsp. aws.; Univ. of Minn., BS, '38; Western Ky. Univ., MA, '68; b. Gilbert, Minn., 1915; p. John and Elin Olson Carlson; h. Jameson D. Gorin (dec.); c. Walter C.; res: 206 W. Columbia, Greensburg, Ky. 42743.

GORMAN, ETHEL MILLER, Info. Specialist, Jefferson County Association for Mental Health, 3600 S. Eighth Ave., Birmingham, Ala. 35222, '59–; Probation Offcr., Jefferson County Juv. and Domestic Rels. Court, '54–'59; Child Welfare Worker, Children's Aid Soc., '53–'54; Auth., "Red Acres" ('56), Nwsltr. Ed., Jefferson County Assn. for Mental Health; Great Bks. Group (Leader, '63), Theta Sigma Phi (Pres., '63–'64), Nat. Cncl. on Crime and Delinquency, Ala. Hist. Soc., Ala. Hist. Assn., Birmingham IEA, Press Club, Mental Health Assn. Staff Cncl. (Bd. of Dirs.), Novel Prize, Ala. Wtrs. Conclave, '53; Howard Col., '28–'29; Rollins Col., AB, '32 (cum laude); b. Birmingham, Ala., 1911; p. Beauregard and Ethel Jungell Miller; h. Thomas C. Gorman (div.); c. Beauregard (dec.), Terry Carroll (Mrs. Raymond J. Salassi, Jr.); res: 409 St. Charles St., Birmingham, Ala. 35209.

GORMAN, KATHERINE BONSEY, Free-lance Wtr.; Auth: "Album" (Olivant Press), Poetry Bk. "Flesh The Only Coin" ('68; 1st prize, Poetry Soc.), NLAPW, PSA, Pa. Poetry Soc.; Who's Who of Am. Wm., Who's Who in Poetry, Dic. of Intl. Biog., Intl. Dic.; b. Phila. Pa.; p. Vernon and Margaret Gilboyne Bonsey; h. William F. Gorman; res: 750 Burlington Ave., N., St. Petersburg, Fla. 33701.

GORNEY, SONDRA KARYL, Dir., Information Center on the Mature Woman, 3 W. 57th St., N.Y., N.Y. 10019, '68–; Pubcty. Coordr., Nat. Multiple Sclerosis Soc., '68; Dir., PR, Inst. of Intl. Educ., '62–'68; Dir., PR, Girls Clubs of Am., '60–'62; Dir., Magazine Svc., '57–'60; Co-chmn., Musical Play Dept., Am. Theatre Wing, '48–'57; Free-lance Wtr., mags., radio, TV, '43–'57; Co-chmn., Musical Play Dept., New Sch., '47–'52; Assoc. Ed., PIC Magazine, '41–'43; various orgs.; U.C.L.A., '43–'45; b. Le Compte, La., 1918; p. David and Tania Reichenbach Kattlove; h. Jay Gorney; c. Karen (Mrs. Kenneth Golden), Daniel; res: 905 West End Ave., N.Y., N.Y. 10025.

GOTH, TRUDY, Free-lance Wtr., art and music criticism, travel; Head, fgn. press rels., European Music, Drama Festivals (Vienna, Athens, Salzburg, Florence, W. Berlin, others); Dir., Founder, Choreographer's Workshop, '47–'54; Cnslt., talent, artistic activities, Intl. Festivals; Bd. of Dirs., "Universal Edition" Music Publ.; Univ. (Florence, Italy), '37; b. Berlin, W. Germany, 1913; p. Ernest and Gisella Schlesinger; res: 159 W. 53rd St., N.Y., N.Y. 10019.

GOTT, GAIL SCHEERE, Wms. Reptr., Stockton Daily Evening Record, P.O. Box 900, Stockton, Cal. 95201, '50–; Wms. Program Dir., Radio Sta. KWG, '45–'50; colmst., daily commls.; wtr. of adv. copy; Stockton Nwsp. Guild (Past Rec. Secy.), Hadassah (Hon. Mbr.), aws. for activity in svc. orgs., cnsl., theatre; b. S. F., Cal., 1919; p. Fred and Marion Kelly Scheere; h. Rudolph Gott; c. Rudolph Joseph; res: 3024 Wallace Ave., Stockton, Cal. 95204.

GOTTLIEB, ANITA, Adv. Mgr., Coulter Electronics, Inc., 590 W. 20th St., Hialeah, Fla. 33010, '68–; Tech. Wtr., '67–'68; Free-lance photog.; Theta Sigma Phi (Univ. of Miami Chptr. Pres.), '65–'66); Univ. of Miami, BA (Mass Commtns. and Philosophy), '67; b. Bklyn. N.Y., 1945; p. Irving and Goldye Krebs Gottlieb; res: 1400 N.W. Tenth Ave., Apt. 5-C, Miami, Fla. 33136.

GOTTLIEB, CAROL MALOYAN, Adv. Prod. Mgr., Western Business Publications, 274 Brannan St., S.F., Cal. 94107, '68–; News, Make-up Ed., Western Banker, '65–'68; Ed., Fed. Reserve Bank of S.F. employee mag.; Asst. to Ed., Monthly Review, '62–'64; Asst. News Librn., AP, '60–'61; Univ. of Cal., BA, '60; b. Oakland, Cal., 1938; p. Maloy and Laura Leich Maloyan; h. Bernon Gottlieb; res: 552 Paco Dr., Los Altos, Cal. 94022.

GOTTLIEB, INEZ BELLOW, Dir. of Commty. Progs., WCAU-TV, City Line and Monument Aves., Phila., Pa. 19131, '65–; Acting Dir., Commty. Progs., '65; Assoc. Prodr., '64; Wtr., '63; Prodr., Pied Piper Prods., '58–'60; Prodr., Wtr., Museum Telemation, Univ. Museum, Univ. of Pa., '63; AWRT, Theta Sigma Phi; Gavel Aw., Am. Bar Assn., '65; Oh. State Aw., '65, '66; NATAS: Golden Gate Aw., '65; Reg. Emmy, '67; Bdcst. Media Aw., '67, '68; Brotherhood Aw., Nat. Conf. Christians and Jews, '66, '67; Donaldson Aw., Pa. Med. Soc., '66; Univ. of Pa., BA (Sociol.), '38; Annenberg Sch. of Commtn, MA (Commtns.), '61; b. Phila., Pa.; h. Jacob Gottlieb; c. Peter, Richard, Vicki; res: 456 Colebrook Lane, Bryn Mawr, Pa. 19010.

GOTTLIEB, ROBIN GROSSMAN, Free-lance Wtr., '57–; Ed., Juv. Dept., Random House, '51–'57; Auth: "Mystery of the Marco Polo Ring" ('68), "Mystery Aboard the Ocean Princess" ('67), six other juv. bks.; Vassar Col., '46–'48; Barnard Col., BA, '50; h. Gerald Gottlieb. res: 210 E. 68th St., N.Y., N.Y. 10021.

GOTWALT, HELEN MILLER, Rsch. Ed., "Action Line," WSBA Radio, Susquehanna Broadcasting Co., Box 910, York, Pa. 17403, '67–; Dir. of Educ. Radio-TV, York Schs., '50–'63; Wtr., Prodr., '45–'55; Cont. Wtr., '42–'48; Auth: "Short Plays for Children" ('69), "Modern Plays for Special Days" ('65), eight other bks. of juv. plays; Freedoms Fndn. aw., '56, '55; Pa. State Col. of Shippensburg; b. Richmond, Ind., 1905; p.

Hanson and Mary Jane McGowan Miller; h. Samuel Gotwalt; res: 828 S. Queen St., York, Pa. 17403.

GOUGH, MARION, Sr. Ed., House Beautiful, 717 Fifth Ave., N.Y., N.Y. 10022, '69–; Gen. Features Ed., Mng. Ed., Textiles Ed., Wtr., Asst. to Decorating Ed., '38–'69; Asst. to Mng. Ed., American Architect, '37; Fashion Group, NHFL, N.Y. Travel Wtrs. Assn. (Pres., '61–'62), Soc. of Am. Travel Wtrs. (Nat. Secy., '66; N.E. Chptr. Chmn., '67–'69); Wellesley Col.; b. Jersey City, N.J.; p. James and Mary Walsh Gough; res: 125 E. 87th St., N.Y., N.Y. 10028.

GOULD, LINDA S., Pubcty. Dir., New American Library, Inc., 1301 Ave. of the Ams., N.Y., N.Y. 10019, '69–; Assoc. Pubcty. Mgr., '68–'69; Assoc. Pubcty. Dir., Dell Publ., '67–'68; Asst. Ed., G. P. Putnam's Sons, '66–'67; Publrs. Pubcty. Assn.; Univ. of Vt., BA, '66; b. Barre, Vt., 1944; p. Isaac and Elsie Goldsmith Gould; res: 45 W. Tenth St., N.Y., N.Y. 10011.

GOULD, NORMA MARMOCI, VP, Compton Advertising, Inc., 625 Madison Ave., N.Y., N.Y. 10022, '63–; Copy Group Head, Grey Adv., '56–'63; Wtr., Benton & Bowles, '55–'56; Wtr., Young & Rubicam, '49–'54; several TV aws.; Univ. of Mo., BA (Eng. Lit.) and BJ (Adv.), '49; h. (div.); res: 111 Waverly Pl., N.Y., N.Y. 10011.

GOULD, RITA J., Local Ed., TV Guide, 310 Grant St., Pitt., Pa. 15219, '61–; Circ. and Prom. Mgr., helped start Television News (first TV mag. in Pitt.), '51; Ed., '53 (when mag. became TV Guide); Pitt. Press Club, Wms. Press Club of Pitt., Pitt. Radio and TV Club (VP, '67–'70), Theta Sigma Phi (Career Conf. Chmn., '69), commty. affairs; Univ. of Pitt., BS, '50; b. Pitt., Pa., '28; p. Samuel and Nelle Goldstein Gould; res: 4601 Fifth Ave., Pitt., Pa. 15213.

GOULD, SANDRA LEE, Staff Wtr., United Press International, 62 E. Broad St., Columbus, Oh. 43215, '68–; News, Wms. Ed., WDLR Radio (Delaware, Oh.), '66–'68; Prod. Dir., WBCO Radio (Bucyrus), '65–'66; AWRT, BPW, Theta Sigma Phi; Kent State Univ., BS (Radio-TV Jnlsm.), '65; b. Columbus, Oh., 1943; p. Weldon and Ollie Edmonds Gould; res: 151-1/2 E. Central Ave., Delaware, Oh. 43015.

GOULDER, GRACE, Auth., Jnlst., Reg. Histrn.; bks: "Ohio Scenes and Citizens" (World, '53), "This Is Ohio" (World, '64); Colmst., Plain Dealer Magazine (Cleve.), Staff Mbr., '14–'17; '40–; Nat. Bd. YWCA (N.Y.C., France, Germany, England), '17–'19; Oh. Hist. Soc. (Hon. Mbr.), Cinn. Hist. Soc., Western Reserve Hist. Soc., Cleve. Aw. for Lit., '64; aws. by Ohioana Lib., Nat. Assn. for State and Local Hist.; Vassar Col. AB; b. Cleve., Oh.; p. Charles and Marion Clements Goulder; h. Robert James Izant; c. Dr. Robert J., Jr., Mary (Mrs. Eugene D. White), Johnathan G. (dec.); res: 250 College, Hudson, Oh. 44236.

GOVAN, CHRISTINE NOBLE, Wtr.; Auth. of 44 bks.,

five adult, several published in fgn. countries; Tchr., Librn., Bk. Reviewer, Lectr.; Short Story "Miss Winters and the Wind" incl. in O. Henry Prize Collection; Auths. Guild, Humane Soc. of U.S.; b. N.Y.C., 1887; p. Stephen and Mary Quintard Noble; h. Gilbert Eaton Govan; c. James F., Emily Govan West, Mary Quintard Steele; res: 400 Laurel Lane, Lookout Mountain, Tenn. 37350.

GOYAK, ELIZABETH FAIRBAIRN, VP, Daniel J. Edelman, Inc., 221 N. LaSalle St., Chgo., Ill. 60601, '68–; AE and Acct. Supvsr., Gardner, Jones & Cowell; AE and Acct. Supvsr., A. Cushman & Assoc.; Reptr., Chgo. Jnl. of Commerce; Reptr., INS; Reptr., Chgo. Tribune; PRSA, Pubcty. Club of Chgo. (Mbr. of Bd., Secy., '58–'60), NHFL (Chgo. Chptr., VP, '67); Who's Who of Am. Wm.; Southern Ill. Univ., BEd., '43; Northwestern Univ., grad. study, '43–'44; b. Chgo., Ill., 1922; p. Lewis and Berenice Bowers Fairbairn; h. Edward A. Goyak; res: 21310 Butterfield Pkwy., Matteson, Ill. 60443.

GRABB, MIGNON STRICKLAND, Dir. Lib. Svcs., Lake Land College, 1904 Prairie, Mattoon, Ill. 61938, '67–; Librn., Lab. Sch., Eastern Ill. Univ., '66–'67; Librn., Unity HS, '63–'66; Tchr., Oakland HS, '62–'63; Beta Phi Mu, Sigma Tau Delta, Phi Delta Kappa, ALA, Assn. of Col. and Rsch. Libs.; Eastern Ill. Univ., BS (Educ.), '62 (cum laude); Univ. of Ill., MS (Lib. Sci.), '66; b. Chickasha, Okla., 1941; p. Augustus and Donna Forehand Strickland; c. Melinda; res: 3312 Prairie, Mattoon, Ill. 61938.

GRABOWSKI, MARILYN, Assoc. Picture Ed., Playboy Magazine, HMH Publishing Co., Inc., 919 N. Michigan Ave., Chgo., Ill. 60611, '65–; Exec. Secy., '64–'65; Standard Oil of Ind., '62–'64; res: 70 E. Walton St., Chgo., Ill. 60611.

GRACE, JACQUELINE HELLYAR, Ed., Bdcst. standards, National Broadcasting Company, 30 Rockefeller Plaza, N.Y., N.Y. 10020, '69–; Mgr., Bdcst. Mgt. Dept., Campbell-Ewald, '65–'69; Asst. TV/Radio Traf. Mgr., Kenyon & Eckhardt, '61–'65; Copywtr., Lintas Ltd. (Sydney, Australia), '48–'49; Copywtr. (London, Eng.), '45–'48; Secy. to War Corrs., Collier's Weekly, London Bur., '42–'44; AWRT; London Sch. of Jnlsm.; Magazine Inst.; b. The Hague, Holland, 1924; p. Frederick and Gwendolyn Grindrod Hellyar; h. Victor Grace; res: 500 Linwood Dr., Fort Lee, N.J. 07024.

GRACE, TEDDEE ELIZABETH, Ed., employee mag. for Stanray Corp., 200 S. Michigan Ave., Chgo., Ill. 60604, '70–; Copywtr., Martin J. Simmons Adv., '69–'70; PR Supvsr., Am. Hosp. Supply (Evanston), '68; PR Asst., '67–'68; Ed., Am. Med. Assn. (Chgo.), '66–'67; Kappa Tau Alpha; Jr. Wms. Adv. Club of Chgo.; Univ. of Mo., BJ, '66; b. Wichita, Kan., 1944; p. Clifford and Vivian Hardy Grace; res: 2970 N. Sheridan Rd., Chgo., Ill. 60657.

GRACZA, MARGARET YOUNG, Auth: "The Hun-

garians in America" (Lerner, '69), "The Bird in Art" ('66), "Ships and the Sea in Art" ('65); Translated bk. from Danish ('64); Asst. in Educ., Mpls. Inst. of Arts, '62–; Dir. of Children's Activities, '56–'62; Tchr., HS, '54–'56; Activities Dir., Intl. Inst. (St. Paul), '50–'52; NLAPW, County Home Sch. Project (Advisory Bd. Mbr.), Mpls. Public Sch. Volunteer Program; Macalester Col., BA, '50; Danish Grad. Sch. for Foreign Students (Fulbright Scholarship, '52–'53); b. St. Paul, Minn., 1928; p. Harold and Amanda Garvick Young; h. Ralph Gracza; c. Susan, Edward; res: 15151 Victor Lane, Minnetonka Village, Minn. 55343.

GRADY, DOROTHY McCORMACK, Media Ctr. Dir., Bedminster Township School, Bedminster, N.J. 07921, '69–; Librn., '60–; Eng. Tchr., '55–'57, '38–'39; Ed., "New Jersey in the Classroom" ('65); NEA, NJEA, SCEA (County), BEA (Local), NJSLA: Kappa Delta Epsilon, Beta Phi Mu; Bedminster-Far Hills Pub. Lib. (Founder, '61, Pres., '67); Bedminster Twp. PTA (Pres., '55–'56); Cornell Univ., BA, '37; Columbia, MA, '38; Rutgers, MLS, '60; b. N. Andover, Mass., 1916; p. John and Gladys Houghton McCormack; h. Allan Grady; c. Lael Lyn (Mrs. Ronald Kirk); res: Bedminster, N.J. 07921.

GRADY, REGINA GEDEON, Prod. Mgr., Feldman, Kahn and Sutton, Inc., Suite 2210, Clark Bldg., Pitt., Pa. 15222, '66–; Corp. Secy., Prod. Mgr., Fourth Allegheny Corp., '60–'66; Prod. Mgr., Sykes Adv., '58–'60; Asst. Prod. Mgr., Bond & Starr, '47–'58; practicing real estate agent; Pitt. Adv. Prod. Assn. (Charter Mbr., Secy.-Treas., '64; VP, '65; Pres., '66), Pitt. Club Printing House Craftsmen (Ed., Bul.); Second Prize Trophy Winner in Intl. Competition of Intl. Printing Craftsmen, '63, '64; Pitt. Adv. Club; active in Humanist Assn. and Ethical Cultural Movement; b. Aspinwall, Pa., 1922; p. Casper and Anna Regina Gedeon; c. Heather Maureen; res: 230 Parker Dr., Pitt., Pa. 15216.

GRAEFF, LILLIAN E., Mag. Ed., The Cleveland Trust Company, 916 Euclid Ave., Cleve., Oh. 44115, '67–; Ed., The Educ. Rsch. Cncl. of Am., '66; News Wtr., Colmst., Edtl. Wtr., The Journal nwsp. (Lorain County), '50–'65; Wtr., poetry; ICIE, Northern Oh. IEA, Wms. Adv. Club (Cleve.), Am. Inst. of Banking; res: 2231 Garden Dr., Avon, Oh. 44011.

GRAF, DONNIE EDWARDS, Media Dir./AE, Andrew M. Weiss Advertising Works, Inc., 595 Madison Ave., N.Y., N.Y. 10022, '62–; Asst. AE, Solow-Wexton; Acc. Coordr., Dancer-Fitzgerald-Sample; Traf. Coordr., Doyle, Dane, Bernbach; Asst. U.S. Bur. Mgr., Newswtr., Reptr., Visnews (Intl. Newsfilm Agcy.); Acc. Coordr., Hixon & Jorgensen (L.A., Cal.); Asst. AE, Robinson & Haynes; Acc. Coordr., Fuller & Smith & Ross; Adv. Prod. Mgr., Western Family Magazine; several aws.; b. Terre Haute, Ind., 1926; p. Ralph and Iva Suttles Edwards; h. Richard Graf; Stepchildren: Stephanie, Mark, Owen; res: 3701 Henry Hudson Pkwy., Riverdale, N.Y. 10463.

GRAFF, MICHELLE, Pres., Avondale Advertising, Inc., 18 S. Northwest Highway, Park Ridge, Ill. 60068, '57–; Wtr., Illus., numerous children's bks.; Publr., Ideas Unlimited mag.; Performer, WTTW, "Make Things with Michelle;" Lectr.; WPA, Ill. WPA, AWRT; 35 aws., '59–'64; Nate Palmer Aws.; Comm. Art and Jnlsm. Col. (Eng.); b. England; p. Dudley-Ward and Elizabeth Halfpenny John; c. Michele, Peter Lloyd; res: 5 N. Home, Park Ridge, Ill. 60068.

GRAHAM, ALICE WALWORTH, Auth: "Lost River" (Dodd, Mead, '38), six other novels (Doubleday, '50–'62); NLAPW, Auths. League of Am.; Miss. State Col. for Wm., '23–'24; La. State Univ., '33; b. Natchez, Miss., 1905; p. John and Alice Gordon Walworth; h. Richard Graham; c. Richard N.; res: 710 N. Union St., Natchez, Miss. 39120.

GRAHAM, BEATRICE, Crtv. Art Dir., Secy.-Treas., Schwartz/Graham Advertising Agency, Inc., 1688 Meridian Ave., Miami Beach, Fla. 33139, '53–; Adv. Dir., Jordan Marsh, '54–'56; Art Dir., Moss & Arnold Adv. (N.Y.C.), '48–'50; Ed., Mayfair Magazine, '46–'48; Nat. Soc. Arts Dirs., Art Dirs. Club of Gtr. Miami, Fashion Group, NHFL, Gtr. Miami Assn. of Adv. Agencies, Nat. Soc. of Communicating Artists; Art Students League, '52–'53; Cooper Union Col., '48–'52; Bklyn. Mus., '45–'46; Pratt Inst., '46–'47; b. N.Y.C.; p. Philip Goldberg and Minnie Lubman Goldberg Graham; res: 3 Island Ave., Miami Beach, Fla. 33139.

GRAHAM, JANE E., Southwest Advertising and Marketing Magazine, Southwest Central Publishing, P.O. Box 8015, Dallas, Tex. 75205; Colmst., California Apparel News, Style For Men; Dallas Ed. California Stylist, Men's Stylist; Owner, Jane Graham Advertising, J & J Productions; Prodr./Talent in bdcst.; Wtr.; Adv. Tchr. Dallas Fashion Merchandising College; Theta Sigma Phi, Fashion Group, Dallas Adv. League, Press Club; winner of many adv. awards for campaigns written for Tracy-Locke and Glenn Adv.; Texas State College for Wm., '38–'39; Abilene Christian College, 39-41; b. Rice, Tex., 1922; p. William Edward and Kathryn Ruth McKay Tidwell; h. Joseph Wesley Graham; c. Kathryn Ann; res: 6010 Glendora, Dallas, Tex. 75230.

GRAHAM, KATHARINE MEYER, Pres., The Washington Post Company, 1515 L St., N.W., Wash., D.C. 20005, '63–; Sunday Circ. and Edtl. Staff, '39–'45; Reptr., San Francisco (Cal.) News, '38–'39; WNPC, Theta Sigma Phi; Vassar Col., '35–'36; Univ. of Chgo., AB, '38; b. N.Y.C., 1917; p. Eugene and Agnes Enrst Meyer; h. Philip Leslie Graham (dec.); c. Elizabeth (Mrs. Yann R. Weymouth), Donald, William, Stephen; res: 2920 R St. N.W., Wash., D.C. 20007.

GRAHAM, VIRGINIA (Virginia Komiss Guttenberg), Actress; Good Will Ambassador, Clairol, '60–'68; Hostess, "Girl Talk," ABC Films, '62–'69;

Co-hostess (with Mike Wallace), "Weekday," NBC, '56–'57; "Food for Thought," Dumont TV, '52–'58; Auth: "There Goes What's-Her-Name" (Prentiss-Hall; Avon); "Don't Blame the Mirror" (Meredith); "Last Day of the World Cook Book" (Avon); AGVA, Theta Sigma Phi; Knights of Pythias Wm. of the Yr.; Cerebral Palsy Wm. of the Yr.; Regency League Emotionally Disturbed Children Hon. Chmn.; Am. Cancer Soc. Chmn.; Intl. Wm. of the Yr.; active in numerous philanthropic groups; Univ. of Chgo., BA; Northwestern Univ., MA (Jnlsm.); b. Chgo., Ill., 1912; p. Davis and Bessie Feiges Komiss; h. Harry W. Guttenberg; c. Lynn K. (Mrs. Seymour Bohrer); res: 1025 Fifth Ave., N.Y., N.Y. 10028.

GRALNICK, BETH BAUMGART, Assoc. Prodr., Dir. of Rsch., News Division, Columbia Broadcasting System, Inc., 524 W. 57th St., N.Y., N.Y. 10019, '68–; Rschr., '64–'68; Univ. of Pitt., BA, '64; b. N.Y.C., 1942; p. Robert and Stella Lacher Baumgart; h. Jeff Gralnick; res: 29 E. 37th, N.Y., N.Y. 10016.

GRAMBS, JEAN DRESDEN, Prof. of Educ., University of Maryland, Secondary Education, College Park, Md. 20742, '67–; Assoc. Prof., '61–'67; Lectr., '55–'61; Supvsr. of Adult Educ., Prince George's County, '55–'58; Visiting Lectr., George Wash. Univ., '52, '54; Asst. Prof. of Educ., Stanford Univ., '49–'53; Instr., '48–'49; Tchr., HS, '41–'43; Auth., bks., articles on educ.; Cnslt.; Reed Col., AB, '40 (Phi Beta Kappa); Stanford Univ., MA, '41 (Pi Lambda Theta); EdD, '48 (Ford Fndn. Fac. Fellow, '52–'53); b. Pigeon Point, Cal., 1919; h. Harold Grambs; c. three; res: 8502 49th Ave., College Park, Md. 20740.

GRAMS, RUTH PFOHL, City Librn., City of Santa Fe Springs, 11700 Telegraph Rd., Santa Fe Springs, Cal. 90670, '67–; Children's Librn., '63–'67; Downey Lib., '62–'63; Head of Harp Dept., Univ. of Mich., '33–'35; Instr., Harp, Hist., Moravian Col., '27–'30; ALA, Cal. Lib. Assn., Nat. Harp Assn., Mu Phi, AAUW, Soroptimist; Dover, Oh. C. of C. aw., '54; Salem Col., BA, '27; Curtis Inst. of Music; Univ. of Southern Cal., MA (Lib. Sci.), '63; b. East Bend, N.C., 1906; p. J. Kenneth and Bessie Whittington Pfohl; h. Roy Grams (dec.); c. Martha (Mrs. Kenneth Williams), Ruth (Mrs. James Uphold); res: 8023 S. Armour Rd., Whittier, Cal. 90602.

GRANGER, DEE ANN, Sr. PR AE, Ruder and Finn, Inc., 20 N. Wacker Dr., Chgo., Ill. 60606; Free-lance PR, '62–'64; PR Dir., Blackhawk Restaurant, '59–'62; PRSA, Pubcty. Club of Chgo.; Crusade of Mercy aw., '63; Northwestern Univ., '43–'46; Roosevelt Univ., '60–'62; b. Hinsdale, Ill., 1925; p. Arthur and Ann Kralek Giesecke; c. Laney Granger, Dawn Granger Titus; res: 201 E. Walton Pl., Chgo., Ill. 60611.

GRANN, PHYLLIS EITINGON, Assoc. Ed., David McKay, 750 Third Ave., N.Y., N.Y. 10017, '63–; Asst. Ed., William Morrow & Co., '60; Oberlin Col., '54–'56;

Barnard Col., '56–'58, BA (cum laude); b. London, Eng., 1939; p. Solomon and Louisa Bols-Smith Eitingon; h. Victor Grann; c. Alison and David Eliot; res: 12 Surf Rd., Westport, Conn. 06880.

GRANT, BESS MYERSON, Commissioner of Consumer Affairs, City of New York, 80 Lafayette St., N.Y., N.Y. 10003, '69–; formerly a TV performer; News Staff, Mutual Broadcasting Co., '61–'62; Panelist, "The Name's the Same," ABC, '54–'55, "The Young Set," ABC, '65; "I've Got a Secret," CBS; Co-commentator, "Tournament of Roses," ABC, '60–'61, CBS, '62–'65; "N.Y. World's Fair Opening," ABC, '64, "Thanksgiving Day Parade Opening," ABC, '64–'65; TV Commentator, "Miss America Pageant," ABC, '54–'56, CBS, '57, '64, '65, "Do You Trust Your Wife," NBC, '56–'57, CBS, '64–'65; Comml. Hostess, "Philco Playhouse," NBC-TV, "Jackie Gleason Show," CBS, '54–'55, Mistress of Ceremonies, "The Big Payoff," CBS-TV, '51–'59, "Premier Playhouse," ABC, '54–'55, "Look Up and Live," '54; began career with WOR-TV, '47, '51, WPIX-TV, '49–'52; Anti-Defamation League, Friends of Music (Trustee), League Sch. of Seriously Disturbed Children (merit aw., '56), Hillside Hosp.; Cunningham League Handicapped Children cit., '55; Multiple Sclerosis Soc. aw., '57; Muscular Distrophy Assn. aw., '58; "Wm. of the Yr.," '65; Metropolitan Museum of Art (Fellow), NATAS (Bd. of Govs.); Lectr., The Distaff Side; Hunter Col., BA, '45; b. N.Y.C., 1924; p. Louis and Bella Podolsky Myerson; h. Arnold M. Grant; c. Barbara C.; res: 25 Sutton Pl., N.Y., N.Y. 10022.

GRANT, EVVA H., Ed.-in-Chief, National Congress of Parents and Teachers, 700 N. Rush St., Chgo., Ill. 60611, '40–; Ed., The PTA Magazine, '40–; Lectr., Northwestern Univ., '45–'46; Tchr., '36–'37; Ed., "PTA Guide to What's Happening in Education" ('65), "Guiding Children as They Grow" ('59); Cnslt. Ed., "Community Life in a Democracy" (Nat. Congress of Parents and Tchrs., '42); Auth., "Parents and Teachers as Partners" ('52); Interpreter, voice of PTA, NBC, '44; EPAA (Pres., '41–'43), NEA, Delta Kappa Gamma; Augustana Col., AB, '34 (Distg. Alumni Aw.); State Univ. of Ia., AM, '37; b. Rock Island, Ill.; p. Morris and Ida Learner Handelman; h. Herman Grant; c. David Alistair; res: 2600 N. Lakeview Ave., Chgo., Ill. 60614.

GRANT, JANE C., Cnslt., The New Yorker, 25 W. 43rd St., N.Y., N.Y. 10036, '43–; Founder, with former husband, Harold W. Ross, '25; Auth., "Ross, The New Yorker, and Me" (Reynad); First Wm. Reptr., gen. staff, N.Y. Times, '19–'29; Ed., Hotel News; Reptr., Fashion, Soc.; occasional bdcsts., synd. colms.; Co-owner, Ed., pubns., White Flower Farm; Contrbr., articles, Saturday Evening Post, Mercury, other pubns.; OPC, Friends of the Whitney Museum, Met. Museum (Life Mbr.), Modern Museum, Lucy Stone League, Nat. Cncl. of Wm., Pan Pacific & S.E. Asia Wms. Assn. of U.S.A.; b. Joplin, Mo., 1895; p. Robert T. and Sophronia Cole Grant; h.

William B. Harris; res: White Flower Farm, Litchfield, Conn. 06759.

GRASZ, LYNNE MORIAN, Prom. Dir., KOLN-TV/KGIN-TV, 40th and "W" Sts., Lincoln, Neb. 68501, '66–; News Reptr., UPI (Detroit, Mich.), '66; Radio Cont., Miller & Paine Dept. Store, '64; AWRT (Cornhusker Chptr. VP, '68–'69), Bdcst. Prom. Assn., Lincoln Ad Club, Cornhuskers Eds. Assn.; Univ. of Neb., BS (Home Econs., Jnlsm.), '66 (Univ. Regents Scholarship; KOLN-TV/KGIN-TV Scholarship; Marie Hulbert Aw., AWRT aw.); b. L.A. Cal., 1943; p. Dale and Marie Bailey Rustermier; h. Mel Grasz; res: 2437 "A" St., Lincoln, Neb. 68502.

GRATTAN, SHEILA MONEEN, AE, Bergen and Lee Public Relations, 1533 Wilshire Blvd., L.A., Cal. 90017, '68–; City Ed., Copley Nswps. (Post-Advocate), '67–'68; Asst. City Ed., '66–'67; Staff Reptr., '66–; Wms. Ed., '65–'66; Youth Pg., Col. Colmst., Pasadena Independent Star News, '57, '58; Gtr. L.A. Press Club, Pubcty. Club of L.A.; Pasadena City Col., AA (Jnlsm.), '59; Immaculate Heart Col., BA (Eng.), '61; U.C.L.A. Grad. Sch. of Bus. Adm.; b. Pasadena, Cal., 1939; p. James H. and Mary B. Moriarty Grattan; res: 2004 Apex Ave., L.A., Cal. 90039.

GRAU, SHIRLEY ANN, Free-lance Wtr., Brandt and Brant, 101 Park, N.Y., N.Y. 10017; Auth: "The Keepers of the House" ('64), "The House on Coliseum Street" ('61), "The Hard Blue Sky" ('58), "The Black Prince" ('55); Pulitzer Prize, fiction, '65; Tulane Univ., '50; b. N.O., La., 1930; p. Adolphe and Katherine Onions Grau; h. James Feibleman; c. Ian, Nora, William, Katherine.

GRAVELLE, MARIAN ELIZABETH, Trade Prom., Adv. Mgr., St. Martin's Press, 175 Fifth Ave., N.Y., N.Y. 10010, '67–; Mgr., Lib. Svc. Dept., Cambridge Univ. Press, '65–'66; Supvsr., Svc. Order Program, Collier-Macmillan Lib. Svc., '63–'64; Submissions Supvsr., G. P. Putnam's Sons Lib. Dept., '60–'62; Sls. Dept., Sheed & Ward, '57–'59; PPA, Publrs. Adv. Club, Children's Bk. Cncl., Publrs. Lib. Prom. Group; St. Lawrence Acad., '41–'53; Marymount Manhattan Col., '54–'57; b. N.Y.C., 1935; p. F. Walter and Lillie Smith Gravelle; res: 81–05 35th Ave., Jackson Heights, N.Y. 11372.

GRAVES, ELEANOR MacKENZIE, Sr. Ed., Life Magazine, 1271 Sixth Ave., N.Y., N.Y. 10021, '68–; Modern Living Ed., Asst. Fashion Ed.; Barnard Col., BA, '48 (cum laude, Phi Beta Kappa); p. Dr. Luther MacKenzie; h. Ralph Graves; c. William W. Parish, Jr., Alexander M. Parish, Sara E., Andrew D.; res: 1158 Fifth Ave., N.Y., N.Y. 10029.

GRAVES, PAULINE BERG, Free-lance, Synd. Nwsp. Feature Wtr., "Try This," 6307 Riggs Pl., L.A., Cal. 90045; Auth: "Distinctive Interiors, Ideas for Small Homes" ('46); Western Rep., Farson, Huff and Northlich, adv., '51–'59; Adv. Copywtr., Barker Bros., '37–'41; Theta Sigma Phi (L. A. Chptr. Pres., '60–'61;

Treas., '58–'59), Pi Beta Phi, Trojan League, Children's Home Soc. (Hostess Guild); Glendale Jr. Col., AA, '34; Univ. of Southern Cal., '37 (cum laude); b. Salt Lake City, Ut., 1914; p. Carl and Blanch Hurlbut Berg; h. Leverne Graves; c. Dennis L., Terry Lou (Mrs. Jim R. Davis); res: 6307 Riggs Pl., L.A., Cal. 90043.

GRAVLEY, ERNESTINE, Auth: "Hang Onto the Willows," "A History of Pottawatomie County"; articles, short stories in nat., reg. mags.; sponsor, annual Ark. Wtrs. Conf.; Lectr. on writing in univs., wtrs. confs.; Bailiff, Assoc. Dist. Court (Shawnee, Okla.), '67–; Who's Who of Am. Wm., South and Southwest, 2,000 Wm. of Achiev., numerous other orgs., aws.; Univ. of Okla.; b. Russellville, Ark.; p. Joseph and Mary Mullins Hudlow; h. Loupe H. Gravely; c. Almalou (Mrs. David Rosenberg), Carol Ann (Mrs. Larry Fugit); res: 1225 Sherry Lane, Shawnee, Okla. 74801.

GRAY, ALBERTA LOUISE, Commentator, Radio Sls. Mgr., WFAR, RD #2, Sharon, Pa., 16146, '60–; Anncr., '57–'59; Wms. Prog. Dir., Anncr., Cont. Wtr., WBBW (Youngstown, Oh.), '54–'56; Anncr., Cont. Wtr., Prog. Dir., WKRZ (Oil City, Pa.), '52–'53; Intl. Platform Assn.; Who's Who of Am. Wm.; Univ. of N.M., '48–'49; b. Chgo., Ill.; p. William and Alberta French Gray; res: RD #2, Reno Rd., Sharon, Pa. 16146.

GRAY, ENID MAURINE, Lib. Dir., Tyrrell Public Library, 695 Pearl, Beaumont, Tex. 77701, '66–; Librn., Caddo Parish Sch. Bd., (Shreveport, La.), '66; Auth, "History of Medicine in Beaumont, Texas" (for C. of C., '69); ALA, Tex. Lib. Assn., Tex. Municipal Librns. Assn.; Beaumont Civic Opera, civic affairs; N.E. La. State Col., BA, '66; N. Tex. State Univ., MA, '69; b. Galveston, Tex., 1943; p. Dr. Willis James and Enid Childress Gray; res: 2815 Westmont Dr., Beaumont, Tex. 77706.

GRAY, FRANCILE du PLESSIX, Auth., essays, fiction and criticism in many mags.; Edtl. Bd., Art in America; Staff Wtr., The New Yorker; Edtl. Asst., Realities, '54–'55; Wtr., UPI, '52–'54; Bryn Mawr Col., '48–'50; Barnard Col., BA (Philosophy), '52 (Putnam Crtv. Writing aw., '52); b. Warsaw, Poland; p. Bertrand and Titiana Jacovleff du Plessix; h. Cleve Gray; c. Thaddeus and Luke; res: Warren, Conn. 16754.

GRAY, MAB, Pubcty. Dir., Hawthorn Books, Inc., 70 Fifth Ave., N.Y., N.Y. 10011, '69–; Dir. of Adv. Prom., Pubcty., Funk & Wagnalls '62–'67; Asst. Dir. of Adv., Prom., Pubcty., Bernard Geis Assoc. '67–'69.

GRAY, NANCY CARPENTER, Pacific Coast Ed., American Home Magazine, Downe Publishing, Inc., 425 California St., S.F., Cal. 94104; Asst. Mng. Ed., Successful Farming, Meredith Publ. Co.; Gen. Assigt. Ed., Better Homes & Gardens; Pubcty., Helena Rubenstein (House of Gourielli); Pubcty., Jacqueline Cochran Cosmetics; AID (Press Affiliate), NHFL;

Swarthmore Col., BA (Eng.), '45; b. Des Moines, Ia., 1923; p. George C., Jr., and Helen Sigler Carpenter; res: 989 Lombard St., S.F., Cal. 94133.

GRAYBILL, MILDRED, Instr., Eastern Mennonite College, Harrisonburg, Va. 22801, '68–; Media Dir., Mennonite Adv. Agcy., '64–'68; AWRT, Natl. Bus. Educ. Assn., Am. Accounting Assn.; 2,000 Wm. of Achiev.; Madison Col., BS, '65; MS, '69; b. Manheim, Pa., 1930; p. Ira and Nora Martin Graybill; res: 1543 College Ave., Harrisonburg, Va. 22801.

GREBE, ZELPHA GROSVENOR, Dir., PR, Columbia Savings and Loan Association, 16th-Broadway, Denver, Colo. 80202, '68–; Asst. Dir. of PR, '64–'68; Savings Supvsr., '61–'64; Asst. Secy., '60; Dir., Fgn. and Personal Shopping, Denver Dry Goods Co., '52–'57; Tchr., Denver Public Schs., '44–'47; Am. Savings and Loan Inst. (Deputy Gov. for Colo., '68–'69), Denver Savings and Loan Inst. (Chmn. of Bd., '66–'68; Pres., '65–'66), AWRT (Rocky Mountain Reg. Chptr. VP, '68–'70; Reg. Conf. Chmn., '69–'70), PRSA; Wm. of the Yr., Am. Bus. Wms. Assn., Denver, '68; Univ. of Denver, BA, '44 (Phi Beta Kappa); b. Aberdeen, S.D., 1922; p. William and Lola Grosvenor; h. Theodore Grebe; res: 1990 Quebec St., Denver, Colo. 80220.

GREEN, ANNE M., Librn. New Hanover County School System, Wrightsboro School, 640 Castle Hayne Rd., Wilmington, N.C. 28401, '67–; Children's Librn., Wilmington Public Lib., '60–'67; Copywtr., Harper and Rowe (N.Y.C.), '53–'57; Eng. Tchr., New Hanover HS (Wilmington), '48–'50; Auth: "Goodby, Gray Lady" (Atheneum Publrs., '64), "The Valley Cup" (Thomas Nelson & Sons, '62), "To Race Again" ('61); N.C. Lib. Assn., N.C. Educ. Assn., NEA, Auths. Guild; Mary Wash. Col., Univ. of Va., BA, '44; courses at Univ. of N.C., E.C. Univ., Univ. of Vt., Univ. of Wis.; b. Wilmington, N.C., 1922; p. Charles and Elizabeth Barnwell Green; res: 3008 Wayne Dr., Wilmington, N.C. 28401.

GREEN, ANNIE LANDER, VP, Guide-Kalkhoff-Burr, 225 Varick St., N.Y., N.Y. 10014, '42–; Secy.-Treas., sls., Kalkhoff Press, '31–'42; Prod. Mgr., William Green, '16–'31; Club of Printing Wm. (Founding Mbr.), AWNY; Vassar Col., '14 (Phi Beta Kappa); b. Bklyn., N.Y., 1893; p. William and Bessie Beebe Green; res: 208 W. 23rd St., N.Y., N.Y. 10011.

GREEN, BEVERLY BRUNTON, Pres. & Gen. Mgr., Green /Associates Advertising, Inc., 1176 W. Seventh, Eugene, Ore. 97401, '63–; Prodr., variety, interview, public svc. program (first local live series), KVAL-TV, '54–'64; Prodr., Talent, KUGN, '48–'51; Prodr., numerous filmed and taped documentaries on civic and health problems; Mid-Ore. Ad Club (Ad Man of the Yr., '69), Very Little Theatre, Lane County Assn. for Mentally Retarded Children and Adults (Pres., '69); active in state, nat. assns. for aid to mentally retarded; Northwestern Univ., summer '42 (scholarship); Plymouth Drama Festival, '44 (scholarship); Univ. of Ore.,

BA (Speech, Drama), '53 (Phi Beta Kappa, Phi Beta; Phi Beta Patroness' Aw., '52–'53; Best Actress Aw.); b. Klamath Falls, Ore., 1925; p. Jacob and Kathryn Bryan Brunton; h. William Howard Green; c. William H., Blakely A.; res: 3505 Dulles Ave., Eugene, Ore. 97401.

GREEN, CAROL, Cont. Dir., Forward Communications, 714 Fifth St., Wausau Wisc. 54401, '61–; MC, "Menu Magic," "Menu Magic Guest Book"; commls., "Bake-Off"; TV Wtr., WSAU, '58–; Radio Show, "Woman Talk," WLIN, '51–'60; AWRT (Pres., Badger Chptr., '68–'69); Sweet Adelines Aw., '68; Shimer Jr. Col., '43; Univ. of Wisc. '43–'44; Milw. Bus. Inst., '46; b. Merrill, Wisc., 1923; p. Edward and Lailla Holstrom Green; res: 508 Pier St., Merrill, Wisc. 54452.

GREEN, CONSTANCE McLAUGHLIN, Free-lance Wtr., '54–; Bks: "The Secret City" ('67), "The Rise of Urban America" ('65), "Washington, Capital City" ('63), others; Pulitzer Prize in Hist., '63; Histrn., Off. Secy. of Defense, Rsch. & Dev. Bd., '51–'54; Chief Histrn., Ordance Corps, U.S. Army, '48–'57; Cnslt. Histrn., Am. Nat. Red Cross, '47–'48; Instr: Smith Col., Mt. Holyoke Col., Univ. of Chgo.; Commonwealth Fund Lectr., Univ. Col., Univ. of London, '51; Atomic Energy Comm. (Hist. Advisory Comm., '64–); Nat. Capital Planning Commn. (Landmarks, Comm., '65–); Univ. of Chgo., '14–'16; Smith Col., AB, '19 (Hon. Dr. of Ltrs., '63); Mt. Holyoke Col., MA, '25; Yale Univ., PhD, '37; Pace Col., Hon Dr. of Humane Ltrs., '68; b. Ann Arbor, Mich., 1897; p. Andrew C. and Lois Angell McLaughlin; h. Donald Ross Green (dec.); c. Lois Angell Green Carr, Donald R., Elizabeth L.; res: 19 Second St. N.E., Wash., D.C. 20002.

GREEN, CORENA CRASE, Ed., Palos Verdes Peninsula News, 700 Silver Spur Rd., Rolling Hills Estates, Cal. 90274, '68–; News Ed., '66–'68; Stringer, '64–'66; San Rafael (Cal.) Independent Journal, '56–'64; Theta Sigma Phi, Cal. Press Wm. (ed. aw.), AAUW, Gtr. L.A. Press Club, Pacific Coast Press Club, NFPW (edtl. aw.); Stanford Univ., AB, '38; b. Grass Valley, Cal., 1917; h. Harold Green; c. Elizabeth, James, Richard; res: 5710 Scotwood Dr., Palos Verdes Peninsula, Cal. 90274.

GREEN, E. ALICE, City Librn., Amarillo Public Library, 1000 Polk St., Amarillo, Tex. 79105, '47–; Asst. Librn., '42–'46; Gen. Asst., '41–'42; Gen. Asst., Tex. State Lib., '39–'41; Librn., Tex. Military Col., '38–'39; ALA, SW Lib. Assn., Tex. Lib. Assn., Tex. Municipal Libs. Assn. (Past Secy.-Treas.), Altrusa, Wms. Div., C. of C.; Amarillo Col., '34–'36; W. Tex. Univ., '36–'37; Univ. of Okla., BS (Lib. Sci), '38; b. Waverly, Kan., 1916; p. Roy and Eliza Carleton Green; res: 3704 Clearwell St., Amarillo, Tex. 79109.

GREEN, JEAN CATHERINE, Ed., Hoosier Doctor's Wife mag.; Contrb. Ed., MD's Wife; Free-lance wtr., non-fiction; Feature Wtr., Washington (D.C.) Times; Washington (D.C.) Post; WNPC, Intl. Platform Assn., NFPA, Wms. Press Club of Ind. (VP, '66–'68; 1st pl. aw.,

best edtl., '68); Ind. Univ., AB, MS; b. Pekin, Ind.; p. William and Jessie Scott Green; h. Frank H. Green; c. David L., William Louis, John C.; res: 516 N. Morgan St., Rushville, Ind. 46173.

GREEN, LUCILLE BRADLEY, Ed. of Religion, Educ. Wtr., Fine Arts Critic, The Greenville News, 305 S. Main St., Greenville, S.C. 29602, '61–; Dir. of PR, Am. Red Cross (Charleston), '61; Wms. Ed., Charleston News & Courier, '56–'61; News Ed., Jacksonville (N.C.) Daily News, '51–'56; Feature Ed., Waverly (N.Y.) Sun-Valley News, '41–'49; Wtr., mag. articles and features; S.C. Press Wms. Assn. (1st pl. aws: features, '69; Criticism, '65–'69); S.C. Chptr. of Am. Inst. of Architects (firsts for architectural writing, '66, '67), S.C. Eds. Assn. (two Sch. Bell Aws., '67–'68); NPWC (first for criticism, '66), Altrusa Club (CharlestonCharter Pres.; Greenville Bd. of Dirs.), Who's Who of Am. Wm.; Who's Who in South and Southwest; Intl. Biogs.; numerous others hons.; Univ. of Rochester, '30–'32; b. Potsdam, N.Y., 1911; p. Eugene and Lula Cole Bradley; c. Mrs. Wilbur L. Lockrow, Mrs. B. P. McWilliams, Eugene Ernest Lunger; res: 107 Broadus Ave., Greenville, S.C. 29601.

GREEN, MARGARET MURPHY, Eng. Tchr., W. T. Woodson High School, Main St., Fairfax, Va. 22030, '65–; Auth: "Defender of the Constitution," "President of the Confederacy," "Paul Revere" (all pub. by Julian Messner); NEA; Am. Univ., '65; b. Lawrence, Mass.; p. William and Margaret Donovan Murphy; h. Francis J. Green; c. Ellen, Frank, William, Mary; res: 6920 Fern Lane, Annandale, Va. 22003.

GREEN, REBA LONG, Bdcstr., "The Reba June Show," WFHG (Bristol, Va.) and WKOY (Bluefield, W. Va.), '52; Free-lance TV, WCYB-TV, '59–; Coord. and advise area Jr. Miss and Miss Am. beauty pageants; Prod., Commentator, fashion shows in Va., Tenn., W. Va.; Prod./Dir., Queen's Pageants, NASCAR, Bristol Intl. Speedway, '59–'62; WOPI Bdcst. Co., '52; Pubcty. Dept., David O. Selznick Studios, '43; AWRT; Will Rogers Aw. for outstanding contrb. to speech educ.; Nat. Champion, Nat. Forensic League Extempore Contest, '38; First. Nat. Extempore winner ('39, '40), and First Nat. Debate winner ('40); Va. Intermont Col., '38–'40 (highest scholastic average on sch. records); Univ. of Redlands, '42 (magna cum laude); b. Yale, Okla., 1920; p. Asa and Ida Allison Long; h. B. J. Green; c. Ralph H. Brumet, Jr., Linda May Brumet, Barbara L. Brumet; res: 101 Haverhill Rd., Bristol, Va. 24201.

GREEN, SHEILA GREENWALD, Free-lance Auth., Illus.; Auth., "A Metropolitan Love Story" (Doubleday, '62); Illus., 43 bks., incl. many for children; Wtr., Harpers Magazine; Sarah Lawrence Col., BA, '56; b. N.Y.C., 1934; p. Julius and Florence Friedman Greenwald; h. George Green; c. Samuel, Benjamin; res: 898 West End Ave., N.Y., N.Y. 10025.

GREENBAUM, MARY REIL, Off. Mgr. and Booker, Blue Ribbon Pictures, Inc., Suite 1400, Two Canal St.,

N.O., La. 70130, '67–; Secy., '64–'67; Metro-Goldwyn-Meyer, '30–'44; Wtr., weekly colm., Box Office Magazine; b. N.O., La., 1913; p. Henry and Johanna Faivre Reil; h. Tilden Greenbaum; c. Mary Louise, Tilden H., III, Bernhard, Jack; res: 2303 Mendez St., N.O., La. 70122.

GREENBERG, BARBARA ELLEN E. Coast Rep., TV Guide, 1290 Ave. of the Americas, N.Y., N.Y. 10019, '65–; Asst. E. Coast Rep., '60–'65; NATAS, IRTS, AWRT (N.Y.C. Chptr. Pres., '67–'68); Elmira Col., '56–'57; Boston Univ., BA (Hist.), '60; b. N.Y.C.

GREENBERG, DOROTHY SEGAL, Secy.-Treas., MBA Music, Inc., 8 E. 48 St., N.Y., N.Y. 10017, '67–; Pres., VP; '60–; Skidmore Col., '41–'42; Columbia Univ., '42–'43; b. N.Y.C., 1923; p. Louis and Stella Friedman Segal; h. Henry Greenberg (div.); c. Robert, Eleanor, Judith; res: 240 W. 75th St., N.Y., N.Y. 10023.

GREENBERG, RITA PHYLLIS, Ed., Recommend Travel Publications, Inc., 1800 N. 20th Ave., Hollywood, Fla. 33020, '68–; Theta Sigma Phi; Univ. of Fla., BS (Adv.), '67; b. Bklyn., N.Y., 1945; p. Sidney and Shirley Greenberg; res: 13395 Arch Creek Rd., Apt. 1, N. Miami, Fla. 33161.

GREENE, ADELE SHUMINER, VP, Ruder & Finn, Inc., 110 E. 59th St., N.Y., N.Y. 10022, '68–; Sr. Assoc., '66–'68; AE, '64–'66; PR Acc. Coordr., Gaynor & Ducas, '63–'64; Asst. to Pres., Cobleigh & Gordon, '62–'63; PRSA; New Sch. for Social Rsch., '44–'47; N.Y.U.; Julliard Sch. of Music; b. Newark, N.J.; p. Adolph and Sara Schubert Shuminer; h. (div.); c. Joshua Michael; res: 30 W. 60th St., N.Y., N.Y. 10023.

GREENE, CARLA, Free-lance Wtr., Auth., children's bks: "Charles Darwin" (Dial Press, '68), "After the Dinosaurs" (Bobbs-Merrill, '68), "Manuel—Young Mexican-American (Lantern '69), 60 others, Wtr., adv. mags., radio plays, short stories; Auths. League of Am., Cal. Wtrs. Guild, Pfsnl. Wtrs. League; network, local, TV, radio interview appearances; b. Mpls., Minn., 1916; p. William and Charlotte Wunderman Greene; res: 570 N. Rossmore, Apt. 612, L.A., Cal. 90004.

GREENE, IRENE BRAFF, Treas., Don Greene Assoc., Inc., 211 E. 43rd St., N.Y., N.Y. 10017, '63–; Biow Co., Grey Adv., '53–'63; Tax Examiner, N.Y.C., '47–'53; Westchester County Dem. Commwm.; Hunter Col., '46; b. N.Y.C., 1926; p. A. J. Braff; h. Don Greene; res: Ardsley, N.Y. 10502.

GREENE, JUDITH M., Media Dir., Promotional Services, Inc., 501 Madison Ave., N.Y., N.Y. 10022, '69–; Pres., Peerless Adv., '68–'69; Media Supvsr., John F. Murray Adv., '68; Media Byr., Grey Adv., '67–'68; Media Byr., Bates, '67; AWNY; Queens Col.; Rutgers Univ., BS; Columbia Univ., MBA; b. N.Y.C., 1945; res: 61 Jane St., N.Y., N.Y. 10014.

GREENE, PAULINE, Pubcty. Dir., Charles J. Charney & Company, Inc., 310 Madison Ave., N.Y., N.Y. 10017, '56–; Adv., Pubcty., Pauline Greene Assocs., '53–'55; Prom. Dir., Namm's, '51–'53; Adv. Mgr., Saks Fifth Ave., '44–'50; Fashion Group, Pubcty. Club of N.Y., Shoe Wms. Exec. Club; b. N.Y.C.; h. Alfred Greene (dec.); res: 303 W. 66 St., N.Y., N.Y. 10023.

GREENE, VIRGINIA OWEN, Ed., Girl Scout Leader, Girl Scouts of the U.S.A., 830 Third Ave., N.Y., N.Y. 10022, '49–; Assoc. Ed., '42–'49; Assoc. Ed. for Girl Scout pubns., '32–'52; Univ. of Ala., AB, '26; b. Montgomery, Ala., 1905; p. Robert H. and Kate Ford Greene; res: N.Y.C.

GREENFELD, IRMA, VP, Copy Supvsr., The Marschalk Co., Time-Life Bldg., N.Y., N.Y., '66–; res: 31 E. 12th St., N.Y., N.Y. 10003.

GREENHOUSE, LINDA JOYCE, Met. Staff Reptr., The New York Times, 229 W. 43rd St., N.Y., N.Y. 10036, '69–; Asst. to James Reston, '68–'69; Free-lance Wtr., New York Magazine, N.Y. Times Magazine; Radcliffe Col., BA, '68; b. N.Y.C., 1947; p. H. Robert and Dorothy Greenlick Greenhouse; res: 15 W. 72nd St., N.Y., N.Y. 10023.

GREER, PHYLLIS JOHNSTON, AE, Nelson Stern and Associates, 530 Hanna Bldg., E. 14th St. and Euclid Ave., Cleve., Oh. 44115, '66–; Sr. Copywtr., Stockton-West-Burkhart (Cinn., Oh.); Copywtr., Higbee's Adv., '56–'58, '62–'66; Edtl. Staff Wtr., Cleveland Shopping News, '44–'47; Cleve. Fashion Group; Mademoiselle Magazine design aw., '47; Mt. Un. Col., Kent State Univ., Darvas Sch. of Fashion Art; b. Alliance, Oh., 1916; p. Hugh and Leah Lansdowne Johnston; h. John Greer; c. Geoffrey Greville; res: 726 Sycamore Dr., Euclid, Oh. 44132.

GREER, REBECCA ELLEN, Articles Ed., Woman's Day Magazine, 67 W. 44 St., N.Y., N.Y. 10017, '68; Features Ed., Bride's Magazine, '65–'68; Ed.-in-Chief, Teen Age Magazine, '62–'63; Asst. Beauty Ed., Ladies Home Jnl., '60–'61; Edtl. Asst., Parents' Magazine, '58–'60; Auth: "Why Isn't a Nice Girl Like You Married?" (Macmillan, '69), "The Bride's Book of Etiquette" (Grosset & Dunlap, '68), "The Book for Brides" (Arco, '65); free-lance articles, McCall's, Mademoiselle, Seventeen, other pubns.; Theta Sigma Phi (N.Y. Chptr. Corr. Secy., '62–'64; VP, '64–'66), Auths. Guild; Univ. of Fla., BS (cum laude; Hall of Fame); b. Wash., D.C.; p. Brig. Gen. Frank U. and May Mann Greer; res: 50 King St., N.Y., N.Y. 10014.

GREER, VIRGINIA BRADFORD, Free-lance Wtr.; Auth., "Give Them Their Dignity" (John Knox, '68); Reptr., Feature Wtr., Press Register (Mobile, Ala.), '62–'65, '55; Mobile NLAPW (VP), Ala. Wtrs. Conclave (VP, '53); Ala. Med. Assn. Aw., '65; Who's Who of Am. Wm.; Who's Who in South & Southwest; Dict. Intl. Biog.; b. Atlanta, Ga.; p. John and Floy Jarrett Bradford; h. John Greer; c. Katherine Greer Looper, John, Jr., Lynn; res: 554 Wisconsin Ave., Mobile, Ala. 36604.

GREESON, GEORGIANA WHITE, Adm. Librn., St. Charles Parish Library, Box 454, Hahnville, La. 70057, '58–; Adm. Librn., Phillips Co. Lib., '55–'57; Children's Librn., L.A. Public Lib., '54; Librn., N. Ark. Reg. Lib., '49–'53; STET; Hendrix Col., '39–'40; Ark. State Tchrs. Col., BA, '43; La. State Univ., BS (Lib. Sci.), '51; Mexico City Col., DF, '51; b. Capps, Ark., 1921; p. James and Agnes Calvert White; h. William H. Greeson (div.); c. Patricia E. (Mrs. Ronald F. Echeté).

GREESON, ROSEMARY ANTOINETTE, Reptr., Photogr., The Mt. Vernon Publishing Co. Inc., 430 Main St., Mt. Vernon, Ind. 47620, '67–; St. Mary-of-the-Woods College, BA (Jnlsm.), '67; b. Evansville, Ind., 1945; p. James Henry and Evelyn Mary Rechtin Greeson; res: 2000 Harmony Way, Evansville, Ind. 47712.

GREGG, Dr. DOROTHY, Asst. to Dir. of PR, United States Steel, 71 Broadway, N.Y., N.Y. 10006, '68–; Asst. Staff Dir. of Educ. Svcs. and Rschr., PR Dept., '60–'68; Asst. Prof., Econs. Dept., Columbia Univ., '42–'58; Assoc. Prof., Grad. School, Pace Col.; Biographer, Men in Business, Harvard Entrepreneurical Studies Ctr., '52; Special Cnslt. to ECA, '52; Speaker before educ., pfsnl., civic, and polit. groups; Co-chmn., Consumer Comm., Wms. Council, N.Y. State Dept. of Commerce (Distg. N.Y. State Wm.); State Advisory Bd., N.Y. State Guidance Ctr. for Wm. in Rockland County Commty. Col.; Special Rsch. Asst. —N.Y. Coordr. for Sen. Jacob K. Javits, '57; AWNY (Pres.), '67–'69; Special Aw., '68), Gamma Alpha Chi (Nat. Hon. VP, '68); Bd. of Dirs.: AAF (Nat. Adv. Wm., '68; Special Governor's Aw., '67), Gtr. N.Y. Safety Cncl., N.Y.C. Cncl. on Econ. Educ., Am. Wms. Assn. and ZONTA Club of N.Y.C.; Univ. of Texas (Phi Beta Kappa and Pi Sigma Alpha), BA, '44; (Grad. Fellow), MA, '45; Columbia Univ. (all-univ. Grad. Fellow), PhD; Salem Col.; Hon Degree of Doctor of Humane Letters; b. Tempe, Ariz.; p. Alfred Tennyson and Mamie Elizabeth Walker Gregg; h. Dr. Paul Hughling Scott; c. Kimerly Scott and Gregg Scott; res: 299 Riverside Dr., N.Y., N.Y. 10025.

GREGORY, DORIS PERRY, Owner, Doris Gregory Public Relations, 412 San Mateo, N.E., Suite 2F, Albuquerque, N.M. 87108, '56–; Exec. Mgr., N.M. Hotel & Motel Assn., '63–; Exec. and Ed., Motel Brokers Assn. of Am. nat. pubn., "Motel Topics," '66–; Ed., N.M. Motor Carriers Mag., "The Transporter," '68–; Travel Cnslt., Tourist Div., N.M. Dept. of Dev.; Dir. and Publicist, Carlsbad Tourist Industries, '59–'66; Exec. Secy. and Pubcty. Dir., U.S. Highway 180 Assn., '66; Pubcty. Dir., Carlsbad C. of C., '60–'66; N.M. Press Wm. (Pres., '64–'65), N.M. PR (Advisory Bd., '65, '66), N.M. Press Assn., PRSA (N.M. Chptr. Pres., '68); Texas Christian Univ., BA; b. Carlsbad, N.M., 1915; p. S. Luther and Edith Nevenger Perry; c. Phillip C., Robert L.; res: 1111 Cardenas SE, Apt. 206, Albuquerque, N.M. 87108.

GREGORY, JANE LOYS, Soc. Ed., Chicago Sun-Times, 401 N. Wabash Ave., Chgo., Ill. 60611, '58–; Asst. Soc. Ed., Chgo. Daily News, '55–'58; Soc. Wtr., Chgo. Herald-Am., '52–'55; Ed.-at-large, Chicagoland mag., '63–; Chgo. Press Club; Printer's Ink Aw., '63; Ill. Club for Catholic Wm. Aw., '63; Welfare PR Forum Aw.; Northwestern Univ., AB, '52; b. Glen Ellyn, Ill., 1929; p. Harold and Clara Johnson Gregory; h. Edward Robert Brooks; c. Edward R. Brooks, Jr., Catharine L. Brooks, Gregory L. Brooks; res: 339 Fullerton Pkwy., Chgo., Ill. 60614.

GREICUS, ALBERTA GUFFIGAN, Gen. Reptr., Music Ed., Educ. Ed., The Munice Star, Adams at High Sts., Muncie, Ind. 47302, '51–; '46–'49; Rsch. Chemist, Beckett Bronze Co., '44–'45; Rsch. Bacteriologist, Methodist Hosp. (Indpls.), '31–'32; Tchr., Habibia Col. (Kabul, Afghanistan), '49–'50; Wms. Press Club of Ind. (VP, '60; three firsts for music criticism, '60's); NLAPW (Muncie Chptr. Pres., '65), Theta Sigma Phi, Nat. Music Critics Assn., Kappa Tau Alpha; DAR; Purdue Univ., '28–'30; Butler Univ., BS (Pharmacy), '31; Ball State Univ., MA (Jnlsm.), '70; b. Muncie, Ind., 1910; p. Michael and Emma Wells Guffigan; h. Sigmund E. Greicus; c. Dr. Michael S.; res: 421 W. Howard St., Muncie, Ind. 43705.

GREVE, DAGMAR, Dir., Sch. and Lib. Programs, John Day-Abelard-Schuman, 257 Park Ave. S., N.Y., N.Y. 10010, '69–; Sch. and Lib. Cnslt., Holiday House, '65–'69; WNBA (N.Y.C. Chptr. Bd. of Mgrs., Term Expiring '71); educ. in Germany; b. Mölln, Germany; p. Ernst and Grete Greve.

GREY, VIVIAN HOFFMAN, Auth., Prof., Mercer County Commty. Col.; Cnslt., Educ. Testing Svc., '64; Cnslt., Creative Playthings, '64; Wtr., "The Betty Crocker Show," D-F-S, '54; Dir. of Pubcty., Oxarardt & Steffner & Co. (Hollywood, Cal.), '52; Wms. Radio, TV, The Borden Co., '50; Auth: "The Invisible Giants: Atoms, Nuclei and Radioisotopes" (Little, Brown & Co., '69), "The Secret of the Mysterious Rays: The Discovery of Nuclear Energy" (Basic Bks.), '62, the First Book of Astronomics (Franklin Watts), others; Nat. Cncl. of Tchrs. of Eng., WNBA, Auths. League of Am., Kappa Delta Pi; N.J. Educ. Assn. aw., '70; Cornell Univ., BS, '48; Columbia Univ., MA, '56; b. Newark, N.J.; p. Harry and Ray Friedlander Hoffman; h. Jerry Grey; c. Leslie Ann, Jacquelyn Eve; res: 61 Adams Dr., Princeton, N.J. 08540; Lovelladies, N.J.

GRIDLEY, MARION ELEANOR, Free-lance Wtr. and Publr.; Auth., numerous bks. for children on Am. Indians; Dir. of PR: Children's Memorial Hosp., Chgo. YWCA, Ill. Heart Assn., Chgo. Med. Sch., Francis W. Parker Sch., Nat. Soc. for Med. Rsch.; Ill. Wms. Press Assn. (Wm. of the Yr. Aw., '65; former VP), NFPW, Chgo. Pubcty. Club, Children's Reading Round Table, DAR, Indian Cncl. Fire (Exec. Secy.); numerous pfsnl. aws.; Northwestern Univ., '54–'55; b. White Plains, N.Y.; p. William T. and Ada Robertson Gridley; res: 1263 W. Pratt Rd., Chgo. Ill. 60626.

GRIEST, ELINOR PRESTON, Assoc. Ed., The Reader's Digest, 200 Park Ave., N.Y., N.Y. 10017, '66–; Reptr., Ed., '60–'66; Reptr. (Wash., D.C. Bur.), '51–'60; Info. Offcr., U.S. Fgn. Aid Program (Paris, France, '49–'51; Wtr., "Offcl. Hist. of Off. of Strategic Svcs." (OSS, Wash., D.C.), '47–'48; Copywtr., Col. Textbk. Dept., Henry Holt & Co. (N.Y.C.), '43–'46; OPC, WNPC (Bd. of Govs. '58–'59), ANWC (Bd. of Govs., '56–'59), WHCA; Swarthmore Col., BA, '43; Sorbonne Univ., '48–'49; b. Lancaster, Pa., 1921; p. Ellwood and Carolyn Hutton Griest; res: 25 E. Tenth St., N.Y., N.Y. 10003.

GRIFALCONI, ANN, Exec. Prodr., Pres., Media Plus, Inc., 60 Riverside Dr., N.Y., N.Y. 10024, '68–; Illus., 25 juv. bks.; Prodr., Educ. Films; New York Times "10 Best Illus. Bks.," '66–'67; Tchr., '54–'66; N.Y.U., Hunter Col., Cinn. Univ.; b. N.Y.C., 1929; p. Joseph and Mary Weik Grifalconi.

GRIFF, BARBARA DANA, Prog. Coordr., "What's My Line" show, Goodson-Todman Productions, 375 Park Ave., N.Y., N.Y. 10022, '68–; Pilots: Don Rickles Show ('68), Celebrity Count Down ('68); Free-lance Crtv. Cnslt., '67–'68; Assoc. Prodr., Helen Gurley Brown Show, '68; Prod. Asst., "What's My Line," '66–'67; "To Tell the Truth," '65–'66; Univ. of Paris, '62–'63; Skidmore Col., BA, '64; Columbia Univ., MA, '65; b. N.Y.C., 1943; p. Morton and Esther Efros Griff; res: 400 E. 85th St., N.Y., N.Y. 10028.

GRIFFIN, C. F. (Eunice Cleland Fikso), Novelist: "Not Without Love," "Nobody's Brother," "Instead of Ashes," "The Impermanence of Heroes"; Columbia Univ. Sch. of Gen. Studies, BS; b. Albany, N.Y.; p. Herdman and Emily Wadsworth Cleland; h. Adam Fikso; c. Theodore Adam, Judith Ann, Lucinda Cleland, Althea Louise; res: 327 Park Ave., Wilmette, Ill. 60091.

GRIFFIN, EMILIE, Sr. Group Supvsr., Compton Advertising, Inc., 625 Madison Ave., N.Y., N.Y. 10022, '68–; VP, '68–; Copy Group Head, '65–'68; Copywtr., '64–'65; Copywtr., Norman, Craig & Kummel, '62–'64; Copywtr., Fuller & Smith & Ross, '59–'62; Copywtr., Swigart & Evans (N.O., La.), '58–'59; Reptr., N.O. Item, '57–'58; aws. for commls: Am. TV Commls. Festival, '62, '67; Venice Film Festival, '62; Newcomb Col., Tulane Univ., BA, '57 (Phi Beta Kappa); b. N.O., La., 1936; p. Norman and Helen Russell Dietrich; h. H. William Griffin; c. Lucy Adelaide; res: 123-40 83rd Ave., Kew Gardens, N.Y. 11415.

GRIFFIN, FRANCES BURKHEAD, Dir. of Info., Old Salem, Inc., Drawer F.-Salem Sta., Winston-Salem, N.C. 27108, '66–; Reptr., Feature Wtr., Colmst., Edtl. Wtr., Winston-Salem Journal-Sentinel, '41–'66; Auth: "Old Salem in Pictures" ('66); N.C. Press Wm. (Pres., '54), AWRT, Arts Cncl. Aw. for svc. to the commty. in field of arts ('50); Greensboro Col., AB, '38 (magna cum laude; Trustee); b. Asheboro, N.C., 1916; p. Carl and Fannie Burkhead Griffin; res: 2005 Buena Vista Rd., Winston-Salem, N.C. 27104.

GRIFFIN, JUNE EVELYN, Copywtr., Grey Advertising Inc., 777 Third Ave., N.Y., N.Y. 10017; Crtv. Dir., Mark Century Corp., '62–'66; Wtr., Mars Bdcst., '61–'62; Wtr., Grant Advertising (Detroit, Mich.; N.Y.C.), '58–'60; Songwtr. (Lyricist); extensive free-lance writing, prod., radio syndication, comml. jingles; Intl. Bdcstrs. Aw., radio, Kent radio comml., '67; Hollywood Ad Club aw., Dodge TV comml., '60; b. Windsor, Ontario, Can., 1933; p. Anthony and Gladys McCauley; c. Brian, Lora-Lynn; res: 344 E. 51st St., N.Y., N.Y. 10022.

GRIFFIN, RACHAEL S., Curator, Portland Art Museum, S. W. Park and Madison Sts., Portland, Ore. 97205, '60–; Curator of Educ., '57–'60; Educ., Pubcty. Asst., Ed., Museum Bul., Museum Art Sch. quarterly, Ore. Artist, '50–'57; Ed., Wtr., catalogs exhbns.; Co-auth., Ed., "The Understanding of Art," course of 18 slide-tape programs; numerous pubns., papers on art; Pacific Arts Assn. (VP, '56); Artists Equity (Ore. Chptr. Bd. of Dirs., '54), numerous others; Cent. Aw. for Distg. Svc. in the Arts, Ore. Art Alliance (Acting Secy., '56); various others; Univ. of Ore., Museum Art Sch. (Portland, Ore.), Reed Col.; b. Portland, Ore., 1906; p. Wilfred and Vida Lewis Smith; h. Richard Griffin; c. Andrew, Mary Lawrence (Mrs. Charles N. Cox); res: 2327 S.W. Market St., Dr., Portland, Ore. 97201.

GRIFFITH, CARRIE McELYA, Asst. Dir. Pers., Ed., The Co-operative Pure Milk Association, 1020 Plum St., Cinn., Oh. 45202, '57–; Intl. Assn. of Pers. Wm. (Exec. Bd. Mbr., '69–'70), Wms. Pers. Assn. of Cinn. (Pres., '67–'68; VP, '66–'67; Secy., '65–'66; Treas., '64–'65; Ed., '63–'64), Cinn. Eds. Assn. (Treas., '60), BPW; Murray State Tchrs. Col.; Univ. of Cinn. Evening Col.; b. Paducah, Ky., 1914; p. Roscoe and Nannie Neal McElya; h. B. Fred Griffith; c. Nancy A. Griffith Klite; res: 8892 Balboa Dr., Cinn., Oh. 45231.

GRIFFITH, JEAN GREEN, Librn., Union Endicott High School, 1200 E. Main St., Endicott, N.Y. 13760, '64–; Librn., Chenango Forks Sch., '50–'51; Librn., Oxford Acad., '49; WNBA (Binghamton Chptr. Treas., '70); State Univ. of N.Y., BS, '49; MS, '68; b. Goshen, N.Y.; p. Fred and Katherine Nelson Green; h. Sidney Griffith; c. Karen, Alan; res: 126 Clifton Blvd., Binghamton, N.Y. 13903.

GRIFFITH, MARICITA BURTON (pseud: Mary Griffith), Free-lance PR, Cnslt., Wtr., Print and Bdcst.; Reptr., 350 news stories, WNUS, '66; Designer's Story, State Street Lights, '58; PR, Govs. Youth Con.; AWRT, Pubcty. Club of Chgo., BPW (Pres., '70–'71); Proofreader, Mkt. Rschr., Analyst, Interviewer, Univ. of Chgo. Press; Chgo. adv. cos.; PR Dir., special promos. & exhbns., Mdse. Mart; pubcty. articles in pfsnl. & educ. mags.; numerous educ., civic & prof. orgs. and aws.; 2,000 Wm. of Achiev.; b. Louisville,

Ky.; p. William and Augusta Pepper Burton; h. Ralph Griffith; c. Mrs. Dorothy Kolb, Ralph B.; res: 2073 W. 107th St., Chgo., Ill. 60643.

GRIFFITH, MARY B. TERRY, Head Librn., White River Regional Library, 110 Broad St., Batesville, Ark. 72501, '45; HS Tchr.; Ark. Lib. Assn. (Pres., '66; Treas., '59); Ark. Col., BA; b. Prescott, Ark., 1905; p. George and Laura Johnson Terry; h. Charles Griffith (div.); c. Charles, Jr. (dec.); res: 658 Boswell St., Batesville, Ark. 75201.

GRIFFITHS, EVELYN PEFFLEY, Reg. Librn., North Arkansas Regional Library, 123 Jaycee Ave., Harrison, Ark. 72601, '58–; Bkmobile., '57; Librn., Woodruff County, '47–'57; Publr., Assoc. Ed., Augusta Advocate, '39–'57; Ark. Lib. Assn. (Pres., '60), ALA, Theta Sigma Phi, WNBA; D. C. Fisher aw., '63; Kan. State Univ., BS (Jnlsm.), '27; L.S.U., BS (Lib. Sci.), '52; b. Whitewater, Kan.; p. Artie and Charlotte Boellner Peffley; h. David Griffiths (dec.); c. two daughters; res: 312 N. Hickory, Harrison, Ark. 72601.

GRIMES, BARBARA CARTER, Chief, Lib. Div., Federal Communications Commission, 1919 M. St. N.W., Wash., D.C. 20554, '64–; FCC Lib., '44–; Univ. of Pitt. Lib., '36–'43; BPW; b. Detroit, Mich., 1916; p. John III and Mae Tompkins Carter; h. Gilbert Grimes; c. Richard Gilbert; res: 725 S. 19th St., Arlington, Va. 22202.

GRIMES, THERESA, PR, Pubcty.; Pubcty. Mgr., Clairol, '55–'69; Pubcty. Dir. Byrde, Richard and Pound, '52, '54; Lynn Farnol PR, '53; Bulova Watch Co., '50–'51; Tchr., grooming course, Bklyn. Col. '66; Wtr., articles on grooming; radio, TV appearances; Theta Sigma Phi; Pubcty. Club of N.Y., Fashion Group, AWRT, Cosmetic Career Wm. (Bd. Mbr., '63); Columbia Univ., '43–'46; Univ. of Ia., BA (Edtl., Radio Jnlsm.); b. Liverpool, Eng.; p. Samuel and Mary Burke Grimes; h. Howard M. Russell; c. Keith Samuel Russell, Laurie Sue Russell, Mrs. Merri-Lynn Siegel; res: 35 W. 81st St., N.Y., N.Y. 10024.

GRISWOLD, DENNY, Ed.-Publr., Public Relations News, 127 E. 80th St., N.Y., N.Y. 10021, '50–; worked with Edward L. Bernays, PR Cnslt.; Benjamin Sonnenberg, PR Cnslt.; and J. Walter Thompson Co.; Edtl. Asst. to B. C. Forbes, Forbes Magazine; Adv. and Prom. Mgr., House & Garden; Edtl. Staff, Business Week; Partner, Glenn Griswold Associates; Cofounder with Glenn Griswold of Public Relations News, '44; Co-ed., Public Relations News, '44–'50; Co-auth. with Glenn Griswold "Your Public Relations—The Standard Public Relations Handbook"; Speaker throughout the country and in many foreign countries; writer of numerous articles on PR and related subjects; Campfire Girls (Pub. Rels. Advisory Comm.), confidential PR advisor to several U.S. Govt. Depts.; member, PRSA, Mayor's PR Advisory Comm. (N.Y.C.); OPC; Intl. PR Assn. (Cncl. Member-at-large), Comm. on Women in PR (Founder and first

Chmn., '46); aws. from Nat. Assn. of PR Cnsl., PRSA (Presidential cit. at annual meeting, '69), Freedoms Fndn., Theta Sigma Phi, Publicity Club of N.Y.; first and only wm. mbr. of U.S. Chamber of Commerce PR Advisory Comm.; honored on 25th anniversary of nwsltr. by Central Pa. Chptr. of PRSA, TWA, Trenton Trust Co., Pubcty. Club of N.Y., ITT Europe, Belgian PR Assn., Canadian PR Soc., Ohio Univ.; Hunter Col., AB; Radcliffe Col., MA; b. N.Y.C., 1910; p. Frank and Rose Lester Prager; res: Kettle Creek Rd., Weston, Conn. 06880.

GRISWOLD, ESTHER DONAT, Wms. Program Dir., Prodr., Hostess, "Of Interest to Women," KOMU-TV, Highway 63 S., Columbia, Mo. 65201, '58–; Cont. Wtr., Bdsctr., Radio Sta. KFNF (Shenandoah, Ia.), '55–'58; Prodr., Hostess, KFEQ-TV (St. Joseph, Mo.); Tchr.; numerous orgs., aws.; Univ. of Neb., '27–'29; Omaha Univ., '53; b. Council Bluff, Ia.; p. John and Mary Jorgensen Jordansen; h. Glenn Griswold; c. Frances Ann (Mrs. William Starke), Diane (Mrs. Tom Dunavant), Ronald Donat; res: 601 Medavista Dr., Columbia, Mo. 65201.

GROARK, DOROTHY KLEESPIES, Librn., Cataloger-Indexer, National Resources Library, Dept. of the Interior, 18th and C Sts., N.W., Wash., D.C., '68–; Cataloger-Indexer, Superintendent of Docs. Lib., Govt. Printing Off., '52–'55; Social Work (Chgo., Ill.), '32–'38; Librn., '30–'32; established Lib., Downtown Col. of Loyola Univ. (Chgo.); Instr. Lib. Sci., Eng.; Free-lance Ed.; Lit. Mkt. Place, ALA, Md. Lib. Assn., various others; Clarke Col., BA (Eng.), '27 (maxima cum laude); Loyola Univ., Chgo., MA (Psych.), '32; grad. work; b. Dubuque, Ia.; p. William and Katherine Sullivan Kleespies; h. Edgar T. Groark; c. Vladimir James, Stephen Mark; res: 1 G Gardenway, Greenbelt, Md. 20770.

GROBER, JUDITH FARRELL, Media Dir., Schaefer Advertising Inc., 317 One Decker Sq., Bala Cynwyd, Pa. 19004, '68–; Media Byr., J. Walter Thompson Co. (L.A., Cal.), '64–'66; Panelist, Lectr. Eastern Indsl. Advs. of Phila.; San Jose State Col., BA (Adv.), '64 (50 Outstanding Wm. Aw., Black Masque); b. L.A., Cal., 1942; p. Joseph S. and Jocelyn McDougall Farrell; h. David T. Grober; res: 570 W. DeKalb Pike, King of Prussia, Pa. 19406.

GROCH, JUDITH, Auth: "You and Your Brain" (Harper and Row, '63), "The Right to Create" (Little, Brown, '70); Thomas Alva Edison Nat. Mass Media Aw., Best Sci. Bk. for Youth, '63; Vassar Col., '46–'48; Columbia Univ. Sch. of Gen. Studies, BS, '52 (cum laude; Phi Beta Kappa); h. Wilbert Minowitz; c. Deborah, Emily, Peter; res: 168 W. 86th St., N.Y., N.Y. 10024.

GRODZINS, RUTH MAIMON, Manuscript Ed., Bulletin of Atomic Scientists, 935 E. 60th St., Chgo., Ill. 60637, '67–; VP, Midway Edtl. Rsch., '64–'67; Univ. of Chgo., BA, '38 (Phi Beta Kappa); b. Chgo., Ill., 1917; p.

Mitchel and Betty Coin Maimon; h. Morton Grodzins (dec.); c. Ann Rose, Marian Kagan; res: 4940 East End Ave., Chgo., Ill. 60615.

GROEBLI, BETTY GALLAGHER POORMAN, Commentator, "The Betty Groebli Show," "Frankley Female," & "Meeting of the Minds," WRC-TV & Radio, 4001 Nebraska Ave. N.W., Wash. D.C. 20016, '62–; TV Modr., "Frankley Female," '69–; "Meeting of the Minds," '68–; TV Modr., "Capital Tie Line," '67–'68; Radio Bdcstr., "Monitor Show," '62–; Bdcstr., KIST (Santa Barbara, Cal.) '54–'61; Commentator, WLAC, WSM (Nashville, Tenn.), '52–'54; Performer, Geddis & Martin Puppet Theater (Santa Barbara, Cal.), '48–'52; WNPC, AWRT, Wms. Adv. Club. of Wash., AFTRA, NATAS, ANWC, League of Wm. Voters, Am. Cancer Soc., TV-Radio Mirror Mag. aw., '68; Univ. of Cal., BA '51 (Alumni of the Year aw., '68–'69); b. Carmel, Cal.; p. J. R. & Mae Gallagher Poorman; h. Dr. John M. Groebli; c. Gregory; res: 3900 Watson Pl. N.W., Wash., D.C. 20016.

GROHSKOPF, BERNICE, Auth: "Seeds of Time" (Atheneum, '63; on Nat. Lib. Assn's. list of outstanding bks. for children, '63), "From Age to Age" ('68), "The Treasure of Sutton Hoo" ('70); Columbia Univ. Press; Dell Publ. Co.; AAUW; Columbia Univ., BA, '48; MA, '54; b. Troy, N.Y.; h. Herbert Grohskpof; c. Peggy; res: New Jersey.

GROOVER, ELOISE TARPLEY, Dir., Educ. Media, State of Florida, State Department of Education, Knott Bldg., Tallahassee, Fla. 32304, '65–; Lib. Cnslt., '64–'65; Instr., Fla. State Univ., '61–'64; Cnslt., Miller County (Ga.) Bd. of Educ., '59–'61; Librn., Miller County HS, '51–'61; Tchr., '56–'60; NEA, ALA, Ga. Lib. Assn. (Pres., '60–'61); Ga. State Col. for Wm., AB, '39; Fla. State Univ., MA, '55; b. Leesburg, Ga., 1918; p. William E. and Annie L. Roberts Tarpley; h. Henry Finn Groover; c. John Edward Jones; res: 2013 Atapha Nene, Tallahassee, Fla. 32301.

GROSECK, JEANNE BOOTH, Owner, Jeanne Booth Public Relations, 4730 Large St., Phila., Pa. 19124, '66–; Dir., PR, Am. Cancer Soc., '60–'66; PR Cnslt. and Wtr., Un. Fund of Gtr. Phila., '56–'60; Asst. Byr., Strawbridge & Clothier, '55–'56; Press and Radio-TV Dir., Indlps. Red Cross, Ind., '52–'55; Dept. Mgr. and Sales Instr., Goldblatt Brothers, Inc. (Chicago), '48–'49; Mgr. (inc. Prom. and PR), Stauffer System Reducing Salon, Chicago, '47–'48; Home Svc. Case Worker, Cook County Red Cross, Chicago, '44–'47; Whittier Col., AB, '43; b. Mt. Airy, N.C., 1921; p. G. Raymond and Garcia D. Booth; h. Stephen Groseck; c. John Booth; res: 4730 Large St., Phila., Pa. 19124.

GROSS, AMY PAULA, Assoc. Ed., Mademoiselle, Conde Nast Publications, Inc., 420 Lexington Ave., N.Y., N.Y. 10017, '69–; Copywtr., '66–'69; Asst. to Arts and Entertainment Ed., '64–'66; Entertainment/Asst. Features Ed., Ingenue, '66; Asst. Reg. News Ed., Glamour, '63–'64; Media Wm.; Conn. Col., BA

(Zoology), '63 (Hons.); b. Bklyn., N.Y., 1942; p. Dr. J. M. and Bernice Friefeld Gross; res: 270 W. 11th St., N.Y., N.Y. 10014.

GROSS, PATRICIA ROBINSON, Corporate Pres., Limited Editions, 1613 N.E. 163rd St., N. Miami Beach, Fla. 33160, '64–; Wms. Apparel Byr., Jordan & Marsh, '60–'63; Coordr. and Wtr: fashion shows, mags. and local nwsps.; Tchr., Miami Dade Jr. Col.; Cnslt.; Univ. of Miami, AB (Jnlsm.-Adv.); b. Balt., Md., 1932; p. S. Manford and Frances A. Clements Robinson; h. Marvin Gross; c. Terri Lee and Michael Robinson; res: 19527 N.E. 22nd Ave., N. Miami Beach, Fla. 33162.

GROSS, REBECCA FLORENCE, Ed., The Lock Haven Express, Lock Haven Express Printing Co., 9 W. Main St., Lock Haven, Pa. 17745, '46–; Mng. Ed., '31–'41; Asst. Mng. Ed., '28–'31; Reptr., summers, '25; Reptr., The Clinton County Times, '22–'23; Nieman Fellow, Harvard Univ., '47; Offcr., WAVES, U.S. Navy, '42–'46; Pa. WPA (Pres., '39–'41), Pa. Soc. Nwsp. Eds. (Pres., '63), Am. Soc. of Nwsp. Eds., Pa. Nwsp. Publrs. Assn. (Distg. Svc. Aw., '67); Distg. Daughter of Pa., '65; Freedoms Medal, Freedom Fndn., '50; Annie Helen-bake Ross Public Lib. (Bd. of Trustees Pres., '47–), Pa. Dept. of Public Welfare (Advisory Comm. Secy., '57), Lock Haven State Col. (Exec. Comm. Chmn., Bd. of Trustees, '59); Temple Univ., '23–'25; Univ. of Pa., AB, '28; b. Lock Haven, Pa., 1905; p. Charles and Susan Ranck Gross; res: 411 Guard Lock Dr., Lock Haven, Pa. 17745.

GROSS, SARAH CHOKLA, Ed., Reviewer, Translator; Tchr., Southern Methodist Univ., Univ. of Tex., Columbia Univ.; Assoc. Ed., Bk. Pg., Dallas Morning News, '33–'34; Radio Prog., '29–'30; Theatre Lib. Assn., WNBA, Zeta Phi Eta; Southern Methodist Univ., BA, '26, MA, '28; b. N.Y.C.; p. Louis and Bassetta Shore Chokla; h. Benjamin Gross; c. Emily Jane (dec.); res: 11 Newkirk Ave., East Rockaway, N.Y. 11518.

GROSS, SUZANNE M., Auth: "Doors into Poetry" (Scribners, Revised Edition forthcoming), "The Honey and the Gall" (Scribners, '67), "Experience and Imagination" (McKay, '65), "Contemporary Religious Verse" ('63), numerous poetry bks., anthologies ('52–), numerous poetry mags. ('55–'69); Film Wtr., U.S. Forest Svc., '62–'66; Cl. and Wtr., '59–'63; Tchr., '61–'62; wrote "Patterns of the Wild," '65–'66 (Mich. Outdoor Wtr's. Teddy Aw., '65; Bronze Medal, Sixth World Forestry Congress, Madrid, '65; Edinburgh Film Festival, '66); Poet-in-Res., St. Norbert Col., conducted lit. seminars and poetry workshops, '63–'67; 1st prize, Sister Madaleva Poetry Contest, '58; 1st prize, "Chicago Choice" poetry contest, '61; poems in Borestone Mtn. "Best Poems," '61–'62, '65–'68; Outstanding Young Wm. of Am., '66; Wis. Wtrs. Cncl. cit., '65; Univ. of Pitt., '51–'52; Univ. of Wis., '54; Beloit Col., BA, '55; b. Janesville, Wis., 1933; p. John and Jessica George Gross; h. Paul

Reed; c. Marguerite Dolores; res: 1648 N. Holyoke, Wichita, Kan. 67208.

GROSSHOLTZ, JEAN, Assoc. Prof., Polit. Sci., Mount Holyoke College, South Hadley, Mass. 01075; Am. Polit. Sci. Assn., Assn. of Asian Studies; AAUP, New England Polit. Sci. Assn., New England Assn. of Asian Studies; Pa. State Univ., BA, '56; Univ. of Denver, MA, '57; MIT, PhD., '61.

GROSSMAN, ELENER NORRIS, Jnlsm. Tchr., Thornridge HS, 15000 Cottage Grove, Dolton, Ill. 60419, '68–; Asst. Prof., Jnlsm., Eng., Grace Col. (Winona Lake, Ind.), '59–'63; Theta Sigma Phi (Bloomington, Ind. Chptr. Pres., '66–'67), Ill. ATJ (Pres.), Jnlsm. Educ. Assn.; Grace Col., BA '58 (summa cum laude); Ind. Univ., MA, '59; b. Mentone, Ind., 1936; p. Leroy and Mabel Sarber Norris; h. Gilbert Grossman; c. Luke; res: 848 172nd St., S. Holland, Ill. 60473.

GROSSO, ELIZABETH GREY, Secy.-Treas., Zane Grey, Inc., 396 E. Mariposa St., Altadena, Cal. 91001, '50–; Univ. of Wis., '30; b. N.Y.C., 1912; p. Zane and Lina Roth Grey; h. George Grosso; c. Mrs. Robert Conan, Mrs. Lewis Murphy; res: Rte. 1, Box 767, Lime Kiln Rd., Grass Valley, Cal. 95945.

GROTE, PENELOPE MORRIS, Bdcst. Coordr., Clinton E. Frank, Inc., 666 Third Ave., N.Y., N.Y. 10017, '69–; Print Traf. Mgr., '69; Radio-TV Prod. Mgr., Wesley Advertising of Shulton, Inc., '68–'69; Asst. to Dir. of Facilities Planning and Scheduling, NBC, '68; Asst. Casting Dir., Benton & Bowles, '67–'68; Asst. Traf. Operator, '66–'67; Sigma Omega Chi, N.Y. Young Repls.; N.J. State Scholarship; Mary Washington Col. of the Univ. of Va., BA, '66; b. Plainfield, N.J., 1944; p. Harry A. and Florence Gilmore Grote; res: 209 E. 52nd St., N.Y., N.Y. 10019.

GROUT, RUTH ELLEN, Prof. Emeritus, University of Minnesota; Auth., Cnslt. in health educ.; AID Cnslt., Jamaica, W. Indies, '69–; Cnslt., World Health Organization in European, S.E. Asia, African, Eastern Mediterranean and Western Pacific Regs., '52–'68; Prof., Sch. of Public Health and Col. of Educ., Univ. of Minn., '52–'67; Assoc. Prof., '43–'52; Cnslt., U.S. Off. of Educ., '42–'43; Cnslt., Health Educ., Tenn. Valley Authority, '39–'42; Dir., Sch. Health Educ. Study, Cattaraugus County, N.Y., '31–'38; Am. Public Health Assn. (Health Educ. Sec. Chmn. and Secy., '51–'53), Soc. of Public Health Educs., Am. Sch. Health Assn., Am. Assn. for Health, Physical Educ. Recreation; AAUW Fellowship, '38; Elizabeth Severance Prentiss Nat. Aw., '58; Mount Holyoke Col., AB, '23; Yale Univ., MPH, '30; PhD, '39; b. Princeton, Mass., 1901; p. Edgar and Laura Miller Grout; res: 6 Brandon Rd., Chapel Hill, N.C. 27514.

GROVER, PAT HINTON, Colmst.-Feature Wtr., Exec. Secy, Mirror Printing Co., P.O. Box 2008, Altoona, Pa. 16602, '43–; Colmst., Pennsylvania Mirror, '68–; NFPW, Pa. Wms. Press Assn. (Pres., '62–'64), BPW (Wm. of the Yr., Achiev., '63), Who's Who of Am.

Wm., Who's Who in the East; Penn. State Univ.; b. Altoona, Pa., 1920; p. Samuel and Anna Marie Buontempo Pincherri; h. (1) Mel R. Hinton (div.); (2) Carl A. Grover; c. Dennis M. Hinton; res: 1035 Grove Hill Rd., Balt., Md. 21227.

GROVES, RUTH CLOUSE, Free-lance Wtr.; Auth., "Harp on the Willow" ('65); Tchr., New Trier Township HS; Theta Sigma Phi, NLAPW; Who's Who of Am. Wm.; Univ. of Neb., AB, '24; Univ. of Chgo., Northwestern; h. Everett C. Groves; c. Everett, Homer, Mrs. Thomas A. Dailey; res: 834 16th St., Wilmette, Ill. 60091.

GROVES, SIBYL MORRISON, Soc. Ed., Lesher Newspapers Inc., 240 W. 17th St., Merced, Cal. 95340, '35–; Merced Soroptimist Club; b. Le Sueur, Minn.; p. Benjamin Abbott and Clara Martin Morrison; h. Fred K. Groves (dec.); c. Fred K., Barbara June (Mrs. David Paxton); res: 2320 K St., Merced, Cal. 95340.

GRUBER, LOUISE J., Fashion Dir., Vanity Fair Mills, Inc., 640 Fifth Ave., N.Y., N.Y. 10019, '67–; Corp. Adv. Mgr., PR, Genesco, Inc., '62–'67; Fashion Coordr., I. Miller; PR AE, Doherty, Clifford, Steers & Shenfield, '59–'61; PR AE, '55–'59; Assoc. Ed., County Gentleman, other edtl. positions, '42–'55; free-lance writing; various orgs.; Univ. of Pa.; b. Wash., D.C., 1925; p. Herbert and Gwendolyn Davis Gruber; res: 20 Beekman Pl., N.Y., N.Y. 10022.

GRUBER, RUTH, Auth.; Colmst., Lectr., Hadassah Mag., '61–; Foreign Corr., New York Herald Tribune, '47–'65; Foreign Corr., New York Post, '46; Special Asst. to Secy. of Interior, '41–'46; Auth: "Israel on the Seventh Day" ('68), "Israel Today: Land of Many Nations" ('63), "Puerto Rico: Island of Promise" ('60), four other bks.; OPC, Wtrs. Guild, Arctic Inst.; Ford Fndn. aw., '64; N.Y.U., BA; Univ. of Wis., MA; Univ. of Cologne, PhD; b. N.Y.C.; p. David and Gussie Rockower Gruber; h. Philip H. Michaels (dec.); c. Celia, David; res: 300 Central Park W., N.Y., N.Y. 10024.

GRUEN, SONIA STRAUSS, Chief Librn., Albert Einstein College of Medicine, 1300 Morris Park Ave., Bronx, N.Y. 10461, '58–; Ref. Librn. and Head Cataloger, Cornell Med. Lib., '53–'55; Supvsr., Young Peoples and Ref. Work, 4 brs. of N.Y. Public Lib., '48–'53; Cataloger, Carnegie Lib. of Pitt., '32–'43; Med. Lib. Assn., Special Libs. Assn.; Univ. of Pittsburgh, BA (magna cum laude), '41; Carnegie Inst., BS (Lib. Sci.), '41; Columbia Univ., BS (Lib. Sci.), '62–'63, Med. Lib. Cert., '58; h. Kurt Gruen; res: 2090 Barnes Ave., Bronx, N.Y. 10462.

GRUHN, CARRIE MYERS, Novelist: "Trumpet in Zion" ('51; retitled "The Lost City," '69), "Unwanted Legacy" ('53), "Happy is the Man" ('63); Ia. State Tchrs. Col., '25–'26; b. Gravity, Ia., 1907; p. Frank R. and Clara Devoe Myers; h. Stanley G. Gruhn; c.

Edward L., Gerald L.; res: 2930 Millers Trunk, Duluth, Minn. 55811.

GRUMBACH, DORIS ISAAC, Assoc. Prof. of Eng., College of St. Rose, 432 Western Ave., Albany, N.Y. 12203, '66–; Lectr., '50–'69; Assoc. Ed., Architectural Forum, Time Inc., '42–'43; Copywtr., Mademoiselle, '41–'42; Title Wtr., M.G.M., '40–'41; Auth: two novels (Doubleday, '62, '64); one non-fiction bk., "The Company She Kept" (Coward-McCann, '67); Modern Lang. Assn., AAUP; N.Y.U., AB, '39 (Phi Beta Kappa); Cornell Univ., MA, '40; b. N.Y.C., 1918; p. Leonard and Helen Oppenheimer Isaac; h. Leonard Grumbach; c. Barbara Wheeler, Jane, Elizabeth, Kathryn; res: 75 Willett St., Albany, N.Y. 12210.

GRUMME, MARGUERITE E., Professional Parliamentarian; Auth., Tchr., Lectr., Parliamentary Procedure; Auth., "Basic Principles of Parliamentary Law & Protocol" ('53); Aids for Organizations ('59); Sls. Adv., Brown Supply Co., '28–'57; WNBA, Am. Soc. of Assn. Execs., Intl. Platform Assn., Intl. Toastmistress Club (Intl. Pres., '48–'49), Nat. Assn. of Parliamentarians; Am. Inst. of Parliamentarians & American Arbitration Assn. (Election Panel), Who's Who of Am. Wm., Who's Who in the Midwest, Dic. of Intl. Biog, Contemp. Auths.; Washington Univ.; b. St. Louis, Mo.; p. August and Mathilda Haller Grumme; res: 3830 Humphrey St., St. Louis, Mo. 63116.

GRYSKA, GLORIA MARSHALL, Tchr., Chicago Board of Education, 3826 W. 58th St., Chgo., Ill. 60629, '60–; Lang. Arts Curriculum Cncl. (Dist. Ten Secy., '67); Sears, Roebuck and Co., '57; Advisory Tchr., Whitney Literary Highlights, '65; Theta Sigma Phi, Gamma Alpha Chi, Delta Zeta, PTA; Univ. of Ill., BS (Jnlsm.), '57; Chgo. Tchrs. Col., MEd, '64; b. Chgo., Ill., 1936; p. Maximilian and Helen Picturna Marshall; h. Eugene Gryska; c. Eugene Mark; res: 728 S. Spring Ave., La Grange, Ill. 60525.

GUARINO, ANN, Asst. Movie Critic, New York Daily News, 220 E. 42nd St., N.Y., N.Y. 10017, '65–; Edtl. Asst. on News Desk; NWC; Hunter Col., BA (Pre-Jnlsm.); b. N.Y.C.; p. Vincent and Adeline Lucia Guarino.

GUENTERT, MARGARET A., Chmn., Eng. Dept., Norwood High School, 2060 Sherman Ave., Norwood, Oh. 45212, '67–; Tchr., Princeton HS; Theta Sigma Phi (Cinn. Chptr. Treas., '66–'67; Alpha Phi Chptr. VP, '61–'62), Eng. Cncl. of Gtr. Cinn. (Pres., '69–'70; VP, '68–'69), Kappa Delta Pi, NEA, Oh. Educ. Assn.; Nat. Cncl. of Tchrs. of Eng.; Oh. Univ., BS (Educ.), '62; Ind. Univ., MS (Educ.), '64; b. Cinn., Oh., 1941; p. Fred and Helen Kramer Guentert; res: 2145 Quatman, Norwood, Oh. 45212.

GUERIN, JUDY K., Dir. of P.R.O.—The Public Relations Organization, 60 E. 42nd, N.Y., N.Y. 10017 and Dir. of PR, Shevlo Advertising Agency, 21 W. 38th St., N.Y., N.Y. 10018; PR, Kelly, Nason, Inc., '65–'67; PR,

Kreda & Assocs., '63–'65; personal appearance tours radio, TV, press, as Fashion, Beauty Dir., The Toni Co. and Educ. Dir., Paper Mate (U.S., Can.), '57–'67; for Kimberly-Clark, Armour, Paraffined Carton Rsch. Cncl., Red. Cherry Inst., Tee-Pak, '57–'64; Mgr., Narrator-Demonstrator, trade shows, convs. (U.S.), '56–'67; AWRT, The Adv. Club of N.Y.; De Paul Univ. (Chgo., Ill.), BA (Speech), '56; b. Chgo., Ill., 1935; p. Thomas P. and Lillian Helgestad Guerin; res: 500 E. 83rd St., N.Y., N.Y. 10028.

GUERIN, POLLY (Pauline Guerin), Polly Guerin Public Relations, 15 Park Ave., N.Y., N.Y. 10016; Apparel Pubcty. Mgr., Monsanto Co., '68–'69; PR/Educ. Dir., The Lovable Co., '65–'68; Fashion Dir., Baar & Beards, Inc., '64–'65; Prom./Adv. Dir., Abaco Fabrics Corp., '61–'64; Assoc. Fashion Dir., Amos Parrish & Co., '58–'61; Fashion Ed., Wms. Wear Daily, '51–'58; Tchr., PR, Pubcty., Fashion Inst. of Tech.; Tchr., Fashion Coord., Pratt Inst.; Lectr., Career Course, Pubcty. Club of N.Y. (Bd. of Dirs., '65–'70); Singer, pfsnl. opera: The Wagner Opera Co., The N.Y. Festival Opera; record, "Pollydate 1965"; entertain Hospitalized Veterans Svc.; various organizations and aws.; Fashion Inst. of Tech. (Apparel Design); City Col. of N.Y. (Bus. Adm.); b. N.Y.C.; p. George and Blanche Ruest Guerin; res: 15 Park Ave., N.Y., N.Y. 10016.

GUIDO, SALLY ANN, Dir. of Mktng. Planning, Disposables Marketing Services Corp. (DMS), 60 East 42nd St., N.Y., N.Y. 10017, '69; Mktng. Planner, ITT Rayonier, '68; Mktng. Analyst, BBDO, '64; VP and Dir. of Mktng., Bramco Intl., '65–'69; Rsch. Assoc., George W. Fotis and Assocs., '62; Auth.—Publr., Govt'l. Rsch. Assn., '59; Admin., N.Y.U., '55; Wtr., assn. and trade publns.; Disposables Assn.; N.Y.U., BS, '62 (cum laude); City Col. of N.Y., MBA, '65 (summa cum laude; Jerome B. Udell Aw. for highest average, '65); b. Flushing, N.Y., 1937; p. Vincent J. and Rose Marie Caruso Guido; res: 100 Bedford St., N.Y., N.Y. 10014.

GUILD, CAROL WILLIAMS, Prod., Telecaster, WVIA-TV, Box 4444, Scranton, Pa., 18509, '66–; Prod., Telecaster, AE, WNEP-TV, '63–'65; Prod., Telecaster, WDAU-TV, '61–'63; Adv. Mgr., Fibercraft Boat Co., '59–'60; Owner, Guild Adv. Agcy., '59–'65; Bdcstr., Telecaster, AE, Prod., KOLO Radio-TV, '52–'55; Bdcstr., AE, KOH Radio, '52–'55; Lectr., M. C., Fashion Commentator; Prod. docs. "Until All Are Free," "History of Lumbering in Pennsylvania," and regular series shows: "Party Line," "Magic Window," "Woman's View," "Carol and Friends," "A Visit with Carol"; Adv. Club, AWRT (N.E. Pa. Pres., '69; VP, '67–'68), b. Minnet, Wash., 1921; p. David and Grace McFadden Williams; h. William Guild; c. Diane (Mrs. Ace Remas), Mrs. William Phelan, Mrs. Ruth Rought, William H., Jr.; res: Rd. #1, New Milford, Pa. 18834.

GUINAN, MABLE HOWLETT, S.W. Field Reptr., Boxoffice, 825 Van Brunt Blvd., Kan. City, Mo. 64124,

'41–; Wm. of Motion Picture Industry (Dallas Pres., '66–'67, '56–'57; Nat. Pres., '59–'60; Nat. VP, '58–'59), Pilot Club Intl.; b. Mena, Ark.; p. Robert and Mary Jane Walker Howlett; h. Thomas Guinan; res: 5927 Winton, Dallas, Tex. 75206.

GUINAN, PATRICIA DAVIDSON, Asst. to Publr., House Beautiful, 717 Fifth Ave., N.Y., N.Y. 10022, '63–; Window Shopping Ed., '38–'56; Ed.-in-Chief, Bride & Home, '56–'63.

GUINEY, ELIZABETH MARIE, Instr. of Eng., North Hennepin State Junior College, Osseo, Minn. 55369, '65–; Librn., Hopkins Public Sch., '62–'65; Univ. of Minn., BS, '62; MA, '66; b. Austin, Minn., 1940; p. Edward and Elizabeth Blowers Guiney; res: 901 Second Ave. N.E., Austin, Minn. 55912; sch. yr: 6500 Phoenix St. N., Mpls., Minn. 55427.

GUINNESS, GLORIA, Contr. Ed., Harper's Bazaar, 717 Fifth Ave., N.Y., N.Y. 10022, '63–; Cnslt., Rschr., Wtr.; Penney Mo. Mag. Aw., '67; b. Mexico; h. Loel Guinness.

GUMMERSON, DORA de WOLFE, Food Ed., The Charlotte News, 600 S. Tryon St., Charlotte, N.C. 28201, '62–; Free-lance Wtr., small pubns.; Tchr., HS (LeRoy, N.Y.), '35–'39; Theta Sigma Phi (Chptr. Secy., '68), Eta Pi Epsilon; Syracuse Univ., BS, '35; b. Boonville, N.Y., 1915; p. Kenneth and Bess Perkins de Wolfe; h. Donald Gummerson; c. Gary, Terry; res: 3801 Barclay Downs Dr., Charlotte, N.C. 28209.

GUNN, Sr. AGNES DAVID, SSJ, Eng. Instr., Chesnut Hill Col., Phila., Pa. 19118, '67–; Tchr., Hallahan HS, '53–'57; '61–'66; W. Phila. Catholic HS, '58–'60; Syllabus Comm., (Eng.) Archdiocese of Phila.; Ed: "A Book of Plays," "Modern American Drama" (Macmillan Pageant of Lit. Series); Contbr., American, Friar, Today; AAUP, Nat. Cncl. of Tchrs. of Eng., Gtr. Phila. Cncl. of Eng. Tchrs.; Delta Epsilon Sigma; Chesnut Hill Col., BA, '49; Univ. of Pa., PhD, '69; b. Phila., Pa., 1928; p. Ernest and Agnes Culliney Gunn.

GUNNING, VIRGINIA FRICK, PR Dir., Young Women's Christian Association of Greater Pittsburgh, Fourth Ave. and Ward St., Pitt., Pa., '69–; Photog. Stringer, UPI; Wtr.-Jnlst., American Red Cross, '58–'69; Self-employed, Va. Gunning, Adv. Designer, '51–'58; dir. mail adv. for Kool Vent Metal Awning Corp., and Buhl Optical Co., '47–'51; U.S. Navy Lt. (j.g.) Commtns. Offcr., '44–'46; Pubcty. Asst., Un. War Fund of Allegheny County, '43–'44; Asst. Adv. Mgr., Triangle Food Stores, '41–'43; News Ed., weekly nwsp., '40–'41; Theta Sigma Phi, Wms. Press Club of Pitt. (Bd. of Dirs., '69), Golden Quill (Exec. Comm. Secy., '68, '69), Beallgrove Horse Show (Secy., '64), Pfsnl. Horsemen's Assn.; Chatham Col., AB (Eng.-Spanish), '39; Duquesne Univ.; Carnegie Inst. of Tech.; Ad Art Studio Sch.; b. Pitt., Pa.; p. Frank and Emma Dornheim Gunning; res: 5624 Forbes Ave., Pitt., Pa. 15217.

GUNTER, BEATRICE BETSY, Media Byr., Young & Rubicam, Inc., 1 E. Wacker Dr., Chgo., Ill. 60601, '69–; Media Byr., George-Savan Adv. (St. Louis, Mo.), '66–'69; Scruggs, Vandervoort & Barney Dept. Store, '65–'66; Frank Block Adv., '65; Weintraub & Assoc. Adv., '59–'65; b. St. Louis, Mo., 1940; p. W. Davis and Jane Lamy Gunter.

GURA, JUDITH JANKOWITZ, Owner, Judith B. Gura Public Relations, 321 W. 78th St., N.Y., N.Y. 10024, '65–; AE, Harold J. Siesel Co., '60–'65; Pubcty., Abraham & Straus, '58–'60; Asst. Prom. Mgr., Ziff-Davis Publ. Co., '56–'58; NHFL (VP, '60), Am. Inst. of Interior Designers, Nat. Soc. of Interior Designers; Cornell Univ., AB, '56; b. N.Y.C., 1935; h. Martin Gura; c. one son, one daughter.

GURRIE, BARBARA PEDOTTI, Prod. Mgr., Jules L. Klein Advertising, Inc., Kimball Towers Penthouse, Springfield, Mass. 01103, '67–; Prod. Mgr., Tech. Reps., Inc. '66–'67; Prod. Mgr., Chambers, Wiswell and Moore, '65–'66; Jr. Adv. Club of Boston, '63–'64; Northeastern Univ., '63–'64; Boston Univ., '66; b. Quincy, Mass., 1943; p. Reno and Elvira DiMartinis Pedotti; h. Francis Edward Gurrie; res: 40 Carew St., S. Hadley, Mass. 01075.

GURWITT, HELEN B., Adv. Dir., Genung's, Inc., 233 S. Fourth Ave., Mt. Vernon, N.Y. 10803, '69–; Adv. Dir., Martin's (Bklyn.), '55–'69; AWNY, Westchester Adv. Club; N.Y.U., BS, '46; b. Bklyn., N.Y., 1925; p. David and Dorothy Garey Gurwitt; res: 60 E. Eighth St., N.Y., N.Y. 10003.

GUSTASON, MILDRED CHVAL, Dir. Mailing Svcs., "The Martha Bohlsen Show" (synd. radio prog.), 1316 N. 56th St., Omaha, Neb. 68132; Owner, Gustason Real Estate Co.; AWRT (Nat. Pres. Cncl. Treas., two yrs.), Quota Club Intl. (Pres., Gov. Seventh Dist.), Status of Wm. Commn. (appointed by Gov. Morrison, '66), Omaha BPW (Dir., Dist. III; Outstanding Wm. of the Yr.), YWCA, Omaha C. of C., Omaha Safety Cncl., Govs. State Safety Comm.; numerous aws. for commty. svc.; Van Sant Sch. of Bus.; Univ. of Omaha, adult educ.; b. Omaha, Neb., 1903; p. Mathias and Aloisie Pavlicek Chval; h. Clifford Gustason; c. Edward W.; res: 4820 Pratt St., Omaha, Neb. 68132.

GUTCH, GLORIA H., TV Comml. Prod. Estimator, Young & Rubicam, 285 Madison Ave., N.Y., N.Y. 10017, '66–; Test Comml. Prodr., MGM Telestudios, '64–'65; Asst. to TV Prod. Mgr., Lever Bros. Co., '61–'64; TV Prod. Asst., McCann-Erickson, '55–'58.

GUTHAT, MABEL OSBORNE, Ed., News-O-Matic, internal monthly mag., and Employee Commtns. Adm., Industrial Lift Truck Division, Eaton Yale & Towne, Inc., 101 W. 87th St., Chgo., Ill. 60620, '54–; Ill. IEA; Northwestern Univ.; b. Belding, Mich., 1904; p. Aaron and Susan Curtis Osborne; h. Guthat; c. Jeanne (Mrs. E. L. Peterson), Joyce (Mrs. John Sampson); res: 7640 Marquette Ave., Chgo., Ill. 60649.

GUTHERY, MADGE COOPER, Dir. of Wms. Activities, WMRN, Marion Broadcasting Co., Box 518, Marion, Oh. 43302, '42–; Wtr., '41–'42; Free-lance Wtr., '38–'41; Tchr., '31–'38; AWRT (Nat. Secy.-Treas., '54–'56; Chptr. Pres., '65–'67), Altrusa Club (Marion Pres.); Oh. State Univ., BS (Educ.), '31; b. Fairbury, Ill., 1910; p. Fred and Selina Howarth Cooper; h. Howard F. Guthery; res: 450 Delaware Ave., Marion, Oh. 43302.

GUTHRIE, JANICE ELAINE, Dir. of PR, Interstate Brands Corp., 12 E. Armour Blvd., Kan. City, Mo. 64111, '54–; Dir. of Pubcty., City of Palm Springs, Calif., '50–'54; Edtl. Prom. Wtr., L.A. Times, '49–'50; PR Rep., Am. Airlines, '42–'49; AWRT (Southern Cal. Chptr. Pres., '60–'62), PRSA; b. Muscatine, Ia., 1925; p. Guy and Mary Yakle Guthrie; res: 7729 Canterbury Prairie Village, Kan. 66208.

GUTMANN, JOAN FENTON, Edtl. Dir., Seventeen Magazine, 320 Park Ave., N.Y., N.Y. 10022, '67–; Art Dir., '58–'67, '51–'52; Asst. Art Dir., '48–'51; Vogue Pattern Bk., '56–'57; Asst. Art Dir., Jr. Bazaar, '45–'46; Lectr., Parsons Sch. of Design; designer of jackets for 17 bks. (Macmillan); graphic designs for Theatre C (Bklyn. Heights); Cooper Union, '43–'45; b. N.Y.C., 1924; p. Joseph M. and Aimee Stark Fenton; h. Karl Gutmann; c. Mrs. Aimee Gage, Linda, Suzanne; res: 10 East End Ave., N.Y., N.Y. 10028.

GUTSTEIN, LINDA ANN, Assoc. Ed., Parade Magazine, 733 Third Ave., N.Y., N.Y. 10017, '68–; Clmst., New York Current, Pop Scene Synd., '67–'68; Rschr., Intl. Affairs Reptr., Newsweek, '62–'67; Contrbr., Encyclopedia Judaica film and theater sec.; Bard Col., BA, '63 (Dean's List); b. N.Y.C., 1942; p. David and Jeanne Felsher Gutstein; res: 142 West End Ave., N.Y., N.Y. 10023.

GYLDENVAND, LILLY MYRTLE, Ed., Scope, American Lutheran Church Women, 422 S. Fifth St., Mpls., Minn. 55415, '59–; Edtl., Adm. Asst., Off. of PR, Evangelical Lutheran Ch., '53–'59; Auth., seven religious bks. ('49–'69); Co-auth., three bks.; numerous mag. articles; Alpha Phi Gamma, Assn. of Statisticians of Am. Religious Bodies, Assoc. Ch. Press (Nat. Aw. of Merit for Scope, '67), Lutheran Daughters of the Reformation (Intl. Pres., '48–'54); Mpls. Star cit., '61; Concordia Col., BA '39; b. La Moure, N.D., 1917; p. Ole and Karen Myhr Gyldenvand; res: 2088 Fry St., St. Paul, Minn. 55113.

H

HAAG, JESSIE HELEN, Auth., col., high sch. textbks.; Prof., Sch. Health Educ., The University of Texas, Sutton Hall 103, Austin, Tex. 78712, '50–; health educ. since '39; Assoc. Ed., Research Quarterly and American Journal of Public Health; Cnslt: Joint Comm. on Health Problems in Educ. of NEA and Am. Med. Assn., Food and Drug Admin.; Rsch. Cncl., AAHPER; Am. Public Health Assn., Am. Sch. Health Assn., Am. Assn. for Advancement of Sci.; Intl. Health Educ. Recipient, Intl. Assn. for Health Educ. of the Public, Rome, Italy, '44; Temple Univ., BS, '39; MS (Educ.), '43; Dr. of Educ., '50; b. Reading, Pa., 1917; p. Charles and Helen Sell Haag; res: 4519 Apache Pass, Austin, Tex. 78745.

HAAS, BARBARA YUNK, PR Dir., Ohio Valley General Hospital, Heckel Rd., McKees Rocks, Pa. 15136, '68–; Free-lance, '63–; Assoc. Ed., PPG Industries, '62–'63; PR Cnslt., Avonworth Sch. Dist.; Adult Educ. Instr., Allegheny County Commty. Col.; Theta Sigma Phi (Pitt. Chptr. Pres., '67–'69), P.R. Soc. Western Pa. Hosps.; BA (Jnlsm.) '62 (cum laude); b. Pitt., Pa., 1940; p. Edward and Bertha Estel Yunk; h. Norbert J. Haas; c. Susan, Craig, Cindy; res: 9000 Willoughby Rd., Pitt., Pa. 15237.

HAAS, DOROTHY F., Auth.; Sr. Ed., Childcraft, Field Enterprises Educational Corporation, Merchandise Mart, Rm. 262, Chgo., Ill. 60654, '68–; Sr. Ed., Whitman Publ. Co., '55–'68; bks: "A Special Place for Jonny," "Maria, Everybody Has a Name," "This Little Pony," 22 other juv. bks.; WNBA, Children's Reading Round Table; Marquette Univ., '55; b. Racine, Wis.; p. Allen and Elizabeth Sweetman Haas; res: 336 W. Wellington Ave., Chgo., Ill. 60657.

HAAS, MARY ODIN, Tchr., Miss. Hist., Biloxi Municipal School District, 501 E. Howard, Biloxi, Miss. 39530, '33–; Orange Grove, '31–'33; NEA (VP, '52), Miss. Educ. Assn. (Pres., '54–'55), Miss. Dept. Classrm. Tchrs. (Pres., '50–'52); BPW Career Wm. of the Yr., '65; Who's Who of Am. Wm., Who's Who in the South and Southwest, Who's Who in Am. Educ., Dic. of Intl. Biog.; Dominican Col., '30; Loyola Univ., PhB, '49; American Col., summer '50; Coe Fndn. Scholar, Tulane Univ., '57; Miss. Col., '63; Reynolds Fellow, Chapel Hill, '65; b. Biloxi, Miss.; p. George and Olympe Roch Haas; res: 644 Lameuse St., Biloxi, Miss. 39533.

HAAS, ROSAMOND EDWARDS, Reptr., University News Service, University of Michigan, Administration Building, Ann Arbor, Mich. 48104, '44–; Auth: three volumes of poetry, "North Portal" (E. P. Dutton, '57), "This Time This Tide" (E. P. Dutton, '50), "Delay is the Song" (E. P. Dutton, '44); Artist, five one-wm. shows: Univ. of Mich., Univ. N.D. and Univ. of Minn.; Ann Arbor Wm. Painters, Ann Arbor Art Assn.; Avery Hopwood Crtv. Writing Poetry Aw., '43; Western Mich. Univ., BA, '29; Univ. of Mich., MA, '34; b. Kalamazoo, Mich., 1908; p. Orley Stephen and Mabel Edwards Haas; res: 1214 Washtenaw Ave., Ann Arbor, Mich. 48104.

HABER, JOYCE BETTE, Synd. Colmst., Los Angeles Times Syndicate, Times-Mirror Sq., L.A., Cal. 90053, '66–; Hollywood Reptr., Time, '63–'66; Rschr., '54–'63;

Auth., "Caroline's Doll Book" (Putnams, '62); free-lance mag. articles; AFTRA, Hollywood Wms. Press Club; Bryn Mawr, '49–'50 (cum laude); Barnard Col., BA, '53; b. N.Y.C.; p. John and Lucille Buckmaster Haber; h. Douglas Schoolfield Cramer, Jr.; c. Douglas Schoolfield, III; res: Beverly Hills, Cal. 90210.

HABERLAND, JODY, Lib. Cnslt. for Adult Svcs., Eastern Massachusetts Regional Library System, Boston Public Library, Boston, Mass. 02117, '68–; Librn., Montgomery County, Md., '65–'68 (Staff Assn. Pres., '67); Prince Georges County, '62–'65 (Staff Assn. Secy., '64); Educ. Tech., U.S. Air Force, Italy, '60–'61; Pubns. Ed., NPVLA and The Prodrs. Cncl., Wash., D.C., '57–'59; Edtl. Tech., HumRRO, George Washington Univ., '55–'57; Bk. Rev. Staff, Library Journal, '70–; ALA, DCLA (Chairman, Book Review Group, '67); Maryland Lib. Assn. (Membership Comm., '68), Mass. Adult Ed. Comm. and New Eng. Lib. Assns., WNBA; Converse Col., BA, '52; grad. study, George Washington Univ., '54–'55; Am. Univ., '55–'57; Catholic Univ. of Am., MS (Lib. Sci.), '63; b. Phila., Pa.; p. Helen DeHart Reher; res: 11 Puritan Rd., Swampscott, Mass. 01907.

HABICHT, EDNA L., Adm. Asst. in PR and Dev., Children's Hospital, 219 Bryant St., Buffalo, N.Y. 14222, '67–; Chief Copywtr., J.G. Kelly Adv.; Asst. Dir., WEBR; Adv. Wm. of Buffalo (Pres.; Adv. Wm. of the Yr., '53), Am. Hosp. Assn. PR (Charter Mbr.).

HACK, KAREN POTTER, Free-lance Wtr., Ed., PR, '69–; Asst. to the Dir. of PR, The American Bankers Assn., 90 Park Ave., N.Y., N.Y. 10016, '68–'69; PR Wtr., The Soap and Detergent Assn., '67–'68; Feature Ed., Toys and Novelties Magazine, Haire Publ. Co., '65–'67; PRSA, Theta Sigma Phi (Treas., '62–'65), East Side Repl. Club, Intl. Soc. of Wine Tasters Ltd., Whitney Museum, Wtr.'s Workshop, Humane Soc.; Univ. of Fla., BS, '65; b. Orlando, Fla., '43; p. George and Dorothy Potter Hack; res: 37 W. 54th St., N.Y., N.Y. 10019.

HACK, PAULA SHAPIRO, Free-lance Adv., Fashion Cnslt., Adv. Copywtr., '67–; Adv., Fashion Cnslt., Fromstein Assocs., '62–'67; Manpower, '62–'67; R. H. Macy (N.Y.C.), '59–'60; BBDO, '54–'59; AWRT, Milw. Adv. Club; Silver Mail Box Aw. for Manpower White Gloves Campaign, '62; Direct Mail Adv. Assn. aw. for White Gloves program for Manpower, '63, '64; numerous aws. from Art Dirs. Club of Milw., '62–'64; Univ. of Wis., BA, '47; Charles Morris Price Sch. of Adv., '49; b. Phila., Pa., 1925; p. Davis and Bertha Shafritz Shapiro; h. Morris Hack; c. Daniel, Jonathan; res: 2567 N. Terrace Ave., Milw., Wis. 53211.

HACKER, NAOMI GORDON, Partner, Partners for Growth, Inc., 1270 Ave. of the Americas, N.Y., N.Y. 10020, '69–; AE, Sanderson Group, '65–'69; PR Staff, Farley Manning, '62–'65; Owner, summer resort, '58–'62; Pubcty. Supvsr., Winter Antiques Show; AWRT; Hunter Col., '52; b. N.Y.C., 1934; p. Joseph

and Lillian Cohen Gordon; h. L. Leonard Hacker; c. Alan, David.

HACKETT, JOAN, Actress; OBie Aw., '60–'61; (distinguished performance); Drama Desk Vernon Rice Aw., '60–'61; (Outstanding achiev.), Emmy Nomination (outstanding supporting actress), '61–'62; Intl. Laurel (Golden Glove), '66; Nomination, Best Fgn. Actress of Yr., British Film Acad., '67; b. N.Y.C.; p. John and Mary Esposito Hackett; h. Richard Mulligan; res: 169 S. Rodeo Dr., Beverly Hills, Cal. 90212.

HACKNEY, ELLEN ELIZABETH, Copy Ed., Hardware Retailer, 964 N. Pennsylvania St., Indianapolis, Ind. 46204, '69–; Assoc. Ed., '67–'69; Chief Edtl. Asst., '61–'67; Edtl. Asst., '60–'61; Theta Sigma Phi; Ind. Univ., AB, '60; b. Indianapolis, Ind., 1938; p. Glendon and Helen Schoelch Hackney; res: 319 N. Graham Ave., Indianapolis, Ind. 46219.

HACKNEY, LOUISE BROADRICK, Wms. Ed., Daily Citizen-News, P.O. Box 1167, Dalton, Ga. 30720, '51–; W. Ga. Col.; b. Dalton, Ga., 1926; p. Glenn and Grace Curtis Broadrick; h. William Clayton Hackney; c. Sandra (Mrs. Larry Joyce), Clayton B., Mitchell J.; res: 1502 Dug Gap Rd., Dalton, Ga. 30720.

HADDAD, BARBARA ANNE, Edtl. Wtr., The Denver Post, 650 15th St., Denver, Colo. 80201, '69–; Music, Art Ed., '64–; Wms. Dept. Reptr., '62–'64; Opera News, '67–; Asst. PR Mgr., N.Y. Med. Col., (N.Y.C.), '61–'62; Rsch. and Dev., Lincoln Center, '60–'61; Corr., Am. Nwsp. Guild, Columbia Univ. Jnlsm. Alumni (Western VP, '62); Who's Who in Am.; Outstanding Young Wm. of Am., Who's Who in the West; Swarthmore Col., BA, '59 (cum laude); Columbia Univ., MS (Jnlsm.), '60 (cum laude); b. Canton, Oh., 1937; p. George and LaVerne Smith Haddad; h. Vincent Ryan; res: One Downing St., Denver, Colo. 82218.

HADDOCK, VIRGINIA ATHEY, Ed.-Publr., Marlinton Journal, 828 Second Ave., Marlinton, W. Va. 24954, '62–; BPW (VP); b. Cumberland, Md., 1907; p. Phillip and Martha Mahaney Athey; h. Paul Haddock (dec.); c. Martha Virginia (Mrs. Charles Shisler), William S. (dec.); res: 1307 Sewell St., Marlinton, W. Va. 24954.

HADLEY, CIS (Alice Beatrice Krick), Wms. Dir., AE, KXMC-TV, P.O. Box 1686, S. Broadway, Minot, N.D. 58701, '53–; Wm.'s Dir., KCJB Radio, '50–'58; Grocery Manufacturers of Am. cit., '53; Prodr., "Cis Hadley Show," '53–'67; Children's Hour, '53–'65; semi-annual fashion shows, '53–; Quota Intl. (Minot Chptr. Pres., '64), AWRT (State Chmn., '53); Gen. Fedn. of Wms. Clubs Short Story Contest 1st Pl., '51; Minot State Col., Univ. of N.D.; b. Berthold, N.D.; p. Walter Edward and Anstis Harries Krick; h. K. H. Swiggum; res: 202 3rd Ave. SE, Minot, N.D. 58701.

HAEBERLY, JANE LAURENS, TV/Radio Prodr., Sullivan, Stauffer, Colwell & Bayles, Inc., 575 Lexington

Ave., N.Y., N.Y. 10022, '70–; Radio-TV Dir., Ingalls Assoc., '69; Bdcst. Supvsr., Geer DuBois, '68; Radio-TV Prodr., Chester Gore Co., '61–'62; TV Prodr., Doherty, Clifford, Steers, Schenfield, '59–'61; TV Prodr., J. Walter Thompson, '51–'55; AWRT, Kappa Kappa Gamma; Northwestern Univ., Columbia Univ.; b. Abbington, Pa., '32; p. Harry and Mabel Cooper Haeberly; h. Thomas Swick; c. Lisbeth Hall, John Hall, Jennifer Hall; res: 63 Park Ave., Bronxville, N.Y. 10708.

HAEGER, PHYLLIS M., VP, PR, Smith, Bucklin and Associates, Inc., 333 N. Michigan Ave., Chgo., Ill. 60601, '63–; PR Dir., '59–'63; PR, '55–'59; Midwest Ed., Tide, '51–'55; Lawrence Univ., BA, '50; Northwestern Univ., MA, '51; b. Chgo., Ill., 1928; p. Milton and Ethel Mohr Haeger.

HAGBERG, MARILYN HOPE, Art Critic, Ed., Architecture Wtr., San Diego Magazine, 3254 Rosecrans St., San Diego, Cal. 92110, '64–; Contrb. Reviewer, Craft Horizons, '66–; Eng. Instr., San Diego City Col., '66–; Rept., Feature Wtr., Critic, Times-Union (Albany, N.Y.), '62–'64; Contrb. Reviewer, Artforum, '65–'67; Tchr., '54–'62; San Diego Contemporary Arts Comm., '68–; San Diego Fine Arts Soc.; Am. Red Cross Aw., '63; State Univ. of N.Y., BS (Educ.), '54; MS (Eng.), '57; b. Bklyn., N.Y., 1933; p. William and Hjordis Mathesen Hagberg; res: 812 Dover Ct., San Diego, Cal. 92109.

HAGE, ELIZABETH B., Dir., Prince George's County Memorial Library, 6532 Adelphi Rd., Hyattsville, Md. 20782, '57–; Dir., Scott County Lib. (Eldridge, Ia.), '50–'57; Ref. Librn., Public Lib. (Appleton, Wis.), '48–'50; Head Librn., Marhsall-Lyon County Lib. (Marshall, Minn.), '45–'48; County Librn., Public Lib. (Va., Minn.), '42–'45; Asst. Supvsr., State WPA (Des Moines, Ia.), '40–'42; Asst., Circ. Dept., Public Lib. (Davenport), '39–'40; Head Librn., Public Lib. (Wahpeton, N.D.), '37–'39; Lib. Cnslt.; Carlton Col., Northfield, Minn., BA, '33; Univ. of Wis. Lib. Sch.; Lib. Sci. Cert., '37; b. Madelia, Minn., 1911; p. George and Hanna Borresen Hage; res: 200 Dorset Rd., Laurel, Md. 20810.

HAGEN, LOIS B., Asst. Wms. Ed., Milwaukee Journal, 333 W. State St., Milw., Wis. 53211, '67–; Home Furnishings Ed., '47–'67; Reptr., Ed., UP, '45–'47; Edtl. Rsch., Time (N.Y.C.), '43.

HAGEN, PAULINE MARIA, Exec. VP, R. H. Alber Co., 439 N. Larchmont Blvd., L.A., Cal. 90004, '50–; Time Byr., '41–'50; Secy., '37–'41; Pacific Pioneer Bdcstrs., Zonta Club of L.A.; L.A. Jr. Col.; b. Willow Springs, Mo.; p. John and Bertha Reichman Hagen; res: 5068 Franklin Ave., L.A., Cal. 90027.

HAGER, LOUISA WILSON, Dir., Bur. of Commtns., Nat. Bd., YWCA of the U.S.A., 600 Lexington Ave., N.Y., N.Y. 10022, '61–; Public Info. Dir., Corp. Agove, '53–'61; PR Dir., N.Y.C. Welfare Cncl., '47–'53; Secy.,

N.Y. State Bd. of Parole, '38–'42; Pubcty. Dir., Wms. Div., Dem. Nat. Campaigns, '36, '44; Reptr., N.Y. Morning World, World-Telegram, '27–'31; PR work, '31–'37; Auth., "Broken Journey" (Harper Bros., '35); N.Y. Nwsp. Wms. Club, PRSA; Wellesley Col., BA, '27; h. Read Hager (dec.); c. Charles, Alan; res: 140 W. 16th St., N.Y., N.Y. 10011.

HAGERTY, MARGARET FREY, Adv.-Prom. Mgr., KOMO-TV, Fishers' Blend Station, Inc., 100 Fourth Ave. N., Seattle, Wash. 98109, '53–; Radio Prom. Mgr., '50–'53; Prom. Asst., '48–'50; Tchr., Newberg, Ia., '48; Off. Mgr., Prod. Mgr., Media Dir., R. L. Sines and Assoc., S.F., '46–'47; Acting City Ed., Fairfield (Ia.) Daily Ledger, '43–'44; NATAS, Bdcstrs. Prom. Assn.; Billboard nat. first place aw. for TV sls. prom., '57; Seattle Adv. and Sls. Club first place aw., '62; Christian Col., '37–'38; Parsons Col., '38–'39; Grinnell Col., BA, '41; b. Moline, Ill.; p. Harry and Helen Somers Frey; h. F. W. Hagerty; res: 6543 46th N.E., Seattle, Wash. 98115.

HAGGIE, HELEN MORROW, Wms. News Ed., and Art Critic, The Lincoln Journal, Lincoln, Neb. 68501, '52–; Reptr., '50–'52; Belleville (Kan.) Telescope, '48–'50; Scottsbluff (Neb.) Star Herald, '33–'34; HS Tchr., '34–'38; Theta Sigma Phi (Neb. Wm. of Yr., '65), Governor's Commn. on the Status of Wm., Volunteer Bur. (Pres.) Catholic Social Svc. (Exec. Comm.); Univ. of Neb., AB, '33; b. Scottsbluff, Neb., 1913; p. William and Philmena Congdon Morrow; h. A. J. Haggie; c. Kate (Mrs. A. L. Ellison); res: 2317 S. 27th, Lincoln, Neb. 68502.

HAHN, BERTHA COCHRAN, Free lance bdcstr., food ed., home econst.; Food Ed., Miami (Fla.) News, '53–'67; Med. Corps., '43–'45; Tower Operator, Bowman Field, Louisville, Ky., '42–'43; dietitian, '39–'42; Dir. Consumer Svc., Gen. Baking Co. (Louisville, Ky. Div.), '38–'39; Home Demonstration Agent, Ind., '29–'38; tchr., '25–'29; Am. Dietetic Assn., Am. Home Econs. Assn., Home Econsts. in Bus., Fla. Wms. Press Club, Theta Sigma Phi; Grocery Manfacturers of Am. Cert. of Hon., '55, '57; Am. Meat Inst. Vesta Aw., '60; WPC aws., '55, '57, '59, '60; Purdue Univ., BS, '25 (Mortar Board); Univ. of Miami, BA, '53; b. Decatur, Ill., 1901; p. E. Burt and Annabelle Ward Cochran; h. Edward A. Hahn; res: 9915 Santos Dr., Miami, Fla. 33157.

HAHN, VERA D., Decorating Ed., American Home Magazine, Downe Publishing, Inc., 641 Lexington Ave., N.Y., N.Y. 10022, '64–; Fashion Reptr., Ed., Home Furnishings Daily; Coordr., World's Fair AID-DuPont Textile Fibers Project; formerly Display Exec., Macy's Bamberger; Asst. to Head of Decorating Dept., Bloomingdale's; Ed: "American Home's All About Decorating" ('69), "How to Buy Home Furnishings" ('66); NHFL (VP, Educ.; Bd. Mbr., '63–'64), Press Assoc., AID, NSID Dallas Mkt. Aw., '60, '66; Parsons Sch. of Design.

HAILEY, MARIAN WALLIS, Actress; Film, "Jenny Makes Three"; TV, "Trials of O'Brien," "Hey Landlord"; Plays: "Keep It In Family," "Best Laid Plans," "Mating Dance," "Evening With Thornton Wilder"; AFTRA, SAG, AEA; Univ. of Wash., BA; b. Portland, Ore., 1941; p. H. Wallis and Elizabeth Kube Hailey; h. John Thackray; res: 210 W. 90th St., N.Y., N.Y. 10024.

HAINFELD, AUDREY, Religion Ed., Hudson Dispatch, 400 38th St., Union City, N.J. 07087, '55–; N.J. Daily Nwsp. Wm. (Secy., '65–'66), NFPW, RPRC (Fellow, '63); Edtl. Cncl., Church Herald; b. West New York, N.J., 1922; p. Charles and Ida Amweg; c. Robin; res: 6 Oak St., Weehawken, N.J. 07087.

HAIR, MARY JANE, Behaviorial Sci. Librn., University of Utah Libraries, University of Utah, Salt Lake City, Ut. 84112, '68–; Asst. Prof., '58–; Instr., Lib. Sci., '47–'58; Educ. Librn., '62–'67; Tchr., Librn., since '40; Co-Auth: "Index of Colored Reproductions in the Univ. of Utah Library," ('55), "Selected Bibliography of the Tillman D. Johnson Collection" ('57), "Handbook to the George D. Thomas Library" ('59); ALA, Mountain Plains Lib. Assn., Utah Lib. Assn. (2nd VP), AAUP (Treas., '62), Beta Phi Mu (Pres., '68–; VP, '66–'67), Faculty Wms. Club (Pres., '58–'59), Theta Alpha Phi (VP), AAUW (Secy., '66–'68); Phi Kappa Phi, '63; Univ. of Ut., BA, '40; MA, '47; Univ. of Wash., MA, '59; b. Salt Lake City, Ut.; p. Thomas and Mary Jane Stewart Hair; res: 31 E. 1 North St., Salt Lake City, Ut. 84103.

HALBARDIER, LYNN I., Pubns. Ed., Employers Insurance of Texas, P.O. Box 2759, 423 S. Akard, Dallas, Tex. 75221, '66–; Ed., Fed. Reserve Bank of Dallas, '62–'66; IEA (Secy., '65; Third VP, '66), ICIE; Freedoms Fndn. at Valley Forge Hon. Cert., '68; George Washington Hon. Medal, '67; Dallas Co. United Fund Pubcty. Aws., '64, '66, '68, '69; U.S. Savings Bond Aw., '66; San Angelo Jr. Col. (Who's Who in Am. Jr. Cols.); E. Tex. State Univ., BA, '62; res: 2727 Hudnall, Apt. 119, Dallas, Tex. 75235.

HALBROOKS, ELIZABETH STAPLES, Bus. Mgr., The Horn Book Inc., 585 Boylston St., Boston, Mass. 02116, '63–; VP, '69–; formerly secy.; WNBA; Wellesley Col., BA, '40; Tufts Univ., MEd, '60; b. Southborough, Mass.; p. Frederick and Elizabeth Flanders Staples; h. William Halbrooks; three children.

HALE, CHANIN, Free-lance Actress, numerous TV appearances, incl. the "Red Skelton Show," "The Dean Martin Show," "Julia," many others; guest appearances on "Truth or Consequences," "The Dating Game," "Girl Talk"; movies incl: "The Night They Raided Minskys," "Synanon," "Guide for the Married Man," others; plays incl: "Little Mary Sunshine," "The Gazebo," "Burlesque"; extensive tours with night club revues, lead in Canadian prods.; Wtr.; b. Dayton, Oh.; p. Harold W. and G. Frances Blakeslee Haney; res: 8724 D, Shoreham Dr., L.A., Cal. 90069.

HALFON, ANN H., Asst. Admin. Dir., Bureau of Libraries, New York City Board of Education, 110 Livingston St., Bklyn., N.Y. 11201, '68–; Acting Asst. Admin. Dir., '62–'68; High Sch. Librn., '54–'62; Librn., Bklyn. Public Lib., '38–'40; N.Y.C. Sch. Librns. Assn., ALA, N.Y. Lib. Assn., WNBA; Hunter Col., BA; Columbia Univ., MLS; h. Raymond Halfon; c. Jerald, Robin; res: 1534 E. Seventh St., Bklyn., N.Y. 11230.

HALL, ADRIENNE KOSCHES, Exec. VP and Co-founder, Hall & Levine Advertising, Inc., 1901 Ave. of the Stars, L.A., Cal. 90067, '59–; Adv. Rsch., Gallup & Robinson, '50–'51; Western States Adv. Agcy. Assn. (Bd. of Dirs., '69–'71), Art Museum Cncl., L.A. County Museum of Art; U.C.L.A., BA; b. L.A., Cal.; p. Arthur and Adelina Immerman Kosches; h. Maurice Arthur Hall; c. Adam, Todd, Stefanie, Victoria; res: Beverly Hills, Cal. 90067.

HALL, ALICE J., Legends Wtr., National Geographic Magazine, 17th and M Sts., N.W., Wash., D.C. 20036, '67–; Ed. Assoc., '65–'67; Secy.-Rschr., '64–'65; Eng. Tchr., Mountain View (Cal.) HS, '59–'62; WNPC; U.C.L.A., '54–'55; Mills Col., BA, '59 (cum laude); b. Spirit Lake, Ia., 1936; p. Glen and Ruth Gable Hall.

HALL, BARBARA ISABELLE, Dir. of Adv., Warner's, 325 Lafayette St., Bridgeport, Conn. 06602, '61–; PR Wtr., Southern New England Telephone Co., '59–'61; Copywtr., Warner Brothers Co., '54–'58; Lectr., Univ. of Bridgeport, '66; Bridgeport Adv. Club, Adv. Club of Fairfield County; 11 adv. aws., '61–'67; Univ. of Conn., BS, '54; b. Fairfield, Conn.; p. James and Barbara Kechkemeti Hall; res: 801 Ellsworth St., Bridgeport, Conn. 06605.

HALL, BARBARA M., Wms. Ed., WHCU, 216 E. State St., Ithaca, N.Y. 14850, '56–; Bdsctr., '53–'56; Wms. Ed., Rural Radio Network, '49–'53; AWRT; Experiment in Intl. Living Commty. Ambassador from Ithaca to Denmark, '49; Cornell Univ., BS, '43; b. Groton, N.Y., 1922; p. Walter and Hazel Jaquette Hall; res: 1209 Mecklenburg Rd., Ithaca, N.Y. 14850.

HALL, CARYL HARMS, PR Dir., Golden Gate District, Children's Home Society of California, 3200 Telegraph Ave., Oakland, Cal. 94609, '67–; Press Dir., Un. Bay Area Crusade (S.F., Cal.), '64–'67; Mng. Ed., The Piedmonter (Oakland, Cal.), '55–'62; Capt., U.S. Marine Corps, '51–'54; Auth.: "Gold on Her Shoulder" ('64), "The Prettiest Politician" ('68); Cal. Wtrs. Club (VP, '68–), S.F. Bay Area Pubcty. Club, Friends of the Oakland Public Lib. (Pres., '66–'68); Stanford Univ., AB (Jnlsm.), '51; b. Berkeley, Cal., 1929; p. Edward and Winifred MacNally Harms; h. (div.); c. Jennifer A., Rebecca J.; res: 5828 Lawton Ave., Oakland, Cal. 94618.

HALL, DORIS JANITSCHEK, PR Mgr., Fashions, Uniroyal, Inc., 1230 Ave. of the Americas, N.Y., N.Y. 10020, '66–; Nwsp. Pubcty. Mgr., Celanese Fibers, '59–'65; Fashion and Pubcty. Dir., Cavendish Trading,

'57–'59; Fashion Coordr., Jonathan Logan, '56–'57; Asst. Prom. Dir., Bates Fabrics, '55–'56; Asst. Sls. Prom. Mgr., Springs Mill, '53–'55; Am. Home Econs. Assn., Home Econsts. in Bus., Fashion Group, Am. Inst. of Interior Designers, Society of Architectural Histrns., NHFL; Skidmore Col., BS (Home Econs.), '53; b. Jersey City, N.J., 1931; p. Rudolph and Viola Geils Janitschek; h. Douglas E. Hall; res: 89 Haddon Pl., Upper Montclair, N.J. 07043.

HALL, ELVAJEAN, Supvsr. of Lib. Svcs., Newton Public Schools, Division of Instruction, 88 Chesnut St., W. Newton, Mass. 02165, '46–; Librn., Stephens Col., (Columbia, Mo.), '44–'46; Lib. Supvsr., Jackson, Mich. Public Schs., '42–'44; Librn., Milw. Univ. Sch., '37–'42; Auth., 11 bks., incl. "Land and People of Argentina" ('60), "Land and People of Norway" ('63), "Land and People of Czechoslovakia" ('66), "The Volga, Lifeline of Russia" ('65), "Hong Kong" ('67); Lib. Cnslt., Hist., Travel Wtr.; ALA, Wms. Nat. Bk. Assn. (Nat. Secy., '60–'62; Boston Chptr. Pres., '57–'59), Auths. Guild, NLAPW, New Eng. WPA, Delta Kappa Gamma, Kappa Delta; Oberlin Col., AB, '30; Univ. of Wis., Lib. Sch., '32; Columbia Univ., MS, '41; b. Hamilton, Ill.; p. Dr. Nelson and Nellie Hyer Hall; res: 233 Commonwealth Ave., Boston, Mass. 02116.

HALL, GUIN B., Deputy Commissioner, Wm.'s Prog., New York State Department of Commerce, 112 State St., Albany, New York and 230 Park Ave., N.Y., N.Y. 10017, '60–; Asst. Deputy Commissioner, '59–'60; Wtr., N.Y. Herald Tribune, '44–'59; served in U.S. Coast Guard, WWII; Asst. Byr., West Coast dept. store; N.Y. State Fair Wm.'s Advisory Comm., N.Y. State Farm-City Cncl., N.Y.S. Bd. of Educ. Consumer Advisory Comm., Governor's Intra-Governmental Advisory Comm. on Prices, Elder Craftsmen Showcase (Bd. of Dirs.), St. Luke's Home of Morningside House (Bd. of Dirs.), Wm.'s City Club of N.Y., Greater N.Y. Safety Cncl., N.Y. State Civil Defense Cncl., N.Y. Nwsp. Wm.'s Club (Pres., '56–'58), AWNY (Hon. Mbr.), N.Y. State Wm.'s Cncl. (Chmn.), Theta Sigma Phi, CWPR, (Nat.) Arts Club, BPW, Pers. Club of N.Y., Repl. Wm. in Industry and Professions, ZONTA, Fashion Group; St. Helen's Hall Jr. Col.; Columbia Univ.; res: 150 E. 18th St., N.Y., N.Y. 10003.

HALL, HELEN, Radio Bdcstr., "The Helen Hall Show," RTF Inc., 43 W. 54th St., N.Y., N.Y. 10019, '65–; Bdcstr., "One Women's New York," WCBS, '62–'65 (Bdcst. Aw., '64); BBC Commentator, "Woman's Hour" and "The World at Ten," '55–; Special Assigts. Reptr., NBC-TV, "Home" and "Today," '56–'57; Roving Reptr., NBC, '55–'62; "Helen Hall Show," MBS Network, '47–'54; Barbara Welles Shows, WOR, '48–'54; Lectr.; Fashion Commentator; AWRT (N.Y. Chptr. Bd. of Dirs., '69–'70; Pres., '57), Wellesley Club of N.Y. Adv. Wm. (Bd. of Dirs., '50–'51); Eng. Speaking Un. Radio Aw., '49; two cits.; Oh. State Univ., '50, '51; Wellesley Col., '37–'38; Tamara Daykarhanava Sch. of Dramatics; b. Kan. City, Mo.; p. Ernest F. and Helena Drees Hall; res: 333 E. 79th St., N.Y., N.Y. 10021.

HALL, HELEN LINNENBERGER, Auth., Rte. 1, Hutchinson, Kan. 67601; Genealogy Bks: Families: Brungardt ('69), Grellner ('68), Strecker ('66), Goetz ('63), Hall ('60), Danler ('58); "These Are Our Religions" (Edition II, '62; Edition I, '59), "Grandfather's Story"; various organizations; Dominican Sch. of Nursing, nursing deg., '36; b. Victoria, Kan., 1912; h. Edwin B. Hall; c. Patrick, Michael; res: Rt. 1, Hutchinson, Kan. 67601.

HALL, MARJORY LUCILE, Travel Ed., Yankee mag.; Auth., Fiction for teen-age girls; AE, VP, H. B. Humphrey, Alley & Richards, '42–'56; Adv. Rsch., Pubcty., Edtl., Ladies' Home Journal, '31–'42; Wellesley Col., BA, '30; b. Pittsfield, Mass.; p. Walter and Lucile Reynolds Hall; h. Taylor B. Yeakley; res: Lincoln House Point, Swampscott, Mass. 01907.

HALL, MARY ROSE, Ed., Daughters of the American Revolution, 1776 D. St., N.W., Wash., D.C., 20006, '65–; Sr. Tech. Ed., Bell Telephone Labs. (New Jersey), '61–'65; Sr. Ed., Western Electric Co. (Winston-Salem, N.C.), '54–'61; Tchr., '52–'54; Beta Sigma Phi, Nat. Trust for Historic Preservation, Smithsonian Assocs.; Freedoms Fndn. aw., '68; Who's Who of Am. Wm.; Univ. of N.C., AB, '52; MA (Eng.), '60; b. Charlotte, N.C.; p. Clarence and Mary Rose Hall; res: 1400 S. Joyce St., Apt. C-609, Arlington, Va. 22202.

HALL, MAYBELLE F., Pres., The Maybelle F. Hall Company, Inc., 625 Madison Ave., N.Y., N.Y. 10022, '51–; VP, Griswold-Eshlemen, '67–; Prom. Dir., Amos Parrish, '40–'50; Cnslt., retail dept. stores; Prodr., Dir., indsl. shows; Mag. Cnslt.; Fashion Cnslt.; Mdsng., Sls. Prom. Csnlt.; Script Wtr.; Fashion Group; War Wtrs. Bd. ('45); NRMA Best Inst. Campaign, '51; Columbia Univ.; N.Y.U.; Pratt Inst.; b. N.Y.C., 1914; p. John and Helen Botschet Froehlich; h. Kirk Shivell (div.); c. Kirk John; res: 333 E. 79th St., N.Y., N.Y. 10021.

HALL, NAN, Bdcst. Svcs. Coordr., Lang, Fisher & Stashower Advertising, Inc., 1010 Euclid Bldg., Cleve., Oh. 44115, '65–; Radio-TV Dept. Traf. Mgr., '53–'65; b. Cleve., Oh., 1925; 27105 Normandy Rd., Bay Village, Oh. 44140.

HALL, NATALIE GRACE, Soc. Ed., Burbank Daily Review, 220 E. Orange Grove Ave., Burbank, Cal. 91502, '70–; Reptr.-Photog., Press-Herald, '67–'70; Soc. Ed., Daily Sun-Post (San Clemente) '66–'67; Soc. Reptr., Citizen-News (Hollywood), '66; Asst. Ed., Building News (L.A.), '64–'65; Soc. Reptr., Evening Outlook (Santa Monica), '64; Theta Sigma Phi, Cosmopolitan Social Club (Secy.); Univ. of the Pacific; Am. Univ., BA, '63; Grad. Work in Jnlsm., U.C.L.A.; b. Bklyn., N.Y., '41; p. Nathan Issac and Margaret Sabelstrom Hall; res: 400 Bonhill Rd., L.A., Cal. 90049.

HALL, ROSA LEE ROSKI, Prod. Mgr., Lowe Runkle Co., 1313 Liberty Bank Bldg., Okla. City, Okla. 73102, '61–; Asst. Prod. Mgr., '57–'61; Asst. Bkkeeper., '56–'57; Bkkeeper., Prod., Industrial Printing Co.,

'44–'56; Okla. City Adv. Club, Okla. City Art Dirs. Club (VP, '68; Dir., '67–'68; Secy., '66); Kan. State Col., '42–'43; b. Okla. City, Okla., 1923; p. Phillip and Helen Synar Roski; h. George Hall; res: 1205 S.W. 58th St., Okla. City, Okla. 73109.

HALL, ROSALYS HASKELL, Free-lance Ed.; Children's Bk., David McKay Company, '61–'68; Children's Bk. Ed., Longmans, Green, '44–'61; Auth: 14 children's bks., incl: "The Bright and Shining Breadboard" (Lothrop, '69), "Miranda's Dragon" (McGraw-Hill, '68); Forum of Jr. Bk. Wtrs., Newport Hist. Soc., Assn. on Am. Indian Affairs; N.J. Col. for Wm.; Columbia Univ.; N.Y.U.; b. N.Y.C.; p. Henry and Alice Haskell Hall; res: 6 Coddington St., Newport, R.I. 02840.

HALL, SIBYL BEEBE, Gen. Mgr., The News Tribune, 1102 S. Fourth St., Ft. Pierce, Fla. 33450, '62–; Off. Mgr., '52–'62; Controller, WIRA, '48–'52; Gen. Mgr., Sunrise Transit, '44–'47; Controller, Cowles Fla. Nwsps., '60–'66; Outstanding Wm., VFW Aux., '50; accounting courses, St. Anastasia Sch., '38; Ext. courses, Univ. of Fla., '45; b. Fountain, Fla., 1920; p. Alvaro and Linnie Daniels Beebe; h. James Hall; c. Mrs. Marvin McKinley; res: 1217 Ormond Ave., Ft. Pierce, Fla. 33450.

HALL, SUE G., Dp, Droke House Inc., 1109 S. Main, Anderson, S.C. 29621, '65–; Actress; Assoc. Publr., Quote Magazine; Ed: "The Quotable Robert F. Kennedy" ('67), "Bobby Kennedy Off-Guard" ('67), "Robert F. Kennedy Allo Scoperto" ('68); Who's Who of Am. Wm; Univ. of Okla.; b. Cedar Rapids, Ia., 1937; h. Wilton E. Hall, Jr; c. Wilton E. Hall, III; Perry Hall; res: Anderson, S.C. 29621.

HALLEY, LOLA STAHLEY, Adv. Mgr., The Daily Leader, 111 W. Sixth Street, Stuttgart, Ark. 72160, '51–; Teletypesetter, Proofreader, '50–'51; Ark. Press Wm. (Pres., '67–'69; Secy., '63–'67; numerous adv. aws.); Stuttgart C. of C.; b. Stuttgart, Ark., 1919; p. Jesse and Margaret Zimmerman Stahley; h. Albert Halley; c. Annette (Mrs. Bill Carper), Robert Lynn, Ray Allen; res: 505 S. Anna St., Stuttgart, Ark. 72160.

HALLIWELL, PATRICIA CROLL, Media Planner/Byr., Reach McClinton & Co., Inc., 505 Park Ave., N.Y., N.Y. 10022, '69–; Media Dir., Hirsch/Tigler/Fried, '68–'69; Sarong, Inc., '67–'68; Adv. Prod., Traf. Mgr., Asst. Ed., Sponsor mag. '63–'66; Canadian Sponsor (Toronto), '62; Jr. League of N.Y.C.; Univ. of Toronto, BA, '62; N.Y. Sch. of Interior Design; b. Toronto, Can.; p. Charles and Sybil Croll Halliwell; h. Lucas Vicens; res: 400 Central Park W., Apt. 3–B, N.Y., N.Y. 10025.

HALLOWELL, JACQUELINE IRENE, Secy.-Treas., Downs and Roosevelt, Inc., Time and Life Bldg., 1271 Ave. of the Americas, N.Y., N.Y. 10020, '68–; Secy., '64–; AE, Selvage and Lee, '61–'64; Radio Free Europe (Munich, Germany), '56–'60; Asst. Prodr.,

Radio-TV, Hardy Burt & Assoc., '53–'56; PRSA; b. Hartford, Conn., 1932; p. Patrick and Helen Schroder Hallowell; res: 326 W. 20th St., N.Y., N.Y. 10011.

HALL-QUEST, OLGA WILBOURNE, Auth., juv. nonfiction; bks: "Conquistadors and Pueblos" (E. P. Dutton, '69), "Guardians of Liberty: Sam Adams and John Hancock" (E. P. Dutton, '63; Lib. of Congress Selected Reading List of Children's Literature on the Am. Revolution, '68), eight others; English Faculty, The Masters Sch., Dobbs Ferry, N.Y., '43–'65; Auths. Guild; Columbia Univ., BS, '33; N.Y.U., MA, '34; b. Willis, Tex., 1899; p. William and Molly Derrick Wilbourne; h. Alfred Lawrence Hall-Quest; res: 311 E. 72nd St., N.Y., N.Y. 10021.

HALM, MARILYN J., Mng. Ed., The Magazine, Meridith Corp., 750 Third Ave., N.Y., N.Y. 10017, '70–; Ed., Mobile Life, Davis Publ., '63–'70; Mng. Ed., Mobile Home Journal, '61–'63; Assoc. Ed., '60–'61; Assoc. Ed., Fawcett Pubns., '58–'60; Rutgers Univ., N.Y.U., New Sch. for Social Rsch.; h. (div.).

HALPERN, ETHEL D., Pres., Montgomery & Co. Inc., 12 Commerce St., Chatham, N.J. 07928, '68–; Corp. Secy., '63–'68; Free-lance Copywtr., '60–'63; Asst. to Prom. Dir., Harper's Bazaar, '58–'60; Copywtr., Bloomingdale's, '50–'56; Assoc. Third Class Mail Users, Friends of the Whitney Museum, Friends of the City Center, Museum of City of N.Y., Museum of Modern Art, Am. Israeli Cultural Fndn.; N.Y.U., BA; b. N.Y.C.; p. Maxwell and Sarah Danziger Halpern; res: 425 W. 23 St., N.Y., N.Y. 10011.

HALPERN, FRANCES ISAACS, Staff Wtr., Polit. Ed., Peninsula News, 900 Silver Spur Rd., Palos Verdes Peninsula, Cal. 90274, '63–; Bdcstr., KKOP-FM Radio, 2257 Hawthorne Blvd., Redondo Beach, Cal. 90277, '68–; AWRT; Am. Press Wm.; Am. Acad. of Dramatic Arts, '43; N.Y.U., '44; b. N.Y.C., 1925; p. Murray Isaacs and Mrs. Ray Hamilton; h. Theodor Halpern; c. Michael, Leslie, Evan; res: 4659 Marloma Dr., Rolling Hills Estates, Cal. 90274.

HAMBLIN, DORA JANE, Staff Wtr., Life, Time Inc., Time-Life Bldg., Rockefeller Ctr., N.Y., N.Y. 10020, '64–; Wtr., N.Y. staff, '61–; Rome Bur. Chief, '56–'60; Corr. (Paris; London; Chgo.), '50–'56; Rschr., '48–'50; PR, Am. Nat. Red Cross (Philippines, Japan, China, Europe), Doughnut Girl (New Guinea, Australia), '44–'48; Reptr.-Photogr., Cedar Rapids (Ia.) Gazette, '42–'44; Free-lance Wtr., Harper's Bazaar, Readers Digest, New Soc. (Britain); Auth: "Pots and Robbers" (Simon and Schuster, '70; Jr. Lit. Guild Selection); Coe Col. (Cedar Rapids, Ia.), BA, '41 (magna cum laude; Phi Beta Kappa); Dr. of Lit. (hon.), '68; Northwestern Univ., MS (Jnlsm., "with highest distinction"); b. Bedford, Ia., 1920; p. Allen and Grace Sailor Hamblin; res: 427 W. 21st St., N.Y., N.Y. 10011.

HAMBRICK, THERA OLLIS, Librn., Valdosta State

Col., Valdosta, Ga. 31601, '61–; Asst. Librn., '46–'61; Librn., Bolles Sch., '43–'46; Tchr., Librn., Gulf HS, '42–'43; Tchr., Librn., Echols County HS, '39–'42; Tchr., St. George HS, '36–'39; ALA; Ga. Lib. Assn., SE Lib. Assn., Ga. Educ. Assn., S. Ga. Academic Libs.; Ga. State Wms. Col., BA, '42; La. State Univ., BS (Lib. Sci.), '46; b. Lowndes County, Ga., 1917; res: Rte. 1, Box 120, Hahira, Ga. 31632.

HAMBY, LOTTIE DERIEUX, Secy.-Treas., Bradley, Graham & Hamby Advertising Agency, Inc., 2520 Devine St., Columbia, S.C. 29205, '51–; pubcty., lyrics, PR, radio-TV writing; polit. speeches, '54–; Columbia Adv. Cncl., Palmetto Outdoor Historical Drama Assn. (Secy.), Richland County Mental Health Assn., Gtr. Columbia C. of C., Un. Fund, Wm.'s Symphony Assn., Citizen's Design for Progress; former Ladies' Doubles Tennis Champion of the Carolinas; Univ. of S.C., AB, '38; Grad. Work, U.S.C.; b. Columbia, S.C. 1918; p. Theoditus and Lottie Derieux Hamby; res: 4429 Reamer Ave., Columbia, S.C. 29206.

HAMEL, MAUREEN QUINN, Soc. Ed., Bristol Press, 99 Main St., Bristol, Conn. 06010, '62–; Edtl. Asst., Aetna Life and Casualty Co., '61–'62; Immaculata Col., Univ. of Hartford; b. Buffalo, N.Y., 1940; p. George and Eleanor Canty Quinn; h. Norman P. Hamel; c. Kevin Michael, Timothy James; res: 78 Cancellaro Dr., Wolcott, Conn. 06716.

HAMER, ELIZABETH EDWARDS, Asst. Librn. of Congress, Library of Congress, Wash., D.C., '63–; Asst. Librn. for Public Affairs, '60–'63; Info. and Pubns. Offcr., '51–'60; Chief, Exhibits and Pubns. Sec., Nat. Archives and Records Svc., '50–'51; Exhibits and Info. Offcr., '47–'50; Nat. Archives, '42–'47; Survey of Fed. Archives in the States, '36–'40; ALA, D.C. Lib. Assn.; Am. Hist. Assn., Soc. of Am. Archivists (Hon. Fellow, '60), Manuscript Soc., S.C. Hist. Soc., Intl. Cncl. on Archives; delegate, White House Conf. on Intl. Coop., '65; Hon. Trustee, Gtr. Wash. Educ. TV Assn.; N.Y.U. Pres. Cncl. for the Grad. Sch. of Arts and Sci., '68–'71; Univ. of Tenn., BA (Hist.), '33 (Phi Kappa Phi; Fellow In Hist., '33–'34); Grad. Work, Am. Univ.; b. Copperhill, Tenn., 1912; p. John Earl and Fanny Wallace Edwards; res: 6620 River Rd., Bethesda, Md. 20034.

HAMER, MARGUERITE BARTLETT, Prof. Emeritus; Prof. of Hist., Univ. of Tenn., '20–'58; Contrbr., Canadian Hist. Review, North Carolina Historical Review, Georgia Historical Review; Auth: "Pennsylvania Politics in the Jacksonian Period" ('19), "Cameos of the South" ('40); articles on Russia, Rhodesia; Tenn. Hist. Soc. (Past Pres.), Dic. of Am. Biog.; Bryn Mawr Col., AB, '13; MA, '15; Univ. of Pa., PhD, '19; b. Phila., Pa. 1890; p. Calvin and Mary Stuart Bartlett; res: 613 20th St., Knoxville, Tenn. 37916.

HAMILTON, DOROTHY HAZEL, Guidance Cnslr.-Publicist, Jane Addams Vocational High School, 2373 E. 30th St., Cleve., Oh. 44115, '59–; Pubns. Advisor,

Collinwood HS, '52–'59; PR, Oh. State Dept. Distributive Educ., '46–'52; Pubcty. Dir., Oh. Div., Nat. War Fund, '43–'46; Pubcty. Wtr., Cleve. Public Schs., '36–'43, '52–; Pubcty. Wtr., Cleve. Commty. Fund, '34–'36; Instr., Annual Oh. Univ. Pubns. Workshop, '59–; Wm.'s Adv. Club of Cleve., Theta Sigma Phi, Jnlsm. Advisors of Greater Cleve. (Pres., '59–'60); Western Reserve Univ., BA, '28; MA (Educ.); Cert. in Guidance '56; b. Cleve., Oh., 1906; p. Clayton and Grace Wilson Hamilton; res: 923 Selwyn Rd., Cleve. Heights, Oh. 44112.

HAMILTON, ELSIE LOUISE, Church Ed., Gastonia Gazette, Freedom Newspapers, 2500 Wilkinson Blvd., Gastonia, N.C. 28052, '60–; Reptr., Belmont Banner, '57–'60; BPW (Belmont Chptr. Charter Pres., '59–'61), N.C. Press Wm.; nwsp. writing aws.; King's Col.; b. Belmont, N.C., 1930; p. Charlie and Madelyn Jordan Hamilton; res: 103 Georgia Belle Ave., Belmont, N.C. 28012.

HAMILTON, EVA NEALON, Staff Wtr., Medford Mail Tribune, 33 N. Fir St., Medford, Ore. 97501, '63–; Corr., Sacramento Bee (Cal.), Oregon Journal, '40–; Reptr., Medford Daily News, '28–'30; Theta Sigma Phi, Delta Kappa Gamma, Southern Ore. Hist. Soc.; Off. of Econ. Opp. aw., '68; Univ. of Ore., BA (Jnlsm.), '27; b. Central Point, Ore., 1904; p. Stephen and Mary Law Nealon; h. Alexander Moore Hamilton (dec.); c. Alexander Moore Jr., Nancy Nealon, Samson, Robert S.; res: 43 Rose Ave., Medford, Ore. 97501.

HAMILTON, ISABEL, Sr. Publicist, J. Walter Thompson Company, 420 Lexington Ave., N.Y., N.Y. 10017, '63–; Assoc. Prom. Dir., Vogue mag., '62–'63; Prom. Dir., Vogue Pattern Svc., '58–'62; Prom. Mgr., Fashion Coordr., Adv. AE, McCall's Pattern Dir., '46–'58; Jr. AE, William Esty Co.; Copywtr., R. H. Macy & Co.; Adv. Sec. Mgr., Kresge Dept. Store (Newark, N.J.); Edtl., Rept., Dry Goods Economist; Fashion Group, NHFL, Wms. Fashion Fabric Assn. (VP; Founding Mbr.); Hunter Col., AB (cum laude); Pratt Inst.; b. N.Y.C.; p. Francis, Jr., and Jeanatte Cunningham Hamilton; h. Earl L. Carver; res: 34 Orchard Farm Rd., Port Washington, N.Y. 11050.

HAMILTON, MARGARET, Actress; veteran of stage, screen, radio, TV; organized and taught Nursery Sch., Presbyterian Ch. (Beverly Hills, Cal.), '48–'51; Bd. of Educ., '47–'51; Tchr. (Cleve., Oh.; Rye N.Y.), '23–'28; AEA (Cncl. Mbr., '54–'69), Episcopal Actor's Guild (Bd. Mbr.), Jr. League of L.A., Cleve. (Children's Theatre); Wheelock Kindergarten Training Sch., grad. '23; b. Cleve., Oh., 1902; p. Walter and Jennie Adams Hamilton; c. Hamilton W. Meserve; res: 34 Gramercy Park, N.Y., N.Y. 10003.

HAMILTON, MARY MILLER, Dir. of Public Info., University of Corpus Christi, P.O. Box 6010, Corpus Christi, Tex. 78411, '66–; Secy. to VP for Dev., '64–'66; Registrar's Off., '63–'64; Secy., '38–'63; Jnlsm. Tchr., Brackenridge HS (San Antonio, Tex.), '30–'38; Theta

Sigma Phi, Tex. Baptist PR Assn., Corpus Christi Press Club; Columbia Scholastic Press Assn. Gold Key, '34; Who's Who Of Am. Wm.; Univ. of Tex., BJ, '30 (Sigma Delta Chi Scholarship Key); b. Beeville, Tex., 1907; p. Rufus and Anna Morey Miller; h. Lawrence E. Hamilton (dec.); res: 2773 Lawnview, Corpus Christi, Tex. 78404.

HAMILTON, NANCY MILLER, Cnslt. to Dept. of Mass. Commtns., New Mexico State Univ., '68–'69; Commtns. Specialist, El Paso (Tex.) Public Schs., '59–'68; Reptr., El Paso Times, '50–'59; Who's Who of Am. Wm.; Who's Who in PR; Univ. of Tex., BA, '49; MA, '54; b. El Paso, Tex., 1929; p. Harold and Corinne Miller Miller; h. Ralph E. Hamilton; c. James R., Jeannie M.; res: 10329 Rushing, El Paso, Tex. 79924.

HAMILTON, SYLVIA WALINOW, Assoc. Dir. in charge of PR, Heart of America United Campaign, 320 E. Tenth St., Kan. City, Mo. 64106, '57–; PR Dir., '50–'59; Public Svc. Dir., KCKN Radio, '45–'48; WAVES, '43–'45; PR Cnslt., Bay Area Un. Crusade, '65; PRSA (Kan. City Chptr. Pres., '60), IEA (Kan. City Chptr. Pres., '61), Wm.'s C. of C., Theta Sigma Phi, Adv. and Sales Execs. Club, Silver Anvil Aw., APRA, '59; Who's Who of Am. Wm., '66; Kan. Jr. Col.; b. Kan. City, Kan., 1919; p. Joseph and Eva Lasik Walinow; h. Ray A. Hamilton; res: 2138 Normandy Lane, K.C., Kan.

HAMM, MARIE NORSTROM, Crtv. Supvsr., Batten Barton Durstine & Osborne, Inc., 383 Madison Ave., N.Y., N.Y. 10017, '60–; Auth: "Money in the Bank Cookbook," "The Second Chafing Dish Cookbook," "The Meat Cookbook," other cookbks.; Byr., accessories, Best & Co.; Assoc. Fashion Ed., Harper's Bazaar; Owner, two Epicure accessory shops; Special Asst., Robinson Hannagan, PR; Auth., mag. articles; Barnard Col., '36–'38; b. Mpls., Minn., 1917; p. Gustave and Marie Anderson Norstrom; h. Frederic J. Hamm (dec.); res: 360 E. 72 St., N.Y., N.Y. 10021.

HAMMAN, ANN LONGLEY, Food Ed., The Evansville Courier, 201 N.W. Second St., Evansville, Ind. 47701, '67–; Consumer Educ. Agt., Coop. Ext. Svc., '57–'65; Home Econst., Monthly Bul., Intl. Harvester Co., '52–'55; 1st Lt., Signal Corps, Wms. Army Corps, '42–'46; Home Econs. in Bus. (Evansville Chptr. Pres., '55), Home Econs. in Homemaking; Univ. of Chgo., PhB, '30; Purdue Univ., MS, '52 (Omicron Nu); b. Pond Creek, Okla., 1907; p. Jeff and Julia Aldrich Longley; h. (div.); c. Henry Longley Hamman; res: 101 Dreier Blvd., Evansville, Ind. 47712.

HAMMER, RUTH, Pres., Ruth Hammer Associates, Inc., 350 W. 51st St., N.Y., N.Y. 10019, '50–; Pubcty. Dir., Lord & Taylor, '41–'50; Wms. Features, UP (Paris, France), '33–'35; Fashion Group (VP, '64–'66), OPC, Shoe Wms. Execs., Pubcty. Club of N.Y.; Sorbonne, License des Lettres, '36; b. Chgo., Ill., 1911; p. Benjamin and Frances Halbren Hammer.

HAMMERSLEY, EVADNA BREDEHOEFT (pseud: Paula Owen), Free-lance Bdcstr., Wtr., for 50 stas.; Dir., Products Prom. Dept., American Sheep Producers Council, Inc., 909-17th St., Denver, Colo. 80202, '54–; previously 20 yrs. with NBC and KOA; Auth., "A Rhapsody of the Rockies" (World Press), two cookbks. under pseud.; Eng. Speaking Union Sterling Aw., '51; Cits., '50, '55; Mark Twain Aw., '45; Adv. Wm. of the Yr., '59; McCall's Golden Microphone Aw., '52; b. Lecompton, Kan., 1911; p. William and Emma Sellers Bredehoeft; h. L. Val Hammersley (dec.); res: 1950 Newton St., Denver, Colo. 80204.

HAMMOND, FAY CORBIN, Fashion Ed., Los Angeles Times, Times-Mirror Sq., L.A., Cal. 90053, '41–; Fashion Group, Theta Sigma Phi, Dante Alighieri Soc. of Southern Cal. (Bd. of Dirs.), L.A. World Affairs Cncl.; Fashion Ed. Aw. from L.A. Wm.'s Div., State of Israel Bonds, '68; Myrtle Wreath Aw., L.A. Hadassah, '67; City of Hope Fashion Aw., '64–'65; Fashion Wm. of the Yr., '61 and Jnlsm. Aw., '59; L.A. Mannequin's Assn., Star of Solidarity from Republic of Italy, '61 and '55; Lily of Florence, Italy, '56; b. Memphis, Tenn.; p. Luther and Naomi Beecher Jones Corbin; h. Harry Hammond Jr.; c. Sonya; res: 436 N. Ardmore Ave., L.A., Cal. 90004.

HAMMOND, MABEL JACKSON, Publr., Ed., Journal Free Press, 520 Market St., Osage City, Kan. 66523; C. of C. (Secy.); Kan. State Tchrs. Col., '26–'28; Washburn Univ., '31–'33; b. Scranton, Kan.; p. Samuel and Mary Barraclough Jackson; h. Edwin Hammond (dec.); c. Charles, Sandra Rogers; res: 703 S. Sixth, Osage City, Kan. 66523.

HAMMOND, TERRY D., Staff Wtr., Wilmington Star-News Newspapers, Murchison Building, Wilmington, N.C. 28401, '66–; Golden Star Aw. for Jnlsm., '68, Nat. Assn. of Nwsp. Publrs., most valuable staffer aw., '68; Wilmington Col.; b. Wilmington, N.C., 1950; p. William Franklin and Elizabeth Bland Hammond Jr.; res: Rte. 1, Box 408B, Wilmington, N.C. 28401.

HAMMONS, SARAH MILDRED, Adm. Asst., '52–; Indsl. Rels. Ed., Pine Chips, Brunswick Pulp and Paper Company, Brunswick, Ga. 31520, '50–; Pers. Mgr., Tidewater Plywood, '47–'50; Pubcty. Asst., State of Ga., '46–'47; Pubcty. Asst., J. A. Jones Constr. Co., '42–'45; Eng. Tchr.; Brunswick Press Club (Pres., VP, Secy., Dir.), Southern Cncl. of Indsl. Eds.; Wesleyan Col., BA (Eng.), '37 (Brunswick Alumnae Assn. Pres.); b. Ft. Payne, Ala., 1914; p. William and Sallie Shook Hammons; res: 1114 Union St., Brunswick, Ga. 31520.

HAMMONTREE, MARIE GERTRUDE, U.S. Department of Justice, 1221 N. Pennsylvania St., Indpls., Ind. 46207, '50–; Auth: juv. bks. incl. "Mohandas Gandhi, A Boy of Principle" ('66), "Walt Disney, Young Movie-Maker" ('69), others; Theta Sigma Phi; Butler Univ., AB, '49; b. Jefferson County, Ind., 1913; p. Harry and Hattie Means Hammontree; res: 930 N. Bosart Ave., Indpls., Ind. 46201.

HAMPTON, NORA GAMBILL, Fashion Ed., The Oakland Tribune, 13th and Franklin, Oakland, Cal. 94612, '63–; Free-lance PR, Prom. Cnslt., reg. and nat. clients, '57–'63; staff, Woodrow Wilson Centennial Commn., Wash., D.C., '55–'56; Honolulu (Hi.) Star Bulletin, '54–'55; Public Info. Staff, Chief of Radio-TV-Film Sec., Defense Mobilization Admin., Wash., D.C., '51–'53; Wtr., Am. Nat. Red Cross staff, '50; TV Wtr.-Prodr., Hollywood, Cal., '47–'50; formerly Adv.-PR Dir., Hockaday Sch., Dallas, Tex.; Assoc., Scott Wilson and Assocs., N.O., La.; UP; Reptr., Borger (Tex.) Dailey Herald; ANWC (Wash., D.C.), PRSA; City of Oakland proclaimed April 27, '67 "Nora Hampton Day"; named Fashion Ed. of Yr. by W. Coast Salesmen; Golden Slipper Aw.; numerous others; Stephens Col., '30 (permanent hon. roll; Nat. Alumnae Bd.); Univ. of Cal. at Santa Barbara; Immaculate Heart Univ., L.A., Cal.; b. Tex.; p. Jesse and Nora Haskins Gambill; h. John Lucien Hampton; c. John M. W.; res: 322 El Toyonal Rd., Orinda, Cal. 94563.

HAMRA, RUBY M., Pres., Hamra Associates, 748 Lexington Ave., N.Y., N.Y. 10022, '69–; Dir., Special Proms., Events, '60–'68; VP, Franklin Simon, '51–'59; AWNY, Fashion Group, PRSA; St. Joseph's Convent Col. (Toronto); b. Toronto, Can.; res: 41 Park Ave., N.Y., N.Y. 10016.

HANAU, STELLA BLOCH, Free-lance Edtl. Svc: mss. criticism and ed., repts. of meetings and confs.; specialize: psychiatric, social work, educ., allied subjects; Info. Specialist (pubcty.), Fed. Govt., War Prod. Bd., Dept. of Commerce, U.S. Public Health Svc., WPA Wtrs. Project; pubcty., Provincetown Playhouse, other experimental theatres; Barnard Col., Columbia Univ., BA, '11; b. N.Y.C., 1890; p. Edward and Elizabeth Long Bloch; c. Richard; res: 360 W. 22 St., N.Y., N.Y. 10011.

HANAUER, JOAN, Feature Wtr., Bk. Rev. Ed., United Press International, 220 E. 42nd St., N.Y., N.Y. 10017, '68–; Rewrite, Feature Wtr., '67–'68; Rewrite, Feature Wtr., World-Journal-Tribune, '66–'67; Journal-American Svc., '52–'58; Reptr., Feature Wtr., Intl. News; Am. Nwsp. Guild, N.Y. Reptrs. Assn.; N.Y.U., BA, '52; b. N.Y.C., 1931; p. Sigfried and Anne Bernard Hanauer; h. Kenneth G. McKenna; c. Megan Marguerite; res: 324 E. 41st St., N.Y., N.Y. 10017.

HANCHETT, BONNY HOWLAND, Publr., Mng. Ed., Clear Lake Observer-American, P.O. Box 218, Lower Lake, Cal. 95457, '56–; Corr., Sacramento Bee; Publr., Ed., Lewis River News, '53–'55; News Reptr., Burbank Herald, '45–'46; Wire Ed., L.A. Times, '44–'45; Soc. Ed., Everett Daily Herald, '42–'43; Theta Sigma Phi, Clear Lake C. of C. (Secy., '58–'60), Soroptimist Club (Clear Lake Pres., '69–'70), Wash. State Univ., BA (Eng., Jnlsm.), '42; b. Muskegon, Mich., 1920; p. Valentine and Dorothy Mitchell Howland; h. Ross Hanchett; c. Val H., Jon Allen, Mary Hanchett Waterman, Roberta

Lee, Kathryn Ann; res: Pt. Lakeview, Lower Lake, Cal. 95457.

HANDFORD, CHARLOTTE CARROLL, Colmst., Guard-Record Co., Inc., 115 N. Fourth St., Batesville, Ark. 72501, '59–; E. Tex. State Col.; b. Newport, Ark., 1910; p. Charles and Hester Phillips Carroll; h. Charles D. Handford; c. Mrs. Mary Jo Baker, Mrs. James Nettles, Mrs. Frank Dunn, Stanley, Charles; res: 828 Broad St., Batesville, Ark. 72501.

HANDY, DRUCILLA, Pres., Drucilla Handy Company, 813 Merchandise Mart, Chgo., Ill. 60654, '54–; Acc. Group Supvsr., Gardner & Jones, '54–'56; PR Dir., Helene Curtis Industries, '52–'54; Acc. Group Supvsr., Mayer & O'Brien, '50–'52; Assoc., Rosemary Sheehan Pubcty., '48–'50; Asst. Adv. Dir., Ronrico Corp., '45–'47; PRSA, Fashion Group, Pubcty. Club of Chgo. (Corp. PR aw., '65); Mary Lyon Jr. Col., '40; Swathmore Col., '40–'42; b. Lynchburg, Va., 1922; p. John and Allen Steele Handy; h. Robert Michel Redinger; res: 2440 Lakeview Ave., Chgo., Ill. 60614.

HANEVOLD, CORAL LOIS, Cont. Dir., Prodr., WSB Radio, 1601 W. Peachtree St., Atlanta, Ga. 30309, '59–; Copy Chief, WCSC-TV (Charleston, S.C.), '56–'58; Asst. Adv. Mgr., Ed., The Weekly Turnstile, Piggly Wiggly Corp., '43–'44; AWRT (Nat. Dir., '67–'69; Atlanta Chptr. Pres., '65–'66, Dir., '64–'65), Atlanta Wms. C. of C. (Dir., '69–'70), Press Club of Atlanta, Pres. Cncl. of Atlanta (Histrn.), '68–'69); Atlanta Ad Club aw., '67, '63–'64; Southeastern Adv. Fedn. aw., '65; Univ. of Ga., BA (Jnlsm.), '40; Emory Univ., '46; b. Birmingham, Ala.; p. Julius and Carrie Reed Lennard; h. Robert B. Hanevold; c. Barbara, Robert Coral; res: 2682 Harrington Dr., Decatur, Ga. 30033.

HANEY, MARGIE AILEEN, Adv., Sales Prom. Dir., J. B. Ivey & Co., 127 N. Tryon St., Charlotte, N.C. 28201, '54–; Adv. Dir., Battelstein's (Houston, Tex.), '52–'54; Asst. Adv. Mgr., Foley's, '48–'52; Fashion Copy Chief, '46–'48; Theta Sigma Phi, Art Dirs. Club, Charlotte Adv. Club; Nat. Retail Merchants Assn. aw., '68, '66, '62–'63; Tex. Wms. Univ., BA, '44; N.Y.U., '48; b. Roscoe, Tex.; p. Austin H. and Burdah Mayes Haney; res: 1623 Purnell Ct., Charlotte, N.C. 28211.

HANFORD, FLORENCE PEIRCE, Supvsr. of Home Econs. Adv., Philadelphia Electric Co., 900 Sanson St., Phila., Pa. 19105, '43–'69; Tchr., Temple Univ., '36–'39; Auth., two cookbks.; Planner, Prodr., Star: "Television Kitchen," '46–'69, and "Television Matinee," '47–'49, WRCT-TV, WFIL-TV; Home Econs. In Bus. (Pres.), AWRT (aws. '58, '59), Electrical Wms. Round Table; PUAA aws., '55, '56, '61; TV Digest aw., '52; WRCV-TV aws., '49–'65; Temple Univ., BS (Educ.), '32; b. Bristol, Pa.; p. Joseph and Gertrude Bannister Peirce; h. Harry Hanford; res: Floharra Farm, Gradyville, Pa. 19039.

HANIFORD, BEATRICE GOLDBERG, TV Dir., Ellis Advertising Company, Suite 1736, Statler Hilton, Buffalo, N.Y. 14202, '56–; Radio Dir., '55–'56; Radio Dir., WEBR, '35–'40; Colmst., Overture Magazine, Auth., children's plays, incl. Alice In Chanukaland, The Formula; Adv. Wm. of Buffalo; Univ. of Buffalo; b. Buffalo, N.Y.; p. Jacob and Nellie Lewis Goldberg; h. Dr. Sidney Haniford; c. David, Linda; res: 110 Devonshire Rd., Buffalo, N.Y. 14223.

HANLEY, MARY DUKE, Head, Biomedical Library Catalog Dept. University of Minnesota, 160 Wilson Library, Mpls., Minn. 55455, '66–; Instr., Librn., '65–'66; Librn., '63–'65; Univ. of Ill. Lib., '59–'63; Info. Specialist, '61–'63; Special Libs. Assn. (Minn. Chptr. VP, Pres.); Phi Kappa Alpha; Beta Phi Mu; Kalamazoo Col., AB, '44; Univ. of Ill., MS (Lib. Sci.), '62; b. Henry, Ill., 1922; p. Clarence and Margaret Jones Duke; h. John T. Hanley; c. Judith, Joan, John, Barbara, Michael; res: 5705 Lawndale Lane, Hamel, Minn. 55340.

HANNA, EDNA KATHRYN, Prom. Mgr., KCTS-TV, University of Washington, Seattle, Wash. 98105, '67–; Radio-TV Copy Dir., Noel Schram & Assoc., '63–'64; Pubcty. Dir., KGUN-TV (Tucson, Ariz.), '62–'63; Sls. Prom. Mgr., KOMO Radio-TV, '58–'62; Radio-TV Dir., Gtr. Seattle, Inc., '57–'58; Prom. Dir., Ch. 13 TV, '54–'56; Radio-TV Copywtr., Dancer-Fitzgerald-Sample and Doherty, Clifford, Steers & Shenfield (N.Y.C.), '51–'54; Dir. of Wms. Programs, WLAN Radio (Lancaster, Pa.), '46–'51; Ed., Radio Wtrs. Lab., '39–'45; AWRT (Wash. Chptr. VP, '62–), Wash. State Press Wm., NATAS, Western Radio and TV Assn., Northwest Adult Educ. Assn., b. Lancaster County, Pa., 1922; p. J. Glenn and Majorie Harvey Hanna; res: 4018 Greenwood N., Seattle, Wash. 98103.

HANNA, LANDY, Actress; former Anncr., Voice of Am., Radio Free Europe, (three yrs.); performed in 14 motion pics., 34 TV shows; b. Budapest, Hungary; res: 939-1/2 N. Sierra Bonita, Hollywood, Cal. 90046.

HANNA, LAVONE A., Prof. Emeritus, San Francisco State College, 1600 Holloway Ave., S.F., Cal. 94132; Prof. of Educ., '47–'61; Dir. of Curriculum, Long Beach Public Schs., '44–'47; Rsch. Assoc., Asst. Prof., Stanford Univ., '39–'44; Auth., "Challenges for a Free People" ('64); Co-auth, two educ. textbks.; Nat. Cncl. for the Social Studies; Assn. for Supervision and Curriculum Dev. (Bd. of Dirs., '47–'60); Cal. Assn. for Supervision and Curriculum Dev. (Bd. of Dirs.; Exec. Comm.; Pres., '50); Pi Lambda Theta, Delta Kappa Gamma; Univ. of Wis., AB, 1919 (Phi Beta Kappa); Univ. of Chgo., MA, '27; Stanford Univ., EdD, '43; Lindenwood Col., LittD, '53; res: 15 Bereuda Way, Menlo Park, Cal. 94025.

HANNA, MARY ANN JONES, Head Sch. Lib. Cnslt., Michigan Department of Education, Bureau of Library Services, 735 Michigan Ave., Lansing, Mich. 48913, '66–; Sch. Lib. Cnslt., Mich. State Lib., '60–'66; Librn., Asst. Librn., '44–'60; Eng. Tchr., Deshler (Oh.) HS, '42–'43; ALA, Mich. Lib. Assn., Mich. Assn. of Sch.

Librns., Mich. Audiovisual Assn., Mich. Assn. For Supervision and Curriculum Dev., Ala, Lib. Assn. (Treas., '56; Secy., '57), Kappa Alpha Theta; DePauw Univ., AB, '42; Univ. of Ill., BS (Lib. Sci.), '44; Western Mich. Univ., MLS, '69; b. Greencastle, Ind., 1920; p. Benjamin and Bernice Allen Jones; h. Albert K. Hanna; c. Susanne, Donovan; res: 323 N. Walnut, Lansing, Mich. 48933.

HANNIGAN, MARTHA MATTINGLEY, Assoc. Ed., Test Engineering and Management, The Mattingley Publishing Co., Inc., 61 Monmouth Rd., Oakhurst, N.J. 07755, '69–; Asst. Ed., '67–'68; Edtl. Asst., '66–'67; Buyers Guide Ed., '67–; Phila. Museum of Art, '62–'64; b. Long Branch, N.J., 1944; p. Ray and Betty Bender Mattingley; h. J. Tyler Hannigan; res: R.D. #1, Box 407, 407 Baileys Corner Rd., Belmar, N.J. 07719.

HANNON, MARY GRACE, VP and Dir. of Rsch., La Roche, McCaffrey & McCall Inc., 575 Lexington Ave., N.Y., N.Y. 10017, '69–; Co.-Dir., '67–'69; Assoc. Dir. of Rsch., '64–'67; Sr. Rsch. Supvsr., Benton & Bowles, '61–'64; Assoc. Rsch. Dir., Sounding Bd. Rsch., '59–'61; Rsch. Asst. Dir., Food Manufacturers', '57–'59; Seminar Lectr., Am. Mgt. Assn.; ARF, Am. Statistical Soc.; Rutgers Univ., BS, '57 (magna cum laude); MBA, '59; b. Scranton, Pa.; p. William and Evelyn Walsh Hannon; res: 26 Perry St., Belleville, N.J. 07109.

HANRAHAN, JACQUELINE HAYES, Edtl. Asst., Adv. Prod. Mgr., Dana Chase Publications, Inc., York at Park Ave., Elmhurst, Ill. 60126, '67–; Edtl. Asst., '65–'67; b. Hampton, Ill., 1941; p. J. S. and Ina Johnson Hayes; h. Edward Hanrahan; c. Edward, Susan, Jefferson.

HANRAHAN, LOIS SIMMONS, Media Supvsr., Dancer-Fitzgerald-Sample, 222 Columbus Ave., S.F., Cal. 94133, '68–; Media Byr., Kenyon & Eckhardt, '67–'68; Net. Byr., BBDO, '66–'67; Asst. to Prodrs., D'Antoni-Baer, '65–'66; Dir. Sales Svc., Mutual Bdcst., '61–'65; MGR Contracts, ABC Radio, '60–'61; Supvr. Special Svcs., CBS TV, '56–'60; Hunter Col.; b. Caguas, P.R., 1931; p. Raymond and Amparo Simmons; h. Robert Hanrahan; c. Jayne; res: 1037 Union, S.F., Cal. 94133.

HANSBROUGH, VIVIAN MAYO, Wtr.; Auth: "History of Greene County, Arkansas" ('46), numerous poems, mag., nwsp. articles; Librn., Jefferson Jr. HS, '61–; Home Ed., Missouri Farmer, '57–'63; Jnlsm. Instr., Stephens Col., '54–'57; Tchr., Ark. HS, '33–'53; Mo. Press Wm. (Pres., '61–'63; Treas., '59–'61); Mo. Wtrs. Guild (Second VP, '68–'69; Secy., '67), NLAPW, Poets' Roundtable of Ark., Ark. Auths., Composers and Artists' Soc., Delta Kappa Gamma, Theta Sigma Phi, Kappa Alpha Mu, Kappa Tau Alpha; Jonesboro Col., '25–'27; Union Univ., BA, '27–'29; Univ. of Chgo., MA, '32–'33; Univ. of Mo., '53–'54; b. Rinard, Ill., 1908; p. Lewis and Elsie Golden Mayo; h. Lewis D. Hansbrough; c. David, Nina (Mrs. James R. McCosh); res: 1840 Cliff Dr., Columbia, Mo. 65201.

HANSEN, CAROL LYNN, Consumer Educ. Dir., S. C. Johnson & Son, Inc., 1525 Howe St., Racine, Wis. 53403, '68–; Asst. Consumer Educ. Dir., '63–'68; Asst. Dir., Dairy Cncl. of Milw., '62–'63; Home Svc. Rep., Wis. Electric Power Co., '60–'62; AWRT (Badger, Wis. Chptr. Pres., '69–'70; Secy.), Home Econsts. in Bus. (Chmn., '68–'69), Am. Home Econs. Assn., Wis. Home Econs. Assn., Electrical Wms. Round Table, Racine Safety Cncl., Wis. Safety Cncl., Nat. Safety Cncl.; Univ. of Wis., BS (Home Econ. Educ.), '60; b. Milw., Wis., 1938; p. Victor and Liane Johannsen Hansen; res: 4046 N. Main St., Apt. B-4; Racine, Wis., 53402.

HANSEN, CHARLOTTE HELGESON, Food Ed., Jamestown Sun, 122 N.W. Second St., Jamestown, N.D. 58401, '49–; Instr., Microbiology, Jamestown Col., '51–'61; Med. Technologist (Wash., D.C.), '47; Serologist, Tex. State Dept. of Health (Wichita Falls), '46; Med. Technologist, Hanford Engine Works (Richland, Wash.), '45; Auth., cookbk., lab. manual; Alpha Delta Tau, ZONTA, Un. Fund (Pres., '67, Bd. of Dirs., '66–'68); Who's Who of Am. Wm.; Univ. of Minn., BS, '44; b. Jamestown, N.D., 1922; p. Louis Helgeson and Ida Clough Helgeson MacDavid; h. Gordon Hansen; c. Jo-Ida Charlotte; res: 309 11th Ave., N.E., Jamestown, N.D. 58401.

HANSEN, KATHRYN GERTRUDE, Ed., College and University Personnel Association, 1205 W. California St., Urbana, Ill. 61801, '55–; Ed., Civil Service Handbook, '62–; NFPW, Colo. Press Wm., Am. Mgt. Assn., NLAPW (Champaign-Urbana Br. Pres., '60–'61, Second VP, '58–'60, Secy., '57–'58), Delta Kappa Gamma (State Pres., '61–'63, Second VP, '59–'61, '57–'59, Secy., '55–'57; Xi Chptr. Pres., '54–'56), AAUW (State First VP, '58–'60), BPW (Champaign-Urbana Club Past Pres., Secy.), numerous other orgs.; Who's Who in Chgo. and Ill., Who's Who in the Middle West, Who's Who of Am. Wm., Who's Who in Am. Educ., Dic. of Intl. Biog., Royal Blue Bk.; Univ. of Ill., BS, '34 (cum laude); MS (Educ.), '36; b. Gardner, Ill., 1912; p. Harry and Marguerite Gaston Hansen; res: 310 W. Charles St., Champaign, Ill. 61820.

HANSL, EVA vom BAUR, Former Wms. Pg. Ed., New York Evening Sun, Parents Magazine; Former Staff Mbr., New York Herald Tribune, New York Sun, New York Times; Auth: "Artists in Music Today," "Minute Sketches of Great Composers," "Trends in Part-time Work for College Trained Women;" Lectr., N.Y.U., Columbia Univ.; Supvsr., three network radio series: "Women in the Making of America," "Gallant American Women," '39–'40, NBC in cooperation with U.S. office of Education, and "Womanpower," '43–'44, CBS in cooperation with War Manpower Commission; reported progress of early feminist movement (1911–1916) for the N.Y. Tribune and Sun; AAUW, BPW; Barnard Col., AB, '09; b. N.Y.C., 1889; p. Carl Max and Elise Urchs vom Baur; h. Raleigh Hansl (dec.); c. Barbara (Mrs. John Van Beschoten Griggs), Raleigh Jr.; res: 240 E. 23rd St., N.Y., N.Y. 10010.

HANSON, BARBARA GAILLARD, Adv. and Sls. Prom. Mgr., Thomas Publishing Co., 461 Eighth Ave., N.Y., N.Y. 10001, '64–; Asst. to Publr., Indsl. Equipment News, '55–'63; Intl. Docs. Svc., Columbia Univ. Press; Assn. of Indsl. Advs., Adv. Club of N.Y.; Columbia Univ.; N.Y. Sch. of Printing; b. Teaneck, N.J., 1929; p. Henry and Marie Hiltenbrand Gaillard; res: 444 E. 84th St., N.Y., N.Y. 10028.

HANSON, BETTE LEE (Bette Lee), Dir. of Wms. Programs, WAPI Radio and TV, Newhouse Broadcasting, Red Mountain, Birmingham, Ala., 35205, '57–; Singer, Violist, Birmingham Symphony, '53–'57; Lectr. on state subjects, Ala. area; aws. for excellence in jnlsm: five AP, two UP, five Adv. Club for TV; one of 12 outstanding Birmingham wm.; Univ. of Ia., B Music, '48; Music Acad. of the West, Santa Berbara, grad. study, '53; Madame Lotte Lehmann, Cal. Tech., grad. study (voice), '52; b. Superior, Wis.; p. Reuben and Dena Knudson Johnson; h. Roger Hanson; c. Heidi Ann, Eric Richard; res: 1734 Woodbine Dr., Birmingham, Ala. 35216.

HANSON, MINNIE HARRIS, PR Dir., Museum of History, Seattle Historical Society, 2161 E. Hamlin St., Seattle, Wash. 98102, '65–; PR, Univ. of Wash., '48–'64; PR, Seattle YWCA, '47–'48; PR, Seattle Hist. Soc., '46–'56; Pubcty., Blood Bank, Minneapolis, '39–'40; Pubcty., Greenwich Settlement House, N.Y., '28; N.Y. Am. and Shopping Colm., '24–'25; Soc. Ed., Seattle Post Intelligencer, '22–'24; Auth., "The Women Build A Museum" ('52); pubns. for Minneapolis Blood Bank; Theta Sigma Phi; Univ. of Wash. BA, '22; b. Seattle, Wash., 1900; p. Otto John and Mary Dinesen Nelson; h. Henry E. Hanson; c. Robin Jean Harris (Mrs. Robert Simpson), Linda Mary Harris (Mrs. George Lamb); res: 3109 E. Laurelhurst Dr., N.E., Seattle, Wash. 98105.

HAPPEL, MARGARET MOUNSEY, Food Ed., Ladies' Home Journal, 641 Lexington Ave., N.Y., N.Y. 10022, '69–; Assoc. Food Ed., '65–'69; Sr. Home Econst., U.S. Testing, '64–'65; Asst. Food Ed., McCall's, '61–'63; Assoc. Head, Home Econs. Dept., Sheldon Heath Sch., Birmingham, Eng., '57–'61; British Home Econs. Assn.; Univ. of Bristol, Gloucester Col. of Home Econs., Grad. with Hons., '57; Univ. of Birmingham, Col. of Food and Fine Arts, '59–'61; b. Derby, England, 1936; p. Eric and Kathleen Viccars Mounsey; h. J. Peter Happel; c. Adrian; res: 86 Huron Rd., Bellerose Village, N.Y., N.Y. 11426.

HAPPER, ANNE ELIZABETH, Wms. Ed., The Elkhart Truth, P.O. Box 487, Elkhart, Ind. 46514, '66–; Wms. Dept. Reptr., '60–'66; Elkhart Civic Theatre; Ind. Univ., '51–'52; Goshen Col., '53–'54; b. Elkhart, Ind., 1933; p. Thomas and Marian Schutt Happer; res: 419-1/2 S. Fourth St., Elkhart, Ind. 46514.

HARBAGE, MARY, Prof. of Educ., Wright State Univ., Colonel Glenn Highway, Dayton, Oh. 45431, '67–; univ. teaching: Miami (Oh. and Fla.), N.Y.U.,

Kent State, Univ. of Va., others; Ed., Wtr., Rsch. Dir.; Chmn., Elementary Educ., Univ. of Ark.; Dir., Lang. Arts, public schs. (Brookline, Mass.); Assn. for Childhood Educ. Intl., Nat. Cncl. Tchrs. of Eng.; Kappa Delta Pi, Pi Lamba Theta, Pi Alpha Theta, Delta Kappa Gamma; other orgs.; Oh. State Univ., AB (hons., Phi Beta Kappa); MA (Elementary Educ.); Ed. D. Tchrs. Col., Columbia Univ. (Curriculum, Teaching); b. Madison County, Oh.; p. Arnett and Helen Postle Harbage; res: 4808 Sunray Rd., Kettering, Oh. 45429.

HARBESON, GEORGIANA BROWN, Free-lance Designer, Own Studio, 41 Ferry St., New Hope, Pa. 18938; Auth., "American Needlework" (Coward McCann, '38; third printing, '67); needlepoint designs, Trinity Cathedral (Trenton, N.J.) and Chapel, Nat. Cathedral (Wash., D.C.); staff, design, Provincetown Players; staged plays & ballets des costumes, John Murray Anderson, Paramount Ballets, others; Magazine Designer, crewel embroideries, House Beautiful, Am. Home Magazine, others; Lectr., Am. Needlework; Tchr. (N.Y.); Dir., exhbns.; solo exhbns.; Nat. Soc. Wm. Artists (N.Y., Past Pres.), Embroiders Guild (America Branch, N.Y. Bd.), Intl. Platform Assn., N.Y. Soc. Artist Craftsmen, Pen & Brush Club, WNPC (N.Y.); active in art, Designing Needlepoint & Crewel Emb. & Lecturing & Teaching & American Arts, hist. groups; Authority, embroideries, Met. Museum of Art, Cooper Un. collections; numerous aws., nat. exhibits; Thouron prizes, composition, Acad. of Fine Arts (Phila.); Honorarium, Hall of Fame, '66; 2,000 Wm. of Achiev.; Moore Col. (Design), '28; studied design Lucien Bernard, '30; Grand Central Sch. of Art (Textile Design); Phoenix Sch. N.Y. Design, '32; b. New Haven, Conn., 1894; p. Charles F. and Caroline W. King Brown; h. John Harbeson (div.), Frank Godwin (dec.); c. son Paul Cret Harbeson; res: Box 6, New Hope, Pa. 18938.

HARDEE, MARTHA HOELL, Ed., Federal Observer, Federal Reserve Bank of Richmond, 8th and Franklin Sts., Richmond, Va. 23213, '67–; Assoc. Bus. Eds. of Va., ICIE; St. Mary's Jr. Col., '65, Univ. of N.C., AB, '67; Va. Commonwealth Univ., '67–'69; b. Graham, N.C. 1945; p. Artis and Martha Hoell Hardee; res: 2126 E. Tremont Ct., Richmond, Va. 23225.

HARDIN, E. ELIZABETH, Prod. Mgr., Editor and Printer Publishing Co., Inc., 470 Atlantic Ave., Boston, Mass. 02210, '63–; Salem State Tchrs. Col.

HARDY, HAZEL NETTLESHIP, Staff Wtr., Broadcasting Magazine, 444 Madison Ave., N.Y., N.Y. 10022, '68–; Edtl. Asst., '67–'68; Direct Mail Asst., Scholastic Mags., '67; Theta Sigma Phi, William Smith Alumnae Assn. (N.Y. Chaptr. Pres., '69–'71); William Smith Col., BA, '65; Univ. of Mo., MA, '67; b. Warsaw, N.Y., 1944; p. Charles and Marion Templin Nettleship; h. Joseph Hardy; res: 615 E. 14th St., N.Y., N.Y. 10009.

HARDY, MARGARET, Prod./Classified Mgr., ANNY Publications, Inc., 12 E. 46th St., N.Y., N.Y. 10017, '69–;

Peat, Warwick, Livingston, '67–'69; Brigham Young Univ., '66; res: 470 W. 24th St., N.Y., N.Y. 10017.

HARFORD, MARGARET, Staff Wtr., Theater Critic, Los Angeles Times, Times Mirror Sq., L.A., Cal. 90053, '62; Music, Theater Critic, L.A. Mirror-News, '55–'62; Music Critic, Hollywood Citizen News, '45–'55; Theta Sigma Phi; Univ. of Cal. Berkeley, '42; b. L.A., Cal.; p. Henry and Margaret Leu Harford; res: 2851 N. Beachwood Dr., L.A., Cal. 90028.

HARGRAVE, VICTORIA ELIZABETH, Head Librn., MacMurray College, Jacksonville, Ill. 62650, '47–; Head Librn., Ripon (Wis.) Col., '44–'46; Ext. Librn., Ia. State Col., '38–'44; Tchr., Brandon (Wis.) HS, '34–'37; ALA, Assn. of Col. and Rsch. Libs., Assn. for Higher Educ., Ill. Lib. Assn.; Who's Who in Am.; Who's Who of Am. Wm.; Who's Who in the Midwest; Ripon Col., AB, '34 (magna cum laude); Univ. of Wis. Lib. Sch., '38; Univ. of Chgo., AM, '47; b. Ripon, Wis.; p. Alexander and Estelle Swanson Hargrave; res: 1017 W. College Ave., Jacksonville, Ill. 62650.

HARGREAVES, MARY MASSEY, Assoc. Prof. of Hist., University of Kentucky, Lexington, Ky. 40506, '69–; Asst. Prof. of Hist., '64–'69; Assoc. Ed., "The Papers of Henry Clay" (Univ. of Ky. Press, '57, '59, '61; three vols. to date), '52–; Rsch. Ed., Harvard Bus. Sch., '37–'39; Auth., "Dry Farming in the Northern Great Plains" (Harvard Univ. Press, '57); articles, revs.; Am. Hist. Assn., Org. of Am. Histrns., Southern Hist. Assn., Agricultural Hist. Soc. (Exec. Cncl., '69–'70), Phi Alpha Theta, Phi Beta Kappa (Chptr. Secy., '64–), AAUP; Bucknell Univ., AB, '35 (summa cum laude); Radcliffe Col., MA, '36; PhD, '51; The Brookings Inst., '39–'40 (Fellow); b. Erie, Pa., 1914; p. Albert E. and Bess Childs Massey; h. Herbert W. Hargreaves; res: 237 Cassidy Ave., Lexington, Ky. 40502.

HARKNESS, GEORGIA ELMA, Prof. Emeritus of Applied Theology, Pacific School of Religion, 1798 Scenic Ave., Berkeley, Cal. 94707, '61–; Prof., Applied Theology, '50–'61; Garrett Theological Seminary, '40–'50; Mount Holyoke Col., '37–'39; Elmira Col., '22–'37; Auth: "Disciplines of the Christian Life" ('67), "A Devotional Treasury from the Early Church" ('68), "Stability Amid Change" ('69), 29 other bks. in the field of religion; Co-winner of Abingdon-Cokesbury aw. for bk. manuscript, "Prayer and the Common Life," '47; Religious Heritage of Am. aw. for Churchwm. of the Yr., '58; Hon. DLitt: Boston Univ., '38; MacMurray Col., '43; Elmira Col., '62; Hon. DD: Wilson Col., '43; Pacific Sch. of Religion, '61; Hon. LLD: Mills Col., '58; educ: Cornell Univ., AB, '12 (Phi Beta Kappa); Boston Univ., MA and MRE, '20; PhD, '23; Yale Univ. Divinity Sch., '28–'29; Union Theological Seminary, '36–'37; b. Harkness, N.Y.; p. J. Warren and Lillie Merrill Harkness; res: 1377 Via Zurita, Claremont, Cal. 91711.

HARKNESS, MARY LOU BARKER, Dir. of Libs.,

University of South Florida, Tampa, Fla. 33620, '68–; Acting Dir., '67–'68; Catalog Librn., '58–'67; Catalog Librn., Ga. Inst. of Tech., '52–'57; Asst. Catalog Librn., Cal. State Polytechnic Col., '50–'52; Jr. Catalog Librn., Law Lib., Univ. of Mich., '48–'50; Cnslt. for Cataloging, Nat. Lib. of Nigeria, '62–'63; ALA (Life Mbr.), Southeastern Lib. Assn., Fla. Lib. Assn.; AAUW; Neb. Wesleyan Univ., BA, '47; Univ. of Mich., BA (Lib. Sci.), '48; Columbia Univ., MS (Lib. Sci.), '58; b. Denby, S.D., 1925; p. Raleigh and Mary Boyd Barker; h. Donald Harkness; res: 2338 Lake Dr., Tampa, Fla. 33612.

HARLAMERT, RUTH EVELYN, Med. Librn., King County Medical Society, 105 Cobb Med. Ctr., Seattle, Wash. 98101, '52–; Librn., '37–'51; Asst. Librn., Tulane Univ. Sch. of Med., '51–'52; Cataloger, Univ. of Neb. Sch. of Med., '30–'37; Med. Lib. Assn. (Bd. of Dir., '66–'68); Spec. Libs. Assn.; Univ. of Neb., BA, '29, Univ. of Wash., BA (Librnship), '48; res: 1000 Eighth Ave., Seattle, Wash. 98104.

HARLAN, IRMA RUTH, Dir., Blue Grass Regional Library, 104 W. Fifth St., Columbia, Tenn. 38401, '64–; Librn., '55–'64; Tchr., '53–'55; ALA, AAUW, Tenn. Lib. Assn., Southeastern Lib. Assn.; Middle Tenn. State Col., BS, '53; George Peabody Col., MA, '62; b. Columbia, Tenn., 1931; p. J. C. and Ducie Mayfield Harlan; res: Trotwood, Apt. 25, Columbia, Tenn. 38401.

HARLOW, JEANERETTE STIETENROTH, News Ed., Natchez Democrat, Natchez Democrat Printing & Publishing Co., 501 N. Canal, Natchez, Miss. 39120, '69–; City Ed., '57–'69; Mng. Ed., Natchez Times, '51–'57; Co-auth., with J. Wesley Cooper, "A Treasure of Louisiana Plantation Homes"; NFPW (Nat. First Pl. Aw., Edtl., Special Edition, '57; Nat. First Pl. Aw., '58), Miss. Press Wm.; First Pl. Miss. Aw., '67; b. Davenport, Ia., 1905; p. John C. and Jennie Stietenroth Harlow; h. Sam J. Eidt (div.); c. Charles Stietenroth Eidt; res: 212 Wensel Ave., Natchez, Miss. 39120.

HARMAN, HELEN BETTY, Ed., Argonne News, Argonne National Laboratory, 9700 S. Cass Ave., Argonne, Ill. 60439, '54–; Theatre of Western Springs (Secy.); Univ. of Ill., Northwestern Univ., Univ. of Chgo.; b. Chgo., Ill., 1910; h. Harry J. Harman (div.); c. Barbara (Mrs. Albert Garvey), Katharine (Mrs. Thomas Pitzer); res: 407 Homestead Rd., La Grange Park, Ill. 60525.

HARMAN, JEANNE PERKINS, Auth: "The Love Junk" (Meredith Press, '51), "Such is Life" (Crowell, '56; Lit. Guild Outstanding selection), "Virgins: Magic Islands" ('62); numerous mag. articles; Co-auth: "Fielding's Guide to the Caribbean and the Bahamas"; Founder-Publr.-Ed., "Here's How: Your Guide to St. Thomas," '57–'68; Prof. of Jnlsm., Univ. of Miami, '53–'54; Corr., Time, Life, Sports Illustrated, '49–; OPC, Intl. Platform Assn., Soc. of Am. Travel Wtrs.; Col. La Perouse (Noumea, New Caledonia), '33; Smith Col., BA '39 (magna cum laude; Phi Beta Kappa); b. Baxter Springs, Kan., 1919; p. Enoch and

Maude Himes Perkins; h. Harry E. Harman, III; c. Jeanne Anne; res: 24–25 King St., St. Thomas, Virgin Islands 00801.

HARMAN, MILDRED BARKER, Legislative Rep., National Woman's Christian Temperance Union, Suite 640 Warner Bldg., 13th and E Sts. N.W., Wash., D.C. 20004, '62–; Wtr., "The Washington Letter," Un. Signal; Reptr., Feature Wtr., daily, weekly nwsps. (W.Va., Md.); rsch., Am. Bus. Men's Rsch. Fndn. (Chgo., Ill.); NLAPW (Ed., The Pen Wm., four yrs.; Chevy Chase Br.), AAUW (Kensington Br. Pres.), BPW, Intl. Platform Assn., WPA, RPRC; Wms. Federated Club of Kensington; Edgar Allen Poe Lit. aw.; Cert. of Merit, State Mother of Yr. aw.; Cit., Am. Legion; W.Va. Univ., AB, '21; Univ. of Md., '43; b. Morgantown, W.Va., 1900; p. William L. and Evalena Brookover Barker; h. Charles N. Harman; c. Alice E., Dr. Charles M.; res: 3908 Baltimore St., Kensington, Md. 20795.

HARMAN, VIRGINIA OWENS, Asst. Prof., Lib. Sci., George Peabody College, Nashville, Tenn. 37203, '68–; Sch. Librn. (Kingsport), '48–'68; Instr., E. Tenn. State Univ., Univ. of Chattanooga; Kingsport Educ. Assn. (Pres., '60), E. Tenn. Lib. Assn. (Chmn., '62), Tenn. Lib. Assn. (Secy., '68), WNBA; Univ. of N.C., BA (Lib. Sci.), '38; Geo. Peabody Col., MA (Lib. Sci.), '53; b. Cinn., Oh.; p. Alfred and May Easton Owens; h. Harrison Harman; c. Joseph H., Betty; res: 112 Haverford Dr., Nashville, Tenn. 37205.

HARMER, RUTH MULVEY, Assoc. Prof., California State Polytechnic College, Pomona, Cal. 91766, '60–; Instr., Lectr., Univ. of Southern Cal., '54–'60; Lectr., U.C.L.A., '52–'58; Reptr., Ed., '42–'51; Free-lance Wtr., mag. articles, '46–; Auth., "High Cost of Dying" (Collier-Macmillan, '63), 'Good Food from Mexico" (Barrows, '51); Am. Fedn. of Tchrs. (Local VP, '66–'67), Nat. Cncl. of Tchrs. of Eng., WNPC, L.A. Press Club, Mexico City Press Club; Barnard Col., AB, '41 (cum laude); Columbia Univ., MA, '42; b. N.Y.C., 1919; p. Charles and Mary Gierloff Mulvey; h. Lowell Harmer; c. Felicia; res: 437 Crane Blvd., L.A., Cal. 90065.

HARNETT, LILA MOGAN, Synd. Colmst., "Week End in New York," '67–; Free-lance Wtr., '63–'67; Ed., Publr., Business Atomics Report, '54–'63; OPC, Met. Opera Guild, N.Y.C. Opera Guild; Bklyn. Col., BA, '46; New Sch. for Social Rsch.; b. N.Y.C., 1926; p. Milton and Claire Merahn Mogan; h. Joel William Harnett; res: 2 Sutton Pl. S., N.Y., N.Y. 10022.

HAROLD, MARGARET PARKER, VP, Allied Publications, Inc., 2900 N.E. 12th Ter., Ft. Lauderdale, Fla. 33304, '50–; Auth., "Daddy Is A Doctor"; Compiler, bk. series on prize-winning printings, water-colors, graphics, sculpture; Univ. of Chattanooga, MA, '50; h. Gilbert Harold; res: 2888 N.E. 24th Pl., Ft. Lauderdale, Fla. 33304.

HARPER, ELY CAROL, Auth., poetry, fiction; Ed., Experiment Magazine, Ed.-Publr., Experiment Press, 6565 N.E. Windermere Rd., Seattle, Wash. 98105, '58–; numerous edtl. positions, '44–'58; Founder, Experiment Theatre, Press, '57; Portland Oregonian, '36–'38; Arena, Intl. Platform Assn., Marquis Biographical Lib. Soc., Centro Studi e Scambi Internazionali, Intl. Aril Soc.; Univ. of Wash., BA, '52; MA (Drama), '59; b. Monroe City, Mo.; p. Aurelius and Annie Adkisson Ely; h. Maurice W. Harper; c. Carol-Maura (Mrs. Charles A. Kiselyak II), Maurice Ely.

HARPER, FAY ROGERS, Ed., Advance Glance; Exec. Secy. to Bd. Chmn., Pres., Advance Transformer Co., 2950 N. Western Ave., Chgo., Ill. 60618, '57–; h. Paul Harper.

HARPER, JOY, Media Dir., Doyle Dane Bernbach Inc., 6399 Wilshire Blvd., L.A., Cal. 90048, '65–; Media Byr., '61–'65; Media Byr., Donahue & Coe, '58–'60; Asst. AE, Erwin Wasey, '56–'57; Asst. to Adv. Mgr., Cue mag. (N.Y.C.), '53–'55; E. Tex. Univ., BA, '45; Cooper Un., '53–'55; b. Wortham, Tex., 1925; p. Robert and Prudence Riley Harper; res: 10370 Rossbury Pl., L.A., Cal. 90064.

HARRAGAN, BETTY LEHAN, Sr. Publicist, J. Walter Thompson Company, 420 Lexington Ave., N.Y., N.Y. 10017, '63–; VP, Ruth Lundgren Co., '57–'63; Wms. Ed., Co. Pubns., N.Y. Telephone Co., '50–'57; AWRT, Marquette Univ., AB (Jnlsm.), '48; Columbia Univ., AM (Am. Literature, Hist.), '50; b. Milw., Wis., 1926; p. Charles and Marie Caswell Lehan; h. David J. Harragan (dec.); c. Kathleen Ann; res: 541 E. 20th St., N.Y., N.Y. 10010.

HARRELL, KAY SUBLETT, Reptr., UPI (Austin, Tex.), '59; Cont. Wtr., KTBC-TV, '58; Cont. Wtr., KCMO-AM, FM and TV (Kan. City, Mo.), '57, '58; Univ. of Mo., BJ, '56; b. Kan. City, Mo., 1934; p. Gilson and Audrey Nixon Sublett; h. Harold Harrell; c. Terry L., Robert G.; res: 4200 Deckard Dr., Bloomington, Ind. 47401.

HARRELL, LAURA D.S., Rsch., Edtl. Asst., Mississippi Department of Archives and History, P.O. Box 571, Jackson, Miss. 39205, '61–; '49–'50; '41–'47; Pubns. Wtr., Med. Scis., Communicable Disease Ctr. (Atlanta, Ga.), '59–'60; Pubns. Wtr., Med. Scis., Army Med. Svc. Sch., (Ft. Sam Houston, Tex.), '52–'58; Asst. Ed., Jnl. of Miss. Hist., '63–; Co-Ed., "Comparative Medicine in Transition" (Ann Arbor, '60); NLAPW, Miss. Hist. Soc., Am. Med. Wtrs. Assn., Miss. Genealogical Soc., Med. Lib. Assn., Soc. of Am. Archivists; Who's Who of Am. Wm.; Who's Who in the South and Southwest; Dir. of Am. Scholars, '69; Gautier Hist. Article Aw., '67; Old Spanish Fort Poetry Aw., '68, '69; Millsaps Col., BA, '34 (magna cum laude); b. Port Gibson, Miss., 1913; p. Milling and Laura Drake Satterfield; h. William Osborne Harrell (dec.); res: 820 Arlington St., Jackson, Miss. 39202.

HARRELL, LAURA FOSTER, News Ed., Parker Brothers, Inc., Ahoskie, N.C. 27910, '57–; staff, '51–'57; N.C. Press Assn. aws., '53, '54, '58, '60, '62, '65–'68; N.C. Educ. Assn. aw., '62; Outstanding Young Wm. of Am.; Bertie County Dev. Assn. aw., '65; E. Carolina Univ.; b. Windsor, N.C., 1932; p. Henry and Genevieve Morris Harrell; res: 205 N. King St., Windsor, N.C. 27983.

HARRIETT, Auth., juv. bks: "First Lady of India" (Doubleday, '69), Auth.-Illus. "Froggie Went a Courtin' " (Harvey House, '67), and childrens bks; many articles; Med. Ed.-Wtr., Macfadden-Bartell Corp., '63–; Writing Instr., Famous Schs., '66–'67; Illus.-Bk. Designer, Harvey House, '65–'66; Asst. Ed., Grolier, '62–'63; Asst. to Art Dir., Grosset and Dunlap, '59–'62; Greeting Card Wtr. and Designer; Tchr., elementary, HS, and Lang. Sch., '41–'66; Actress, theatre, TV, film and radio; various orgs. and aws.; Western Ill. Univ. (Jnlsm., Art, Commerce); Knox Col. (Bible); N.Y.U. (Radio-TV); drama and art schs.; b. Lewistown, Ill.; p. George and Sylvia Black Wilcoxen; h. (div.); c. Brett G. (Mrs. Richard J. Bell); res: 135 East 54 Street, New York, New York 10022.

HARRIMAN, JOAN FRYE, Cnslt., Joan Frye Harriman, 1 Sherwood Terr., Yonkers, N.Y. 10704; consumer educ. for home econs. products; dev. sewing courses; Consumer Cnslt., dept. stores, Dir. of Field Activities, Coats & Clark Inc. (N.Y.C.), '36–'63; David Hale Fanning Vocational Sch. (Worcester, Mass.), '35–'36; dept. store PR; Originator, Clothing Aw. Program, Nat. 4-H Clubs; Judge, nat. sewing contests, Nat. Grange, Wool Cncl.; Judge Bankers' Trust Doll Contest; AWNY (Dir., '55), Am. Home Econs. Assn., Canadian Home Econs. Assn. (Life Mbr.), Camp Fire Girls; aws: for originating ideas in demonstrations, home econs., use of products, U.S. Dept. of Agriculture, Commonwealth of Mass., N.Y. State; Pratt Inst., '30; Mass. State Tchrs. Col., '35; h. Roger L. Harriman.

HARRINGTON, DENYSE KATHERINE, Mgr., WCBS-TV Traffic, Columbia Broadcasting System, 51 W. 52nd St., N.Y., N.Y. 10019, '68–; Asst. Mgr., '68; Adm. Asst. '67; Asst. Mgr., Opns., '66; Adm. Asst., '64–'66; Stephens Col., AA, '59; Northwestern Univ., '59–'60; b. Chgo., Ill., 1939; p. J. Earl and Katherine Sweeney Harrington; res: 32-05 Newtown Ave., Astoria, N.Y. 11102.

HARRINGTON, GERRY, Partner, Don Harrington Associates, 10 E. 49th St., N.Y., N.Y.; Free-lance Wtr., PR assigts.; Info. Specialist, Inter-Am. Affairs, U.S. Govt. (Wash., D.C.); Study Dir., Ted Bates; Wtr., Analysts, Bur. of Applied Social Rsch., Columbia Univ.; Copywtr., Grey Advertising, Doherty, Clifford & Shenfield; Smith Col., BA; h. Don Harrington; c. Peter T., John Jeffrey; res: Merwin Lane, Wilton, Conn. 06897.

HARRINGTON, KATHERINE SPOORE, Wms. Ed., Knickerbocker News, 24 Sheridan Ave., Albany, N.Y.

12201, '55–; Gen. Reptr. '43–'55; N.Y. State Wms. Cncl., N.Y. Couture Group Advisory Comm.; Delmar BPW Wm. of the Yr.; Who's Who of Am. Wm.; N.Y. State Univ., BA, '37 (Alumna aw., '69); b. Albany, N.Y., 1917; p. James and Katherine Fridy Spoore; h. John F. Harrington; res: 266 Lark St., Albany, N.Y. 12210.

HARRINGTON, PATRICIA ADDISON, Assoc. Librn., Rockford College, 5050 E. State St., Rockford, Ill. 61101, '65–; Humanities Ref. Librn., Humboldt State Col. (Arcata, Cal.), '62–'65; Ed., George Washington Univ. Human Rsch. Unit (Monterey, Cal.), '58–'60; Asst. Ed., Ed., free-lance, Dun & Bradstreet Mkt. Rsch. Div. (N.Y.C.), '48–'51; Lectr.; AAUP (Campus Chptr. Secy., '68–'70), ALA, Ill. Lib. Assn.; Wells Col., BA, '48; Univ. of Cal. (Berkeley), MS (Lib. Sci.), '62; b. Columbus, Oh., 1926; p. Hugh and Mary Porter Addison; h. George F. Harrington (div.); c. David L., Hilary Anne, Elaine; res: 732 Garfield Ave., Rockford, Ill. 61103.

HARRIS, BERNICE KELLY, Auth., "Purslane" (Mayflower Cup Aw., '39), "Portulaca," "Sweet Beulah Land," "Sage Quarter," "Janey Jeems," "Hearthstones," "Wild Cherry Tree Road"; NBC-TV play, "Yellow Color Suit"; Christmas bks: "The Very Real Truth about Christmas," "Santa on the Mantel"; bk. of plays, "Folk Plays of Eastern Carolina"; autobiog., "Southern Savory"; Crtv. Writing Tchr., Chowan Col., '63–; Eng. Tchr., schs., insts.; State Lit. and Hist. Assn. (Pres.), Pen and Brush, Delta Kappa Gamma (Hon.), Roanoke-Chowan Group (Convener); The Governor's Aw. for lit. distinction, '66; Meredith Col., AB, '13 (Distg. Svc. Aw., '18); Univ. of N.C., Hon. DLett, '60; Wake Forest Univ., Hon. DLett, '59; b. Clayton, N.C., 1892; p. William and Rosa Poole Kelly; h. Herbert Harris; res: Box 115, Seaboard, N.C. 27876.

HARRIS, BETH NORMAN, Colmst., Bk. Reviewer, Herald-Enterprice-American Newspapers, P.O. Box 2568, Palm Springs, Cal. 92262, '60–; Interviewer, KFI, KABC Radio (L.A., Cal.), '55–'61; KYA (S.F., Cal.), '50–'55; Prodr., bk. show, KOO-TV; Emcee, "Stag at Eve," panel show, TV, KPIX, '50–'55; aw., best feature colm. in Cal., Cal. Press Wm., '64; b. Balt., Md.; p. John and Pauline Seligman Mendes; h. Maurice Harris; res: 699 Regal Dr., Palm Springs, Cal. 92262.

HARRIS, BEVERLY, Free-lance Publicist, Wtr., '54–; PR, Blue Cross of Mass., Sheraton Hotel Corp., N.Y. Hosp. Svc., Dartmouth Col.; short stories, articles in nat. mags., '48–; Co-auth., several bks. on sailing incl. "Sail In A Day" (Grosset & Dunlap); Lasell Jr. Col., Boston Univ.; b. Lyndon Center, Vt., 1924; p. William and Grace Harris; res: 2 S. Cedar Pl., Boston, Mass. 02116.

HARRIS, CAROLYN HUEY, Exec. VP, Crtv. Dir., Harris & Weinstein Assoc., Inc., 1069 Spring St., N.W., Atlanta, Ga. 30309, '53–; Copy Chief, Tucker Wayne & Co., '49–'53; Copy Chief, Rich's, '45–'49; Copywtr., Michael's Dept. Store; Reptr., Carlsbad Current Argus; Lectr., Henry Grady Jnlsm. Sch. Univ. of Ga.; Atlanta Adv. Club (Dir.-VP, '48–'52), Fashion Group (Reg. Dir.), AWRT, Theta Sigma Phi Gamma Alpha Chi (Univ. of Ga. Chptr. Hon. Mbr., Wm. of Yr. in Adv., '57); Am. Mgt. Assn.; Univ. of Ga., AB, '41; b. Atlanta, Ga., 1919; p. John and Frances Wilson Huey; h. J. Rodney Harris; res: 2965 Pharr Ct. South NW, Atlanta, Ga. 30305.

HARRIS, COLEEN THOMAS, Hostess, "Open House With Coleen Harris," WCYB-TV, Appalachian Broadcasting Corp., Reynolds Arcade Bldg., Bristol, Va. 24201, '67–; Comml. Talent, '64; AWRT, Bristol Assn. Retarded Children; Bristol Evening Lions Club aw., '69; b. Walhalla, S.C., 1926; p. John and Inez Crenshaw Thomas; h. Jack Harris; c. Tom, Scott; res: 211 Forest Dr., Bristol, Tenn. 37620.

HARRIS, ELEANOR TOWLES, Ed., The Rand Corporation, 1700 Main St., Santa Monica, Cal. 90406, '60–; Ed., Huntington Lib. Pubns., '56–'60; Henry E. Huntington Lib. and Art Gallery (San Marino), '50–'55; Auth: "A Guide for the Preparation of Indexes," ('65), "The Rocky Mountain Journals of William Marshall Anderson: The West in 1834," ('67); Second Lt., USMC Reserve, '50–'59; Smith Col., BA, '50; Univ. of Paris, '54; b. N.Y.C., 1928; p. Oliver and Cecile Long Towles; h. J. Wayne Harris; res: 428 Mesa Rd., Santa Monica, Cal. 90402.

HARRIS, ELISABETH ALTSCHUL, Copy Chief, Willis/Case/Harwood, Inc., 3411 Office Park Rd., Dayton, Oh. 45439, '67–; Copy Chief, Butler Assoc., '65–'67; Feature Wtr., Dayton Daily News, '63–'65; Auth., bk. on obesity; Dayton Ad Club (Dir., '68–'70); Northwestern Univ., '44–'45; b. Dayton, Oh., 1926; p. Malcolm and Mildred Kusworm Altschul; h. Samuel Harris; c. Scott, Kent, Megan; res: 2524 Elsmere Ave., Dayton, Oh. 45406.

HARRIS, ETTA CALDWELL, Auth., 17 bks. of poetry, two of folklore; Talent, 30-minute poetry program, KAGH (Crossett, Ark.); Poetry Cnslt.; Staff, Southern States Wtrs. (Nashville, Tenn.); Co-founder-Publr.-Ed., poetry mag. Challenger; Sponsor, numerous local, state, nat. poetry contests; Tchr.; Feature Wtr.; News Corr.; Artist; Lectr.; numerous orgs., aws.; Ark. A. & M. Col.; Ark. State Tchrs. Col.; b. Hamburg, Ark., 1898; p. David King and Cora Goyne Caldwell; h. William Edward Harris; c. William E., Jr., Mrs. Jack Burchfield, Mrs. Wm. C. McMurray, Mrs. Travis Maxwell; res: 411 S. Cherry St., Hamburg, Ark. 71646.

HARRIS, FRAN ALVORD, Special Features Coordr., WWJ Stations, 622 Lafayette Blvd., Detroit, Mich. 48231, '64–; Wms. Ed., Bdcstr., WWJ-TV, '47–'64; Wms. Ed., Bdcstr., WWJ, '43–'64; "Nancy Dixon Show," Young & Rubicam, '39–'43; "Julia Hayes Show," Robert Gust & Co., '30–'34; Theta Sigma Phi (Pfsnl. Chptrs. VP, '68–; Detroit Chptr. Pres., '51–'52; Headliner Aw., '52), Wms. Adv. Club, AFA (Detroit Club Pres., VP Wms. Activities, '63–'67), AWRT (Detroit

Chptr. Pres., '56), Detroit Press Club; Soroptimist Wm. of the Yr., '65; "Ten Top Wm.," Detroit, '64; Detroit Adv. Wm. of the Yr., '58; Detroit Civic Aw., '57; Mich. Soc. for Mental Health aw., '58; Ferris State Col. Bd. of Control, '68–; Govs. Commn., Status of Wm., '63–'69; Mich. Wms. Commn., '69–; Grinnell Col., BA, '29 (Alumni Aw., '59); b. Detroit, Mich., 1909; p. William and Edith Vosburgh Alvord; h. Hugh W. Harris; c. Patricia (Mrs. Floyd Metz), Hugh W., Jr., Robert A.; res: 8925 E. Jefferson Ave., Detroit, Mich. 48214.

HARRIS, JEAN BACHMAN, Wms. Ed., Ch. Ed., Ludington Daily News, N. Rath Ave., Ludington, Mich. 49431, '67–; Proofreader; Choir Dir.; b. Pottsville, Pa., 1920; p. Robert L. and Lillian Kummerer Bachman; h. Walter Harris; c. Richard L., Laurie (Mrs. Richard Barnett), Brian R.; res: 318 N. Lewis St., Ludington, Mich. 49431.

HARRIS, JEANNE DURAN (Jeanne Duran), Special Events Dir., WJR Radio, 2100 Fisher Bldg., Detroit, Mich. 48202, '69–; Partner, Podium Personalities Lecture Bureau; Wms. Ed., daily program, '67–'69; Feature Wtr., Detroit Free Press, '65–'67; Daily Sunday Soc. Colmst., '60–'65; Free-lance Wtr.; Crtv. Writing Instr.; Staff Mbr., Oakland Univ. Annual Wtrs. Conf., six yrs.; special Brotherhood Month bdcsts., four yrs.; Theta Sigma Phi, Detroit Wm. Wtrs., AWRT, Detroit Press Club; nat. Catherine L. O'Brien Aws., Top Ten, two nwsp. series, '66, '67; Cert. of Merit, Family Circle Magazine, '69; Western Mich. Univ., OTR, '33; Univ. of Mich. (Psychotherapy), '35; Columbia Univ. (Writing), '39; Univ. of Okla., Special Cert. (Indsl. Psych.), '42; b. Detroit, Mich.; p. Howard A. and Laura B. Titus Steele; h. George Stafford Harris; c. John Duran, Debra Duran, Maria Duran; res: 31990 Bingham Rd., Birmingham, Mich. 48010.

HARRIS, JUDITH L., Head of Consumer Svcs., PR Dept., Borden, Inc., 350 Madison Ave., N.Y., N.Y. 10017, '68–; PR, '59–; Asst. Food Ed., Parents' Magazine, '58–'59; med., nutrition ed., cnslt.; Nutrition, Diet Therapy Instr., sch. of nursing; Am. Med. Wtrs. Assn., AWNY, Am. Dietetic Assn.; Case Western Reserve Univ., BA, '54; b. Cleve., Oh., 1932; p. Samuel and Jennie Strom Harris; res: 500 E. 77th St., N.Y., N.Y. 10021.

HARRIS, LINDA, Adv. Mgr., Dana Perfumes Corp., 625 Madison Ave., N.Y., N.Y. 10022, '67–; Wtr., Almay Cosmetics, '67; Media Dir., AE, Leonard Stein Adv., '62–'67; AWNY; Bklyn. Col., BA, '60; b. N.Y.C., 1940; p. Harold and Irene Horowitz Harris; res: 345 E. 56th St., N.Y., N.Y. 10022.

HARRIS, LINDA BARTON, Prod. Mgr., Glenn Advertising, Inc., Continental Nat. Bank Bldg., Ft. Worth, Tex. 76102, '65–; Traf. Mgr.; AWRT (Treas., '69), Beta Sigma Phi (Secy., '69); b. Handley, Tex., 1937; p. W. C. and Zavala Swift Barton; h. Rex Harris; res: 104 Hunt St., Mansfield, Tex. 76063.

HARRIS, LOUISE, Rschr.; Auth., four biog.-hist. bks.; Founder, C. A. Stephens Collection, Brown Univ.; Am. Guild of Organists (R. I. Chptr. Treas., '35–'39), Hymn Soc. of Am.; Brown Univ., AB, '26; b. Warwick, R.I., 1903; p. Samuel and Faustine Borden Harris; res: 15 Jay St., Rumford, R.I. 02916.

HARRIS, MAJORIE BRINK, Rsch. Dir., Gray & Rogers, Inc., 12 S. 12th St., Phila., Pa. 19107, '67–; Adv. Rsch. Mgr., Atlantic Richfield, '66–'67; Acc. Rsch. Supvsr., N.W. Ayer & Son, '57–'66; Am. Mktng. Assn. (Phila. Chptr. Secy., '69–'71); Pa. State Univ. BA (Jnlsm.), '52.

HARRIS, MARY ELLEN, Copywtr., Grey Advertising, Inc., 777 Third Ave., N.Y., N.Y. 10017, '66–; Copy Secy., '65; Hollywood Intl. Bdcst. aw., '68; Fla. State Univ., BA, '63; N.Y.U.; b. Seattle, Wash., 1942; p. Guy and Maude Juelson Harris; res: 31 Gramercy Park S., N.Y., N.Y. 10003.

HARRIS, MILDRED VerSOY, Wtr., poetry, non-fiction; Tchr., '15–'60; Auths. League of Am., Wms. Press Club of N.Y.C., Kappa Delta Pi, Sr. Citizens of Am.; Auths. of N.J., Who's Who of Am. Wm., Who's Who in the East, Dic. of Intl. Biog.; Newark State Tchrs. Col., '15; N.Y.U., BS (Educ.), '36; MA, '45; b. Newark, N.J., 1896; p. Charles and Emily Williams VerSoy; h. Russel Harris (div.); res: 29 Park Ct., Verona, N.J. 07044.

HARRIS, NELL H., Assoc., Bering Realty Corporation, 6002 Woodway, Houston, Tex. 77027, '69–; Freelance PR Cnslr., '64–; Pres., Hosp. Adv. Svcs., '62–; AWRT, Adv. Club of Am., Houston Real Estate Bd., Intl. Assn. of Concert Mgrs., Houston C. of C.; Who's Who in Am., Who's Who in the Southwest; Who's Who of Am. Wm., Distg. Wm. in Tex., Intl. Dic.; Rice Univ., AB; b. Palestine, Tex.; p. Tom and Nellie Hester Harris; h. (div.); c. Mrs. C. E. Richards, Jr., Charles H. Swartz, Tom B. Swartz; res: 7114 Captain St., Houston, Tex. 77036.

HARRIS, ORA ELIZABETH, Ed., Bus. Mgr., The Boonville Standard, 204 W. Locust St., Boonville, Ind. 47601, '66–; Bus. Mgr., Asst. Ed., '46–'66; Acting Ed., '42–'46; Bookkeeper-Secy., '40; Secy., '32; First Baptist Ch. (Tchr., Treas.), Boonville C. of C., Repl. Wms. Club; Lockyear Bus. Col.; Univ. of Evansville; b. Boonville, Ind., 1912; p. William and Octavia Poole Harris; res: Rural Rte. 1, Boonville, Ind., 47601.

HARRIS, PATRICIA ASBURY, Asst. Dir., News Bur., University of Arizona, 116 Administration Bldg., Tucson, Ariz. 85721, '68–; Asst., Press Bur., '51–'59; Wms. Ed., Ariz. Daily Star, '59–'63; Mng. Ed., W. Allis (Wis.) Star, '47–'51; Reptr., Evening News (Sault Ste. Marie, Mich.), '43–'47; Theta Sigma Phi (Fac. Advisor, Beta Upsilon Chptr.), Tucson Press Club; Univ. of Ariz.; b. Wheeler, Wis., 1911; p. Lucius and Helen Finley Asbury; h. A. Kingsley Harris (dec.); c. Virginia H.

Knebel, Majorie H. Zismann, Linda H. Kelley; res: 4026 E. Hayne St., Tucson, Ariz. 85711.

HARRIS, SUSANNE SEGAL, Dir. of Rsch., TV Prog. Ctr., McCann-Erickson, 485 Lexington Ave., N.Y., N.Y. 10017, '66–; Rsch. Analyst, Needham, Harper & Steers, '65–'66; Traf. Coordr., Foote, Cone & Belding, '64–'65; Univ. of Wis., BA, '64; b. Springfield, Ill., 1942; p. Arthur and Marion Hasterlik Segal; h. David A. Harris; res: 21 Barstow Rd., Great Neck, N.Y. 11021.

HARRIS, VIOLA SAINER, Actress; Broadway "Zelda"; films, "Funny Girl"; TV shows, "Family Affair"; others; Dir., commty., ch. groups; Tchr., Eng., Drama, L.A. HS; AMPAS, AEA, AFTRA, SAG; Theatrical Aw., Paul Hoffman Sch.; Hunter Col., BA, '40 (Phi Beta Kappa); Northwestern Univ., MA (Theatre), '41; Dramatic Workshop (Scholarship Aw.), '41–'43; b. N.Y.C.; p. Lazarus and Sophia Rosenberg Sainer; h. Robert H. Harris; c. Steven Lee, Sunny Dee; res: 138 S. Anita Ave., L.A., Cal. 90049.

HARRISON, BARBARA SARLE, Free-lance Wtr., Prodr., '69–; Copywtr., Louis Benito Adv. (Tampa, Fla.), '61–'69; Partner, Crtv. Dir., Shelmerdine & Harrison Adv. (Anchorage, Alaska), '58–'60; Cont. Dir., Midnight Son Bdcst. Corp., '55–'58; Radio-TV Copy, Cole & Weber Adv. (Portland, Ore.), '54–'55; Theta Sigma Phi (Fla. W. Coast Pfsnl. Chptr. Pres. '66–'67), AWRT, Hillsboro County Heart Assn. (Bd. of Dirs., '61–; Exec. Bd., '66–'68); Tampa Adv. Club aw., '65; Fla. PR Assn. aw., '67; Univ. of Ut.; Portland Col.; Univ. of Alaska; b. Salt Lake City, Ut., 1924; p. Joseph and Josephine Woodruff Sarle; h. Albert N. Harrison; c. Mary Jane (Mrs. R. D. Stortroen), Caroline (Mrs. Frank Padgett), Linda Sue, Thomas Albert; res: Rte. 1, Box 414-J, Valrico, Fla. 33594.

HARRISON, BETTY DODGE, Coordr., Education Center, Brigham Young University, 120 Col. Hall, Provo, Ut. 84601, '66–; Tchr., Educ. Psych., '60–'67; Tchr., Univ. of Hi.; '67–'68; Cl.-Interviewer, Ut. State Dept. of Employment Security, '58–'59; '46–'52; Ut. County Dept. of Public Welfare, '55–'57; private practice, Psychologist; Special Educ., cnslt., '61–; cnslt., learning disabilities (Ut., Hi.); Cnslt., Title I projects; contbr., pfsnl. pubns.; Edtl. Bd., BYU Studies, '65–'69; various orgs., aws.; Univ. of Ut., '52–'53; Brigham Young Univ., BS, '59 (High Hons.); MS, '60 (High Hons.); Ph.D., '65; b. Kemmerer, Wyo., 1928; p. Harold and Marion Holden Dodge; h. formerly Garth Harrison; c. Rosemary, Brent; res: 1495 N. 1880 West, Provo, Ut. 84601.

HARRISON, ELIZABETH CAVANNA, Free-lance Wtr.; Auth: "Mystery in Marrakech" (William Morrow, '68), "The Country Cousin" (William Morrow, '67), 58 other bks. for young adults; Auths. League, Auths. Guild; Douglass Col., BL, '29 (Phi Beta Kappa); b. Camden, N.J., 1909; p. Walter and Emily Allen Cavanna; h. George Russell Harrison; c. Stephen

Cavanna Headley; res: 170 Barnes Hill Rd., Concord, Mass. 01742.

HARRISON LORENE CUTHBERTSON, Bdcstr.; Owner, The Hat Box, 300 E St., Anchorage, Alaska 99501, '48–; Wtr., Spokeswm., radio, TV commls.; Hostess, "Lorene's Scrapbook" (Alaska Press Club Aw. of Merit, '55), '54–'58; "Hat Box Fashion Show," '54–'60, KENI-TV; Anchorage City Welcoming Hostess, '45–'48; Emergency Housing Bur. Dir., '44–'45; Tchr., '25–'29; Chmn., Performing and Fine Arts Commn., Alaska Centennial, '66–'67 (Svc. Aw., '67); AWRT, Intl. Platform Assn., Beta Sigma Phi (Intl. Hon. Mbr.), Delta Kappa Gamma (Hon. Mbr.); active in many civic orgs., numerous local aws.; b. Pittsburg, Kan., 1905; p. Matthew and Margaret Dunlap Cuthbertson; h. Jack Harrison; c. Margaret Lee (Mrs. Joseph F. Veilbig), Carol Anne (Mrs. Robert V. Dodd); res: 1242 W. Tenth Ave., Anchorage, Alaska, 99501.

HARROP, NORMA, Publicist, Talent, 10 E. 49th St., N.Y., N.Y. 10017; BBDO; Ketchum, MacLeod & Grove, Inc.; NHFL (organized Pitt. Chptr.); Nat. Assn. of Social Workers; AWRT; Camp Fire Girls (Cleve. Dist. Dir.); active in Pitt. civic groups; Hunter Col., BA (Eng.), '50; Columbia Univ. (Jnlsm.), '51; Univ. of Pitt., MSW (Commty. Org.); b. N.Y.C.; p. Frederick and Nina Paget Harrop; res: 22 W. 17 St., N.Y., N.Y. 10011.

HARSHE, FLORENCE ELIZABETH, Dir., Southern Adirondack Library System, 22 Whitney Pl., Saratoga Springs, N.Y. 12866, '59–; Dir., N. Country Lib. System (Watertown, N.Y.), '57–'59; Chief of Advisory Svcs., Asst. Dir., '51–'57; Lib. of Hi., '47–'51; Lima (Oh.) Lib., '41–'47; AAUW, N.Y. Lib. Assn., ALA, Hudson Mohawk Lib. Assn., BPW; Oh. State Univ., BS (Educ.), '39; Western Reserve Univ., BS (Lib. Sci.), '41; b. Lima, Oh., 1917; p. Carl and Maud Meyers Frank res: R.D. 2, Loughberry Rd., Saratoga Springs, N.Y. 12866.

HARSTICK, ALICE HENRIKSEN, Publr., Cuming County Democrat, 228 S. Main St., West Point, Neb. 68788, '68–; with husband, purchased, operated nwsp., Co-publr., '45–'68; Tchr., rural schs., four yrs.; Neb. Press Assn.; civic groups; outstanding commty. svc. aw., Ak-sar-ben (Omaha, Neb.), '65; b. West Point, Neb., 1907; p. Jacob and Marie Hansen Henriksen; h. Raymond T. Harstick (dec.); c. Rosemary (Mrs. Darold Lierman).

HART, CAROLYN GIMPEL, Auth., juv. fiction: "The Secret of the Cellars" (Dodd, Mead, '64), "Dangerous Summer" (Four Winds Press, '68); Univ. of Okla., BA, '58 (Phi Beta Kappa); b. Okla. City, Okla., 1936; p. Roy W. and Doris Akin Gimpel; h. Philip D. Hart; c. Philip D., Jr., Sarah Ann; res: 4612 N. Indiana, Okla. City, Okla. 73118.

HART, MARTHA W., Prom. Mgr., George Braziller, Inc., 1 Park Ave., N.Y., N.Y. 10016, '69–; Mgr., Vassar Cooperative Bookshop, '68–'69; '64–'69; Hollins Col., '53–'56; Vassar Col., BA, '64; b. Roanoke, Va., 1935; p.

James and Clare Stone White; c. Sheila, James Alan; res: 333 E. 30th St., N.Y., N.Y. 10016.

HART, MARY TOLEN, Asst. to Adv. Dir., Florida State Theatres, Inc., 128 E. Forsyth St., Jacksonville, Fla. 32202, '54–; Wm. of the Motion Picture Industry Intl. (Jacksonville Club Pres., '69, '67, '59; Intl. VP, '60–'61), Pres., Cncl. of Jacksonville (Treas.) Wm. of the Motion Pic. Industry, Intl. (Intl. Pres., '69–'70); Radio WMBR Bus. Wm. of the Yr., '69; Jacksonville Univ.; b. Kearny, N.J., 1915; p. Thornton and Estella Pepper Tolen; h. John Hart; c. John, Jr., Patricia Ann, Mrs. Marilyn Burke (Dec.); res: 4852 Princess Anne Lane, Jacksonville, Fla. 32210.

HARTER, HELEN O'CONNER, Auth: "Carmelo," (Follett, '62), "English Is Fun," (Harter); Auth., Illus., "Goldilocks y Los Tres Osos y Otros Cuentos" (Nat. Textbk.); Ariz. State Tchrs. Col., AB, '36; Ariz. State Univ., MA; b. Tempe, Ariz., 1905; p. Andrew and Ida Woolf O'Connor; h. Tom J. Harter; c. Susan Ann, Mrs. Eduarda Yates; res: 320 Roosevelt St., Tempe, Ariz. 85281.

HARTER, MARGARET BURTON, bk. revs., program papers, "History of Woman's Auxiliary to Kentucky State Medical Association" ('48–'49; revsd., '53); Case Hist. Wtr., Family Welfare Soc. (Cambridge, Mass.), '32–'36; Bibliographical Asst., Alumni News Dir., Univ. of Ill., '31; Asst. Ed., Ill. Alumni News Magazine, '27–'30; Soc. Ed., Kokomo (Ind.) Dispatch, '27; News Asst., Kokomo (Ind.) Tribune, '25, '26; sponsoring fgn. students, corr. with visiting foreigners, other work, Intl. Ctr., past 10 yrs.; Kappa Tau Alpha (Charter Mbr.), Theta Sigma Phi; Univ. of Ill., AB, '27 (with hons. in jnlsm.; Phi Beta Kappa); b. Chgo., Ill., 1906; p. James S. and Fleda Blair Burton; h. Dr. John S. Harter; c. J. Burton; res: 1410 Castlewood Ave., Louisville, Ky. 40204.

HARTLEY, ELDA VOKEL, Pres., Hartley Productions, Inc., 279 E. 44th St., N.Y., N.Y. 10017, '55–; VP, '40–'55; Dir. of Visual Educ., State of N.C., '38–'40; Free-lance Ed., Wtr., '36–'38; Actress, contract, Fox, '31–'32; Assn. of Doc. Film Prodrs. (One of Founders), NHFL, AWNY; film aws. incl: blue ribbon, Am. FF, '67, and Gold Eagle, Cine, '69, for "Mood of Zen"; blue ribbon, Columbus FF, '69, for "The Flow of Zen"; others; U.C.L.A., BA, '36; Columbia Univ., MA, '40; b. Brownwood, Tex., 1911; p. Leo and Emily Lockwood Voelkel; h. Irving Hartley; c. Keith, Monty, Donn; res: Cat Rock Rd., Cos Cob, Conn. 06807.

HARTMAN, JOYCE FRANKEL, N.Y. Ed., Houghton Mifflin Company, 53 W. 43rd St., N.Y., N.Y. 10036, '61–; '45–'49; Asst. Ed. (Boston, Mass.), '44–'45; Asst. Ed., Look, '42–'44; Soc. of Wm. Geographers; Smith Col., BA, '42; b. N.Y.C., 1921; p. Joseph and Sylvia Roth Frankel; h. Dr. Daniel Hartman; c. Gail, Alison.

HARTMAN, JUDI SWEETON, Free-lance Wtr., talent, adv.; Crtv. Dir., Asst. VP, Vance Adv. & PR Agcy.,

'67–'69; Media Dir., Wtr., Bozell & Jacobs, '66–'67; KTHT Radio '66; KILT Radio, '65–'66; AWRT, Galveston Bay Cruising Assn., Lake House Yacht Club; b. Kokomo, Ind., 1940; p. William C. O'Brien and Gertrude Vonderahe; h. Dr. David E. Hartman; res: The Lake House, 3325 Nasa Road One, Seabrook, Tex. 77586.

HARTRICK, DOROTHY BECK, Assoc. Media Dir., Lang, Fisher & Stashower, Inc., 1010 Euclid Ave., Cleve., Oh. 44115, '68–; Asst. Media Byr., Time Byr., Supvsr.; Wayne State Univ.; b. Balt., Md.; p. Samuel and Janet Clarkson Beck; h. Howard W. Hartrick; c. Patricia (Mrs. John D. Hunter); res: 520 Sandalwood Dr., Bay Village, Oh. 44140.

HARTWIG, MARIE DOROTHY, Acting Chmn., Dept. of Physical Education for Women, University of Michigan, N. University St., Ann Arbor, Mich. 48104, '68–; Tchr., '30–' Co-auth., four children's bks.; Pi Lambda Theta; ZONTA, Wm. of the Univ. Fac. (Pres.); other orgs. in field; Univ. of Mich., AB, '29 (Mortar Bd.); BS, '32; MA, '38; b. East Orange, N.J.; p. Frank and Fannie Koch Hartwig; res: 2650 Geddes Ave., Ann Arbor, Mich. 48104.

HARVEY, ANNIE ELIZABETH, PR Dir., Pennsylvania Association for the Blind, 308 S. Craig St., Pitt., Pa. 15213, '60–; Young Repls. of Pa.; PRSA; Univ. of Pitt.; b. Ehrenfeld, Pa., 1923; p. William and Annie Gray Harvey; res: 2 Mellon Ter., Pitt., Pa. 15206.

HARVEY, MARY KERSEY, Sr. Ed., McCall's Publishing Co., 230 Park Ave., N.Y., N.Y. 10036, '65–; Dir., Edtl. Comm., McCall Corp., '62–'65; Special Asst. to Ed.-in-Chief, Saturday Review, '58–'62; VP, Ver Standig, Inc., '52–'58; Coordr., U.S.-U.S.S.R. "Dartmouth" Confs., '60, '61, '62, '64, '69; Edtl. Advisory Bd., Journal of Learning Disabilities ('68–), Vista ('67–); Contrbr., numerous pubns.; Wms. Adv. Club of Wash., D.C. (Pres., '56–'57), AWNY (Dir., '60–'61), Nat. Cncl. of Wm., OPC; active in intl. peace orgs.; Occidental Col., BA, '44; b. L.A., Cal.; p. Merlin Kersey; h. Paul Harvey; c. Pamela Joyce; res: 60 E. Eighth St., N.Y., N.Y. 10003.

HARVILL, ELEANOR K., Rsch. Asst.-PR, United States Steel Corporation, 525 William Penn Pl., Pitt., Pa. 15230, '56–; Rsch. Dir., other positions, Hill and Knowlton, '46–'56; Military Intelligence Svc., Wms. Army Corps., '43–'46; Spanish Tchr., Riverdale Country Sch. for Boys, '42–'43; PRSA, AAPOR, Nat. Fgn. Trade Cncl.; Barnard Col., BA, '41; Columbia Univ. Tchrs. Col., MA, '42; b. Yonkers, N.Y., 1919; p. Peter and Anna Rodak Harvill; res: Gateway Towers, Apt. 7-G, Pitt., Pa. 15222.

HARWELL, BARBARA ANN, VP, Crtv. Dir., Rominger Advertising Agency, Inc. 3627 Howell St., Dallas, Tex. 75214, '69–; Crtv. Dir. Copy chief, '66–'69; Copywtr., Tracy Locke Co., '64–'67; Adv. Mgr., Volk Bros. Co., '59–'64; Asst. Adv. Mgr., '55–'59; Copywtr.,

A. Harris & Co., '54–'55; Dallas Adv. League (aws., '67–'68, '65); Who's Who of Am. Wm., '69; Univ. of Ark., BSJ (Jnlsm.), '54; b. San Angelo, Tex., 1933; p. George and Irene Holland Harwell; res: 6429 Lontos Dr., Dallas, Tex. 75214.

HARWOOD, SIFLIN HARRIET, Exec. Prodr., Secy.-Treas., Mbr. Bd. of Dirs., Harwood Advertising, Inc., Suite 1507, Tucson Fed. Savings Tower, Tucson, Ariz. 85701, '52–; Mbr. Bd. of Dirs., H & G Enterprises; previously Brokerage Mgr., John P. Witt & Company (Cleve., Oh.); Cleve. Col.; b. Cleve., Oh., 1923; p. Nat and Clara Kangisser Siflin; h. Elk Harwood; c. Bobette Harwood Sipes; res: 1122 E. Via Lucerna, Tucson, Ariz. 85718.

HARWOOD, SKIPPY DUNCAN, PR, Delaware Inn, 56 Main St., Stamford, N.Y. 12167, '69–; Interiors Magazine, '65–'69; Palm Beach Daily News, '63–'64; Wtr., educ. movies, Ray Waters Inc.; Reptr., Wheaton Daily Jnl.; Copywtr., Boston Store (Milw., Wis.), Adv. Mgr., Scruggs, Vandervoort and Barney (St. Louis, Mo.), Soc. Ed., Tallahassee (Fla.) Daily Democrat; Tchr., Jnlsm., '57–'59; AWNY; Univ. of Wis., BS (Home Econs., Jnlsm.); b. Cochrone, Wis.; h. James Harwood.

HASERODT, ETHEL MILLER, Free-lance Cnslt.; Y.W.C.A. of Passaic and Clifton (N.J.), '42–'67; Advisory Secy., Nat. Bd. of Y.W.C.A., '35–'42; Y.W.C.A. of Lawrence (Mass.), '30–'35; ZONTA Club of Passaic and Clifton (Pres., '67–); NAACP aw.; · B'Nai Brith aw.; Wechsler aw. for public svc.; Who's Who of Am. Wm.; Northwestern Univ., BS; N.Y.U., MA; b. Milw., Wis., 1902; p. Robert and Dorothy Richardson Miller; h. E. Oliver Hasserodt; c. Mrs. Richard Shaffner; res: 4 Addison Pl., Fair Lawn, N.J. 07410.

HASKIN, DOROTHY CLARK, Staff Wtr., World Vision International, 919 W. Huntington Dr., Monrovia, Cal. 91016, '59–; Free-lance Wtr., '40–; Auth., 34 published bks.; Ghostwtr., Ed., 37 bks.; Hostess, radio prog., "Dorothy and Her Friends"; Biola Col.; b. Boston, Mass., 1905; p. William and Evelyn Howard Clark; res: 2573 Glen Green, Hollywood, Cal. 90028.

HASLEY, LUCILE HARDMAN, Auth: "Reproachfully Yours," "The Mouse Hunter," "Saints and Snapdragons," "Mind If I Differ?;" Lectr.; Milw.-Downer Col.; Univ. of Wis.; b. South Bend, Ind., 1909; p. H. Monroe and Charlotte Rennoe Hardman; h. Louis Hasley; c. Daniel, Mrs. Robert Avery, Mrs. Paul Lombardi; res: 3128 Wilder Dr., South Bend, Ind. 46615.

HASSO, SIGNE, Actress, Composer, Lyricist; Intl. Star, theatre, motion pics., TV (U.S., Europe); prods. incl: "Cabaret," "The Mountain Giants," "Uncle Vanya"; films: "House on 92nd Street," "A Double Life," "Heaven Can Wait," others; tours with Nat. Repertory Co., '64–'65, '59–'60; Wtr., short stories; wrote music, lyrics for one-wm. show (Europe); some 40 songs in Swedish, Eng., German; lyrics,

album, "Scandinavian Folk Songs—Sung and Swung" (Grand Prix Edison Intl. Aw., '65); brought to U.S. by RKO; motion pics. (Stockholm, Paris, Vienna), (first Scandinavian Acad. Aw.); plays (Sweden, Scandinavian countries); aws. incl: first Scandinavian Theatre Aw., '39; Royal Dramatic Acad. (Swedish govt. grant); b. Stockholm, Sweden, 1918; p. Kefas and Helfrid Lindström Larsson; c. (dec.); res: 215 W. 90th St. Apt. 7F, N.Y., N.Y. 10024.

HASTINGS, JUDITH ANNE, PR Dir., Chesapeake Bay Girl Scout Council, Inc., 1503 W. 13th St., Wilmington, Del. 19806, '67–; Adv. Coordr., Etienne Dupuch Jr. Pubns. (Nassau, Bahamas), '65–'67; Freelance Copywtr., Indsl. Ed. (St. Louis, Mo.), '64–'65; Copywtr., Famous-Barr Co., '62–'64; Ed., Store Chat., '60–'62; Pubns. Supvsr., Assoc. Credit Burs. of Am., '59–'60; Pa. State Univ., BA (Jnlsm.), '56; b. Phila., Pa., 1934; p. Barnard and Helen Young Hastings; res: Woodstream Gardens Apts., 902 Peachtree Rd., Claymont, Del. 19703.

HASTINGS, MARY LUCILLE, Archivist, State of Colorado: Division of State Archives and Public Records, 1530 Sherman St., Denver, Colo. 80203, '68–; staff, '62–'69; Info. Wtr., Colo. State Planning Div., '57–'62; staff, Colo. State Depts. of Educ., Vocational Educ. and Agriculture, '51–'57; Copywtr., Harold Walter Clark Advertising Agcy., '49–'51; Radio News Ed., KLZ, '44–'49; Ed., Brighton (Colo.) Blade, '41–'44; free-lance writing, pubcty., bus. rept., '40–'41; teaching crtv. writing, Denver Opp. (adult) Sch., Denver Public Schs., '51; rsch. projects, Colo. subjects, '60–'69; NLAPW (Central Colo. Br. Pres., '64–'66, '56–'58; numerous aws., writing, ed.), NFPW (Colo. Pres., '54–'55), Denver Wms. Press Club (Secy., '46–'47), Theta Sigma Phi (Denver Pres., '40), BPW; svc. aw., Denver Tuberculosis Soc., '65; active in civic orgs.; Univ. of Colo., BA (Jnlsm.), '40; Univ. of Denver; b. Belle Plaine, Kan.; p. Ruby E. and Frances E. Helme Hastings; res: 760 Marion St., Denver, Colo. 80218.

HASTINGS, SYBIL BUTLER, Art. Dir., Columbia Mills, Inc., 101 Park Ave., N.Y., N.Y. 10017, '54–; Color Cnslt., Adv. Mgr., Holliston Mills, '34–'54; Dodd, Mead & Co., '19–'33; WNBA, Am. Inst. of Graphic Arts; b. Farmington, Kan.; p. Charles and Mary Wright Butler; h. Milo Hastings (dec.); c. Edith (Mrs. John C. Callaham), Warren; res: White Plains Rd., Tarrytown, N.Y. 10591.

HATCH, CLAUDIA, Guidance Bk. Ed., Scholastic Magazines, Inc., 50 E. 44, N.Y., N.Y. 10036, '69–; Assoc. Ed., '62–'69; Dept. Ed., Young Living Dept., Seventeen, '54–'58; Assoc. Ed., 2-to-5 World, '52–'54; Asst. Ed., Charm, '50–'52; Dir., Lilliput Play Sch. (Poundridge, N.Y.), '39–'42; Ed., Co-auth., "What You Should Know about Sex and Sexuality" ('69); many articles in nat. mags., incl., Harper's Bazaar, Co-ed., others; Playwright: "The Prophecy," "Three Heads in 4 Acts" ('50); chptr., "Dynamo" (by Hallie

Flanagan, '42); Cosmopolitan Club; Vassar, AB, '29; b. Waterville, N.Y.; p. Charles T. and Annabel Wilson Hatch; h. Walter Clare Stearns, Jr. (dec.); c. David G. Stearns, John Noble Stearns II, Annabel Stearns Manly; res: 108 E. 91, N.Y., N.Y. 10028.

HATCH, LUCILE, Prof., School of Librarianship, University of Denver, University Park, Denver, Colo. 80210, '65–; Acting Dean, '66–'68; Assoc. Prof., '56–'65; Librn., Sharples Jr. HS (Seattle, Wash.), '55–'56, '52–'54; Visiting Prof., Sch. of Librnship., Univ. of Wash., '54–'55; Tchr., Librn., various Wash. high schs., '35–'52; frequent lectr., reviewer; numerous articles; ALA (Div. Pres., '62–'63; VP, '61–'62), various other lib. assns., Lib. Assn. (Eng.), Wms. Educ. Club, Wms. Fac. Club, Am. Assn. of Higher Educ.; State Col. of Wash., BA (Fgn. Lang.), '35 (Phi Beta Kappa, Phi Kappa Phi); Univ. of Denver, BS (Lib. Sci.), '46; Univ. of Ore., MEd, '54; b. Walla Walla, Wash., 1913; p. Arthur and Blanche Craft Hatch; res: 2350 E. Iliff Ave., Apt. 4, Denver, Colo. 80210.

HATCH, MARIAN ADAMS, Adv. and Sls. Prom. Mgr., Matthey Bishop, Inc. (Malvern, Pa.), '53–'68; Dir. of Special Events, PR, John Wanamaker Stores, '53–'68; Wtr.-Dir., WTIC (Hartford, Conn.), '45–'46 (Bdcst. Magazine PR-Radio aw., '46); Prom. Dir., Dell Pubns. (N.Y.C.), '43; Chester County Adv. Club (Dir.); BPW ('66–'68), Theta Sigma Phi, Sls. Prom. Exec. Club, PRSA; Trans-Am. Adv. Agcy. Network aw., '66; 3 Freedom Fndn. aws.; Columbia Univ.; Univ. of Pa.; b. Haverford, Pa., 1909; p. Franklin and Marian Townsend McAllister; h. Earl Chester Hatch (div.); c. Sandra (Mrs. Philip J. Griffin), David T. (dec.); res: Wessex House, St. Davids, Pa. 19087, 358 11th St., Atlantic Beach, Fla. 32233.

HATCH, RUTH STREETER, Wash. Rep., International Science News Features, 2771 Woodley Pl., Wash., D.C., 20008, '69–; Free-lance Wtr., NANA, '65–; Mgr., own real estate, '45–; Pres., Millstone Farm Day Camp, '47–'67; Wash. Ed., Film News Magazine, '63–'65; Wash. Ed., Palm Beach Life Magazine, '55–'56; Free-lance Wtr. (Europe), '49; works published: "Lobby, a Capital Game," "Alice in Merger Land," "When Are You Dead?"; Nat. Assn. of Sci. Wtrs., Am. Med. Wtrs. Assn., N.Y. Acad. of Sci., Am. Assn. for the Advancement of Sci., Smithosonia Assn., ANWC, OPC, Nat. Lawyer's Club; dirs., Phi Kappa Phi, Cap and Scroll; Dominican Col.; Univ. of Nev., BS; Univ. of Cal., George Washington Univ., Catholic Univ., Colo. Col.; Columbia Univ., A.S.W.P., '68 (Hon. Fellowship, '68); b. Elko, Nev.; p. Oscar J. and Jessie DeLar Streeter; h. Douglas Lorenzo Hatch; c. Douglas L., Jr., Mrs. Ruth Hatch Vinogradov, Mrs. Annette Hatch Norton; res: Millstone Farm, Burke, Va. 22015.

HATFIELD, EILEEN BUSTEED, Family Living Ed., Courier-Tribune, P.O. Box 369, Curry Pike, Bloomington, Ind. 47401, '67–; City Ed., Times-Herald, Wash., Ind., '60–'66; Soc. Ed., '46–'60; AP aw. for best wms. feature wtr. in Ind.; Univ. of Ill.; b. Wash., Ind., 1924; p. William E. and Edith White Busteed; h. Marion W. Hatfield; c. Lt. Eugene Merrill Maresca.

HAUBRICH, ALICE CLARK, Wtr., '57–; Auth: "Becky—Grandmother of New Hampshire," ('66); "200-Year History of Congreational Church in Claremont, N.H.," ('64); Intl. Platform Assn., N.H. Hist. Soc., Claremont Wms. Club (Pres., '69), Piscataqua Pioneers (Pres., '69); b. Haverhill, Mass., 1915; p. John and Ruth Parker Clark; h. William Palmer Haubrich; c. Carol Anne; res: 9 Lindy Ave., Claremont, N.H. 03743.

HAUGH, DOLORES GEORGE, Wms. Pg. Ed., Day Publications, 117 S. Main St., Mount Prospect, Ill. 60056, '66–; Feature Wtr., Paddock Pubns., '59–'66; Ill. Wms. Press Assn. (Meta Palmer Aw.), Mount Prospect BPW, Mount Prospect Art League, Mount Prospect Hist. Soc. (Secy., '68–'69); Ill. Sesquicentennial aw.; Wright Jr. Col., '43; Art Inst. of Chgo., '43–'45; b. Chgo., Ill., 1923; p. Sanford and Norma Leonard George; h. Robert W. Haugh; c. Cheryl Eileen, Sandra Alison; res: 7 S. Edward St., Mount Prospect, Ill. 60056.

HAUPT, ENID A., Ed.-in-Chief, Seventeen Magazine, 320 Park Ave., N.Y., N.Y. 10022, '54–; Asst. to Publr., Philadelphia Inquirer, '53; Corr., '42–'53; aws. for work with young people: Govt. of the Netherlands, '56; French Republic, '58; Pan Am. Union, '57; U.S. Comm. for UNICEF, '59; Ladies Aux., Veterans of Fgn. Wars, '65.

HAUTZIG, ESTHER RUDOMIN, Fiction, Non-fiction Wtr.; Free-lance Pubcty. Cnslt. for children's bks.; Dir. of Prom. of Children's Bks., Thomas Y. Crowell Co., '54–'60; Pubcty. Asst., Children's Bk. Cncl., '52–'54; G. P. Putnam, '51–'52; Spring Bk. Festival Hon. Bk., '68; Boston Globe Bk. Aws. Hon. Bk., '68; Nat. Bk. Aw., Nominee, '69; Hunter Col., '48–'50; b. Vilna, Poland, 1930; p. Samuel and Chaja Cunzer Rudomin; h. Walter Hautzig; c. Deborah Margolee and David Rudomin; res: 505 West End Ave., N.Y., N.Y. 10024.

HAVENS, SHIRLEY ELISE, Assoc. Ed., Library Journal, R. R. Bowker Co., 1180 Ave. of the Americas, N.Y., N.Y. 10036, '67–; Asst. Ed., '66; Mng. Ed., '59–'66; Edtl. Asst., '57–'59; Ed., Annual Architectural Issues, '62–'66; Asst. to Librn., Carnegie Endowment for Intl. Peace, '54–'57; Asst. to Bursar, Tchrs. Col., Columbia Univ., '47–'52; articles in School Library Journal, other pubns.; N.Y. Lib. Club (Ed., Bul.), '65–'67), President's Comm. on Employment of the Handicapped (Commendation, '69); Hunter Col., BA, '47 (cum laude, Phi Beta Kappa); Tchrs. Col., Columbia Univ. (Grad. Program in Eng.), '47–'52; b. N.Y.C.

HAVERFIELD, BETTY LUKER, Ed., The Crescent, Gamma Phi Beta Sorority, 507 Medavista Dr., Columbia, Mo. 65201, '65–; Pioneer Pubns. (Chgo., Ill.), '44–'46; Edtl. Asst., Indsl. Medicine, '42–'44; Theta Sigma Phi, Gamma Alpha Chi, Mid-Mo. Press Club,

Univ. of Mo. Jnlsm. Wms. Assn. (Pres., '53), Nat. Pan-hellenic Eds. Conf., Gamma Phi Beta aw., '66, '68; Who's Who of Am. Wm.; Univ. of Mo., BJ, '42; b. Chgo., Ill., 1920; p. George and Florence O'Conner Luker; h. Robert Walter Haverfield; c. Judith Ann, Robert David; res: 507 Medavista Dr., Columbia, Mo. 65201.

HAVILAND, LEONA, Ref. Librn., U.S. Merchant Marine Academy, Kings Point, N.Y. 11024, '52–; Librn., Smithsonian Inst., Wash., D.C., '48–'50; Asst. to Cata-loguer, U.S. Nat. Museum, '44–'48; Sr. Asst., Chil-dren's Dept., Ferguson Lib., '43–'44; Ref. Dept., '40–'44; ALA; Special Libs. Assn.; Long Island Hist. Soc.; N.Y. Genealogical and Biographical Soc.; Who's Who of Am. Wm.; Univ. of Ala., BS (Educ.), '40; Univ. of Ill., MS (Lib. Sci.), '51; b. Stamford, Conn., 1916; p. Howard and Ada Jewell Haviland; res: 10 Welwyn Rd., Great Neck, N.Y. 11021.

HAWES, EVELYN JOHNSON, Wtr., c/o Publr. Har-court, Brace and World, Inc., 757 Third Ave., N.Y., N.Y. 10017; "The Happy Land"; "A Madras-Type Jacket"; "Proud Vision" (Thomas Y. Crowell); Tchr; Fac., Univ. of Wash. and Univ. of Cinn.; Guest Speak-er, Pacific N.W. Wtrs. Conf., '68; AAUW, NLAPW (Western N.Y. Br. Pres.), '64–'66; Founder's Medal, Distinction in Writing; Nat. Aw. for Best Published Novel, Wash., D.C.): 3rd Prize, Nat. Fiction Contest, Tommorrow Magazine; Cited, Martha Foley, Best Short Stories; Univ. of Wash. (Liberal Arts; Fellow-ship), N.Y. State Univ. at Buffalo, Purdue Ext., Univ. of Cinn.; b. Colville, Wash.; p. Judge W. Lon and Iva Dickey Johnson; h. Nat H. Hawes; c. Linda Hawes Clever, M.D. (Mrs. James A. Clever); res: 59 Mea-dowstream Dr., Snyder, Buffalo, N.Y. 14226.

HAWK, DOROTHY WILKINSON, News. Ed., Daily Globe, 37 W. Main St., Shelby, Oh. 44875, '67–; Soc. Ed., Feature Wtr., '55–'67; Gen. Reptr., '53–'55; Ash-land Col.; Oh. State Univ.; b. Jackson Twp., Oh., 1913; p. Chet and Amy Gilchrist Wilkinson; h. H. Stewart Hawk; c. Stewart P., Mary Jo (Mrs. Victor Huffman); res: 93 E. Main St., Shelby, Oh. 44875.

HAWKINS, ELINOR DIXON, Librn., Craven-Pamlico-Carteret Regional Library, 400 Johnson St., New Bern, N.C. 28560, '58–; Head of Circ., Greensboro Public Lib., '51–'56; Children's Librn., Enoch Pratt Free Lib. (Balt., Md.), '50–'51; Storyteller, "Tele-Story Time," WNBE-TV, '63–; WFMY-TV, '52–'58; N.C. Lib. Assn., Pilot Intl. (Pres., '57–'58, VP, '62–'63), N.C. Lives, Dic. of Intl. Biog.; Who's Who of Am. Wm.; Who's Who Among Students in Am. Univs. and Cols.; Fairmont State Col., AB, '49; Univ. of N.C., BS (Lib. Sci.), '50; b. Masontown, W. Va., 1927; p. Thomas and Susan Reed Dixon; h. Carroll W. Hawkins; c. John Carroll; res: P.O. Box 57, Cove City, N.C. 28523.

HAWKINS, SARAH MARGARETT, Wms. Dir., WCAO, Plough Broadcasting Co., Inc., 40 W. Chase

St., Balt., Md. 21201; Radio Bdcst., Prod., Dir., 15 yrs.; AWRT (Md. Chptr. Secy., '67–'68), DAR, Pilot Club of Balt. (Pres., '56); Catholic Univ. of Am., BS, '45; Md. Gen. Hosp. Sch. of Nursing, '36; b. Newport News, Va., 1915; p. James and Barbara Barclay Hawkins; res: 6801 Alter St., Balt., Md. 21207.

HAWKINS, VALERIE FRANCES, On-Camera Spokes-wm., Texaco; '66–; Spokeswm., Proctor and Gam-ble, '65; Talent, more than 50 TV commls.; AFTRA, SAG; St. Louis Univ. (Eng.), '61; b. Wash., D.C., 1942; p. Barnard and Eugenia MacDonald Hawkins; h. Robert Weber (div.); c. Laura Katherine; res: 2035 Thayer Ave., L.A., Cal. 90025.

HAWLEY, MARGARET DENGLER, News Ed., Bailey Meter Co., 29801 Euclid Ave., Wickliffe, Oh. 44092, '68–; Northern Oh. IEA, ICIE; State Univ. of N.Y. (Psych.); b. Dunkirk, N.Y., 1931; p. Gerald and Mar-garet Cobbe Dengler; h. Rodney Hawley; c. Patricia, Michael, Brad, Randy, Gerald; res: 7970 Mentor Ave., Apt. G-11, Mentor, Oh. 44060.

HAY, ALEXANDRA LYNN, Film Actress, Columbia Pictures Corp., 1438 N. Gower St., Hollywood, Cal. 90028, '66–; Movies incl. "The Greatest Mother of 'Em All" ('69), "Guess Who's Coming to Dinner" ('67); "Skidoo" ('68), "Model Shop" ('68); Co-star, CBS Playhouse, "Shadow Game" ('69); b. L.A., Cal., 1947; p. Alexander and Allie Rydalch Hay; res: 20910 Ban-dera, Woodland Hills, L.A., Cal. 91364.

HAY, MABEL LOUISE, Bus. Mgr., News & Journal, Inc., 221 Spring St., Jeffersonville, Ind. 47130, '33–; b. Jeffersonville, Ind., 1908; p. Oscar and Florence Coyle Hay; res: 510 E. Market St., Jeffersonville, Ind. 47130.

HAY, SARA HENDERSON, Poet, Lit. Critic, Lectr.; Edtl. Asst., Oxford Univ. Press (N.Y.C.), '43–'44; Asst. to Head, Rare Bks. Dept., Charles Scribner's Sons, '35–'43; Auth: six vol. poetry, incl. "The Stone and the Shell" (Univ. of Pitt. Press, '59; Pegasus aw.); "The Delicate Balance" (Scribner's, '51; Edna St. Vincent Millay Mem. aw.); PSA (Exec. Bd., '35–'40), Crafts-man's Group, Wm. Poets, Sigma Alpha Iota, Alpha Gamma Delta; David Leitch Memorial Prize, '55; Lyric Memorial Prize, '59; Brenau Col.; Columbia Univ.; b. Pitt., Pa., 1906; p. Ralph and Daisy Baker Hay; h. Niko-lai Lopatnikoff; res: 5448 Bartlett St., Pitt., Pa. 15217.

HAYDEN, ELAINE LAWSON, Feature Wtr., Athens Banner Herald, Athens, Ga. 30601, '68–; Ed., Sunday mag., '67–'68; Jackson Herald (Jefferson); Hartwell Sun; Lenoir Rhyne Col., BA, '60; b. Montclair, N.J., 1939; p. Eldon and Gota Wikstrom Lawson; h. Neil S. Hayden; c. Stephanie Charlotte, Jennifer Elaine, Aaron Alexander; res: 190 Plum Nelly Rd., Athens, Ga. 30601.

HAYENGA, LOIS WELLS, Ed., Eagle Bend News, Box L, Eagle Bend, Minn. 56446, '59–; Minn. Nwsp. Assn.

(Adv. Vigor Aw., '59); b. Redwood Falls, Minn., 1931; p. Fred and Helen Champion Wells; h. Lester F. Hayenga; c. Keith L., Julie Ann.

HAYES, ANNIE GREEN, Librn., Walker College, Jasper, Ala. 35501, '61–; Tchr., Prin., Librn., '23–'61; Ala. Lib. Assn., ALA, NEA, Ala. Educ. Assn., AAUW (Treas.), BPW (Pres., Dist. Dir.), Toastmistress Intl. (Pres.); Who's Who of Am. Wm.; Dic. of Intl. Biog.; Who's Who in Lib. Svc.; Livingston State Col., BS, '47; Univ. of Ala., MS, '58; b. Guin, Ala., 1903; p. William and Bettie Allman Green; h. William E. Hayes; c. William T., Betty; res: Rte. 5, Box 344, Jasper, Ala. 35501.

HAYES, BLANCHE SHIRLEY, Volunteer Rsch. Svcs., Civilian and National Defense; Volunteer Health, Welfare and Education Svcs., Reptr., Feature Wtr., Benton (Ill.) Standard; Tchr. (Champaign, Ill.); Theta Sigma Phi (Matrix Table Founder), AAUW, Pi Beta Phi (50 Yr. Svc. Aw., '69); Nat. Civilian Defense Aw., '44; Lindenwood Col., '17–'18; Univ. of Ill., AB, '21; b. Benton, Ill., 1899; p. Charles T. and Malinda G. Jones Shirley; h. Col. William Hayes; c. William B. Hayes; res: 1002 W. Healey St., Champaign, Ill. 61820.

HAYES, DIXIE HILL, Food. Ed., The Kokomo Tribune, 300 N. Union St., Kokomo, Ind. 46901, '67–; proofreader, dispatch employee, '63; b. Council Bluffs, Ia., 1945; p. Ronald and Fern Edenburn Wells; h. Phillip Hayes; c. Ginger L., Patrick Michael; res: 5904 Monona Dr., Kokomo, Ind. 46901.

HAYES, MARGARET (Maggie), Dir. of Special Events, Bergdorf Goodman, 754 Fifth Ave., N.Y., N.Y. 10019; Fashion Ed., Life; Actress, films, TV, theatre (nominated, Acad. Aw., Best Supporting Player, "Black Board Jungle," '56); Co-prod., "Fortune and Men's Eyes," "An Ordinary Man," both off-Broadway; NATAS, AFTRA, SAG, AEA; Mirror News Annual Aw., "Best Dressed for Her Life" (Cal.), '59; outstanding aw., Cerebral Palsy, charity work, '66, '67, '68; Johns Hopkins Tchrs. Col.; b. Balt., Md., 1924; p. Jack and Clara Bussy Ottenheimer; h. Herbert Swope Jr.; c. Herbert III, Margaret Tracy Brooks Swope; res: 150 E. 72nd St., N.Y., N.Y. 10021.

HAYES, MARI, Copy Group Head, J. Walter Thompson, 420 Lexington Ave., N.Y., N.Y. 10017, '65–; Assoc. Copy Group Head, '60–'65; Group Head, SSC&B, '57–'59; Sr. Wtr., Y&R, '52–'57; Benton and Bowles, '49–'52; AWNY (Dir., '63–'68), Copy Club of N.Y.; Printers Ink/Marketing Communications Silver Medal, '69; N.Y.U.; b. Hoboken, N.J.; p. Frank and Mari Borneque Hayes; h. James Wettereau (dec.); c. James; res: 22 E. Eighth St., N.Y., N.Y. 10003.

HAYES, Sr. MARY ALMA, P.B.V.M., Asst. Prof.; Dir., Lib. Sci. Program, University of San Francisco, '58–; Coordr., Workshops and Insts., '54–; Tchr.-Librn., '38–'58; Lectr., Cnslt. to numerous pfnsl. orgs.; Contrbr., pfnsl. jnls.; Nat. Cncl. Tchrs. of Eng., Cal. Assn. Tchrs. of Eng. (Exec. Bd.), Cal. Central

Cncl. Tchrs. of Eng. (Exec. Bd., '63–'67), Catholic Audio-Visual Educs. Assn., NEA-DAVI, Audio-Visual Educs. Assn. of Cal., ALA, Catholic Lib. Assn. (Co-Founder, Northern Sec.; Chmn. several yrs.), Cal. Assn. of Sch. Librns. (Exec. Bd.); NAEB; Lib. Binding Inst. Nat. Silver Bk. Aw., '61; Who's Who in Lib. Sci., Dic. of Intl. Biog.; S.F. Col. for Wm., AB (Eng., Educ.), '47; Rosary Col., MA (Lib. Sci.), '47; b. Oakland, Cal., 1912; p. Michael and Catherine Burke Hayes; res: Presentation Convent, 281 Masonic Ave., S.F., Cal. 94118.

HAYES, MARY HEALY, Hostess, Radio Prog., WOR, '63–; CBS; NBC; ABC; h. Peter Lind Hayes; res: 103 Mt. Tom Rd., New Rochelle, N.Y. 10805.

HAYNES, DOROTHY FRANCES, Dir., Public Info., PR, Connecticut Institute for the Blind, 120 Holcomb St., Hartford, Conn. 06112, '58–; Dir., Public Info., Gtr. Hartford Easter Seal Drive, '60, '57; Free-lance Wtr., Artist, '49–; Asst. Dir., Robotham & Co., '42–'49; NLAPW (Gtr. Hartford Br. Pres.), '62–'64, VP, '60–'62), Conn. Cncl., VP, '68–'70), Secy., '64–'66), Hartford Soc. Wm. Painters (VP, '56–'58; aw., '53), Hartford Citizens Charter Comm. (Bd. of Dirs., '58–'61); numerous art aws.; b. Hartford, Conn.; p. Henry and Hattie Blake Haynes; res: 1256-D Farmington Ave., W. Hartford, Conn. 06107.

HAYNES, GRETCHEN WINTERHOFF, Ed., Justice, United Farm Workers Organizing Committee, AFL-CIO, 343 Winthrop St., Westbury, N.Y. 11590, '68–; Ed., State Coordr., Ariz. Consumers Cncl., '66–'68; Ed., L.I. CORE Nwsltr., '64–'65; Assoc. Ed., Bks. from the USA, Announcement Ed., Lib. Jnl., R. R. Bowker Co. (N.Y.C.), '58–'61; Ed., The Inst., for Commty. Dev. & Svcs., Mich. State Univ., '61; Am. Nwsp. Guild; Oberlin Col., AB, '55; London Sch. of Econs., '55–'56; New Sch. for Social Rsch., '56–'57; b. Detroit, Mich., 1934; p. Frederick and Virginia Burger Winterhoff; h. John Haynes; c. Karen Elizabeth, Julia Ruth.

HAYNES, VIRGINIA ELLYN, Adv. and PR VP, Kenneth Beauty Salons and Products, Inc., 19 E. 54th St., N.Y., N.Y. 10022, '68–; PR Dir., '65–'68; Asst. PR Dir., Helena Rubinstein, '63–'65; Assoc. Beauty Ed., Good Housekeeping Magazine, '62–'63; Instr. of Good Grooming, Adult Educ. Sch. (Caldwell, N.J.); Actress; Fashion Group Inc. ('66–), AWRT (N.Y. Chptr.); Outstanding Young Wm. of Am., '68; Am. Univ., '55–'57; Univ. of Colo., BA (Speech and Drama), '59; b. Mathews, Va., 1936; p. Jennings Wade Dorsey and Clara Virginia Miller Haynes; res: 15 E. 71st St., N.Y., N.Y. 10021.

HAYS, ELINOR RICE, Auth., biogs: "Morning Star," "Those Extraordinary Blackwells"; novels (as Elinor Rice): "The Best Butter," "Action in Havana," "Mirror, Mirror," "Take the Cash"; articles, short stories in New Yorker, Reader's Digest, Holiday, Seventeen, Woman's Day, others; h. Paul Hays; res: 276 Riverside Dr., N.Y., N.Y. 10025.

HAYS, JEAN MARIE, Public Info. Asst., University of Nebraska Medical Center, 42nd and Dewey Ave., Omaha, Neb. 68105, '66–; Public Info. Specialist, U.S. Army Engineers (Omaha Dist.), '64–'66; PR Asst., St. Catherine's Hosp., '58–'63; Am. Med. Wtrs. Assn., Omaha Cncl. of Indsl. Eds.; Mid-West Hosp. Assn. aw., '68; ACPRA aw., '67; Hosp. Mgt. aw., '59; Creighton Univ., BS, '55; b. Omaha, Neb.; p. Leo and Patricia Costello Hays; res: 4159 Chicago St., Omaha, Neb. 68131.

HAYS, WILMA PITCHFORD, Wtr., children's bks., incl: "PilgrimThanksgiving" (Coward McCann, '55), "Cape Cod Adventure" (Coward McCann, '64), "Little Horse That Raced a Train" (Little Brown, '59), "The Goose Who Was a Watchdog" (Little Brown, '67), "Drummer Boy for Montcalm" (Viking Press, '59), "Samuel Morse And The Electronic Age" (Franklin Watts, '66), "The French Are Coming" (Colonial Williamsburg Press, '65), "Pontiac" (Houghton Mifflin, '65), "The Apricot Tree" (Ives Washburn, David McKay, '68), "Rebel Pilgrim" (Westminster Press, '69); Cape Cod Wtrs. Workshop (Charter Mbr.), Auths. Guild; several Jr. Lit. Guild choices, '55, '61, '63; numerous bk. club choices; Univ. of Neb., '28–'32; b. Nance County, Neb., 1909; p. Clarence and Grace Lull Pitchford; h. R. Vernon Hays; c. Grace A. (Mrs. Elliott Kone); res: 660 La Gorce Dr., Venice, Fla. 33595; summers: Thimble Farms, Branford, Conn. 06405.

HAYWARD, OLGA HINES, Head, Ref. Dept., Southern University, Southern Univ. Br., P.O., Baton Rouge, La. 70807, '48–; Br. Librn., N.O. Public Lib. System, '46–'48; Head Librn., Grambling Col., '44–'46; Tchr. Marksville (La.) HS, '41–'42; ALA, La. Lit. Assn., Nat. Assn. of Col. Wm. (Secy., '49–'54), Dillard Univ., BA, '41; Atlanta Univ., BS (Lib. Sci.), '44; Univ. of Mich., MA (Lib. Sci.), '59; b. Alexandria, La.; p. Samuel and Lillie George Hines; h. Samuel Hayward; c. Anne Elizabeth, Olga Patricia; res: 1632 Harding Blvd., Baton Rouge, La. 70807.

HAYWOOD, CAROLYN, Auth., Illus., 30 children's bks., incl. "Eddie and His Big Deals" (Boys' Clubs of Am. Jr. Bk. Aw., '55); Auths. Guild, Phila. Art Alliance, Phila. Water Color Club, Cosmopolitan Club of Phila., Fellowship of the Pa. Acad. of the Fine Arts; "Distinguished Daughter of Pennsylvania," '69; b. Phila., Pa.; p. Charles and Mary Cook Haywood; res: 210 Lynnebrook Lane, Phila., Pa. 19118.

HAZZARD, GENEVIEVE CATHERINE, Central Reg. Dir., Project HOPE, 8102 E. Jefferson Ave., Detroit, Mich. 48214, '69–; VP, Campbell-Ewald Co., '50–'68; Asst. Mgr., Century Adv. Agcy., '45–'50; Theta Sigma Phi, Fashion Group (Reg. Dir., '65–'66; Bd. Mbr., '66–), Vista Maria Sch. (Bd. Mbr., '53–), Detroit Adv. Wm. of the Yr., '59; Nat. Adv. Wm. of the Yr., '60; Acad. of Achiev. aw., '60; Gamma Alpha Chi aw., '60; St. Theresa's Convent, BA.

HEAD, AGNES KASTNER, Publr., Hobbs Flare, Box

1095, 114 E. Dunnam, Hobbs, N.M. 88240, '48–; Lovington Daily Leader, '44–'58; Auth: "Hobbs Sketchbook," "Twelve Years Hard Life"; BPW (Charter Mbr., '38); numerous press aws.; subject of Nation's Business article, '65; Southeast Mo. State Tchrs. Col.; b. Dexter, Mo., 1904; p. Herman and Mary Wise Kastner; h. J. C. Head; c. Mrs. Mary Gene Schubert, Mrs. Joe Gallegos, C. J. Head; res: 1826 N. Jefferson, Hobbs, N.M. 88240.

HEAGNEY, ANNE, Colmst., Word of God, 2187 Victory Blvd., S. I., N.Y. 10314, '60–; Auth., juv. hist. bks., incl., "De Toni of the Iron Hand," (Colonial Dames of 17th Century aw., '61); Am. Catholic Hist. Assn., Hot Springs (Ark.) Wtrs. Workshop, Nat. Cncl. of Catholic Wm.; Little Rock Col., BA, '21; b. N.Y.C., 1901; p. Denis and Mary Masterson Heagney; res: 400 Bayles Ave., Hot Springs Ark. 71901.

HEALD, PHYLLIS WARDE, Ed., Your Digest, Home Econs. Dept., University of Arizona, Tucson, Ariz. 85721, '68–; Auth., five prod. plays; Past Dir., Southwest Workshop and Conf. at Univ. Northern Ariz.; Ariz. Press Wm. (Past Pres.; Wm. of the Yr., '67–'68), Theta Sigma Phi (Tucson Club Past Pres.); NFPW aw., '60; b. New Rochelle, N.Y., 1902; p. Ernest and Justine Bible Warde; h. Weldon F. Heald (dec.); res: 351 Smoot Pl., Tucson, Ariz. 85705.

HEALY, JULIA DAVIS, Auth., fiction, non-fiction, 18 bks.; incl. "Mount Up" ('67), "Legacy of Love" ('61); Wellesley Col., '21; b. Clarksburg, W. Va.; p. John W. and Julia McDonald Davis; h. Charles Healy; res: 115 Brookstone Dr., Princeton, N.J. 08540.

HEALY, MEG, Radio Commentator, KIXL, 1401 S. Akard St., Dallas, Tex. 75215, '49–; "The Healy's at Home," WFAA (Dallas), '46–'47; Theta Sigma Phi (aw., '66), ZONTA (Dallas Club Pres., '65), AWRT (Dallas Chptr. VP, '69), Catholic Bus. Wm. of Dallas (Pres., '60), Red Cross Media Aw., '68; Who's Who of Am. Wm.; p. Francis and Margaret Peurifoy Vaeth; h. Tim Healy (dec.); c. Dr. Tim Healy S.J., Mary Dean Dumais, David, Peggy Beauvois; res: 2920 Dyer St., Dallas, Tex. 75215.

HEAPS, JUNE FISHER, Head, Domestic Trade Sls., Williams & Wilkins Company, 428 E. Preston St., Balt., Md. 21202, '61–; Johns Hopkins Univ., '57–'58; b. Balt., Md. 1930; p. William and Elsie Stambaugh Fisher; h. Edgar Heaps; res: 3930 Kimble Rd., Balt., Md. 21218.

HEARD, A. LaRUE, Consumers Reptr., WINS Radio, Group W., 90 Park Ave., N.Y., N.Y. 10016, '68–; Detroit Free Press, '66–'67; John B. Russworm aw., '69; Pulitzer team aw., '67; Univ. of Mich., AB, '66; Columbia Univ. Sch. of Jnlsm., MS, '68; b. Detroit, Mich., 1944; p. Andrew and Corlee Williams Heard; res: 200 Claremont Ave., Apt. 44, N.Y., N.Y. 10029.

HEARST, AUSTINE McDONNELL, Colmst., Washington Times Herald, Washington, D.C. '43–'54; King

Features Syndicate, '48–'54; Radio Commentator, guest panelist NBC, CBS. Am. Newspaperwomen's Club, Wms. Nat. Press Club; Graduated, Convent of Notre Dame, '39; King-Smith Studio Sch., '39–'41; p. Austin and Mary Belt McDonnell; h. William Randolph Hearst, Jr.; c. William Randolph Hearst, III, and John Augustine Chilton Hearst; res: 810 Fifth Avenue, N.Y., N.Y. 10021.

HEATHCOTE, LESLEY MURIEL, Dir. of Libs., Prof., Montana State University, Bozeman, Mont. 59715, '65–'70; Librn., Prof., '52–'65; Librn., Assoc. Prof., '47–'52; Lib. Asst., '46–'47; Rsch. Asst., Intl. Labour Off., '45–'46; Serials Librn., Univ. of Wash., '29–'44; Asst. to Registrar, Univ. of Alberta, '24–'28; Ed., Montana Library Quarterly, '55–'63; Mont. Lib. Assn. (Pres., '53–'54, Hon Life. Mbr., '69), Pacific Northwest Lib. Assn. (Pres., '51–'52; Hon. Life Mbr., '68), ALA, Phi Alpha Theta; Univ. of Alberta, BA, '24 (first rank hon.); MA, '28; Univ. of Wash., BS (Lib. Sci.), '29; b. Edmonton, Alberta, Can., 1904; p. Henry and Annie Hilton Heathcote; res: 9236 SE 23rd, Mercer Is., Wash. 98040.

HEATHMAN ANN FISHER, Wms. Program Dir., Mitchell Broadcasting Company, 909-1/2 Main St., Grinnell, Ia. 50112, '67–; Copywtr., '64–'67; BPW; Carroll Col.; b. Phila., Pa., 1920; p. Mark and Lenora Northey Fisher; h. Fred Heathman; c. Judy, Linda, William; res: 603 Main St., Grinnell, Ia. 50112.

HEATLEY, MURIEL ROTH, Mgr., Commentary Library, 165 E. 56th St., N.Y., N.Y. 10022, '68–; Adv. Mgr., Seven Arts Bk. Soc. and Bk. Find Club, '67; Dept. Group Head, Macmillan Co., '64–'65; Adv. Mgr., Marboro Bks., '60–'63; Mgr., Hudson Bk. Club; AE, Friend-Reiss, '57–'60; Free-lance Wtr.; Hunter Col., BA (Eng.); Columbia Univ.; New Sch. for Social Rsch.; N.Y.U.; b. N.Y.C., 1922; p. John and Frances Gellert Roth; h. Herbert Heatley; c. Katherine Frances (Mrs. Paul Schwartz); res: 142-10 Hoover Ave., Jamaica, N.Y. 11435.

HEAVENRIDGE, JANET HOWES, Prod. Mgr., East-West Center Press, 1777 East-West Rd., Honolulu, Hi. 96822, '65–; Asst. Prod. Mgr., Univ. of Mich. Press, '60–'65; Univ. of Mich., AB, '50; Univ. of Conn., '50–'52; b. Ridgefield, Conn., 1928; p. Robert and Phyllis Greene Howes; h. Jerome Heavenridge; c. David C., Charles G.; res: 612 Poipu Dr., Honolulu, Hi. 96821.

HEBENSTREIT, JANET BLACK, Copy Chief, Gerald F. Selinger Co., Barclay Bldg., City Line Ave., Bala-Cynwyd, Pa. 19004, '69–; PR Dir., Ed., Am. Tile News, American Olean Tile Co., '61–'69; Assoc. Ed., Sun Publ. Co. (Naperville, Ill.), '59–'61; AAIE, Del. Valley Assn. of Communicators, Suburban PR Club; Hofstra Univ., BS, '46; b. Bklyn., N.Y., 1925; p. Foster and May Howard Black; h. Ferdinand Hebenstreit; c. Douglas B.; res: Oak Hill, Hagy's Ford Rd., Narberth, Pa. 19072.

HEBSON, ANN HELLEBUSCH, Dir. of Info. Svcs., Mary Baldwin College, Staunton, Va, 24401, '69–; Staff Wtr., News Bur., University of Miami (Coral Gables, Fla), '67–'69; Dir of PR, Nat. Bus. Col. (Roanoke, Va.), '65–'67; Auth: "The Lattimer Legend," (Macmillan fiction aw., '61), "A Fine and Private Place" (Macmillan, '58); Theta Sigma Phi, EWA; 1962 Yrbk. of Ency. Britannica; Contemporary Auths.; Intl. Dic. of Biog.; Who's Who Among Auths.; Burke's Peerage; Grinnell Col., BA, '47 (cum laude); b. Montgomery, Ala., 1925; p. Charles and Lucille Atherton Hellebusch; h. William J. Hebson (div.); c. William Jr., Annie Laurie, Andrew C; res: 21 Prospect St., Staunton, Va. 24401.

HECHT, LUCILLE ELIZABETH, Ed., International Altrusan, Altrusa International, Inc., 332 S. Michigan Ave., Chgo., Ill. 60604, '43–; Theta Sigma Phi, Ill. Wms. Press Assn. (numerous jnlsm. aws.), Soc. of Typographic Arts, Old Town Triangle Assn. (Pres., svc. aw., '68), Sr. Ctrs. of Met. Chgo. (Bd. Mbr.); numerous NFPW aws., President's Comm. on Employment of the Handicapped aw., '63; Univ. of Wis., BA '37; b. Rockford, Ill.; p. Robert and Anna Hanke Hecht; res: 1915 N. Lincoln Ave., Chgo., Ill. 60604.

HECK, BESSIE HOLLAND, Auth., "Millie" (World Publ. Co., '61; Runner-up, Sequoyah Children's Bk. Aw., '63), "Captain Pete" (World Publ. Co., '67), "The Year at Boggy" (World Publ. Co., '66), others; L. Corr: Southern Florist & Nurseryman (Ft. Worth, Tex.) '51–'61; Florist Exchange (N.Y.), '54–'59; Florist Rev. (Chgo. Ill.), '58; Nwsp. Inst. of Am. (N.Y.), Wtrs. Course), '46; b. Coalgate, Okla., 1911; p. John and Martha Ann Lemons Holland; h. Jack Heck; c. Ronald, Lillian, Roberts, LaFern Parker, Gaylia Knox, Naomi Wenzel; res: 3321 E. Fourth St., Tulsa, Okla. 74112.

HECTOR, SHIRLEY, Dir., Shirley Hector Agency, 29 W. 46th St., N.Y., N.Y. 10036, '50–; Rep. World-Union Press; Wtrs. Cnslt.; World Traveller; Lectr.

HEENEY, MARY ELLEN BURGER, Local Ed., South Haven New Era, South Haven, Kan. 67140, '47–; News Wtr., Wellington (Kan.) Daily News, '39; Corr., Radio KLEY (Wellington), '68; Sumner County Fedn. Wms. Clubs (Past Pres.), Sumner County Hist. Soc.; 1st prize, N.Y. Herald Tribune Press Contest, '38; Kan. Press Wm. aws., '69, '67, '64; Kan. Nwsp. Contest aw., '67–'68; Phillips Univ.; b. Portland, Kan., 1903; p. John and Fannie Aker Burger; h. David Gesslin Heeney (dec.); c. Mary Lous Heeney Boettcher, Patricia Ann Heeney Reich, John David; res: Box 98, South Haven, Kan. 67140.

HEFFINGTON, VIRGINIA KATHERINE, Homemaking Ed., Miami Herald, One Herald Plaza, Miami, Fla. 33101, '63–; Assoc. Food Ed., Better Homes & Gardens, '54–'63; Reptr., Freeman-Journal (Webster City, Ia.), '47–'51; Auth: "The Amos Rutledge New England Cookbook as told to Virginia Heffington" ('69),

"Food With a Florida Flair" ('68); Theta Sigma Phi (Des Moines, Ia. Chptr. Pres., '58), Home Econsts. in Bus.; Vesta aw., '66; Ia. State Univ., BS (Home Econ., Jnlsm.), '54; b. Webster City, Ia., p. Fred and Margaret Filloon Newman; h. Jack Cochrane; res: 2660 Tigertail Ave., Miami, Fla. 33133.

HEGEMANN, DOLORES ANN, Educ. Cnslt., WHA Radio, Ext. Div., University of Wisconsin, Radio Hall, Madison, Wis. 53706, '68–; Tchr., 18 yrs.; Nat. Cncl. for Social Studies; Holy Family Col., BA, '60 (magna cum laude); Marquette Univ., MA (European Hist.), '65; b. Lindsay, Neb., 1929; p. Bernard and Emma Otterpohl Hegemann; res: 2209 Cypress Way, Madison, Wis. 53713.

HEIDBREDER, MARGARET ANN, Staff Assoc., National Book Committee; Dir., School and Library Services, American Book Publishers Council, One Park Ave., N.Y., N.Y. 10016, '64–; Sch., Lib. Cnslt., Random House, Knopf, Pantheon, '63–'64; Sch., Lib. Cnslt., Henry Z. Walck, '60–'63; Sch., Lib. Asst., McGraw-Hill Bk. Co., '59–'60; Asst. Ed., Sch. Dept., Holt, Rinehart & Winston, '57–'59; Asst. Ed., Col. Dept., Alfred A. Knopf, '56–'57; Edtl. Asst., Tech. Bk. Dept., Macmillan Co., '55–'56; WNBA (VP, '69–; Bd. Mbr., '60–), Publrs. Lib. Prom. Group (Past VP), ALA, Am. Assn. of Sch. Librns., Intl. Reading Assn.; Univ. of Mich., BA, '55 (Phi Beta Kappa, cum laude); b. Mpls., Minn., 1933; p. H. Willis and Margaret Hislop Heidbreder; res: 433 W. 21st St., Apt. 2-A, N.Y., N.Y. 10011.

HEIDEN, STELLA, Mng. Ed., Dir., Universe Books, 381 Park Ave. S., N.Y., N.Y. 10003, '69–; Import Mgr., Dir. of Subsidiary Rights, Frederick A. Praeger; Asst. to Mng. Dir., Andre Deutsch Ltd. Publrs. (London); N.Y. Rep: Verlap Fritz Molden (Vienna), Calmann-Levy, Editeurs (Paris); Almqvist & Wiksell/Gebers (Stockholm); res: 58 W. 12th St., N.Y., N.Y. 10011.

HEIDERSTADT, DOROTHY, Librn., Prospect Branch, Kansas City Public Library, 4821 Prospect St., Kan. City, Mo. 64130, '68–; Librn., Paseo Br., '67–'68; Ref. Librn., Westport Br., '65–'67; Librn., Louis George Br., '42–'65; Children's Supvsr., Bethlehem (Pa.) Public Lib., '37–'42; Auth., 11 juv. non-fiction books, incl: "Stolen by the Indians" (McKay, '68), "Marie Tanglehair" (McKay, '65); Radio & TV Cnsl. of Gtr. Kan. City (Pres., '55–'56), ALA, Okla. Hist. Soc., Auth. Guild; Univ. of Kan. AB '36 (Phi Beta Kappa); Simmons Col., BS (Lib. Sci.), '37; b. Geneva, Neb., 1907; p. Charles and Florence Kilmer Heiderstadt; res: 3028 Sheley Rd., Independence, Mo. 64052.

HEILY, KATHRYN ANN, AE, Merrill Lynch, Pierce, Fenner & Smith, 300 California St., S.F., Cal. 94104, '69–; Adv. Mgr., Automobile Club of Wash.; Dir., Adv., Mktng., U.S. Projector Corp.; Asst. Dir., Audio-Visual Aids, Bank of America; Wtr., Prodr., Dir., Vista Prodns.; Theta Sigma Phi, Fin. Wms. Club of S.F., Adv. Assn. of the West; Univ. of Wash., BA (Jnlsm.); b.

Seattle, Wash., 1935; p. Raymond and Mary Armstrong Heily; res: 46 Forest Lane, San Rafael, Cal. 94903.

HEIN, LUCILLE ELEANOR, Free-lance Wtr., '50–; Program Specialist, Camp Fire Girls, '45–'50; Instr. in Eng., Wagner Col., '40–'44; Lectr. at wtrs. workshops, Tch., Crtv. writing, Ed. of many bks.; Auth: articles, reports, manuals; bks: "Thinking of You" (Association Press, '69), "We Talk With God" (Fortress Press, '68), "Enjoying the Outdoors With Children" (Association Press, '66), others; Univ. of Wis., BA, '37; MA, '38; b. Chgo., Ill., 1915; p. Ernest and Sena Midthun Hein; res: 33 Central Ave., S.I., N.Y. 10301.

HEINS, ETHEL YASKIN, Bk. Reviewer, Horn Book Magazine, 585 Boylston St., Boston, Mass. 02116, '63–; Elementary Sch. Librn. (Lexington), '62–; Children's Librn., '57–'62; '38–'43; Tchr., Children's Lit., Boston Col., '68–; ALA, Mass. Tchrs. Assn., Lexington Educ. Assn., Am. Assn. of Sch. Librns., New England Round Table of Children's Librns.; Douglass Col., BA, '38; Columbia Univ., '39; Harvard Grad. Sch. of Educ., '64; b. N.Y.C., 1918; h. Paul Heins; c. Peter S., Margery E.; res: 18 Warwick Rd., W. Newton, Mass. 02165.

HEINZ, CATHARINE FRANCES, Librn., Television Information Office, 745 Fifth Ave., N.Y., N.Y. 10022, '59–; Rsch. Librn., Mutual Of N.Y., '56–'59; Dir., Hosp. Lib. Bur., Un. Hosp. Fund, '48–'56; Asst. Dir., '47–'48; Med., Crew Librn., U.S. Naval Hosp. (Bklyn., N.Y.), '47; Ensign to LTJG, U.S.N.R., '43–'46; Librn., Tchr. (Cal., La.), '41–'43; Auth., bibliographies on TV, '60–; bk. revs.; ency. work; AWRT, ALA (Hosp. Libs. Div. Pres., '50–'51; Co-ed., "Objectives & Standards for Hospital Libraries," '53), Special Libs. Assn. (N.Y. Chptr. Secy., '62–'63; Exec. Ed., "Special Libraries of Greater New York Directory," '63), LPRC (Bd., '66–'68), N.Y. Lib. Club, Radio and TV Nwsp. Dirs. Assn., NAEB; Chm., PR Svcs. to Libs. Radio-TV-Film Festival, '66–'67; Rosary Col., BA, '41; Columbia Univ., MS, '52 (Sch. of Lib. Svc. Alumni Assn. Pres., '67–'68; Bd., '66–'69); b. Anaheim, Cal.; p. William J. M. and Genevieve Rolling Heinz; res: 100 W. 57th St., N.Y., N.Y. 10019.

HEINZE, BESSIE NEUBERG, Partner/Exec. Dir., Heinze and Penfound, 22 W. Monroe St., Chgo., Ill. 60603, '32–; Exec. Dir., Blessed Event PR program, '64–; Copywtr., Arrow Bus. Svc., '28–'32; Wms. Adv. Club of Chgo., Mothers' Aid, Am. Red Cross; Helen Cody Baker aw., '66; b. Chgo., Ill., 1909; p. Benjamin and Ghisela Braunstein Neuberg; h. Walter William Heinze; c. Ernest Gerson, William John; res: 247 E. Chesnut St., Chgo., Ill. 60611.

HEINZE, LINDA HOLLI, Asst. Prod., Mgr., McCall's Magazine, 230 Park Ave., N.Y., N.Y. 10017, '69–; Dir. of Adv. Make-Up, '64–; Dept. Asst., Look; Make-Up Coordr.; Lectr., Baruch Sch. of Bus., other schs.; Prod. Systems Cnslt.; Artist; N.Y. City Commty. Col. (Adv. Prod. Mgt.); Pace Col. (Bus.); b. Bklyn., N.Y., 1939; p.

Rudolph and Jessica Babcock Heinze; res: 145 E. 27th St., N.Y., N.Y. 10016.

HEISE, ARDYS, TV Coordr., University of California and Public Affairs Officer, School of Medicine, University of California, San Diego; TV, Radio Coordr., San Diego campus, '67; TV-radio Coordr., Barnes Champ Advertising, three yrs.; organized Ardys Heise & Assocs., PR, '64; TV Weather Girl, KFME-TV, one yr.; prod. shows, starting with "Here's to Women," her radio, TV show (Ontario, Cal.), beginning '48; Tchr., Commtns., Upland Col., two yrs.; PRSA (accredited), Theta Sigma Phi, AWRT, San Diego PR Club; top aw., ACPRA, '69; active in PTA; Upland Col., BA; San Diego State Col.; b. Upland, Cal.; h. Clarence Heise; res: 6014 Dira St., San Diego, Cal. 92122.

HEISEL, JOAN MAPLE, Wms. Dir., KOBI-TV, Prodr., Talent, "Woman's World," California-Oregon Broadcasting Inc., 2000 Crater Lake Hyway., Medford, Ore. 97501, '65–; Free-lance PR; Fashion Dir., Meier Frank Co. (Salem, Ore.); BPW, Jackson County Cncl. on Alcoholism, AWRT; Rose Festival (Portland, Ore., Hon. Mbr., '67); Providence Hosp. Sch. of Nursing, '51–'53; Univ. of Ore., '54–'55; S. Ore. Col. of Educ., '60–'61; b. Baker, Ore., 1934; p. James and Claire Oliver Maple; h. Manville Heisel; c. Mary Kate, Clare Marie, Michael John, Kevin Paul, James Matthew, Samantha Susan; res: 905 Oakgrove Rd., Medford, Ore. 97501.

HEITMAN, ELLEN A., Librn., Local Hist. Div., Finkelstein Memorial Library, Spring Valley, N.Y. 10977, '69–; Children's Librn., '62–'69; Librn.-in-Charge, '46–'62; N.Y. Lib. Assn., ALA, Rockland County Public Librns. Assn., BPW, Friends of Lib., Rockland County Conservation, Nat. Wildlife Fedn., Rockland County Hist., Museum Spring Valley, Valley Garden Club; New Paltz Col.; b. Spring Valley, N.Y.; p. Chester and Mabel DeBaun Heitman; res: 35 S. Madison Ave., Spring Valley, N.Y. 10977.

HELFMAN, ELIZABETH SEAVER, Auth., juv. nonfiction; bk., "Signs and Symbols around the World," 11 others; former tchr.; Teaching Guide Ed., NewsTime, '59–'66; Rsch. Dept., Bank St. Col. of Educ., '56–'68; Auths. Guild, Forum of Wtrs. for Young People; Mt. Holyoke, AB, '33; Radcliffe, MA, '34; Bank St. Col. of Educ., '39; b. Pittsfield, Mass., 1911; p. Henry and Alice Wentworth Seaver; h. Harry Helfman; c. Robert; res: 70 Prospect St., New Paltz, N.Y. 12561.

HELLER, DEANE FONS, Non-fiction Auth: "Ataturk"; "Paths of Diplomacy"; "The Cold War"; "The Berlin Wall"; Wtr., Miami Herald, '69; Wtr., Chicago Sun, '42–'44; Soc. of Am. Travel Wtrs. (founding mbr., '56), Old Island Restoration Fndn.; Univ. of Chgo., '42–'44; Univ. of Md., '47–'48; b. Milwaukee, Wis., 1924; p. Edmond and Delphine Fons; h. David Heller (dec.); c. David Fons and Douglas Bruce; res: 1502 Vernon Ave., Key West, Fla. 33040.

HELLER, GOLDIE, VP, AE, Dir. of Fashion, Wms. Svcs., Clinton E. Frank, Inc., 666 Third Ave., N.Y., N.Y. 10017; h. Edward W. Greenberg.

HELLER, JUDITH SULECKI, Ed., Forum in Medical Sciences, University of California, School of Medicine, Center for the Health Sciences, L.A., Cal. 90024, '67–; Assoc. Ed., Title Insurance & Trust Co., '63–'65; Tech. Ed., Hughes Aircraft Co., '63; Reptr., Santa Monica Evening Outlook, '63; Theta Sigma Phi (Beta Rho Chptr. Pres., '60–'61); U.C.L.A., AB, '61; Univ. of Ia., MA, '63; b. Erie, Pa., 1939; p. John and Mary Raskin Sulecki; h. Albert Heller; c. Naomi; res: 12117 Maxwellton Rd., Studio City, Cal. 91604.

HELLMAN, DORIS R., Free-lance Publicist; Pubcty Dir., L.A. County Museum, '58–'65; L.A. Philharmonic Orchestra, '45–'48; Pubcty. Club of L.A., Assn. of Theatrical Press Agents and Mgrs.; Barnard Col., BA, '28; b. N.Y.C., 1908; p. Dr. Milo and Helen Michelson Hellman; res: 1354 N. Harper Ave., Hollywood, Cal. 90046.

HELLMAN, LILLIAN, Auth., c/o Little, Brown and Company, 34 Beacon St., Boston, Mass. 02106; bk: "An Unfinished Woman" ('69); 12 plays incl. "The Children's Hour" ('34), "Watch on the Rhine" (N.Y. Drama Critics' Circle Aw., '41), "The Little Foxes" ('39), and "Toys in the Attic" (N.Y. Drama Critics' Circle Aw., '61); ed: "The Selected Letters of Anton Chekhov," "The Big Knockover: Selected Stories and Short Novels" of Dashiell Hammett; U.S. State Dept. cultural mission to Soviet Union, '44; Script Reader, MGM (Hollywood); Horace Liveright, publr.; educ: N.Y.U.; b. N.O., La.; h. Arthur Kober (div.).

HELM, MARGIE MAY, Librn., Western Kentucky University, Bowling Green, Ky., '20–'65 (Retired '65; Margie Helm Lib. named in hon.); Asst., N.Y. Public Lib., '19–'20; Rschr. in Ky. church history; auth., lib. articles in pfsnl. mags.; tchr., high sch., '16–'19; Ky. Lib. Assn. (Pres., '28–'30), S.E. Lib. Assn. (Secy.-Treas., '34–'36), ALA, BPW (local outstanding wm. cit.), other lib. and civic orgs.; Randolf Macon Wms. Col., AB, '16; Pratt Inst., Grad., '22; Univ. of Chgo., Grad. Lib. Sch., AM, '33; Fellowship, '30–'31); b. Auburn, Ky., 1894; p. Thomas and Nellie Blakey Helm; res: 1133 Chestnut St., Bowling Green, Ky. 42101.

HELMER, CONSTANCE ALLEN, Chief Nwsp. Librn., Columbus Dispatch, 34 S. Third St., Columbus, Ohio 43215, '66–'68; '69–; Chief Librn., Mansfield News Journal, '68–'69; instituted rapid retrieval system for Horvitz Newspapers (Ohio) and Columbus Dispatch; listings of ideas in ANPA Librn. Bul.; Ohio State Univ.; Kent State Univ.; h. Raymond G. Helmer, Jr.

HELMING, ANN, Auth: "To the Farthest Island" (Coward-McCann, '69), "A Woman's Place" (Coward McCann, '62), Asst. Drama Critic, Hollywood Citizen News, Chicago Tribune; colm., N.Y. Times Sybd, seven years; Hollywood Press Club; U.C.L.A., MA, '69

(Phi Beta Kappa); b. Bismarck, N.D., 1924; p. Grant and Helen Galloway Helming; res: 1516 N. Fairfax Ave., L.A., Cal. 90046.

HELZBERG, SHIRLEY BUSH, Pres., Bush, Burk & Morris Advertising, 1600 Baltimore Ave., Kan. City, Mo. 64108, '69–; Sls. Svc. Mgr., KLAC Radio (L.A., Cal.), '67; Prom. Mgr., KMBZ Radio (Kan. City, Mo.), '66–'67; Time Byr., Potts-Woodbury Advertising, '64–'66; AWRT; Cottey Col. (Nevada, Mo.), '59–'60; b. Kan. City, Mo., 1941; p. Geo. H. and Eulah M. Bush; h. Barnett C. Helzberg, Jr.; res: 5740 Cherokee Dr., Shawnee Mission, Kan. 66205.

HEMENWAY, JOAN ELIZABETH, Mgr., Sls. Adv. and Prom., Board of Publication, Lutheran Church in America, 2900 Queen Lane, Phila., Pa. 19129, '69–; Assoc. Ed., Youth mag., '62–'65; Free-lance Wtr. for various Protestant jnls.; Bksellers. Assn. of Phila.; Phila. Club of Adv. Wm.; Conn. Col. for Wm., BA, '60; Union Theological Seminary, BD, '68; b. Phila., Pa., 1938; p. Seymour and Katherine McKown Hemenway; res: 20 W. Tulpehocken St., Phila., Pa. 19144.

HEMENWAY, PATRICIA O'DONNELL, Feature Wtr., The Hartford Times, 10 Prospect St., Hartford, Conn. 06103, '65–; Wms. Ed., '59–'65; Soc. Ed., '55–'59; NLAPW, Symphony Soc. of Gtr. Hartford, Wadsworth Athenaeum; Green Mountain Col., '48; Hillyer Col.; Univ. of Hartford; b. Naugatuck, Conn., 1927; p. Edward and Edith Edquist O'Donnell; h. Allyn W. Hemenway, Sr.; res: 156 W. Main St., Avon, Conn. 06001.

HEMINGER, GOLDA McCLELLAND, VP, Findlay Publishing Company, 308 Broadway, Findlay, Oh. 45840, '41–; Owner, Repl. Courier, Radio WFIN; Owner, Radio WCSI (Columbus, Ind.); Nat. Camp Fire Girls (Hon. Bd. Mbr., '56–'56; Bd. VP, '55–'56; Bd. Mbr., '46–'56; WO-HE-LO aw., '56); Carnegie Inst., BS, '16; b. Rawson, Oh., 1893; p. James and Emma Holmes McClelland; h. Russell Lowell Heminger; c. Harold H., Edwin L.; res: 214 Glendale Ave., Findlay, Oh. 45840.

HEMINGWAY, MARY MOON, Free-lance Wtr., Tchr.; Colmst., "Notes for the Hostess," House & Garden, '59–; Tchr., New Canaan Country Sch., '64–; Copy Ed., House & Garden; AE, Carl Reimers Agcy.; Stamford Museum (Dir., '35–); Bryn Mawr Col., AB, '40; Manhattanville Col., MAT, '67, MA (Theology), '69; b. Dorset, Vt., '17; p. John and Charlotte Lucas Moon; h. Booth Hemingway; c. Ann (Mrs. Peter Tarlton), John M., Booth Roy; res: 353 Old Long Ridge Rd., Stamford, Conn. 06903.

HEMINGWAY, MARY WELSH, Auth: recollections on experiences shared with Ernest Hemingway; Former Reptr., Lord Beaverbrook London Daily Express; four Life magazine articles during WWII; Chptrs., "Their Finest Hour" ('41, Harcourt, Brace &

World) and "I Can Tell It Now" ('64, Dutton); guest on "Today," "Mike Douglas," "Girl Talk," "Dick Cavett" TV shows; h. Ernest Hemingway (dec.); res: 27 E. 65th, N.Y., N.Y. 10021.

HEMLOCK, ANN CAROL, Accounting/Bus. Mgr., de Martin, Marona & Associates, Inc., 33 W. 54th St., N.Y., N.Y. 10019, '69–; Bus. Mgr., MBA Music, Inc., '65–'69; VP, Dir., MBA Music of Can., Ltd., '67–'68; Asst. Controller, Philips Electronics, Inc., '63–'65; Licensed Notary Public, State of N.Y.; Soc. of Wm. Accountants, Spanish Inst., Inc.; Spencer Bus. Col., Univ. of Mich., Hunter Col., New Sch. Social Rsch.; b. N.Y.C.

HEMPEL, DIANE PERLOW, Assoc. Ed., University: A Princeton Quarterly, Stanhope Hall, Princeton Univ., Princeton, N.J. 08540, '69–; Asst. Ed., '63–'69; h. Carl G. Hempel.

HEMPHILL, HELEN ALBERTA, City Ed., Hastings Daily Tribune, Seaton Publishing Company, 908 W. Second St., Hastings, Neb. 68901, '52–; Feature Wtr., Drama Critic; Telegraph Ed., '38–'44; Tchr., Kan. State Univ. Sch. of Jnlsm., '30–'33; Theta Sigma Phi (Mu Chptr., Pres., '30), Am. Col. Quill Club (Pres., '29); Who's Who of Am. Wm.; Kan. State Univ., BS (Indsl. Jnlsm.), '30; Colo. State Col.; b. Clay Center, Kan.; p. Benjamin and Mattie Stewart Hemphill; res: 728 N. Lincoln Ave., Hastings, Neb. 68901.

HEMPHILL, JEANETTE FRANKE, Sr. Librn., Instr. in Bibliography, Univ. of Colo., 1100 14th St., Denver, Colo. 80202, '56–; Ref. Asst., Denver Public Lib., '54–'55; Asst. Instr. in German, Univ. of Ia., '51–'53; Cnslt., Delfi, Inc., '68–'69; various orgs., aws; Univ. of Ia., BA, '53; Univ. of Denver, MA, '56; b. Amana, Ia., 1932; p. William and Elizabeth Erzinger Franke; h. William Hemphill; c. D. Tristan and Joanna Lynn; res: 7061 Beach St., Westminster, Colo. 80030.

HENDERSON, DANNA KUSIANOVICH, Asst. to Ed., Airline Management and Marketing including American Aviation, Ziff-Davis Publishing Co., 1156 15th St. N.W., Wash., D.C. 20005, '69–; Mng. Ed., American Aviation, '68–'69; Ed., Business Aviation, '66–'68; Assoc. Ed., American Aviation, Aviation Daily, '60–'66; Rsch. Asst., Sen. Clinton P. Anderson, '59–'60; Reptr./Photogr., Albuquerque (N.M.) Journal, '54–'59; Aviation/Space Wtrs. Assn., Nat. Aviation Club, Am. Helicopter Soc., Nat. Bus. Aircraft Assn., Whirley-Girls (Secy.-Treas., Scholarship Chmn., '59–), Theta Sigma Phi, Aircraft Owners and Pilots Assn., Periodical Press Gallery; Univ. of N.M., BA, '55; b. Roswell, N.M., 1934; p. Daniel and Marguerite Blankenship Kusianovich; h. Jack A. Henderson; c. Lisa; res: 16208 Laurel Ridge Dr., Laurel, Md. 20810.

HENDERSON, JESTINA TUTT, Supvsr. of Lib.-Media Ctrs. Marshallton School District, 2916 Duncan Rd., Wilmington, Del. 19808, '67–; Assoc. Librn., Del. State

Col., '60–'67; Librn., S.C. State Col., '52–'60; Librn., Elizabeth City State Col., '47–'49; Comm. on Standards for Media Ctrs. in State of Del., ALA, Del. Lib. Assn. (Secy., '65–'66), Del. State Educ. Assn., NEA; Shaw Univ., BS; Catholic Univ., MS, '53; Rutgers Univ., post-grad., '62; h. Romeo Henderson.

HENDERSON, SYBIL VENNETTE, Pres., Henderson Publications, 6057 Melrose Ave., L.A., Cal. 90038, '67–; Partner, Gordon-Henderson Prods., '64–; Owner, Henderson Assoc., '59–; Auth.: "Lake, Stream and Seafood Cookbook—The Western Way" ('67), "Astrological Party Cookbook", other cookbks.; Prodr., films on cooking, safety in the kitchen; Cnslt., dev., Papaya Industry of Hi.; Lectr., Cal. Polytechnic Col.; Program Dir., Southern Cal. Produce Cncl.; AWRT, Western States Adv. Agcy. Assn., L.A. Adv. Wm.; L.A. Mdsng. Execs. Club aw., '66; b. Hot Springs, S.D., 1917; p. Ray and Dora Thomas Houghton; c. Michael Peck, Mrs. Ralph Kopald, Judy Peck; res: 176 N. Orange Dr., L.A., Cal. 90036.

HENDERSON, WANDA RAWATHA, Social and Environmental Cnslt.—Corporative Programming, Wanda Henderson Affiliates, 4121 Wilshire Blvd. Suite 212, L.A., Cal. 90005; prod. special events for corps.; West Coast Rep., Christian Sci. Monitor; Soc. Ed., Featured Colmst., L.A. Times-Mirror, '60's; Wms. Ed., Citizen News (Hollywood, Cal.), '50's; Wms. Ed., Citizen News (Tucson, Ariz.), '40's; Theta Sigma Phi, Fashion Group; Les Dames de Champagne of L.A., Intl. Hospitality Corps (Exec. Dir., founded, dev.); Statham House (Exec. Dir., established); Univ. of Ariz., Phoenix Jr. Col., Theater Arts Inst.; h. William E. Holzhauser.

HENDERSON, ZENNA CHLARSON, Auth. "Pilgrimage: The Book of the People" (Doubleday in U.S.; Gollanz in Eng.; Verlag in Germany), "The People: No Different Flesh," "The Anything Box"; Tchr., Eloy (Ariz.) Public Schs., '61–; Tchr., U.S. Air Force dependents, France; Tchr., Seaside Hosp. for Children, Waterford, Conn.; Sci. Fiction Wtrs. of Am., NEA, Ariz. Educ. Assn.; Ariz. State Univ., BA, '40, MA, '54; b. Tucson, Ariz., 1917; p. Louis and Emily Rowley Chlarson; h. (div.); res: Box 499, Eloy, Ariz. 85231.

HENDRA, BARBARA JANE, Pubcty. Dir., Trident Press, Pocket Books, Washington Square Press, Essandess Special Editions, Simon & Schuster, Inc., 630 Fifth Ave., N.Y., N.Y. 10020, '69–; Pubcty. Dir., Fawcett World Lib., '61–'69; Asst. to the Pubcty. Dir., '60–'61; PPA; Vassar Col., BA, '60; b. Watertown, N.Y., 1938; p. Frederick and Irene Rotundo Hendra; h. Eugene Gervasi; res: 142 Sterling Pl., Bklyn., N.Y. 11215.

HENDRICKS, SUE CAROLYN, Ed., Co. Pubns., Atlas Van-Lines, Inc., 1212 St. George Rd., Evansville, Ind. 47711, '67–; Secy. to VP, Fin.; Ky. Real Estate Broker, '67; Apt. Mgr., Secy., Frank Metts Realtors (Louisville, Ky.), '66–'67; free-lance writing, brochures, prom. for Nashville entertainers; ICIE, IEA (Ind. Chptr., Best

Magazine of Month, '69; Pres. Aw. of Merit, '69), Indsl. Eds. of Chgo. Assn.; Univ. of Evansville Evening Col.; b. Evansville, Ind., 1940; p. Henry and Margie Trent Hendricks; res: 1028 S. Lincoln Park Dr., Evansville, Ind. 47714.

HENDRIX, MARGARET WILLIAMS, Edtl. Assoc., Writer's Digest, 22 E. 12th St., Cinn., Oh. 45210, '53–; Gospel Light Press (Hollywood, Cal.); Am. Horseman mag. (Lexington, Ky.); Radio Interviewer, WDET (Wayne State Univ.); Auth: Writer's Digest Correspondence Courses textbooks; Theta Sigma Phi, Detroit Wm. Wtrs., Wm. Nat. Book Assn.; Oh. State Univ., BA (Edtl. Jnlsm.), '49; b. Columbus, Oh., 1927; p. Walter and Eva Johnston Williams; h. James Hendrix; c. Holly Lee, Susan Brooke; res: 24 Brucewood Dr., Pitt., Pa. 15228.

HENDRY, GAY, Premium Byr., Grey Advertising Inc., 777 Third Ave., N.Y., N.Y. 10017, '67–; Pres., Hendry House and Subsidiaries (Mail Order); b. Passaic, N.J., 1925; p. Joseph Rowinski; h. William Hendry; c. William, Jr., Robert, Elizabeth, Brian, Barbara; res: 35 Woodlawn Terr., Cedar Grove, N.J. 07009.

HENKE, ESTHER MAE, Assoc. Dir., Oklahoma Department of Libraries, 109 State Capitol, Okla. City, Okla. 73105, '68–; Ext. Librn., Okla. State Lib., '55–'68; Field Librn., '54–'55; Reference Librn., '53–'54; Head Librn., Ray County Lib. (Richmond, Mo.), '48–'51; Bookmobile Librn., '47–'48; Ed., Public Library Services Branch Nwsltr., '53–; various offs. in ALA, Southwestern Lib. Assn., Okla. Lib. Assn.; Theta Sigma Phi Aw., Outstanding Wm. of the Yr. in the Field of Lib. Svcs., '66; St. John's Jr. Col., '43–'44; Univ. of Okla., BA (Lib. Sci.), MA (Hist.), '53; b. Orlando, Okla., 1925; p. Emil and Marie Weber Henke; res: 4316 Woodland Dr., Okla. City, Okla. 73105.

HENKEL, MARGARET NOONAN, Assoc. Ed., Harper's Bazaar, 717 Fifth Ave., N.Y., N.Y. 10022, '69–; Asst. Beauty Ed.

HENNE, FRANCES, Prof., School of Library Service, Columbia University, N.Y., N.Y. 10027, '61–; Assoc. Prof., '55–'61; Visiting Assoc. Prof., '54–'55; Acting Dean, Grad. Lib. Sch., Univ. of Chgo., '51–'52; Assoc. Dean and Dean of Students, '47–'50; Assoc. Prof., '49–'54; Asst. Prof., '46–'49; Instr., '42–'46; Univ. HS Lib., '39–'42; N.Y. State Tchrs. Col. Lib. (Albany), '35–'38; Springfield (Ill) Public Lib., '30–'34; extensive work for sch. lib. standards and lib. and sch. media programs, projects and dev.; Co-auth., "Youth, Communication, and Libraries," and numerous articles in pfsnl. jnls.; Wms. Nat. Bk. Assn., AAUP, N.Y. Lib. Assn., Am. Assn. of Sch. Librns. (Pres., '48–'49; Dir., '45–'48), ALA, NEA, others; Carnegie Fellowship, '38–'39, Lippincott Aw., '63; Univ. of Ill., AB, '29 (Mortar Bd., '28), MA, '34; Columbia Univ., BS (Lib. Sci.), '35; Univ. of Chgo., PhD, '49; b. Springfield,

Ill., 1906; p. J. Z. and Laura Taylor Henne; res: 345 E. 50th St., N.Y., N.Y. 10022.

HENNIGER, JEAN FLOYD, Wms. Ed., The Oregonian, 1320 S.W. Broadway, Portland, Ore. 97201, '66–; Home Decoration Ed., '59–'66; PR Dir., Portland Symphony, '50–'59; Mgr., Portland Chamber Orchestra, '46–'50; First East-West Wtrs. Conf. (Hi.); Theta Sigma Phi, Fashion Group, Am. Interior Designers; 2 Am. Laundry Assn. AHLMA aws.; Chefs de Cuisine Aw., '66–'67; Ore. State Univ., BS, '43 (Distg. Achiev. Cit., '64); b. Texline, Tex., 1921; p. William and Bertha Floyd; h. Carl Henniger; c. Michael, Peter, Jan, Gayle (Mrs. Tony Karol); res: 3150 S.W. 108th St., Beaverton, Ore. 97005.

HENNINGE, ROSE ESZTERHAZY, Dir., Fairport Public Library, 335 Vine St., Fairport Harbor, Oh. 44077, '67–; Instr. in elementary educ., Supvsr., Student Teaching, Lake Erie Col., '60–; Asst. Librn., '40–'47; WNBA, AAUP, AAUW (VP), Delta Kappa Gamma (VP), League of Wm. Voters (Secy.), Intl. Reading Cncl.; Lake Erie Col., BA (Educ.), '60; (summa cum laude); Case Western Reserve Univ., MS (Lib. Sci.), '67; b. Fairport Harbor, Oh.; p. Alexander and Wilma Dunkler Eszterhazy; h. Bradford J. Henninge; res: 9771 Old Johnnycake Ridge, Mentor, Oh. 44060.

HENNINGS, JOSEPHINE SILVA, Info. Specialist-Govt. Liaison Offcr., U.S. Dept. of Defense, Pentagon, Wash., D.C., '61–; Delegate Liaison-Radio and TV, UN, N.Y.C.; Fgn. Corr., St. Louis (Mo.) Globe Democrat; Features Ed., St. Louis Star-Times; Colmst.-Edtl. Wtr., Honolulu (Hi.) Advertiser; Stringer, AP; News Analyst-TV Panelist-Special Events, ABC (N.Y.C.); News Analyst-Fgn. Corr. CBS; News Analyst-Special Events, WINS; Dir. of Radio for Civil Defense, WKAQ (San Juan, Puerto Rico); OPC, WNPC, AWRT; Who's Who of Am. Wm.; Who's Who in the East; Intl. Biog.; UN-U.S. Dept. of Labor Top Wm. in Intl. Bdcst. aw.; Wash. Univ., BA; George Wash. Univ. (Jnlsm., Polit. Sci.); b. St. Louis, Mo.; p. Francois and Josephine Barrick Silva; h. Senator Thomas C. Hennings (div.; dec.); c. Mrs. Joan King, Breen Halpin; res: 2501 Calvert N.W., Wash., D.C.

HENRY, ANNE GRACE WIRTSCHAFTER, PR; Secy.-Treas., Henry's Marine Buying Service, Inc., P.O. Box 301, Coconut Grove, Fla. 33133, '65–; free-lance pubcty. writing, Pan Am. Bank (Miami, Fla.), Andros Mgt. Ltd. (Bahamas), others, '61–'69; pubcty. writing, PR, Leo Burnett Co., Inc. (N.Y.C.), '58–'60; pubcty. writing, PR, The Franklin Inst. (Phila., Pa.), '57–'58; free-lance pubcty. writing, through agcys., The Borden Co., others, '56–'57; free-lance mag. writing, Dell Publ. Co., '56–'57; copyreading, Offcl. Detective Stories Magazine (Triangle Pubns.), '50–'56; Assoc. Ed., Nat. Sports Rev. (Atlantic City, N.J.), '49–'50; Temple Univ. (Home Econs., Bus. Adm.), '44–'47; Charles Morris Price Sch. of Adv. and Jnlsm., '47–'48; b. Atlantic City, N.J., 1925; p. Charles M. and Mabel

Steinhart Wirtschafter; h. Joseph Henry; res: Houseboat VASA, Miami, Fla.

HENRY, HELEN GORHAM, Mgr., Commtns. Dept., Louisville Area Chamber of Commerce, 300 W. Liberty St., Louisville, Ky. 40202, '67–; Ed., Louisville Magazine, '63–; '53–'60; Edtl. Asst., '51–'53; Dir., Pubns. Div., '63–'67, '53–'60; Dir., News Svcs. Div., Ky. Dept. of Public Info., '61–'62; Nwsp. Reptr., Adv. Copywtr., '48–'51; Part Owner, Amster & Associates, Louisville PR Cnslts.; Am. Assn. of Commerce Pubns. (Pres., '60), PRSA (Bluegrass Chptr. Past Dir.), Am. C. of C. Execs.; Ky. Colonel; Western Ky. Univ., BS, '46 (cum laude); Univ. of Ky., ABJ (Jnlsm), '48; b. Central City, Ky., 1925; p. J. Broadus and Bertha Gorham Henry; res: 7 Hawthorne Hill, Louisville, Ky. 40204.

HENRY, HELEN KINCAID, Pres., Daily News, Chester Ave., Middlesboro, Ky. 40965, '60–; Wms. Ed., '51–'64; Pres., Cumberland Gap, '60–; Retail Bus., '47–'50; Nurse, '40–'45; Vanderbilt Univ., BS (Nursing), '39; b. Cumberland Gap, Tenn.; p. Robert and Beulah Chance Kincaid; h. Maurice Henry; c. Kay Henry Ballard; res: N. 24th St., Middlesboro, Ky. 40965.

HENRY, MARY ROBLEE, Feature Assoc. Ed., Vogue Magazine, 420 Lexington Ave., N.Y., N.Y. 10017, '55–; Auth., "A Farmhouse in Provence" (Alfred A. Knopf, '69); Wtr., travel articles in nat. pubns.; N.Y. Travel Wtrs. Assn.; res: 301 E. 47th St., N.Y., N.Y. 10017.

HENRY, MURIEL CROTHERS, Dir., Info. Svcs. and Assoc. Gen. Dir., National League for Nursing, 10 Columbus Circle, N.Y., N.Y. 10019, '56–; Dir. of Program, Nat. Comm. on Careers in Nursing, '48–'56; PR Dir., Travelers Aid Soc. of Chgo., '45–'47; Assoc. Ed., Robbins Publ. Co., Am. Perfumer, '39–'42, and Gas Age and Indsl. Gas, '42–'45; Staff Assoc., Nat. Travelers Aid Assn., '37–'38; Radio, Pubcty. Wtr., J. Walter Thompson (L.A., Cal.), '33; Pubcty. Dir., Seattle Gas Co., '31–'33; Pubcty. Wtr., Pacific Tel. & Tel. Co. (Seattle, Wash.), '30–'31; booklet, "Story of Gas" (Am. Gas Assn., '38); articles; AAUW, Theta Sigma Phi (Nat. VP, '40–'46; N.Y.C. Chptr. Pres., '37–'38; VP, '55–'56; Secy., '36–'37), AIGA, Nat. PR Cncl. for Health and Welfare Svcs.; Univ. of Wash., BA (Jnslm.), '29; N.Y.U., '36–'37; Univ. of Chgo., '46–'47; Columbia Univ., '57–'58; b. Pryor, Okla., 1906; p. I. James and Katherine M. Freeman Crothers; h. Donald A. Henry (dec.); c. Dr. Helen I., Douglas A., Donald A., Jr.; res: 200 E. 36th St., N.Y., N.Y. 10016.

HENSEL, JANET WAGNER, Catalog Librn., Rose Memorial Library, Drew University, Madison Ave., Madison, N.J. 07940, '66–; Librn., Claude O. Markoe Sch., (St. Croix, U.S. Virgin Islands) '66; Catalog Librn., various Cols. and Univs., '62–'65, '55–'59; Catalog, Reference Librn., Engineering Lib., IBM Corp. (Kingston, N.Y.), '59–'62; Librn., Museum Asst., Schenectady (N.Y.) Museum, '52–'54; Librn. and Asst. Librn., '46–'52; Who's Who of Am. Wm.; Allegheny Col. (Meadville, Pa.), BA (Eng. Lit.), '45; Syracuse Univ.

Lib. Sch., BS (Lib. Sci.), '46; b. Cleve., Oh., 1923; p. Trace and Sara Davison Wagner; h. Robert E. Hensel; res: 851 Springfield Ave., Apt. 14-J, Summit, N.J. 07901.

HENSELL, HESTER E., PR Cnsl. in Educ., Hester E. Hensell, Inc., 5 Tudor City Pla., N.Y., N.Y. 10017; VP, OPC, '45–'50; Ed., several OPC bks: "Deadline Delayed" ('47), "Men Who Made Your World" ('49), and others; Polish Govt. Info. Ctr., '44–'45; Fgn. Dept., First Nat. City Bank, '41–'44; Fgn. Corr., Un. Press, '35–'40; Ed., "Who's Who in Foreign Correspondence" ('47); Auth., "Would You Call It Feudal?" ('44); Wtr., mag. articles; PRSA (Bd. Mbr.), AAUW (Bd. Mbr.), BPW (Dist. Bd. Mbr.); Temple Univ., BS (hons.); N.Y.U., MA; Univ. of Lyon (France) Fellow, '32–'34; Univ. of Perugia (Italy), '35; b. Hagerstown, Md.; p. Walter S. and Cora C. Chenoweth Hensell.

HENSLEY, ATHENE ORME, Asst. VP, Indsl. Rels., United States National Bank, 190 Broadway, San Diego, Cal. 92112, '69–; Asst. VP, Adv. and Bus. Dev., '65–'69; Indsl. Relations Dir., '62–'65; Asst. Dir., Adv., PR, '59–'62; Loan Offcr., '52–'62; Natl. Assn. of Bank Wm. (Educ. Chmn., '68), Bank PR & Mktng. Assn., Am. Inst. of Banking, Bank Adm. Inst., San Diego Clearing House; many citizenship aws; Southern Ore. Col., BA, '33; Am. Inst. of Banking, Cert., '66; b. Grants Pass, Ore., 1913; p. Alex and Majorie Orme; h. Glen Hensley; res: 6763 Eldridge St., San Diego, Cal. 92120.

HENTHORN, MAXINE WELLS, Head, Dept. of Jnlsm., Angelo State University, 2200 W. Ave. N, San Angelo, Tex. 76901, '65–; Dir. of Jnlsm., '63–'65; numerous articles; W. Tex. Jnlsm. Educ. Assn. (Pres., '68–'69); Aw., outstanding achiev. in jnlsm. educ., Nwsp. Fund, Inc., '65–'66; Stephen F. Austin State Univ. (Nacogdoches, Tex.), BS, '61; MA, '62 (Alpha Chi; top scholarship aw. for grad. study); Univ. of Wis., '62–'63; Syracuse Univ., '65 (Nwsp. Fund Fellow); Univ. of Mo. (Kappa Tau Alpha, Tri-Penta, Chi Omicron Mu); b. Garrison, Tex.; p. A. H. and Bessie Barrett Bird; h. Dr. David Wilson Henthorn; c. Albert Durward Wells, Brenda Bess Wells; res: 3101 Oak Forest Dr., San Angelo, Tex. 76901.

HEPP, SIGRID HÉLÈNE, TV Prodr., J. Walter Thompson Co., 420 Lexington Ave., N.Y., N.Y. 10016, '64–; Asst. Prodr., '62; Secy., '61; Edtl. Asst., Translator, Atlas Magazine, Eleonor Davidson Worley Publ. Co., '67; Art Dirs. Club of Chgo. Aw., Religion in Am. Life TV comml. "God's Work" ('60), '59–'60; Univ. of Munich, '60–'61, '57–'59; Colo. Col., BA, '61; b. N.Y.C., 1938; p. Ernst and Frances Fulenwider Hepp; res: 300 E. 33rd St., N.Y., N.Y. 10016.

HEPPINSTALL, CYNTHIA OUTLAW, Exec. Dir., Heppinstall Enterprises, 328 Winona Ave., Phila., Pa. 19144, '60–; PR AE, '56–'59; PR Cnsl., Mktng. Advisor to beauty industry product manufacturers, svc. cos.; PR Cnsl., Contrb. Ed., Goodway Total Commtns., Inc., '67–; Mng. Ed., Beauty Fair Magazine, '65–'68;

Wms. Ed., Deadline Exclusive, radio show, '59–'61; live coverage of "March on Wash." for network of five radio stations; NAMW (Del. Valley Chptr. Secy., '67–'68), Nat. Assn. of Mkt. Developers (Phila. Chptr. PR Dir., '67–'68), various others; Temple Univ., Phila. Col. of Textiles and Sci.; b. Phila., Pa., 1931; p. W. Oscar and Floretta Tyree Outlaw; h. Frank Heppinstall; c. Erie V., Marcus V.; res: 328 Winona Ave., Phila., Pa. 19144.

HERBST, (LILA) DEAN FINLEY, Exec. Dir., Theta Sigma Phi, 106 Lantern Lane, Austin, Tex. 78731, '67–; Free-lance PR, Ed., Wtr., '53–'67; Public Affairs Asst., USIA, Dept. of State, Kabul, Afghanistan, '50–'53; Wms. Ed., Austin American-Statesman, '47–'50; Asst. Prod. Ed., Tide Magazine, N.Y.C., '45–'47; PR, BBC, '44–'45; Auth., "Flight to Afghanistan" (Steck-Vaughn Co., '69), teenage suspense novel; Writers Roundup (Best Tex. Bks. of Yr.), '69; Univ. of Tex., BJ, '44; active in commty., church orgs.; b. Houston, Tex., 1923; p. Frank and Lila McCullar Finley; h. Harvey Herbst; c. Frederick, Marian; res: 5705 Bulard Dr., Austin, Tex. 78731.

HERBST, MARGARET MARY, Owner, Margaret Herbst, Public Relations, 101 Park Ave., N.Y., N.Y. 10017, '51–; Press Chief, Associated Bulb Growers of Holland, '46–'51, '38–'40; Asst., Press Dept., Netherlands Info. Bur., '40–'46; weekly synd. colm. on gardening; radio recs.; first wm. to speak at Intl. Horticultural Congress, '62; numerous orgs., aws.; Hunter Col., BA, '37 (Phi Beta Kappa); b. N.Y.C.; p. Louis and Harriet Klein Herbst; res: 642 Locust St., Mt. Vernon, N.Y. 10552.

HERD, BETTY WEST, Real Estate Ed., Evening Star, 4043 Irving Pl., Culver City, Cal. 90230, '62–; Wm's. Cncl., Culver City Bd. of Realtors Emblem Club; Copley Jnlsm. Aw. ('63, '67); b. Wales, Eng., 1920; p. Ernest and Amelia Purnell West; h. William Herd; res: 10733 Farragut Dr., Culver City, Cal. 90230.

HERFURTH, HILDEGARDE JEANETTE, Dir., PR, Southeast Asia Area, American Red Cross, Saigon, Vietnam, APO 96309, '69–; Hollywood Rep., '67–'69; Mag. Specialist, '63–'67; Dir., Public Info. (Minn.-Hennepin Chptr.), '57–'62; Wtr., Photogr. (European Area), '55–'57; Reptr., Ed., Washington Post, Washington Times Herald, Alexandria (Va.) Gazette, Portsmouth (Va.) Star, '46–'55; AWRT, Toastmistresses Intl. (D.C. Last Word Club Pres., '65–'66), Alpha Psi Omega; Valparaiso Univ., AB, '46; Univ. of Pa., MA, '63; b. Alexandria, Va., 1923; p. Paul and Jeannette Fuchs Herfurth; res: Saigon, Vietnam, APO 96309.

HERMAN, M. JEAN, PR Cnslt., Wtr., self-employed, 134 E. 60 St., N.Y., N.Y. 10022, '50; rsch., writing, PR cnslt. work for clients incl: academic insts., wms. groups, Variety Clubs of Am., Seven Cols. Vocational Workshops; colm., Cape Ann Summer Sun; booklet, "The Bells Aren't Ringing"; specializing, consumer groups, civil liberties; Barnard Col. (Govt., Econs.), '46 (Dean's List, '45–'46); Columbia Grad. Eng. Dept., '50–'53; b. Newburgh, N.Y.; p. Henry R. and Mildred E. Heyman Herman.

HERMANN, MILDRED M., Special Asst. to the Gen. Secy., Board of National Missions, United Presbyterian Church, U.S.A., 475 Riverside Dr., N.Y., N.Y. 10027, '66–; Dir. of Press Rels., '60–'66; Gen., Feature Wtr., '53–'60; Dir. of Christian Educ. (Indian chs.; S.D.), '48–'53; articles in various ch. pubns.; three bks. (Friendship Press); PRSA; Hunter Col., AB, '46 (summa cum laude; Phi Beta Kappa); Columbia Univ., AM, '47; Union Theological Seminary, BD, '67; b. N.YC., 1924; p. John and Mildred Erbe Hermann; res: 619 Wilcox Ave., Bronx, N.Y. 10465.

HERNANDEZ, AILEEN C., Free-lance PR and Industrial Cnslt., 680 Beach St., Rm. 342, San Francisco, Cal. 94109, '66–; Equal Employment Opportunity Commission, Wash., D.C., '65–'66; formerly Asst. Chief of Cal. Fair Employment Practice Commission; Educ. and PR Dir, Intl. Ladies Garment Workers Union, Pacific Coast Region; NOW (Nat. Pres., '70–), Nat. Comm. Against Discrimination in Housing (Western Representative), Nat. Urban Coalition (Nat. Steering Comm.), Am. Civil Liberties Union (Nat. Advisory Comm.), Bay Area Urban League (Bd. of Dirs.); Howard Univ., BA (Govt.), '47; Cal. State Col., MA (Political Sci.), '61; b. N.Y.C., 1926; h. (div.).

HERNANDEZ, PATRICIA ORRELL, Media Dir., Witherspoon & Associates, Inc., 321 S. Henderson, Ft. Worth, Tex. 76101, '67–; AWRT (Treas., '68–'69); Wichita Univ.; b. Nakoosa, Wis., 1937; p. Dale and Evelyn Rapier Orrell; h. Danny Hernandez; c. Cynthia, Deborah; res: 4224 Grand Lake Dr., Ft. Worth, Tex. 76135.

HEROLD, FLORENCE NELL, Wms. Program Dir., WTTN Watertown Radio, Inc., 104 W. Main St., Watertown, Wis. 53094, '55–; Prodr. of German program, '53–'55; various organizations and aws.; Northwestern Col.; b. Watertown, Wis., 1926; p. Elmer and Esther Degner Nell; h. Howard Herold; c. Gail (Mrs. Brian Theide), Glenn Elliott, Lynn Ellen; res: 608 Elm St., Watertown, Wis. 53094.

HERR, MARILYN HUBBARD, Performer, Children's Show, WHEN-TV, 980 James St., Syracuse, N.Y. 13214, '55–; Cont. Dir., '54; AWRT; Am. Acad. of Dramatic Arts, '48; b. Watertown, N.Y., 1928; p. Amos and Anita Persons Hubbard; h. Edmund Herr; c. Corliss Alexandra, Charles Haskell II; res: 135 Sunnyside Park Rd., Syracuse, N.Y. 13214.

HERRIDGE, FRANCES, Drama and Movie Ed., New York Post, 75 West St., N.Y., N.Y. 10001, '54–; Dance Critic, '50–; Smith Col., BA; h. Frances Karns.

HERRMANN, EDITH MARIE, Sr. Librn., Head, Tech. Svcs., Hillside Public Library, John F. Kennedy Plaza,

Hillside, N.J., 07205, '52–; Br. Librn., West Hartford (Conn.) Public Lib., '51–'52; various librn. positions, '43–'51; ALA, N.J. Lib. Assn. (Oh. Bd. its Techn. Svcs. Sect. 1957–'61, '62–'63; Pres., '59–'60), BPW (Hillside Club Bd. Mbr., '69–'70, '64–'65, '56–'59), Intl. Platform Assn.; Who's Who of Am. Wm., 2,000 Wm. of Achiev., Royal Blue Bk., numerous others; Pembroke Col., AB, '42; Columbia Univ., BS (Lib. Sci.), '43; MS, '49; b. Berlin, Germany, 1920; p. Alfred and Elisabeth Bernhard Herrmann; res: 204 Westfield Ave., Elizabeth, N.J. 07208.

HERSHEY, A. ARLENE, Free-lance Publicist, Wtr., '69–; Mgr., Consumer Products Pubcty., Educ., Hamilton Watch Co., '56–'68; Free-lance Travel Lectr., '53–'56; U.S. Army Special Activities Div., Entertainment Dir., overseas, '48–'53; APRA, PRSA, AAUW; Univ. of Rochester, BM, '38; Eastman Sch. of Music, '39; Julliard Sch. of Music, '40; New Sch. of Social Rsch., '42; b. Harrisburg, Pa., 1915; p. Eli and Carrie Hershey Hershey; res: 332 N. Duke St., Lancaster, Pa. 17602.

HERSHEY, LENORE O., Mng. Ed., Ladies' Home Journal, 641 Lexington Ave., N.Y., N.Y. 10022, '69–; Special Projects Ed., McCall's; Sr. Ed.; Special Prom. Dir.; Wtr., short stories, several mags.; Lectr., Radcliffe Col., '68–'69; AWNY, Child Study Assn., Riverdale Neighborhood House Bd.; Riverdale Commty. Good Neighbor Aw.; Hunter Col., BA; p. Max and Frances Oppenhiemer; h. S. G. Hershey; c. Jane; res: 750 Ladd Road, N.Y., N.Y. 10471.

HERZEL, CATHERINE WILLIAMS, Ed. (children), Board of Parish Education, Lutheran Church in America, 2900 Queen Lane, Phila., Pa. 19129, '69–; Free-lance Wtr.; Librn., public sch., sch. of nursing; Wilson Col., AB; h. Frank Herzel; res: 7148 Crittenden St., Phila., Pa. 19119.

HERZIG, DORIS, Reptr., Newsday, 550 Stewart Ave., Garden City, N.Y. 11530, '59–; PR Dir., Lamp and Shade Inst. of Am., '51–'59; NHFL; Hunter Col., BA (Phi Beta Kappa); b. Bklyn., N.Y.; res: 34–15 74th St., Jackson Heights, N.Y.

HERZINGER, NORMA MARTIN, Wms. Pg. Ed., Twin Falls Times News, 132 Second St. W., Twin Falls, Idaho 83301, '63–; Idaho Press Wm., NPWC, Altrusa Club (Corr. Secy., '68–'69); Nat. Fedn. of Music Clubs aws.; Who's Who of Am. Wm.; local aws. for wms. coverage; b. Twin Falls, Idaho, 1936; p. Ben and Gladys Bigley Martin; h. Stanley Herzinger; c. Vicki Jo, Susan Jean; res: 1037 Sunrise Blvd., Twin Falls, Idaho 83301.

HESSEL, EDITH BELL, Secy.-Treas., Cambist Films, Inc., 850 Seventh Ave., N.Y., N.Y. 10019, '64–; Actress, '45–; IFIDA, AEA, AFTRA, SAG; Univ. of Wn. '44–'45; b. Seattle, Wash., 1923; p. Everett and Edith Swan Bell; h. Lee Hessel; c. Brad E., Jill R.; res: 15 Oak Ave., Tarrytown, N.Y. 10591.

HESTER, GRACE COX, Ed., Forest Press, Inc., Box 366, Elm St., Tionesta, Pa. 16353, '65–; started as typist, '60; active in civic activities; b. Grafton, W. Va., 1928; p. Clifford and Eva Campbell Cox; h. Richard Hester; c. Richard A., Donald L., Linda Sue; res: Box 422, Elm St., Tionesta, Pa. 16353.

HESTER, LORRAINE HAYS, Ed., Photogr., Dallas Power and Light Co., 1506 Commerce, Dallas, Tex. 75201, '59–; Feature Wtr., Photogr., Garland Daily News, Texas Mesquiter, '57–'58; Dallas IEA (Third VP, '64; Bd. of Dirs., '65; Ed. of the Yr., '68), ICIE, Theta Sigma Phi; Dallas Adv. League Aw. of Merit, '67; Southwest Conf. of Indsl. Eds. Aw. of Merit, '64, '65; Aw. of Excellence, '67; Kan. City Univ., '45; Southern Methodist Univ., '57–'58; b. Crawford County, Ark.; p. Frederick and Margaret Weaver Hays; h. (div.); c. Bruce Hays Gibson; res: 4411 Westway, Dallas, Tex. 75205.

HETZELL, MARGARET CAROL, Assoc. Dir. of PR, General Conference of Seventh-day Adventists, 6840 Eastern Ave., N.W., Wash., D.C. 20012, '62–; Asst. Dir. of PR, '54–'62; Ed., Tell, monthly PR jnl., '51–; Auth. of numerous PR and religious bks. and articles; Wtr. and Dir. of several PR and religious films; Dir. of denomination's exhbn. at N.Y. World's Fair; conducted commtns. workshops in U.S. and other countries; Assoc. Ch. Press, '67–; RPRC (Wash., D.C. Chptr. Treas., '63), Columbia Union Col. Alumni Assn. (VP, '67, '69); Columbia Union Col., BA, '40; b. Vineland, N.J., 1917; p. Albert and Elizabeth Atwood Hetzell; res: 7211 Trescott Ave., Takoma Pk., Md. 20012.

HETZNER, BERNICE M., Librn., Prof. of Lib. Sci., University of Nebraska College of Medicine, 42nd and Dewey Ave., Omaha, Neb. 68105, '63–; Assoc. Prof., '48–'57; Film Librn., Univ. of Omaha, '46–'47; Adm. Asst., Lincoln Public Lib., '44–'46; Contrbr., "Handbook of Medical Library Practice"; Cnslt., VA Hosp. Libs., '56; ALA, Med. Lib. Assn. (Bd. of Dirs., '59–'62), Special Lib. Assn., Neb. Lib. Assn., Mountain-Plains Lib. Assn.; Murray Gottlieb Prize Essay Aw., '58; Univ. of Denver, AB (Lib. Sci.), '34; Colo. State Univ., MA, '35; h. Ralph Hetzner; res: 327 S. 92nd St., Omaha, Neb. 68114.

HEUSINKVELD, HELEN GEORGE, Co-auth: (with Noverre Musson) "Best Places to Live When You Retire" (Fell, '69), "1001 Best Places to Live When You Retire" (Dartnell, '64), "Buildings for the Elderly" (Reinhold, '63), Theta Sigma Phi; Knox Col.; Univ. of Ia.; b. Clinton, Ia., 1898; p. Calvin and Goldie Reno George; h. David Heusinkveld; c. David, Kennon Dunham; res: 1673 Cedar Ave., Cinn., Oh. 45224.

HEWITT, PENELOPE PEARMAN, Prodr.-TV Dept., Doyle Dane Bernbach, 20 W. 43rd St., N.Y., N.Y. 10025, '66–; Asst. Prodr., doc. series, "Intertel," NET, '64–'66 (Peabody Aw. winning series); Prodr., Ogilvy-Mather (London), '59–'63; Prod. Coordr., Lintas Limited (London), '54–'59; Cannes Film Festival first prize, '62;

Am. Inst. Graphic Artists Outstanding Commls. of '68; Benenden Sch. (Kent, Eng.), '50; St. Martins Sch. of Art (London), Nat. Design Diploma, '53; b. Broxbourne, Eng.; h. Robert Hewitt; res: 645 West End Ave., N.Y., N.Y. 10025.

HEYA, MARIA ELIZABETH, Serials Librn., Gannon College, Perry Sq., Erie, Pa. 16501, '53–; Auth., "Hungarian Classical Literature in U.S. Libraries" (Catholic Univ. of Am., '53); ALA, Catholic Lib. Assn., Pa. Lib. Assn., ZONTA; Gannon Col. medal, '63; Villa Maria Col., BA (magna cum laude); Catholic Univ. of Am., MS (Lib. Sci.); b. Budapest, Hungary; p. Zoltan and Maria Nikolich Heya; h. Milivoj Karcic; c. Julia; res: 223 W. Seventh St., Erie, Pa. 16501.

HEYDUCK, MARJ, Asst. to Ed., Dayton Journal Herald, 37 S. Ludlow St., Dayton, Oh. 45402, '66–; Daily Colmst., '44–; Ed. of Wms. Dept., '49–'66; Lectr. on wms. pages for Am. Press Inst. Seminars; UPI aw. for best colm. in Oh., '66; Penney Aw. for excellence in wms. pages, '64; Nat. Headliner's Aw., '46; Salvation Army Advisory Bd.; Oh. State Univ. (Jnlsm.), '32–'34; b. Dayton, Oh., 1913; p. Robert Carl and Helen Rhodes Evers; h. E. C. Heyduck (dec.); res: P.O. Box 66, Arcanum, Oh. 45304.

HICKEY, MARGARET, Public Affairs Ed., Ladies' Home Journal, 641 Lexington Ave., N.Y., N.Y. 10022, '46–; Cnslt., Rockefeller Bros. Fund, '67–; Lawyer (St. Louis, Mo.), '28–'33; Founder, Miss Hickey's Sch. for Secys., '33; Theta Sigma Phi, Kappa Beta Pi, ANWC, Nat. Fedn. BPW (Pres., '44–'46), Nat. Conf. of Social Welfare (Pres., '54–'56), Am. Nat. Red Cross, Social Sciences Commission of Nat. Sci. Fndn., Brandeis Univ. Bd. of Overseers, '65–; Trustee, Am. Youth Fdn., '55–; Trustee, Tuskegee Inst., '52–'64; Benjamin Franklin Aw. for Public Svc. Jnlsm., '58; Univ. of Mo. Sch. of Law, J. D., '28; Culver-Stockton Col., EdD, '66; Hon. Degs.: St. Mary's Col., LittD, '64; Wilson Col., DHL, '62; Mac Murray Col., LLD, '57; Cedar Crest Col., LLD, '52; b. Kan. City, Mo.; p. Charles and Elizabeth Wynne Hickey; h. Joseph T. Strubinger; res: 6808 Washington Blvd., St. Louis, Mo. 63130.

HICKEY, MARY ANN, Media Dir., E. G. White Advertising, Inc., 1117 N. 19th St., Suite 806, Arlington, Va. 22209, '55–; Prod., Media Dir., Calloway Assocs. (Boston, Mass.), eight yrs.; Media Dir., S. Gunnar Myrbeck & Co. (Quincy, Mass.), eight yrs.; WAC, two yrs. svc.; Artist, State Health Dept. (Tex.), two yrs.; Wms. Ad Club of Wash. (Wash., D.C.); b. Ft. Worth, Tex.; h. (div.).

HICKS, HELEN SIMMONS, Head, Info. Svcs. Branch, Naval Radiological Defense Laboratory, S.F., Cal. 94135, '60; Info. Specialist, '54–'58; Sustained Superior Accomplishment Aw., '57; Info. Specialist, Naval Supply Ctr., '58–'60; Rep., Display World mag., '52–'54; Free-lance Wtr., mag. articles; Bay Area Soc. of Indsl. Communicators (Secy.-Treas., '65), Armed Forces Wtrs. League (S.F. Chptr., Prog. Chmn., '65).

HICKS, LINDA MORRIS, PR, Dublin Progress, Box R, 116 W. Blackjack, Dublin, Tex. 76446, '69–; PR with H. L. Hunt, Inc.; Youth Freedom Speaker Cnslt.; b. Jefferson, Tex., 1940; p. Tom and Verna Bramlett Morris; h. Tommy Hicks.

HIESTAND, EMILY WATKINS, Adv. Mgr., The Mortgage Banker, 1707 H St., N.W. Wash., D.C. 20006, '68–; Copywtr., Foote, Cone & Belding, '46–'47; Copywtr., Grant Adv., '43–'45; Catalog Copywtr., Sears, '42–'43; Univ. of Ala., BS, '42; Northwestern Univ., MBA, '43; b. Tuscaloosa, Ala.; h. Orris Sidney Hiestand; c. Emily Lucille, Andrew, Peter; res: 7828 Hampden St., Bethesda, Md. 20014.

HIGGINS, DIANA LURVEY, Ed., The Woman, Reese Publishing Company, 201 Park Ave., S., N.Y., N.Y. 10003, '67–; Edtl. Dir., Ideal Publ. Co., '63–'66; Ed., '49–'63; OPC; Middlebury Col., BA, '44 (Mary Dunning Thwing Aw.); b. Waterville, Me.; p. Preston and Alice Packard Lurvey; h. George E. Higgins; c. Timothy Preston, Michael Peter; res: 37-22 68th St., Woodside, N.Y. 11377.

HIGGINSON, MARGARET VALLIANT, Rsch. Prog. Dir., American Management Association, 135 W. 50th St., N.Y., N.Y. 10017, '69–; Sr. Rsch. Assoc., '65–'69; Rsch. Assoc., '64–'65; Org. Specialist, Girl Scouts, U.S.A., '63; Rsch. Mgr., Collier Bks., '62; Glover Assoc., '53–'62; Auth., several bks.; Am. Sociological Assn.; Univ. of N.M., BS (Psych.), '47; MA, '49; Syracuse Univ., '50; New Sch. for Social Rsch., '52–'56; b. Georgetown, Del., 1923; p. William and Emma Friedel Valliant; h. William J. Higginson; res: 2 Tudor Pl., Apt. 10-CN, N.Y., N.Y. 10017.

HIGUERA, CONSUELO, Asst. VP, Adv. and PR Offcr., Banco de Ponce, 1030 Southern Blvd., Bronx, N.Y. 10459, '68–; Mgr., '63–'68; Mgr., Manhattan Br., '61–'63; Asst. Agt., '61; Nat. Assn. of Bank Wm., CWPR, Repl. Wm. in Industry and Professions, Bronx Cncl. on the Arts (Treas.); educ. in Ponce, Puerto Rico; b. Santo Domingo, Republic Dominican; p. Fidel and Julia M. Higuera; res: 541 E. 20th St., N.Y., N.Y. 10010.

HILGER, Sr. MARY IONE, O.S.B. (pseuds: Elizabeth Terres, Beth Hilione, "Sheen"), Auth., Rschr., Histrn.; bk., "First Sioux Nun" (Bruce Publ. Co., '63: Nat. Fedn. of the Press Assn. Second Pl., U.S.; First Pl., N.D., '63; Cit., Nat. Congress of N. Am. Indians, '63; in appreciation of bk., adopted into Sioux tribe as "Princess Morning Star," '63); many writings, periodicals, nwsps. incl., Daily Tribune (Dubuque, Ia.); poems, articles, features; Ed., Advisor, Publr., sch. pubns., '35–'46; Tchr., 42 yrs., 21 admin., elementary and secondary in Wis., Minn., and N.D.; Admr.; NLAPW (Nat. Bd. of Ltrs., '66; N.D. Pres., '66; The Esther Dixon State-Br. Aw., '67), NFPW, Nat. Wtrs. Club, Inc., Canadian Auths. Assn.; hist., cultural groups; personal aws., aws. for writings, incl., Wm. of Achiev. for N.D., N.D. Press Wm. Assn., '63;

London citation for portrayal of North American Indian, Dic. of Intl. Biog.; State Tchrs. Col. (St. Cloud, Minn.), '20; St. Benedict's Col. (St. Joseph, Minn.) and Univ. of Minn. (Mpls., Minn.), BA, '31; Marquette Univ. (Milw., Wis.) and Catholic Univ. of Am., summers, '38–'46; b. Roscoe, Minn., 1897; p. Frederick W. and Elizabeth Terres-Scharle Hilger; res: Annunciation Priory, Apple Creek Rd., Bismarck, N.D. 58501.

HILKER, HELEN-ANNE, Interpretive Projects Offcr., Library of Congress, Wash., D.C. 20540, '69–; Info. Offcr., '60–'69; Press Offcr., '54–'60; Asst. Info. Offcr., '46–'51 (cit., '51); Edtl. Rschr., Scripps-Howard Nwsp. Alliance, '51–'54; News Wtr., Am. Nat. Red Cross, '45–'46; Nwsp. Reprtr., '37–'41; Ed., Lib. of Congress Info. Bul., '54–'69; WNPC (VP, '61–'62), Am. Hist. Assn., Renaissance Soc. of Am., Kappa Tau Alpha, Kappa Delta Epsilon; Oh. Nwsp. Wms. Assn. aw., '45; Educ. Press Assn. aw., '45; Educ. Press Assn. aw., '66; Allegheny Col., AB (Hist., Polit. Sci.), '41 (Phi Beta Kappa; cum laude); State Univ. of Ia., MA (Jnlsm.), '42; b. Springfield, Oh., 1920; p. Albert and Mary Shanahan Hilker; res: 4201 Cathedral Ave., N.W., Wash., D.C. 20016.

HILL, BETTY HEINZ, Info., Educ. and Training Coordr., Laramie County/Cheyenne Civil Defense Agency, 318 W. 19th St., Cheyenne, Wyo. 82001, '67–; Wtr., Prodr., radio programs aired weekly over Cheyenne radio stations; AWRT, Wyo. Press Wm.; b. Denver, Colo., 1926; p. Fred and Rose Dean Heinz; h. Marion D. Hill; c. Dale Eugene, Dianne Lyn; res: 750 Melton St., Cheyenne, Wyo. 82001.

HILL, CAROL, Tchr. of Speech and Bdcst., Announcer Training Studios, 25 W. 43rd St., N.Y., N.Y. 10036, '61–; Free-Lance Talent, Ch. 6 (N.Y.C.); WNHC-TV (New Haven, Conn.), '58; WGLV-TV (Easton, Pa.), '56–'57; Poetry Soc. of London (Eastern Centre Secy., '68–), AWRT, Intl. Platform Assn.; Dic. of Intl. Biog., '67–'69; Royal Blue Bk., '68–'69; Bklyn. Col.; b. Oakland, Cal.; p. Preston and Melinda Culliard Hill; res: 388 State St., Bklyn., N.Y. 11217.

HILL, ELIZABETH STARR, Auth., fiction, non-fiction, c/o Brandt and Brandt, 101 Park Ave., N.Y., N.Y. 10017; juv. bks: "Evan's Corner" (Holt, Rinehart and Winston, '67; ALA Notable Bk. for Children, '67; color film, '69), "Pardon My Fangs" (Holt, Rinehart and Winston, '69), four others; Contrbr., New Yorker, Good Housekeeping, Harper's Bazaar, other Am., British, European pubns.; Finch Col.; p. Raymond and Gabrielle Wilson Cummings; h. Russell Gibson Hill; c. Andrea van W., Bradford W.

HILL, ESTHER POTTERF, Reprtr., Central Montana Publishing Co., 521 W. Main St., Lewistown, Mont. 59457, '64–; Poetry Ed., '63–; Circ. Mgr., '62–'64; Mont. Press Wm. (aws., '66–'69), NFPW, Lewistown City-County Planning Bd. (Secy., '68–); Mont. Press Assn. aw., '68; b. Lewistown, Mont., 1924; p. Dee Roy and Lena Jenni Potterf; h. Leonard Hill; c. George, Karen

296

(Mrs. Dale Wensinger), Jeannette, Beth (Mrs. Larry Wakeford), Lenora, Sherry, Susan; res: 307 Prospect Ave., Lewistown, Mont. 59457.

HILL, FERN BERRY, Character Actress, all studios, TV; Double for Helen Hayes; doubled hands, feet, legs, handwriting for: Bette Davis, Olivia De Havi-land, Lauren Bacall, Doris Day; Dancer for Busby Berkeley; contract, Warner Bros. Studios; acting contract; free-lance Character Actress, comls.; SAG, AFTRA; photog. hon. (London, Eng.), '30; b. Fairview, Okla., 1909; p. Benjamin and Dorothy Mae Shephard Berry; h. Donald E. Hill; res: 1927 N. Ever-green, Burbank, Cal. 91505.

HILL, FLORENCE EDNA, Ed., Brief Views, '62–'67; Tchr., '25–'61; NEA, Oh. Educ. Assn., Nat. Re-tired Tchrs. Assn., Oh. Retired Tchrs. Assn., Nat. Thespian (Sponsor, '38–'61, Oh. Dir., '50–'62); Who's Who of Am. Wm.; Dic. of Intl. Biog.; Oh. State Univ., BA, BSC (Educ.), '23 (Phi Beta Kappa); Northwestern Univ., MA, '36; b. Canton, Oh., 1900; p. Harry and Ida English Hill; res: 261 W. Vivian Lane, Hemet, Cal. 92343.

HILL, JOHANNA DOUGHERTY, AE, AC&R Adver-tising, Inc., 437 Madison Ave., N.Y., N.Y. 10022, '67–; Gaynor & Ducas, '63–'67; Sls. Prom. Mgr., Loft Candy Corp., '61–'63; Gruen Watch Co., '57–'61; Nat. Assn. of Suggestion Systems (Secy., '53); N.Y.U., Nat. Acad. of Dramatic Arts; b. Freeport, N.Y.; p. John and Frances McShea Dougherty; c. David Sean Hill; res: 235 E. 57th St., N.Y., N.Y. 10022.

HILL, LOIS, Dir. of PR, St. Luke's Episcopal Hospital, Texas Children's Hospital, Texas Heart Institute, 6621 Fannin St., Houston, Tex. 77025, '59–; Pers. Dept., '58; Assoc. Ed., Med. Arts Publ. Co., '50–'55; Info., Special-ist, Military Intelligence Dept., U.S. Army, '44–'45; PR, Wms. Auxiliary Army Corps, '42–'44; Nat. Hosp. Assn., Tex. Hosp. Assn., Houston Hosp. PR Assn. (Pres., '66), Am. Soc. For Hosp. PR Dirs; Tex. Med. Assn. Anson Jones Aw., '61; articles in medical pubns.; Rice Univ., BA, '35; b. Victoria, Tex., 1914; p. John and Lucille Lane Peters; h. Lambert O. Pearson; c. Rodney Hill; res: 5630 Reamer St., Houston, Tex. 77035.

HILL, MABEL EDITH, VP, Westchester Rockland Newspapers, Inc., '27–'68; Who's Who of Am. Wm.; b. Ossining, N.Y., 1905; p. George and Maud Acker Hill; h. James J. Boyle; res: 36 Wolden Rd., Ossinning, N.Y. 10562.

HILL, MARGARET DONALD, Bdcst. Media Supvsr., Sr. Media Byr., Henderson Advertising Agency, Inc., P.O. Box 5308, Greenville, S.C. 29606, '69–; Media Byr., '66–'68; Adm. Asst., Media Byr., '58–'65; Secy. to Pres., '52–'54; Univ. of N.C. (Greensboro, N.C.), BA (Econs.), '48; b. Asheville, N.C.; p. John Clinton and Elizabeth Robertson Donald; h. Lawrence K. Hill; c. Lawrence K., Jr., James Wm.; res: 307 McCarter Ave., Greenville, S.C. 29607.

HILL, MIRIAM GANN, Asst. Prof. of Jnlsm., University of Alabama, Box 1709, University, Ala. 35486, '60–; Copy Ed., Reptr., Feature Wtr., Asst. Wms. Ed., The Birmingham News, '45–'59; Auth, Sci. Articles for Americana Ency., Numerous mag. Articles; Theta Sigma Phi (Birmingham Pfsnl. Chptr. offcs.; Beta Gamma Chptr.-Univ. of Ala. Advisor; Nat. Scholarship Aw., '60); Nwsp. Fund, Inc. Aw., '60; Nieman travel grant for writing and study in Japan, '57; var. scholar-ship and civic aws.; Samford Univ., AB, '46; Univ. of Ala., MA, '60; b. Jasper, Ala., 1925; p. Claude and Gena Johnson Gann; res: 103 Frederick Ct. Apts., Tuscaloosa, Ala. 35401.

HILL, PAMELA, Field Prodr., NBC News, National Broadcasting Company, 30 Rockefeller Plaza, N.Y., N.Y. 10020, '69–; Dir., Assoc. Prodr., '68–'69; Auth., "United States Foreign Policy" ('66); Bennington Col., BA, '60; b. Winchester, Ind., 1938; p. Paul and Mary Frances Abel; h. (div.); c. Christopher Abel Hill; res: 1160 Fifth Ave., N.Y., N.Y. 10029.

HILL, RUTH K., Prodr. (Assoc.) Wtr., WOR-TV, 1481 Broadway, N.Y., N.Y. 10036; Assoc. Prodr., "Stock Market Observer"; Assoc. Prodr., Reptr., WNEW-TV; UN Corr., WNEW; NBC Corr., Monitor; Prodr., Corr., "Flair" Program, ABC; Prodr., Wtr., Commen-tator, own program, UN, Algonquin Hotel, WEVD, nine yrs. (aw., for producing "Best in Local News Programming", Mayor Wagner, Commn. Human Rights, '63); Prodr., "Non Proliferation Program"; Press Cnslt., Disarmament Comm.; UNA; Reptr.-Prodr., Brinkleys Jnl., NBC; articles; Broadway appearances; Dramatist Guild, AFTRA, OPC, Actors Studio; cit., March of Dimes, '62; Stephens Col. (Kappa Alpha Theta); Univ. Col. (Vancouver, British Columbia); b. Seattle, Wash.; h. (div.); c. Joshua and Erik Lazar; res: 49 E. 96th St., N.Y., N.Y. 10028.

HILL, SARAH SHARPE, Corporate Secy., Pilot Freight Carriers Inc., P.O. Box 615, Winston-Salem, N.C. 27102, '67–; Dir. of PR and Adv., '64; VP, Craft Shop Inc.; PR Round Table of Winston-Salem (Secy.), PRSA, Winston-Salem C. of C., Piedmont Craftsmen Inc. (Bd. of Trustees, '68–'71); numerous aws. from Am. Trucking Assn. Sls. Cncl., S. Atlantic Conf. of Indsl. Eds.; Briarcliff Col., AA; Univ. of Pa.; b. Win-ston-Salem, N.C., 1940; p. Ruel and Eileen Lackey Sharpe; h. James Hill; c. Sarah Berry Benedict, James King, Jr.; res: 640 Yorkshire Rd., Winston-Salem, N.C. 27106.

HILLERY, MARY JANE LARATO, Ed.-in-Chief, The Sudbury Citizen, Beacon Publishing Co., Inc., Main St., Acton, Mass. 01776, '67–; Pan Am. Airways, '55–'61; U.S. Navy, '50–'54; Nat. Edtl. Assn., Nat. Nwsp. Assn., League of Wm. Voters (Bd. of Dirs.), '64–'68); Northeastern Univ., AS, '50; b. Boston, Mass., 1931; p. Donato and Porzia Avellis Larato; h. Thomas Hillery; c. Thomas Jr.; res: 66 Willow Rd., Sudbury, Mass. 01776.

HILLEY, DONNA WHITTEN, Secy.-Treas., Bill Hudson and Associates, Inc., 708 17th Ave. S., Nashville, Tenn. 37203, '68–; Asst. to Pres., WKDA Radio, '60–'67; Legal Counsel Am. Investors Life Ins. Co.; Exec. Asst., Bdcst. Cnslt.; AWRT; b. Montevallo, Ala., 1940; p. James Truman and Janie Mae Whitten; h. Rayford Hilley; c. Vickie Diane and Debbie Carol; res: 736 Brookhollow Rd., Nashville, Tenn. 37205.

HILLIARD, GRACE JOHNSON, Garden Ed., Pratt Tribune, 319 S. Ninnescah, Pratt, Kan. 67124, '53–; Great Bend (Kan.) Daily Tribune, '68–; Ed., Kansas Gardener, 7 yrs.; articles in Am. Rose Soc. Mag. and Am. Rose Soc. Annual; Apprentice Judge, Rose Shows; Garden Wtrs. Assn. of Am.; Kan. Assoc. Garden Clubs (Past State Pres.); Kan. Wm. of the Yr., '57; Southwestern Col.; b. Freeport, Kan., 1902; p. H. H. and Maude Collins Johnson; h. Ernest Hilliard; c. Ernest, Kenneth, Barbara (Mrs. William L. Foust), Lawrence; res: 316 S. Pearl, Pratt, Kan. 67124.

HILLIER, HELEN RUTH, Home Furnishings Ed., Flint Journal, 200 E. First St., Flint, Mich. 48502, '62–; Wms. Ed., Flint News Advertiser, '34–'56; Tchr., Eng., Hist., '57, '28–'29; Univ. of Mich., AB, '27; MA, '62; b. Flint, Mich., 1905; p. Harry and Amelia Kettelhut Ruth; h. (div.); res: 1907 E. Second St., Flint, Mich. 48503.

HILLMAN, CHARLENE HAMILTON, PR Cnsl., 4120 N. Keystone Ave., Indpls. Ind. 46205, '64–; PR Dir., Clowes Memorial Hall for the Performing Arts, '63–'64; PR Dir., Paul Lennon Adv. Agcy., '62–'63; PR Staff, Bob Long Assocs., '59–'62; Ed., The Hoosier Independent; PRSA (Accredited Mbr., Hoosier Chptr. Pres., '67), Ind. IEA (VP), Adv. Club of Indpls. (Adv. Wm. of Yr., '69), Theta Sigma Phi, AWRT, Mayor's Task Force on Commtns.; Ind. Univ.; b. Akron, Oh., 1921; p. Charles and Laura Anderson Hamilton; h. Robert E. Hillman; c. Robert E. Jr.; res: 3226 Barnard St., Indpls., Ind. 46220.

HILLPOT, MAUREEN TOOMEY, Adv. Dir., Travel Div., American Express, 65 Broadway, N.Y., N.Y. 10006, '68–; formerly Group Head, J. Walter Thompson; Copywtr., Y&R; Ed., ABC Radio; Wtr., TV programs, mktng. articles; Auths. Guild, Auths. League of Am., Kappa Gamma Pi; Good Counsel Col. (magna cum laude); Columbia Univ., PhD Candidate; b. N.Y.C.; p. Timothy and Bina Sullivan Toomey; h. William Hillpot; res: 295 Central Park W., N.Y., N.Y. 10024.

HILLS, CAROL LECHTHALER, Assoc. Prof., Boston University—School of Public Communication, 640 Commonwealth Ave., Boston, Mass. 02265, '63–; Gen. Electric Co., '51; Borden Co. (N.Y.C.), '50; Cnslt., PR, nonprofit, governmental, military orgs., '51–; PRSA (Accredited), Am. Sociological Assn., Soc. for Psychological Study of Social Issues, Assn. for Educ. in Jnlsm.; Tufts Univ., AB, '47 (cum laude); Boston Univ., MS, '49 (Alumni Assn. Aw., Outstanding Svc. to Sch. and Commty., '58); b. Quincy, Mass.; p. Frederick C. Lechthaler; h. Kenneth M. Hills Jr.

HILLS, VIRGINIA CARTER, Librn., National Geographic Society, 16th and M Sts., N.W., Wash., D.C. 20016, '65–; Asst. Librn., '57–'65; Cataloger, Ref. Asst., '51–'56; Periodicals Asst., '43–'50; Special Libs. Assn., D.C. Lib. Assn. (Bd. of Dirs., '68–), Assn. of Am. Geographers, AAUW, Am. Soc. for Info. Scis., ZONTA (Wash., D.C. Chptr. Bd. of Dirs., '69; Secy., '68–'69); Radford Col., BS, '42; Catholic Univ. of America, BS (Lib. Sci.), '51; b. Essexville, Mich., 1920; p. Charles and Emma T. Carter; h. Benjamin O. Hills; res: 4004 49th St., N.W., Wash., D.C. 20016.

HILLYARD, KAY ABBOTT, Free-lance Wtr., Ed.; Colmst., Am. Home on Cal. Cookery, '66–; Home Econs. Ed., Assoc. Ed., Harvest Years, '61–'66; Home Econs. Ed., Sunset, '48–'57; Info. Specialist, Prod., Mktng., U.S. Dept. Agriculture, '46–'47; Head Script-Traf., Overseas Br., OWI, '42–'46; Script Wtr., CBS, '36–'38; Wtr., Home Econst., '30–'35; Am. Home Econs. Assn., Home Econsts. in Bus.; Who's Who of Am. Wm.; Dic. of Intl. Biog.; Colo. State Univ., BS (Home Econs., Educ.), '29; b. Denver, Colo., 1907; p. Stephen and Kate Locke Abbott; h. Coyle Hillyard (dec.); c. Steven A.; res: P.O. Box 3564, Carmel, California 93921.

HILLYER, ELIZABETH, Home Furnishings Ed., Chicago Tribune, 435 N. Michigan Ave., Chgo., Ill. 60611, '66–; Synd. Colmst., "Designing Woman," Nat. Nwsp. Synd., '48–'65; Home Furnishings Ed., Modern Bride mag., '49–'51; Independent Interior Designer; radio, TV, decorating shows; answering decorating questions, WBBM (Chgo., Ill.), '65; Am. Inst. of Interior Designers (Assoc., '52), Fashion Group, NHFL (Nat. Dir., '59); Dorothy Dawe Aws: Distg. Home Furnishings Jnlsm., '58; Special Aw., Innovation, '68; Louise Thompson Bolender Aw., '60; Lindenwood Col., Univ. of Neb., Univ. of Colo., Univ. of Mo., Parsons.

HILSINGER, JUDITH LOUISE, Exec. Prodr., "Comment," WWDC Radio, Avco Broadcasting Corporation, P.O. Box 4068, Wash., D.C. 20015, '67–; PR Dir., '66–'67; Mkt. Rsch., Proctor and Gamble, '64–'66; Children's Intl. Summer Villages (U.S. Bd. of Trustees, '69–'71); 2000 Wm. of Achiev.; Univ. of Cinn., BA, '64; Northwestern Univ. Grad. Sch. of Radio-TV-Film, '66; Am. Univ. Sch. of Commtns., '67; b. Cinn., Oh., 1942; p. Dr. Raymond and Angelese Hayes Hilsinger; res: 4970 Battery Lane, Bethesda, Md. 20014.

HILTON, DORIS SEDERHOLM (Pseud: Jane Sterling), Nwsp. Colmst., Radio and TV Personality, Retired; Staff Colmst., The Denver (Colo.) Post, '50–'60; Dir.-Prodr., "These Kids of Ours," KOA Radio, TV, 10 yrs.; Free-lance Wtr., radio (Hollywood, Cal.); Cont. Wtr., KOMO, KJR (Seattle, Wash.); Copywtr., Bon Marche Dept. Store; Co-sponsor, five recreational clubs for young and old people (Denver); promoted Code of Conduct program in Denver High Schs.; Leader, patient-finding survey, Multiple Sclerosis Soc.; Pioneer, Leader, prom. of adequate legislation to deal with deserting fathers; La Sertomo Intl. Wm. of the Yr., '57; Denver Juv. Ct. Gold Cup Aw., outstanding svc. to youth, '55; Civic Leader; Jamestown Col.; Cornish Sch. of the Arts; b. Jamestown, N.D.; 1919; p. Alfred and Agnes Anderson Sederholm; h. John P. Hilton, M.D.; c. James M., Jill Elizabeth, Jon R.; res: 6235 Montview Blvd., Denver, Colo. 80207.

HIMELSTEIN, MIRIAM NEUSTADTER, Comptroller, Fleet Press Corp., 156 Fifth Ave., N.Y., N.Y. 10010, '67–; Comptroller, Arts Inc. Publrs., '62–'67; New Sch., '26; b. N.Y.C., 1907; p. Peter and Hannah Herzig Neustadter; h. Harry Himelstein; c. Thelma (Mrs. Steinberg), Honey (Mrs. Sungolowsky), Ephraim, Rita (Mrs. Schneier) res: 1701 45th St., Bklyn., N.Y. 11204.

HIMES, KATHRYN E., Controller, Bd. of Dirs., FilmFair, 10900 Ventura Blvd., Studio City, Cal. 91604, '60–; Controller, Bd. of Dirs., Ray Patin Prodrs., '54–'60; Bd. of Dirs: Newell Film Lab, Festival Films; Davis Bus. Col. (Bus. Adm.); b. Defiance, Oh., 1919; p. Clifford and Ethel Breese Himes; res: 3483 N. Knoll Dr., L.A., Cal. 90028.

HIMMELFARB, GERTRUDE, Wtr.; Prof. of Hist., City University of New York, 33 W. 42nd St., N.Y., N.Y. 10036, '65–; Auth: "Victorian Minds" ('68), "Darwin and the Darwinian Revolution" ('59), "Lord Acton" ('52); Am. Hist. Assn., Conf. on British Studies; Fellowship, Nat. Endowment for the Humanities, '68–'69; Rockefeller Fndn. Fellowship, '62–'63; Guggenheim Fellowships, '55–'56; '57–'58; Am. Philosophical Soc. Fellowship, '53–'54; AAUW Fellowship, '51–'52; Bklyn. Col., BA, '42; Univ. of Chgo., MA, '44; PhD, '50; b. N.Y.C., 1922; p. Max and Bertha Lerner Himmelfarb; h. Irving Kristol; c. William, Elizabeth.

HINCKLEY, JUNE BENEFIELD, Colmst., The Houston Chronicle, 512-20 Travis St., Houston, Tex. 77002, '55; Free-lance PR, '48–'49; City Reptr., Houston Press, '43–'46; Soc. Ed., The Brady Standard, '38–'41; Theta Sigma Phi (Houston Chptr. Headliner Aw., '65); Tex. Mng. Eds. aw., '65; AP aw., '65; Howard Payne Col., '38–'39; Univ. of Tex., '45–'48; b. Gorman, Tex., 1921; p. Malcolm and Gay Neill Benefield; h. Kenneth R. Hinckley; c. Carolyn, Nancy, Bill; res: 811 Monte Cello St., Houston, Tex. 77024.

HINDERSTEIN, JUDITH CORTELL, Free-Lance Wtr., Publicist, '69–; Ed., The Employers' Owl, Employers' Group of Ins. Cos. (Boston, Mass), '60–'68; Employee Commtns. Ed., S. S. Pierce Co., '59; Ed., Avis News, Avis Rent-A-Car Co., '58; Mass. IEA (Secy., '64), Madison Art Assn., Boston Univ., ACS, '58; b. Rochester, N.H., 1939; p. Benjamin and Lillian Nesbitt Cortell; h. Allan Hinderstein; c. Toby Rachel, Rina Tara; res: Rte. Two, Stebbinsville Rd., Stoughton, Wis. 53589.

HINDLIN, PAUIA LEE, Casting Dir., CBS-TV, 530 W. 57 St., N.Y., N.Y. 10019, '59–; Asst. Casting Dir.; Exec. Secy.; Bklyn. Col., '50–'51; City Col. of N.Y., '58;

N.Y.U., '60–'61; New Sch., '67; b. N.Y.C., 1931; p. Norman and Rebecca Ediss Hindlin; res: 166 E. 63rd St., N.Y., N.Y. 10021.

HINDMAN, JANE FERGUSON, Ed., Catholic Library World, Catholic Library Association, 461 W. Lancaster Ave., Haverford, Pa. 19041, '63–; Holy Family Col., '59–'63; Phila., Pa. Bd. of Educ., '24–'59; Auth., "Mathew Carey, Pamphleteer for Freedom" ('60); Catholic Lib. Assn., ALA, Pa. Lib. Assn., Lib. PR Assn. of Gtr. Phila., Ch. and Synagogue Lib. Assn.; Drexel Inst. Sch. of Lib. Sci., '24; Temple Univ., BS (Educ.), '29; b. Phila., Pa., 1905; p. William and Mary Eslen Hindman; res: The Mermont, 207, Bryn Mawr, Pa. 19010.

HINEK, ERMA ALBRIGHT, Corp. Secy.-Treas., Mng. Ed., Consumer Bulletin, Consumer's Research, Inc., Bowerstown Rd., Washington, N.J. 07882, '64–; Ed., '49–'64; Warren Messenger, '59; "Health Survey of Warren County, N.J., 1956–1958," N.J. Farm Bur. and N.J. State Dept. of Health; several edtl. projects for League of Wm. Voters; Wash. Township Cent. Hist., Commemorative Pubn. Comm., '49–; Warren County Welfare Cncl. (Pres., '58–'60), Warren County Guidance Ctr. (Pres., '60–'62), numerous other educ., health, welfare orgs.; Cornell Univ., '31–'32; b. York, Pa., 1914; p. Benjamin and Nell L. Boyle Albright; h. Frank Hinek; c. Robert R.; res: R.R. 4, Box 155, Washington, N.J. 07882.

HINSHAW, HELEN ELSIE, Pubcty. Dir., Grand Canyon College, 3500 W. Camelback Rd., Phoenix, Ariz. 85017, '69–; Intl. Ed., Delta Kappa Gamma Soc., Intl. (Austin, Tex.), '57–'69; Tchr., Ind. Schs., '36–'57; Delta Kappa Soc. (Ind. State Rec. Secy., '50–'53; State Ed., '47–'52; Rho Chptr. Pres., '56–'57), Theta Sigma Phi (Austin Pfsnl. Chptr. Pres., '67–'68), Hobart Classroom Tchrs. Assn. (Pres., '55–'56), Ind. HS Press Assn. (Pres., '53–'54), Nat. Assn. of Jnlsm. Dirs., Nat. Educ. Assn., Ind. State Tchrs. Assn., AAUW, Austin Cerebral Palsy Ctr. (Secy. of Bd.), Altrusa; b. Thornton, Ind., 1911; p. Raymond B. and Mayme E. Hanson Hinshaw; res: 337 W. Pasadena St., Phoenix, Ariz. 85013.

HIRSCH, REBA B., Adv., PR Cnslt., Reba Hirsch Advertising, 223 W. Commerce St., Shamokin, Pa. 17872, '56–; Auth: "250 Ways to Say Please Pay" ('65), "Political Vocabulary Guide" ('64), "The Writer's Companion" ('62); other pubns., articles; Copy Dir., Michener and O'Connor, Inc., '52–'56; Copy Dir., Ed Shapiro, Inc., '50–'52; Crtv. Dir., Deane, Klein, Davidson Co., '48–'50; AE, Julian G. Pollock Co., '45–'47; several aws. for inst., ins. adv.; annual rept., PR, programming; b. Burlington, N.J.; p. David and Eva Rubenstein Hirsch.

HIRSCHL, BEATRICE PAUL, Free-lance Wtr., nonfiction; PR Dir., Carnegie Lib. of Pitt., '62–'68; PR Reptr., Pitt. Post-Gazette, '57–'61; Mng. Ed., Am.-Jewish Outlook, '54–'57; Gen. Assigt. Reptr., Homestead Daily Messenger, '53–'54; Wms. Press Club of

Pitt. (Bd. of Dirs., '65–'67), Theta Sigma Phi (Bd. of Dirs., '66–'69); ALA commty. svc. aw., '67; Univ. of Pitt., AB, '53 (Mortar Bd.); b. Pitt., Pa.; p. Solomon and Freda Rabinowitz Paul; h. Kenneth L. Hirschl; c. Susan Eileen; res: 574 Crystal Dr., Pitt., Pa. 15228.

HITCHCOCK, JOANNA GOODMAN, Asst. Adv. Mgr., Exhibits Mgr., Princeton University Press, 41 William St., Princeton, N.J. 08540, '68–; Asst. Prom. Mgr., '66–'68; Pubcty. Asst., Oxford Univ. Press (London, Eng.), '62–'66; PPA, Publrs. Adv. Club; Oxford Univ., BA, '60; MA, '66; b. London, Eng., 1938; p. Christopher and Joan Whybrow Goodman; h. Martyn Hitchcock; res: 22 Church St., Kingston, N.J. 08528.

HITE, CAROLYN HARVILL, Supvsr., Rights and Permissions, Methodist Publishing House, 201 Eighth Ave. S., Nashville, Tenn. 37203, '63–; Wms. Nat. Bk. Assn.; George Peabody Col. for Tchrs., BA, '59; b. Nashville, Tenn., 1937; p. Durand and Carolyn Cartwright Hite; res: 2204-B Hobbs Rd., Nashville, Tenn. 37215.

HITE, KATHLEEN, Free-lance Wtr., TV Fiction, '53–; Staff Wtr., CBS Radio, '43–'50; Creator, "Empire" TV series, '63; Contrbr., "Gunsmoke," "Wagon Train," "The Monroes," "Guns of Will Sonnett" (Cowboy Hall of Fame Best TV Script aw., '68); WGA, Theta Sigma Phi (Headliner Aw., '64); Univ. of Wichita, BA (Jnlsm., Hist.), '38; b. Wichita, Kan., 1917; p. Frank and Mary Worrell Hite; res: 5035 Odessa Ave., Encino. Cal. 91316.

HITTER, TINA, Media Byr., Needham, Harper & Steers, 909 Third Ave., N.Y., N.Y. 10022, '68–; Intl. Media Byr., Nat. Export Adv. Svcs., '67–'68; Media Trainee, Doyle Dane & Bernbach, '66–'67; Queens Col., BA (Social Scis.), '65.

HITZ, MAURINE CAMPBELL, Past Gen. Chmn., Anderson Women's Committee, Clowes Memorial Hall, 4600 Sunset Ave., Indpls., Ind. 46208, '67–'68; Theta Sigma Phi; Butler Univ., AB, '36; b. Thorntown, Ind., 1915; p. Arch and Elsie Bratton Campbell; h. George Hitz; c. Mary Pat, Barbara Jean, Mrs. Daniel E. Hussong, Mrs. George W. Sasser; res: 3506 Nichol Ave., Anderson, Ind. 46011.

HIVELY, SUZANNE LEE, Wms. Ed., Sandusky Register, 314 W. Market St., Sandusky, Oh. 44870, '64–; Feature Wtr., Jnl. Gazette (Ft. Wayne, Ind.); Artist, Intl. Harvester Co. (Chgo., Ill.); Airplane Flight Instr.

HOAG, MIMI, Chief Cataloger, Bucks County Free Library, 50 N. Main St., Doylestown, Pa. 18901, '68–; Commty. Col. Cataloger, '66–'68; Mgr.-Chmn., Co-operative Art Gallery (Upstairs Art Gallery); WNBA, Pa. Lib. Assn., ALA; Univ. of Cal., Berkeley, BA (Decorative Arts), '49; Drexel Univ., MS (Lib. Sci.), '69 (Fine Arts Librn.); b. Santa Maria, Cal.; p. Charles and Emilie Havenor Laubly; h. James Richmond Hoag; c.

Jeffrey R., Lorraine D., Mark T.; res: Fordhook Farms, Doylestown, Pa. 18901.

HOBART, LOIS ELAINE, PR Dir., Escuela Ecuesstre SMA, Apdo. 185, San Miguel de Allende, Gto. Mexico, '63–; Colmst., Mexico City News, Mexico City Times, Times Week; Free-lance Wtr., Photogr., '54–; Assoc. Ed., Head of Job Dept., Glamour, Conde Nast, '45–'53; Assoc. Ed., Esquire, '43–'45; bks: "What Is a Whispery Secret?" "Mexican Mural," "Behind the Walls," "Strangers Among Us," "Patriot's Lady," "Elaine Forrest, Visiting Nurse," "Katie and Her Camera," "Palette for Ingrid," "Laurie, Physical Therapist"; Univ. of Minn., BA, BS, MA (cum laude); b. Mpls., Minn.; p. Evan and Alveda Gjertsen Hobart; h. Harold Black; c. Anthony H. Black; res: Huertas 19A, San Miguel de Allende, Gto. Mexico.

HOBART, ROSE, Actress, plays incl: "The Legend of Hannah Senesh," "Critics Choice," "The Cocktail Party," many others, starting with first appearance on stage, '20; motion pics. incl. starring roles in: "A Night at Earl Carrolls," "I'll Sell My Life"; featured roles, "Bride of Vengence," many others; active in PTA (Hon. Life Membership, '61); b. N.Y.C., 1906; p. Paul and Marguerite Buss Kefer; h. Barton H. Bosworth; c. Judson Hopkins Bosworth; res: 4030 Oakfield Dr., Sherman Oaks, Cal. 91403.

HOBBS, DOROTHY JAMES, Asst. Dir., Winthrop Rockefeller Public Relations, 222 Nat. Old Line Bldg., Little Rock, Ark. 72201, '64–; Ed., Press Rels., WR Campaigner mag., '64; Asst. Dir., Employee Commtns., Schlumberger Well Surveying Corp., '50–'61; Ed., employee pubns., Shell Oil Co., '46–'50; Adv. Asst., Kilgore News Herald, '45–'46; SAIE (Gulf Coast Chptr. Secy.-Treas. '47–'48; Life Mbr., '54; Bd. Mbr.; '49; Treas.; '51–'52), ICIE (Mbr. Exec. Bd., '55–'57; Southwestern Area Dir., '53–'54), Theta Sigma Phi; Univ. of Tex., BJ, '45; b. Groveton, Tex., 1923; p. Carl and Luna Allen James; h. W. Lester Hobbs (dec.); c. Yvonne (Mrs. R. Leiland Jaynes); res: 11600 Rivercrest Dr., Little Rock, Ark. 72207.

HOBBY, OVETA CULP, Ed., Chmn. of Bd., The Houston Post Company, Houston, Tex., '65–; Dir., Corporation for Public Broadcasting; Pres., Ed., Lit. Ed., Rsch. Ed., '31–'53; Dir., KPRC, KPRC-TV, '55, '45–'53; Secy., Dept. HEW, '53–'55; Fed. Security Admr., '53; Commd. Col., U.S. Army, Dir., WAC, '43–'45; Dir., WAAC, '42; Chief, Wms. Interest Sec., War Dept., Bur. PR, '41–'42; Parliamentarian, Tex. House of Reps., '26–'31;, '39, '41; Auth; distinguished positions of leadership; Philippine Military Merit Medal, '47; Hon. Aw. for Distg. Svc. in Jnlsm., Univ. of Mo., '50; Publr. of the Yr. Aw., Headliners Club, '60; Living Hist. Aw., Rsch. Inst. of Am., '60; Hon. Aw., Nat. Jewish Hosp., '62; Carnegie Corp. Aw. for the Advancement and Diffusion of Knowledge and Understanding, '67; Cnslt.-Alternate, UN Freedom of Info. Conf., '48; Cnslt., '48 Comm. on Org. of the Exec. Br. of the

Govt.; educ: Mary Hardin-Baylor Col.; numerous hon. degrees; b. Kileen, Tex., 1905; p. I. W. and Emma Hoover Culp; h. Wm. P. Hobby (dec.); c. William, Jessica (Mrs. Henry E. Catto, Jr.); res: Houston, Tex.

HOBSON, SHEILA SMITH, Free-lance Wtr.; Black hist. filmstrips, records, (Pitman Publ. Co., Buckingham Learning Corp., '69); monthly colm. in Tuesday mag. ('69); Commtns. Workshop for commty leaders, '68; Asst. Prodr., WABC-TV, '68–'69; Graphic Coordr., Rschr., Assoc. Prodr., NET-TV, '68; Asst. Prodr., Channel 13, '67–'68; Ed., John Wiley & Sons, '66–'67; Ed., Medical Tribune, '63–'66; Mundelein Col., BA (Jnlsm.), '63; N.Y.U., MA (TV), '66; b. Chgo., Ill., 1942; p. Leonard and Ethel Johnson Smith; h. Charles Hobson; res: 784 Columbus Ave., N.Y., N.Y. 10025.

HOCKER, MARGARET LOUISE, Assoc. Prof. of Lib. Educ., Wisconsin State University, 17th and State Sts., La Crosse, Wis. 54601, '67–; Ref. Librn., '50–'67; Ref. Librn., Univ. of Cinn., '47–'49; HS Librn. (Central City, Ky.), '43–'47; HS tchr., Librn. (Bremen), '41–'43; ALA, Wis. Lib. Assn., Beta Phi Mu, Delta Kappa Gamma, AAUW, Wis. Educ. Assn.; Western Ky. State Univ., AB, '41; Univ. of Ky., BS (Lib. Sci.) '46; Univ. of Mich., AM (Lib. Sci.), '50; b. S. Carrollton, Ky.; p. Asbury and Fannie Brown Hocker; res: 1525 State St., La Crosse, Wis. 54601.

HODGE, BEULAH WILEY, Prodr., Talent, "Men and Ideas," KLRN-TV, Ch. 9, Box 7158, Univ. Sta., Austin, Tex. 78712, '65–; Interviewer, "Faces of Self," '65; Hostess, "High Noon," '63–'65; Dir., Intercultural Rel. Workshops, Am. Friends Svc. Comm., '57–'59; Eng., Speech, Theatre Tchr., Carroll Col., '42–'43; League of Wm. Voters, Delta Sigma Nu, Sigma Tau Delta, Theta Alpha Phi, Pi Kappa Delta; Carroll Col., BA, '41 (summa cum laude; Who's Who in Am. Cols. and Univs.); Cornell Univ., MA (Dramatic Prod.), '42; b. Galesville, Wis., 1919; p. Guilford and Beulah Arnold Wiley; h. Francis Hodge; c. Elizabeth Jean; res: 1109 Bluebonnet Lane, Austin, Tex. 78704.

HODGE, VIRGINIA LEE FRAPS, Wms. Ed., The Arizona Daily Star, 208 N. Stone Ave., Tucson, Ariz. 85703, '66–; Reptr., Wms. Dept., '62–'66; Stringer, Upper Darby (Pa.) News; Theta Sigma Phi, Ariz. Press Wm.; Jr. League of Tucson; Univ. of Ariz., '58–'62; b. Darby, Pa., 1940; p. Junius and Margaret Burges Fraps; h. Carle Hodge; c. Margaret O.; res: 4500 W. Speedway Blvd., Tucson, Ariz. 85705.

HODGES, ELIZABETH JAMISON, Wtr.; Asst. Librn. and Supvsr. of Adult Svcs., Robbins Library, 700 Massachusetts Ave., Arlington, Mass. 02174, '61–; Auth: "Free as a Frog" (Addison-Wesley, '69), "Serendipity Tales" (Atheneum, '66), "The Three Princes of Serendip" (Atheneum, '64; revsd., Constable Young Bks. Ltd., '65); Lectr., Univ. Col. of Northeastern Univ.; Tchr., juv. writing, Boston Area Wtrs. Conf., '69; Radcliffe Col., AB; Simmons Col., Sch. of Lib. Sci., BS; b.

Atlanta, Ga.; p. William and Elizabeth Hodges Hodges.

HODGES, MARGARET MOORE, Asst. Prof., Graduate School of Library and Information Science, University of Pittsburgh, 135 N. Bellefield Ave., Pitt., Pa. 15213, '68–; Lectr., '64–'68; Storyteller, "Tell Me A Story," ETV, WQED, '54–; Story Specialist, Head Start, '64–'68; Children's Librn., '53–'64; Auth., 11 children's bks.; Univ. of Pitt. Wms. Assn. (Pres.), '49–'50), ALA, Pa. Lib. Assn., Am. Assn. of Lib. Schs.; Vassar Col., AB, '32 (cum laude); Carnegie Inst. of Tech., MS (Lib. Sci.), '58; b. Indpls., Ind., 1911; p. Arthur and Anna Mason Moore; h. Fletcher Hodges, Jr.; c. Fletcher III, Arthur C., John Andrews; res: 5812 Kentucky Ave., Pitt., Pa. 15232.

HODGIN, ALLIE AUSTIN, Ref. Librn., Appalachian State University Library, Boone, N.C. 28607, '34–; Tchr., '28–'32; ALA, Southeastern Lib. Assn., N.C. Lib. Assn., AAUP, AAUW, BPW, Delta Kappa Gamma, Appalachian State Univ. Fac. Senate (Secy., '68–'69); Bus. Wm. of the Yr., '56; Appalachian State University BS, '34; George Peabody Col. for Tchrs., BS (Lib. Sci.), '40; MLS, '65; b. Marshville, N.C., 1908; p. Ennis and Cora Rushing Austin; h. David Reid Hodgin; res: Rte. 1, Box 120, Boone, N.C. 28607.

HOENSHELL, MAXINE YOUNG, Pubns. Ed., Freightliner Corporation, 5400 N. Basin St., Portland, Ore. 97217, '65–; Asst. Ed., Esco Corp., '60–'65; Mng. Ed., Sawyer's Newsreel, '56–'59; Photogr. and Nwsp. Wtr., '53–'55; Theta Sigma Phi (Archivist, '67–'68), Ore. Assn. of Eds. and Communicators (Secy.-Treas., '61–'63; Treas. for reg. conf., '63; Dir., '61–'65); Hon. Mention in Ill. Press Photogrs. Contest ('55); Northwest Schs. (Radio-TV Prod.), '55; b. Green County, Wis., 1918; p. Milton Henry and Vera Gertrude Brereton Young; c. Donya Lynnette Burmeister; res: P.O. Box 3874, Portland, Ore. 97208.

HOFF, MARILYN GAYLE, Auth: "Dink's Blues" (Harcourt, Brace and World, '66), "Rose" (Harcourt, Brace and World, '69); McKnight Fndn. Humanities Aw., '64; Macalester Col., BA (summa cum laude), '64; Syracuse Univ., MA (Crtv. Writing Fellow), '68; b. Iowa Falls, Ia., 1942; p. J. C. and Gayle Hoff; res: 323 W. Alcott Ave., Fergus Falls, Minn. 56537.

HOFFERBERT, ELIZABETH MANIS, Pubns. Ed., The Mead Corporation, W. Main St., P.O. Box 769, Kingsport, Tenn. 37660, '50–; Asst. News Ed., TEC News, Tennessee Eastman, '46–'50; Indsl. Rel. Cnslr., Manhattan Project (Oak Ridge), '44–'46; Supvsr., Goodall Co., (Roanoke, Ala.), '39–'44; (Knoxville, Tenn.), '35–'39; Reptr., Knoxville Journal, '23–'24; AAIE (Bd. of Dirs., '69–'70, '54–'56), Appalachian IEA (Pres., '67–'69, '58–'59), AAUW, Kingsport Forum on Human Rel. (Dir., '67–'68), Tenn. Soc. for Crippled Children (Sullivan County Chptr. Bd. of Dirs., '54–), Palmer Memorial Ctr. (Secy., Bd. Mbr., '54–); Freedom Fndn.

aw., '54; Who's Who of Am. Wm.; Univ. of Tenn., '21–'23; b. Tazewell, Tenn., 1905; p. Horace and Elizabeth Brooks Manis; h. (div.); c. Mrs. John E. Webb, Louis E. Hofferbert, Jr., Mrs. David F. Marples; res: 333 W. Ravine Rd., Kingsport, Tenn. 37660.

HOFFERT, JEANELLE RYE, Edtl. Asst., Mallinckrodt Chemical Works, Second & Mallinckrodt Sts., St. Louis, Mo. 63160, '61–; Indsl. Press Assn. of Gtr. St. Louis (Secy., '66–'67); b. London, Ark., 1932; p. Corbett and Mildred Wade Rye; h. Fred Wm. Hoffert Jr.; c. Fred Wm. III, Dennis Keith, Cindy Lea; res: 272 Coburg Dr., St. Louis, Mo. 63137.

HOFFINE, LYLA, Auth: "Carol Blue Wing" (David McKay, '67), "Eagle Feather Prize" (David McKay, '62), six other juv., young adult bks.; Prof. Emeritus, State Col., Minot, N.D., '67–; Dir. of Verbal Commtns., '54–'65; Auths. League of Am.; Univ. of N.D., BA, MA; b. Highland, Wis., 1897; p. Frank and Isabelle Smith Hoffine; res: 421 9th Ave. N.W., Apt. 4, Minot, N.D. 58701.

HOFFMAN, BETTYE KING, Mgr. of Corporate Info., National Broadcasting Co., 30 Rockefeller Plaza, N.Y., N.Y. 10020, '68–; AWRT; N.Y.U., BA, '61; b. Tewksbury, Mass.; h. Randall W. Hoffmann; res: 2023 Hendricks Ave., Bellmore, N.Y. 11710.

HOFFMAN, ELIZABETH ELLEN, Adv. and PR Dir., Brennan's Restuarants Corporation, 417 Royal St., N.O., La. 70130; Adv. Dir., Acc. Supvsr. Fitzgerald Adv., '67–'69; N.O. Ad Club, Nat. Restaurant Assn. Traveler's Aid (Bd. Mbr.), Bethlehem-House of Bread; Loyola Univ. of the South.

HOFFMAN, GENE KNUDSEN, Dir., Southern California Counselling Center, Santa Barbara Branch, 3 W. Carillo St., Santa Barbara, Cal. 93101, '68–; Cnslr.-in-Training (L.A., Cal.), '67–'68; Contrbr., Liberation Magazine; Manas; textbook, "Dialogue on Women"; Prodr., Narrator, radio program, "Stories Children Love"; records; Actress, plays, "The Return of Ulysses," "The Ugly American"; Contrbr., anthology, "Seeds of Liberation"; poetry, Thrust Magazine; short story, Contrbr., Friends Jnl. on religion & Psych.; Drama Critic, Goleta Gazette Citizen, '64–'68; AFTRA, AEA, Am. Assn. for Humanistic Psych., Soc. of Friends, Fellowship of Reconciliation; Pasadena Playhouse Col. of Theatre Arts, '36–'40; b. L.A., Cal., 1919; p. Thorkild and Valley Filtzer Knudsen; h. Hallock Hoffman; c. Nikolas, Valley, Paul, Erik, Kristian, Nina-Kiriki, Kai; res: 1375 Schoolhouse Rd., Santa Barbara, Cal. 93103.

HOFFMAN, HELEN EVANGELINE, Exec. Dir., Chicago Maternity Center, 737 N. Michigan Ave., Chgo., Ill. 60611, '48–; Ketchum Inc. (Pitt., Pa.); Hartwell, Jobson & Kibbie (N.Y.C.); Salvation Army; Commty. Fund (Bd. of Dirs.) Welfare PR Forum (Pres.), Visiting Nurse Assn.; Columbia Univ.; b. Niagara Falls, N.Y.,

1909; p. Edmund and Helen Kimball Hoffman; res: 166 E. Superior, Chgo., Ill. 60611.

HOFFMAN, MARY CALLAWAY, Ed., Edtl. Pg., The Gadsden Times, Locust St., Gadsden, Ala. 35902, '66–; Assoc. Ed., '65–'66; Staff Wtr., '60–'65; Tchr., '36–'40; NLAPW, Freedom Fndn. (State Bd. Mbr.), DAR; Who's Who of Am. Wm.; Gadsden Educ. Assn. aw., '68; b. Americus, Ga., 1912; p. Timothy and Tallulah Brown Callaway; h. James Lawrence Hoffman; c. James Lawrence, Katherine C., Jane; res: 1100 Sixth Ave., Gadsden, Ala. 35901.

HOFFMANN, PEGGY, (Margaret Jones Hoffmann), Auth: "My Dear Cousin" (Harcourt, Brace & World, '70), "The Money Hat" (Westminster, '69), "A Forest of Feathers" ('66), "Shift to High!" ('65), "The Wild Rocket" ('64), others; Longview Wtrs. (Bd. Mbr., '67–), Night Wtrs., Am. Guild of Organists, Mensa; Miami (Oh.) Univ., AB, '34; Chgo. Theological Seminary, '34–'35; b. Delaware, Oh., 1910; p. Miles and Renee Roberts Jones; h. Arnold E. Hoffmann; c. Theodore C., Bruce F., Rosemary B.; res: 2609 Wade Ave., Raleigh, N.C. 27607.

HOFFMEIR, MIRIAM FLORENCE, Mgr. of Program Analysis Dept., National Broadcasting Company, 30 Rockefeller Plaza, N.Y., N.Y. 10020, '54–; Supvsr., '42; Asst. Supvsr., '38; Cont. Dept., '33; AWRT (Bd. Trustees Chmn., '68–; Nat. Bd. Secy. Treas., '65–'67; N.Y.C. Chptr. Pres., '59–'60), IRTS; Wilton Playshop (Pres., '56–'58; VP, Prodr., '54–'56; Bd. Trustees, '62–), Mid-Fairfield Child Guidance (Bd. Trustees, '61–), Un. Fund (Wilton, Conn., Bd. Dirs., '68–); Columbia Univ., N.Y.U.; b. N.Y.C.; p. Harry J. and Ann Florence Kimberly Hoffmeir; h. Edward Brother; c. Kathe (Mrs. Roland J. Allen), Elizabeth; res: 56 Grumman Hill Rd., Wilton, Conn. 06897.

HOFHERR, WILLIMIENE RICH, Dir. of Pfsnl. Pubns., Pubcty., Muncie Community Schools, 328 E. Washington St., Muncie, Ind. 47305, '59–; Eng. Tchr., 19 yrs.; Theta Sigma Phi (Treas.), NPC, Ind. Press Club, Delta Kappa Gamma, Muncie Tchrs. Assn., NEA, Ind. State Tchrs. Assn., Altrusa (Pres.); Ball State Univ., BS, '42; b. McMinnville, Tenn., 1919; p. William and Musie Rich; h. Philip Hofherr; c. Mrs. Robert Ten Eyck, Jr., Philip, Jr.; res: 1002 W. North St., Muncie, Ind. 47303.

HOGAN, ALICE HAMILTON, Wtr., fiction stories in gen. mags., incl. "The Night Mrs. Kent Quit" (Saturday Evening Post, '56; Christopher Aw.); Chmn., Eng. Dept., James Hillhouse HS, New Haven, Conn., '61–; represented in anthologies: "On My Honor," "First Date Stories"; Auths. Guild of Am., AAUW, Radcliffe Club, League of Wm. Voters, Nat. Cncl. of Tchrs. of Eng., NEA; Columbia Univ., BS, '32; Radcliffe Col., MA, '42; b. New Haven, Conn.; p. John and Mary Gormley Hogan; res: 49 Osborn Ave., New Haven, Conn. 06511.

HOGAN, BERNICE HARRIS, Auth: three juv. bks.,

eight adult non-fiction; Remedial Reading, Abingdon Grade School, W. Latimer St., Abingdon, Ill. 61410, '66–; AAUW, Ill. Educ. Assn., Abingdon Educ. Assn., Intl. Reading Assn.; Bethany Col., AB, '51; b. Phila., Pa., 1929; h. Donald Hogan; c. Carol Louise, Robert Lawrence, Susan Lynn; res: 710 W. Jackson St., Abingdon, Ill. 61410.

HOGG, JOAN KATHERINE, House Organ Ed., Hercules Corporation, Edgemont Dr., Covington, Va. 24426, '66–; Typist-Clerk, '64–'66; AAIE; DSL Commty. Col.; b. Rocky Mount, N.C., 1946; p. Milton and Fanny Daniel Hogg; res: 321 E. Trout, Covington, Va. 24426.

HOGUE, HELEN MARIE, Librn., South Side Branch Library, Oshkosh Public Library, 106 Washington Ave., Oshkosh, Wis. 54901, '57–; Staff, '44–'57; HS Tchr: Rosholt, '43–'44; Norway, Mich., '41–'42; ALA, Wis. Lib. Assn., Wis. State Hist. Soc., Alpha Xi Delta (Pres., '49–'51), active in numerous civic groups; Wis. State Univ., BS, '41; b. Oshkosh, Wis., 1918; p. Harvey and Frances Graessle Hogue; res: 1115 Winnebago Ave., Oshkosh, Wis. 54901.

HOHN, HAZEL STAMPER, Auth., Children's Fiction and Non-fiction, Adult Non-Fiction; Wms. Air Force Svc. Pilot, WWII; Reno Pen Wm., Ninety-Nines (Secy.), League of Wm. Voters (Bd. of Dirs., '66–'67); Who's Who of Am. Wm.; Who's Who in Wm. in the West; b. Bklyn, N.Y.; p. Hamilton and Hazel Walker Stamper; h. Werner Hohn; c. Jim, John, Carol, Susan; res: 605 Jeanell Dr., Carson City, Nev. 89701.

HOLAHAN, JEWEL BRAUN, Exec. Ed., Language Arts, Follett Educational Corp., 1010 W. Washington Blvd., Chgo., Ill. 60607, '67–; Mng. Ed., Educ. Div., Follett Publishing Co., '64–'67; Mng. Ed., Dir. of Edtl. Svcs., '60–'62; Asst. Mgr., Engineering Presentations, Goodyear Aircraft Corp. (Akron, Oh.), '54–'60; Ed., '52–'54; Prod. Ed., Ency. Britannica (Chgo., Ill.), '46–'52; Proofreader, '42–'43; Chgo. Bk. Clinic (VP, '69–'70; Dir., '66–'69), NEA, Cncl. for Exceptional Children, Nat. Cncl. Tchrs. of Eng., Am. Mgt. Assn.; Pa. State Univ., BA (Jnlsm.) '40; b. Hamilton, Oh., 1920; p. Walter and Ruth Sheley Braun; h. David Holahan (div.); c. Charmian (Mrs. Keith Goudy), Janice (Mrs. Paul Westerhouse III); res: 712 Jefferson St., Hinsdale, Ill. 60521.

HOLAHAN, URSULA ANN, Cooperative Ext. Agt., Schenectady County Cooperative Extension, 620 State St., Schenectady, N.Y. 12309, '62–; Ext. Home Econ. (Rochester), '54–'62; Asst. Prom. Dir., United Piece Dye Works, '52–'54; Assoc. Ed., Textile Lab., Good Housekeeping Inst., '49–'52; Borden Test Kitchen, '47–'49; AWRT, N.Y. State Assn. Ext. Home Econsts. (State Pres., '68–'69; Dist. Chmn., '66–'67), Am. Home Econs. Assn., N.Y. State Home Econ. Assn., Soroptimist; Distg. Svc. Aw., Nat. Assn. of Ext. Home Econsts., '67; Cornell Univ., BS (Home Econ.), '47; Univ. of Minn., MS (Home Econ.), '62; b. Bronx, N.Y., 1921; p.

Joseph and Florence Kelleher Holahan; res: Concord Apts., Apt. B6, Concord Rd., Anderson, S.C. 29621.

HOLCOMB, CAROLYN JENSEN, Staff Reptr., Waterloo Daily Courier, W. H. Hartman Co., Box 540, Commercial St., Waterloo, Ia. 50704, '64–; Theta Sigma Phi, Kappa Tau Alpha, Gamma Phi Beta, Panhellenic Assn.; Voice of Democracy aw., '58; Freedoms Fndn. aw., '59; Univ. of Ia., BA, '62 (Phi Beta Kappa; Alpha Lamda Delta; cum laude); b. Davenport, Ia., 1940; p. Charles and Catherine Cooper Jensen; h. Thomas Joel Holcomb; c. Scott, Kellie; res: 1510 E. Ridgeway Ave., Waterloo, Ia. 50702.

HOLCOMB, ELIZABETH COLEMAN, Dir., Lee-Itawamba Regional Libraries, 219 Madison, Tupelo, Miss. 38801. '57–; Librn., Lee County Lib., '53–'56; Librn., Tupelo HS, '31–'37; articles in lib., hist. pubns.; ALA, Miss. Lib. Assn., NE Hist. Soc., Lee County Mental Health Assn., Dorothy Canfield Fischer Aw., '61; Outstanding Citizen of Tupelo Aw., '66; Miss. State Col. for Wm., BA, '31; Univ. of Ill., BLS '36; b. Memphis, Tenn. 1909; p. James and Laura Holt Coleman; h. Gene Holcomb; c. Gene, Jr.; res: 642 N. Madison, Tupelo, Miss. 38801.

HOLDEN, SARAH McCORDIC, Sr. Staff Wtr., American Education Publications, A Xerox Company, 55 High St., Middletown, Conn. 06498, '68–; Staff Wtr., Ed., Read mag., '51–; Oh. State Univ., BA, '47; MA (Eng.), '48 (Phi Beta Kappa); b. Thunder Hawk, S.D., 1910; p. N.R. and Lulu Bishop McCordic; h. Oliver Holden; c. Mrs. H.-W. Wendt, Mrs. Morton Leonard; res: Pond Meadow Rd., Westbrook, Conn. 06457.

HOLDING, VERA ZUMWALT, Free-lance Poet.; "Listen the Prairies Speak," "Dim Trails," three other bks.; Auth. of teenage novels: "Love Has Silent Wings," "Run Far, Run Fast, Run Scared;" Wtr. of hist. articles; Ed., Tipton (Okla.) Home Magazine, '61–; Co-Ed., Publr., Tipton Tribune, 27 yrs.; Instr., crtv. writing, Okla. Univ.; crtv. writing workshop; various orgs., aws.; Daniel Baker Col. (voice and piano), '14; Am. Conservatory, '17–'18; b. Sansaba, Tex., 1894; p. William and Sarah Favers Zumwalt; h. Chester Allen Holding; c. Robert Lyle, Mrs. Caroll Joy Tucker; res: 516 Clearview, Norman, Okla. 73069.

HOLETON, SUZANNE, Prod. Exec., Mercury Newsfilm/Associated Film Consultants, 501 Madison Ave., N.Y., N.Y. 10022, '65–; Copywtr., Prod. Coordr. Dir., WBFM, '61–64; Pubcty., Filmex, '61; Prodrs. Asst., Arthur Lodge Prods., '53–'60; NBC-TV News, '51–'53; Pubcty., Prom. Asst., WINS, '47; Copywtr., Bdcstr., WCHS, '46; AWRT, NATAS; Oh. Wesleyan Univ., AB, '46; DePauw Univ.; Columbia Univ.; N.Y.U.; Theodora Irvine Sch. of Theatre; b. Warren, Oh., 1924; p. Charles and Mildred Fording Holeton; res: 71 Irving Pl., N.Y., N.Y. 10003.

HOLL, ADELAIDE HINKLE, Ed., sch., lib. bks., Western Publishing Company, 850 Third Ave., N.Y., N.Y.

10022, '69–; Auth., children's bks., "Magic Tales," "The Runaway Hat," "Journey to the Sea," many others; Ed., Random House, '67–'69; Staff Wtr., Artists' and Wtrs. Press, '61–'67; Tchr., '48–'61; Pi Lambda Theta, Auths. League of Am., NEA, Intl. Reading Assn.; Classroom Tchrs. Aw., Freedom Fndn. (Valley Forge), '60; Capital Univ. (Columbus, Oh.), BA, BS, '40 (Outstanding Alumna A., '67); Oh. State Univ., MA, '59; b. Pitt., Pa., 1920; p. Lester and Bertie Van Dean Smith Hinkle; h. (div.); c. Linda Holl Segel, Thomas Richard; res: 5 Tudor City Pl., Apt., 1905, N.Y., N.Y. 10017.

HOLLAND, EDNA WU, Head Librn., Gail Borden Public Library, 200 N. Grove Ave., Elgin, Ill. 60120, '62–; Field Librn., Wis. Free Lib. Comm. (Madison), '60–'62; Head Librn., Antigo (Wis.) Public Lib., '47–'60; Children's Librn., '44–'47; Ill. Lib. Assn. (Secy., '67–'68), AAUW, ZONTA (Pres., '69–'70; VP, '68–'69; Secy., '65–'66); John Cotton Dana Lib. Pubcty. aw., '66; Northland Col., BA, '44 (cum laude), Western Reserve Univ., BS (Lib. Sci.), '47; b. Antigo, Wis., 1921; p. John and Margaret Funck Wu; h. Arthur Holland; res: 550 Barrett St., Elgin, Ill. 60120.

HOLLAND, HILDA, Adv. Mgr. and Dir. of Bk. and Conv. Exhibits Dimension mag., 838 Fifth Ave., N.Y., N.Y. 10021, '59–; Auth., "Why Are You Single?" (Farrar and Strauss); France Forever Magazines; Publr: "Travel With Me" and "Guide Industriel Americain"; WNYC Radio; Wtr., mag. articles; Colmst., Palestine Post; aw. for article in Coronet; h. (dec.)

HOLLAND, KRISTINA, Actress, c/o Wm. Cunningham & Assoc., 9000 Sunset Blvd., Suite, 911, L.A., Cal. 90069; Commls., on-camera, voice-over, radio spots, musical comedy ("The Fantasticks," S.F. prod.); TV shows incl: "The Courtship of Eddie's Father"; AFTRA, SAG, AEA; S.F. State; b. Fayetteville, N.C., 1944; p. Mel and Jacque Hermansen; h. Ronald Poindexter; res: 2125 No. Beverly Dr., Beverly Hills, Calif., 90069.

HOLLAND, PHYLLIS HAMILTON, Wtr., PR and Adv., Phyllis Holland Public Relations and Advertising, 1030 N. Main St., Fairmont, Minn. 56031, '67–; Farm Ed., Fairmont Sentinel, '66–'68; Staff Wtr., '63–'66; Adv., PR Mgr., Lundell Mfg. Co., '52–'61; b. Washta, Ia., 1927; p. Ray and Winnifred Conley Hamilton; h. Orlin Holland; c. Jeffrey; res: 1030 N. Main St., Fairmont, Minn. 56031.

HOLLANDER, SOPHIE SMITH, State Supvsr. in Educ., Massachusetts Dept. of Education, 182 Tremont St., Boston, Mass. 02111, '67–; Ed., Bur., pubn.; Auth., "Impressions of the United States" (Holt, Rinehart, & Winston, '65); Nat. Cncl. of Tchrs. of Eng., Intl. Reading Assn., Assn. for Suprvsn. and Curriculum Dev., Assn. of State Supvsrs. of Eng. and Reading; Hunter Col., BA, '31; Columbia Univ., MA, '32; h. A. Gerson Hollander M.D.; c. Mrs. Rina Humphers, Mrs. Edith

Michelson, Robert, Jonathan; res: 150 S. Huntington Ave., Boston, Mass. 02130.

HOLLETT, RUTH DUKES, Ed., synd. colm., "Anti-Query," '46–; Cert. Appraiser, Funiture, Fine Arts, Antiques; Seminar Tchr.; Auth., textbk.; Prodr., TV program on antique Porcelains, Time-Tribune (Tampa, Fla.); Participant, Wtr., Wedgwood Intl. Seminar (Eng.), '69; Wtr., Tchr., courses, Antiques, Americana, St. Petersburg Jr. Col.; St. Petersburg Hist. Soc. Museum, '50–'61; Lectr.; studio, shop, Ceramics (St. Petersburg, Fla.), '46; various orgs.; b. Phila., Pa., 1903; p. George and Laure Nelson Dukes; h. George L. Hollett; c. Frank W. Harris 3rd, Nelson G. Harris, Ruth Hollett Brownely; res: 1000 23rd Ave., N. St. Petersburg, Fla. 33704.

HOLLINS, VIOLA VAN DUYNE, Copyreader, Headline Wtr., Reptr., Desk, The Bakersfield Californian, Bin 440, Bakersfield, Cal., '62–; Wire Ed., '44–'58; Former Food, Ch., Farm, Home, Garden Ed.; Bakersfield Nwsp. Guild (Charter Mbr.); Univ. of Okla. Sch. of Jnlsm., '40; b. Weatherford, Okla., 1914; p. John and Phoebe Johnston Van Duyne; h. Harry H. Hollins; c. Sandi, John; res: 2717 Ardee Circle, Bakersfield, Cal. 93304.

HOLLOWAY, IRMAGENE NEVINS, Asst. for Consumer Educ., Office of Product Safety, Consumer Protection and Environmental Health Services, 200 "C" St., S.W. Wash., D.C. 20204, '68–; Asst. to Chief, Injury Control Prog., '66–'68; Safety Prog. Specialist, Div. of Accident Prevention, '61–'66; Gtr. Cinn. Safety Cncl., '52–'54; Gtr. N.Y. Safety Cncl., '49–'51; Dir., Accident Prevention, Am. Nat. Red Cross, '42–'48; Dept. Head, Health & Physical Educ. for Wm., Kan. State Col. of Pittsburg, '28–'42; Conslt., numerous orgs.; Tchr. Fellow, N.Y.U. '38–'39, '41; Dir., Special Project, Blueprint for Life (Cleve., Oh.), '61–'63; NBC-Educ. Exchange Prog. Coordr., '67–'68; AWRT, Intl. Dev. Comm., Nat. Safety Cncl. (Outstanding Achiev. Aw., '68), Am. Acad. of Safety Educ. (Pres., '65–'66), ZONTA, BPW Pfsnl. Wm. of Yr., D.C. Club, '66; Am. Museum of Safety and GNYSC Plaque, '52; ARC Achiev. Aw., '48; Zeta Tau Alpha Achiev. Aw.; Baker Univ., BA; PhD (Hon.) '46; Columbia Univ., MA, '28; N.Y.U., EdD, '41; b. Dodge City, Kans.; p. O. Newton and Martha Griffith Nevins; h. Hubert Holloway (dec.); res: 1600 S. Joyce St., Arlington, Va. 22202.

HOLLOWAY, TERESA BRAGUNIER, Free-lance Wtr.; Adm. Aide, Florida Senate; '65–; Attache, '47–; Auth., 28 young adult novels; Mgr., Apalachicola C. of C., '47–'50; Owner, Herring Ginger Ale Co., '40–'43; Off. Mgr., '37–'39; Lectr., Crtv. Writing, Tallahassee Jr. Col., '69; Tchr., Crtv. Writing, Fla. Jr. Col. (Jacksonville), '66–'67; Photogr., TV features, documentaries; NLAPW (Jacksonville Br. Past Pres.; nat. aw., '66, '68), MWA; Sears Fndn. aw. '58; Cit., President Truman, '51; Cit., Gen. Louis Hershey, '47; Who's Who of Am. Wm., Contemporary Auths.; Dic. of Intl. Biog.; Fla. State Col. for Wm., LI, '25; b. Apalachicola, Fla., 1906; p. David and Mordina Floyd Bragunier; h. John Calvin Holloway; c. John (dec.); res: 4349 Irvington Ave., Jacksonville, Fla. 32210.

HOLMES, ANN HITCHCOCK, Fine Arts Ed., Houston Chronicle, 512 Travis, Houston, Tex. 77002, '48–; gen. reptr., '42–'48; Contrbr., Opera News, N.Y. Times, Art in Am., others; Municipal Art Commn. (Houston, Tex.; Charter Mbr.), Univ. of Tex. Fine Arts Advisory Cncl.; Ogden Reid grant, European study of arts, '53; Guggenheim Fellowship, '60; Ford Fndn. grant, Critics program, '64; hon. mention, nat. competition for architectural jnlsm., Am. Inst. of Architects; Whitworth Col. (Brookhaven, Miss.), (Drama); Georges Bridges Studio (Birmingham, Ala.), (Sculpture); Southern Col. of Fine Arts (Houston, Tex.), (Musicology); b. El Paso, Tex.; p. Fred and Joy C. Holmes.

HOLMES, BETTY JEAN, Asst., Abilene Free Public Library, Fourth and Broadway, Abilene, Kan. 67410, '47–; ALA, Mt. Plains Lib. Assn., Kan. Lib. Assn.; b. Abilene, Kan., 1929; p. Emery and Ada Brown Holmes; res: 911 N. Mulberry, Abilene, Kan. 67410.

HOLMES, LEILA B., Colmst., "Today in Science," The Indianapolis Star, 307 N. Pennsylvania St., Indpls., Ind. 46225, '69–; Colmst., Indianapolis Star, '59–'67; Wtr., Ind. Univ. Med. Ctr., '67–; Indpls. Press Club, Theta Sigma Phi, Nat. Soc. of Arts and Letters; Agnes Scott Col., BA, '45; b. Macon, Ga.; p. William and Ethel McKay Holmes; res: 25 E. 40th St., Indpls., Ind. 46205.

HOLMES, LUCY MARIA, Prom. Mgr., The Seabury Press, 815 Second Ave., N.Y., N.Y. 10017, '52–; Asst. Ed., MacMillan, '46–'51; Prod. Asst., Little, Brown, '43–'45; Librn., Nichols Jr. Col., '41–'42; WNBA, Publrs. Adv. Club (Treas., '66–'68), Religious Publrs. Group; Boston Univ., '35–'37; Pembroke Col., BA, '39; b. Plymouth, Mass.; p. Edwin and Emma Holmes.

HOLMES, MARA FIORATOS, Wtr., Ed., Voice of America, U.S. Information Agency, Room 2300, 330 Independence Ave. S.W., Wash., D.C. 20025, '65–; Bdcstr., "Agriculture U.S.A.," '65–; "Science Newsfront," '69–; Fiction Wtr., '62–'65; AWRT; b. Harbin, China, 1927; p. Andrew and Vera Baboushkina Fioratos; h. Louis Clifford Holmes; res: 301 South Carolina Ave. S.E., Wash., D.C. 20003.

HOLMES, MARJORIE ROSE, Colmst., Washington, D.C. Evening Star, Second and Virginia Ave., S.E., Wash., D.C., '58–; Auth: "I've Got to Talk to Somebody, God" (Doubleday, '69), "Writing the Creative Article" (The Writer, '69), "Love & Laughter" (Doubleday, '67), others; many mag. articles; lectr., wtr. confs.; WNPC, ANWC, Children's Bk. Guild; Buena Vista Col., '27–'29 (Hon. Iowans Aw., '66); Cornell Col. (Mt. Vernon, Ia.), BA, '31 (Alumni Achiev. Aw., '63); b. Storm Lake, Ia., 1910; p. Samuel and Rosa Griffith Holmes; h. Lynn Mighell; c. Majorie

(Mrs. Stanley Croner), Mark, Mallory, Melanie; res: 1110 Shipman Lane, McLean, Va. 22101.

HOLMES, MARY HELEN, Dir., Madison Heights Public Library, 240 W. Thirteen Mile Rd., Madison Heights, Mich., '58–'66; League of Wm. Voters, Altrusa Club of Gtr. Birmingham; Who's Who in Am. Educ.; Who's Who of Am. Wm.; Who's Who in Am. Lib. Sci.; Univ. of Mich., AB, '20; Univ. of Wis., Lib. Cert., '34; b. Northville, Mich., 1896; p. Hiram and Jane Blackwood Holmes; res: 875 S. Bates St., Birmingham, Mich. 48009.

HOLMES, SANDRA GLENDALIN, Film Ed., McGee Report, National Broadcasting Co., 30 Rockefeller Plaza, N.Y., N.Y. 10020; N.Y.U., BS, '63.

HOLMQUIST, KAY (Katherine Northcut Holmquist), Wms. Ed., Fort Worth Star-Telegram (Morning and Sunday), 400 W. Seventh St., Ft. Worth, Tex. 76102, '68–; Reptr. (Evening) '67–'68; Copywtr., Sears-Detroit Group (Troy, Mich.), '66–'67; Copy Chief, Tandy Corp. (Ft. Worth, Tex.), '63–'65; Librn., San Diego Un.-Tribune, '61–'63; Theta Sigma Phi; nomination, Pulitzer Prize in Jnlsm., '68; Mng. Eds. Aw., Tex. AP, '69; Harding Col. (Searcy, Ark.), BA (Eng., Jnlsm.), '64; T.C.U. (Ft. Worth); Mich. State Univ. (Rochester); b. Ft. Worth, Tex., 1939; p. Huey and Bonnie Langdon Northcut; res: 3855 Medford Rd., Ft. Worth, Tex. 76103.

HOLSCHUH, JOLANDA HUELLEIN-DUCHENE, Comptroller-Treas., Springer-Verlag New York Inc., 175 Fifth Ave., N.Y., N.Y. 10010, '66–; Assoc., Asst., Cert. Public Accountant, '56–'65; educ: equivalent to C.P.A. (Germany), '63; b. Germany, 1935; res: 23 Mansfield Pl., Lynbrook, N.Y. 11563.

HOLSINGER, JANE LUMLEY, Auth., "The Secret of Indian Ridge" (Bobbs-Merrill); Children's Reading Round Table; Ind. Univ., Univ. of Cal.; b. Woodstock, Ill.; p. Vincent and Neva Bunker Lumley; h. Arthur Holsinger; c. Mrs. Nouroilah Rowhani; res: 4919 E. Lake Shore Dr., Wonder Lake, Ill. 60097.

HOLT, MARY BROWN, Wms. Dir., Bdcstr., WABQ, Booth Broadcasting, 2644 St. Clair Ave., Cleveland, Oh. 44114, '66–; WJMO, '50–'66; WJW, '50–'52; WSRS, '45–'50; AWRT (Western Reserve Chptr. VP, '62–'66; Oh. Chptr. Secy., '58–'60), AFTRA (Radio-TV Best Comml. Anncr. Aw., '61); Street Club's Coveted Aw., '67; Salvation Army aw., '68; Black Draught aw., '66; Fla. A. and M. Col., '39–'42; Western Reserve Univ. (Drama), '43–'45; b. Fremont, Oh., 1921; p. Walter and Matilda Warren Brown; c. Carole Driggins, Clifford Holt; res: 12615 Cornado Ave., Cleve., Oh. 44108.

HOLT, SHARON K., Media Dir., Lumpp & Fillman, Inc., One Henson Pl., Champaign, Ill. 61820, '67–; Adv. Club of Champaign-Urbana, Gamma Alpha Chi, Graduate Adv. Assn.; Univ. of Ill., BS, '66; b. Champaign, Ill., 1944; p. Perry and Eva Holt.

HOLTZMAN, ELEANOR FENSTER, VP-Dir. of Mkt. Svcs., Delehanty, Kurnit & Geller, Inc., 733 Third Ave., N.Y., N.Y. 10017, '68–; VP-Dir. of Rsch., McCann-Erickson, '66–'68; VP-Dir., of Rsch., Marplan, '58–'66; h. Alexander Holtzman.

HOLZHAUSER, KRIN CRAWFORD, VP-Dir. of Air Media, Goodwin Dannenbaum Littman & Wingfield, Inc. (Advertising & Public Relations), 2400 W. Loap S., Houston, Tex. 77027, '57–; On-air Bdcstr., CBS, 17 yrs.; AWRT (Nat. Pres., '67–'68; Pres.-elect, '66–'67; Nat. VP, '64–'66; Houston Chptr. Pres., '64–'65; Educ. Fndn. Trustee), BPW (First VP, '69–'70; Wm. of Achiev., '68), Radio Free Asia (Advisory Bd. Dirs.), AWARE Educ. Program (Advisory Bd.); Nat. Cystic Fibrosis (Advisory Bd. Dirs.), Heart Assn. (Bd.); Robt. Eastman Aw., outstanding wm. in bdcst., '67; La. State Univ., BA, MA, '36 (summa cum laude; Belasco Nat. Drama Scholarship, '32); b. N.O., La., 1911; p. William A. and Mattie Mai Barker Crawford; h. Leland Louis Holzhauser; c. Dennis L.; res: 7518 Edna St., Houston, Tex. 77017.

HONEYWELL, EUGENIA HUBBARD, Pres., Nixon Newspapers, Inc., 123 W. Canal St., Wabash, Ind. 46992; VP, Honeywell Fndn., Inc.; VP, Hoosier Salon Patrons Assn.; Met. Opera Nat. Cncl., Soc. of Friends of Music; Distg. Citizen of Wabash, '59; Hon. Deg., Tri-State Col., '69; Educ: Ind. State Col.; b. Clay City, Ind., 1896; p. Wallace and Della DeCoursey Hubbard; h. 1. Don M. Nixon (dec.) 2. Mark C. Honeywell (dec); c. John R. Nixon; res: 720 N. Wabash St., Wabash, Ind. 46992.

HOOBLER, MAJORIE JEAN, Dir. of Consumer Svcs., Gardner, Jones & Crowell Inc., 79 W. Monroe St., Chgo., Ill. 60603; Acct. Supvsr., Philip Lesly Co., '61–'68; PR Grant Adv., '53–'61; Free-lance Wtr., Chicago Tribune, '68–'69; AWRT (Chgo. Chptr. VP, '69–); Hope Col.; Univ. of Ill., BS (Jnlsm.), '46; b. Detroit, Mich., 1927; p. Dartt Hoobler and Mrs. Alvin P. McMecken; res: 30 E. Elm St., Chgo., Ill. 60611.

HOOD, CAROLINE, VP, Rockefeller Center, Inc., 50 Rockefeller Plaza, N.Y., N.Y. 10020, '64–; Dir., PR, '44–'64; Asst. Dir. PR, '42–'44; Rep., '37–'42; Sls. Rep. '34–'37; PRSA, AWNY (Past Pres.); CWPR (Past Pres.); N.Y. State Wms. Cncl.; The Hemisphere Club, N.Y. Convs & Visitors Bur. Bd. of Dirs., Radio City Music Hall Bd. of Dirs.; Repl. Wm. in Industry and the Professions aw., '64; Columbia Univ., New Sch. for Social Rsch.; b. Pawtcuket, R.I., 1909; p. John and Martha Briggs Hood; h. John H. Carlin; res: 400 E. 58th St., N.Y., N.Y. 10022.

HOOD, FLORA MAE, Free-lance Wtr.; Auth: "Something for Medicine Man" (a Jr. Literary Aw. book of documentary fiction, '61), "The Longest Beard in the World" (Children's Press, '62), "Uncle Sam" (biography of Samuel Wilkson), "One Luminaria for Antonio," "Pink Puppy," "Living in Navajoland"; teaching three tribes of Indians for the gov-

ernment (Cherokee, Pueblos, and Navajos); Radio Ed.-Wtr., Press Assn. (Charlotte, N.C.); News Bureau Asst., Stetson Univ. (Deland, Fla.); Asst. Ed., Univ. Press, Wash. State Univ. (Pullman, Wash.); WWII Radio Ed., News Bureau and Press; Chowan Col. (Murfreesboro, N.C.), BA; William and Mary, '55–'56; UCLA, '59; San Miguel (Mexico), '60; b. Louisville, Ky.; p. Claudius W. and Ada Word Hood; res: Baldwin, Ga. 30511.

HOOGASIAN-VILLA, SUSIE, Asst. Prof. of Eng., Oakland Community College, 27055 Orchard Lake Rd., Farmington, Mich. 48024, '69–; Home Econ. Educ. Tchr., Wayne State Univ., '66–'68; Home Econ. Tchr., Detroit Public Schs., '59–'61, '49–'55; Clawson Public Schs., '44–'47; Auth., "100 Armenian Tales and Their Folkloristic Relevance," (Chgo. Intl. Folklore Contest aw., '66); Am. Home Econs. Assn., Mich. Folklore Soc., Am. Folklore Soc., Detroit Armenian Wms. Club; Wayne State Univ.; BS, '44; MA, '48; Merrill-Palmer Inst., Ind. Univ.; b. Detroit, Mich., 1921; p. Kazar and Hripsima Demerjian Hoogasian; h. John J. Villa; c. John K. Villa, Nancy Emelyn Villa, James David Villa; res: 32550 Plumwood Lane, Birmingham, Mich. 48010.

HOOK, INGA RUNDVOLD, Free-lance Prodr., '68–; Prodr., Wtr., Commentator, NBC, '50–'67; Fashion Ed., Colmst., Washington (D.C.) Times Herald, '45–'50; WNPC, AWRT, ANWC, AFTRA, Soc. of Am. Travel Wtrs.; svc. aw., D.C. Bar Assn., State of Md. svc. aw., others; b. Styrn, Norway; p. Torger and Malene Nesjheim Rundvold; h. Lester James Hook; c. Ingrid Hook Davis; res: 9719 Bexhill Dr. W., Kensington, Md. 20795.

HOOK, PENNY ANN, Asst. Cont. Dir., WESH-TV, 1501 Minnesota Ave., Orlando, Fla. 32804, '68–; Asst. Byr., J. B. Ivey & Co., Charlotte, N.C., '66–'67; AWRT (Secy., '69); Barry Col., '62–'63; Stetson Univ., AB, '66; b. Park Ridge, N.J., 1944; p. August and Doris Berg Hook; res: 1636 Oakmont Lane, Orlando, Fla. 32804.

HOOKS, ELEANOR WRIGHT, Librn., Public Library of Johnston County and Smithfield, 305 Market St., Smithfield, N.C. 27577, '57–; staff '54–'57; N.C. Lib. Assn., N.C. Lit. and Hist. Assn., Smithfield Wms. Club; Brenau Col., AB, '35; b. Raleigh, N.C., 1914; p. William and Jennie Ellis Wright; h. J. Thel Hooks; c. J. Thel, Jr., Ellis W., William R.; res: 108 Johnston St., Smithsfield, N.C. 27577.

HOOS, IDA RUSSAKOFF, Research Sociologist, University of California, Berkeley, Cal. 94707, '65–; Cnslt., U.S. Health Education and Welfare, Dir., Vocational Svc. (Boston, Mass.); Auth: "Automation in the Office" (Public Affairs Press, '61), "Retraining the Workforce: Analysis of Current Experience" (Univ. of Cal. Press, '67); numerous mag. articles; Radcliffe Col., AB, '33 (magna cum laude); Univ. of Cal., PhD (Sociology), '59; b. Skowhegan, Me.; p. Susman and Manya Simkin Russakoff; h. Sidney S. Hoos; c. Phyllis

(Mrs. Richard DeLeon), Judith; res: 868 Arlington Ave., Berkeley, Cal. 94707.

HOOVER, HELEN BLACKBURN, Free-lance Wtr., c/o Brandt & Brandt, 101 Park Ave., N.Y., N.Y. 10017, '54–; non-fiction, some juv. fiction, "Great Wolf and the Good Woodsman" ('67; GA 50 Bks., '67–'68), "The Gift of the Deer," four other nature bks. ('63–'69); numerous articles in nature and gen. mags.; metellurgist '43–'54; Proofreader, ABC, '30–'43; Auths. Guild, MWA, Intl. Platform Assn., numerous conservation orgs.; Oh. Univ., '27–'29; DePaul Univ., Univ. of Chgo., '43–'49; b. Greenfield, Oh., 1910; p. Thomas and Hannah Gomersall Blackburn; h. Adrian Hoover.

HOOVER, KATHLEEN O'DONNELL, Chmn. of Museum Comm., Metropolitan Opera Guild, Inc., 1865 Broadway, N.Y., N.Y. 10023, '46–; Chmn., Lects. Comm., '37–'40; Auth: "Makers of Opera" ('48; Inst. of Graphic Arts slection), "Virgil Thomson: His Life" ('58; Eng. Speaking Un. aw., '59'); Ed., "Liszt's Weimar" ('61'); Wtr. of articles in pfsnl. jnls.; various orgs.; Univ. of Vienna, 1900–10; Academia Santa Cecilia (Rome, Italy), '11–'12; Sorbonne, '13–'14; Columbia Univ. Ext. Dept., '43–'45; b. Wash., D.C., 1895; p. James and Sarah George O'Donnell; h. Edwin Keith Hoover; c. Gordon Phillips Hoover (dec.); res: 120 E. 79th St., N.Y., N.Y. 10021.

HOPE, BETTY, Ed., Employee Pubn., The Singer Company, 30 Rockefeller Plaza, N.Y., N.Y. 10020, '62–; Edtl. Asst., Exec. Secy. to Dir. of PR, '53–'62; Free-lance TV and play-writing; Pubcty. Club of N.Y., N.Y. Assn. of Indsl. Communicators; Fairleigh Dickinson Univ., BA, '53 (cum laude, Liberal Arts Hon. aw.,); b. Garfield, N.J.; p. Theodore Frank and Anna Kardash Wislotski; res: 756 Linden Ave., Elizabeth, N.J. 07202.

HOPE, ELEANOR SCHORER, Auth., "The Wishing Ring" (Harcourt, Brace & Howe, '19); play prod., '18; Free-lance Feature Wtr.-Artist, chief clients: Phila. Inquirer, St. Louis Globe Democrat, Toronto Star, starting '31; Wtr., Cartoonist, Dir. of children's activities, "Cousin Eleanor" of Kiddie Klub, N.Y. Evening World, '10–'30; "Judy," '26–'27 teenage comic; "Tumble Tom," comicstrip; Travelogs; The Wm. Pays Club (Pres., '43–'44, '44–'45), OPC; Nat. Acad. of Design, '06; Columbia (Writing, Eng.), '13; Art Students League; Julian's Acad. (Paris), '30–'31; b. N.Y.C., 1891; p. William B. and Martha F. Dohm Schorer; h. Lieut. Chester Raines Hope, U.S.N.R. (dec.); res: 345 W. 86th St., N.Y., N.Y. 10024.

HOPE, MARJORIE CECELIA, Free-lance Wtr., numerous mag. articles on social revolution, youth revolt, problems of war and peace, psych.; social work, refugees in hosp. (Harlem); Head Start program; lib. work, '51–'53; Tchr., grade, HS (France, U.S.); Soc. of Mag. Wtrs.; Sarah Lawrence Col., BA, '44; Columbia Univ., MA (Sociol.), '54; N.Y.U., MSS (Social Work), '59; b. Lakewood, Oh., 1923; p. Carl

and Marguerite Jones Hope; h. (div.); res: 117 W. 13th St., N.Y., N.Y. 10011.

HOPF, ALICE LIGHTNER, Auth., juv. sci. fiction, non-fiction; Grey Matter Secy., Grey Advertising, Inc. 777 Third Ave., N. Y., N.Y. 10017, '54–; bks: "The Day of the Drones" (W. G. Norton, '69), "Butterfly and Moth" (G. P. Putnam's Sons, '69); numerous other bks., mag. articles, short stories; Auths. Guild, Sci. Fiction Wtrs. of Am., N.Y. Entomological Soc., Lepidopterists Soc.; Vassar Col., '23–'27; b. Detroit, Mich., 1904; p. Clarence and Frances McGraw Lightner; h. Ernest Hopf; c. Christopher; res: 136 W. 16th St., N.Y., N.Y. 10011.

HOPKINS, DOROTHY FRANCES AE, Cunningham and Walsh, Inc., 260 Madison Avenue, N.Y., N.Y., 10016, '68–; Dir. of Consumer Info., Pan-American Coffee Bur., '64–'68; Pubcty. Assoc., '60–'64; Copywtr., J. Walter Thompson, '56–'60; AWRT, NHFL, Theta Sigma Phi (N.Y. Chptr. Pres., '64–'65, '67–'68); Syracuse Univ., BA (Jnlsm.), '53; b. N.Y.C., 1931; p. Harris and Frances Strache Hopkins; res: 243 W. 70th St., N.Y., N.Y. 10023.

HOPKINS, JEANNETTE E., Exec. Ed., Urban Affairs Program, Ed., Trade Dept., Harper & Row, 49 E. 33, N.Y., N.Y. 10017; Trade Ed., '64–; Dir. of Pubns., Metropolitan Applied Research Center, Inc., 60 E. 86th St., N.Y., N.Y.; Auth: "Racial Justice and the Press" (Met. Applied Rsch. Ctr., '68), "A Relevant War Against Poverty" (with Kenneth B. Clark; Harper & Row, '69), "14 Journeys to Unitarianism" (Beacon Press, '53); Ed., Harcourt, Brace & World, '56–'64; Sr. Ed., Beacon Press, '51–'56; News Ed., Am. Unitarian Assn., '51–'56; Nwsp. Reptr., New Haven Register, Providence Bul., Okla. City-Times, '45–'51; Vassar Col., AB, '44; Columbia Univ. Sch. of Jnlsm., MS, '45; Okla. City Col. of Law, '50; b. Camden, N.J., 1922; p. Carleton R. and Gladys E. Hull Hopkins; res: 301 E. 47, N.Y., N.Y. 10017.

HOPKINS, JO M., Nat. Fashion Pubcty. Coordr., Sears Roebuck and Co., 360 W. 31st St., N.Y., N.Y. 10001; PR, Pubcty. Dir., Capezio Inc., '65–'67; Fashion Coordr., Lanz Originals, '55–'64; Wtr., Theatrical Costume Hist. booklet; Wtr., TV series for charm sch. program; various organizations; Columbia Univ., '52; N.Y.U. '54; b. Morristown, N.J., 1931; p. Patrick and Kathleen McCabe Hopkins; res: 130 W. 57th St., N.Y., N.Y. 10019.

HOPKINS, MARILYN R., Asst. Dir. of Adv., PR, First Federal Savings and Loan Association of Chicago, 1 S. Dearborn, Chgo., Ill. 60603, '66–; Asst. to Adv. Mgr., House organ Ed., '60–'66; Copywtr., Cone and Confeld Adv. (Cleve., Oh.), '59–'60; Asst. to Adv. Mgr., Viking Air Products, '57–'59; Theta Sigma Phi; IEA of Chgo., Chgo. Fin. Advs.; Marquette Univ., BS (Jnlsm.), '57.

HOPKINS, MARY BRANDEL, Wms. Ed., The Capital

Times, 115 S. Carroll St., Madison, Wis. 53701, '27–; Theta Sigma Phi (Treas., '26–'27), Coranto Sigma Iota, NLAPW ('32–'36); Univ. of Wis., BA, '27; MA, '28; b. Randolph, Wis., 1907; p. Edward W. and Mary J. Jones Brandel; h. James D. Hopkins; c. James Edward, Mrs. Laurence C. Baker; res: 807 Butternut Rd., Madison, Wis. 53704.

HOPKINS, MARY L., Entertainment Ed., Norfolk Ledger Star, 150 W. Brambleton Ave., Norfolk, Va. 23501, '58; Edtl. Staff, '42 '58; Va. Press Assn. aw. for feature writing and excellence of page one layout.

HOPKINS, PATRICIA LAGOW, Wms. Ed., Athens Daily Review, 214 S. Palestine St., Athens, Tex. 75751, '67–; NFPW, Tex. Press Wms. Assn.; Lion's Intl. (Hon. Mbr.); Cooke County Jr. Col., '64; b. Kaufman, Tex., 1944; p. Jack Lagow and Mrs. Helen Taylor; c. Jodie L., Loretta Ann; res: 803 Mission St., Athens, Tex. 75751.

HOPKINS, WILMA KIMBLE (Wilma Sohl), City Desk Asst., Tucson Daily Citizen, 208 N. Stone, Tucson, Ariz. 85703, '67–; Assoc., PR New York, Inc., '62–'67; Asst. Press Rel. Dir., Am. Mgt. Assn., '56–'62; Photogr., Feature Wtr., Columbus (Oh.) Citizen, '43–'56; Oh. Nwsp. Wms. Assn. (former mbr.), Pubcty. Club of N.Y., Theta Sigma Phi, Ariz. Press Wms. Assn. (1st Prize for feature story, '68), NFPW; Ariz. Nwsp. Assn. Aw. for writing, '68; b. Bellefontaine, Oh., 1917; p. Edward and Hazel Beatrice Kimble; h. Bruce Hopkins; res: 350 N. Silverbell Rd., Tucson, Ariz. 85705.

HOPPER, JEAN GOLDMAN, Head. Librn., Bus., Sci. and Industry Dept., Free Library of Philadelphia, Logan Sq., Phila., Pa. 19103, '54–; Librn. III, Bklyn. Public Lib., '49–'53; Ed: ALA/AFL-CIO Lib. Service to Labor Groups Nwsltr.; ALA, Special Lib. Assn., Pa. Lib. Assn., Am. Assn. for the Advancement of Sci., Am. Soc. of Information Sci.; Hunter Col., BA, '33; Columbia Univ., MS (Lib. Sci.), '51; b. N.Y.C. 1912; p. Max and Bertha Skulsky Goldman; h. Terrell W. Hopper (div.); res: 2101 Walnut St., Apt. 1111, Phila., Pa. 19103.

HOPPER, MARJORIE BIVINS, Exec. Dir., Chicago Area School Television, Inc., 5400 N. St. Louis Ave., Chgo., Ill. 60625, '66–; Exec. Secy., '64–'66; Prin., Arcadia Elementary Sch., '62–'64; Tchr., Flossmoor Public Schs., '55–'62; AE, Dir. Mail Div., R. R. Donnelley, '44; Cnslt., NAEB Project For Improvement of TV; Cnslt., Curriculum Advisory Svc.; Delta Kappa Gamma, Ill. Cncl. of Educ. Telecommunications (Secy.-Treas.), NEA, AWRT, Am. Assn. of Sch. Adm.; Who's Who of Am. Wm.; Univ. of Chgo., AB, MA; b. Chgo., Ill., 1924; p. Frederick and Anna Fox Bivins; h. Frank Hopper; c. James Vaseff, Carol Vaseff, Patricia (Mrs. Frank Liebert); res: 6101 N. Sheridan Rd. E., Chgo., Ill. 60626.

HORN, JEANNE DAVIS, Free-lance Wtr., Rschr., Lectr. on Antiques; bks: "Hidden Treasure," "You Can Find a Fortune"; Rsch. Cnslt., CBS; radio, TV appearances; Treasure Hunters of Northern Cal.,

Prospectors Club Intl.; Univ. of Chgo.; b. Canon City, Colo., 1925; p. Cecil and Wanda Willis Davis; h. John Horn; c. John, Daniel W., Mrs. Robert T. Baker; res: 801 Maine St., Vallejo, Cal. 94590.

HORN, LEE, PR Coordr., 3M Company, 135 W. 50th St., N.Y., N.Y. 10020, '69–; Sr. Publicist, '68–'69; Radio-TV Supvsr., PR, BBDO, '59–'68; Radio-TV Publicist, '58–'59; Radio-TV Cnslt., Bozell & Jacobs, '58; AWRT (N.Y.C. Chptr. VP, '68–'69, Secy., '66–'67), NATAS; Univ. of Mich., BA, '44; b. N.Y.C.; p. David and Ray Kornberg Horn; h. Bert Kaye (dec.); res: 340 E. 64th St., N.Y., N.Y. 10021.

HORNADAY, MARY, Free-lance Jnlst., c/o Overseas Press Club of America, 54 W. 40th St., N.Y., N.Y. 10018; formerly Christian Science Monitor Staff Corr., Wash., D.C., London, L.A., Boston, N.Y.C.; Contrbr., Life, Look, Diplomat; WNPC (Pres., '35–'36), OPC (Secy., '66–'67; VP, '68–'69); UN Observer, Wms. Intl. League for Peace and Freedom; Order of Beneficence, King Paul of Greece; Goodwill Ambassador to Switzerland, Soc. for Friendship with Switzerland, '50; Assembly of Captive Nations Cit. for balanced reporting on East Europe; Swarthmore Col., AB (Phi Beta Kappa); b. Wash., D.C., 1906; p. James and Gertrude Hornaday; res: One Gracie Terrace, N.Y., N.Y. 10028.

HORNBAKER, ALICE GOLDER, PR Dir., Children's Home Society, 530 N. First St., San Jose, Cal. 95112, '69–; San Jose Mercury-News, '49–'55; Free-lance Wtr., Photogr.; b. Cincinnati, Oh., 1927; p. Albert and Ida Frisch Golder; h. Joseph B. Hornbaker; c. Christopher, Holly Jo, Joey; res: 6390 Camden Ave., San Jose, Cal. 95120.

HORTON, MARILYN BAGLEY, Ed., Firing Line, Lamar Life Insurance Co., P.O. Box 880 , Jackson, Miss. 39205, '67–; Ed., agcy. pubns., '67; Secy. to Dir. of Adv. and Sls. Prom., '65–'67; Miss. State Col. for Wm., BS, '63; b. Wyandotte, Mich., 1941; p. William O. and Christina Ford Bagley; h. William Horton Jr.; res: 410 Broad St., Apt. A, Jackson, Miss. 39203.

HORVATH, BETTY, Auth. of children's bks: "The Cheerful Quiet" (Franklin Watts, '69), "Will the Real Tommy Wilson Please Stand Up" (Franklin Watts, '69), "Jasper Makes Music" (Franklin Watts, '67), "Hooray for Jasper" (Franklin Watts, '66); Phillips Univ.; b. Jefferson City, Mo., 1927; p. Brans Bolton and Augusta Kapell Ferguson; h. John Horvath; c. Sally Hope, Polly Lynne, John Charles; res: 2340 Waite Ave., Kalamazoo, Mich. 49001.

HORWICH, DR. FRANCES R., Free-lance Educ., Lectr., Wtr., TV Personality, "Miss Frances," Wtr., Prodr., Ding Dong Sch., nat. syndication, Independent TV Corp. (N.Y.C.), '59–; WGN-TV (Chgo., Ill.), '57–'59; NBC Network, '52–'56 (numerous aws.) Dir. Children's Programming, WFLD-TV (Chgo., Ill.), '66–; Educ. Cnslt., Field Enterprises Educ. Corp., '65–'66;

Cnslt., Curtis Publ. Co. (Phila., Pa.), '65; Educ. Dir., '64; Dir. of Children's Activities, '62–'63; Wtr., Prodr., Talent, radio program, NBC Network (N.Y.C.), '56; Supvsr., Children's Programs, NBC, '55–'56; Talent, Wtr., Prodr., TV program, '55; Chmn., Prof., Dept. of Educ., Roosevelt Univ. (Chgo., Ill.), '47–'52; Assoc. Prof., '46–'47; Tchr., other positions, '29–'46; Univ. of Chgo., PhB, '29 (Alumni Medal, '57); Tchrs. Col., Columbia Univ., MA, '33; Northwestern Univ., PhD, '42 (Alumni Aw. of Merit, '54; Frances R. Horwich Scholarships, '55); Bowling Green State Univ. (Oh.), Dr. of Pedagogy (hon.), '54; b. Ottawa, Oh.; p. Samuel and Rosa Gratz Rappaport; h. Harvey L. Horwich.

HOSKINSON, MILDRED PUTNAM, Wms. Ed., Creston News Advertiser, 503 W. Adams St., Creston, Ia. 50801, '57–; Tchr., '33–'42; Ia. Poetry Assn. (Area Chmn., '58–), Ia. Daily Press Assn.; Simpson Col., '30–'32; b. Prescott, Ia., 1913; p. Harry and Daisy Boyer Putnam; h. Robert Hoskinson; c. Mrs. L. S. Reeves, Robert, Andrew; res: 1300 N. Maple St., Creston, Ia. 50801.

HOSMER, BARBARA J., Wms. Ed., California Newspapers, Inc., Independent-Journal, Box 330, San Rafael, Cal. 94901, '61–; Weekend Mag. Ed., Independent-Journal; Feature Wtr., Santa Barbara News-Press; Auth. of travel series on U.S.S.R., India, E. Africa, S. Africa and Rhodesia; Univ. of Cal., AB (Jnlsm.); Columbia Univ., MA (Jnlsm.); b. S.F., Cal.

HOSTETLER, JUANITA, Admin. Asst., WHP, Inc., 216 Locust, Harrisburg, Pa. 17108, '66–; Staff, '40–'66; AWRT (Mid-Eastern Area Dir.-at-Large, '69–), Art Assn. of Harrisburg (Treas., '69–); b. Everson, Pa., 1911; p. Gideon and Mary Long Hostetler; res: 125 Pine, Harrisburg, Pa. 17101.

HOUGHTON, RUTH ADAMS, Dir. of Public Info., Andover Newton Theological School, 210 Herrick Rd., Newton Centre, Mass. 02159, '68–; Dir., PR, Mass. Heart Assn., '66–'67; Dir., PR, Elm Farm Foods Co., '62–'66; PRSA (accredited), Pubcty. Club of Boston, ZONTA; Centenary Col. for Wm., AA, '37; Radcliffe Col., BA, '39; b. East Orange, N.J., 1918; p. Richard and Maude Lyle Mortensen; h. Evans F. Houghton; c. Stanley, Evalyn, Charles, Eleanore, John, Richard; res: 56 Norwood Ave., Newton Centre, Mass. 02159.

HOUP, DEBORAH DALEHITE, Ed., Texas LP Gas Association, P.O. Box 9925, 8408 N. Interregional Hwy., Austin, Tex. 78757, '68–; Theta Sigma Phi, Beta Sigma Phi, Univ. of Tex. Law Wives, Phi Mu Alumnae; Univ. of Fla., BA (Polit. Sci.), '66; BS (Jnlsm.), '67; b. Starkville, Miss., 1945; p. Thomas and Catherine Green Dalehite; h. Kenneth Houp, Jr.; res: 607-B Thrush Ave., Austin, Tex. 78753.

HOUSE, HONOR GREGORY, Pres., Founder, Gregory House Advertising, 1621 Euclid Ave., Cleve., Oh. 44115, '38–; Prodr., weekly radio program, "One World Living"; AFA (VP, '48–'50), Gamma Alpha Chi

(Nat. Pres.), Wms. Adv. Club of Cleve. (Pres.), Theta Sigma Phi (Cleve. Chptr. Pres.); Zeta Tau Alpha (Hon. Ring Aw., '35), ZONTA (Cleve. Chptr. Pres.); Univ. of Chgo., '28; Butler Univ., BS (Jnlsm.), '31; b. Indpls., Ind., 1910; p. Everett and Eva Benson Gregory; h. Bromley House; res: 10423 Lake Ave., Cleve., Oh. 44102.

HOUSE, LAURICE MOSELEY, Copy Ed., Proofreader, Ohio University Press, Athens, Oh. 45701; Free-lance Ed., '43–; Nat. Bk. Assn., Am. Med. Wtrs. Assn.; The Literary Market Place; Case-Western Reserve Univ., '28; b. Painesville, Oh., 1906; p. Everett and Alice Hendricks House; res: 463 W. Main St., Kent, Oh. 44240.

HOUSSELL, JUDITH SAUNDERS, Commty. Rels. Dir., Cincinnati Human Relations Commission, Room 158, City Hall, Cinn., Oh. 45202, '68–; PR Dir., Great Rivers Girl Scout Cncl., '65–'68; PR Dir., Girl Scout Cncl. of the Nation's Capitol, '63–'65; PR Dir., Greater Cinn. Girl Scout Cncl., '59–'61; PR workshops for commty. leaders and students; PRSA, Cinn. Eds. Assn. (Bd. Mbr., '67), Theta Sigma Phi, Marketeers Investment Soc., Nat. Assn. of Intergroup Rels. Offcrs.; Baldwin-Wallace Col., BA (Who's Who Among Students in Am. Cols. and Univs.; Outstanding Sr. Wm.; Jnlsm., Forensic and Psych. Hons.); b. Batesville, Ind., 1936; p. David Rodman and Anne Kohles Saunders; h. (div.); res: 5720 Winton Rd., Cinn., Oh. 45232.

HOUTZ, SARA JANE, Rsch. and Educ. Cnslt., Detroit Orthopaedic Clinic, 5447 Woodward Ave., Detroit, Mich. 48202, '55–; Instr., Asst. Prof. Physical Med. and Rehabilitation, Univ. of Ill., Rsch. and Educ. Hospitals, '51–'55; Inst., Asst. Prof., Med. Col. of Va., '45–'51; Physical Therapist, U.S. Army, '42–'45; High School Tchr., '39–'41; Auth: 49 papers in Med. Jnls., 2 books; Rsch., Teaching, Cnslt.; Wayne State Univ., '67–, Univ. of Wash. (Seattle) Summer Session, '63; Am. Med. Wtrs. Assn. (Mich. Chptr. Secy.-Treas., '58–'60), educ: Neb. State Tchrs. Col., '32–'34; Univ. of Colo., B.S., '39; Med. Col. of Va., MS, '49; b. Sioux City, Ia., 1913; p. Howard and Mabel Bach Houtz; res: 9595 Mettetal, Detroit, Mich. 48227.

HOVEY, KEZIA KEEBLE, Fashion Ed., Vogue, Conde Nast Publications, Inc., 420 Lexington Ave., N.Y., N.Y. 10017, '68–; Fashion Ed., Glamour, '63–'68; h. Chandler Hovey III.

HOWARD, ANN, Prodr., Bdcstr., "Ann Howard Show," WDBJ Radio, P.O. 150, Roanoke, Va. 24002, '66–; Prodr., Personality, "Panorama," WDBJ-TV, '56–'62; Point of Sale Prom. Dir., Parents Magazine, '53–'56; Ed., My Baby, '50–'53; Eastern Ed., Modern Beauty Shop, '45–'50; AWRT, AAUW, Roanoke Fine Arts Ctr., Wms. Auxiliary of Roanoke Symphony; Nat. Safety Cncl. aw., '59; Bklyn. Col., BA, '44; b. N.Y.C., 1921; p. Alf and Nani Nyman Howard; h. Cyril

C. Morgan; c. Elizabeth Ann, Cyril Charles Jr.; res: 3630 Penarth Rd. S.W., Roanoke, Va. 24014.

HOWARD, CHRISTINA (TINA) COLE, Actress, Singer; CBS King family Prods., TV Lead Singer with "4 King Cousins," "King Family Show," '64–'69; TV Female Lead, "My Three Sons," '66–; TV Female Lead, "Hawaiian Eye." '62; Contract Player, Warner Bros. Studios, '62; SAG, AFTRA, AGVA; "Most Promising Actress," Photoplay mag., '67–'68; Nomination "Stars of Tomorrow 1968," female in comedy TV; Brigham Young Univ., '61; Warner Bros. Sch. of Dramatics, '59, '60; b. Hollywood, Cal. 1943; p. Buddy and Yvonne King Cole; h. Volney Howard, III; c. Volney Erskine, IV.

HOWARD, HELEN ADDISON, Free-lance Wtr.; Radio, TV Monitor, Ed., Radio Reports, Inc., (L.A., Cal.), '43–'56; Daily Missoulian (Missoula, Mont.), '23–'29; Auth., three bks. on Western Am.; Contrb. Ed., "Frontier Omnibus" (Mont. State Univ. Press, '62); Contrbr., hist. mag.; Bk. Revr.; Mont. Hist. Soc., Equestrian Trails (Bd. of Dirs.); Univ. of Mont., BA, '27; Univ. of Southern Cal., MA, '33; b. Missoula, Mont., 1904; p. Albert and Helena Cullenan Howard; h. Ben Overland; res: 410 S. Lamer St., Burbank, Cal. 91506.

HOWE, MARION RITA, Assoc. Ed., American Historical Review, 400 A St., S.E., Wash., D.C. 20003, '69–; Asst. Ed., '64–'69, Edtl. Asst., '60–'64; Co-compiler, "Index to Am. Hist. Rev. (1955-1965)" (Am. Hist. Assn., '68); Am. Hist. Assn.; Phi Alpha Theta; Pa. State Univ., BA '58; MA '60; b. Philipsburg, Pa., 1936.

HOWERTON, CANDACE, Actress; Old Globe Theatre aw., '64; SAG, AFTRA, AEA; San Diego State Col., San Fernando Valley State Col.; b. San Diego, Cal.,1946; p. Leroy and Marguerite Griffin Howerton; h. John Bell; res: 4209 Radford Ave., Studio City, Cal. 91604.

HOWES, BARBARA, Auth., four bks. of poetry; Ed., two bks. of stories; Runner-Up, Nat. Bk. Aw., '67; Brandeis Univ. Crtv. Arts Poetry Grant, '58; Guggenheim Fellowship, '55; Bennington Col., AB, '38; b. N.Y.C., 1914; p. Osborne and Mildred Cox Howes; h. William Jay Smith (div.); c. David E., Gregory Jay; res: Brook House, North Pownal, Vt. 05260.

HOWIE, MILDRED CARTER, Acc. Supvsr., Public Relations Pacific Division, Lennen & Newell, Inc., 353 Sacramento St., S.F., Cal. 94111, '66–; Head of Prom., Adv. and Pubcty., KGO/KGO-TV, '57–'58; Pubcty. Wtr., '49–'56; Wtr.-Prod., '56–'57; Radio Dir., S.F. Chptr. of Am. Red Cross, '48–'49; Free-lance PR for Suicide Prevention Inc.; Bi-weekly bdcsts, KQED-FM, educ. radios; AWRT (Golden Gate Chptr. Pres. Elect, '69), S.F. Adv. Club (Wm. of Yr., '68), S.F. Adv. Club (Secy., '69); Univ. of Cal. (Jnlsm.), '43; b. S.F., Cal., 1922; p. John and Blanche Roddick Carter; h. (div.); c.

Linda Ramey, Jan Howie; res: 212 Granada Dr., Corte Madera, Cal. 94925.

HOXIE, JANE STEAGALL, TV/Radio Log Ed., Independent Press-Telegram, 604 Pine Ave., Long Beach, Cal. 90801, '49–; TV Ed., '49–'60; Adv. Dir., Columbia, '46–'50; Asst. Adv. Mgr., Lipman's (Portland, Ore.), '43–'46; Theta Sigma Phi, Orange County Press Club, Cal. Press Wm.; active in numerous civic groups (Outstanding Civic Svc. Aw., '59); Ore. State Univ., BS, '41; N.Y.U. Sch. of Retailing, MS, '42; b. Portland, Ore.; p. Dr. John R. and Gertrude Still Steagall; h. (div.); c. Susan Terry, Sharon Lynne; res: 12821 Valencia Way, Garden Grove, Cal. 92641.

HOY, MARY ANN COLLINS, Bus. Wtr., Dayton Journal Herald, Dayton, Ohio, '69–; Grad. Asst., University of Dayton, '67–'69; Dir., Public Info., Am. Red Cross, '65–'67; Staff Wtr., Chase Manhattan Bank (N.Y.C.), '62–'64; Free-lance Wtr., Publicist; Miami Valley IEA, Theta Sigma Phi; Outstanding Young Wm. of Am.; Duquesne Univ., '58–'60; Syracuse Univ., BS (Jnlsm., Home Econ.), '62; Univ. of Dayton, MBA, '69; b. Clifton Forge, Va., 1940; p. Edward and Helen Woods Collins; h. Robert J. Hoy; res: 1002 Manhattan Ave., Dayton, Oh. 45406.

HRUSKA, MILLI HEFFERNAN, Colmst., Advisor, 915 Highway 35, Middletown, N.J. 07748, '49–; Colmst., Daily Register (Red Bank); Radio Personality, WFHA, WHTC (New Shrewsbury); OPC, Monmouth Players, Monmouth Col., Lib. Assn.; Skidmore Col.; Monmouth Col.; Columbia Univ.; b. N.Y.C., 1917; p. John and Harriet Murray Heffernan; h. Albert J. Hruska; c. Harriet M. Fahey, George A. Middleton, Michael B.; res: 13 Sailer's Way, Rumson, N.J. 07760.

HUBBARD, CAROL RESINGER, Reptr., Entertainment Ed., Columbia Daily Tribune, Seventh and Cherry Sts., Columbia, Mo. 65201, '69–; Assoc. Dir., Pubns., Univ. of Mo. Med. Ctr., '67–'69; Adv. Prod. Mgr., Columbia Daily Tribune, '66–'67; Asst. Ed., University Pubns., Univ. of Mo., '65–'66; Asst. Ed., Leisure World News (Laguna Hills, Cal.), '65; Reptr., Kan. City (Mo.) Star; Theta Sigma Phi, Kappa Tau Alpha; Univ. of Mo., BJ, '64; b. Ironton, Mo., 1942; p. Clifton and Lorinne Harris Resinger; h. Barry F. Hubbard; res: Route 1, Hallsville, Mo. 65255.

HUBBARD, CHARLOTTE MOTON, Deputy Asst. Secy., Bureau of Public Affairs, Department of State, Wash., D.C. 20025, '64–; Offcr. in charge, Community Meetings on Foreign Policy, '63–'64; PR Asst., United Givers Fund, '58–'63; Dir., Commty. Svcs., WTOP-TV, '53–'58; Nat. Rep., CIO-PAC, '52–'53; Field Rep., Tuskegee Inst., '49–'51; Commty. Rel. Advisor, Girl Scouts of the U.S.A., '45–'50; Nat. Field Rep., Fed. Security Agcy., '42–'45; Instr., Assoc. Prof., Hampton (Va.) Inst., '34–'42; AWRT, Am. Wms. Club, ANWC, Cosmopolitan BPW, Tuskegee Inst. Jr. Col., '31 (Alumni aw., '65); Boston Univ., BS (Phys. Ed.), '34 (Alumni aw., '68); b. Hampton, Va., 1912; p. Robert and Jennie Booth Moton; h. Maceo William Hubbard; res: 1830 16th St., N.W., Wash., D.C. 20009.

HUBBELL, PATRICIA ANN, Auth: Non-Fiction and Poetry for Children; Colmst., Bridgeport (Conn.) Sunday Post, '60-'68; Ed. Asst., Westport Town Crier, '51-'54; Ed. Asst., Newtown Bee, '50-'51; Auths. Guild, Dog Wtrs. Assn. of Am.; Univ. of Conn., BA, '50; b. Bridgeport, Conn., 1928; p. Franklin H. and Helen Osborn Hubbell; h. Harold Hornstein; c. Jeffrey, Deborah; res: R.F.D. 1, Norton Rd. Easton, Weston, Conn. 06880.

HUBER, ETHEL STEVENS, Music Supvsr., Columbia Broadcasting System Television Network, 518 W. 57th St., N.Y., N.Y. 10019, '57-; CBS Music Supvsr. for: "Armstrong Circle Theater" ('57-'63), WWI Series ('65), "Trials of O'Brien" ('65-'66), "Love Is A Many Splendored Thing" ('68); Music Supvsr., "Walt Whitman," "Lewis Carroll," "Edgar Allan Poe," "John Donne," Ch. 13, '69; Other Credits: "A View from Space" (ABC, '69), "Fireball Jungle" (independent film, '68), "The Patty Duke Show" (ABCm '63-'65), "Play of the Week" ('60-'61), "I Cover Times Square" (prod. by and starring husband, '52-'53); Emmy aw. nomination, "Signposts on a Merry-Go-Round," (CBS, '68); Chgo. Musical Col.; N.Y.U.; h. Harold Huber (dec.); c. Margaret (Mrs. Marshall Minor); res: 225 E. 57th St., N.Y., N.Y. 10022.

HUBIK, DOLORES HELEN, Dir., Off. of Doctrine and Literature, Wms. Army Corps (Ft. McClellan, Ark.), '68-'69; Instr., '67-'68 Info. Offcr., Defense Lang. Inst., Presidio of Monterey (Cal.), '64-'66; Command Info. Offcr., (Fort McClellan, Ala.), '64; Info. Offcr., Asst. Info. Offcr., Army Air Defense Command (Fort Totten, N.Y.), '62-'64; Feature Wtr., Reptr., Wms. Ed., '51-'61; Theta Sigma Phi; Army Commendation Medal, '64; U.S. WAC, '61-'69; Univ. of Southern Cal., BA (Jnlsm.), '51; Long Beach State Col., '56; Univ. of Wis., '67; San Jose State Col., '69-; b. L.A., Cal., 1929; p. Edward and Helen Gerlich Hubik; res: 2529 W. 157th St., Gardena, Cal.

HUBLEY, FAITH, Co-prodr., Hubley Studios, 815 Park Ave., N.Y., N.Y. 10021, '55-; Artist, Film Ed., Script Cl., numerous studios, '44-; 55; Free-lance Script Cl., "12 Angry Men;" Acad. Aws. for cartoons: "Tijuana Brass Double Feature," "The Hole;" Art Students League; b. N.Y.C., 1924; p. Irving and Sally Gronich Chestman; h. John Hubley; c. Mark, Emily, Ray, Georgia; res: 114 E. 72nd St., N.Y., N.Y. 10021.

HUCK, A. VIRGINIA, Free-lance Wtr., '43-; Auth., "Brand of the Tartan" ('55); Ed., Cent. Edition, Winona Daily News, '55; Rsch. Dir., Minn. Statehood Cent. Commn.,'55-'58; Reptr., Minneapolis Tribune, '46; Theta Sigma Phi (Nat. Rsch. Grant, '50), NLAPW; Univ. of Minn., BA (Jnlsm.), '50 (Phi Beta Kappa); BS (Eng.), '60; b. Ipswich, S.D., 1919; res: 534 Otis Ave., St. Paul, Minn. 55104.

HUDSON, ELINOR JANSON, Theatre Dir., Valley Players Fireside Theatre, Santa Cruz Civic Light Opera Co., Box 91, Felton, Cal. 95018; Wtr., New York Herald Tribune (Berlin); Wtr., Prodr., "Paris Holiday," "Dear Friends and Gentle Hearts" (operettas); Coloratura Singer; BPW; Univ. of San Marco, Conservatory Dresden; b. Dresden, Germany; p. Arne and Blanche Barney Janson; h. Raymond Hudson; res: Valley Dr. 5834, Felton, Cal. 95018.

HUDSON, LOIS PHILLIPS, Asst. Prof. of Eng., Univ. of Wash.; Asst. Prof. of Eng., N.D. State Univ., '67-'70; Auth: "The Bones of Plenty" (Atlantic-Little, Brown, '63); "Reapers of the Dust" ('65); short stories, poems, articles in numerous mags.; various organizations and aws.; Univ. of Puget Sound, BA, '49 (with hons.); Cornell Univ., AM, '51; Honorary Doctorate, N.D. State Univ., '65; b. Jamestown, N.D., 1927; p. Carl W. and Mary Aline Runner Phillips; h. Randolph Hudson; res: 11629 N.E. 70th Pl., Kirkland, Wash. 98033.

HUDSON, PEGGY DILTS, Radio-TV Ed., Scholastic Magazines, 50 W. 44th St., N.Y., N.Y. 10036, '61-; Wtr., '60; Auth., bks., mag. articles; NATAS; Syracuse Univ., BA (Jnlsm., Eng.), '59 (Phi Beta Kappa); b. Hamburg, Ia., 1936; p. Virgil and Eva Rood Dilts; h. James A. Hudson; res: 23 University Dr., Setauket, N.Y. 11733.

HUFF, BARBARA A., Mng. Ed., Junior Literary Guild, Doubleday and Company, 277 Park Ave., N.Y., N.Y. 10017, '54-; Mng. Ed., '69-; poetry publ. in U.S., Can., Sweden; U.C.L.A., BA, '52; b. L.A., Cal., 1929; p. Robert and Irene Lawton Huff; res: 1 Christopher St., N.Y., N.Y. 10014.

HUFF, Sr. J. ELLEN, Dir. of Lib., Spalding College, 853 Library Lane, Louisville, Ky. 40203, '46-; Instr., '45-'46; Tchr., Librn., St. Andrew HS (Roanoke, Va.), '38-'45; Tchr., Librn., Sacred Heart HS (Helena, Ark.), '33-'38; Tchr., Librn., Sacred Heart HS (Memphis, Tenn.), '32-'33; Carnegie Lib., (Okla. City, Okla.), '27-'30; ALA, Catholic Lib. Assn., Southeastern Lib. Assn., Ky. Lib. Assn., AAUP, AAUW, Ky. Hist. Assn., Spalding Col., AB, '38; Col. St. Catherine, BS (Lib. Sci.), '38; b. Harrodsburg, Ky., 1904; p. James and Ellen Spalding Huff; res: 851 S. Fourth St., Louisville, Ky. 40203.

HUGGARD, MARGARET EFFINGER, Pubns. Ed., Homelite Division, Textron, Inc., Port Chester, N.Y. 10573, '56-; Curator of Art, Univ. of Mich., '27-'30; N.Y. Assn. of Indsl. Communicators (Bd. Mbr: '60-'63; '65-'68), ICIE (Reg. Dir., '63-'65), Conn. IEA (Bd. Mbr., '58-'60); Univ. of Mich., AB, '26 (summa cum laude); Radcliffe Col., MA, '27; b. Ann Arbor, Mich., 1905; p. John and Margaret Thain Effinger; h. Cecil W. Huggard; c. Richard, Susan Huggard West; res: 19 Buena Vista Dr., Glenville, Conn. 06830.

HUGH, S. ELIZABETH, Dir., Off. of PR, New

Orleans Chapter, American National Red Cross, 2000 Tulane Ave., N.O., La. 70112, '52–; Prodr., Dir., Wtr., Originator, "The Game" program, WDSU-TV, '50–'52; Talent, "Food for Champions" program, '50–'51; Brown's Velvet Dairy Products, Inc., '50; Tichner's Antiseptic, '49–'50; "On Stage" radio series, WWL, '48–'50; Staff, Dir. of Radio Pubcty., Gtr. N.Y. Cncl., Boy Scouts of Am. (N.Y.), '47–'48; Staff, Dir. of Radio Pubcty., Girl Scout Cncl. of Gtr. N.Y., '47–'48; Staff Wtr., March of Dimes, '47; Staff., Wtr., World Bdcst. System, Inc., '44–'46; Staff Wtr., "Night Clubs for Victory," CBS, '42–'44; AWRT (N.O. Chptr. VP, '61), Press Club of N.O. (Charter Mbr.), ICIE (N.O. Chptr. Secy., Treas., '66); active in civic groups; N.Y.U. Radio Workshop, '40–'41; b. London, Eng., 1915; p. Ralph and Grace Tout Hugh; res: 8125 Hickory St., N.O., La. 70118.

HUGHES, BARBARA JEAN, Adv. Mgr., Columbia University Press, 440 W. 110th St., N.Y., N.Y. 10011, '66–; Sls. Prom. Mgr., MacMillan, '65–'66; Sls. Prom. Coordr., Doubleday, '61–'65; Asst. Adv. Mgr., Interscience Publishers, '59–'61.

HUGHES, GEORGIA HOLLANDER, Supvsr., Employee Pubns., Wyandotte Chemicals Corporation, 1609 Biddle Ave., Wyandotte, Mich. 48192, '69–; PR Staff Asst., '61–'69; Mng. Ed., Wyandotte Tribune, '58–'61; Copywtr., Kaiser-Frazer Sls. Corp., '48–'50; Edtl. Supvsr., Spencer Corset Co. (New Haven, Conn.), '42–'46; IEA of Detroit (Pres., '65–'66; achiev. aws., '67, '65), Wms. Adv. Club of Detroit, BPW; Keystone Jr. Col., '37; b. Scranton, Pa.; p. Charles and Ella Morgenstern Hollander; h. H. Richard Hughes (dec.); c. Nancy Louise; res: 494 North Dr., Wyandotte, Mich. 48192.

HUGHES, JOAN KIRKBY, Instr., IBM, 3424 Wilshire Blvd., L.A., Cal. 90005, '65–; Programmer, Process Control Computer Div., Thompson Ramo Woolridge Co., '62–'65; Tchr., Eng., Hist., '59–'62; Ed., Woodland Hills Reporter, '54–'59; Auth: "Programming the IBM 1130" (John Wiley & Sons, '69); Theta Sigma Phi; U.C.L.A., BA (Eng.), '59; p. Raymond and Eleanor Horsey Kirkby; h. William Hughes; res: 13906 Wyandotte St., Van Nuys, Cal. 91405.

HUGHES, MARY BROWNE, Librn., University of Michigan, 60 Farnsworth St., Detroit, Mich. 48202, '51–; Detroit Inst. of Arts, '50–'51; Ross Roy Advertising, '48–'49; Fisher Body, Experimental & Dev. Div., '47–'48; Chrysler Corp. Engineering Lib., '43–'47; Engineering Soc. of Detroit, Spec. Libs. Assn., ALA, Altrusa Intl. Platform Assn., various other orgs. and volunteer wk.; Top 10 Working Wm. in Met. Detroit, '68; Wayne State Univ., BA, '40; Simmons Col., BS (Lib. Sci.), '43; b. Detroit, Mich., 1918; p. Michael and Victoria Soloski Browne; h. George A. Hughes; c. Mary Christina; res: 5751 Yorkshire St., Detroit, Mich. 48224.

HUGHES, MARY ELIZABETH, Intl. PR Cnslr., Rad-

cliffe Chautauqua Circuits; PR Cnslr., U.S. Navy and Marine Band Concert Tours; Organizer, Mothers' Comm., U.N., '50–'51; Dir., Am. Mother's Comm., '37–'51; Organizer, Dir., numerous nat. orgs; Auth. of numerous handbks. and manuals for civic, educ. and religious insts.; Intl. Platform Assn., Nat. Planning Assn., Nat. Rsch. Inst., Am. Inst. of Mgt.; Nat. Dir., Wms. Div., Nat. Recovery Adm. (Appointed by Pres. Roosevelt); Ky. Univ.; b. Lexington, Ky.; p. Clifton M. and Effie Gilbert Hughes; c. (adopted): June (Mrs. William Keller Cooper), Lt. Col. Charles M.; res: 405 E. 63rd St., N.Y., N.Y. 10021.

HUGHES, PAULA DeMENNA, Stockbroker, Shields & Co., 44 Wall St., N.Y., N.Y. 10004, '62–; Exec. Sls., Brown and Bigelow, '54–'62; Lectr., schs., civic orgs.; AWNY (Dir., '65–'67), FAA (N.Y. Chptr. Secy., '61), Assn. of Customers Brokers; The Greenwich House (Dir.), Park East Corp. (Dir.); N.Y. Inst. of Fin.; opera training with Ruth Shaffner; h. William Hughes; c. Catherine Louise; res: 406 Grace Church St., Rye, N.Y. 10580; and 4 E. 88 St., N.Y., N.Y. 10028.

HUGHES, SANDRA M., Asst. AE, Rominger Advertising Agency, Inc., 3627 Howell St., Dallas, Tex. 75204; Prod. Mgr., Rogers & Smith Adv.; Adv. Mgr., W. A. Green Co.; Dallas-Ft. Worth Art Dirs. Club (Secy., '68), Dallas Adv. League (Bd. of Dirs., '69–); Southern Methodist Univ.; b. Deport, Tex.; p. William and Alma Hughes; res: 4141 Newton, Apt. 101, Dallas, Tex. 75219.

HULBERT, JEWEL GENTRY, Social Ed., Memphis World News, 210 Auburn Ave., Atlanta, Ga., '44–; Hist. Instr., Memphis Schs., '42–; Memphis Educ. Assn., Tenn. Educ. Assn., NEA, Link, Inc. (Secy.); Lemoyne Col., AB (Sociol.), '41; b. Trinidad, Colo., 1913; p. James and Gertrude Johnson Gentry; h. James Hulbert; res: 1032 S. Lauderdale St., Memphis, Tenn. 38126.

HULIN, BERNICE SCHMIDT, Educ. Dir., Benson Optical Company, 1812 Park Ave. S., Mpls., Minn. 55440, '61–; PR Dir., Pick Nicollet Hotel, '58–'60; TV Ed., Ia. State Univ., '53–'57; Bdcstr., Wtr., "What's Cookin'," KSTP-TV, '48–'52; AWRT (Chptr. Pres., '69–'70), Wms. Adv. Club of Mpls. (VP, '60–'61), BPW, Mpls. Wms. C. of C., Altrusa Press Club, Minn. Press Club; h. Norman Hulin; res: 2701 Park Ave. S., Mpls., Minn. 55407.

HULL, DOROTHY HOLLAR, Ed., The News-Chronicle Company, Box 100, Shippensburg, Pa. 17257, '61–; Tchr., Lurgan Twp., '57–'61; City Ed., News-Chronicle, '56–'57; Reptr., '48–'56; Tchr., Lurgan Twp., '28–'29; Tchr., Linden Hall (Lititz), '27–'28; Pa. Wms. Press Assn. (aws., '64–'65), BPW (Shippensburg Club Pres., '67–'69), AAUW, Pa. Rural Ltr. Carriers Auxiliary (State Pres., '43–'45); Keystone Press aws. '66–'68, '63; Wilson Col., AB, '27 (summa cum laude); b. Lurgan Twp., Pa., 1906; p. Irvin and Mary Stouffer Hollar; h. Donald F. Hull; c. Donald F., Jr., Lois (Mrs. Keller Thorne),

Irvin S.; res: 215 S. Queen St., Shippensburg, Pa. 17257.

HULL, ELEANOR HORNER, Free-lance Wtr.; Assoc. Ed., Fashion Digest, '56–'67; Instr., Trophagen Sch. of Fashion, '56–'67; Pres., Shoulderite, '46–'50; AE, Gussow-Kahn, Adv., '45–'46; Gov. Ed., U.S. Army, '44–'45; Wtr., Sterling Adv., '42–'44; AWNY, Wms. Press Club of N.Y., Intl. Platform Assn.; Who's Who of Am. Wm., Dic. of Intl. Biog.; Southern Methodist Univ., Columbia Univ.; b. Dallas, Tex.; p. Lee and Frances Connor Horner; h. Leon G. Hull (div.); c. Carol (Mrs. J. R. Clark); res: 3131 N. Seventh Ave., Phoenix, Ariz. 85013.

HULL, ELEANOR MEANS, Auth: Variety of fiction and non-fiction; Caseworker, Westchester County Dept. of Soc. Svcs., '65–'68; N.Y.C. Dept. of Social Svcs., '64; Univ. of Denver, BFA, '34, Univ. of Redlands, BA, '32; b. Denver, Colo. 1913; p. Carleton and Florence Crannell Means; h. Angus Hull; c. Angus Crannell, Stephen Carleton, Peter Henrich, Jeremy Robert, Mary Margaret; res: 41 Healy Ave., Hartsdale, N.Y. 10530.

HULL, HELEN R., Prof. Emeritus, Columbia University, N.Y., N.Y.; Prof., Assoc. Prof., Asst. Prof.; Instr.; Instr., Wellesley Col.; Auth.; mystery stories; Auths. League (Past Pres.), Who's Who; Univ. of Mich., Univ. of Chgo., b. Albion, Mich.; p. Warren and Louise McGill Hull; res: 872 West End Ave., N.Y., N.Y. 10025.

HUMPHREY, BARBARA, Dir., Writing Dept., Cooper & Golin, Inc., 360 N. Michigan Ave., Chgo., Ill. 60601, '68–; Dir., Edtl. Svcs., The Fin. Rel. Bd., '67–'68; VP, Dir., Writing Dept., The PR Bd., '52–'67; Ed., PRB Nwsltr., '63–'67; PR Dir., Ill. Commerce Commn., '50–'52; Reptr., Chgo. Sun, '44–'48; Pubcty. Club of Chgo.; Univ. of Kan., BA, '38; U.C.L.A.; b. Junction City, Kan., 1917; p. Arthur and Anne Malott Humphrey; res: 61 E. Cedar St., Chgo., Ill. 60611.

HUMPHREY, SYLVIA WINDLE, Food Ed. and Corr., Bell-McClure Syndicate, 1501 Broadway, N.Y., N.Y. 10036, '60–; Contrbr., N. Am. Nwsp. Alliance, '47–'55; Reg. Ed., PWB (London), '44–'45; Ed., OWI (N.Y.C.), '43–'44; Trade Bks., Oxford Univ. Press, '36–'37; bks., articles; Lectr.; Project Cnslt., Hueblein, Inc.; Owner and Pres., Stenlia Specialities, Inc.; OPC; Cit. for Crtv. Achiev., New Haven Festival of Arts, '66; Swarthmore Col., BA; b. W. Chester, Pa.; p. Ernest and Sylvia Moore Windle; h. Robert Gwynne Humphrey (dec.); c. Anne Chalfant, Sylvia Kay; res: "Stenlia," Amity Rd., Bethany, Conn. 06525.

HUNT, AUDREY GEITZ, Bdcstr., WIS Radio, 1111 Bull St., Columbia, S.C., 29201, '58–; Comml. Copywtr., '56–; Special Assigts., WIS-TV, '54–; various radio stations, '46–'52; Free-lance Wtr., Talent; AWRT (Palmetto Chptr. Pres., '66–'68; Southern Area VP, '69–'70); b. San Jose, Cal.; p. Homer N. and Helen Rhenquist Geitz; h. Samuel Arthur Hunt, Jr.; c. David,

Andrew, Steven; res: 6821 Crosfield Rd., Columbia, S.C. 29206.

HUNT, BARBARA, PR Cnslr., Owner, Barbara Hunt Associates, 606 Executive Bldg., 35 E. Seventh St., Cinn., Oh. 45202, '62–; Asst. Dir., Campus Union, Univ. of Cinn., '57–'62; Asst. to PR Dir., '56–'57; PR Cnslt., '52–'56; Auth., "A History of the Alumanae of the Jewish Hospital of Cincinnati School of Nursing" ('61); PRSA, Theta Sigma Phi; Nat. Assn. of Col. Uns. aw., '61–'62; h. J. R. Schwing; res: Johnswood Farm, RR #2, Loveland, Oh. 45140.

HUNT, BILLIE ELEANORA HARRISON, Commty. Rels. Cnslt., Family Service Association of San Diego, 7645 Family Circle, San Diego, Cal. 92111, '62–; AE, Eves Adv. Agcy., '53–'61; Cont. Ed., KFSB (Joplin, Mo.), '46–'50; Fashion Coordr., Newmans, '46; Program Dir., WMBH, '41–'46; Family Svc. Assn. of Am., Theta Sigma Phi, Southern Cal. Press Wm.; b. Joplin, Mo., 1923; p. Joseph and Ruby Haley Harrison; h. Ezra O. Hunt, Jr.; c. Robert Bret, Nancy Brienn; res: 1756 Shady Crest Pl., El Cajon, Cal. 92020.

HUNT, ELIZABETH MULLEN, Publr., Prodr. of children's operettas, radio progs., Houston Independent School District, 4901 Simsbrook, Houston, Tex. 77045, '60–; Sch. Prin., '60–; Tchr., '55–'60; Nat. Platform Assn., Freedom Fndn. aw., '64; Oxidental Col., BA (Speech); Univ. of Southern Cal., MA (Speech); b. Long Beach, Cal., 1912; p. William and Anna Hepp Mullen; h. Andrew William Hunt; c. Lacy, Andrew, William; res: 5154 Jackwood St., Houston, Tex. 77035.

HUNT, ELSIE HEALZER, Artist, 523 Sixth St., Filer, Idaho 83328; VP, Buhl Art Guild, '62–; Auth., "The Ship of Peace," ('57); several mag. articles; Idaho Art Assn. (Exec. Cncl. Mbr.), Idaho Wtrs. League (Pres., '55); Who's Who of Am. Wm.; Dic. of Intl. Biog.; Who's Who in the West; Univ. of Idaho; b. Ness City, Kan., 1909; p. John and Katherine Kurbs Healzer; h. Vaughn Hunt; c. Thomas Vaughn; res: Box 55, 523 Sixth St., Filer, Idaho. 83328.

HUNT, GLENDA MARGARET, Tchr., Allan Junior High School, 4900 Gonzales, Austin, Tex. 78702; Auth., Ed., Mathematics textbks. (S.W. Educ. Dev. Lab., '68); Theta Sigma Phi (VP, '68–'69); Univ. of Tex., BJ, '64; M.Ed., '69; b. San Antonio, Tex., 1942; p. John and Mabelle Harn Hunt; res: 705 E. 43rd St., Austin, Tex. 78751.

HUNT, MARGARET MAYBERRY, Free-lance Wtr.-Illus.; Publicist, Sacramento-Sierra Heart Assn., '61–'63; Asst. Mng. Ed., Kan. Govt. Jnl. (Topeka, Kan.), '59–'60; Arts and Crafts Dir., Shawnee County Day Sch., '57–'59; Asst. Dir., Art Dept., Winfield State Training Ctr. (Winfield, Kan.); Special Features Wtr., Topeka State Jnl. nwsp., '57–'60; Colmst., Wellington (Kan.) Daily News, '45–'49; Kan. State Tchrs. Col. of Emporia, '27–'29; State Univ. of Ia., '32–'33; special study in art with Birger Sandzen, S. J. Covacevich;

wtrs. confs: Kan., '58, '59; Cal., '65, '67; b. Okla. City Okla.; p. James W. and Louise S. Adams Mayberry; h. Harold Seymore Hunt; c. Harold Seymore, Jr., Mignon, Janet (Mrs. Bill Hiebert); res. and studio: 2901 27th St., Sacramento, Cal. 95818.

HUNT, MARY ALICE, Asst. Prof., Florida State University, School of Library Science, Tallahassee, Fla. 32304, '66–; Instr. '58–'59; Asst. Prof., Art Educ. and Constructive Design, Asst. Librn., Univ. Sch., '62–'66; Instr., Audio-Visual Educ., '59–'62; Librn., Materials Ctr., '55–'58; Photogr.-engraver, Tallahassee Democrat, '51–'52; numerous articles in pfsnl. jnls.; Cnslt., educ. media, N. Fla. Jr. Col. prog., "Strenthening Existing Institutions," spring '68, '69; Cnslt., non-print reviewing prog. Booklist and Subscription Books Bulletin, '69–; Fla. Lib. Assn. (Ed., Florida Libraries, '61–'67), Fla. A-V Assn., Fla. ASL, Southeastern Lib. Assn.; Kappa Delta Pi, Beta Phi Mu; Fla. State Univ., AB (Jnlsm.), '50; MA (Lib. Sci.), '53; b. Lima, Oh., 1928; p. Blair and Grace Henry Hunt; res: 1603 Kolopakin Nene, Tallahassee, Fla. 32301.

HUNT, MARY CECILIA, Librn., Creighton University, 25th and California Sts., Omaha, Neb. 68131, '28–; Tchr., '27–'28; Catholic Lib. Assn. (Midwest Sec. Secy., '42–'45); Col. of St. Catherine, AB, '26; b. Arlington, Minn., 1904; p. Bartley and Ellen Trimbo Hunt; res: 507 N. 28th Ave., Omaha, Neb. 68131.

HUNT, SYLVIA INEZ WHITAKER, Auth: (poetry) "Windows Through the Wall," "High Country" ('62); Co-auth: "Lightning in His Hand, The Life Story of Nikola Tesla" ('64; NLAPW Aw., '66), "Horsefeathers and Applesauce" ('59), "To Colorado's Restless Ghosts" ('60); numerous nwsp. features; Tchr., Adult Educ. in commtns., speech techniques, crtv. writing; Colo. Springs Poetry Fellowship, Poetry Soc. of Colo., Quill Club, Colo. Auths. League, NLAPW; Jnl. of Outdoor Life Nat. Aw. for mystery story contest; Colo. State Col.; Colo. Univ.; b. Willow Hill., Ill., 1899; p. Andrew B. and Minnie Steers Whitaker; h. Nelson V. Hunt; c. Dorothy Frances (Mrs. Kenneth Kiester); res: 707 Prospect Pl., Manitou Springs, Colo. 80902.

HUNTER, BEATRICE TRUM, Auth., three bks. on natural foods, gardening; Tchr., '40–'55; Lectr., ecology, conservation, pollution; Fedn. of Homemakers (Hon. Bd. Mbr.), Am. Acad. of Applied Nutrition (Hon. VP, '62–'63), Natural Food Assoc. (N.H. Chptr. Bd. of Dirs.), Soil Assn.; Friends of Nature aw., '62; Bklyn. Col., BA, '40; Columbia Univ., MA, '42; b. N.Y.C., 1918; p. Gabriel and Martha Engle Trum; h. John Frank Hunter; res: R.F.D. One, Hillsboro, N.H. 03244.

HUNTER, D. JEANNE, Free-lance Wtr.; Charleston Gazette, '50; Theta Sigma Phi, Commty. Health Assn.; Oh. Univ., '52–'55; Morris Harvey Col.; b. Gasaway, W. Va., 1934; p. Russell and Margaret Oldham Staats; h. James M. Hunter; c. Russell, Margaret Helen, Jim Luke; res: 127 Fairview Dr., Ripley, W. Va. 25271.

HUNTER, KRISTIN, Free-lance Wtr., '66–; PR Offcr., City of Phila., '65–'66, '63–'64; Copywtr., Wermen & Schorr, '62–'63; Copywtr., Lavenson Bur. of Adv., '52–'59; Auth: "God Bless the Child" (Athenaeum aw., '64), "The Soul Brothers and Sister Lou" (Scribners, '68, Cncl. on Interracial Bks. for Children aw.); Auths. Guild of Am.; Univ. of Pa., BS, '51; b. Phila., Pa.; p. George and Mabel Manigault Eggleston; h. John Lattany.

HUNTER, LORA NESBITT, Librn., St. Petersburg Junior College, Clearwater Campus, 2465 Drew St., Clearwater, Fla. 33515, '65–; Boca Ceiga HS, '64–'65; Librn., Blanton & Bear Creek Elementary Schs., (St. Petersburg, Fla.), '63–'64; Lib. Cnslt., Fla. State Dept. of Educ., Talahassee, '62–'63; Librn., Corbin Elementary Sch. (Ormond Beach, Fla.), '61–'62; Librn., Mainland HS, '55–'61; Bus. Tchr., Asst. Librn., Mainland Jr.-Sr. HS, '49–'55; Bus. Tchr., Altha (Fla.) HS, '47–'48; Asst. Librn., Ouachita Col., '46–'47; Instr. Gen. Ext., '60–'62; Visiting Instr., Univ. of Fla., '61; Exec. Dir., Nat. Lib. Week, Fla., '67; Fla. Assn. Sch. Librns. (Pres., '59–'60; VP, '59–'60); Volusia County Classroom Tchrs. Assn. (Pres., '60–'61), Fla. Educ. Assn., Delta Kappa Gamma Soc. (Alphi Phi Chptr. Secy., '60–'68; VP, '68–), D.A.V.I., Fla. Assn. Jr. Cols., Beta Phi Mu; Ouachita Col., BA, '46; Fla. State Univ., MA, '52 (Lib. Sci.); b. Little Rock, Ark., 1926; p. Clifton and Opal Welch Nesbitt; h. Robert Hunter; c. Stephen Ray, Susan Kay (dec.), Robert Thomas; res: 4500 9th Ave. N., St. Petersburg, Fla. 33713.

HUNTER, MARJORIE ROSE, Congressional Corr., The New York Times, 1920 L St., N.W., Wash., D.C., 20036, '64–; Wash. Bur., '61–; Polit. Reptr., Winston-Salem (N.C.) Jnl., '50–'61; Raleigh (N.C.) News and Observer, '42–'48; WNPC (Pres., '69–'70, Secy., '68–'69); N.C. Press Assn. aws., '50–'61; Elon Col., BA, '42; b. Bethany, W. Va., 1922; p. Joshua and Minnie Gilliland Hunter; res: 1711 Massachusetts Ave., N.W., Wash., D.C. 20036.

HUNTINGTON, DOROTHY PHILLIPS, Tchr., Short Story Writing, YWCA, 610 Lexington Ave., N.Y., N.Y., '59–; Auth., short stories (Dorothy Sanburn Phillips); Pen and Brush Club (N.Y.C. Bd. Mbr., Pres., '58–'62, '51–'56); Vassar Col., BA, '14 (cum laude; Phi Beta Kappa); Radcliffe Col., '14–'16; b. N.Y.C., 1893; p. John and Jennie Peterson Phillips; h. Richard Huntington; c. Samuel P.; res: 1470 Parkchester Rd., Bronx, N.Y. 10462.

HUNTINGTON, LOUISE BURGENER, Mgr., Co-owner, Lovell Chronicle, 234 E. Main St., Lovell, Wyo. 82431, '55–; Wyo. Press Assn., Lovell BPW, Private Pilot; J. E. Hanway commty. svc. plaque, '65; several aws. for color work in offset field; Sisters of Charity Sch. of Nursing, '51; b. Powell, Wyo., 1930; p. Albert and Lottie Moore Burgener; h. Burton Huntington; res: Rural Rte., Lovell, Wyo. 82431.

HUNZIKER, PAT SISSONS, Owner, Pat. L. Hunziker,

Public Relations, 221 Loma Alta Ave., Los Gatos, Cal. 95030, '66–; Pubns. Ed., PR Dir., Northern Div., Am. Savings & Loan, '59–'65; Assoc. Ed., trade pubn., Howard Publ. Co., '55–'57; Adv. Copywtr., Benet Hanau & Assocs., '52–'53; PRSA (Peninsula Chptr. Dir., '66–'67), San Jose Adv. Club (Dir., '66–'67), PR Roundtable, Pfsnl. Photogrs. of Northern Cal., Northern Cal. Indsl. Eds., Intl. Platform Assn., Santa Clara Valley Sci. Fair Assn. (Dir.), Intl. Student Ctr. (past Pres.), World Affairs Cncl. of San Jose, Pacific Neighbors; Art Ctr. Sch. (L.A., Cal.), '45–'46; Northwestern Univ., '56; b. Phoenix, Ariz., 1925; p. Robert and Mina Mantel Sissons; h. Clarence Hunziker.

HURD, EDITH THACHER, Auth., 50 children's bks.; Radcliffe Col., AB; Bank St. Col. of Educ.; h. Clement Hurd; c. J. Thatcher Hurd; res: 80 Mountain Lane, Mill Valley, Cal. 94941.

HURLEY, MARIE VIRGINIA, Dir., The Ferguson Library, 96 Broad St., Stamford, Conn. 06901, '65–; Asst. Librn., '54–'65; Librn., Cuyahoga County (Cleve., Oh.), '51–'54; Librn., S. Euclid-Lyndhurst (Oh.), '48–'50; Asst. Librn., U.S. Info. (Sydney, Australia), '46–'47; Librn., Riverdale (N.Y.C.), '41–'46; First Asst. Br. Librn., '40–'41; Sch., Ref. Librn., '33–'40; Wms. Nat. Bk. Assn. (Secy.), Columbia Univ. Lib. Sch. Alumni Assn. (Bd. Mbr.), '68), ALA, New England Lib. Assn., Conn. Lib. Assn. (Pres.), '68–'69); Elmira Col., BS, '32; Columbia Univ., LS, '33; b. Elmira, N.Y.; p. Daniel and Olga Hauenstein Hurley; res: 154 Cold Spring Rd., Stamford, Conn. 06905.

HUSTED-ANDERSEN, ADDA, Edtl. Bd., Metal, Craft Horizon, 887 First Ave., N.Y., N.Y. 10022; Instr., Craft Students League; res: 349 E. 49th St., N.Y., N.Y. 10017.

HUTCHENS, ELEANOR NEWMAN, Prof. of Eng., University of Alabama, Box 1247, Hunstville, Ala. 35807, '67–; Assoc. Prof. of Eng., Agnes Scott Col., '61–'67; Publicist, '47–'54; '40–'43; Ed., Agnes Scott Alumnae Quarterly, '47–'54; Ed., Mortar Board Quarterly, '45–'50; Asst. Ed., Huntsville Times, '44–'47; News Ed., DeKalb New Era (Decatur, Ga.), '42–'43; Auth: "Writing to be Read," ('69), "Irony in Tom Jones," ('65); Modern Lang. Assn. of Amer.; Agnes Scott Col., BA, '40 (Phi Beta Kappa, Mortar Bd.); Univ. of Pa., MA, '44; PhD, '57; b. Huntsville, Ala., 1919; p. Morton and Susie Newman Hutchens; res: 300 Williams Ave., S.E., Huntsville, Ala. 35801.

HUTCHESON, DOROTHY FRANCIS, Inst., Consumer Dir., Rice Council for Market Development, 3917 Richmond Ave., Houston, Tex. 77027, '55–; Mary Carter, TV Talent Program, KTRK, KGUL-TV, '52–'55; Reg. Dir., Dulane Co. (River Groves, Ill.), '45–'47; Mgr., North Am. Aviation Co., '43; AWRT, Am. Sch. Food Svc., Univ. of Tex. Mktng. Assn. (hon. mbr.); Univ. of Houston, '50–'52; b. Mart, Tex. 1916; p. Oscar and Eva Ingram Francis; c. Wayland Thomas; res: 5703 Wyandott Blvd., Houston, Tex. 77040.

HUTCHINS, ELIZABETH MARIE, Dir. of Lib. Svcs., Young & Rubicam, Inc., 285 Madison Ave., N.Y., N.Y. 10017, '67–; Asst. Librn., '56–'64; Lib. Dir., Fremont Public Lib., '64–'67; SLA, Newaygo County Lib. Assn. (Chmn., '64–'66), Mich. Lib. Assn. (Chmn., Dist. IV, '66–'67), Beta Phi Mu, Phi Kappa Phi; Drake's Bus. Col., Bus. Cert., '36; Duke Univ., BA, '41 (magna cum laude, Phi Beta Kappa); Univ. of Mich., MA (Lib. Sci.), '56; b. E. Brunswick, N.J., 1917; res: 122 Summerhill Rd., E. Brunswick, N.J. 08816.

HUTMACHER, BARBARA PRICE, Ed., Living Pages, News-Chronicle, P.O. Box 1346, Thousand Oaks, Cal. 91360, '67–; Southwestern Corr., Richmond (Va.) News-Leader, '64–; Ventura County Press Club; Theta Sigma Tau Southern Cal. Chptr. jnlsm. aw., '68; Cal. State Gold Medal, '67; Nat. Headliners Club aw., '68; Cal. Publrs. Assn. aw., '67; Rockford Col. for Wm., '44–'45; Western Mich. Col., '45–'46; b. Toledo, Oh., 1926; p. Norman and Betty Wilkinson Price; h. Donald A. Hutmacher; c. Clay, Dave, Cary, Darcy, Beth; res: 450 Tuolumne St., Apt. 2, Thousand Oaks, Cal. 91360.

HUTTON, EDNA RAIT, Nat. Ed., Sigma Alpha Iota, '44–; (Ring of Excellence, '44; Cert. of Merit, '62; Nat. Leadership Aw., '65); Epsilon Province Pres., '41–'44; Field Worker, Ia. Cncl. Christian Educ., '23–'40; Head, Piano, Theory Depts., Hastings (Neb.) Col., '18–'20; Sterling (Kan.) Col., '09–'18; Dir., SAI Sigma Alpha Iota, Memorial Music Lib., Univ. of Mich., '68–; Auth: "Carols of the Ages" (Bethany Press, '43), "Sigma Alpha Iota—1903–1963" (George Banta, '64); Des Moines BPW (Wm. of Achiev., '63), Marquis Biographical Lib. Soc. (Advisory Mbr.); Nat. Fedn. of Music Clubs Individual Three-Star Aw., '67; Monmouth Col., '09; Am. Conservatory of Music; Columbia Univ., grad. study; b. Morrison, Ia.; p. Alexander and Mary Wyatt Rait; h. Walter Hutton (dec.); res: 2305 Grand Ave., Des Moines, Ia. 50312.

HUTTON, JANE BIRD, Ed., Harrodsburg Herald, 101-107 W. Broadway, Harrodsburg, Ky. 40330, '51–; Asst. Ed., Adv. Mgr., '47–'51; Adv. Mgr., '37–'47; Reptr., '35; NFPW, Nat. Nwsp. Assn., Ky. Press Assn.; Trustee: Ky. Wesleyan Col., Ft. Harrod Drama Prods., Shakertown at Pleasant Hill; Ky. Wesleyan Col.; b. Harrodsburg, Ky., 1914; p. Daniel and Grace Linney Hutton; res: 111 W. Broadway, Harrodsburg, Ky. 40330.

HUTTON, ROSALIA, Prog. Dir., X-TRA/KOST, Nat. Music Dir., The McLendon Corporation, 5670 Wilshire Blvd., Suite 940, L.A., Cal. 90036, '68–; Gen. Mgr., X-TRA/KOST, '67–'68; Off. Mgr., '61–'66; Asst. to Pres., McLendon Corp., '66–'67; Singles Mdsng. Mgr., Capitol Records, '59–'61; AWRT, Radio Adv. Slsmen. of L.A.; b. McGehee, Ark., 1936; p. Theodore and Ruth Neeley Dexter; h. Frederick E. Hutton (div.); c. John Frederick; res: 7654 Fountain Ave., Apt. 10, L.A., Cal. 90046.

HUUS, HELEN, Prof. of Educ., University of Missouri, 5100 Rockhill Rd., Kansas City, Mo. 64110, '67–; Univ. of Pa., '47–'67; Wayne State Univ., '45–'47; Waves Offcr., U.S. Navy, '44–'45; Mediapolis (Ia.) Public Schs., '36–'38; Worth County (Ia.) Public Schs., '33–'35; Auth: numerous bks., articles on educ.; Intl. Reading Assn. (Pres., '69–'70); Nat. Cncl. on Rsch. in Eng. (Pres., '67–'68), AAUW, AAUP, Nat. Cncl. of Tchrs. of Eng., Comparative Educ. Soc., Am. Folklore, ALA; Univ. of Northern Ia., BA, '40 (magna cum laude); Univ. of Chgo., MA, Ph.D, '44; Univ. of Oslo (Fulbright Rsch. Scholarship); b. Northwood, Ia., 1913; p. Jacob and Mary Tiffany Huus; res: 5000 Oak St., Kansas City, Mo. 64112.

HYDE, HELEN PATTERSON, Free-lance Wtr.; Former Prof. of Jnlsm., Univ. of Wis.; Theta Sigma Phi (Past Nat. Treas.), Ariz. Press Club for Wm.; Univ. of Kan., '17; Univ. of Wis., '26; b. Osage City, Kan.; h. Grant M. Hyde; res: 107 El Encanto Apts., 2820 E. Sixth St., Tucson, Ariz. 85716.

HYDE, NINA SOLOMON, Fashion and Beauty Ed., The Washington Daily News, 1013 13th St., N.W., Wash., D.C. 20005, '62–; Fashion Ed., Tobe & Assoc., '60–'61; Reptr., Wms. Wear Daily, '58–'59; Asst. Dir. of Rsch., Maidenform Bras, '57–'58; Rsch. Project Dir., McCann-Erickson, '54–'57; Lectr., Smithsonian Inst., Marymount Col.; Auth., articles on col. life and fashion; Fashion Group, WNPC, ANWC; Nat. Footwear Inst. first prize, '68; Smith Col., BA, '54; b. N.Y.C., 1932; p. Dr. Harry and Ruth Wulfsohn Solomon; h. Lloyd Hyde; c. Jennifer, Andrea; res: 3035 Oliver St., N.W., Wash., D.C. 20015.

HYER, ANNA LAURA, Dir., Division of Educational Technology, NEA, 1201 16th St., Wash., D.C. 20036, '57–; Assoc. Exec. Secy., DAVI, '51–'57; Admr., Overseas Film Project (Iran, Turkey), '51; film prod., Syracuse Univ., '48–'51; Pers. Dir., Ind. Univ., '42–'45; Guidance Cnslr., Muncie (Ind.) Schs., '39–'41; Purdue Univ., BS, '32; Northwestern Univ., MA, '41; Ind. Univ. EdD., '52; b. Wheeling, Ind., 1911; p. Ralph and Ethel Shaffer Hyer; res: 7613 Wiley Dr., Lorton, Va. 22079.

HYLAND, DIANE, Actress; "Look Back in Anger" (Broadway, '58); "Sweet Bird of Youth" (Broadway, '59–'60); NTA "Play of the Week" ("No Exit," "Climate of Eden"); TV guest star roles: "Dr. Kildare," "Naked City," "Peyton Place," "The F.B.I.," "The Fugitive," "Name of the Game," others; Films: "Jigsaw," "One Man's Way"; AEA, AFTRA, SAG, NATAS (best actress nomination, '62); Actors Studio; b. Cleve. Hgts., Oh.; p. John and Mary Gorman Gentner. h. Joseph Goodson; res: L.A., Cal.

HYMAN, BILLIE, Pres., AE, Continental Associates, Div. of Continental Advertising Agency, Inc., 1955 Merrick Rd., Merrick, N.Y. 11566, '67–; Musicians Local 802 Bkg. Agent; L.I. PR Assn., L.I. Adv. Club; Assn. of Indsl. Advs.; Hunter Col., BA, '46.

HYMAN, FRIEDA CLARK, Auth: "Jubal and the Prophet," ('58), "Builders of Jerusalem," ('60); numerous stories, poetry on Judaism; Dir., Midrasha HS (Hartford, Conn.), '68; Jewish Educs. Cncl. of Gtr. Hartford; Tchr. of Yr. aw., '58; William F. Krevit lit. aw., '61; Hunter Col., BA, '32; Jewish Theological Seminary, Trinity Col.; b. N.Y.C., 1913; p. Jacob and Mary Brody Clark; h. Israel Hyman; c. Salo H., Judith C. Rosenheim; res: 37 Colebrook St., Hartford, Conn. 06112.

HYMON, MARY WATSON, Head. Librn., Grambling College, P.O. Box 3, Grambling, La. 71245, '47–; Librn., '43–'47; ALA, La. Educ. Assn., La. Lib. Assn., Adult Educ. Assn.; Pi Lambda Theta, Ford Fndn. Fellowship Training aw.; Who's Who of Am. Wm.; Who's Who in Am.; Ky. State Col., AB, '40; Univ. of Denver, BS (Lib. Sci.), '41; MA, '54; Ind. Univ., EdD, '60; b. Hagerstown, Md., 1918; p. Ralph and Georgia Reed Watson; h. George Hymon; c. Nolan Jerome; res: P.O. Box 448, Grambling, La. 71245.

I

IANNIELLO, LYNNE YOUNG, Asst. PR Dir., Ed., Anti-Defamation League of B'nai B'rith, 315 Lexington Ave., N.Y., N.Y. 10016, '62–; PR Dir., Oceanside Public Sch., '61–'62; Free-lance Wtr., '52–'61; Reptr., Feature Wtr., Long Island Press, '50–'52; Asst. Ed., R. H. Macy pubns., '47–'50; PR, Colonial Airlines, '46–'47; Theatrical Publicist, '45–'46; Auth., "Milestones Along The March" (Praeger, '65); Ed., "The \ Axe-Grinders, Critics of Our Public Schools" (Macmillan, '63); Polk Edtl. Writing aw.; N.Y.U. Sch. of Jnlsm., BS, '46; b. N.Y.C., 1927; p. Joseph and Gertrude Goodman Young; h. Paul Ianniello; c. Geoffry D., Richard G.; res: 21 South Kensington Ave., Rockville Centre, N.Y. 11570.

IKERMAN, RUTH C., Free-lance Wtr., non-fiction; Bk. Reviewer, "Books for The Family," L.A. Times; devotional bks., religious articles; Auth: "Golden Words for Every Day" ('69), "Devotional Thoughts From the Holy Land" ('68); NLAPW, Cal. Wtrs. Guild; three George Washington Medals, Freedom Fndn., Valley Forge for mag. writing; Univ. of Redlands, BA, '31 (Alumni Assn. Distg. Svc. Aw., '66); b. Redlands, Cal., 1910; p. Clarence C. and Sophie H. Doll Percival; h. Lawrence H. Ikerman; res: 11 Panorama Dr., Redlands, Cal. 92373.

ILACQUA, ALMA AQUILINO, Free-lance PR, Tchr., Lemoyne Col. (Syracuse, N.Y.), '69–; Merchandising Group, N.Y., N.Y. '59–; Ruder & Finn, N.Y.C. and Chgo., '66–; Bauer, Tripp, Hening & Bressler, N.Y.C., '66–; Barlow-Johnson and Conklin, Labs & Beebe (Syracuse), '40–'46; Auth., short stories, articles and poems for numerous pubns.; Theta Sigma Phi (Syracuse Chptr. Treas., '58–'60; Pres., '60–'62; Nat.

Comm. Chmn., '63–'65), NLAPW, Pi Lambda Theta, N.Y. Auths. League; Syracuse Univ., AB (Jnlsm.), '40 (cum laude); MA (Educ., Literature), '43; b. Syracuse, N.Y., 1919; p. Achille and Josephine Caluori Aquilino; h. Joseph M. Ilacqua; c. Laurel, Mary, Joseph, Michael, Carol; res: 326 Wendell Terr., Syracuse, N.Y. 13203.

ILOTT, PAMELA CAADWAL, Wtr., Exec. Prodr., Columbia Broadcasting System, 524 W. 57th St., N.Y., N.Y. 10019; Dir. of Religious Bdcsts., '57; Script Ed., '54.

IMMEL, MARY BLAIR, Asst. to the Curator, Tippecanoe County Historical Association & Museum, 10th and South St., Lafayette, Ind. 47901, '67–; Auth., over 70 stories, items of curriculum, articles, poems; and four bks: "Men of God," "Keys to Many Doors," "Two-Way Street" (Bethany Press, '65), "Call Up The Thunder" (Bethany Press, '69); Chapman Col., BA (Educ.), '52; Purdue Univ., MA (Am. Hist.), '67; b. Wichita, Kan. 1930; p. Clinton C. and Bernice H. DeVore Blair; h. Rev. Daniel M. Immel; c. Daniel C., Michael V., Douglas B.; res: 2610 Summerfield Dr., Lafayette, Ind. 47905.

IMPARATO, MARYLOU LUTHER, Fashion Ed., Los Angeles Times, Times-Mirror Sq., L.A., Cal., '69–; Feature Wtr., '60; Partner, Imparato-Luther Associates, '68–'69; Ed., McCall Corp., '61–'68; Fashion Ed., Chicago Tribune, '56–'59; Des Moines Register and Tribune, '52–'56; Wtr., Lincoln (Neb.) Journal, '51–'52; Contrbr., Ladies Home Journal, Quest, other mags.; Fashion Group, Theta Sigma Phi; Who's Who of Am. Wm.; Univ. of Neb., '51 (Phi Beta Kappa, high distinction); b. Cambridge, Neb., 1930; p. Walter and Zola Beddeo Luther; h. Arthur Imparato; c. Walter, Andrew; res: 707 N. Hillcrest, Beverly Hills, Cal. 90210.

INDORF, ERIKA, Free-lance Talent; Dir., Drama Coach, voice and diction; Dir., Summer Seminar, Poetry Interpretation and Pantomine for Norfolk Theater Center, '69; three other pantomimes, '69; Dir., Christmas festival, seven children's programs, '69; Guest of Marionetteatern (Stockholm, Sweden), '68; assisting cultural events, Oberhausener Film Festival, '68; '67; Dir., Script Wtr., Children's Theatre Summer Workshop, Caracas Theatre Club, '67; film prod. (Caracas, Venezuela), '67; Film Ed., Zenith Cinema Svc., Inc., '66; Dir.-Asst., Script-Girl, Altschul Prods., '66; Radio, TV & Film Dept., Northwestern Univ. (Evanston, Ill.), '65; Assoc. Prodr., doc. film, '64–'65; Prod. Asst., WGBH-TV (Boston, Mass.), '64; AWRT; Bus. Col.; b. Magdeburg, Germany, 1912; p. Joseph and Anna Bley Schiffer; h. (div.); c. Marlice, Dieter; res: c/o Mrs. Jean Behrend, 2147 Ewing, Evanston, Ill. 60201.

INERFELD, JACQUELINE BIRON, AE, Daniel & Charles, Inc., 261 Madison Ave., N.Y., N.Y. 10016, '66–; Assoc. Adv. and Design, '62–'66; N.Y.U., BA, '56; b. Antwerp, Belgium, 1938; p. David and Bellina Biron;

h. David Inerfeld; res: 21 Glendale Rd., Harrison, N.Y. 10528.

INGALLS, CHARLOTTE ELIZABETH, Wms. Ed., Hollywood Sun-Tattler, 2028 Tyler St., Hollywood, Fla. 33020, '59–; Asst. Mkt. Ed., AP (Chgo.); News Wtr., CBS; Wms. Wear Daily; Haire Pubns., '40–; Hollywood C. of C., BPW (Wm. of Yr., '68); Ward-Belmont Jr. Col.; b. Chgo., Ill., 1914; p. Clarence E. and Gertrude Reader Ingalls; res: 2122 Plunkett St., Hollywood, Fla. 33020.

INGRAM, BETTY ELAM, Adm. Asst., Birmingham Area Chapter, American Red Cross, 2316 4th Ave. N., Birmingham, Ala. 35203, '69–; Dir. PR, '62–'68; Asst. Dir. PR, '59–'62; Wms. News Ed., Kingsport (Tenn.) Times-News, '58–'59; AWRT (Pres., '69–'71), Theta Sigma Phi (Pres., '67–'68), Birmingham Press Club (Bd. of Dirs., '68–'70), PR Cncl. of Ala., Am. Bus. Wms. Assn., ZONTA; Distg. Young Wm. Aw., Eastwood Jayceettes, '69; Photo Aw., Un. Commty. Funds and Cncls. of Am., '60; Birmingham's Intl. Fair Svc. Aw., '66; Univ. of Tenn., BS (Jnlsm.), '58; b. Birmingham, Ala., 1938; p. James W. and Bettie Bates Elam; h. Bill Ingram; res: 1780 Murray Hill Rd., Birmingham, Ala. 35216.

INGS, MARVEL Y., Ed., The Credit Union Executive, CUNA International, Inc., 1617 Sherman Ave., Madison, Wis. 53701, '64–; Asst. Ed., Everybody's Money, '64–; Contrb. Wtr., The Credit Union Magazine, '64–; Dir., PR, United Commty. Chest and Welfare Cncl., '60–'64; Dir., PR, Wis. Motor Carriers Assn. and Wis. Truckers Safety Cncl., '49–'59; Instr., Univ. of Wis. Eng. Dept., '46–'49; Curator, PR and Educ., Wis. State Hist. Soc., '42–'46; Auth: children's bk., "Our Own Wisconsin" ('44); prize-winning play, "Blackhawk" ('48); Theta Sigma Phi, Wis. Press Wm., Madison Press Club, Madison Adv. Club, Wis. State Hist. Assn.; Free-lance Wtr., reg. hist. and geology, study of Indian problems; Univ. of Wis., BA, '38; b. Antigo, Wis., 1915; p. William and Beth Horn Ings; res: 4219 Doncaster Dr., Madison, Wis. 53711.

INMAN, JULIA DAUGHERTY, Radio-TV Ed., Indianapolis Star, 307 North Pennsylvania St., Indpls., Ind. 46206, '54–; Petersburg (Va.) Progress-Index, '53–'54; Theta Sigma Phi; Wheaton Col., '47–'49; Col. William & Mary, BA, '51 (Phi Beta Kappa); b. Fort Benning, Ga.; p. Joseph B. and Martha Oliver Daugherty; res: 8825 River Rd., Indpls., Ind. 46240.

INNIS, PAULINE LEE, Free-lance Auth., Lectr.; Auth: "Fire From the Fountains" (Harcourt Brace, '68), "Wind of the Pampas" (David McKay, '67), "The Ice Bird" (Luce, '66), "The Wild Swans Fly" (David McKay, '64), and many other bks.; Am. Nwsp. Wms. Club (Secy., '68–'69; VP, '69–), Capital Speakers Club (VP, Treas., Nwsltr. Ed.), Children's Bk. Guild (Pres., '67), Auths. League, Intl. Platform Assn.; Ind. State Soc. Wm. of the Yr., '66; Univ. of

London and Manchester; b. Eng., 1918; p. Charles and Florence Jones; h. Walter D. Innis.

INSKEEP, LUCINDA KLEMEYER, Asst. Wms. Ed., The Columbus Dispatch, 34 S. Third St., Columbus, Oh. 43216, '69–; Wms., Soc. and Teen Feature Wtr., '64–'69; Edtl. Asst., Viking Press, '62–'63; Holiday Magazine, '58–'62; Theta Sigma Phi; The Press Club of Oh.; Oh. Nwsp. Wms. Assn.; Centenary Jr. Col., '54; b. N.Y.C., 1935; p. Robert G. and Anna Moore Johnson Klemeyer; h. Robert L. Inskeep; res: 2073 Zollinger Rd., Columbus, Oh. 43221.

IRVIN, ALISE REID, Dir., East Albemarle Regional Library, 205 E. Main St., Elizabeth City, N.C. 27909, '66–; HS Librn., '65–'66; Tchr., Vocational Home Econs. (Cleveland County, Shelby, N.C.), '45–'65; AAUW, NEA; Univ. of N.C., BS (Home Econs.), '45; b. Elizabeth City, N.C., 1924; p. Horace and Maude Stanton Reid; h. Abram V. Irvin (dec.); c. Addison Vann, Benjamin Reid; res: 1712 Crescent Dr., Elizabeth City, N.C. 27909.

IRVING, MARY BREWSTER, Edtl. Cnslt., '68–; Auth: "Flags" (Golden Press, '64), "Dogs" (Golden Press, '63), with Maurice Robbins, "The Amateur Archaeologist's Handbook" (Crowell, '65); Assoc. Ed., Am. Mgt. Assn., Grolier, Inc. (N.Y.), '63–'68; Mng. Ed., Beacon Press (Boston, Mass.), '60–'62; Assoc. Ed., Fodor's Modern Guides, (The\Hague, Netherlands), '57–'59; Social Studies Ed., Allyn & Bacon, Inc. (Boston, Mass.), '53–'57; Vassar Col., BA, '36; Oxford Univ., B. Litt. (Anthropology), '38; b. Boston, Mass., 1914; p. Frederick and Mary Chapman Irving; res: 2221 Limpet Lane, Largo, Fla. 33540.

IRWIN, CONSTANCE FRICK, Auth: "Fair Gods and Stone Faces" ('63; Black Hawk Aw., Midland Booksellers Assn., '64; Ella Victoria Dobbs Aw., Pi Lambda Theta aw., '65), "Jonathan D" ('59), "The Comeback Guy" ('61), others; Asst. Prof., Lib. Sci., Univ. of Ia., '61–'67; Librn., '46–'54, '37–'42; Bk. Ed., Columbia Univ. Press (N.Y.), '47; Auths. League of Am., NLAPW (Ia. City Br. Treas., '64–), Wms. Press Club (Evansville, Ind., Pres., '40–'42, '48–'50), ALA, various others; Ind. Univ., AB, '34 (with distinction, Phi Beta Kappa); MA, '41; Columbia Univ., BS in Lib. Svc., '47 (with high hons.); b. Evansville, Ind., 1913; p. Herman and Minnie Laurenstein Frick; h. W. R. Irwin; c. William Andrew; res: 415 Lee St., Iowa City, Ia. 52240.

ISAAC, MARIJEAN, Pres., Radio-TV Pubcty. Assocs., 335 E. 54th St., N.Y., N.Y. 10022, '59–; Radio-TV Pubcty. Dir., BBDO, Grey Advertising, Gaynor & Ducas; Program Dir. and Pubcty. Dir., Louis G. Cowan Inc. (Chgo); AWRT, Northwestern Univ., BS (Speech); b. Canton, Oh.; p. Charles and Gula Welsh Isaac; res: 335 E. 54th St., N.Y., N.Y. 10022.

ISAACS, FLORENCE SATOW, Prom. Mgr., Ed., Newsletters, Dell Publishing Co., Inc., 750 Third Ave., N.Y., N.Y. 10017, '61–; Prom. Asst., '59–'61; Asst. Adv. Mgr., Cosmair, '58–'59; Adv. Asst., Fisher Radio,

'57–'58; Bernard M. Baruch Sch., City Col. of N.Y., BBA, '57; b. Bklyn., N.Y., 1937; p. Joseph and Sylvia Tanklow Satow; h. Harvey A. Isaacs; c. Jonathan S.; res: 13 W. 13th St., N.Y., N.Y. 10011.

ISELE, ELISABETH WOODWARD, Wms. Ed., Kent Record-Courier, 206 E. Erie St., Kent, Oh. 44240, '66–; Soc. Ed., Norwalk (Oh.) Reflector-Herald, '35–'40, '27–'30; Oh. Press Wm.; b. Collins, Oh., 1909; p. Charles and Bessie Hassard Woodward; h. Frederick W. Isele; c. Ronald; res: 463 W. Main St., Kent, Oh. 44240.

ISELY, HELEN PEARSON, Auth., bk. of verse, "The Moon Is Red" (Alan Swallow, '62; 1st pl. rating, Midland Booksellers Assn., '62); 590 poems published in 150 mags., nwsps., incl. McCall's, Farm Jnl.; articles on arthritis for nwsps.; Asst. Ed., Lyrical Ia., '59; Public Speaking Tchr., '55–'57; Tchr., Gravette (Ark.) HS, '38–'40; Critic, Alpha group of poets (Des Moines, Ia.), '64–'69; NLAPW; Theta Sigma Phi aw., '64; Univ. of Ark., '38; b. Fayetteville, Ark., 1917; p. Herbert and Nettie Ingalls Pearson; h. Duane Isely (div.);¡c. Deanna Nilsson, Karl; res: 126 S. Franklin Ave., Ames, Ia. 50010.

ITO, DIANNE E., Copy Supvsr., McCann-Erickson International, 485 Lexington Ave., N.Y., N.Y. 10019, '68–; Copywtr., '65–'67; Wtr., Assoc. Prodr., Jantone Prod., '64–'65; Free-lance Wtr., '62–'63; Wtr., "Capt. Kangaroo" show, R. Keeshan Assoc., '61–'62; Prod. Asst., CBS, '60; Am. Film Festival aw., '66–'67; Art. Dir. Club cit., '69; Oh. State Univ., AB (Speech, Eng.), '59; b. L.A., Cal., 1937; p. Soze and Mitsue Morikawa Ito; h. Marshall Arisman; res: 314 W. 100th St., N.Y., N.Y. 10025.

IVAN, MARTHA PFAFF, Wtr.; Asst. to Pres. in charge of PR, Kilgore College, 1100 Broadway, Kilgore, Tex. 75662, '68–; Dir. of Guidance, '46–'68; Chmn., Eng. Dept., '35–'46; Co-auth., (pseud: Gus Tavo) five juv. bks.; Auth: (pseud: Martha Miller) "Timberline Hound" (Knopf, '63); Tex. Jr. Col. Tchrs. Assn., Tex. Press Wm., NPWC; Tex. Inst. of Ltrs. Cokesbury Aw., '69; Tex. Technological Col., BA, '30; MA, '31; b. St. Louis, Mo., 1909; p. Albert and Margaret Harris Pfaff; h. Gustave E. Ivan (dec.); res: 624 Leach St., Kilgore, Tex. 75662.

IWAMOTO, RANKO, Sr. Assoc., Dir., Japan Desk, Ruder and Finn, Inc., 110 E. 59th St., N.Y., N.Y. 10022, '63–; Rsch. Asst., Boston Univ., '61–'63; monthly feature articles, "N.Y. Happening," for Fukuso, Japanese wms. mag., '67–; Whitworth Col., BA (Jnlsm.), '60 (cum laude); Boston Univ. Sch. of Public Commtns., MS (Jnlsm.), '63; b. Tokyo, Japan; p. Torajiro and Seiko Iwamoto.

IZAKSON, ERIKA, Rsch. Dir., Business International Corporation, 757 Third Ave., N.Y., N.Y. 10017, '65–; European rsch., European Ed., '57–'65; Columbia Univ., BS, '54; MA (Polit. Sci.), '56; h. Zuss Izakson; c. Orna.

J

JACKER, CORINNE LITVIN, Story Ed., Station WNDT, W. 58th St., N.Y., N.Y. 10019, '69–; Auth., bks. incl., "The Black Flag of Anarchy: Antistatism in America" ('68), "Window on the UnKnown: "A History of the Microscope" ('66), "Man, Memory & Machines: An Introduction to Cybernetics" ('64); plays incl., "Pale Horse, Pale Rider" ('59); TV shows incl., "A Picture of Love" (CBS-TV, '59); others; poetry; Fellow, Macdowell Colony, '60; Auths. Guild; ALA list of 25 best bks. for young readers, '68; Lib. Jnl. recommended list, '69; AAAS list, 50 best bks. published in sci. for lay readers; Stanford, '50–'52; Northwestern, BS, '54; MA, '55; b. Chgo., Ill., 1933; p. Thomas and Theresa Bellak Litvin; h. Richard Jacker (div.); res: 110 W. 86th St., N.Y., N.Y. 10024.

JACKSON, BABETTE, VP, Dir. of Rsch., Dancer-Fitzgerald-Sample, Inc., 347 Madison Ave., N.Y., N.Y. 10017, '68–; VP, Assoc. Rsch. Dir., '62–'68; Sr. Project Dir., '56–'63; Asst. Rsch. Dir., Biow Co., '46–'56; Am. Mkt. Assn., ARF, AAPOR, AWNY; Barnard Col., BA (magna cum laude, Phi Beta Kappa), Grad. Work, Columbia Univ.; h. Murray Sommer.

JACKSON, CHARLOTTE COBDEN, Children's Bk. Ed., San Francisco Chronicle, and Chicago Sun-Times, '55–; yearly roundup revs. of children's bks., Atlantic Monthly, '56–'67; Revs. of children's bks., L.A. Times, early 1960's; Auth: "Tito, The Pig of Guatemala" ('40), "Sara Deborah's Day" ('41), "Roger and The Fishes" ('43), "Round The Afternoon" ('46), "Mercy Hicks" ('49), "The Story of San Francisco" ('55), "The Key to San Francisco" ('61); Friends of the Bancroft Lib. of Univ. of Cal. (Cncl. Mbr., Secy., '67–'68); S.F. State Tchrs. Col., '21; Univ. of Cal.; b. Big Oak Flat, Cal.; p. Edward G. and Louise Alice Marconi Codben; h. Joseph Henry Jackson; c. Marion Jackson Skinner; res: 2626 Buena Vista Way, Berkeley, Cal. 94708.

JACKSON, CLARA OSTROWSKY, Assoc. Prof., Lib. Sci., Kent State University, Kent, Oh. 44240, '63–; Tchr., Streetsboro Public Schs., '59–'63; Librn., Agnes Russell Ctr., Tchrs. Col., Columbia Univ., '58–'59; Nursery Sch. Tchr., N.Y.C., '51–'58; Serials Cataloger, Columbia Univ. Libs., '39–'45; Educ. Seminars Asst., Univ. of Minn. Lib., '37–'39; Encyclopedia Britannica Sch. Lib. Aws. (Oh. Liaison, '66–'69), Oh. Assn. of Sch. Librns. (Secy., '68–'69), Oh. Lib. Assn., WNBA; Univ. of Minn., BS, '37; Columbia Univ. Sch. of Lib. Svc., MLS, '59; Tchrs. Col., MS, '58; b. N.Y.C.; p. Joseph and Anna Novorodsky Ostrowsky; h. Sidney Jackson; c. Miriam Ruth, Joseph Walter; res: 424 E. Summit St., Kent, Oh. 44240.

JACKSON, EILEEN DWYER, Social Colmst., "Straws in the Wind," San Diego Union Tribune, Copley Press, 943 Third Ave., San Diego, Cal. 92112, '52–; Soc. Ed., San Diego Journal, '48–'50; Soc. Ed., Colmst., Feature Wtr., San Diego Union, '30–'48; Social Colmst., Court Reptr., Gen. Assigt., San Diego Sun, '22–'25; Galley Slave Aw., Theta Sigma Phi, San Diego Chptr., '69; Wm. of Valor in San Diego, '59; Wm. of Elegance, '68; Comite Pro Sinfonica of Tijuana, Mexico, plaque; San Diego State Col., '25; Univ. of Ariz., '26, b. San Diego, Cal. 1906; p. Edward and Vera Morse Dwyer; h. Everett Gee Jackson; c. Mrs. Thomas Thole Williamson; res: 1234 Franciscan Way, San Diego, Cal. 92116.

JACKSON, GRETCHEN FLIPPIN, Pers. Supvsr., Dept. of Health and Hosp., City of Boston, '68–; Asst. Dir., Off. of Public Info., Dept. of Health and Hosps., City of Boston, Sept., '68–; Founder-Dir., Gretchen Jackson Model Agcy., '65; Lectr., A & M Univ., '63; Colmst., Fame mag. (Bermuda monthly), '63; Special Events Advisor, WRIB (Providence, R.I.), '60; AWRT, Pubcty. Club of Boston, N.E. Wms. Press Assn.; press and PR staff for Gubernatorial Candidate, Foster Furcolo, '58; Governor's press staff; Kiwanis (two aws.), Nat. Urban League Svc. Aw., Zeta Phi Beta Wm. of the Yr., Pseudora Cunningham Radio and Jnlsm. Aw., YWCA and Clairol Citizen's Aw.; b. New Rochelle, N.Y.; p. Robert J. and Clara Johnson Flippin; h. Clarence Jackson; c. Toussaint Noel and Carlton Flippin; res: 15 Reedsdale St., Boston, Mass. 02134.

JACKSON, KATHERINE GAUSS, Contrb. Ed., Bk. Rev. Ed., Harper's mag., 2 Park Ave., N.Y., N.Y. 10016, '38–; Assoc. Ed., '38–'44; Sr. Ed., '44–'68; Co-Ed., "The Papers of Christian Gauss," '57; Nat. Judge, Avery Hopwood fiction aws., Univ. of Mich.; Asst. Treas., Freedom House; Smith Col., '24; b. Bethlehem, Pa., 1904; p. Christian and Alice Hussey Gauss; h. Andrew Jackson; c. Stuart; res: 17 E. 97th St., N.Y., N.Y. 10029.

JACKSON, MARY, Actress; Broadway: "Kiss & Tell," "Eastward in Eden," "Flowering Cherry"; TV: "Run for Your Life," "My Three Sons," "Do Not Go Gentle into That Good Night;" Film: "Airport;" SAG, AFTRA, AEA; b. Milford, Mich.; p. Thomas and Lela Stephens Jackson; res: 2055 Grace Ave., Hollywood, Cal. 90028.

JACKSON, TOMI, Wms. Ed., "Recipes For Living" daily prog., WCHD-FM, Bell Broadcasting, 278 E. Forest, Detroit, Mich. 48202, '60–; Disc Jockey, '60; Free-lance TV Prodr., docs., '60–'67; PR Dir., Cnslt., Architectural Barriers Comm.; Wtr.-Prodr., PR Dir. Sales Training Inc.; YWCA, Un. Fndn. (Demmy Speaker Aw.), Wm.'s Adv. Club (Secy.), AWRT (Nat. VP), Theta Sigma Phi, Detroit Press Club, Media Wm., New Detroit Comm.; Wayne State Univ., Mich. State Univ.; b. Dallas, Tex., 1923; p. Thomas and Ida Alexander Stephens; h. (div.); c. Linda; res: 17300 Pontchartrain Blvd. Detroit, Mich. 48238.

JACOBS, COLETTE J., AE, Doremus & Company, 1111 Wilshire Blvd., Suite 305, L.A., Cal. 90017, '64–; Acc. Coordr., Hixson & Jorgensen, '60–'63; Media Estimator-Byr., Foote, Cone & Belding, '57–'60;

Chmn., Bus. in Action-Adv., with L.A. City Sch. System for educs. in L.A. area, '67; L.A. Jr. Ad Club (Pres., '61), L.A. Adv. Club (Secy., '67-'68; Dir., '68-'69; Secy., '69-'70); Univ. of Ariz., BBA (Adv.), '57; b. Oak Park, Ill., '35; res: 10912-1/2 Wilshire Blvd., L.A., Cal. 90024.

JACOBS, FLORA GILL, Wtr., fiction and non-fiction, juv. and adult; Reptr., Wms. Dept., Wash. Post, '50-'52; Wms. Ed., Wash. Times-Herald, '42-'43; Asst. Wms. Ed., '40-'42; bks. incl: "A History of Dolls' Houses" (Scribners, '53, '65), "The Doll House Mystery" (Coward McCann, '58) "The Toy Shop Mystery" (Coward McCann, '60), "A World of Doll Houses" (Rand McNally, '65), "A Book of Dolls and Doll Houses" ('67), "The Haunted Birdhouse" ('70); WNPC, ANWC, Mystery Wtrs. of Am., Children's Bk. Guild of Wash., D.C. (Pres., '65); George Wash. Univ., '36-'40; b. Wash., D.C., 1918; p. Morris and Dora Seidenman Gill; h. Ephraim Jacobs; c. Amanda Bolling; res: 16 W. Kirke St., Chevy Chase, Md. 20015.

JACOBS, MARIANNE JEAN, Supervising Ed., Empire State Weeklies, Inc., 2010 Empire Blvd., Webster, N.Y. 14580, '58-; Adv. Mgr., Better Business Bureau (Rochester), '56-'58; Asst. to PR Dir., Am. Red Cross, '56-'58; Reptr., Rochester Sun, '53-'56; Bittner Pubns., '52-'53; b. Rochester, N.Y., 1934; p. Adolph and Alma Singer Jacobs; res: 1101 Parkside Dr., Webster, N.Y. 14580.

JACOBS, NATALIE TRUNDY, Actress, Apjac Productions, 20th Century Fox Studios, Box 900, Beverly Hills, Cal.; Broadway: "Girls of Summer" ('57), "By the Beautiful Sea" ('54), "A Girl Can Tell" ('53); Films: "Beneath the Planet of the Apes" ('70), "Mr. Hobbs Takes a Vacation" ('62), "The Careless Years" ('57), "The Monte Carlo Story" ('56); Briarcliff Col.; b. Boston, Mass.; p. Francis and Natalie Trundy Campana; h. Arthur P. Jacobs; res: 713 N. Beverly Dr., Beverly Hills, Cal. 94710.

JACOBSEN, ELLEN MARIE, Pres., Ellen Jacobsen & Co., Inc., 299 Madison Ave., N.Y., N.Y. '63-; PR Mgr., Cluett, Peabody & Co., Inc., '54-'62; Adv. Sales Prom., PR Mgr., Lady Arrow Div., '62; AWRT, PRSA, Altrusa Intl. (Bd. of Dirs., '67-'68), Kappa Gamma Pi; Outstanding Young Wm. of Am., '66; Misericordia Col., AB, '54 (cum laude), N.Y. Univ. Grad. Sch. of Arts and Scis., '54-'56; b. N.Y.C., 1932; p. Arthur and Gladys Callahan Jacobsen; h. Frederick H. Parenteau Jr.; c. Frederick, Suzanne; res: 70 Beechtree Dr., Larchmont, N.Y. 10538.

JACOBSON, RUTH KRAUSÉ, Dir. of Special Events, Fleishman, Hillard, Wilson & Ferguson, Inc., One Memorial Dr., St. Louis, Mo. 63102, '68-; Free-lance, '55-'57; Crusade for Freedom acct., Harshe-Rotman & Druck, '51-'52; Midwest Dir., CARE, Inc., '48-'51; Howard G. Mayer and Assoc., '47-'48; Sales Prom., B. Forman Co., Free-lance Col. Bd and Guest Ed.,

Mademoiselle, '45; Nat. Trust for Historic Preservation (PR Advisory Bd.), Nat. Park Svc. (Info. Advisory Comm.), and numerous other commty. groups; PRSA (Pubcty. Chmn., '66-'69), Press Club of Met. St. Louis, Theta Sigma Phi; Northwestern Univ., Medill Sch. of Jnlsm., BS, '47; Grad. Work: Univ. of Chgo., Northwestern Univ.; b. Watertown, N.Y.; p. Thomas and Ruth Parmalee Krause'; h. (div.); c. Anne; res: 12 Burroughs Lane, St. Louis, Mo. 63124.

JACOBSON, SUSAN LYNN, Assoc. Ed., Ladies' Home Journal, Downe Publishing, Inc., 641 Lexington Ave., N.Y., N.Y. 10022, '67-; Edtl. Asst., '65-'66; McCall's, '66-'67; Wells Col., BA, '64 (Dean's List); Columbia Univ./Union Theological Seminary Masters Program, '64-'65; b. Hackensack, N.J., 1942; p. Allan and Lucile LeMaitre Jacobson, Jr.; res: 369 Graydon Terrace, Ridgewood, N.J. 07450.

JACOBSON, SUSAN ROSENBERG, Mng. Ed., Paperback Library, Coronet Communications, Inc., 315 Park Ave. S., N.Y., N.Y. 10010, '69-; Sr. Ed., '65-'69; Assoc. Ed., '63-'65; Edtl. Asst., '63; Syracuse Univ., BA (Jnlsm.), '63; b. N.Y.C., 1942; p. Harold and Dorothy Rosenberg; h. Joel Jacobsen; res: 80 East End Ave., N.Y., N.Y. 10028.

JACQUES, SHIRLEY JONES, Ed., Co. Pubns., Howard Johnson Company, 222 Forbes Rd., Braintree, Mass. 02184, '67-; PR Asst., '65, Adv. Asst., '64; PR, Waldorf Assoc.; Art Dept, BBDO; Radio-TV Asst., Harold Cabot; Traf. Dir., Sutherland-Abbott; Copywtr., Holland, Barta; Adv. Mgr., Stoneham Independent; ICIE, Mass. Indsl. Eds. Assn. (aw., '68); Pubcty. Club of Boston, Adv. Club of Boston; Boston Univ., BS, '54; b. Melrose, Mass., 1931; p. Sherman and Marion Duffill Jones; h. William Jacques; res: 20 Maxim Pl., Quincy, Mass. 02169.

JAFFA, AILEEN RABY, Artist; Auth., poetry; bks. incl: "Tiptoe to the Wind" ('67), "Word out of Time" ('65), "Three Dragons Easily" ('63); Head, Agriculture Lib., Univ. of Cal. (Berkeley), '56-'62; Librn., Agricultural Ref. Svc., '33-'62; Jr. Asst., '28-'33; various organizations and aws.; Univ. of Cal. (Berkeley), AB, '22; Sch. of Librarianship, Cert., '28; b. Oakland, Cal., 1900; p. Myer E. and Adele Solomons Jaffa; h. (div.); c. Lawrence Marvin Jaffa, Joan Elizabeth Jaffa (dec.); res: 126 Pomona Ave., El Cerrito, Cal. 94530.

JAFFE, JAN PAYNTER, AE, Mgr., Rsch./Mktng. Info., Tatham-Laird & Kudner, Inc., 605 Third Ave., N.Y., N.Y. 10016, '68-; Mgr., Rsch./Mktng. Info., '69-; Asst. AE, '68; Exec. Dev. Program (Chgo.), '66-'67; Univ. of Chgo., BA, '64; MBA, '66; b. Chgo., Ill., 1944; p. Gilman and Helen Hepner Paynter.

JAFFE, NICOLE S., Actress; parts incl: Broadway Stage, "This Was Burlesque"; Hollywood Stage, "You're A Good Man, Charlie Brown"; Movies, "The Trouble with Girls" (MGM); TV, "Scooby-Doo, Where Are You?" (Hanna-Barbara); McGill Univ.; b.

Montreal, Canada; p. Bernard and Irma Jaffe; res: 3764 Grey Ave., Montreal, Quebec, Can.

JAFFE, YVONNE UMLAND, Ed., "Interstatements," ISC Industries, Inc., 3430 Broadway, Kan. City, Mo. 64141, '69–; Ed., "Young America Today," Sears Roebuck Gen. Off., '68–'69; Dir., Public Info., Parks & Recreation Dept., '66–'68; Free-lance bk. revs., Kansas City Star, '63–'67; Instr., Eng. Dept., Willamette Univ. (Salem, Ore.), '60–'61; Mo. Parks & Recreation Assn., PR Cncl. of Health & Welfare Svcs., ICIE; Univ. of Neb., BA (Polit. Sci.), '60; b. Lincoln, Neb., 1939; p. Rudolph and Elsie Rochenbach Umland; c. Michael A., Sara Ann; res: 1208 W. 39th St., Kan. City, Mo. 64111.

JAHODA, GLORIA, Auth., fiction, non-fiction, c/o Paul Reynolds and Co., 599 Fifth Ave., N.Y., N.Y. 10017; Auth: "Annie" (novel, '60), "Delilah's Mountain" (novel, '63), "The Other Florida" ('67), "The Road to Samarkand: Frederick Delius and His Music" (Biog., '69); also articles and poetry; Va. Hist. Soc., Fla. Hist. Soc., Tallahassee Hist. Soc. (Pres., '67–'68), Delius Assn. of Fla., Intl. Sir Thomas Beecham Soc., Norfolk and Norwich Archaeological Soc., Norfolk Rec. Soc., Fla. Audubon Soc.; Northwestern Univ., BA, '48; MA, '50; Univ. of Wis., '50–'52; b. Chgo., Ill., 1926; p. Chase W. and Adelaide Peterson Love; h. Gerald Jahoda.

JAIMES, RUTH MARSH, Wms. Ed., Newton Daily News, 200 First Ave. E., Newton, Ia. 50208, '61–; b. Spirit Lake, Ia., 1925; p. Herbert and Florence Bullough Marsh; h. Albert E. Jaimes; c. Marsha, Alberta, Albert Jr.; res: 1113 E. 15th St. S., Newton, Ia. 50208.

JAMES, BEATRICE BOSTWICK, Lib. Dir., Bergenfield Public Library, 50 W. Clinton Ave., Bergenfield, N.J. 07621, '55–; Asst. Librn., '25–'55; ZONTA (Pres.-elect, '70), N.J. Lib. Assn. (Pres., '69–'70), ALA, Cncl. Nat. Lib. Assn. (Chmn., '70–'71, Secy.-Treas., '68–'69), WNBA; B'nai B'rith aw., '58; Unico Nat. (Bergenfield Chptr.) citizen aw., '65; Sarage Col.; b. Union City, N.J.; p. John and Elnora Chamberlain Bostwick; h. Edward A. James; res: 90 Harcourt Ave., Bergenfield, N.J. 07621.

JAMES, CONNIE HOOVER, Dir., PR, Oregon Tuberculosis and Health Association, 830 Medical Arts Bldg., Portland, Ore. 97205, '48–; Dir., Volunteer Svcs., Off. of Price Adm.; Dir. of Wms. Projects, Nat. Youth Adm., Ore.; Nat. Campfire Girls (Butte, Mont.); Ore. Press Wm. (Aw. for Journalistic Effort; Pres., '67–'69), Ore. Assn. of Eds. and Communicators, Theta Sigma Phi, Portland PR Round Table, Nat. Respiratory Disease Conf., (Chmn., Christmas Seal Campaign Comm., '58, '61), Ore. Conf. Tuberculosis Workers (Pres., '62–'64), Ore. League for Nursing (Bd. of Dir.); Intermountain Union Col., '24–'28 (Helena, Mont.; Cert. in Commty. Affairs); Univ. of Ore.; h. Donald H. James; res: 2550 N.W. Marcia St., Portland, Ore. 97210.

JAMES, MILDRED V., Rsch. Dir., Sales Prom., Off. Mgr., Farm Journal, Inc., 777 Third Ave., N.Y., N.Y. 10017; AWNY; N.Y.C. Columbia Univ., '30; b. N.Y.C.; h. Leo F. James (dec.); c. Robert; res: Vista Towers, 65 Glenbrook Rd., Stamford, Conn. 06902.

JAMES, ROWENA GABLE, Mng. Ed., Iowa State University Press, Press Bldg., Ames, Ia. 50010, '64–; Prom. Mgr., Assoc. Ed., '58–'64; Instr., Tech. Jnlsm. Dept., Ia. State Univ., '53–'55; Edtl. Wtrs. Staff, Register and Tribune (Des Moines), '50–'53; Theta Sigma Phi (Ames Chptr. Pres., '68–'69), Zeta Phi Eta; Univ. of Ia., AB, '51; Ia. State Univ., MS, '58; b. Hastings, Ia., 1919; p. Mearl Arthur and Ethelyn McKie Gable; c. Margaret Elizabeth James; res: 2004 Greeley, Ames, Ia. 50010.

JAMES, SYLVIA KOMITO, Dir., TV-Radio-Films Div., PR Dept., United Fund of the Philadelphia Area, 450 Suburban Station Bldg., Phila., Pa. 19103, '50–; Staff, '47–; Bdcstr., Wtr., Prodr., Dir.; AWRT, Phila. PR Assn., TV Radio Adv. Club, Phila. Club of Adv. Wm.; Bdcst. Pioneers; numerous bdcst. script aws.; b. N.Y.C.; h. Hyman James (dec.); res: 3170 Merriel Ave., Camden, N.J. 08105.

JAMESON, FLORENE BROWN, Nat. Sales Asst., WOAI-TV, 1031 Navarro, San Antonio, Tex. 78206, '66–; Sales Asst., KENS-TV, '65–'66; Traf. Dir., KONO Radio, '63–'65, '56–'57; Traf. Dir., KONO-TV, '57–'63; Traf. Dir. KENS-TV '51–'57; AWRT (San Antonio Chptr. Pres., '63); b. Wayside, Tex., 1923; p. Carl and Zora Wesley Brown; h. John Jameson; c. Richard C., Mrs. Franklin J. Parks, Martha Jean, Janice Florene; res: 927 Utopia Rd., San Antonio, Tex. 78223.

JAMISON, ELEANOR POYNTER, Publr., Sullivan Daily Times and Sullivan Union, 115 W. Jackson St., Sullivan, Ind. 47882, '50–; Bus. Mgr., '33–'50; Hoosier State Press Assn. (Bd. of Dirs., '52), Ind. Democratic Edtl. Assn. (Pres., '59), WPC of Ind., BPW, NFPW, Theta Sigma Phi (Fanny Wright Memorial Aw., '49); Ind. Univ., AB, '22; Wellesley Col., '23; b. Sullivan, Ind., 1901; p. Paul and Alice Wilkey Poynter; h. William C. Jamison; c. Mary Alice (Mrs. Robert M. Griffin, Jr.), Anne P. (Mrs. Dan L. Parker); res: 244 W. Washington St., Sullivan, Ind. 47882.

JANE, MARY CHILDS, Auth: "Mystery of the Red Carnations" ('68, Lippincott), "Mystery at Shadow Pond" ('58, Lippincott), 14 other juv. mysteries; Boys Club bk. aw., '67; Bridgewater State Col., BS (Educ.); b. Needham, Mass., 1909; p. Henry and Grace Dyer Childs; h. William Jane; c. Stephen, Thomas; res: Pump St., Newcastle, Me. 04553.

JANES, BARBARA BECKETT, Dir. of Commty. Rels. and Dev., The Jewish Hospital of St. Louis, 216 S. Kings Highway, St. Louis, Mo. 63110, '67–; Dir. of PR, '64–'67; Prodr., Wtr., KMOX Radio, '64; Wtr., Dir., Condor Film, '64; Free-lance Wtr., Dir., KTVI-TV, '62–'64; Free-lance Wtr., Prodr., WIIC-TV (Pitt., Pa.),

'60-'62; PR Asst., Wms. Pers. Dir., Alcoa (Cleve., Oh.), '55-'56; Club Dir., Special Svcs. USAF (Germany), '52-'53; NATAS, Theta Sigma Phi; Pa. Golden Quill Aw., numerous others aws.; Univ. of Mo.; AB, '52 (Phi Beta Kappa); b. Boonville, Mo., 1930; p. Theodore and Gladys Watson Beckett; h. Richard S. Janes; c. Sally, Lisa, Susan; res: #9 Terryhill Lane, St. Louis, Mo. 63131.

JANOW, DOROTHY ADELE, Asst. Media Dir., Black Russell Morris, 231 Johnson Ave., Newark, N.J. 07108, '69-; b. Gorsee, France, 1950; p. Walter and Mildred Adamska Janow; res: 737 Adams Ave., Elizabeth, N.J. 07208.

JANOWSKI, BARBARA EDGECOMBE RAY, Camera Pg. Colmst., The Gary Post-Tribune, 1065 Broadway, Gary, Ind. 46402, '56-; Instr., Beginning and Advanced Photog., Ind. Univ., Gary Center, '48-'52; Owner and Operator, Barbara Ray Studio, portraiture, '43-'52; Proofreader, Ed., Cost Estimator, Chgo. printing plants, '29-'41; articles, various hist. pubns.; Pfsnl. Photogrs. of Ind., Pfsnl. Photogrs. of Am., NLAPW, WPC of Ind., NFPW; Good Citizenship Medal, Ind. Sons of the American Revolution, '63; b. E. Liverpool, Oh., 1912; p. Arthur E. and Elizabeth B. Ripley Edgecombe; h. Joseph E. Janowski; c. Jan Joel, Joel Justin; res: 149 Morningside Ave., Gary, Ind. 46408.

JARVIS, KAY HOGAN, Food Ed., Evening Tribune, Union-Tribune Publishing Co., 919 Second Ave., San Diego, Cal. 92112, '67-; Orgs. Ed., San Diego Union, '64-'67; Military Social News Ed., '61-'64; Feature Wtr., San Clemente Sun, '57-; Theta Sigma Phi, Cal. Press Wm. (1st Pl. Aw., Features, '65); NPWC 2nd Pl. Aw., Features, '65; Chaffey Col., '51-'53; L.A. State, '53-'54; b. Denver, Colo., 1934; h. Roy Stuart Jarvis; c. Christopher; res: 3052 Curlew St., San Diego, Cal. 92103.

JARVIS, LUCILE HOWARD, Prodr., NBC News, 30 Rockefeller Plaza, N.Y., N.Y. 10020, '60-; Co-prodr., "Capitol Close-up" (Radio); Wms. TV Ed., Pathe News; Assoc. to Prodr., Talent Assoc.; Assoc. Food Ed., McCall's; Copywtr., Beechnut Foods; WNPC, OPC, NATAS, AWRT, SRTCA; "The Louvre" show, 6 Emmys, Peabody aw., Radio-TV Critics aw., Thomas Alva Edison aw., Am. Film Festival aw., '64-'65; "The Kremlin" show, Emmy, McCall's Golden Mike aw., '63; Cornell Univ., BS, '38; Columbia Tchrs. Col., MS, '41; b. N.Y.C., 1919; p. Herman and Sophie Howard; h. Serge Jarvis; c. Barbara, Peter; res: 116 Central Park S., N.Y., N.Y.

JASON, ADELINE L., AE, Penny Baker, Inc., 341 Madison Ave., N.Y., N.Y. 10017, '68-; AE, Virginia Burdick Assoc.; PR Dir., Knudsen-Moore, Inc.; PR Dir., Baumritter Corp.; Home Furnishings Pubcty., Abraham & Straus; Asst. Sls. Prom. Dir., Lit. Bros.; Home Furnishings Ed., Bride-to-Be (Curtis Publ.); Phila. Wms. Adv. Club, NHFL; Nat. Retail Merchants

Assn. aws., '49; Univ. of Pa.; Columbia Univ., BA (Jnlsm.); b. Atlantic City, N.J.; p. Michael and Louise Lensh; h. Lewis N. Jason; res: 47 Gary Rd., Stamford, Conn. 06903.

JASOUS, JACQUELINE MARIE, Asst. Fashion Ed., Bride's Magazine, Conde Nast Publications, Inc., 420 Lexington Ave., N.Y., N.Y. 10017, '67-; Staff, '65; U.S. Steel Fndn., '63-'65; Free-lance Wtr., Song-Wtr.; City Col. of N.Y., '63-'65 (Dean's List; Mosesson Aw. for Excellence in Col. Jnlsm.); b. N.Y.C., 1946; p. George amd Viola Samra Jasous; res: 336 E. 86th St., N.Y., N.Y. 10028.

JAUSS, ANNE MARIE, Free-lance Artist, Auth.; Auth. and Illus: "Wise and Otherwise" ('53), "Legends of Saints and Beasts" ('54), "Discovering Nature the Year Round" ('55), "The River's Journey" ('57), "Under a Green Roof" ('60), "The Pasture" ('68, Auths. Aw., N.J. Assn. of Tchrs. of Eng.), many others; Art Sch., Munich, Germany; b. Munich, Germany, 1907; p. Georg and Caroline Hegeler Jauss; res: R.D. 1, Box 82H, Stockholm, N.J. 07460.

JAYCOX, BETTY LOOKER, Wms. Ed., Akron Beacon Journal, 44 E. Exchange St., Akron, Oh. 44309, '53-; Jr. League (Past Pres.), Akron Art Inst. (Bd. Mbr.); numerous aws. from Oh. Nwsp. Wms. Assn., NPWC, Oh. Press Wm., Theta Sigma Phi; Smith Col., BA, '34; h. Edward Van K. Jaycox; c. Jill (Mrs. Carl Dietrich), Edward Jr.; res: 2252 E. Waterloo Rd., Akron, Oh. 44312.

JAYMES, GRAYCE ELLSWORTH, Secy.-Treas.-Dir., Young American Enterprises, Inc.; VP/Partner, G. & J. Inc., The Pavilion, Suite 3119, 500 E. 77th St., N.Y., N.Y. 10021.; Ed., SoundBlast News, SoundBlast Publishing Corporation, '69-; VP, Gen. Mgr., Promotion Consultants, Inc., '66-'68; Adv. Mgr., Bldg. Stone Inst., '65-'66; Radio Commentator, WHBI, '66; Dir. of PR, TeleRadio Corporation, '64-'66; Adv. Club of N.Y., AWNY, AFA, N.Y.; b. Rochester, N.Y. 1927; p. Peter and Mary Cusumano Bosaits; c. John E.; res: 104-60 Queens Boulevard, Forest Hills, N.Y. 11375.

JEFFERS, LUCIE SPENCE (MURPHY), Advisor, Med. Writing; Cnslt., Occupational Therapy; Ed., American Journal of Occupational Therapy, '48-'62; Co-auth., "Medical Writing"; Ed., "Four Corners Cookbook"; Am. Occupational Therapy Assn. (VP, '44-'46; Aw. of Merit, '65), Wis. Occupational Therapy Assn. (VP, '69-'70); Lindenwood Col., '27-'29; Northwestern Univ., BS, '31; Milw. Downer Col., OT Cert., '34; b. LaCrosse, Wis., 1910; p. Harry and Lottie Beckett Spence; h. C. A. Jeffers; res: Box 256, Rte. 2, Wautoma, Wis. 54982.

JEFFERSON, DOROTHY CAMPBELL, Owner, Public Relations Services, '60-; Dir. PR, Capitol Court Shopping Ctr., '56-'60; Commentator, WOKY-TV, '54-'56; Ed., "Spyglass" colm., Milwaukee Journal, '40-'53; Asst. Ed., Morehouse Publ. Co., '35-'39; Cnslt., Easter Seal Soc. of Milw., City, State Fair of Wis., Milw. Mental Health Assn.; PR Tchr., Univ. of Wis.-PRSA course; Theta Sigma Phi, PSRA, Who's Who Of Am. Wm.; Who's Who In PR; Marquette Univ., PhB, '34; b. Milw., Wis., 1912; p. James and Mathilda Reichmann Campbell; h. Dr. Roland A. Jefferson; res: 1260 N. Prospect Ave., Milw., Wis. 53202.

JEFFREY, MILDRED MESURAC, Asst. Prof. of Eng., Hofstra University, Hempstead, N.Y. 11550; Nwsp. Reptr., Feature Wtr.; Auth., novel, "Daughter Oh My Daughter!"; poetry in lit. quarterlies, short stories; Linguistic Soc. of Am., Nat. Cncl. of Tchrs. of Eng.; Hunter Col., A.B.; Adelphi Univ., AM; Grad. courses, New Sch.; Columbia Univ.; City Univ. of N.Y.; Univ. of Colo.; h. George Jeffrey.

JELM, HENRIETTA, PR, Clean Air Council, '69–; PR, Viewpoint Books, '67–'69; Adv., PR, Lit. Rep., Henrietta Jelm & Associates (L.A., Cal.), '60–'67; W. Coast Dir. and PR and Prom., Doubleday and Co., '60–'67; NFPW (Reg. Dir., '67–'69; Radio Prom. Aw., '63), Cal. Press Wm. (Radio-TV Prom. Aws., '63–'66), AWRT (Southern Cal. Dist. Pres., '68–'69; VP, '66–'67), Radio TV Wm. of Southern Cal. (Bd. of Dirs., '62–'67; VP, '67–'68), L.A. Adv. Wm (two Golden Lulus, '66), Hollywood Wms. Press Club; b. Fresno, Cal., 1900; p. William D. and Mary Catherine Hughes Foote; h. Carl Jelm (div.); c. Carlotta Diana (Mrs. Roger Starrett Williams); res: 1256 Devon Ave., L.A., Cal. 90024.

JENKINS-VAITEKUNAS, KAY T., Dir. of Sales Dev., WLOS-TV, 288 Macon Ave., Box 2150, Asheville, N.C. 28802, '68–; Prog. Sales Supvsr., '63–'66; Nat. Sales Asst., '63–'65; Exec. Sales Secy., '58–'64; Copywtr., WLOS Radio-TV, '54–'57; Time Study, Cost Accountant, Mich. Dimension Co. (Manistique), '38–'53; AWRT, Am. Bus. Wm. Assn., Asheville Sales and Mkt. Exec. Club (Sls. Aw.); Capital Univ.; b. Morrow County, Oh., 1918; p. Dale and Marie Rood Jenkins; h. Felix Francis Vaitekunas; c. Felix Francis, II; res: 101 Cumberland Circle, Asheville, N.C. 28801.

JENKS, MARY ELLEN, Dir. of Home Svcs., Green Giant Co., 8000 Normandale Blvd., Mpls., Minn. 55431, '62–; Wtr., Am. Dairy Assn., '61–'62; Dir. of Home Svcs., Salada Foods, '57–'61; Hostess, "Mary Ellen Jenks Show," WKOW-TV, '54–'55; Alice in Dairyland (goodwill ambassador), Wis. Dept. of Agriculture, '53–'54; AWRT, Inst. Food Edtl. Cncl., Consumer Svcs. Comm., Grocery Manufacturers of Am.; Am. Home Econs. Assn., Home Econs. Comm., Nat. Assn. of Frozen Food Packers; Univ. of Wis., BS, '56 (Phi Kappa Phi; cum laude); Univ of Wis., MS (Speech), '57; b. Milw., Wis., 1933; p. Frank and Emma Sweitzer Jenks; h. Douglas R. Jordal; c. Joyellyn Jenks; res: 6405 Cherokee Trail, Edina, Minn. 55435.

JENNER, NADINE NEWBILL, Adv., PR, Non-fiction Wtr.; Auth., HS Adv. Text; Agencies: Radio Adv.; Rogers & Smith; Ed. of House Organ, and Mktng. Rsch., National Dairy and Food Bureau; Adv. Copy,

PR, Mandel Brothers; for Oh. Sesquicentennial radio series; Theta Sigma Phi (Col. Pres., Past VP, Prof. Chmn., Matrix Corr.), DAR (Past Nat. Chmn., Radio; Ill. State Chmn., Radio), ADPi (Past Alumni Ed., Adelphean); Rockford Col.; Univ. of Ill., AB, '28; Art Inst.; Chgo. Academy of Fine Arts; Portland, Ore., 1907; p. T. J. Newbill and Leona Hopper Newbill; h. Albert E. Jenner, Jr.; c. Cynthia Lee, Nancy (dec.); res: 119 Tudor Pl., Kenilworth, Ill. 60043.

JENNINGS, AMY REBECCA, Chief Librn., Federal Trade Commission, Sixth St. at Pennsylvania Ave., N.W., Wash., D.C. 20580, '47–; Nat. Labor Rels. Bd., Wash., D.C., '44–'47; Ref. Librn., Social Security Bd. Lib., U.S. Dept. of Agriculture Lib., Wash., D.C., '43–'44; Head Librn., Grenada, Miss. City Sch., '42–'43; Watertown, Tenn. HS, '36–'41; Tchr., Prin., Wilson Co. Tenn. Schs., '27–'35; articles in various prof. pubns.; Law Librns. Soc. (Secy., '46–'48), Special Libs. Assn.; Cumberland Univ., AB, '40; George Peabody Col. for Tchrs., BS (Lib. Sci.), '42; b. Murfreesboro, Tenn., 1907; p. Esrom Bertram and Lillian Lee Jordan Jennings; res: 417 Poplar Dr., Falls Church, Va. 22046.

JENNINGS, GERTRUDE FEDER, Dir. of Bibliography, R. R. Bowker Co., 1180 Ave. of the Americas, N.Y., N.Y. 10036, '69–; Asst. to Pres. of Bowker, '65–; formerly Asst. Dir., Am. Booksellers Assn.; WNBA (Dir.); Ed., Bookwoman; Univ. of Chgo., BA; b. Chgo., Ill; p. Louis and Pauline Feder; res: 62 Perry St., N.Y., N.Y. 10014.

JENNINGS, JANET SURDAM, Coordr. of Tech. Svcs., Binghamton Public Library, 78 Exchange St., Binghamton, N.Y. 13901, '65–; Head, Catalog Dept., '32–'60; First Asst., Catalog Dept., '32; Head of Catalog Dept., Head of Processing, Four County Lib. Syst., '60–'65; ALA, N.Y. Lib. Assn., WNBA (Chptr. Secy., '67–); Cornell Univ., '26–'30 (Phi Beta Kappa, Phi Kappa Phi); Drexel Inst. of Tech., '31–'32; b. Candor, N.Y.; p. James and Alvena Surdam Jennings; res: 99 Oak St., Binghamton, N.Y. 13905.

JENNISON, FLORENCE TYE, Bay City Corr., United Nations, '46–; UN Charter Conf. (S.F.), '45; Dumbarton Oaks, '44; League of Nations, '23; Co-auth., "Movement of Money Earnings and Real Earnings in the U.S." ('31); Goucher Col., BA, '23; John Marshall Law Sch., JD, '41; b. Bay City, Mich., 1900; p. George and Lillian O'Connor Jennison; res: 1251 Esplanade Ave., N.O., La. 70116.

JENSEN, ARLENE KNUTSON, Staff Wtr., Kenosha News Publishing Corp., 715 58th St., Kenosha, Wis. 53140, '64–; Cont. Dir., WAXO Radio, '63–'64; PR cnslt. for civic orgs.; Am. Nwsp. Guild (Local Secy., '66–'68); active in civic groups; b. Elroy, Wis., 1937; p. Carl and Olga Ormson Knutson; h. Donald Jensen; c. Steven Bolint, Rhanda Bolint, Erik Jensen; res: 5204 70th St., Kenosha, Wis. 53140.

JENSEN, H. JUNE ANDERSON, City Ed., Sunnyvale

Daily Standard, Community Publications, Inc., 155 S. Taaffe St., Sunnyvale, Cal. 94086, '64–; Pubcty. Dir., Redwood City Rodeo, '51–'64; Courthouse Reptr., S.F. Chronicle, '55–'56; Ed., Solano Republican (Fairfield, Cal.), '47–'48; News Ed., KLSM Radio, (San Mateo), '46–'47; Courthouse-City Hall Reptr., Redwood City Tribune, '44–'46; AAUW; Univ. of Cal., AB (Jnlsm.), '44; b. Riga, Latvia, 1924; p. H. Dewey and Erma Sams Anderson; h. Paul B. Jensen; c. Chris, Kimberley, Paul, Lars, Thor; res: 708 Laurel Ave., Menlo Park, Cal. 94025.

JENSEN, IDA-MARIE CLARK, Assoc. Librn., Head Ref. Librn., Utah State University, Logan, Ut. 84321, '69–; Assoc. Prof., '61–; Head Librn., Sci. and Engineering Div., '64–'68; Ref. Librn., '47–'63; Instr., Eng. Dept., '47–'49; Rsch. Asst., Cornell Univ., '41–'44; Am. Assn. for the Advancement of Sci., AAUW, Mountain Plains Lib. Assn., Ut. Lib. Assn., Phi Kappa Phi, Delta Kappa Gamma, Intl. Platform Assn.; Jasper Aw., Bibliographical Ctr. for Rsch., Denver, Colo.; Cert. of Recognition, Ut. State Univ., '67; Ut. State Univ. MS (Eng.); '56; Univ. of Denver, MA (Lib. Sci.), '60; b. Logan, Ut.; p. Prof. Samuel E. and Ida Andersen Clark; h. Lyman Jensen; res: 1461 Sumac Dr., Logan, Ut. 84321.

JENSEN, JANE SAYRE, Bk. Ed., International Development Review, Society for International Development, Center for Developmental Change, University of Kentucky, Lexington, Ky. 40506, '66–; Rsch. Assoc. '66–; Lectr., Dept. of Polit. Sci., '67–; Univ. of Fla., BAE, '60 (with hons.); MA, '61; Univ. of Ill., PhD, '67; b. Charleston, W. Va., 1938; p. Denver and Edith Cain Sayre; h. Lloyd Jensen; res: 1236 Indian Mound Rd., Lexington, Ky. 40502.

JENSEN, JEAN RYERSON, Fashion Ed., Indianapolis News, 307 N. Pennsylvania, Indpls., Ind. 46206, '68–; Fashion Copywtr., Wm. H. Block dept. store, '66–'68; Chas. A. Stevens, Chgo., '44–'46; Wieboldts, '43–'44; Press Wm. of Ind. (State Aws.: first place for feature, second place for fashion, '68); Wright Jr. Col.; b. Chgo., Ill., 1921; p. Richard and Laura Grenig Ryerson; h. Bertram Jensen; c. Clay, Carla, Pamela, Pirie, Christine Butler; res: 6028 Harlescott Rd., Indpls., Ind. 46220.

JENSEN, PAULINE LONG, Auth., juv. bks.: "Out of House and Home" (Bobbs-Merrill, '65), "Thicker Than Water" (Bobbs-Merrill, '66); articles, stories; Critic, Anna Phelan Seminar, '65–; Am. Assn. of Univ. Pen Sec., '68–; Fac., Northstar Wtrs. Conf., '68; Tchr., Crtv. Writing, YWCA, '63–'66; NLAPW (Mpls. Br. Pres., '64–'66; State Pres., '66–'68), Minn. Auths. Guild (Pres., '60–'61; aw., '61, '62); ext. courses; private study, Dr. Anna Phelan, Univ. of Minn.; b. Gretna, Neb., 1900; p. Albert and Lavinia Manley Long; h. Dewey Martin Jensen; c. Marilynn Ann, Jeanne Jensen Cagle; res: 5220 Abbott Ave. S., Mpls., Minn. 55410.

JEROME, BETTE, Prodr.-Modr., panel discussion programs, Docs. Narrator, Comml. Spokeswoman, '53–; Concert Artist, Choral Dir., '42–'53; Child Actress, stage, radio, N.Y., '30–'40; AWRT (V.P., '69–'70), Intl. Platform Assn., NATAS, AFTRA, SAG, "Teen Talk" (aws., AAUW, '56–'60; McCall's Golden Mike; Dept. of Indian Affairs) "Tell-Us-Scope" (D.C. Bd. of Educ. aw.); Who's Who of Am. Wm.; Julliard Sch. of Music, '40–'42; b. Newport News, Va., 1925; p. Elias and Sophie Harris Jerome; h. Samuel M. Bialek; c. Alan Rafel, Lisa Rafel (Mrs. Ian Haim), Donald Bialek, Joan Bialek, Barry Bialek; res: 1200 N. Nash St., Arlington, Va. 22209.

JETER, LIESELOTTE (LEE) KLINGER, Asst. Mgr. and Wms. Dir., KFLJ, 10th and Russell Sts., Walsenburg, Colo. 81089, '57–; Radio, TV Personality; Wtr., Prodr., Radio Free Europe Progs. for U.S.A. radio stations, '62–'63; Lectr., schs., civic orgs., '62–; Tchr., voice and expression in Dallas and Stephenville, Tex., '50–'56; Beta Sigma Phi, Governor's Comm. on Arts and Music; Nat. Radio Free Europe Aw., '62, '63; The Freedom Bell, presented by Mayor Willy Brandt, Berlin, '63; nominated Colo. Wm. of the Yr., '66, '67; active in numerous civic groups; Western Reserve Univ., '42–'45 (Ranney Hon. Music Aw.); b. Cleve., Oh., 1924; p. John and Wilhemina Mauler Klinger; h. Floyd Jeter; c. Kristy-Lee; res: Cloud Nine, Walsenburg, Colo. 81089.

JEVAS, RENA J., Soc. Ed., Daily Chief Company, 111 West Wyandot Ave., Upper Sandusky, Oh. 43351, '67–; Oh. State Univ., '66–'67; b. Marion, Oh., 1948; p. Thomas and Ruth Hoffhein Jevas; res: 209 S. Fifth St., Upper Sandusky, Oh. 43351.

JEWETT, ALYCE WILLIAMS, Wtr., non-fiction; Public Affairs Offcr. and Instr., Agricultural Econs., Univ. of Cal., '61–'62; Instr., '34–'36; Dir. of Info., Agricultural Cncl. of Cal., '55–'61; Special Asst. to Gen. Mgr., Poultry Producers of Central Cal., '45–'55; Auth., "Agricultural Cooperatives: Strength in Unity," (Interstate Printers, Danville, Ill., '63); Wtr., Cooperative Movement, Ency. Brittanica; Yolo Co. Hist. Soc., (Pres.), '65–'67), Conf. of Cal. Hist. Socs. (Dist. VP, '67–'69); First Wm. Recipient, Distg. Svc. Plaque, Nat. Assn. Future Farmers of Am., '64; Who's Who of Am. Wm.; Univ. of Cal., BS, '31; Univ. of Cal., MS, '34; Harvard, Radcliffe, '36–'37; b. Oakland, Cal., 1908; p. Robert and Ethel De Maranville Williams; h. Lindsay Jewett; res: 788 Elmwood Dr., Davis, Cal. 95616.

JINKS, JOAN METZNER, Jnlsm. Instr., Miami-Dade Junior College-South, 11011 S.W. 104th St., Miami, Fla. 33156, '68–; PR Wtr., Hanke Meyer Assoc., '67–'68; Fashion Ed., Miami News, '64–'66; Reptr., Copy Ed., Miami Herald, '60–'63; Reptr., Fashion Ed., Charlotte (N.C.) Observer, '58–'60; Ed. Asst., Seventeen, '56–'57; Theta Sigma Phi, Fla. Wms. Press Club (writing aw.), Nat. Cncl. of Col. Pubns. Advisers; N.C. Press Club Writing Aw., Am. Trucking Assn. Safety Writing Aw.,

Queens Col., BA (Eng.), '56; Columbia Univ. Grad. Sch. of Jnlsm., MS, '58; b. N.Y.C., 1936; p. Jerome and Jeanne Silberman Metzner; h. Larry Jinks; c. Laura Beth, Daniel C.

JOBERT, EDITH CAVELL, Free-lance Talent; Weather Forecaster, WHNB-TV (W. Hartford, Conn.), '53–'68; AFTRA; Boston Univ.; b. Manchester, Conn; p. Arthur and Dorothy Greenwood Jobert; h. Ralph G. Nappi; c. Lisa, Noelle, Gina; res: 213 Cherry Hill Dr., Newington, Conn. 06111.

JOBES, GERTRUDE BLUMENTHAL, Auth., fiction, non-fiction; bks: "One Happy Family" ('55), "Motion Picture Empire" ('66), others; Literature Tchr., Milford (Conn.) YMCA, '61; Asst. to Ed.-in-Chief, Hearst Metrotone News, '32–'45; Warner Bros. Theatres, '29–'31; Aborn Operas, '25–'29; New Haven Poetry Soc., Fla. Poetry Soc., Auths. Guild; 2,000 Wm. of Achiev.; Dic. of Intl. Biog.; Columbia Univ.; New Sch. for Social Rsch.; N.Y.U.; Cert. in Gen. Educ.; b. N.Y.C., 1907; p. Henry and Frances Scheff Blumenthal; h. James Jobes (dec.); res: Park Sheraton Hotel, 870 Seventh Ave., N.Y., N.Y. 10019.

JOBSON, MARIAN, Chmn. of the Bd., Jobson Associates, Inc., 9 Rockefeller Plaza, N.Y., N.Y. 10020, '60–; Chmn. of the Bd., Carriere and Jobson, Inc., '54–'60; Partner and Founder, Hartwell, Jobson and Kibbee, '37–'54; AE, Harold Strong, Inc.; AE, Tamblyn and Brown; Asst. to Pres., Chatham Col.; PRSA, Chatham Col. Club, The Seeing Eye (VP, '42–), Am. Assn. of Workers for the Blind; Chatham Col., Pitts., Pa., AB; Katharine Gibbs Sch., N.Y.; b. Chgo., Ill.; p. George and Almira Giddings Jobson; res: 253 E. 49th St., N.Y., N.Y. 10017.

JOHANSEN, JANET MALONE, Rsch. Dir., Parents' Magazine Enterprises, 52 Vanderbilt Ave., N.Y., N.Y. 10017, '68–; Asst. Rsch. Dir., '64–'68; Prom. Rsch. Dir., American Legion Mag., '62–'64; House & Garden, '52–'59; AWNY, Media Rsch. Dirs. Assn., Mag. Prom. Group; Univ. of Ala., N.Y.U.; b. Mobile, Ala.; p. Price and Anna Delahunty Malone; h. Harry B. Johansen (dec.); res: 315 E. 69th St., N.Y., N.Y. 10021.

JOHN, ALMA VESSELLS, Dir. Wm.'s Activities, WWRL, 41-30 58th St., Woodside, N.Y. 10037, '53–; Former Home Arts Specialist, Grey Advertising Co.; Educ. Cnslt., Personal Products Co., Milltown, N.J.; League for Mutual Aid, AWRT; Nat. Assn. of Mkt. Developers, NAMW, Key Wm. Of Am.; Nat. Assn. of Radio and TV Announcers (Wm. of the Yr. Aw.); Who's Who Of Am. Wm.; McCall's Golden Mike Aw. (Best Youth Prog. in U.S., "What's Right with Teenagers," '58); numerous aws., cits. in nursing, public health, human rels., radio bdcst.; Harlem Hosp. Sch. of Nursing, '29; N.Y.U. Sch. of Educ., BS, '46; b. Phila., Pa.; p. Joseph and Hattie Taylor Vessells; h. C. Lisley John; res: 2190 Madison Ave., Apt. 10-D N.Y., N.Y. 10037.

JOHN, ELIZABETH BEAMAN, Colmst., World Book Encyclopedia Science Service, Inc., 516 Travis St., Houston, Tex. 77002, '67–; Tchr., crtv. writing, Cuyahoga Commty. Col., '66–'68; War Corr. (European Theater), Cleveland News, '45; Auth: "Seloe" (World, '55), "Hummingbirds" (Follett, '60); Co-auth: "Flak Bait" ('48); Free-lance Wtr., natural hist., sci. articles; NLAPW (Cleve. Br. Pres., '56–'57) several art and ltr. aws.; Univ. of Cinn.; Cleve. Inst. of Art; Cleve. Col. of Western Reserve Univ.; active in numerous civic groups; b. Cinn., Oh., 1907; p. Dr. Charles and Laura Bogue Beaman; h. Henry John; res: 6815 Mayfield Rd., Cleve., Oh. 44124.

JOHNSEN, GRACE M., Dir., Bdcst. Standards and Practices, American Broadcasting Companies, Inc., 1330 Ave. of the Americas, N.Y., N.Y. 10019, '47–; Dir., Wms., Children's Religious Progs., '42–'45; Asst. Dir., Public Svc. Progs., NBC, '45–'47; Supvsr., Educ. Progs., '40–'42; AWNY (Secy., '45; Pres., '48–'50; Dir., '56–'57), AFA (Secy., '50–'52), AWRT (Dir., '57–'59); b. Bklyn., N.Y. 1911; p. Vidkunn and Astrid Andersen Johnsen; h. Walter Holt; res: 160 E. 48th St., N.Y., N.Y. 10017.

JOHNSEN, JENNY ALVILDE, Founder, Ed., Publr., Minnesota Posten, The Friend Publishing Company, 1455 W. Lake St., Mpls., Minn. 55408, '56–; Ed., Minneapolis Posten, '50–'56; Ed., Dotre av Norge, '47–'50; Ed., Publr., The Friend, '32–'50; Minn. Nwsp. Assn., Wms. Intl. League for Peace and Freedom (Mpls. Chptr. Pres., '51–'52); Univ. of Minn., '19–'21; b. Warren, Minn.; p. Peter and Ida Holt Storbakken; res: 2040 Upton Ave. S., Mpls., Minn. 55405.

JOHNSON, ALICE FREIN, East Coast Corr., Seattle Times, Capital Bureau, 720 Nat. Press Bldg., Wash., D.C. 20004, '43–; Wms. News Reptr., Gen. News and Features, City Desk (Seattle off.), '42; Wms. News Ed., '42–'43; Secy., Univ. of Wash. Sch. of Jnlsm., '23–'25; Contrbr., N. Am. Nwsp. Alliance; Wash. D.C. Corr., Alaska nwsps: Anchorage News, Fairbanks News-Miner, Ketchikan News, Juneau Empire, '50–'56; WNPC (Pres., '56–'57), ANWC (Bd. Mbr., '56–'58), Theta Sigma Phi (Wm. of Achiev., '57), Univ. of Wash., AB (Romantic Langs.), '22 (cum laude); AB (Jnlsm.), '23; b. Palo Alto, Cal., 1900; p. Pierre Joseph and Emma Blanche Macleod Frein; h. Jesse Charles Johnson; c. Mary Virginia (Mrs. Joseph B. Jeffers, Jr.); res: 5900 Bradley Blvd., Bethesda, Md. 20014.

JOHNSON, BARBARA PRITCHARD, Co-dir., Publishing Division and Ed., "International" (Braniff inflight mag.), Kelly Nason, 300 E. 42nd St., N.Y., N.Y. 10017, '70–; Staff Wtr., Advertising Age, '69–'70; Asst. Ed., Missouri Alumnus (Columbia, Mo.), '67–'68; Staff Wtr., Institutions (Chgo., Ill.); Instr., Mag. Ed., Univ. of Mo. Sch. of Jnlsm.; Co-prodr., "The Making of Europe" ('68, doc.); Theta Sigma Phi, Kappa Tau Alpha; J. C. Penney Co. Fellowship, '68; Brussels, Belgium, Graduate Fellowship, '68; John W. Jewell Jnlsm. Fellowship, '66; Univ. of Mo., BJ, '67; MA,

'69; b. Chgo., Ill., 1945; p. Irving and Virginia Baker Pritchard; h. P. J. Johnson; res: 333 E. 75th St., N.Y., N.Y. 10021.

JOHNSON, DOROTHY LOU, Ed. and Rept. Coordr., Touche Ross & Co., 208 S. La Salle St., Chgo., Ill. 60604, '69–; Designer, Mfr., Greeting Cards; Chgo. Mgr., Crossroads of Sport, '68; PR Mgr., Ill. Soc. of CPA's, '65–'67; Mdsng. AE, Edward H. Weiss Adv., '62; Mdsng. Exec., Foote, Cone & Belding, '47–'61; The Fashion Group; Who's Who in Am. Cols. and Univs.; Augustana Col., BA, '46; b. Sioux Falls, S.D., 1924; p. Melvin M., and Minnie Aassen Johnson; res: 1400 Lake Shore Dr., Chgo., Ill. 60610.

JOHNSON, DOROTHY M., Free-lance Wtr.; previously: Edtl. Staff, Business Education World (N.Y.C.); Exec. Ed., The Woman; Ed., Montana Fourth Estate; Mgr., Mont. Press Assn.; Asst. Prof. of Jnlsm., Univ. of Mont.; Auth., 10 bks., specializing in ancient Greece, western frontier; Auths. Guild; hon. Blackfeet Indian, hon. police chief, Whitefish, Mont.; Spur Aw., '56; Univ. of Mont., BA, '28; b. McGregor, Ia.; p. Lester and Mary Louisa Barlow Johnson; res: 2309 Duncan Dr., Missoula, Mont. 59801.

JOHNSON, DOROTHY SYLVESTER, Sr. Ed., Reading, The Macmillan Company, 866 Third Ave., N.Y., N.Y. 10022, '70–; Dir. of Lang. Arts and Humanities, Encyclopaedia Britannica Educ. Corp., '68–'70; Sr. Ed., '67–'68; Staff Ed., Sci. Rsch. Assoc., '65–'67; Sr. Ed., Soc. For Visual Educ., '62–'63; Asst. Ed., Lang. Arts., Scott, Foresman & Co., '61–'62; Instr., French, Nat. Col. of Educ., '60; Tchr., '45–'58; NEA, Nat. Assn. for Childhood Educ.; Kan. City Jr. Col., AA, '38; Kan. City Tchrs. Col., BS, '40; Univ. of Kan., BA, '48; MA, '50; b. Kan. City, Mo., 1920; p. Frederick and Edna Hall Sylvester; h. Richard Johnson; c. Mrs. Kathleen Hanna, Mrs. Martha Phillips; res: 406 W. 20th St., N.Y., N.Y. 10011.

JOHNSON, EDNA RUTH, Acting Ed., The Churchman, 1074 23rd Ave. N., St. Petersburg, Fla. 33704, '68–; Mng. Ed., '48–'68; Chmn., Arts Ctr., '67–; Assoc. Church Press aw., '62; Univ. of Wis., Northwestern Univ., Univ. of S. Fla.; b. Sturgeon Bay, Wis., 1918; p. Charles and Georgia Knutson; res: 1074 23rd Ave. N., St. Petersburg, Fla. 33704.

JOHNSON, ELEANOR MURDOCH, Ed.-in-Chief, American Education Publications, 55 High St., Middletown, Conn. 06457, '40–; Edtl. Dir., '34–'40; Wtr., '27–'34; Co-founder, "My Weekly" ('28); Asst. Superintendent of Schs., '30–'34; Dir., Elementary Schs., '18–'30; Tchr., '13–'18; Auth: "Treasury of Literature" (Chas. E. Merrill, '56), "Word Mastery Spellers" (Chas. E. Merrill, '53), others; numerous juv. paperbacks (Am. Educ. Pubns., '41–); Altrusa (VP, '51–'52), Theta Sigma Phi (Headliner Aw., '48); Univ. of Chgo., PhB, '25 (cum laude); Columbia Univ. Tchrs. Col., MA, '32; b. Hagerstown, Md., 1892; p. Richard and Emma Shuff Johnson; res: 121 Record, Frederick, Md. 21701.

JOHNSON, ELIZABETH BALUSS, Asst. Prof. and Program Dir., KEBS-FM, San Diego State College, San Diego, Cal. 92115, '66–; Exec. Secy., Seattle C. of C., '62–'64; Timebyr., J. Walter Thompson, and BBDO (S.F.) '59–'61; PR and Prom., KIRO and KIRO-TV (Seattle), '56–'58; Prodr., several radio series, distributed nat. through Nat. Educ. Radio; Theta Sigma Phi, NAEB, Assn. for Pfsnl. Bdcst. Educ.; Univ. of Wash., BA, '57; Syracuse Univ., MS, '66; b. Madison, Wis., 1936; p. Roy S. and Virginia Baluss Johnson; res: 4750 70th St., No. 53, La Mesa, Cal. 92041.

JOHNSON, ELIZABETH REISTROFFER, Librn., Stepan Chemical Co., Edens and Winnetka Rd., Northfield, Ill. 60093, '68–; Chief Assoc. Ed., Wtr., The United Educators, Inc. '59–'68; Am. Chemical Soc., Am. Inst. of Biological Sci.; St. Ambrose Col., BS, '42; b. Grand Mound, Ia., 1921; h. Harry Johnson; res: 130 Prospect Ave., Lake Bluff, Ill. 60044.

JOHNSON, EVELYN STEIL, Adv. Mgr., Harvey Publications, Inc., 1860 Broadway, N.Y., N.Y. 10023, '57–; Program Dir., WABF-FM and Dir., Records-from-Abroad, '52–'57; Fund Campaign Asst., Met. Opera Guild, '50–'51; Registrar, N.Y. Col. of Music, '45–'50; Adv. Club (Cert. of Hon. Mention); Hunter Col., BA (cum laude; Phi Beta Kappa); Columbia Univ., MA (Fine Arts); b. N.Y.C., 1921; p. William and Martha Roehm Steil; h. Thruston Johnson; res: 600 W. 116th St., N.Y., N.Y. 10027.

JOHNSON, HARRIETT, Music Critic, Ed., New York Post, 75 West St., N.Y., N.Y. 10016; Auth: "Your Career in Music" (Dutton); ASCAP, NLAPW, Sigma Alpha Iota, Music Critics Assn., Who's Who of Am. Wm., Who's Who in Am.; Univ. of Minn., BA (Music); h. (div.); c. Craig H. Norville; res: 162 W. 54th St., N.Y., N.Y. 10019.

JOHNSON, JOSEPHINE WINSLOW, Auth.; fiction: "Now In November" ('34), "Jordanstown" ('37), "Years End" ('39), "Winter Orchard" ('36), "Wildwood" ('47), "Dark Traveler" ('63), "Sorcerers Son" ('65); non-fiction, "The Inland Island" ('69); articles in nwsps., mags.; Auths. Guild, Breadloaf Wtrs. Conf.; Pulitzer Prize for fiction, '35; O'Henry Memorial Aw., short shories, '35; Ohioana Lib. Aw. for best fiction, '63; Cinn. Fine Arts Assn. Aw., '64; incl. several yrs., Best Am. Short Stories; Washington Univ. (St. Louis, Mo.), '33 (Alumnae Cit., '55); b. Kirkwood, Mo., 1910; p. Benjamin H. and Ethel Franklin Johnson; h. Grant Cannon; c. Terence, Ann, Carol: res: 4907 Klatte Rd., Cinn., Oh. 45244.

JOHNSON, JOYCE GLASSMAN, Sr. Ed., Dial Press, 750 Third Ave., N.Y., N.Y. 10017, '68–; Assoc. Ed., '67–'68; William Morrow, '66–'67; Auth., "Come and Join the Dance" (Atheneum, '62); Barnard Col., '51–'55; b. N.Y.C., 1935; p. Daniel and Rosalind Ross Glassman; h. Peter Pinchbeck; c. Daniel; res: 60 St. Marks Pl., N.Y., N.Y. 10003.

JOHNSON, LADY BIRD (Claudia A. Taylor Johnson), First Lady of the United States, '63–'68; speeches, travel, welcoming and receiving Heads of State, leadership in nat. program of conservation and beauty (organized Comm. for a More Beautiful Capital), Project Headstart Hon. Chmn.; Former Chmn. of Bd., KTBC radio and TV (Austin, Tex.); cited for contrb. to public interest through media of airwaves, Theta Sigma Phi, AWRT; George Foster Peabody Bdcst. Aw., TV program, "A Visit to Washington on Behalf of a More Beautiful Capital"; St. Mary's Episcopal Sch. for Girls (Dallas, Tex.); Univ. of Tex., BA, '33; BJ, '34; LittD (hon.); Tex. Wms. Univ. (Denton), LLD (hon.); b. Karnack, Tex., 1912; p. Thomas J. and Minnie Patillo Taylor; h. Former President Lyndon Baines Johnson; c. Lynda Bird (Mrs. Charles Robb), Luci Baines (Mrs. Patrick J. Nugent); res: LBJ Ranch, Stonewall, Tex.

JOHNSON, LILA JONES, Ed., Pubcty. Dir., Women's City Club of Detroit, 2110 Park Ave., Detroit, Mich. 48070, '64–; Free-lance PR, '57–'64; Reptr., The Berkley Advance, '56; Pers. Asst., Michigan Bell Telephone Co., '49–'50; Asst. Pers. Mgr., Sears Roebuck and Co., '48–'49; PRSA, PR Soc. of Mich.; Univ. of Ill., '44–'48; Col. of Commerce and Bus. Adm., '48; Soc. of Arts and Crafts, '60–'61; Wayne State Univ., '61–'62; Oakland Commty. Col. (Vice Chmn. of Bd., '66–; Secy., '64–'66); b. Mattoon, Ill., 1926; p. Robert and Ruth Pinkard Jones; h. Leonard Johnson; c. Douglas Alan, Steven Robert, Paul Leonard, Susan Ruth; res: 12726 LaSalle Blvd., Huntington Woods, Mich. 48070.

JOHNSON, LUCY C. TRENT, Tchr., Librn., Archivist, Bibliographer; Tchr., Librn., D.C. Public Schs., '65–'67, '53–'57; Librn.: Catholic Univ., '56–'57; Hunter College 1959–60; St. Clare's Hosp. Nursing Sch., '62–'65; Hofstra Col. (evenings), Brentwood HS, '60–'62 (Sponsor, Eugene G. Hoyt Chptr., Nat. Hon. Soc.); Queens Public Ref. Lib., '57; American Univ. Grad. Sch., '55–'56; Bklyn. Public Ref. Lib., '52; Howard Univ., '45–'52; U.S. Govt., '35–'45; Archivist and Bibliographer, Union Theological Seminary, '63–'64; Contrbr., bibliographies, bk. revs. to various jnls., nwsps.; Member ALA, D.C. Lib. Assn., WNBA, NEA, other pfsnl. orgs.; Frelingluysen Univ., Diploma (Embalming), '33; Howard Univ., AB (Hist.), '45; Catholic Univ. of Am., BS (Lib. Sci.), '49; N.Y.U., AM (Guidance), '52; Columbia Univ. (Lib. Svc.), '62, '63; b. W.Va.; p. Robert H. and Martha A. Payne Trent; c. Loretta A., Henry T.; res: P.O. Box 3274, Wash., D.C. 20010.

JOHNSON, M. ELIZABETH, Ed., Bus. Mgr., The Franklin Times, Inc., P.O. Box 119, Louisburg, N.C. 27549, '52–; Chmn., Mathematics Dept. Louisburg Jr. Col., '47–; NCEA, AAUW (Chptr. Pres., '50–'52, '52–'66; State Parliamentarian, '62–'64), Delta Kappa Gamma (Chptr. Pres., '61–'62; VP, '60–'61), Nat. Nwsp. Assoc.; Who's Who; Louisburg Jr. Col., Liberal Arts Diploma, '28; Univ. of N.C., BA; '30; MA, '37; b. Louisburg, N.C., 1909; p. Asher F. and Sadie N. Thomas Johnson; res: P.O. Box 119, Louisburg, N.C. 27549.

JOHNSON, MAL, Dir. of Commty. Rels., Hostess, "Let's Talk About It" and "For Your Information," WKBS-TV, 3201 S. 26th St., Phila., Pa. 19129; Colmst., Citizens-Times, Post Observer, Greater Phila. Publics, Cnslt. Tchr., Chmn. Bd. of Dirs. Young Communicators; Univ. of Pa. & Temple; AWRT (Bd. of Dirs., '66–: Educ. Fndn. Bd. of Trustees, Dir. Public Info.), TV and Radio Adv. Club of Am., Phila. Adv. Wm.; Bd. Mbr., 26 civic orgs.; Wm. of Yr. (England, '57; McGuire Air Force Base, '68); Temple Univ.; Springfield College Sch. of Intergroup Rel.; b. Phila., Pa. 1924; p. Bishop and Johnnie Reeves Hooser; h. Frank Johnson (Dec.); res: 6115 W. Oxford St., Phila. Pa. 19151.

JOHNSON, MARGARET GELTZ, Exec. Dir., Cleveland Senior Council, 1066 Hanna Bldg., Euclid Ave. and E. 14th St., Cleve., Oh. 44114, '67–; Reviewer, Jr. Bks., and Dir., World Friends Club, The Cleveland Press, '37–'66; tchr., Lincoln Sch. (Lakewood), '17–'19; Oh. Nwsp. Wms. Assn. (1st Prize for bk. revs.), Wms. Nat. Bk. Assn., volunteer work; Lake Erie Col., BA, '17; Western Reserve Univ., grad. work in jnlsm., '38–'39; b. Mansfield, Oh.; p. William and Helen Dewees Geltz; h. Lawrence R. Johnson (dec.); c. Mrs. Stephen J. Knerly, Mrs. William L. Atwell, David M.; res: 1447 W. 101st St., Cleve., Oh. 44102.

JOHNSON, MARGOT, Auths. Rep., Margot Johnson Agency, 405 E. 54th St., N.Y., N.Y. 10022, '54–; Head Lit. Dept., Bernard Schubert, '50–'54; A. & S. Lyons, '45–'50; VP, Ann Watkins, Inc., '37–'45; Rsch. Asst., '36–'37; Smith Col., AB (Hist.), '30 (Hons.); Sorbonne, '30–'32; b. Kan. City, Mo., 1909; p. J. Henry and Edna Gordon Johnson.

JOHNSON, MARGUERITE LOUISE, Contrb. Ed., Time, Time & Life Bldg., Rockefeller ctr., N.Y., N.Y. 10020, '69–; Art Wtr., '63–'69; Waldorf Col., '51–'53; St. Olaf Col., BA, '55 (magna cum laude); Columbia Univ., MA, '63; res: 116 Central Park S., N.Y., N.Y. 10019.

JOHNSON, MARJORIE JANE, Librn., New Castle-Henry County Public Library, 296 S. 15th St., New Castle, Ind. 47362, '63–; Ref. Cataloguer, '56–'63; ALA, Ind. Lib. Assn., BPW, Altrusa Intl. (VP, '68–'70); Ball State Univ., BA, '59; Univ. of Ill., MS (Lib. Sci.), '62; b. New Lisbon, Ind.; p. Omer and Madie Jeffers Johnson; res: 1313 H Ave., New Castle, Ind. 47362.

JOHNSON, MARTIE KRAYER, Newswm., WTVD-TV, Box 2009, Durham, N.C. 27702, '66–; Dir. of Public Info., Durham's Anti-Poverty Program, '65–'66; Eng. Tchr., Durham HS, '49–'60; AWRT; NEA, N.C. Educ. Assn., Duke Univ., AB, '49; b. St. Petersburg, Fla., 1928; p. Alfred and Pauline Lyon Krayer; h. Cecil Johnson; c. Sherron Patricia, Jana Lynne, Cecil, Jr.; res: 2609 Glendale Ave., Durham, N.C. 27702.

JOHNSON, MAXINE L., Adv. and PR AE, Media Dir., Bozell & Jacobs, Inc., 1100 Glendon Ave., L.A., Cal. 90024, '69–; PR and Adv. AE, Copywtr., Bozell & Jacobs, (Omaha, Neb.), '66–'69; Ed., Show & Tell, '68–; Asst. Cont. Dir., KMTV, '65–'66; Bdcstr. and Copywtr., KHAS-TV, '63–'65; Rptr., KHAS Radio, '63; PR AE, Nat. Alliance of Businessmen; AWRT, Omaha Press Club, Omaha Adv. Club, NAB, civic opera and drama groups; Hastings Col., BA, '65; b. Oakland, Neb., 1942; p. Vinton and Thelma Stromquist Johnson; res: 4474 Murietta Ave., Sherman Oaks, Cal. 91403.

JOHNSON, MINNIE REDMOND, Librn., West Center, Chicago State College, 500 N. Pulaski Rd., Chgo., Ill. 60612, '58–; Head Librn., Hampton Inst., '52–'58; Asst. Librn., Fisk Univ., '50–'52, '46–'49; Instr., Atlanta Univ., '45–'46; Librn., '37–'43; Tchr., '33–'37; ALA, Ill. Lib. Assn., Chgo. Lib. Club, Assn. of Col. and Rsch. Libs.; Fisk Univ., BA, '32; Atlanta Univ., BS (Lib. Sci.), '44; Univ. of Chgo., MA, '45; b. Clarksville, Tenn., 1910; p. Robert and Julia Thomas Redmond; h. E. Milton Johnson; res: 501 E. 32nd St., Chgo., Ill. 60615.

JOHNSON, NANCY BRADY, Cont. Dir., WBIG, Greensboro, N.C. 27420, '70–; Media Dir., Porter-Ward, Inc., '68–'70; Copywtr., WBIG; Prom., WFMY-TV; Media, Copy, Hege-Middleton & Neal; Traf. Dir., WPET; Piedmont Triad Adv. Club; b. Greensboro, N.C., 1940; p. W. H. and Raytanza Brady; h. Donald Johnson; c. Fred H. Alton III, Jeffrey H. Alton; res: 2717 Shady Lawn Dr., Greensboro, N.C. 27408.

JOHNSON, NATALIE GANDRUD, Wms. Dir., Prom. Dir., Central Minnesota Television Co., 720 Hawthorne, Alexandria, Minn. 56308, '68–; Wms., Dir., '61–'67; Exec. Secy., '59–'68; AWRT (Northstar Chptr. Secy., '67–'68), Alexandria Press Club (Secy.-Treas., '67–'68); Gustavus-Adolphus Col., Univ. of Manitoba (Can.); b. Glenwood, Minn., 1931; p. G. M. and Ida Disrud Gandrud; h. Arthur Johnson; c. Arthur Craig, Kathryn, Gary, Teresa; res: Rte. 3, E. Lake Latoka, Alexandria, Minn. 56308.

JOHNSON, PATRICIA JOHNSTONE, Public Info. Offcr., University of California, University Hospital, 225 W. Dickinson St., San Diego, Cal. 92103, '67–; Wtr., Reptr., San Diego Union, '64–'67; Publr., Del Mar Surfcomber, '60–'63; Wtr., Stockton Record, '52–'60; Wtr., UP, '49–'52; Theta Sigma Phi, Cal. Press Wm.; Univ. of Mo., BJ; Univ. of Cal., MA.

JOHNSON, PEARL PATTERSON, Assoc. Ed., Farm Journal, Inc., 230 W. Washington Sq., Phila., Pa. 19105, '41–; poetry published in leading mags., material in Reader's Digest; Theta Sigma Phi; Drexel Inst. of Tech., '16–'18; Waterbury Art Sch., '27–'30; Univ. of Pa. Sch. of Jnlsm., '39–'41; b. Waterbury, Conn., p. Samuel H. and Margaret Sitser Patterson; h. C. Haldane Johnson (dec.); res: Alden Park Manor, Phila., Pa. 19144.

JOHNSON, ROLANDA STONEBACK, Asst. Corr., ZDF-West German TV 2, 2914 M St., N.W., Wash., D.C. 20007, '63–; Asst. Corr. and Prod. Asst., ARD German TV, '61–'63; Free-lance; AWRT; Mount Holyoke Col., BA, '59 (magna cum laude; Phi Beta Kappa); Mainz Universitaet, '59–'61; Middlebury Col., MA, '60; b. Allentown, Pa., '37; p. Roland and Elizabeth Williams Stoneback; h. Maurice Johnson; c. Keith Erik; res: 3804 Raymond St., Chevy Chase, Md. 20015.

JOHNSON, RUBY VALENTINE, Bdcstr., WHOK, N. Memorial Dr., Lancaster, Oh. 43130, '48–; AWRT; b. Fairfield County, Oh., 1917; p. Sumner and Merle Pierce Valentine; h. Wayne Johnson; c. Judy Ann, Janet Lynn, Wayne C., Jr.; res: 345 Kaye Dr., Pickerington, Oh. 43147.

JOHNSON, SHIRLEY KING, Wtr., fiction and non-fiction; "Lookin' Around," colm. for Lincoln (Neb.) Sun papers, '67–'68; Children's bk., "A Dog Named Chip" ('63); "Stuck in the Country" (David C. Cook Co., '66); Shirley K. Johnson Collection of manuscripts and papers, Univ. of Southern Miss., Hattesburg; b. Adair, Ia., 1927; p. Roland and Gladis Evans King; h. Thomas Johnson; c. Elaine, Evan, Barry, Bryan; res: 4118 Randolph St., Lincoln, Neb. 68510.

JOHNSON, THEODORA LUCIA, City Librn., Azusa Public Library, 729 N. Dalton Ave., Azusa, Cal. 91702, '62–; City Librn., Lompoc (Cal.) Public Lib., '60–'62; Adult Svcs. Coordr., Palo Alto Public Lib., '59–'60, Order Librn., '54–'59, Asst. Cataloger, Ref. Librn., '53–'54, Lib. Asst., '51–'52; Ed., Campbell Press, Saratoga Observer, '46–'51; Reptr., San Jose Mercury-News, '45–'46; Reptr., Sunnyvale Standard, '44–'45; Reptr., Bethesda (Md.) Journal, '39–'41; ALA, Cal. Lib. Assn., Public Lib. Execs. Assn. of Southern Cal. (Pres., '70; VP, '69; Secy.-Treas., '65–'66); George Washington Univ., AB (Eng. Lit.), '41; San Jose State Col., Lib. Cert., '53; b. Wash., D.C., 1918; p. Lucius and Margaret Brooks Johnson; res: 1309 N. San Gabriel Ave., Azusa, Cal. 91702.

JOHNSON, TOKI SCHALK, Colmst., Feature Wtr., New Pittsburgh Courier, 315 E. Carson St., Pitt., Pa. 15219, '43–; Wtr., fiction, prior to '43; Pitt. Press Club (1st Black mbr.; Charter Mbr.), Wms. Press Club (VP, '69–; Mary Shine Aw., '69), Media Wm. of N.Y.; Feature aws., Nat. Nwsp. Publrs., '65–'67, '69; numerous cits.; Boston Univ.; b. Boston, Mass.; p. Theodore Otto and Mary Eleanor Wilkinson Schalk; h. John W. Johnson; res: 3510 Iowa St., Pitt., Pa. 15219.

JOHNSON, VICKI LYNNE, Indsl. Ed., Great Northern Oil Company, P.O. Box 3596, St. Paul, Minn. 55432, '67–; Knox Reeves Adv. Agcy., '66–'67; Northwestern IEA; Univ. of Minn., '62–'66; b. Richmond, Va., 1944; p. Kenneth and Dorothy Drews Johnson; res: 80 Logan Pkwy., Mpls., Minn. 55432.

JOHNSON, WINIFRED MacNALLY, Auth., articles

and poetry, four jr. novels (Westminster Press and Macrae Smith); NLAPW (Piedmont-Oakland Br., Pres., '52); Cal. Wtrs. Club (Dir., '62–'65), Auths. Guild, Intl. Platform Assn., Ina Coolbrith Circle (Grand Prize, '51); winner numerous poetry contests; Univ. of Cal., '26–'27; b. Louisville, Ky.; p. Winfield and Mayme Gilmore MacNally; h. Harold Johnson; c. Mrs. Caryl Hall, Mrs. Laurie Heil; res: 145 Stonecrest Dr., Napa, Cal. 94558.

JOHNSTON, BETTY JEANNE, Exec. Dir., Arizona Society for the Prevention of Blindness, Inc., 1515 E. Osborn Rd., Phoenix, Ariz. 85014, '66–; Dir. of Public Info., & Educ., Ariz. Div., Am. Cancer Soc.; PRSA, Ariz. Soc. of Assn. Execs.; Phoenix Press Club; Youngstown Univ., BS (Bus. Adm.), '60; Grad. Work, Ariz. State Univ., '68–; b. Cleve., Oh., 1932; p. Dwight and Adeline Girard Johnston; res: 904 W. Mission Lane, Phoenix, Ariz. 85021.

JOHNSTON, ELISE ENDLING, Off. Mgr., Johnston & Associates, P.O. Box 3493, Baton Rouge, La. 70821, '66–; Secy.-Treas., '64–'66; Owner, Mgr., Book Store, '68–; Altrusa; La. State Univ., BA, '59; b. San Jose, Cal., 1936; p. R. A. F. and Lillian Endling; h. Robert E. Johnston, Jr.; res: 815 W. Johnson St., Baton Rouge, La. 70802.

JOHNSTON, JANE, Dir., Wm.'s Activities, KSTP Radio-TV, 3415 University Ave., Mpls., Minn. 55414, '63–; Talent, WCCO-TV, WTCN-TV, KMSP-TV, Mpls., Minn., '60–'63; Talent, WDAY Radio-TV, '54–'60; WAVE Radio (Louisville, Ky.), '39–'42; AWRT (Northstar Chptr. VP, '66), Mpls. C. of C., Fashion Group; Who's Who of Am. Wm.; Univ. of Louisville, '39–'41; b. Anderson, Ind., 1922; p. George and Irene Gustin Johnston; c. Lynn J. Anderson, Scott N. Sheryak; res: 1300 Mt. Curve Ave., Mpls., Minn. 55403.

JOHNSTON, JESSIE ELIZABETH, Field Home Econst., Corning Glass Works, Corning, N.Y. 14830, '45–; Reg. Home Econst., Continental Baking Co., '43–'45; Nutritionist, Infant Welfare of Chgo., '42–'43; Supvsr., Ia., '41; Electrical Wms. Round Table (Nat. Treas., '68–'70, Nat. VP, '62–'64), AWRT, Wms. Adv. Club of Chgo., Am. Home Econs. Assn., Home Econsts. in Bus.; Ia. State Univ., BS (Home Econs.), '40; b. Chgo., Ill.; p. Theodore and Lee Summersby Johnston; res: 210 E. Pearson, Chgo., Ill. 60611.

JOHNSTON, MARGARET MIMS, Instr., Henry W. Grady School of Journalism, University of Georgia, Athens, Ga. 30601, '68–; Tchr., '66–'68; Edtl. Asst., Southern Baptist Fgn. Mission Bd. (Richmond, Va.), '65; '60–'64, '55–'59; Edtl. Asst., America's Textile Reporter, '59; Theta Sigma Phi, Assn. for Educ. in Jnlsm.; Mars Hill Col., AA, '53; Furman Univ., BA, '55 (magna cum laude); Syracuse Univ., MA (Jnlsm.), '65; b. Chester, S.C., 1933; p. John and Edith Mims Johnston; res: 235 Sycamore Dr., Athens, Ga. 30601.

JOHNSTON, MARGUERITE, Wtr., The Houston Post, 4747 Southwest Freeway, Houston, Tex. 77001, '68–; Colmst., '47–'68; Corr., Birmingham News, London Daily Mirror, '45–'46; Reptr., '39–'45; Auth: "A Happy Worldly Abode" ('64); WNPC, Press Club of Houston; Houston Cncl. on Alcoholism aw., '57; Planned Parenthood aw., '68; Theta Sigma Phi Headliner aw.; Birmingham-Southern Col., BA (cum laude); b. Birmingham, Ala., 1917; p. Robert and Marguerite Spradling Johnston; h. Charles W. Barnes; c. Susan, Patricia, Steven, Polly.

JOHNSTON, MYRNA MORNINGSTAR, Food Cnslt., Better Homes and Gardens, Meredith Corporation, 1716 Locust, Des Moines, Ia. 50303, '66–; Foods and Equipment Ed., '37–'66; Contrbr., Cookbks: "Better Homes and Gardens Cook Book" ('40), "Jr. Cook Book" ('55), "Barbecue Book" ('56), "Salad Book" ('58), "Meat Cook Book" ('59), "Holiday Cook Book" ('59), Tchr.; '23–'35; Theta Sigma Phi, WNPC; Drake Univ., BS, '23 (Distg. Svc. Alumni Aw., '59; b. Des Moines, Ia.; p. Edward R. and Ella Kimball Morningstar; h. Warren Johnston; c. Joed Johnston Steinberg; res: 3450 S.W. 31st St., Des Moines, Ia. 50321.

JOHNSTON, PAMELA, Mgr., PR, U.S. Consumer Product Division, The Singer Company, 30 Rockefeller Plaza, N.Y., N.Y. 10020, '68–; Mdsng. Distrb., J. C. Penney, '65–'68; Fashion Coordr., Retail Sls. Mgr., Tiger Fabrics, '63–'65; Adv. Club, Pubcty. Club, N.Y. Jaycees (Wms. Div. VP, '66–'68); Univ. of Conn., BS (Home Econs.), '63; b. Coatesville, Pa., 1940; p. David and Katherine McCall Johnston; res: 425 E. 63rd St., N.Y., N.Y. 10021.

JOHNSTON, WINIFRED, Dir., Open-Door Idea Agency, 516 Chautauqua Ave., Norman, Okla. 73069; '51–; Offcr. (in charge of progs.), Okla. State Soc. (Wash., D.C.), '49–'51; Tech. Ed., U.S. Naval Ordnance Lab., '45; Ed., Dir., Coop. Bks., '39–; Lectr., Wtrs. Workshops and Aesthetics, Univ. of Okla., '27–'45; Asst. in Eng., '23–'27; U.S. Signal Corps, '18–'20; Contrbr., news and mag. periodicals; Modern Lang. Assn. of Am., Shakespeare Assn., Auths. Guild, Southwest Wtrs. (Pres., '38), Norman (Okla.) Forum (Secy., '42–'45), Wash., D.C. Film Cncl., '46–'51; Wms. Nat. Bk. Assn.; Martha Foote Crow Poetry Aw., '24, '26; Central State Col., Teaching Cert., '14; N.Y. Inst. of Photog., '20; Univ. of Okla., BA, '24; Grad. Work, '25–'26; b. Topeka, Kan.; p. J. H. and Sophia Doonan Johnston; h. Charles M. Perry (dec.).

JOHNSTONE, KATHLEEN YERGER, Auth: "Collecting Seashells" (Grosset & Dunlap, '69), "Sea Treasure—A Guide to Shell Collecting" (Houghton Mifflin Co., '57); Lectr., hist., volunteer svc.; Miss. State Col. for Wm.; BA (Eng.), '27; b. Mobile, Ala., 1906; p. Arthur and Kathleen Williamson Yerger; h. Harry Inge Johnstone; c. M. Inge, Yerger, Douglas; res: 2209 River Forest Rd., Mobile, Ala. 36605.

JOINER, VERNA J., Auth., non-fiction; Contrb. Wtr., Reach Magazine, Warner Press, '68–; Col.,

"Teen Topics," '55–'68; Contrb. Ed., The Gospel Trumpet (now Vital Christianity), '50s; Auth: "From Papa and Me" ('56), "This Home We Build" (Warner, '57), "Growing Steady" (Warner, '59), "Five Minutes to Four" (Beacon, '60), "Your Dating Data" (Warner, '62), "What Teens Say" (Warner, '62), "When Love Grows Up" (Warner, '66); Southeastern La. Col., '25–'26, '51–'53; Anderson Col., '52; b. Covington, La., 1896; p. Alexander and Emma Spiers Jones; h. Charles Joiner; c. Charles, Ronald, Howell, Joyce (Mrs. Lloyd Baker), Marie (Mrs. LaNoyette Mayo), Lydia (Mrs. Dalton Martin); res: 212 N. Chesnut, Hammond, La. 70401.

JOLOWICZ, KATHRYN ANN, Home Furnishing Stylist, Doyle Dane Bernbach Inc., 20 W. 43rd St., N.Y., N.Y. 10036, '62–; Residential and Contract Decorator, '61–'62; Charlotte Brown Interiors; Consolidated Hotel; Lectr., Parsons Sch. of Design, '68; Sets and Hist. Adv. Cnslt.; Free-lance Showroom Decorator; NHFL, Parsons Alumnae; N.Y.U., BFA, '61; Parsons Sch. of Design, '61; b. N.Y.C., 1939; p. Paul and Ruth Eltzsch Jolowicz.

JONAS, MERRILL, Casting Supvsr., Ogilvy & Mather, Inc., 2 E. 48th St., N.Y., N.Y. 10017, '67–; Talent Agt., TV Comml. Dept., Ashley-Famous Agcy., '64–'67; TV Actress, '58–'64; Registrar, Am. Musical & Dramatic Acad., '62–'63; Assoc. Dir., Radio-TV Pubcty., Radio Free Europe, '55–'59; N.Y. Sch. of Interior Design; Neighborhood Playhouse.

JONES, BARBARA, Bus. Mgr., The Albany Herald, Treas., Gray Communications Systems, Inc., P.O. Box 48, Albany, Ga. 31702; Albany BPW (Past Pres.), AAUW (Albany Chptr. Past Pres.), Albany C. of C., Adv. Media Credit Execs. Assn., Nat. Assn. Nwsp. Purchasing Execs. Albany Commty. Cncl. (Pres.), Albany Assn. of Retarded Children (Dir.); Wesleyan Col., '37 (magna cum laude); b. Waycross, Ga.; p. Tillman and Kate Bowles Jones; res: 1112 Peachtree Terr., Albany, Ga. 31705.

JONES, BEA, Ed., Garden and Home, Newsday, Garden City, N.Y. 11530, '68–; Ed., Special Editions, Garden Colmst., '51–'67; Rewrite, '44–'51; Reptr., Nassau Daily Rev.-Star, '42–'44; articles, Winter Haven (Fla.) Chief; Co-auth., "Smash the Political Machine" (Brentano's, '32); Contrbr., Crowell-Collier Ency., '69; Garden Wtrs. Assn. of Am. (Pres., '70, '71; Dir., '68, '69); NWC of N.Y. (VP, '68, '69); Columbia Univ.; b. Bklyn., N.Y.; p. William and Eve Fiske McCree; h. Richard Wainwright Wyse; c. Dr. Ian Robertson Jones; res: 41 Belton Rd., Babylon, N.Y. 11702.

JONES, BEATRICE WASHBURN, Bk. Ed., Miami Herald, Herald Sq., Miami, Fla. 33101, '57–; Reptr., New Orleans (La.) Times Picayune, '35–'37; New York Sun; San Francisco (Cal.) Examiner; Minneapolis (Minn.) Tribune; h. Charles P. Jones.

JONES, BESS HARRIS, Public Info. Dir., Texas Tuberculosis and Respiratory Disease Association, 2406 Manor Rd., Austin, Tex. 78702, '56–; Pubcty., United Fund, '52; Reptr., Austin American Statesman, '49–'52; Info. Wtr., Tex. Centennial (Dallas) '36; Southwestern Banker, Texas Weekly, '35–'36; Theta Sigma Phi, Soc. of Austin Indsl. Eds., Austin Cerebral Palsy Center (Founding Pres., '48), Volunteer Cncl. of Austin State Sch. for Retarded Children (First Pres., '55), Governor's Advisory Comm. on TB Control, President's Comm. on Mental Retardation; Austin Col., '30; Univ. of Tex., BJ, '34; b. Smithville, Tex., 1913; p. Robert K. and Bess Nichols Harris; h. Herman Jones; c. Mrs. M. L. Cooper, Harris, Mark; res: 3303 Greenlee Dr., Austin, Tex. 78703.

JONES, BETTY ARLENE, PR Dir., Richard Roby Advertising Associates, Inc., 3209 N.W. 63rd St., Okla. City, Okla. 73116, '68–; Wms. Reptr., The Daily Oklahoman, Oklahoma City Times, '66–'68; '64–'65; Pubcty. Dir., Salvation Army of Tex., '65–'66; Theta Sigma Phi; Univ. of Okla., BA (Jnlsm.), '64; Currently attending Okla. City Univ., Sch. of Law; Southern Methodist Univ.; b. Ardmore, Okla., 1942; p. Oran and Ava Armstrong Jones; res: 3527 N.W. 54, Okla. City, Okla. 73112.

JONES, CLARA STANTON, Dir., Detroit Public Library, 5201 Woodward Ave., Detroit, Mich. 48202, '70–; Lib. Neighborhood Cnslt., '68–'70; Chief of Dept., Hubbard Br., '62–'68; Chief of Div. of Conely, Lothrop & Knapp branches, '51–'63; First Asst. and Young Adult Librn., Butzel Br., '49–'50; Young Adult Librn., Parkman Br., '48–'49; Adult Librn., Main Lib., '46–'48; Children's Librn., Detroit Public Lib., '44–'45; Librn., Booker T. Washington HS, New Orleans, La., '43; Assoc. Librn., Southern Univ. Lib., Baton Rouge, '40–'41; Ref. Librn., Dillard Univ., '38–'40; ALA (Administrative Sec.; Adult Svcs. Div. Planning Comm. for '70 Conf.; Social Responsibilities Roundtable), WNBA; First Recipient of "Aw. for Distinguished Librnship," ALA Black Caucus, '70; "Cert. of Merit," Detroit West Side Human Rels. Cncl., '56; Spelman Col., AB, '34; Univ. of Mich., AB, '38; b. St. Louis, Mo., 1913; p. Ralph Herbert and Etta C. James Stanton; h. Albert D. Jones; c. Stanton William, Vinetta Black (Mrs. Albert), Kenneth Albert; res: 16631 Princeton, Detroit, Mich. 48221.

JONES, DAISY, Garden Ed., The Cincinnati Post and Times Star, 800 Broadway, Cinn., Oh. 45202, '58–; Military Ed., Food Pg. Ed., Garden Ed., and Gen. Reptr., Cinn. Times Star, '35–'58; Weekly Garden Col., Cinn. Enquirer, '34–'35; Weekly Garden Prog., WLW, '33–'35; Weekly Garden Col., Western Hills Press, '33–'34: Am. Horticultural Soc., Royal Horticultural Soc.; Achiev. aw., Federated Gardens Club, '63; Cit., Oh. Assn. of Garden Clubs, '66; b. Falmouth, Ky., 1897; p. Walker and Elizabeth Pettit Woodhead; c. Florence Elizabeth Rentschler, George M.; res: 7344 Clovernook Ave., Cinn., Oh. 45231.

JONES, DAISY MARVEL, Prof. of Educ., Arizona

State University, College of Education, Forest Ave., Tempe, Ariz. 85281, '63–; Dir. of Elementary Educ. (Richmond, Ind.), '46–'63; Asst. Supvsr. (Muncie), '42–'46; Assoc. Prof. of Educ., Central Normal (Danville), '34–'42; Tchr. (Marion County), '24–'31, '33–'36; Critic Tchr., Ind. State Univ., '31–'33; Auth., Harper & Row, Basic Reading Series; Wtr., various educ. pubns.; Assn. for Supervision and Curriculum Dev. (Bd. of Dir. Mbr. at large, '69–'73), AAUW (Secy., '66–'68), Reading Cncl. (local chptr. Pres., '67–'68); Ind. State Univ., BS, '31; MS, '33 (Distg. Alumni Aw., '63); Ind. Univ., EdD, '47; b. Brownsburg, Ind., 1906; p. Harlen and Nannie Mark Marvel; h. Vivian L. Jones; res: 928 Terrace Rd., #102, Tempe, Ariz. 85281.

JONES, DOROTHY HOLDER, Auth., fiction: "The Wonderful World Outside" (Dodd, Mead, '59; winner of Dodd, Mead 17th Summer Lit. Competition), and "The Oldest One" ('63), "Those Gresham Girls" ('65), "Dress Parade" ('66), "An Understanding Heart" ('67), "Abbie Burgess: Lighthouse Heroine," ('69), all publ. by Funk & Wagnalls; articles and stories in more than 50 mags.; Children's Bk. Guild of Wash., D.C. (Treas.), '68–'69); Ga. Evening Col.; b. Houston, Tex.; h. Thomas A. Jones, Jr.; c. Bryan K., Vicki L.; res: 1300 Tracy Pl., Falls Church, Va. 22046.

JONES, FLORENCE KEUPP, Corp. Secy., Asst. to Pres., Bevel & Winthrop, Inc., 360 Lexington Ave., N.Y., N.Y. 10017, '64–; Asst. to Dir., Renault News Bur., '61–'64; Owner, Pres., Reed-Jones, Inc., Am. News Svc., '58–'61; VP, '49–'58; Colmst., Modern Science; BPW (Intl. Chptr. Pres.), OPC, PRSA cit.; b. Bklyn., N.Y., 1917; p. Frank and Elizabeth Frische Keupp; h. (div.); c. Judd Kent Jones, Jeffrey Peter Jones; res: 2900 NE 30 St., Fort Lauderdale, Fla. 33306.

JONES, GEORGIA L., Wms. Ed., KOTV, 302 S. Frankfort, Tulsa, Okla. 74120, '67–; AWRT; Scripps Col. (Phi Beta Kappa); b. Tusla, Okla., 1941; p. Jenkin Lloyd and Juanita Carlson Jones; h. Kenneth Snoke; res: 4107 E. 51st St., #114, Tulsa, Okla. 74135.

JONES, JANE C. B., Asst. PR, North American Rockwell Corp., Automotive Divisions, Clifford at Bagley, Detroit, Mich. 48231, '65–; Dir. of PR, Shatterproof Glass Co., '60–'65; Dir. of PR, Mercy Col., '56–'58; Edtl. Staff, Detroit News, '45–'53; Prodr., Dir., Educ. TV, WTVS (Detroit, Mich.); News Announcer, (Detroit, Mich.); News Announcer, WPAG (Ann Arbor); PRSA, Pilot, Intl. (Detroit Chptr. Bd. Mbr., '66, '68, '69) Pequaming Svc. Fndn.; Masonic Order (Great Falls, Mont. Chptr. Hon. Mbr.); U.S. Marine Corps, Reserve '52–; Detroit Press Club, Wms. Economic Club of Detroit; Univ. of Minn., PhB, '58; Grad. Work, Univ. of Detroit; b. Detroit, Mich.; p. John A. and Eda Moormann Beetham; h. C. P. Jones.

JONES, JANICE PERRY, Mgr., Dow Consumer Information Service, The Dow Chemical Co., 2030 Building, Abbott Rd. Midland, Mich. 48640, '66–; Tchr.,

Midland (Mich.) Public Schs., '66; Boulder Valley Public Schs. (Boulder, Colo.), '64–'65; AWRT, MCA Wms. Activities Comm., GMA Consumer Svcs. Comm.; Ball State Univ., BS (Jnlsm.), '64 (Mortar Board, Alpha Phi Gamma, Sigma Tau Delta, Alpha Chi Omega, Kappa Delta Pi); b. Anderson, Ind., 1942; p. Clifton and Doris Catt Perry; h. Curtis R. Jones; res: 1907 Eastlawn Dr., Midland, Mich. 48640.

JONES, JOAN WEBER, Ed., Employee Communications, Warner-Lambert, 201 Tabor Rd., Morris Plains, N.J. 07950; Mng. Ed., Lipton Magazine; Ed., Smith, Kline and French Labs; Caldwell Col., BA ('53); h. Paul M. Jones.

JONES, JUANITA PIPKIN, Asst. Reg. Dir., American Society Composers, Authors and Publishers, 806 17th Ave., S., Nashville, Tenn. 37203, '62–; Rec. Div., RCA Victor, '54–'62; Country Music Fndn. (Offcr., '69–), Country Music Assn. (Offcr., '64–'65), Acad. of Country and Western Music, NARAS (Dir., '67), Gospel Music Assn. ('65–'66), PRSA, AFA, AWRT (Nat. Eligibility Chmn., '67–'69); Wm. of the Yr., '67; Southern Missionary Col.; Draughn's Bus., Col.; Harris Sch. of Adv. Art; b. Nashville, Tenn.; p. Dewey and Helene Phillips Pipkin; h. J. Paul Jones; res: 1911 Lone Oak Circle, Nashville, Tenn. 37215.

JONES, JUNE ELEANOR, Traf. Mgr., Talent, KODA AM/FM, Taft Broadcasting Co. 4808 San Felipe, Houston, Tex. 77027, '61–; Traf. Mgr., KXYZ, '53–'61; Traf. Mgr., KNUZ, KQUE, '48–'53; Gen. Adv., Gregory Giezendaner Adv., '45–'48; AWRT; Univ. of Houston, '45–'47; b. Latexo, Tex., 1928; p. M. C. and Bethel Parsley Sims; h. (div.); c. Clara Elizabeth, June Eleanor; res: 3910 University Blvd., Houston, Tex. 77005.

JONES, LILLIAN FREUND, Media Dir., Sykes Advertising, Inc., 411 Seventh Ave., Pitt., Pa. 15219, '69– Media Dir., Bond & Starr, Inc., '68–'69; Media Byr., BBDO, '64–'65; Pitt. Adv. Club, NIAA; b. Hamburg, Germany, 1923; p. Kurt and Odette Furth Freund; h. Leonard E. Jones (div.); c. Dale C., Christopher D.; res: 589 Briarwood Ave., Pitt., Pa. 15228.

JONES, MADELINE ADAMS, Ed., Cowles Book Co., 488 Madison Ave., N.Y., N.Y. 10003, '69–; Prom. Mgr., Arco Publ. Co., '66–'69; Ed., Crown Publrs., '63–'66; Col. of William and Mary; Univ. of Ill., AB; b. Wash., D.C.; p. Leason and Jeannette Blaisdall Adams; h. K. Jones; c. Mrs. Anthony Prisendorf, Mrs. Jeffrey Casdin, Margot K.; res: 21 E. 10th St., N.Y., N.Y. 10003.

JONES, MARY ALICE, Auth., non-fiction, Apt. 908, 3415 West End, Nashville, Tenn. 37203; Cnslt. Bk. Ed., Rand McNally & Co., '63–; Auth: "Tell Me About God," "Tell Me About Jesus," "Bible Story of Creation," "Prayers for Young Children," "My First Book About Jesus," "Know Your Bible" (all for children), "The Faith of Our Children," "The Christian Faith Speaks to Children"; Auths. League, Theta Sigma Phi;

AAUW; Univ. of Tex., BA; Northwestern Univ., MA; Yale Univ., PhD; b. Dallas, Tex.; p. Paul and Mamir Henderson Jones; res: Apt. 908, 3415 West End, Nashville, Tenn. 30203.

JONES, NANCY CAROL, Asst. Prof. of Jnlsm., The Pennsylvania State University, School of Journalism, 216 Carnegie Building, University Park, Pa. 16802, '67–; Ed., AP (Louisville, Ky.), '61–'65; Melbourne (Fla.) Bur. Chief and Hollywood (Fla.) City Hall Reptr., Miami Herald, '59–'61; Reptr., The Newport News (Va.) Daily Press, '56–'58; articles in prof. pubns.; Theta Sigma Phi (Fac. Advisor to Student Chptr.; Founding Mbr. of State Col. Pfsnl. Club), Pa. Wms. Press Assn.; Univ. of Pitt., BA (Jnlsm.), '56 (magna cum laude); Northwestern Univ., MS (Jnlsm.), '59; Univ. of Mo., PhD (Jnlsm.), '67 Sci. Grant); b. Pitt., Pa., 1934; p. Eugene E. and Mary Jane Cassilly Jones; res: Apt. 5, 204 E. Hamilton Ave., State College, Pa. 16801.

JONES, OLGA ANNA, Auth., non-fiction; Ed. in Chief, U.S. Off. of Educ., 20 yrs.; Assoc. Dir., Cncl. of Social Agcys. (Columbus, Oh.), '23–'28; Ed., Oh. League of Women Voters, '22–'23; Edtl. Staff, Columbus Citizen, '18–'22; Auth, two editions of "Churches of the Presidents in Washington"; Wash. Altrusa Club (Pres.), WNPC, NEA (Life Mbr.); "Golden Circle Cert.", Ohio State Univ. Assoc.; Earlham Col.; Oh. State Univ.; b. Hollansburg, Oh., 1888; p. Amos and Elizabeth Jane Harrison Jones; res: 3133 Connecticut Ave., N.W., Wash., D.C. 20008.

JONES, ROMELLE RANKIN, Prod. Mgr., MAC Publications, 6565 Sunset Blvd., L.A., Cal. 90028, '59–; Northern Montana Col., '48–'50; b. Great Falls, Mont., 1930; p. Walter and Virginia West Rankin; h. John Jones; c. John Charles, Theresa Romelle, Maria Virginia; res: 12952 Fernmont, Sylmar, Cal. 91342.

JONES, RUBY A., Eng. and Jnlsm. Tchr., Madison Heights Senior High School, 4610 Madison Ave., Anderson, Ind. 46013, '59–; Colmst, "As I See It," Middletown News, '58–; Alexandria Times-Tribune, '64–; Auth: "The Searching Wind," "Notes of A Journey," "Westward Ho!"; Contrbr., articles, religious pubns., several anthologies; Wtr., "The Hoosier Schoolmaster" (Jnl. of Dept. of Educ.); Poet, appearing in "Encore" (Poetry quarterly, Albuquerque, N.M.) and two prof. mags.; AAUW, Nat. Cncl. of Tchrs. of Eng.; Published winner, Nat. Poetry Anthology Contest, '63–'64; '65, '66; Poetry Aw., Poets of Ind., '63; Who's Who of Am. Wm.; Who's Who in the Midwest; Earlham College, AB, '30; Butler Univ.; Ind. Univ.; Ball State Univ.; b. Fortville, Ind., 1908; p. James W. and Ora C. James Hiday; h. Harry Paul Jones; c. James, David, Jon; res: Maplestone Farm, R.R. 1, Box 53, Daleville, Ind. 47334.

JONES, SHARON TUOR, Ed., State Farm Mutual Insurance Companies, 4600 25th Ave. N.E., Salem, Ore. 97303, '65–; Policy Issue and Med. Sec., '63–'65;

Ore. Assn. of Educators and Communicators, ICIE; Ore. State Univ.; b. Earlville, Ill., 1944; p. Frank A. and Viola C. Franta Tuor; h. Gordon Wayne Jones; res: Rte. 1, Box 246, Hubbard, Ore. 97032.

JORDAN, ALEXANDRA SLOSSON, Asst. Customer Rels. Dir., Professional Color Laboratories, 306 W. First Ave., Roselle, N.J. 07203, '68–; Asst. Ed., Better Homes and Gardens Magazine, '65–'68; Asst. to the Dir. of News Svcs., N.Y. World's Fair Corp., '64–'65; Asst. to the Dir. of PR, Pocono Summer Playhouse (Mountainhome, Pa.), '63; Copy Trainee, Time Magazine, '61–'62; Free-lance Photogr.; Theta Sigma Phi; Stephens Col., AA, '58; Pa. State Univ., BA (Jnlsm.), '60; Boston Univ. (Photojnlsm.); b. Buffalo, N.Y., 1939; p. John S. and Emily V. Broaddus Slosson; h. Alexander Jordan; res: 414 Walnut Ave., Cranford, N.J. 07016.

JORDAN, BARBARA ALDRICH, Dir., Morrill Memorial Library, Norwood, Mass. 02062, '68–; Ref. Dept., Reader Svcs., Carnegie Lib. (Pitt., Pa.), '51–'68; Instr., Carnegie Lib. Sch., '51; Dir., Plymouth (Mass.) Public Lib., '47–'48; other libs., '34–'47; AAUW, ALA, Pitt. Lib. Club (Pres., '63, VP, '67–'68), Mass. Lib. Assn.; Wheaton Col., AB (Eng. Lit.), '30; Simmons Col., BS (Lib. Sci.), '45; b. Boston, Mass., 1908; p. Sydney and Ruth Elliot Jordan; res: 99 Day St., Norwood, Mass. 02062.

JORDAN, GRACE EDGINGTON, Free-lance Auth., fiction, non-fiction, Fac. in Jnlsm., Univ. of Wash., '17–'20; Fac. in Jnlsm., Alumni Sec., Univ. of Ore., '17–'24; Fac. Jnlsm., Univ. of Cal., '22; Reptr., Eugene (Ore.) Guard Register, '16–'17; Auth: "Home Below Hell's Canyon" ('54), "Canyon Boy" ('60), "King's Pines" ('61), "Idaho Reader" ('63); Weekly Colm., Idaho nwsps., '64–; Monthly Colm., Republican Call (Seattle), '65–; many short stories; Theta Sigma Phi (Nat. Organizer, '19–'23), NLAPW, AAUW; Univ. of Ore., BA, '16 (magna cum laude; Phi Beta Kappa); b. Wasco, Ore.; p. Dr. Jesse and Martha Ann Hartley Edgington; h. Leonard B. Jordan; c. Patricia Jean Story, Joseph L., Stephen E.; res: Boise, Idaho 83705.

JORDAN, HENRIETTA, VP, Assoc. Prodr., Format Productions, Inc., 12754 Ventura Blvd., Studio City, Cal. 91604, '62–; Adm., Prod., Sales '59–'62; Asst. to VP and Exec. Prodr., UPA Pictures, '50–'59; NATAS, AWRT, Pacific Pioneer Bdcstrs.; b. Bklyn., N.Y., h. Edward Jordan; res: 12100 Valley Spring Lane, Studio City, Cal. 91604.

JORDAN, JENICE ANN KRESSER, Wms. Feature Wtr., Columbus Dispatch , 34 S. Third St., Columbus, Oh. 43216, '61–; Homes Wtr., '56–; Local Corr., Fairchild Publ., '53–'56; Soc. Dept., Sandusky Register, '48–'50; Theta Sigma Phi, Oh. Nwsp. Wms. Assn., Nat. Soc. of Interior Designers, Design Wtrs. Intl.; Marygrove Col. (Detroit, Mich.), '46–'48; b. Findley, Oh., 1928; p. Arthur and Margaret Burton Kresser; c. Abbe, Cynthia, Jenifer; res: 1164 Shady Hill Dr., Columbus, Oh. 43221.

JORDAN, JOYCE SMITH, Bd. of Dirs., Secy. of Radio Columbus, Inc. (WDAK), Columbus, Ga.; Adm. Asst., Radio WDAK '65–; Past Mbr., Bd. of Dirs., Secy., Radio Albany Inc., Albany, Ga.; AWRT (Chattahoochee Valley Chptr. Pres.); Univ. of Ga.; b. Pine Mountain, Ga., 1935; p. Dennis and Ida Sturdivant Smith; h. Joe Jordan; c. Lisa Denise, Angela Louise; res: 5909 Sherborne Dr., Columbus, Ga. 31904.

JORDEN, ELEANOR HARZ, Visiting Prof., Div. of Modern Languages, Cornell University, Ithaca, N.Y., '69–; Chmn., Dept. of East Asian Languages, Fgn. Svc. Inst., Dept. of State (Wash., D.C.), '69, '61–'67; Chmn., Vietnamese Lang. Div., '67–'69; Scientific Linguist, '59–'61; Dir., Fgn. Svc. Inst. Japanese Lang. Sch., Am. Embassy (Tokyo), '50–'55; Instr. in Japanese, Yale Univ., '47–'48; '43–'46; Auth., nine lang. textbks.; Linguistic Soc. of Am., Assn. of Tchrs. of Japanese; Dept. of State Superior Hon. Aw., '65; Bryn Mawr Col., AB, '42; Yale Univ., MA, '43; PhD, '50; b. N.Y.C.; p. William and Eleanor Funk Harz; h. William Jorden; c. W. Temple, Eleanor H., M. Telva; res: 119 N. Sunset Dr., Ithaca, N.Y. 14850.

JORGENSON, MARY LOUISE, Adm. Asst., Bethesda Hospital Association, 320 S. Hubbard St., Crookston, Minn. 56716, '67– Dir. PR, Dir. of Volunteers, Printing Dept. Chief, Secy. to Admr., Special Projects Dir., '60–'67; PR Dir., N.W. Educ. Improvement Assn., '60–'67; BPW (Pres.), '61), Am. Soc. for Hosp. PR (Chapter Mbr.), PRSA; Patient Rels. Prog. aw., S. M. Edison Chemical Co., '63; Nat. Hon. Mention for external bul., MacEachern aws., '63; Hosp. Aux. Nwsltr. aw., Minn. Hosp. Assn. Aux., '63; b. International Falls, Minn., 1926; p. Martin David and Clemye Alberta Dahl Jorgenson; res: 109 Lincoln Ave., Crookston, Minn. 56716.

JOSTEDT, MARGARET, Sr. Copywtr., William Esty Company, 100 E. 42nd St., N.Y., N.Y. 10016, '69–; VP, Avery, Hand & Co. (Westport, Conn.), VP, Gardner Adv. Co.; Educ. Dir., KWK-TV (St. Louis, Mo.); AWNY, Wms. Adv. Club of St. Louis (Past Pres.), Theta Sigma Phi, NATAS, St. Louis Adv. Wm. of Yr., '66; First Pl., Intl. TV Film Festival at Cannes, '67; First Pl., Am. TV Film Festival, '61; Adv. Wtrs. Club of St. Louis aws., '64–'66; Who's Who Among Students in Am. Cols. & Univs.; Webster Col., AB (Eng.), '47 (Morton J. May Aw.); b. St. Louis, Mo.; p. Theodore and Catherine Egan Jostedt; res: 225 E. 36th St., N.Y., N.Y. 10016.

JOSTEN, MARGARET MARY, Commty. Rels. Wtr., Cincinnati Enquirer, 617 Vine St., Cinn., Oh. 45202, '68–; Staff Reptr., '50–'68; Theta Sigma Phi; Oh. Assoc. Press commty. svc. aw. for series on the Negro commty., '67; AP Mng. Eds. Assn. cit. for coverage of riot in Cinn., '67; Oh. Univ., BS (Jnlsm.), '45; b. Athens, Oh., 1923; p. Martin and Isabelle Fraser Josten; h.

G. E. Mitchell (dec.); res: Edgecliff Apts., 2200 Victory Pkwy., Cinn., Oh. 45206.

JOYNER, LOUISE YURT, Ed., Krispy Kreme Doughnut Corp., 1820 Ivy Ave., Winston-Salem, N.C. 27102, '57–; Bakers Assn. of Carolinas (Secy., '47–'57), Western Carolinas Retail Bakers Assn. (Secy., '42–'47); b. Louisville, Ky., 1907; p. Alois and Amelia Scherer Yurt; h. F. Leon Joyner; c. Jimise (Mrs. Douglas Hunt); res: 4211 Kings Ct., Jacksonville, Fla. 32217.

JUNAS, LILLIAN M., Instr., Photojnlsm., Ball State University, Center for Journalism, Muncie, Ind. 47306, '67–; Asst. Dir. Public Info., Col. Photogr., Ed., Coordr. of audio visual aids, Sports Info. Dir., Juniata Col., '64–'67; Asst. Prof. Jnlsm., Eng. Composition, Lock Haven (Pa.) State Col., '61–'63; Photog. Lectr., S.D. State Univ.: Reptr.-Photogr., Hazleton Standard-Speaker, '57–'59; pic.-stories, various pubns.; three one-man photo. exhbns.; Theta Sigma Phi, Nat. Press Photogrs. Assn., Am. Nwsp. Guild, Univ. Photogrs. Assn. (Commtns. VP, '69), Nat. Cncl. of Col. Pubn. Advisers, Soc. for Photographic Educ., Assn. for Educ. in Jnlsm.; Pa. State Univ., BA (Jnlsm.), '57; MA (Photojnlsm.), '61; Country Sch. of Photog., Pfsnl. Cert., '64; Banff (Can.) Sch. of Fine Arts, '67–'68; Center of the Eye, Aspen, Colo., '69; b. Hazelton, Pa., 1938; p. Paul and Elizabeth Wargo Junas; res: 936 Peace St., Hazleton, Pa. 18201.

JURGENSEN, BARBARA BITTING, Auth., non-fiction: "Leaping Upon The Mountains" ('60), "All The Bandits of China" ('65), "Oh, Please . . . Not Bethlehem" ('66), "Men Who Dared" ('67), "Parents, Ugh!" ('68), "Quit Bugging Me" ('68), "The Lord Is My Shepherd, But" ('69); several hundred mag. articles; St. Olaf Col., BA, '50; b. Excelsior, Minn., 1928; p. W. H. and Ethel Nesbitt Bitting; h. L. Richard Jurgensen; c. Janet, Marie, Peter; res: 216 Fairmont Dr., De Kalb, Ill. 60115.

JURMA, MALL KUUSIK, Asst. Ed., Wtr., Voice of America, Estonian Service, U.S. Information Agency, Wash., D.C. 20547, '51–; Inspector, Public Libs., Ministry of Educ., Estonia; Sr. Librn., Central Lib., City of Tallinn, Estonia; PEN, AAUW; Tartu Univ. (Estonia), MA; Columbia Univ. Writers' Sch.; b. Tallinn, Estonia; p. Juhan and Pauline Kassik Kuusik; h. Endel Jurma; res: 24 Central Ave., Ridgefield Park, N.J. 07660.

JURNEY, DOROTHY M., Wms. Ed., Detroit Free Press, 321 W. Lafayette, Detroit, Mich. 48231, '59–; Wms. Ed., Miami Herald, '49–'59; Asst. Wms. Ed., Miami News, '46–'49; '43–'44; Asst. City Ed., Washington D.C. News, '44–'46; Asst. Press Rep., Panama Canal, '41–'42; Wms. Ed., Gary Post Tribune, '39–'41; Reptr., Photogr., Ed., Michigan City (Ind.) News, '30–'39; Fla. WPC (Life Mbr.), Mich. WPC, Theta Sigma Phi (Nat. Headliner aw., '56); Twice winner, second pl. gen. excellence, J. C. Penney-Univ. of Mo. contest; Western Col. for Wm., '26–'28; Northwestern Univ.

Medill Sch. of Jnlsm., BS, '30; b. Michigan City, Ind., 1909; p. H. Roy and M. Zeola Hershey Misener; h. (sep.) res: 16258 Parkside, Detroit, Mich. 48221.

JUSTICE, KATHERINE, Actress, c/o Mark Levin Associates, 332 S. Beverly Dr., Beverly Hills, Cal. 90212; Films: "The Way West," "Five Card Stud."

JUSTIS, NELLIE RIDDLE, Dept. Ed., Scottsbluff Daily Star-Herald, 1405 Broadway, Scottsbluff, Neb. 69361, '52–; Soc. Wtr., News-Blade, (Bridgeport, Neb.), '45–'46; Soroptimists (Scotts Bluff County PR Chmn., '66–'67; Secy. '68); b. Bridgeport, Neb., 1914; p. Rolland and Myrtle Middleton Riddle; h. Gale Justis; c. Royce Plummer, Larry Plummer, Mrs. Rodney Kister, Sue Justis; res: 1114 E. 15th St., Scottsbluff, Neb. 69361.

JUSTUS, MAY, Juv. Auth., 50 bks, incl: "The Complete Peddler's Pack" (Univ. of Tenn. Press, '67), "New Boy In School (Hastings House, '62; chosen Ambassador Bk., Eng. Speaking Un.); 5 Jr. Lit. Guild Selections; Tchr., 25 yrs.; Univ. of Tenn., '28–'35; b. Del Rio, Tenn., 1898; p. Stephen and Margaret Brooks Justus; res: Rte. 1, Tracy City, Tenn. 37387.

K

KAEHELE, EDNA DYKES, Auth: "Triumph Over Cancer," "Training the Family Dog," "Sealed Orders," and numerous poems and articles for nat. mags.; b. Oh.; p. John and Maud Dykes; h. Robert Kaehele (div.); c. Jerry, Dean, Richard, Sharon Kaehele German; res: 55 W. Lakeview Ave., Columbus, Oh. 43202.

KAEL, PAULINE, Movie Critic, The New Yorker, 25 W. 43 St., N.Y., N.Y. 10036, '68–; Auth: "I Lost it at the Movies" ('65), "Kiss Kiss Bang Bang" ('68), "Going Steady" ('70); Univ. of Cal. (Berkeley), '36–'40; b. Sonoma County, Cal., 1919; p. Isaac Paul and Judith Friedman Kael; c. Gina James.

KAHN, FLORENCE GOLDEN, VP, George N. Kahn Company, 212 Fifth Avenue, N.Y., N.Y. 10010, '49–; Pres., Landmark Industries, '60–; VP, Stafford Assoc., '58–'68; VP, Rsch. Cncl., '60–'64; VP, Gift Cncl., '59–'60; Gussow-Kahn Adv., '42–'48; Tchr: Baruch Grad. Sch. of Bus., CCNY, Fordham Univ.; Cnslt.; Lectr.; AWNY, N.Y. League BPW, Beta Gamma Sigma, AAUP, AAUW; Bklyn. Col., BA, '33; Columbia Univ. MA (Fine Arts), '42; MBA (Mkt., Mgt.), '58; p. Bernard and Sophia Cotlow Golden; h. George N. Kahn; c. Phyllis, Bruce; res: 20 Park Ave., N.Y., N.Y. 10016.

KAHN, HANNAH, Poetry Rev. Ed., Miami Herald, 1 Herald Plaza, Miami, Fla., 33101, '58–; Auth., "Eve's Daughter" (bk. of poems, '62); poetry published in Harper's, Saturday Review, N.Y. Times, McCall's,

Ladies Home Journal, other mags.; Theta Sigma Phi (Commty. Headliner Aw., '59), Poetry Soc. of Great Britain and Am. (winner, Intl. Sonnet Competition, '57), Poetry Soc. of Am., Poetry Soc. of Va., Poetry Soc. of Ga.; Acad. of Am. Poets; Dade County Assn. for Retarded Children (past Pres.); b. N.Y.C., 1911; p. David and Sarah Abrahams; h. Frank M. Kahn; c. Melvin A., Daniel L., Vivian Dale; res: 40 N.E. 69th St., Miami, Fla. 33138.

KAHN, LUCILLE HAVILL, City Ed., Daily and Sunday Times, Waverly Pl., Melbourne, Fla. 32901, '69–; Wms. Ed., '61–'69; PR, State of Ill.; Prog. Dir., Radio WMBB (Melbourne); Fla. Press Wms. Club; Northwestern Univ.; b. Chgo., Ill.; p. Frederick and Ogla Solberg Havill; h. Karl Kahn (dec.); res: 2335 St. Andrews Circle, Melbourne, Fla. 32901.

KAIDEN, NINA, Pres., Ruder & Finn Fine Arts, 110 E. 59th St., N.Y., N.Y. 10022, '69–; VP, '64–'69; Dir. of Fine Arts, '59–'64; Graphics Dir., '58–'59; Dir. of Special Projects, Am. Fed. of the Arts, '51–'57; Cnslt., Lincoln Ctr. for the Performing Arts; Jesse H. Jones Hall for the Performing Arts; Cleveland Playhouse; Harsen Hall, Harvard Univ. Sch. of Educ.; Ed., art bks.; Museum of Graphic Arts (Adv. Cncl.), N.Y. Bd. of Trade (Arts Adv. Cncl.); Emerson Col., BA, '51; b. N.Y.C., 1931; p. Frank and Janice Feldman Nirenberg; h. Norman Wright; c. Thomas Faulds Kaiden; res: 15 W. 81st St., N.Y., N.Y. 10024.

KAISER, INEZ YEARGAN, Owner, Inez Kaiser & Associates, Suite 1108, 928 Grand Ave., Kan. City, Mo. 64106; Tchr., Home Econs., '50–'64; Civil Svc. employee and Tchr., '44–'50; Tchr., elementary sch., '40–'44; PR Cnslt. and Free-lance Wtr.; Am. Home Econs. Assn., Home Econsts. in Business, Publicity Club of N.Y., Adv. Club of N.Y., Wash., D.C. Press Club, AWRT, PRSA, PR Soc. of Kan. City, NAMW, NAMD (Secy., '69–'70; Betty Jayne Everett Aw., '69), Am. Soc. for Hosp. PR; Media' Wm. of the Yr., '67; Conf. of Nat. Real Estate Brokers Assn. Aw., '68; Nat. Shoe Inst. Golden Slipper Aw., '65; West Coast Area Golden Mike Aw., '68; AIMBW Aw.; Auth., "Soul Food Cookery"; Kan. City Jr. Col., '35–'37; Kan. State Tchrs. Col., BS (Home Econs.); Columbia Univ., MA; b. Kan. City, Kan., 1918; p. Leroy and Louise Menser Yeargan; h. Richard Kaiser; c. Richard S., Jr.; res: 2705 Garfield, Kan. City, Mo. 64109.

KAISER, JOAN, Fashion, Beauty Ed., Los Angeles Herald-Examiner, 1111 S. Broadway, L.A., Cal. 90015, '65–; Fashion Wtr., '60–'65; Fashion Wtr., L.A. Herald Express, '55–'60; Theta Sigma Phi, Fashion Group; Fashion Circle West (Chmn., '68–'70); Costume Cncl., L.A. County Museum of Art; Comm. of Pfsnl. Wm. of Southern Cal., Symphony Assn.; Opera Assn. of Music Center; Univ. of Southern Cal., BS, '56; b. L.A., Cal.; p. Irvin and Florence Michaelson Kaiser.

KALISON, ADRIENNE, Assoc. Prod., CBS Television Network, 524 W. 57th St., N.Y., N.Y. 10019, '66–;

employed as clerk-typist, '50; NATAS; b. Bklyn., N.Y., 1930; p. William and Bertha Kronengold Kalison; res: 372 Central Park W., N.Y., N.Y. 10025.

KALMBACH, MARGARET HAWKINS, Adm. Asst., South Carolina Educational TV Network, 2712 Millwood Ave., Columbia, S.C. 29205, '65–; Tchr., Florence HS, '38–'39; AWRT (Palmetto Chptr. Pres., '68–'69), BPW (Carolina Chptr. 2nd VP, '69–'70); Col. Who's Who, '37–'38; Pi Beta Phi (S.C. Alpha Chptr. Pres.); Univ. of S.C., BS, '38; b. Ft. Wayne, Ind., 1919; p. Joseph and Maude Miller Hawkins; h. R. Lynn Kalmbach (dec.); c. Jo Ann (Mrs. James Y. Campbell, Jr.), Roberta (Mrs. Roger K. Mahaffey), Betty Jane; res: Hawkinshurst, Hopkins, S.C. 29061.

KAMENITSA, MAXINE ELLIOTT, Early Childhood Curriculum Specialist, Southwest Educational Development Laboratory, Suite 550, Commodore Perry Hotel, Austin Tex., '68–; Ft. Worth, Ind. Sch. Dist., '60–'68; Tex. Christian Univ., '58–'60; Ft. Worth Children's Museum, '55–'60; Tex. Wm.'s Univ., '51–'56; U.S. Govt., '46–'48; City of Denton, '48–'49; Conslt., Fndn. Visually Handicapped Children, '54; Ed., numerous childhood educ. handbks.; Theta Sigma Phi (Denton Chptr. Pres., '45–'47), Alpha Delta Kappa, Who's Who in Am. Cols. and Univs., '45; N. Tex. State Univ., BS, '50; Tex. Wm.'s Univ., MA, '68; b. Noedesha, Kan.; p. William and Beulah Morrow Elliott; h. William Kamenitsa; c. Dennis, Laura, Cindy; res: 2017 David Dr., Ft. Worth, Tex. 76111.

KAMINKOWITZ, GRACE, Adv., Fashion Coordr., Helene Curtis, 4401 W. North Ave., Chgo., Ill. 60639, '63–; Copy Chief, '61–'63; Copywtr., May Co., '57; Retail Adv. Mgr., Montogomery Ward & Co., '55–'61; Theta Sigma Phi (Chgo. Chptr. Pres., '66–'67); Univ. of Iowa, BA, '55; grad. work, Northwestern Univ.; b. N.Y.C., 1935; p. Louis and Gertrude Noachs Kaminkowitz; res: 505 N. Lake Shore Dr., Chgo., Ill. 60611.

KAMINS, JEANETTE, Wtr., Radio, TV, Stage; Auth: "A Husband Isn't Everything" (St. Martin's, '66), "Everything But A Husband" (St. Martin's, '62); Auths. Guild of Am.; N.Y.U., Univ. of Colo.; b. Boston, Mass.; p. Samuel and Bessie Bikman Kamins; res: 350 W. 55th St., N.Y., N.Y. 10019.

KAMISHER, MARCIA, Beauty Ed., Teen mag., Petersen Publishing Co., 770 Lexington Ave., N.Y., N.Y. 10021, '69–;

KANE, BEATRICE COLLINS, Eng. Tchr., Edgewood High School, 1000 Edgewood Ave., Madison, Wis. 53711, '48–'69; Eng. Tchr., Univ. of Wisconsin, '43–'48; Theta Sigma Phi (Col. Chptr. Cup, '33; Charter Mbr., Madison Chptr.); Univ. of Michigan, BA, '34; Wayne State Univ., MA, '39; b. Detroit, Mich. 1913; p. Raymond W. and Margaret Jane Deppe Collins; h. Kenneth J. Kane; c. Kathleen Margaret; res: 501 S. Midvale, Madison, Wis. 53711.

KANE, DOROTHY NOYES, Asst. Prof., Educ., Southern Connecticut State College, 501 Crescent St., New Haven, Conn. 06515, '66–; VP, Treas., Noyes & Sproul (N.Y.C.), '37–'60; AWNY (Past Treas.), NEA, Planned Parenthood League; AFA Adv. Wm. of the Yr., '57; Auth., "Your Child" (Doubleday, '63); Goddard Col., BA, '64; Yale Univ., MPH, MUS, '66; b. Balt., Md., 1906; p. Selden and Flora Keily Noyes; h. Lawrence Kane; c. Barbara Chamberlain Sproul; res: 14 Charlton Hill, Hamden, Conn. 06518.

KANE, ELINOR MARGARET, Copy Ed., Atlantic Monthly, 8 Arlington St., Boston, Mass. 02116, '63–; Asst. Copy Ed., Proofreader, '61–'63; Rsch. Tech., Harvard Col., '59–'60; Rsch. Asst., Eye and Ear Infirmary, '58–'59; Wheaton Col., '58; b. Lawrence, Mass., 1937; p. Henry and Elinor Moore Kane; res: 26 Juniper Rd., Andover, Mass. 01810.

KANTOR, KATHERINE PEDELL, Fashion Ed., Suffolk Sun, 303 Marcus Blvd., Deer Park, N.Y. 11729, '66–; Free-lance Wtr., mags., adv. agcys.; Staff Wtr., TV Guide, '52–'56; Nwsp. Wms. Club of N.Y.; Hunter Col., BA (Eng.), '46; b. N.Y.C., p. Boris and Mary Solovey Pedell; h. Leonard Kantor; c. David John, William Matthew; res: 44 Spring Ct., Muttontown, P.O. Syosset, N.Y. 11791.

KAPLAN, HARRIET ATLASS, Gen. Mgr., WAYS, 400 Radio Rd., Charlotte, N.C. 28214, '65–; Dir., Radio-TV, Cushman Veeck & Samuel (Chgo., Ill.), '61–'65; Dir., Public Affairs Prog., WBBM Radio-TV (Chgo.), '56–'61; Prod. Staff, WBBM-TV, '55–'56; h. Stanley Kaplan.

KAPLAN, SYLVIA K., Librn., Dept. of Mental Health, State of Illinois, 160 N. La Salle St., Rm. 1500, Chgo., Ill. 60601, '67–; Librn., '53–'66; AAUW (Secy., Chgo. Chptr.), Special Libs. Assn., ALA, Med. Lib. Assn. (Cert., '68), NEA, Am. Assn. of Intl. Semantics; Northwestern Univ., PhB, '56; Rosary Col., MA (Lib. Sci.), '61; Univ. of Ill., Post-masters Work, '65–; b. Chgo., Ill., 1921; p. Max and Gertrude Yalowitz Kaplan; h. Milton I. Kaplan; res: 5541 S. Everett St., Apt. 815, Chgo., Ill. 60637.

KAPLOVITZ, SUSAN ENID, Wtr., PR, State Street Bank and Trust Company, 225 Franklin St., Boston, Mass., '70–; Tchr., Russian and Eng., Acton-Boxborough Reg. HS, '67–'69; Tchr., Eng. and Speech, Southwick HS, '66–'67; Mass. Indsl. Eds. Assn., Bellringer Aw. from Boston Pubcty. Club, '70; Mt. Holyoke Col., BA (Eng.), '66; b. Norfolk, Va., 1944; p. Maxwell and Fay Ediss Kaplovitz; res: 180 Holworthy St., Cambridge, Mass. 02138.

KAPST, MARY IRETON, Adult Svcs. Librn., Hawaii Public Library, Waianuenue St., Hilo, Hi. 96720, '69–; Librn., Am. C. of C. (Manila, The Philippines), '63–'66; Librn., U.S. Naval Base Dependents Sch. (Sangley Point, Philippines), '58–'62; Dir., USIS Libs. (Manila), '53–'57; Librn., USIS (Cebu, Philippines), '51–'53; Librn., U.S. Public Health Svc., (Cinn., Oh.), '49–'51;

Librn., Delphos (Oh.) Public Lib., '46–'49; ALA, Philippine Lib. Assn. (Bd. of Dirs.), Assn. of Special Libs. of The Philippines (Bd. of Dirs.); Wilmington (Oh.) Col., BS, '33; Univ. of Illinois, BS (Lib. Sci.), '42; h. Michael R. Kapst.

KAPSTEIN, DOROTHY MELTZER, Fashion Ed., Seventeen, 320 Park Ave., N.Y., N.Y. 10022, '64–; own art gallery, '55–'64; Ed., Tobe and Assocs., '45–'55; Lectr., sch. groups; fashion show planning, direction; TV appearances; extensive youth activities; N.Y.U. Sch. of Retailing, '44 (Hall of Fame, Class Pres.); b. Bayonne, N.J., 1923; p. Samuel and Pauline Pollock Meltzer; h. John J. Kapstein; c. Matthew, Ethan; res: 29 E. Ninth St., N.Y., N.Y. 10003.

KAPUSTA, BARBARA NICHOLS, Asst. to Dir., Cosmopolitan Professional Placement, Inc., 2007 Investment Bldg., 239 Fourth Ave., Pitt., Pa. 15222, '67–; Employment Cnslr. in charge of med. placement, '65–'67; part-time PR, Am. PR Assocs., '64–'65; Allegheny Bus. and Pfsnl. Wms. Club (2nd VP, '69–); Theta Sigma Phi; Duquesne Univ., BA (Jnlsm.), '64; b. Pitt., Pa., 1942; p. Dr. Thomas and Berniece Jacobs Nichols; res: 2104 Wendover Pl., Pitt., Pa. 15217.

KARABAICH, MARY L., PR Dir., American Red Cross, Pacific Northwest Division, 2106 Second Ave., Seattle, Wash. 98121, '63–; Pers., The Boeing Company, '61–'63; Wtr., Catholic Northwest Progress, '57–'61; Hosp. Recreation Worker, Am. Nat. Red Cross, '52–'56; U.S. Fgn. Svc., '51; Wtr., Northwest Airlines, '48–'50; Theta Sigma Phi (Seattle Prof. Chptr. Treas., '68–'69); Univ. of Washington, BA, '48; MA (Commtns.), '58; b. Seattle, Wash.; p. John and Mary Orlic Karabaich; res: 6433 Flora Ave. S., Seattle, Wash. 98108.

KARL, JEAN EDNA, VP, Dir., Children's Bk. Dept., Atheneum Publishers, 122 E. 42nd St., N.Y., N.Y. 10017, '65–; Dir., Children's Bk. Dept., '61–; Children's Bk. Ed., Abingdon Press, '56–'61; Jr. Edtl. Asst., Asst. Ed., Scott, Foresman & Co., '49–'56; Co-dir., Case Western Reserve Lib. Sch. seminar on publ. for children, '69; ALA-Children's Bk. Cncl. Joint Comm., '62–'64; Auth., "From Childhood to Childhood" (John Day, '70); Contrbr., pfsnl. pubns.; Mt. Union Col., BA, '49, LettD, '69; b. Chgo., Ill., 1927; p. William and Ruth Anderson Karl; res: 300 E. 33rd St., N.Y., N.Y. 10016.

KARNS, FRANCES HERRIDGE, Drama and Movie Ed., New York Post, 75 West St., N.Y., N.Y. 10001, '54–; Dance Critic, '50–; Smith Col., BA; h. Frances Karns.

KASDAN, SARA MOSKOVITZ, Auth: "Mazel Tov, Y'All" ('68), "So It Was Just a Simple Wedding" ('61), "Love and Knishes," ('56); Univ. of Louisville; b. Fort Smith, Ark. 1911; p. Morris and Leah Chmarov Moskovitz; h. James Kasdan; c. Mrs. Arnold Zegart, Mrs. Alan Moskovitz, Mrs. Michael Rosenberg; res: 2171 Millvale Rd., Louisville, Ky. 40205.

KASHUBA, JUDITH ANN, Music Coordr., Experimenta Phantasmagoric, Actor's Theatre School, University of Houston, Box 72, Houston, Tex. 77004, '69–; Asst. Dir., Actor's Theatre Sch., '63; Exec. Dir., Experimenta Phantasmagoric, '63; Auth., non-fiction and fiction; AWRT, NLAPW; Univ. Miami (Pre Med.), '61; S. Conn. State Col. and Yale Univ. Drama Sch., '62; Theatre in Rink Apprentice, '65; Univ. of Houston, BBA, '69; b. Derby, Conn., 1944; p. Joseph Michael and Anna Mary Rostocki Kashuba; res: 2502 Bammel Timber Lane, Houston, Tex. 77040.

KASMAN, ALICE JOY, Partner, Partners for Growth, Inc., 1270 Ave. of the Americas, N.Y., N.Y. 10020, '68–; former high sch. tchr., S.F., N.Y.C.; Barnard Col., AB, '64 (cum laude); Univ. of Notre Dame, MA; b. N.Y.C., 1943; p. H. Larry and Helen Sweet Kasman; res: 13 W. Ninth St., N.Y., N.Y. 10011.

KASS, BABETTE, Owner, Babette Kass Creative Research, One Rockefeller Plaza, N.Y., N.Y. 10020, '60–; Tech. Dir. of Rsch., Young & Rubicam, Inc., '55–'60; Dir., Adv., Mkt. Rsch., Bur. of Applied Soc. Rsch., Columbia Univ., '48–'55; AAPOR, Am. Sociological Assn., Who's Who Of Am. Wm., Who's Who In Adv.; Auth., bks., articles in field; Columbia Univ., MA; Hunter Col.; b. N.Y.C.; p. David and Sadie Fischel Kass; h. Jacob M. Miller; res: 930 Fifth Ave., N.Y., N.Y. 10021.

KASSEWITZ, RUTH BLOWER, Dir. of Commtns., Frendino/Grafton/Pancoast/Architects, 2575 S. Bayshore Dr., Miami, Fla. 33133, '67–; Acct. Supvsr., Asst. to the Pres., The Venn Corp., '64–'67; Acct. Supvsr., Venn-Cole & Assocs., '59–'64; Copywtr., Publicist, Grant Adv., '57–'59; Copywtr., Merritt Owens Adv. Agcy., '55–'57; Copywtr., Oh. Fuel Gas Co., '51–'55; PRSA (S. Fla. Chptr. Pres., '69), Theta Sigma Phi (Gtr. Miami Chptr. Pres., '62–'63; Treas., '60–'62), Adv. Club of Gtr. Miami (Dir., '59–'62), Gamma Alpha Chi, Fla. PR Assoc. (Secy.-Treas., '62–'64), AWRT, Theta Sigma Phi (Gtr. Miami Chptr. Headliner Aw., '65); Am. Inst. of Architects Aw., '60; Crusade for Freedom Svc. Aw., '60; Un. Cerebral Palsy Svc. Aw., '67; Miami Univ., '46–'49; Oh. State Univ., BS, '49–'51; b. Columbus, Oh., 1928; p. E. Wallett and Helen Daub Blower; h. Jack Kassewitz; c. Jack; res: 1136 Aduana Ave., Coral Gables, Fla. 33146.

KAST, CAROLINE SUE, Key Precinct Supvsr., ABC News Polit. Unit, American Broadcasting Company, 1330 Ave. of the Americas, N.Y., N.Y. 10019, '66–; Reg. Mgr. of Adm., Applied Rsch. and Mgt. Scis. Div., C-E-I-R, Inc., '62–'64; Edtl. Asst., Am. Diabetes Assn., '59–'62; N.Y. Adv. Club, AWRT, NATAS; Mt. Holyoke Col., '50–'51; Hood Col., '51–'54; b. Muncie, Ind., 1932; p. Harold and Ruth Lindoerfer Kast; res: 235 E. 22nd St., N.Y., N.Y. 10010.

KASTBERG, ALICE WINIFRED, Assoc. Decorating Ed., Ladies' Home Journal, 641 Lexington Ave., N.Y., N.Y. 10022, '62–; edtl. work, '42–'62; Virginia Aiken

Decorating Shop, '42; AID (Press Affiliate, '56–); McLane Art Inst., '38–'41; b. Farmingdale, N.Y., 1920; p. William and Nora Fariel Kastberg; res: Comly Ave., Byram, Conn. 06473.

KATES, JOAN B., TV Bdcst. Field Supvsr., Parkson Adv., Inc., 767 Fifth Ave., N.Y., N.Y. 10023, '68–; Asst. to Mng. Ed., "Today Show," NBC, '66–'68; Asst. to Unit Mgr., '65–'66; Prod. Asst., WGBH-TV (Boston, Mass.), '62–'63; Tape Ed. Asst., Municipal Bdcst. System, '62; Alpha Epsilon Rho (VP, Treas., '63–'65); Outstanding Young Wm. of Am., '68; Who's Who in Am. Cols. and Univs., '65; Emerson Col., BA (Bdcst.), '65; b. Elizabeth, N.J., 1943; p. Leonard and Frances Temkin Kates; res: 1 University Pl., Apt. 11-0, N.Y., N.Y. 10003.

KATO, KAY, Colmst., Cartoonist, Star Ledger, Star Ledger Plaza, Newark, N.J. 07101; Contrbr., New York Times Magazine, Nation's Business, others; OPC; Am. Art Week aw., '55; Pa. Acad. of Fine Arts, Am. Acad. of Dramatic Arts; res: 60 Chapman Pl., Glen Ridge, N.J. 07028.

KATZ, CHARLOTTE KAUFMAN, Self-employed Educ. Cnslt., Wtr., Milton S. & Charlotte S. Katz, Consultants, 2 Horizon Rd., G-11, Fort Lee, N.J. 07024, '65–; Co-auth., "Systems for Education: "Theory and Use" (in progress); Co-auth., Auth., pseud. C. B. Stauffer, tech. writing for GE Co.; Nat. Soc. for Programmed Instr., Nat. Inst. for Applied Behavioral Sci.; Oh. State Univ., econs., '45–'47; Temple Univ., statistics, '63; b. Columbus, Oh., 1928; p. William and Blanche Gladfelter Kaufman; h. Milton S. Katz; c. Richard F. Betts, Barbara A.

KATZANDER, SHIRLEY SALTZMAN, Owner, Shirley Katzander PR, 1133 Sixth Ave., N.Y., N.Y. 10036, '69–; Prom. Dir., The Reporter, '54–'69; PR Dir., Jacob K. Javits, '54; AE, PR, J. J. H. Lawrence, '53–'54; AE, James Jones & Co., '51–'52; Copy Ed., Stars & Stripes (Germany), '47–'51; Reptr., PM, '44–'46; Reptr., Wtr., Chicago (Ill.) Sun and Sun Radio News, '42–'44; Reptr., Philadelphia (Pa.) Inquirer, '39–'41; Colmst., Madison Avenue mag.; Contrbr., New York mag.; Mag. Prom. Group (Secy., '63–'69), AWNY, OPC, PRSA; b. Phila., Pa., 1921; p. Benjamin and Jennifer Sahn Saltzman; h. (div.); res: 35 E. Ninth St., N.Y., N.Y. 10003.

KAUFFMAN, DOROTHA STRAYER, Free-lance Wtr., poetry, songs, novels, articles; Auth: "The Singing Pen" (poetry, '55), "Dark Side of Nowhere" (novel, '65); Eurekan Lit. Soc., Christian Auths. Guild; Marion·Col., '47; Moody Bible Inst., '51; Evangelical Tchr. Training Inst., '51; b. Zanesfield, Oh., 1925; p. Forrest and Helen Hildreth Strayer; h. Glen Kauffman; c. Linda Kauffman Turner, Glenna Lee, Garold James; res: 4571 W. 245, W. Liberty, Oh. 43357.

KAUFFMAN, HELEN RITA, Pres., Helen Kauffman

Public Relations, 9017 Rangely Ave., L.A., Cal. 90048, '59–; Free-lance Wtr.; Fashion Group; Hunter Col., '52–'53; N.Y. Phoenix Sch. of Design, '54; Columbia Univ., '55; Univ. of Southern Cal., '57; UCLA, '55–'57, '65–'68; Santa Monica City Col., '68; b. Phila., Pa.; p. Jacob and Mollie Futterman Kauffman.

KAUFFMANN, KATHRYN A., Prod. Mgr., Madison Advertising Agency, 804 Watterson City Bldg., Louisville, Ky. 40218, '66–; Artist, Baer, Kemble & Spicer (Cinn., Oh.), '65; Artist, Asst. Prod. Mgr., Schindler-Howard Adv. Agcy., '63–'65; Prod. Mgr., Strauchem & McKim, '59–'63; Univ. of Cinn., BS (Design), '60; b. Buffalo, N.Y., 1937; p. William and Ruth Sherwood Kauffmann; res: 1031 Everett Ave., Louisville, Ky. 40204.

KAUFMAN, BEL, Auth., "Up the Down Staircase"; Lectr., Educ.; Adjunct Proff., English Literature, Borough of Manhattan Commty. Col.; TV, radio appearances; Auths. League, Dramatists Guild, PEN (Exec. Bd.), Columbia Univ. English Grad. Union, Sholom Aleichem Fndn. (Exec. Bd.); Plaques from Anti-Defamation League, United Jewish Appeal; Paperback-of-the-Yr. Aw.; Bell Movie Prize; Hunter Col., BA (magna cum laude, Phi Beta Kappa); Columbia Univ., MA (highest hons.); Nasson Col., LLD (Hon.); b. Berlin, Germany; p. Dr. Michael and Lola Rabinowitz Kaufman; c. Jonathan Goldstine, Thea Goldstine; res: 1020 Park Ave., N.Y., N.Y. 10028.

KAUFMAN, EVALYN DARROW, Wms. Svc. Copy Ed., Redbook Magazine, McCall Publishing Company, 230 Park Ave., N.Y., N.Y. 10017, '66–; Copywtr., '58–'62; Sr. Ed., Hairdo Magazine, '64–'66; Free-lance Ed., Wtr., '62–'64; p. Maurice and Lulu Benham Darrow; h. Joseph Kaufman; res: 18 W. 70th St., N.Y., N.Y. 10023.

KAUFMAN, SUE ELAINE, Free-lance Wtr., '47–; Asst. to Fiction Ed., Mademoiselle, '47–'49; Auth: "Diary of a Mad Housewife" (Random House, '67), "Green Holly" (Scribner's, '61), "The Happy Summer Days" (Scribner's, '59), many short stories, articles; Vassar College, BA, '47; b. Lawrence, N.Y., 1926; p. Marcus and Anna Low Kaufman; h. Jeremiah Barondess; c. James Barondess; res: 544 E. 86th St., N.Y., N.Y. 10028.

KAUFMAN, YVONNE HECHLER, Prog. Dir., Radio Station WVSC, Inc., Box 231, Somerset, Pa. 15501, '68–; Public Svc. Dir., '67; Wms. Dir., '58–'67; Cont. Dir., '53–'58; Soroptimist (Pres., '68–'69; VP, '64–'68); Who's Who of Am. Wm.; Ind. Univ. of Pa., '39–'40; b. New Lexington, Pa., 1918; p. Harry and Lucretia Hechler; h. Harry Kaufman; c. Lucretia Joan, Donna Lynne; res: R.D. 6, Somerset, Pa. 15501.

KAUFMANN, ANN ELIZABETH, Mgr., Employee Pubns., Dayton's, 700 On The Mall, Mpls., Minn., 55402, '59–; PR Asst., Un. Fund of Hennepin County; Northwestern IEA; Carleton Col., BA, '50.

KAUFMANN, MADELINE MAYBELLE, Pres., The Kaufmann Press, Inc., 132 W. 14th St., N.Y., N.Y. 10011, '56–; Secy. to Pres., '48–'56; Actress, radio programs, '40–'42; Actress, Provincetown Players, '38–'39; numerous organizations and aws.; N.Y.U., BA, '42; Am. Acad. Dramatic Arts, '46; Pimny, Columbia, Western Univ. (GA); b. Westfield, N.J., 1918; p. Henry and Anne Mary David Kaufmann; res: Troy Towers, 380 Mountain Rd., Union City, N.J. 07087.

KAUNITZ, RITA DAVIDSON, Adviser, Model Cities, City of Bridgeport, Conn., '69. Coordr., Urban Affairs Study, Fairfield Univ., '68; Cnslt., Ctr. for Housing, Building & Planning, United Nations, '60–'66; Wtr., Lectr., on urban affairs; Nat. Cncl. of Wm. of U.S. (Ch., Urban Affairs Committee, '69–; State of Conn: Clean Air Cmmsn., Adv. Cncl. on Cmmty. Affairs, Governor's Comm. on Environmental Policy, others; Bridgeport Mayor's cit., '69; N.Y.U., BA, '42 (magna cum laude); Columbia Univ., MA (Public, Govt.), '46; Harvard Univ., PhD (Reg. Planning), '51; b. N.Y.C., 1922; p. David and Bessie Golden Davidson; h. Paul E. Kaunitz; c. Jonathan, Andrew; res: 14 Red Coat Rd., Westport, Conn. 06880.

KAWATZKY, VIVIAN THERESE, Fashion Ed., The Milwaukee Sentinel, 918 N. Fourth St., Milw., Wis. 53201, '65–; Fashion Wtr., Reptr., '62–'65; Wms. Dept. Reptr., '53–'62; Theta Sigma Phi; J. C. Penney-Univ. of Mo. Aw. for Fashion Writing, '67; Mount Mary Col., BA, '51; b. Milw., Wis., 1929; p. Raymond J. and Anne Delany Kawatzky; res: 1260 N. Prospect Ave., Milw., Wis. 53202.

KAY, HELEN, Auth., 25 juv. bks. incl: "Lion for a Sitter" ('69), "Man and Mastiff: The Story of the St. Bernard Dog Through History" ('67), "Name for Little—Noname" ('68); Auths. League, PEN, Am. Ctr., Wms. City Club of N.Y., WNBA; b. N.Y.C.; p. Hyman and Tessie Herman Colodny; h. Herbert Goldfrank; c. Lewis R., Deborah, John L.; res: 435 E. 87th St., N.Y., N.Y. 10028.

KAY, MARA V., Wtr.; Auth: "In Place of Katia," "The Burning Candle," other bks. for young adults; Auths. League; Queen Mary's Col. For Girls (Yugoslavia); res: 2 Lent Ave., Hempstead, N.Y. 11550.

KAY, VIRGINIA, Colmst., Star News, 525 Colorado, Pasadena, Cal. 91109, '38–; Pasadena Interracial Club (hon. life mbr.); Pasadena Wms. Civic League Wm. of the Yr., '54; p. William and Noma Bentley Osman; h. Frederick Powers.

KAYA, OLGA, Actress, motion pic. and TV; classical ballet dancer, Munich Opera House; appeared in "Clambake," "Dayton's Devils," "Mannix," "Mission: Impossible," "Family Affair" and others; SAG, AFTRA; b. Berlin, Germany; p. Alexander and Raisa Bandzevicius Korzeniauskas; res: 1550 W. Laurel Ave., Hollywood, Cal. 90046.

KAYE, LIBBY, Pubns. Mgr., Eaton Yale & Towne Inc., 100 Erieview Plaza, Cleve., Oh. 44114, '68–; Ed., '56–'68; Asst. Ed., '54–'56; Edtl. Asst., '52–'54; Theta Sigma Phi, Cleve. Press Club, Northern Oh. IEA (Pres. '57), AAIE, PRSA; 13 aws., Freedoms Fndn.; Four aws., N.Y. Stock Exchange (Nat. Invest-In America Week), '61–'64; Seven Aws., SCORE, Distg. annual repts., to Employees, '60–'68; Fin. World Aw. for Distg. annual rept. to shareholders, '67; Ohio Univ., BSJ, '52; b. Cleve., Oh. 1930; p. Sarkas and Rose Benneian Kalousdian; h. Don Zadnik; c. Christie, Kimberly; res: 10102 Edgepark Dr., Cleve., Oh. 44125.

KAZICKAS, JURATE C., Feature Wtr., Associated Press, 50 Rockefeller Plaza, N.Y., N.Y. 10020, '69–; Free-lance Jnlst. (Vietnam), '67–'68; Rschr., Look, '66–'67; Tchr. (Kenya), '64–'66; Outstanding Young Wm. in Am., '68; Sports Illustrated aw., '65; Trinity Col., BA, '64; b. Vilnius, Lithuania, 1943; p. Joseph and Alexandra Kalvenas Kazickas; res: 56 Lyncroft Rd., New Rochelle, N.Y. 10804.

KEAGY, IRVANA SUE, Wtr., short stories; Wms. Ed., Press-Citizen, 319 E. Washington St., Iowa City, Ia. 52240, '67–'69; Gen. Reptr., State Corr., Wichita (Kan.) Eagle, '64–'67; Theta Sigma Phi; Univ. of Kan., William Allen White School of Jnlsm., BS, '67; b. Valley Ctr., Kan., 1945; p. Irvin B. and A. LaVerne Guthrie Keagy; h. Alan Wilks; c. Jolin Rai Wilks; res: 1982 Algonquin Road, Apt. 4B, Mt. Prospect, Ill. 60056.

KEAHBONE, CAROL STRANGE, Wms. Ed., Anadarko Daily News, 117–119 E. Broadway St., Anadarko, Okla. 73005, '67–; articles in many other pubns.; Okla. Press Assn.; N. Tex. State Col., '49–'52; b. Oceanside, Cal., 1932; p. Roy P., Sr., and Berniece Fannin Strange; h. Ernie Keahbone; c. David Bruce Holloway, Cameron; res: Rte. 2, Box 141, Anadarko, Okla. 73005.

KEANE, BARBARA G., Treas., Motion Pic. Prodr., Beacon Television Features, Inc., 708 Washington St., Dedham, Mass. 02026, '51–; Radio/TV Dir., Boston-N.Y. Agency; Bdcst. Execs. Club (Boston-Charter Mbr.), AWRT (Trustee, Bd. of Educ. Fndn., '69–'71; Pres., New England Chptr., '67; Nat. Chmn., Seminars Educ. Fndn.); b. Boston, Mass., 1916; p. William H. and Barbara E. Brown Keane; res: 29 Standish Rd., Milton, Mass. 02187.

KEANE, LEONTINE RITA, Dir. of Info., Div. of Urban Extension, Wayne State University, Detroit, Mich. 48202, '66–; Dir. of Radio-TV Pubcty., '58–'66; Asst. to Exec. Secy., WTVS, '55–'58; Wtr.-Prodr.-Bdcstr., Detroit Public Schs., '53–'54; Wm.'s Ed., WJLB, '51–'53; Eng. Instr., Univ. of Detroit, '47–'51; PRSA (Mich. Chptr. Dir.); Theta Sigma Phi (Detroit Chptr. Pres.); Am. Red Cross (Southeastern Mich. Chptr. Dir.); AWRT (Detroit Chptr. past Pres.); Prodr., Modr., synd. radio prog., "Writing With Writers"; Prodr., Host, "Searchlight" TV series; Manhattanville Col., BA; Univ. of Detroit, MA; b. Grosse Pointe, Mich.; p.

William and Leontine D'Haene Keane; res: 1007 Harvard Rd., Grosse Pointe, Mich. 48230.

KEATING, ANNE S., Circ. Dir., Smithsonian Magazine, Smithsonian Institution, 420 Lexington Ave., N.Y., N.Y. 10017, '69–; Prom. Dir., Am. Museum of Natural Hist., '57–'69; Cnslt., Doubleday, '63–'69; Cnslt., Interplay mag., '66–; Dir. Mail Adv. Assn. (aw., '69, '63), Nat. Assn. of Dir. Mail Wtrs., Prom. Round Table; Hunter Col., BA, '53; b. N.Y.C., 1931; p. William and Anne Clayton Keating; res: 320 Central Park W., N.Y., N.Y. 10025.

KEATING, GERALDINE THOMAS, Exec. Dir., International Council of Industrial Editors, 2108 Braewick Circle, Akron, Oh. 44313, '56–; Akron Gen. Hosp., '53–'56; Ahlberg Bearing Co., '38–'40; Home Owners Loan Corp., '35–'37; Am. Soc. of Assn. Execs., Akron Area Bus. and Indsl. Eds., Akron Civic Theatre; Who's Who of Am. Wm.; Univ. of Akron, BS, '35; b. Akron, Oh., 1913; p. John Armstrong and Elizabeth L. Russ Thomas; h. William C. Keating; c. Judith Faye (Mrs. Douglas E. Cameron), William C., III; res: 2062 Wyndham Rd., Akron, Oh. 44313.

KEATING, MARIANNE BIER, Corporate PR Wtr., J. Walter Thompson Co., 420 Lexington Ave., N.Y., N.Y. 10017, '63–; Fin. Wtr., Ed., '59–'63; Exec. Secy., Copy Dept., '56–'59; Auth., non-fiction mag. articles; AWNY, AEA, '47–'50; SAG, '47–'50; Univ. of Wash., '44–'47; b. Ritzville, Wash., 1928; p. Philip and Amanda Ott Bier; h. John Keating (dec.); res: 39 Fifth Ave., N.Y., N.Y. 10003.

KEATING, MICHELINE, Feature Wtr., Movie, Drama Critic, Tuscon Daily Citizen, 208 N. Stone Ave., Tucson, Ariz. 85703, '68–; Ed., Tucson Daily Citizen weekend mag., '55–'68; Reptr., '51–'55; Ed., Magazine Tucson, '48–'51; Staff Wtr., Collier's, '40–'43; Reptr., New York Journal, '38–'40; Reptr., New York Mirror, '34–'38; Auth: "Fame" (Putnam), "City Wise" (Long & Smith), two other novels; Theta Sigma Phi, Ariz. Press Wm., NFPW; b. N.Y.C.; p. Michael and Pearl Murphy Keating; res: 7301 E. 19th St., Tucson, Ariz. 85710.

KEATS, SHEILA, Auth., non-fiction (music); Wtr., Prog. Notes, Carnegie Hall Concerts of Am. Symphony Orchestra, '68–; Staff Wtr., Lincoln Ctr. for the Performing Arts; Mgr. and PR, The Goldman Band, '60–'68; Independent Concert Mgr. and Musical Publicist, '62–'66; Dir. of Alumni Affairs, Julliard Sch. of Music, '56–'60; Ed., The Julliard Review, '56–'60; Wtr., Musical Heritage Soc., catalog of the Manhattan Sch. of Music, Knopf Ency. of Music & Musicians; Am. Fedn. of Musicians; Radcliffe Col., '47–'48; Syracuse Univ.; '48–'50; Julliard Sch. of Music, BS, '54; b. Bayonne, N.J., 1929; p. Irving and Helen Saskin Keats; res: 565 West End Ave., N.Y., N.Y. 10024.

KEAVENY, JEAN DIXON KYHL, Asst. to Dir., Corp. Rel., Adv., International Telephone and Telegraph

Corp., 320 Park Ave., N.Y., N.Y. 10022, '65–; Admr., Edtl. Svcs., '60–'65; Ed., Wtr., '46–'60; Wms. Army Corps., '43–'45; PRSA, Wis. State Col., '30–'32; b. Bangor, Wis., 1914; p. Harvey and Doris Esch Kyhl; h. Norbert J. Keaveny (dec.); res: 155 W. 68th St., N.Y., N.Y. 10023.

KEAY, LOU CARTER, PR Dir., Museum Field Rep., West Texas Museum, Texas Technological College, Box 4210, Lubbock, Tex. 79409, '65–; Lou Keay PR, '64–'65; PR Dir., Un. Fund of Lubbock, '62–'65; Cont. Dir., KDUB-TV, '59–'62; Ed.-Wtr., Bernard Brister PR (Dallas), '57–'59; Pubcty. Wtr., WBAP-TV (Ft. Worth), '52–'56; AAF, Adv. Club of Lubbock, AWRT (Lubbock Chptr. Pres., '66–'68), Gamma Alpha Chi, Theta Sigma Phi, Zeta Phi Eta; Mensa; active in various civic groups; Tex. Wm.'s Univ., '44–'46; Emerson Col., '47–'48; Tex. Christian Univ., Univ. of Tex. Ext. Div.; b. Oceanside, Cal., 1927; p. Leslie and Ota Belle McCain Carter; h. (div.); c. Monica, David Leslie; res: 3507—22nd Pl., Lubbock, Tex. 79410.

KEEFE, MILDRED JONES, Dir. of Dramatic Art, Greenbrier College, Lewisburg, W. Va. 24901, '45–; Dir., Fine Arts Dept., '52–; Dir. of Speech Arts Dept., St. Mary's Jr. Col., '43–'45; Musical Dir. and Asst. Prof. of Fine Arts in Religion, Boston Univ., '34–'40; Founder and Coordr., Crtv. Arts Festival of W. Va., '55–'68; Auth., "Choric Interludes" (Expression Co., '42), "White Beauty" and other poems; AAUP, AAUW, Am. Educ. Theatre Assn., NEA, W. Va. Educ. Assn., NLAPW, W. Va. Poetry Soc., W. Va. Speech Assn., Intl. Platform Assn., Marquis Biog. Lib. Soc., Centro Studi E Scambi Intl. (Řome); Nat. Register of Prominent Ams.; Pi Lambda Theta and Pi Gamma Mu cit., '34; Crtv. Arts Festival, '59; (Hon Life Mbr., '65); Boston Univ., BS (Educ.), '34; AM, '36; b. Boston, Mass., 1896; p. John and Eliza Jones Keefe; res: 10 Pearl St., Mattapoisett, Mass. 02739.

KEEL, MARY ANN CAUGHRAN, Wms. Dept., Boise (Idaho) Statesman, '58–'62; Area Ed., Twin Falls (Idaho) Times News, '57–'58; Stringer, Salt Lake City (Ut.) Tribune, '50–'56, and News Ed., Northside News (Jerome, Idaho), '50–'56; Drama Ed., Tacoma (Wash.), News Tribune, '43; Wms. Ed., Mt. Vernon (Wash.) Herald, '37–'38; Theta Sigma Phi, Idaho Press Wm. (aw., '61); Northwestern Univ., '34; Univ. Puget Sound, '35; Univ. of Wash., BA (Jnlsm.), '37; b. Tacoma, Wash., 1914; p. Gilbert and Esther Russ Caughran; h. James Stanley Keel, Jr.; c. John R., Patrick G., Michael L., Carolyn Sue Good; res: 8811 Valhalla Dr., Everett, Wash. 98201.

KEELER, JULIA ANNETTE, Acting Librn., Des Moines (Ia.) Art Ctr., '67–'68; Art Lectr., Ia. State Univ. (Ames) '64; Artist, Tchr., Des Moines Independent Commty. Sch. Dist., '31–'64; Art Tchr., Theodore Roosevelt Sr. HS, '42–'64; Art Tchr., Callanan Jr. HS, '31–'42; Tchr., Art, Jnlsm., Eng., various Kan. HS, '21–'29; Theta Sigma Phi, Delta Phi Delta, Artists Equity; Fort Hays Kan. State Col., '15–'18; Kan. State Univ., BS (Indsl.

Jnlsm.) '19; Pratt Inst., '24–'25; Colo. Springs Art Ctr., '26–'28; Kan. Univ., BFA, '31; Des Moines Art Ctr. summer sessions under Cowles Fndn., '56–'68; b. Garden City, Kan. 1895; p. Lewis and Sadie David Keeler; res: 5011 Pleasant St., Des Moines, Ia. 50312.

KEENAN, MARY EVAN, Asst. to Radio-TV Dir., Kalish, Spiro, Walpert & Ringold, Chestnut East Bldg., Ninth and Chestnut, Phila., Pa. 19107, '68–; Prom. Wtr., WFIL-TV, '68–'69; Ithaca Col., BS (Radio-TV), '68; b. Doylestown, Pa., 1946; p. Martin and Joan S. Keenan; res: 930 Stony Lane, Gladwyne, Pa. 19035.

KEENE, REBECCA R., PR Dir., Strong Memorial Hospital, University of Rochester, 260 Crittenden Blvd., Rochester, N.Y. 14620, '45–; Wm.'s Army Corps, '43–'45; Univ. of Rochester, '30–'43; PRSA, Rochesterians aw., '64; Gamma Phi Beta, Pi Gamma Mu; N.D. State Univ., '27; b. Fargo, N.D.; p. Edward and Myrtle Pearman Keene; res: 83 Brunswick St., Rochester, N.Y. 14607.

KEESHAN, MILDRED PRITCHARD, Colmst., Free-lance Wtr., '47–'65; Colmst., Manhattan (Kan.) Mercury, '52–'65; KJCK (Junction City), '50–'52; Junction City Republic, '47–'50; Kan. Press Wm., Kan. Auths. Club, NLAPW, (Topeka Br. Rec. Secy.), '64–'66), Soroptimist Club (Manhattan, Kan., Pres., '54), NFPW Aws., '56, '58; numerous State Aws. for colm.; Kan. State Univ., '19–'21; b. Junction City, Kan., 1900; p. Henry and Lena Ford Pritchard; h. H. Hawley Keeshan; c. Marilyn Mildred; res: 1721 Dotsero Ave., Loveland, Colo. 80537.

KEHM, FREDA S., Radio Personality, "Call Dr. Kehm," WBBM 630 N. McClurg Ct., Chgo., Ill. 60611, '62–; Lectr., Northwestern Univ., '57–; Assoc. Prof., Dept. of Sociol. and Anthropol., Carlton Col.; Instr., Social Work, Univ. of S.D.; Supvsr., F.E.R.A., S.D.; Acting Dir., S.D. Public Health Assn.; Exec. Dir., S.D. Child Welfare Commn.; Dir., Assn. for Family Living; Auth: "World Book Childcraft," "Let Children Be Children" (Association Press, '68), "Health and Safety for Teenagers," and numerous articles for adults, children; Alpha Pi Zeta, Am. Sociological Soc., Nat. Cncl. on Family Rels., Ill. Cncl. on Family Rels., Am. Assn. of Marriage Cnsls.; Who's Who of Am. Wm., Am. Men of Sci., 2,000 Wm. of Achiev., Ill. Lives; Univ. of Ill., BA (Psych.; Phi Beta Kappa); Univ. of S.D., MA (Sociol., Psych.); Northwestern Univ., PhD (Sociol.), '41; h. Harry C. Kehm (dec.).

KEHOE, CONSTANCE DE MUZIO, Assoc. Prof. of Eng., Wheelock College, 200 Riverway, Boston, Mass. 02215, '60–; Co-auth., "Enjoying Ireland" ('66); Col. Eng. Assn.; Ford Fndn. Fellowship, '55; Mt. Holyoke Col., BA, '55; Yale Univ., MA, '56; Middlebury Col., MA, '59; Trinity Col., Dublin, PhD, '67; b. Malden, Mass., 1933; p. Hector and Elizabeth Antico De Muzio; h. William F. Kehoe; c. John William.

KEISER, JESSIE LIEB, VP, Leigh Charell Studios, Inc.,

2 W. 37th St., N.Y., N.Y. 11018, '58–; AE, '45–'57; Park Ave. Fashion Studios, '37–'43; Lazarnick Photogrs., '21–'37; AWNY, Fashion Group, N.Y. Pubcty. Club; b. N.Y.C., 1902; p. Henry and Bertha Shoenlank Liebeskind; h. Leo Keiser; c. Henry B.; res: 333 E. 34th St., N.Y., N.Y. 10016.

KEITH, JUDITH, Free-lance Wtr., Lectr.; Auth., "I Haven't a Thing to Wear" (Tandem Press, '68); PR Cnslt., '59–'69; Cnslt., Un. World Federalists, '60–'67; Pa. Ballet Co., '64–'67; PR Dir., Wermen & Schorr Adv., '56–'59; Publr., Ed., Pursestrings, '55–'56; Adv. Dir., PR Dir., Glamorene, Inc., '52–'55; res: 1919 Chestnut St., Phila., Pa. 19103.

KELIHER, ALICE V., Cnslt., Bur. of Indian Affairs; Distg. Prof., Wheelock Col., '64–'69; Distg. Prof., Jersey City State Col., '60–'64; Prof., N.Y.U., '40–'60; Instr., Yale Univ., '30–'33; Lectr.; Wtr., Auth., three bks.; numerous monographs, more than 300 articles in pfsnl. jnls.; various orgs.; Columbia Univ., BS, '28; MA, '29; PhD, '30; Jersey City State Col., Litt. D (hon.), '64; Lesley Col., LHD (hon.), '67; Wheelock Col., DSE (Hon.), '69; b. Wash., D.C., 1903; p. James and Ida Crow Keliher; res: Box 307, Peterborough, N.H. 03458.

KELLER, EUGENIA, Mng. Ed., Chemistry, American Chemical Society Publications, 1155 16th St., N.W., Wash., D.C., 20036, '67–; Assoc. Ed., '65–'67; Assoc. Ed., Industrial and Engineering Chemistry, five yrs.; Auth., many works in chemistry field; Am. Assn. for the Advancement of Sci.; Purdue Univ., BS, '37; George Washington Univ., '52–'54; b. Houston, Tex., 1914; res: 1711 Massachusetts Ave., N.W., Wash., D.C. 20036.

KELLER, JUDITH PALM, Copywtr., Bryant Radio and Television Co., 5600 Ave. A, Lubbock, Tex. 79408, '69–; Copy Dir., Martin Masters Assoc. (New London, Conn.), '67–'68; Cont. Dir., KCBD (Lubbock), '65–'67; Traf. Mgr., KBAT (San. Antonio), '63–'65; Cont. Dir., '62–'63; AWRT (Lubbock Chptr. Pres.), '66; San Antonio Chptr. Secy., '65) Southwest Tex. State Col., '60–'62; b. San Antonio, Tex., 1942; p. Blake and Doris Farris McCreless; h. Charles Keller; res: 3506—23rd St., Lubbock, Tex. 79410.

KELLER, JUNE, Owner, June Keller Public Relations, '58–; AE, Miami Mgr., Alan Bell PR, '57; Miami Mgr., Allied PR, '56; Reptr., Miami Beach Sun, '49–'51; Reptr., St. Louis (Mo.) Star Times, '47–'48; Theta Sigma Phi (Miami Chptr. Pres.), '68–'69); Univ. of Mo., BJ, '47; b. Buffalo, N.Y.; res: 710 N.E. 160 St., N. Miami Beach, Fla. 33162.

KELLER, LOIS J., Soc. Ed., Decatur Publishing Co., Inc., 141 S. Second St., Decatur, Ind. 46733; res: Homestead #25, Decatur, Ind. 46733.

KELLEY, FAY EVANS, VP, Crtv. Dir., Pidcock & Co.,

Inc., 126 W. Bay St., Savannah, Ga. 31401, '59–; Dir., Downtown Merchants Assn., '55–'59; Assoc. Copy Supvsr., Kenyon & Eckhardt, '52–'55; Sr. Copywtr., Cecil & Presbrey, '51–'52; Client-contact, copy, Hewitt, Ogilvy, Benson & Mather, '48–'51; Copywtr., Benton & Bowles, '46–'48; Copywtr., Compton Adv., '45–'46; Pubcty. Dir., Radio Sta. WPTF (Raleigh, N.C.), '43–'45; Fashion Group, Oglethorpe BPW (Charter Mbr.), Savannah Adv. Club; "Silver Medal Aw." for outstanding excellence in Adv., '63; numerous other aws.; Jr. Col. (Glendale, Cal.); Univ. Ext. (Milw., Wis.); b. Elvins, Mo., 1914; p. William and Emma Myers Evans; h. Chauncey Kelley; res: 52 E. Broad St., Savannah, Ga. 31401.

KELLEY, HELEN HAM, Asst. Prof., Photojnlsm., California State Polytechnic College, San Luis Obispo, Cal. 93401, '66–; Free-lance Wtr., Photogr.; Pfsnl. Photogrs. of Am., Cal. Press Photogrs. Assn.; Kan. Univ. (Jnlsm.), '62–'63; Brooks Inst. of Photog., '63–'66 (1st pl. aw., movie, '65); Grad. Work, San Jose State Col. (Mass. Commtns.), '69; b. Buell, Mo., 1922; p. Simeon and Almeda Miller Ham; h. George Kelley; c. Nancy Jo Coburn, Almeda Ann Jenkins; res: 184 Highland Dr., San Luis Obispo, Cal. 93401.

KELLEY, MARY RUTH, Prod. Ed., University of Illinois Press, University Press Bldg., Urbana, Ill. 61801, '52–; Sr. Proofreader, '41–'52; Proofreader, Champaign-Urbana News-Gazette, '37–'41; Univ. of Ill., BS (Educ.), '33; b. Kelso, Wash., 1913; p. Edward and Olive Phelps Kelley; res: 1422 Cambridge Dr., Champaign, Ill. 61820.

KELLEY, SARA WRIGHT, PR Dir., National League for Nursing, 10 Columbus Circle, N.Y., N.Y. 10019, '54–; Asst. Dir., Comm. on Careers, '50–'54; PR Cnslt., N.Y. State Dept. of Commerce, '50–'51; Info. Specialist, U.S. Public Health Svc., '42–'45; PRSA; Mississippi State Col. for Wm., BA, '38; Columbia Univ. Sch. of Jnlsm., '41; b. Meridian, Miss., 1915; p. Charles M. and Minnie T. Wright; h. Welbourn Kelley; c. Page; res: 26 Kinderkamack Rd., Park Ridge, N.J. 07656.

KELLOGG, CYNTHIA, Mng. Ed., Venture Magazine, Cowles Communications, 488 Madison Ave., N.Y., N.Y. 10022, '63–; Decorating Ed., Ladies Home Journal, '61–'63; Reptr., Home News Ed., Asst. to Wms. Ed., N.Y. Times, '43–'61; N.Y. Nwsp. Wms. Club (Prize for story on wm., '56); Radcliffe Col., BA, '43; h. William Jensen; res: 185 West End Ave., N.Y., N.Y. 10023.

KELLY, BELLA SHAFF, Special Feature Wtr., Miami News, 1 Herald Plaza, Miami, Fla., '64–; News and Feature Wtr., '53–'61; Educ. Wtr., '47–'53; Reptr., '45–'47; Wtr., Univ. of Miami News Bur., '61–'63; Theta Sigma Phi; Civic Merit Aw., Miami Jr. C. of C., '58; Univ. of Miami, '42–'44; b. Miami, Fla.; p. Louis Shaff; h. Herbert Kelly, Jr.; res: 498 S.W. 27th Rd., Miami, Fla. 33129.

KELLY, CAROLE TACKETT, News Ed., Starkville Daily News, 101 S. Washington, Starkville, Miss. 39759, '67–; Pubcty. Dept., Mid-South Fair, Early Maxwell Assoc.; Corr., Jackson Daily News; N.E. Miss. Press Assoc.; Univ. of Miss., BA (Liberal Arts), '64; b. Tupelo, Miss., 1942; p. Yale and Althea Jeffreys Tackett; h. George M. Kelly; c. Cameron Lee; res: Roselawn Terr., Starkville, Miss. 39759.

KELLY, KAREN, Mag. Specialist, American National Red Cross, National Headquarters, Wash., D.C. 20006, '68–; Adv. Dir., Tempco (Detroit, Mich.), '68; Asst. Dir., PR, Southeastern Mich. Chptr. Am. Red Cross, '64–'68; PR Dir., Multiple Sclerosis Soc. of Mich., '63–'64; Special Cnslt. to Nat. Prog. for Voluntary Action, '69–; AWRT, Wms. Adv. Club of Wash., Mid-Atlantic Assn. of Indsl. Eds.; 2,000 Wm. of Achiev.; Mich. State Univ., BA, '60; b. Highland Park, Mich., 1938; p. William and Agnes Gillette Kelly; res: 950 25th St., Wash., D.C. 20037.

KELLY, KATHLEEN, Modern Living Ed., The Wichita Eagle and The Wichita Beacon, 825 E. Douglas, Wichita, Kan. 67201, '55–; Gen. Assigt. Reptr., '52–'55; Am. Home Econs. Assn., Sedgwick County Home Econs. Assn. (Pres. '60–'61), Witchita Home Economists in Bus. (Pres. '60–'61), Theta Sigma Phi (Wichita Club Pres., '62–'64; Kan. Wm. Jnlst. of Yr., '60), NFPW, Kan. Press Wm. (2nd VP), Wichita Press Wm.; Vesta Aw. for excellence in food pgs., Nat. Livestock and Meat Bd., '65; Reed and Barton Silversmiths Aw., '67; numerous other writing aws.; Kan. State Univ., BS (Home Econs., Jnlsm.), '55 (Mortar Bd.); b. Manhattan, Kan., 1933; p. Lawrence L. and Ida Comstock Kelly; h. 1. Gary A. Humphries (dec.); 2. John W. Whalen; c. Kelly O'Neil Humphries, John Peter Whalen, Harold Gibbs Whalen, Patricia Kay Whalen, Mrs. Richard H. Wedel; res: 3001 Cornelison, Wichita, Kan. 67203.

KELLY, MARION BRADLEY, Dir. of PR., Cleveland Young Women's Christian Association, 3201 Euclid Ave., Cleve., Oh. 44115, '59–; Colmst: "Working Mothers" and "Day by Day," Cleve. Plain Dealer, '56–; Oberlin News Tribune, '50–; Am. Red Cross, '53–'56; PRSA, Press Club, AWRT, Theta Sigma Phi, Fashion Group; Lect. Club Cncl. Wm. of Achiev. Aw., '69; Univ. of Wis., BA, '38; b. Cleve., Oh., 1917; p. Arthur E. and Marion Chute Bradley; h. (dec.); c. Mrs. Guy Powers, Mrs. David D. Wise, Ralph, William B., Margaret L.; res: 214 W. College, Oberlin, Oh. 44074.

KELLY, REGINA Z., Auth., juv. bks. incl: "Abigail Adams, The President's Lady," "Chicago: Big-Shoul-dered City" (Friends of Literature aw. for both, '63), others; Univ. of Chgo. grad.; Northwestern Univ.; b. N.O., La.; h. Norman H. Kelly.

KELLY, VENITA M., Fashion Ed., Cincinnati Post and Times Star, 800 Broadway, Cinn., Oh. 45202, '52–; "The Venita Kelly Show" (TV), '59–'60; Adv., E. W. Scripps Co., '40–'52; Lectr., Fashion Show Commentator and TV Personality; Oh. Nwsp. Wms. Assn., Theta Sigma Phi, Fashion Group, Paris Fgn. Corrs. Club;

Rogers Sch. of Dramatics, '28; Univ. of Cinn. Evening Col., '48; b. Kokomo, Ind.; p. Frederic and Cecile Budd Kelly; res: Phelps Town House, 506 E. Fourth St., Cinn., Oh. 45202.

KELLY, VIOLA M., Adv. Mgr., National Science Teachers Association, 1201 16th St., N.W., Wash., D.C. 20036; Nat. Sci. Tchrs. Assn., NEA.

KELSEY, ALICE GEER, Auth., Childrens bks., religious educ. materials; "Land of the Morning" (Friendship Press, '68), many others; Curriculum Conslt., Philippine Fedn. of Christian Churches, '56–'58; Social Worker, Near East Fndn. Program for Crippled Children with Greece Mission of UN Relief and Rehabilitation Adm., '45; Orphanage Dir., Near East Relief (Turkey), '19–'20; Settlement Work (Hartford), '18–'19; Ithaca Writers' Assn., Children's Commn. of Christian Educ. Dept. of N.Y. State Cncl. of Churches; Mount Holyoke Col., BA, '18; Cornell Univ.; b. Danvers, Mass., 1896; p. Curtis Manning and Mary Louise Gillett Geer; h. Lincoln Kelsey (dec.); c. Paul M., Edith (Mrs. Norman F. Lewis), Olive (Mrs. George L. Gallaher), Martha (Mrs. Gordon K. Davenport); res: 109 Comstock Rd., Ithaca, N.Y. 14850; summer res: Coreys RFD, Tupper Lake, N.Y. 12986.

KEMBLE, DOROTHY A., Free-lance Cnslt.; Dir. of Cont. Acceptance; Mgr., Supvsr., religious, educ., public svc. programs; adm. of lit. rights; Prodr.; Wtr., radio, TV shows; Auth., articles on bdcst.; Supvsr., Field Pers., C. E. Hopper, Inc., TV, Rsch., '60–'65; Mutual Bdcst. System, '45–'54; ABC, '42–'45; NBC, '37–'42; Head, Adv. Investigation dept., Macfadden Pubns. Inc.; Lectr.; N.Y.U., Barnard Col. (Playwriting); b. N.Y.C.; p. Edmund and Mary Mead Kemble; res: Westbrook Apts. 4B, Westbrook, Conn. 06498.

KEMP, NANCY MARGARET, Librn., H. J. Heinz Co., 1062 Progress St., Pitt., Pa. 15230, '54–; Carnegie Free Lib. of Allegheny; Special Libs. Assn. (Pitt. Chptr. Pres., '55–'56), Pa. Libs. Assn., Am. Col. & Rsch. Libs.; Carnegie Inst. of Tech., '43–'47; Univ. of Pitt.; b. Pitt., Pa.; h. James A. Wright; res: Spruce Haven Dr., RD4, Box 1405, Wexford, Pa. 15090.

KEMP, ROSE BLYTH, Dir. of TV, Radio & Films, California Institute of Technology, 1201 E. California Blvd., Pasadena, Cal. 91109, '65–, '58–'62; Asst. PR Dir., '55–'58; Dir., Commty. Rels. and Founder, KCET (L.A.), '62'–'65; AWRT (Nat. Dir., '65–'68), Western Radio & TV Assn. (Dir., '60–; Secy.-Treas., '63–'65), Univ. Film Assn. (Treas., '62–'64; Fndn. Advisory Bd., '65–), NAEB; Robert Eastman Aw., '64; CINE Golden Eagle Aw., '68; Univ. of Southern Cal., '34–'36; b. Salem, Oh., 1917; p. Robert and Rose Mullins Modisette; h. Bradley Kemp; c. Sheriden Bentley, Michaela Gonzalez, Andrew Blyth, Ian Blyth, Donna Blyth, Duncan Blyth, Susan, Bradley Jr.; res: 11000 Wrightwood Pl., N. Hollywood, Cal. 91604.

KEMP, VIRGINIA JO HIGGINBOTHAM, News Ed., Milford Advertiser, '61–'65; Reptr., '59–'61; Educ. Ed., The Cinn. Times-Star, '57–'58; City Reptr., '57, '56, '55; Pubcty., Old Milford Area, Inc.; Milford Better Schools Committee; Theta Sigma Phi Lectr., pubcty. workshops; Kappa Tau Alpha; Oh. Univ. Sch. of Jnlsm., '53–'57; BSJ, '61 (magna cum laude); Univ. of Cinn., '59–'61; b. Hamilton County, Oh., 1935; p. James and Frances Brackett Higginbotham; h. John W. Kemp; c. Deborah Sue, John Thomas, Andrew William, Rebecca Jo; res: 25 Apple Lane, Milford, Oh. 45150.

KEMPER, ELISE WEIL, Prodr., Modr., WMAR-TV, 6400 York Rd., Balt., Md. 21212, '57–; McCall's Golden Mike aw., '57; Vassar Col., AB, '15; b. Atlanta, Ga., 1894; p. Arthur and Lala Hirsch Weil; h. Armand Kemper; c. Elinor K. Wolf, David (dec.), Marion K. Harris; res: 2616 Talbot Rd., Balt., Md. 21216.

KEMPER, INEZ, Auth., P.O. Box 2011, Wash., 13, D.C., 20013, "Highways to the Hills" (Loizeaux Bros.), "Doorway to Heaven" (Baker Bk. House), "In Touch with Heaven" (Wm. B. Eerdman Publ. Co.); b. Blocton, Ala., 1906; p. Charles and Lottie Wilson Kemper; res: Cottondale, Ala.

KEMPNER, NAN SCHLESINGER, Contrb. Ed., Harper's Bazaar, 717 Fifth Ave., N.Y., N.Y. 10022, '67–; Fashion Feature Ed., '66–'69; b. S.F., Cal., 1930; p. Albert and Irma C. Schlesinger; h. Thomas J. Kempner; c. Thomas L., Adeline F., James L.; res: 895 Park Ave., N.Y., N.Y.

KENDALL, CAROL SEEGER, Auth., juv., adult fiction; bks: "The Baby-Snatcher" (Bodley Head, England, '56), "The Gammage Cup" (Harcourt, Brace, '59; Ohioana Aw., '60; Runner-up, Newbery Aw., '60), others; Oh. Univ., AB, '39 (Phi Beta Kappa; Mortar Bd.); b. Bucyrus, Oh., 1917; p. John and Laura Price Seeger; h. Paul Kendall; c. Gillian M., Carol S. (Mrs. Kerry Ahearn); res: 30 Forest St., Athens, Oh. 45701.

KENDALL, DONNA JOYCE, Supvsr., Int. Commtns., Title Insurance & Trust Co., 433 S. Spring St., L.A., Cal. 90054, '66–; Staff Asst., PR, '63–'66; Asst. Mgr. PR, Modern Woodmen of Am., '61–'63; Adv. and Pubcty. Supvsr., '59–'61; Staff Asst. PR, '57–'59; L.A. Adv. Wm. (Bd. of Dirs., '66–'69; Golden Lulu Achiev. Aw., '68); PRSA, Cal. Assn. of Real Estate Tchrs., L.A. Area C. of C.; Stephens Col., AA; State Univ. of Ia., BA (Jnlsm.); b. Milan, Ill., 1929; p. O. D. and Ragnhild Hansen Kendall; res: 419 S. Rexford Dr., Beverly Hills, Cal. 90212.

KENDALL, ELIZABETH ANTOINETTE, Reptr., Austin (Tex.) American, Wtr., Scottish Rite News Bulletin; Drake's Freedom Press; Soil and Water Magazine; Ed., Am. Inst. of Crop Ecology; Theta Sigma Phi (cit., '64), Panhellenic Assn. (D.C. Chptr. Secy., '67–'69); Minn. DAR cit.; Univ. of Tex., BJ, '32; b. Rushford,

N.Y.; p. Charles and Elizabeth Mullen Kendall; res: 4550 Connecticut Ave., Wash., D.C. 20008.

KENDRICK, ROSEMARY, Reptr., The Capital Times, 115 S. Carroll St., Madison, Wis. 53703, '67–; Ed., "University Record," Univ. of Rochester, '65–'67; Theta Sigma Phi, Nwsp. Guild of Madison (Treas.), Phi Kappa Phi; Utica Col. of Syracuse Univ., BA, '62 (magna cum laude); Univ. of Wis., MA (Jnlsm.), '65; b. Utica, N.Y., 1940.

KENISTON, ROBERTA CANNELL, Assoc. Dir., Eastern Michigan University Library, Ypsilanti, Mich. 48197, '63–; Head, Ref. Dept., Asst. Librn., '52–'57; Head, Undergrad. Lib., Univ. of Mich., '57–'63; Fiction Librn., Ann Arbor Public Lib., '51; Mich. Lib. Assn., ALA, AAUP, Phi Kappa Phi; Univ. of Chicago, PhB, '27; Univ. of Mich., AM (Lib. Sci.), '51; b. Rockford, Ill., 1908; p. Robert J. and Anastasia Barth Cannell; h. Hayward Keniston; c. Kenneth, Mrs. Marjorie McIntosh; res: 1507 E. Park Pl., Ann Arbor, Mich. 48104.

KENNAN, CLARA B., Tchr., Eng., Crtv. Writing: Ouachita Univ., '52–'55; Univ. of Ark. at Little Rock, '46–'50; Ark. A&M, '30–'46; Southern State, '28–'30; El Dorado Jr. Col., '26–'28; Free-lance Wtr., articles, poems; Co-auth. with Dr. T. M. Stinnett of cent. hist. of Ark. Educ. Assn., "All This and Tomorrow Too" ('69); AAUW (Ark. Div. Treas., '43–'46), NLAPW (Ark. Pioneer Br. Treas., '48–'50), WNBA, Ark. Retired Tchrs. Assn. (Bd. Mbr., Histrn., '57–'70); Ark. Wtrs. Conf. aws., '52, '48; Univ. of Ark., BS, '24, MS (Educ.), '27; b. Rogers, Ark.; p. Alvero and Rosella Reeves Kennan; res: 1200 Commerce St., Apt. 615, Little Rock, Ark. 72202.

KENNEDY, BERENICE CONNOR, Pres., Feminine Forecast, Inc., 200 E. 66th St., N.Y., N.Y. 10021, '66–; Ed., Girl Talk, '69–; Sr. Ed., McCall's, '62–'66; Assoc. Ed., Ladies' Home Journal, '61–'62; Dir., Edtl. Prom., '51–'60; Dir., Radio-TV, Buckley Org., '50–'51; Jr. AE, Geare-Marston Agcy., '48–'50; Cnslt., Life, '67; Cnslt., American Cyanamid Co., '68–; AFA, AWNY (VP, Dir., '62–'64), Phila. Club of Adv. Wm. (VP, '58–'60), Phila. Fashion Group (Dir., '59), OPC; Repl. Wm. in Bus. and Industry, Salute to Wm. Aw., '66; Phila. Adv. Wm. of Yr., '60; Univ. of Pa., AB, '47; (major honors, Polit. Sci.); h. Jefferson Kennedy, Jr.

KENNEDY, DOROTHY DOUGHERTY, AE, PR Dept., The Griswold-Eshleman Company, 55 Public Sq., Cleve., Oh. 44113, '63–; Reptr., UPI (Bangkok, Thailand), '56–'59; (Tokyo), '53–'55; Colmst., Columbus (Oh.) Citizen, '46–'51; Hostess daily TV show, WTVN (Columbus), '49–'50; Rptr.-Rewrite, Phila. Inquirer, '43–'46; Feature Wtr., Cedar Rapids (Ia.) Gazette, '42–'43; Reptr., Louisville Courier-Journal, '41; Univ. of Ark., BA, '41 (Phi Beta Kappa); b. Ft. Smith, Ark., 1921; p. Ord and Edith Barnett Dougherty; h. Edward Ridgway Kennedy; c. Samuel Ridgway, III, Jean B.; res: 6185 Seminole Trail, Mentor, Oh. 44060.

KENNEDY, EVELYN KIRK, Instr., Long Beach City College, 1305 E. Pacific Coast Highway, Long Beach, Cal. 90805; Group Tour Coordr., Fenwick Travel Svc., '67–; Colmst., "Cooking With Ev," Un. Features, '67–'68; Theta Sigma Phi (Club Pres., '68), AAUW, BPW (Local Pres., '58–'59); Mills Col., BA, Oh. Univ., MS, '54; b. L.A., Cal.; p. William and Ethel Michael Oldenburger; h. Robert Kennedy; res: 3115 E. Fifth St., Long Beach, Cal. 90814.

KENNEDY, FLORYNCE R., Atty., '57–; Dir., Media Workshop, 8 E. 48th St., N.Y., N.Y. 10017; Guest, "Opinions" (Peabody Aw. Winning Commty. Show, '66), WLIB-AM, '64–'66; Colmst., "Once Upon a Week," Queens Voice; Hostess, "Queens Voice Show," WWRL Radio, '63–'64; Colmst., Phila. Independent; Contrbr., "The Hand that Cradles the Rock"; Actress: "The Landlord" (with Diana Sands, Pearl Baily) and "Black Roots"; NAMW, NATAS, Nat. Assn. of Radio Anncrs.; Columbia Univ. Sch. of Law, LLB, '51; b. Kan. City, Mo., 1916; p. Wiley and Zella Jackman Kennedy; h. Charles Dye (dec.).

KENNEDY, FRANCES MIDLAM, Sr. VP, Crtv. Dir., Admr. of Crtv.-Mgt. Rev. Bd., Dancer-Fitzgerald-Sample, Inc., 347 Madison Ave., N.Y., N.Y. 10017, '69–; VP, Crtv. Group Head, Mbr. Crtv Rev. Comm., '62–'68; VP, Copy Chief, '47–'62; Wtr., Copy Supvsr., Compton Adv., '39–'47; Wtr., numerous articles, bklets., ltrs. for ch. and charitable orgs.; Chgo. Adv. Wm. of Yr., '60; Emma Proetz Aw. for outstanding adv. prod. by a wm., '57; Golden Kay Chgo. Copywtrs. Aw., '58; Goldey Bus. Col., Wilmington, Del.; b. Wilmington, Del., 1913; p. Edward West and Annie Bullen Midlam; h. Joseph C. Kennedy (dec.); c. Edward C., Stephen D., Katharine (Mrs. David C. Treadway); res: Hawk Mountain, Pittsfield, Vt. 05762.

KENNEDY, JEAN MARIE, Prodr., "David Susskind Show," Talent Associates, Ltd., 444 Madison Ave., N.Y., N.Y. 10022, '59–; formerly adv. and PR, Fox Michigan Corp.; Emmy for producing "Open End"; Univ. of Detroit, PhB; b. Detroit, Mich.; p. Mark and Helen Sweeney Kennedy.

KENNEDY, JULIA, Reptr., News Features, Associated Press, 50 Rockefeller Plaza, N.Y., N.Y. 10020, '69–; Reptr., Milwaukee Journal, '68–'69; Reptr., Rochester Times-Union, '68; Univ. of Wis., BA, '69; b. Santa Barbara, Cal., 1947; p. Edward and Lyn Crost Kennedy; res: 520 E. 72nd St., Apt. 3-K, N.Y., N.Y. 10021.

KENNEDY, MARY JO, TV Actress, "Lancer" 20th Century Fox, '69; "Here Come The Brides," Screen Gems, '69; "Paddy," Dun Laoghaire Prod., '68; "Outsider," Universal, '68; "High Chapparral," Paramount, '67, "Run for Your Life," Universal, '67; SAG, U.C.L.A., BA (Theater Arts), '68; b. Akron, Oh. 1945; p. Donald L. and Elizabeth Manchester Weir; res: 1520 N. Beverly Glen Blvd., L.A., Cal. 90024.

KENNEDY, MARY LOUISE, Mng. Ed., Elementary Book Clubs, American Education Publications, 55 High St., Middletown, Conn. 06457, '67–; Dir., Weekly Reader Children's Bk. Club, '66–'67; Ed., '58–'66; Ed., My Weekly Reader, '51–'57; Edtl. Asst., Charles E. Merrill, '50; Field Secy., Kappa Kappa Gamma, '49; Copy Ed., Harcourt, Brace, '48; Corr., Bk.-of-the-Month Club, '47; Ed., "Paperbacks in the Elementary School" ('69); Wms. Nat. Bk. Assn.; Oh. State Univ., BA, '46 (summa cum laude, Phi Beta Kappa); Northwestern Univ., MA, '47; b. Columbus, Oh., 1924; p. John and Anne Long Kennedy; res: 390 Pine St. Ext., Middletown, Conn. 06457.

KENNEDY, MURIEL MATSON, Wms. Prog. Hostess, "The Woman's Way," WWNY, Box 211, Watertown, N.Y. 13601, '69–; Radio Coordr., Commty. Clubs Aws., '66–'67; Wtr., Prodr., Performer, TV Series on Pregnancy, '55; Instr., various areas of nursing; Nat. League of Nursing (Vice Chmn., Cncl. of Public Health Agencies, '58–'59); Columbia-Presbyterian Sch. of Nursing, RN and BS, '43; b. Corning, N.Y., 1921; p. Leon R. and Mildred Scudder Matson; h. Dr. John A. Kennedy; c. John, Thomas, James, Timothy, Mary; res: 742 Ives St., Watertown, N.Y. 13601.

KENNEDY, RUTH O'KEEFE, Colmst., Morning-Telegraph and Daily Racing Form, '61–; Secy.-Treas., Va. Horse Shows Assn. (Warrenton), '54–; Field Secy., Virginia Horsemen's Association (Warrenton) '56–; Contrbr., sports articles on races, hunt racing and horse shows in Va.; Am. Horse Shows Assn., Un. Hunts and Nat. Steeplechase and Hunt Assn.; Sweet Briar College, '44; b. N.Y.C., 1923; p. Francis and Julia deHayes O'Keefe; c. Frances Elizabeth, Mary Dandridge; res: Rte. 1, Warrenton, Va. 22186.

KENNEDY, SHIRLEY RUTH, Rsch. Dir., Cranford/Johnson & Associates, Suite 300, First Nat. Bank Bldg., Little Rock, Ark. 72201, '66–; Prom. Dir., KARK and KARK-TV, '54–'66; Adm. Asst., Brooks-Pollard Co., '47–'54; Adv. Dept., Sports Afield Magazine, '46–'47; Wtr., mag. feature articles; Broadcast Promotion Assn. ('60–'66); Who's Who of Am. Wm.; Southwest Mo. State Col., '38–'40; b. Springfield, Mo., 1921; p. Brownlow and Ida Gugel Kennedy; res: 212 Vernon E., Little Rock, Ark. 72205.

KENNETH, CLAIRE, Auth., 5800 Arlington Ave., Riverdale, N.Y., N.Y. 10471; Auth: "Night in Cairo," "Randevu in Rome," "Light Over the Nile," "The Love Riddle," "May in Manhattan," "Countess for Sale," "Diary of Egon," "Pirouette"; Auths. Guild, PEN; Cit. for Gallant Svc. from Pres. Dwight D. Eisenhower; Univ. of Budapest, BS, '42; b. Budapest, Hungary, 1923; p. Ivor and Vilma Vargha de Koelcsey-Kende; h. Paul de Bardossy; c. Thomas; res: 5800 Arlington Ave., Riverdale, N.Y., N.Y. 10471.

KENNEY, BRIGITTE SCHNEIDER, Rsch. Assoc., University of Mississippi Medical Center, Dept. of Psychiatry, Jackson, Miss. 39211, '68–; Systems Analyst, Med. Lib., '66–'68; Dir., Info. Svc. Div., Miss. R & D Ctr., '62–'66; Asst. Librn., Transportation Ctr., Northwestern Univ. (Evanston, Ill.), '59–'62; Readers Advisor, '59; Prof. Student Asst., Joint Ref. Lib. (Chgo.), '58; Ref. Asst., Miss. Lib. Commn., (Jackson), '55–'57; Lib. Asst., Tombigbee Regional Lib. (West Point, Miss.), '52–'53; ALA, AAUP, Special Libs. Assn., Am. Soc. for Info. Sci., Southeastern Lib. Assn., Miss. Lib. Assn.; Univ. of Chgo., MA (Lib. Sci.), '59; b. Halberstadt, Germany, 1927; p. Dr. Alexander and Irmgard Schneider; h. B. Higdon Kenney; c. Veronica Irmgard; res: 1686 Winchester St., Jackson, Miss. 39211.

KENNY, BARBARA GARRIGUES, Comml. Artist, Ross Jurney Associates, Inc., 140 Social Hall Ave., Salt Lake City, Ut. 84111, '68–; Tchr., Painting, '67–'68; Artist, '60–'69; Three annual art shows; 2nd pl., Art Festival, Ut., '67; Univ. of Ut., '56–'57; Choyinard Art Inst., '59–'60; b. Hollywood, Cal., 1938; p. Alfred and Ross Jurney Garrigues; res: 2726 Grandview Circle, Salt Lake City, Ut. 84106.

KENOYER, NATLEE PEOPLES, Auth., four bks. incl. "Firehorses of San Francisco" ('70); many articles on horses, animals; Reg. Nurse, '32–; Western Wtrs. of Am., Cal. Wtrs.; Valley Wtrs. Conf. aw.; Jr. Literary Guild selection, '60 Gold Spur aw.; b. Modesto, Cal., 1907; p. Nathan and Laura Wichman Peoples; h. Franci O. Kenoyer; c. Michael, Patrick, James; res: 88 La Paz, Campbell, Cal. 95008.

KENT, GRACE TEED, Dir. of Adv., Longchamps Inc., 230 Park Ave., N.Y., N.Y. 10017, '67–; formerly Therapeutic Dietician, Florence Crittenden Hosp.; Range Cnslr., Detroit Edison; Asst. Dir. Home Svc. Whirlpool; Dir. of Home Econs., Leo Burnett; Colgate-Palmolive; Charm, Grooming Instr., Berkeley Schs.; Alexander's; Free-lance Cnslt., adv. agcys., PR firms; Home Econsts. in Bus. (Detroit Chptr. Pres., '60), AAUW, Wms. Adv. Club, N.Y. Adv. Club, Am. Home Econs. Assn., Electrical Wms. Round Table, DAR, Alpha Chi Omega; Wheaton Col., '47–'49; Mich. State Univ., BS, '51; b. Ann Arbor, Mich., 1929; p. Dr. Reed and Florence Schleicher Teed; h. Alan Bradley Kent; c. Deborah Grace; res: 413 E. 50th St., N.Y., N.Y. 10022.

KENT, JOAN ARNOLD, Program Comml. Coordr., Columbia Broadcasting System, Inc., CBS Bdcst. Ctr., 524 W. 57th St., N.Y., N.Y. 10019, '61–; Exec. Secy. to Prodr., "Person to Person," '60; Asst. to Prodr., "Playhouse 90," '58–'60; Adm. Asst. to Prodr., "Studio One," '56–'57; Placement Supvsr., CBS-N.Y., '53–'55; theater, nightclub, recital work, Chandra Kaly dance group; two Pacific U.S.O. tours entertaining troops; Eastman Bus. Sch.; b. Havana, Cuba; p. Benjamin Arnold and Claire Arnold Stiles; h. (div.); res: 40 E. 73 St., N.Y., N.Y. 10021.

KENT, LILLIAN JAFFE, Pres., Kent/Jaffe, Inc., 50 E. 42nd St., N.Y., N.Y. 10017, '68–; VP, Dolan-Kent, '51–'68; AWNY; Bklyn. Col., BA, '36 (cum laude);

Univ. of Mich., MA, '37; b. N.Y.C., 1916; p. Ellis and Anna Blumberg Jaffe; h. Jack Kent; res: 225 W. 106th St., N.Y., N.Y. 10025.

KENT, MARGUERITE KIRTSINGER, Adv. Mgr., American Marketing Association, 230 N. Michigan Ave., Chgo., Ill. 60601, '65–; Prodr., Wtr., Publicist.; Univ. of Chgo., PhB., '47; b. Chgo., Ill., 1905; p. Charles and Maude Fountain Kirtsinger; h. Leonard Kent (div.); res: 1235—12th St., Northfield, Ill. 60094.

KENT, PAULA, PR and Mktng. Cnslt., 515 BonAir St., LaJolla Cal. 92037, '70–; Prom. Dir., Union-Tribune Publishing Co., San Diego, Cal. '49–'70; Fashion Ed., '48–'49; Pers. Mgr., Fashion Ed., San Diego Daily Jnl., KSDJ, '46–'48; U.S. Navy Wms. Reserve, U.S. Coast Guard (Lt., Sr. Grade), '42–'46; Methods Engineer, IBM, '41–'42; Sls. and Mktng. Execs. Club (VP, '69–'70, Bd. of Dirs., '64–'66; svc. aw., '63, '66–'68), Intl. Nwsp. Prom. Assn. (Bd. of Dirs., '68–'70), Altrusa Club, Am. Cancer Soc. (Bd. of Dirs., '63–'65), Sls. Prom. Execs. Assn. L.A. (Man of the Yr. aw., '65), Pers. Mgt. Assn. (Hon. Mbr.), Cal. Press Wm., NFPW; Who's Who of Am. Wm., Who's Who in the West, World Who's Who in Finance and Industry, Intl. Biog. Dic.; Nat. Fedn. BPW aw., '66; Cal. BPW "Achievement Award, '66; San Diego BPW aw., '65; San Diego "Wm.-of-Achiev.", '63, '64; San Diego Wm. of the Yr., '65; Outstanding Citizen aw., '61; San Diego "Wm.-of-Valour," '58; "Walter O'Malley/Theta Sigma Phi (L.A.) Unique Coverage aw., '68; City of San Diego 200th Anniversary" Don Award (Legion of Portola)" '69; "Distinguished Service Award" by Investment Education Institute of Detroit, '69. In national, regional and state competitions in public relations, advertising, publicity, news and feature writing has won 149 awards, '49–'70; Boston Univ., BS, '39, MS, '41; h. Dr. Stanley J. Lloyd; c. Diane Adrienne Noel, Robin Michele Cheri, Kevin Christopher, Gisele Nicolette Jolie; res: 515 Bon Air St., La Jolla, Cal. 92037.

KENT, PRUDENCE, Adv. Copy Dir., The Strathmore Agency, 575 Madison Ave., N.Y., N.Y., '64–; VP, Gen. Mgr., Gresh & Kramer Ad Agency; Asst. Mdsng. Mgr., General Foods Corp.; Adv. Mgr., Community Opticians; AWRT, AWNY, PRSA, Theta Sigma Phi (Phila. Chptr. Pres., '63–'64); N.Y.U., BS, '34 (cum laude); b. N.Y.C.; h. (dec.); c. Geoffrey; res: 15 W. 72nd St., N.Y., N.Y. 10023.

KENTZLER, CLAIRE PROTHERO, Coordr., Wisconsin School of the Air, WHA-Radio, University of Wisconsin Extension, Radio Hall, Madison, Wis. 53706, '68–; Script Wtr., '58–'68; Prod. Asst., '55–'58; Cont. Ed., '51–'54; Oh. State aw., '68, '65; Univ. of Wis., BS (Eng.), '51; b. Baraboo, Wis., 1928; p. Rolla and Mable Bauer Prothero; h. James Kentzler; res: RR #1, Lacy Rd., Verona, Wis. 53593.

KEOWN, KAREN DRAPER, Wtr., Prodr., J. Walter Thompson Co., 420 Lexington Ave., N.Y., N.Y. 10017,

'67–; Assoc. Prodr., '67; Copywtr., '63–'67; Mich. State Univ., BA (Commtn. Arts), '63; b. Millington, Mich.; p. LaVerne and Vivienne McPherson Draper; h. John T. Keown; res: 230 E. 48th St., N.Y., N.Y. 10017.

KERMAN, GERTRUDE LERNER, Actress, Dir., Wtr.; Dir., off-Broadway, Commty. Theatres, '50–; Instr., Great Neck Sch. of Drama, '55–; Instr., Adelphi Univ., '48–'54; Auth: "Shakespeare For Young Players" ('64), "Plays and Creative Ways With Children" ('61); McGill Univ., BA, '29 (summa cum laude); The New Sch. For Social Rsch., Columbia Univ., N.Y.U.; b. Quebec City, Que., Can., 1909; p. Leon and Deborah Ortenberg Lerner; h. (1) Joseph Kerman (dec.); (2) LeRoy S. Furman; c. Patricia Clare, Julie Beth Adelman; res: 105 W. 13th St., N.Y., N.Y. 10011.

KERMEEN, DONNA CAROL, Pubcty. Mgr., Clairol, 345 Park Ave., N.Y., N.Y. 10022, '69–; Product Publicist, '67–'69; AE, Rowland Co., '66–'67; Edtl. Mgr., Planned Communications Svcs., '64–'66; PRSA, AWRT; The Principia Col., BA, '59; b. N.Y.C., 1938, p. Leonard and Gertrude Jackson Kermeen; h. Gerald Multer; res: ·400 E. 56th St., N.Y., N.Y. 10022.

KERN, CECELIA CARPENTER, Ed., The Liberty Press, East St., Liberty Center, Oh. 43532, '66–; b. Henry County, Oh., 1929; p. Roy and Gertrude Meyer Carpenter; h. Clifford Kern; c. Barry Eugene, Thomas Alan, Debra Anne; res: W. Maple St., Liberty Center, Oh. 43532.

KERR, ADELAIDE, Free-lance Wtr.; AP Newsfeatures Svc., 17 yrs.; AP Corr. (Paris, France), five yrs.; OPC; Univ. of Kan., State Univ. of Mont., N.Y.U.; res: 130 E. 39th St., N.Y., N.Y. 10016.

KERR, FRANCES WILLARD, Supervising Wtr., Ed., U.S. Information Agency, 1776 Pennsylvania Ave., Wash., DC. 20547, '53–; Feature Wtr., U.S. Dept. State, '47–'53; Econs. Wtr., U.S. Dept. Labor, '46–'47; Pubns. Wtr., U.S. Signal Corps., '43–'46; PR, YMCA, '39–'43; Free-lance Wtr., '36–'39; WNPC, ANWC; b. Independence, Mo.; p. Rector and Lucy Whitney Kerr; res: 4305 Murdock Mill Rd. N.W., Wash., D.C. 20016.

KERR, JOAN BALLINGER, PR Rep., Scandinavian Airlines System, Inc., 8929 Wilshire Blvd., Beverly Hills, Cal. 90211, '64–; Feature Ed., Teen Magazine, '60–'64; Ed. of House Organ, Union Bank, '58–'60; Reptr., West L.A. Independent, '57–'58; Wtr., travel articles for numerous publs.; Theta Sigma Phi; Univ. of Southern Cal., BA (Jnlsm.), '57; b. Honolulu, Hi., 1934; p. Homer and Catherine Sabella Ballinger; h. Robert E. Kerr; c. Robert James; res: 1441 Princeton St. #5, Santa Monica, Cal. 90404.

KERR, LOIS FIEDLER, Auth: "The Many Faces of Love" (Fleming H. Revell, '68), "The Sound of Silence," (Fleming H. Revell, '65); Matrix Aw., Dallas Chptr., Theta Sigma Phi, '65; Kent State Univ., BS, '50, Austin Presbyterian Theological Seminary, '67–'68; b.

Homer, Oh. 1928; p. Frederick and Bertha Wright Wagner; h. William Kerr; c. James, Louis, Kurt; res: 6708 Haney Dr., Austin, Tex. 78723.

KERSHAW, HELEN SEARS, Wms. Pg. Ed., Keene Evening Sentinel, 60 West St. Keene, N.H. 03431; b. Milford, N.H., 1901; p. Frank N. and Lilla M. Pike Sears; h. Joseph Kershaw; res: Troy Rd., RFD 1, N. Swanzey, N.H. 03431.

KESEG, EVELYN FERRELL, Mgr., Commty. Svcs., Nationwide Communications Inc., 246 N. High St., Columbus, Oh. 43215, '66–; Asst. Corporate Secy., '57–; Secy. to Pres., '42–'66; AWRT (VP, '69–'70; Secy., '68–'69), NATAS (Columbus Chptr. Membership Secy., '68–'70); Oh. State Univ.; b. Chapmanville, W. Va., 1919; p. Peter M. and Milford Seaman Ferrell; h. Andrew Keseg; res: 1744 Westwood Ave., Columbus, Oh. 43212.

KESSEL, MARIAN LUCILLE, Staff VP and Ed., Home Life, Advertising Division, Inc., 211 N. LaSalle St., Chgo., Ill. 60601, '43–; Asst. Wms. Ed., Chgo. Sun, '41–'42; Home Econ., Jewel Tea Co., (Barrington), '36–'41; Tchr., home econ. and commerce (Plymouth, Ind.), '29–'34; Altrusa (Chgo. Group Corr. Secy., '60–'61; Bd. Dir., '60–'61, '62–'63; State St. Cncl. Aw.); Chgo. Sun Publrs. Aw. for Enterprise, '42; Ind. State Univ., BS, '29; b. near Terre Haute, Ind.; p. Andrew and Lora Parrish Kessel; res: 720 Gordon Terr., Chgo., Ill. 60613.

KESSELMAN, ANNETTE G., Pers. Mgr., Waring and LaRosa, Inc., 555 Madison Ave., N.Y., N.Y. 10022, '64–; formerly Placement Mgr., Archer East Assoc.; Radio Rsch., Adam Young.

KESSLER, GLORIA RUBIN, Dir., Exec. Placement, Columbia Broadcasting System, Inc., 51 W. 52nd St., N.Y., N.Y. 10019, '69–; Mgr. Compensation, '66–'68; Mgr. Non-Exempt, '64–'66; Salary Analyst, '60–'64; Interviewer, '59–'60; NBC, '56–'58; Guest Lectr. on Compensation, Am. Mgt. Assn.; Am. Compensation Assn., several salary survey groups; Syracuse Univ., BA (Psych.), '56 (magna cum laude; Psi Chi); h. Bertram Kessler.

KESTEN, DOROTHY KAY, VP, Mng. Ed., Army Aviation Magazine, Army Aviation Publications, Inc., 1 Crestwood Rd., Westport, Conn. 06880, '56–; Aviation/Space Wtrs., Assn., Army Aviation Assn. of Am., Am. Helicopter Soc., Assn. of the U.S. Army; Cornell Univ., BS, '43; b. Rochester, N.Y., 1923; h. Arthur H. Kesten; c. Dale, Lynn; res: 1 Crestwood Dr., Westport, Conn. 06880.

KETTEMAN, KAY, Colmst., "Creative Cooking," "A Thought For Today," Am-Ton Journal; Colmst., "Today's Play," Magnificat nwsp.; Former Hostess, WGR-TV, WNED-TV: Buffalo BPW (Past Pres.), AWRT (W. N.Y. Chptr. Past Pres.), Am. Bus. Wms. Assn. (Buffalo Chptr. Past Pres., Wm. of the Yr., '65), Wms. Adv. Club

of Buffalo, NLAPW; Who's Who of Am. Wm., 2,000 Wm. of Achiev.; Outstanding Civic Leaders of Am.; D'Youville Col., BA; b. Buffalo, N.Y.; h. Fred C. Ketteman; res: 400 Starin Ave., Buffalo, N.Y. 14216.

KEUSCH, BEVERLYE, Pres., Beverlye Keusch Assoc., 605 Lincoln Rd. Mall, Miami Beach, Fla. 33139, '53–; Soc. Ed.; Assoc. Ed., S. Fla. TV Guide; Colmst., Anglo Jewish Press; Colmst., Miami Beach Sun; City of Miami Beach PR Bd., Theta Sigma Phi, AFA, BPW (VP, '68–'69); Am. Osteopathic Assn. jnlsm. aw., '62; Univ. of Miami, BA, '54; b. Bronx, N.Y., 1934; p. Nathan and Gertrude Elinsky Keusch; h. Edward Weinberger; res: 8000 West Dr., Apt. 107, N. Bay Village, Fla. 33141.

KEWLEY, LaDONNA HUTTON, Dir. of Cont., WCCO-TV, 50 S. 9th St., Mpls., Minn. 55402, '56–; all media depts., Knox Reeves Adv., '44–'56; AWRT, Adv. Club of Minn.; active in civic groups; Univ. of S.D., '44 (Jnlsm. Achiev. aw.); b. Flandreau, S.D., 1922; p. Howard and Ada Freshney Hutton; h. William J. Kewley; res: 2230 Selby Ave., St. Paul, Minn. 55104.

KEY, GENE, Sr. VP, Goodwin, Dennenbaum, Littman & Wingfield, Inc., 2400 West Loop, S., Houston, Tex. 77027, '67–; VP, Air Prod. Dir., '65–'67; AE, TV Prod., '60–'63; Owner, Key Assoc., Dallas, '57–'60; Partner, W. W. Sherrill Co., Dallas, '54–'57; Fashion Group of Houston (Secy., '64–'66), Tex. Wms. Univ., BS, '45; b. Vernon, Tex., 1924; p. Oran and Mina Claer Key; h. Barre Monigold; res: 11718 Longleaf Lane, Houston, Tex. 77024.

KEZERIAN, LILLIAN NANCY, Supvsr. of Pubns., Connecticut General Life Insurance Company, Hartford, Conn. 06115, '68–; PR Asst., '60–'68; Adv. and PR Dept., '55–'60; Claim Dept., '53–'55; ICIE; Wheaton Col., BA, '53 (cum laude); Trinity Col., MA, '61; b. Hartford, Conn., 1931; p. Albert and Mary Malootian Kezerian; res: 156 Manchester St., Hartford, Conn. 06112.

KIBBEE, KATHERINE KIRK, former Reptr., Post-Gazette, Pitt., Pa.; Staff Wtr., Jewish Chronicle, '66; PR Aide, Montefiore Hosp., '65–'66; Daily Messenger (Homestead), '65; Rsch. Advisor, Children's Hosp. of Pitt., '63; Theta Sigma Phi (Nat. Chmn., Div. of Hospitalized Veterans Writing Project, '66–'68), Wms. Press Club of Pitt. (Gertrude Gordon contest, 1st prize, '65), Kappa Tau Alpha, Pitt. Press Club, Soc. of Tech. Wtrs. and Publrs.; Pa. Nwsp. Publrs. Assn. plaque for outstanding student internship, '65; Randolph-Macon Wms. Col.; Am. Acad. of Dramatic Arts; Duquesne Univ., BA, '65; Oh. State Univ., MA, '69; h. Robert Kibbee; c. Robert, Jr., Katherine, Douglas Alan; res: 242 W. 18th Ave., Columbus, Oh. 43210.

KIDNEY, DOROTHY BOONE, Auth: "Come and See" (Moody Press), "Lively Youth Meetings" (Moody Press), "Away from It All" (A. S. Barnes and Co.), many articles, short stories and poems; Public Sch. Tchr: Yarmouth (Me.) Intermediate School,

'64–'69; Gray, Me., '60–'63; b. Presque Isle, Me., 1919; p. Frank and Bertha Libby Boone; h. Milford Kidney; res: Box 106, Yarmouth, Me. 04096.

KIESER, HENRIETTA F., Crtv. Dir., Jocelyn & Gross, Inc., 6404 Maple, Omaha, Neb. 68104, '67–; Copywtr., Knox Reeves Adv. (Mpls., Minn.), '64–'67; Crtv. Dir., VP, Savage-Dow (Omaha), '63–'64; Copy Chief, VP, Bozell & Jacobs, '44–'61; AWRT (Omaha Chptr. VP, '69; Pres., '59; N. Star Chptr. Pres., '66–'67), Omaha Adv. Club (Adv. Wm. of Yr., '56), Alpha Gamma Chi; AFA 9th District Adv. Wm. of Yr., '56; Univ. of Omaha, BA, '40; b. Omaha, Neb., 1919; p. Henry and Sophia Grau Kieser; res: 1203 Marbee Dr., Omaha, Neb. 68124.

KILEY, MARY ELIZABETH, Free-lance Rschr.; Readers Digest Assn.; Smith Col., BA; Radcliffe Col.; res: 127 E. 90th St., N.Y., N.Y. 10028.

KILEY, NANCIE JEAN, Media Supvsr., Grey Advertising, 9025 Wilshire Blvd., Beverly Hills, Cal. 90211, '69–; Media Supvsr., Erwin Wasey Adv., '67–'69; Media Dir., Wyman Anderson McConnell, '65–'67; Media Dir., M. B. Scott Adv., '58–'60; b. L.A., Cal., 1933; p. Phil and Winifred Ray Sutton; c. Clark, Brent, Craig; res: 5039 Buffalo, Sherman Oaks, Cal. 91403.

KILGORE, MARGARET A., Congressional Reptr., United Press International, National Press Bldg. 315, Wash., D.C. 20004, '63–; Statehouse Bur. Chief, Trenton, N.J., '59–'63; Newark, N.J., Bur., '59; Columbus, Oh., Bur., '57; WNPC (Pres., '68–'69); Stephens Col.; Syracuse Univ.; b. Ravenna, Oh.; p. Alfred Kilgore and Donna Voorhees Kilgore Hall; res: 301 G St., S.W., Wash., D.C. 20024.

KILIAN, MARGARET ALICE, Exec. Dir. of PR, Georgia Education Association, 197 Central Ave., S.W., Atlanta, Ga. 30303, '66–; Program Dir., WABE, Atlanta Bd. of Educ., '63–'66; Coordr., Educ. Radio Programs, '48–'63; U.S. Army Training Aid, Signal Corps, '43–'46; Tchr., Atlanta Pub. Schs., '30–'43; Ga. Educ. Assn., NEA, Assn. of Childhood Educ., NAB, AWRT (Atlanta Chptr. Pres., '53; Dir. at Large, '65–'67; Distg. Svc. Aw., '67); BPW (Dogwood Chptr. Pres., '68–'69); Third Army aw. for commty. svc., '65; Oglethorpe Univ., AB (educ.), '30; Columbia Univ., MA (Educ.), '48; Grad. Work, Emory Univ., '63; b. Seattle, Wash.; p. Justus and Margaret Cornell Kilian; res: 4261 Rickenbacker Way N.E., Atlanta, Ga. 30305.

KIMBALL, HELEN STRYKER, Wms. Dir., KIRO, 3rd and Broad, Seattle, Wash. 98121, '57–; Wms. Talent Programmer, TV-Radio, '41–'57; AWRT (Dir. at Large, '67–'68); McCall's Golden Mike Aw., '63; Matrix Table, '65; Wash. Press Wms. Sugar Plum Aw., '66; Youth Ctr. Cert. of Hon., '64; Govt. of South Korea cit. for svc. to orphanages in Seoul; b. Galena, Ill., 1905; p. Henry and Bertha Moser Stryker; h. Charles D. Kimball; c. Mrs. Charles E. Bradley, III; res: Highlands, Seattle, Wash. 98177.

KING, ANDREA, Free-lance Actress; Warner Bros., Universal, Paramount, Fox, MGM., Nat. Gen. Corp.; Broadway theater: "Growing Pains," '33; "Fly Away Home," '36; "Boy Meets Girl," '39; road companies: "Life with Father," "Angel Street"; AEA, AFTRA, SAG, AMPAS, Who's Who of Am. Wm., Blue Book (L.A. register); Madam Dakahanaka Drama Sch., N.Y.C.; b. Paris, France, 1919; p. Douglas and Belle Hart McKee; h. Nathaniel Willis; c. Deborah Anne Willis; res: 260 S. Rodeo Dr., Beverly Hills, Cal. 90212.

KING, ANNIE GREENE, Head Librn., Tuskegee Institute, Tuskegee Institute, Ala. 36088, '66–; Chief Librn.; Ref. Librn.; Librn., Fla. Memorial Col. (St. Augustine); Tchr.-Librn., Public Schs. (N.C.); ALA, Southeastern Lib. Assn., Ala. Lib. Assn., AAUP, AAUW; N.C. Col., BA, '42; BS (Lib. Sci.), '47; Univ. of Ill., MS (Lib. Sci.), '52; b. Trenton, N.C., 1922; p. L. T. and Annie Williams Greene; h. Jay King; c. Jay, Jr., Wayne, M. Denise, Cheryl; res: 207 Johnson St., Tuskegee Institute, Ala. 36088.

KING, ELIZABETH LEONE, Wms. Prom. Dir., New York Mets, Shea Stadium, Flushing, N.Y. 11368, '63–; Adm. Asst., New York Yankees, '32–'60; AWNY, Pubcty. Club of N.Y.; b. Galeton, Pa.; p. Harry and Bessie Bristol King; res: 219 W. 13th St., N.Y., N.Y. 10011.

KING, ESTELLA MAY GOODHART, Ed., Alumni Magazine, The College of Wooster, Galpin Hall, Bever St., Wooster, Oh. 44691, '68–; Ed., Assoc. Dir., Alumni Assn., '60–'68; Assoc. Dir., Assoc. Ed., '55–'60, Assoc. Secy., '52–'55; Wayne County Reptr., Canton Repository, '50–'52; Eng. HS Tchr. (Garfield Hgts., Cleve.), '26–'31; Eng. HS Tchr. (Creston), '25–'26; AAUW, Am. Alumni Cncl. (two Certs. of Achiev., '66); Who's Who of Am. Wm.; Col. of Wooster, BA, '25; b. Orrville, Oh., 1903; p. Ulysses and Ordina Shoup Goodhart; h. Howard King; c. Howard D., Jr., James G., Elizabeth A.; res: Tuckahoe Circle, Wooster, Oh. 44691.

KING, JOANNE JOHNSON, Wms. Dir., KHOU-TV, Corinthian Broadcasting Company, 1945 Allen Pkwy., P.O. 11, Houston, Tex. 77001; Fashion Ambassadoress to Europe World's Fair, '68; b. San Antonio, Tex.; p. Dunlap and Maelean McGill Johnson; h. Robert King; c. Beaufort E., Robin D.; res: 38 Rivercrest Dr., Houston, Tex. 77042.

KING, LANORA GENE, Free-lance Wtr.; News-Feature Staff Wtr., Daily Review, '66–'68; Soc. Ed., Post Dispatch, '65–'66; Assoc. Ed., Claremont Press, '62–'63; TV and radio scriptwtr.; Oh. Jr. Col. Commty. Svc. Aw., '68; U.S. Marine Corps Commty. Svc. aw. for patriotism, '67; active in political interest groups, educ. programs and commty. svc. events; Cal. State Col., '63–'65; b. New Castle, Ind., 1924; p. John Sr., and LaVerne Williams King; res: 4400 Sandalwood Dr., Pleasanton, Cal. 94566.

KING, LIS PETERSEN, Pres., Lis King, Inc., 427

Bloomfield Ave., Montclair, N.J. 07042, '69–; VP, Keyes, Martin & Co. (Springfield), '68, PR Dir., '64–'67; Wtr., The Advance (Dover), '62–'63; Wtr., Daily News (U.S. Virgin Islands), '60–'62; PRSA; b. Copenhagen, Denmark; p. C. O. and Gerda Petersen; h. John R. King; c. Dorte, David, Barbaree; res: 63 Prospect Ave., Montclair, N.J. 07042.

KING, MARIAN, Free-lance Wtr.; hist., religious biogs., short stories, juv. art bks.; Auth: "Kees" (Harper Brothers, '30; Jr. Lit. Guild Selection), "Kees and Kleintje" (Albert Whitman, '34; Jr. Lit. Guild Selection), "Mary Baker Eddy: Child of Promise" (Prentice Hall, '68), "Piccolino" (A. Whitman, '39), "A Gallery of Children" (Acropolis Bks., '67), many others; Lectr., bk. revs.; Rschr.; Auths. Guild of Am., Nat. Wms. Cncl. of Am., Children's Bk. Guild of Wash., D.C.; ANWC; Who's Who in Am.; b. Wash., D.C.; p. Joseph and Jeannette Michel King; res: 4501 Connecticut Ave., Wash., D.C. 20008.

KING, MARION MAY, Head Librn., Lorain Public Library, 351 Sixth St., Lorain, Oh. 44052, '37–'67; Head Librn., Stow (Oh.) Public Lib., '32–'37; Asst., Oberlin Col. Lib., '26–'31; Asst., Dayton (Oh.) Public Lib., '24–'26; ALA, Oh. Lib. Assn. (Pres., '59–'60), Wms. Nat. Bk. Assn., AAUW, Delta Kappa Gamma (Beta Gamma Chptr. Pres., '62–'63; Secy., '49–'52), Lorain County Mental Health Assn., Lorain County Family Svc. Assn.; Oh. Mental Health Assn. cit., '67; Univ. of Mich., AB, '32; b. Wellington, Oh., 1902; p. Harry and Iva Townsend King; res: 1110 11th St., Lorain, Oh. 44052.

KING, PEGGY CAMERON, Auth: "Ladies, Please Come to Order" (Grosset and Dunlap, '68), "Ladies, Let's Travel" (Grosset and Dunlap, '70), over 200 mag. and nwsp. articles; Staff Mbr., Oakland Univ. Wtrs. Conf., eight yrs.; Lectr., other wtrs. confs.; Tchr., adult educ. courses in writing; Detroit Wm. Wtrs. (numerous offs.; Wtr. of the Yr., '61; Bk. Auth. of the Yr., '68), Theta Sigma Phi, WNBA; Univ. of Toronto, BA, '32; Ontario Col. of Educ., '33; b. Midland, Ontario, Canada; p. Angus and Ada Millar Cameron; h. Harry King; c. Garrison, Patricia King Mullett, Susan King Rabick; res: 16140 Reedmere Rd., Birmingham, Mich. 48009.

KING, RETA ELIZABETH, Head Librn., Chadron State College, Chadron, Neb. 69337, '61–; Co-librn., '56–'61; High Sch. Librn., '47–'56; Tchr., '31–'40; NEA, Neb. State Educ. Assn. (Dist #1 Pres., '45), Neb. Assn. of Col. Libs. (Pres., '62), AAUW (Br. Pres., '59, Treas., '65–'69), ALA; Peru State Col., AB, '37; Univ. of Denver, MA, '55; b. Edgar, Neb., 1914; p. John and Pearl Hattan King; res: 828 Bordeaux St., Chadron, Neb. 69337.

KING, VERNE ELSENBOSS, Mgr., Corporate Employee Commtns., Warnaco, Inc., 350 Lafayette St., Bridgeport, Conn. 06602, '69–; Ed., Warnaco News, '62–'69; Ed., Olin, '61–'62; Ed., Columbia Records, CBS, '51–'62; Ed., Chance Vought (United Aircraft), '44–'45; Lectr., Jnlsm., indsl. commtns., and PR,

Conn. Credit Union League and Bunnell HS, Stratford, Conn., '66–'69; ICIE (Dir. of Nat. Affairs from Conn., '67–'69), Conn. IEA (Pres., '66–'67); Boston Univ., BS (Jnlsm.), '43; b. Danbury, Conn.; p. Vernon and Mildred Roswell Elsenboss; h. Gerald King (dec.); c. Susan V., Gerald G., Jr.; res: 1 Barrows St., Stratford, Conn. 06497.

KINGHAM, ELISABETH SLATTER, Ed., house mag., Harris, Kerr, Forster & Company, 420 Lexington Ave., N.Y., N.Y. 10017, '44–'47, '69–; Pers. Dir., '44–'47; Asst. to Exec. Dir., Harvard Bus. Sch. Club, '65–'68; b. Wilkes-Barre, Pa.; p. Frank and Mary Rutledge Slattery; h. T. Victor Kingham; c. Thomas B; res: 309 Ave. C., N.Y., N.Y. 10009.

KINGMAN, LEE, Auth., Free-lance Ed.; over 20 children's bks., incl: "The Year of the Raccoon," "The Best Christmas"; Ed., Children's Bks., Houghton Mifflin Co., '44–'46; Gen. Ed., Illustrators of Children's Books, '57–'66; Newbery and Caldecott Medal Books, '56–'65; Colby Jr. Col., '38; Smith Col., BA, '40; b. Reading, Mass., 1919; p. Leland W. and Genevieve Bosson Kingman; h. Robert Natti; c. Peter, Susanna; res: Blood Ledge, Lanesville, Gloucester, Mass. 01930.

KINGSFORD, JOAN ELIZABETH, Ed., The Bulletin, The Travelers Insurance Companies, One Tower Sq., Hartford, Conn. 06115, '62–; Asst. Ed., '60–'62; Soc. Ed., The Meriden (Conn.) Record, '49–'60; Conn. IEA (Pres. '67–'69; VP, '66–'67, '65–'66; Treas. '64–'65; Rec. Secy., '63–'64; Mbr., Bd. of Dirs., '61–'63); Nat. Civil Defense Photog. Aw., 1st Pl., '58; b. Meriden, Conn. 1930; p. Allen and Florence Weisgraber Kingsford; res: 206 Broad St., Meriden, Conn. 06450.

KINGSTON, LENORE, Actress, Anncr., Prodr., Wtr.; Prodr., MC, "Purely Personal" spots, KFWB (Hollywood), '57–'66; Mrs. Weeks in "General Hospital," '63–'65; Prodr., Talent daytime TV (Hollywood): "Classfied Column," "Mailing of Household Tricks," "Key to the Kitchen," '47–'63; Pioneered in TV, NBC (NY) with interview shows, '41; Radio actress in serials (Chgo.), '37–'40; (N.Y.) '40–'42; Tchr. TV Prod., Pasadena Playhouse, '63–'65; Wtr., Travel Tapes, Nat. Parks; AWRT, Pacific Pioneer Bdcstrs., AFTRA, SAG; many Army, Air Force, Navy Svc. Cits.; Merit Aw., Radio and TV Wm. of Southern Cal., '59; L.A. City Col.; b. L.A., Cal.; p. Walter Kingston and Geneva Henrick Bourgeotte; h. Robert R. Jensen.

KINNEY, JEAN BROWN, Adv. Cnslt. and Auth., Squash Hollow Rd., New Milford, Conn. 06776, '47 and '63–; Cnslt., Knox Reeves Adv., '65–'69; Cnslt., Grey Agcy., (Paris), '64; VP, Benton & Bowles, '59–'64; Copy Supvsr., Grey Agcy., '57–'59; Copy Supvsr., Lennen & Newel, '56–'57; Copy, Biow Agcy., '51–'56; bks: "Start with an Empty Nest" ('68); "How to get 20 to 90% Off on Everything You Buy" ('66); 3 children's bks.; AWNY (2nd VP, '65), Adv. Club of Minn., The Fashion Group, Intl. Platform; Jane Arden Aw., Des Moines Chptr., Theta Sigma Phi (Hon. Mbr., '69); State Univ. of Ia., Cert. of Jnlsm., '34; Coe Col., '28; b.

Waukon, Ia., 1912; p. Dr. C. A. and Bernadette Mooney Stout; h. C. Cleland Kinney; c. Susan and Dina; res: Squash Hollow Rd., New Milford, Conn. 06776.

KINS, GLORIA STARR, Soc. & Diplomatic Ed., Status Magazine, 641 Lexington Avenue, N.Y., N.Y. 10022; New York Ed., Boletin Diplomatico of Mexico, since '63 (and currently); Assoc. Prodr. for Intl. Affairs and Celebrities, Sandy Lesberg Productions., WOR, '64–'67; Assoc. Prodr.; The Caspar Citron Show, WQXR, '60–'64; Asst. to Charles Van Rensselaer, Soc. Colmst. of Journal American, '62–'66; F.P.A.; Pan-American Soc., Dame of the Chaine des Rotisseurs; "Gran Maestre de la Orden National del Merito," rank of Commander by Pres. of Paraguay Alfredo Stroessner, '63; State of N.Y. Cert., "Outstanding Public Service, Bd. of Dirs. of the Stanley M. Isaacs Neighborhood Center and the U.S. Comm. for Refugees, Inc; many other cits.; N.Y.U.; Born N.Y.C. 1927; p. Frank and Claire Elias Starr; h. Richard J. Kins; c. Debora S., Victoria S.; res: 131 East 66 Street., N.Y., N.Y. 10021.

KINTER, ONA LEE, Free-lance Publicist; Labor Rels., Pers., U.S. Steel (Braddock, Pa.), '55–'59; Adv., Frank M. Gallagher Assocs. (Wilmington, Del.), '54; PR Dir., Nwsltr. Ed., Hampton Township, Pa.; Pubcty. Dir., Ed., Hampton Repl. Comm., '67–'69; Theta Sigma Phi; Pa. State Univ., BS, '54; b. Elkton, Md., 1932; p. F. Curtis and Gertrude Benjamin Lee; h. William Kinter; c. Lee Ann, Cydney, Eleanor; res: 4443 Greengrove Dr., Allison Park, Pa. 15101.

KIPLINGER, JOAN REED, Pubns. Ed., Blue Cross of Northeast Ohio, 2066 E. Ninth St., Cleve., Oh. 44115, '66–; Rsch. Ed., Booz, Allen & Hamilton, '64–'66; Asst. Adv. Mgr., Chemical Rubber Co., '57–'58; Asst. Ed., Stouffer Corp., '56–'57; Theta Sigma Phi (life mbr.), Northeast Ohio IEA (Asst. Secy., '66–'67, Secy., '67–'69); Kent State Univ., BA, '55; b. New Philadelphia, Oh., 1933; p. George J. and Emma L. Cattani Reed; c. Martin, Terrence; res: 8177 Stockbridge Rd., Mentor, Oh. 44060.

KIRCHOFF, V. SUE SLAYTON, Free-lance Adv. Copywtr., '65–; Adv. Copywtr., Jordan Marsh (Miami, Fla.), '62–'65; Adv. Copywtr., John Wanamaker (Phila., Pa.), '60–'62; Adv. Copywtr., TV Wtr., Food Fair, '59–'60; Sls. Prom., Procter & Gamble (Pitt.), '58–'59; Theta Sigma Phi (Greater Miami Chptr. Rec. Secy., '66–'67), Univ. of Mo. Sch. of Jnlsm., BJ, '58; b. Chillicothe, Mo., 1936; p. William and Helen Anderson Slayton; h. Glenn Kirchhoff; c. William S., Anne L.; res: 1420 N.W. 173 Terr., Miami, Fla. 33169.

KIRK, CHRISTINA, Feature Wtr., New York Daily News, 220 E. 42nd St., N.Y., N.Y. 10017, '63–; Fin. Reptr., Herald Tribune, '60–'63; Asst. Ed., Dun's Review, '58–'60; Cable Ed., INS, '55–'58; Wms. Page Reptr., Gary (Ind.) Post-Tribune, '52–'54; Reptr., Hays (Kan.) Daily News, '51–'52; Guest Lectr., Blair Acad.

Summer Sch. of Jnlsm., '65, '67, '69; Nwsp. Wms. Club of N.Y. (Treas.; Past Pres.; Best Series aw., '61; Best News Story aw., '66); Reptrs. Association Cultural Interest Aw., '64; Loeb Special Achiev. aw. for Bus. Rept., '61; Paul Tobenkin Cit., '61; Ind. Univ., AB (Jnlsm.), '50; b. Gary, Ind., 1928; p. Peter and Mary Hotchkiss Kirk; h. Joseph De Mul; res: 235 E. 22nd St., N.Y., N.Y. 10010.

KIRK, CLARA MARBURG, Visiting Prof. in Eng., University of Illinois, Chicago Circle, Chgo., Ill. 60680, '67–; Lectr., Prof., Rutgers Univ., '37–'63; Assoc. Prof., Bryn Mawr Col., '33–'36; Instr., Vassar Col., '23–'26, Asst. Prof., '29–'33; Auth., non-fiction, 16 books, incl: "The Altrurian Romances of William Dean Howells" (with R. Kirk, Indiana Press, '68), "Oliver Goldsmith" (Twayne Publrs., '67), "W. D. Howells & Art in His Time," (Rutgers Univ. Press, '65), also many articles and revs.; Fulbright Scholar in Belgium and Rome, '55–'56; Vassar, BA, '20 (Phi Beta Kappa); Univ. of Pa., MA, '21; Univ. of Chgo., PhD, '29; b. Phila., Pa., 1898; p. Edgar and Fanny Moncure Marburg; h. Rudolf Kirk; c. Susanne B., Donald; res: 4037 Rear, Baltimore Ave., Phila., Pa. 19104.

KIRK, LUCILE DVORAK, Free-lance Wtr., Edtl. Cnslt.; Assoc., Dept. Ed., Parents' Magazine, '35–'67; Ed., School Management, '35–'51; Co-owner, Chelsea Bk. Shop (N.Y.C.), '27–'37; Copywtr., McCann-Erickson, '25–'27; Reptr., Feature Wtr., Sch. Page Ed., Cleve. Press, '22–'24; Asst. Dir. Pubns., Cleve. Bd. of Educ., '20–'22; Theta Sigma Phi (VP, '66–'69, '58–'60; N.Y.C. Chptr. Pres., '56–'58; Distg. Svc. Aw., '62; Camp Fire Girls, Soc. of Am. Travel Wtrs. (Bd. '62–'65; Northeast Chptr. VP, '66–'67), ZONTA; Alpha Omicron Pi Distg. Svc. Aw., '67; AIGA Cert. of Merit, '58; Western Reserve, BA, '19 (Cits. '62, '69); Tchrs. Col., Columbia Univ., MA, '44; b. Cleve., Oh.; p. Joseph and Ada Ackley Dvorak; h. George W. Kirk; c. Catherine Ada (Mrs. Richard L. Stauffer), Mary Daler (Mrs. Ray Smith); res: 1 Hillside Ave., Pelham, N.Y. 10803.

KIRK, PHYLLIS, Actress, Commentator, Wtr., Lectr., represented by Intl. Famous Agcy.; Nora in TV series, "The Thin Man," for 2-1/2 years (Emmy nominee); various plays on Broadway, Chgo. and other cities; Guest TV appearances; Motion pictures; Corr., News, WBKB; Modr., Wtr., "The Young Set," ABC-TV; Guest Interviewer, NBC's "Monitor"; Guest Lectr. at various univs.; AFTRA, SAG, AEA, WGA; b. Laurens, N.Y.; p. Theodore and Adele Kroohs Kirkegaard; h. Warren Bush.

KIRK, RUTH KRATZ, Wtr., Photogr.; Auth: "Olympic Rain Forest" (Univ. Wash.), "Japan, Crossroads of East and West" (T. Nelson), 10 other non-fiction bks.; Tchr., Photog., Peninsula Col.; Lit. Guild aw., '66; Governor's writing aw., '67; Northwest Bksellers. aw., '67, Wash. Press Wms. aw., '69; Occidental Col., '43–'44; Tenn. State Col., '45–'46; b. L.A., Cal., 1925; p. Reginald and Esther Cumberland Kratz; h. Louis Kirk; c. Bruce G., Wayne L.; res: 1420 Mt. View S., Tacoma, Wash. 98465.

KIRKENDALL, NORMA A., Dir. of Prom., Woman's International Bowling Congress, 1225 Dublin Rd., Columbus, Oh. 43215, '64–; Ed., Woman Bowler; PR; articles, religious educ.; ICIE, Central Oh. Indsl. Eds. (Pres., '66); NBC Pubcty. Aw., '65; Oh. State Univ., BS, '39; Chgo. Theological Seminary, ThD, '57; b. Ashland, Ky., 1918; p. Gard and Ethel Kirkendall; res: 1037 Hardesty Pl. E., Columbus, Oh. 43204.

KIRSCHNER, MADELINE, Fgn. Lang. Specialist, Brooklyn Public Library, Ingersoll Building, Grand Army Plaza, Bklyn., N.Y. 11238, '67–; Sr. Librn., '67–; Librn., Lang. and Literature Dept., '66–'67; Librn., Telephone Ref. Dept., '64–'66; Librn., Kings Highway Br. Lib., '63; ALA, N.Y. Lib. Club, Gamma Sigma Sigma Nat. Svc. (Nat. Second VP; Svc. Coordr.; Ed., svc. publns, '67–'69; Nat. Third VP, PR; Ed., "Gamma Gossip", '65–'67; Nat. Secy., '63–'65); Who's Who of Am. Wm.; Who's Who in the East; Who's Who in Lib. Svc.; Dic. of Intl. Biog.; Bklyn. Col., BA, '62 (cum laude); Columbia Univ., MS (Lib. Sci.), '63; b. N.Y.C., 1941; p. Max and Esther Weiner Kirschner; res: 399 Ocean Pkwy., Bklyn., N.Y. 11218.

KIRSHNER, DARLENE CARRON, Free-lance Actress, c/o Robert Longnecker Agency, 1369 Warner Ave., L.A., Cal. 90024; Miss Mo., '54; Miss. Intl. Air Parcel Post; Miss Advertising-St. Louis; Miss Aviation; TV show, Channel 11, St. Louis; TWA Airline Stewardess; Univ. of Mo.; b. St. Louis, Mo., 1936; p. Anthony L. and Mary C. Gamewell Carron; h. Mervyn Edward Kirshner; c. Shaun Patrick, Shea Timothy; res: 1369 Warner Ave., L.A., Cal. 90024.

KIRSHNER, GLORIA I., Educ. Cnslt., Ed., Teachers Guides to Television, P.O. Box 564, Lenox Hill Sta., N.Y., N.Y. 10021, '68–; Educ. Cnslt., '62–; Ed., Tchrs. Guides to the 21st Century, '67–'69; Asst. to the Exec. Prodr., Wtr., "Animal Secrets," NBC, '66–'68; Educ. Cnslt., Robert Sudek Assoc., '65–; Educ. Cnslt., Ideal Toy Co., NBC, '62–'64; Ed., NBC Tchrs. Guides, '62–'65; Wtr., "Exploring," '63–'64; Tchr. (N.Y.C.), Free-lance Cnslt., '55–'62; Auth., "From Instinct to Intelligence" (Grosset & Dunlap, '69); Guest Ed., Mademoiselle, '53; steering comm., Mass Media Feasibility Study, '67; articles, Family Circle, pfsnl. pubn.; various orgs.; Barnard Col., AB, '53; Columbia Univ., Tchrs. Col., MA, '58.

KISH, FRANCES, Free-lance Wtr.; presently affiliated with New England Writing Assoc.; former Ed., Movies, Photoplay; Prodr., Wtr., Wendy Barrie TV show; Contrb. Ed., Macfadden Pubns.; OPC, NATAS, Am. Soc. for Psychical Rsch.; res: 400 E. 57th St., N.Y., N.Y. 10022.

KISH, HENRIETTE, Colmst., Corr., North American Newspaper Alliance, Inc., '58–; Assoc. Ed., Lifetime Living, '51–'55; Asst. Ed., Look, '42–'51; Auth., "Questions Older People Ask" (E. P. Dutton, '55); OPC, NWC of N.Y.; res: 400 E. 57th St., N.Y., N.Y. 10022.

KISLING, FRANCES RITA, Librn., Vestal Central School, Vestal, N.Y., '55–; Southern Tier Librns. Assn. (Past Pres., Past Secy.), WNBA, PTA (Life Mbr., for svc. to sch.); State Univ. of N.Y. at Geneseo, BS; ext. courses, Syracuse Univ., Cortland, Oneonta, Geneseo; b. Binghamton, N.Y.; p. Herman and Gladys Taylor Kisling; res: 307 June St., Endicott, N.Y. 13760.

KISS, MARY CLEMENT, Staff Wtr., Kingsport Times-News, E. Market St., Kingsport, Tenn. 37660, '67–; Reptr., '50–'55; Theta Sigma Phi; Univ. of Mich., BA (Jnlsm.), '50; h. Alvin Kiss.

KISTER, HANNA SILBER, Pres., Roy Publishers, Inc., 30 E. 74th St., N.Y., N.Y. 10021, '42–; Pres., '58–; worked in publishing with husband in Warsaw, Poland ('24–'42) and N.Y.C.; Am. Bk. Publrs. Cncl., PEN Am. Ctr., WNBA; b. Poland; h. Marian Kister (dec.); c. Mrs. C. Lombrogis, Mrs. G. W. Clark.

KITCHEN, HELEN ANGELL, Wtr., Ed.; Ed.-in-Chief, Africa Report (Wash., D.C.), '60–'68; Special Asst. to Dir. of Rsch. for Near East, Africa, S. Asia, Dept. of State, '50–'58; Asst. Ed., Middle East Journal, '48; Edtl. Asst., Readers Digest, '42–'44; Auth: "Footnotes to the Congo Story" (Walker & Co., '67), "A Handbook of African Affairs" (Praeger, '64), others; Theta Sigma Phi; Secy. of State outstanding svc. aw., '57; Sigma Delta Chi aw., '42; Univ. of Ore., BA, '42 (Phi Beta Kappa, cum laude); b. Ore.; p. Lloyd and Hilda Miller Angell; h. Jeffrey C. Kitchen; c. Jeffrey Jr., Erik, Lynn; res: 10401 Riverwood Dr., Potomac, Md. 20854.

KITTRELL, HELEN HAND, Dir., Clinch-Powell Regional Library Center (Clinton, Tenn.) '52–'69; Regional Librn. (Bryson City, N.C.) '45–'52; Organized Lib. Svc., Fontana Dam, N.C., '42–'45; In charge of Adult Lib. Svc., TVA School and Commty. Library (Norris, Tenn.), '39–'42; Organized the TVA Sch. Library, '35–'39; Revisor, Emory Univ. Lib. Sch. (Atlanta, Ga.), '31–'34; Tenn. Lib. Assn., Southeastern Lib. Assn., ALA; Univ. of Kan., AB, '24; Emory Univ. Lib. School; BA (Lib. Sci.), '31; b. Topeka, Kan. 1903; p. Maynard Fletcher and Ada Grabendike Hand; res: 5354 Brook Way, Apt. 3, Columbia, Md. 21043.

KIYAK, ALEXIS JOAN, Media Dir., Johnson & Dean, Inc., 302-G Waters Bldg., Grand Rapids, Mich. 49502, '69–; Time Byr., Acc. Asst.

KLAGSBRUN, FRANCINE LIFTON, Auth., Ed. Cnslt.; Exec. Ed., Cowles Bk. Co., '65–'68; Mng. Ed., Hart Publ. Co., '65; Exec. Ed., Ency. Americana, Grolier, '64–'65; Assoc. Ed., World Bk. Ency., '57–'64; Auth: "Sigmund Freud" (Watts, '67), "Psychiatry: A Book for Young People" (Watts, '69), "The Story of Moses" (Watts, '68), "The First Book of Spices" (Watts, '68); Modern Lang. Assn., Intl. Platform Assn.; Bklyn. Col., BA, '52 (magna cum laude; Phi Beta Kappa); Inst. of Fine Arts, N.Y.U., MA (Art Hist.), '59; Jewish Theological Seminary of Am., BHL, '52; b. Bklyn., N.Y.; p. Benjamin and Anna Pike Lifton; h. Samuel C. Klagsbrun; res: 45 East End Ave., N.Y., N.Y. 10028.

KLARK, PEGGY JEAN (Peggy Klotz), PR, Contact Rep., Jack Waltzer Orchestra, '59–; former model; Pubcty. Club of N.Y. (Outstanding Achiev. Aw., '63), Intl. Debutante Ball Comm., Intl. Rescue Comm., Intl. House, Kidney Disease Fndn. (Bd. Mbr.), Easter Seal Comm. (Bd. Mbr.); Spanish Inst. Aw., '66; Duke Univ., AB; Latin Am. Inst.; b. Staunton, Va.; p. Morris and Dorothy Rosenthal Klotz; res: 240 Central Park S., N.Y., N.Y. 10019.

KLASS, BLOSSOM MARCUS, Wms. Ed., New York & Brooklyn Daily, 2427 Surf Ave., Bklyn., N.Y. 11224, '56–; Bklyn. Col., BA, '51; MA, '54; b. Bklyn., N.Y.; p. Max and Anette Marcus; h. Lionel Klass; res: 1444 E. 23rd St., Bklyn., N.Y. 11210.

KLEIN, AGATHA LINDNER, Chief, Central Library, St. Paul Public Library, 90 W. Fourth St., St. Paul, Minn. 55102, '58–; Coordr., Adult Svcs., '52–'58; Instr., Univ. of Minn. Lib. Sch., '48–'49; Supvsr., Public Libs. Dept. of Educ., '42–'48; Librn., '38–'42; ALA, Minn. Lib. Assn. (cit., '68); Aurora Col., BA, '35; Univ. of Minn., BS (Lib. Sci.), '38 (magna cum laude); b. Sandwich, Ill.; p. Philip and Ethel Harrison Lindner; h. John A. Klein; c. Harrison J.; res: 1476 N. Grotto St., St. Paul, Minn. 55117.

KLEIN, CHARLOTTE CONRAD, Sr. VP, Harshe-Rotman & Druck, Inc., 300 E. 44th St., N.Y., N.Y. 10017, '68–; VP, Group Supvsr., '65–'68; Exec. VP, Flanley & Woodward, '62–'65; VP, Edward Gottlieb & Assoc., '50–'62; David O. Selznick Studios; CBS Radio; UP; Lectr., Boston Univ., New Sch. For Social Rsch.; PRSA (Secy.-Treas., '68; Cit., '67), CWPR; U.S. Trademark Assn. cit., '63; U.C.L.A., AB, '44; New Sch. For Social Rsch.; res: 138 E. 36th St., N.Y., N.Y. 10016.

KLEIN, ESTHER MOYERMAN, Publr., Philadelphia Jewish Times, 1530 Spruce St., Phila., Pa. 19102, '53–; Staff Mbr., '25–; Ed., Phila. Art Alliance Bul., '45–'49; Commentator, WPEN Radio, '49–'53; Auth: "A Guidebook to Jewish Philadelphia" ('65), "International House Celebrity Bookbook I" ('64; II, '66); Phila. Jewish Times Inst. (Pres. and Founder), Rittenhouse Sq. Wms. Comm. Phila. Orchestra (Pres. and Founder), Long Beach Island Fndn. for Arts and Scis. (Founder), "Today's Concert" Lect. Series for Phila. Orchestra (Dir., '59–'69); Wm. of the Yr. Aw., B'nai Brith Wms. Cncl., '69; Temple Univ., '29 (Distg. Grad. Aw., '64); Univ. of London, '54; b. Phila., Pa., 1907; p. Louis and Rebecca Feldman Moyerman; h. Philip Klein; c. Arthur, Karen (Mrs. Paul Mannes).

KLEIN, LEONORE GLOTZER, Librn., White Plains Schools, Eastview Avenue Junior High School, White Plains, N.Y., '62–; Pleasantville, N.Y., Schs., '59–'62; Ref. Librn., Fla. Southern Col. (Lakeland, Fla.), '53–'59; Librn., Eng. Tchr., N.Y.C. Sch. System, '50–'53; Auth., 17 published juv. pic. bks., incl. "Brave Daniel"

(Young Scott, '58; Jr. Lit. Guild selection); N.Y. State Lib. Assn., Authors Guild; Barnard Col., BA, '36; Wellesley Col., MA, '37; Columbia Univ. Sch. of Lib. Sci., MS (Lib. Sci.), '64 b. N.Y.C., 1916; p. Isidor and Sadie April Glotzer; h. Joseph M. Klein; c. Robert, Judith Stenn; res: 7 Barbara Lane, Hartsdale, N.Y. 10530.

KLEIN, MIRIAM BENOWITZ, Asst. Pubns. Ed., Holder, Kennedy Company, Inc., 712 Baker Building, 110 21st Ave., S. Nashville, Tenn. 37203, '69–; Secy. to Gen. Sls. Mgr., WLAC-TV, '61–'62; Wtr., Med. Nwsltr. and Mags. Dept., William Douglas McAdams (N.Y.C.), '59–'60; Asst. Wms. Pg. Ed., Perth Amboy (N.J.) Evening News, '58; Theta Sigma Phi (Nashville Chptr. VP, Treas., '63–'69; Archivist, '61–'62); Syracuse Univ., BA, '59 (Phi Beta Kappa); b. Perth Amboy, N.J., 1937; p. Max and Fannie Lipack Benowitz; h. Jerome S. Klein; c. Lawrence Neil, Regina Beth, Risa Lynn; res: 4414 Sunnybrook Dr., Nashville, Tenn. 37205.

KLEIN, SHIRLEY ELIZABETH, Cnslt. for Nwsps. and Am. Conslt., International Publishing Corporation, Ltd., of London, Eng.; Exec. Asst., Westchester Rockland Nwsp., '55–'64; Cnslt., ANPA, '51–'55; Asst. Ed., Commerce Clearing House, '48–'50; Theta Sigma Phi, Pi Beta Phi, DAR; DePauw Univ., BA, '46 (Mortar Bd.); Kent Col. of Law, Chgo.; b. Blue Island, Ill., 1924; p. Alden J. and Hazel Airey Klein; res: 95 A Granite St., Rockport, Mass. 01966.

KLEINHENZ, LOUISE ELEANOR ROSS, Ed., The Hoosier Schoolmaster and The Communicator, Office of State Supt. of Public Instruction, Room 110 State House, Indpls., Ind. 46204, '68–; Edtl. Asst., Adv. Mgr., The Ind. Tchr., '54–'67; Pubcty: Marion County His. Soc., '65–; Southside Civic Org., '59–'61; PTA, '47, '56–'58; Easter Sunrise Svc., '45–'46; Home Show, '41; Local Ed., Marion County Mail, '28–'40; Pubcty., Palace Theatre, '24–'27; Co-auth., "The First 50 Years of the Indiana Congress of Parents and Teachers, Inc." ('62), other pubns.; various orgs; Butler Univ., AB, '28; b. Indpls., Ind.; p. Henry and Mabel Morton Ross; h. John E. Kleinhenz; c. Christopher; res: Indpls., Ind.

KLEMESRUD, JUDY LEE, Reptr., Wms. News Dept., The New York Times, 229 W. 43rd St., N.Y., N.Y. 10036, '66–; City Desk Reptr., Chgo. Daily News, '62–'66; Free-lance articles, Cosmopolitan, This Week, Glamour; N.Y. Nwsp. Wms. Club Annual Aw. for Best Wms. Page Story, '68; Univ. of Ia., BA (Jnlsm.), '61; Columbia Univ., MS (Jnlsm.), '62; b. Thompson, Ia., 1939; p. Theo and Glee Florence Klemesrud; res: 222 E. 75th St., N.Y., N.Y. 10021.

KLESH, CAROLINE BUNTING, Ed., Publr., The Observer, Inc., 115 Front St., Massapequa Park, N.Y. 11762, '59–; Secy.-Treas., Klesh & Klesh Cnslts., '56–'59; PR, N.Y. Public Lib., '51–'54; N.Y. Press Assn., Farmingdale Village Hist., '63–; Vassar Col., '44 (cum laude); b. Pontiac, Mich., 1922; p. George and Marion Searight Bunting; h. Frank Klesh; c.

Christopher, Michael; res: 33 Merritt Rd., Farmingdale, N.Y. 11735.

KLIJN, TRUDI S., Assoc. Ed. of Lit., The United Methodist Board of Missions, 475 Riverside Dr., N.Y., N.Y. 10027, '69–; Asst. Ed., The Methodist Wm./response, '67–'69; RPRC; Univ. of Utrecht (Holland), BA, '62; Boston Univ. Sch. of Theology, BD, '66 (cum laude); b. Terschelling, Holland, 1938; p. Gerard and Everdina de Koning Klijn; res: De W. Pfisterlaan 55, Driebergen, Holland.

KLINE, CECELIA TILLEY, Pres., Kline, Inc., Advertising & Public Relations, P.O. Box 15012, Phoenix, Ariz. 85018, '68–; Ed., Heard Museum of Anthropology & Primitive Arts, Newsltr., '69–; Pres., Ed., Star Times, '68–; Cecelia Kline & Assoc., '60–'68; Feature Wtr., The Phoenix Gazette, '56–'59; Dir., PR and Adv., The Ebco Mfg. Co., '47–'50; Ed., Ohio Jersey News, '48–'49; Visiting Lectr., Univ. of Ariz., Phoenix Col.; PRSA (Charter Mbr., Cnslrs. Section, Ariz. Chptr.), Ariz. Press Wm., Nat. Soc. of Arts and Letters (Nat. Bd. Mbr.), NFPW, Phoenix Press Club; more than 60 aws. in PR and Adv., '57–'69; Oh. State Univ., '38–'40, George Washington Univ., '42–'44; b. Portsmouth, Ohio; p. William Benjamin and Minnie Belle Seel Tilley; h. Doil Kline; c. Donna Cecelia; res: 4515 E. Cheery Lynn Rd., Phoenix, Ariz. 85018.

KLINGERMAN, ETHEL, Lib. Dir., Moorestown Free Library, 16 E. Main St., Moorestown, N.J. 08057, '66–; Librn., Eastern Baptist Col. (St. Davids, Pa.), '56–'66; Field Dir., Lycoming County Girl Scout Cncl. (Williamsport), '55–'56; Cataloger, James V. Brown Public Lib., '54–'55; Cataloger, Univ. of Pa. (Phila.), '51–'54; ALA, AAUP, N.J. Lib. Assn., Libs. Unlimited of South Jersey (Secy.-Treas., '68–'69), Assn. of Col. & Rsch. Libs., (Del. Valley Chptr. Secy.-Treas., '65–'67); Wilson Col., BA, '50; Grad. Sch. of Lib. Sci., Drexel Inst. of Tech., MS (Lib. Sci.), '51; Muncy, Pa., 1929; p. Foster J. and Ida Black Klingerman; res: 505 Camden Ave., Moorestown, N.J. 08057.

KNAGGS, BONNIE LOU, Corr., Republican·Courier, 308 Broadway, Findlay, Oh. 45840, '69–; Ed., North Baltimore News, '65–'69; Adv. Mgr., '61–'65; Reptr., '59–'61; Soc. Ed., Advertiser Press, '58–'59; BPW, C. of C.; b. Wood County, Oh., 1930; res: 223 East St., North Baltimore, Oh. 45872.

KNAPIK, DIANNE M., Prod. Mgr., Gralla Publications, 7 E. 43rd St., N.Y., N.Y. 10017; Asst. to Prod. Mgr., '65–'67; N.Y. Public Lib., '64–'65; Librn., Newman Club Lib., N.Y.U., '64; N.Y.U, '63–'64; b. Yonkers, N.Y., 1946; p. Joseph and Dolores Fariello Knapik, res: 26-60 College Point Causeway, College Point, N.Y. 11354.

KNIGHT, ALICE TIRRELL, Rep., Hillsborough Dist. 4, New Hampshire General Court, '67–; Reg. Home Econst., Frigidaire Sls. Corp., '48–'64; Home Econst., Boyd Corp. (Portland, Me.), '46–'47; Mt. Ida Jr. Col.,

(Newton Centre, Mass.), '40–'45; Prin., Bartlett Sch. (Goffstown), '38–'40; AWRT (New England Chptr. Dir.), Am. Home Econs. Assn., NHFL (New England Chptr. Pres., '61), BPW, Soroptimist Club; Univ. of N.H., BA, '25; b. Manchester, N.H., 1903; p. Nathan and Clara Stiles Tirrell; h. Norman Knight; res: Addison Rd., RFD 2, Goffstown, N.H. 03045.

KNIGHT, CHARLOTTE WILLIAMS, Dir., Univ. Lib., Wisconsin State University, Platteville, Wis. 53818, '55–; Visiting Lectr., Univ. of Wis., '52–'55; Hosp. Lib., Hines Hosp., (Hines, Ill.), '46–'52; Bus. and Sci. Lib. Br. Supvsr., Rockford (Ill.) Public Lib., '45–'50; Lib. Asst., '32–'34; Lib. Asst., Lawrence Univ., '28–'30; ALA, Ill. Lib. Assn., Wis. Lib. Assn. (Pres., '67–'68; Secy. Exec. Bd., '56–'57), AAUW, AAUP, NEA, WEA; Univ. of N.D., '25–'26; Lawrence Univ., BA, '31 (cum laude); Univ. of Ill. (Lib. Sci.); Univ. of Wis., BA (Lib. Sci.), '51 (cum laude); b. Camp Douglas, Wis., 1909; p. Curtis John and Ermina Irene Pettis Williams; h. R. C. Knight; c. Richard C., Enola Jean Woodard, Geraldine Carol Manhan, Janet Ermina Wisner, Susan Charlotte Seaver; res: 1190 N. Eastman St., Platteville, Wis. 53818.

KNIGHT, GERALDINE PARKER, Pres. and Owner, Verified Audit Circulation Corporation, 1801 Ave. of the Stars, Gateway West, Century City, L.A., Cal. 90067, '64–; VP, '52–'63; VP, Knight and Parker, '46–'52; Assoc., Cal. Assocs., '43–'46; Beta Gamma Sigma, '55–'60, Order of Artus, USC (Pres., '63), Am. Econ. Assn.; Who's Who of Am. Wm.; Univ. of Iowa, BA, '33, U.C.L.A., MBA (Bus. Adm.), '55; PhD candidacy in Econ. at University of Southern Cal., '64; b. Memphis, Tenn., 1911; p. Abe and Vallie Wilson Parker; h. John Knight; res: 1744 Midvale Ave., L.A., Cal. 90024.

KNIGHT, MARIAN EBERSON, PR Dir., The Cincinnati Historical Society, Eden Park, Cinn., Oh. 45202, '65–; Promotion/Mdsng. Dir., WSAI Radio, '57–'61; Wtr., Employee-Plant Commty. Rels., General Electric Company (Cinn.), '54–'56; PRSA, Theta Sigma Phi; Rollins Col., '48–'50; Univ. of Ky., AB, '52 (cum laude); Univ. of Cinn., '54–'55; res: 4926 LeBlond Ave., Cinn., Oh. 45226.

KNIGHT, RUTH ADAMS, Auth., '43–; Radio Script Wtr., '35–'58; Bk. Reviewer, New York Sun, '30–'35; Reptr., Bk. and Drama Ed., Toledo (Oh.) Times, '20–'30; Auth: "Certain Harvest" (Doubleday and Co.), "Queen of Roses" (Doubleday), "The Treasured One" (E. P. Dutton), "Halfway to Heaven" (McGraw-Hill), "Women Must Weep" (Dell) "The Land Beyond" (McGraw-Hill), numerous other novels, non-fiction books; PEN, Auths. League, Auths. Guild, Radio Wtrs. Guild (Co-founder), Woman Pays Club, Oh. NWC ('25–'30); Toledo Univ.; b. Defiance, Oh.; p. John and Lucy Shead Yingling; c. Elizabeth Lou Bixby (Mrs. William Courtney), John Adams Knight; res: 1430 Oak St. Studio B., S. Pasadena, Cal. 91030; Roxbury, Conn. 06783.

KNORR, LYNN HORTENSE, Data Info. Supvsr., Midwest Graphics, Inc., Box 3457, Sioux Falls, S.D. 57108, '68–; Downwind Pubns., '67; Asst. Film Dir., KORN-TV (Mitchell, S.D.), '65–'67; Dept. of Telecommtns., Southern State Col. (Springfield), '62–'65; Brownie film aw., '65; Southern State Col., '63–'65; b. Bison, S.D., 1944; p. Hector and Eleanor Kozcheckie Knorr; res: 501 S. Phillips, Sioux Falls, S.D. 57108.

KNOWLES, ALISON, Artist; Special Projects Ed., Something Else Press, '68–'69; one-man show, Nonagon Gallery, N.Y.C., '58; Judson Gallery, '62; group shows, Cologne (Germany), L.A., N.Y., '63–'64; Middlebury Col.; Pratt Inst., BFA, '56; Manhattan Sch. of Printing; Guggenheim Grant, '68; b. N.Y.C., 1933; p. Dr. Edwin and Lois Beckwith Knowles; h. Richard C. Higgins; c. Hannah, Jessie; res: 238 W. 22nd St., N.Y., N.Y. 10011.

KNUDSON, ROZANNE, Media Cnslt., Media Plus, 60 Riverside Dr., N.Y., N.Y. 10024, '68–; Tchr., Adelphi Univ., Purdue Univ.; Supvsr., Eng., Hicksville (L.I.) Schs., '67–; Auth: "Selected Objectives in the English Language Arts" (Houghton Mifflin), other textbks.; Brigham Young Univ., BA, '54; Univ. of Ga., MA, '58; Stanford Univ., PhD, '67; b. Wash., D.C., 1932; p. James and Ruth Ellsworth Knudson; res: 73 Blvd., Sea Cliff, N.Y. 11579.

KOBALLA, LOUISE HINKSON, Prod. Mgr., Belden & Frenz & Lehman Inc., 1400 Keith Bldg., Cleve., Oh. 44115, '55–; Burlington (Ia.) Jr. Col., '38–'40, Univ. of Iowa, BFA, '42; Parsons Sch. of Design, N.Y.C., '46–'48; Cert.; b. Burlington, Ia., 1920; p. Harry M. and Ethel Penney Hinkson; h. (div.); res: 3219 Rocky River Dr., Apt. 16, Cleve., Oh. 44111.

KOBER, BODIL OXENVAD, PR Exec., Chicago Chamber Orchestra Tours, 332 S. Michigan Ave., Chgo., Ill. 60604; h. Dieter Kober.

KOCH, ALICE M., Program Dir., KMOX, One Memorial Dr., St. Louis, Mo. 63102, '66–; Wms. Adv. Club, AWRT, Theta Sigma Phi, Adult Educ. Cncl., Press Club of St. Louis, Mo. Bdcst. Assn., Bdcst. Prom. Assn.; Who's Who in Midwest, Who's Who of Am. Wm., Who's Who in Bus. and Industry, Downtown St. Louis Aw., '65; Northwestern Univ., BS (Jnlsm.), '46 (magna cum laude); b. St. Louis, Mo., 1925; p. E. R. and Frances Mary Kricker Methudy; c. John Thomas; res: 200 Mansion House Ctr., Apt. 310, St. Louis, Mo. 63102.

KOCH, DOROTHY CLARKE, Wtr., fiction; Auth: "I Play at the Beach," "Gone Is My Goose," "Let It Rain," "When the Cows Got Out," "Monkeys Are Funny That Way," "Up the Big Mountain"; Owner, Private Sch., "The Fives"; Who's Who of Am. Wm.; Who's Who in the South; Contemporary Auths.; British Biographical Dic., Blue Bk. of London; Meredith Col., BA, '47; Univ. of N.C., Grad. Sch.; b. Ahoskie, N.C., 1924; p. David Arthur and Agnes

Jones Clarke; h. William Julian Koch; c. Patricia Koch Cribb, David, Jean, Deborah; res: 401 Clayton Rd., Coker Hills, Chapel Hill, N.C. 27514.

KOCHA, JUNE HAGGSTROM, KMO, Broadcast House, Inc., P.O. Box 1651, Tacoma, Wash. 98401, '45–; b. Tacoma, Wash., 1928; p. Olaf and Margaret Pearson Haggstrom; h. John Kocha; c. Pamela; res: 2009 Brookdale Rd. E., Tacoma, Wash. 98445.

KOCIN, IOLA GRIMM, Asst. Prof. of Art, Adelphi University, Garden City, N.Y. 11530, '65–; New Products Ed., American Grocer Publication, 21 Ontario Rd., Bellerose, N.Y. 11426, '50–; Art Tchr., Homer (N.Y.) Acad. and HS; Art Tchr., N.Y.C. Sch. System; Free-lance Artist, Designer: fashion, adv., illus.; AWNY, AAUW; Who's Who of Am. Wm.; Harriet T. Leavenworth Painting Aw., '37; art prizes, N.Y. State Fair, '37, '38; Schenectady Art League Show prize, '40; Syracuse Univ., BFA, '37; Cert. in Art Educ., '40; Otis Art Inst., '39; b. Syracuse, N.Y., 1917; p. Benjamin and Anna Elstien Grimm; h. Sidney Kocin; c. Ann Flam; res: 21 Ontario Rd., Bellerose, N.Y. 11426.

KOERSELMAN, GLADA REICHERT, Ed., LeMars Daily Sentinel, LeMars, Ia. 51031; h. Dick Koerselman.

KOESTER, DOROTHY ANN, VP, Media Planning & Production, Inc., 1346 Connecticut Ave. N.W., Wash., D.C. 20036, '64–; Retail Wtr., Elder & Johnson Co. (Dayton, Oh.); Wtr., Asst. Prog. Dir., WHIO TV; Radio/TV Wtr., Fed. Civil Defense Adm.; AWRT; Several Retail Adv. Aws. for copy; Adv. Club Aws. in Oh., Mich., for best television copy and prod.; Mount St. Joseph Col. (Cinn., Oh.), BA, '50; b. Dayton, Oh., 1929; p. R. J. and Della Phillips Koester; res: 4000 Tunlaw Rd., Wash., D.C. 20007.

KOESTLER, FRANCES A., PR Cnslt., Ed., Free-lance Wtr., specializing in welfare, health, commty. rel.; Wms. Pg. Wtr., Nat. Jewish Monthly, '59–; Dir. of Commty. Rels., Jewish Child Care Assn. of N.Y., '57–'63; Dir. of PR, Nat. Travelers Aid Assn., '52–'57; Overseas Pubcty. Dir., Am. Joint Distrb. Comm. (Paris, France), '46–'47; Dir. of PR, Welfare Cncl. of N.Y.C., '43–'46; Auth: "Creative Annual Reports" ('69), "Careers in Social Work" ('64); Nat. PR Cncl. for Health and Welfare Svcs. (Secy., '69–'70), Nat. Conf. on Soc. Welfare; Bklyn. Col., BA, '36; b. N.Y.C.; p. Louis and Minna Rindner Adlerstein; h. Milton Koestler; res: 135 Ashland Pl., Bklyn., N.Y. 11201.

KOHLENBERG, HELEN ETHEL, VP and Mng. Ed., The Western Spirit, Miami County Publishing Co., Inc., 113 S. Pearl, Paola, Kan. 66071, '56–; Ed., '51–'56; Assoc. Ed., '38–'51; Reptr., '28–'38; NFPW, Kan. Press Wm.; Ottawa (Kan.) Bus. Col., '22–'23; Jr. Col. of Paola, '36; b. Louisburg, Kan., 1907; p. August H. and Maude Wren Kohlenberg; res: 406 E. Peoria, Paola, Kan. 66071.

KOLBA, BEATRICE MOORE, Ed., Copywtr., Victor Comptometer Corporation, Business Machines Group, 3900 N. Rockwell, Chgo., Ill. 60618, '62–; Ed., "Comptometer Circle," '59–'61; Copy Ed., "American Business Magazine," Dartnell Corp., '51–'59; BEMA Indsl. Jnlsm. Aw., '67; Northwestern Univ., '43–'47; b. Chgo., Ill., 1918; p. William F. and Anna G. Sahlin Moore; h. Stanley Kolba; res: 4120 N. California Ave., Chgo., Ill. 60618.

KOLLER, ANNE HESSE, Adv. and Sls. Prom. Dir., Lenco Photo Products Inc., Subs. of GAF Corp., 140 W. 51st St., N.Y., N.Y. 10019, '69–; Pres., Exec. Prodr., Rossmore Prods. and Selling Methods, '59–; Prodr., Roger Wade Prods., '55–'59; Asst. to Mdsng. Ed., Look, '52–'55; Cnslt., sls. prom., teaching, and educ. programs; Am. Soc. of Travel Agts. Pubcty. Comm.; Hunter Col., BA, '70; b. N.Y.C., 1931; p. Gustave and Kathleen Flaherty Heese; h. Karl Koller; c. Suzanne Elizabeth, Karl Gerard, Miriam Thérèse, Stephen Lawrence; res: 54 Rossmore Ave., Bronxville, N.Y. 10708.

KOLTUN, FRANCES LANG, Travel Ed., Mademoiselle, Conde Nast Publications, Inc., 420 Lexington Ave., N.Y., N.Y. 10017, '59–; Travel, Vacation Ed., Charm, '55–'59; Edtl. Staff, '50–'55; Fashion Mdse. Ed., American Girl, '46–'50; U.S. Govt. Svc., '45–'46; Abraham & Strauss, '42–'45; Colmst., Publrs. Hall Synd.; Auth: "Complete Book for the Intelligent Woman Traveler"; Fashion Group, Am. Soc. of Travel Agts., Discover Am. Travel Org., Travel Wtrs. of N.Y. (Past Pres.), Soc. of Am. Travel Wtrs., Intl. Union of Offcl. Travel Orgs.; Bklyn. Col., BA (magna cum laude); Columbia Univ., MA, '45; b. N.Y.C.; p. Samuel and Rebecca Lang Koltun; res: 55 W. 55th St., N.Y., N.Y. 10019.

KOMINIK, E. NIKI, VP, Grey Advertising, Inc., 777 Third Ave., N.Y., N.Y. 10017, '65–; Dir., Crtv. Rsch., '62; Supvsr., '57; Rschr., Dancer, Fitzgerald, Sample, '54; Tchr.; Free-lance Wtr.; Auth. brochure, "Sense and Nonsense in Creative Research" ('62), Guest Wtr., adv. colm., N.Y. Times, '67; Speaker, careers, job seeking, confs., cols., convs.; AWNY, N.Y. Adv. Club; Cornell Univ., AB, MA, PhD (Phi Beta Kappa, Phi Kappi Phi); b. Utica, N.Y.; h. Otto Peter Kominik; res: 5220 S.W. 60th Pl., Miami, Fla. 33155.

KOMISAR, LUCY, Free-lance Wtr., '69–; Reptr., Assoc. Prodr., NET, '68–'69; Special Asst., Deputy Admr., Human Resources Adm., '67–'68; Ed., Mississippi Free Press, '62–'63; Press Secy., Political Campaigns, for Elinor Guggenheimer (May–June, '69), and Rep. Allard Lowenstein (May–June, '68); NOW; articles in New York, Saturday Review, Village Voice; Queens Col., City Univ. of N.Y., BA, '64; b. N.Y.C., 1942; p. David and Frances Munshin Komisar; res: 100 W. 12th St., N.Y., N.Y. 10011.

KONER, SILVIA TOPP, Asst. Articles Ed., Redbook, 230 Park Ave., N.Y., N.Y. 10017, '68–; h. Marvin Koner.

KONKLE, JANET EVEREST, Auth.; Kindergarten Tchr., Hillerest Sch., Grand Rapids Board of Education, 143 Bostwick N.E., Grand Rapids, Mich. 49502, '60–; Primary Tchr., Dickinson and W. Leonard Schls., '52–'60; Alexander Sch., '39–'41; Auth., "J. Hamilton Hamster" ('57; Eng. Speaking Un. overseas ambassador bk.), other juv. bks.; Mich. Assn. for Childhood Educ., (Pres. '69–'71); Cncl. of Performing Arts for Children (VP '67–'69), Wms. Nat. Bk. Assn., Delta Kappa Gamma (Pres. '68–'70); Contemporary Auths.; many nat. photog. aws.; Western Mich. Univ., BS, '39; b. Grand Rapids, Mich., 1917; p. Charles Arthur and Minnie Koegler Everest; h. Arthur J. Konkle; c. Kraig E., Dan J., Iil Marie (Mrs. David Gahsman); res: 1360 Oakleigh Rd. N.W., Grand Rapids, Mich. 49504.

KONNER, JOAN WEINER, Prodr.-Wtr., National Broadcasting Company, 30 Rockefeller Plaza, N.Y., N.Y. 10020, '68–; Wtr.-Reptr., NBC News, '65–'68; Prodr., Wtr., Talent, WNDT-TV, '63–'65; Edtl. Wtr., Colmst., Asst. to Ed., Feature Reptr., The Record (Hackensack, N.J.), '61–'63; NATAS; N.J. Press Wm.'s Aw., '61; Vassar Col., '49; Sarah Lawrence Col., B.A., '51; Columbia Grad. Sch. of Jnlsm., M.S., '61; b. Paterson, N.J., 1931; p. Martin and Tillie Frankel Weiner; h. Jack A. Konner; c. Rosemary, Catherine; res: Sneden's Landing, Palisades, N.Y. 10964.

KONRAD, EVELYN, Owner, Evelyn Konrad Associates, 750 Park Ave., N.Y., N.Y. 10021, '58–; Sr. Ed., Sponsor, '52–'58; Assoc. Ed., Today's Woman; Colmst., United Nations World, '51–'52; Auth., "Marketing Research: A Management Overview" (Am. Mgt. Assn., '67); over 200 gen. bus. and mktng. articles in trade pubns.; PRSA, IRTS, OPC; Stanford Univ., BA (Intl. Rels.), '48; MA (Hist., Polit. Sci.), '49; N.Y. Sch. of Interior Design, '65; N.Y.U. Grad. Sch. of Bus. Adm., PhD Candidate, '65; b. Vienna, Austria, 1930; p. Eugene and Margaret Dukler Konrad; h. Bernard Jereski; c. Laura Diane, Elisabeth Merrilee, Robert William, Richard Perry; res: 955 Park Ave., N.Y., N.Y. 10028.

KOOLWYK, LOIS LOWMAN, County Librn., Monterey County, 26 Central Ave., Court House Annex, Salinas, Cal. 93901, '51–; County Ext. Librn., (Santa Barbara), '46–'51; Acting County Librn. (Chemung County, N.Y.), '43–'46; Jr. Librn., Steele Memorial Lib. (Elmira), '41–'43; ALA, Cal. Lib. Assn., Public Lib. Execs. of Central Cal. (Pres.), '61); Elmira Col., BA, '40; Syracuse Univ., BLS, '41; b. Elmira, N.Y., 1917; p. Malden C. and Gertrude G. Aldridge Lowman; h. John Koolwyk; c. Louise M.; res: 12 Corral De Tierra Rd., Salinas, Cal. 93901.

KOPEL, EVE ANDERSON, New England Sls., Fashion Rep., Ironwear Hosiery Co., Div., Burlington Hosiery Co., 1345 Ave. of the Americas, N.Y., N.Y. 10019; Model, Tchr., Allen Agcy. (Boston, Mass.); AWRT; h. Bernard Kopel; c. Robin Alice; res: 159 Ipswich St., Topsfield, Mass. 01983.

KOPELAND, ELLEN GAIL, News Prod. Asst., Wtr., WIP, Metromedia, 135 S. 19th St., Phila., Pa. 19103, '67–; AWRT; Emerson Col., '62–'64; Temple Univ., BS, '68; b. Phila., Pa., 1945; res: Park Towne Pl. W., 22nd and The Pkwy., Phila., Pa. 19130.

KOPELMAN, JEAN RAPAPORT, Prodr., "The Match Game," Goodson-Todman, 375 Park Ave., N.Y., N.Y. 10022, '63–; "Number Please," '61–'62; "Beat the Clock," '55–'62; Prod. Mgr., '50–'54; Middlebury Col., '44–'46; b. N.Y.C., 1927; p. E. H. and Dorothea Zeigel Rapaport; h. Mel Kopelman; c. Butch Hollander, Eddie Hollander, Elizabeth Kopelman; res: 965 Fifth Ave., N.Y., N.Y. 10021.

KOPMAN, EDYTHE H., Mng. Ed., Weight Watchers Magazine, 1790 Broadway, N.Y., N.Y. 10019, '67–; Bus. Mgr., Prod. Mgr., Signature mag., '58–'67; Bus. Mgr., Cheetah mag., '67; Skidmore Col., BS, '54.

KORD, JOAN M., Asst. Mgr., Doubleday Syndicate, Doubleday & Company, Inc., 277 Park Ave., N.Y., N.Y. 10017, '67–; Asst. to Ed.-in-Chief, Trade Dept., '63–'67; Edgewood Park Jr. Col.

KORDA, REVA FINE, Crtv. Dir., Ogilvy & Mather, Inc., 2 E. 48th St., N.Y., N.Y. 10017; with co. since '53; Macy's, '51–'53; Gimbels, '49–'51; Hunter Col., BA, '47 (magna cum laude, Phi Beta Kappa); b. N.Y.C., 1926; p. Louis and Yetta Fine; h. William Korda; c. Natasha, Joshua; res: 271 Central Park W., N.Y., N.Y. 10024.

KORDSMEIER, BEVERLY BREESE, Free-lance Cnslt., '69–; AE, Jack Drury Assoc. PR, '65–'68; Wtr., Mexican Nat. Tourist Cncl. (N.Y.C.), '63–'64; U.S. PR Dir., Guest Airways, '60–'63; Ed., Nat. Airlines pubn., '59; Theta Sigma Phi, Soc. of Am. Travel Wtrs., S. Fla. Cncl. Bd. Comm. on PR For Girl Scouts; Univ. of Okla., BA (Jnlsm.), '55; h. Joseph Kordsmeier; res: 1975 Broad Causeway, N. Miami, Fla. 33161.

KOREY, LOIS BALK, Sr. VP, Crtv. Supvsr., McCann-Erickson Advertising, 485 Lexington Ave., N.Y., N.Y.; Wtr., Jack Tinker and Partners, '61–'63; Wtr., Andy Griffith show, Peter Lind Hayes-Mary Healy show, '59–'61; Wtr., Steve Allen Tonight show, Ernie Kovacs show, Sunday Night Comedy Hour; '54–'61; Adv. Club of N.Y., Wtrs. Guild; Clio, '66–'69; Andy aw., '69; Barnard Col., '52–'54; b. N.Y.C., 1933; p. Samuel and Lillian Balk; h. Stanton Korey; c. Susan, Christopher; res: 145 Central Park W., N.Y., N.Y. 10023.

KORLE, ERTUGRUL SARA, Commentator, Voice of America; Corr., Hayat, Ses; '61–; Corr., Anatolian News Agcy., '54–'58; Corr., Vatan Istanbul, '49–'54; Auth., "Gecmis Zaman Olur ki" (Turkey, '50); FPA (Asst. Secy. Gen., '67–'68); Istanbul Univ., BA, '45; b. Berlin, Germany, 1922; p. Ertugrul and Munire Celaleddin Ertugrul; h. Sinan Korle; res: 411 E. 53rd St., N.Y., N.Y. 10022.

KORNETZ, MITZI, Dir. of PR, The Medical Founda-

tion, 29 Commonwealth Ave., Boston, Mass. 02116, '69–; Edtl. Cnslt., '68; Dir. of Commty. Rels., Family Svc. Assn. of Gtr. Boston, '61–'66; Radio-TV Dir., Boston Univ., '57–'60; Cnslt., Mass. Bay Telecasters, '54–'55; Radio-TV Dir., Un. Commty. Svcs. of Met. Boston, '46–'54; Pubcty. Dir., WTAG (Worcester), '43–'46; Cont. Dir., '39–'43; Cnslt., exec. training, behavorial scis., media commtns.; NATAS, PRSA, AWRT, Intl. Platform Assn.; Variety aw., "Sex Guidance for Today's Youth," radio series, '46; Oh. State Univ. hon. mention, '59; Simmons Col., BS, '39; b. Boston, Mass.; p. Max and Sarah Crosby Kornetz; res: 60 Babcock St., Brookline, Mass. 02146.

KOSCINA, SYLVA, Actress, CMA, 9255 Sunset Blvd., L.A., Cal. 90069; Films: "The Hornet's Nest" (Un. Artists, '69), "The Secret War of Private Frigg" (Universal, '67), "A Lovely Way to Die" (Universal Int., '67), others; SAG, Academia Italiana Del Cinema; Univ. of Naples; b. Zagreb, Yugoslavia, 1937; p. Ivan and Valeria Orduly Koscina; res: 00047 Marino Laziale, Rome, Italy.

KOSKOS, CATHERINE, Asst. Dir., United Fund of Greater Chattanooga, P.O. Box 509, Chattanooga, Tenn. 37401, '69–; PR Dir., '59–'69; Chattanooga Times; AWRT, Adv. Club, Bus. Eds. Assn. (Pres., '67–'68, Treas., '60, '65), C. of C., Univ. of Tenn., BA, '48; b. Chattanooga, Tenn., 1926; p. Harry and Sophia D. Koskos.

KOSSOFF, ROSALIND, Motion Pic. Cnslt., Radim Films Inc., 220 W. 42nd St., N.Y., N.Y. 10036, '69–; own bus., VP, '64–'69; Pres., Film Images Inc., '53–'64; Dir., Les Actualities Francaises, French Govt. (N.Y.), '46–'53; Assoc. Head of Distrb., Nat. Film Bd. of Can. (N.Y. Off.), '43–'46; cnslt., special projects, 16mm cultural-educ. motion pics.; various orgs.; Columbia Univ., '27; Am. Acad. of Dramatic Art, '31; b. N.Y.C., 1910; p. Jacob and Fannie Markowitz Kossoff; h. Harry J. Bimberg; res: 357 W. 55th St., N.Y., N.Y. 10019.

KOSTKA, DOROTHY PARMENTER, Colmst., "Freedom After Fifty," Contemporary Sunday mag., Denver Post, 16th at Cal., Denver, Colo. 80201, '64; Contrbr., nat. mags.; Auth., "Climb to the Top" (Doubleday, '63); Colo. Auths. League (VP, '56–'57, Treas., '62; Top-Hand aw., '53, '59, '61–'63, '65–'66), Denver Wms. Press Club (VP, '62), Theta Sigma Phi; Littleton's Most Valuable Citizen, '59; numerous other aws.; Knox Col., AB, '28 (magna cum laude; Alumni Achiev. aw., '64); b. Ft. Smith, Ark., 1906; p. Robert and Lillian Bollinger Parmenter; h. William Kostka; c. William Jr., Stefan Matthew; res: 1836 W. Lake Ave., Littleton, Colo. 80120.

KOVEL, TERRY HORVITZ, Wtr., Register and Tribune Syndicate, Des Moines, Ia., '54–; Synd. Colmst., "Know Your Antiques," '54–; Auth. (with husband): "Complete Antiques Price List" ('69), "Know Your Antiques" ('67), "American Country Furniture" ('65), others; various bks., mag. articles; Educ. TV Series with husband, "Know Your Antiques"; Oh. Nwsp. Wms. Assn. (Hon.), Nat. Penwns. Assn., Board Soc. of Collectors, Silver Museum of Art; Wellesley Col., BA, '50; Univ. of Ill., '61; b. Cleveland, Oh., 1928; p. Isadore and Rix Osteryoung Horvitz; h. Ralph Kovel; c. Lee, Karen; res: 22000 Shaker Blvd., Shaker Heights, Oh. 44122.

KRAFT, MARY, Dir., Home Building and Decorating, Good Housekeeping Magazine, 959 Eighth Ave., N.Y., N.Y. 10019, '52–; formerly, Palmer & Riley, Cleve., Oh.; Mgr., Interior Design Dept., Armstrong Cork, Lancaster, Pa.; Nat. Assn. of Home Builders (Cert. for Meritorious Svc., '64, '65, '66), Design Wtrs. Intl., AID, NSID (Distg. Svc. Cit., '60), Architectural League; Dorothy Dawe aw., '53, '58, '63, '68; Dallas Mkt. Ctr. Edtl. aw., '68; Hon. Cotton Picker, Order of the Long Leaf Pine, State of N.C.; Cleve. Sch. of Art (Interior Design); John Huntington Polytech. Inst. (Architecture); b. Canton, Oh.; p. Lee and Anna Koch Kraft; h. Erwin M. Frey (dec.); res: 220 Central Park S., N.Y., N.Y. 10019.

KRAFT, VIRGINIA, Assoc. Ed., Sports Illustrated, 110 W. 51st St., N.Y., N.Y. 10020, '66–; Staff Wtr., '59–'66; Reptr., '54–'59; Wtr., Ed., Field & Stream, '52–'54; Auth: "Sports Illustrated Book of Dog Training" (Lippincott, '60), Sports Illustrated Book of Shotgun Sports" (Lippincott, '68), two other sports bks.; Nobel One-World Fellowship, '50; Headliners' aw., '67; Barnard Col., AB, '51; Columbia Univ., MA, '52; b. N.Y.C., 1932; p. George and Jean Gillis Kraft; h. Robert Dean Grimm; c. Tana A., Tara K., Robert Jr., Jill C.; res: Gipsy Trail Club, Carmel, N.Y. 10512.

KRAKAUER, ELIZABETH GOTTSCHALK, Assoc. Prof. of Research Methods, Librn., Prescott Col., P.O. Box 2299, Prescott, Ariz. 86301, '68–; Bibliographer, Sterling Lib., Yale Univ., '67–'68; Bibliographer, Lockwood Memorial Lib., '65–'67; Ref. Librn., State Univ. of N.Y. (Buffalo), '62–'67; Univ. of Buffalo, BA (Psych.), '63; State Univ. of N.Y., MA (Anthropology), '65; MS (Lib. Sci.), '66; b. Hanover, Germany, 1911; h. Hans S. Krakauer; c. John L., Thomas H.; res: 501 S. Cortez St., Apt. 2-D, Prescott, Ariz. 86301.

KRAKOWSKI, LILI H., Dir. of Bk. Prom., March Advertising, Inc., 15 W. 44th St., N.Y., N.Y. 10036, '68–; formerly Prom. Asst., Lib. Sls., World Publ.; AE, Wtr., Sussman & Sugar; Sr. Copywtr., Macmillan; Copy Chief, Adv. Mgr., McGraw-Hill; Translator, German novel (McGraw-Hill); fluent French, German, Portuguese; Critic; Rochester Inst. of Tech. Sch. for Am. Craftsmen, AAS; res: 249 E. Houston St., N.Y., N.Y. 10022; Summer res: Box #1, Constableville, N.Y. 13325.

KRAL, MARY ANN, Systems Analyst Manual Wtr., Korvette Retail Chain, 450 W. 33rd St., N.Y., N.Y. 10001, '69–; Sls. Prom. Wtr., Prod. Coordr., Blue Cross, '65–'69; Training Materials Specialist, Penneys, '63–'65; Packaging Coordr., '62–'63; Copywtr., '60–'62;

AWNY, BPW; Sigma Tau Delta; Marquette Univ., BS (Lib. Arts), '56 (Delta Sigma Epsilon Aegis Aw.); N.Y.U., special courses; b. Kenosha, Wis., 1935; p. Rudolph and Josephine Mikulski Kral; res: 430 W. 34th St., N.Y., N.Y. 10001.

KRAMER, ESTHER COHEN, Asst. Dir., Pratt Institute Graduate School Library and Information Service, 110 Livingston St., Bklyn., N.Y. 11201, '59–; Lectr., '64–'69; Librn., Eli Whitney Vocational HS, '46–'59; N.Y. Lib. Assn., ALA; Hunter Col., BA, '29; State Univ. of N.Y., BS (Lib. Sci.), '40; Columbia Sch. Lib. Svc., '39, '59; b. N.Y.C.; p. David and Rose Shapiro Cohen; c. Nancy Ellen Paige, Fredrica D.; h. Martin Kramer; res: 1035 Washington Ave., Bklyn., N.Y. 11225.

KRAMER, NORA, Dir., The Bookplan, Cnslt., Scholastic's Arrow Book Club, '58–; Dir., Bookplan, '43–; Cnslt. as Eleanor Brent in Macy's Little Bookshop, '43–'53; Auth: "The Grandma Moses Story Book" (Random, '61), "The Cozy Hour Story Book" (Random, '60), five other juv. bks.; Co-auth. with Dr. K. R. Kramer of "Coppercraft and Silver Made at Home" (Chilton, '57), WNBA, Auths. Guild, Child Study Assn. of Am. (Children's Bk. Comm.), Conf. of Christian and Jews Bk. Comm., Chmn. of English-Speaking Unions Children's Bks.-Across-The-Sea Comm.; Beaux Arts Inst., Sch. of the Museum of Fine Arts (Boston), City Col. of N.Y.; b. Pendleton, England; p. Harris and Rachel Wolf Atkin; h. Dr. Sidney D. Kramer; c. Karl Robert, Virginia (Mrs. Jerome D. Stein Jr.), Joan (Mrs. Arthur P. Stoliar); res: 46 Jane St., N.Y., N.Y. 10014.

KRANIDAS, KATHLEEN COLLINS, Wtr., fiction, poetry; "One Year in Autumn" (Lippincott, '65; Barker, '65); Tchr.; Barnard Col., BA, '52; h. Thomas Kranidas; c. Stephen, Thomas, Anne, Mary Caroline; res: 5 Silverspruce Lane, Stony Brook, N.Y. 11790.

KRANTZ, HAZEL NEWMAN, Auth.; Elementary Tchr., N. Bellmore Schs., '64–'68; Bks: "Tippy" ('68), "The Secret Raft" ('64), "Freestyle for Michael" ('62), "100 Pounds of Popcorn" ('60); Fashion Coordr., Felix Lilienthal, '43–'45; N.Y.U., BS, '42, Hofstra Univ., MS, '59; b. Bklyn., N.Y., 1920; p. Louis and Eva Newman Newman; h. Michael Krantz; c. Laurence, Vincent, Mrs. Margaret Risi; res: 875 Leeds Dr., N. Bellmore, N.Y. 11710.

KRASNER, JOAN DANZIG, Wms. Pg. Ed., The Buffalo Evening News, 214-218 Main St., Buffalo, N.Y. 14240, '56–; Asst. Feature Ed., '52–'56; Soc. Ed., The Evening Times (Sayre, Pa.) '48–'51; Page One aws., '57, '61; Elmira Col., '46–'48; b. Elmira, N.Y.; p. George Hamilton and Estelle Saqui Danzig; h. Dr. Joseph Krasner; c. Susan Starr, Karin Alison.

KRATZMIER, PEGGY THORNE, Wms. Ed., Daily Star Progress Newspaper, 600 S. Palm Ave., La Habra, Cal.

90631, '65–; b. Seattle, Wash., 1924; p. Harry Ashley and Mary Loud Thorne; h. August Kratzmier; c. John T. Robbins, Debra Sue Robbins, Candace (Mrs. Clifford Souza); res: 800 W. Florence Ave., La Habra, Cal. 90631.

KRAUS, BARBARA, Special Asst. to Dir., Peace Corps, 806 Connecticut Ave., N.W., Wash., D.C. 20006, '69–; (N.Y. off: 321 E. 43rd St., N.Y., N.Y.); own PR bus., non-profit orgs., '66–'69; PR Dir., UN Assn. of U.S.A., '57–'66; Auth: "Cookbook of the United Nations," "Compliments to the Chef," others.

KRAUS, HAZEL L., Dir., Home Furnishings Div., Metro Newspaper Service, Metro Associated Services, Inc., 80 Madison Ave., N.Y., N.Y. 10016, '37–; formerly Adv. Mgr., Martin's, Bklyn.; Co-Auth., "Newspaper Advertising" (Prentice-Hall, '47); numerous articles, home furnishings trade pubns.; NHFL, Intl. Design Wtrs., Fashion Group, AID (Press Affiliate), Museum of Contemporary Crafts (Press Affiliate), Victorian Soc. in Am., Intl. Design Wtrs.; Freedoms Fndn. aw., '58; Dorothy Dawe aw., '69; N.Y.U., BCS; b. Chgo., Ill., 1896; p. Samuel and Esther Lyons Ludwig; h. Raymond Kraus (dec.); c. Allan Daniel; res: 440 E. 20th St., N.Y., N.Y. 10009.

KRAUSHAAR, DIANA ANGUIANA, Asst. Radio/TV Dir., Eisaman, Johns & Laws, 6290 Sunset Blvd., L.A., Cal., 90028, '66–; Traf./Opn. Mgr., KTLA-TV, '57–'66; Traf./Opn. Dept., KCOP-TV; '55–'57; b. L.A., Cal., 1933; p. Jose and Soledad Corona Anguiano; h. Richard Kraushaar; c. Laura V., Roderick G.; res: 1181 Old Mill Rd., San Marino, Cal. 91108.

KRAUSS, RUTH, Auth: 32 bks. for children, 4 bks. of poems, Conductor, poetry workshop; b. Balt., Md.; p. Julius and Blanche Rosenfeld Krauss; h. Crockett Johnson; res: 74 Rowayton Ave., Rowayton, Conn. 06853.

KRAVITZ, GLORIA, Assoc. Ed., Film and TV Daily International Yearbook of Motion Pictures and Television, 330 W. 58 St., N.Y., N.Y. 10019, '61–; Asst. Ed., '54–'61; Adv. Dept., Sacony, '52–'54; Collegiate Secretarial Sch., '51–'52; b. Worcester, Mass.; p. Samuel and Sarah Kravitz; res: 8900 Blvd. E., North Bergen, N.Y. 07047.

KRAWITZ, RUTH LIFSHITZ, Exec. Asst., New York City Board of Education, Office of Superintendant, 1377 Jerome Ave., Bronx, N.Y. 10452, '66–; Instr., Grad. Inst., Fordham Univ.,'69; Cnslt., Instr., Lehman Col., '65–; Auth., Ed., Oceana Pubns.; Bank Street Col., '68; Curriculum Asst., '59–'66; Tchr., Common Brs., '49–'59; Owner-Dir., Blue Rill Day Camp, '50–; Fordham Univ. Sch. Admrs. Assn. (Pres., '68–'70), Assoc. Sup. and Curriculum Dev., Intl. Reading Assn.; Cncl. Supervisory Assns.; Hunter Col., BA, '49; Yeshiva Univ., MS, '65; b. N.Y.C., 1929; p. Samuel and Dora Zawel Lifshitz; h. Irving Krawitz; c. Eileen, Stephen; res: 22 W. Allison Ave., Pearl River, N.Y. 10965.

KREBS, BETTY DIETZ, Fine Arts Ed., Dayton Daily News, Dayton, Oh. 45419, '65–; Wms. Pg. Ed., Music and Art Ed., '40–'64; "The Betty Dietz Show," WHIO-TV, '51–'52; Wms. Pg. Ed., Dayton Herald, '39–'40; Theta Sigma Phi (Dayton Club Pres., '66–'69), Dayton Wms. Press Club (Past Pres.), Adventures in Movement for the Handicapped (Pres.); Oh. Nwsp. Wms. Assn. aws: Wm. of Yr., '49; numerous writing, editing aws.; Wm. of Distinction aw., NFPW; School of Dayton Art Inst.; b. Dayton, Oh.; p. Robert C. and Elizabeth Breidenbach Dietz; h. William J. Krebs; res: 1126 Oakwood Ave., Dayton, Oh. 45419.

KREHBIEL, BECKY FALCONER, Edtl. Cartoonist, Chicago Tribune, 435 N. Michigan Ave., Chgo., Ill. 60611, '41–; Illstr., Whitman Publishing Co., Jack & Jill mag.; WNBA, Geneva Garden Club (Pres., '67–'68); Chgo. Acad. of Fine Art, Chgo. Art Inst.; b. Rochester, N.Y.; p. Donald and Rebecca Courtney Falconer; h. Evans Krehbiel; c. Courtney, David, Reebie, Linda; res: 601 Forest View Dr., Geneva, Ill. 60134.

KREIG, MARGARET, Wtr., Sci., Med.; Auth: "Green Medicine: The Search for Plants That Heal" (Rand McNally, '64), "Black Market Medicine" (Prentice-Hall, '67); numerous articles pub. in nat. mags.; Former Med. Ed., Staff Wtr., Parents Magazine; Soc. of Mag. Wtrs., OPC, Nat. Assn. of Sci. Wtrs., PEN, Auths. Guild, Auths. League, MWA (Chgo. Reg. VP, '50–'51, aw., '68); Midwestern Wtrs. Conf. bk. aw., '51; Univ. of Ill., Univ. of Chgo., Northwestern Univ., Columbia Univ.; h. Boccioletti Lauro.

KREITZ, HELEN MARIE, Contrbr., bibliography of children's hist.; number of stories, The Arithmetic Tchr., '60; Elementary Tchr., Temple Public Schools, '52–; Adv. Saleswm., Taylor (Tex.) Times, '52; Mary Hardin-Baylor Col., BA, '50; Univ. of Tex., M. Ed., '59; b. Taylor, Tex., 1929; p. Joe Jr. and Mary Miller; res: 1818 S. 35th St., P.O. Box 3446, Temple, Tex. 76501.

KREMER, HELEN E., Public Lib. Cnslt., Michigan Department of Education, Bureau of Library Services, 735 E. Michigan Ave., Lansing, Mich. 48913, '51–; Public Lib. Cnslt., Wis. Free Lib. Commn., '47–'51; Br. Librn., Akron (Oh.) Public Lib., '41–'47; Children's Librn. (Fond du Lac, Wis.), '34–'41; Conductor of workshops, seminars; Speaker, Panelist, educ. groups; Contrbr., articles to pfsnl. lib. periodicals, govt. pubns.; ALA, Mich. Lib. Assn., Adult Educ. Assn. of Mich.; Univ. of Wis., BA, '32; BLS, '32; b. Fond du Lac, Wis., 1910; p. Berthold and Esther Gardner Kremer; res: 1676 Algoma Dr., Okemos, Mich. 48864.

KRESICH, HELEN MARIE, Ed., Illinois Banker mag., Dir. of Commtns., Illinois Bankers Association, 188 W. Randolph St., Chgo., Ill. 60601, '68–; Mng. Ed., '64–'68, '61–'62; Rsch. Asst., Inst. for Philosophical Rsch., '64; Investigator-Analyst, Nat. Conf. of Bar Examiners,

'62-'64; Jr. Copywtr., Bozell & Jacobs, '57-'61; Free-lance Cnslt., Speech Wtr.; Illinois Press Assn., Chgo. Press Club, Chgo. Fin. Advs., Am. Inst. of Banking, Assn. of Chgo. Bank Wm.; State Univ. of Ia., '56-'57, Univ. of Chgo., '58-'59, Am. Inst. of Banking, '64-'65; Northwestern Univ., '68; b. Chgo., Ill., 1938; p. Marko and Mary Zaborac Kresich; res: 452 Oakdale, Chgo., Ill. 60657.

KRETZER, CAROLE LEIGH, Info. Offcr., California Public Utilities Commission, 107 S. Broadway, L.A., Cal. 90012, '66-; Asst. Info. Offcr., Div. of Highways, '62-'66; Ed., Union Bank, '62; Assoc. Ed., FM & Fine Arts Magazine, '61-'62; Theta Sigma Phi; Univ. of Ala., BA, '55 (Phi Beta Kappa; Mortar Bd.); b. Lincoln, Ill., 1933; p. Dan G. and Mary Mowrey Kretzer; res: 315 California Terr., Pasadena, Cal. 91105.

KRETZMER, BERNICE FREIBERG, Exec. VP, Paul Venze Associates, Inc., 295 Madison Ave., N.Y., N.Y. 10017, '65-; VP, '60-'65; PRSA, AWNY, AWRT; Who's Who Of Am. Wm; Am. Red Cross, Motor Svc.; Boys Town, Md.; John Hopkins Univ., McCoy Col.; b. Balt., Md., 1923; p. David and Jenny Reis Freiberg; h. Frank Kretzmer; res: 516 B Beaconscourt, Salem Harbor Andalusia, Pa.

KRIEG, LAUREL L., Dir., Martins Ferry Public Library, 20 S. Fifth St., Martins Ferry, Oh. 43935, '48-; Librn., Ocean County (N.J.) Lib., '37-'48; Children's Librn., '29-'37; ALA, Oh. Lib. Assn.; Western Reserve Univ., AB, '28; BS (Lib. Sci.), '29; Univ. of Chgo., AM, '43; b. Burton, Oh., 1907; p. John and Josephine Brainard Krieg; res: 20 S. Fourth St., Martins Ferry, Oh. 43935.

KRIEGER, JUDITH GEARY, AP Telegraph Ed., Ottumwa Courier, 213 E. Second, Ottumwa, Ia. 52501, '68-; State Ed., '66-'68; Asst. News Ed., Decorah (Ia.) Nwsps., '65-'66; Ia. Press Wm. (1st pl. aw, pg. makeup, and 2nd pl. aw., Critic's rev., '69), Ia. Assn. of AP Telegraph Eds., (Pres., '69-'70); Drake Univ. (Des Moines, Ia.), BA (Jnlsm.), '65; b. Burlington, Ia., 1943; p. Ralph C. and Lorraine Gruver Geary; h. Bernard Krieger; res: 145 E. Maple, Ottumwa, Ia. 52501.

KRIPKE, MADELINE FAITH, Asst. Ed., Children's Bk. Dept., E. P. Dutton & Co., Inc., 201 Park Ave. S., N.Y., N.Y. 10014, '70-; Asst. Ed., Children's Bk. Dept., Bobbs Merrill Publ. Co., '69-'70; Caseworker, Waverly Welfare Ctr., '67-'69; Barnard Col., BA, '65; b. New London, Conn., 1943; res: 317 W. 11th St., N.Y., N.Y. 10014.

KROEBER, THEODORA KRACAW, Auth., four bks., incl. "Ishi in Two Worlds" ('61 Commonwealth Club S.F. Medal); Co-auth., "Almost Ancestors" ('68); Wm. Geographers; Univ. of Cal., BA, '19; MA (Psych.), '20; b. Denver, Colo., 1897; p. Charles and Phebe Johnston Kracaw; h. Alfred Kroeber; c. Clifton, Theodore, Karl, Ursula; res: 1325 Arch St., Berkeley, Cal. 94708.

KROFSKY, JEAN, Mng. Ed., "Agway Cooperator," Agway, Inc., Box 1333, Syracuse, N.Y. 13201, '61-; Reptr., Springfield Republican, '44-'45; Ed., "Servicer," Eastern States Farmers' Exchange; Auth., "The Gardener's Cookbook" ('52).

KRONE, GLADYS LOUISE, Head Librn., Carnegie City Library, 1415 N. Ninth St., Ft. Smith, Ark. 72901, '53-; Staff, '49-'53; Ark. Lib. Assn. (Past Secy.), WNBA, Soroptimist Club (Past, Pres., Treas.), Ft. Smith Symphony Assn. (Past Bd. Mbr., Secy.); Golden Deeds commty. svc. aw., '68; Who's Who in Ark. Educ.; Coe Col., Northwestern Univ.

KRONENBITTER, ANN WILLIAMSON, Pubcty. Dir., Western Insurance Information Service, 4050 Wilshire Blvd., L.A. Cal. 90005, '60-; Adm. Asst., McFadden & Eddy Assoc., '60; Publicist, Walter E. Kline & Assoc., '58-'60; Indsl. Ed., Bendix Corp. (Kan. City Div.), '53-'58; Pubcty. Club of L.A.; PRSA, Wilshire BPW, Insurance Wm. of L.A.; Cottey Col., AA, '49; Drury Col., BA, '53; b. Rich Hill, Mo., 1930; p. Russell and Constance Emerson Williamson; res: 405 S. Old Ranch Rd., Arcadia, Cal. 91006.

KRUEGER, CARYL WALLER, AE, W. S. Myers & Associates, Inc., 830 Ala Moana Blvd., Honolulu, Hi. 96813, '66-; Adv. Mgr., Island Federal Savings and Loan Assn., '62-'66; PR, Adv., Caryl Krueger Assocs. (Chgo., Honolulu), '60-'64; Asst. AE, Advertising Division, Inc. (United States Savings and Loan League, Chgo.), '52-'60; PR Dept., Toni Co., '51-'52; Cont. Dept., WGN, WGN-TV, '50-'51; Contrbr., articles on real estate, adv., PR, family life, gardening and travel, various mags.; Theta Sigma Phi (Hon. Mbr.); NLAPW Aw., '68; Who's Who of Am. Wm.; Wm. of the Yr., Panhellenic of Hi., '67; Northwestern Univ., Sch. of Speech, BS, '50; h. Cliff W. Krueger; c. Claire, Chris, Carrie, Cameron; res: 4433 Kahala Ave., Honolulu, Hi. 96815.

KRUMEICH, DOROTHY MAHON, Reptr., Feature Wtr., Peekskill Star, 824 Main St., Peekskill, N.Y. 10566, '69-; Wms. Ed., '49-'69; Wtr., features, Westchester-Rockland nwsps. and U.S.I.A.; Wms. Press Club of N.Y.; U.S. Bur. of Nat. Guard aw.; Columbia Sch. Gen. Studies, '50-'53; h. Edwin A. Krumeich (dec.).

KRUUSE, ELSA, Ed., Religious Newsweekly '58-; Assoc. Ed., Tempo, '68-; National Council of Churches, 475 Riverside Dr., N.Y., N.Y. 10027; Mng. Ed., Interchurch News, '59-'68; United Church Herald, '54-'58; Edtl. Staff, other mags., '49-'54; Special Corr., Christian Science Monitor, Scandinavia, '47-'49; PR, Church World Svc., Children to Palestine, '45-'47; Edtl. Staff, U.S. Off. of War Info., Sweden, '41-'45; Translator, Swedish bks., short stories, articles; OPC, Am.-Scandinavian Fndn.; Who's Who of Am. Wm.; Smith Col., '27-'28; Cass Tech., '28-'29; Sorbonne, '29-'31; Univ. of Stockholm, '41-'42; b. Catskill, N.Y., 1909; p. Roscoe and Grace Hazard Conkling; c. Robin C., Sigrid K. (Mrs. Larimore Toye), Monika K. (Mrs.

Douglas E. Mitchell); res: 334 Riverside Dr., N.Y., N.Y. 10025.

KRYL, SUSAN FREESTONE, Media Dir., Asst. VP, Maxwell Sroge Company, Inc., 333 N. Michigan Ave., Chgo., Ill. 60601, '69-; Media Dir., '67-; Roland Assoc., '64-'67; h. Robert Kryl.

KU, AH JOOK LEONG, Info. Specialist, Dept. of Educ., State of Hawaii, P.O. Box 2360, Honolulu, Hi. 96804, '66-; Pubns. Ed., Hi. Employers Cncl.; PR Dir., Salvation Army, Hi.; PR Secy., C. of C. of Honolulu; Eng. Ed., Chinese Govt. Info. Off., Nationalist China; Tech. Pubns. Ed., Bur. of Comml. Fisheries, U.S. Dept. of Interior; Adv. Asst., Hi. Telephone Co.; Pers. Asst., Hi. Electric Co.; Reptr., Honolulu Star-Bulletin; Staff Wtr., AP, Honolulu Bur.; Theta Sigma Phi (Pres., '60; Secy., '58), PR Wm. of Honolulu (VP, '56), Honolulu Press Club, IEA of Hi. (Secy., '60); Univ. of Mo. Sch. of Jnlsm., BJ, '34 (Exchange Scholar); Univ. of Hi., BA, BEd, '33; b. Kailua, Oahu, Hi.; p. Ah Hoy and Dung Shee Leong; res: 258 Wai Nani Way, Honolulu, Hi. 98615.

KUEHLTHAU, MARGARET WILLIAMS, Gen. Assigt. Rptr. and Feature Wtr., Tucson Daily Citizen, 208 N. Stone Ave., Tucson, Ariz, 85701, '60-; Theta Sigma Phi (Tucson Chptr. Secy., Treas.), Ariz. Press Wm. (Wm. of Achiev., '66; 17 1st pl. writing aws.), NFPW (two 1st pl., two 2nd pl. writing aws.), Best Writing aw., Ariz. Nwsp. Assn., '67; Aw. of Merit for Exceptional Prof. Svc., Tucson Educ. Assn., '69; Univ. of Wis. Sch. of Jnlsm., '42; b. Barneveld, Wis.; p. Edward and Nettie Rundell Williams; h. Arthur E. Kuelthau; c. James F., William E., Nancy (Mrs. Richard Clevinger), Anne (Mrs. Roger Masa); res: 2227 E. First St., Tucson, Ariz. 85719.

KUFTINEC, JEAN GUYTON, Free-lance Ed.; Ed., Sylvania News, Sylvania Electronic Systems (Waltham, Mass.), '61-'62; The Nestle News, The Nestle Co. (White Plains, N.Y.), '57-'60; Jnlsm.-Eng. Tchr., Northwest Jr. Col. (Senatobia, Miss.), '57; Corr., Bur. Chief., The Memphis (Tenn.) Commerical Appeal, '55-'57 (Outstanding Corr. Aw., '55, '56); HMI ('57-'60), Mass. IEA ('61-'62), Theta Sigma Phi (N.Y. State Coordr., '57-'60; New England Regional Coordr., '67-; Boston Club Pres., '67-); Univ. of Miss., BA, '56 (with special distinction); MA, '57; b. Memphis, Tenn., 1935; p. Milburn and Anna Yarbrough Guyton; h. Dubravko Kuftinec; c. Alexandra, Sonja, Steven; res: 15 Mansion Dr., Topsfield, Mass. 01983.

KUH, JOYCE DATTEL, Asst. Ed., Ladies' Home Journal, 641 Lexington Ave., N.Y., N.Y. 10022; Edtl. Asst., McCall's, '63-'65; Newcomb Col. (Tulane Univ.), BA, '59; b. Greenville, Miss., 1937; p. Milton and Hannah Marks Dattel; h. Richard Kuh; res: 14 Washington Pl., N.Y., N.Y. 10003.

KUH, KATHARINE, Art Ed., Saturday Review, 140 Madison Ave., N.Y., N.Y. 10017, '59-; Art Cnslt., S. Ill.

Univ., '63-'68; Auth., four bks. on art, including "Break-Up: The Core of Modern Art" (N.Y. Graphic Soc., '65); report on Alaska Indian carvings, '46; series, adult discussion of Modern Art, Fund for Adult Educ. of Ford Fndn., '55; curator, Chgo. Art Inst., '43-'59; Ed., Bul., '45-'53; Visiting Prof., Univ. of Fine Arts, San Miguel (Mexico), summers, '38-'40; Owner, Dir., Katharine Kuh Gallery, Chgo., '35-'42; Vassar Col., AB, '25; Univ. of Chgo., AM, '28; N.Y.U., Grad. Work, '29; b. St. Louis, Mo., 1904; p. Morris and Olga Weiner Woolf; h. George E. Kuh (div.); res: 140 E. 83rd St., N.Y., N.Y. 10028.

KUHLMAN, MARY E., Dir. Consumer Svc., Dr Pepper Company, 5523 E. Mockingbird Lane, P.O. Box 5086, Dallas, Tex. 75222, '63-; Am. Inst. of Baking, '53-'63; U.S. Dept. Agriculture-FHA, '36-'53; HS Home Econs. Tchr., '32-'36; Am. Home Econs. Assn., AWRT, Confrerie de la Chaine des Rotisseurs (Dallas Chptr.); Who's Who of Am. Wm.; Personalities of the South; Intl. Biogs.; Univ. of Okla., BS, '32; Nutrition Grad. Study; b. Norman, Okla., 1909; p. J. H. and Mary Joe Lessly Kuhlman; h. Lawrence E. Smith; res: 4409-1/2 Cole Ave., Dallas, Tex. 75205.

KUHN, IRENE CORBALLY, Free-lance Wtr.; Travel Ed., Am. Labor Magazine; Synd. Colmst., "It's My Opinion," Columbia Features; Auth: "Assigned to Adventure," "Inside Story," "Deadline Delayed," "The Enemy Within" (collaborated with Raymond J. de Jaegher); Fgn. Corr. (Europe, Far East); Commentator, Mutual Bdcst. Co., '50-'51; '39; Asst. Dir. of Info., NBC, '39-'49; Commentator, "Irene Kuhn's Program"; War Corr. (China-in Chungking), '45; Prodr., show in series, "Down Mexico Way," '42; various orgs.; Marymount Col., Columbia Univ.; b. N.Y.C.; p. Patrick J. and Josephine Connor Corbally; h. (dec.); c. Rene (Mrs. Douglas W. Bryant); res: 45 Christopher St., N.Y., N.Y. 10014.

KUHN, RENI R., Assoc. PR Dir., Arndt, Preston, Chapin, Lamb & Keen, 375 Park Ave., N.Y., N.Y. 10022, '68-; Acc. Mgr., '66-'67; Acc. Supvsr., Rowland Co., '67-'68; PR Dir., W. & J. Sloane, '62-'67; Home Furnishings Publicist, Macy's, '55-'62; NHFL (N.Y. Chptr. Bd. Mbr., '68-'69); Wellesley Col., BA, '55; h. W H. Kuhn; c. Phillip W., John H., Peter M.

KULP, NANCY JANE, Actress, c/o Filmways Television, 1040 N. Les Palmas, Hollywood, Cal.; Currently on "Beverly Hillbillies" (Emmy nominee, '66-'67); Free-lance Actress: "A Star Is Born," "Three Faces of Eve," "Playhouse 90," many others; AMPAS, NATAS, Pi Beta Phi; Humane Society Aw., '68; Who's Who of Am. Wm.; Fla. State Univ., BA; Grad. work, Univ. of Miami; b. Harrisburg, Pa.; p. Robert and Marjorie Snyder Kulp; h. (div.); res: 3611 Longridge Ave., Sherman Oaks, Cal. 91403.

KUMIN, MAXINE WINOKUR, Wtr., fiction and poetry; Cnslt., children's literature, Central Atlantic Reg. Educ. Lab. (Wash., D.C.), '67-'69; Lectr., Eng.,

Tufts Univ., '65–'68; Auth., 14 children's bks.; also: "The Passions of Uxport" (novel, '68), "Through Dooms of Love" (novel, '65), "The Privilege" (poetry, '65), "Halfway" (poetry, '61); Auths. Guild, PSA (Lowell Mason Palmer aw., '61; William Marion Reedy aw., '68); Grant, Nat. Cncl. on the Arts and Humanities, '67–'68; Radcliffe Col., BA, '46; MA, '48; b. Phila., Pa., 1925; p. Peter and Doll Simon Winokur; h. Victor Kumin; c. Daniel, Jane, Judith; res: 40 Bradford Rd., Newton Highlands, Mass. 02161.

KUNIAN, MARJORIE, Asst. Pubcty. Dir., Plaza Hotel, 59th St. and Fifth Ave., 10019, '69–; Regional Mktng Admr., Honeywell Inc., '68–'69; organized Ambassadorial Reception to promote intl. relations, '68; Theta Sigma Phi, Hotel-Motel Greeters Intl.; Syracuse Univ., Jnlsm. degree and BA (Social Psychology), '65; res: 420 E. 64th St., 10021.

KUNZELMANN, LINDA ADAMI, Mgr., Clearance Dept., Wells, Rich, Greene, 767 Fifth Ave., N.Y., N.Y. 10022, '69–; h. Philip Kunzelmann.

KUPPER, LORRAINE HOLLAND, List Rental Mgr., Christian Herald mag., 27 E. 39th St., N.Y., N.Y. 10016, '68–; Prod. Mgr., '66–; h. George Kupper.

KURSH, CHARLOTTE OLMSTED, Wtr., Anthropologist; Rsch. Conslt., Stanford Rsch. Inst. (Menlo Park, Cal.), '68–'69; Mental Rsch. Inst. (Palo Alto), '58–'68; Auth., "Heads I Win, Tails You Lose," (Macmillan, '63); Am. Anthropological Assn., Southwestern Anthropological Assn.; Sweetbriar Col., BA; Stanford Univ., MA, PhD, '65; b. Brookline, Mass.; p. Frederick Law and Sarah Sharples Olmstead; h. Maurice Kursh; c. Dr. Stephen Paschall Gill, Dr. Sarah Gill, Mrs. William Beighley, Mrs. Gayland Jordan; res: 80 Valencia Ct., Portola Valley, Cal. 94025.

KURTZMAN, BETTE LOUISE, PR Dir., National Conference of Christians and Jews, 203 N. Wabash Ave., Chgo., Ill. 60601, '66–; PR Dir., Little City Fndn., '64–'67; PR Dir., Monticello Realty Corp., '63; SHOW Magazine, '61–'63; Pubcty. Club of Chgo.; De Paul Univ., BA, '50; b. Chgo., Ill., 1927; p. Louis and Grace Jackson Kurtzman; res: 2400 Lake View, Chgo., Ill. 60614.

KUSEK, RITA BLANAN, Head Librn., Chicopee Public Library, Market Sq., Chicopee, Mass. 01013, '63–; First Asst. Librn., '58–'63; Lib. Asst., '47–'58; Article on Chicopee, Americana Ency., '68; New England Lib. Assn., Mass. Lib. Assn., Western Mass. Reg. Advisory Cncl., Western Mass. Lib. Assn., Round Table of Young Adults Librns., Young Adult Cooperative Book Review Group of Mass.; Cit., meritorious svc. in dev. of Chicopee, '65; Westfield State Col., '32–'35; Prof. Lib. Cert., '50; Col. of Our Lady of the Elms, BA, '66; b. Chicopee, Mass. 1915; p. Robert A. and Albina Deslauriers Blanan; h. John J. Kusek; c.

John David, Robert M., Judith Ann (Mrs. John Wass); res: 89 Taylor St., Chicopee, Mass. 01020.

KUSHNER, TRUCIA D., Reptr., Mkt. Ed., Women's Wear Daily, Fairchild Publications, 7 E. 12th St., N.Y., N.Y. 10003, '69–; Asst. Ed., Eye, '69; Reptr., Patriot Ledger (Quincy, Mass.), '67–'68; Dir. of Pubns., Manhattan Commty. Col., '65–'66; Media Wm.; Simmons Col., BS, '65; Boston Univ., MS, '68; b. N.Y.C., 1945; p. Elias and Leah Zank Kushner; res: 410 W. 24th St., N.Y., N.Y. 10011.

KUSKIN, KARLA SEIDMAN, Auth.-Illus: "Watson, The Smartest Dog in the U.S.A." ('68), "The Walk the Mouse Girls Took" ('67); 13 other juv. bks.; AIGA aws., '60, '58, '56; Yale Univ., BFA, '55; b. N.Y.C., 1932; p. Sidney and Mitzi Salzman Seidman; h. Charles Kuskin; c. Nicholas, Julia; res: 96 Joralemon St., Bklyn., N.Y. 11201.

KUTLER, JOYCE STERN, Dir. of PR, Allens Lane Art Center, '69–; Asst. Ed., Food Distributor, '66–; Ed., Penn Fruit Co.; Theta Sigma Phi; Syracuse Univ., BA, '52 (Phi Beta Kappa); b. Phila., Pa., 1930; p. Joseph and Dorothy White Stern; h. Gordon E. Kutler; c. Barry Scott, Bruce Robert; res: 8312 Rodney St., Phila., Pa. 19150.

KUTZ, MARGARET LENGEL, Publr.-Ed., The Oakland News, 234 Meyran Ave., Pitt., Pa. 15213, '59–; Colmst., '57–'58; Rehabilitation Cncl. of S. Oakland (Chmn.), Oakland C. of C. (Dir.; Humanitarian Aw.); Who's Who of Am. Wm., Dic. of Intl. Biog.; b. Cresson, Pa., 1915; p. John and Magda Stephania Lengel; h. Frank Kutz (dec.); c. Richard J., Frank M., James, Robert (dec.), John F. (dec.); res: 3274 Parkview Ave., Pitt., Pa. 15213.

KWEDER, ADELE NELSON, Hist. Feature Wtr., Waukegan News Sun, 100 Madison St., Waukegan, Ill. 60085, '69–; Auth: "Keep Calm Cook Book" (Prentice-Hall, '63; Pocket Books, '66), articles, various Med. Jnls., '65–; Lectr., early med superstitions and charm cures, '65–; Aux. to Am. Soc. of Abdominal Surgeons (Pres., '63), Aux. to Intl. Col. of Surgeons (VP, '69), Ill. State Med. Aux., Lake Co. Med. Soc. (Pres., '67); Ill. State Med. Soc. Public Affairs Aw., '69; Ill. Press Wms. Nate Palmer Aw., '69; b. Chgo., Ill., 1910; p. Carl and Hannah Chalstrom Nelson; h. David J. Kweder; c. Dourelle Jay (Mrs. Ron Griesheimer), Rae Lynne (Mrs. Richard Plodzien); res: 1432 N. Sheridan Rd., Waukegan, Ill. 60085.

KYLE, MARY J., Ed. and Publr., Twin Cities Courier, Minnesota Sentinel Publishing Company, 84 S. Sixth St., #501, Mpls., Minn. 55402, '68–; Pres., Minn. Sentinel Publ. Co., '68–; Co. VP, '67–'68; Ed. and Assoc. Publr., '67–'68; Ed., Twin City Observer-Sun Publ. Co., '63–'66; Colmst. and Reptr., '47–'52; TV Edtl. Commentator and Radio Communicator; Rsch.; Minn. Hist. Soc. for "Negro in Minnesota"; Minn. Press Wm., NPWC, Minn. Press Club; Edtl. Writing aw., Herman Roe Memorial Aw., '67; "Good Guy" Aw., Minn. Nwsp. Assn., '68; Human Rights Svc. Aw., Jewish Labor Commn., '68; Who's Who of Am. Wm.; Univ. of Minn., '25–'27, '33–'35; b. St. Paul, Minn., 1908; p. Ernest B. and Edith Mae Burnett James; h. Earle F. Kyle; c. Shirley M., Robert C., Mrs. Ray Walker, Earle F., Jr.; res: 3637 Fourth Ave. S., Mpls., Minn. 55409.

KYPER, BETTINA BEALS, Soc. Ed., Brockton Daily Enterprise, 60 Main St., Brockton, Mass. 02401, '58–; Reptr., Feature Wtr., '36–'58; Copy Desk, '42–'45; Boston Press Club, New England Wms. Press Assn.; b. Brockton, Mass., 1914; p. Arthur and Helen Andrews Beals; h. Edwin C. Kyper Jr.; res: 37 Ettrick St., Brockton, Mass. 02401.

L

LaCAILLE, JOAN B., Partner, Rich-LaCaille, 140 E. 81st St., N.Y., N.Y. 10028, '59–; VP of PR, Dawson & Royal Inc., '66–'68; Cnslt., Fred Rosen Assoc., Edward Gottlieb & Assoc. Monsieur Henri Wines, DuPont, '67–'68; Radio-TV Prom. Cnslt., Am. Express Co., '65–'66; Radio-TV Lectr. on Africa, '56–'65; Photogr.-Jnlst., Africa; APA-Phoenix Theater, many charity orgs.; Sarah Lawrence Col., BA, '50; b. Worcester, Mass., 1928; p. William D. and Dorothy Crane Kelleher; h. C. Wilson LaCaille (dec.).

LACHER, FRANCES RUTLAND, Copy Supvsr., Schwab, Beatty & Porter, Inc., 660 Madison Ave., N.Y., N.Y. '68–; Crtv. Dir., Hirsch/Tigler/Fried, '67–'68; Copy Group Head, Foote, Cone & Belding, '64–'65; VP, Crtv. Supvsr., Dancer-Fitzgerald-Sample, '59–'63; Copy Group Head, Compton Adv., '53–'59; Copy Cnslt., '65–; Fine Arts Cnslt., '68–; Auth., Publr., "The Brides Book" ('49); AWNY, AAF; Printers Ink aw., '61; Newsfront aw., '61; This Week aw., '61; b. Bklyn., N.Y.; h. Samuel Lacher; c. Dorothy Alison, Irene Melanie; res: 650 Ocean Ave., Bklyn., N.Y. 11226.

LADD, NANCY LEWIS, Publicist, Wtr.; '58–; Mdsng. Ed., Furniture Retailer; Midwest Reptr., Gift & Tableware Reptr.; Decorating Ed., Institutions Mag., '50–'58; NHFL, Theta Sigma Phi, Am. Inst. of Interior Designers (PR assoc.); Who's Who of Am. Wm.; Vassar Col., BA, '46; Univ. of Wis., MA (Jnlstry.), '47; Art Inst. of Chgo., '47–'49; b. Milw., Wis., 1926; p. Thomas and Leone Anderson Lewis; h. Frank Ladd; c. Thomas L., Geoffrey N.; res: 2742 Prairie Ave., Evanston, Ill. 60201.

LADD, SUE CAROL, Pres., Ladd Enterprises, Jaguar Productions, 9250 Wilshire Blvd., Beverly Hills, Cal. 90212; grad., Nat. Park Seminary; b. Chgo., Ill.; h. Alan Ladd; c. Alan Jr., David Alan, Carol Lee Ladd Veitch, Alana Sue Ladd Jackson; res: 323 N. Mapleton Dr., L.A., Cal. 90024.

LAFRANCO, CLAUDIA J. RAUSCH, Copywtr., Intl. Creative Div., Dentsu Advertising Ltd., 11, 1-Chome, Tsukiji, Tokyo, Japan, '70–; Copywtr., Allen & Dorward, Inc. (Cal.), '67–'69; Asst. AE, Pub. Comm. Bur. (PR affiliate A&D), '68–'69; Adv. Mgr., Amax Aluminum-Mill Products and Hunter Engineering, '66–'67; Asst. Adv. Mgr., '65–'66; Adv. Asst., '63–'65; Sls. Advisor, Jr. Achievement Co., '62; Public Info. Offcr., U.S. Naval Electronics Reserve Univ., '54; L.A. Adv. Wm., Exec. Secys; Mt. San Antonio Jr. Col., AA, '55; b. Bismarck, N.D.; p. Andrew and Veronica L. Rausch; res: Sanei Heights, 43-4 Oyama-cho, Shibuya-ku, Tokyo, Japan.

LAGER, THELMA, Owner, Lager & Associates, 1800 N. Argyle Ave., Hollywood, Cal. 90028, '64–; Copywtr. and AE at numerous adv. agcys.; Cnslt., Cal. Fashion Designers; Mbr. of Bd., Richard J. Neutra Inst.; LAAW, AAF, Radio-TV and Rec. Charities, Inc. (founding mbr.), Jr. Achievers (Judging Comm.); Lulu Aws., '61–'63; Wesleyan Univ. (Music); b. Danville, Ill.; p. S. Nathan and Rose Aron Lager; h. Maurice O. Huebsch; c. Hilary, Mark J.; res: 320 de la Fuente Ave., Monterey Pk., Cal. 91754.

LaHATTE, PATRICIA NOOT, Prom. Dir., The Atlanta Journal and The Atlanta Constitution, 10 Forsyth St., Atlanta, Ga. 30303, '54–; News Pic. Ed., The Atlanta Jnl., '43–'54; Art Dir., Sun. Atlanta Jnl. Magazine and Rotogravure Sec., '40–'42; Discussion Leader, Am. Press Inst.; Co-auth., "Discover Atlanta" (Simon & Schuster, '69); Artist, oils and watercolors; Intl. Nwsp. Prom. Assn. (Pres., '69–'70; Past Bd. of Dirs.; Southern Reg. Past Pres.; 1st VP, '68–'69; 2nd VP, '67–'68), Ga. C. of C., Atlanta Wms. C. of C.; Atlanta Wm. of the Yr. in Bus., '58; 1st pl. annual Ed. and Publr. Nwsp. Prom. Contest aws. in nat. adv. and newspaperboy categories; Certs. of Merit in public svc., retail adv., and PR; Intl. Circ. Mgrs. Assn. '64; Atlanta Sch. of Art; b. Port Townsend, Wash.; p. William and Elsie Forbes Noot; res: 834 Valley View Lane, City of Lake Berkeley, Rte. 2, Duluth, Ga. 30136.

LaHAY, WAUHILLAU, Staff Wtr., Scripps-Howard Newspaper Alliance, 1013 13th St., N.W., Wash., D.C., 20005, '63–; Dir. of Wm's Activities, Kenyon & Eckhardt Adv.; Free-lance, '60–'63; '53–'60; Dir. of Radio-TV Pubcty., N.W. Ayer & Son (N.Y.C.), '43–'53; Okla. State Col., '28–'29; b. Claremore, Okla., 1909; p. Joseph and Ann Russell LaHay; c. Phillip M. Lohman, III; res: 1070 30th St., N.W., Wash., D.C. 20007.

LAHRMER, PATRICIA, Free-lance Wtr., Bdcstr., '68–; Colmst., "The Passionate Shopper," New York, '68; Consumer News Reptr., WINS, '66–'68; PR Offcr., "University of the Seven Seas," '64–'65; Ed., "The Bellevuer," Bellevue Hosp., '62–'64; PR Adv., N.Y.C. Commn. to the UN, '67; Theta Sigma Phi (Oh. Univ. Chptr. Pres., '61), AWRT, AFTRA; Oh. Univ. Sch. of Jnlsm., '61 (cum laude); b. Newark, Oh., 1939; p. Frederick and Mary Lahrmer; h. Robert H. Ross; res: 72 Courtfield Gardens, London, S.W. 5, England.

LAIB, JANET, PR Cnslr., Janet Laib Public Relations and Publicity, 214 E. 70th St., N.Y., N.Y. 10021, '54–; Beauty Ed., Seventeen, '54; American Druggist, '47–'49; PR Dir., Hathaway Shirt Co., '53; OPC; Fashion Group; Univ. of Mich., '43–'46; New Sch. for Social Rsch., BA (PR), '54; b. Detroit, Mich., 1926; p. Walter and Jeanne Lewenthal Laib; c. Margo Amgott.

LAIRD, JEAN RYDESKI, Auth., 11 bks., numerous fiction, nonfiction articles published in major mags.; Nwsp. Colmst.; Writing Tchr., Oak Lawn HS Adult Evening Sch., '64–; Canterbury Club of Chgo. (Pres., '63–'65); b. Wakefield, Mich., 1930; p. Chester and Agnes Petranek Rydeski; h. Jack E. Laird; c. John, Jane, JoanAnn, Jerilyn, Jacquelyn; res: 10540 S. Lockwood Ave., Oak Lawn, Ill. 60453.

LAKLAN, CARLI (Virginia Laughlin Aiello), Auth: "Olympic Champions" ('68), "Surf With Me" ('67), numerous other bks.; many with pseud. John Clarke; Free-lance Mag. Wtr., '51–; Radio Scriptwtr., WOR (N.Y.C.), '41–'51; Dir., Am. Apprentice Theatre; summer stock, '38–'40; Instr., Univ. of Wash., '36–'37; Who's Who of Am. Wm.; Contemporary Auths.; Stanford Univ., '32–'33; Univ. of Wash., MA, '36; N.Y.U., Columbia Univ., '38–'39; b. Paoli, Okla.; p. John and Elizabeth Crawford Laughlin; h. 1. George Vogt (div.) 2. James J. Aiello; res: 14 Bay Ave., Sea Cliff, L.I., N.Y. 11579.

LAKRITZ, ESTHER HIMMELMAN, Wtr. of children's fiction and non-fiction, incl. "Randy Visits the Doctor" (Broadman Press, '62); Tchr., Caledonia (Mich.) HS, '49–'50; Univ. of Wis., BS (Secondary Educ.), '49; b. Milw., Wis., 1928; p. Alex and Mildred Hoffman Himmelman; h. Dr. Leo Lakritz; c. Simeon, Naomi, David; res: 2661 E. Collingwood Dr., Beloit, Wis. 53511.

LAM, GWEN L., Wtr., Educ. Cnslt., '69–; Sr. VP, Glick & Lorwin, Inc., '59–'69; Pres., Educ. Materials Corp., '54–'59; Edtl. Dir., Wheat Flour Inst., '48–'54; Wms. Army Corps, '45–'46; Home Econs. Tchr., '43–'46; Mbr., White House Conf. on Food, Nutrition, Health, '69; Am. Home Econs. Assn. (VP), AWNY, N.Y. Home Econsts. in Bus.; Tex. Tech. Univ., BS (Home Econs. Educ.), '43; Ia. State Univ., MS (Tech. Jnlsm.), '48; b. Tahoka, Tex., 1922; p. E. and Inez Hitt Lam; res: 165 W. 66th St., N.Y., N.Y. 10023.

LaMARRE, LINDA A., Home Furnishings Ed., The Detroit News, 615 W. Lafayette Blvd., Detroit, Mich. 48231, '69–; Soc. Reptr., Wms. Zones Supvsr., '63–'69; Reptr., The Pontiac Press, '62–'63; Theta Sigma Phi, Sigma Delta Chi; Univ. of Mich., BA (Jnlsm.).

LAMB, GLADYS JOHNSON, Owner and Partner, Kelly & Lamb Advertising Agency, 1480 West Lane Ave., Columbus, Oh. 43221, '46–; Theta Sigma Phi, Columbus Adv. Club; Outstanding Pilot Trophy, '49 and '52, Adv. Wm. of the Yr., '66; Ohio State Univ.; h.

J. Loel Lamb; c. Trent Owen and Harriet Gayle (Mrs. Rex Allen); res: 2379 Club Rd., Columbus, Oh. 43221.

LAMB, MYRNA, Playwright; Auth., "Mod Donna," Am. Shakespeare Theatre prod., '70, and three segments of "Scyklon Z": "In the Shadow of the Crematoria," "The Serving Girl and the Lady," "But What Have You Done for Me Lately?"; res: 211 Satterthwaite Ave., Nutley, N.J. 07110.

LAMBERT, CELIA FLORIO, PR Dir., The Atlantic Companies, 45 Wall St., N.Y., N.Y. 10005, '60–; Indsl. Ed., '47–'60; Auth., bks., trade mag. articles; tchr., indsl. jnlsm., Radcliffe; N.Y. Assn. of Indsl. Communicators (Pres., '60–'61); ICIE; PRSA; Katherine Gibbs Sch.; N.Y.U. Sch. of Jnlsm.; b. Fitchburg, Mass.; h. George Lambert; res: 3 Peter Cooper Rd., N.Y., N.Y. 10010.

LAMBERT, ELEANOR, Pres., Eleanor Lambert, Inc., 32 E. 57th St., N.Y., N.Y. 10022; Originator, Coordr., Coty Am. Fashion Critics' aws., Cotton Fashion aws.; Originator, N.Y. Couture Groups Nat. Press wks., annual Intl. Best Dressed polls; Colmst., "She," Pubs. Hall Synd.; Special Cnslt., WAC, U.S. Army Corps, '43–'45; mbr., Nat. Cncl. on Arts, '65–'66; AWRT, Fashion Group (VP, '61–'63); Theta Sigma Phi Wm. of the Yr., '63; N.Y. Bd. of Trade aw., '60; John Herron Art Inst., Chgo. Art Inst.; b. Crawfordsville, Ind.; p. Henry and Helen Craig Lambert; h. Seymour Berkson (dec.); c. William Craig; res: 1060 Fifth Ave., N.Y., N.Y.

LAMBERT, HAZEL MARGARET, Prof., Educ., Fresno State College, Fresno, Cal. 93726, '55–; Tchr., Univ. of Tenn., Plymouth Tchrs. Col.; Tchr.; Auth., three educ. textbks.; Prodr., film, "Montessori Education"; AAUW, Am. Psych. Assn., Nat. Assn. for Educ. of Young Child, Kappa Delta Pi, Pi Lambda Theta; Rsch. Grant, Fresno State Col., '68; Univ. of Minn., MA, '44; Univ. of N.C., PhD, '54; b. Baudette, Minn.; p. Aristide and Ann Doncet Lambert; res: 1300 W. Escalon St., Fresno, Cal. 93705.

LAMBERT, JOYCE, VP, MacManus, John & Adams, Inc., 437 Madison Ave., N.Y., N.Y. 10019, '65–; AE, '54–: Film Critic, Feature Wtr., Australian Assoc. Nwsps.; NHFL; b. Harrow-on-the-Hill, England; p. Charles and Sophy Holt Lambert; res: 101 W. 55th St., N.Y., N.Y. 10019.

LAMBERT, KAREN ANN, Reprtr., Salina Journal, 333 S. Fourth St., Salina, Kan. 67401, '69–; '66–'67; VISTA Svc. (S.D.), '67–'68; Theta Sigma Phi, Central Kan. Girl Scout Cncl.; Kan. Press Assn. aw., '67; Kan. Univ., BS (Jnlsm.), '66 (with distinction).

LAMBERT, VIRGINIA VAN HOUTEN, Wms. Ed., The Morning Call, 33 Church St., Paterson, N.J. 07505, '69–; Reptr., '67–'69; Seton Hall Univ., BS, '59; Montclair State Col., '60–'62; b. Paterson, N.J., 1938; p. Edward and Virginia McAleer Van Houten; h.

Raymond J. Lambert Jr.; c. Eileen, Patrick, Kathleen; res: 29 Lincoln Pl., Waldwick, N.J. 07463.

LAMBKA, MARY LOU, Asst. to Pres., Prom. Mgr., Wheeler Communications, Inc., 280 Columbine St., Denver, Colo. 80206, '69–; Prom. Mgr., KTLN Radio, '67–'69; Copywtr., KOY Radio, '67; Traf. Mgr., KHEY Radio, '66–'67; Traf. Mgr., KTSM Radio, '63–'66; Bdcstrs. Prom. Assn., AWRT, Adv. Club of Denver; Univ. of Tex.; Southwest Tex. State; b. Sioux Falls, S.D., 1943; p. Irwin and Dorothy Rouse Lambka.

LAMBRECHT, EUNICE GROBE, Free-lance Ed., '68–; Mng. Ed., Industrial Medicine & Surgery (Chgo., Ill.), '65–'68; Circ. Mgr., Hi-Time Publrs. (Elm Grove, Wis.), '63–'65; Asst. to Owner, Saxton Adv. Agcy. (Milw.), '49–'63; Cont. Dir., Radio WMAM (Marinette), '48–'49; Theta Sigma Phi; Civil Air Patrol aw., '61; Marquette Univ., Ph.B. (Jnlsm.), '48; b. Tomahawk, Wis., 1926; p. Walter and Ottilia Dunkel Grobe; h. Marshall Edgar Lambrecht; res: 5229 N. Sherman Blvd., Milw., Wis. 53209.

LAMPERT, ZOHRA, Actress, Kaplan-Veidt, 667 Madison Ave., N.Y., N.Y. 10021; Theatre: "Look, We've Come Through," "Mother Courage," "Nathan Weinstein's Daughter," "The Natural Look," "Lovers and Other Strangers" (Broadway); "After the Fall," "Marco Millions" (Lincoln Ctr. Repertory); Films: "Pay or Die," "Splendour in the Grass," "Posse from Hell," "A Fine Madness," "Bye Bye Braverman," "The One with the Fuzz"; TV: "Dr. Kildare," "I Spy," "The Defenders," "Trials of O'Brien," "The Man From U.N.C.L.E."; Variety Poll aw.; Critics aw.; twice nominated for Tony aw.; Univ. of Chgo., AB; b. N.Y.C., 1937; p. Morris and Rachil Eriss Lampert; res: 165 E. 49th St., N.Y., N.Y. 10017.

LAMPMAN, NATHALIE ELIZABETH, Dir., Info. Svcs., State University of New York at Albany, 1400 Washington Ave., Albany, N.Y. 12203, '65–; Asst. Ed., Business Week, '57–'61; Forbes mag., '54–'57; Mng. Ed., City Ed., Reptr., Colmst., Hudson Daily Star, '40–'53; Corr., UPI, N.Y. Herald Tribune; OPC, State Univ. of N.Y. PR Cncl., BPW, Pi Gamma Mu, Columbia County Hist. Soc. (Bd. of Dirs.), Columbia Mem. Hosp. Aux. (former mbr. Bd. of Dirs.); Eye Rsch. Fndn. aw., '59; Un. Fund, Commty. Chest aw., '58; State Univ. of N.Y., BA, '65 (cum laude); MA, '68; b. Hudson, N.Y.; p. Frank and Eugenia Raymond Lampman; res: 3 Stonehenge Lane, Albany, N.Y. 12203.

LAMPORT, FELICIA, Auth: "Cultural Stage" (Houghton Mifflin, '66), "Scrap Irony" ('61), "Mink on Weekdays" ('50); articles, verse, bk. revs. in major mags.; formerly dialogue subtitles, MGM; Reptr., N.Y. Jnl.; Auths. Guild, PEN, ASCAP, Am. Chess Fedn. (Dir.), The MacDowell Colony (Dir.); Vassar, BA, '37; b. N.Y.C., 1916; p. Samuel and Miriam Divorsky Lamport; h. Benjamin Kaplan; c. James L., Nancy L.; res: 2 Bond St., Cambridge, Mass. 02138.

LANCASTER, EDITH EARLE, Head Librn., Northwest Nazarene College, Nampa, Idaho, 83651, '57–; Asst. Librn., '56–'57; Asst. Librn., Trevecca Nazarene Col., '53–'56; ALA, BPW, Idaho Lib. Assn., Pacific Northwest Lib. Assn., Delta Kappa Gamma; Who's Who in Am. Educ.; Trevecca Nazarene Col., BA, '52; George Peabody Col. for Tchrs., MA; b. Fulton, Ky., 1927; p. Leslie and Bertha Burgess Lancaster; res: 116 10th Ave., S. Ext., Nampa, Idaho, 83651.

LANCASTER, PEGGY WILSON, Assoc. Crtv. Dir., Gumpertz, Bentley & Dolan, 6380 Wilshire Blvd., L.A., Cal. 90048, '69–; Sr. Copywtr., '67; Sr. Copywtr., Reach, McClinton, '67; Copywtr., MacManus, John & Adams, '64–'67; News Commentator, U.S.I.A. Voice of Am. (Wash., D.C.), '58–'60; Wtr., Talent, Serial, Radio WCAU, WCAU-TV (Phila., Pa.) '55–'57; L.A. Adv. Wm. (Bd. Mbr.), '68; certs., Lulu aws., '65–'69; certs., '65–'67); Phila. Fashion Group; Phila. Adv. Wm. aw., '54; Radio Adv. Bur. aw., '55; Univ. of Pa., BA (summa cum laude); b. Reading, Pa.; p. Ray and Ella Fry Wilson; h. William Lancaster (dec.); res: 4016 Via Opata, Palos Verdes Estates, Cal. 90274.

LANDAU, GENEVIEVE HERSHSON-MILLET, Exec. Ed., Parents' Magazine, 52 Vanderbilt Ave., N.Y., N.Y. 10017, '68–; Articles Ed., '61–'68; Assoc. Ed., '58–'61; Wtr., numerous articles in Parents' Magazine, pfsnl. jnls., encys.; Med. Wtrs. Assn.; Smith Col., BA, '54 (summa cum laude); Columbia Univ., MA (Lit.), '55 (highest hons. in Eng.; Phi Beta Kappa); b. Dallas, Tex., 1927; p. Harry and Elsie Lazarus Hershson; h. Sidney Landau; c. Elizabeth Millet, Jessica Millet; res: 17 Bank St., N.Y., N.Y. 10014.

LANDAU, IDA BIENSTOCK, Bd. Chmn., West Coast Dir., Transworld Feature Syndicate, Inc., 141 E. 44th St., N.Y., N.Y. 10017, '62–; Founder, Pres., Mng. Dir., '51–'62; Delta Phi Epsilon; N.Y.U. Sch. of Law, LLB, '20; b. Hartford, Conn., 1899; p. Samuel and Sophia Bisko Bienstock; h. Jacob Landau; c. Albert, Paula; res: 13250 Chandler Blvd., Van Nuys, Cal. 91401.

LANDAU, LUCY UNDERWOOD, Actress, '56–; Broadway: "Separate Tables," "The Thrill of it All," "Strange Bedfellows;" TV: "Name that Tune," Jack Paar, Phil Silvers, Merv Griffin shows; featured roles in "Omnibus," "Defender," numerous other TV dramatic shows; theatre group, summer stock, commls.; pre-WWII career as tchr., child psychologist; three yrs. a gunner in British army; AEA, AFTRA, SAG, Actors Fund, Intl. Bdcst. Aw., '68; League of Wm. Voters, Nat. Cncl. of Jewish Wm., Hadassah; Leeds (Eng.) Univ.; Univ. of London, BA; b. Eng.; h. Abram Landau; res: 83-80 118th St., Kew Gardens, N.Y. 11415.

LANDEN, FRANCES PATTON, Supvsr. of Commtns., Peoria Pleasure Driveway and Park District, Glen Oak Park Pavilion, Peoria, Ill. 61603, '69–; Dir. of Pubns., Lakeview Ctr. for the Arts and Scis., '63–'69; Educ. Asst., Arts and Sci. Fedn., '56–'63; Rsch. Assoc., State

Hist. Soc. of Mo., '39–'42; Assoc. Ed., Monroe City (Mo.) News, '33–'38; Univ. of Mo., BJ, '33; MA, '38; b. Mount Vernon, Mo., 1913; p. George and Cora Brown Patton; h. Ernest W. Landen; c. Selma (Mrs. Herbert Odom), Karlynn H.; res: 4111 N. Hawthorne Pl., Peoria, Ill. 60614.

LANDERS, ANN (Esther Friedman Lederer), Human Rels. Colmst., Publishers-Hall Syndicate, 30 E. 42nd St., N.Y., N.Y. 10017, '55–; AMA (Advisory Bd.), Harvard Med. Sch. Resources and Dev. Comm., Meninger Fndn. (Bd. of Trustees); one of ten most influential wm. in U.S., 1967 UP Intl. poll; one of 20 most admired wm. in the world, 1969 Gallup poll; Adolf Meyer Aw., Assoc. for Mental Health, '65; Golden Stethoscope Aw., Ill. State Med. Soc., '67; Golden Plate Aw. Academy of Achiev., Dallas, '69; Nat. Plaque of Honor by Americans Friends of the Hebrew Univ., '68; Auth: "Since You Asked Me" ('62), "Teen-Agers and Sex" ('64), "Truth Is Stranger," ('68); Morningside Col., '36–'40.

LANDGARD, JANET A., Actress, TV, motion pic., Columbia Pictures, 1801 Ave. of the Stars, Century City, Cal. 90067, '63–; b. Pasadena, Cal., 1947; p. George and Marjorie Klos Landgard; h. Neil Wilson; c. Shaw Janet.

LANDIS, JESSIE ROYCE, Actress, c/o Peter Witt, 37 W. 57th St., N.Y., N.Y. 10019; stage, film and TV performances; Auth., autobiog., "You Won't Be So Pretty but You'll Know More" (W.H. Allen, '64); AEA, AFTRA, SAG; Film's Daily Favorite Five ('55); Laurel Aw. for film, "To Catch a Thief" ('56); Blue Ribbon Aw. for films, "The Swan" ('54), "North by Northeast" ('62), "Gidget Goes to Rome" ('63); b. Chgo., Ill.; p. Paul and Ella Gill Medbery; h. J.F.R. Seitz; res: Box 214, Ridgefield, Conn. 06877.

LANDO, EUNICE JUDY, Public Info. Coordr., Community College of Allegheny County, 711 Allegheny Bldg., 429 Forbes Ave., Pitt., Pa. 15219, '67–; Programmed Instr., Xerox's Educational Subsidiary, '62–'65; PR Asst. Dir., N.Y. Inst. of Technology, '58–'59; AWRT, ACPRA, Assoc. Eds. Soc. of Pitt.; Univ. of Cal.; S.F. State Col.; Hunter Col.; b. Pitt., Pa., 1929; p. Joseph and Pauline Rosenshine Lando; res: 4909 Centre Ave., #16, Pitt., Pa. 15213.

LANDON, MARGARET MORTENSON, Auth: "Anna and the King of Siam," "Never Dies the Dream;" Wheaton Col., BA, '25; b. Somers, Wis., 1903; p. Annenus and Adelle Estburg Mortenson; h. Kenneth Perry Landon; c. Margaret (Mrs. Charles W. Schoenherr), William Bradley, Carol (Mrs. Lennart Pearson), Kenneth Perry; res: 4711 Fulton St. N.W., Wash., D.C. 20007.

LANDRETH, LUCINDA KREIDER, Mgr., National Educational Radio Network Div., National Assn. of Educational Broadcasters, 1346 Connecticut Ave., N.W., Wash., D.C. 20036, '69–; Adm. Asst., '65–'69; Div. of Educ. Planning and Financing, UNESCO, '64–'65; HS Hist. Tchr., '63–'64; Rschr., educ. radio; AWRT, NAEB, Who's Who of Am. Wm., Assn. of Jr. Leagues of Am.; Pa. State Univ., BA (Hist.); b. Lancaster, Pa., 1941; p. W. Gordon and Kathryn Kreider Landreth; res: 1829 Summit Pl., N.W., Apt. 102, Wash., D.C. 20009.

LANE, DOROTHY GARTLEY (Dotty Lane), Fashion Ed., WKNT, AM, FM, Kent, Oh.; Fashion Ed., Record-Courier; Kent Am. Field Svc., Kent Un. Fund, Robinson Memorial Hosp. Bd.; Oh. Press Wm. fashion aw., '69; Kent State Univ.; b. Rayland, Oh., 1916; p. Roy and Alva Frycklynd Gartley; h. James H. Lane; c. J. Marsh, Priscilla, Suzanne, Mrs. Charles Garrett; res: 7389 St., Rte. 43, Kent, Oh. 44240.

LANE, LAURA, Wms. Ed., Farm Journal, Inc., Washington Sq., Phila., Pa. 19105, '69–; Assoc. Ed., '55–'69; Assoc. Ed., Country Gentleman, '47–'55; Ext. Svc. Ed., Tex. A. & M. Univ., '46–'47; Ext. Svc. Assoc., '39–'46; Reptr., Vernon Daily Record, '36–'39; WNPC, Theta Sigma Phi (Headliner Aw., '51), Epsilon Sigma Phi (Outstanding Contrb. to Rural Life Aw., '51), Assoc. Country Wm. of the World (Life Mbr.); Tex. Wms. Univ., BS, '33; Grad. Work, Columbia Univ., '44; b. Vernon, Tex., 1913; p. William, III and Martha Conner Lane; res: 2018 Spruce St., Phila., Pa. 19103.

LANE, MARILYN C., Publicist, 140 S. Hibiscus Dr., Hibiscus Island, Miami Beach, Fla. 33139, '66–; Dir. PR Dept., E. J. Scheaffer Adv.; '66–'69; Staff Wtr., Photogr., Sunday mag. sec., Miami News, '61–'66 (six aws. for excellence of work); Fla. WPA, Theta Sigma Phi, Daguerre Pieterialists; Univ. of Miami; b. Chgo., Ill., 1930; p. Wallace and Evelyn Winters Hurter; h. Edward Gadinsky; c. Glenn Edward Lane, Pamela Gadinsky, Brian Gadinsky, Seth Gadinsky; res: 140 S. Hibiscus Dr., Hibiscus Island, Miami Beach, Fla. 33139.

LANE, MARION THORNBERRY, Wms. Pg. Ed., Lodi News-Sentinel, 127 N. Church St., Lodi, Cal. 95420, '69–; Farm Ed., Police-Court Reptr., '68–'69; Copy Ed., Crescent City American, '66–'68; Feature Wtr., Del Norte Triplicate; Auth., children's play, Plays Inc., '65; Nwsp. Inst. of Am. Grad., '64; b. Boulder, Colo., 1932; p. Amy Smith Ritchie; h. (div.); c. Lawrence L., Dale E.; res: 451 Pioneer Dr., Lodi, Cal. 95420.

LANE, MARSHA, Wms. Mktng. Cnslt., Schenley Industries, 1290 Avenue of the Americas, N.Y., N.Y. 10019, '67–; Bdcstr., WBAB Radio, '65–'67; Assoc. Ed., Offcl. Sports, Inc., '63–'65; Free-lance PR, Rsch., '60–'63; Assoc. Dir., Fndn. for the Study of Primitive Culture; PR Dir., Doctors' Hosp. (Freeport, N.Y.); AWRT, Assn. for the Help of Retarded Children; Univ. of Mich., BA (Eng., Speech); b. N.Y.C., 1929; p. Samuel and Blanche Schecter Chosed; h. William Lannik; c. Susana, David, Elizabeth; res: 200 S. Merrick Ave., Merrick, N.Y. 11566.

LANE, MARY BEAUCHAMP, Prof. of Educ., San Francisco State College, 1600 Holloway Ave., S.F., Cal. 94132, '59–; Staff, N.Y.U. and Ctr. for Human Rels. Studies, '51–'58; Educ. Asst., Pasadena City Schs., '48–'50; Curriculum Cnslt., Mpls. Public Schs., '45–'48; Co-auth: "Human Relations in Teaching" ('55), "Understanding Human Development" ('59); Wtr., many articles for Childhood Educ. and Educ. Leadership; Nat. Assn. for the Educ. of Young Children (Bd. of Governors, '67–), Northern Cal. Assn. for the Educ. of Young Children (Pres., '67–'69), Assn. for the Supervision and Curriculum Dev. (Bd. of Governors, '59–'61), Assn. of Childhood Educ. Intl.; Northeastern Mo. State Tchrs., Col., BS, '30; Northwestern Univ., MA, '45; N.Y.U., EdD, '50; b. Edwardsburg, Mich., 1911; p. Hugh and Carrie Scott Beauchamp; h. Howard Lane; c. Jay, Kelley; res: 10 Lundy Lane, San Mateo, Cal. 94402.

LANE, NANCY, Assoc. Ed., Political Science Quarterly, Columbia University, 321-M Fayerweather Hall, N.Y., N.Y. 10027, '62–; Assoc. Ed., Proceedings of the Acad. of Polit. Sci., '62–'67; Staff, N.Y. Times, '59–'61; Barnard Col., AB, '60; b. N.Y.C., 1938; p. Morton and Lillian Gelb Lane; res: 45 W. 10th St., N.Y., N.Y. 10011.

LANEY, NINA INGRAM, Librn., Panhandle Publishing Co., Box 471, 209 Main St., Borger, Tex. 79007, '60–; Edtl. Asst., '52–'60; b. Coles County, Ill., 1914; p. Thomas and Fanny Davis Ingram; h. Joe C. Laney; c. J. Thomas, Mrs. Leo Smith, Mrs. B. L. Bybee; res: 214 Mackenzie St., Stinnett, Tex. 79083.

LANG, DOREEN, Actress, Kingsley Colton & Assoc., Inc., 321 S. Beverly Dr., Beverly Hills, Cal. 94712; Theatre: "Blithe Spirit," "Make Way for Lucia," "I Know My Love," "Season in the Sun," "Faithfully Yours" (N.Y.C.); "The Women," "The Marriage of Blood" (London, England); Films: "The Wrong Man," "North by Northwest," "The Birds"; Auth., "Needle & Thread" (prod. Phoenix Theatre, London, England, '39); AEA, SAG, AFTRA; Cornish Theatre Sch., BA; h. Arthur Franz; c. Ann Wilder; res: 32960 Pacific Coast Highway, Malibu, Cal. 90265.

LANG, JOYCE BURNETT, Pubns. Coordr., E. C. Brown Center for Family Studies, University of Oregon, 1802 Moss St., Eugene, Ore. 97403, '69–; Pubn. Asst., Pacific Sociological Review, '67–'69; Adv. Copywtr., Bon Marche, '66–'67; Owner, Write-It-Right, '66; Ed., Co-Publr., Hebron (N.D.) Herald, '57–'65; Wtr., Reptr., Ed., '40–'57; N.D. Press Wm. (Charter Pres., achiev. aw., '65; 27 writing aws.), BPW (Enderlin Chptr. Pres., '49), Theta Sigma Phi; Univ. of N.D., BA (Jnlsm.), '40; b. Cummings, N.D., 1918; p. Mack and Bertha Carver Burnett; h. Irvin W. Lang; c. Michael, Patricia; res: 4679 Barger Dr., Eugene, Ore. 97402.

LANG, LILLIAN A., Radio Prog. Dir., The British Broadcasting Corp., 630 Fifth Ave., N.Y., N.Y. 10020, '59–; joined PR Dept. during WWII; AWRT (Dir. at Large, '56–'57; N.Y.C. Chptr. Treas., '55; 1st VP, '65–'66; Pres., '66–'67); Eng. Speaking Un. Better Understanding aw., '55; Chateau de Marnand (Switzerland), French Teaching Cert.; b. London, Ontario, Can., 1917; p. Dr. Charles and Mary Hodgins Lang; res: 29 Claremont Ave., N.Y., N.Y. 10027.

LANG, MIRIAM MILMAN, Co-Auth., "Doctors to the Great" (Dial Press, '62); Eng. Tchr., Port Chester High School, Tamarack Road, Port Chester, N.Y. 10573, '66–; Instr., Writing, Scarsdale Adult Sch., '66; Instr., Eng. and Drama, Westchester Commty. Col., '56–'62; Prodr.-Dir., Commty. Players, E. Rockaway Jewish Commty. Ctr. (Hewlett, L.I.), '49–'54; Dramatists Guild, Port Chester Tchrs. Assn., Westchester Tchrs. Assn.; Wellesley Col., BA, '36; Columbia Univ., MA, '38; b. Chgo., Ill., 1915; p. Barnet and Rose Smoleroff Milman; h. Theodore Lang; c. Rosemary, Jonathan, Patricia; res: 18 Sammis Lane, White Plains, N.Y. 10605.

LANG, NANCY, Music Specialist, Voice of America, U.S. I.A., Wash., D.C. 20547, '65–; Dir. of Pubcty., Command Records, '63; Music Dir., Station WTFM, '62; Dir., Recorded Music, Heritage Stations, '60–'61; Assoc. Ed., Hi-Fi/Stereo Review, '59; WQXR, '52–'59; AWRT, Music Critics Assn., Assoc. Cncls. of the Arts; Skidmore Col., BM, '50; Columbia Univ., MA, '51.

LANGBORT, POLLY, Media Group Supvsr., Young & Rubicam, Inc., 285 Madison Ave., N.Y., N.Y. 10017, '67–; Secy., Coordr., Spot TV; Byr.; Sr. Byr.; Supvsr.; Adelphia Univ., BA, '54; res: 340 E. 64th St., N.Y., N.Y. 10021.

LANGDALE, SHARRY HOFER, Assoc. Ed., Computers and Automation, 815 Washington St., Newtonville, Mass. 02160, '67–; Univ. of S.D., BA (Phi Beta Kappa); b. Freeman, S.D., 1940; p. J. L. and Marianne Lammers Hofer; h. Daniel Langdale; c. Shelley Rae; res: 743 Watertown St., Newtonville, Mass. 02160.

LANGDON, AUDREY, Sr. Wtr., Pritchard Wood Associates, 1345 Ave. of the Americas, N.Y., N.Y. 10009, '66–; Sls. Prom. Mgr., Diamond-Shamrock, '63–'66; Adv. Mgr., Air Reduction, '59–'62; Press Offcr., Soc. Cosmetic Chemists, '58; PR Mgr., Colgate-Palmolive, '53–'57; Fashion Coordr.; Beauty Ed., My Baby; numerous articles, speeches on beauty, fashion, mktng.; Cosmetic Career Wm. (Charter Mbr.), Fashion Group; Carnegie Inst., '41–'45; Univ. of Pitt., BA, '47; b. McKeesport, Pa., 1927; p. Thomas and Ruth Mandel Langdon; c. Jawaid Hanid Awan, Sarah Hanid Awan; res: 22 Upper Mountain Ave., Montclair, N.J. 07042.

LANGDON, PATRICIA MARIE, Adv. Dir., Let's Live Magazine, 444 N. Larchmont Blvd., Hollywood, Cal. 90004, '68–; Ed., TV Star Parade, Ideal Publ., '66–'68; Publr., Teen Scene, Media 3, '62–'66; Publicist, Milton Blackstone, '60–'62; Adv. Club of N.Y., Hollywood Wms. Press Club, West L.A. Heart Fund (Co-chmn.);

Sacred Heart of Mary Col. (N.Y.); b. N.Y.C., 1933; p. John D. and Alma Knothe Langdon; c. Ellyn, Arien, Heather; res: 178 Crescent Dr., Beverly Hills, Cal. 90210.

LANGDON, SUE ANE, Actress, c/o APA, 9000 Sunset Blvd., Hollywood, Cal. 90069; starred on Broadway in "The Apple Tree"; co-starred, movies: "A Guide for the Married Man," "A Fine Madness," "The Rounders," "The Cheyenne Social Club" six others; TV appearances in many series, incl. "Mannix," "Ironside," "Bonanza"; Tex. State Tchrs. Col.; Idaho State Col.; Mont. State Col.; b. Paterson, N.J.; p. Albert and Grace Huddle Lookhoff; h. Jack Emrek; res: 24115 Long Valley Rd., Hidden Hills, Cal. 91302.

LANGE, DONNA JEAN, Entertainment Ed., Edtl. Staff, The Valley Independent, Eastgate 19, Monessen, Pa. 15062, '61–; Chatham Col., BA (Eng.), '61; Famous Wtrs. Sch., cert., '68; b. North Charleroi, Pa., 1938; p. Henry and Viva Mae Kerr Lange; res: 724 Edwards Ave., Belle Vernon, Pa. 15012.

LANGE, JEAN RUTHVEN, Wtr., Prodr., KLRN-TV, Box 991, San Antonio, Tex. 78206; Who's Who of Am. Wm.; h. Hans A. F. Lange (dec.).

LANGENFELD, ELIZABETH GROEPPNER, Prom. Rep., TV Guide Magazine, Triangle Publications, PO Box 500, Radnor, Pa. 19088, '58–; Interpreter, Investigator, overseas, U.S. Govt., '54–'58; AWRT, Ia.-Ill. PR Cncl. (Pres., '69–), Faculty Wives Club of Black Hawk Col. (Pres., '68–'69), Miss. Press Club; Loretto Col. (Rosenheim, Germany), Grad., '48; Univ. of Munich (Germany), '56–'57; h. Frank J. Langenfeld; c. Mary Elizabeth; res: 5021 35th Ave., Moline, Ill. 61265.

LANGEVIN, DOROTHY SMEAD, Sr. Public Info. Specialist, N.Y. State Department of Commerce, 112 State St., Albany, N.Y. 12207, '66–; VP, R. L. Bliss (N.Y.C.), '62–'66; AE, Adv. and PR (Rutland, Vt.), '60–'62; Indsl. Ed., Warner Bros. (Bridgeport, Conn.), '57–'60; Asst. Ed., Boats Magazine (Milford), '54–'57; Indsl. Ed., Remington Arms (Bridgeport), '41–'44; PRSA, N.Y. State PR Assn., League of Wm. Voters; Cedar Crest Col., BA, '31; Univ. of Pa., '32; Univ. of Bridgeport, '57; b. Buffalo, N.Y., 1909; p. George and Hepsey Allen Smead; c. Eleanor B. (Mrs. Earle F. Robinson); res: 3442 Gari Lane, Schenectady, N.Y. 12303.

LANGNER, MILDRED CROWE, Librn., Prof., University of Miami School of Medicine Library, Box 875, Biscayne Annex, Miami, Fla. 33152, '68–; Librn., Assoc. Prof., '63–'68; Chief, Ref. Svc. Div., Nat. Lib. Med. (Bethesda, Md.), '61–'62; Librn., Asst. Prof., Miami and Ala.; '45–'61; Lectr., Librnship., '45–; Bk. Reviewer, Library Journal, others; '57–; Med. Lib. Assn. (Pres.), Am. Med. Wtrs. Assn., Fla. Lib. Assn., Special Libs. Assn. (Ala. Chptr. Pres.), Univ. of Chattanooga, BA (Eng.), '33; Peabody Col. for Tchrs., BS (Lib. Sci.), '45; b. Chattanooga, Tenn., 1911; p. Patrick

and Anna Costello Crowe; h. Julian Langner (dec.); res: 1408 S.E. Bayshore Dr., Miami, Fla. 33131.

LANGTON, JANE GILLSON, Fiction Wtr., children's bks.: "The Majesty of Grace" ('61), "The Diamond in the Window" ('62), "The Swing in the Summerhouse" ('67); adult bk, "The Transcendental Murder" ('64); Wellesley Col., '40–'42; Univ. of Mich., BS, MA, '42–'45 (Phi Beta Kappa); Radcliffe Col., MA, '48; Boston Museum Sch., '58–'59; b. Boston, Mass., 1922; p. Joseph L. and Grace Brown Gillson; h. William Langton; c. Christopher, David, Andrew; res: Sandy Pond Rd., Lincoln, Mass. 01773.

LAPHAM, GEORGIE MOORE, Colmst., Gold Coasting, Palm Beach Post-Times, Perry Newspapers, 291 S. Federal Highway, Delray Beach, Fla. 33444, '59–; VP, Bede Aircraft, '56–'59; Head, Intl. PR, Schine Hotels & Enterprises, '54–'56; Ed.-Publr., Delray Beach News and County News, '51–'54; Fgn. Corr., Perry Nwsp., '59–; BPW (Delray Beach Pres., '46), OPC, Fla. Gold Coast Press Club (Pres., '62–'63); Epilepsy Fndn. of Am. (Palm Beach County Chptr., Exec. Dir.); aws. for gen. and edtl. excellence, '51–'54; Highest Air Force Aw. to Wm. Civilian, '46; b. Chgo., Ill., 1910; p. George and Kittie Packard Moore; h. (div.); res: 609 S.E. 3rd St., Delray Beach, Fla. 33444.

LARABEE, LOTTIE B., VP for Academic Affairs, Drake College of Florida, Ft. Lauderdale, Fla. 33301, '68–; Academic Asst. to Pres., Prof. of Higher Educ., '67–'68; Rschr., Cnslt., col. and univ. adm., '55–'67; former Sch. Dir. (Chgo., Ill.); former Fac. Mbr., Lock Haven (Pa.) State Col., Southern State Col. (S.D.), Albion (Idaho) Normal; Auth., three bks. on col., univ. adm.; Am. Assn. for the Advancement of Sci., Sigma Alpha Iota, Kappa Delta Pi, New England His. Genealogical Soc., American Assn. for Higher Educ., Am. Assn. of Independent Col. and Univ. Pres. aw., '68; N.Y.U., MA (Col., Univ., Adm.), '45; PhD (Col., Univ. Adm.), '55; b. Sprague, Neb.; p. Arthur and Anna Bartels Larabee; res: 1201 S.E. Second St., Ft. Lauderdale, Fla. 33301.

LARKEN, SHEILA ANN, Res. Actress, Assn. of Producing Artists, Front St. Playhouse, Seattle Repertory; TV roles, "Bonanza," "The Virginian," "It Takes a Thief," "Marcus Welby M.D.," others; Bennington Col., BA, '65; b. N.Y.C., 1944; p. Alexander and Pearl Rosenberg Diamond; res: 822 N. Harper Ave., Hollywood, Cal. 90046.

LaROCQUE, GERALDINE ELIZABETH, Assoc. Prof. of Eng., Teachers College, Columbia University, 525 W. 120th St., N.Y., N.Y. 10027, '65–; Tchr., '47–'62; Prom. Adv., Mdsng. Mgr., WTCN Radio-TV (Mpls., Minn.), '53–'55; Cnslt., sch. systems; Speaker, pfsnl. meetings; Dir., workshops; AAUP, Am. Educ. Rsch. Assn., N.Y. State Cncl. of Eng. Tchrs., Nat. Cncl. of Tchrs. of Eng., numerous other educ. groups, Pi Lambda Theta, Phi Alpha Theta, Lambda Alpha Psi; John Hay Fellowship at Harvard, '60–'61; Univ.

of Minn., BS (Phi Beta Kappa; high hons.), '47; MA (scholarship), '52; Stanford Univ., PhD (scholarship), '65; b. Duluth, Minn., 1926; p. Weldon and June LaRocque; res: 88 Morningside Drive, N.Y., N.Y. 10027.

LARREMORE, LUCILE ERNSON, News Ed., Llano News, 813 Berry St., Llano, Tex. 78643, '59–; Ed., '55–'59; Corr., KTBC-TV (Austin), '60–'65; Corr., Austin (Tex.) American-Statesman, '53–'68; b. Monroe, Ut., 1910; p. Joseph and Mabel Bates Ernson; h. Wilma Sylvester Larremore; c. Frederick Kassell, David, Lynn, Gary, Brian, Jacqueline Larremore Sessions; res: Valley Spring Rte., Llano, Tex. 78643.

LARSEN, BEVERLY NAMEN, Colmst., "Farm Flavor," Audubon News-Advocate, Audubon, Ia.; colm. began in another nwsp., '58–; Wtr., two religious bks. (Augsburg Publ., Mpls., Minn., '64, '65), more than 50 articles in religious mags., others; Tchr., Exira (Ia.) Schs.; Dana Col., BS (Sci.); b. Dodge, Ia., 1929; p. Louis and Lucille Skuldt Namen; h. Edwin Larsen; c. Stephen Peterson, Christine Peterson, Rachel; res: Rte. 2, Exira, Ia. 50076.

LARSEN, CAROL STROLL, PR Dir., Peck & Peck, 521 Fifth Ave., N.Y., N.Y. 10017, '62–; Publicist, Jos. Bancroft & Sons, '60–'62; Publicist, Chrysler Corp., '59–'60; Edtl. Wtr., Street & Smith Pubns., '58–'59; Fashion Group; Rollins Col., BA, '58; b. N.Y.C., 1936; p. George and Helen Wrentmore Stroll; h. Leslie H. Larsen; res: 399 E. 72nd St., N.Y., N.Y. 10021.

LARSEN, DOROTHY MURPHY, Food Svc. Dir., Passaic County Manchester Reg. High School District, 70 Church St., Haledon, Paterson, N.J. 07508, '60–; Mdsng. Dir., Hot Shoppes (Wash., D.C.); Consumer Svc. Dir., Gen. Baking Co.; Bakery Div., A&P; Contrbr., numerous food svc. pubns.; Prod., moving pics. for Cherry Growers Assn., Peanut Growers Assn.; Food Mdsng. Cnslt.; TV-Radio Cooking Demonstrator; AWRT, Food Svc. Execs. Assn., N.J. Sch. Food Svc. Assn. (Pres.); b. Jersey City, N.J., 1912; p. Joseph and Emma Becker Murphy; h. Arthur Larsen; c. Bernard L.; res: Box 464, 42 Merrie Trail, Denville, N.J. 07834.

LARSEN, MARY JOAN, Wtr.; Tchr., Granite HS (Salt Lake City, Ut.), '63–'67; Tchr., Granger (Ut.) HS, '60–'62; PR, Brigham Young Univ. Adult Educ., '58–'59; Thesis: "A Survey of Journalism in Utah Secondary Schools" ('63); material in Intermountain Industry mag.; Ut. Assn. of Jnlsm. Dirs. (Pres., '61–'62); Kappa Tau Alpha, Theta Sigma Phi (Univ. of Ut. Chptr. Adviser, '60–'65; Pres., '58–'59); Univ. of Ut., BS, '59 (Wms. Press Club Pres., '58; aw. for "Outstanding Svc. in Jnlsm.," '59); MS, '63; PhD Study, '68–'69; b. Salt Lake City, Ut., 1937; p. Nils K. and Johanne Nygaard Larsen; res: 607 Eighth Ave., Salt Lake City, Ut. 84103.

LARSEN, PAT LOPER, Wms. News Ed., Beatrice Daily Sun, Seventh and Ella Sts., Beatrice, Neb. 68310,

'68–; Wms. Ed., '47; Neb. Press Wm. (aws., '69), NPWC; Tex. Wms. Univ., '47–'48; b. Fairbury, Neb., 1928; p. H. A. and Thelma Clough Loper; h. Leon Larsen (dec.); c. Linda, Pam, Clark, Debbie, Teresa; res: 821 N. 11th St., Beatrice, Neb. 68310.

LARSON, JOAN PROSS, Dir. Photog., Peace Corps, 806 Connecticut Ave. N.W., Wash., D.C. 20525, '68–; Deputy Dir., Commty. Rels., VISTA, OEO, '64–'68; Auth., Bk, "Visit With Us in Japan" ('64); nwsp., mag. articles; appeared nat. TV, radio; Dir., Special Eng. Prog., The Am. Sch. in Japan, '63–'64; AWRT, ANWC, NLAPW, Theta Sigma Phi, Nat. Press Photogrs. Assn., WNPC; Who's Who of Am. Wm.; Dic. of Intl. Biog.; The 2000 Wm. of Achiev.; Univ. of Toledo, BE, '49 (cum laude; Who's Who of Am. Cols.); R. H. Macy Jr. Exec. Training Program, '50; Sophia Univ. (Tokyo, Japan; Far E. Hist.); Am. Univ. (Photo-jnlsm.); Univ. of Mo., '67; b. Platteville, Wis., 1927; p. Irving and Willah Johnson Pross; res: 4201 Cathedral Ave. N.W., Apt. 807-E, Wash., D.C. 20016.

LARSON, KATHRYN KEIPER, Wms. Svc. Dir., WHEN Broadcasting, 980 James St., Syracuse, N.Y. 13203. '58–; On-air Hostess; AWRT (Past Pres.), Theta Sigma Phi (Pres.; Former VP), NLAPW; GMA Lifeline of Am. Aw., '62; Eastwood BPW Wm. of the Year, '62; Syracuse Univ.; b. Binghamton, N.Y., 1917; p. Calvin and Eleanor Meaker Keiper; h. Kenneth Larson; c. Linda Bothwell, Eric; res: 215 DeWitt St., Syracuse, N.Y. 13203.

LARSON, LOISELDA HOWARD, Jnslm. Dir., Tchr., Laurel Sr. HS, 203 E. 8th St., Laurel, Mont. 59044, '42–; Eng. Tchr., Missonla County HS, '39–'41; Tachr., '34–'39; Mont. Jnlsm. Dirs. (Pres., '64–); Recipient of Gold Key as Outstanding Jnlsm. Tchr. in Mont.; Chmn., State Commn. Comm. on Jnlsm. Textbks.; Am. Bus. Wms. Assn., AAUW (Life Mbr; Mont. Wm. of Achiev., '66–'68), NEA (Life Mbr.), Nat. Press Wm. (Life Mbr.), Mont. Press Wm. (Treas., '65–'69), Nat. Cncl. of Eng. Tchrs. (Life Mbr.), Nat. Dir., '69–'72), Mont. Assn. of Eng. Tchrs. (Pres., '59–'60), Kan. State Univ., BS, '34; MS, '38; Wall Street Journal Fellow, Univ. of Mont.; b. Colby, Kan.; p. Lester Carlton and Margaret Snellbacher Howard; h. William Roseberry Larson; c. MarlesBea (Mrs. Edward C. Nicholls); res: 2510 Rimrack Rd., Billings, Mont. 59102.

LARSON, MARGARET A., VP, Bell & Stanton, Inc., 909 Third Ave., N.Y., N.Y. 10022; Acc. Supvsr., AE; Head, Wms. PR, Mogul Williams & Saylor; Acc. Supvsr., AE, Lynn Farnol Group; AWRT, Fashion Group, NHFL; Bennington Col., BA, '44; Johns Hopkins Sch. of Advanced Intl. Studies, MA, '47; b. N.Y.C., 1923; p. N. H. and Mary Leckie Larson; res: 411 E. 85th St., N.Y., N.Y. 10028.

LARSON, MARGARET HAMILTON, Feature Wtr., Bremerton Sun, 545 Fifth St., Bremerton, Wash. 98310, '68–; Pubns. Ed., Asst. to Dir., Univ. of Wash., Off. of HS and Col. Rels., '56–'58; Theta Sigma Phi, Olympic Col. (Trustee), Kitsap Day Care Assoc. (Originated,

'66; Past Pres.), Un. Good Neighbor Fund (Bd. Mbr.); Univ. of Wash., BA, '56; b. Nampa, Idaho, 1934; p. William and Helen Wood Hamilton; h. Stuart Manning Larson; c. Christian Mark, Kevin William, Kathryn Ann; res: Rte. 4, Box 2506, Bremerton, Wash. 98310.

LARSON, MARIAN LOUISE, Jnl. Ed., American Society of Safety Engineers, 850 Busse Hwy., Park Ridge, Ill. 60668, '67–; Asst. Ed., Hosp. Topics, '65–'67; Ed., Together Magazine, '58–'65; Free-lance Wtr., '54–'58; active in Inter-Am. field; Cnslt., Latin-Am. Affairs; Founder, Chgo. Partners of Alliance, '64; NFPW, NATAS, AWRT, Soc. of Tech. Wtrs. and Publrs., IEA, Am. Soc. of Bus. Press Eds., Mensa; seven nat. aws. in writing; Diploma of Distg. Visitor to Mexico, '55; Hon. Citizen, City of Puebla, Mex. '55; Northwestern Univ. Sch. of Jnlsm.; b. Remsen, Ia., 1918; p. David and Flora Johnson Anderson; c. Robert, Jr.; res: 4954 N. Kentucky Ave., Chgo., Ill. 60630.

LARSON, W. CAROLYN, Edtl. Asst., Social Education Journal, National Council for the Social Studies of the National Education Association, 1201 16th St. N.W., Wash., D.C. 20036, '69–; Free-lance Wtr., '66–; Feature Wtr., Nat. Cowboy Hall of Fame, '65; Wms. Staff Wtr., Oklahoman and Times, '64–; Theta Sigma Phi (Okla. City Chptr. Archivist, '65), Avalanche Ski Club; Univ. of Okla., BA (Jnlsm.), '64; b. Okla. City, Okla., 1942; p. Roy and Eleanor Hanson Larson; res: 1129 New Hampshire Ave., N.W., Wash., D.C. 20037.

LaRUE, ARLENE CATHERINE, Wms. Ed., Herald-Journal and Herald-American Post-Standard, 220 Herald Pl., Syracuse, N.Y. 13201, '47–; City Ed., Rome Sentinel, '41–'47; Reptr., Daily Sentinel, '35–'41; Reptr., Geddes News, '34–'35; Jnlsm. Tchr., Syracuse Univ. Ext. Sch., '55, and Syracuse Adult Educ., '56; Theta Sigma Phi (Eastern Reg. Dir., '55–'58; Syracuse Chptr. Pres., '51–'53), ZONTA; N.Y. State Fair Playwriting Contest (1st Prize, '54), Hadassah Commty. Svc. Aw., ('53), WAGE (Radio) Commty. Svc. Aw. ('52); Syracuse Univ., BS (Jnlsm.), '34; res: 107 Whedon Rd., Syracuse, N.Y. 13219.

LaSALLE, DOROTHY MARGUERITE, Auth., nine bks. on physical educ., play, dance, health, dev., incl. "Guidance of Children Through Physical Education," "Health Instruction for Today's Schools"; articles in jnls. and mags.; Emeritus Prof., Wayne State Univ., '65–; Prof., Health and Physical Educ., '46–'65; Visiting Lectr: Univ. of Colo., Univ. of Mich., Univ. of Tenn., Univ. of Pitt., Univ of Wis.; Wayne State Univ. (Col. of Educ. Svc. Aw., '44); Tchrs. Col., Columbia Univ., BS (Hygiene and Physical Educ.), '17; MA, '31; EdD, '43; b. Lake Geneva, Wis., 1895; p. Charles and Mary Lawson LaSalle; res: 866 Roslyn Rd., Grosse Pointe, Mich. 48236.

LASCOLA, ELIZABETH WHITE, Free-lance Wtr.; State Dept. of Mental Hygiene, '68–'69; News Wtr., Sacramento State Col. News Bur., '67; Feature Wtr.,

state employees pubn., '66; Ed., Colmst., Sacramento Suburban Nwsps., '57–'64; Theta Sigma Phi, Foster Families Info. Svc.; Univ. of Cal., Berkeley, BA, '48; b. L.A., Cal., 1924; p. Lewis and Irma Linn White; h. Raymond Lascola; c. Ellen, Julia; res: 1412 Meredith Way, Carmichael, Cal. 95608.

LASSEY, ANNE FREDERICK, Librn., West Plains Rural Library, 1404 Second Ave. W., Williston, N.D. 58801, '58–; N.D. Farmers Un. (Jamestown), '44–'53; U.S. Post Off. (Spring Brook), '25, '28; educ: courses in lib. sci. (Madison, Wis.; Dickinson, N.D.; Grand Forks, N.D.); b. Xenia, Oh., 1904; p. Frank and Carrie Darner Frederick; h. Julius Lassey; res: 1418 Seventh Ave. W., Williston, N.D.

LASSWELL, SHIRLEY BASSO, Pres., Stephen Slesinger, Inc., Red Ryder Enterprises, Inc., Hawley Publications, Tele-Comics, Inc., 1111 N. Westshore Blvd., Tampa, Fla. 33607; Owner, comic strips "Red Ryder," "Little Beaver," "King of the Royal Mounted," "Ozark Ike," U.S.-Canadian rights to "Winnie-the-Pooh mdsng., '29 (under license to Walt Disney Prods., '66–); Assoc., Zane Grey, Inc., motion pics., prom. sls., comic bks. based on famous Western stories by Zane Grey, all related pubns. sold world-wide; Krewe of Venus; b. Detroit, Mich., 1924; p. Michael and Clara Leasia Basso; h. Fred D. Lasswell, Jr.; c. Patricia Ann Slesinger; res: 5108 Longfellow Ave., Tampa, Fla. 33609.

LATANIOTIS, DOLORES ANGEVINE, Librn., Forbes, Inc., 60 Fifth Ave., N.Y., N.Y. 10011, '68–; Reptr., '67–'68; Rschr., '63–'67; Edtl. Asst., Inst. Radio Engineers, '61–'62; b. Detroit, Mich., 1932; p. Byron and Myrtle Herriot Angevine; h. Nikos Lataniotis; res: 1729 Montgomery Ave., Bronx, N.Y. 10453.

LATHAM, EMILEIGH MAXWELL, Free-lance Wtr., '63–; special project for Southern Reg. Educ. Bd. (scripts for radio series on higher educ.), '64–'66; Public Info. Wtr., Ga. Gov. Carl Sanders' Commn. to Improve Educ., '63–'64; Tchr., writing, Emory Univ. Evening Sch., '63; PR Asst., Ga. State Col., '61–'63; News Dir., WTAR-Radio (Norfolk, Va.), '47–'51; TV, '50–'51; Theta Sigma Phi (Cinn. Chptr. VP, '66; Atlanta Chptr. Rec. Secy., '64), Nat. Assn. Radio News Dirs. ('48–'51), AAUW; Univ. of N.C., AB (Jnlsm.), '44; b. Pink Hill, N.C., 1923; p. Hugh and Emily Turner Maxwell; h. Herald Latham; c. Lynn, Diann, Jeffrey; res: 5918 Julian Ct., Memphis, Tenn. 38117.

LAUB, GERTRUDE JELINEK, Sr. Byr., Brentano's, 586 Fifth Ave., N.Y., N.Y. 10036, '50–; N.Y. Bksellers League (Pres., '68–'70); Univ. of Vienna; b. Vienna, Austria; p. Felix and Alice Weintraub Jelinek; h. Eric Laub; res: 86-10 34th Ave., Jackson Heights, N.Y. 11372.

LAUBENHEIMER, BOBBYE DUREN, Ed., Mutual Benefit Life Insurance Co., 520 Broad St., Newark, N.J. 07101, '63–; PR Cnslt., Un. Commty. Fund (Aws., '67,

'68); N.J. Assn. of Communicators (VP, '69–; Secy., '63–'65; Aw., '67), IEA, Delta Psi Omega, Newark Museum Assn., Jr. Wms. Club; Vt. Col., AA, '62; b. Newark, N.J., 1943; p. Harry, Jr., and Muriel Schultz Duren; h. Russell J. Laubenheimer; res: 8 Ridge Rd., Upper Saddle River, N.J. 07458.

LAUBER, PATRICIA DONOVAN, Mng. Ed., Dunedin Times Publishing Co., 591 Main St., Dunedin, Fla. 33515, '68–; Pres., Publr., Marcis Enterprises, Suburban Living and Suburban Rev. (S. Plainfield, N.J.), '59–'67; Ed., S. Plainfield Weekly News Rev., '57–'59; Features and Proms. Ed., Beverage Retailer Weekly (N.Y.C.), '53–'55; Reptr., Matzner Pubns. (Passaic, N.J.), '51–'53; Newscaster, WERA-Radio Sta. (Plainfield), '67–'68; Free-lance PR, Seymour Malkin and Assocs. (Maywood), '51–'55; Dunedin C. of C. (Dir., '69–), Clearwater BPW PR Chmn.; important civic activities in N.J.; Who's Who of Am. Wm., Chestnut Hill Col., Seton Hall Univ.; b. Newark, N.J., 1933; p. Joseph and Frances K. Culnan Donovan; h. Edward C. Lauber; c. Mark Edward, Christopher Joseph; res: 437 Leeward Island, Island Estates, Clearwater, Fla. 33515.

LAUBER, PATRICIA GRACE, Auth., children's bks., fiction and non-fiction, incl: "Restless Earth" and "Who Discovered America" (Random House, '70), 40 others, '54–'69; Chief Ed., sci. and mathematics, The New Bk. of Knowledge, Grolier, Inc., '61–'67; Ed.-in-chief, Science World, Street & Smith, '56–'59; Wtr., Ed., Scholastic Magazines, '46–'55; Wtr., Look, '45–'46; Auths. Guild; Wellesley Col., BA, '45 (Wellesley Col. Scholar); b. N.Y.C., 1924; p. Hubert Crow and Florence Walker Lauber; res: 165 E. 60th St., N.Y., N.Y. 10022.

LAUDA, FRANCES SHAVER, Food Ed., Seventeen, Triangle Publications Inc., 320 Park Ave., N.Y., N.Y. 10022, '56–; Free-lance Wtr., home econs., '54–'56; Food Pubcty. Wtr., J. Walter Thompson, '50–'54; Assoc. Homemaking Ed., Macfadden Pubns., '48–'50; Home Econs. orgs.; Cornell Univ. (Home Econs.), '44–'45; Pratt Inst., BS (Home Econs.), '48; b. Evanston, Ill., 1926; p. George J. and Elizabeth Siddall Shaver; h. Francis Charles Lauda; c. Betsy Louise, Susan Ann, Cindy Jane; res: Tudor Lane, Sands Pt., N.Y. 11050.

LAUER, ELEANOR ANDERSON, Copywtr., Timebyr., Henry J. Kaufman & Associates, Inc., 1050 31st St., N.W., Wash., D.C. 20007, '61–; Crtv. Dir., Robert M. Gamble, '59–'61; Copywtr., Erwin, Wasey, Ruthrauff & Ryan, '55–'59; Ed. Asst., Farm Journal (Phila., Pa.), '54–'55; Copywtr., Virgil A. Warren Adv. (Spokane, Wash.), '53–'54; Copywtr., Sears, Roebuck & Co., '51–'52; AWRT (Rec. Secy., '68–'69), Theta Sigma Phi (Nat. Capital Chptr. VP, '61–'62); Nat. Adv. Agcy. Network Premier Aws., '66, '68; Phila. Club of Adv. Wm. aws., '57, '58; Univ. of Idaho, BA, '54; b. Spokane, Wash., 1931; p. Elliot and Alice Beck Anderson; h. Norman Lauer; c. Douglas Fredrick, Nancy Delores; res: 1008 N. Daniel St., Arlington, Va. 22201.

LAUER, SUE KEITH, Mgr., Paige Palmer Enterprises, Inc., 920 W. Market St., Akron, Oh. 44313. h. Frank Lauer; c. Steven Keith, Roger Michael; res: 21855 Cottonwood Dr., Rocky River, Oh. 44116.

LAUGHLIN, FLORENCE, Wtr., fiction, non-fiction; Auth., eight juv. bks.; Lectr., Tchr., San Diego State Col. Wtrs. Workshop, '67; San Diego State Col., '28–'30; b. Crosby, N.D., 1910; p. Richard and Ida Morgan Young; h. (div.); c. Andrea Laughlin Conley, William R.; res: 2925 E. Fifth St., Tucson, Ariz. 85716.

LAURANCE, MARGARET DICK, Ed., Pubcty. Dir., Farmers New World Life Insurance Company, 9611 Sunset Highway, Mercer Island, Wash. 98040, '62–; Ed. Pubns., Univ. of Wash., '62; Edtl. Asst., Sunset Magazine, '52–'53; ICIE, Pacific N.W. IEA, Theta Sigma Phi, Seattle C. of C. (Wms. Div.); Univ. of Ore., BA, '40 (Sigma Delta Chi Aw.); b. Fairfield, Idaho, 1918; p. Robert and Trella Lamson Dick; h. Erwin Laurance; c. James D. and Stephen D. res: 7247 S.E. 29th, Mercer Island, Wash. 98040.

LAURITZEN, ELIZABETH MOYES, Tchr., Secondary Literature, Department of Interior, Bureau of Indian Affairs, Intermountain School, Brigham City, Ut., '56–; Tchr., '31–'56; Ut. Lib. Assn., NLAPW (Ut. Chptr. Secy., '68–'69), AAUW (Rec. Secy., '69); Auth., "Shushima" (Caxton, '64); Sons of Ut. Pioneers Story Contest gold medal, '66; Dept. of Interior svc. aw., '66; Univ. of Northern Ariz., BA, '34; Ut. State Univ., MS, '61; b. Thatcher, Ariz., 1909; p. Joseph and Anna Plumb Moyes; h. Richard Dawn Lauritzen; c. JoAnn, Richard, Hope, Theodore, Karl, Arthur; res: 686 S. Fourth St. W., Brigham City, Ut. 84302.

LAUSTED, EDITH M., VP, Gordon J. Weisbeck, Inc., 5555 Main St., Buffalo, N.Y. 14221, '58–.

LAUX, JEAN AMELIA, Ed., Cats Magazine, 10 California Ave., Pitt., Pa. 15202, '58–.

LAVAGNO, DORITA LABADIE, Layout Dir., Eng. edition, Realites, 13 Rue Saint Georges, Paris, France, '61–; Layout Designer, Connaissance des Arts, '61–; Layout Dir., Vogue, '56–'60; Co-designer, record jackets, "Cycnus"; aw. for stand "Liqueur Izana," Lausanne Exhbn.; Ecole Nat. Superieure des Arts Decoratifs, Paris, Diploma, '56; Ecole Tech. du Livre Estienne, Diploma, '60; b. Madrid, Spain, 1925; p. Rene and Maria Llandres Labadie; h. Pierre Lavagno; res: 35 Rue Gallieni, Malakoff 92, Paris, France.

LAVERY, BEE CANTERBURY, PR, Adv. Cnslt.; PR, Thomas Bradley for Mayor campaign, '69; Wms. Products Mdsng., Compton Adv., '66; Dir. Prom., Merle Norman Cosmetics, '65; Adv., PR Dir., Rose Marie Reid Swimsuit Co., '63–'65; Fashion Dir., Bullocks Dept. Stores, '60–'63; Free-Lance Wtr., '52–'59; Wms. Ed., Hollywood NBC Press Dept., '49–'52; Publicist, Pubcty. Pfd., '47–'49; Reptr., S.W. Wave Pubns., '44–'46; Ed., Whittier Reporter, '43; Theta Sigma Phi

(Pres., '50), Hollywood Wms. Press Club, L.A. Adv. Wm. (LULU, '65), Fashion Group (Bd. of Dirs., '62–'63), Univ. Southern Cal., AB, '48 (Sch. of Jnlsm. Bd. of Dirs., VP); b. L.A., Cal., 1926; p. Charles and Bernice Peacock Canterbury; h. Emmet Lavery, Jr.; c. Geoffrey W., Tracy Elizabeth; res: 5120 Encino Ave., Encino, Cal. 91316.

LAVIN, PATRICIA, Auth., Entertainer, Lectr. on graphology, handwriting analysis; Auth: "The Pen is Mightier Than the Couch"; Wtr., articles, Today's Speech (Univ. of Pitt.), Manage mag., others; Lectr. on words (speech entitled "Performance on Words"); Rep., Sheaffer Pen Co., Nat. stationery show; Owner, Lavin Secretarial Svc.; Intl. Platform Assn., Wms. Lit. Club of Chgo., Am. Handwriting Analysis Fndn.; Northwestern Univ.; b. St. Louis, Mo., 1918; p. Morris and Rachel Lowenberg Lavin; res: 535 N. Michigan Ave., Apt. #405, Chgo., Ill. 60611.

LAWLER, LILLIAN BEATRICE, Prof. Emeritus, Hunter College, City University of New York, 695 Park Ave., N.Y., N.Y. 10021, '59–; Prof. of Classics, Assoc. Prof., Asst. Prof., Instr., '29–'59; Asst. Prof. of Classics, Instr., Univ. of Kan., '26–'29; Instr., Univ. of Ia., '23–'25 (Visiting Prof., '61–'66); Auth., "The Dance in Ancient Greece" (Wesleyan Univ. Press, '65), others; frequent contrbr. to pfsnl. jnls.; Bk. Reviewer; Classical Assn. of the Atlantic States (Pres., '47–'49), Am. Classical League (Hon. VP, '57–), Classical Soc. of the Am. Acad. in Rome (VP, '45, '47), Eta Sigma Phi (Nat. Trustee, '49–'55), Am. Philological Assn., Archaeological Inst. of Am., Classical Assn. of Middle West and South, Auxilium Latinum, Pi Lambda Theta; Univ. of Pitt., BA, '19 (Phi Beta Kappa, summa cum laude, Mortar Bd.); Univ. of Ia., MA, '21; PhD, '25; b. Pitt., Pa., 1898; p. Thomas and Ellen Nuttridge Lawler; res: 14 W. Court St., Iowa City, Ia., 52240.

LAWLESS, DOROTHY KENNEDY, Auth.; Bk., "Rug Hooking & Braiding—For Pleasure & Profit" ('52, revsd. '62); mag. contrbr., handicraft articles; Tchr., Centinela Valley Union High School District, Adult Education, 4500 Lennox Blvd., Lennox, Cal. 90304, '50–; Ed., The Hookers Delight (L.A.), '50–'67; Real Estate, Sentinel Realty Co. (Inglewood), '38–'48; Central Tchrs. Col. (Edmond, Okla.), tchrs. cert., '24; U.C.L.A., '52–'54; b. Okla. City, Okla., 1906; p. James and Ethel Tole Kennedy; h. Phillip Lawless; c. John; res: 4501 Valdina Pl., L.A., Cal. 90043.

LAWNER, LYNNE, Wtr.; edtl. work, Encyclopedia Britannica (Italy); c/o Georges Borchardt, Inc., 145 E. 52nd St., N.Y., N.Y. 10022; Translator, Ed., "Letters from Prison by Antonio Gramsci" (Harper's, '70); poems incl: "Triangle Dream" (Harper and Row, '69), "Wedding Night of a Nun" (Atlantic Little-Brown Press, '64); various aws.; Wellesley, BA, '58 (Phi Beta Kappa, Jr. Phi Beta Kappa, Jr. Durant Scholar); Cambridge Univ. (Eng.), '58–'59 (Henry Fellowship, '57–'58); Univ. of Rome; Columbia Univ., Ph.D., '69; b.

Dayton, Oh., 1935; p. Harry and Irene Fuchs Lawner; res: 802 Otterbein Ave., Dayton, Oh.; also, via Adelaide Ristori, 42, Rome, Italy.

LAWRENCE, CYNTHIA, Assoc. Crtv. Dir., Eisaman, Johns & Laws, Inc., 6290 Sunset Blvd., L.A., Cal. 90028, '69–; Copy Group Head, '66–'69; Copy Chief, Carson-Roberts, '60–'65; Retail Copywtr., May Co., '57–'59; Agcy. Copywtr., Smith, Hagel & Knudsen (N.Y.C.), '55–'57; Space Byr., W. H. Hunt & Assocs. (L.A., Cal.), '53–'55; Auth: five "Barbie" children's fiction bks. (Random House, '63–'65), "Barbie-Easy-As-Pie" cookbk. (Random House, '65); MWA, L.A. Adv. Wm. (Bd. of Dirs., '67; Annual Lulu Adv. Achiev. Aws., '58, '59, '61, two in '62, two in '63), Am. TV Commls. Festival aws., '61, '62; U.C.L.A., AB, '50 (Phi Beta Kappa); b. Bklyn., N.Y.; p. Joseph and Mae Bloomberg Lawrence; h. Robert A. Lowry; c. Charlotte Ann, Robert A., Jr.; res: 11012 Fruitland Dr., Studio City, Cal. 91604.

LAWRENCE, GEORGENE MARY, Crtv. Dir., La Grave Advertising, 924 Des Moines Bldg., Des Moines, Ia. 50309, '69–; Cont. and Prod. Mgr., KCBC, '68–'69; Cont. Dir., '67–'68; Cont. Dir., WANE-TV (Fort Wayne, Ind.), '67; Reprtr., Valley Advance; Lectr. on adv. to bus. and sch. groups; AWRT (Hawkeye-Ia. Chptr. Pres.-Elect, '69–'70; Secy., '68–'69), Des Moines Wms. Adv. Club (Treas., '69–'70), Alpha Xi Delta, Theta Sigma Phi; Vincennes Univ., AA, '64; Drake Univ., BA, '66 (Ranking Sr. Wm.); b. Vincennes, Ind., 1944; p. Woodford and Thelma Larson Lawrence; res: 1306 34th St., Des Moines, Ia. 50311.

LAWRENCE, ISABELLE, Free-lance Wtr., Lectr.; Tchr., '33–'69; Auth., eight jr. hist. fiction bks.; WNBA, Chgo. Soc. of Midland Auths.; Children's Reading Round Table (Pres., '62; VP, '61); Chgo. Children's Reading Roundtable aw., '68–; Jr. Literary Guild aw., '55; Freedoms Fndn. aw., '60; Radcliffe Col., AB, '14, AM, '21; b. Cambridge, Mass.; p. George and Belle Richmond Lawrence; res: 2970 Sheridan Rd., Chgo., Ill. 60657.

LAWRENCE, JOSEPHINE MACK, Free-lance Wtr., '67–; PR, YWCA, '65–'67; Program Dir., Dist. Advisor, San Antonio, Bexar County Cncl. of Girl Scouts of Am., '62–'65; Program Dir., Youth Dept., YWCA, '60–'62; Program Asst., Pubcty., Denver Camp Fire Girls, '59–'60; PR Dir., San Antonio Symphony, '53–'54; Mng. Ed., Southwest Technical Journal, '51–'53; Assoc. Ed., Southwestern Musician Magazine, '47–'51; Tchr.; Asst. to Ed., Household mag., '42–'45; Theta Sigma Phi, San Antonio Art League, Nat. Wtrs. Club, Panhandle State Col., AB (Eng., Speech), '31; Univ. of Colo., Grad. Work, '33; b. Wichita, Kan., 1911; p. Bert and Eva Hall McGinnis; h. Henry H. Lawrence; res: 123 Marchmont Lane, San Antonio, Tex. 78213.

LAWRENCE, KAY, Wms. Ed., Bdcst., Associated Press, 50 Rockefeller Plaza, N.Y., N.Y. 10020, '43–;

NWC (Pres., '60–'62), AWRT, ZONTA; Lesley Col. grad., '28; b. Burlington, Vt., 1908; p. Howard and Helene Harding Lawrence; h. Barry Faris (dec.); res: Turtle Bay House, 249 E. 48th St., N.Y., N.Y. 10017.

LAWRENCE, MARY BERG WELLS, Pres., Wells, Rich, Greene, Inc., 767 Fifth Ave., N.Y., N.Y. 10022, '66–; Jack Tinker & Partners, '64–'66; Doyle Dane Bernbach, '57–'64; McCann-Erickson; Macy's; Carnegie Tech.; b. Youngstown, Oh., 1928; p. Waldemar and Violet Berg; h. (1) Burt Wells (div.); (2) Harding Lawrence; c. Kathryn Wells, Pamela Wells.

LAWRENCE, MERLOYD LUDINGTON, Treas., Ed., Translator, Seymour Lawrence, Inc., 90 Beacon St., Boston, Mass. 02108, '65–; Copywtr., Houghton Mifflin Co., '55–'57; published translations incl: "The Dinner Party" (Claude Mauriac; '64), "Eugenie Grandet," "The Cure of Tours" (Honore de Balzac; '64), "Madame Bovary" (Flaubert; '69), "Mad Shadows" (Marie-Claire Blais; '60); articles in pubns. incl: The Atlantic Monthly, Mademoiselle, The Christian Science Monitor; Am. Translators Assn.; Radcliffe Col., BA, '54 (Phi Beta Kappa); MA, '57; b. 1932; h. Seymour Lawrence; two children.

LAWRENCE, MILDRED ELWOOD, Free-lance Wtr.; fiction for children and young people; 23 bks. (Harcourt, Brace & World, '40–'69); VP, Reptr., Eustis (Fla.) Publ., '45–'47; Soc. Ed., Flint (Mich.) Jnl., '28–'29; Wtr., Reptr., and Art, Music, Bk. Reviewer, '29–'37; Auths. League of Am., AAUW, Theta Sigma Phi, Delta Kappa Gamma; Flint Jr. Col., AA, '26; Lawrence Univ., BA, '28 (magna cum laude, Phi Beta Kappa); Yale, MA, '31; b. Charleston, Ill., 1907; p. DeWitt and Gertrude Jefferson Elwood; h. Clarence Lawrence; c. Mrs. James T. Schermerhorn; res: 1044 Terr. Blvd., Orlando, Fla. 32803.

LAWRENCE, NANCY JEAN, Copy Chief, Mathison/Ress Advertising, 200 Madison Ave., N.Y., N.Y. 10016, '69–; Copywtr., Needham, Harper & Steers, '67–'69; Copy Chief, Howard Marks Adv., '58–'67; Tchr., Am. Cncl. for Emigres in the Professions; AWNY; N.Y. Art Dirs. Club aw., '68; Cleve. Adv. Club aw., '62, '63; Cleve. Art Dirs. Club aw., '63; Balt. Art Dirs. Club Best in Balt. aw., '68; Dir. Mail aw., '68; Kent State Univ., BA (cum laude; Cardinal Key), '57; b. Youngstown, Oh., 1935; p. William and Edith Hurtig Swimmer; c. Dinah; res: 363 E. 76th St., N.Y., N.Y. 10021.

LAWRENCE, VIVIAN, Bdcstr., Interviewer, Modr., WLIW-TV, Garden City, L.I., N.Y., '69–; PR Cnslt., Am. Red Cross Nassau County Chptr., '67; Lectr., many PR workshops, seminars, various orgs.; Wms. Dir., WFYI-Radio and WHLI-Radio; Commentator, Interviewer, Modr., Radio Stas. WFYI, WROR, WEGO, WHLI; Wtr., Prod., daily programs, WHLI-AM-FM, '59–'60; daily interview "Vivian Lawrence on Long Island," '64–'69; Dir., PR, N.Y. State Congress of Parents and Tchrs.,

'61–'64; Free-lance PR; tchr.; Free-lance Wtr., poetry, short stories; numerous orgs.; L.I. Univ., BA (Eng., Jnlsm.), '38; b. N.Y.C., 1917; p. Samuel and Faye Resnick; h. Paul S. Lawrence; c. Richard Stuart, Wendy Deirdre; res: 165 Gerard Ave., New Hyde Park, N.Y. 11040.

LAWS, RUTH MITCHELL, Dir., Adult Continuing Education, Delaware Dept. of Public Instruction, P.O. Box 6971, Dover, Del. 19901, '68–; Supvsr., Planning, Rsch., Vocational Educ., '65–'68; State Supvsr., Home Econs., '56–'65; Asst. Supvsr., Home Econs., '47–'55; Dir., Home Econs., Del. State Col., '42–'55; Home Econs. Tchr., Smyrna Jr. HS, '37–'41; Supvsr., Adult Educ. (Wilmington), '35–'37; Cnslt.; Auth., migrant educ. pubns., Dover Dept. Public Instr.; Del. Commn. on Children and Youth (Chmn., '65–), Del. Commn. on Aging ('60–), NEA, Assn. for Supervision and Curriculum Dev.; Am. Home Econs. Assn., Nat. Assn. for Public Sch. Adult Educ., Del. Assn. for Sch. Admrs., Nat. Cncl. on Family Rel.; Nat. Cncl. Negro Wm. cit., '52; Future Homemakers of Am. cit., '63; Newark (Del.) Kiwanis aw., Service to Aging '67; Kappa Delta Pi, '65; Pi Lambda Theta, '66; Omicron Nu, '67; Hampton Inst., BS, '33 (alumni aw., '65); Cornell Univ., MS, '43; EdD, '56; N.Y. Univ. Alumni Aw., '56; b. Gatesville, N.C., 1912; p. Charles and Claire Delk Mitchell; h. William Laws; c. Cherritta Laws Matthews; res: 844 Forest St., Dover, Del. 19901.

LAWSON, CAROLINE SAMPSON, AE, Diener & Dorskind Advertising Agency, 1501 Broadway, N.Y., N.Y. 10036; AE, Equity Adv.; Owner, Caroline Sampson Interiors; Leber, Katz, Paccione Adv. Agcy.; Allied Bd. of Trades; N.Y.U; N.Y. Sch. of Interior Design; b. N.Y.C.; p. Michael and Helen Sampson; c. Dara Colbrette Lawson; res: 785 West End Ave., N.Y., N.Y. 10025.

LAWSON, KATE DRAIN, Costume Designer, Hope Enterprises, '51–; Lectr., stage scenery, Cal. State Col. (L.A.); Lectr., costume design, Cal. Inst., '60–; theatre designing, Equity Players on Broadway, '22; numerous N.Y. prods., Berkshire Playhouse, Katherine Cornell Touring prods. ('32–'33), W. Coast prods., L.A. Civic Light Opera ('39–'42); Exec. Dir. of Pelican Prods. for John Houseman (L.A.); '47–'48; org. NBC-TV Costume Dept. (W. Coast, '51); designed prod. "Oedipus Rex" (R.T.T., '67); dancer, '21, Guild prods. ('26, '30), motion pictures (32–'53); AEA (W. Coast Advisory Bd., '56–), SAG, AFTRA, ANTA (Nat. Bd., '58–; Dir. Reg. One, '58–; Greater L.A. Chptr. Secy., '60–'61; Special Aw., '66), AETA (Monte Meacham Aw.), Who's Who in the Theatre, AWRT, NATAS Aw., '65–'66; numerous others; Paris Art Schs., '21–'30; b. Spokane, Wash., 1894; p. James and Ethel Marsland Drain; h. John Howard Lawson (div.); c. Alan Drain Lawson; res: 1126 N. Gower St., L.A., Cal. 90038.

LAYLAND, KAREN JEAN, Adm. Dir., National Association of FM Broadcasters, 665 Fifth Ave., N.Y., N.Y.,

'69–; Dir., Commtns. System, National Council of Churches of Christ, '68–'69; Mkt. Svcs. Assoc., Div. of Mass Media, Un. Presbyterian Ch., '65–'68; Cont. Dir., Public Svc. Coordr., John Poole Bdcst. (Hollywood, Cal.), '63–'64; Cont. Dir., Prom., Pubcty Wtr., Prod. Coordr., KBEA/KBEY-FM (Kan. City, Mo.), '62–'63; AWRT, Alpha Epsilon Rho, Commty. Svc. Soc. of N.Y.C.; Ottawa Univ., '60–'62; Univ. of Kan., BS (Jnlsm.), '65 (Outstanding Wm. in Bdcst.); b. Independence, Mo., 1942; p. Max and Relia McMullen Layland; res: 327 W. 87th St., N.Y., N.Y. 10024.

LAYMAN, PATRICIA FRANCES, Prodr., Young & Rubicam, 285 Madison Ave., N.Y., N.Y., '65–; Prodr., Doyle, Dane, Bernbach, '64; Prodr., Elliot, Unger & Elliot, '63; AE, Pritchard, Wood & Partners (London, England), '53–'60; Prom. Mgr., Esquire mag. (England), '52; two Clio aws., Art Dirs. Gold Medal; b. London, England, 1933; p. Herbert and Lilian Layman; res: 17 E. 82nd St., N.Y., N.Y. 10028.

LAZAR, ELAINE LAVIN, TV-Radio Ed., Press Publishing Company, Ohio & Atlantic Aves., Atlantic City, N.J. 08401, '67–; Free-lance publicist, amusement prom.; Atlantic City Wtrs. Guild, Atlantic City PR Chptr., Pen Wm. of Atlantic City, Wms. Press Club of Atlantic City; b. Phila., Pa., 1931; p. Irving and Pauline Smith Lavin; h. William Lazar; c. Lisa Beth, Alan, Gary; res: 17 N. Gladstone Ave., Margate, N.J. 08402.

LEAMAN, JUNE TURNER, VP, Crtv. Dir., Nat. Adv. Dir., Estee Lauder, Inc., 767 Fifth Ave., N.Y., N.Y. 10022, '66–; Adv., Prom. Dir., Bergdorf Goodman; Adv. Mgr., Salon Div., Charles of the Ritz; Wtr., Ogilvy, Benson & Mather; Copy Chief, Saks Fifth Ave.; Fashion Group; L.I. Adv. Club aw., '69; State Univ. of Ia., BA (Jnlsm.), '45; b. N.Y.C.; p. Morton and Rhea Herman Turner; h. John I. Leaman; res: 3 E. 76th St., N.Y., N.Y. 10021.

LEAPER, RAE ADELBLUE, Asst. Dir., Public Information, California Division, American Cancer Society, 875 O'Farrell St., S.F., Cal. 94109, '64–; Ed., employee pubn., Hospital Care Corp., Cinn., Oh., '60–'62; Fashion Press Agt., Shillito's, Cinn., Oh., '59–'60; Staff Wtr., Convair Astronautics Div. of Gen. Dynamics, San Diego, Cal., '58–'59; Asst. to Ed., San Diego County Medical Soc. bul., '55–'57; numerous mag. articles; Bay Area Soc. of Indsl. Communicators; Aw. of Merit, ICIE, '65; San Diego State Col., AB, '57; Northwestern Univ., Medill Sch. of Jnlsm., MSJ, '58 (Kappa Tau Alpha); b. Sioux City, Ia., 1936; p. Leo and June Taylor Adelblue; h. Norman Leaper; res: 445 Collingwood St., S.F. Cal., 94114.

LEARNED, MICHAEL, Actress; American Conservatory Theatre, 450 Geary St., S.F., Cal. 94102, '67–; Can. Bdcst. Co., Nat. Film Bd., Can., '61–'66; "Coriolanus" (Stratford, Ontario, '60), "A God Slept Here" (Off-Bdwy., '57), "Three Sisters" (Off-Bdwy., '59, Act '69); AEA, Assn. Can. TV and Radio Performers, AFTRA; b.

Wash., D.C., 1939; p. Bruce and Betti Hooper Learned; h. Peter Donat; c. Caleb, Christopher, Lucas.

LEATHERBEE, MARY LOGAN, Travel Ed., Life Magazine, Time Inc., Rockefeller Ctr., N.Y., N.Y. 10020; Movie Ed.; Asst. Entertainment Ed.; Wms. Air Force Svc. Pilot, WW II.

LeBAR, LOIS EMOGENE, Auth.; Chmn. of Grad. Christian Educ., Wheaton Col., Wheaton, Ill., 60187; '49–; three bks. on religion, incl. "Focus on People in Church Education" (Fleming H. Revell, '68); Sun. Sch. and Bible Lessons for Primaries (Scripture Press, '36–'69); Contrbr. to bk. on Christian educ.; Tchr., Moody Bible Inst. (Chgo., Ill.), '34–'41; Tchr., (Perry, N.Y.), '28–'33; Rsch. Commn. of Nat. Sun. Sch. Assn., Nat. Cncl. of Chs. (Profs. Sec. of Div. of Ch. Educ.), Sr. Mary Alumni, Moody Bible Inst. ('59); Geneseo State Normal, '28; Roosevelt Col., BA, '43; Wheaton Col., MA, '45; N.Y.U., PhD, '51.

LeBAR, MARY EVELYN, Chmn., Dept. of Christian Education, Wheaton College, Wheaton, Ill. 60187, '63–; Prof., '60–; Instr., '45–'60; Tchr., '30–'33, '35–'43; Auth., religious textbks.; Roosevelt Univ., AB, '43; Wheaton Col., MA, '45; N.Y.U., PhD, '51; b. Olean, N.Y., 1910; p. Roscoe and Alta Hathaway LeBar; res: 703 Howard St., Wheaton, Ill. 60187.

LEBOWITZ, SARAJANE, Fashion Copywtr., Jordan Marsh, 1501 Biscayne Blvd., Miami, Fla. 33132, '65–; Press Ed., Mademoiselle, '63–'64; Asst. Feature Ed., Bk. Reviewer, Balt. Sun, '60–'63; Theta Sigma Phi (Rec. Secy., '68–'70, Treas., '67–'68); Art Dirs. Club of Gtr. Miami aw., '66; Univ. of Md., BA; b. Balt., Md.; p. Jack and Winifred Caplan Lebowitz; res: 700 Biltmore Way, Coral Gables, Fla. 33134.

LECHNER, MARIAN GERTRUDE, Librn., Connecticut General Life Insurance Co., Hartford, Conn. 06115, '55–; Librn., U.S. Naval Air Dev. Ctr. (Johnsville, Pa.), '50–'55; Librn., Butler County Traveling Lib., '43–'50; Special Libs. Assn., Conn. Lib. Assn. (Pres.), '68; AAUW (Gtr. Hartford Div. Secy., '67–'69); Grove City Col., AB, '37; Columbia Univ., BS (Lib. Sci.), '47 b. Butler County, Pa., 1915; p. John and Henrietta Graham Lechner; res: 60 Robin Rd., W. Hartford, Conn. 06119.

LeCOCQ, RHODA PRISCILLA, Public Info. Offcr., Sacramento County Department of Social Welfare, '69–'70; Auth: "The Radical Thinkers" (Cal. Inst. of Asian Studies, '69); short stories, incl., "Behold a Pale Horse" (Stanford Press Anthology, best short stories in 20 yrs., '66); "The Shadow Outside", G.E. TV Theatre, '57; Ed., Cal. State Dept. of Educ., '68–'69; Educ. and Info., City and County of Honolulu, '61–'63; Lectr. on bus. repts., Univ. of Honolulu, '60; PR Dir., Honolulu Acad. of Arts, '57–'59; Lt., Chief of Info., Magazine and Bk. Sec., U.S. Navy, Wash., D.C., '43–'46; PRSA, Theta Sigma Phi (Col. Chptr. Pres.), various others; Stanford Univ., MA (Crtv. Writing),

'50; The Sorbonne, '51; Univ. of Cal., MA (Philosophy), '67; Cal. Inst. of Asia Studies, PhD (Philosophy), '69; b. Lynden, Wash., 1926; p. Ralph and Nellie Straks Le Cocq; h. (div.); res: 603 P St., Capital Towers, Sacramento, Cal. 95814.

LEE, CARVEL BIGHAM, Artist, Auth., '41–; Adv. Mgr., Strutwear Knitting Co., '31–'41; Intl. Platform Assn., Richfield Hist. Soc.; Who's Who of Am. Wm., Who's Who in the Midwest, Contemporary Auths.; Univ. of Minn.; b. Mpls., Minn., 1910; p. Abraham and Rebecca Lung Bigham; h. Kermit A. Lee (dec.); c. Kermit Jr., Lorita Lee Nelson; res: 7329 Colfax Ave. S., Mpls., Minn. 55423.

LEE, DOLORES STUMP, Co-ed., Pine Bluffs Post, 106 Main St., Pine Bluffs, Wyo. 82082, '59–; various positions, '46–'59; Wyo. Press Assn.; b. Pharr, Tex., 1923; p. Joseph and Mary Ellen Murphy Stump; h. James H. Lee; c. Lawrence Edward, Michael Duane, Dale Scott; res: 106 Main St., Pine Bluffs, Wyo. 82082.

LEE, ELIZABETH HADDOCK, News Ed., Grenada Newspapers, Inc., 158 Green St., Grenada, Miss. 38901, '56–; b. Waycross, Ga., 1916; p. Edgar and Nell Page Wilmot; h. Joseph Lee; c. Joseph III; res: 57 Thomas St., Grenada, Miss. 38901.

LEE, FLORENCE HENRY, Coordr., Tchr. Educ., Douglass College, Rutgers University, George St., New Brunswick, N.J. 08903, '66–; Prof., '69–; Assoc. Prof., '57–'69; Educ. Lectr., '49–'57; Sch. Psychologist, Maplewood-South Orange Public Schs., '42–'43; Tchr. (Highland Park), '35–'42; Dir. Religious Educ., Christ Episcopal Ch. (New Brunswick), '30–'35; Auth., educ. articles; Ed., "Principles and Practices of Teaching in Secondary Schools—A Book of Readings" (David McKay, '65); Am. Psychological Assn., N.J. Psychological Assn., NEA, AAUP, Am. Educ. Rsch. Assn., Nat. Cncl. of Measurement in Educ., Kappa Delta Pi, Pi Lambda Theta; Douglass Col., AB, '29 (Phi Beta Kappa); Rutgers Univ., MA, '32; Columbia Univ., MA, '40; Rutgers Univ., EdD, '43; b. New Brunswick, N.J., 1910; p. William and Frances May Henry; c. Alfred William, Dorothy H.; res: 23 Delevan St., New Brunswick, N.J. 08902.

LEE, FRAN (pseud: Mrs. Fix-It), Actress; Consumer Ed., Metromedia, 205 E. 67th St., N.Y., N.Y., 10021; TV, stage, film dramatic roles; commls.; TV cooking shows, household hints; mag., nwsp. articles; Lectr.; public appearances; more than 1,000 appearances for civic, charitable orgs.; SAG, AFTRA, AEA, AWRT; Heckscher Theatre Scholarship, '25; Distg. Svc. Aw., Pubcty. Club of N.Y., '63; N.Y.C. Tchrs. Training Grad.; b. N.Y.C, 1910; p. Max and Anna Siegelbaum Laderman; h. Samuel Weiss; c. Barry, Gene; res: 15 W. 81st St., N.Y., N.Y. 10024.

LEE, FRANCES HELEN, Edtl. Asst., Industrial Water Engineering Magazine, Select Publications, 373 Fifth Ave., N.Y., N.Y. 10016, '69–; Edtl. Asst., AEP Operating

Ideas, Am. Electric Power Svc. Corp., '66–'69; Edtl., Gordon & Breach Sci. Publrs., '64–'66; Edtl. Asst., Christian Herald Family Bookshelf, '57–'62; Wms. Nat. Bk. Assn., Marquis Biographical Lib. Soc. (Advisory Mbr.); Who's Who of Am. Wm.; N.Y. State Civil Defense svc. cert.; Queens Col., BA, '57; N.Y.U., MA, '62; b. N.Y.C., 1936; p. Murray and Rose Rothman Lee; res: 170 Second Ave., N.Y., N.Y. 10003.

LEE, JULIA McEACHIN, VP, Woodward & Lothrop, Inc., Wash., D.C., '66–; Asst. VP, '65–'66; Dir. of Sls. Prom., '57–'65; Asst. to PR VP, '49–'57; Mgr. of PR, '48–'49; Dir. of PR, Ala. State Col., '45–'48; Cryptanalyst, FBI (Wash., D.C.), WWII; Adv. Club of Wash., D.C., Fashion Group (Wash., D.C. Chptr. Bd. of Dirs.), Wms. Adv. Club (Adv. Wm. of the Yr., '67, '62), PRSA, NATAS, Nat. Retail Merchants Assn., Bd. of Trade; Multiple Sclerosis Soc. aw., '67; Oglethorpe Univ., AB, '42; George Washington Univ., MA (Adm. Educ.), '45, MA (Public Adm.), '50.

LEE, KATHLEEN WILSON, Co-ed., Staff Wtr., Marissa Messenger, Scanographer Operator, D. L. Lee Publishing Company, 118 S. Main St., Marissa, Ill. 62257; Tchr., Decatur Schs.; Pres. of Marissa Public Lib.; Marissa Wms. Club; Eastern Ill. Univ.; '30; b. Coulterville, Ill., 1908; p. William and Luvena Fullerton Wilson; h. Thomas J. Lee; c. Richard W., Nancy Graves, Marilyn Boschert; res: 224 E. Glenn St., Marissa, Ill. 62257.

LEE, LILLIAN FRANCES, Coordr., Commty. Rel., Atlanta Public Schools, 224 Central Ave. S.W., Atlanta, Ga. 30303, '65–; Program Dir., '57–'65; Script Ed., '48–'57; Tchr., '34–'48; Wtr., Bdcstr., WABE Radio, '48–'57; AWRT (Atlanta Chptr. Pres.), '52; Southern VP, '54–'56), Atlanta Press Club, PRSA, Delta Kappa Gamma, Atlanta Tuberculosis Assn. (Pres.); Inst. for Educ. by Radio and TV aws., '50–'56; McCall's Gold Mike, '55; Shorter Col., BA, '32; Emory Univ., MEd, '51; b. Atlanta, Ga., 1911; p. John and Frances Thrasher Lee; res: 525 Carol Way N.W., Atlanta, Ga. 30327.

LEE, MARIANNA HASSOL, Free-lance Wtr., Ed., Yale Univ. Press, McGraw-Hill, Berlitz Sch. of Langs. (Wash., D.C.), articles for Parade; Mng. Ed., Univ. of Tex. Press (Austin, Tex.), '68–'69; Mng. Ed., Johns Hopkins Press (Balt., Md.); Assoc. Ed., Parade (N.Y.C.); Mng. Ed., Portfolio; Copy Chief, Grolier Inc.; Smith Col., '48–'52; Univ. of Geneva, '50–'51; Columbia Univ., '52–'53; Oxford Univ., '57; b. N.Y.C., 1930; p. Isaac and Charlotte Steiner Lubow; h. Edward Lee; res: 803 Avondale Rd., Austin, Tex. 78704.

LEE, MILDRED, Auth: young adult fiction, "The Skating Rink" ('69; Bk. World hon. aw.), "Honor Sands" ('66), "The Rock and the Willow" ('63; Child Study of Am. aw.), '64); adult novel, "The Invisible Sun" ('46); Tift Col.; Columbia Univ.; N.Y.U.; Univ. of N.H.; b. Blocton, Ala., 1908; p. Dallas and Aeolian Spear Lee; h. James Scudder; c. Barbara Schimpff

DuLac, Robert Donald Schimpff, Jane Powell Scudder; res: 1361 Fifty-second Ave. N., St. Petersburg, Fla. 33703.

LEE, MURIEL LOCKROW, Commtns. Assoc., TV Prodr., Church Federation of Greater Indianapolis, 1100 W. 42nd St., Indpls., Ind. 46208, '64–; Exec. Prodr., docs., '62–'64; Exec. Prodr., Children's Progs., '56–'62; Script Wtr., '54–'56; Prof. of Speech, Purdue Univ., '69–; WLWI-TV svc. aw., '61; Wayne State Univ., BA, '50; Butler Univ., MA, '68; b. Highland Park, Mich.; p. Virgil and Ruth McAlpine Lockrow; h. Ralph L. Lee; c. Sandra, Christopher; res: E-40 Chester Rd., RR #1, Carmel, Ind. 46032.

LEE, NORMA AUDREY, Educ. Rels. Dir., Clairol, 345 Park Ave., N.Y., N.Y. 10022, '70; Trade Pubcty Mgr., '67–'70; Pubns. Mgr., '61–'66; Dir. of PR, Sheraton Atlantic, '60–'61; PR Cnslt., '58–'60; PR Coordr., U.S. Lawn Tennis Assn., '57; Lectr., career groups; PRSA, Comm. of Wm. on PR, AAIE (Dir., '62–'67), Cosmetic Career Wm., Fashion Group Inc., Nat. Cncl. of Wm., Intl. Platform Assn.; Johns Hopkins Univ.; Peabody Inst.; b. Balt., Md., 1935; p. Harry and Edna Lee; res: 135 W. 79th St., N.Y., N.Y. 10024.

LEE, REBECCA SMITH, Rschr., Wtr., '29–; U.S. Navy, '43–'45; Head, Eng. Dept., Tex. Christian Univ., '31–'43; Dept., '19–'43; Auth: "Mary Austin Holley: A Biography" (Univ. of Tex. Press, '62); "The Great Elm Tree: Heritage of the Episcopal Diocese of Lexington" (Co-auth.; Faith House Press, '69); Carr Collins aw., '63; Univ. of Ky., AB, '16 (Phi Beta Kappa); Columbia Univ., MA, '18; Univ. of Chgo., PhD, '32; b. Paducah, Ky., 1894; p. Frank and Caroline Weaks Smith; h. Owen S. Lee (dec.); res: 1166 Indian Mound Rd., Lexington, Ky. 40502.

LEE, ROSE MARIE, Wms. Ed., Parsons Sun, 220 S. 18th., Parsons, Kan. 67357; Marquette Univ., '64–'66; Univ. of Kan., BS (Jnlsm.), '68.

LEE, RUTA, Actress, Armed Forces TV & Radio Service, c/o Barbara Best, 6565 Sunset Blvd., Hollywood, Cal. 90028; Films: "Seven Brides For Seven Brothers," "Sergeants Three," "Operation Eichman;" TV: 500 network shows; Lectr., Am. Cancer Soc.; L.A. City Col.; b. Montreal, Can.; p. Joseph and Mary Kamandulis Kilmonis; res: 2623 Laurel Canyon Blvd., Hollywood, Cal. 90046.

LEE, VIRGINIA ANN, Asst. Choreographer, Petersen Production, 8490 Sunset Blvd., L.A., Cal., '69–; Asst. Choreographer, "Hollywood Palace," "Something Else," TV shows; Dancer, "Something Else," "Dick Van Dyke Special," "Laugh-In," "Jonathan Winters," "Smothers Bros.," "Jim Nabor Show"; Actress: "Flower Drum Song," "The Hawaiians," "King and I" "Dimension-5," "The Cool Ones"; Stage: "Kismet," "South Pacific," "King and I" (L.A. Civic Light Opera); AFTRA, SAG, AEA, AGVA, Chinese Optimist Club (Hon. Mbr., '68); Miss China-

town of L.A., '68; U.C.L.A., L.A. City Jr. Col.; b. L.A., Cal., 1946; p. Dr. A. Edward and Holly Leung Lee; h. Jeffrey Scott Latimer; res: 2410 W. Silverlake Dr., L.A., Cal. 90039.

LEE, VIRGINIA HILL, Reptr., News Journal, 70 W. Fourth St., Mansfield, Oh. 44901, '57–; Wtr., Daily Telephone, Evening World (Bloomington, Ind.), '30's; Oh. Nwsp. Wms. Assn. (aws: News, '56; Features, '67), Oh. Press Wm. (News aw., '68), Delta Kappa Gamma (hon. mbr.); Chalk and Slate aw., Mansfield Educ. Assn.; Ind. State Univ.; b. Owen County, Ind. 1909; p. John P. and Maude Crowe Hill; h. Dr. Paul J. Lee (dec.); c. Carol (Mrs. A. A. Bernheimer); res: Lucas, Oh. 44843.

LEE, VIRGINIA YEW, Auth., fiction, non-fiction; Am. Wildlife Fedn.; Commonwealth Club of Cal. gold medal, "Best Fiction by Cal. Auth.," '63; S.F. State Col., BA, '67; b. S.F., Cal., 1927; p. S. N. and S. Jone Yew; h. Howard F. Lee; c. Roberta Lee, Dee Dee Moy; res: 1232 Fifth Ave., S.F., Cal. 94122.

LEE-BENNER, LORRAINE FISHER, Copywtr., Talent, WCSC-TV, 485 E. Bay St., Charleston, S.C. 29402, '66–; Prom. Dept., '59–'66; Film Ed., '54–'57; b. Charleston, S.C., 1936; p. Walter and Edna McCaffer Fisher; h. Lord Lee-Benner; c. Elizabeth; res: 6 S. Adgers Wharf, Charleston, S.C. 29401.

LEECH, CAROLYN SHUBART, Asst. PR Dir., American Sheep Producers Council, 909 17th St., Denver, Colo. 80202, '67–; Owner, Harry E. Shubart Co. (PR), '49–'65; Colmst., Dayton Daily News, '43–'45; Tchr., '32–'33; Publr., '49–'65; Corr. for trade pubns., '49–'60; AWRT, PRSA (Colo. Chptr. Third VP, '62), Adv. Club of Denver (Wms. VP, '55–'56; Dir., '53–'56); Denver Adv. Wm. of the Yr., '56; Who's Who in PR; Who's Who of Am. Wm.; Univ. of Colo., BA, BE '29 (Kappa Delta Pi); Am. Acad. of Dramatic Arts; b. Trinidad, Colo., 1908; p. Arthur and Sallye Burger Sanders; h. John Leech; c. Harry, Carita, Mary, Virginia, Sister Helen Patrice, Patricia; res: 2172 Ridge Rd., Littleton, Colo. 80120.

LEEK, SYBIL, Colmst. Ladies Home Journal, 641 Lexington Ave., N.Y., N.Y. 10022, '66–; Auth: "The Sybil Leek Book of Fortune Telling" (MacMillan), "The Astrological Cookbook" (Pyramid), many others; Reptr., BBC (Eng.) and Southern TV Studios (Eng.); featured in docs. and films; SAG, AFTRA, PEN, Wm. of Am.; N.Y. Guild of Dirs. Aw., '66; b. Hanley, Eng., 1924; p. Christopher Edwin and Louisa Ann O'Brien-Booth Falinski-Fawcett; c. Stephen and Julian; res: 709 Riverside Dr., Melbourne Beach, Fla. 32951.

LEHMAN, LESLIE MITTMAN, Copywtr., Batten, Barton, Durstine & Osborne, 383 Madison Ave., N.Y., N.Y. 10017, '69–; Copy Trainee, Doyle, Dane, Bernbach, '68–'69; Asst. Soc. Ed., The Athens Messenger,

'66–'67; Life, '66; Theta Sigma Phi, Kappa Tau Alpha, Pi Gamma Mu; Oh. Univ., BSJ (Eng.), '67 (Phi Beta Kappa; Phi Kappa Phi); b. N.Y.C., 1947; p. Bernard and Phyllis Klinger Mittman; h. John Lehman; res: 70–20 108 St., Forest Hills, N.Y. 11375.

LEHMAN, RUTH GILLESPIE, Edtl. Pg. Ed., Times-Call Publishing Co., 717 Fourth Ave., Longmont, Colo. 80501, '65–; Controller, Secy.-Treas., '57–; Secy.-Treas., Loveland Publ. Co., '67–; Colo. Press Assn., Inst. of Nwsp. Controllers and Fin. Offcrs., Nat. Conf. of Edtl. Wtrs., Colo. Bar Assn., Am. Bar Assn., Denver Symphony Soc. (Bd. of Dirs.); Univ. of Colo.; Columbia Law Sch., LLB; b. Denver, Colo.; p. Dean and Lillie Baldwin Gillespie; h. Edward Lehman; c. Ruthann, Dean; res: 68 Stanford Lane, Longmont, Colo. 80501.

LEHNUS, OPAL HULL, Art. Dept. Head and Tchr., Logansport High School, 1301 E. Broadway, Logansport, Ind. 46947, '53–; "Creative Crafts for Churches" and "Creative Art Crafts for Churches"; Art Tchr., '50–'53; work with Ch. of God Religious Educ., teaching crafts in ch. camps and chalk talk progs.; Art Educ. Assn. of Ind. (Cncl. Mbr.; 2nd VP, '67–'68), Ind. State Tchrs. Assn., NEA, Religious Ed. Comm. of Ch. of God (Assoc. Mbr.); Anderson Col.; Ball State Univ., BS, '51; MA, '58; b. Summitville, Ind., 1920; p. John and Ida Clary Hull; h. Lyle Lehnus; c. Roger, Roland, Gloria; res: 76 15th St., Logansport, Ind. 46947.

LEIBELL, MARIE LOUISE (MOLLY), Adv. Sls. Rep., Time Magazine, 3545 Wilshire Blvd., L.A., Cal. 90005, '62–; joined Time, Inc. as typist, '41; L.A. Adv. Club, L.A. Adv. Wms. Club, Wilshire Country Club; Col. of New Rochelle, BA, '39; Katherine Gibbs Secretarial Sch., '40; b. N.Y.C., 1918; p. Vincent and Marie Kavanagh Leibell; res: 316 N. Rossmore Ave., L.A., Cal. 90004.

LEIBSON, PAULA PATTON, Bk. Ed., El Paso Times, P.O. Box 20, El Paso, Tex. 79999, '59–; Adv., Lord & Thomas (Chgo., Ill.); Univ. of Ill.; b. Terre Haute, Ind., 1911; p. Paul and Nettie Royer Patton; h. Arthur Leibson; c. David, Vicky, Mark; res: 1000 Kelly Way, El Paso, Tex. 79902.

LEIDERMAN, ANNETTE LOUISE, Press Rep., WCBS, 51 W. 52nd St., N.Y., N.Y. 10019, '69–; Publicist, "That Show," Trans-Lux TV Corp., '68–'69; Pubcty. Asst., WNEW-TV, '67–'68; Copywtr., Franznick-Meden Adv., '67; Young & Rubicam, '65–'66; Jr. Wtr./Trainee, J. Walter Thompson, '63–'65; Theta Sigma Phi; Am. Univ., BA (Jnlsm.), '63; b. Hempstead, N.Y., 1942; p. Samuel and Lee Chapnick Leiderman.

LEIGH, CARMA RUSSELL, State Librn., California State Library, Sacramento, Cal. 95814, '51–; Cnslt., State Librn., State of Victoria, and Lib. Cncl. of Victoria (Melbourne, Australia), '69; State Librn., Ed., Bul., Wash. State Lib. (Olympia, Wash.), '45–'51; Librn., San Bernardino County (Cal.) Free Lib., '42–'45; Librn., Orange County Free Lib. (Santa Ana), '38–

'42; Librn. Watsonville Public Lib., '32–'35; Asst. Circ. Dept., Berkeley Public Lib., '30–'31; Nat. Bk. Comm. (Nat. Bd., '54–), Univ. of Southern Cal. Grad. Sch. Lib. Sci., Sacramento State Col., Univ. of Cal. at Berkeley Sch. Librnship.; Okla. Col. for Wm., AB, '25; Univ. of Cal. at Berkeley, Cert. (Librnship.), '30; AM, '32; Univ. of the Pacific, LHD (hon.), '65; b. McLoud, Okla., 1904; p. William and Ida Jenkins Russell; h. 1. E. F. Zimmerman (div.) 2. Robert D. Leigh (dec.); c. Rita (Mrs. Boyd D. Collier); res: 3353 11th St., Sacramento, Cal. 95818.

LEIGHTON, FRANCES SPATZ, Wash. Corr., Metropolitan Sunday Newspapers, 1035 National Press Bldg., Wash., D.C. 20004, '65–; Wash. Corr., This Week mag., '63–'69; Wash. Corr., American Weekly, '50–'63; Auth: "My Life With Jacqueline Kennedy" (with Mary Gallagher), "White House Chef" (with Francois Rysavy), 12 other bks.; WNPC, NLAPW, ANWC, Art League; Edgar aw., '61; Oh. State Univ.; b. Thompson, Oh.; res: 3636 16th St. N.W., Wash., D.C. 20010.

LEIKLIND, MIRIAM, Librn., University Circle and Silver Park, Cleve., Oh. 44106, '31–; Cleve. Public Lib., '31–'37; Ed., "Index to Jewish Periodicals"; organized Jewish Lib. Assn. in Cleve. and Nat. Jewish Lib. Assn.; Pres. of Jewish Lib. Assn. and Lib. Assn. of Jewish Librns.; Western Reserve Univ. Lib. Sch.

LEIMER, MYRT, Circulation Mgr., World Vision, Inc., 919 W. Huntington Dr., Monrovia, Cal. 91016, '68–; Prod. Mgr., Dir. of Mdse. Design, Asst. Dir. of Pubns., Regal Bks.; Adv. Dir., Group Dept., Pacific Mutual Life Ins. Co.; U.C.L.A., BA, '46 (with hons.); Inst. of Design (Chgo.); Chouinard Art Institute, (L.A.); Univ. of Calif. Ext.; b. LaHabra, Cal., 1924; p. O. J. and Wilhelmine Kleine Leimer; res: 718 W. Foothill Blvd., Apt. 13, Monrovia, Cal. 91016.

LEINHAUSER, JEAN, Exec. VP, Aaron D. Cushman and Associates, Inc., 333 N. Michigan Ave., Chgo., Ill. 60601, '67–; VP, '65–'67; Acc. Supvsr., '65; AE, '61–'65; Acc. Supvsr., The PR Bd., '61; AE, '58–'61; Guidance Svc. Ed., Sci. Rsch. Assoc., '58; Asst. News Ed., Modern Beauty Shop mag., '56–'58; PR Dir., Hobby Industry Assn., '55–'56; Auth., "Teach Yourself to Knit" ('68); Theta Sigma Phi (Chgo. Chptr. Pres., '65–'66), Pubcty. Club of Chgo. (Golden Trumpet aw., '68, '61), NHFL, Chgo. Assn. of Commerce and Industry, Kappa Kappa Gamma; GA Cncl. of Chgo. aw., '69, '67; Seventeen mag. Rose Aw., '68; Univ. of Ia., BA (Jnlsm.), '55; b. Ottumwa, Ia., 1933; p. Peter and Ruth Daggett Leinhauser; res: 1150 Lake Shore Dr., Chgo., Ill. 60611.

LEIPER, MARIA, Sr. Ed., Simon & Schuster, Inc., 630 Fifth Ave., New York, N.Y. 10020; Auth., "A Treasury of Hymns and Carols," '53; Vassar Col., AB (hons.), '28; b. New Florence, Pa., 1906; p. Callender and Beatrice Marley Leiper; h. David Millar, Jr.; res: 460 W. 24th St., N.Y., N.Y. 10011; and Meriden, N.H. 03770.

LEITHAUSER, GLADYS GARNER, Instructional Asst., Wayne State University English Dept., Detroit, Mich., '68–; Eng. Instr., Highland Park Jr. Col., '67–'68; Rsch. Asst., biochemistry, Detroit Inst. of Cancer Rsch., '62–'67; Co-Auth., "The Dinosaur Dilemma," children's fiction; Wayne State Univ., BS, '46; MA, '69; b. Detroit, Mich., 1925; p. Herbert and Caroline Speer Garner; h. Harold Leithauser; c. Lance, Mark, Brad, Neil; res: 122 Elm Park, Pleasant Ridge, Mich. 48069.

LeJEUNE, DOROTHY TAYLOR (Pseud: Dorothy Darling), PR, Philadelphia Area United Fund, 450 Suburban Station Bldg., John F. Kennedy Blvd., Phila., Pa. 19103, '68–; Cont. Dir., WDEL (Wilmington, Del.); Prom. Coordr., Bloomingdale's (N.Y.C.); Mng. Dir., Nat. Hand-Knitting Yarn Assn.; Asst. to Prom. Dir., B. Altman & Co. (N.Y.C.); Adv. Dir., Rich's (Atlanta, Ga.); Fashion Prom. Dir., Wm. H. Block Co. (Indpls., Ind.); Fashion Group, Adv. Club of Wilmington, AWRT, Pilot Intl.; George Washington Univ., AB, '47; b. Altoona, Pa., 1929; p. Isaiah and Ruth Patterson Taylor; h. Malcolm LeJeune; res: 3213 Naaman's Rd., Wilmington, Del. 19803.

LEMANI, TANYA, Actress, Singer, Dancer, c/o Mitchell Gertz Agency, 338 N. Rodeo Dr., Beverly Hills, Cal. 90210; appearances as singer at International, Tropicana Hotels, Las Vegas, Nev.; TV: "It Takes a Thief," "Elvis Presley," "Flying Nun," others; motion pics: "Big Daddy," "Some Kind of Nut," "The Hell with Heroes," others in Hollywood and Iran; Court Interpreter, Russian, Persian, Eng. langs.; SAG, AEA, AGVA, Melrose Theatre Assn.; S.F. City Col., Pasadena Playhouse; b. Sari, Iran, 1944; p. George and Valentina Sbitnev Soleimani; res: 342 N. Orange Dr., L.A., Cal. 90036.

LEMBO, DIANA MacDONOUGH, Assoc. Prof., Lib. Sci., Palmer Grad. Lib. Sch., Long Island University, Greenvale, N.Y. 11548, '65–; Sch. Librn., '58–'65; Adjunct Asst. Prof., '64; Ed., monthly filmstrip rev. colm., "Screenings," Sch. Lib. Jnl., '67–; Co-auth: "Juniorplots" (R. R. Bowker, '67), "Library Learning Laboratory" (Fordham Publ., '69), "Introducing Books" (Bowker, '70); Cnslt.; Speaker; NEA-DAVI, Nassau-Suffolk Sch. Lib. Assn., ALA, N.Y. Lib. Assn., Kappa Delta Pi, Pi Lambda Theta; Cornell Univ., BS, '45; L.I. Univ., MS (Educ.), '59; MS (Lib. Sci.), '61; N.Y.U., PhD; b. Waterbury, Conn., 1925; p. Thelma Fava Spirit; c. Stephen J., Jarron L., Deirdre J.; res: 96 Forest Ave., Locust Valley, N.Y. 11560.

LEMKE, ANTJE BULTMANN, Assoc. Prof. of Lib. Sci., Syracuse University, Syracuse, N.Y. 13210, '65–; Asst. Prof., '63–'65; Instr., Asst. Dean, '61–'63; Guggenheim Fellowship, '60–'61; Music Librn., '52–'59; h. Rudolf Lemke (dec.).

LENARD, KATHRYN PASSILIA, Dir. of Rsch., Metromedia Radio, 485 Lexington Ave., N.Y., N.Y. 10024, '69–; Media Rsch. Mgr., Metromedia, Inc., '59–'69; Bklyn. Col., BA, '55; b. N.Y.C., 1934; p. Benjamin and Henrietta Nelson Passilia; h. Jay Lenard; c. Jennifer, Dena; res: 325 W. 86 St., N.Y., N.Y. 10024.

LENCI, MARGARET ZELLERS, Travel Wtr.; Asst. to Auth., "All the Best in . . ." series; Colmst., New Bedford (Mass.) Standard Times; Colmst., Travel mag.; Assoc. Ed., Bon Voyage mag.; Dir. of Virgin Islands Info. Ctr., Rockefeller Ctr., '60–'65; PR, Wendell P. Colton Co., '56–'60; Soc. of Am. Travel Wtrs.; Conn. Col. for Wm., BA, '56; b. Bridgeport, Conn., 1934; h. Gordon Kent Lenci; res: 5414 Cherry St., Kan. City, Mo. 64110.

LENGELSEN, RUTH E., Librn., Mt. Carmel Public Library, 120 E. 5th St., Mt. Carmel, Ill. 62863, '48–; Asst. Librn., '41–'44; HS Librn., '33–'38; Colmst., weekly "Library Notes"; Weekly Bdcstr., Radio WVMC "Story Time"; ALA, Ill. Lib. Assn., Mt. Carmel Wms. Club, Delta Theta Tau, BPW (Wabash Chptr. Secy.); Univ. of Ill., '36; b. Wabash County, Ill., 1911; p. Charles T. and Florence Buchanan Lengelsen; res: 1210 Mulberry St., Mt. Carmel, Ill. 62863.

L'ENGLE, MADELEINE CAMP, Auth: "A Wrinkle in Time," ('62), "The Moon by Night" ('63); "The Arm of the Starfish" ('65), "Dance in the Desert" ('69), many others; Auths. Guild, Wtrs. League; Newbery Medal, '63; Austrian State Prize for Lit., '69; Lewis Caroll Shelf aw., '66; Sequoya Aw; Smith Col., '41 (hons.); b. N.Y.C., 1918; p. Charles and Madeleine Barnett Camp; h. Hugh Franklin; c. Josephine (Mrs. Alan W. Jones), Maria, Bion; res: West St., Goshen, Conn. 06756.

LENGYEL, ELIZABETH ANN, Wms. Ed., The Day, 27 Green Hill Pl., Madison, Conn. 06443, '67–; Feature Wtr., New Haven (Conn.) Register, '65–'67, Reptr., '63–'65; Soc. Ed., New Britain (Conn.) Herald, '61–'63; Outstanding Young Wm., '67; Duke Univ., BA (Sociology), '61; b. Waterbury, Conn., 1939; p. John and Margaret Dubiel Lengyel; res: 21 Oakley St., New Haven, Conn. 06512.

LENNON, FLORENCE TANENBAUM, Free-lance Wtr., Tchr. of Poetry, Unincorporated University of the University of Colorado, Boulder, Colo.; Auth: "Victoria Through the Looking-Glass, the Life of Lewis Carroll" ('45); Poetry: "Farewell to Walden" ('39), "Forty Years in the Wilderness" ('61); Poetry published in nwsps., mags., anthologies (U.S., Can., Eng.), '16–; Wtr., "The Broken Column," Town and Country Rev. (weekly, Boulder, Colo.); Free-lance work, Boulder Camera, '46–; Directress, Conductor, Poetry Tchr., Educ. Wtr., Reptr.; Auths. Guild, PSA, New Eng. Poetry Soc., Denver Nwsp. Guild, OPC, Intl. Platform Assn.; Poetry Prize, Bread Loaf Wtrs. Conf., '38; Manuscript Prize (poetry), Nat. Wtrs.' Club (Denver, Colo.), '55; Fellowship, MacDowell Colony, '62; Fellowship, Huntington Hartford Colony, '62; active in Boulder civic groups; Training Sch. for Montessori Tchrs. (N.Y.), diploma, '21; Columbia Univ., BS, Univ. of Colo., MA, '47; b. N.Y., 1895; p. Leon and Johanna

Beran Tanenbaum; h. 1. Samuel Becker; 2. John Lennon (div.); c. Mrs. Robert Melton, Mrs. Philip Oppenheim; res: 1074 Rose Hill Dr., Boulder, Colo. 80302.

LENNON, MARY LOUISE, Educ. Dir., Life Cycle Center, Kimberly-Clark Corporation, N. Lake St., Neenah, Wis. 54956, '69–; Commty. Health Cnslt., Metropolitan Life Insurance Co., (N.Y.C.), '63–'69; Tchr., '59–'63; Rosemary Hall, Greenwich, Conn.; Emanuel Col., BA, '57; Wellesley Col., MA, '59; b. Boston, Mass., 1936; p. Edward and Amber Murphy Lennon; res: 318 E. Doty Ave., Neenah, Wis. 54956.

LEONARD, EDITH MARIAN, Prof. Emeritus, University of California, '64–; Prof., '44–'64; Prof., Santa Barbara State Col., '42–'44; Assoc. Prof., '32–'42; Primary Supvsr., '25–'32; Primary Supvsr., San Bernardino City Schs., '22–'25; Tchr., '20–'22; Co-auth., six non-fiction bks.; NEA, Delta Phi Upsilon, Delta Kappa Gamma, Intl. Platform Assn., various educ. orgs.; Who's Who in the West; Dic. of Intl. Biog.; Nat. Col., BA, '24; Claremont Col., MA, '30; b. San Bernardino, Cal.; p. Willis and Nettie McCullough Leonard; res: P.O. Drawer FF, c/o Trust Dept., Santa Barbara, Cal. 93102.

LEONARD, JEAN, Assoc. Ed. of Pubns., Metropolitan Museum of Art, Fifth Ave. and 82nd St., N.Y., N.Y. 10028, '49–; Asst. Ed., '40–'49; Ed., Edmund Bergler Fndn., '62–; Bryn Mawr Col., AB; b. Nashville, Tenn.; p. Norris and Susanna Black Leonard; res: 120 E. 64th St., N.Y., N.Y. 10021.

LEONARD, MARGERY BRAUER, Asst. Mgr., PR Dir., Washington Athletic Club, 1325 Sixth Ave., Seattle, Wash. 98111, '58–; Wms. Secy., '46–'58; Ed., Wash. Athletic Club News, '43–'46; Adv. Mgr., I. Magnin, '42–'43; Copywtr., Sears Roebuck, '39–'42; Lectr., Univ. of Wash. Hotel Sch.; Soroptimist Club of Seattle Met. (Pres., '67–'68, Dir., '64–'66), Theta Sigma Phi (Past Pres., Col. Chptr.), Seattle Adv. Club, AAUW; Club Mgrs. Assn. of Am. aws., Who's Who of Am. Wm., '69–'70; Grinnell Col., AB, '37; Northwestern Univ., Univ. of Wash.; b. Kan. City, Kan.; p. Rudolph and Marjorie Clark Brauer; h. Arthur F. Leonard (div.); c. John R.; res: 3620 31st St. W., Seattle, Wash. 98199.

LEONARD, NONNA THELMA, Tech. Pubns. Ed., U.S. Army School/Training Center, Fort McCellan, Anniston, Ala. 36201, '62–; Govt. Svc: Ill., Hi., Japan, Wash., D.C., '42–'62; Theta Sigma Phi (Beta Gamma Student Chptr. VP, '49), Soc. of Tech. Wtrs. and Publrs., Am. Assn. for Adv. of Sci., Intl. Platform Assn., Intl. Toastmistress Clubs (Histrn., '65–'66), Anniston BPW (Pres., '68–'70); Bradley Univ., BA (Jnlsm.), '52; b. Ill.; p. John and Callie Wims Leonard; res: Apt. 14, 1130 Christine Ave., Anniston, Ala. 36201.

LEONARD, SHERYL, Dir. of PR, Educ., American Jewish Committee, 105 W. Adams St., Chgo., Ill. 60603, '66–; Mgr. PR, Adv., Goodman's Discount Dept. Stores; Colmst., Nat. Post and Opinion, '64–'65; Dir., PR, Commty. Discount Corp., '59–'63; Colmst., Wtr., Skokie News and Villager News Magazine, '56–'58; Wtr., Performer, WBKB-TV, WAIT, WMOR, '48–'52; Tchr., PR Central YMCA Commty. Col.; Guest Colmst., Chgo. Daily News; Actress, Yiddish Theatre Group of Chgo.; Lectr.; Auth., "Lovingly Yours"; WPA, Ill. Wms. Press Assn. (Mate E. Palmer Aw., '69, '64), Pubcty. Club of Chgo., BPW, PRSA; Medill Sch. of Jnlsm., Northwestern Univ.; b. Chgo., Ill.; c. Robert Clyde Lentzner, Mrs. Bernie Alan, Davida Shapiro, Denise Shapiro; res: 4726D Main St., Skokie, Ill. 60076.

LEONARD, SUZANNE PADILLA, Reptr., Times-Press, 122 S. Bloomington St., Streator, Ill. 61364, '69–; Asst. Wms. Pg. Reptr., '59'; b. Streator, Ill., 1941; p. Lawrence and Marion Obenhin Padilla; h. Lawrence Leonard; c. Curtis John, Jayne Anne; res: 1439 E. Broadway, Streator, Ill. 61364.

LePINE, IDA RYAN, Soc. Ed., Oswego Palladium-Times, 174 W. First St., Oswego, N.Y. 13126, '57–; Intl. Affairs Cnslt., U.S. Dept. of HEW; b. Utica, N.Y., 1900; p. John and Mary Queenan Ryan; h. Fred C. LePine; c. Frederick P., Thomas J.

LERNER, CAROLINE STEINHOLZ, VP, Fine Arts, Ruder & Finn Inc., 110 E. 59th St., N.Y., N.Y. 10022, '69–; Pres., Gallery Passort Ltd., '60–'68; PRSA; Cornell Univ., BA, '46; b. N.Y.C., 1925; p. Reuben and Gladys Garf Steinholz; c. Lawrence Richard Lerner, David Lawson Lerner; res: 375 West End Ave., N.Y., N.Y. 10024.

LERNER, SARETTE GOULD, Wms. Ed., Antioch Ledger, 1700 Cavallo Rd., Antioch, Cal. 94509, '69–; Contra Costa Times, '67–'68; Washington Scroll, '57–'59; Univ. of Wis., BA, '57; b. Milw., Wis., 1936; p. Jack and Mildred Wasserman Gould; h. Eugene Lerner; c. Jack Lawrence, David Ross, Ellen Beth, Andrew Martin; res: 42 E. Lake Dr., Antioch, Cal. 94509.

LERNER, SHARON GOLDMAN, Pres., Carol Rhoda Books, Inc. 241 First Ave. N., Mpls., Minn. '69–; Art Ed., Lerner Publications Company, '62–; Art Tchr. and Tour Guide, Walker Art Ctr., '62–'66; Tour Guide, Mpls. Inst. of Art, '62; Art Tchr., Whitebear Public Schs., '61–'62; Art Tchr., Univ. of Minn., '60–'61; Auth. and Illus.; ten children's bks. (Lerner Pubns., non-fiction, verse, art), Mamamore, Chgo. Bk. Clinic Design Aw. for "The Horse in Art" and "Self-Portrait in Art," local art exhbns.; Univ. of Minn., BS, '60; Grad. Work, '60–62; b. Chgo., Ill., 1938; p. Julius and Ethel Kremen Goldman; h. Harry J. Lerner; c. Adam and Mia; res: 1020 Ives Lane, Mpls., Minn. 55427.

LERNOUX, PENNY MARY, Bur. Chief for S. Am., Copley News Service, Corrientes 456, Off. 181, Buenos Aires, Argentina, '67–; Caracas Bur. Chief, '64–;

Fgn. Svc. Offcr., U.S.I.A. (Gogata and Rio de Janeiro), '61–'63); Reptr., Hollywood Citizen News, '61; OPC, Argentine Fgn. Corrs. Assn.; CNS Aw. for best fgn. feature, '68; Univ. of Southern Cal., BA (Spanish and Jnlsm.), '61 (Cal. State Scholarship, '60; Theta Sigma Phi Scholarship, '60; Inter-Am. Press Assn. Scholarship, '62; Phi Beta Kappa, '61; Phi Kappa Phi, '61); b. L.A., Cal. 1940; p. Maurice and Beatrice Lernoux; res: Ave. Alvear 1640, Piso 8, Buenos Aires, Argentina.

LeSHAN, EDA GROSSMAN, Psychologist, Auth: "Sex and Your Teenager" (David McKay Co., '69), "The Conspiracy Against Childhood" (Atheneum, '67), "How to Survive Parenthood" (Random House, '65); numerous mag. articles, pamphlets; Commentator, "Newsfront," Channel 13; Cnslt. Psychologist, Pengilly Sch., New Rochelle, N.Y.; Dir. of Educ., Manhattan Soc. for Mental Health, '60; Guidance Ctr. of New Rochelle, '56; Family Life Educ., '50–'56; Child Psychologist, '46; Child Welfare Worker, Nursery Sch. Dir., '40–'45; Am. Psychological Assn.; Columbia Univ. Tchrs. Col., BS (Early Childhood Educ.); Clark Univ., MA (Child Psych.); b. N.Y.C., 1922; p. Max and Jean Schick Grossman; h. Lawrence Le Shan; c. Wendy; res: 322 Central Park W., N.Y., N.Y. 10025.

LeSIEUR, HELEN E., PR Dir., The Arthritis Foundation, Southern California Chapter, 4311 Wilshire Blvd., L.A., Cal. 90005, '61–; Arthritis Fndn., Ill. Chptr., '60–'61; Sr. AE, Aaron D. Cushman & Assoc., '54–'60; Free-lance Publicist, seasonal projects, '52–'54; PRSA, Pubcty. Club of L.A. (Pres., '66–'67, 1st wm. pres.), PIRATES (wm. in Radio-TV public svcs.); S.E. Mo. State Col.; Wash. Univ.; Northwestern Univ.; b. Coffeyville, Kan.; p. Frank and Grace Koon LeSieur; res: 5709 Fallsgrove St., L.A., Cal. 90016.

LESKO, RUTH GARLAND, VP, Lesko Inc., One Oliver Plaza, Pitt., Pa. 15222, '70–; AE, Ketchum MacLeod & Grove, Inc., '67–'70; Copywtr., '62–'64, TV Wtr., Prodr., Lando, Inc., '65–'67; Crtv. Dir., Jay Reich, Inc., '64–'65; AWRT (Gateway Chptr. VP, '68), Theta Sigma Phi; Chatham Col., BA (Eng.), '56; Yale Univ., '56–'57; b. Pitt., Pa., 1934; p. William and Esther M. Garland; h. George Lesko; c. Tanya, Hud; res: 9463 Doral Dr., Pitt., Pa. 15237.

LESLIE, ALEEN, Auth: "Windfall" (novel; New Am. Lib.), "The Scent of the Roses" (novel), "Slightly Married" (Broadway play); Auth., Originator, Owner, "A Date with Judy," radio-TV situation comedy; Screen Wtr., Columbia, Universal, R.K.O., 20th Century-Fox, M-G-M; b. Pitt., Pa.; h. Jacques Leslie; c. Jacques, Jr., Mrs. Diane Leslie Huffman; res: 1700 Lexington Rd., Beverly Hills, Cal. 90210.

LESLIE, GAY GIFFORD, Staff Wtr., The Wisconsin State Journal, 115 S. Carroll St., Madison, Wis. 53711, '67–; Pubns. Ed., Univ. of Wis. summer sessions off., '66–'67; Theta Sigma Phi, Madison Press Club, Madison BPW Outstanding Young Career Wm. aw., '68;

Univ. of Wis., BS, '66 (Sigma Epsilon Sigma; Crucible; Mortar Bd.; Phi Kappa Phi); h. Harry Leslie.

LESLIE, KAY DALY, VP, Crtv. Svcs., Revlon, Inc., 767 Fifth Ave., N.Y., N.Y. 10022, '60–; VP, Crtv. Dir., Norman, Craig and Kummel, '49–'60; AE, Foote, Cone and Belding (S.F., Cal.), '45–'49; Fashion, Beauty Ed., Chicago (Ill.) Herald American, '43–'45; Fashion Coordr., Gimbels (Milw., Wis.), '41–'43; Fashion Group; Gimbels-Schusters aw., '63; Cal. Apparel Assn. aw., '45; numerous copywriting, art aws.; Rosary Col., BA, '40; b. County Tyrone, Ireland; p. Joseph and Margaret Daly; h. Warren Leslie; c. Kelly Bradford, Peter Bradford, Richard Bradford; res: 220 Central Park S., N.Y., N.Y. 10019.

LESSER, JEREMIE LEE, PR Dir., Program Guide Ed., AE, and Dir. of Syndication, WNCN, 2 W. 45th St., N.Y., N.Y. 10036, '67–; Ext. Svcs. Prods., BBC (London, Eng.), '65–'67; Wellesley Col., BA, '65; b. N.Y.C., 1943; p. Albert Lee and Norma Sharfman Lesser; res: 7-1/2 W. 75th St., N.Y., N.Y. 10023.

LesSTRANG, JEAN MENTZER, VP, Treas., Les Strang Advertising, Inc., 2082 S. State Rd., Ann Arbor, Mich. 48104, '53–; Ed., The Reporter, '52–'53; Freelance Wtr., '49–'52; AWRT, Wms. Adv. Club, ZONTA; Who's Who in the Midwest, Who's Who in Commerce and Industry, Who's Who of Am. Wm.; Univ. of Mich. grad., '47; b. Balt., Md., 1926; p. John and Marguerite Paul Mentzer; c. Michelle, Diane Jean, Paul Jacques, David Matthew; res: 2427 Londonberry Rd., Ann Arbor, Mich. 48104.

LETOWSKY, RUTH, Dir. of Pubcty. and PR, WQXI-TV, 1611 W. Peachtree St., N.E., Atlanta, Ga. 30309, '66–; Prom. Coordr., '63–'66; Secy.-Wtr., Life of Ga. '62–'63; Am. Cancer Soc. (Ga. Chptr. Dir. TV Activities, '67–'69), AWRT (Rec. Secy., '68–'69); Fla. State Univ., '59–'60; Univ. of Fla., '60–'62; b. Peekskill, N.Y., 1941; p. Manuel and Ethel Kanner Letowsky; res: 5320 Roswell Rd., Atlanta, Ga. 30305.

LETTS, LOU MESSENGER, Adv. Mgr., Houston Bank & Trust, 1801 Main St., Houston, Tex. 77001, '56–; Secy., Pubcty. Dir., Bdcst. Dir., Copywtr., AE, Brennan Adv. Agcy., '54–'56; AAF (10th Dist. Dir., '65–; '57–'59; distg. svc. aw., '58; Gov., '67–'68; Second Lt. Governor '66–'67), Houston Adv. Club (Dir., '59–'63; 2nd VP, '57–'59; "Wm. of the Yr.", '58), Houston C. of C., AWRT, Tex. PR Assn., Press Club of Houston, Am. Inst. of Banking, Gamma Alpha Chi (Nat. Pfsnl. Dir., '69–; Nat. VP, '66–'69; Southwest Reg. VP, '64–'66), Who's Who of Am. Wm., Who's Who in the South and Southwest, Dic. of Intl. Biog., Who's Who in the South and Southwest, Dic. of Intl. Biog., Who's Who in Commerce & Industry; Northern Ill. Univ., BE (Eng.), '36 (cum laude); b. St. Paul, Minn., 1915; p. Wiley and Helen Robinson Messenger; h. Dale Letts; c. David A., Sarah R.; res: 1535 Antoine Dr., Houston, Tex. 77055.

LETZIG, MARGARET HIMSTEDT, PR, Pubcty., Prom., Free-lance Wtr.; Rsch. and Clinical Social Worker, Univ. of Ark. Medical Sch., '56–'61; District Mgr., Educational Eiv., Marshall Field Enterprises, Inc., Chgo., '45–'51; Dir. of Social Svc., St. John's Hospital, St. Louis, '44–'45; Adm. Offcr., Wms. Army Corps., U.S. Army, '42–'44; District Dir. and Asst. State Supvsr., Wms. and Professional Projects, Fed. Works Agency, '33–'42; Tchr., Little Rock Public Schs. and St. Mary's Academy, '19–'23; Marquis Publications, Inc. Advisory Comm., '69–; in charge of pubns. for Federal Works Agency; articles in National Recreation Magazine, Arkansas Gazette, Arkansas Democrat Magazine Sections; Pioneer Branch, Nat. League of Am. Pen Wm., Nat. Bkwms. Assn., Friends of the Lib.; Ark. Lives, Who's Who in Ark., Who's Who of Am. Wm., Who's Who in South and Southwest; Dic. of Intl. Biog., Dic. of British and Am. Wtrs., 2,000 Wm. of Achiev., Commty. Leaders of Am., Intl. Platform Assn.; Trinity College, BA, '19; Tulane University, Masters (Social Work), '56; b. Little Rock, Ark.; p. Henry and Margaret Hickey Himstedt; h. Frank William Letzig; c. Margaret Ellen (Mrs. E. Ray Kemp, Jr.), Frank William Letzig, Jr., res: 4816 Crestwood Dr., Little Rock, Ark. 72207.

LEUBBERT, KAREN MERRITT, Librn., Webster College, 470 E. Lockwood, St. Louis, Mo. 63119, '68–; Acting Librn., '67–'68; ALA, Beta Phi Mu; Webster Col., BA, '64; Case Western Reserve Univ., MS (Lib. Sci.), '67; b. St. Louis, Mo., 1942; p. Joseph and Lorene Amrhein Merritt; h. Jack Luebbert; res: 8529 Wyndhurst, St. Louis, Mo. 63134.

LEUBNER, SYLVIA E., Ed., Garrett Publications, Parapyschology Foundation, 29 W. 57th St., N.Y., N.Y. 10019, '68–; Edtl. Asst., '68; Duke Univ., BA, '63 (Phi Beta Kappa); b. Louisville, Ky.; p. Samuel and Mary Nevius Shearer; res: 207 W. 106th St., N.Y., N.Y. 10025.

LEUDERS, HERMINE HALL, VP, Group Head, Sullivan, Stauffer, Colwell & Bayles Inc., 575 Lexington Ave., N.Y., N.Y. 10022, '60–; Group Head, '56–'59; Key Wtr., '54–'55; Copywtr., Benton & Bowles, Inc., '49–'54; Tchr. of fiction, Harvard Summer Sch.; Radcliffe Col., BA (Philosophy; cum laude); c. Stephanie, Cynthia, Alison, Duane; h. Duane Leuders.

LeVAN, SHARON K., AE, The Marschalk Co., Inc., 1271 Ave. of the Americas, N.Y., N.Y. 10020, '68–; AE, Johnstone, Inc., '68; Lasell, AS, '66; b. Carbondale, Pa., 1946; p. Theodore and Mary LeVan; res: 222 E. 75th St., N.Y., N.Y. 10021.

LEVECK, RUTH ARNOLD, Librn., Baptist Medical Center, 1700 W. 13th St., Little Rock, Ark. 72207, '62–; Librn., J. T. Robinson HS, '59–'62; PR, J. H. Leveck & Sons, '42–'58; Tchr., '25–'29; WNBA (Little Rock Charter Mbr., Exec. Bd.), PEN (Ark. Pioneer Br. Pres., '44–'46; State Pres., '46–'48), Ark. Lib. Assn., Med. Lib. Assn., Intl. Platform Assn.; Midwest Wtrs. Conf. aw.;

Who's Who of Am. Wm.; PEN aw., '48; Univ. of Ill., BA, '25; Univ. of Ark., MA, '55; Peabody Col., MA, '62; b. Little Rock, Ark.; p. Joseph and Catherine Dotterer Arnold; h. Donald Leveck; res: 121 Normandy Rd., Little Rock, Ark. 72207.

LEVENSTEIN, ROSLYN, Copy Supvsr., Young & Rubicam, 285 Madison Ave., N.Y., N.Y. 10017, '64–; Copywtr., '62–'64; Creator, "Adventures of Terry Tell-Time" TV show, '57; Wtrs. Guild; numerous adv. aws. for "Excedrin" commls., '68, '67; others, '66, '65; N.Y.U., BA (Adv.); b. N.Y.C.; p. Leo Rapoport and Mrs. Stella Rosenberg; h. Lawrence Levenstein; c. Leland Seides; res: 403 Tryon Ave., Englewood, N.J. 07631.

LEVI, Sr. MARY CAROLISSA, Auth.; Librn., St. James School, 1120 Caledonia St., LaCrosse, Wis. 54601; bk: "Chippewa Indians of Yesterday and Today;" ('56), mag. and nwsp. articles; Nat. Wtrs. Club; numerous writing aws.; LaCrosse State Tchrs. Col., Diploma, '33; Viterbo Col., BE; Loras Col., '31; Gonzaga Univ., '60; b. Genoa, Wis.; p. John and Elizabeth Fanetti Levi; res: St. Rose Convent, 912 Market, LaCrosse, Wis. 54601.

LEVI, SHONIE BIEGELSEN, Wtr., Talent, "Today's Woman," WEVD, Advertisers Broadcasting Co., 117 W. 46th St., N.Y., N.Y. 11432, '63–; Auth., "Across the Threshold," Co-auth., "A Guide to the Jewish Homemaker"; Past Prin., Temple Emanuel Hebrew Sch.; Lectr., U.S. and Can.; Educ. Cnslt., Nat. Hadassah; active in Jewish wms. and religious orgs., recipient of aws.; Tchrs. Inst., Jewish Theological Seminary, '26 (Past Pres., Alumni Assn.); Cooper Union, '32; Columbia Univ., Grad. Work; b. N.Y.C., 1907; p. Nathan and Sara Grosshard Biegelsen; h. S. Gershon Levi; c. Don S., Victoria M.; res: 164 11 Highland Ave., Jamaica, N.Y., N.Y. 11432.

LEVIN, ALEXANDRA LEE, Free-lance Wtr., biogs: "The Szolds of Lombard Street" ('60), "Vision" ('64); numerous mag. and nwsp. articles, '56–; Phila. Hadassah Bk. of the Yr. Aw., '61; Bryn Mawr. Col., '29–'32; b. Wash., D.C. 1912; p. Lawrence and Alexandra McDannold Lee; h. M. Jastrow Levin; c. Betsy, Lawrence Lee, Sally, Mrs. Lexie L. Cohen; res: 3712 Chesholm Rd., Balt., Md. 21216.

LEVIN, BEATRICE S., Asst. Prof., Texas Southern University, Wheeler St., Houston, Tex. 77004, '64–; Tchr., Crtv. Writing, Benedictine Heights Col. (Tulsa, Okla.); '56–'58; Instr., Univ. of Wis., '45–'49; Edtl. Asst., Encyclopedia Americana, '42–'43; Free-lance Auth, numerous bks., short stories and articles in mags. and educ. jnls., nwsps.; AAUP, Tex. Assn. of Col. Tchrs., Tex. Assn. of Tchrs. of Col. Eng.; R.I. Col., BA (Educ.), '42; Univ. of Wis., MS (Drama), '48; b. Providence, R.I., 1920; h. Franklyn K. Levin; c. Michael Jonathan, Alan Robert, Philip Lincoln.

LEVIN, FELICE MICHAELS, Cnslt., Office of Reports,

Ford Foundation, 320 E. 43rd. St., N.Y., N.Y. 10017, '68–; Coordr. of Pubns., Off. of Admission Svcs., City Univ. of N.Y., '67–'68; Rsch. Asst. to Prof. Scott Cutlip, Univ of Wis., '65–'67; Instr., PR courses; Staff Wtr., Wis. State Jnl., '57–'65; Dir. of Pubns., Univ. of Wis. Ext. Div., '53–'57; Theta Sigma Phi (Madison Chptr. Pres., '51–'52), OPC, Govs. Commn. on Status of Wm. (1st Wis. Commn., '64–'65), Wis. Wms. Legislative Cncl. (Pres.), Univ. of Wis., BA, '49 (Phi Kappa Phi, Mortar Bd.); MA, '67; b. Chgo., Ill., 1928; p. Harry and Fannie Litz Michaels; h. Harry C. Levin; res: 360 E. 72nd St., N.Y., N.Y. 10021.

LEVIN, KIM, Edtl. Assoc., Art News, 444 Madison Ave., N.Y., N.Y. 10022, '63–; Tchr., Phila. Col. of Art, '67–; articles: Am. Jnl. of Archeology ('64), Art News ('64–'69), Art News Annual ('69); exhbns., Poindexter Gallery, '64, '67; Vassar Col., AB; Columbia Univ., MA.

LEVIN, MARCIA OBRASKY, Auth: 18 juv. bks. (Wonder Bks., Grosset and Dunlap); seven novels for teen-age girls (Whitman); math., diet and grooming bks. (McGraw-Hill); Temple Univ., Univ. of Ind.; b. Phila., Pa., 1918; p. Abraham and Elizabeth Lauter Obrasky; h. Martin P. Levin; c. Jeremy, Wendy (Mrs. Pedro Sanchez), Hugh; res: 370 Grace Church St., Rye, N.Y. 10580.

LEVINE, BETTIJANE, Crtv. Dir., Coty Cosmetics, 235 E. 42nd St., N.Y., N.Y. 10017; Sr. Wtr., Carson/Roberts Advertising (L.A., Cal.); Ed., Wms. Wear Daily (N.Y.C.); Pubcty. Mgr., The Broadway Stores (L.A.); Mademoiselle mag. (N.Y.C.); articles in trade and consumer pubns.; Belding Aw. for Crtv. achiev. in adv., N.Y.U., BA; b. N.Y.C.

LEVINE, SUZANNE BRAUN, Assoc. Ed., McCall's Magazine, 230 Park Ave., N.Y., N.Y. 10017, '69–; Feature Ed., Mademoiselle, '67–'69; Photo Rschr., Time-Life Bks., '66–'67; Reptr.-Wtr., Seattle Magazine, '63–'65; Contrbr., Cosmopolitan, '69; Radcliffe Col., BA, '63 (cum laude); b. N.Y.C., 1941; p. Dr. Imre and Esther Bernson Braun; h. Robert F. Levine; res: 22 E. 36th St., N.Y., N.Y. 10016.

LEVINSON, MURIEL PARKER, Free-lance Artist, Adv. Cnslt., '68–; Adv. Prod. Mgr., McGreevey, Werring & Howell, '65–'68; Asst. Sls. Prom. Mgr., Spartan Stores, '65; Fashion Coordr., Adv. Dir., Sls. Prom. Mgr., S. Iren Johns, '54–'65; Art Dir., Chernoff-Herman, '52–'54; Fashion Artist, '50–'52; Asst. Prod. Dir., Metrotone, '47–'49; Am. Mensa Soc., Intl. Platform Assn., Suburban Artists Guild; Fashion Inst. of Tech. and Design, AA; b. N.Y.C., 1928; p. Harry and Rebecca Grossman Perlman; h. Samuel Levinson; c. Robert; res: 1356 Kearney Dr., New Brunswick, N.J. 08902.

LEVINTHAL, SONIA, Assoc. Dir., Public Info., Scholastic Magazines, 50 W. 44th St., N.Y., N.Y. 10036, '69–; Dir., Public Info., McGraw-Hill, '63–'69; Dir.

Pubcty., '55–'63; Wtr., articles in trade mags.; Publrs. Adv. Club (Pres., '61–'63), Publrs. Pubcty. Assn. (Co-Founder; Pres., '63–'64), N.Y. Assn. of Indsl. Communicators (Bd. of Govs., '66); Smith Col., '42; b. N.Y.C.; res: 110 East End Ave., N.Y., N.Y. 10028.

LEVITT, FAITH MANDEL, Wms. News Dir., WISH-TV Indiana Broadcasting Corp., 1950 N. Meridian, Indpls., Ind. 46202, '64–; Free-lance: WEWS-TV, '49, WTAM, WHK, tchr., nwsp. colmst.; Western Reserve Univ., BS, '49; Columbia Tchrs. Col., '49–'50; b. Cleve., Oh.; h. Eugene Levitt; c. Hope, Lisa, Tod, Russell, Jason; res: 5430 Hawthorne Dr., Indpls., Ind. 46226.

LEVY, BARBARA WEXNER, Wms. Fashion Ed., Boot & Shoe Recorder, 100 E. 42nd St., N.Y., N.Y. 10017, '68–; Fashion, Shoe Ed., Window Shopping the World, '67–'68; Reader Svc., Scholastic Mags. (N.J.), '66–'67; Houston-Miami Corr., Modern Retailer, Reg. Ed., Boot & Shoe Recorder, '58–'65; Theta Sigma Phi, Shoe Wm. Execs.; Lindenwood Col., AA, '45; Univ. of Houston, '58–'59; b. Hot Springs, Ark., 1927; p. Henry and Helen Loeb Wexner; h. Herb Levy; c. Barbara Levy Stern, Richard, Lauren; res: 3 Horizon Rd., #610, Fort Lee, N.J. 07024.

LEVY, MARION MURPHY, PR Dir., Rehabilitation Institute of Chicago, 410 E. Ohio, Chgo., Ill. 60611, '69–; Dir. of PR, Arlington Park Towers (Arlington Heights), '69; Mgr. of Employee Commtns., Alberto-Culver, '67–'69; Supvsr. of Employee Commtns., Libby, Mc Neill & Libby, '67; AE, Daniel J. Edelman & Assoc., '66; PR, Morton Salt, '65–'66; Ed. of Agts. Pubns., Kemper Ins., '62–'65; Ed. of Employee Pubns., Zurich Am. Ins., '54–'62; ICIE (Secy., '65–'66; Area Dir. Ill., Wis., '63–'64), Indsl. Eds. Assn. of Chgo. (Pres., '62; Dir., '59–'64), Pfsnl. Photogrs. of Am., Pubcty. Club of Chgo., PRSA, numerous graphic and writing Chgo., Ill.; p. Joseph and Ruth Olson Murphy; h. Harold F. Levy (div.); res: 3550 Lake Shore Dr., Apt. 2524, Chgo., Ill. 60657.

LEVY, PHYLLIS SARI, Assoc. Fiction Ed., Ladies' Home Journal, Downe Communications, Inc., 641 Lexington Ave., N.Y., N.Y. 10022, '65–; McCall's, '62–'65; Assoc. Ed., Viking Press, '59–'62; Simon & Schuster, '55–'59; Freelance Ed., Rschr.; Poetry Judge, Scholastic Magazine annual contest; Radcliffe Col., BA, '52; b. N.Y.C., 1931; p. Dr. Milton and Ruth Halpern Levy; res: 23 Washington Sq. N., N.Y., N.Y. 10011.

LEVY, RALENE, Print Mgr., Allied Artists Pictures Corporation, 230 W. 41st St., N.Y., N.Y. 10036, '66–; Asst. Fgn. Svc. Mgr., '52–'66; Syracuse Univ., '45; Latin Am. Inst., '46–'47; b. Bayonne, N.J., 1927; p. Sydney and Jennie Taub Levy; res: 65 W. 29th St., Bayonne, N.J. 07002.

LEVY, RUTH, Asst. to Exec. VP, Pergamon Press Inc., Maxwell House, Elmsford, N.Y. 10523, '65–; Dir.,

Customer Svc., '62; Asst. to VP, Maxwell Scientific Intl., '63–'65; Founder and Partner, Rsch. Info. Svc., '46–'61; Am. Translators Assn. (Past Secy.-Treas.); Cornell Univ., BA, '34; Columbia Tchrs. Col., MA, '35; p. David Levy and Clara Vos Morgenstern; res: 365 W. 25th St., N.Y., N.Y. 10001.

LEWIN, MERRIAM EVE, Auth: "The Inner City Mother Goose" (Simon & Schuster, '69), "After Nora Slammed the Door: American Women in the 1960'; —The Unfinished Revolution" (World Publ. Co., '64), others; Crtv. Writing Instr., City Col. of N.Y., '65–'69; Lectr., N.Y.U. and Central Wash. State Col.; Soc. of Mag. Wtrs. (VP, '68), Auths. Guild, ASCAP; CBS-TV Fellowship, '59; Colliers Star Fiction Aw., '47; Yale Younger Poets Prize, '46; Univ. of Pa., AB, '37.

LEWIN, SUSAN GRANT, Design Ed., House Beautiful, 717 Fifth Ave., N.Y., N.Y. 10022, '70–; Design Ed., Fairchile Pubns., Inc., '66–'70; Design Reptr., Home Furnishings Daily, '63–'66; Edtl. Asst., IEEE, '61–'63; Am. Inst. of Int. Designers, Nat. Soc. of Int. Designers (Edtl. Distinction Aw., '67), NHFL, Design Wtrs., Intl. (East Coast VP, '69); Univ. of Pa., BA, '60; b. Phila., Pa., 1939; p. Benjamin and May Lipsky Winig; h. Harold Lewin; res: 173 Ws. 78th St., N.Y., N.Y. 10024.

LEWIS, ALICE GENE SALE, Head Librn., Public Library, 450 Griffith Ave., Owensboro, Ky. 42301, '65–; Asst. Librn., Alice Lloyd Jr. Col., '64–'65; Head, Ref., Ky. State Lib. (Frankfort), '59–'64; Hosp. Librn. (Ft. Knox), '56–'58; ALA, Southeastern Lib. Assn., Ky. Lib. Assn., League of Wm. Voters; Univ. of Ky., AB, '49; MS (Lib. Sci.), '59; b. Morganfield, Ky., p. Herschel and Ruth Galbraith Sale; h. Ralph Lewis; c. Mrs. George Siewers, Lucinda; res: 1312 Parrish Ave., Owensboro, Ky. 42301.

LEWIS, ANN, Sr. Copywtr., Grey Advertising, 777 Third Ave., N.Y., N.Y. 10017; Wtr.; Sr. Wtr., Reach McClinton Inc.; Sr. Wtr., Wesley Assocs.; Artist, Wtr., J. Kaufman & Assoc. (Wash., D.C.); Artist, Chgo. Tribune; Mills Col. (Cal.), Colo. Col., Art Inst. of Chgo.; b. Indpls., Ind.; p. Charles S. Jr. and Clara Hodge Lewis; res: 173 Riverside Dr., N.Y., N.Y. 10024.

LEWIS, ANN E., Owner, Publr., Ed., Georgia Magazine, Box 1047, Decatur, Ga. 30031, '57–; The Whitmire News, '49–'52; Country Corr. from Whitmire for daily nwsps.; free-lance hist., travel articles; NLAPW (Atlanta Br. Pres., '62–'63), Theta Sigma Phi (Atlanta Pfsnl. Chptr.), Atlanta Press Club, Pilot Club of Decatur; Cit., resolutions, Ga. Legislature Hist. Commn.; Atlanta Wtrs. Club Wtr. of the Yr., '64; Atlanta Wm. of the Yr. in Bus., '62; Ga. Wtrs. Assn. aw. for excellence, '68; Columbia Col., AB, '22; b. Clinton, S.C., 1903; p. Robert and Eleanor Beard Hatton; h. William W. Lewis; c. Robert S., Elisabeth (Mrs. Robert S. Crutchfield), Eleanor (Mrs. Robert J. Corley), Ann H., William W., Jr.; res: 605 Ridgecrest Rd., N.E., Atlanta, Ga. 30307.

LEWIS, BETTY BLAKE, Co-ed., Co-publr., Proscenium Publications, (Theatre Critics' Reviews, '63–; Theatre Information Bulletin, '44–); 4 Park Ave., N.Y., N.Y. Edtl. Dept., Newsweek, '43–'44; Co-Auth: "Broadway—Inside The Last Decade" ('54), "The Keys to Broadway" ('51); Drama Desk, Outer Critics' Circle (Treas., '61–); Columbia Univ., '41–'42; b. N.Y.C.; p. Frederic and Violet Fisher Gibbs; h. Glyn Lewis; res: 61 Jane St., N.Y., N.Y. 10014.

LEWIS, BETTY JESSEL, VP, Co-prodr., "The Wondrous World of Betty and Bob," nat. synd., 23 Barry Dr., Glen Cove, N.Y., '64–; Tchr., Cumbres (Dublin, N.H.), '69–; Publr., Suburban Mirror (Tucson, Ariz.), '61–'64; Edtl. Staff, '54–'61; Co-prodr., "Thru' the Looking Glass," KTVC, KOLD (Tucson, Ariz.), '61–'64; "Betty Jessel Show" (Providence, R.I.), '50; Auth., "Who Flung That Gauntlet?" ('68); OPC; Wash. Univ., '43; b. N.Y.C., 1922; p. Jack and Blanche August Jessel; h. Robert Lewis; c. Lauri, Diane; res: Dublin, N.H.

LEWIS, CAROLE SARA, Dir., Rights and Permissions, Dell Publishing Co., Inc., 750 Third Ave., N.Y., N.Y. 10017, '65–; Mng. Ed., The Dial Press, Inc., '63–'65; Asst. Ed., The Dial; Rights, Permission, '60–'63; Edtl. Asst., '58–'60; Rights, Permissions Ed., Julian Messner, div. of Simon and Schuster, '65; Doubleday & Co., Inc., '57–'58; Cornell Univ., BA, '57 (Phi Beta Kappa; Kappa Delta Epsilon); b. Bklyn., N.Y., 1935; p. Joseph and Ruth Feinsilber Lewis; h. Edward Stoddard; res: 210 E. 11th St., N.Y., N.Y. 10003.

LEWIS, CLAUDIA LOUISE, Wtr., specialist in children's literature, social anthropology emphasizing studies of children and families; '43–; Tchr., Children's Literature, Pubns. Cnslt., Bank St. Col.; Nat. Cncl. of Tchrs. of Eng., Am. Anthropological Assn., Assn. For Childhood Educ. Intl.; Reed Col., BA, '30; Univ. of Minn., MA, '43; Columbia Univ., PhD, '59; b. Corvallis, Ore., 1907; p. Claude and Marie Berry Lewis; res: 259 W. 11th St., N.Y., N.Y. 10014.

LEWIS, DIANE COPELAND, Wms. News Ed., Wichita Eagle and Beacon, 825 E. Douglas Ave., Wichita, Kan. 67202, '69–; Copy Ed., '68; PR Cnslt., Kan. Assn. For Mental Health, '68; PR Dir., YWCA, '65–'67; Public Info. Dir., St. Joseph Hosp., '62–'66; PR Asst., Wichita Un. Fund, '62–'65, '59–'60; News Bur. Dir., Wichita State Univ., '61, Reptr., Wichita Beacon, '59; Wichita Eagle, '56–'57; Theta Sigma Phi (Wichita Pfsnl. Club Pres., '68–'69), PRSA (Kan. Chptr. Pres., '67; Mid-West Reg. Secy., '67), NFPW (Bd. Mbr., '68–), Kan. Press Wm. (Bd. Mbr., '66–), Wichita Press Wm. (Pres., '65–'66); Volunteer Bur., Panel of Am. Wm.; Wichita State Univ., BA, '59 (Mortar Bd., Alumni Bd., '65–'68); b. Wichita, Kan., 1937; p. John and Winogene Lawhorn Copeland; h. Richard V. Lewis; res: 3903 E. Central Ave., Wichita, Kan. 67208.

LEWIS, DOROTHY MOORE, Pres., American Mothers Committee, Inc., Room 2226 Waldorf-Astoria, N.Y., N.Y. 10022, '63–; Bd. Mbr., 19 yrs.; Auth., bks. on bdcst., mag. articles; Dir., World Study on Wm. in Radio and TV, UNESCO, '59–'60; Composer, hymns and children's songs; Exec. Dir., UN Press Svc., '56–'59; Ed., UN News for Bdcstrs., '47–'56; Liaison Offcr., UN Off. of Pub. Info., '54–'56; Coordr., Am. Bdcsts. for UN, '48–'54; Coordr. of Listener Activity, NAB, '42–'47; Founder, Radio Cncl. on Children's Programs, '39–'42; Mgr., radio sta., '29; Nat. Cncl. of Wm. U.S.A. (Wm. of Conscience Aw., '68), Intl. Assn. of WRT (Pres., '56; Hon. Pres., '64–), AWRT (Hon. Life Mbr., '52–), AWNY (VP, '43–'45), Wm. Un. for UN (Pres.), George Peabody Aws. Commn. 30 yrs., Comm. on Wm. in PR (Past Pres., Advisory Bd.), Theta Sigma Phi Wm. of Achiev., '52, N.Y. State BPW Wm. of Yr., '56, Wms. Mdse. Cnsl. Svc., numerous other orgs., on many bds., aws.; Univ. of Vt., Univ. of Colo.; b. Albany, N.Y., 1896; p. Howard and Annie Hoyt Moore; h. Edwin C. Lewis; c. Charlotte (Mrs. Thomas A. Gage), Barbara (Mrs. Dean M. Schmitter, dec.); res: 414 E. 52nd St., Apt. 4B, N.Y., N.Y. 10022, and Winnisquam, N.H.

LEWIS, DOROTHY ROE, Asst. Prof. of Jnlsm., School of Journalism, University of Missouri, Columbia, Mo. 65201, '64–; Colmst., Chgo. Tribune–N.Y. News Synd., '60–; Gen. Wms. Ed., AP (N.Y.C.), '41–'60; Asst. Wms. Ed., King Features Synd., '40; Nat. Assigt., INS, '30–'37; Auth., "The Trouble with Women Is Men" (Prentice-Hall, '60); Co-auth., "Talking Through My Hats," (Coward McCann), and "Lilly Dache's Glamour Book" (Lippincott); Collaborator and Ghost Wtr. for numerous celebrity bks. in wms. field; Theta Sigma Phi, Kappa Tau Alpha, ZONTA Nwspwm. of the Yr. ('57); Univ. of Mo., BJ, '24 (Medal Aw. for Distg. Svc. in Jnlsm., '58); b. Alba, Mo.; p. Daniel and Anna Tibbs Roe; h. John B. Lewis; c. Mrs. P. Turner, Mrs. Charles J. Schreiber; res: 2806 W. Rollins Rd., Columbia, Mo. 65201.

LEWIS, ELOISE C., Librn., Ross Roy, Inc., 2751 E. Jefferson Avenue, Detroit, Mich. 48207, '57–; Special Libs. Assn.; b. Iron River, Mich., 1919; p. Edwin and Mary Cooper Stohl; c. Robert Charles Lewis; res: 4164 Lakewood, Detroit, Mich., 48215.

LEWIS, FLORA, Colmst., Newsday Syndicate, Stewart Ave., Garden City, N.Y. 11530, '67–; Washington Post, '57–'66; McGraw-Hill, '55; Free-lance; The Observer, The Econst., France-soir, and others, '47–'54; AP, '42–'46; OPC (best fgn. mag. reporting, '56; best fgn. news interpretation, '60), Golden Slipper Club Wm. of the Yr., '68; U.C.L.A., BA, '41 (summa cum laude); Columbia Sch. of Jnlsm., MS, '42; b. L.A., Cal.; p. Benjamin and Pauline Kallin Lewis; h. Sydney Gruson; c. Kerry Gruson, Sheila Gruson, Lindsey Gruson.

LEWIS, FRANCES H., Dir. of PR, Beaver College, Easton and Church Rds., Glenside, Pa. 19038, '51–; Asst. Dir., '48–'51; Reptr., Times Chronicle, '44–'48; Beaver Col. Fac. Club (Pres., '58–'59); Suburban PR Club (Pres., '60–'61); AAUW; York Rd. Area Commty.

Cncl. (Dir., Pres., '69–'70); ACPRA (Special Merit Cert., '64); PRSA; Beaver Col. Alumnae Assn. (First VP, '62–'64, Second VP, '58–'60); Dic. of Intl. Biog., Who's Who of Am. Wm., Who's Who in the East, Who's Who in PR, Who's Who in Educ.; Beaver Col., BA, '39; b. Montclair, N.J.; p. Walter and Esther Harman Lewis; res: 721 Fairfield Rd., Glenside, Pa. 19038.

LEWIS, JACQUELINE BAILEY, Sch. Sec. Ed., Herald-Mail Publishing Co., 25 Summit Ave., Hagerstown, Md. 21740, '67–; b. Hagerstown, Md., 1947; p. David C. and Vivian Stouffer Van Voorhis; h. David Lewis; res: 110 S. Main St., Boonsboro, Md. 21713.

LEWIS, JANE WARING, Acc. Supvsr., Chirurg & Cairns, Inc., 641 Lexington Ave., N.Y., N.Y. 10022, '61–; AE, Chester Gore Adv., '57–'60; Art Dir., '55–'57; Syracuse Univ., BFA, '52; b. Metuchen, N.J., 1931; p. Charles and Marybelle Tribble Waring; h. Daniel Lewis; c. Daniel T.; res: 34 Gramercy Park, N.Y., N.Y. 10003.

LEWIS, JANET, Crtv. Writing Lectr., Stanford University, Stanford, Cal., '69–; '60–'67; Auth., six novels, incl. "The Trial of Soren Quist" ('47; S.F. Commonwealth Club Gold Medal); Shelley Mem. Aw. for poems, '24–'44, '47; Guggenheim Fellow, '50–'51; Lewis Inst., AA, '18; Univ. of Chgo., PhB, '20; b. Chgo., Ill., 1899; p. Edwin and Elizabeth Taylor Lewis; h. Yvor Winters; c. Mrs. Donald E. Thompson, Daniel L.; res: 143 W. Portola Ave., Los Altos, Cal. 94022.

LEWIS, LUCIA (Elizabeth Hoolihan Larkin), Wtr., Bdcstr., radio travel shows, news programs for wm.; Wtr., Bdcstr., "Radio Answer Series" (Clearwater, Fla.), '68–'69; Wtr., Bargain Corner Show, WTAN, '66–'69; AE, Comml. Rep., Copywtr., WTAN-AM/FM, '66–'69; radio travel show, '65–'67; Bdcstr., Progs., commls. (Evanston, Ill.), '56–'61; Travel Cnslt., N. Shore, travel lects., Midw., '55–'64; travel show, "Faraway Places with Elizabeth H. Larkin," '55; N. Shore Rep., Student Travel Cnslr., Northwestern Univ., for Olson Campus Tours, '51–'54; Pilot Club, Nomad Club, Edgewater Drama Club of Chgo., AWRT; Northwestern Univ., Sch. of Speech; b. Dayton, Oh.; p. Clifton and Mabel Rice Hoolihan; h. (div.); c. Mrs. Charles Pearson, Sheila Larkin; res: 1598 S. Haven St., Clearwater, Fla. 33516.

LEWIS, MARGUERITE GARBER, Prodr. and Moderator, "Parents in Action" TV show; Tchr. (Oh.), '33–'37; Nat. Fedn. of Motion Pic. Cncls. (Nat. Pres., '65–'67), AAUW, Am. Field Svc., Am. Film Festival; Col. of Wooster, AB (Speech, Eng.); Univ. of Mich., MA (Speech); b. Richland County, Oh., 1911; p. Horatio and Sylvia Swank Garber; h. Leroy Lewis; c. Sylvia (Mrs. David Rauppius), Thomas, David, Catherine, Linda; res: 3521 Suffolk Dr., Fort Worth, Tex. 76109.

LEWIS, MAXINE WILSON (pseud: Mary Milo), Health Ed., Beauty Ed., Family Circle, 488 Madison

Ave., N.Y., N.Y. 10022, '50–; Fiction Ed.; Auth., "The Magic Key to Successful Writing" (Prentice-Hall, '55), Family Circle beauty bk.; Co-auth., two others; Cosmetic Career Wm. (Bd. of Governors, '67), N.Y. Acad. of Scis.; Univ. of Cal.; b. Unalaska, Alaska; p. Will and Alma Anderson Wilson; h. Alfred Lewis (div., dec.); res: Divinity Hill, Shelter Island Heights, N.Y. 11965.

LEWIS, NAOMI, Free-lance Actress, '45–; major radio and TV shows, title role and two others daily on "Rootie Kazootie Clubs" (NBC-TV, ABC-TV, '51–'56); children's records (RCA Victor, Golden Records), comedy record albums (Crescendo, Capitol, Tower), numerous radio and TV commls.; AFTRA, SAG, NARAS, NATAS, Pacific Pioneers Bdcstrs.; Special Cit., Am. TV Commls. May Festival on-Camera Spokeswm. ('64); Recognition Performance Aw., May Am. TV and Radio Commls. ('68); numerous radio aws. for commls.; "Library of Achievers" interviews accepted in Rogers and Hammerstein Library of Recorded Sound, Lincoln Center; Middlesex Jr. Col.; b. N.Y.C.; p. Sander and Fannie Itzkowitz Lippman; h. Richard Mack (dec.); c. Daniel, Jonathan; res: 11628 Chenault St., L.A., Cal. 90049.

LEWIS, REBECCA AINES, PR Svcs. Dir., Mid-Continent Council of Girl Scouts, Inc., 1114 Grand Ave., Kansas City, Mo. 64106, '61–; Staff, The Independent, '53–'62; Crtv. Asst., "Happy Home," KMBC-TV, '55–'61; PRSA (Kansas City Chptr. Bd., '70–), AFTRA, AWRT (Kansas City Chptr. Pres., '61), Assn. of Girl Scout Pfsnl. Workers (Nat. Bd.), PR Soc. of Kan. City (Treas.-Secy., '68), Radio-TV Cncl. of Gtr. Kan. City (Past Pres.); Who's Who of Am. Wm., Marquis Biog. Lib. Soc., (Advisory Mbr., '69); Kan. City Jr. Col., AA, '35; Kansas Univ., BA, '37; b. Kan. City, Mo., 1916; p. Lewis and Chloe Mays Aines; h. Charles Emmit Lewis, Jr.; c. Bettina Anne, Laurie Jane; res: 406 Homestead Dr., Shawnee Mission, Kan. 66208.

LEWIS, VIVIAN OPPENHEIM, Paris Corr., London Sunday Times, Thomson Newspapers, 200 Grey's Inn Rd., London, England, '67–; Paris Corr., The Economist, '66–'67; Brussels Corr., Business Week, '65–'66; Radcliffe Col., BA, '62 (magna cum laude); Univ. of Cal., MA, '63; b. N.Y.C., 1941; p. Julius and Erna Oppenheim; h. Paul Lewis; c. Malia Rachel, Raphael Ario; res: 16 Rue Henri Barbusse, Paris 5, France.

LI, LORETTA MAE JUN, Art Dir., Basic Books, Inc., 404 Park Ave., S., N.Y., N.Y. 10016, '62–; Graphic Designer, '54–'62; Prod. Asst., Viking Press, '53–'54; Graphic Arts U.S.A. Exhibit (Moscow, U.S.S.R.), '63; AIGA aw., 50 best-designed bks. of yr., '60, '67; Turck and Renfeld aw., best bk. jacket of yr., '62, '65–'66; Bravo aw., '68; Oberlin Col., BA, '52; b. Honolulu, Hi., 1931; p. Min Hin and Minnie Chan Li; res: 342 E. 15th St., Apt. 3B, N.Y., N.Y. 10003.

LIBBEY, FLORENCE ELIZABETH, Assoc. Prof., Assoc. Librn., Colby College, Waterville, Me. 04901, '56–;

Instr., Lib. Sci. Workshop, Summers, '61–'64; Asst. Librn., Instr. of Bibliography, '45–'47; Librn., Farmington (Me.) State Tchrs. Col., '42–'45; Dir., Bur. of Lib. Ext. State Lib. (Augusta), '30–'42; Asst. Dir., Sch. Librns. Workshop, Univ. of Me., Summer, '50; Ed., Wtr., pfsnl. pubns.; Lib. assns., Alpha Delta Pi, Delta Kappa Gamma, AAUW, AAUP; Dir. of Am. Scholars; Who's Who in Lib. Svc.; Who's Who of Am. Wm.; Colby Col., AB, '29; Columbia, BS-LS, '30; MS-LS, '66; Alliance Francaise (Paris), '68; b. Augusta, Me., 1906; p. Benjamin F. and Anne E. Young Libbey; res: 45 Winter St., Waterville, Me. 04901.

LIBERMAN, DORIS GORDON, Ed., Replay Publications, Inc., 7036 Clayton Ave., St. Louis, Mo. 63117, '69–; The Mdsng. Group, '65–; Publ. new amateur sports mag., May 28, '69–; Asst. News Dir., KLPM (Minot, N.D.); Ed., Strictly Personnel and Supervisor's Digest, USAF civilian pubns., Wright Patterson AFB; Theta Sigma Phi, Greater St. Louis Bk. Fair, Cncl. of Jewish Wm. Bul. (St. Louis Sec., Past Ed.); Univ. of Mo., BJ, '53 (Dean's List); b. Minot, N.D., 1931; p. Sol and Fanny Sgutt Gordon; h. Pierce Liberman; c. Keith, Richard, Nancy; res: 13 Dromara Rd., St. Louis, Mo. 63124.

LIBMAN, MYRNA, Ed., American Baby Publishing Co., 10 E. 52nd St., N.Y., N.Y. 10022, '68–; Fashion Reptr. and Cnslt., Tobe Assocs., '66–'67; Assoc. Ed., Sls-Mktng. Today, '66; News and Feature Ed., Hotel Mgt. Rev., '62–'65; Ed., nwsltr. of Revitalization Corps; Bklyn. Col., '55–'57.

LICHT, JOYCE FERRY, AE, DeGarmo, McCaffery, Inc., 605 Third Ave., N.Y., N.Y. '65–; Daniel & Charles, '56–'65; Dowd, Redfield, Johnstone; Bambergers; Stern's; Tobe-Coburn Sch.; b. N.Y.C.; h. Morris Licht; c. Christopher Claypool, Kathleen Claypool, Lise Claypool; res: 250 W. 94th St., N.Y., N.Y. 10025.

LICHTENSTEIN, GRACE ROSENTHAL, Reptr., New York Times, 229 W. 43rd St., N.Y., N.Y. 10036, '70–; Radio News Script Wtr., '68–'70; Prom. Wtr., '66–'68; Prom. Wtr., R. R. Bowker Co., '65–'66; Copywtr., Cambridge Univ. Press, '62–'64; numerous mag. articles incl. New York, Village Voice, Christian Science Monitor; Nwsp. Guild; Bklyn. Col., AB, '62 (Phi Beta Kappa, magna cum laude); b. Bklyn., N.Y., 1941; p. Alvin and Rose Smith Rosenthal; h. Stephen Lichtenstein; res: 61 Jane St., N.Y., N.Y. 10014.

LIDDELL, ALICE M., VP, Media Dir., Kenyon & Eckhardt, Inc., 535 Boylston St., Boston, Mass. 02116, '68–; Media Dir., '56–'68; VP, Media Dir., Ingalls-Miniter Co., '48–'56; Media Asst., Loudon Adv., '44–'48; Bdcst. Exec. Club of New Eng. (Secy., '58; Treas., '59; VP, '61), New Eng. Media Evaluators Assn. (Secy.-Treas., '63); Simmons Col., Assoc. in Adv., '59–'62; b. Milton, Mass., 1923; p. David and Jessie Anderson Liddell; res: 294 Beacon St., Boston, Mass. 02116.

LIEBELER, DOLORES OLSON, Staff Wtr. and Youth

Page Ed., South Bend Tribune, 223 W. Colfax, South Bend, Ind. 46626, '62–; Wtr., new math mag.,*Modern Math for Parents,* published by Tribune for distrb. and sls. to cols., used by govt. teaching prog.; numerous articles to nwsps.; Ed., Red Cross nwsp., Nat. Red Cross Camp, '45; South Bend Press Club, Am. Contract Bridge League, PTA (Past Pres.), Univ. of Minn., '45–'47; b. Mpls., Minn., 1926; p. Cecil and Esther Pederson Olson; h. John R. Liebeler; c. John R., Jr., Carol, Nancy, Joanne; res: 1816 Hass Dr., South Bend, Ind. 46635.

LIEBERS, RUTH LAMPERT, Auth., non-fiction for tchrs., six easy-to-read fiction bks. for children; Contrbr., Bk. of Knowledge, '66, Humpty Dumpty's Magazine, '58–; Tchr., Ed., Scholastic Pubns. "Newstime," '55–'58; Tchr., Bd. of Educ., '38–'52; Resource Cnslt., Elementary Sch. Study, '52–'62; Cnslt., Bank St. Col. of Educ., '62–; N.Y.U., Hunter, City Col., Bank St. Col.; b. N.Y.C., 1910; p. Samuel and Lena Langman Lampert; h. Arthur Liebers; res: Halsey Lane, Remsenburg, N.Y. 11960.

LIEPMAN, RUTH, Lit. Agt., Niederdopher 43, Zurich, Switzerland 8001; started lit. agcy. with husband (Hamburg), '48; journalistic work; specialized, intl. private law, copyright law; educ: Univ. Hamburg, Dr., '34; Univs. Berlin, Amsterdam, Zurich; studied law; b. Polch, Germany, 1909; p. Dr. Theo and Hilde Stern Lilienstein; h. Heinz Liepman (dec.).

LIFTON, BETTY JEAN KIRSCHNER, Auth., "The One-Legged Ghost" (Jr. Lit. Guild Selection, '68; Graphic Design Aw., '68), 11 other children's bks. (Atheneum Publrs., '62–'69; W. W. Norton, '62–'69; William Morrow, '56–'62); plays prod. at Provincetown (Mass.) Playhouse, Act IV, Fisherman's Players (Wellfleet); two movies, "A Thousand Cranes" (doc. of children of Hiroshima), and "The Unborn"; articles in Mademoiselle, N.Y. Times Magazine; Reptr., Tokyo Evening News, '52–'56; Prod. Asst., Proctor Prods., '51–'52; Script Wtr., Goodson Todman, '50–'51; Auths. Guild, Tokyo Press Club, New Haven Festival of the Arts Aws. ('67, '68), Herald Tribune "Kap the Kappa" Aw. ('60); Barnard Col., BA, '48; h. Robert Jay Lifton; c. Karen, Kenneth; res: Rimmon Rd., Woodbridge, Conn. 06525.

LILLARD, MADELINE BERG, Ed., Spot News, Finishes First, E.I. du Pont de Nemours & Co., Inc., '36–'46; Maryland and Prince Georges County Hist. Socs., Life Member, Women's Committee of the Washington National Symphony, Who's Who of Am. Wm., Dic. of Intl. Biog.; Bucknell Univ., BA, '35; b. Wilmington, Del., 1913; p. Frederick and Isabella Strebb Berg; h. John F. Lillard, Jr.; c. John III, Deborah B.; res: 3904 Calverton Dr., College Heights Estates, Hyattsville, Md. 20782.

LILLARD, PATRICIA LOUISE, Ed., Intercom, Meharry Medical College, 1005 18th Ave. N., Nashville, Tenn. 37208, '66–; Young Adult Chptr., Negro Bus. and Prof. Wm.; Tenn. A & I State Univ., Univ. of Tenn. (currently); b. Nashville, Tenn., 1948; p. Mrs. Mary E. Lillard; h. William Phillips; c. William F. Phillips, Jr.; res: 548-A 17th Ave. N., Nashville, Tenn. 37203.

LINCOLN, MARJORIE FALLS, Lib. Dir., Wheaton Public Library, 225 N. Cross St., Wheaton, Ill. 60187, '50–; Univ. of Chgo. Lib., '48–'50; Des Moines (Ia.) Public Lib., '39–'41; State Univ. of Ia. Lib., '36–'38; Lib. Admrs. Conf. of Northern Ill. (Secy.-Treas., '61–'62), W. Suburban Lib. Club (Pres., '60–'61), Ill. Lib. Assn. (Chmn., Pub. Libs., '69–'70), ALA, AAUW, Wheaton Drama Club; Who's Who of Am. Wm.; Who's Who in the Midwest; Who's Who in Lib. Svc.; State Univ. of Ia., BA, '37 (cum laude; Phi Beta Kappa); Univ. of Chgo., BLS, '48; b. Des Moines, Ia.; h. S. A. Lincoln.

LINCOLN, VICTORIA, Wtr., Fiction, Non-Fiction; Auth: "A Private Disgrace: Lizzie Borden by Daylight" (MWA Edgar Aw., '67), "Out From Eden," "A Dangerous Innocence," "February Hill," others; numerous mag. articles, short stories; many works translated into six langs. and Braille; Auths. League, Wtrs. Guild, PEN; p. Jonathan Thayer and Louise Cobb Lincoln; h. Victor Lowe; c. Penelope (Mrs. Donald McKay), Thomas Lowe, Louise (Mrs. Robert Kittredge); res: 3947 Cloverhill Rd., Balt., Md. 21218.

LIND, MELVA, Dean of Students, Prof. of French, Gustavus Adolphus College, St. Peter, Minn. 56082, '53–; Dean of Wm., Prof. of French, Miami Univ. (Oxford, Oh.), '50–'53; Assoc. in Higher Educ., AAUW (Wash., D.C.), '48–'50; Asst. Prof., Mt. Holyoke Col., '36–'48, Dir., French Lang. House, '43–'48; Dept. of French, Smith Col., '29–'36; Auth., bk. on French poetry, numerous articles; Theta Sigma Phi (Nat. VP; Reg. Dir.), Alliance Francaise of Minn. (Pres.), numerous educ., hist. wmn. orgs.; French govt. hon., Palmes Academiques; Univ. of Minn., BA, '25; MA (Pers. Psych.), '43; Univ. of Lyon, France, MA, '26; Sorbonne, Doctorate, '29; MacPhail Sch., M Music, '37; res: 3104 45th Ave. S., Mpls., Minn. 55406.

LINDAHL, LORRAINE GRIFFITH, Manuscript Ed., Ausberg Publishing House, 426 S. Fifth St., Mnpls., Minn. 55415, '62–; Edtl. Div., '60–; Ed., Gould Battery News (St. Paul, Minn.), '45–'46; Edtl. and News Wtr., Plentywood (Mont.) Herald, '40–'42; Proofreader, Williston (N.D.) Daily Herald, '39–'40; Lib. Asst., James Memorial Lib., '34–'40; Theta Sigma Phi, Mont. State Univ., BA (jnlsm., cum laude) '45; b. Cinn., Oh., 1921; p. Edward and Emma Borger Griffith; h. Murlin S. Lindahl; c. David Mark, Marcia Gail, Sandra Jean; res: 4904 Park Ave. S., Mpls., Minn. 55417.

LINDEMANN, REGINA, Design and Pubns. Mgr., Benjamin Moore & Co., 548 Fifth Ave., N.Y., N.Y. 10036, '69–; Asst. Adv. Mgr., '55–'69; Dir. of Decorating Dept., '45–'55; Interior Decorator, Chgo. Br.

LINDEN, KATHRYN BERTHA, Dir., ANA-NLN Film

Service, American Nurses Association and National League for Nursing, 10 Columbus Circle, N.Y., N.Y. 10019, '53–; established film svc., incl. prod. and distrb. film lib., '53, videotape lib., '68; Exec. Prod., Cnslt., three filmstrips, 21 16mm. films, '54–'69; Project Dir., Audio Visual Survey in Nursing, '68–'70; Dir., Audio Visual Educ., East and West Assn., '44–'46; Audio Visual Cnslt; Wtr., articles in nursing, film pubns.; Audiovisual Conf. of Med. and Allied Scis. (VP, '59; Chmn., '60–'62); Am. Film Festival, Film Cncl. (Bd. Mbr., Corr. Secy., '60–'67); Who's Who of Am. Wm.; Dic. of Intl. Biog.; Blue Bk. (London); Tarknath Das Fndn. (Bd. of Dirs. and Exec. Secy.); Columbia Univ., BS (Hist. of Fine Arts), '53 (hons.; Alumni Assn. Bd. of Dirs.: Corr. Secy., '69–'70; Secy., '60–'63); Columbia Univ. Tchrs. Col., MA (Social Psych.), '56; b. Bklyn., N.Y., 1905; p. Robert and Anna Jaehns Linden; res: 504 W. 110th St., N.Y., N.Y. 10025.

LINDEN, PATRICIA (Patricia Fink Nutting), Ed., Epicure, 180 Beacon St., Boston, Mass. 02116, '68–; Adv. Cnsl., Imagination Inc., '62–; Boston Contrb. Ed., Art Direction Magazine, '68–'70; ghost wtr., speeches and articles; cnslt., crtv. and copy dir., various N.E. adv. agcys., '68–'70; Colmst., "The Soft Cell" monthly, N.E. Adv. Wk., '67–'69; Lectr., Northeastern Univ., '68; Copywtr., AE, Arnold & Co., '58–'62; AE, radio WILD, '58; Librn., Reilly Brown & Tapply, '57–'58; photogr's. asst., '57–'58; fashion model, '56–'57; Art Dirs. Club of Boston (Secy., '69–'70; aws., '57–); Ad Club of Boston ('62–'69; 1st wm. nominated Ad Man of Yr., Jr. Ad Club), Hatch Aws. for excellence in adv., various other aws. and orgs.; Leland Powers Sch. of Radio and Drama, '44; Cambridge Jr. Col., '45; Boston Univ. ext.; '46–'50; b. Boston, Mass., 1926; p. Nathan and Estelle Kaufman Fink; h. Philip Nutting; c. Peter Linden.

LINDER, HELEN McDADE, Wms. News Ed., The Dispatch, E. First Ave., Lexington, N.C. 27292; Wms. Program Dir., Traf. Coordr., WBUY, five yrs.; h. Dozier Linder; c. Larry C., Martha L., Ellen M.; res: 1220 Greensboro St., Lexington, N.C. 27292.

LINDER, JOANN JORDAN, Reg. Ed., TV Guide Magazine, Triangle Publications, 899 Logan St. Suite 305, Denver, Colo. 80203, '60–; Asst. Reg. Ed. (Kan. City, Mo.), '59–'60; Okla. Edition, '58–'59; Ed., Kan. State Edition, '56–'58; AWRT; Independence (Kan.) Commty. Col.; Univ. of Kan.; b. Neodesha, Kan.; p. Edwin L. and Eula E. Anderson Jordan; h. Gene Linder; res: 800 Washington, Denver, Colo. 80203.

LINDLOFF, JUDY SHORT, AE, James Jeffords Associates, 2040 W. Wisconsin, Milw., Wis. 53217, '69–; "Miss Alabama," '64; Finalist, "Miss America Pageant"; Houston Baptist Col., BME; b. Birmingham, Ala., 1944; h. Darol Lindloff.

LINDMANN, MARCIA RICE, VP, The Matthews Agency, Inc., 610 W. 25th St., Norfolk, Va. 23517, '62–;

Eng. Tchr., Old Dominion Col., '53–'58; Tidewater Arts Cncl. (PR Dir.) AAUW (Norfolk Chptr. Bd. of Dirs.), Norfolk C. of C., Linguistic Soc. of Am., Univ. of N.C., BA, MA, '53; b. Huntington, W. Va, 1931; p. Lloyd and Beatrice Odell Rice; h. Charles J. Lindemann; c. Kirstine, Anna Margrethe, Carla; res: 5201 Studeley Ave., Norfolk, Va. 23508.

LINDSAY, JUNE McKEE, Coordr., Being Unlimited, 2339 S. Circle Dr., Ann Arbor, Mich. 48103, '57–; rsch., writing, edtl. svcs., numerous commty., univ., ethnic orgs.; special issues of "The History of the Negro in Michigan," Michigan Challenge mag., '68–'69; The Univ. Record Quarterly ('64–'66); "50 Years of Curricular Theatre at the Univ. of Mich." ('65); program for prod. of "Langston Hughes Looks at Dark America" ('68–'69); Coordr., McKee Prods., WXYZ-TV ABC (Detroit), '51–'56; various orgs., aws.; Bethany Col., '38–'39; Univ. of Mich., BA (Speech), '43 (hons.); b. Detroit, Mich., 1920; p. Maitland and Josephine Campbell McKee; h. Powell Lindsay; c. Kristi Costa-McKee.

LINER, REBA WATKINS, Ed., Mercantile National Bank, Box 5415, Dallas, Tex. 75222, '56–; Soc. Ed., Dallas Times Herald, '46–'52; Dallas IEA, ICIE; b. Farmersville, Tex. 1928; p. Allen and Ivy Mankins Watkins; h. div.; c. Michael, Elaine; res: 5730 Kenwood, Dallas, Tex. 75206.

LING, MONA, Commtns. Cnslt., Free-lance, 1029 Vermont Ave., N.W., Wash., D.C. 20005, '54–; designed program for bus., industry; Tchr., bus., industry, 15 yrs.; work in many areas, U.S., Can.; Auth., bks. for bus., industry; Am. Soc. for Training and Dev., Intl. Platform Assn. (Past Pres., 12 Western states), NLAPW, Intl. Soc. for Gen. Semantics, Soroptimist Club; "The Golden Apple," Cal., for outstanding work in clubs; Univ. of Cinn.; Univ. of Mich.; Univ. of Southern Cal.

LININGTON, B. ELIZABETH, (pseuds: Dell Shannon, Lesley Egan, Anne Blaisdell), Novelist: "The Long Watch" (Gold Medal Aw., Cal. Commonwealth Club, '56), "Knave of Hearts" (Runner-up for Best Mystery, '62), detective-novels; John Birch Soc.; Glendale Col.; b. Aurora, Ill., 1921; p. Byron G. and Ruth Biggam Linington; res: 721 South St., Glendale, Cal. 91202.

LINK, MARILYN CALMES, Special Asst., PR, Mohawk Airlines, 80 E. 42nd St., N.Y., N.Y. 10017, '61–; Adm. Asst., Gen. Precision Equipment Corp., '57–'61; Collaborator, Smithsonian Inst., Nat. Air Museum, '54–'58; Instr., Univ. of Neb., '51–'53; Tchr., '49–'51; Contrb. Ed., Flying mag., '64–; Aviation/Space Wtrs. Assn., Nat. Pilots Assn., Nat. Aviation Educ. Cncl.; Univ. Aviation Assn. aw., '62; Wms. Intl. Assn. of Aeronautics aw., '65; Syracuse Univ., N.Y.U., BS (Educ.), '46; Univ. of Ill., MS (Educ.), '49; b. Glendale, Cal., 1924; p. Edwin and Marie Calmes Link; res: 110 E. 57th St., N.Y., N.Y. 10022.

LINK, MARION CLAYTON, Free-lance Wtr.; Reptr., Binghamton Evening Press, '29–'31; Auth., "Sea Diver, a Quest for History Under the Sea" (Rinehart & Co., '59); Theta Sigma Phi, ZONTA, Soc. of Wm. Geographers, WNBA; Syracuse Univ., BS, '29 (Phi Kappa Phi); b. Ilion, N.Y.; p. Floyd and Elma Gray Clayton; h. Edwin A. Link; c. William M., Edwin C.; res: 10 Avon Rd., Binghamton, N.Y. 13905.

LINN, ANN EMBREY, Acc. Supvsr., Reach, McClinton & Co., 505 Park Ave., N.Y., N.Y. 10022; h. William Linn.

LINN, JANICE MELLINGER, Free-lance Wtr., Colmst., Cinn. Enquirer, '65–'68; Food Ed., '58–'61; Home Econst., Procter & Gamble Co., '55–'58; Theta Sigma Phi, Omicron Nu, Phi Upsilon Omicron; Ia. State Univ., BS, '55 (Mortar Bd.); b. Springfield, Oh., 1933; p. Flenner and Janice Kauffman Mellinger; h. Alan Linn; c. Louis C., Flenner M., Rachel E.; res: 195 Cleveland Dr., Croton-on-Hudson, N.Y. 10520.

LIPMAN, JEAN, Ed., Art in America, 635 Madison Ave., N.Y., N.Y.; Auth., Lectr., Collector, early, contemporary Am. art; six bks., Am. folk art field; articles in nat., art mags.; b. N.Y.C.; h. Howard Lipman.

LIPPINCOTT, SARAH LEE, Rsch. Assoc., Lectr., Sproul Observatory, Swarthmore College, Swarthmore, Pa. 19081, '61–; Rsch. Assoc., '50–; Visiting Prof., Am. Astronomical Soc., '60–; Cnslt., AAAS Commn. on Sci. Educ., elementary sch. curriculum, '65; Participant, NATO summer course on Galactic Structure (Nijenrode, Netherlands), '60; Tenth Gen. Astronomical Un. (Moscow, U.S.S.R.), '58; French Solar Eclipse Expedition Mbr., Oland, Sweden, '54; Fulbright, Kovalenko Fellowships, Paris Observatory, '53–'54; Co-auth: "Point to the Stars" (McGraw-Hill, '63; Revsd., '67), "Philadelphia, the Unexpected City" (Doubleday, '65), articles in popular mags.; Kappa Kappa Gamma, Sigma XI (Swarthmore Chptr. Pres., '59–'60; VP, '59; Secy.-Treas., '68–); Univ. of Pa., BA, '42; Swarthmore Col., MA, '50; b. Phila., Pa., 1920; p. George and Sarah Evans Lippincott; res: 510 Elm Ave., Swarthmore, Pa. 19081.

LIPPMAN, ADELE THIER, Secy.-Treas., Lippman Advertising Association, Inc., 520 Genesee Bldg., 1 Genesee St., Buffalo, N.Y. 14202, '48–; Nat. Cncl. of Jewish Wm., B'nai Brith, Buffalo Hadassah; b. Bklyn., N.Y., 1919; p. Jacob and Bertha Heller Thier; h. Albert Lippman (dec.); c. Wayne, Marc; res: 735 Parkside Ave., Buffalo, N.Y. 14216.

LIPSCOMB, AUDRE LOFLAND, Cont. Dir., KCBD-TV, 5600 Ave. A, Lubbock, Tex. 79408, '56–; Copywtr: KCBD-Radio, '53–'56, KLYN-Radio, Amarillo, '50–'53, KFDA-Radio, '39–'42; Co-auth., "Radio and Television Continuity Writing" (Pitman Publ. Corp., N.Y.C., '62); Theta Sigma Phi, AWRT (Lubbock Chptr. VP, '68–'69); Tex. Tech. Univ., '36–'37; h. Lloyd Lipscomb; res: 2116 55th, Lubbock, Tex. 79412.

LIST, CLAIRE, Asst. Prog. Offcr., The Ford Foundation, 320 E. 43rd St., N.Y., N.Y. '67–; Project Specialist, '66–'67; Rsch., Prom., Harper-Atlantic Sls., '65–'66; Copy Rsch. Mgr., D-F-S, '60–'65; Rsch. Analyst, Benton & Bowles, '59–'60; Adv., Rsch., Tatham-Laird (Chgo., Ill.), '54–'60; Am. Econ. Assn., NAEB, NEA; Smith Col., BA (Eng.), '54; N.Y.U., MBA (Econs.), '66; b. Rochester, N.Y., 1932; p. Stuart and Claire Wrightson List; res: 444 E. 82nd St., N.Y., N.Y. 10028.

LIST, ILKA KATHERINE, Auth., juv. non-fiction; Sculptor; bks: "Let's Explore the Shore" (Obolensky, '62), "Tide Pools" (MacMillan, '70), "Questions and Answers About the Shore" (Scholastic Bks.), '70); Sculpture exhibit, Environment Gallery, private collections; Cornell Univ., '53–'54; Reed Col., '54–'55; St. Andrews Univ., '56–'57; b. Orange, N.J., 1935; p. Albert and Phyllis Carrington List; c. Natasha Katherine Maidoff, Jonah Asher Maidoff, Lee David Maidoff; res: 201 W. 89th St., N.Y., N.Y. 10024.

LISTER, ROSEMARY, City Ed., Reptr.-Photogr., Ottawa Herald, 104 S. Cedar, Ottawa, Kan. 66067, '64–; ed. three annual special nwsp. editions, '65–; Kan. Press Wm. (aws.), Kan. Press Assn.; Univ. of Kan., '63–'64; b. Ottawa, Kan., 1945; p. Robert and Dorothy Jackson Lister; res: RFD 2, Ottawa, Kan. 66067.

LITT, IRIS, Free-lance Wtr., Adv., Pubcty., '69–; Sr. Copywtr., Clinton E. Frank Adv., '64–'69; Copywtr: Benton & Bowles, '62–'64; Norman, Craig & Kummel, '61–'62; Ellington & Co., '59–'61; Doherty, Clifford, Steers & Shenfield, '58; N.Y. Mkt. Ed., The Writer, '50–'55; Assoc. Ed., Miss Am., '49; Contrbr., poetry mags.; PSA; Universidad de las Americas (Mexico City); Oh. State Univ., BA, '48 (with hons. in Eng.; Atlantic Monthly aw.); h. Gilbert Burris (dec.); c. Jonathan, Dean; res: 255 W. 11th St., N.Y., N.Y. 10014.

LITT, JOYCE SHIELA, Copy Chief, Sweet & Company Advertising Inc., 757 Third Ave., N.Y., N.Y. 10017, '67–; Copy Chief, Sweet & Artley, '65–'66; Copy Chief, Jamian Advertising & Publicity, '56–'64; NHFL; Cert. of Merit, N.Y. Art Dirs. Club, '69; N.Y.U., '47–'51 (Wm. of Yr.; Eng. Hons.; Wms. Hon. Soc.); b. N.Y.C., 1930; p. Samuel and Edna Lipshitz Litt; h. Nathan Lubow; c. Susan Marjorie, Andrew Michael; res: 465 West End Ave., N.Y., N.Y. 10024.

LITTIKEN, BARBARA L., Supvsr., Sls. Prom. Div., Mutual Trust Life Insurance Company, 77 S. Wacker Dr., Chgo., Ill. 60606, '67–; Ed., Edtl. Asst., '63; Sls. Prom. Asst., Ill. Mid.-Continent Ins. Co., '60–'63; Mail Adv. Club of Chgo. (Bd. of Dirs., '67–; Oscar aw. Judging Comm., '69), IEA of Chgo., Life Ins. Advs. Assn.; DePauw Univ., BA, '60.

LITTLE, MARY ENGLAND, Dir. of Caney Fork Regional Library, Caney Fork Regional Library Center, 209 Rhea St., Sparta, Tenn. 38583, '57–; Tchr., '38–'56; mag., nwsp. articles; radio programs; Mid-State Eng.

Cncl. (Pres., '50–'51), NEA (Life Mbr.), Nat. Lib. Week (State Dir., '62), Tenn. Congress of Parents and Tchrs. (Life Mbr.), Parents and Tchrs. of Tenn. (Bd. of Mgrs.; Treas., '69–'72), AAUW (State Bd., '67–'69; Cookeville Br. Pres., '67–'69), Delta Kappa Gamma (Alpha Delta Chptr. Pres., '68–'70); Tenn. Tech., BS (Eng.), '38 (Pres., Nat. Alumni Assn., '65–'67); George Peabody, MA (Eng.), '46; MA (Lib. Sci.), '57 (Phi Gamma Nu); b. Sparta, Tenn., 1916; p. Dallas and Althea Alcorn England; h. Joe Little; c. Joe, Jr., Bettye.

LITTLE, MARYBELLE CORDELL, Off. Mgr., The Hanford Sentinel, 418 W. Eighth, Hanford, Cal. 93230, '69–; Head Bkkeeper., Adv. and Legal Cl., Nat. Adv. Mgr., Radio Sta. Bkkeeper., '55–'69; h. J. Warren Little (div.).

LITTLEFIELD, KATHRYN, Media Mgr., Cole & Weber, Inc., 220 S.W. Morrison, Portland, Ore. 97204, '65–; Media Byr., '64–'65; U.S. Info. Svc. (India, France), '61–'63; Asst. to Pubcty. Dir., Gump's (S.F., Cal.), '58–'60; Stanislaus Adv., '56–'58; AWRT (VP, '66), Ore. Adv. Club; Univ. of Ore., BA, '51; b. Portland, Ore., 1929; p. Forrest and Isabelle Kidd Littlefield; res: 2235 S.W. Vista, Portland, Ore. 97201.

LITTLES, CLARICE REEVES, Soc. Ed., The Miami Times, 6530 Northwest 15th Ave., Miami, Fla. 33147, '65–; elementary tchr., Bd. of Public Instr. Dade County, 27-1/2 yrs.; Theta Sigma Phi; Dade County Assn. for Early Childhood Educ. (Pres., '53–'55; '59–'61), NEA, NRTA, FEA, ACEI (Life Mbr.), Assn. for Childhood Educ. Intl., AAUW (Miami Br.), active in ch. and civic orgs.; St. Augustine's Col., Raleigh, N.C., AB, '37; N.Y.U., MA, '48; b. Nassau, N.P. Bahamas, 1915; p. Henry and Rachel Cooper Reeves; h. William Littles; res: 1291 Northwest 68th St., Miami, Fla. 33147.

LITZEL, GENEVA DOROTHEA, Mng. Ed., Charles City Press, 100 N. Main, Charles City, Ia. 50616, '68–; Gen. News Ed., Photogr., '66–'68; News Ed., Photogr., Mason City Globe-Gazette, '60–'66; Accountant, Frank J. Enbusk Co., '56–'59; Reptr., Photgr., Clear Lake Mirror-Reporter, '51–'55; Reptr., Clear Lake Reporter, '46; Clear Lake Mirror, '45; Ia. Press Photgrs. Assn., C. of C., AP Mng. Eds. Assn., Charles City Art Assn., Floyd County Hist. Soc., Clear Lake VFW Aux. (Past Pres.), Charles City Wms. Club; Who's Who of Am. Wm.; Who's Who in the Midwest; b. Mason City, Ia., 1928; p. Jacob and Marie Guther Maassen; h. (div.); c. Phyllis Marie, Philip D., Lewis F.; res: 407 Fourth Ave., Charles City, Ia. 50616.

LIVINGSTON, CAROLE ROSE, Pubcty., Prod. Dir., Lyle Stuart, Inc., 239 Park Ave. S., N.Y., N.Y. 10003, '66–; Secy. to Pres.; Bklyn. Col., BA, '68 (magna cum laude, Alpha Sigma Lambda); b. N.Y.C., 1941; p. Frank and Sally Stern Rose; h. Hyman Livingston; res: 140 E. Second St., Bklyn., N.Y. 11218.

LIVINGSTON, JOYCE SAMPSON, Wms. Dir. and

Bdcstr., KTVH-TV, Box 12, 2815 E. 37th N., Wichita, Kan. 67201, '67–; Free-lance talent; Physical Fitness Dir. and TV Talent, YMCA, '66–'67; Realtor, '66–; Home Econst., '65; Interior Decorator, Sears, '64–'65; Home Econst., Continental Baking Co., '61–'64; Freelance PR and Comml. Demonstrations, '53–'61; AWRT, Heart Assn. (Bd. of Dirs.); b. St. Joseph, Mo., 1930; p. Louis and Dorothy Goodman Sampson; h. Don Livingston; c. Dawn Lee Johnson, Don, Jr., Mark, Dari Lynn, Matthew, Luke; res: 1029 McLean Blvd. N.W., Wichita, Kan. 67201.

LIVINGSTON, KATHRYN ZAHONY, Feature Ed., Town & Country, 717 Fifth Ave., N.Y., N.Y. 10022, '68–; Copy Ed., Harper's Bazaar, '65–'68; Copy Ed.-Wtr., Vogue Pattern Bk., '63–'64; Copywtr., Montgomery Ward, '61–'63; articles, World Bk. Yr. Bk., '67, '68, '69; Marquette Univ., BA, '61; b. Budapest, Hungary, 1938; res: N.Y., N.Y.

LIVINGSTON, LIDA ELSPETH, Pres., Lida Livingston, Inc., 572 Madison Ave., N.Y., N.Y. 10022, '67–; VP, Infoplan, '57–'67; VP, N.Y. Mgr., The Ettinger Co., '51–'57; Hollywood Mgr., '45–'51; Publicist, MGM, '43–'45; Feature Wtr., Hollywood Citizen News, '38–'43; Ed., "Dali, A Study of His Art-in-Jewels"; Auth., "Photography for Public Relations"; Founder, Dir., Intl. Commtns. Cncl., Intl. Youth Cncl.; Theta Sigma Phi (Nwsp. Feature Aws., '41), Hollywood Wms. Press Club, PRSA; Wms. Assn., Allied Beverage Industries; U.C.L.A., N.Y.U., New Sch. for Social Rsch.; b. Victoria, British Columbia, Canada; p. John and Edith Bull Livingston; c. Peter Perutz; res: 20 W. 86th St., N.Y., N.Y. 10024.

LLOYD, DOROTHY DAVIS, Dir. of Pubns., Maryland State Teachers Association, 344 N. Charles St., Balt., Md. 21201, '68–; Mng. Ed., '62–'68; Assoc. Ed., '57–'62; Asst. Ed., '56–'57; Cnslt: State Dept. of Educ. pubn. on sch. law revision ('67), bk. on Md. in "Enchantment of America" series (Children's Press, '66), Md. Cncl. on Educ. pubn. "Handbook for Citizens School Advisory Committees" ('66); NEA (Life Mbr.), '56), Wms. Adv. Club of Balt. (Pres., '61–'63; Bd. of Dirs., '63–'64), Middle Atlantic AIE (Bd. of Dirs., '56–'58), Nat. Assn. of State Educ. Eds. (Secy.-Treas., '66–'68), NSPRA, Edpress Assn., Kappa Kappa Gamma, Delta Kappa Gamma (hon. life mbr.); cits. for commty. activities; Duke Univ., AB (Phi Beta Kappa); b. Enfield, N.C.; h. 1. Thomas Murray; 2. Robert Lloyd; c. James Thomas Murray; res: Ruxton Towers, 8415 Bellona Lane, Balt., Md. 21204.

LLOYD, NORRIS, Auth., "A Dream of Mansions" (Random House), three bks. for children; Soc. of Midland Auths., Friends of Lit. Aw., '62; b. Greenwood, S.C.; p. Robert and Corrie Van Diviere Norris; h. William B. Lloyd, Jr.; c. William III, Robin N., Lola Lloyd Horwitz, Christopher; res: 806 Rosewood Ave., Winnetka, Ill. 60093.

LLOYD, PATRICIA ANN, Fashion Ed., Colmst.,

Pensacola News-Journal, 101 E. Romana, Pensacola, Fla. 32501, '46–; Stephens Col.; b. Mobile, Ala., 1920; p. Thomas and Ola Wardlaw Lloyd; res: 2023 East Scott St., Pensacola, Fla.

LOACH, JEAN, Owner, Jean Loach and Associates, 50 Sutton Pl. S., N.Y., N.Y. 10022, '62–; Pres., Future Record Co., '62–; Wms. Ed., Talent, "The Jean Loach Show," WXYZ-TV (Detroit, Mich.), '50–'60; Performer, '45–'50; Band Leader, '41–'45; toured eight countries as good-will ambassador, apptd. by Pres. Eisenhower; AWRT, AFTRA, N.Y. Fedn. of Musicians, Chgo. Fedn. of Musicians, Detroit. Fedn. of Musicians, SAG; Mundelein Col.; b. Chgo., Ill.; p. George and Mary Sipes Loach; res: 50 Sutton Pl. S., N.Y., N.Y. 10022.

LOBSENZ, AMELIA FREITAG, Pres., The Lobsenz Public Relations Co., Inc., 745 Fifth Ave., N.Y., N.Y. 10022, '55–; Dir., Mag. Dept., Edward Gottlieb and Assocs., '50–'55; Auth, juv. fiction incl: "Kay Everett Calls CQ" ('52, Jr. Lit. Guild aw.), "Kay Everett Works DX"; non-fiction articles to major mags.; Soc. Mag. Wtrs., Nat. Assn. Sci. Wtrs., Am. Med. Wtrs. Assn., PRSA, Pubcty. Club Chgo., OPC, AWRT; Agnes Scott Col.; b. Greensboro, N.C.; p. Leo and Florence Freitag; h. Dr. Harry Abrahams; c. Kay, Michael; res: The Columns, 10 Red Ground Rd., Old Westbury, N.Y. 11568.

LOBSENZ, DOROTHEA HARDING, Adm. Secy., Society of Magazine Writers, Inc., 54 W. 40th St., N.Y., N.Y. 10018, '65–; Ed., Brearley Bulletin, '68–; Bennington Col., BA, '52; b. N.Y.C., 1930; p. William Barclay and Constance Fox Harding; h. Norman M. Lobsenz; c. Robin Chotzinoff, Jennifer Chotzinoff; res: 300 West End Ave., N.Y., N.Y. 10023.

LoCASCIO, S. PAT MINSHULL, Reprtr., Baltimore News American, South and Lombard Sts., Balt., Md., '68–; Reptr: Evening Capital, Annapolis, '67–'68; Hagerstown Morning Herald, '66–'67; Fauquier Democrat, Warrenton (Va.), Ledger Star and Virginian Pilot, Norfolk, '65–'66; Free-lance polit. speech writing, PR; Photogr.; Va. Press Assn. photog., jnlsm. aws.; Sch. of Photographic Modeling, N.Y.C.; b. Norfolk, Va.; p. Wallace and Olive McEnally Minshull; h. Charles Lo Cascio; c. Diane, Donna, Jaime, Patrick Gonzalez; res: 205 Gibson Rd., Annapolis, Md. 21401.

LOCKE, SONDRA, Actress; Films: "The Heart is a Lonely Hunter" (Warner Bros.-Seven Arts, '68; Acad. Aw. nomination, Golden Globe nomination); "Run Shadow Run" (20th Century Fox, '69); Cleve. Critics and Motion Pic. Theatre Owners "Most Promising New Star," '68; Mademoiselle aw., 68; Cinema aw., '68; b. Shelbyville, Tenn., 1947; p. Stefamand Margaret Leigh Locke; h. Gordon Anderson.

LOCKEN, LISA DUCKSTAD, Ed., "Bemistory," Bemis Co., Inc., 800 Northstar Center, Mpls., Minn., 55402, '66–; Asst. Ed., '63–'66; special Bemis survey projects, '67–'69; N.W.I.E.A. (Special Achiev. Aw., '68; Inst. Aw., '66), ICIE; Newcomb & Sammons Special Aw., '69, Score Aw., '67; N.D. State Univ., '54–'56; Univ. of Minn., BA, '58; b. Fargo, N.D., '36; p. John and Althea Reed Duckstad; h. John Locken; res: 3300 Girard S., Mpls., Minn. 55408.

LOCKETT, MARIAN WORKMAN, Media Byr., Lewis & Gilman, Inc., 1700 Market St., Phila., Pa. 19103, '66–; Asst. Media Byr., '66; Asst. to Rsch. Dir., Triangle Pubns., Radio and TV Div., '64–'66; Asst. to Media Dir., Noble-Dury (Nashville, Tenn.), '63–'64; Traf. Mgr., WNBS-Radio (Murray, Ky.), '62–'63; AWRT (Treas., '68–'69), TV Radio Adv. Club (Secy., '69–'70), Mrs. Kentucky ('54), Govs. Comm. for Pubcty. ('63); Murray State Univ., '62–'63; b. Murray, Ky., 1931; p. Otis and Myrtle Jones Workman; h. D. Barker Lockett; c. Ella Potts, Jennifer Potts, George Potts, Cynthia Potts, Elizabeth, Douglas; res: 109 Lee Circle, Bryn Mawr, Pa. 19010.

LOCKHART, AILEENE SIMPSON, Cnslt. Ed., William C. Brown Company, Publishers, 135 S. Locust St., Dubuque, Ia. 52001, '52–; Prof., Univ. of Southern Cal.; Auth: "Anthology of Contemporary Readings" ('66), "Modern Dance" ('65), "Music for the Modern Dance" ('61), "Toward Excellence in College Teaching" ('63); Ed., 100 health, physical educ. bks.; active in health, educ. orgs.; Who's Who in Educ., Who's Who of Am. Wm., Dic. of Intl. Biog.; Tex. Wms. Univ., BS, '32; Univ. of Wis., MS, '37, PhD, '42, DSc (Hon.), Univ. of Neb., '67; b. Atlanta, Ga., 1911; p. Thomas and Aileene Simpson Lockhart; res: 5460 Weatherford Dr., L.A., Cal. 90008.

LOCKHART, HELEN DeLOISE, Commty. Rels. Librn., Memphis Public Library, Memphis, Tenn., '69–; Dir., Shiloh Reg. Lib. Ctr. (Jackson), '57–'69; Asst. Dir., '53–'57; Librn., Belfry (Ky.) HS, '50–'52; Tenn. Lib. Assn. (Pres., '67–'68, VP, '66–'67), Southeastern Lib. Assn., ALA (Cncl. Mbr., '69–'73), AAUW (VP), Delta Kappa Gamma (Corr. Secy.); Union Univ., AB, '46; George Peabody Col. for Tchrs., MA, '53; b. McVeigh, Ky., 1923; p. Delmon and Amanda Helvey Lockhart; res: 5286 Boswell, Memphis, Tenn. 38117.

LOCKHART, PATRICIA KENNEDY, Head, Visitor and Tour Svcs., Merck & Co., Inc., Merck Sharp and Dohme, West Point, Pa. 19486, '67–; Free-lance Corr., '47–'64; Ed., Hahnemann Med. Col. and Hosp. of Pa. (Phila.) '63–'67; Asst. Ed., INA World, '58–'63; Asst. PR, Adv. Mgr., Theodore Presser, '56–'58; Svc. Rep., Bell Telephone Co. of Pa., '55–'56; Del. Valley Assn. of Communicators (Pres., '62–'63; Secy., '61–'62; Svc. Aw. '65), Nat. Multiple Sclerosis Soc. (Pres., Wms. Div., Eastern Pa. Chptr.; Bd. Mbr., '66–'68), U.S. Sr. Lawn Tennis Championships Comm. (Secy.); Denison Univ., '53–'55; b. Phila., Pa. 1935; p. George and Margaret Cortright Kennedy; res: "Northfield," Sunneytown Pike, N. Wales, Pa. 19454.

LOCKWOOD, LUCILLE PETERSON, Mgr., "Top of

the Week," Newsweek Magazine, 444 Madison Ave., N.Y., N.Y. 10021, '67–; formerly Restaurant Cnslt., London, England; Auth., cookbk.; AWNY; b. Worcester, Mass., 1914; p. Hugo and Grace Cavanaugh Peterson; h. Warren Lockwood; c. Charles Monahan, III, Gayla Wright, Lynn Monahan, Kerry Phillips, Molly Ludlow, Helen Lockwood: res: 219 E. 69th St., N.Y., N.Y. 10022.

LOCKWOOD, MARY-ANN ADEMINO, Dir. of Pubns., University of Oregon Medical School, 3181 S.W. Sam Jackson Park Rd., Portland, Ore. 97201, '56–; Asst. Prof., '65–; Unit Head, Am. Nat. Red Cross (Tokyo, Japan, Korea), '55–'56; Asst. Dir. of Admissions, Whitman Col. (Walla Walla, Wash.), '53–'55; Asst. to Dir., Off. of High Sch. Student Rels., Univ. of Wash.; Am. Col. PR Assn., Theta Sigma Phi (Portland Pfsnl. Chptr. Secy.), Ore. Assn. of Eds. and Communicators (Pres., '66; Dir. of Nat. Affairs, '66–'67; First VP, '65; Second VP, '64; Secy., '63; Adair Aw., '68), ICIE (Reg. VP, '66), Portland Art Assn., Univ. of Wash., BA (Jnlsm., Educ.), '51; b. Seattle, Wash., 1930; p. John and Marion Sullivan Ademino; h. Virgil Baasch Lockwood; c. Craig Stephen, Kirt Owen; res: 2770 S.W. Montgomery Dr., Portland, Ore. 97201.

LOCKWOOD, MOLLY, Adv. Dir., Status Magazine, 641 Lexington Ave., N.Y., N.Y. 10022, '68–; Adv. Mgr., '66–'68; Asst. Adv. Dir., '65–'66; Assoc. Mdsng. Ed., House & Garden, '60–'65; Exec. Training Program, Lord & Taylor, '58–'59; VP, Treas., Penobscot Aviation Svc. Corp., '68–; AWNY, Kappa Kappa Gamma; Pa. State Univ., BS, '58 (outstanding student leader); b. London, Eng., 1936; p. Warren S. and Ann Gleason Lockwood; h. G. Richard Ludlow; res: 120 E. 38th St., N.Y., N.Y. 10016.

LOEBER, MARY (LIZ), Bdcst. Buying Supvsr., Post Keyes Gardner, Inc., 633 Battery St., S.F., Cal. 94111, '62–; Bdcst Byr., BBDO, three yrs.; Head Byr., Brisacher, Wheeler & Staff, eight yrs.; Drake Univ.; res: 90 Terradillo Ave., San Rafael, Cal. 94901.

LOESER, KATINKA, Auth: "The Archers at Home" ('68), "Tomorrow Will Be Monday" ('64); Free-lance Wtr.; Poetry Magazine's Young Poets aw. ('43); Univ. of Chgo., AB, '36; h. Peter DeVries; c. Jan, Peter Jon, Derek; res: 170 Cross Highway, Westport, Conn. 06880.

LOEWE, JUDITH BARBARA, Audience Prom. Dir., WKBG-TV, Kaiser Globe Broadcasting, 75 Morrissey Blvd., Boston, Mass., '68–; Sr. On-air Prom. Prodr., WNEW-TV, '68; Asst. Adv. Mgr., On-air Prom. Supvsr., On-air Prom. Wtr., WPIX-TV, '63–'68; Smith Col., AB, '63; b. Bklyn., N.Y., 1942; p. Milton and Minna Wolf Loewe; res: 133 Marlborough St., Boston, Mass. 02116.

LOFFT, VIRGINIA MARY, Ed., Suburban Newspaper Group, 1111 Union Ave., Cherry Hill, N.J. 08034, '66–; Wms. Ed., '61–; News Ed., '61–'66; Edtl. Dir.,

Hobby Industry Assn. of Am., '59–'61; Assoc. Ed., County Agt. and Vo-Ag Tchr. Mag., '56–'59; PR Cnslt., Haddon Township Public Schs.; PR Cnslt., private home builders; Rschr. and Wtr. on ecology; Crtv. Writing Instr., Haddon Township Adult Sch.; N.J. State Press Assn.; numerous aws. for jnlsm.; Suburban Press Fndn. (Chgo., Ill.), Mayor's Comm. on Juv. Concerns; St. Joseph's Col., '56; Charles Morris Price Sch. (Adv., Jnlsm.), '61; b. Phila., Pa., 1934; p. George and Josephine Binder Lofft; res: 343 Richmond Ave., Blackwood, N.J.

LOFTUS, MARGARET THORNBERRY, Prod. Mgr., California Continuing Education of the Bar, University of California, 2490 Channing Way, Berkeley, Cal. 94704, '60–; Indexer, '57–'60; Mng. Ed., Oh. Law Reptr., W. H. Anderson Co. (Cinn., Oh.), '53–'57; Edtl. Proofreader, Yrbk. Publrs. (Chgo., Ill.), '47–'49; Edtl. Proofreader, Commerce Clearing House, '44–'47; Free-lance indexing, cnslt. on bk. mfg., design; Western Bk. Publrs. Assn., Printing Hist. Soc., Bookbuilders West, Wm. Nat. Bk. Assn.; Mills Col., '34–'37; res: 1612 Oxford St., Berkeley, Cal. 94709.

LOGAN, LILLIAN STERN, Prof. of Educ., Brandon Univ., 18th St., Brandon, Manitoba, Can., '69–; '65–; Univ. of Victoria, '65, '66, '67; Univ. of Alberta, Calgary, '63, '64; Findlay Col. (Oh.), '58–'62; Co-auth., bks. on educ.; Pi Lambda Theta (Nat. VP, '61–'63; Rsch. Aw. for Wm., '62), Delta Kappa Gamma; Can. Speech Assn., ACEI, Can. OMEP; Univ. of Wis., BS (Educ.), '39, MS (Educ.), '50, PhD, '53; res: 602 15th St., Brandon, Manitoba, Can.

LOGAN, SUSIE TITUS, Mgr., Classified National Advertising Department, Wichita Eagle and Beacon, 825 E. Douglas, Wichita, Kan. 67201, '56–; McCormick-Armstrong, '20–'25; NPWC, Kan. Press Wm., Wichita Press Wm. (Treas., '69), Wichita Hist. Soc., Intl. Platform Assn.; Who's Who of Am. Wm.; Who's Who in Midwest; World's Who's Who in Commerce and Industry; Manchester Centra; Ref. Lib. (Eng.); b. Waldo, Kan., 1902; p. Casper and Lona Titus; h. (div.); c. Mrs. Peggy Logan Sandergard, Samuel; res: 741 Pippin Court, Wichita, Kan. 67203.

LOHRER, MARY ALICE, Prof., Graduate School of Library Science, University of Ill., Urbana, Ill. 61801, '41–; Fulbright Lectr., Univ. of Tehran, Iran, '66–'67; Visiting Prof., Japan Lib. Sch., Tokyo, Japan, '59; Foreign Assigts., Chulalongkorn Univ., Bangkok, Thailand, '55–'56; Librn., Hindsale Township HS, '34–'41; Asst. Librn., Oak Park & River Twsp. HS, '28–'38; rsch. studies, articles; Ill. Assn. of HS Librns. (Pres., '40–'41), Ill. Lib. Assn. (Pres., '46–'47), Beta Phi Mu (Pres., '54–'55); ALA, AALS, AAUW; Univ. of Ill., BS (Lib. Sci.), '38; Univ. of Chgo., AM, '44; PhB, '28; b. Chgo., Ill., 1907; p. Hugo and Mary Nyman Schultz; res: 1905 N. Melanie Lane, Champaign, Ill. 61820.

LOIZEAUX, FREDDIE HILL, PR Dir., Controlled Demolition, Inc., 15 Burnbrae Rd., Balt., Md. 21204,

'56–; PRSA, Balt. PR Cncl., Wms. Adv. Club of Balt. (2nd VP, '65–'66), Intl. Platform Assn., NEA, NSPRA, Delta Kappa Gamma, Md. Congress of Parents and Tchrs. (Pres., '66–'69; Gold Apple Aw., '62; Univ. of Ga., BS, '39; b. Carnesville, Ga., 1917; p. Fred and Ruth Addison Hill; h. John D. Loizeaux; c. Mrs. George W. Chapman III, Mrs. Thomas F. Bryant, Jr., John Mark, Douglas Kevin.

LOIZEAUX, MARIE DUVERNOY, Ed., Loizeaux Brothers, Inc., 1238 Corlies Ave., Neptune, N.J. 07753, '59–; Ed., Publicist, H. W. Wilson Co., '39–'59; Staff, New Rochelle Public Lib. (N.Y.), '24–'39; Founder, Dir., Public Relations Planner; Auth., "Publicity Primer: An ABC of 'Telling All' About the Public Library;" Columbia Univ. Ext.; b. Plainfield, N.J., 1905; p. Elie and Elise Duvernoy Loizeaux; res: 418 Redmond Ave., Oakhurst, N.J. 07755.

LOLLOBRIGIDA, GINA, Actress, 49 motion pics., incl. "Trapeze," "Solomon and Sheba," "Come September," "Mistress Campbell"; Aws: three French Oscars, four German Oscars, one FGA aw., three David di Donatello, one Grolla d'oro, two Nastri d'argento; c. Milko; res: 223 Via Appia Antica, Rome, Italy.

LOMAX, BETTY FRANK, PR Dir., Exec. Ed., Right Now mag., National Society of Afro-American Police, 308 Lenox Ave., N.Y., N.Y. 10027, Assoc. Prodr., "Louis Lomax Speaks" (Ch. 31), '63; Rsch. Asst. to TV Prodr., '62; Prodr., Dir., "Frankly Speaking" daily prog., '58–'62; Prodr., Dir., "Mid-Nite Rocket" prog., Radio WADO, '57–'58; Cnslt., PR Dept., Shaw Artists Agcy., '56–'57; Media Wm. (Past VP); Harlem Sr. Citizens aw.; Queens Col., '49–'51; b. Toronto, Ont., Can., 1932; p. Harry and Mabel Bell; c. Omar H.; res: 398 E. 152nd St., Bronx, N.Y. 10455.

LONERGAN, PAULINE JOY, Auth.; employee, United Transformer, Div. TRW, 150 Varick St., N.Y., N.Y. 10013; children's bks., "Brian's Secret Errand" (Doubleday, '69), four others; Children's Bk. Dept., Brentano's, '49–'51; Pubcty. Dir., Prentice-Hall, '42–'44; HS Tchr., '34–'38; Auths. Guild; Denison Univ., BA, '32; Syracuse Univ., MA, '33; b. Toronto, Ont., Can., 1909; p. Charles and Jean McGillivray MacLean; h. John Lonergan; res: 651 E. 14th St., N.Y., N.Y. 10009.

LONG, HELEN HALTER, Pres., Books of the World, Inc., Roxbury Bldg., Sweet Springs, Mo. 65351, '63–; Co-auth., "Social Studies Skills" (Inor Publ. Co., '64), Auth: "Society in Action" (Inor Publ. Co., '36), Nat. Safety Cncl. Lesson Units ('44–'52); Dir. of Curriculum Studies, Inst. for Instructional Improvement (N.Y.C.), '62–; Asst. Superintendent of Schs., Mamaroneck, N.Y., '54–'61; Prin., Jr. HS, '49–'54; Prin., Chatsworth Sch. (Larchmont, N.Y.), '42–'49; Assoc. Ed., The Clearing House, '35–'55; Pi Gamma Mu, Kappa Delta Pi; Alpha Xi Delta Diamond Jubilee Outstanding Wm. Aw., '68; Wash. Univ., AB, '27 (Phi Beta Kappa); AM,

'28 (magna cum laude); N.Y.U., PhD, '37; b. St. Louis, Mo., 1906; p. Charles and Ida May Halter; h. Forrest E. Long; res: 107 Medallion Dr., Sweet Springs, Mo. 65351.

LONG, LOIS, Fashion Ed., The New Yorker, 25 W. 43rd St., N.Y., N.Y. 10036, '25–; Colmst., '24–'28; Dramatic Ed., Vanity Fair, '24–'25; Copywtr., Vogue, '22–'24; Fashion Group; Sylvania aw., '53; Vassar Col., BA, '22 (cum laude); b. Stamford, Conn., 1901; p. William and Frances Bancroft Long; h. Harold A. Fox; c. Mrs. Robert Maxwell; res: 2190 Gateway Terr., Easton, Pa. 18042.

LONGMEYER, JUDTIH SHULMISTRAS, Mgr., Commty. Rels. and Employee Commtns., Skil Corporation, 5033 N. Elston Ave., Chgo., Ill. 60630, '69–; Commtns. Specialist, '68; Ed., '65; Edtl. Asst., '64; Iota Sigma Epsilon (VP, '69–'70), IEA, Jr. Wms. Adv. Club of Chgo.; Indsl. Mgt. Soc. Film Competition Aw., '68; Chgo. City Col., AA, '62; b. Chgo., Ill., 1943; p. John and Ann Jakaitis Shulmistras; h. Joseph F. Longmeyer; res: 7654B N. Sheridan Rd., Chgo., Ill. 60626.

LONGO, MARJORIE HIGGINS, PR, Adv. Dept. Ed.-Wtr., Mercantile Trust Company N.A., 721 Locust St., St. Louis, Mo., '64–; Pers. Div., '59–'64; Am. Inst. of Banking, Indsl. Press Assn., ICIE; Indsl. Press-U.F. aws: 1st pl., cover design, '62, '63; 2nd pl., feature story, '63; 1st pl.; Wash. Univ., (St. Louis); b. Detroit, Mich., 1931; p. Cleo R. and Alma Henegar Higgins; h. Samuel J. Longo; res: 905 N. Woodlawn Ave., Kirkwood, Mo. 63122.

LONGO, PATRICIA GERARD, VP, Harvey Probber, Inc., 979 Third Ave., N.Y., N.Y. 10022, '67–; Exec. Asst. to Pres., Dir. of PR, '63–'67; pers. Asst., Ethicon, '58–'63; NHFL, Self-Dynamics Group; Douglass Col., '55–'58; Rutgers Univ. (Jnlsm., Pers., PR); b. Somerville, N.J., 1937; p. Gerald and Mae Hagaman Mecco; h. Joseph F. Longo; res: 125 Heritage Hill Rd., New Canaan, Conn. 06840.

LONGO, ROSALIE FROHLICH, Wms. Ed., Paterson News, News Printing Co., News Plaza, Paterson, N.J. 07509, '59–; Asst. Wms. Ed., '56–'59; Staff Wtr., '54–'56; Wtr., feature articles: Editor and Publisher, '62; Family Circle, '69; Nwsp. Reptrs. Assn. of N.Y.C.; Paterson Wms. Club (hon. mbr.); Who's Who of Am. Wm.; state, reg., nat. aws. for nwsp. articles and free-lance writing; Seton Hall Univ.; b. Paterson, N.J., 1936; p. Julius and Anita Hocker Frohlich; h. James Longo; c. Lauren Mary, Linda Mary; res: 798 Franklin Lakes Rd., Franklin Lakes, N.J.

LOO, BEVERLY JANE, Dir. Subsidiary Rights Dept., McGraw-Hill Book Co., Inc., 330 W. 42nd St., N.Y., N.Y., '62–; Fiction Ed., McCall's, '59–'62; Subsidiary Rights Dir., Prentice-Hall, '57–'59; Asst. to Ed.-in-chief, Farrar Straus & Cudahy, '56–'57; Wms. Nat. Bk. Assn., OPC; Univ. of Cal., Berkeley, AB, '53; b. L.A., Cal., 1931; c. Richard Y., Bessie (Sue); res: 300 E. 57th St., N.Y., N.Y. 10022.

LOOG, VIRGINIA ANDERSON, Wms. Ed., Winter Park Regional, Orlando Sentinel Star Co., 120 E. Morse Blvd., Winter Park, Fla. 32789 (Orlando Sentinel Star Co., 633 N. Orange Ave., Orlando, Fla. 32802), '69–; Staff Wtr., Orlando Sentinel Star, '67–'69; Freelance Wtr., '62–'67; Reptr., Asbury Park Press, '43–'47; Reptr., Long Branch (N.J.) Daily Record, '37–'43; reprints of features in Grit, Fla. State Educ. Magazine; one act plays prod. by Wms. clubs; Photogr.; Fla. Wms. Press Club, Monmouth County Wms. Press Club (Pres., '45–'47), Altrusa Club of Winter Park, Winter Park Wms. Club (hon.); St. Petersburg Jr. Col., '28–'30; Cedar Crest Col., '30–'31; Rutgers Univ., '31; b. Englewood, N.J., 1909; p. John C. and Jeannette Mager Anderson; h. Roland H. Loog (dec.); c. John Ellsworth Tilton, Roland H.; res: 2810 Eastern Pkwy., Orlando, Fla. 32803.

LOOMIS, CAROL JUNGE, Bd. of Eds., Fortune Magazine, Time Inc., Time & Life Bldg., N.Y., N.Y. 10020, '68–; Assoc. Ed., '58–'68; Rsch. Assoc., '54–'58; Ed., house organ, The Maytag Co., '51–'54; John Hancock Aw. for excellence in bus. and fin. jnlsm., '68, H. Hentz fin. jnlsm. aw., '68, G. M. Loeb Achiev. aw., '69; Drury Col., '47–'49; Univ. of Mo., BJ, '51; b. Cole Camp, Mo., 1929; p. Harold and Mildred Case Junge; h. John Loomis; c. Barbara C., Mark H.; res: 32 Bonnie Briar Lane, Larchmont, N.Y. 10538.

LOPER, MARY LOU BRION, Wtr., Los Angeles Times, Times-Mirror Sq., L.A., Cal., '59–; Ed. Wms. Pgs., The Phoenix (Ariz.) Gazette, '56–'59; Jr. League of L.A., Opera Assocs. of the Music Ctr., KCET Wms. Cncl. Bd., Pasadena Jr. Philharmonic Comm.; Ariz. State Univ., BA, '55; b. Chandler, Ariz., 1932; h. Dr. James L. Loper.

LOPEZ, BARBARA BOYLE, Adm. Asst., Chiat/Day Inc., Advertising, 1300 W. Olympic Blvd., L.A., Cal. 90015, '68–; Staff, '66–'68; b. Detroit, Mich., 1943; p. James and Daisy Porter Boyle; h. Pete Lopez; c. daughter; res: 11332 Montana Ave., L.A., Cal. 80049.

LOPEZ, MARY GARDNER, Wms. Ed., Queens Voice, 170-11 Hillside Ave., Jamaica, N.Y., '59–; Reg. Dir., Commn. of Human Rights, '64–'68; Dir., Ophelia DeVore Charm Sch., '57–'58; Ed., Nashville (Tenn.) Sun; Commentator, Radio WWRL (commty. svcs. aw., '63), Col. Instr., '48–'52; Nat. Media Wms. Assn. (Queens Chptr. Pres.), Alpha Kappa Alpha (commendation), Doll League (Pres.), Elmhurst Civic Assn., NAACP (Outstanding Svc. aw.); Tenn. State Univ., Univ. of Mich.; Newark Univ.; b. Nashville, Tenn.; p. Kossie Gardner and Mrs. Jean Chandler; h. Dr. George A. Lopez; c. Sharon, Adrienne; res: 105-11 Ditmars Blvd., E., East Elmhurst, N.Y. 11369.

LoPRETE, TERE, Art Dir., Book Division, The McCall Publishing Company, 230 Park Ave., N.Y., N.Y. 10017, '69–; Dir. of Design and Prod., Juvenile Books, J.B. Lippincott Company, '66–'69; Dir. of Design for Alfred A. Knopf, Random House, Vintage Books, Modern Library and College Divisions of Knopf and Random House, '61–'69; Design and Prod. Mgr., Juvenile Books, Knopf, '58–'59; began as Designer, Adv. Dept., McGraw-Hill, '47; designs small pamphlets of literature for home printing; book design aws: Philadelphia Book Show, Juvenile Section, '67, '68; AIGA 50 Books of the Year Show, '59, '67; AIGA Children's Book Show, '58–'60, '61–'62; Art Student's League and Sch. of Visual Arts; b. Jersey City, N.J.; p. John and Nellie DiRoma LoPrete; res: 49 W. 12th St., N.Y., N.Y. 10011.

LORANGER, JANET A., Ed.-in-chief, Bks. for Young Readers, Charles Scribner's Sons, 597 Fifth Ave., N.Y., N.Y. 10017, '65–; Assoc. Ed., Bks. for Young Readers, Harper & Row, '60–'65; Chmn., Eng. Dept., A.O. Davis HS (Mt. Vernon, N.Y.), '56–'58; Tchr. (Minn., Ill., N.Y.), '49–'56; Children's Bk. Cncl., PEN, Wms. Nat. Bk. Assn., ALA, N.Y. Lib. Assn.; Carleton Col., BA, '49; Univ. of Minn., MA, '54; b. Duluth, Minn., 1927; p. Donald and Frances Coit Loranger; res: Box 113, W. Redding, Conn. 06896.

LORBERG, AILEEN DOROTHY, Colmst., Jackson Post and Cash-Book, 214 W. Main, Jackson, Mo. 63755, '69–; Auth: "Lookout Summer" (Lothrop, Lee and Shepard, '60), "Otahki, Trail of Tears Princess" (Ramfre Press, '67), 200 short stories, articles; Tchr., Cape Girardeau Public Schs., '34–'36; Dir., Poetry Playhouse; Sch. Psychologist, Eng. Tchr. (Clayton), '36–'41; Mo. State Eng. Assn., Cape Girardeau Wtrs. Guild (Pres., '54–'55), Mo. Wtrs. Guild (Juv. Fiction Aws., '53, '56; Non-Fiction Aw., '53); S.E. Mo. State Col., BS (Educ.), '34; Univ. of Southern Cal., MA (Eng.), '38; Bread Loaf Sch. of Eng., grad. studies, '39; b. Cape Girardeau, Mo., 1910; p. Martin and Flora Wolters Lorberg; res: 821 Broadway, Apt. 2, Cape Girardeau, Mo. 63701.

LORCH, ELSE BEYLEGAARD PETERSEN, Asst. to Pres., Permissions Ed., Head, Royalty Dept., New Directions Publishing Corp., 333 Sixth Ave., N.Y., N.Y. 10014, '65–; Adm. Asst., Columbia Univ. Med. Ctr., '60–'65; Registrar, St. David's Sch., '59–'60; Dept. Secy., English, Fgn. Langs., Columbia, '56–'59; French Tchr., Calhoun Sch., '54–'56; Univ. of Norway, License in French; Columbia Univ., MA (Romance Langs.); Univ. of Grenoble, Diplôme Premier Degré; b. Bergen, Norway; p. Severin and Ingrid Olsen Petersen; h. (div.); c. Duncan, Madeleine Louise (Mrs. Alvin Philip Tramm), Ingrid Jacqueline (Mrs. Brian J. Turner); res: 39 Claremont Ave., N.Y., N.Y. 10027.

LORY, BARBARA BANNER, Free-lance Wtr. and Publicist; AE, Bell & Stanton, '67–'68; VP-Adv./PR/Mktng., Decorative Adventures, '66–'67; Mgr.-Adv./Mdsng./PR, Riekes Crisa, '65–'66; AE, Arndt, Preston, Chapin, Lamb & Keen, '60–'65; NHFL; currently teaching English to Libyans; Douglass Col., '57–'59; b. Phila., Pa., 1940; p. Allen and Nancy Torelli Shaw; h. Robert Lory; res: P.O. Box 385, Tripoli, Libya.

LOSEE, H. MADELEINE WECKEL, Program Coordr., National Aeronautics & Space Administration, 300-Seventh St. S.W., Wash., D.C. 20546, '68–; Chief, Lib. Programs Br., STID, '64–'68; Chief, Legislative Ref. Br., '62–'63; Chief, Hq. Lib., '61–'62, Atomic Energy Commn.; '61–'62; Chief, Legislative Ref. Svc., '59–'61; Law Librn., '51–'59 (Ed., AEC Doorway to Legal News); Acting Chief, Am. & British Exchange, Lib. of Congress, '51; Evaluation Offcr., '46; Chief, Am. Law Sec., Law Lib., '45–'46; Contrbr., pfsnl. jnls.; Cnslt., Fed. Dept. Lib. Survey, '59; FID, Am. Soc. for Info. Sci., Law Librns. Soc. (Wash., D.C. Pres., '59–'61); Special Libs. Assn., other pfsnl. orgs.; Univ. of Ill., BS, '33; MA, '36; grad. work; p. John and Flossie McCullough Weckel; h. Gordon Carroll Losee; c. Carol Ann; res: 6166 Leesburg Pike, Falls Church, Va. 22044.

LOTKO, ANN L., Media Dir., Bruce B. Brewer Co., Inc., 1221 Baltimore Ave., Kan. City, Mo. 64105, '64–; Adv. Media Byr., '50–'60; Media Dir., Holland Dreves Adv. (Omaha, Neb.), '61–'64; Media Dir., Savage-Dow Agcy., '55–'60; Lectr., adv. classes, Univ. of Kan., '67–'69; Contrbr., Oil Painting Exhibits; Central Bus. Col., '43–'44; art study under Frank Sepousek (Omaha, Neb.); b. Tonganoxie, Kan., 1925; p. William and Emma Scheidt Oelschlaeger; c. C. Thomas II, William; res: 2402 Nebraska, Kan. City, Kan. 66102.

LOTT, HELEN J., Media Dir., Nelson Stern & Associates, 530 Hanna Bldg., Cleveland, Oh. 44115, '65–; Bdcst. and Print Byr., Griswold-Eshleman; VP, TV-Radio Prodr., Commls. Wtr., Leech Adv.; AE, Carr Liggett Adv.; Musical Dir., WEWS Television Sts.; Acc. Expediter, Copywtr., Fuller & Smith & Ross; Pfsnl. Orchestra Musician, Hanna Theater, Broadway, nat. cos. of musical shows, Musicarnivel, Cleve. Summer Symphony, Ice Follies, ballet, opera, celebrity personal appearances; Cleve. Fedn. of Musicians, AFM, Cleve. Adv. Club PR Cert., '50; Lakeside Yacht Club; Cleve. Inst. of Music, BM; res: 12505 Edgewater Dr., Lakewood, Oh. 44107.

LOTT, LAURIE ANN, Asst. Ed., Surfing Illustrated Magazine, 1454 Fifth St., Santa Monica, Cal. 90406, '67–; Asst. Ed., Hot Boat Magazine, '67–'68; Santa Monica City Col.; b. Santa Monica, Cal., 1951; p. Davis and Arlene Peterson Lott; res: 13222-B Admiral Ave., Marina del Rey, Cal. 90291.

LOUCKS, OPAL MELTON, Wms. Ed., Joy Publishing Co., 232 E. Broadway, Centralia, Ill. 62801, '34–; Wms. Ed., Centralia Evening and Sunday Sentinel; Reptr.; Colmst., "Opal Opines," past five yrs.; aws. for Best Story of Yr. and Best Feature Story; b. Orchardville, Ill., 1911; p. John and Ora Burkett Melton; h. Arthur Loucks; res: 304 Melrose, Centralia, Ill. 62801.

LOUVIERE, DOT (Dorothy Picard Louviere), Ed. and Classified Mgr., Daily Iberian TV Preview, Daily Iberian, 926 E. Main, New Iberia, La. 70560, '64–; Classified Asst., '61; Wrote TV Colm.; Mu Sigma, Woodman of the World Am. Hist. Aw.; b. N.O., La., 1930; p. Alfred and Lorena Romero Picard; h. Antoine Louviere; res: 714 Railroad Ave., New Iberia, La. 70560.

LOVE, BARBARA J., Pres., Foremost Americans Publishing Corporation, Suite 628, Empire State Building, 350 Fifth Ave, N.Y., N.Y. 10001, '69–; Ed.-Wtr., CBS Television Network, '67–'69; Sr. Ed., Sponsor mag., '65–'67; Assoc. Ed., '63–'65; Prod. Ed., '62–'63; Assoc. Ed., N.Y. Lumber Trade Journal, '61–'62; Free-lance Wtr., PR; AWNY, Theta Sigma Phi, Organization for the Great Arts (Coordinating Dir., '70), NOW; Who's Who of Am. Wm., World Who's Who in Finance and Industry; Purdue Univ., '55–'57; Syracuse Univ., BA, '59 (Commtns. Alumni Soc., '64–); b. Montclair, N.J., 1937; p. Egon Love and Lois Ashley Crane; res: 43 Fifth Ave., N.Y., N.Y. 10003.

LOVE, NANCY, VP, Mike Merrick Co., Inc., 1414 Avenue of the Americas, N.Y., N.Y. 10019, '69–; AE, '67–'69; Prom. Wtr. and liaison, nwsps. and mags., Hearst Publ. Co.; Wtr., Free-lance Publicist; Prodr.-Wtr., TV, L.A. (Cal.), '54–'55; Auth., screenplay, "The Auctioneer," '67; U.C.L.A. (Jnlsm.); b. S.F., Cal.; h. (div.); res: 229 E. 79th St., N.Y., N.Y. 10021.

LOVEITT, HAZEL SCOTT, Wm's Pgs. Ed., Guy Gannett Publishing Company, 390 Congress St., Portland, Me. 04104, '67–; Wtr., Wm.'s Sports Ed., Feature Wtr., '54–'69; Governor's Comm. on Children and Youth; Portland Toastmistress Club (Pres.); Maine Press and Radio Wm. aw., '56–'57; Portia Law School; b. Boston, Mass., 1920; p. James and Fannie Ireland Scott; h. (1) Reginald B. LeMoine (dec.); (2) Melvin Loveitt; c. Stephen, Frank LeMoine, Robert LeMoine; res: Chute Rd., S. Windham, Me.

LOVELACE, ELLEN O'CONNELL, Media Dir., Hilton Advertising Agency, Inc., 3315 Memorial Hwy., Tampa, Fla. 33609, '65–; Mechanical Artist, Copywtr., '64–'65; Hon. Ky. Colonel; Fla. State Univ., BS (Bus., Adv.); b. Pitt., Pa., 1941; p. John and Ernestine Sullivan O'Connell; h. Winston Lovelace; res: 909 Druid Rd. W., Clearwater, Fla. 33516.

LOVELL, EMILY KALLED, Free-lance Wtr., '48–; Ed., N.M. pioneer interviews, '67–'69 (now with publr.); Auth: "Weekend Away" ('64), "Personalized History of Otero County" ('63); Sierra Vista Corr., Arizona Republic, '65–'66; Co-founder, Ed., Publr., Otero County Star (Alamogordo, N.M.), '61–'65; Local Newscstr., KALG, '64–'65; Corr., Fairchild Pubns., '59–'63; (Sierra Vista and Tucson), '65–'68; Corr. (Alamogordo), El Paso Herald-Post, '54–'65; Tularosa Basin Times, '57–'59; INS (Denver), '50–'54; City Ed., Alamogordo News, '48–'51; Dir., Star Publ. Co., '61–'65; Pres., '64–'65; Traf. Mgr., KOPO (Tucson, Ariz.), '46–'47; Copywtr., Asst. Traf. Mgr., WOOD (Grand Rapids, Mich.), '44–'46; Theta Sigma Phi (Nat. VP for mbrs.-at-large, '68–'70) Ariz. Press Wm., N.M. Press Wm., NFPW aws.; Mich. State Univ., BA, '44 (hons., Phi Kappa Phi), Univ. of Ariz. Ext., '66; Cal.

State Col. at Hayward, '68; b. Grand Rapids, Mich., 1920; p. Abdo and Louise Claussen Kalled; h. Robert Lovell; res: Box 4035, Tucson, Ariz. 85717.

LOVETT, LINDA LADD, Asst. Ed., Computers and Automation, 815 Washington St., Newtonville, Mass. 02160, '62–; Co-auth., "Glossary of Terms in Computers and Data Processing" (Berkeley Enterprises, '60); b. Arlington, Mass., 1926; h. Robert F. Lovett; c. Curtis L., Gregory B.; res: 45 Moore Rd., Wayland, Mass. 01778.

LOVRIEN, PHYLLIS ANN, Supvsr., Consumer Svcs., Oscar Mayer & Co., 910 Mayer Ave., Madison, Wis. 53701, '63–; Madison Press Club (Offcr., Dir., '65–'68), Am. Home Econs. Assn., Home Econsts. in Bus. (Nat. Exec. Bd., '69; Wis. Chmn., '68), AWRT, Theta Sigma Phi, GMA Consumer Svc. Comm.; Who's Who of Am. Wm.; Who's Who in the Midwest; Ia. State Univ., BS, '63.

LOW, JACQUELYN, VP, Adv., PR, Cabot, Cabot & Forbes Company, 28 State St., Boston, Mass. 02109, '56–; Asst. PR, Adv. Dir., Reach, McClinton & Humphrey, '52–'56; Boston Adv. Club (Past Dir.), PRSA (New England Chptr. 1st VP, '68; Treas., '63–'65); Boston Zoological Soc. (Dir., '67); Boston Adv. Woman of the Year, '66; Simmons Col., BA, (Outstanding Alumna Aw., '69), '52; b. Brookline, Mass., 1930; p. Edmund and Marjorie Nutting Low; res: 265 Commonwealth Ave., Boston, Mass. 02115.

LOWE, BEVERLY WINETTE, Free-lance wtr.; Interviewer, motion pic. and TV stars, for radio prom.; Doubleday and Co.; Disc Jockey, KSFV; Pubcty., Universal Pictures, '60–'67; Tech. Wtr., Marty Semans and Chic Donchin; AWRT; Oh. State Univ., BA, MA; b. Cleve., Oh., 1928; p. Benjamin and Gladys Winette; c. Gregory, Fred; res: 3255 Longridge Ave., Sherman Oaks, Cal. 91403.

LOWE, FLORENCE SEGAL, Coordr. of Special Projects, Metromedia, Inc., 5151 Wisconsin Ave. N.W., Wash., D.C. 21116, '63–; Wash. Corr., '61–'63; PR, Press Cnslt., WIP (Phila., Pa.), '58–'60; Wash. Colmst., Phila. Daily News, '55–'58; Wash. Colmst., Manchester (N.H.) Un. Leader, '48–'58; Wash. Colmst., TV Guide, '54–'57; Wash. Corr., Variety, Daily Variety, '42–'58; AWRT (D.C. Chptr. Pres., '54–'55; Bd., '65–'66), WNPC (Bd., '64–'67; Secy., '57; Treas., '55), ANWC (Bd., '63; VP, '56), NATAS (Wash. Chptr. VP, '67–'68), Intl. Platform Assn.; Univ. of Pa., BS (Educ.), '31; Temple Univ., '32–'34; Phila. Sch. of Social Svc., '35; b. N.Y.C., 1912; p. Samuel I. and Rose Kantor Segal; h. Herman Albert Lowe (dec.); c. Lesley Lowe Israel, Roger Barnard; res: 2727-29th St. N.W., Wash., D.C. 20008.

LOWELL, JULIET, Auth: "Dear Doctor" ('70), "Dear Candidate" ('68), "Boners in the News" ('66), 11 other bks.; Lectr.; OPC, Auths. League of Am.; Vassar Col., BA, '22; b. 1901; p. Max and Helen Kohut Lowenthal; h. (dec.); c. Margot (Mrs. Leonard Einstein), Ross

Lowell; res: Hampton House, 28 E. 70th St., N.Y., N.Y. 10021.

LOWRIE, JEAN ELIZABETH, Head, Dept. of Librnship., Prof., Western Michigan University, Kalamazoo, Mich. 49001, '61–; Assoc. Prof., '58–'61; Asst. Prof., '51–'56; Auth., "Elementary School Libraries" (Scarecrow Press, '61); articles on sch. lib. materials ctrs., pers. needs, rsch. in educ. jnls., '66–'68; ALA (Exec. Bd., '69–), U.S. Delegate to World Confedn. of Orgs. of Teaching Profession (Paris, '64; Vancouver, '67; Dublin, '68; Abidjan, '69); Keuka Col., BA, '40; Western Reserve Univ., BS (Lib. Sci.), '41, PhD, '59; Western Mich. Univ., MA, '56; b. Northville, N.Y., 1918; p. A. Sydney and Edith Roos Lowrie; res: 1006 Westmoreland Ave., Kalamazoo, Mich. 49001.

LOWRY, CYNTHIA COLEMAN, Colmst.-TV, Associated Press, 50 Rockefeller Plaza, N.Y., N.Y. 10020, '59–; Feature Wtr., '48–'59; Corr., France, Germany, '45–'47; Reptr.-Ed., N.Y. Bur., '42–'45; Reptr., Macy-Westchester Nwsps., '36–'42; Syracuse Univ., BS, '33; b. Mt. Vernon, N.Y., 1912; p. Robert and Elsie Newell Lowry; res: 175 Bedford Rd., Pleasantville, N.Y. 10570.

LOWRY, MARTHA RYAN, Auth., "Floral Art for America" (M. Barrows & Co.), '64); Lectr., exhbn. of floral art at N.Y. Intl. Flower Show, Pa. Flower Shows; Pa. Garden Club Fedn. (Past 1st VP; Aw. of Merit for literary effort, '68), Guild Flower Arrangers (1st Pres.), NLAPW, Fashion Group, Bethel Garden Club (Past Pres.), Countryside Bk. Club (Past Pres.), amateur flower show judge; b. Lancaster, Pa.; p. George and Martha Stroman Ryan; h. William Fleming Lowry; c. William F., III, John C.; res: 5021 Highland Ave., Bethel Pk., Pa. 15102.

LUBAR, REA, Owner, Rea Lubar Associates, 15 W. 38th St., N.Y., N.Y. 10018, '67–; VP and Crtv. Dir., Arnold Constable, '65–'67; Dir. of Fashion Prom., Bonwit-Teller, '60–'63; Dir. PR, Lord and Taylor, '44–'56; Auth., poetry and articles in numerous mags.; Lectr. on PR, cols. and univs.; Fashion Group, Home Fashions League; Cornell Univ., BA, '42 (cum laude); b. N.Y.C., 1922; p. Dr. David and Fannie Socol Lubarsky; h. Kenneth Duncan; c. Laura Jacobs, Nicholas Jacobs; res: 21 E. 83rd St., N.Y., N.Y. 10028.

LUCAS, DIAL K., Adm. Asst., Rodgers, Newman & Cauthen, Inc., 2730 Devine St., Columbia, S.C. 29205, '65–; '60–; The State-Record Publ. Co., '47–'58; Columbia Adv. Club (Secy., '68–'69), AWRT (Palmetto Chptr. Secy., '68–'69), Sears Career Cncl.; b. Columbia, S.C., 1930; p. Benjamin and Lillie Arledge Kaigler; h. L. C. Lucas (div.); c. Lynda D.; res: 4215 Mimosa Rd., Columbia, S.C. 29205.

LUCAS, GEORGIA BRIGGS, Free-lance Wtr., Poet, Auth., "Prelude"; Theta Sigma Phi, NLAPW, Acad. of Am. Poetry, Poetry Soc. of Tex. (several aws.); Who's Who of Am. Wm.; Who's Who in Tex. Today; Dic. of

Intl. Biog.; Univ. of Tex.; b. Austin, Tex.; p. George and Addie Hocutt Lucas; res: 1801 Lavaca St., Apt. 7C, Austin, Tex. 78701.

LUCAS, HELEN, Acc. Supvsr., Richard K. Manoff, 845 Third Ave., N.Y., N.Y. 10018, '67–; AE, Cunningham & Walsh; Coty; Helena Rubinstein; Young & Rubicam; Boston Univ., BS; Wharton Sch. of Fin. and Commerce, MBA, '58; b. Boston, Mass.; p. Charles Lucas; res: 233 E. 69th St., N.Y., N.Y. 10021.

LUCAS, KAREN ERICKSON, Media Dir., Edward Spilman and Associates, Liberty Towers, Tulsa, Okla. 74119, '67–; Univ. of Tulsa; h. Ronald D. Lucas.

LUCAS, ROSEMARY DEAN, Hostess, "Mid-Day" and Weather Girl, WAPI-TV, Box 1310, Birmingham, Ala. 35201, '62–; "Mid-Day," '65–; WAVE-TV, Louisville, Ky., '54–'56; AWRT, Birmingham Press Club; aws.; Ind. Univ., '53; b. L.A., Cal.; p. Roy and Juarita Damer Dean; c. Kim, Jim.

LUCIER, VIRGINIA MARY, Wms. Ed., News Publishing Co., 375 Cochituate Rd., Framingham, Mass. 01701, '52–; Soc. Ed., '48–'52; Wtr., Reprtr., '46–'48; Wtr., Critic, opening nights, plays, musicals, opera, ballet, mot. pics. in Boston area: Contrbr., articles, Boston Record Am., Boston Globe, Amusement Business, UPI; Speaker on Jnlsm., clubs and schs.; Framingham BPW (Wm. of the Yr., '62); Pubcty. Chmn., civic groups; Framingham Bus. Col., '47; Boston Univ., '48–'50; b. Framingham, Mass., 1928; p. Casimirro and Margaret Scansaroli Rossi; c. Deborah Jane Lucier; res: 586 Hollis St., Framingham, Mass. 01701.

LUCKE, GRETCHEN, Ed., "The Norton Spirit," and PR Staff, Norton Company, 1 New Bond St., Worcester, Mass. 01606, '63–; Mng. Ed., '60–'63; Assoc. Ed., '58–'60; PR Staff, '57–; employee, '29–; Worcester County Eds. Cncl. (Pres., '62–'63; "Ralph M. Hall" aw. as mbr. best typifying devotion to indsl. ed. profession), Mass. IEA, ICIE, Quota Club Intl. (Worcester Br. of Dirs., 1st VP, '66–'67); Becker Jr. Col., '28; b. Worcester, Mass., 1909; p. Hermann and Sarah Kean Lucke; res: 175 Lincoln St., Worcester, Mass. 01605.

LUCKHARDT, MILDRED CORELL, Lectr., Auth., Compiler, Abingdon Press, 201 Eight Ave., S., Nashville, Tenn. 37202, '60–; Staff, Rye (N.Y.) Lib., '55–'64; Nwsp. Colmst., '28–'31; Wtr., N.Y. Sun, '23–'27; Ed., PR, Met. Trust Co., '19–'21; Auth: "Story of St. Nicholas," "Christmas Comes Once More," "Good King Wenceslas," 18 other bks.; Auths. Guild, NLAPW, ALA, Westchester County Lib. Assn.; Columbia Univ.; b. N.Y.C., 1898; p. Philip and Mildred McCaffrey Corell; h. Gustav George Luckhardt; c. Philip, Mrs. Lewis Robbins, Mrs. David Kenney; res: 86 Grandview Ave., Rye, N.Y. 10580.

LUCKHARDT, VIRGINIA ETHEL, Head Librn., Reed Library, California State College, California, Pa. 15419, '49–; Tchr., '38–'48; ALA, AAUP; Univ. of Pitt., AB, '36

(summa cum laude, Phi Kappa Phi), MA, '45 (summa cum laude); Carnegie-Mellon Univ., MLS, '49 (summa cum laude, Phi Kappa Phi); b. Pitt., Pa., 1915; p. John Henry and Ethel Henderson Luckhardt; 3254 Wainbell Ave., Pitt., Pa. 15216.

LUDLAM, YVONNE de JOURNO, Ed., The New York State Banker, New York State Bankers Assn., 405 Lexington Ave., N.Y., N.Y. 10017, '66–; Secy., Bd. of Dirs., '58–; Wtr./Ghost Wtr., '55–; Auth: "P.R. Prompter" ('62), "Simon and His Family Bank" ('60), "Why a Commercial Bank?" ('57); PR Cnslt., Cantan-Rose Inst. of Art (Jamaica, N.Y.), '55–; various orgs., aws.; N.Y.U., '33–'36; Syracuse Univ., Bankers Inst. of PR, cert., '59; West Point Bankers Inst. for Exec. Dev., '63; Cornell Univ. Sch. of Agriculture, '67; b. Allentown, Pa.; p. Ernest and Estelle Labe de Journo; h. John Louis Ludlam; c. John Louis, Jr., Barbara Reneé (Mrs. Tad Danz); res: 39 Tuckahoe Rd., Southampton, N.Y. 11968.

LUDLOW, JEAN HODGES, Feature Wtr., The Ridgewood Newspapers, 30 Oak St., Ridgewood, N.J. 07450, '68–; Free-lance Wtr., '67–'68; Colmst., Orange County (Cal.) Evening News, '63–'67; nwsp. colmst. aw., '66; hist. writing aw., '67; Occidental Col., '53–'55; b. Statesville, N.C., 1935; p. John and Lucille Pounds Hodges; h. Richard Ludlow; c. Susan, Elizabeth; res: 3246 Front Rd., Jacksonville, Fla. 32217.

LUDLUM, JUDITH PENNEBAKER, Fashion Ed., Pittsburgh Post-Gazette, 50 Blvd. of the Allies, Pitt., Pa. 15230, '69–; Wms. Dept., '67; E. I. duPont de Nemours & Co., '64–'66; Asst. to Sunday Ed., Nashville Tennessean, '61–'64; Off. of Info. and Pubns., Vanderbilt Univ. (Nashville, Tenn.), '60–'61; Fashion Group, Pitt. Press Club, Theta Sigma Phi, Wms. Press Club, Chi Omega Alumnae; Univ. of Ky., BA, '60; b. Murray, Ky., 1938; p. Gordon and Dorothy Printz Pennebaker; h. Alfred Clay Ludlum II; c. Alfred III; res: 178 Mohawk Dr., Pitt., Pa. 15228.

LUDORF, PATRICIA JOAN, Dir., Consumer Rels., J. C. Penney Co., Inc., 1301 Ave. of the Americas, N.Y., N.Y. 10019, '68–; formerly Reprtr., Gannett, U.S., Europe; Adv. AE, Con Edison; PR Exec., M. W. Kellogg; Auth., Publr., "National Handbook for First Voters" ('56); articles in nat. mags.; OPC, PRSA (Silver Anvil Aw.; N.Y.C. Bd. Mbr.), CWPR (First VP), Inst. of the Press (Secy.), AWNY, Theta Sigma Phi (Pres., two terms), Am. Mgt. Assn., polit., charitable orgs.; Mayor's Key of the City of N.Y.; Cert. of Special Merit, Graphic Arts Industries; Who's Who of Am. Wm.; Who's Who in Intl. PR; Who's Who in the East; Barnard Col., BA; Medill Sch. of Jnlsm., Northwestern Univ., MS; Certs. L'Institut d'Etudes Politiques, Sorbonne, N.Y.U. Mgt. Inst.; b. Farmington, Conn., p. Henry and Norene McMahon Ludorf; res: 110 East End Ave., N.Y., N.Y. 10028.

LUDWIG, JANE M. (Luckii Ludwig), News-Edtl. Staff, Antioch (Cal.) Daily Ledger; Dept. Asst., Marshall University, Huntington, W. Va.; Tchr., news-edtl. classes; Rsch. new techniques in TV docs.; Dir., educ. TV jnlsm. programs; Sports Ed., Record-Chronicle (Renton, Wash.), '66–'67; Reptr., Lewiston (Idaho) Morning Tribune, '65–'66; NFPW, Wash. Press Wm., Theta Sigma Phi, various others; Sigma Delta Chi aws. for sports writing, '67; Univ. of Mont., BA (Jnlsm.), '65; Marshall Univ., MA (Jnlsm.), '69 (magna cum laude); b. Albany, Ore., 1943; p. Myles and Roberta Dawson Ludwig; res: 821 W. Seventh Ave., Albany, Ore.

LUEG, LENA FONG, Art Dir., Walker & Company, 720 Fifth Ave., N.Y., N.Y. 10019, '67–; Barry Col., BA (GA), '64; Pratt Inst., BFA (Adv. Design); h. Brock L. Hor; res: 42–49 Colden St., Apt. 8M, Flushing, N.Y.

LUELOFF, JORIE ANN PAYNE, Newscstr., News Reptr., NBC News, Merchandise Mart, Chgo., Ill. 60654; Feature Wtr., AP (N.Y.C.), '64–'65; Secy., CIA, '62–'63; NATAS, Chgo. Press Club; Mills Col., BA, '62; Univ. of Geneva (Switzerland), '61–'62; Grad. Inst. of Intl. Affairs (Geneva), '61–'62; Georgetown Sch. of Fgn. Svc., '63; b. Milw., Wis.; p. R. T. and Marjorie Kaltenbach Lueloff.

LUGLIANI, CLAUDIA SHELL, Catalog Ed., Yosemite Junior College District, 835 Glenn Ave., Modesto, Cal. 95353, '67–; Wms. Dept. Staff Wtr., Modesto Bee, '65–'66; Reptr., The Dalles (Ore.) Chronicle, '61–'63; Theta Sigma Phi; Univ. of Ore., BS (Jnlsm.), '61 (T. Neil Taylor aw.); b. Hamburg, Ia., 1940; p. John and Mary Aspedon Shell; h. Kenneth J. Lugliani; res: 1210 Crescent Dr., Modesto, Cal. 95350.

LUKAS, ELEANOR SIKORA, Pubns. Ed., Grand Union Co., East Paterson, N.J., '56–; Edtl. Training Cnslt., City of N.Y., '67–; ICIE (Mgt. Achiev. Aw., '68, '62), N.Y. Assn. of Indsl. Communicators (Treas., '60–'62), Drew Univ. Alumni Assn. (Secy., '53–'54), Pi Gamma Mu, Tau Kappa Alpha, Mensa; Bergen County Un. Fund aw., '65; numerous cits. for employee pubns.; Who's Who of Am. Wm.; Drew Univ., BA (Econs.), '48 (cum laude); Columbia Univ., N.Y.U.; b. N.Y.C.; p. Paul and Lillian Albrecht Sikora; h. Walter E. Lukas.

LUKENS, CHRISTINE LUCILE, Assoc. Prof. of Lib. Sci., Sterling College, Sterling, Kan. 67579, '67–; Head Librn., '50–'67; HS Tchr., '23–'50; AAUP, AAUW, ALA, MPLA, KLA, KASL; Delta Kappa Gamma Scholarship, '50; Sterling Col., AB, '23 (Alumni Aw., '67); Stanford Univ., MA, '26; Denver Univ., MA, '54; b. Beloit, Kan., 1901; p. Samuel and Leota Tice Lukens; res: Campbell Hall, Sterling, Kan. 67579.

LUMPKIN, ANNE CRAIG, Adm. Asst., KLRA, 1755 Union National Plaza, Little Rock, Ark. 72201, '58–; KTLN, Denver (Colo.), '54–'58; KGKO, Dallas (Tex.), '52–'54; KVLC, Little Rock (Ark.), '48–'52; AWRT; Univ. of Colo. Ext., '57; b. De Valls Bluff, Ark.; p. Claude and Lou Craig Lumpkin, Sr.; res: 2909 Fair Park Blvd., Little Rock, Ark. 72204.

LUMPKIN, THELMA SANTORO, Free-lance Graphic Designer, '67–; Adv. Mgr., Waterbury Nat. Bank, '60–'67; PR Dir., St. Mary's Hosp., '55–'60; Partner, Korant Agcy., '49–'55; Mgr., Nu-Tone Studio, '47–'49; Dir., Waterbury Family Svc. Assn., '62–'64; Dir., Waterbury Mental Health Assn., '60–'62; Auth., two one-act plays, "Shadow of Reason" prod. ('50), "Susanne's Room" prod. ('52); Central Conn. Cncl. on Hosp. PR (Pres., '57–'59), Am. Red Cross, Waterbury Area Un. Cncl. and Fund ('57; svc. aws., '61, '62); Fin. World Annual Rept. Nat. Survey 1st Pl. aw., '63, 2nd Pl., '60; Conn. State Drama Tournament Best Play Aw., '50; various other aws.; Simmons Col., BS (Eng.), '47; Yale, Graphic Arts and Design, '59; Harvard Grad. Sch. of Bus., Mkt. Mgt. and Adv., '65; b. Waterbury, Conn., 1925; p. Quirino and Flora Di Napoli Santoro; h. G. Thomas Lumpkin; res: Sperry Rd., Bethany, Conn. 06525.

LUND, DEANNA PHYLLIS, Actress, TV series "Land of the Giants," Irwin Allan Co., PO Box 900, Beverly Hills, Cal.; Free-lance TV shows, incl. "Batman"; Movie, "Tony Rome"; Weather Show, Ch. 10 (Miami, Fla.); Theatre roles; started own modeling sch. and agcy. in Fla.; commls. and independent prods.; Entertainer for GI's (radio, TV, Vietnam, hosps.); SAG, AFTRA; Rollins Col.; b. Oak Park, Ill., 1942; p. Arnold and Phyllis Lund; c. William Randall Upson, Kimberlee Arlund Upson.

LUND, DORIS HEROLD, Free-Lance Wtr., Artist, '47–; Copywtr., William Esty, '46–'47; Copywtr., Young & Rubicam, '40–'46; Auth., children's bks; Bk. Illus.; Tchr., Head Start, Norwalk, Conn.; Auths. Guild; Swarthmore Col., '39 (high hons.); b. Indpls., Ind., 1919; p. Don and Katharine Brown Herold; h. Sidney Lund; c. Meredith Lund Cohen, Eric, Mark, Lisa; res: 9 Sunwich Rd., Rowayton, Conn. 06853.

LUND, ELIZABETH LESLIE, Partner, Lund Associates, 12 Sunset Hill Ave., Norwalk, Conn. 06851; Dir. Commty. Planning PR, Edtl. Svcs. Dir., Un. Commty. Funds and Cncls. of Am.; PR and Dev. Dir., Nat. Conf. on Social Welfare; Dir., Commty. Rels. and Convention Mgr., Camp Fire Girls, Inc.; Eastern Seaboard Field Rep., Am. Wms. Voluntary Svcs.; Reg. Dir., Girl Scouts of U.S.A.; PRSA, Nat. Assn. of Social Workers, Nat. PR Cncl. of Health & Welfare Svcs.; Barnard Col.; b. Cleve., Oh.; p. Paul and Florence Fletcher Webster; h. John Lund; c. Mrs. Martin L. Schechtman, Mrs. Philip L. Hahn, John Ronald Leslie.

LUND, EMMA COWDEN, AE, Copywtr., Emma Lund, Inc., 987 Wagon Wheel Rd., St. Paul, Minn. 55118, '64–; AE, E. T. Holmgren, '56–'64; Ed., The Minnesotan, Univ. of Minn., '58–'59; Copywtr., Schuneman's, '54; PR, John Withy, '52–'54; Lay Cnslt., Jnlsm. Careers, Macalester Col.; Adv. Club of St. Paul (Dir., '65–'67; VP, '66–'67), AAUW (VP); Nat. Retail Copywriting Aw., '55; Macalester Col., BA, '54 (hons.); b. Chgo., Ill., 1931; p. Joseph and Elsie Remley Cowden; h. Richard Lund; c. Rachel Joy, Laurel Jean.

LUND, G. HELENE LEACH, Asst. Ed., Bus. Mgr., A. A. Lund Associates, East Rd., Sheffield, Mass. 01257, '56–; Med. Rschr., N.Y.C., '43–'44; Textbk. Ed., Macmillan Co., '37–'39; textbk. prom., '35–'37; Tchr., High Sch. Eng.; George Washington Univ., MA, '30; N.Y. State Col. for Tchrs., AB, '23; b. Gloversville, N.Y., 1902; p. Arthur and Helena Titcomb Leach; h. Albert A. Lund.

LUND, WANDA SMITH, Print Media Analyst, Goodwin, Dannenbaum, Littman & Wingfield, Inc., 2400 W. Loop St., Houston, Tex. 77027, '68–; Print Media Byr.; Adv. Asst., Navy Point Stores (Pensacola, Fla.); Display Adv. Rep. (Bryan, Tex.); b. Bryan, Tex., 1935; p. R. L. Sr., and Eva Dodson Smith; h. Walter Lund; c. Lawrence S., Angela Gail; res: 2015 Mardel Ct., Houston, Tex., 77042.

LUNDGREN, RUTH, Pres., Ruth Lundgren, Ltd., 320 Fifth Ave., N.Y., N.Y. 10001, '68–; Founder and Pres., The Ruth Lundgren Company, '48–'68; Dir. PR, Pan. Am. Coffee Bur., '45–'48; PR Staff Exec., J. M. Mathes, Inc., '42–'45; Assoc. Ed., Everywoman's Magazine, '40–'42; Wtr., monthly colm., Motor Boating Magazine, '62–; daily colm., St. Petersburg Times, '56–'60; Publr., The Ruth Lundgren Newsletter, '50–'58; Contrbr., popular and pfsnl. pubns.; Pubcty. Club of N.Y.; Bklyn. Col., '36–'41; Columbia Univ., '42; b. Bklyn., N.Y.; p. John and Hanna Carlson Lundgren; h. W. F. Williamson (dec.); c. John R., Mark W.; res: 3311 Bay Front Dr., Baldwin Harbor, N.Y. 11510.

LUNEY, LILLIAN GALITZ, Mng. Ed., The Union Signal, The Young Crusader, National Woman's Christian Temperance Union, 1730 Chgo. Ave., Evanston, Ill. 60201, '60–; The Union Signal, '51–; free-lance pubcty.; Theta Sigma Phi (Northwestern Univ. Chptr. Secy., '47–'48); Northwestern Univ., BS (Jnlsm.), '48; b. Evanston, Ill.; p. Ernest and Mary Teufert Calitz; h. Edmund A. Luney; c. Preston T.; res: 1866 Sherman Ave., Apt. 1 N.E., Evanston, Ill. 60201.

LUNNON, BETTY S., Spvsr. of Libs., Department of Educ., Government of American Samoa, Pago, Pago, Am. Samoa, 96920, '68–; Lib. Supvsr., Dade County Fla. Schs., '54–'68; Librn., Fairlawn Elementary Sch., '52–'54; Librn., Miami Edison Sr. HS, '38–'42; Cataloger, U.S. Govt. (Wash., D.C.), '36–'38; Auth: "Jacarezinno Vadico" ('46), mag. and jnl. articles, short stories; part-time Prof., Univ. of Miami, '61–'68; Dir. of Bk. Selection Workshop, Drexel Inst. (Phila., Pa.), '64; Cnslt. of Materials Workshop, Univ. of Ala., '68; many lib. and educ. orgs.; Delta Kappa Gamma, Kappa Delta Pi, Quota Club, DAR; Theta Sigma Phi Headliner Aw., '66; Britannica Aw.; Fla. Lib. Assn. (Pres., '61–'62), Am. Assn. of Sch. Librns. (Bd. of Dirs., '62–'64), Sch. Lib. Supvrs. (Nat. Chmn.), Lib. Comm., Field Enterprises, '64–'68; George Washington Univ., BS, '38; Appalachian Univ., MA (LS), '59; b. Montgomery, Ala., 1908; p. Merrill Ashurst and

Martha T. Guice Sheehan; h. James Lunnon (dec.); c. Penelope (Mrs. Darrell F. Fleeger); res: 1002 Granada Blvd., Coral Gables, Fla. 33134.

LUNZ, LOIS MARILYN, Supvsr., Div. of Relationships, Milw. Public Schs., Milw., Wis., '69–; Mng. Ed., Catholic Sch. Jnl., Bruce Publ. Co., '65–'69; Assoc. Ed., '62–'65; New Products Ed., Am. Sch. Board Jnl., '56–'62; Assoc. Ed., Founding Ed., Catholic Management Jnl., '56–'62; VP, Assoc. Ed., The Confectioner Magazine, '54–'56; Mng. Ed., Prod. Ed., Hobby-Model Merchandising News, '50–'54; Theta Sigma Phi (Milw. Chptr. Treas.) St. Bernardine's Guild (PR), NSPRA, Milw. County Radio and TV Cncl., Inst. Food Edtl. Conf. (Cert., '62); Marquette Univ., BA (Jnlsm.), '45; Milw. Sch. of Engineering, Cert. (Graphic Arts), '51; Laubach Literacy Tutor, Cert., '67; b. Milw., Wis., 1924; p. Ralph and Lora Plutte Lunz; res: 3235 N. 50th St., Milw., Wis. 53216.

LURIE, DIANA MARGARET, Assoc. Ed., Ladies Home Journal International, 641 Lexington Ave., N.Y., N.Y. 10022, '68–; Life, '61–'67; Oh. Univ., BFA, '61 (hons.); b. Johannesburg, S. Africa, 1941; p. Harold and Rose Brasch Lurie; res: 333 E. 34th St., N.Y., N.Y. 10016.

LUSKY, LOIS FREESE, VP, Acc. Supvsr., Sam Lusky Assoc., 550 First Nat. Bank Bldg., Denver, Colo. 80202, '65–; AE, '63–'65; PR Dir., U.S. Nat. Bank of Denver, '60–'63; Asst. PR Dir., '58–'60; PR Asst., '53–'58; PR Cnslr., Boys' Clubs of Denver; PRSA (Colo. Chptr. VP, '66), Govs. Commn. on Status of Wm., Bank PR and Mktng. Assn., Colo. Indsl. Press Assn. (Dir., '60–'63); several pfsnl. aws.; Who's Who in Colo.; N.D. State Sch. of Sci., AA (Eng.) '52; b. Wahpeton, N.D., 1931; p. James and Edna Eckes Freese; h. Sam Lusky; c. Mark; res: 3106 S. Newport, Denver, Colo. 80222.

LUTER, YVONNE, Bur. Chief, Stern Magazine, 1349 Lexington Ave., N.Y., N.Y. 10028, '51–; Bryn Mawr Col., BA, '49; Columbia Univ., MA, '58; b. Hamburg, Germany, 1928; p. Ernest and Marie-Louise Mankiewicz Spiegelberg; h. John Luter; c. Linda Penny; res: 1185 Park Ave., N.Y., N.Y. 10028.

LuTOUR, LOU, Dir., PR, Dist. 4, New York City Board of Education, 433 W. 123rd St., N.Y., N.Y. 10027; Pres., Founder, Global News Synd.; Free-lance Bdcstr.; Synd. Colmst., "Global Portraits," "Black Profiles of Courage;" AWRT, Intl. Platform Assn., Am. Poets League, World Poets Resource (Founder), Nat. Guild of Career Wm. (Co-Founder, Pres.), AAUW, Nat. Cncl. of Negro Wm.; Who's Who of Am. Wm., Who's Who in Poetry, Am. Poets Fellowship Soc. aw., '68; LittD, Free Univ. of Asia, '68; Harris Tchrs. Col., AB; Douglass Univ., MFA, '41; Columbia Univ., MA (Special Educ.) '62, Great China Arts Col., DHL (hon.), '69; b. St. Louis, Mo.; p. Henry and Amanda Boone Schwartz; res: 1270 Fifth Ave., N.Y., N.Y. 10029.

LUTZ, LAURA ANDERSON, PR Asst., The Coleman

Company, Inc. 250 N. St. Francis, Wichita, Kan. 67201, '67–; PR Dept., Associated Advertising Agency; PR, Paul Dannelley; NFPW, Kan. Press Wm., Wichita Press Wm. (VP, '69–'70), AWRT; h. Ed W. Lutz; c. Maryanne (Mrs. W. F. Griffin), Laura Lee (Mrs. Alan E. Crow); res: 965 Emerson, Wichita, Kan. 67212.

LUXFORD, NOLA, Fgn. Corr.; Fashion Show Prodr.-Commentator, '49–'58; Rep., NBC "Monitor," S. Pacific, '57–'58; Programs to Australia and New Zealand, OWI, NBC, '41–'45; "Four Star News," NBC, '41–'44; N.Y. World's Fair, '39–'40; "Fashion Show of the Air," '35–'36; Prodr., Commentator, KFI (L.A., Cal.), '32–'36; Auth., "Kerry Kangaroo" (McGraw Hill, '57); OPC, Town and Country Fine Arts Club, Adv. Wm., UN Speakers Bur., BPW, Anzac Club (N.Y.C. Founder, Pres., '41–'45), AEA, SAG; OBE from King George, '47; Cert. of Merit from Pres. Harry S. Truman, '47; U.S. Navy Achiev. Aw., '47; Fine Arts Club Wm. of the Yr., '63; Who's Who in Am.; Who's Who of Am. Wm.; Who's Who in New Zealand and other listings; b. New Zealand; p. Ernest and Adelaide McGonagle Pratt; h. Glenn R. Dolberg; res: 5167 Angles Crest, La Canada, Cal. 91011.

LYDON, PAULETTE le CORRE, Pres., Pol Lydon Inc., 16 Sidney Pl., Bklyn. Heights, N.Y. 11201, '49–; Publr., "The Polychart Graphic Primer"; Chief Chartist, Nat. Indsl. Conf. Bd., '28–'63; Am. Statis. Assn., DAR; Who's Who of Am. Wm.; Who's Who in the East; Royal Bluebook, Dic. of Intl. Biogs.; Beaconsfield Col. (Plymouth, Eng.), '13–'16; Brevet Superieur d'Institutrices (France), '17; b. Pont-l'Abbe-Lambour, Sud-Finistere, France, 1898; p. Francois-Michel-Marie and Therese-Josephe-Marie Janvier le Corre; h. George Lydon; res: 16 Sidney Pl., Bklyn. Heights, N.Y. 11201.

LYNCH, DOROTHEA PATRICIA, Copy Chief, AE, Stone & Manning Advertising, Inc., 1405 Statler Office Bldg., Boston, Mass. 02116, '68–; Copywtr., Kennedy's of Boston, '67–'68; First Prize, Joyce Glueck Poetry Competition, '67; Northeastern Univ., AB, '67; b. Boston, Mass, 1944; p. William and Dorothea Tierney Lynch; res: 2 Ashmont Park, Dorchester, Mass. 02124.

LYNCH, ELEANOR MARY, Home Econs. Dir., Reynolds Metals Company, 19 E. 47th St., N.Y., N.Y. 10017, '47–; Product Publicist, J. Walter Thompson, '43–'47; Home Econs. Dir., L.I. Lighting, '39–'43; Wtr., numerous articles on food prep.; "Crtv. Cooking With Aluminum Foil;" Am. Home Econs. Assn., AWRT, Electrical Wm's. Round Table; Simmons Col., BS, '32; h. James Terry.

LYNCH, M. ELIZABETH, Prof. Emeritus, Jnlsm., Marygrove College, Detroit, Mich. 48221, '65–; Prof., '49–'65; '38–'49; Fulbright Prof. of Jnlsm. and PR, eight univs. in Brazil, '62–'63; Soroptimist Fdn. grant, '62; PR cnsl., rsch., lect., all media; advisory work for pubns.; Founder and Dir., Marygrove Col. Feature Svc.; AAUP, PRSA, Assn. for Educ. in Jnlsm., AAUW, Intl.

Fedn. of Univ. Wm., Theta Sigma Phi (Nat. Rsch. Aw.; Mich. Headliner Aw.); Ind. Univ., AB, '32; AM, '38; Grad. Work; b. Oil City, Pa.; p. John and Jessie Webster Lynch; res: Apt. 147, 650 Pinellas Pointe Dr. S., St. Petersburg, Fla. 33705.

LYNCH, MARY BRIDGES, Dir., Prod. Adm., Monument Record Corporation, 530 W. Main St., Hendersonville, Tenn. 37075, '69–; Adm. Asst., Chet Atkins, RCA Victor Record Div., '68–'69; Personal Secy., '63–'68; Wtr, liners for record albums on 12 rec. artists; AWRT, Am. Fedn. of Musicians, Country Music Assn., NARAS, Beta Sigma Phi; Watkins Inst. (Bus.); b. Franklin, Tenn.; p. Leo D. and Fannie M. Stephens Lynch; res: 3010 Louise Dr., Nashville, Tenn. 37211.

LYNCH, MARY CAROLYN, Adv., PR Mgr., Ed., Norfolk & Dedham Mutual Fire Ins. Co., 222 Ames St., Dedham, Mass. 02026, '63–; Ed., state magazine for the Mass. Assn. of Insurance Wm., '69; ICIE, Mutual Ins. Communicators (edtl. aws., '67, '68), Nat. Assn. of Ins. Wm., Nat. Secys. Assn. (Fairbanks Chptr., Charter Mbr.; Corr. Secy., '61–'63); Ins. Lib. Assn. of Boston, '57; Am. Inst. of Banking, '55; b. Providence, R.I.; p. James and Grace Hackett Lynch; res: 42 Winslow Ave., Norwood, Mass. 02062.

LYNCH, PATRICIA KATHLEEN, Wtr.; Assoc. Prodr., CBS News, 524 W. 57th St., N.Y., N.Y. 10019, '67–; Assoc. Prodr., '69–; Gen. Assignment Reptr., Gannett Nwsps., West Chester, N.Y., '66–'67; English Tchr., East Meadow HS, '60–'65; Auth., "What's It All About, Charlie Brown" (Holt, Rinehart and Winston, '67); "The Air Jam," CBS News documentary, '69; Wtr., Assoc. Prodr., "Man on the Moon: The Epic Journey of Apollo 11" (CBS News, '69); Wtrs. Guild; Col. of New Rochelle, AB (English), '59; Boston Col., MA (English), '60; b. Jamaica, N.Y., 1938; p. Harold and Violet Carman Lynch; res: 416 E. 85th St., N.Y., N.Y. 10028.

LYNCH, SHEILA, Free-lance Bk. Designer, Random House, Harper and Row, Simon and Schuster, Meredith Press, Farrar, Straus and Giroux, others, Art Dir., children's bks., Harcourt, Brace and World; AIGA, 50 Bks.; Children's Bk. Show; Cooper Union, '47; b. Paterson, N.J.; p. Charles and Marie Kearns Lynch; res: 365 W. 20th St., N.Y., N.Y. 10011.

LYND, DR. HELEN MERRELL, Auth: "England in the 1880's," "On Shame and the Search for Identity," "Toward Discovery"; Co-Auth: "Middletown," Middletown in Transition"; Prof. Emeritus, Sarah Lawrence Col. ('29–'64); formerly Prof., Vassar, N.Y.U.; Cnslt: Genl. Educ. Bd., Rockefeller Fndn.; ACLU (Academic Freedom Comm), Am. Hist. Assn.; Cowell Col., Univ. of Cal. at Santa Cruz (Hon. Fellow); Wellesley Col. Fellowship; Grant Squires Prize; Columbia Univ.; educ: Wellesley Col., AB (Phi Beta Kappa); Columbia Univ., MA, PhD; Ripon Col. Hon. Dr. Litt.; b. LaGrange, Ill.; p. Edward and Mabel Waite

Merrell; h. Robert S. Lynd; c. Staughton, Andrea L. Nold; res: 420 W. 116th St., N.Y., N.Y. 10027.

LYNE, LIZ, Amusements Ed., Critic, The Shreveport Times, 222 Lake, Shreveport, La. 71102, '67–; Fine Arts Ed., The Odessa (Tex.) Am., '65, '67; Tchr., Colegio Panamericano (Bucaramanga, Colombia), '66; Shreveport Press Club (Treas., '68–'69); Librettist for opera, "The Hinge-Tune", 1st pl. winner, Nat. Opera Contest, '65; 2nd pl., NFPW mag. colms., '68; La. Press Wms. Competition, 1st pl., mag. colms., '68; La. Press Wms. Competition, 1st pl., mag. colms., 3rd pl., features, '68; Tex. Tech., BA, '65 (hons. program for superior students); b. Kermit, Tex., 1943; p. Raymond and Caleista Benton Lyne; res: 529 E. 43rd St. Odessa, Tex. 79760.

LYNN, SUE GOLDMAN, Asst. Dir. PR, E. J. Scheaffer and Associates, 1090 N.E. 79th St., Miami, Fla. 33138, '67–; Coordr., Men's and Boy's Apparel Club, '65–'67; Free-lance Wtr., Atlanta, Ga., '66–'67; Staff Wtr., Frosted Food Field, N.Y.C., '51–'53; Toastmistresses Intl., Fashion Group (Secy.), Fla. PR Assn.; L.I. Univ., '48–'50; New Sch. for Social Rsch., '50–'51; b. N.Y.C., 1930; p. Joseph Goldman and Jennie Kornhouser Goldman Gittleman; h. Charles Lynn; c. Toby Ruth, Lori Faye, Dian Michelle; res: 855 N.W. 170th Terrace, Miami, Fla. 33169.

LYON, BARBARA ANN, Ed., Numismatic Information Service, PO Box 282, Pleasant Valley, N.Y. 12569, '62–; Wtr., Synd. Colms., "The World of Coins" and "Coin Counting"; Am. Numismatic Assn. #48783, Intl. Org. of Wooden Money Collectors (Hon. #434), Rossica Soc. of Russian Philately #705, British Soc. of Russian Philately; b. Bklyn., N.Y., 1938; p. William and Sonja Kowha Lyon; res: Rossway Rd., Pleasant Valley, N.Y. 12569.

LYON, SUE, Actress; Pres., Sue Pax Inc., c/o Stuart Wechsler, 122 E. 42nd St., N.Y., N.Y. 10017; motion pics: "Lolita" (Seven Arts, '62), "Night of the Iguana" (Seven Arts, '64), "Seven Women" (MGM, '66), "The Flim Flam Man" (20th Century, '67), "Tony Rome" (20th Century, '67), "Four Rode Out" (Saggitarius, '68); TV: "Arsenic and Old Lace," ABC-TV, '68; active in vol., fund-raising work for Orthopedic Hosp., Synanon Fndn., ACLU, Shalom Inc., Adv. Cncl., N.Y. Inst. for Consumer Educ. and Dev.; Cnslr., E. Harlem Youth Employment Svc.; Golden Globes, '62, '63; Santa Monica City Col. (Dean's Hon. List); b. Davenport, Ia., 1946; p. Jack and Sue Karr Lyon; h. Hampton Fancher III (div.); res: Park Ave., N.Y., N.Y.

LYONS, DOROTHY MARAWEE, Wtr., teenage fiction; bks: "Smoke Rings" ('60), "Bright Wampum" ('58), "Java Jive" ('55), "Blue Smoke" ('53), others, all published by Harcourt Brace and World; State of California, Department of Industrial Relations, 411 East Canon Perdido, Santa Barbara, Cal. 93101, '60–; Am. Red Cross, Santa Barbara Chptr., '43–'48; Hawaii Chptr., '37–'42; Honolulu Star-Bulletin, '37; Nat. Assn.

of Bk. Publrs., N.Y.C., '31–'37; Delta Zeta, Am. Connemara Soc. (Bd. Mbr.), Dorothy Lyons Horsemanship Sch. (Pres.); Univ. of Mich., BA, '29; b. Fenton, Mich., 1907; p. Daniel and Mary Louise Adams Lyons; res: 740 Puente Dr., Santa Barbara, Cal. 93105.

LYONS, HELEN PADGHAM, Engineering Librn., Millikan Memorial Library, California Institute of Technology, 1205 E. California Blvd., Pasadena, Cal. 91109, '68–; Librn., Nat. Engineering Sci. Co., '64–'68; Engineering Librn., Hoffman Electronics Corp., '63–'64; Corporate Librn., Cannon Electric Co., '56–'63; Lib. Asst., Pasadena Public Lib., '43–'56; Special Libs. Assn. (Southern Cal. Chptr: Assoc. Ed., Chptr. Bul., '68–'70; Aw. for special svcs., '68 Annual Conf.), Cal. Lib. Assn., Nat. Mgt. Assn. (Cannon Electric, Secy., '58); Pasadena Jr. Col., '37; Univ. of Southern Cal., '57–'63; b. Gooding, Idaho, 1917; p. George W. and Grace M. Diddy Padgham; h. Robert L. Lyons; c. Mrs. Anita L. Jones, Robert L., Jr., Barbara L. (Mrs. Wm. H. Mojnnier), Beverly L. (Mrs. James R. Doolittle); res: 3335 Rida St., Pasadena, Cal. 91107.

LYONS, JOSEPHINE, Crtv. Dir., Ted Bates & Company, 666 Fifth Ave., N.Y., N.Y. 10019, '70–; VP, Crtv. Dir., Woman's World-Kenyon & Eckhardt, and Special Feature Br., Westinghouse Broadcasting, '67–'70; Reptr., NBC News, NBC Today Show, '65–'67; Copywtr., Group Head, Benton & Bowles, '60–'65; Wtr., TV commls. (Gold Key Adv. Aw., '63); Reptr., Dem. and Repl. Convs., CBS WINS, '60, '64, '65; Reptr., Am. Expsn., Russia, CBS, '61; Copywtr., J. Walter Thompson, '55–'58; Instr., TV Course, N.Y.U., '56; TV Wtr.-Prodr., Public Affairs, CBS (Hon. Mention, Peabody Aws. for "It's Up to You," '53), '52–'55; Adv. Wtrs., Wms. Adv. Club of N.Y., OPC, Univ. of Cinn., '47; Wellesley, '49; Sorbonne, '51; b. Cinn., Oh.; p. Phillip and Sonia Chase; res: 930 Fifth Ave., N.Y., N.Y. 10021.

LYTEL, JUNE WALDO, Instr., Eng. Dept., Villanova University, Villanova, Pa. 19085, '69–; Grad. Teaching Asst., Freshman Eng., '68–'69; Rsch. Asst., Eng. Dept., '68; Tchr., Akiba Acad., '67; Ed., Towers, Perrin, Forster & Crosby, '53–'55; Textbk. Ed., John C. Winston Co., '51–'53; Theta Sigma Phi (Life Mbr.; Dir. of PR Clinic, '57), Modern Lang. Assn.; Temple Univ., BS, '51 (Hon. Grad.; Outstanding Sr., '51; Sigma Delta Chi Jnlsm. Scholarship Prize, '51); Villanova Univ., MA (Eng.), '69 (high hons.); b. Philadelphia, Pa., 1930; p. Paul and Shirley Bishoff Waldo; h. Frederick Lytel; c. Craig R., Leslie M.; res: 117 E. Fourth Ave., Conshohocken, Pa. 19428.

LYTLE, RUBY COKER, Auth, "What Is the Moon?" (Charles E. Tuttle Co., Tokyo, Japan, '65); own pen and ink illus.; monthly 1200 wd. essay in Home Forum of Christian Sci. Monitor ('66–), short stories, children's mags.; articles, Western Family; more than 200 poems, nat. mags.; bk. revs., "The World in Bks."; Contemporary Auths.; Glendale Jr. Col., AA (Eng.), '38 (hon soc.); b. Glendale, Cal., 1917; p. Edgar and

Effie Myers Coker; h. Marcus Zearing Lytle; c. Monica Hope; res: 3147 Pontiac St., La Crescenta, Cal. 91214.

M

MacBEAN, DILLA WHITTEMORE, Edtl. Bd. Mbr., Jr. Literary Guild, Doubleday & Company, Inc., 277 Park Ave., N.Y., N.Y. 10017, '58–; Lib. Cnslt., Signal Bks. Series, '59–'69; Ency. Britannica, '55–'63; Spencer Press, Inc., '55–'59; Tchr., Lib. Sci.; DePaul Univ. at Chgo., '38–'45; Chgo. Tchrs. Col., '36–'43; Dir., Div. of Libs., Chgo. Public Schs., '35–'55; Auth., "Picture Book Dictionary" (Children's Press, '47); Co-auth., "What Book is That?" (Macmillan, '48); ALA (Councilor, '49–'56), Am. Assn. of Sch. Librns. (Pres., '55–'56), Ft. Lauderdale Friends of the Lib. (Bd. Dir., '63–'68), NEA, Ill. Lib. Assn., Wms. Nat. Bk. Assn., Chgo. Children's Reading Round Table aw., '56; Northwestern Univ., BA, '19; Carnegie Inst. of Tech., MA (Lib. Sci.), '21; Chgo. Tchrs. Col., ME, '39; b. Sioux City, la., 1895; p. James and Jennie Weed Whittemore; h. Alex G. MacBean; c. Donald A., John W.; res: 2160 Imperial Point Dr., Ft. Lauderdale, Fla. 33308.

MACDONALD, NONA MARY, Dir., Radio-TV Pubcty., Time Incorporated, Time & Life Bldg., Rockefeller Ctr., N.Y., N.Y. 10020, '66–; Radio Prodr., UN Info. Svc., '64–'66; Pubcty. Coordr., Screen Gems (Can.), '63–'64; Features Ed., UPI (Montreal, Can.), '57–'58; Colmst., Feature Wtr., The Vancouver Province, '52–'54; Radio, TV Prod., Canadian Broadcasting Corp., '54–'64; IRTS, AWRT; Univ. of Toronto, Ba; b. Saskatoon, Sask., Can.; p. Ronald and Nona Hutcheson Macdonald; h. Richard Burgheim (div.); res: 110 W. 69th St., Apt. 9D, N.Y., N.Y. 10023.

MACDONALD, ZILLAH KATHERINE, Auth., juv. bks. for many publrs.; taught at Columbia Univ., '19–'49; many Juv. Bk. of the Month selections; Dalhousie Univ., Columbia Univ., Harvard Univ. Summer Sch.; p. Charles and Annie McLearn Macdonald; h. Colin Macdonald; res: 468 Riverside Dr., N.Y., N.Y. 10027.

MacDOUGALL, MARY KATHERINE SLATE, Tchr.-Sponsor of Pubns., Austin Independent School District, 1212 Rio Grande, Austin, Tex. 78701, '59–; Wms. Ed., Austin Am.-Statesman, '58–'59; Tex. Assn. Mutual Ins. Agts., '56–'58; TV progs., A. C. Greene Bk. Store, '55–'56; Wms. Ed., Abilene Reptr.-News, '50–'55; Tricounty Ed., Pt. Huron (Mich.) Times-Herald, '43–'45; Auth: "Black Jupiter" (Broadman Press, '60), "What Treasure Mapping Can Do for You" (Unity Books, '68), "Prosperity Now" (Unity Books, '69); "Making Love Happen," (Doubleday, '70); Theta Sigma Phi, AP Aws. at Abilene; Wall St. Jnl. Nwsp. Fund Fellow, '60; Nwsp. Fund Top 50 Best Jnlsm. Tchrs., '66; Univ. of

Mich., BA, '30; b. Mt. Auburn, Ill.; p. Fay and Kittie Alexander Slate; h. 1. Wayne F. McMeans (dec.), 2. H. Alexander MacDougall (dec.); c. David McMeans, Nancy McMeans (Mrs. Charles Richey), Alexander MacDougall, Kent MacDougall, Alan Ross MacDougall; res: 2511 Hartford Rd., Austin, Tex. 78703.

MacDOUGALL, RUTH DOAN, Auth., "The Lilting House" ('65); Outstanding Young Wm. of Am., '66; Bennington Col., '57–'59; Keene State Col., BE, '61; b. Laconia, N.H., 1939; p. Daniel and Ernestine Crone Doan; h. Donald MacDougall; res: 10 Arch Street, Dover, N.H. 03820.

MACHETANZ, SARA BURLESON, Auth., Photogr.; Juv. Bks: "Robbie and the Sled Dog Race" (Scribner, '64), "A Puppy Named Gih" (Scribner, '57), two others; Adult Non-fiction: "Howl of the Malemute" ('61), "Where Else But Alaska" ('55); Co-Photogr: "Alaska Sled Dog," "Alaska U.S.A."; Auths. League of Am.; Jr. Lit. Guild aw., '50; Who's Who in the West, Who's Who of Am. Wm., Who's Who in Am. Art, Contemporary Auths.; Alaska Hall of Fame; E. Tenn. State Univ., BS, '40; b. Johnson City, Tenn., 1918; p. Horace and Sadie Ward Burleson; h. Fred Machetanz; c. Traeger; res: High Ridge, Str. Rte., A, B 56, Palmer, Alaska. 99645.

MacINNES, HELEN, Auth., c/o International Famous Agency, 1301 Sixth Ave., N.Y., N.Y. 10019; novels; "Above Suspicion" ('41), "Decision at Delphi" ('60), "The Salzburg Connection" ('68), 11 others; play, "Home Is the Hunter," '64; Auths. Guild Cncl., '66; Columba Prize in Literature, Iona Col., '66; Glasgow Univ., MA (French, German), '28; London Univ., Diploma in Librnship., '31; b. Glasgow, Scotland, 1907; p. Donald and Jessica McDiarmid McInnes; h. Gilbert Highet; c. Gilbert K. MacI.; res: 535 Park Ave., N.Y., N.Y. 10021.

MACK, CAROLINE TYSON, Publr.; Pa. State Univ. (Jnlsm.), '38; b. Butler, Pa., 1917; p. George and Mary Shearer Tyson; h. David Mack (dec.); c. David, Jr., Caroline (Mrs. Don DeMarino); res: 133 Craig Dr., Greensburg, Pa. 15601.

MACK, SARA ROHRBACH, Asst. Prof., Kutztown State College, Kutztown, Pa. 19530, '58–; Adjunct Prof., Grad. Sch. of Lib. Sci., Drexel Inst. of Tech., '68; Librn., Mt. Penn HS, '49–'58; Tchr., Chalfont Public Sch., '43–'45; Auth., "Inspirational Readings for Elementary Grades" (Kutztown Pub. Co., '64); ALA, Am. Assn. for Higher Educ., Pa. Lib. Assn., Pa. State Educ. Assn., Pa. Sch. Libs. Assn., Kappa Delta Pi, Alpha Beta Alpha; Kutztown State Col., BS, '43 (President's Aw. for superior teaching '62); Columbia Univ., MA, '55; Grad. Work: Temple Univ., Univ. of Pa.; b. Topton, Pa., 1921; p. Jonathan and Alda Heffner Rohrbach; h. Rev. George Mack; c. Carol; res: 125 W. Palm Dr., Topton, Pa. 19562.

MACKEN, MARY CATHERINE, Coordr. for State

Bdcst. Svcs., University of Wisconsin Radio-Television, Radio Hall, Madison, Wis. 53706, '63–; Adm. Asst. to Dir., State Hist. Soc. of Wis.; extensive rsch., writing for various pubns.; Univ. of Wis., BA; b. Madison, Wis.

MACKESY, LILLIAN SONNTAG, Food Ed., Feature Wtr., The Post-Crescent, 306 W. Washington St., Appleton, Wis. 54911, '53–; Free-lance Wtr., '33–'57; Feature Wtr., Wisconsin Magazine, '46–'48; Badger Legionaire, '44–'46; Adv. Mgr., Secor Co., '29–'31; Ed., Co-auth., "Land of the Fox, Saga of Outagamie County" ('49); Wis. Acad. of Sci., Arts and Letters (Vesta Aw., '65, '67); State Hist. Soc. of Wisc., Menasha Hist. Soc., Outagamie County Hist. Soc.; Univ. of Toledo, '26–'27; Univ. of Wis., '28–'29; b. Toledo, Oh., 1907; p. Albert and Clara Dieball Sonntag; (Stepfather Louis Plotkin); h. James J. Mackesy (dec.); c. James J., Janet Warren (Mrs. David Wiggins), Joan Claire (Mrs. Darrell Dorschner); res: 907 Bell Ave., Appleton, Wis. 54911.

MACKIE, JEANETTE ROSELYN, PR Dir., Gulf Life Insurance Co., 1301 Gulf Life Dr., Jacksonville, Fla. 32207, '66–; Dir. of PR Dev., '63–'66; Sales Pubns. Ed., '59–'63; Adv., PR Wtr., '53–'59; Asst. Adv. Dir., Mgr., P. Deisroth & Sons (Hazleton, Pa.), '42; Asst to Adv. Mgr., Furchgott's, '48; Fla. PR Assn. (Silver Image Aw., '68); Pilot Club (Dist. Governor, '68–'69; Jacksonville Club Pres., '63); Who's Who of Am. Wm.; World Who's Who in Commerce and Industry; Who's Who in the South and Southwest; Lasell Junior Col.; b. Hazleton, Pa., 1918; p. Frank and Arreca Belding Mackie; res: 5568 Fair Lane Dr., Jacksonville, Fla. 32210.

MACKIN, CATHERINE PATRICIA, News Corr., National Broadcasting Company, Wash., '69–; Corr., Hearst Nwsps., '63–'69; Polit. Wtr., Balt. News Am., '60–'63; WNPC, Wash. Soc. Nieman Fellows; Univ. of Md., BA, '60; Harvard Univ., '67–'68 (Nieman Fellowship), b. Balt., Md., 1939; p. Francis and Catherine Gillooly Mackin; res: 2320 20th St., N.W., Wash., D.C. 20009.

MacLACHLAN, JANET, Actress; Films: "Up Tight!", "Change of Mind," "Halls of Anger," "Darker than Amber," ". . . tick . . . tick . . . tick;" TV: guest roles on "My Friend Tony," "Ironside," "The F.B.I.," "Name of the Game," "Mod Squad"; Theatre: "Raisin' Hell in the Son," "Tiger, Tiger Burning Bright;" Actors Studio; Hunter Col., BA, '60; b. N.Y.C.; p. James and Ruby MacLachlan; res: 2428 Gower St., Hollywood, Cal. 90028.

MacLAINE, SHIRLEY (Shirley MacLaine Beaty), Actress, c/o Benjamin Neuman, 211 S. Beverly Dr., Beverly Hills, Cal. 94712; Cal. delegate, Dem. Nat. Conv. (Chgo.), '68; nominated three times for Acad. Aws., best actress category, "Some Came Running," "The Apartment," "Irma La Douce"; Theatre Owners of Am. Star of the Yr. aw., '67; Venice Film Festival Best Actress aw., '60; Italian Film Festival Best Actress aw., '64; Hollywood Fgn. Press Assn. Intl. Stardom aw., '54; Fgn. Press aw. for best actress, '58, '61, '63; toured Roumania at request of State Dept. on cultural exchange visit; assisted in financing an orphanage in Calcutta and Tokyo; Am. Film Inst. Bd. Dir.; Wash. Sch. of Ballet; b. Richmond, Va., 1934; p. Ira and Kathlyn MacLean Beaty; h. Steve Parker c. Stephanie Sachiko.

MacLEAN, JANE TOWNSEND, Family Ed., Daily Times-Advocate, 226 E. Valley Pkwy., Escondido, Cal. 92025, '65–; Soc. Ed., '57–'59; Classified Adv. Mgr., '52–'55; part-time, Palomar Col., San Marcos, '65; Classified Cl., San Diego Independent, '65; North County Press Club, '67; b. Estherville, Ia., 1934; p. William and Vivian Sorenson Townsend; h. (div.); c. Debra Lynn Miller, Ronald L. Miller, Jr., Kathleen MacLean, Matthew MacLean. res: 3958 Grandon, San Marcos, Cal. 92069.

MacLEOD, BEATRICE BEACH, Drama Critic, Ithaca Journal, 123 W. State St., Ithaca, N.Y. 14850, '61–; Telluride Assn., '59–; Asst. Prof. of Drama, Ithaca Col., '49–'51; Dir., Montreal Negro Theatre Guild, '46–'48; Theater Dir., Swarthmore Col., '34–'36; Publr., "On Small Wings" (Westminster Press, '59); Swarthmore Col., BA, '31 (Phi Beta Kappa); Yale Drama Sch., MFA, '34; b. Brentwood, L.I., N.Y., 1910; p. William D. and Edith Waldo Beach; h. Robert MacLeod; c. Alison Stuart, Ian; res: 957 E. State St., Ithaca, N.Y. 14850.

MacLEOD, MARION McLEAN, Auth. (all published by C. R. Gibson Co.): "All About You—An Adopted Child's Memory Book" ('59), "Cradle to College" ('60), "Let's Talk with Adoptive Parents" ('59); poems, articles, various pubns.; Lectr., radio, TV, '59–; bdcsts. incl: "Tempo Boston," "Today Show," "American Profile," "Mike Douglas Show"; Authority on adoption; Auths. Guild, Boston Auths. Club, Poetry Soc. of Vt., NLAPW (Br. Pres., '58–'60), several social welfare groups; WEEI Radio Edtl. Aw., '67; "Advocate Rose Aw.," The Jewish Advocate, '68; "Portrait of the Month," Un. Ch. Herald, '62; "First Person Profile," WBZ-TV (Boston, Mass.), '67; many aws. for svc. to adoption progs.; Who's Who of Am. Wm.; Who's Who in the East; Dic. of Intl. Biog.; The 2,000 Wm. of Achiev.; Notable Boston Auths.; educ: Cleve. Col.; Babson Col.; Univ. of N.H.; others; b. Hamilton, Ontario, Can.; p. John W. and Agnes H. Zealand McLean; h. Glenn MacLeod; c. Dianne MacLeod Brayton; res: 43 Glen Rd., Wellesley Hills, Mass. 02181.

MACMILLAN, NORMA KATHLEEN, Wtr., films and TV; Wtr., Recording Artists, Actress, CBC Radio-TV, Canada, 10 yrs.; SAG, AFTRA, AEA, WGA; Trinity Col., London, Eng., ATCL, LTCL (speech and drama); b. Vancouver, B.C., Can.; p. Lachlan and Harriet Nicholas MacMillan; h. Thorn Arngrim; c. Stefan Arngrim, Alison Arngrim.

MacMINN, ALEENE BARNES, Asst. Entertainment Ed., Los Angeles Times, 202 W. First St., L.A., Cal. 90053, '68–; Exec. TV Ed., '65–'68; Asst. TV Ed., '60–'65; Asst. Family Ed., '57–'60; Wms. Page Wtr., '53–'57; Wms. Page Reptr., Glendale (Cal.) News Press, '48–'52; Theta Sigma Phi, Alpha Gamma Delta; Univ. of Southern Cal., BA (Jnlsm.), '52; b. Salt Lake City, Ut., 1930; p. Harold and Allie Rasmussen Barnes; h. Fraser K. MacMinn; c. Margaret Aleene, Gregor Geordie; res: 1753 N. Pacific Ave., Glendale, Cal. 91202.

MACRAE, ELIZABETH, Actress, c/o Kumin-Olenick Agency, 400 S. Beverly Dr., Beverly Hills, Cal. 94712; "General Hospital," ABC-TV, '69–; three seasons, "Gomer Pyle, U.S.M.C.," recurring character; roles in numerous other live, filmed TV programs; many appearances in summer stock, Off Broadway; SAG, AFTRA, AEA; Herbert Berghof Studio, Art Students League, Otis Art Inst.; b. Columbia, S.C.; p. James and Dorothy Hendon MacRae; h. Nedrick Young (dec.); res: N.Y.C. and L.A.

MADAFFER, RUTH MADSEN, Exec. Dir., San Diego County Council of Camp Fire Girls, 2067 First Ave., San Diego, Cal. 92101, '56–; Exec. Dir., Compton (Cal.) Cncl. of Camp Fire Girls, '52–'56; Publicist, Commty. Chest of L.A. Area, '50–'52; Asst. Ed., Western Livestock Journal, '49–'50; U.S. Dept. of State Fgn. Svc. (Bern, Switzerland), '46–'49; Theta Sigma Phi, ZONTA (San Diego Club Past Pres.); Univ. of Southern Cal., BA (Jnlsm.), '46 (magna cum laude, Phi Beta Kappa, Phi Kappa Phi); b. Maywood, Cal., 1925; p. Hans and Rachel Bisbey Madsen; h. James V. Madaffer; c. James V. Jr., Jon Anthony, Mary Ann; res: 3879 Auburndale St., San Diego, Cal. 92111.

MADDEN, BETTY SIEGMUND, Home Econs. Cnslt., Abrahams Assoc., 1121 Nat. Press Bldg., Wash., D.C. 20004, '70–; Dir., PR and Pubcty., Sheraton-Park Hotel & Motor Inn., '67–'70; Public Info., Food and Drug Adm. DHEW, '63–'65; PR, Home Econst., Colmst., Continental Baking Co., '59–'63; Pubcty., Southern Cal. Gas Co., '39–'41; ANWC, AWRT, PRSA, Adv. Club of Wash., Am. Home Econs. Soc., Kappa Alpha Theta; Purdue Univ., BS (with distinction), '37; Univ. of Md., MS '67; b. Vincennes, Ind., 1916; p. Robert and Harriet Simpson; h. (1) T. C. Siegmund (dec.); (2) Wm. F. Madden (dec.); c. Suzanne Siegmund Nessel, Judith Siegmund Gardner; res: 2727 29th St., N.W., #538, Wash., D.C. 20008.

MADDENS, JEAN LAWRENCE, Pubns. Ed., Atlantic Research Corporation, Shirley Highway at Edsall Rd., Alexandria, Va. 22314, '66–; Cost Analyst, Redeye Project Team, '64–'66; Secy., Head of Documentation & Info. Svcs., '62–'64; Secy., Supvsr. of Pers. Training, S. S. Kresge Co. (Detroit, Mich.) '46–'50; AAIE, ICIE, Mid-Atlantic Assn. of Indsl. Eds.; Adrian Col., '44; Wayne Univ., '45–'46; Am. Univ., '69; b. Detroit, Mich., 1926; p. William and Mary Alexander Lawrence; h. Fred Maddens; c. Cynthia Jean, Nancy Ann,

David Frederick, Robert Douglas; res: 5309 Juxon Place, Springfield, Va. 22151.

MADDOX, VIVIAN, Asst. City Librn., Milwaukee Public Library, 814 W. Wisconsin Ave., Milw., Wis. 53233, '59–; Rsch. Asst., Rutgers Grad. Sch. of Lib. Svc., '58–'59; Public Lib. Cnslt., Mo. State Lib., '58; Chief Librn., Springfield (Mo.) Public Lib., '52–'57; Head Librn., Garland County Lib. (Hot Springs, Ark.), '49–'52; AAUW, ALA; Adult Educ. Assn., Beta Phi Mu, Delta Kappa Gamma, active in numerous commty. educ. groups; Milw. Municipal Wms. Club Achiev. Aw., '63; Ark. State Col., BA, '39; La. State Univ.; BS (Lib. Sci.), '46; Rutgers Univ., MLS, '59; b. Harrisburg, Ark., 1916; res: 3447 N. Hackett Ave., Milw., Wis. 53211.

MADDOX, YVONNE T., Mgr. of Pfnsl. Svcs., Comtact Corporation, 477 Madison Ave., N.Y., N.Y. 10022, '67–; Asst. to Dir. of Adv., Syntex Labs. (Palo Alto, Cal.), '65–'67; Sr. Secy. to Dean, Baylor Univ. Col. of Med. (Houston, Tex.), '64–'65; Asst. to Dean, Colo. Univ. Sch. of Med. (Denver), '62–'64; Asst. to Dir. of Pers., Univ. of Okla. Med. Col. (Okla. City), '59–'61; Educ. Fndn. Comm., AWRT, Pharmaceutical Adv. Club; 2,000 Wm. of Achiev.; Okla. State Univ., '54–'57; San Antonio Jr. Col., Cert.; b. Paducah, Tex., 1936; p. James and LaVonne Tarlton Maddox; res: 37 W. 76th St., N.Y., N.Y. 10023.

MADDUX, RACHEL, Auth: "Turnip's Blood," '37, "The Green Kingdom" (Simon & Schuster, '57), "Abel's Daughter" (Harpers, '60), "A Walk in the Spring Rain" (Doubleday, '66), and many short stories; Univ. of Kan., BA; b. Wichita, Kan., 1912; p. Harry and Malisa Morison Maddux; h. King Baker; c. Melissa Ruth Baker; res: Rte. 1, Tennessee Ridge, Tenn. 37178.

MADFIS, MIRIAM GOSIAN, Adv., Prom. Mgr., The Writer, Inc. and Plays, Inc., 8 Arlington St., Boston, Mass. 02116, '44–'50; '59–; Edtl. Asst., The Technology Review, '40–'44; Lectr., Lesley Col., '43; Simmons Col. Club of Boston (staff, Simmons College Review, '64–'68; Treas., '66–), numerous other alumnae activities; Simmons Col., BS, '40 (Class Secy., '65–); b. Brockton, Mass., 1920; p. Maurice and Dorothy Aronson Gosian; h. Bernard M. Madfis; c. Elaine Roberta, Meredith Joan; res: 21 Farmington Rd., W. Roxbury, Mass. 02132.

MADIGAN, MARGARET M., Copy Ed., George Braziller, Inc., 1 Park Ave., N.Y., N.Y. 10016, '69–; Copy Ed., Cosmopolitan; Moore Col. of Art, BFA, '66; b. N.Y.C., 1944; p. Martin and Kathleen Hassett Madigan; res: 1441 York Ave., N.Y., N.Y.

MADLEE, DOROTHY (Dorothy Haynes Madle), Feature Wtr., Boston Sunday Advertiser, 5 Winthrop Sq., Boston, Mass. 02106, '66–; Free-lance Wtr., Univ. of Wis: "Wisconsin Tales and Trails," "Exclusively Yours," "Better Camping," "Repertory Theatre";

Reptr., Feature Wtr., Art Ed., Milw. Sentinel, '42–'62; Auth., "Miss Lindlow's Leopard" (W. W. Norton, '65): MWA, New Eng. Wms. Press Assn.; Boston Press Club; Milw. Press Club William Pohl Humor Aw., '59; Boston Youth Activities Commn. Svc. Aw., '67; Oh. Northern Univ.; Univ. of Wis.; Harvard Univ.; b. Springfield, Mo., 1917; p. Robert and Grace Lapsley Haynes; h. Alain Madle (dec.); res: 122 Bowdoin St., Boston, Mass. 02124.

MADLEY, GRACE MARCIA, Home Furnishings Ed., The Philadelphia Inquirer, 400 N. Broad St., Phila., Pa. 19101, '52–; Feature Wtr., Sunday Magazine; Fashion Reptr.; Gen. Wms. Features; Am. Inst. of Interior Designers, NHFL (Phila. Chptr. VP), Nat. Soc. of Interior Designers; Dorothy Dawe Aw. for Home Furnishings Jnlsm., '62; Am. Inst. of Men's and Boys' Wear Lulu Competition Aws. (four plaques for men's fashion reporting); Univ. of Pa.; b. Phila., Pa.; p. Morris and Fannie Mafchir Madley; res: 415 S. Van Pelt St., Phila., Pa. 19146.

MADOW, PAULINE REICHBERG, Hist., Columbia University's Oral History Research Office, Butler Library, 116th St. and Broadway, N.Y., N.Y. 10026, '68–; Chief Copy Ed., Grolier Intl. Ency., Grolier, Inc., '61–'63; Assoc. Ed., Current Biog., H. W. Wilson Co., '59–'61; Ed: "The Peace Corps" and "Recreation in America" (H. W. Wilson, 2nd editions, '66 and '67); auth. of bk. revs. and articles in notable pubns.; Rutgers Univ., BA; MA; p. Jacob and Sonja Goldin Reichberg; h. Seymour Stephen Madow; c. Patricia Leslie Madow; res: 72 Park Terr. West, N.Y., N.Y. 10034.

MAGARET, HELENE, Eng. Prof., Marymount College, Tarrytown, N.Y., '44–; Col. of St. Teresa (Winona, Minn.), '40–'44; Rockford (Ill.) Col., '40–'41; Auth., numerous non-fiction and fiction bks.; Neb. Wtrs. Guild (Hon. Mbr.), Gallery of Living Catholic Auths.; Col. Eng. Assn., AAUW (Fellowship), '37; Mariana Griswold Van Rensselaer Poetry Prize, '32; educ: Barnard Col., BA, '32 (cum laude; Phi Beta Kappa); State Univ. of Ia., MA, '38; PhD, '40; b. Omaha, Neb., 1906; p. Ernst Friedrick and Celia Wolcott Magaret; res: 126 N. Broadway, Tarrytown, N.Y. 10591.

MAGEE, LOIS C., Kern County Librn., Kern County Library, 1315 Truxtun Ave., Bakersfield, Cal. 93301, '67–; Coordr. Ext. Svcs., '62–'67; Adult Ext. Supervising Lib., '59–'62; Ref. Librn., '56–'57; Asst. State Ext. Librn., State of Ariz., '57–'58; Cal. Lib. Assn. (Dist. Pres., '67–'68), ALA, Beta Phi Mu, Am. Soc. of Public Adm., AAUW, Bakersfield C. of C.; Univ. of Wash., '29–'30; U.C.L.A., BA, '34; Univ. of Southern Cal., MS (Lib. Sci.), '56 (Grolier Aw., '56); b. De Smet, S.D., 1912; p. Dr. Charles and Julia Tenney Cowgill; h. John Paul Magee; c. Marie (Mrs. Ross A. Stone), Paul T.; res: 3907 Noel Pl., Bakersfield, Cal. 93306.

MAGER, JANINE AMY, Fashion Credits Ed., The Hearst Corporation, 717 Fifth Ave., N.Y., N.Y. 10022,

'69–; Asst. Byr., Bloomingdale's, '68; Fashion Stylist, Fabiani (Rome), '67; Pubcty. Asst., Bonwit Teller, '66; Finalist, Vogue's "Prix de Paris," '68, Glamour's "10 Best Dressed" contest, '65; Univ. of Rochester, '64–'65; Univ. of Pa., BA, '68; b. N.Y.C., 1946; p. M. F. and Emmy Leo Mager; res: 355 E. 72nd St., N.Y., N.Y. 10021.

MAGGARD, CHARLOTTE CROUSE, Co-Publr., Reminder Publishing Company, 711 Grand Ave., Glenwood Springs, Colo. 81601, '63–; Adv. Sls., Aurora Star; Reptr., Rocky Ford Daily Gazette; Univ. of Colo., BA, '59; b. Carroll, Ia., 1937; p. Wayne and Elinor Halloran Crouse; h. Allan Maggard; c. Lucy, Ann; res: P.O. Box 339, Glenwood Springs, Colo. 81601.

MAGID, NORA LOUISE, Free-lance Wtr. and Ed., c/o Max Ascoli, 660 Madison Ave., N.Y., N.Y. 10021; Lit. Ed., The Reporter, until dissolution in '68; tchr., literature and crtv. writing at univs.; Nwsp. Guild, PEN; McGill Univ., BA; Columbia Univ., MA; b. Montreal, Quebec, Can.; p. Solomon and Valentina Bieber Magid; res: 510 W. 112th St., N.Y., N.Y. 10025.

MAGIERA, MARY ANNE, Educ. Wtr., Worcester Telegram, 20 Franklin St., Worcester, Mass. 01601, '67–; City Govt. Reptr., Norwich (Conn.) Bul., '66–'67; Wms. Page Ed., Webster (Mass.) Times, '63–'66; Advisor, high sch. page reprs., '63–'66; EWA, Boston Press Club; Who's Who in Am. Cols. and Univs.; Boston Univ., BS (Jnlsm.), '63 (Sorority Wm. of the Yr., '63; Scarlet Key, '62–'63); b. Webster, Mass., 1942; p. Charles and Mary Kralik Magiera; res: 48 Myrtle Ave., Webster, Mass. 01571.

MAGNUSON, DORIS SMITH, Teen Page Ed., Portland Evening Express, 390 Congress St., Portland, Me. 04102, '57–; Theta Sigma Phi ('51–'58); Univ. of Mo. Sch. of Jnlsm., BJ, '52; b. East Orange, N.J., 1930; p. Drury and Florence Watlington Smith; h. Henry Magnuson; c. Elaine S., Henry A., III; res: 1832 Congress St., Portland, Me. 04102.

MAGRUDER, BETTIE LOU, Wms. Ed., Wichita Eagle & Beacon Publishing Company, 825 E. Douglas, Wichita, Kan. 67201, '66; Wms. News Ed., '65–'66; Reptr. and Feature Wtr., Wms. Dept., '62–'65; Jnlsm. Advisor, St. Mary's HS, '62–'63; Kan. Press Wm., NFPW, Wichita Press Wm., Soroptimist Club of Wichita, Theta Sigma Phi (Wichita Club Pres., '69), Alpha Phi; various aws. for wms. pages and state and nat. press wms. writing contests; Wichita State Univ., BA (Jnlsm) '58; b. Wichita, Kan., 1935; p. Ira and Rose Hults Magruder; res: 1849 S. Glendale, Wichita, Kan. 67218.

MAHAR, DULCY ANN MORAN, Commtns. Offcr., United States National Bank of Oregon, 309 S.W. Sixth Ave., Portland, Ore. 97208, '69–; Commtns. Specialist, '66–'69; Ed., employee pubns., Meier & Frank Co., '64–'66; Wtr., Pitts. Post Dispatch, '61–'63; (summers between col. semesters); Chi Delta Phi (Pres., '63),

Ore. Jr. Adv. Club (Secy., '67–'68), Ore. Assn. of Eds. and Communicators (2nd VP, '69–'70; 1st pl. aw., '68); Pacific Indsl. Communicators Assoc. Aw. of Excellence, '68; Univ. of Ore., BS, '63; b. Stockton, Cal., 1941; p. John and Genevieve Sanguinetti Moran; h. Ted Mahar; res: 3356 N.E. Alameda Dr., Portland, Ore. 97212.

MAHONEY, HELENE MULLER, VP, Acc. Supvsr., Jerry Della Femina & Partners, Inc., 635 Madison Ave., N.Y., N.Y. 10022, '67–; Delehanty, Kurnit & Geller Inc., '64–'67; Genesco Inc., '58–'64; William Douglas McAdams, Inc., '56–'58; Rogers & Cowan PR, '55–'56; Fashion Group, AWNY; Parsons Sch. of Design; N.Y.U., BA; b. N.Y.C., 1935; p. Henry and Augusta La Blotier Muller; h. Robert Mahoney; res: 345 E. 73rd St., N.Y., N.Y.

MAHOOD, RUTH I., Chief Curator of History, Los Angeles County Museum, L.A., Cal., '58–; Curator of Hist., '54–'57; Instr. in Hist., '46–'54; Tchr., L.A. City and County Schs., '42–'46; High Sch. Hist. Tchr., (Verden, Okla.), '38–'42; Jr. High Sch. (Buckingham, Ill.), '25–'31; Auth., numerous hist. articles; Conf. of Cal. Hist. Socs. (Reg. 14A VP, '59–), Pilot Intl. (Dist. 18 Lt. Governor, '65–'66; Governor, '66–'67), Western Museums League (Pres., '61–'62), Cal. Hist. Commn., Cal. Heritage Preservation Comm., Jr. Hist. Socs. (Chmn., '63–'65); Cal. Hist. Soc. Aw. of Merit, '64; Civil War Centennial Commn. Aw. of Achiev., '65; L.A. City Sch. Dist. Cert. of Appreciation, '66; Central State Col., AB (Hist.), '33; Colo. Univ., MA, '42; b. Buckingham, Ill., 1908; p. Samuel and Sarah Bulington Mahood.

MAILMAN, VIRGINIA SHEVLIN, Sr. VP and Partner, Addison, Goldstein & Walsh, Inc., 635 Madison Ave., N.Y., N.Y. 10022, '61–; Asst. N.Y. Bur. Chief and Pic. Ed., Show Business Illustrated, '60–'61; Reptr., Life, '52–'60; Stanford Univ., BA, '51 (Cal. Scholarship Fedn.); b. Bronxville, N.Y., 1929; p. Matthew and Virginia McMillan Shevlin; h. Norton Mailman; c. Bruce Addison, Matthew Addison, Christopher Mailman; res: 109 E. 69th St., N.Y., N.Y. 10021.

MAINA, JILL DIANE, Free-lance Actress, Dancer, Anncr., Wtr., Communicaster; Prodr., Anncr., Communicaster, KLAC Radio; Anncr., KMET-FM; Wtr., Newsline Pubns.; SAG, AFTRA, Garrick Players, Alpha Psi Omega, Cellar Theatre, Actors Den; Pasadena Playhouse Col. of Theatre Arts, BA (Theatre Arts, '63; MA, '65; b. Chgo., Ill., 1942; p. Paul and Edna Burke Maina; res: 11625 La Maida, N. Hollywood, Cal. 91601.

MAJOR, GERALDYN HODGES, Sr. Staff Ed., Johnson Publishing Company, Inc., 1270 Ave. of the Americas, N.Y., N.Y. 10020, '67–; Chief, Paris Bur., '67–'68; Soc., Assoc. Ed., '53–'67; Wms. Ed., Amsterdam News, '47–'53; Adm. Asst., Bur. of Public Health, Educ., and Info., N.Y.C. Dept. of Health, '34–'46; Wms. Ed., Daily Citizen, '33–'34; N.Y. Soc. Ed., Pittsburgh Courier,

'24–'27; Dir., Geraldyn Dismond Bur. of Specialized Pubcty., '24–'34; Mng. Ed., Interstate Tattler, '27–'32; AWRT, Urban League of Gtr. N.Y., NAACP, Nat. Cncl. of Negro Wm., Negro Actors Guild, Alpha Kappa Alpha (cit., '66); Negro BPW cit., '63; Media Wm. cit., '53; Hon. Citizen, Boys' Town, '52; Nat. Assn. of Fashion and Accessory Designers cit., '62; Republic of Haiti Nat. Decoration of Honneur et Merite, '52; African Cultural Soc. of the Dominican Republic cit., '59; Dominican Press Assn. cit., '59; Frontiers of Am. cit., '50; Nat. Assn. of Colored Wms. Clubs cit., '66; Two Thousand Wm. of Achiev.; Who's Who of Am. Wm.; Univ. of Chgo., PhD, '15; b. Chgo., Ill., 1894; p. Herbert and Mae Powell Hodges; h. John Major; res: 2235 Fifth Ave., 10C, N.Y., N.Y.

MAJTHENYI, KLARA, Mng. Ed., N.Y. and London, Col. Dept., Appleton-Century-Crofts, 440 Park Ave. South, N.Y., N.Y. 10016, '68–; Fgn. Lang. Ed.; Special Projects Ed.; previously with The Macmillan Co. and G. P. Putnam's Sons; free-lance translation, ed., bk. design; Manhattanville Col., BFA; b. Budapest, Hungary; p. Ladislaus and Gabriella Roboz Majthenyi; res: 84 Sterling Ave., White Plains, N.Y., and 142 E. 33rd St., N.Y., N.Y. 10016.

MALAMUD, PHYLLIS CAROLE, Asst. Ed.—Feature Reptr., Newsweek Magazine, 444 Madison Ave., N.Y., N.Y. 10022, '64–; Back of Bk. Rschr., '62–'64; Pubcty. Asst., '60–'62; Rschr., Pres. Commn. on the Causes and Prevention of Violence, '68; Am. Bar Assn. Gavel Aw., '68; Russell Sage Fndn. Fellow at Wash. Univ. and Trans-Action mag., '68–'69; City Col. of N.Y., '56–'60; Wash. Univ., '68–'69; b. N.Y.C., 1938; p. Louis and Hannah Unterman Malamud; res: 7 Lexington Ave., N.Y., N.Y. 10010.

MALE, MARILYN HELEN, Stock Broker, E. F. Hutton & Company Inc., N.Y., N.Y., '67–; Tchr., Sls. Seminars, Training Sch.; Stockbroker Trainee, '66–'67; Adv. AE, Village Voice, '63–'66; Social Worker, Veterans Adm., '59–'60; Turtle Bay Assn., Assn. of Investment Brokers, N.Y. Pubcty. Club; Childrens Welfare Special Scholarship Aw., '56–'57; Veterans Adm. Special Scholarship Aw., '59–'60; Hunter Col., MS (Social Work), '63; N.Y. Inst. of Fin., '66; b. N.Y.C.; p. Samual and Celia Berk Tepper; res: 327 E. 50th St., N.Y., N.Y. 10022.

MALKIN, MARY ANN O'BRIAN, Assoc. Publr., A. B. Bookman's Weekly, Newark, N.J., '62–; Bk. Rev. Ed., '55–; Asst. to Dir. Am. Inst. Physics, '49–'55; Asst. to Ed., Publisher's Wkly., '45–'49; Adm. Asst. Chem. Warfare, Rockefeller Inst., Columbia Univ. (N.Y.C.), '41–'45; ALA, Am. Music Lib. Assn., Am. Theatre Lib. Assn., Special Libs. Assn. (Div. Chmn., '66–'67; Treas., '66–), Wms. Nat. Bk. Assn. (Chptr. Secy., '60–'66), Bksellers League N.Y.C. (Dir., '60–), Nat. Assn. Bk. Eds., Delta Gamma, Soroptimist Club (Secy., '66–); Penn. State Univ., BS, '37; Columbia, N.Y.U., grad. work; b. Altoona, Pa., 1913; p. Lawrence and Anges Lynch O'Brian; h. 1. Donal W. Lee (div.) 2. Sol M. Malkin; res: Box 1100, Newark, N.J. 07101.

MALLICOAT, LOIS EVELYN, Prod. Mgr., Parker Advertising, Inc., 609 Deep Valley Dr., Palos Verdes Peninsula, Cal. 90274, '66–; Asst. Prod. Mgr., McCann-Erickson (L.A.), '60–'66; Prod. Mgr., Tempo, Inc. (Chgo., Ill.), '58; Univ. of Chgo., BS (Jnlsm.); b. Oak Park, Ill.; p. Metford and Lorene Davis Mallicoat; res: 2045 Anza Ave., Torrance, Cal. 90503.

MALLON, PEARL, Wms. Ed., Valley Courier, 401 State Ave., Alamosa, Colo. 81101, '62–; Auth., "Wagons to Jets" ('69), poetry, non-fiction; Wms. Ed., Park City Daily News (Bowling Green, Ky.); Colo. Press Wm. (Secy., VP; Southcentral Dist. Pres., '67–'69), BPW (Secy., '59); many aws. for writing, photog.; Who's Who of Am. Wm.; Marymount Col., '44; b. Wakeeney, Kan., 1911; p. William and Jennie Hardin Law; c. James L., Larry C., Mrs. Wallace Holloway, Mrs. Glenn Rife, Mrs. G. W. Metz; res: 212 Alamosa Ave., Alamosa, Colo. 81101.

MALMGREN, LOYS CAROLINE, Radio-TV Coordr., General Foods Corp., 250 North St., White Plains, N.Y., 10602, '69–; Radio-TV Coordr., N. W. Ayer & Sons, '66–'69; Publicist, '56–'66; AE, two yrs.; Commentator, '56; Wtr., Prodr., Talent, on-camera TV, Radio shows, '48–'56; AWRT, Zenith TV Aw. for commty. interest programming, '56; Boston Univ., Col. of Practical Arts & Ltrs., '46; Bryant Col.; N.Y.U., Sch. of Gen. Educ., '62 (Assn. of Wms. Law Class); N.Y. Sch. of Interior Design, '64; b. New Britain, Conn., 1924; p. Alexander Lambert and Anna Stabert Malmgren; res: 7 Wildem Rd., Berlin, Conn. 06037, and 200 E. 66th St., N.Y. N.Y. 10021.

MALONE, MARY KILLILEA, Ed., Technical Review, Western Union Telegraph Co., 60 Hudson St., N.Y., N.Y. 10013, '61–; Tech. Wtr., '29–'42; Evaluation Mgr., McGraw-Hill Bk. Co., '59–'60; Computer Engineer, Royal McBee Corp., '58–'59; Tch. Ed., Sutton Publ. Co., '57–'58; Staff Ed., General Precision Lab., '51–'56; Patent Engineer, IT&T, '48–'51; Engineer, Eclipse-Pioneer, '42–'48; Soc. of Tech. Wtrs. and Publrs., N.Y. Assn. of Indsl. Communicators; Hunter Col., BA (Math, Physics); b. N.Y.C.; p. Michael and Katherine Killilea; h. William J. Malone; res: Horizon Towers S., Ft. Lee, N.J. 07024.

MALONE, NANCY, Actress; TV: "Naked City" (NATAS nomination, Best Performance), "Long Hot Summer" (Am. Cinema Eds. Best Performance by an Actress Aw.); "U.S. Steel Hour," "Dr. Kildare," "77 Sunset Strip," "Bonanza," "The Fugitive," and many others; Stage: "Major Barbara," "Seven Year Itch," "The Chalk Garden," "Requiem For a Heavyweight"; films include: "The Violators," "I cast No Shadow," "Intimacy," "The Outsider;" b. Queens Village, L.I., N.Y.; p. James and Bridget Shields Maloney; res: 2808 Laurel Canyon, Canyon Pl., L.A., Cal. 90046.

MALONE, RUTH MOORE, Auth., "Swiss Holiday Recipes," '66; Free-Lance Wrtr: Am. Home, Good Housekeeping, Parents, weekly syndicated feature (6

newspapers, S Ark. Palmer Media) '59–'65; Ed., "Holiday Inn International Cook and Travel Book," '62–; Food Ed., Holiday Inn Magazine, '62–; Assoc. Ed., Arkansas Today, '60; Auth: "Dogpatch USA Cookbook" ('70), "Where to Eat in the Ozarks, How It's Cooked" ('61–'63); Camden Dist. Wms. Club (Past Pres.) Ark. Federation Womens Clubs, WNBA, Ark. Press Women, Natl. League Amer. Penwomen, (Past Pres., L.R. Branch), Pi Beta Phi (past Alumna Pres.); Ward Belmont Col. (Nashville, Tenn.); b. Clarendon, Ark.; p. John and Bessie Branch Moore; h. Charles Malone; c. Margaret (Mrs. Hubert de Marcy), Bess (Mrs. Dick Lankford); res: 1 River Ridge, Little Rock, Ark. 72207.

MALSAM, MARGARET HULA, Free-Lance Wtr.; Adv. Copywtr., Holiday Gifts; Ed., "La Paloma" for Denver Archdiocese, Cursillo Movement; h. George Malsam.

MALTBY, FLORENCE GARLAND, Asst. Prof. in Lib. Sci., Southwest Missouri State College, Springfield, Mo. 65802, '63–; Teaching Asst., Univ. of Ill. Grad. Sch. of Lib. Sci., '66–'67; Grad. Asst., '59–'60; Ref. Asst. and Instr. of Lib. Sci., Central Mich. Univ., '61–'63; Elementary Librn: USAFE Dependents Sch., Wiesbaden, Germany, Ramstein, Germany, Sculthorpe, Eng.; Barrington (Ill.) Elementary Schs.; ALA, Ia. Lib. Assn., Ill. Lib. Assn., Mich. Assn. Sch. Librns., AAUP, Alpha Beta Alpha, Alpha Xi Delta, Kappa Delta Pi, Beta Phi Mu; Univ. of Northern Ia., BA, '54; Univ. of Ill., MS (Lib. Sci.), '60; Cert. of Advanced Study in Librarianship, '67; b. Sumner, Ia., 1933; p. Harold and Blanche Gritzner Garland; h. George R. Maltby; c. Patricia; res: 819 E. Linwood Dr., Springfield, Mo. 65804.

MALUSO, CLAIRE SAUNDERS, Training Dir. and Ed. Photogr., Strouss Hirshberg Company (May Company), W. Federal St., Youngstown, Oh. 44501, '67–; Youngstown Univ., '64–'66; Time-Life Prog., '66; Tchr., Pers. Qualifications, Youngstown Public Schs., two yrs.; Quota Intl., BPW, Am. Soc. for Training and Dev., Youngstown Educ. Wives, Fedn. of Wms. Clubs, Chi Epsilon; active in numerous civic groups; Youngstown Univ., '47–'50; b. Youngstown, Oh., 1929; p. John, Sr., and Florence Fitch Saunders; h. John J. Maluso; c. John J. Jr., Mary Jo; res: 2818 DeCamp Rd., Youngstown, Oh.

MAMALAKIS, MARIE J., Dir. of Pubns. and Prof., University of Southwestern Louisiana, Lafayette, La. 70501; Univ. Librn., '41–'65; Ed., Lafayette Progress, '54–'62; Public Sch. Tchr., Librn., St. Landry Parish, '34–'41; Publicist, Gas. Sch., Gulf Coast Drilling Sch. and other groups; Free-lance Wtr., articles in jnls., nwsps., periodicals; La. Lib. Assn., Phi Kappa Phi, Omicron Delta Epsilon, Beta Phi Mu, Pi Gamma Mu, Phi Alpha Theta; spotlighted by BPW; Univ. of Southwestern La., BA, '33; La. State Univ., BS (Lib. Sci.), '41; Grad. Work; Univ. of Chgo., '48; Tulane, '53; La. State Univ., '62; b. Shreveport, La., 1913; p. John and

Demetria Passadakis Mamalakis; res: 1018 Auburn Ave., Lafayette, La. 70501.

MAMPE, M. SCOTT, Dir. of Pubcty., Artist Rels. and Reviewer Service, Classical Division, Mercury Record Productions, Inc., 110 W. 57th St., N.Y., N.Y. 10019, '68–; Music Dir., WRVR-FM, '66–'67; Asst. Program Dir., WFLN-FM (Phila., Pa.), '64–'66; TV Specialist, U.S.I.A.-ITV (Wash. D.C.), '63; Acting Music Dir., WKAR, Mich. State Univ., '62–'64; Pi Kappa Lambda, Alpha Epsilon Rho (Corr. Secy., '61–'62); Who's Who of Am. Wm.; Ithaca College, BFA, '62 (magna cum laude; Oracle, '62; Zeta Sigma Nu, '59); Mich. State Univ., E. Lansing, MA, '64 (Grad. Asstship.); b. Lahaska, Pa., 1940; p. Charles D. and Mildred Schmidt Mampe, Sr.; res: 312 W. 90th St., N.Y., N.Y. 10024.

MANBECK, AGNES LUTERAN, Pres., Agnes Manbeck Advertising & Public Relations, 431 W. 61st St., Kan. City, Mo. 64113, '68–; Radio/TV Dir., Allmayer Adv.; Media Byr., Winius-Brandon Co.; AWRT (Kan. City Chptr. Pres., '67–'69), Radio/TV Cncl. of Greater Kan. City, Adv. & Sales Exec. Club; active in many civic groups; b. Kan. City, Mo., 1927; p. John and Rose Erdelyi Luteran; h. Buford L. Manbeck; c. Sharon Ann Himes, Liesa Jo, Buford L., Jr.

MANCEWICZ, BERNICE WINSLOW, Art Ed., Feature Wtr., The Grand Rapids Press, Vandenberg Center, Grand Rapids, Mich. 49502, '67–, '55–'65; PR Dir., United Fund, '65–'67; Fashion Ed., Feature Wtr., Grand Rapids Herald, '48–'55; Auth., Photogr., "Alexander Calder" (Eerdmans Publ. Co., '68); WNBA, Civic Theatre (Bd. Mbr.); Chgo. Art. Inst.; b. Racine, Wis.; p. John and Edna Gelmuss Winslow; h. John Mancewicz; c. Marcia, Mark, Carol; res: 229 Covell Rd. N.W., Grand Rapids, Mich. 49504.

MANDELL, BABETTE DONIGER, Acc. Mgr., Lando, Inc., 725 Liberty Ave., Pitt., Pa. 15222, '69–; Mgr., Progs. and Public Affairs, Gateway Broadcasting Enterprises; Sls. and Prom. Coordr., Catalina Inc. (L.A., Cal.), '58–'60; Asst. to VP, Grey Adv.; Pres., Editorial Films, Inc. (N.Y.C.), '52–'57; Prodr., Kathi Norris Inc., '50–'52; Prog. Dept. Asst., WPIX-TV, '48–'50; AWRT (Pres. Elect, '69–'70), AAUW (VP, '66–'67); Wms. Press Club, Adv. Club of Pitt., Pitt. Radio-TV Club; Who's Who of Am. Wm.; Pa. State Univ. BA, '44; Grad Work, New Sch. and Columbia Univ. Radio Workshop, '45–'48; b. Paterson, N.J.; p. Harry and Roselyn Lewis Doniger; h. David Mandell; c. Clifford, Sara, Cynthia; res: 428 Glaids Dr., Pitt., Pa. 15243.

MANDES, CLEO, Ed. and PR Asst., Fruit Growers Express Company, Western Fruit Express Company, Burlington Refrigerator Express Company, 1101 Vermont Ave., N.W., Wash., D.C. 20005, '53–; PR Asst., '66–; Legal Secy., '43–; Assn. of Railroad Eds. (Pres.); Strayer Bus. Col., Grad., '40 (highest distinction); b. Wash., D.C., 1922; p. Charles and Zoi Christopoulos Mandes; res: 1416 Fifteenth St., N.W., Wash., D.C. 20005.

MANDIGO, HELEN JEDLICKA, Supvsr. Home Econs., Baltimore Gas & Electric Co., 1300 Gas & Electric Bldg., Balt., Md. 21203, '62–; Eastern Reg. Field Coordr., Am. Sheep Prodrs. Cncl. (Denver, Colo.), '58–'62; Home Svc. Dir., The Gas Svc. Co. (Kan. City, Mo.), '48–'58; Home Econst., '42; home econs. cnslt., '58; Am. Home Econs. Assn. (Nat. Pres., '66–'68), Home Econsts. in Bus. (Nat. Chmn., '56–'58), Wms. C. of C. of Kan. City (Pres., '55–'56), ZONTA (Kan. City Pres., '54–'55), Wms. Adv. Club of Balt., AWRT, Intl. Platform Assn.; Univ. of Kan., AB, '35; b. Kan. City, Mo.; p. Joseph and Lottie Vincent Jedlicka; h. James Allen Mandigo; c. James A., Jr.; res: 112 Martingale Rd., Lutherville, Md. 21093.

MANDLER, JEAN MATTER, Assoc. Rsch. Psychologist, Lectr., University of California, San Diego, Department of Psychology, La Jolla, Cal. 92037, '65–; Rsch. Assoc., Dept. of Psych., Univ. of Toronto, '61–'65; Rsch. Assoc., Lab. of Social Rels., Harvard Univ., '57–'60; U.S. Public Health Svc., Postdoctoral Fellow, Harvard Univ., '56–'57; Co-auth: "Thinking: From Association to Gestalt" ('64); "The Diaspora of Experimental Psychology" from "Perspectives in American History," Vol. II ('68); rsch. articles, pfsnl. jnls.; Am. Psychological Assn., The Psychonomic Soc.; San Diego Parents Assn. for the Gifted (Pres.); Swarthmore Col., BA, '51 (summa cum laude; Phi Beta Kappa); Harvard Univ., PhD, '56; b. Oak Park, Ill., 1929; p. Joseph A. and May R. Finch Matter; h. George Mandler; c. Peter C., Michael A.; res: 1406 La Jolla Knoll, La Jolla, Cal. 92037.

MANES, NELLA CELLINI, Sr. VP, Ehrlich-Linkins & Associates, 4926 Wisconsin Ave., N.W., Wash., D.C. 20016, '68–; Stock-holder, Co-founder, '68; VP in charge of media, Kal, Ehrlich & Merrick, Inc., Media Dir., Time Byr., Asst. Time Byr., '49–'68; Adv. Club of Met. Wash. (Wash. Adv. Wm. of Yr., '62); AWRT, NATAS, Fashion Group; b. Steubenville, Oh.; p. Benvenuto and Liberata DeMarco Cellini; h. (div.); c. Mrs. Michele Cellini Broadfoot; res: 8144 Eastern Ave., N.W., Wash., D.C. 20012.

MANHART, SHARON RUH, Vice-Chmn., Wisconsin Citizens For Family Planning; Theta Sigma Phi; Oh. State Univ., BA (Radio-TV Jnlsm.), '54; b. Columbus, Oh., 1933; h. Harold E. Manhart; c. Grant, Scott, Anne; res: 5425 Trempealeau Trail, Madison, Wis. 53705.

MANION, MARION HEMSTREET, Mgr. of Corporate Pubns., Sprague Electric Company, 87 Marshall St., N. Adams, Mass. 01247, '64–; Assoc. Ed., '58–'64; Pers. Dept., '55–'58; AAIE (Dir., '68), ICIE, Mass. IEA, North Adams Un. Commty. Fund (Dir.); Cortland State Col., '36–'37; b. Ilion, N.Y., 1918; p. Adelbert and Emma Schultz Hemstreet; h. (div.); c. Barbara (Mrs. Bruce Whitman), Robert, Jr., Patricia (Mrs. Philip Mower), J. David; res: 889 Massachusetts Ave., N. Adams, Mass. 01247.

MANN, JOAN JACOBSEN, Free-lance Wtr.; articles, Seattle Times; Theta Sigma Phi, Am. Med. Wtrs. Assn.; Univ. of Wash., BA (Jnlsm.), '53; currently working for BFA; Cornish Sch. of Allied Arts, Seattle; b. Seattle, Wash., 1931; p. H. H. and Jeanetta Baker Jacobsen; h. Hugh Mann; c. Susan, Kristi, Steven, Nancy, Roy; res: 4025 N.E. 92nd, Seattle, Wash. 98115.

MANN, PEGGY LAVINDER (Evelyn Lavinder Mann), Wms. Dir., WTVD-TV, Capital Cities Broadcasting, 2410 Broad St., Durham, N.C. 27702, '57–; Prodr.,-Bdcstr., wms. show, '54–; Auth., "Peggy Mann's Idea Book"; Panelist, "A Visit with Franz Winkler, M.D."; AWRT (N.C. Chptr. Chmn.; Panelist, seminars for bdcst. media students, Univ. of N.C.), Durham Cancer Soc. Bd. Dir., Quota Club Bd. of Trustees; Durham Mother of the Yr. '61; Nat. Winner, Best Commercials for Formula 409, '65; Duke Univ., AB; b. Roanoke, Va., 1909; p. Thomas and Norma Price Lavinder; h. Glenn E. Mann; c. Beverly (Mrs. Stanley Shores, Jr.), Lesley; res: Rte. 2, Box 43, Cole Mill Rd., Durham, N.C. 27705.

MANNES, MARYA, Free-lance Wtr., TV and Radio Commentator, c/o Harold Ober Associates, 40 E. 49th St., N.Y., N.Y. 10017; Auth: novels, "They" ('68), "Message from a Stranger" ('48), non-fiction "More in Anger" ('58), others; Staff Wtr., The Reporter, '52–'63; Contrbr: N.Y. Times, McCall's, TV Guide, others; PEN, Auths. League, Dramatists Guild; George Polk Memorial Aw. for radio and TV mag. rept., '58; Hood Col., DHL, '60; Theta Sigma Phi Aw. of Hon., '62; b. N.Y.C.; p. David and Clara Damrosch Mannes; c. David Blow.

MANNING, DOROTHY FRANKLIN, Golf Colmst., Houston Post, 2410 Polk Ave., Houston, Tex. 77001, '66–; Staff Wtr., The Lady Golfer; Golf Writers Association of America, Theta Sigma Phi (Houston Chptr., Nwsltr. VP, '66–'67; Histrn., '65–'66); Press Club of Houston; active in commty. golf groups; Tex. Wms. Univ., BA (Jnlsm.), '39; b. Jourdanton, Tex., 1919; p. John and Louise Martin Franklin; h. Arthur E. Manning; res: 7217 Staffordshire, Houston, Tex. 77025.

MANNING, ELEANOR ROBERTS, Inst. Sls. Mgr., Broadcasting Publications, Inc., 444 Madison Ave., N.Y., N.Y. 10022, '49–; Radio-TV AE, Kudner Agcy., '43–'49; IRTS, Bdcst. Pioneers, Pitt. Adv. Club, AWRT, AWNY, Sigma Alpha Iota; Univ. of Rochester, BM, '30; b. Montclair, N.J., 1908; p. John and Elsie Roberts Manning; res: The Maples, Mendham Rd., Bernardsville, N.J. 07924.

MANNING, MARTHA ANN, VP and Owner, Mitchell & Manning Advertising, Inc., 1402 Davis Building, Dallas, Tex. 75202, '69–; Media Dir., Crook Adv. Agcy., '66–'69; Air Media Dir., Norsworthy-Mercer, '65–'66; Adm. Asst., Clyde Melville Co., '61–'64; Assn. of Bdcst. Execs. of Tex. (Bd. of Dirs., '68–'69; Secy., '67–'68), AWRT (Dallas Chptr. Pres., '64–'66); Southern Meth-

odist Univ., '52–'54; b. Dayton, Oh., 1934; p. Sam and Clyde Enix Manning; res: 10015 La Prada Dr., Dallas, Tex. 75228.

MANNING, MARY FRANCES, Wtr., Las Vegas Review Journal, 737 N. Main St., Las Vegas, Nev. 89102, '65–; Univ. of Nev.; b. Marlboro, Mass., 1947; p. John and Mary Bordeleau Manning; res: 1110 Toni Ave., Apt. 3, Las Vegas, Nev. 89109.

MANNING, REBECCA, VP, James F. Fox, Inc., 500 Fifth Ave., N.Y., N.Y. 10036, '68–; Dir. of Consumer Rels., '67–'68; PR AE, Harold J. Seisel Co., '64–'67; Press Assoc., Alfred Auerbach Assocs., '60–'64; Free-lance Wtr., '59–'60, '50–'54; Fashion Publicist, Joseph Bancroft & Sons Co., '54–'59; Fashion Ed., Dallas (Tex.) Fashion and Sportswear Magazine, '48–'50; wtr., numerous mag. articles; Fashion Group, NHFL, PRSA, Electrical Wms. Round Table, PR Assoc. of Am. Inst. of Interior Designers; Commtns. Offcr., U.S.N. Lt. (jg), WWII, '43–'46; Lander Col., BA, '43; Grad. Work: Smith Col., Columbia Univ., Mt. Holyoke Col., N.Y.U.; b. Leesville, S.C.; h. Jerome L. Kresch.

MANSFIELD, CATHERINE COHOLAN, Supvsr. Rating Svcs., Columbia Broadcasting System, 51 W. 52nd St., N.Y., N.Y. 11019, '67–; Mgr. Circ., TV & Radio coverage studies, NBC, '57–'67; Sr. Analyst, A. C. Nielsen Co., '56–'57; Ratings Analyst, Cunningham & Walsh Adv.; Rsch. Librn., Fuller & Smith & Ross Adv., '52–'54; Radio, TV resch. comms.; Manhattanville Col., BA; b. New Britain, Conn.; p. William and Dorothy Colling Coholan; h. Richard Mansfield; res: 139 E. 35th St., N.Y., N.Y. 10016.

MANSFIELD, PATRICIA LOUISE, AE, Batz Hodgson Newoehner Inc., 411 N. Tenth, St. Louis, Mo. 63101, '57–; free-lance, '55–'57; AE, Olian Adv., '53–'55; Byr., Famous Barr Co., '51–'53; Adv. Mgr., Prince Gardner Co., '46–'51; U.S.N.R., Lt. (jg), '44–'46; AWRT (St. Louis Chptr. Pres., '63–'64; Nat. Bd., '64–'66); NATAS (St. Louis Chptr. Bd. of Governors, '66–'68), Theta Sigma Phi, Wms. Adv. Club of St. Louis (Pres., '68–'69; Adv. Wm. of the Yr., '66); AAF Ninth Dist. Adv. Wm. of Yr., '67; Wash. Univ., AB, '42; b. St. Joseph, Mo.; p. Earl and Vera Douglass Mansfield; res: 329 E. Jefferson, Kirkwood, Mo. 63122.

MANSFIELD, RUTH E., AE, Compton Advertising, Inc., 625 Madison Ave., N.Y., N.Y. 10022, '65–; Mgr., New Bus., '56–'65; Mgr., Intl. Mkt. Rsch.; Colgate-Palmolive, '53–'56; Domestic Consumer Rsch.; b. Omaha, Neb., 1917; p. Henry and Clara Havlik Hansen; h. (div.); res: 450 E. 63rd St., N.Y., N.Y. 10021.

MANSFIELD, SALLY SMYTH, Media Cnslt., 128 Market St., Saugerties, N.Y. 12477, '60–; Tchr., '63–'69; Media Dir., C. J. LaRoche Adv., N.Y.C., '47–'59; Ridgeway, Ferry & Yocum, '45–'47; Wildrick & Miller, '43–'45; AWNY; active in politics; N.Y.U., BS (Mathematics); b. Saugerties, N.Y.; p. Edwin and Charity L. Mansfield; c. Edwin.

MANSON, PAULA, VP, Eddy Manson Productions, Inc., 16915 Donna Ynez Lane, Pacific Palisades, Cal. 90272, '61–; Prodr., music for films, commls., recs. (numerous Am. Commls. Festival Aws); former dancer, actress, comedienne (pseud: Paula Dorne); extensive USO tours, '43–'48 (numerous cits.); sportswear shop, N.Y.C., '48–'49; Am. Fedn. of Musicians, AGVA, ASCAP; private dance studies; City Col. of N.Y.; b. Ind.; p. Leonard and Lucinda Milligan Douse; h. Eddy Manson; c. David Joseph.

MANTHORNE, MARY ARNOLD, Pres., The Horn Book, Inc., 585 Boylston St., Boston, Mass. 02116, '62–; Chmn., Bd. of Trustees, Stevens Public Lib. (Ashburnham), '54–; Pres., Mass. Lib. Aid Assn., '62–; Russell Sage Col., AB, '32; b. Haverhill, Mass., 1909; p. Asher and Elizabeth Cooke Arnold; h. Gordon Manthorne; c. Arnold, William D.; res: 121 Main St., Ashburnham, Mass. 01430.

MANTIUS, MARJORIE ELLIS, Corp. VP, Dir. of PR, Gift-Pax, Inc.; Adv. and PR Dir., Peugeot, Inc. (Forest Hills, N.Y.), '64–'69; AE, Ted Worner Assocs., '63–'64; Accs. Supvsr., '59–'61; PR Dir., Gift-Pax, Inc., '61–'63; Intl. Motor Press, Intl. Platform Assn., Gamma Phi Beta; Who's Who of Am. Wm., Dic. of Intl. Biog.; Randolph-Macon Wms. Col., Univ. of N.C. Sch. of Jnlsm.; b. Roanoke, Va.; p. Clarence and Ana Sanderson Ellis; h. Philip Mantius; c. Edward S. Lebens, David E. Lebens, Bruce P. Lebens; res: West Meadow Rd., Setauket, N.Y. 11733.

MAPLES, EVELYN PALMER, Copy Ed., Proofroom Supvsr., Herald Publishing House, 3225 S. Noland Rd., Box 1019, Independence, Mo. 64051, '63–; Head Proofreader, '53–'63; Tchr., '37–'38; Poet; Auth: "Norman Learns About the Sacraments," "Jomo, The Missionary Monkey," "What Saith the Scriptures"; Who's Who of Am. Wm.; Contemporary Auths.; S.W. Mo. State Col., '36–'38; b. Ponce de Leon, Mo., 1919; p. Thomas and Bertie Dalby Palmer; h. William Maples; c. Norman, Matthew, Mrs. Billi Jo Carroll; res: 16216 E. Sea, Independence, Mo. 64050.

MARA, THALIA, Pres., National Academy of Ballet, 257 W. 93rd St., N.Y., N.Y. 10025, '63–; Pfsnl. Dancer, '30–'52; Choreographer, "The Seasons," "The Nutcracker"; Auth: "First Steps in Ballet" (Doubleday), "On Your Toes" (Doubleday), "So You Want to be A Ballet Dancer" (Pitman), "The Language of Ballet" (World), numerous other bks. and contrbs. to pubns. in the field of dance; h. Arthur Mahoney.

MARCHBANK, FRANCES ADELIA, Project Asst. Admr., Page Communications Engineers, Inc., 3300 Whitehaven Ave., N.W., Wash., D.C. 20007, '66–; in Libya, oil cos., '68–'69; in Vietnam, '66–'68; Fed. Electric Co., ETA (Germany), '65–'66; Gen. Electric Co., 412L Project, '65, Tech. Ed. (Syracuse, N.Y.), '59–'60; Asst. Prodr., Met. Opera Bdcsts., Asst. to Music Critic Edward O. D. Downes, free-lance wtr. for Airlanes mag. (N.Y.C.), '60–'65; Delta Delta Delta; Syracuse Univ., BA, '59; b. Paterson, N.J., 1939; p. Frederick and Frances Witbeck Marchbank; res: 2100 Linwood Ave., Apt. 23K, Fort Lee, N.J. 07024.

MARCORDES, HELEN I., Dir. TV-Radio Prod. Dept., Assoc. Partner, Jack Tinker & Partners, 1414 Sixth Ave., N.Y., N.Y. 10019, '69–; TV-Radio Prodr., '66–'68; Dir., TV Prod., Smith-Greenland, '68–'69; TV-Radio Legal, Grey Adv., '65–'66; TV-Radio Prod. and Traf., Hockaday Assoc., '64–'65; TV Traf., Papert, Koenig, Lois, '62–'64; N.Y.U., BS, '61; Parsons Sch. of Design, Cert. (Fashion Illus.), '60; b. N.Y.C., 1941; p. Arthur and Louise Herfurth Marcordes; c. Mary Lou Hawkins; res: 111 E. 81st St., N.Y., N.Y. 10028.

MARCUM, LILLIAN LOUISE, Librn., Public Library, Oconee County, 301 S. Spring St., Walhalla, S.C. 29691, '65–; Public Sch. Tchr., '56–'64; Art Instr., Anderson Col., '54–'56; ALA, S.C. Lib. Assn., Southeastern Lib. Assn., Pilot Club of Walhalla; Furman Univ., BA, '64; La. State Univ., MLS '65; b. Easley, S.C., 1931; p. Eldon and Cecil Maples Marcum; res: 100 Glazner St., Easley, S.C. 29640.

MARCUS, HELEN, Casting Dir., "What's My Line," Goodson-Todman Productions, 375 Park Ave., N.Y., N.Y. 10022, '68–; Advisor, Smith College Theatre Dept., '65–; Casting Dir., "To Tell the Truth," '62–'68; Assoc. Prodr., "Number Please," '61; Assoc. Prodr., "Beat the Clock," '58–'61; Program Coordr., "Two for the Money," '55–'57; Program Coordr., "Name's the Same," '55; in charge of subsidiary rights, Play Dept., MCA Mgt., '52–'54; TV Casting, CBS, '51; freelance photogr.: candid portraits, travel, bk. jackets, mags.; Phoenix Theatre (Pres. of Cncl., '68–;); Smith Col., BA, '47; b. N.Y.C.; p. Joseph and Augusta Hittleman Marcus; res: 66 E. 83rd St., N.Y., N.Y. 10028.

MARDIS, JANET CAROLYN, Pubns. Ed., Miami Valley Hospital, 1 Wyoming St., Dayton, Oh. 45409, '66–; Special Wtr., '65–'66; Soc. Ed., The Dayton Daily News, '60–'64; Fashion Ed., '56–'64; Feature Wtr., '53–'64; Oh. Nwsp. Wms. Assn., Am. Soc. for Hosp. PR Dirs.; nwsp. aws. for features and stories; Oh. Univ., BA, '53; b. Dayton, Oh., 1931; p. Chauncey and Marguerite Hearne Mardis; h. James F. Clarke; c. Jeffrey M.; res: 3824 Elmira Dr., Dayton, Oh. 45439.

MARENUS, FAY NEMIROW, Media Dir., Gary F. Halby Associates Inc., 55 W. 42nd St., N.Y., N.Y. 10036, '68–; Secy. Asst. to VP, Markland Inc., '64–'68; Asst. to Media Dir., Norman D. Waters Assoc., '52–'57; Rsch. Project, Corporacentrics Commtns. Controls Corp.; Univ. of Mo., BJ, '52; b. Phila., Pa., 1930; p. Maurice and Adeline Sianne Nemirow; h. Joseph Marenus; c. Mitchell, Judith; res: 16 Birch Lane, Green Acres, Valley Stream, L.I., N.Y. 13502.

MAREZ, JOANNE COKER, Wms. Ed., Idaho Free Press, 316 Tenth Ave. S., Nampa, Idaho 83651, '67–; Feature Wtr., '67; Display Adv. Clerk, '66; Religious

Ed., '65; Proofreader, '64; Idaho Press Wm.; state writing aws., '67, '68, '69; b. Nampa, Idaho, 1946; p. Robert Coker and Lorraine Redinger Payne; h. (div.); c. Steven Michael; res: 508 Garland, Nampa, Idaho 83651.

MARGETTS, MONTY (MARY), Free-lance Actress, c/o Ivan Green Agcy., 1800 Ave. of the Stars, L.A., Cal. 90067; films, '64–; TV dramas, comedies, '54–; "Monty Margetts Show," TV; "This Woman's Secret," NBC, '45–'53; radio (S.F., Cal.); began pfsnl. career, radio, stage (Seattle, Wash.), '29; b. Vancouver, B.C., Can., 1912; p. Roland and Marjorie Davies Margetts; h. Harold Manville McDonald; c. Hilary (Mrs. Robert Alan Costley); res: Parklabrea 556 S. Fairfax Ave., L.A., Cal. 90036.

MARGOLIS, ELLEN, Free-lance Wtr., fiction and non-fiction; articles in nat. and trade mags.; children's bk., collection of stories based on Oh. folklore, "Idy, the Fox-chasing Cow" (World); Tchr., crtv. writing, Univ. of Akron, Oh.; Children's Librn., Akron Public Lib., '56–'57; NFPW; Kent State Univ., BS, '55; Case-Western Reserve Univ., MS (Lib. Sci.), '56; b. Cleve., Oh., 1934; h. Matthew A. Margolis; c. Joel, Ann, Sarah Kim; res: 651 Treecrest Dr., Akron, Oh., 44313.

MARGOLIS, ESTHER MOLLY, Dir. of Pubcty., Bantam Books, Inc., 666 Fifth Ave., N.Y., N.Y. 10019, '65–; Asst. Prom. Dir., Ingenue; Founder and Co-Dir., Bridge East Inc.; PPA (Dir., '67–), AWRT ('67); Univ. of Mich., BA, '58; MA, '62; b. Detroit, Mich., 1937; p. Hyman and Tillie Rachael Kowall Margolis; res: 225 E. 79th St., N.Y., N.Y. 10021.

MARIAUX, HERMINE LOUISE, Home Furnishings Ed., House and Garden, 420 Lexington Ave., N.Y., N.Y. 10017, '70–; Ed., Decoration & Architecture and Town & Country Magazine, Hearst Magazines, '66–'70; Home News Ed., The New York Times; At Home Ed., Glamour; Assoc. Ed., Interior Design; Feature Ed., Home Furnishings Daily; Furniture Ed.; Home Furnishings Cnslt.; Guest Instr. on Design Mdsng.; N.Y.U.; Feature Wtr., stories on social and indsl. leaders in fgn. countries; various organizations; Cols. in Cologne, Germany and Lausanne, Switzerland (Fine Arts); Col. for Fgn. Trade and Commerce (Econs. and Fgn. Langs.); Cologne Acad. of Music; b. Cologne, Germany; p. Dr. Jur Hermann and Louise Ermertz Mariaux; h. Josef Head.

MARILLEY, JANE ELLEN, Pres., Courtesy Associates, Inc., 1629 K St., N.W., Wash., D.C. 20006, '47–; Edtl. Asst., Aviation News, McGraw-Hill Publ. Co.; Pres., Atlantic States Telephone Answering Assn.; Advisory Bd., Madison Nat. Bank; radio, TV appearances; many speaking engagements; Am. Mgt. Assn., Am. Soc. of Assn. Execs., Wash. Soc. of Assn. Execs., Aerospace Wtrs. Assn., ANWC, PRSA (accredited rating), Health & Welfare Cncl., D.C. Comm. on the Status of Wm., Met. Wash. Bd. of Trade, Interracial Cncl. for Bus.

Opp.; Trinity Col., A.B., '44 (Trustee): Am. Univ. (Jnlsm.), '45–'46; b. Wash., D.C., 1923; p. Anselm and Margaret Collins Marilley; res: 1750 M St., N.W., Wash., D.C. 20036.

MARINE, SHIRLEY JULIA, PR Dir., Milwaukee Public Museum, 800 W. Wells St., Milw., Wis. 53233, '65–; WTMJ Public Svc. Cncl., '69–; Asst., Pubns., Radio-TV Exhibits, Milw. Public Lib., '53–'65; PR Dept., Un. Commty. Svcs., '52–'53; Milw. Art Ctr., Milw. County Hist. Soc., Wis. Humane Soc., Mayor's Beautification Comm., '65–; Milw.-Downer Col., BA, '52; b. Milw., Wis., 1930; p. Richard and Helen Cyganek Marine; res: 1321 N. Prospect Ave., Apt. 10, Milw., Wis. 53202.

MARJOLLET, JANINE ELIZABETH, VP, Dir. of Bdcst. Opns., Carl Ally, Inc., 437 Madison Ave., N.Y., N.Y. 10022, '68–; Dir. of Bdcst. Opns., '64–; Prodr., Programmer, Bus. Mgr., Traf. Mgr., Secy., Campbell-Ewald, '55–'64; AWRT, Simmons Col., BS; N.Y.U.; b. Boston, Mass.; p. Leon and Leona Leglize Marjollet; res: 141 E. 56th St., Apt. 2C, N.Y., N.Y. 10022.

MARK, PAULINE DAHLIN (pseud: Polly Mark), Nurse-Tchr., Penfield Central School, Penfield, N.Y. 14526, '58–; '48–'50; Nurse-Tchr., Chautauqua Central Sch., '56–'58; Educ. work, Methodist Mission (Singapore, Borneo), '50–'55; Auth: "Tani" (David McKay, '63), "The Way of the Wind" ('65); N.Y. State Tchrs. Assn., N.Y. State Sch. Nurse-Tchrs. Assn., Penfield Educ. Assn. (Past Secy.); Clifton Springs Sanitarium and Clinic, RN, '34; Syracuse Univ.; Univ. of Rochester; b. Mayville, N.Y., 1913; p. Charles and Nettie Dearing Dahlin; h. Herman J. Mark; c. Charles B., Kathleen A.; res: 2176 Five Mile Line Rd., Penfield, N.Y. 14526.

MARKEL, HELEN, Article Ed., McCall's Magazine, 230 Park Ave., N.Y., N.Y., '66–; Sr. Ed., Ladies Home Journal; Contrb. Ed., Woman's Day; Smith Col., BA; Columbia Univ. Scho. of Jnlsm., MA; b. N.Y.C., 1925; p. Lester and Meta Edman Markel; h. John G. Stewart; c. Jenny, Mark; res: Two W. 67th St., N.Y., N.Y. 10023.

MARKEL, SELMA ROBINSON, Sr. Ed., McCall's, 230 Park Ave., N.Y., N.Y. 10017, '56–; Travel Ed.; Ed., Junior McCall's; Geyer Adv. Agcy., '53–'56; Staff Wtr., New York Star, '48–'49; Staff Wtr., PM, '40–'48; Head, Selma Robinson Assoc., PR, '34–'39; Free-lance Contrbr., articles, poems, stories; N.Y. League for the Hard of Hearing (Bd. of Dirs.), French Inst., Am.-Italy Soc., Met. Museum; O. Henry short story aw., '34; Geist jnlsm. aw., '46; N.Y.U., Columbia Univ., Sch. of Sci. Rsch.; b. N.Y.C.; p. Benjamin and Jenny Rudich Robinson; h. Howard Markel (dec.); c. Robinson, Lael (Mrs. James Lawrence); res: 1025 Fifth Ave., N.Y., N.Y.

MARKHAM, MARGARET, Exec. Dir., Vitamin Information Bureau, 575 Lexington Ave., N.Y., N.Y. 10022, '67–; Ed., Am. Baby Magazine; Ed., Mother-to-be Magazine; Contrb. Ed., Med. World News; Contrbr., mags.; Exec. Ed., Medicom; Ed., Sci. Info., Albert Einstein Col. of Med.; Ed., GU Rev.; Nat. Assn. of Sci. Wtrs., Am. Assn. for Advancement of Sci.; Radcliffe Col., BA; b. Budapest, Hungary; res: 146 S. Cypress Lane, Westbury, N.Y. 11590.

MARKO, ELEANOR, Wms. News Ed., The Daily Register, 105 Chestnut St., Red Bank, N.J. 07701, '68–; Asst. Wms. News Ed., '64; Staff Reptr., '58; News Corr., '52; Art Ed., weekly colm. "Palette Talk," '59–; NFPW, N.J. Nwsp. Wm. (aws., '69, '65), Monmouth Museum (Bd. of Dirs.), Beta Sigma Phi; Webster Inst., '38; N.Y.U., '39; b. Lyndhurst, N.J., 1920; h. Theodore Marko; c. Renee, Robert M.; res: 85 Alexander Dr., Middletown Twp., Red Bank, N.J. 07701.

MARKS, BETTY, Dir. of Mktng Svcs., Funk & Wagnalls Company, Div. of Reader's Digest, 380 Madison Ave., N.Y., N.Y. 10017, '67–; Pubcty. Mgr., Grosset & Dunlap, '65–'67; Lily Tulip Cup Corp., '61–'64; PR Dir., Audio Fidelity Records, '59–'61; Adv. & Prom. Mgr., Holt Rinehart & Winston, '64–'58; PPA; Univ. of Vt., BA, '48; b. N.Y.C., 1928; p. Dr. Rudolph and Bessie Rosenfeld Levy.

MARKS, EDITH BOBROFF, Co-Dir., Career Blazers Agency, Inc., 36 W. 44th St., N.Y., N.Y. 10036, '57–; Ghost Wtr., Eugene Gilbert & Co., '56–'57; PR, "Do It Yourself" Show, '55–'56; Publicist, Segy Gallery., '54–'55; Co-auth: "From College to Career" (Bobbs-Merrill, '61), "From Kitchen to Career" (Bobbs-Merrill, '63); Sigma Alpha Lambda; Bklyn. Col., BA '66 (cum laude); Columbia Tchrs. Col., MA, '70; b. Maynard, Mass.; p. Samuel and Rebecca Weber Swartz; h. Jason Marks; res: 35 W. 90th St., N.Y., N.Y. 10024.

MARKS, MARCIA BLISS, Wtr., Ed., Woman's Day, 67 W. 44th St., N.Y., N.Y. 10036, '66–; Contrb. Ed., Dance Magazine, '61–; Assoc. Ed., Grolier, '60–'66; Copy Ed., Little, Brown & Co., '54–'58; Pubns. Supvsr., U.S.I.S. (Singapore), '51–'52; Edtl. Trainee, Christian Sci. Monitor, '48–'50; Cnslt. on dance for N.Y. State Cncl. on the Arts; Auth., children's bk. "Swing Me, Swing Tree" ('58); Soc. for Asian Music, Wilderness Soc., Appalachian Mt. Club, Woodland Trail Walkers, Principia Col., BA, '48; Univ. of Geneva, '46–'47; Middlebury Col. French Sch., '48; Harvard-Yenching Inst., Harvard Univ., '52–'53; b. Cleve., Oh., 1927; p. Lloyd and Blanche Beal Marks; res: 116 W. 75th St., N.Y., N.Y. 10023.

MARKS, ROWENA McLEAN, Consumer Svcs. Mgr., Spice Islands Co., div. of Leslie Salt Co., 505 Beach St., S.F., Cal. 94133, '62–; Dietitian, Harriman Jones Clinic, '57–'58; Dist. Home Econst., S. Cal. Edison, '59–'60; Food Pubcty., Cal. Foods Rsch. Inst., '60–'62; Tchr., S.F. Sate Col.; Auth., "How California Cooks" (Ward-Pitcher, '69), "International Dining with Spice Islands" ('63), Home Econsts. in Bus. (S.F. Chptr. Chmn., '64–'65), AWRT (Golden Gate Chptr. Secy., '68–'69), Inst. of Food Technologists, Am. Dietetic Assn.; 17 mag. "Rose" aws., '66; Who's Who of Am. Wm.; Who's Who in the West; Royal Blue Bk.; Dic. of Intol.

Biog.; b. Winnipeg, Manitoba, Can., 1935; p. Sidney and Katherine Meckling McLean; h. George Marks; res: 142 Midcrest Way, S.F., Cal., 94131.

MARKSBERRY, MARY LEE, Auth., "Foundation of Creativity" (Harper and Row, '63); Chmn., Division of Elementary Education, University of Missouri—Kansas City, 5100 Rockhill Rd., Kan. City, Mo. 64110, '64– (Outstanding Prof., Sch. of Educ., '65); Tchr. of Educ., Psych. in cols. and univs. since '42; numerous rsch. repts., articles, revs.; numerous pfsnl. orgs.; Pi Lambda Theta, Kappa Delta Pi, Kappa Omicron Phi; Central Mo. State Col., BS (English), '35; Univ. of Mo., MA (Curriculum, Supervision), '39; Univ. of Chgo., PhD (Curriculum), '51; b. Blairstown, Mo.; p. James and Mary McDonald Marksberry.

MARLOWE, JOAN, Co-Publr., Co-Ed., (Theatre Information Bulletin & New York Theatre Critics Reviews) Proscenium Publications, Tower Suite 21D, 4 Park Ave., N.Y., N.Y. 10016, '44–; Edtl. Dept., Newsweek, '43; Actress, "Mr. and Mrs. North" (Broadway, '41); Co-Auth: "The Keys to Broadway" ('51), "Broadway—Inside the Last Decade" ('54); Drama Desk (Treas., '58–'60), Outer Circle (Secy., '57–); Stephens Jr. Col., AA, '38; Cornell Univ., '39; b. Ithaca, N.Y.; h. Roderic W. Rahe; c. Ward Morehouse III, Roderic W. Rahe Jr., Christopher W. Rahe; res: 18 Tory Hole Rd., Darien, Conn. 06820.

MARMUR, MILDRED ROSENBERG, Dir. of Subsidiary Rights, Simon & Schuster Inc., 630 Fifth Ave., N.Y., N.Y. 10020, '68–; Dir. of Fgn. Film Serial Rights, '59–'68; Ed., '58–'59; Secy., '53–'58; Translator: "Madame Bovary" (New Am. Lib., '64), "Tender and Violent Elizabeth" (Simon & Schuster, '60), others; Am. Bk. Publrs. Cncl., Mensa, Pi Delta Phi; Bklyn. Col., BA; Univ. of Minn., MA; b. Bklyn., N.Y.; p. Louis and Esther Holtzman Rosenberg; h. Julius Marmur; c. Alexander George and Nathaniel Zachary; res: 420 West End Ave., N.Y., N.Y. 10024.

MAROSSI, RUTH, Partner, Page Proofs Literary Agency, 25 E. 10th St., N.Y., N.Y. 10003, '62–; Co-auth: "Investing Abroad" (Harper and Row, '65) and "Money Makes Money and the Money Money Makes Makes More Money" (World Publ., '70); Cooper Un., '52; Yale Univ., BFA, '54; Columbia Univ., MA (Polit. Sci.), '59; b. Vienna, Austria, 1931; p. Maurice and Alice Eichberg Marossi; h. Gerald Krefetz; c. Nadine Carol and Adriene Dara.

MARQUARDT, DOROTHY ANN, Auth., juv. nonfiction; Jr. Lib. Asst., Quincy Free Public Library, Fourth and Maine Sts., Quincy, Ill. 62301, '51–; Public Lib. since '47; two bks.; Who's Who in Lib. Sci., Contemporary Auths.; Washington Univ.; Quincy Col.; b. Edina, Mo., 1921; p. John and Beatrice Franz Marquardt; res: 3421 Lawrence Rd., Quincy, Ill. 62301.

MARQUARDT, ELAINE MEYER, Mng. Ed., Colmst., The Tigerton Chronicle, Cidar and Alder Sts., Tigerton, Wis. 54486, '64–; Reg. Corr., Appleton Post Crescent; Edtl., News Wtr., Clintonville Press Gazette, '57–'64; Wtr., Marion Advertiser, '34; Milwaukee Journal, '32–'34; active in numerous civic orgs.; Univ. of Wis.; b. Marion, Wis., 1914; p. Harvey and Teresa Zaug Meyer; h. Lester Marquardt; c. Otto L., Dr. Bernard, Rev. Michael, T. Patrick, Virginia Mae (Mrs. Daniel Berger), Mary Alice (Mrs. James Power), Eileen, Rosemary (dec.); res: R.R. #2, Tigerton, Wis. 54486.

MARQUIS, ELVIRA T., Special Cnslt. to the Pres., Council of Graduate Schools in the United States, 1785 Massachusetts Ave., N.W., Wash., D.C. 20036, '63–; Free-lance Educ., Cultural PR Cnslt., '65–; Lectr. in U.S. under mgt. of Columbia Lect. Bur., '56–'65; Free-lance Jnlst., pubns. in U.S., Paris and Geneva, '55–'63; Am. Specialist (Lectr. on univ.-commty. rels), U.S. Dept. of State, '55–'60; NATAS, AWRT, OPC, Greater L.A. Press Club, RPRC, Am. Bus. Commtn. Assn.; Lutheran Tchrs. Col., Altona, Germany; Acad. of Dramatic Arts, N.Y.C.; Nwsp. Inst. of Am.; Grad. Work, U.C.L.A. (Jnlsm., Educ.); b. Hamburg, Germany, 1918; p. Frederick and Emely Geveke Trabert; h. Leonard J. Marquis (dec.); res: 865 Comstock Ave., L.A., Cal. 90024, and 2837 29th Place, N.W., Wash., D.C. 20008.

MARSH, SUSAN RAYMOND, Free-lance Wtr., Photogr.; over 60 articles in N.Y. Times; seven bks. about maps; Colo. Coordr., Nat. Cncl. for Geographic Educ.; Smith Col., AB, '35; Univ. of Denver, grad. work; b. Jersey Shore, Pa., 1914; p. Allen and Marietta Persch Raymond; h. Thompson G. Marsh; c. Nancy (Mrs. Loy Banks), Alice (Mrs. Wilder K. Abbott), Lucy (Mrs. Leland Yee), Mary; res: 199 Ash St., Denver, Colo. 80220.

MARSHALL, BETTY, Nat. Dir. of Mags., McFadden, Strauss, Eddy & Irwin, 509 Madison Ave., N.Y., N.Y. 10022, '68–; Mgr., NBC Mag. Sec., '62–'68; Asst. Bur. Chief, Newsweek (L.A. Bur.), '52–'59; Asst. to Colmst., Florabel Muir, N.Y. News, '49–'53; Entertainment Ed., Colmst., Mexico City Herald, '47–'48; Gtr. L.A. Press Club (VP, '57–'59), Hollywood Wms. Press Club, Aviation Space Wtrs. Assn., Cal. Assn. of Nwsp. Wm. Flame Aw., '59; h. Richard D. Spaulding-Marshall; res: 186 Riverside Dr., N.Y., N.Y. 10022.

MARSHALL, GLORIA, Home Econs. Dir., Myers Infoplan International, 1345 Ave. of the Americas, N.Y., N.Y. 10019, '61–; AE, Theodore Sills and Co., '52–'61; Home Econs. Dir., '51–'52; Assoc. Food Ed., Am. Home Magazine, '51–'52; Asst. to Home Econs. Dir., What's New in Home Econs. Magazine, '50–'51; Am. Home Econs. Assn., Home Economists in Bus., N.Y. State Home Econs. Assn.; N.Y.U., BS, '49; b. Bridgeport, Conn., 1927; p. Lawrence and Ellen Walsh Marshall; c. Marshall Thomson; res: 58 W. 58th St., N.Y., N.Y. 10019.

MARSHALL, VIRGINIA BOGAR, Jr. Partner, William

A. Marshall & Associates Advertising Agency, W. 1005 Gardner Ave., Spokane, Wash. 99201, '53–; Crtv. Dir: Miller, Ogle & Myers; Tomowske Adv.; McLean, Ogle & Myers, '49–'52; Head Fashion Copywtr., Bon Marche Dept. Store, '48–'49; Fashion Coordr., Palace Dept. Store, '46–'47; Display and Adv. Trainee, Sears Roebuck & Co., '42–'43; Spokane Adv. and Sales Assn. ('54–'64), C. of C., Adv. Assn. W., Am. Acad. Adv., AAF, Intl. Toastmistress; Ft. Wright Col., Holy Names, '39–'42; b. Deary, Idaho, 1921; p. Chester and Sarah Drury Bogar; h. William A. Marshall; c. G. X. Bayes, Jaye B.; res: W. 2838 Hoffman Ave., Spokane, Wash. 99205.

MARSTON, LOUISE CAROL, Soc. Ed., The Wisconsin State Journal, 115 S. Carroll St., Madison, Wis. 53701, '34–; extensive public speaking engagements; Theta Sigma Phi, NPWC; Milwaukee-Downer Col., '27–'29; Univ. of Wis. Sch. of Jnlsm., BA, '31; b. Appleton, Wis., 1909; p. Roy and Frances Ballard Marston; res: 1 Langdon St., Madison, Wis. 53703.

MARTENS, GRACE E., Mgr., PR Dept., Chirurg & Cairns, Inc., 641 Lexington Ave., N.Y., N.Y. 10022, '69–; PR AE, '62–'69; Publicist, Dir. of Men's fashions, '59–'62; Asst. to Dir. of Pubcty., Adv. and Prom., McGregor-Doniger, Inc., '56–'59; Prom. and Pubcty. Cooordr., '54–'56; Prom. Coordr., '53–'54; b. Teaneck, N.J., 1928; p. Peter and Anna Stein Martens; res: 34 Garden St., Teaneck, N.J. 07666.

MARTIN, ALLIE DENT, Dir., Tulsa City-County Library, 400 Civic Ctr., Tulsa, Okla. 74103, '63–; Head, Children's Dept., '49–'61; Assoc. Prof., Lib. Sci., Univ. of Okla., '58–; Librn., Miss. County Lib., '42–'43; Asst. to Exec. Secy., Ark. Lib. Commn., '37–'39; Librn., Little Rock Jr. Col. Lib., '36–'37; Librn., Batesville Public Lib., '35–'36; Ark. Lib. Assn. (Pres.), Okla. Lib. Assn. (Pres., svc. aw.), Southwestern Lib. Assn., ALA, Public Lib. Assn. (Exec. Bd. Mbr.), WNBA; Ark. Col., BA (Eng.), '35; George Peabody Col., BS (Lib. Sci.), '39; Columbia Univ., MS (Lib. Sci.), '49; b. Annieville, Ark., 1914; p. Carleton and Ethel Dent; h. Ralph Martin; c. Elizabeth M. Siggins; res: 120 E. 26th St., Tulsa, Okla. 74114.

MARTIN, BETTY S., Dir., Wms. Div., Institute of Life Insurance, 277 Park Ave., N.Y., N.Y. 10017, '60–; Asst. Dir., '46–'60; CWPR; Pomona Col., AB; Univ. of Paris, Sorbonne; Claremont Cols., MA.

MARTIN, BEVERLY R., Consumer Mktng. Specialist, Colorado Department of Agriculture, 1525 Sherman St., Denver, Colo. 80203, '69–'70; Trainee, '67–'69; Home Econs. Tchr., '61–'67; Interviewer, Guest Speaker, Demonstrator; Am. Home Econs. Assn., Colo. Home Econs. Assn., AWRT (Corr. Secy., '69–'70), Nat. Educ. Assn.; Univ. of Mass., BS (Home Econs.), '61; Simmons Col., MS (Home Econs.), '67; b. Worcester, Mass., 1939; p. Reuben and Mary Kabian Martin; res: Rte. 1, Little Ponderosa, Plymouth, Wis. 53073.

MARTIN, ELIZABETH CLARK, Lib. Dir., Englewood Lib., 31 Engle St., Englewood, N.J. 07632, '57–; Asst. Dir., '46–'57; Children's Librn., N.Y. Public Lib., '32–'46; h. Nathan Barnert Martin.

MARTIN, ELSIE STARK, Food Cnslt., Judge, numerous exhibits, contests; Bd. of Dirs., Wms. Mdse. Cnsl. Svc. (N.Y.C.), '66–'69; Nat. Hq. Dir. of Consumer Educ. and PR, Best Foods, '36–'58; first wm. in industry to dir. wms. activities in PR, Dir. of Home Econs., R. B. Davis Co. (Hoboken, N.J.), '26–'36; State Rels. Svc., U.S. Dept. of Agriculture (Fargo, N.D., and Mpls., Minn.), '17–'26; Supvsr., eight Southern Minn. schs.; org. depts. of Home Econs., Chatfield, '15–'17; Wtr., N.D. State Univ., BS, '15 (Distg. Alumni Achiev. Aw., '65); b. Glen Ullin, N.D.; p. Dr. George A. and Anna Knox Stark; h. Dr. William H. Martin (dec.); res: 2 Delaware St., New Brunswick, N.J. 08902.

MARTIN, EVELYN TEW, Radio & TV dir., Nelson Stern Associates, 530 Hanna Bldg., Cleve., Oh. 44115; Prom. and Pubcty. Dir., WJW Radio; Cont. Dir., WKYC Radio; Cont. Dir., KYW Radio; Fashion Copy Chief, Higbee's Dept. Stores; Auth: "Reluctant Eve" (Other Worlds Magazine Jules Verne Aw., '56), "Ghost Planet," "Narkeeta," and many other sci. fiction novels; Auth., "Year of the Rainbow" (sci. fiction drama prod. by KYW-TV); Prodr., Mng. Dir., Muse Summer Theatre; Cleve. Wtrs. Club; Univ. of Ala.; Western Reserve Univ.; b. Faunsdale, Ala., 1923; p. James and Ethel Knight Tew; h. Joseph L. Martin; c. Katheryn Martin Kiel, Robert L., Eleanor C.; res: 17601 Chagrin Blvd., Shaker Heights, Oh. 44120.

MARTIN, JANET ROUSE, Wms. Ed., Daily Press —Panax Corp., 600 Ludington St., Escanaba, Mich. 49829, '65–; Escanaba Public Sch. System, '64–'65; Northern Mich. Univ.; b. Escanaba, Mich., 1941; p. Raymond and Linella Fallmer Rouse; h. Gerald Martin; c. Stephen Lee, Christine Beth; res: 1030 S. 16th St., Escanaba, Mich. 49829.

MARTIN, JOYCE M., Radio and TV PR, Eastern Airlines, 10 Rockefeller Plaza, N.Y., N.Y. 10020; Dir., News and Mag. Coordr., N.Y. World's Fair Corp. (Flushing Meadow), '62–'65; Dir. PR, N.Y. State Dem. Comm. (N.Y.C.), '49–'62; AWRT, Alpha Delta Pi; Queens Col., BA, '49 (Scholar; hons.; Alumnae Assn.); b. N.Y.C., 1928; p. Albert and Jewel Woolley Martin; h. Charles Bowden; c. Charles M.

MARTIN, JUDITH SYLVIA, Reptr., The Washington Post, 1515 L St., N.W., Wash., D.C. 20005, '60–; WNPC, WHCA, State Dept. Corrs. Assn.; Wellesley Col., BA, '59; b. Wash., D.C., 1938; p. Jacob and Helen Aronson Perlman; h. Robert Martin; c. Nicholas Ivor; res: 1651 Harvard St., N.W., Wash., D.C. 20009.

MARTIN, KATHRYN KELTNER, Asst. Dir. Home Econs., Swift & Company, 1919 Swift Dr., Oak Brook, Ill. 60521; Dir. of Wms. Activities, Wms. Show, WCOL (Columbus, Oh.), '43–'46; Home Econst., radio work,

Oh. Fuel Gas Co., '41–'43; Head of Stock, F. & R. Lazarus Co., '40–'41; AWRT (Chgo. Chptr. Pres., '65–'67), Home Econsts. in Bus., AHEA, Ill. Home Econs. Assn.; Oh. Wesleyan Univ.; b. Stantontown, Oh., 1918; p. Clyde and Amelia Keltner; h. Howard L. Martin; res: 1360 N. Lake Shore Dr., Chgo., Ill. 60610.

MARTIN, LAURA KATHERINE, Assoc. Prof., Lib. Sci., University of Kentucky, Lexington, Ky. 40506, '40–; Instr., Univ. of Denver, '52, Ind. Univ., '40; Fac., San Jose State Col.; Librn., Cal. schs., '25–'38; Chmn., Ky. State Cert. Bd. for Public Libs., '58–'67; Edtl., Mags. for Sch. Libs., lib. studies, Bul. of Nat. Assn. of Sec. Sch. Prins., conf. proceedings; Contrbr. to pfsnl. jnls.; Am. Assn. of Sch. Librns. (Pres., '51–'52), ALA (2nd VP, '52–'53), Lexington Librns. Assn. (Pres., '61–'62), ALA, Ky. Lib. Assn., Southeastern Lib. Assn., AAUP, active in local orgs.; U.C.L.A., AB, '29; Stanford Univ., MA, '40; Univ. of Chgo.; b. Springfield, S.D., 1906; p. Michael and Rena Alderman Martin; res: 442 Oldham Ave., Lexington, Ky. 40502.

MARTIN, LUCILLE STUSSY, Publr., Sawyer County Gazette, Winter, Wis. 54896, '49–; Elementary Tchr., '42–'63; Eau Claire State Univ., ext. classes, '50–'60; b. Eau Claire, Wis., 1898; p. Karl and Martha Hanck Stussy; h. Roy Martin; c. Mrs. Edward Strout; res: Winter, Wis. 54896.

MARTIN, MARGARET ANN, Educ., Medical Wtr., The Shreveport Times, 222 Lake St., Shreveport, La. 71102, '66–; Educ. Wtr., '65–; Religion Wtr., '64–'66; Theta Sigma Phi, Shreveport Press Club (Treas., '65); Univ. of Tulsa, BA, '62; La. State Univ., MA, '64; b. Shreveport, La., 1940; p. Robert and Sabra Brown Martin; res: 3512 Lakeland St., Shreveport, La. 71109.

MARTIN, MARTHA DUCE, Adm. Asst., School of Home Econs., University of Missouri, 114 Gwynn Hall, Columbia, Mo. 65201, '64–; PR, all media; Theta Sigma Phi (Columbia Pfsnl. Chptr. State Coordr., '67–'68; Pres., '68–'69; VP, '66–'67), Phi Upsilon Omicron (Fac. Advisor, '64–'68), Am. and Mo. Home Econs. Assn., NPWC, Mo. Press Wm.; Am. Assn. of Agri. Col. Eds., Outstanding Young Wm. in Am., '67; Univ. of Mo., BS (Home Econs. Jnlsm.), '64; MS (Cmmtns.), '69; b. Maysville, Mo., 1941; p. Clifford and June Gaskell Duce, 1941; h. James A. Martin; c. Gregory L.; res: 170 Crestvale Ct., Columbia, Mo. 65201.

MARTIN, MARY ANN McGRATH, Film Ed., National Broadcasting Company, 30 Rockefeller Plaza, N.Y., N.Y. 10020, '68–; Asst. Film Ed.; 1st Asst. Film Ed.; NATAS; College of New Rochelle, BA (Hist.), '62; b. N.Y.C., 1941; p. Edward J. and Irene P. Murphy McGrath; h. John Martin; res: 446 W. 51st St., N.Y., N.Y. 10019.

MARTIN, NANCY LEE, VP, Martin Partners, Inc., 300 S. Beverly Dr., Beverly Hills, Cal. 90212, '68–; Owner, NLM PR, '67–'68; VP, PR Dir., Recht & Co., '63–'67; PR Cnslt., Housing Opps. Ctr. div., Commty. Rels. Conf.

of Southern Cal.; Theta Sigma Phi (L.A. Pfsnl. Chptr.), Pubcty. Club of L.A., N.Y. Type Dirs. Spectra Aw., '63; Phoenix Col., AA, '52; Univ. of Cal., Berkeley, AB, '54; b. Phoenix, Ariz.; p. Donald and Mary Wilson Martin; res: P.O. Box 5221, Beverly Hills, Cal. 90210.

MARTIN, NINA NIX, State Sch. Lib. Cnslt., Alabama State Department of Education, Dexter Ave., Montgomery, Ala. 36104, '66–; Librn., Tchr., '51–'66; Cnslt., Univ. of Southern Miss., Miss. State Col., Purdue Univ.; Wtr., articles, filmstrips; Ala. Educ. Assn., Ala. Sch. Librns. Assn. (Corr. Secy., '67–); Beta Phi Mu, numerous others; Univ. of Southern Miss., BS, '55; Springhill Col.; La. State Univ., MS (Lib. Sci.), '65; b. Laurel, Miss., 1932; p. George and Lillian Seward Nix; h. Gerald Martin; c. Florence D., Gerry L.; res: 3809 D Meadowview Dr., Montgomery, Ala. 36105.

MARTIN, NORENE DANN, Exec. VP and Wtr., National Parking Association, 1101 17th St., N.W., Wash., D.C. 20036, '65–; Exec. Dir.; Exec. Asst., '55–; Ed., '53–; Ed. and Copywtr., MacMillan Publ. Co., '43–'46; Co-auth., "The Parking Industry" ('69); Greater Met. Wash. Bd. of Trade ('65), Am. and Wash. Socs. of Assn. Execs.; Black Mountain Col.; Columbia Univ., MA, '40; Insts. for Org. Mgt.; b. Fulton, N.Y.; p. Lee and Grace Brown Dann; h. Joseph W. Martin; c. David, Martha, Sara; res: 3705 McKinley St., N.W., Wash., D.C. 20015.

MARTIN, PATRICIA J., Mgr., Prom. Svcs., Warner-Chilcott Laboratories Division, Warner-Lambert Pharmaceutical Company, 201 Tabor Rd., Morris Plains, N.J. 07950; AAF, Adv. Club of N.Y., Pharmaceutical Adv. Club, AWNY (Pres., '69–'70; VP, '67–'69; Treas., '65–'67; Asst. Treas., '63–'65; President's aw., '68); New Sch. of Soc. Rsch.; Col. of New Rochelle, BA (magna cum laude).

MARTIN, PATRICIA MILES, Auth., children's fiction, non-fiction, and biog: "Hoagie's Rifle-Gun" (Atlantic-Little Brown, '70), "That Cat! 1-2-3" (Putnam's), "Nobody's Cat" (Atlantic-Little Brown, '69), "Jacqueline Bouvier Kennedy" (Putnam's), "The Pointed Brush" (Lothrop); N.Y. Herald Tribune Spring Festival Hon. Bk., '59), many others; Sch. Tchr., '18–'20; Wms. Nat. Bus. Assn.; 10 Jr. Lit. Guild selections; b. Cherokee, Kan., 1899; p. Thomas and Nell White Miles; h. Edward Martin; res: 910 Bromfield Rd., San Mateo, Cal. 94402.

MARTIN, RACHEL SANGSTER, Ref. and Serials Librn., Furman University Library, Poinsett Highway, Greenville, S.C. 29613, '58–; Librn., Wms. Col., Furman, '57–'58; Head, Humanities Div., Fla. State Univ. Lib. (Tallahassee), '56–'57; Librn., Mary Baldwin Col. (Staunton, Va.), '51–'56; Asst. Ref. Librn., Auburn (Ala.) Univ., '49–'51; Librn., Lindley Jr. HS (Greensboro, N.C.), '46–'49; Tchr., '39–'46; S.C. Lib. Assn., Southeastern Lib. Assn., ALA, AAUP (Furman Univ. Chptr. Pres., '62–'63), Beta Phi Mu, Altrusa Club (Greenville Club Pres., '66–'68); Brenau Col., BA, '39;

Univ. of N.C., BS (Lib. Sci.), '49; Univ. of Ia., MA, '55; b. Mt. Olive, N.C.; p. Leon and Bertha Reaves Forrest; res: 219 Courtney Circle, Greenville, S.C. 29609.

MARTINEZ, ELIZABETH RUSCH, Brand Mgr., Chesebrough-Ponds, 485 Lexington Ave., N.Y., N.Y. 10017; Brand Mgr., Lehn & Fink, Dorothy Grey/Tussy Div., '65–'68; Asst. to Mkt. VP, Coty, '63–'64; Harvard-Radcliffe Program in Bus. Adm., Cert., '63; Northwestern Univ., BA, '62; b. Madison, Wis., 1940; p. Forrest and Thelma Berner Rusch; h. Arthur Martinez; res: 305 E. 72nd St., N.Y., N.Y. 10021.

MARTINEZ, HOPE G., Sr. VP, U.S. Media-International, 375 Park Ave., N.Y., N.Y. 10022, '69–; VP, BBDO, '68–'69; Staff, '46–'68; AWRT, Bedside Network (Bd. of Dirs.), AAAA; Time Byr. of Yr. Aw., '61; Mu Kappa Tau Mktng. Aw., N.Y.U.; Benjamin Franklin Bus. Sch.; b. Madrid, Spain; p. Anthony and Dolores Bejarano Martinez; c. Claudia.

MARTINI, TERI, Auth: "The Fisherman's Ring" (St. Anthony Guild), "True Book of Indians" (Children's Press), "What a Frog Can Do" (Reilly and Lee), four other juv. bks.; over 30 stories and articles in juv., educ. pubns.; Tchr.; Auths. Guild, WNBA; Who's Who of Am. Wm., Contemporary Auths.; Trenton Tchrs. Col., BS, '52; Columbia Univ., MA, '61; b. Teaneck, N.J.; p. Charles and Irene Martini; res: 216 Overlook Ave., Leonia, N.J. 07605.

MARTONE, BARBARA ANN, Prom. Mgr., Sch. and Lib. Cnslt., Holiday House, Inc., 18 E. 56th St., N.Y., N.Y. 10022, '69–; Asst. to Dir., Sch., Lib. Dept., World Publ., '66–'69; Publrs. Lib. Prom. Group (Secy., '69–) Rivier Col., BA (Eng.), '65; b. N.Y.C., 1944; p. Henry and Bianca Briganti Martone; res: 62 W. 12th St., N.Y., N.Y. 10011.

MARTZ, JoHANNE ZERBEY, Asst. Secy., Asst. Treas., J. H. Zerbey Newspapers, Inc., P.O. Box 57, Orwigsburg, Pa. 17961, '58–; Asst. Atty. Gen., Pa. Dept. of Public Welfare, '62–'69; Tchr. (Doylestown), '56–'58; Tchr. (San Benito County, Cal.), '54–'56; Theta Sigma Phi, BPW, Pa. Nwsp. Publrs. Assn., Pa. Press Wms. Assn., Schuylkill County Bar Assn., Pa. Bar Assn.; Stanford Univ., AB (Jnlsm.), '53; San Jose State Col., Tchr. credential, '54; Univ. of Pa. Law Sch., LLB, '61; b. Pottsville, Pa.; p. Uzal and Elizabeth Zerbey Martz; h. William R. Mosolino; c. William, Geoffrey; res: Quarry House, Box 57, Orwigsburg, Pa. 17961.

MARVIN, JANIS ELIZABETH, Traf. Supvsr., WOI-TV, WOI Bldg., Ames, Ia. 50010, '63–; Cont. Dir., Traf. Mgr., '56–'63; Cont. Wtr., KRNT & KRNT-TV, '54–'56; AWRT (Nat. VP, '68–; Chptr. Past Pres., VP); Wms. Adv. Club of Des Moines (Pres., '67–'68; Past VP), Theta Sigma Phi; Ia. State Univ., Grinnell Col., BA, '53; b. Ia. City, Ia., 1930; p. Kenneth and Eleanor Morning Marvin; res: 1822 Duff Ave., Ames, Ia. 50010.

MASLOW, PHYLLIS FELDMAN, Art Dir., La Roche

McCaffrey McCall, 575 Lexington Ave., N.Y., N.Y. 10022, '67–; Photogr.-Designer, Nesbitt Reynolds-Film Presentations, '64–'67; Pratt Inst., '60–'64; b. N.Y.C., 1942; p. Harry and Sarah Taback Feldman; h. Edward Maslow; res: 165 West End Ave., N.Y., N.Y. 10023.

MASON, LINDA SUE, Wtr., Assoc. Prodr., "CBS News With Joseph Benti," CBS News, 524 W. 57th St., N.Y., N.Y. 10019, '69–; Desk Asst., Rschr., '66; Newswtr., WCBS-TV, '67–'69; Apprentice Film Ed., Proferes-Desmond Films, '65–'66; Assoc. Prodr., WCNY-TV (Syracuse), '64–'65; Reptr., Providence (R.I.), Jnl., '61–'64; Wtr., Prodr., doc. on Am. Indian, "The Vanishing Warrior"; Brown Univ., BA, '64 (hons.); Syracuse Univ., MS (Univ. Fellow); b. Middletown, N.Y., 1942; p. Dr. Harry and Betty Sanders Mason; res: 314 W. 81st St., Apt. 2B, N.Y., N.Y. 10024.

MASON, LUCILE G., Dir., Public Affairs Div., Girl Scouts of the U.S.A., 830 Third Ave., N.Y., N.Y. 10022, '69–; Special Asst. to Nat. Exec. Dir., Conv. Coordr., '69; Exec. Dir., Assn. of the Jr. Leagues of Am., '66–'68; Conf. Mgr., Camp Fire Girls, '65–'66; Casting Dir., Dept. Head, Compton Adv., '51–'65; Prom. Wtr., Script Ed., Asst. Dir., ABC, '47–'51; Lectr., Am. Theatre Wing, '51–'58; PRSA, Intl. Platform Assn., AWRT (N.Y.C. Chptr. Pres., '58–'59), Kappa Delta Pi, Pi Lambda Theta, Intl. Commtn. Assn., Alpha Kappa Delta; Who's Who of Am. Wm.; Who's Who in the East; Smith Col., AB (Theatre), '47; N.Y.U., MA (Commtns. in Educ.), '69; b. Montclair, N.J.; p. Mayne and Rachel Entorf Mason; res: 770 Park Ave., N.Y., N.Y. 10021.

MASON, MADELINE, Tchr., Crtv. Writing Workshops, School of Eurythmy, Anthroposophical Society of New York, 211 Madison Ave., N.Y., N.Y.; Auth., fiction, "Riding for Texas"; Poet: "Journey in a Room," "The Cage of Years," others; Translator; Visiting Poet at many schs. and cols. in U.S. and Eng.; radio readings; various organizations; p. J. and Maude Fredericka Mason Manheim; h. Malcolm Forbes McKesson; res: 22 E. 29th St., N.Y., N.Y. 10016.

MASON, NADINE, Free-lance Wtr., '61–; Reptr., Special Wtr., Los Angeles Times, 29 yrs.; superior court beat, '43–'61; city gen. assigt., '38–'43; seven towns, San Gabriel Valley, '33–'38; Orange County Corr., '32–'33; Reptr., Spokane Press, '21; Gamma Delta Upsilon (Beta Chptr. Pres., '33), Theta Sigma Phi (L.A. Pfsnl. Chptr. Past VP, Secy., Treas.; Best News Story, Southern Calif., '40); Fullerton Jr. Col., '32–'33 (hon. student; created news bur.); b. Spokane, Wash., 1905; p. Charles and Della Crowe Cole; h. Tom Bickmore; c. Bobbie'dine (Mrs. Clinton Rodda), Audrey (Mrs. James R. Wheeler); res: 1886 Silverlake Blvd., L.A., Cal. 90026.

MASON, ZULA HAMILTON, Reg. Dir., Bureau of Teaching Materials and Asst. Prof., Library Science, Madison College, Box 225, Harrisonburg, Va. 22801, '66–; Asst. Prof., Lib. Sci., '58–; Librn., Laboratory Schs., '58–'66; tchr., public and high schs., '50–'58, '41–'43; librn., '46–'47, '49–'50; Va. Educ. Assn. (Madison Col. Chptr. Secy., '69–), ALA, Va. Lib. Assn., NEA; Blue Mountain Col., BA, '41; Appalachian State Univ., MA (Lib. Sci.), '60; b. Louisville, Ky., 1921; p. Dr. Wistar and Martha Watson Hamilton; h. Howard E. Mason; c. James Edward Herring, Martha Anne Herring, David Wister Herring; res: 220 Ohio Ave., Harrisonburg, Va. 22801.

MASSEY, JOAN LOIS, Prodr.-Talent Coordr., Paul S. Webb Productions, 9000 Sunset Blvd., Hollywood, Calif. 90069, '69–; Talent Coordr: "Donald O'Connor Show," Metro-Media TV, '68; Ralph Edwards Prods. (L.A.), '67; Alex Dreier News, KTTV, '66; "Paul Condylis Show," KABC Radio, '65; Talent, fund raising for YMCA; AWRT; Columbia Col. of Bdcst.; b. Portland, Ore., 1927; h. Bill Massey; c. Billey M.; res: 6607 Fair Ave., N. Hollywood, Cal. 91606.

MASSEY, RUTH L., Asst. Ed., Vista, The United Nations Association of the U.S.A., 833 UN Plaza, N.Y., N.Y. 10017, '65–; Edtl. staff, Holiday, Curtis Publ. Co., '45–'64; Swarthmore Col., AB, '41; b. Beverly, N.J., 1919; p. Maurice and Olive Wilson Massey; res: 5 Tudor City Pl., N.Y., N.Y. 10017.

MASSING, HERTA HERZOG, Partner, Jack Tinker & Partners, Inc., 1414 Sixth Ave., N.Y., N.Y. 10019, '61–; Chmn. of Bd., Marplan, Rsch. Div. of Interpublic, '62–'64; Rsch. Cnslt., McCann-Erickson (Germany), '59–'61; (N.Y.C.) Mgr. Radio-TV Rsch., Mgr. Motivational Rsch., Dir. of Rsch., '43–'59; Assoc. Dir. Mkt. Rsch., Bur. of Applied Social Rsch., Columbia Univ., '39–'43; Asst., Dept. of Sociology, '35–'37; Asst. Prof., Univ. of Vienna, '32–'34; Am. Psychological Assn., Am. Sociological Assn., World Assn. for Public Opinion Rsch., Am. Mktng. Assn., Am. Assn. for Public Opinion Rsch., ARF; Univ. of Vienna, Austria, '31 (Social Psych.); h. Paul W. Massing.

MASSOW, ROSALIND, Wms. Ed., Parade Publications, 733 Third Ave., N.Y., N.Y. 10017, '61–; Gen. Assgts. Reptr., Feature Wtr., Colmst., New York Journal American; Governor Rockefeller's Comm. on Minorities in Media, '68; Pres. Comm. on Status of Wm., '62; Nwsp. Wms. Club of N.Y. (Pres., '64–'66; Front Page Aw., '56, '60, '66), OPC (Governor, '66–'67), Reptrs. Assn. of N.Y.; Hearst Headline Svc. Writing Aw., '61; Hunter Col., Columbia Univ., N.Y.U.; b. N.Y.C.; p. Morris and Ida Massow; h. Norton M. Luger; res: 420 E. 23rd St., N.Y., N.Y. 10010.

MASTERS, ANN V., Feature Wtr., Copy Ed., Bridgeport Sunday Post, 410 State St., Bridgeport, Conn., '55–; Dir., Sch. Savings Dept., Drydock Savings Bank (N.Y.C.); Wtr., "Cognac for Breakfast," Atlantic Monthly; OPC, Assn. of Bank Wm. New Eng. Wm's. Press Assn. Aw., '62; Conn. Med. Press Aw., '64; N.Y.U., BA, '46; Am. Inst. of Banking, Grad.; res: RFD 1, Plumtrees Rd., Newtown, Conn.

MASTERSON, IOLA JOSEPHSON, Soc. Ed., Independent and Press-Telegram, Twin Coast Newspapers Inc., 604 Pine Ave., Long Beach, Cal. 90801; Colmst., "Wild Waves Say," '42–; Wtr., synd. radio scripts; Ed., "Letters From Home," World War II period; Radio Talent; Cal. Press Wm. (3rd pl., daily colm., '68; 2nd pl., pg. edited by a wm., '65; 1st pl., '64), NPWC (1st pl. for wms. sec., '64); Long Beach Jr. Col., AA, '34; b. Vanguard, Saskatchewan, Can., 1914; p. Oscar E. and Mary Gilchrist Josephson; h. Norman Whitfield Masterson; c. Mark W.; res: 510 Monrovia Ave., Long Beach, Cal. 90814.

MATCHINGA, CARYN (AKA) TOIAN, Screen Wtr., "79 Park Avenue," Paramount Pictures, Harold Robbins Productions, '69–; Feature Film Wtr., Film Project Inc., '68; Actress, motion pic., "Madigan"; Guest roles, numerous TV shows incl. "Iron Horse," "Big Valley," "Wackiest Ship in the Army;" Cartoonist; WGA, SAG, AEA; Barter Aw., '61; Carnegie Inst. of Tech.; b. Painesville, Oh., 1944; p. Rudolph and Alma Witt Matchinga; res: 1447 N. Clark St., L.A., Cal. 90069.

MATEER, SHIRLEY ANN, Acct. Supvsr., Bozell & Jacobs, 575 Lexington Ave., N.Y., N.Y. 10022, '69–; AE, '67–'69; Ed. Advisor Publicist, Scott Paper Co., '62–'67; Asst. Pers. Dir., John Wanamaker, '60–'62; Mkt. Rsch., Proctor & Gamble, '58–'60; AWNY, AWRT, Phila. Club of Adv. Wm., Un. 100,000 Mile Club, Punxsutawney C. of C. Merit Aw.; Oh. Univ., BA, '57; Northwestern Univ., MA, '58; b. Punxsutawney, Pa., 1935; res: 77 W. 55th St., N.Y., N.Y. 10019.

MATHERS, CAROLYN, Media Dir. and Traf. Coordr., Love & Anctil, Inc., 5051 Westheimer, Houston, Tex. 77027, '68–; Med. Mycology Rsch. Coordr., Univ. of Oklahoma, '62–'68; Intermarket Assn. of Adv. Agcys., Houston Assn. of Indsl. Advs.; Univ. of Okla., BA, '68; b. Miami, Fla., 1945; p. Gaylord A. and Rosemary Fendley Mathers; res: 3131 Cummins Lane, Houston, Tex. 77027.

MATHESON, PEGGY DURHAM, Dir. of Public Info., Saint Gregory's College Shawnee, Okla. 74801, '69–; Dir. of Public Info., Univ. of Tulsa, '68–'69; Assoc. Ed., Okla. Gas & Electric Co., '63–'64; Reptr., Ed., The Okla. Jnl., '66–'68; Ed., Bristow News & Record-Citizen, '66; Asst. PR Dir., World Neighbors, Inc., '65–'66; Tulsa Press Club, Gamma Alpha Chi, Southeast Tulsa County Dem. Club; Southwestern State Col. (Okla.), '59–'61; Univ. of Okla., BA (Jnlsm.), '63; b. Boise City, Okla., 1941; p. John and Mildred M. Durham; h. Mandell Matheson; res: 4024 Bismarc Dr., Del City, Okla. 73115.

MATHEWS, ELEANOR MUTH, Wtr., juv. fiction curricular material for Parish educ., '55–; Lectr., Dept. of Educ., Hunter Col., '50–'54; HS Tchr., '47–'50; Story Parade, '45–'47; Hunter Col., BA '45 (magna cum laude; Phi Beta Kappa); Tchrs., Col., Columbia Univ., MA, '50; b. N.Y.C.; p. Harry and Paula Fingerle Muth;

h. William Mathews; c. Patricia, John, Paul; res: 169 Circle Dr., Millington, N.J. 07946.

MATHEWS, MARCIA MAYFIELD, Auth., fiction, non-fiction; bks: "Richard Allen" (Helicon Press, '63), "Henry Ossawa Tanner, American Artist" (Univ. of Chgo. Press, '69); mag. articles; Tchr., Art Hist., Morehouse Col., '58–'61; Duke Univ., '35–'38; Wellesley Col., '32–'35; grants from Carnegie Fndn., Am. Philosophical Soc., '32, '34, '63, '67; Sophie Newcomb Col., Bachelor of Design; Wellesley Col., BA (Fine Arts); Inst. of Art and Archaeology, Brevet (Art. Hist.); b. N.O., La.; p. Robert and Marie Allen Mayfield; h. Joseph J. Mathews; c. Timothy M.; res: 924 Clifton Rd., N.E., Atlanta, Ga. 30307.

MATHEWS, VIRGINIA H., Staff Assoc., National Book Committee, 1 Park Ave., N.Y., N.Y. 10016, '57–; Ed., Dir. of Adv., Pubcty., Longmans, Green & Co., David McKay Co., '50–'57; Free-lance Edtl. Scouting, J. B. Lippincott Co., others, '50; Brentano Bk. Stores, '44–'49; Auth., Chptr. in "Libraries at Large" ('69); Co-Ed., "The Development of Lifetime Reading Habits;" Cnslt., numerous lib., reading projects; Exec. Prodr., "Gateways to Ideas" educ. radio progs., '64; Creator, tchrs. curricular, trade bks. for children in-svc. course, N.Y. Bd. of Educ., '54; Radio Prog., "Books Bring in the World" (WNYC); Contrb. Ed., Publisher's Weekly, Reviewer, New York Times Sunday Book Review, New York Herald Tribune, '45–'50; ALA, Conn. State Comm. on Sch. Lib. Dev. (Chmn., '64–), Nat. Cncl. of Tchrs. of Eng.; Constance Lindsay Skinner aw., '65; Am. Assn. of Sch. Librns. cit., '67; Goucher Col., Columbia Univ., Univ. of Geneva.

MATHEWSON, ESTHER LOUISE, Free-lance Wtr., Lectr.; Tchr., Adult Demonstration Sch., '48–; Ed., Mgr., L.A. Sch. Jnl., '48–'60; PR Dir., St. Vincent's Hosp., '60–'65; Mathewson Pubns., '44–'48; Adv., Pubtcty. Mgr., Avion, '43–'44; Engineer, Aerodynamics, '38–'43; established Nat. Assn. Nurse Aides, '68; Cnslt. in race rels., electronics firm, '67; NATAS, Intl. Platform Assn., Soroptimist Intl. (Past VP, Treas.), Assn. Better Radio-TV, BPW (Past Bd. of Dirs.), Greater L.A. Press Club; Army-Navy E., '45; Southern Cal. Independent Eds. best mag. layout, '45; active in public svc. orgs., Dic. Intl. Biog., 2,000 Wm. of Achiev., Who's Who in Am. Educ.; Who's Who of Am. Wm., Royal Blue Bk.; U.C.L.A. (Pre-Med.); b. Mansfield, Oh., 1914; p. Arthur and Edith Capen Mathewson; res: P.O. Box 57277, L.A., Cal. 90057.

MATHIAS, C. SUE, PR Dir., Opns. Mgr., Sky Harbor, Inc., 7700 W. 38th St., Indpls., Ind. 46254, '67–; Prom. Wtr., WLW-I TV, '65–'67; prog. Dept., '64–'65; Copywtr., Strobe and Assocs., '63–'64; Theta Sigma Phi (Indpls. Chptr. Secy., '69); Univ. of Cinn., '59–'61; Butler Univ., BS (Commtns., Jnlsm.), '63; b. Indpls., Ind., 1941; p. C.A. and Geraldine Longest Mathias; res: 5509 Portsmouth Ave., Indpls., Ind. 46224.

MATHIS, BETTY, Partner, Mathis and Bondurant,

1628 N.E. 15th Ave., Ft. Lauderdale, Fla. 33305, '45–; Colmst., Sportswtr., Atlanta (Ga.) Constitution; Theta Sigma Phi (Broward County chptr. Pres., '67–'69, Treas., '65–'67), Am. Soc. for Hosp. PR Dirs., PR Cncl. of Fla. Hosp. Assn.; Agnes Scott Col., '34–'36; b. Atlanta, Ga., 1918; p. Walter and Evelyn Epting Mathis.

MATHIS, TREVA WILKERSON, Assoc. Dir. of Libs., Guildford College Library, Greensboro, N.C. 27410, '66–; Acting Librn., '60–'66; Cataloger, Quaker Room Asst. Curator, '50–'66; Asst. Circ. Librn., Univ. of N.C. (Greensboro), '34–'45; Greensboro Lib. Club (all offs.), N.C. Lib. Assn.; Wms. Col., Univ. of N.C., AB (Lib. Sci.), '33; b. Randleman, N.C.; p. Charles and Lula Phillips Wilkerson; h. William Sam Mathis; c. Treva Lynne (Mrs. John E. Kasey), William Brantley; res: 1200 Double Oaks Rd., Greensboro, N.C. 27410.

MATICKA, MARIE CHECKI, AE, Chirurg & Cairns, Inc., 641 Lexington Ave., N.Y., N.Y. 10022; Fashion Group; Fairleigh Dickinson Univ., Katharine Gibbs Sch., N.Y. Sch. of Int. Design; b. Hackensack, N.J., p. J. and T. Checki, h. Jerry Maticka; res: 404 E. 66th St., N.Y., N.Y. 10021.

MATIN, DOROTHY HORWITZ, Dir. of Special Attractions, Sterling Recreation Organization, 975 John St., Seattle, Wash. 98109, '58–; Prom., Hamrick Theatres, Fox Evergreen Theatres, MGM, 20th Century Fox, Universal, Warner Bros., A.I.P., Paramount, Columbia; Colmst., "What's Smart in the Mart," '39–'42; Tchr. (Mercer Island, Wash.), '48–'58; Northwestern Univ.; b. Chgo., Ill., 1920; p. Harry and Eva Light Horwitz; h. Harmon Matin; c. Lowell R.; res: 9711 Mercer Wood Dr., Mercer Island, Wash. 98040.

MATTHEOS, ELIZABETH RODOUSAKIS, Mng. Ed., Children's Digest, 52 Vanderbilt Ave., N.Y., N.Y. 10017, '67–; Edtl. Asst., Staff Wtr., Scholastic Magazines, '65–'67; Editing Asst., McGraw Hill, '63–'65; WNBA; Syracuse Univ., BA, '63; h. Constantin Mattheos.

MATTHEW, JEANNETTE MORROW, Head of Social Svc. and Reg. Campus Libs., Indiana University, 518 N. Delaware St., Indpls., Ind. 46024, '56–; Librn: Adjutant Gens. Sch. Lib. (Ft. Harrison, Ind.), '51–'56; N.Y. Public Lib., '50–'51; Columbia Univ. Zoology/Geology Lib., '48–'51; Denver Public Lib. Bkmobile., '46–'48; St. Louis Public Lib., '42; Adult Educ. Cncl. of Indpls. (Founder, '53; 1st Wm. Pres., '56–'57; Past Pres. Aw., '61), Mayor's Comm. on Commty. Manpower (Founder and Secy., '60–'62), numerous lib. assns. and offs.; Park Col., BA, '46; b. St. Louis, Mo., 1922; p. Harry Wylie and Ruth Wilkinson Morrow; h. Neil Matthew; res: 212 E. 49th St., Indpls., Ind. 46205.

MATTHEWS, ANNE McILHENNEY, Feature Colmst., Buffalo Courier-Express, '64–; Prom. Dept., '60–'64; Art Critic, '59; Reptr., Wms. Pgs. Ed., Colmst., '25–'42; PR Offcr., Major, Wms. Army Corps, '42–'47; Niagara Frontier Press Club (Dir.), OPC, Saturn Club;

Who's Who of Am. Wm., Who's Who in the East, Dic. of Intl. Biog., Bronze Star aw.; Univ. of Buffalo; b. Phila., Pa.; h. Burrows Matthews (dec.); res: 9293 Sisson Highway, Eden, N.Y. 14057.

MATTHEWS, MARGARET HENRY, Midwest Ed., Mademoiselle, 65 East South Water, Chgo., Ill. 60611, '53–; Fashion Dir., Field Schlick; Fashion Dir., Young Quinlan; Fashion Group, Red Cross Bd. of Dirs., Pan Pacific and S.E. Asia Assn., Chgo. Cncl. on Fgn. Rels.; Macalester Col., Univ. of Minn., BS; b. St. Paul, Minn.; p. Albert and Vena MacDonald Henry; h. Robert M. Matthews; c. Priscilla; res: 2608 N. Lakeview, Chgo., Ill. 60614.

MATTINGLY, ALETHEA SMITH, Prof., Dept. of Speech, University of Arizona, Tucson, Ariz. 85721, '54–; Asst. to Prof., '34–; Visiting Prof. and Lectr. at many univs.; Auth., "Interpretation: Writer, Reader, Audience" (Wadsworth Publ., Second Edition, '70); Wtr., jnl. articles, bk. reviews; numerous speech orgs. Zeta Phi Eta; Who's Who of Am. Wm.; Who's Who in the West; Univ. of Ariz. Meritorious Instr. Aw., '60; Univ. of Wis., BA, '24 (with hons.); MA, '31; Northwestern Univ., PhD, '54; b. Chgo., Ill., 1904; p. Albert and Mary Elizabeth Randall Smith; h. Charles Mattingly; res: 1312 E. Adams St., Tucson, Ariz. 85719.

MAUNU, HELEN J., Head, Book Order Dept., Cleveland Public Library, 325 Superior Ave., Cleve., Oh. 44114, '57–; Asst. Head, Philosophy and Religion, '49–'56; Asst., Lib. Dept., '45–'48; Asst., Intercultural Lib., '44–'45; Ref. Asst., N.Y. Public Lib., '43–'44; Asst., Carnegie Public Lib. (Aberdeen, S.D.), '28–'38; Oh. Lib. Assn., ALA, Northern Oh. Tech. Svcs. Librns., Wms. Nat. Bk. Assn., Altrusa; Western Reserve Univ., BA, '42; Columbia Univ. Sch. of Lib. Svc., BS (Lib. Sci.), '43.

MAXSON, HELEN WRIGHT, Dir., Southern Area Publisher-Writer Administration, Broadcast Music, Inc., 710 16th Ave. S., Nashville, Tenn. 37203, '65–; Wtr. Adm., '62–'65; free-lance radio, TV, agcys., '57–'62; WSM, WSM-TV, '49–'57; Country Music Assn., NARAS, AWRT (Treas., '69); b. Nashville, Tenn., 1930; p. William and Dora Walker Wright; h. R. H. Maxson, III; c. Sheryl Lea, Evelyn Ann, Ralph Howard, IV, Carole Marie; res: 211 Wauford Dr., Nashville, Tenn. 37211.

MAXTON, L. PAULINE, Asst. Dir., Reading Public Library, Fifth and Franklin Sts., Reading, Pa. 19602, '61–; Head of Ref. Dept., '49–'61; Asst. Ref. Librn., '47–'49; Tchr., '42–'47; ALA, Pa. Lib. Assn.; Kutztown State Col., BS (Educ.), '42; Drexel, MS (Lib. Sci.), '50; b. Birdsboro, Pa., 1920; p. Claude and Ruth Moser Maxton; res: 815 Main St., Birdsboro, Pa. 19508.

MAXWELL, JOANNE DUTCHER, Exec. Asst., Rep. John N. Erlenborn, Congressional District Office, 108 N. Main St., Wheaton, Ill. 60187, '66–; Theta Sigma Phi (Nat. Legislative Chmn., '67–'68), Sigma Tau Delta, Pi

Kappa Delta, Phi Alpha Theta, Kappa Kappa Gamma, NEA, Ill. Press Assn. (Ed. of the Yr., '61), DuPage Press Assn.; Japanese Am. Citizen League Good Neighbor Aw., '59; Who's Who of Am. Wm.; Monmouth Col., AB, '53 ('Who's Who among Students, Student Leaders'); b. Chgo., Ill., 1931; p. William and Phoebe Hirshey Dutcher; h. Donald P. Maxwell; c. Donna Jo, Barbara Lee; res: 30 Maple Lane, Naperville, Ill. 60540.

MAXWELL, MARTHA ANN, Coordr., Semo Library System, Courthouse Pk., Cape Girardeau, Mo. 63701, '65–; Dir., Cape Girardeau Public Lib., '67–; Asst. Lib., Scenic Reg. Lib., '63–'64; Ref. Librn., '61–'63; Instr., Mo. State Lib. Workshop, '67; AAUW, BPW, Mo. Lib. Assn., Southeast Mo. Round Table (Pres., '68); Outstanding Young Wm. of Am. '69; Ark. State Col., BSE, '60; George Peabody Col. for Tchrs., MA (Lib. Sci.), '61; b. Paragould, Ark., 1938; p. Lloyd and Jessie Fairchild Maxwell; res: 410 Themis, Cape Girardeau, Mo. 63701.

MAXWELL, Sr. MARY H., Auth., non-fiction; Tchr., Cardinal Mindszenty High School, 717 Central Ave., Dunkirk, N.Y. 14048, '54–; bks: "Like a Swarm of Bees" (Fathers of St. Paul, '57), "Witness to Christ" (Newman Press, '65); mag. articles, poetry, short stories; Nat. Cncl. Tchrs. of English, N.Y. State English Cncl., AAUW; Wtrs. Confs: Georgetown, LaSalle Col., Iona Col. (speaker); Medaille Col., MS (Educ.), '54; Rosary Col. Lib. Sch.; courses, Notre Dame Univ., Univ. of Buffalo, Canisius Col.; b. Buffalo, N.Y.; p. Dr. John and Elizabeth Dwyer Maxwell; res: 634 Central Ave., Dunkirk, N.Y. 14048.

MAXWELL, NICOLE HUGHES, Auth: "Witch Doctors Apprentice" (Houghton Mifflin, '61; Victor Galancz, London, '62; Hoffman & Campe, Hamburg, '63), "Guide to Lima" (for Peruvian govt.); Collaborator, bk. on Peru; Bolivian Corr. for Vision Bks., numerous mag. articles in U.S.A. and S. Am.; Fellow of Royal Geog. Soc., Founder of Ecuadorian Inst. Ethnology and Geog., Intl. PEN, Soc. Magazine Wtrs., Inst. Human Studies, OPC; Univ. of Manila, Radcliffe; Oh. State Med. Sch., b. S.F., Cal.; p. George and Pearl Aurys Hughes; res: 150 E. 30th St., N.Y., N.Y. 10016.

MAY, ALETHA BARRETT, VP, Don May Advertising, Inc., 1111 Davis Bldg., 1309 Main St., Dallas, Tex. 75202, '58–; b. Trenton, Tex., 1911; p. James and Lois Adams Barrett; h. Donald Wright May; c. Janis Susan; res: 6149 Brandeis Lane, Dallas, Tex. 75214.

MAY, ELIZABETH, Specialist in Children's Music, Santa Monica United School District, 1723 Fourth St., Santa Monica, Cal. 90404, '58–; U.C.L.A., '54–'55; San Jose State Col., '50–'53; Sacramento State Col., '48–'50; Auth., "The Influence of the Meiji Period on Japanese Children's Music" (Univ. of Cal. Press, '63); Contrbr., pubns. of many articles in the field of music; Soc. for Ethnomusicology, Music Educs. Nat. Conf., Southern Cal. Recorder Soc.; Mills Col., AB, '35; Univ.

of Cal., MA, '40; U.C.L.A., PhD, '58; Univ. of Western Australia (Fulbright Lectureship), '65; b. Denver, Colo., 1907; p. Henry and May Rickard May; res: 1658-1/2 Malcolm Ave., L.A., Cal. 90024.

MAY, JANIS SUSAN, Rsch. Dir., Don May Advertising, Inc., 1111 Davis Bldg., Dallas, Tex. 75202, '58–; Portrait Photogr., '69–; Dallas Adv. Club; active in civic musical groups; Trinity Univ.; Southern Methodist Univ.; Dallas Acad. of Speech and Drama; b. Amarillo, Tex., 1946; p. Donald and Aletha Barrett May; res: 6149 Brandeis Lane, Dallas, Tex. 75214.

MAY, MARJORIE, AE, Thomas J. Deegan Company, Time and Life Bldg., N.Y., N.Y. 10020, '69–; Cnslt., food, cosmetics, fashion, '64–'69; PR Dir., World's Fair-Restaurant Assoc., '64–'65; PR Dir., Kikkoman Intl., '61–'64; PR Dir., Exquisite Form Ind., '60–'61; Press Rels. Mgr., Intl. Latex Corp., '54–'60; Instr., Fashion Inst. of Tech., '66–'67; PRSA, Lucy Stone League, Wm. Pays Club, Wine and Food Soc.; Syracuse Univ., BA, '49 (Phi Beta Kappa, cum laude); b. Schenectady, N.Y.; p. Lawrence and Florence Messing May; res: 325 E. 79 St., N.Y., N.Y. 10021.

MAYBERRY, GENEVIEVE, Auth., non-fiction; formerly Primary Tchr., Ore., Alaska; bk., "Eskimo of Little Diomede" (Follett); hist. writing, Sheldon Jackson Jr. Col.; mag. articles; NLAPW (Alaska Pres., '55), Delta Kappa Gamma (Juneau Chptr. Pres., '58), Pacific Northwest Wtrs. Conf., Willamette Wtrs.; Ore. Col. of Educ., '26; Univ. of Ore., '41; b. Lebanon, Ore., 1900; p. Winfield and Adeline Smith Mayberry; res: 624 S. Elizabeth, Milton-Freewater, Ore. 97862.

MAYER, JANE ROTHSCHILD, auth: "The Year of the White Trees" ('58), "Dolly Madison" ('54), "Betsy Ross and the Flag" ('52), "Getting Along in the Family" ('49), others; former ed., Field Enterprises; Soc. of Midland Auths. (former VP, Treas.), Auths. League, Chgo. Press Club, Arts Club of Chgo.; b. Kan. City, Mo., 1903; p. Louis and Nora Westheimer Rothschild; h. David Mayer; c. David, III, Philip, Mary Jane Bezark; res: 1445 N. State Pkwy., Chgo., Ill. 60610.

MAYER, MARY ALICE, Supvsr., Behavorial and Social Science Studies, Management Sciences Division, American Telephone and Telegraph, 195 Broadway, N.Y., N.Y. 10007, '69–; Asst. to Exec. Dir., Chgo. Area Sch. TV, Inc., '67–'69; Tchr., '62–'69; AWRT, BPW, Ill. Cncl. on Educ. Telecommunications, Kappa Tau Alpha, 2,000 Wm. of Achiev. NAEB; Clarke Col., BA (Speech, Theatre), '62; Univ. of Ill., MS (Radio-TV), '63; Northwestern Univ., PhD (Speech), '69; b. Chgo., Ill., 1941; p. John and Annamarie M. Mayer; res: 270 Henderson St., Jersey City, N.J. 07302.

MAYER, TERRY, Free-lance Publicist, Fashion, Home Furnishings, '70–; Fashion Dir., Farley Manning Assoc., '67–'70; Terry Mayer Assoc., '64–'67; Mogul, Williams, Saylor, '63–'64; Fashion Coordr., J. C. Penney, '61–'63; VP, Fashion Dir., Amos Parrish & Co., '59–'61; Pubcty., Adv. Dir., David Crystal Inc., '50–'59; Press Publicist, Gimbel Bros., '48–'50; Fashion Publicist, Macy's, '45–'48; Jr. Copywtr., Aldens, '44–'45; Wtr., mag. articles; various orgs., aws.; L.I. Univ., BS, '44; b. N.Y.C., 1923; res: 165 E. 35th St., N.Y., N.Y. 10016.

MAYERSON, CHARLOTTE LEON, Sr. Ed., Random House, 201 E. 50th St., N.Y., N.Y. 10022, '69–; Sr. Ed., Holt, Rinehart, Winston, '63–'69; Edtl. Asst., Harper's mag., Harper & Row, '61–'63; Rsch. Dir., Book-of-the-Month Club; Auth: "Two Blocks Apart" ('65), "Shadow & Light" ('64); Am. Acad. of Polit. and Social Sci.; Queens Col., BA; b. N.Y.C.; p. Victor and Hilda Leon; h. Burton Mayerson; c. Robert Henry.

MAYES, ALEXANDRA, Mktg. Ed., Glamour, Conde Nast Publications, 420 Lexington Ave., N.Y., N.Y. 10017, '69–; Accessories Ed., '65–'69; Eastern Mdsng. Ed., '62–'65; Coty Aws. Comm., Shoe Wm. Execs., Nat. Handbag Assn.; Conn. Col. for Wm.; b. N.Y.C., 1941; p. Herbert and Grace Taub Mayes; res: 151 E. 83rd St., N.Y., N.Y. 10028.

MAYES, ROBERTA LYNDON, Ed., The Jekyll Islander, P.O. Box 143, Jekyll Island, Ga. 31520, '68–; Wms. Ed. and Feature Wtr., North Side News (Atlanta, Ga.); Info. Specialist with U.S. Govt. PR during World War II; Reptr., La Grange Daily News, '38–'40; Newman Herald, '34–'38; poems published, '30–'40; Theta Sigma Phi; Wms. Col. of Ga., '32–'34; b. Newman, Ga., 1915; p. Lewis Leibrandt and Sarah Buchanan Lyndon; h. William A. Mayes (dec.); c. Sarah Buchanan, Evelyn Lyndon; res: 8 B Forest Ave., Jekyll Island, Ga. 31520.

MAYES, VERCA L., Retired Nwsp. Owner, Publr.; Formerly Owner, Publr., Sand Springs (Okla.) Leader, for 25 yrs.; Mng. Ed., Laddonia (Mo.) Herald; Vandalia (Mo.) Mail; Rsch. Assigt., for Sand Springs, Okla; Treas., City of Sand Springs, '49–'51; Tulsa Press Club, NFPW, Beta Sigma Phi, Theta Sigma Phi, Gamma Alpha Chi; C. of C. (Past Dir.); numerous civic, public svc. orgs.; Who's Who of South and Southwest; State Polit. hons.; b. Mexico, Mo., 1909; p. Benjamin and Eudora Hamilton Mayes; res: 1105 N. Main, Sand Springs, Okla. 74063.

MAYHALL, Dr. M. MILDRED PICKLE, Auth: "The Kiowas" (Univ. of Okla. Press., '62), "Indian Wars of Texas" (Texian Press, '65); Co-ed., "This Is Austin—Capital of Texas" ('64), Rschr., Wtr., Lectr. on ethno-history; Tchr., Social Studies, Austin HS, '56–'64; Instr. in Anthropology, Univ. of Tex., '27–'45; Tex. State Hist. Assn., W. Tex. Hist. Assn., Am. Anthropological Assn., Mont. Hist. Soc., Western Hist. Assn., Nat. Geog. Soc.; Theta Sigma Phi Wtrs. Round-up Aw., '66; Assoc. for State and Local Hist. Aw. for film strip, "The Indians of Texas," '60; Chi Upsilon; Kappa Delta Pi; Pi Lambda Theta; Sigma Xi; Am. Men of Sci.; Univ. of Tex., BA, '24 (Phi Beta Kappa); MA, '26; PhD, '39; Grad. Work, Univ. of Chgo., '29, '30, '33; b. Aus-

tin, Tex., 1902; p. David and Birdie Givens Pickle; h. Temple B. Mayhall; c. David, William; res: 1906 Raleigh Ave., Austin, Tex. 78703.

MAYHEW, JEAN BINKLEY, Assoc. Prof. of Speech, Central Michigan University, Mt. Pleasant, Mich. 48858, '61–; Instr., '52–'61; TV lect. series, Queens Col. (N.Y.C.), '65; Commtns. Cnslt. to Mgt., industry; Auth., "Handbook for Speech 101" (Wm. Brown & Co.); articles in pfsnl. jnls.; AWRT, AAUP, NAEB, Nat. Soc. for Study of Commtn., many educ. orgs.; Commty. Leaders of Am.; Dic. of Intl. Biog.; Dir. of Am. Scholars; 2,000 Wm. of Achiev.; Mich. State Univ., BA (Speech, Drama, Radio Dramatic Prod.), '41; Univ. of Mich., MA (Speech Educ.), '51; b. Gratiot County, Mich. 1919; p. Paul and Mary Mallory Binkley; h. LaVern Mayhew; c. David E., Rebecca Lynne; res: 803 W. Preston Rd., Mt. Pleasant, Mich. 48858.

MAYNARD, IDLYE COTHRON, Asst. Media Dir., Noble-Dury & Assoc., Inc., Life & Casualty Tower, Nashville, Tenn. 37219, '68–; Media Byr., '67; Traf. Mgr., '66–'67; Cont. Dir., '65; b. Gallatin, Tenn., 1942; p. Jimmy and Anna Butts Cothron; h. Douglas Maynard; res: 1104 Shiloh Dr., Nashville, Tenn. 37205.

MAYNARD, MIRIAM CLARK, City Ed., The Kinston Daily Free Press, Drawer 129, North St., Kinston, N.C. 28501, '65–; Wms. Ed., '62–'65; Feature Ed., '53–'65; Reptr., '52–'65; Public Affairs Inst., Wash., D.C.; Navy Disbursing Dept., Cherry Point, N.C., WW II; Tchr., Writing for News Media, Lenoir Commty. Col.; N.C. Press Wm. (2nd pl., Colm. Div., '57; Hon. Mention, '56), N.C. Press Assn.; School Bell Aw., '69; Greensboro Col.; American Univ.; b. Kinston, N.C., 1922; p. Thomas and Ione Lane Maynard; res: 310 Sherwood Pl., Kinston, N.C. 28501.

MAYO, MARGOT BOOTH, Tchr., music and folklore, Mills College of Education, 66 Fifth Ave., N.Y., N.Y. 10011, '45–; WAC, '43–'45; Tchr: Woodward Sch., '54–, Walden Sch., '36–'40, Little Red Sch. House, '36–'39, Founder-Leader, Wtr., Am. Sq. Dance Group, '33–'58; Ed., Promenade, Am. Folklore, '38–'54; Founder, Wtr., Margot Mayo Folk Singers, '45–'58; rschr., wtr., articles on folklore; Am. Folklore Soc., N.Y. Folklore Soc., Soc. for Ethnomusicology; Inst. of Musical Art, Dalcroze Sch. of Music; Martha Graham Sch. of Dance, New Sch. of Soc. Rsch., Columbia Univ.; b. Commerce, Tex., 1910; p. William and Etta Booth Mayo; res: 550 Riverside Dr., N.Y., N.Y. 10027.

MAZEFSKY, GERTRUDE MESSEROFF, AE, William H. Mazefsky Associates, (Pitt., Pa.), '40–'44; Lib. Ref., Acquisitions, Univ. of Pitt. Lib., '56–; Carnegie Lib. of Pitt.; Theta Sigma Phi, ALA, Pa. Lib. Assn.; Univ. of Pitt., BA, '40; Carnegie Inst. of Tech., MLS; b. Rezina, Bessarabia, 1918; p. Rev. David and Bluma Weisman Messeroff; h. William H. Mazefsky; c. Janet, Judith, Martin, res: 5548 Wellesley Ave., Pitt., Pa. 15206.

McADAM, ELIZABETH WICKHAM, Auth., three non-fiction bks. ('42, '44, '68); Free-lance Wtr., PR, colmnst., numerous mag. articles, '19–; Wtr.-Ed., Music Magazine, '42–'52; Auths. League of Am.; Intl. Music League, Red Cross (Aw. of Merit, '20), Wms. Assn. Cleve. Col.; Beaver Col., '15–'16; Oberlin Conservatory and Col., '16–'17; Columbia Univ., '18–'19; Western Reserve Univ., '40–'50; b. Wheeling, W. Va., 1896; p. James and Katherine Graham Wickham; h. Will McAdam (dec.); c. Will, Betty McAdam Berens. res: 3560 Fairmount Blvd., Cleve., Oh. 44118.

McANDREW, MARIANNE CHRISTINE, Actress: Film: "Hello Dolly" (20th Century Fox); Nat. Soc. of Arts and Ltrs., Acting Aw., '64; Northwestern Univ., BS, '64; b. Cleve., Oh., 1942; p. Frank and Mary Ann Stempien McAndrew; h. Stewart Moss; res: 3270 Primera Pl., L.A., Cal. 90028.

McBAIN, DIANE ︱JEAN, Actress; motion pics. (Warner Bros.): "Claudelle English," "Parrish," "Ice Palace"; "Surfside Six," Warner Bros. TV series, '60–'61; Interior Decorator; Make-up Cnslt.; bd. of Dirs., USO, '68–'69; b. Cleve., Oh., 1941; p. Walter and Cleo McBain; res: 4617 Willis Ave., Sherman Oaks, Cal. 91403.

McBRIDE, ESTELLE SAFIER, Free-lance Wtr., Adv. Cnslt., '68–; VP, Cnslt., Special Assignment Wtr., Grey Adv. Agcy., '63–'68; Copy Group Head, '50–'55; articles, Seventeen Magazine; Adv. Copy and Programs, WOR Radio; Feature Wtr., N.Y. Times Magazine, '44–'49; Group Head, Adv., R. H. Macy, '36–'41; Billboard Aw. for radio adv. copy, '47; Adv. Wtrs. of N.Y. Aw., '64; Carnegie Inst. of Tech. (Voice), '30–'33; b. Monessen, Pa.; p. Joseph and Sarah Safier; h. Matthew B. McBride; c. James M.; res: 230 Riverside Dr., N.Y., N.Y. 10025 and Sherman, Conn.

McBRIDE, MARIAN DUNNE, Staff Wtr., The Milwaukee Sentinel, 918 N. 4th St., Milw., Wis. 53213, '42–; Staff Wtr., Milw. Journal, '45–'46; PR Dir., Bruce Publ. Co., '43–'45; WNPC, ANWC, Assn. of Marquette Univ. Wm. (Bd. Mbr., '52–'58), Theta Sigma Phi (Milw. Pfsnl. Chptr. Pres., '46–'47; Wis. Outstanding Wm. Jnlst Aw., '68); Gamma Phi Epsilon; Univ. of Wis. Wm. in Action Aw., '63; Marquette Univ., BA (Jnlsm.), '43; b. Wallace, Idaho, 1923; p. Pierce and Julia Flynn Dunne; h. Raymond E. McBride; c. Joseph, Genevieve, Michael, Patrick, Dennis, Mark, Timothy; res: 7631 Rogers Ave., Wauwatosa, Wis. 53213.

McCAFFERTY, AUDREY JANE, Mgr., Press and Pubcty., The Kroger Co., 1014 Vine St., Cinn., Oh. 45201, '70–; PR Asst. '55–'70; Feature Wtr., '51–'55; Press and Radio News Wtr., '51; Secy., '47–'51; ZONTA (Cinn. Club Pres., '64–'65), PRSA, Theta Sigma Phi (Cinn. Pfsnl. Chptr. VP, '69–'70); Xavier Univ., Univ. of Cinn.; b. Batavia, Oh.; p. H. J. and Lillian Berger McCafferty; res: 4408 Ashland Ave., Cinn., Oh. 45212.

McCAFFERTY, LEE, VP, W and B Public Relations Division, Waldie and Briggs, Inc., E. Wacker Dr., Chgo., Ill. 60601, '69–; '66–; VP of Pubns., Wyatt & Morse, Mgt. Cnslts.; Adv. and Sls. Prom. Div., Crane Co. Gen. Offs.; newsp. rept.; Ed., Cost Reduction Newsletter, '61–; edtl., bks: "Cost Reduction Guide for Manufacturing Management," "Numerically Controlled Machine Tools—The Breakthrough of Autofacturing"; Northern State Tchrs. Col., (Educ., Eng.); h. John K. McCafferty; res: 6055 N. Kilpatrick, Chgo., Ill. 60646.

McCAIG, NANCY PROSSER, Copy Chief, Eby & Everson, Inc., 1637 Marion, Denver, Colo. 80218, '50–; Copy Chief, Marshall Robertson Agcy., '35–'64; Copywtr.; Asst. Wm's. Ed., Denver Post, '30–'34; Denver Wm's. Press Club; Monticello Col., '26–'28; Wash. Univ., St. Louis, Mo., AB, '30; b. Fayette, Mo.; h. Donald McCaig; c. Dr. Nancy C., Mrs. James R. Hunter, Jr.; res: 9003 E. Nassau Ave., Denver, Colo. 80237.

McCAIN, NINA JUNE, Educ. Ed., Boston Globe, Boston, Mass. 02107, '68–; Wtr., N.Y. World Journal Tribune, '67–'68; N.Y. World Telegram, '63–'67; Religious News Svc., '61–'63; Religion Ed., Dallas (Tex.) Morning News, '59–'61; Stanford Pfsnl. Jnlsm. Fellowship Program, '68; Univ. of Tex., BJ, '59.

McCALL, ELIZABETH BARTOW, Chestnut Hill Corr., Philadelphia Inquirer, Society Dept., 400 N. Broad St., Phila., Pa. 19101, '67–; Nwsp. Reptr., '19–'33; League of Wm. Voters (Past. Pres.); Pa. Nwsp. Publrs. Assn. aw., '53; b. Phila., Pa., 1900; p. Josiah and Margaret Allen Bartow; h. Shirley Carter McCall; c. S. Carter Jr., J. Bartow; res: 101 Rex Ave., Phila., Pa. 19118.

McCALL, JOAN C., Actress: "Any Wednesday" (Broadway, '69), "Star Spangled Girl" (Broadway, '67; nat. tour, '68–'69), "Don't Drink the Water" (tour, '68); "Barefoot in the Park" (Broadway, '67; nat. tour, '65–'66), "A Race of Hairy Men" (Broadway debut, '65); AEA, SAG, AFTRA, Outstanding Young Wm. of '67; Berea Col., BA (Fine Arts); h. David Shedon.

McCALL, VIRGINIA NIELSEN, Auth., c/o Lenniger Lit. Agcy., 11 W. 42nd St., N.Y., N.Y. 10036: "The Mystery of Secret Town" (David McKay Co., '69), "Keoni, My Brother" (David McKay Co., '65), "Dangerous Dream" (LaSelva, '64), many others; Auths. Guild, Auths. League of Am., Cal. Wtrs. Club; Univ. of Idaho, '27–'29; Ut. State Agricultural Col., '30–'31; b. Idaho Falls, Idaho, 1909; p. Jesse H. and Florence Kingston Nielsen; h. Joseph R. McCall; res: Johnsville Star Rte., Blairsden, Cal. 96103.

McCALLUM, MARJORIE HUDSPITH, Wm's. Ed., Great Bend Daily Tribune, 2012 Forest, Great Bend, Kan. 67530, '69–; Asst. Wm's. Ed., '65–'69; Corr., Woonsocket (R.I.) Call, '56–'59; Wtr., short stories in Wm's. Magazine (London); Kan. Press Wm.; Ch. Wm.

Un. plaque and WICS cert. for faithful rept.; active in ch. and civic affairs; Harrow Art Sch., England, '34–'46; Kilburn Polytech. Sch., London, '36–'38; b. London, Eng., 1921; p. Herbert and Florence Forman Hudspith; h. (div.); c. Brenda (Mrs. Tom Kelley), Rosalind, Peter John; res: 2300 Jefferson, Great Bend, Kan. 67530.

McCALMONT, LUCRETIA ANNE, Rsch. Assoc., Fortune Magazine, Time Inc., Time & Life Bldg., Rockefeller Ctr., N.Y., N.Y. 10020, '64–; social worker; Tchr. of Eng., Adult Educ. Program, N.Y.C.; educ: Smith Col., Univ. of Geneva, Univ. of Cinn.; BA (Polit. Sci.); b. Cinn., Oh., 1938; p. Samuel and Jean Chappell McCalmont; res: 211 E. 73rd St., N.Y., N.Y. 10021.

McCANCE, JEAN DAVIS, Wms. Ed., News-Dispatch, 121 W. Michigan Blvd., Michigan City, Ind. 46360, '69–; Asst. Wms. Ed., '66–'69; Asst. Ed., New Buffalo (Mich.) Times, '62–'66; Entertainment and Wms. Ed., The Globe (Camp Lejeune, N.C.), '57; Ind. AP newswriting contest, 2nd pl. aw., '68; b. Chgo., Ill., 1936; p. Henry and Anna Perkins Davis; h. (div.); c. Arick David, Terry Dale; res: 228 Monroe, New Buffalo, Mich. 49117.

McCANDLESS, STEPHANIE LEE, Exec. Dir., Pacific and Asian Affairs Council, 2004 Univ. Ave., Honolulu, Hi. 96822, '68–; Prog. Dir., '63–'68; Tchr., Punahou Acad., '62–'63, '58–'59; Asst. Dean of Students, State Univ. of N.Y., '60–'61; Prog. Specialist, Inst. of Intl. Educ. (N.Y.C.), '60; Theta Sigma Phi, Hi. Assn. for UN (Dir., '66–), Nat. Cncl. for Social Studies, Hi. Cncl. for Social Studies, Cncl. for Econ. Educ. for Hi.; Outstanding Young Wm. of the Yr. for Hi., Outstanding Ams. Fndn., '67; Nat. Registry of Prominent Ams., Who's Who of Am. Wm., Who's Who in the West, Nat. Social Dir.; Principia Col., BA, '56 (cum laude; Sch. of Nats. Scholarship, '54); Univ. of Wash., MA, '62 (Paul Ashley Scholarship in Jnlsm., '58–'59); b. St. Louis, Mo., 1934; p. Lee and Mary Glor McCandless; res: 2877 Kalakaua Ave. Apt. 207, Honolulu, Hi. 96815.

McCARDLE, DIANE M., Bdcst. Prod. Coordr., Needham, Harper & Steers, Inc., Advertising, 909 Third Ave., N.Y., N.Y. 10022, '62–; Casting, '66–; Asst. Fashion Coordr., Julius Garfinkel (DePinna); NATAS; Marymount Jr. Col. of Va., Assoc. (Applied Sci.), '59; res: Charcoal Rd., South Norwalk, Conn. 06854.

McCARTHY, DOROTHY GREENLEAF, Wtr., nonfiction; Tchr., Elementary, Col. Educ. courses, Wis. Public Schs., State Univ.; nwsp. col.; Wis. Reg. Wtrs. Assn. (Bd. Mbr.), State Hist. Soc. Wms. Aux. (Bd. Mbr.); Contrbr., "Badger History" pubn. for upper elementary grades, "Famous Women of Wisconsin" series; Aw. of Merit, '63); Madison Area Wtrs. (First Prize, Article Category, '69); Mills Col., BS, '24; Univ. of Wis., MA, '36; Univ. of Chgo., '32; b. Savanna, Ill., 1901; p. Francis and Margaret Kenney Greenleaf; h. John R. McCarthy; res: 917 W. Pleasant, Portage, Wis. 53901.

McCARTHY, JOSEPHINE VERCELLI, Home Econst., Radio-TV (Ret.), National Broadcasting Company, 30 Rockefeller Plaza, N.Y., N.Y. 10019; Instr., Home and Family Life Dept., Miami Dade Jr. Col., '61–'64; Home Econ. Ed. and Hostess, food demonstration shows, WNBT, '50–'61; radio audience participation shows, WMCA, WHN, WOR, '40–'49; Chmn. of Foods, N.Y. Inst. of Dietetics, '46–'48; Auth., "Josephine McCarthy Favorite TV Recipes" ('58); Co-auth., "Soy Beans Soup to Nuts" ('44); Am. Home Econ. Assn., AWRT, AFTRA, UN Assn. of Hawaii (Bd. Mbr.); TV Guide Best Homemaking Show Aw., '51; helped launch June Dairy Month in London for Dairy Industry of Eng., '56; Cal. State Tchrs. Col., '15–'18; Univ. of Cal., BA; b. Bellota, Cal., 1897; p. Charles and Adelaide Boera Vercelli; h. John McCarthy (dec.); c. Mrs. Millicent Meaney; res: 32 Kailua Rd., Kailua, Oahu, Hi. 96734.

McCARTHY, MARY BETH, TV-Radio Ed., Worcester Telegram and Gazette, Inc., 20 Franklin St., Worcester, Mass. 01601, '64–; Asst. to TV-Radio Ed., '62–'64; Secy., '61–'62; b. Worcester, Mass., 1943; p. Martin and Agnes Hanlan McCarthy; res: 57 Camp, Worcester, Mass. 01603.

McCARTHY, NOBU, Actress, all major studios, nine motion pics., six stage prods., ten commls., more than 60 TV shows (incl. "Love, American Style," ABC), '59–; "To Catch a Thief"; starred in "Geisha Boy"; Japan's top fashion model at age 16; "Miss Carnival" (Tokyo, Japan), age 14; SAG, AFTRA, AEA; Pavlova Ballet Sch., Kamakura, Japan, '47–'53; b. Ottawa, Can.; p. Masaji and Yuki Kano Atsumi; h. David McCarthy; c. Marlan, Serena.

McCARTHY, RUTH CONSTAD, Exec. Ed., Vogue Magazine, 420 Lexington Ave., N.Y., N.Y. 10017, '70–; Mktng. Dir., '67–'70; Mktng. Ed., Harper's Bazaar, '60–'67; Corr., ABC Radio, TV (Havana, Cuba), '53–'59; Feature Wtr., UP, '45–'49; Fashion Group, Urban League of N.Y.; Pa. State Univ., AB, '45; b. N.Y.C., 1925; p. Irving and Irene Klein Constad; h. Francis McCarthy; c. Kyle Susan, Keith John; res: 336 Central Park W., N.Y., N.Y. 10025.

McCARTY, JUDI ANDERSON, Copywtr., Gelders, Holderby & Smith, Inc., 515 N. Robinson Suite 215, Okla. City, Okla. 73127, '67–; Svc. Rep., Southwestern Bell, '62–'67; Corr., Okla. Publ. Co., '59–'61; Beta Sigma Phi, AWRT; Univ. of Okla., '61–'62; Okla. City Univ., '63–'64; b. Waukegan, Ill., 1943; p. John and Marjorie Doser Anderson; h. Bruce McCarty; res: 1417 N. Holly, Okla. City, Okla. 73127.

McCARTY, MYLREA KING, Wms. Ed., Torrington Broadcasting Co., 52 S. Main St., Torrington, Conn. 06790, '58–; Bdcstr., '48–'50; Dir. of Radio-TV, Nat. Audubon Soc., '51–'58; Prodr.-Emcee, "Wildlife Unlimited," WOR-TV and "Songs of the Wild," NBC, '51, "Explorers of the Wild," WTIC (Hartford), '51–'58; AWRT (offs.), Torrington Quota Club Pres.; Lectr. on conservation and travel; Breeder of Morgan horses;

St. Johnsbury Acad., '19–'23; b. Burke, Vt., 1906; p. Theodore and Mary Nutt King; h. Clinton McCarty; c. Mrs. Searle Spangler, Mrs. Wesley M. Vandervliet; res: Starks Rd., Winsted Conn. 06098.

McCARTY, REGA LUCILE, Tchr., Ft. Steilacoom Community College, 4601 Sixth Ave., Tacoma, Wash., 98406, '59–; workshops; Colmst., Suburban Times, '68–; Free-lance Wtr.; Auth: "Brenda Becomes a Buyer," "Lorna Evans, Social Worker" (Julian Messner), 10 plays (Rodeheaver Hall Mack), poetry, 100 confession stories; PR; Mdse. Byr.; Store Exec.; NLAPW (Tacoma Br. VP, '66–'68), Tacoma Wtrs. Club (Past Pres.), various others; Monmouth Col., '21–'22; Ia. State Tchrs. Col., '25; b. Batavia, Ia., 1904; p. James and Allie Walker Kramer; h. F. Neal McCarty; c. Mark T.

McCAULEY, ELFRIEDA BABNEY, Coordr., Secondary School Libraries, Greenwich Public Schools, Greenwich, Conn. 06380; Reptr., Religious News Svc.; Secy.-Treas., McCauley Enterprises; free-lance publicist; ALA, NEA, Beta Phi Mu; Univ. of Wis., BS, '48; Columbia Univ., MS, '65; Grad. Work, '68–'69; b. Milw., Wis., 1925; h. Leon McCauley; c. Brian, Christopher, Matthew, Kevin; res: 32 Longmeadow Rd., Riverside, Conn. 06878.

McCLAIN, IONE WILLIAMS, Gen. Ref. and Humanities Librn., University of Wyoming Library, Laramie, Wyo. 82070, '66–; Free-lance Wtr., Bk. Reviewer; Librn., Sheridan Col.; Librn., Sue Bennett Col. (London, Ky.); Librn., Faulkner County Lib. (Conway, Ark.); Mountain Plains Lib. Assn. (Past Treas.), Wyo. Lib. Assn. (Pres. three times), ALA, NEA, Delta Kappa Gamma, AAUW, Beta Phi Mu, NPWC; Hendrix Col., BA, '25 (magna cum laude); Univ. of Ill., BS (Lib. Sci.), '31 (hons.); h. Barney McClain.

McCLARY, JANE STEVENSON (Jane McIlvaine), Auth., eight juv. bks., four non-fiction adult bks.; Ed., Publr., Downington (Pa.) Archive, '46–'54; Fortune Ltrs. Dept., '41–'43; Colmst., Washington Times-Herald, '39–'41; Pa. WPA (Pres., '52), OPC, Theta Sigma Chi (Hon.); b. Pitt., Pa., 1919; p. William and Elizabeth Walker Stevenson; h. Nelson McClary; c. Stevenson McIlvaine, Mia (Mrs. Van Santvoord Merle-Smith, III), Christopher; res: Eglinton, Middleburg, Va. 22117.

McCLELLAND, JANE SUDEKUM, Owner, McClelland Agency (PR and Adv.), 1642 El Dorado, San Jose, Cal. 95126, '61–; Rewrite, S.F. News, '44–'51; Reptr., Palo Alto Times, '43–'44; Phoenix Republic, '41–'42; Cont., KTAR Radio, '41; Stringer, Phoenix Gazette, '40–'41; PRSA, San Jose Adv. Club, Theta Sigma Chi, San Jose Parks and Recreation Commn., San Jose Day Nursery (Bd. of Dirs.), Happy Hollow Corp. (Bd. of Dirs.), San Jose Goals Comm.; Stanford Univ., BA; h. Bruce A. McClelland.

McCLENDON, IDA ALICE Jr., News Coordr./Ed.,

Reed College, Information Services Office, 3203 S.E. Woodstock Blvd., Portland, Ore. 97202, '68–; News Librn., Rschr., Radio Music Dir., King Bdcst. Co., KGW AM and TV, '66–'68; Prom. and Pubcty. Asst., '66; Asst. to Pers. Dir., '65–'66; Rschr., TV doc., "Albina: Portland's Ghetto of the Mind," '67, (NATAS Reg. "Emmy," '68); Co-prod., Co-hostess, "Black Is," '68; Ore. Assn. of Eds. and Communicators, PR Round Table, AWRT (Willamette Rose Chptr. Pres., '68–'69; Secy.-Treas., '67–'68); Cert. of Appreciation, Tillamook Job Corps Ctr. and U.S. Bur. of Land Mgt., '68; Board Member, YMCA, '68–'70; Governor's Appointment to Oregon State Law Enforcement Council, '69–'70; Portland State Univ., BS (Humanities), '66; b. Portland, Ore., 1941; p. William H., Sr., and Ida A. Edwards McClendon; res: 2303 N.E. 12th Ave., Apt. #4, Portland, Ore. 97212.

McCLINTON, KATHARINE MORRISON, Auth: "Collecting American 19th Century Silver" (Chas. Scribners Sons, '69), "Collecting American Victorian Antiques" ('67), 12 other bks. on furnishings, antiques, related subjects ('29–'65); numerous mag. and nwsp. articles; art criticism colm., San Diego Sun, three yrs.; Edtl. Staff, McCall's, '38–'39; Lectr., Univ. of Cal. Ext., three yrs.; Artist, exhbns., numerous Cal. shows; San Diego Wms. Federated Clubs County Art Chmn., '29; Who's Who in the East; Who's Who; Stanford Univ., AB, '21; Columbia Univ., MA (Fine Arts), '22; Wheaton Col., LittD (hon.), '61; b. S.F., Cal., 1899; p. Robert and Leila Perry Morrison; h. Harold L. McClinton; c. Julianna M. Ashley, Robert B.; res: 25 East End Ave., N.Y., N.Y. 10028.

McCLOSKEY, EUNICE LonCOSKE, Artist, Auth.; 400 paintings exhibited in 14 states; Auth: "So Dear To My Heart," "The Golden Hill," six illus. vols. poetry, five art bks.; NLAPW, Intl. Inst. of Arts and Letters, Delta Kappa Gamma, Assoc. Artist; numerous poetry, art aws.; Columbia Univ.; b. Johnsonburg, Pa., 1906; p. Fredrick and Ada Nelson LonCoske; h. Lewis McCloskey; c. Mimi Minteer; res: 403 Oak St., Ridgway, Pa. 15853.

McCLOSKEY, KATHERINE, Staff Wtr., gen. assigt. rept. and educ., Santa Barbara News-Press, De la Guerra Plaza, Santa Barbara, Cal. 93101; Prodr., "Trade Winds," five day a week radio program, five yrs.; Santa Barbara Bd. of Educ., 11 yrs., Delta Kappa Gamma, Cal. Tchrs. Assn. John Swett Aw. for excellence in rept.; '67; h. Haddon McCloskey (dec.); c. Donald V., Haddon H.; res: 1937 Laguna St., Santa Barbara, Cal. 93101.

McCLURE, ELEANOR BROWN, Ed., The National Gardener, 4401 Magnolia Ave., St. Louis, Mo. 63110, '65–'69; Garden Wtr., St. Louis Post-Dispatch, '47–'65; Landscape Designer, Contractor, '53–; Free-lance Horticultural Wtr., Photogr., '42–; Advisory Comm., Crops and Soils, Univ. of Mo., '54–'59; Mo. Botanical Garden Horticultural Cncl., '48–'52; Am. Horticultural Soc., Am. Hemerocallis Soc., Garden Wtrs. Assn.,

Federated Garden Clubs of Mo. (Bd. Mbr., '42-'54), Nat. Cncl. of State Garden Clubs; Wellesley Col., AB, '24; b. Kan. City, Mo., 1903; p. Charles and Lucinda Jones Brown; h. James N. McClure; c. James N., Jr., Henry Dixon, Mary Lou; res: 2 Sappington Spur, Kirkwood, Mo. 63122.

McCOLLUM-BLUNT, MARY CLYDE, Staff Stylist, H. G. Peters & Co., Inc., 525 Mildred Ave., Primos, Pa. 19018, '67-; Staff Stylist, Still Photog., Mel Richman, Inc. (Bala-Cynwyd, '65-'67); Phila. Art Alliance (Pfsnl. Mbr.), Buten Museum of Wedgwood (Curator), NHFL; Phila. Col. of Art, '39-'41; res: "Parkview," 33 Price Ave., Narberth, Pa. 19072.

McCOLM, CONSTANCE LEE, Prin. Librn., Reader Svcs., California State Library, 900 Capital Mall, Sacramento, Cal. 95809, '60; Supervising Librn., '55-'60; Head, Am. & British Sec., '52-'55; Special Recruit, Lib. of Congress, '51-'52; Tchr., A to Zed Sch. (Berkeley), '47-'48; Co-auth., "Business and Population Statistics" (Cal. Senate Fact-finding Comm. on Commerce and Econ. Dev.); ALA, Cal. Lib. Assn., Standards and Dev. Comm., Sierra Club of Cal.; Univ. of Cal., AA, '45; MA, BLS, '51; Reed Col., BA (Econ.), '47; Berkeley, Cal., 1926; p. Charles and Evelyn Grundy Lee; h. George McColm.

McCONNELL, BONNIE KERR, Free-lance Bk. Reviewer, Poetry Cnslt., '60-; Ed., Tempo mag. (Can.); Bk. Reviewer, Scrivener Magazine, '66; State Pres., Composers, Auths. and Artists of Am., '60-'64; Auth: "Dark Tigers of my Tongue" ('57), "Season of the Golden Dragon" ('60), "Leopard on a Topaz Leash" ('61), "A Pride of Lion-Noons" ('64); over 3,000 poems; Mich. Poetry Soc., Lansing Poetry Soc., N.H. Poetry Soc., Catholic Poetry Soc. of Am., N.J. Poetry Soc., Versewriters Guild of Oh., Idaho Poets and Wtrs. Guild, Composers, Auths. and Artists of Am., Ariz. State Poetry Soc., Danae; Driftwood Nat. Contest first prize, '68; N. Am. Mentor Nat. Contest aws., '67, '68, '69; Clover Pubns. aw. and golden cert., '69; several other aws.; Wayne State Univ., '62-'64; b. Detroit, Mich.; p. Rosmer and Evelyn Hauer Kerr; h. Ralph McConnell; c. Judith L. Parker, Holly S. Parker; res: 11551 Roxbury, Detroit, Mich. 48224.

McCONNELL, DIANE Du BOIS, Artist, Ex. Prodr., Presson Productions & Stone Fox Music Co., 8293 Presson Pl., L.A. Cal. 90069, '68-; Artist, Actress, '57-; Free-lance work, studios; Child Actress, Universal Pics., 20th Century Fox; SAG, AEA, AFTRA; U.C.L.A., Col. Drama and the Arts (Debating Hons., French and Eng.); b. Brussels, Belgium, 1940; p. Joques and Josie Du Bois; h. Keith W. G. McConnell; c. Kevin W. G.

McCORMACK, MARIE W., Educ. Dir., Information Center on The Mature Woman, 3 W. 57th St., N.Y., N.Y. 10019; Commentator, "Woman's Circle," ABC Radio, '53-'54; Prog. Dir., Am. Theatre Wing, '44-'47; Supvsr., Health & Recreation, Poughkeepsie (N.Y.) Bd. of Educ., '41-'44; Auth., "Songs and Games of Physical Fitness for Boys and Girls" ('65); AWRT, Catholic Actors Guild; U.S. Army cit., '47; Am. Red Cross aw., '47; N.Y. State Tchrs. Col., BS (Health, Recreation), '41; Columbia Tchrs. Col.; b. Poughkeepsie, N.Y.; p. Thomas and Mary Ann McCormack; h. Alfred Gentilcoeur; res: 245 E. 63rd St., Apt. 422, N.Y., N.Y. 10021.

McCORMACK, PATRICIA SEGER, Colmst., United Press International, 220 E. 42nd St., N.Y., N.Y. 10017, '59-; Med. Sci. Ed., INS, '57; Health and Welfare Ed., Pittsburgh Sun Telegraph, '52-'57; Adm. Rsch. Analyst, Legislative Rsch. Commn. (Ky.), '51-'52; Comml. Rsch. Div., U.S., Steel, '49-'51; Nat. Assn. of Sci. Wtrs., NWC; Freedoms Fndn. aw., '55; Family Svc. Assn. of Am. aw., '65; Boys Club of Am. aws., '66, '65; Pitt. Wms. Press Club aw., '50; Univ. of Pitt., '49; b. Pitt., Pa., 1927; p. Arthur and Anna McCaffrey Seger; h. Donald P. McCormack; c. Christopher Paul; res: 29 Treadwell Ave., Westport, Conn. 06880.

McCOY, ANN WILSON, Mistress of Ceremonies, "The Ann McCoy Show," Jefferson Standard Broadcasting, 1006 Edista Dr., Florence, S.C. 29501, '67-; Dietary Cnslt.; Pubcty. Chmn., Un. Fund; wtr., pfsnl. articles; George Peabody Tchrs. Col.; b. Aurora, Ind.; p. Marvin and JoElla Marshall Wilson; h. Singletary McCoy; c. Boyce Allen Brasington, John Williams Brasington.

McCRACKEN, BETSY NICHOLS, Contrb. Ed., Special Interest Pubns., Meredith Publishing Co., 1716 Locust, Des Moines, Ia. 50303, '69-; Free-lance Wtr., '52-'69; Assoc. Ed., Better Homes and Gardens, '48-'52; Contrb. Ed., Des Moines Register and Tribune, '54-'57; Theta Sigma Phi; Ia. State Univ., BS, '48 (Mortar Bd., Phi Kappa Phi, Omicron Nu); b. Topeka, Kan., 1927; p. Floyd and Nell Beaubien Nichols; h. Scott McCracken; c. Scott B., Robert G., Richard C., Janet S.; res: 314 52nd, Des Moines, Ia. 50312.

McCULLOCH, MARY HERCULES, Dir., Fairfax County Public Library, 3915 Chain Bridge Rd., Fairfax, Va. 22030, '58-; Children's Librn., Cleve. Heights (Oh.) Public Lib., '48-'49; Hosp. Librn., Lansing (Mich.) Public Lib., '43-'45; Supvsr., Children's Work, Hamtramck Public Lib., '39-'41; Br. Librn., Flint Lib., '37-'39; Cnslt. on Lib. Construction; ALA (Cncl.-at-large, '64-'68; Bd. of Dirs., '64-'68), Va. Lib. Assn. (Secy.; Pres., '63), Southeastern Lib. Assn., Dist. of Columbia Lib. Assn.; active in civic and cultural orgs.; Youngstown Col., AB (Biological Scis.), '34; Carnegie Inst. Tech., BS (Lib. Sci.), '37; b. Union City, Ind., 1913; p. A. Neil and Carrie Sumner Hercules; h. William R. McCulloch; res: 3607 Woodhill, Pl., Fairfax, Va. 22030.

McCULLOUGH, FRANCES MONSON, Assoc. Ed., Harper & Row, 49 E. 33rd St., N.Y., N.Y. 10016, '69-; Asst. Ed., Reader, '64-'69; Asst. Ed., Harcourt, Brace & World, '61-'63; Ed., "The Light Around The Body" (Nat. Bk. aw., '67), "House Made of Dawn" (Pulitzer

Prize, '69); Auth., "Earth, Air, Fire & Water" (Coward-McCann, '70); Stanford Univ., BA, '60; b. Quantico, Va., 1938; p. George and Frances Fouché Monson; h. David McCullough; c. Benjamin, Katherine; res: 156 Berkeley Pl., Bklyn., N.Y. 11217.

McCULLOUGH, MARIE MOORE, Pres., McCullough Associates, Convention Hall, Atlantic City, N.J. 08401, '41–; Dean, Atlantic City Sch. of Modeling, '45–; Exec. Dir., Atlantic City Models' Guild, '44–; Prodr., "Fashions, Fads & Facts" (daily radio prog., WFPG); Fashion Group, AWRT, Am. Bus. Wms. Assn., Hotel Sls. Mgt. Assn., Jr. Wms. Club; Mbr., Atlantic City Convention Hall Commission, '57–; b. Atlantic City, N.J., 1917; p. Sterling and Marie Ruffu Moore; h. James J. McCullough; c. James J. Jr., William J., Maria; res: Hanover at 8 South, Margate Station, Atlantic City, N.J. 08402.

McCULLOUGH-THOMPSON, JANE FISKE, Edtl. Dir., Benjamin Thompson Assocs., One Story St., Cambridge, Mass. 02138; Trustee and Edtl. Dir., Kaufmann Intl. Design Aw., '57–'66 (grant for Bauhaus rsch., '65–) Auth., articles on design, design educ., '60–; Founder-Ed.-in-chief, Industrial Design mag., '54–'59; Architectural Ed., Interiors, '50–'54; Harvard, Bennington, Marlboro, Pratt Inst., Ill. Inst. of Tech.; Soc. of Architectural Histrns.; APB Aw. for Outstanding Jnlsm., '62; Vassar Col., AB, '47; N.Y.U. Inst. of FA; b. Urbana, Ill., 1927; p. David and Ahna Anderson Fiske; h. Benjamin Thompson; c. Jill McCullough, Allen McCullough, Sheila McCullough; res: 27 Willard St., Cambridge, Mass. 02138.

McCUNE, PATRICIA, Food Ed., Pasadena Star-News, 525 E. Colorado Blvd., Pasadena, Cal. 91109, '56–; U.C.L.A., BE (Educ.).

McCUNE, SARA MILLER, Publr. and Pres., Sage Publications, Inc., 275 S. Beverly Dr., Beverly Hills, Cal. 90212, '64–; Publ. Cnslt., '64; Trade Sls. Mgr., Pergamon Press Ltd. (Oxford, Eng.), '63–'64; Asst. to VP for Sls., The Macmillan Co., '61–'63; Queens Col., BA, '61 (dean's list; N.Y. State Regents scholarship; Pi Sigma Alpha); b. N.Y.C., 1941; p. Nathan and Rose Glass Miller; h. George D. McCune; res: 312 S. Reeves Dr., Beverly Hills, Cal. 90212.

McCURDY, MARILYN BROWNLEE, TV Tchr., KQED, 525 Fourth St., S.F., Cal. 94107, '67–; Lafayette Sch. Dist., '65–'67; Tchr., Laguna Salada Un. Sch. Dist. (Pacifica), '62–'65; Guest Lectr: Cal. State Col., S.F. State Col., Hi. Public Schs., 17th Dist. Cal. Congress of Parents and Teachers, elementary sch. dists. throughout northern Cal.; Cal. Tchrs. Assn., AAUW, Pi Lambda Theta; Univ. of Southern Cal., BS, '62 (cum laude); Grad. Work, S.F. State Col.; b. L.A., Cal., 1940; h. William T. McCurdy; c. Michael William; res: 1410 Via Don Jose, Alamo, Cal. 94507.

McDANIEL, AUDREY, Wtr., religious bks., music; Bdcstr.; bks: "The Greatest of These is Love" (C. R.

Gibson Co., '62), "Forget-M-Nots of Love" (C. R. Gibson Co. '64), "Garden of Hope" (C. R. Gibson Co., '69); Hymnbook, "Hymn Gems from Sacred Memory Time" (Harold Flammer, Inc., '67); radio program, 15 stations; NLAPW (Nat. Chaplain '66–'68; Nat. Aw., '66); Poetry Soc. of London, Intl. Platform Assn., Intl. Who's Who in Poetry; b. Wash., D.C.; p. Dwight and Jennette Nolan Stansell; h. Valrie McDaniel; c. Val; res: 5800 N. 11th St., Arlington, Va. 22205.

McDERMOTT, ANGELA, Dir., Div. of Instructional TV, Maryland State Department of Education, 600 Wyndhurst Ave., Balt., Md. 21210; Ch. 67, Owings Mills, Md. 21117, '68–; Free-lance Cnslt., closed circuit TV, '67–'68; Dir. of TV, Nat. Svcs., Parlons Français, Una Aventura Español, Heath deRochemont Co. (Boston, Mass.), '61–'66; Exec. Dir., "The 21 Inch Classroom," WGBH-TV, '59–'61; Assoc. Dir., Cncl. for a TV Course in Humanities (Ford Fndn.), '57–'59; Exec. Prodr., Mohawk Hudson Cncl. on ETV, WRGB-TV (Schenectady, N.Y.), '53–'56; Tchr., Librn., Cnslt., Commtns. Cnslt.; Lt., U.S. Naval Reserve; NEA, DAVI, NAEB, Boston Pubcty. Club, AWRT (New Eng. Past Pres.; Educ. Fndn. Bd. of Trustees), Cncl. for Humanities (Boston, Bd. of Trustees); "Golden Mike" TV Aw., McCalls, '55, '60; DAR Aw. for N.Y. Hist. series, '56; Ithaca Col., BS (Eng. Speech, Drama); Syracuse Univ., MS (Radio, TV); State Col. (Albany, N.Y.), Lib. Certification; Elementary Certification; Univ. of Buffalo; Smith Col.; b. Lockport, N.Y.; p. Patrick F. and Helena E. Carberry McDermott; res: 22 Cross Keys Rd., Cross Keys Village, Balt., Md. 21210.

McDERMOTT, BETTY FOBAIR, Owner, Dir., The Creative Kitchen, 10303 Whipple St., N. Hollywood, Cal. 91602, '62–, and VP, Flax & Flax, Inc., mfgs. and designers, 10214 Riverside Dr., N. Hollywood, Cal. 91602, '69–; Dir. of Consumer Svc., Western Growers Assn. (L.A.); Dir. of Home Svc., Bay Area Div., Southern Counties Gas Co. (Santa Monica); Home Econst., Gas Light Co. (Wash., D.C.); Dietitian and Tchr., Kamehameha Schs. (Honolulu, Hi.); Cnslr.-Coordr., Herbert Hoover HS (San Diego) student tour of Mexico; Home Econs. Tchr., Covina Un. HS; Co-auth., bk. "How California Cooks" (Ward-Ritchie Press, '70); Wtr., articles on food and features; Univ. of Cal., Santa Barbara, BA (Home Econs.), '51; b. Butte, Neb., 1930; p. Roscoe and Annette Anderson Fobair; h. Thomas J. McDermott, Jr.; c. Robert Bruce; res: 10303 Whipple St., Toluca Lake, N. Hollywood, Cal. 91602.

McDONALD, CERYL ALEXANDRA, Media Dir., Grant Advertising, Inc., 500 Empire Life Bldg., Dallas, Tex. 75201, '67–; Radio Asst., Edward Petry & Co., '65–'66; Adm. Asst., KBOX, '64; Prod. Coordr., WFAA-TV, '58–'64; Traf. Mgr., KENS-TV, '54–'58; Alpha Epsilon Rho; Univ. of Tex., Austin, BFA (Radio, TV Bdcst.), '54; b. San Antonio, Tex., 1929; p. Alexander and Ceryl Potts McDonald; res: 3206 Lemmon East, Two, Dallas, Tex. 75204.

McDONALD, JEANNE GRAY, Free-lance Bdcstr.;

Prodr., travel films, '54–'65; Commentator, Prodr., KNXT, '50–'54; KTTV, '50; KMPC Radio, '47–'50; Lectr., wms. orgs.; Freedoms Fndn. (Founder, Wms. Div.; Nat. Pres., '69–'70; George Washington Medal, '68); Radio and TV Wm. of Southern Cal. (Founder and Pres., '52–'53), AWRT (Hon.), Emmy, Best Cultural Program, '51; LULU, L.A. Adv. Wm., '52; Silver Mike Aw., '49; Morale Aw., '68; Francis Holmes Achiev. Aw., '49; Hon. Pres., Wms. Div., L.A. C. of C.; Columbia Univ., '40–'42; Art Students League, '42–'43; Nat. Acad. of Dramatic Art, '45; b. Seattle, Wash., 1917; p. George and Mary Gray Murphy; h. Dr. John Bowen McDonald; c. Gregory Roland Stoner, Jeanne Eve; res: 910 Stradella Rd., Bel Air, L.A., Cal. 90024.

McDONALD, JOSEPHINE K., Coordr. of Sch. Libs., Longmeadow Public Schools, Williams Middle School, Longmeadow, Mass. 01106, '60–; Instr., Boston Univ. Inst. for Sch. Librarianship, '69–'70; State Col. at Westfield, '65–; Librn., Westover AFB, '51–'60; War Dept., Europe, '45–'46; Watertown (Mass.) Arsenal, '44–'45; Camp Edwards, '42–'44; Lib. Asst., Worcester Free Public Lib., '37–'42; Auth., "School Library and You," '64; NEA, other educ. orgs.; ALA, Mass. Sch. Lib. Assn., New England Sch. Lib. Assn.; State Tchrs. Col., Worcester, BS (Educ.); Simmons Col. Sch. of Lib. Sci., MLS; b. Branford, Conn., 1916; p. Simon and Agnes Tamulevich Kasketa; h. William C. McDonald; c. William Michael, Ann Marie; res: 79 Roosevelt Ave., Springfield, Mass. 01118.

McDONALD, LUCILE SAUNDERS, Auth., Free-lance Wtr.; Seattle Times Sunday Magazine, '43–'66; New York Times, UP, Portland Oregonian, Buenos Aires Herald, Cordova Daily Times, Salem Statesman, others; Auth., 20 teenage and adult bks.; Theta Sigma Phi (Past Reg. Dir., Nat. Headliners Aw., '59), Seattle Free Lances, Auths. Guild. of Am.; Wash. State Press aws.; Univ. of Ore.; b. Portland, Ore., 1898; p. Frank and Rosa Wittenberg Saunders; h. Harold D. McDonald; c. Richard K.; res: 11855 Holmes Pt. Dr., N.E., Kirkland, Wash. 98033.

McDOWELL, AUDREA ADAMS, Free-lance Wtr., non-fiction and adv. copy, '65–; Copy Dir., Fessel, Siegfriedt and Moeller Adv. Agcy., '64–'65; Copy Dir., The Mullican Co., '58–'63; Cont. Dir., WAVE (Louisville, Ky.), '56–'58; Ed., Talking Bk. Dept., Am. Printing House for the Blind, '53–'56; Univ. of Louisville, '46–'49; b. Hibbing, Minn.; p. Ralph and Carrie Meers Adams; h. Robert Emmett McDowell; c. Robert E., Jr.; res: 2212 Fairland Ave., Louisville, Ky. 40218.

McDOWELL, JULIA LOOMIS, Artist, Designer, Associated Advertising Agency, Inc., 22 W. Luck Ave., Roanoke, Va. 24001, '69–; WSLS-TV, Shenandoah Life Stations, '64–'69, '53–'55; C. N. Snead Adv., '55–'56; drawings published in Gourmet, America, Flower Grower, '60–'64; AWRT; Roanoke Valley Adv. Club Aw. of Excellence, '69; Cit., Roanoke City Cncl., '69; Sch. of Art, Richmond Pfsnl. Inst., Va. Commonwealth Univ., '49–'52; b. Norfolk, Va., 1931; p. James and

Catherine Guthrie Loomis; h. Charles B. McDowell, Jr.; c. Charles James, John Edmond; res: 1815 Langdon Rd., S.W., Roanoke, Va. 24015.

McDUFF, MARJORIE McLEAN, Mng. Ed., Crowell Collier and Macmillan Directory Corporation, Suite #110, Humble Bldg., Hattiesburg, Miss. 39401, '68–; Assoc. Ed., Who's Who in Am. Educ., Inc. '55–'68; b. N.O., La., 1918; p. Clarence and Leah Briede McLean; h. Joseph McDuff; c. Mrs. Rebecca Lynn Kramer; Alan Rea, Nancy Gail; res: 800 S. 17th Ave., Hattiesburg, Miss. 39401.

McDUFFIE, ANN GREER, Food Ed., The Tampa Tribune, 505 E. Kennedy Blvd., Tampa, Fla. 33602, '60–; Home and Fashion Ed., Beauty Ed., Feature Wtr., Etiquette Colmst., '56–'60; State Wms. Ed., '55–'56; Soc. Ed., Tampa Times, '52–'55; Fla. Wms. Press Club (Secy. and Pubn. Ed., four yrs.; Bd. Mbr., '56–; numerous aws., '56–), Theta Sigma Phi (Fla. W. Coast Pfsnl. Chptr.: Pres., '68–'69; VP, '67–'68; Treas., '66–'67); Am. Meat Inst. Vesta aw. for excellence in food presentation, '62, '63; b. Macon, Ga.; p. Aden L. and Ruth Morgan Greer; h. William King McDuffie; res: 4208 Barcelona St., Tampa, Fla. 33609.

McELDERRY, MARGARET KNOX, Ed. of Bks. for Children, Harcourt Brace Jovanovich, Inc., 757 Third Ave., N.Y., N.Y. 10017, '45–; Children's Librn., N.Y. Public Lib., '34–'44; Children's Bk. Cncl. (Pres., '50); Mt. Holyoke Col., BA, '33; Carnegie Lib. Sch., BS (Lib. Sci.), '34; b. Pittsburgh, Pa.; p. William and Evelyn Bronte McElderry; h. Storer B. Lunt; res: 184 Sullivan St., N.Y., N.Y. 10012.

McELDOWNEY, PAULINE ELIZABETH, Asst. Ed., VP and Treas., The Harlem Valley Times, Inc., PO Box H, Amenia, N.Y. 12501, '59–; Asst. Pers. Dir., Cal. Consumers Corp., '43–'45; Ins. Reptr., N.Y. Jnl. of Commerce, '43; Dutchess County Dem. Wms. Club, Amenia Dem. Club; Pasadena Jr. Col., '44; Cal. Tech., '44; b. N.Y.C., 1920; p. Dr. George G. and Pauline Dusenbury Starke; h. Elliott H. McEldowney, Jr., c. Elliott Henry, III, G. Phillip, Gregory R.; res: E. Main St., Amenia, N.Y. 12501.

McELROY, ROSALIE FARRAGE, AE, KWIZ Radio, 3101 W. Fifth St., Santa Ana, Cal. 92703, '69–; Fashion Cnslt. and Coordr., Flair Modeling Sch. (Tucson, Ariz.), TV Spot Talent, '54–'66; Newscaster, KVOA-Radio, '56–'64; AE, '54–'66; Wm. Newscaster, KYOR, '49–'52; h. Paul McElroy (div.).

McENTEE, HELEN S., Asst. Prof., Dept. Lib. Sci., Graduate School, St. John's University, Jamaica, N.Y. 11532, '65–; Librn., Woodside Sch., Peekskill, N.Y., '69–'70; Adj. Prof., '59–'65; Librn., Glen Rock (N.J.) Sr. HS, '56–'65; Instr., Paterson State Col., '64; Librn., various schs., '48–'56; Cnslt., Paramus (N.J.) Catholic HS, '67; Educ. Rschr.; Catholic Lib. Assn. contributing Ed., basic ref. bks.; (Secy. HS Libs., '69–'71); Nat. Poetry Therapy Assn; ALA, NEA, N.Y. Lib. Assn.,

AAUW, AAUP: Eastman Sch. of Dental Hygiene, RDH, '37 (hons.); Ladycliff Col., BA, '46; St. John's Univ., BLS, '48 (Fac. Aw. for Scholarship, '48); Tchrs. Col., Columbia Univ., MA (Developmental Psych.), '54; b. Bklyn., N.Y., 1915; p. Henry and Mary Fuchs Schroeder; h. Col. Girard L. McEntee (dec.); res: 2 Weyant Terr., Highland Falls, N.Y. 10928.

McEVOY, MARGARET (PEGGY) SANTRY, Edtl. Staff, Readers Digest, 231 E. 48th St., N.Y., N.Y. 10017; past positions, Ladies' Home Jnl., Life, Town and Country, Diplomat, N.Y. Mirror, INS-UPI, Wash. Post features; radio shows, CBS, NBC, WRC (Wash., D.C.); WNPC, N.Y. Wms. Press Club, OPC; N.Y.U. (Jnlsm.); b. N.J.; h. J. P. McEvoy (dec.); c. Margaret Michele (Mrs. Peter Doty), Patricia (Mrs. Roger Greenwalt).

McFADDEN, RUTH MAUZY, Wms. Ed., Muncie Evening Press, Muncie Newspapers, Inc., 125 S. High St., Muncie, Ind. 47305, '25–; NLAPW (Muncie Br. Pres.) Theta Sigma Phi (Past. Pres.), Wms. Press Club of Ind., DAR; Radio WLBC cit.; b. Rushville, Ind.; p. Homer and Rose White Mauzy; h. William H. McFadden; res: 200 Alden Rd., Muncie, Ind. 47904.

McFADDEN, WILMOT C., Dir. Lib., Carnegie Public Library, 300 Blair Ave., Rock Springs, Wyo. 82901, '53–; Asst. Librn., '47–'48; Wyo. Sch. Dist. Number Four, elected Bd. of Educ., '66–'69, '69–; Wyo. Advisory Cncl., Fed. Commn. Civil Rights '63–'70; ALA, Am. Lib. Trustee Assn., Wyo. Lib. Assn. (Pres., '58; VP, '57), Mountain Plains Lib. Assn. (Chmn.); Dorothy Canfield Fisher Aw. to small libs., '65; Compiled "Handbook for Wyoming Library Trustees," '62, Nat. Grolier Aw. for Best Nat. Lib. Wk. Program, '69; S.D. State Univ., '38–'42; b. Lead, S.D., 1919; p. William and Ingeborg Christianson Curnow; h. John McFadden; c. Christina Hamm, Susan McFadden, Mrs. Ron Parmely.

McGAREY, MARY, Wms. Ed., Dispatch Printing Company, 34 S. Third St., Columbus, Oh. 43215, '67–; Reptr., Educ. Wtr., Colmst., Asst. City Ed.; Oh. Nwsp. Wms. Assn. (Past Pres.), Press Club of Oh. (Past Pres.), Theta Sigma Phi (Past Pres.), Oh. Legislative Corrs. Assn., EWA, Nat. Assn. of Sci. Wtrs.; Oh. Univ., BS (Jnlsm.), '42; b. Junction City, Oh., 1921; p. William and Marie McGonagle McGarey; res: 5020 Dublin Rd., Columbus, Oh. 43220.

McGAUGHEY, FLORENCE HELEN, Auth.; Prof. of English, Indiana State University, 217 N. Sixth St., Terre Haute, Ind. 47809, '46–; English Tchr., '26–'46; six poetry bks.; nwsp., mag. essays; Modern Lang. Assn., Delta Kappa Gamma, Alpha Phi Gamma, NLAPW, Nat. Arts Club, World Poetry Soc., Wabash Valley Press Club; Italian orgs. and hons.; Intl. Aw. of Hon., Poets Corner, Inc., '59; Talisman Key Intl., '60; Western Col. for Wm., '22–'23; DePauw Univ., AB, '26 (Alumni Cit., '59); Middlebury Col., AM, '32; Ind. Univ.; Ind. State Univ.; b. Roachdale, Ind., 1904; p. Charles and Sallie Brumfield McGaughey; res: 136 S. 25th, Terre Haute, Ind. 47803.

McGAW, JESSIE BREWER, Auth., juvs. bks.; Asst. Prof. of Eng. and Latin, Univ. of Houston, Cullen Blvd., Houston, Tex. '52–; Tch., Ward Belmont Sch., '38–'40; bks: "Little Elk Hunts Buffalo" ('61), "Painted Pony Runs Away" ('58), "How Medicine Man Cured Paleface Woman" ('56); Cncl. of Tchs. of Fgn. Langs. (Houston Area Treas.), Tex. Inst. of Letters (Best Juv., '56), Tex. Folklore Soc., Am. Classical League, Modern Lang. Assn., Delta Kappa Gamma, AAUP; "Today Show" Merit Aw., '56; Theta Sigma Phi Juv. Auth. of Yr., '58; Duke Univ., BA, '35; Peabody Col., MA, '40; Columbia Univ. grad. sch., '48–'50; Am. Acad., Rome (Fulbright Scholar), '58; Univ. of Colo., '51; b. Montgomery County, Tex., 1913; p. L. Vernon and Birdie Basford Brewer; h. Harold L. Geis; c. Miriam Katherine McGaw, Vernon Howard McGaw; res: 2405 Dickey Pl., Houston, Tex. 77019.

McGEE, PATRICIA S., Exec. Dir., National Multiple Sclerosis Society, Northeastern Connecticut Chapter, 104 Asylum St., Hartford, Conn. 06103, '64–; Radio Bdcstr., Wms. Program Dir., Asst. Station Mgr. for five yrs.; AWRT (New England Chptr. Pres., '68–'69), Quota Intl., Newington Wms. Club; Univ. of Hartford; b. Beacon Falls, Conn., 1921; p. John and Sabyna Flynn Malone; h. James Michael McGee; res: 217 Brookside Rd., Newington, Conn. 06111.

McGIFFIN, LEE SHAFFER, Free-lance Wtr.; juv. fiction, non-fiction, E. P. Dutton; short stories, Saturday Evening Post, wms. mags.; network radio, TV; Reptr., Syracuse (N.Y.) Post-Standard, Buffalo Evening News; Herald Tribune Hon. Aw.; Tex. Inst. of Ltrs. Aw.; Theta Sigma Phi Aw.; Who's Who of Am. Wm.; DePauw Univ.; Syracuse Univ.; Univ. of Ala., BA; b. Delphi, Ind.; h. Norton McGiffin (dec.); c. Donald N.; res: 300 S. Davis Dr., Arlington, Tex. 76010.

McGILLIVRAY, KATHERINE F., Dir. PR and Adv., Allied Chemical Canada, Ltd., 1155 Dorchester Blvd. W., Montreal 102, Quebec, Can., '62–; Adm. Asst. to Pres., Lake Ontario Portland Cement Co. (Toronto), '57–'61; Off. Mgr., Dir., Canadian Charcoal Corp., '53–'57; Exec. Asst., Manton Bros., '51–'53; Rep'd. Nurses Assn. of Ontario, '45–'51; Free-lance PR Cnslt., '45–'61; Reptr., Der Courier (Regina, Sask.), '37–'41; Pfsnl. Child Actress (Vienna, Austria, '26–'31; Adv. and Sls. Execs. Club of Montreal (VP, '66–'68), Assn. of Indsl. Advs. (VP, '66–'68), Can. PR Soc., Fedn. of Can. Adv. and Sls. Clubs (Treas., '69), Sls. Mktng. Execs. of Montreal (Secy., '69), Central Collegiate Inst., '37 (hons. grad.); b. Vienna, Austria, 1922; p. Ernest and Frances Von Kollmann Pollak; h. (div.); c. Frank, Stanley; res: 3555 Cote des Neiges Rd., Apt. 1504, Montreal 109, Quebec, Can.

McGINNIS, JACKLYN MURPHY, Media Dir., Larry Painter & Associates, "The Quarter," Jackson, Miss. 39216, '68–; Media Buyer, Kinro Adv., Atlanta, Ga., '63–'68; b. Memphis, Tenn., 1938; p. John and Audrey Kerr Murphy; h. James H. McGinnis, Jr.; c. John K.,

Kathleen D., James S.; res: 1160 Winnrose, Jackson, Miss. 39211.

McGOVERN, Sr. ANNE M., Dir. of Lib., Mercy Col., 555 Broadway, Dobbs Ferry, N.Y. 10522, '63–; Tchr.-Librn., Pius X Central Sch., '59–'63; Met. Catholic Lib. Librns. (Chmn., '69–'71; Vice-Chmn., '67–'69), Cath. Lib. Assn., ALA, AAUP (Mercy Col. Chptr. Treas., '69–'70); Marymount Col., BA, '57; Rosary Col., MA (Lib. Sci.), '63; b. N.Y.C., 1934; p. Patrick and Elizabeth Leydon McGovern; res: 545 Broadway, Dobbs Ferry, N.Y. 10522.

McGOVERN, MARY JANE FORSTER, VP, Duncan-Brooks, Inc., 600 Old Country Rd., Garden City, N.Y. 11530, '68–; AE, Gamut, '67–'68; Copywtr., PR, Mineola Theatre, '65–'68; PR, Dir., Theatre Sch. Island-Wide Pubns., '63–'68; Colmst., Reptr., Ed., WBAB Radio, '63–'65; Copywtr., PR, Air Interviews, '63–'65; PR Cnslt., Mineola Sch. Dist.; L.I. PR, L.I. Adv. Club; St. John's Col., '52–'54; b. Bklyn, N.Y., 1934; p. Anthony and Kathryn McDermott Forster; h. John McGovern; c. Kathleen Mary, Maureen Ann, Lizabeth Jane, Terence Raymond; res: 164 Meadowsweet Rd., Mineola PO, Williston Pk., N.Y. 11501.

McGOWAN, BARBARA KILBRIDE, Adv. Coordr., Springfield Gas Light Company, 2025 Roosevelt Ave., Springfield, Mass. 01101; also Copy Coordr., "The Gas Jet," house organ; copywtr., layouts, photogr., art; free-lance for major printing firms; direct assigts. for cos. in Greater Springfield area; Talent, TV interviews; Public Utilities Adv. Assn. (nat. aws. for prom.), Am. Gas Assn., ICIE, N. Eng. Gas Assocs., Mass. Indsl. Eds. Assn., Valley Press Club, Adv. Club of Springfield (numerous adv. aws., all media), civic agcys., ZONTA, Jr. Achiev. Advisor; biogs.; Bay Path Jr. Col., Western N. Eng. Col., Univ. of Hartford; b. Springfield, Mass., 1940; p. Everett and Irene Kelly Kilbride; h. Terence E. McGowan; res: 1218 Mountain Rd., W. Suffield, Conn. 06093.

McGRATH, PHYLLIS KETLER, PR Dir., The Greeley National Bank, 8th Ave. and 8th St., Greeley, Colo. 80631, '67–; Exec. Secy to City Mgr., City of Greeley, '65–'67; Bank PR and Mktng. Assn., AWRT, Greeley C. of C.; Greeley Jayceettes Girl of the Yr., '63; Santa Ana (Cal.) Jaycee Anns Girl of the Yr., '64; Colo. State Univ., '57–'59; Northwestern Univ., '69–'70; b. Benkelman, Neb., 1937; p. Merle and Eva Marie Cooley Ketler; h. John McGrath; c. John Robert, Jefferey Allen; res: 1616 Montview Blvd., Greeley, Colo. 80631.

McGRAW, MARIETTA HORTON, Dir., Amherst Public Library, 770 Hopkins Rd., Williamsville, N.Y. 14221, '61–; Buffalo and Erie County Public Lib., Head of Kensington Br., '58–'60; Coordr., storytelling, schs., '52–'58; Head of Jefferson Br., '51; Head of William St. Br., '49–'50; Jr. Librn., '46–'49; tchr., Hornell, N.Y., '27–'29; Tchr., State Univ. Col. at Geneseo, '58; N.Y. State Lib. Assn., Buffalo and Erie County Public Lib.

Librns. Assn., Library Staff Assoc. (Pres., '59–'61); Geneseo Normal Sch., '27; N.Y. State Univ. Col. at Geneseo, BS (Lib. Sci.), '51; Alfred Univ.; b. Whitesville, N.Y., 1908; p. Bert and Clara Spicer Horton; h. Harold McGraw; c. Jean (Mrs. Leon Riker); res: 39 Argonne Dr., Kenmore, N.Y. 14217.

McGRIFF, VERNICE BROWN, Product Mgr., Beech-Nut, Inc., 460 Park Ave., N.Y., N.Y. 10022, '69–; Mkt. Rsch. Supvsr., '68–'69; Sr. Mkt. Rsch. Analyst, Warner-Lambert, '65–'68; Rsch. Proj. Dir., Ted Bates & Co., '63–'65; Am. Mktng. Assn., AWNY, NBPW; GAP; N.Y.U., BS (Mktng.), '59; Seton Hall Univ., BS (Educ.), '62; p. James and Lonie Davis Brown; h. R. McGriff; c. Lori G.; res: Newark, N.J. 07112.

McGUCKIN, PATRICIA GARDINER, Ed., Capital Finance Corporation, 100 E. Broad St., Columbus, Oh. 43215, '63–; Wtr., Make-up, Columbus Dispatch; Central Oh. Bus. and Indsl. Eds.; Oh. State Univ.; b. Columbus, Oh.; p. Fred and Julia Newkirk Gardiner; h. (div.); c. Julia G., Malcolm L.; res: 1746 E. Broad St., Columbus, Oh. 43203.

McGUINN, M. PATRICIA, Pres., Maxwell-Hamilton Corp., 52 Vanderbilt Ave., N.Y., N.Y. 10017, '69–; Media Dir., Bill Suitt Agcy., '68–'69; Assoc. Media Dir., Clinton E. Frank, '67–'68; Assoc. Media Dir., Needham and Grohman, '64–'67; Agcy. Cnslt., Gaynor and Ducas, '63–'64; Media Supvsr., Fletcher Richards, Calkins and Holden, '57–'63; Cnslt., travel industry; Adv. Agcy. Cnslt., '63–'64; St. John's Univ., BBA, '60; b. N.Y.C., 1931; p. William and Mildred McGuinn; res: 47–46 50th St., L.I. City, N.Y. 11104.

McGUIRE, ALICE BROOKS, Assoc. Prof., University of Texas, 2607 Main Bldg., Univ. Sta., Austin, Tex. 78712, '68–; Librn., Casis Elementary Sch., '51–'68; Instr. and Dir., Children's Bk. Ctr., Univ. of Chgo., '44–'49; Asst. Prof., Drexel Inst. of Tech., '28–'44; Cnslt., sch. libs.; Dir., workshops; Auth., articles in pfsnl. periodicals; Contrbr. to jr. encys.; ALA, AASL (Pres., '54–'55), Intl. Reading Assn., Tex. Lib. Assn. (Librn. of the Yr., '68), Grolier aw., '62; Smith Col., AB, '23; Drexel, BS (Lib. Sci.), '26; Columbia Univ., MS, '32; Univ. of Chgo., PhD, '58; b. Phila., Pa.; p. John and Anna Brooks; h. J. Carson McGuire; res: 3415 Foothills Terr., Austin, Tex. 78731.

McGURN, BARBARA ANN, Ed., The Theatrical Calendar, Celebrity Service, Inc., 171 W. 57th St., N.Y., N.Y. 10019, '68–; Adm. Asst., Collins Tuttle Real Estate, '65–'68; Ed., Scientific Dics.-SETI/Western Publ., '61–'64; Ed., Scientific Dics.-SETI/Western Publ., '61–'64; Copy Dept., Lennen & Newell, '58–'61; Edtl. Asst., Nat. Underwriter (Life edition), '56–'59; Wtr., travel and fiction; Rsch. and PR, Repl. presidential elections, '64, '68; Chestnut Hill Col., AB, '55 (Mademoisselle Mag. Col. Bd., '53–'57); Columbia Univ.; b. Boston, Mass., 1934; p. James and Theresa Norwicke McGurn; res: 2500 Kennedy Blvd., Jersey City, N.J. 07304.

McHALE, JOAN NIELSEN, Soc., Fashion Ed., Miami News, 1 Herald Plaza, Miami, Fla. 33132, '66–; Soc. Ed., '61–; '54–'60; Wash., D.C. Corr., Women's Wear Daily, '60–'61; Theta Sigma Phi (Pres., '56–'57), Fla. Wms. Press Club (six aws., '67–'68); Univ. of Miami, '47–'48; '51–'53; b. Dobbs Ferry, N.Y., 1930; p. Kay and Lilly Robinson Nielsen; h. (div.); c. Billy Jr., Emily, Elise, Dorothy; res: 2420 San Domingo St., Coral Gables, Fla. 33134.

McHARRY, ELIZABETH POSTON, Mng. Ed., Town & Village Newspaper, 614 E. 14th St., N.Y., N.Y. 10009, '68–; Reptr.-Ed., '65–'68; Ed., UP (N.Y.C.), '41–'51; Night Bur. Mgr. (Cleve.), '44; Rewrite, '43; Reptr., News Adv. (Creston, Ia.), '40–'41; Reptr., Times Republican (Corydon), '35–'37; Theta Sigma Phi; Stephens Col.; Drake Univ., BA, '40; b. Corydon, Ia.; p. Eugene and Kathryn Ballew Poston; h. Charles K. McHarry; c. Mark Kirwan, Lucinda Laney; res: 441 E. 20th St., N.Y., N.Y. 10010.

McHUGH, RUTH JONES, Ed.-Owner, Northridger, 18137 Parthenia St., Northridge, Cal. 91324; Ed., Ariz. Range News (Willcox, Ariz.), '60–; Ed., '40–'59; Ed. San Pedro Valley News (Benson, Ariz.), '34–'46; Ed., Attica Independent (Attica, Kan.), '32–'34; Feature Wtr., Ariz. Daily Star, '36–'59; Feature Wtr., Ariz. Stockman, '36–'59; Ariz. Mother of the Yr., '54; Who's Who of Am. Wm.; Who's Who of the West; Advisory Bds: Mayor Sam Yorty, San Fernando Valley Salvation Army, Shooting Star Fndn. for the Indians; Wichita State; Kan. State Tchrs. Col.; b. McCook, Neb.; p. Robert and Mary F. Kincaid Jones; h. Matthew O. McHugh; c. Jill Mellenbruch Boyd; res: 18137 Parthenia St., Northridge, Cal. 91324.

McINTIRE, VIRGINIA ALLEN, Owner, Virginia McIntire Photography, 308 N. Doheny Dr., Beverly Hills, Cal. 90211, '54–; L.A. Adv. Wm., Nat. Home Fashions League, Pfsnl. Photogs. W., Beverly Hills Art League (Pres., '67–'68); Omaha Univ.; b. Omaha, Neb.; p. Daniel and Julia Sherwood Allen; h. Harlan McIntire.

McINTOSH, SHIRLEY HUPP, Pres., SM Advertising Associates, 7315 Wisconsin Ave., Bethesda, Md. 20014, '65–; Adv., PR Dir., Walker & Dunlop, '63–'64; Nat. Adv. Dir., Undersea Tech. Magazine, '60–'63; AWRT (Bd. of Dirs.), Adv. Club of Wash.; Univ. of Md., '55–'57; currently, Am. Univ.; b. Keyser, W.Va., 1937; p. James and Evelyn Fleek Hupp; h. Donald McIntosh; res: 5101 River Rd., Bethesda, Md. 20016.

McIVER, VIVIAN DOWNES, Librn., Needham Free Public Library, 1139 Highland Ave., Needham Heights, Mass. 02194, '60–; Asst. Librn., '57–'60; Cataloger, '43–'57; ALA, New Eng. Lib. Assn., Mass. Lib. Assn., Greater Boston Lib. Admin. (Pres., '62–'63); Simmons Col., BS, '43; b. Needham, Mass., 1921; p. George and Fanny Collishaw Downes; h. Gavin McIver; c. Carolyn R., Gavin R., Jr.; res: 70 Pickering St., Needham, Mass. 02192.

McKECHNIE, MARGARET A., Customer Svcs. Mgr., Computer Image Corp., 2145 S. Platte River Dr., Denver, Colo. 80223, '69–; PR Asst., Ed., House organ, First Nat. Bank, 111 E. Fourth St., Cinn., Oh., '66–'69; Theta Sigma Phi; Oh. Univ., BS (Jnlsm.; cum laude); b. Niagara Falls, 1944; res: 945 Ogden St., Denver, Colo. 80218.

McKEE, ALICE, Fashion and Soc. Ed., Ft. Lauderdale News, 101 W. New River Dr. E, Ft. Lauderdale, Fla. 33302, '63–; Wms. Section Reptr., '61–'63; Asst. to Mng. Ed., Living for Young Homemakers, '60; Theta Sigma Phi, Fla. Wms. Press Club (Aw., '68); writing aws., Fla. Assn. for Retarded Children, '64, '68; Duke Univ., BA (Hist.), '58 (Dean's List); b. Keokuk, Ia., 1936; p. Thomas and Mary Lynch McKee; res: 317 Hendricks Isle, Ft. Lauderdale, Fla. 33301.

McKEE, MARY JEANNE, Wtr., Edtl. and Information Svcs. PR, Business Products Group, Xerox Corporation, Xerox Sq., Rochester, N.Y. 14603, '69–; Newswtr., Part-time, WOKR-TV, '69–; Reptr., Dem. and Chronicle, '57–'69; Pers. Asst., Graflex, Inc., '56–'57; Svc. Asst., N.Y. Telephone Co., '54–'56; Jr. Exec. Training Program, The Higbie Co. (Cleve., Oh.), '53–'54; Rochester Corr., Approach, '68–; Rochester Corr., Religious News Svc., '61–'69; Pubcty. Cnslt., Virginia Wilson Interracial Ctr., '68–; Ed., Rochester Commty. Music Nwsltr., '55–'59; Theta Sigma Phi, Rochester Nwsp. Guild (Secy., '63–'64), ZONTA; Heidelberg Col., BA (Eng.), '53 (Silver Key for Excellence in Jnlsm.); Eastman Sch. of Music (Flute), '52, '61; Rochester Inst. of Tech. (Jnlsm.), '56–'57; B. Rochester, N.Y., 1931; p. Rev. William and Faustina Dresser McKee; res: 11 Buckingham St., Apt. 3, Rochester, N.Y. 14607.

McKELVY, TRUDI, Free-lance PR, Pubcty., Talent, 3630 St. Elizabeth Rd., Glendale, Cal. 91206; NBC, '56–'61; Boy Scouts of Amer., fin., TV, radio, '54–'55; Educ. TV, '53–'54; Pers. Work, May Co. (Wilshire), '52–'53; Staff Artist, Singer, KEHE Radio, '37; NATAS (Nat. Aws. Comm., '67–'68; Nat. Monitoring Comm., '68–'69), AWRT, Radio & TV Wm. of Southern Cal. (Offcr.), W. Coast Pioneer Bdcstrs.; active in numerous civic and cultural orgs.; U.C.L.A.; pfsnl. schs., dance, music; b. Hillsboro, Tex., 1912; p. William T. and Margaret Hendrix McCullar; h. Volney Lewis McKelvy; c. Gerald Aubrey Kemp; res: 3630 St. Elizabeth Rd., Glendale, Cal. 91206.

(Offcr.), W. Coast Pioneer Bdcstrs.; active in numerous civic and cultural orgs.; Wm. of the Yr., Town and Country Fine Arts Club, '70; Hon. Mayor, Higashi-Osaka, Japan, '70; U.C.L.A.; pfsnl. schs., dance, music; b. Hillsboro, Tex., 1912; p. William T. and Margaret Hendrix McCullar; h. Volney Lewis McKelvy; c. Gerald Aubrey Kemp; res: 3630 St. Elizabeth Rd., Glendale, Cal. 91206.

McKENZIE, BARBARA, Auth., Photogr.; Assoc. Prof., Radio-TV-Film, School of Journalism, University of Georgia, Athens, Ga. 30601, '69–; Assist. Prof., Eng. Dept., Drew Univ., Madison, N.J., '64–'69; bks: "Mary McCarthy" (Twayne, '66), "The Process of Fiction" (Harcourt, Brace and World, '69); Am. Film Inst., Soc. for Photographic Educ.; Rockford Col., '52–'55; Univ. of Miami, BA, '56; MA, '58; Florida State Univ., PhD, '63; b. Mt. Vernon, N.Y., 1934; p. Leslie and Euphemia Anderson McKenzie; res: 111 Coventry Rd., Athens, Ga. 30601.

McKENZIE, ELIZABETH ADAMS, Ed., Dean of Students' Office, University of Illinois, 610 E. John, Champaign, Ill. 61820, '66–; Pubns. Ed., NAEB, '59–'66; Pubns. Coordr., Univ. of Wis. Ext. Div., '56–'58; Edtl. Secy., Trains, '53–'55; Assoc. Ed., L.S. Ayres and Co. (Ind. pls., Ind.), '46–'48; Theta Sigma Phi; Ind. Univ., BS, '46; b. Carlton, Ga., 1926; p. Robert and Evelyn Colson Adams; h. Leonard J. McKenzie (dec.); res: 1515 W. Charles, Champaign, Ill. 61820.

McKIBBIN, BARBARA CULLEY, Mktng. Dir., Vogue, 420 Lexington Ave., N.Y., N.Y. 10017, '69–; Fashion Projects Ed., '67–'69; Mktng. Ed., '63–'67; Fashion Coordr., J. Walter Thompson, '56–'62; h. Wm. McKibbin.

McKILLOP, ANNABELLE, Head, Children's Svc., Windsor Public Library, 434 Victoria Ave., Windsor, Ont., Can., '37–; Br. Librn., Walkerville Public Lib., '29–'37; Contributor, prof. jnls., Can. Lib. Assn.; Ontario Lib. Assn. (Chmn., Children's Librns. Section, '41–'42), Canadian Assn. Children's Librns. (Vice-chmn., '46–'47), Inst. of Pfsnl. Librns. of Ont., ALA, WNBA; Queens Univ., BA; Univ. of Toronto, BLS (Lib. Sci.), '41; b. W. Lorne, Ont., Can.; p. Malcolm and Margaret Ferguson McKillop; res: 1616 Ovellette Ave., Apt. 214, Windsor, Ont., Can.

McKIM, RUBY SHORT, Ed., Doll Talk, Kimport Dolls, 1212 W. Lexington, Independence, Mo. 64051; '36–; Ed., Publr., "One Hundred and One Patchwork Patterns," '31; Staff Wtr., Better Homes & Gardens, seven yrs.; Art Tchr., Manual Training HS (Kan. City), '15; Art Supvsr., Independence Sch. System, '11–'14; Auth., many articles on artcraft and home beautifying; Nat. Fedn. of Doll Clubs; Who's Who of Am. Wm.; N.Y. Sch. of Fine and Applied Arts, '11; Kan. City Art Inst.; b. Millersburg, Ill., 1891; p. Morris and Viola Vernon Short; h. Arthur E. McKim; c. Mrs. W. B. Fullerton, Jr., Mrs. H. T. Galvin, Kim; res: 1210 W. Lexington St., Independence, Mo. 64051.

McKINLEY, ALICE E., Exec. Dir., DuPage Library System, P.O. Box 826, Wheaton, Ill. 60187, '67–; Lib. Ext. Specialist, USOE, BAVE, DLSEF, LSCA (Wash., D.C.), '65–'67; Gen. Cnslt., Mich. State Lib., '56–'65; Armed Forces Librn., U.S. Army (Europe), '47–'55; Young People's Asst., Kan. City Public Lib., '46–'47; Asst. Librn., Park Col. (Parkville, Mo.), '44–'46; Children's Librn., Minot (N.D.) Public Lib., '43; Tech. Cnslt., Macomb County (Mich.) Planning Commn., '59–'60; conducted various workshops for public lib.

employees, '55–'64; ALA, ILA, Adult Educ. Assn., Am. Soc. for Public Admin., Ill. Lib. Assn.; Blackburn Univ. (Carlinville, Ill.), Assoc. BA, '40; Park Col., BA, '42; Univ. of Denver, BS (Lib. Sci.); b. Champaign County, Oh., 1921; p. Herman and Sarah Siebert McKinley; res: P.O. Box 682, Wheaton, Ill. 60187.

McKINNEY, JUDY LEWIS, Bdcstr., WOAY-TV, 110 Professional Park, Beckley, W. Va. 25801; AWRT; Montreat Col., BA; h. Dr. Worthy McKinney; c. David S.; res: 200 MacArthur St., Beckley, W. Va. 25801.

McKINNEY, MARGERY MULKERN, Sr. Ed., University of Missouri Press, 103 Swallow Hall, Columbia, Mo. 65201, '69–; Ed., '62–'69; Edtl. Asst. '60–'62; Wtr., short stories in New College Writing No. 2, Midlands; articles, Parents' Magazine, Redbook; Who's Who of Am. Wm.; Univ. of Mo., BA, '58 (with distinction); Phi Beta Kappa; Mortar Bd.; McAnally Prize, '56; 1st prize, Mahan Short Story Contest, '56; hon. mention, '57); MA, '65; b. Big Timber, Mont., 1906; p. James and Helen Williams Mulkern; h. Fred McKinney; c. Megan (Mrs. Robert William Whitfield, Jr.), Kent J., Molly (Mrs. Carliss Coleman Farmer), Doyne (Mrs. William Sherman McKenzie); res: 710 Thilly Ave., Columbia, Mo. 65201.

McKINNIE, PATRICIA TROTTER, Adm. Asst. to Exec. Dir., St. Paul Housing and Redevelopment Authority, 55 E. 5th St., St. Paul, Minn. 55102, '69–; Copy Ed., Mpls. Tribune, '66–'69; Indsl. Pubns. Ed., Univac, '60–'66; Copywtr., '58–'60; Copywtr., St. Paul dept. store, '56–'57; Free-lance Wtr.; PR activities, commty. and civic orgs.; PRSA, Twin Cities Nwsp. Guild, ICIE (Hon. Mention Aw., '64), Northwest IEA (Secy., '64–'65; Outstanding Pubn. Aw., '65); Univ. of Ill., BS (Jnlsm.), '55; advanced courses, Univ. of Minn.; b. Chgo., Ill., 1934; h. Cato McKinnie; c. Karen Lynn; res: 1315 Zealand Ave., N., Mpls., Minn. 55427.

McKNEELY, SHIRLEY CRAIN, VP, Carmichael & Company, Corner Chapel Hill & Roney Sts., Durham, N.C. 27702, '68–; Asst. AE, C. Knox Massey & Assocs., Adv. and Mktng., '63–'67; Prod. Mgr., '58–'63; volunteer crtv. cnslt., Durham county elementary and jr. high schs.; AAF; Univ. of N.C. at Greensboro, '48–'50; b. Durham, N.C., 1930; p. Clyde and Nellie Crain; h. Arthur McKneely; c. Michael T., Melisa Ann; res: Rte. 1, Cornwallis Rd., Durham, N.C. 27703.

McKNIGHT, ELIZABETH EVANS, Asst. City Ed., Stockton Daily Record, Box 900, Stockton, Cal. 95202, '69–; Central Cal. News Ed., 20 yrs.; Wtr., weekly colm., "The Back Road"; Nwsp. Guild, Stockton Press Club, Stockton Redev. Agcy. (Pres., '59–'60), Cal. BPW, Stockton Wm. of the Yr., '67; Col. of the Pacific, '24–'29; b. Balt., Md.; p. Robert W. Evans; h. Charles McKnight; c. David Chapman, Arthur Chapman, Betty Dyck; res: 332 E. Robinhood, Stockton, Cal. 95207.

McLANE, HELEN J., Asst. to the PR Dir., International Harvester Co., 401 N. Michigan Ave., Chgo., Ill. 60611, '69–; Cnslt., '66–'69; VP, Beveridge Org., '61–'66; Assoc., '56–'61; Press Dir., Commty. Fund of Chgo., '53–'56; PR Wtr., Chgo. Assn. of Commerce and Industry, '52–'53; Co-Auth., "The Investment Club Way to Stock Market Success" (Doubleday, '63); PRSA (Accredited), Trustee, Natl. Assn. of Investment Clubs; Northwestern Univ., BS, '51 (with distinction); MBA (Finance), '65; b. Indpls., Ind.; p. Alvin and Ethel Ranck McLane; res: 1360 Lake Shore Dr., Chgo., Ill. 60610.

McLAREN, LYNN, Free-lance Photogr: assigts. for many mags., annual repts., col. catalogs; Wtr.-Photogr: "Berlin and Berliners," "The Village—The People" (All-India prize for excellence); many one-man shows in U.S. and abroad; Ed., Middle East Newsletter; Asst. Ed., Foreign Service Journal; Am. Soc. of Mag. Photogrs.; numerous aws.; Tanzania exhbn. shown at UN, Newsweek Gallery, N.Y.C.; Vassar Col., BA (Contemporary Hist., Econs.), '44; b. Bklyn., N.Y., 1922; p. James and Gwendolen McLaren; h. John Y. Millar (div.); c. Gwendolen, David, Bruce; res: 42 W. Cedar St., Boston, Mass. 02114.

McLARTY, MARY ADELAIDE, Dir., Davidson County Public Library, 221 S. Main St., Lexington, N.C. 27292, '67–; Onslow County Public Lib., '57–'67; Wilson County Public Lib., '53–'57; ALA, Southeastern Lib. Assn., N.C. Lib. Assn., BPW; John Cotton Dana Aw., '60; Jaycee Commty. Wm. of the Yr., '64; Stephens Col., AA, '45; Univ. of N.C., BA (Hist.), '47 (Hons.); MA, '49; BS (Lib. Sci.), '53; b. Memphis, Tenn., 1925; p. John Robert and Edith Wiggins McLarty; res: P.O. Box 249, Lexington, N.C. 27292.

McLAUGHLIN, MARY ANN, Dir. of Adv. and Prom., Col. Div., The Bobbs-Merrill Co., Inc., 4300 W. 62nd St., Indpls., Ind. 46260, '69–; Off. Mgr., Media Dir., Copywtr., MacGill-Ross, '66–'69; Copywtr., Caldwell, Larkin & Sidener-Van Riper, '64–'66; Copywtr., Media Dir., Shaw-Hagues Inc., '63–'64; Adv. Sls. Trainee, Chicago (Ill.) Tribune, '61–'63; Wtr., Greensburg (Ind.) Daily News, '59–'60; Theta Sigma Phi; Ind. Univ., AB (Jnlsm.-Eng.), '61; b. Greensburg, Ind., 1939; p. James and Mary Link McLaughlin; res: 4811 Round Lake Rd., Indpls., Ind. 46205.

McLEAN, BARBARA MALAN, Dir. of Instr., University of Kansas, Ext. Building, Lawrence, Kan. 66044, '66–; Auth., non-fiction: "The Risk Takers: A Good Gamble for the Schools" (Univ. of Kan. Bul. of Educ., '66), "Willa Cather, A Study Syllabus" (Univ. of Kan. Extramural Independent Study Ctr., '68), others; Poet: "Fidepoems," "Chokecherry Monstrosity," others; Ind. Univ., BA (Jnlsm. and Eng.), '50; Univ. of Kan., MA (Eng.), '65; PhD; b. Pinckneyville, Ill., 1929; p. W. Russell and June Hume Malan; h. James E. McLean; c. James Malan and Thomas Albert; res: 1418 Grand, Parsons, Kan. 66044.

McLENDON, WINZOLA POOLE, Wtr.; Staff Reptr.,

Washington Post, '54–'67; Colmst., Philadelphia Inquirer, '51–'53; Honolulu Advertiser, '50–'51; Wms. News Dir., Hubert Humphrey campaign, '68; Contrbr., Diplomat, The Washingtonian, Venture, others; WNPC, ANWC, WHCA; Who's Who of Am. Wm.; b. Cardwell, Mo.; p. Mactie and Ethel Romines Poole; h. Capt. John Benjamin McLendon; c. Martha Elizabeth (Mrs. Charles H. Beardsley); res: 414B The Westchester, 4000 Cathedral Ave., N.W., Wash., D.C. 20016.

McLOUD, MARY, Dir. PR, Sheraton-Palace Hotel, Market and New Montgomery Sts., S.F., Cal. 94119, '64–; Dir. PR, Hilton Hotels in Hi., '63–'64; Dir. PR and Pubcty., Waldorf-Astoria Hotel (N.Y.C.), '57–'62; AE, Am. Soc. of Travel Agts., and Wms. Dir PR, The Caples Co., '55–'57; Staff, Madison Sq. Travel Bur., '52–'55; Prom., George Peabody and Assocs., '51–'52; Dir., Pubcty., Prom., PR, Herald Tribune Fresh Air Fund, '50; Coordr., Pubcty., PR, Prom., Bermuda News Bur. (Hamilton, Bermuda), '48–'49; Am. Field Svc. (N.Y.C.), '47–'48; edtl., rsch., Time, Inc., '42–'46; Soc. of Am. Travel Wtrs., Comm. of Wm. in PR, S.F. Press Club, AWRT, Bay Area Pubcty. Club (Dir.), S.F. Adv. Club; Skidmore Col.; b. Lima, Peru (Am. parents); res: 1938 Taylor St., S.F., Cal. 94133.

McLUCAS, GRACE BEEZLEY, Dir. of P.R., Young Women's Christian Association of Metropolitan Chicago, 1001 N. Dearborn St., Chgo., Ill. 60610, '69–; Nat. Program Coordr., Cncl. on Religion and Intl. Affairs, '67–'69; Dir. of PR, Visiting Nurse Assn. of Chgo. (Helen Cody Baker Aw. for annual rept.), '64–'67; PRSA, Pubcty. Club of Chgo., Soc. of Typographic Arts, Welfare PR Forum (Bd. Dir., '66–'69); Wellesley Col., BA, '33; Grad. Work, Northwestern Univ.; b. Oak Park, Ill., 1911; p. Charles, Jr., and Leah Van Blarcom Beezley; h. (div.); c. Don H., Bruce B., William S. (dec.); res: 314 Oxford Rd., Kenilworth, Ill. 60043.

McMAHAN, VETA ELIZABETH, Police Reptr., Van Nuys Publishing Co., 14519 Sylvan St., Van Nuys, Cal. 91408; Corr., Ed. & Publr. (San Fernando Valley), '48–; Asst. Ed., House Organ, Beech Aircraft Corp., '46–'47; Court Reptr., St. Louis Globe-Democrat, '44–'46; Gen. Reptr., Milw. Sentinel, '42–'44; Wms. Club Ed., Wichita (Kan.) Beacon, '30–'42; Corr., Variety, '38–'42; San Fernando Valley Press Club (Secy., '48–'49); Cal. Nwsp. Publrs. Assn. Better Nwsp. Contest Aw. for mental health series, '63; Kan. City Jr. Col., '24; Kan. Univ., '27; Wichita State Univ., BA, '30; b. Kingman, Kan., 1904; p. Albert and Gertrude Pro McMahan; res: 14033 Burton St., Van Nuys, Cal. 91402.

McMANUS, MAUREEN ELEANOR, Pubcty. Dir., Cowles Book Company, 488 Madison Ave., N.Y., N.Y. 10022, '68–; Pubcty. Dir., Holt, Rinehart and Winston, '56–'68, '51–'54; Pubcty. and Rsch., Reader's Digest, '54–'56; Pubcty. for pubn. of American Heritage, paperback edition of "The Family of Man," '54; Pubcty. Dir., G. P. Putnam's Sons, Coward-McCann, John Day Co., '45–'51; Head of Appointments Div.,

Am. Red Cross Blood Donor Svc., Bklyn. Br., '42-'45 (U.S. Navy Cit.); Lectr., Bk. Pubcty., Radcliffe Col., Georgetown Univ.; Cnslt. to Intl. Publrs. meeting, Wash., D.C., '64; WNBA (Bd. of Dirs.), Nat. Bk. Aw. Pubcty. Comm., Publrs. Adv. Club (former Offcr.), Publrs. Pubcty Assn.; Marymount Col., Am. Acad. of Dramatic Arts; b. N.Y.C.; p. Terence and Eleanor Lynn McManus; res: 131 E. 93rd St., N.Y., N.Y. 10028.

McMASTER, FLORENCE RIMAN, Law Librn., Assoc. Prof. of Law, Indiana University Indianapolis Law School, 102 W. Michigan St., Indpls., Ind. 46204; Asst. Librn., Col. of Law, Univ. of Ill., '44-'46; Asst., Docs., Univ. of Ill., '43-'44; Asst. to Librn., Univ. of Toledo, '37-'43; wtr., jnl. articles, bk. chptrs.; Am. Assn. of Law Libs., Chgo. Assn. Law Libs., Special Libs. Assn. (Ind. Chptr. Pres., '57-'58), Am. Bar Assn., Ind. State Bar Assn., Am. Judicature Soc., admitted to practice Supreme Ct. of U.S., '69, Ind. and Fed. Cts., '61; Univ. of Toledo, PhB, '37; Univ. of Ill., BS (Lib. Sci.), '44; Ind. Univ., LLB, '61; h. (div.).

McMILLAN, PRISCILLA JOHNSON, Auth., non-fiction; Moscow Corr., North American Newspaper Alliance, '58-'60; Ed., Translator, Current Digest of the Soviet Press, N.Y.C., '54-'58; bk., "Khrushchev and the Arts: The Politics of Soviet Culture 1962-64" (M.I.T. Press, '65); Translator, Svetlana Alliluyeva's "Twenty Letters to a Friend" (Harper and Row, '67); mag. articles; h. George E. McMillan; res: Coffin Point, Frogmore, S.C. 29920.

McMILLEN, BETTIE MILLER, Asst. to Pres., Patricia Brown's Reading System, Inc., 146 Seventh Ave. N., Nashville, Tenn. 37202, '69-; Exec. VP, Commtns. in Art, '66-'68; Partner, Saver, Kerr & McMillen, '65-'68; VP, Doyne Adv., '53-'65; Crtv. Dir., WKDA, '50-'53; Nashville Adv. Fedn. (Secy., '60; VP, '66); AWRT (Southern Area VP, '67-'68); AFA Gold Medal Aw., '65; Outstanding Print Campaign Aw., '63; BPW Nashville Outstanding Businesswoman Aw., '63; 2,000 Wm. of Achiev.; Averett Jr. Col., '43-'45; Univ. of Mo. (Jnlsm.), '45-'47; b. Nashville, Tenn., 1926; p. George and Clara G. Miller; h. John McMillen; c. Michael John; res: 3927 Woodlawn Dr., Nashville, Tenn. 37205.

McMILLEN, ELEANOR EVA, Exec. Dir., The Fashion Group, Inc., 9 Rockefeller Plaza, N.Y., N.Y. 10020, '58-; Kenyon and Eckhardt, '49-'58; Berkshire Knitting Mills, '45-'49; Montgomery Ward, '43-'45; Lord and Taylor, '40-'43; Friends Univ., BA, '37; Boston Univ., MA, '39; N.Y.U., MS (Retailing), '40; b. Goddard, Kan.; p. Claude and Ida Woolworth McMillen; h. Niels Olsen; c. Andrew, Peter; res: 22 Fraser St., Pelham, N.Y. 10803.

McMULLAN, PENELOPE EAKINS, Reptr.-Wtr., Newsday, 550 Stewart Ave., Garden City, N.Y. 11530, '69-; Youth Ed., Richmond (Va.) Times-Dispatch, '69; Reptr., Rschr., Newsweek, '67-'69; Vassar Col., AB (Eng.), '66; b. Bklyn., N.Y., 1944; p. William and Jean Pickup Eakins; h. C. G. McMullan (div.); res: 313 E. 85th St., N.Y., N.Y. 10028.

McMULLEN, CATHERINE ELIZABETH, Ed., Better Camping, Kalmbach Publishing Co., 1027 N. Seventh St., Milw., Wis. 53233, '63; edtl. work on Better Camping, Ships and the Sea, Model Trains, Trains, '51-'63; Asst. News Ed., Candian Register, Kingston, Ontario, '49-'51; Family Camping Fedn. (Bd. Mbr., Past Secy.), Outdoor Wtrs. Assn. of Am., Theta Sigma Phi; Marquette Univ., BA (Jnlsm.), '49; grad. work, '59-'61; Queen's Univ., summer courses, '46-'50; b. Toronto, Ontario, Can., 1927; p. Francis and Harriet Ford McMullen; res: 9528 W. Metcalf Pl., Milw., Wis. 53222.

McMULLEN, CLAIRE D., PR Dir., Press Assoc., One Belmont Ave., Bala-Cynwyd, Pa. 19004 and 521 Fifth Ave., N.Y., N.Y. 10017, '67-; Sls. Prom. Specialist, WFIL-TV (Phila., Pa.), '66-'67; Asst. Dir. of Adv. and Prom., '45-'60; Dept. Store Econst. and Home Fashions Ed., '60-'66; Non-fiction wtr. of speeches, articles, radio and TV scripts, colm.; NHFL, Electrical Wms. Roundtable, Nat. Repl. Wms. Cl. ('60-'64), TV-Radio Adv. Club; Col. of Chestnut Hill, '43-'44; N.Y.U., '44-'45; b. Phila., Pa.; p. Enos and Margaret Kielt McMullen; res: Wessex House, St. Davids, Pa. 19087.

McMURRER, MARY CATHERINE, Asst. Ed., Modern Manufacturing, McGraw-Hill, 330 W. 42nd St., N.Y., N.Y. 10036, '66-; News Ed., Inst. of Electrical and Electronics Engineers, '63-'66; Tchr., '62-'63; Freelance ed. and writing; Bdcst. Jnslm. Aw., '63; Modern Manufacturing Edtl. Achiev. Aw., '68; Trinity Col., AB, '63; Univ. of N.H., '63; b. N.Y.C.; p. Louis and Rita Maxwell McMurrer; res: 333 E. 89th St., N.Y., N.Y. 10028.

McMURRIA, MARY GORDY, Ed., Bradenton Herald Sunday Magazine, The Bradenton Herald, 401 13th St., W., Bradenton, Fla. 33505, '65-; Wms. Ed., '60-'65; Asst. Wms. Ed., '55-'60; Wms. Ed., Enquirer (Columbus, Ga.), '44-'45; City Ed., Columbus (Ga.) Ledger, '40; Asst. Wms. Ed., '39-'41; Assoc. Ed., News (Dalton), '37; Fla. Wms. Press Club (writing aws., '62, '64, '65), Theta Sigma Phi, Who's Who of Am. Wm., Univ. of Ga., BJ (Jnlsm.), '37 (Phi Beta Kappa, Phi Kappa Phi); b. Columbus, Ga., 1916; p. James and Frances Ellison Gordy; h. Henry B. McMurria; c. Patricia, Frances; res: 3200 Ave. A, W., Bradenton, Fla. 33505.

McNABB, KATHERINE C., Assoc. Univ. Librn., University of California, Santa Barbara, Cal. 93106, '68-; Asst. Univ. Librn., '59-'68; Head, Catalog Dept., '47-'59; Chief, Catalog Dept., Kan. City (Mo.) Public Lib., '45-'47; First Asst., '31-'45; Cataloger, Queensborough Public Lib. (Jamaica, N.Y.), '30-'31; ALA, Cal. Lib. Assn., Southern Cal. Tech. Processes Group (Vice Chmn., '62-'63; Chmn., '63-'64); Hood Col., BA, '27; Columbia Univ., BS (Lib. Sci.), '30; b. Wewoka, Okla.,

1904; p. James and Alice Long McNabb; res: 3647 Sunset Dr., Santa Barbara, Cal. 93105.

McNAMARA, DOLORES LA COUME, Assoc. Ed., American National Insurance Company, Moody at Market St., Galveston, Tex. 77550, '46–; Secy., '32–'46; Altrusa Intl. (Galveston Club Corr. Secy., '66–'67); b. Galveston, Tex., 1913; p. James and Lucille Rizzo La Coume; h. Robert J. McNamara; c. Linda Ann Polivka; res: 2714 John Dr., La Marque, Tex. 77568.

McNAMARA, RITA A., Owner, Rita McNamara Advertising, 370 Lexington Ave., N.Y., N.Y. 10017, '67–; AE, Pubcty. Supvsr., Sls. Prom. Div. of Interpublic, SCI, '66–'67; VP, Crtv. Svcs., Grant Adv., '64–'66; AE, Wesley Assocs., '60–'64; Grant Adv./Abbott Kimball Co., '58–'60; Fashion Group; Tobe Coburn Sch. for Fashion Careers; N.Y.U.; res: 35 Park Ave., N.Y., N.Y. 10016.

McNAMEE, NITA D., Asst. Rsch. Dir., Aylin Advertising Agency, Inc., 2737 Buffalo Speedway, Houston, Tex. 77006, '64–; Gamma Alpha Chi (Houston Chptr. VP, '68); Univ. of Tex., BBA, '63; b. Higgins, Tex., 1941; p. Dwight and Blanche Vom Hoff McNamee; res: 7600 Highmeadow, Apt. 78, Houston, Tex. 77042.

McNEAR, BETTE H., Wms. Ed., News-Journal Co., 813 Orange St., Wilmington, Del. 19899, '68–; Asst. Wms. Ed., '64–'68; Wms. Wtr., Albany (N.Y.) Times-Union, '57–'61; Syracuse Post-Standard, '57–'61; Publr., wkly., Cazenovia, N.Y., '52–'57; Colmst., Delmarva Dialog; Del. Press Club (Bd. Mbr.); Soroptimist, Salvation Army (Advisory Bd.); Md.-Del. Press Assn. Contest Second Prize, '67; Third Prize, '68; St. Lawrence Univ., '46; b. Norristown, Pa., 1925; p. C. Burt and Emma Watkins Hitchcock; h. James J. McNear (div.); c. Frank, Mrs. Kevin Wright, Mrs. David Fischbach; res: 926 Longview Ct., Wilmington, Del. 19899.

McNEESE, GRETCHEN GRONDAHL, Assoc. Ed., VIP mag., 919 N. Michigan Ave., Chgo., Ill. 60304, '67–; Ed., Sunday Mag., San Juan Star, '63–'65; Staff Wtr., The Oregonian (Portland), '52–'61; Theta Sigma Phi (Univ. of Ore. Chptr. Pres., '51–'52); Univ. of Ore., BA (Jnlsm.), '52 (Phi Beta Kappa; T. Neil Taylor Aw., outstanding Jnlsm. student, '49, '50); b. Portland, Ore., 1931; p. Jack and Alice Wells Grondahl; h. James McNeese; c. Amy, Terence James; res: 1006 S. Euclid Ave., Oak Park, Ill. 60304.

McNEILLY, ELLEN JANE, Prod. Mgr., Alfred A. Knopf, Inc., 201 E. 50th St., N.Y., N.Y. 10022, '69–; Prod. Supvsr., A. A. Knopf/Random House, '66–'69; AE, American Book Stratford Press, '64–'66; Prod. Asst., '63–'64; Art Ed., Harcourt, Brace & World '62–'63; Free-lance Photogr.; Assoc. Mbr., Soc. for the Scientific Study of Religion, '62; Mbr., Action Comm. Publrs. for Peace, '70; Wellesley Col., BA (Sociology), '62; N.Y. Univ., '62–'63; b. Winchester, Mass., '39; p. Samu-

el and Dorothy Bond McNeilly; res: 31 W. 84th St., N.Y., N.Y. 10024.

McPHILLIPS, MARY, Bdcstr., WOR Radio, 1440 Broadway, N.Y., N.Y. 10018, '65–; CBC Radio, TV (Toronto, Can.), '60–'65; CFPL TV (London, Can.), '54–'60; Univ. of Western Ontario, BA (Liberal Arts); b. London, Ontario, Can., 1931; p. Paul and Blanche Molloy Sweeney; h. George W. Snowden; c. Michelle; res: 439 W. 43rd St., N.Y., N.Y. 10036.

McQUEEN, MARGARET WARNKEN, Assoc. Dir., Community Council of Austin and Travis County, 430 Littlefield Bldg., Austin, Tex., 78701, '64–; Health Planning Specialist, Tex. State Health Dept., '63–'64; Rsch. and Info. Dir., Tex. Social Welfare Assn., '61–'63; Rsch. Ed., Analyst, Tex. Rsch. League, '54–'61; Co-ed., "Schools in Transition" (Univ. of N.C. Press, '54); Wtr., numerous social sci. rsch. studies; Theta Sigma Phi; Univ. of Tex., BA, '33 (summa cum laude); MA, '34; La. State Univ., '35–'36; Radcliffe, '36–'38; b. Austin, Tex., 1912; p. Edwin and Louise Walton Warnken; h. R. C. McQueen (div.); c. Bruce Ryan; res: Rte. 7, Box 815, Austin, Tex. 78703.

McQUOWN, PATRICIA TAYLOR, Asst. to Prog. Mgr., KUAT-TV & AM, Radio-TV Bureau, University of Arizona, Tucson, Ariz. 85721, '67–; Traf. Mgr., Cont. Dir., Public Svc. Dir., Asst. Mgr., KTAN Radio, '61–'67; Feature Wtr., Talent, Cont., KMMJ Radio (Grand Island, Neb.), '59–'61; Cont. Dir., KRGI Radio '53–'58; b. Shreveport, La., 1921; p. Wirt and Grace Simms Taylor; h. Edmund McQuown; c. Michael, Kathleen, Colleen; res: 7433 Princeton Dr., Tucson, Ariz. 85710.

McRAE, MARGARET CLARK, Treas., McRae & Bealer, Inc., 873 Spring St. N.W., Atlanta, Ga. 30308, '66–; Off. Mgr., '64–'66; Atlantic Christian Col., B.A., '63; b. Wilson, N.C., 1940; p. Badie and Margaret Smith Clark; h. Floyd W. McRae, Jr.; res: 3037 Rockingham Dr., N.W., Atlanta, Ga. 30327.

McRAE, SHIRLEY WILSON, PR AE, Food Svc. Div., Theodore R. Sills, Inc., 26 Windward Rd., Belvedere, Cal. 94920, '69–; Dir., Food Svc. Div., California Foods Rsch. Inst. (S.F.), '57–; Dir., Consumer Svcs., Foremost Dairies, '54–'57; '43–'49; Instr., Lux Col., '49–'51; Cal. Assn. Med. Lab. Technologists (State Pres., '46–'47); AWRT (Chmn.-Elect, '69–'70); Univ. of Saskatchewan, Liberal Arts deg., '40; Lib. Sci. deg., '42; b. Moose Jaw, Saskatchewan, Can., 1922; p. John and Amy Goldberg Wilson; h. (div.); res: 26 Windward Rd., Belvedere, Cal. 94920.

McRAE, VERA MARIE, Asst. to the Pres., Stern, Walters & Simmons, Inc., 155 E. Superior St., Chgo., Ill. 60611, '67–; Ill. Normal Univ., '58 (Acad. Scholarship); b. Moline, Ill., 1939; p. Melford and Inez Edwards McRae; res: 2234 N. Cleveland, Chgo., Ill. 60614.

McSHERRY, ELIZABETH ANN, Bk. Ed., The Hartford Courant, 285 Broad St., Hartford, Conn. 06101, '54–;

Eng. Tchr., Bulkeley HS, '23–'54; NLAPW; Who's Who of Am. Wm.; Blackburn Col., AB; Bates Col., MA; b. Carlinville, Ill.; p. Thomas and Elizabeth Dennison McSherry; res: 232 Farmington Ave., Hartford, Conn. 06105.

McSTEA, ELIZABETH MORROW, Free-lance PR Cnslt.; 3333 N.E. 34th St., Ft. Lauderdale, Fla. 33308, Committee on Women in Public Relations; RSA (Silver Anvil Aw., '61), AWNY, AWRT, Theta Sigma Phi, Nat. Bd. of Rev. of Motion Pics, Crusade for Freedom Cit., '54; Who's Who of Am. Wm., Who's Who in PR, Who's Who in Commerce and Industry, Who's Who in the East; N.Y.U., BS (Jnlsm.); MA (Eng. Lit.); Columbia Univ., Hunter Col., Grad. Work; b. Paisley, Scotland; p. William J. and Elizabeth Ann Grogan McStea.

McVEIGH, BARBARA W., Wms. Page Ed., Medina County Gazette, Public Sq., Medina. Oh. 44256 '68; Colmst., '53–'56; Sales, Halle Bros. (Cleve.), '66–'68; Jr. Exec., '58–'63; Red Cross Grey Ladies Aw., '62; Flora Stone Mather Col.; b. Cleve., Oh; h. (div.); res: 230 W. Worth St., Medina, Oh. 44256.

McWHIRTER, MILLIE, Free-lance Wtr.; Auth: "Hushed Were the Hills" (Abingdon Press, '69), "A Magic Morning With Uncle Al" (World Publ., '69); Auths. Guild, Theta Sigma Phi, NLAPW, Oh. Press Wm.; Lambuth Col., BS; res: 1350 Custer Rd., Cinn., Oh. 45208.

McWILLIAMS, ELIZABETH MARSHALL, Public Svc. Dir., CKLW AM-FM, CKLW-TV, 1450 Guardian Bldg., Detroit, Mich. 48226, '66–; P.B.X. Club (Pres.); b. Walkerville, Ontario, Can., 1918; p. Frank and Agnes McCrae Marshall; h. Joseph McWilliams; c. Kenneth Frank, Gerald William; res: 1939 Balfour Blvd., Windsor, Ontario, Can.

McWILLIAMS, MARGARET EDGAR, Chmn. Home Econ. Dept., and Prof., Food and Nutrition, California State College, 5151 State College Dr., L.A., Cal. 90032, '68–; Assoc. Prof., '66–'68; Asst. Prof., '61–'66; Auth: "Food Fundamentals" (John Wiley and Sons, '66), "Nutrition for the Growing Years" ('67); Co-auth., "Understanding Food" ('69); Auth., radio vignettes, "Food for Health and Happiness"; Col. Tchrs. of Food and Nutrition (Pacific-South Reg. Chmn.), Inst. of Food Technologists, Am. Home Econs. Assn., Cal. Home Econs. Assn. (Ed., Cal. Home Econst.), Am. Dietetic Assn., AAUP, Phi Upsilon Omicron, Omicron Nu, Iota Sima Pi, Sigma Delta Epsilon, Phi Kappa Phi, Sigma Alpha Iota; Phi Upsilon Omicron Founders Fellowship, '64–'65; Home Econsts. in Bus. Fndn. Fellowship, '68–'69; Ia. State Univ., BS, '51; MS, '53; Ore. State Univ., PhD, '68; b. Osage, Ia., 1929; p. Alvin and Mildred Lane Edgar; h. Don McWilliams; c. Roger, Kathleen; res: 1916 N. Gilbert, Fullerton, Cal. 92633.

MEAD, MARGARET, Auth.; Lectr.; Curator of Ethnology, American Museum of Natural History, N.Y., N.Y., '64–; Adjunct Prof. of Anthropology, Columbia Univ., '54–; bks: "Anthropologist and What They Do," "Anthropology: A Human Science," "Continuities in Cultural Evolution," "People and Places," "An Anthropologist at Work: Writings of Ruth Benedict," "New Lifes for Old: Cultural Transformation—Manus, 1928–1953," "Soviet Attitudes Toward Authority," "The School in American Culture," "Male and Female," "And Keep Your Powder Dry," "From the South Seas," "Sex and Temperament in Three Primitive Societies," "The Changing Culture of an Indian Tribe," "Growing Up in New Guinea," "Coming of Age in Somoa"; Ed., Co-ed., and Co-auth. of many other writings; numerous expeditions; Fellow: Am. Acad. of Arts and Scis., Am. Anthropological Assn. (Pres., '60), AAUW, Am. Ethnological Soc., Am. Soc. of Clinical Hypnosis (Charter), Am. Orthopsychiatric Assn., Royal Soc. for Encouragement of Arts, Manufacturers and Commerce (Benjamin Franklin Fellow), Postgrad. Ctr. for Mental Health (Hon.), Am. Assn. for the Advancement of Sci. (Past Dir.); Barnard Col., BA, '23 (Phi Beta Kappa); Columbia Univ., MA, '24; PhD, '29; Hon. Degs.; from 17 colleges.

MEAD, PEARL EDELMANN, Media Dir., William Douglas McAdams, Inc., 150 E. 59th St., N.Y., N.Y. 10022, '55–; Asst. to Media Dir., '54–'55; Pharmaceutical Adv. Club, Inc. (Bd. of Dirs. and Secy., '66–'67), AWNY (VP, '63–'64); Gamma Alpha Chi (Pres., '64–'65); Adv. Wm. of Yr., '64); Bklyn. Col., BA, '35; b. N.Y.C., 1914; p. Alfred and Rebecca Abramowitz Edelmann; h. Daniel S. Mead; res: 185 E. 85th St., N.Y., N.Y. 10028.

MEADOWS, JEANNE CHRISTAKOS, Adv. Copywtr., Sears, Roebuck, Heart of Huntsville, Huntsville, Ala. 35805, '69–; PR Dir., Flerrissant Valley Commty. Col. (Ferguson, Mo.), '69; Adv. Copywtr., Sears (Chgo., Ill.), '68–'69; Nwsp. Reptr., Columbia Tribune (Columbia, Mo.), '67–'68; Univ. of Mo., BJ, '67.

MEADOWS, LOUISE HALL, Co-owner, VP, Critique Publishing Associates, Inc., Hotel Ohio Suite 214, W. Boardman St., Youngstown, Oh. 44503, '67–; Off. Mgr., Buckeye Rev. Publ. Co., '64–'67; Secy., Reptr., Dickerson Publ. Co., '61–'64; Nat. Assn. of Negro BPW, NAMW, (Nat. Treas., '68–'70); McGuffey Ctr. Svc. Aw. for Special Pubcty., '60–'64; Gilead House Commty. Ctr. (Bd. of Dirs.); b. E. Liverpool, Oh.; p. Dr. Isaac R. and Charlotte Powe Hall; h. William D. Meadows; res: 276 W. Scott St., Youngstown, Oh. 44502.

MEALEY, CATHERINE CRUM, Ed., Laramie Sentinel, 121 Ivinson, Laramie, Wyo. 82070, '69–; Assoc. Prof. of Law, Law Librn., Univ. of Wyo., '62–; practicing lawyer, '58–'60; Am. Bar Assn., Wyo. Bar Assn.; Univ. of Ia., BA (Psych.), '50; MA (Special Educ.), '51; JD (Law), '57 (with distinction); Univ. of Wash., MA (Law Librnship.), '62; b. Ames, Ia., 1928; p. Lloyd and Katherine Parry Crum; h. (div.); c. Gwen, Karen Kay Voight.

MEANS, FLORENCE CRANNELL, Free-lance Wtr.,

Lectr., '28–; Auth: "Our Cup Is Broken" (Houghton Mifflin, '69), 39 other bks.; Lectr: Wtrs. Conf., Univ. of Colo., Univ. of Denver, Temple Buell Col. (Denver, Colo.); Denver Wms. Press Club, Colo. Auths. League; Child Study Assn. of Am. aw., "The Moved-Outers," '45; Nancy Bloch Aw. for Intercultural Rels., "Knock At the Door, Emmy," '57; McPherson Col. (Kan.); Central Baptist Seminary; Univ. of Denver; Henry Read Sch. of Art, Denver; b. Baldwinsville, N.Y., 1891; p. Philip and Fannie Grout Crannell; h. Carl Means; c. Eleanor (Mrs. Angus C. Hull); res: 595 Baseline Rd., Boulder, Colo. 80302.

MEANS, MARIANNE, Synd. Nat. Affairs Colmst., King Features Syndicate, 690 Mills Bldg., Wash., D.C. 20006, '66–; White House Corr., Hearst Newspapers, '61–'65; Wash. Corr., '59–'61; Wms. Ed., Northern Virginia Sun, '57–'59; Copy Ed., Lincoln (Neb.) Journal, '55–'57; Auth., "The Woman in the White House" (Random House, '63); mag. articles, speeches, TV appearances; Delta Delta Delta, Theta Sigma Phi, Kappa Tau Alpha, Gamma Alpha Phi; Univ. of Neb., BA (Phi Beta Kappa); b. Sioux City, Ia., 1934; p. Ernest and Else Andersen Hansen; h. Emmet Riordan; res: 1518 32nd St., N.W., Wash., D.C. 20007.

MEDFORD, KAY, Actress, Co-star with John Forsyth, "To Rome With Love" TV series, Don Federson CBC, Studio City, N. Hollywood, Cal.; Musicals on stage: "Paint Your Wagon," "Funny Girl" (Tony and Oscar nominations, '64, '68), three others; 20 comedies, including "Hole in Head" and "Don't Drink the Water"; Dir. in Special Svcs., Hi. and Japan, '46–'47; Theatre World Aw. for "Lullabye," '54.

MEDGESY, LOIS JACOBSEN, PR Asst., Jacobsen Manufacturing Co., 1721 Packard Ave., Racine, Wis. 53403, '66–; Santa Barbara News-Press, '61; Asst. Ed., Package Engineering, '58; Asst. PR Dir., Am. Dietetic Assn., '58; Jnl. of Am. Anthropologists, '57; Wms. Adv. Club of Chgo. ('60), Adv. Club of Racine; Wis. Indsl. Eds., ICIE; Mich. State Univ., '52–'54; Northwestern Univ., BA, '56; b. Racine, Wis., 1934; p. Einar and Elsa Paur Jacobsen; h. (div.); c. Laura L.; res: 3329 Chatham St., Racine, Wis. 53402.

MEEHAN, KATHLEEN MARY, Eng. Tchr., Central HS, Muncie Community Schools, 311 S. High St., Muncie, Ind. 47305; Supvsr., pfsnl. pubns., '55–'60; Jnlsm. Tchr., Sponsor sch. paper, '31–'55; Tchr., '25–'31; Soc. Ed., Muncie Star, '24–'25; Wtr., children's stories, articles in mags.; Ind. HS Press Assn. (Pres., Advisors Sec.), Ind. Cncl. of Tchrs. of Eng. (Past Secy.), Delta Kappa Gamma, Muncie Tchrs. Assn. (Secy., '35), Ind. State Tchrs. Assn., Theta Sigma Phi (Muncie Chptr. Past Pres., Past VP, Past Secy.), NLAPW (State Pres., '62–'64; Muncie Br. Past Pres.); Muncie Wm. of the Yr., '57; Muncie BPW Civic Aw., '63; Wms. Press Club aws., '65–'68; Who's Who of Am. Wm.; Ball State Univ., AB, '25; MA, '49 (Distg. Alumni Aw., '63); b. Muncie, Ind., 1904; p. Michael and Dora Conroy Meehan; res: 410 S. Madison St., Muncie, Ind. 47305.

MEEKER, HELEN FALKENSTEIN, Soc. Ed., Hamilton, Oh., Journal-News, Court St. at Journal Square, Hamilton, Oh. 45012, '66–; Gen. News Wtr. and Asst. Soc. Ed., 13 yrs.; b. Hamilton, Oh., 1925; p. Albert and Russie Landon Falkenstein; h. Howard E. Meeker; c. Kathleen, Alan; res: 1074 New London Rd., Hamilton, Oh.

MEESE, MILDRED FOULKE, Auth., Instr., Crtv. Writing, Amherst Senior High School, 4301 Main St., Snyder, N.Y. 14226, '56–; Auth: four novels (Bobbs-Merrill Co.), short stories; NLAPW (numerous writing aws.), Scribblers Club; Cornell Univ., AB, '24 (Phi Beta Kappa); b. Ellington, N.Y., 1902; p. Roescoe and Pluma Alexander Foulke; h. Harold Frederick Meese; c. Harold II, Dorothy, Richard; res: 102 Keswick Rd., Buffalo, N.Y. 14226.

MEGGERS, BETTY J., Rsch. Assoc., Smithsonian Institution, Wash., D.C. 20560, '54–; Auth., pubns. on archeology, cultural theory, incl. "Ecuador" (Thames and Hudson, '65); Am. Anthropological Assn., Soc. for Am. Archaeology, Anthropological Soc. of Wash. (Pres., '66–'68, VP, '65–'66, Treas., '55–/60); Intl. Congress of Americanists gold medal, '66; Eduador Order of Merit, '66; Univ. of Pa., AB, '43 (Phi Beta Kappa); Univ. of Mich, MA, '44 (Sigma Xi); Columbia Univ., PhD, '52; b. Wash., D.C., 1921; p. William and Edith Raddant Meggers; h. Clifford Evans; res: 1227 30th St. N.W., Wash., D.C. 20007.

MEIGS, CORNELIA LYNDE, Prof., Emeritus, Bryn Mawr College; Auth: "The Trade Wind" (Little, Brown Co.), "Invincible Louisa" (ALA Newbery Medal); other children's bks.; Bryn Mawr Col., AB, '08; b. Rock Island, Ill., 1884; p. Montgomery and Grace Lynde Meigs; res: Sion Hill, Havre de Grace, Md. 21078.

MEILACH, DONA ZWEIGORON, Auth., non-fiction; ten art bks., three med. bks., four juv. bks.; mag. articles; Lectr., Chgo. area; Photogr.; Tchr., adult educ., '58–'65; Nat. Assn. of Sci. Wtrs., Intl. Speaker's Platform, Children's Reading Roundtable, Auths. League; Contemporary Auths.; Who's Who in Am. Wm.; Who's Who in the Midwest; Who's Who in Ill.; Dic. of Intl. Biog.; Univ. of Chgo., PhB, '46; Student at Large, Chgo. City Jr. Cols., Art Inst. of Chgo., '58–'64; Northwestern Univ., MA, (Art Hist.), '69; b. Chgo., Ill., 1926; p. Julius and Rose Don Zweigoron; h. Dr. Melvin M. Meilach; c. Susan, Allen; res: 4001 W. Chase, Lincolnwood, Ill. 60646.

MEINHARDT, MAVIS ELAINE, Print Media Dir., Wildrick & Miller, Inc., 1 Rockefeller Plaza, N.Y., N.Y. 10020, '66–; Mkt. Rsch., '64–'66; Asst. to Treas., '62–'64; Employee Rel., Inc., '60–'62; AWNY, Nat. Agricultural Adv. & Mktng. Assn.; Columbia Univ.; b. Center, Tex., 1928; h. John Ahearn; c. Diana Elaine, Jerry W.; res: Apt. 17C, 97–30 57th Ave., Rego Park, N.Y. 11368.

MEISTER, ANTOINETTE BAURNES, Lectr., Allegheny County Community College, 250 Lebanon Sch. Rd., W. Mifflin, Pa. 15122, '69–; PR Cnslt., DAR Pitt. Chptr., '68–'69; Reptr., Pitt. Post Gazette, '66–'67; Feature Wtr., '65–'66; Reptr., Homestead Daily Messenger, '60–'61; Theta Sigma Phi (Pitt. Pfsnl. Chptr. Secy., '65–'66), Pa. State Univ., BA (Jnlsm.), '65; b. Pitt., Pa., 1942; p. Joseph and Rita Armstrong Baurnes; h. Robert C. Meister; c. Bridget Marie, Rebecca Helene, Heather Lynn; res: 129 W. Virginia Ave., Munhall, Pa. 15120.

MELFORD, DOROTHY ALLISON, Pres., PTA Ltd., 25 W. 43rd St., N.Y., N.Y. 10036, '62–; Prodr., TV and Film; Fashion Designer; Theatrical Mgt.; Foreign TV Rep.; AWRT, Fashion Group, 2,000 Wm. of Achiev.; Columbia Univ.; N.Y.U.; b. N.Y.C.; p. Daniel and Murielle MacKay Schiffmacher; c. Jean Allison, Marilyn Sue Koenig, Dudley Richard Martin; res: 301 E. 47th St., N.Y., N.Y. 10017.

MELHADO, PHYLLIS ACKERMAN, Copywtr., Media Byr., Ad Graphics, Inc., 200 Madison Ave., N.Y., N.Y. 10016, '66–; PR, Edtl. Wtr., Nabisco, '64–'66; Copywtr., Adm. Asst., Hollywood Pavilion N.Y. World's Fair, '64; Asst., Copywtr., Martin Weiner & Co.; Theta Sigma Phi; Temple Univ., BS (Commtns.), '64 (Sch. of Bus. Alumni Assn. Aw., Senior Wms. Honor Soc., Dean's List, Ed.-in-Chief—Temple News); N.Y. Univ., MA (Commtns.), '70; b. Phila., Pa., 1942; p. Carl and Patricia DeMarco Ackerman; h. Seth Melhado; res: 400 E. 73rd St., N.Y., N.Y. 10021.

MELLEN, HARRIETTE ALLEN, Fashion Ed., Vogue, Conde Nast Publications, Inc., 420 Lexington Ave., N.Y., N.Y. 10017, '66–; Fashion Ed., Harper's Bazaar, '63–'66, '50–'52; Jr. Fashion Ed., Mademoiselle, '50; Prom., Saks Fifth Ave., '49–'50; Prom., Lord & Taylor, '47–'49; b. Hartford, Conn., 1924; p. Walter and Leslie Smith Allen; h. Henry Mellen; c. Leslie Irene Bell, Louis Baker Bell Jr.; res: 85 Park Row, Cedarhurst, N.Y. 11516.

MELLEN, JENNIFER, Ed.-Wtr., United Nations Association of the United States of America, 345 E. 46th St., N.Y., N.Y. 10017; '69–; Ed., Am. RDM Corp., '68–'69; Ed.-in-Chief, Edtl. Lydsa (Mexico City, Mexico), '67–'68; Subjects Ed., Sterling Publ., '65–'67; Free-lance Wtr., mags. and songs (Chilean Song Festival 2nd pl., '69); Univ. of Mexico, BA (Eng. and Psych.), '61; b. Pitt., Pa., 1941; p. Arthur J. and Frances Peckham Mellen; res: 40 W. 75th St., N.Y., N.Y. 10023.

MELLEN, KATHLEEN DICKENSON, Auth: "Hawaiian Heritage," "In a Hawaiian Valley," other bks., published by Hastings House; "Hawaiian Heart Throbs" (poetry, '36); Honolulu Wms. Press Club; Sullins Col.; b. Castlewood, Va.; p. Robert W. and Rose Earnest Dickenson; h. George Mellen; res: 2998 Makalei Pl., Honolulu, Hi. 96815.

MELTON, VERA BOLICK, Coordr. Lib. Svcs., Department of Community Colleges, 100 S. Harrington, Raleigh, N.C. 27602, '69–; Lib. Supvsr., Haywood County Consolidated Schs. (Waynesville), '65–'69; Head Librn., Needham B. Broughton Sr. HS (Raleigh), '55–'65; Supvsr., Libs., Caldwell County (Lenoir), '53–'55; Librn., Hudson HS, '51–'53; Tchr., '44–'51; Auth., handbks. for student lib. assts.; Contrbr., World Bk. Ency.; N.C. Lib. Assn. (Chmn., '57–'58), NEA, N.C. Lib. Assn. (Chmn., '58–'61), Southeastern Am. Lib. Assn., other lib. assns., Beta Sigma Phi (Pres., '53–'54), Appalachian State Tchrs. Col., BS, '49; MA, '53; b. Lenoir, N.C., 1924; p. Jessie and Ethel Miller Bolick; h. Jerome Melton; res: 4315 Leesville Rd., Raleigh, N.C. 27609.

MELVIN, Sr. M. CONSTANCE, Chmn., Marywood Col., Scranton, Pa. 18509, '60–; HS Librn., '41–'46; Librn., Marywood Col., '46–'48; Librn., Columbia Univ., '41; Auth. of numerous bks. on lib. subjects; ALA, Catholic Lib. Assn., ALA-CLA joint comm., '63–'65; CNLA Joint Comm. of Lib. Educ., '68–; Pa. Lib. Assn. (Exec. Bd., '65–'66); Who's Who in Lib. Svc. ('66), Who's Who of Am. Wm., Dic. of Intl. Biog.; Marywood Col., AB (Social Sci.), '40; Columbia Univ., BS (Lib. Sci.), '41; Univ. of Chgo., PhD., '62.

MELVIN, SARAH GUTHRIE, Adv. and Pubcty. Dir. and Fashion Coordr., Triumph Hosiery Mills, Inc., 437 Fifth Ave., N.Y., N.Y. 10016, '67–; Adv. Mgr., Spode, Inc., '65–'67; Art Assoc., United Bus. Pubns., '64; Art Dir., YEAR Inc., '62–'64; Asst. Art Dir., NewsFront, '61–'62; Hosiery Fashion Execs.; Pratt Inst.; b. N.Y.C.; p. Dennis and Ruth Adams Guthrie; h. Walter B. Melvin; c. John David; res: 94 Macdougal St., N.Y., N.Y. 10012.

MELZER, HELENE LICHT, Reptr., Wall Street Journal, 245 National Press Bldg., Wash., D.C. 2004, '68–; Asst. Wms. Ed., The Washington (D.C.) Post; Soc. Ed., Los Angeles (Cal.) Mirror; WNPC; U.C.L.A.; h. Leo Melzer; res: 4836 Drummond Ave., Chevy Chase, Md. 20015.

MENDENHALL, RUTH DYAR, Auth., bks., mag. articles on mountaineering, outdoor activities; Theta Sigma Phi; Univ. of Wash., BA (Jnlsm.), '34 (Sigma Delta Chi Scholarship Aw.); b. Kiesling, Wash., 1912; p. Ralph and Else Kiesling Dyar; h. John Mendenhall; c. Vivian, Valerie M. Cohen; res: 335 Sequoia Dr., Pasadena, Cal. 91105.

MENNELL, CONSTANCE JACKSON, Media Dir., Wilton, Coombs & Colnett, Inc., 927 La Cienega Blvd., L.A., Cal., 90069, '69–; AE, Don Frank & Associates; '68–'69; Adv. Mgr., Lake Tahoe Assoc. (S.F.), '67–'68; Asst. AE, Cancilla, Wren & Knapp, '65–'67; Jr. Ad Club, S.F.; Skidmore Col., BA (Psych.), '62; b. Boston, Mass., 1940; p. Frederick and Josephine Peters Jackson; h. Michael Mennell; res: 948 Seventh St., Santa Monica, Cal. 90403.

MENNINGER, JEANETTA LYLE, Ed., Bulletin of the Menninger Clinic, The Menninger Foundation, Box 829, Topeka, Kan. 66601, '36–; Dir., Div. of Pubns., '46–'64; Rsch. Asst., Carnegie Fndn. Project (Hollywood, Cal.), '37–'41; PR Dept., Columbia Univ., '30; Reptr., Feature Wtr.; Ed., Bk. Page, Music Page, '26–'30; numerous mag. articles; Collaborator, "Love Against Hate," '42; Chgo. Cncl. on Fgn. Rels., Am. Med. Wtrs. Assn., Theta Sigma Phi (Cal. Chptr. aw., '39), NFPW mag. aw., '64), Kan. Press Wm. (mag. aw., '63), active in civic affairs; Park Col., Parkville, Mo., AB, '23 (Distg. Alumna); Grad. Work, Columbia Univ., '30–'31; Central Col. for Wm. (Lexington, Mo.); Washburn Univ., Kan. City Art Inst.; b. St. Louis, Mo., p. Edward and Jeanetta Patterson Lyle; h. Karl Menninger; c. Rosemary Jeanetta; res: 1819 Westwood Circle, Topkea, Kan. 66604.

MENTZ, LaROUX, Ed., Rocky Fork Enterprise, Rocky Fork Press, Inc., 76 Mill St., Gahanna, Oh. 43230, '64–; Founder, '62–; Tchr., Home Econs., Oh. State Univ.; Dress Designer (N.Y.C.), Mechanical Engineer, Sperry Gyroscope Co.; Omicron Nu, Phi Upsilon Omicron, Adv. Club of Columbus (recognition, '63); Oh. State Univ., BS (Home Econs.), '39; b. Columbus, Oh., 1920; p. J. Hamilton and Anice Goodman Roebuck; h. Frederic Mentz; c. Susan, Diana, Nancy; res: 377 Granville St., Gahanna, Oh. 43230.

MENTZER, ANNABELLE BROWNE, City Hall Reptr., Soc., Feature Wtr., Huntington Herald-Press, 7 N. Jefferson St., Huntington, Ind. 46750; Wtr., La Prensa (Tampa, Fla.); Corr., News-Sentinel (Ft. Wayne); Delta Theta Tau, Am. Bus. Wms. Assn.; b. New Castle, Ind., 1908; p. Charles and Carrie Compton Cain; h. Harry Mentzer; c. Patricia (Mrs. John Dalton); res: 1401 Dayton Ct., Huntington, Ind. 46750.

MENZIES, ELIZABETH GRANT CRANBROOK, Photogr., published in numerous nat. mags.; Auth,: "Before the Waters: The Upper Delaware Valley" (Rutgers Univ. Press, '66), "Millstone Valley" (Rutgers Univ. Press, '69), Co-auth., "Princeton Architecture: A Pictorial History of Town and Campus" (Princeton Univ. Press, '67); Articles in Encyclopedia Americana; Artist, wood cuts in the Graphic Collection of Princeton Univ.; Soc. of Architectural Histrns.; N.J. Hist. Soc., Stoney Brook-Millstone Watersheds Assn.; N.J. Tercentenary Medal ('64); Am. Assn. for State and Local Hist. Aw. of Merit ('68); b. Princeton, N.J., 1915; p. Alan W.C. and Mary Isabella Dickson Menzies; res: 926 Kingston Rd., Princeton, N.J. 08540.

MENZIES, HEATHER MARGARET, Actress c/o Nora Sanders Agency, 12069 Ventura Pl., Studio City, Cal., '63–; motion pics: "Hail Hero" "The Sound of Music" (20th Century Fox, '64), "Hawaii"; Broadway, "We Have Always Lived in the Castle" ('66); TV: "My Three Sons," "Ed Sullivan," "Dragnet," "Farmers Daughter"; SAG, AFTRA, AEA, Nat. Forensic League (Deg. of Merit); Pierce Col.; ballet student, nine yrs.; b.

Toronto, Can., 1949; p. George and Mary Brotherston Menzies.

MERCER, MARILYN, Feature Ed., Glamour, Conde Nast Publications, 420 Lexington Ave., N.Y., N.Y. 10017, '60–; Reptr., New York Herald Tribune, '56–'59; Ed., Wtr., Bell Synd., '48–'55; Co-Auth., "Adultery for Adults" (Coward McCann, '68); NWC, Auths. Guild.; Smith Col., BA, '45; b. White Plains, N.Y., 1923; p. Harold and Clara Whelpley Mercer; res: 340 E. 64th St., N.Y., N.Y. 10021.

MERCHANT, JANE HESS, Auth: "The Greatest of These" (Abingdon Press, '54), "Every Good Gift" (Abingdon Press, '68), seven other poetry bks.; poems in Saturday Evening Post, numerous other pubns.; NLAPW (twice voted outstanding mbr., Knoxville Br.; Best Bk. of Poetry, '54–'56), Poetry Soc. of Tenn., Tenn. Wms. Press and Auths. Club; aw. from The Lyric, '61; b. Knoxville, Tenn., 1919; p. Clarence and Donia Swann Merchant; res: 2034 Emoriland Blvd., Knoxville, Tenn. 37917.

MERCHANT, MARY ANDERSON, Mgr.-Ed., Washington Afro-American Newspaper, 1800 11th St. N.W., Wash., D.C. 20001, '66–; City Ed., '64–'66; Reptr., '53–'64; tchr.; Capital Press Club; Pa. Nwsp. and Publrs. Assn. two hon. mentions, ct. rept. and spot news; Johnson C. Smith Univ. (cum laude); h. Colston Merchant; res: 4404 Illinois Ave. N.W., Wash., D.C. 20011.

MERCIER, JEAN DOYLE, Auth., novel, "Whatever You Do, Don't Panic" (Doubleday, '61; also in Eng.; TV rights sold), second in progress; Young People's Art course for Famous Schs. Intl. ('67); short stories in nat. mags.; evaluate and ed. work of applicants to Famous Wtrs. Sch., Westport, Conn.; Tchr., crtv. writing course three yrs.; Asst. Fashions Ed., Holiday Magazine, '45–'49; b. Cleve., Oh., 1916; p. Harry and Catherine Masterson Doyle; h. Louis F. V. Mercier; c. Madeleine Zoe, Catherine Louise, Jean Evangeline; res: 15 Long Lots Rd., Westport, Conn. 06880.

MEREDITH, SHEILA V., Asst. VP., Commtns., National Association of Mutual Insurance Companies, 2611 E. 46th St., Indpls., Ind. 46205, '69–; Commtns. Dir., '65–'69; Edtl. Asst., '61–'65; Secy., Commtns. Dept., '58–'61; Ind. Soc. of Assn. Execs., Mutual Ins. Communicators (outstanding achiev. and disting. edtl. excellence aw., '68), Ind. Assn. of Indsl. Eds.; Who's Who of Am. Wm.; Ind. Central Col., '50–'52; b. Warsaw, Ind., 1933; p. Edwin and Virginia Caywood Meredith; res: 2801 Barbary Lane, Indpls., Ind. 46205.

MERIWETHER, LEE ANN, Actress; movies: "Legend of Lylah Clare," "Angel in my Pocket," "The Undefeated"; various TV dramatic shows, regular on "The Time Tunnel"; Wms. Ed., Dave Garroway's "Today Show"; Theatre West (Exec. Bd., '61, '68, '69), NATAS, Child Guidance Aux.; City Col. of S.F., '53–'54; b. L.A., Cal.; p. C. Gregg and Ethel Mulligan Meriwether; h. Frank Aletter; c. Kyle Kathleen, Lesley Anne.

MERO, ANNE H., Pubns. Ed., East Bay Municipal Utility District, 2127 Adeline St., Oakland, Cal. 94623, '67–; Dir., Intl. Child Art Ctr., S.F., Cal., '66; Pubcty. Dir., S.F. Museum of Art, '64–'66; Prog. Dir., S.F. Heart Assn., '61–'64; ICIE; Bay Area Soc. of Indsl. Eds.; Mills Col., BA, '52.

MERRELL, KAREN DIXON, Auth., children's bks: "Tithing" ('65) and "Prayer" ('63); Instr., Brigham Young Univ., '65; Elementary Sch. Tchr., '59; educ. orgs.; Brigham Young Univ., BS (Hon. Soc.); b. Payson, Ut., 1936; p. Jack V. and Mary Jean Carter Dixon; h. Victor Dallas Merrell; c. Ann, Kay, Joan, Paul, Mark; res: 2211 Greenery Lane, Silver Spring, Md. 20906.

MERRIAM, EVE, Free-Lance Wtr., non-fiction and poetry; Tchr., Crtv. Writing, City Col. of N.Y., '65–'69; Lectr. on status of wm., N.Y.U., '66; Tchr., Poetry Inst., Central Wash. State Col., '66; Soc. of Mag. Wtrs. (VP, '68), ASCAP, Auths. Guild; AGAC; Yale Younger Poets Prize, '46; Colliers Star Fiction Aw., '48; CBS-TV Fellowship, '59; Univ. of Pa., AB, '37; b. Phila., Pa., 1916; h. Leonard C. Lewin; c. Guy Michel, Dee Michel; res: 548 Riverside Dr., N.Y., N.Y. 10027.

MERRILL, JEAN FAIRBANKS, Auth: "The Black Sheep" (Pantheon, '69), "The Pushcart War" (William R. Scott, '64; Lewis Carroll Shelf aw., Boys Club of Am. Jr. Bk. aw., Wm. Allen White Children's Bk. aw., all '65), "The Superlative Horse" (Scott, '61; Lewis Carroll Shelf Aw., '63), 14 other children's bks. ('51–'68), TV drama "The Claws in the cat's Paw" (Republic Aw., '57); Assoc. Ed., Bank St. Readers, '65–'66; Ed., Lit. Cavalcade, '56–'57; Assoc. Ed., '50–'51; Feature Ed., Scholastic Magazines, '46–'49; Auths. Guild, N. Am. Mycological Assn.; Allegheny Col., BA, '44 (first rank in class; Phi Beta Kappa, '43); Wellesley Col., MA, '45; Univ. of Madras, '52–'53 (Fulbright grant for rsch. in Indian folk lit.); b. Rochester, N.Y., 1923; p. Earl and Elsie Fairbanks Merrill; res: 313 E. 10th St., N.Y., N.Y. 10009 (Nov.–May), and P.O. Box 3, Washington, Vt. 05675 (May–Nov.).

MERRILL, MARION, Asst. Mgr. Press Rels., Consumer Info., Union Carbide Corporation, 270 Park Ave., N.Y., N.Y. 10017, '60–; Ed., '48–'60; Ed., Eldridge Publ. Co., '47–'48; Info. Specialist, Ed., Colmst., U.S.A.F., '41–'47; Ed., Dell Publ. Co., '39–'41; Wtr., Whitman Publ. Co., '38; Edtl. Asst. Stage Publ. Co., '37–'38; Mfg. Chemists Assn. Wms., CWPR, NHFL, AWNY; Vassar Col., BA, '37; b. Chgo., Ill., 1916; p. George and Anna Darby Merrill; res: 44 W. 69th St., N.Y., N.Y. 10023.

MERRITT, HELEN HENRY, Asst. Prof., Northern Ill. Univ., DeKalb, Ill. 60115, '65–; Instr., '63; tchr., DeKalb Schs.; guiding Free Expression in children's art, '64; Ill. Craftsmen's Cncl.; Ill. Art Educ. Assn.; Univ. of Hi.; Colby Col., BA; Rockford Col., MA; Northern Ill. Univ., MFA, '63; b. Norfolk, Va., 1920; p. J. Crockett and Mabel Richards Henry; h. James Merritt; c. Deborah B.; res: 419 Garden Rd., DeKalb, Ill. 60115.

MERSEY, ELIZABETH HARRIS, Copy Chief, Edward M. Meyers Association, 39 W. 55th St., N.Y., N.Y. 10022, '69–; AE, '61–'64; Adv. Dir., R.A.M. Div., Genesco, '66–'69. Free-lance Copywtr., incl. nat. adv. campaign for Norman Hilton, '66–; Barnard Col., BA, '41; b. N.Y.C.; p. Mitchell and Rose Reiss Harris; c. James, William; res: 3 E. 78th St., N.Y., N.Y. 10021.

MESROBIAN, ARPENA SACHAKLIAN, Assoc. Dir. and Ed., Syracuse University Press, Box 8, University Sta., Syracuse, N.Y. 13210, '68–; Acting Dir., '65–'66; Asst. Dir., '61–'68; Exec. Ed., '58–'60; Bk. Rev. Ed., The Armenian Rev., Auth., articles on hist. of Armenian literature; Theta Sigma Phi, Intl. Platform Assn.; Armenian Col. of Beirut, '38; Syracuse Univ., AA, '59; b. Somerville, Mass.; p. Aaron and Eliza Der Melkonian Sachaklian; h. William J. Mesrobian; c. William Stephen, Marian Elizabeth (Mrs. Bruce MacCurdy); res: 108 Winkworth Pkway., Syracuse, N.Y. 13215.

MESSENGER, RUEY SIEGER, Dir. of Pubcty., PR and Fashion, Julius Garfinckel & Co., 1401 F St., N.W., Wash., D.C. 20004, '53–; Fashion Coordr., '49–'53; Dir. of Svc., Am. Retail Fedn., '43–'49; Free-lance Radio and Platform Fashion Commentator, '39–'49; Fashion Byr., Wm. Hengerer (Buffalo, N.Y.), '33–'39; Pers. Dept., W. T. Grant Co., '28–'31; Round Table, Wms. Civil Defense, Fashion Group, Wms. Adv. Club of Wash., Delta Sigma Rho, AAUW (Jr. Group Pres.), numerous charitable, svc. orgs.; Star of Solidarity (Italy, '56), Cit. from Dist. of Colmbia for war and social svc. work, Who's Who of Am. Wm.; Swarthmore Col., AB (Econs.), '28; b. Lancaster, Pa., 1910; p. P. George and Emma McCreary Sieger; h. Theodore Ives Messenger (dec.); c. Ruey (Mrs. Seth Warfield), Saliann; res: The Dorchester House, 2480 16th St., N.W., Wash., D.C. 20009.

MESSICK, VIRGINIA FALLIN, Head Librn., Wesley College, College Sq., Dover, Del. 19901, '64–; Lib. Commn. of the State of Del., '53–'64; Cnslt., Collier's Ency.; 20th Century Club, DAR (State Vice-Regent, Chptr. Regent), AAUW (Pres.), Beta Phi Mu, '60, Delta Kappa Gamma; Wilson Col., AB, '31; Rutgers Univ., MLS, '59; b. Phila., Pa., 1909; p. Ira and Elizabeth Colton Fallin; h. Samuel Messick; res: 616 N. State St., Dover, Del. 19901.

MESSING, DOROTHY, Assoc. Ed., Dell Publishing, 750 Third Ave., N.Y., N.Y. 10017, '69–; Tchr., '65–'69; Bklyn. Col., BA, '65; b. N.Y.C.; res: 1385 York Ave., N.Y., N.Y. 10021.

METCALF, DOROTHY, Media Dir., Charles Advertising, 400 N. Michigan Ave., Chgo., Ill. 60611, '69–; Media Dir., Burton Browne Adv.; Prod., William Byrd Press (Richmond, Va.); Circ. Asst., Nat. Future Farmer Magazine (Alexandria); Ark. State Tchrs. Col. (educ., psych.); b. Lamar, Ark., 1934; p. John and Lois Metcalf; res: 561 W. Stratford Pl., Chgo., Ill. 60657.

MEUDT, EDNA KRITZ, Auth.; poetry bks., "Round River Canticle" (Wake-Brook House, '60), "In No Strange Land" ('64), "No One Sings Face Down" ('69), poems in numerous mags., several short stories, one play; Permanent Teaching Staff, poetry, Rhinelander School of Arts, '64–; col. poetry workshops; judge, nat. groups; Wis. Fellowship Poets (Pres., '52–'54, '60–'62), Nat. Fedn. of State Poetry Assns. (Pres., '63–'65), NLAPW (Milw. Br. VP, '56–'58; 1st Prize, '59); 1st prizes, state poetry contests; Theta Sigma Phi Wtr's. Cup for Wis., '65; various others; b. Wyoming Valley, Wis., 1906; p. John and Kristine Neilsen Kritz; h. Peter Meudt; c. Richard E., Howard E. (dec.), Mrs. Kathy Ipsen, Mrs. Christine Parkinson; res: RFD 3, Dodgeville, Wis. 53533.

MEYER, CAROLINE HANSEN, Staff Wtr., Broadcasting Magazine, 444 Madison Ave., N.Y., N.Y. 10022, '68–; Staff Wtr., Television Magazine, Bdcst. Pubns., '66–'68; Boston Univ., BA, '66; b. Middlesex County, N.J., 1945; p. Henrik and Elizabeth Layburn Hansen; h. John Meyer; res: 46 W. 73rd St., N.Y., N.Y. 10023.

MEYER, CATHARINE, Sr. Ed., Harper's Magazine, Two Park Ave., New York, N.Y. 10016, '46–; News Ed., Off. of War Info., '43–'46; Asst. Ed., Free World Magazine, '42–'43; Asst. Prof., Eng., Vassar Col. '36–'42; Instr., Eng., Stephens Col., '29–'32; Flora Mather Col., Case Western Reserve Univ., AB (Phi Beta Kappa); Radcliffe Col., AM; PhD; b. Cleveland, Oh.; p. Henry C. and Leonie Claudon Meyer.

MEYER, DOROTHY CAMPBELL, Indsl. Ed., HRB-Singer, Inc., Box 60, Science Park, State College, Pa. 16801, '65–; Ed., Proofreading Supvsr., '60–'64; Proofreader, '60; Clmst., Centre Daily Times, '51–; AAIE (Exec. Comm., '69; Nat. Placement Chmn., '61–'68), Theta Sigma Phi; Governor's Safety aw., '65; active in numerous civic groups; Lock Haven State Normal Sch., '27; b. Spring Mills, Pa., 1905; p. Warren and Bertha Keefer Campbell; h. Randall W. Meyer; c. Randall William, Jr., Robert C.; res: 323 Bradley Ave., State College, Pa. 16801.

MEYER, ELISE LANDAUER, Auth: "The Art of Cooking with Spirits ('64), "You Can Be a Better Cook Than Mama Ever Was" ('68; Culinary Soc. selection; Cook Bk. Guild of Canada Selection, '68; Alternate Selection, '69); active in polit., civic orgs.; Hon. Citizen, Magnolia, Miss., '68; Newcomb Col., Tulane Univ.; b. N.O., La., 1912; p. Nick and Alma Landauer Meyer; res: 120 Quinlivan Rd., Magnolia, Miss. 39652.

MEYER, GENEVIEVE F., Free-lance Wtr., Ed.; Ed., interior decorating colm., Bell-McClure Syndicate;

Cnslt. Ed., Fawcett Pubns.; Ed: "Ethan Allen Treasury," "New Ideas for Decorating 1970 Annual" (Pyramid Pubns.); NHFL; Smith Col., '45–'47; Barnard Col., BA, '49; b. N.Y.C., 1927; p. Abraham and Alice Silver Fisch; h. (div.); c. Elizabeth Jane, Katherine Amy; res: 44 Graham Rd., Scarsdale, N.Y. 10583.

MEYER, HELEN HONIG, Pres., Dell Publishing Co., Inc., 750 Third Ave., N.Y., N.Y. 10017, '57–; Dir.; Popular Sci., McCall's, '23–'24; Pres., Dial Press; Pres., Noble and Noble Publrs.; Intl. Bk. and Lib. Programs Govt. Advisory Comm.; b. Bklyn., N.Y. 1907; p. Bertolen and Esther Greenfield Honig; h. Abraham Meyer; c. Adele (Mrs. Roger H. Brodkin), Robert; res: 231 Montrose Ave., S. Orange, N.J. 07079.

MEYER, JANE, Copy Grouphead, Eisaman, Johns & Laws Advertising, 6290 Sunset Blvd., L.A., Cal. 90028, '67–; Copywtr., Grey Advertising (Beverly Hills), '62–'67; Sr. Wtr., May Co., '59–'62; Riverside Press-Enterprise, '59; Fashion Group, L.A. Adv. Wms., six lulus, '65–'69; four certs., '60–'69, Bleding Aws. (2nd, 3rd, '67; 2nd, 3rd, '68); Northwestern Univ. Medill Sch. of Jnlsm., BS (Jnlsm.), '53; Univ. of Heidelberg (Germany), Diploma, '58; b. Seward, Neb.; res: 11677 Montana Ave., Number Three, L.A., Cal. 90049.

MEYER, JANICE POPE, Dir. of PR, Kentucky TB and Respiratory Disease Assn., 4100 Churchman Ave., Louisville, Ky. 40215, '62–; Reptr., The Louisville Times; Free-lance Wtr.; Theta Sigma Phi; Stephens Col., '40; Ind. Univ., AB, '42; b. Franch Lick, Ind., 1920; p. George and Cornelia Wulfman Pope, 1920; h. Welles Meyer; c. Welles Thomas; res: 4318 Kinloch Rd., Louisville, Ky.

MEYER, JO CALDWELL, Exec. Asst., School of Communication, University of Texas at Austin, Austin, Tex. 78712, '65–; Sch. of Jnlsm., '49–'65; Nat. Exec. Secy., Theta Sigma Phi, '40–'64 (Life Mbr.; Jo Caldwell Meyer Hon. Scholarship initiated in '64; Achiev. Aw., '57; San Antonio Pfsnl. Chptr. Headliner Aw., '57); London Sch. Memorial Assn., Henderson, Tex., '37; Wtr., Ed., State Reclamation Dept., '32–'37; free-lance jnlst., speaker; NFPW, Tex. Press Wm.; Cit. of Hon., Incarnate Word Col.; Univ. of Tex., BJ, '31; b. Ennis, Tex., 1910; p. Robert and Jo Rowland Caldwell; h. Bruce G. Meyer; c. Bruce G., Jr., Mary Jo (Mrs. Rodney C. Richburg); res: 1604 Northwood Rd., Austin, Tex. 78703.

MEYERS, MILDRED BUSH, Prof., Harrisburg Area Community College, Cameron St., Harrisburg, Pa.; former Fulbright Exchange Prof., Anatolia Col., Salonika, Greece; Col. Tchrs. of English, Pa. Tchrs. of English; Univ. of Ky., AB, '31; MA, '32; grad. work, Harvard, Breadloaf, Pa. State Univ.; b. Colesburg, Ia.; p. Wilbur and Fannie Hyde Bush; h. William Koontz Meyers (dec.); c. Dr. Marshall G. Guthrie, Mrs. Joyce von Schmid; res: 406 15th St., New Cumberland, Pa. 17070.

MEZEI-DELBOL, VERA, Copywtr., Grey Advertising, Inc., 777 Third Ave., N.Y., N.Y. 10017, '69–; Copy Supvsr., Cunningham & Walsh, '62–'68; Sullivan, Stauffer, Colwell & Bayles, '59–'62; Copy Dir., Needham & Grohmann, '56–'59; Young & Rubicam, '54–'56; Adv. Club of N.Y., Adv. Wtrs. of N.Y., AWNY; London Sch. of Econs. and Polit. Sci., Univ. of London, BCom.; b. Budapest, Hungary, 1930; p. Alexander and Ilona Kallos Mezei; h. Robert E. Delbol; res: 63–11 Queens Blvd., Woodside, N.Y. 11377.

MICHAEL, PHYLLIS CALLENDER, Auth.; Tchr., Northwest Area High School, R.D. #2, Shickshinny, Pa. 18655, '66–; Tchr., Pa. Schs., '28–'33; '43–; five bks.; poetry hymns, songs, mag. articles; Intl. Platform Assn., Hymn Soc. of Am., Marquis Biog. Lib. Soc.; Who's Who of Am. Wm.; Who's Who in the East; Dic. of Intl. Biog. (Cert. of Merit, '67); Royal Blue Bk.; 2,000 Wm. of Achiev. (Diploma for Distg. Achiev., '69); Contemporary Auths.; first place, Nat. Favorite Hymns Contest, '53; Bloomsburg State Col., '28; Univ. Ext. Conservatory, BMus., '53; b. Briar Creek Twp., Pa., 1908; p. Bruce and Emma Harvey Callender; h. Arthur Michael; c. Robert B., Keith W.; res: Oak Haven, R.D. #3, Shickshinny, Pa. 18655.

MICHAELIS, DIANA TEAD, TV Prdr.; U.S. Rep., International Association for Cultural Freedom, 2100 Pennsylvania Ave., N.W., Wash., D.C. 20037, '68–; Dir., TV-Film Off., VISTA, OEO, '65–'68 (Acad. Aw.; '67; nomination, '68); TV Film Cnslt., Project Head Start, '63–'64; Pres. Commn. on Status of Wm., '62–'63; Prodr., NET, '59–'61; Asst. Rsch. Dir., Am. Comm. on Race, '53–'54; Asst. Public Affairs Dir., "The Search," CBS, '52–'53; Exec. Asst. Dir., Mass Commtns., UNESCO, '48–'52; Auth., "What Is Race" (UNESCO, '52); Interviewer, Oral Hist. Project, John F. Kennedy Archives; Wash. Film Cncl.; Who's Who in the South; Dic. of Intl. Biog.; Nat. Gold Bk.; Smith Col., AB; Oxford; b. N.Y.C., 1925; p. Ordway and Clara Murphy Tead; h. Michael Michaelis (div.); c. David T., Ordway P., res: 3316 Volta Pl., N.W., Wash., D.C. 20007.

MICHAELIS, INGRID KROSCH, Edtl. Rschr., Time Inc., Time and Life Building, Rockefeller Ctr., N.Y., N.Y. 10020, '64–; Elmira Col., BA, '63; b. N.Y.C., 1941; p. Otto and Marie Nahrmann Krosch; h. Martin Michaelis; res: 67 Park Ave., N.Y., N.Y. 10016.

MICHAELS, LINDA ANN, Dir. PR, Carnegie Code Enforcement Program, Dept. of Housing and Urban Dev., 110 E. Main St., Carnegie, Pa. 15106, '68–; Exec. Secy., Commty. Org. Specialist, Dir. PR; wtr., pubcty., campaign material, Borough of Carnegie; Pitt. Press Club, Theta Sigma Phi, Comm. for Better Jnlsm., Jnlsm. Aw. in Pa.; numerous other civic, svc. orgs., aws.; Duquesne Univ., BA (Jnlsm.), '67; b. Pitt., Pa., 1945; p. Stanley and Anne Michaels; res: 741 Washington Ave., Apt. 2, Carnegie, Pa. 15106.

MICHAELS, MARILYN BROOKS, Ed., Sun Oil Company, DX Division, Box 141, Tulsa, Okla. 74102,

'57–; Feature Wtr., Tulsa Daily World, '56–'57; Soc. Ed., '51–'55; Assoc. Ed., Am. Mercury Magazine (N.Y.C.), '55–'56; PR Dir., Philbrook Art Ctr. (Tulsa), '50–'51; Indsl. Eds. of Tulsa, Theta Sigma Phi; Univ. of Wichita, '46–'48; Univ. of Mo., BJ, '50; Grad. Work, Univ. of Tulsa; b. Okmulgee, Okla.; p. Clifford and Catherine Tumy Michaels; res: 1625 S. Elwood, Tulsa, Okla. 74119.

MICHAUD, MARGARET M., Mgr., Treasury Affairs, American Broadcasting Company, 1330 Ave. of Americas, N.Y., N.Y. 10019, '64–; Payroll Supvsr., '63–'64; Bus. Mgr., '57–'63; Sls. Svc. Mgr., '53–'56; Becker Bus. Col., Worcester, Mass., '40–'42; p. Patrick and Phoebe Martin Michaud; res: 2 Kaywood Rd., Port Washington, N.Y. 11050.

MICHEL, JOAN HESS, Contrb. Ed., American Artist Magazine, Billboard Publications, 165 W. 46th St., N.Y., N.Y. 10036, '59–; Mng. Ed., '57–'59; Asst. Ed., '56–'57; Edtl. Asst., '55–'56; Asst. Copy Ed., Town and Country, '53–'54; Sweet Briar Col., Ba, '51; George Peabody Col. for Tchrs., MA, '52 (Carnegie Fellowship, '51–'52), b. Bklyn., N.Y., 1929; p. James and Mildred Horak Hess; h. Frederick Michel; c. Jennifer, Frederick, Christopher; res: 108 Manhasset Woods Rd., Manhasset, N.Y. 11030.

MICHEL, MARGARET G., Pers. Mgr., The Times-Picqyune Publishing Corporation, 3800 Howard Ave., N.O., La. 70140, '43–; own art studio, private classes, comml. and FA, adults and children, exhbns. in Vieux Carré; Art Tchr., N.O. high schs., camp; freelance comml. art; Pers. Mgt. Assn. of N.O. (Secy. of Bd.); Tulane Univ., B Design, '24; Art Sch.; b. Harriman, Tenn.; p. Robert and Roxie Brown Goodman; h. Francois Raoul Michel (dec.); c. Margaret Michel (Mrs. David Bernhardt, Jr.); res: 1428 Second St., N.O., La. 70130.

MICHEL, MARY LOU, PR Dir., Magee-Womens Hospital, Forbes and Halket St., Pitt., Pa. 15213, '65–; Asst. PR Dir., West Penn Hosp.; Placement Cnslr., Liken Employment; Exec. Dir., Evelyn Wood Reading Dynamics; Staff Wtr., Pittsburgh Press; Staff of internal sls. pubn., Westinghouse Electric Corp.; Am. Hosp. Assn., PRSA (Pitt. Chptr. Treas., '67–'70), numerous hosp. PR orgs., Theta Sigma Phi, WNPC, Pitt., Press Club; Hosp. PR cit., Mac Eachern Competitions, '68; b. Pitt., Pa., 1931; p. Martin and Emma Beck Michael; res: 1410 E. Elfinwild Rd., Allison Pk. Pa. 15101.

MICHELFELDER, PHYLLIS R. DEVENEAU, Dir. of Dev., Finch College, 52 E. 78th St., N.Y., N.Y. 10022, '69–; Fund Raising Cnslt., Bennington Col., '66–'69; Fund Raising Cnslt., Tamblyn and Brown, '64–'66; Dir. of Col. Rels., Columbia Univ., '61–'64; Assoc. Dir., Independent Col. Funds of Am., '59–'61; Dir. of PR, Barnard Col., '51–'59; Dir. of PR, Douglass Col., '47–'51; Ed., The New Hampshire Alumnus and Asst. Dir. of Public Info., Univ of N.H. '44–'47; AP, '43–'44;

Univ. of N.H., AB, '43; b. Chgo., Ill., 1921; p. George and Gertrude Proctor Deveneau; h. William F. Michelfelder; res: 204 Thunder Hill Dr., Stanford, Conn. 06902.

MICHELS, MARCIA ANN, Ed., Colmst., Amusement Features Syndicate, 218 W. 47th St., N.Y., N.Y. 10036, '60–; Mount Mary Col., '55–'57; Am. Acad. of Dramatic Arts, '57–'58; b. Milw., Wis., 1937; p. Victor and Irene Mevis Michels.

MICHELSON, DVORA, Head of Radio, TV Sec., British Information Services, 845 Third Ave., N.Y., N.Y. 10022, '68–; Head of Radio and TV Programming, '61–'68; Films Offcr., '60–'61; Mkt. Rsch., Corsets Silhouette (London, Eng.), '58; AWRT; Univ. of London, BA, '58 (hons.); New Sch. for Social Rsch., '64, '66; b. Riga, Latvia, 1936; p. Herman and Ethel Atkin Michelson; res: 330 E. 52nd St., N.Y., N.Y. 10022.

MIDDAUGH, GENEVIEVE LAMPSON, Wms. Ed., The Bismarck Tribune, 224 Fourth, Bismarck, N.D. 58501, '64–; Soc. Ed., '28–'30; N.D. Crippled Children's Svcs., '43–'50; Phillips" Petroleum Co. (Bartlesville, Okla.), '41–'43; Soc. Ed., Daily Sun (Parsons, Kan.), '26–'28; Free-lance Wtr.; NLAPW (Medora Br. Secy.-Treas., '65–'69), NPWC, N.D. Press Wms. Club (Dist. Pres., '67–'68; 2nd VP, '69–'70; writing aws.); Parsons Jr. Col., '26; b. Parsons, Kan., 1906; p. George and Genevieve Johnston Lampson; h. Richard E. Middaugh; c. Richard E., Roger L., David A.; res: 108 W. Turnpike Ave., Bismarck, N.D. 58501.

MIDDIONE, ELIZABETH DERBY, Assoc., Blum & Middione, 1355 Market St., S.F., Cal. 94102; PR Cnslt. in S.F. '58–; Nat. Wholesale Sls. Mgr.: Georg Jensen (N.Y.C.), '52–'57; Vaco Co., '47–'52; Cal. Hist. Soc., Cal. Col. of Arts and Crafts (Advisory Bd.), S.F. Chamber Music Soc. (past Bd. Mbr.), Aspen Intl. Design Conf., '52–'57; Who's Who of Am. Wm.; Juilliard Inst. of Music, '44; b. Jackson Springs, N.C., 1923; p. Roger and Elizabeth Harlan Derby; h. Carlo Middione; res: 131 Delmar St., S.F., Cal. 94117.

MIDDLETON, MARIE DIXON, Reg. Dir., Fort Loudoun Regional Library Center, Box 146, Athens, Tenn. 37303, '64–; Adm. Asst., '62–'64; Librn., Jefferson Sch., Alexandria, Va., '58–'62; Polk County HS, Benton, Tenn., '51–'58; AAUW, Tenn. Lib. Assn., Southeastern Lib. Assn., Pilot Club; E. Tenn. State Univ., BS, '51 ('who's Who among Students); George Peabody Col. for Tchrs., MA, '54; b. Englewood, Tenn.; p. Earl and Martha Shepherd Dixon; h. Robert H. Middleton; res: Box 254, Englewood, Tenn. 37329.

MIEL, ALICE, Auth.; Prof. of Educ., Teachers Col., Columbia Univ., N.Y., N.Y. 10027, '42–; Curriculum Coordr., Mt. Pleasant, Mich., Public Schs., '39–'42; Elementary Prin., Ann Arbor, '37–'39; Tchr., '24–'39; numerous bks., pamphlets; Cnslt.; curriculum progs., U.S., Japan; Staff Mbr., Horace Mann-Lincoln Inst. of Sch. Experimentation, '45–'48; Dir., "Study of Schs. in

Changing Communities," '58–'62; Assn. for Childhood Educ. Intl. (Chmn., '49–'51), NEA Assn. for Supervision and Curriculum Dev. (Exec. Comm.; Pres., '53–'54; First VP, '54–'55); World Educ. Fellowship (Secy.-Treas., '68–'69).

MIELKE, MARGARET GUSTAFSON, Poet; Lectr. to student assemblies on Alaska Poets and Poetry, Poetry Ed., Anchorage Times, '54–'56; Tchr., Mont., '33–'42; compiler, three anthologies of contemporary Alaska poetry; poems in "Haiku of America," "American Mosaic," "100 Years of Alaskan Poetry," other collections; active in commty. orgs.; WNBA; first Poet Laureat of Alaska; Alaska Methodist Univ. First Poetry Aw., '63; Centennial Aw. for Poetry, '67; Hon. Life Mbrship., ESA; World Congress of Poets, Academy of Am. Poets; Cnslr. to Alaska Poetry Soc.; Who's Who in Intl. Poetry, Who's Who of Am. Wm., Wm. of the West, Blue Bk. of Alaska 49ers; Eastern Mont. Normal Sch., Univ. of Mont., Mont. Univ.; Univ. of Alaska, '30–'34, '60 (Degree Equivalent); b. Kandiohi, Minn., 1912; p. William and Alice Klint Gustafson; h. John Mielke; c. Susan M. Noyes, Marnice M. Diggins, John R., James W., Gertrude M. Keller, Frank G.; res: The Three Bushes, Box 74, Chugiak, Alaska 99567.

MIGALA, LUCYNA JOZEFA, TV News Prodr., TV and Radio Reptr., NBC News, Mdse. Mart, Chgo., Ill. 60654, '68–; News Wtr. and Prodr., '66–'70; Prod. Asst. and Rschr., '63–'66; Wtr., Prodr., Anncr., WOPA, '62–'66; AWRT; Loyola Univ., '62–'63; Northwestern Univ., BSJ, '66; Chgo. Conservatory Col., '63–'66; Washington Jnlsm. Ctr. Fellow, '69; b. Krakow, Poland, 1944; p. Joseph and Estelle nee Suwala Migala; res: 300 N. State St., Chgo., Ill. 60610.

MIKE, GLADYS MARY, Assoc. Ed., monthly mag., National Wool Growers Association, 600 Crandall Bldg., Salt Lake City, Ut. 84101, '59–; formerly secy.; Intermountain Assn. of Indsl. Eds. (Treas., '67–'69; Secy., '62; Ed. of the Yr., '66; Best Fulfillment of Stated Purpose of Pubn., '67, '68); Ut. Press Wms. Assn. (Corr. Secy., '67, '68).

MIKES, FREDREKA WILBUR, Commtns. Coordr., Millers Group, 900 Monroe St. (PO Box 2269, Ft. Worth 76101—mail), Ft. Worth, Tex. 76102, '62–; Ed., PR, adv., '40, '43–'45; Wms. Page, Ft. Worth Press, '61; PR Off., Lake Charles Army Air Base, '42; Ed., co. pubns., Shell Oil Co. and Pipe Line Co., '41; Jnlst.-Secy. to M.D. abroad and traveling, '38–'39; Asst. to Ed., Radiology Magazine, Radiological Soc. of N. Am., '37–'38; Ed., Mustang, Southern Methodist Univ., '36–'37; Pubcty., Dallas Commty. Chest, '35–; Ed., Southwestern Horseman (Dallas), '34; Reptr., Tex. Catholic, nine yrs.; Theta Sigma Phi, Mutual Ins. Communicators (cert. for distg. edtl. excellence, '68), ICIE, AAUW (past Pres.); Southern Methodist Univ., BS (Jnlsm), '34 (Mortar Bd.; four gold "M" aws.); b. Marshalltown, Ia., 1911; p. Fred and Edith Woodward

Wilbur; h. Edward J. Mikes; c. Helen Elizabeth; res: 817 Lake Charles Ave., Ft. Worth, Tex 76103.

MIKKANEN, MILDRED IRENE ELLSTROM, Family Dept. Ed., Times-Union, 55 Exchange St., Rochester, N.Y. 14614, '64–; Wms. Ed., Telegram and The Evening Gazette (Worcester, Mass.), '55–; Reptr., Gazette, '47–'55; Workshop Leader, wtrs. confs.; Theta Sigma Phi, Altrusa Club; b. Shrewsbury, Mass., 1919; p. Edwin and Edna Nilson Ellstrom; h. T. R. Mikkanen (dec.); res: 585 Highland Ave., Rochester, N.Y. 14620.

MILES, BETTY BAKER, Auth., juv. bks: "A Day of Fall" ('68), "A Feast on Sullivan Street" ('63), seven others, '58–'61 (all Alfred A. Knopf); Co-auth., "Joe Finds a Way" (Carousel Bks.); mag. articles; Film for children, "Elephants" (Richard Kaplan Prods.); Assoc. Ed., The Bank Street Readers, Macmillan, '66–'68; Pubns. Assoc., Bank Street Col., '64–'66; Auths. League; Antioch Col., BA, '50; b. 1928; h. Matthew Miles; c. Sara, David, Ellen; res: 94 Sparkill Ave., Tappan, N.Y. 10893.

MILES, JOSEPHINE, Prof., University of California, Berkeley, Cal. 94720, '40–; Auth: "Poems 1930–'1960" (Ind., '60), "Style and Proportion" (Little Brown, '67), Am. Acad. of Arts and Scis., Guggenheim Fellowship, '48–'49, Inst. of Arts and Ltrs. Aw., '56; U.C.L.A., BA; Univ. of Cal., Berkeley, PhD.

MILES, LEE, Home Sewing Ed., Redbook, 230 Park Ave., N.Y., N.Y. 10017, '66–; Asst. Fashion Ed., '64–'65; Fashion Group; Bennett Col., AA, '60; res: 181 E. 73rd St., Apt. 11-G, N.Y., N.Y. 10021.

MILES, TICHI WILKERSON, Pres., Publr., The Hollywood Reporter, 6715 Sunset Blvd., Hollywood, Cal. 90028, '62–; Cinema Circulus (VP), L.A. Mayor's Cncl. for Intl. Visitors and Sister Cities, AWRT, Delta Kappa Alpha, Cncl. of Support Orgs., NATAS, Merchants and Manufacturers Assn., Printing Industries Assn. of Southern Cal., Wm. of Mot. Pic. Industry; h. William Miles.

MILES, VERA, Actress, numerous motion pics., incl. "Wild Country" ('70), "Mission Batangos" and "Hellfighters" ('69), "Kona Coast" ('67), "Gentle Giant" ('65), "FBI Story" ('58), "Man Who Shot Liberty Valance" ('60), "Psycho" ('58), "The Searchers" ('55); b. Boise City, Okla., 1930; p. Thomas and Burnice Wyrick Ralson; h. Keith Larsen; c. Debra, Mrs. Kelley Casanova, Michael, Keith.

MILES, VIRGINIA GOLDMAN, VP, Special Planning, Young & Rubicam, Inc., 285 Madison Ave., N.Y., N.Y. 10017, '64; Special Projects, '61–'64; VP, Rsch. Positions, Interpublic, '51–'61; Dir. of Adv. Rsch., Alexander Smith Inc., '49–'51; Psychology Instr., City Col. of N.Y., '46–'51; AWNY, Am. Mktng. Assn., Am. Assn. of Public Opinion Rsch., Am. Psychological Assn.; Wellesley Col., BA, '36; Columbia Univ., MA, '38, PhD, '40 (Sigma Xi); b. N.Y.C., 1916;

p. Samuel and Jeanette Shalet Goldman; h. Fred Miles; c. Erica (Mrs. Bernard Boring); res: 91 Glenbrook Pkwy., Englewood, N.J. 07631.

MILKS, MAXINE GOTTMEIER, Mkt. Analyst, Chicago Tribune, 435 N. Michigan Ave., Chgo., Ill. 60011, '65–'67; Space Sls., '64–'65; Chgo. Wms. Adv. Club; Univ. of Mo., BJ, '64 (Kappa Tau Alpha); b. Youngstown, Oh., 1942; p. Richard and Walentyna Schossler Gottmeier; h. Patrick Milks; c. Catherine Bridget; res: 835 17th St., Wilmette, Ill. 60091.

MILLANE, JEANE E., Dir. of Info. Svcs., Gloucester County College, Tanyard and Salina Rds., Sewell, N.J. 08080, '68–; Educ. Ed., Woodbury (N.J.) Daily Times, '62–'68; Free-lance Wtr.; Asst. Ed., Veterans of Fgn. Wars Wms. Auxiliary Nat. Mag., '52–'55; Radio Wtr., WHB (Kan. City, Mo.), '48–'52; Educ. Wtrs. Assn.; NSPRA; Univ. of Neb. (Liberal Arts), '45–'48; Univ. of Ariz. (Linguistics), '61–'62; b. Chester, Neb., 1925; p. William and Grace Breden Millane; res: 651 N. Glassboro Rd., Wenonah, N.J. 08090.

MILLAR, LEOLA FAUDREE, Adm. Librn., Rolla Public Library, Box 248, Rolla, Mo. 65401, '54–; Librn., Rolla HS, '50–'53; Mo. Lib. Assn. (Secy.), '61; Chmn., Public Lib. Div., '63), ALA; Stephens Col., '23–'25; Univ. of Mo., Rolla; Univ. of Mo., Columbia; b. Evansville, Ind., 1905; p. Thomas and Martha Harris Faudree; h. Charles Millar; c. Nancy Lee (Mrs. William Kenneth Mengel), James Bruce; res: 1400 Pine St., Rolla, Mo. 65401.

MILLER, ALICE McCARTHY, Free-lance Wtr., assigts. for Harper & Row, '69–; Assigts., NBC, "Today Show," '52–'53; Auth., several fiction bks. for young people and adult non-fiction bks.; Instr., Psych. and Sociol., Julliard Sch. of Music, '65–'66; Instr., Pratt Inst., Psych., '61–'63; Instr., Commtn. Arts and Skills, N.Y.C. Commty. Col., '60–'61; Auths. Guild of Auths. League of Am.; U.S. Delegate to Intl. Psychological Congress in Moscow, U.S.S.R., '66; Levittown (L.I.) Public Lib. (Founder, 1st Bd. of Trustees Mbr., '50–'52); b. Lynn, Mass.; p. William and Julia McCarthy McCarthy; h. Warren Miller; c. Nancy Lynn, Jacqueline; res: 1370 St. Nicholas Ave., N.Y., N.Y. 10033.

MILLER, ANN, Ed., employee nwsp., Stouffer Foods Corp., Division of Litton Industries, 1375 Euclid Ave., Cleve., Oh. 44115, '65–; Ed., Cleveland Engineering, '64–'65; Bedford (Oh.) Times-Register, '59–'64; City Ed., '57–'59; Northern Oh. IEA (Secy.), '65–'66; Treas., '66–'67; Second VP, '67–'68; First VP, '68–'69; Pres., '69–'70; Mbr. of the Yr. Aw., '68), ZONTA, Theta Sigma Phi; prizes for indsl. jnlsm., '65, '67, '68; b. Cleve., Oh., 1928; p. Clarence and Margaret Stephens Fitch; h. (div.); c. Stephen Arthur, Jeffrey Charles; res: 25 Blaine St., Bedford, Oh. 44146.

MILLER, BARBARA JOAN, Commtns. Specialist, University of Washington, Seattle, Wash. 98105, '63–; Copywtr., Radio-TV Prodr., Publicist, Advertising

Cnslrs., '55–'63; Circ. Prom. Asst., Family Circle Magazine (N.Y.C.), '50–'54; Auth., one-act play prod. by Anchorage (Alaska) Little Theatre, '58–; Co-auth., TV shows,KING-TV for N.W. Auto Show, '59; Radio-TV Offcr., Wing Staff, Civil Air Patrol, '56–'59; AWRT, NFPW (Wash. Bd. Mbr.); Univ. of Wash., BA (Eng.), '49; b. Longview, Wash., 1926; p. William and Olive Bayley Miller; res: 4018 Greenwood Ave. N., Seattle, Wash. 98103.

MILLER, CATHARINE RYALL, PR Dir., Edinboro State College, Edinboro, Pa., '63–; working on TV series, "Edinboro"; Mt. Lebanon Sr. HS, '58–'63; Instr., Univ. of Pitt., '53–'58; Robert Morris Jr. Col., '47–'53; Army, Navy, Air Force Wms. Magazine (Wash., D.C.), '42–'43; Dart Ellsworth Assoc., '38–'41; Head, Eng. Dept., Morton Sch. of Bus (Wilkinsburg, Pa.), '36–'40; PSEA, NEA, AAUP, Nat. Cncl. of Tchrs. of Eng., Theta Sigma Phi, Nat. Cncl. of Col. Pubns. Advisors, Phi Delta Epsilon (Edinboro State Col. Chptr. Founder-Adviser; Medal of Merit Faculty Aw., '68), DAR, Ind. Univ., AB, '32; Univ. of Pitt., MA, '57; b. Pitt., Pa. 1910; p. J. Milton and Catharine Stahl Ryall; c. John Ryall Miller; res: Box 357, Garden Terr. Dr., Edinboro, Pa. 16412.

MILLER, CHRIS (Dorothy June Chrisman), Free-lance PR Cnslr.; Adv. Rep. and Contrb. Ed., Texas Metro Magazine (Arlington, Tex.), '69–; Progs. and Svcs. Coordr., Greater Ft. Worth and Tarrant County Commty. Action Agecy., '68–'69; Adv. Mgr., Ft. Worth Magazine, Ft. Worth C. of C., '67–'68; TV-Radio Coord., Tarrant County League of Wm. Voters, '64–'68; Special Colmst., Ft. Worth Star-Telegram, '66; AWRT, Adv. Club of Ft. Worth, Press Club of Ft. Worth, C. of C., League of Wm. Voters, Mensa; Mills Col., '44; Tex. Christian Univ., '64–'66; b. Boston, Mass., 1926; p. Rev. Charles and Dorothy Noyce Chrisman; h. (div.); c. Louis C., Gerald L., res: 2528 Ridgmar, Ft. Worth, Tex. 76116.

MILLER, CORA MATHILDA, Ref. Librn., University of Portland, 5000 N. Willamette Blvd., Portland, Ore. 97203, '65–; Assoc. Prof. of Lib. Sci., '64–; Asst. Head Dept. of Lib. Sci., '59–'64; Asst. Librn., Acting Librn., '44–'45; Eastern Ore. Ext. Librn., '57–'59; Librn., Ore. State Bd. of Health, '55–'57; Circ. Dept., Denver Public Lib., '43–'44; ALA, Pacific N.W. Lib. Assn., Ore. Lib. Assn. Pres., '56–'57; Secy., '69–'70, '53–'54), Am. Bus. Wms. Assn. (Sentinel of the West Chptr. Pres., '69–'70; Corr. Secy., '66–'67); AAUW, Univ. of N.D., BA, '26; Univ. of Denver, BS (Lib. Sci.), '44; Univ. of Ore., MEduc., '49; b. McHenry County, N.D.; p. Axel and Rosan Knudtson Miller; res: 6939 N. Portsmouth Ave., Portland, Ore. 97203.

MILLER, DONNA MYERS, ITV Studio Tchr., Dade County Board of Public Instruction, 1410 N.E. 2nd Ave., Miami, Fla. 33132, '62–; Lang. Arts curriculum projects; ITV summer workshops; Classroom Tchr., Miami Sr. HS, '59–'62; Orlando Jr. Col., '57–'59; Bronson Sr. HS, '56–'57; Ft. Lauderdale Naval Air Jr. HS,

'55–'56; Fla. Assn. of Educ. TV (Corr. Secy.-Treas.), Nat. Cncl. of Tchrs. of Eng., Classroom Tchrs. Assn., Fla. Educ. Assn., NEA, other pfsnl. orgs.; Kent State Univ., '49–'52; Univ. of Fla., BA (Educ.), '54; M Educ., '55; h. Robert Miller.

MILLER, ELEANORA LILJEGREN, News Corr., Register & Tribune, Des Moines, Ia. 50144, '56–; Free-lance Wtr., Poet.; High Sch. Tchr., Eng. and Speech, '38–'41; Ia. Poetry. Assn., NLAPW (State Pres., '68–'70), Am. Red Cross Public Info. Cnslt.; Augustana Col., BA; Univ. of Ia.; b. Gowrie, Ia., 1916; p. Alfred and Minnie Carlon Liljegren; h. Forest Miller; c. Carolin (Mrs. Larry Gibson), Loring; res: 208 S. Church St., Leon, Ia. 50144.

MILLER, FRANCES FOX, Free-lance Wtr., Rschr.; former Tchr., Jnlsm. and English, Ind. Univ., Anderson Col., Ball State Univ.; TV prog., "That Which Never Dies," prod. by WLBC-TV, Muncie, Ind., '67; Nat. Assn. of Jnlsm. Educs., NEA, Theta Sigma Phi, NFPW, Pi Delta Kappa, AAUW; Who's Who in Am. Wm.; Outstanding Jnlsm. Tchr. Prize, '66; Ball State Univ., BS; Ind. Univ., MS; Doctorate, '69; Univ. of Mich. (Wall St. Jnl. PR Fellowship); Schenectady, N.Y., 1922; p. Clarence and Minnie Fox; h. Guy Miller; c. Marlene M. Greenwalt, Norman; res: 420 S. College Ave., Muncie, Ind. 47303.

MILLER, GENEVIEVE, Dir., Howard Dittrick Museum of Historical Medicine; Assoc. Prof., Med. Hist., Case Western Reserve University, 11000 Euclid Ave., Cleve., Oh. 44106, '67–; Curator, '62–'67; Asst. Prof., '53–'67; Instr., Johns Hopkins, '45–'48; Auth: "Bibliography of the History of Medicine of the U.S. and Canada, 1939–1960" (Johns Hopkins Press,' 64), "The Adoption of Inoculation for Smallpox in England and France" (Univ. of Pa. Press, '57); mbr., many sci., hist. orgs.; William H. Welch medal, '62; Goucher Col., AB, '35 (Phi Beta Kappa); Johns Hopkins Univ., MA, '39; Cornell Univ., PhD, '55; b. Butler, Pa., 1914; p. Charles and Genevieve Wolford Miller; res: 2235 Overlook Rd., Cleve. Heights, Oh. 44106.

MILLER, GLADYS, Assoc. Publr., Hudson Publishing Co., 175 S. San Antonio Rd., Los Altos, Cal. 94022; Interior Designer, 30 yrs., including Blair and Blair Lee Houses, President Roosevelt's Adm.; Decorating Ed., Mademoiselle, Family Circle; Ed., New Homes Guide and Home Modernizing; Wtr., synd. colm., Consolidate, six yrs.; Radio Program, Bigelow Sanford, two yrs.; Inst. of Am. Interior Designers (Fellow, '62), NHFL (Trailblazer, '68); Fashion Group, Inter Soc. Colo. Cncl., Theta Sigma Phi, Kappa Kappa Gamma (Achiev. Aw., '57); Ore. State, BA, '22 (Centennial Alumni Aw., '69); N.Y.U., MA, '57; Moore Inst. of Art, Sci. and Industry, '57 (Hon. DFA); b. 1896; p. George and Carrie Graves Miller.

MILLER, HAZEL SAMUELSON, Exec. Secy., Nat. Treas., Ladies Auxiliary to the Veterans of Foreign Wars, 406 W. 34th St., Kan. City, Mo. 64111, '57–; Off.

Mgr., Secy., Tchr., '27–'28; Reptr., The Evening Sentinel (Shenandoah, Ia.), Cedar Rapids Gazette, Omaha World Herald; Theta Sigma Phi, Kan. City C. of C., VFW Aux. (Nat. Pres, '45; Ia. State Pres., '34–'35; Secy., '35–'42); President's Comm. Employment of the Handicapped, '66–'71; Govs. Comm. Employment of the Handicapped (Mo.), '68–'69; Univ. of Ia. (Jnlsm.), '21–'26; b. Shenandoah, Ia.; p. August M. and Alvidia M. Johnson Samuelson; h. Alex M. Miller; res: 300 W. Armour Blvd., Kan. City, Mo. 64111.

MILLER, HEATHER ROSS, Auth.; English Instr., Southeastern Community College, Whiteville, N.C., '69–; Lectr., Pfeiffer Col., '65–'67; three novels, poetry collection, short stories, mag. articles; AAUP; Nat. Cncl. on the Arts Grant, '68–'69; Univ. of N.C. at Greensboro, BA (English), '61 (Phi Beta Kappa); MFA (English, Writing), '69; b. Albemarle, N.C., 1939; p. Fred and Geneva Smith Ross; h. Clyde Miller; c. Melissa, Kirk; res: Singletary Lake State Park, Elizabethtown, N.C. 28337.

MILLER, HELEN HILL, Free-lance Wtr., 2810 P St. N.W., Wash., D.C. 20007 also Tamasee, Kitty Hawk, N.C., '53–; bks. on Greece; contrbr. to nat. mags.; Contrb. Ed., The New Republic, '58–'66; Sr. Tutor, Am. Univ., '65; Cnslt., U.S. Dept. of Labor, '62–'63; staff wtr., '34–'40; Exec. Secy., Edgar Stern Family Fund, '56–'63; Exec. Dir., Nat. Policy Commn., '41–'47; '38–'41; Corr., Wash. Bur. of Newsweek, '50–'52; Corr., The Economist (London), '40–'50; Lectr., St. John's Col., '39–'40; Am. Assn. Adult Educ. Rsch. Grant, '26–'27; WNPC (Pres., '55–'56), Am. Polit. Sci. Assn.; Am. Archaeological Inst., Bryn Mawr Col., AB, '21 (Tutor, summer schs., '21, '23, '26; Dir. of Col., '48–'52); Oxford (Eng.) Univ., Diploma (Econs., Polit. Sci.), '22; Univ. of Chgo., PhD, '28; Inst. Univ., Geneva (Switzerland), Cert., '28; b. Highland Park, Ill., 1899; p. Russell and Lucia Green Hill; h. Francis Pickens Miller; c. Andrew P., Robert D.

MILLER, HELEN PRISCILLA, Publr., West Schuylkill Press and Pine Grove Herald, 1 Good Spring St., Tremont, Pa. 17981, '60–; Ed., Mgr., '36–'60; Pa. BPW (State Bd. Mbr., VP, '50–'60), Pottsville BPW (Orchid Aw. for Commty. Svc.; Pres., '58); Tremont Wms. Club (Pres., '44); active in public svc. orgs.; Pottsville Bus. Col., '22; b. Tremont, Pa., 1904; p. Samuel and Ruth Coxon Miller; res: 134 Clay St., Tremont, Pa. 17981.

MILLER, HELENE CHURCH, Pres., Helene C. Miller Associates, '67–; Dir., Mkt. Aides, Kelly Girl Svc. (Boston), '64–'66; Media Wtr., Clare Crawford Adv., '63–'64; Dir., Commty. Svcs., Continental Baking (Hartford, Conn., Boston), '57–'63; Am. Mktng. Assn. (Secy., '65–'67), AWRT, Pubcty. Club of Boston; Who's Who in Am. Mktng.; New Haven Jr. Commty. Col., '35–'37; Northeastern Univ., '63–'66; Harvard Univ., '67; b. Middletown, Conn., 1916; p. William and Lillian Charlesson Church; h. (1) Richard Lord (dec.); (2) Joseph Miller (dec.); c. Richard Lambert Lord Jr.,

Suzanne Yale Lord Hovey, Joanne St. Denis Lord Lavender; res: 61 Foster Rd., Belmont, Mass. 02178.

MILLER, HOPE RIDINGS, Auth., non-fiction; Prod. Cnslt., Metromedia Television, 5151 Wisconsin Ave., N.W., Wash., D.C. 20016, '67–; bks: "Embassy Row, The Life and Times of Diplomatic Washington" (Holt, Rinehart and Winston, '69), "Great Washington Houses" (Clarkson N. Potter, '69); formerly Soc. Ed., Colmst., The Washington Post; Wash. Corr., Town and Country; Synd. Colmst.; Ed.-in-Chief, Diplomat Magazine; WNPC (Pres., '38–'39), ANWC (VP, '37–'38), Soc. of Am. Travel Wtrs.; Nat. Bd. of Governors, USO (apptd. by Pres. Johnson, '67); Who's Who in Am.; Univ. of Tex., BA; Columbia Univ., MA; b. Bonham, Tex.; p. Dr. Alfred and Grace Dupree Ridings; h. Dr. Clarence Lee Miller (dec.); res: 1868 Columbia Rd., N.W., Wash., D.C. 20009.

MILLER, JANE, Dir. of Feature Events, Abraham & Straus, 420 Fulton St., Bklyn., N.Y. 11201, '59–; Home Furnishings Publicist, '53–'59; Publicist, Helen Sprackling, '50–'52; Acc. Wtr., Dudley, Anderson & Yutzy, '48–'50; Guest Lectr., Tobe-Coburn Sch.; Bklyn. Arts and Culture Assn., NHFL; John B. Stetson Univ., '37–'39; Rollins Col., '39–'41; b. Buffalo, N.Y., 1919; p. William and Theodora Sevin Miller; res: 2 Grace Ct., Bklyn., N.Y. 11201.

MILLER, JOY M., Free-lance Wtr., '69–; Wms. Ed., AP, '60–'69; '44–'60; Univ. of Kan., BA, '44; res: 161 W. 75th St., N.Y., N.Y. 10023.

MILLER, JUNE CAMP, Wtr.; Staff Asst., Rsch., Veterans Administration, 819 Vermont Ave., N.W., Wash., D.C. 22070, '68–; Wtr., Ed., '65–'68; Dir. Special Supplements Dept., Congressional Quarterly, '57–'67; nwsp. work, '48–'57; Auth., "Code of an American Mother," '56; Edtl. Cnslt., AMVETS; Wms. Adv. Club of Wash.; Jeffersonian Medal, Freedoms Fndn., '57; Who's Who of Am. Wm.; Zeith Bus. Sch., '42; b. Richmond, Va., 1923; p. Harry and Laura Siverson Camp; h. Marshall E. Miller; c. April Lee, Harry Michael Abendshein; res: 1616 Wainwright Dr., Reston, Va. 22070.

MILLER, KAY JOHNS, AE, Larry Manzo Public Relations, 6725 Sunset Blvd., L.A., Cal. 90028, '68–; Dir. PR, Bryan Hardwick Agcy., '68 Dir. PR Larwin Co., '68; Ed., Homebuyers Magazine, '66–'67; Kay Miller Advertising, '63–'66; Free-lance Wtr., mag. articles; NHFL, L.A. Beautiful, L.A. Art Dirs. Club (Past), Project '5–'9 (Dir.); Univ. of N.M., '40–'42; b. Shreveport, La., 1921; p. Walter and Lucile Simpson Jackson; h. Josef Miller; c. Victoria R., Laurie R., res: 108 S. Almont Dr., L.A., Cal. 90048.

MILLER, LORENA, Dir., Lexington County Circulating Library, Box 187, Batesburg, S.C. 29006, '48–; County Librn., '48–; Librn., Batesburg Public Lib.; Tchr.; ALA, S.C. Lib. Assn., Batesburg-Leesville BPW; Batesburg-Leesville Wm. of Yr., '63; Coker Col., BA;

b. Batesburg, S.C.; p. James and Lydia Sturkie Miller; res: 213 Line St., Batesburg, S.C. 29006.

MILLER, MARION FREED, Hostess, "Time For The Truth," KTYM Radio, 6803 West Blvd., Inglewood, Cal. 90302, '66–; Cnslt., Tchr., Lectr.; Auth., "I Was a Spy" (Bobbs-Merrill); Reader's Digest First Person Aw. Am. Inst. of Fine Arts medal and cit. for heroism; Pres. Dwight D. Eisenhower Commendation for Patriotism; Pres. Richard M. Nixon Commendation for Courage; Delta Phi Epsilon Wm. of the Yr.; Who's Who of Am. Wm.; numerous other aws.; proclaimed "Most Decorated Wm. in Am." by Congress; Univ. of Miami, BMusEd (cum laude); b. N.Y.C., 1920; p. Harry and Ida Sweetwine Freed; h. Paul Miller; c. Paul, Jr., Betsy Lou, Robert Bruce; res: 10591 Cushdon Ave., L.A., Cal. 90064.

MILLER, MINETTA AUDRAE, Owner, Minetta A. Miller Public Relations, Suite 212, Johnson Bldg., 509 17th St., Denver, Colo., 80202, '62–; Prom., PR, Henritze's Restaurant, '60–'62; Ernest S. Baker, Atty., '53–'59; Asst. Secy., Sioux Oil Co., '48–'53; Pubcty., PR, Colo. Central Power Co., '43–'48; Nat. Secys. Assn (Northwest Dist. Rep., Inst. for Certifying Pfsnl. Secys., '51–'55), Desk and Derrick Clubs of Denver (Pres., '52) and N.A. (Reg. Dir., First VP, '54–'55), AWRT (Chptr. Pres., '68–'69); Oil Wm. of the Yr., '54; Denver Secy of the Yr., '55; Third Place, Intl. Secy. of the Yr. Contest, '56; Morningside Col., BA (Econs.), '40 (Hon. Soc.); Grad. Study, Univ. of Denver; b. Parker, S.D.; p. Harry and Edna Brereton Miller; res: 333 E. 16th Ave., Apt. 701, Denver, Colo. 80203.

MILLER, NAN COURTNEY, Pres., Nan Miller & Associates, Inc., 55 E. Washington St., Chgo., Ill. 60612, '63–; Nan Miller Prods. and Theatrical Agcy., '45–'53; President's Club, Small Bus. Cncl., Public Safety Cncl., Chgo. YWCA (Dist. Dir.), Chgo. Assn. of Commerce and Industry, Pubcty. Club of Chgo., PRSA; Northwestern Univ., BA, '57; (with highest distinction; Phi Beta Kappa); Sch. of Law, Juris Dr., '61.

MILLER, NATALIE, Wms. Ed., Ithaca Journal, 123 W. State St., Ithaca, N.Y. 14850, '65–; Auth. of non-fiction juv. hist. bks. and articles incl. "Cornerstones of Freedom" series (Children's Press, '66–'67), "Give Me Liberty" (Meredith Press, '67); Tchr.; Ithaca Wtrs. Club (Prose Dept. Chmn., '66), Ithaca Wms. Club; Beaver Col., BA, '37 (cum laude); Syracuse Univ. (Lib. Sci.); b. Sanford, Me., 1917; p. Nathaniel and Jessie Littlefield Hanson; h. Josiah Miller; c. Judith (Mrs. James Merry), Nancy (Mrs. Bosko Milinic), Richard, Eris; res: 46 Cornell St., Ithaca, N.Y. 14850.

MILLER, NORMA ROSS, City Ed., The Herald-American, 554 McKean Ave., Donora, Pa. 15033, '57–; Donora C. of C., '50–'57; Donora Commty. Chest, '50–'57; Off. Mgr., Donora Golden Jubilee, '51; Wtr., Universal Trade Press Synd. (N.Y.C.); numerous civic activities; Pa. Nwsp. Eds. Assn., Pa. Wms. Press Assn.; Wash. County Poetry Soc. (Pres.; many aws.); Pa. State

Univ.; b. Butler, Pa., 1920; p. William and Doris Ferguson Ross; h. Alden F. Miller, Jr.; c. Alden F. III; res: Overlook Terr., Donora, Pa. 15033.

MILLER, PATRICIA SKINNER, Copywtr., Frank F. Sawdon, Inc., 555 Madison Ave., N.Y., N.Y., '67–; Copywtr., DuBarry Cosmetics, '66–'67; Group Head Pubcty. Dept., J. Walter Thompson, '56–'66; Pubcty. Wtr., Cunard Line, '52–'56; Beauty Ed., Canadian Home Jnl. (Toronto), '49–'52; Auth., short stories and articles in Canadian mags., comic strip in "Teen Magazine," early 60s; AWNY; b. Edmonton, Alberta, Can., 1929; p. George and Mabel Maxwell Skinner; h. George Miller; res: 25 Fifth Ave., N.Y., N.Y. 10003.

MILLER, RETILLA COOK, Wms. Ed., Jackson County Floridan, 144 E. LaFayette St., Marianna, Fla. 32446, '56–; Circ. Mgr., '30–'41; Tchr., '28–'29; b. Grapeland, Tex., 1911; p. James and Clarissa Ray Cook; h. Floyd Miller; c. Wilton R., Margaret C., Marilyn B., Jeanette, Kathryn; res: 610 Pine St., Marianna, Fla. 32446.

MILLETT, KATE, Assoc. Prof., Dept. of Sociology, Bryn Mawr College, Bryn Mawr., Pa.; Auth., "Sexual Politics" (Doubleday, '70); Sculptor, numerous exhbns.; Depts. of Eng. and Philosophy, Barnard Col., Columbia Univ. (N.Y.C.), '64–'68; Eng. Dept., Hunter Col., '63–'64; Waseda Univ. (Tokyo, Japan), '61–'63; educ: Univ. of Minn. (Phi Beta Kappa), Oxford Univ. (1st Class Hons.), Columbia Univ., PhD; b. St. Paul, Minn., 1934; p. James and Helen Feely Millett; res: 307 Bowery, N.Y., N.Y. 10003.

MILLIGAN, DELLA BATES, Dir. of PR, Chatham College, Pitts., Pa. 15232, '66–; Asst. Dir., '63–'65; Secy., Asst. PR, KDKA-TV, '63–'65; Wtr., Pitt. Suburban Nwsp. Assn., '60–'61; Theta Sigma Phi (Pitt. Chptr. Pres., '69–'70; VP, '66–'67), Wms. Press Club (Pitt.), Pitt. Press Club, ACPRA, EWA; Bethany Col., '56–'58; W. Va. Univ., BS, '60; b. Upland, Pa., 1938; p. Davis and Alice Bentley Bates; h. Jack Milligan; res: 1150 Bower Hill Rd., Pitt., Pa. 15243.

MILLING, EILEEN, Pres., Public Relations Analysts Inc., 210 E. 47th St., N.Y., N.Y. 10017, '68–; VP, Lobsenz Public Relations Co., '62–'68; Pres., Communicators, PR Div., Smith-Greenland Adv., '59–'61; VP, Chester Gore Adv. PR Div., '57–'59; tchr.; TV commentator; nwsp. reptr.; mag. wtr.; AWRT, NATAS, IRTS, Fashion Group, NHFL; aw. for commty. affairs-educ., '59; L.I. Univ., BS, '42; Temple Univ., '43–'44; N.Y.U. Sch. of Bus., candidate for MBA (Mgt.), '69; b. Bklyn., N.Y. 1922; h. Leonard J. Milling; c. Mrs. Susan Jo Mayer; res: 12 Colony Lane, Roslyn Heights, N.Y. 11577.

MILLS, ALICE CATHERINE, Dir., Wms. Dept., National Safety Council, 425 N. Michigan Ave., Chgo., Ill. 60611, '46–; org. as separate dept., '54–; Traf. Safety Dept., Field Dept., five mos. in pers., '43–; PR and renting, Edgewater Beach Apts., five yrs.; The Principia, St. Louis, Mo., two yrs.; Northwestern Univ., three yrs.; b. Chgo., Ill.; p. Walter and Floy Mills; res: 1247 Judson Ave., Evanston, Ill. 60202.

MILLS, ALYCE E., Classified Adv., Press Enterprise Newspaper, 1534 N. Palm Canyon, Palm Springs, Cal. 92262, '59–; Desert Sun Nwsp., 3 yrs.; Limelight News, 2 yrs.; ZONTA; Who's Who of Am. Wm.; b. Krebs, Okla., 1912; p. Walter and Mary De Jackamo Hokey; h. Edward Barnum; c. Kathryn (Mrs. Thomas Rhodes), Marilyn (Mrs. Richard Haviken); res: 4113 Calle San Antonio, Palm Springs, Cal. 92262.

MILLS, ANN FOMIN, TV-Radio Prodr., Campbell-Ewald Company, 3044 W. Grand Blvd., Detroit, Mich. 48202, '65–; Art Dir., Young & Rubicam, '62–'64; Wms. Adv. Club of Detroit; Wayne State Univ., BFA, '62; b. Detroit, Mich., 1941; h. John Mills; res: Dearborn, Mich.

MILLS, BETTY LIDSTROM, Free-lance Wtr.; Co-auth., "Mind If I Differ" (Sheed & Ward, '64); N.D. Educ. Bdcst. Cncl., '69–; Veterans Memorial Lib. (Pres., '69–; VP, '68–'69; Secy., '64–'67), N.D. Lib. Assn., NLAPW; Univ. of Minn., '44–'47; Mary Col., BA, '67 (cum laude); b. Bismarck, N.D., 1926; p. Leonard and Crystal Sletmoen Lidstrom; h. William R. Mills; c. Randa L., Sherry Ann, William L.; Nancy J.; res: 1019 Ave. C. West, Bismarck, N.D. 58501.

MILLS, MARION LAURA, AE, PR Dir., William Eisner & Associates, 176 W. Wisconsin Ave., Milw., Wis. 53203; Consumer Copy Dir., PR Dir.; Copywtr., Contact, PR, McCann-Erickson (Honolulu, Hi.); Copy, Contact, PR, Cramer-Krasselt (Milw., Wis.); Adv. Copy Dir., Oscar Mayer & Co. (Madison); Copy Chief, AE, Arthur Towell; Tchr., Adv., Univ. of Wis.; Milw. Adv. Club (Bd. of Dirs., '68–'70), AWRT (Secy., '69), Theta Sigma Phi (Milw. Alumnae Chptr. Pres., '67; Honolulu Alumnae Chptr. Past Pres.; Madison Alumnae Chptr. Past Pres.), ZONTA, Cerebral Palsy of Greater Milw. (Bd. of Dirs.); Honolulu Adv. Wm. of the Yr., '65; Univ. of Wis., BA, '32; Ind. Univ., grad. work; b. Lake Mills, Wis., 1907; p. Eugene and Fannie Everson Mills; res: 2612 N. Maryland, Milw., Wis. 53211.

MILLSPAUGH, DORIS RINTELMANN, Assoc. Ed., Ed.-Rschr. Students' Information Service, Illustrated World Encyclopedia, Inc., 26 The Place, Glen Cove, N.Y. 11542, '67–; Secy. (to Pres. & Chairman of the Board) '60–'69; Music Tchr., '34–'40; Wis. Col. of Music, Milw.; St. Louis Inst. of Music, '35; Prospect Hall Secretarial School, '39; b. Milw., Wis., 1916; p. Walter and Elsa Gathmann Rintelmann; h. Abbott Millspaugh; c. Susan, Judy Doris (Mrs. Michael Connell).

MILNE, MARGERY GREENE, Lectr., University of New Hampshire, Durham, N.H. 03824, '67–; Auth., most with husband, of 25 bks. in nature, zoology, biology, natural hist.; numerous articles, bk. revs. in major jnls.; lectr., '48–; Cnslt.-Wtr., Dept. of Educ.,

New Zealand, '66; Univ. of Colo., '60, '62, '67; Prof., numerous other cols. and univs., '36–'61; numerous lit. and sci. hons., aws., rsch. grants, Phi Beta Kappa, Phi Sigma, Sigma Xi; Hunter Col., AB, '33; Columbia Univ., MA, '34; Radcliffe Col., MA, '37; PhD, '39; rsch. at Woods Hole Marine Labs., Scripps Inst. Oceanography, extensive field study; b. N.Y.C.; p. S. and Beatrice Gutman Greene; h. Lorus J. Milne; res: One Garden Lane, Durham, N.H. 03824.

MILNER, SHARON ANN, Photogr.-Reptr., The Sheldon Mail, 227 Ninth, Sheldon, Ia. 51201, '66–; The Monday Sun; Ed., The Lake Park, '63–'66; Soc. Ed., The Spirit Lake Beacon, '54–'63; Adv. Dept., Cedar Rapids Gazette, '54; Theta Sigma Phi (Mbr.-at-Large, '53–), BPW (Spirit Lake and Sheldon Chptr. VP, '69–; Secy.); Drake Univ., BA, '53; b. Cedar Rapids, Ia., 1931; p. John and Effie Safley Milner; res: 918-1/2 Fifth Ave., Sheldon, Ia. 51201.

MILTON, SHIRLEY FUCHS, Prof., Fashion Institute of Technology, 227 W. 27th St., N.Y., N.Y. 10002, '67–; VP, Al Paul Lefton Adv.; Sls. Prom. Asst., Grand Union (N.J.); Owner, Farrand Agcy. (L.A., Cal.); Cnslt. on adv. plans, campaigns; Auth., "Advertising Copywriting" ('69); bks. on pubcty. and on copywriting, in progress; Eta Mu Phi, N.Y. Assn. of Jr. Cols., Fashion Group, Awny, Pubcty. Club of N.Y.; Cornell Univ., BA, '32 (Phi Beta Kappa); N.Y.U., MA, '33; N.Y.U., Sch. of Retailing, grad. work; Columbia Univ.; b. N.Y.C.; p. Emanuel and Helen Hyams Fuchs; h. Bruce Milton (div.); c. Gabriel B., David H.; res: 140 West End Ave., N.Y., N.Y. 10023.

MINER, CAROLINE EYRING, Eng. Tchr., Salt Lake City School District, 2166 S. 17 E., Salt Lake City, Ut. 84106, '45–; Tchr., '30–'32, '39–'43; Auth., six bks., fiction, non-fiction, poetry ('61–'68); NPWC (Salt Lake City Br. Pres., '68–'70), Delta Kappa Gamma (Eta Chptr.; Pioneer Wm., '69), Kiwanis Tchr. of Yr., '66; Brigham Young Univ., AB, '29 (Distg. Svc. Aw., '69); Ut. State Univ., MS, '43; Univs. of Ut., Hi., Cal., Alaska, grad. work; b. Colonia Juarez, Mexico, 1907; p. Edward and Caroline Romney Eyring; h. Glen B. Miner; c. Bryant A., Caroline M. Morgan, Rosemary M. Fairbourn, Edward G., Henry L., Camilla V., Joseph K., Steven E.; res: 2429 Kensington Ave., Salt Lake City, Ut. 84108.

MINER, RUTH ALLAN, Ed. of Juv. Bks., Macrae Smith, 225 S. 15th St., Phila., Pa. 19118; '68–; '63–'65; Edtl. Asst., Copy Ed., Asst., Assoc. Ed., Ladies' Home Journal, John C. Winston Co.; Phila. Booksellers Assn.; Univ. of Pa., AB, '40 (Phi Beta Kappa); b. Phila., Pa., 1918; p. Allan and Ethel Knowles Huckins; h. Richard Miner (dec.); c. Mrs. Craig N. Canning, Mrs. Nicholas A. Robinson, Allyn Jane; res: 41 W. Gravers Lane, Phila., Pa. 19118.

MINNEY, MARY ALICE, Dir., Dept. of Educ., International Consumer Credit Association, 375 Jackson Ave., St. Louis, Mo. 63130 and Society of Certified

Consumer Credit Executives, 7405 University Dr., St. Louis, Mo. 63130, '67–; Special Asst., Intl. Consumer Credit Assn., '64–'67; PR Supvsr., Assoc. Credit Burs. of Am., '62–'64; Pubns. Supvsr., '60–'62; Assoc. Ed., '55–'60; Secy., '49–'55; ICIE, Indsl. Press Assn. of Gtr. St. Louis (Past VP, Secy.); Wash. Univ., BS, '64; b. St. Louis, Mo., 1926; p. Peter and Alice Sollberger; res: 4100 Arsenal St., St. Louis, Mo. 63116.

MINSKY, BETTY JANE TOEBE, Bur. Chief, Clinton County, The State Journal, Lansing, Mich., '67–; Wtr., on assigt., Nationwide Trade Synd.; Corr., northern Mich., Fairchild Pubns., four yrs (Aw., '65); Free-lance Wtr., bus., trade pubns., 16 yrs.; Mgr., C. of Cs., Cheboygan (Mich.), St. Johns, six yrs.; Auth., "Gimmicks Make Money in Retailing" (Fairchild Pubns., '63); Mich. Wms. Press Club (Photog. Aw., '69); b. Woodville, Wis., 1932; p. Wilburt and Lucille Lopas Toebe; h. John A. Minsky; c. Gregg, Jennifer, Kenneth, Jack; res: 4958 N. U.S. 27, Rte. 3, St. Johns, Mich. 48879.

MINTZ, JUNE MIRKEN, Assoc. Ed., Parents Magazine, 52 Vanderbilt Ave., N.Y., N.Y. 10017, '67–; Former Fiction Ed., Charm Magazine.

MINUDRI, REGINA U., Project Coordr., Federal Young Adult Library Services Project, 655 Castro St. #5, Mountain View, Cal. 94040, '68–; Reg. Librn., Santa Clara County, '62–'68; Ref. Librn., Menlo Park Lib., '59–'62; Ed., School Library Journal, Bks. for Young Adults, '67–; ALA, Cal. Lib. Assn., Bay Area Young Adults Librns. (Pres., '66–'68); S.F. Col. for Wm., BA, '58; Univ. of Cal., Berkeley, MA, '59; b. S.F., Cal., 1937; p. John and Molly Halter Minudri; res: 470 Wraight Ave., Los Gatos, Cal. 95030.

MIRSKY, JEANNETTE R., Auth: "To the Arctic!" ('34, Knopf, '70, U. of Chicago); "The Westward Crossings" ('50, Knopf, '70; U. of Chicago), "The Gentle Conquistadors" ('69, Pantheon); "Balboa, Discoverer of the Pacific," ('64), "Houses of God," ('65), other books, articles; Soc. of Wm. Geographers, Soc. for the Hist. of Discovery, Asia Soc., PEN, Royal Central Asian Soc.; Am. Specialist, USIA (Mexico, Guatemala, Costa Rica, '65; Africa, '67); Soc. Sci. Rsch. Cncl. grant, '35; Guggenheim Fellowship, '47–'48, '49–'50; Rockefeller Fndn. Grant, '64–'68; Visiting Fellow, Dept. of Oriental Studies, Princeton Univ., '64–'68; Visiting Fellow, E. Asian Studies, Princeton Univ., '69–'70; Barnard Col., BA, '24 (Phi Beta Kappa); Columbia Univ., (Anthropology), '35–'39; b. Bradley Beach, N.J., 1903; p. Michael and Frieda Ittleson Mirsky; h. Edward Bellamy Ginsburg (dec.); res: 230 Nassau St., Princeton, N.J. 08540.

MISCALLY, MILDRED LOIS, Dir. of PR, Queens College, 1900 Sedwyn Ave., Charlotte, N.C. 28207, '46–; Asst. Prof. of Jnlsm., '53–'68; Tchr., Charlotte City Schs., '32–'45; Pubcty. Dir., Kanuga Confs. (Hendersonville), summers '35–'44; Teaching Asst.,

Henry W. Grady Sch. of Jnlsm., Univ. of Ga.; Theta Sigma Phi, Delta Kappa Gamma, ACPRA, Southern Col. Placement Assn., Phi Kappa Phi; Am. Bus. Wms. Assn., Carolina Heritage Chptr. Boss of the Yr. Aw., '69; Univ. of Ga., AB (Jnlsm.), '30 (summa cum laude; Phi Beta Kappa); MA, '46; b. Savannah, Ga., 1909; p. James and Edna Middleton Miscally; res: 1020 Arosa Ave., Apt. 2, Charlotte, N.C. 28203.

MISCH, NANCY SCOTT, Special Assigts. Reptr., Coffeyville Publishing Co., Eighth & Elm Sts., Coffeyville, Kan. 67337, '69–; Wms. Ed., '67–'69; Reptr., '66–'67; Clay Ctr. Kan. Dispatch, '65; NPWC, Theta Sigma Phi, Gamma Alpha Chi, Epsilon Sigma Alpha, P.E.O. Sisterhood, Kan. Press Wm. (daily page makeup aw., '68; daily edtl. competition aw., '66), Outstanding Young Wm. of Am.; Cottey Col. for Wm.; Univ. of Kan.; b. Council Grove, Kan., 1944; p. Willard Scott and Betty Kennedy Scott Strom; h. Gary Misch; res: 102 Ohio, Coffeyville, Kan. 67337.

MISHKIN, LEAH YABLONSKY, Head Librn., Saul Silber Memorial Library, Hebrew Theological College, 7135 N. Carpenter Rd., Skokie, Ill. 60076, '38–; Asst. Librn., '27–'31, '35–'38; Published various bibliographies; Lewis Inst., BHL; Hebrew Theological Col.; b. Slobodko, Lithuania, 1909; p. Nisson and Czippe Klebansky Yablonsky; h. Leonard C. Mishkin; c. Mrs. Annette Linzer, Marguerite; res: 3530 Lake Shore Dr., Chgo., Ill. 60657.

MISKE, FAE R., Pres., Joseph Burstyn Inc., 165 W. 46th St., N.Y., N.Y. 10036, '55–; Gen. Sls. Mgr., '46–'55; Secy., '36–'46; Intl. Film Importers and Distributors of Am.; City Col. of N.Y., '36–'37; Hunter Col., '38–'39; '56–'57; b. N.Y.C., 1917; p. Morris and Ida Cooperman Miske; c. Gerald Norman and Arthur Lauren; res: 1562 Unionport Rd., N.Y., N.Y. 10462.

MITCHEL, CLAIRE FURMAN, Dir. PR, Community Action Commission, 820 Linn Mall, Cinn., Oh. 45214, '65–; Cnslr., Claire Mitchel Public Relations, '55–; Dir. PR, Schindler-Howard Advertising Agcy.; Feature Wtr., Lakeland News (Dover, N.J.); Free-lance Wtr., mags., nwsps.; PRSA; Oh. State Univ. (Jnlsm.); b. N.Y.C., 1921; p. Bernard and Yetta Israel Furman; h. Arnold Mitchel; c. Madelaine (Mrs. Ronald Miller), Jeffrey F.; res: 4514 Perth Lane, Cinn., Oh. 45229.

MITCHELL, BARBARA STEPPER, Owner, Mitchell Design, 1923 Sylvan St., Eugene, Ore. 97403, '65–; Dir. of Pubns., Univ. of Ore., '63–'65; Adv. Dir., Field Emission Corp. (McMinnville), '62–'63; Pubns. Ed., Univ. of Ore., '61–'62; News Ed., Univ. of Ore. Med. Sch., '60–'61; News Wtr., Yakima (Wash.) Daily Republic, '59–'60; Theta Sigma Phi (Eugene Club Pres., '68–'69; Treas., '66–'68), Ore. Assn. of Eds. and Communicators (two Excellence Aws., '68; Sweepstakes Aw., '69), ACPRA (Merit Aw., '66; three Excellence Aws., '66); Univ. of Ore., BS (Jnlsm.), '59 (cum laude; Phi Beta Kappa); b. Eureka, S.D., 1937; p. John and Mabel

Helmer Stepper; h. Tom B. Mitchell; c. Dayna, Stuart, Derek.

MITCHELL, CATHERINE CECELIA, Rschr., CBS News Election Unit, CBS News, 524 W. 57th St., N.Y., N.Y. 10019, '69–; Adm. Asst. to Walter Cronkite, CBS News, '66–'69; Exec. Secy. to Pres. of CBS News, Fred Friendly, '66; Volunteer Tchr. for retarded readers; N.Y. Coord. Cncl., Volunteer's Shelter, French Inst.; Fordham Univ., BS, '60; Hunter Grad. Sch. of Polit. Sci., '62 (dean's list; two partial scholarships); b. N.Y.C.; p. Timothy and Catherine Lavery Mitchell; res: 48–36 47th St., Woodside, N.Y. 11377.

MITCHELL, ELIZABETH HELENE, Ed., Sanford Tribune, Sanford Publishing Co., 201 A Main St., Sanford, Me. 04073, '51–; Asst. Ed., Rochester (N.H.) Courier, '50–'51; City Ed., Franklin Journal-Transcript, '44–'50; Ed., Vermont-Standard, '43–'44; Ed., Springfield Reporter, '37–'43; Reptr., '30–'37.

MITCHELL, HESTER LOUISE, Librn., Addison-Wesley Publishing Company, Inc., Reading, Mass. 01867, –67; Head Librn., Public Lib. (Ipswich, Mass.), '51–'67; Head, Children's Dept., Public Lib. (Everett, Mass.), '48–'51; in lib. work since '33; Contrbr., periodicals, nwsps.; ALA, New Eng. Lib. Assn., New Eng. Sch. Lib. Assn., Mass. Lib. Assn., Mass. State Aid, Boston Bk. Rev. Club (Treas., '57), Merrimack Valley Lib. Assn. (Pres., '52–'54; Exec. Bd., '51–'60), Wms. Nat. Bk. Assn., Special Libs. Assn., Intl. Platform Assn.; Who's Who in Lib. Sci.; Who's Who of Am. Wm.; Who's Who in the East; Dic. of Intl. Biog.; The 2,000 Wm. of Achiev.; active in hosp., civic groups; educ: Univ. of Va.; Regent Inst. (London); Univ. of N.H.; Boston Univ.; Mass. Dept. of Educ.; Univ. of Okla.; b. Plainfield, N.J., 1915; p. Henry S. and Maude F. Raymond Mitchell; res: Holten Gardens Apts., Danvers, Mass. 01923.

MITCHELL, JACQUELINE A., Dir. of Pubcty. and Prom., Parfum Marcel Rochas, 730 Fifth Ave., N.Y., N.Y. 10019, '68–; Pubcty. Dir., Coty; Dir., Radio-TV Opns., Edward Gottlieb & Assoc.; Asst. PR Dir., Miradel; Composer; Free-lance Wtr.; Fashion Group; AWRT; Queens Col., '47–'49; b. N.Y.C., 1930; p. James and Margaret Arvay Adams; res: 500 E. 77th Str., N.Y., N.Y. 10021.

MITCHELL, LUANA VONDEREMBS, Asst. Ed., Los Altos Town Crier, Foothill Printing and Publishing Company, 354 Second St., Los Altos, Cal. 94022, '67–; Wms. Page Ed., Gen. Assigt. Reptr., Los Altos News, '57–'67; Gen. Assigt. Reptr., Hollister Evening Freelance, '56; Theta Sigma Phi (Peninsula Chptr: VP, '67–'68; Secy., '57–'58); Soroptimist Club (Secy., '67–'68); Who's Who of Am. Wm.; San Jose State Col., BA (Jnlsm.), '57; b. L.A., Cal., 1935; p. Arthur and Harriet Riley Vonderembs; h. David A. Mitchell; res: 10249 Ainsworth Dr., Cupertino, Cal. 95014.

MITCHELL, MARTHA JOY, Head Librn., Franklin High School, Franklin, Tenn. 37064, '66–; Librn.,

Dalewood Jr. HS, '64–'66; Head Librn., Temple Col., '60–'64, '54–'58; NEA, Tenn. Educ. Assn., Tenn. Lib. Assn., WNBA; Temple Col., BA, '54; Peabody Col., BA, '59; MA (Lib. Sci.) '60; b. Rome, Ga.; p. John and Edith Torrell Mitchell; res: 2406 Blair Blvd., Nash, Tenn. 37212.

MITCHELL, MARY FRIEDRICH, Interim Assoc. Dir., Detroit Public Library, 5201 Woodward Ave., Detroit, Mich. 48202, '68–; Ref. Svcs. Dir., '67–'68; Pers. Dir., '63–'67; Chief, Gen. Ref., '53–'63; Chief, Municipal Ref. Lib., '49–'53; Tchr., Univ. of Minn. Lib. Sch. '42–'44; ALA, Mich. Lib. Assn. (Pres., '65–'66), Adult Educ. Soc. of Met. Detroit, ZONTA; Univ. of Minn., BLS, '41; St. Olaf Col., BA, '40; b. Jasper, Minn., 1919; p. Otto and Alma Berdan Friedrich; h. James Mitchell; res: 850 Whitmore Rd., Detroit, Mich. 48203.

MITCHELL, MARY MAHONEY, Chief, Lib. Svc., Veterans Administration Hospital, N. Main St., Northampton, Mass. 01053, '58–; Librn., '49–'58; Descriptive Cataloger, NASA, '47–'49; Librn.; Cambridge Public Lib., '38–'47; ALA, Med. Lib. Assn., Mass. Lib. Assn. Hosp. Group; Simmons Col., '37–'38; b. Cambridge, Mass.; p. James and Norma Richards Mahoney; h. John Mitchell; res: 71 Leonard St., Leeds, Mass. 01053.

MITCHELL, MELBA BROOME, Traf. Dir., Goodwin Dannenbaum Littman & Wingfield, Inc., 80 Interstate 10 N., Beaumont, Tex. 77706, '67–; BPW, AWRT (Secy.-Treas., VP, '69–'70); Lamar State Col. of Tech., '68–'69; b. Brookhaven, Miss., 1933; p. Burton and Carrie Fore Broome; h. Herman Mitchell; c. Becky, Doy; res: 805 Tannahill, Vidor, Tex. 77662.

MITCHELL, MEMORY FARMER, Hist. Pubns. Ed., North Carolina State Department of Archives and History, Box 1881, Raleigh, N.C. 27602, '61–; Asst. State Archivist, '56–'61; Judge, Cabarrus County Domestic Rel. Court, '54–'55; Adm. Asst., N.C. Dept. of Public Welfare, '50–'54; Instr., Meredith Col., '49–'50; Auth., "Legal Aspects of Conscription and Exemption in North Carolina, 1861–1865" (Univ. N.C. Press, '65); Ed., "Messages, Addresses, and Public Papers of Terry Sanford, Governor of North Carolina, 1961–1965" (State of N.C.: 1966) Org. of Am. Hists., Southern Hist. Assn., Hist. Soc. of N.C., N.C. Lit. and Hist. Assn., Wake County Hist. Soc. (Past Secy.), N.C. State Bar, AAUW (Raleigh Br. Pres., '61–'63); Raleigh Wm. of the Yr., '61; Meredith Col., AB, '44 (cum laude); Univ. of N.C., LLB, '46; AM, '49; b. Raleigh, N.C., 1924; p. James and Foy Johnson Farmer; h. Thornton W. Mitchell; c. James T., David W.; res: 2431 Medway Dr., Raleigh, N.C. 27608.

MOBLEY, PEGGY HINDMAN, Ed. and Gen. Mgr., Suburban Publishers, Cedar Hill Chronicle, 307 Houston St., Cedar Hill, Tex. 75104, '65–; Corr., S.W. Dallas County Suburban (Duncanville); Tex. Press Assn., Nat. Press Assn., S. and E. Tex. Press Assn.; b. Hale Center, Tex., 1932; p. Earl and Ethel Berry Hindman; h.

Howard L. Mobley; c. Joyce, William, Julia LeeAnn, Jeannie, Patti Lu, Lorri; res: 214 Bennett, Cedar Hill, Tex. 75104.

MOCK, JOANNE McKESSON, Prodr.-Dir., KQED-TV Educational Services, 525 Fourth St., S.F., Cal. 94107, '64–; Asst. Prodr., Dir., Asst. to Dir. of Instructional TV, '61–'64; Asst. Prodr., Queen-B Prods., Radio-TV (N.Y.C.), '60–'61; Asst. to Prog. Sls. Mgr., Prod. Asst., ABC-TV Network, '54–'58; TV Prodr., "The Eyes Have It" (Nat. Educ. TV Aw., '66); Bdcst. Preceptor Aw., S.F. State Col. Radio-TV-Film Dept., '66; Western Radio TV Assoc.; U.C.L.A., BA, '52; b. Buffalo, N.Y., 1930; p. Harold and Ruth Straight Mock.

MOCK, LAURIE CLAR, Free-lance Actress, theatre, motion pics. and TV, '62; SAG, AFTRA, AEA, Assn. for Rsch. and Enlightenment (Virginia Beach, Va.), b. Orange, Cal.; p. Sanford and Flora Clar Mock.

MODE, RUTH ROSENTHALER, Dir. of PR, Ted Menderson Company, 1077 Celestial St., Cinn., Oh. 45202, '59–; Baer, Kemble & Spicer; Frederic W. Ziv, Inc.; Theta Sigma Phi (Past Pres.), PRSA (Cinn. Chptr. Past Offcr.); Oh. State Univ., BS (Jnlsm.); b. Cinn., Oh.; p. Louis and Amelia Levy Rosenthaler; h. Arthur S. Mode; c. Dr. Arthur S., Robert L.; res: 1106 Egan Hills Dr., Cinn., Oh. 45229.

MODELL, JUDY, AE, National Public Relations Counsel, 60 E. 42nd St., N.Y., N.Y. 10017, '57–; Owner, Judy Modell Designs, '52–'57; NHFL, SAG, Phila. Museum Sch. of Art; b. Phila., Pa.; p. Paul and Sara Bellack Wintrob; res: 235 E. 73rd St., N.Y., N.Y. 10021.

MOELLER, PEARL L., Supvsr. of Special Collections, Museum of Modern Art Library, 11 W. 53rd St., N.Y., N.Y. 10019, '69–; Supvsr. of Rights and Reproductions, '59–'69; Supvsr. of Photographic Svcs., '54–'59; Asst. in charge of negatives and slides, '44–'54; Secy., Film Lib., '41–'44; articles in lib. jnls.; assists auths. with art rsch.; Special Libs. Assn. (N.Y. Chptr.); Mount Holyoke Col., BA, '38 (hons. in course); William and Mary Col., BFA, '40.

MOERS, ELLEN, Adjunct Asst. Prof., Barnard College, Columbia University, N.Y., N.Y. 10027, '69–; Lectr., Columbia Univ., Hunter Col.; Auth: "Two Dreisers" (Viking, '69), "The Dandy: Brummell to Beerbohm" (Viking, '60); Lit. Critic articles in N.Y. Times Bk. Rev., Bk. World, Harper's, Am. Scholar, Commentary, N.Y. Rev. of Bks., others; Guggenheim Fellow, '62; Vassar Col., BA, '48 (Phi Beta Kappa); Harvard Univ., MA, '49; Columbia Univ., PhD, '54; h. Martin Mayer; res: 33 East End Ave., N.Y., N.Y. 10028.

MOFFAT, FRANCES AYRES, Soc. Ed., Colmst., San Francisco Chronicle, Fifth and Mission Sts., S.F., Cal. 94103, '63–; Soc. Ed., Colmst., S.F. Examiner, '52–'63; Soc. Stringer, N.Y. Times, '66–; S.F. Wms. Press Club (Founder; Pres.), '64–'68), Stanford Univ., BA (Jnlsm.), '39; b. Sonora, Cal., 1914; p. Robert and Kate O'Neil

Ayres; c. Stephen, Gerie; res: 1227 Montgomery St., S.F., Cal. 94133.

MOFFITT, HELEN REED, Founder, Ed., Publr., Writer's Council, 633 N. Grant, Pocatello, Idaho 83201, '57–; Auth., three bks., short stories and poetry ('50–'62); Gem State Auths. Guild (Founder; 1st Pres.), '58; Auth. of the Yr., '68), Idaho Wtrs. League (Pres.), '54–'55), Nat. Wtrs. Club, N.Y. Wtrs. Guild, Soc. of N. Am. Poets, Mark Twain Soc. (Hon. Mbr.), Who's Who of Am. Wm., Dic. of Intl. Biog.; Albion Normal, Grad., '20; Idaho State Univ., '54–'56; b. Sanford, Colo., 1904; p. Thomas and Elizabeth Miller Reed; h. Dewitt Moffitt; c. Robert L.

MOGAVERO, JANICE NITSCH, Ed., East Aurora Advertiser, 710 Main St., E. Aurora, N.Y. 14052, '64–; Ed., Buffalo Alumnus (distg. cit. for special writing, '63); Asst. Ed.; Free-lance Wtr. for educ. pubns.; Am. Alumni Cncl. aws. in layout and design; State Univ. of Buffalo, BA (Eng.), '58; b. Buffalo, N.Y., 1936; p. Robert A. and Twylah V. Hurd Nitsch; h. Joseph S. Mogavero; c. Michael Joseph; res: 81 Ch. St., E. Aurora, N.Y. 14052.

MOHLER, JUNE FOSTER, Pubcty., Sls. Training Mgr., Fieldcrest Mills Inc., 60 W. 40th St., N.Y., N.Y. 10018, '65–; Asst. to Pres., Financial Planning Corp., '60–'65; VP, Lee Ballard Assocs., '57–'60; Home Svc. Dir., Bendix Home Appliances, '49–'57 (Home Svc. Dir. Aw., '52); Tchr., '46–'47; various orgs.; Univ. of Md., BS, '46; N.Y.U., MA, '68 (hons.); b. Brunswick, Md., 1925; p. John and Edna Deaner Foster; c. R. Douglas Mohler Jr.; res: 60 E. Eighth St., N.Y., N.Y. 10003.

MOHLMAN, MARGARET ANN, Copy Group Head, Needham, Harper & Steers, Inc., 909 Third Ave., N.Y., N.Y. 10022, '65–; Copywtr., Foote, Cone and Belding, '62–'65; Copywtr., Compton Adv., '57–'62; Sweet Briar Col., BA; b. Lafayette, Ind.; res: 333 E. 49th St., N.Y., N.Y.

MOHR, BERTA, Owner-Ed., Berta Mohr Fashion Syndicate, 185 E. 85th St., N.Y., N.Y. 10028, '46–;Synd. Nwsp. Fashion Colmst.; Retail Fashion Adv.; Contrbr., fashion resumes, Funk & Wagnall's New Intl. Yrbk., '54–'66; Speaker, Fifty-third annual conv. of Jewish wms. Orgs. of Md., '69; Fashion Group, OPC; AIMBW-MRA "Lulu" aws. for edtl. excellence, incl. 1st, '59–'62, '67 and 2nd, '63; Special Achiev., '64, '66; First Runner Up, '68; Who's Who of Am. Wm.; Univ. of Mo., BJ (Kappa Tau Alpha); b. Vienna, Austria; p. Josef and Rosa Kramer Mohr; h. (div.); res: 185 E. 85th St., N.Y., N.Y. 10028.

MOHRENWEISER, ROSABELLE BARTELT, News Ed., Kanabec County Times, 101 S. Union St., Mora, Minn. 55051, '59–; Soc. Ed., Proofreader, '56–'59; Tchr.; Minn. Press Wm., b. Pease, Minn., 1912; p. Frank and DeMorna Rathbun Bartelt; h. Milton Mohrenweiser;

c. Mary Ann (Mrs. Don Winge); res: Rte. 3, Mora, Minn. 55051.

MOLAN, DOROTHY LENNON, Ed., Nursery Publications, American Baptist Board of Education and Publication, Valley Forge, Pa. 19481, '65–; Assoc. Dir. of Missionary and Stewardship Educ., '63–'65; Assoc. Dir. of Missionary and Stewardship Educ., '63–'65; Special Assigts. Wtr.; Auth: "Land of the Lighthouse" (aw.), and several bks. on Christian educ.; Ed., "American Baptist With a Spanish Accent" (aw.); Dir. of Children's Work, N.J. Baptist Conv., '51–'54; Public Sch. Tchr. (Delaware Township, N.J.), '44–'45, '48–'50; Dir. of Pers., Toccoa Falls (Ga.), '40–'43; Tchr., Christian educ.; Am. Baptist Wm. (Nat. VP); Trinity Col., '32–'35; Toccoa Falls Bible Col., AB, '38; b. Tampa, Fla., 1911; p. Luther and Agnes Hardee Lennon; h. Rev. Horace Molan; c. Elma (Mrs. John Aumick); res: 356 Crossfield Rd., King of Prussia, Pa. 19406.

MOLLOY, ANNE BAKER, Wtr., juvenile bks. and mag. articles; Auth: "The Girl From Two Miles High," "Blanche of the Blueberry Barrens," "Captain Waymouth's Indians," others; Mount Holyoke Col.; b. Boston, Mass., 1907; p. Lawrence and Lila Nichols Baker; h. Paul Molloy; c. John S., Mrs. Eliot F. Porter, Jr.; res: 3 Edward, Portsmouth, N.H. 03801.

MOLONY, MARY MOORE, Mng. Ed., The American Scholar, United Chapters, Phi Beta Kappa, 1811 Que St. N.W., Wash., D.C., '60–; Edtl. Cnslt., various auths., publrs., '51–; Asst. to Dir., Comm. for UN Day, '50–'51; Adm. Asst. to Dir., Nat. Planning Assn., '41–'50; Eng. Tchr., '35–'37; Georgetown Univ. Wtrs. Conf., '61–; Adm. Staff Mbr., Bread Loaf Wtrs. Conf., '52– (Fellowship, '52), Co-Dir., Reston Wtrs. Conf., '69; Nat. Assn. of Arts and Ltrs. (Rec. Secy. '69–), Univ. of Ky., AB, '32; MA, '34; b. Versailles, Ky., 1912; p. John and Elizabeth Samuels Nash; h. Charles Molony; res: 314 S. Fairfax St., Alexandria, Va. 22314.

MOLTER, RITA JEAN, Food Ed., The Family Circle, Inc., 488 Madison Ave., N.Y., N.Y. 10022, '65–; Food Copywtr., '60–'65; PR AE, Gen. PR, '56–'60; Product Publicist, The Pillsbury Co., '54–'56; Asst. Bk. Ed., The Meredith Publ. Co., '50–'54; Theta Sigma Phi (N.Y. Chptr. Treas., '63–'65); Ind. Univ., AB, '45–'49.

MONAGHAN, CLAIRE I., Secy. to the Cncl., New York State Council on the Arts, 250 W. 57th St., N.Y., N.Y. 10019, '68–; Exec. Prodr., Riverside Radio WRVR, '62–'67; Asst. Prodr.-Ed., "We Shall Overcome;" Asst. Coordr. Educ. Radio-TV, York (Pa.) City Schs., '60–'62; AWRT; Col. of New Rochelle, BA; b. York, Pa.; p. Charles and Mary McVaugh Monaghan; res: 626 West End Ave., N.Y., N.Y. 10024.

MONAGHAN, LUCILE MERRIFIELD, Adv. Mgr., Fibers Div., Eastman Chemical Products, Inc., 1133 Ave. of the Americas, N.Y., N.Y. 10036, '68–; Copywtr., Asst. Adv. Mgr., '41–; Fashion Copywtr.; Free-lance Wtr.; Collector of Victorian children's bks.; Theta

Sigma Phi; Syracuse Univ., AB, '27; b. Martindale, N.Y., 1906; p. Chester and Matild Nash Merrifield; h. Robert Monaghan (dec.); c. Roberta (Mrs. Patrick M. Yarker), Stephen; res: 211 E. 52nd St., N.Y., N.Y. 10022.

MONAHAN, JANET McWHORTER, Wms. Ed., Sun-Sentinel, Gore Newspapers Co., 2501 N. Fed. Highway, Pompano Beach, Fla. 33061, '68–; Feature Wtr.; Pi Delta Epsilon, Sigma Sigma Sigma; numerous aws. from Fla. Wms. Press Club, '68; Western Mich. Univ.; Fla. Southern Col., BS (Jnlsm.), '65; b. Wash., D.C. 1943; p. Charles A. and Barbara Stead McWhorter; h. Thomas A. res: 2625 N. Andrews Ave., Ft. Lauderdale, Fla. 33311.

MONAHAN, MARIAN, AE, McCann-Erickson, 44 Montgomery, S.F., Cal. 94104, '68–; Bdcst. Media Dir., '63–'68; Stanford Univ., BA (Sociol.), '54.

MONROE, FLORENCE M., Asst. Adm. Dir., WNYE-FM-TV, 112 Tillary St., Bklyn., N.Y. 11201, '67–; TV Supvsr., WNYE-TV, '53–'67; TV Tech., WABD Dumont, '45–'47; Instr., Workshop for Instructional TV, N.Y.U., '61–'65; AWRT (N.Y.C. Chptr. Pres., '63–'64), NAEB, N.Y. State Educ. Radio and TV Assn., Kappa Delta Pi, NATAS ("Emmy," '69, '56); Oh. State Univ. Inst. for Educ. by Radio and TV, '57, '55, '54; N.Y.U., BS, '45 (cum laude); MA, '53; PhD, '67.

MONROE, JOYCE CULBERTSON, Mgt. Asst., Communications Hawaii, Inc., KGU Radio, 605 Kapiolani Blvd., Honolulu, Hi. 96813, '68–; Prog. Dir., WJLB (Detroit, Mich.), '65–'67; VP, Nat. Prog. Dir., Rounsaville Radio Chain, '57–'65; AWRT; Columbia Univ.; Univ. of Hi.; b. Shreveport, La., 1924; p. Jackson and Lillian Jacoby Culbertson; h. (div.); c. Peter; res: 645 Elepaio St., Honolulu, Hi. 98616.

MONTAGUE, RUTH DuBARRY, Artist, Wtr., Lectr. Educator; Nat. Gallery of Art, Met. Museum of Art, Smithsonian Inst., Am. Museum of Natural Hist., Intl. Platform Assn.; Who's Who of Am. Wm., Who's Who in Am. Art, Who's Who in the South and Southwest, Am. Art Dir., Dic. of Intl. Biog.; many intl. art honors; b. Paris, France (Am. citizen); res: c/o Ecole Marson, Chalet deBizy, 4 Rue de la Cote BP 149, 27 Vernon (Eure), France.

MONTGOMERY, CHARLOTTE NICHOLS, Colmst., "Speaker for the House," Good Housekeeping, 959 Eighth Ave., N.Y., N.Y. 10019, '55–; non-fiction wtr.; Cnslt., Speaker; Soc. of Magazine Wtrs., Theta Sigma Phi, AWNY (Adv. Wm. of Yr.), '54); Vassar Col., '27 (Phi Beta Kappa); h. Harry Montgomery; res: 240 Watchung Fork, Westfield, N.J. 07090.

MONTGOMERY, ELIZABETH RIDER, Free-lance Wtr., '40–; Auth., 21 juv. textbks., two plays published; many prods., aws.; nine bks., juv. fiction ('40–'66); 22 bks., juv. non-fiction ('44–'70); numerous stories, articles in children's mags.; Staff Wtr., Scott,

Foresman and Co., '38–'63; Tchr., Wash. and Cal. schs.; Seattle Free-lance Wtrs. (Pres., '55–'56), NLAPW, NPWC, Who's Who of Am. Wm., various others; Western Wash. Col., '24–'25; U.C.L.A., '27–'28; b. Huaras, Peru, S. Am.; p. Charles and Lula Tralle Rider; h. Arthur Julesberg; c. Janet Montgomery Small, Robin A. Montgomery; res: 4801 Beach Dr. S.W., Seattle, Wash. 98116.

MONTGOMERY, GLADYS T., Free-lance govt. repts in sci. field, '62–; McGraw-Hill Wash., D.C., Off. '42–'62: Staff Wtr., '57–'62; Wash. Ed., Electronics, '44–'57; Wash. Corr., '43–'44; Wash. Corr., Nucleonics, '47–'52; Wash. Ed., Textile World, '43–'46; Wash. Staff Wtr., Bus. Week; U.S. Rep., briefing for wm. wtrs., NATO, '58; invited to Mexico by outgoing Pres. Aleman, '52; WNPC (Pres., '57–'58), AAAS, Nat. Assn. Sci. Wtrs., Armed Forces Commtns. and Electronics Assn. (cit. for distinguished svc. as sci. and tech. wtr., '70); Inst. Electrical and Electronic Engineers (Assoc. Mbr.); Wellesley Col., BA; b. Natick, Mass.; p. Charles and Myrtle Cates Taylor; h. Alexander Montgomery; res: 2725 Twenty-ninth St. N.W., Wash., D.C. 20008.

MONTGOMERY, JUDITH JOHNSON, Art. Dir., Doyle Dane Bernbach, 6399 Wilshire Blvd., L.A., Cal. '66–; N.Y. off. '65–'66; AIGA, '67, Belding Aw.; L.A. Adv. Club, L.A. Art Dirs. Club, N.Y. Adv. Club, AWLA, Crtv. Nwsp., '68; Scripps Col., '55–'57; Chovinard Art Inst., BFA, '65; b. Long Beach, Cal., 1938; p. Paul Randel and La Verna Dugas Johnson; h. Donald Montgomery.

MONTGOMERY, LOIS, Wms. Program Dir., WLBK AM-FM, DeKalb Radio Studios, Inc., 711 N. First St., DeKalb, Ill. 60115, '47–; Ill. BPW (Radio Chmn., '55), AWRT; Northern Ill. Univ.; Northwestern Univ.; h. (div.); c. Roger F. Still, Gary M. Still; res: 348 South Third St., DeKalb, Ill. 60115.

MONTGOMERY, PATRICIA HOY HANCOCK, Mgr., Wms. Progs., American Airlines, Inc., 633 Third Ave., N.Y., N.Y. 10017, '60–; Assoc. Ed., House & Garden, '57–'59; Feature Wtr., Home Furnishings Ed., Beauty Ed., Chgo. Daily News, '51–'56; Reptr., News and Feature Wtr., UP; Cnslt., special projects, works prod., '69–; Fashion Group, AWRT, Soc. of Am. Travel Wtrs.; Inst. of Men's and Boy's Wear cit. for outstanding writing, '56; Am. Furniture Mart Dorothy Dawe Aw. for excellence in home furnishings coverage, '54; Univ. of Mo., BJ; Stephens Col., AA; b. Evanston, Ill.; p. Kenneth and Margaret Wood Hoy; c. Diane Hancock; res: 415 E. 52nd St., N.Y., N.Y. 10022.

MONTGOMERY, RUTH SHICK, Auth: "A Gift of Prophecy," "'Flowers at the White House," "Mrs. LBJ," other non-fiction bks.; Synd. Colmst., King Features, '56–'68; Wash. Corr., INS, '56–'57; Wash. Corr. and Colmst., N.Y. Daily News, '44–'56; Reptr: Chgo. Tribune, Detroit News, Detroit Times, Waco (Tex.) News-Tribune; WNPC (Bd. of Governors,

'51–'54; Pres., '49–'50), WHCA, State Dept. Corrs. Assn., Mrs. Roosevelt's Press Conf. Assn. (Pres., '44–'45), Congressional Press Gallery, Theta Sigma Phi (Madison and Cal. Chptrs. Wm. of the Yr., '66–'67), George R. Holmes Aw., '57; Pall Mall Jnlsm. Aw., '47; Indpls. Press Club Frank Page Aw., '57; other aws.; Baylor Univ., DL (Hon.), '56 (Most Outstanding Alumna Aw., '66–'67); Ashland Col., DL (Hon.), '58; b. Sumner, Ill.; p. Ira and Bertha Judy Shick; h. Robert H. Montgomery; res: 1324 E. Bay Shore Dr., Virginia Beach, Va. 23451.

MONTGOMERY, SUZANNE, Assoc. Ed., Compass Publications, Inc. 1117 N. 19th St., Arlington, Va. 22209, '69–; Mng. Ed., Oceanology, Am. Aviation Pubns.; '67–'69; Assoc. Ed., Aerospace Tech. Magazine, '65–'68; Univ. of Ia., BA, '63; Cert. Sch. of Jnlsm.; b. Osceola, Ia., '40; p. L. W. Montgomery; res: 1717 20th St., N.W., Wash., D.C. 20009.

MONTI, MINNIE S., Free-lance Tech. Translator, for Eaton Yale & Towne, Inc., Lubrizol, Basic Incorporated, Goodyear Tire & Rubber Co., Owens-Illinois Rsch. Libr. (Toledo), others, '56–; Visiting Lectr. on bks., Case Western Reserve Univ., '54–'60; Wms. Nat. Bk. Assn. (Cleve. Chptr. Pres., '43–'44), Who's Who of Am. Wm.; h. (dec.); res: 2556 Overlook Rd., Cleve. Heights, Oh. 44106.

MONTOOTH, MARJORIE BINNEY, Wms. Dir., Interviewer, Binney Montooth Show; Free-lance Copywtr., Radio Station WYRM, 1056 Willard Ave., Newington, Conn. 06111, '63–; WEXT (W. Hartford, Conn.), '63; Time Sales, radio; AWRT; Public Svc. aw., Red Cross; Bill Savitt Friendly Town aw., stimulating brotherhood, '67; Yale Sch. of Drama, '40; Radio City Sch. of Radio and Drama; b. Bklyn., N.Y., 1916; p. William C. and Florence Wolmuth Binney; h. Charles Montooth; c. Charles Byron Montooth, IV; res: 167 Moseley Terr., Glastonbury, Conn. 06033.

MONTZ, WANDA JOSEPHINE, Dir. of Cont., KCAU-TV, Seventh and Douglas, Sioux City, Ia. 51101, '69–; Prom. Mgr., WMTV (Madison, Wis.), '54–'69; Asst. Sun. Ed., Portland, (Ore.) Oregonian; Reptr., Boise (Idaho) Statesman; Theatre Ed., Cedar Rapids (Ia.) Gazette; Theta Sigma Phi, Madison Adv. Club, Madison Press Club, Cedar Rapids Wms. Club, Altrusa Intl., Sioux Wms., AWRT; Rhinelander (Wis.) Wtrs. Workshop playwriting aw., '66, poetry aw., '67; State Univ. of Ia.; b. Arlington, Ia.; p. J. J. and Sophia Büchel Montz; res: 3017 Douglas St., Sioux City, Ia. 51104.

MOODREY, DOREEN LORETTA, Commtns. Mgr., Chatham Super Markets, Inc., 2300 E. Ten Mile, Warren, Mich. 48091, '65–; Copywtr., TV Prodr., W. B. Doner Adv. Agcy. (Detroit), '65; Asst. to Crtv. Dir., Soloman-Sayles Adv. Agcy., '64; Copywtr., Crowley's Dept. Store, Grinnell's Music Store, CKLW-TV, '62; Free-lance Adv. Wtr.; commtns. cnslt.; Detroit Press Club, Indsl. Eds. Assn. of Detroit (aw.), Indsl. Eds.

Assn. of Chgo. nat. aw. for Chatham News; Univ. of Detroit, BS (Mktng.); b. Windsor, Can., 1939; p. Michael and Bernadette Cotch Moodrey; res: 17130 Second, Detroit, Mich. 48203.

MOONEY, JEAN MARIE, Dir. of Wms. Svcs., Newspaper Enterprise Association, 1200 W. Third St., Cleve., Oh. 44113, '51–; Wms. Div., '47–'51; Asst. to Exec. VP, Cuyahoga Abstract Title and Trust Co., '39–'47; monograph, "What Women Read," ('61); Seminar Lectr., Am. Press Inst., Columbia Univ., '51–; U.S. Delegate, Asian Am. Wtrs. Conf., East West Ctr. (Honolulu, Hi.), '67; various orgs., aws. and hons.; Cleve. Col. of Western Reserve, '40, '41, '48; b. Cleve. Oh., 1921; p. John and Elsie Longabaugh Mooney; res: 19413 Argyle Oval, Rocky River, Oh. 44116.

MOORE, ALMA CHESNUT, Free-lance Wtr., Ed.; Articles, mag., newsps., and nwsp. synds.; Auth: "How to Clean Everything," "The Friendly Forests," and "The Grasses"; Wms. Ed., Transradio Press, '35–'42; Wms. Ed., Pitt. Press, '29–'30; Edtl. Staff, Am. Forests, '28–'29; Pubcty., Am. Nat. Red Cross, '25–'28; Reptr., Balt. American, '22–'25; Goucher Col., AB, '22; b. Wash., D.C., 1901; p. Victor King and Olive Spohr Chesnut; h. (div.); c. Peter, Anthony, Christopher; res: 5 Rockledge Rd., Hartsdale, N.Y. 10530.

MOORE, BERNICE MILBURN, Asst. for Commty. Programs, The Hogg Foundation for Mental Health, Will C. Hogg Bldg., University of Texas, Austin, Tex. 78712, '55–; Cnslt., '41–'55; Dir., Seminars for Chaplains, U.S.A.F., '56–'64; Advisor to teaching staff, '64–'66; Assoc. Dir., Philanthropy in S.W., '64; Cnslt., Tex. Educ. Agcy., '41–'64; Asst. Dir., Reg. Pfsnl. Projects WPA, '38–'41; Rsch. Asst., Inst. for Rsch. in Social Sci., Univ. of N.C., '34–'37; Dir., Tex. State Child Welfare Study, '33–'34; Nwsp. Reptr., Austin Am.-Statesman, '24–'25; Auth., bks., monographs, pamphlets on family and mental health; cnslt., dir., advisor on many health and social dev. projects, '55–; Theta Sigma Phi (Nat. Headliner Aw., '56; Austin Chptr. Past Pres.), numerous other orgs. and aws., biogs; Univ. of Tex., Grad. Work, '30–'34; Univ. of N.C., PhD, '37; b. San Antonio, Tex., 1904; p. Ted and Carrie Coley Milburn; h. Harry Estill Moore (dec.); res: 1215 W. 22-1/2 St., Austin, Tex. 78705.

MOORE, BONNIE ENOCH, Ed., Rex Hospital, 1311 St. Mary's St., Raleigh, N.C. 27603, '69–; Cnslt., Occidental Life Ins. Co., '69–; Ed., co. pubns., '39–'69; Free-lance Wtr., articles in ins. mags., org. hists.; Lectr.; Southern Cncl. Indsl. Eds. (Secy. and Bd. Mbr., '64), ICIE, Raleigh Adv. Club (Hon. Life Mbr., '68; 1st VP, '55; Secy., '56–'63), Southern Round Table Life Adv. Assn. (nat. aw. for best mag., '40s; reg. aw., best edtl. in indsl. pubn., '60), Pilot Club of Raleigh (past Pres.); greensboro Col., Art Grad., '23; Univ. of N.C.; N.C. State Univ.; b. Greensboro, N.C., 1904; p. William and Louisa Smith Enoch; h. Roger Moore; res: 1512 Greenwood Dr., Raleigh, N.C. 27608.

MOORE, CHARLOTTE FISHER, Conslt., pageants, festivals, special events; Ed., The DownTowner, '38–'67; Asst. Mgr., DownTown Assn. of S.F., '40–'67; Founder, 49-Mile Scenic Dr. ('38), Christmas Eve in S.F. ('46); Promotor, DownTown Wk. in S.F. ('58, '59, '60), Nat. Aw. of Merit, '58–'59); Conslt., Miss S.F. World Beauty Pageant, '68–; numerous other civic proms. in S.F. area; b. S.F., Cal.; p. Paul and Barbara Segers Fisher; h. Edwin Webb Moore (dec.); res: 2280 Pacific Ave., S.F., Cal. 94115.

MOORE, CHRISTINE WALHOOD, Ed., Publr., The McClusky Gazette, 303 Main St., McClusky, N.D. 58463, '56–; Assoc. Ed., Bus. Mgr., '48–'56; Instr., McClusky HS, '39–'49; Auth., four travel bks.; Col. Educ. Club (Pres., '26–'27), NEA, Nat. Nwsp. Assn. (aws., '56–'58), NPWC, N.D. Press Wm. (numerous aws., '57–'69), N.D. Press Assn. (aw., '69), McClusky Boosters Club, N.D. Hist. Soc., Gtr. N.D. Assn., Intl. Platform Assn.; Who's Who in North Dakota; Who's Who of Am. Wm.; N.D. State Univ., BS, '27; p. Ole and Christine Aarestad Walhood; h. Raymond Patrick Moore (dec.); c. Thomas E.; res: 302 W. Second St., McClusky, N.D. 58563.

MOORE, CONSTANCE GOODRIDGE, Dir. Wms. Svcs., VP, Doherty Assocs., Inc., 551 Fifth Ave., N.Y., N.Y. 10017, '63–; Pubcty. Dir., Quaker Lace and N. Am. Lace; NHFL; h. James B. Moore, Jr.

MOORE, CULLEN SULLIVAN, Wtr., features, Epoque, Ltd. (London, England); Colmst., Mobile Press Register, New Orleans Times Picayune, Los Angeles Herald Examiner, more than 50 nwsps. in U.S.; Series, "Truth About Men," pub. '66–'69; OPC, NWC of N.Y., Am. Fedn. of Astrologers; Greenville Wms. Col., Furman Univ., Anderson Jr. Col.; b. Anderson, S.C.; p. G. Cullen and Frances Lanius Sullivan; h. Wickliffe Moore; res: 775 Park Ave., N.Y., N.Y. 10021.

MOORE, DEANIE FRAZIER, Free-lance Talent, 3908 Deborah Dr., Monroe, La. 71201; Tchr., Rsch. Asst., '57–'68; Wms. Ed., WHBC Radio (Canton, Oh.); Navy Lt., Off. of PR (Wash., D.C.); News Ed., Wms. Ed., KWKH-KTBS; AWRT, Phi Beta, Alpha Kappa Delta, Am. Sociol. Assn., Navy League, AAUW; L.A. Cncl. on Family Recs., Mayor's Comm. on Urban Renewal, Jr. League; Gen. Fed. of Wms. Clubs aw., '65; Jaycee Cert. of Appreciation, '63–'66; Dic. of Intl. Biog.; La. State Univ., BA, '42 (Who's Who in Am. Cols. and Univs.; Mortar Bd.); Univ. of Akron, MA (Commtns., Sociol.-Psych.), '69; b. Dallas, Tex., 1921; p. Clifton L. and Marie Montgomery Frazier; h. Dan M. Moore; c. Milton, Marguerite Marie Bauer, John Montgomery Bauer.

MOORE, ELIZABETH DuPREE, Dir., Oconee Regional Library, 801 Bellevue Ave., Dublin, Ga. 31021, '57–; Ref. Librn., Middle Ga. Reg. Lib. (Macon); tchr., public schs., Gordon and Twin City; ALA, Southeastern Lib. Assn., Ga. Lib. Assn. (VP, '63–'64;

Secy., Public Col. for Wm., BS (Educ.), '42; Emory Univ., MLibranship., '53; b. Wilkinson County, Ga., 1922; p. John and Effie Douglas DuPree, Jr.; c. Du-Pree, George, Melanie; res: 207 Coney St., Dublin, Ga. 31021.

MOORE, ELIZABETH POWER, PR AE, Asst. to Pres., Bauerlein Inc., 1026 Hibernia Building, N.O., La. 70112; Adm. Asst. to VP, '57–'60; Press Club of N.O., PRSA (N.O. Chptr. VP, '67–'69; Secy., '67–'68; Treas. '66–'67); St. Mary's Dominican Col. Gold Medal Comm., '67; Who's Who of Am. Wm.; b. Boston, Mass.; p. Joseph and Ann McDonough Power; h. Paul Moore; c. Mark P., Ann Elizabeth; res: 5432 Gen. Diaz, N.O., La. 70124.

MOORE, ETHEL MAE, Mdsng. Coordr., Amalgamated Publishers Inc., 310 Madison Ave., N.Y., N.Y. 10017, '65–; copy dept., Wm. N. Scheer Adv. Agcy. (Newark, N.J.), '57–'65; Adv. Mgr., N.J. Afro Am. Nwspr., '48–'55; Cl.-Sls., '42–'48; PR Cnslt., own firm; Auth., "Ethel's Cookery," synd. food colm.; Newark Bus. Col. (Bus. Adm.); Rutgers Univ. (Adv., Mktng. courses); b. Vaux Hall, N.J., 1917; p. Martin and Laura Monger Marshall; c. Chester, Leroy; res: 89 Spruce St., Newark, N.J. 07108.

MOORE, GLENDA SUE, VP, Lennen & Newell, Inc., Wyatt & Williams Div., 1900 LTV Tower, Dallas, Tex. 75201, '61–; Texas Instruments, '60–'61; Reptr., Dallas Morning News, '59–'60; Dallas Adv. League; N. Tex. State Univ., BA, '59; b. Roscoe, Tex., 1937; p. Weldon and Oda Roberts Moore; res: 3451 Chaparral Dr., Dallas, Tex. 75234.

MOORE, HELEN JEAN, Dir. of Libs., Prof. of Eng., Point Park College, 201 Wood St., Pitt., Pa. 15222, '62–; Ref. Asst., Univ. of Pitt. Lib., '55–'62; Eng. Instr., '41–'45; Modern Lang. Assn., ALA, Pa. Lib. Assn.; Univ. of Pa., BA, '37; Univ. of Pitt., MA, '41; PhD, '52; Carnegie Lib. Sch., MS (Lib. Sci.), '58; b. Falls Creek, Pa.; p. William and Olive Zeigler Moore; h. Robert J. Asquine (div.); c. Helen-Jean Asquine; res: 228 Parkman Ave., Pitt., Pa. 15213.

MOORE, M. JOSEPHINE, Librn., Longview Public Library, 1600 Louisiana, Longview, Wash., 98632, '64–; County Librn., Plumas County Free Lib. (Quincy, Cal.), '61–'64, Field Librn., U.S. Army Special Svcs. (Europe), '59–'61; Br. Supvsr., Adm. Asst., Yakima (Wash.) Valley Reg. Lib., '54–'59; Br. Librn.; Multnomah County Lib. (Portland, Ore.), '52–'54; Wash. Lib. Assn. (Exec. Dir.; Bd. Mbr., '64–'66), Nat. Lib. Week for Wash., '66; ALA, Pacific N.W. Lib. Assn.; Soroptimist (Longview Club Pres., '65–'67), Delta Kappa Gamma, League of Wm. Voters, AAUW, Lower Columbia Commty. Action Cncl. (Chmn., '67–'69); Western Col. for Wm., AB, '49; Univ. of Ill., MS (Lib. Sci.), '52; b. Portland, Ore., 1928; p. Jesse and Madge Guthrie Moore; res: 1806 Florida, Longview, Wash. 98632.

MOORE, MARGARET STEPHENSON, Polit. and Feature Wtr., The Indianapolis News, 307 N. Pennsylvania St., Indpls., Ind. 46206, '68–; Asst. PR Dir., '53–'68; Copy Ed., '52–'53; Head, Jnlsm. Dept., Franklin Col., '42–'52; Colmst., Indpls. Star, '38–'43; Ed., Mooresville Times, '33–'38; Reptr., Logansport Press, '31–'33; Ed., La. State Univ. Reveille, '30–'31; Co-auth., "The Law Breakers," '68; Free-lance Wtr., polit. articles; Contrbr., numerous pubns.; BPW, Altrusa, Theta Sigma Phi (Nat. Secy., '47–'53; La. State Univ. Chptr. Pres., '30; Indpls. Chptr. Frances Wright aw., '46; Wm. of the Yr., '68; Nat. Headliner aw., '68); Wms. Press Club of Ind. (Pres., '49–'51; Kate Milner Rabb aw.,'67); NPWC (VP, '40–'41); Indpls. C. of C. Wm. of the Yr., '67; Nat. Cncl. of Wm. "Wm. of Conscience" aw., '68; Nat. Recognition aw., Freedoms Fndn., '69; many other aws.; active in numerous civic groups; La. State Univ., BA (Jnlsm.), '30; Grad. Work, Univ. of Mich.; b. Plainfield, Ind., 1909; p. Robert and Virginia Rupe Stephenson; h. Everett L. Moore (dec.); c. Sue Ellen (Mrs. M. Stanton Evans), Jo Ann (Mrs. David Long); res: 4429 Brookline Place, Indpls., Ind. 46220.

MOORE, MARIANNE CRAIG, Auth., 15 bks. of poetry, '21–, incl: "Tell Me, Tell Me," '66, "The Fables of La Fontaine (transl.), '54, "Collected Poems," '51; Contrbr., mag. poetry and criticism; Visiting Lectr., Bryn Mawr Col., '53; Ed., The Dial, '25–'29; Asst. N.Y. Public Lib., '21–'25; Tchr., '11–'15; Am. Acad. Arts and Ltrs., Nat. Inst. Arts and Ltrs. (Aw., '46; Gold Medal, '53), Dial Aw., '24, Helen Haire Levinson Prize, '33, Ernest Hartstock Memorial Prize, '35, Shelley Memorial Aw., '40; Contemporary Poetry's Patrons' Prize, '44; Harriet Monroe Poetry Aw., '44; Guggenheim Memorial Fellowship, '45; Bollingen Prize, '51; Nat. Bk. Aws., '51, '68; Pulitzer Poetry Prize, '51; M. Carey Thomas Aw., '53; Poetry Soc. of Am. Gold Medal, '60, '67; Brandeis Univ. poetry aw., '63; Acad. of Am. Poets Fellowship, '65; Bryn Mawr, AB, '09; Carlisle Comml. Col., '10; Hon. Litt D: Wilson Col., '49; Mt. Holyoke Co., '50; Univ. of Rochester, '51; Dickinson Col., '52; L.I. Univ., '53; Douglass Col., '55; Rutgers Univ., '55; Wash. Univ., '67; N.Y.U., '67; Hon. LHD: Smith Col., '50, Pratt Inst., '58; b. St. Louis, Mo., 1887; p. John and Mary Warner Moore; res: 35 W. Ninth St., N.Y., N.Y. 10011.

MOORE, REBECCA DAVIS, PR Rep., Southern Airways, Inc., Atlanta Airport, Atlanta, Ga. 30320, '67–; Tour Mgr., Maid of Cotton, Nat. Cotton Cncl. of Am. (Memphis, Tenn.), '67; Tour Secy., '66; AWRT, Atlanta Wms. C. of C.; Southwestern at Memphis, BA, '65; b. Rolling Fork, Miss., 1942; p. Dudley and Rebecca Davis Moore; res: 3499 Paces Ferry Rd. N.W., Atlanta, Ga. 30327.

MOORE, ROBERTA J., Chmn., Journalism Department, Walla Walla College, College Place, Wash. 99324, '62–; Assoc. Prof. of Eng., '57–'62; Head, Eng. Dept., Canadian Union Col. (Alberta), '52–'57; Head, Eng. Dept., Union Springs Acad. (N.Y,), '51–'52; Dean of Wm., Campion Acad. (Loveland, Colo.), '48–'49; Assn. for Educ. in Jnlsm., Modern Lang. Assn., AAUW;

Atlantic Union Col., BA, '48 (high hons.); Boston Univ., MA, '53; Syracuse Univ., PhD, '68; b. Wallingford, Vt., 1920; p. John and Edna Williams Moore; res: Box 333, College Place, Wash. 99324.

MOORE, RUTH E., Reptr., Chicago Sun-Times, 400 N. Wabash, Chgo., Ill. 60611, '50–; Auth., bks. on evolution, natural scis. (five Knopf; one Time-Life); Wms. Bd., Univ. of Chgo. Bd., Ill. Children's Home and Aid Soc. Bd., The Thresholds; Wash. Univ., AB; MA (Trustee); Alumni Cit., '66); McMurray Col., D Litt., '55; b. St. Louis, Mo.; p. William and Ethel Sledd Moore; h. Raymond W. Garbe; res: 860 Lake Shore Dr., Chgo., Ill. 60611.

MOOREHEAD, AGNES, Actress, TV, radio, motion pics., stage; Endora, "Bewitched," ABC-TV (nominated five times, TV Acad. "Emmy"); TV appearances incl: "Studio One," "Playhouse 90," "Wild, Wild West" (TV Acad. "Emmy"); motion pics., Incl: "Citizen Kane" ('41), "The Magnificent Ambersons" (N.Y. Critics aw., Best Actress; Acad. Aw. nomination), "All That Heaven Allows" "Hugh, Hush Sweet Charlotte," "Johnny Belinda," "Magnificent Obsession," "Mrs. Parkington" (Acad. Aw. nominations, all five); many other films; radio appearances, '29–; one-wm. prog., "That Fabulous Redhead," U.S.A., Europe, Middle East; Lectr.; toured U.S. with shows incl. "The Rivalry"; concert recital, "Don Juan in Hell," U.S., Europe (also a rec.); albums incl: "Psalms of David," "Nancy Hanks," "Sorry-Wrong Number"; Drama Tchr., private and Univ. of Southern Cal.; Founder, Charter Mbr., Mercury Theater Players; Muskingum Col., BA; Univ. of Wis., MA (Eng., Public Speaking); PhD; Am. Acad. of Dramatic Arts; three Hon. Doctorates; b. Boston, Mass.; p. Rev. and Mrs. John H. Moorehead; res: 1023 N. Roxbury Dr., Beverly Hills, Cal. 90210.

MORAN, IRENE E., Dir. of PR, Brooklyn Public Library, Grand Army Plaza, Bklyn., N.Y. 11238, '65–; PR Asst., '62–'65; Exec. Asst., Maurice Feldman PR (N.Y.C.), '59–'62; Asst. PR Dir., WOR Radio-TV, '55–'59; Pubcty. Dept., Du Mont TV, '51–'55; Edtl. Asst., The American Banker, '44–'51; PRSA, PR Offcrs. Soc. of N.Y., LPRC, ALA, N.Y. Lib. Assn.; N.Y.U., BS (Jnlsm.), '51; b. Jersey City, N.J., 1927; p. Walter and Mary Watson Moran; res: 2770-A Kennedy Blvd., Jersey City, N.J. 07306.

MORAN, RILLA ROBERTSON, Pres., Moran Associates, Inc., 2004 20th Ave., S., Nashville, Tenn. 37212, '67–; Free-lance PR, 15 yrs.; Wtr., nwsps., local radio, TV progs.; Polit. Cnslt., senators, congressmen, gubernatorial candidates; active in various civic groups; BPW (Nashville Pres., '58–'59), Radio and TV Cncl. of Middle Tenn. (Pres., '58–'60), PRSA, AWRT, Credit Wm. of Nashville (Pres., '56), Citizens for TVA (first wm. named to bd. dirs.); Tenn. Rep., Southern Assembly on Higher Educ. sponsored by Columbia and Tulane Univs., '55; George Peabody Col. for Tchrs.; Univ. of Tenn.; Univ. of Ind.; b. Smith County, Tenn., 1924; p. Ward and Lydia Shoemake Robertson.

MORAN, SHEILA KATHLEEN, Sports Wtr., Associated Press, 50 Rockefeller Plaza, N.Y., N.Y. 10020, '69–; Bdcst. News Wtr., '68–'69; Newsman, UPI Wash. Bur., '66–'67; State House Reptr., Newark (N.J.) Star Ledger, '64–'66; Fashion Ed., The Sun Sentinel (Pompano Beach, Fla.), '62–'64; Wire Svc. Guild, N.Y. Nwsp. Wms. Club; 3rd Prize feature writing category for exclusive interview with Beatles, Fla. AP Mng. Eds.; Manhattanville Col., BA (Hist.); b. Norwalk, Conn.; res: 29 W. 76th St., N.Y., N.Y. 10023.

MORASCO, LOIS M., Asst. to Dir., PR, Governmental Rels., Reading Company, Room 405, Reading Terminal, Phila., Pa. 19107, '68–; Ed., Reading Railroad News, '67–; Mgr., PR, Adv., Southeastern Pa. Transportation Authority, '65–'67; Free-lance Wtr., '63–'64; Asst. Mng. ed., Germantown Courier, N.W. Suburban Adv., '58–'61; Assn. of Railroad Eds. (Exec. Bd., '69), Am. Mktng. Assn., Assn. of Railroad Adv. Mgrs., Am. Cncl. of Railroad Wm.; Pa. Nwsp. Publrs. Assn. aws., '60, '61; Temple Univ.; b. Phila., Pa., 1933; p. Louis and Jean Cerino Morasco; res: 8133 Ardleigh St., Phila., Pa. 19118.

MORASKO, RAMONA (NONI) BAUDIEN, Bdcstr., KXGN TV and Radio, Box 58, Glendive, Mont. 59330, '68–; Prodr., "Noni's Early Morning Roundup," Radio; "Eastern Montana Today," TV; Salesman, Copywtr., Newscaster; ZONTA (Glendive Club Pres., '64–'66; Dist. Public Affairs Chmn.; Chmn., Dist. 12 Annual Conf., '66), State O Mok See (Chmn., '66), AWRT; NFPW, Mont. Press Wm.; local civic, political activities; b. Mandan, N.D., 1928; p. Mike and Elizabeth Schoonover Baudien; h. Frank J. Morasko; c. Vicki Lee (Mrs. Mike Clark), Kerry Lynn Flaten, Dale Flaten, Mike Flaten.

MORCH, SYS T., AE, The Marschalk Co., Time-Life Bldg., N.Y., N.Y. 10020, '67–; Benton & Bowles, '67; Knox Reeves Adv., '64–'66; Ottoson & Co. (Chgo.), '63–'64; Shimer Col., BA, '63 (cum laude); Harvard, Sorbonne; b. Copenhagen, Denmark; p. E. Trier and Eritta Hansen Morch; res: 51 W. 16th St., N.Y., N.Y. 10011.

MOREAU, LORRAINE MARIE, Prod. Assoc., Dun's Review, Dun & Bradstreet Publications Corp., 466 Lexington Ave., N.Y., N.Y. 10017, '67–; Prod. Asst., '63–'66; The Productioneers (Secy., Treas.); Hartford Sch. of Music, Columbia Univ., N.Y.U.; b. Springfield, Mass., 1927; p. Alfred and Alice Moreau; res: 98-01 67th Ave., Forest Hills, N.Y. 11374.

MOREHEAD, JEANNE BELLEW, Owner, Jeanne Morehead Advertising & Public Relations, 1111 N. Westshore Blvd., Suite 208 D, Tampa, Fla. 33607, '67–; VP, AE, Tampa Adv. Agcy., '64–'67; Prom., Talent, WRAL-TV (Raleigh, N.C.), '58–'63; Press Wtr., ABC-TV (N.Y.C.), '57; Press Wtr., WBKB (Chgo., Ill.), '54–'56; Talent, WTAR-TV (Norfolk, Va.), '52–'54; "Nancy Dixon Show," Young & Rubicam (St. Louis, Mo.), '51; AWRT (Hurricane Chptr. Pres., '67–'68; Mbr. of Yr.

aw., '66–'67), Theta Sigma Phi, Fla. PR Assn. (Dir., '67–'68, '65–'66), Tampa Adv. Club; Univ. of Mo., BJ, '48; b. Des Moines, Ia., 1928; p. Chellis and Ethel Cook Bellew; h. Harry T. Morehead; c. Harry Jr., Julie Jeanne; res: 4707 Leona, Tampa, Fla. 33609.

MORELAND, GUYLA WALLIS, Soc. Ed., Colmst., News Wtr., Photgr., Cairo Evening Citizen, 713 Washington Ave., Cairo, Ill. 62914, '61–; Info. Wtr., Dept. of Info., State of Ill., '60–; Programming, WKRO, '60; Colmst: "Garden Club Gleanings," '58–; "Country Cousin," '48–'58; BPW (Nwsp. Wm. of the Yr., '58), NLAPW (Egypt Br. Pres., '56), Cairo Hist. Assn., Cairo Bus. and Pfsnl. (Pres., '67–'68), Cairo Camera Club (Pres., '58–'59); Governor's aw. as Sesquicentennial Chmn.; Who's Who of Am. Wm.; b. Benton, Ky., 1908; p. Burnett and Annie West Wallis; h. T. Henry Moreland; c. Mrs. Edna Irene Day, Mrs. Mary Virginia Whitis, Wallis Henry, Franklin Edward, Harry Lee; res: 3213 Park Ave., Cairo, Ill. 62914.

MORELLI, ADALINE BIANCA, Dir. of Adv., Sls. Prom., Jantzen Intimate Apparel, 666 Fifth Ave., N.Y., N.Y. 10019, '63–; Adv., Sls. Prom. Dir., Bali Brassiere Co., '60–'63; Adv., Sls. Prom. Dir., Blue Swan, Div. McKay Products, '52–'60, Asst. to Sls. Mgr., '47–'53; Copywtr., Asst. Art Dir., Calkins & Holden, '43–'47; Fashion Group, Underfashion Club; Who's Who of Am. Wm., Who's Who in Adv.; Mercyhurst Col., BA (magna cum laude); b. Parma, Italy; p. Cesare and Amalia Agresti Morelli; res: 715 Park Ave., N.Y., N.Y. 10021.

MORGAN, CYNTHIA GENEVIEVE, Head, Information Service, and Ed., Agri-Record, State Department of Agriculture, 635 Capitol St., N.E., Salem, Ore. 97310, '39–'69; Reptr., Valley News Ed., Ore. Statesman, '28–'39; Secy., State Dept. of Agriculture's Consumer Advisory Comm.; Wtr. of various special articles for farm pubns. serving Ore. area; Theta Sigma Phi (Portland Pfsnl. Chptr. Ore. Wm. of Achiev. aw., '61), Ore. Press Wm. (Pres., '63–'65), ZONTA (Salem Club Pres., '42–'43; Dist. VIII Sec.-Treas., Lt. Gov., Gov., '50–'52), Govs. Comm. on Farm Safety; various press wm. writing aws.; Univ. of Ore., BA, '27; b. Allison, Ia., 1904; p. M. D. and Lola Michael Morgan; res: 1098 "E" St., N.E., Salem, Ore. 97301.

MORGAN, ELIZABETH GREGORY, Pres., Owner, Morgan Research Associates, P.O. Box 66404, Houston, Tex. 77006, '51–; Exec. Reg. Mgr., Daniel Starch, N.Y.C., '42–'51; articles in Journal of Marketing, Houston Magazine, others; Co-Chmn., Seminar on Bus. Rsch., '56; Am. Mktng. Assn. (Houston Chptr. Pres., '56–'57); Nat. Assn. of Home Builders Certs.; Speaker; Phi Sigma Alpha (Hon.); active in commty. orgs.; Hackley Col.; b. Cadillac, Mich., 1916; p. Harry and Edna Gregory Morgan.

MORGAN, GWEN, Fgn. Corr., Chicago Tribune, 85 Fleet St., London, England, '46–; Staff Corr., UP (Wash., D.C.), '43–'46; UP (Chgo., Ill.), '42–'43; Omaha (Neb.) World-Herald, '41; Kan. City (Kan.) Kan., '39–'40; WNPC, Edward S. Beck Fgn. Corr. aw., '63, '51; Smith Col., BA; b. Chgo., Ill.; p. Edgar and Ethel Yarick Morgan; h. Arthur Veysey; res: 10 Cumberland Terr., Regent's Park, London, England.

MORGAN, IRENE FRANCES, Ed., National Messenger, National Life Insurance Co., National Life Dr., Montpelier, Vt. 05602, '57–; Coordr. of Field Svcs., '56; Ed., training material, '44; Cont. Dept. Head, Talent, WLAW Radio (Lawrence, Mass.); WNAC Radio (Boston); Life Ins. Advs. Assn. (Past Secy.-Treas.); aws. of excellence for mag., '63, '64; McIntosh Bus. Sch., '29; b. Methuen, Mass., 1911; p. Frank and Agnes Mushet Morgan; res: Rd. #1, Spring Hollow Lane, Montpelier, Vt. 05602.

MORGAN, LOUISE, Dir. Wms. Programs WBOS, 275 Tremont St., Boston, Mass. 02215, '65–; Dir. Wms. Programs, WNAC, '42–'65; Speech Faculty: Nat. Park Jr. Col., Leland Powers Sch., Southern Seminary; currently, Chamberlain Sch. of Retailing, Sch. of Fashion Design, Academic Moderne; Fashion Group of Boston (Past Dir.), AWRT (N.E. Past Treas.), NHFL (N.E. Past VP; Aw. of Merit, '62), Easter Seal Soc. Trustee; Lasell Jr. Col., Leland Powers Sch. of Speech; b. Salem, Mass.; p. Jesse and Beda Nord Woolley; res: 11 Park Dr., Boston, Mass. 02215.

MORGAN, SALLY C., Wms. Ed., The Daily Ardmoreite, Box 1328, Ardmore, Okla. 73401, '67; Reptr., '66; Display Designer and Adv. Cnslt., Seng Jewelers (Louisville, Ky.), '65–'66; Kappa Kappa Gamma (Ardmore Alumnae Treas., '68–'69); Trinity Univ., '61–'62; Univ. of Okla., '62–'65; b. Okla. City, Okla., 1944; p. David, Jr., and Dora Willis Morgan.

MORGENSTERN, LUCILE CAMPBELL, Publr.-Ed., Times-Reporter Printing Co., Adams, Wis. 53910, '62–; Proofreader, Brown & Bigelow (St. Paul, Minn.), '45–'62; Society Ed., Bookkeeper (Hector), '35–'43; h. Marvin Morgenstern.

MORGENTHALER, ANNE KONET, Rptr., Evening Outlook, 1540 Third St., Santa Monica, Cal. 90406, '57–; Religion Ed., '60–'67; Suburban Ed., Cleve. Press, '48–'53; Oh. Wms. Nwsp. Assn., '48–'53; Mt. Olive Lutheran Ch.; Community Svc. Aw., Santa Monica Bay Cncl. of Chs., '69; Cal. Nwsp. Publrs. Assn. commty. svc. aw., '68; active in commty. groups; Western Reserve Univ., BA, '47 (Phi Beta Kappa); b. Cleve., Oh., 1924; p. John and Theresa Jakymetz Konet; h. Z. George Morgenthaler; c. Bruce; res: 3409 Club Dr., L.A., Cal. 90064.

MORHAIM-KELRICH, VICTORIA (Victoria Kelrich Reiter), Free-lance Wtr.; PR, Bleeden, Morhaim & Switzer, '57–'58; Auth: "Casebook: Nymphomania" (Dell, '64), "The Girl Who Had Everything" (NAL, '62), "Girl in the Gold Leather Dress" (NAL, '60); stories for mags.; Film Wtr. (ghostwtr. and several pseuds.); b.

Chgo., Ill., 1937; p. Michael and Fira Kaciff Kelrich; h. Arthur P. Reiter.

MORICONI, JANIE McKELVEY, Wms. Ed., Pittsburg Publishing Company, 701 N. Locust, Pittsburg, Kan. 66762, '66–; Reptr., Feature Wtr., Record Publ. Co. (Roswell, N.M.), '64–'66; Pittsburg Wtrs. Club (VP, Program Chmn.); active in civic orgs.; 3rd pl. aw., Large Dailies Category, Kan. Better Nwsp. Contest for Special Pgs., '68; Tex. Technological Col., '61–'63; b. Tyler, Tex., 1943; p. Samuel and Frankie Duke McKelvey; h. John Joseph Moriconi; c. Charlotte Ann, Jana Maria; res: Rte. 1, Box 437, Pittsburg, Kan. 66762.

MORLEY, FRANKIE PETERSON, Owner, Morley Media Svcs., 109 Lexington, Suite 208, San Antonio, Tex. 78205, '69–; Gen. Mgr., Karcher Adv., '68–'69; Media Byr., The Pitluk Group, '66–'68; Bus. Mgr., Westberry/Le Messurier Adv., '64–'66; Cont. Dir., KITE Radio, '62–'64; Traf., KONO Radio, '60–'62; AWRT (Past Secy.), civic, svc. orgs.; b. Devine, Tex., 1934; p. Frank and Bessie Dennis Peterson; h. Robert E. Morley; c. Joel B., Mark E.; res: 1019 Cerro Alto Dr., San Antonio, Tex. 78213.

MORRA, MARION ELEANOR, Dir. of Public Info., New Haven Redevelopment Agency, 157 Church St., New Haven, Conn. 06510, '65–; Mayor Lee's Campaign Staff, '65, '67; Adv. Supvsr., maj. media, Southern New Eng. Telephone Co.; Ed., Employee and External Magazines; Hamden's Commty. Ambassador to Mexico, Expt. in Intl. Living; New Haven Col., AA (hons.); b. Hamden, Conn.; p. Italo and Eleanor Tirone Morra; res: 22 James St., Hamden, Conn. 06518.

MORRIS, ANN ZADORKA, Art Dir., NR Advertising Inc., 1666 Newbridge Rd., N. Bellmore, N.Y. 11710, '68–; Staff, '60–'62; Sadowsky Assocs. (Hicksville), '64–'68; Independent Art Soc. (Acting Treas.); exhbns. at outdoor shows, galleries; Pratt Inst. (Adv. Design), '44–'47; Traphagen Sch. of Design (Illus.) '66–'69; b. Hicksville, N.Y., 1926; p. Alexander and Justyna Bordiuk Zadorka; h. George Morris; c. Georgeann; res: 85 Duffy Aven., Hicksville, L.I., N.Y. 11801.

MORRIS, EFFIE LEE, Coordr., Children's Svcs., San Francisco Public Library, Civic Ctr., S.F., Cal. 94102, '63–; Children's Specialist, Lib. for the Blind, N.Y. Public Lib., '58–'63; Children's Librn., '55–'58; Children's Librn., Cleve. Public Lib., '46–'55; Instr., Sch. of Lib. Sci., Atlanta Univ. (Ga.); Special Lectr., Western Reserve Univ. Sch. of Lib. Sci. (Cleve., Oh.), '53–'55; Field Work Supvsr., '49–'55; Lectr., Sch. of Educ., Univ. of S.F., '66–'68; articles, pfsnl. jnls.; various orgs., aws.; Univ. of Chgo., '38–'41, Case-Western Reserve Univ., BA, '45; Sch. of Lib. Sci., BS (Lib. Sci.), '46; MS (Lib. Sci.), '56; Richmond, Va.; p. William and Erma Caskie Morris; res: 100 Terra Vista Ave., Apt. 3, S.F., Cal. 94115.

MORRIS, ELIZABETH LIPPITT, PR Asst., New York State Historical Association, Fenimore House, Cooperstown, N.Y. 13326, '60–; Secy., '55–'60; Sls. Prom., NBC, '40–'43; PR Lectr., Cooperstown Grad. Sch.; N.Y. Folklore Soc. (Treas.), Central N.Y. Commty. Arts Cncl. (Bd. Mbr.), AWRT (Capitol Dis. Chptr. Pres., '68–); Who's Who of Am. Wm.; Duke Univ., '33–'35; b. Cooperstown, N.Y., 1915; p. Ceylon K. and Florence R. Phillips Lippitt; h. Robert E. Morris; c. Michael Lippitt, Robert Ricks, Stephen Sloat; res: 87 Chestnut St., Cooperstown, N.Y. 13326.

MORRIS, GAY ANNE GREENHALGH, Fashion Ed., Brides Magazine, Conde Nast, 420 Lexington Ave., N.Y., N.Y. 10017, '68–; Asst. Byr., Lord & Taylor, '62–'63; Skidmore Col., BA, '62; b. Bridgeport, Conn., 1940; p. Milton and Ruth Wuttina Greenhalgh; h. Jonathan Morris; res: 229 E. 79th St., N.Y., N.Y. 10021.

MORRIS, HELEN ISABEL, Asst. Mgr. of Corp. Rels., PR Dept., Union Carbide Corporation, 270 Park Ave., N.Y., N.Y. 10017, '69–; Mgr., Bus. and Fin. Pubns., '68–'69; Mgr., Stockholder Rels., '67–'68; Sr. Copywtr., '63–'67; Copy Chief, '61–'63; Asst. to Dept. Mgrs., '55–'61; Rschr., '37–'39, Edtl. Asst., Ed., '39–'55; Fin. Rels. Soc., Chemical PR Soc., AAUW; Rutgers Univ., BL (Jnlsm.), '37; b. Paterson, N.J.; p. Walter Scott and Isabel Robertson Morris; res: 779 11th Ave., Paterson, N.J. 07514.

MORRIS, JEAN AARON, Bdcstr., WINQ Radio, P.O. Box 1010, Tampa, Fla. 33601, '68–; Sls. Mgr., WALT, '66–'68; Bdcstr., Prodr., Sls., WFLA Radio-TV, '57–'65; Tchr., Cnslt., Patricia Stevens Career Col., '69–; Lectr., civic clubs; AWRT (Fla. Chptr. Charter Mbr.; Pres., '65–'66; VP, '64–'65); Fla. Wm. of Distinction; Who's Who of Am. Wm.; Ten Best Dressed Career Wm., '67; Jaycee Civic aw., '64; Tampa Univ., BS, '59; Univ. of S. Fla., MA, '69; b. Athens, Ga., 1929; p. Ralph and Ruth Llewallyn Aaron; h. Joe Morris; c. Susan, Terry, Mrs. Karen Matches; res: 9323 Forest Hills Dr., Tampa, Fla. 33612.

MORRIS, MARGARET SINCLAIR, Head Librn., Galesburg Public Library, 40 E. Simmons St., Galesburg, Ill. 61401, '63–; Cataloger, '46–'62; Circ. Asst., '44–'45; ALA, Ill. Lib. Assn. PEO, Pi Beta Phi, Altrusa; Frances Shimer Col., '25–'27; Knox Col., BS, '29; b. Pontiac, Ill., 1908; p. Robert and Maude Thompson Sinclair; h. Warren Morris; c. Ann (Mrs. Allan L. Harshbarger); res: 170 W. North St., Galesburg, Ill. 61401.

MORRIS, MITZI, Owner-Dir., Mitzi Morris Agency, 527 Madison Ave., N.Y., N.Y. 10022, '68–; Partner, Principal, Placement Assocs., '67–'68; Art Dept. Mgr., Jerry Fields Assocs., '68–'69; Artists Rep., '57–'59; Art Byr. and Art Secy., Hicks and Greist, '56–'57; Lectr; Wtr., articles on adv. art, design educ.; AIGA, AWNY, Type Dirs., Club, Intl. Ctr. for Typographic Arts; Art Students League, '42–'46; Hans Hoffman Sch. of Art, '46–'47; New Sch. for Social Rsch., '45–'47; b. N.Y.C.; p. Morris and Freda Frajer Fox.

MORRIS, NELL, Mgr., Consumer Svc., Frito-Lay, Inc., P.O. Box 35034, Dallas, Tex. 75235, '50–; formerly Assoc. Prof., Chief Dietitian, Tex. Wms. Univ.; Tex. Dietetic Assn. (twice Pres.), N. Tex. Home Econsts. in Bus. (past Chmn.), Inst. of Food Technologists (past Pres., Secy., Treas.), Am. Sch. Food Svc. Assn. (Exhibitors Advisory Bd.), Dallas Restaurant Assn. Ladies Aux., Kappa Kappa Iota (Pres., '69; past Treas.), ZONTA (past Treas.), AAUW, AWRT, Grocers Manufacturers of Am.; Tex. Home Econst. of the Yr., '61; Who's Who of Am. Wm.; Who's Who in the South and Southwest; Tex. Wm. of Distinction; Who's Who in Am. Educ.; 2000 Wm. of Achiev.; Dic. of Intl. Biog.; Tex. Wms. Univ., BS, MA; Univ. of Chgo., work toward PhD; b. Hillsboro, Tex.; p. James and Nellie Wright Morris; res: 3131 Maple Ave., The Terrace House, Dallas, Tex. 75201.

MORRIS, W. KATHRYN KIRKHAM, Sunday and Feature Ed., Hobbs Daily News-Sun, 201 N. Thorp, Hobbs, N.M. 88240, '65–; Amarillo News-Globe, '49–'52; News-Jnl. (Clovis, N.M.), '46–'49; Am. Red Cross Field Svc., '43–'46; Okmulgee (Okla.) Times, '29–'41; N.M. Press Wms. Club (Pres., '53–'54) N.M. Press Assn., numerous writing and photo aws. from above and from NFPW and N.M. Med. Assn.; NPWC, Nat. Press Photogrs. Assn., U.S.A.F. hons.; Okmulgee Jr. Col., Northeastern State Col., Tahlequah, Okla.; b. Newark, Tex., 1908; p. Walter and Ode Cravens Kirkham; h. (div.); res: 520 Seco Dr., Hobbs, N.M. 88240.

MORRISON, BARBARA, Actress; movie, TV appearances in U.S., '43–, following Shakespearean repertory career in England; TV shows: "Red Skelton Show," "Here's Lucy," numerous others; movies: "From Here to Eternity," "Airport," others; AEA (Cncl. Mbr.), SAG, AFTRA, Theatre Forty Classical Repertory Co. (Bd. of Dirs.); Ursuline Convent, '24–'26; Royal Acad. of Dramatic Art, '26–'27; b. Weston-Super-Mare, Somerset, England, 1909; p. John and Augusta Palmer Aspinall; res: 8710 Hollywood Hills Rd., L.A., Cal. 90046.

MORRISON, JOY SOUTH, Wms. Ed., Idaho State Journal, 305 S. Arthur, Pocatello, Idaho, 83202, '55–; Reptr., '48–'50; Cont. Dir., KWIK Radio, '53–'55; Jnlsm.-Eng. Tchr., East HS (Salt Lake City, Ut.), '51–'52; Off. Mgr., Uncle Ray Publ. Co. (Madison, Wis.), '47–'48; Theta Sigma Phi; Idaho State Univ., '41–'43; Univ. of Wis., BA (Jnlsm.), '47 (cum laude); b. Montpelier, Idaho, 1924; p. Edward and Ruth Heath South; h. Thomas L. Morrison; c. Michele Ann; res: 1015 E. Elm, Pocatello, Idaho. 83202.

MORRISON, LAURA EMILY, Pres., Morrison-Gottlieb, Inc., 40 E. 49th St., N.Y., N.Y. 10017, '62–; Partner, '47–'62, '38–'43; Exec. Ed., Modern Plastics Magazine, '43–'47; PRSA, Pubcty. Club of N.Y., NHFL, Theta Sigma Phi; Univ. of Mo., AB, '32; Columbia Grad. Sch. of Jnlsm., MS, '34; b. Kan. City, Mo.; p. Lacey and Emma Snow Morrison; h. William H. Gottlieb; c. William P. Gottlieb; res: 7 Woodland Dr., Sands Point, N.Y. 11050.

MORRISON, LOUISE BECK, Dir., Timberland Regional Library, Seventh and Franklin, Olympia, Wash. 98501, '68–; Timberland Lib. Demonstration, '67–'68; S. Puget Sound Reg. Lib., '66–'68; Coordr. of Adult Svcs., Pierce County Lib., Tacoma, '65–'66; PR Librn., '64–'65; Special Svcs. Librn., U.S. Army, Europe, '62–'64; ALA, Pacific Northwest Lib. Assn., Wash. Lib. Assn., AAUW; Univ. of Puget Sound, BA, '61 (Mu Sigma Delta, '60; Myra E. Dupertuis French Lang. aw., '61); Univ. of Wash., ML, '62; b. Melrose, N.M., 1923; p. Lindsay and Blanche Porter Beck; h. DeWitt T. Morrison (div.); c. Mrs. Kurt Farnham; res: Rte. 11, Box 430-B, Olympia, Wash. 98501.

MORRISON, MARGARET CAUDLE, Dir. of Radio-TV Dept., The Piluk Group, 100 Richmond, San Antonio, Tex. 78205, '62–; Copywtr., '51–'62; Theta Sigma Phi (San Antonio Chptr. Pres., '63–'64), AWRT (San Antonio Chptr. Pres., '63), San Antonio Adv. Club (Bd. of Dirs., '68–'69), San Antonio Assn. for the Blind (VP, '60–); Va. Intermont Col., '31–'33; Meredith Col., BA, '35; b. Louisville, Ky., 1915; p. Arthur Ivy and Anne Bright Caudle; h. (div.); c. R. L. Morrison; res: 8401 N. New Braunfels Ave., San Antonio, Tex. 78209.

MORRISON, NAN R., Sr. VP, Dir. of Pubcty., Harold J. Siesel Co., Inc., 845 Third Ave., N.Y., N.Y. 10022; Publicist, Mdse. Mart (Chgo.); Staff Wtr., Carl Byoir Assocs.; Harold J. Siesel Co., '49; AWRT, Nat. Soc. of Interior Designers, NHFL, Am. Inst. of Interior Designers; Univ. of Okla., BS (Jnlsm.); b. Norwalk, Oh.; p. Lee and Irma Modell Morrison; h. A. Mitchell Silverman; res: 510 E. 77th St., N.Y., N.Y. 10021.

MORRISON, NYLEEN NEWTON, Wms. Ed., Gen. Reptr., Concord Daily Monitor, Monitor Publishing Co., 3 N. State St., Concord, N.H. 03301, '47–; Gen. Reptr., '34–'36; poetry published in Humanist, Massachusetts Review, other mags.; Exec. Bds.: Concord Family Svc., Concord Arts Cncl.; Hist. Dist. Commn. (Clerk); Tufts Univ., AB, '33; b. Concord, N.H., 1912; p. Earl and Dr. Ethel Mitchell Newton; h. Robert D. Morrison (dec.); c. Helen (Mrs. Stanton P. Goldstein); res: 50 N. Spring St., Concord, N.H.

MORRISON, VIOLET SYMONS, Pubcty. Dir., Gimbels, Pitt., Pa., '30–'54; Wms. Adv. Club (Pres., '27', Pitt. Adv. Club (Wm. of the Yr., '53), Theta Sigma Phi (First Pres., Pitt. Pfsnl. Chptr.), Fashion Group (First Reg. Dir., '46), ZONTA (Charter Mbr.); Eta Mu Pi (Hon.); Pitt.'s Outstanding Bus. Wm., '35; Syracuse Univ., Pa., 1901; p. Walter and Mary Tamblyn Symons; h. Greyson W. Morrison (dec.); res: 3038 Marshall Rd., Pitt., Pa. 15214.

MORRISSEY, SALLY TUCKER, Wms. Page Ed., Durango Herald, 1275 Main Ave., Durango, Colo. 81301, '64–; RN for many years; active in local med.

groups; St. Joseph Hosp. Sch. of Nursing, '41; b. Sunnyside, Utah, 1924; p. Frank and Ruth Martin Tucker; h. John J. Morrissey, Jr.; c. Cecilia (Mrs. Pat Cugnini), John J., III, Mary (Mrs. George Thompson), Frank; res: 80 Riverview Dr., Durango, Colo. 81301.

MORROW, JOYCE KNOEDLER, VP, Cooper & Beatty, Ltd., 200 Park Ave., N.Y., N.Y. 10017, '70–; Henry Holt & Co.; Copy Chief, Life; Am. Inst. of Graphic Arts, Soc. Typographic Arts, Pa. Breeder's Assn.; Wellesley Col., BA, '38; b. Gloucester City, N.J., 1917; p. Elmer and Carolyn Gentry Knoedler; h. Richard S. Morrow (dec.); res: Goshen Rd., R.D. 2, Sugartown, Pa. 19355.

MORROW, PATRICIA, Actress, 20th Century Fox, 10201 W. Pico St., Beverly Hills, Cal.; TV: Co-Star, "Peyton Place" (ABC, '64–'69); Nat. Youth Chmn., Crippled Children's Soc., '70; San Fernando State Col.; b. L.A., Cal.,1944; p. Robert and Margaret Lynch Morrow; res: 4623 Cartwright Ave., North Hollywood, Cal. 91602.

MORSICATO, YVONNE M. LIPIRA, AE, Chief Copywtr., Finley H. Greene Advertising Agency, 429 Franklin St., Buffalo, N.Y. 14202, '69–; Copywtr., Manhardt Adv., '67–'69; Accountant, local firms, '59–'66; Bryant and Stratton Bus. Inst. (Bus. Adm., Accounting), '59; active in numerous commty. projects; b. Buffalo, N.Y., 1940; p. Vincent and Mary Nicosia Lipira; h. Nelson A. Morsicato; c. Vincent A., Steven N., Andrea M.; res: 3032 George Urban Blvd., Depew, N.Y. 14043.

MORTELL, PAULINE STRAMARA, Fashion Copywtr., Arndt, Preston, Chapin, Lamb & Keen, Inc., 1528 Walnut St., Phila., Pa. 19102, '65–; Gimbels, '58–'64; Lazarus Dept. Store, (Columbus, Oh.), '57–'58; Adv. Mgr., Allen's Dept. Store (Phila.), '53–'57; Adv. Sls., Stephenson Bros., '48–'53; four copy aws., Phila. Club of Adv. Wm. '69 Ad Competition; Pa. State Univ., BA, '47; b. Pottsville, Pa., 1926; p. Samuel and Verna Rovnak Stramara; h. Emmett F. Mortell; res: 347 Hatboro Rd., Ivyland, Pa. 18974.

MORTIMER, CHARLOTTE PFAU, Owner, Publicite, P.O. Box 11153, Palo Alto, Cal. 94306, '63–; PR Cnsl., Deafness Rsch. Fndn., Peninsula Children's Ctr.; Corr., Med. World News (N.Y.C.), '63–'64; Pubcty. AE, Arndt, Preston, Chapin, Lamb & Keen, '61–'63; Copywtr., William Douglas McAdams, '60–'61; Copywtr., Paul Klemtner, '59–'60; Open Heart Surgery Nurse, Columbia Presbyterian Med. Ctr., '57–'60; Pubcty. Club of N.Y., Am. Med. Wtrs. Assn., Columbia-Presbyterian Hosp. Alumnae Assn.; Douglass Col., '52–'54; Columbia Univ., Columbia Presbyterian Med. Ctr., Sch. of Nursing, BS, RN, '57; Columbia Univ.; N.Y.U.; Grad. Work; b. Newton, N.J., 1933; p. Karl and Auguste Otterbach Pfau; h. John A. Mortimer; c. Meredith Elizabeth; res: 700 Kings Mountain Rd., Woodside, Cal. 94062.

MORTON, ELIZABETH, Free-Lance Ed.; Cnslt., Chilton Bks., '59–'64; Trade Bk. Ed., John C. Winston Co., '50–'58; Assoc. Ed., '45–'49; Edtl. Asst., '22–'45; Presbyterian Bd. of Pubn., '14–'22; PR, YWCA, '62–'64; Children's Bk. Cncl. (Past Pres., VP), Phila. Bksellers. Assn. (Hon., '59), WNBA; Pa. SPCA Svc. Aw., '68; Drexel Inst., '14; b. Media, Pa.; p. William and Annie Wray Morton; res: Apt. L-4, 150 W. Evergreen Ave., Phila., Pa. 19118.

MORTON, JEAN, Dev. Coordr., Meharry Medical College, Nashville, Tenn., '68–; PR Cnslt; Panelist, "What Do You Think," "Books in Black Print," WVOL Radio; Asst. to Exec. Secy., PR/Commtns., Met. Nashville Educ. Assn., '67; PR Dir., San Diego (Cal.) Tchrs. Assn. (NEA Pacemaker Aw.) '65–'67; Loan Offcr., Central Savings and Loan Assn. '58–'65; PR and Adv. Dept., First Nat. Trust and Savings Bank, '51–'58; Supvsr., Billing Dept., Howard Nat. Bank (Burlington, Vt.), '46–'51; Mng. Ed., Crowley Ridge Chronicle (Forrest City, Ark.), '45; PRSA, AWRT, League of Wm. Voters, Bus. Press Club, NEA, Am. Press Club, BPW; Univ. of Vt.; U.C.L.A.; b. Oxford, Miss.; h. John H. Morton (div.); c. Melanie; res: 3000 Hillsboro Rd., Nashville, Tenn.

MORTON, LENA BEATRICE, Chmn., Division of Humanities, Head of Department of English, Texas College, Tyler, Tex. 75701, '62–; Prof. of Eng., Southern Univ., '55–'62; Prof. of Eng., Academic Dean, Lane Col., '50–'55; Prof. of Eng., Langston Univ., '48–'50; Public Sch. Tchr., coop. with Univ. of Cinn., '22–'48; Auth: four bks., incl: "My First Sixty Years—Passion for Wisdom" ('65), "Negro Poetry in America" ('25); articles in jnls.; Cnslt. in educ.; Guest Lectr., E. Tex. State Univ.; Intl. Platform Assn., Modern Lang. Assn. of Am., AAUP, Acad. of Am. Poets, Marquis Biog. Lib. Soc. (Advisory Mbr.), Intl. Mark Twain Soc., Intl. Inst. of Arts and Ltrs.; Piper Prof. of '67; Cert. of Aw. for Lit. and Humanitarian Endeavors, '69; Univ. of Cinn., BA, '22; MA, '25; Western Reserve Univ., PhD, '47; Univ. of London, Eng., Cert., '56; Harvard Univ., post-doctoral study, '59; b. Flat Creek, Ky., 1901; p. William and Susie Stewart Morton; res: 3256 Beresford Ave., Cinn., Oh. 45206.

MOSELEY, ABIGAIL STURGES, Bk. Designer, Thomas Y. Crowell Co., 201 Park Ave. S., N.Y., N.Y. 10003, '70–; Bk. Designer, Doubleday & Co., '68–'69; Asst. Art Dir., Progressive Architecture mag., Reinhold Publ. Co., '66–'68; Museum of Modern Art Exhibition, Graphic Design: Spring, '70, Fall, '68; Museum of Primitive Art, Exhibition Design, Winter, '69–'70; Vassar Col., BA, '66; Tufts Univ., Pratt Inst. of Graphic Arts; b. N.Y.C., 1944; p. Hollister and Elizabeth Betz Sturges; h. Ralph Moseley; res: 458 Greenwich St., N.Y., N.Y. 10013.

MOSELEY, ALICE-KAREN LEWIS, VP, Assoc. Crtv. Dir., Grey Advertising Co., 777 Third Ave., N.Y., N.Y., '66–; VP, Assoc. Crtv. Dir., McCann-Erickson, '52–'66; Clio aws., '64; Art Dirs. Club aws., '65, '61–'63; '59;

Copy Club aw., '69; b. Mpls., Minn.; p. Charles and Karen Larsen Lewis; h. Paul Moseley; c. Alexandra Alice, Paul William IV; res: Norfield Woods, Weston, Conn. 06880.

MOSELEY, ELIZABETH ROBARDS, Cnslr., Fayette County Board of Education, 400 Lafayette Pkwy., Lexington, Ky., '51–; Tchr., '45–'51, '39–'42; Sch. Prin. (Versailles, Ky.), '44–'45; Music Supvsr. (Shelbyville, Ky.), '43–'44; Auth., "Davy Crockett—King of the Wild Frontier" ('67); Co-auth., numerous bks.; NLAPW (State Pres., '66–'68; Br. Pres., '64–'66), Am. Pers. and Guidance, NEA, Ky. Educ. Assn.; Kappa Delta Pi ('61), Who's Who of Am. Wm.; Who's Who in the South and Southwest; Univ. of Ky., BS (Music), '39; MA, '42; b. Robards, Ky.; p. Thomas Marshall and Pearl Brooks Robards; h. Cabell L. Moseley; c. Thomas Robards, Wynn Glass; res: 416 Dudley Rd., Lexington, Ky. 40502.

MOSER, RETA CAROL, Tech. Wtr., Northrop Corp., Aircraft Division, 3901 W. Broadway, Hawthorne, Cal., '65–; Publicist, Space Exposition, U.S.A., '64; VP, Sec.-Treas., Rekell Industries, '63; free-lance tech. wtr., '59–'64; Ed.-in-Chief, Galva (Ill.) News, '58; Auth., "Space-Age Acronyms" (Plenum Publishing, '64; updated '69; Library Journal top 100 tech. bks., '64); Theta Sigma Phi (Secy., '57–'58), Sigma Beta Gamma, Angel Flight; Southern Ill., Univ., BS (Jnlsm.), '58; Grad. Schs.: Southern Ill. Univ., U.C.L.A., Univ. of Southern Cal., '58–'59; b. Waterloo, Ia., 1936; p. Merle and Elizabeth Eighmey Moser; res: 1048 Harrison Ave., Venice, Cal. 90291.

MOSESSON, GLORIA RUBIN, Ed. of Bks. for Children and Young Adults, Thomas Nelson and Sons, 250 Park Ave., N.Y., N.Y. 10019, '70–; Ed. of Bks. for Children. Young Adults, Meredith Press, '64–'70; Auth: "Breeding Laboratory Animals" ('68), "Holly Books" ('66); Juv. Ed., Bobbs-Merrill, '61–'63; Textbk. Ed.: Educ. Publ. Corp., '56–'61, Chartwell House, '48–'55; Tech. Ed., Chemical Publ. Co., '47–'48; Chemist, '45–'47; Cnslt. to various publrs.; ALA, Children's Bk. Cncl.; Bklyn. Col., BA, '43 (cum laude); Cornell Univ., MS, '45; b. N.Y.C., 1924; p. Louis and Regina Greenfield Rubin; h. Norman D. Mosesson; c. Eric, Neil, Roger, Carl, Carol; res: 290 West End Ave., N.Y., N.Y. 10023.

MOSHER, MARJORIE E., Circ. Dir., Your New Baby, Parents' Magazine Enterprises, Inc., 52 Vanderbilt Ave., N.Y., N.Y. 10017, '55–; Sls. Prom., Pubcty., Central Feature News; Adv., Circ. Dir., Etude Magazine; Adv. Dir., Quality Premium Co.; Wtr., articles on bus.; AWNY, Adv. Club of N.Y., NHFL; Bucknell Univ.; N.Y.U.; Dale Carnegie Public Speaking Course; b. Glens Falls, N.Y.; p. Hugh and Ethel Conklin Mosher; res: 880 Mountain Ave., Springfield, N.J. 07081.

MOSIER, SUE, M. Dir. of Wms. Programs, Radio Station KFKA, 1025 Ninth St., P.O. Box K, Greeley, Colo. 80631, '49–; Owner, Western Welcome Hospi-

tality Svc., 15 yrs.; Volunteer State Dir., Nat. Fdn. March of Dimes, nine yrs.; AWRT (Secy., '61; Treas., '59), Altrusa (Secy., '60), State Speakers Bur., '51–'54, Toastmistress Intl., Colo. Press Wm. (Pres., '60), other civic and svc. orgs. and aws.; Gainesville Jr. Col., '30; Colo. State Col., '32; b. Portales, N.M., 1910; p. John and Ina McWhirter Wilson; h. George Mosier; c. Margaret Sue (Mrs. Wendell Scott), Mary Jeannette (Mrs. Thomas A. Connell); res: 2439 11th St. #12, Greeley, Colo. 80631.

MOSLEY, JEAN BELL, Auth: "Wide Meadows" (Caxton Printers, Ltd., '60; Family Bookshelf Bk. Club; English Speaking Union Am. Ambassador Bk.), two other bks., short stories, mag. articles, booklets for Know-Your-Bible Prog.; wkly. newsp. col.; Mo. Wtrs. Guild (Pres., '55–'56; Bk. Aw., '53; Best Short Story, '54), Sigma Tau Delta (Hon.), Mag. Wtrs. of Am., Working Press of the Nation; Reader's Digest First Person aws., '64, '67; Flat River Jr. Col., '31–'34; Southeast Mo. State Col., BS (Educ.), '37; b. Elvins, Mo., 1913; p. Wilson and Myrtle Casey Bell; h. Edward Mosley; c. Stephen P.; res: 703 E. Rodney Dr., Cape Girardeau, Mo. 63701.

MOSS, MARILYN, Copy Ed., Federated Publications, Lafayette Journal-Courier, 211 N. Sixth St., Lafayette, Ind. 47901, '66; TV Colmst., '66–'69; Asst. Pubcty. Mgr., TV Guide (Radnor, Pa.), '58–'66; Judge, Atlantic City (N.J.) Press Clubs news competition, '68; Delta Zeta, Theta Sigma Phi, Wms. Press Club of Ind.; Nat. Headliner Aw. for TV colms., '68; Merit Aw. of AAIE-N.Y.U.-Ed Stern & Co. co. pubns. competition, '65; PR Coordr., Delta Zeta; Who's Who of Am. Wm.; Ind. Univ., AB, '54; b. Spencer, Ind.; p. William G. and Marie Million Moss; res: 1001 Calley Dr., Monticello, Ind. 47960.

MOSS, RUTH, Feature Wtr., Chicago Tribune, 435 N. Michigan Ave., Chgo., Ill. 60611, '55–; Gen. Assigt. Reptr., '50–'55; Ed., The Trib, employees' pubn., '47–'50; econ. rsch., '45–'46; booklets: "New Math" ('62), "New Science" ('63), "The Early Readers" ('66); with Lola May, PhD, "New Math For Adults Only" (Harcourt, Brace & World, Inc., '66); Contrbr., Ency. Britannica's Pre-Reader; various aws. and hons.; Northwestern Univ. (Evanston, Ill.), BS, '45 ("with distinction," with hons. in econs., Phi Beta Kappa); b. Dyersburg, Tenn., 1924; p. David W. and Ruth Luscombe Moss; h. John Thomas Buck; c. Mary-Moss, Thomas L.; res: 2655 Sheridan Rd., Evanston, Ill. 60201.

MOTE, ANNIE-CLAIRE IRVINE, AE, Herbert S. Benjamin Associates, Inc., 2736 Florida Blvd., Box 2151, Baton Rouge, La. 70821, '65–; Radio-TV Dir., '58–'65; Bauerlein Adv. (N.O.), '56–'57; Charles A. Rawson Assocs. (Atlanta, Ga.), '55–'56; Baton Rouge Adv. Club (Pete Goldsby Aw.), '69; VP, Bd. Mbr., Pres., '62–'65), AAF (many offs.), '64–; Otis Dodge Aw., '68); Outstanding Young Wm. in U.S., '65; Gamma Alpha Chi Wm. of the Yr. Aw., '68; Fla. State Univ., BA

(Jnlsm.); b. Orlando, Fla., 1931; p. Arthur and Doris Daniels Irvine; h. William Mote; res: 12273 Goodwood Blvd., Baton Rouge, La. 70815.

MOTTIN, LINDA BALLOU, Ed., Campus Pubns., University of Missouri, 8001 Natural Bridge Rd., St. Louis, Mo. 63121, '67–; Adv. Copywtr., St. Louis Globe Democrat, '67; Assoc. Ed., Decorating Retailer, '64–'67; Free-lance edtl., mags., '67–; Theta Sigma Phi, Indsl. Press Assn. of Greater St. Louis; Southern Ill. Univ., BS (Jnlsm.), '64; b. Huron, S.D., 1942; p. Harvey and Virginia Ballou; h. Thomas D. Mottin; res: 440 G Chapel Ridge Dr., Hazelwood, Mo. 63042.

MOTZ, MINNE ROSENBAUM, Asst. Dir., School Library Service, New York City Board of Education, 110 Livingston St., Bklyn., N.Y. 11201, '63–; Supvsr., Sch. Libs., '60–'63; Sch. Librn., '54–'59; WNBA (N.Y. Chptr. VP, '64–'65), ALA-CBC Joint Committee, N.Y. Lib. Cncl.; Bklyn. Col., BA, '36; Columbia Univ., MS (Lib. Sci.), '57; b. N.Y.C.; p. Samuel and Toba Lerner Rosenbaum; h. Lloyd Motz; c. Robin Owen, Julie Ann; res: 815 W. 181st St., N.Y., N.Y. 10033.

MOWER, PAULINE (Pat) GRIFFITH, Dir. of Info., Future Homemakers of America, U.S. Office of Education, Wash., D.C. 20202, '66–; Press Asst. to U.S. Congressman, '63–'65; Dir. of PR, AARP, NRTA, '61–'63; AE, Richards Assocs., '59–'61; Partner, Pat Dee Assocs., '54–'59; Radio-TV Offcr., Army (WAC) CIN-FO, '51–'54; PR Offcr., '42–'46; Dir. Commty. Svc., WHO (Des Moines, Ia.), '50–'51; Asst. Dir. Commty. Svc., '39–'42; Dir. Wms. Activities, NAB, '48–'50; News Commentator, WINX (Wash., D.C.), '46–'48; Asst. Dir. Commty Svc., WLS (Chgo., Ill.), '34–'39; AWRT, ANWC (Secy., '62–'63), WAC Offcrs. Assn.; Intl. Platform Assn., Assn. of U.S. Army; Bronze Star Medal, '45; DePauw Univ., AB, '31; b. Scottsburg, Ind., 1909; p. William and Minnie Carlisle Griffith; h. DeWitt C. Mower (dec.); res: 3736 Military Rd., N.W., Wash., D.C. 20015.

MOYER, CLAIRE INCH, Auth., non-fiction; Tchr., Algonac Community Schools, Gilbert Junior High School, Algonac, Michigan 48001, '68–'70; bks: "Silver Domes" (Big Mountain Press, Denver, '54), "Ke-weenaw" (Swallow Press, Chgo., '65); Tchr., '53–'69; Nat. Educ. Assn., Mich. Educ. Assn., Algonac Educ. Assn.; Wayne State Univ., '24–'25; Univ. of Ut., '47–'50; Univ. of Denver, BA, '53; Univ. of Wash., '56; b. Calumet, Mich., 1905; p. James and Elizabeth Jones Inch; h. Roy Donald Moyer; c. Mrs. John Winterhouse, Jr., Mrs. William Kirk Crane, Mrs. Phillip C. Christner; res: 463 Ballantyne Apts., El Cajon, Cal. 92020.

MOYER, MARIE ANTONIO, Asst. Sls. Dev.; Ed., Currents Magazine, Southern Life Insurance Co., 330 S. Greene St., Greensboro, N.C. 27402, '60–; Life Underwriter Training Cncl.; Carolina Bus. Communicators (Bd. of Dirs.; Past Secy., Secy.-Treas.); b. Albany, N.Y., 1928; h. Joseph Moyer; c. Joseph, Christine, Vicki-Ann; res: 4508 Graham Rd., Greensboro, N.C. 27410.

MUDD, EMILY HARTSHORNE, Auth., bks., papers on marriage, family rels. mental health; Prof. Emeritus, Family Study in Psychiatry, University of Pennsylvania School of Medicine, Stauffer Bldg., Phila. Gen. Hosp., Phila., Pa. 19104; mbr. of many pfsnl. orgs.; Intl. Platform Assn.; Distg. Daughter of Pa., '59; Resolution of Congratulations, Phila. City Cncl., '61; Medaille d'Honneur, Societe d'Encouragement au Progres, Paris, '66; many other pfsnl., civic hons.; Univ. of Pa., MSW, '36; PhD, '50; Hobart and William Smith Col., DSc (Hon.), '58; b. Phila., Pa., 1898; p. Edward and Clementine Rhodes Hartshorne; h. Stuart Mudd; c. Emily (Mrs. James Mitchell), Margaret C., Stuart H., John H.; res: 734 Millbrook Lane, Haverford, Pa. 19041.

MUDD, Sr. JAMES EDWARD, Head Librn., Brescia College, 102 W. Seventh St., Owensboro, Ky. 42301; Ky. Lib. Assn., ALA, Catholic Lib. Assn.; St. Mary of the Woods, AB; Catholic Univ. of Am., BS (Lib. Sci.); b. New Haven, Ky.; p. Edward and Estelle Howard Mudd; res: Brescia Col., Owensboro, Ky.

MUECKE, MADELINE M., Asst. Ed., McGraw Hill, 330 W. 42nd St., N.Y., N.Y. 10036, '68–; Asst. Ed., International Textiles (Amsterdam, Holland), '64–'65; Asst. Ed., Bruce Humphries Publrs. (Boston, Mass.), '63–'64; Theta Sigma Phi; Mount Holyoke Col., AB, '63; Syracuse Univ., MA (Jnlsm.), '67; b. N.Y.C., 1941; p. Berthold and Eleanor Thalmann Muecke Jr.; res: 108 W. 15th St., N.Y., N.Y. 10011.

MUEHL, LOIS BAKER, Auth., juv. fiction, non-fiction; Reading Supvsr., Rhetoric Program, University of Iowa, OAT, Iowa City, Ia. 52240, '64–; bks: "My Name Is _____" (Holiday House, '59; Jr. Lit. Guild), "Worst Room in School" (Holiday House, '61; Parents Bk. Club; N.Y. Times 100 Bks. for Children); Tchr., '58–'68; '41–'42; Adv., Radio, TV Wtr., '43–'45; Oberlin Col., BA (English), '41 (Phi Beta Kappa); Univ. of Ia., MA (English Educ.), '67; b. Oak Park, Ill., 1920; p. Arthur and Mary Hull Baker; h. Siegmar Muehl; c. Erika, Sigrid, Torsten, Brian; res: 430 Crestview Ave., Iowa City, Ia. 52240.

MUELLER, ELIZABETH ANN, Adm. Svcs. Librn., Suburban Library System, 903 W. Burlington Ave., Western Springs, Ill., '69–; Head Librn., La Grange Public Lib., '65–'69; Ref. Librn., J. Walter Thompson, '62–'65; Lib. Adm. of Northern Ill., Ill. Lib. Assn., ALA; AAUW, League of Wm. Voters; Valparaiso Univ., BS (Educ.), '56; Univ. of Chgo., MLS, '64; b. Hinsdale, Ill., 1934; p. William L. and Lillie A. Daiss Mueller; res: 341 S. Spring, LaGrange, Ill. 60525.

MUELLER, ESTHER LOUISE, Wtr.; Tchr., Retired; Tchr., Eng., Jnlsm., Fredericksburg, Tex., '54–'64; Am. Dependants Schs., Germany, '51–'53; Tchr., Jnlsm., Tex. Wms. Univ., '45–'47; Tchr., first grade, Fredericksburg, Tex., 17 yrs.; Wtr., hist. bks. and Tex. folklore; Delta Kappa Gamma, Theta Sigma Phi, Phi Kappa Phi, Gillespie County Hist. Soc.; Esther Mueller

Day proclaimed by Mayor, May 21, '64; Univ. of Tex., BA, '37; BJ, '42; MA, '43; b. Fredericksburg, Tex., 1902; p. William and Emma Wehmeyer Mueller; res: 603 W. Schubert St., Fredericksburg, Tex. 78624.

MUELLER, LUCYANN, Soc. Ed., St. Louis Globe-Democrat, 12th and Delmar Blvds., St. Louis, Mo. 63101, '67–; Feature Wtr., '66–'67; part-time bdcst., KMOX Radio; speaking engagements; Ed., C. V. Mosby Co., publrs., '65; Theta Sigma Phi (Rec. Secy., '67; Ladies of the Press chmnships.), Met. St. Louis Press Club (Bd. of Dirs., 2nd VP), Who's Who in Am. Wm.; Northwestern Univ., BS (Jnlsm.), '65; b. St. Louis, Mo., 1943; p. Arthur and Lucy Scott Mueller; res: 12 Armin Pl., Webster Groves, Mo. 63119.

MUFFOLETTO, ANNA, Free-lance Home Econst. and Wtr., two cookbks. in progress, 444 E. 82nd St., N.Y., N.Y. 10028; Cnslt. to Dorothy Rogers, "The House in My Head"; Wtr., articles; photogr.; comml. dietitian; PR; tchr., 11 yrs.; Lectr., Lehman Col.; Am. Home Econs. Assn.; Univ. of Buffalo, BS, '55; Hunter Col., MA, '62; S.F. State Col., Columbia Univ.; Intl. Fgn. Cooking Schs.; b. Buffalo, N.Y., 1933; p. Charles and Lucia Greco Muffoletto.

MUGNO, MARJORIE JANE, Info. Specialist, Texas Highway Department, 11th and Brazos, Austin, Tex. 78701, '69–; Ed. Highway News, '58– (ICIE Aws. of Achiev., '60, '64; Southwest Conf. of Indsl. Eds. Merit Aw., '65, '64), Asst. Ed., Texas Highways, '67–; Soc. of Austin Indsl. Eds., Theta Sigma Phi, Tex. Fine Arts Assn., Laguna Gloria Art Museum patron; active in various civic groups; Univ. of Tex., BJ, '57; res: 2808 Townes Lane, Austin, Tex. 78703.

MUILENBURG, GRACE METCALF, Asst. Prof. of Tech. Jnlsm. and Asst. Agricultural Ed., Kansas State Univ., Waters Hall, Manhattan, Kan. 66502, '69–; Ed., Tech. Wtr., University-Wide Adm. Univ. of Mo. (Columbia), '66–'69; PR Dir., Kan. Geological Survey (Lawrence, Kan.), '55–'66; Info. Wtr., '47–'55; Engineering Draftsman, N. Am. Aviation, '43–'45; Tchr., Chautauqua County, '39–'41; Cowley County, '33–'37; Auth., "The Kansas Scene" (Kan. Geological Survey, '53); Geological Soc. of Am., Theta Sigma Phi, Kan. Press Wm., Kan. Hist. Soc.; Univ. of Kan., BS (Jnlsm.), '47; Univ. of Mo., MA (Jnlsm.), '70; b. Dexter, Kan., 1913; p. Guy and Lucy Sinclair Metcalf; h. Virgil Muilenburg (dec.); c. George N.; res: 2075 College View, Manhattan, Kan. 66502.

MUIR, HELEN, Non-fiction Auth., "Miami USA" (Henry Holt, '54); Free-lance Mag. Wtr., '44–; Drama Critic, Miami News, '60–'65; Children's Bk. Ed., Miami Herald, '49–'56; Colmst., '41–'42; Wms. Ed., Miami Daily News, '43–'44; Synd. Colmst., Universal Svc., '35–'38; Radio Bdcstr., WIOD, '35; Radio Bdcstr., WQAM, '42; Carl Byoir & Assocs., '34–'35; New York Evening Journal, '33–'34; New York Evening Post, '30–'31; Yonkers Herald Statesman, '29–'30, '31–'33; various orgs., aws.; b. Yonkers, N.Y., 1911; p. Emmet

and Helen Flaherty Lennehan; h. William Whalley Muir; c. William Torbert, Mary (Mrs. Frederick W. Burrell); res: 3855 Stewart Ave., Coconut Grove, Miami, Fla. 33133.

MUIR, JEAN, Auth., bks., mag. articles; Feature Wtr., Oregon Journal (Portland), '40–'45; Auth: "The Smiling Medusa" (Dodd, Mead, '69), The Adventures of Grizzly Adams" (Putnam, '69), two others; MWA, WNBA (Secy., '69–'70), Armed Forces Wtrs. League; Reed Col., Sorbonne; b. Portland, Ore.; p. William and Jane Whalley Muir; res: 1120 Taylor St., S.F., Cal. 94108.

MULAC, MARGARET E., Owner, Recreation Consultant Service, 3141 Scarborough Rd., Cleve. Heights, Oh. 44118, '45–; Supvsr., Girls and Wms. Activities and Playgrounds, Recreation Dept., City of Cleve.; Program Dir., Univ. Settlement; Lectr., recreation, Case-Western Reserve Univ.; Arts and Crafts Dir., The A. M. McGregor Home; Conductor, recreation insts., Special Svcs., U.S. Army, Germany, France, '58; Cnslt., Reg. Planning Commn. of Cleve.; Auth: "The Game Book," "Family Fun," "Leisure-Time for Living and Retirement," many other bks. on recreation; Wms. Nat. Bk. Assn., Cleve. Wms. Physical Educ. and Recreation Assn., Am. Recreation and Parks Assn., Am. Assn. Physical Educ., Health and Recreation Assn., Soc. of Park and Recreation Educs., People to People, active in numerous nature and wildlife groups; Who's Who of Am. Wm.; Who's Who in the Midwest; Western Reserve Univ., BA, '34; MA, '53; Nat. Recreation Sch., Cert., '35; b. Parma, Oh., 1912; p. James and Anna Teska Mulac.

MULANEY, KATHLEEN ELIZABETH, Public Info. Asst., University of San Francisco, 2130 Fulton St., S.F., Cal. 94117, '67–; Prod. Mgr., San Francisco Magazine, '65–'67; Adv. Prod. Coordr., '63–'65; Circ. Mgr., Traveler Magazine, '62–'63; Theta Sigma Phi; Marquette Univ., AB (Jnlsm.), '62 (Who's Who among Students in Am. Cols. and Univs.); Univ. of S.F., Cal. Secondary Teaching Credential, '68; Masters Candidate (Polit. Sci.), '70; b. Milw., Wis., 1940; p. Charles and Elizabeth McLaughlin Mulaney, Sr.; res: 2010 Vallejo St., S.F., Cal. 94123.

MULBERY, E. LENORE DONER, Social and Ch. Ed., Lamar Tri-State Daily News, 310 S. Fifth, P.O. Box 930, Lamar, Colo. 81052; Corr., Pueblo Chieftain and Star Jnl.; Univ. of Colo., BA, BE, '44; b. Denver, Colo., 1923; p. Harold and Annie Sanders Doner; h. Truman Mulbery; c. Ronald, Donald; res: Rte. 2, Box 159, Lamar, Colo. 81052.

MULCAHY, LUCILLE BURNETT, Asst. Acquisitions Librn., Albuquerque Public Library, 423 Central Ave., N.E., Albuquerque, N.M. 87105, '63–; N.M. Bk. Co., '59–'62; Auth: "Magic Fingers," ('58), "Blue Marshmallow Mountains" ('59), "Natoto" ('60), "Fire on Big Lonesome" (ELK Grove Press, '67; N.M. Press Wms. ZIA Aw., '67) and many other children's bks.; NFPW;

N.M. State Univ., '47; b. Albuquerque, N.M., 1918; p. Harry and Grace Lomax Burnett; h. Clemons D. Mulcahy, Jr. (div.); c. Dee Ann Eileen, Burnette Mulcahy Grega.

MULDER, F. JEANETTE, Asst. Secy., Asst. Treas., Beaumont Television Corp., 2955 Interstate 10 E., Beaumont, Tex. 77706, '69–; Adm. Asst., '64–'69; KFDM Radio, '45–; Radio-Bdcst. Pioneers; AWRT (Golden Triangle Chptr. Pres., '67–'68); active in local civic, charitable orgs.; Duquesne Univ., '41–'42; Lamar State Col., special courses, '47–'49; b. Beaumont, Tex., 1924; p. Herbert and Anne Colichia Mulder, Sr.; res: 575 24th St., Beaumont, Tex. 77706.

MULDOON, NANCY DALE, Free-lance Bk. Designer, '55–; Art Dir., Georgeson & Co., N.Y.C., '52–'54; Bk. Designer, Oxford Univ. Press, '50–'52; AIGA; designs in Publishers' Choice Exhibitions, 50 Bks. of Yr., Textbook Shows; R.I. Sch. of Design, BA, '46–'50; b. Melrose, Mass., 1929; p. Irving and Mildred Hubbard Dale; h. Edward Muldoon; c. Marilyn, Kevin, Lauretta, Karen; res: High Ridge Rd., Brookfield Ctr., Conn. 06805.

MULHAUSER, RUTH ELIZABETH, Prof. of Romance Langs., Case Western Reserve University, Cleve., Oh. 44106, '56–; Assoc. Prof., '46–'56; Instr., then Asst. Prof., Hollins Col., '42–'46; Instr., Hiram Col., '41–'42; Instr., Col. of Wooster, '38–'39; Auth., "Sainte-Beuve and Greco-Roman Antiquity"; Ed., "Sainte-Beuve Coliers de Notes Grecques"; Co-auth., two French lang. bks.; Renaissance Soc. of Am., Modern Lang. Assn., AAUW (Founders Fellowship), Medival Soc., Amer. Assoc. of Teachers of French, Palmes Académiques; Oberlin Col., BA, '35 (Phi Beta Kappa); Western Reserve Univ., MA, '37; Radcliffe Col., MA, '40; PhD, '41; b. Cleve., Oh., 1913; p. Frederick and Helen Fletcher Mulhauser.

MULHERN, SANDRA FLORENCE, Prom. Asst., Fitchburg Gas and Electric Light Co., 125 High St., Boston, Mass. 02110, '65–; Lumber Mutual Ins. Co., '64–'65; Employers' Group of Ins. Cos., '60–'63; AAIE (Safety Edtl. Aw., '63, '64), ICIE (Achiev. for Mgt. Aw., '63); Independent Mutual Ins. Agts. Assn. of New England Adv. aw., '65; Nat. Assn. of Mutual Ins. Agts. First Adv. aw., '65; Hood Col., AB, '60; b. Brookline, Mass., 1938; p. John F. and Katherine White Mulhern, Jr.; res: 51 Curve Hill Rd., S. Yarmouth, Mass. 02664.

MULL, JANE ADDAMS, Art Rschr., Fortune Magazine, Time Inc., Time & Life Bldg., Rockefeller Ctr., N.Y., N.Y. 10020, '46–; Am. Cncl. of Learned Socs. and Am. Commn. for the Protection and Salvage of Artistic and Hist. Monuments in War Areas (Roberts Commn.), '43–'46; Index of Christian Art, Princeton Univ., '38–'43; Asst. Ed., The Art Bul., Col. Art Assn., '44; Wellesley Col., BA, '36; MA, '38; Inst. d'Art et d'Archéologie, Univ. of Paris, Cert., '38; res: 455 E. 51st St., N.Y., N.Y. 10022.

MULLANEY, FAITH L., Media Specialist, Quincy Public Schools-Library Services, Coddington St., Quincy, Mass. 02169, '68–, '66–'67; Librn., Pfsnl. Lib., '67–'68; Walpole Public Schs., '65–'66; Town of Milton, '63–'65; Lib. Inst., summer '68; Comm. for Selection of Multi-Media Materials; WNBA, Quincy Educ. Assn., Mass. Tchrs. Assn., S. Shore Sch. Librns.; State Col. at Bridgewater, '59–'63; Sch. Lib. Cert.; b. Quincy, Mass.; p. Elmer and Ruth Cornish Peterson; h. John Mullaney; c. Hope, Kristin; res: 11 Arthur St., Quincy, Mass. 02169.

MULLEN, MARY, Wtr., non-fiction; Asst. to Pres., National Retired Teachers' Association, 215 Long Beach Blvd., Long Beach., Cal., '65–; formerly Tchr., Admr., Buffalo, N.Y., Alhambra, Cal.; Ed., Neighborhood School, Guidebook for Elementary School; Auth., "Guide for Retired Teachers of California"; AAUW, Cal. Elementary Admrs. (Pres., '46–'47), Nat. Retired Tchrs. (VP, '65–), Cal. Retired Tchrs. (Pres., '63–'65); numerous teaching, civic aws.; BA, '23; MA, '30; grad. work, seven univs., '30–'56; b. Buffalo, N.Y., 1900; p. Nicholas and Katherine Carroll Mullen; res: 2011 San Remo Dr., Laguna Beach, Cal. 92651.

MULLER, MARGIE HELLMAN, Asst. VP, PR, Tompkins County Trust Company, 110 N. Tioga St., Ithaca, N.Y. 14850, '66–; Dir. of PR, '60–'66; Adv., PR Mgr., Theodore Presser Co. (Bryn Mawr., Pa.), '57–'59; Sr. Assoc., Conant & Co. (N.Y.C.), '54–'57; Copywtr., Lee Hamrick Adv. (Ithaca), '51–'54; Sls. Prom., Joyce (Cal.) Ltd. (London, England), '50–'51; Bank PR & Mktng. Assn.; Who's Who of Am. Wm.; U.C.L.A., BA, '49; b. L.A., Cal., 1927; p. S. Jack and Marjorie Hellman; h. Steven Muller; c. Julie, Elizabeth; res: 125 Cayuga Park Rd., Ithaca, N.Y. 14850.

MUMBAUER, RUTH K., Supvsr., Test Kitchen, Family Circle Magazine, 488 Madison Ave., N.Y., N.Y. 10022, '56–; Ed., Gen. Foods Corp., '51–'56; Nurse Corps, AUS (Hawaii) '41–'46; Private Institutional nursing, '32–'41; Home Econsts. in Bus., AHEA, Theta Sigma Phi (N.Y.C. Chptr. Pres., '55–'57), Pi Lambda Theta, Kappa Delta Pi; Hospitalized Veterans Writing Project, AAAS, VFW, Grand View Nursing Sch., Diploma, '35; Univ. of Mo., BA, '49; BJ, '50; Columbia Univ., MA, '57; b. Bucks County, Pa., 1914; p. Robert R. and Rebecca Kehs Mumbauer; res: 2 E. 12th St., N.Y., N.Y. 10003.

MUNGER, NANCY TERRY, Dir. of Info. Ctr., J. Walter Thompson Company, 420 Lexington Ave., N.Y., N.Y. 10017, '61–; Ref. Librn., '58–'61; Librn., Compton Adv., '56–'58; Lib. Asst., '54–'55; Jr. Accountant, Gerry Bros., '52–'54; Tchr., '50–'52; Special Libs. Assn. (N.Y. Chptr. Pres., '68–'69), AWNY; Conn. Col., BA (Psych.), '50; Univ. of Cal., MS (Lib. Sci.), '65; b. Waterbury, Conn., 1928; p. Robert and Nancy Templeton Munger; res: 404 E. 66th St., N.Y., N.Y. 10021.

MUNHALL, DIANE SHEWAN, Prodr., Pres., Shewan

Production, Inc., 145 E. 49th St., N.Y., N.Y. 10017, '60–; Prodr., Pres., Reilly, Shewan & Co., '54–'60; Gen. Mgr., Huber Hoge & Sons, Adv. Agcy., '50–'54; Prodr., Jacques Frey Enterprises, '47–'50; Co-founder, AFC-NABET, Local 15, film div. of NABET; ATVAS (N.Y. unit); many aws.; b. N.Y.C.; p. Edwin and Anne Hansen Shewan; h. John Munhall (div.); c. John, Jr., Leslie Carson.

MUNRO, BETTE JONES, Mgr. Bdcst. Prod., Colle & McVoy Advertising Agency, 1400 Park Ave., Mpls., Minn. 55404, '59–; TV Wtr.-Prodr., Campbell-Mithun Adv. Agcy., '55–'58; Pubcty. Dir., Wms. Activities, Minn. Centennial Commn., '58; TV Wtr.-Prodr., Olmstead & Foley Adv. Agcy., '53–'55; TV-Radio Copywtr., BBDO, '50–'52; Bdcstr. and Wtr., WENY Radio (Elmira, N.Y.), '48–'49; WKJG Radio (Ft. Wayne, Ind.), '47–48; Minn. Adv. Club, AWRT, Theta Sigma Phi (Twin Cities Chptr. past-Pres.); Univ. of Minn, BA (Jnlsm.), '47 (Jnlsm. Sch. Bd. of Dirs.); b. St. Paul, Minn., 1925; p. Erwin and Myrtle Healey Jones; h. John Munro (div.); c. Susan Marie; res: 13709 Wood Lane, Minnetonka, Minn. 55343.

MUNTZ, MARGARET MILLS, Coordt., Beachwood Libraries, 24601 Fairmount Blvd., Beachwood, Oh. 44124, '68–; Librn., Hilltop Schs., '62–'68; Asst. Librn., Cleve. Heights HS, '60–'62; Akron Cataloguer, Firestone Tire & Rubber Co., '38–'39; Resident Tchr., Hudson Country Day Sch., '36–'37; Oh. Assn. of Sch. Librns. (Pres.-elect, '69–'70), Hilltop Beachwood Tchrs. Assn. (Pres., '65), Oh. Lib. Assn.; Wooster Col., AB, '36 (Math, Soc. Scis.); Case Western Reserve, MS (Lib. Sci.), '64; Insts., Western Mich., '67, Loughborough, Eng., '68; b. Cinn., Oh.; p. Charles and Luella Hatherley Mills; h. Ralph Muntz; c. Donna, Charles, Marilyn, Marlene; res: 105 Meadowhill Lane, Chagrin Falls, Oh. 44022.

MURDOCH, FAITH TOWNSEND, Dir. of Sch. Libs., Detroit Board of Education, 5057 Woodward Ave., Detroit, Mich. 48202, '63–; Supvsr. of Sch. Libs., '57–'62; Sch. Librn., '28–'56; Contrbr., pfsnl. lib. jnls.; Cnslt., workshops; Wayne State Univ., '68, '69; Western Mich. Univ., Cinn. Public Schs., '68; Univ. of Wis., '67; Mich Assn. of Sch. Librns. (VP, '51–'52) Am. Assn. of Sch. Librns. (2nd VP, '67–'68), ALA, Mich. Lib. Assn., Delta Kappa Gamma; Detroit Tchrs. Col., '25–'27; Wayne State Univ., BS, '34; MA, '38; Univ. of Mich., MLS, '64; b. Sault Ste. Marie Mich., 1909; p. Dr. Wesley and Mina MacNeil Townsend; h. J. Roderick Murdoch; res: 16545 Kentfield Ave., Detroit, Mich. 43219.

MURDOCK, CECILE KIRBY, WTVJ Channel 4, '58; WQAM Radio, '57; Stephens Col., '54–'55; Univ. of Miami grad., '57; b. Miami, Fla., 1935; p. Cecil and Gwendolyn Smoak Kirby; h. (div.); c. Martha Suzanne, Merri Melody; res: 3551 E. Galbraith Rd., Cinn., Oh. 45236.

MURPHREE, JOYCE TILL, Info. Specialist, Alabama

Department of Public Health, State Office Bldg., Montgomery, Ala. 36104, '67–; Ed., Ala. Sunday Magazine, '65–'67; State Ed., Ala. Journal, '64–'65, Asst. Wm.'s Ed., '63–'64; Reptr., Troy Messenger, '62–'63; ICIE, (Montgomery Chptr. VP, '69); Univ. of Ala., Montgomery Ctr.; b. Monroe County, Ala., 1938; p. Hurley and Era Johnson Till; h. (div.); c. Rodney Kyle; res: 125 Ingle Dr., Montgomery, Ala. 36110.

MURPHY, CHRISTAL MASTON, TV Prodr., Wtr.; PR, Oakland Public Schools, 1025 Second Ave., Oakland, Cal. 94606; TV series on KPIX; formerly taught news (Gold Key Aw., Columbia Univ., '56; Black Cat Aw., S.F. Press Club); Theta Sigma Phi (Far Western Dir.; East Bay Chptr. Pres.); Columbia Scholastic Press Assn. (VP, '53–'57); Univ. of Cal., Berkeley, Tchrs. Credential, '27; Stanford Univ., Masters (Educ. TV), '54; b. Palmyra, Mo., 1905; p. John and Pearl Kempf Maston; h. Joseph Murphy (dec.); res: 2211 Santa Clara Ave., Alameda, Cal. 94501.

MURPHY, ESTHER MARIE, Mgr., News Bur., Seattle-First National Bank, 1001 Fourth Ave., Seattle, Wash. 98124, '69–; Pubns. Offcr., '66–'69; Ed., Bankoscope, '56–'66, '49–'53; Ed., offcl. pubns., Univ. of Wash., '54–'56; Ed., Opns. Manual, Bramwell Construction Co., '53–'54; News Ed., Puyallup Valley Tribune, '48–'49; Theta Sigma Phi (Seattle Pfsnl. Chptr. VP, '68–'69) ICIE (Pacific N.W. Pres., '64), bank orgs.; Wash. State Press Wm. Sugar Plum Aw., '69; civic orgs.; Wash. State Univ., '44–'46; Univ. of Wash., BA, '46–'48; b. Seattle, Wash., 1926; p. Patrick and Mary Kearins Murphy; res: 3218 N.W. Esplanade, Seattle, Wash. 98107.

MURPHY, GRETA WERWATH, VP for PR, Dev., Milwaukee School of Engineering, 1025 N. Milwaukee St., Milw., Wis. 53201, '66–; Corp. Mbr., '49; Dir. of PR, Dev., '45; Mbr., Milw. County Planning Comm., '66–; PRSA (Nat. Dir., '52–'53; Wis. Chptr. Pres., '57; Svc. Cit., '60), ACPRA (Nat. Dir., '54–'56, '60–'61; Dist. Dir., '63–'64; Trustee, '64–'67), Theta Sigma Phi, AFA (Wms. Adv. Club of Milw. Pres., '51), ZONTA (Milw. Club Pres., '59–'60; Dist. Gov., '61–'63), Milw. Univ. Sch., '38; Oh. State Univ., '43–'45; b. Milw., Wis., 1910; p. Oscar and Hannah Seelhorst Werwath; h. John H. Murphy; res: S. Cedar Beach Rd., Belgium, Wis. 53004.

MURPHY, JONNE FURMAN, Dir. Sls. Svcs., Radio Advertising Bureau, 555 Madison Ave., N.Y., N.Y. 10022, '69–; Special assistance projects for local radio stations and advertising agencies; Dir. Large Mkts. Mbr. Svc., '68–'69; Dir. Media Svcs., '66–'68; Media Group Buying Supvsr., BBDO, '64–'66; Bdcst. Media Supvsr., Gumbinner Agcy., '58–'64; Bdcst. Pioneers, IRTS, AWNY; Skidmore Col., BS, '35 (cum laude); b. White Plains, N.Y., 1914; p. Eugene and Esther M. Patterson Furman; h. Ray T. Murphy; (dec.) c. Stephen D. and Kent C.; res: 72 Chatterton Pkwy., White Plains, N.Y. 10606.

MURPHY, KAY, Home Furnishings Ed., Miami Herald, 1 Herald Plaza, Miami, Fla. 33101, '50–; Feature Wtr., '42–'50; Feature Wtr., Columbus (Oh.) Dispatch, '36–'42; Feature Wtr., Athens (Oh.) Messenger, '34–'36; Cnslt. Ed., Florida Architecture, '66, '65; Theta Sigma Phi, Am. Inst. of Interior Designers, NHFL; Dorothy Dawe Aw., '62, '54; Nat. Summer Furniture Manufacturers Assn. aw., '57; Euster Mdse. Mart aw., '69; Nat. Assn. of Real Estate Eds. aw., '66, '60; Nat. Assn. of Home Builders aw., '68, '60; Univ. of Oh., BA (Jnlsm.), '36; b. Chillicothe, Oh., 1916; p. John and Haldee McCune Murphy; res: 35 S.W. 24th Rd., Miami, Fla. 33129.

MURPHY, LAVINIA ELLEN, Dir. of Instructional Material and Resources Belmont Public Sch. Belmont, Ma.; Asst. Dir., Institute for Media Personnel, Boston University School of Education; Sr. Supvsr. of Sch. Lib. Dev., Mass. Dept. of Educ.; Elementary Librn., Marshfield Public Schs.; Cnslt., ALESCO; Instr., Bridgewater State Col.; Instr., Swampscott Public Schs.; Instr., Lynnfield Public Schs.; ALA, NEA, Mass. Audio-Visual Assn. (Bd. of Dirs., '69–; Secy., '67–'69), Pi Lambda Theta; Bridgewater State Col., BS (Educ.), '60; Boston Univ., MS, '65; b. Medford, Mass., 1938; p. Edward Gordon and Irene Ceclia McNamara Murphy; res: 152 Cester St., Hanover, Mass. 02239.

MURPHY, MARY E., in charge product pubcty., PR Dept., Borden, Inc., 350 Madison Ave., N.Y., N.Y. 10017, '51–; PR Dept., Ted Bates, adv. agcy., '48–'51; Nat. Dairy Products, '39–'48; Staff, WSAN (Allentown, Pa.), '36–'37; Talent, TV, "For Your Information"; lectr., consumer pubcty. courses, Pubcty. Club of N.Y. (Pres., '55–'56), PRSA, AWRT (N.Y.C. Chptr. Treas., '68–'69; Nat. PR. Chmn., '63–'64) Am. Home Econs. Assn., NHFL, food industry aw., '63; Boston Univ., '37–'38; b. Catasauqua, Pa.; p. Henry and Bessie Flemming Fox; h. (div.); res: 325 E. 41st St., N.Y., N.Y. 10017.

MURPHY, ROSEMARY, Actress, c/o Ashley Famous Agency Inc., 9255 Sunset Blvd., L.A., Cal. 90069; plays: "A Delicate Balance," "Any Wednesday," "Weekend," "A Night of the Iguana," "Look Homeward, Angel", others; films: "To Kill a Mockingbird," "King Lear," "Comedy of Errors"; TV: Amer. Shakespeare Festival; Wtr., "Shakespeare for Children"; AEA (Cncl. Mbr., '69–), SAG, AFTRA; Tony Aw. nominations and Variety Critics Poll: "Period of Adjustment," '61; "A Delicate Balance," '67.

MURPHY, VIRGINIA LEWIS, Traf. Dir., WHA, Radio Hall, University of Wisconsin, Madison, Wis. 53706, '67–; Teaching Asst., Pers. and Labor Rels., Wash. State Univ., '65–'67; Independent Econ. study, Fluor Corp. (L.A., Cal.), '65; Teaching speech and reading clinics, Occidental Col., '64–'65; Occidental Col., AB, '65 (hons. in Econs.; Wm. R. Staats Aw. Scholar in Econs., '65); Cal. State Col. at L.A., '65; Wash. State Univ., '65–'67; b. Pasadena, Cal., '43; p. Donald and Claire

Kingman Lewis; h. Avon Murphy; res: 1116 Ann St., #16, Madison, Wis. 53713.

MURPHY, WINIFRED SCHMALE, Prodr., Dir., KQED Television, 525 Fourth St., S.F., Cal. 94107, '57–; joined KQED as secy.-receptionist, '54; numerous series for NET, including "Conversations with Eric Hoffer," "Once upon a Japanese Time" (Oh. State Aw., Inst. for Educ. by Radio-TV, '59; Special Aw., Network Classification, for Cultural Programming); Wtr., mag. articles, wkly. nwsp. cols.; S.F. City Col., AA (Bus.), '51; BA (TV), '54; S.F., Cal., 1931; p. John and Ida Drady Schmale; h. Owen J. Murphy; c. Dana Catherine, Megan Elizabeth; res: 633 Woodbine Dr., San Rafael, Cal. 94903.

MURRAY, ALICE CATHERINE, Ed., indsl. house organ, "On the Beam," Leckenby Company, 2745 Eleventh Ave. S.W., Seattle, Wash. 98134, '57–(Freedoms Fndn. aw., '68); Cont. Wtr., Pubcty. Dir., Radio Sta. KOL, '34–'36; various orgs., aws.; Univ. of Wash., BA (Jnlsm.), '34; b. Seattle, Wash., 1912; p. Joseph and Alice Johnston Murray; res: 317 N. 150th St., Seattle, Wash. 98133.

MURRAY, CAROL ORLOWSKY, Dir. of Commtns., Touche Ross & Co., 1345 Ave. of Americas, N.Y., N.Y. 10019, '63–; Adv. Dir., Am. Surety, '61–'63; VP, Gene Murray Adv., '58–'61; ICIE, OPC, N.Y. Assn. of Indsl. Eds., AWNY, George Wash. Univ., MBA, '50; b. Cinn., Oh., 1929; p. Joseph and Carol Brown Orlowsky; h. Gene Murray; c. Charles, David, Philip, Eugene, Joan; res: Litchfield Way, Alpine, N.J. 07624.

MURRAY, DENE RATERMANN, Exec. Dir., American Association of Medical Assistants, 200 E. Ohio St., Chgo., Ill. 60611, '66–; Info. Assoc., Nat. 4-H Svc. Comm., '51–'65; Dir. of PR, Ed., The Zontian, '48–'51; Ed., Nat. Congress of Parents and Tchrs., '44–'48; Employee Rels., Shure Bros., '42–'43; AWRT (Chgo. Chptr. Pres., '61–'63, Dir., Nat. Bd.) Pubcty. Club of Chgo. (svc. aw., '65), PRSA, Met. BPW (Pres.), Wms. Adv. Club of Chgo. (VP); Huron Col., BA (cum laude); b. Haynes, N.D.; p. John and Minnie Dempsey Curtis; h. 1. William F. Ratermann (dec.); 2. Jay Murray (sep.); res: 900 N. Lake Shore Dr., Chgo., Ill. 60611.

MURRAY, IRENE, Asst. Ed., The Link, The Chaplain, 122 Maryland Ave., N.E., Wash., D.C. 20002, '60–; Edtl. Asst., '57–'60; Auth: "The Green Olive Tree" (Zondervan, '59), "The Yielded Heart" (Zondervan, '57); Instr., short story, Judson Workshop for wtrs. and artists (Elgin, Ill.); Auths. Guild, RPRC, Assoc. Ch. Press; Northwestern Univ.; Am. Univ.; b. Silvis, Ill.; p. Michael and Grace Tubbs Murray.

MURRAY, JANE ELLEN, VP, Assoc. Crtv. Dir., Adv. Wtr., J. Walter Thompson Co., 875 N. Mich. Ave., Chicago, Ill. 60611, '69–; Group Head; Wtr., '59; Chgo. Soc. of Communicating Arts (Bd. of Dirs., '69), Copy Club of Chgo. (Secy., '61), Wms. Adv. Club of Chgo. (Rec. Secy., Corr. Secy., '53–'55; Rep. to Intl.

Adv. Conf. in London, '51), Jr. Wm's. Adv. Club (Pres., '52); Vogue Prix de Paris Aw., '48; Adv. Club of N.Y. Andy Aw., '68; Chgo. I Aw. Cert., '68; Am. TV Comml. Festival Aw., '64; Vassar, Grad., '48; Northwestern Univ., '48, '49; b. Chgo., Ill., 1927; p. Thomas and Mildred Spacek Murray; res: 1120 Lake Shore Dr., Chgo., Ill. 60611.

MURRAY, JO ANNE GREER, Ed., The Moore County News, P.O. Box 207, Lynchburg, Tenn. 37352, '63–; Gen. Mgr., Reprtr., '56–'63; Soc. Ed., Court Reptr., '53; Tchr., Moore County Sch. System; Moore Selective Svc. Bd.; Tenn. Press Assn., Nat. Nwsp. Assn., Moore County C. of C.; b. Shelbyville, Tenn., 1934; p. Joe and Pauline Raby Greer; h. Bobby Murray; c. Zachary G., Jason S.; res: Valley View, Lynchburg, Tenn. 37352.

MURRAY, JOAN ELIZABETH, Corr., WCBS-TV, 51 W. 52nd St. (or 518 W. 57th), N.Y., N.Y., '65–; Co-hostess, "Opportunity Line" (local Emmy Aw.); Co-hostess, news, current events series, "2 at One," 27 months; Hostess, high sch. equivalency examination preparatory bdcsts., educ. TV stations; synd. radio interview program, black wm. of accomplishment; Exec. VP, Zebra Assocs. Inc., adv. agcy.; On-air interviewer, Hostess, Wtr., Prod. Asst., "Women on the Move," NBC, '64; radio, TV commls., indsl., feature films, docs., TV programs, CBS; Prod. Asst., Script Girl, "Candid Camera"; corporate affairs staff; Secy., TV network press info. dept.; court rept.; numerous speaking engagements, appearances; autobiog., "The News" (McGraw-Hill, '68); various orgs.; Ithaca Col., '56–'57; New Sch. for Social Rsch., '58–'60; Hunter Col., '65–'66; b. Ithaca, N.Y.; p. Isaiah and Amanda Pearl Yates Murray; res: 536 E. 79th St., N.Y., N.Y. 10021.

MURRAY, LEE LANE, Radio Talent, Prodr., Lee Murray Productions, 1418 Wrenwood, Troy, Mich. 48084, '66–; Wms. Dir., WJR, '48–'66; Wms. Dir., WJRT, '57–'58; Wms. Dir., WNEM-TV, '56–'57; Wtr., Dir., Workshop Marionettes, '49–'51; numerous orgs., aws.; b. Dowagiac, Mich., 1920; p. Jerry and Betty Ross Lane; h. George Murray; c. William, Robert, Richard.

MURRAY, LOIS SMITH, Prof. of Eng., Baylor University, Waco, Tex. 76703, '31– (Tchr. aw., '62); Cnslt., human rel., Cooper Fndn., Hogg Fndn. (Austin); Lectr., Univ. of Tex., Univ. of Del., Univ. of Wis., Univ. of Chgo.; AAUP, Modern Lang. Assn., Tex. Assn. of Col. Tchrs. of Eng., Sigma Tau Delta, PSA, Waco Citizenship aw., '46; Baylor Univ., AB, '30; (magna cum laude), MA, '31; b. West, Tex., 1909; p. Walter and Cora Casey Smith; h. John D. Murray; c. Lowell Clarence Douglas, Dell Ilene Douglas Everton; res: Rte. 2, McGregor, Tex. 76657.

MURRAY, MARY PAULINE, Home Econst., Publicist, McCormick & Co., Inc., 11350 McCormick Rd., Cockeysville, Md. 21030, '66–; Home Econst., '62–'66;

Home Econst., Westinghouse, '51–'62; selected by U.S. Dept. of Commerce for Intl. Trade Fair, Zagreb, Yugoslavia, '59; Am. Home Econs. Assn., Home Econsts. in Bus. (Nat. Exec. Bd., '68–), Md. Home Econs. Assn., AWRT (Chptr. Treas., '69–'70), Wms. Adv. Club of Balt.; Who's Who of Am. Wm.; Who's Who in the East; Dic. of Intl. Biog.; Pi Beta Phi; Univ. of Tenn., BS, '50; b. Knoxville, Tenn., 1928; p. James and Myra Mims Murray; res: 221 Ridgemede Rd., Balt., Md. 21210.

MURRAY, NATALIA DANESI, VP, Rizzoli Editore Corp., 712 Fifth Ave., N.Y., N.Y. 10019, '65–; U.S. Rep., Mondadori Publ. Co., '50–'65; Free-Lance Wtr., '46–'50; Chief, Special Project Div., USIS, Rome, Italy, '45–'46; Chief, Press Reading Bur., PWB, '44–'45; Chief, Italian Short Wave Div., NBC, '38–'44; Translator; Auth., juv. bk.; Actress; Auths. Rep.; originated Foster Parents Comm. for Italian War Orphans; WNBA; Amita Aw., '61; b. Rome, Italy; p. Giulio and Ester Traversari Danesi; h. William Murray; c. William.

MURRELL, MARGARET FAYE, Crtv. Dir., Carlocke Langden, Inc., Exec. VP, Whitmark Associates, 505 N. Ervay, Suites 714, 716, Dallas, Tex. 75201; Bdcst. Wtr.-Prodr., BBDO; Wtr., Prod. Mgr., Key Assocs.; Wtr.-Prodr., Erwin Wasey, Ruthrauff & Ryan; Sr. Copywtr., Southern Union Gas Co.; Adv. Sls., Carlsbad (N.M.) Current Argus; AWRT (Dallas Chptr. VP, charter mbr.), AAUW (Past Carlsbad, N.M. Chptr. VP), Theta Sigma Phi (Dallas Chptr. Matrix Aw., '67), various others; Dallas Adv. League Adv. wm. of the yr., '68; Tyler Jr. Col.; Tex. Wms. Univ., BA/BS, '47; b. Tyler, Tex., 1926; p. Hugh and Oman Hudson Murrell; res: 5446 Druid Lane, Dallas, Tex. 75209.

MURSET, SUSIE J., VP and Secy., Nan Miller & Associates, Inc., 55 E. Washington St., Chgo., Ill. 60602, '63–; Asst., Nan Miller Prods., '50–'53; Registered Nurse, '34–'69; Owner, Band Box Beauty Salon, '37–'40; Chgo. Assn. of Commerce and Industry, 1st Dist. Nurse's Assn., Ill. Nurse's Assn., Am. Nurses' Assn.; St. Luke's Hosp. Sch. of Nursing, '34; PR courses.

MURTHA, JOHANNA MARY, Commtns. Specialist, City National Bank & Trust Co., 100 E. Broad St., Columbus, Oh. 43215, '69–; Ed., PR Asst., '60–'69; Central Oh. Bus. & Indsl. Eds. (Treas., '66, Secy., '65), Capital City Young Repl. Club; Oh. State Univ., BA (Jnlsm.), '60; b. Columbus, Oh., 1938; p. Thomas and Hedwig Bangert Murtha; res: 100 N. Edgevale Rd., Columbus, Oh. 43209.

MUSGROVE, VIRIGINIA DUDLEY, Prod. Coordr., WSOC-AM-FM-TV, Cox Broadcasting Co., Inc., 1901 N. Tryon St., Charlotte, N.C. 28201, '67–; Talent, "Clown Carnival," '65–; TV News Prod. Coordr., '65–; TV Prom. Asst. and Pubcty., '62–'65; Carolina Sch. of Bdcst., WYFM, '61; Instr.; Asst. Mgr. and Secy.-Treas., Mecklenburg Election Tabulating Svc.; Theta Sigma

Phi, AWRT, Am. Fedn. of Musicians; Outstanding Young Wm. of Am.; High Pt. Col., BS (Bus. Adm.), '57–'61; Carolina Sch. of Bdcst., '61–'62; b. Catawba, N.C., 1940; p. William M. and Christine Reaves Musgrove; res: 420A W. Craighead Rd., Charlotte, N.C. 28206.

MUSTRIC, FLORENCE, PR Dir., Fairview General Hospital, 18101 Lorain Ave., Cleve., Oh. 44111, '68–; Sr. Ed., World Publ. Co.; Acting Dir. PR, Goodwill Industries; ICIE (All-Oh. Aws., Best Photojnl., '69), Northern Oh. Indsl. Eds. Assn.; Oberlin Col., AB, '61; MA (Teaching), '62.

MUTH, DIANA, Radio-TV Dir., Houston Symphony, Jones Hall, 615 Louisiana St., Houston, Tex. 77005, '66–; Copy Chief, Nahas-Blumberg Adv., '51–'66; Radio Show "Around the Art World with Diana Muth," KXYZ; AWRT; Pagefield Col., Llanelly, Wales, BA (Lit.), '45; b. Cardiff, Wales, 1924; p. Watcyn and Alice Evans; h. Henri Muth; res: 3790 Purdue St., Houston, Tex. 77005.

MUTO, SUSAN ANNETTE, Asst. Dir., Institute of Man, Duquesne University, Pitt., Pa. 15219, '65–; Tchr.; Mng. Ed., Envoy, inst. mag., Humanitas, inst. jnl.; Asst. Dir., PR, Un. Jewish Fedn., '65; Soc. Ed., Jewish Chronicle, '65; Co-Auth., "The Emergent Self" (Dimension Bks., '68), Co-Auth., "The Participant Self" ('69); Theta Sigma Phi, Outstanding Young Wm. of Am., '68; Duquesne Univ., BA, '64 (Gold Medal in Jnlsm., '64; Who's Who Among Students, '64); Univ. of Pitt., MA (Eng. Lit.), '67; b. Pitt., Pa., 1942; p. Frank and Helen Muto; res: 229 Grandview Ave., Pitt., Pa. 15211.

MYER, ELIZABETH G., Dir., Department of State Library Services, 95 Davis St., Providence, R.I. 02908, '64–; Supvsr. of Public Lib. Svcs., Rural Areas, '58–'64; Ref. Librn., Morrill Memorial Lib., '50–'53; Tchr.-Librn., Newton, Mass. Public Schs.; Librn., Phoebe Griffin Noyes Lib. (Old Lyme, Conn.); Lieutenant, U.S. Navy; Enoch Pratt Free Lib.; Providence Public Lib.; Supvsr., State W.P.A. Lib. Project; articles in pfsnl. periodicals; ALA, Am. Assn. of State Libs. (Exec. Bd., '65–'67), R.I. Lib. Assn. (Pres., '62–'64), Conn. Lib. Assn., Mass. Lib. Assn., AAUW, R.I. Hist. Soc.; Barnard Col., AB; Brown Univ., MA (Eng.); Simmons Sch. of Lib. Sci., BS (Lib. Sci.); Grad. Work, Wayne State Univ.; b. Boston, Mass.; p. Otto J. and Edith Geer Myer; res: 3 Sunset Dr., Barrington, R.I. 02806.

MYER, JO ANN, Dir. of Tourism and Prom., Brevard County, Fla. Brevard Economic Development Council, Holiday Office Ctr., Cocoa Beach, Fla. 32931, '69–; Ed., University of Florida Alumni Magazine, College of Journalism and Communications, University of Florida, '68–'69; Wtr., Rschr., Radio Ctr. and Second One Hundred TV series, '68–'69; Ed., Fla. Wms. Magazine, '67; Ed., Union Brochure, '66–'67; Asst. Ed., Enjay Chemical Co. (N.Y.C.), '67–'68; Asst. Ed., Corn Products, '68; Theta Sigma Phi, Kappa Tau

Alpha; Univ. of Fla., BS (Jnlsm.), '67 (Outstanding Wm. Grad., '67); MA (Commtns.), '69; b. Miami, Fla., 1945; p. Isaac and M. Cecile Myer; res: 134 E. Alachua Lane, Cocoa Beach, Fla. 32931.

MYERS, ELISABETH PERKINS, wtr., Heritage Woods, R.R. 2, Box 211, Bloomington, Ind. 47401; Auth., 12 biogs. for young people ('61–'69); articles on travel, ch. concerns, child care; short juv. fiction; various orgs., aws.; Vassar Col., AB, '40; b. Grand Rapids, Mich., 1918; p. Edward and Lili Zimmermann Perkins; h. John Holmes Myers; c. Thomas P.

MYERS, HORTENSE, Ind. Statehouse Reptr., United Press International, 113 N. Capitol St., Indpls., Ind. 46204, '58–; INS, '42–'58; Rptr. and Ed., Old Trail News, '34–'42; Co-auth: "Carl Ben Eielson, Young Alaskan Pilot," '61; "Cecil DeMille, Boy Dramatist," '63; "Vilhjalmur Stefansson, Young Artic Explorer," '66; "Edward R. Murrow, Young Newscaster," '69; and others; NFPW (Pres., '62–'65; Wm. of Achiev., '66), Wms. Press Club of Ind. (Pres., '54–'56; Kate Milner Rabb Aw., '64), Theta Sigma Phi (Indpls. Chptr. Pres., '57–'58; Frances Wright Aw., '60; Nat. Headliner Aw., '67), Indpls. Press Club (aw. of hon., '63), EWA (Sch. Bell Aw., '67); Butler Univ., BS, '53; b. Indpls., Ind., 1913; p. Walter and Stella Smith Powner; h. Stanley M. Myers; c. Mark P.; res: 9055 Rockville Rd., Indpls., Ind. 46234.

MYERS, JOAN FLECK, Assoc. Ed., Girl Scout Leader, Girl Scouts of the U.S.A., 830 Third Ave., N.Y., N.Y. 10022, '65–; Features Ed., American Girl, '65–'68; Ed., Newsletter for Girl Scout Pfsnl. Workers, '64–'65; PR Dir., Girl Scout Cncl. of Central Md. (Balt.), '60–'64; PR Staff, Commty. Chest-Red Cross Un. Appeal, '60–'63; various orgs.; Temple Univ., BS (Jnlsm.), '57; b. Balt., Md.; p. A. C. and Madeline Bloch Fleck; h. Richard A. Myers, Jr.; c. Kevin Mark, Deborah Ann, Cheryl Lynn; res: 197 Dartmouth Ave., Fair Haven, N.J. 07701.

MYERS, SHIRLEY F., Adv.-Pubns. Dir. Mgr., Arkwright-Boston Insurance, 225 Wyman St., Waltham, Mass. 02154, '67–; Supvsr., Pubns. Div., '64–'67; Asst. to Mgr. Pubns. Div., '63–'64; Field Dir., Mistick Side Girl Scout Cncl., '63; Dist., PR Advisor, Southern Oakland Girl Scouts, '58–'62; Dist. Advisor, Cleve. Girl Scout Cncl., '56–'57; Assoc. Ed., Willard Storage Battery Co., '55; Asst. AE, Ad Enterprise Adv. Agcy., '54–'55; Sr. Verse Wtr., Am. Greetings Corp., '51–'54; Adv. Cnslt., '68–; Free-lance Verse Wtr., Copywtr., Artist '54–; Interior Decorating Cnslt., '69; slide film artwork, prod., '61; Adv. Club of Greater Boston, Mass. IEA, Wms. Adv. Club of Detroit; Case Western Univ., BA, '51; Mich. Univ., '60; Boston Univ. Sch. of PR and Commtns., '62; b. Akron, Oh., 1931; p. Irving and Lillian Granatstein Myers; res: 260 Tremont St., Melrose, Mass. 02154.

MYLLER, LOIS WESTERDAHL, VP, School and Library Division, Simon & Schuster, Inc., 630 Fifth

Ave., N.Y., N.Y. 10020, '66–; Dir., Sch. and Lib. Dept., World Publ. Co., '58–'65; Asst. Dir., Educ. Dept., E. P. Dutton, '52–'58; WNBA (Treas.), Publrs. Lib. Prom. Group (Pres.), Children's Bk. Cncl. (Pres., '70–'71); Hunter Col., BA; b. N.Y.C.; p. Rev. Clifford and Elsie Olson Westerdahl; h. Rolf Myller; c. Elise and Corinne; res: 1165 Fifth Ave., N.Y., N.Y. 10029.

MYRENE, MARY ELLEN, Feature Wtr., Associated Press, 50 Rockefeller Plaza, N.Y., N.Y. 10020, '65–; Theta Sigma Phi (Univ of Mont. Chptr. Pres., '64–'65; Univ. of Mont. jnlsm. aw., '64; Univ. of Mont., '61–'65; b. Spokane, Wash., 1943; p. Elmer and Jennie Botman Myrene; res: 401 E. 74th St., N.Y., N.Y. 10021.

MYRICK, IDA MARIE, PR Rep., National Airlines, Inc., P.O. Box 2055, A.M.F., Miami, Fla. 33159, '65–; Adv. and PR Dept., Howard Johnson, Inc. of Fla.; Theta Sigma Phi (Greater Miami Chptr: Treas., '68–'69; Corr. Secy., '69–'70), Fla. PR Assn.; Wms. Cancer Assn.; volunteer in commty. projects, incl. Un. Fund of Dade County; Univ. of Fla. Sch. of Jnlsm. and Commtns., BS, '64 (hons.); b. Pitt., Pa., 1942; p. Costa and Alma LaFace; res: 700 N.E. 29th Terr., Miami, Fla. 33137.

MYRICK, JEAN LOCKWOOD, Wtr., children's poetry, fiction; Auth., "Ninety-Nine Pockets" (Lantern Press, '65); Sioux Falls Col., '46; Seattle Pacific Col., '46–'50; b. Sioux Falls, S.D., 1924; p. Russell and Nellie Buswell Lockwood; h. Patrick L. Myrick; c. Mary Nell, Ann, Alexander, Jonathan, Geordie, Monica, Gwyneth, Gareth; res: 11800 86th St., Snohomish, Wash. 98290.

N

NADLER, FREDA KAPLAN, Alumnae Ed., Wesleyan College, Forsyth Rd., Macon, Ga., '63–; Features Wtr., Sunday Magazine of Atlanta Journal-Constitution, '55–; Features Wtr., Cleveland (Oh.) Plain Dealer, '34–'36; Wtr., "Chicago Life" radio program, '34; Feature Wtr., Midweek mag., Chicago Daily News, '31–'34; Ed., Oakland Outlook, '31–'32; Macon Cncl. on World Affairs (Pres., '57–'58), Phi Kappa Phi; Who's Who of Am. Wm.; Wesleyan Col., AB, '26 (Alumnae Assn: Pres., '52–'55; Trustee, '58–'61; Phi Delta Phi; Distg. Svc. Aw., '62); b. Macon, Ga., 1906; p. Henry and Mary Doctor Kaplan; h. Charles Elihu Nadler; c. George Eldon (Stepson); res: 560 Wesleyan Dr., Macon, Ga. 31204.

NAFZIGER, CHARLOTTE HAMILTON, Publicist, Jnlst.; Asst. Ed., Pubcty. Wtr., Wis. Power and Light Co., '30–'32; Soc. Ed., The Capital Times (Madison, Wis.), '29–'30; Asst. Soc. Ed., '28–'29; Pubcty. Wtr., Wis. Sch. of Music, '28–'29; Theta Sigma Phi, Coranto, NLAPW (Minn. Br. VP, '48–'49); Univ. of Manitoba (Winnipeg, Can.), '23–'24; Toronto Conservatory of Music, ATCM, '25; Univ. of Wis. (Madison, Wis.), BA, '28; b. Winnipeg, Manitoba, Can.; p. E. William and Ida Pearl Richmond Hamilton; h. Ralph O. Nafziger; c. Ralph Hamilton, James A. Richard; res: 3405 Crestwood Dr., Madison, Wis. 53705.

NAGY, HESTER WORTHINGTON, Sls. Mgr., WMBS, 82 W. Fayette St., Uniontown, Pa. 15401, '68–; Program Dir., '66–'68; Traf. Mgr., '60–'66; Bdcstr., four features daily, '55–; discussions on radio and wms. roles in commtns., with civic groups; Free-lance rec. radio series for Intl. Packers, Assoc. Release Svcs. of Chgo.; AWRT (Pitt. Gateway Chptr. Pres.-elect, '69–'70; VP, '68–'69), Pitt. Radio and TV Club, Pitt. Press Club; Waynesburg Col.; b. Uniontown, Pa., 1927; p. Albert and Claudia Stumpf Worthington; h. Stephen J. Nagy; c. Alan Charles, Beth Ann; res: Box 32, Farmington, Pa. 15437.

NAHAS, ANN NELSON, Wms. Ed., Joliet Herald-News, 78 Scott St., Joliet, Ill. 60431, '52–; Am. Assn. of Nwsp. Food Eds. (Advisory Bd.), '64), Tri-Ex League (Pres. '63–'64), Joliet Jr. Wms. Club; Copley Jnlsm. aw., '59; Caswell-Massey Fashion aw.; Who's Who of Am. Wm.; Who's Who in Midwest; Nat. Social Register; Am. Conservatory of Music, '51–'52; b. Joliet, Ill., 1932; p. Otto and Marie Boughton Nelson; h. George Edward Nahas; res: 111 Woodlawn Ave., Joliet, Ill. 60435.

NAISMITH, GRACE, Assoc. Ed., Reader's Digest, 200 Park Ave., N.Y., N.Y. 10017, '38–; U.S. Dept. of Agriculture Info. Svc.; Rocky Mountain News, '30; Auth., "Private and Personal," ('66); numerous mag. articles; OPC (Gov.), Theta Sigma Phi; William Woods Col. (Hon. DSci., '69); b. Ft. Collins, Colo., 1904; p. A. I. and Nellie Taylor Akin; h. John C. Devlin; c. James Naismith, Stuart Naismith; res: Westview Lane, S. Norwalk, Conn. 06854.

NALLEY, LORIE MOLNAR, Attorney, Partner, Molnar and Gammon, Law Firm, 2011 Eye St., N.W., Wash., D.C. 20006, '63–; admitted to practice before U.S. Supreme Court, U.S. Court of Appeals (D.C. Circuit), U.S. Dist. Court (D.C.), Supreme Court of Oh.; field of commtns. law; licensed real estate broker; Assoc. Atty., Frieda B. Hennock, '59–'60; sole practitioner, '60–'63; Fed. Commtns. Bar Assn., Dist. of Columbia Bar Assn., Am. Bar Assn., AWRT (Wash., D.C. Chptr. Bd. of Dirs.), W. Montgomery County Citizen's Assn.; various aws. for educ. and musical activities; Ursline Col., BA, '56 (magna cum laude; first in class ranking); Georgetown Univ. Law Ctr., BL, '59, (Bd. of Eds., Law Jnl.); Catholic Univ. of Am., Grad. Work, '68–; b. E. Canton, Oh., 1934; p. Mr. and Mrs. Paul J. Molnar; h. Donald F. Nalley.

NANCE, MAXINE DeVANEY, Radio Cont. Dir., Wms. Dir., Gilmore Broadcasting Corp., KODE-TV/AM, 1928 W. 13th St., Joplin, Mo. 64801, '58–; Commty. Club Aws. Dir., KODE-Radio, '59–'61; Cont.

Dir., Wms. Dir., Prom. Mgr., Radio Sta. WMBH, '46–'57; Lighting Advisor and PR, Empire Dist. Electric Co., '39–'46; Dir., Radio-TV pubcty., Joplin's First Fall Festival of the Arts, '67; Prod., Emcee, fashion shows, Joplin C. of C., '54–'55; Dir., Queen contests, '56–'57; Emcee, '57; AWRT, Am. Bus. Wms. Assn. (Charter Mbr., '52; Pres., '53–'54), NRPW, Mo. Press Wm., Joplin C. of C., Beta Sigma Phi (Life Mbr.; Order of the Rose, '58), Joplin Little Theatre; Kan. State Col., '34–'35; La Salle Univ., '39; b. Joplin, Mo., 1916; p. Galen and Zella Jordan DeVaney; h. Kirby A. Nance; res: 3218 Oak Ridge Dr., Joplin, Mo. 64801.

NAREL, DOROTHY MILLER, Wms. Program Commentator, Mid-Hudson Publications and WGHQ, Freeman Sq., Kingston, N.Y. 12401, '68–; Wms. Page Ed., '55–; Wms. Program Dir., WKNY-TV; Employee Rels. Dept., GE (N.Y.C.); Lectr.; Free-lance PR, Fashion Show Commentator; Am. Nwsp. Guild (Kingston Unit Pres., '62–'67), Empire State Dist. Cncl. of Guilds (VP, '63–'66); BPW (Ulster County Pres., '65–'67), Am. Guild of Organists (Hon. Mbr.), various commty. orgs., Montclair State Tchrs. Col., '42–'44; Columbia Univ., '44–'46, b. Newark, N.J., 1924; p. Rheinhardt and Alma Kalkowski Miller; h. Aleksander Narel; c. Mrs. Daniel B. Elkins, Mrs. Keith F. Jordan; res: Mosher Pl., West Hurley, N.Y. 12491.

NARELL, IRENA PENZIK, Auth.; Secy.-Treas., Steel Bands Productions, Inc., 152-32-1/2 12th Rd., Whitestone, N.Y., 11357, '69–; non-fiction bk., "Ashes to the Taste" (Univ. Publrs., '61); Rsch. on ancient Israel, one vol. hist.-fiction completed, "Son of a Star"; Co-owner, Dir., Art Originals Gallery (N.Y.C.), '58–'61; Staff, Polish Delegation to U.N., '46–'52; Columbia Univ., BS, '46; b. Sanok, Poland, 1923; p. Dr. Abraham and Antonina Katz Penzik; h. Murray Narell; c. Jeff, Andrew.

NARODICK, BLANCHE GORDON, Free-lance Publicist, Ghost Wtr.; Am. Col. of Surgeons; Tchr., high sch. jnlsm.; Edtl. Cnslt., Doctor's Hosp.; Speaker, pubcty. clinics; Theta Sigma Phi (Seattle Chptr.: Past Pres., Treas.), Tau Kappa Alpha; Univ. of Wash., BA (Jnlsm.), '30 (Phi Beta Kappa); Northwestern Univ., MA (Jnlsm.), '32; b. Seattle, Wash.; h. Philip H. Narodick; c. Kit G.; res: 6008 Princeton Ave., N.E., Seattle, Wash. 98115.

NASH, JULIE GRAFF, Adv. Dir., Whitehall Furniture Galleries, 1501 W. 86th St., Indpls., Ind. 46260, '67–; Reptr., Indpls. News Bur. of Fairchild Pubns., '63–'64; Adv., Indpls. Times, '62; Auth., Harper & Row publrs.; Theta Sigma Phi, Ind. Univ. Sch. of Med. Faculty Wms. Club (Pubcty. Chmn., '65–'70); Northwestern Univ., '60; Univ. of Wis., '61–'62; Butler Univ., '63–'64; b. Peoria, Ill., 1943; p. Marvin and Dorothy Blanton Graff; h. Dr. Franklin Nash; c. David, Jennifer; res: 3433 W. 46th, Indpls., Ind. 46208.

NASH, MARTHA NASH, Adm. Asst., Storer Television Sales, Inc., 1375 Peachtree St., N.E., Suite 552,

Atlanta, Ga. 30309, '67–; Advertising Time Sales, Inc., '61–'67; spot sls., CBS-TV, five years; AWRT (Atlanta Chptr. Past Secy.); b. Hapeville, Ga., 1924; p. John and Mabel Clair Nash; h. Edwin B. Nash; res: 2779 Knollview Dr., Decatur, Ga. 30034.

NASH, RUTH COWAN, Free-lance Wtr.; Asst. to Under-Secy. HEW, Wash., D.C., '58–'61; Cnslt., PR, Wms. Div. Repl. Nat. Comm., '57–'58; Reptr., Wash., D.C. AP, '45–'56, '40–'43; (Chgo.), '29–'40; War Corr., N. Africa, Gt. Britain, Europe, '43–'45; UPI, '29; Reptr., San Antonio (Tex.) Evening News, '28; WNPC (Pres., '47–'48), OPC, Am. Nwsp. Wms. Club of Wash., Defense Advisory Commn. on Wm. in Svcs., '58–'61; Univ. of Tex., AB; b. Salt Lake City, Ut.; p. William and Ida Baldwin Cowan; h. Bradley D. Nash; res: High Acres Farm, Harpers Ferry, W. Va. 25425.

NASH, VIRGINIA LEE WADLEY, Soc. Ed., Starkville Daily News, P.O. Box 321, 101 S. Washington, Starkville, Miss. 39759, '66–; Tchr., elementary grades; Miss. Press Wms. Assn. (Feature Writing aw., 3rd pl., '68), Oktibbeha County Genealogical Soc.; Memphis State Univ., BS, '56; b. Memphis, Tenn., 1918; p. Dr. Samuel Lewis and Bertha Elizabeth Rahm Wadley; h. Sherrill Nash; c. Carolyn, Suzanne; res: 400 Linden Circle, Starkville, Miss. 39759.

NASON, NANCY COLE, Educ. Ed., The Peekskill Evening Star, 824 Main St., Peekskill, N.Y. 10566, '65–; Panel Modr., Ctr. for Rsch. in Mktng. (N.Y.C.), '65–; Cnslt., Rsch. Inst. of Am., '62–'63; Asst. Dir., Public Svc.-Rsch. Inst. of Am., '59–'62; Ed., "Life with Liberty," Lib. Mutual Ins. Co., '56–'59; Reptr., Lewiston (Me.) Daily Sun, '53–'56; First annual scholarship, Me. Press-Radio Wm., '56; Bates Col., AB, '55; Columbia Grad. Sch. of Jnlsm., MS, '56; b. Lewiston, Me., 1933; p. Samuel and Mabel Lewis Cole; h. Donald Wentworth Nason (dec.); c. Caroline Elizabeth; res: P.O. Box 132, Putnam Valley, N.Y. 10579.

NATCHEZ, GLADYS, Assoc. Prof., City College, 135th St., Convent Ave., N.Y., N.Y. 10031, '63–; Remedial Reading Specialist, Bd. of Coop. Svcs. (Westchester); Psychotherapist, private practice; Auth: "Children with Reading Problems" (Basic Bks., '68), "Reading Disabilities: Diagnosis and Treatment" ('64); Am. Psychological Assn., Am. Orthopsychiatric Assn., Am. Acad. Psychotherapists, Intl. Reading Assn.; Columbia Univ., MA, '39; N.Y.U., PhD, '58; Adelphi, Postdoctoral Cert. '68; b. N.Y.C., 1915; p. Sidney and Hortense Stern Worms; h. Benjamin Natchez; c. Peter, Daniel, Meryl; res: 617 Parkway, Mamaroneck, N.Y. 10543.

NATHAN, ADELE GUTMAN, Free-lance Juv. Auth., non-fiction, c/o Anita Diamant Berke, 51 E. 42nd St., N.Y., N.Y. 10017: "Major John Andre—Gentleman Spy" (Franklin Watts, '70), "When Lincoln Went to Gettysburg" (Dutton), "Building the First Transcontinental Railroad" (Random House, '52; rev., '69), many others; Wtr., articles and interviews for mags.

and nwsps.; Colmst.; numerous nwsps., '32–'53; Radio series for NBC, WOR, ABC, '40–'48; Goucher Col., BA; Johns Hopkins Univ.; Columbia Univ.; b. Balt., Md.; p. Louis Kayton and Ida Newburger Gutman; res: 118 W. 57th St., N.Y., N.Y.

NATHAN, EMILY S., Owner, Emily Nathan Public Relations Counsel, 128 Central Park S., N.Y., N.Y. 10019, '34–; Special Events and Press, WOR Radio, '31–'34; Feature Wtr., The Sun, '29–'31; Nwsp. Wms. Club of N.Y. (Pegasus Aw., '65), PRSA, AWRT, Columbia Univ. Jnlsm. Alumni Assn.; Columbia Univ., B. Lit. (Jnslm.), '29; b. N.Y.C.; p. Edgar J. and Sara Solis Nathan.

NAUGHTON, LOUISE HECK, Asst. Mgr., Info. Retrieval, Society of Manufacturing Engineers, 20501 Ford Rd., Dearborn, Mich. 48128, '67–; Dir., Bacon Mem. Public Lib., '62–'66; Librn., Wayne County Public Lib., '60–'62; Lib. Aide, '54–'59; ALA, SLA, Mich. Lib. Assn.; Wayne State Univ., BS, '48; Univ. of Mich., AM (Lib. Sci.), '60; h. (div.).

NAUMANN, DOROTHY S. C., Ed., P.G.A. News, Pennsylvania Gas Association, 3450 Beechwood Blvd., Pitt., Pa. 15217, '69–; Ed., Equitable News, Equitable Gas Co., '50–'68; PR Specialist, '45–'50; Dir. PR, Methodist Church Un., '40–'45; Contrbr., articles, indsl. pubns.; Assoc. Eds. Soc. of Pitt., ICIE; Univ. of Pitt., BA, '24 (magna cum laude; Pi Lambda Theta).

NAUNTON, ENA ANNE, Med. Wtr., The Miami Herald, 1 Herald Plaza, Miami, Fla. 33101, '70–; Fashion Ed., '65–'70; Copy Ed.; Feature Wtr.; Gen. News Reptr., Sunday Courier and Press (Evansville, Ind.); Gen. News Reptr., The Evening News (Portsmouth, Eng.); Theta Sigma Phi, Fla. Wms. Press Club (10 aws.); Nat. aw., Am. Inst. of Men's and Boy's Wear, '68; Portsmouth (Eng.) Col. of Art and Tech.; British Nat. Cncl. for the Training of Jnlsts. (Cert.); b. Portsmouth, Eng.; p. Frederick and Anne Marshall Naunton; res: 333 University Dr., Coral Gables, Fla. 33134.

NEAL, BETTY DEEL, Pubns. Supvsr., Texas Society of Certified Public Accountants, 200 Corrigan Tower, Dallas, Tex. 75201, '64–; Ed., Tex. CPA News; Mng. Ed., Tex. CPA, tech. mag.; Asst. to Pres., Defenders of Am. Liberties; Off. Mgr., Commty. Svc. Bur.; Dallas IEA (Treas., '67); Press Club of Dallas (Secy., '67–'68); Nat. Repl. Conv. (alternate, '60); ICIE Aw. of Merit, '68; b. Roanoke, Va., 1930; p. Coy and Cecil Kirby Deel; h. (div.); res: Apt. 107, 3111 Douglas, Dallas, Tex. 75219.

NEAL, FRANCES POTTER, Librn., Exec. Secy., Arkansas Library Commission, 506-1/2 Center St., Little Rock, Ark. 72201, '52–; Circ., Ref. Librn., '47–'51; Librn., Warren Elementary Sch., '41–'47; Tchr., '24–'31; AAUW, BPW (2nd VP, '56), WNBA, Ark. Lib. Assn. (Pres., '50), ALA, Southwestern Lib. Assn. (Pres., '66); Progressive Farmer Wm. of Yr. aw., '56; Ark. Wm. of Yr., Democrat aw., '57; Univ. of Ark., BS (Educ.), '45; Univ. of Denver, MA, '49; b.

Strong, Ark.; p. Finis and Lucy Richardson Potter; h. Karl Neal; res: 108 Brown St., Little Rock, Ark. 72205.

NEAL, GEORGIANNE DAVIS, VP, Noblesville Daily Ledger, 957 Logan St., Noblesville, Ind. 46060; Bd. of Dirs.; Ed.; numerous volunteer pubns. and brochures, '55–'60; Feature Wtr., Asst. Wms. Ed., Indpls. News, '51–'55; Marion County Child Guidance Clinic (Bd. Mbr.), Central Ind. Cncl. of Camp Fire Girls (Bd. Mbr.), Orchard Country Day Sch. (Bd. Mbr.), Indpls. Wms. Club, Jr. League of Indpls.; Dorothy Dawe Cits., '53, '54; Radcliffe Col., AB, '51; Univ. of London, Grad. Work, '51; b. Indpls., Ind., 1930; p. Herschel and Ruth Fifer Davis; h. James Neal; c. Anne de Hayden Neal, Andrea D.; res: 7670 E. 126th St., Noblesville, Ind. 46060.

NEAL, HELEN SMITH, Free-lance Wtr., articles in more than 70 mags.; Free-lance Ed., several publrs., '67–'69; Psych. Tchr., Marymount Col., Boca Raton, Fla. 33432, '69–; Tchr., St. Ann's (Palm Beach); numerous positions in various univs.; Chief, Old Age Pension Commn. (Boston); social work and ed., house organ, Little Wanderers' Home, '20s; started several workshops; NLAPW (Palm Beach Br. VP, Treas., '65–'68; Madison Br. Treas., '38–'40), Mo. Wtrs. Guild (Pres., '46–'47; org., Columbia Br.), AAUW, AAUP, Am. Social. Soc., Danforth Fellowship, Michigan Univ., '60, numerous others; Mt. Holyoke, AB, '21; Miami Univ., Oxford, Oh., '23–'24; Univ. of Wis., '39; Univ. of Mo., '46; '53, '56–'64; b. Lynn, Mass., 1900; p. Fred Andrew and Frances Knowland Smith; h. Robert Miller Neal (dec.); c. Margaret (Mrs. A. Franklin Anderson), Ruth (dec.), Robert S., Elizabeth (Mrs. Donald E. Neitz), Carolyn (Mrs. Jack C. Hannah); res: 322 Westminster Rd., W. Palm Beach, Fla. 33405.

NEAL, MARGARET F., Free-lance Copywtr., Copy Ed.; TV commls.; previously, Copy Group Head, Grey Adv.; pfsnl. cellist; Stephens Col.; Univ. of Wis.; Univ. of Tulsa; Yale Summer Music Sch.; b. Springfield, Mass., 1933; p. Robert and Helen Smith Neal; h. A. Franklin Anderson; c. Dorcas Alicia, Keith Lowell; res: 499 Old Town Rd., Terryville, N.Y. 11776.

NEAL, PATRICIA LOUISE, Actress, c/o The Wm. Morris Agency, 151 El Camino Dr., Beverly Hills, Cal. 90212; Plays: "Another Part of the Forest," (N.Y. Critics aw., '46), "Children's Hour," "Roomful of Roses," "Suddenly Last Summer," "The Miracle Worker"; Films: "The Fountainhead," "Hasty Heart," "The Day the Earth Stood Still," "Face in the Crowd," "In Harm's Way," "Hud," (Best Fgn. Actress, '64; N.Y. Critics Aw., '64; Oscar, Acad. Aw., '64); "The Subject Was Roses"; Valiancy Aw., Wm. Un. for Cerebral Palsy, '67; Heart of the Yr. Aw., Am. Heart Assn., '68; Spirit of Achiev. Aw., Albert Einstein Col. of Medicine, '68; Northwestern Univ.; The Actor's Studio; b. Packard, Ky., 1926; p. William B. and Eura Mildred Neal; h. Roald Dahl; c. Tessa, Theo, Ophelia, Lucy; res: "Gipsy House," Gt. Missenden, Buckinghamshire, Eng.

NEALE, JUDITH ROBERTS, Pubcty. Mgr., University of Chicago Press, 5750 S. Ellis Ave., Chgo., Ill. 60637, '69–; Dir. of N.A. Prom. and Subscriptions, Apollo Magazine, '69; Edtl. Asst., Asst. Ed., '65–'68; Asst. Export Sls. Mgr., Edtl. Asst., New Am. Lib., '64–'65; Edtl. Trainee, Asst., Doubleday, '62–'64; Smith Col., BA (Hist.), '61; b. Cambridge, Mass., 1939; p. Arthur and Janice Banner Roberts; h. (div.); res: 5707 S. Kimbark Ave., Chgo., Ill. 60637.

NEALIN, PATRICIA LORETTO, Dir. of Films, WGN-TV, WGN Continental Broadcasting Company, 2501 W. Bradley Pl., Chgo., Ill. 60618, '59–; Asst. to Film Dir., '55–'59; Film Ed., Booker, '52–'55; Bdcst. Pioneers, AWRT (Nat. Dir.-at-large, '65–'68; Nat. Secy.-Treas., '68–'70; Chgo. Chptr. Pres., '63–'65); Mundelein Col., BA, '49 (Ed., col. nwsp.; Kappa Gamma Pi); b. Chgo., Ill., 1927; p. Daniel and Elizabeth Hallisey Nealin; res: 7301 N. Ridge Blvd., Chgo., Ill. 60645.

NEBEN, JACQUELINE, Dir., Mdsng. and Prom., Harper's Bazaar, 717 Fifth Ave., N.Y., N.Y. 10022, '64–; Mdsng. Mgr., Crtv. Prom. Dir., McCall's, '61–'64; Fashion and Beauty Prom. Mgr., '53–'61; Prom. Mgr., Photoplay, '48–'53; Fashion Group, AWNY; Art Dirs. Club aw., '61, '66; NAMA, '67; Soc. of Illus. aw., '66; Pratt Inst.; Columbia Univ.; b. N.Y.C.; p. Ernest and Emily Guck Neben; h. John A. Bolster; res: 8531 88th St., Woodhaven, N.Y. 11421.

NECK, G. YVONNE BRUCE, Media Dir., Advertising Incorporated, 4238 S. Peoria, Tulsa, Okla. 74105, '68–; Media Dir., Whitney Adv., '63–'67; Exec. Asst., '57–'63; AWRT (Tulsa Chptr. Pres., '68–'69; VP, '66–'67; Secy., '64–'65); Univ. of Tulsa; Tulsa Bus. Col.; b. Bridgeport, Okla., 1933; p. Lloyd and Madge Belyeu Bruce; h. Ted Neck; c. Linda Elaine, Deborah Sue, Vicky Ann; res: 5149 E. 45th St., Tulsa, Okla. 74135.

NECKER, ALICE F., Film Dir., WBBM-TV, 630 N. McClurg Court, Chgo., Ill. 60610, '61–; Asst. to Film Dir., WCBS-TV, '54–'60; Secy., '53; WABD-TV, '52; Registrar, Franklin Sch. (N.Y.C.), '44–'51; AWRT (Chgo. Chptr. Secy., '68–'70; Altrusa Club of Chgo. (Dir.-at-large, '67–'69; VP, '69–'70); Who's Who of Am. Wm.; Queens Col., BA, '43; b. N.Y.C., 1921; p. William and Louise Burke Necker; res: 1400 Lake Shore Dr., Chgo., Ill. 60610.

NEHRLING, IRENE DAHLBERG, Co-auth., seven bks. on gardening (Hearthside Press, '58–'68); mag. and nwsp. articles, buls., bks., on gardening; Wtr., food articles in mags., '21–'27; Ed., Contrbr., Am. Cookery Magazine, WWII; Asst. Prof., Dept. Head, Inst. Mgt. Dept., Cornell Univ. (Ithaca, N.Y.), '24–'27; Instr., Asst. Head, '21–'24; New Eng. Wild Flower Preservation Soc. (Bd. of Dirs.); Univ. of Minn., BS, '21 (Phi Upsilon Omicron Scholarship, '19–'20; Caleb Doerr Scholarship, '20–'21; Omicron Nu); b. Curtiss, Wis., 1900; p. Oke and Eleonora Jensen Dahlberg; h. Arno H. Nehrling; c. A. Herbert, Dorothy Irene (Mrs. War-

ren P. Higgins); res: 3 Carey Rd., Needham Heights, Mass. 02194.

NEIDLINGER, NANCY, Public Info. Dir., Vermont Heart Association, Box 596, Rutland, Vt., 05701, '66–; Conn. GOP, '65–'66; Wtr., doc., forthcoming prod.; cnslt.; special proms., Vt. Assn. of Bdcstrs., AWRT; Wells Col., BA, 1962; b. Hartford, Conn., 1940; p. Dr. William and Nancy Pickering Neidlinger; res: P.O. Box 16, Killington, Vt. 05751.

NEIGOFF, ANNE, Mng. Ed., The Child's World, Standard Educational Corporation, 130 N. Wells St., Chgo., Ill. 60606, '57–; Ed., Children's Activities Magazine, '56–'57; Ed., Supplementary Bks., Benefic Press, '54–'56; Free-lance Wtr., Edtl. work; Children's Reading Round Table (Pres., '60–'61), Wms. Nat. Bk. Assn. (Chgo. Chptr. Pres., '64–'65), Chgo. Bk. Clinic (Secy., '68–'69), Chgo. Lib. Club; b. Chgo., Ill., 1911; p. Joseph and Esther Lichtenstein Neigoff; res: 6547 N. Kedzie Ave., Chgo., Ill. 60645.

NEILL, ARLENE MONROE, News Reptr., Feature Ed., Entertainment Ed., Boulder Daily Camera, P.O. Box 591, Boulder, Colo. 80302, '45–; Dir., part-owner, '66–'69; News Reptr., '42–; '36–'37; Classified Adv. Asst., '34–'36; News Ed., Rawlins, Wyo., '39–'41; Theta Sigma Phi, Boulder Pow Wow Assn. (Pubcty. Dir., '45–'57, Kappa Kappa Gamma, Am. Legion Aux., Boulder Country Club (Charter Mbr.); Univ. of Colo., BS (Jnlsm.), '34; b. Boulder, Colo., 1913; p. Dr. Charles and Edna Paddock Monroe; h. James W. Neill; res: 501 Aurora Ave., Boulder, Colo. 80302.

NELMS, DOROTHY LEE, Media Dir., Burton-Campbell, Inc., 1800 Peachtree Rd., N.W., Atlanta, Ga. 30309, '66–; Media Byr., Liller Neal Battle and Lindsey, '60–'66; Br. Media, '58–'60; Asst. Media and Rsch. Dir., Lindsey & Co. (Richmond, Va.), '46–'58; Atlanta Media Planners Assn. (Charter Mbr.), Atlanta Bdcst. Execs. Club (Charter Mbr.); Univ. of N.C., BA (Sociol.), '46; b. Oxford, N.C., 1925; p. Lonnie Sr., and Effie Lee Nelms; res: 1582 Walthall Ct., N.W., Atlanta, Ga. 30318.

NELSON, ALIX R., Sr. Ed., Simon and Schuster, 630 Fifth Ave., N.Y., N.Y. 10020, '69–; Prom., Pubcty. Wtr., '67–'69; Asst. Ed., '60–'61; Vassar Col., BA, '60; Columbia Univ.; b. N.Y.C., 1938; p. George and Shirley Polykoff Halperin; h. Gerald Nelson; c. Shawn Elizabeth, Corin Alexandra; res: Moriches Rd., St. James, N.Y. 11780.

NELSON, CAROL S., Art Dir., Geer DuBois Inc., 220 E. 42nd St., N.Y., N.Y. 10017, '68–; Art Dir: Warren, Muller, Dolobowsky Adv., '67–'68; Johnstone Adv., '66–'67; Fashion Intl., '66; West, Weir & Bartell, '65–'66; Revlon, '62–'65; Andy Aw. hon. mention, '68; Art Dirs. Club Distinctive Merit Aw., '68; Univ. of N.Y. at Farmingdale, AAS, '57; b. Westchester, N.Y., 1938; p. W. W. and Elsie Bauer Sourbeck; res: 241 E. 17th St., N.Y., N.Y. 10003.

NELSON, CATHERINE BYRNES, Intl. PR Cnslt., 5 Via Altino, Milan, Italy 20144, '66–; accounts incl. Norman, Craig & Kummel—Italy; PR, Fibramianto S.r.i., '63–'65; Accounting and Dir. of Client Contracts, Mary Wells, CPA, '55–'62; Federazione Relazioni Pubbliche; Fondazione "Pro Juvente" Aw., Don Carlo Gnocci, '68; Univ. of Milan Aw. for work at Intl. Congress on Muscle Diseases, '69; Univ. of Richmond, Va. (Modern Language Scholarship); attended RPI Ext. of Col. of William and Mary, Richmond; b. Phila., Pa., 1936; p. Francis Thomas and Marion Kathryn Brown Byrnes; h. Nelson; c. Marion Ruth Nelson.

NELSON, EDNA DEU PREE, Free-lance Wtr.; Assoc. Ed., Am. Water Works Assn.; Ed., PR, Air Reduction Co.; Auth: "The California Dons" (Appleton, '62), "O'Higgins & Don Bernardo" (Dutton, '54); numerous mag. articles; PEN; Univ. of Cal.; Columbia Univ.; b. Oberlin, Kan.; p. Edward and Anora Nelson Deu Pree; h. (dec.); res: 614 Blvd. Way, Oakland, Cal. 94610.

NELSON, EVE AMIGONE, VP, Spartans Industries, Inc., 450 W. 33rd St., N.Y., N.Y. 10001, '68–; VP, Nat. Adv., Sls. Prom., E. J. Korvette, Inc.; VP, Nat. Adv., Sls. Prom., Meyer Bros. (Tex.), '52–'59; Divisional Adv. Mgr., R. H. Macy's (N.Y.), '50–'52; Tchr., Adv., Univ. of Houston, '57–'58; Auth., "Take It from Ever" ('68); Univ. of Buffalo, Sch. of Jnlsm.; Studio Theater Sch. of Playwriting, Prod.; h. Warren Nelson; res: 136 E. 56th St., N.Y., N.Y.

NELSON, HAZEL FOWLER, Nelson Mortgage Company, Inc., 299 S.W. 27th Ave., Miami, Fla. 33135, '41–; Military Svc. Ed., The Miami Herald, '42–'45; Reptr., Feature Wtr., Okla. City Times, '37–'41; Reptr., Norman Transcript, '30–'37; Tchr., Eng. and Jnlsm., Chickasha HS, '27–'30; Intl. Platform Assn., Marquis Biographical Lib. Soc. (Advisory mbr.), Theta Sigma Phi (Greater Miami Chptr. Charter Mbr. and Pres., '52–'53), Active in civic affairs; Am. War Brides Silver Aw. for nwsp. series, '46; Who's Who of Am. Wm.; Who's Who in Commerce and Industry; Who's Who in South and Southeast; Dic. of Intl. Biog.; Univ. of Okla., BA (Eng., Jnlsm.), '27; Univ. of Wis., grad work, '28; b. Mulhall, Okla., 1905; p. Oscar and Belle Lowe Fowler; h. Bowen Nelson; c. Creston Annette; res: 10255 S.W. 53rd Ave., Miami, Fla. 33156.

NELSON, ILSE NETTER, Educ. Cnslt., Consultants on European Schools; N.Y.C. Sch. volunteer; Cncl. on Basic Educ., Am. Assn. for Friendship with Switzerland, Cosmopolitan Club of N.Y.C.; Oxford Univ.; Univ. of Vienna, '36; N.Y.U. Inst. of Fine Arts, '39; b. Mannheim, Germany, 1914; p. Arthur and Kate Netter; h. George Nelson; c. Gerald, Irene Bareau, Ingrid; res: 12 E. 93rd St., N.Y., N.Y. 10028.

NELSON, JANET WAGNER, Free-lance Wtr.; Gen. Ed., Ski Magazine, Universal Publishing and Distributing Corp., 235 E. 45th St., N.Y., N.Y. 10017, '68–; Mng. Ed.; Articles Ed., Parade; Asst. Ed., Good Housekeeping; Assoc. Ed. and Pic. Ed., AT&T; Ed., Mich. Bell Telephone; Auth., "How to Ski" (Charlton Pubns., '63); OPC, Theta Sigma Phi; NET Sch. Bell Aw., '64; Mich. State Univ., BA, '53 (hons.); b. Detroit, Mich., 1931; p. Robert and Isabell Taylor Wagner; h. Ted Nelson; res: Finney Farm Rd., Croton-on-Hudson, N.Y. 10520.

NELSON, JOSEPHINE BJORNSON, Assoc. Prof., Info. Specialist, University of Minnestoa, Institute of Agriculture, St. Paul, Minn. 55101, '61–; Daily Program on KUOM (Univ. of Minn.); Asst. Prof., Asst. Ext. Ed., '57–'61; Instr., '49–'57; Pubcty. Asst., '42–'49; Instr., '33–'42: Concordia Col. (Moorhead), Menaul Sch. (Albuquerque, N.M.), Windom (Minn.) HS, Clifton (Tex.) Jr. Col.; Free-lance Wtr.; NLAPW (Pres. Minn. Br., '68–'70; 1st VP, '66–'68; 2nd VP, '58–'60); Minn. Press Wm., Minn. State Nutrition Cncl. (Secy., '55–'59), Epsilon Sigma Phi (Pi Chptr. Pres., '60), AWRT (N. Star Chptr. Bd. of Dirs., '69–), Am. Assn. of Agricultural Col. Eds., AAUW (Moorhead Chptr. Pres., '40–'42); Minn. Educ. Assn. Sch. Bell aw.; Minn. Safety Cncl. Aws. of Merit; Gamma Sigma Delta; St. Olaf Col., BA, '27 (summa cum laude); Univ. of Ia., MA, '30; b. Twin Valley, Minn., 1906; p. Lars and Georgina Herreid Bjornson; h. John S. Nelson; res: 2222 Hendon Ave., St. Paul, Minn. 55108.

NELSON, KRISTIN HARMON, Artist, Kristin, Inc. (Studio and Gallery), 723-1/2 N. La Cienega Blvd., L.A., Cal. 90069; First one-wm. show in L.A., Sari-Heller Gallery, (Beverly Hills, '67); V.P., newly formed Ballet Soc. of L.A.; b. N. Hollywood, Cal., 1945; p. Tom and Elyse Knox Harmon; h. Rick Nelson; c. Tracy Kristine, twins Gunnar Eric and Matthew Gray.

NELSON, MARY JO, Courthouse Reptr., Oklahoma City Times, Oklahoma Publishing Co., 500 N. Broadway, Okla. City, Okla. 73125, '61–; Reptr., '54–'61; Asst. State Ed., '51–'54; Copy Messenger, '45–'51; Theta Sigma Phi (Reg. Dir.; Past Okla. City Chptr. Pres.), Religious Newswtrs. Assn. (Nat. Treas., '60–'62); Am. Col. PR Assn. aw., '65; Am. Chess Fedn. aw., '57; Okla. Jr. City Col.; b. Maysville, Okla., 1927; p. Harlan and Alma Cowan Nelson; res: 3308 N. Utah Ave., Okla. City, Okla. 73112.

NELSON, SUSAN HOLTZ, Pubns. Ed., Personnel and Public Affairs Dept., Towmotor Corporation, subsidiary of Caterpillar Tractor Co., 16100 Euclid Ave., Cleve., Oh. 44112, '64–; Reptr., Evansville (Ind.) Press, '64; Copy Desk Ed., '63; Northern Oh. Indsl. Eds. Assn., Theta Sigma Phi (Purdue Univ. Chptr. Pres., '63–'64); Purdue Univ., BS (Eng. Literature), '64; b. Evansville, Ind., 1942; p. Albert and Helen Ziss Holtz; h. Walter M. Nelson; res: 276 E. 244th St., Apt. 210, Euclid, Oh. 44123.

NEMEYER, CAROL ANMUTH, DLS Candidate, Columbia Univ., Sls., Asst. Librn., McGraw-Hill, Inc., '61–'66; WNBA, SLA, ALA, ISIS, Private Libs. Assn.; N.Y. Tech. Svc. Librns.; Beta Phi Mu (Nu Chptr. Pres.,

'67–'69); Berea Col.; L.I. Univ., BA, '49; Columbia Univ., MLS, '60; b. N.Y.C.; p. Archie Anmuth and Betty Anmuth Rosalin; h. Sheldon Nemeyer; res: 415 W. 23rd St., N.Y., N.Y. 10011.

NEMY, ENID, Reptr., New York Times, 229 West 43rd St., N.Y., N.Y. 10036, '63–; Wtr., Ed., The Canadian Press; Wtr., Bdcstr., Canadian Bdcst. Corp.; Freelance Wtr., mags., incl. New York Magazine, McCalls; Canadian Wms. Press Club (Past Pres.) NWC of N.Y. (Past VP); United Col., Winnipeg, Manitoba; Univ. of Manitoba; b. Winnipeg, Manitoba, Can.; p. Benjamin and Frances Nemy; h. S. Ralph Cohen; res: 1040 Park Ave., N.Y., N.Y. 10028.

NESBIN, ESTHER WINTER, Dir. of Lib. Svcs., Palomar Col. Lib., San Marcos, Cal. 92069, '65–; Head, Dept. of Lib. Sci., '62–'65; Librn. and Instr. in Lib. Sci., '47–'65; Librn., Temple of the Jewelled Cross (L.A.), '42–'46; Instr. in Lib. Sci., Univ. of Buffalo (N.Y.), '39–'42; Lib. Asst., Grosvenor Lib., '31–'42; Auth., "Shaker Literature in the Grosvenor Library"; Cnslt., Camp Pendleton Law Lib., Monterey Jr. Col., Palo Verde Jr. Col. Lib.; Instr., Flower Arrangement, Palomar Col., '65; Advisory Comm., Cal. Lib. Tech. Program; Cal. Lib. Assn. (Jr. Col. Librns. Round Table: Pres., '66; VP, '65; Secy., '64); Cal. Lib. Assn. of Sch. Libs., Cal. Tchrs. Assn., Delta Kappa Gamma; Univ. of Buffalo, BA, '31; Lib. Sci. Cert., '32; San Diego State Col., '48; b. Denver, Colo., 1910; p. Oscar and Helen Schmandt Winter; h. Anthony Nesbin (dec.); res: P.O. Box 102, San Marcos, Cal. 92069.

NESTLER, ALICE THERESA, Analyst, State Office of Economic Opportunity, 100 Arlington Ave., Nashville, Tenn. 37210, '67–; Indsl. Communicator, S.E. Massengill Co., '48–'66; Ed., Makeup, Reptr., Smyth County News (Marion, Va.), '47–'48; Reptr., Providence (R.I.) Jnl. and Bul., '44–'46; PR, Pubcty., News Bur., Mt. Holyoke Col. (S. Hadley, Mass.), '42–'44; Reptr., Makeup, ed., Daily Record (Long Branch, N.J.), '39–'42; Appalachian IEA (past Secy., Treas., Pres., Rep. to Nat. Assn.); AAIE (Bd. of Dirs.; VP; Secy.); Mt. Holyoke Col., BA, '39; Univ. of Pitt., OEO Training Prog. Inst., '66–'67; b. Montclair, N.J., 1918; p. Peter and Helen Cook Nestler; res: PO Box 7125, Nashville, Tenn. 37210.

NEU, JOANN BRT, Publr., Wausa Gazette, Wausa, Neb. 68786, '65–; Tchr., '48–'53; Neb. Press Assn.; Univ. of Neb.; Wayne State Col., BA, '48; b. Lincoln, Neb., 1927; p. Otto K. and Leona Nuernberger Brt; h. Dillon Neu (dec.); c. Patricia, Bradley; res: Wausa, Neb. 68786.

NEUMAN, SUSAN CATHERINE, Dir. of Communications, Ferendino/Grafton/Pancoast, 800 Douglas Entrance, Coral Gables, Fla., '69–; Ed., The Miamian, '65–'69; Reptr., Colmst., North Dade Journal, '64–'65; Wtr., Miami Herald, '62–'64; Reptr., Colmst., North Dade Hub, '59–'61; ICIE, Fla. Mag. Assn., Mag. Publrs. Assn., Theta Sigma Phi (Headliner aw., '64), Am. Soc.

of Mag. Eds., Adv. Club of Gtr. Miami; Who's Who of Am. Wm.; Univ. of Miami, AB, '64; b. Detroit, Mich., 1942; p. Paul and Elsie Goetz Neuman; res: 4080 N.W. 165th St., Miami, Fla. 33054.

NEUMANN, RUTH VENDLEY, Pres., Neumann Associates, 980 Greenwood Ave., Winnetka, Ill. 60093, '58; Ed., Orchestra News Magazine; Adv. Mgr., Chgo. Musical Instrument Co.; Auth: "You Need Music," "Cooking with Spirits," "Conversation Piece Recipes"; articles on music; Rosary Col., AB, '27; b. Chgo., Ill., 1907; p. Anton and Margaret Hastings Vendley; h. Arthur Neumann; c. Ruth (Mrs. Thomas Burkhart), Barbara (Mrs. John P. Donlan).

NEUMANN, SYLVIA SIMMONS, VP, Young & Rubicam, Inc., 285 Madison Ave., N.Y., N.Y. 10017, '62–; Asst. to Bd. Chmn., '68–; Asst. to Pres., '62–'68; Prom. Specialist, special projects group, '60–'62; Assoc. Crtv. Dir., dir. mail and contests, McCann-Erickson (N.Y.C.), '55–'60; Crtv. Dir., Amos Parrish Adv. Agcy., '55; Prom. Copy Chief, Grey Adv. Agcy., '52–'54; Copywtr., '50–'52; Clubmobile Group Head, ARC (Italy), '42–'45; Auth: "Successful Contests and How to Create Them," "The Creative Approach to Premiums," numerous articles in bus. jnls.; AWNY, Adv. Wtrs. Assn. of N.Y.; Medal of Freedom, '45; Purple Heart, '44; various aws. from bus. groups for best indsl. film of yr.; Bklyn. Col., BA, '40 (cum laude); Columbia Univ., MA (Eng. Lit.), '41; b. N.Y.C.; h. 1. Alexander L. Harvey (div.) 2. Hans H. Neumann, M.D.; res: 74 Old Belden Hill Rd., Wilton, Conn. 06897.

NEUWIRTH, PATRICIA TREIB, Asst. Ed., Esquire Magazine, 488 Madison Ave., N.Y., N.Y. 10022, '69–; Edtl. Rschr., manuscripts; Free-lance Rschr., gathering material for Esquire Wtrs., others; Bklyn. Col., '65; b. N.Y.C., 1943; p. Aaron and Birdie Adler Treib; h. Alan Neuwirth; res: c/o B. Neuwirth, 1 Elm Lane, Great Neck, N.Y. 10020.

NEVILLE, EMILY CHENEY, Auth., fiction, Harper & Row, 49 E. 33rd St., N.Y., N.Y. 10017; five bks. incl. "Fogarty" ('69), "Berries Goodman" ('65); Jane Addams aw., '66), "It's Like This, Cat" ('63); John Newbery Medal, '64); N.Y. Mirror, '41–'42; N.Y. Daily News, '40; Bryn Mawr Col., AB, '40; b. Manchester, Conn., 1919; p. Howell and Anne Bunce Cheney; h. Glenn Neville (dec.); c. Emily Tam, Glenn H., Dessie Louise, Marcy Ann, Alec; res: Keene Valley, N.Y. 12943.

NEW, ANNE LATROBE, Cnslt. on Commty. Rels., National Accreditation Council for Agencies Serving the Blind and Visually Handicapped, 79 Madison Ave., N.Y., N.Y. 10016; Asst. to Gen. Dir., Am. Br. of Intl. Social Svc., '66–'68; Asst. to Exec. VP. Nat. Recreation and Park Assn., '57–'66; Coordr. of Public Info. Svcs., Girl Scouts of the U.S.A., '47–'57; Cnslt. to non-profit health and welfare agcys., '68–'69, various orgs.; Univ. of S.C., AB (Educ.), '30 (Phi Beta Kappa); b. Evanston, Ill., 1910; p. Charles and Agnes Bateman New; h. John

Timmerman; c. Jan (Mrs. Harris G. Abbott); res: 235 S. Barry Ave., Marmaroneck, N.Y. 10543.

NEWCOMB, DORIS DOYLE, Head Librn., Central High School, 31 Main St., Binghamton, N.Y. 13905, '57–; Ref. Librn., Lab. Sch. Librn., Colo. State Col., '35–'45; AAUW, WNBA, N.Y. Lib. Assn.; Univ. of Denver, BA, '34; Colo. State Col., MA, '35; Syracuse Univ., summers '59, '60; b. Buffalo, S.D.; p. William and Dora Doyle; h. Josiah Newcomb; res: R.D. 5, Brooks Rd., Binghamton, N.Y. 13905.

NEWELL, DEBORAH FUHS, Reptr., Ocean County Daily Observer & Ocean County Sun, 530 Brick Blvd., Brick Township, N.J. 08723, '69–; Trenton State Col.; Ocean County Col., AA (Educ.), '68; b. Cheyenne, Wyo., 1948; p. Paul and Norma Glockler Fuhs; h. Roger Newell; res: Terrace Garden Apt. 7A, Toms River, N.J. 08753.

NEWELL, DOROTHY JAMES, Gen. Assigt. Reptr., Religion Ed., The Patriot Ledger, 13 Temple St., Quincy, Mass. 02169, '63–; TPL Reviewer, arts page, '63–; Asst. Ed., Soc. and Ch. Ed., Gen. Assigt. Reptr., Butler County News-Record (Zelienople, Pa.) '55–'63; News Dir., New Eng. Nazarene Dist., '63–; News Dir., Pitt. Nazarene Dist., '55–'63; Religious News Wtrs. Assn. (Secy., '68–'70), BPW, RPRC (Assoc., '69–); Keystone Press aw., PNPA Spot News 2nd wkly. cit., '63; Nazarene Col., '45–'46; Met. Jr. Col. (Kan. City, Mo.), '52–'53; b. Brockton, Mass., 1928; p. Locke and Katharine Alger James; h. Rev. J. Scott Newell; c. John S., Kerry J., Thomas M., Herbert L., Scott R.; res: 138 Vassall St., Wollaston, Mass. 02170.

NEWELL, VERNA B., TV Hostess and Prodr., WDAY-TV, 207 N. Fifth St., Fargo, N.D. 58102, '56–; On-the-Air Personality, WDAY, '66–'69; Comml. Wtr. and On-the-Air Personality, KFGO, '53–'56; Comml. Wtr. and On-the-Air Personality, WKBH, (La Crosse, Wis.), '51–'52; AWRT (North Star Chptr. Charter Mbr.), Sweet Adelines, Inc. (PR Dir. of Nat. Bd. of Dirs.); Valley City State Tchrs. Col.; b. Fargo, N.D.; p. Edward and Anna Hanson Bekken; c. Bill Edward, Robert Dale; res: 2821 Eighth St. N., Fargo, N.D. 58102.

NEWMAN, CLYDE GREENHAW, City Ed., Times Publishing Co., 111 W. Rush, Harrison, Ark. 72601, '36–; Reptr., '26–'36; News Corr., Ark. Gazette, '27–; Corr., Little Rock Bur. of AP and Atlanta (Ga.) INS, many yrs.; Wtr., features, trade jnl. articles; Am. Legion Aux. (Secy.), Harrison BPW, Am. Red Cross, active ch., commty. work; Ark. "Top Ten Stories" AP aw., '41; Harrison Bus. Col.; b. Valley Springs, Ark., 1896; p. Breck and Lizzie Huffman Greenhaw; h. John Robert Newman, Jr.; res: 1512 Park Ave., Harrison, Ark. 72601.

NEWMAN, HELEN WILSON, Radio-TV Dir., Barber & Drullard Inc., 633 Delaware Ave., Buffalo, N.Y. 14202, '57–; Copywtr., Prodr., adv. agcys., '49–'57;

Radio Dir., Wtr., Prodr., network docs.; Wtr., one-act plays for ch. group prod., Ch. World Svc. (N.Y.C.), '46–'48; WACs, sergeant in PR, Wtr., Prodr., radio plays for recruiting, Staff Reptr., Ft. Dix Post, '43–'46; Tchr., adult educ. class in adv., Buffalo YMCA; numerous public svc. pubcty. campaigns; Adv. Wm. of Buffalo (Bd. of Dirs; Pres., '62–'63; Jr. Achiev., '67–'68; Adv. Wm., '58–'65; Wm. of the Yr. Aw., '61–'62); Columbia Univ.; b. Middletown, N.Y., 1916; p. John and Hildred Wilson; h. Robert E. Newman; res: 947 Delaware Ave., Buffalo, N.Y. 14209.

NEWMAN, JEANETTE, Pres., Community Relations Counselors, 78 Hall Ave., New City, N.Y. 10956; PRSA, Pubcty. Club of N.Y., Am. Assn. for the Advancement of Sci., Am. Geriatrics Soc.

NEWMAN, LILLIAN J. TESSER, Mng. Ed., Wall Street Transcript, 54 Wall St., N.Y., N.Y. 10005, '63–; Fed. of Arts; Commty. Svc. Soc.; Hunter Col., BA; N.Y. Inst. of Finance, Cert. in Security Analysis; b. N.Y.C.; p. Max and Sadie Crystal Tesser; h. Elias Newman; res: 215 Park Row, N.Y., N.Y. 10038.

NEWMAN, MAXINE WISE, Supvsr. of Info. Svcs., Columbia Broadcasting System, CBS-Washington Bureau, 2020 M St., N.W., Wash., D.C. 20036, '69–; Secy., Assgt. Desk, CBS News-Wash. Bur., '68; Adm. Asst., PR, Wash., D.C., Urban League, '67–'68; Exec. Secy., Compton Advertising, Inc. (L.A., Cal.), '66–'67; Howard Univ., '62–'63; U.C.L.A., '63–'66; b. L.A., Cal., 1945; p. Percy and Janet Berry Wise; h. Samuel Newman; res: 5600 Chillum Pl., N.E., #102, Wash., D.C. 20011.

NEWMAN, NANCY BLITZSTEN, Asst. Dir. Commty. Rels., Michael Reese Hospital and Medical Center, 2929 S. Ellis Ave., Chgo., Ill. 60616, '66–; PR Dir., Wtr., Univ. of Chgo. Hosps. and Clinics, '64–'66; Staff Wtr., Prom. Dept., Chgo. Sun-Times and Chgo. Daily News, '58–'64; edtl. writing; Prod. Cnslt., Prodrs. Film Studios, '58; Assoc. Ed., Bus. Screen Magazine, '57–'58; Film Cnslt., Ed., Nat. Dir. of Safety Films, Nat. Safety Cncl., '52–'57; Faculty Mbr., PR Inst. of Am. Hosp. Assn., '66; Featured Speaker, Am. Hosp. Assn. 69th Annual Meeting, '67; PR Cnslt., Roosevelt Univ. and Pro Musica Soc. of Chgo.; Scriptwtr., "Ether Trail Hazards" (U.S. Dept. of Health, '56); PRSA, Pubcty. Club of Chgo. (Secy.), Am. Soc. of Hosp. PR Dirs., Hosp. PR Dirs. of Chgo., Chgo. Hosp. Cncl., Arts Club of Chgo., Chgo. Press Club; Welfare PR Forum Helen Cody Baker aw. for fund raising piece, '66; Univ. of Chgo., BA, BS, '52; b. Chgo., Ill., 1931; p. Harry and Alice Karno Blitzsten; h. Morton Newman; res: 433 W. Briar Pl., Chgo., Ill. 60657.

NEWMAN, SHIRLEE PETKIN, Auth: "Liliuokalani: Young Hawaiian Queen," "About the Men Who Run Your City," "Folk Tales—Latin America," 8 other juv. bks., fiction and non-fiction; Assoc. Ed., Child Life Magazine; Copywtr., adv. and PR; AE; b. Boston, Mass., 1924; p. Isreal and Ida Goldstein Petkin; h.

Jackson Newman; c. Paula, Jeff; res: 34 Roosevelt Rd., Newton Centre, Mass. 02159.

NEWMAN, THELMA R., Exec. Dir., Classroom Renaissance, 930 Stuyvesant Ave., Union, N.J. 07083, '68–'70; Ed.-Designer, Robert Zeidman, '66–'67; Cnslt: J. L. Hammett Co., '67–'69; Cormac Corp., '62; Esso, '61–'62; Instr., Art and Art Educ., N. Tex. State Col., '48–'49; N.J. State Col., '50–'52; '47–'48; Lectr.; onewm. shows of photog., other exhbns.; Inventor of Poly-Mosaic, art-craft material; Auth., two bks. on art form, ency. contrb., numerous mag articles on art, educ., travel; rschr.; City Col., BBA (Adv.), '46; N.Y.U., MA (Art in Higher Educ.), '48; Columbia Univ. Tchrs. Col., Ed D (Art Educ.), '63; h. Jack Newman; c. two sons.

NEWMARK, SANDI EHRLICH, Feature Ed., The Pet Dealer Magazine, '69–; Edtl. Asst., Jewish News (Newark, N.J.), '68; Asst. Articles Ed., Ingenue Magazine, '67–'68; Feature Wtr., Suffolk Sun, '66–'67; Edtl. Asst., Look Magazine, '66; Theta Sigma Phi; Syracuse Univ., BA, '65; b. Newark, N.J., 1944; p. Milton and Jean Geltman Ehrlich; h. Alan Newmark; res: 66–36 Yellowstone Blvd., Forest Hills, N.Y. 11375.

NEWSOME, RUTH TAPLIN, VP, Newsome & Company, Inc., 4300 Prudential Tower, Boston, Mass. 02199, '68–; Treas., '57–'68; Dir., '57–'62; Dir. of Wms. Div., Dir. of New Eng. Consumer Panel, '63–; Special Project Dir., Carling Brewing Co. (Natick), '60–'63; Area Dir., New Eng. States, Radio Free Europe, '66–'69; Dir., Special Events for New Eng. States Exhbn., N.Y. World's Fair, '64–'65; AWRT (Mass. Chmn., '62–'65), Boston Pubcty. Club, Boston Wellesley Club; Wellesley Col., BA, '29; b. Boston, Mass., 1908; p. George and Grace Bachelder Taplin; h. Paul A. Newsome; c. Patricia (Mrs. Clare C. Leiby, Jr.), Nancy (Mrs. Bruce G. Bailey); res: 35 Meadowbrook Rd., Needham, Mass. 02192.

NEWSON, NAOMI SISK, Prog., Sls. Traf. Mgr., WGHP-TV, Sheraton Hotel Bldg., High Point, N.C. 27260, '68–; Sls. Coordr., '66–'68; Asst. Bus. Mgr., '63–'66; Traf. Mgr., WSJS-TV (Winston-Salem), '60–'63; Sls. Coordr., WFGA-TV (Jacksonville, Fla.); '55–'60; Tchr., '43–'53; AWRT; State Col., Nat. Bus. Col., Roanoke, Va.; h. (div.); c. Nicky Newson; res: Dalton Rd., King, N.C. 27201.

NEWTON, BETTY WRIGHT, Elementary Sch. Tchr., Anton Schools, 100 Ellwood Blvd., Anton, Tex. 79313, '51–'54, '63–'69; Tchr., Project Head Start, summers, '68, '69; Panel Mbr. and Physical Educ. Demonstrator, Head Start Workshop, '68, '69; Adult Basic Educ. Instr., '67–'69; Phi Kappa Phi (grad. mbr.), Tex. State Tchrs. Assn., NEA, Mortar Bd. Alumnae, Tex. Fedn. of Wms. Clubs (past Pres., Secy., Treas.) Theta Sigma Phi; Tex. Tech. Col., BA (Jnlsm.), '51; MA (Educ.), '68 (Grad. Fellowship); b. Anton, Tex., 1930; p. Henry and Mary Van Dyke Wright; h. Madison Newton; c. Kimberly Kay, Monty; res: Box 566, Anton, Tex. 79313.

NEWTON, HAZEL TOMSON, Home Svc. Dir., Public Service Company of Colorado, P.O. Box 551, 1155 Canyon Blvd., Boulder, Colo. 80301, '68–; (Grand Junction, Colo.), '60–'68; Food Econst., Safeway Stores, Inc., '57–'60; Dickinson Bus. Col. (Topeka, Kan.), '36–'37; Colo. State Univ. (Ft. Collins, Colo.), BS, '41 (Omicron Nu, Phi Kappa Phi); b. Dover, Kan., 1918; p. Joseph and Nina Flickinger Tomson; h. Harold Newton (dec.); c. Douglas, Kathleen Woeber, Nina Jo; res: 4440 Laguna Pl., Apt. #306, Boulder, Colo. 80303.

NEWTON, LUCELLE SMITH, Soc. Ed., The Camden News, 113 Madison Ave., Camden, Ark., '61–; Pianist, Reptr., Rotary and Kiwanis; Charter Organizer, Pianist for Jaycee Minstrels, 25 yrs.; Chaperone for Miss Camden to state pageant, '55–'61; Tchr., piano and voice, 20 yrs.; Ouachita Baptist Col., BA, '27; b. Lapile, Ark., 1908; p. William and Ida Cobb Smith; h. Jack Jay Newton; c. William J., James L.; res: 1246 Moses N.W., Camden, Ark. 71701.

NEY, ELEANOR MARGARET, Wms. Ed., Westchester Rockland Newspapers Inc., 8 Church St., White Plains, N.Y. 10602, '61–; Educ. Ed., Food Ed.; Soc.; Sch. News Ed., The Standard Star, New Rochelle (N.Y.); Asst. Wms. Ed., Westchester County Publrs. Inc.; Co-dir., Staff Mbrs., '59–; Dir., WRN "A Way With Words" Conf., '56–; taught Adult Educ., crtv. writing; various orgs., aws.; b. N.Y.C.; p. William and Effie MacDonald Ney; h. Joseph C. Bergin; res: 37 Davis Ave., New Rochelle, N.Y. 10805.

NICCUM, GRACE PECHER, VP, Richard T. Clarke Company, 96 Jessie St., S.F., Cal. 94105, '69–; Media and Prod. Mgr., '64–'69; Off. Mgr., Miller Freeman Publ. (N.Y.C.), '62–'64; Corr., Dept. Mgr. (S.F.), '59–'62; S.F. City Col.; Golden Gate Col.; New Sch. of Social Rsch.; b. West Branch, Ia., 1935; p. Rudolph and Ruth Ploog Pecher; h. Richard Niccum (div.); res: 128 Carlotta Circle, Mill Valley, Cal. 94941.

NICHOLL, JANE, Assoc. Prodr., CBS News, 524 W. 57th St., N.Y., N.Y. 10019, '67–; Prod. Asst., Assoc. Dir., Assoc. Prod., Granada TV (Manchester, Eng.), '56–'66; Felixstone Col., Suffolk, Eng.; b. Harrogate, Yorks., Eng., 1935; p. John and Ruth Watson Green; h. Bernard Sahlins; res: 36-1/2 E. 75th St., N.Y., N.Y. 10021.

NICHOLS, CECILIA FAWN, Auth., "The Goat Who Ate a Cow" (Bruce, '64), articles, short stories, poetry, two plays; currently writing three bks: sci.-fiction, biog. of Blind Boone, and psychic experiences; Tchr., Neb., Cal., Ariz., U.S. Air Force Bases, '29–'60; Tchr., writing, San Gabriel Valley Schs., '60–'63; Movie Critic and Feature Wtr., Omaha (Neb.) Bee News, '26–'29; Mgr., Classified Adv., Wms. Page Ed., Tucson (Ariz.) Daily Citizen, '34–'35; recognized for teaching methods; active in theatrical work; appearances in operas; Cal. Retired Tchrs. Assn.; Univ. of Omaha; Univ. of Neb.; Grad. work, Univ. of Southern Cal.; b. Bellevue, Neb., 1906; p. Robert and Ellen McGinley Nichols;

res: 74039 Playa Vista Dr., Twentynine Palms, Cal. 92277.

NICHOLSON, EVA CONSTANTINE, Co-owner, Gen. Mgr., Radio Augusta, Inc., 2605 Walton Way, Augusta, Ga. 30904, '61–; Tchr., '35–'38; Former Co-owner, Gen. Mgr., WAUG; Current Dir., Secy-Treas., Radio WANS; Agnes Scott Col., AB, '35; h. George C. Nicholson; c. Mrs. Michael Papapavalou, Mrs. Nicholas Frangias, Christopher, Sam.

NICHOLSON, MARGARET KATHERINE, Corp. Secy., Head of Contract and Copyright Dept., Farrar, Straus and Giroux, Inc., 19 Union Sq. E., N.Y., N.Y. 10003, '64–; Corp. Secy., '69–; Head of Contract and Copyright Dept., MacMillan Co., '54–'64; Head of Publ. Dept., Oxford Univ. Press., '30–'52; bks: "Manual of Copyright Practice" ('45, '56, Reissue '70), "A Practical Style Guide for Authors and Editors" ('67), others; frequent guest lectr.; contrbr. to encys. on usage, spelling, copyright; Copyright Soc. of U.S.A. (Asst. Secy., '67); Univ. of Cal., Berkeley, AB, '25; grad. work, '26; b. S.F., Cal., 1904; p. William and Abigail Cochrane Nicholson; h. Laurence D. Smith (dec.); c. Kathryn Smith Miller; res: 96 Fifth Ave., N.Y., N.Y. 10011.

NICKERSON, GERTRUDE SAMPSON, Assoc. Ed., The Beanstalk, Burnham & Morrill Div., Wm. Underwood Co., One Bean Pot Circle, Portland, Me. 04104, '57–; Employee, '35–; AAIE, OES; b. Turner, Me., 1914; p. Charles and Rosa Willard Sampson; h. (div.); c. William L.; res: 225 Evans St., S. Portland, Me. 04106.

NICKS, IDA CLEMENT, Safety Cnslt., Tennessee Department of Highway Safety, C2-242 Cordell Hull Bldg., Nashville, Tenn. 37210, '65–; Lectr. on safety, numerous orgs.; Wms. Dir., daily shows "Ida Views and News," "Memories and Melodies," WDKN (Dickson, Tenn.), '50–'65; Speech Tchr.; AWRT (Nashville Chptr. Pres., '65–'66); Memphis-Shelby County Safety Cncl. special aw. for "Outstanding Work in Safety," '67; Future Homemakers of Am. (Hon. Mbr., '69); Am. Airlines cit. "Fair Lady" for safety prom.; many civic certs.; Martin Col. grad.; Nashville Conservatory of Music; b. Dickson, Tenn.; p. James and Agnes Work Clement; h. Carl Nicks (dec.); c. Anne (Mrs. J. O. Williams, Jr.), Betty Lou (Mrs. Bob Wolcott); res: 3415 West End Ave., Apt. 602, Nashville, Tenn. 37203.

NICOT, SUZANNE LOUISE, Asst. Dir., Cary Memorial Library, 1874 Massachusetts Ave., Lexington, Mass. 02173, '66–; Ref. Librn., '62–; Ref. Librn., Winchester Public Lib., '61–'62; Cataloger, Fogg Museum, Harvard Univ., '60–'61; Cataloger, Harvard Law Sch. Lib., '54–'60; Mass. Lib. Assn., New Eng. Lib. Assn.; Simmons Col., BS (Lib. Sci.), '54; b. Montreal, Quebec, Can.; p. Simon and Jeanne Arlaud Nicot; res: 1384 Commonwealth Ave., Boston, Mass. 02134.

NIDA, JANE BOLSTER, Dir., Arlington County Department of Libraries, 1015 N. Quincy St., Arlington, Va. 22201, '57–; Asst. Dir., '54–'57; Dir., Public Lib. (Falls Church, Va.), '51–'54; rsch. lib. work, Order Librn.; lib. lit. contrbs.; various organizations; Aurora Col. (Aurora, Ill.), BA, '42; Univ. of Ill. (Urbana, Ill.), BS (Lib. Sci.), '43; b. Chgo., Ill., 1918; p. Chalmer and Elsie Sonderman Bolster; h. Dow Hughes Nida; c. Janice (Mrs. Richard G. Thatcher); res: 4907 29th St., N., Arlington, Va. 22207.

NIELSEN, HELEN BERNIECE, Auth., mystery and suspense, Wm. Morrow & Co., Inc., 425 Park Ave. S., N.Y., N.Y. 10016, '51–; 15 bks., incl: "Verdict Suspended," "Darkest Hour"; mag. fiction; TV Wtr.; Auths. Guild, ACLU, NAACP; aws: Best Detective Stories (Cook), '55, '59; Ellery Queen's Double Dozen, '64; "Decision," Manhunt Anthology, '58; "Hunch," Magulies Anthology, '59; Ellery Queen Anthology, '68; Chgo. Art Inst., '32–'34 (scholarships); U.C.L.A., ext. courses; b. Roseville Twp., Ill.; p. Christian and May Christensen Nielsen; res: 2622 Victoria Dr., Laguna Beach, Cal., 92651.

NIELSEN, HELEN REIS, Free-lance PR Cnslt., Nielsen Associates, L.A., Cal., '70–; AE, Allan, Ingersoll and Weber, '68–'70; PR Cnslt. and Wms. Activities, P. Ballantine & Sons (Newark), '60–'66; Restaurant Assocs., '63–'67; special proms., Am. Shakespeare Theatre (Stratford, Conn.); polit. campaign, Wms. Div. for Sen. Abraham A. Ribicoff, '62; special writings, Mayor Hugh Curran (Bridgeport, Conn.), '64; Wtr., brochures, City of Bridgeport, '66; City of New Haven, '64; Wtr., "Beer Party USA," for U.S.B.A., '64 (Edgar Aw., '66); various organizations, aws., and hons.; Depauw Univ., '42–'45; h. (div.); res: 14918 Pampas Ricas Blvd., Pacific Palisades, Cal. 90272.

NIN, ANAIS, Auth: "The Diary of Anais Nin" (Vol. I, '66; Vol. II, '67; Vol. III, '69; Harcourt, Brace & World), "Collages," "D. H. Lawrence: An Unprofessional Study," "House of Incest," "The Novel of the Future," "Under a Glass Bell" (Swallow Press), and numerous others; Mark Twain Soc.; b. Paris, France; p. Joaquin and Rosa Culmell Nin; res: c/o Gunther Stuhlmann, 65 Irving Pl., N.Y., N.Y. 10003.

NISSENSON, MARILYN CLASTER, Film Wtr., Film Prodr., Learning Corp. of America, 711 Fifth Ave., N.Y., N.Y., '68–; Film Wtr., Ency. Britannica Films, '68; Assoc. Prodr., CBS News, '63–'68; WGA; Wellesley Col., BA, '60; Columbia Univ., MA, '61; b. Bellefonte, Pa., 1938; p. Milton and Beatrice Berman Claster; h. Hugh Nissenson; res: 411 West End Ave., N.Y., N.Y. 10024.

NIXON, MARIE MARKS, Adm. Asst. in Pubns. and PR, Akron Jewish Center, 220 S. Balch St., Akron, Oh. 44302, '54–; Comm. Mbr., "Civic Forum of the Air," wkly. Telecast of public interest, radio rebdcst., '60–; Assoc. Ed., The Akron Jewish News, '55–; Ed., Akron Jewish Ctr. Yrbk., '54–; Publicist, Dev. Corp. for Israel, '58, '59; Assoc. Ed., The Mill Line, Midwest Rubber

Reclaiming Co. (E. St. Louis); All-Oh. Eds. (Exec. Bd., '60, '61), Un. Fund PR Cncl. (Exec. Bd.), ICIE (Pres., '60; Secy., '50, '58; aws., '62, '63) Nat. Assn. of Jewish Ctr. Workers, Am. Jewish PR Soc., '67; Univ. of Akron, '38–'40; (Friends of Akron Univ. Lib.); b. Kiev, U.S.S.R., 1921; p. Charles and Rose Soulla Marks; h. Glen T. Nixon; c. Glen G., Richard T.; res: 1749 Kingsley Ave., Akron, Oh. 44313.

NOBLE, RUTH VERRILL, Ed., Dir., Berkshire Publishing Company, '50–; Librn., R.I. Sch. of Design, Providence, '42–'46; Asst. Librn., Fogg Museum, Harvard, '40–'42; Auth., "Maine Profile," '54; Ed., "A Guide to New England Dining," '60; Dir., Charlotte Cushman Charitable Fndn.; Wellesley Col., BA; Columbia Univ., BS (Lib. Sci.), '46; b. Portland, Me.; p. Ernest and Marion Verrill; h. Richard Heathcote Heindel; res: 269-D N. Arlington Ave., Harrisburg, Pa. 17109.

NOBLE, VALERIE, Self-employed Bus. Rschr., Analyst, Wtr., Designer, '68–; Rsch. Librn., Upjohn Assn., '63–'68; Free-lance Adv., PR (Honolulu, Hi.), '62–'63, '60–'61; Commtns. Dir., Woodrum and Staff, '61–'62; Adv. Dir., Spencecliff Restaurants, '58–'60; Retail Adv. Dept., Honolulu Star Bul., '55–'58; Designer, record covers, nat. prom., adv., '58–'68; Exec. Retail Trainee, The Emporium (S.F., Cal.), '53–'55; Ed., Special Libs. Assn. Adv. and Mktng. Div. Bul., '67–'69; extensive rsch. on mutual funds; Owner, "Bookstamp," mail-order bkplates.; articles on libs. and adv.; bk., "The Effective Echo: Dictionary of Advertising Slogans"; Special Libs. Assn., Honolulu Adv. Club (Dir., '61), PR Wm. of Honolulu (Secy., '59), PR Cnslt. to Mich. Inter-Lib. Scholarship Assn.; ANPA Aw. for nwsp. tabloid, '59; Riverside Col., AA, '51; Pomona Col., BA, '53; Western Mich. Univ., MA (Lib. Sci.), '65; b. Bakersfield, Cal., 1931; p. Orland and Audrey Sauer Noble; res: 313 Solon, Kalamazoo, Mich. 49007.

NOEL, CHRIS, Radio Personality, Armed Forces Radio Service, 1016 N. McCadden Pl., L.A., Cal. 90038, '66–; Motion Pics., TV; Rec. Artist (Monument Records); NAB recognition cit. for work in behalf of GI's, '68; numerous military aws.; b. W. Palm Beach, Fla., 1941; p. Dave and Louise Truax Botz; h. Ty Herrington (dec.); res: 399 E. 72nd St., N.Y., N.Y. 10021.

NOEL, MARY ROSE, PR Mgr., American Airlines, Inc., Box 66065, O'Hare Intl. Airport, Chgo., Ill. 60666, '42–; PR Dir., Chgo. Cncl., Boy Scouts of Am., '38–'42; AWRT, Theta Sigma Phi, Pubcty. Club of Chgo., PRSA, North Pk. Alumni Assn. (Bd. of Dirs.), NFPW (1st pl. "Other Pubns." aw. won twice; Ill. Chptr.); Who's Who of Am. Wm.; North Pk. Jr. Col., AA, '34–'36; Northwestern Univ., BA (Jnlsm.), '36–'38; b. Chgo., Ill.; p. Philip E. and Marie G. Ward Noel; h. Russell Vincent Ray; res: 516 Linden Lane, Libertyville, Ill. 60048.

NOGUCHI, SUZAN, Free-lance Illus.; Staff Artist, Sch. Nature League (N.Y.C.); Auth.-Illus: "Double-

day's First Guide to Insects" ('64), "Plants of Woodland & Wayside" ('58); "Insects in Their World" ('55); Illus. of many bks.; N.Y. Entomological Soc. (Hon. Life Mbr.), Delta Phi Delta; Who's Who of Am. Wm.; Univ. of Colo., BFA, '38; b. Iliff, Colo., 1916; p. Minosuke and Tomi Noguchi; h. (1) Ralph B. Swain (dec.); (2) William K. Firmage; c. Tom Alfred, Ralph Adrian; res: 74 Fuller Ave., Chatham, N.J. 07928.

NOHLQUIST, BETTY GRAMS, Asst. Dir. PR, St. Joseph's Hospital, 5000 W. Chambers St., Milw., Wis. 53210, '63–; Coordr., social and scientific functions; Ed., house organ, doctors nwsltr., brochures, pamphlets; Asst. Dir. Adm. Rsch., '61–'63; Asst. Pers. Dir., Public Info. Offcr., '59–'61; Lakewood Corr., Jamestown Sun News, '55; Secy. to Chief Pathologist, Milw. County Hosp., '41–; Wis. Anti-TB Assn.; Wis. Indsl. Eds. Assn.; b. Milw., Wis., 1924; p. Melvin and Annabelle Morton Grams; h. Lester Nohlquist; c. Janice, Mrs. Dena Nohlquist Adamson; res: 2848 N. 47th St., Milw., Wis. 53210.

NOKES, JACQUELINE WHITE, Wms. Dir. and Hostess "Midday," KSL-TV, Broadcast House, Salt Lake City, Ut. 84111, '61–; weather show, '61–'62; Staff Tchr., "Romper Room," '59–'60; Miss Nancy, "Romper Room," '57–'59; Special Lectr., sociol., high schs., career schs.; AWRT (Nat. VP, '66–'68; Ut. Chptr. Pres., '63–'64), Freedom Fnd. Aw., '68; U.C.L.A., AA; Univ. of Utah; b. Salt Lake City, Ut., 1929; p. James and Edna Hansen White; h. Andrew Grey Nokes; c. Patricia, Larry, Jimmy, Tony; res: 2075 Lincoln Lane, Salt Lake City, Ut. 84117.

NOLAN, BARBARA PAULSON, Exec. Secy., PR Dir., Detroit Historical Society, 5401 Woodward, Detroit, Mich. 48202, '68–; Commty. Rels., '52–'68; Wms. Adv. Club of Detroit (VP and Dir., '69–; Corr. Secy. and Dir., '65–'67), Greater Mich. Fndn. Mich. Week, Detroit Hist. Soc. Guild, Detroit Cultural Ctr. Assn., PRSA, Hist. Soc. of Mich., Am. Assn. for State and Local Hist., Detroit Press Club (Adv. Wm. of Yr., '68); named one of Detroit's top ten working wm. by Central Bus. Dist. Assn., '63; Mich's. list of outstanding wm., '64; Un. Fndn. of Detroit aws. for commty. svc., '50–'66; Custer Elementary Sch. Alumni Aw., '68; April 29, '68, proclaimed Barbara "Bobbie" Nolan Day in Detroit by Mayor J. P. Cavanagh; Wayne State Univ., (Speech, Radio Drama) '47–'51, (Bronze, Silver, Gold Key aws., '47–'51); b. Detroit, Mich., 1930; p. Edwin and Edna Heliste Paulson; h. Edward Nolan; res: 18311 Mansfield, Detroit, Mich. 48235.

NOLAN, JEANNETTE COVERT, Auth: 47 bks. (biog., hist. novels, juv.), short stories; formerly nwsp. reptr., feature wtr.; Theta Sigma Phi, Wms. Press Club of Ind., NFPW; Ind. Univ. Aw. for Most Distg. Juv. Bk., '54, '60; Ind. Univ. Wtrs. Conf. Hall of Fame, '68; Dr. of Ltrs. (Hon.), Ind. Univ., '67; b. Evansville, Ind.; p. Charles and Grace Tucker Covert; h. Val Nolan (dec.); c. Val, Jr., Alan T., Kathleen C. (Mrs. Alan H. Lobley); res: 25 Northview Dr., Indpls., Ind. 46208.

NOLAN, MARY CATHERINE, Media Byr., Dodson, Craddock & Born Advertising, P.O. Drawer "A," Pensacola, Fla. 32502, '65–; Escambia Treating Co., '64–'65; Nat. Beta Club; Pensacola, Jr. Col., AA, '60–'62; Fla. State Univ., BS, '64 (dean's list); b. Pensacola, Fla., 1942; p. Ernest and Merle Nowell Nolan; res: 1026 E. Strong St., Pensacola, Fla. 32501.

NOLAN, SARA STAFFORD, Dir. of Pubns., Mng. Ed., The Tennessee Teacher, Tennessee Education Association, 598 James Robertson Pkwy., Nashville, Tenn. 37219, '60–; PR Staff, Assoc. Ed., Reflector, George Peabody Col. for Tchrs., '58–'59; Copy Dir., C. P. Clark, '44–'57; Co-auth., words and music, "Alice-in-Wonderland" operetta prod. by Nashville Children's Theatre and Yuha Col. (Cal.); Auth., "Borrowed Angel" rec. (Decca and RCA), three others; poetry; children's stories, incl. "The Star that Wanted to Shine"; articles; Artist; AAUW, EDPRESS (Dir., Reg. 6, past four yrs.), ICIE, Middle Tenn. Bus. Press Club, NEA, Middle Tenn. Educ. Assn., Nashville Symphony Guild, Tenn. Art League; Davidson County BPW Wm. of the Yr., '60; Memphis State Univ., BS; George Peabody Col. for Tchrs., MA, '58; Univ. of Tenn.; b. Franklin County, Tenn.; p. Joseph and Mary Grigsby Stafford; h. (dec.); res: 2017 Sweetbriar Ave., Nashville, Tenn. 37212.

NOLAND, BETTY LEE, Ed., Sears, Roebuck and Co., 3625 Truman Rd., Kan. City, Mo. 64127, '66–; ICIE, OES, Beta Sigma Phi, Xi Beta Kappa; Univ. of Kan., '37–'39; b. Kan. City, Mo., 1920; p. James and Lorena Joy Lee; h. Merle D. Noland.

NOLTE, JUDITH A., Ed.-in-Chief, American Baby and Mothers-to-Be Magazines, American Baby, Inc., 10 E. 52nd St., N.Y., N.Y. 10022; Assoc. Mdsng. Dir., The Bride's Magazine; Asst. Fashion Ed., '64–'65; Tchr. of Eng., HS of Commerce, '62–'64; Tchr. of Eng., Drama, Middletown HS; Univ. of Minn., BS (Educ.), '60; N.Y.U., MA (Eng.), '65.

NORDSTROM, URSULA, Sr. VP, Publr., Harper Junior Books, Harper & Row, 49 E. 33rd St., N.Y., N.Y. 10016, '67–; Head of Jr. Bk. Dept., '41–'67; Asst. to Head of Dept., '40; Auth., "The Secret Language" ('60); Children's Bk. Cncl. (Pres., '54), ALA, Cosmopolitan Club; b. N.Y.C.; p. William and Marie Nordstrom Litchfield; res: 870 UN Plaza, N.Y., N.Y. 10017.

NORELL, IRENE PALMER, Assoc. Prof., Dept. of Lbrnship., San Jose State College, San Jose, Cal. 95114, '65–; Asst. Prof., '59–'65; Asst. Prof., Northern Ill. Univ., '58–'59; Lectr., Univ. of N.D., '52–'56; Head Librn., N.D. Public Lib. (Grand Forks) '50–'56; Auth: "Prose Writers of North Dakota" (Univ. of N.D., '68), "Geographical Literature" ('69); Cal. Lib. Assn., ALA, Special Libs. Assn., WNBA, Delta Kappa Gamma; Who's Who of Am. Wm.; Univ. of Minn., MA, '57; b. Springfield, N.H.; p. Ernest and Irene Palmer; h. William Norell; c. Andrew E., William E.; res: San Jose, Cal.

NORIN, GARLAND BAKER, Tchr., Drama, Speech, ·Vashon Island High School, Rte. 1, Box 359, Burton, Wash. 98013, '60–; Engineering Librn., Boeing, '59–'60; Brunswick-Balke-Colender Co., '57–'58; Tchr., Burton Elementary Sch., '52–'57; Nat. Cncl. of Tchrs. of Eng., Intl. Platform Assn., WNBA, Am. Educ. Theatre Assn., Speech Assn. of Am.; Wash. State Nwsp. Assn. aw., '58; Wash. State Univ., BA, '35; b. Tacoma, Wash.; p. Robert and Alice Holgerson Baker; h. Lawrence S. Norin; c. Robert, William; res: Rte. 2. Box 37, Burton, Wash. 98013.

NORMAN, BEVERLY, Owner, Beverly Norman Public Relations, 9704 W. 105th Terr., Overland Pk., Kan. 66212, '62–; Fennell-Gibson, '59–'62; Fennell, Quinn & Gibson, '57–'59; Jim McQueeny Assocs., '55–'57; Asst. PR Dir., Un. Campaign, '53–'55; Hostess, two radio shows; Gamma Alpha Chi (VP), AWRT (Past. Pres.), PRSA; Univ. of Mo., BS, '53; b. Kan. City, Kan., 1931; p. George and Helen Neisler Reeder; h. Fletcher Norman.

NORMAN, ELVA KUYKENDALL, Ed., The Suburban Educator, PR Dir., St. Louis Suburban Teachers Association, 10330 Old Olive St. Rd., St. Louis, Mo. 63141, '64–; PR Dir., '42–'64; St. Louis YWCA, '55–'64; St. Louis County Library; Feature Wtr., Reptr., The Mineral Wells (Tex.) Index, '30–'31; PR for ALA, Natl. Fed. Garden Clubs; Wtr., articles, feature, short stories, various pubns.; Univ. City Adult Evening Sch. Bd.; Theta Sigma Phi (Nat. PR Dir., '58–'61); St. Louis Chptr. Treas., '53–'56), Pi Gamma Mu, Met. St. Louis Press Club, AWRT, Indsl. Press Assn., Delta Kappa Gamma, Mo. Nat. Press Wm.; numerous press aws.; Baylor Col., BJ; Grad. Work; b. Waxahachie, Tex.; 1911; p. The Rev. Thomas and Laura Martin Kuykendall; h. Isaac Daniel Norman; c. John K., Eric J., Daniel T., res: 7407 Melrose Ave., St. Louis, Mo. 63130.

NORMAN, ESTHER MARX, Free-lance Ed., Auth., Wtr., '30–; Ed., The Jr. Times, full page children's feature for 15-1/2 yrs.; News Ed., Wtr., KCLO (Leavenworth, Kan.), two yrs.; over 2,000 juv. fiction stories and hundreds of short features; Kan. Press Wm., Mo. Press Wm., NPWC (58 writing aws. from the above three orgs., '51–), NLAPW, Kan. Fedn. of Humane Socs. (Charter Mbr.; Secy., '57–'68), organized Leavenworth Humane Soc. ('47) and Good Samaritan Humane Soc. (St. Joseph, Mo., '69); Who's Who of Am. Wm.; b. St. Joseph, Mo., 1906; p. Joseph and Electa Worthwine Marx; h. Hubert Norman; res: 1833 N. 29th St., St. Joseph; Mo. 64506.

NORMAN, JANE, Creator, Talent, Pixanne Show, WNEW-TV, 205 E. 67th St., N.Y., N.Y. 10021, '69–; Creator, Wtr., Talent, Pixanne Show, WCAU-TV (Phila., Pa.), '60–'69; Tchr., '56–'60; conducted seminars on drama, music for young children; Composer, Wtr., children's songs, stories; Wtr., Prodr., Talent, children's records, '68; educ. radio, TV shows; summer stock; TV, Radio Adv. Club; TV-Radio Mirror aw., Best Children's Program in East, '65–'66; Temple

Univ., BS (Educ.), '56; b. Phila., Pa., 1935; p. Stanley and Jeanette Einfeld Lazarus; c. Richard L. Norman; res: B524 Park Dr. Manor, Phila., Pa. 19144.

NORMAN, JOHNNIE, AE, Diener & Dorskind Advertising Agency, 1501 Broadway, N.Y., N.Y. 10036; Asst. to AE, '65–'66; Rsch. Cl., N.Y. Public Lib., '62–'65; Cnslt. to indsl. cos. on hiring minority groups; Group for Adv. Progress ('68); interviewed for radio and mag. coverage; City Col. of N.Y. (Fine Arts), '59–'61 (Mayor's Cert. for Excellence); b. Augusta, Ga., 1941; p. John and Elenora Stokes Bennings; h. Walter L. Jones; c. David Norman; res: 860 Riverside Dr., N.Y., N.Y. 10032.

NORRIS, FLORA CREECH, Adm. Asst., Sls. Coordr., WTVD Television, PO Box 1326, Raleigh, N.C. 27602, '67–; Sls. Secy., '65–'67; Traf. Mgr., WNAO, '49–'51; Bdcstr., '50; Traf. Mgr., WRC-NBC (Wash., D.C.), '45–'46; WWDC (Wash., D.C.), '44–'45; Cont. Wtr., WPTF (Raleigh, N.C.), '43–'44; League of Wm. Voters, AWRT; Wake County Democratic Wm., Wake County Hist. Soc.; St. Mary's Jr. Col., Raleigh, N.C., '41; Peace Jr. Col., '42–'43; b. Raleigh, N.C., 1923; p. Herbert and Minnie Huntt Ransom Norris; res: 107 E. Lane St., PO Box 1141, Raleigh, N.C. 27602.

NORTH, FLORA d'ILLE, Pres., Howell-North Books, 1050 Parker St., Berkeley, Cal. 94710, '61–; Co-founder, '38–; Univ. of Cal., '40.

NORTH, JEANNE B., Rsch. Assoc., Information General Corporation, 999 Commercial St., Palo Alto, Cal. 94303, '69–; Rsch. Assoc., Programming Svcs., Inc., '67–'68; Chief Librn., Govt. Doc. Div., Stanford Univ., '65–'67; Head Librn., Engineering Lib., '63–'65; Supvsr., Palo Alto Lib., Lockheed Missiles & Space Co., '61–'63; Rsch. Info. Specialist, '61; Head Librn., Un. Aircraft Corp., '56–'61; Ref. Librn., '48–'56; Jr. Liaison Engineer, Wilson Chemical Feeders, '45; Jr. Liaison Engineer, Curtiss-Wright Corp., '44; Lectr: Univ. of Tex., New Haven State Tchrs. Col., Univ. of Okla.; Special Libs. Assn. (Nat. Secy., '60–'63; S.F. Chptr. Pres., '67–'68; Conn. Valley Chptr. Pres., '54–'55), Soc. of Tech. Wtrs. and Eds. (Nat. Secy., '59–'61; Exec. Bd., '55–'58), Am. Soc. for Info. Sci., Am. Soc. of Indexers, ALA, Am. Soc. for Engineering Educ.; Cornell Univ., Aeronautical Engineering Cert., '43; State Univ. of Ia., BA (Eng.). '47; Columbia Univ., BS (Lib. Svc.), '48; b. Independence, Mo., 1922; p. Harry G. and Alice V. Weed Barto; h. John North; c. Barbara V. (Mrs. Robert Hirsch); res: 742 Southampton Dr., Palo Alto, Cal. 94303.

NORTHRUP, SHIRLEY M., Area Mgr., Dorothy Carnegie Course, Dale Carnegie Courses, 2025 Nicollet Ave., Mpls., Minn. 55404, '67–; Course Instr., '64–; Area Mgr. (Des Moines, Ia.), two yrs.

NORTON, ESTHER G., Prod. Mgr., Phillipps Associates, Inc., 7654 W. Boncroft, Toledo, Oh. 43617, '68–; Davis Bus. Col., Stautzenberger Bus. Sch.; b. Toledo,

Oh., 1925; p. Franz and Esther Galbraith Norton; h. (div.); c. Patricia Ann Bevington, Dennis Richard Bevington; res: 4804 N. Arvilla, Toledo, Oh. 43623.

NORWOOD, LINDA STEWART, Staff Wtr., Dept. of Public Relations, Loyola University, 6363 St. Charles Ave., N.O., La. 70118, '69–; Copywtr., Star Adv. Agcy. (Houston, Tex.), '68–; Mng. Ed., The Cotton Digest, '65–'67; Edtl. Asst., Tenn. Gas Transmission, '64–'65; Theta Sigma Phi; Baylor Univ., BA (Eng., Jnlsm.), '64 (Ed., col. mag.); b. Waukegan, Ill., 1943; p. Coy and Dorothy Perkins Stewart; h. Larry Norwood; res: 358 Millaudon St., N.O., La. 70118.

NOTEWARE, BETTY HARPEL, City Ed., Manistee News-Advocate, 75 Maple St., Manistee, Mich. 49660, '64–; Wms. Commentator, WMTE, '55–'56; Bur. Mgr., UP (Herrin, Ill. and Fort Wayne, Ind.), '43–'44; Tchr., Jnlsm., W. Shore Commty. Col. (Scottville, Mich.), '69–'70; Manistee Area Sch. Dist. Bd. of Educ., '60–'68; Mich. State Repl. Central Comm. '56; State Univ. of Ia., BA (Jnlsm.), '41; b. Chgo., Ill., 1919; p. Gates and Margaret Sutton Harpel; h. Max Marshall Noteware; c. Margaret Esther; res: 3506 Lakeshore Rd., Manistee, Mich. 49660.

NOTT, GOLDIE TILMAN, Librn., Ferris State College, 901 S. State St., Big Rapids, Mich. 49307, '46–; Head Librn., Sch. and Public Lib. (Greenville), '43–'46; Soc. Ed., Proofreader, Big Rapids Pioneer, '42–'43; Children's and Br. Librn., Dayton (Oh.) Public Lib., '35–'42; ALA, Mich. Lib. Assn. (Dist. IV Chmn.), '55) Cncl. Mich. Academic Librns.; Miami Univ. (Oxford, Oh.), BS (Educ.), '34 (Phi Beta Kappa); Univ. of Ill., BS (Lib. Sci.), '42 (high hons.; Beta Phi Mu); MA (Lib. Sci.), '56; Univ. of Mich., MA (Educ.), '62; b. Eugene, Ore., 1913; p. Charlie and Lillian Hoffman Tilman; h. George W. Nott; res: RFD #1, Rodney, Mich. 49342.

NOVACK, EVE, VP, Diener & Dorskind Inc., 1501 Broadway, N.Y., N.Y. 10036, '70–; AE, '67–; AE, Hokar Adv. Agcy.; Fin. Space Salesman, Vanderbilt Enterprises; Broker, ENA Assocs.; Cnslt. to industry in adv. and sls. prom.; Tech. Wtr.; Assn. of Indsl. Advs.; Packer Collegiate Inst., '58; Hunter Col.; Univ. of Nev.; b. Antwerp, Belgium, 1941; p. Frederick and Hanna Guttshabas Novak; res: 300 E. 74th St., N.Y., N.Y. 10021.

NOVAK, GLORIA HEINKEL, Religion Ed., Calumet Publishing Co., 9120 Baltimore Ave., Chgo., Ill. 60617, '68–; Ed. Wms. Cooking Colm., '67; Staff Wtr., '67; Volunteer Recognition Aw., '69; Northwestern Univ., '45–'46; Chgo. Acad. of Fine Arts, '46–'49; b. Chgo., Ill., 1926; p. Emil and Valerie Kosak Heinkel; h. John Novak; c. Linda, James, Lori; res: 10712 Ave. B, Chgo., Ill. 60617.

NOVER, NAOMI GOLL, Jnlst., Nwsp. Reptr., Colmst., Educator, "Washington Dateline," Denver (Colo.) Post, '53–; off: Wash. Bur., Nat. Press Bldg., Wash., D.C. 20004, '49–; Music Critic, Aspen Festival,

'49; Edtl. Asst., Buffalo (N.Y.) Times; Wtr., synd. features, mag. articles; Photogr.; Corr. to Eur. war zones, Portland (Ore.) Oregonian; Wtr., Dir., plays, Buffalo; participated in radio, TV plays; christened S.S. Syosset, Balt., Md., '45; active in Red Cross, U.S. War Bonds (aw. pin), Girl Scout Cncl. (Silver Eagle Recipient), Wms. Bd. of George Washington Univ. Hosp., Columbian Wm. of George Washington Univ., Goodwill Embassy Tour (Originator), Welcome to Wash., Commty. Chest (Chmn., three areas); Congressional Press Galleries, White House Corrs. Assn., AAUW, Pi Lambda Theta (Past Corr., offcl. pubn.), Wms. Nat. Press Club, ANWC; Univ. of Buffalo and Tchrs. Col., BA; George Washington Univ., MA, '51; b. Buffalo, N.Y.; p. B. B. and Rebecca Shane Goll; h. Barnet Nover; res: 4545 Connecticut Ave., N.W., Wash., D.C. 20008.

NOVINA, TRUDI, Dir., Home Furnishings Pubcty., Donald Degnan Associates, 511 Fifth Ave., N.Y., N.Y. 10017, '64–; Free-lance mag. articles and bklets., one paperback bk., wms. interests, mostly Fawcett Pubns., '60–'66; Wms. Page Reptr., Home Furnishings Ed., N.Y. World Telegram and Sun, '51–'60; NHFL, Am. Soc. of Interior Designers, OPC; Bklyn. Col., BA (Eng.); b. N.Y.C.; p. Isidor and Lillian Greenberg Novina; h. 1. Leo Papazian (dec.), 2. Charles Coakley; c. Lyssa Papazian, Gregory Papazian; res: 34 W. 89th St., N.Y., N.Y. 10024.

NOWAK, JEAN McDUFFIE, Dir. of Info., Indian Health Service, U.S. Dept. of Health, Education & Welfare, 330 C. St. S.W., Wash., D.C. 20025, '62–; Dir. of Info., Div. Health Mobilization, '59–'62; Dir. PR, First Aid and Water Safety, Am. Nat. Red Cross, '56–'59; Dir., Radio and TV, '52–'56; Free-lance adv. and PR, '50–'52; Reptr., Feature Wtr., Radio Personality, '41–'52; WNPC, AAUW (Bd. of Dirs.), AWRT, League of Wm. Voters (Bd. of Dirs.); Dept. of HEW Superior Svc. aw., '65; U.S. Public Health Sv. Special Aw., '68; Lake Forest Col., '35–'38; Univ. of Wis., BA, '39; b. Sheboygan, Wis.; p. Raymond and Leila Stephen McDuffie; h. Francis Jefferson Nowak (div.); c. Francis J., Jr., Nancy (Mrs. Murray Bishop), Robert C.; res: 3223 Volta Pl. N.W., Wash., D.C. 20007.

NOYES-KANE, DOROTHY, Asst. Prof., Southern Connecticut State College, 501 Crescent St., New Haven, Conn. 06515, '66–; Cnslt., J. Walter Thompson Co.; Pres., Dir., John Slade Ely Center for Health Educ. Rsch., '60–'66; VP, Treas., Noyes & Sproul, Inc., '37–'60; VP, Redfield-Johnstone Agcy., '34–'36; Org., The Medical Market, '33; Copy Wtr., Lewis-Waetjen Agcy., '30–'33; Dr's. lit. asst., '27–'30; Auth., one bk.; Librn., Kings County Med Soc., '24–'27; AFA (Adv. Wm. of Yr. Aw.), '57), Assn. Med. Adv. Agcys. (Org., 1st Pres., '53–'54), AWNY (Past Treas., Dir., Life Mbr.), World Med Assn. (Found. Mbr.); Am. Med. Wtr's. Assn., Nat. Assn. Sci Wtrs.; NEA, mbr. and dir. several public health and civic orgs.; Goddard Col., BA, '64; Yale, MPH, MUS, '66; b. Balt., Md., 1906; p. Selden G. and Flora Keily Noyes; h. 1. A. E. Sproul, Jr. (div.)

2. Lawrence James Kane; c. Christopher Noyes, Barbara Chamberlain Spraul; res: 14 Charlton Hill, Hamden, Conn. 06518.

NTI, SHIRLEY DUNN, Dir. of Pubns., Office of University Relations, University of Maryland, College Park, Md. 20742, '69–; Ed., Univ. pubns., Off. of PR, Howard Univ. (Wash., D.C.), '66–'69; Ed., Fac./Staff Nwsltr.; Calendar of Events; Assoc. Ed., The Howard Magazine; Edtl. Asst. Traf. Engineering and Safety Div., Am. Automobile Assn. Hq., '64–'66; Ed., Credit Un. Nwsltr.; Ed., master's theses, doctoral dissertations; ACPRA, Am. Alumni Cncl., Am. Assn. of Univ. Profs., Prince Georges County PR Assn., Trinity Col., AB (Eng.), '64; b. Snow Hill, N.C., 1942; p. Claude Dunn and Mildred Dunn Edwards; h. Robert K. Nti; res: 4235 Hayes St., N.E., Wash., D.C. 20019.

NUCCIO, SALLIE KREDA, Pres., Kreda Associates, Inc., 1681 Second Ave., N.Y., N.Y. 10028, '64–; VP, Gen. Mgr., Wyatt & Allen, Inc., Time-Life Bldg., '62–'64; Cnslt: Puerto Rican Dev. Program, Am. Chess Fdn., Bobby Fisher, Wallpaper Cncl. of Am.; NHFL; Chgo. Art Inst., '47–'48; b. Sheffield, Ia., 1929; p. Edwin and Frances Quinell Peters; h. John Nuccio; c. Mimi, Carol, Kathy Kreda, Karen Kreda, Helvi.

NUNN, ALICE ELIZABETH, Actress; AEA, SAG, AFTRA, AGVA; Wesleyan Conservatory of Music and Sch. of Fine Arts, BFA in Drama (Radio), '49 (Col. Paper Ed., Sr. Yr.); b. Jacksonville, Fla., 1927; p. Nathan and Alice Brush Nunn; res: 710 Westmount Dr., L.A., Cal. 90069.

NURNEY, GERALDINE LATHAM, City Librn., San Jose Public Library, 180 W. San Carlos St., San Jose, Cal. 95113, '43–; Librn., '31–'43; Lib. work, '27–'30; Wtr., articles; weekly lib. program, Radio KEEN Adult Educ. Senate, San Jose Unified Sch. Dist., '50–'54, '55–'59; '47–'50; various orgs., aws.; Sacramento Jr. Col., JC, '27; Univ. of Cal. (Berkeley), AB, '30; San Jose State Col. (Cal.), Teaching Credential, '31; Lib. Cert., '31; b. Toledo, Oh., 1907; p. Roy and Harriet Stolberg Latham; h. Ray Nurney (dec.); res: 3584 Irlanda Way, San Jose, Cal. 95124.

NYDELE, ANN, Exec. Dir. Industrial Design Society of America, 60 W. 55th St., N.Y., N.Y. 10019, '70–; Dir. of PR, ISD Incorporated, '68–'70; Dir. of PR, Royal Worcester Porcelain Co., '67; PR Dir., Walter Dorwin Teague Assoc., '62–'67; Free-lance PR, '60–'62; Asst. to PR Dir., Lippincott & Margulies, '58–'60; Pubcty. Dir., Tussy Cosmetics, '57–'58; Wms. Interest Publicist, Kenyon & Eckhardt, '56–'57; Prom., Pubcty., Family Circle mag., '55–'56; Asst. to Prom., PR Dir., Ellington & Co., '51–'55; Cnslt. to indsl. designers; PRSA, Adv. Club of N.Y., Soc. of Architectural Histrns.; Adelphi Col., BA, '49; b. Chgo., Ill., 1926; p. Lt. Col. Victor and Anna Bertram Nydele; res: 142 E. 16th St., N.Y., N.Y. 10003.

NYE, SARAH LITSEY, Instr., Famous Writers School,

54 Wilton Rd., Westport, Conn., '60–; Poet: "Legend," "For the Lonely," "The Oldest April;" Auth: "There Was a Lady" ('45), "The Intimate Illusion" ('55), "A Path to the Water" ('60); Tchr., seminars, workshops; b. Ky.; p. Edwin Carlile Litsey; h. Frank W. Nye (dec.); c. Christopher; res: R.F.D. 2, W. Redding, Conn. 06896.

O

OAKLEY, HELEN McKELVEY, Free-lance Wtr.; Auths. Guild, L.I. Re-wtrs.; Bryn Mawr Col., AB; b. N.Y.C.; p. Ralph and Helen Fairchild McKelvey; h. Walter T. Oakley; c. Valerie Thurston (Mrs. Charles Atherton Jr.), Deborah Huntington; res: 128 Park Ave., Manhasset, N.Y. 11030.

OAKLEY, MARJORIE RAMSEY, Asst. Prof. of Counseling, Foods and Nutrition, Logan Br., Marshall University, Logan, W.Va. 25601, '68–; Guidance Cnsl., Cabell County Schs., '67–'68; VP, PR, Nugget Foods, '66–'67; Exec. VP, Cnslt., '64–'66; Cnslt. and PR, '59–'64; Nutritionist, '58–'59; Public Speaker and Info. Rep., Columbia Gas System, '56–'58; Talent and Home Econst., WSAZ-TV, '54–'56; Tchr., '52–'54; Contrbr. to cookbk. of TV personalities, "Cooking with the Experts" ('55); Wtr., articles; Lectr.; Logan County Planning Commn. (Chmn., '69–'72), PRSA, numerous food orgs., Delta Kappa Gamma, Kappa Omicron Phi, NEA (Life Mbr.), AAUW (Logan County Pres., '50–'51); Who's Who of Am. Wm.; Who's Who of Commerce and Industry; b. Huntington, W. Va., 1924; p. Thomas A. and Goldia V. Ramsey; h. Harvey Oakley; c. Michael; res: c/o Circuit Judge, Logan, W. Va. 25601.

OATES, JOYCE CAROL, Auth., "Them" (Vanguard Press, '69; Nat. Bk. Aw., '70); "Expensive People," "Garden of Earthly Delights" (both novels; Vanguard Press); "Anonymous Sins and Other Poems" (poetry); O. Henry Prize aws., '67, '65, '64, '63; "Fifty Best American Stories 1915–1965," "Best American Short Stories" ('70, '69, '67, '65, '64, '63); "Literary Anthology" ('68, '67); Assoc. Prof. of Eng., Univ. of Windsor; Syracuse Univ., BA, '60 (Phi Beta Kappa); Univ. of Wis., MA, '62; b. Lockport, N.Y. 1938; h. Raymond J. Smith, Jr.; res: 6000 Riverside Dr. E., Ontario, Windsor, Canada.

OBERLE, MARCELLA, Assoc. Prof., California State College, 515 State College Dr., L.A., Cal. 90032, '66–; Asst. Prof., '60–'66; Instr., Northwestern Univ., '54–'60; Instr., State Univ. of N.Y., '50–'51; Tchr., High Schs., '42–'47; Am. Educ. Theatre Assn., WNBA, AAUW, AAUP, Assn. of Cal. State Col. Profs., Central States Speech Assn., Western Speech Assn. (Pres., '70, VP, '66, Exec. Secy.-Treas., '66–'69); Northern Ill. Univ., BE, '42; Northwestern Univ., MA, '48, PhD,

'65; b. Propitatorin, Ill.; p. Floyd and Loretta Murphy Oberle; res: 838 De La Fuente, Monterey Park, Cal. 91754.

OBERMIRE, NOLA A., Mgr., Sls. Prom. and Rsch., CBS Television Stations Division, KMOX-TV, One Memorial Dr., St. Louis, Mo. 63102, '69–; Mgr., Audience Prom., '64–'69; Asst. Prom. Dir., KOLN-TV/KGIN-TV, '63–'64; AWRT; Univ. of Neb., '56–'61.

OBRE, SALLY MURPHY, Beauty Ed., Ladies' Home Journal, 641 Lexington Ave., N.Y., N.Y. 10022, '69–; Fashion Ed., Ingenue, '67–'69; Fashion Coordr., Plymouth Shops, '66–'67; Merchandise Ed., Glamour, '61–'65; Fashion Group; Ind. Univ., '50–'54; b. Quincy, Mass., 1932; p. Phillip and Mary White Murphy; h. Paul Obre; c. David R.; res: 24 E. 81st St., N.Y., N.Y. 10028.

O'BRIEN, ELIZABETH BUTTON, Sr. Assoc., Drake Sheahan/Stewart Dougall, Inc., 330 Madison Ave., N.Y., N.Y. 10017, '69–; Sr. Assoc., Stewart Dougall & Assocs., '56–'68; '43–'51; Partner, O'Brien Assocs. (Litchfield, Conn.), '54–'55; Rsch. Dir., House of Herbs (Salisbury), '52–'53; AWNY (Bd. of Dirs., '65–'66); Wellesley Col., BA, '35; b. Stonington, Me., 1914; p. Max and Mabel Goss Button; h. John Edward O'Brien; c. Carol (Mrs. Allen A. Whittlesey), Joan (Mrs. William G. McGloughlin); res: HoshieKon Farm, R.D. 2, Litchfield, Conn. 06759.

O'BRIEN, ESSE FORRESTER, Auth., 14 non-fiction, juv. bks., incl: "Circus—Cinders to Sawdust" (The Naylor Co., '59; hon life mbr. of Clown Club of Am.), "Poems" ('67); "Elephant Tales" (The Steck Co., '41; AIGA list of 60 outstanding textbks., '41), nine transcribed into braille; and in the Lib. of Congress; Reviewer, mags. and Tex. nwsps.; Lectr., religious subjects, travel, writing, reviewing; conducted seminars in juv. writing, W. Tex. State Col., Univ. of Houston, others; Nat. Bd. of Lectrs., Theta Sigma Phi (One of Tex. outstanding auths., '59), Intl. Mark Twain Soc. (Hon. Mbr.), The Eugene Field Soc. (Hon. Mbr.), Tex. Wms. Press Assn. (aws., '57, '60, '62), AAUW, Tex. Poetry Soc., Am. Poetry League, Waco (Tex.) Poetry League, NFPW (aws., '60, '65, '66); Baylor Univ., Art degree, '13; BA, '34 (Wm. of the Yr., '63); Univ. of Mo.; N.Y.C. Art League; b. Waco, Tex.; p. William and Esse Clay Forrester; h. John L. O'Brien; c. William F.; res: Rte 10, Box 228, Waco, Tex. 76708.

O'BRIEN, M. HELEN LYNCH, Dir. of Taylor Kitchens, The Taylor Wine Company, Inc., Hammondsport, N.Y. 14840, '64–; PR, recipe dev., menu planning, prom.; Lectr., demonstration programs for TV, radio, groups; Am. and N.Y. Home Econs. Assns., AWRT (Central N.Y. Chptr. Liaison Offcr. and Bd. Mbr., '66–'68), BPW, AAUW, numerous others; Syracuse Univ., BS (Food and Nutrition), '44; Grad. Work, '46–'47; b. Syracuse, N.Y., 1923; p. Dr. George and Irene Hughes Lynch; h. Richard C. O'Brien (dec.); c.

Irene A., Richard C., Kristen M., Jeffrey J.; res: 112 Cook St., Bath, N.Y. 14810.

O'BRIEN, MARY ELIZABETH, Ed., The Garden Journal, The New York Botanical Garden, Bronx Park, Bronx, N.Y. 10458, '69–; Ed., Popular Gardening & Living Outdoors, Holt, Rinehart and Winston, '58–'69; Mng. Ed., Popular Gardening, '50–'58; Asst. to Ed., Flower Grower, '40–'50; Am. Soc. of Magazine Eds., Garden Wtrs. of Am., numerous horticultural orgs.; b. N.Y.C., 1917; p. Patrick and Elizabeth Donovan O'Brien; res: 314 W. 22nd St., N.Y., N.Y. 10011.

O'BRIEN, MIMI ELIZABETH, Assoc. Prodr., "To Tell the Truth," Goodson-Todman Television Productions, 375 Park Ave., N.Y., N.Y. 10022, '69–; Talent Coordr., "Dick Rickles Show," 69–; Assoc. Prodr., "Call My Bluff"; Casting Dir., "Missing Links"; Crtv. Special Material, "Play Your Hunch"; Prod., "Two for the Money" and "It's News to Me"; Univ. of Pa., BS; b. N.Y.C.; p. Edward J. and Miriam Schofield O'Brien; h. Arthur Maturo; c. Arthur L., III, Elizabeth; res: 240 E. Palisade Ave., Englewood, N.J. 07631.

O'CONNOR, JEAN K., AE, Ruder & Finn Inc., 110 E. 59th St., N.Y., N.Y. 10022, '67–; Assoc. Edward Thomas Assocs., '64–'67; AE, Roy Bernard Assocs., '64; Wtr.-Ed., Bur. of Intl. Commerce, U.S. Dept. of Commerce, '63–'64; various organizations; Am. Univ., BA, '58 (hons.; Mortarboard); b. Chester, Pa.; p. Arthur D. and Margaret A. Hawkins O'Connor; res: 45 Sutton Pl. S., N.Y., N.Y. 10022.

ODDO, GENEVIEVE GRILLO, Secy., Bd. of Dirs., Oddo Publishing, Inc., Box 68, Beauregard Blvd., Fayetteville, Ga. 30214, '67–; VP, '64–'67; Co. Secy., Firmenich & Co., '47–'52; ALA; b. Bklyn, N.Y., 1917; p. Alfred and Celeste Quadrino Grillo; h. Paul C. Oddo; c. Paul Jr., Charles, Warren; res: Beauregard Blvd., Fayetteville, Ga. 30214.

ODELL, JANET OBERNDORFER, Wms. Ed., Food Ed., The Pontiac Press, P.O. Box 9, Pontiac, Mich., 48056, '62–; Tchr., Jr. HS, Sr. HS, Bus. Col., '37–'53; Girl Scout Exec. (Saginaw), '36; Theta Sigma Phi (VP, '66–'67; '68–'69), AAUW, YWCA (Pontiac Bd. Mbr., six yrs.), ZONTA; Mich. State Univ. Ext. Svc. Golden Coop. Aw. ('66); Milw.-Downer Col., BA, '34; Univ. of Mich., '34–'35; b. Milw., Wis., 1912; p. Arthur and Elsie Foote Oberndorfer; h. Carmi Odell; c. Mrs. Roger Clough, John; res: 163 Ogemaw, Pontiac, Mich. 48053.

ODMARK, MARION J., Nwsp. Colmst., "Working Girl's Notebook," Chicago Today, 445 N. Michigan Ave., Chgo., Ill. 60611; res: 201 E. Walton Ave., Chgo., Ill. 60611.

ODOM, MARY MARGARET, Instructional TV Studio Math Tchr., Dade County Public Schools, 1410 N.E. Second Ave., Miami, Fla. 33132, '67–; Secondary Mathematics Tchr., '60–'69; Sci. Tchr., Broward and Pinellas County Public Schs., '57–'59; Co-Auth., "Introduction to Exponents" (Holt, Rinehart and Winston, '64), Fla. Textbk. Selection Comm. (Math Chmn., '67–'68), Dade County Cncl. of Tchrs. (Pres., '66–'67; VP, '65–'66; Secy., '63–'65), Fla. Cncl. of Tchrs. of Mathematics (Dir., '69–'70), Nat. Cncl. of Tchrs. of Mathematics, Delta Kappa Gamma; Fla. Star Tchr. aw., '68; Fla. State Univ., BS (Math, Sci. Educ.), '57; MS (Math), '65 (Nat. Sci. Fndn. Scholarship); Mexico City Col., '58; Cornell Univ., '66 (Shell Fellowship); Mich. State Univ., '68 (Nat. Sci.Fndn. Scholarship); b. Bartow, Fla., 1935; p. Earnest and Ruby Mathews Williams; h. Aubrey Odom; c. Alan Lee; res: 2340 N.W. 191st St., Miami, Fla. 33054.

ODOM, RETHA B., Mgr., PR, Rsch. and Dev., Shell Oil Co., 50 W. 50th St., N.Y., N.Y. 10020, Dir., Public Info. and Educ., N.Y.C. Dept. Air Resources; Dir. PR, Assoc. Commty. Teams; Asst. Dir. PR, N.Y. Acad. Scis.; PR Cnslt: WCBS-TV, State of N.Y. Exec. Chamber, N.Y. Urban League; NAMW; Syracuse Univ., MA; res: 215 W. 78th St., N.Y., N.Y. 10024.

OEFINGER, MYRTLE HEATH, Wms. Ed., Express Publishing Co., Ave. E and Third, San Antonio, Tex. 78228, '54–; Staff Mbr., '52; Sch. Ed., '53; Theta Sigma Phi (VP, '69–'70; Headliner Aw.), '63; Tex. Assoc. Press Mng. Eds. Assn. (aws: 1st pl., '58, '62, '66; 2nd pl., '60; Hon. Mention, '61, '59; Catherine L. O'Brien aw., 2nd pl., '59; Mex. Govt. Tourist Dept. aw., 1st pl., '67), Am. Bus. Wm., Tejas Chptr. Boss of the Yr., '66; OES, Wms. Soc. of Christian Svc. (Life Mbr.), ZONTA, YMCA (N.W. Br. Bd. of Mgrs.); BPW Wm. of Achiev., '69; Westmoorland Col., '34–'35; Trinity Univ., '68; b. San Antonio, Tex., 1917; p. Barney and Mamie Perrin Heath; h. Roy Donald Oefinger (dec.); c. Janet (Mrs. R. E. Bickle), Roy Donald, Cheryl Ann; res: 918 Alexander Hamilton, San Antonio, Tex. 78228.

OERTEL, ALICE GASKILL, Owner, Gaskill-Oertel Advertising Agency, P.O. Box 206, Boynton Beach, Fla. 33435, '46–; Ed., Publr., Rental Svc. Forecaster, '56–; AE, Melvin F. Hall Adv. Agcy. (Buffalo, N.Y.), '41–'46; Retail Adv. Copywtr., '36–'41; Boynton Beach C. of C.; Univ. of Kan., BA, '28 (Mortar Bd., Alpha Sigma Mu); Grad. Work, La. State Univ.; b. El Dorzdo, Kan., 1909; p. Terry and Eva Worswick Gaskill; h. Oran Lee Oertel; res: The Windward, Adams Rd., Ocean Ridge, Boynton Beach, Fla. 33435.

OFFORD, LENORE GLEN, Mystery Reviewer, San Francisco Chronicle, Fifth and Mission Sts., S.F., Cal. 94119, '50–; Auth: 11 novels, incl. eight mysteries ('38–'59); two collaborations; essays; MWA (Northern Cal. Chptr. Reg. VP, '48–'49; "Edgar" Aw. for criticism, '51); Crime Wtrs. Assn. (Eng.), The Baker Street Irregulars (Titular Investiture, '63); Mills Col., BA, '25 (cum laude); Univ. of Cal. '25–'26; b. Spokane, Wash., 1905; p. Robert and Catherine Grippen Glen; h. Harold Offord; c. Judith Marie (Mrs. James Kennedy); res: 641 Euclid Ave., Berkeley, Cal. 94708.

OGLE, LUCILE E., Cnslt., Western Publishing Company, 850 Third Ave., N.Y., N.Y. 10022; Bd. of Dirs., Odyssey Press, '59–'68; VP, Bd. of Dirs., Artists & Writers Press, '48–'68; VP, Golden Press, '57–'68; Western Publishing Company, '36–'68; Ed., Harter Publishing Co., Cleve., '26–'35; Co-originator of Golden Books with George Duplaix; Am. Inst. of GA (Bd. of Dirs., '50–'56), League Sch. for Seriously Disturbed Children (Bd. of Dirs., '65–'70); annual Lucille E. Ogle literary aw. established by Western Publishing; Western Reserve Univ., BEd., '36; N.Y. Univ., M (Merchandising), '37; b. Cleve., Oh.; p. John and Maud Johnston Ogle; res: R.D. 1, Lower Mountain Rd., New Hope, Pa. 18938.

O'GORMAN, MARY WILSON, Ed., Smith-Reynolds Advertising, 244 Jackson Sq., S.F., Cal. 94111, '69–; Prod. Mgr., '64–'69; Prod. Mgr., J. L. Hunt Publr., '63–'64; Grade Sch. Tchr. (Scotland), '57–'58; Adv. Prod. Wms. Club (S.F. Chptr. VP; Pres., '68); Jordanhill Tchrs. Col., '56; night sch. (adv.), '60–'63; San Mateo Col. (Bus. Law), '68; b. Kilmarnock, Scotland, 1938; p. Alexander and Margaret Thompson Wilson; h. Brian O'Gorman; res: 403 Diamond St., S.F., Cal. 94114.

O'HARA, HELENE, Cnslt., fashion, specializing in footwear and color, '62–; Wtr., non-fiction articles, scripts, dir. mail; articles in nat. mags.; non-fiction novel in progress; Dir. of Fashion and Prom., Allied Kid Co., '48–'62; Free-lance for Hanes Hosiery; Footwear Ed., Mdsng. Motivation; on cnslt. basis at present; Shoe Wm. Execs. (Pres., Chmn. of Bd., '56–'58), Fashion Group (Gov., '60–'62; Pres. Comm., '60–'63), AWNY (Chmn. Shop Talks, '61), 210 Assocs.; Marygrove Col., '29–'32; Simmons Col., BS, '33; N.Y.U.; Pratt Inst.; b. Canton, Oh., 1911; p. James and Sadie McCrossin O'Hara; h. Dr. Robert O. Parker; res: 330 W. 12th St., N.Y., N.Y. 10014.

O'HARA, JUANITA ARNOLD, Wms. Pg. Staff Wtr., Peoria Journal Star, One News Plaza, Peoria, Ill. 61601, '62–; Reptr., Pekin Daily Times, '61–'62; Ill. Press Wms. Assn., NPWC; Ill. State Univ., '46–'47; Univ. of Minn., '47–'48; Bradley Univ., Bus. Mgt. Deg., '67; b. Sparta, Ga., 1924; p. Byron and Carlena Hutchins Arnold; h. John O'Hara; c. John, Jr., Maureen, Janet, Michael, Mark; res: 101 North Ct., Marquette Heights, Ill. 61554.

O'HARA, R. E. MARY, Assoc. Ed., Children's Pubns., Friendship Press, Dept. of National Council of Churches, 475 Riverside Dr., N.Y., N.Y. 10027, '68–; Asst. Ed., '67–'68; Compiling multimedia kit, "The See-Sound Show" (Friendship Press, '70); Theta Sigma Phi, Riverside Ch. tutorial prog. for children, Phi Kappa Phi; Syracuse Univ., BA, '65 (cum laude); MA (Jnlsm.), '69; b. Londonderry, Northern Ireland, 1944; p. The Rev. Francis and Joyce Bell O'Hara; res: 322 W. 75th St., N.Y., N.Y. 10023.

OHLIGER, GLORIA ANN, Wms. Page Ed., The Washington Daily News, 1013 13th St., N.W., Wash., D.C. 20036, '63–; WNPC, ANWC; George Washington Univ., '45–'46; b. Brownsville, Tex., 1925; p. Frederick and Evangeline Anzaldua Ohliger; res: 1330 New Hampshire Ave. N.W., Wash., D.C. 20036.

OHRN, ELINOR HENRY, Copywtr., D'Arcy Advertising Company, One Memorial Dr., St. Louis, Mo. 63102, '56–; Copywtr., Rutledge & Lilienfeld, '55–'56; Cont. Dir., KXOK, '41–'55; Copywtr., KCKN (Kan. City), '40; Copywtr., KDRO (Sedalia), '39–'40; Tchr., adult educ. class in crtv. writing; Wms. Adv. Club of St. Louis (Bd. Mbr., '60–'61; Wtr., Gridiron shows), Adv. Wtrs. Club of St. Louis; various aws. for adv. and TV commls., '57–; Wash. Univ. (dean's list; soph. hons.); b. St. Louis, Mo.; p. Frederick and Helene Buss Henry; h. Gus Ohrn (dec.); res: 1342 E. McCutcheon, Richmond Heights, Mo. 63144.

OILER, BETTY PRESTON, Wms. Ed., Glendale News-Press, 111 N. Isabel St., Glendale, Cal. 91209, '48–; Assoc. Wms. Ed., '45–'48; News-Ed., Wyandotte News-Herald, '42–'45; Theta Sigma Phi (L.A. Pfsnl. Chptr. 1st VP, '64–'65), Univ. of Mo.—J. C. Penney Aws. for Wms pages, '62, '64, '67; Copley Nwsprs. Ring of Truth Aws., '62, '66, '67; Mich. State Univ., BA (Jnlsm.), '41; b. Petoskey, Mich., 1920; p. Earl and Lillian Emrey Preston; h. Philip R. Oiler; c. Pamela (Mrs. William R. Beauer); res: 4030 Lehman Rd., La Crescenta, Cal. 91214.

OKUN, LILIAN, Radio-TV Specialist, New York Public Library, 8 E. 40th St., N.Y., N.Y. 10017; Auth., "Let's Listen to a Story"; WMCA; Wtr: WOR Radio, '33, and mag. articles for children and juv.; TV Acad. (former Pres.), AWRT, Radio Pioneers, ANTA, AFTRA, RTD Guild; Peabody Aw. for teenage bk.; Am. Acad. (Dramatic Arts); Columbia Univ.; b. N.Y.C., 1907; p. David and Henrietta Okun; res: 307 E. 44th St., N.Y., N.Y. 10017.

OLAR, LIBBY LEVCOVITCH, Prodr. and Hostess, "American-Jewish Variety Show," WXFM, 333 N. Michigan, Chgo., Ill. 60645, '63–; AWRT, Bdcst. Adv. Club; Jewish War Veterans aw.; WEBH aw.; b. Winnipeg, Can., 1915; p. Ben-Zion and Anna Freedland Levcovitch; h. Richard Olar; c. Linda Warnick, Ruby; res: 6207 N. Richmond, Chgo., Ill. 60645.

OLDS, HELEN DIEHL, Free-lance Wtr.; Tchr., Juvenile Writing, Queens Col., '57–; bks: "Miss Hattie and the Monkey" (Follet), "Detour for Meg" (Messner), "Christopher Columbus" (Putnam); Tch., writing, summer confs.; Auths. League, Wms. Nat. Bk. Assn., Rewriter Club (L. I., founder); Univ. of Tex.; Wittenberg Univ., BA, '21; b. Springfield, Oh., 1895; p. William and Henrietta Zammert Diehl; h. Phelps Olds (dec.); c. Howard, Jerry Phelps; res: 251-32 43rd Ave., Little Neck, N.Y. 11363.

OLENDER, TERRYS T., Auth: "My Life in Crime" (Holloway House pocketbk. edition, '66; 1st Place, Cal. Press Wm., '67), "For the Prosecution: Miss

Deputy D.A.'' (Chilton; best seller list several weeks), ''Delitto e Preguidizio'' (Longanesi, Italy); Deputy Dist. Atty., five yrs.; **Defense Atty.; Film-Drama Ed.,** Cal. Jewish Press; Film Reviewer, The Am. Zionest; Feature Colmst., L.A. Daily Jnl.; Colmst., ''Hollywood Oddities,'' World Un. Press Synd.; Overseas Corr. for ONA; Am. Bar Assn., Wm. Lawyers Assn., Greater L.A. Press Club, NFPW, Hollywood Fgn. Press, NATAS, AWRT, Cal. Press Wm. (Wm. of Achiev., '67–'69); Mills Col.; Univ. of Cal. at Berkeley, BA (Anthropology); Univ. of Southern Cal. (Law deg.; Law Review); admitted to Cal. Bar and Fed. Bar; b. S.F., Cal.; h. Edward Glick.

OLER, MERIAM MATTHAI, Media Dir., Knudsen Moore, Inc., 777 Summer St., Stamford, Conn. 06901, '68–; Media Byr., Planner, Analyst, Estimator, Van Sant Dugdale & Co., (Balt., Md.), '62–'66; h. R. Wayne Oler; c. one daughter; res: 2 Washington Ct., Stamford, Conn. 06902.

OLICK, ALICE WEISS, Educ. Wtr., The Record, 150 River St., Hackensack, N.J. 07602, '67–; Reptr., '64–'67; Reptr., The Sunday Post, Paramus, '61–'63; N.Y.U.; b. Weehawken, N.J., 1932; p. Louis and Anna Kohn Weiss; h. Marvin Olick; c. Karrie, Eric; res: 806 Arbor Rd., Paramus, N.J. 07652.

OLIS, RUTH, Fashion Ed., Courier-Post, Camden, N.J., '59–; N.J. Daily Nwsp. Wm. (Pres., '68–'70), Fashion Group of Phila., WNPC, NFPW; Rider Col., BS; b. Providence, R.I.; res: Kings Highway Towers, Maple Shade, N.J. 08052.

OLIVER, SYLVIA BASSETT, Admr., Little Dixie Regional Library, 111 N. Fourth, Moberly, Mo. 65270, '62–; Tchr., Springfield Sch. (Mich. City, Ind.), '58; Huntsville (Mo.) HS, '55–'57; Moberly Jr. HS, '54–'55; Mo. Lib. Assn., ALA; S. W. Tex. State Tchrs. Col., BS, '42; Univ. of Mo., MS (Lib. Sci.), '69; b. South Bend, Ind., 1921; p. Clark and Lillian Geer Bassett; h. Willard Oliver; c. Mrs. Jill Pilkington, Jeffrey; res: 103 Elm, Huntsville, Mo. 65259.

OLIVER, TONI FRANCES, Sr. Home Fashions Coordr. and Publicist, Macy's, Herald Sq., N.Y., N.Y., '68–; Home Furnishings Publicist, '66–'68; Asst. to Sr. VP of PR, Raymond Loewy-William Snaith, Inc., '63–'65; Finch Col., BA, '63.

OLMSTEAD, BETTY C., Media Byr., Venet Advertising Inc., 820 Second Ave., N.Y., N.Y. 10017, '67–; Media Asst., '65–'67; Asst. to Rsch. Dir., '63–'65; Programmer, Chubb & Son, '62–'63; Upsala Col., AB (Econs.), '62; b. Plainfield, N.J., 1940; res: 1011 Oakland Ave., Plainfield, N.J. 07060.

OLSEN, FLORENCE J., Secy. of Corp., Kensol-Olsen Mark Inc., 40 Melville Park Rd., Melville, L.I., N.Y. 11746, '66–; Bur. of Adv., Nwsp. Copy Rsch., ANPA, '48–'65; Copy and TV Rsch., BBDO, '44–'48; Outdoor Advertising, '43–'44; AWNY, AAF; N.Y.U. Sch. of

Commerce; N.Y.U.; res: 896 Lincoln Ave., Baldwin, L.I., N.Y. 11510.

OLSEN, MARY HUCK, Home Econ. Cnslt., '69–; Dir., Consumer Svcs., Frigidare Div., General Motors, '68–'69; Dir., Home Econ., '56–'68; Gen. Home Svc. Dir., Ohio Fuel Gas Co., '48–'56; Dir. of Rsch., '44–'48; Home Econsts. in Bus. (Nat. Chmn., '63–'64); Am. Home Econ. Assn., Oh. Home Econ. Assn. (Pres., '54–'56), Electrical Wms. Roundtable, AWRT; Oh. Univ., BS (Home Econ.), '44; b. Lowell, Oh., 1923; p. Clemence and Eulalia Schilling Huck; h. James H. Olsen; res: 2591 Charing Rd., Columbus, Oh. 43221.

OLSEN, NORMA T., TV Opns. Mgr., American Broadcasting Company, 4151 Prospect Ave., Hollywood, Cal. 90027, '50–; Asst. to Dir. of Tech. OPNS, Blue Network Co., '42–'50; NBC (N.Y.C.), '37–'42; Hollywood BPW, Acad. of Magical Arts (Assoc. Mbr.); L.A. County Art Museum (Charter Mbr.); Drake Bus. Col., N.Y.C.; b. Bklyn., N.Y.; p. John Olsen; res: 10840 Lindbrook Dr., L.A., Cal. 90024.

OLSEN, WINNIFRED CASTLE, Teaching Specialist in Northwest History, Tacoma Public Schools, PO Box 1357, Tacoma, Wash. 98401, '67–; Asst., State Capitol Museum (Olympia), 5 yrs.; Radio Program Prod., KGY, 8 yrs.; Ins. Agt., one yr.; Sls. Rep., World Bk. Ency., 18 yrs.; Ed., ''Suggested Activities and Resources for Teaching the History of Negro Life in America'' (NEA Aw., '68); Auth: ''Before Tacoma—What? Puyallup and Nisqually Indians'' ('68), ''Tacoma Beginnings'' ('69); Theta Sigma Phi, Wash. State Public Info. Cncl., Wash. State Hist. Soc., AAUW (Wash. Div. State Pres.; Olympia Br. Fellowship Grant, '65); Delegate, White House Conf. on Children and Youth, '60; Wash. State Univ., BA (Sociol., Jnlsm.), '38 (Phi Beta Kappa; Mortar Bd.; Alumni of Month, '44); b. Olympia, Wash., 1916; p. Lewis and Minnie Klumb Castle; h. Walter H. Olsen; c. Walter H., Jr., Wayne L.; res: 133 N. Foote, Olympia, Wash. 98501.

OLSHANSKY, ROBERTA HANKES, (pseud: Marie Gifford), Prom. Home Econst., Armour and Company, 401 N. Wabash, Chgo., Ill. 60611, '67–; Home Econs. Corr., '65–'67; Therapeutic and Rsch. Dietitian, Peterson Med. Clinic, '64–'65; Cnslt., adv. agcys., food photogrs.; food photog. and TV comml. food layouts; Am. Home Econs. Assn., Am. Dietetic Assn., Chgo. Dietetic Assn., Ill. Home Econs. Assn., Home Econsts. in Bus. (Chgo. Chptr. Exec. Bd., '66–'69, Top Ed. of Nwsltr. aw., '67–'69); Mount Mary Col., BS, '63; Baylor Univ. Med. Ctr., Dietetic Internship, '63–'64; b. Aurora, Ill., 1941; p. Robert and Marie Leick Hankes; h. Melvin A. Olshansky; res: 3920 N. Lake Shore Dr., Chgo., Ill. 60613.

OLSON, EDNA HOWARD, Librn., Library Georgia Sta., University of Georgia, Experiment, Ga. 30212, '49–; Wtr., papers for trustee groups; Flint River Reg. Lib. (Chmn. Trustees, '69–); Intl. Assn. of Agricultural Librns. and Documentalists, ALA (Trustees Assn.),

Southeastern Lib. Assn., Ga. Lib. Assn. (Secy., '61–'63); volunteer tchr. of exceptional children; active in civic orgs.; Ga. State Col., BCS, '50 (Delta Mu); Emory Univ., ML (Lib. Sci.), '55; b. Dawson County, Ga.; p. Dr. William and Estey Dooley Howard; h. Lawrence Carroll Olson (dec.); c. Margaret, Wayne, Howard; res: 733 E. College St., Griffin, Ga. 30223.

OLSON, GLORIA ANN SONDRA, Deputy Chief of Command Info., Military Assistance Command, Saigon, Vietnam, '69–; Chief, Radio-TV News Br., Off. of Asst. Secy. of Defense and Public Affairs, '67–'69; Chief, TV Br., Defense Info. Sch. (Ft. Harrison, Ind.), '65–'67; Public Info. Offcr., Bdcst. Off., Northern Area Command (Frankfurt, Germany), '59–'61; Public Info. Offcr., Bdcst. Off., Milw. NIKE Defense, '56–'59; several Army Commendation and Joint Svcs. Commendation Medals for radio-TV and military svcs.; Oswego Tchr. Col., BS, '51; Syracuse Univ., MS (Radio-TV), '53; Univ. of Wis. (Adv., PR), '65; Defense Info. Sch., '64; b. Rome, N.Y., 1928; res: 4215 W. Fifth Lane, Hialeah, Fla.

OLSON, JANE VIRGINIA, Mng. Ed., American Scientist, Society of the Sigma Xi, 155 Whitney Ave., New Haven, Conn. 06510, '69–; Ed., Yale Univ. Press, '58–'69; Tech. Ed., Ill. State Geological Survey, '49–'55; Copy Ed., Vogue, '46–'49; Copy Ed., Atlantic Monthly, '42–'46; League of Wm. Voters; Univ. of N.M., BA, '39; Univ. of Chgo., grad. study; b. Chgo., Ill., 1916; p. Oscar W. and Mary Bowles Olson; res: 130 Everit St., New Haven, Conn. 06511.

OLSON, LAURA MAXINE, Public Info. Offcr., National Endowment for the Humanities, 1800 F St., N.W., Wash., D.C. 20506, '69–; Legislative Asst. to Senator Ernest Gruening, '66–'69; Asst. Legislative Asst., '62–'65; Special Cnslt., population, Senate Govt. Opns. Subcomm. on Fgn. Aid. Expenditures; Press Asst. to Senator Maurine B. Neuberger, '61–'62; Rsch. Asst. to Rep. Charles O. Porter, '57–'60; Reptr., Polit. Wtr., Roseburg (Ore.) News-Rev., '54–'56; News Ed., Cottage Grove (Ore.) Sentinel, '53–'54; Cnslr. for Wm., Univ. of Ore., '52–'53; Prom. Wtr., N.Y. Herald Tribune Synd., and Wtr., N.Y. Herald Tribune News Svc., '50–'52; Line-Up Ed., True Detective, '49–'50; Theta Sigma Phi, Senate Press Secys. Assn., Fed. Eds. Assn., Who's Who of Am. Wm.; Univ. of Ore., BS (Jnlsm.), '49; b. Baker, Ore., 1927; p. Arthur and Retta Mercer Olson; res: 607 Massachusetts Ave., N.E., Wash., D.C., and McKenzie Highway, Leaburg, Ore.

OLSON, MARTHA ANNETTE, VP, Farley Manning Associates, 342 Madison Ave., N.Y., N.Y. 10021, '65–; AE, '60–'65; Owner, Schram, Reiner, Olson, Inc. (St. Louis, Mo.), '55–'60; AE, Fleishman-Hillard, Inc., '50–'55; PRSA, Theta Sigma Phi; Parsons Jr. Col.; res: 39 E. 67th St., N.Y., N.Y. 10021.

OLSON, ROBERTA MALCHESKI, Ed., The Fertile Journal, Mill St., Fertile, Minn. 56540, '68–; City Ed., News Ed., Reptr., St. Cloud Daily Times, '64–'68; Cont.

Wtr., KROC Radio, '61–'63; Asst. to PR Offcr., Bemidji State Col., '63–'64; Radio Newscaster; BPW (Minn. State Top Hat aw., '68), Minn. Press Wm. (Feature Writing aw., '69), ZONTA, Pi Delta Epsilon, active in local orgs.; Northland Col. (Key scholarship); Bemidji State Col., BA, '64; b. Washburn, Wis., 1940; p. Edmund and Beverly Peterson Malcheski; h. John J. Olson; res: Top Notch Trailer Ct., Fertile, Minn. 56540.

OLTEN, CAROL MARIE, Staff Wtr., San Diego Union, Union-Tribune Publishing Co., 940 Third Ave., San Diego, Cal., '64–; Reptr., San Diego Tribune, '64; Columbia Missourian, '62–'64; Wash. Missourian, '58–'62; Kappa Tau Alpha, Theta Sigma Phi; Webster Col., '60 (cash scholarship); Univ. of Mo. Sch. of Jnlsm., BJ '64 (Hearst Scholarship; Frank Scott aw., '64); b. Wash., Mo., 1942; p. William and Edna Brinker Olten; res: 6548 La Jolla Blvd., La Jolla, Cal. 92037.

O'MEARA, MARY ELIZABETH, Wtr. and Edtl. Cnslt., '68–; Sr. Ed., "Plan for New York City", '68–'69; VP, Assoc. Crtv. Dir., Young & Rubicam, '62–'68; (Photog. aw., '66); VP, Copy Dir., '57–'62; Assoc. Copy Dir., '51–'56; Copywtr., '46–'51; Copywtr., Supvsr., Compton Adv., '43–'46; Art Asst., Copywtr., J. Walter Thompson, '34–'43; Vassar, BA, '34; Art Students League, '36–'38; N.Y.U. Flight Ground Sch., '42; Hunter Col., '69; b. New Haven, Conn., 1913; p. Edward and Helen Sheehan O'Meara; res: 135 E. 71st St., N.Y., N.Y. 10021.

O'MEARA, SUSAN, Prodr., BFB Productions Inc., 422 Madison Ave., N.Y., N.Y. 10017, '68–; Prod. Mgr.; Prod. Coordr.; Prodr., TV commls. (Am. TV Commls. Festival runner-up for Best Concept, '69); Actress, TV, theater, '56–'66; Bradley Univ., BA, '54; b. Peoria, Ill., 1932; b. Don and Ruth Manning O'Meara; res: 77 Park Ave., N.Y., N.Y. 10016.

OMMERMAN, BETTY, Fashion Ed., Newsday, 550 Stewart Ave., Garden City, N.Y. 11530, '57–; Wms. Feature Wtr., '55; Entertainment Feature Wtr.; Fashion Reptr., Womens Wear Daily; Wire Ed., Daily Messenger (Canandaigua, N.Y.); Feature Wtr.; Fashion Lectr.; Fashion Advisor, TV appearances; Nwsp. Wms. Club of N.Y.; Am. Inst. of Mens and Boys Wear edtl. aw., '68; Greater N.Y. Wms. Div. of State of Israel Bonds aw. for distg. svc. and rept., '67; Caswell-Massey fashion rept. aw.; Fur Fashion excellence aw., '65; Hunter Col., BA (Liberal Arts); Univ. of Wis. (Jnlsm.); b. N.Y.C.; p. Morris and Gussie Heller Ommerman.

OMOHUNDRO, DELIGHT DIXON, VP, Marcello, Inc., 180 E. State St., Westport, Conn. 06880, '68–; Adv. Dir., Warner's; Adv. Mgr.; Colmst., Bpt Post-Telegram; Cnslt., mktng., beauty, adv. for maj. corps.; Am. Mgt. Assn., Assn. Nat. Adv., AFA, Adv. Club of Bpt. (Treas.), AWRT, IRTS, Fashion Group; Andy, '66, '67; Who's Who in Adv., other dirs.; Cornell, BA, '54; Univ. of Perugia; h. William A. Omohundro.

O'NEIL, CECILIA, Pres., National Retired Teachers Association, Western Headquarters, 215 Long Beach Blvd., Long Beach, Cal., '67–; VP, '58–'67; Bd. of Dirs., Am. Assn. of Retired Persons, '67; Pres., Cal. Retired Tchrs. Assn., '57–'59; Pres., Cal. Tchrs. Assn., Bay Sec., '45–'46; Tchr., San Mateo and San Jose; Dean of Girls and Vice Principal, San Jose, '32–'52; Intl. Sr. League Tchr. of the State, '58, Delta Kappa Gamma; San Jose State Col. Grad.; Univ. of Cal.; res: San Jose, Cal.

O'NEIL, DORIS CONSTANCE, Chief, Picture Collection, Time Inc., Time and Life Bldg., Rockefeller Ctr., N.Y., N.Y. 10020, '59–; '48–'59; Cnslt., pic. lib. systems and standards; Pic. Rschr., several bks. and publrs.; Evaluator of pic. collections; Lib., R.I. Sch. of Design, '45–'48; Art Dept., Providence Public Lib., '39–'45; Special Libs. Assn., Pic. Pfsnls.; Educ: R.I. School of Design; b. Pawtucket, R.I., 1916; p. Edgar and Catherine Sullivan O'Neil; res: Pumpkin Hill Rd., New Milford, Conn. 06776.

O'NEIL, MARY KERRIGAN, Exec. Dir., Western Reserve Girl Scout Council, 108 Fir Hill, Akron, Oh. 44309, '67–; PR Specialist and Supvsr. of Employee Pubns., The Firestone Tire & Rubber Co., '50–'67; Auth., many bklets. for Firestone; Dir., 12 periodicals; Theta Sigma Phi (Akron Chptr. Pres., '66–'67), ICIE (Akron Chptr. Founder and Pres.; Reg. Dir., two terms); Who's Who of Am. Wm.; Univ. of Neb., BA, '42; b. Primghar, Ia.; p. John and Estelle Bray Kerrigan; h. Walter P. O'Neil; res: Apt. 1, 172 S. Miller Rd., Akron, Oh. 44313.

O'NEILL, EILEEN, Actress, TV and film, c/o William Morris Agency, 151 El Camino, Beverly Hills, Cal.; "Burke's Law," "Get Smart," "Smothers Brothers," many others; Thalians.

O'NEILL, MARY L., Auth: "Hailstones & Halibut Bones" (Doubleday, '61; two educ. motion pics.), "Fingers Are Always Bringing Us News" (Doubleday, '69; Jr. Guild Selection, fall, '69), eight others; Copywtr., Copy Chief, Higbee Co. (Cleve., Oh.); Copywtr., McCann-Erickson; VP, Partner, Gibbons-O'Neill Adv. Agcy.; Lectr., elementary, high schs., cols.; Speaker, Institutes on Crtv. Writing, Univ. of Minn.; Auths. Guild, formerly; b. N.Y.C., 1908; p. James and Marie Galarneau le Duc; h. John A. O'Neill (dec.); c. Mrs. John F. Kelly, John R., Mrs. Benjamin L. Hagler; res: 173 Riverside Dr., Apt. 7C, N.Y., N.Y. 10024.

OPATOW, LORNA, Pres., Opatow Associates Inc., 527 Madison Ave., N.Y., N.Y. 10022, '63–; Rsch. Dir., Hearst Magazines; Public Speaker in mktng., packaging, and rsch.; NHFL (N.Y. Chptr. Pres., '69–'71; Bd. of Dirs.), Am. Mktng. Assn., AWNY, Am. and World Assns. for Public Opinion Rsch., AWRT, Am. Sociol. Assn., Municipal Art League; Beta Gamma Sigma; Univ. of Pa., BA (Econs.); Temple Univ., MA (Bus. Adm.); b. Phila., Pa.

OPPENHEIM, CAROL, Special Assigt. Reptr., Chicago Today, 441 N. Michigan Ave., Chgo., Ill. 60611, '66–; Chgo. Am., '57–'62; Public Info. Offcr. (New Haven, Conn.) Redev. Agcy., '62–'65; Theta Sigma Phi; Chgo. Nwsp. Reptrs. Assn.; Univ. of Mich., BA, '57; b. Chgo., Ill., 1936; p. Nathan and Helen Freshman Oppenheim; h. Richard C. Fogelson; res: 431 W. Oakdale Ave., Chgo., Ill. 60657.

OPPENHEIMER, EVELYN, Auth: "The Articulate Woman, Public Speaking Fashioned for Women" (Droke House, '68), "Red River Dust" (Word Books, '68), "Book Reviewing for an Audience" (Chilton, '62), "Legend and Other Poems" (Naylor, '51); Radio Bk. Reviewer, sponsored by Doubleday Bk. Shops (KRLD, Dallas and Ft. Worth; KPHO, Phoenix; KKHI, S.F.); Lit. Agt.; Instr., Univ. of Dallas ('59), U.C.L.A. ('58), Univ. of Tex. ('58, '60), Tex. Technological Col. ('57); Univ. of Chgo., PhB, '29 (Phi Beta Kappa); b. Dallas, Tex.; p. Louis and Gertrude Baum Oppenheimer; res: 4505 Fairway Ave., Dallas, Tex. 75219.

ORDONEZ, BRENDA WAGNER, Mgr., Tri-Ocean Inc., bk. publishing, 62 Townsend, S.F., Cal. 94107, '69–; h. Mario Ordonez.

O'REILLY, ROSE MARIE, Mgr. of TV Ratings, Columbia Broadcasting System, 51 W. 52nd St., N.Y., N.Y. 10019; Radio and TV, '38–; Guest Lectr. on TV at local cols.; Radio and TV Rsch. Cncl. (Secy.-Treas., '62–'64); Catholic Apostolate Radio, TV and Adv. ('66–'68); St. Joseph's Col. for Wm., BA, '36; N.Y.U. Grad. Sch. of Bus. Adm.; b. N.Y.C.; res: 111-10 75th Ave., Forest Hills, N.Y. 11375.

ORENTE, ROSE J., Dir., Owner, Rose Orente, Publicity, 225 E. 79th St., N.Y., N.Y. 10021, '62–; Pubcty. Dir., John Wiley & Sons, '51–'62; Pubcty. Dept., Harper & Bros., '44–'50; Auth: verse-play, "Carlotta's Serape," CBS Radio Workshop (1st Place, Acad. of Am. Poets Contest, '57); poems, stories, articles in jnls.; PSA, PPA, Am. Interlingua Soc.; Hunter Col., BA, '38; b. N.Y.C.; p. Israel and Minnie Chasin Orenstein.

ORFANOS, MINNIE A., Librn., Northwestern Univ. Dental School, 311 E. Chicago Ave., Chgo., Ill. 60611, '50–; Asst. Librn., '45–'50; Lib. Asst., '43–'45; Lib. Asst., Chgo. Public Lib., '40–'43; Auth., buls., articles, bk. revs. on dental and lib. subjects; Med. Lib. Assn. (Midwest Reg. Group: Pres., '68; Secy., '65–'67, '57), Sigma Phi Alpha, Northwestern Univ., Evening Div., PhB, '54; Univ. of Mich., MS (Lib. Sci.), '63; b. 1921; res: 45 Wilmette Ave., Glenview, Ill. 60025.

ORMSBY, JEANNE LOUISE, AE, Dix & Eaton Incorporated, 1010 Euclid Ave., Cleveland, Oh. 44115, '69–; PR Dir., Cuyahoga County Lib. System, '62–'68; PR Dir., St. John's Hosp., '56–'62; PR Dir., Lutheran Hosp., '55–'56; Staff Asst., PR Dept., Un. Appeal, '51–'55; PRSA (N.E. Oh. Chptr. Pres., '66); YWCA (Cleve. Bd. of Trustees, '67–), Welfare Fedn. of Cleve. (PR, '66–'67), Cleve. Hosp. Cncl. PR Advisory Comm.

(Founder), ZONTA (Cleve. Bd. Mbr., '66–'69); Best Article aw. in bul., Oh. Lib. Assn., '67; Case Western Reserve Univ., AB, '49 (Encampment for Citizenship Scholarship, '48); b. Detroit, Mich., 1926; p. Irwin and Lucille Cooke Ormsby; res: 4550 Van Epps Rd., Cleve., Oh. 44131.

ORMSBY, VIRGINIA H., Lang. Arts Specialist, Geo. W. Carver Elementary Board of Public Instruction, Lindsey Hopkins Bldg., Miami, Fla.; Tchr., Ga. and Fla.; Auth., Illus., pic. and reg. bks. for children (J. B. Lippincott Co., '55–; Crown Publrs.); Delta Kappa Gamma (recognition at intl. conv., '60); Oglethorpe Univ., AB; High Museum of Art; b. Atlanta, Ga.; p. Robert and Juliet Milmow Haire; h. (div.); c. Eric Linn, Alan Robert; res: 1336 Obispo Ave., Coral Gables, Fla. 33134.

ORNISH, NATALIE GENE, Pres., Dallas Records, 6031 Sherry Lane, Dallas, Tex. 75225, '57–; Crtv. Wtr., PR Exec., Rogers & Smith Adv., '47; Ed., Reptr., AP (Omaha, Neb.), '45; Lectr.; Playwright, "Just Twelve" musical theatre; Composer, Auth., songs, educ. records for children; ASCAP, Who's Who of Am. Wm., Dallas Mot. Pic. Classification Bd., '65–'69; Sam Houston State Col., BA, '43; Northwestern Univ., MS, '45; b. Galveston, Tex., 1926; p. George and Bess Shapiro Moskowitz; h. Edwin P. Ornish; c. Laurel Ann, Dean Michael, Steven Andrew, Kathy April; res: 7146 Currin Dr., Dallas, Tex. 75230.

ORR, CAROL WALLACE, Exec. Asst. to Dir., Princeton University Press, 41 William St., Princeton, N.J. 08540, '69–; Asst. to Assoc. Dir., '68–'69; Ed., Paperbacks, '67–'68; Permissions Mgr., '66–'67; Adm. Asst., U.S. Govt., '55–'56; Pers. Interviewer, John Hancock Mutual Life Ins., '53–'55; Boston Univ., '51–'53; Douglass Col., BA, '66 (Phi Beta Kappa); Harvard Univ., '61–'64; b. Newton, Mass., 1933; p. Barton and Mary Stigler Wallace; c. Brett Amanda, Ross W.; res: 19 Bank St., Princeton, N.J. 08540.

ORR, ELLEN (Lillian Ellis Hester), Colmst., Delta Farm Press, Clarksdale, Miss. 38614, Bolivar Commercial, Cleve., Miss. 38774, '48–; Colmst., Progressive Farmer (Memphis); Co-Auth., "Delta Decameron;" NLAPW, Miss. Press Wm. (writing aws.); Miss. Wms. Col., '29; b. Ackerman, Miss., 1907; p. William and Mamie Hames Ellis; h. Thomas A. Hester; c. Thomas III, John William; res: Box 242, Honey Bayou Rd., Shelby, Miss. 38774.

ORR, LORRAINE BATE, Bdcstr., Wtr., Co-prodr., Orr Production Services, Inc., Campus Radio Voice, Inc., 178 E. 70th St., N.Y., N.Y. 10021, '58–; Publicist, BBDO, Ted Bates, Benton & Bowles; Copywtr., Gene Walker Assocs. (S.F., Cal.); Actress: Broadway, films, radio, TV; Co-prodr., TV films, "Welcome Mat"; AWRT, NFHL; Soc. for Prevention of Cruelty to Children aw., '67; N.Y.U.; City Col. of N.Y., special courses; b. Ottawa, Can.; p. Llewellyn and Dorothy Walters Bate; h. John Dean Orr; res: 178 E. 70th St., N.Y., N.Y. 10021.

ORR, MARY CASWELL, Actress, numerous roles in stock theatre, Broadway (debut as Rosemary in "Bachelor Born," '38), on tour in U.S. and overseas, '64; TV part in "Suspect" (NBC, '42; first full-length play on TV); Auth., two novels, short stories in nat. mags., original story, "The Wisdom of Eve" (basis for movie "All About Eve," which won an Oscar Aw., '50, and basis for musical "Applause"; Screen wtrs. Guild Aw. for original story); Co-auth., with husband, 40 TV scripts, also plays; AEA, SAG, AFTRA, Dramatists Guild, ALA, Gamma Phi Beta; Mrs. Dow's Sch., Briarcliff Manor; Syracuse Univ.; b. Bklyn., N.Y.; p. Chester and Jessica Hawks Orr; h. Reginald Denham; res: 100 W. 57th St., N.Y., N.Y. 10019.

ORSBORN, NICKI NICKERSON, Owner, Nicki Orsborn, Public Relations and Advertising, 503 Arizona Land Title Bldg., Tucson, Ariz. 85701, '66–; PR Dir., Nat. Fndn. for Asthmatic Children, '64–; PR Dir., Tucson C. of C., '62–'64; Ed., Tucson Progress, nwsp. (C. of C. nat. aw. for objectivity, '64); Reptr., Ariz. Daily Star, '61–'62; HS Tchr., '52–'54; Copywtr., Prod. Mgr., Asst. Adv. Mgr., Sears, Roebuck and Co. (Kan. City; Denver, Colo.), '45–'48; Cnslt., PR, Adv.; Ariz. Press Wm., PRSA, NFPW; Kan. State Univ., BS, '52 (with hons.); b. Syracuse, Kan., 1928; p. Hiram E. and Anna M. Quinby Nickerson; c. Kris, Lisa, Tina Marie; res: 4342 E. Sixth, Tucson, Ariz. 85711.

ORTIZ, SILVIA M., Head of Crtv. Adv., Spanish Advertising and Marketing Services, 1501 Broadway, N.Y., N.Y. 10036, '61–; Crtv. Head, Intl. Mktng. (Puerto Rico), '61–'67; Copywtr., Publicidad Alvarez (Perez, Cuba), '59–'60; Copywtr., Godoy & Cross, '54–'59; Mktng. Cnslt. and Rschr. in Puerto Rico, '64–'67; Pfsnl. Advs. Nat. Assn. (Havana, Cuba, '56–'60); El Mundo Nwsp. adv. aw; Univ. of Havana, Master of Philosophy and Arts, '54; Master of Adv., '56; b. Havana, Cuba.

ORTNER, RUTH RINDZUNER, PR Dir., Intercontinental Parking Systems and Auto Baby Sitters of New York, 827 Sterling Pl., Brooklyn, N.Y. 11216; Pres., Chatterbox for PR; Cnslt., Parking and Travel Industry, Military Parking and Auto Shipping; AWRT, N.Y. Conv. and Visitors Bur.; b. N.Y.C., 1916; p. Harry and Clara Nudelman Rindzuner; h. Louis Ortner; c. Charles, Michael; res: 17 Radnor Rd., Great Neck, N.Y. 11023.

ORTON, WANDA JONES, Gen. Assigt. Reptr., Baytown Sun, 1301 Memorial Dr., Baytown, Tex. 77520, '57–; Wms. Ed., '54–'57; Wms. News, '52–'54; Corr., '51–; Wtr., articles, Seventeen; Tex. Press Wm. (two state 1st Pl. aws., '68), NFPW, several pubcty. aws.; Lee Col., '52–'54 (Phi Theta Kappa); Univ. of Houston (dean's list; outstanding Latin student aw., '68); b. Baytown, Tex., 1934; p. Clyde and Bennie Nelson Jones; h. Walter Orton; c. Jan Kay; res: 113 Lakewood, Baytown, Tex. 77520.

OSBORN, BARBARA MONROE, Prof., California State College at Los Angeles, 5151 State Col. Dr., L.A., Cal. 90032, '56–; Instr., E. L.A. Commty. Col., '55–'56;

Dir., Supvsr., Nursing, Cal., '44–'55; Cnslt., health; Auth., textbk. "Introduction to Community Health" (Allyn & Bacon, '64; revsd., '70); Co-auth., "Foundations of Health Science" ('69); Text Reviewer in health educ.; active in health orgs.; Am. Red Cross Chmn. of Nursing Svcs. in L.A., '67–; Univ. of Cal., Berkeley, BS (Nursing), '43; Cal. State Col., MA, '56; U.C.L.A., Educ. Degree, '60; b. Oakland, Cal., 1921; p. Russell and Ruth Watson Monroe; h. William Henkel; c. Patricia Joan McClean, Robert S.; res: 236 N. Windsor Blvd., L.A., Cal. 90004.

OSBORN, IRENE CHARLES, Pres., Osborn/Charles Associates, Inc., 1212 Ave. of the Americas, N.Y., N.Y. 10036, '69–; VP, Secy., Co-founder, '58–'69; Crtv. Dir., Lester Harrison Adv., '55–'58; Crtv. Dir., Daniel & Charles Adv., '53–'55; Art Dir., Butterick Pattern Co., '50–'53; Art Dir., Simplicity Pattern Co., '47–'50; Dir., Farsight Corp.; N.Y. Art Dirs. Club, Soc. of Illus., numerous graphic design, packaging aws.; Parson's Sch. of Design; b. N.Y.C.; h. Jack R. Osborn; c. John Charles; res: 65 E. 76th St., N.Y., N.Y. 10021.

OSBORN, STELLANOVA, a Founder and VP, International Movement for Atlantic Union; Corresponding Secy., Federal Union, Inc.; Contrb. Ed., Freedom & Union, 1736 Columbia Rd., N.W., Wash., D.C. 20009, '65–; Secy. for N. Am., IMAU, '58–'65; Cncl. 2nd Bd. Mbr., Atlantic Union Comm., '50–'61; Auth., 7 bks., '41–'62; Co-auth., 4 others, '39–'45; Ed., Univ. of Mich. Offcl. Pubn., '25–'30; Asst. Ed., Good Health Magazine, '25; Contrb. Ed., sociol. and econs., New Intl. Ency. Supplement, '24; Staff Ed., New Intl. Yrbk., '23; Co-sponsor, Co-exec. bks. for Meiji Univ., Tokyo, after earthquake, '24; Capital Bus. and Pfsnl. Wms. Club (Most Valuable Mbr., '66); Upper Peninsula of Mich. Wtrs. poetry cit., '66; Univ. of Mich., AB, '22 (magna cum laude; Phi Beta Kappa); MA (Medieval Eng.), '30 (Outstanding Achiev. Aw., '67); b. Hamilton, Can., 1894; p. Edward and Rosa Lee Brunt; h. Chase Salmon Osborn; res: Possum Poke, Possum Lane, Poulan, Ga. 31781, and Sugar Island Star Rte., Sault Ste. Marie, Mich. 49783.

OSBORNE, MARY CHRISTINE, Partner, Osborne Assocs., 180 Madison Ave., N.Y., N.Y. 10016, '54–; Selvage & Lee (N.Y.C.), '50–'54; PR Dept., Quaker Oats Co. (Chgo.), '46–'50; Theta Sigma Phi (N.Y. Chptr. Pres., '58–'60; Reg. Dir., '69–'70), NHFL (N.Y. Chptr. Pres., '67–'69), PR Assoc., Am. Inst. of Interior Designers; State Univ. of Ia., BA (Jnlsm.), '46 (Phi Beta Kappa); b. Ottumwa, Ia., 1925; p. Glenn and Jennie Johnson Osborne; h. John C. Conover; res: 32 E. 39th St., N.Y., N.Y. 10016.

OSGOOD, ESTHER E., Dir. of Pubns., National Association of Independent Schools, 4 Liberty Sq., Boston, Mass. 02109, '64–; '62–'64; Ed., The Independent Sch. Bul., '41–; Independent Schs. Educ. Bd., '30–'62; Shattuck Sch. Cent. Aw. for svc. to secondary educ. ('58); Radcliffe Col., AB, '30; b. Boston, Mass., 1908; p. Frederick and Elizabeth McArthur Osgood; res: 360 Randolph Ave., Milton, Mass. 02186.

OSTERWALD, BIBI, Actress, TV commls., six Broadway shows, starring 41 times as understudy, incl. "Golden Apple" (Aw. for best supporting player); talent on folk-music recs.; TV shows; three motion pics.; AEA (Cnslr., '55–'62), SAG, AFTRA; Wash. Catholic Univ.; Wash. Sch. for Secys.; b. New Brunswick, N.J., 1920; p. Rudolf and Dagmar Kvastad Osterwald; h. Justin Arndt; c. Christopher J.

OSTMAN, ELEANOR, Food and Home Furnishings Ed., St. Paul Dispatch-Pioneer Press, Northwest Publications, 55 E. Fourth St., St. Paul, Minn. 55101, '67–; Home Furnishings Ed., '65–; Wms. Dept. Wtr., '62–'65; Dorothy Dawe Aw., '68; Judge of '69 Pillsbury Bake-Off; Jr. League of St. Paul; Macalester Col., BA (Jnlsm.), '62; b. Hibbing, Minn., 1940; p. Ero and Ellen Lapinoja Ostman; h. Ronald T. Aune; c. Aric Bruce; res: 853 Lincoln Ave., St. Paul, Minn. 55105.

OSTRANDER, KATHERINE ANDRE', Media Dir., Dailey & Associates, 3807 Wilshire Blvd., L.A., Cal. 90005, '63–; Media Dir., Donahue & Co., '61–'63; Media Dir., Heintz & Co., '60–'61; Exec. Time Byr., Dan B. Miner/Honig Cooper, '50–'58; b. Fullerton, Cal., 1922; p. William and Mildred Shryock Andre'; c. Kathrina, Ann; res: 2046 Sanborn Ave., L.A., Cal. 90027.

OSTROM, DORIS ANNE, Copy Group Head, J. Walter Thompson Co., 420 Lexington Ave., N.Y., N.Y., '61–; Copywtr., '56–'58; Copywtr., Lambert & Feasley, '59–'60; Copywtr., D'Arcy Adv., '58–'59; Copywtr., BBDO, '51–'56; Guest Lectr., Tobe Coburn Fashion Inst.; AWNY; Film Festival certs., TV commls., '61, '63, '66; Addy aw., A.A.F., '67; Ad Age 100 Best Print Ads, '67; Stockholm, Sweden "Successful Am. Adv." Exhbn., '67; Univ. of Wis., BS (high hons.).

O'SULLIVAN, JOAN, Wms. Ed., King Features Syndicate, 235 E. 45th St., N.Y., N.Y. 10017, '66–; formerly Reptr., New York Sun; Home Ed., Sunday Mirror Magazine; currently auth. of six wkly. photo features by Joan O'Sullivan and six beauty and charm colms. as Jeanne D'Arcy; Auth., "100 Ways to Popularity" (Mcmillan, '63); Lectr., Fordham Univ., '55–'56; Trustee, Anne O'Hare McCormick Jnlsm. Scholarship Fund; N.Y. Nwsp. Wms. Club (Twice Pres.; Distg. Writing Aw. '50); Fordham Univ. night courses, two yrs.; b. N.Y.C.; p. Timothy and Edna D'Arcy O'Sullivan; h. Archie Vassiliadis; c. Darcy, Demitra; res: 360 First Ave., N.Y., N.Y. 10017.

OTCHIS, ETHEL HERBERG, Auth., "At the Top of the Hill" (Youth Educ. Svcs., Inc., '69), "The Boy Who Shook Hands With the President" (Golden Gate Jr. Bks., '64); Tchr., '59–; Intl. Reading Assn.; San Fernando Valley State Col., BA, '59 (cum laude); MA, '69; h. Jack Otchis; res: 4132 Ellenita Ave., Tarzana, Cal. 91356.

OTIS, ELIZABETH RICHARDS, Lit. Agt. and Pres., McIntiosh and Otis, Inc., 18 E. 41st St., N.Y., N.Y. 10017; Vassar Col., '23.

OTIS, MAXINE WATSON, Home Svc. Advisor, Great Falls Gas Co., 725 Central Ave., Great Falls, Mont. 59401, '62-; Home Demonstration Agt., Shasta County (Cal.), '46-'48; Head, Home Econs. Dept., Macalester Col., '44-'45; Home Econs. Tchr., '40-'41; '43-'44, '50-'61; radio cooking prog.; other home econs. progs.; past; Home Econs. orgs., State 4-H Alumni Aw., '68, '69; active in svc. orgs.; Mont. State Univ., BS (Home Econs. Educ.), '40 (Phi Upsilon Omicron Life Mbr.); b. Hobson, Mont., 1917; p. Vernon and Edna Barrick Watson; h. Clayton Otis; c. Jacqueline Elaine Gingery, Larry E., Donald E., Clayton M.; res: 315 20th St., S.W., Great Falls, Mont. 59401.

OTT, BETTY STEINHAUER, Bdcstr., Wms. Dir., WGAR, Hotel Statler Hilton, Euclid Ave., Cleve., Oh. 44101, '60-; Darvis Fashion Sch., Gregory House Adv., WJW, WNOB; ext. work, three counties; ZONTA, Theta Sigma Phi, Gamma Alpha Chi (Nat. Pres.), Wms. Adv. Club (Cleve., Past Pres.), AWRT (Western Reserve Chptr. Past Pres.), Fashion Group, Zeta Tau Alpha (Past Nat. VP); Silver Medal aw., AAF; Cleve. Adv. Wm. of Yr., '65; various other aws.; Miami Univ., BS; Cleve. Marshall (Law.); b. Newport, Ky.; p. Walter V. and Agatha Hagemeyer Steinhauer; h. David Ott; c. SoAnn; res: Box 55, Chime Hill Music St., Novelty, Oh. 44072.

OTT, NANCY GAIL, Eastern Clearance Supvsr., Mutual Broadcasting System, 135 W. 50th St., N.Y., N.Y.; Newswm., AP (Miami, Fla.), '67-'68; Makeup and News Ed., Southern Methodist Univ. nwsp. (Dallas, Tex.), '66-'67; Park Cities Weekly, '67; Theta Sigma Phi, Expt. in Intl. Living (Exchange Student to Ireland, '62); Vogue Prix de Paris, semi-finalist; Bennett Col., AA, '65; Southern Methodist Univ., BA (Jnlsm.), '67; b. N.Y.C., 1945; p. Gilbert and Bettina Ferrel Ott; res: 120 Oxford Blvd., Garden City, N.Y. 11530.

OTTEMILLER, FRANCES TOMPSON, Pres., Treas., The Shoe String Press, Inc., 995 Sherman Ave., Hamden, Conn. 06514, '68-; Partner, '52-'58; Secy.-Treas., '58-'68; Secy.-Treas., Tompson Malone, '68-; Dir. edtl. work on Who's Who in Lib. Svc.; Asst. to Ed., "Index to Plays in Collections"; Printing Industries of Conn., Hamden Hist. Soc.; Pembroke Col., BA (Hist.), '41 (magna cum laude; hons. in hist.; Phi Beta Kappa); h. John H. Ottemiller (dec.).

OTTENBERG, MIRIAM, Reptr., Washington Star, 225 Virginia Ave. S.E., Wash., D.C. 20003, '37-; Reptr., Akron (Oh.) Times-Press, '37; Copywtr., Neisser-Meyeroff (Chgo., Ill.), '35-'36; Auth., "The Federal Investigators" (Prentice-Hall, '62); WNPC (Pres., '64-'65); Pulitzer Prize for local rept., '60; many Wash. Nwsp. Guild aws.; Goucher Col., '31-'33; Univ. of Wis., BA, '35; b. Wash., D.C., 1914; p. Louis and Nettie Podell Ottenberg; res: 2939 Van Ness St. N.W., Wash., D.C. 20008.

OTWAY, RITA, Retired; PR educ. programs for AWNY (Pres., '23), Electrical Wms. Round Table-N.Y. (Pres., '25), Pubcty. Club of N.Y. (Hon. Mbr., '47-'66; Exec. Secy.); theater career in Eng., U.S., incl. D'Oyley Carte (Eng.); Am. Wms. Assn. of N.Y.; Royal Acad. of Music (London; Silver, Bronze Medals); b. London, Eng., 1887 (U.S. Citizen, '41-); Harold and Adelaide Ashton Glover Otway; h. Wilfrid Seagram (dec.); c. Barbara Seagram Vivian; res: 16 Edgewater Dr., Old Greenwich, Conn. 06870.

OUSTECKY, MARIANNE STEWART, Ed., Business Education World, Gregg Div., McGraw-Hill Book Co., 330 W. 42nd St., N.Y., N.Y. 10036, '69-; Ed., Business Teacher, '68-'69; Scientific American, '65-'68; Edtl. Asst., NEA, '64; Mary Washington Col., '60-'62; Oh. State Univ., '62-'63; Univ. of Md., BS (Bus. Adm.); b. Greenville, Miss., 1943; p. Nathaniel and Amelia Silverman Stewart; h. Henry Oustecky.

OVESEY, REGINA HAIMO, Pres., Ovesey and Company Inc., Advertising, 50 E. 58th St., N.Y., N.Y. 10022, '67-; Pres., Regina Ovesey; Crtv. Dir., Sr. VP, Mogul, Williams & Saylor; various orgs., aws.; Stanford Univ., BA (Phi Beta Kappa); p. Samuel Frederick and Rose Haimo; h. Dr. Lionel Ovesey; c. Candace, Michele; res: 935 Park Ave., N.Y., N.Y. 10028.

OWEN, BETTY MEEK, Ed., Teen Age Book Club, Scholastic Magazines, Inc., 50 W. 44th St., N.Y., N.Y. 10036, '61-; Asst. Ed., '58-'60; Asst. Ed., Campus Book Club, '58-'59; Asst. Ed., Science World Book Club, '60-'61; Kappa Beta Pi; Kan. Jr. Col., '30-'32; Kan. City Sch. of Law, LLB (cum laude), '36; b. Kan. City, Kan., 1913; p. James and Mary Dobbins Meek; h. Claude M. Owen, II; c. Rebel, James; res: 362 W. 19th St., N.Y., N.Y. 10011.

OWENS, ANGELA BOYKINS, Reptr.-Newscaster, Metromedia Radio-Philadelphia, WIP, 19th and Walnut Sts., Phila., Pa. 19103, '68-; The Evening and Sunday Bulletin, '67-'68; Nat. Geog. Soc., '66-'67; Sigma Delta Chi Speakers Bur.; Eastern Baptist Col., BA; Columbia Univ. Sch. of Jnlsm. Cert.; b. Wilmington, N.C., 1944; p. Lennon and Daisy Bell Boykins; h. Robert Owens; res: 155 E. Godfrey Ave., #D-104, Phila., Pa. 19120.

OWENS, NORA, VP, Lowe Runkle Advertising Co., 1313 Liberty Bank Building, Okla. City, Okla. 73102, '69-; Copywtr.; Ed., Petroleum Club News; Assoc. Ed., Country Club News; HS Speech Tchr.; radio and TV shows; Central State Col., BA, '53; b. Okla. City, Okla., 1931; p. Ray and Ruth Smith Owens; res: 3000 Hemingford Lane, Okla. City, Okla. 73120.

OWENS, ROCHELLE BASS, Auth., bk. of five plays, "Futz and What Came After" (Random House, '68); three bks. of poetry; translator, critic, wtr., short fiction publ. in numerous anthologies, mags., jnls.; Playright, prod. off-Broadway N.Y.C., Europe and Asia; Lectr., poetry readings, univs. and cols.; grants from Ford Fndn., Rockefeller Fndn., Yale Sch. of Drama;

Obie aw. for "Best Play," '67–'68; New Sch. for Social Rsch.; b. Bklyn., N.Y., 1936; p. Maxwell and Molly Adler Bass; h. George Economou; res: 606 W. 116th St., N.Y., N.Y. 10027.

OWENSBY, MARY POYNOR, County Librn., Harris County, 2502 Crawford, Houston, Tex. 77004, '51–; Librn., '38–'51; Tchr.; Tex. Lib. Assn. (past State Treas.), ALA, BPW (Local Pres., Secy.); Coker Col., '33–'35; Flora MacDonald Col., AB, '37; Univ. of Ala., '38; Univ. of S.C.; b. Columbia, S.C., 1915; p. Wilmer and Mamie Squier Poynor; h. Othell Owensby; res: 4406 Grass Valley Dr., Houston, Tex. 77018.

OWETT, TRUDY HILSENRAD, Fashion Ed., Ladies' Home Journal, 641 Lexington Ave., N.Y., N.Y. 10022, '64–; Prodr., Dir., own fashion articles; Studio Mgr., Mark Shaw, '57–'63; Art Byr., Ruthrauff & Ryan Adv., '53–'57; Free-lance fashion articles, New York mag.; Fashion Group, Coty Aws. Jury; Cooper Un., Art Sch. degree; b. Vienna, Austria; h. Bernard Owett; c. Margot, Adam; res: 323 E. 18th St., N.Y., N.Y. 10003.

OZICK, CYNTHIA, Auth., "Trust" (New Am. Lib., '66; Signet, '69); fiction, poetry, translations, essays, revs. in numerous mags.; contrbr. to five anthologies ('65–'69); Nat. Fndn. on the Arts and the Humanities aw. ('68); N.Y.U., BA (Eng.), '49 (cum laude; Phi Beta Kappa); Oh. State Univ., MA, '50; b. N.Y.C., 1928; p. William and Celia Regelson Ozick; h. Bernard Hallote; c. Rachel Sarah; res: 34 Soundview St., New Rochelle, N.Y. 10805.

P

PACE, CAROLINA JOLLIFF, Tex. Rep., Educational Reading Service, Inc., '67–; Publrs. Trade Rep., Don R. Phillips Co., '65–'67; Prom., Inst. Cnslt., H. Regnery-Reilly & Lee Publ. Co., '62–'65; Exec. Secy., Dallas Book and Auth. Luncheon, '59–'63; WNBA; Who's Who of Am. Wm.; Southern Methodist Univ., '60; b. Dallas, Tex.; p. Lindsay and Carolina Juden Jolliff; h. John M. Pace; res: 4524 Lorraine Ave., Dallas, Tex. 75205.

PACIGA, ALICE WOODS, Adv. Mgr., The Willett Company, 700 S. Desplaines St., Chgo., Ill. 60607, '64–; Secy., Howard Willett Charitable Fndn., '64–; Secy., Solar Liquid Heating Co., '65–; Secy., Mayor Richard J. Daley's Venetian Night Yachting Festival in Chgo., '59–'65; Jr. Wms. Adv. Club of Chgo. (former VP), Wms. Adv. Club of Chgo., IEA of Chgo., ICIE; Am. Trucking Assn. of Am. Best Internal Pubn. aw., '65; Chgo. Col. of Commerce, '52–'54; b. Chgo., Ill., 1935; p. Paul and Irene Lisowski Wodarczyk; h. Peter Paciga; res: 9154 W. 89th St., Hickory Hills, Ill. 60457.

PAGAN, RUBELINA (Ruby), Bdcst. Media Supvsr.,

N.W. Ayer-Jorgensen-Macdonald, Inc., 3540 Wilshire Blvd., L.A., Cal. 90005, '68–; Radio-TV Time Byr., '63–'68; from Secy. to Radio-TV Time Byr., Young and Rubicam (N.Y.C. and L.A.), '58–'63; b. N.Y.C., 1941; p. Paul and Monseratte De Clet Rosado Pagan; res: 9913 E. Lampson St., Whittier, Cal. 90601.

PAGANO, ELLEN BLAKELY, News Ed., Graphic Arts Technical Foundation, Inc., 4615 Forbes Ave., Pitt., Pa. 15213, '67–; Polit. Reptr., New Castle (Pa.) News, '66–'67; Theta Sigma Phi; Pa. State Univ., BA, (Jnlsm.), '66; b. Dedham, Mass., 1944; p. Thomas Hugh and Mary Ann Quinn Blakely; h. Louis Andrew Pagano; res: 141 N. Dithridge, Pitt., Pa. 15213.

PAGE, BEVERLY ANDERSEN, Prom., Pubcty. Dir., WLW, Avco Broadcasting, 140 W. Ninth St., Cinn., Oh. 45202, '67–; PR Dir., Fashion Fair, '65–'67; Adv. Coordr., Polk Bros. (Chgo., Ill.), '64–'67; Discount Adv. Mgr., Gurnee (Waukegan), '59–'62; Prom. Dir., Goldblatt Bros., '57–'59; Owner, Mayfair Agcy., '52–'57; PRSA; Cinn. Enquirer Wm. of the Yr., '68; Waukegan Sun Best Ad of the Yr. aw., '60; N. Pk. Col., AA, '46; Univ. of Ill., BS, '48; b. Chgo., Ill., 1926; p. Edward and Margaret Rankin Andersen; h. Clarence Page (dec.); c. Carol Lynn, Edward; res: 3153 Portsmouth Ave., Cinn., Oh. 45208.

PAGE, FRANCES ELEANOR, Music Supvsr., Communication Center, University of Texas, P.O. Box 7158, Austin, Tex. 78712, '49–; Asst. Music Supvsr., '47–'49; Copyist, Asst. Orchestra and Chorus Dir., '45–'47; Accompanist and Orchestra Pianist, '43–'45; Asst. Prof., Univ. of Tex., '66–; Lectr., '54–'66; Composer, Conductor, musical scores for radio series: "Poet's Playhouse," "The Child Beyond," many others (all 1st aws. from Oh. State Inst. for Educ. Radio and TV); Prodr., instructional TV, "Intermediate Music" 1st aw., Oh. State Inst.), "A Song Unfurled" (Freedoms Fndn. Aw.); Austin Outstanding Svc. aw., '61; Univ. of Tex., Austin, BA, '42 (Phi Beta Kappa); B Music, '43; M Music, '51; Un. Theological Seminary, '52; b. Austin, Tex., 1921; p. Sam and Nina Jennings Page; res: 601 W. 12th, Austin, Tex. 78701.

PAGE, HENRIETTA MARIA, Librn.-Cnslt., Roger Williams College (Providence, R.I.), '68–'69; Auth: "The Fertile Crescent," "The Moslem World," others; Librn.-Cnslt., Foxboro Co., '68–'69; Head of Lib. Div., U.S. Naval Underwater Weapons Rsch. and Engineering Station (Newport, R.I.); active in lib., rsch. fields since '27; Special Libs. Assn.; Queens Col.; Columbia Univ.; Am. Inst. of Banking; b. Queens County, L.I., N.Y., 1900; p. William and Maria Weinig Wutz; h. Henry N. Page (dec.); c. Lois Ann (Mrs. Wendell E. Bennett), Natalie (Mrs. John F. Krause); res: P.O. Box 323, Foxboro, Mass. 02035.

PAGE, RUTH WOLF, Ed., Essex Publishing Co., 44 Park St., Essex Junction, Vt. 05452, '58–; Asst. to Exec. Offcr., Bk. Publrs. Bur. (N.Y.C.), '43–'45; articles in Vermont Life; bk. revs. in nat., local pubns.; Vt. State

Col. System (Trustee; Secy. of Bd.); New Eng. Nwsp. aws., '68; '66; '62; Swarthmore Col., '42 (summa cum laude; Phi Beta Kappa); b. Phila., Pa., '21; h. Proctor H. Page Jr.; c. Candace (Mrs. Ronald Herring), Patti, Robert; res: Appletree Point, Burlington, Vt. 05401.

PAGE, TONY, Ed.-Publr., Cross Country News, Meacham Field, Fort Worth, Tex. 76106, '52–; Auth., "Personal, Please" ('57); Feature Wtr. for various wms. mags.; Colmst., Aviation News Beacon, '45–'47; Aviation Ed., The Valley Times, '45–'47; Flight Magazine, '40–'45; Theta Sigma Phi, Fort Worth Press Club, Aviation/Space Wtrs. Assn., many other aviation assns.; James J. Strebig Memorial Aw. for outstanding aviation rept., '62; Wms. Nat. Aeronautical Assn. Wm. of the Yr. in Aviation, '60; numerous other aviation aws.; b. Moscow, Idaho, '10; p. C. M. and Ruby Slee Edgett; h. (div.); res: Box 9661, Ft. Worth, Tex. 76107.

PAIGE, DOTTIE, Corp. Secy.-Treas., Patterson Advertising Agency, Inc., 2900 Plass Ct., Topeka, Kan. 66604, '61–; Copy, Media Dir., '61–'69; Copywtr., '59–'61; Prom. Dir., WIBW Radio-TV, '57–'59; Wms. Dir., '55–'59; Wms. Dir., WREN Radio, '51–'54; Guest Lectr., Copywriting, Media Buying, Washburn Univ., '63; Prom. Comm., Un. Fund; Pfsnl. Adv. Cl. of Topeka (Silver Medal Aw., '68; Adv. Wm. of the Yr., '64; Secy., '61–'62), AWRT (Heart of Am. Chptr. VP, '59), Topeka Press Wm. (Pres., '64), Topeka C. of C., Theta Sigma Phi (VP, '67); Kan. State Univ., BS, '51; b. Topeka, Kan.; p. Warren and Vivian Neiswender Paramore; res: 1731 Randolph, Topeka, Kan. 66604.

PALADINO, JEANNETTE E., PR Dir., Warwick & Legler, Inc., 375 Park Ave., N.Y., N.Y. 10022, '68–; PR Acct. Supvsr., BBDO, '63–'68; Staff Wtr., L.I. Comml. Rev., '61–'63; PRSA, AWRT; Hofstra Univ., BA (Eng.), '62 (Ed., Evening Forum; Pi Delta Epsilon; Eng. Hon. Soc.).

PALAIA, CAROL THORESON, Food and Trade Pubcty., General Mills, Inc., 9200 Wayzata Blvd., Mpls., Minn. 55440, '65–; Intl. Milling, '64–'65; Prudential Ins. Co. of Am., '63–'64; Am. Home Econs. Assn., Minn. Home Econs. Assn., Twin Cities Home Econsts. in Bus.; Univ. of Minn., BS (Food and Jnlsm.), '63; h. Nicholas A. Palaia; res: 849 24th Ave. S.E., Mpls., Minn. 55414.

PALCIC, JUDITH ANN, Ed., Spotlight, Group Hospitalization, Inc., 550 12th St., S.W., Wash., D.C., '68–; Edtl. Cnslt., Branislav Maksomovich; Auth., "Justice in Violation" and several children's stories; Staff Assoc., PR Dept., Un. Fund of Allegheny County (Pitt., Pa.), '67–'68; Theta Sigma Phi (Secy., '67), Chi Omega; Pa. State Univ., BA (Jnlsm.), '67; b. Greensburg, Pa., 1945; p. Gilbert and Ann Lucas Palcic; res: 3601 S. Fifth St., Arlington, Va. 22201.

PALEN, JENNIE MAY, Auth: "Report Writing for Accountants" (Prentice-Hall, '55), "Moon Over Manhattan" (Wings Press, '49), "Good Morning,

Sweet Prince" (Am. Weave, '57), "Stranger, Let Me Speak" (Golden Quill Press, '64); Ed., Compiler, Contrbr., Ency. of Auditing Techniques ('66); Contrbr., numerous other bks.; CPA (N.Y. State); Rsch. projects in accountancy; ghost wtr.; speaker; Sr. Ed., Prentice-Hall, '63–'66; Accountant, Ed., Rschr., Instr. in accountancy, Baruch Sch. of Bus. and Civic Adm., '57–'62; Rept. Reviewer, prin., Haskins and Sells, '18–'49; Pen and Brush Club (VP, '66–), Query Club, Am. Inst. of CPAs, N.Y. State Soc. of CPAs, PSA (Poetry Prizes), Am. Wms. Soc. of CPAs (Hon. Mbr., '56; Pres., '46–'47), NLAPW (Nat. Advisory Bd., '56–'58; Bklyn. Poetry Circle (Pres., '60–'66), Wms. Press Club of N.Y.C. (Dir., '65–'67), Phi Chi Theta (Hon. Mbr.), Poetry Soc. (London) Greenwood Prize, numerous state and poetry soc. prizes; N.Y.U., BCS (summa cum laude); p. Frank and Mary Every Palen; res: 26 E. 10th St., N.Y., N.Y. 10003.

PALMER, PAIGE (Paige Rohrer Freeman), Dir. of Wms. Activities; Hostess, "Paige Palmer Show," WEWS-TV, 3001 Euclid Ave., Cleve., Oh. 44115, '48–; W. Coast Fgn. Fashions Ed., The Californians, '46; Dir. Retail Prom., Colin-Hall-Marx fabric house, '44; Dir., one cosmetic line, Madam Helena Rubinstein, '43; Asst. Dir., Richard Hudnut Success Sch., '42; Auth., three bks. on health; AWRT (Western Reserve Chptr. Pres.), NATAS, Fashion Group; numerous aws., incl. AFTRA Best Wms. TV program, FRANY, various others; Univ. of Akron Phys. Educ. degree; b. Akron, Oh.; p. Paul and Katharine Grisbraun Rohrer; h. Arthur Freeman; c. Richard Roush, Paul Roush, Perry Brown; res: 2750 N. Revere Rd., Akron, Oh. 44313.

PALMOUR, CLAIRE TORRIBLE, Special Asst. to Dir. of Recruitment, VISTA, 1111 18th St. N.W., Wash., D.C. 20506, '69–; Recruitment Br. Chief, S.E. Reg., (Atlanta, Ga.), '67–'69; Comml. Mgr., WDUN Radio, (Gainesville), 13 yrs.; AWRT (Atlanta Chptr. Pres.); b. Green Cove Springs, Fla., 1922; p. William and Margaret Conway Torrible; h. Evans Palmour; c. Evans, Jr., Jody; res: 2510 Virginia Ave. N.W., Apt. 907N, Wash., D.C. 20037.

PANITZA, YVONNE FOURCADE, Assoc. Ed., The Reader's Digest Inc. (Pleasantville, N.Y.), The Reader's Digest European Editorial Office, 216 Boulevard Saint Germain, Paris 7eme, 75 France, '66–; Head of Rsch. Dept., in charge of rsch. on continent, '65; Rschr., Gen. Reptr., '53; UN Info. Offcr. (Paris and N.Y.); Rsch., Reader's Digest articles, bk. projects incl. "The Longest Day," "Great Wits and Grand Horizontals," "Madam Sarah," "Or I'll Dress You in Mourning," "Twelve Cities"; Univ. of Paris, Baccalaureate; Inst. of Polit. Sci., BA; Cambridge Univ., Proficiency Cert.; b. Paris, France, 1929; p. Jean Fourcade and Christiane Mainfroy; h. John D. Panitza; res: 16 rue de Chazelles, Paris, 17eme, France, 75.

PAOLUCCI, BRIDGET RIZZO, Free-lance Network Corr., Canadian Broadcasting Corp., 245 Park Ave., N.Y., N.Y., '62–; Prod., WNDT, '61–'62; Wtr., Bdcstr., on Fulbright Grant, Radio Italia (Rome, Italy), '60–'61; Wtr., Dir., TFI Prods. (N.Y.C.) '59–'60; Prod., Dir., WTVS (Detroit, Mich.), '55–'59; AWRT (Detroit Chptr. Treas., '57–'58); NAEB Scholarship ('55); Manhattanville Col., BA, '53 (Bd. of Dirs., Alumnae Assn.; Pubns. Chmn.); Univ. of Mich., MA, '58 (Speech Fellowship, '56); b. Detroit, Mich., 1932; p. Frank and Dora Lenzini Rizzo; h. Umberto Paolucci; c. Anne Marie, John Christopher; res: 22 Euclid Ave., Mt. Vernon, N.Y. 10552.

PAPANGELIS, PATRICIA CUTHBERTSON (Pat Pappas), Adm. Asst., HMH Publishing Co., Inc. (Playboy), 919 N. Michigan Ave., Chgo., Ill. 60611, '65–; Rights and Permissions, '63–; Asst. Mng. Ed., VIP Magazine, '63–'65; Asst. Mng. Ed., Playboy Press, '62–'63; Edtl. Asst. to Ed., Publr. Hugh M. Hefner, Playboy, '54–'59; volunteer work for Hull House Assn., Jane Addams Ctr.; Am. Inst. of Banking, '51–'52; Art Inst. of Chgo., '54–'55; b. Gibson County, Tenn., 1932; p. Henry and Mollie Clayton Cuthbertson; h. Charles Papangelis; c. Dena, Stacy; res: 551 Roscoe, Chgo., Ill. 60657.

PAPE, GERTRUDE HASDORFF, Co-publr., The Burleson County Citizen, Corner Buck and Main Sts., Caldwell, Tex. 77836, '55–; Asst. Ed., beginning '52; Elementary Sch. Tchr., '35–'37; Tex. Lutheran Col. (Seguin, Tex.); b. Nixon, Tex., 1915; p. August and Frieda Hausmann Hasdorff; h. A. C. Pape; c. Allan Craig, James Mark, Carol Anne Pape Duncan; res: 301 W. Stone, Caldwell, Tex. 77836.

PAPPAS, GWENDOLYN BENNETT, Auth., five bks.; VP, PR Dir., Super Chef Manufacturing Co., Hodges St., Houston, Tex.; Portrait Artist; Past Poet Laureate of Tex. (elected by Tex. Congress, '63), aws. from city of Houston: Ten Outstanding Wm., Homemaker of Yr., Mother of Yr., all '61; b. Birmingham, Ala., 1919; p. Brooke and Lily Mildred Sparks Bennett; h. Phillip Miller Pappas; c. Even B., Phillip, Jr., Sewell B., Christopher C., Gwendolyn, Jr., Regina F.; res: 2318 Bluebonnet Blvd., Houston, Tex. 77025.

PAPPAS, IRENE, PR Dir., Lutheran Hospital Society of Southern California, 1414 S. Hope St., L.A., Cal. 90015, '61–; PR Dir., Edward J. McElroy Adv., '59–'61; News Dir., City of Hope Med. Ctr., '57–'59; Free-lance Pubcty., '52–'59; Am. Soc. for Hosp. PR Dirs., L.A. Adv. Wm. (Lulu Aw.), '60), Hosp. Cncl. of Southern Cal. (PR Sec. Secy., '64), Gtr. L.A. Press Club, L.A. C. of C.; Mont. State Univ., BA, '41 (cum laude; Sigma Delta Chi Scholarship Key; Alpha Lambda Delta Nat. Scholarship Aw.); b. Butte, Mont., 1919; p. Peter and Maria Drakaki Pappas; res: 2620 Ivan Hill Terrace, L.A., Cal. 90039.

PAQUETTE, LUCILLE LEEMEZA, Songwtr., Entertainer, Singer; appearances: Royal Box (N.Y.C.), Merv Griffin Show; Eden Roc (Miami, Fla.), Caesar's Palace (Las Vegas, Nev.), Johnny Carson, Joey Bishop, Steve Allen, Pat Boone Shows, Century Plaza Hotel (L.A.,

Cal.), Eammon Andrews TV Show (London), two TV Specials, others; AGVA, AFTRA; Best New Female Vocalist Aw., '68; b. N.Y.C., 1943; p. Mel and Florence Grosso Paquette; c. Mark, Mike, Mitchell, Matthew, Monti; res: 6316 N. Mockingbird Lane, Paradise Valley, Ariz. 85253.

PARCHE, M. CONSTANCE, Librn., Carborundum Co., R & D, P.O. Box 337, Niagara Falls, N.Y. 14302, '44–; Chemist, '38–'44; European Tour Conductor, '33–'38; Actuaries Dept., Mutual Life Ins. Co. of N.Y., '30–'32; Wtr., tech. articles in bks., pfsnl. jnls.; Am. Chemical Soc. (Western N.Y. Sec. Secy., '64–'66), Special Libs. Assn. (Western Chptr. Pres., '58–'59); active, local orgs.; Bryn Mawr Col., AB (Chem.), '30; Univ. of Berlin, '34; Univ. of Buffalo; b. Niagara Falls, N.Y., 1907; p. Edwin and Sarah Rombough Cole; h. William Henry Wilder Parche; res: P.O. Box 275, Niagara Falls, N.Y. 14302.

PARDIECK, ELIZABETH LEWIS, Wms. Page Ed., Burbank Daily Review, 220 E. Orange Grove, Burbank, Cal. 91503, '59–; Reptr., '59; Cal. Nwsp. Publrs. Assn. Merit Aw., '64, '66; L.A. Valley Col., AA, '59; San Fernando Valley State Col., Sr., part-time student; b. Lorna Linda, Cal. 1938; p. J. William and Jean Satterlee Lewis; h. John Richard Pardieck; c. Diana Marie; res: 10357 Leolang Ave., Sunland, Cal. 91040.

PARHAM, MARJORIE BROWER, Publr., Cincinnati Herald, Porter Publishing Co., Inc., 863 Lincoln Ave., Cinn., Oh. 45206, '63–; Publrs. Conf. aw., '68; Iota Phi Lambda aw., '70; Univ. of Cinn., Wilberforce Univ.; b. Batavia, Oh., 1918; p. James and Estella Harvey Brower; h. Hartwell Parham; c. William M. Spillers, Jr.; res: 4503 Sunnyslope Terr., Cinn., Oh. 45229.

PARIS, M. JEANNE, Dir. of Home Econs., Swift & Company, 1919 Swift Dr., Oak Brook, Ill. 60525, '57–; Asst. Dir., '55–'57; Dir. of Home Econs., The Kroger Co., '48–'55; Asst. Prof. of Home Mgt., W. Va. Univ.; HS Home Econs. Tchr. (Rugby, N.D.), '40–'41; Auth., "Your Future as a Home Economist" (Richards Rosen Press, '64); Co-auth., "The Young Woman in Business" (Ia. State Univ. Press), '60); Altrusa Intl., Altrusa Club of Chgo. (Pres., '64–'66), Am. Home Econs. Assn., Home Econs. in Bus. Sec. (Nat. Chmn., '60), active artist; N.D. State Univ., BS, '40 (Alumni Achiev. aw., '64); Univ. of Neb., MA, '45; b. Bismarck, N.D., 1918; p. Frank and Elida Couch Paris; res: 1255 N. Sandburg Terr., Chgo., Ill. 60610.

PARISE, FLORENCE M., Adm. Asst. to Exec. VP and Gen. Mgr., KCET, 1313 N. Vine St., L.A., Cal. 90028, '64–; Mktng. Rsch. Asst., Doyle-Dane-Bernbach Adv., '62–'64; Rschr., Program Dept., CBS-TV, '57–'62; Dir. of Mdsng., WFIL (Phila.), '55–'57; Bus. Affairs, CBS-TV (N.Y.C.), '53–'55; Cont., Music, Prod., Dir., WAER Syracuse Univ., '51–'53; AWRT (L.A. Chptr. Rec. Secy., '67–'68), NATAS, Alpha Epsilon Rho, Theta Beta Phi; Syracuse Univ., BA (Philosophy and Bdcst.), '53 (magna cum laude; Phi Beta Kappa); b. Bklyn., N.Y.;

p. Joseph Thomas and Eugenia Gallo Parise; res: 6782 Milner Rd., L.A., Cal. 90028.

PARISH, BERTIE GAMMELL, Ed. and Publr., The Clayton Record, 109 E. College Ave., Clayton, Ala. 36016, '60–; Tchr., '37–'39; Ch. organist and Choir Dir., '39–; Ala. Press Presidential Cit., '67; Ala. Col., BM, '36; b. Dothan, Ala., 1915; p. William and Peanie Ennis Gammell; h. Thomas William Parish; c. Dr. Thomas W., Jr., Joseph E., Rebecca S.; res: 227 Eufuala Ave., Clayton, Ala. 36016.

PARISH, PEGGY, Auth., 17 children's bks., incl: "Costumes to Make," "Play Ball Amelia Bedelia," "Snapping Turtle's All Wrong Day" ('70), others, '61–'69; several educ. articles; Tchr., part-time, crtv. dancing, '48–'52; Tchr., '48–'67; Auths. Guild; Univ. of S.C., '44–'48; Peabody Col., grad. work, '50; b. Manning, S.C., 1927; p. Herman and Cecil Rogers Parish; res: 160 E. 88th St., N.Y., N.Y. 10028.

PARK, N. LEE BAUMAN, Adv. Dir., Peck & Peck, 521 Fifth Ave., N.Y., N.Y. 10017, '70–; Copy Chief, Lane Bryant, '67–'70; free-lance wtr: TV commls., print adv., TV and show fashion commentary, mag. article; Wtr., Prodr., Talent, KSL-TV (Salt Lake City, Ut.), Wtr., Talent, WBNS-TV (Columbus, Oh.); Kent State Univ., BA (magna cum laude); b. Granville, Ph.; p. Lester and Viola Weekly Bauman; h. Hugh Winston Park (div.); c. Vanessa K.; res: 305 W. 86th St., N.Y., N.Y. 10024.

PARKER, ANN ELIZABETH, Ed., "The Little Trib," Chicago Tribune, 435 N. Michigan Ave., Chgo., Ill. 60611, '55–; Free-lance Photogr., '53; Ed., Inland Steel, '54; Ed., Blue Cross Commn., '50; Photog. Tchr., '67–'69; published non-fiction and photos. in Chgo. Tribune Magazine, '67; Chgo. Press Club, Chgo. Cncl. on Fgn. Rels., IEA of Chgo., ICIE, best feature story for indsl. ed. for Chgo. Crusade for Mercy, '59, '61; Chgo. Jr. Achiev., '59, '60; Pembroke Col., Brown Univ., BA (Eng., Am. Lit.), '49; b. Chgo., Ill., 1927; p. Woodruff and Ruth Ballantine Parker; res: 527 W. Aldrine Ave., Chgo., Ill. 60657.

PARKER, BERTHA MORRIS, Auth. (Houghton-Mifflin, Harper Row, and Golden Press), non-fiction bks., brochures, monographs, incl. "The Golden Treasury of Natural History" ('52; revsd., '68), Golden Bk. Ency. Vol. 1–16 ('59; revsd., '69), 85 brochures in Harper Row Basic Sci. Educ. Series; Translations of various bks. into more than 30 langs.; Rsch. Assoc., Field Museum of Natural Hist., '55–; Tchr. of Sci., Univ. Lab. Schs., Univ. of Chgo., '16–'55; Nat. Assn. for Rsch. in Sci. Teaching (Assoc. Ed., Sci. Educ., '38–'45; Sigma Delta Epsilon, various others; Oberlin Col., '08–'09; Columbia Univ., '09; Univ. of Chgo., SB, '14 (Phi Beta Kappa); SM, '23; b. Rochester, Ill., 1890; p. Homer D. and Margaret Lawrence Parker; res: 1700 E. 56th St., Chgo., Ill. 60637.

PARKER, CHARLOTTE TEMPLE, Auth: "An ABC for

Mothers" (Simon & Schuster), "How to Amuse and Outwit Important People under Ten" (Grosset & Dunlap; serialized in S. African Press, '68); Free-lance Wtr., Publicist; Reprtr., Feature Wtr., local nwsps. and nat. Chronicle of the Horse, '66–; Founded Greenwich Hosp. Aux. Nwsltr., "Volunteer Life," '60; Synd. Colm., "Tips to Mothers," N.Y. Herald Tribune and Publr. Nwsp. Synd., '52–'63; Owner, pubcty., adv. agcy., 444 Madison Ave. (N.Y.C.), '46–'50; Copy Chief and Bdcstr., WHCU (Ithaca), '43–'44; PR Dept., N.W. Ayer & Son (N.Y.C.), '40–'42, '44–'46; Staff Wtr. for WCBS Commentator, '38–'40; Mt. Holyoke Col., AB, '35; h. Robert Karl Heimann; c. Mark, Karla; res: Gilliam Lane, Riverside, Conn. 06878.

PARKER, EDNA JEAN, Sun. Wms. Sec. Ed., Akron Beacon Jnl., 144 E. Exchange St., Akron, Oh. 44309, '61–; Free-lance, under name Stori-Art; former Pan Am. Stewardess and purser; Tchr., HS Jnlsm., Speech, Eng.; NFPW (Oh. Press Wm. Pres., '68–'70), Oh. Nwsp. Wms. Assn. (Exec. Bd.); Home Fashions League, Nat. Soc. of Interior Designers (Press), Theta Sigma Phi, more than 25 writing aws. past six yrs.; Delta Zeta, Un. Fndn. Wm. of Summit County (Charter Mbr.), OES; Oh. State Univ., BA (jnlsm.), '52–'55 (Alumni Club); Univ. of the Ams. (Mexico City), '54; Univ. of Akron, BA (Educ.), '61; b. Akron, Oh., 1935; p. Murray S. Parker; res: 74 Maplewood Ave., Akron, Oh. 44313.

PARKER, ESTHER HANLON, Public Info. Asst., University of Cincinnati, Cinn., Oh. 45221, '61–; Ed., GE Aircraft Nuclear Propulsion Dept. News, weekly nwsp., GE (Evendale), '57–'61; Commtns. Specialist, '56–'57; Ed., "And-30," pubn. of Cinn. Eds. Assn. '59–'60; Nat. Assn. of Sci. Wtrs., Theta Sigma Phi, AAAS, Oh. Conf. of IEA; Carling 1st aw. for best edtl. '60; Wheaton Col., Norton, Mass., AB, '29 (PR Dir., '29–'30); b. Hudson, Mass., 1907; p. Joseph and Gertrude Alcorn Hanlon; h. Henry M. Parker; c. Ruth V., Mrs. Harold F. Bartz; res: 895 Greenville Ave., Cinn., Oh. 45246.

PARKER, ETHEL MAX, Cnslt., Public Info., American Red Cross, Southwestern Wis. Territory, Dane County Chptr., 1202 Ann St., Box 603, Madison, Wis. 53701, '66–; Public Info. Dir., Dane Chptr., Am. Red Cross, '52–'66; Educ., Adult and Secondary Public Schs. (Sheboygan, Wis.), '36–'49; Cont. Dir., WHBL-Radio, '38–'39; Feature Wtr., Theater Ed., Reprtr., Capital Times (Madison), '26–'33; Theta Sigma Phi (Madison Chptr. Pres., '61–'63; Wtrs. Cup, '61), Wis. Mental Health Assn. (Chmn., Public Policy Comm.), Madison Press Club (Treas., '58–'59; Pubn. Ed., '67–'68), Pi Lambda Theta; Sigma Delta Chi Scholarship Key, '28; Red Cross Feature Story aw., '59, '60, '61; Univ. of Wis., BA (Jnlsm.), '28; MA (Eng. Educ.), '51; b. Sheboygan, Wis.; p. Mayer and Jennie Zion Max; h. Cedric M. Parker; res: Box 320, Waubesa Beach Rd., Madison, Wis. 53711.

PARKER, FAYE MITCHELL, Interviewer, WQED (TV), Fifth Ave., Pitt., Pa. 15213, '50–; Prodr., Dir., Pitt.

Children's Theatre, '50–; Wms. Dir., KDKA-TV, '50–'55; KDKA, '39–'52; Auth., "Adventure in the Arts"; numerous articles in wms. mags.; Children's Theatre Conf., Theatre Assn. of Pa., Pitt. Cncl. for the Arts, Platform Assn.; Dorothy Clifford Aw. for outstanding contrbr. to educ. theatre; Rockford Col.; c. James Allan Youngling, George Mitchell Youngling, Molly Jo Youngling.

PARKER, JEAN BARGOS, Dept. Head, Edtl. Promo., Special Projects, Time Inc., Rockefeller Center, N.Y., N.Y. 10020, '49–; Asst. Dept. Head, '42–'49; Rsch. Cnslt., Volunteer Blood Bank, Am. Red Cross; Smith Col., BA, '40; Rutgers Univ.; b. Cranford, N.J., 1920; p. Juan and Beatrice Sherman Bargos; h. Richard Parker (dec.); c. Mathew, Christopher; res: 20 Norman Pl., Cranford, N.J. 07016.

PARKER, JEWEL GRAY, Librn., The Hutchison School for Girls, 1740 Ridgeway Rd., Memphis, Tenn. 38117, '68–'69; Sch. Librn., '59–'68, '46–'58; Ref. Librn., Southwestern Col., '58–'59; Tchr., Lausanne Sch. for Girls, '41–'46; ALA, Southeastern Lib. Assn., Tenn. Lib. Assn., AAUW, Beta Phi Mu; Who's Who of Am. Wm.; Dic. of Intl. Biog.; Who's Who in Lib. Svc.; Two Thousand Wm. of Achiev.; Miss. Southern Univ., '22–'23; Memphis State Univ., BS, '33; George Peabody Col., BS (Lib. Sci.), '50; MA (Lib. Sci.), '55; b. Counce, Tenn., 1902; p. Joseph and Linna Jones Gray; h. Jesse L. Parker; c. Joan Louise (Mrs. William P. Sutherland); res: 1185 Marcia Rd., Memphis, Tenn. 38117.

PARKER, LORE LIONEL, VP, Copy Supvsr., Doyle Dane Bernbach Inc., 20 W. 43rd St., N.Y., N.Y. 10036, '67–; Copy Supvsr., '64–; Copywtr., '59–'64, '52–'56; Copywtr., Dowd, Redfield & Johnstone, '58–'59; Copywtr., Robert Orr, '56–'58; Copy Club; Intl. Film and TV Festival of N.Y. Gold Aw., '68; Cannes Film Festival Special Cert., '67; Am. TV Commls. Festival, '67; Hollywood Radio and TV Soc. Intl. Bdcst. Aw., '67; Art Dirs. Club of N.Y. Cert. of Merit, '66, '67; Gold Medal, '66.

PARKER, MARY JANE, Free-lance Wtr., 140 E. Broad St., Fairburn, Ga. 30213, Mary Jane Parker & Assocs. (N.Y.C., Atlanta, Ga.); Radio and TV Dir., Burke Dowling Adams Division B.B.D. & O.; Ed. of trade mags. (Chgo., Ill.; N.Y.C.); Asst. State Sch. Supvsr., Ga. State Dept. of Educ.; Poet; AWRT (Atlanta Chptr. past Pres.; Charter Mbr.), Fashion Group (Atlanta Chptr. past Pres.; Charter Mbr.), Fashion Group (Atlanta Chptr. past Secy.); Who's Who of Am. Wm., '68–'69; Ga. Col. at Milledgeville, AB; Columbia Univ., Teachers Col., MA; b. Fairburn, Ga.; p. James and Mary Wilson Parker; h. Pierce Wilson Seal (dec.); c. Robert Parker Seal, Mrs. Allen Wooddall; res: 140 E. Broad St., Fairburn, Ga. 30213.

PARKER, MARY LEWIS GRAY, Head Librn., State University of New York, Agricultural and Technical College, Canton, N.Y. 13617, '49–; Tchr., Madrid Central Sch., '48–'49; ALA, Special Libs. Assn., N.

County Ref. and Rsch. Resources Cncl. (Trustee, '66; Pres., '67–'68; Secy., '68), N.Y. Lib. Assn. (Col. and Univ. Lib. Sec. VP, Pres.-elect, '68–'69), Delta Kappa Gamma, Pi Beta Phi, Canton Town Repl. Comm. (Secy.); St. Lawrence Univ., BS, '35; MEduc., '48; Syracuse Univ., MS (Lib. Sci.), '55; b. Canton, N.Y., 1913; p. Charles and Margaret Chapman Lewis; c. Charles Lewis Gray, Margaret Adelaid (Mrs. John F. Caneen); res: 18 Pine St., Canton, N.Y. 13617.

PARKER, PATRICIA KOOB, Adv. and Prom. Mgr., Holden-Day, Inc., 500 Sansome St., S.F., Cal. 94111, '68–; Dir., Adv. and Prom., Scott, Foresman and Co., Col. Div., '65–'68; Dir., Adv. and Prom., Macmillan Co., '62–'64; Adv. Copy Dir. and Ed., Wiley Bulletin, John Wiley and Sons, Inc., '56–'62; Cnslt., Scott, Foresman, '68–'69; Mail Adv. Club of Chgo.; Univ. of Mont., Missoula BA, (Drama), '54; b. Humboldt, Ia., 1933; p. Donald and Eva Parsons Koob; h. Thomas E. Parker; res: 29 Lupine Ave., S.F., Cal. 94118.

PARKER, VIRGINIA, Health Scis. Librn., Queen's University, Old Arts Building, Kingston, Ontario, Can., '67–; Librn., Tex. Med. Ctr. Lib. (Houston), '57–'67; Assoc. Librn., Univ. of Tex. Med. Br. (Galveston), '56–'57; Librn., Am. Cancer Soc. (N.O., La.), '46–'49; Cataloger, Detroit News, '43–'46; Librn. Asst., Wayne Univ. Col. of Med., '42–'43; articles on med. hist.; MLA, various others; Newcomb Col. of Tulane Univ., BA, '37 (Phi Beta Kappa); La. State Univ., BS (Lib. Sci.), '42 (Phi Kappa Phi; Beta Phi Mu); b. Brookhaven, Miss., 1916; p. Elmer Clifford and Amelia Sebastian Parker; res: 237 Bath Rd., Kingston, Ontario, Can.

PARKER, VIRGINIA SALUS, Sls., WIPC, Mountain Lake Rd., Lake Wales, Fla., '68–; Sls. Mgr., Sls., Copy Wtr., WJCM Radio (Sebring), '67–'68; Adv. Mgr., Avon Park Sun, '65–'67; Wtr., Palm Beach Post Times, '64–'65; Lighting Cnslt., Verd-A-Ray Corp. (Miami), '60–'63; Free-lance, '59–'60; Mdsng. Coordr., WGBS Radio, '57–'59; Sls., Ralph B. Rose Poster Printing, Park East Pubn., Vita Vision; Pubcty., Elizabeth Arden, and Special Proms., Schiaparelli cosmetics, '46–'47; Sls. and Supvsr., Reuben H. Donnelley; Bryant and Stratton Col.; courses at Columbia Univ., Elizabeth Arden Salon and Madam Tovar; b. Brockton, Mass., 1918; p. John and Jennie Krusas Salus; h. (div.); c. Deborah Anne Parker; res: 412 Persimmon St., Sebring, Fla. 33870.

PARKS, ALTA, Asst. Dir., Gary Public Library, 220 W. Fifth Ave., Gary, Ind. 46402, '55–; Head of Ext., '51–'55; Head Librn., Ingham County Lib. (Mason, Mich.), '43–'51; Sch. Librn., Tchr., '34–'43; ALA (Cncl., '61–'66), Public Lib. Assn. (Pres., '65–'66), Lib. Adm., Lib. Org. and Mgt. Sec. (Secy., '58–'60), Mich. Lib. Assn. (Pres., '49–'50; County Librns. Sec. Pres., '44–'45), Ind. Lib. Assn. (Pres., '56–'57), Altrusa (Gary Chptr. Pres., '60–'62), Gary Neighborhood House Bd. ('61–'64); b. Southfield, Mich., 1910; p. Charles and Emma Brooks Parks; res: 3654 Polk St., Gary, Ind. 46408.

PARKS, JANITH FINLEY, Radio-TV Dir., Gulf State Advertising Agency, 2714 Southwest Freeway, Houston, Tex. 77005, '68–; Radio Anncr., WENZ (Richmond, Va.), '65–; Instr. of Psych., Va. Union Univ.; Elementary Sch. Tchr.; Nwsp. Ad Model; Radio Ad Voice; AWRT, Alpha Kappa Alpha; Who's Who Among Am. Cols. and Univs. ('61); Va. Union Univ., BA, '61; Wayne State Univ., MA, '65; b. Detroit, Mich., 1941; p. Benjamin Harrison and Yvonne Allen Lucas Parks.

PARKS, MARTHA SMITH, Pubns. Coordr., Autonetics Division, North American Rockwell Corp., 3370 Miraloma Ave., Anaheim, Cal. 92803, '64–; Sci. Wtr., '64–'69; Prom.-Tech. Copy Supvsr., '58–'64; Tech. Wtr., '56–'58; Specifications Wtr., Hughes Aircraft Co., '55–'56; Test Equipment Design Engineer, Instr.; Auth.; Adv. Assn. of the West, L.A. Adv. Wm., Mensa; Stephens Col., AA (Jnlsm.), '36; Univ. of Miss., BA (Eng., French), '38; Univ. of Cinn., '42–'43; Electronics Engineering Aircraft Radio Engineering Sch., '43; Long Beach City Col., '68–'69; b. Holly Springs, Miss., 1917; p. Miss. Supreme Court Justice Lemuel and Emma Robertson Smith, Jr.; H. James G. Parks (div.); res: 360 Carpio Dr., Diamond Bar, Cal. 91766.

PARR, MARY YOHANNAN, Assoc. Prof., St. John's University, Grand Central and Utopia Pkwys., Jamaica, N.Y. 11432, '69–; Assoc. Prof., Pratt Inst., '63–'69; Asst. Prof., Villanova Univ., '62–'63; Asst. Dir., Newark State Col., Lib., '55–'62; Librn., San Antonio Public Lib., '53–'54; Cost Analyst, Miller Paper Co., '52–'53; Luna County Bd. of Educ., '51–'52; Head Librn., Willard Memorial Lib., '50–'51; Children's Librn., Cuyohoga County Lib., '49–'50; ALA, N.Y. Lib. Assn., N.Y. Lib. Club, WNBA, AAUP; Col. of Wooster, AB, '48; Western Reserve Univ., MS (Lib. Sci.), '49; b. Cleve., Oh.; h. Wendell Parr; res: 63 Essex Ave., Montclair, N.J. 07042.

PARR, SALLY CARMICHAEL, Dir., Radio-TV, Richard W. Pemberton Advertising, 1310 W. El Paso, Ft. Worth, Tex. 76102, '67–; Anncr., Prodr., KTVT-TV, '62–'63; KFJZ Radio and TV, '55–'58; Actress, leading roles, "Sun Sets at Dawn" (Un. Artists, '51), "A Model Young Lady" (TV Film, '51); AWRT, Ft. Worth Commty. Theatre; Univ. of Tex., BFA, '47 (summa cum laude); b. Dallas, Tex., 1925; p. J. Bryan and Winnefred Warren Carmichael; res: 5113 Birchman, Fort Worth, Tex. 76107.

PARRY, BETTY WIDDER, Pres. and Owner, Betty Parry Associates, 4814 Falstone Ave., Chevy Chase, Md. 20015, '64–; Mkt. Rsch. Analyst, Young & Rubicam, '58–'59; New Products Rsch. Analyst, Colgate-Palmolive Co., '57–'58; Social Rsch. Interviewer: Columbia Univ., Nat. Opinion Rsch. Center, '51–'55; Social Worker, N.Y.C. Dept. of Welfare, '49–'51; Cnslt., State Univ. of N.Y. (Wash., D.C. Off.), '66; Bur. of Social Sci. Rsch., '69; Am. Sociological Assn., Am. Assn. for Public Opinion Rsch.; Who's Who of Am. Wm.; Dic. of Intl. Biog.; 2000 Wm. of Achiev.; Mar-

quis Biographical Lib. (Advisory Mbr.); Queens Col., BA, '48; New Sch. for Social Rsch., '58–'59; b. N.Y.C., 1927; p. Jacob and Blanche Gardner Widder; h. Hugh J. Parry; c. John, Stephen Brawer, Roberta Brawer, Brian; res: 4814 Falstone Ave., Chevy Chase, Md. 20015.

PARSON, MARY JEAN, Mgr., Program Controllers, ABC News, 7 W. 66th St., N.Y., N.Y. 10023, '69–; Unit Mgr., ABC-TV, '65–'69; Dir., Prod. Exhibits, Better Living Ctr., World's Fair, '64–'65; Gen. Mgr., freelance, nat. tours, '63–'64; Asst. to Pres., Nat. Performing Arts, '63; Bus. Mgr., Mineola Playhouse, '62–'63; Creator of Inst. for Cultural Studies, O'Neill Fndn.; Founder, Mineola Sch. of Theatre for Children; Freelance Wtr. on theatre, UPI; Auth., Ala. Sesquicentennial music-drama, '69; Auth., Assoc. Prodr., benefit for Kennedy Cultural Ctr., Wash., D.C., '66; NAEB, AETA, ANTA, Alpha Psi Omega (life mbr.); Outstanding Young Wm. of Am.; Who's Who of Am. Wm.; Birmingham-Southern Col., BA, '56 (cum laude); Yale Sch. of Drama, M.F.A., '59 (scholarship); b. Houston, Tex., 1934; p. Guy Virgil and Ursula Clark Parson; res: 215 W. 91st St., N.Y., N.Y. 10024.

PARSONS, CYNTHIA, Free-lance Wtr., educ. subjects, '68–; Auth., "Schools Can Change"; Educ. Ed., The Christian Science Monitor; Cnslt., Newton Public Schs., '69; Lectr. in New Math, '60; EWA (1st prize for educ. writing, '62–'68); Travel grant winner to Indonesia, '68; Secy.-Treas., '66–'68)); Carnegie Corp. Rsch. Grant ('66); Principia Col., BA, '48; Antioch-Putney Grad. Sch., MA (Educ.), '56; b. Cleve., Oh., 1926; p. Sanford and Elenore Mann Parsons; res: The Schoolhouse, Gassetts, Vt. 05145.

PARSONS, EILEEN E., Consulting Ed.; Head of Edtl./Prod. Dept., Sterling Institute, Prudential Tower, Boston, Mass. 02199, '66–'70; Free-Lance PR Wtr., '66; Edtl. Asst. United Presbyterian Church Commn. on Ecumenical Mission and Rels., '65–'66; Barnard Col., AB (British Civilization), '65 (Hon. Soc. Jr. Yr.); N.Y.U. Writing Seminar, '65; res: 655 Powell St., San Francisco, Cal. 94108.

PARSONS, RUTH DWYER, Educ. Reptr., Waterbury Republican-American, 389 Meadow St., Waterbury, Conn., '60–; Gen. Reptr., Soc. Wtr., Critic, '50–'60; Ed., Intermission mag., '50; EWA, Waterbury Arts Cncl. (Bd. of Dirs.), Mattatuck Commty. Col. Advisory Cncl. (Secy.); Oh. State Univ.; Univ. of Conn.; p. John and Gladys Whitehouse Dwyer; h. Howard Parsons; c. Beth, Patricia (Mrs. David Bailey); res: 329 Grandview Ave., Waterbury, Conn. 06720.

PARSONS, VIOLET J., Secy.-Treas., Prod. Mgr., Mail-O-Graph, Inc., 206 W. Fourth St., Kewanee, Ill. 61443, '41–; Prod., '32–; Pilot Club Intl. (Pres.); Knox Conservatory of Music.

PARTINGTON, SUSAN TROWBRIDGE, Free-lance Wtr., Fashion and Fine Arts Commentator; Auth.,

"The Model's Way, a Guide for Teenage Girls" (Hawthorn, '69); Co-auth. "Teenage Beauty, Charm & Personality" (Prentice-Hall); Ghost-Wtr., four bks. in charm and beauty field; Wtr., Ed., TV Commentator, Prentice-Hall, Young & Rubicam, Hawthorn Bks., '54–'69; Commentator, Wtr., Cnslt., John Robert Powers, '52–'54; Prodr., Publicist, Special Events, Abraham & Straus, '47–'52; Who's Who of Am. Wm.; Univ. of Wis., '42–'43; Univ. of Wash., '44; b. Milw., Wis.; p. John and Elsa Gumz Trowbridge; h. James H. M. Partington; c. Marshall, Bartholomew; res: Southfield Point, Stamford, Conn. 06902.

PARTON, VIRGINIA, Mng. Ed., Texas Bar Journal, Box 12186, Capitol Station, Austin, Tex., 78711, '44–; Off. of Price Adm. (San Antonio), '43–'44; Off. of War Info., '42; U.S. Dept. of State (Wash., D.C.) '41–'42; All-Church Press (Ft. Worth and Dallas, Tex.), '40; Theta Sigma Phi (Assoc. Ed., The Matrix, '48–'58; Austin Alumna Chptr. Pres., '49–'50), Austin IEA (Pres., '59); Univ. of Tex., BJ, '39; b. Mobeetie, Tex., 1916; p. Agus Tremain and Maye Durham Parton; res: 1206-A Lorrain, Austin, Tex. 78703.

PARTRIDGE, DOROTHY GARRETSON, PR Exec., Sun Oil Company, 1608 Walnut St., Phila., Pa. 19046, '52–; Mng. Ed., Etude Music Magazine, '49–'51; Ed., Philadelphia Magazine, '45–'49; Ed., The Extract, Sharp & Dohme, '43–'45; Tchr., '38–'43; Wtr., articles, petroleum indsl. mags.; Soroptimist Club of Phila. (Pres., '62), Girl Scout Cncl. of Phila. (PR, '62–), Theta Sigma Phi, Desk & Derrick Club; Am. Petroleum Inst. Oil Info. Comm. Gold aw., '56, and Silver aw., '54; Dir. Mail Advs. Assn. cits., '43, '44; Phila. Art Alliance; Bryn Mawr Col., AB, '38; Grad work: Univ. of Pitt., Temple Univ., '39–'43; Charles Morris Price Sch. (Adv.), '44; b. Phila., Pa., 1917; p. LeRoy and Jessie Fox Garretson; h. H. Kelsey Partridge, Jr.; step-children: Ronald K., Mrs. Barry G. Rogers; res: 1018 The Benson East, Jenkintown, Pa. 19046.

PASANEN, JANE SMITH, Pubcty. Dir., McCall Publishing Company Book Division, 230 Park Ave., N.Y., N.Y. 10017, '69–; Macmillan Co., '66–'69; John Wiley & Sons, '63–'66; Asst. Pubcty. Dir., David McKay Co., '61–'63; Publrs. Pubcty. Assn. (Offcr.); h. Glenn Pasanen.

PASCAL, NAOMI BRENNER, Exec. Ed., University of Washington Press, 1416 N.E. 41st St., Seattle, Wash. 98105, '63–; Ed., '53–'63; Assoc. Ed., Univ. of N.C. Press, '48–'53; Asst. Ed., Vanguard Press (N.Y.C.), '46–'58; Phi Beta Kappa ('45); Wellesley Col., BA, '46 (Durant Scholar, '45); b. Bklyn., N.Y., 1926; p. Mortimer and Sylvia Freehof Brenner; h. Paul Pascal; c. David Morris, Janet Brenner; res: 9927 232nd St. S.W., Edmonds, Wash. 98020.

PASCHAL, NANCY (Grace Trotter), Auth., Three Jr. novels: "Clover Creek" ('46), "Magnolia Heights" ('47), "Promise of June" ('55), all published by Nelson, all Jr. Lit. Guild selections; eleven other books; Bk.

Reviewer; Speaker on crtv. writing; Dallas Story League; b. Dallas, Tex.; p. William and Nancy Paschal Trotter; res: 2028 Whitedove Dr., Dallas, Tex. 75224.

PASCHALL, JEANETTE, Mktng. Rsch. Mgr., McGraw-Hill, Inc., 330 W. 42nd St., N.Y., N.Y. 10036, '57–; Chemical Engineer, Ling-Temco-Vought, Inc., '56; Owner, Cnslt., Flavor Hall, '53–'55; Chief Chemist, Parade Extract Co., '49–'53; Asst. Chemist, Dr. Pepper Co., '45–'49; Rsch. Chemist, Humble Oil & Refining Co., '43–'44; Auth., numerous articles on mktng.; Am. Chemical Soc., Am. Mktng. Assn., Chemical Mktng. Rsch. Assn., Adv. Rsch. Fndn., Phi Theta Kappa, Iota Sigma Phi; Univ. of Tex., BA (Chemistry), '43; Southern Methodist Univ., '46; Alexander Hamilton Inst., '54–'55; New Sch. of Soc. Rsch., '63–'64; Am. Mgt. Assn., '64; b. Marlin, Tex., 1921; p. Fred and Irene Cable Paschall; res: 215 E. 68th St., N.Y., N.Y. 10021.

PASHKIN, RONA L., Prodr., The Marschalk Co., Div. of Interpublic, 1271 Ave. of the Americas, N.Y., N.Y. 10009, '69–; Prodr., McCann-Erickson; Assoc. Prodr., Mijas Prodns.; State Univ. of N.Y.; b. N.Y.C., 1946; p. Lester and Mildred Leifer Pashkin; res: 11 W. 82nd St., N.Y., N.Y. 10024.

PASSINI, MARY WALLIS, Soc. Ed., The Napa Register, P.O. Box 150, 1615 Second St., Napa, Cal. 94558, '69–; News and Feature Wtr.; Secy. to Ed. and Publr.; S.F. State Col., BA (Crtv. Writing), '65; b. Cal., '43; res: P.O. Box 235, 1319 Linden St., Napa, Cal. 94558.

PATAKY, JUDY ROSENMAN, Asst. to Publr. and Ed., Coast FM and Fine Arts Magazine, 291 S. La Cienega Blvd., Beverly Hills, Cal. 90211, '68–; Tchr., jnlsm.; public speaking, lit.; Wtr., bk. reviews and contrbr. to Jersey City State Col. literary jnl., '60–'62; Chmn., N.J. State Col. Cultural Lect. series, '60–'61; Jnlsm. Key for nwsp. writing; Jersey City State Col., BA, '62; Yeshiva Univ. (lang., speech, commtns.), '62–'64; b. N.Y.C., 1940; p. Sara Sharlin; h. Tom Pataky; c. Aaron, Jenny Sue.

PATE, MARGARET FARHA, PR, Adv. Sec., The Pate Organization, Nichols Hills Exec. Bldg., 6403 N.W. Grand Blvd., Okla. City, Okla. 73116, '47–; Co-Founder, Partner; Dir. PR, U.S. Recruiting and Induction Hqs., '41–'45; Dir. Adv., Carroll, Brough & Robinson, '40–'41; Dir. PR, Griffith Amusement Co., '31–'40; Tchr., PR and Adv. Career Conf., annually, Okla. Univ.; Cnslt., Advisory projects: Okla. City C. of C., Frontiers of Sci. Fndn., numerous others; three cits. for pubn. "Immutable Images of Oklahoma"; Governor of Okla. special aw., '61; Okla. City C. of C. special aw., '57; various other aws.; Williams Woods Col., '32–'34 (Mbr. Pres. Soc., '69); Univ. of Mo., '34–'37 (Phi Beta Kappa); b. Wichita, Kan.; p. Merhige and Saidy Mattar Farha; h. Stanton Stanton Pate, Jr.

PATE, PSYCHE LAWTON, Chmn. of the Bd., Secy.-Treas., KPRS Broadcasting Corp., 2301 Grand Ave.,

Kan. City, Mo. 64108, '52–; Chmn. of the Bd., '62–; AWRT, Radio-TV Cncl., C. of C. of Greater Kan. City, Wms. C. of C.; active in local charitable, civic orgs.; Fisk Univ.; b. Birmingham, Ala., 1913; p. Eugene and Minnie Lee Lawton; h. Edward H. Pate; c. Edward H., III, Patricia Eugenia, Penny Bernadette; res: 3444 E. 46th St., Kan. City, Mo. 64130.

PATE, VIRGINIA FORWOOD, Pres., Gen. Mgr., WASA AM/FM, The Chesapeake Broadcasting Corporation, P.O. Box 97, 1605 Level Rd., Havre de Grace, Md. 21078, '60–; VP, '55–'60; Bd. of Dirs., Secy.-Treas. Cash Loan Co., '60–; Treas., WKEN, Inc. (Dover, Del.), '56–'57; PR, Irwin & Leighton, '41–'42; Standard Oil Co. of Pa., '40–'41; various orgs.; Col. of William and Mary (Williamsburg, Va.), AB, '40; b. Havre de Grace, Md., 1919; p. Walter and Bennita Charshee Forwood; h. Jason Thomas Pate (dec.); c. David, Kennon, Barbara; res: 1000 Chesapeake Dr., Havre de Grace, Md. 21078.

PATRICH, LOIS M., Adv. Mgr., Carson Pirie Scott & Company, One S. State St., Chgo., Ill. 60690, '63–; Asst. Adv. Mgr., '61–'63, Copy Supvsr., '60–'61, Asst. Adv. Mgr., Mandel Brothers Dept. Store, '58–'60; Lectr. (retail adv.), Columbia Col. (Chgo.), '67–'68; Chgo. Adv. Club, Fashion Group of Chgo., Fndn. of Univ. of Ill.; Adv. Wm. of the Yr., Chgo., '68; Univ. of Ill., BS.

PATRICOF, PAT E., AE, Morris Silver Associates, 310 Madison Ave., N.Y., N.Y. 10017, '59–; Free-lance Wtr., articles; AE, Jules Berens Org., '55–'57; AE, Steve Hannagan Assn., '42–'54; Pubcty. Dir. and Ed., mag. WGN Concert Bur., '40–'42; AE, Radio Features, '36–'40; Pubcty. Wtr., Spot Comml Wtr., Benton & Bowles, '33–'36; Pubcty. Club of N.Y. (Charter Mbr.), Theta Sigma Phi; Oh. State Univ., Col. of Commerce and Jnlsm., BS, '32 (Alumni Assn. of N.Y. Bd. of Govs., 20 yrs.); N.Y. Inst. of Fin., '57; b. Middletown, Oh.; p. Leon and Dora Rosenfeld Patricof; res: 319 E. 50th St., N.Y., N.Y. 10022.

PATTERSON, ALLENE SEALY, Librn. and Assoc. Soc. Ed., Olean Times Herald, 104 Times Sq., Olean, N.Y. 14760, '65–; Eastern Star; b. Shinglehouse, Pa., 1910; p. Paul and Bessie De Remer Sealy; h. Darold D. Patterson; c. Nancy (Mrs. Robert Dimicco), Paul; res: Bolivar, N.Y. 14715.

PATTERSON, EVELYN ROELOFS, Dir., Evelyn Patterson Cooking School, 128 Fitz Randolph, Princeton, N.J. 08540, '58–; Cnslt., TV and Radio food commls.; Lectr., Food Demonstrator; Auth: cookbks., "Meal for Guests" ('54), "Gourmet's Kitchen" ('58), "Recipes for Simple but Elegant Dining" ('63), articles on food; Univ. of Mich., AB, '40; b. Prinsburg, Minn., 1917; p. Evart and Tchitska DeVries Roelofs; h. Gardner Patterson; c. Eliza Ruth; res: 128 Fitz Randolph Rd., Princeton, N.J. 08540.

PATTERSON, MARGARET JONES, Feature Wtr., Pittsburgh Press, 34 Blvd. of the Allies, Pitt., Pa. 15230,

'67–; internship, '66; Asst. Ed., suburban nwsp.; Theta Sigma Phi (Pubcty. Chmn. for Annual Nat. Mtg., '69; Pitt. Chptr. Mbrship. Chmn., '68–'69); Oh. Univ., BSJ, '67 (cum laude; Outstanding Sr. Aw.); b. Pitt., Pa., 1945; p. Robert and Ruth Wilson Jones; h. George Patterson, Jr.; res: 5510 Kentucky St., Pitt., Pa. 15232.

PATTERSON, ODETTE WALLING, Free-lance PR Cnslt.; Adv.-PR Mgr., First Fed. Savings & Loan Assn. of St. Petersburg, '55–'69; various positions, '45–'55; Stone and Webster Engineering (Oak Ridge, Tenn.) '44–'45; Ed., Fact & Fancies, '53–'69; articles in nat. savings and loan pubns.; participated in savings and loan conv. progs. and workshops; St. Petersburg Wms. Press Club (Pres., '69), Suncoast Adv. Club (VP, '64), Reg. 11 PR and Adv. Cncl. of Savings & Loans (Pres., '64–); Fourth Dist. AFA (Printer's Ink Silver Medal aw., '59; Corr. Secy., '59–'60), Wms. Adv. Club of St. Petersburg (Pres., '59–'60), Suncoast BPW (VP, '62–'63), Gamma Alpha Chi, Theta Sigma Phi; Northwestern Univ., Grad. Sch. of Fin. PR Assn., '62; b. Pau, France, 1914; p. William and Francoise Laulhe Walling; h. Charles A. Patterson; res: 732 Hillside Dr., S., St. Petersburg, Fla. 33705.

PATTERSON, POLLY REILLY, Staff Assoc., Bell Telephone Company of Pennsylvania, 201 Stanwix St., Pitt., Pa. 15222, '65–; various mgt. positions; Assn. of Pitt. Bus. Wms. Clubs (Past Pres., Bd. of Dirs; "Salute of Yr.," '52–'53 for personal svcs. to commty.), Pitt. Adv. Club (VP, Secy.; Bd. of Dirs.; "Addie Oscar," Adv. Wm. of Yr., '56), Allegheny County Soc. for Crippled Children (VP, Bd. of Dirs.) Assn. of Indsl. Advs. (Pitt. Chptr. Bd. of Dirs., Life Mbr.), Allegheny Chptr. of Nat. Fndn. for Infantile Paralysis (Secy.; Nat. Cit. for 18 yrs. volunteer svc., '58; Bd. of Dirs.), Altrusa Intl. (Pres., '50–'51; Governor-elect of Second Dist.), BPW (Bd. of Dirs.; Dist. and State Aws. for program planning) Oscar for PR, one of Pitts. outstanding wm., '59; Bell Telephone's Good Neighbor aw.; Nat. Soc. for Crippled Children and Adults (Nat. Trustee), Univ. of Pitt.; b. Wilkinsburg, Pa., 1906; p. Thomas and Margaret Coughey Reilly; h. W. Ray Patterson; res: 402 Olympia Rd., Pitt., Pa. 15211.

PATTERSON, SALLY H., Wtr., Ogilvy & Mather, Inc., 2 E. 48th St., N.Y., N.Y. 10017, '64–; Compton, '62–'64; Warwick and Legler, '60–'62; Adv. Age "100 Best," '67, '68; Intl. Bdcst. aw., Hollywood, '68; Cannes Film Festival Gold Lion, '68; Univ. of N.C., BA (Eng.); res: 430 E. 63rd St., N.Y., N.Y. 10021.

PATTERSON, SUZANNE FAUCHER, Staff Wtr., Réalites Magazine, 13 rue St. Georges, Paris, France (and 301 Madison Ave., N.Y., N.Y.), '68–; Edtl. Asst., Wtr., '64–'68; Translator, J. Walter Thompson (Paris), '62–'64; Jr. Copywtr. (N.Y.C.), '59–'62; Interpreter, VIP Guide, World's Fair (Brussels, Belgium), '58; Colmst., weekly "Our Girl in Paris," Dayton (Oh.) Journal-Herald, '63–; Wtr., articles in Cleve. Plain Dealer, London Sun. Telegraph, Mpls. Times Star; TV spots from Paris, WHIO-TV (Dayton, Oh.), '66–'68; Vassar,

BA (French Lit.), '57 (Jr. Yr. abroad, Paris Univ., '55–'56); b. Wash., D.C., 1935; p. William Prior and Suzanne Welch Patterson; res: 32 Rue de Turin, Paris 8e, France.

PATTERSON, VIRGINIA HICKOK, Pubcty. and Adv. Mgr., Cambridge University Press, 32 E. 57th St., N.Y., N.Y. 10022, '64–; Pubcty. Dir., The Macmillan Co., '47–'64; Trade Adv. Mgr., '43–'45; Asst. Ed., Longmans, Green & Co., '35–'37; Rschr., Prom. Dept., Bank of N.Y. and Trust Co., '32–'35; free-lance manuscript conslt., edtl. work, Lane Publ. Co. (S.F., Cal.), '46–'47; free-lance and special projects, Nat. Press Bur., '40–'41; Nat. Bk. Aws., Nat. Cncl. Wm. in U.S., Publrs. Adclub of N.Y. (Dir., '55–'57; Secy.-Treas., '45–'46), PPA; Hood Col., BA, '30; b. Zelienople, Pa., 1909; p. James and Estelle Dindinger Hickok; h. Richard O. Patterson (div.).

PATTON, EVVE JOHNSON, Mgr., Ogilvy & Mather, Inc., 6565 Sunset Blvd., Hollywood, Cal. 90028, '65–, '59–'65; KTTV, Inc., '53–'59; AWRT (Cal. Chptr. Corr. Secy., '68), NATAS, AAF, L.A. Adv. Mgr., Pacific Pioneer Bdcstrs., Hollywood Radio and TV Soc., L.A. Adv. Club, Variety Club; Univ. of Ore.; b. Hollywood, Cal., 1932; p. S. Elmer and Lottie Fite Johnson; h. George Patton; res: 1220 Sunset Plaza Dr., L.A., Cal. 90069.

PATTON, JANE VanDIKE, Dir. Librn., Northwest Regional Library System; Dir., Bay County Public Library, 25 W. Government, Panama City, Fla. 32401, '57–; Building Cnslt. for County and Hq. Libs.; AAUW (Educ. Comm., '61–'66), ALA, S.E. Lib. Assn., Fla. Lib. Assn. (Secy.-Treas., Public Lib. Secy., '60–'62); Univ. of Ia., '34–'36, Fla. State Univ., BA (Lib. Sci.), '57; MS (Lib. Sci.), '67; b. Elberon, Ia.; c. Mrs. John Conness, Mrs. John Lotas, Jon.; res: 1613 Dewitt St., Panama City, Fla. 32401.

PATTON, JOANNE SMOOT, PR Dir., The Patton Agency, 1800 N. Central Ave., Phoenix, Ariz. 85004, '62–; Reptr., The Arizona Republic, '60–'62; Media Coordr: Mayor's Cncl. on Youth Employment (Phoenix), Nat. Alliance of Businessmen (Ariz.); Phoenix Press Club, Ariz. Press Wm. (numerous best of yr. aws., '62–'65), NFPW, PRSA (Counselor Sec.-Ariz. Chptr.), Alpha Phi; eight "Lulu" first aws., '65–'69; Ariz. State Univ., BA (Jnlsm.), '60 (Top 100 Club; Gamma Alpha Chi; Pi Delta Epsilon); b. Phoenix, Ariz., 1939; p. Glenn and Virginia George Smoot; h. Kenneth Patton; c. Jennie Ann, Corey; res: 7611 N. Invergordon Rd., Scottsdale, Ariz. 85251.

PAUL, CHARLOTTE, United States Board of Parole, 107 Indiana Ave., N.W., Wash., D.C., '64–; Auth. of numerous bks., short stories and articles; Wash. State Bd. of Prison Terms and Paroles, '62–'64; Lit. Critic, The Argus, '61–'62; Wash. State Cncl. for Children and Youth, '57–'61; Ed. and Co-Publr. of two weeklies in Wash., '49–'61; Edtl. Asst., Esquire-Coronet, '42–'45; Asst. Fgn. News Ed., Chgo. Sun Times, '40–'43; Theta Sigma Phi (Matrix Table honors, '56), Nat. Cncl. of Crime and Delinquency, Assn. of Paroling Authorities, Wms. Nat. Democratic Club, BPW, Western Correctional Assn., AAUW (Wash., D.C. Chptr.); NFPW Wm. of the Yr., '56; numerous writing and reporting aws.; Wellesley Col., BA, '38 (Wellesley Scholar); b. Seattle, Wash., 1916; p. Charles Henry and Alice Paine Paul; h. Robert Winter Reese; c. Hiram Paul Groshell, John Paine Groshell; res: 2500 Turbridge Lane, Alexandria, Va. 22308.

PAULEY, GAY, Wms. Ed., United Press International, 220 E. 42nd St., N.Y., N.Y. 10022, '57–; formerly UPI Polit. Reptr., Charleston, W.Va.; Ky. Mgr.; UPI; News Reptr., Huntington (W.Va.) Advertiser; conducted radio news program on Mutual Network; former panelist on "Ladies of the Press," WOR (N.Y.C.) news show; Nwsp. Wms. Club of N.Y. (Pres.), Theta Sigma Phi (Nat. Headliner Aw., '65); Hon. by Foremost Wm. in Commtns., '69; FRANY from Am. fashion industry for fashion coverage, '68; Marshall Univ., '42; courses at Colo. Univ.; b. Poca, W.Va.; p. James and Diana Pauley; h. John L. Sehon; c. John L. VI, Edward H., Redd G.; res: 410 E. 57th St., N.Y., N.Y. 10022.

PAULI, HERTHA E., Auth: "The Secret of Sarajevo" ('65), "Sojourner Truth" ('62), "Cry of the Heart" ('57), "I Lift My Lamp" ('42), 24 Children's books; PEN; Silver Medal of Honor, Fed. Republic of Austria, '67; Student Gymnasium, Acad. of Dramatic Arts, Vienna, Austria; b. Vienna, Austria, 1909; p. Wolfgang and Bertha Schuetz Pauli; h. E. B. Ashton; res: 102 Woodhull Rd., Huntington, N.Y. 11743.

PAVIA, NATALIE EDGAR, Edtl. Assoc., Art News, 444 Madison Ave., N.Y., N.Y. 10022, '59–; Art Hist. Instr., Queens Col.; Artist; Artists Club, Col. Art Assn.; Bklyn. Col., AB, '57 (magna cum laude); Columbia Sch. of Art and Archeology; b. N.Y.C., 1937; p. Paul G. and Eugenie Ruppell Edgar; h. Phillip Pavia; c. Louis Edgar; res: 3 Great James St., N.Y., N.Y. 10012.

PAXSON, CAROLIN GOYNE, Dir. of Radio, TV, White & Shuford Advertising, Inc., 1821 Wyoming, El Paso, Tex. 79999, '66–; Exec. Prodr., Copy Chief, Mithoff Adv., '64–'66; Adv. Wtr., Prodr., Sanders Co., '63–'64; Copywtr., McCormick Adv., '62–'63; Cont. Dir., Prom. Mgr., KFDA-TV (Amarillo), '58–'62; Adv. Club of El Paso (Secy., '67; over 50 aws., '64–), BPW, League of Wm. Voters; many aws., '61–; Stephens Col., '55–'56; Tex. Tech. Col., '57–'58; b. Amarillo, Tex., 1939; p. F. C. and Marie Thomsen Goyne; h. David Paxson; c. Michael, Steffani, Patricia, Audian; res: 9280 McCabe, El Paso, Tex. 79925.

PAXSON, MARJORIE BOWERS, Newsfeatures Ed., The St. Petersburg Times, 490 First Ave. S., P.O. Box 1121, St. Petersburg, Fla. 33731, '69–; Wms. Ed., '68–'69; Ed., Matrix, '67–; Asst. Wms. Ed., Miami Herald, '56–'68; Wms. Ed., Houston (Tex.) Chronicle, '52–'56; Soc. Ed., Wms. Ed., Houston Post, '48–'52; AP

Omaha, Neb., '46–'48; UPI (Lincoln), '44–'46; Theta Sigma Phi (Nat. Pres., '63–'67; Nat. 1st VP, '60–'63), Fla. Wms. Press Club (Treas., '67–'69), Kappa Tau Alpha, Fashion Group; Rice Inst., '40–'42; Univ. of Mo., BJ, '44; b. Houston, Tex., 1923; p. Roland and Marie Bowers Paxson; res: 5342 Bayou Grande Blvd., N.E., St. Petersburg, Fla. 33703.

PAYE, Sr. MARY PAUL, R.S.M., Dir of Pubcty., Asst. Prof., Jnslm., College Misericordia, Dallas, Pa. 18612, '67–; Tchr., Gate of Heaven Sch.; Central Catholic HS (Johnstown, Pa.); Theta Sigma Phi, Assn. for Educ. in Jnslm.; Col. Misericordia, BA, '52; Catholic Univ., MA (Eng.), '56; Syracuse Univ., PhD (Mass Commtns.), '65; b. Wilkes-Barre, Pa., 1930; p. Charles and Margaret McCarthy Paye; res: College Misericordia, Dallas, Pa. 18612.

PAYETTE, VIRGINIA ELLIS, Colmst., United Feature Syndicate, Inc., 220 E. 42nd St., N.Y., N.Y. 10017; Colmst., UP, Hollywood, Cal., '42–'52; Theta Sigma Phi; Univ. of Southern Cal., (Jnlsm.), '42 (Phi Beta Kappa; Phi Kappa Phi; Outstanding Wm. in Jnlsm.); b. L.A., Cal., 1920; p. Dwight and Kathryn Smith Ellis; h. William C. Payette; c. Bruce, Susie (Mrs. James McDougal); res: 4 Bacon Ct., Bronxville, N.Y. 10708.

PAYNE, ALMA SMITH, Auth., non-fiction: "Jingle Bells and Pastry Shells" ('69), "Partners in Science" ('68), numerous others; Supvsr. of Parent Educ., Parent-Nursery Sch. and Child-Care Ctrs., Berkeley Public Schs., '40–'47; Instr., Ext. Div., Univ. of Cal., '42–'44; Supvsr., Emergency Nursery Schs., '36–'40; Theta Sigma Phi, numerous lib. assns. and offs., numerous civic orgs.; Univ. of Cal., AB, '22 (Phi Beta Kappa); MA, '38; b. Oakland, Cal.; p. Robert Russell and Neva Palmer Smith; h. William R. Ralston; c. Robert Warner Chambers, James Warner Chambers, Jr., Margaret Payne Ferris, Richard M. Payne, William R. Ralston, Jr., Donald H. Ralston.

PAYNE, EMILY CLEMENT, Dir., Tri-County Regional Library, 606 W. First St., Rome, Ga. 30161, '64–; Librn., '59–'64; Eng. Tchr., '58–'59; NEA, Ga. Educ. Assn., ALA, S.E. Lib. Assn., Ga. Lib. Assn.; Shorter Col., AB, '58; Emory Univ., ML, '63; b. Walker County, Ga., 1920; p. W. M. and Leona Davis Clement; h. Albert S. Payne; c. William, LeAnn (Mrs. Robert Strom); res: Rte. 2, Rome, Ga. 30161.

PAYNE, ETHEL L., Wash., D.C., Corr., Sengstacke Publications, 2400 S. Michigan Ave., Chgo., Ill. 60616, '62–, '53–'58; Polit. Wtr., Staff, Dem. Nat. Comm., '62; AFL-CIO (Comm. on Polit. Educ., '58–'61; Feature Wtr., Chgo. Defender, '51–'53; WNPC, Capital Press Club; Newsman's Newsman aw., '56, '67; Chgo. Cncl. on Fgn. Relations World Understanding aw., '56; Ill. Press Assn. aw., '52; Medill Sch. of Jnlsm., '40–'41; b. Chgo., Ill.; p. William and Bessie Austin Payne; res: 1712 16th St., N.W., Wash., D.C. 20009.

PEABODY, BARBARA KEATING, Copy Group

Head, J. Walter Thompson Co., 420 Lexington Ave., N.Y., N.Y. 10017, '60–; Cunningham & Walsh, '58–'60; N. W. Ayer, '54–'58; Wtr., CBS; Am. TV Commls. Festival judge, '63–; ANDY aws. judge, '68; Radio Clio aw., '62–'63; print aw., '66; Clio recognitions, '67, '66; Wellesley Col., '44; b. Bklyn., N.Y., 1922; p. Ralph and Carolyn Kirwin Keating; h. George Peabody; c. Christopher, Carolyn; res: 21 E. 90th St., N.Y., N.Y. 10028.

PEACOCK, MARY WILLA, Ed., Rags magazine, 30 East 20 St., N.Y., N.Y. 10003, '70–; Staff Ed., Innovation Magazine, '69–'70; Assoc. Lit. Ed., Harper's Bazaar, '65–'69; Wtr., mag. articles; Fiction Eds. Panel, Ia. Col. Wtrs. Conf., '67–'68; Panelist, "Guess My Sign," WPIX-TV, '68; Vassar Col., BA, '64; b. Evanston, Ill., 1942; p. William G. and Mary W. Young Peacock Jr.; res: 46 Grand St., N.Y., N.Y. 10013.

PEAKE, MIRAED, PR Acc. Rep., J. Walter Thompson Company, 420 Lexington Ave., N.Y., N.Y. 10017, '65–; Assoc. Ed., Co-ed Magazine, '60–'65; Dir. of Wms. Activities, Dodge Div., Chrysler Corp., '51–'60; Pubcty. Mgr., McCall's Patterns, '53–'57; Publicist, Elizabeth Maher Assocs., '50–'53; Co-auth., "Co-ed Book of Charm and Beauty" ('63); Free-lance Wtr.; N.Y. Fashion Group, NHFL (N.Y. Chptr. Secy., '68–'71); Bryn Mawr Col., '45–'48, '49; b. Chgo., Ill., 1927; p. Junius and Miriam Morrison Peake; h. R. Leigh Smith, Jr.; c. L. Randall, S. Wilson; res: 225 E. 66th St., N.Y., N.Y. 10021.

PEARCE, JANET C., Edtl., Union College, Lamont House, Schenectady, N.Y., 12308, '65–; Secy. to News Dir., '62–'64; Secy. to Deputy Chief Engineer, N.Y. State Dept. of Construction, Bridges Div., '64–'65; U.S. Eastern Amateur Ski Assn.; Univ. of Buffalo, AAS, '62; b. Macomb, Ill., 1942; p. Clifford and Esther Wood Pearce; res: 1436 Via Del Mar, Schenectady, N.Y. 12309.

PEARCE, KATHERINE, Pres., National Retired Teachers Association, 215 Long Beach Blvd., Long Beach, Cal. 90802; VP of Area VII; Tchr. and Supvsr., Fort Worth Public Schs., '15–; NEA, Tex. State Tchrs. Assn., Fort Worth Classroom Tchrs. Assn., AAUW, Delta Kappa Gamma; numerous aws. and cits.; West Tex. Tchrs. Col.; Tex. Christian Univ., BM; Columbia Univ. (Music); Northwestern Univ., MA (Music).

PEARLMAN, EVE BERGER, Secy.-Treas., New York Institute of Advertising, Inc., 280 Madison Ave., N.Y., N.Y. 10016, '64–; VP, M. B. Pearlman, five yrs.; Pers., Paramount Pics., six yrs.; Tchr.; AWNY, AAF, IAA, Adv. Club of N.Y.; Hunter Col., BA; b. N.Y.C.; p. Charles and Manya Absel Berger; h. Max Pearlman; c. Dorothy Coxe, Arthur; res: 199 Johnson Rd., Scarsdale, N.Y. 10583.

PEARSON, ANN THOMAS, Feature Events Dir., Burdine's Division, Federated Department Stores, Inc., 22 E. Flagler St., Miami, Fla. 33101, '65–; Copy Supvsr., Stockton-West-Burkraet (Cinn., Oh.), '62–'63;

Copy Dir., Edwin C. Huster (Knoxville, Tenn.), '59–'62; AE, Botsford-Constantine-Gardner (Portland, Ore.), '56–'59; Div. Adv. Mgr., Bullock's (L.A., Cal.), '49–'56; Adv. Club of Gtr. Miami, Fla. PR Soc., Fashion Group; b. Nashville, Tenn.; p. John and Nelle Henderson Thomas; c. John Welshan; res: 3156 Virginia St., Miami, Fla. 33133.

PEARSON, HELEN R., Auth., seven mathematics textbks., '58–'70; Lectr., Purdue Univ., Indpls. Campus, '66–'68; Head, Math. Dept. Arlington HS, '61–'65; Tchr., math., Arsenal Tech. HS, '42–'61; Nat. Cncl. of Tchrs. of Math., Central Assn. of Sci. and Math Tchrs., NEA, AAAS, Pi Lambda Theta (Nat. Treas., '52–'56; Indpls. Chptr. Outstanding Wm. in Educ., '56), Delta Kappa Gamma (State Corr. Secy., '56–'58), Adm. Wm. in Educ., Ind. Sch. Wm.; Ind. Univ., AB, '26 (with distinction); Phi Beta Kappa); MA, '31; Univ. of Chgo., '38–'42; b. Amboy, Ind., 1898; p. Theodore and Olive Resler Pearson; h. Russell S. Parks; res: 6246 N. Olney St., Indpls., Ind. 46220.

PEARSON, SANDRA NEEDHAM, Project Dir., The Commercial Analysts Company, 211 E. 43rd St., N.Y., N.Y. 10017, '70–; Asst. Product Mgr., Corn Products, '66–'68; Rsch. Analyst, '64–'66; Syracuse Univ., BA, '60; h. Robert Pearson; res: 430 Warburton Ave., Yonkers, N.Y. 10701.

PECK, HELEN ESTELLE, Auth., children's books; Tchr.; Delta Kappa Gamma (Pres.); Boston Univ., BS, '36; b. Hamden, Conn., 1910; p. Gilbert and Mary Penn Peck; res: 3 Francisco Dr., Santa Barbara, Cal. 93105.

PEDEN, CAROL (Laura), Ed., Teen Gazette, The Phoenix Gazette, 120 E. Van Buren, Phoenix, Ariz., '67–; Edtl. Dept., Ind. Univ. Press, '65–'66; DePauw Univ., '61–'63; Ind. Univ., AB (Eng.), '65 (Phi Beta Kappa); Grad. work, Univ of Ariz., '66; b. Bloomington, Ind., 1943; p. Richard and Rachel Mason Peden; h. Paul J. Schatt, res: 5250 N. 20th St., Apt 209, Phoenix, Ariz. 85016.

PEDEN, MARIE McKINNEY, Wms. Ed., Greenville Piedmont, Box 1688, S. Main St., Greenville, S.C. 29602, '58–; Asst. Wms. Ed., '55–'58; Substitute Tchr., Greenville City Schs., '53–'54; Bookkeeper, Ivey's and Cabiniss Gardner, '34–'42; Local USO Volunteer Corps; S.C. Press Assn. (Wms. Div. Bd. of Dirs., '68–'70), ZONTA (Charter Mbr.), Greenville Wms. Club (Charter Mbr.), Wm. in C. of C. (Charter Mbr.); State aws. in field, '60–'68; Nswp. Wm. of the Yr., '60, '67; Greenville BPW Career Wm. of Yr., '63; Nat. Fedn. of Music Clubs Special Aw., '64, '67, '69; Salvation Army Commty. Svc. Aw., '65; Greenville Gen. Hosp. Commty. Svc. Aw., '67; Brenau Col., BA, '32; b. Greenville, S.C., 1912; p. Marvin Ansel and Lillie Barton McKinney; h. Ralph Hutchings Peden; c. Patricia Elaine, Ralph H., Jr.; res: 18 Tomassee Ave., Greenville, S.C. 29605.

PEDERSEN, ELSA KIENITZ, Auth., bks. for young people, incl. 12 fiction (Abingdon Press, Atheneum Publrs., Ives Washburn, Inc.), one textbk. (Coward McCann, Inc.); Colmst., Anchorage Daily Times; Off. Mgr., Wakefield Fisheries (Seldovia, Alaska), '63–'68; Bkkeeper, Seldovia Bay Packing Co., '52–'63; The Alaska Sportsman, '43; Auths. Guild, Alaska Press Wm.; "Cook Inlet Decision" on N.Y. Times list of 100 Best juv. bks., '63; "Fisherman's Choice" and "House Upon A Rock", Jr. Lit. Guild Selections '68; Latter Day Saints Col., '35; b. Salt Lake City, Ut., 1915; p. William and Else Stark Kienitz; h. Theodore Pedersen; res: Bear Cove, Box 113, Homer, Alaska 99603.

PEELER, ELIZABETH HASTINGS, Assoc. Dir. for Tech. Svcs., University of West Florida Library, Pensacola, Fla. 32504, '67–; Head, Catalog Dept., State Univ. of N.Y. (Stony Brook), '65–'67; Chief, Catalog Sec., UN Lib. (N.Y.C.), '64–'65; Sr. Lectr., Inst. of Librarianship (Ibadan, Nigeria), '60–'64; Head, Catalog Dept., Univ. of Miami (Fla.), '46–'60; Cataloger, Agnes Scott Col., '44–'46; Cataloger, Birmingham-Southern Col., '42–'44; Asst. to Acting Librn., Southwestern At Memphis, '39–'42; Ed., "Florida Libraries" ('59–'60); Fla. Lib. Assn. (Pres., '55–'56), Southeastern Lib. Assn., ALA; Vanderbilt Univ., BA, '35; MA, '36; Emory Univ., BA (Lib. Sci.), '39; Columbia Univ., MS (Lib. Sci.), '50; b. Nashville, Tenn., 1914; p. John and Luna Hastings Peeler; res: B3 English Cove Apts., Gulf Breeze, Fla. 32561.

PEELLE, VERA C., Publr. and Owner, National Road Traveler, Printers and Publishers Newspaper, 51 E. Church St., Cambridge City, Ind. 47327, '61–; Co-Publr. with husband, '36–'61; b. Frankfort, Ind.; p. Abner and Ella Campbell; h. Omar S. Peelle (dec.); res: 402 S.W. Third St., Cambridge City, Ind. 47327.

PEEPLES, BARBARA CAPLES, PR Dir., Emanuel Hospital, Portland, Ore., '69–; Owner, Barbara C. Peeples, Public Relations Counsel, '64–'69; AE, Goodrich and Snyder, '60–'64; Adm. Asst., PR, Instr., Longview Public Sch., '57–'60; Reptr., Camas Post-Record, '50–'51; AE, Milt Bona and Assoc., '49; Freelance PR: Polit., indsl., comml. and commty. orgs.; articles for specialized pubns.; Theta Sigma Phi (Portland Chptr. Pres. '66–'67; Univ. of Wash. Chptr., VP, '48); Ore. Nwsp. Publrs. Assn., PR Roundtable, PR Org. Portland Hosps.; Univ. of Wash., BA, '49; b. Vancouver, Wash., 1927; p. D. Elwood and Martha Glass Caples; h. (div.); c. Douglas Laurence, Lizbeth Stephanie; res: 8175 S.W. Fairway Dr., Portland, Ore. 97225.

PEERSON, ETHEL, Dir., Muscle Shoals Regional Library, 218 N. Wood Ave., Florence, Ala. 35630, '57–; Cnslt., Ala. Public Lib. Svc. (Montgomery, Ala.), '57–'58; Dir., Flint River Reg. Lib. (Griffin, Ga.), '51–'57; Ref., Adult Svcs., Kingsport (Tenn.) Public Lib., '47–'50; Librn., TVA Lib. (Wilson Dam, Ala.), '42–'47; Hish Sch. Librn., '35–'41; Exec. Dir., Nat. Lib. week for Ala., one yr.; Adult Educ. Assn. of the U.S.,

Film Cncl. of Am., Literacy Cncl.; various other orgs.; Florence State Col., '25; Athens Col., '27–'28; Radford Col., BS, '34; Emory Univ., (Lib. Sci.), '35; b. Florence, Ala., 1906; p. James and Sarah Darby Peerson; res: 217 E. Irvine Ave., Florence, Ala. 35630.

PEET, LOUISE JENISON, Prof., Family Environment Department, Iowa State University, Ames, Ia. 50010, '30–; Auth.: "Young Homemakers' Equipment Guide" ('67); Co-Auth.: "Household Equipment"; Am. Home Econ. Assn., Phi Sigma Phi, Sigma Xi, Omicron Nu, Wellesley Col., BA, '08 (Phi Beta Kappa; Mortar Bd.); MA, '11; Iowa State Univ., PhD, '29; b. Cambridge, Mass., 1885; p. Frank and Jean Mac-Quarrie Jenison; h. William Peet; c. William, Jr.; res: 2833 Ross Rd., Ames, Ia. 50010.

PELKEY, CAROLYN CONSTANT, Media Dir., Karcher Advertising Agency, 1017 Camden St., San Antonio, Tex. 78215, '68–; Cont. Dir., KONO and KITY-FM Radio, '67; Traf. Dir., Public Svc. Dir., '66; Traf. Dir., '65; public svc. projects for hosps. and veterans; AWRT (San Antonio Chptr. Secy., '68–); active in youth affairs; Ill. State Normal Tchrs. Col. (scholarship); b. Decatur, Ill.; h. Francis Pelkey; c. James L., Michael D., Diane L., Daniel C., Valerie G.; res: 8007 Latigo, San Antonio, Tex. 78227.

PELLATON, JACQUELINE, Feature Wtr., Trenton Times Newspapers, 500 Perry St., Trenton, N.J., '62–; Reptr. and Deskman, Geneva (N.Y.) Times, '59–'62; Edtl. Rschr., Time, '48–'54; Free-lance PR; N.J. Daily Nwspwms. 1st prize for layout, '68; Mt. Holyoke Col., BA, '48; Columbia Univ. Am. Press Inst. seminary, '67; b. Paris, France; h. div.; c. Roger Imre Pellaton and Nicole C. Pellaton; res: 37 Maple St., Princeton, N.J.

PELLEGRINO, VICTORIA YURASITS, Articles Ed., Pageant Magazine, 205 E. 42nd St., N.Y., N.Y. 10017, '68–; Wtr.-Ed., Civic Educ. Svc. (Wash., D.C.), '66–'68; Free-lance Wtr., med. stories and interviews; Am. Optometric Assn. writing aw., '68; Am. Univ. Sch. of Intl. Svc., BA, '66; b. N.Y.C., 1944; p. Steven F. and Elsie Schmitt Yurasits; res: 30 East End Ave., N.Y., N.Y. 10028.

PELTZ, MARY OPDYCKE, Archivist, Metropolitan Opera Association, Lincoln Center, N.Y., N.Y. 10023, '57–; Ed., Opera News, '36–'57; Asst. Music Critic, N.Y. Evening Sun, '20–'24; Chmn., In-Svc. Course, and Speakers Bur., Met. Opera Guild; Barnard Col., '16–'20; b. N.Y.C., 1896; p. Leonard and Edith Bell Opdycke; h. John DeWitt Peltz; c. John D., Mary Ellis Nevius, Henry S.; res: 169 E. 78th St., New York, N.Y. 10021.

PELUSO, CAROL ANN, Off. Mgr., KJOE, 526 Lane Bldg., 610 Marshall St., Shreveport, La. 71101, '68–; Traf. Mgr., '65–'68; U.S. Air Force, '59–'62; b. Auburn, N.Y., '41; p. Joseph and Georgianna Wood Peluso Sr.; res: 2143 Portland Ave., Shreveport, La. 71103.

PELUSO, PAULINE SMITH, Colmst., Valley Publications, 17025 Ventura Blvd., Sherman Oaks, Cal. 91403, '68–; Talent Agt., Dorothy Shreve Agcy., '66–; Wtr., mag. articles; Pubcty. Dept., Columbia Pictures (Hollywood, Cal.), '46; Continuity Wtr., KGNC Radio (Amarillo, Tex.), '44; Screen Actors Guild; Amarillo Bus. Col.; L.A. City Col., '50; b. Amarillo, Tex., '25; p. Jack and Eurapha Williams Smith; h. Walter Peluso; c. Andrew, Joy (Mrs. Mader), Cynthia; res: 10435 Haskell, Granada Hills, Cal. 91344.

PEMBERTON, MARGARET MILLER, Wms. Ed., Feature Wtr., Ashland Times-Gazette, Ashland Publishing Company, 46 E. Second St., Ashland, Oh. 44805, '66–; Oh. Nwsp. Wms. Assn. (aws., '67–'69); Univ. of Cinn.; b. Fort Recovery, Oh., '27; p. Earl and Anna Warnock Miller; h. Ray F. Pemberton; c. Steve R., Barbara Lee; res: 629 Bruce Ave., Ashland, Oh. 44805.

PENDERGAST, MAE BELLE LeMASTER, Wms. Ed., The Sacramento Union, 301 Capitol Mall, Sacramento, Cal. 95812, '57–; '48–'51, '40–'44; Soc. Reptr., '37–'40; Wms. Ed., KCCC-TV, '53–'55; Cal. Press Wm., NPWC, Sacramento Press Club, Cal. Congress of Parents and Tchrs. (Hon. Mbr.); Jr. Museum Guild (First Pres.), Mercy Children's Hosp. Guild (Charter Mbr.); Cal. Nwsp. Publrs. Assn. best wms. page, '49, '51, '68; Reed & Barton aw., '68; Penney-Missouri Aw., '69; Stanford Univ., '36, '37; b. Fresno, Cal., 1918; p. Charles and Gertrude Floydstead LeMaster; h. Bernard Patrick Pendergast; c. Mrs. Dale William Mahon, Mrs. Gary Lee Wilson; res: 2272 Tenth Ave., Sacramento, Cal. 95818.

PENDLETON, NANCY GRAHAM, Reptr., Ed. Asst., Tri-Village Publishing Co., 1302 Grandview Ave., Columbus, Oh. 43212, '64–; Reptr., Photogr., Copy Ed., Hartley Nwsps., '59–'60; Cont. Ed., WOSU-Radio, '55–'57; originated, wrote script, talent, on two shows, "Leisure-Time Previews" and "Time for Fun," WOSU-Radio; Theta Sigma Phi (2nd VP, '60–'61); Oh. State Univ., BA (Jnlsm.), '55; h. Dean Pendleton.

PENMAN, RUTH H., Employee Dev. Mgr., Fisher-Price Toys, Inc., 606 Girard Ave., E. Aurora, N.Y. 14052, '67–; Pers. Dir., '50–'67; AAIE, Indsl. Rels. Assn. of Buffalo (Treas., '67, Secy., '66); BPW, Who's Who of Am. Wm.; Univ. of Buffalo, BA, '34; Millard Fillmore Col., Univ. of Colo.; b. Avalon, Pa., 1913; p. James and Ethel Weller Penman; res: 97 Hirschfield Dr., Buffalo, N.Y. 14221.

PENNELL, RUTH HOWARD, Wtr., Prodr., KUDO, 760 Harrison St., S.F., Cal. 94107, '69–; Wtr., Dir., Prodr., Host, "United Nations' Story," 8 yrs. on air; Kaiser Industries (Oakland), '55–'62; UNICEF (N.Y.C.), '54; Univ. of Cal., 15 yrs.; UN Ctr. (Alameda County Bd. of Dirs.), 10 yrs.; AWRT; Who's Who of Am. Wm.; Who's Who in the West; Berkeley Wms. City Club UNICEF Aw., '60; b. S.F., Cal., 1903; p. Luther D. and Laura Mathis Howard; h. Frank Pennell (dec.); c. Donn, Robert Howard; res: 2730 Buena Vista Way, Berkeley, Cal. 94708.

PENNEY, ALEXANDRA DRACOS, Beauty Ed., Glamour Magazine, Conde Nast Publications, 420 Lexington Ave., N.Y., N.Y., '68–; Copywtr. and Fashion Prom., Vogue; Adv. and Pubcty., Part-time Byr., Bonwit Teller; Copywtr., Simplicity Patterns; Col. Bd., Lord & Taylor; Fashion Group; Smith Col., BA; b. Boston, Mass., 1940; p. Harry and Helen Dore Dracos; h. Richard Penney; c. John B.; res: 50 E. 72nd St., New York, N.Y.

PENNEY, ANNETTE CULLER, Jnlst., Int. Design Cnslt.; Auth., "Dirksen, the Golden Voice of the Senate" (Acropolis Press, '68); Dir. of Press Info. and Pers., Steadman Security Corporation, 1730 K St., N.W., Suite 904, Wash., D.C. 20006, '67–; Press Aide to Dir. of Public Housing Admin., '64–'66; free lance PR, '61–'64; Reptr., Fairchild Pubns., '46–'61; numerous nwsp., mag. articles; contrbr. to "This Generation" colm., Chgo. Tribune and N.Y. News Synd.; HLF (Wash., D.C. Chptr. Pres., '51–'52), WNPC (VP, '57–'58), ANWC, Va. Press Wm., Intl. Platform Assn.; S. Ga. Col. (Bus. Adm.); American Univ. (liberal arts), George Washington Univ.; b. Cordele, Ga., 1916; h. Robert Adam Penney; res: 1320 Pine Tree Rd., McLean, Va. 22101.

PENNIMAN, GWENDOLEN BROOKS, Colmst., Saratoga News, Saratoga, Cal., '56–; Drama Dir., Playwright, '25–; Auth: "Goona-Goona" ('50), "Poems of Japan" ('65); Ed: "Winged Pegasus" ('65); "A Day at Montalvo" ('64); NLAPW (Santa Clara Br. Poetry Sec. Chmn., '56–'57), AAUW, Quadrennial Contests in The Arts (Founder, '56; Nat. Secy.); Hon. MHD, Free Univ. of Asia, '68; Phillipine Republic Gold Laurel Wreath, '68; Academia Internationale Gold Medal, '67; San Jose State Col., AB (Speech), '44; AB (Eng.), '50; Grad. Work, Stanford Univ., '47; b. Lincoln, Neb.; p. Harrington and Florence Brooks Emerson; c. Beatrice Penniman Frazier, Arthur; res: 22100 Mt. Eden Rd., Saratoga, Cal. 25070.

PENNINGTON, EUNICE RANDOLPH, Reg. Librn., Current River Regional Library System, Van Buren, Mo. 63965, '63–; Auth: "Ozark National Scenic Riverways" ('67), "Perry the Pet Pig" ('66), others; ALA, Mo. Lib. Assn.; Ark. State Univ., BS, '62; Peabody Lib. Sch., MS (Lib. Sci.), '67; b. Fremont, Mo., 1923; p. Charley and Hattie Pritchard Randolph; h. Daniel Douglas Pennington; c. Mary Anna (Mrs. Kenneth McDowell), Albert Joe; res: Fremont, Mo. 63941.

PENSON, BETTY BUTLER, Travel, Wms. Ed., Idaho Statesman Newspapers, Bannock at Sixth St., Boise, Idaho 83701, '48–; Wms. Ed., '37–'43; overseas travel, govt. rsch. projects, '56–; Continuity Dir., KVMV (Twin Falls, Idaho), '43–'46; Wms. Ed., The Seattle (Wash.) Times, '46–'47; Wms. Ed., The Boise Capital News, '34–'37; Theta Sigma Phi (Boise Chptr. Pres., '60), Idaho Press Club (Pres., '64), Idaho Press Wm., Soc. of Am. Travel Wtrs., hist. orgs.; NFPW nat. aws.; b. Boise, Idaho, '14; p. H. B. and Maybelle Tingley Butler; h. George Penson (dec.); c. Mrs. Brock

O'Leary, Kelly C. Matthews; res: 1014 N. 18th, Boise, Idaho 83702.

PENTLAND, MARY ELLEN, Pres., Pentland Gift Sources, Inc., 225 Fifth Ave., N.Y., N.Y. 10010, '66–; Pentland Assocs., '45–'66; Rsch. Assoc., Can Manufacturers Inst., '43–'45; VP, Amos Parrish Agcy., '41–'43; Nat. Wms. Dir., Finnish Relief Fund, '40–'41 (decorated by Finnish Govt., '40); Asst. to Publr., Parents Magazine, '39–'40; Lectr., '38–'39; Head, Pentland Advertising Agcy., Portland, Ore. and Seattle, Wash., '31–'37; Pentland News Bur., '31–'36; Adv. Mgr., PR Dir., First Nat. Bank of Portland, '30–'31; AE, Botsford, Constantine and Gardner, '29–'30; Wtr., KJR, Seattle, '27–'29; Ed., Wms. Pg. Feature, Seattle Spokesman Review, other nwsps., '25–'27; Am. Mktg. Assn., AWRT, Comm. of Wm. in PR, Gift and Decorative Accessories Assn., NHFL, Theta Sigma Phi, Kappa Kappa Gamma; First Nat. Josephine Snapp Trophy, '37; Portland Adv. Club Special Achiev. Aw., '33; Allied Linens and Domestics Assn. display aws., '53–'54; Northwestern Univ., BS (Jnlsm., Drama, Mktg.); b. Newberry, Mich.; p. William and Margaret Davidson Pentland; h. John Sutton (div.); res: 330 Third Ave., N.Y., N.Y. 10010.

PEREIRA, Dr. I. RICE, Artist, Poet., Auth.; more than 70 one-man. exhbns., incl. London, Rome, Barcelona, Paris, Berlin, Venice, Tokyo; paintings owned by more than 100 museums; Wtr., philosophy of space, optics, light, and related subjects; Bks: "The Poetics of the Form of Space, Light and the Infinite" ('69), "The Finite Versus the Infinite" ('62), numerous others; Un. Poets Laureate Intl. (Hon. Philosopher Poet Laureate, '69), Centro Studi and Scambi Intl. (Rome), Intl. Platform Assn., Mark Twain Soc., James Joyce Soc.; Hon. PhD, L'Univ. Libre (Asie) and Intl. Fedn. of Rsch. Socs. of Europe, Asia, Africa, '69; Greatness and Leadership Aw., UN Day, Philippines, '68; b. Boston, Mass.; p. Emanuel and Hilda Vanderbilt Rice; res: 121 W. 15th St., N.Y., N.Y. 10011.

PERKINS, LALLA HALL, Adv. Mgr., Frederick Daily Leader, 304–06 W. Grand, Frederick, Okla. 73542, '68–; Reptr., City Ed., News Ed., Adv. Mgr., 20 yrs.; UP Intl. Bur. (Okla. City), '44–'45; News Dept., Radio KOMA; Frederick Jr. Col., '41–'42; Southwestern State (Okla.); b. Frederick, Okla., 1923; p. Thomas and Lorena Cotton Hall; h. Robert Perkins; c. Robert L., Jr., Merry Helen (Mrs. Lawrence B. Nulty), Merrle Holly; res: 911 S. Twelfth St., Frederick, Okla. 73542.

PERKINS, NORMA JEAN SULLIVAN, Free-lance Ch. Sch., Curriculum Wtr., '55–; Ed., Children's Story Papers and Fellowship Hour Materials, The Evangelical United Brethren Ch. Bd. of Pubn., The Otterbein Press, '58–'65; Asst. in Christian Educ., Bound Brook, N.J. Presbyterian Ch., '56–'57; Tchr., Ft. Wayne, Hoagland, Ind., '52–'55; Ed., The Spokesman, Fern Hill United Methodist Ch., Tacoma, Wash., '69–'70; McChord Air Force Base NCO Wives Club news reptr. for local nwsps., '69–'70; Who's Who of Am. Wm.,

Dic. of Intl. Biog.; Ind. Univ., '48–'50 (Dean's Hon. Roll); Manchester Col., BS, '52; Princeton Theological Seminary, MRE (Prin.), '58; b. Ft. Wayne, Ind., 1930; p. John L. and Lottie May Martin Sullivan; h. Laurence G. Perkins; c. Marjorie Marie, Laurena Linda; res: 1515 Crescent Ave., Ft. Wayne, Ind. 46805.

PERKINSON, GRACE ELEANOR, PR Offcr., The Free Library of Philadelphia, Logan Sq., Phila., Pa. 19103, '67–; PR Cnslt., World Affairs Cncl. of Phila., '67; Nat. Info. Secy., Am. Friends Svc. Comm., '62–'65; Info. Wtr., '57–'61; Philosophy Instr., Mount Holyoke Col., '47–'51; educ: Mount Holyoke Col., BA (Philosophy), '47 (with honors; Mary E. Woolley Fellowship); Oxford Univ. Fulbright Scholar, '51–'52; Univ. of Pa., MA (Commtns.), '67 (NBC Scholarship); b. Phila., Pa., 1923; p. Boyd and Mary McMichael Perkinson; res: 408 E. Gravers Lane, Phila., Pa. 19118.

PERL, ELLEN FREU, Owner, Ellen-Perl Publicity and Public Relations, 405 E. 63rd St., N.Y., N.Y. 10021, '58–; Fashion Coordr. for weekly fashions shows, Barbetta Restaurant; N.Y. Pubcty. Club; N.Y.U., New Sch. for Social Rsch.; b. Stuttgart, Germany; p. Richard and Meta Freu; h. Lothar Perl.

PERMAR, ELISE JOHNS, Wms. Page Ed., Brunswick Daily News, Newcastle St., Brunswick, Ga., '66–; Co-ed., Wms. World Shopping Svc., '69–; Reptr., Fairchild's Pubns. Inc. (N.Y.C.), '63–'68; Free-lance Wtr., fiction and non-fiction in many minor mkts.; Dixie Cncl. of Auths. and Jnlsts., Brunswick Press Club; New Paltz State Tchrs. Col., '34–'37; N.Y.U., '38; Univ. of S. Miss., '54; b. N.Y.C.; p. Victor and Elise Perron Johns; h. Edward Permar; c. Mrs. Harold Hubbard, Andrew J., Matthew J.; res: 520 Wesley Oaks Circle, St. Simons Island, Ga. 31522.

PERPICH, MARY JANE, Youth Beat Ed., The State Journal, 120 E. Lenewee St., Lansing, Mich. 48933, '65–; Lansing Commty. Col.; Mich. State Univ.; b. Marshall, Tex., '44; p. Joseph B. and Flora Mae Perpich; res: 2817 Harwick Dr., Lansing, Mich. 48917.

PERRIN, GAIL, Wms. Ed., Boston Globe, 135 Morrissey Blvd., Boston, Mass. 02107, '65–; Gen. Assigt. Reptr., '65; Reptr., Washington Daily News, '60–'65; Reptr., Honolulu Star Bulletin, '59; WNPC; Wellesley Col., BA, '60; b. Boston, Mass., '38; p. Hugh and Helen Baxter Perrin; res: 245 Commonwealth Ave., Boston, Mass. 02116.

PERRY, BARBARA, Actress; Owner, Perry's Studios of the Theatre, 6757 Hollywood Blvd., Hollywood, Cal. 90028; star, Palace Theatre, '52; Palladium and Hippodrome, London; Broadway prods.; numerous live TV credits; 21 filmed TV shows; four motion pics.; seven W. Coast stage shows; stock; SAG, AFTRA, AEA; Royal Acad. of Dramatic Art, London (RADA Aw.); b. Norfolk, Va., 1924; p. Wm. and Victoria Gates Perry; h. Arthur Babbitt; c. Laurel Lee James; res: 6926 La Presa Dr., Outpost Estates, Hollywood, Cal. 90028.

PERRY, JEAN WEAVER, Reptr., Educ. Wtr., Meridian Star, 814 22nd Ave., Meridian, Miss., '63–; Reptr., Drama, Music Critic, Lorain (Oh.) Journal, '37–'60; Miss. Press Wm. (Secy., '68), EWA, Oh. Nwsp. Wm's. Assn. (VP, '58–'60; Secy.); numerous writing aws.; b. Lorain, Oh., 1918; p. Floyd and Nellie Clements Weaver; h. Cecil B. Perry; res: 2925 15th Pl., Meridian, Miss. 39301.

PERRY, JOAN PONDER, Adm. Exec., Frank M. Taylor, Advertising, 716 S. 37th St., Birmingham, Ala. 35222, '65–; Media Dir., '62–'65; Exec. Secy. to Pres., Royal Cup, Inc., '58–'61; AWRT (Ala. Chptr. Dir., '69–'70; Pres., '67–'69; Am. Red Cross (Public Info. Comm.); b. Birmingham, Ala., 1941; p. Hubert and Sybil York Ponder; h. Curtis Perry; c. Michael, Christine; res: 909 Reedwood Lane, Birmingham, Ala. 35235.

PERRY, M. JEANNETTE HOCUTT, Secy.-Treas., Specialized Agricultural Publications, Inc., 600 Capital Club Bldg., Raleigh, N.C. 27601, '64–; Zebulon Jr. Wms. Club; b. Raleigh, N.C., 1945; p. Earlie and Dorothy Davis Hocutt; h. Larry D. Perry; res: Rte. 4, Box 213-A, Zebulon, N.C. 27597.

PERRY, PENNIE ELLENE, Chief Librn., James E. Shepard Memorial Library, North Carolina Central University, Durham, N.C. 27707, '65–; Asst. Prof., Sch. of Lib. Sci., summers '64–'65; Visiting Prof., Fla. A.M. Univ., summers '56–'63; Librn., Second War H.S. (Charlotte, N.C.), '46–'65; Cnslt., workshop in Lib. Sci., S.C. State Col. (Orangeburg, S.C.), summers '59–'60; ALA, N.C. Lib. Assn., NEA, Shaw Univ., BS (Biology); Univ. of Mich., MS (Lib. Sci.), '57; Univ. of Chgo., PhD (Librnship.), '60–'61, '67–'68; b. Wendell, N.C.; p. Guyon and Eliza Jones Perry; res: 523 Nelson St., Durham, N.C.

PERRY, PORTIA, Dir., Public Info., Camden County Council on Economic Opportunity, Inc., 500 Broadway, Camden, N.J. 08103, '67–; Radio Anncr., Commentator, WCAM, '63–'67; WDAS, '59–'63; WHAT, '56–'59 (Achiev. Aw., '58); Dir. of PR, Camden Co. Highway Dept., '65–'66; Mng. Ed., N.J. Chronicle, '64–'65; Long Distance Telephone Operator, '52–'54; Case Worker, Phila. Dept. of Public Assistance, '49–'51; Field Inspector, U.S. Signal Corps, '45–'49; AWRT, BPW (Outstanding Achiev. Aw., '54), Nat. Media Wm. (local Pres.), Nat. Assn. of Mkt. Developers, NAACP (Freedom Fund Comm. Aw., '62), Prison Svc. Comm. of S. Jersey; Richard Taylor Aw. for Commty. Svc. and Vocal Artistry; Am. Heart Assn. Cert. of Merit, '61; numerous other aws.; Morgan State Col., BA (Psych./Sociol.); Additional Study, Temple Univ.; D.D., Phila. Theological Seminary, '58 (Hon.); b. Balt., Md., 1925; h. Calvin L. Dempsey; res: 1610 Park Blvd., Camden, N.J. 08003.

PERSONS, MADELYN, Owner, The Persons Company, national PR, 3205 Whittier St., San Diego, Cal. 92106.

PERSSON, ESTHER EKBERG, Editorial Consultants, 2000 40th St. N., St. Petersburg, Fla. 33713; Volunteer Ed., Pharos, Museum of Fine Arts; '63–; Free-lance Ed., various N.Y. publrs.; Ed., Tchrs. Col. Press, Columbia Univ., '58–'62; Ed., Twentieth Century Fund, '48–'53; Nat. Assn. of Bk. Eds.; Hunter Col., BA, '28; Columbia Univ., Grad Work; b. Lund, Sweden, 1907; p. Albin and Hanna Gibson Ekberg; h. L. Nathanael Persson; c. Lorens.

PESKIN, SHEILA PERLMAN, Ed., Shure Brothers, Inc., 222 Hartrey, Evanston, Ill. 60204, '66–; Adv. Girl Friday, Am. Photocopy Equipment Co., '64–'67; AAIE; Mich. State Univ., '53–'54; Northwestern Univ., '54–'55; U.C.L.A., '55–'56; Loyola Univ., '58–; b. Chgo., Ill., 1935; p. Morris and Florence Sherman Perlman; h. Gerald Peskin; c. Cheryl Ann, Marla, Mitchell; res: 1034 Antique Lane, Northbrook, Ill. 60062.

PESMEN, SANDRA ZUCKERMAN, Reptr., Chicago Daily News, 401 N. Wabash, Chgo., Ill., '69–; Reptr., Lerner Chgo. N. Side Nwsps., '61–'69; Reptr., Wayne (Mich.) Eagle, '58–'61; Reptr., Commty. News Svc., '52–'55; State of Ill. Golden Key Aw., '66; Nat. Edtl. Assn. feature writing aw., '67; Univ. of Ill. (BS (Jnlsm.), '52; b. Chgo., Ill.; p. Benjamin and Emma Lipschultz Zuckerman; h. Harold Pesmen; c. Bethann, Curtis; res: 2811 Fern Ave., Northbrook, Ill.

PETAL, BEVERLY DOBRY, Fashion Publicist, Petal and Associates, 804 N. Whittier Dr., Beverly Hills, Cal. 90210, '68–; PR Dir., Comml. Carpet Co., '57–'67; Fashion Cnslt.; AWRT; Univ. of Wash.; b. Tacoma, Wash., 1933; p. Leo and Jean Samuelson Dubry; h. Lawrence Petal; c. Erica; res: 804 N. Whittier Dr., Beverly Hills, Cal. 90210.

PETER, LILY, Auth., poetry bks: "The Green Linen of Summer" ('64), "The Great Riding" ('66; Kenneth Beaudoin Gemstone Aw.; First Aw., Poetry Soc. of Okla.); poems and articles on hist. and music in nat. mags.; poetry readings, lects. at numerous cols., univs., writing groups; Chmn. of Music, Ark. Territorial Sesquicentennial Comm., '69; Ark. Arts Ctr. (Bd. of Dirs.), Moravian Music Fndn. (Hon. Trustee); active in DAR, numerous other commty., cultural, farming orgs.; Moramus Aw., Friends of Moravian Music, '64; Hon. Dr. of Humane Ltrs., Moravian Col., '65; Memphis State Univ., BS; Vanderbilt Univ., MA (Distg. Alumni Aw., '64); Music Study, Chgo. Musical Col., Juilliard Inst. of Musical Art, Columbia Univ.; b. near Marvell, Ark.; p. William and Florence Mobrey Peter; res: Marvell, Ark. 72366.

PETERS, JOAN ALLEN, Ext. Ed., Asst. Prof of Home Econs., Cooperative Extension Service, University of New Hampshire, Schofield House, Durham, N.H. 03824, '61–; Ext. Nutritionist, N.H. Coop. Ext. Svc., '60; Home Svc. Rep., Iroquois Gas Corp., '58; Home Econs. Instr., Univ. of Hi., '57; Ext. Nutritionist, Univ. of Del., '55–'56; Dietitian, Wernersville (Pa.) State Hosp., '54; Am. Home Econs. Assn., AWRT, Am. Assn.

of Agricultural Col. Eds., Omicron Nu; N.H. Fedn. of Wms. Clubs Public Svc. Aw., '64; Am. Home Laundry Manufacturer's Assn. Aw., '64; Acadia Univ., '53; Pa. State Univ., MS, '55; b. Amherst, Nova Scotia, Can., 1933; p. Kenneth and Dora Jones Allen; h. (div.); c. Karl; res: 62 Madbury Rd., Durham, N.H. 03824.

PETERS, LAURI, Actress, Repertory: Guthrie Theatre, '68–'69; Manitoba, '68; San Diego Shakespeare Festival, '66; Arena Stage, '65–'66; motion pics., "For Love of Ivy" and two others; five Broadway shows; TV parts; Daniel Blum Theatre World Aw., '59; Am. Sch. of Ballet (scholarship, '56); b. Detroit, Mich., 1943; p. Harold and Emily Caldwell Peterson; res: 345 Riverside Dr., N.Y., N.Y. 10025.

PETERS, MARY E., Br. Librn., Cleveland Public Library, 3706 W. 25th St., Cleve., Oh. 44109, '65–; Head, Children's Dept., Lima Public Lib., '58–'65; Cinn., Hamilton County Public Lib., '37–'57; ALA, Delta Kappa Gamma, Children's Lib. Assn. (Treas. '55–'56), Oh. Lib. Assn. Catholic Lib. Assn., WNBA; Col. of the Sacred Heart, BA, '33; Columbia Univ., BS (Lib. Sci.), '37; b. Cinn., Oh.; p. William and Ida Spence Peters.

PETERSEN, ALICE L., Food Ed., News Syndicate Co., Inc., 220 E. 42nd St., N.Y., N.Y. 10017, '53–; Co-auth: "The Sunday News Family Cook Book" ('62); Assoc. Food Ed., McCall's; Home Econs. Lectr., Bklyn. Union Gas Co.; Home Econs. in Bus., Am. Home Econs. Assn., NHFL; Delmarva Poultry Industry Cit., '58; Jersey Fruit Coop. Assn. Cit., '60; Col. of St. Catherine, BA, '27; b. Omaha, Neb.; p. Walter and Frederrika Paulsen Petersen; res: 75 Bank St., N.Y., N.Y. 10014.

PETERSEN, ELOISE WALTON, PR Cnslt., Community Research Associates, 124 E. 40th St., N.Y., N.Y. 10017, '67–; formerly AE, Persian Lamb Inst., Rogers and Cowan, Pennoyer Assocs.; PR Dir., Bergdorf-Goodman; Assoc. PR Dir., United Commty. Funds and Cncls.; PR Assoc., Nat. War Fund; Partner, Advertising Assocs., Indpls., Ind.; Dev. Dir., Nat. Travelers Aid Assn., Music Rsch. Fndn.; Owner, Eloise Walton Assocs.; Reptr., Wms. Pg. Ed., Indpls. Star and Indpls. Times; Feature Wtr., Portland (Me.) nwsps.; Auth: radio dramatizations, TV shorts, public affairs pamphlets; AWNY, AWRT, Fashion Group, Theta Sigma Phi; Ind. Univ. Ext.; b. Princeton, Ind., 1902; p. Charles and Agnes Grigsby Kimball; h. Harold G. Petersen; res: 301 E. 21st St., N.Y., N.Y. 10010.

PETERSEN, GAIL M., Crtv. Group Head, J. Walter Thompson Company, 410 N. Michigan Ave., Chgo., Ill. 60611, '68–; Copywtr., '67–'68; Copywtr., Edward H. Weiss Adv., '64–'67; Copywtr., Sears Roebuck and Co., '62–'64; Theta Sigma Phi (Northwestern Univ. Chptr. Secy., '61); Northwestern Univ., BS (Jnlsm.), '62; b. Fertile, Minn., 1940; p. Jerry and Norma Hendricks Petersen; res: 1360 N. Lake Shore Dr., Chgo., Ill. 60610.

PETERSEN, NANCY KAY WOODBRIDGE, Edtl. Wtr., Rschr., National Broadcasting Co., Burbank, 3000 W. Alameda Ave., Burbank, Cal. 91505, '69–; Pubcty., KFI Radio; PR Asst., Braille Inst.; Edtl. Asst., Popular Ceramics; Staff Wtr., Santa Monica (Cal.) Evening Outlook; Gtr. L.A. Press Club; San Diego State Col., BA (Jnlsm.), '65; b. L.A., Cal.; p. Cyril and Virginia Van Norden Woodbridge; h. Kenneth William Petersen; res: 4107 National Ave. Burbank, Cal. 91505.

PETERSON, ESTHER EGGERTSEN, Wash. Rep., Amalgamated Clothing Workers of America, 815 16th St. N.W., Wash., D.C. 20006, '69–; Legislative Rep., '45–'48; Asst. Dir. of Educ., '39–'44; Asst. Secy. of Labor for Labor Standards, '61–'69; Special Asst. to the Pres. for Consumer Affairs and Chmn. of the Pres., Comm. on Consumer Interests, '64–'67; Exec. Vice-Chmn., Pres. Commn. on the Status of Wm., '61–'63; Dir. of Wms. Bur., U.S. Dept. of Labor, '61–'64; Legislative Rep., Indsnl. Un. Dept., AFL-CIO, '58–'61; Lectr., Winsor Sch. (Boston, Mass.), '30–'36; Lectr., Bryn Mawr Summer Sch. of Wm. Workers in Industry, '32–'39; Wms. Nat. Democratic Club (Pres., '69–'70), Nat. Capital Democratic Club, AAUW, League of Wm. Voters, ANWC, Am. Home Econsts. Assn.; Brigham Young Univ., AB, '27; Columbia Tchrs. Col., MA, '30; b. Provo, Utah, '06; p. Lars E. and Annie Nielsen Eggertsen; h. Oliver A. Peterson; c. Karen (Mrs. Gene Wilken), Lars, Eric, Iver; res: 7714 13th St. N.W., Wash., D.C. 20012.

PETERSON, JULIA JENNIE, Asst. to Dir., Iowa Testing Programs, N101, E. Hall, University of Iowa, Ia. City, Ia.; Assoc. Ed.; Test Auth; Theta Sigma Phi, Univ. of Ia., BA, '32 (magna cum laude, Phi Beta Kappa); res: 1429 Yewell St., Ia. City, Ia. 52240.

PETERSON, MARY ANN CATHERINE, Ed., Montana-Dakota Utilities Co., 400 N. Fourth St., Bismarck, N.D. 58501, '64–; Theta Sigma Phi (Mpls. Chptr. VP, '67–'68; Secy., '65–'66), Northwestern IEA (Bd. of Dirs., '67–'68; Secy., '66–'67; 3rd pl. aw. for excellence in indsl. ed., '67), Bismarck BPW (Bismarck's Young Careerist, '69); Univ. of Minn., BA (Jnlsm.), '64; b. Mpls., Minn., 1942; p. Leonard and Marie Waselak Peterson; res: 1422 N. 22nd St., Bismarck, N.D. 58501.

PETERSON, MARY BURROWS, Public Svc. Dir., KTRK-TV, Capital Cities Broadcasting Corp., 3310 Bissonnet, Houston, Tex. 77005, '63–; Exec. Asst., '62–'63; b. Ranger, Tex., 1931; p. Arthur and Isabelle Allred Burrows; h. Marvin T. Peterson; res: 2226 Brooktree, Houston, Tex. 77008.

PETERSON, MILDRED OTHMER, Wtr., Lectr., Librn., Civic Leader; Ed., Book Marks, '29–'35; Wtr. for N. Ill., Drug Topics, Drug Trade News, others, '35; Bdcstr., wkly. bk. programs, Ia.; Colmst., Mid-West News Synd., Des Moines Register and Tribune, Chicago Tribune; Pan Am. Bd. of Educ. (Founder; Pres., '55–'58; Merit Aw., '66; Distg. Svc. Aw., '68), Hospital-ity Ctr. of Greater Chgo., for Fgn. Students and Visitors (Founder; Pres., '54–'58; Distg. Svc. Aw., '58); ALA, Ill. Lib. Assn., Alpha Delta Pi (Past Chptr. Pres.; Ed., Adelphean, '38–'39; Wm. of Yr. for U.S., Can., '55), Ia. Auths., numerous other commty., charitable, intl., travel orgs. and activities; decorated by Uruguay, '52; Cuba, Panama, '56; Cited by Chgo. Sun; numerous other hons., aws.; with husband, travelled and photographed in 115 countries; Univ. of Neb. (Distg. Svc. Medal, '63), Univ. of Ia., Univ. of Chgo. (Scholarship in Latin-Am. Field), Northwestern Univ.; b. Omaha, Neb., 1902; p. Frederick and Freda Snyder Othmer; h. Howard R. Peterson; res: Vista Homes, 5834 Stony Is. Ave., Chgo., Ill. 60637.

PETERSON, MIRIAM ELIZABETH, Dir., Division of Libraries, Chicago Public Schools, 228 N. La Salle St., Chgo., Ill. 60640, '55–; Princ., Elementary Schs., '50–'55; Supvsr., HS Libs., '48–'50; Tchr., Librn., '38–'48; Contrbr. to pfssnl. jnls.; Augustana Col., Rock Island, Ill., AB, '29 (Alumni Achiev. Aw., '63); Univ. of Chgo., BS (Lib. Sci.), '47; Northwestern Univ., MA, '37; MA, '46; PhD, '55 (Pi Lambda Theta, Beta Pi Mu); b. Chgo., Ill.; p. Carl and Hannah Johnson Peterson; res: 5422 Wayne Ave., Chgo., Ill. 60640.

PETERSON, MONICA D., Actress, c/o Wm. Morris Agcy., 151 El Camino Dr., c/o Wayne Weisbart, Beverly Hills, Cal.; Contract, 20th Century Fox Studios, Jeff Corey Studio, Look; performed in theatrical orgs. in Sweden, Finland, Italy, Eng., Spain ('63–'67) incl. three motion pics. "Escala in HiFi," "Gibraltar," "Roman Empire"; Special project, Vietnam; teaching guidance, underprivileged children; Actress Star of Tomorrow aw. ('68); three aws. of appreciation and bravery from Gen. Abramson in Saigon, '68, '69; Overseas Comm. aw., '69; Univ. of Southern Cal. (Sociol.); Univ. of Stockholm (Sweden); b. Loundoun County, Va., 1938; res: 1226 N. Laurel Ave., L.A., Cal. 90069.

PETERSON, VIVIAN ALICE, Head Librn., Midland Lutheran College, Fremont, Neb. 68025, '60–; Catalog Librn., Luther Col. (Decorah, Ia.), '52–'60; Serials Cataloger, Ia. State Univ. (Ames, Ia.), '49–'52; Tchr.-Librn., Minn. Public Schs., '41–'48; Auth., "An Audio-Visual Program in a Medical Sch. Lib." ('49); pubns. in pfssnl. periodicals; ALA, Neb. Lib. Assn. (Treas., '65–'67), various others; Augsburg Col., BA, '37–'41; Univ. of Denver, MA, '47–'49; Columbia Univ., '55, '68; b. Blooming Prairie, Minn., 1919; p. Hans and Alice Hansen Peterson; res: 1434 N. Platte, Fremont, Neb. 68025.

PETKOVSEK, MARIAN LORAINE, Public Info. Cnslt., Easter Seal Society for Crippled Children and Adults of California, 228 McAllister St., S.F., Cal. 94102, '63–; Staff Wtr., Ed., PR (Chgo., Ill., off.) '51–'63; Freelance Wtr., numerous articles in med., educ., reference and religious pubns.; Theta Sigma Phi; Univ. of Ia., BA (Jnlsm.), '51; b. Peoria, Ill., 1929; p. Andrew and Anna Herrick Petkovsek; res: 1765 Vallejo St., S.F., Cal. 94123.

PETRIE, YVONNE ELAINE, Fashion Ed., The Detroit News, 615 W. Lafayette, Detroit, Mich. 48231, '54–; Reptr., '53–; Reptr., Wms. Dept., The Hammond (Ind.) Times, '48–'53; Fashion Group, Theta Sigma Phi; state and nat. aws.; Who's Who of Am. Wm.; Univ. of Chgo., '46–'47; ext. courses, Ind. Univ., Univ. of Mich.; b. Hammond, Ind., 1927; p. Harold Francis and Elizabeth Margaret Nuttall Petrie; h. Charles L. Nevins; c. Noel Victoria, Charles Preston, II; res: 1353 Nicolet Pl., Detroit, Mich. 48207.

PETROSKY, GEORGIANNE KAY, PR Dir., Carnegie Library of Pittsburgh, 4400 Forbes Ave., Pitt., Pa. 15213, '68–; PR, Fund Raising Specialist, State Lib. PR Ctr. (Western Pa.), '66–'68; Radio, TV News Wtr., UP Bur. (Pitt.), '65; Assoc. Ed. of Pubns., H. J. Heinz Co., '64–'65; PR Cnslt., Musicians Club of Pitt.; Tutor, col. students from culturally disadvantaged areas; Auth.: "Library Public Relations Manual" ('67); Wms. Press Club of Pitt., Theta Sigma Phi (Treas., '68–'69; Histrn. '67), Kappa Tau Alpha, Pa. Lib. Assn., Westmoreland County Girl of Yr., '60, Who's Who in Outstanding Young Wm. of Am., Duquesne Univ., BA (Jnlsm., Eng.), '64 (Dean's List; Jnlsm. Internship aw.); b. Greensburg, Pa., 1942; p. George T. and Kathryn Messich Petrosky; res: 406 N. Neville St., Apt. #208, Pitt., Pa. 15213.

PETTEYS, ANNA FEDDERSEN, Publr., Sterling Journal-Advocate, 117 S. Third St., Sterling, Colo. 80751, '52–; Auth, "Doctor Portia" ('64); State Bd. of Educ. (Colo.), '50–'68; State Bd. of Trustees, Colo. State Cols., '42–'52; Phi Beta Kappa, Pi Lambda Theta, '43; Liberty Bell, '69, Colo. Educ. Assn. Aw., Nat. Assn. State Bds. of Educ. Aw., Alpha Delta Kappa, Theta Sigma Phi; Grinnell Col., BA, '12; Colo. State Col., MA, '43; b. Bryant, Ia., 1892; p. John and Julia Ingwersen Feddersen; c. Mrs. Helen Watrous, Mrs. Anna Mae Pattee, John Alden (dec.), Robert Alonzo; res: 112 Park, Sterling, Colo. 80751.

PFEIFFER, SARAH SHIELDS, Corr., Photo Weekly, 165 West 46th St., N.Y., N.Y. 10036; Lectr. on investments and on interviewing celebrities; Taught "Investing for Wm.," Emory Univ. (Atlanta, Ga.) night sch., '68; organized 24 wms. investment clubs (article by Time, Dec. 29, '58); Atlanta TV Show "Riches in Your Home," '52; wrote, appeared on "Womens Radio Jnl." '45–'47; Feature Wtr., Newton (Mass.) Graphic and Newton Villager; Reptr., Colmst., Asheville (N.C.) Citizen-Times, '30–'32; New Eng. Wms. Press Assn. (past Pres.; Life Mbr.); NLAPW (past Ga. State Pres.; past Atlanta Br. Pres.); Theta Sigma Phi; aws. from NLAPW, NFPW; Agnes Scott Col., BA; b. Dawson, Ga., 1906; p. John and Marie Cheatham Shields; h. John Pfeiffer; c. John, Jr., Peggy (Mrs. Robert E. Bass, Jr.); res: 3784 Vermont Rd., N.E., Atlanta, Ga. 30319.

PFENNIG, GLENADINE RUSSELL, Assoc. Ed., Wms. News, The Baytown Sun, P.O. Box 90, Baytown, Tex. 77520, '68–; Wtr., '67–; Public Info., Adj. General's Dept. (Austin), '65–'67; Copywtr., Scarbrough's Dept.

Store, '64; PR, Assoc. Enterprises, '63–'64; Wtr., articles in nwsps. and house organs; Theta Sigma Phi, Tex. Press Wm. (four 1st pl. aws., '68); Univ. of Tex., Austin, BJ (Jnlsm.), '64 (Tex. PR Assn. Scholarship, '64); b. Kilgore, Tex., 1942; p. Glenn and Nadine Bell Russell; h. Jon Pfennig; res: 510 William, Apt. 66, Baytown, Tex. 77520.

PHELAN, MARY KAY, Wtr., "Probing the Unknown" ('69), eight other juv. bks.; Free-lance Wtr., mags.; Copywtr., Marshall Field & Co., '37–'42; De Pauw Univ., AB, '35; Northwestern Univ., MA, '37; b. Baldwin City, Kan., 1914; p. Thomas and Adah Shafer Harris; h. Martin Phelan; c. Richard H., Jerry D.; res: 2524 Lorton Ave., Davenport, Ia. 52803.

PHELPS, FLORA LEWIS, Sr. Ed., Americas, Pan American Union, Wash., D.C. 20006, '63–; Assoc. Ed., '60–'63; Auth., numerous articles on archaeology, anthropology, art and educ.; Photogr.; Lectr. in Anthropology, Univ. Col. of Rutgers Univ., '54–'55; various orgs. and aws.; Bryn Mawr, AB (cum laude), '38; Columbia Univ., AM, '54; b. S.F., Cal., 1917; p. George Chase and Louise Manning Lewis; h. C. Russell Phelps; c. Andrew Russell, Carol Lewis, Gail Bransford.

PHELPS, JUDITH KAY, Feature Ed., Centralia Sentinel, 232 E. Broadway, Centralia, Ill. 62801, '63–; Reptr., Ill. State Register (Springfield); Reptr., Springfield Sun.

PHELPS, MARY ELLIOTT, Dir., Lexington Public Lib., 251 W. Second St., Lexington, Ky. 40507, '68–; Conducted TV and Radio Programs for Lib.; Asst. Dir. for Tech. Svcs., Lib. of State Univ. of N.Y. (Stony Brook), '68; Head of Acquisitions Dept., '65–'68; Head of Agriculture Lib., Univ. of Ky., '62–'65; Asst. Head of Acquisitions Dept., '59–'62; Guest Lectr. in Lib. Sci., Univ. of Ky.; ALA, Ky. Lib. Assn., Lexington Lib. Assoc., Friends of Ky. Libs.; Sweet Briar Col., '29–'31; Univ. of Ky., AB, '33; MS (Lib. Sci.), '59; b. Lexington, Ky., 1911; p. Nathan and Marie Powell Elliott; h. William Phelps; res: 432 W. Second St., Lexington, Ky. 40508.

PHELPS, NANCY ANN WEIDEMAN, Acc. Coordr., Andrews Advertising Inc., 2040 W. Wisconsin Ave., Milw., Wis. 53233, '67–; Adv. Dept., The New Yorker Magazine, '63–'64; AAUW, theatrical and cultural orgs.; Carroll Col., BA, '63; Univ. of Birmingham (Eng.), '61–'62; b. Waukesha, Wis., 1941; p. Gilbert and Ruth Alldredge Weideman; h. Richard Phelps; c. Lori Faye, Libby Lee; res: 10141 W. Forest Home Ave., Hales Corners, Wis. 53130.

PHELPS, WILMA AHRENS, Dir. Lib. Svcs., Phoenix College Library, 1202 W. Thomas Rd., Phoenix, Ariz. 85013, '58–; Asst. Librn., '35–'57; Circ., Phoenix Public Lib., '35; Self-employed, '32–'35; Head Cataloger, Maricopa County Free Lib., '29–'32; Assoc. Ed., "Bibliography for Junior College Libraries" ('68); ALA,

Ariz. Lib. Assn., Salt River Lib. Assn., Delta Kappa Gamma, Kappa Delta Pi, Phoenix Altrusa Club, Ariz. Pioneers Hist. Soc.; U.C.L.A., AB (Hist., Polit. Sci.), '28; Riverside Lib. Sch. Cert., '29; Ariz. State Univ., MA (Educ., Lib. Sci.), '58; Grad. Work, '66; Univ. of Ariz., Grad Work, '61; b. Ft. Smith, Ark., 1907; p. Charles and Elizabeth Snyder Ahrens; h. Arthur Lee Phelps; res: 7549 N. 16th Lane, Phoenix, Ariz. 85021.

PHILBRICK, ETHEL COMPTON, Ed., The Wyckoff News Corp., 629 Wyckoff Ave., Wyckoff, N.J. 07481; Assoc. Ed., Colmst., Reptr., Soc. Ed., Printer's Asst., 35 yrs.; b. Hohokus, N.J., 1917; p. Roy and May Vanderbeck Compton; b. Robert N. Philbrick; c. James, David; res: 232 Brookside Ave., Ridgewood, N.J. 07450.

PHILLIPS, BETH HEURING, Free-lance Wtr., currently assisting in prep. of bk. on Gen. Dwight D. Eisenhower; Tchr., Jr. HS, '43–'44; DePauw Univ., AB, '43 (Phi Beta Kappa); b. Freeport, Ill., 1922; p. Benjamin and Hortense Hale Heuring; h. Austin Phillips; c. Beth Anne; res: 596 Dryad Rd., Santa Monica, Cal. 90402.

PHILLIPS, EDITH CROWL, Asst. Prof., Wayne State University Department of Library Science, Detroit, Mich. 48202, '68–; Bk. Selection Coordr., Mich. State Lib., '65–'68; Head, Cataloging Sec., '62–'65; Sch. Librn., Grandville, '58–'62; Asst. Dir. and Cataloger, Kent County Lib., '53–'55; Sch. Librn., Chgo. Jewish Acad., Chgo., Ill., '61–'62; Staff Librn., Univ. of Mich. Gen. Lib., '45–'49; ALA, Mich. Lib. Assn., WNBA; Eastern Mich. Univ., BA, '42; Univ. of Mich., MA (Lib. Sci.), '49; h. Clarence A. Phillips.

PHILLIPS, ELEANORE ROBERTS, West Coast Ed., Vogue Magazine, 3921 Wilshire Blvd., L.A., Cal. 90005, '54–; Glamour, '48–'54; W. Coast Ed., Jr. Bazaar, '46–'48; W. Coast Fashion Ed., Look, '44–'46; Paramount Pics., '43–'44; Colleagues (Pres.), Liason between Fashion Group and L.A. County Museum of Art Costume and Textiles Dept., Hollywood Wms. Press Club, L.A. Adv. Wm.; Mt. Vernon Jr. Col.; b. 1910; p. Wesley and Ivy Gardner Roberts; h. Franklyn Phillips; c. Eleanore (Mrs. John Valianos), Frank, Jr.; res: 505 S. Irving Blvd., L.A., Cal. 90005.

PHILLIPS, ESTHER MOORE, Nwsp. Ed., PR Dir., Adv. Exec., Arcade Publications, 8630 St. Charles Rock Rd., St. Louis, Mo. 63114, '69–; Ed., '57–'60; Gen. Mgr., Donnelly Pubns., '68–'69; Ed., '60–'67; PR Offcr., Bank of St. Ann, '67–'68; Northwest BPW (VP, '68), Beta Sigma Phi (Xi Gamma Epsilon Chptr. Pres., '56, '63); White House Conf. on Educ., '63; Governor's Conf., '68; Sch. Bell Aw. nomination, '65–'67; Univ. of Ill., '43–'44; b. Kan. City, Mo., 1924; p. Thomas and Emma Heins Moore; h. Clyde Randol Phillips; c. David L., Ann E., Bethany J., Margaret S., Mrs. Kay Phillips Pretorius; res: 11029 St. Francis Lane, St. Ann, Mo. 63074.

PHILLIPS, FLORENCE McALLISTER, Free-lance Wtr.,

PR Cnslt.; Dir., Wms. News Dept., Carl Byoir & Assoc., '62–'64; Assoc. Dir., '51–'62; Mng. Ed., Haire Publ. Co., '47–'51; Ed., Bay Shore Sentinel and Islip Press, '42–'47; NHFL, Fashion Group, Catholic Inst. of the Press, Repl. Wm. in the Professions and Industry; Manhattanville Col., BA, '39; b. Bklyn., N.Y., 1918; p. Logan and Florence McAllister Phillips; res: 301 E. 22nd St., N.Y., N.Y. 10022.

PHILLIPS, JEAN BROWN, Dir., Jean Phillips Associates, PR, 360 W. 22nd St., N.Y. N.Y., '69–; Free-lance Wtr.; Circ. Prom. Mgr., Cowles Commtns., '68–'69; PR Mgr., Frank G. Shattuck Co., '64–'68; AE, Theodore Sills, Inc., '62–'64; Wms. News Dir., WTVT-TV (Tampa, Fla.), '59–'62; Copywtr., N.W. Ayer and Son (Phila., Pa.), '55–'58; OPC, PRSA, AWRT, AWNY, Am. Mgt. Assn., Am. Home Econs. Assn.; Who's Who of Am. Wm.; Drexel Inst., BS (Home Econs., Eng.); b. Phila., Pa.; p. T. Harold and Elizabeth Ulrich Brown; h. John Phillips; c. Barbara Jean; res: 360 W. 22nd St., N.Y., N.Y. 10011.

PHILLIPS, JEAN-RAE TURNER, Staff Wtr., Daily Journal, 295 N. Broad St., Elizabeth, N.J. 07207, '45–; PR, Nat. State Bank, '52; Tchr., Hillside HS, '42–'45; Reptr., Trenton Times, '42; Tchr., Jersey City State Col., '68; Am. Nwsp. Guild (N. Jersey Guild Secy., '68; Second VP, '69–'70), N.J. Daily Nwsp. Wm., (Treas. '68–'70), BPW, Photographic Soc. of Am.; numerous aws. for civic orgs.; Trenton State Col., BS (Educ.), '42; Tchs. Col., Columbia Univ., MA, '44; Newark State Col., '64–'67; New Sch. for Soc. Rsch., '68; b. Newark, N.J., 1922; p. William and Jessie MacRae Turner; h. N. S. Phillips; c. Margaret-Ann; res: 517 Madison Ave., Elizabeth, N.J. 07201.

PHILLIPS, JOSEPHINE FRYE, Auth: Supplementary Readers, "Wagons Away" (American Bk. Co., '41), "On the Airways" (Row, Peterson, '42), "Rufus Putnam" ('50); many children's stories, Rand McNally's Child Life, '26–'38; Free-lance non-fiction articles, hist. quarterlies; Owner-Mgr., Ft. Harmar Lib. Svc., Americana, '59–'67; Staff, Oh. Wtrs. Conf., '55, '56; Instr., Eng. Dept., Marietta Col., '52–'55, '60–'61; Wtr., home dept. features, Travelers Protective Assn. Magazine, '22–'26; Cnslt., owner of collection used by rschrs. on Revolutionary War, Critical Period and opening of Old Northwest to settlement; Nat. Wtrs. Club, Nat. Soc. of Arts and Letters, ZONTA; Marietta Col., AB, '34; Univ. of Conn., Grad. Sch. (Munson Inst. of Maritime Hist.), '62; b. Orange, Mass., 1896; p. George and Aurie Andrews Frye; h. Thomas D. Phillips (dec.); c. Gwyneth Josephine (Mrs. F. Howard Rexroad), Elizabeth (dec.), Marcia (Mrs. James Thornton, Jr., dec.), Mary (dec.); res: 228 Fifth St., Marietta, Oh. 45750.

PHILLIPS, MARGOT GOOCH, Owner, Margot Phillips Public Relations, 2422 Tracy Pl. N.W., Wash., D.C. 20008, '59–; Playreader, Nat. Bdcst. Co.; Adv. Copy Chief, Julius Garfinckel & Co.; Radio and TV Dir., Robert J. Enders Adv.; Free-lance Wtr., Bdcstr.;

AWRT, PRSA, Fund Raisers Soc. of Am.; Erskine Jr. Col.; b. Bronxville, N.Y., 1922; p. Joseph Low and Edith Albert Gooch; h. Jewett O. Phillips Jr.; c. Peter Gooch.

PHILLIPS, MARY ELIZABETH, Head Librn., Library Association of Portland, 801 S.W. 10th Ave., Portland, Ore. 97205, '64–; Chief Assoc. Librn., '60–'64; Acting Head Librn., '59–'60; Assoc. Librn., '53–'59; Head, Ext. Dept., '50–'53; Br. Librn., '37–'50; Gen. Asst., '31–'37; Lib. Cnslt., Ore. State Lib., '62; Auth., "Public Libraries in Oregon" ('62); Ore. Lib. Assn. (Pres., '48), Pacific N.W. Lib. Assn. (Pres., '67–'69), ALA (Cncl., '69–'71); Univ. of Ore., BA, '30; Univ. of Wash. Lib. Sch., BS (Lib. Sci.), '31; b. Portland, Ore., 1909; p. Richard and Katheryn Rodgers Phillips; res: 1414 N.E. Hancock St., Portland, Ore. 97212.

PHILLIPS, RUBY HART, Colmst. on Latin Am., 3020 S.W. 95 Ct., Miami, Fla. 33165, '63–'68; Auth: "The Cuban Dilemna" ('63), "Cuba: Island of Paradox" ('59); Corr., New York Times; Newsday; OPC; Inter-Am. Press Assn. Tom Wallace Aw., '69; h. James Doyle Phillips (dec.).

PHIPPS, SUZANNE WOODIN, Prod. Ed., Modern Bride Magazine, Ziff-Davis Pubns., 1 Park Ave., N.Y., N.Y. 10016, '67–'70; Gift and Boutique Ed.; Prod. Dir., New York Jr. League Magazine, '67–; Copy Ed., Factory Magazine, '66–'67; Prod. Ed.; Asst. Prod. Mgr., '65–'66; Asst. to Adv. Prod. Mgr., Electrical Construction and Electrical Wholesaling mags., '61–'62; Photogr., N.Y. Jr. League; Univ. of Miami; N.Y. School of Printing Industries, '67; b. Englewood, N.J., 1940; p. William Hamilton and Anne Miner Phipps; h. A. deForest Keys; res: 7 Rue Theodore de Bouville, Paris 17, France.

PHLEGER, MARJORIE TEMPLE, Auth., juv. fiction, "Pilot Down Presumed Dead" (Harper & Row); Co-auth: "You Will Live Under the Sea," "Off to the Races" (Random House); Nwsp. Colmst., La Jolla Light, '58–'62; Dir. of PR, La Valencia Hotel (La Jolla, Cal.), '58–'62; Drama Dir., The Bishop's Sch., '51–'57; Soc. Reptr., San Diego Union, '55–'59; Theatre Dir., Lectr.; Univ. of Southern Cal. BS, '29; Cal. Sec. Cred., '30; Smith Col., MA (Theatre), '48; b. Glendale, Cal., 1909; p. Charles and Flora Morrell Temple; h. Fred Phleger; c. Charles Frederick, Audrey Anne Phleger McElmury; res: 8593 La Jolla Shores Dr., La Jolla, Cal. 92037.

PHOENIX, ANNA LORRAINE, Bus. Coordr. J. Walter Thompson Company, 420 Lexington Ave., N.Y., N.Y. 10017, '68–; Screening Girl, '67; Bdcst. Coordr., '66; Secy. Asst., '64; Secy., '62; Berkley Secretarial Sch., '62; b. Hackensack, N.J., 1943; p. Charles and Camille Heard Phoenix; res: 247 Second St., Hackensack, N.J. 07601.

PICKEN, MARY BROOKS, Auth., Ed., Mary Brooks Picken Studio, Quaker Hill, Pawling, N.Y. 12564; Auth.

of 96 bks., sewing, tailoring, needlecraft; fashion dic.; 46 bks. for Wms' Inst., subsidiary of ICS (Scranton, Pa.); 32 bks., VP Dir. of Instr., Singer Co.; 10 bks. (Harper Row), two (Funk & Wagnalls), one (Chgo. Mail Order); educ. and writing, '11–; Fashion Ed., Pictorial Rev.; Fashion, Home Making Ed., Everywoman's Magazine; Advisor, Stephens Col. (Columbia, Mo.); Univ. of Pa.; Columbia Univ. (Tchr., Econs. of Fashion, Sch. of Bus.); Albion Col. (Albion, Mich.), LittD (Hon.); b. Arcadia, Kan., 1886; p. Christopher C. and Mattie E. Buchanan Brooks; h. G. Lynn Sumner (dec.); c. June Sumner Birdsong, George Warren Sumner.

PIÉ, VIRGINIA HUGHES, Dir., Commty. Rels., Baltimore Regional Red Cross, St. Paul and 23rd Sts., Balt., Md. 21218, '68–; Dir., Radio and TV, Eastern Area, Am. Red Cross; Public Info. Dir., Richmond, Va. Chptr.; Cont. Dir., WEZL Radio; Reptr., Richmond News Leader; Mid-Atlantic IEA (Bd. Mbr.), Md.-Del. Press Assn.; PRSA; Stratford Jr. Col.; Univ. of N.C.; b. Charlottesville, Va., 1935; p. Roy and Virginia Thomas Hughes; h. Robert S. Pié; c. Robert S., Jr.; res: 337 Paddington Rd., Balt., Md. 21212.

PIERCE, PONCHITTA, Special Corr., CBS News, 524 W. 57th St., N.Y., N.Y. 10019, '68–; N.Y. Edt. Bur Chief, Johnson Publ. Co., '67–'68; N.Y. Ed., Ebony, '67–'68; Assoc. Ed., '65–'67; Asst. Ed., '64–'65; Guest speaker at workshops, orgs.; Theta Sigma Phi, NATAS, AFTRA, N.Y. Urban League (John Russwurm Aw., '68), Governor Rockefeller's Comm. on Minority Groups in News Media; Wms. Jnlsm. Aw., J. C. Penney-Mo. Contest, '67; Who's Who of Am. Wm.; Pictorial Hist. of Negro in Am.; Univ. of Southern Cal., BA, '64 (cum laude); Cambridge Univ., '62; b. Chgo., Ill., 1942; p. Alfred and Nora Vincent Pierce; res: 780 Madison Ave., N.Y., N.Y. 10021.

PIERCE, TIMATHA STONE, Mgr., Adv. and Prom., WRC, 4001 Nebraska Ave., N.W., Wash., D.C. 20016, '64–; Asst. to Dir. of Info., WTOP, AWRT (D.C. Chptr. Pres., '69–'70), Adv. Club of Met. Wash. (Bdcst. Colmst., The Ad Clubber, '64–'69; many pubcty. offs.; Aw. of Excellence, '68), numerous orgs. and aws.; Mary Wash. Col., Univ. of Va., BA (Dramatic Arts and Speech), '62; b. Hartford, Conn., 1940; p. Franklin and Elizabeth Stone Pierce; res: 4813 N. 20th Pl. Arlington, Va. 22207.

PIERCY, JOSEPHINE KETCHAM, Prof. Emeritus and Auth. of books on lit. and lit. hist., Indiana University, Ballantine Hall, Bloomington, Ind. 47401, '66–; Prof., '64–'66; Assoc. Prof., '50–'64; Instr., '26–'40; Grad. Asst., Univ. of Ill., '22–'26; Theta Sigma Phi (Treas. currently; past Pres.), Nat. Soc. of Arts and Letters ('67), Modern Lang. Assn., AAUP; Ind. Univ., BA, '18; MA, '19 (Phi Beta Kappa); Columbia Univ., MA, '22, Yale Univ., Ph.D., '37; b. Indpls., Ind. 1895; p. Joseph William and Mary Ketcham; res: 708 Ballantine Rd., Bloomington, Ind. 47401.

PIERRE, DORATHI BOCK, Press and PR Dir., Bus.

Agt., Ed., Admr., '46–'69; Nat. Advance Agt. and Press Rep., Ballet Russe de Monte Carlo, S. Hurok Attractions, Am. Ballet Theatre, Nat. Phoenix Theatre, Royal Dramatic Theatre of Sweden, Columbia Artists Management, Hollywood Bowl, Nat. Repertory Theatre, and Am. tours of Comedie Francaise, The Old Vic Co., Royal Shakespeare Co.; Adm. Dir. of theatre school; Co-auth., "Only A Few Can Tell" ('44); Contrbr., World Bk. Ency.; Pi Epsilon Delta, Nat. Collegiate Players (Hon. Mbr.), Citizens Comm. of Dance Arts, Las Fiestas de Las Americas (Founding Mbr.; Bd. of Dirs., '41; Pres., '46–'49), ANTA, BPW, Intl. Platform Assn., Nat. Assn. for Music and Related Arts (Mbr. Advisory Bd., '43–'51), Opera Guild of Southern Cal., Nat. Collegiate Players, Southern Cal. Folklore Soc. (Charter Mbr., '52–), Assn. of Theatrical Press Agts. and Mgrs., The Publicists Assn.; The Dance Ency.; Univ. of Ore.; b. Chgo., Ill.; p. Richard W. and Martha Methven Bock; h. Jacques Pierre (dec.); res: 4136 Mammoth Ave., Sherman Oaks, Cal. 91403.

PIKE, RUTH SCHAD, Asst. to Reg. Dir., U.S. Bureau of Outdoor Recreation, 1000 Second Ave., Seattle, Wash. 98104, '68–; Staff, '64–'68; Seattle Urban Renewal Off., '62–'64; Wash. State Parks & Recreation Cmmsn., '50–'61; Rsch. Assoc., Wash. State Univ., '48–'50; Ed., Colorado Municipalities, '45–'48; Dir. of Pubns., Trinity Univ. (San Antonio, Tex.), '43–'45; Ed., Neb. Univ. Ext. Div., '31–'42; Theta Sigma Phi (Seattle Chptr. Pres., '62), Wash. Recreation and Park Soc., Honor Fellow Aw., '67; Am. Park and Recreation Soc. (Bd. of Dirs., '67–; svc. aw., '69); Nat. Camp Fire Girls aw., '69; Univ. of Neb., AB (Jnlsm.), '26, MA (Sociology), '31; h. Lawrence Pike; res: 3527 Wallingford Ave. N., Seattle, Wash. 98103.

PINE, BERTHA RADLAUER, PR Dir., United Fund, 1515 E. Osborn Rd., Phoenix, Ariz. 85014, '57–; Exec. Dir., Maricopa Mental Health Assn., '55–'57; Talent on daily cooking show, KTVK-TV, '55; Food Colmst., Evening Bulletin (Providence, R.I.), '48–'53; PRSA (Ariz. Chptr. 1st wm. Dir., '63–'69; Pres., '67), Intl. Cncl. of Indsl. Eds. (Ariz. Dir.), Theta Sigma Phi, Ariz. Press Wm.; b. Phila., Pa., 1915; p. Kurt and Hilda Edelschein Radlauer; h. div.; c. Charles A., Elinor R.; res: 5118 N. 32nd Pl., Phoenix, Ariz. 85018.

PINE, RUE COREY, Tchr., St. Johns Presbyterian Church, 11000 National Blvd., L.A., Cal. 90064, '67–; Dir., Christian Educ., St. Pauls Presbyterian Church, '64–'67; Theta Sigma Phi; Stephens Col., '48–'50; U.C.L.A., BA (Sociology); MS (Jnlsm.); b. Evanston, Ill., 1931; p. Hal and Dorothy Hauck Corey; h. Benjamin Pine; c. Pamela, Paul; res: 10549 Clarkson Rd., L.A., Cal. 90064.

PINKERTON, JANE DENNIS, Pres., Pinkerton Public Relations, Inc., 527 Madison Ave., N.Y., N.Y. 10022, '62–; Sales, Prom., Edtl. Mgt., Sponsor Pubns.; Sr. Presentation Wtr., Radio Adv. Bur.; Midwest Ed., Bdcst. Pubns.; Adv. Club of N.Y., AWNY, AWRT, IRTS, NHFL, Pubcty. Club of N.Y., PRSA, Soc. of Professional Mgt. Cnslts.; Nat. Busmens. Cncl.; Medill Sch. of Jnlsm., Northwestern Univ., BJ, '46; b. Chgo. Ill., 1923; p. George and Edith Dennis Pinkerton; res: 235 E. 22nd St., N.Y., N.Y. 10010.

PINSKER, ESSIE LEVINE, Pres., Essie Pinsker Associates, Inc., 110 W. 40th St., N.Y., N.Y. 10018, '60–; Press Dir., Am. Symphony Orchestra, '62–'64; Fashion Cnslt., Claire Lang Assocs., '59–'60; Sportswear Ed., Wms. Wear Daily, '53–'59; Byr., Arkwright Inc., '41–'42; '44–'49; Guest Ed., Infants & Childs Rev. and Teen Merchandiser, '46–'48; Byr., Ohrbachs, '42–'44; Guest Lectr./Instr., Fashion Inst. of Tech., '62–'65; Fashion Group, Fashion Coalition; Bklyn. Col., BA; grad. courses at numerous schs.; b. N.Y.C., 1918; p. Harris and Sophia Feldman Levine; h. Sidney Pinsker; c. Susan Harris, Seth Howard; res: 8 Peter Cooper Rd., N.Y., N.Y. 10010.

PINTER, ELIZABETH LEES, Exec. Dir., Study Abroad Inc., 1748 S. Escondido Blvd., Escondido, Cal. and 250 W. 57th St., N.Y., N.Y., '56–, '50–'56; Wtr., Lectr. on Europe, '49–'50; Lectr., PR, Okla. State Col., '47–'48; Wtr., Lectr. on Latin Am., '46–'47; frequent lects., articles, educ. and intl. educ., orgs. and pubns.; AAUW, Theta Sigma Phi, Nat. Cncl. of Tchrs. of Eng., Intl. Reading Assn.; Univ. of Okla., SB, '45; Pulitzer Grad. Sch. of Jnlsm., Columbia Univ., MS, '46 (Phi Beta Kappa); Univ. of Cal., Berkeley, grad. work; b. Weleetka, Okla., 1924; h. Anthony Pinter; c. Stephanie Ann, Claudia Louise; res: 2636 Loma Vista Dr., Escondido, Cal. 92025.

PIRK, HARRIET, VP, Shaller-Rubin Advertising, 909 Third Avenue, N.Y., N.Y., '70–; Adv. and Crtv. Dir., Almay Cosmetics, 562 Fifth Ave., N.Y., N.Y. 10009, '65–'70; Crtv. Supvsr: C. J. LaRoche and Norman, Craig & Kummel; L. W. Frohlich; Guest Lectr. and Seminar Speaker at adv./cosmetic confs.; Fashion Group Inc.; Flora Stone Mather Col. for Wm., BA (Eng.); b. Cleveland, Oh.; h. Herbert Pirk; res: 41 Fifth Ave., N.Y., N.Y. 10003.

PITCHER, EVELYN GOODENOUGH, Prof. and Chmn., Eliot Pearson Dept. of Child Study, Tufts University, Medford, Mass. 02155, '64–; Dir., NDEA Inst. for Training Tchrs. for new Public Sch. Kindergartens, '68; Summer Head Start Orientation Prog., '65; Summer Pre-sch. Supvsr., NDEA Inst. for Disadvantaged Youth, Lincoln Filene Ctr., '65; Lectr., Psychology, '59–'64; Co-dir., Nursery Sch., Pre-sch. Examiner, Dir. Pre-sch. Svcs., Gesell Inst. of Child Dev. (New Haven, Conn.); Co-auth., "Helping Young Children Learn" (Charles E. Merrill Bks., '66), "The Guidance Nursery School" (Harper & Row, '64), "Children Tell Stories; An Analysis of Fantasy" (Intl. Univs. Press, '63), "Gesell Institute Party Book" (Harper, '65); Wilson Col., BA, '37; Yale Univ., MA, '39; PhD, '56; N. Eng. Col., LLD, '62; b. Lansing, Oh., 1915; p. Bert and Edna Jackson Wiltshire; h. Robert B. Pitcher; c. Ursula Goodenough, Daniel Goodenough; res: 91 Somerset St., Belmont, Mass. 02178.

PITRONE, JEAN MADDERN, Auth., "Trailblazer" (Harcourt Brace and World, '69; Friends of Am. Wtrs. First Prize Aw. for Teenage Biog.); Assoc. Ed., Writer's Digest, '67–; Free-lance Wtr., mag. and nwsp. articles and stories; Staff Speaker, Oakland Univ. Wtrs. Conf., '64–'70; Theta Sigma Phi, Detroit Wm. Wtrs., WNBA; Detroit Inst. of Musical Art, '54; b. Ishpeming, Mich.; p. Courtney and Gladys Maddern; h. Anthony Pitrone; c. Joseph, Jill, Anthony, Joyce, John, Janet, Julie, Jane, Cheryl; res: 8244 Riverview, Dearborn Heights, Mich. 48127.

PITT, HARRIETT PHILMUS, Acc. Supvsr., Harshe-Rotman & Druck, Inc., 300 E. 44th St., N.Y., N.Y. 10017, '64–; (PRSA Silver Anvil aw., Coffee House Prog. for Nat. Coffee Assn., '66); AE; Free-lance PR Cnslt., largely non-profit orgs., 18 yrs., incl. civil rights conf. for secondary schs.; youth and commty. volunteer wk.; Wtr., W.W. II hist. of Girl Scouts, and Girl Guides in underground, mags., nwsps., radio, TV; Tchr.; PRSA (Silver Anvil Aw., '63), Nat. Social Welfare Assembly; b. New Haven, Conn., 1924; p. Morris and Eva Philmus; h. James Eldon Pitt; c. David, Timothy, Debra; res: 500 E. 77th St., N.Y., N.Y. 10021.

PITTS, ELAINE HALLEAD, Dir. of Consumer Rels., Sperry and Hutchinson Company, 330 Madison Ave., N.Y., N.Y. 10017, '64–; Dir. of Consumer Svcs., '59–'64; Mgr. of Packaging Svcs., '53–'59; Sr. Packaging Engineer, Spiegel Inc., '46–'53; Lectr. on packaging, materials handling, and PR at many univs.; Wtr. of articles in U.S., fgn. trade pubns.; Packaging Fndn. (Bd. of Trustees); various orgs.; Ill. Inst. of Tech., '38–'40; Art Inst. of Chgo. (design), '47–'48; b. Chgo., Ill., 1917; p. Harry and Ethel Waring Hallead; h. Paul Pitts; res: 77 E. 12th St., N.Y., N.Y. 10003.

PLACE, DIANE McLANE, Consumer Specialist, Consumer Protection and Environmental Health Service, Public Health Service, Dept. of Health, Education and Welfare, 1560 E. Jefferson, Detroit, Mich. 48207; Consumer Specialist, U.S. Food and Drug Adm., Dept. of HEW (cit., '69), '64–'69; County Agt., Mich. State Univ., '64; News Ed., Shamie Pubns., '63; Reptr., Grocers' Spotlight, '61–'62; active in various health orgs.; Am. Home Econs. Assn., Detroit Press Club, Theta Sigma Phi; Wayne State Univ., BA, '61 (with distinction); b. Detroit, Mich., 1918; p. Arthur and Harriet Evans McLane; h. Tyrus Place; c. Tyrus Wilson; res: 1322 Nicolet, Detroit, Mich. 48207.

PLAIN, ELEANOR, Head Librn., Aurora Public Lib., One E. Benton St., Aurora, Ill. 60504, '39–; Head Cataloger, '37–'39; Asst. Ref. Librn., '34–'36; Gen. Asst., '31–'34; Asst. and Instr. of Lib. Sci., Ind. State Tchrs. Col. Lib. (Terre Haute, Ind.), '36–'37; ALA (Cncl.), '54–'58, '65–'69; Public Libs. Div: Exec. Secy., '48–'51; Bd. of Dirs. '65–'69); Ill. Lib. Assn. (VP, '47–'48; Pres., '48–'49), Univ. of Ill. Grad. Sch. of Lib. Sci. (Advisory Cncl.), Ill. Librn. Cit. ('62), Aurora Hist. Soc. (Dir.), Ill. Hist. Soc., AAUW, Univ. of Mich., AB, '25; AB (Lib. Sci.), '36; Grad. Lib. Sch., Univ. of Chgo., MA, '50; b.

Aurora, Ill.; p. Frank and Jennie Guinang Plain; res: 305 W. Downer Pl., Aurora, Ill. 60506.

PLANTHOLD, MILDRED A., Owner, Mildred Planthold Associates, R.R. #1, St. Clair, Mo. 63077, '57–; Assn. Exec., Allied Florists of Greater St. Louis, '57–; Wms. Ed. and Fashion and Food Ed., St. Louis Globe Democrat, '42–'56; Ch. Ed., '41–'43; Tchr., Notre Dame Acad. (Quincy and Belleville, Ill.), '40–'41; Speech Arts Tchr., Chautauqua (N.Y.) Summer Schs., '37–'38; Auth./Dir., "God's Career Women" doc. film (Sierra Aw., '53); NFPW (Pres., '69–'71), Florist Assn. Execs. Cncl. (Nat. Pres., '68–'70), numerous other orgs. and aws.; N.Y.U., '35; Wash. Univ., '36–'37; b. St. Louis, Mo., 1913; p. Fred F. and Amanda Marie Rook Planthold; h. Louis Cardinal Michie; res: R.R. #1, St. Clair, Mo. 63077.

PLANTS, MARJORIE SOUDERS, Assoc. Crtv. Dir., Avery, Hand and Co., Westport, Conn., '69–; Assoc. Crtv. Dir., Hodes-Daniel Adv. (Elmsford, N.Y.), '65–'69; VP, Assoc. Crtv. Dir., Lennen & Newell, Adv. (N.Y.C.); Assoc. Crtv. Dir., Compton Adv.; Free-lance Copywtr.; music composer, pianist; AWNY, Kappa Kappa Gamma; Univ. of Neb. (Eng., Music); b. Auburn, Neb.; c. Kenneth, Martha, David; res: Stony Ridge Lane, Riverside, Conn. 06878.

PLAUT, GLORIA ATANAS, Asst. Fashion Ed., Look Magazine, 488 Madison Ave., N.Y., N.Y. 10022, '64–; Life, '56–'61; Fashion Group; Skidmore Col., BA, '55; b. N.Y.C.; h. Richard L. Plaut, Jr.; c. Christopher, Alexandra.

PLAUTZ, GAIL, Press Rep., Columbia Broadcasting System, 51 W. 52nd St., N.Y., N.Y. 10019, '67–; Asst. to Mgr. of Photo Unit, '66–'67; Secy., '66; Univ. of Mich., BA (Speech), '65 (Zeta Phi Eta); b. Detroit, Mich., '43; p. John and Alberta Phelps Plautz; res: 42 E. 75th St., N.Y., N.Y. 10021.

PLEASANT, JANIE RUTH, Exec. Dir., Dairy Council of High Point and Greensboro, Inc., 914 N. Elm St., Greensboro, N.C. 27401, '63–; Exec. Dir., Dairy Cncl. of Savannah (Ga.), '56–'63; Home Econst., Westinghouse Electric Supply Co., '51–'56; Home Agt., Ext. Svc. of N.C. State Univ., '48–'51; Asst. Home Agt., '46–'48; Home Econs. Tchr., '44–'46; guest appearances, radio and TV; N.C. Foods and Nutrition Cncl. (VP, '65–'67); home econs. assns.; AWRT, N.C. Wm. in Radio and TV; Who's Who of Am. Wm.; Appalachian State Tchrs. Col., BS, '44; Grad. Work; b. Yanceyville, N.C., 1923; p. Major and Laura Stephens Pleasant; res: 301 E. Lake Dr., Greensboro, N.C. 27401.

PLEUNE, B. JOYCE, Dir., Kent County Library, 726 Fuller Ave. N.E., Grand Rapids, Mich, 49503, '58–; Head of Sch. Svc. Dept., '52–'58; Bkmobile Librn., '51–'52; Tchr., Diamond Sch., '45–'50; Mich. Lib. Assn. (Secy. to Exec. Bd., '68), ALA; Calvin Col., AB (Educ.), '45; Western Mich. Col., Cert. in Lib. Sci., '51; Univ. of Mich., MA (Lib. Sci.), '59; b. Grand Rapids, Mich., '21;

p. Edward and Jessie Van Dellen Pleune; res: 785 Knapp St. N.E., Grand Rapids, Mich. 49505.

PLUMMER, AGNES DUNCAN, Asst. Treas., Tri-State Advertising Company Inc., 307 S. Buffalo St., Warsaw, Ind. 46580; Secy., '54; Zimmer Mfg. Co., '39–'44; Creighton Bros., '35–'39; Warsaw Area Bd. of Realtors; Tri Kappa ('31–); Intl. Col.; LaSalle Ext.; b. Warsaw, Ind., 1913; p. James and Norah Syphers Duncan; h. Edward Lynn Plummer; c. Sharon Lynn (Mrs. Louis C. Notter, Jr.); res: Rte. 2, Goose Lake, Warsaw, Ind. 46580.

PLUNKETT, OLIVE M., Cnslt., Batten, Barton, Durstine & Osborn, Inc., 383 Madison Ave., N.Y., N.Y. 10017, '66–; VP, Crtv. Supvsr., TV, Copywtr., '46–'65; Guest Lectr., Tobe Coburn Sch. for Fashion Careers; AWNY (Bd. of Trustees, '61–'65), Fashion Group; Bd. of Trustees, Hofstra Univ., '62–'65; educ: N.Y.U., AB, '39; N.Y.U. Grad. Sch. of Bus.; b. Bklyn., N.Y., 1917; p. J. Oliver and Catherine Crombie Plunkett; h. Dr. Morris E. Rose (dec.); res: Midstream Rte. 3, Charlottesville, Va. 22901.

PODENDORF, ILLA E., Chmn., Sci. Dept., Laboratory School, University of Chicago, 1362 E. 59th, Chgo., Ill. 60637, '54–; Auth., children's non-fiction sci. bks.; Lectr. on teaching sci.; workshops for tchrs.; helped dev. curriculum; Am. Assn. for Advancement of Sci., Nat. Sci. Tchrs. Assn., Central Assn. of Sci. and Math Tchrs., Cncl. Elementary Sci. Inst.; Drake Univ., BS, '34; Univ. of Ia., MS, '42; res: 5550 Dorchester, Chgo., Ill. 60637.

POGANY, HORTENZIA LERS, Chief Catalog Librn., Assoc. Prof., Seton Hall University, S. Orange, N.J. 07079, '69–; Chief Catalog Librn., '65–'69; Cataloger, '60–'65; Asst. Librn., Albertus Magnus Col. (New Haven, Conn.), '58–'60; Rschr., Medieval Inst., Nat. Archives (Budapest, Hungary), '51–'55; Catholic Lib. Assn., ALA, N.J. Lib. Assn., Classical League of U.S.A.; Szilagyi Erzsebet Gymnasium (Budapest), BA, '37; Pazmany Peter Univ. (Budapest), Tchr. Diploma, '42; Rutgers Univ., MLS, '65; b. Budapest, Hungary; p. Dr. Vilmos and Elvira Reischl Lers; h. Dr. Andras Pogany; c. Andras, Jr., Csaba Antal, Orsolya Maria, Balazs, Mrs. Aniko DePierre, Mrs. Ildiko DeAngelis; res: 201 Raymond Ave., S. Orange, N.J. 07079.

POGREBIN, LETTY COTTIN, VP in Chg. of Adv., Prom. and Subsidiary Rights, Bernard Geis Assoc., 128 E. 56th St., N.Y., N.Y. 10022, '61–; VP, '70–; Asst. Dir., '60–'61; Copywtr., Sussman and Sugar, '60; Edtl. Asst., Coward McCann, '59–'60; Secy., Simon and Schuster, '57–'59; Reptr., Peekskill (N.Y.) Evening Star, '56; Auth., "How to Make It in a Man's World" (Doubleday, '70); Publrs. Pubcty. Assn. (Secy., '69–'70; Bd. Mbr., '67–'69), WNBA; Phila. PR Assn. Key, '70; Who's Who of Am. Wm., Outstanding Young Wm. of Am.; Brandeis Univ., BA, '59 (cum laude, hons. in Eng. and Am. Lit.); b. N.Y.C.; p. Jacob and Cyral Halpern Cottin; h. Bertrand Pogrebin; c.

Abigail, Robin, David; res: 12 St. Lukes Pl., N.Y., N.Y. 10014.

POHLMANN, LILLIAN GRENFELL, Auth., fiction for children and young adults; sch. lib. work, 12 yrs.; Auths. Guild, Auths. League of Am., Cal. Wtrs. Club; Student, Univs. of Cal., Okla., Colo., Mex.; Free Univ. (The Netherlands); b. Grass Valley, Cal., 1902; p. William and Myrtle Massie Grenfell; h. George Pohlmann; c. Iris MacInnes, Hal Grenfell Twigg; res: 388 Hillside Ave., Mill Valley, Cal. 94941.

POISKER, DOROTHY MYERS, Publr., Owner, Indian Valley Echo, 706 S. County Line, Telford, Pa. 18969, '55–; Bdcstr., "Dorothy Poisker Show," WBUX (Doylestown), '60–; Elementary Sch. Tchr., '51–'54; operated nursery sch., '48–'51; AWRT, Pa. Assn. of Adv. Publrs., Phila. Club of Adv. Wm.; Lutheran Training Sch. for Christian Workers; Temple Univ.; b. Phila., Pa., 1907; p. William Kickline and Anna Heinz Myers; h. John Thomas Poisker; res: 125 Green Hill Rd., Telford, Pa. 18969.

POJEFKO, JOANNE TRAVNIK, Prod. Mgr., Collateral Dept., Griswold-Eshleman Company, 55 Public Sq., Cleve., Oh. 44113, '67–; Adv. Prod. Club of Cleve. (Bd. of Dirs., '69–'70); b. Cleve., Oh., 1929; p. Anton and Jennie Tomsic Travnik; h. James Pojefko; res: 4929 Broadview Rd., Cleve., Oh. 44109.

POLAKOWSKI, PATRICIA KUHNS, Deputy Public Affairs Offcr., U.S. Naval Electronics Laboratory Center, Code CO40, San Diego, Cal. 92152, '67–; Sta. Nwsp. Ed. and Public Affairs Specialist, '60–'67; Reptr. for weeklies, dailies, govt. secs.; Cal. Press Wm. (VP, '69; Southern Dist. Pres., '67–'68), Theta Sigma Phi, San Diego PR Club, AWRT, PRSA, 28 writing aws. from pfsnl. affiliations ('60–'69), San Diego PR Club (Best Continuing PR Program, '69; Best Short Term PR Program, '69; Mont. State Univ., BA (Jnlsm.), '49; h. William A. Polakowski; res: 4510 Mt. Alifan Dr., San Diego, Cal. 92111.

POLASKY, CORNELIA (Connie), Pubns. Ed., Miami University, 103 Roudebush Hall, Oxford, Oh. 45056, '62–; Milw. Bur. Chief, Fairchild Pubns., '61–'62; Pubns. Ed., Ball State Univ., '59–'61; Asst. Dir., Coe Col., '51–'59; Theta Sigma Phi, Am. Col. PR Assn.; Stephens Col. (Mo.), '46–'47; Univ. of Ia., BA, '50 (Jnlsm.).

POLKING, KIRK, Ed., Writer's Digest, F and W Publishing Co., 22 E. 12th St., Cincinnati, Oh. 45210, '63–; Free-lance Wtr., '57–'63; Circ. Mgr., Farm Quarterly, '52–'57; Ed. Asst., Writer's Digest, Modern Photog., '48–'52; Lectr. on writing, Univ. of Cinn., Xavier Univ., Ind. Univ., Univ. of Mo.; Auth., mag. articles; four children's bks., incl. "Let's Go To an Atomic Energy Town" (G. P. Putnams Sons, '68); Auths. Guild, NLAPW, Theta Sigma Phi, Cinn. Eds. Assn. (Pres., '68–'69); Univ. of Cinn.; Xavier Univ.; Am. Univ.; b. Covington, Ky., 1925; p. Henry and Mary Hull Polking; res: 2701 Lehman Rd., Cinn., Oh. 45204.

POLL, GENE (Argentine Pollarolo Lombardi), Partner, Dudley-Anderson-Yutzy, 551 Fifth Ave., N.Y., N.Y. 10021, '68–; AE, '64–'69; Dir. of Home Fashions Prom., '63–'68; Dir., Radio-TV Dept., '53–'63; AWRT, NHFL (Nat. Dir.), Am. Inst. of Interior Designers; St. Louis Univ., BJ; b. Italy; p. Giacomo and Ida Laguzzi Pollarolo; h. Dr. Alfonso A. Lombardi; c. Melinda, Mary, Laura, John; res: 435 E. 79th St., N.Y., N.Y. 10021.

POLLACK, BEATRICE JEFFE, VP, McCann-Erickson, Inc., 485 Lexington Ave., N.Y., N.Y. 10017, '70–; Acc. Dir., Fashion Dir.; AE, Daniel & Charles Adv.; Fashion Group; N.Y.U., BS (Mktng.); Univ. of Mich.; h. Stanley E. Pollack.

POLLARD, FRANCES MARGUERITE, Assoc. Prof. of Lib. Sci., Adm. Asst., Booth Library, Eastern Illinois University, Charleston, Ill. 61920, '63–; Dir. of Lib. Sci. grad. program; Head Librn., Chmn. of Lib. Sci. Dept., Ala. State Col., '61–'63; Asst. Librn., '49–'61; Lib. Asst., '46–'48; Student Aide, Sterling Br., Cleve. Public Lib., '48–'49; Lib. Asst. (Fort McClellan, Ala.), '43–'46; Tchr., elementary, H.S., '38–'43; Contrbr., "Major Problems in the Education of Librarians," '54; ALA, NEA, Ill. Lib. Assn., AAUW, AAUP, numerous other educ., lib. assns.; Gen. Educ. Bd. Fellowships, '52, '53; Selma Univ., Jr. Col. Diploma, '38; Ala. State Col., BS (Educ.), '41; Western Reserve Univ., MS (Lib. Sci.), '49; Ph.D., '63; Columbia Univ., grad. study; b. Florence, Ala., 1920; p. Lorenzo and Carrie Mayfield Pollard; res: 1330 A St., Charleston, Ill. 61920.

POLSON, DOROTHEE SINGER, Food Ed., The Arizona Republic, 120 E. Van Buren, Phoenix, Ariz. 85004, '62–; Wms. Ed., Kansas City Kansan, '59–'62; Feature Wtr., Minneapolis Star, '57–'59; various orgs., aws.; Univ. of Minn., BA (Jnlsm.), '49; b. Mpls., Minn., 1927; p. Charles Sr. and Marie E. Sorkin Singer; h. Paul E. Polson Sr.; c. Paige Elizabeth, Dorian L.; Paul E. Jr.; res: 6608 N. 13th St., Phoenix, Ariz. 85014.

POLYKOFF, SHIRLEY, Sr. VP, Bd. of Dirs., Foote, Cone & Belding, 200 Park Ave., N.Y., N.Y.; Copywtr., '55–; Creator, Clairol "Does she . . . or doesn't she?", "Is it true blondes have more fun?", "The closer he gets the better you look", "If I've only one life, let me live it as a blonde," "Every Woman should be a redhead at least once in her life," other campaigns; Guest Prof., Adelphi Univ., Syracuse Univ. Grad. Sch., New Sch. of Social Rsch.; Fashion Group (VP, '69), AWNY, Copy Club of N.Y. (VP, '63); Nat. Adv. Wm. of the Yr., '67; Intl. Film Festival 1st prize, '68; 54 other adv. aws.; N.Y.U.; b. N.Y.C.; p. Hyman and Rose Leiberman Polykoff; h. George Halperin (dec.); c. Mrs. Alix R. Nelson, Mrs. Laurie R. Zucker; res: 969 Park Ave., N.Y., N.Y. 10028.

POMEROY, RUTH FAIRCHILD, Wms. Svc. Ed., Redbook, McCall Publishing Company, 230 Park Ave., N.Y., N.Y. 10017, '56–; Homemaking Ed., '53–'56; Food Ed., Today's Woman, '51–'53; Wms. Svc. Pubcty. Dir.,

Kenyon and Eckhardt, '47–'53; Home Econs. Tchr., Berwick HS, '40–'42; AWNY (Bd. Mbr., '63–'65; Corr. Secy., '69–'70), Am. Home Econs. Assn., Home Econs. Wm. in Bus.; AAF Printer's Ink Silver Medal aw., '68; Ind. Univ., BS, '40; Grad. Work, Univ. of N.C., '41; N.Y.U., '47; b. Berwick, Pa., 1919; p. William and Mary Croop Fairchild; h. Richard W. Pomeroy (div.); c. Mary D., Anne F.; res: 1361 Madison Ave., N.Y., N.Y. 10028.

POMPIZZI, CARLA TOLOMEO, Assoc. Ed., TV Guide, Radnor, Pa. 19088, '68–; Asst. Ed., Amalgamated News, '66–'67; Theta Sigma Phi, Alpha Sigma Alpha, Young Repl. Club; Temple Univ., BS (Jnlsm.), '66; b. Phila., Pa., 1945; p. Ralph and Valborg Van Pelt Tolomeo; h. Ermin M. Pompizzi; res: 264 N. Radnor and Chester Rds., Radnor, Pa. 19087.

POMPONIO, FAITH, Secy. for Info. and PR, World Council of Churches, 475 Riverside Dr., N.Y., N.Y. 10027, '65–; PR Dir., Protestant Cncl. of City of N.Y., '62–'64; Dir. of Press Rels., Am. Baptist Conv., '56–'61; Secy.-News Wtr., '53–'56; Contract Dept., Young & Rubicam, '49–'53; RPRC (Nat. secy., '66–), PRSA, Cncl. of Religious Bdcstrs.; Who's Who of Am. Wm.; City Col. of N.Y., BBA; b. N.Y.C., 1927; p. Domenico and Sophia Ferrar Pomponio; res: 2441 Seebode Ct., Bellmore, N.Y. 11710.

PONDER, CATHERINE, Auth.; Minister, Unity Church, San Antonio, P.O. Box 32110, San Antonio, Tex. 78216, '56–; bks: "The Dynamic Laws of Prosperity," "Healing Secret of the Ages" (Prentice-Hall), "How to Live a Prosperous Life" (Unity Sch.), six others; The Ministerial Sch., Unity Sch. of Christianity, ordained '58; h. Robert K. Ponder (dec.).

PONDER, LINDA CROW, Bdcst. Media Asst., Luckie & Forney, Inc., #11 Off. Pk. Circle, Birmingham, Ala. 35223, '68–; Bdcst. Media Asst., Media Byr., Frank M. Taylor, Adv., '65–'67; AWRT (Corr. Secy., '68–'69; Rec. Secy., '69–'70); Univ. of Ala., '64–'65; b. Moody, Ala., 1945; p. James and Opel Tucker Crow; h. James Ponder; c. Julie Lynne; res: 1305 44th St. W., Birmingham, Ala. 35208.

PONLEITHNER, ROMAYNE RICHARDSON, Ed., Pacific Books, Publishers, 2435 Birch St., Palo Alto, Cal. 94302, '66–; Free-lance Ed., Col. and Sch. Depts., Rand McNally, '58–'68; Edtl. Wtr., Copy Ed., "Handbook of Research on Teaching" ('63); Special Asst. in prep., "Public Higher Education in Illinois," Ill. Joint Cncl. on Higher Educ., '61; Edtl. Wtr., Bur. of Educ. Rsch., Univ. of Ill., '61–'63; Asst. to Dir., Inst. of Govt. and Public Affairs, special project for Ill. State Legislature, Univ. Of Ill., '60; Edtl. Wtr., Univ. of Ill. Press, '57–'60; Edtl. Asst., Commerce Clearing House (Chgo.), '50–'51, '54–'57; Theta Sigma Phi, Kappa Tau Alpha; Univ. of Ill., BS, '50 (hons.); h. Henry Ponleithner; c. Alice, Paul, Thomas, David; res: 3427 Cork Oak Way, Palo Alto, Cal. 94303.

PONSELL, MARY LOUISE, Wtr., Ed.; Edtl. Dir., Delaware Today, 835 Tatnall St., Wilmington, Del. 19801, '66–'69; Free-lance PR, Bur. of Adv., Am. Nwsp. Publrs. Assn., N.Y., '64–'65; Mng. Ed., Sponsor mag., '63–'64; Assoc. Ed., '62–'63; Sr. Ed., U.S. Radio mag., '61; Adv., PR, Ketchum, MacLeod & Grove, Inc., '58–'60; Cont. Wtr., WDEL, '57–'58; NLAPW, Adv. Club of Wilmington, Commtns. Alumni Soc. of Syracuse Univ. (VP, '63–'64); AAUW, League of Wm. Voters; Brandywine Arts Festival; Syracuse Univ., BA, '56; b. Wilmington, Del., 1935; p. Mazie Campbell and Francis Irenee Ponsell; res: 13 Rock Manor Ave., Wilmington, Del. 19803.

PONSOT, MARIE BIRMINGHAM, Lectr., Department of English, Queens College of the City University of New York, Flushing, N.Y., '67–; Lectr., EXCEL Program, '69–; Lectr., SEEK Program, '66–'68; Freelance Wtr.; poetry, criticism, TV, radio, juvs.; Archivist, UNESCO (Paris), '48–'50; WGA, James Joyce Fndn.; Contemporary Auths.; Who's Who of Am. Wm.; St. Joseph's Col., BA, '40; Columbia Univ., Grad. Sch. of Philosophy, MA, '41; Univ. of Paris, '47–'48; b. N.Y.C., 1922; p. William and Marie Condee Birmingham; h. Claude Ponsot; c. Monique Rudnytsky, Denis, Antoine, William, Christopher, Matthew, Gregory; res: 8329 169th St., Jamaica, N.Y. 11432.

PONTIUS, ELEANOR H., Exec. Ed., The Bride's Magazine, 420 Lexington Ave., N.Y., N.Y. 10017, '66–; Fashion Pubcty. Mgr., Monsanto Textiles, '66; Teaching Assoc., Fashion Inst. of Tech., '65–'66; Fashion Dir., B. Altman, '63–'64; Fashion Prom. Dir., Ladies Home Journal, '53–'63; Fashion Group, NHFL, AID (Assoc.); Phila. GA Soc. aws. for prom. art dir., '56–'62; Best Poster of Yr. aw., '62; Phila. Art Alliance; Col. of William and Mary, BA; b. Upland, Pa.; p. J. Minshall and Elizabeth Jones Holden; c. Frederick Holden Gernerd; res: 77 Park Ave., N.Y., N.Y. 10016.

POOL, TAMAR HIRSHENSON, Ed., Hadassah Magazine, Shearith Israel Congregation, 8 W. 70th St., N.Y., N.Y.; Auth: "An Old Faith in the New World" ('55), "Israel and the United Nations" ('48), "Is There An Answer?"; Playwright; "In the Spirit of '76" ('26); Nat. Pres., Hadassah, '39–'43 (Hon. VP for life); Instr., French, Latin and Greek, Hunter Col., '14–'17; various organizations; Hunter Col.; Univ. of Paris (Intl. Fellowship to France); Columbia Univ.; b. Jerusalem, Israel; p. Rabbi Haim and Eva Cohen Hirshenson; h. David de Sola Pool; c. Dr. Naomi (Mrs. Manuel Rodstein) and Ithiel de Sola Pool.

POPERNIK, CATHERINE H., Assoc. Prodr., Alan Burke Productions, 211 E. 51st St., N.Y., N.Y. 10022, '69–; Assoc. Prodr. and Rsch. Dir., WNEW-TV, '65–'69; Theta Sigma Phi (N.Y. Chptr.); Oh. Univ., BSJ, '61; b. Wilkes Barre, Pa., 1939; p. Max M. and Rose Mary Hunyadi Popernik; res: 206 E. 70th St., N.Y., N.Y. 10021.

POPHAM, DR. ESTELLE L., Prof. and Chmn. of Dept.

of Bus. Educ., Hunter College, 695 Park Ave., N.Y., N.Y., '50–'69; Cnslt. on Effective Commtn., Krey & Metzler and Harcourt Brace, '68; Chmn. of Pubns. Comm., Nat. Bus. Educ. Assn., '65–'68; Second Dean, Inst. for Certifying Secys., '50–'52; Co-auth., "Effective Secretarial Procedures and Administration" ('68); AAUW (Former State Bd. Mbr.), Nat. Secys. Assn. (hon. Mbr.); Univ. of Wis., AB, '29; Univ. of Ia., MA, '47; N.Y.U., PhD, '49 (Delta Pi Epsilon); b. Chillicothe, Mo., 1906; p. Walter B. and Lucy Story Popham; res: 210 E. 68th St., N.Y., N.Y. 10021.

POPICK, FRANCES GLASSMAN, VP of Finance, Bernard Popick Associates Inc., 311 Landis Ave., Vineland, N.J. 08360, '69–; Controller, Asst. Controller, '58–'69; AAAA, PRSA; b. Phila., Pa., 1932; p. Nathan and Molly Waldorf Glassman; h. Bernard Popick; c. Marsha Susan, Lynne Fern; res: 1866 Greenwillows Dr., Vineland, N.J. 08360.

POPLIS, NOEL THOMPSON, Press Offcr., U.S. Naval Ordnance Laboratory, White Oak, Silver Spring, Md. 20910, '67–; Ed., Oak Leaf (house organ), '64–'67; Tour Dir., '62–'64; Middle Atlantic IEA, Montgomery County (Md.) Press Assn.; Univ. of Miami, '34–'35; Univ. of Md.; b. Wash., D.C., 1916; p. William and Alice Putnam Thompson; h. Alexander Poplis; res: 1309 Millgrove Pl., Ednor, Md. 20904.

POPPER, HILDEGARDE, Ed., Consumer Magazine Services, Sumner Rider and Associates, 355 Lexington Ave., N.Y., N.Y. 10017; PR Cnslt.; Pubcty. for GE, Young & Rubicam, '57–'61; Household Equipment Ed., House & Garden Magazine, '42–'57.

PORCHER, ELIZABETH LONG, Dir., Abbeville-Greenwood Regional Library System, 106 N. Main St., Greenwood, S.C. 29646, '65–; Librn., Greenwood City and County Public Lib., '50–'65; Circ. Librn., Univ. of Denver (Colo.), '46–'49; Circ. Librn., Univ. of S.C., '43–'46; Hosp. Visitor, Am. Red Cross in N. Africa, '43–'44; Librn. of Caroliniana Collection, Univ. of S.C., and Tchr., Lib. Sci., '36–'43; Librn., Charleston HS, '28–'36; S.C. Lib. Assn., Crusade for Freedom 1st prize for essay; two nat. aws. as librn. of Greenwood Lib.; Col. of Charleston, BA, '28; Columbia Univ., BS (Lib. Sci.), '32; b. Charleston, S.C., 1905; p. Dr. Walter Peyre and Mary Porcher Porcher; res: 105 W. Henrietta St., Greenwood, S.C. 29646.

PORTER, ELLA WILLIAMS, Wtr., Dodd, Mead and MacMillan; Critic Cnslt., Scott Foresman Health Series; Tchr., Crtv. Writing, Donners Grove Adult Sch.; Tchr., Public Schs.; Delta Kappa Gamma, Midland Auths., PEO; Coe Col., BEd., '24; h. Rex Porter; res: 4817 Bryan Pl., Downers Grove, Ill. 60515.

PORTER, JEAN HASLER, Dir., Communications Center, Board of Cooperative Educational Services, Salt Works Rd., Medina, N.Y., 14103, '62–; Sch. Tchr. and Librn., '41–'62; Cnslt.; Auth., four lib. svc. bks.; Niagara-Orleans Area Assn. of Sch. Librns. (Pres., '60–

'61), N.Y. State Tchrs. Assn. (Sole Supervisory Dist., Niagara County Pres., '59–'61; V. Chmn., Lib. Sec., Northwestern Zone, '65–'68), N.Y. Lib. Assn. (Bd. of Dirs., '61–'64; Governing Cncl., '69–'70); Univ. of Buffalo, BA (Eng.), '41; Lib. Sci. courses; b. Buffalo, N.Y., 1922; p. Henry and Ida Hasler; h. Charles Porter; c. Charles Henry, II; res: 3739 Hartland Rd., Gasport, N.Y. 14067.

PORTER, JUDY WISEMAN, Ed., C-E News, Combustion Engineering Inc., 911 W. Main St., Chattanooga, Tenn. 37401, '55–'60, '67– (Chattanooga Bus. Eds. Assn. aw., '60); Univ. of Chattanooga; b. Chattanooga, Tenn., p. J. A. and Ruth Goins Wiseman; h. Garland A. Porter Jr.; res: 3011 Lancaster Circle, Chattanooga, Tenn. 37415.

PORTER, KATHERINE ANNE, Auth., c/o Seymour Lawrence, Inc., 90 Beacon St., Boston, Mass. 02108; "Collected Short Stories of Katherine Anne Porter" ('65; Bk. of Month Club), "Ship of Fools" ('62; Bk. of Month Club), "Holiday" (O'Henry Aws. for short stories), "The Days Before" ('52), "The Leaning Tower" (short stories, '44), "Preface to Fiesta in November" (S. Am. short stories, '42), "The Itching Parrot" (translation from Spanish, '42), "Pale Horse, Pale Rider" (three short novels, '39; 1st annual gold medal for lit., Soc. for Libs. of N.Y.U., '40), "Noon Wine" ('37), "Hacienda" ('34), "Floweing Judas" ('30), Compiler and Translator, "KAP's French Song Book" ('38); First Glasgow Prof., Wash. and Lee Univ.; Wtr.-in-residence: Univ. of Va., Stanford Univ.; Lectr., Univ. of Mich., Univ. of Liege, Belgium; Ford Fndn. grant in lit., Fellow of Reg. Am. Lit. (Lib. of Congress), Am. Acad. of Arts and Ltrs., Guggenheim Fellowship for Crtv. Writing, Bk. of Month Club Aw., Annual Prize for lit. work (Tex. Inst. of Lit., Dallas) Emerson-Thoreau Bronze Medal of Am. Acad. of Arts and Scis., Nat. Bk. Aw. for fiction, Pulitzer Prize for fiction, Nat. Inst. of Arts and Ltrs. (VP, '50–'52; Gold Medal for fiction, '67); Wms. Col., Univ. of N.C., LittD, '49; Smith Col., LittD, '58; Univ. of Mich., '54, LHD; Univ. of Md., '66, LHD; b. Indian Creek, Tex., 1890; p. Harrison and Mary Jones Porter; h. Albert Russel Erskine (div.); res: 3601 49th St., N.W., Wash., D.C. 20016.

PORTER, MARGARET McFARLAND, Asst. to Publr., Porter Publishing Company, 2285 Peachtree Rd., N.E., Atlanta, Ga. 30309, '64–; Treas., '67–; Dir. Rsch., Annual Rev. issue, Southern Adv. and Publ., '61–'64; Ed., Merita Family Magazine for Am. Bakeries, Jr. AE, Tucker Wayne & Co., Atlanta Adv. Agcy., '53–'54; PR Staff, Queen for a Day (Hollywood, Cal.), '44–'45; Southern Nwsp. Publrs. Assn. (Assoc. Mbr.), Atlanta Adv. Club, Atlanta Hist. Soc., High Museum of Art, Mag. Reps. of the South; b. Atlanta, Ga., 1914; p. Robert, Sr., and Nettie Hume McFarland; h. Garland Burns Porter; c. William W., Margaret Tracy; res: 69 Mobile Ave., N.E., Atlanta, Ga. 30305.

PORTER, PATRICIA, Publicist, Celanese Fibers Co.,

75 St. Alphonsus St., Boston, Mass. 02120, '62–; Makeup Ed., Boston Record American, '56–'59; Wms. Ed., Boston Herald Traveler, '50–'56; Makeup Ed., Boston Sunday Advertiser, '47–'50; Copy Ed., San Francisco (Cal.), '40–'45; Fashion Writing Tchr., Academic Moderne; Fashion Group (Regional Dir., '70–'71) NHFL; Univ. of Cal., BA, '39; b. Antioch, Cal., 1915; p. William and Ellen Beede Kelley; h. Philip Bronstein; c. Patricia.

PORTER, STELLA PORTER, Pres., Owner, Stella Z. Porter/Media Consultant Services, 116 Winchester Rd., P.O. Box 132, Merion Sta., Pa. 19066, '69–; VP, Media, Bauer Tripp Hening and Bressler (N.Y.C., Phila.); h. Francis N. Porter.

PORTER, SYLVIA F., Synd. Fin. Colmst., Publishers-Hall Syndicate, 30 E. 42nd St., N.Y., N.Y. 10017, '47–; Auth: "How to Get More For Your Money," "Managing Your Money," "Sylvia Porter's Income Tax Guide" (annual); Ed., "Reporting on Governments"; Monthy Colmst., Ladies' Home Jnl.; Hunter Col., '32 (magna cum laude; Phi Beta Kappa); N.Y.U.; eight hon. degs.; h. G. Sumner Collins.

PORTRAIT, EVELYN, Fashion and Beauty Ed., Cue Magazine, 20 W. 43rd St., N.Y., N.Y. 10036, '65–; TV Actress; TV Commentator; commls.; Fashion Group (N.Y. Chptr.); Syracuse Univ., BA; b. Newark, N.J.; h. Robert Loeb.

PORTTEUS, ELNORA MANTHEI, Dir. Supvsr., Cleveland Public Schools, 1380 E. Sixth St., Cleve., Oh. 44114, '65–; Asst. Prof., Kent State Univ., '58–'65; Librn., Findlay, Oh., '49–'58; Indsl. Rels. Cnslrs. (N.Y.C.), '47–'48; Asst. Librn., Fed. Reserve Bank (Cleve.), '43; Tchr., Librn., Racine-Kenosha (Wis.) Normal Sch., '41–'42; Conslt., Educ. Planning Svc., '60–; Children's Bks., (Rand, McNally) '66–'68; Dir., NDEA Inst., '65; Advisory Bd., Cuyahoga Commty. Col., '66–; ALA (John Cotton Dana Aw., '67), Oh. Assn. of Sch. Librns. (Pres., '57–'58), Oh. Lib. Assn., Delta Kappa Gamma, AAUW (Oh. Div. Bd. Mbr., '55–'58); Ency. Britannica Aw., '67; Oshkosh State Col., '37–'39; Univ. of Wis., BS, '41; Kent State Univ., MA, '54 (Distg. Alumna, '67); b. Rosendale, Wis.; p. Herman and Anna Kentop Manthei; h. Paul Portteus; c. Andre, Mrs. Carrie-Jo Haas, Lane; res: 7357 W. Lake Blvd., Kent, Oh. 44240.

PORTUGAL, ROSE PODWELL, Dir., Ed., Fountainhead Publishers, 475 Fifth Ave., N.Y., N.Y. 10017, '60–; Free-Lance Lit. Agt., '48–'60; Bus. Mgr., Am. Bksellers. Assn., '40–'47; Greenberg Publrs., '28–'39; Columbia Univ. Adult Educ. Courses in Lit., Advanced Accounting, '20–'23; p. Max and Sarah Kaufman Podwell; h. John Portugal (dec.); res: 65 W. 95th St., N.Y., N.Y. 10025.

POSNER, IRINA GABRIELLA, Assoc. Prodr., CBS News, 524 W. 57th St., N.Y., N.Y., '65–; Wolper Prods., '65; NET, '64; Mt. Holyoke Col., BA, '60; b. N.Y.C.,

1939; p. George and Naja Bermannis Posner; res: 119 E. 89th St., N.Y., N.Y. 10028.

POST, ANNABEL DOROTHY, Home Econs. Ed., Sunset Magazine, Lane Magazine and Book Company, Menlo Park, Cal. 19025, '59–; Staff, '57–; Assoc. Food Ed., Woman's Home Companion, '53–'56; Asst. Ed., '50–'53; Tchr.; Home Econs. in Bus., Am. Home Econs. Assn.; Univ. of Wash., BS, '45; Tchr. Credential, '48; b. Sumner, Wash., 1922; p. Leslie and Mildred Bothwell Post; res: 569 Addison Ave., Palo Alto, Cal. 94301.

POSTELL, PATRICIA L., Dir., Oak Ridge Public Library, Kentucky and Broadway, Oak Ridge, Tenn. 37830, '60–; Cataloger, Acting Dir., '57–'60; Librn., Ext. Div. Univ. of Ala. (Montgomery), '49–'51; St. Margaret's Hosp., '48–'50; Librn., Xavier Univ. (N.O., La.), '33–'36; ALA, Tenn. Lib. Assn., Southeastern Lib. Assn., Staff City of Oak Ridge; b. N.O., La., 1911; p. William and Eugenie Grosch Luck; h. Paul E. Postell; c. Paul E., Jr., Patricia P. Roberts, Kathleen P. Stephens, Virginia P. Gaylor, Rebecca M., Mark W.; res: 502 Michigan Ave., Oak Ridge, Tenn. 37830.

POTTER, CAROLE LIPSHAY, Sr. Publicist, American Broadcasting Company, 1330 Ave. of the Am., N.Y., N.Y. 10019, '69–; Assoc. Ed., Info. Off., National Association of Broadcasters, '68–'69; Free-lance Wtr., non-fiction stories in mags.; Story Ed., Dell Pubn., '64–'65, '67–'68; Guidette, NBC, '62; AWRT, TV Acad. of Arts and Scis.; Boston Univ., BS (Bdcst.), '62; b. N.Y.C., 1940; p. Theodore and Beatrice Lipshay Weinberger; h. Allan R. Potter (div.); res: 355 E. 72nd St., N.Y., N.Y. 10021.

POTTER, CLIFFORDEAN HAMMOND, Prog. Dir., WOMI, 3121 Frederica St., Owensboro, Ky. 42301, '40; Vocalist, Anncr., '38–'69; Tutor, voice and drama; Org. two chptrs. of Beta Sigma Phi, Alexis Club, Ky. Bdcstrs. Assn. (Ky. Mike); Hon. Marine, '61; Hon. Boy Scout, '67; Duchess of Paducah Aw., '56; First Wm. on Broadcast Music, Inc. Prog. Clinic Panels, '53–'54; Owensboro Army Reserve Aw. of Merit; Owensboro Sat. Musicale (Radio Chmn., '38–; Mbr., 40 yrs.; TV Chmn., '60), Ky. Fedn. of Music Clubs (Bd. Mbr., '56–'58); b. Tell City, Ind., 1908; p. Winfield and Anna Dietrich Hammond; h. Hugh O. Potter; c. Hugh O., Jr.; res: 3100 Frederica St., Owensboro, Ky. 42301.

POTTER, DOROTHY MAY, Owner, Dorothy Potter Associates, 333 Prospect St., Northampton, Mass. 01060, '58–; Exec. Dir., PR, Pioneer Valley Assn., '66–; Dir. of PR: Franklin County Public Hosp., '65; Cooley Dickinson Hosp., '56–; Williston Acad., '57–; Field Dir. and Admr., ARC Blood Prog., '49–'51; Colms. and Features, Capital Times, State Jnl. (Madison, Wis.), '30–'31; Daily Hampshire Gazette '51–; News Ed., Univ. of Wis. Daily Cardinal Jnl.; Creator, Prodr., progs. on WHAI, WHYN, WHMP, WIBA, WHA, TV-WHYN; PRSA, AHA, PR Directors Assn., New Eng. Hosp. PR Assn., Valley Press Club; FETO as ARC

Cnslt., '46–'49; Univ. of Wis. (Polit. Sci.; Law), '31; b. Madison, Wis., 1907; p. Harry and Susanne Burnham Potter.

POTTER, JACQUELINE RILEY, Pres., Jacqueline Potter Advertising Agency, Inc., 608 W. Highland, Carthage, Mo. 64836, '67–; Adv. Mgr., Carthage Marble Corp., '62–'67; Copywtr., '53–'62; Cont. Ed., Radio Sta. KSWM (Joplin), '53–'54; Copywtr. Trainee, Spiegels (Chgo., Ill.), '52–'53; Tchr., '51–'52; Construction Industry Adv. and Prod. Lit. aw., '66; Bldg. Prod. Lit. aw., '62, '58; Adv. Club of Wichita Adv. Excellence aw., '62; Univ. of Cal., Berkeley, AA, '49; Univ. of Ill., BA, '51 (hons.); b. Joplin, Mo., 1929; p. Perry and Lorraine Hammons Riley; h. E. Elliott Potter; c. Jamey N., Lisa Gail.

POTTKER, OLGA SOMENZI, Wms. Ed., Waukegan News-Sun, 100 Madison St., Waukegan, Ill. 60085, '69–; Colmst., Feature Wtr., Reptr., all '62–'69; Adv., Peoria Journal-Transcript, '40–'44; Northwestern Univ., '35–'37; b. Oglesby, Ill.; h. Ralph Pottker; c. Mrs. Ned Rosenbaum and Mrs. Andrew Stuart Fishel; res: 2559 Ravenswood Ave., Highland Pk., Ill. 60035.

POUNDS, JESSIE L., Tchr., Librn., Quinault High School, Amanda Park, Wash. 98526, '58–; Tchr., '32–'58; Co-Auth., "Okla. State Physical Education Syllabus" ('52); active in local, nat., intl. track and field progs.; Northwestern Tchrs. Col., BS, '37; A&M Col., MS, '42; b. Elmwood, Okla.; p. Francis and Louisa Tchergi Pounds; res: Box 68, Quinault, Wash. 98575.

POUNDSTONE, SALLY HILL, Dir., Mamaroneck Free Library, Library Lane, Mamaroneck, N.Y. 10543, '66–; Instr., Lib. Sci., Col. of New Rochelle, '70–; Regular Bk. Reviewer, Lib. Jnl., '62–; Instr., Lib. Sci., N.Y.U. Ctr. for Continuing Educ., '68; Librn., Bedford Hills Sch., '65–'66; Chief, Acquisitions, White Plains Public Lib., '60–'62; Asst., Folger Shakespeare Lib., '59–'60; Asst. Head, Ref. Dept., Louisville (Ky.) Free Public Lib., '55–'59; ALA (Staff Orgs. Round Table, Bd. Chmn., '59–'60), Ky. Lib. Assn. (Secy., '57–'59), Westchester Lib. Assn. Dirs. Sec. (Vice Chmn., '69–), N.Y. State Lib. Assn.; Univ. of Ky., BA, '54; MA, '55 (Phi Beta Kappa; Beta Phi Mu); h. R. Bruce Poundstone; c. Nancy, Holly, Angus.

POWDERLY, BARBARA KATHRYN, Media Dir., Adm. Asst., Stern, Hays and Lang, Inc., 5601 Biscayne Blvd., Miami, Fla. 33138, '67–; VP, Treas., Media Dir., Harold Gardner Assocs. '63–'67; Asst. Controller, Oak Ridge Inc., '59–'63; Adv. Club of Gtr. Miami; Who's Who of Am. Wm.; Who's Who of the South and Southwest; Who's Who of Commerce and Industry; Advisory Mbr., Marquis Biographical Lib. Soc.; b. Scranton, Pa., 1940; p. Eugene and Kathryn Loftus Powderly; res: 12601 N.W. 27th Ave., Miami, Fla. 33167.

POWELL, ANGELA MARIA, Pers. Mgr., Doyle Dane Bernbach, Inc., 20 W. 43rd St., N.Y., N.Y. 10036, '66–;

Mgr., Corwin Consultants, '64–'66; Mgr., Kellogg Agcy., '61–'64; AWNY, Museum of Modern Art; Hunter Col., BA; h. Charles Powell.

POWELL, DOROTHY BLANKENSHIP, Ed. of House Organs and Pers. Asst., The Lowe Brothers Company, Div. of Sherwin-Williams Company, 424 East Third St., Dayton, Oh. 45402, '54–; Am. Soc. of Training and Dev. (Western Oh. Chptr.), IEA; Jacobs Bus. Col. (Miami, Oh.), '46–'47; b. Ashland, Ky. 1929; p. William M. and Carrie Pack Blankenship; h. Charles Powell; c. Steven D., William C., Mark J.; res: 3508 Valleywood Dr., Kettering, Ph. 45429.

POWELL, ENID LEVINGER, Free-lance Wtr., fiction and essay; Bd. of Dirs., Consol. Clnrs., Inc., Des Plaines, Ill., '57–; Verse Wtr., Barker Greeting Card Co., '52–'54; Copywtr., S.C. Baer Co. (Cinn., Oh.), '50–'52; Sigma Delta Tau, Suburban Wtrs. (Pres., '69–'70), Writer's Digest Short Story contest winner '67–'69; Univ. of Cinn. (Poetry Prize, '50); b. Bklyn., N.Y., 1931; p. Herbert and Selma Sherman Levinger; h. Bert Powell; c. Patti Irene, Jon Lawrence; res: 1209 Green Bay Rd., Highland Park, Ill. 60035.

POWELL, MARCIA L., Home Ed., Electricity on the Farm Magazine, 466 Lexington Ave., N.Y., N.Y. 10017, '67–; Eastern Ed., Housewares Buyer, '66–'67; Asst. AE, Edward Gottlieb & Assocs., '64–'65; PR Asst., Parsons-Jurden, '65–'66; Club Ed., The Phoenix Gazette, '62–'64; Assn. of Home Appliance Manufacturers Edtl., Theta Sigma Phi (N.Y. Chptr. Program VP, '69–'70), Alpha Xi Delta (N.Y. Alumnae Pres., '68–'70), Alpha Omicron Chptr. Dir., '66–), NHFL, Electrical Wms. Round Table (N.Y. Secy., '68–'69), NPWC; numerous Ariz. Press Wm. feature aws.; Enwood Chamber Opera Players; Project Head Start Cultural Program, '66; Univ. of Ga., AB (Jnlsm.), '62; N.Y. Sch. of Interior Design; b. Opelika, Ala., 1941; p. Clyde and Leonora Stowe Powell; h. John-Jerome Gallagher; res: 54 W. 74th St., N.Y., N.Y. 10023.

POWELL, MARION SMITH, Wtr., Marschalk Co., Inc. 601 Rockwell Ave., Cleve., Oh. 44114. '69–; Wtr., Meldrum and Fewsmith, Inc., '65–'69; Wtr., Lang, Fisher & Stashower Adv., '58–'65; Wtr., Fuller & Smith & Ross Adv., '49–'58; Wms. Adv. Club of Cleve., Cleve. Soc. Commtns. Arts; AAF Printers' Ink Silver Medal aw. '68.

POWERS, ANNE L., Instr., crtv. writing, Marquette Univ., College Journalism, Milw., Wis. 53233; Auth., eight novels, Bobbs-Merrill Co. Inc., 1720 E. 38th St., Indpls. 7, Ind., '46–'60; Allied Auths., Fictioneers, Wis. Reg. Wtrs. Assn., Press Club Aux., Wis. Cncl. of Wtrs.; Sigma Kappa aw. for best gen. bk. by NFPW, Theta Sigma Phi Wtrs. aw., '51; Univ. of Minn., '32–'33; b. Cloquet, Minn., 1913; p. John and Maud Lynch Powers; h. Harold A. Schwartz; c. Weldon, Lynn (Mrs. Michael Donoghue); res: 3800 N. Newhall St., Milw., Wis. 53211.

POWERS, DOROTHY ROCHON, Feature Wtr., Edtl.

Wtr., The Spokesman-Review, Monroe and Riverside Ave., Spokane, Wash. 99210, '43–; Repl. nominee for U.S. Congress, '66; Gen. Colm. "Our Town," '54–'66; most beats, educ., med., courts, '47–'54; Gen. Assigt. Reptr., '43; Corr., Nashville (Tenn.) Banner, '46; State Ed., The Clarksville Leaf-Chronicle, '46; Ed., weekly Maryville Enterprise, '46; Dean Stone Visiting Lectr. in Jnlsm., Univ. of Mont. (Missoula), '62; Lectr., Jnlsm., Univ. of Tex., Syracuse Univ.; clinics at Univs. of Wash., Wash. State, Idaho, Ill., Ind., Ore.; Ernie Pyle Mem. aw. '60 (only wm. winner); Nat. Headliner, Theta Sigma Phi, '59; Nat. Headliner, Nat. Headliners Club, '58; Nat. Merit aw., Am. Municipal Assn., '64; numerous other aws. and honors; Univ. of Mont., Missoula, BA (Jnlsm.), '43 (cum laude; Sigma Delta Chi aw.) b. Erskine, Alberta, Can., 1921; p. C. G. and Edna Waterbury Rochon; h. Ethridge Elwood Powers; res: 2340 W. First Ave., Spokane, Wash. 99204.

POWERS, MARCELLA (pseud: Bayes Branham), Free-lance Wtr.; New Mexico Magazine Staff Wtr., '63–'68; Marcella Powers Agcy., '46–'60; Leland Hayward, '45; Good Housekeeping, '42–'45; N.M. Press Wm.; NPWC Aw., '66; Univ. of Wis.; b. Orange, N.J., 1921; p. Francis and Kathryn Dauth Powers; c. Michael Edward Amrine Emily Pigeon, Alexander Pigeon; res: 433 San Antonio St., Santa Fe, N.M. 87501.

POWERS, MARGARET M., Consumer Rels. Rep., Sperry and Hutchinson Co., 30 Superior Dr., Natick, Mass. 01760, '65–; Admr., PR Daystrom, '57–'60; Alumnae PR, Wellesley Col., '44–'57; AWRT, BPW, Pubcty. Club of Boston, Quota Intl.; Simmons Col., '41–'43; Katherine Gibbs Sch., '43–'44; res: 1406 Windsor Dr. South, Framingham, Mass. 01701.

PRACHT, GRETCHEN MARPLE, Ed., Exec., Lawyer, Wtr., 906 National Bldg., Mpls., Minn. 55402; VP, Dir. PR and Adv., Ed., Lutheran Brotherhood Bond, '55–'67; Nat. Fraternal Congress (Pres., PR), Adv. Club of Minn., PRSA, ICIE, NFPW, Minn. Press Wm.; Minn. Col. of Law, LLB, '30; b. Waterville, Minn., 1909; p. Ezra and Ida Krause Marple; h. Howard Pracht; c. Patricia (Mrs. Richard Jesperson); res: 5912 Ewing Ave. S., Edina, Minn. 55410.

PRAGER, ALICE H., Exec. VP, Mng. Dir., SESAC, Inc., 10 Columbus Circle, N.Y., N.Y. 10019; Founder, Pres., The Personal Touch, Inc., product prom.; ZONTA, Radio and TV Execs. Soc., AWRT (Adv. Bd.), Ed., News and Views), AIM, Bdcst. Pioneers, NAB; Russell Sage Col., Grad., '51; N.Y.U., grad. work; b. N.Y.C., 1930; p. Paul and Ruth Collin Heinecke; h. George L. Drescher; res: 300 Central Park W., N.Y., N.Y. 10024.

PRATT, VIVIANE MANUEL, Contrb. Ed., San Diego Magazine, 3254 Rosecrans St., San Diego, Cal. 92110, '64–; Asst. Ed., '64–'68; Rsch. Asst., Edward Petry (N.Y.C.), '55; Rsch. Asst., Foote Cone and Belding, '52–'55; NFPW 1st pl. aw. for page regularly edited by a wm.; wtrs. contest, '66; Cal. Press Wm. 1st pl. for editing, '66; 1st pl. for colm., '66; b. LaBaulle, France, 1932; h. H. Lee Pratt III; c. Nicholas Frederick and Andrea Lee; res: 2628 Hidden Valley, LaJolla, Cal. 92037.

PREECE, BETTY PETERS, Adj. Prof. of Graphic Sci., Florida Institute of Technology, County Club Rd., Melbourne, Fla. 32901, '65–; Fac. Advisor for student nwsp. Crimson; Ed., Indian River Engineer, Inst. Electrical and Electronics Engineers, '59–'67; Chief, Surveillance Systems Sec., Air Force Missile Test Center, Patrick AFB, Fla., '51–'54; Electrical Engineer previously; Svc. Shop Engineer, GE, '47–'50; Ed., Univ. of Ky. Col. of Engineering mag., Ky. Engineer; Rsch., early hist. of S. Brevard County, Fla., '66–; IEEE, AIAA, Soc. of Wm. Engineers, Wms. Engineering Soc. (Eng.), Missile, Space and Range Pioneers, DAR, Delta Kappa Gamma (Hon. Mbr., '64), Fla. Hist. Soc., S. Brevard Hist. Soc.; Who's Who of Am. Wm.; Dic. of Intl. Biog.; Univ. of Ky., BS (Electrical Engineering), '47; b. Decatur, Ill., p. George and Margaret Stock Peters; h. Raymond G. Preece; c. J. Eric, B. George.

PREISSER, BERNICE GOLDMAN, VP, Lando, Inc., 725 Liberty Ave., Pitt., Pa. 15222, '62–; Copy Supvsr., Consumer Mkting. Dir., Ketchum, MacLeod & Grove, '56–'62; Copy Supvsr., Wade Adv. (L.A.), '50–'55; Dir., Special Events, May Co. (L.A.), '47–'50; Owner, adv. agcy., '42–'45; Tchr., radio writing, NBC (L.A.); Tchr., adv., Univ. of Pitt., Carnegie-Mellon; Pitt. Adv. Wm. of Yr., '65; Intl. Bdcst. Aw. for TV, '68; Pitt. Adv. Club (Dir., '63–'68), Pitt. Press Club; Univ. of Wis., '37–'38; Univ of Pitt., '36–'37; b. Pitt., Pa., 1917; p. Maurice and Ethel Rosenstein Goldman; h. Thomas Preisser (dec.); c. Thomas Edwards III; res: 4927 Wallingford St., Pitt., Pa. 15213.

PREMINGER, MARION MILL, French Educ. Radio, Consul General of the Republic of Gabon, 550 Park Ave., N.Y., N.Y. 10021; French Educ. Radio in Africa; Auth: "All I Want is Everything" (Funk and Wagnall), "The Sands of Tamanrassett" (Hawthorne); AWRT, OPC, Wms. News Svc. Radio Brazzaville; Chevalier of French Legion of Honor, Hon. PhD, numerous other aws.; b. Arad, Hungary, 1913; p. Andreas Deuth and Maria Deuth Mill; h. Albert Mayer.

PRESBERG, MIRIAM GILBERT, Dir., Authors' and Publishers' Service, 146–47 29th Ave., Flushing, N.Y. 11354, '49–; Mng. Dir., Island Press, '46–'48; Pubcty. Dir., Arco Publ., '45–'46; Mng. Ed., Didier Publ., '43–'45; Auth., children's fiction, non-fiction; Nat. Conf. of Christians and Jews Brotherhood Aw., Best Mag. Fiction of the Yr., '62; Hunter Col., BA, '40; b. N.Y.C., 1919; p. Charles and Kate Kinstler Goldstein; h. Abe Presberg; c. Karen Laurie; Andrea Claire.

PRESCOTT, RUTH VANBUREN, Dir., Info. Svcs., Grinnell College, 1202 Park St., Grinnell, Ia. 50112, '55–; PR Asst., '44–'55; Wms. Commentator, Bangor (Me.) Radio Station WABI, '37–'39; Wms. Ed., Daily Commercial, '37–'39; State Ed., Daily News, '41; Soc. Ed., '34–'37; Sch. Ed., '33–'34; ACPRA (Mid-Am. Dist.

Secy., '66–'67; Vice Chmn., '67–'68; Chmn., '68–'69; Dist. and Nat. Pubns. aws., '57–) PRSA, Am. Alumni Cncl. (Dist. and Nat. aws., '57–), Theta Sigma Phi (Outstanding Adviser aw., '63); Cornell Col., BA (Phi Beta Kappa), '33; b. Kearney, Neb., 1912; p. George J. and Eda M. Cramer VanBuren; h. Herbert L. Prescott (div.); c. Joel, Jane; res: 1416 East St., Grinnell, Ia. 50112.

PRESNICK, LORRAINE COOPER, VP, Assoc. Rsch. Dir., Foote, Cone & Belding, Inc., 200 Park Ave., N.Y., N.Y. 10017, '68–; Group Mgr., '66; Acct. Rsch. Supvsr., '65; Project Dir., '64; Project Dir., Satterthwhite Rsch., '62–'64; AMA, AAPOR; Queen's Col., BA, '62; b. N.Y.C., 1938; p. Irving and Sophie Harrison Cooper; h. Michael C. Presnick; c. Christopher Andrew, Joshua Michael; res: 60 Sutton Pl. S., N.Y., N.Y. 10022.

PRESSLY, HARRIET BYRNE, Free-lance Reptr., WPTF, 410 S. Salisbury St., Raleigh, N.C. 27602, '61–; Wms. Ed., Wtr., Prod., Talent for daily show, '43–'60; Speaker, young people groups and orgs., wms. clubs; Guest Lectr., Dept. Radio, TV, Motion Pics., Univ. of N.C. (Chapel Hill), '42–'69; AWRT (N.C. Pres., '61–'63); nat. cits. for Bond prom., '45, '55; N.C.A.P. Aw. for excellence in bdcst., '55–'56; N.C. Dairy Products. Aw. of Appreciation to Wm. in Commtns., '68; Wake County Wm. of Yr., '62; N.C. Parks and Recreation Outstanding Svc. aw., '69; FHA Hon. Mbr., '54; N.C. Mother of Yr., '48; Delta Kappa Gamma; Who's Who of Am. Wm.; active in public svc. orgs.; Goucher Col., AB, '18; b. Houston, Tex., 1895; p. George and Lulu Haynie Byrne; h. William C. Pressly; c. Harriet (Mrs. Charles L. Tucker), Lt. Cmdr. James M., Mary Lou, Cmdr. George B., Dorothy (Mrs. E. Jack Fulghum); res: E. 2 Grosvenor Gardens Apts., Raleigh, N.C. 27603.

PRESTON, AMY ELIZABETH, Dir., Bethlehem Public Library, 11 W. Church, Bethlehem, Pa. 18017; '41–; Abington Libr., '37–'41; Wilmington (Del.) Public Schs.; Delta Kappa Gamma, ALA, Pa. Lib. Assn. AAUW, League of Wm. Voters; Ursinus Col., AB, '30; Drexel Inst., BLS, '32; p. Benjamin and Mary Walker Preston; res: RD 3, Bethlehem, Pa. 18015.

PRESTON, RUTH, Fashion-Beauty Ed., New York Post, 75 West St., N.Y., N.Y., 10006, '46–; Partner, Levin Corp., '37–; Asst. Prom. Dir., Harper's Bazaar, '44–'45; Dist. Dir., Temporary Emergency Relief Assn., '32–'33; Adv. Dept., Macy's, '30; Caseworker, Fed. of Jewish Philanthropies, '29–'30; various orgs.; Syracuse Univ., BA, '27 (Phi Beta Kappa); Sorbonne '29; Columbia Univ., MA, '30; b. Bklyn., N.Y., 1906; p. Joseph and Augusta Stadler Levin; h. A. Robert Peskin; c. Abbey Sara (Mrs. Rubin Klein), Stephen David; res: 2 Fifth Ave., N.Y., N.Y. 10011.

PRESTOPINO, ELIZABETH DAUBER, Free-lance Artist, Estelle Mandel Co., Inc., 65 E. 80th St., N.Y., N.Y. 10021; Illus. for Follett Pubns., Golden Bks., Grossett & Dunlap, Holt, Rinehart & Winston, William Morrow & Co.; Hon. Mention, N.Y. Watercolor Soc.;

Third Prize, N.J. Watercolor Soc.; Hon. Mention, N.J. Tercentenary, N.Y. Soc. of Illus.; b. Brooklyn, N.Y., 1910; p. Benjamin and Fanie Glaser Dauber; h. Gregorio Prestopino; c. Paul, Gregory; res: 20 Farm Lane, Roosevelt, N.J. 08555.

PREUSS, ANNE MacDOUGALL, Assoc. Ed., The Metropolitan Museum of Art, Fifth Ave. and 82nd St., N.Y., N.Y. 10028, '68–; Asst. Ed., '62–'68; Edtl. Asst., '59–'62; Edtl. Asst., Mademoiselle, '58–'59; Free-lance Ed.; Swarthmore Col., BA, '56; Courtauld Inst., London Univ., '56–'57; h. Jack Preuss.

PRICE, JEANIE COSSE, VP, Treas., Dora-Clayton Agency, Inc., 820 Carnegie Bldg., 133 Carnegie Way, Atlanta, Ga. 30303, '68–; Mkt. Rsch. Dir., AE, '54–'68; AWRT, Atlanta Rep. Assn., Atlanta Bdcst. Execs. Assn., Atlanta Adv. Club; Univ. of Ga.; b. Atlanta, Ga., 1938; p. C. Ray and Dora Cox Dodson; h. Albert Alonzo Price, Jr.; c. Allan Monroe Chandler, Dora Claire Price, Patrick Clayton Price; res: 7095 Faunsworth Drive, N.W., Atlanta, Ga. 30328.

PRICE, JO-ANN ELIZABETH, Free-lance Reptr., Photogr., '65–; Reptr., N.Y. Herald Tribune, '55–'65; Religious News Ed., '51–'55; Religious News Ed., Milw. Jnl., '46–'51; Reptr., Photogr., Amarillo Times, '46; Theta Sigma Phi, OPC, Nwsp. Reptrs. Assn., N.Y.C., Religious Newswriters Assn. (Secy.-Treas. '51–'54), Canadian Wms. Press Club; Nat. Conf. of Christians and Jews (Recognition Cert. '68), Supple Religious Memorial Aw. '65; Faith and Freedom Aw. '64, Nat. Religious Pubcty. Cncl. fellow '61, George Polk Memorial Aw. '52; Northwestern Univ. BSJ (with distinction) '45; MSJ, '46; b. Calgary, Canada, 1924; p. Josiah Frampton and Elizabeth Bailey Price; h. Harry William Baehr; res: 135 Willow St., Bklyn., N.Y. 11201.

PRICE, JUDITH MITNICK, Asst. to Dir. of Acquisitions, Time Inc., 50th St. and Sixth Ave., N.Y., N.Y. 10020, '69–; Bus. Reptr., Time, '66–'69; Econ. Analyst and Wtr., Chase Manhattan Bank, '65–'66; Econ. Analyst, Nat. Bur. of Econ. Rsch., '64–'65; Am. Econ. Assn., Young Concert Artists (Advisory Bd.), Museum of Modern Art; Univ. of Pa., BA, '64 (hons.); Columbia Univ., grad. facs., PhD prog. in Econs., '64–'65; b. Phila., Pa., 1942; p. Larry and Sylvia Snyder Mitnick; h. Peter Price; res: 157 W. 13th St., N.Y., N.Y. 10011.

PRICE, MARIE BUCK, Radio Newsman, Associated Press, 50 Rockefeller Plaza, N.Y., N.Y. 10020, '63–; Newsman, AP Newsfeatures Dept., '62–'63; Sls. Prom. Wtr., IBM, '58; Reptr., The Reporter Dispatch (White Plains, N.Y.) '54–'58; Theta Sigma Phi, N.Y. Nwsp. Wms. Club, Am. Acad. of Polit. and Social Sci.; Mich. State Univ., BA (Jnlsm.), '54 (cum laude); b. Scotia, N.Y., 1933; p. Henry and Edna Gode Buck; c. Eric D.; res: 450 E. 20th St., Apt. 6A, N.Y., N.Y. 10009.

PRICE, WILLADENE ANTON, Asst. Ed., Social Education Magazine, National Council for the Social Studies, 1201 16th St., N.W., Wash., D.C. 20036, '68–; Edtl. Asst., '68; Lectr., Flora Frame Agcy., '62–'64;

Teaching Staff, Star Island Wtrs. Conf. (Isle of Shoals, N.H.), '62; Ed., Univ. Publ. Co., (Lincoln, Neb.), '40–'42; Adv. Mgr., '34–'40; Assoc. Ed., '33–'39; Auth: "For All Time to Come" (SRA, '64), "Gutzon Borglum, Artist and Patriot" (Rand McNally, '61), "Bartholdi and the Statue of Liberty" (Rand McNally, '59; 1st aw. in Biog., NLAPW, '60); Authors League of Am., NLAPW (1st VP, '68–'70; Pubcty. Chmn., '64–'66), Manuscript Club of Boston, Intl. Platform Assn., Alexandria YWCA (Dir., '56–'58; VP, '57–'58); George Peabody, '39; Univ. of Neb.; b. Omaha, Neb., 1914; p. August and Ethel Heater Anton; h. John Price; c. Jon DeAlanson; res: 2916 Mayer Pl., Alexandria, Va. 22302.

PRICKETT, RUTH EMELINE, Assoc. Ed., Oklahoma Natural Gas Company, 401 N. Harvey Ave., Okla. City, Okla. 73101, '62–; Bldg. Mgr., Land and Geological Dept., and Ed., Okla. Dist. pubn., '62; Customer Accounting, '48; Central Okla. IEA (Bd. of Dirs., '65–'67; Secy.-Treas., '67–'68), Oh-En-Gees (Pres., '49–'50); Okla. Univ., BFA (Music, Eng.), '48; b. Okla. City, Okla.; p. Hunter and Zeta Denniston Prickett; res: 2909 Moulton Dr., Okla. City, Okla. 73127.

PRIDE, JOY, Prod. Supvsr., The Christian Science Publishing Society, One Norway St., Boston, Mass. 02115, '66–; Art Dir., Prod. Ed., McCormick-Mathers Publ. Co., '61–'66; Sr. Art and Prod. Ed., textbks., The Macmillan Co., '56–'61; Asst. Art Ed., Am. Bk. Co., '54–'56; Free-lance Artist, Wtr., Tchr., '35–'54; Col. Art Instr., '32–'35; Auth., two bks. of Am. folk songs; numerous articles; radio scripts incl. folk song series for CBS network, WQXR, Voice of Am.; Exhbns. of painting, N.Y. shows, Argent Gallery, Nat. Acad.; one-wm. show, Hollywood, Cal.; Univ. of Ky., AB; MA; Art Acads., Paris, others in Europe; N.Y.U., Art Student League; b. Lexington, Ky., 1909; p. James and Grace Conn Pride; res: 2 Everette Dr., Newburyport, Mass. 01950.

PRIEST, MARJORIE McQUISTON, PR Dir., League of Women Voters of Los Angeles, 1134 Crenshaw Blvd., L.A., Cal. 90019, '67–'69; Mercury Adv. Agcy., '50–'51; Asst. Adv. Mgr., Fireman's Fund Ins. Co. (S.F.), '49; Ed., Hotel Greeters Guide, '47–'48; Reptr., Pitt. Post Dispatch, '46–'47; Asst. Ed., Sausalito News, '44–'46; Theta Sigma Phi (S.F. Alumni Chptr. past Pres.; L.A. Alumni Chptr. VP, '69–'70), Reg. Plan Assn. of Southern Cal. (Dir.), League of Wm. Voters (L.A. Dir., '66–'69); Dir. Mail Adv. aw. for prods. at Fireman's Fund; Southern Cal. Bdcstrs. Assn. Silver Radio aw. for crtv. spot announcements on League of Wm. Voters, '68; Univ. of Hi., '40–'42; Univ. of Cal., Berkeley, BA (Jnlsm.), '44; b. Long Beach, Cal., 1923; p. Capt. Edward and Dorothea Brewer McQuiston; h. Bennett W. Priest; c. Leslie, Mark, Randall; res: 3959 Franklin Ave., L.A., Cal. 90027.

PRIESTLEY, OPAL SHORE, Pres., Sunshine Press, 241 N. Water St., Las Cruces, N.M. 88001, '49–; Secy.-Treas., '47–'48; Secy.-Treas., Artesia Advocate, '45–'54;

Secy.-Treas., Crowley Sigmal (La.), '30–'45; Secy.-Treas., Perry Jnl. (Okla.), '26–'30; Tchr., '23–'30; '45; Auth., five fact and fiction bks. ('52–'65), five small pic. bks. ('66–'69); Okla., La., N.M. Press Assns.; Scholastic Magazines Fiction Aw., Martha Foley Hon. Mention, Univ. of N.C. Fiction Aw.; Okla. Central Univ., '23–'24; Univ. of Okla., '24–'26 (Staff Mbr., Sch. for Pfsnl. Wtrs., '56); N.M. State Univ., BA, '50 (Wm. of Achiev., '68); b. Iola, Kans., 1904; p. Edmond and Elizabeth Dorsa Shore; h. Orville E. Priestley; c. Joseph S., Orville E., Jr.; res: 426 N. Miranda, Las Cruces, N.M. 88001.

PRIETO, MARIANA BEECHING, Free-lance Wtr., more than 700 published pieces, in Mademoiselle, The New York Times, others; Auth: "When the Monkeys Wore Sombreros" (Harvey House, '69), "Johnny Lost" (The John Day Co., '69), "A Kite for Carlos" (Bk. for Brotherhood, Nat. Cncl. of Christians and Jews, '67), beauty bk., Spanish lang. bks., seven juv. bks. (some dual lang., Spanish and Eng.); Tchr., '59–; Archeological rsch., painting, studying ancient civilizations in Latin Am., Mexico, Caribbean; Nat. Assn. of Public Sch. Adult Educs., Fla. Auths. Club; Colegio Sagrada Corazon (Havana, Cuba), Univ. of Miami; Univ. of Fla.; b. Cinn., Oh., 1912; p. Charles and Sylvia Beck Beeching; h. Martin Prieto; c. Mrs. Ralph Maercks; res: 2499 S.W. 34th Ave., Miami, Fla. 33145.

PRIGMORE, JOAN CRAWFORD, AE, Ward Hicks Advertising, P.O. Box 2108, 315 Gold Ave. S.W., Albuquerque, N.M. 87102, '64–; Space Byr., '62–'64; Prom. Dir., KCBD-TV (Lubbock, Tex.), '54–'62; News Reptr., Lubbock Avalanche-Journal, '52–'54; Co-auth: "Radio and Television Continuity Writing," (Pitman, '62); Theta Sigma Phi; Albuquerque Adv. Club Silver Medal, '67; Gold Medals, '68; N.M. Bdcstrs. Assn. aw., '68; Board of Directors, Albuquerque Symphony Orchestra; Hardin-Simmons Univ., BA (Jnlsm.) '52; b. Hobbs, N.M., 1931; p. William and Ora Boone Crawford; res: 5805 Goliad NW, Albuquerque, N.M. 87107.

PRINCE, JUDY LYNN ELLIS, Asst. Dir., Cigar Institute of America, 1270 Ave. of Americas, N.Y., N.Y., '69–; AE, Harshe-Rotman & Druck, '66–'69; Tourist Prom., State of Fla. Dev. Commn., Fla. Showcase, '65–'66; PR Dir., TV Hostess, WEDU-TV (Tampa, Fla.), '64–'65; Weather Girl, News Reptr., WUFT-TV (Gainesville), '64; AWRT, Theta Sigma Phi, Zeta Phi Eta, Alpha Epsilon Rho; Am. Cancer Soc. aw., '63; Who's Who of Am. Wm.; 2,000 Wm. of Achiev.; Univ. of Fla., BS (Jnlsm.), '64 (Outstanding Svc. aw., '63), Instituto de Technilogico (Monterrey, Mex.), '59; Univ. of S. Fla., '61; b. Babylon, N.Y., 1942; p. Malcom and Madeline Eistrat Ellis; res: 85 East End Ave., N.Y. N.Y. 10028.

PRINCE, LUCILLE CROCKETT, Staff Wtr., Florence Times Tri-Cities Daily, 219 W. Tennessee St., Florence, Ala. 35631, '40–; b. Sheffield, Ala. 1920; p. Edward F. Sr., and Willie B. Williams Crockett; h. F. L. Prince; c.

William David, Carol Ann, Dinah Sabrina; res: 102 Park Blvd., Sheffield, Ala. 35660.

PRINDLE, KAREN, Prodr., Dir., WTTW-TV, 5400 N. St. Louis Ave., Chgo., Ill. 60625, '65–; Asst. Dir., WNDT-TV (N.Y.C.), '64–'65; Asst. to Prodr., WNEW-TV, '64; Prodr., Dir., WNED-TV (Buffalo), '62–'63; Prod. Asst., '60–'62; Chgo. Area Emmy for Prod. and Dir. of "Requiem for a Slave" ('66–'67); Ithaca Col., BS (TV and Radio), '60; res: 629 W. Fullerton Pkwy., Chgo., Ill., 60614.

PRINS, RUTH BALKEMA, Prodr., "Wunda Wunda," KING-TV, 320 Aurora, Seattle, Wash. 98199, '53–; Story Lady, "Telaventure Tales," '51–'68; Wtr., Talent, "Compass Rose" series for NET, nationwide, '58; Prodr., Dir., "Children's Theatre of the Air" weekly program, Univ. of Wash. KCTS and comml. outlet KOMO, '48–'52; Dir., The Ruth Prins Primary Sch.; NATAS, NEA, AWRT (Seattle Chptr. Charter Mbr.); Univ. of Wash., BA, '42 (cum laude, Gamma Phi Beta Scholarship for Outstanding Wm. in Eng.); MA, '50; b. Sioux City, Ia., 1920; p. Peter and Oma Foster Balkema; h. Robert Prins; c. Robert Peter, Debra; res: 4735 W. Roberts Way, Seattle, Wash. 98199.

PRITCHARD, SHEILA EDWARDS, Wtr., poetry; "Michigan Signatures" ('69), "Ten from Detroit" ('68), "In Rainwater Evening"; Auth., "Poets of Today V"; Tchr., crtv. writing courses, Wayne State Univ., '65–'67; Fed. Poverty Progs., "Poets Visit the Schools," '66–'68; WDET-TV (Wayne State Univ.) "Writing with Writers," '64–'65, Panels with Seymour Riklin; WDET-Radio, Detroit Adventure Progs., readings, '64–'68; Staff, Oakland Univ. Wtrs. Conf., '60–'68; Detroit Wm. Wtrs. (Hon. Mbr.; Wtr. of the Yrs., '54–'57), Wms. Nat. Bk. Assn., Mich. Poetry Soc.; Wayne State Univ.; b. Detroit, Mich., 1909; p. Calita and Mabel Cobb Edwards; h. Robert Otis Pritchard, Sr.; c. Robert Otis, Jr., Neil Edwards; res: Rte. One, Box 92, Bonita Springs, Fla. 33923.

PRITCHETT, ELAINE HILLYER, Jnlsm. Dir., Memorial High School, 935 Echo Lane, Houston, Tex. 77024, '62–; Pubcty. Dir., Houston Museum of Fine Arts, '59–'61; Comm. Club Aws. Dir., KXYZ, '58–'59; Prom. Dir., Radio WFAA-KGKO, '43–'45; Photolithographer, '42; Adv. Dir., Ben Griffin Auto Co., '42; Copywtr., Abe Berger Adv., '41; Publicist, State Fair of Tex., '41; Corr., Dallas Times Herald, '38–'41; Summer Instr., High Sch. Pubns. Workshops: Tex. A & M Univ., '64–'69; Trinity Univ., '68; Northwood Inst., '68; various orgs., aws.; Southern Methodist Univ., BS (Jnlsm.), '41; b. Ft. Worth, Tex., 1920; p. G. Ballard and Adela Kerr Hillyer; h. Henry L. Pritchett, Jr., c. Henry L. III, Ballard H.; res: 11710 Longleaf Lane, Houston, Tex. 77024.

PROCTOR, NANCY NILES, Client Svc. Coordr., Sieber & McIntyre, Inc., 108 N. State St., Chgo., Ill., '68–; Print Prod. Mgr., Grant Adv., '67–'68; Ed., Township Times, Pioneer Suburban Nwsps., '66–'67; STP

Div., Studebaker Corp., '66; Burton Browne Adv., '63-'65; Chissold Publ. Co., '63; Patterson Publ. Co., '60-'62; Chgo. Adv. Prod. Wms. Club (Founder, '68; Pres.); b. La Crosse, Wis., 1939; p. William and Margaret Pendleton Niles; h. Kenneth Proctor; c. Keith, Angela, Natalie; res: 76 Petrie Circle, Streamwood, Ill. 60103.

PROCTOR, VILMA, Chief Med. Librn., Prof., Med. Bibliography, Univ. of Southern Cal. Med. Sch., 2025 Zonal Ave., L.A., Cal. 90033, '46–; Tchr. of Med., Sci. Bibliography, Sch. of Lib. Sci.; Cnslt., bk. publ.; AAUP, Med. Lib. Assn., Special Lib. Assn., Iota Sigma Pi; Hamburg, Germany, Ph.D. (Organic Chemistry), '30; Denver, Colo., BS (Lib. Sci.), '40; Harvard Sch. of Med., post grad. work; b. Hamburg, Germany; res: 701 S. Harvard Blvd., L.A., Cal. 90005.

PROCTOR, VIRGINIA RICHMOND, Adv. Mgr., Huron Daily Tribune, 211 Heisterman, Bad Axe, Mich. 48413, '66–; Adv. Slswm., '65-'66; Mich. Press Assn. (Adv. Mgrs. Div., 3rd pl. for best color and offset reproduction, '69), Child Study Club 4 (Pres., '68-'69); Central Mich. Univ. off campus courses, '57; b. Bay City, Mich., '35; p. Kenneth and Sara Sadtler Richmond; h. Lee Proctor; c. Vickie, Brook Ann, Beth Laraine, Holly Lee, Christopher, Clay Alan; res: Box 118, Bad Axe, Mich. 48413.

PROPST, MARY THOMAS, Head Librn., Southside Regional Library, Boydton, Va. 23917, '48–; Hist. Rsch. Librn., Colonial Williamsburg; Tchr., Va. Public Schs., '39-'45; BPW (Dist. Rec. Secy., '68–), Va. Lib. Assn., Delta Kappa Gamma, numerous civic clubs; Longwood Col., BS (Educ.), '39; William and Mary Col., AB (Lib. Sci.), '46; b. Skipwith, Va., '17; p. John and Lucy Woltz Thomas; h. Noel L. Propst; c. Noel Jr.; res: R.F.D. 1, Boydton, Va. 23917.

PROTAS, JUDITH C., VP and Copy Supvsr., Doyle, Dane, Bernbach, Inc., 20 W. 43rd St., N.Y., N.Y. 10036 (aw.-winning campaigns for Levy's, Ohrbach's, Cracker Jack); Copy Club of N.Y., Adv. Club of N.Y. (Andy aw., '65; Andy aws. judging comm.; Clio aws. judging comm.); aws: Art Dirs. Club of N.Y., Am. TV Commls. Festival, many others; Barnard Col., BA, '43; Yale Grad. Sch., MA, '45; b. N.Y.C.; p. Julius and Anne Atkins; res: 310 E. 74th St., N.Y., N.Y. 10021.

PROTHRO, LOUISE GRAY, Consumer Products Specialist, Farley Manning Assoc., Inc., 342 Madison Ave., N.Y., N.Y. 10017; Group Mgr., PR, Pet, Inc. (St. Louis, Mo.), '62-'68; Pubcty., '51-'62; Instr., Fla. A & M Univ., '48-'51; Newark (N.J.) Urban League, '43-'45; AWRT, Wms. Adv. Club, Home Econsts. in Bus.; Nat. Assn. of Mkt. Dev. aw., '65; Framingham State Col., BA, '41; Columbia Univ., MA, '51; b. Macon, Ga.; p. Charles and Louise Hill Gray; h. Robinson Prothro (div.); c. Jeanne; res: 120–11 199 St., St. Albans, N.Y. 11412.

PROWSE-PARSONS, BEATRICE, Wms. Ed., Enfield Press, 71 Church, Enfield, Conn., '62–; Assoc. Ed., Nat. Grange Monthly, '49-'62 (Lifeline of Am. nat. aws., '54, '56); Founder and Publr.-Ed., Acton (Mass.) Beacon, now the Assabet Valley Beacon, '43-'49; Ed., Hudson (Mass.) News Enterprises, '42-'43; Corr., AP and UPI; Colmst., "Bea Liner"; Wtr., nwsp. and mag. edtls.; Soroptimist (Past Public Affairs Chmn.; New England Reg. Mbr.-at-Large; Springfield, Mass. Chptr. past Pres.), Nat. Grange; Fisher Jr. Col.; special courses at Boston Tchrs. Col.; Harvard Univ.; b. Upton, Mass.; p. Cornelius J. and Florence E. Van Iderstine Prowse; h. Norman Parsons (div.); c. Donn Winthrop; res: 22 Elmshade Way, Springfield, Mass. 01119.

PRUITT, EVELYN, Program Dir., Geography Programs, Office of Naval Research, Wash., D.C. 20360, '59–; Geographer, Scientific Offcr., Coastal Geography, '48-'59; Cartographic Engineer, Aeronautical Charts, U.S. Coast and Geodetic Survey, '42-'47; Ed., The Professional Geographer, '57-'59; Co-auth., "Culture Worlds: Brief Edition" (Russell, Kniffen and Pruitt, '61; revsd.); Assn. of Am. Geographers, Soc. of Wm. Geographers (Asst. Treas., Treas., '65–); numerous aws.; Univ. of Cal., MA, '43; res: 1817 N. Quinn St., Apt. 304, Arlington, Va. 22209.

PRZYWARA, Sr. MARY BENICE, Head Librn., Trustee, Villa Maria College, 240 Pine Ridge Rd., Buffalo, N.Y. 14225, '64–; ALA, Catholic Lib. Assn., Nat. Cncl. of Tchrs. of Eng.; Who's Who of Am. Wm.; Who's Who in Lib. Svc.; Dic. of Intl. Biog.; Canisius Col., AB, '42 (magna cum laude); State Univ. of N.Y., BS (Lib. Sci.), '44; Niagara Univ., MA, '51; State Univ. at Buffalo, doctoral candidate; b. Windber, Pa.; p. Stanley and Hedwig Liss Przywara; res: 600 Doat St., Buffalo, N.Y. 14211.

PUCKETT, MARLENE SKAGEN, Media Dir., Gaynor & Ducas of California, 1800 Ave. of Stars, L.A., Cal. 90067, '67–; Media Dir., Rullman & Munger, '66-'67; Media Byr., Cole Fischer Rogow, '61-'66; Jr. Adv. Club of L.A., CORANTO; Univ. of Wis., BS, '60; b. Baldwin, Wis., 1938; p. Earl and Marie Wenger Skagen; h. Ray Puckett (dec.); c. Jill; res: 1225 Harvard St., Santa Monica, Cal. 90404.

PUDNEY, BETTY ANN, Public Info. Dir., Division of Employment Opportunities, Mobilization for Youth, 214 E. Second St., N.Y., N.Y. 10001, '65–; Wtr., Rschr., Cunningham and Walsh, '64; Educ. Ed., Nat. Instructional TV Lib., '62-'64; Asst. Pubcty. Dir., Harper and Bros., '59-'62; Rschr., Time, '56-'58; Reptr., Binghamton Sun, '54-'55; Reptr., Endicott-Bul., '53-'54; prepared news features on corporate accts., Ray Josephs Assocs.; Rschr., Interviewer, wtr. for various auths.; hist., theological, sociological rsch. for ABC show "The First Christmas" ('66); Eng.-Speaking Un.; Northwestern Univ., Medill Sch. of Jnlsm., BS, '53; Cornell Univ., Grad. Work (Grad. Asst.); b. Oneonta, N.Y., 1931; p. Cecil and Harriet Lawless Pudney; res: 315 East 77th St., N.Y., N.Y. 10021.

PULLIAM, NINA MASON, Secy.-Treas. and Dir., Phoenix Newspapers, Inc., Central Newspapers, Inc., Indianapolis Newspapers, Inc., 120 E. Van Buren St., Phoenix, Ariz. and 307 N. Pennsylvania St., Indpls., Ind.; VP and Dir., Muncie (Ind.) Newspapers, Inc.; Auth., "I Traveled a Lonely Land" (Bobbs-Merrill, '55), Nat. Soc. for Prevention of Blindness (Bd. of Dirs.), Franklin Col. Bd. of Trustees, Franklin Col. Alumni Cncl. VP Dir. ('52–'55), NFPW, Wms. Press Club of Ind., BPW, Theta Sigma Phi (Headliner Aw., '54); Univ. of N.M., '26–'27; Ind. Univ., '25–'26; '27–'28 (D.H.L., '67); Univ. of Ariz., '63; b. Martinsville, Ind., 1906; p. Benjamin and Laura Gesaman Mason; h. Eugene C. Pulliam; res: 5702 Palo Christi Rd., Paradise Valley, Ariz. 85251.

PULLING, HAZEL ADELE, Wtr., non-fiction, Lib. Sci. jnls.; Rsch., "What Happens to the Books in Circulation"; Head Librn., Cal. Western Univ., San Diego, '60–'65; Prof., Sch. of Lib. Sci., Immaculate Heart Col. (L.A.), '55–'60; Assoc. Prof., Univ. of Southern Cal., '40–'50; Head, Lib. Sch., Tex. Wm's. Univ., '50–'53; ALA, Am. Hist. Assn., local orgs., Special Libs. Assn. Nat. Conv. Chmn. (L.A.), '49; Phi Beta Mu, Phi Alpha Phi, Phi Alpha Theta; Univ. of Chgo., PhB, '30; MA, '31; Univ. of Southern Cal., BS (Lib. Sci.); PhD, '44 (Phi Beta Kappa); b. Edmonton, Alberta, Can., 1902; p. Edward and Leonora Miller Pulling; res: 910 Cornish Dr., San Diego, Cal. 92107.

PULVERMACHER, MARIE B., Ed., The Green (feature sec.), The Capital Times, 115 S. Carroll St., Madison, Wis. 53703, '54–; Reptr., '42–'47; Ed., Copy Reader, '47–'54; Theta Sigma Phi (Chptr. Pres., '66–'67; Treas., '63), Madison Press Club (VP, '69; Bd. of Dirs., '62, '59); Univ. of Wis., BS, '42; b. Sauk City, Wis., 1919; p. Carl and Theresa Geier Pulvermacher; res: 111 W. Wilson St., Madison, Wis. 53703.

PUNDT, HELEN MARIE, Free-lance Ed., Wtr.; Assoc. Ed. of Pubns., Am. Home Econs. Assn., Wash., D.C., '61–; Asst., Ida Jean Kain, Synd. Colmst., '51–'53; Auth: juvs., "Spring Comes First to the Willows," "Zenty," "The Judge's Daughters," "Mystery of the Castle Coins" (all Thomas Y. Crowell); Sr. Ed., Gen. Foods Corp., '53–'61; Asst. Ed. for Ext. Svc., Cornell Univ., '49–'51; former tchr., feature writing, Ia. State Univ.; Info. Specialist, Dept. of Agriculture, '43–'47; Theta Sigma Phi, MWA, ANWC, Auths. League, Auths. Guild; Ia. State Univ., BS, '43; b. Rochester, N.Y.; p. Adolph E. and Elizabeth Kehm Scharf; res: 2929 Connecticut Ave. N.W., Wash., D.C. 20008.

PURDY, SUSAN GOLD, Auth., Illus., juv. bks.; Free-lance Designer, '63; Textile Designer, Wamsutta Mills, '62–'63; Auth: "Jewish Holidays" (J. B. Lippincott, '69), "Festivals for You to Celebrate" (Lippincott, '69), seven others; Vassar Col., N.Y.U.; b. N.Y.C.; p. Harold and Frances Joslin Gold; h. Geoffrey Purdy; res: Wilton, Conn. 06897.

PURRINGTON, ANN MEDER, Cont. Dir., WTVJ, Division of Wometco Enterprises, 316 N. Miami Ave.,

Miami, Fla. 33128, '65–; Wtr., Asst. Cont. Dir., '52–'59; Free-lance Wtr.; Wtr., Wms. Prog. Dir., On-Air Bdcstr., "Homemaker's Exchange" and "After Breakfast Show," WICH-Radio Sta. (Norwich, Conn.), '49–'52; Cont. Wtr., WHYN-Radio (Holyoke, Mass.), '46–'49; Theta Sigma Phi, AWRT; Adv. Club of Greater Miami Cit. of Excellence for 30" TV Comml., '66; Smith Col., AB, '43; b. Northampton, Mass.; p. Jacob and Petranela Rawska Meder; h. John Purrington; c. Cynthia Jean; res: 16400 S.W. 95th Ave., Miami, Fla. 33157.

PUSTARFI, BETTY ANN, Mgr. of Adv. and PR, Vacu-Blast Corporation, Box 885, Belmont, Cal. 94002, '65–; PR Dir., '64–'65; AE, Kossack and Assoc., '63–'64; Exec. Dir., Ariz. Soc. Am. Inst. of Architects, '58–'63; Assn. of Indsl. Advs. (N. Cal. Chptr. Bd. of Dirs., '68–'69), Peninsula Adv. Club (Treas., '68–'69; Secy., '67–'68); L.A. Adv. Wm. Competition for wm. in adv. in 13 western states, Lulu aw. for Prom. Lit., and Aw. of Merit for Nat. Pubcty. Campaign, '68; Ariz. State Univ., BA (Eng.), '55 (with distinction); Masters Program, '58 (Teaching Fellowship); b. Newark, N.J., 1931; p. Theodore and Jeanette Kisch Pustarfi; res: 185 Graystone Terr. #5, S.F., Cal. 94114.

PUSZCZ, ARLENE VICTORIA, Fashion Ed., The Times-Union, Capital Newspapers, 24 Sheridan Ave., Albany, N.Y. 12201, '67–'69; Reptr., Wms. Dept., '66; PR, Macy's Colonie, '66; Copywtr., Beckman Assoc., Adv. Agcy., '64–'65; Reptr., Schenectady Gazette, '63–'64; Col. of St. Rose, BA, '63; b. Schenectady, N.Y. 1941; p. Joseph and Victoria Buturla Puszcz; res: One Andrews Rd., Troy, N.Y. 12180.

PUZAK, GAIL SCOTT, News Reptr., Co-hostess "Today at Home," The WSJS Stations, Box 3018, 700 Coliseum Dr., Winston-Salem, N.C. 27102, '66–; AWRT (Nat. Special Svcs. Comm.; N.C. Chptr. Publicist); Phi Rho Pi (Hon. Mbr.); Amicus aw., Sr. Citizens, '68; Sch. Bell aw., N.C. Schs., '69; Wake Forest Univ., AB (Speech; Outstanding Freshman Actress; Who's Who in Am. Cols. and Univs.); b. Wash., D.C., 1944; p. Dr. Michael and Elizabeth Kurtz Puzak; res: 1843 Hawthorne Rd., Winston-Salem, N.C. 27103.

Q

QUA, ELLEN HUGHES, Ed., Ballston Journal, Grose Publications, Ballston Spa., N.Y. 12020, '62–; News Commentator, WKAJ (Saratoga Springs); Feature Wtr., Albany Times Union; Reptr., Glens Falls Post Star, '50–'54; Reptr., N.Y. Herald Tribune, '50–'54; Ed., Wms. Page, Troy Record, '45–'50; Reptr., '42–'45; Sch. Tchr., '29–'30; Wms. Press Club of N.Y. State (Charter Mbr.), AWRT, N.Y. State Press Assn., Nat. Nwsp. Assn., ZONTA, BPW; Granville (N.Y.) Tchrs. Training, '28–'29; Cornell Univ., '42–'43; Skidmore Col., '52–'53; New Sch. for Soc. Rsch., '53; b. Bethesda, Wales, 1910;

p. William and Mary Griffith Hughes; h. Arthur Garfield Qua (dec.); res: 156 Caroline St., Saratoga Springs, N.Y. 12866.

QUATTLEBAUM, LOIS FISCHER, Social Ed., Prod., Bdcstr., "World of Women," WNOK-TV, 6027 Devine St., Columbia, S.C. 29205, '62–; "Teen Talk," '62–'64; Wms. Ed., Soc. Ed., Colmst., Bk. Reviewer, The Record Nwsp., '51–'62; Rschr., '45–'50; Caroliniana Hist. and Genealogical Soc., Eng. Speaking Un. (Secy., '59), NPWC, S.C. Press Assn. Wms. Div. (past Pres., Secy.), Altrusa (past Pres.; Wm. of the Yr.), Quill-Wtrs. (past Pres.), AWRT (Treas.), Wms. Club of Columbia (Wm. of the Yr.); numerous scriptwriting aws.; Who's Who of Am. Wm.; Royal Blue Bk.; Nat. Social Reg.; 2000 Wm. of Achiev.; Several other dirs.; Univ. of S.C., '27, '29, '30; Butler Univ.; Draughon's Bus. Co.; Huckelberry Crtv. Arts, '45; b. Charleston, S.C.; p. Louis M. and Genevieve deGafferelly Fischer; h. George Edwards Quattlebaum (dec.); c. George Edwards, Jr. (dec.); res: 1314 Devonshire Dr., Columbia, S.C. 29204.

QUILLIN, ELLEN SCHULZ, Dir. Emeritus, Witte Memorial Museum, 3801 Broadway, San Antonio, Tex. 78209, '62–; Dir., '26–'62; Dir., San Antonio Public Schs. Dept. of Sci. and Nature Study, '23–'50; Lectr. '26–'50; Auth., "Texas Wild Flowers" ('28); Co-auth., seven bks. on nature study; Univ. of Mich., AB, '10, MS, '18; b. Saginaw County, Mich., 1892; h. Roy W. Quillin; res: 422 W. Kings Highway, San Antonio, Tex. 78212.

QUINLAN, KARIN ANN, Prodr., Jack Tinker & Partners, 1414 Sixth Ave., N.Y., N.Y. 10019, '67–; Secy., '64–'66; Georgetown Visitation Jr. Col., AA; b. Port Chester, N.Y.; p. Edward and Anne Haffmans Quinlan; res: 63 Betsy Brown Rd., Port Chester, N.Y. 10573.

QUINLAN, LIZ WEXLER, Pubns. Ed., Association of Junior Leagues of America, 825 Third Ave., N.Y., N.Y. 10022, '68–; Assoc. Ed., Readers Digest Almanac, '65–'67; Assoc. Ed., Trade Dept., Macmillan Co., '63–'65; Asst. to Ed.-in-Chief, Trade Dept., McGraw-Hill Bk. Co., '60–'63; Free-lance Ed., Wtr.; DAR; Vassar Col., AB, '59; b. N.Y.C., 1937; p. A. Ralph and Mary Darbee Wexler; h. Robert J. Quinlan; res: 200 East End Ave., N.Y., N.Y. 10028.

QUINN, ESTHER CASIER, Assoc. Prof., Fordham University, Lincoln Ctr. Campus, N.Y., N.Y. 10023, '68–; Asst. Prof., Hunter Col., '63–'68; Instr., '60–'63; Lectr., '48–'60; Fellow, '46–'48; Auth., "The Quest of Seth" (Univ. of Chgo. Press, '62); articles, reviews, editing.

QUINN, MELICENT BROWN, Free-lance Wtr., '20–; Wms. Ed., Gleaner-Journal (Henderson, Ky.), '24–'67; Auth., bk. of poems, "Jonquils" ('44–'45); poetry in many U.S. and Eng. anthologies; pfsnl. pianist, '13; NLAPW, Western Ky. Bishop's Ltr., Wms. Club of Henderson, Henderson County Hist. Soc., Henderson Music Club, Garden Club of Henderson, Who's Who

in South and Southwest; Who's Who of Am. Wm.; Dic. of Intl. Biogs.; Intl. Who's Who in Poetry; private schs. and conservatories; p. Stephen and Melicent Parker-Plumb Brown; h. Walter Cannon Quinn (dec.); c. Walter, Melicent (Mrs. John Alexander Wall, Jr.); res: 301 Third St., Henderson, Ky. 42420.

QUINN, Sr. M. BERNETTA, O.S.F., Prof. of Eng., The College of Saint Teresa, Winona, Minn. 55987, '53; Visiting Prof., Allen Univ. (Columbia, S.C.), '68–'69; Tchr., '37–'40, '42–'46, '52–'53; summer teaching, various cols.; Auth., non-fiction, four bks. on poetry, col. hist., religious biogs.; Am. Studies Assn., Modern Lang. Assn.; several grants for study; Col. of St. Teresa, '42; Cath. Univ. of Am., Wash., D.C., MA, '44; Univ. of Wis., PhD, '52; Univ. of Denver; b. Lake Geneva, Wis., 1915; p. Bernard and Ellen Foran Quinn.

QUINT, RUTH J. Wms. Ed., New Haven Register, 367 Orange St., New Haven, Conn. 06503; Eds. Advisory Bd., N.Y. Couture Bus. Cncl., Fashion Reptrs. Aw., City of N.Y., '68; Eastern Mink Breeders Assn. cits.; New Haven Cancer Soc. (Bd. of Trustees), Yale-New Haven Hosp. Wms. Auxiliary; Brandeis Univ. Nat. Wm.'s Comm. (New Haven Chptr. Co-founder); b. New Haven, Conn.; p. Louis and Bessie Clark Quint; res: 153 Cold Spring St., New Haven, Conn. 06511.

QUINTAL, CLAIRE, Acting Chmn., French Dept., Assumption College, 500 Salisbury St., Worcester, Mass. 01609, '69–'70; Assoc. Prof.; Affiliate Assoc. Prof., Clark Univ.; Prof., Am. Col. in Paris; Auth: "The Letters of Joan of Arc" (Pitt., '69), collaborator on "The First Biography of Joan of Arc" ('64; one of 50 best bks. of yr. by AIGA); Lectr., nationwide, '64–'65; numerous learned socs.; exhbn. of art, Paris, '68; Silver Medal, City of Paris; Outstanding Young Wm. of Am.; Anna Maria Col., AB (first Joan of Arc Medal); Univ. of Montreal, MA; Univ. of Paris, doctorate (Comparative Lit.), '61; res: 50 Franklin St., Worcester, Mass. 01608.

QUIRK, JANE WAGNER, Commtns. Specialist, the Buehler Corporation, 9000 Precision Dr., Indpls., Ind. 46236, '69–; PR Mgr., '61–'69; Ed., '55–'60; Employee Pubns. Mgr., ITT-Kellogg (Chgo.), '60–'61; Ed., Monument Engineering, '52–'55; Pers. Cnslr., Western Electric, '46–'49; Overseas Svc., Am. Red Cross, '45–'46; Employee Rel. Cnslr., Selective Svc. System (Wash., D.C.), '42–'45; Ind. IEA (Dir., '54–'55, '57–'59, '67; VP, '59; Pres., '60, '64–'65), ICIE (Dir. of Nat. Affairs, '65–'66; Exec. Bd., '60, '64–'65); Ind. Manufacturers Assn. (Co-auth. and Ed., "Public Relations Handbook," '68), Indpls. C. of C., Commty. War Fund (Vice-Chmn., '44), Un. Fund Campaign ('68), U.S. Savings Bonds (Govt. Unit Chmn., '43–'44; Cert. of Merit); Svc. aw., Nat. Fndn., March of Dimes, '68; Oshkosh State, '35; Am. Univ., '44; Univ. of Chgo., '47; Purdue Univ. Ext., '63; b. Eagle River, Wis., 1915; p. William and Sarah Carter Wagner; h. (div.); c. Sarah Jane; res: 7023 Indian Lake, N. Dr., Indianapolis, Ind. 46236.

R

RAASCH, HARVIAN, Special Talent, The Journal Company, WTMJ-TV, 720 E. Capitol Dr., Milw., Wis. 53212, '67–; Cont. and Traf. Dir., WISM (Madison, Wis.), '61; Cont. and Traf. Dir., '60; Edtl. Staff, Torch; Chmn. of Wms. Activities, AFA Conv.; Radio and TV Chmn., Commtns. Milw. Month, '70; Milw. Adv. Club, (Bd. of Dirs.), Theta Sigma Phi (Milw. Chptr. Pres., '69–'70); Beta Sigma Phi Wm. of the Yr. Aw., '68; Univ. of Wis., BS (Jnslm.), '60 (Eta Sigma Phi); b. Milw., Wis., '39; p. Harvey A. and Vivian Schmidt Raasch; res: 14775 Beechwood, Brookfield, Wis. 53005.

RABBIA, ANGELA MARIE, Rsch. Assoc., Fortune Magazine, Time-Life Building, N.Y., N.Y. 10020, '66–; Wtr.-Ed., Investor's Reader, '63–'66; Lang. Instr., UN, '62–'64; Instr., Hunter Col., '62–'64; Free-lance; Elmira Col., BA, '60 (summa cum laude; Phi Beta Kappa); Univ. of Leicester, '58–'59; Ind. Univ., MA, '62; b. Utica, N.Y., 1938; res: 460 E. 79th St., N.Y., N.Y. 10021.

RABBITT, WINIFRED THERESE, Free-lance PR; Press Rep., UNIVAC; AE, Rumrill Agcy.; PR, Gen. Foods; AWRT; N.Y.U.; Fordham; Armed Forces Info. Sch.; b. New Rochelle, N.Y.; p. Thomas S. and Agnes Thompson Rabbitt; res: 162 Stephenson Blvd., New Rochelle, N.Y. 10801.

RABITCHEFF, JUDITH GILMAN, Free-lance Wtr., Prodr., '69–; Prodr., Allegro Film Productions, '65–'69; Admr., Allegro Film Svcs.; Wtr. Columbia Records, '64–'65; Actress, Broadway and TV; Bklyn. Col., BA; Univ. of Conn.; b. N.Y.C.; h. Aaron Rabitcheff; res: 315 W. 70th St., N.Y. 10023.

RADFORD, RUBY LORRAINE, Free-lance Wtr., fiction, biog., for children and young adults, '21–; Tchr., eight yrs.; Auth: "Prelude to Fame" (Geron-X, '69), "Robert Fulton" (Putnam, '70), many others; Ga. Wtrs. Assn., Dixie Cncl. Auths.; & Jnlsts.; Columbia Univ., Univ. of Ga.; b. Augusta, Ga.; p. Walter and Elizabeth Bailey Radford; res: 1422 Johns Rd., Augusta, Ga. 30904.

RADIN, HELEN KRISTT, VP, Vision Associates, Inc., 680 Fifth Ave., N.Y., N.Y. 10019, '59–; Asst. Dir., Dynamic Films, '57–'59; Prodr., "The Odds Against" (Acad. Aw. nominee, doc. short subjects); Hunter Col.; b. N.Y.C., 1933; p. David and Olga Lewit Kristt; h. Harris Radin; c. Jennifer Mora; res: 390 West End Ave., N.Y., N.Y. 10024.

RADKE, KATHERINE WOERPEL, News Ed., Waterloo Courier, Royle Publishing Company, Professional Bldg., Waterloo, Wis., '57–; PR Off., Wms. Army Air Corp. (Ft. Oglethorpe), '43.

RADMACHER, CAMILLE J., Exec. Dir., Western Illinois Library System, and Warren County Librn., '60–'62 W. Side Public Sq., Monmouth, Ill. 61462, '65–; Dir., Western Ill. Film Cooperative, '60–'65; Circulation Librn., Warren County Lib., '39–'48; Exec. Dir., Ill. Nat. Lib. Week, '59–'60; Dir., Warren-Henderson County Lib. Project, '57–'59; ALA (Ill. Chmn.), Ill. Lib. Assn., Ill. Librn. Cit. Comm. (Chmn., '69; aw., '67); Monmouth Col., '35–'37; b. Monmouth, Ill., '17; p. Harry and Esther Greenleaf Radmacher; res: 500 N. First St., Monmouth, Ill. 61462.

RADMACHER, MARY, Chief Librn., Skokie Public Lib., 5215 Oakton, Skokie, Ill. 60076, '56–; Head, Ref. Dept., Gary Public Lib. (Gary, Ind.), '51–'56; Ref. Librn., '46–'51; Asst. Agriculture Librn., Univ. of Ill. Lib. (Urbana, Ill.), '46; Catalog Dept., '43–'46; Librn. (Monmouth, Ill.), '36–'43; various orgs.; Monmouth Col., '34–'36; Univ. of Ill., BA, '45; Lib. Sch., BS (Lib. Sci.), '46; b. Monmouth, Ill., 1915; p. Harry and Esther Greenleaf Radmacher; res: 1209 Sherwin, Chgo., Ill. 60626.

RADTKE, DOLLEE EHRHARDT, Media Dir., AE, Robert S. Block Advertising Inc., 777 W. Glencoe Pl., Milw., Wis. 53217; TV, Fiction Wtr., '59–'60; Ad-Craft Agcy., '52–'59; Milw. Adv. Club.

RADTKE, LORRAINE MARION, PR Dir., Wisconsin Heart Association, 205 W. Highland Ave., Milw., Wis. 53203, '68–; Ed., Badger Lutheran, '56–'68; Owner, Radtke Reports, '56–'68; Adv. Specialist, Wis. Gas Co., '50–'56; Asst. Prof., Oh. Wesleyan Univ., '49–'50; Instr., '48–'49; Instr., Marquette Univ., '46–'48; Part-time Lectr., '44–'45; State Ed., Milwaukee Sentinel, '44–'45; Auth., "The Story of the Wilhelm Friedrich Radtke Family" ('57); Milw. Sch. Bd. (Pres., '63–'65; Dir., '55–), Theta Sigma Phi, Phi Alpha Theta, Milw. Adv. Club, Wis. Indsnl. Eds. Assn., PRSA, Delta Zeta, AAUW; Univ. of Minn., MA, '46; Marquette Univ., Ph.B., '44; b. Milw., Wis., '22; p. Fred and Ella Patzke Radtke; res: 2654 N. 57th St., Milw., Wis. 53210.

RAEBECK, LOIS RUPP, Auth: "Who Am I?" (Follett Publ., '70); "New Approaches to Music in the Elementary Schools" (W. C. Brown Publ., '69); Singing Talent; Tchrs. Col., MA, '48; h. (dec.); res: 31 Joralemon St., Bklyn., N.Y. 11201.

RAEPPEL, JOSEPHINE EUGENIA, Librn., Albright College, Reading, Pa. 19604, '45–; Assoc. Prof., Marshall Col., summers, '53, '58, '60; Librn., Bergenfield Jr.-Sr. HS, '43–'45; Librn., War Prisoners Aid (YMCA), '42–'43; Lib. Asst., Union Theological Seminary, '35–'42; Lib. Asst., Univ. of Rochester, '30–'35; Special Libs. Assn. (Pres., '42–'43), AAUW, AAUP (Reading Chptr., Secy. and Treas., '60–), Altrusa Club of Reading (Pres., '68–'70; VP, '67–'68; Secy. '66–'67); Kappa Delta Pi; Univ. of Rochester, AB, '30; Columbia Univ., BS (Lib. Sci), '37; MS (Lib. Sci.), '49; N.Y.U., MA, '38; Ore. State Univ. EdD, '55; b. Rochester, N.Y., 1903; p. L. Alfred and Augusta Hoff Raeppel; res: 920 N. Fourth St., Reading, Pa. 19601.

RAFFERTY, KATHLEEN KELLY, Ed.-in-Chief, Dell

puzzle pubns., Dell Publishing Co., Inc., 750 Third Ave., N.Y., N.Y. 10017, '42–; Bd. of Dirs., '68–; Auth: six-million copy "Dell Crossword Dictionary," "Big Dell Crossword Puzzle" ('65), "Dell Challenger Crosswords" ('67), "Hard Crosswords" ('69); Intl. Platform Assn.; Who's Who of Am. Wm., Dic. of Intl. Biog. 2,000 Wm. of Achiev.; Univ. of Ia.; b. Chester, Ia., 1915; p. Patrick and Elizabeth O'Haire Kelly; h. James Thomas Rafferty; c. Kathleen Ellen, Brigit Elizabeth, James Thomas Jr.; res: 4669 Palisade Ave., Riverdale, N.Y. 10471.

RAHM, VIRGINIA MARTIN, Ed., Chicago Police Star, Chicago Police Department, 1121 S. State St., Chgo., Ill. 60626, '65–'69; Asst. Ed., '64–'65; Asst. Ed. Triad, house organ, Continental Nat. Am., '63–'64; Radio Wtr., UPI, '62–'63; Asst. to PR Dir., Mpls. Public Lib. (Mpls., Minn.), '60–'62; Univ. of Minn., BA (Intl. Rels.), '57 (cum laude); Grad. Work (Jnlsm.); b. Mpls., Minn., 1935; p. Norman and Merle Murphey Martin; h. Mark Rahm; res: 5617 42nd Ave. N., Minneapolis, Minn. 55422.

RAINEY, JEAN OSGOOD, Exec. VP, Rainey McEnnoe and Manning Inc., 1750 Pennsylvania Ave. N.W., Wash., D.C. 20006, '62–; VP for PR, Manchester Orgs., '60–'61; Dir. of PR, Nat. Assn. of Food Chains, '54–'59; Dir. of Press Rels., '50–'54; Staff Asst., '46–'49; PRSA, ANWC (VP, '69–'70), AWRT (Nat. Dir.-at-Large, '62–'64; Wash. Chptr. Pres., '61–'62); Lansing Bus. Univ., '42; b. Lansing, Mich., '25; p. Earl and Blanche Eberly Osgood; h. John L. Rainey; c. Cynthia, John, Jr., Ruth; res: 3127 N St. N.W., Wash., D.C. 20007.

RAINIE, DOROTHY ESTILL, Soc., Wms. Ed., The Toledo Times, Blade Building, Toledo, Oh. 43604, '55–; Soc. Ed., '30–'32; Soc. Ed., News Bee, '28; b. Toledo, Oh., '07; p. Frank and Mary Dull Estill; h. Walter J. Rainie; c. Patricia (Mrs. William Alverson); res: 2241 Townley Rd., Toledo, Oh. 43614.

RAINIER, PATRICIA ANNE, Actress, Model, Rumrill-Hoyt, Inc., 380 Madison Ave., N.Y., N.Y. 10017, '69–; Comml. Model, Lee & Assocs. (L.A., Cal.); Actress, motion pics: "Death Scene," "Sex and the Single Girl," "Gavilon," "Tony Rome"; in 18 stage prods. (Milw., Wis.); TV drama roles; Singer, incl. four Criteria Albums; Poet; Lyricist, "Love"; Top Actress aw., Eastern U.S., NBC, '68; Zeta Phi Eta; Marquette Univ., BA (Speech, Drama, Eng.), '62; b. Ft. Lauderdale, Fla., 1940; p. Robert and Anne Dempsey Rainier; res: 2308 N.E. 13th St., Coral Ridge, Ft. Lauderdale, Fla. 33304.

RAINONE, NANETTE, Prodr., Reptr., Interviews and Documentaries, WBAI-FM, 30 E. 39th St., N.Y., N.Y. 10016, '68–; Prodr., "Womankind," wkly. series on feminist commty.; Reptr. for 15-minute closeup of news event on "City"; active in Wms. Liberation, N.Y. Radical Feminists; Queens Col., BA (Eng. Lit.), '65; b. Bklyn., N.Y., 1942; h. Ralph L. Blumenfeld; c. Bruno R.; res: 784 Columbus Ave., N.Y., N.Y. 10025.

RAKESTRAW, CAROLINE LEIDING, Exec. Dir., Episcopal Radio-TV Foundation, Inc., 2744 Peachtree Rd., N.W., Atlanta, Ga. 30305, '59–; Exec. Secy., '54–'59; Exec. Secy., Diocese of Atlanta, Episcopal Ch., '45–'54; Trustee, Protestant Radio and TV Ctr. (Atlanta, Ga.); AWRT; Ohio State TV aw., "The Endless Thread", '69; Univ. of Ga., '30–'34; b. Atlanta, Ga., 1912; p. Christopher Boone and Caroline Adkins Leiding; h. Emmett Rakestraw (dec.); c. Catherine (Mrs. Huisdean Evan J. MacLeod); res: 750 Longwood Dr., N.W., Atlanta, Ga. 30305.

RALEIGH, SALLY SANDERSON, Wms. Ed., Seattle Post-Intelligencer, Sixth Ave. and Wall St., Seattle, Wash. 98111, '65–; Fashion Ed., '60–'65; Staff, '54–'60; Reptr., '40–'42; Soc. Ed., Wenatchee Daily World, '38–'40; Theta Sigma Phi (Pres., '64–'65), Fashion Group of Seattle (Reg. Dir., '65–'67), Wash. Press Wm. (many aws.); Sigma Delta Chi-Wash. State Press aws: 2nd, wms. features, '63; 1st, wms. colms., '64, '66; wms. cover page, '66; special interest colms., '67; Univ. of Pitt., BA, '35; b. Freewater, Ore.; p. Stanley and Henrietta Young Sanderson; h. Robert Raleigh; c. Mrs. Dennis Proctor; res: 4613 S. 168th St., Seattle, Wash. 98188.

RAMBACH, PATRICIA SCHARLIN, Ed.-in-Chief, Carnegie Endowment for International Peace, 345 E. 46th St., N.Y., N.Y. 10028, '69–; Exec. Ed., '66–'69; Am. Polit. Sci. Assn., OPC, Middle East Inst.; Univ. of Pa., BA, '50; b. N.Y.C., '28; p. Nathan and Gloria Marks Scharlin; h. Harvey W. Rambach; c. Wendy, Janet, Amy, Peggy.

RAMEY, MARY RAGLAND, Dir., Danville Public Library, 975 Main St., Danville, Va. 24541, '66–; Head, Catalog Dept., '29–'66; Tchr., '27–'28; Va. Lib. Assn., Southeastern Lib. Assn., ALA; Univ. of N.C., BA, '27; Emory Univ. (Lib. Sci. deg.) '29; b. Salisbury, N.C., 1906; p. Dr. Marcus and Attie White Ragland; h. Vernon Ramey; res: Rt. 1, Box 457, Danville, Va. 24541.

RAMEY, WANDA, Public Affairs Newscaster, KQED-TV, 525 Fourth St., S.F., Cal. 94107, '67–; Newscaster, KPIX-TV, '58–'67; Newscaster, KCBS, '54–'57; Newscaster, KGO-TV, '51–'53; Newscaster-Interviewer, KROW, '50–'52; Founder, Chmn. Bd. of Dirs., San Quentin Prison Inmate Film Workshop (Hon. Inmate, '65); S.F. Press Club, AFTRA (Bd. of Dirs.; Pres., '52–'54), S.F. Examiner Bdcst. Wm. of the Yr., '56; AP aw. for outstanding news show, '60; Ind. State Univ., BA, '41–'45 (outstanding alumnus, '68); b. Terre Haute, Ind.; p. H. L. and May Stuart Ramey; h. Richard Queirolo; c. Kristi Louise; res: 25 Castle Rock Dr., Mill Valley, Cal. 94941.

RAMMEL, HELEN C., Corr., Correspondance Diplomatique, Vienna, Austria, '68–; RNS, '58–'67; Auth., "Austrian Teachers and their Education Since 1945" ('57); OPC; Fulbright aw., '54–'55; Boston Univ., BS, '35; MS, '42; Fordham Univ., PhD, '49; b. Stoneham, Mass., 1913; p. James and Grace Doherty Lahey; h. Otto Rammel; res: 28 E. 95th St., N.Y., N.Y. 10028.

RAMSEY, DONNA GOLZ, Free-lance Wtr. and Copy Ed., The Waukegan News-Sun, 100 W. Madison St., Waukegan, Ill. 60085, '70–; Ed., Weekend Life edition, '66–'70; Soc. Ed., North Shore Life (News-Sun Who's Who of Am. Wm.; Northwestern Univ.-Medill Sch. of Jnlsm., BS, '60; b. Waukegan, Ill., 1938; p. Earl August and Elizabeth Macaitis Golz; h. Bill D. Ramsey; c. Deborah Lynn; res: 411 Mawmann Ave., Waukegan, Ill. 60085.

RAMSEY, MARY ANN, Owner, Medical Public Relations Consultant, 170 Lakeside Rd., Ardmore, Pa. 19003, '64–; Dir. PR and Alumni, Temple Univ. Med. Ctr., '59–'64; Dir. PR, '56–'58; Dir. PR and Health Educ., Lankenau Hosp., '58–'59; Dir. PR and Volunteer Svc., Children's Hosp. of Phila., '51–'56; PR Cnsl., John La Cerda Agcy., '49–'50; Assoc. Ed., Ed., Philadelphia Magazine, '48–'49; Del. Valley Hosp. PR Assn. (Pres., '60, '69), PR Soc. of Hosp. Assn. of Pa. (Pres., '69; VP, '68), Phila. PR Assn., Del. Valley Assn. of Communicators, Am. Med. Wtrs. Assn., Am. Assn. for Advancement of Sci.; Who's Who of Am. Wm.; World's Who's Who of Commerce and Industry; Who's Who in the East; Dic. of Intl. Biog; PR Blue Bk.; 2,000 Wm. of Achiev.; Univ. of Hi., '41–'42; Univ. of Pa., AB Eng.), '46; b. Norfolk, Va., 1925; p. Rear Adm. Logan and Harriet Kilmartin Ramsey.

RANCE, JACQUELINE PATRICIA, Commtns. Dir., Sweetheart Cup Corporation, 7575 S. Kostner Ave., Chgo., Ill. 60652, '67–; Indsl. Ed., Nat. Biscuit Co., '61–'67; Asst. Indsl. Ed., Libby, McNeill & Libby, '56–'61; ICIE, IEA of Chgo.; St. Xavier Col., BA, '56 (Who's Who Among Students in Am. Univs. and Cols.); b. Chgo., Ill., 1934; p. Jack and Helen Kulak Rance; res: 1612 W. 87th St., Chgo., Ill. 60620.

RAND, ABBY, Free-lance Wtr., 44 E. 63rd St., N.Y., N.Y. 10021, '66–; Auth: "Ski Guide to Europe," "Ski North America"; Travel Ed., SKI mag., '64–; VP, Wolhandler PR, '59–'66; Rogers & Cowan PR, '57–'59; Mng. Ed., Television Magazine, '51–'57; NATAS; Univ. of Chgo., AB.

RAND, AYN, Auth: "Atlas Shrugged" (Random House, '57), "Night of January 16th" (The World Publ. Co., '68), "The Romantic Manifesto" (The World Publ. Co., '69); Ed., The Objectivist, '62–; Lectr., Harvard Univ., Columbia Univ., many other cols. and univs. '60–; Screen Wtr., '32–'34, '44–'49; Univ. of Leningrad, '24; Lewis and Clark Col., Dr. of Humane Letters (hon.), '63; b. Leningrad, Russia, '05; h. Frank O'Connor; res: c/o The Objectivist, 201 E. 34th St., N.Y., N.Y. 10016.

RANDALL, ELIZABETH, Adv. and Prom. Mgr., Radio Div., National Broadcasting Company, 30 Rockefeller Plaza, N.Y., N.Y. 10022, '69–; "Monitor" Prod. Asst., '67–'69; Chief Wtr. for "Reach for the Stars," Merv Griffin Prods.; Film Ed. and Prod. Asst., Q.B.A. Adv.

Bur.; Free-lance Copywtr., Omega Adv.; Prom., Robert G. Jennings Corp.; Wtr., Hugh Downs radio program; Univ. of Wis., '61–'62 (Phi Beta); N.Y.U., BS, '65 (Eclectic Soc.); b. N.Y.C., '44; p. Ralph Batsley and Maxine Kuhn Randall; res: 315 E. 54th St., N.Y., N.Y. 10022.

RANDALL, PRISCILLA RICHMOND, PR Cnslt., Rochester Methodist Hospital, 201 West Center, Rochester, Minn. 55901, '67–; Pubcty., Pubns. Coordr., '60–'66; PRSA, Am. Soc. for Hosp. Assn. Intl. Platform Assn.; Wellesley Col., '43–'44; Winona Col. Ext. Div., '67–'69; b. Arlington, Mass. 1926; p. Harold B. and Florence Hoefler Richmond; h. Dr. Raymond V. Randall; c. Raymond Richmond, Priscilla, Susan; res: 611 Memorial Pkwy., Rochester, Minn. 55901.

RANDALL-MILLS, ELIZABETH WEST, Poet: "Words and Silences," ('59), "Country of the Afternoon," ('64); Co-auth., "Servants of the Altar" (a devotional); Borestone Mountain Aws. (Best Poems of '67); Vassar Col., '24–'28 (Phi Beta Kappa); b. St. Louis, Mo., 1906; p. Walter and May Scott West; h. Horace Randall-Mills; res: RFD 2, Old Lyme, Conn. 06371.

RANDLE, AMANDA S., Coordr., Sch. Libs., Harvey Rice School, Materials Examination Center, 11529 Buckeye Rd., Cleve., Oh. 44104; Sch. Librn., Eglin AFB (Fla.); Asst. Librn., Elemendorf AFB (Anchorage, Alaska), Tchr., Greenville S.C.; Cleve.; ALA, WNBA, Oh. Assn. of Sch. Libs., Media Cncl. of Oh.; Fla. A&M Univ., BS, '57; Western Reserve Univ., MS (Lib. Sci.), '62; b. Greenville, S.C.; p. Wesley and Delarion Sullivan; res: 3460 E. 142nd St., Cleve., Oh. 44120.

RANES, RUBY VINES, Soc. Ed., Mt. Vernon Democrat, 430 Main, Mt. Vernon, Ind. 47620, '48–; DAR, Tri-Kappa, Dem. Party; Univ. of Evansville; b. Mt. Vernon, Ind., 1915; p. Percy Lee and Amy Ashworth Vines; h. John Kenneth Ranes; res: 320 E. Second St., Mt. Vernon, Ind. 47620.

RANKIN, LUTRELLE TIFT (pseud: "Weetie" Rankin), Assoc. Ed., The Daily Tifton Gazette, 211 Tift Ave., Tifton, Ga. 31794, '52; former Mng. Ed.; Wire Ed., Wms. Ed., '50s; Colmst. for Gazette and Macon Telegraph; Ed., The Star, St. Simons, Sea Island, Brunswick; Co-ed., The Shipworker, Blyn. Navy Yard, '44; Co-ed., Anti-Submarine Warfare Bul. (Wash., D.C.), '43; WAVES, WW II; Poetry, features, edtls.; Aide to Commander-in-chief Adm. King, USN, Wash., D.C.; Off. of Secy. of Navy Knox; Aide to Adm. Kelley, Commander of Bklyn. Navy Yard, '42–'44; Theta Sigma Phi (past VP); Univ. of Ga., AB (Jnlsm.); Smith Col., Offcr. Training, Commn. of Ensign; b. Tifton, Ga., 1919; p. Amos and Lutrelle McLennan Tift; h. Homer Rankin; c. Lutrelle Rankin Quinn, Royal F., Anne Rankin Willis, Lyn L., Thomas L., Meade M., Shine F., John D.; res: Lake Wisteria, Rte. 4, Tifton, Ga. 31794.

RAPPAPORT, CARMEN, Wtr., Computer Systems

Analyst, U.S. Gov., Bldg. 6, Directorate of Data Systems, Oakland Army Base, Cal., 94626, '67–; Eng. Tchr., Public Schs., (Richmond Hill, Ga.); Social Case Aide, Family and Children's Svc. (Altoona, Pa.); Pa. State Univ., BA, '63; b. Altoona, Pa., 1941; p. Paul and Mary Pearce Zetler; h. Arthur Rappaport; res: 22 Deerhaven Pl., Pleasant Hill, Cal. 94523.

RASKIN, EDITH LEFKOWITZ, Free-lance Wtr.; Auth: "Fantastic Cactus" (Lothrop, Lee & Shephard, '68), "Pyramid of Living Things" (McGraw Hill, '67); Co-auth., with Joseph Raskin, "Indian Tales" (Random House, '69); other bks.; Sci. Tchr., N.Y.C. high schs., Auths. Guild; Hunter Col., BA, '30; N.Y.U., MA, '41; b. N.Y.C., 1908; p. Maximillian and Sara Brown Lefkowitz; h. Joseph Raskin; res: 59 W. 71st St., N.Y., N.Y. 10023.

RATCLIFF, ONA MAE MINNICK, Wtr., non-fiction, poetry; Co-owner, Ratcliff Real Estate, 416 State St., Atwood, Kan. 67730; Ed., Prairie Schooner; Kan. Fedn. of Music Clubs (Pres., '69–'71), other orgs.; Who's Who of Am. Wm.; Fort Hays State Col., Kan. State Col. of Emporia, Univ. of Kan. Ext.; b. Yakima, Wash.; p. Charles and Maggie Biddle Minnick; h. Dewey J. Ratcliff; c. Mrs. Jane Shull, Anne (Mrs. David Schalker); res: 507 Plumb Pl., Atwood, Kan. 67730.

RATHER, SHEILA BALLS, Coordr. of Placement Svcs., Seven Berkeley and Berkeley-Claremont Secretarial Schs., U.S. Industries, 420 Lexington Ave., N.Y., N.Y., 10017, '69–; Exec. VP, Brook Street Bureau of Mayfair Ltd., '66–'69; Casting Dir., Goodson-Todman, '63–'66; Program Ed., Associated TV (London, Eng.) '55–'60; Prod. Asst. BBC '52–'55; Drama Prodr., Tchr., Reading Educ. Comm. (Reading, Eng.); Wtr., TV sec., Jr. Ency Britannica; AWRT, N.Y.C. C. of C. of Brit. Am. C. of C.; Nat. Employment Assn.; Royal Acad. of Music; Royal Col. of Music, A.R.C.M. Guildhall Sch. of Music and Drama, L.G.S.M. Reading Univ. b. Newcastle-on-Tyne, Eng. 1930; p. Leonard H. and Jane T. Mayes Balls; h. Hal Rather; c. Julian Stephen, Jonathan Massey; res: 36 Brewster Road W., Massapequa, N.Y. 11758.

RATHGEB, MARLENE MASINI, Crtv. Dir. of Prom., Mademoiselle Magazine, 420 Lexington Ave., N.Y., N.Y. 10017, '70–; Asst. Prom. Dir., '68–'70; Prom. Copy Chief, '64–'68; Ed., Complete Shopper in Manhattan, '60–'61; Adv. Mgr., Georg Jensen Inc., '55–'59; Asst. Adv. Mgr., '53–'55; Wellesley Col., BA (Eng. Literature), '53 (cum laude); b. Newark, N.J., 1932; p. Ernest and Amy Caruso Masini; h. Robert Rathgeb; c. Lisa, Amy; res: 343 E. 30th St., N.Y., N.Y. 10016.

RATHMANN, DOROTHY M., Dir. of Nutrition, CPC International, 343 Winter St., Waltham, Mass. 02154, '68–; Asst. Dir. of Nutrition, Corn Products Co., '64–'67; Info. Coordr., '57–'64; Fellow, Mellon Inst. (Pitt., Pa.), '44–'57; Wtr., Zein, An Annotated Bibliography ('54), "Vegetable Oils in Nutrition" ('57), "Unsaturated Fats and Serum Cholesterol" ('58), rsch. repts. and buls.; Am. Assn. for Advancement of Sci.,

Am. Chemical Soc., Am. Oil Chemists Soc., Inst. of Food Technologists, Sigma Xi, Soroptimists, Nat. Audubon Soc.; Grinnell Col., BA, '39 (Phi Beta Kappa); Univ. of Rochester, PhD, '44; b. Chgo., Ill., 1917; p. John and Ella Auer Rathmann; res: 260 Mt. Auburn St., Watertown, Mass. 02172.

RATLIFF, SHERRIE LEE, Asst. Ed., Playboy, 919 N. Michigan Ave., Chgo., Ill. 60611, '70–; Secy. to Articles Ed., '69–'70; Saturday Evening Post, N.Y.C., '68–'69; Pubns. Asst. for ALA Bulletin, Am. Lib. Assn., Chgo., '68; Oh. State Univ., BA (Jnlsm.), '67; b. Middletown, Oh., 1946; p. Farris and Wilma Duff Ratliff; res: 1624 N. LaSalle St., Chgo., Ill. 60614.

RATNY, RUTH LUCILLE, Mktng. Colmst., Chicago Daily News, 401 N. Wabash Ave., Chgo., Ill. 60611, '65–; Owner, Ruth L. Ratny Enterprises, '65–; Pres., Wash. Video Prods., '64; Crtv. VP, Fred Niles Commtns. Ctr., '54–'64; Wtr., Prodr., Motion Pics. for TV and Theatre; Chgo. Unlimited; Chgo. Film Cncl. (Bd. of Dirs.); DePaul Univ.; b. Chgo., Ill., 1930; p. Herman Joseph and Bertha deLee Ratny; res: 70 E. Walton St., Chgo., Ill. 60611.

RATZESBERGER, ANNA, Ed., The Delphian Quarterly, The Delphian Society, 53 W. Jackson Blvd., Chgo., Ill. 60604, '56–; Auth., juv. bks.; WNBA; Univ. of Ill., BA, '24; Univ. of Mich., Sherwood Music Sch.; b. Milford, Ill.; p. Louis and Edna Stimpson Ratzesberger; h. Peter P. Lagoonoff; res: 4046 N. Kildare Ave., Chgo., Ill. 60641.

RAUSCH, HILDA EDNA, Publr., Owner, The Monroe County Beacon, 103 E. Court St., Woodsfield, Oh. 43793, '46–; Monroe BPW; b. Woodsfield, Oh., 1907; p. Clem J. and Mary A. Weisend Rausch; res: 105 E. Court St., Woodsfield, Oh. 43793.

RAVESON, BETTY RICH, Exec. Ed., The Palm Beach Voice, 323 Worth Ave., Palm Beach, Fla. 33480, '69–; Colmst., Feature Wtr., Palm Beach News and Life, '62–'69; "Winner's Circle" TV Show, Ch. 12, '67; Wtr., articles for Asheville Citizen-Times, '65–; All Florida mag., '64–; Colmst., Delray Beach News Jnl., '63; Delray Ed., Palm Beach Illustrated, '59–'62; Feature Wtr., Albany (N.Y.) Times-Union, '43–'46; Night Bur. Mgr., UPI, '42–'43; Eastchester Ed., Yonkers Herald Statesman, '40–'42; Atlanta Press Club, Fla. Wms. Press Club, Gold Coast Press Club (aw., '62), Delray Beach Playhouse PR Dir., '59–'61; Columbia Sch. of Jnlsm., '34; b. Schenectady, N.Y., 1913; p. Edwin and Florence Nutree; h. Sherman H. Raveson; res (summer only): Wayah Valley Rd., Franklin, N.C. 28734.

RAWLS, CHARLINE JONES, Publr.-Ed., The Cadiz Record, P.O. Box 311, Cadiz, Ky. 42211, '62–; Ed., '56–; Established first lib. in Trigg County, Ky., '53; Ky. Press Assn. ('56–'69), Nat. Edtl. Assn. ('56–'69), Ky. Lib. Assn. ('53–'56), Cadiz-Trigg C. of C. (Pubcty. Dir., '60–'69), numerous certs. of appreciation (local), Cadiz Improvement Cncl., civic activities; Univ. of Ky.; Murray State Univ.; b. Hopkinsville, Ky., 1922; p.

Jolly and Pearl Routen Jones; h. William H. Rawls, Jr.; c. Mrs. Margaret Jo Cozine, Mrs. Mary Gay Cooke; res: 60 Cunningham, Cadiz, Ky. 42211.

RAWSON, ELEANOR STIERHEM, Sr. Ed., David McKay Company, 750 Third Ave., N.Y., N.Y. 10017; Fiction Ed., Collier's, Today's Woman; Assoc. Ed., American Magazine, Standard mags.; Tchr., Columbia Univ., '56–'57; Guest Lectr., Columbia, N.Y.U.; PEN, Wms. Nat. Bk. Assn., OPC; b. Atlantic City, N.J.; h. Kennett Rawson; c. Linda Cynthia, Kennett Jr.

RAY, ALICE KUNZ, Asst. PR Dir., Community Fund of Chicago and Metropolitan Crusade of Mercy, 123 W. Madison St., Chicago, Ill. 60602, '46–; Instr. in Sociol., Univ. of Tex., '45–'46; Adoption Caseworker, Chgo. Child Care Soc., '42–'45; Caseworker, Family Welfare Assn. (Springfield, Ill.), '41–'42; Reptr., Ill. State Register, '39–'41; PRSA; Univ. of Mo., BJ, '39; Univ. of Chgo., MA, '45; b. Springfield, Ill., 1917.

RAY, RUTH GILL, Dir., Wms. Activities, WKST, Scott Broadcasting Co. of Pa. Inc., 219 Savannah Gardner Rd., New Castle, Pa. 16101, '53–; Dir., Wms. Activities, WRYO (Rochester, Pa.); Commentator, fashion shows, '53–; Lectr., fashion and travel, Wms. Clubs. '53–; AWRT (Charter Mbr.); Fashion Industry of N.Y.C. FRANY aw., '68; Geneva Col., '25–'27; Pitt. Art Inst., '37; b. Beaver Falls, Pa.; p. David and Nellie Reeher Gill; h. John Ray (dec.); c. Mrs. Robert Schimeck, Mrs. Burnette Bordelon, Atty. John David; res: 227 Oakville Rd., Beaver Falls, Pa. 15010.

RAYBORN, PEG MacKINNON, Wms. Dir., WSOC-TV, and WSOC Radio, AM and FM, Cox Broadcasting Co., 1901 N. Tryon St., Charlotte, N.C. 28201, '67; Prod., Wtr., 30 vignettes weekly for "Woman's World"; Prod., Dir., TV specials; Free-lance Comml. Talent, TV and Radio (Miami, Fla.), '62–'66; Prodr., Talent, "Miami's Animal of the Week," Educ. Ch., '64; Newscaster, WCKT-TV, '63; Theta Sigma Phi (Treas., '69–'70; Charlotte Chptr. Treas., '70–'72), Adv. Club of Charlotte, AWRT (Tarheel Chptr. Pres., '70–'72); Charlotte's Wm. of the Yr. in field of communicating arts, '68; Best local vignettes on radio, N.C., for "Women's World"; Radio-TV Magazine aw., best local TV prog. in N.C., "Today in the Carolinas," '69; active in civic affairs; Columbia Univ., BA, '55; b. Cleve., Oh., 1935; p. Alexander and Ella Stanley MacKinnon; h. Robert Rayborn; c. Robert Scott, Stephen Michael, Christopher William; res: 1331 Abbey Pl., Charlotte, N.C. 28209.

RAYN, LOUANN SCHERZER, Cnslt., Nelson Advertising, 705 Brush Creek, Kan. City, Mo. 64141, '67–; Owner/Mgr., Salesmaker Associates Adv. Agcy., 9 yrs.; Crtv. Dir./Copy Chief, Litman Stevens, 3-1/2 yrs.; Acc. Secy. (copy), Merritt Owens Agcy., 2 yrs.; Copywtr., Harzfeld's Inc., 2 yrs.; Adv. Round Table (VP, '67–'68); Bd. of Dirs., '66, '68), Am. Fedn. of Adv. (Secy., 9th Dist.), Kan. City (Kan.) C. of C. (1st Wm. Lifetime Mbr.), Soroptimist (Kan. City, Kan. Pres., '69–'70); Univ. of Kan. City; b. Kan. City, Kan., 1931; p.

Louis and Anita Gaydess Scherzer; h. Robert Rayn; c. Edith Ann; res: 2017 Freeman, Kan. City, Kan. 66102.

RAYWID, MARY ANNE, Prof. of Educ., Hofstra University, Hempstead, N.Y. 11550, '59–; Tchr., Evanston (Ill.) HS, '56–'58; Tchr., Americanization Sch. (Wash., D.C.), '54; Edtl. Assoc., NEA, '50–'54; Auth., "The Ax-Grinders" ('62); NEA, AAUP, Philosophy of Educ. Soc.; Univ. of N.C., AB, '49; Univ. of Ill., MA, '50; PhD, '59; b. Wash., D.C.; p. Leo and Vivian Thrift Raywid; h. Raymond L. Scheele; c. Scott Alan Scheele; res: Woods Rd., Westbury, N.Y. 11590.

READ, GLORY, Pres., Public Relations Counsel, Inc., 18 E. 41st St., N.Y., N.Y. '67–; VP, '64–'67; AE, '58–'64; Wtr., PR Off., News Bur., Duke Univ., '54–'57; Feature Wtr., Reptr., Herald-Sun (Durham, N.C.), '49–'51; Co-Auth., "New Hairstyle and Beauty Ideas" (Fawcett, '66); PRSA, Cosmetic Career Wm., Adv. Club of N.Y.; Duke Univ., AB, '49; b. Balt., Md.; h. William M. Read III; c. William M., IV, Philip Mark; res: 87 Anderson Dr., Clifton, N.J. 08113.

READE, PRISCILLA HAGUE, Ed., Union County Journal, 337 Market St., Lewisburg, Pa. 17837, '67–; Wms. Ed., '66; Bus. Mgr., '65; Pa. Nwsp. Publrs. Assn., Pa. Wms. Press Assn., Pa. Soc. of Nwsp. Eds., Nat. Nwsp. Assn.; Keystone Feature News Story (2nd pl., '69); Stephens Col., '41–'42; b. Seattle, Wash., 1924; p. Wesley and Priscilla Redgrave Hague; h. John Reade; c. John M. IV, Robert L., Priscilla A., Corinne M., Wesley H.; res: 231 Market St., Lewisburg, Pa. 17837.

READY, ELIZABETH, Exec., PR, Lord & Taylor, 424 Fifth Ave., N.Y., N.Y. 10016; Radio Wtr., Prodr.; NHFL (VP); Univ. of Vt., BS (Econs.); b. Burlington, Vt.; p. William J. and Mary Donlin Ready; res: Mt. Philo Rd., Shelburne, Vt.

REAGAN, CORNELIA ANN, VP, Conant & Company Public Relations, Inc., 500 Fifth Ave., N.Y., N.Y. 10036, '69–; AE, Hank Meyer Assoc., '68–'69; AE, Ruder & Finn, '67–'68; Wtr., New York Times, '66; Cnslt., Woodrow Wilson Nat. Fellowship Fndn. (Princeton, N.J.), '63–'66; Network News Ed., Telenews, ABC & CBS, '51–'61; OPC, Radio-Newsreel-TV Working Press Assn., EWA, ACPRA; Univ. of Mich., AB, '47; b. N.Y.C., 1926; p. Richard and Cornelia Carney Reagan; res: 55 E. Ninth St., N.Y., N.Y. 10003.

REARDON, MARTHA BOOTH, Sls. Traf. Mgr., WPIX-TV, 220 E. 42nd St., N.Y., N.Y. 10017, '68–; Traffic Mgr., KRLD-TV (Dallas, Tex.), '63–'68; Exec. Secy., Couchman Adv. Agcy., '62–'63; Traf. Mgr., KWTX Bdcst. (Waco, Tex.), '52–'53, '55–'62; Copywtr., KSWO (Lawton, Okla.), '53–'55; AWRT (Corr. Secy.; Treas.; '65–'68); Baylor Univ., (Speech-Radio), '48–'52; h. Paul Reardon; res: 405 E. 54th St., N.Y., N.Y. 10022.

REARICK, KATHLEEN MOUGEY, Fashion, Home-furnishing Prom. Dir., Good Housekeeping Magazine, 959 Eighth Ave., N.Y., N.Y. 10019, '68–; Mdse. Prom. Dir., EYE Magazine, '67; Prom. Dir., Bride and

Home Magazine, '65; Asst. Byr., Wm. Van Buren Res. Byrs., '63; AWNY; Va. Intermont Col.; b. Wooster, Oh., 1943; p. Kenneth E. and Mary F. Mougey Rearick; res: 416 E. 78th St., N.Y., N.Y. 10021.

RECK, ALMA KEHOE, Copywtr., American Furniture Company, 1601 Lawrence St., Denver, Colo. 80202, '55–; Asst. Adv. Mgr., The May Co., '30–'35; Copywtr., '25–'30; Auth., numerous mag. articles, eight juvenile bks; Denver Wms. Press Club, Colo. Auths. League ("Top Hand" Aw., '60); Socrates Aw., '64; b. Washington, Ind., 1901; p. John and Helen Reister Kehoe; h. Warren Dart Reck (div.); c. Marjorie Rebecca; res: 606 Corona St., Denver, Colo. 80218.

RECKERT, CLARE M., Fin. News Reptr., The New York Times, 229 W. 43rd St., N.Y., N.Y. 10036, '40–; Wall St. off.; free-lance projects; N.Y. Reptrs. Assn.; N.Y. Times aw., story, fin. news sec.; William & Mary Col., Columbia; b. N.Y.C., 1921; p. John Baptist and Rosa Wolfe Reckert; res: 66 Ft. Washington Ave., N.Y., N.Y. 10022.

REDDICK, NANCY CAROL, Adv. Coordr., Southwestern Drug Corporation, 8000 Carpenter Freeway, Dallas, Tex. 75247, '66–; Art Dir., Riverside Press; Southern Methodist Univ., BFA; b. Dallas, Tex., 1937; p. W. G. and Carol Shands Reddick; res: 4535 Cedar Springs, Dallas, Tex. 75219.

REDDING, ANITA REMMER, Adv., Prom. Mgr., Princeton University Press, Princeton, N.J. 08540, '65–; Dir., Mail Adv. Mgr., '64–'65; Prom. Mgr., '62–'64; numerous articles on boating, '60–'62; Rutgers Univ. (Sch. of Jnlsm.), BL, '36; b. Bklyn., N.Y.; p. Henry and Anna Hinck Remmer; h. John Redding; c. David, Katherine, John; res: 39 Linden Lane, Princeton, N.J. 08540.

REDDING TRUDY GLENN, Actress-Model, Theatrically with George Hunt Agency 8350 Santa Monica Blvd. Suite 104, L.A., Calif. 90069; Commercially with Bernard Sandler's Commercial Talent Agency (C.T.A.) 6922 Hollywood Blvd. Hollywood, Calif., 90028; Films: "Billie Boy" ('67), "Pride and Joy" ('67); TV: "My Three Sons," "Gunsmoke," others; b. Bell, Cal.; p. Glenn and Erma Weir Redding; res: 6537 Live Oak, Bell Gardens, Cal. 90201.

REDENIUS, JOSEPHINE LOUISA, Lt. Colonel, U.S. Army (Ret'd.); Dir. of PR and Dev., Valley Forge Military Academy and Junior College, Wayne, Pa. 19087, '67–; Chief, Coord. Br., U.S. Army Command Info. Off. (Wash., D.C.), '66–'67; Chief of WAC Recruiting, U.S. Army, '63–'66; Info. Offcr., Chief of Info., '58–'63; Pubcty. and Army Recruiting (N.Y.), '56–'58; Adm. Asst. to Chief of Staff, Armed Forces (Japan), '54–'56; Commanding Offcr., Basic Training Co. (Ft. Lee, Va.), '53–'54; Intelligence Offcr., Atomic Energy Comm. and Armed Forces Special Weapons Project, '44–'53; Model in War Bond Drives and Recruiting Movies, '43–'44; U.S. Army Legion of Merit; U.S. Army Commendation with Oak Leaf Cluster; Pa. Merito-

rious Svc. aw.; Assn. of U.S. Army Nat. Svc. aw., '68; Am. Univ., AB (Jnlsm.) (Distg. Alumnus aw.); MA, '63; Temple Univ., Dr. of Humane Letters (hon.), '64; b. Oceanville, N.J., 1920; p. Jacob and Josephine H. Palmer Redenius; res: 15 N. Cornwall Ave., Ventnor, N.J. 08406.

REDFORD, RUBY, Ed., Illuminating Engineering, 345 E. 47th St., N.Y., N.Y. 10017, '42–; Engineering Div., General Electric (Cleve., Oh.), '30–'42; Illuminating Engineering Soc., Theta Sigma Phi, Commission Internationale de l'Eclairage (U.S. Nat. Comm.); IM Aws. for Edtl. Excellence, '59, '66; Western Reserve Univ., '27–'29; Columbia Univ., '42–'44; b. Wallassey, Cheshire, Eng., 1907; p. Septimus and Daisy Winter Redford; res: 30 W. 60th St., N.Y., N.Y. 10023.

REDMAN, HELEN FIELD, Head Librn., University of California Los Alamos Scientific Laboratory, P.O. Box 1663, Los Alamos, N.M. 87544, '53; Rept. Librn., '49–'52; Asst. Librn., Tech. Lib., '47–'49; Ref. Asst., Western Reserve Univ. Lib., '46–'47; Lib. Circ. Cl., rare bks., Houghton Lib., Harvard Univ., '44–'46; Auth., Ed., various editions, "Weapon Data Subject Heading List" (Joint Atomic Weapons Tech. Info. Group, AEC-DOD); Dir., Tech. Info. Ctr., Atomos en Accion exhibit, AEC (San Salvador, El Salvador), '65; AEC Tech. Info. Panel, '56–; Special Libs. Assn. (Rio Grande Chptr. Pres., '56–'58), N.M.LA; Ed., "Dictionary of Report Series Codes"; Wellesley Col., AB, '44 (Phi Beta Kappa); Western Reserve Univ., BS (Lib. Sci.), '47; b. Boston, Mass., 1923; p. Robert F. and Grace Hager Field; h. Leslie Redman; res: Rte. 1, Box 177, Santa Fe, N.M. 87501.

REED, DONNA, Asst. Program Mgr., WFIU, Indiana University, Department of Radio-TV, Bloomington, Ind. 47401, '67–; Wtr., Prodr., WHAS (Louisville, Ky.), '62–'64; Cont. Dir., WCPO-TV (Cinn., Oh.), '61; AE, WAXU, WBLG (Lexington, Ky.), '59–'61; Talent, WKYT (Lexington), '58–'60; NAEB, Theta Sigma Phi (Bloomington Chptr. VP, '69–'70), AWRT (Hoosier Chptr. VP, '69–'70); Univ. of Ky., BA, '59; b. Ghent, Ky., 1937; p. William and Lillian Beach Reed; res: 1819 Arlington Rd., Bloomington, Ind. 47401.

REED, JANICE JOPLIN, News Ed., Oakland City Journal (owned by Cochrane Newspaper, Inc.), 314 N. Main St., Oakland City, Inc. 47560, '54–; BPW (Pres., '49), Wms. Rsch. Club (Pres., '69–'70), DAR, many civic activities; Franklin Col. (Franklin, Ind.), BA (Hist.), '25; Oakland City Col. (Music), '62; b. Franklin, Ind. 1901; p. Joseph and Lillie Clark Joplin; h. George A. Reed (dec.); c. Joseph C., Jeri (Mrs. George M. Fettinger), Jarvis J.; res: 330 N. Main St., Oakland City, Ind. 47560.

REED, JUDITH HARTLIEB, Bus. and Adv. Mgr., The Drama Review, 32 Washington Pl., N.Y., N.Y. 10003, '68; Circ. Mgr., '64–'67; Stetson Univ., BME, '64 (Pi Kappa Lambda); b. Balt., Md., 1942; p. Julian and Marie Glover Hartlieb; h. Marvin Reed; res: 71 Ridgedale Ave., Madison, N.J. 07940.

REED, RUTH KIRBY, Wms. Ed., Piqua Daily Call, 121 E. Ash. St., Piqua, Oh. 45356, '60–; Proofreader, '47–'60; Wittenberg Univ.; b. Conover, Oh., 1927; p. Webster and Florence Long Kirby; h. Richard W. Reed; res: 1322 Maplewood Dr., Piqua, Oh. 45356.

REESE, ELOUISE (SKIPPY), Soc. Ed., Bozeman Daily Chronicle, 32 S. Rouse, Bozeman, Mont. 59715, '69–; News Room; PR, Farm Bur. wm. (Helena, Mont.); State Capitol; Douglas Air Craft; BPW (Pres.); Oh. State Univ.; b. Antwerp, Oh., '17; p. Edward and Minnie Knapp Willit; h. Paul Reese; res: R.R. 2, Box 197, Belgrade, Mont. 59714.

REESE, FRAN CHARLOTTE, Owner, Fran Reese Public Relations/Promotion Consultants, 1104 64th St., Des Moines, Ia. 50311, '68–; PR Dir., Gtr. Des Moines United Way, '66–'68; Public Svc. Dir., Educ. Svcs. Dir., Employee Pubns. Ed., Info. Dir., Des Moines Register and Tribune Co., '56–'66; Savings Info. Head, Un. Fed. Savings and Loan Assn., '53–'55; Copywtr., Fashion Coordr., Younkers of Ia., '50–'53; Wms. Adv. Club of Des Moines (Pres., '55, VP, '54), AWRT (VP, '68, Secy., '67), Ia. Indsl. Eds. Assn. (Pres., '59, VP, '58, Secy.-Treas., '57), Theta Sigma Phi, Des Moines Press and Radio Club (Secy., '56–'61); numerous adv. aws.; Who's Who of Am. Wm.; State Univ. of Ia., '34–'35; Albia (Ia.) Jr. Col., '35–'36; b. Chgo., Ill.; p. Egon and Helen O'Neil Reese.

REESE, VIRGINIA JANE, Coord. Librn. of Residence Hall Libs., University of Michigan, 3011 Student Activities Bldg., Ann Arbor, Mich. 48104, '68–; ALA; Millersville State Col., BS, '67; Univ. of Mich., MA (Lib. Sci.), '68.

REEVES, JO ANN WILLIAMS, Supvsr., Div. of Instructional TV, Maryland State Department of Education, 600 Wyndhurst Ave., Balt., Md. 21210, '67–; Tchr., on camera, WEDU-TV (Tampa, Fla.); Tchr.; Prodr., Wtr., Curriculum Dev. for TV, Cnslt., Social Studies and Lang. Arts, (Sarasota); numerous articles in educ. jnls.; AWRT, DAVI, NAEB (Nat. Prog., '68), AAUW, Kappa Kappa Iota (Gamma Chptr. Pres., '65), Nat. Elementary Prins. Conv. Prog. ('65), Phi Theta Kappa, Kappa Delta Pi, Pi Kappa Delta; East Tenn. State Univ., BA (Eng., Hist., Educ.; first hons.); MA (Eng. and Hist.); b. Coleman, Tex., 1935; p. Otto and Alice Rainey Williams; h. Billy Reeves; res: The Mending Wall, Columbia, Md. 21043; 3520 Beal Rd., Franklin, Oh. 45005.

REGENSBURG, ALICE BRESCHEL, Pres., The Lynn Farnol Group Inc., 50 Rockefeller Plaza, N.Y., N.Y. 10020, '62–; VP, '59–'62; Dir. of Crtv. Svcs., '56–'59; AE, '53–'56; Dir., Am. Footwear Inst.; Lectr.; PRSA, Comm. on Wm. in PR (Chmn., '68–'69), AWRT, Fashion Group, Electrical Wms. Roundtable, Shoe Wm. Execs. (Pres., '67); Columbia Univ., '37–'39; b. N.Y.C., '18; p. Gustav and Ann Doherty Breschel; h. Charles P. Regensburg; c. Mrs. Alan Bomser; res: 875 Park Ave., N.Y., N.Y. 10021.

REHME, JOAN CLARK, Ed., Family Pg., The Shelbyville News, 123 E. Washington St., Shelbyville, Ind. 46176, '66–; Soc. Reptr., '44–'45; Reptr., Ch. Ed., TV Ed., '64–'66; Secy.-Treas., Dir., The Stanley Jones Agcy., '61–; Kappa Alpha Theta, Kappa Kappa Kappa, PEO; Vassar Col., '38–'40; DePauw Univ., AB, '42; b. Indpls., Ind., 1920; p. Frank G. and Helen Henderson Clark; h. Frank J. Rehme; c. Christopher G.; res: 2017 S. Riley Highway, Shelbyville, Ind. 46176.

REHMEYER, SHARON SAWYER, Free-lance Wtr.; Eng. Tchr., Los Altos HS at Hacienda Heights, La Puente Un. HS Dist., Cal., '69–'70; Substitute Tchr., '67–; Reptr.-Photogr., The Daily News, Whittier, Cal., '61–'65; Theta Sigma Phi (U.C.L.A. Beta Rho Chptr. Pres., '61–'62), AAUW (Whittier Br. Pubcty. Chmn. '64); Univ. of Cal., BA (Eng.), '61; MS (Jnlsm.), '63; b. L.A., Cal. 1939; p. Marion Bell, Sr., and Dorothy Kathleen McGraw Sawyer, Jr.; h. Ted Rehmeyer; c. David Michael, Kimberly Ann; res: 15631 E. Tetley St., Hacienda Heights, Cal. 91745.

REICE, SYLVIE SCHUMAN, Wtr.; Youth Ed., McCall's, 230 Park Ave., N.Y., N.Y., '67–; Synd. Colmst., "The Swinging Set," Publishers Hall, '67–; Ed.-in-Chief, Ingenue, '59–'67; Edtl. positions, Today's Woman, Deb, Co-Ed, '46–'59; three bks., mag. articles, short stories; Cnslt., numerous youth orgs.; Citizens Advisory Bd., Press. Cncl. on Youth Opp., '67–'69; Fashion Group, NHFL, Auths. Guild, AWNY; Care Public Svc. Cit. for initiating Teen-Agers Care, '67; Bur. of Intercultural Educ. short story prize, '57; Hunter Col., BA (summa cum laude; Phi Beta Kappa); New Sch. for Social Rsch.; b. N.Y.C.; p. Samuel and Dora Weinstock Wolshine; h. Albert Reice; c. Milo, Seth, Naomi.

REICHENBACH, ALICE, Asst. Dir. of Fashion Pubcty., Sears, Roebuck and Company, 360 W. 31st St., N.Y., N.Y. 10001, '59–; Dir., "Staten Island Today," WNYC Radio, '49–'50; P.R. Dir., Staten Island Museum, '48–'50; Copy-wtr., W. T. Grant Co., '43–'47; AWNY (Dir.), BPW (S.I. Club Pres., '51–'53); Bklyn. Col., BS (Educ.), '40; b. N.Y.C., 1920; p. Jacob and Jane Barry Elzer; h. E. J. Reichenbach; c. Elinor Monaghan; res: 15 W. Raleigh Ave., S.I., N.Y. 10310.

REICHMANN, JEAN VAN VRANKEN, Mng. Ed., Bureau of National Affairs Inc., 1231 25th St., N.W., Wash., D.C. 20037, '70–; Asst. Mng. Ed. '64–'69; Ed., '57–'64; Ed., Georgetown Univ. Grad. Sch., '54–'57; Staff Corr., INS, '45–'54; WNPC; Westminster Col., BA, '42; b. Bellevue, Pa.; p. Stephen and Helen Van Vranken; h. John A. Reichmann.

REID, BETTY GRANGER, Ed.-Publr., New York Courier; Wms. Program Dir., Bdcstr., WLIB Radio, 310 Lenox Ave., N.Y., N.Y.; formerly edtl. positions with Bronze America, L.A., Cal.; N.Y. Amsterdam News; Broomall (Pa.) Record; California Voice; Bdcstr., Jamaica (West Indies) Broadcasting Co.; OPC, Intl. Press Club, Alpha Kappa Alpha, BPW; extensive civic, civil rights activities; Hon. Commissioner, N.Y.C. Dept. of Public Events; three Nat. Nwsp. Publrs. Merit aws., '66; N.Y. Urban League Merit aw., '67; numerous nwsp., radio aws.; Hunter Col., BA, '39; N.Y.U. Sch. of Jnlsm., '44; Temple Univ., '45; b. Rocky Mount, N.C., 1921; p. Dr. Jesse and Romayne Smith Adams; h. Wendell A. Reid; c. Betty Granger, Mrs. Patricia G. Lawson, William R. R. Granger, III, Wyndelle E. Reid; res: 101-25 W. 147th St., N.Y., N.Y. 10039.

REID, CORINNE, Pres., Corinne-Darby Personnel Agency Inc., 50 E. 42nd St., N.Y., N.Y. 10017, '67–; Partner, Palmer DeMeyer, '62–'65; Placement Counselor, '55–'62; Univ. of Wis., BS; res: 320 E. 58th St., N.Y., N.Y. 10022.

REID, DARBY, VP, Corinne Darby Personnel Agency, Inc., 50 E. 42nd St., N.Y., N.Y. 10017, '67–; Placement Counselor, Palmer De Meyer, '65–'67; N.Y.U., BS (Adv.), '60; res: 305 E. 40th St., N.Y., N.Y. 10016.

REID, EUGÉNIE CHAZAL, Wtr., children's fiction, c/o Bertha Klausner, 130 E. 40th St., N.Y., N.Y. 10016; bks: "Mystery of the Carrowell Necklace" (Lothrop, Lee, & Shepard Co., '65), "Mystery of the Second Treasure" (Lothrop, Lee, & Shepard Co., '67); Fla. State Univ., BA, '45; Univ. of N.C., BS (Lib. Sci.), '47; b. Woodbury, N.J., 1924; p. Philip M. and Mabel Batten Chazal; h. George K. Reid; c. Louise, Philip; res: 2928 DeSoto Way S., St. Petersburg, Fla. 33712.

REID, FRANCES PUGH, Eng. Tchr., Borah High School, Independent District #1, 6001 Cassia, Boise, Idaho 83705, '58–; Boise Jr. Col., '54–'58; High Sch. Tchr., '31–'40; Auth: "None So Small" ('58), "Thy Word in My Heart" ('62); Wtr., articles, poems, short stories; Delta Kappa Gamma ('59–), NEA, Idaho Educ. Assn., Boise Educ. Assn., Idaho Wtrs. League (Twin Falls Chptr. Treas., Secy., VP, '45–'47; many writing aws.; '51–'69); Drury Col., AB, '31; b. LaGrange, Mo., '10; p. Bert and Johanna Schroeter Pugh; h. Garth O. Reid; c. Garth, Jr., James Allison; res: 6117 Lubkin, Boise, Idaho 83704.

REID, HELEN ROGERS, Chmn. of Bd., New York Herald Tribune, '53–'55; Pres., '47–'53; VP, '22–'47; Trustee, Barnard Col., '14–; numerous nat. govt. aws.; Barnard Col., AB, '03; Yale Univ., LittD (hon.), '50; Mt. Holyoke Col., LittD (hon.), '54; 15 other hon. degs.; b. Appleton, Wis., 1882; p. Benjamin and Sarah Johnson Rogers; h. Ogden Mills Reid (dec.); Whitelaw, Elisabeth (dec.), Ogden R.; res: 834 Fifth Ave., N.Y., N.Y. 10021.

REID, MARGARET GRAGG, Librn., Pikes Peak Regional Library District, 20 N. Cascade, P.O. Box 1579, Colorado Springs, Colo. 80901, '64–; City Librn., '49–'63; Ref. Librn., '47–'49; Librn., U.S. Air Sea Rescue Agcy., '43–'47; Jr. Librn., U.S. Army War Col. (Wash., D.C.), '42; Jr. Librn., Fed. Works Agcy., '39–'42; Asst., Deering Lib., Northwestern Univ., '37–'39; High Sch.

Librn. (LaJunta, Colo.), '36; Colo. Lib. Assn. (Pres., '58–'59), Colo. Cncl. for Lib. Dev., NLAPW, AAUW, Wms. Educ. Soc. of Colo. Col., hist. orgs.; Colo. Col., '27–'31; Univ. of Denver, BA (Eng. Lit.); BS (Lib. Sci.), '36; b. Centralia, Ill., '09; h. N. Stanley Reid; res: 25 Cragmor Village, Colo. Springs, Colo. 80907.

REID, MILDRED I., Auth: "Over Fool's Hill," "The Devil's Handmaiden," textbks. for wtrs.; Owner, Wtrs. Colony; Lectr.; Tchr., crtv. writing; Who's Who of Am. Wm.; Who's Who in the Midwest; Who's Who in the East; Who's Who in Illinois; res: Contoocook, N.H. 03229.

REID, RITA JOYCE, Assoc. Corp. Secy., Bus. Mgr., Mktng., Acc. Servicing Paxson Advertising, Incorporated, 822 Highland Ave., St. Joseph, Mich. 49085, '58–; Off. Mgr., Asst. Prod. Mgr., Media Mgr., '50–'58; VP, Dir., Reid Products, Inc.; Am. Cancer Soc. (Berrien County Div. Dir., '55–'67), Cancer Svc. Inc. (Dir. and Budget Chmn., '67–), Twin Cities Un. Commty. Fund, BPW; DePaul Univ.; b. Chgo., Ill., 1922; p. Earl J. and Elizabeth Cleary Joyce; h. Harrison J. Reid; c. Thomas J., II; res: 390 Lake Shore Dr., Stevensville, Mich. 49127.

REID, VIRGINIA MORTON, Supvsr., Elementary Eng., Oakland Public Schools, 1025 Second Ave., Oakland, Cal. 94606, '47–; "The Instructor," TV program for NCTE; films on poetry and individualized reading; Chmn., 5th Ed., "Reading Ladders for Human Relations"; Tchr., schs., many univs.; Contbr., prsnl. jnls.; NCTE (Pres. Elect), WNBA; S.F. State Col., AB, '31; Columbia Univ., MA, '40; b. Alameda, Cal.; p. James Bairnson Morton and Louisa Butcher Morton Reid; res: 5939 Mazuela Dr., Oakland, Cal. 94611.

REID, W. KATHLEEN, Prom. Mgr., Herder and Herder, 232 Madison Ave., N.Y., N.Y. 10016, '68–; Dev. Asst., Nat. Cncl. of Catholic Men, '65–'68; Instr., Immaculate Col. for Wm. (Wash., D.C.), '63–'65; LeMoyne Col., AB (cum laude), '62; Catholic Univ. of Am., MA, '64; b. Red Creek, N.Y., '40; p. S. Webster and Loretta Maroney Reid; res: 320 E. 42nd St., N.Y., N.Y. 10017.

REIF, RITA MURPHY, Reptr., The New York Times, 229 W. 43rd St., N.Y., N.Y. 10036, '56–; Cl., News Asst., '47–'56; Copy Girl, N.Y. Journal-American, '46–'47; Auth: "Living With Books" (New York Times, '68); "The Antique Collector's Guide to Styles and Prices" (Hawthorn Bks., '70); Dorothy Dawe aw.; Fordham Univ., BS; Columbia Univ., MA, '51; b. N.Y.C., 1929; p. Henry and Louise Becker Murphy; h. Paul Reif; c. L. Leslie, Timothy Mark; res: 57 W. 58th St., N.Y., N.Y. 10019.

REILLY, M. HAPPIE, VP/Fashion Dir., Ruder and Finn, 110 E. 59th St., N.Y., N.Y., '65–; Adv. Dir., Jack Winter, '59–'65; Fashion Lectr.; Fashion Group (N.Y. Governor); Acad. of the Sacred Heart, '40–'44; b.

N.Y.C., '27; p. John and Estelle Mulqueen Reilly; res: One Lexington Ave., N.Y., N.Y. 10010.

REINERT, B. JEANNE, Contrb. Ed., Science Digest, '67–; Asst. Ed., '65–'67; Amusements Ed., Beaumont (Tex.) Journal, '62–'63; Nat. Assn. of Sci. Wtrs., Theta Sigma Phi; Hearst Jnlsm. Writing Aw., '62; Univ. of Tex., BJ, '58–'62; N.Y.U., '65; Columbia Univ., '65–'66; b. Memphis, Tenn., 1941; p. John Carl and Helen Barnett Reinert; h. Charles Graves; c. Barbara Michelle, John Justin; res: 326 River Bend Rd., Berkeley Heights, N.J. 07922.

REINERT, CATHERINE (KATE) ELLEN, Reptr., Star-Gazette, Elmira, N.Y., '69–; Wms. Ed., Schenectady Union-Star, '66–'69; Legislative Corr., Cuyler News Svc. (Albany); Corr., Wilkes-Barre Record (Pa.), '61–'64; Wilkes-Barre Sunday Independent, '63–'64; Dallas (Pa.) Post, '63–'64; U.S. Rep. for Canadian Wms. Press Club (Canadian Cent. intl. press tour), '67; Wms. Press Club of N.Y. State (Pres. '67–'69; Founding Offcr., '66), Theta Sigma Phi, Am. Nwsp. Guild; Lambda Iota Tau, '63; Who's Who in Am. Cols.; Who's Who of Am. Wm.; Col. Misericordia, BA; Grad. Asst., Syracuse Univ., '64–'66; b. Wilkes-Barre, Pa., 1942; p. John Joseph and Catherine Josita Davis Reinert; h. Mark Fleisher; res: 515 W. Water St., Elmira, N.Y. 14905.

REINHARDT, DOROTHY PEDERSON, Adv. Sls. Analyst, Western Farm Publications, Inc., 251 Kearny St., S.F., Cal. 94108, '69–; Adv. Prod. Mgr., '66–'69; Sls. Prom. Mgr., Western Farm Equipment, '57–'66; Adv. Sls. Prom. Mgr., King Pubns., '51–'57; Adv. Mgr., Implement Record, '46–'51; Northern Cal. Indsl. Adv. Club (S.F., '51–'57); Minn. Sch. of Bus., '35; Univ. of Minn. Ext. Sch., '43; Univ. of Cal. Ext. Sch., '46; b. Willmar, Minn.; p. Alfred C. and Nanna Meyer Pederson; h. Robert T. Reinhardt (dec.); res: 3731 Fillmore St., S.F., Cal. 94123.

REINHART, ALICE JOAN, Actress, c/o Kingsley Colton Assocs.; currently, "Heartbeat Theater" Hollywood, Cal.; N.Y. Radio: created and played Chichi 11 yrs. in "Life Can Be Beautiful"; parts in every radio show originating in N.Y.C., '29–'51; own interview show, Mutual; five motion pics. and series of shorts; Talent, TV cmmls.; numerous TV roles and parts (N.Y.C. and Hollywood); leads, S.F. and Cleve. stock theater; starred on Broadway, Berlin and Hollywood; SAG, AFTRA, AEA, AMPAS, NATAS, AWRT; Who's Who of Am. Wm.; Univ. of Cal., Berkeley; Columbia Univ.; U.C.L.A.; b. S.F., Cal.; res: 8907 Dorrington Ave., L.A., Cal. 90048.

REINHART, MARY BAYLOR, Exec. Asst., San Francisco Aid Retarded Children, 1362 Ninth Ave., S.F., Cal. 94122, '67–; PR Cnslt., Cal. Dept. of Public Health, S.F. Med. Ctr., Western Interstate Cmmsn. on Higher Educ., Am. Orthopsychiatric Assn., S.F. Econ. Opportunity Cncl., '65–'67; Dir. of Public Info., Child Study Assn. of Am., '62–'65; Asst. Dir. of Public Info.,

Boys' Clubs of Am., '58–'62; Free-lance Wtr., '57–'58; Edtl. Asst., Gen. Dynamics Corp., '56–'57; Edtl. Rschr., Time, '51–'56; PRSA, Coord. Cncl. on Mental Retardation; Who's Who in Am. Cols. and Univs. '36–'37; Beaver Col., BA, '37 (Magna cum laude); b. Cumberland, Md.; p. Boyd and Henrietta Wellington Reinhart; h. (div.); res: 940 Union St., S.F., Cal. 94133.

REIS-EL BARA, MARGOT ANNE, TV Ed.; Feature Wtr., Sunrise mag., colm., "Brevard after Dark"; Gannett Florida Newspapers, 308 Forest Ave., Cocoa, Fla. 32922, '66–; Adv. Dept., '65–'66; Pilot Club of S. Brevard, Indian River Players; Univ. of Conn., '59–'60; George Wash. Univ., '61; b. Wareham, Mass., 1941; p. Henry and Helen Ludwig Reis-El Bara; res: 106 River Dr., Melbourne, Fla. 32901.

REMILLARD, MARY GALLAGHER, Wms. Ed., Pomona Progress-Bulletin, 300 South Thomas St., Pomona, Cal. 91766, '59–; News Ed., Montclair Tribune, '59; Wms. Ed., Duluth (Minn.) Herald and News-Tribune, '56–'58; PR Dir., Col. of St. Scholastica, '42; Reptr., Ed., Duluth News-Tribune, '35–'40; Tchr., St. Mary's Acad. (Silver City, N.M.), '55; Jnlsm. Tchr., Col. of St. Scholastica '43; AAUW, Soroptimist Club of Pomona (1st VP, '69–'70, Secy., '67–'68); Col. of St. Scholastica, BA, '35; b. Luck, Wis.; p. Henry and Adelaide Conklin Gallagher; h. Alfred Remillard; c. Jeanne (Mrs. L. N. Ayers), Renee (Mrs. K. G. Kent), Page; res: 2282 Sixth St., LaVerne, Cal. 91750.

REMKE, MARIAN HANNA, PR Coordr., Adv. and Mktng. Svcs., and Ed., Special Products Div., National Cash Register Company, S. Main and K Sts., Dayton, Oh. 45409, '67–; Owner, Hadley Hanna Assocs., '62–; Mgr., News and Info. Dept., and Assoc. Ed., Michigan Challenge, Mich. State C. of C. (Lansing), '61–'62; PR Dir., Miami Valley Cncl., Boy Scouts of Am. (Dayton), '57–'61; Dayton Adv. Club (Bd. of Dirs., Secy., '66–'68), Miami Valley Assn. of Indsl. Eds. (Bd. of Dirs., Treas., '65); Dayton Art Inst.; Org. Mgt. Inst.; b. Noblesville, Ind., 1920; p. Forest and Janie Thompson Hanna; c. Charlotte (Mrs. Paul K. Kahl), Paul Arthur; res: 4514 Croftshire Dr., Dayton, Oh. 45440.

RENAULT, BARBARA PRITCHARD, Prodr., Bishopric/Green/Fielden, Inc., 3361 S.W. Third Ave., Miami, Fla. 33145, '64–; Cont. Dir., Public Svc. Dir., Asst. Prod. Engineer, WINZ Radio, '62–'64; Opns. Mgr., WNOG Radio, '57–'62; Display Adv., Lakeland Ledger, '52–'54; Soc. Ed., Collier County News, '50–'54; AWRT (Bd. Mbr.), Pilot Club Intl.; Southern Dist. AFA aws: writing and producing, '64; Prodr. '66; Prodr. '67; Prodr. and Wtr., '68; 3 Big Mike aws. for Prod., '68; Fla. Southern Col., BA, '56; b. N.Y.C., 1934; p. William and Margaret Ford Seeley; h. Lawrence Renault; c. Leslie Diane Pritchard; res: 5725 S.W. 117th Ave., Miami, Fla. 33143.

RENFRO, KATHRYN R., Assoc. Dir. of Libs. for Gen. Svcs., University of Nebraska, Lincoln, Neb. 68508,

'68–; Assoc. Dir. of Libs. for Tech. Svcs., '64–'68; Asst. Dir. of Libs. for Tech. Svcs., '53–'64; Tech. Svc. Librn., '50–'53; Catalog Librn., '49–'50; Sr. Asst. Librn., Catalog Dept., '46–'50; in lib. svc., various univs., since '39; Contrbr., lib. pfsnl. jnls.; ALA (Cncl.), '65–'69, '57–'61), Assn. of Col. and Rsch. Libs. (Bd. of Dirs., '65–'69), Neb. Lib. Assn. (Pres., '63–'64), Mountain Plains Lib. Assn., AAUP, AAUW, Beta Phi Mu; Colo. Col., '35–'38; Univ. of Denver, AB (Lib. Sci.), '39; b. Horse Cave, Ky., 1918; p. Edmund and Rose Strader Renfro.

RENO, DORIS SMITH, Music-Dance Ed., The Miami Herald, 1 Herald Plaza, Miami, Fla. 33101, '40–; Theta Sigma Phi; DePauw Univ., BA, '28, Mills Col. MA, '29; b. Aurora, Ind. 1907; p. George and Blanche Shutts Smith; h. Paul Halvor Reno; c. Susanna Clare, Elisabeth Margret (Mrs. John V. Hardeman, Jr.); res: 3672 Douglas Rd., Miami, Fla. 33133.

REOTT, EILEEN M., Ed., Notes of Interest; News, Feature Wtr., Photogr., First National Bank of Louisville, The Kentucky Trust Co., P.O. Box 1019, Louisville, Ky. 40201, '68–; Adv. mgr., Ky. Banker, '60–'65; Exec. Secys., Inc.; Alfred Univ., '40–'41; Univ. of Ky., Ky. Sch. of Banking, '61–'65; b. Wellsville, N.Y. 14895.

REPALONE, ALICE LATRONICA, Prod. Mgr., McGraw-Hill Publishing Co., Inc., 330 W. 42nd St., N.Y., N.Y. 10036, '60–; Asst. Prod. Mgr.; Statistician; b. N.Y.C., 1919; p. Vincent and Mary Ongar Latronica; c. two sons; res: 28–15 34th St., L.I. City, N.Y. 11103.

REPPERT, B. HOLLY SHUMWAY, Adv. Mgr., The New Republic Magazine, 1244 19th St. N.W., Wash., D.C. 20036, '67–; Mgr., New Republic Bk. Club; h. Laurence Reppert; res: 1100 Carson St., Silver Spring, Md. 20901.

REU, SOPHIE HOHNE, Sr. VP, Sterling Communications, Inc., 375 Park Ave., N.Y., N.Y. 10022, '65–; started co. as Movies USA, '50; N.Y. Film Cncl. (lifetime Pres.), AWRT; Hunter Col., '38–'40; b. Hamburg, Germany; p. William and Luise Poehlson Hohne; h. Rudolf Reu; c. Andrea S., Lorelei L.; res: 30 Barnsdale Rd., Short Hills, N.J. 07078.

REUTHER, RUTH E., Tchr. of Lang. Arts, Wichita Falls Independent School District, Barwise Jr. H.S., 3907 Grant, Wichita Falls, Tex. 76308, '58–; Auth: "Gray C, Circus Horse" (Houghton Mifflin), "Wife of Four Hobbies" (Pageant); Tex. State Tchrs. Assn., NEA, Poetry Soc. (Tex. Chptr. Pres., '66–'68), Delta Kappa Gamma, Wms. Forum; Who's Who of Am. Wm.; Intl. Biog.; Kappa Delta Pi; Gainesville Jr. Col., AA; N. Tex. State Univ., BS; Okla. Univ., grad. work; b. Gainesville, Tex., '17; p. Edwin and Grace Huffaker; h. James R. Reuther; c. Mrs. B. E. Richardson; res: 4450 Phillips, Wichita Falls, Tex. 76308.

REVILLON, LEONE, Mng. Dir., Language Guild Institute, Inc., 75 E. 55th St., N.Y., N.Y. 10022, '69–; Dir., '42–'69; Assoc., Trans-Ocean Public Relations, '59–'62; Edtl. Bd., So You're Going to Be Married, Conde Nast, '34–'35; Auth., "Traveller's Conversational Grammar" ('54); Translator, Free-lance Ed., Painter; Am. Translators Assn.; Who's Who of Am. Wm.; Who's Who in the East; Dic. of Intl. Biog.; Translators and Translation; College de Groslay, France, Diplome, '32; b. Paris, France; p. Theodore and Kate Vidler Revillon; h. Nikanov de Fedor; res: 57 E. 88th St., N.Y., N.Y. 10028.

REX, HARRIET, VP and Copy Group Head, J. Walter Thompson, 420 Lexington Ave., N.Y., N.Y., '60–; Copy Group Head, '57–; Sr. Wtr., '53–'57; Jr. Wtr., '49–'53; Radio and Direct Mail Wtr., Swift and Co., '48–'49; conducts copy seminar, Adv. Club of N.Y., '66–'69; Adv. Wm. of N.Y. (2nd VP; Bd. of Dirs., '68–'69), Copy Club of N.Y.; Univ. of Mo., BJ (Jnlsm.), '48 (Kappa Tau Alpha); b. New Bedford, Mass., '28; p. Frederick and Stella Hay Rex; h. Andrew Feeney; c. Andrew, Brian; res: 15 Lockwood Dr., Old Greenwich, Conn. 06870.

REY, SISTER MARIA DEL REY, PR Dir., Maryknoll Sisters, Maryknoll, N.Y. 10545; Tchrs., St. James Acad. (Philippines), '38–'45; Reptr., Pittsburgh (Pa.) Press, '31–'33; Auth: "Prospero Strikes It Rich" (Harper & Row, '68), "No Two Alike" (Dodd Mead, '65), seven other books; Theta Sigma Phi; Who's Who of Am. Wm., Ill. Club of Catholic Wm. aw., '65; Univ. of Pitt., BA (Jnlsm.), '31; Columbia Univ., MS (Jnlsm.), '64; b. Pitt., Pa. 1908; p. George and Anna Caraher Danforth.

REYNOLDS, CAROLE CARPENTER, Librn., Capistrano Unified School District, San Juan Capistrano, Cal., '67–; Colmst., Pasadena Star-News, '60–'65; Secy., George Murphy (U.S. Senator), '45; Theta Sigma Phi, Stanford Univ., AB, '41–'45; Immaculate Heart Col., MLS, '66; b. Balt., Md.; p. Fred J. and Marion O'Keefe Carpenter; h. John Stanford Reynolds; c. Kimberly, Kathleen, Ralph, John; res: 2173 Ocean Way, Laguna Beach, Cal. 92651.

REYNOLDS, DOROTHY M., Sls. Svc. Mgr., Columbia Broadcasting System, Television Network, 630 N. McClurg, Chgo., Ill. 60611, '69–; Asst. Sls. Svc. Mgr., '57–'69; Sls. Svc. Mgr., Mutual Bdcst. System, '47–'57; AWRT (Nat. Dir., '61–'63; Chgo. Chptr. Pres., '57–'59), Bdcst. Adv. Club; Ia. State Univ., BS, '39; b. Ames, Ia., 1916; p. Charles and Vada Yates Reynolds; res: 107 Kenilworth, Prospect Heights, Ill. 60070.

REYNOLDS, HELEN LANCASTER, Co-publr., Green River Star, Box 592, Green River, Wyo. 82935, '51–; Corr., Salt Lake Tribune, AP, Denver Post, '38–'51; Reptr., Rock Springs Daily Reminder, '36, Thermopolis Independent-Record, '27–'28; Wyo. Press Assn., Wyo. Press Wm. (VP, '58–'59, Treas., '57), NFPW, Green River C. of C., Green River Wms. Club (Pres., '59–'60); Univ. of Kan., BA, '22; b. Junction City, Kan.; p. George and Anna Kummer Lancaster; h. Adrian W. Reynolds; res: 290 N. First West St., Green River, Wyo. 82935.

REYNOLDS, JEAN E., Sr. Ed., Children's Bks., The McCall Publishing Company, 230 Park Ave., N.Y., N.Y. 10017, '69–; Prentice-Hall, Inc., '66–'69; Trade Bk. Div., '63–'66; WNBA, Nat. Sci. Tchrs. Assn., ALA, Cncl. on Interracial Bks. for Children, Children's Bk. Cncl.; Wells Col., BA, '63; City Col. of the City Univ. of N.Y., MA, '66; b. Saginaw, Mich., 1941; p. F. Perry and Katherine Reynolds; h. Ernest Goldstein; res: 1385 York Ave., N.Y., N.Y. 10017.

REYNOLDS, WANIA JEAN McGINNIS, Staff Asst., Dept. of Med. and Surgery, Veterans Administration, 810 Vermont Ave., Wash., D.C. 20420, '68–; Acting Info. Offcr. and Asst. Info. Offcr., Div. of Health Mobilization, Dept. of Health, Educ. and Welfare, '63–'68; Public Info. Specialist, Off. of Surgeon Gen., PHS, DHEW, '61–'63; Free-lance Wtr., rschr., ed., '58–'61; Copy Ed., U.S. Lady Magazine, '57–'58; Reg. Ed., TV Guide, '56–'57; professionally active in TV, radio, mags., nwsps., since '47; AWRT, Fed. Eds. Assn.; Stephens Col., AA, '48 (Beta Phi Gamma; Delta Sigma); Stanford Univ., BA (Eng.), '50; Am. Univ.; b. Duncan, Okla., 1928; p. William Earl and Ima Armstrong McGinnis; h. (div.); res: 209 N. Royal St., Alexandria, Va. 22314.

RHEAY, MARY LOUISE, Asst. Dir., Atlanta Public Lib., 126 Carnegie Way, Atlanta, Ga. 30303, '63–; Head, Children's Dept., '56–'63; Asst. Head, '53–'56; Supvsr. Sch. Work, '42–'53; Lib. Asst., '41–'42; Part-time Instr., Ga. State Col., '60–; Emory Univ. Lib. Sch., '60–'68; ALA (Staff, exhbn., Seattle World's Fair, '62), Ga. Lib. Assn., Southeastern Lib. Assn., Met. Atlanta Lib. Assn. (Pres.), '64–'65), ZONTA (Secy.), '69–'70); Atlanta Wm. of Yr. in Pfsns., '62; Ala. Col., AB, '40; Emory Univ., AB (Lib. Sci.), '41; MS (Lib. Sci.), '59; b. Montgomery, Ala., 1920; p. Ross and Maria Cunningham Rheay; res: 4555 Meadow Valley Dr. N.E., Atlanta, Ga. 30305.

RHOADS, GERALDINE E., Ed., Woman's Day, Fawcett Publications, Inc., 67 W. 44th St., N.Y., N.Y. 10036, '66–; Exec. Ed., McCall's, '63–'66; Mng. Ed., Ladies' Home Journal, '62–'63; Assoc. Ed., '57–'63; WNPC, Fashion Group, Am. Soc. of Mag. Eds. (Exec. Comm., '67–), Mag. Publrs. Assn., NEA, Consumers Research Inst. (Chmn., Pubns. Comm.); Bryn Mawr Col., AB, '35; b. Phila., Pa., 1914; p. Lawrence and Alice Rice Rhoads; res: 865 First Ave., N.Y., N.Y. 10017.

RHODES, VIVIAN NEUBERG, Actress, '51–; numerous TV, motion pic., radio, theatre roles, N.Y.C., Chgo., Hollywood; Tchr., '52–; Nat. Forensic League, Nat. Thespian Soc., SAA, Am. Educ. Theater Assn., SAG, AFTRA, AEA; Oh. Radio Anncrs. Aw., '51; Evanston Drama Club Scholarship, '55; Northwestern Univ. grad.; Cal. State Col. at L.A., MA (Drama); b. Springfield, Oh., 1934; p. Dr. Maurice and Beulah Rhodes Neuberg; res: 4160 Fair Ave., North Hollywood, Cal. 91602.

RIBNICK, GLORIA ROSENZWEIG, Off. Supvsr., Ribnick & Associates, 2444 Times Blvd., Houston, Tex.

77005, '64–; Ed., "Bank Notes," Tex. Nat. Bank; Edtl. Wtr., Pasadena (Cal.) News; Soc. Ed., Houston News Citizen; Radio Copywtr., Adv. Wtr.; Univ. of Tex., BA (Jnlsm.), '49; h. Jerry J. Ribnick.

RICCA, ALICE CAREY, Partner, Impact Public Relations, 740 N. Rush St., Chgo., Ill. '64–; VP, Alan Mann Co., '60–'62; VP, Philip Lesly Co., '50–'59; Ed., California Stylist, '46–'50; U.S. Marine Corps., '44–'46; Asst. Dir., "Ma Perkins" (NBC Radio), '39–'40; Radio Casting Dir., Blackett-Sample-Hummert, '31–'38; PRSA, Am. Inst. of Interior Designers, NHFL; Chgo. Pubcty. Club aw., '69; h. James Ricca; res: 23 Salem Lane, Evanston, Ill. 60203.

RICE, ANITA WILLSON, Corp. Secy.-Treas., William W. Matthews and Company, Inc., 130 Seventh St., Pitt., Pa. 15222, '67–; Wtr., non-fiction film scripts, TV commls., pubcty.; PR, Three Rivers Arts Festival, '59–'68; Assoc. Artists of Pitt., '55–'59; Am. Red Cross Blair County Chptr., '47–'51; h. Phillip Rice.

RICE, ELIZABETH, Free-lance Illus., Auth.; Illus., 35 children's bks.; Auth.-Illus: "I'm Alvin," "Benje," "Jacki;" Univ. of Tex. grad., '36; b. Marshall, Tex., 1913; p. Eddie and Stella Wilbourn Rice; h. E. L. Bauknight (dec.); c. Stella Lynn; res: 1305 Alta Vista, Austin, Tex. 78704.

RICE, JOAN ANN, Teen Wtr., Akron Beacon Journal, 44 E. Exchange St., Akron, Oh. 44309, '66–; Reptr., Kent-Ravenna Record-Courier, '63–'65; Wms. Dept. Ed., '66; Wtr.-Bdcstr., "Polsky's Hi-School Salute," WAKR, '66–'69; Theta Sigma Phi (Akron Club Pres., '69–'70), Oh. Press Wm. (numerous writing aws.), Oh. Nwsp. Wms. Assn.; Veterans of Fgn. Wars hon. for svc. to youth progs.; Firestone Pk. Br. YMCA aw.; numerous certs. of merit for writing and press coverage; Kent State Univ., BA, '64; b. Akron, Oh., 1942; p. John, Sr., and Nancy Zeig Rice; res: 3117 Industry Rd., Rootstown, Oh. 44272.

RICE, LILA, Lib. Cnslt., Georgia Department of Education, 156 Trinity Ave. S.W., Atlanta, Ga. 30303, '68–; Dir., Pine Mt. Reg. Lib. (Manchester), '55–'68; Staff Wtr., LaGrange Daily News, '48–'51; ALA, Ga. Lib. Assn., Southeastern Lib. Assn., Ga. Adult Educ. Cncl; Beta Sigma Phi Wm. of the Yr., '54; LaGrange Col. (Eng.), '39–'40; Tift Col., AB, '42; Peabody Col., MA (Lib. Sci.), '51–'54; Emory Univ., '66–'69; b. Wadley, Ala., 1921; p. John Benjamin and Elvie Elizabeth Moncus Rice; res: 4110 Windsor Oak Dr., Doraville, Ga. 30040.

RICE, LOIS MARSHALL, PR Dir., Milwaukee Art Center, 750 N. Lincoln Memorial Dr., Milw., Wis. 53202, '68–; PR-Prom. Dir., Bdcst. Div., Bartell Media, '59–'68; Fgn. Advisor, educ. programming; Advisor, Milw. Educ. TV stations WMVS/WMVT, '68; AWRT (Secy.), '67–'68), Milw. Adv. Club, numerous cultural orgs.; Univ. of Wis., '37–'40; b. Evansville, Wis.; p. Ray A. and Vera Dowse Marshall; h. John Spence Rice; c.

Jeffrey Marshall; res: 905 E. Hyde Way, Fox Pt., Wis. 53217.

RICE, TERESSA HARRIS, Dir. Press Info., Sports Illustrated, Time, Inc., Time-Life Bldg., Rockefeller Ctr., N.Y., N.Y. 10020, '54–; Free-lance PR Cnclr., '52–'54; Actress, '42–'52; Duke Univ., BA (English); b. Dover, N.J.; p. Charles and Dora Graubert Harris; h. Robert Rice (div.); c. Susan Andrea, David Joshua.

RICH, ELIZABETH MARGARET, VP, A. A. Schechter Associates, Inc., 551 Fifth Ave., N.Y., N.Y., '67–; AE, '61–'62; AE, Hill & Knowlton, '62–'67; AE, Rowland Co., '59–'61; Ed., Reptr., Chgo. Tribune Press Svc., '47–'59; Jnlsm. Lectr., Dominican Col. for Wm., '61; Nat. Assn. of Wm. Lawyers, Am. Bar Assn.; OPC; St. John's Univ., BA, LLB; b. N.Y.C., 1930; p. Louis Anthony and Margaret Ann Gilchrist Rich; h. William N. Provenzano; res: 59 Kings Highway, Tappan, N.Y. 10983.

RICH, LORETTA COOPER, Traf. Mgr., WMNY-TV, Box 211, Watertown, N.Y. 13601, '54–; AWRT, BPW (Watertown Chptr. Pres., '66–'68; N.Y. PR Chmn., '68–'70); active in ch. and svc. orgs.; Watertown Sch. of Commerce, '42–'43; b. Fulton, N.Y., 1922; p. Leon and Bertha DeMott Cooper; h. Hampton Rich; c. Michael, Shane; res: Star Rte., Watertown, N.Y. 13601.

RICH, LUCILLE C., Reptr.-Assigt. Ed., WCBS-TV News, 524 W. 57th St., N.Y., N.Y. 10019, '68–; Special Projects Cnslt., '66; Non-fiction Wtr.; Talent; YMCA (Bd. of Mgrs.), N.Y. Comm. of Young Audiences (Bd. Mbr.); Queens Col., BA; Columbia Univ., Grad. Work.

RICH, SHANI WALLIS, Actress, motion pics., "Oliver"; stage: "Bells Are Ringing," "Wonderful Town," "Wish You Were Here," "Bus Stop," "Finian's Rainbow," "Irma La Douce," "Call Me Madam," "A Time for Singing"; supper clubs; TV shows; AGVA, AFTRA, SAG; dramatic studies at Aldershot Repertory Co.; Royal Acad. of Dramatic Arts (scholarship); b. London, Eng., 1941; p. James and Ethel Darlison Wallis; h. Bernard Rich.

RICHARD, JENNIE McBRIDE, Auth., eight novels, numerous Short Stories; Advisory Mbr., The Marquis Biographical Library Society, 200 E. Ohio St., Chgo., Ill. 60611; Wtr. (songs), "Put Your Eyes Back In," "Sagittarius Jug"; Wtr., Short Story, "Green Moss Hills" (aw. winner); many poems publ. in Arizona Highway, California Farmer, and other pubns.; Poetry bk., "Medley"; Un. Poetry Soc. of Am., Centro Studi E Scambi (Diploma of Merit, '68); Am. Poets League, Intl. Poetry Assn.; b. Fillmore, Ut., 1884; p. John and Mary Thornton McBride; h. Irving Richard; c. Marion C. Richards, Lura R. Anderson, Anna F. Moon; res: 552 Second Ave., San Bruno, Cal. 94066.

RICHARD, ST. CLAIR SMITH, PR Dir., Westchester Library System, 285 Central Ave. White Plains, N.Y.

10606, '66–; Exec. Ed., Halo House, '44–; Ed., Independent Herald of Westchester, '65–'66; Feature News Wtr.: N.Y. News, '55–'65; UPI, '56–'67; World-Tele-Sun, '63–'64; Jnl.-Am., '64; World-Jnl.-Tribune, '66; Municipal Rels. Asst. to Mayor P. Raymond Sirignano, '61–'62; Press Asst., Wilma Rogalin, V.-Chmn., GOP State Comm., '64; Lectr. in Jnlsm., Adv., Oral Interpretation, Good Cnsl. Col., '59–'60; Ed., The Commentator, '44–'46; Ed., Arcade, '40–'43; Lib. PR Cncl., numerous other state and local orgs. and aws.; Univ. of Ia., '29–'30; Barnard Col., '30–'31; Columbia Univ., B. Lit. (Jnlsm.), '33; b. Newton, Ia., 1910; p. William Walter and Nelle Van Dusseldorp Smith, h. George Charles Richard 2nd; c. Thomas Lane, Randall St. Clair, D. du Chane; res: 60 the Blvd., New Rochelle, N.Y. 10801.

RICHARDS, ELIZABETH A., Asst. Dir. of Rsch., Grey Advertising, Inc., 777 Third Ave., N.Y., N.Y. 10017, '69–; Group Head, Audits & Surveys, Inc., '67–'69; Assoc. Dir. of Rsch., BBDO, '59–'67; Mgr. Copy Rsch., '59–'62; Acc. Rsch. Supvsr., Keyes, Madden & Jones (Chgo., Ill.), '56–'59; Rsch. Supvsr., Leo Burnett, Inc., '53–'56; Asst. Dir. of Rsch., Newsweek, '46–'49; Lectr. in Mktng., De Paul Univ., N.Y.U., and Bernard Baruch Sch. of Bus. and Public Adm., '53–'66; Lt. Commdr., USNR, '42–'46; Co-auth., "The Institute for Advanced Marketing Studies: Organization and Administration," '66; Am. Econ. Assn., Am. Mktng. Assn.; Bryn Mawr Col., AB (cum laude), '41; Univ. of Mo. Sch. of Jnlsm., BJ, '42; Northwestern Univ., PhD (Bus. Adm.), '54; b. Chgo., Ill., 1920; res: 905 West End Ave., N.Y., N.Y. 10025.

RICHARDSON, FRANCINE MARIE, Prod. Mgr., Melvin F. Hall Advertising Agency, Inc., 584 Delaware Ave., Buffalo, N.Y. 14202, '67–; Traf. Mgr., '67; Adv. Wm. of Buffalo, Nat. Hon. Soc.; b. Buffalo, N.Y., 1945.

RICHARDSON, SABRA HALL, Public Info. Supvsr., Houston Natural Gas Corporation, PO Box 1188, Houston, Tex. 77001, '65–; Public Info. Asst., '63–'65; Radio Sta. KILT (while univ. student), '60–'62; Houston Adv. Club (Dir., '68–'70), Gamma Alpha Chi (Houston Chptr. Pres., '65–'66), S.E. Tex. IEA, ICIE Achiev. for Mgt. Aw., '68; Univ. of Houston, BS (Jnlsm.), '63 (Top Ten Student); b. Houston, Tex., 1941; p. James and Susie Jageman Hall; h. (div.); res: 419 Stratford #9, Houston, Tex. 77006.

RICHARDSON, SHIRLEY KEITH, News Ed., Mayhill Publications, 27 N. Jefferson St., Knightstown, Ind. 46148, '66–; b. Oh. County, Ind., '31; p. Fenton and Mary Keith; h. Arthur Richardson; c. Mary Jane, Jo Dee, Steven; res: 366 E. Carey, Knightstown, Ind. 46148.

RICHEY, DOROTHY HILLIARD, Pres., Richey-Bosch Associates, Public Relations, P.O. Box 5201, Beaumont, Tex. 77707, '63–; Bdcstr., KLVI, synd. radio show, "Today's Woman in Today's World"; TV specials; nat. lects. on motivation; Auth., "Road to San

Jacinto," "How to be Rich and Beautiful"; articles in trade mags., syndicated column; Theta Sigma Phi; AWRT (Nat. Dir.-at-large, '68–'69, '69–'70); Golden Mike Aw., '69; 2000 Wm. of Achiev., Contemporary Auths., Who's Who of Am. Wm.; Univ. of S.W. La., BA, '47; Univ. of Okla.; b. Norphlet, Ark.; p. Albert and Ruth Hilliard; h. Noyes Richey; c. Noyes, Jr., Dorothy R., Kenneth A., Jeanne E., William H.; res: 129 Berkshire Lane, Beaumont, Tex. 77706.

RICHMOND, SYLVIA BEATRICE, Lit. Ed., Chelsea Record, 18 Fourth Street, Chelsea, Mass. 02150, '41–; Chief Librn., Chelsea Public Lib., '47–'67; Lectr.; NLAPW (Treas., '48–'50), New Eng. Wms. Press Assn. (VP, '50–'52); U.S. Treasury Dept. Cit. for War Bond Sales; Am. Red Cross Cit.; Am. Cancer Rsch. Fndn. Cit.; Columbia Univ.; Boston Univ.; Mass. Inst. of Tech.; Simmons Col.; b. Chelsea, Mass., 1903; p. Louis I. and Sarah Kabat Richmond; res: 72 Tudor St., Chelsea, Mass. 02150.

RICHTER, ANNE J., Ed.-in-Chief, Bk. Dept., R. R. Bowker, 1180 Ave. of the Americas, N.Y., N.Y. 10036, '47–'70; Secy., R. R. Bowker, '67–'70; Bd. of Dirs. R. R. Bowker, '56–'67; Secy. to Pres., R. R. Bowker, '37–'47; Secy. to Pres., Harper & Bros., '25–'31; Contrbr., professional mags. in book and lib. fields; Wms. Nat. Bk. Assn. (Pres., '58–'60, '68–'70; Constance Lindsay Skinner Aw., '57; N.Y. Chptr. Pres., '46–'48), Special Libs. Assn.; Mary Baldwin Col., '23–'24; b. Pitt. Pa., 1905; p. Herbert D. and Edith Brown Jones; h. Eugene Richter; c. Eugene D.; res: 222 Valley Rd., Montclair, N.J. 07042.

RICHTER, HARVENA, Auth., "The Human Shore" (Little, Brown, '59); Lectr. in English, University of New Mexico, Bandelier Hall, Albuquerque, N.M., '69–; Col. Tchr., '52–'66; Free-lance Wtr., '48–'52; Copywtr., '43–'48; poetry, short stories in numerous pubns.; Auths. Guild, Modern Lang. Assn., N.Y.U. English Grad. Assn.; AAUW Fellowship, '64–'65; resident fellowships for writing, Yaddo, MacDowell Colony, Wurlitzer Fndn.; Univ. of N.M., BA; N.Y.U., MA, PhD; b. Reading, Pa., 1919; p. Conrad and Harvena Achenbach Richter; res: 11 Maple St., Pine Grove, Pa. 17963.

RICHWAGEN, ELLEN EUGENIA, Chief Librn., Boston State College, 625 Huntington Ave., Boston, Mass. 02115, '58–; Asst. Librn., '57–'58; Children's Librn., Boston Public Lib., '50–'57; Asst. in Children's Rooms, '39–'43; Children's Librn., Needham Public Lib., '43–'50; ALA, Mass. Lib. Assn.; Who's Who in Am.; Who's Who of Am. Wm.; numerous other dirs.; Bridgewater State Tchrs. Col., BS, '36; Simmons Col., 5th Yr. Deg. (Lib. Sci.), '57; Boston State Col., MEduc, '62; b. Needham, Mass.; p. Paul and Ellen Guilfoy Richwagen; res: 544 Washington St., Brighton, Mass. 02135.

RICKETTS, VIVA LEONE, Auth., dog and pets bks., Howell Book House, 845 Third Ave., N.Y., N.Y. 10022,

'54–; Wtr., articles and fiction for 7 N.Y. publrs., '32–'44; Eng. publr., Robert Hale, Inc., '69; PR, '32–'44; Radio Anncr., WAIU (Columbus, Oh.), '30–'32; Martha Kinney Cooper Ohioana Lib. Assn., Nat. Sci. Fndn., numerous wildlife orgs.; b. LaRue, Oh., 1900; p. John Elmer and Anna Dell McClintick Harris; h. Van Ricketts; c. Lawrence Ervan; res: 10167 Windfall Rd., Rte. 2, LaRue, Oh. 43332.

RIDGWAY, FRANCES STEVENS, Chief, Atlanta News Bureau, McGraw-Hill Publications Co., 1375 Peachtree St., N.E., Atlanta, Ga. 30309, '65–; Edtl. Asst., '54–'64; Asst. to Pres., Turner E. Smith and Co., '48–'54; Who's Who of Am. Wm.; Georgia Col., AB, '44 (Who's Who among Students in Am. Univs. and Cols.; Alumnae Achiev. aw., '67); Woodrow Wilson Col. of Law, LLB, '48; b. Athens, Ga., 1922; p. Cronner and Ada McConnell Ridgway; res: 270-E Peachtree Hills Ave., N.E., Atlanta, Ga. 30305.

RIDINGS, NORMA SANDERS, Ed., News-Democrat, 102 E. Main, P.O. Box 111, Waverly, Tenn. 37185, '67–; Asst. Ed., '64–'67; Public Info. Chmn., County Unit, Am. Cancer Soc.; b. Paris, Tenn., 1938; p. Rev. Floyd and Vera Ellis Sanders; h. William C. Ridings, Jr.; c. Angela Dawne; res: 122 Circle Dr., Waverly, Tenn. 37185.

RIEDINGER, RUTH WILLSTAEDT, Exec. VP, Riedinger & Riedinger Limited, 135 Ferry St., Schenectady, N.Y. 12305, '63–; Owner, Riedinger Advertising, '46–; Secy.-Treas., Vernoy Assoc., '35–'37; Gen. Mgr., Hynes & Cox Electric Corp., '31–'35; Adm. Staff, Albany Times-Union, '25–'30; PRSA (Cnslrs. Section), ZONTA (Past Schenectady Chptr. VP), Schenectady County Hist. Soc.; b. Kan. City, Mo., 1903; p. Theodore and Theresa Kiefner Willstaedt; h. Albert Riedinger (dec.); c. Noel, Theodore Albert; res: 219 Union St., Schenectady, N.Y. 12305.

RIEDMAN, SARAH R., Coord. Ed., "The Pediatric Patient" (an annual vol., under name of Sarah R. Gustafson); Cnslt., Hoffmann-LaRoche Inc., Kingsland Park, Nutley, N.J. 07110, '63–; Dir., Dept. of Med. Literature, '58–'67; Asst. Prof., Dept. of Physiology, Bklyn Col., '30–'52; Auth: "How Man Discovered His Body" (Abelard-Schuman, '47), (24 other sci. bks.); Auths. Guild, Am. Med. Wtrs. Assn. (Med. Commtns. Aw., '67), World Fedn. of Scientific Workers, Am. Assn. for Advancement of Sci.; Aws: Sigma Xi ('35), RESA ('59), N.J. Assn. of Tchrs. of Eng. ('64); Hunter Col., AB, '26; N.Y.U., MS, '28; Columbia Univ., PhD, '35; b. Kishinev, Rumania, 1902; p. Benjamin and Hilda Gdansky Regal; h. Elton T. Gustafson; c. Olin Riedman, Eric Riedman; res: 7 Palmetto Way, Sewalls Point, Jensen Beach, Fla. 33457.

RIEGER, BETTY JANE, Print Prod. Mgr., Goodwin, Dannenbaum, Littman & Wingfield, Inc., 2400 W. Loop St., Houston, Tex. 77027, '60–; Space Byr., McCann-Erickson, '55–'59; Traf. Mgr., KTRH Radio, '50–'55; Univ. of Houston; b. Mexia, Tex. 1927; p.

Herman and Willie Adams Rieger; res: 2503 McCue #15, Houston, Tex. 77027.

RIEGLE, BARBARA RICKARD, Wms. Ed., Bdcstr., Reptr., KNX Radio, Columbus Broadcasting System, 6121 Sunset Blvd., Hollywood, Cal. 92801, '67–; Colmst., "On the Mark," The Downtowner, L.A.; '68–; polit. wtr., Colmst., "Women and Politics," L.A. (Cal.) Herald-Examiner, Hearst Corp., '63–'67; Wtr., Ed. on "Big News," KNXT, '66–'67; Polit. Ed., Wtr., Esquire Publ. Co., WQXI, and Polit. Commentator, WAII-TV (Atlanta, Ga.), '62–'63; Morning News Dir., Anchorman TV-Radio News Bdcsts., WRBL-AM-FM-TV (Columbus, Ga.) '58–'62; Ed., weekly nwsp., Phoenix City, Ala., '57; radio prod., "Queen of Battle," U.S. Army Info. Ctr. (Columbus); Ed., Publr., weekly nwsltr., U.S. Army (Germany), '53–'55; nominated for McCalls Golden Mike aw. for Wm., '63; NPWC (aw. for Radio, TV News Writing, '67–'68), Cal. Press Wm. (State Bd., L.A. Chptr. Bd. Mbr.; many 1st pl. writing aws., '66–), AWRT (Southern Cal. Chptr. Bd. Mbr.); b. L.A., Cal.; c. Katherine, Karen, Chris, Melissa, Rick.

RIEKER, JANE LOUISE, Wtr.; Deputy Chief of Corrs., Life (Wash., D.C.), '50–'54; Legislative Asst., Carl T. Curtis (R-Neb.), U.S. House of Reps., '48–'49; Co-auth: "Woman Into Space" (Prentice-Hall, '63) "Black Man in Red Cuba" (Univ. of Miami Press, '70); Cnslt., Citizens' Comm. on Transportation Quality, Off. of Secy. of Transportation (Wash., D.C.); Fla. Gold Coast Press Club (Pres., '60–'61), D.C. WNPC, Theta Sigma Phi; Univ. of Akron, AB; h. (div.); res: 4057 Malaga Ave., Coconut Grove, Miami, Fla. 33133.

RIGBY, BARBARA, TV Prom., KTSM, 801 N. Oregon, El Paso, Tex., '69–; Traf. Dir., Univ. of Tex.

RIGLER, RUTH L., Corporate VP, Adolph's Ltd., 1800 W. Magnolia Blvd., Burbank, Cal. 91503, '67–; Head, Pubcty. and PR, '59–; Dir., Consumer Educ. Dept., '51–; Dir., Jeannette Frank Test Kitchens, '51–; '49–; Visiting Nurse, Chgo. Health Dept., '43–'45; Instr., Supvsr., Evanston (Ill.) Hosp., '37–'41; Auth., "The Modern Meat Cookbook" ('58; Revsd., '68); AWRT (Southern Cal. Chptr. VP); Univ. of Minn., BS (Nursing Educ.), '33; b. Mpls., Minn., 1911; p. Frank and Jeannette Rosen Rigler; h. (div.); c. Rae (Mrs. Jon Brent), Terry; res: 11926 Goshen Ave., L.A., Cal. 90049.

RIKER, ELLA MARGARET, Pubcty. Dir. of Cosmetic Div., Lehn and Fink, Subsidiary of Sterling Drug, Inc., 225 Summit Ave., Montvale, N.J. 07645, '68–; Pubcty. Dir., John H. Breck, '59–'68; Wms. Dir., J. Walter Thompson (Chgo., Ill.), '56–'59; Cosmetic Career Wm. (Bd. of Governors, '69–'70), AWRT; St. Mary's Col., BA (Jnlsm.); b. 1930; p. William and Ella Benitz; c. Vincent, Mark; res: 53 Ridge Pl., Wayne, N.J. 07470.

RILEY, FRAN, Sr. AE, Dir. of Wms. Div., Mekler/Ansell Associates, Inc., 279 E. 44th St., N.Y., N.Y. 10017, '68–; Pres., McColl-Riley Assocs., '59–'68;

AE, Ted Bates, '56–'59; Pubcty., Pubns. Mgr., NAB, Wash., D.C., '52–'56; Lectr.; Pubcty. Club of N.Y. (Pres., '63–'65; Most Valuable Mbr. aw., '65–'66; Distg. Svc. aws., '67, '68), PRSA, AWRT (Nat. Advisory Cncl., '56–'58); Int. Platform Assn.; Yale Achiev. Key; Pace Col. Alumna; b. Suffern, N.Y., 1921; p. William and Helen Byrne Riley; res: 61 Jane St., N.Y., N.Y. 10014.

RILEY, NAN, Dir., Wms. News Dept., Carl Byoir and Associates, 800 Second Ave., N.Y., N.Y. 10017, '65–; Wms. Affairs Specialist, Eastern Airlines, '65; PR Dir., Bamberger's (Cherry Hill, N.J.), '63–'65; Asst. PR Dir., Franklin Inst. (Phila., Pa.), '62–'63; Reptr., S.F. Examiner, '59–'62; UPI, '58–'59; Miami Daily News, '56–'58; PRSA, Fashion Group, Theta Sigma Phi, NHFL; Key of City of Miami, '58; Univ. of Miami, BA, '55 (cum laude); h. Paul E. Eberhardt, Jr.; res: 670 West End Ave., N.Y., N.Y. 10025.

RIMMER, MARGRET KING McDONALD, Owner, Margret Rimmer Specialty Shop, Westchester Fashions, One Summit Ave. and 1506 Pennsylvania, Ft. Worth, Tex. 76104, '59–; Dr. Home Econs., Dir. Pubcty. and Prom., WBAP-TV, '49–'59; Free-lance Colmst., Ft. Worth Star Telegram; Fashion Coordr., Am. Fashion Assocs. (Dallas), '63; Free-lance Radio-TV Commls., Fashion Commentary; Theta Sigma Phi, Kappa Kappa Gamma, AWRT (Southwestern Area VP, '58, '59); Zenith Aw., '54–; Who's Who of Am. Wm.; Who's Who in Bus. and Commerce; Who's Who in Southwest; Tex. Wm. of Distinction; Christian Col., Assoc. Deg. (Music), '36; Univ. of Mo., BA, '40; Tex. Christian Univ., '64–; b. Hitchcock, Okla.; p. William and Loretta Truscott King; h. Dr. Raymond J. Rimmer; c. Lance King McDonald, Lt. Raymond J., Karen (Mrs. Donald Hatchett); res: 3209 Overton Park E., Ft. Worth, Tex. 76109.

RINDLAUB, JEAN WADE, Cnslt., Adv. and New Products, '65–; VP and Dir., BBDO, '30–'64; Ed., N.Y. State Status of Wm. Rept.; Colm., "What One Woman Can Do," Nat. Cncl. of Wm. bul.; articles, mags.; Speaker, bus., home econ., consumer groups; Nat. Cncl. of Wm. (VP), AWNY (Life Mbr.), Fashion Group, N.Y. State Cncl. of Wm. (retired mbr.); AFA Adv. Wm. of Yr.; Printers' Ink Medal; b. Lancaster, Pa., 1904; p. Robert and Lola Hess Wade; h. Willard W. Rindlaub; c. John, Anne (Mrs. Frank B. Dow, Jr.); res: 1156 Kensington Rd., W. Englewood, N.J. 07666.

RINGEL, HARRIET COOK, Adv. and Pubcty. Supvsr., Central Illinois Light Company, 300 Liberty St., Peoria, Ill. 61602, '66–; Ed., CILCO News, '59–'66; Instr. in Interior Decoration, Bradley Univ., '62–; Central Ill. Eds. Assn. (Pres., '65), Ill. Press Assn., Public Utilities Adv. Assn; Peoria PR Soc. (Pres., '67), civic orgs; Bradley Univ., BS, '38 (grad. with distinction; Pi Beta Phi); b. Peoria, Ill., 1916; p. Joseph E. and Eleanor M. Fisher Cook; h. Charles Ringel; c. Kathryn (Mrs. Richard Riegler), Margaret; res: 1600 W. Columbia Terr., Peoria, Ill. 61606.

RINGER, BARBARA ALICE, Asst. Register of Copyrights, Copyright Office, Library of Congress, Wash., D.C. 20540, '66–; Asst. Register of Copyrights for Examining, '64–'66; Chief, Examining Div., '60–'64; Asst. Chief, '56–'60; Head, Renewal and Assigt. Sec., '51–'56; Copyright Examiner, '49–'51; Adjunct Prof. of Law, Georgetown Univ. Law Ctr., '63–; Auth. of numerous articles on copyright, pfsnl. mags.; Co-auth. of bk., "Copyrights" ('63; revsd. '65); Fed. Bar Assn., AAUW, various others; Superior Svc. Aw. ('51, '58); Wm. A. Jump Meritorious Aw. for Exemplary Achiev. in Public Adm. ('58); George Wash. Univ., AB, '45 (with distinction; Phi Beta Kappa); Columbia Univ., MA, '43; LLB, '49; b. Lafayette, Ind., 1925; p. William and Gladys Ringer; res: 5102 Fairglen Lane, Chevy Chase, Md. 20015.

RINGOLD, FRANCINE LEFFLER, Ed.-in-Chief, Nimrod Magazine, Univ. of Tulsa, 7th and College, Tulsa, Okla., '68–; Script Ed., Dir., Univ. of Mich. TV; Instr. of Eng., Univ. of Tulsa, '66–'69; four TV dramas prod.; short stories published; Univ. of Mich., BA (Eng.), '55 (high hons.); Phi Beta Kappa; Zeta Phi Eta; Phi Kappa Phi; Univ. of Tulsa, MA, '64; b. N.Y.C., 1934; p. Saul and Lillian Lieberman Leffler; h. Anthony Ringold; c. Leslie, John, James, Suzanne; res: 122 E. 25th St., Tulsa, Okla. 74114.

RIOS, TERE, Auth., "The Fifteenth Pelican" (adapted for "The Flying Nun," ABC-TV); Instr., Crtv. Writing, Univ. of Wis.; Contrbr., 60 stories, articles to nat. mags.; Wis. Reg. Wtrs. Assn., Madison Area Wtrs., Wtrs. Sodality of Am.; Univ. of Wis.; Univ. of Pitt.; Johns Hopkins; b. Bklyn., N.Y.; h. Col. Humbert J. Versace (U.S.A., Ret.); c. Capt. Humbert Rocque Versace, Stephen Vincent, Richard Patrick, John Michael, Teresa Dominicque; res: Black Earth, Wis. 53515.

RIPP, JUDITH ELLEN, Movie Ed., Parents' Magazine, 52 Vanderbilt Ave., N.Y., N.Y. 10017, '67–; Asst. Movie Ed., '64–'67; Rschr., Colliers Ency., '62–'64; Co-auth., movie script, '68; Asst. Prodr., movie short, '69; Cornell Univ., BA (Comparative Literature), '61; b. N.Y.C., 1940; p. Max and Gertrude Roth Seelenfreund; h. (div.); res: 276 Riverside Dr., N.Y., N.Y. 10025.

RIPS, RAE ELIZABETH, Chief, Hist. and Travel Dept., Detroit Public Library, Detroit, Mich. 48202, '48–; Ref. Asst., '42–'48; Auth., "United States Government Publications" (Wilson, '50); ALA, Special Libs. Assn., WNBA; Detroit Lib. svc. aw., '69; Univ. of Chgo., AB, '36; AM, '38; Univ. of Ill., BS (Lib. Sci.), '40; b. Omaha, Neb.; res: 630 Merrick, Detroit, Mich. 48202.

RITACCO, JOANNE MARIE, Free-lance Prod. Asst. for Public Bdcst. Lab., NET, Eli Prods., Washington, D.C.; Adm. Asst., Unit Mgr., Prod. Asst., WETA, '63–'68; h. Paul Anthony.

RITTENHOUSE, HARRIET HARRIS, Acting Librn., City-County Public Library, 700 Fifth St., Moundsville,

W. Va. 26041, '68–; Cataloguer, '62–'68; Librn., Ordnance Rsch. Lab., Pa. State Univ., '46–'49; Asst. Librn., Elmhurst Col., '45–'46; Circ. Asst., Pa. Univ. Lib., '43–'45; W.Va. Lib. Assn.; Knox Col., '38–'40; Univ. of Ill., AB, '42; BS (Lib. Sci.), '43; b. Tampico, Ill., 1920; p. William and Vara Gray Harris; h. Ellwood Rittenhouse, Jr.; c. William Charles; res: Box 57, Moundsville, W.Va. 26041.

RITTER, NATALY STENZLER, Free-lance TV Wtr., Metro-Goldwyn-Mayer, (Culver City, Cal.), '66–'67; Copywtr., McCann-Erickson (S.F.), '65–'66; Copywtr., BBDO (N.Y.C.), '62–'65; Copywtr., Young & Rubicam, '59–'61; Wtr., Prodr., film on child art for U.C.L.A.; TV scripts for "Man From U.N.C.L.E.," '67; WGA, Theta Sigma Phi; volunteer work, Albert Einstein Col. of Med.; Syracuse Univ., BA (Jnlsm.), '58; b. Phila., Pa., 1936; p. Benjamin and Gertrude Naphtaly Stenzler; h. Toby G. Ritter; c. Victoria Beth, Lianne, Louis; res: Pirates Cove, Mamaroneck, N.Y. 10543.

RIVERS, PAULINE WOLLY, Special Staff Cnslt., U.S. Committee for UNICEF, 331 E. 38th St., N.Y., N.Y. 10016, '68–; Dir., Speaker Svcs. for UN-UN Assn.-USA, '58–'67; Dir., Org. Activities, New York Times, '55–'58; Asst. Dir., Dir., Club Svc. Bur., New York Herald Tribune '43–'55; Tchr., Eng., UN Secretariat Wives, UN Hospitality Comm.; various orgs.; Elmira Col., BA; Columbia Univ., Grad. Sch., '30–'32; b. N.Y.C.; h. (dec.); res: 2 W. 67th St., N.Y., N.Y. 10023.

RIVLIN, HELEN ANNE BLOOM, Prof. of Hist., State University of New York at Binghamton, N.Y., '69–; Visiting Assoc. Prof., '68–'69; Asst. to Assoc. Prof., Univ. of Md., '57–'69; Rsch. Assoc., Middle East Ctr., Harvard Univ., '56–'57; Rsch. Fellow, '54–'56; Auth., "The Agricultural Policy of Muhammad Ali in Egypt" (Harvard Univ. Press, '61), other articles, revs., specializing in Middle East hist.; Middle East Inst., Middle East Studies Assn., Am. Hist. Assn., AAUP, AAUW; Who's Who of Am. Wm.; Univ. of Rochester, BA, '49 (Phi Beta Kappa; high hons.); Radcliffe Col., MA, '50; Oxford Univ., DPhil, '53; b. Rochester, N.Y., 1918; p. William and Sarah Bernstein Bloom; h. Ephraim Rivlin (div.); res: 3141 Cornell Ave., Vestall, N.Y. 13850.

RIXON, BARBARA SPENCER, Pres., PR Cnslt., Barbara Rixon Associates, 103 E. 75th St., N.Y., N.Y. 10021, and P.O. Box 17734, Charlotte, N.C., '64–; Wms. Ed., Mecklenburg Times, '64; Colmst., '60–'62; Home Furnishings Ed., Feature Wtr., Charlotte News, '62–'63; Polit. PR Cnslt., '52–'62; PR Asst. (A.I.D.), PRSA (N.C. Bd. Mbr.), '68; (1st Wm. Mbr.), Charlotte PR Soc., (1st Wm. Mbr.), N.C. Hist. Soc., N.C. Press Wms. Assn. (three aws., '63, one aw., '64), Theta Sigma Phi; Smith Col., BA, '43; b. Cheyenne, Wyo.; p. Percy Craig and Joan Maloney Spencer; h. W. E. Rixon (div.); c. Mrs. Kay J. Jennell, Jr., Patricia Anne, Joanne Scofield; res: 103 E. 75th St., N.Y., N.Y. 10021.

RIZNIK, CHARLOTTE BARNES, Dir. of PR, Save-Our Seashore, San Rafael, Cal. 94901, '69–; Staff Corr.,

Marin Co., S.F. Chronicle, '52–'69; Ed., Marin Magazine, '50; Reptr., Independent Journal, '46; Ed., Reptr., Marin Journal, '45–'46; Fgn. Press Liaison Offcr., State Dept., '43–'45; Asst. to West Coast Dir., OWI, '41–'43; Adm. Asst., Overseas Br., '40–'41; Adv. Dir., Stylist, Botany Worsted Mills, N.Y.C., '30–'31; Stylist, Fashion Cnslt., D. Roditi Commissionaires, Paris, '27–'29; Fashion Reptr., Womens Wear Daily, N.Y.C., '26; Reptr., S.F. Examiner, '25; Jr. Clerk, Packard Motor Co., '15; Am. Nwsp. Guild, ZONTA (Dir.); Univ. of Cal., Berkeley, '25; b. N.Y.C., 1901; p. T. Roy and Mary Mahu Barnes; h. Joseph Quentin Riznik; c. Dr. Barnes Riznik; res: 360 Redwood Rd., San Anselmo, Cal. 94960.

RIZZO, ANGELYN RENA, Reptr., Educ. Wtr., Lafayette Journal and Courier, Federated Publications Inc., 221 N. 6th St., Lafayette, Ind. 47901, '61–; Ed. of employee pubn., PR, Johnson and Johnson (Chgo., Ill.), '60–'61; Asst. Sls. Mag. Ed., Intermediate Adv. Mgr., Continental Casualty Ins. Co., '59–'60; Freelance Feature Wtr.; Ind. Assn. of Press Wm., NAPW, Lafayette Press Club; Marquette Univ., '54–'57; Purdue Univ., BS (Eng., Jnlsm.), '59; Northwestern Univ.; b. Chgo., Ill., '37; p. Reno and Anna Loro Rizzo; res: 508 Perrin Ave., Lafayette, Ind. 47904.

RIZZO, FRANCINE JEAN, Pres., Rizzo Associates, Inc., 153 Fifth Ave., N.Y., N.Y. 10010, '68–; Computer Field Express, Inc., '68; Market Fact-N.Y., Inc., '66–'68; Erdos & Morgan, Inc., '64–'66; Sarah Lawrence Coll.; b. N.Y.C., 1943; p. Felix and Marion Christadora Rizzo; res: 444 Central Park West, N.Y., N.Y. 10025.

ROACH, HELEN P., Assoc. Prof. (Retired), Speech and Theatre Dept., Brooklyn College, Bklyn., N.Y. 11210, '64–; Asst. Prof., Instr., '31–'64; Founder, Supvsr., Listening Room, '54–'69; Speech Tchr., Arena Stage (Wash., D.C.), '65–'66; Prodr., record album, "The Hungarian Revolution," '69; Auth., non-fiction; Talent, Spoken Records (Scarecrow Press, '63, '66, '70); Visiting Rsch. Fellow, Radcliffe, '60–'61; Assn. for Recorded Sound Archivists (Charter Mbr.), SAA, Soc. for Theatre Rsch. (London), AAUP, Newman Hon. Soc.; Hunter Col., AB, '24; Tchrs. Col., Columbia, AM, '28; Columbia Univ., PhD, '48; b. St. Joseph, Mo., 1903; c. Marcus, Mary McConville; res: 333 E. 41st St., N.Y., N.Y. 10017.

ROACH, MIRIAM MARSHALL, Studio Tchr., Secondary Social Scis., WDCN-TV, PO Box 12555, Acklen Sta., Nashville, Tenn. 37212, '68–, '62–'67 (Aw. of Merit, '67: Freedoms Fndn. Aw., '64, '66); Tchr., Met. Nashville Schs., '37–; Wtr., Prod., TV quiz progs. "Let's Find Out," WSM-TV, '52; Instr., Special Educ., Univ. of Tenn., '47; In-Svc. Cnslt., ITV, '63–; Tchr.-Designer "Inquiries in Sociology," ASA, '67; ITV Cnslt., Demonstration Tchr., Vanderbilt Univ., '66–'68; Wtr., "Matthew Paris," Speculum, '34; film "Plus is for True"; Univ. of Chattanooga, '28–'30; Vanderbilt, BA, '32 (Owen Medal in Hist., '32); MA, '33 (Teaching Fellow, '33–'35); Wayne State Univ., grad. work, '41; b. Chattanooga, Tenn.; p. Daniel, Sr., and Percy Johnson

Marshall; c. Marc E., Karen Deirdre; res: 414 E. Iris Dr., Nashville, Tenn. 37204.

ROACH, STELLA, Dir. of News Bur., PR, Los Angeles Home Furnishings Mart, 1933 S. Broadway, L.A., Cal. 90007, '60–; W. Coast Ed., Globe News Photo Synd., '52–'59; Pubcty. Wtr., Paramount Studios, '39–'49; Warner Bros., '36–'39; Reptr., Wms. Pg. Ed., Colmst., Caller-Times (Corpus Christi, Tex.); Hollywood Wms. Press Club (Pres., '56–'57), NHFL (Southern Cal. Chptr. Pres., '69–'70); b. Laredo, Tex., 1909; p. Norman and Eugenia Dodier Roach; res: 104 N. LaPeer Dr., L.A., Cal. 90048.

ROADEN, JOYCE THOMAS, Reg. Librn., Kentucky Department of Libraries, 305 E. Center, N.E., Corbin, Ky. 40701, '66–; Librn., Corbin City Schs., '65; Ky. Lib. Assn., Friends of Ky. Libs. (Scenic Chptr. Charter Mbr.); Ark. Tech., BS, '65; b. Okla. City, Okla., 1938; p. Earl and Jewell Graham Thomas; h. Ralph Roaden; c. Ralph, Earl, Beverly, Calvin; res: Falls Rte., Box 47, Corbin, Ky. 40701.

ROBB, IZETTA WINTER, Free-lance Ed., '69–; Mng. Ed., Naval Aviation News, '54–'69; Ed., '50–'54; Edtl., Naval Aviation Bul., '43–'50; Wms. Page Ed., Washington Daily News, '40–'41; WNPC, Fed. Eds. Assn.; Navy Civilian Svc. Aw., '68; Univ. of Minn., BA, '26 (summa cum laude); MA, '28; res: 1711 Massachusetts Ave., N.W., Wash., D.C. 20036.

ROBBINS, JUNE STUMPE, Free-lance Wtr., '46–; Jnlst., Pageant, '46–'47; Newsweek, '44–'46, London Daily Mirror, '44; N.Y. Herald Tribune, '43–'44; St. Louis Globe Democrat, '42; Auth., "Eight Weeks to Live—the Last Days of Senator Taft" (Doubleday); Jnlsm. Lectr.; OPC, Soc. of Mag. Wtrs.; mag. aw. for brotherhood, Nat. Assn. of Christians and Jews, '64; 1st prize, mag. writing, Am. Med. Assn., '65; Washington Univ., AB, '43; Columbia Univ., MS, '44; b. St. Louis, Mo., 1921; p. Oscar and Constance Wagon Stumpe; h. Jhan Robbins; c. Penelope, Thomas, Margaret, David; res: Box 65, Cornwall, Conn.

ROBBINS, MILDRED BROWN, Colmst., San Francisco Chronicle, 5th and Mission Sts., S.F., Cal., '56–; Soc. Ed.; radio prog.; Aw. of Merit, Cal. Hist. Soc., '64; Laura Bride Powers Memorial aw., '66; Exalted order of the Grizzly, Cal. Heritage Cncl., '69; Univ. of Cal., AB; b. S.F., Cal.; p. Alexander M. and Frida Herrmann Brown; h. Theodore Robbins; c. Alexandra; res: 2154 32nd Ave., S.F., Cal. 94116.

ROBBINS, MILDRED ELOWSKY, Hon. Pres., National Council of Women, U.S.A., 345 E. 46th St., N.Y., N.Y. 10024, '68–; Pres., '64–'68; UN Rep., '56–'64; Ed., "Measure of Mankind"; Chmn., Wms. Conf. on War Against Poverty, '68; Intl. Peace Acad. Bd., Un. Cerebral Palsy; N.Y.U., BA, '42; b. N.Y.C., 1922; p. Samuel and Isabella Zeitz Elowsky; h. Louis J. Robbins; c. Jane Marla, Aileen; res: 54 Riverside Dr., N.Y., N.Y. 10024.

ROBERSON, PATT FOSTER, Bus. Mgr., The Southern Review, Drawer D, University Station, Baton Rouge, La. 70803, '64–; La. Reptr., Canal Record, quarterly pubn. of Panama Canal Soc., '67–; Ed., Lake Echoes, Our Lady of the Lake Hosp., '63 (Life mbr., aux.); Published "Survey of Foreign, English-Language Literary Quarterlies Available for Exchange," '65; Ghost Wtr.; Asst. Ed., base nwsp., U.S. Navy, Rodman, Canal Zone, '54–'55; Theta Sigma Phi, Assn. for Educ. in Jnlsm., Friends of the La. State Univ. Lib.; Canal Zone Jr. Co., AA, '54; La. State Univ., BA, '57 (Life mbr., alumni assn.); b. Middletown, N.Y., 1934; p. Gilbert and Mildred O'Neal Foster; h. Murray Ralph Roberson, Jr. (dec.); res: 4875 Maribel Dr., Baton Rouge, La. 70812.

ROBERTS, ANNE HARTLEY, Ed., First National Bank, 248 E. Capitol St., Jackson, Miss. 39201, '68–; Am. Inst. of Banking; Belhaven Col., '56–'57; b. Jackson, Miss., 1938; p. Richard and Ann Hartley Roberts; res: 624 Raymond Rd., Jackson, Miss. 39204.

ROBERTS, FRANCES, Chmn. of Dept. of Hist., University of Alabama, P.O. Box 1247, Huntsville, Ala. 35807, '66–; Prof., '61–; Assoc. Prof., '59–'61; Asst. Prof., '56–'59; Instr., '50–'56; Tchr. in public schs., '35–'52; Auth: "Shadows on the Wall," "The Life and Works of Howard Weeden," "Civics for Alabama Schools"; Wtr., pamphlets and articles; Social Studies Cnslt. to Ala. High Schs.; AAUW (Huntsville Br. past Pres., '49–'51), Ala. Educ. Assn., Ala. Cncl. for Social Studies (past Pres.); Livingston State Col., BS, '37; Univ. of Ala., MA, '40; PhD, '56; Vanderbilt Univ.; b. Gainesville, Ala., '16; p. Richard and Mary Watson Roberts; res: 603 Randolph Ave. S.E., Huntsville, Ala. 35801.

ROBERTS, JOSEPHINE PAMP, Wms. Ed., Feature Wtr., Morning News, News Observer Company, 13666 E. 14th St., San Leandro, Cal. 94577, '69–; S.F. Press Club, E. Bay Wms. Press Club; numerous writing aws.; S.F. City Col., AA, '52; Stanford Univ., BS, '54 (cum laude); b. Omaha, Neb., 1912; p. Carl and Elsie Williams Pamp; h. Wilbur Carlos Roberts (dec.); c. William Carl, Robert L., Marjorie Roberts Dohrman; res: 104 Broadmoor Blvd., San Leandro, Cal. 94577.

ROBERTS, JOY, Media Dir., Sheldon Marks Associates, 9025 Wilshire Blvd., Beverly Hills, Cal. 90211, '64–; Selders, Jones and Covington; Winius-Brandon; Free Lance Photgr.; b. Kan. City, Mo.; c. Paula.

ROBERTS, LEILA-JANE SMITH, Head Librn., Winchester Public Library, 80 Washington St., Winchester, Mass. 01890, '67–; Asst. Librn., '63–'67; Young Adult Librn., '60–'63; Asst., '57–'60; Publr., Bus. Mgr., YA Coop. Bk. Revs., '69–; Tchr., '54–'56, '45–'49; New England Lib. Assn. (Dir., '69–'70), Mass. Lib. Assn., Gtr. Boston Public Lib. Admrs. (Secy., '68–'69), BPW, League of Wm. Voters; Oberlin Col., BA, '45; b. Syracuse, N.Y., 1923; p. Reveley and Ruth Mallory Smith; h. Russell D. Roberts; c. Jane G.; res: 14 Fairview Terr., Winchester, Mass. 01890.

ROBERTS, MARGUERITE, Auth: "Tess in the Theatre" (Univ. of Toronto Press, '50; Daiaka, sha., Tokyo, Japan), "Hardy's Poetic Drama in the Theatre" (Pageant Press, N.Y., '65); Chmn., Eng. Dept., University of Richmond, Richmond, Va. 23173, '65–; Dean, Westhampton Col., '47–'65; Lectr., Univ. of Toronto (Can.), '46–'47; Dean of Wm., McMasters Univ., '37–'46; Assoc. Ed., Dean's Jnl., '42–'50; AAUW, Fellowship of Radcliffe Rsch. grants for Univ. of Toronto and Univ. of Richmond, various others; Univ. of Evansville, BA, '24; Radcliffe Col., MA, '28; PhD, '43 (Area Rep.), b. Rockport, Ind.; p. Ralph and Alice Saunders Roberts; res: 15 Towand Rd., Richmond, Va. 23226.

ROBERTS, MARY D., Auth: "Don's Great Discovery" (Ives Washburn), "Hurricane Mystery" (Ives Washburn), "Get with It, Joan" (Ives Washburn), "Trailmakers" (Ives Washburn), "Promises to Keep" (Meredith Press), "The Ghost of the Fifth Door" (Macrae Smith); N.Y.U., Univ. of the Ams. (Mex.); b. N.Y.C.; p. Lawrence James Duffy and Mary D'Villiers; c. Christia; res: 150 E. Adams St., Brownsville, Tex. 78520.

ROBERTS, NANCY CORRELL, Auth: "Where Time Stood Still" ('70), "This Haunted Land" ('70), "Sense of Discovery: The Mountain" ('69); "A Week in Robert's World" ('69); numerous other bks.; mag. articles; Ed. and Publr., The Scottish Chief, '55–'58; Auths. Guild; Univ. of N.C., BA, '47; Univ. of Miami, post grad. work, '47–'48; h. Bruce Roberts; c. Nancy Lee and David Roberts; res: 6624 Sunview Dr., Charlotte, N.C. 28210.

ROBERTS, RUBY ALTIZER, Ed., Lyric mag., '52–; Poetry Colmst., Newport News Times Herald; Poet Laureate of Va. (Gen. Assembly, '50); Who's Who of Am. Wm., Who's Who in the South and Southwest, Intl. Who's Who in Poetry, Bellamann aw., '52; Col. of William and Mary (Hon. deg.), '61; b. Sowers, Va., 1907; p. Waddie and Dana Cummings Altizer; h. Laurence L. Roberts; c. Heidi Anne; res: 301 Roanoke St., Christiansburg, Va. 24073.

ROBERTS, SUSAN F., Wtr.; Cnslt., Family Service Association of America, 44 E. 23rd St., N.Y., N.Y., '63–; PR Dir., L.S.U. Med. Ctr. (N.O., La.), '53–'63; Nwsp. Reptr., '43–'53; Auth., "Witch America" (Delacorte/Dell, '70), Co-auth., "The Yogi Cookbook" (Crown, '68); OPC, PRSA; Sophie Newcomb Col. grad.; b. N.O., La., 1919; p. Frank and Margaret Jackson Bryson; c. Susan M., Laura S.; res: 170 Carroll St., Bklyn., N.Y. 11231.

ROBERTSHAW, SARAH JOANNE, Adv. Copywtr., McCann-Erickson, Inc., 485 Lexington Ave., N.Y., N.Y. 10017, '67–; LaRoche, McCaffrey & McCall, '65–'67; Daniel & Charles, '65; West, Weir & Bartell, '64–'65; Ellington & Co., '62–'64; ASIFA E. animation aw., '69; two Clio nominations, '69; Rosary Col., BA (Speech, Drama), '62; b. St. Paul, Minn., 1940; p.

Charles and Enes Marinucci Robertshaw; res: 132 W. 80th St., N.Y., N.Y. 10024.

ROBERTSON, LAURA, Reptr., Albuquerque Tribune, 701 Silver St., Albuquerque, N.M. 87103, '68–; Wms. Ed., Arizona Daily Sun (Flagstaff); Auth., "How to Start a Money Making Business at Home" (F. Fell, '69); NLAPW; N.M. State Tchrs. Col.; b. Atoka, Okla., 1924; p. Robert and Adna Timberlake Ridgway; h. Harry Jamharian; c. John Kenneth Dembowski; res: 624 Kentucky S.E., Albuquerque, N.M. 87108.

ROBERTSON, SYLVIA VICK, Wtr., Staff of North Carolina Governor Robert W. Scott, State Capitol, Raleigh, N.C. 27602, '69–; Staff Wtr., Photogr., Acting Mng. Ed., Richmond County Daily Journal (Rockingham, N.C.), '64–'69; Wtr., Greenville (N.C.) Daily Reflector, '64; N.C. Press Wm. (writing, photog. aws., '68), N.C. Press Assn. (reptr. aw., '68), N.C. Press Photogrs.; E. Carolina Univ., '60–'63; b. Sanford, N.C., 1942; p. Charles and Ilene McFayden Vick; h. Fred Robertson (sep.); c. Lisa Michelle; res: 4130 Camelot Dr., Apt. C-4, Raleigh, N.C. 27609.

ROBERTSON-RIEHL, KATE, Actress, theater, TV, film, radio, '20–; Colmst. and Acting Tchr., '53–'54; Radio Commentator, '36–'48; Pacific Pioneer Bdcstrs., AEA, SAG, AFTRA; Carnegie Inst. of Tech. Sch. of Drama; b. Edinburgh, Scotland; p. George and Jane McPherson Robertson; h. August Riehl; c. Donald, David; res: 10402 Bloomfield St., Toluca Lake, N. Hollywood, Cal. 91602.

ROBICHAUD, BERYL, VP, McGraw-Hill, Inc., Princeton Rd., Hightstown, N.J. 08520, '46–; Mgr. Contract Termination System, Sperry Gyroscope, '42–'46; Secy. of Educ., IBM, Endicott, N.Y., '40–'42; Auth. of two bus. bks.; Sigma Xi, N.J. Acad. of Sci., Data Processing Mgt., Inst. of Mgt. Scis.; Mount Holyoke Col., BA (cum laude; trustee); Columbia Univ., MA; Trustee, Mercer County Commty. Col.; b. N.Y.C., 1919; p. Walter and Marjorie Hunekee Robichaud; res: Fairway Dr., Princeton, N.J. 08540.

ROBIN, TONI, Vice-chmn., Bd. of Dirs., The Marschalk Company, 1271 Ave. of the Americas, N.Y., N.Y. 10020, '68–; Pres., Chief Exec. Offcr., Johnstone Inc., '66–'68; Sr. VP, Assoc. Crtv. Dir., Norman Craig & Kummel; Crtv. Dir., Ellington; Adv. Prom. Dir., The Wool Bur.; Assoc. Ed., Holiday mag.; The Fashion Group; Traphagen Sch. of Design; Art Students League; b. Wilmington, Del.; h. Martin Snyder; res: 390 West End Ave., N.Y., N.Y. 10024.

ROBINETTE, VIVIEN BROOKER, Poet, Auth.; b. Rogers, Tex.; p. William and Anne Smith Brooker; h. James F. Robinette; res: 2021 Primrose Ave., S. Pasadena, Cal. 91030.

ROBINSON, ALICE GRAM, Pres., Congressional Digest Corp., 3231 P St., N.W., Wash., D.C. 20007; Founder, '22–; Dir., Wms. Div., Repl. Nat. Comm.,

'28; Edtl. Dept., Commty. Ctr.; Press Dept., Nat. Wms. Party; PR, Brewer, Taylor, Gram Co.; Special Wash. Wtr., Good Housekeeping, Fashion Art, Farmer's Wife, others; Auth., one textbk.; Am. Acad. of Polit. Sci., Kappa Alpha Theta, WNPC (a Founder); Univ. of Ore., Univ. of Cal.; b. Omaha, Neb.; p. Andrew and Carrie Jensen Gram; h. Norborne Thomas Nelson Robinson, Jr.; c. Norborne Thomas Nelson, III; res: 3210 Q. St., N.W., Wash., D.C. 20007.

ROBINSON, ANNE DURRUM, Copywtr., David G. Benjamin, Inc., 1201 W. 24th, Austin, Tex. 78705, '65–, '46–'48; Free-lance Wtr., Talent, '65–; Talent, KHFI, '57, '69; Ed., mag., '63–'65; Cont. Ed., Public Svc. Dir., KASE, '61–'63; Talent, KTBC-TV, '57; Cont. Ed., '42–'44; Talent, KLRN-TV, '57; Copywtr., John Henry Faulk Agcy.; Cont. Ed., KNOW, '48–'50; Staff Wtr., NBC (Hollywood), '44–'45; Special Lectr., radio writing, Univ. of Tex., '52, '57; Univ. of Tex. radio, TV workshops; Co-auth., light verse, "Never the Twain Shall Eat" ('40); Auth., verse coloring bk., "Symphony for Simple Simon" ('57); Wtr., Univ. of Tex. Sch. of the Air; Theta Sigma Phi; Tex. Wms. Univ., BJ (Jnlsm.), '35 (summa cum laude); Univ. of Tex., MJ, '58; b. Hugo, Okla., 1913; p. William and Effie Lear Durrum; h. Harold G. Robinson; c. Lear; res: 2309 Shoal Creek Blvd., Austin, Tex. 78705.

ROBINSON, DORIS JAMISON, Reg. Home Econst., U.S. Dept. of the Interior, Bureau of Commercial Fisheries, 300 South Ferry St., Terminal Island, Cal. 90731, '65–; Food and Fashion Ed., Home Svc. Dir., Ebony Magazine, '62–'64; Home Economics Tchr., L.A. City Bd. of Educ., '52–'62; Educ. TV fishery presentations, '65–; homemakers colm., Las Vegas Review Jnl., '67–'68; Am. Home Econs. Assn., Home Economists in Bus., Am. Sch. Food Svc. Assn., AWRT; Outstanding Contrb. in Homemaking Educ. aw., L.A. City Bd. of Educ., '62; Pepperdine Col., BS (Homemaking Educ.), '52; b. Portland, Ore.; p. James D. and Catherine M. Cash Jamison; h. John M. Robinson, Jr., M.D. (dec.); res: 2813 Fifth Ave., L.A., Cal. 90018.

ROBINSON, HAZEL GODWIN, Wms. Ed., Daily Highlander, 37 W. Orange Ave., Lake Wales, Fla. 33853, '65–; Colmst., "Leave It To Hazel"; Adv. Mgr., '60–'64; Nat. Music Club aws. for coverage of Nat. Music Week, '67, '68, '69; b. Cairo, Ga., '19; p. Joseph Alex and Pearl Jarvis Godwin; h. Sam P. Robinson; c. Larry and Gary; res: 915 Hesperides, Lake Wales, Fla. 33853.

ROBINSON, HELENE M., Assoc. Prof., Music, Arizona State University, Tempe, Ariz. 85281, '67–; Head, Piano Dept., Ariz. State Col. (Flagstaff); Head, Piano Dept., Southern Ore. State Col. (Ashland); Asst. Prof., Cal. State Col. (Fullerton); Assoc. Prof., Piano, Univ. of Cal. (Santa Barbara); presented workshops, lect.-demonstrations; Auth: col. textbks., "Basic Piano for Adults" (Wadsworth Publ., '64), "Intermediate Piano for Adults" ('69); Coordr., Co-ed., Co-auth., "Teaching Piano in Classroom and Studio" ('67; Music

Educs. Nat. Conf., '67); Univ. of Ore., BA (Music) (Phi Beta Scholarship); Northwestern Univ., MMUS.; Univ. of Southern Cal., grad. work; b. Eugene, Ore.; p. Kirkman and Emily Robinson; res: 1625 E. Malibu Dr., Tempe, Ariz. 85281.

ROBINSON, MARGARET CECILIA (Sister Marian Dolores), Prof. of Psych. and Commtns., Marylhurst College, also Tektronix Inc., Box 324, Marylhurst, Ore. 97036, '65–; '48–'59; Sorbonne (Paris, France), '63–'65; Univ. of Windsor (Ontario, Can.), '59–'63; Ft. Wright Col. (Spokane, Wash.), '47–'48; Loyola Univ. (Chgo., Ill.), '43–'47; Psychological Cnslt., '65–; rsch., personality and commtn., '65–; "Creative Personality in Religious Life" (Sheed & Ward Inc., '63); group sessions, workshops in commtn.; Ore. Psych. Assn (Secy.-Treas.), '53–'55), Portland Psych. Assn. (Pres.-elect, '69), Am. Psych. Assn., Am. Assn. for Advancement of Sci., other pfsnl. groups in psych.; Fulbright Post-doctoral Rsch. Aw., Univ. of Louvain (Belgium), '55, '56; Fulbright Cultural Aw., France, '56; Post-doctoral Rsch. Aw., Univ. of Detroit, '63–'64; Tektronix Grantee, '66; educ: Loyola Univ. (Chgo., Ill.), MA, '44; PhD, '47; Columbia Univ. (N.Y.) and Univ. of Chgo., Post-doctoral Rsch.; Am. Bd. of Examiners in Pfsnl. Psych., Diplomate (Clinical Psych.), '58; b. Astoria, Ore., 1925; p. James J. and Mathilda Carlson Robinson.

ROBINSON, PAMELA, Sr. Copywtr., Prom., Mademoiselle, 420 Lexington Ave., N.Y., N.Y. 10028, '68–; Jr. Copywtr., '66–'67; Chief Copywtr., Ann Taylor Sportswear, '69–; Auth., "Mademoiselle's ABC's of Beauty" ('69); Univ. of Fla., BS (Jnlsm.), '64; Ray-Vogue Sch. of Design, '66; b. Knoxville, Tenn., 1943; b. Brooks and Alice Hendrick Robinson; res: 401 E. 89th St., N.Y., N.Y. 10028.

ROBINSON, WILHELMENA SIMPSON, Assoc. Prof., Central State University, Box 262, Wilberforce, Oh. 45384, '56–; Instr., '46–'53; Cnslt., Yellow Springs Public Schs., '68–'69; Toledo Bd. of Educ., '68; Fac., Univ. of Louisville, '68; Catherine Spalding Col., '67; Oh. State Univ., '56–'57; Le Moyne Col., '46–'47; Edward Water Col., Fla. Normal Col., and Ala. State Tchrs. Col., '34–'36; Phi Alpha Theta, NEA (Life Mbr.), AAUW; STET; Columbia Univ., MA, '34; various other cols.; b. Pensacola, Fla., 1912; p. Joseph and Mattie Riley Simpson; h. Collins Robinson; c. Antoine L.; res: 535 W. South Col., Yellow Springs, Oh. 45387.

ROBNETT, ALYCE L., Prod. Mgr., Art Dir., Humphrey, Williamson & Gibson, Inc., 1400 Skirvin Tower, Okla. City, Okla. 73102, '59–; Layout Artist and Asst. Adv. Mgr., Kerr's Dept. Store, '50–'58; Okla. City Art Dirs. Club (Treas., '66), Southwestern Water Color Soc. (Okla. City Chptr.), Annual Art Dirs. Show (3rd pl. for Bklets., '66); b. Okla. City, Okla., 1932; p. Roscoe and Wildred Mitchell Robnett; res: 2840 Clermont Pl., Okla. City, Okla. 73116.

ROBOTTI, FRANCES VON SCHORNSTEIN, Ed.-in-Chief, Fountainhead Publishers Inc., 475 Fifth Ave.,

N.Y., N.Y. 10007, '63–; Auth: "French Cooking in the New World" ('68), "Key to New York" ('64), "Much Depends on Dinner" ('61), "Whaling and Old Salem" ('50), "Chronicles of Old Salem" ('49); AAUW, other orgs., Commanderie des Cordon Bleus de France Medal for lit. contrb., '66; Hunter Col., BA, '38; b. L.A., Cal., 1916; p. Maxmilian Von Schornstein and Helen Jacob Bunting; h. Peter Robotti; c. Armando V.; res: 155 E. 55th St., N.Y., N.Y. 10022.

ROBSON, MARJORIE REYNOLDS, AE, Creamer, Trowbridge, Case & Basford, Incorporated, 212 Dyer St., Providence, R.I. 02903, '67–; New Zealand Bdcst. Corp., '66–'67; Ladies' Home Jnl., '64–'65; J. Walter Thompson, '62–'64; Smith Col., BA, '62; b. Greenwich, Conn., 1940; p. Dr. Whitman M. and Phebe E. Root Reynolds; h. J. Michael Robson; res: 263 Benefit St., Providence, R.I. 02903.

ROCHAMBEAU, SHEILA MACKINTOSH, Contrb. Ed., Vogue U.S.A., Condé Nast Publications, 4 place du Palais, Bourbon, Paris, France, '51–; Am., European educ.; b. London, Eng., 1931; p. Alastair and Lela de Talleyrand Mackintosh; h. Count de Rochambeau; c. Eric, Mark, Nicholas; res: 20 Rue de l'Université, Paris, France.

ROCHE, MARY McDERMOTT, Mng. Ed., House and Garden, Condé Nast Publications, Inc., 420 Lexington Ave., N.Y., N.Y. 10017, '58–; Charm, '55–'58; News Ed., House Beautiful, '50–'53; Home Ed., N.Y. Times, '44–'50; articles, Harper's, N.Y. Times Magazine, Woman's Day, others; h. (div.).

RODEKOHR, SHARON KAY, Media Supvsr.; Barickman and Selders Advertising, Inc., 427 W. 12th St., Kan. City, Mo. 64105, '67–; AWRT; Kan. City Bus. Col., '58–'59; b. Lexington, Mo., 1940; p. Maurice and Helen Kessler Rodekohr; res: 538 N. 17th St., Lexington, Mo. 64067.

RODENWOLD, ZELTA FEIKE, Home Econs. Cnslt., Agricultural Research Service, United States Department of Agriculture, '50–'62; Info. Specialist, Bur. of Home Econs., '48–'50; Ed. of Pubns., Am. Home Econs. Assn., '46–'48; Dir., Wms. Progs., KOAC, '32–'46; Ore. Home Mgt. Spec., '30–'32; Ed., Ore. State Alumni mag., '21–'27; Theta Sigma Phi (Past Wash., '24; Chptr. Treas.), AWRT, Am. Home Econs. Assn. (D.C. Pres., '50), Press Club of Ore., Phi Kappa Phi (Corvallis Chptr. Pres., '37–'38), Omicron Nu (Nat'l. Treas.); Ore. State Univ., BS, '19; Ia. State Univ., MS, '29; b. Bayard, Ia., 1895; p. Ferdinand and Anna Peterson Feike; h. Benjamin William Rodenwold (dec.); res: 1717 S.W. Park Ave., Portland, Ore. 97201.

RODGERS, ELIZABETH STUART, Partner, Stuart-Rodgers Studio, 2504 Greenbay Rd., Evanston, Ill., '45–; Instr., Photojnlsm., Northwestern Univ., '61–'69; Auth., "Altar-Bound" ('58); Northwestern Univ., BS (Jnlsm.), '44; b. Indpls., Ind., 1922; p. William and

Gertrude Ellinwood Stuart; h. John Boyd Rodgers; c. Betsy, Holly, John B., III, Wm. S.; res: 138 Eddy Lane, Northfield, Ill. 60093.

RODINI, EMA LOU BIRELINE, Commty. Corr., News of Delaware County, 7416 W. Chester Pike, Upper Darby, Pa. 19018, '60–'69; Free-lance Wtr., The Evening Bulletin (Phila., Pa.); Commty. Corr., Chester (Pa.) Times, '55–'60; Edtl. Wtr., Industrial Maintenance, '48; Continuity Wtr., KSAL Radio (Salina, Kan.), '42–'44, '45–'47; Control Operator, Waves, '44–'45; Theta Sigma Phi (Phila. Pfsnl. Chptr. Treas., '65–'67; VP, '69–'70); Kan. State Univ., BS (Jnlsm.), '42; b. Lewis, Kan., '19; p. Frank and Eleanor Montgomery Bireline; h. Robert J. Rodini; c. Elizabeth, Kenneth, Nanette; res: 5237 Springfield Rd., Clifton Heights, Pa. 19018.

RODMAN, MAIA WOJCIECHOWSLCA, Auth: "Shadow of a Bull" (Atheneum, '64; Newbery aw., Deutzcher Fugend Buchpzeis); "Hey What's Wrong With This One?" (Harper, '69); "Tuned Out" (Harper, '68); six other children's bks.; Polish Acad. of Art and Letters; b. Warsaw, Poland, 1927; p. Zygmunt and Zofia Rudakowska Wojciechowslca; h. Selden Rodman (div.); c. Oriana; 659 Valley Rd., Oakland, N.Y.

RODMAN, NORMA CONNOLLY, Actress; Theatre: "A Streetcar Named Desire," others; TV: "The Eleventh Hour," "Studio One," others; Films: "The Wrong Man," "Winning"; Entertainment Chmn., Eugene McCarthy Presidential Campaign; The Actor's Studio; b. Boston, Mass., '30; p. Archibald and Beulah Dyer Connolly; h. Howard Rodman; c. Adam Dyer, Nancy Ann, Phillip Samuel; res: 626 S. Lorraine Blvd., L.A., Cal. 90005.

ROEBLING, MARY GINDHART, Chmn. of the Bd., Trenton Trust Company, 28 W. State St., Trenton, N.J. 08605, '51–; first elected Pres., '37–'41; Public Speaker, Nationwide; formerly Customer's Wm., Smith Barney Co., brokers (Phila., Pa.); numerous public svcs., organizations, comms. and aws. incl. assoc. mbr. OPC, assoc. mbr., Amer. Nwsp. Wm.'s Club, Print Club of Philadelphia, Pres. Comm. on Status of Wm., apptd. by President Kennedy; Univ. of Pa. Wharton Sch. and N.Y.U., advanced study in econs. and fin.; Hon. Degrees: Rider Col., DFA; Ithaca Col., DL, Bryant Col., DS, Muhlenberg Col., DS; Wilberforce Univ., DH; b. West Collingswood, N.J., 1905; p. Isaac D. and Mary Simon Gindhart, Jr.; h. Siegfried Roebling (dec.); c. Elizabeth (Mrs. David J. Hobin), Paul; res: 40 W. State St., Trenton, N.J. 08608.

ROEDER, GLORIA BROOKS, "Gloria" of nationally synd. TV series, "Exercise with Gloria," Triangle Publications, Inc., TV/Radio Division, 4100 City Line Ave., Phila., Pa. 19131, '64–; "Exercise with Gloria," WRCV-TV, '61–'64; "Exercise with Gloria," WTAR-TV (Norfolk, Va.), '61; Exercise, Posture Instr., Richard Hudnut's DuBarry Success Sch. (N.Y.C.), '44–'45; Instr. WAVES, WACS, retarded children, Armed Forces wives; Co-prodr., "Exercise with Gloria" record album; Co-auth., "Exercise with Gloria" booklet;

guest appearances on network TV programs, incl. "What's My Line," "To Tell the Truth"; Treas., GLORED, Inc. (Pa.); Lectr.; ATVAS, AFTRA; Wm. of Yr: Phila., '64; Atlantic City, '63; Who's Who of Am. Wm.; Colby Jr. Col., AA, '43 (Key Club); Univ. of N.H., BS (Phys. Educ.), '44; b. Lowell, Mass., 1923; p. John and Edna Brundin Brooks; h. Edward F. Roeder; c. Mrs. Kent E. Hoisington, Donna M., Gail J., Pamela F., Karen S., Michelle P.; res: 432 Timber Lane, Devon, Pa., 19333.

ROGERS, CAROLINE, Assoc. Ed., Reader's Digest, 200 Park Ave., N.Y., N.Y. 10017; Lectr., Univs., Cols. on writing, jnlsm. and Reader's Digest; NATAS, Am. Inst. of Aeronautics & Astronautics, WNPC; Univ. of Ore.; Dominican Col.; b. Roseburgh, Ore.; res: 20 E. 74th St., N.Y., N.Y. 10021; 455 Worth Ave., Palm Beach, Fla. 33480.

ROGERS, DOROTHY, Prof. of Psych., State University of New York, College at Oswego, State University College, Oswego, N.Y. 13126, '50–; Asst. Prof., Psych., '48–'50; Instr., Psych., '46–'58; Wtr: travel bks., textbks., "Jeopardy and a Jeep" ('57), "Mental Hygiene in Elementary Education" ('57; best bk. in educ. by a wm. for '55–'57, $1,000 aw.), "Fountainhead of Teacher Education" ('61), "Psychology of Adolescence" ('62), "Highways Across the Horizon" ('66), "Issues in Adolescent Psychology" ('69), "Extension Manual for Adolescent Psychology" ('69), "Child Psychology" ('69), "Issues in Child Psychology" ('69), "Readings in Child Psychology" ('69), "Issues in Child Psychology" ('69), "Readings in Child Psychology" ('69); Co-auth., Test Manual for "Issues in Adolescent Psychology" ('69); N.Y. Psychological Assn., Am. Psychological Assn.; Univ. of Ga., AB, '34 (Phi Beta Kappa); MA, '36; Duke Univ., PhD, '46 (Fellowship); b. Ashburn, Ga., 1914; p. Edwin and Ella Mae Evans Rogers; res: Franklin Ave., Oswego 17, N.Y. 13126.

ROGERS, GEORGIA McMAHON, Assoc. Ed., New Jersey Equine Industry News, Department of Civil Service, Trenton, N.J., '69–; Sr. Asst., Public Info., '69; PR Dir., Douglas/Sarpy Red Cross (Omaha, Neb.), '64–'68; Substitute HS Tchr. (Athens, Pa.), '68; Wtr. of several mag. articles; AWRT (Omaha Chptr. Secy.-Treas., '67); AIE (Omaha Chptr. Secy., '66), Neb. Press Assn., Neb. Press Photogrs., Radio-TV Cncl. of Omaha; City Col. of S.F., AA, '51; Wash. Univ., '54–'56; Univ. of Md., '60–'62; Univ. of Neb. at Omaha, BS (Jnlsm.), '64 (grad. with distinction); b. Lewiston, Idaho, 1924; p. Frank C. and Belle Eleta Wheeler McMahon; h. Clifford Rogers; c. Erin, Clifford; permanent res: 226 Bridge St., Athens, Pa. 18810. Current res: 3802D Falcon Courts N., McGuire AFB, N.J. 08641.

ROGERS, HELEN JEAN, VP, Dir., John H. Secondari Productions Ltd., 212 W. 48th St., N.Y., N.Y. 10036; Prodr., ABC-TV; Radcliffe Col., MA; h. John H. Secondari; c. John Gerry, Linda Helen.

ROGERS, KASEY, Wtr., Lewis Company Ltd., 8741 Sunset Blvd., L.A., Cal. 91316; Free Lance Wtr.; Film Actress in 25 pictures including "Samson and Delilah"; TV Actress in 750 programs including "Bewitched" and "Peyton Place"; b. Morehouse, Mo.; p. Eben E. and Ina Mae Mocabee Rogers; h. W. Winston Lewis III; c. Jay, Mona, Monika, Michael; res: 17457 Sumiya Dr., Encino, Cal. 91316.

ROGERS, KATE ELLEN, Prof., Chmn., Housing and Interior Design, School of Home Economics, University of Missouri, 140 Stanley Hall, Columbia, Mo. 65201, '58–; Assoc. Prof. and Chmn., '56–'58; Asst. Prof., '54–'56; Auth., "Modern House, U.S.A.," (Harper & Row), '62); VP, Co-Owner, Design Today, Inc., '51–'54; Instr., Tex. Tech., '47–'53; Cnslt., Dept. of Health, Educ. and Welfare, '63; Am. Home Econs. Assn., Am. Assn. of Housing Educs., Am. Inst. of Interior Designers, Interior Design Educs. Cncl., Soc. of Architectural Histrns., Phi Lambda Theta, Kappa Delta Pi, Gamma Sigma Delta; George Peabody Col., BA (Fine Arts), '46; MA (Fine Arts), '47; Columbia Univ., EdD (Fine Arts, Educ.), '54; b. Nashville, Tenn., 1920; p. Raymond and Louise Gruver Rogers; res: 1844 Cliff Dr., Columbia, Mo. 65201.

ROGERS, MARGARET DWYER, Dir. of PR, Overlook Hosp., 193 Morris Ave., Summit Ave., Summit, N.J. 07901, '59–; Press Rep., Met. Museum of Art (N.Y.C.); Reptr., Feature Wtr., Cape Cod and New Bedford Standard Times (Hyannis, Mass.); Radio Newscaster, WOCB; Co-auth., "Favorite Paintings from the Metropolitan Museum of Art"; N.J. Hosp. PR Assn. (Pres., '68–'70); Pulse PR aw., large hosp. patient rels., '63; McEachern aw., '67; Summit BPW Wm. of the Yr., '68; numerous aws., N.J. Art Dirs. Club; Oberlin Col., '40–'42; Mount Holyoke Col., BA, '44; Columbia Univ. Grad. Sch. of Jnlsm., MS, '45; b. N.Y.C., 1922; p. Walter and Geraldine McKeown Dwyer; h. (div.); c. Brian; res: 27, The Crescent, Short Hills, N.J. 07078.

ROGERS, ROSEMARY FREY, Dir.-Design Guild and Adv., The Globe Wernicke Company, Division of Sheller-Globe Corporation, 1505 Jefferson Ave., Toledo, Oh. 43524, '68–; Cinci., Oh., '49–'68; Ed., Kroger Co., '43–'45; Head, Col. Div., American Bk. Co., '36–'43; Auth., radio script, "I Am Unafraid"; Co-Auth., "Labor Legislation in the South"; Jnlsm. Tchr., Salmon Chase Col.; Inst. of Bus. Designers (Nat. Bd. Mbr.), Toledo Adv. Club; Phi Kappa Epsilon Aw., Univ. of Cinci., '35; Sweet Briar Col., AB, '34; Grad. Scholar in Econs., Univ. of Cinci.; Accounting Cert. with Lambda Aw.; b. Cinci., Oh., 1912; p. Clarence and Charlotte Altmeyer Frey; h. Robert Witherbee Rogers (dec.); res: 2251 Robinwood Ave., Toledo, Oh. 43620.

ROGERS, RUTH JONES, Histrn., Air Force, Air Reserve Personnel Center, 3800 York St., Denver, Colo. 80205, '60–; Librn., Air Force Accounting and Fin. Ctr., '52–'60; Librn., Denver Public Lib., '48–'52;

Tchr., Sterling Jr. Col., '44–'48; Prin., Chadron HS (Neb.), '42–'44; Special Libs. Assn. (Colo. Chptr. Pres., '59–'60); BPW (Sterling, Colo. Pres., '46); Intl. Toastmistress Clubs (Alpha-Jets Pres., '62); Pi Mu Epsilon, '29; Delta Kappa Gamma, '46; Who's Who of Am. Wm.; Who's Who in Lib. Sci.; Univ. of Neb., BS (Educ.), '30 (Phi Beta Kappa); MA (Latin), '32; Univ. of Denver, BS (Lib. Sci.), '46; b. Fairmont, Neb., 1909; h. Laurence Rogers; res: 610 S. Alton Way, Denver, Colo. 80231.

ROGERS, SUSAN, Home Furnishings Ed., New York Post, 75 West St., N.Y., N.Y. 10006, '67–; Reptr., Women's Wear Daily, '66; Fashion Asst., Elle, '65; Fashion Asst., British Vogue, '64; Press Asst., Harrods, '64; Nwsp. Wm. of N.Y. (Bd. of Dirs., '68–); Nwsp. Reptrs. Assn.; Nwsp. Guild; Guest Mng. Ed., Mlle., '64; Seven Col. Conf. Scholar, '59; Radcliffe Col., BA, '63; b. Bklyn., N.Y., 1942; p. Dr. Lawrence S. Rogers and Tessie Deich; res: 201 E. 19th St., N.Y., N.Y. 10003.

ROGERS, VIRGIE EVANS, Dir. of PR, Swan Cleaners, 247 S. High St., Columbus, Oh. 43215; Theta Sigma Phi, PRSA, Columbus Adv. Club; Oh. State Univ., BA (Jnlsm.), '60; b. Cleveland, Tenn., 1912; p. Richard and Minnie Johnson Evans; h. Clyde N. Rogers; c. Joel C.; res: 5990 Flora Villa Dr., Worthington, Oh. 43085.

ROGGERS, JANE, VP, Dept. Store Sls., Bureau of Advertising ANPA, 485 Lexington Ave., N.Y., N.Y. 10017, '69–; VP, Sls. Prom. Dir., Halle's (Cleve., Oh.), '68–'69; Adv. Dir., Kaufmann's (Pitt., Pa.), '65–'68; Adv. Dir., Neiman Marcus (Dallas, Tex.), '62–'65; Sls. Prom. Dir., Bonwit Teller (Phila., Pa.), '57–'62; Fashion Group; Phila. Adv. Club aw., '61; Dallas Adv. Club, aw., '64; Ind. Univ., BA (Lang.), '48; b. Greenville, Ill., 1924; p. Leon and Irene Kennedy Babcock; h. Edward B. Renner; res: 45 E. 89th St., N.Y., N.Y. 10028.

ROHALY, REGINA KAY, Club Ed., Wms. Dept., Pittsburgh Post-Gazette, Blvd. of the Allies, Pitt., Pa. 15222, '65–; Reptr., Wms. Ed., Homestead Daily Messenger, '62–'63; Copywtr., Adv. Dept., Joseph Horne Co.; Pitt. Wms. Press Club (Bd. Mbr., '68–'69), Theta Sigma Phi (Secy., '69–); Duquesne Univ., BA, '62; Univ. of Pitt. (grad. sch.), '65; b. Duqesne, Pa., 1940; p. Michael J. and Anna Kushner Rohaly; h. Robert F. Reitmeyer; res: 4927 Oakridge Dr., Pitt., Pa. 15227.

ROHATS, HELEN MARIE, Traf./Cont. Dir., WLS Radio, 360 N. Michigan Ave., Chgo., Ill. 60601, '69–; Asst. to Opns. Dir., '68–'69; Cont. Dir., '62–'68; AWRT; DePaul Univ., '61–'63; b. Chgo., Ill., 1943; p. Joseph and Helen Brady Rohats; res: 1230 W. Jarvis, Chgo., Ill. 60626.

ROHN, MARY JANE TURLEY, Crtv. Dir., Page/ Schwessinger Advertising Agency, Inc., 2433 N. Mayfair Rd., Milw., Wis. 53226, '63–; Copy Dir., William Eisner & Assocs., '59–'63; Asst. Set Designer, Miller Theater, '59; Copywtr., Baker/Johnson & Dickinson, '50–'57; Copywtr., Madison Advertising Agcy. '48–'50; Guest Lectr: Univ. of Wis., Milw., '65–'69, Theta Sigma Phi, Marquette Univ., '68; Guest Panelist, Marquette Univ., '62; AWRT (Badger Chptr. Pres., '64–'65; Educ. Fndn. Dir., '66–'69), Milw. Adv. Club (Brace Fund Bd. of Dirs., '68–'70; Gulf Park Col., '44–'46 (Phi Theta Kappa); Univ. of Wis., BA (Jnlsm.-Adv.), '48; MA (Jnlsm.), '49; b. Norfolk, Va., 1928; p. Robert E. and Lydia Elmore Turley; h. (div.); c. Mary L.; res: 8627 Ludington Ct., Milw., Wis. 53226.

ROLLIN, BETTY, Auth.; Sr. Ed., Look, 488 Madison Ave., N.Y., N.Y. 10022, '66–; Asst. Ed., '66–'68; Assoc. Features Ed., Vogue; bks: "I Thee Wed" (Doubleday, '61), "Mothers Are Funnier Than Children" ('64), "The Non-drinkers Drink Book" ('66); Sarah Lawrence Col.; b. N.Y.C.; p. Leon and Ida Silverman Rollin; res: 300 E. 49th St., N.Y., N.Y. 10017.

ROLLINS, CHARLEMAE HILL, Children's Librn., Chicago Public Library, 78 E. Washington, Chgo., Ill. 60616, '26–'69; Tchr., children's lit., Roosevelt Univ., 15 yrs.; summers, Rosary Col. (River Forest) and Fisk Univ. (Nashville, Tenn.); Auth: "Christmas Gif' " (Follett), "They Showed the Way" (Thos. Y. Crowell), "Famous Negro Poets and Famous Negro Entertainers" (Dodd Mead); ALA (Pres., Children's Div.), Ill. Lib. Assn. (Chmn., Children's Sec.), Jane Addams Bk. Aw. Comm., WILPF, '63–'65; WNBA Aw., '70; Rust Univ., Western Univ. at Quindaro, Kan.; b. Yazoo, Miss.; p. Allen and Birdie Tucker Hill; h. Joseph W. Rollins; c. Joseph W., Jr.; res: 500 E. 33rd St., Chgo., Ill. 60616.

ROLLINS, OTTILIE HIRT, Head Librn., Assoc. Prof., Clarkson College of Technology, Harriet Call Burnap Memorial Library, Potsdam, N.Y. 13676, '67–; Acting Librn., '66–'67; Asst. Librn., Asst. Prof., '61–'66; Cataloger, '56–'61; Asst. Cataloger, '55; Secy., '48–'50; Physical Educ. Instr., Russell Sage Col. (Troy, N.Y.), '45–'48; Asst. in German Dept., '42–'48; German Tchr., Academic Secy., Putney Sch., '35–'42; AAUP, ALA, Special Libs. Assn., N.Y. Lib. Assn., AAUW (Pres., '54–'56), Russell Sage Col., BS (Physical Educ.), '45 (cum laude); Western Reserve Univ., MS (Lib. Sci.), '60; b. Vienna, Austria, '15; p. Alfred and Christine Cepelak Hirt; h. John Rollins; c. Alfred Hirt, Christopher John; res: 44 Bay St., Potsdam, N.Y. 13676.

ROM, MARGUERITE EUSTICE, Ed., Publr., Crystal Lake News and McHenry County Guide, 404 Virginia, Crystal Lake, Ill. 60014, '47–; Corr., Sun Times, Daily News, UPI; Ed., Garden Glories for Garden Club of Ill., '50–'53; Auth: "Hong Kong from a Woman's View Point" ('65), "Las Vegas from a Woman's View Point" ('67), "Paradise Island from a Woman's View Point" ('70), "Puerto Rico from a Woman's View Point"; Tchr., '30–'37; N. Ill. Edtl. Assn.; Gov. of Ill. and Ill. House of Reps. cit. for shoreland preservation on Crystal Lake, '67; Knox Col., BA, '27; Univ. of Chgo., BS, '30; Northwestern Univ., grad. work, '47; b. Clinton, Ia.; p. William and Blanche Neisslie Eustice; h.

George J. Rom; c. Quin O'Brien; res: 1411 Liano Vista, Crystal Lake, Ill.

ROMAN, GAIL SUNNYE, Retail Salesman, WCBS-TV, 51 W. 52nd St., N.Y., N.Y. 10019, '68–; Media Dir., Diener, Hauser, Greenthal, '66–'68; Asst. to Media Dir., Charles Schlaifer and Co., '65–'66; Mich. State Univ., '60–'61; City Col. of the City Univ. (English), '64 (cum laude; Phi Beta Kappa); b. N.Y.C., 1942; p. Louis and Anne Kartz Gottlieb; res: 600 West End Ave., N.Y., N.Y. 10024.

ROMANO, CLARE CAMILLE, Artist, Instr., Pratt Inst., '63–; New School for Social Research, '60–; Manhattanville Col. (Purchase, N.Y.), '64–'65; Art Ctr. of Northern N.J. (Tenafly), '61–'65; Artist-in-res., GA U.S.A. exhbn., U.S.I.A. (Yugoslavia), '65; '66; numerous grants, prizes, aws., commns.; 18 one-wm. exhbns.; four bks., woodcuts, collographs and etchings; Auth: textbk. "Printmaking—Innovations and Traditions" (Macmillan, '69); Cooper Un. Sch. of Art, '43 (Cit. for Pfsnl. Achiev., '66); study in Europe; b. Palisade, N.J., 1922; p. Anthony and Luisa Cafara Romano; h. John Ross; c. Christopher, Timothy; res: 110 Davison Pl., Englewood, N.J. 07631.

ROMANOW, BERTHA ELIZABETH, PR Dir., Greater Utica Community Chest & Planning Council, 208 Paul Bldg., Utica, N.Y. 13501, '62–; Pubns. Ed., Gen. Electric Co., '60–'62; PR Asst., Carl Spitzer Assocs., '58–'60; Asst. to AE, Rumrill-Hoyt Co. Adv., '54–'58; Advisor, Utica Col. Student Chptr., PRSA; articles, trade pubn.; YWCA (Bd. of Dirs.; Bus. & Pfsnl. Club Pres., '58; Delegate, Intl. Conf., '59); Utica Col. of Syracuse Univ.

ROME, AVERY PHILLIPS, Manuscripts Ed., Daedalus, 7 Linden St., Cambridge, Mass. 02138, '69–; Asst. Copy Ed., Presbyterian Life Magazine (Phila., Pa.), '68; Swarthmore Col., BA, '69 (High Hons. degree; Phi Beta Kappa); b. Phila., Pa., '47; p. Edwin P. and Chloe Denham Rome; res: 57 Wendell St., Cambridge, Mass. 02138.

ROMERO, PATRICIA WATKINS, Chief Ed., United Publishing Company, 1413 K St. N.W., Wash., D.C. 20005, '69–; Rsch. Assoc., Assn. for the Study of Negro Life and Hist. Inc., '65–'69; Visiting Lectr., Findlay Col. (Findlay, Oh.), '69; Instr., Central State Univ. (Wilberforce, Oh.), '64–'65; Assoc. Ed., Negro History Bulletin, '67–; Co-Auth., "Negro In the Civil War" ('67); Ed: "I, Too, Am America" ('68), "In Black America" ('69); Am. Hist. Assn., Southern Hist. Assn. (Negro Hist. Rsch. grant, '65–'66); Ford Fndn. Grant, '69; Central State Univ., BA (Hist.), '64 (Phi Alpha Theta; Alpha Gamma Rho); Miami Univ., MA, '65; Oh. State Univ., '68–; b. Columbus, Oh., '35; h. div.; c. Stephen, Arthur, Jeffrey; res: 912 Middlebury Dr., Worthington, Oh. 43085.

ROMMEL, (Mimi) DAYTON, Copy Supvsr., Foote, Cone & Belding, Inc., 401 N. Michigan Ave., Chgo., Ill.

60611, '69–; Crtv. Group Head, Campbell-Mithun Adv., '68–'69; Copywtr., Leo Burnett, '64–'68; Freelance Wtr., Louisville Courier Jnl., Chgo. Daily News, Chgo. Tribune, Mademoiselle, others; Reviewer, Chgo. Daily News Panorama; Tchr., crtv. writing seminars; Novels: "Run for the Roses" (Cassell, Eng., '64), "Cry of Peacocks" (Dodd Mead, '63); Music-Drama, "Our Bright Summer Days Are Gone" ('60); Auths. Guild, Filson Club; Rosary Col., '38–'40; Univ. of Chgo., '40–'42; Centre Col., BA (Justice McReynolds Hist. Prize; several scholastic scholarships); p. Victor and Faith Keenan Dayton; h. Irvine Rommel; c. Lylas D., Park H.; res: The Seneca, 200 E. Chestnut, Chgo.; Starlings, Cox's Creek, Ky.

ROMNEY, BETH, Free-lance Spokeswoman, Publicist; AWRT, AFTRA; Univ. of Ky., '60–'62; b. Manchester, N.H., 1943; p. Howard and Sallie Castle Gaul; res: 4478 Via Marina, Marina Del Rey, Cal. 90291.

RONTOWSKY, DORIS HELEN, Art Dir., Lance Studios, 151 W. 46th St., N.Y., N.Y. 10036, '63–; Artist, Bob Stewart, '57–'59; one-wm. show, Tempo 78 Gallery, '68; Werblin Gallery, '69; Am. Film Festival Blue Ribbon, '64; Intl. Film and TV Festival Bronze aw., '68; Pratt Inst., BFA, '63; N.Y.U. film-making course, '63–'64; b. N.Y.C., 1941; p. John and Ethel Hall Rontowsky; res: 419 E. 78th St., N.Y., N.Y. 10021.

ROONEY, RUTH, Graphic Designer, 307 N. Michigan Ave., Chgo., Ill. 60601, '60–; Publishing and Adv. Design; Artists Guild of Chgo., Bk. Clinic, Children's Reading Round Table, WNBA; Art Inst. of Chgo.; b. Chgo., Ill.; p. George and Nanette Rooney; res: Chgo., Ill.

ROOSEVELT, EDITH KERMIT, Synd. Colmst., Wtr., Distrb., "Between the Lines", 800 Fourth St., S.W., Wash., D.C. 20024, '63–; Wash. Corr., Manchester Union Leader, '67; Feature Wtr., Newark Star Ledger '59–'63; Assoc. Ed., Spadea Syndicate, '57–'59; UPI (Wash., D.C.), '53–'55; S.F. and L.A. Burs., '50–'53; Barnard Col., BA, '50; b. N.Y.C.

ROOT, LIN SEGAL, Free-Lance Wtr.; Sci. and Med. Ed., Time; Distg. Visiting Prof., The Pennsylvania State University, English Department, 228 Burrowes S., University Park, Pa.; formerly Asst. Bacteriologist, La. Sugar Experiment Sta., N.O., La; Rsch. Biochemist, Psychiatric Inst. of the Manhattan State Hosps.; Assoc. in Special Problems, Oceanographic Expedition to Galapagos Is.; articles in numerous nat. mags.; Broadway play, "One Good Year"; movie scripts for Paramount, Columbia, others; OPC (Exec. Secy., '68–'70; Past VP; Bd. of Dirs.), Nat. Assn. of Sci. Wtrs., Soc. of Mag. Wtrs., Nuclear Energy Wtrs. Assn.; b. Boston, Mass.; p. Samuel and Jennie Kader Segal; h. Wells Root; c. Jonathan S.; res: 44 W. 44th St., N.Y., N.Y. 10036.

ROOT, SUSAN PRICE, Reptr., Chicago Daily News, 401 N. Wabash, Chgo., Ill., '67–'68; Colmst., Sally

O'Hare colm., '67–'68; Ed., Gen. Motors house organs, '66; Edtl. Asst., Skiing mag., '65–'66; Rutgers Univ., BA (Eng.), '65; h. Clayton Dyer Root III.

ROSBOROUGH, JEAN L., Ref. and Interloan Librn., Four County Library System, Clubhouse Rd., Binghamton, N.Y. 13803, '65–; George F. Johnson Lib., Endicott, '61–'65; Tchr., Union-Endicott Sch. Syst., '58–'61; Soc. Ed., Detroit (Mich.) News, '31–'34; Sr. Clerk, Pontiac Public Lib., '29–'31; WNBA (VP, '67–'69), South Central Ref. and Rsch. Cncl., N.Y. Lib. Assn.; Beta Phi Mu; Russell Sage Col., AB, '29; Mich. State Univ., '27; Syracuse Univ., MLS, '66; b. Pontiac, Mich.; p. Rollin Washington and Grace Reid Clark; h. James B. Rosborough (dec.); c. Ruth E. (Mrs. Donald L. Duttweiler); res: 17-C Andrea Dr., Vestal, N.Y. 13850.

ROSDAL, GLORIA SACKS, AE, Solow/Weston Inc., 600 Madison Ave., N.Y., N.Y. 10022, '64–; Asst. AE, '60–'64; Asst. Adv. Mgr., Turner Hall Corp., '54–'57; Hofstra Col., '43–'46; b. N.Y.C., 1926; p. Jack and Anna Nathanson Sacks; h. Joseph Rosdal (div.); c. Steven, Richard; res: 69–24 Exeter St., Forest Hills, N.Y. 11375.

ROSE, DOROTHY BLASSER, Ed. of Parents and Children's Colm., The News and Chicago Tribune Syndicate, 220 E. 42nd St., N.Y., N.Y. 10017, '66–; Freelance Wtr., fiction and articles, '53–'66; Pubcty. Dir., Oceanside, L.I. Public Schs., '63; Crtv. Writing Tchr., L.I. Schs. adult educ. classes, '58, '61; NLAPW (Secy.; Best Published Short Story Aw., '59); Nwsp. Guild, NWC (N.Y., '67–); N.Y.U. writing courses; b. Phila., Pa., '13; p. George and Jean O'Brien Blasser; h. Robert Rose; c. Dr. Robert Vance and Gary Francis; res: 24 Madison Ave., Oceanside, L.I., N.Y. 11572.

ROSE, ELINOR K., Synd. Light-verse Feature Wtr.; Pfsnl. Speaker, Conv. Programs, Unltd. (Detroit, Mich.); Daily Synd. Wtr., Allied Features (Cleve., Oh.); Free-lance Wtr., daily nwsps., mags.; bks: "Relax, Chum," "Sugar and Spice," "Rhyme & Reason"; Anthologies: "Childhood in Poetry," "Fun and Laughter"; Staff, Oakland Univ. Wtrs. Conf. (Mich.), '62–; Theta Sigma Phi, Mich. Poetry Soc., Detroit Press Club, Intl. Platform Assn., Am. Acad. of Polit. and Social Scis., Kappa Kappa Gamma (Nat. Achiev. aw., '68); Wtr. of the Yr. aw., Detroit Wm. Wtrs., '59; AAUW, Who's Who in the Midwest; Hillsdale Col., AB (cum laude; Bd. of Wm. Commissioners; Achiev. Aw., '55); b. Edon, Oh.; p. David T. and B. Laura Twichell Kiess; h. Dana Rose; c. Stuart R., Douglas D., Bruce G.; res: 25560 Dundee Rd., Royal Oak, Mich. 48070.

ROSE, LAURA MAY, Ed., Publr., The Piedmont Herald, Herald Printing House, 34 Railroad St., P.O. Box 68, Piedmont, W.Va. 26750; Sole Owner, '68–; Partner, '33–'68; Worker, '11–; W.Va. Press Assn. (50 Yr. Mbr.); Masthead aw. from Beta Beta Chptr., Theta Sigma Phi; Western Md. Col.; Frostburg State Col.; b. Westernport, Md., 1892; p. Frank W. and Eliza Pearce Rose; res: 33 E. Fairview St., Piedmont, W. Va. 26750.

ROSE, MAUREEN J., Adv. Traffic Mgr., R. R. Bowker, 1180 Ave. of the Americas, N.Y., N.Y. 10036, '57–; Copy Ed., Boy Scouts of Am., '56–'57; Prod. Expediter, Rsch. Inst. of Am., '55–'56; WNBA; Cornell Univ., BA, '55 (High Hons. in Govt.); b. Newark, N.J.; p. Maurice and Adelaide Rose; res: 313 E. 61st St., N.Y., N.Y. 10021.

ROSE, THELMA MAY, Head, Fgn. Literature Dept., Cleveland Public Library 325 Superior Ave., Cleve., Oh. 44114, '66–; Staff, '60–'66; N.Y. Public Lib., '38–'40; ALA, Oh. Lib. Assn., WNBA (Cleve. Chptr. VP, '69–'70); Case Western Reserve Univ., BA, '32; BS, LS, '37; b. Cleve., Ph.; p. Samuel and Blanche Nyer May; h. Harold R. Rose; c. Jane (Mrs. D. L. Salem), James; res: 2301 Delaware Dr., Cleve. Hgts., Oh. 44106.

ROSEN, DENA L., Dir. of Rsch., Ruder and Finn, Inc., 1812 K St., N.W., Wash., D.C. 20006, '67–; Adm., Legislative Asst., Campaigns U.S.A., '66–'67; American Univ., BA (Government), '65 (Dean's List); b. Jersey City, N.J., 1943; p. Ned and Helen Weisenfeld Rosen; res: 7333 New Hampshire Ave., Hyattsville, Md. 20783.

ROSEN, JOYCE ANN, Dir., Dev. and PR, Child Welfare League of America, 44 E. 23rd St., N.Y., N.Y. 10010, '69–; PR Dir., Nat. Fund for Med. Educ., '52–'69; Cnslt., various health and welfare agcys.; Hunter Col., BA, '45; Columbia Univ., MA, '47; b. N.Y.C., 1925; p. Ben and Martha Wolfe Rosen; res: 415 E. 52nd St., N.Y., N.Y. 10022.

ROSENBAUM, M. VIRGINIA, Ed.-Publr., The Citizen Newspaper, P.O. Box 360, Frostburg, Md. 21532, '61–; Mgr., WTBO Radio (Cumberland, Md.), '45–'61; Henry J. Kaufman Adv. (Wash., D.C.), '42–'45; Bdcstr. Commentator; Md.-Del.-D.C. Press Assn., Nat. Nwsp. Assn.; Broker, Roselanl Real Estate; Co-owner, Roseland speedway; b. Suffolk, Va., 1921; p. John and Mildred (Hinebaugh) Fike; h. Fred Rosenbaum; c. Frances Kay Yates; res: 611 N. Third St., LaVale, Md. 21502.

ROSENBERG, NANCY SHERMAN, Free-lance Wtr., c/o Collins-Knowlton-Wing, 60 E. 56th St., N.Y., N.Y. 10022; Tchr. of Mathematics, past 11 yrs.; Auth: bks. for children and bks. dealing with medicine, mathematics; 1st Prize, Children's Spring Bk. Festival, N.Y. Herald Tribune, '61; Bryn Mawr Col., BA, '52; b. N.Y.C., 1931; p. Monroe and Gertrude Horn Sherman; h. Dr. Lawrence C. Rosenberg; c. Eric, Mark, Constance, Elizabeth; res: 28 Fanshaw Ave., Yonkers, N.Y. 10705.

ROSENBLATT, ALICE A., Free-lance Artist, Tybee Pl., Yonkers, Mohegan Heights, N.Y. 10710; Tchr., N.Y. High Schs., '16–'62; Tchr., Fordham Univ., '29–'30; mural in Jr. High Sch. 55, '26; works with gifted children; Mt. Vernon Art Assn. (Bd. of Dirs.), Yonkers Art Assn. (numerous prizes for painting, '50–'54), Westchester Arts and Crafts Guild; Sch. Art League ('33–'34); Westchester County Fair and Flower

Show 1st prize for water color, '49; Columbia Univ., BS; MA, '38; Supvsr. of Fine Arts Diploma, '34; Univ. of Madrid, Spain, '58; b. N.Y.C.

ROSENGREN, FLORENCE K., Pres., Rosengren's, 312 Bonham St., San Antonio, Tex. 78205, '35–; Pres., '49–; ZONTA, Am. Bkseller's Assn., WNBA; Headliner Aw., '60; b. Milwaukee, Wis.; p. John and Blanche Cannon Kednay; h. Frank Rosengren; c. Frank D.; res: 104 Anastacia Pl., San Antonio, Tex. 78212.

ROSENHAUSE, SHARON, Urban Affairs Wtr., The Record, 150 River St., Hackensack, N.J. 07602, '69–; Reg. Reptr., Gen. Assigt., '66–'69; 1st Prize, N.J. Press Assn., '68; Queens Col., BA (Eng.), '65; Boston Univ., grad. work; Stanford Univ., '68–'69 (Pfsnl. Jnlsm. Fellow); b. Bronx, N.Y., 1943; p. Philip and Fay Zucker Rosenhause; res: 330 Third Ave., N.Y., N.Y. 10001.

ROSENQUEST, BARBARA UNGERLEIDER, Exec. VP, FMH Company, 3525 Berry Dr., Studio City, Cal. 91604, '66–; Assoc. Mdse. Ed., Harper's Bazaar, '62–; Fashion Dir. and Commentator, Kay Windsor (L.A., Cal.), '57–; VP, Robert S. Howell Assocs., '62; TV-Motion Picture Dept. Dir., Mary Webb Davis Agcy., '55–'57; Assoc. Prodr., DuMont TV, '50–'52; Visiting Lectr., Cal. State Col., '67; U.C.L.A., '69; AWRT, Fashion Group, L.A. Wms. C. of C.; Smith Col., BA, '49; Columbia Univ.; U.C.L.A.; b. Phila., Pa., 1920; p. Harry and Marian Rice Ungerleider; h. Donald Rosenquest; c. Nils Christopher and Elin Jordis.

ROSENWASSER, DOROTHY ECKMAN, Free-lance Artist, 414 Hawthorne Ave., Yonkers, N.Y., 10705; Bk. Illus: Oceana Publns., Meredith Press, Bobbs Merrill, '60–; Art Students League, Yonkers Art Assn., Kent Art Assn.; Nat. Acad. of Design; h. Milton Rosenwasser.

ROSMOND, BABETTE, Auth.; Fiction Ed., Seventeen, Triangle Publications, 320 Park Ave., N.Y., N.Y. 10022, '57–; bks: "Robert Benchley, His Life and Good Times" (Doubleday, '70), "Shut up, He Explained: A Ring Lardner Study" (Scribner, '62), "The Lawyers" (Walker, '62), "The Children" (Harcourt Brace, '50), other novels; Better Living Magazine, '54–'57; Street and Smith, '40–'47; short stories, New Yorker, Mademoiselle, other mags.; b. N.Y.C.; h. Henry Stone; c. James M., Eugene R.; res: 232 Eastland Ave., Pelham, N.Y. 10803.

ROSS, BETSY, name owned by Radio WSNY/1240, Inc., 144 Lafayette St., Schenectady, N.Y. 12305; currently five wm., one the radio voice of wms. info., the other four women used for personal appearances.

ROSS, BETTY, Dir. PR, Shoreham Hotel and Motor Inn, 2500 Calvert St., N.W., Wash., D.C. 20008, '62–; Free-lance Wtr., PR, '50–'62; Asst. Prog. Mgr., Station WTOP, '48–'50; D.C. delegate to Democratic Nat. Conv., '64; Soc. of Am. Travel Wtrs. (Middle Atlantic Chptr. Secy., '64–), Wms. Nat. Democratic Club (Mbr.

Governing Bd., '63–'69), PRSA, ANWC, AWRT; Smith Col., AB, '46 (cum laude); b. Hartford, Conn.; p. Harry H. and Frances Horowitz Beckanstin; h. Richard S. Ross (div.); c. Elisabeth Hewitt; res: 3516 Albemarle St., N.W., Wash., D.C. 20008.

ROSS, CAROL JOY, Mgr., Office Research Institute, P.O. Box 744, South Miami, Fla. 33143, '60–; Staff Wtr., Bahamas Dev. Bd. News Bur. (Nassau, Bahamas), '57–'59; Staff Wtr., Wms. Dept., Miami (Fla.) News, '55–'57; Free-lance Wtr.; Theta Sigma Phi; Univ. of Miami at Coral Gables, AB, '57 (Who's Who Among Col. and Univ. Students); b. Chestnut Hill, Mass., 1936; p. H. John and Kathryn Perkins Ross; res: 4540 S.W. 62nd Ct., Miami, Fla. 33155.

ROSS, CORINNE MADDEN, Free-lance Wtr., 1330 N. State Pkwy., Chgo., Ill. 60610; Prom. Dir., New Horizons Publrs., '67–'68; Mng. Dir., Auth., several children's bks., Mid-American Publ. Co., '65–'66; Prom. Dir., Childrens Press, '64–'66; Chgo. Bk. Clinic, Chgo. Press Club; Mt. Ida Jr. Col. (Newton, Mass.), AB, '51; b. Newton, Mass., 1931; p. Alphonsus L. and Corinne Bodwell Madden; h. Charles K. Ross (div.); res: 1330 N. State Pkwy., Chgo., Ill. 60610.

ROSS, ELEANOR DOUDAY, Casting Dir., Grey Advertising, Inc., 777 Third Ave., N.Y., N.Y., '65–; Asst. Casting Dir., govt. doc. and training films for Armed Forces, Army Pictorial Ctr. (L.I. City), '59–'65; Free-lance, theatre, films; NATAS; b. N.Y.C.; p. Salo and Anne Kantor Douday; h. Robert Ross (sep.); c. Babette Louise, Denise Marjorie; res: N.Y.C.

ROSS, ISHBEL, Auth., fiction, non-fiction; bks: "Sons of Adam, Daughters of Eve" ('69), "Taste in America" ('67), "Charmers and Cranks" ('65), 18 others; Wtr., OWI, '41–'44; Edtl. Staff, N.Y. Herald Tribune, '19–'33; mag. articles, lectures, TV appearances; b. Sutherlandshire, Scotland; p. David and Grace McCrone Ross; h. Bruce Rae (dec.); c. Catriona; res: 155 E. 76th St., N.Y., N.Y. 10021.

ROSS, JAYNE FREEMAN, Aws. Mgr., American Broadcasting Co., 1330 Ave. of the Americas, N.Y., N.Y. 10019, '67–; Asst. Ed., Farm and Ranch Guide, '66–'67; Exec. Dir., Netherland-American Fndn., '57–'66 (Ambassadress of Intl. Brotherhood, Municipality of Sneek, The Netherlands, '64); Advisory Cncl., Am. Scholarship Assn., '64–'66; AWRT, NATAS; Drake Bus. Col., '50; h. George Matsuda.

ROSS, LOIS I., Home Econs. Dir., The Quaker Oats Company, Mdse. Mart Plaza, Chgo., Ill. 60654, '53–; Test Kitchen Supvsr., '47–; Test Kitchen Home Econst., '44–; ZONTA, AWRT, Home Econsts. in Bus. (Chgo. Chptr. Past Chmn.), other home econs. assn.; Univ. of Kan., BA, '41 (Omicron Nu; Pi Lambda Theta); res: 360 Ridge Ave., Evanston, Ill. 60202.

ROSS, MADELINE DANE, Free-lance Jnlst.; formerly Svc. Ed., Delineator; Mng. Ed., Jnl. of the Am.

Inst. of Homeopathy; Ed., Publr., UNNRA Team News; Info. Specialist, State Dept., Brussels World's Fair, '58; Public Info. Offcr., UNNRA, '45–'46 (Cit. for Pubn., '45); articles in numerous nwsps., mags.; OPC (six two-year terms on Bd. of Governors; VP, '63; Distg. Svc. Plaque, '55); Cornell Univ.; Columbia Sch. of Social Work; b. N.Y.C.; res: 136 E. 36th St., N.Y., N.Y. 10016.

ROSS, PHYLLIS E., Sls. Prom. Mgr., I.S.M. Publishing Co., 80 William St., N.Y., N.Y. 10038, '68–; AE, Sr. Media Byr., S.S.C. & B., '66–'68; All Media Byr., K & E, '65–'66; Media Supvsr., W. B. Doner & Co. (Balt., Md.), '63–'65; Media Supvsr., S. A. Levyne & Co. (Balt., Md.), '60–'63; Wall St. Adv. & PR Assn., AWNY; Baruch Col., Univ. of Md.; b. N.Y.C.; res: 321 E. 54th St., N.Y., N.Y. 10022.

ROSS, RUTH N., Asst. Ed., Newsweek, 444 Madison Ave., N.Y., N.Y. 10022, '66–; Rschr., '64–'66; Asst. Ed., Hayden Publishing, '61–'63; Edtl. Asst., '58–'60; American Book Co., '57–'58; free-lance articles, Urban West, Cosmopolitan; Black Perspective (Vice Chmn., '69); Advisory Bd., N.Y. Urban Coalition Commtns. Skills Bank, '69–; Hunter Col., BA, '57; b. N.Y.C.; p. Edgar and Florence Pickens Ross; res: 190 Lexington Ave., N.Y., N.Y. 10016.

ROSS, VIRGINIA LOUISE, County Librn., San Mateo County Library, 25 Tower Rd., Belmont, Cal. 94002, '54–; Asst. County Librn., '52–'54; Supv. Branch Librn., '50–'52; Jr. Librn., Oakland Public Lib., '48–'50; Librn., USAFIK (Seoul, Korea), '46–'48; Hosp. Librn., U.S. Naval Hosp. (Bethesda, Md.), '44–'46; Librn., U.S. Naval Training Station (Farragut, Idaho), '42–'44; Asst. Ref. Librn., Univ. of Cal., '41–'42; ALA, AAUW, WNBA, Cal. Lib. Assn. (Pres., '65); Stanford Univ., BA (Hist.), '37; Yale Univ., MA (Anthropology), '39; Univ. of Cal., '41; b. Covina, Cal.; p. Verne and Isabel Bumgarner Ross; res: 3648 Jefferson Ave., Redwood City, Cal. 94062.

ROSS, WENDY SORTWELL, Wtr./Ed., Voice of America, 330 Independence Ave. S.W., Wash., D.C., '64–; Radio Prod. Asst., '63–'64; Intelligence Analyst, CIA, '62–'63; AWRT; Smith Col., BA, '62; Univ. of Munich, W. Germany '62 (Teaching Scholarship from W. German Govt.); b. Syracuse, N.Y., 1940; p. James and Elizabeth Sortwell Ross; res: 2700 Q St., N.W., Wash., D.C. 20007.

ROSSE, ALLIANORA, Artist; Staff Illus., Flower Grower mag., The Home Garden, '53–; Free-lance Illus. for Ladies' Home Journal, Life, Woman's Day; Bk. Illus: "A Treasury of American Gardening," "A Sense of Seasons," others; Co-auth: "The Best Day for Every Little Girl"; Garden Wtrs. Assn. of Am.; Art Acad. of The Hague, '42–'46; b. Clarkstown, N.Y.; p. Herman and Sophia Luyt Rosse; h. Don Munson; res: 78 Macdougal St., N.Y., N.Y. 10012.

ROSSI, SHIELA McKEON, Acc. Supvsr., The Rowland Co., 415 Madison Ave., N.Y., N.Y. 10017; AE; NHFL; St. John's Univ., BA; b. N.Y.C.; p. Owen and Cecelia Winters McKeon; h. John Paul Rossi; c. Christopher; res: 330 E. 33rd St., N.Y., N.Y. 10016; Aesop's Neck Lane, Quogue, L.I., N.Y.

ROSSNAGEL, NANCY LEE, Dir. of Radio & TV Adv., Phillipps Assoc., 7654 W. Bancroft, Toledo, Oh. 43617, '66–; Copywtr., Hadley Miller Adv., '66; Home Econst., Toledo Edison Co., '63–'65; Prod. Coordr., WSPD-TV, '61–'63; Copywtr., WJIM-TV (Lansing, Mich.), '59–'61; Jr. AE, Simons-Michelson Co. (Detroit), '57–'59; Adv. Club of Toledo, Wms. Adv. Club of Toledo, Theta Sigma Phi, Alpha Epsilon Rho; adv. aws.; Wayne State Univ., BA (Home Econs., Radio-TV), '57; b. Cleve., Oh., 1934; p. Earl and Lois Harter Harnden; res: 354 Mellington Dr., Toledo, Oh. 43610.

ROSS-SKINNER, JEAN, Mgr., European News Bureau, Dun & Bradstreet Publications Corp., 42 Gresham St., EC 2, London, England, '66–; Mng. Ed., Dun's Review, '63–'66; Sr. Ed., '61–'63; Assoc. Ed., Forbes, '60–'61; Edtl. Asst., Business Week, Toronto, '54–'60; Assn. of Am. Corrs. in London; h. John Gilbert.

ROSTENBERG, LEONA, Auth.; Partner, Leona Rostenberg—Rare Books, 152 E. 179th St., N.Y., N.Y. 10453; bks: "English Publishers in the Graphic Arts: 1599–1700" ('63), "Publishing, Printing and Bookselling in England, 1551–1700" ('65); numerous articles, trade pubns.; Antiquarian Booksellers Assn. of Am., England; Renaissance Soc., Bibliographical Soc. of Am.; N.Y.U., BA, '30; Columbia Univ., MA, '33; b. N.Y.C., 1908; p. Adolph and Louisa Dreyfus Rostenberg.

ROTCHSTEIN, JANICE A., Media Dir., Pierce Promotions, 420 E. 51st St., N.Y., N.Y. 10022, '68–; Asst. AE, Alexander Co., '67–'68; Prodr., Dir., Bdcstr., KFMB Radio, San Diego, Cal., '64–'66; KEBS-TV, Radio, '62–'66; Theta Sigma Phi; San Diego State Col., BA (Educ., Social Studies), '66 (cum laude; Who's Who among Students in Am. Univs. and Cols.); numerous bdcst., jnlsm. aws.); Northwestern Univ., MSJ, '67; b. Coronado, Cal., 1944; p. Morris and Elizabeth Wolke Rotchstein; res: 339 E. 57th St., N.Y., N.Y. 10022.

ROTH, CLAIRE JARETT, Free-lance Lib. and Guidance Cnslt., 28 Edgemont Ave., Summit, N.J. 07901, '64–; Co-auth: "Art Careers" (Walck, N.Y., '63), "Hospital Health Services" (Walck, '64); Rsch. Asst., special projects, E. Orange Schs., '67–'68; Fac. Mbr., Inst. for Librnship., Am. Hosp. Assn., '62; Librn., Sch. of Nursing, '56–'64; Asst. Dir., Bellmore Memorial Lib., '53–'54; Supvsr., Educ. Reading Room, N.Y.U., '49–'51; Ref. Asst., N.Y.U. Wash. Sq. Lib., '46–'49; Asst. Young People's Librn., Bklyn. Public Lib., '43–'46; N.Y. Lib. Club (Bd. Mbr., '49–'54), ALA, Assn. Hosp. Insts. and Libs., various others; Univ. of N.C., BA, '43; Columbia Univ., Sch. of Lib. Svc., BLS,

'45; N.Y.U., Sch. of Educ., MA (Guidance and Pers. Adm.), '50; b. N.Y.C., 1923; p. Jack and Selma Falb Jarett; h. Harold Roth; c. Elizabeth Terry, Amy Jarett; res: 28 Edgemont Ave., Summit, N.J. 07901.

ROTH, JANE STEPHENSON, Print Prod. Supvsr., North Advertising Incorporated, 2100 Merchandise Mart, Chgo., Ill. 60654, '63–; Prod., Reach McClinton, '58–'63; Traf. and Prod., J. R. Pershall, '46–'58; Wms. Adv. Club of Chgo. (Treas., 3 yrs.); h. Donald Roth.

ROTH, JUNE SPIEWAK, Auth., many cookbks., incl. "How to Cook Like a Jewish Mother," ('69); Auths. League of Am., Intl. Platform Assn.; Contemporary Auths.; Who's Who of Am. Wm.; Pa. State Univ., '42–'44; Tobé-Coburn Sch., '45; b. Haverstraw, N.Y., 1926; p. Harry I. and Ida Glazer Spiewak; h. Frederick Roth; c. Nancy (Mrs. Tomas Bjorkman), Robert; res: 1057 Oakland Ct., Teaneck, N.J. 07666.

ROTHCHILD, SYLVIA ROSNER, Colmst., Jewish Advocate, 251 Causeway St., Boston, Mass., '62–; Freelance Wtr., short stories, articles, revs. for Jewish mags., Boston Globe, others; Auth., novels: "Sunshine and Salt" (Simon and Schuster, '64), "Keys to a Magic Door" (Farrar Straus & Cudahy, '60); Artist; Cellist with Newton and Boston Civic Orchestras; Brookline Art Assn., Copley Soc.; Jewish Bk. Aw., '60; b. N.Y.C., 1923; p. Samuel and Bertha Neuberger Rosner; h. Seymour Rothchild; c. Alice, Judith, Joseph; res: 19 Hilltop Rd., Brookline, Mass. 02167.

ROTHMAN, RUTH GOLDHABER, Assoc. Rsch. Dir., Batten, Barton, Durstine & Osborne, 383 Madison Ave., N.Y., N.Y. 10014, '68–; Projects Supvsr., '66–'68; Jr., Sr. Rsch. Analyst, '59–'62; VP, Asst. to Rsch. Dir., Applied Mktng. Rsch., Inc., '62–'66; Am. Mktng. Assn.; Univ. of Md., BA, '53; Univ. of Mich., MA, '59; b. Phila., Pa., 1932; p. Jacob and Esther Bolen Goldhaber; h. Richard Rothman; res: 50 Commerce St., N.Y., N.Y. 10014.

ROTMAN, SHEILA LOIS, Commtns. Coordr., ITT Bell & Gossett, 8200 N. Austin Ave., Morton Groves, Ill. 60653, '68–; Ed., '66–'68; U.S. Savings Bond Dr. Chmn., Fluid Handling Div. of ITT, '66–'68; AMA Seminars, others; IEA of Chgo.; Pair Sch. of Bus., '59; Evanston Bus. Col.; b. Chgo., Ill., 1940; p. Harry and Rea Altman Rotman; res: 8528 N. Lotus, Skokie, Ill. 60076.

ROTTMANN, BETTY COOK, Info. Specialist, Office of Public Information, University of Missouri, 223 Jesse Hall, Columbia, Mo. 65201, '69–; News Wtr., '58–'69; Corr., Fairchild Pubns., '61–'62; Colmst., Missouri Ruralist & Kansas Farmer, '57–'58; Colmst., Ste. Gen. Herald, '55–'57; Children's Radio Series, '49–'50; AAUW, Theta Sigma Phi, Mo. Press Wm. (Pres., '65–'67), Mo. Wtrs. Guild, NFPW, Inst. of Gen. Semantics, Kappa Tau Alpha, Kappa Alpha Mu; numerous writing aws.; Central Wesleyan Jr. Col., AA; Univ. of Mo., BJ, '58; b. Longton, Kan., 1922; p.

Fred and Ora Mae Allen Cook; h. Leroy Rottmann; c. Larry, Tina; res: 1200 Coats St., Columbia, Mo. 65201.

ROUNDS, GERTRUDE WINSOR, Librn., James M. Milne Library, State University College, Oneonta, N.Y. 13820, '49–; Asst. Librn., '46–'49; Supply Librn., N.Y. Public Lib., '42–'44; Sch. Librn., '35–'46; Lib. Cnslt., Walkerbilt Woodwork, '60–; ALA, S. Central Rsch. Lib. Cncl.; Syracuse Univ., BS (Lib. Sci.), '34; N.Y.U., MA, '46; b. Buffalo, N.Y.; p. Floyd and Esther Wade Rounds; res: 6 Roosevelt Ave., Oneonta, N.Y. 13820.

ROUNTREE, ELIZABETH COFFEE, Librn., Dir., Northeast Georgia Regional Library, Green and Jefferson Sts., Clarkesville, Ga. 30531, '65–; Librn., Piedmont Col., '57–'65; BPW (Pres., '69–'70); Demorest Wms. Club (Pres., '64–'65); Beta Phi Mu; Piedmont Col., AB, '58 (summa cum laude); Univ. of Ill., MA (Lib. Sci.), '59; b. Banks Co., Ga., 1937; p. Troy and Bessie May Moss Coffee; h. George Rountree; res: Box 325, Demorest, Ga. 30535.

ROWE, JO ANN OSBORN, Wms. Dir., Ridder Publications, KSSS, 3939 E. San Miguel, Colorado Springs, Colo. 80901, '65–; Wms. Dir., KRDO Radio-TV, '60–'65; Wms. Dir., KKTB-KVOR, '54; Free-lance, KKTV, '56–'67; Colmst., Colo. Springs Free Press, '63–'65; Auth: "The Party Line Cook Book" ('63), "The Best of Party Line" ('68); AWRT, Pikes Peak Press Club, Nat. Cncl. on Alcoholism (Bd. Mbr.), Civil Defense Cncl. (Bd. Mbr.); Distg. Svc. Aws. for work in special fields of Alcoholism, Mental Retardation and Rehabilitation, Mental Health, Colo. State Penitentiary; Colo. Col., '43–'47, Tulsa Univ., '47–'50; b. Colo. Springs, Colo. 1924; p. Carl Ransom and Zoe Ella Smith Osborn; h. Prentiss Rowe; c. Carl, Prentiss Tomblin, David Lee, Melanie Ann; res: 1009 Parkview Blvd., Skyway Park, Colorado Springs, Colo. 80906.

ROWLEY, BETTY WHALEN, Media Dir., Ricks Ehrig, Inc., 1500 Tower Bldg., Seattle, Wash., '68–; Media Mgr., Cole & Weber, '64–'68; Media Byr., '55–'64; Cl., Seattle First Nat. Bank, '50–'55; Univ. of Wash., '45–'47; b. Bellingham, Wash.; p. Edward and Lucile Wright Whalen; h. David Rowley; res: 2831 W. Elmore Pl., Seattle, Wash. 98199.

ROWLEY, KATHRYN WOODWARD, Traf. and Media, Aylin Advertising Agency, P.O. Box 19262, Dallas, Tex. 75219, '69–; Sls. Svc./Traf. Mgr., WBAP AM-FM-TV, '66–'69; Cont. Dir., KNOK, '63–'64; Traf. Mgr., '60–'61; Off. Mgr., KPCN, '62; AWRT (Ft. Worth Chptr. Pres., '68–'69); Arlington State Col.; b. Wash., D.C., 1941; p. O'Conner and Grace Wilson Schultz Woodward; h. Jim Rowley (div.); c. Mark Christopher, Tammi Lynne, Terry Noelle; res:3459 McFarlin, Dallas, Tex. 75205.

ROY, LOUISE THOMASON, AE, Dir. of PR, Rolfe C. Spinning, Inc., 725 S. Adams Rd., Birmingham, Mich. 48011, '66–; Adv. AE, A. R. Closter, '44–'65; rsch., dev. of case hists. for indsl. clients; published in numerous trade media; Engineering Soc. of Detroit, Theta Sigma Phi, Detroit Press Club; Wayne State Univ., BA; b. Erwin, Tenn., 1920; p. William F. and Ellena Emerson Thomason; h. Nelson J. Roy; c. Thomas N., Patricia; res: 2464 St. Joseph, W. Bloomfield Twp., Mich. 48053.

ROYAL, JULIANNA, Dir. of Bus. Affairs, TV Bdcst. Div., Chris Craft Industries, L.A., Cal., '69–; C.P.A., Bus. Mgr., KCOP Television, '60–'69; Arthur Young and Co., '53–'58; Lightfoot Studio, '50–'53; Occidental Life, '48–'50; Wtr., articles, accounting pubns.; Am. Wms. Soc. of Cert. Public Accountants (Nat. Dir., '63–'64), Am. Soc. of Wm. Accountants (L.A. Chptr. Past Pres.; Most Valuable Mbr., '61, '62), IBFM (Charter Mbr., Former Dir.), AWRT (Southern Cal. Chptr. Pres., '69–'70; Merit aw., '68), L.A. C. of C. Wms. Div. (Dir., '69), Urban League; Pomona Col., BA (Econs.), '48; b. E. Aurora, N.Y., 1926; p. Osmon II, and Carolyn Merritt Royal; h. Charles A. Shiner (div.); res: 2232 Beachwood Dr., Apt. 12, L.A., Cal. 90028.

RUBENSTEIN, EVE SCHMOLL, Gen. Mgr., Northwest Broadcasting Company, Warden Bldg., Ft. Dodge, Ia. 50501, '69–; Gen. Sls. Mgr., '63–'69; Sls. Staff, '57; Cont. Wtr., hostess for "Eve's Kitchen," '53; Lectr., Ia. Central Col. '68–'69; Catholic Daughters of Am., ('58–'59), AWRT (Heart of Am. Chptr., Bd. Mbr., '56–'58; Hawkeye Chptr., Pres., '65–'66; Secy., '67–'68); Golden Slipper aw. for Nat. Fashion Press, '67; Denver Univ., '28–'29; b. Fort Dodge, Ia. 1909; p. Jacob and Mary Elizabeth Thie Schmoll, Jr.; h. Charles Rubenstein; res: 1630 13th Ave. N., Ft. Dodge, Ia. 50501.

RUBIN, HILDA HARMEL, Artist, Instr., '53–; Tchr., Suburban Fine Arts Ctr. (Highland Park); North Shore Art League, Arts Club of Chgo., Artists Equity Assn.; Union League aw., '64; Purchase aws., '69, '65; Art Inst. of Chgo., Ray Vogue Sch. of Design, Haydn Real Gymnasium; b. Vienna, Austria; p. Julius and Evelyne Kohn Harmel; h. Charles Rubin; c. Diana R. Daly; res: 1460 N. Sandburg Terr., Chgo., Ill. 60610.

RUBIN, JUDITH, Acc. Mgr., Arndt, Preston, Chapin, Lamb & Keen Inc., 1528 Walnut St., Phila., Pa. 19102, '65–; Special Projects Dir., Phila. Nat. Bank, '62–'64; AE, Adelphia Assocs., '56–'62; Phila. PR Assn.; Univ. of Pa., BA, '56; b. Phila., Pa.; p. Richard I. and Dorothy Shaltz Rubin; res: 2401 Pennsylvania Ave., Phila., Pa. 19130.

RUBIN, MARLYN ANN, Wms. Ed., Miami Beach Sun, P.O. Box 180, Miami Beach, Fla. 33139, '69–; Theta Sigma Phi, Kappa Tau Alpha, Phi Kappa Phi; Stephens Col., AA; Univ. of Fla., BS (Jnlsm.), '69 (cum laude); b. Waycross, Ga., 1947; p. Ralph and Louise Rubin; res: 641 Fourth Key Dr., Ft. Lauderdale, Fla. 33304.

RUBIN, SYRIL IVLER, Pres., Founder, S-CAR-GO Inc., 103 Pleasant Ave., Upper Saddle River, N.J. 07458, '63–; Publicist, Uniplan, '60; Home Econst. Pubcty., Bordeaux Wine Assn., '54; Pubcty., Am. Spice Trade and Fresh Fruit and Vegetables, '51; Sls. Prom., Lever Bros., '49; Sls. Prom., Intl. Milling Co., '47–; Am. Home Econs. Assn., AWRT, Founder of Ramsey Am. Field Svc. Chptr., Chaine des Rotiseurs, Sommelier Soc.; Univ. of Wis., '36–'37; Pa. State Col., BS (Sci.), '37; Columbia Univ.; New Sch. for Social Rsch.; b. N.Y.C., 1919; p. Isidore and Lily Freystadt Ivler; h. Mark I. Rubin; c. Isa L., Eric I.; res: 15 Fen Ct., Ramsey, N.J. 07446.

RUCKER, JOAN MAXINE, Food Publicist, Home Econst., Rainey, McEnroe & Manning, 1750 Pennsylvania Ave. N.W., Wash., D.C. 20006, '69–; State Home Econst., Ga. Egg Commn., '66–'69; Colmst., Ga. nwsps., '66–'69; Am. Home Econs. Assn., Home Econsts. in Bus., AWRT; Univ. of Ga., BS (Home Econs.), '65; b. Elberton, Ga., 1943; p. Carl and Cynthia Smith Rucker; res: 1310 34th St. N.W., Wash., D.C. 20007.

RUDOLPH, JEAN BURIANEK, Prod. Asst., Swanson, Sinkey, Ellis Advertising Agency, 1222 "P" St., Lincoln, Neb. 68508, '65–; Publ. Asst., Thos. D. Murphy Co., '63–'65; Off. Mgr., Baker Printing Co., '60–'63; b. Lincoln, Neb., 1943; p. Louis and Lucille Brt Burianek; h. Dr. Roger Rudolph; res: 1840 W. Que St., Lincoln, Neb. 68528.

RUDOV, FLORENCE HERLICK, Media Byr., Fuller & Smith & Ross, Inc., 1 Oliver Plaza, Pitt., Pa. 15222; AWRT, Veterans Hsop. Radio and TV Guild, Pitt. Radio and TV Club (Bd. of Dirs., '70–71; Secy., '63–'65); Bus. Training Col., '44–'45; Univ. of Pitt. Evening Sch., '57.

RUE, ELOISE, Assoc. Prof., School of Library & Information Science, University of Wisconsin, Chapman Hall, Room 303, P.O. Box 413, Milw., Wis. 53201, '65–; Assoc. Prof., Chmn., Dept. of Lib. Sci., Sch. of Educ., '64–'65; Asst. Prof., Chmn., '62–'64; Asst. Prof., '58–'62; Librn., Lectr., Prof., '26–'58; ALA, Am. Assn. of Sch. Librns., many other lib., educ. orgs.; Who's Who in Lib. Sci.; Who's Who of Am. Wm.; Who's Who in the Midwest; Univ. of Mich., BA (Lib. Sci.), '29; Univ. of Chgo., MA, '46; b. Peoria, Ill., 1907; h. Ivan H. Trevor; res: 8525 N. 59th St., Brown Deer, Wis. 53223.

RUEHLIN, POLLY REED, Public Info. Offcr., Los Angeles City School District, 1210 Magnolia Ave., Gardena, Cal., '68–; Dir. of PR, Boy Scouts of Am., L.A. Area Cncl., '62–'68; Public Info. Dir., '57–'62; Lectr. on PR, Univ. of Southern Cal., '67; U.C.L.A., '66, '67; Theta Sigma Phi, PRSA, Public Interest Radio and TV Educ. Soc. (Offcr. and Bd. of Dirs., '57–); Jr. Speakers Bur. for Un. Way, Adv. Club of L.A. (Offcr. and Bd. of Dirs.), Who's Who in PR; Syracuse Univ., BA, '56 (cum laude); Stanford Univ., MA, '57; b.

Camden, N.J., 1935; p. G. Elmer and Helen Coyle Reed; c. Holly Ann, Rex James; res: 1301 Wycliff Ave., San Pedro, Cal. 90732.

RUELLAN, ANDREE, Painter, Graphic Artist, Kraushaar Galleries, 1055 Madison Ave., N.Y., N.Y. 10028; numerous one-man exhbns., U.S., Europe; works in many museums, U.S., Europe; murals for public bldgs., Va. and Ga.; Phila. Watercolor Club, Woodstock Artists Assn.; 3rd Prize, Worcester Museum, '38; Pa. Acad., Phila., Pennell Medal, '45; Dawson Medal, '50; Am. Acad. and Inst. of Arts and Ltrs. $1000 grant, '45; Pepsi-Cola Medal of hon. and purchase, '48; N.Y. State Fair Print Purchase Prize, '51; Guggenheim Fellowship, '50–'51; Ball State Tchrs. Col. aw., '58; numerous other aws.; educ: Art Students League, N.Y.C. (current mbr. also); Maurice Sterne, Rome, Italy; Academie Suedoise, Academie Grande Chaumiere, Paris, France; b. N.Y.C., 1905; p. Andre and Louise Lambert Ruellan; h. John Taylor; res: Shady, N.Y. 12479.

RUETHER, ROSEMARY RADFORD, Wtr., non-fiction; Instr., Hist. Theology, School of Religion, Howard University, Wash., D.C. 2001; formerly Prof. of Hist., Immaculate Heart Col., L.A., Cal.; Soc. for Religion in Higher Educ.; Danforth Grant, '60; Kent Fellowship, '62–'65; Scripps Col., BA, '58; Claremont Grad. Sch., MA, '60; PhD, '66; b. St. Paul, Minn., 1936; p. Robert and Rebecca Ord Radford; h. Herman Ruether; c. Rebecca, David, Mary Elizabeth; res: 1438 Montague St., N.W., Wash., D.C. 20011.

RUGGLES, ELEANOR, Auth., non-fiction, c/o W. W. Norton and Co., Inc., 55 Fifth Ave., N.Y., N.Y. 10003; bks: "The West-Going Heart: A Life of Vachel Lindsay" ('59), "Prince of Players: Edwin Booth" ('53), two other biogs.; Vassar Col., AB, '38 (Phi Beta Kappa); b. Boston, Mass.; p. Daniel and Alice Morrill Ruggles; h. Robert S. O'Leary; res: 16 Martin St., Cambridge, Mass. 02138.

RUGH, BELLE DORMAN, Auth: "Crystal Mountain," "Path Above the Pines," "The Lost Waters"; formerly Asst. Prof. of Eng.; N.Y. Herald Tribune Spring Bk. Festival Aw., '55; Vassar Col., BA, '29; Tchrs. Col., Columbia Univ., MA, '32; b. Beirut, Lebanon, 1908; p. Dr. Harry and Mary Dale Dorman; h. Douglas Rugh; c. Elizabeth, Molly (Mrs. Theodore M. Newcomb, Jr.), June; res: 25 Clarridge Rd., Wethersfield, Conn. 06109.

RUKEYSER, MURIEL, Poet, c/o Monica McCall, 1301 Sixth Ave., N.Y., N.Y. 10019; bks: ten poetry, four prose, four juv.; two short films; one play; Translator, four bks.; Tchr: Sarah Lawrence, Columbia, N.Y.U., City Col. of N.Y.; Bd. Mbr., Tchrs. and Wtrs. Collaborative Rsch.; Nat. Inst. of Arts and Ltrs.; Vassar Col.; Columbia Univ.; Hon. DLitt., '61; b. N.Y.C., 1913; c. William L.

RULE, BETTY-JO BOYLE, Public Info. Offcr., Denver Public Library, 1357 Broadway, Denver, Colo. 80203, '61–; PR Dir., Adult Educ. Cncl., '60–'61; Freelance PR, '59–'60; Public Info. Dir., E. Griffith Sch., '56–'59; Asst. to Dir. of PR, Denver C. of C., '56; ALA, PRSA, Colo. Lib. Assn.; Colo. Indsl. Press Assn.; Allegheny Col., BA (Eng.), '53 (Phi Beta Kappa); b. Chgo., Ill., 1931; p. Joseph and Nell Hughes Boyle; h. Lloyd W. Rule; res: 9027 E. Floyd Pl., Denver, Colo. 80231.

RUMPLE, CAROL ANN SAMPSON, Ed., Harbridge House, Inc., 11 Arlington St., Boston, Mass., '66–'68; Asst. Ed., Little, Brown & Co., '65–'66; Asst. Ed., Industrial Research Magazine (Ind.), '64–'65; Theta Sigma Phi (Delta Chptr. Treas., '63–'64); Scholarships: Delta Theta Sigma Phi ('62–'63), Bloomington Profession Theta Sigma Phi ('63–'64); Purdue Univ., '60–'61; Ind. Univ., AB, '61–'64; b. Wash., D.C., 1942; p. Raymond and Anne Widmar Sampson; h. John Rumple; c. Anne Marie; res: R.R. 2, Box 130, Chesterton, Ind. 46304.

RUNGE, ALIS, Assoc. Ed., Progressive Architecture, 600 Summer St., Stamford, Conn. 06904, '67–; formerly Asst. Ed.; Asst. Ed., Dell Publishing; Univ. of Denver, BA, '50.

RUSH, ANNA FISHER, Household Equipment Ed., McCall's, 230 Park Ave., N.Y., N.Y. 10017, '64–; Assoc. Ed., '52–'64; Asst. Ed., '48–'52; Home Econs. Dir., Met. Edison Co., '46–'48; Home Econst., Phila. Elec. Co., '43–'46; Cnslt., Nat. Comm. on Household Employment; AWNY (Secy., '68–'70), Electrical Wms. Round Table (Nat. Secy., '68–'70), Intl. Platform Assn., Am. Home Econs. Assn., Home Econsts. in Bus.; J. C. Penney-Univ. of Mo. aw., '67; Assn. of Home Appliance Manufacturers aw., '69, '65, '64; Syracuse Univ., BS (Home Econs.), '43; b. Norristown, Pa., 1921; p. Jacob and Blanche Hoffman Fisher; h. Harry Rush; res: 100 Hepburn Rd., Clifton, N.J. 07012.

RUSKAMP, JUDITH SARA, Assoc. Ed., Chicago Review, 5757 S. Drexel, Chgo., Ill. 60637, '66–; Univ. of Chgo., BA (Philosophy), '69; b. Chgo., Ill., 1946; p. John and Mildred Schneider Ruskamp; res: 8345 S. Kostner, Chgo., Ill. 60652.

RUSKEY, NICOLE WALLER, Fashion Coordr., California Fashion Creators, L.A., Cal., '66–'68; Asst. Fashion Dir., Joske's, Houston, Tex., '65–'66; Edtl. Asst., Bride's Magazine, N.Y.C., '65; Theta Sigma Phi (SMU Student Secy., '63–'64); Stephens Col., AA, '62; Southern Methodist Univ., BA (Jnlsm.), '64; Fashion Inst. of Tech., AAS, '65 (Glamour Scholarship); b. Huntsville, Tex., 1942; p. Jim and Lesal Brandes Waller; h. John Ruskey; c. Lesal Nicole; res: 2288 Bronson Hill Dr., Hollywood, Cal. 90028.

RUSSELL, ANNA LOE, Head Ref. Librn., The Library, George Peabody College for Teachers, Nashville, Tenn. 37203, '47–; Librn., Henderson State Tchrs. Col., '46–'47; Asst. Ref. Librn., Wms. Col. of Univ. of N.C., '45–'46, Asst. Cataloger, '43–'45; Asst. Librn., Greens-

boro Col., '43; Asst. Librn., Little Rock Public Lib., '38–'42; Tchr., '29–'34; ALA, WNBA, Tenn. Lib. Assn. (Treas., '66–'67, '57–'58), AAUW (Greensboro Br. Treas., '46), Pi Gamma Mu, Kappa Delta Pi, Southeastern Lib. Assn.; Ark. State Tchrs. Col., AB, '26–'29; G. Peabody Col. for Tchrs., BS in LS, '38, MA, '42; b. Belleville, Ark.; p. Samuel Hix and Anna Huckaby Russell; res: Forrest Hills Apts., 2600 Hillsboro Rd., Nashville, Tenn. 37212.

RUSSELL, ARLENE A., Chief of Ext. Svcs., Hennepin County Library, 300 Nicollet Mall, Mpls., Minn. 55401, '60–; Gen. Asst. Librn., bkmobile svcs. and bk. selection, '54–'60; Head Librn., Waverly, Ia., '43–'54; Ia. Lib. Assn. (Treas.; planning and legislative comms.), Minn. Lib. Assn. (Pres., '61–'62; VP, '60–'61; Mbrshp. Comm.), ALA (State Exec. Dir., Nat. Lib. Wk., '68); Wartburg Col., BA (Alumni Cit.); Univ. of Minn., BS (Lib. Sci.), '43; b. Waverly, Ia., 1910; p. Joseph and Pyrle Knapp Russell; res: 5521 Newton Ave. S., Mpls., Minn. 55419.

RUSSELL, BETTY J., Lit. Agent, R.R. 1, Box 118, Valparaiso, Ind. 46383, '50–; Tchr., '22–'27; Auth: "Chick, Chick Here" ('57), "Big Store—Funny Door" ('55), two other bks.; AAUW (Chgo. Br. Pres., '52–'54), Chicago Children's Reading Round Table (Pres. '49–'50), WNBA (Pres., '60–'61, Nat. Pres., '62–'63); Geneva Col., AB, '22; b. New Brighton, Pa.; p. William and Lida Boyd Cunningham; h. George Russell.

RUSSELL, BEVERLY ANNE, Copy and Features Ed., The Bride's Magazine, 420 Lexington Ave., N.Y., N.Y. 10017, '68–; Reprtr., Feature Wtr., London (Eng.) Evening News, '60–'67; Wms. Pg. Colmst., Manchester Evening News, '58–'60; Asst. Ed., Fashion Forecast, '57–'58; Asst. Fashion and Beauty Ed., Good Housekeeping, '54–'57; b. London, Eng., 1934; p. Leslie and Maude James Russell; h. Roger Houghton Beardwood; c. Benjamin R. P.; res: 227 Central Park W., N.Y., N.Y. 10024.

RUSSELL, JANICE FISHER, PR Dir., St. Luke's Hospital, 101 Page St., New Bedford, Mass. 02742, '58–; Asst. Dir., '56–'58; PRSA, Am. Soc. for Hosp. PR Dirs., New Eng. Hosp. PR Assn., New Bedford Visiting Nurse Assn.; Wheaton Col., AB; b. New Bedford, Mass., 1917; h. Clayton B. Russell; c. Judith (Mrs. Charles V. F. DeMailly, Jr.); res: 123 Rotch St., New Bedford, Mass. 02470.

RUSSELL, M. ELSA, Assoc. Ed., The Reader's Digest, 200 Park Ave., N.Y., N.Y. 10017, '52–; formerly Edtl. Asst., G. and C. Merriam Publ. Co.; Staff Wtr., NBC; Eng. Tchr., N.Y.C. and Conn. high schs.; Lectr., Georgetown Univ. and Cape Cod Wtrs. Confs., N.Y.U., City Col.; OPC, WNBA (Bd. of Mgrs.), Theta Sigma Phi; Mt. Holyoke Col., BA; Columbia Univ., MA; b. Springfield, Mass.; p. Patrick and Mary Russell; res: 45 Tudor City Pl., N.Y., N.Y. 10017.

RUSSELL, MARVEL BROTHERTON, Wms. Ed., daily radio show, KWTX Broadcasting Co., 4520 Bosque

Blvd., Waco, Tex. 76710, '53–; b. Joplin, Mo., 1912; p. Walter and Lottie Anderson Brotherton; h. Albert Russell; c. Susan (Mrs. James Monroe), William E., Mary Elizabeth (Mrs. William Wilson); res: 1509 Northcrest Dr., Waco, Tex. 76710.

RUSSELL, MARY E., Pers. Mgr., Carson Pirie Scott & Co., 124 Southwest Adams St., Peoria, Ill. 61601, '66–; Employment Mgr.-Training Dir., '62–'66; Employment Mgr., '60–'62; Jubilee BPW; h. Emmett M. Russell; c. Laurence A., Linda I.; res: 2821 W. Bacon Dr., Peoria, Ill. 61614.

RUSSELL, NORMA HOUSTON, Wms. Ed., Bellevue American, 10112 N.E. 10th St., Bellevue, Wash. 98004, '52–; Overlake Outlook, '49–'52; Tchr.; Theta Sigma Phi (Seattle Chptr., '61); Wash. State Press Wm. (Secy., '62–'63; Pres., '63–'65); recipient 80 newswriting aws.; Moose Jaw Normal Sch. grad., '30; Univ. of Wash., '36–'37; b. Moose Jaw, Can., 1911; p. Robert E. and Amanda Rimmington Manley; h. Arthur M. Russell; c. Robert Paul; res: 4212 Hunt's Point Rd., Bellevue, Wash. 98004.

RUSSELL, PHEBE GALE, Pres., PGR Enterprises, Inc., Suite #705, Ring Bldg., 18th and M Sts. N.W., Wash., D.C. 20036, '63–; Pres., Ellensburg (Wash.) TV Cable Co., '61–'68; VP, WICO-Radio (Salisbury, Md.), '58–'62; Pubcty. Dir., NBC (Wash., D.C.), '33–'39; Nat. Commty. TV Assn.; Radio Corrs. Assn.; b. N.Y.C., 1910; p. George and Marian Hyde Gale; h. Frank M. Russell; c. Gale, Morgan Niles; res: 6401 Garnett Dr., Chevy Chase, Md. 20015.

RUSSELL, RUTH RUMMLER, Wtr., Chestnut Hill Local, 8434 Germantown Ave., Phila., Pa. 19118, '68–; Adviser, student nwsp., '68–'69; Free-lance articles for Cliff Dweller mag., '66–'67; Reptr., The Herald, '55; Assoc. Ed., The Spectator, '55–'57; Ed., Penn Mutual Magazine, '57; Theta Sigma Phi (Nwsltr. Ed., '57–'59; VP, '60; Treas., '69–'70), active in sch. and civic orgs.; Temple Univ., BA (Jnlsm.), '55 (hons.; outstanding Sr.); b. Phila., Pa., 1933; p. William and Doris Ellwanger Rummler; h. Edward E. Russell; c. Ann J., Edward E., Jr., Robert J., Mary E.; res: 34 E. Chestnut Hill Ave., Phila., Pa. 19118.

RUSSELL, VERA HOOD, Wms. Ed., Miami News-Record, Box 940, Miami, Okla. 74354, '55–; N.E. Okla. Wtrs. Guild; h. Pete Russell; res: 401 E. F St., Picher, Okla. 74360.

RUTHERFORD, KAY LYON, Ed., Foremost Americans Publishing Corporation, Empire State Bldg., 350 Fifth Ave., N.Y., N.Y. 10001, '68–; Planning Asst., Planned Parenthood Fedn. of Am., '69–; Asst. Ed., Sponsor Magazine, '66–'68; Exec. Secy., The Katz Agcy., '56–'64; Asst. Nat. Sales Coordr., Radio-TV Stas., Time-Life Inc., '55–'56; Retail Sls. Mgr., Countess Mara, Inc., '48–'54; civilian employee (commtns., intelligence), U.S. Army (SWPA), '42–'45; Univ. of Alberta, AB, '41; b. London, Eng.; p. Henry and Florence Franks Emmett; h. Robert Lyon Rutherford (div.); c. Dr. Robert B. Rutherford; res: 30 East End Ave., N.Y., N.Y. 10028.

RUTHERFORD, MILDRED CARLSON, VP, Massachusetts Society for the Prevention of Cruelty to Animals, 180 Longwood Ave., Boston, Mass. 02115, '63–; VP, C. F. Hutchinson, Inc., '55–'63; Bdcstr., Radio-TV, 25 yrs. (WBZ); AFTRA, Wms. Edtl. & Indsl. Union (Trustee), Parade mag. aw., Adv. Wm. of the Yr.; Who's Who of Am. Wm., Who's Who of Wm. of Achiev.; Univ. of Conn., BS; b. Hartford, Conn.; p. Gustave and Mathilda Carlson; h. Rondall Rutherford; res: 21 Herrick Rd., Newton Centre, Mass. 02109.

RUTZ, KAREN BECRAFT, Ed., The Torch of Beta Sigma Phi, Walter W. Ross and Co., Inc., 1800 W. 91st Pl., K.C., Mo. 64114, '69–; News Ed., Scout-Sun Nwsps. of Johnson County, '68–'69; Wtr., Ed., Hallmark Cards, Inc., '63–'68; Theta Sigma Phi (Secy., '65–'66; Histrn., '66–'67; Second VP, '67–'68); K.C. Indsl. Eds.; Univ. of Hi., '59–'61; Univ. of Mo., BJ, '63 (Kappa Tau Alpha); b. Portland, Ore., 1942; p. Clinton and Bertha Olson Becraft; h. George H. Rutz; c. Mark Rutz; res: 10908 W. 66th St., Apt. 101, Shawnee Mission, Kan. 66203.

RYAN, ELLEN MARIE, Ed., Wtr., Publicist; Ed., Ebasco Svcs., '54–'66; Mng. Ed., Intl. House Quarterly, '50–'54; Ed., NBC Chimes, NBC, '49; PR Offcr., Histrn., Staff Offcr., U.S. Army, WAC (New Guinea, Philippines), '42–'45; UNNGO, AAIE, Pfsnl. Indsl. Communicators Assn.; Col. of St. Elizabeth, N.J., '38; Sorbonne, '47; Columbia Univ., '47; b. Madison, N.J.; p. Francis and Ida Keefe Ryan; res: 4601 Henry Hudson Pkwy, Riverdale, N.Y. 10471.

RYAN, FRAN, Actress, Lew Sherrell Agency, 8961 Sunset Blvd., Hollywood, Cal.; also: William D. Cunningham & Assocs., 9000 Sunset Blvd., Hollywood, Cal.; TV: "Green Acres," "Beverly Hillbillies," "Tonight Show," others; Theatre: "The Impossible Years" (Melodyland, '68), "Nobody Loves An Albatross" (Drury Lane, '67), "Bells Are Ringing" (Hyatt Music Theatre, '65), others; numerous TV commls.; SAG, AFTRA, AEA, AGVA; Col. of San Mateo, '46–'48; b. L.A., Cal., 1918; p. John and Mary Burton Ryan; h. Howard C. Shafer (dec.); c. Christopher; res: 341 N. Kenwood, Burbank, Cal. 91505.

RYAN, G. JACQUELINE, Dir., PR, Streisand, Zuch and Freedman, Inc., 37 W. 57th St., N.Y., N.Y. 10019, '67–; formerly AE, Public Relations Progs.; Vernon Pope, Inc.; Asst. to PR Dir., Avon Products; articles, fashion and fabric trade pubns.; AWRT; William and Mary Col., '53–'54; Green Mountain Col., AA, '56; b. Meadville, Pa., 1935; p. John and Helen Corrigan Ryan; res: 69 Cedar Grove Pkwy., Cedar Grove, N.J. 07009.

RYAN, LINA LEWIS, PR Dir., St. John's Hospital, 1923 S. Utica, Tulsa, Okla., 74104, '69–; Media Dir.,

Public Relations International, Ltd., '69; Prod. Dir., White Adv. Agcy., '67–'68; Dir. of Adv. and Prom., KOTV-TV, '64–'66; Dir. of Sls. Rsch., '61–'63; Traf. Dir., '58–'60; Traf. Dir., WJTV-TV (Jackson, Miss.), '55–'57; Guest Lectr., bdcst. prom.; Univ. of Tulsa, '64; Bdcstrs. Prom. Assn. past mbr., AWRT (Okla. State Pres., '61–'62; Tulsa Pres., '63–'65; Bd. of Dirs., '60–'65), 2,000 Wm. of Achiev.; Various other dirs.; Okla. State Univ., BS (Bus. Adm.), '41; b. St. Louis, Mo.; h. Ken Ryan; c. Jay Patrick, David Lloyd; res: 14 S. 74th East Ave., Tulsa, Okla. 74112.

RYAN, LORETTA DOLORES, Col. Librn., Cleveland State University, 2400 Euclid Ave., Cleve., Oh. 44115, '70–; Undergrad. Librn., '67–'70; Head, Ref. Dept., '62–'67; Librn., Max S. Hayes Sch., '58–'62; Librn., Cleve. Public Lib., '46–'58; Publr., "Rudiments of Research" ('66); ALA (various comms.), Special Libs. Assn. (Chptr. Pres., other offs., '58–'66), AAUW, WNBA; Case Western Reserve Univ., BS, '35; BS (Lib. Sci.), '43; b. Cleve., Oh.; p. Miles and Loretta Wagner Ryan; res: 13910 Larchmere Blvd., Cleve., Oh. 44120.

RYAN, MARION E., Dir. of Electric Living, Detroit Edison Company, 2000 Second Ave., Detroit, Mich. 48226, '56–; Asst. to Dir. of Home Svc., '38–'56; Home Svc. Advisor, '32–'38; AWRT (Detroit Chptr. Past Pres.), Theta Sigma Phi (Headliner aw., '69), Electrical Wms. Round Table (Nat. Pres., '58–'60), Wms. Adv. Club of Detroit, Soroptimist Club (Wm. of the Yr., '69); Alex Dow aw., '69; Wayne State Univ., Univ. of Detroit.

RYAN, PHYLLIS JUNE, Wms. Dir., Tomah Mauston Broadcasting Co., Inc., 1016-1/2 Superior Ave., Tomah, Wis. 54660, '64–; Comml. Mgr., Cont. Dir., '60–'64; Sls. Mgr., '58–'60; Bdcstr., '54–'58; AWRT, BPW; Univ. of Idaho, '48; b. Billings, Mont., 1928; p. Ralph Daniel and Marguerite Wax Ryan; c. John Ryan Rice; res: R.R. #1. Tomah, Wis. 54660.

RYAN, SHIRLEY, Partner, Sinclair & Ryan, 150 E. 49th St., N.Y., N.Y. 10017, '68–; VP, Abbott Kimball Co., '67–'68; AE, Delehanty Kurnit & Geller, '66–'67; Adv., Prom. Dir., Intl. Silk Assn., '65–'66; Mdsng. Dir., Bride's Magazine, '63–'65; PR Ed., Mademoiselle, '61–'63; Asst. Fashion Coordr., Vogue Pattern Svc., '58–'61; Prom. Dept., Glamour, '54–'58; Fashion Group, NHFL; Wellesley Col., BA, '54; b. Canton, China; p. Millard and Gertrude Kicker Ryan.

RYCKMAN, MARIE MAGUIRE, Food Ed., Feature Wtr., Dayton Journal Herald, Fourth and Ludlow, Dayton, Oh. 45401, '64–; Ed., Publr., The Community Times (Wayne Twp.), '62–'64; Asst. Soc. Ed., Bangor (Me.) Daily News, '54–'59; Faculty, Univ. of Me., '40–'43; Rsch. Asst., State Univ. of N.Y., '39–'40; Rsch. Asst., Bennington Col., '38–'39; Feature Wtr., Boston (Mass.) Post, '37–'38; AAUW, Theta Sigma Phi, Oh. Nwsp. Wms. Assn.; numerous writing aws.; Bennington Col., AB, '37; Univ. of Me., MA, '48; h. S. James Ryckman; c. Jane, Christopher, Gary, S. James Jr.; res: 127 Dixon Ave., Dayton, Oh. 45419.

RYDEN, HOPE E., Auth., bk. in progress (E. P. Dutton); articles in Look; ABC doc. III, "To Love a Child," '68–'69; ABC Evening News, '66–'68; Hope Ryden Prods., "Operation Gwamba-CBS," '65; Film Prod., Wtr., Dir., Drew Assocs., "Susan Starr," "Jane," "Mission to Malaya," others, '61–'65; Lectr: Univ. of Chgo., Univ. of Ia.; Light House, Humane Soc.; Who's Who of Am. Wm.; Who's Who in the East; Univ. of Ia., BA; b. St. Paul, Minn.; p. E. E. and Agnes Johnson Ryden; res: 345 E. 81st St., N.Y., N.Y. 10028.

RYDEN, SUSAN HARDIN, Media Dir., Bill Bailey Communications, 8200 Center Dr., La Mesa, Cal. 92041, '69–; Who's Who in Am. Cols., Univ. of Denver, BA, '67 (Phi Beta Kappa, Mortar Bd.); b. Hastings, Neb., 1945; p. Robert F. and Marjorie Harman Hardin; h. Edwin Ryden.

S

SAARINEN, ALINE, News Corr., National Broadcasting Company, 30 Rockefeller Plaza, N.Y., N.Y. 10020; Art Critic, N.Y. Times, '49–56; Art News, '45–'49; Auth., "The Proud Possessors" (Random House); articles in nat. mags.; Fine Arts Commn., N.Y. State Cncl. on the Arts; Guggenheim Fellowship, '56; numerous hon. degrees, aws.; Who's Who in Am.; Vassar Col., BA, '35; N.Y.U. Inst. of Fine Arts, MA, '40; b. N.Y.C., 1914; p. Allen and Irma Lewyn Bernstein; c. Donald Louchheim, Hal Louchheim, Eames Saarinen; res: 190 E. 72nd St., N.Y., N.Y. 10021.

SABO, PAT PATTERSON, Wms. Ed., Tribune Publishing Co., 120 W. First Ave., Mesa, Ariz. 85201, '58–; The Arkansas Gazette (Little Rock), '48–'49; The Times Herald (Wash., D.C.), '47–'48; various organizations and aws.; Univ. of Miss., '47–'48; b. Hunter, Ark. 1931; p. Cecil and Edna Crutchfield Patterson; h. Louis Sabo; c. Lynn Michelle; res: 1010 W. Fourth Pl., Mesa, Ariz. 85201.

SACHS, ALICE, Ed., Crown Publishers, Inc., 419 Park Ave. S., N.Y., N.Y. 10016, '40–; active in numerous polit., urban affairs orgs.; Wellesley Col., BA (Phi Beta Kappa); Sorbonne, Certificat d'Etudes Francaises; b. Kan. City, Mo.; p. Charles and Flora Weil Sachs; res: 140 E. 63rd St., N.Y., N.Y. 10021.

SACHS, HILDA GOTTLIEB, Dir. of Pubcty., Window Shade Manufacturers Association, 230 Park Ave., N.Y., N.Y. 10017, '61–; PR, Pubcty., Hill and Knowlton, '56–'58; Ed., House and Garden, '51–'56; Auth., four non-fiction bks.; NHFL (VP, '64), AWRT, Am. Inst. of Interior Designers, Resources Cncl. (Advisory Bd., '67–'69); Sorbonne, Art Students League; b. N.Y.C.; p. Arnold and Beatrice Schiff Gottlieb; h. Edgar Sachs; c. Stephen; res: 1111 Park Ave., N.Y., N.Y. 10028.

SACHS, PATRICIA SUSAN, Copywtr., Daniel and Charles, 261 Madison Ave., N.Y., 10016, '70–; Ed., The McCann Magazine, McCann-Erickson, Inc., '70; also a Copywtr. on Westinghouse, Hilton, Look; Ed., Universal Publishing; Asst. Ed., Cosmopolitan magazine; The Copy Club; N.Y.U., '60–'64; b. N.Y.C., 1944; p. Louis and Renee Meinhardt Sachs; res: 2 Sutton Pl. South, N.Y., N.Y. 10022.

SADLER, LENA EITEL, Ed., Wetterau News and Views; Mgr., Wetterau Employees Credit Union, 7100 Hazelwood Ave., Hazelwood, Mo. 63402, '69–; Layout Artist, Wetterau Foods; Am. Bus. Wm., Indsl. Press Assn., Mo. Credit Union Mgrs.; N.E. Mo. State Col.; b. Kirksville, Mo., 1932; p. John and Amy Harris Eitel; h. Joe Sadler; c. Deborah Lynn, Terry Vaughn; res: 620 Brendan St., Florissant, Mo. 63031.

SADTLER, BARBARA KOLTES, Fashion Ed., Newshouse Newspapers, 950 Fingerboard Rd., S.I., N.Y. 10305, '66–; Fashion Coordr., Jordan Marsh (Boston, Mass.), '63–'66; Fgn. Affairs Analyst, Defense Dept. (Wash., D.C.), '61–'63; Guest Lectr., Syracuse Univ. students' abroad program (Amsterdam, Holland); accredited, Chambre Syndicale de La Couture Parisienne (Paris, France); Alliance Francaise (N.Y.), Univ. of Minn., BA (Psych.), '61 (Hons. Program); b. Hutchinson, Kan., 1940; p. Edwin M. and Rose Marie Meyers Koltes; h. David Roth Sadtler; res: Putnam Green, 330, Greenwich, Conn. 06830.

SAFRAN, CLAIRE, Ed., Coronet, 315 Park Ave. S., N.Y., N.Y. 10010, '68–; Assoc. Ed., Family Weekly, '66–'67; Ed., In, '65–'66; Ed., TV Radio Mirror, '61–'65; Assoc. Ed., '54–'58; Mng. Ed., Photoplay, '58–'61; News Ed., Photo Dealer, '51–'53; Bklyn. Col., BA, '51, b. N.Y.C.; p. Simon and Flora Rand Safran; h. John Milton Williams; c. Scott; res: 361 E. 50th St., N.Y., N.Y. 10022.

SAGER, SUE LEVEN, AE, Harshe, Rotman and Druck, Inc., 108 N. State St., Chgo., Ill. 60602, '59–; Founder, People Reaching Productions, '70; Freelance Wtr., '56–'59; Adv., PR div., Futorian Mfg., '54–'56; Owner, PR firm, '51–'54; Home Furnishings Ed., Chgo. Am., '50–'51; various organizations; Drake Univ., BFA, '50; Grad. Work, Art Inst. of Chgo.; b. Evanston, Ill. 1928; p. Benjamin and Rose Goldsmith Leven; h. (div.); c. Sally, Shawn, Scott; res: 1460 Sandburg Terrace, Chgo., Ill. 60610.

SAGINAW, ROSE BLAS, AE, Associated Advertising, 1798 E. Lancaster, Ft. Worth, Tex., '63–; mktng.; PR, polit. candidates, retail accs.; Copywtr., TV, radio, dir. mail; Guest lectr., Ft. Worth Art Ctr., '67; Theta Sigma Phi, Dir. Mail Assn. of Am.; Who's Who of Am. Wm.; Wayne Univ. (Detroit, Mich.), '47; b. Detroit, Mich., 1926; p. Harry and Lillian Sher Blas; h. Sol Saginaw; c. Harry, Jane; res: 10227 Woodford Dr., Dallas, Tex. 75229.

ST. JOHN, WYLLY FOLK, Staff Wtr., Atlanta Journal and Constitution Magazine, Box 4689, Atlanta, Ga. 30302, '41–; Auth: "The Christmas Tree Mystery" (Viking, '69), "The Mystery of The Gingerbread House" (Viking, '69), two other bks.; Theta Sigma Phi, Auths. Guild, Atlanta Press Club, Atlanta Plot Club; Ga. Auth. of the Yr., '68; Univ. of Ga., ABJ, '30 (summa cum laude, Phi Beta Kappa); b. Bamberg County, S.C., 1908; p. William and Annie Mattox Folk; h. Thomas F. St. John; c. Anne (Mrs. Charles H. Dyer); res: 198 Dogwood Ave., Social Circle, Ga. 30279.

ST. JOHNS, ADELA ROGERS, c/o Doubleday & Company, Inc., 277 Park Ave., N.Y., N.Y. 10017; Auth: "Honeycomb" (50 yrs. of nwsp. experience, '69), "Tell No Man" (religious novel, '66), "Final Verdict" (account of her father's life, '62); magazine serials, over 200 short stories; started on San Francisco Examiner and Los Angeles Herald; res: Santa Monica, Cal.

ST. MARIE, SATENIG SAHJIAN, Mgr. of Educ. & Consumer Rels., J. C. Penney Co., Inc., 1301 Ave. of the Americas, N.Y., N.Y. 10019, '63–; Home Econst., '59–'63; Home Econst., Conn. Ext. Svc., Mass. Ext. Svc.; Am. Retail Fedn. (Consumer Rels. Comm., only wm. mbr.), Am. Home Econs. Assn. (VP, '68–'70), Conn. Home Econs. Assn. (Pres., '58–'60), Fashion Group, AWNY, Cornell Univ. Col. of Human Ecology Advisory Cncl.; Simmons Col., BS, '49; Columbia Univ., MA, '59; b. Brockton, Mass., 1927; h. Dr. Gerald L. St. Marie.

SAK, ELIZABETH J., Entertainment, Educ. Ed., Photogr., Brattleboro Daily Reformer, 71 Main St., Brattleboro, Vt. 05301; Windham Col., BA; b. Montague City, Mass., 1939; p. Anthony and Beatrice Cembalisty Sak; res: 4 North St., Box 472, Brattleboro, Vt. 05301.

SAKOL, JEANNIE, Auth., "Gumdrop, Gumdrop, Let Down Your Hair" (Prentice-Hall, '69), two other bks.; Weekly Colm., N. Am. Nwsp. Alliance; Contrbr., Cosmopolitan, Harper's Bazaar, Punch, others; Lectr.; Dramatists Guild; N.Y.U., Hunter Col.; b. N.Y.C.; p. Henry and Helen Abrahams Sakol; res: 230 E. 48th St., N.Y., N.Y. 10017.

SALAUN, MARY-MATHILDA, Reptr., WFAA-TV, Commtns. Cntr., Dallas, Tex. 75202, '66–; AWRT (Dallas Chptr: Corr. Secy., '69; Treas., '67), Dallas Press Club (Hon. Mention, Features, '68); Newcomb Col. of Tulane Univ., BA (Polit. Sci.), '65 (Pi Sigma Alpha); b. N.O., La., 1943; p. Clifford and Edwina Richards Salaun; res: 14418 Hague Dr., Farmers Branch, Tex. 75234.

SALB, JOAN HERMAN, Pres., Joan Salb Associates, 11 Riverside Dr., N.Y., N.Y. 10023, '66–; Copy Chief, Ad. Sales Prom., Assoc. Mdsng. Corp., '60–'66; Copywtr., Larabee Assoc. Adv. (Wash., D.C.), '59–'60; Presentation Wtr., Parents Magazine, '59; Copywtr., McCann-Erickson, '55–'59; AWNY, N.Y. Inst. of Adv., AAF (ADDY Aw., '67); Bklyn. Col., BA (Jnlsm.), '55;

grad. work, Columbia Univ., '57; b. N.Y.C., 1934; p. Aaron and Florence Sisenwein Herman; h. Jack B. Salb; res: 11 Riverside Dr., N.Y., N.Y. 10023.

SALE, VIRGINIA, Actress; Films: 300 character roles; TV: guest star in 200 shows; Radio: "Martha" role in "Those We Love"; Concert tour: appearances in 1,500 cities; Auth., monologue material, used as textbk. in drama schs. (Samuel French, publr.); Zeta Phi Eta; Who's Who of Am. Wm.; Univ. of Ill., Am. Acad. of Dramatic Arts; b. Urbana, Ill.; p. Frank and Lillie Partlow Sale; h. Sam Wren (dec.); c. Virginia Wren Moore, Christopher Sale Wren; res: 1990 N. Sycamore Ave., Hollywood, Cal. 90028.

SALISBURY, ANNE TOWNSEND, Sr. Pubcty. Specialist, J. C. Penney Co., Inc., 1301 Ave. of the Americas, N.Y., N.Y. 10019, '68–; Publicist, Best Foods, '65–'68; Fashion, Educ. Wtr., McCall's Corp., '61–'65; Exec. Trainee, Lord and Taylor, '59–'61; Am. Home Econs. Assn., Home Econsts. in Bus., NHFL, AWRT; N.Y. State Col. of Home Econs., Cornell Univ., BS, '59; b. Penn Yan, N.Y., 1937; p. James and Eileen Murphy Townsend; h. Kent Salisbury; res: 51 E. 93rd St., N.Y., N.Y. 10028.

SALLIS, ULDINA WALL, Reptr., Photogr., Daily Journal, S. Green St., Tupelo, Miss. 38801, '55–; poems published in Greenville (S.C.) News, Daily Jnl.; BPW, N. Miss. Press Assn.; extensive civic activities, hons.; b. Smithville, Miss., 1915; p. Benny and Pruda Myatt Wall; h. (div.); c. Mrs. James Rikard, Jack D.; res: 300 Highland Dr., Tupelo, Miss. 38801.

SALOMON, ANNIKA L., Prodr., Joshua Tree Productions, Inc., 15 W. 46th St., N.Y., N.Y. 10036, '68–; b. Solna, Sweden, 1940; p. Otto and Viveka Brising Salomon; res: 514 E. 83rd St., N.Y., N.Y. 10028.

SALTER, ADELINE, Prog. Mgr., KJAC-TV, 17th & Woodworth Blvd., Port Arthur, Tex. 77640, '62–; Asst. to Opns. Mgr., '58–'62; Asst. Prod. Mgr., Asst. Prog. Mgr., '57–'58; AWRT, S.E. Tex. Press Assn., Jr. League of Beaumont, Beaumont Heritage Soc., DAR, Beaumont Commty. Players; Lamar Jr. Col., '34–'36; b. Kountze, Tex., 1917; p. John and Catherine Rankin Salter; res: 6550 Lexington Dr., Apt. 16, Beaumont, Tex. 77706.

SALTER, CAMILLA ATKISON, Ed., Publr., The Kerrville Mountain Sun, 731 Water St., Kerrville, Tex., '21–; Theta Sigma Phi, S. Tex. Press Assn. (Pres.); many press hons., incl. Dallas News Cup, most outstanding weekly paper, Tex., twice; active in ch., civic groups; Univ. of Okla., Okla. Presbyterian Col., State Col. (Durant, Okla.); b. Durant, Okla., 1894; h. Winfred A Salter; c. Forrest; res: 517 Elm St., Kerrville, Tex.

SALTER, PRISCILLA HENDRYX, Sr. Ed., Wtr., PR, Westinghouse Electric Corp., 1 Maritime Plaza, S.F., Cal. 94111, '68–; PR Asst., '56–'68; AE, PR, Ketchum, MacLeod & Grove, '53–'56; Reptr., Colmst., Pittsburgh (Pa.) Post-Gazette, '46–'53; Chatham Col., BA, '46;

Univ. of Pitt., Univ. of Cal., S.F. State Col.; h. Jack Salter; res: 440 Lombard St., S.F., Cal. 94133.

SALVATO, JACQUELINE DANELLE, Lib. Dir., Seaford Public Library, 2234 Jackson Ave., Seaford, N.Y. 11783, '68–; Asst. Dir., '61–'68; Dir., Garden City Public Lib., '56–'58; Reg. YA Librn., Bklyn. Public Lib., '54–'56; Librn., '53–'54; Bookmobile Librn., Pierce County Public Lib. (Tacoma, Wash.), '53–'54; ALA, N.Y. Lib. Assn., local lib., hist. groups; Adelphi Col., BA, '48 (Pi Gamma Mu); Columbia Univ., Sch. of Lib. Svc., MS, '51; b. N.Y.C., 1927; p. George and Beatrice Leipziger Danelle; h. Jerome Salvato; c. Joanne.

SALZBERG, EMILY MIKSZTO, Copy Ed., Fortune, Time & Life Bldg., Rockefeller Ctr., N.Y., N.Y. 10020, '47–; Ed., Omgus, U.S. Army (Berlin, Germany), '44–'47; Copywtr., Gen. Electric, '42–'43; Russell Sage, BA, '41; Columbia Col., '50–'53; b. Schenectady, N.Y., 1921; p. William and Emilia Nacewicz Mikszto; h. Hugh Salzberg; res: 250 W. 94th St., N.Y., N.Y. 10025.

SAMACHSON, DOROTHY MIRKIN, Free-lance Wtr.; Auth: "Let's Meet the Ballet" (Henry Schuman), "The First Artists" (Doubleday & Co.), six other nonfiction bks.; Hunter Col., '32–'34; b. N.Y.C.; h. Joseph Samachson; c. Michael, Miriam Berkley; res: 185 N. Marion St., Oak Park, Ill. 60301.

SAMEK, STEFANIE, Copywtr., Dodge and Delano Advertising, Inc., 655 Madison Ave., N.Y., N.Y. 10021, '67–; McCann-Erickson, '64–'67; Centenary Col., AA, '63; Tobe-Coburn Sch. for Fashion Careers, Cert., '64 ("T" Aw., '67); b. L.A., Cal., 1943; p. Stefan and Genevieve McGuire Samek; res: 222 E. 75th St., N.Y., N.Y. 10017.

SAMMONS, MARGARETTE BLACKBURN, Mgr., Pubcty., Adm., and Commty. Rel., Friden Division, The Singer Company, 2350 Washington Ave., San Leandro, Cal. 94577, '68–; Mgr., Commty. Rel., '69–; Exec. Asst., '67–'68; Staff Asst., Pubns., '64–'67; Theta Sigma Phi (Secy., '69–'70), East Bay Wms. Press Club; Ore. State Univ., BS (Home Econs.), '62; Tobe-Coburn Sch. for Fashion Careers, '63; b. Albany, Ore., 1940; p. J. Lewis and Lily Wellington Blackburn; h. Keith Sammons; res: 4328 Circle Ave., Castro Valley, Cal. 94546.

SAMPOGNA, ADAIR DuFINE, Ed., Shell Oil Co., 700 White Plains Rd., Scarsdale, N.Y. 10583, '65–; Reptr., Asst. to Wms. Pg. Ed., White Plains Reporter Dispatch, '64–'65; Theta Sigma Phi; Lambda Sigma Sigma; N.Y. Assn. of Indusl. Commtns.; Syracuse Univ., BA, '64 (cum laude); N.Y.U.; b. N.Y.C., 1942; p. Irving and Doris Meyer DuFine; h. Frank A. Sampogna; res: 2221 Palmer Ave., New Rochelle, N.Y. 10801.

SAMSON, IRENE GRIFFITH, City Librn., Anchorage Public Library System, 427 F. St., Anchorage, Alaska 99501, '46–; Stillwater Co., Mont.; St. Louis (Mo.) Public Lib.; Tchr., Neosho (Mo.) Public Sch. System; various orgs.; Southwest State Coll., BS; George Peabody Col., MS (Lib. Sci.); b. Norwood, Mo.; p. Martin and Lillie McKinley Griffith; h. Roy S. Samson; res: 1835 13th Ave., Anchorage, Alaska 99501.

SAMUELS, GERTRUDE, Staff Wtr., The New York Times Magazine, The New York Times, 229 W. 43rd St., N.Y., N.Y. 10036, '46–; N.Y. Times, '43–; Newsweek, Time mags., '41–'43; N.Y. Post, '37–'40; Adm. Asst., Dept. of Agriculture (Wash., D.C.), '33–'37; Auth: "The Secret of Gonen" (Avon, '69), "The People Vs. Baby" (Doubleday, '67; Avon, '69), "The Story of David Ben-Gurion" (Crowell, '61), "The Corrupters" (a play, published in "The Best Short Plays 1969," ed. by Stanley Richards, Chilton); articles, nat. mags. incl: Harper's, The Nation, The Saturday Review, others; Special Observer (Europe), UNICEF, '48; various orgs.; George Wash. Univ., '35–'37; b. Manchester, Eng.

SAMUELSON, MARY BOLLINGER, Wms. Ed., Covina Valley Newspapers, Inc., 128 E. College St., Covina, Cal. 91790. '61–; Wms. Ed., San Gabriel Valley Newsps., '56–'61; Who's Who of Am. Wm., Who's Who in the West; Kent State Univ., Oh. State Univ.; h. James A. Samuelson; c. Linda Diane Jagger Roberts; res: 315 S. Grand Ave., W. Covina, Cal. 91790.

SÁNCHEZ, ERIKA KRAEMER, Educ. Rschr., Time, Incorporated, Time & Life Bldg., Rockefeller Ctr., N.Y., N.Y. 10020, '62–; Hunter Col., BA, '60 (Phi Beta Kappa, cum laude); Columbia Univ., Univ. of Madrid; b. N.Y.C., 1940; p. Helmut and Ruth Shearer Kraemer; h. José Antonio Sanchez; res: 401 E. 81st St., N.Y., N.Y. 10028.

SANDBURG, HELGA, Auth: novels, short stories (Virginia Quarterly Review Prize, Best Short Story, "Witch Chicken," '59), poetry (Second Prize, Borestone Mountain Poetry Aw., "The Woman," '62), nonfiction; Lectr., '60–; Adm. Asst., The Papers of Woodrow Wilson, N.Y.C., '58–'59; Lib. of Congress., Wash., D.C., '52–'56; personal secy. to father, Carl Sandburg, '44–'51; Auths. Guild, PSA, Am.-Scandinavian Fndn., Nat. Nubian Club, Am. Milk Goat Record Assn., Save the Dunes; Mich. State Col., '39–'40; Univ. of Chgo., '40; b. Maywood, Ill., 1918; p. Carl and Lillian Steichen Sandburg; h. George Crile, Jr., M.D.; c. John Carl Steichen, Karlen Paula Steichen; res: 2060 Kent Rd., Cleve., Oh. 44106.

SANDERS, ANNE MADDOX, City Ed., Laurel Leader-Call, 130 Beacon St., Laurel, Miss. 39440, '65–, '53–'57, '44–'46; Manhattan (Kan.) Mercury-Chronicle, '46–'48; features in other Miss. pubns.; NFPW (First Prize, Wtrs. Contest, '67); Miss. Press Wms. Assn. (three times state prize winner); active in local civic orgs.; Blue Mountain Col., '43–'44; b. Stringer, Miss., 1925; p. James and Terrie Copeland Maddox; h. Philip Sanders; c. James, Suzell, Shana; res: 1753 Lake Park Dr., Laurel, Miss. 39440.

SANDERS, CLEMA DELORES, Gen. Mgr., Apache Enterprises & Co., Inc., 5062 Matilda, Dallas, Tex. 75206, '68–; Wtr., WADK; Tchr., Newport Independent Sch. Dist.; PR, Newswtr., WACO, KWTX radio, TV; PR Exec., SMI; Asst. to Pres., PBI; Asst. to Pres., Exec. Club; Cnslt.; articles, speciality, trade pubn.; pubcty.; Press Club of Waco (Secy.-Treas.), PRSA; Beta Sigma Phi; Baylor Univ., BA, '61; Sorbonne, Univ. of Paris, MA, '62; b. Waco., Tex., 1939; h. G. W. Sanders; c. Cindy Delores.

SANDERS, DOROTHY JENKINS, VP, Co-owner, Prog. Dir., Sanders Enterprises, Inc. (WPXE), Lee-San Corporation (WBGC), P.O. Drawer 520, Starke, Fla. 32091, '59–; Off. Mgr., Mid-South Bdcst. Co. (Chattanooga, Tenn.), '55–'59; AWRT, Starke Lib. Bd.; b. Charleston, S.C.; p. Stephen and Kitty Linder Jenkins; h. John Sanders; res: P.O. Drawer 520, Starke, Fla. 32091.

SANDERS, EMILY C., Lib. Dir., Charleston County Library, 404 King St., Charleston, S.C. 29403, '40–; Pratt Inst. Lib. (Bklyn., N.Y.), High Sch. Lib. (Summerville, S.C.), Timrod Lib.; ALA (Cncl., '56–'60), S.C. Lib. Assn. (Pres., '47–'48), Southeastern Lib. Assn. (Exec. Comm., '60–'64); AAUW, BPW, League of Wm. Voters; Univ. of N.C., AB; Pratt Inst. Lib. Sch., Grad.; b. Beaufort, S.C., 1905; p. William Meek and Grace Tonking Sanders; res: Ashley House, Charleston, S.C. 29401.

SANDERS, JOAN ALLRED, Auth.; English Instr., Utah State University, Logan, Utah. 84321; numerous novels, biogs. and stories incl: "La Petite: Louise de la Valliere," "Baneful Sorceries"; PEN; Univ. of Ut., BA; b. Three Forks, Mont.; p. M. Thatcher and Pearl Oberhansley Allred; h. Raymond T. Sanders; c. Raymond Craig; res: 815 Canyon Rd., Logan, Ut. 84321.

SANDERS, MARION K., Sr. Ed., Harper's Magazine, 2 Park Ave., N.Y., N.Y. 10016, '60–; Chief, Mag. Br., USIS, '46–'52; News Wtr., Off. of War Info., '44–'46; Asst. Dir. PR, Port of N.Y. Auth., '37–'44; Adjunct Asst. Prof., N.Y.U., '65–; Auth: "The Lady and the Vote" ('56), "The Professional Radical" (with Saul Alinsky, '70); Auths. Guild, Assn. of Sci. Wtrs.; Wellesley Col., AB, '25; b. N.Y.C., 1905; p. Leo and Lillian Rouse Klein; h. Theodore M. Sanders (dec.); c. T. Michael Jr., Mary (Mrs. Leo von Euler); res: 35 E. 30th St., N.Y., N.Y. 10016.

SANDERS, MARLENE, News Corr., American Broadcasting Co., Seven W. 66th St., N.Y., N.Y. 10023, '64–; Asst. News Dir., WNEW, '62–'64; Prodr.-Wtr., WBC, '61–'62; Assoc. Prodr.-Wtr., WABD-WNEW TV, '55–'60; AFTRA, Theta Sigma Phi, AWRT; Wtrs. Guild of Am. aw., '63; McCall's Golden Mike aw., '63; Robert Sherwood aw. for "Night Beat," '58; Brotherhood aw., '64; Oh. State Univ., '48–'49; Cleve. Col., '49–'50; b. Cleve., Oh.; p. Mac Sanders and Evelyn Fisher; h. Jerome Toobin; c. Jeffrey, Mark; res: 175 Riverside Dr., N.Y., N.Y.; Candlewood Echoes, Sherman, Conn.

SANDERS, TIANNE GABRIEL, Tchr., Drama Workshop, College of the Desert, Palm Desert, Cal.; League of Wm. Voters; Critics choreography aw., '69; Col. of the Desert; p. Frances and Victoria Gabriel; h. Shepard Sanders; c. Kimberly Jeanne, Trinza Ann.

SANDOR, VICTORIA IVANOVNA KOCHUROVA, (pseud: Alla Ktorova), Asst. Prof. of Russian, George Washington University, H St., N.W., Wash., D.C., '63–; U.S.I.A. Voice of Am., '65–; Intourist Guide, '56–'58; Tchr. of Eng. HS, Moscow, '54–'56; Auth: "The Face of the Fire Bird" (in Russian, '69), "Jurius Gasse (in German, '64), "Jurius Stroede" (in Danish, '63), also many articles, essays, short stories and novels; PEN (Intl.), Dobro Slovo (Russian); Leningrad Theatre Inst., '45–'47; U.S.S.R. Moscow Inst. of Fgn. Langs., '48–'54; Georgetown Univ., '62; b. Moscow, U.S.S.R., 1926; p. Ivan V. and Rebecca E. Voronova Kochurov; h. John Henry Sandor; res: 395 O Street, S.W., Wash., D.C. 20024.

SANDOW, LYN A., Educ. Media Ed., Grolier Incorporated, 575 Lexington Ave., N.Y., N.Y. 10022, '69–; Wtr., Grolier Educ. Corp., '66–'68; Project Supvsr. Resources Dev. Corp. (East Lansing, Mich.), '61–'66; Wtr., article "Teaching With Conceptual Models," Educ. Tech. Magazine, Aug., '68; 20 self-instructional courses; Designer, educ. toys and games; Nat. Soc. for Programmed Instruction, NEA, Nat. Soc. for the Study of Educ., Modern Lang. Assn.; Univ. of Conn., BA, '59; Southern Conn. State Col. and Mich. State Univ., grad work.

SANDUSKY, MARUTH QUARLES, Media Dir., Bill Hudson and Associates, Inc., 708 17th Ave. S., Nashville, Tenn. 37203, '69–; TV Ed., Cummings Press, '68–'69; Prod. Mgr., Savage, Kerr & McMillen, '67–'68; Prom. Mgr., WLAC-TV, '56–'67; Traf. Mgr., WKDA Radio, '54–'56; Auth., TV colm., Middle Tenn. area nwsps., '65–'67; TV articles, '66; Ed., TV prog. booklet, '68; org., musical shows, TV prom., '65, '66; AWRT (Nashville Chptr.), Radio & TV Cncl. of Middle Tenn. (Secy., '65–'66); Who's Who of Am. Wm., various others; Watkins Inst., '48; Famous Wtrs. Sch., '65–'67; b. Cookeville, Tenn., 1929; p. Stephen B. and Lottie Phillips Quarles; h. Floyd Sandusky; c. Margaret Kathleen (Mrs. Jim Cooper); res: 2815 Barclay Dr., Nashville, Tenn. 37206.

SANEHOLTZ, BETTY JEAN, Dir., Consumer Svc., Parents' Magazine, 52 Vanderbilt Ave., N.Y., N.Y. 10017, '67–; Assoc. Dir., '64–'67; Instr., Kent State Univ., '60–'64; Columbus & Southern Ohio Electric Co., '59–'60; Ind. Mich. Electric Co., '57; Co-auth., "Fifty Years of Laundry Writings—An Annotated Bibliography" ('64); Am. Home Econs. Assn., N.Y. State Home Econs. Assn., N.Y. Home Econsts. in Bus., Electrical Wms. Round Table; Bowling Green State Univ., BS, '56; Oh. State Univ., MS, '58; b. Napoleon, Oh.; p. Arthur and Helen Bittikofer Saneholtz.

SANGER, JOAN OYAAS, Free-lance Ed. and Nonfiction Wtr.; Mng. Ed., Physical Therapy, Am. Physical Therapy Assn., '62–'69; Assoc. Ed., Nat. Assn. of Social Workers, '60–'61; Ed., Personal Efficiency, LaSalle Ext. Univ. (Chgo., Ill.), '57–'59; Edtl. Dept. Dir.; Prod. Ed., Leland Publrs. (St. Paul, Minn.), '53–'57; Asst. Dir. of Sch. and Col. Activities, Am. Red Cross, '50–'53; Nwsp. Reptr.; Theta Sigma Phi, N.Y. Assn. of Indsl. Communicators, Am. Studies Assn., Douglaston Civic Assn. (Secy., '65–'68), Univ. of Wis. Alumni Club of N.Y. (Dir., '67–); Univ. of Wis., BA, '46 (hons.); b. Eau Claire, Wis., 1924; p. John and Martha Arnsdorf Oyaas; h. Frank Sanger; res: 73 Poplar St., Douglaston, N.Y. 11363.

SANGUINETTI, ELISE AYERS, Auth: "The Dowager" (Scribner, '68), "The New Girl" (McGraw-Hill, '62), "The Last of the Whitfields" (McGraw-Hill, '62); Univ. of Ala., AB, '47; b. Anniston, Ala.; p. Harry and Edel Ytterboe Ayers; h. Phillip Sanguinetti; res: 412 Keith Ave., Anniston, Ala. 36201.

SANNER, ALICE MATHILDA, Adv. Mgr., Rockford Machine Tool Co., 2500 Kishwaukee St., Rockford, Ill. 61101, '46–; Ed., Hot Chips, '51–; Rockford Adv. Club, Rockford Indsl. Eds. (Pres., '60; VP, '69); b. Dubuque, Ia., 1913; p. Louis and Emma Gross Sanner; res: 122 N. Chicago Ave., Rockford, Ill. 61107.

SANTI, TINA AIDA, VP-Radio/TV, Grey and Davis, Inc., 777 Third Ave., N.Y., N.Y., '66–; formerly Acc. Supvsr., Combine Corp.; Staff Wtr., Western Electric; Bdcstr., WHER, Memphis, Tenn., '60–'61; WMCT-TV, '59–'60; Maryville Col., '57–'58; Memphis State Univ., BA, '61 (Dean's List); b. Memphis, Tenn., 1939; p. Clement and Dale Pendergrast Santi; res: 220 E. 60th St., N.Y., N.Y. 10022.

SARA, DOROTHY, Graphologist, Wtr.; Tchr., Henry George Sch. of Social Sci.; Wms. Nat. Bk. Assn.; Adv. Club of N.Y.; b. Bklyn., N.Y.; res: 11 E. 32nd St., N.Y., N.Y. 10016.

SARE, MARY LATHAM, Free-lance Wtr.; Social Caseworker, The Salvation Army, '64–; Edtl. Asst., The Ind. Tchr. Magazine; Ed., U.S. Naval Avionics Facility; Radio Cont. Wtr., Indpls. WIRE; News, Feature Reptr., Vincennes Sun-Comml.; Wtr., children's mags.; Free-lance poetry; bks.: "Ind. Sesquicentennial Poets" ('66), "Versatile Verse" ('29); Penny Poetry, Univ. of Colo., '59–'60; Tchr.; Ed., Nyhart Co.; Ind. Univ., AB, '29; b. Indpls., Ind., 1907; p. Harry T. and Mary C. Dunn Latham; h. Dale W. Sare; c. John W., Wm. B., Sally (Mrs. Delbert Michel); res: 1728 Cross Dr., Woodruff Pl., Indpls., Ind. 46201.

SARETT, ALMA JOHNSON, Prof. of Speech, University of South Florida, Tampa, Fla. 33620, '64–; Assoc. Prof., '60–'64; Asst. Prof. of Speech, Univ. of Fla., '55–'60; Univ. of Northern Ia., '45–'46; Fla. Southern Col., '36–'40; Auth., "Jo's Boys," "Basic Principles of Speech" ('58, '66); Ed., "Covenant With Earth: A Selection From the Poems of Lew Sarett" ('56); Auth. of several monographs and articles in professional jnls.; Speech Assn. of Am. (Delegate, Constitutional

Conf., '69; Delegate, Legislative Assembly, '61–'64, '66–'69), Southern Speech Assn., Fla. Speech Assn. (Pres., '39–'40), Zeta Phi Eta (aw., '60); Fla. Southern Col., BS, '34; Northwestern Univ., MA, '38; PhD, '42; b. Durant, Fla., 1908; p. Joseph and Elizabeth Barnes Johnson; h. 1. Lew Sarett (dec.), 2. Clarence W. Anderson; c. Lewis H., Mrs. John Stockdale; res: 11005 Carrollwood Dr., Tampa, Fla. 33618.

SARGENT, SHIRLEY, Ed., Flying Spur Press, Box 278, Yosemite National Park, Cal. 95989, '67–; Colmst., Mariposa Gazette, '55–; Ed., Mariposa Sentinel, '67–; Tchr., '48–'61; Auth., 12 bks., 6 with Yosemite subjects; James D. Phelan Aw., '64; Henry E. Huntington Lib. Rsch. aw., '68; Mariposa Soroptimists "Wm. of the Yr." aw., '68; Pasadena City Col.; b. L.A., Cal., 1927; p. Robert and Alice Fletcher Sargent; res: Yosemite National Park, Cal. 95989.

SARLAT, GLADYS, Pres., Gladys Sarlat Public Relations; Pima Bldg., 149 N. Stone Ave., Tucson, Ariz. 85701, '70–; PR Dir., VP, Waller & Sarlat Advertising, Inc., '68–'70; VP for PR, Harwood/Garland Adv., '59–'68; Asst. Prod. Mgr., Cunningham & Walsh (S.F., Cal.), '58; Asst. Fashion Dir., Emporium-Capwell Dept. Store, '55–'56; Fashion Dir., Warsaw & Co. (N.Y.C.), '50–'54; PR Lectr., Univ. of Ariz., Glendale Commty. Col.; PRSA, Tucson Press Club, Fashion Group; L.A. Wms. Adv. Club cit., '62; Woman of the Year, for Bus., Arizona Daily Star, '63; Who's Who of Am. Wm.; Univ. of Wash., BS, '46; Columbia Univ.; b. Elizabeth, N.J., 1923; p. Max and Dorothy Levin Sarlat; res: 3239 E. Third St., Tucson, Ariz. 85716.

SARMENTO, ANNA MARIA DE MORAES, Coordr. of Intl. Rsch., Marplan Research Inc., 1414 Ave. of the Americas, N.Y., N.Y. 10019, '69–; Sr. Project Dir., '69; Project Dir., '67–'68; Study Dir., '65–'66; Rsch. Analyst, Inst. of Commtns. Rsch., '63–'64; cslt.; AAPOR, Grad. Facs. of Columbia Univ.; Catholic Univ. of Rio De Janeiro, BA (Romance Langs.) '60; Columbia Univ. MA (Sociol.) '63; b. Rio De Janeiro, Brazil, 1938; p. Armando and Elza Correa Sarmento; res: 114 E. 78th St., N.Y., N.Y. 10021.

SARTAIN, GERALDINE, Free-lance Wtr., '60–; Publicist, Nat. Cncl. of Chs., '53–'59; Publicist, YWCA Nat. Bd., '49–'53, '42–'44; King Features, '37–'39; Feature Wtr., New York World Telgram, '31–'37; New York World, '29–'31; Paris (France) Times, '27; Shanghai (China) Times, '26; Honolulu (Hi.) Star-Bulletin, '24–'25; Reptr., Wtr., S.F. (Cal.) Chronicle, '20–'24; OPC, N.Y. Nwsp. Wms. Club (Pres., '31–'32), Univ. of Cal., AB, '15; b. S.F., Cal.; p. Alfonzo and Karen Lawson Sartain; res: 1400 Geary Blvd., S.F., Cal. 94109.

SARTAIN, SHIRLEY COPPEDGE, VP, Dir. of PR, Louis Hertz Advertising, 148 Cain St., N.E., Atlanta, Ga., '63–; Owner-Ed., Monthly Ctr., Svc.; Mfg. Agt., '56–'63; Exec. Dir., Ga. Assn. for Mental Health, '53–'54; various organizations; Univ. of Ga.; b. Atlanta, Ga. 1928; p. Clarence and Bonnie Barnard Cop-

pedge; h. William F. Sartain; c. William F., Jr.; res: 288 The Prado, N.E., Atlanta, Ga. 30309.

SARVIS, SHIRLEY JEAN, Food Wtr., Cnslt., '62–; Auth., several cook bks., Cnslt., Time-Life cook bks.; Staff Home Econst., Sunset Magazine, '57–'62; Theta Sigma Phi, Am. Home Econs. Assn., Home Econsts. in Bus.; Kan. State Univ., BS, '57 (summa cum laude); Univ. of Colo.; b. Norton, Kan., 1935; p. George and Wilhelmina Koch Sarvis; res: 1100 Filbert, S.F., Cal. 94109.

SASNETT, MARTENA TENNEY, Coordr., Intl. Educ. Studies, University of California, 405 Hilgard Ave., L.A., Cal. 90024, '64–; Fgn. Student Asst., Univ. of Southern Cal., '47–'51; Fashion Wtr., Coordr., '45–'47; Radio Script Wtr., '44–'45; Auth: "Financial Planning for Study in the United States" ('67), "Educational Systems of the World" ('52); Co-auth: "The Country Index" ('70), "Graduate Study in the United States" ('66) "Educational Systems of Africa ('66); Nat. Assn. of Fgn. Student Affairs; Boston Univ. commtns. aw., '58; Bradford Jr. Col. grad., '25; Acad. of Speech Arts grad., '27; b. Patchogue, N.Y., 1908; p. Henry and Grace Kelley Tenney; h. J. Randolph Sasnett; res: 2829 Miradero Dr., Santa Barbara, Cal. 93105.

SATTERFIELD, CAROLYN HOOPER, Wms. Ed., The Durham Sun, Durham Herald Co., 115 Market St., Durham, N.C. 27702, '65–; Wms. Ed., Durham Morning Herald, '43–'45; N.C. Press Wm. (aws., '67, '69); Duke Univ., '43–'45; b. Durham, N.C., 1925; p. Connie and Elizabeth Overton Hooper; h. John Satterfield; c. Carolyn H., Carlotta Elizabeth; res: 1518 Hermitage Ct., Durham, N.C. 27707.

SATTERTHWAITE, TINA NOBLE, Home Furnishings Ed., Toledo Blade, Superior and Orange Sts., Toledo, Oh., '49–; Wms. Feature Ed., Toledo Times, '47; Who's Who of Am. Wm., Dorothy Dawes aw., '66, '62, '59; h. James Satterthwaite; res: 3456 River Rd., Toledo, Oh. 43614.

SAUKKONEN, MIRJAM A., Cnslt., School Library Services, Ohio Department of Education, 22 E. Gay St., #444, Columbus, Ohio 43215, '66–; Wtr., "Library Aides," (Ohio Dept. of Educ.), '68); Librn., Pepper Pike Sch., Orange Local Schs., '56–'66; Tchr., '52–'56; Lakewood City Sch. District, '46–'52; various organizations; Kent State Univ., BS (Educ.), '46, MS (Lib. Sci.), '62; Univ. of Wis., MS (Elem. Educ.), '54; b. Cleve., Ohio, 1925; p. John and Mary P. Saukkonen; res: 1335 Crestwood Ave., Columbus, Ohio 43227.

SAUL, MARGARET, free-lance publishing cnslt., 228 Grove St., Montclair, N.J. 07042, '63–; Educ. Rsch. Dir., R. R. Bowker, '61–'63; Ed., Sch. Lib. Jnl., '55–'61; tchr., Omaha Public Schs., '54–'55; Hastings Col., AB, '54; b. North Platte, Neb., 1933; p. Ralph and Margaret Priest Saul; h. Daniel Melcher; c. Frederic.

SAUNDERS, BETTY HUEY, Free-lance Wtr., 165 E.

Third St., Oswego, N.Y. 13126; Colmst., The News-Champion (St. Louis, Mo.), '31–'37; Agt.; Ed., The Grail, '28–'30; Adv. Wtr.-Salesman, The News-Champion, summer '27; Oswego Palladium Times; numerous articles, poetry, plays; various organizations and aws.; Univ. of Mo., BJ, '31 (Sch. of Jnlsm. Honor Cncl., Jay L. Torrey Scholarship Aw., '30); b. St. Louis, Mo. 1909; p. Leslie and Kathryn Hyer Huey; h. Aulus Saunders; c. Alan Ward, Susan (Mrs. William Harry Cook); res: 165 E. Third St., Oswego, N.Y. 13126.

SAUNDERS, CARYL HEYDE, Dir. of PR, Western Iceberg Lettuce, Inc., P.O. Box 9123, S.F., Cal. 94129, '64–; Adv. Dir., Wm. Timmer Real Estate (San Rafael), '63–'64; Free-lance Wtr., '60–'63; Tech. Wtr., Douglas Aircraft (El Segundo, Long Beach), '53–'55; Adv. Club of S.F., Pubcty. Club of S.F. (nwsltr. aw., '68), PRSA, Nat. Agricultural Adv. and Mktng. Assn. (Secy., '68, '69), Adv. Wms. Prod. Club, AWRT, Inst. Food Eds. Cncl.; Col. of Pacific, '48–'51; b. Grand Island, Neb., 1931; p. Budd and Sarabeth Jones Heyde; h. R. Charles Saunders; c. Craig, Brian; res: 389 Riviera Dr., San Rafael, Cal. 94901.

SAUNDERS, DORIS EVANS, Wtr., Assoc. Prodr., "Our People," WTTW, '68–; Colmst., "Confetti," Chigo Daily Defender, '66–; Dir., Inst. Dev. Public Info., Chgo. State Col., '68–; Staff Assoc., Off. of Chancellor, Univ. of Ill.; Edtl. Colmst., "My Point of View," Chicago Courier Newsp.; Owned and Operated Plus Factor, PR, '66–'68; Librn., Dir. of Bk. Div., Johnson Publishing, '49–'66; compiled and edited "The Negro Handbook," '66; currently working on profile of Congressman William L. Dawson; Nat. Assn. of Media Wm., Chgo. Wms. Adv. Club, The Black Academy of Arts and Letters (Secy., Bd. of Dirs., '69–'71); Alpha Gamma Pi; Chgo. Pub. Lib. Training Class, Certificate, '42; b. Chgo., Ill., '21; p. Alvesta and Thelma Rice Evans; h. Vincent Ellsworth Saunders, Jr.; c. Ann Camille, Vincent E. III; res: 9718 S. Indiana Ave., Chgo., Ill. 60628.

SAUNDERS, MARJORIE INEZ, Dir., PR, Baylor University Medical Center, 3500 Gaston, Dallas, Tex. 75246, '52–; '45–; practiced civil law; PR Cnslt. Hospital PR, Volunteer Programs; Lectr.; papers published, pfsnl. pubns.; numerous organizations, aws. and hons.; Southern Methodist Univ.; Jefferson Univ. Sch. of Law (Dallas, Tex.), LL.B.; b. Dallas, Tex.; p. Claude W. and Cordelia Croxdale Saunders; res: 6208 Malcolm Dr., Dallas, Tex. 75246.

SAUNDERS, RUBIE AGNES, Edtl. Dir., Parents' Magazine Enterprises, Inc., 52 Vanderbilt Ave., N.Y., N.Y. 10017, '67–; Ed., Mng. Ed., Edtl. Secy.; Auth: "The Calling All Girls Party Book" (Parents Magazine Press, '66); "Marilyn Morgan, R.N." (Signet, '69); NAMW; Hunter Col., BA, '50 (alumni aw., '60); b. N.Y.C., 1929; p. Walter and Rubie Ford Saunders; res: 218 Jefferson Ave., Bklyn., N.Y. 11216.

SAURO, REGINA CALDERONE, Wtr., juvenile stories, poems, plays for mags.; bks: "The Too-Long

Trunk" (Lantern Press, '64), "Read Aloud Stories from Child Life" (Wonder Bks., '60), "Stories from Jack and Jill" (Wonder Bks., '60), "My English Book" (Sadlier, '62); b. Altoona, Pa., 1924; p. Augustine and Clory Martini Calderone; h. Thomas Sauro; res: 1529 La Salle Ave., Niagara Falls, N.Y. 14301.

SAVAGE, KATE, Free-lance Wtr.; Colmst., Baltimore (Md.) Post; rsch. for radio program "Fashion Was Fate"; Colmst., Home News; Auth. "Una Abroad;" Johns Hopkins Univ.; b. Balt., Md.; p. Harry and Lena Savage; res: 3607 Springdale Ave., Balt. Md. 21216.

SAVAGE, KAY, Food Ed., Detroit Free Press, 321 W. Lafayette, Detroit, Mich. 48231, '45–; Feature Wtr., Macomb Daily News, '41–'45; Auth., three food bks.; Theta Sigma Phi (Detroit Chptr. Past Pres.; Headliner of the Yr., '63), AWRT, Electrical Wms. Round Table; Vesta aw., '67; Nat. Pressure Cooker aw.; numerous certs. of merit; Mich. State Univ.; b. Conneaut, Oh., 1907; p. Francis and Nina Hall Hanratty; h. Howard E. Kennedy (dec.); res: 1528 Chateaufort Pl., Detroit, Mich. 48207.

SAVAGE, M. ANIA, Rewrite Reptr., The Record, 150 River St., Hackensack, N.J. 07602, '68–; Legislative Corr., (Trenton Bur.), '67–'68; Polit. Reptr. (N.Y. edition), '66–'67; Reptr., Rockland County (N.Y.) Jnl.-News, '64–'66; Free-lance bk. manuscript Ed.; Barnard Col., BA, '63 (English; N.J. Scholarship; Barnard Scholar); Columbia Grad. Sch. of Jnlsm., MS, '64; b. Wolcniw, Ukraine, 1941; p. Iwan and Anna Vlasenko Bojcum; h. Charles F. Savage; res: 344 W. 72nd St., New York, N.Y. 10023.

SAVAGE, PEG, Co-auth., "Sex and the Senior Citizen" (Frederick Fell, '68); Adm. Asst., Sr. Aides Prog., National Council of Senior Citizens, 1627 K St., N.W., Wash., D.C. 20006, '69– (Nat. Nwsp. Writing aw., '68); Edtl. positions, mags. and nwsps., '57–'69; Theta Sigma Phi; City of Miami Beach Aw. of Merit; Univ. of Miami, BA, '56 (Outstanding Sr. Wm. Jnlst., Mortar Bd., other hons.); b. Girardville, Pa., 1935; p. Simon and Stella Stack Savage; c. Steven S. Grey; res: 1704 Abingdon Dr., Alexandria, Va. 22314.

SAVARESE, JULIA ROSE, Prom. Wtr., McCall's, 230 Park Ave., N.Y., N.Y. 10017, '69–; Mgr. of Special Projects, Holiday mag., '66–'68; Exec. Ed., California Home, '63–'66; Asst. to Ed., American Home, '59–'63; Auth: "The Weak and the Strong" (fiction, Putnam's, '52); "Dreaming Spires" (poetry, '50); "How to Book the Boss" (non-fiction, Corinthian, '68); TV Scripts: "Ring Around Rosey" (NBC, '64); "Houses" (Omnibus, '50); Actor's Studio Wtrs. Wing, New Dramatists Comm., Auths. League, Dramatists Guild; Ford Fndn. grant, '61; Albert Ralph Korn poetry aw., '50; Catholic fiction aw., '60; Hallmark TV aw., '62; Hunter Col., BA, '52; Times Sch. of Jnlsm., '52–'54; b. N.Y.C., 1930; p. Francis and Rose Volpe Savarese; res: 200 E. End Ave., N.Y., N.Y. 10028.

SAVELL, TARIS ISABEL, Special Events Dir., Wms. Commentator, WNVY, 1415 N. Spring St., Pensacola, Fla. 32501, '58–; Prodr., "Canerama" show, WEAR-TV, '62–; Prog. Dir., '56–'58; TV-Radio Mirror aw., '65; UP cert., '62; U.S. C. of C. aw., '63; Who's Who of Am. Wm.; Who's Who in the South; Dic. of Intl. Biog.; 2,000 Wm. of Achiev.; Personalities of the South; La. State Univ., BA, '54; b. Selma, Ala.; p. Bernard and Minnie Savell; res: 1415 N. Spring St., Pensacola, Fla. 32501.

SAVITCH, JESSICA BETH, Adm. Asst., Free-lance On-air Talent, Columbia Broadcasting System, 51 W. 52nd St., N.Y., N.Y. 10019, '69–; Prom. Asst., '68–'69; Staff Anncr., WBBF Radio (Rochester, N.Y.), '66–'68; Assoc. Prodr., Trans Media, Inc., '66–'68; Staff Anncr., WOND Radio (Atlantic City, N.J.), '62–'64; Alpha Epsilon Rho (Alpha Omega Chptr. Rec. Secy.); Ithaca Col., BS (TV-Radio), '68; b. Wilmington, Del., 1947; res: 34–41 71st St., Jackson Heights, N.Y. 11372.

SAVOLA, JUDITH BABICH, Reptr., Radio KUIK (Hillsboro, Ore.), '67; PR, News Dir., Wash. County Fair, '67; Reptr., Hillsboro (Ore.) Argus, '56–'63; Theta Sigma Phi; Univ. of Ore., BA (Jnlsm.), '67 (Theta Sigma Phi Matrix Table aw., '59); b. Berwyn, Ill., 1940; p. George and Helen Thompson Babich; h. Vernon Victor Savola, Jr.; c. Thomas, Kathryn; res: 2132 Balsam Blvd., Port Orchard, Wash. 98366.

SAVOYA, EDNA HICKS, Head Ref. Librn., Miami Public Library, 1 Biscayne Blvd., Miami, Fla. 33132, '51–; Br. Librn., '47–'50; Librn., Manhasset (N.Y.) HS, '36–'47; Librn., Port Jervis (N.Y.) HS, '34–'36; Law Librn., N.Y. State Supreme Ct. (Elmira), '34; Ed., "Diabetes for Diabetics" ('68, '65); ALA, Fla. Lib. Assn., Dade County Lib. Assn.; N.Y. State Col., BS (Lib. Sci.), '33; N.Y.U., Hunter Col.; b. Hornell, N.Y., 1911; p. Walter and Mabel Walrath Hicks; h. Charles Savoya; res: 97 Campina Ct., Coral Gables, Fla. 33134.

SAYERS, ELLISEVA, Wtr., Ed., PR Cnslt.; PR for many fgn. govt. agencies: Japan, Portugal, etc., Cnslt., wines; OPC, FPA; Wine & Food Soc., Trinity Col. (Dublin, Ireland), BA; b. Cork, Ireland; p. Jacob and Hilda Talpis Sayers; res: 727 Park Ave., N.Y., N.Y. 10021.

SAYLOR, NEVILLE SWAIM, Tchr., Poet; Colmst., Ed., "Poetry Review," Southern Standard; WNBA, Poets Round Table of Ark., Auths., Composers, and Artists Soc. of Ark., Nat. Fedn. of State Poetry Socs.; various prizes, state, local poetry contests; Ouachita Univ., BA, '44; Henderson State Col., MSE, '69; b. Ark.; p. Neval and Eunice Bennett Swaim; h. Earney Saylor (dec.); c. Cheryll, Anita, Jeanne, Allen, Jack; res: 1303 Wilson St., Arkadelphia, Ark. 71923.

SAYRE, CHARLOTTE C., Assoc. Prod. Mgr., American Chemical Society, 1155 16th St., N.W., Wash., D.C. 20036, '69–; Assoc. Ed., Prod., '53–'69; Asst. Ed., Prod., '45–'53; Edtl. Asst., Prod., '36–'45; Proofreader, Mack Printing Co. (Easton, Pa.), '33–'36; active in civic, ch. groups; Wilson Col., AB, '32; b. Easton, Pa., 1912; p. George B. and Margaret J. Cowling Sayre; res: 2001 N. Adams St., Arlington, Va. 22201.

SCANLON, MARION STEPHANY, Prof. of Health Educ., Marygrove College, 8425 W. McNichols Rd., Detroit, Mich. 48221, '51–; Auth: "Trails of the French Explorers" ('56); seven stories in light verse for children; two children's prose stories; Am. Assn. for Health, Physical Educ. and Recreation, NLAPW (aw., '61), AAUW, Theta Upsilon; Univ. of Mich. drama aw., '43; Ripon Col., Bph; Univ. of Wis., MS, '36; b. Lanesboro, Minn.; p. Cornelius and Margaret Rafferty Scanlan; res: Box 246, Lanesboro, Minn. 55949.

SCARBROUGH, LINDA CLAIRE, Sci. Wtr., New York Daily News, 220 E. 42nd St., N.Y., N.Y. 10017, '67–; Publr., Owner, The Granger (Tex.) News; Univ. of Okla., '62–'64; George Wash. Univ., BA, '66; b. Austin, Tex., 1945; p. Don and Clara Sterns Scarbrough.

SCHACHNE, MIRA, Pic. Rschr., Cowles Communications, 488 Madison Ave., N.Y., N.Y. 10022, '59–; CBS, '57–'59; N.Y. Public Lib., '56–'57; Bklyn. Public Lib., '52–'56; free-lance pic. rsch., photog.; Am. Soc. of Pic. Pfsnls.; Bklyn. Col., BA (English); b. Bklyn., N.Y., 1935; p. Henry and Sally Cohen Schachne; res: 8900 Boulevard East, North Bergen, N.J. 07047.

SCHACHT, BEULAH M., Assoc., Lemoine Skinner, Jr. Public Relations, Inc., 111 N. Fourth St., St. Louis, Mo. 63102, '67–; Feature Wtr., Colmst., St. Louis Globe-Democrat, '44–'67; various organizations; b. St. Louis, Mo. 1920; p. Milford and Beulah Brown Schacht; res: 4933 McPherson, St. Louis, Mo. 63108.

SCHACHT, JOY CRITCHETT, Wtr., Ed.; Asst. in pubns., Univ. Rels. Off., Univ. of Northern Ia., '66–'68; Asst., News Info. Svcs.; Copy Ed., Physical Educ. for Elementary Schs., '65–'66; Free-lance Copy Ed., bk. manuscripts, Ia. State Univ. Press (Ames), '63; Proofreader, '61–'62; Staff Wtr., Wms. Dept., Des Moines (Ia.) Register & Tribune, '56–'58; Theta Sigma Phi (Ia. State Univ. (Ames) Student Chptr. Adviser, '61–'62); civic groups; Grinnell Col.; Am. Inst. of Bus., '53; Univ. of Colo., '57; Drake Univ., BA, '59; b. Carroll, Ia., 1934; p. George and Gretchen Joy Critchett; h. Carroll J. Schacht; res: 1212 W. Seventh St., Cedar Falls, Ia. 50613.

SCHAEFER, DORIS MARIE, Mgr., Info. Svcs., AAI Corporation, P.O. Box 6767, Balt., Md. 21204, '58–; Staff Asst., Pers., '53–'58; Supvsr., Film Lib., Radiology Dept., Johns Hopkins Hosp., '50–'53; Asst. Byr., Stewart's, '47–'50; Staff Asst., Pers., Glenn L. Martin Co., '43–'47; U.S. Employment Svc., '41–'43; Contrbr., "Practical Supervision," Palmer J. Kalsem (McGraw Hill, '45); various orgs.; Goucher Col., AB (Eng., French), '38; b. Chesapeake City, Md., 1917; p. William and Marie Chambers Schaefer; res: 802 Mockingbird Lane, Towson, Md. 21204.

SCHAEFER, RUTH CRANE, Dir., Wms. Activities, WMAL-AM, TV, '44–'55; Dir., Wms. Activities, WJR (Detroit, Mich.), '28–'44; daily scheduled TV prog.; Pioneer, comml. radio, rated one of foremost wm. on air; work, patterns of prod., govt. agcys., civic orgs., bus., others; Guest Instr., radio, TV, schs., univs., other groups; collaborated, several bks.; Wms. Adv. Club of Wash. (Pres., '45–'46), ANWC (Pres., '53–'55), WNPC (First VP, '49–'50), Nat. Assn. of Wm. Bdcstrs. (Nat. Pres., '47–'48); Florence Crittenton Home (Bd.); Northwestern Univ., '21–'24; courses, other univs.; b. Springfield, Mo., 1902; p. A. M. and Nora Belle O'Neal Franklin; h. William H. Schaefer; res: 3901 Connecticut Ave. N.W., Wash., D.C. 20008.

SCHAEFFER, HENRI-BELLA, Artist-Painter, 111 Bank St., N.Y., N.Y. 10014; represented in permanent collections, Norfolk (Va.) Museum of Art and Scis.; Butler Inst. of Am. Art, Youngstown, Oh.; LeMoyne Col., Memphis, Tenn.; Fla. Southern Col.; one-man, group, travelling shows; Am. Fedn. of Arts, Nat. Artists Equity Assn. (Secy., '62–'66); Advisory Mbr., Marquis Biographical Lib. Soc.; listed in numerous dirs.; b. N.Y.C.; p. Leon and Luba Tchleschew Schaffer; h. Themis DeVitis.

SCHAFER, PATRICIA GAYLE, Ed., Bank Pubn., PR Asst., First National Bank, #1 Burnet Plaza, Ft. Worth, Tex. 76102, '64–; PR Asst., '63–; Sr. Transit Cl., '62; Pers. Asst., '61; Control Cl., Proof Dept., '58–'60; IEA (Ft. Worth Chmn. of Bd.; Pres., '68), Bus. Builders (Pres.), Ft. Worth Press Club, Am. Inst. of Banking (completed col. level bank courses); b. Ft. Worth, Tex., 1940; p. Harry A. and Ella Mae Schafer; res: 6900 Meadowbrook Dr., Ft. Worth, Tex. 76112.

SCHAFRAN, LYNN HECHT, Art Critic, Auth.; Project Assoc., Department of Exhibitions, Museum of Modern Art, 11 W. 53rd St., N.Y., N.Y. 10019, '66–; Edtl. Assoc., Art News, '67–; Instr., Art Hist., Smith Col., '65–'66; Asst. to Curator, Gallery of Modern Art, '64–'66; Smith Col., BA (magna cum laude), '62; Columbia Univ., MA (Art Hist.), '65; b. N.Y.C.; p. David and Gery Schaeffer Hecht; h. L. G. Schafran; c. David Spencer.

SCHANZER, BEVERLY M., Prodr.-Wtr., CBS News, Columbia Broadcasting System, 524 W. 57th St., N.Y., N.Y. 10021, '63–; Assoc. Prodr., Macy's Thanksgiving Parade, '69; Wtr., Cotton Bowl Parade, '69; "Dimension at Home," '69–; Polit. Rsch., '68; "Ask Betty White," '67; "Ask Betty Furness," '65–'67; Sound Reptr., Xerox Indsl. Film, '65; Co-ed., "The United States—An Aerial Close-up," '68; Wtrs. Guild of Am., Who's Who of Am. Wm.; Syracuse Univ. (Hons.), '56–'60; Hunter Col.; b. N.Y.C., 1939; p. Howard and Frances Maybaum Schanzer.

SCHARDING, GERTRUDE SEIDLER, Asst. Mgr., Press Rels., Union Carbide Corp., 270 Park Ave., N.Y.,

N.Y. 10017; active in press rels. since '44; Kappa Tau Alpha; Am. Nwsp. Publrs. Assn. Jnlsm. aw., '46; N.Y.U., BS (Bus. Adm.), '50; b. Bklyn., N.Y., 1913; p. Francis and Emma Heege Seidler; h. Raymond F. Scharding (dec.); res: 120 E. 37th St., N.Y., N.Y. 10017.

SCHARF, FLORENCE C., Dir. of Adv. Packaging, and PR, Teenform, Inc., 112 W. 34th St., N.Y., N.Y. 10001, '63–; Dir. of Customer Rels., Bi-Flex Inc., '53–'63; Free-lance Cnslt.; contrbr. of articles to wms. apparel mags.; Underfashions Club, Adv. Club of N.Y., AWNY, Fashion Group; ADDY Aw., for sls. prom. material; Brandeis Univ., BA; N.Y.U.; City Col.; New Sch. for Soc. Rsch.; res: 2 Horatio St., N.Y., N.Y. 10014.

SCHAUER, CATHARINE GUBERMAN, Coordr. of Public Info., Macon Junior College, Macon, Ga., '69–; Co-Adviser, yrbk., nwsp., '69; Ed., Fac. Nwsltr., '69; Tchr., '67, '68; Sponsor, lit. mag., jr. high sch.; Nwsp. Colmst., Dade County Times Un., '62–'63; Theta Sigma Phi (col. scholarship), Nat. Educ. Assn., Nat. Cncl. of the Tchrs. of Eng., Ga. Educ. Assn.; Miami Dade Jr. Col., Assoc. of Arts, '65 (Co-ed., col. nwsp., '64; 1st pl., news, feature writing, Fla. Jr. Col. Press Assn., '65); Univ. of Miami, BEduc., '67 (Nwsp. Copy Ed., Staff Wtr., '66); b. Woodbury, N.J., 1945; p. Jack and Anna Felipe Guberman; h. Irwin Schauer; res: 255 Hartley Ave., Macon, Ga. 31204.

SCHEIBLA, SHIRLEY HOBBS, Auth., "Poverty Is Where the Money Is" (Arlington House, '68); Wash. Ed., Barron's Weekly, '59–; Lectr.; Wash. Corr., Newport News (Va.) Daily Press, Richmond News Leader, '48–'52; Wash. Staff Corr., Wall Street Journal, '43–'48; numerous mag. articles; WNPC, ANWC (Corr. Secy., '51); Col. of William and Mary, '38–'39; Univ. of N.C., BA (Jnlsm.), '41 (Chi Delta Phi); b. Newport News, Va., 1919; p. Wade and Maude Bean Hobbs; h. Louis Scheibla; c. Louis, III; res: 6630 Tansey Dr., Falls Church, Va. 22042.

SCHEIFELE, KATHLEEN SAYRE, Assoc. Ed., University of Arizona Press, Box 3398, College Station, Tucson, Ariz. 85700, '67–; Asst. Ed., '60–'67; Phi Alpha Theta; Univ. of Ariz., BA (Hist., Anthropology), '51; b. Royal Oak, Mich., 1930; p. Webster and Lucilla Porter Scheifele; res: 3025 N. Dickson Dr., Tucson, Ariz. 85716.

SCHEIRMAN, MARIAN THOMSON, Wtr., Union of Independent Colleges of Art; Poet, "The Gaylon Stacy TV Show" (Okla. City); Theta Sigma Phi (Okla. City Chptr. Pres., '54–'56), Okla. Wtrs. Club, Okla. Poetry Soc.; Univ. of Kan., BS (Jnlsm.), '46; b. Irving, Kan.; p. R. G. and Irl Browning Thomson; h. William Schierman; c. David, John, Margaret, Kathleen; res: 5201 W. 99th St., Overland Park, Kan. 66207.

SCHELL, CAROL ELBIN, Prom., Pubcty Mgr., WNYS-TV, Shoppington, Syracuse, N.Y. 13214, '62–;

Asst. Prom. Mgr., WCPO-TV (Cinn., Oh.), '60–'61, '56–'59; Asst., Adv.-Prom. Dept., KRCA-TV (Hollywood, Cal.), '59; AWRT (Central N.Y. Chptr. VP, '65–'66), Am. Cancer Soc.; U.S. Air Force recruiting aw., '63, '69; Cinn. Col., BFA, '59; b. Morgantown, W. Va., 1937; p. Harry and Gertrude Simms Elbin; h. Charles Schell; c. Karen Denise; res: 113 Rutledge St., Syracuse, N.Y. 13214.

SCHELLENBERG, HELENE CHAMBERS, Crtv. Writing Tchr., Fremont & San Lorenzo School Districts, 36119 Fanshawe Ct., Fremont, Cal. 94536, '61–; Auth: "Breath of Life" ('68), "Nurse's Journey" ('64), two other bks.; Cal. Wtrs. Club, Fremont Wtrs., Pacifica Wtrs.; Who's Who of Am. Wm.; San Diego State Col., '34–'37; b. Saskatoon, Can.; p. Stanley and Lillian Lancaster Chambers; h. Carl Schellenberg (dec.); c. Carl S.

SCHENKER, TILLIE ABRAMSON, Head Librn., East Baton Rouge Parish Library, 700 Laurel St., Baton Rouge, La. 70802, '47–; Asst. Librn., '39–'46; Field Worker, La. State Lib., '34–'39; ALA, La. Lib. Assn. (Pres., '62–'63), Baton Rouge Lib. Club; La. State Univ., BS, '30; BS (Lib. Sci.), '34; b. Baton Rouge, La., 1910; p. Abraham and Mathilde Mendelsohn Abramson; h. Max Schenker (dec.); res: 220 Steele Blvd., Baton Rouge, La. 70806.

SCHERLING, MARILYN BEASON, Partner, Adv., Osborne County Farmer, 210 W. Main St., Osborne, Kan. 67473, '64–; Adv. Sls., '58–; Theta Sigma Phi; Kan. State Univ., BS (Tech. Jnlsm.); b. Athol, Kan., 1930; p. Harold and Murle Munson Beason; h. Christian Scherling; c. Deborah, Susan, Sydney, Dane; res: 121 N. Fifth St., Osborne, Kan. 67473.

SCHERMAN, BERNARDINE KIELTY, Edtl. Dept., Book of the Month Club, 280 Park Ave., N.Y., N.Y. 10017, '38; Auth: "Girl from Fitchburg" (Random House, '64), "Jenny Lind Sang Here" (Houghton Mifflin), three others; Ladies Home Journal, '43–'61; Story Magazine, '33–'38; h. Harry Scherman.

SCHERR, BARBARA JEAN, Free-lance Wtr., Ed., PR, '69–; Pub. Rel. Wtr., Blue Cross, '68–'69; Ed., house organ, '66–'68; Edtl. Asst., Promenade Magazine, '65–'66; Boy Scouts of Am., '63–'65; Corr., Approach nwsp., '69; Ed., Guiding Eyes for Blind's Guide Lines nwsltr., '69; Contrbr., Off. Supvsrs. Bul.; Theta Sigma Phi, N.Y. Assn. of Indsl. Communicators, ICIE (Hon. Mention, Evaluation and Aw. Program, '67), Jr. Friends of Ch. 13 (Educ. TV); Univ. of Cal., Berkeley, BA (Social Sci.), '63; N.Y.U., grad. studies (human rel.), '69; b. Richmond Hill, N.Y., 1941; p. James and Ruth November Scherr; res: 431 E. 87th St., N.Y., N.Y. 10028.

SCHETTERER, JUNE TRAVER, Reptr., The Standard-Star, 251 North Ave., New Rochelle, N.Y. 10801, '48–; Free-lance Artist, '63–; Lectr., children's bk. illus., N.Y.U., '68; PBA of New Rochelle aw., achiev. in

Jnlsm. and commty. svc., '66; Alleghany Col., BA, '48 (cum laude; Phi Beta Kappa; hons. in English; Kappa Kappa Gamma Prize, Doan Prize); post-grad., N.Y.U., Col. of New Rochelle; b. Beaver Falls, Pa., 1926; p. Harry and Ruth Gowell Traver; h. George Schetterer; res: 60 Locust Ave., New Rochelle, N.Y. 10801.

SCHEXNAYDER, CHARLOTTE TILLAR, Ed., Co-publr., The Dumas Clarion, Clarion Publishing Co., 136 E. Waterman, Dumas, Ark. 71639, '54–; Ed., The McGehee (Ark.) Times, '48–'53, '44–'46; Edtl. Asst., La. State Univ. Ext. Svc., '43; various organizations; Ark. A & M Col., '40–'42 (Alumni Bd.); Univ. of Chgo., '42; La. State Univ., BA, '44; Grad. work, '46–'47; b. Tillar, Ark., 1923; p. Jewell and Bertha Terry Tillar; h. Melvin J. Schexnayder, Sr.; c. Melvin John, Jr., Stephen Maurice, Sarah Elizabeth; res: 322 Court St., Dumas, Ark. 71639.

SCHIELD, MARGARET STEWARD, Circ. Mgr., Cody Publications, Verona, Kissimmee, Fla. 32741, '64–; Secy., '61–'64; Ia. State Dept. of Social Welfare; Wartburg Col. (Waverly, Ia.), (Bus.), '40–'41; b. Waverly, Ia., 1922; p. Roy and Gertrude E. Flin Steward; h. Preston T. Schield; c. Susan Kay (Mrs. Allen Kowalsky, Kathleen, Steven, Annette; res: 207 Marion Ave., Kissimmee, Fla. 32741.

SCHIFF, DOROTHY, Ed.-in-Chief, Publr., New York Post Corp., 210 South St., N.Y., N.Y. 10002, '62–; Publr., '42–; Owner, VP, Treas., '39–; 1969 Citizens Un. Cit. "in recognition of her distg. svc. in the field of journalism"; Brearley Sch., '12–'20; Bryn Mawr, '20–'21; b. N.Y.C., 1903; p. Mortimer and Adele Neustadt Schiff; c. Mortimer W. Hall, Mrs. Adele Leopold, Mrs. Werner H. Kramarsky.

SCHIFFELER, MARJORIE WINTERMUTE, Chmn., Art Dept., Tuller College, 5870 E. 14th St., Tucson, Ariz. 85711, '67–; private art work; Art Cnslt., commty. events, (Carmel, Cal.); Guest Exhibitor, Legion of Honour (S.F., Cal.), State Capital of Va.; Carmel (Cal.) Art Assn.; N.Y. Art Students' League Scholarship, '18, '19; "Prixe Rome," Paris, '21; 1st, Tucson (Ariz.) Art Festival, '66–'69; private tutoring (Europe); b. S.F., Cal., 1904; p. Dr. George P. and Ida L. Culver Wintermute; h. Charles Schiffeler; c. John William; res: 50 Pine Terr., Tiburon, Cal. 94920.

SCHIFMAN, YSOBEL SANDLER, Pres., Ysobel Sandler Advertising, Inc., 1 Gramercy Park, N.Y., N.Y. 10003, '53–; Acct. Exec., Shaller Rubin Co., '50–'53; D. H. Ahrend Co., '43–'50; Partner, Universal Stenographic Svc., '39–'43; WNBA, League of Adv. Agcys. (Treas., '58–'60; Bd. of Dirs., '60–'68); City Col.; b. N.Y.C.; p. Max and Alice Rosenfield Gundersheimer; h. Harold Schifman; res: 90 Boulder Rd., Manhasset, N.Y. 11030.

SCHILDT, SYLVIA, Copy Chief, Sls. Prom. Supvsr., Interstate Department Stores—RMA Division, 76 Ninth Ave., N.Y., N.Y. 10011, '66–; Sr. Wtr., W. T.

Grant, '64–'66; Adv. Dir., Loweth National, '62–'64; Asst. Adv. Dir., Steinberg-Kass, '60–'62; Wtr., Macy's, '59–'60; AWNY slogan aw.; City Col. of N.Y., '55 (poetry aw.); b. Bklyn., N.Y., 1934; p. Isidore and Esther Basson Siegel; h. Frank J. Schildt; c. Christiaan C.

SCHILLER, SUE ANN, Art Dir., Nadler & Larimer Advertising, 225 Madison Ave., N.Y., N.Y. 10016, '69–; Art Dir., Daniel & Charles, '68–'69; Art Dir., Kenyon & Eckhardt, '65–'66; Asst. Art Dir., Van Brunt & Co., '64–'65; Adv. Age selection of top 100 nat. ads, '67; Mich. State Univ., BA, '60; Art Ctr. Sch. (L.A.), BPA, '63; res: 280 Riverside Dr., Apt. 7-K, N.Y., N.Y. 10025.

SCHILLING, REAN A., Ed., Reeves Instrument Div. of DCA, East Gate Blvd., Garden City, N.Y. 11530, '67–; Prom. Dir., Walt Whitman Shopping Ctr. (Huntington, N.Y.); Staff Wtr., Sportsmens Life Magazine; L.I. Communicators Assn. (VP, '68–); Douglas Col., '46; Hofstra Univ., BA, '49; c. Peter, Carroll; res: 88 W. Shore Dr., Massapequa, N.Y. 11578.

SCHIMELFENIG, GRACE O'MALLEY, Exec. Secy., WVIA-TV, Box 4444, Scranton, Pa. 18509, '67–; ABWA (Lackawanna Chptr. Rec. Secy.), AWRT (Rec. Secy.; Northeastern Pa. Chptr. Mbrship. Chmn.); b. Scranton, Pa.; p. William and Ann O'Malley; h. John Schimelfenig; c. John, Mari; res: 1217 Linden St., Scranton, Pa. 18510.

SCHINDLER, CRIS HALL, Ed., Maison Blanche, P.O. Box 60820, N.O., La. 70160, '53–; UP, '52–'53; Clarion-Ledger (Jackson, Miss.), '49–'52; ICIE, Southern Cncl. of Indsl. Eds.; Millsaps Col., BA, '49; h. John Schindler; c. two sons; res: 3501 River Oaks Dr., N.O., La. 70114.

SCHLANSKER, JANE TURK, Wtr., Witherspoon & Associates, Inc., 321 S. Henderson St., Ft. Worth, Tex. 76101, '67–; Engineering Wtr., Gen. Dynamics Corp., '66–'67 (Good Design/Fine Worksmanship aw.); Adm. Asst., TV Dept., Univ. of Colo., '65–'66; Adm. Asst., NAEB, '65; Teaching Asst., Univ. of Kan., '63–'64; AWRT (Fort Worth Chptr. Corr. Secy.), Alpha Epsilon Rho, Theta Sigma Phi; Who's Who of Am. Wm.; DePauw Univ., BA, '63; Univ. of Kan., '63–'64; b. Indpls., Ind., 1940; p. Laurel and Esther Liebig Turk; h. William B. Schlansker; res: 2822 Princeton St., Ft. Worth, Tex. 76109.

SCHLATTER, JANET McNAUGHTON, Free-lance Wtr.; NLAPW, Theta Sigma Phi; Milw.-Downer Col., BA, '34; Univ. of Wis., MA, '36; b. Wausau, Wis.; p. George and Irma Hackendahl McNaughton; h. Edward Bunker Schlatter; c. Carol, James, Charles; res: 1143 Amherst Dr., Madison, Wis. 53705.

SCHLEIGER, GLADYS SOMMERS, Ed., State Farm Insurance Companies, 5901 O St., Lincoln, Neb. 68510 '64–; ICIE; Univ. of Neb.; b. Lincoln, Neb., 1936; p. Christian and Ada Kriegar Sommers; h. Robert Schleiger; c. James Lee, Karen Jo, Nancy Ann; res: 7251 Kearney Ave., Lincoln, Neb. 68507.

SCHLOSS, SYLVIA SHEATH, Acc. Mgr., Arndt, Preston, Chapin, Lamb and Keen, Inc., 375 Park Ave., N.Y., N.Y. 10022, '68–; Assoc. Ed., Home Furnishings Daily, '66–'68; Publicist, Macy's, '64–'66; Foote, Cone and Belding (London, England); Asst. Fashion Byr., Farmer's Dept. Store (Sydney, Australia); NHFL; Univ. of Sydney, BA; Julian Ashton Art Sch.; N.Y. Sch. of Interior Design; b. Auckland, New Zealand, 1937; p. Alan and Marjorie Palmer Sheath; h. Stuart Schloss; res: 4 East 89th St., N.Y., N.Y. 10028.

SCHMID, LINDA McCAUSLAND, Conslt., Art Educ., KQED-TV, 525 Fourth St., S.F., Cal. 94107; Instr. of Art, Col. of Notre Dame (Belmont), '67–; Asst. Prof. of Art, S.F. State Col., '69; Tchr., Cal. and Tex. Schs., '56–'67; Wtr., Talent, Children's Art Series, KLRN-TV (Austin, Tex.), '62–'64; Wtr.-Talent, three nationally distrb. children's TV series (Art Studio, '65–; You & Eye, '67–; Art Studio Too, '68–); Published: NAEB Jnl., '63; The Educ. Digest, '63; Lectr., Conslt. for various art assns.; Aws: NET for excellence in childrens programming, '66; Am. Legion, '68; U.C.L.A., BA, '56; Univ. of Tex., MFA, '64 (Phi Kappa Phi); b. Union Town, Pa., 1934; p. Joseph Vanderlin and Laurette Rachael Scott McCausland; h. John Schmid; c. Ann V.; res: 61 Central Ave., S.F., Cal. 94117.

SCHMIDT, AGATHA G., Rsch. Dir., National Review Magazine, "Firing Line" TV Show, 150 E. 35th St., N.Y., N.Y. 10016, '65–; rsch. on "The Unmaking of a Mayor" (Viking, '66), "Did You Ever See A Dream Walking" (Bobbs-Merrill, '70) and other bks. by William F. Buckley, Jr.; Manhattanville Col., BA (Philosophy), '59; b. N.Y.C., 1940; p. Godfrey and Grace Hunt Schmidt; res: 250 E. 63rd St., N.Y., N.Y. 10021.

SCHMIDT, AUDREY MARIE, Ed., Geigy Division, McGraw Hill Book Company, 330 E. 42nd St., N.Y., N.Y. 10036, '69–; Tchrs. Sec. Ed., Today's Secretary, Educ. Dir., '62–'69; High Sch. Tchr., L.I., '54–'62; Gregg Shorthand Tchrs. Assn. (Pres., '62–'63; Exec. Secy., '63–), Supvsrs. and Admrs. Assn., BPW, Nat. Bus. Educ. Assn., Bus. Educ. Assn. of N.Y.; Bus. Educ. Index; N.Y.U., BS (Bus. Educ.), '54; MA (Intl. Rels.), '61; b. Springfield Gardens, N.Y., 1929; p. Joseph and Marion Bruna Schmidt; res: 200 E. 74th St., N.Y., N.Y. 10021.

SCHMIDT, MARIAN H., Radio Sls., KARR & KOPR, FM Radio Station, 1900 Third St. N.W., Great Falls, Mont. 59401; Radio KFBB; AWRT (Treas., '69), Adv. Club; b. Great Falls, Mont., 1917; p. T. Charles and Lillian Pappin Hibbard; c. Mrs. Vicki Buffington; res: 2018 Fifth Ave. N., Great Falls, Mont. 59401.

SCHMIDT, VICTORIA DABROWSKI, Exec. VP, Communications Council, Inc., Seven Park St., Montclair, N.J. 07042, '58–; AE, Roy Bernard Co. (N.Y.C.), '57–'58; PR, Fashion Coordr., Owens Corning Fiber Glass, '53–'57; Fashion Ed., Wms. Day Magazine, '50–'53; Pubcty., Sls. Prom., L. Bamberger & Co. (Newark, N.J.), '48–'50; Fashion Group, NHFL, various others; Douglass Col., BA (Eng.), '42 (Alumnae Assn. Dir., '61–'66; Pres., '66–'67); b. E. Orange, N.J.; p. Eugene and Emily Gocek Dabrowski; h. Ralph Schmidt; c. Lisa Karen; res: Post Kennel Rd., Bernardsville, N.J. 07924.

SCHNEIDER, CAROL EITINGON, Pubcty. Dir., Praeger Publishers, Inc., 111 Fourth Ave., N.Y., N.Y. 10003, '65–; Pubcty., John Wiley & Sons; McGraw-Hill; Wellesley Col., BA, '63 (Phi Beta Kappa); h. William J. Schneider.

SCHNEIDER, JANE ELEANOR, Dir. of Pubns., Cincinnati Symphony Orchestra, 1313 Central Trust Tower, Cinn., Oh. 45202, '68–; Asst. Dir. of PR, '67–; Copywtr., Un. Central Life Ins., '66–'67; PR Asst., Paul Werth Assocs., '65–'66; Public Info., Oh. Highway Dept., '64–'65; Theta Sigma Phi (Columbus Chptr. Secy., '65–'66), Who's Who of Am. Wm.; Oh. State Univ., BA, '64; b. Dayton, Oh., 1942; p. Robert C. and Mildred E. McManaman Schneider; res: 3017 Montana Ave., Cinn., Oh. 45211.

SCHNEIDER, M. J. WEBER, Ed., The Boyertown Times, Berks-Mont Newspapers, Inc., 52 S. Reading Ave., Boyertown, Pa. 19512, '66–; Keystone Press Aw. for best edtl. in Pa. weekly nwsp., '68; Albright Col. (Reading, Pa.), BS, '45; h. Robert H. Schneider; c. Martha, Marcus, Henry, Michael, Lars, Brian, Stephanie, David, Douglas; res: RD 1, Boyertown, Pa. 19512.

SCHNEIDER, RITA MARIE, Edtl. Dir., Equipment & House Ed., What's New in Home Economics, Reuben H. Donnelley Corp., 466 Lexington Ave., N.Y., N.Y. 10017, '68–; Equipment & House Ed., '66–; N.E. Field Home Econst., Housewares Div., GE Co., '64–'66; Better Homes and Gardens, '62–'64; Home Econst., Major Appliance Div., GE Co., '56–'62; Home Econst., Graybar Electric Co., '52–'56; Home Svc. Rep., Appalachian Power Co., '49–'52; Am. Home Econs. Assn., Home Econsts. in Bus. (N.Y.C. Group Chmn., '68–'69), NHFL, Electrical Wms. Round Table (N.Y.C. Group Treas., '65–'66), Am. Assn. of Housing Educs.; consumer info. aws., '69, '67; Seton Hill Col., BS (Home Econs. Educ.), '49; b. Cleve., Oh., 1928; p. Edward and Marie Byrne Schneider; res: 300 E. 33rd St., N.Y., N.Y. 10016.

SCHNEIDER, SARAH JULIAN, PR Dir., St. Margaret Memorial Hospital, 265 46th St., Pitt., Pa. 15201, '67–; PR Asst., '66–'67; Staff Wtr., Jewish Chronicle Nwsp., '66; Feature Ed., Suburban Commty. Nwsps., '66; PR Soc. of Western Pa. Hosps., Theta Sigma Phi (Pittsburgh Chptr. Secy., '68–'69); Duquesne Univ., BA (Jnlsm.), '67; b. Detroit, Mich., 1945; p. John and Theresa Cavallaro Julian; h. Charles J. Schneider, III; res: #307, 9802 Presidential Dr., Allison Park, Pa. 15101.

SCHNURMANN, ERIKA, Dir., Kearny Public Library, 318 Kearny Ave., Kearny, N.J. 07032; Formerly Dir., Little Falls (N.J.) Public Lib., Hawthorne (N.J.) Public Lib., Wayne (N.J.) Public Lib.; Head of PR Dept., Paterson (N.J.) Public Lib.; N.J. Lib. Assn. (Past Treas.), Lib. PR Cncl., ALA, NLAPW, AAUW, Intl. Platform Assn.; Pembroke Col., AB, '37; Columbia Univ., MS (Lib. Sci.), '47; b. Paterson, N.J.; p. Karl and Martha Buegen Schnurmann; res: 234 E. 18th St., Paterson, N.J. 07524.

SCHOEN, EILEEN FICKS, Ed., The National Humane Review, The American Humane Association, P.O. Box 1266, Denver, Colo. 80201, '57–; Asst. Ed., Fed. Reserve Bank of N.Y., '56–'57; Asst. Ed., Fawcett Pubns., '56; Edtl. Asst., Cosmopolitan, '55–'56; Colo. Indsl. Press Assn. (Pres., '66–'67; VP; Treas.), ICIE, Intl. Platform Assn., Theta Sigma Phi; W. Va. Univ., BSJ, '55; N.Y.U., '55–'56; b. Brownsville, Pa., 1933; p. I. J. and Hanna Silver Ficks; h. Kenneth Shoen; res: 1841 S. Ivanhoe St., Denver, Colo. 80222.

SCHOENBERGER, PODINE, Sci. Ed., Times-Picayune, 3800 Howard Ave., N.O., La.; formerly Fashion Ed., Religious Ed., Gen. Assign. Reptr.; Theta Sigma Phi, Delta Delta Delta, Press Club of N.O. (former 2nd VP, Bd. Mbr.), La. Press Women; Who's Who of Am. Wm.; Who's Who in Southwest; numerous writing aws.; Am. Cancer Soc. (nat. aw.), NFPW (two nat. aws.), Am. Dental Assn. (nat. aw.), Arthritis Fndn. (reg. aw.); Orleans Club (hon. mbr.); La. State Univ., BA; Columbia Univ.; b. Baton Rouge, La.; p. George and Podine Pope Schoenberger; res: 622 Audubon Street, N.O., La.

SCHOENTHAL, HARRIET GORDON, AE, Harold J. Siesel Co., 845 Third Ave., N.Y., N.Y., '62–; formerly Dir., Adv. and PR, Harvey Probber; PR Dir., Heywood-Wakefield Co.; Wtr., articles for Budget Decorating, '69; NHFL (N.Y. Chptr. Membership VP, '68–'69), AWRT; b. Albany, N.Y.; p. Martin and Minna Landau Gordon; res: 207 E. 74th St., N.Y., N.Y. 10021.

SCHOONMAKER, EMMA FARRIS, Mng. Ed., Copublr., Schoonmaker Publishers, 307 E. Main St., Sentinel, Okla. 73664, '58–; Co-publr., '55–; Okla. Press Assn., Sentinel C. of C.; various edtl. aws.; Okla. Sch. of Nursing, '51–'52; Southwestern State Col., '66–'67; h. Wayne Schoonmaker; c. Kenneth Wayne, Mark Lynn, Dan Allan, Brian Scott; res: 122 N. Seventh St., Sentinel, Okla. 73664.

SCHOONOVER, JEAN WAY, Partner, Dudley-Anderson-Yutzy, 551 Fifth Ave., N.Y., N.Y. 10017, '50–; Partner, '68–; formerly News and Packaging Ed., Food Field Reporter; Pennsylvania Railroad rep.; High Sch. English Tchr., Librn., Castleton, N.Y.; AWRT (Pres. Cabinet), PRSA; Cornell Univ., BA, '41 (Kappa Delta Epsilon; Pi Lambda Theta); N.Y. State Col. at Albany; b. Richfield Springs, N.Y., 1920; p. Walter and Hilda Greenawalt Way; h. Raymond Schoonover; c. Katherine, Charles D., James A.; res: 25 Stuyvesant St., N.Y., N.Y. 10003.

SCHOR, RHEA KAY, Sculptor, 22 E. 17th St., N.Y., N.Y. 10003; Auth., non-fiction, poetry bks.; Sculpture Tchr., Buswick HS, '63–'66; Ed., Poetry Press, '54–'60; represented in many permanent collections; one-man show, Barzansky Galleries, '56; Nat. Assn. of Wm. Artists, Cosmopolitan Artists (Founder, First Pres.), Intl. Exhibtns. (Founder, Dir.), Sculpture Ctr. of N.Y. (Life Mbr.), NLAPW; Who's Who in Am. Art; Who's Who of Am. Wm.; other dirs.; Huntington Hartford Fndn. Fellowship, '59; Intl. Arts and Ltrs. Fellowship, '60; New Sch. for Social Rsch., '58–'61; Sculpture Ctr., '53–'63; b. N.Y.C., 1906; p. Harry and Rose Veprik Kay; h. Aaron Jacob Schor; c. Dr. Joseph M., Robert H.; res: 255 W. 90th St., N.Y., N.Y. 10024.

SCHORR, THELMA MERMELSTEIN, Sr. Ed., American Journal of Nursing, 10 Columbus Circle, N.Y., N.Y. 10019, '62–; Assoc. Ed., '53–'62; Asst. Ed., '50–'53; Head Nurse, Bellevue Hosp., '45–'50; Am. Nurses Assn., Med. Comm. for Human Rights; Columbia Univ., BS; Bellevue Sch. of Nursing; b. New Haven, Conn., 1924; p. Simon and Rebecca Katz Mermelstein; h. Norman Schorr; c. Susan, Marjorie, Elizabeth; res: 470 West End Ave., N.Y., N.Y. 10024.

SCHOTT, BARBARA JO WOERNER, Publr., Owner, Medina Valley & County News Bulletin, Schott's Publishing Service Co., P.O. Drawer D, Castroville, Tex. 78009, '68–; Owner, '58–; Copywtr., Rucker-Rosenstock (Petersburg, Va.), '56–'57; Tex. Press Assn. (numerous aws.); b. San Antonio, Tex., 1939; p. Martin and Lillie Lipke Woerner; h. Joseph L. Schott; c. Robert Joseph, Kathryn Anne; res: P.O. Drawer D, Castroville, Tex. 78009.

SCHOVILLE, EILEEN PURDY, Ed. and Publr., Kickapoo Scout, Main St., Soldiers Grove, Wis. 54655, '67–; Prod., Copy, Howard H. Monk and Assocs. (Rockford, Ill.), '58–'67; Adv. Mgr., Yates-Am. Machine Co. (Beloit, Wis.), '55–'58; Wms. Ed., WNAR Radio (Norristown, Pa.), '51–'55; Army PR, WACs, '42–'45 (Bronze Star, '45); Bryant and Stratton Bus. Col., Buffalo, N.Y., '32–'34; b. Middleport, N.Y. 1915; p. Phillip and Mable Giles Purdy; h. Gerald Schoville; res: Rte. 3, Soldiers Grove, Wis. 54655.

SCHRAM, JOAN ISAM, Volunteer Pubcty. Chmn., Seattle Art Museum Guild, Volunteer Park, Seattle, Wash. 98102, '68–; Ed., Brighton (Colo.) Blade, '36–'39; Reptr., '35–'36; Theta Sigma Phi; extensive volunteer activities, local civic, charitable orgs.; Colo. State Univ., '30–'32; Northwestern Univ., BS, '34; Univ. of Wash., '40–'41; b. Denver, Colo., 1912; p. Alfred and Mary Hunter Isham; h. Lloyd W. Schram; c. Mrs. Deanne McBride, Brent H.; res: 5528 55th Ave., N.E., Seattle, Wash. 98105.

SCHREIBER, FLORA RHETA, Auth.; Asst. Prof. of English and Speech, Dir. of PR, John Jay College of Criminal Justice, 315 Park Ave. S., N.Y., N.Y. 10010, '64–; bks: "Your Child's Speech" (Putnam's, '56), "William Schuman" (G. Schirmer's, '54); Tchr. of speech, radio, TV in cols. since '44; Psychiatry Ed., Science Digest; Colmst., Bell McClure Synd.; Dir., Film, Radio and TV Workshop, New Sch. for Social Rsch.; numerous mag. articles on polit. personalities, psychiatry, speech, criminology, commtn., lit. criticism; Cnslt., NBC, BBDO, others; Soc. of Mag. Wtrs., Intl. Soc. of Gifted Children (Bd. Mbr.), Auths. League of Am., AAUW; Columbia Univ., '34–'39; Univ. of London, '37; N.Y.U. Radio Workshop, Museum of Modern Art Film Lib., '42; b. N.Y.C., 1918; p. William and Esther Aaronson Schreiber; res: 32 Gramercy Park S., N.Y., N.Y. 10010.

SCHREIBER, JOANNE L., Sewing Ed., Newspaper Enterprise Association, 230 Park Ave., N.Y., N.Y., '66–; PR, Y&R, '53–'65; Forstmann Woolens, '51–'53; Freelance Wtr., Publicist; Auth., "Homemaker's Handbook" (Conso Publ. Co.); NHFL (VP, '62–'63); Vassar Col., AB, '48; b. El Dorado, Ark.; p. John and Dorothy Roe Lewis; h. Charles J. Schreiber; c. Catherine, Laurie, Christopher; res: 41 Rowayton Ave., Rowayton, Conn. 06853.

SCHREIBER, NEICE, Music and Art Ed., Times/Guide Publishing Co., 4627 Ponce de Leon Blvd., Coral Gables, Fla., '67–; Gen. Assigt. Wtr., Miami Herald Publ. Co., '68; Assoc. Ed., Lowe Museum New Letter, '67–'68; Assoc. Ed., Young Democratic Monthly; Asst. Instr. of Art Hist., Univ. of Miami; Theta Sigma Phi, Fla. Wms. Press Club; Kappa Pi, Young Democratic Clubs of Fla. (Presidential Svc. Aw., '66; Young Democratic Club Svc. Aw., '67); Univ. of Miami, BA, '67 (Art Hist.); b. Miami, Fla, 1943; p. Maurice and Ann Yane Schreiber; res: 2823 S.W. 36 Ave., Miami, Fla. 33133.

SCHREPEL, CONCETTA THERESA MASCOLO, Freelance Wtr., poetry, pubcty., nwsp. features, adv.; Prodr., TV commls.; Cnslt.; Auths. Guild, Auths. League of Am.; Newark Col. of Engineering; Seton Hall; b. Bloomfield, N.J.; p. Domenick and Vincenzina Ruglio Mascolo; h. William J. Schrepel; c. John William; res: 119 Golf Rd., Bloomfield, N.J. 07003.

SCHRITT, KATHERINE SZYMECZEK, Librn., Mason City Globe-Gazette, 300 N. Washington, Mason City, Ia. 50401, '62–; b. Mason City, Ia.; p. Lawrence and Hedwega Kuscinska Szymeczek; h. Gust Schritt (div.); c. Mary Jo Ann, Frances Katherine (Mrs. J. David Watson Jr.); res: 1305 N. Carolina Pl., Mason City, Ia. 50401.

SCHROEDER, ETHEL SCHULTZ, Auth: "Science of Christianity, the Education of the Future," ('64), "Science of Christianity Syllabus" ('68); Pres., Intl. Adv. Cncl., N.Y.C., '56–; U.S.I.A., '52–'56; Psychological Strategy Bd., Wash., D.C., '51–'52; Asst. to VP, Time, Inc., '45–'49, '33–'43; Psychological Warfare Div., Allied Force Headquarters; SHAEF, Algiers, London, Paris, '43–'45; Asst. Dir., Artistic Mornings, Inc., '31–'33; Nat. City Bank, '30–'31; Travel Asst., En Route Svc., '26–'30; Ltrs. Abroad (Bd. of Dirs.); Lamb's

Bus. Col., '24–'25; Oxford Univ., Eng., summers, '48, '49; b. N.Y.C.; p. Peter and Louise Meier Schultz; h. William A. Schroeder; res: 20 E. 68th St., N.Y., N.Y. 10021; 25 Webb Rd., Westport, Conn. 06880.

SCHROEDER, EVA I. A., Assoc. Dir., Heidelberg College Library, Heidelberg College, Greenfield St., Tiffin, Oh. 44883, '68–; Prof. of Lib. Sci., State Univ. Col. (Geneseo, N.Y.), '59–'68; Visiting Librn., Tech. Svcs., Univ. of Rochester (N.Y.), '65–'66; Visiting Lectr., Univ. of Ill. (Urbana), summer '64; Visiting Librn., State Univ. of N.Y. (Buffalo), summer '63; Librn., N.Y. Public Lib., '56–'59; Instr., Univ. of Vt. (Burlington), '52–'55; Auth., articles in pfsnl. jrnls., translator of German bk.; various orgs.; Univ. of Griefswald, Germany; Univ. of Graz, Austria; Univ. of Vt.; Univ. of Berlin, PhD, '42 (cum laude); Univ. of Mich. AM (Lib. Sci.), '56; b. Belgard, Germany; p. Ernst and Elfriede Rudolph Schroeder; res: 229 Mohawk St., Tiffin, Oh. 44883.

SCHROEDER, MARCIA STEFFEN, Asst. Art Dir., WFBM Stations, 1330 N. Meridian St., Indpls., Ind. 46202, '63–; Art. Dirs. Club of Ind. (Rec. Secy., '67–'68; '68–'69); John Herron Art Sch. of Ind. Univ., '59–'63; b. Indpls., Ind., 1941; p. Anthony and Eva White Steffen; h. Carlyle Schroeder; res: 599 W. Westfield Blvd., Indpls., Ind. 46208.

SCHROEDER, MARIA DUNKL, Actress, Tech. Advisor, Script Translater, Thomas/Spelling Paramount, 780 N. Gower St., Hollywood, Cal. 90038, '69–; 20th Century Fox, '68; Nat. Gen., '68; MGM, '68; SAG; b. Vienna, Austria 1942; p. Josef and Maria Glassl Dunkl; res: 7607 Fountain Ave., Hollywood, Cal. 90046.

SCHROEDER, ZEIMA HAY, Pres., Wendt Advertising Agency, 401 Third Ave. N., Great Falls, Mont. 59401, '68–; Copywtr.; AAUW (Past Pres.), Soroptimist Club (Great Falls Past Pres.), civic, hosp. groups; Univ. of Mont., BA (Jnlsm), '28; b. Belt, Mont., 1906; p. Charles W. and Martha Beatty Hay; h. George L. Schroeder; res: 1710 Meadowlark Dr., Great Falls, Mont. 59401.

SCHUBER, MILLI ANTLER, Actress; Model; Tchr., L.A., Cal.; SAG; Univ. of Southern Cal., '54; U.C.L.A., '55; L.A. State Col., BS, '56; MS, '57; b. Newark, N.J.; p. Otto and Else Fehlauer Antler; h. Eric Schuber (div.); c. Mark Richard, Karen Jeanne; res: 312 S. Reeves Dr., Beverly Hills, Cal. 90212.

SCHUBERT, HELEN C., VP, R. S. Weeks and Associates, 2 N. Riverside Plaza, Chgo., Ill. 60606, '68–; PR, Helen Schubert, '67–'68; Adm. Dir., Nat. Design Ctr., '63–'67; PR Dir., Un. Cerebral Palsy, '62–'63; PR Rep., Smith-Bucklin, '61–'62; Wms. Dir., Philip Lesly Co., '58–'61; Wtr., tennis mags.; Contrbr., "World Bk. Yrbk."; Theta Sigma Phi (Pres., '69–'70; VP, '61–'62), Wms. Ad Club of Chgo. (Second VP, '69–'70), NHFL (Ill. Chptr. Educ. VP, '68–'69, '67–'68; Pubcty. VP,

'62–'63), AWRT, PRSA, numerous others; Univ. of Wis., BS, '52; b. Cedarburg, Wis., 1930; p. Paul H. and Edna Schmidt Schubert; res: 21 E. Bellevue Pl., Chgo., Ill. 60611.

SCHUDA, JOSEPHINE MARIE, PR Dir., Home Builders Association of Metropolitan Pittsburgh, 1105 Standard Life Bldg., Pitt., Pa. 15222, '67–; Wtr., Ed., Pubcty., Fox Grocery Co., '66–'67; Theta Sigma Phi, Associated Eds. Soc. of Pitt., Kappa Tau Alpha, Young Repls. of Mt. Lebanon; Duquesne Univ., BA, '66; b. Richmond, Va., 1944; p. Joseph and Sylvia Ronsse Schuda; res: 2391 Whited St., Pitt., Pa. 15226.

SCHULDER, DIANE BLOSSOM, Adjunct Lectr., New York University Law School, Washington Sq., N.Y., N.Y.; Lawyer; Auth., "Does the Law Oppress Women?" chptr. in Robin Morgan's "The Hand That Cradles the Rock"; Nat. Lawyers Guild; Columbia Law Sch., LLB; res: 15 W. 12th St., N.Y., N.Y. 10011.

SCHULTHEIS, BARBARA EASTWOOD, Pubcty. Mgr., R. R. Bowker Co., 1180 Ave. of Americas, N.Y., N.Y. 10036, '65–; Pubcty. Mgr., Univ. of Cal. Press, '64–'65; Sls., Prom. Asst., Holden-Day, '63–'64; Sls., Prom. Asst., Beacon Press, '60–'62; PPA, ALA; Wells Col., BA, '60; b. Englewood, N.J., 1938; p. James and Barbara Kirkby Eastwood; h. Albert Schultheis.

SCHULTHEIS, ELLEN ENGELSON, Gen. Mgr., University of Colorado Press, Regent Hall, Box 22, Boulder, Colo. 80302, '68–; Copy Ed., "Scientific Study of Unidentified Flying Objects," '68; RCA Educ. System Dept., '68; Asst. to Artist in Residence, Aspen, Colo., Summer Inst., '65; Nat. Univ. of Mexico, '63; Univ. of Wis., '64–'65; Univ. of Colo., '67–; b. Bklyn., N.Y. 1946; p. Howard and Miriam Turner Engelson; h. Robert Schultheis; c. Alexandra W.; res: 215 Chautauqua Park, Boulder, Colorado. 80302.

SCHULTZ, EDNA MOORE, Radio Bdcstr., "Thoughts Along the Way," WDCX-FM (Buffalo), Wtr., Lancaster Enterprise and Depew Herald, Clark St., Lancaster, N.Y. 14086, '53–; Auth: "They Said Kathy Was Retarded," "Mother and Daughter Banquet Ideas;" numerous published poems; Who's Who of Am. Wm., Intl. Biog. Dic.; Western N.Y. Pen Wm. light verse aw.; b. Ellettsville, Ind., 1912; p. Emerson and Anna Hinshaw Moore; h. Charles Schultz; c. C. David, Nancy (Mrs. Raymond Morningstar), Janice (Mrs. Thomas Dalbo), Christine (Mrs. Darwin Overholt), Kathleen (dec.); res: 113 Zurbrick Rd., Depew, N.Y. 14043.

SCHULTZ, EILEEN HEDY, Art Dir., Good Housekeeping, 959 Eighth Ave., N.Y., N.Y. 10019, '59–; Paradise of the Pacific Magazine, Honolulu, Hi., '58–'59; Comml. Artist, C. A. Parshall Studios, '57–'58; Nat. Soc. of Art Dirs., Art Dirs. Club of N.Y. (Exec. Bd., '69–'71; Judge, Annual Exhbn., '63, '65, '67, '69; Adv. Design aw.), Soc. of Illus., AIGA; First Prize, Adv. Design, SVA; Gilbert Paper Co. Design Aw.; Advertising and Sales Promotion Design Aw.; Sch. of Visual Arts, '57; Grad. Studies: Columbia Univ., Art Students League, Academie des Beaux Arts (Paris); b. Yonkers, N.Y.; p. Harry and Hedy Morchel Schultz; res: 244 S. Broadway, Yonkers, N.Y. 10705.

SCHULTZ, ELEANOR NINMAN, Club Ed., Feature Wtr. Photogr., Wms. Dept., The Arizona Republic, Box 1950, 120 E. Van Buren, Phoenix, Ariz. 85001, '68-; Home Ed., Colmst., The Phoenix Gazette, '63-'68; Ed., Reptr., Brooks Publrs. (Apache Junction), '61-'63; Summer Soc. Ed., Kan. City (Kan.) Kansan, '61; Asst. to Ed., Western Auto Co. mags. (Kan. City, Mo.), '59-'61; Wtr., Brown and Bigelow (St. Paul, Minn.), '54; Free-lance Greeting Card Artist, '45-'50; Artist, Hallmark Greeting Card Co. (Kan. City, Mo.), '42-'45; Theta Sigma Phi (Phoenix Chptr. Secy.), Ariz. Press Wm. (VP, '66-'67; numerous aws.), NLAPW; 1st pl. aw., NPWC; Okla. Col. for Wm., '37-'39; Okla. State Col., BA (Art, Jnlsm.), '42; Kan. City Art Inst.; Mesa Commty. Col.; b. Peoria, Ill., 1919; p. L. T. and Annie Smith Ninman; h. Waldo Schultz (dec.); c. Thomas John, Patricia Ann, Paul Richard; res: 716 S. Lewis, Mesa, Ariz. 85201.

SCHULTZ, IRENE B., Asst. Dir. of Crtv. Svcs., Mutual Of New York, 1740 Broadway, N.Y., N.Y. 10019, '69-; Ass. Dir. of Commtns., '64-'69; Ed., Co. nwsp., '62-'64; Asst. Ed., '60-'62; Edtl. Asst., '59-'60; Sls. Prom., '58-'59; BPW, Life Adv. Assn., Pubcty. Club of N.Y.; City Univ. of N.Y., BBA (Adv.), '63; b. N.Y.C., 1933; p. Herman and Amelia Adolfson Schultz; res: 784 Columbus Ave., N.Y., N.Y. 10025.

SCHULTZ, JOY ROBINSON, Pres., Quill Associates, Inc., 1118 Metropolitan Federal Savings Bldg., 1407 Main St., Dallas, Tex. 75201; Read-Poland, '66-'68; Free-lance Publicist, '54-'66; Auth., "The West Still Lives;" Press Club of Dallas, Tex. Press Wm.; Tex. Tech. Col.; b. Post, Tex., 1923; p. Louie and Hettie McElroy Robinson; h. David W. Schultz; c. Marianne (Mrs. Stephen Arnold), Elizabeth Ann; res: 3019 Clydedale Dr., Dallas, Tex. 75220.

SCHULTZ, JUDITH LEE, Educ. Reptr., San Jose Mercury, 750 Ridder Park Rd., San Jose, Cal. 95131, '69-; Wire Copy Ed., '68-'69; Acting Wire Ed., Decatur (Ill.) Herald, '67-'68; Asst. City Ed., '66-'67; Educ. Reptr., '65-'66; Am. Newsp. Guild; Curtis Publ. Co. Aw. for Outstanding Wm. Jnlsm. Grad., '65; Ohio Wesleyan Univ., BA (Jnlsm.), '65; b. Marietta, Ohio 1942; p. Gary and Violet Cherdron Schultz; res: 698 N. Santa Cruz Ave., Apt. 16, Los Gatos, Cal. 95030.

SCHULTZ, SIGRID, Free-lance Wtr., '54-; Lect. tours, European writing assigts., Collier's, Mutual Bdcst. System, '46-'54; War Corr., Chgo. Tribune, MBS, McCall's, '44-'46 (European Theatre Ribbon); Auth., "Germany Will Try It Again" ('43); Bdcst. for MBS, '38-'41; Corr.-in-chief for Central Europe, Chicago Tribune, '26-'41; Asst. Corr., Berlin, '19-'26; OPC (Gov., '58-'59), War Corrs. Club, Pen Club, Berlin

Foreign Press Club; The Sorbonne, Paris; Berlin Univ., '17-'18; b. Chgo., Ill.; p. Herman and Hedwig Jaskewitz Schultz; res: 35 Elm St., Westport, Conn. 06880.

SCHULTZ, SUSAN A., Acting Dir. of Lib. Svcs., B. L. Fisher Library, Asbury Theological Seminary, Wilmore, Ky. 40390, '69-; Assoc. Dir., '67-'69; Librn., '49-'67; Lib. Asst., Univ. of Ill. Lib. Sch. Lib., '47-'49; Asst. Librn., Bethany (Okla.) Col., '46-'47; Dean of Wm., John Fletcher Col. (Univ. Park, Ia), '40-'45; Lib. Cnslt., Union Biblical Seminary (Yeotmal, India), '61-'62; Ky. Lib. Assn. (VP, '57-'58), Am. Theological Lib. Assn. (Exec. Secy., '67-); Ky. Lib. Trustees Assn. cit., '67; John Fletcher Col., BA, '40; Univ. of Ill., BS (Lib. Sci.), '46; MS (Lib. Sci.), '49; b. Mt. Lake, Minn., 1911; p. David and Anna Eitzen Schultz; res: 201 W. Linden St., Wilmore, Ky. 40390.

SCHULZE, LORRAINE E., VP and Dir. of Media, Venet Advertising, 820 Second Ave., N.Y., N.Y. 10017, '67-; Media Dir., '64-; Media Byr., Riedl & Freede Adv., '56-'64; Univ. of Miami, '55-'56; b. Passaic, N.J., 1937; p. Ludwig and Ilse Kramer Schulze; res: 331 Summit Ave., Hackensack, N.J. 07601.

SCHUMACHER, BOBBIE LOU, Ed., Blue Cross and Blue Shield, Liberty Building, Des Moines, Ia. 50307, '59-; Reptr., Wms. Sec., Waterloo (Ia.) Daily Courier, '56-'59; Ed., co. publns., Ia.-Ill. Gas and Electric Co. (Davenport), '48-'56; Ia. IEA (Pres., '67-'68), ICIE (Dist. Four VP, '69; Sec.-Treas., '67), Wms. Adv. Club of Des Moines, Theta Sigma Phi, Kappa Delta; Okla. State Univ., BA (Jnlsm.), '47; b. Crowder, Okla., 1924; p. Robert and Alma Hall Schumacher; res: 3109-1/2 Woodland, Des Moines, Ia. 50312.

SCHUMAN, JACQUELINE WILSDON, Free-lance Bk. Designer; Harper and Row, '59-'62; Doubleday, '58; Cooper Union, '53-'57 (Best Fine Artist aw.); b. Windsor, Eng., 1935; p. Albert and Elizabeth Goften Wilsdon; h. (sep.); c. Katherine A.; res: 838 West End Ave., N.Y., N.Y. 10025.

SCHUR, ENID KAISER, Sr. Media Supvsr., Bozell and Jacobs, Inc., 575 Madison Ave., N.Y., N.Y. 10022, '67-; McCann-Erickson, '55-'61; Edward Petry, '53-'55; Cunningham and Walsh, '50-'53; Syracuse Univ., BS (Jnlsm.), '50; b. N.Y.C., 1930; p. Charles and Claudia Silverson Kaiser; h. A. Schur; c. Leslie A.; res: 3000-59 Stevens St., Oceanside, N.Y. 11572.

SCHUR, SUSAN ELISABETH, Pres., AE, Susan E. Schur, One Emerson Pl., Boston, Mass. 02114, '63-; Pres., The Schur Co., '62-; Tech. Cnslt., Deutsch & Shea, '62-'63; Partner, Sculptor's Workshop, '61-; Rsch. Metallurgist, Advanced Metals Rsch. Corp., '60-'62; One-man art shows at Harvard, M.I.T., '65-'67; Soc. of Wm. Engineers (Nwsltr. Ed., '61-), Am. Inst. of Mining, Metallurgical & Petroleum Engineers, Soc. of Tech. Wtrs. & Publrs., Am. Assn. for the Advancement of Sci., Sigma Xi; Mass. Inst. of Tech., BS, MS (Metallurgy), '60; b. N.Y.C., 1939; p. George and Martha Salzer Schur.

SCHURMACHER, SUSAN JEANNE, Wms. and Soc. Ed., Binghamton Press Company, Vestal Pkwy. E., Binghamton, N.Y. 13790, '68–.

SCHUSTER, ISABEL, Assoc. Adv. Mgr., The National Observer, Dow Jones & Co., Inc., 30 Broad St., N.Y., N.Y. 10004, '69–; Classified Adv. Mgr., '66–'69; Wall Street Journal, N.Y.C., '57–'61; Pitt., '55–'57; Owner, retail bus., Coral Gables, Fla., '52–'54; former fashion model, N.Y.C., Palm Beach, Fla.; AWNY; b. Bklyn., N.Y., 1909; h. (dec.).

SCHUTZ, NANCY JEANNE, VP, Group Head, Dancer-Fitzgerald-Sample, Inc., 347 Madison Ave., N.Y., N.Y. 10017, '69–; Group Head, Ogilvy & Mather, '64–'68; Supvsr., Kenyon & Eckhardt, '61–'64; Wtr., Knox Reeves, '55–'61; Am. TV & Radio Commls. Festival aw., '68; Venice Film Festival aw., '68; Univ. of Minn., BA, '55 (magna cum laude, Phi Beta Kappa); b. Mpls., Minn.; p. Earl and Ida Mellum Schutz; res: 440 E. 62nd St., N.Y., N.Y. 10021.

SCHWABACHER, ETHEL KREMER, Artist, Auth.; five shows, Betty Parsons Gallery, '53–'64; others; bk., "Arshile Gorky" (Whitney Museum/MacMillan, '57); active in commty. affairs; Who's Who of Am. Wm.; Who's Who in Am. Art; Intl. Dir. of Art; Archives of Am. Art, others; b. N.Y.C., 1903; p. Eugene and Agnes Oppenheimer Kremer; h. Wolfgang S. Schwabacher (dec.); c. Christopher, Brenda Webster; res: 1192 Park Ave., N.Y., N.Y. 10028.

SCHWAGER, GLORIA De VORE, Weather Bdcstr., WBRZ-TV, Baton Rouge, La., '64–; Bdcstr., Dir., Prodr., KFDM-TV (Beaumont, Tex.), '55–'62; Theta Sigma Phi (Treas.), Altrusa Club (Past Pres.); Who's Who of Am. Wm.; U.C.L.A., '37–'41; El Capital Col. of Theatre; b. Ft. Worth, Tex., 1920; p. Fred and Olive Green De Vore; h. H. R. Schwager; c. Mark C. Rochester; res: Jack Tar Capitol House, Baton Rouge, La. 70821.

SCHWARTZ, DIANNE DRUCKER, Asst. Dir., Community Relations Dept., Michael Reese Hospital & Medical Center, 2929 S. Ellis St., Chgo., Ill. 60616, '66–; Pubns. Ed., '62–'66; Assoc. Ed., Telephony mag., '58–'62; Reptr., Skokie (Ill.) News, '57–'58; Chgo. IEA, ICIE, Ladies of the Press, Theta Sigma Phi; Helen Cody Baker aw.; Northwestern Univ., BS (Jnlsm.), '57; b. Chgo., Ill.; p. Adolph and Faye Beezy Drucker; h. Howard Schwartz; res: 6136 N. Damen, Chgo., Ill. 60645.

SCHWARTZ, FRANCES BELL, VP, Ed.-in-Chief Juv. Bks., Abelard-Schuman Ltd., 257 Park Ave. S., N.Y., N.Y. 10010, '69–; VP, '65–; Ed., Children's Bks., '61–'69; Free-Lance Ed., '45–'61; Bd. Mbr., Westchester County Campaign Chmn., Wms. Div., Fedn. of Jewish Philanthropies, '59–; WNBA, Children's Bk. Cncl. (Bd. of Dirs.); McGill Univ., '32–'33; Columbia Univ., '58; N.Y.U., '63; b. Mariupol, Russia; p. Aaron and Jennie Bell; h. Lew Schwartz; c. Edward Arthur; res: 12 Park Rd., Scarsdale, N.Y. 10583.

SCHWARTZ, HANNAH GEISEN, Film Broker, Schoenfeld Film Distributing Corp., 220 W. 42nd St., N.Y., N.Y. 10036, '63–; Harrison Pictures Corp., '58–'63; b. N.Y.C., 1923; p. Morris and Ethel Katcher Geisen; h. George Schwartz; c. Barbara May Landy, Janet Lee Benedetto; res: 110 Seaman Ave., N.Y., N.Y. 10034.

SCHWARTZ, LAVINIA SCHULMAN, Dir. of Midwest Opns., The Advertising Council, Inc., 203 N. Wabash Ave., Chgo., Ill. 60601, '46–; Reg. Chief, Midwest area, Deputy Chief, O.W.I. Domestic Radio Bur., '43–'46; Midwestern Dir., Educ. Dir., Public Svc., WBBM, '38–'43; Wms. Adv. Club; Chgo. Fed. Adv. Club, AWRT, numerous others; Chgo. Adv. Wm. of Yr., '59–'60; Annual Welfare PR Forum aw., '67; Vassar Col., AB, '20 (Phi Beta Kappa); Univ. of Chgo.; b. Cinn., Oh., 1898; p. Alexander and Pauline Leopold Schulman; h. Charles Schwartz; c. Mrs. Polly Hertz, Robert A. D., Charles P., Jr.; res: 5135 S. Woodlawn Ave., Chgo., Ill. 60615.

SCHWARTZ, LEE CRANE, Free-lance Nwsp. Feature Wtr., '61–; Reptr., Syracuse (N.Y.) Herald-Journal, '47–'54; PR, Onondaga County Easter Seal Soc., '63–'67; Theta Sigma Phi (Central N.Y. Chptr. VP, '66); Syracuse Univ., AB, '47; b. Syracuse, N.Y., 1924; p. Louis and E. Sarah Freeman Crane; h. Harry Schwartz; c. Paul Louis, Joyce Melissa; res: 3 Deborah Dr., S. Burlington, Vt. 05401.

SCHWARTZ, MARJORY REED, Prodr.-Dir., WEDU (TV), 908 S. 20th St., Tampa, Fla. 33605, '67–; AWRT (Secy., '69–'70), Alpha Epsilon Rho, Alpha Gamma Delta, Kappa Tau Alpha; Univ. of Fla., BS (Bus. Adm.), '63; BS (Bdcst.), '66; b. Ithaca, N.Y., 1941; p. James and Marion Head Schwartz; res: 207 N. Trask St., Tampa, Fla. 33609.

SCHWARTZ, MONETT SPECTOR, Pres., Monett Schwartz Creative Services, 8455 Beverly Blvd., Suite 407, L.A., Cal. 90048, '68–; Media Cnslt.; AWRT; b. Kan. City, Mo., 1922; p. Barney and Mollie Litman Spector; h. Robert E. Schwartz; c. Michael Steven, Paul David, Susan Yetta; res: 911 N. Havenhurst Dr., L.A., Cal. 90046.

SCHWARTZ, RONNY RAVITCH, Dir., Adv., Prom., PR, Patchogue Plymouth Co., 555 Fifth Ave., N.Y., N.Y. 10017, '64–; East Coast Mgr., Alicia K. Smith, L.A., Cal., '62–'64; NHFL; Bryn Mawr Col., '44; h. Bernard Lee Schwartz.

SCOBEY, MARY-MARGARET, Auth. of Educ. bks.; Prof. of Educ., San Francisco State College, 1600 Holloway Ave., S.F., Cal. 94132, '54–; Asst. Prof., Syracuse Univ., '52–'54; Supvsr. of Instr., Merced County Schs., Cal., '47–'50; Officer, WAVES, '43–'46; Tchr., '37–'43; Assn. for Supervision and Curriculum Dev. (Nat'l. Assn., Cal. Assn. Bds. of Dirs.); Editor, *California Journal for Instructional Improvement*; S.F. State Col., AB, '37; Tchrs. Col., Columbia Univ., MA, '46; Stanford Univ., Ed.D., '52; b. S.F., Cal., 1915; p. Marshall and

Susan Thompson Scobey; res: 1335 Ridgewood Dr., Millbrae, Cal. 94030.

SCOFIELD, NATALIE WORTHINGTON, Radio-TV Dir., Carr Liggett Advertising, Inc., 815 Superior Ave., Cleve., Oh. 44114, '62–; Radio-TV Prod. Coordr., Fox Video Prods., '60–'62; Asst. to AE, Lang, Fisher & Stashower, '58–'60; Tchr., '50–'54; NATAS; AFTRA aw., '60–'61; Cleve. Soc. of Communicating Arts aw., '68; Nat. Adv. Agcy. Network aws.; Cleve. Inst. of Art, '44–'46; Western Reserve Univ.; b. Balt., Md., 1925; p. N. Ainsworth and Dorothy Smith Worthington; h. Norman Scofield (div.); res: 12010 Lake Ave., Lakewood, Oh. 44107.

SCOFIELD, SUNSHINE COLE, Prodr., Hostess, "Sunny Today," Wms. Dir., KERO-TV, 321-21st St., Bakersfield, Cal. 93303, '67–; Co-prodr., "Speaking of Music" series, '64–; Dir. of Commty. Club Aws. Program, hostess of "The Sunny Scofield Show," KBAK-TV, '61–'67; various organizations and aws.; Bakersfield Col., U.C.L.A.; b. San Angelo, Tex. 1916; p. Cullen and Minnie Taylor Cole; h. James LaMonte Scofield; c. David Gregory Lane; res: 1612 Hillside Dr., Bakersfield, Cal. 93306.

SCOMA, SHIRLEE NANSIN, Pres., Color Lithographers, Inc., 225 Varick St., N.Y., N.Y. 10014, '56–; h. Salvatore F. Scoma; c. Candace, Salli; res: 40 Fifth Ave., N.Y., N.Y. 10011.

SCOTT, ANGELINE THOMPSON, Free-lance Sales Prom. Wtr., R. H. Macy & Co., N.Y., '66–; Morton Advertising Agcy, '66–; Home Furnishings Wtr., Stern Brothers, '65–'66; Adv. Copywtr., W. T. Grant, '64–'65; Free-lance Wtr., adv., pubcty., publ., '47–'60; Concept Wtr., Sterling Advertising Agcy., '45–'46; Asst. Sls. Supvsr., Montgomery Ward, '42–'45; Asst. Adv. Dir., E. M. Scarbrough & Sons (Austin, Tex.); Theta Sigma Phi; A.A.U.W.; Univ. of Tex., BJ (permanent teaching cert.); Tobé-Coburn Sch., Cert. of Graduation (with distinction); N.Y.U.; b. Albuquerque, N.M.; p. Oscar N. and Seppie L. Gibson Thompson; h. James C. Scott, Jr.; c. Christopher Lawrence; res: 12 Dowsing Pl., Amityville, L.I., N.Y. 11701.

SCOTT, ANN CRITTENDEN, Rsch. Assoc., Fortune, Time-Life Bldg., N.Y., N.Y. 10020, '67–; Instr., Hist., Douglass Col., '64–'66; Southern Methodist Univ., BA, '59 (Phi Beta Kappa, magna cum laude), MA, '62; Columbia Univ., MA (Intl. Affairs), '67; b. Dallas, Tex., 1937; p. Norman and Mary O'Banion Crittenden; res: 14 W. 86th St., N.Y., N.Y. 10024.

SCOTT, ANN LINDSEY, Asst. in Public Info., Instr., Mississippi State College for Women, Columbus, Miss. 39701, '69–; Jnlsm. Instr., Miami-Dade (Fla.) Jr. Col., '66–'68; Theta Sigma Phi, AAUP, Am. Bus. Wms. Assn.; Kappa Tau Alpha; Univ. of Mo., BJ, '65; MA (Jnlsm.); b. Florence, Ala., 1943; p. Alf and June Lindsey Scott; res: 310 12 St. N., Apt. 7, Columbus, Miss. 39701.

SCOTT, BARBARA WALTERS, Reptr., Corbin Times-Tribune, Corbin, Ky. 40701, '67–'69; Ed., Clay City (Ky.) Times, '64–'67; Reptr., City Ed.; Winchester Sun, '60–'64; b. Winchester, Ky., 1936; p. Robert Walters and Cynthia Walters Thurman; h. Gene Scott; c. Cynthia Jane, Leslie Grace, Gene Paul; res: 605 Ford St., Corbin, Ky. 40701.

SCOTT, BESS WHITEHEAD, Publicist, Gulf State Advertising Agency, 2714 S.W. Freeway, Houston, Tex. 77005, '44–; Reptr., Colmst., Dept. Ed., Dallas Times Herald, Houston Press, Houston Post, '28–'44; Adv., Hulsey Theatres, '16–'18; Wtr., Bdcstr., "Show Business" radio prog.; '45; BPW (Houston Chptr. Pres., '47–'48; Wm. of the Yr. aw., '54), Theta Sigma Phi (Headliner aw., '55), Houston Press Club, Houston Adv. Club, Alpha Gamma Chi; Who's Who of Am. Wm.; Baylor Univ., BA, '12; b. Blanket, Tex., 1890; p. William and Sarah Barnett Whitehead; h. Hubert Clark Scott; c. Hubert C., Mrs. Lila Bess Ready (dec.); res: 12014 Susquehannah Dr., Houston, Tex.

SCOTT, JANE MARIE, Young Ohio Ed., The Plain Dealer, 1801 Superior Ave., Cleve., Oh. 44114, '54–; Wms. Ed., The State News Bur., '50–'52; Soc. Ed., Chagrin Valley Herald, '46–'47; Theta Sigma Phi, Press Club of Cleve., Oh. Nwsp. Wms. Assn. (aw.), '64); Univ. of Mich., AB, '41; b. Cleve., Oh.; p. Clarence and Nelle McGee Scott; res: 1375 Bunts Rd., Lakewood, Oh. 44107.

SCOTT, JANE TONER, VP, Publr., Colmst., The Anderson Herald, Anderson Newspapers, 1133 Jackson St., Anderson, Ind. 46015; Wms. Press Club, Cancer Bd., Mayor's Comm. on Pollution, Ind. Univ. Alumna Club (Secy.); Ind. Univ.; b. Anderson, Ind., 1909; p. Edward and Harriet Williams Toner; h. John E. Scott; c. John Toner Scott, Nancy (Mrs. Daniel Mulvihill), Lucinda (Mrs. Jon Shafer); res: 212 W. Eighth St., Anderson, Ind. 46016.

SCOTT, JUDITH UNGER, Wtr., teenage non-fiction, 10 bks. incl. "Manners for Moderns," "Cues for Careers," "The Book of Dating"; Free-lance Wtr.; staffs, Ladies' Home Jnl., Jack and Jill Magazine; radio program; Tchr., Christian Wtrs. Conf. (Green Lake, Wis.), '62; Col. of S. Jersey, Temple Univ., '38–'42; b. Phila., Pa., 1916; p. Ernest and Elsie Cheeseman Unger; h. Gilbert H. Scott; c. Meredith U.; res: 576 Walnut St., Audubon, N.J. 08106.

SCOTT, LENORE, Artist, Auth.; Owner, Kurtz Art Associates, 147 W. 42nd St., N.Y., N.Y. 10036, '52–; bks: "The Shakespeare Game" (Avalon Hill), "Egyptian Hieroglyphics for Everyone" (Funk and Wagnall); AWNY; Australian Cup aw., Assn. of Ad Men and Wm., '58; Fashion Coordinates Inst. Annual aw., '59; Cooper Union Sch. of Fine Arts, '41–'45; b. N.Y.C.; p. Arthur and Jessie Kurtz; h. Henry Joseph Scott; res: 47 E. 87th St., N.Y., N.Y. 10028.

SCOTT, LOUISE BINDER, Auth: children's and elementary, filmstrips, textbooks (McGraw-Hill);

Tchr., Cal. State Col., L.A., Cal.; Zeta Phi Eta, Intl. Reading Assn., Am. Speech and Hearing Assn., Nat. Assn. For the Educ. of Young Children; Who's Who of Am. Wm.; Emerson Col., BLI; Boston Univ., EdM; b. Hamburg, Ia.; p. Stephen and Emma Binder Scott; res: 623 N. Monterey St., Apt. 10, Alhambra, Cal. 91801.

SCOTT, LUCILE McALLISTER, Nat. Circ. Mgr., Assoc. Soc. Ed., Atlanta Daily World, 210 Auburn Ave. N.E., Atlanta, Ga. 30303, '34–; Nat. Cncl. of Negro Wm., Nat. Screen Guild, Alpha Kappa Alpha; Nat. Designers Assn. aw., '59; Albany State Col. Jnlsm. aw., '65; A & I State Univ., AB, '32; b. Jackson, Miss., 1901; p. Robert and Florence Johnson McAllister; h: William Scott (div.); c. William Alexander, 3rd, Robert Lee; res: 1377 Hunter St. N.W., Atlanta, Ga. 30314.

SCOTT, NATALIE ANDERSON, Free-lance Wtr.; Auth: "So Brief the Years," "The Sisters Livingston," "The Story of Mrs. Murphy" (Bk.-of-the-Month Club selection, '47; best seller), other novels; short stories for mags., articles; b. Ekaterinoslav, Russia, 1906; p. Boris and Nadjeshda Mochugoreskaya Sokoloff.

SCOTT, ROSE PETERS, Anchorman, Ed., KGW-TV, King Broadcasting Co., 1501 S.W. Jefferson, Portland, Ore. 97201, '67–; Newscaster, KGW Radio, '65–'66; Eng. Instr., Univ. of Ore., '62–'65; Ed., Rschr., Ore State Dept. of Educ., '61–'62; AFTRA (Portland Bd. of Dirs.), Portland Civic Theater (Bd. of Dir.), Govs. Comm. on Employment of the Handicapped; Ore. BPW Golden Torch aw., '69; Willamette Univ., BA (Eng.), '58; Univ. of Ore., MA (Eng. and Am. Lit.), '64; b. N.Y.C., 1928; p. Fred and Rose Muller Peters; h. (div.); res: 2243 N.W. Flanders, Portland, Ore. 97210.

SCOTT, RUTH BOYER, Pubns. Wtr., National Institute of Neurological Diseases and Strokes, Bldg. 31, Room 8A18, Bethesda, Md. 20014, '57–; Free-lance Wtr., '47–'57; Tchr., Univ. of Wash.; Guest Lectr., George Washington Univ.; WNPC, Nat. Assn. of Sci. Wtrs., Soc. of Mag. Wtrs.; Who's Who of Am. Wm., Who's Who in the East; Univ. of Wash., BS (magna cum laude; Phi Beta Kappa); b. San Diego, Cal.; p. Harvey and Jean Cook Boyer; h. Morris R. Scott (dec.); c. Jean (Mrs. Howard Shipley), Carol (Mrs. C. T. Ireland); res: 4536 Fairfield Dr., Bethesda, Md. 20014.

SCOTT, RUTH FORD, Actress; Broadway: Star, "The Milk Train Doesn't Stop Here Anymore," '64; "Dinner at Eight" '66–'68; Off-Broadway, London, Italy, Mass., Fla., motion pic.; Wtr: adapted Faulkner's "Requiem for a Nun" for stage; Intl. Celebrity Register; Univ. of Miss., BA, MA (Philosophy); h. Zachary Scott (dec.); res: One W. 72nd St., N.Y., N.Y. 10023.

SCOTT, SHELBY ANNE, Newscaster-Reptr., WBZ-TV, Westinghouse Broadcasting, 1170 Soldiers Field Rd., Boston, Mass. 02134, '65–; Reptr., KIRO Radio-TV (Seattle, Wash.), '58–'65; Traf. Mgr., KVI, '57–'58; AWRT, Theta Sigma Phi; UPI Tom Phillips aw. for Rept., '67; Univ. of Wash., BA (Commtns.), '57; b. Seattle, Wash., 1936; p. Harry and Inga Ring Schuck.

SCOTT, SHIRLEY CLEARY, Gen. Mgr., WSYL, Sylvania Broadcasting System, Inc., P.O. Box 519, Sylvania, Ga. 30467, '66–; Station Mgr., '63–'66, Prog. Dir., '59–'63, News Dir., '56–'59; numerous AP bdcst. aws., '60–'67; Sylvania Gen. Wms. Club, Beta Sigma Phi (Pres.), Sylvania Jr. Wms. Club (Secy.); Univ. of Ga.; Ga. Southern Col.; b. Sylvania, Ga., 1937; p. Howard and Reba Humphrey Cleary; h. Eugene Scott; c. Angel, Cleary Eugene; res: P.O. Box 83, Sylvania, Ga. 30467.

SCOTT, TIRSA SAAREDRA, Wtr., educ. materials, textbks.; Auth: "Como se Dice?" "Como se Escribe?" "Somos Amigos I, II;" Pomona Col., BA; h. David Winfield Scott; c. Tirsa Margaret, Edith Elizabeth; res: 3016 Cortland Pl. N.W., Wash., D.C. 20008.

SCOTT, WILLODENE ALEXANDER, Supvsr. of Materials, Lib. Div., Metro Nashville-Davidson County Public Schools, 2601 Bransford Ave., Nashville, Tenn. 37204, '66–; tchr., librn., elementary, jr. high and high schs.; Southern Assn. Evaluation comms. for six high schs.; Cnslt., in-svc. training meetings, Ala., Tenn.; Visiting Fac. Mbr., Peabody Lib. Sch.; part-time instr., Univ. of Tenn. Nashville Ctr.; ALA, NEA (Life Mbr.), Tenn. Lib. Assn., Tenn. Educ. Assn., S. E. Lib. Assn., Wms. Nat. Bk. Assn., Met. Nashville Educ. Assn.; George Peabody Col. for Tchrs., BA, '46; BS (Lib. Sci.), '47; MA (Lib. Sci.), '49; Grad. Work; b. Ethridge, Tenn.; p. Jesse Cary and Maud Goff Alexander; h. Ray D. Scott; c. Pamela D.; res: 525 Clematis Dr., Nashville, Tenn. 37205.

SCOVEL, MYRA SCOTT, Free-lance Wtr., 37 Farley Dr., Stony Point, N.Y. 10980, '68–; Children's Ed., Dir. of Children's Dept., Friendship Press, '67–'68; Coordr. for Med. Emphasis Program, United Presbyterian COEMAR, '59–'67; Librn., Christian Med. Col., Ludhiana, Punjab, India, '53–'59; Med. Missionary Work, Peking, China, Tsining, Shantung, Huai Yan, Anhwei Province, Canton, '30–'51; Bks: "The Weight of a Loaf" poetry, (Westminster), "Chinese Ginger Jars," "Richer by India," "To Lay A Hearth" (Harper & Row); numerous juvs.; various organizations; b. Mechanicville, N.Y. 1905; p. Robert and Myrtle Fox Scott; h. Dr. Frederick G. Scovel; c. James K., Carl R., Mrs. Anne Fitch, Thomas S., Mrs. Judith Robinson, Mrs. Victoria Harris; res: 37 Farley Dr., Stony Point, N.Y. 10980.

SEABOLT, BETTY ROACH, Controller-Treas., Capital Film Laboratories, Inc., 470 E St. S.W., Wash., D.C. 20024, '65–; Asst. Treas., '54–'65; Bkkeeper., '53; Wm. of the Motion Picture Industry (D.C. Club Pres., '68–'69; VP, '69–'70), Soroptimist Club (D.C. Treas., '69–'70); b. Joplin, Mo., 1924; p. Harry and Bertha Biggs Roach; res: 5911 Cherrywood Terr., Greenbelt, Md. 20770.

SEAGOE, MAY V., Prof. of Educ., University of California, L.A., Cal. 90024, '34–; Tchr. and Cnslr., various sch. dists. (So. Cal.), '25–'34; Auth., non-fiction bks.; contr., bk. review sec. of L.A. Times; Am. Psychological Assn. (Div. Pres., '58–'59), S. Cal. Educ. Rsch. and Guidance Assn. (Pres., '52–'53), Pi Lambda Theta (Nat. Pres., '43–'47), Am. Educ. Rsch. Assn.; U.C.L.A., Ed. B, '29 (highest hons.); Stanford Univ., MA, '31, PhD; b. Pomona, Cal., 1906; p. George Jacob and Ada Phillips Seagoe; h. (div.); c. Brent Phillips, Amy Mildred.

SEAMAN, BARBARA ROSNER, Free-lance Wtr., specializing in med., psychology, marriage; Auth., "The Doctor's Case Against the Pill" (Peter H. Wyden, '69); Colmst., "Understanding Your Marriage" (Brides Magazine), '65–'67; Colmst., Contrb. Ed., Ladies' Home Journal, '65–'69; AAUW, Nat. Assn. of Sci. Wtrs., Soc. of Mag. Wtrs., Am. Sociological Assn., Soc. for the Scientific Study of Sex, OPC; Col. Univ. Advanced Sci. Writing Fellow, '67–'68; Oberlin Col., BA, '56; Ford Fndn. Early Admissions Scholar; b. N.Y.C., 1935; p. Henry and Sophie Kimels Rosner; h. Dr. Gideon Seaman; c. Noah Samuel, Elana Felicia, Shira Jean; res: 300 West End Ave., N.Y., N.Y. 10023.

SEAMAN, EDNA LIZBETH, Adm. Asst., Multimedia Broadcasting Company, P.O. Box 788, 505 Rutherford St., Greenville, S.C. 29602, '68–; Prom. Mgr., PR Dir., WFBC-TV, '60–'68; Public Svc. and Prog. Mgr., '58–'60; Prom. and Public Affairs Mgr., '56–'58; AWRT (Piedmont Chptr: Pres., '59; VP, '67; Palmetto Chptr. Pres., '69); PRSA (Greenville Chptr. Sec. '67), C. of C. (Greater Greenville Pres., Wms. Div.; Cert. of Merit, '67); Creole Petroleum Co. Hon. Merit for Special Svcs.; NBC Prom. Daytime Contest, '59, '60; Furman Univ., '55; Univ. of S.C., '58; b. Spartanburg, S.C., 1924; p. Joseph and Amelia Latuf Seaman; res: 111 Batesview Dr., Greenville, S.C. 29602.

SEARS, BARBARA PLUMER, Coordr., College Relations, Pima College, '69–; City Ed., Arizona Daily Star, 208 N. Stone Ave., Tucson, Ariz., '68–'69; Wms. Ed., Educ. Wtr., Asst. City Ed.; Tucson Press Club (Secy., '68, reptr. aw., '67); Wellesley Col., BA, '43; b. Florence Villa, Fla.; p. Bowdoin and Elinor Caldwell Plumer; c. William R., George B.; res: 3654 N. Cactus Blvd., Tucson, Ariz. 85716.

SEARS, VIRGINIA LA COSTE, Sls. Mgr., KFKA, RG, Inc., 1025 Ninth St., P.O. Box K, Greeley, Colo. 80631, '52–; Sales Rep., '50–'52; Dir., Religious Educ., Congregational Ch., '46–'50; Asst. Registrar, Colo. State Col., '28–'32; Tchr., '24–'27; AWRT (Bd. of Dirs., '66–'69; Treas., '65–'67), Soroptimist (VP, '65–'66); Human Rels. aw., Dale Carnegie Sales Div., '61; Life Master, Am. Contract Bridge League; Colo. State Col., '24–'32; b. Denver, Colo., 1906; p. Leon and Louena Dunbar LaCoste; h. Roy Sears; c. Roger Douglas, Gary Roy, Larry Edward; res: 1832 Montview Blvd., Greeley, Colo. 80631.

SECREST, MERYLE DOMAN, Cultural Reptr., Washington Post, 1515 L St. N.W., Wash., D.C. 20005, '69–; Wms. Features, '65–'69; Food Ed., Columbus (Oh.)

Citizen; Wms. Ed., Hamilton (Ontario) News; Reptr., Bristol (England) Post; Can. Wms. Press Club cit., '50; Hamilton (Ont.) Press Club Wm. of the Yr., '51; b. Bath, England, 1930; p. Albert and Olive Love Doman; h. David Secrest (div.); c. Cary, Martin, Gillian; res: 4444 Greenwich Pkwy. N.W., Wash., D.C. 20007.

SEE, RUTH DOUGLAS, Asst. Prof. of Hist., Virginia Commonwealth University, 901 W. Franklin St., Richmond, Va. 23220, '67–; Auth: "That the World May Know" (CLC Press, '65), "Make the Bible Your Own" (John Knox Press, '61), "What Can We Do?" (Friendship Press, '65); Ed. of Youth Materials, Presbyterian Bd. of Christian Educ., '49–'67; Visiting Tchr., Nat. Taiwan Univ. (Taipei, Taiwan), '56–'57; Instr. in Bible and Eng., Stillman Col. (Tuscaloosa, Ala.), '36–'45; Religious Educ. Assn., AAUP, ZONTA; Mary Baldwin Col., BA, '31 (Alumni aw., '65); N.Y. Theological Seminary, MRE, '34; N.Y.U., PhD, '53; b. Balt., Md., 1910; p. R. Gamble and Louisa Spear See; res: 3607 Chamberlayne Ave., Richmond, Va. 23227.

SEEBACHER, SOPHIE SMOLIAR, Ed. and Publr., Photo Industry News, Inc., 165 W. 46th St., N.Y., N.Y. 10036, '56–; Free-lance Wtr., Ed., PR, '45–'56; Reptr., PM, '42–'45; Ed., Master Plumber, '36–'42; b. N.Y.C.; p. Max and Pauline Smoliar; h. Ira Seebacher; c. Jay; res: 48 Knollwood Rd. S., Roslyn, N.Y. 11576.

SEELE, HELEN MARIE, Media Svcs. Mgr., Marsteller, Inc., 866 Third Ave., N.Y., N.Y. 10022, '65–; Asst. Media Dir., '58–'65; Assn. of Indsl. Advertisers (N.Y. Chptr. VP, '68–'69, '69–'70; Secy., '67–'68); Scudder Sch. of Bus.; b. Long Branch, N.J.; p. Edward and Sara Ludwig Seele; res: 33 E. 43rd St., N.Y., N.Y. 10017.

SEELY, JERI BUSHONG, Ed., The Mail-Journal, Box 188, Milford, Ind. 46542, '61–; Eastern Star; b. Goshen, Ind., 1940; p. Jerord and Kathryn Huber Bushong; h. D. G. Seely; res: 405 W. Catherine, Milford, Ind. 46542.

SEGAL, JOSEPHINE AHERN, Fashion Ed., Look Magazine, 488 Madison Ave., N.Y., N.Y. 10022, '64–; Wms. Fashion Ed., Sports Illustrated, '54–'64; Sportswear Fashion Ed., Wms. Wear Daily, '51–'54; Fashion Group (Bd. Dir., '64), Theta Sigma Phi; Ia. State Univ., BS (Tech. Jnlsm.), '45; b. Wayne, Neb.; p. John and Nelle Thorndike Ahern; h. Marvin B. Segal; res: 131 E. 70th St., N.Y., N.Y. 10021.

SEGAL, MARILYN MAILMAN, Auth: "Run Away Little Girl" ('66) Random House; Admr., University Sch., 3330 College Ave., Ft. Lauderdale, Fla., '67–; Wellesley Col., BA; McGill Univ. BS; Nova Univ. PhD candidate; h. Myron Segal.

SEGELKE, EDITH REEVES, Bus. Mgr., KOAA-TV and KCSJ, Broadcasting Corp., 2226 Television Lane, Pueblo, Colo. 81003, '68–; Bus. Mgr., Campbell-Roy & Assocs., '64–'68; Accounting and Traf. Mgr., Metropolitan TV Co., '62–'64; Bus. Mgr., Star Bdcst. Co., '57–'62; Lincoln Sch. of Bus.; b. Sidney, Ia., 1908; p.

Orval and Icadora Hayes Reeves; h. Floyd Segelke (dec.); c. Marcia Lee, Janet Ruth, David Floyd, Jo-Ellen; res: 512 W. 18th St., Apt. 3, Pueblo, Colo. 81003.

SEGRE, ANN WHITE, Pres., Audio-Visual School Service, 155 W. 72nd St., N.Y., N.Y. 10023, '69–; Ann Segre Associates, '61–'69; Ed., Journal of Lifetime Living, '55–'60; PR Dir., J. B. Williams Co., '49–'55; formerly Edtl., Prom. Cnslt.; Colmst., Scholastic Publications; Auth., four children's bks.; Collaborator, six food, nutrition bks.; h. Alfredo Segre.

SEIDENBERG, BERYL E., VP, Media Dir., Smith/Greenland Co., Inc., 1414 Ave. of the Americas, N.Y., N.Y. 10019, '61–; VP, Bdcst. Media, Kastor, Hilton, Chesley, Clifford and Atherton, '58–'61; Beaver Col.; b. Phila., Pa., 1928; p. Herman and Lona Pensler Seidenberg; res: 400 E. 57th St., N.Y., N.Y. 10022.

SEIDMAN, JEANNETTE KAPLAN, Chmn. of the Bd., Inter Racial Press of America, Inc., 305 Madison Ave., N.Y., N.Y. 10017, '56–; adv. rep. for more than 1,000 fgn. lang. nwsps., mags., radio stations; BPW, numerous civic and charitable orgs.; aws. for prom. of U.S. Savings Bonds sls., other hons.; Who's Who of Am. Wm.; Who's Who in World Jewry; Nat. Reg. of Important Ams.; b. Russia, 1887; h. Nathan H. Seidman (dec.); c. Lloyd, Bert, Dick; res: 320 E. 42nd St., N.Y., N.Y. 10017.

SEIFERT, ELIZABETH, Novelist, Dodd, Mead and Co.; Auths. Guild, WNBA, Soc. of Auths and Dramatists; Redbook-Dodd, Mead First Novel aw., '38; pocketbks. by Dell, foreign publication in many countries; Washington Univ., AB, '18; b. Washington, Mo.; p. Richard and Anna Sanford Seifert; h. John J. Gasparotti; c. John J., Richard S., Paul A., Anna G. Felter; res: 511 Fort St., Moberly, Mo. 63570.

SEIFERT, SHIRLEY LOUISE, Auth., hist. fiction, '19–; Theta Sigma Phi (Nat. Headliner Aw., '65); St. Louis Group Action Cncl. aws: Wm. of Achiev., '48, '49; Cit. of Special Merit, '61; Wash. Univ., BA (Phi Beta Kappa; summa cum laude; distg. alumni, '55); Univ. of Wis.; b. St. Peters, Mo.; p. Richard and Anna Sanford Seifert; res: 505 S. Clay, Kirkwood, Mo. 63122.

SELBY, JOYCE McNEAL, Media Dir., Shirey & Rynas, Inc., 1700 Pennsylvania Ave. N.W., Wash., D.C. 20006, '68–; Off. Mgr., R. W. Briggs Food Brokerage, '66–'67; Off. Mgr., Chaimson Food Brokerage, '58–'66; Exec. Secy., Homer A. Ray Jr., '52–'58; Am. Bus. Wms. Org. (Charter Mbr., Treas.); Trophy, outstanding broker, '66; b. Caribou, Me. 1926; p. Donald P. and Carolyn Bishop McNeal; h. Elmer Edward Selby; c. Larry Estin Braley; res: Silver Spring Towers, 816 Easley St., Silver Spring, Md. 20910.

SELCER, JOYCE RITA, Media Dir., Rapp and Collins, Inc., 90 Park Ave., N.Y., N.Y. 10016, '65–; Media Byr., '65; BBD&O, '64–'65; Wunderman, Ricotta and Kline, '62–'64; Sls. Prom. Exec., Copywtr., Barton's Candy Co., '61; Asst. to Retail Adv. Mgr., Living for Young

Homemakers, '56–'60; article, "Media in Advertising," Direct Marketing, June '69; AWRT; N.Y.U., '44–'47; b. N.Y.C., 1928; p. David and Lillian Bresnick Weinberg; h. (div.); c. Andrew, Kenneth; res: 1177 E. 98th St., Bklyn., N.Y. 11236.

SELLERS, NAOMI WHITE, Tchr., Burlingame High School, Oak Grove and Carolyn Aves., Burlingame, Cal. 94401, '54–; Tchr., Okla. State Univ., '43–'45; Auth., "Cross My Heart" (Doubleday); many short stories for McCall's, Cosmopolitan, others; AAUW, Delta Kappa Gamma, Kappa Delta Pi; Univ. of Okla., BA, MA; b. Dustin, Okla.; p. John and Annie Rice White; h. Elbert Eugene Sellers; res: 312 Midvale, San Mateo, Cal. 94403.

SELSMAN, MARLENE SIGNE, Talent (Motion Pics., TV); Tchr., L. A. City Schs., Evergreen Stage Workshop; Dir., U.C.L.A.; SAG, AGVA, AFTRA; U.C.L.A. (Dean's List, Best Dir.), '63–'68; b. Miami, Fla., 1946; p. Victor and Rose Goldstein Selsman; res: 9344 W. Olympic Blvd., Beverly Hills, Cal. 90212.

SELSNIK, ANN BERTOLUCCI, Media Dir., Robert E. Burger Adv., 722 Montgomery St., S.F., Cal. 94111, '67–; City Col. (S.F., Cal.), Assoc. of Arts, '33.

SELTZER, GLADYS MARKS, Free-lance Wtr., Publicist; PR Cnslt., Covered Bridge Girl Scout Cncl., '66–'68; Dir. of Info. Svcs., Rose Polytechnic Inst., '59–'64; Reptr., Terre Haute Star, '54–'58; Reptr., Phila. (Pa.) Evening Bulletin, '39–'42; Wms. Ed., 69th St. News (Upper Darby, Pa.), '39; Theta Sigma Phi (Pres., undergraduate Chptr., '37–'38), AAUW (Terre Haute Br. Secy., '67–'69), Ind. Col. PR Assn. ('62–'64), Terre Haute Pen & Brush Club (Pres., '68–'69); Temple Univ., BS, '38; Ind. State Univ., MS (Eng.), '67; b. N.Y.C., 1915; p. Allen and Dorthea Matthews Marks; h. Robert D. Seltzer; c. David, Ann, Ruth; res: R.R. 24, Box 429, Terre Haute, Ind. 47802.

SEMROW, ELLEN HARTLEV, Dir., Nutrition, Continuing Educ., American Institute of Baking, 400 E. Ontario St., Chgo., Ill. 60611, '52–; Dir., Consumer Svc., '43–'45; Dir., Consumer Svc., Nat. Assn. Margarine Mfrs., '51–'52; Asst. Dir., Hotpoint Inst., Hotpoint, Inc., '49–'51; Dir., Consumer Svc., The Glidden Co., '42–'43; Edtl. Asst., The Wheat Flour Inst., '41–'43; numerous bklets., articles, speeches; AWRT (Chgo. Secy., '66–'68), Home Econs. in Bus. (Exec. Bd., '55–'58; Chgo. Chmn., '52–'53); Ia. State Univ., BS (Nutrition), '41 (Phi Kappa Phi; Iota Sigma Pi; Omicron Nu); Univ. of Chgo., '60; b. Chgo., Ill., 1915; p. Louis and Julie Pedersen Jensen-Hartlev; h. Harry H. Semrow (div.); c. Harry H., Jr.; res: 4937 W. Montana St., Chgo., Ill. 60639.

SENG, MINNIE A., Head Cataloger, St. Ambrose Col., 518 W. Locust, Davenport, Ia. 52803, '67–; Ed., "Education Index," H. W. Wilson Co., '59–'66; Head Cataloger, Fresno State Col. (Cal.), '44–'59; N.Y. Lib. Club, ALA, CLA; AAUW; Univ. of Mich., AB, '32; AB

(Lib. Sci.), '35; AM (Lib. Sci.), '43; b. Muskegon, Mich., 1909; p. Edward and Ella Pattie Seng; res: 328 W. Columbia, Apt. 2, Davenport, Ia. 52803.

SENIOR, KATHLEEN ANN, PR Dir., Stevens & Wilkinson Architects & Engineers, 157 Luckie St. N.W., Atlanta, Ga. 30303, '67–; Commty. Rel. Dir., Mead Packaging, '65–'67; AE, Gregory Dawson Inc., N.Y., '64–'65; Dept. Store Merchandising Mgr., '61–'64; Prom. Dir., Conde Nast Pubns., N.Y., '58–'61; U.S. C. of C. (Wash., D.C., Consumer Issues Comm., '67–), Atlanta Wms. C. of C. (Bd. of Dirs., '68–; Current Interest Chmn., '68–'69; PR Chmn., '67–'68; Asst. to Pres.), Atlanta Arts Festival (VP, '69–'70), Atlanta Ballet Guild (VP, '66–'67); Life Magazine Nat. Retail Merchants Assn. nat. aw., '62; Pa. State Univ., BA, '52; b. Summerville, N.J., 1930; p. Raymond and Anne O'Neill Senior; res: 4256 Powers Ferry Rd. N.W., Atlanta, Ga. 30305.

SENTNER, MARY STEELE, Wash. Rep., Good Housekeeping, '56–; Owner, Rsch. Bur., '37–'56; Bk. Reviewer, 20th Century Fox (London, England), '35–'37; Fashion Wtr., New York World, '25; ANWC, Theta Sigma Phi; Peace Col., BA, Columbia Sch. of Jnlsm.; b. Mt. Olive, N.C.; p. William and Kate Southerland Steele; h. David P. Sentner; c. Joyce (Mrs. R. G. Daly Jr.); res: 2601 Woodley Pl. N.W., Wash., D.C. 20008.

SERAFIN, DOLORES KOHLER, VP-Adm., The Herald-News, 988 Main Ave., Passaic, N.J. 07055, '64–; Asst. to Pres., '62–'64; Adm. Asst., '60–'62; Secy., '58–'60; Cert. Pfsnl. Secy.; Rutgers Univ., BS, '55; Am. Mgt. Assn. (Mgt., Exec. Courses); b. Hazelton, Pa., 1928; p. Michael and Anna D. Kohler; h. Charles J. Serafin; res: 17 Yorkshire Rd., Clifton, N.J. 07013.

SERBUS, PEARL DIECK, Mng. Ed., Calumet Index Newspapers, 11242 Michigan Ave., Chgo., Ill. 60628, '68–; Food Wtr., Suburban Index Ed.; Ill. Wms. Press Assn. (Pres., '62–'63; Wm of the Yr., '68), Riverdale C. of C. (past VP; Outstanding Mbr. Plaque), Roseland BPW, PTA (Distg. Mbr. Aw., '57); Ill. Educ. Assn. Sch. Bell Aw., '65; b. Riverdale, Ill., 1915; p. Emil and Pearl Kaiser Dieck; h. Gerald Serbus; c. Allan, Bruce, Curt; res: 13811 Edbrooke Ave., Riverdale, Ill. 60628.

SERVIS, SUSAN DE LUCA, Chief Reptr., The Record, 150 River St., Hackensack, N.J., '66–; Reptr., '64; special police news work, special labor rept.; Speaker, civic groups, sch. comms.; gold badge, N. Bergen Local 18, '66; commended, Fairview Mayor, Cncl., outstanding work in news field, '63; Fairview Wms. Club (Founder, past Pres.); N.Y.U.; Bergen Jr. Col.; b. Fairview, N.J., 1928; p. Enrico and Frances Pistilli De Luca; h. Walter Servis (dec.); c. Susan Eva, Anthony; res: 400 Cliff St., Fairview, N.J. 07022.

SETON, CYNTHIA PROPPER, Colmst., The Berkshire Eagle, Pittsfield, Mass. 01201, '57–; Auth: "I Think Rome Is Burning" (Doubleday, '62), "A Special and Curious Blessing" (Norton, '68); Smith Col., BA, '48; b. N.Y.C., 1926; p. Karl and Charlotte Janssen Propper; h. Paul Seton; c. Anthony M., Julia M., Margaret P., Jennifer R., Nora J.; res: 34 Harrison Ave., Northampton, Mass. 01060.

SEURAT, PILAR HERNANDEZ, Free-lance Actress, '59–; Group Dancer, '58–'59; b. Manila, Phillipine I., 1938; p. Al and Ceferina Whitte Hernandez; h. Aka Seurat (div.); c. Dean Devlin; res: 3908 Carpenter Ave., Studio City, Cal. 91604.

SEVAGIAN, HELEN HAIG, Info. Off. Chief, Boston Public Library, P.O. Box 286, Boston, Mass. 02186, '58–; Offcr.-in-Charge, '54–'58; Pfsnl. Asst., '47–'54; Co-Prodr. and Talent, weekly segment of "Big Brother's World," WBZ-TV, '64–'66; Co-Prodr., weekly prog. on lib. bks., WBUR-FM, '57–'60; Ed., BPL News, '54–'58, Je. '66; ALA (Bd. Mbr., '65–'67), New Eng. Lib. Assn., Mass. Lib. Assn. ('69), Pubcty. Club of Boston ('55–), Armenian Relief Soc. (Mbr. of Bd., '65–'67; Secy., '65–'66); several civic, cultural orgs., aws.; Boston Univ., BS, '47 (alumni aws., '60, '62); Simmons Col., BS (Lib. Sci.), '49; b. Boston, Mass., 1926; p. Haig and Surpoohy Tarbassian Sevagian; res: 104 Hilltop St., Milton, Mass. 02186.

SEVERN, SUE, Prod. Supvsr., Consumer Publications, Billboard Publications, Inc., 165 W. 46th St., N.Y., N.Y. 10036, '66–; Edtl. positions with co. since '61; Co-auth: "The State Makers" ('62), "Highways to Tomorrow" ('60), two others; Free-lance Wtr., Ed., Corr., '47–'61; small trade mags., '41–'46; b. Balt., Md., 1918; p. Charles and Beatha Hill Schulz; h. William Severn; c. Ellen Sue (Mrs. James F. Coulter); res: 135 E. 54th St., N.Y., N.Y. 10022.

SEVY, BARBARA SNETSINGER, Librn., Philadelphia Museum of Art, 26th and Benjamin Franklin Pkwy., Phila., Pa. 19101, '68–; Asst. Librn., '65–'67; Librn., Pa. Horticultural Soc., '64–'65; Cataloguer, Am. Philosophical Soc., '55–'57; Librn., Commn. on Financing of Hospital Care, Chgo., Ill., '51–'54; various organizations; Univ. of Vt., BS, '47 (Mortar Bd.); Drexel Inst. of Tech., MS (Lib. Sci), '55; b. Montpelier, Vt. 1926; p. Cecil and Florence Barber Snetsinger; h. Roger Sevy; c. Pamela, Jonathan; res: 242 Mather Rd., Jenkintown, Pa. 19046.

SEWARD, BARBARA SCHOFIELD, AE, WPRO, 24 Mason St., Providence, R.I. 02902, '66–; WWSC Radio (Glens Falls, N.Y.), '63–'66; Grad. Asst., Dale Carnegie Courses; AWRT, AAUW; Wellesley Col., BA, '39; Katharine Gibbs, '40; Brown Univ. (Philosophy); b. Ipswich, Mass. 1918; p. George A. and Hilda M. Joyce Schofield; h. (div.); c. Joseph W. Epply, III, Diana R. Epply, Mark C. Epply; res: Natick Rd., Oaklawn, R.I. 02920.

SEWELL, SALLIE WIMBERLY, Ed., Journal of Retailing, New York University, 432 Commerce Bldg., Washington Sq., N.Y., N.Y. 10003, '60–; Mng. Ed., '55–'60; Asst. Ed., '54–'55; formerly Ed., Polly Pigtails;

Asst. Ed., National Carbonator and Bottler, Textile Industries; Instr. in English, Univ. of N.C. Wms. Col., Greensboro, N.C.; Free-lance Wtr., '40–; Wms. Press Club, Intl. Platform Assn., Query Club, Pen and Brush Club, AAUW; Hollins Col., '32–'34; Barnard Col., AB, '36; Univ. of N.C., Chapel Hill, MA, '39; N.Y.U., writing, psych., lang. courses, '50–; b. Macon, Ga.; p. Frank and Julia Patterson Sewell; res: 1 University Pl., N.Y., N.Y. 10003.

SEXTON, ANNE HARVEY, Poet: "To Bedlam and Part Way Back" ('60), "All My Pretty Ones" ('62), "Live or Die" ('66), "Love Poems" ('69), "Selected Poems" ('64); PSA, Royal Soc. of Literature (Eng.); Radcliffe Inst. aw., '61–'63; Am. Acad. of Arts and Letters, '63–'64; Ford Fndn., resident poet for plays, '65; Lit. Mag. Travel aw., '66; Pulitzer Prize for Poetry, '67; Guggenheim Aw., '69; b. Newton, Mass., 1928; p. Ralph and Mary Staples Harvey; h. Alfred Sexton; c. Linda, Joyce; res: 14 Black Oak Rd., Weston, Mass. 02193.

SEYBOLD, GENEVA, Free-lance Wtr., Ed.; Sr. Specialist, Employee Commtn., Nat. Indsl. Conf. Bd., '42–'65; Assoc., Raymond Rich Assocs., '38–'42; Staff Mbr., National Municipal Review, '32–'35; Ed., S.W. Straus and Co., '26–'27; Assoc. Ed., Popular Science Monthly, '24–'26; Auth., 23 bks. on bus.; Theta Sigma Phi (N.Y.C. Pfsnl. Chptr. Pres., '26; Past VP, Treas.); Washburn Col., AB, '21 (summa cum laude); Distg. Svc. aw., '58); Columbia Univ. Sch. of Jnlsm., BLitt., '23 (Pulitzer Traveling Scholarship, Europe, '23–'24); courses, London Univ., Sorbonne, Univ. of Geneva; b. Topeka, Kan., 1900; p. George and Rose Abels Seybold; res: 225 E. 66th St., N.Y., N.Y. 10021.

SEYMOUR, BARBARA JACOBSON, Inf. Offcr., Supvsr. Manuals and Info. Svcs., '69–; Oregon Public Welfare Division, 401 Public Service Bldg., Salem, Ore. 97310; Adm. Asst. '63–'69; Staff Asst., Plans and Manuals, '61–'63; Caseworker, '51–'61; various orgs.; Univ. of Chgo., PhB, '48; MA, '62 (with honors); b. Chgo., Ill. 1930; p. Louis and Amelia Potasch Jacobson; h. Douglas Seymour; c. Kim Louis Colin, Leif Mardan; res: 1234 Heather Lane S.E., Salem, Ore. 97302.

SHAFFER, ANN MARNELL, Wms. Dir., KBOL, 2928 Pearl, Boulder, Colo. 80302, '62–; Singer, Traf. Cl., Copywtr., KANS, Wichita, Kan., '36–'40; Staff Vocalist, KFEQ, St. Joseph, Mo., '33–'36; AWRT (Rocky Mt. Chptr: VP, Bd. of Dirs., '67–'68); b. St. Joseph, Mo., 1919; p. John and Nellie Toohey Marnell; h. Russel Shaffer; c. Stephen, Rusty, Jeffrey; res: 1330 King Ave., Boulder, Colo. 80302.

SHAFFER, ELLEN KATE, Rare Bk. Librn., Free Library of Philadelphia, Logan Sq., Phila., Pa. 19103, '54–; Auth: "Fray Gilberti and His Books" ('63), "The Garden of Health" ('57), "The Nuremberg Chronicle" ('50); Antiquarian Bkseller, Dawson's Bk. Shop (L.A., Cal.), '46–'54, '29–'44; WAC, AC, Far East Air Svc.

Command, '44–'45; Librn., Anaheim (Cal.) Elementary Sch. System; Lectr., Lib. Sci., Columbia, '60–; ALA, Manuscript Soc. (Pres.), Bk. Club of Cal., lib., art, hist. orgs.; Riverside Lib. Svc. Sch., cert.; U.C.L.A., BA, '29; Mexico City Col., '51; Univ. of Southern Cal., MA, '54; b. Leadville, Colo.; p. Frank H. and Nellie Maguire Shaffer.

SHAFFER, PAT SLAYBACK, Free-lance Wtr. of hist. novels; Wtr., Prodr., Anncr., two TV series, daily radio interview show, WLBC Radio-TV, Muncie, Ind.; Reptr., Feature Wtr., Muncie Evening Press; Feature Wtr., Cinn. Enquirer, '65; Cnslt., high sch. jnlsm.; Instr., Univ. of Cinn. Evening Col.; various organizations; Ind. Univ., BA; b. Dayton, Ind. 1907; p. Melvin and Grace Lee Slayback; h. John Hoagland Shaffer; c. Dr. William Lee; res: 10102 W. Kelso Dr., Sun City, Ariz. 85351.

SHAFFER, WILMA L. HATFIELD, Ed., The Christian Mother, Standard Publishing, 8121 Hamilton Ave., Cinn., Oh. 45231, '63–; Auth: three devotional bks. for wm., eight nursery-rhyme Bible storybooks for children; Wtr., '54–'57; Cinn. Wms. Press Club, NLAPW, Intl. Platform Assn., Phi Kappa Epsilon, Eastern Star, Delta Criterion Wms. Club (Pres., '47), Beatrice (Neb.) Wms. Club (VP, '54); Univ. of Neb., '53–'54; Univ. of Cinn., assoc. deg., '65; b. Warrensburg, Ill., 1916; p. Jasper and Ethel Thomas Hatfield; h. Bruce H. Shaffer; c. Janice (Mrs. Charles H. Smith), Dr. Lawrence B., Roger A.; res: 9984 Lake Park Dr., Cinn., Oh. 45231.

SHAFTER, ANNETTE ETHEL, Print Media Byr., Arnold & Company Inc., 1111 Park Square Building, Boston, Mass. 02116, '66–; Leland Powers Sch. of Radio, TV and Theater, '56; b. Rockland, Me. 1938; p. Samuel and Diane Rossman Shafter; res: 101 Monmouth St., Brookline, Mass.

SHALLEY, DORIS PARKER, Free-lance Ed.; Asst. Ed., J. B. Lippincott Co., 10 yrs.; Swarthmore Col., BA, '44; h. John Shalley; res: General Sullivan Rd., Washington Crossing, Pa. 18977.

SHAMBURGER, A. PAGE, Contrb. Ed., Air Progress Magazine, 420 Lexington Ave., N.Y., N.Y. 10017, '66–; Auth., non-fiction bks. incl: "Classic Monoplanes" ('66), "Tracks Across the Sky" ('64); Co-auth: "Command the Horizon" ('68), "World War I Aces & Planes" ('68); over 500 articles, mags.; Auths. Guild, Aviation/Space Wtrs. Assn., Ninety-Nines, Aircraft Owners and Pilots Assn., other aviation groups; cit., State of N.C., '64, '66, '67, '68; cit., U.S.A.F., '67; Doris Mullen Memorial Scholarship, helicopter flying; Wms. Advisory Comm. on Aviation; St. Mary's Jr. Col.; Marjorie Webster Col.; b. Aberdeen, N.C.; res: Page Hill, Aberdeen, N.C. 28315.

SHAMBURGER, PEARL GORDON, Librn., Montgomery County Public Library, Troy, N.C. 27371, '60–'68; Tchr., '41–'59, '20–'31, '10–'14; Nat. Tchrs. Assn., ALA, Sandhill Lib. Assn., N.C. Tchrs. Assn., Delta Kappa

Gamma; Guilford Col., BS, '10; Univ. of N.C., MA, '49; b. Guilford County, N.C., 1890; p. James and Mary Idol Gordon; h. Charles Lewis Shamburger; res: Star, N.C. 27356.

SHANAHAN, SHIRLEY, Info. Specialist, Voice of America, U.S. Information Agency, 330 Independence Ave. S.W., Washington, D.C., '63–; Prod. Asst., '59–'63; Secy. to Asst. Program Mgr., '57–'59; Media Analyst, Young and Rubicam, '56–'57; Media Asst., VanSant Dugdal, '52–'56; AWRT (Wash. D.C. Chptr. Secy., '67–'68); Md. Inst., Col. of Art; b. Baltimore, Md.; p. Arthur and Gladys Turner Shanahan; res: 800 Fourth St. S.W., Wash., D.C. 20024.

SHANK, DOROTHY ROTH, Bdcstr., Wms. Dir., WJJL, Hotel Niagara, Niagara Falls, N.Y. 14303, '59–; Fashion Ed., Niagara Falls Gazette, '57–'59; WEBR (Buffalo, N.Y.), '46–'57; WHLD (Niagara Falls, N.Y.), '44–'45; AWRT (Western N.Y. Chptr.'s First Pres.), Zonta Club (Pres., '66–'68), BPW (Pres., '63–'65), College Club, Assn. of Pfsnl. Wm. Wtrs. (Pres., '44), NLAPW (Western N.Y. Chptr. VP), Niagara Area C. of C. Wms. Div. (Bd. Chmn., '65–'67), Nia-Cap (Bd. of Dirs., Chmn., '66–'68); Pubcty. Dir., Niagara Falls Winter Festival, '67, '68; civic work; Who's Who in the East, Who's Who of Am. Wm., 2000 Wm. of Achiev.; Brown Univ., AB, '29; R.I. Sch. of Design; Albright Col., '30–'31; W. Chester State Tchrs.' Col., '34; b. Turbotville, Pa., 1907; p. Rev. William H. and Bessie H. Lotz Roth; h. Lawrence S. Shank; res: 205 59th St., Niagara Falls, N.Y. 14304.

SHANK, MARGARETHE ERDAHL, Eng. Instr., Glendale Community College, 6000 W. Olive Ave., Glendale, Ariz. 85301, '65–; Phoenix (Ariz.) Col., '59–'65; Tchr., various high schs.; Auth: "The Coffee Train" (Doubleday, '52), "Call Back the Years" (Augsburg Publ., '66) AAUP (Secy., '65), Auths. Guild, Nat. Cncl. of Tchrs. of Eng., Alpha Delta Kappa; Hon. Mbr., Intl. Mark Twain Soc.; Who's Who in the West; Contemporary Auths.; Dic. of Intl. Biog.; Univ. of Ariz., BA (Educ.), '31; Univ. of Cal. at Berkeley, '37; Ariz. State Univ., MA (Eng.), '59; b. Turtle Lake, N.D., 1910; p. Bertinus and Gyda Jaastad Erdahl; h. Oliver Shank; c. Stephen Henry; res: 9860 N. 29th Pl., Phoenix, Ariz. 85028.

SHANNON, ALICE ADAMS, Free-lance Wtr., Collaborating Auth., "Resin & Glass Artcraft" (M. Barrows Publ. Co., '66; first prize for non-fiction, NIAPW, '68 Biennial); Tchr., Crtv. Writing, Adult Educ. of San Jose Unified Sch. Dist.; PR, March of Dimes, County Mental Health Assn., Un. Funds; NLAPW (Santa Clara County Br. Pres., '68–'70; VP, Secy.), Cal. Fedn. Chapparral Poets (Robert Frost Chptr. Dir., '64–'65), Cal. Wtrs. Club, Nat. Wtrs. Club, PR Round Table, BPW (Corr. Secy., Secy., '53–'62), Who's Who of Am. Wm., Who's Who in the West, Dic. of Intl. Biog.; b. Fort Madison, Ia., 1916; p. Charles and Isobel Fuller Adams; h. Elwood W. Shannon; c. Laurence M. (dec.); res: 4834 MaryJane Way, San Jose, Cal. 95124.

SHANNON, SHIRLEY McWILLIAMS, Prom. Dir., Mademoiselle mag., Conde Nast Publications, 420 Lexington Ave., N.Y., N.Y. 10017, '66–; Partner, Dickson & Shannon PR, '64–'66; Adv., Prom., PR, VP, Rose Marie Reid (Cal.), '50–'63; Fashion Group (L. A. Chptr. Treas., '62–'63), Sls. Prom. Execs. Assn. (L.A. Club Pres., '61–'62); Western Adv. Wms. Assn. aw., '57; U.C.L.A., BA, '50; h. James V. Shannon; res: Greenwich, Conn. 06830.

SHAPIRO, ETHEL BRONSTEIN, Radio-TV Dir., AE, Hameroff & Associates Advertising & Public Relations, Inc., Suite 1990, 88 E. Broad St., Columbus, Oh. 43215, '70–; Asst. Radio-TV Dir., AE, '69–'70; Copywtr., Prodr., Parker/Berlo Adv., '65–'66; Wtr., Prodr., Host, WOSU-TV, '62; Traf. Mgr., Wtr., '61–'65; Off. Mgr., Copywtr., Lazarus Display Dept., '60–'61; Adv. Club of Columbus; First pl. aw., TV Bureau of Adv. competition among retail advertisers, Furniture stores category, '69; Oh. State Univ., '46–'47; b. Columbus, Oh.; p. Joseph and Sophie Dworkin Bronstein; h. Ralph Shapiro; c. Anita Joye, Michael Alan; res: 2714 Burnaby Dr., Columbus, Oh. 43209.

SHAPIRO, HELEN, VP, Harshe-Rotman & Druck, Inc., 300 E. 44th St., N.Y., N.Y. 10017, '61; Wms. Interest AE, '53–; NHFL, Fashion Group, Pubcty. Club of N.Y.; b. Boston, Mass.

SHAPIRO, LILLIAN LADMAN, Asst. Prof., Dept. of Lib. Sci., St. John's University, Jamaica, N.Y. 11427, '69–; Head Librn., N.Y.C. Bd. of Educ., '65–'67, '48–'63; Acting Asst. Dir. in Chg. of Sr. High Sch. Libs., '63–'65; Lib. Asst., '40–'48; Latin Tchr., '33–'40; panelist, speaker, reviewer; contrbr. to pfsnl. jnls.; ALA, N.Y.C. Sch. Librns. Assn. (VP, Pres., '56–'58), N.Y. Lib. Club (VP, '68; Pres., '69), WNBA, A.S.C.D., N.Y. Film Cncl., Dept. of Audio-Visual Instr.; Eta Sigma Phi, Beta Phi Mu, Who's Who of Am. Wm., Dic. of Intl. Biog.; Hunter Col., BA, '32; Columbia Univ. Sch. of Lib. Svc., BLS, '40; MLS, '69; Additional course work, Columbia Univ., New Sch. for Social Rsch., Queens Col., C. W. Post Col., St. John's Univ.; b. N.Y.C.; p. Julius and Manya Duckerevich Ladman; h. Herman Shapiro; c. Judith R., Mrs. Brian R. Skea; res: 70 E. 10 St., New York City, N.Y. 10003.

SHAPP, MARTHA SEGALL, Ed.-in-Chief, The New Book of Knowledge, Grolier, Inc., 575 Lexington Ave., N.Y., N.Y. 10022, '60–; Curriculum Coordr. for N.Y.C. Elementary Schs., '49–'60; Curriculum Cnslt., N.Y. State Educ. Dept., '49; Tchr., '33–'48; Co-Auth. (with Charles Shapp), "Let's Find Out" series (30 bks.; Franklin Watts); numerous educ. orgs.; Auths. Guild, Nat. Cncl. for the Social Studies; Barnard Col., AB, '29; Columbia Univ., MA, '40; b. N.Y.C., 1910; p. Charles and Anna Mendelson Segall; h. Charles Shapp; c. William Donald Glauber; res: 400 E. 56th St., N.Y., N.Y. 10022.

SHARP, A. CAMILLA, Librn., Technology Campus Library, University of Arkansas, 1201 McAlmont, Box

3017, Little Rock, Ark. 72203, '62–; Asst. Librn., MacMurray Col. (Jacksonville, Ill.), '59–'62; Asst. Librn., Ark. State Univ., '49–'59; Asst. Librn., Henderson State Col., '45–'49; Asst. Librn., Memphis State Univ., '44–'45; WNBA (Little Rock Chptr. Secy., '68–'69), Ark. Lib. Assn. (Secy., '64), ALA; Ark. State Univ., BA, '40; Peabody Col., BS (Lib. Sci.), '44; b. Jonesboro, Ark.; p. Edward and Corinne Mackey Sharp; res: 1620 N. Pierce, Little Rock, Ark. 72207.

SHARP, JANE PRICE, Owner, Ed., The Pocahontas Times, 810 Second Ave., Marlinton, W. Va. 24954, '57–; W. Va. Press Assn. (Dir., Pres., '67), Pocahontas Hist. Soc. (Pres.), C. of C. (Dir.), Wms. Club (Past Pres.), Am. Legion Aux.; Davis and Elkins Col.; b. Marlinton, W. Va., 1919; p. Calvin and Mabel Milligan Price; h. Basil Sharp (dec.); c. Basil P., John C., Mrs. Russell D. Jessee, Jr.; res: 1119 Second Ave., Marlinton, W. Va. 24954.

SHARPE, EILEEN, Assoc., Philip Lesly Co., 33 N. Dearborn St., Chgo., Ill. 60602, '69–; Acc. Rep., J. Walter Thompson Co., '64–'69; AE, M. Collins PR, '60–'63; "Journal About Town," "How America Lives," Ed., Ladies' Home Journal, '52–'60; Mng. Ed., My Baby, '50–'51; Sr. Ed., Sch. and Career Ed., Seventeen, '47–'50; Prod. Ed., Wtr., Glamour, '45–'47; Auth., "How to Promote Your Retail Drugstore;" Benjamin Franklin aw.; res: 1207 W. 97th St., Chgo., Ill. 60643.

SHARPE, RUTH COLLIER, Poet, several bks. and anthologies of poetry, incl: "Tristram of Lyonesse" ('49), "When Falcon from the Wrist & Other Poems" ('49); Penn & Brush Intl. Platform Assn., Marquis Biographical Lib. Soc.; aws: Olcott Fndn., for "Song of the Paramahamsa," '40; 2,000 Wm. of Achiev.; Assn. of Am. Philosophers Seminar; Cert. of Merit for Distg. Svc. to Literature from Dic. of Intl. Biog., '67; Nat. Register of Prominent Ams.; b. Gladstone, Mich., 1897; p. Parrie and Harriet McGannon Collier; h. Richard Sharpe; res: El Morya, 956 West Point Rd., Lake Oswego, Ore. 97034.

SHATTUCK, CYNTHIA JEAN, Media Dir., Edward M. Hechtman Adv./Marketing, 100 E. Ohio St., Chgo., Ill. 60611, '68–; Media Byr., Campbell-Ewald Adv.; Chgo. Bdcst. Adv. Club; Chgo. Adv. Club.

SHAW, BEA, Exec. Prodr., Bea Shaw Productions, 10527 Sarah St., N. Hollywood, Cal. 91602, '63–; Actress, Comml. Spokeswm. on radio, TV, '58–'63; Wms. Prog. Dir., WFAA-TV (Dallas, Tex.), '53–'58; Actress, Margo Jones Theatre (Dallas), and Lake Whalom Playhouse (Fitchburg, Mass.), '50–'53; Hollywood Radio and TV Soc., L.A. Adv. Wm., Adv. Assn. of the West (seven aws.), '67, '68), SAG, AFTRA, AEA, Intl. Platform Assn., Dallas Wms. Club; Aws: 12 Intl. Bdcst., '63–'68; seven Lulu, '64–'68; Southern Cal. Bdcst., '68; six Clio, '66–'68; Don Belding, '67; Dallas Adv. League, '66, '68; Univ. of Tex.; b. Dallas, Tex., 1927; p. Charles and Estelle Goldstein Shaw; h. (div.); c. Donald Shaw Passman; res: Toluca Lake, Cal.

SHAW, ELIZABETH A., Adm. Asst., Alabama Association of Independent Colleges and Universities, Suite 107, 6 Office Park Circle, Birmingham, Ala. 35203, '64–; Secy. to Exec. VP, '63–'64; Secy. to PR Dir. and Sr. VP, Military Svc. Co., Div. of EBSCO Industries, Inc., '48–'63; Birmingham Assn. of Indsl. Eds. (Second VP), Southern Cncl. of Indsl. Eds., Intl. Cncl. of Indsl. Eds., PR Cncl. of Ala.; Samford Univ., '50.

SHAW, ELIZABETH LEWIS, Assoc. Ed., University of Arizona Press, Box 3398, College Station, Tucson, Ariz. 85700, '59–; Free-lance Ed., Wtr., '49–'59; Wms. Ed., Fine Arts Ed., Ariz. Daily Star, '41–'49; Articles and bk. revs: Ariz. Highways, N.M. Historical Magazine, Point West, Phoenix; Wms. Press Club; Univ. of Ariz., BA, (Philosophy) '41; MA (Philosophy) '67; b. Mpls., Minn., 1919; p. Albert L. and Edna Raymond Lewis; h. Ellsworth Shaw; c. Victoria, Franklin, Rebecca, Thomas, John, Mary; res: 3602 E. Flower St., Tucson, Ariz. 85716.

SHAW, ELIZABETH ROBERTS, Dir., Public Info., Museum of Modern Art, 11 W. 53rd St., N.Y., N.Y. 10015, '54–; New York Times, '53; Holiday mag., '51–'53; Citizens Cncl. on City Planning, '49–'51; Phila. Housing Assn., '43–'45; Publrs. Pubcty. Assn.; Smith Col., AB, '42; b. N.Y.C., 1921; p. Lawrence and Margaret McClain Roberts; h. Samuel Parkman Shaw Jr.; c. Chris Anne Boldt, Linda Boldt; res: 162 E. 93rd St., N.Y., N.Y. 10021.

SHAW, GRACE GOODFRIEND, Mng. Ed., Peter H. Wyden, Inc., 750 Third Avenue, N.Y., N.Y., '69–; Ed., Adult Bks., The World Publishing Company, '68–'69; Dir., ed. svcs., '67–'68; Supvsr., '65–'66; Mng. Ed., Bobbs-Merrill Co., '63–'65; Ed., col. dept., '61–'65; Free-lance Ed.-Wtr., '50–'61; Assoc. Ed., C. L. Barnhart and Co., '50; Edtl. Coordr., The World Scope Ency., '46–'50; Reptr., Port Chester (N.Y.) Daily Item, '42–'45; Series Ed., "Americans All" (series, Garrard Publ. Co., '68–); Nat. Assn. of Bk. Eds. (Treas., '68–'69); Bennington Col., '38–'39; b. N.Y.C.; p. Henry B. and Jane Stone Goodfriend; h. Herbert F. Shaw; c. Brandon H.; res: 85 Lee Rd., Scarsdale, N.Y. 10583.

SHAW, IOLA, PR Cnslr., Prin., Shaw Associates, 579 N.E. 79th St., Miami, Fla. 33138, '59–; Instr., PR and Adv., N.Y.C. Commty. Col., '59–'63; Harry Graff PR, '56–'59; Arthur Gasman PR; Am. Soc. of Assoc. Execs., PRSA; PR Soc. (Accredited Mbr.); Hunter Col.; b. Bridgeport, Conn.; c. Deborah Tina; res: 15201 N.E. 6th Ave., N. Miami, Fla.

SHAW, JOY REESE, Dir. of Public Info., Dade County School System, Greater Miami, 1410 N.E. Second Ave., Miami, Fla. 33132, '64–; Special Assigt. Reptr., The Miami Herald, '56–'64; Reptr., Feature Wtr., Colmst., The Jacksonville Jnl., '46–'56; Edtl. Advisory Bd., Educ. USA, '67–'68, '68–'69; Dir., one of four nat. pilot projects on Student Involvement, Project Public Info., '66–'67, '67–'68; Lectr., Auth.; Theta Sigma Phi; NSPRA (VP-at-Large, Exec. Comm., '67–'68,

'68–'69) Southern Assn. of Cols. and Schs. (four public svc. aws.); Associated Dailies of Fla.; 12 1st pl. aws., Fla. Wms. Press Club; numerous other aws.; Who's Who of Am. Wm.; John B. Stetson Univ., AB; Fla. State Univ.; b. Marbury, Ala.; p. Dr. T. O. and Nancy Jane Benson Reese; h. Jerry Shaw; c. Stacey Coleman; res: 3992 Utopia Ct., Coconut Grove, Miami, Fla. 33133.

SHAW, MARY TODD, Artist, Tchr., Mint Museum of Art; One-man shows: Mint Museum of Art (Charlotte, N.C., '67), Furman Univ. ('65), Columbia Museum of Art ('66), others; Exhbns: Nat. Acad. (N.Y.C.), Riverside Museum (N.Y.C.), Royal Scottish Acad. (Edinburgh), many others; Nat. Assn. of Wm. Artists; Who's Who of Am. Wm., Dic. of Intl. Biog., Who's Who of South and Southwest; numerous painting aws.; High Museum Sch. of Art, '41; Ga. Tech., Queens Col.; b. Gadsden, Ala.; p. Oscar and Jennie Harris Todd; h. Edward H. Shaw; c. Barbara T., George N.; res: 6611 Burlwood Rd., Charlotte, N.C. 28211.

SHAW, MILDRED HART, Chief Edtl. Wtr., Bk. Ed., The Daily Sentinel, Grand Junction, Colo. 81501, '46–; Soc. Ed. '35–'40; News Reptr.; Rifle Telegram, '32–'35; Nat. Conf. of Edtl. Wtrs.; top Colo. edtl. aw., '66; Hon. mention, '67; Dir., HS Great Bks. Seminar; Grand Junction Comm. for Gifted Child; Co-chmn., Dist. 51 Project Bookshelf; Univ. of Wash., '27–'30; b. Casaus, N.M., 1909; p. William L. and Pearl Barker Hart; h. J. Earl Shaw; c. James S.; res: 2778 Patterson Rd., Grand Junction, Colo. 81501.

SHAW, RAY, Free-lance Wtr., Photo-Jnlst.; Photo Assigts. in '70: Russia, Alaska, Mexico; former Sculptor, hand portraits of Bernard Baruch, Irving Berlin, George Washington Carver, Jack Dempsey, Gen. James Doolittle, Albert Einstein, Franklin D. Roosevelt, others; Auth: "Week in Lateef's World," (Macmillan Co., '70), "Week in Tooran's World" (Kashmir; Macmillan Co., '70), "Week in Charlene's World" (Zuni, N.M.; Macmillan), "The Nutcracker" (Prentice-Hall, '70); Wms. Press Club, OPC; Northwestern Univ., N.Y.U.; b. Lithuania; h. (dec.); c. Faith, Lee; res: 255 W. 90th St., N.Y., N.Y. 10024.

SHAW, RETA, Actress, "The Ghost and Mrs. Muir" TV series, 20th Century Fox Production, Beverly Hills, Cal.; stage appearances incl: "The Pajama Game," "Picnic"; TV shows incl: "Red Skelton," "I Spy," others; screen appearances, 15 films, incl: "Mary Poppins," "Pollyanna"; Tchr., Bishop-Lee Sch. (Boston, Mass.); Tchr., Buffalo Little Theatre, one yr.; AEA, SAG, AFTRA (Credit Un. Bd. of Dirs. Secy.); Zeta Phi Eta, Cal. PTA (Hon. Life Mbr.); Leland Powers Sch. of the Theatre (Boston, Mass.), '33; b. S. Paris, Me.; p. Howard W. and Edna M. Easson Shaw; h. (div.); c. Kathryn Forester; res: 12403 Addison St., N. Hollywood, Cal. 91607.

SHAW, TERRI (CHARLOTTE ANN), Reptr., Asso-ciated Press, 50 Rockefeller Plaza, N.Y., N.Y. 10020, '65–; Buffalo Courier-Express, '62–'64; Wire Svc. Guild; Inter-Am. Press Assn. Scholarship, S.A., '66–'67; Antioch Col., BA, '63; Columbia Univ. Grad. Sch. of Jnlsm., MS, '65 (hons.); b. Wash., D.C., 1940; p. Richard and Kathleen Penn Shaw; res: 110 Sullivan St., N.Y., N.Y. 10012.

SHAY, MYRTLE QUICK, Free-lance Wtr.; juv. bks: "Adventures of Ricky and Chub" (Lantern Press, '65), "Two on the Trail" (Bobbs-Merrill, '67); fiction, articles, poetry in numerous pubns.; Ind. State Normal, '10; Ind. Bus. Col., '20; Okla. Univ., '45–'46; Maren Elwood Col., '52–'53; b. Columbus, Ind., 1889; p. Tunis and Emma Harris Quick; h. Edward B. Shay; res: P.O. Box 6314, Phoenix, Ariz. 85005.

SHEA, ELEANOR BENSON, Wms. Ed., Bk. Reviewer, Art Ed., Holyoke Transcript-Telegram, 180 High St., Holyoke, Mass. 01040, '68–; Bk., Reviewer, Art Ed., '64–; Soc. Ed., '64–'68; Social Reptr., '61–'64; Substitute Art Tchr., Holyoke public schs., '60; Asst. Ed., Wms. Home Companion Magazine (N.Y.C.), '40–'42; various orgs.; b. N.Y.C., 1915; p. Charles and Mary Newbranch Benson; h. Stephen R. Shea; c. Maureen Lois, Kathleen B., Stephen C.; res: 275 Franklin St., Holyoke, Mass. 01040.

SHEA, RITA SCHIFF, Prod. Mgr., George Roman Advertising, Inc., 810 N. Calvert St., Balt., Md. 21202, '62–'68; Brager Gutmans Adv. Dept., '60–'62; Bahms, Birnbaum, Gerber & Wolf Adv. '59–'60; Irvins Dept. Store Adv., '58–'59; b. Balt., Md., 1939; p. Louis B. and Lena Genovese Schiff; h. James Morrow Shea; res: 118 So. Eaton St., Balt., Md. 21224.

SHEAR, MARIAN MARGOLIN, Partner, Margolin-Shear & Assoc., 2201 Grand Ave., Kan. City, Mo. 64108, '58–; VP, Litman-Stevens & Margolin, '54–'58; Copy Chief, Litman-Bremson & Assoc., '51–'54; Pubcty. Cnslt., various groups incl: Jewish Commty. Ctr., '51–; Dems. of Johnson County, Kan., '63–; various organizations and aws.; Univ. of Ill., BS (Jnlsm.), '51 (Mortar Bd., Phi Beta Kappa, Torch, Alpha Lamba Delta); b. Kan. City, Mo., 1931; p. Louis and Lillian Mnookin Margolin; h. Brad Shear; c. Lisa Meredith, Barbara Jill; res: 8212 Dearborn St., Prairie Village, Kan. 66208.

SHEETS, PHYLLIS VAN METER, Sci. Wtr., Instr., University of Nebraska Medical Center, 42nd and Dewey Ave., Omaha, Neb. 68105, '68–; Biomedical Commtns. Instr., grad. program '68, '69, '70; Pubns. Ed., Bishop Clarkson Memorial Hospital, '63–'68; Rsch. Asst., Ill. State Geological Survey, '59; Asst. to Dir., Kan. State Univ. News Bur., '57–'58; Reptr., Coffeyville (Kan.) Daily Jnl., '44–'47; various organizations; Kan. State Col., BS (Indsl. Jnlsm.), '43; b. Ada, Kan. 1921; h. Norman Sheets; c. Sara, Marla; res: 4119 Monroe, Omaha, Neb. 68107.

SHEARIN, ROSE ANN, VP, Crtv. Dir., Geyer,

Oswald, Inc., 555 Madison Ave., N.Y., N.Y. 10022, '67–; Benton & Bowles, '62–'67; J. Walter Thompson, '56–'62; Young & Rubicam, '51–'56; Printer's Ink Club of the Yr. Aw., '52; several Clios and Reg. Radio aws.; Univ. of N.C., AB, '51; b. Rocky Mount, N.C., 1930; p. Claude and Nina Kitchen Shearin; res: 9 Appletree Lane, Great Neck, N.Y. 11024.

SHECTER, LYNN HOLLANDER, Mgr., Adv. and PR, Gelman Instrument Company, 600 S. Wagner Rd., Ann Arbor, Mich. 48106, '67–; Pubns. Ed., '66–'67; Pres., Penguin Assocs., '63–'66; Copy Ed., Coronet Magazine, '64–'65; Assoc. Ed., Majestic Publ. Co., '63–'64; Ed., Magazine Mgt. Co., Inc., '61–'63; Wtr., magazine articles; Wms. Adv. Club of Detroit, League of Wm. Voters; N.Y.U., BS, '60 (cum laude; Kappa Delta Phi hon. scholarship); MA, '61; Univ. of Mich., '69–; b. N.Y.C.; h. Robert Joseph Shecter; res: 521 N. Division, Ann Arbor, Mich. 48104.

SHEEHAN, BARBARA ANN, Dir. of PR, Metromedia Producers Corporation, 485 Lexington Ave., N.Y., N.Y. 10017, '68; Prod. Coordr., Allen Funt Prods., '67–'68; AE, Bill Doll & Co., '62–'67; S.F. State Univ.; b. N.Y.C., 1941; p. Andrew and Eleanor Garrett Sheehan; res: 141 E. 56th St., N.Y., N.Y. 10022.

SHEEHAN, MARIE-LOUISE McINTOSH, Dir., Chillicothe & Ross County Public Library, 140–46 S. Paint St., Chillicothe, Oh. 45601, '69–; Librn., '58–'68; Cnslt., Pickaway Co. Lib., '68–; Bk. Reviewer, Chillicothe Gazette, '68–; Contrbr., Americana Ency., '68; Instr. Lib. Sci., Oh. Univ., '60–'66; Librn., Perry Co. Public Lib. (New Lexington, Oh.), '54–'56; Asst. Dir., John McIntire Public Lib., '50–'52; Linden Public Lib. (Linde, N.J.), '42–'46; Children's Lib., N.Y. Public Lib. '41–'42; Oh. Lib. Assn.; Douglass Col., Rutgers Univ., BA (Lib. Sci.), '41; Grad. Sch. Educ. '43–'46; b. Roselle, N.J., 1916; p. Stanley and Aurore Panciatichi McIntosh; h. Francis X. Sheehan; c. Christopher, Joe, Frances; res: 167 W. 2nd St., Chillicothe, Oh. 45601.

SHEEHY, GAIL HENION, Contrb. Ed., New York Magazine, 207 E. 32nd St., N.Y., N.Y., '68–; Cosmopolitan, '66–'68; Feature Wtr., N.Y. Herald Tribune, '63–'66; NWC Best Feature Writing Aw., '64; Rockefeller Rsch. Fellowship, Race Rels. Reporting, Columbia Univ., '69; Univ. of Vt., BS; courses, N.Y.U., New Sch. for Social Rsch.; b. Mamaroneck, N.Y.; p. Harold Henion and Lillian Henion Paquin; h. Albert Sheehy (div.); c. Maura; res: 26 W. 86th St., N.Y., N.Y. 10023.

SHEETZ, ALYCE ROGERS, Asst. Prof. of Jnlsm., Univ. of Oregon, Pubns. Dir., Univ. of Oregon, Exec. Secy., Oregon Scholastic Press, '69–; Pubns. Advisor, Jnlsm. Tchr., South Eugene High School, '58–'69; Prom. Mgr., KVAL-TV; Reprtr., Springfield (Ore.) News; Wtr., Ed., Jaffe Pubns. (L.A., Cal.); Theta Sigma Phi, Kappa Tau Alpha, NEA, Eugene Press Club, Columbia Scholastic Press Assn., Nat. Scholastic Press Assn., Ore. Scholastic Press Assn., Jnlsm. Educ. Assn.; Univ. of Ore., BS (Jnlsm.), MS (Jnlsm.); b. Wilkeson, Wash.; p.

Mr. and Mrs. Albert E. Rogers; h. (div.); c. John R. Sheetz; res: 1642 Hilyard St., Eugene, Ore. 97401.

SHEETZ, ANN KINDIG, Ed., Akron/Mentone News, Box 277, Akron, Ind. 46910, '68–; News and Feature Ed., Akron News, '62–'68; Ed., Mentone News, '65–'68; short stories and articles: Highlights for Children, Light and Life Evangel, Story Time, Teen Time; Hoosier State Press Assn. (adv. aw., '68); Ind. Univ., '52–'53; Manchester Col., '66–'67; b. Kosciusko County, Ind., 1934; p. F. Leon and Margaret Hammerel Kindig; h. Loren Sheetz; c. Todd Kevin, Douglas Brian; res: R.R. 2, Akron, Ind. 46910.

SHEFFIELD, ANN WALKER, Soc. Ed., The Times-Recorder, 415 W. Forsyth St., Americus, Ga. 31709, '31–; Fla. State Univ.; b. Americus, Ga., 1908; p. James and Jessie Daniel Walker; h. Wallace B. Sheffield (dec.); res: 234 Taylor St., Americus, Ga. 31709.

SHELBY, LILA NORMA, Artist; one-man shows at Aregnt Galleries, N.Y.C., '40; La. Art. Commn., (Baton Rouge), '40; Southern Galleries (Shreveport), '63; many group shows; portraits incl. Billy Graham, Vice President Alben Barkley; Nat. Assn. Wm. Artists, NLAPW, Arts Student League; Who's Who of Am. Wm., Who's Who in the South; Dic. of Intl. Biog.; Columbia Univ., '40–'41; b. Simsboro, La., 1900; p. Jesse and Ola Calahan Shelby; h. Matthew Mark Wallace; res: 718 Green Acres Rd., Metairie, La. 70003.

SHELLEY, SALLY SWING, Chief Info. Offcr., United Nations Educational, Scientific and Cultural Organization, United Nations, N.Y., N.Y. 10017, '57–; Chief Info. Offcr., '69–; Mgr., Am. Soc. of Indsl. Designers, '52–'57; Radio News Ed., Voice of Am., '52; U.S. Army Field Svc. for Japan, '50–'52; Fgn. Corr., UP, '49–'50; Feature Wtr., Boston Globe, '44–'46; Visiting Lectr. in Polit. Sci., Col. of the City of N.Y., '61–'62; UNCA; Who's Who of Am. Wm.; Who's Who in the East; Smith Col., AB (English, Hist.); Grad. Studies: Univ. of Paris (Philosophy), Columbia Univ. (Film, TV); b. Kent, England, 1929; p. Raymond and Betty Gram Swing; h. James M. Shelley; c. Sidney S.; res: 510 E. 23rd St., N.Y., N.Y. 10010.

SHEMANSKI, FRANCES, Assoc. Ed., Travel Weekly, One Park Ave., N.Y., N.Y. 10016, '67–; Travel Wtr. and PR, Lufthansa Airlines, '66–'67; Assoc. Travel Ed., World-Journal-Tribune, '66; Travel, Religious, Educ. Ed., N.Y. Journal American, '49–'66; conducted adult educ. in travel, N.Y.U., '63; Theta Sigma Phi (N.Y. Chptr. VP Programs, '66–'68), Soc. of Am. Travel Wtrs. (Nat. Secy., '60–'61; N.Y. Chptr. Pres., '65), Medal from Israeli Tourist Office for columns. on Israel, '63; Hunter Col., BA (Jnlsm.), '47; b. Arena, N.Y., 1925; p. John and Helen Goleneski Shemanski; res: 2716 Gunther Ave., The Bronx, N.Y. 10469.

SHEPARD, ELAINE ELIZABETH, Wtr., Bdcstr., Actress; bks: "Forgive Us Our Press Passes" (Prentice-

Hall, '62), "The Doom Pussy" (Schuster, '67), both nominated for OPC Best Bk. Aw.; Fgn. Corr., N. Am. Nwsp. Alliance, '59–; Combat Corr., Mutual, Vietnam, '65–'66 (two cits., 145th Aviation Battalion); White House Press Corps, '59–'60; WINS, Dem. Conv., '56; Modr., "Hollywood Reporter," WITG-TV, Wash., D.C.; "Free Ride," WNBW-TV; numerous theatre, motion pic. roles; AEA, SAG, AGVA, AFTRA, OPC; Offcl. Commendation, Mayor Sam Yorty, L.A., Cal.; b. Olney, Ill.; p. Thomas and Bernice Shadle Shepard; res: 12 E. 62nd St., N.Y., N.Y. 10021.

SHEPARD, JOAN, Wms. Ed., WINS, 90 Park Ave., N.Y., N.Y. 10016, '69–; Fashion Reprtr., Women's Wear Daily, '64–'69; Drexel Inst. of Tech., BS, '64; b. Phila., Pa., 1941; p. David and Olivia Shepard Walker.

SHEPARD, M. JOAN, Free-lance Prodr./Dir., Network for Continuing Medical Education, Distrbr. Viviane Woodward, '69–; Adm. Asst. to Pres., TV Stations, Inc. (N.Y.C.), '69; Prodr., Public Bdcst. Lab., '67–'69; Prodr.-Dir., Instr., Bklyn. Col. TV Ctr., '65–'67; Dir., WNDT, '62–'65; Asst. to Prog. Mgr., NET, '61–'62; Prod. Staff, CBS News, '60; Public Affairs Prog. Cnslt. to 115 stations; Dirs. Guild of Am., NATAS, NAEB; Who's Who of Am. Wm.; Syrcause Univ., BS (Radio-TV), '51; MS (TV), '60; b. Erie, Pa., 1929; p. Samuel and Margaret D. Shepard; res: 210 E. 73rd St., N.Y., N.Y. 10021.

SHEPHARD, GERALDINE, Pres., Geraldine Shephard Assoc., 1199 Park Ave., N.Y., N.Y. 10028, '66–; AE, Marianne Strong Assoc., '64–'66; AE, Universal PR, '61–'64; Asst. Ed., Vogue; PR Cnslt., John V. Lindsay mayoral campaign; Jr. League of N.Y., River Club of N.Y.; Principia Col., BA; b. S.F., Cal.; p. C. A. and Vera H. Shephard.

SHEPHERD, BETTY BONNET, PR, Dev. Secy., National Conference on Social Welfare, 22 W. Gay St., Columbus, Oh. 43215, '63–; Pubcty. Dir., Public Svc. Coordr., WLWC-TV, '54–'63; Alumni Record, Oh. State Univ., '30–'44; PRSA, ICIE, NATAS; Who's Who of Am. Wm.; Oh. State Univ., BA, '30 (cum laude; Phi Beta Kappa); b. Columbus, Oh., 1909; p. Alvin and Katherine Early Bonnet; h. Frank Shepherd (dec.); c. Douglas, India Katherine (dec.); res: 2430 Brentwood Rd., Columbus, Oh. 43209.

SHEPHERD, ELEANOR LOUISE, Wms. News and Fashion Dir., KUSN, Howitt Bldg., Eighth and Frederick, St. Joseph, Mo. 64501, '55–; KFEQ and KFEQ-TV, '45–'55; Air Transport Command, '43–'45; AWRT (Kan. City, Mo. Chptr. Treas., '65–'66), C. of C., St. Joseph Civic Ballet (Secy.-Treas. '68–'69); Golden Slipper Radio-TV Aw., Nat. Footwear Inst., '65; Mo. Press Wm. writing aws., '68; Who's Who of Am. Wm., Who's Who in Food and Lodging; Platt Bus. Univ.; res: 624-1/2 No. 7th St., St. Joseph, Mo. 64501.

SHEPHERD, EMALENE SHERMAN, Free-lance Wtr., Ed. Assoc., Writer's Digest, 22 E. 12th St., Cinn., Oh.

45210, '68; Asst. Supvsr., TV-Radio Dept., Univ. of Cinn., '63–'68; Bk., "The Student Journalist and Freelance Writing," (Richards Rosen Press, '67); many mag. articles; Theta Sigma Phi (Cinn. Chptr. Secy., '68–'69), NLAPW; Univ. of Cinn., PhB, '54 (Phi Kappa Epsilon Scholarship Key); b. Cinn., Oh., 1920; p. George and Dulcie Wentworth Sherman; h. Justice Shepherd; c. John Alan; res: 8251 Cheviot Rd., Cinn., Oh. 45239.

SHEPPARD, JUDITH HELENE, VP, Assoc. Rsch. Dir., The Marschalk Company, Inc., 1271 Ave. of the Americas, N.Y., N.Y. '69–; Assoc. Rsch. Dir., '65–; Rsch., Gen. Foods, '54–'65; Am. Mktng. Assn.; Queens Col., BA (Psy.); b. N.Y.C.; p. George and Grace Wollenberg Silverburgh; res: 245 E. 63rd St., N.Y., N.Y. 10021.

SHEPPARD, SARA LANDIS, Mgr., Prom. and Adv., Chilton Book Co., 401 Walnut St., Phila., Pa. 19106; formerly Prom. Mgr., Reinhold Trade Bk. Dept.; Prom. Cnslt., Watson-Guptill Pubns.; Dir., Prom. and Adv., Oceana Pubns.; Edtl. Asst., Doubleday; Univ. of N.C., '42; b. Badin, N.C., 1923; p. Thomas and Ouida Watson Sheppard; h. (div.); c. Susan Sheppard Landis, Timothy Joseph Landis, Margaret Carol Landis; res: 222 W. Rittenhouse Sq., Phila., Pa. 19103.

SHERARD, MARY MORRISON, Dir., Vicksburg Public Library, 1420 Monroe St., Vicksburg, Miss. 39180, '52–; Reprtr., Miss. Lib. News, '65–; weekly bk. col., Vicksburg Evening Post; State Chmn., Nat. Lib. Week, '58; Lib. plays; Miss. State Col. for Wm., '38–'42; La. State Univ., '52; b. Vicksburg, Miss.; p. Harry G. and Louise Hagan Sherard; res: Rte. 3, Box 5, Vicksburg, Miss. 39180.

SHERBURNE, ZOA MORIN, Free-lance Wtr., William Morrow & Company, 425 Park Ave. S., N.Y., N.Y.; 12 bks., young adults; about 300 short stories; poems; Lectr., sch. confs.; wtrs. convs.; Tchr., short story writing, Cornish Sch. of Allied Arts, '57; Speaker, C.L.A. conv., '68; Phi Delta Nu, Free-lance Wtrs., NLAPW; Matrix Table, Wm. of Achiev., '50; Child Study Assn. aw., bk., "Jennifer," '59; b. Seattle, Wash., 1912; p. Thomas and Zoa Mae Webber Morin; h. Herbert N. Sherburne; c. Marie (Mrs. Steven Brumble), Norene (Mrs. Frank Perdue), Zoa (Mrs. Arnold Holte), Anne, Herbert, Thomas, Philip, Robert; res: 5420 Kirkwood Pl. N., Seattle, Wash. 98103.

SHERF, TERRY (Harriet N. Sherf), President, Terry Sherf & Associates, Inc., Advertising and Public Relations, 13415 Ventura Blvd., Sherman Oaks, Cal. 91403, '63–; TV Wtr., NBC-TV "Queen for a Day" series, '58–'60; articles, edtl. contrbs. published in numerous nat. mags.; Ed. for publrs., incl. Prentice-Hall; Nwsp. Colmst.; AWRT, Am. Publicists' Guild, Am. Soc. of Fin. Wtrs. and Publicists; Univ. of Cal. (Berkeley), BA, '57; U.C.L.A. Grad. Sch. of Jnlsm.; b. Chgo., Ill., 1934; p. Mortimer and Beatrice Flamm Sherf; res: Sherman Oaks, Cal.

SHERMAN, JAYNE BARON, Ed., American Telephone & Telegraph Co., 123 William St., N.Y., N.Y. 10038, '69–; Tech. Wtr.-Ed., First National Bank of Miami, '67–'69; Free-lance Wtr.; Cnslt. (PR, Adv.), Dev. Corp. of Am.; Bus. Mgr., Tempo Magazine; Mng. Ed., Ed.-in-Chief, Miami Hurricane; Theta Sigma (Miami Chptr. VP, '66–'67); Orange Key, '66–'67; Shimer Col., '64–'65; Univ. of Miami, BA, '67; Am. Inst. of Banking, '68; b. Bklyn., N.Y., 1946; p. Alvin and Gloria Sherman; res: 4 E. 10th St., N.Y., N.Y. 10003.

SHERMAN, MARGOT, Sr. VP, McCann-Erickson, Inc., 485 Lexington Ave., N.Y., N.Y. 10017, '64–; Copy Wtr., '37; Adm. Dir., Crtv. Div., '57–'63; VP, '49–'64; Chmn., Crtv. Plans Bd., '57–; Plans Rev. Bd., '60–; Sr. VP, Asst. to Pres., Bd. of Dirs., '64–; Wms. Ed., Colmst., "Shopping with Polly"; Adv. Dept., J. L. Hudson dept. store; Copy Staff, Montgomery Ward (N.Y.C.); Reptr., N.Y. World-Telegram; AWNY (VP, '59–'60); Adv. Wm. of Yr., '58; various other organizations and aws.; Univ. of Mich., BA (summa cum laude; Phi Beta Kappa; Phi Kappa Phi; Theta Sigma Phi; Outstanding Achiev. aw., '65); b. Detroit, Mich.; p. Harry and Elise Stackel Sherman; h. Charles D. Peet (dec.); c. Charles D., Jr., Margaret; res: 944 Kimball Ave., Bronxville, N.Y. 10708.

SHERMAN, MARJORIE W., Soc. Ed., The Boston Globe, Boston, Mass. 02107, '35–; Lectr., Radcliffe Col.; Wms. Press Club, World Affairs Cncl.; Boston Cncl. for Intl. Visitors, UNICEF Bd.; Wms. Press Assn. aws.; Boston Univ., London Sch. of Econs.; b. Boston, Mass., 1912; p. Albert and Bessie Goulding Watts; h. (div.); c. Samuel W., Frederick T.; res: 176 Main St., Hingham, Mass. 02043.

SHERMAN, SARA JO BERRY, Free-lance Wtr., Bdcstr., PR Dir.; currently PR Dir. of Holiday Hills Resort, Crossville, Tenn.; Fashion Reptr. for Sunday Gleaner and Evening Star, Kingston, Jamaica, West Indies; Freeport News (Bahamas); formerly Fashion Wtr.-Colmst. for Pawtucket (R.I.) Times, North Attleboro (Mass.) Evening Chronicle; Wms. Ed., Nashville Magazine; formerly Bdcstr., numerous stations; Voice of America; American Services Radio, Europe; Who's Who of Am. Wm.; McCall's Golden Mike aw. for Most Outstanding Wm. Bdcstr., '59; b. Monterey, Tenn.; p. Everett and Lula Sehon Berry; c. John; res: Mountain Manor, Monterey, Tenn. 38574.

SHERR, LYNN BETH, Wtr., Associated Press, 50 Rockefeller Plaza, N.Y., N.Y. 10020, '69–; Ed., Filmstrip Div., '65–'69; Edtl. Asst., Wtr.; Conde Nast Pubns., '63–'65; Educ. Film Lib. Assn. aw., '67–'69; Wellesley Col., BA, '63.

SHERRILL, JOSEPHINE PRICE, Head Librn., Livingstone College Carnegie Library, Monroe St., Salisbury, N.C. 28144, '28–'70; Tchr., '16–'28; ALA, N.C. Lib. Assn., Assn. of Col. and Rsch. Libs., N.C. Tchrs. Assn.; Livingston Col., AB, '16; Hampton Inst., BS (Lib. Sci.), '28; b. Salisbury, N.C., 1893; p. Joseph and Jennie Smallwood Price; h. Richard Sherrill; c. Charles, Richard, Jennie (dec.); res: 828 W. Monroe St., Salisbury, N.C. 28144.

SHERRILL, SARAH BARKER, Asst. Ed., Antiques Magazine, 551 Fifth Ave. N.Y., N.Y. 10017, '67–; Asst. Ed., Prod. Mgr., The Public Interest, '66–'67; Asst. Ed., Shorewood Press, '65–'66; G. P. Putnam's, '64–'65; Asst. Ed., Mng. Ed. Atlantic Monthly Press, '58–'64; Houghton Mifflin Co., '57–'58; Smith Col., BA, '57 (Phi Beta Kappa).

SHERTZER, MARION PETERSEN (Marion Corwell), Educ. Affairs Rep., Ford Motor Company, The American Rd., Dearborn, Mich. 48121, '66–; Dir., Sch. Relations, Dearborn Public Schs., '62–'66; Mgr., Educ. TV, Henry Ford Museum and Greenfield Village, '54–'62; Asst. Film Dir., '53; Prod. Asst., WMSB-TV (E. Lansing, Mich.), '52–'54; Public Speaking Instr., Henry Ford Commty. Col., '62–'66; Cnslt., Conf. on Educ. Dissemination, Univ. of Ill., '68; Cnslt., Midwest Airborne TV Workshop, Wayne State Univ. (Detroit), '57; Cnslt., Seminar and Workshop for Tchs., Univ. of Wis., '58; Bd. of Trustees, Andrews Univ., '68–; AWRT (Nat. Pres., '69–'70; Detroit Chptr. Pres., '59–'61, Five-to-Watch Aw., '64; E. Central Area. VP, '61–'63; Pres.-Elect '68–'69), Theta Sigma Phi (Headliner Aw., '69), Mich. Sch. PR Assoc., Met. Detroit Sch. PR Assn. (Founder; Pres., '65–'66), PRSA, Mich. Wms. Commn., Nat. Educ. Bdcstrs. Assn.; Inst. for Educ. by Radio-TV Aw., '59; Detroit Advisory Cnsl. Aw., '58; Mich. State Univ., BA, '53; MA, '54; Univ. of Cal., Tokyo branch, '51; b. Hillsdale, Ill., 1926; p. Andrew and Ellen Knudsen Petersen; h. William Shertzer; c. Ann Elizabeth; res: 28911 W. Huron River Dr., Flat Rock, Mich. 48135.

SHERWOOD, ALTA PINKERTON, Circ. Dir., Quarter Horse Journal, 2736 W. 10th, Amarillo, Tex. 79105, '64–; Circ. Dept., '59–'64; Dague Col., '39; b. Kingman, Kan., 1920; p. Frank and Anna Johnson Pinkerton; h. Karl L. Sherwood; c. Mrs. Patricia J. Jones; res: 2717 Curtis Dr., Amarillo, Tex. 79109.

SHERWOOD, JEAN SWIHART, Children's Librn., Redwood City Public Library, 881 Jefferson Ave., Redwood City, Cal. 94063, '57–; WNBA (S.F. Chptr. Org. Chmn., '68), Assn. of Children's Librns. of Northern Cal. (Pres., '61), ALA, Cal. Lib. Assn. (Children's Svcs. Div. Pres., '67); Abbot Acad., '28; Ecole Vinet, Lausanne, Switzerland; Cas Alta, Florence, Italy; Vassar, '33; b. Elyria, Oh.; p. Homer and Hazel Spurrier Swihart; h. Norman Sherwood; c. Norman E., Jr., Daniel R.; res: 12 Duane St., Redwood City, Cal. 94062.

SHIBE, HELEN BORDEN, Artist, Interior Designer; exhbns. incl: Brian Gallery (Santa Monica, Cal.), '64–'67; Jane Freeman Gallery (W. L.A., Cal.); many others; represent sculptor; Art Tour, Europe, TWA, Am. Express; Head, Group Ins., Douglas Aircraft Co. (Santa Monica, Cal.), '36–'38; Intl. Platform Assn., Westwood Art Assn., Japan-Am. Soc.; featured, Better

Homes & Gardens, House Beautiful, L.A. Times, '53–'58; Cert. of Merit, Distg. Svc., Art, Interior Design; Dic. of Intl. Biog.; 2,000 Wm. of Achiev.; Layton Art Sch.; Chgo. Art Inst., '28–'29; Univ. of Wis., BA, '34; U.C.L.A., '48–'49; b. Kaukauna, Wis.; p. Charles J. and Amanda Lindauer Borden; h. Ray Carlton Shibe (dec.); res: 11361 Ovada Pl., L.A., Cal. 90049.

SHINN, EUNICE A., Lib. Cnslt. to State Insts., Arkansas Library Commission, 506-1/2 Center, Little Rock, Ark. 72201, '67–; Ref. Librn., '62–'67; High Sch. Librn., '47–'62; Elem. Sch. Tchr., '29–'47; Delta Kappa Gamma, AAUW (Chptr. Secy.), '55), WNBA, Ark. Lib. Assn. (Secy., '62–'63); Ark. Polytechnic Col., '27–'29; State Col. of Ark., BS (Elem. Educ.), '45; La. State Univ., BS (Lib. Sci.), '54; b. Russellville Ark.; p. Nathaniel and Elizabeth Thompson Shinn; res: 205 Country Club Rd., N. Little Rock, Ark. 72116.

SHINN, MARGARET ANN, Actress, Diamond Artists Agency, 8400 Sunset Blvd., L.A., Cal. 90069, '65–; Films: "Valley of the Dolls," "Conception 3," "The Night of the Beast," "Hush, Hush, Sweet Charlotte"; TV: "Ben Casey," "Bonanza," "The Beverly Hillbillies," "Love of Life"; AFTRA, SAG, AEA; La. State Univ., BA, '62; Am. Acad. of Dramatic Arts; HB Studio; Columbia Film Ind. Workshop; b. N.O., La., 1940; p. William and Verna Carpenter Shinn; h. Frederick Cooper Gray; c. Erik Jon.

SHIPMAN, DOROTHY MIDDLEBROOK, Dir., Shipman Library, Adrian College, Williams St., Adrian, Mich. 49221, '54–'64; Librn., St. Joseph's Hosp. Nursing Sch. (Ann Arbor), '53–'54; Librn., Manistique Sch. and Public Lib., '18–'53; Tchr., '15–'18; ALA, Mich. Lib. Assn., Upper Peninsula Lib. Assn., Marquis Biog. Lib. Soc.; Adrian Col. Lib. named in her hon., '63; Who's Who in Mich.; Who's Who in the Midwest; Who's Who of Am. Wm.; Wells Col., '14; Univ. of Mich., MS (Lib. Sci.), '53; b. Manistique, Mich., 1892; p. William and Dora James Middlebrook; res: 412 Walnut St., Manistique, Mich. 49854.

SHIRCLIFF, JOYCE SMITH, Exec. Opns. Dir., KPPC AM/FM, Crosby-Avery Broadcasting, 585 E. Colorado Blvd., Pasadena, Cal. 91101, '67–; Adv. Dir., KADS, McLendon Corp., '65–'66; AWRT; b. Tulsa, Okla., 1930; p. Walter and Edith Richardson Smith; h. Edward Shircliff; c. Toni D., Mrs. Carol Ann Willis, Skipper; res: 12633 S. La Reina, Downey, Cal. 90242.

SHIRLEY, BETTY E., TV, Radio Casting Dir., LaRoche, McCaffrey and McCall, Inc., 575 Lexington Ave., N.Y., N.Y. 10022, '66–; Casting Dir., "The Doctors" (NBC-TV), '66; Casting Dir., Papert, Koening, Lois, '64–'65; Casting Dir., Doyle, Dane Bernbach, '62–'64; Zeta Phi Eta; Fla. State Univ., BA, '48; N.Y.U., MA, '51; b. Tampa, Fla.; p. Lyman and Betty Bridges Shirley; res: Sylvan Blvd., Alpine, N.J. 07620.

SHIRLEY, VIRGINIA L., VP, Media Mgr., S.M.Y. Inc., 676 N. St. Clair St., Chgo., Ill. 60611, '69–; Media Dept.

Mgr., Don Kemper Co., '62–'69; Northwestern Univ.; b. Kankakee, Ill. 1936; p. Glenn and Virginia Ritter Shirley; res: 1501 N. State Pkwy., Chgo., Ill. 60610.

SHOEMAKER, VIVIEN B. KEATLEY, Free-lance Wtr., PR; Ed., Manhattan Eye, Ear and Throat Hospital (N.Y.C.), '64–'65; PR Dept. Nat. Assn. for Mental Health (N.Y.C.), '63–'64; PR Dir., Tucson (Ariz.) Estates, '61–'63; Ed., Western Ways Features, '50–'59; Edtl. Rsch. Dir., Farm Mgt. Magazine (L.A., Cal.), '51; Reptr., Tucson Daily Citizen, '50; Auth., bks., over 200 articles and feature stories; Ariz. Press Wm. (Pres., '60–'61), Tucson and Phoenix Press Clubs, OPC, PRSA, NFPW (Reg. Dir., '64–'68; 1st Pl. Hon. aw., '59); Who's Who in Ariz.; Who's Who of Am. Wm.; Univ. of Mich., AB (Jnlsm., Rhetoric, Philosophy), '32 (with distinction); b. Hillsboro, Tex., 1909; p. Charles and Nora Smith Bulloch; h. Perry Monroe Shoemaker; c. Linda C., Kent P., Karen A., Craig M.; res: 5202 Neptune Way, Tampa, Fla. 33609.

SHONTZ, PATRICIA O'DONNELL, Edtl. Wtr., Econst., The Detroit News, 615 W. Lafayette St., Detroit, Mich. 48226, '66–; Econ. Commentator, WWJ-TV News, '68–; Cnslt. Econst., Manufacturers Nat. Bank, '68–; Partner, R. A. Helling & Assocs., '66–; Adjunct Prof., Univ. of Mich. (Dearborn), '66–'67; Asst. Prof., Univ. of Windsor, '63–'66; Grad. Asst., Wayne State Univ., '61–'63; Instr., Univ. of Detroit, '55–'60; various orgs.; Univ. of Detroit, BS, '55 (summa cum laude); MBA, '56; Wayne State Univ., PhD, '63; b. Milw., Wis. 1933; p. James and Erma Graap O'Donnell; h. Peter M. Shontz, Jr.; c. Deborah Jane; res: 1015 Bedford Rd., Grosse Pointe Park, Mich. 48230.

SHORE, WILMA, Wtr., short stories in major mags.; Auth., "Women Should Be Allowed" (Dutton); Wtrs. Guild of Am.; rep., "Best Short Stories 1941," "Prize Stories, 1958;" b. N.Y.C., 1913; p. William and Viola Brothers Shore; h. Louis Solomon; c. Hilary (Mrs. Albert M. Bendich), Dinah (Mrs. Edward P. Stevenson); res: 229 W. 78th St., N.Y., N.Y. 10024.

SHOREY, KATHARINE ABIGAIL, Dir., Martin Memorial Library, Martin Library Association, 159 E. Market St., York, Pa. 17401, '35–; Dir., York-Adams County Dist. Lib. System, '61–; Green County Dist. Lib., Xenia, Ohio, '31–'35; Night Supvsr., Circ., Columbia Univ. Lib., N.Y.C., '25–'31; Asst., Public Lib., Davenport, Iowa, '20–'31; Honored by Nat. Bd., Am. Bus. Wms. Assn. as one of Top Ten Bus. Wm., '69–'70; Western Reserve Univ., Cert. in Lib. Sci., '24; Barnard Col., BA, '31; Univ. of Edinburgh, Scotland, '49; b. Davenport, Iowa; p. Albourne and Ida McCulloch Shorey; res: 153 E. Market St., York, Pa. 17401.

SHORT, BARBARA WILLARD, VP, Chief AE, Inform, Inc., P.O. Box 2627, Club Blvd., Durham, N.C. 27705, '69–; Wms. Ed., Durham Morning Herald, '61–'69; Staff Wtr., '58–'60; Ed., Popular Government (Chapel Hill); N.C. Press Wm., NFPW; numerous writing aws.;

Outstanding Young Wm. of Am., Who's Who of Am. Wm.; Univ. of N.C., BA (Jnlsm.), '56 (Phi Beta Kappa); b. High Point, N.C., 1934; p. William and Estelle Presnell Willard; h. Joseph Short; c. Penny R., Allison P., Lori A.; res: 2717 Cedar Creek Dr., Durham, N.C. 27705.

SHORT, MARJORIE KEATING, AE, Dailey & Associates, 574 Pacific Ave., S.F., Cal. 94133, '68–; Asst. AE, '64–'68; Secy., '61–'64; San Diego State Col., '47–'49; b. Coronado, Cal., 1932; p. H. S. and Gladys Jones Keating; h. John Patrick Short; res: 66 Pleasant St., S.F., Cal. 94108.

SHOUSE, LOUISE P., Sls. Svc. Mgr., Woman's Day mag., 67 W. 44th St., N.Y., N.Y., '69–; Copy Coordr., L. W. Frohlick, '68; Asst. to Dir. of Sls. Prom., Cunningham & Walsh, '64–'68; Kappa Phi Kappa; Kent State Univ., BS, '62 (magna cum laude); b. Spencer, Ind., 1940; p. Robert and Mary McCoy Shouse; res: 1275 Third Ave., N.Y., N.Y. 10021.

SHRADER, GLADYS LINTON, Librn., Head of planned instructional materials ctr., Mooresville High School, Mooresville, Ind., '69–; Tchr., Head of Dept. of Fgn. Langs., Perry East Jr. HS, Indpls., '64–'69; Supervising Tchr. in German and French, Ind. Central Col., Franklin Col., Purdue Univ., '65–'69; Librn., W. Newton and Stephen Decatur Schs., Marion County, Ind.; '57–'64; Lib. Asst. (pfsnl. educ., nursing, med. educ.), Ind. Univ., '50–'57; Instr., '46–'47; Miss. State Col., '47–'50; Tchr., Spanish, Broad Ripple HS, Indpls. Ind., '45–'46, sponsor of high sch. weekly free newsp. and tchr. of Jnlsm. and Eng., Bloomington (Ind.) HS; '24–'31; innovator in methods of teaching fgn. langs.; NEA, Ind. State Tchrs. Assn., Theta Sigma Phi, DAR, Disciples of Christ; Am. Cncl. of Fgn. Lang. Tchrs. (Charter Mbr.), Am. Assn. Tchrs. of German, ALA; Who's Who of Am. Wm.; Who's Who in the Midwest; Tchrs. Svc. Aw., '69; Ind. Univ., AB, '23; MS, '51; b. Johnson County, Ind., 1903; p. Prof. Ernst Marshall and Minnie Smith Linton; h. Carl Ernest Shrader; c. Dr. Carl, Mrs. Bryce Rohrer; res: 1400 Atwater Ave., Bloomington, Ind. 47401 and RR4 Franklin, Ind. 46131.

SHREVE, IRENE MACY, Lib. Cnslt.; Purdue Univ. Faculty, Univ., Univ. Ext. Adm., '69; Archivist, Eli Lilly and Co., '56–'59; Chief Librn., '34–'56; in fields of Rsch., PR, Libs., Tchr., since '16; Fac., Sch. of Lib. Svc., Columbia Univ., '57; Auth. and Collaborator of numerous pfsnl. articles; Joint Auth: "Scientific and Technical Libraries" ('64); ALA, numerous lib. assns. and aws.; Indpls. C. of C. "Salute to Wm. Who Work" aw., '58; Brenau Col., AB '16 (Trustee, '63–'66); U. of Wis. (Summer Sch. Cert. in Lib. Sci.), '30; Univ. of N.C., BS (Lib. Sci.), '33; b. Converse, Ind., 1894; p. Milton D. and Mary Hunt Macy; h. 1. A. Wright Strieby (dec.) 2. Dr. R. Norris Shreve; c. Robert M. Strieby; res: 715 Northridge Dr., W. Lafayette, Ind. 47906.

SHRIVER, MARYLOUISE WARD, Teen Pg. Ed., Winter Haven Publishing Company, P.O. Box 1440,

Winter Haven, Fla. 33880, '67–; Proofreader, Colmst., Staff Wtr.; Aws., Boy Scouts, Girl Scouts; Friendship Aw., Future Home Makers of Am., Winter Haven HS chptr.; b. Phila., Pa., 1904; p. Rev. Samuel and Kate Tilge Ward; h. Robert Shriver; c. Walter E. Ferguson, Robert T. Ferguson; res: 1433 N. Lake Howard Dr., P.O. Box 502, Winter Haven, Fla. 33880.

SHROPSHIRE, RUTH MILLER, Wms. Program Dir., "About Town" Hostess, Sls. Wm., WLAQ, Mt. Alto Rd., P.O. Box 228, Rome, Ga. 30161, '65–; AWRT (Atlanta Chptr. Rec. Secy., '69–'70); AP aw., wms. prog., '68; Nat. Fedn. of Music Clubs hons., '65, '66, '68, active in civic groups; Shorter Col. (Rome, Ga.), '38–'41; b. Baconton, Ga., 1921; p. James and Ruth Wilson Miller; h. Forrest H. Shropshire; c. Salli E., Ruth M., Forrest H., Jr.; res: Rte. 5, Horseleg Creek Rd., Rome, Ga. 30161.

SHROYER, MARY SEABURY, Wms. Pg. Ed., Fairbanks Daily News-Miner, Illinois St., Box 710, Fairbanks, Alaska. 99701, '68–; Univ. of Alaska; b. Boston, Mass., 1936; p. Mortimer and Marg Peck Seabury; h. Peter Shroyer (div.); c. Frida Semler, Eva Gardin, Eric, Mary Peck; res: 413 Eighth Ave., Fairbanks, Alaska 99701.

SHULER, LUCILLE WINKEY, Ed., Jay Shuler Co., Inc., 2650 E. Bayshore, Palo Alto, Calif. 94303, '61–; Ed., Arabian Horse World (monthly); Syracuse Univ., BA, '47 (magna cum laude; Phi Beta Kappa); b. N.Y., 1924; p. Albert and Anna Hanewinckel Winkey; h. Jay Shuler; c. Janalin Margaret; res: 110 Russell Ave., Portola Valley, Cal.

SHUMSKY, ELLEN, Free-lance Photogr., (Publ. in Win mag., others) Photog. Tchr.; March Hoffman Aw., '70; b. N.Y.C.; p. Philip and Ida Metrick Shumsky; res: 25 Leroy St., N.Y., N.Y. 10014.

SHURA, MARY FRANCIS (Mary Young Craig), Wtr.; Commty. Rels. Dir., Kan. City Area Cncl. of Girl Scouts, '60–'61; Tchr: Col. of St. Theresa, Univ. of Kan.; Bks: "Simple Spigott," "Garrett of Greta McGraw," "Mary's Marvelous Mouse," "Nearsighted Knight," "Runaway Home," "Backwards for Luck," "Shoefull of Shamrock," "A Tale of Middle Length," "Pornada"; Theta Sigma Phi, Auths. Guild, Auths. League of Am.; Northwest Mo. State Col., '41–'43; b. Pratt, Kan., 1923; p. Jack and Mary Milstead Young; h. Raymond C. Craig; c. Minka (Mrs. William Sprague), Daniel C. Shura, Jr., Alice B. Craig, Mary F. Craig; res: 134 Hacienda Dr., Tiburon, Cal. 94920.

SHURLING, SUSAN CRAWFORD, Wms. Ed., The Macon News, 120 Broadway, Macon, Ga. 31208, '68–; Wesleyan Col., BA (Eng.), '67, Walter F. George Sch. of Law (Mercer Univ.), '67–'68; b. Atlanta, Ga., 1945; p. William C. and Mary Evans Crawford; h. William M. Shurling, III; res: 233 College St., Macon, Ga. 31201.

SHURPIT, JoANN JEAN, Dir. of Home Econs., Libby,

McNeill & Libby, 200 S. Michigan Ave., Chgo., Ill. 60604, '53–; Test Kitchen Home Econst., '51–'53; "Mary Hale Martin," Portfolio, '65; Am. Home Econs. Assn., Am. Meat Inst., Home Econsts. in Bus., Nat. Assn. Frozen Food Packers, AWRT, Wms. Adv. Club of Chgo., Electrical Wms. Round Table, Grocery Manufacturers of Am.; Univ. of Wis., BS (Home Econs., Jnlsm.), '51; b. Montello, Wis., 1929; p. Leon and Merle Krahenbuhl Shurpit; res: 260 E. Chestnut St., Chgo., Ill. 60611.

SHUTE, ALBERTA VAN HORN, Ed., Star In The East, Maine Woman's Christian Temperance Union, R.F.D. 5, Augusta, Me. 04330; Auth: "A Year and a Day from My Kitchen Window" ('65), "Or Even the Silver Cord" ('57); Who's Who of Am. Wm.; Dic. of Intl. Biog.; Colby Col.; Gorham State Tchrs. Col.; Univ. of Me.; b. E. Boothbay, Me., 1906; p. Simeon and Julia Dodge Van Horn; h. Donald Shute; c. Leon, Sarah, Daniel; res: Manchester, Me.

SHUTTLESWORTH, DOROTHY EDWARDS, Wtr., bks. incl: "All Kinds of Bees" (Random House), "The Wildlife of South America" (Hastings House), "Clean Air—Sparkling Water" (Doubleday & Co.), other nature bks.; Ed., Jr. Natural Hist. Magazine, '36–'48; Staff, Natural Hist. Magazine, '34–'36; N.J. Citizens for Clean Air, Inc. (VP, '67–); b. Bklyn., N.Y.; p. James and Anna Wall Edwards; h. Melvin Shuttlesworth; c. Gregory, Lee Ann Phillips; res: 406 N. Walnut St., E. Orange, N.J. 07017.

SIBONGA, DOLORES ESTIGOY, Ed., Filipino Forum, 524 S. King, Seattle, Wash. 98104, '69–; Prodr., Wtr., KOMO-TV, '67–'69; Asst. Prom. Mgr., '65–'67; Ed., Loomis Armored Car Svc., '62–'65; Theta Sigma Phi (Chptr. VP, '51–'52), NATAS; Prodr., Wtr., two TV docs. (nominated for local Emmy aws.); Univ. of Wash., BA, '52; p. Victor and Maria Dasalla Estigoy; h. Martin J. Sibonga; c. Martin Jr., Randi Maya; res: 4627 43rd Ave. S., Seattle, Wash. 98118.

SIDEBOTHAM, PHYLLISS JACOBSEN, Wms. Ed., The Decatur Daily, 101 Johnston St., Decatur, Ala. 35601, '66–; Decatur Wms. C. of C. (Pres., '65–'67), Morgan County March of Dimes Chmn., '60–'64; Wm. of the Yr., '65; Moravian Col. for Wm., '44–'46; Pa. State Univ.; b. Aretesian, S.D., 1924; p. Jacob and Lauretta Lynch Jacobsen; h. Norman C. Sidebotham; c. David Norman, Mrs. Claud Lavender, Jay Phillip, Neill Stephen; res: 2016 Pennylane S.E., Decatur, Ala. 35601.

SIDES, PATRICIA ANN, Assoc. Prodr., John M. Secondari Productions, Ltd., 212 W. 48th St., N.Y., N.Y. 10056, '68–; ABC-TV, '63–'68; Rschr., '62; Pubcty. Dir., Cncl. on Student Travel; Rsch: "The Agony and The Ecstasy," "Italians in America"; Ed., Contact Magazine; NATAS; Peabody Aws. for "1492," Saga of Western Man, '64; "Visit to Washington with Mrs. L.B.J.," '65; Emmy for "Leonardo da Vinci," '65; Oh. State Aw., "Christ is Born," '67; Pomona Col., BA, '53; Stan-

ford Univ. grad study, '54; Univ. of Florence, special studies, '55; b. Pendayia, Cyprus, 1932; p. Claude and Dorothy Smith Sides; res: 53 E. 67th St., N.Y., N.Y. 10021.

SIDLER, HELEN ANNA, Project Supvsr., Rsch. and Dev. Dept., Clark County School District, 2832 E. Flamingo Rd., Las Vegas, Nev. 89109, '67–; Rsch. and Dev. Coordr., Nev. ETV, '66–'67; Adm. Asst., Commty. TV of Southern Cal., '62–'64; AWRT, AAUW, League of Wm. Voters; Univ. of Rochester, BA, '47; Eastman Sch. of Music, BMus, '49; Grad. Studies, Middlebury Summer Italian Lang. Sch., '46–'50; b. Danville, Pa., 1925; p. William and Minnie Roberts Sidler; res: 1187 Maryland Circle, Apt. 4, Las Vegas, Nev. 89109.

SIDNEY, STEFFI (Steffi Skolsky), Free-lance Prod. Asst. and Wtr.; TV Progs and Commls., Datebook Magazine, '62–; Actress, '53–'62; Asst. to Prodr., King Bros., Inc., '55–'60; Pubcty. Wtr., James Byron & Assoc., '53–'55; AWRT.

SIEBERT, MARILYN ANNE, Ed., M.A.C. Gopher Magazine, 615 Second Ave. S., Mpls., Minn. 55402, '62–; Adv. Copywtr., Gamble-Skogmo, '60–'61; Univ. of Minn., BA, '59; b. Dayton, Oh., 1936; p. Richard and Marie Schoening Siebert; res: 4804 W. 70th St., Mpls., Minn. 55435.

SIEGEL, DORIS TAYLOR, Auth., "How Still My Love" ('57), four other novels under pseud: Susal Wells; Cal. Wtrs. Guild, Chi Omega, Chi Delta Phi, active in civic, cultural, genealogical orgs.; U.C.L.A., BA (Alumni Assn.; Founders Club); b. N.Y.C.; p. Russell and Cora Davis Taylor; h. William E. Siegel; c. Richard T.; res: 1520 San Remo Dr., Pacific Palisades, Cal. 90272.

SIEGEL, DOROTHY SCHAINMAN, Free-lance Wtr., 168–20 127th Ave., Jamaica, N.Y. 11434; "Checklist for a Perfect Home," "The Big Town for Teens," articles in Redbook, McCall's, and other mags.; Staff Wtr., Good Housekeeping mag. '60, '62; Soc. of Mag. Wtrs.; U.C.L.A., AA, BA (Theater Arts); b. N.Y.C., 1932; p. Phillip and Anne Keats Schainman; h. Jerome Siegel; c. David M., Irene R.; res: 168–20 127th Ave., Jamaica, N.Y. 11434.

SIEGEL, EVE, Pres., Eve Siegel Associates, 35 W. 53rd St., N.Y., N.Y. 10019, '59–; Warner Bros.; AWRT, Fashion Group; Coronet aw.; Hunter Col.; b. N.Y.C.; p. Abraham and Rose Dick Siegel; h. Louis Weiner; res: 405 E. 54th St., N.Y., N.Y. 10022.

SIEGEL, LOIS P., Commtns. Atty., Haley, Bader & Potts, Suite 700, 1730 M St., N.W., Wash., D.C. 20036, '65–; Atty. Advisor, FCC, '63–'65; AWRT, Am. Bar Assn., Fed. Commtns. Bar Assn., N.Y. State Bar Assn.; Barnard Col., BA, '60; N.Y.U. Sch. of Law, LLB, '63; b. Bklyn., N.Y., 1939; p. Irving and Lillian Rakusin Siegel; res: 1245 Fourth St. S.W., Wash., D.C. 20024.

SIEGEL, MARGOT AUERBACHER, Free-lance Wtr., Bk. Reviewer; Auth, "A Career in Fashion" (Dillon Press, '70); Free-lance Corr., Fairchild Pubns.; European coverage; bk. revs: Mpls. Sunday Tribune, Mpls. Star; special project, N.Y. Daily Mirror; numerous fashion prods., Munsingwear, others (N.Y.; Mpls., Minn.); Pubcty. Dir., Walker Art Ctr. (Mpls., Minn.), '62–'66; own free-lance firm, '50's; special projects, Eleanor Kairalla Agcy.; Fashion Ed., Wms. Wear Daily, '46–'48; Pubcty. Dir., Alvin Gardner Agcy., '45; News, Feature Wtr., Am. Red Cross, '44–'45; Teaching Asst., Am. Studies Program, Univ. of Minn., '47; lects., PR, City Col. (N.Y.); Fashion Group (Reg. Dir., '64–'66), OPC, Theta Sigma Phi, Minn. Press Club; Univ. of Minn., BA (Jnlsm., Adv.), '44; Am. Studies; b. St. Paul, Minn., 1923; p. William and Jeanne Braunschweig Auerbacher; h. Harold Siegel; c. William, Sandra; res: 25 Park Lane, Mpls., Minn. 55416.

SIEGEL, MICKI, Ed.-in-Chief, Screenland, Silver Screen, Macfadden-Bartell, 205 E. 42nd St., N.Y., N.Y. 10017, '68–; Free-lance Wtr., '67–'68; Ed.-in-Chief, In mag., '66–'67; Assoc. Ed., Photoplay, '64–'66; N.Y.U., BS (Jnlsm.); New Sch. for Social Rsch., MA (Eng.); b. Jersey City, N.J.; p. Herman and Claire Singer Siegel.

SIEGELMAN, MARY KLYCE, Exec. VP, Outstanding American High School Students, 500 Farley Bldg., Birmingham, Ala., '69–; Copywtr., Prod. Supvsr., Frank M. Taylor, Adv., '63–'68; articles, Ext. Magazine; AWRT (Secy., '68), Alpha Gamma Delta; The 2,000 Wm. of Achiev.; Ala. Homemaker aw., '60; Spring Hill Col., '59–'60; Univ. of Ala., BS, '63 (Theta Sigma Phi Jnlsm. aw.); b. Birmingham, Ala., 1940; p. Martin and Grace McGeever Klyce; h. Les Siegelman; c. Bonnie Lache'; res: 2507 Lane Park Rd., Birmingham, Ala. 35223.

SIEMEK, SHIRLEY L., Media Dir., Kolb, Tookey & Assoc. Inc., 435 N. Michigan Ave., Chgo., Ill. 60611, '57–; Gourfain-Cobb Adv., '50–'51; Wm. Adv. Club of Chgo.; Northwestern Univ.; res: 414 Homestead Rd., LaGrange Park, Ill. 60525.

SIEMON, MARGARET WILHELMINA, Br. Mgr., The Book House for Children, 801 Green Bay Rd., Lake Bluff, Ill. 60044, Des Moines Off., '52–; New Eng. Field Mgr., '48–'52; Field Trainer, Midwest Area, '42–'48; Elementary and High School tchr., Eng. and Social Studies, '36–'42; Field Staff, Prairie Farmer, '32–'36; Auth., "Science Study Guide," "Curriculum Correlations, '66; Wms. Nat. Bk. Assn., Assn. for Supervision and Curriculum Dev., AAUW, Nu Pi Sigma, scholarships; Univ. of Chgo., PhB, '32; Univ. of Ill., Univ. of Colo., grad. work, '39, '40; b. 1910; p. Emil and Emma Scharff Siemon; res: 601 48th St., Des Moines, Ia. 50312.

SIEMS, BONNIE COLLEEN, Ed., The Mazeppa Journal, Mazeppa, Minn. 55956, '62–; one-man art show, Rochester, Red Wing, '57; Minn. Edtl. Assn., Mazeppa Commty. Club; Mpls. Sch. of Art, BFA, '57; b. Mazeppa, Minn., 1935; p. F. John and Mildred Clemens Siems; res: Mazeppa, Minn. 55956.

SIFF, NANCY K., Tchr., Board of Education, 110 Livingston St., N.Y., N.Y. 11201, '66–; Independent TV Prodr., '64–; Free-lance Wtr., liners for Columbia Masterworks Albums; TV Prodr., SSC&B, '63–'64; BBDO, '50–'63; Mgr., New Friends of Music, Inc., '50; Program Coordr., WABF-FM, '48–'50; AWRT, Musical groups; Who's Who of Am. Wm.; Who's Who in the East; N.Y.U. Washington Sq. Col., BA; Grad. Sch. of Arts and Scis., MA; b. N.Y.C.; p. Philip and Bertha Karpas Siff; res: 39 Fifth Ave., N.Y., N.Y. 10003.

SIGISMUND, RITA ST. JOHN, Owner, Rita Sigismund Advertising & Public Relations, '57–; Prom., Adv. Mgr., The Bon Marche, '49–'57; Wtr., J. L. Hudson Co. (Detroit, Mich.), '46–'49; Lectr., Univ. of Wash.; Fashion Group (Treas., VP, '61–'65), AWRT, NATAS; Socrates honors, '49–'57; Univ. of Wash., Seattle Univ.; b. Everett, Wash., 1927; p. Hugo and Mary Zmuda Sigismund; res: 1933 Clise Pl. W., Seattle, Wash. 98199.

SIGRIST, HELEN QUIST, Assoc. Ed., Intl. Editions, The Reader's Digest, Pleasantville, N.Y. 10570, '48–; Univ. of Wash.

SILBERBERG, ELSA, Librn. II, Bibliographer, University of California, Acquisition Department, Berkeley, Cal. 94704, '65–; Phi Beta Mu, Cal. Arts Soc., Wms. Faculty Club, Cal. Alumni Assoc. (Life Mbr.); Stockholms Högskola, '48–'50; Mt. Allison Univ., '48–'50; Univ. of Toronto, '50–'51; Univ. of Cal. (Berkeley), BA, '53; MLS, '61; Univ. of Denver, '53–'54; Maywood Col., '58–'59; b. Tallin, Estonia; p. Juri and Elisabeth Linkvest Silberberg; res: 2720 Piedmont Ave., Berkeley, Cal. 94705.

SILLS, LEONA GALIN, Prom. Dir., House & Garden, 420 Lexington Ave., N.Y., N.Y. 10017, '67–; Prom. Mgr., '64–'67; Prod. Mdsng. Mgr., '60–'64; Mdsng. Specialist, House Beautiful, '57–'60; Copywtr., Hirshon Garfield, '55–'57; New Haven Col.; b. New Haven, Conn.; p. Henry and Rose Wood Galin; c. Joshua Wood Sills; res: 7 E. 75th St., N.Y., N.Y. 10021.

SILVA, RUTH CARIDAD, Prof., Polit. Sci., Pennsylvania State University, 133 Sparks Bldg., University Park, Pa. 16802, '59–; Fac., '48–; Instr., Wheaton Col. (Norton, Mass.), '46–'48; Teaching Fellow, Univ. of Mich. (Ann Arbor), '44–'46; Fulbright Prof., Cairo (Egypt) Univ., '52–'53; Visiting Prof., Johns Hopkins Univ., '65; Rsch. Cnslt: on Legislative Apportionment, Robinson, Silverman, et al (N.Y.C.), '61–'62; N.Y. State Constitutional Comm., '59–'60; U.S. Atty. Gen. H. Brownell, '57; and Speech Wtr., Ill. Sen. Paul Douglas, '56; Auth: "Presidential Succession" ('51, '68), "Legislative Apportionment in New York" ('60), "Rum, Religion, & Votes: 1928 Re-Examined" ('62); Wtr., over 30 articles; Univ. of Mich., AB, '43 (Phi Kappa Phi; other univ. hons.); AM, '43; PhD, '48;

b. Lincoln, Neb.; p. Ignatius D. and Beatrice Davis Silva.

SILVERMAN, JACLYN ARMSTRONG, Exec. Asst., Prom., IOS Foundation, 405 Park Ave., N.Y., N.Y. 10028, '68–; Ed., City East, '67–'68; Pubcty Dir., Ingenue, '63–'66; Pubcty Dir., Ben B. Bliss Co., '61–'62; b. N.Y.C., 1925; p. John and Lillian Rosenberg Armstrong; c. Constance, Michael; res: 439 E. 88th St., N.Y., N.Y. 10028.

SILVIAN, LEONORE, Free-lance Wtr.; Assoc. Ed., Signature, '65–'68; Sr. Press Wtr., WCBS, '64–'65; Founder, Ed., TV Channels, '60–'62; Ed., TV Star Parade, '55–'60; Radio-TV Ed., Look, '51–'54; Mgr., mag., public affairs pubns., ABC, '47–'51; OPC; Northwestern Univ., BS, '40; MS, '41; b. Duluth, Minn.; p. William and Mollie Silvian; res: 340 E. 52nd St., N.Y., N.Y. 10022.

SIMA, SANDRA ELIZABETH, Industry Rels. Home Econst., National Live Stock & Meat Board, 36 S. Wabash, Chgo., Ill. 60603, '65–; Field Home Econst., '63–'65; Free-lance Talent; Am. Home Econs. Assn., Home Econsts. in Bus. (Chgo. Secy., '69–'70), AWRT, Theta Sigma Phi; Ia. State Univ., BS, '63; b. Webster City, Ia., 1941; p. Irven Guy and Elizabeth Maley Sime; res: 1360 N. Sandburg Terr., Apt. 1401, Chgo., Ill. 60610.

SIMENDINGER, MARGARET RING, Free-lance Wtr.; Wtr., 187 stories, nat. mags., British pubns., '54–; Reptr., Newark (N.J.) News, '45–'53; Reptr., Newark Sunday Call, '41–'45; Co-auth: "Childbirth" ('62); Theta Sigma Phi, Charlotte Wtrs. Club, Civinettes; Sorbonne, Paris, '30–'31; b. Elizabeth, N.J. 1911; p. Frederick and Grace Higbie Ring; h. William H. Simendinger; c. William H., Jr., Richard F.; res: 1001 Scalybark Rd., Charlotte, N.C. 28209.

SIMISTER, FLORENCE PARKER, Free-lance Wtr.; Auth: "Streets of the City, an Anecdotal History of Providence" ('68), "Streets of the City, an Anecdotal History of Newport" ('69), others; "Streets of the City" radio program (cit., '57, '69), '52–; Wtr., Providence Public Lib., '48–'53; Exec. Secy., R.I. Refugee Svc., '42–'48; Auth.'s League, R.I. Yearbook (Bd. of Dirs., '67), Friends of the Lib. of Brown Univ., Assocs. of the John Carter Brown Lib., R.I. Hist. Soc., Newport Hist. Soc.; Brown Univ.; Univ. of Conn.; b. Providence, R.I., 1913; p. George and Bertha Zinner Parker; h. Robert Simister; res: 100 Angell St., Providence, R.I. 02906.

SIMMONDS, GAIL BALDWIN, Media Byr., Ramsdell, Buckley & Co., Inc., 3 Penn Center Plaza, Phila., Pa. 19102, '66–; Asst. to Sls. Mgr., Aiton & Co. Ltd. (Westminster, London, Eng.), '65–'66; Asst. to Investment Offcr., Boston Safe Deposit & Trust Co. (Boston, Mass.), '63–'65; Pharmaceutical Adv. Club; Centenary Col. for Wm., AA, '62; b. Phila., Pa., 1942; p. Seward and Barbara Bishop Baldwin; h. David F. C. Sim-

monds; res: "Between Streets," 2111 Rodman St., Phila., Pa. 19146.

SIMMONS, JOAN HOGLUND, Music Critic, The Times-Union, 24 Sheridan Ave., Albany, N.Y. 12201, '66–; Reptr., Feature Wtr., '65–'66; Ed., descriptive guide to civic orgs., Capital Nwsps., '66; Ed., teaching aid on manners, N.Y. State Educ. Dept., '69; Music Critics Assn.; Nat. Fedn. of Music Clubs Special aw., '68, Hearst Newsps. Writing aws., '67–'69; St. Joseph's Col., AB, '64; b. Portland, Me., 1942; p. Edward C. and Louise Thorndike Hoglund; h. Paul B. Simmons; c. Charles; res: 12 Freeman Rd., Albany, N.Y. 12208.

SIMMONS, MARY ANN, Free-lance Wtr., Ed.; Reptr., Ed., St. Petersburg (Fla.) Times, '65–'68; Wtr., Ed., Electronic Commtns., '61–'64; Colmst., Smithfield (N.C.) Herald, '54–'55; speech writing, rsch., Repl. Party, '63–; Duke Univ., '55–'58; N.C. State Col., '57; b. St. Petersburg, Fla.; p. George and Pearl James Simmons; res: 6205 Seventh Ave. N., St. Petersburg, Fla. 33710.

SIMMONS, SYLVIA H., Asst. to Chmn. of the Bd., Young & Rubicam, Inc., 285 Madison Ave., N.Y., N.Y. 10017, '68–; VP, '62–; Asst. to Pres., '62–'68; Prom. Specialist, '60–'62; Assoc. Crtv. Dir., McCann-Erickson, '55–'60; Crtv. Dir., Amos Parrish Co., '55; Prom. Copy Chief, Grey Adv., '52–'54; Copywtr., '50–'52; Staff Asst., Am. Red Cross (Italy), '42–'45; Auth: "Successful Contests and How to Create Them," "The Creative Approach to Premiums"; contrbr., numerous articles to bus. pubns.; AWNY, Adv. Wtrs. Assn. of N.Y., Dir. Mail Adv. Assn., Sales Prom. Execs. Club, Sigma Tau Delta; Medal of Freedom, '45; Purple Heart, '44; various aws. for best indsl. film of yr. from bus. groups.; Bklyn. Col., BA (cum laude), '40; Columbia Univ., MA (Eng. Lit.), '41; b. N.Y.C.; h. Hans H. Neumann, M.D.; res: 74 Old Belden Hill Rd., Wilton, Conn. 06897.

SIMON, MINA LEWITON, Auth., juv. fiction incl: "First Love" (McKay), "The Divided Heart" (McKay), "That Bad Carlos" (Harper), others; Writing Instr., New Sch. For Social Rsch.; Hudson Valley Philharmonic Soc.; New Sch. For Social Rsch., '36–'40; b. N.Y.C., 1914; p. Leonard and Sara Cass Lewiton; h. Howard Simon; c. Dr. Bettina Simon Niederer; res: Lilac Hill, Stanfordville, N.Y. 12581.

SIMON, NORMA FELDSTEIN, Auth. of bks. for children, '53–; Ctrv. Rsch. Cnslt., Dancer-Fitzgerald-Sample (N.Y.C.), '69–; Skills and Materials Dev. Cnslt., Bank St. Col. of Educ., '66–; Cnslt., Sch. Dept., The Macmillan Co., '68–'69; Therapist to Children, '65–'69; Cnslt. in Lang. Arts, Pre-sch. prog., (Stamford, Conn.), '64–'69; Tchr. training, '49–'51, '62–'63; Tchr., '48–'53; Auths. Guild, Nat. Assn. for the Educ. of Young Children; Bklyn. Col., BA, '47; Bank St. Col. of Educ., MS (Educ.), '48; New Sch. for Soc. Rsch., '48–'51; b. N.Y.C., 1927; p. Nathan and Winnie Lepselter Feldstein; h. Edward Simon; c. Stephanie, Wendy, Jonathan; res: Old County Rd., S. Wellfleet, Mass. 02663.

SIMON, RITA MINTZ, Auth., Ed.; Prof. of Commtns., Sociol., University of Illinois, Urbana, Ill. '63–; Visiting Prof., Yale Univ., '62–'63; Rsch. Assoc., Colo. Univ. Sch. of S.W., '61–'63; Asst. Prof., Rsch. Assoc., Univ. of Chgo. Law Sch., Sociol. Dept., '58–'61; Auth: "The Jury and the Defense of Insanity" (Little, Brown and Co., '67); "As We Saw the Thirties," ('67); Ed., "The Sociology of Law" ('68); Am. Sociological Assn.; Guggenheim Fellowship, '66–'67; Univ. of Chgo., PhD, '57; b. N.Y.C., 1931; p. Abraham and Irene Waldman Mintz; h. Julian Simon; c. David Meyer, Judith Debs, Daniel Hillel; res: 1105 S. Busey, Urbana, Ill. 61801.

SIMON, SHIRLEY SCHWARTZ, Free-lance Wtr.; Staff Wtr., Educational Dimensions, Inc., 3592 Lee Rd., Cleve., Oh. 44120; Auth: "Best Friend" (Lothrop, Lee & Shepard), "Cousins At Camm Corners;" three other juv. bks.; Lectr.; John Carroll Univ., '70–; Shaker Heights Bd. of Educ., '67–'69, '63–'65; Western Reserve Univ., '65–'67; Mt. Union Col., Cleve. Children's Bk. Fair; Auths. Guild, Wms. Nat. Bk. Assn.; Cleve. Col., '39–'41; b. Cleve., Oh.; p. Bernard and Sylvia Silberman Schwartz; h. Edgar Simon; c. Allen H., Ruth E.; res: 3630 Cedarbrook Rd., Cleve., Oh. 44118.

SIMON, VIVIEN WEINBERGER, Adm. Secy., Houston Chapter of the Texas Society of Certified Public Accountants, 606 C & I Bldg., Houston, Tex. 77002, '64–; PR, Adv. Asst., Tex. Med. Assn., '62–'64; Off. Mgr., Pfsnl. Planning Svc., '59–'62; Dept. Asst., Sch. of Commtns., Univ. of Tex., '61–'62; Ed., Dept. of Zoology, Univ. of Tex., '57–'59; Theta Sigma Phi (Univ. of Tex. Chptr. and Houston Pfsnl. Chptr., Pres. '70–'71, Corr. Secy. '66–'68), Southeast Tex. Indsl. Eds., Gamma Alpha Chi; Univ. of Tex., BJ, '61; b. Chgo., Ill. 1939; p. Melvin and Corinne Himelstein Weinberger; h. R. J. Simon; c. Robert James; res: 818 Piedmont Dr., Sugar Land, Tex. 77478.

SIMONS, ELLEN A., D.K.G., Inc., 733 Third Ave., N.Y., N.Y., '69–; Sr. Adv. Copywtr., Jerry Della Femina & Partners; Copywtr., Art Dir., Gilbert Advertising Inc.; Asst. Art Dir., Cadwell Davis Co.; Julliard Sch. of Music, '57–'59; Adelphi Col., '59–'61; Sch. of Visual Arts, '61–'63; b. N.Y., N.Y., 1941; p. Leon and Netty Rothenberg Simons; res: 160 E. 55th St., N.Y., N.Y. 10022.

SIMONTON, CAROL GAWRYLA, Bdcst. Copywtr., Radio-TV Prod., Cole and Weber, Inc., 220 S.W. Morrison, Portland, Ore. 97204, '69–; Copywtr., Prod., Copy Chief, Bozell Jacobs, Inc., Atlanta, Ga., '63–'68; Radio-TV Dir., Alfred L. Lino and Assocs., St. Petersburg, Fla., '60–'63; Continuity-Traffic, WABR, Orlando, '59; Traffic Mgr., WLOF-TV, '58–'59; Continuity/Opns., WSUN-TV, St. Petersburg, '56–'58; AWRT (Chptr. Pres., '69–'70; '62–'63); St. Petersburg Jr. Col., AA, '60; b. N.Y.C., 1936; p. Raymond and

Cathleen Loftus Gawryla; h. William J. Simonton; res: 10570 S.W. Barnes Rd., Portland, Ore. 97225.

SIMPSON, DEBORAH SCHWARZ, Jnlsm. Tchr., White Sulphur High School, '59–'62; Asst. Dir. Pubcty., The Greenbrier, '55–'59; Stringer, AP, UPI, '57–'59; Theta Sigma Phi, AAUW, Greenbrier County Hist. Soc.; Jr. Wms. Club (Wm. of Yr., '58–'59), Outstanding Young Wm. of Am., '65; Univ. of Ky., BA, '55; b. Covington, Va., 1933; p. Henry and Beatrice Robinson Schwarz; h. Emmett Lawrence Simpson; c. Henry Beryl, Emily Beatrice, Emmett Darin; res: Fair Oaks, D935, White Sulphur Springs, W. Va. 24986.

SIMPSON, JEAN IRWIN, Auth.; Emeritus Prof. of Foods, Syracuse University, Syracuse, N.Y. 13210, '62–; Prof. of Foods, '49–'62; Chief of Rsch. Kitchens, Frozen Food Fndn., '45–'49; Assoc. Prof., Univ. of Ill., '41–'45; Asst. Prof., Univ. of Toronto, '39–'41; Food Specialist, Ladies Home Jnl., '30–'34; Instr., Cornell Univ., '27–'30; McGill Univ., '23–'26; Bks: "The Frozen Food Cookbook" (Simon & Schuster, '48), "The Frozen Food Cookbook and Guide to Home Freezing" (The Avi Publ. Co., '62); numerous articles; Inst. of Food Technologists, Am. Home Econs. Assn., NLAPW; Univ. of Toronto, BA, '21; Univ. of Chgo., MS (Foods, Nutrition), '27; PhD (Food Chemistry, Nutrition), '39; b. Buffalo, N.Y.; p. Irwin and Mary Segsworth Simpson; res: 1235 Westmoreland Ave., Syracuse, N.Y. 13210.

SIMPSON, JOAN ULRICH, Wms. Ed., Stockton Record, 530 E. Market, Stockton, Cal. 95202, '67–; Reptr., '61–'67; Asst. Dir., PR, Univ. of the Pacific, '59–'61; Theta Sigma Phi; Univ. of Va., Mary Washington Col., '54–'55; Univ. of the Pacific, BA, '58 (summa cum laude); Stanford Univ., MA, '59; h. James Simpson; c. Kenneth S.; res: 616 Morada Lane, Stockton, Cal. 95207.

SIMPSON, JO-ANN KATSON, Asst. Ed., American Home Magazine, Downe Publishing Co., 425 California St., S.F., Cal. 94104, '67–; Free-lance Edtl. Asst., '63–'67; Free-lance Wtr., '57–'63; Media Rep., French Nat. Tourist Off. (S.F., Cal.), '55–'57; Exec. Secy., French Consulate Gen. (Denver, Colo.), '52–'55; NHFL, Marin Soc. of Artists, League of Wm. Voters (Marin County, Cal., Bd.); Univ. of Geneva (Switzerland), '50–'51; L'Institut pour les Hautes Etudes Internationales (Geneva); Smith Col., AB, '52; b. Albuquerque, N.M., 1931; p. Robert and Frances Bell Katson; h. C. D. Simpson; c. Sabrina S.; res: 66 Ivy Dr., Ross, Cal. 94957.

SIMPSON, LOUISE GARDINIER, Wms. Ed., Laurel Leader-Call, 130 Beacon St., Laurel, Miss. 39440, '67–; Soc. Ed., '61–'67; '32–'37; Reptr., Clarion-Ledger (Jackson), '55–; Miss. Press Wms. Assn. (aws., '69, '65), NPWC; b. Laurel, Miss., 1914; p. Dewey and Anice Halsell Gardinier; h. George Simpson.

SIMPSON, NORMA LUCILLE, Modr., "Accent on

Living," WHA Radio, Radio Hall, University of Wisconsin, Madison, Wis. 53706, '68–; Grad. Asst. to Prog. Modr., '66–'68; Ext. Home Econs. Agt. (Clark and Teton Counties, Idaho), '57–'62; Home Svc. Advisor, Idaho Power Co. (Pocatello); Idaho Home Econs. Assn. (Dist. Dir., '58–'60), Am. Home Econs. Assn., Am. Assn. of Agricultural Col. Eds., Intl. Farm Youth Exchange (spent 6 mos. in Peru, '62–'63); Outstanding Young Wm. in Am.; Idaho State Univ., BA (Home Econs.), '57 (sophomore wms. scholastic hon.); Univ. of Wis., MS (Home Econs. Jnlsm.), '69 (Omicron Nu); b. Idaho Falls, Idaho, 1935; p. C. Weston and Gladys Simpson; res: 2130 University Ave., Apt. 107, Madison, Wis. 53705.

SIMPSON, PATRICE LOUISE, Asst. PR Mgr., Playboy Magazine & Playboy Clubs International, Inc., 919 N. Michigan Ave., Chgo., Ill. 60611; Playboy Enterprises, Inc: Exec. Secy., Asst. to VP in Charge of Prom., Off. Mgr., Traf. Mgr., Media Mgr., promotional mailings, 11 yrs.; free-lance modeling; Substitute Tchr., Art, Eng.; Wms. Adv. Club of Chgo.; Univ. of Miami, BS (Educ.), '57; b. Evanston, Ill., 1936; p. M. Chapman and Florence Pries Simpson; res: 70 W. Burton Pl., Apt. 1803, Chgo., Ill. 60610.

SIMPSON, VIRGINIA STATLER, Supvsr. Librn., Bks. for Blind and Physically Handicapped, California State Library, Library and Courts Building, Sacramento, Cal. 95809, '41–; Librn., Intl. House, Univ. of Cal. (Berkeley), '41; Cataloger, Tchrs. Pfsnl. Lib. (Oakland, Cal.), '36–'39; ALA, Cal. Lib. Assn., AAUW, Delta Zeta; Univ. of Cal., AB, '34; Cert. in Librarianship, '35; b. Chgo., Ill., 1910; p. Clarence R. and Leah Hoke Statler; h. Charles M. Simpson; res: 2331 Irvin Way, Sacramento, Cal. 95822.

SIMS, FRANCESCA ANN, Actress, Jonanthan Winters Show, '68; commls., '68 (Arts Dirs. Aw., Best Comml. of Yr., Pontaic, Bonnie & Clyde Comml., '68); Co-wtr., film screenplays; SAG, AFTRA; L.A. City Col.; b. Glendale, Cal., 1945; p. Francis J. and Virginia M. Jeffers Sims; res: 1919 N. Beverly Glen, L.A., Cal. 90024.

SIMUNICH, MARY HEDRICK, Owner, Mary Simunich Public Relations, P.O. Box 15178, Phoenix, Ariz., 85018, '66–; PR Dir., Walter O. Boswell Mem. Hosp. (Sun City), '69–; PR Dir., Phoenix Playboy Club, '65–; PR Dir., Ed., St. Luke's Reptr., St. Luke's Hosp., '60–'68; Co-founder, VP, Paul J. Hughes PR, Inc., '60–'66; Pubcty. Dir., Phoenix Symphony, '57–'63; AE, Tom Rippey & Assocs., '55–'57; Exec. Secy. to Mgrs., KPHO-Radio, KPHO-TV, '50–'54; PRSA, ICIE (Ariz. VP, '69–'70), Am. Soc. of Hosp. PR Dirs. (Ariz. Chptr. Bd. of Dirs.), various other organizations; Phoenix Adv. Wm. of Yr., '62; b. Chgo., Ill., 1918; p. Tubman K. and Mary St. Clair McCamish Hedrick; h. Dr. William A. Simunich; res: 4133 N. 34th Pl., Phoenix, Ariz. 85018.

SINCLAIR, DOROTHY TUTT, Dir. of Development, Radio-TV-Film Center, University of Houston, 4513 Cullen Blvd., Houston, Tex. 77004, '67–; Dir., GRETA (ITV Svc.), '65–; Supvsr., Radio-TV-Film Prod., Houston Public Schs., '52–'65; Copywtr., Foley's, '50–'52; Colmst., Free-lance Wtr., Adv., Winston-Salem, N.C., '47–'50; Adv. Dir., Sosnik's, '46; Talent and Continuity, WDAK, '45; Reptr., Columbus (Ga.) Enquirer, '44; Auth. of textbook; various organizations; Converse Col., Mars Hill Col., Wms. Col. of the Univ. of N.C., BA; Univ. of Houston, MA; b. Spartanburg, S.C.; p. George and Maude Yarborough Tutt; h. Brownlow Sinclair; c. George Lott II, Brownlow W., Jr., Douglas Elliott, Diane Y.; res: 5101 Brae Burn Dr., Bellaire, Tex. 77401.

SINCLAIR, EDNA ROSS, Dramatist-Lectr.; Intl. Platform Assn. (Nat. Secy., '69), ZONTA (Bloomington-Normal Chptr. VP), Ill. Fed. of Wms. Clubs, active in civic affairs; Who's Who of Am. Wm.; Who's Who in the Midwest; Ill. Wesleyan Univ., Southwest Fine Arts Sch., Bradley Univ.; b. Bloomington, Ill., 1924; p. Oscar F. and Delia Ross; h. Duane Sinclair; c. Gary Lee, Stephen Ross; res: 302 W. Cooper St., Colfax, Ill. 61728.

SINDORF, GERALDINE, Corp. Secy., Dir., James A. Shanahan & Assoc., Inc., PR, Intl., 21 E. Van Buren, Chgo., Ill. 60605, '56–; General Monorail Corp., Aquinaldo Fndn. AngBalita Enterprises, Inc.; Asst. to Ed., Bon Appetif, Chgo. Mkt. News, Prof. Beauty News, '56–'63; Rsch.-Stylist, Motorola, '49–'56; Int. Designer, John Smith Co., '48–'49; Carroll Col., BA, '33; b. Hartland, Wis.; p. William and Agnes Kenney Service; h. (dec.).

SINGER, EVELYN, Lit. Agt., Reading Cnslt., 41 W. 96th St., N.Y., N.Y. 10025, '51–; Assoc., Jeanne Hale Agcy., '50; Cadmus Bks., E. M. Hale & Co., '49; WNBA, Intl. Reading Assn.; N.Y.U., MA, '67; h. Joseph Haber.

SINGER, JANE SHERROD, Edtl. Dir., B. P. Singer Features, 3164 West Tyler, Anaheim, Cal. 92801, '55–; Co-auth: anthologies, biographies, mystery and sea books (with husband); Tchr., Whittier Col., Univ. of Cal., S.F. State Col.; Fullerton Jr. Col., '34–'36; U.C.L.A., BE, '40; Univ. of Cal., MA (Psych., Ed.); b. Wichita Falls, Tex., 1917; p. St. Clair and Nina Bean Sherrod; h. Kurt Singer.

SINGER, MARILYN R., Assoc. Ed., School Library Journal Book Review, R. R. Bowker, 1180 Ave. of the Americas, N.Y., N.Y. 10036, '69–; Asst. Ed., E. P. Dutton, '67–'69; Edtl. Asst., W. W. Norton, '65–'67; ALA, WNBA; Simmons Col., BS, '65; b. Hartford, Conn.; p. Abraham and Sylvia Singer; res: 271 W. 11th St., N.Y., N.Y. 10014.

SINGER, NIKI SARACHAN, VP, Vernon Pope Co., Inc., 1270 Ave. of the Ams., N.Y., N.Y. 10020, '69–; Dir. of Wms. Interest, '65–'69; Asst. Prom. Mgr., Fairchild Pubns., '62–'65; Univ. of Mich., BA (cum laude), '59; b. Rochester, N.Y., 1937; p. Judge Goodman A. and

Evelyn Simon Sarachan; h. Warren Singer; res: 310 West End Ave., N.Y., N.Y. 10023.

SINGER, PHYLLIS WHEELER, Wms. Ed., Waterloo Daily Courier, Box 540, Waterloo, Ia. 50704; Gen. Assigt. Reptr., Bldg. Ed., Daily Colmst.; Sports Ed., Gen. Assigt. Reptr., Boone News Republican (Boone, Ia.); NPWC, Ia. Press Wm., NLAPW (Waterloo-Cedar Rapids Br. Secy.), Intl. Platform Assn.; Jane Arden (Ia.) Aw. for contrb. to commtns., U.S. Marines, U.S. Air Force cit., Press Wm. aws.; MacMurray Col. (Jacksonville, Ill.), '49; b. Boone, Ia., 1927; p. Jesse J. and Florence Ostrand Wheeler; h. John D. Singer; c. Pamela, Julie; res: 320 Lillian Lane, Waterloo, Ia. 50701.

SINKEY, BURNETTA FRANTZ, Soc. Ed., Cherokee Daily Times, S. Second St., Cherokee, Ia. 51012, '54–; Piano Instr. (Cherokee, Ia.), '27–'52; Tchr. (Ida Grove, Ia.), '26–'27; Tchr. (George, Ia.), '25–'26; Tchr. (Ute, Ia.), '24–'25; Eastern Star; Ia. State Tchs. Col., '22–'24; Morningside Col.; b. Omaha, Neb., 1904; p. William M. and Frances Price Frantz; h. Boyd J. Sinkey; c. Boyd W.; res: 441 Ash St., Cherokee, Ia. 51012.

SINNEN, JEANNE, Sr. Ed., University of Minnesota Press, 2037 University S.E., Mpls., Minn. 55455, '57–; Ed., '52–'57; Edtl. Asst., '49–'52; Am. Studies Assn.; Univ. of Minn., BA, '48 (Phi Beta Kappa; summa cum laude); MA, '49; b. St. Paul, Minn., 1926; p. Frank and Myrtle Fredericksen Sinnen; res: 967 Wakefield Ave., St. Paul, Minn. 55106.

SINZ, DOROTHY CLAIRE, Food Ed., Dallas Times Herald, Dallas, Tex. 75202, '45–; Asst. Wm.'s Ed., '46–'50; Garden Ed., Beauty Ed., '45–'48; Pubcty. Dir., Baker Hotel, '36–'41; Staff, Dallas Morning News, '36; First Place Aw., Grocery Manufacturers, '57; Aws: Vesta-Am. Meat Inst., '47, '54; Dairy Cncl., '54; Beef Cncl. '58, Am. Dairy Assn., '54; Aw., Press Club, '62; Nat. Judge, Mrs. Am. contest, '59–'63; Judge, Pillsbury Bake-off, '50; Cert. de Hon., L'Escole Du Cordon Bleu, Paris, France, '63; Theta Sigma Phi (Matrix Aw.), Fashion Group (Reg. Dir.), Confererie de la Chaine des Rotisseurs (dame de la chaine), Gamma Phi Beta (Pres.), Kappa Tau Gamma, Zonta (Pres., '56–'57), Dallas Soc. Crippled Children Bd. Dirs., '61–'62; Southern Methodist Univ., BS, '36; b. Chgo., Ill.; p. Pius and Marie Ankele Sinz; res: 6337 Ellsworth St., Dallas, Tex. 75214.

SIOUSSAT, HELEN JOHNSON, Mgt. Cnslt.; Dir., Talks Public Affairs Dept., CBS, '37–'64; Auth., "Mikes Don't Bite" (L. B. Fischer, '43); AWRT (Co-founder); Peabody aw., '54; Radio-TV Daily aw., Freedoms Fndn. aw.; numerous others; Goucher Col.; b. Balt., Md., 1902; p. Maurice J. T. and Helen Johnson D'Oylé Sioussat; h. (dec.); res: 2126 Connecticut Ave. N.W., Wash., D.C. 20008.

SITLEY, DOROTHEA WIELLAND, Dir., Consumer Rels., Gimbels' Phila., Ninth and Market Sts., Phila.,

Pa. 19105. '47–; BPW, Fashion Group, Hist. Soc. of Pa., NHFL, Phila. Club of Adv. Wm., PRSA; numerous civic aws., cits.; Who's Who in PR, Who's Who in the East, Who's Who of Am. Wm., Dic. of Intl. Biog.; b. W. Collingswood, N.J., 1900; p. Mr. & Mrs. George F. Wielland; h. (dec.); c. Gloria, Ralph; res: Parkway House, 2201 Pennsylvania Ave., Phila., Pa. 19130.

SITWELL, PHRONSIE MARSH, Educ. Wtr.; Real Estate Mgr., Lynchburg, Va.; published articles, poetry, features, drama, analyses of fgn. and domestic news; Lectr.; 30 yrs. in educ.; Dir., student drama, crtv. writing; radio script wtr.; De Bretts and Burke's Peerage; Lynchburg Col., '24–'26; Mary Washington Col., BS, '27; Columbia Univ., MA, '32; Inst. on World Affairs, Geneva, '35; N.Y.U., '41 (Fellowship); Univ. of Pa., '57 (Fellowship); Va. Polytech Inst., '67–'68; b. Campbell County, Va., 1907; h. 1. Erik Solling Mouberg (Div.), 2. Capt. Herbert Cecil FitzRoy Sitwell (dec.); c. Edmund Mouberg; res: Three Otters Estate, Bedford, Va. 24523.

SIVELLS, WANDA KELLAR, Dir., Learning Center, Wharton County Junior College, 911 Boling Highway, Wharton, Tex. 77488; Dir. of Lib. Svcs., Librn.; Bldg. Cnslt., Strake Jesuit Lib., '67; Contrb. Auth., Bibliography on Lib. Development ('68); Tex. Jr. Col. Tch. Assn. (Chmn., Lib. Sec., '68–'69), Delta Kappa Gamma (Chmn., Legislative Comm., '68–'69), Southern Assn. Cols. and Schs. Visitation Comm., Tex. Lib. Assn. (Col. and Univ. Sec. Secy., '61, Dist. Treas., '62), Southwestern Lib. Assn., ALA, ACRL, AAUW, TSTA; N. Tex. State Univ., BS (Lib. Sci.), '46; Tex. Wms. Univ., MLS, '65; Grad. Studies: Univ. of Tex., Tex. A & M., Univ. of Okla., Univ. of Houston; b. Cross Plains, Tex., 1925; p. Harvey and Loren Graves Kellar; h. Charles Graves Sivells; c. Patricia Ann (Mrs. Leslie E. White), Michael Patrick; res: 511 Lazy Lane, Wharton, Tex. 77488.

SIZEMORE, MARGARET DAVIDSON, Dean of Wm., Samford University, 800 Lakeshore Dr., Birmingham, Ala. 35209, '50–; Assoc. Prof. of French, '47–; Auth.: (with N. S. Graydon) "The Amazing Marriage" ('65), "Wake Me When It's Over" rec.; Edtl. Asst., U.S. Air Force; Ala. Wtrs. Conclave (Pres., '61–'62), NLAPW (Birmingham Br. Pres., '66–'68), Birmingham Festival of Arts Chmn., ('61), Intl. Platform Assn., various educ. assns., Birmingham Wm. of the Yr. ('62), Wms. Comm. of 100 (Pres., '68–'70), Monterey (Mex.) Tech. Bd. of Visitors ('57–), Contemporary Auths., Who's Who of Am. Wm., Who's Who in Educ., Dic. of Intl. Biog., Lib. of Ala. Lives, Am. Millinery Inst. Aw., "Ami de Paris" by City of Paris ('51), Archbishop of Canterbury cit. ('51), Salon de France ('47–), Samford Univ., AB, '28; MA, '30; Univ. of Paris, Normal Deg., '29; Western Reserve Univ.; b. Birmingham, Ala.; p. Julius W. and Ruth Lee Davidson; h. James M. Sizemore; c. James M., Ruth L.; res: 3084 Sterling Rd., Birmingham, Ala. 35213.

SIZEMORE, PATRICIA ANN, Publr., The Peoples Journal, P.O. Box 278, Booneville, Ky. 41314, '64–;

Pres., Publr., Leslie County (Ky.) news; Ky. Press Assn., NPC, Ky. Hist. Soc., Owsley County Dem. Wms. Club (Pres.); Tampa Univ. grad.; b. Middlesboro, Ky., 1941; h. T. C. Sizemore; c. Pam, Tim; res: Booneville, Ky.

SKANTZ, PATRICIA BOWERS, Talent, c/o Dorothy Day Otis, 511 N. La Cienega Blvd., L.A., Cal. 90048; Actress, NBC-TV, '67–'68; bdcst., Metromedia Radio, '66–'68; Actress-Interviewer, TV (Wash., D.C.), TV, '61–'65; TV comls., '61–'65; Fashion Show Commtr., Fashion Model; Tchr., Fashion, Finishing Sch.; AWRT, SAG (L.A. Chptr. Bd. of Dirs.), AFTRA; Birmingham, (Ala.) S. Col., '46–'50; Univ. Ala., '50–'51; b. Birmingham, Ala., 1934; p. William and Ellen Foster Bowers; h. Lawrence Skantz; c. Lawrence Michael, Patricia Ann, Vanessa Maria; res: 28105 Ambergate Dr., Palos Verdes Peninsula, Cal. 90274.

SKEEN, EVELYN DELANEY, VP, Wms. Dept. Dir., Zigman-Joseph Associates, 208 E. Wisconsin Ave., Milw., Wis. 53202, '66–; Wms. Dept. Dir., '63–; Wms. Ed., Let's See mag., '58–'63; Reptr., The Chronicle (Middleburg, Va.), '56–'60; Talent, Radio KALB (Alexandria, La.), '39–'40; Coordr., Heritage-Milw. Fashion Show, '64–'69; PRSA, Milw. Jr. League (Pres.); Distributive Educ. Clubs of Am. aw., '68; Am. Fedn. of Adv. aw., '66; La. State Univ., BA (Eng.), '39; b. Alexandria, La., 1918; p. John and Frances Burroughs Delaney; h. Richard B. Skeen; c. Sally (Mrs. John Searle); res: 205 Green Bay Rd., Thiensville, Wis.

SKELLEY, GLADYS, Wms. Ed., Burlington Hawk-Eye, Box 10, 800 S. Main St., Burlington, Ia. 52601, '59–; Wms. Ed., Waverly Democrat, Bremer County Republican, '54–'59; Wtr., Prodr., Radio WLS (Chgo., Ill.), '46–'53; Home Ed., Prairie Farmer (Chgo.), '46–'54; Assoc. Ed., Asst. Dir. of Info. Ia. Farm Bur. (Des Moines), '45–'46; Feature Wtr., Cedar Rapids (Ia.) Gazette, '42–'45; Soc. Ed., Iowa City Press-Citizen, '39–'42; Muscatine Journal, '39; Reptr., Daily Iowan (Ia. City), '35–'38; Ia. Press Wm., Nat. Farm Home Eds. Assn. (Pres.), '53–'54); numerous writing aws.; Who's Who of Am. Wm.; Univ. of Ia., BA (Jnlsm.); b. Monticello, Ia., 1909; p. James and Anna Lubben Skelley; res: 935 N. Seventh St., Burlington, Ia. 52601.

SKELLY, FLORENCE R., VP, Daniel Yankelovich Inc., 575 Madison Ave., N.Y., N.Y. 10022, '61–; Sr. Assoc., Stewart Dougall & Assoc., '52–'61; Analyst, Housing Div., Bur. of Census, '50–'52; h. Eugene Altman.

SKIFF, MARGARET SARA, Coordr. of Children's Svcs., Cuyahoga County Library, 4510 Memphis Ave., Cleve., Oh. 44144, '40–; Cleve. Public Lib., '38–'40; Park Sch. of Cleve., '36–'38; ALA, Oh. Lib. Assn. WNBA (Pres.), '56–'57); Univ. of Rochester, BS (Educ.), '34; Case Western Reserve Univ., MS (Lib. Svc.), '56; b. Gainesville, N.Y.; p. John and Winifred Skiff; res: 2173 Oakdale Dr., Cleve., Oh. 44118.

SKILLMAN, HOPE CHRISTIE, Secy., Membership Chmn., National Council of Women of United States,

Inc., 345 E. 46th St., N.Y., N.Y. 10017, '68–; Textile Designer; Pres., Skillman, Inc., '44–; Pres., Hope Skillman, Inc., '42–'44; Dir., Assoc. Ed., Fine Arts, '32–'33; Assoc. Ed., Parnassus, '30–'31; Tchr., textiles, Tobe-Coburn Sch.; Cnslt., Goucher Col.; Bd. Govs., Phila. Col. of Art; Fashion Group (Pres., '58–'60), Inner Circle; Lord & Taylor Achiev. aw., '60; Maid of Cotton aw.; Goucher Col., AB, '61; Grad. Work; b. Grand Rapids, Mich.; p. Frederic and Julia Christie Skillman; h. Saul Schary; res: 56 W. 10th St., N.Y., N.Y. 10011.

SKINNER, ELIZABETH ABRAMS, Jnlsm., Eng. Tchr., North Marion High School, Rte. 1, Box 269 A, Aurora, Ore. 97002, '67–; Tchr., Molalla Union HS; Theta Sigma Phi, Nat. Cncl. of Tchrs. of Eng., NEA, Ore. Educ. Assn.; Univ. of Wash., BA, '38; Ore. Col. of Educ., MAT, '66; b. Salem, Ore., 1916; p. Carle and Myrtle Duncan Abrams; h. G. L. Skinner (dec.); c. David Leslie, Susan Carol; res: 805 Kingwood Dr. N.W., Salem, Ore. 97304.

SKINNER, OLIVIA LITTLE, Feature Wtr., Everyday Magazine, St. Louis Post-Dispatch, 1133 Franklin Ave., St. Louis, Mo. 63101, '60–; Tchr., '58–'60; Free-lance Wtr., '43–'53; Feature Wtr., Colmst., Co-ed., 1948 Guide to Europe of Paris Herald-Tribune, '48–'50; Tchr., N.Y.C. '43–'45; Theta Sigma Phi, Mo. Press Wm. (VP, '69); NFPW state, nat. aws.; Multiple Sclerosis Soc. Aw. for Family and Children's Svc. of Greater St. Louis; Nat. Col. of Educ.; b. Evanston, Ill., 1919; p. Charles and Myra Wilson Little; h. Claiborne Skinner; c. Charles C. C., Claiborne, Jr.; res: 484 Lake Ave., St. Louis, Mo. 63108.

SLACK, SARA LOUISE, Wms. and Soc. Ed., N.Y. Amsterdam News, 2340 Eighth Ave., N.Y., N.Y. 10027, '70–; Educ. Ed., '61–'70; Sch. Reptr., '58–'61 (cited by 28 Harlem schs. for sch. rept.); '56–'58; TV Talent, "Ladies of the Press," "Page One"; Auth., play "Melody" ('45; first black student to receive DAR Silver Platter Aw. for Playwriting); Media Wm., N.Y. Nwsp. Reptr's. Assn., commty. svc. aws.; Northfield Seminary for Girls; Howard Univ., '47 (alumni club); b. Stratford, Conn., 1924; p. Arthur and Mamie Rogers Slack; res: 30 E. 30th St., N.Y., N.Y. 10016.

SLADE, LYNN ANDREA, PR Pers. Placement Cnslr., Toby Clark Agency, Inc., 18 E. 48th St., N.Y., N.Y. 10017, '69–; Asst. Pubcty. Dir., Seventeen, '68–'69; Press News Ed., '67–'68; Theta Sigma Phi, AWRT; Univ. of Wash., BA, '65; b. Chgo., Ill., 1944; res: 421 E. 81st St., N.Y., N.Y. 10028.

SLATER, HELENE SOUTHERN, Pres., Southern-Slater Enterprises, '55–; NAMW (N.Y. Chptr. VP, '67–), Lambda Kappa Mu (N.E. Reg. Dir., '68–), Am. Acad. of Polit. and Social Sci., Am. Sociological Soc.; Radio WWRL commty. aw., '65; New Sch. for Social Rsch., BA (Pubns.), '55; MA (Sociology), '59; b. Phila., Pa.; p. William and Henrietta Ford Southern; h. (div.); res: 485 W. 22nd St., N.Y., N.Y. 10011.

SLATER, MARJORIE T. Media Dir., Ingalls Associates, Inc., 137 Newbury St., Boston, Mass. 02116, '65–; Exec Secy., Mktng. Asst., '63–'65; Mktng.-Rsch. Asst., Harold Cabot & Co., '58–'62; Bdcst. Execs. Club (Bd. of Dirs.), Am. Mktng. Assn.; Simmons Col., BS, '54–'58; res: 115 Langley Rd., Newton Center, Mass. 02159.

SLAUSON, MARILYN, Rschr. and Adm. Asst., Channing, Rothbard & Weinberg, Inc., 33 Rector St., N.Y., N.Y. 10006, '68–; Free-lance editing; New Student Prom., Col. of New Rochelle, New Rochelle, N.Y.; Assoc. and Wtr., Glick & Lorwin Educ. PR, (N.Y.C.); Wtr. and Asst. to VP for Adv.-PR, Manpower/Travelpower (Milw., Wis.); Pubcty. Dir., Northwestern Mutual Life Ins.; AE, Baker, Johnson & Dickinson Adv.; Copywtr.; Free-lance TV panelist; Copy Chief and On-Air Proms., WMAW; Copywtr.; Theta Sigma Phi (Milw. Chptr. Exec. Bd.), Adv. Wm. of Milw., Life Advs. Assn., Phi Beta Kappa (Milw. Chptr. Exec. Bd.), Alpha Phi, Polit. Volunteer; Standard & Poor's Outstanding Fin. Adv.-PR Nat. Aw.; DePauw Univ., BA (cum laude; Pulliam Radio-TV Scholarship); b. Wauwatosa, Wis.; p. Eugene and Sara Fitzgerald Slauson; res: 534 E. 85th St., N.Y., N.Y. 10028.

SLINGSBY, PHYLLIS CRUM, Wms. Ed., Contra Costa Times, 1940 Mt. Diablo Blvd., Walnut Creek, Cal. 94596, '49–; East Bay Wms. Press Club (Pres., '69–'70), Walnut Creek Soroptimist Club (Pres., '62–'63), BPW (Walnut Creek Pres., '64–'65); b. Bakersfield, Cal.; p. Marion and Stella Hughes Crum; h. Perk Slingsby; c. Mrs. Gerald Wayne Johnson; res: 134 Jackson Way, Alamo, Cal. 94507.

SLOAN, FYCHELENE ADKINS, Ed., weekly newsp., Herring Publishing Co., Munday, Tex. 76371; Reptr., Proofreader; Eastern Star, Am. Legion; b. Rule, Tex.; p. Dallas and Edna Harris Adkins; h. Howard Sloan; c. Dickie, Tommy, Becky, Sherry; res: Box 387, Rochester, Tex. 79544.

SLOANE, PATRICIA, Artist; One-man shows: Grand Central Moderns ('68), Fordham Univ. ('68), Univ. of R.I. ('68); Auth., "Color: Basic Principles and New Directions (Reinhold/Studio Vista, '68); Tchr: Mercer County Commty. Col., Univ. of R.I., N.Y.U., Kingsborough Commty. Col.; Col. Art Assn., AAUW, Inst. for the Study of Art and Educ., Am. Soc. for Aesthetics and Art Criticism; R.I. Sch. of Design, BFA, '55; Hunter Col., MA, '68; b. N.Y.C., 1934; p. David and Marian Frauenthal Sloane; h. Kenneth Campbell; res: 79 Mercer St., N.Y., N.Y. 10012.

SLOBODKINA, ESPHYR, Wtr. of numerous children's bks., Artist, Sculptor, Illus., Lectr., Owner, Art Development Co., 20 W. Terrace Rd., Great Neck, N.Y. 10021; Several one-man art shows, '42–; art in various museums in Am., Israel; Tchr. of art; Lectr. on art of writing and illustrating children's bks.; various organizations; Nat. Acad. of Design in N.Y.C.; b. Cheliabinsk, Siberia, Russia; p. Solomon and Itta

Agranovich Slobodkin; h. William Lester Urquhart (dec.); res: 20 W. Terrace Rd., Great Neck, N.Y. 11021.

SLOCUM, GRACE PAYSON, Asst. Dir., Enoch Pratt Free Library, 400 Cathedral St., Balt., Md. 21201, '64–; Pers. Offcr., Free Lib. of Phila. (Pa.), '59–'64; Coordr., Young Adult Svcs., Bklyn. (N.Y.) Public Lib., '53–'59; Young Adult Librn., Pratt Lib., '47–'53; Eng. Tchr. (Wilmington, N.C.), '43–'46; ALA, Md. Lib. Assn. (Pres., '67–'68); Univ. of N.C., AB, '43; Columbia Univ. Lib. Sch., BS (Lib. Sci.), '47; b. Wilmington, N.C., 1922; p. Robert and Annie H. Slocum; res: 159 W. Lanvale St., Balt., Md. 21217.

SLONIM, RUTH, Prof., Dept. of Eng., Washington State University, Pullman, Wash. 99163, '64–; '47–'64; Visiting Prof., Univ. of Puerto Rico, '46–'47; Central Wash. State Col., '44–'45; Univ. of Minn., '38–'44; Auth: "London: An Appreciation" (Humphries, '54), "San Francisco: 'the City' in Verse" (Wash. State Univ. Press., '65); numerous orgs., aws.; Duluth State Col., BA, '38; Univ. of Minn., MA, '42; grad. study, also, Univ. of Cal., Berkeley; b. Chgo., Ill., 1918; p. S. M. and Lena Slonim; res: 1813 C St., Pullman, Wash. 99163.

SLOSBERG, MILDRED DIZON, Free-lance Travel Wtr., '33–; Painter, Sculptor, '24–; Adv. Copywtr., Sears Roebuck (L.A., Cal.), '33–'35; various orgs.; Univ. of Wis., BA (Jnlsm.), '33; Boston Univ. Sch. of Public Commtns., MA (PR, Mass Commtns.), '66; b. Wonewoc, Wis. 1911; p. Philip and Helen Blumenthal Dizon; h. Charles Slosberg (dec.); c. Myles J., Ellen May Rosenthal, Barry M.; res: 280 Boylston St., Chestnut Hill, Mass. 02167.

SLOSBURG, BERNICE LIPSCHUTZ, PR, AE, Bofinger-Kaplan Advertising, Inc., 1601 Church Rd., Glenside, Pa. 19038, '62–; PR Dir., St. Christopher's Hosp. for Children; AE, C. Robert Gruver Assoc.; Asst. to Pres., Cherry Sportswear; Phila. PR Assn., Montgomery County PR Club, Del. Valley Hosp. Assn. PR Soc., Hosp. Assn. of Pa. (aw.); b. Phila., Pa., 1931; p. Harry and Sylvia Glayman Lipschutz; h. Philip Slosburg; c. Harvey S., Stephen L., Michael H.; res: 7943 Jenkintown Rd., Cheltenham, Pa. 19012.

SLOVER, BONNIE, Pres., Brown-Stone East, Ltd., 43 W. 12th St., N.Y., N.Y. 10011, '68–; Dir. of Adv. Svc., Fashion Mktng. Mgr., Holiday mag., '58–'68; East Ed., Charm, '57; Asst. Fashion, Adv. Dir., Burlington Industries, '56; Fashion, Adv. Dir., Margot, Arkey, Jr., '55; Assoc. Mdse. Ed., Glamour, '51–'54; Midwest Ed., '50; Fashion Group, AWNY; Who's Who of Am. Wm.; William Smith Col., AB, '45; b. Bath, N.Y., 1925; p. Oliver and Jessie Millspaugh Watkins; res: 43 W. 12th St., N.Y., N.Y. 10011.

SMALL, ANNIE LEE STAGG, Owner, Mgr., WYTH, Beacon Heights, Madison, Ga. 30650, '60–; Talent, Exec., WCSC-TV, '52–'59; Commentator, KFRU, '47–'50; Anncr., '38–'40; Anncr., Wtr., WSB, '43–'45;

Anncr., WMBR, '42–'43, '32–'35; Anncr., WFMJ, '41–'42; Tchr., Stephens Col., '47–'50; BPW (State VP, '66); numerous bdcst. aws.; Stephens Col., '38–'40; Northwestern Univ., '40–'41; b. Elba, Ala., 1920; p. Olin and Madalia Lee Stagg; h. James Small; c. James Jr., Preston W.; res: Dixie Ave., Madison, Ga. 30650.

SMALL, JANE MANN (Carol Lane), Wms. Travel Dir., Shell Oil Co., 1008 W. Sixth St., L.A., Cal. 90054, '64–; Pubcty. Dir., Union County (N.J.)'¹Citizens for Goldwater-Miller, '64; Colmst., Elizabeth (N.J.) Daily Journal, '47–'53; Pubcty. Dir., March of Dimes, Union County, '47; AWRT, other orgs.; 2,000 Wm. of Achiev.; Webber Col., '46; Pubcty. Club of N.Y., Cert., '63; b. Chgo., Ill. 1926; p. George and Angeline Malhiot Mann; h. John Small (div.); c. Mrs. Candis Keilman; res: 691 Irolo St., L.A., Cal. 90005.

SMALL, MIRIAM ROSSITER, Prof. Emeritus of Eng., Wells College, Aurora, N.Y. 13026, '64–; Chmn. of Dept., Prof., Instr., '27–'64; Chmn. of Am. Studies; Auth., two biogs: "Charlotte Ramsay Lennox (Yale Studies in Eng., '35, reissued, '69), "Oliver Wendell Holmes" (Twayne's U.S. Auths. series, '62); pfsnl. articles, incl. one for Ency. Americana; Instr., Tchr., Eng., '20–'27; Tchr., French, Exeter (N.H.) HS, '19–'20; Fulbright Lectr., Am. Lit., Univ. of Vienna (Austria), '56–'57; Col. Eng. Assn. (Central N.Y. Chptr. Secy., Pres., '50s), Modern Lang. Assn., Am. Studies Assn. (Central N.Y. Chptr. Pres., '63–'64; Secy., '45–'47); Wellesley Col., '19 (Phi Beta Kappa; Durant Scholar, '16–'19; scholarships); Yale Univ. Grad. Sch. in Eng., MA, '23 (scholarship '23–'24); PhD, '25 (largest fellowship for wm. at Yale, '24–'25); b. Goshen, Conn., 1899; p. Rev. Harry E. and Bertha Bartlett Small; res: N. Berwick, Me. 03906.

SMARGON, ANDREA, Andrea Smargon, Publicity, 325 E. 57th St., N.Y., N.Y. 10022, '62–; Pubcty. Dir., The Dial Press, '60–'62; Pubcty. Dir., Cadence Records, '58–'59; Public Info. Dir., Am. Social Health Assn., '56–'58; Campaign Pubcty. Dir., Un. Cerebral Palsy of N.Y.C., '55, '53; Div. Pubcty. Mgr., Fedn. of Jewish Philanthropies Campaign, '54; Nat. Radio, TV Pubcty. Dir., Citizens for McCarthy, '68; Radio, TV Pubcty. Cnslt., Nat. Citizens Comm. Concerned about Deployment of the A.B.M., '69; Univ. of Wis., BA, res: 325 East 57th St., N.Y., N.Y. 10022.

SMART, MAY FERNE, Adv. Wtr., Batz-Hodgson-Neuwoehner, Inc., 411 N. 10th St., St., Louis, Mo. 63101, '59–; Wtr., Frank Block Assoc., '55–'59; Wtr., Maurice Hirsch Adv., '45–'55; Wms. Adv. Club of St. Louis, AWRT (St. Louis Chptr. Pres., '67–'68, VP, '66–'67, Secy., '65–'66), NATAS; Wash. Univ.; b. Clarksville, Mo.; p. J. Jay and Edith Fern Whiteside; c. William Edward Smart; res: 4475 W. Pine St., St. Louis, Mo. 63108.

SMILEY, JANE TOWLER, Fashion and Retail Adv. Cnslt., The New Yorker Magazine Inc., 25 W. 43rd St., N.Y., N.Y. 10036, '59–; Adv. Sls., '53–'59; Asst. Byr.,

Lord & Taylor, '51–'53; Off. Mgr., PIB, '50–'51; Statis. Decoder, C. E. Hooper, '49–'51; Asst. Byr., R. H. Macy, '47–'49; Fashion Group (Bd. Dir., '62–'63); Trends (Pres., '68–'60); Smith Col., BA, '47; b. Syracuse, N.Y., 1925; p. Eugene and Lucile Hagen Towler; h. Richard H. Smiley; res: Two Tudor City Pl., N.Y., N.Y. 10017.

SMITH, ALICE GULLEN, Chmn., Lib. and AV Educ. Dept., Univ. of Southern Fla., SSO Bldg. 245, Tampa, Fla., '66–; Instr., Asst. Prof., Dept. of Lib. Sci., Wayne State Univ., '57–'65; Librn., Detroit Pub., Adjunct Teaching for Wayne State Univ., '46–'57; Dir., Congressional Churches Religious Education Cncl. of Churches, '41–'46; Instr., Eng. Tchr. and Librn., '33–41; Free-lance Wtr: professional jnls., poems, articles; ALA (YASD), Comm. for the Identification of Children's Libs. in Continental America, ALA (AASL), Guidelines for Inner City Sch. Libs., AASL, NCTE, ACEI, NEA, AAUP, Fla. Lib. Assn. (Secy., '68–'69), Friends of the Lib. of Hillsborough County (Pres., '68–'69); Wayne State Univ., BA (Eng. and Speech), '32; Univ. of Mich., MA (Lib. Sci.), '48; Wayne State Univ., MS (Lib. Sci.), '59; EdD, '66; (Wm. of Wayne Alumnae Aw., '67; Alumni Aw., '68); b. Farmington, Mich.; h. Norma Smith; res: 10912 B, 22nd St., Tampa, Fla. 33605.

SMITH, BARBARA E., Ed., Thomas Y. Crowell Co., 201 Park Ave. S., N.Y., N.Y. 10003, '69–; Prod. Ed., '66–'68; Asst. Ed., '64–'66; Asst. to Pic. Ed., Look, '63–'64; Alpha Phi, Theta Sigma Phi (VP, '69–); De Pauw Univ., BA, '62; (N.Y. Alumnae Pres., '69–); b. Schenectady, N.Y., 1940; p. J. Stanford and Elaine Showater Smith; res: 301 E. 64th St., N.Y., N.Y. 10021.

SMITH, BARBARA HERRNSTEIN, Auth., Ed.; Eng. Instr., Bennington College, Bennington, Vt. 05201, '62–; Eng. Instr., Brandeis Univ., '61–'62; Bks: Ed., "Discussions of Shakespeare's Sonnets" ('64), "Shakespeare's Sonnets" ('69); Auth., "Poetic Closure: A Study of How Poems End" (Christian Gauss aw., '68); NOW; City Col. of N.Y., '50–'52; Brandis Univ., BA, '54 (summa cum laude); MA, '55; PhD, '64; b. N.Y.C., 1932; p. Benjamin and Ann Weinstein Brodo; h. 1. Richard Herrnstein (div.) 2. Thomas Smith; c. Julia Herrnstein, Deirdre Maud Smith; res: Bennington Col., Bennington, Vt. 05201.

SMITH, BARBARA J., Adv. Mgr., Fanning Personnel Agency, 180 Broadway, N.Y., N.Y. 10038, '68–; Met. Adv., '66–'68; J. Howard Fink Adv., '64–'66; Queens Col.

SMITH, BARBARA JOHNSON, Auth.; Asst. Exec. Dir., Assoc. Proj. Dir., Colorado State College Foundation, Colorado State College, Frasier Hall 108, Greeley, Colo. 80631, '68–; PR Cnslt., Weld County Bank, '68–; Mktng. Offcr., '67–'68; Instr., Aims Jr. Col. Fine Arts, '67–'69; Colo. State Col. Fine Arts, '67; Media Specialist, Rocky Mountain Special Ed. Instr. Matl. Cntr., '66–'67; Adv. Mgr., Jrnl. Publ., '65–'66; Wms. Ed., Broomfield Star, '64–'65; Tech. Illus., Martin-Marietta Corp., '69–'61; Staff Artist, KRMA-TV,

'59–'60; Program Dir., Radio KYOU, '59; various orgs.; Univ. of Denver, BFA, '60 (cum laude); Univ. of Colo., '63–'64; Colo. State Col., MA (fine arts), '67; b. Scottsbluff, Neb. 1938; p. Howard and Robbie Twiggs Johnson; h. (div.); c. Brian Richard; res: 2112 Sixth Ave., Greeley, Colo. 80631.

SMITH, BEULAH FENDERSON, Colmst., Portland Press Herald, Portland, Me.; York County Star, Kennebunk, Me., '64–; Free-lance poet, short stories; Lectr., Star Is. and Me. Wtrs. Confs.; Me. State Poetry Contest Winner; Me. Wtrs. Conf. Contest Winner; Recchia Medal for Verse; Contemporary Auths.; Who's Who of Am. Wm.; Colby Col., BA '36; b. Ogunquit, Me., 1915; p. Archie and Sarah Clark Fenderson; h. Robert Smith; c. Kaaren Wright, Daniel Thurston, Stephen Morrill, Susan Lee; res: The Elmere, Wells, Me. 04090.

SMITH, CAMILLA PARKER, Co-owner, Sydney R. Smith Sporting Books, Canaan, N.Y. 12029, '66–; Staff, '49–'53; authority on bks. about horses and related subjects; Prod. Mgr., Harper's Magazine, '59–'66; Asst. Prod. Mgr., '53–'59; Antiquarian Booksellers Assn. of Am.; Blackstone Jr. Col., '47–'49; b. Pittsfield, Mass., 1929; p. Sydney R. and Margery Parker Smith; res: Bouldernol West, Canaan, N.Y. 12029.

SMITH, CHARLOTTE ANNETTE, Librn., Howey Academy, Howey-in-the-Hills, Fla. 32737, '69–; Librn. in charge of Docs., Stetson Univ., '68–'69, '58–'64; Chief Librn., duPont-Ball Lib., '40–'58; Asst. Cataloger, '39–'40; Librn., State Tchrs. Col. (Troy, Ala.), '33–'38; Tchr., HS and Jr. Col. (Ga.), '25–'30; Cnslt., Volusia County Lib.; ALA, Southeastern Lib. Assn., Fla. Lib. Assn. (Treas.), '51–'52; DKG (Rec. Secy., '47–'48), AAUW (DeLand Br. Pres., '51–'53), BPW (Pres., '52–'53); active in Episcopal church work; Agnes Scott Col., BA, '25; Emory Univ., MA, '27; BA (Lib. Sci.), '31; Greeneville, Tenn., 1902; p. Russell K. and Onie Campbell Smith; res: 615 N. Hayden Ave., DeLand, Fla. 32720.

SMITH, DOROTHY ALDEN, Art Dir., Westminster Press, 929 Witherspoon Bldg., Walnut and Juniper Sts., Phila., Pa. 19107, '44–; Asst. Adv. Dir., Thedore Presser Co.; Artist, Lotz Engraving Co.; Photogrammetric Engineer, U.S. Dept. of Interior; Free-lance Illus., Designer, '39–; Lectr: Phila. Col. of Art, Moore Col. of Art, Hussian Sch. of Art, Studio Sch. of Art and Design, Buten Wedgewood Museum; Gold Medal, Art Dirs. Club of Phila., Freedoms Fndn. Bronze Medal, '58; Bk. Clinic of Phila., Phila. Art Alliance, Phila. Booksellers Assn.; N.Y. Sch. of Pfsnl. Art; N.Y. Sch. of Fine and Applied Art (Parsons); b. Atlantic City, N.J., 1918; p. Paul R. and Mary A. McCloskey Smith; res: 608 Weadley Rd., Strafford, Wayne, Pa. 19087.

SMITH, DOROTHY KATHMANN, Partner, Media Dir., Farson & Huff Advertising Agency, 1110 Republic Bldg., Louisville, Ky. 40202, '48–; Prod. Mgr., '42–'48; Secy., '35–'42; b. Louisville, Ky., 1916; p. Garfield and Amelia Emrich Smith; res: 2200 Valley Vista Rd., Louisville, Ky. 40205.

SMITH, DOROTHY MARJORIE, Telegraph Ed., Waycross Journal-Herald, 400 Isabella St., Waycross, Ga., '44–; Corr., Atlanta (Ga.) Journal, '52–; Pilot Club of Waycross (Pres., '48–'49), AAUW; several AP writing aws.; Ga. State Col. for Wm., AB, '39; b. Waycross, Ga., 1916; p. Isaac and Lorena Godwin Smith; res: 622 McDonald St., Waycross, Ga. 31501.

SMITH, DRUE H., Info. Offcr., State of Maryland, 301 W. Preston St., Balt., Md. 21201, '67–; Dir., Public Affairs, Commentator, WDEF-TV; Corr., CBS, NBC, ABC; Wm.'s Ed., Chattanooga Times; Colmst., News, Free Press, The Sun Papers, The Examiner, D.C.; WNPC (Chattanooga Pres.), President's Comm. on Consumer Affairs (Tenn. Chmn.), AWRT, BPW (Wm. of Achiev.), ANWC, Quota Club Wm. of Yr., Who's Who of Am. Wm., DACOWITS (Hall of Fame), Tenn. Heart Assn. Chmn., United Cerebral Palsy Southeastern Chmn., Commty. Leaders in Am., Univ. of Chattanooga; b. Chattanooga, Tenn.; p. Jesse C. and Sara Muxen Henderson; h. Roy B. Smith; c. Drucilla; res: 1709 Golf St., Chattanooga, Tenn.; Bendabout Farms, Bedford County, Tenn.; 1028 Connecticut Ave. N.W., Wash., D.C.

SMITH, ELEANOR SPINDEN, Feature Wtr., North Iowa Farmer, Charles City Press, 100 N. Main St., Charles City, Ia. 50616; Univ. of Northern Ia.; b. Fredericksburg, Ia., 1937; p. Edwin and Lucille Niemann Spinden; h. Roger Smith; c. Michael Allen, Michelle Kay; res: Highway 218 W., Charles City, Ia. 50616.

SMITH, ELEANOR TOUHEY, Lib. Svc. Program Offcr., U.S. Office of Education, Region II, 26 Federal Plaza, N.Y., N.Y. 10007, '67–; Coordr. of Adult Svcs., Bklyn. Public Lib., '53–'67; Head of Extension, Ferguson Library, Stamford, Conn. '49–'51; Asst. Dir., Santa Monica, Cal. Public Lib., '45–'49; Dir., Vanport, Ore. Public Lib., '43–'45; Readers Advisor, Lib. Assn. of Portland, '32–'43; Asst. Prof. U. of Washington Summer 1964, Critic; Auth., "Psychic People" (Morrow, '68); Contrbr. to TV, Radio pfsnl. bks., periodicals, newspapers; ALA (Adult Svcs. Div. Pres., '64–'65), N.Y. State Lib. Assn. (Pres., '69–'70), Bksellers. League of N.Y. (Pres., '66–'68); WNBA (Nat. Secy., '64–'68; Chptr. Pres., '63–'64), Lib. PR Cncl. (Pres., '55–'56), N.Y. Lib. Club (Pres., '60–'61), N.Y. Adult Educ. Assn. (Bd. Mbr.); Friends of the Bklyn. Public Lib. Aw. for Distg. Librnship., '61; Univ. of Ore., BA, '30 (Phi Beta Kappa); Univ. of Southern Cal., Cert. of Librnship., '32; Columbia Univ. Sch. of Lib. Svc., MS, '52 (Alumni Pres., '62–'63); b. Portland, Ore.; p. Thomas and Sarah Ford Touhey; h. S. Stephenson Smith (dec.) res: 201 Eastern Parkway, Bklyn., N.Y. 11238.

SMITH, ELIZABETH JANE, Dir. of Air Media Pubcty., Liberty Mutual Insurance Co., 175 Berkeley St., Boston, Mass. 02135, '69–; Radio-TV Press Rep., '67–'68;

Asst. PR Dir., WBZ-TV, '62–'67; PR Staff, Boston Univ., '61–'62; PR Coordr., N. Adams (Mass.) Hosp., '60; Lectr. in Radio-TV-PR for wms. groups, cols., and high schools; AWRT (Mass. State Rep., '68–'69), New England WPA, Boston Press Club, Big Sister Assn. (Bd. of Dirs., Advisor in PR), Tau Mu Epsilon, Boston Commty. Media Comm.; volunteer PR work: Col. of New Rochelle (N.Y.), AB (Eng.), '60; Boston Univ., MS (Commtns.), '61; b. N. Adams, Mass.; p. Francis P. and Elizabeth Mulcare Smith.

SMITH, EUNICE YOUNG, Auth.-Illus., bks. for young people, Painter; AAUW, Children's Reading Round Table, Auths. League of Am.; S. Bend Art Ctr., Longboat Key-Fla. Art Ctr.; Univ. of Ind. juv. bk. aw.; Rosary Col., '20; Lakeview Comm. Art Sch., '21; Ind. Univ. Ext., '35–'36; Acad. of Fine Arts (Chgo., Ill.), '45; b. LaSalle, Ill., 1902; p. Arthur M. and Katherine Whitmarsh Young; h. Stuyvesant C. Smith; c. Chad, Sharon (Mrs. Herbert Kane); res: 15026 Dragoon Trail, Mishawaka, Ind. 46544.

SMITH, FRANCES C., Free-lance Wtr.; Assoc. Ed., Boys' Life, '44–'66; Auth: "World of the Arctic" (Lippincott), "Men at Work in Alaska," six others; Soc. of Am. Travel Wtrs., Outdoor Wtrs. Assn. of Am.; Univ. of Kan., AB; Columbia Univ., MA; res: 10 Park Pl., Cranbury, N.J. 08512.

SMITH, FRANCES MARY, AE, J. Walter Thompson Co., 420 Lexington Ave., New York, N.Y. 10017, '47; Non-Fiction Ed., Ace Pubns., '45–'47; Assoc. Ed., Business Education World, '42–'45; N.Y. Assn. of Indls. Commtns. (Pres., '58–'59), AWNY; Columbia Univ., BS, MS; b. Mpls., Minn.; p. Ralph and Lottie Aves Smith; res: 2 Tudor City Pl., N.Y., N.Y. 10017.

SMITH, GRACE BERNIER, Wms. Ed., The Morning Call, 33 Church St., Paterson, N.J. 07509, '68–'69; Asst. Wms. Ed., '65–'68; Wms. Ed., The Jnl.-News, '63–'65; Staff Wtr., Nat. Assn. Credit Mgt., '61–'63; Dir., Owner, Smith PR & Adv., '59–'61; Co-ed., Publr., Ramapo Valley Independent, '41–'57 (many aws.); Soroptimist (Rockland County Club); Penney-Mo. aw., excellence of wms. sec., '68; Hampden-Sydney Col.; b. Laconia, N.H., 1914; p. Charles A. and Grace Logue Bernier; h. Lamson Smith (former); c. Mrs. Robert S. Yeaple, Todd M., Steven C.; res: 33 Bon Aire Circle, Suffern, N.Y. 10901.

SMITH, HAZEL BRANNON, Ed., Publr., The Lexington Advertiser, 110 Yazoo St., Lexington, Miss. 39095, '43–; Ed., Publr: The Durant (Miss.) News, '36–; Banner County Outlook, '54–; Northside Reporter, '58–; Theta Sigma Phi (Nat. Headliner aw., '62), Miss. Press Wm. (past State Pres.), NFPW (edtl. aws.), Miss. Press Assn., Intl. Conf. of Weekly Nwsp. Eds., Nat. Nwsp. Assn. (past State Dir.); Pulitzer Prize, edtl. writing, '64; Elijah Parish Lovejoy aw., '60; Who's Who in Am., '68–'69; Univ. of Ala., BA, '35 (Alumna aw., Jnlsm., '66); b. Gadsden, Ala.; p. Dock and Georgia Freeman Brannon; h. Walter D. Smith; res: P.O. Box 180, Hazelwood, Lexington, Miss. 39095.

SMITH, HAZEL SWANSON, Personal Librn. for pres. of Missouri-Kansas-Texas R.R. Co.; Asst., Tripoli Leader, '43–'46; Colmst., Waverly Democrat; Theta Sigma Phi (Des Moines Alumnae Pres., '46), Gtr. Des Moines C. of C. aw., '65; Zeta Tau Alpha; active in civic groups; Univ. of Ia., BA (Jnlsm.), '27; b. Des Moines, Ia., 1904; p. John G. and Hulda Anderson Swanson; h. Walter H. Smith; c. Kenneth E., Edgar L., res: 5312 Ingersol, Des Moines, Ia. 50312.

SMITH, HELEN EIWEN, Dir., Greece Public Library, 125 Mitchell Rd., Rochester, N.Y. 14626, '59–; ALA, N.Y. Lib. Assn.; Hunter Col., BA; Columbia Univ., BS (Lib. Sci.); h. James J. Smith.

SMITH, HELEN MAXWELL, Owner, A-One Advertising Agency, 616 Jefferson Tower, 351 W. Jefferson Blvd., Dallas, Tex. 75208, '63–; Univ. of Tex.; Southern Methodist Univ., BA, '57; b. Dallas, Tex., 1918; p. R. Norman and Lorena Maxwell Smith; h. Russell L. Smith (dec.); c. Helen Hope Hall; res: 835 Wood River Rd., Dallas, Tex. 75232.

SMITH, HELEN MILLER, Free-lance Auth.; Legal Secy., Gallagher & Bewick, Attorneys, 14 W. Main St., Evansville, Wis. 53536, '33–; juv. bks. incl. "Laughing Child" (Bks. I, II, III, '46, '47, '48); poetry bks. incl: "Chiaroscura" ('63), "Windfalls" ('55); poetry, articles, humorous pubns., nat., fgn.; poetry in many anthologies, translated fgn. langs.; Instr.; numerous organizations and aws.; Contemporary Poets Intl. Hall of Fame, Manila, '69; Rock County Normal (Teaching Cert.), '22; Univ. of Cal., BA, '26; Univ. of Wis., MS, '56; Oh. Christian Col., PhD, DD, '68; Juris. Dr. (hon.), '69; hon. degs: Free Univ. of Asia, PhD, '67; Intl. Acad. of Leadership, Philippines, LitD, '68; St. Olav's Acad., Sweden, PhD, '69; Great China Arts Col., Hong Kong, DLib Arts, '69; Intl. Univ., Ecuador, DLib Arts, '69; b. Chgo., Ill., 1903; p. J. A. and DeEtte Gericke Miller; h. Charles Harmon Smith; c. Glen D., DeEtte Ellen Amdahl, George D.; res: 409 Lincoln St., Evansville, Wis. 53536.

SMITH, JACQUELINE BYARS, Asst. Station Mgr., Pacific & Southern Broadcasting, 1611 W. Peachtree, N.E., Atlanta, Ga. 30309, '68–; Adv. Tchr., Massey Jr. Col.; Film Dir., Crosley Bdcst.; News Reptr., WIBC; Prodr., "The Snooky Lanson Show," WIBC; AWRT, Wms. C. of C., Atlanta Press Club; Univ. of Ala., AB, '58; b. Atlanta, Ga.; p. Franklin and Anne Byars Smith; res: 97 Peachtree Park Dr., N.E., Atlanta, Ga. 30309.

SMITH, JANET, Dir., Highland Rim Regional Library, 2102 Mercury Blvd., Murfreesboro, Tenn. 37130, '62–; Asst. Reg. Librn., '60–'62; Bookmobile Librn., '55–'59; Beta Phi Mu, ALA, Tenn. Lib. Assn., Southeastern Lib. Assn., Delta Kappa Gamma, Xi State-Beta Epsilon (Corr. Secy.); Martin Jr. Col., '51–'53; Middle Tenn. State Univ., '53–'55; Peabody Col., MA (Lib. Sci.); b. Aspen Hill, Tenn., 1932; p. Urban H. and Nelle Jones Smith.

SMITH, JANICE RHODES, Media Dir., Martin,

White & Mickwee Advertising, 614 S. 38th St., Birmingham, Ala. 35222, '69–; Media Dir., '66–'69; Media Byr., Union Adv. '63–'66; Traf., WAFG-TV (Huntsville, Ala.), '60–'61; AWRT (Heart of Dixie Chptr. Bd. of Dirs. '68–'69; Pres.-elect, '69–'70; Pres., '70–'71); b. Union City, Tenn., 1942; p. Charles and Geneva Smith Rhodes; h. Robert Smith; c. Terianne, James Douglas, Patricia Lynn; res: 4243 Clairmont Ave., Birmingham, Ala. 35222.

SMITH, JEAN FREAS, TV News Reptr., WRC-TV, 4001 Nebraska Ave., N.W., Wash., D.C. 20012, '65–; Ed., Voice of Am., '63–'65; Edtl. Asst., King Features, '51–'52; WNPC, AWRT; Va. AP Aw., '68; Adv. Club (Wash., D.C.) Aw., '68; Sarah Lawrence Col., BA, '50; Nat. Defense Fgn. Lang. Fellowship, '61; B. Wash., D.C., 1929; p. Samuel and Katherine Rheinhardt Freas; c. Rebecca, Candida; res: 4805 Bending Lane, N.W., Wash., D.C. 20007.

SMITH, JEAN LORRAINE, Ed. of Pubns., Natural Gas Pipeline Co. of America, 122 S. Michigan Ave., Chgo., Ill. 60603, '66–; ICIE.

SMITH, JEANETTE HIGBIE, Prom. Mgr., Dir. of Commty. Svcs., Evening Outlook, United Western Newspapers, Inc., 1540 Third St., Santa Monica, Cal. 90401, '65–; Public Affairs Pubcty. Coordr., Special Projects Ed., Mktng. Mgr.-Wms. Activities, Subscription TV, Inc. (Santa Monica/L.A., Cal.), '64; Radio-TV Dir., Asst. to Pres., Michael W. Gradle, Inc. (L.A., Cal.), '63–'64; Cont. Dir., Prom. Dir., W. Tex. TV Network, '61–'63; Wtr., Ed., Asst. Prog. Dir., Inst. for Intl. Rsch. and Dev., Educ. Materials Div., '60–'61; PR Dir., Am. Home Security Life Ins. Co. (N.M.), '58–'60; Publicist, The Ettinger Co. (L.A., Cal.), '51–'52; Owner, Pubcty. Pfd., '46–'51; Rsch. Cnslt., Topanga Malibu Bdcst. Co., '65–; Theta Sigma Phi (L.A. Chptr. Pres., '67–'69; Exec. VP, '66), Intl. Nwsp. Promotion Mgrs. Assn., Nat. Soc. for Programmed Instr.; res: 1112 Franklin St., Santa Monica, Cal. 90403.

SMITH, JESSICA, Ed., New World Review, 156 Fifth Ave., N.Y., N.Y. 10010, '36–; Auth: "Women in Soviet Russia" ('28), "People Come First" ('48); Ed., Soviet Union Rev. (Wash., D.C.), '29–'33; Russian Reconstruction Farms (USSR), '26–'28; Pubcty., Am. Friends Svc. Comm. in Russia, '22–'24; Wtr., Phila. N. Am., '11–'12; Rsch., Edtl. Asst., Nat. Cncl. of Am.-Soviet Friendship; Rsch. Dir., joint New World Rev.-Nat. Cncl. of Am.-Soviet Friendship Lib.; Swarthmore Col., AB, '15; b. Madison, N.J., 1895; p. Walter and Jessie Stout Granville-Smith; h. John Abt; c. David Ware; res: 444 Central Park W., N.Y., N.Y. 10025.

SMITH, JOANNE, Traf. Opns. Mgr., WAGA-TV, Storer Broadcasting Company, 1551 Briarcliff Rd., N.E., Atlanta, Ga. 30302, '63–; Traf.-Cont. Coordr., '59–'61; Sls. Svc. Coordr., WITI-TV (Milw., Wis.), '61–'63; Traf. Mgr., WAKE Radio (Atlanta), '58–'59; Special Cnslt., WLBW-TV (Miami, Fla.), '69; AWRT (Atlanta Chptr. Rec. Secy., '67–'68; Treas., '69–'70); Tift Col., '54–'55;

Univ. of Ga., Henry W. Grady Sch. of Jnlsm., '58; b. Barnesville, Ga., 1936; p. Curtis M. and Kathryn R. Smith; res: 979 Canterbury Rd., N.E., Atlanta, Ga. 30324.

SMITH, KATHERINE SCHMITTOU, Arizona Newspapers Association, 3443 N. Central Ave., Suite 905, Phoenix, Ariz. 85012, '57–; Mgr., Weekly Nwsps. of Ariz.; Feature Wtr., Reptr., The Ariz. Republic, '55–'57; Free-lance Wtr., '49–'54; Fashion Dir., Goldsmith's (Memphis, Tenn.), '48–'49; Copywtr., Gerber's, Goldsmith's, adv. agcys., '45–'48; PR, Curtis Wright Aircraft, '43–'45; Indsl. Engineering, Curtis Publ. Co. (Phila., Pa.), '42–'43; Theta Sigma Phi (Phoenix Chptr. Pres., '64–'66), Gamma Alpha Chi (Hon. Mbr.), Phoenix Adv. Club (Bd. Mbr.), Phoenix Press Club Ariz. Press Wm., Newsp. Assn. Mgrs., Am. Soc. Assn. Execs., Intl. Newsp. Prom. Assn.; Memphis State Univ., '38–'41; Univ. of Tenn. at Memphis; b. Memphis, Tenn., 1921; p. Suall and Iva Lou Spears Schmittou; h. John Clemons Smith; res: 570 W. Tam O'Shanter Dr., Phoenix, Ariz. 85023.

SMITH, KATHLEEN MACOUBRIE, Tchr., writing, lit. composition, jnlsm., Olathe, Kan. H.S., other Schs., students widely published '23–'60; wtr., public-opinion clms.; Theta Sigma Phi, Am. Col. Quill Club; Kan. Univ., AB, '16; MA, '30; b. Yates Center, Kan., 1894; p. A. E. and Laura Banister Macoubrie; h. John Smith; c. Laura Margaret Smith Huggins; res: 320 N. Cherry, Olathe, Kan. 66061.

SMITH, LAURA SNYDER, Librn., Readers Svc. Dept., St. Louis Public Library, 1301 Olive St. St. Louis, Mo., '69–; Cnslt., Inst. and Handicapped Lib. Svcs., Fla. State Lib. (Tallahassee), '68–'69; Asst. Dir., Gadsden (Ala.) Public Lib., '67–'68; Head Librn., James S. Rickards Jr. Sr. HS (Tallahassee, Fla.), '65–'67; Am. Assn. of Workers for the Blind, S.E. Correctional Educ. Assn., S.E. Lib. Assn. (Public Lib. Sec. Secy., '68–'70), Fla. Lib. Assn. Ala. Lib. Assn., Phi Alpha Theta; Fla. State Univ., BA, '64 (magna cum laude; Phi Kappa Phi; Phi Beta Kappa; Alpha Lambda Delta); MS, '65 (Beta Phi Mu); b. Hartford, Conn., 1943; p. Mary Snyder.

SMITH, LIZ, Free-lance non-fiction wtr., Zanden Associates, 38 E. 38th St., N.Y., N.Y. 10016; Film Critic, Cosmopolitan; Wtr., Sports Illustrated, '66–'67; Entertainment Ed., Cosmopolitan, '64–'66; Assoc., Cholly Knickerbocker colm., '57–'62; Assoc. Prodr., "Wide Wide World" (NBC-TV), '54–'56; Colmst., Palm Beach Pictorial; Univ. of Tex., BJ, '59; b. Ft. Worth, Tex.; p. Sloan and Elizabeth McCall Smith; h. (div.).

SMITH, MARGARET PHYLLIS, Staff Wtr., RCA Laboratories, David Sarnoff Research Center, Princeton, N.J. 08540, '58–; Pers. Asst., '55–'58; Asst. Prof., Bucknell Univ., '52–'55; Instr., '47–'52; AAUW, AAUP, Mod. Lang. Assn., Nat. Cncl. of Tchrs. of Eng., Kappa Delta Epsilon, Sigma Delta Pi, Sigma Tau Delta; Bucknell Univ., AB (Eng.), '47 (magna cum laude; Phi Beta Kappa); MA (Eng.), '47; b. Plymouth, Pa., 1925; p.

Harold and Mae Bittenbender Smith; res: 276 Nassau St., Princeton, N.J. 08540.

SMITH, MARGARET RUTH, Educ. Cnslt.; '64–; Field Reader, Bur. of Rsch., U.S.O.E., '67–; Visiting Prof., Michigan State Univ., '68–'69; Rsch. Analyst Emeritus, Wayne State Univ., '64; Rsch. Analyst, '52–'64; Assoc. Admissions Offcr., '46–'52; Dir. of Student Activities, '40–'46; Auth., articles in pfsnl. pubns.; Pi Lambda Theta (VP, '50–'52; Detroit Alumnae Chptr. Pres., '48–'50), Am. Pers. and Guidance Assn., Am. Col. Pers. Assn. Am. Assn. for Higher Educ., Am. Assn. for Inst. Rsch., Southern Col. Pers. Assn., Mich. State Assn. of Wm. Deans and Cnslrs. (VP, '49–'51), Delta Kappa Gamma (Zeta Chptr. VP, '52–'56), Comm. for the Interchange of Tchrs. of the Fed. Security Agcy., '48–'64; Mich. Col. Pers. Assn. (Pres., '57–'58; VP '56–'57), Kappa Delta Pi, Nat. Assn. of Wm. Deans and Cnslrs.; Am. Educ. Rsch. Assn., AAUW, Zonta; Who's Who in Am. Educ., Who's Who of Am. Wm., Dic. of Intl. Biog., Who's Who in the South and Southwest, Personalities of the South, Contemporary Auths., Royal Blue Bk.; Sigma Sigma Sigma Emily Gates Achiev. Aw., '67; one of the Top Ten Working Wm. of Detroit, '64; Goucher Col., AB, '24 (Southeastern Mich. Alumnae Pres., '62–'64); Columbia Univ., AM, '29; PhD, '37; b. W. Va; p. Flavius and Mary Alice Meredith Smith; res: 3060 Pharr Ct., North, N.W., Atlanta, Ga. 30305.

SMITH, MARGARETH, KELL, Secy. and Treas., Modern Sound Pictures, Inc., 1410 Howard St., Omaha, Neb. 68102, '43–; NAVA, Nat. Fedn. Independent Bus., Omaha C. of C.; b. Wausau, Wis., 1915; p. Ernest and Margaret Helke Kell; h. Keith Traviss Smith; c. Sandra Louise; res: 1501 N. 59th St., Omaha, Neb. 68102.

SMITH, MARGOT HAGEMAN, Food Ed., Red Bank Daily Register, 105 Chesnut St., Red Bank, N.J. 07701, '67–; h. James H. Smith; res: 86 Rumson Rd., Rumson, N.J. 07760.

SMITH, MARGUERITE R., Colmst., Indianapolis News, Indpls., Ind., '66–; Free-lance Wtr., Photogr.; Colmst., Feature Wtr., Photogr., Indianapolis Times, '45–'66; Theta Sigma Phi, Ind. Wms. Press Club, Nat. Wms. Press Club; Oberlin Col., AB, '20 (Phi Beta Kappa); h. Leland Rooy Smith; res: 1903 Parkview Dr., Alhambra, Cal. 91803.

SMITH, MARIE D., Staff Wtr., White House beat, The Washington Post, 1515 L St., N.W., Wash., D.C. 20005, '54–; Auth: "The President's Lady: An Intimate Biography of Mrs. Lyndon B. Johnson" ('64), "Entertaining in the White House" ('67); Lectr., "What Goes on in the White House," "The Challenge to Women Today"; ANWC (Pres., '68), WNPC, Auths. Guild, Va. Press Wm., NLAPW; Catherine L. O'Brien news rept. aw., '66; Sons' and Daughters' Fndn. wrtr. aw.; '62; Univ. of Ga.; b. Canton, Ga.; p. David P. and Dessie Marr Smith; res: 8913 Little River Turnpike, Fairfax, Va. 22030.

SMITH, MARION McGILL, Librn., Dir. Jackson Library, Graduate School of Business, Stanford Univ., Stanford, Cal., '57–; Acting Dir., '53–'54; Chief Circ. Librn. and Curator, Hopkins Transportation Collection, '54–'57; Rsch. Assoc., Nat. Mediation Bd., '48; Wash. Ed., Rsch. Inst. of Am., '44; Head, NLRB Lib. (Wash., D.C.), '38–'44; McKinsey Fndn. Aws. Comm., '63–'65; ALA, Cal. Lib. Assn., Special Libs. Assn., Am. Soc. Information Sciences; Univ. of Mont., AB (Lib. Sci.), '39; George Washington Univ., '37–'38; Columbus Law Sch., Grad. Work, '40; b. St. Louis, Mo., 1914; p. Thomas and Agnes Barlowe McGill; h. H. Albert Smith (div.); res: 819 Esplanada Way, Stanford, Cal. 94305.

SMITH, MARY ALICE, Ed. and Publr., Handweaver & Craftsman Magazine, 220 Fifth Ave., N.Y., N.Y. 10001, '50–; Prom., Nat. Ceramic Exhbn., Everson Museum (Syracuse), '45–'49, '37–'41; PR, Rsch., Kan. Emergency Relief Adm., '32–'37; Asst. Ed., Jnl. of the League of Kan. Municipalities, '44–'45; Instr., Jnlsm., Univ. of Kan., '21–'23; Pen and Brush Club, Needle and Bobbin Club, Theta Sigma Phi, Phi Beta Kappa, Who's Who of Am. Wm.; Univ. of Kan., AB, '19; AM, '29; b. Abilene, Kan.; p. Samuel and Alice Beltzhoover Smith; res: 79 Barrow St., N.Y., N.Y. 10014.

SMITH, MARY ANN, Commtns. Cnslt., Iowa Department of Public Instruction, 801 Bankers Trust Bldg., Des Moines, Ia. 50302, '66–; Pres., SAM and Associates, Inc., '65–; Ed., Publr., Solon Economist and Coralville News, '61–'65; Ed., Northwestern National Banks, Minn., '59–'61; Ed., Midland Cooperatives, '57–'59; Assoc. Ed., Popular Science, N.Y.C., '54–'57; PRSA, Ia. Indsl. Eds. (Bd. Mbr.), Theta Sigma Phi (Bd. Mbr., '68); Who's Who in Midwest; Drake Univ., BA, '50 (Who's Who among Am. Cols. and Univs.); Univ. of Kan., '51; N.Y.U., '53; b. Cedar Rapids, Ia., 1921; res: 3103 Grand Ave., Des Moines, Ia. 50312.

SMITH, MARY ELLEN SHULL (pseud: Mike Smith), Free-lance Wtr.; prod. weekly radio program on industry in S. Fla., '47–; Auth., bks., articles on Fla.; Theta Sigma Phi (VP, '60; Miami Chptr. Headliner Aw.); Rollins Col.; Chgo. Acad. of Fine Arts; b. Malabar, Fla.; p. Charles and Addie Wallace Shull; h. Tom Q. Smith (dec.); res: 2740 S.W. 31st Pl., Miami, Fla. 33133.

SMITH, MARY KATHARINE DAVIS, Auth., Reviewer, Lectr.; bks: "Hands," "Symbolism of O.E.S."; Intl. Platform Assn. (Dir.), DAR (Regent); P.G.M., Tex. O.E.S. State Bd.; T.F.W.C.; Past Pres., Wms. Missionary Union; Charter Mbr. and Past Pres., Tues. Bk. Club; Nationally Accredited Flower Show Judge (Life); First 500 Families of Am., Royal Blue Bk., 2,000 Wm. of Achiev., Dic. of Intl. Biog., other dirs.; Gainesville Col., Tchrs. Cert., '36; N. State Univ.; b. Glenn, Ga., 1917; p. Alonzo and Ruby Garvey Davis; h. Gordon B. Smith, Sr.; c. Gordon B., Jr.; res: 924 S. Denton St., Gainesville, Tex. 76240.

SMITH, MILDRED CATHARINE, Ed.-in-Chief Emeritus, Publishers' Weekly, R. R. Bowker Co., 1880 Ave. of the Americas, N.Y., N.Y. 10036, '67–; Ed.-in-Chief, '59–'67; Asst. Ed., '20–'59; Secy., '36–'67; Dir., '33–'67; Constance Lindsay Skinner Wms. Aw., Nat. Bk. Assn., '44; Van Doren Aw. for many contrbs., bk. as instrument of Am. culture, '68; Wellesley Col., AB, '14; MA, '22; b. Smithport, Pa., 1891; p. Charles A. and Jane Haskell Smith; res: 557 E. Shore Rd., Great Neck, L.I., N.Y. 11204.

SMITH, NANCY R., PR Mgr., American Can Company, 100 Park Ave., N.Y., N.Y. 10017, '69–; Asst. Dir. of PR, Sears, Robuck, '67–'69; Fashion Publicist, J. C. Penney Co., '65–'67; Fashion Coordr., "Say When," Edward E. Finch & Co., '64–'65; Pubcty. Dir., Joseph Bancroft & Sons, '62–'64; Asst. Ed., Glamour and Mademoiselle, '62–'64; Free-lance Script and Feature Wtr.; AWRT, Outstanding Young Wm. of Am., '68; Grinnell Col., BA; '60; b. Elgin, Ill., 1938; p. Oramel and Frances McEnery Smith; res: 117 E. 71st St., N.Y., N.Y. 10021.

SMITH, NINA TREADAWAY, Dir., Kinchafoonee Regional Library, Main St., Dawson, Ga. 31742, '54–; Tchr., '49–'53, '30–'43; ALA, Southeastern Lib. Assn., Ga. Lib. Assn., Ga. Educ., BPW; Univ. of Ga., AB (Educ.), '38; George Peabody Col. for Tchrs., MS (Lib. Sci.); h. S. Jay Smith; c. S. Jay Jr.

SMITH, NOELLE GAY, Mgr., PR Dept., Patt Patterson and Associates, Inc., 333 Queens St., Suite 700, Honolulu, Hi. 96813, '69–; AE, '68; Copywtr., '68; PR Asst., Leffingwell/Assoc., '67–'68; Public Info. Dir., Ariz. State Dept. of Educ., '66–'67; Honolulu Jr. Ad Club; Universidad de las Americas (Mexico City), '65; Ariz. State Univ., BA, '66; b. Phoenix, Ariz., 1943; p. Noel G. and Marjorie Riffel Smith; res: 1655 Kanunu St. #204, Honolulu, Hi. 96814.

SMITH, NORA O'LEARY, Patterns Ed., Ladies' Home Journal, Downe Publishing Co., 641 Lexington Ave., N.Y., N.Y. 10022, '46–; Fashion Group; Mass. Col. of Art; b. Sharon, Mass.; h. John J. Smith; c. Stephen, Wendy, Nancy, Richard; res: 308 E. 50th St., N.Y., N.Y. 10022.

SMITH, OPHIA SMITH, Co-auth., hist bks. incl. "Johnny Appleseed," "A Voice in the Wilderness," "Colonial Inventions," "Colonial Labor," "Contributions of the Puritans"; Contrbr. to pfsnl. hist. mags; church mags.; retired music tchr.; NLAPW (hist. writing aw.); Ohioana Fellowship, '49; Butler County, Oh. cit.; other awards; Gimbel Sch. of Music (Bolivar, Mo.); Kan. City Conservatory of Music; Oxford (Oh.) Col. for Wm.; Drury Col., Miami (Oh.) Univ.; b. Walnut Grove, Mo., 1891; p . Joseph N. and Emma Bradshaw Smith; h. William E. Smith; c. Joseph W.; res: 329 W. Chestnut St., Oxford, Oh., (winter) 235 Lyell St., Los Altos, Cal. 94022.

SMITH, PATRICIA LINDEN, Ed., University of Washington Press, 1416 N.E. 41st St., Seattle, Wash. 98105,

'63–; Ed., Off. of Scholarly Jnls., '61–'63; Wash. State Univ., BA, '60 (summa cum laude; Phi Beta Kappa); MA (Eng.), '61; b. Tonasket, Wash., 1939; p. William and Harriet Hundall Linden; h. Payton Smith; res: 2003 Franklin E., Seattle, Wash. 98102.

SMITH, PAULINE S., Ed., The Scout, Finch, Pruyn and Co., Inc., 1 Glen St., Glens Falls, N.Y. 12801, '65–;.

SMITH, PHYLLIS McQUEEN, PR, Bd. of Trustees, Florence Crittenton Home, 3235 42 Ave. W., Seattle, Wash. 98199, '66–; Publicist, Seattle Chptr., March of Dimes, '68–; Co-Publr., Whidbey Press Nwsps., Whidbey News-Times, (Oak Harbor), '39–'65; Publicist, Boeing Aircraft (Seattle), '37–'39; Theta Sigma Phi, various organizations and aws.; Wash. State Univ., BA (Eng.), '33; b. Kaslo, B.C., 1912; p. Alfred and Margaret McCallum McQueen; h. A Glenn Smith; c. Shelley (Mrs. Paul Pierce), Glenn M., Craig W.

SMITH, REA WATERS, Asst. to Exec. Dir., Public Relations Society of America, Inc., 845 Third Ave., N.Y., N.Y. 10022, '57–; AE, PR Cnslr., Shirley D. Smith & Assocs. (Memphis, Tenn.), '47–'57; Time study accountant, Am. Aviation Co. (Jamestown, N.Y.), '41–'45; NLAPW, Fndn. for PR Rsch. & Educ.; PRSA cit., '60; Allegheny Col.; b. Jamestown, N.Y., 1918; p. F. Coy and Rena Schultz Waters; h. Shirley D. Smith; res: 4 Peter Cooper Rd., Apt. 11-F, N.Y., N.Y. 10010.

SMITH, REBECCA BOSWELL, Free-lance Wtr., Marietta Daily Journal, Marietta, Ga. 30060, '68–; Wms. Ed., '67–'68; News staff, '65–'67; Reptr., Winston Salem (N.C.) Jnl., '64–'65; Outstanding Young Wm. of Am.; Outstanding Personalities of the South; Salem Col., AB, '63 (Outstanding Eng. Student; Who's Who in Am. Cols. and Univs.); b. Charlotte, N.C., 1941; p. James and Lena Fowler Boswell; h. Robert Smith; c. Robert Bruce, Elizabeth Dudley; res: 1746 Kimberly Dr., Marietta, Ga. 30060.

SMITH, RITA IRENE, Wms. Ed. and Travel Colmst., Courier-Express, 785 Main St., Buffalo, N.Y. 14240, '66–; Asst. Wms. Ed., Reptr.; many aws. from Buffalo Nwsp. Guild, Nat. Nwsp. Guild; D'Youville Col., BA (Eng., Hist.); b. Olean, N.Y.; p. Christopher and Dorothy Considine Smith; res: 2 Osgood Ave., W. Seneca, N.Y. 14224.

SMITH, ROBERTA FRY, Free-lance Wtr.; Ed., Scholastic Magazines and Books, '63–'66; Fac., Oh. State Univ., '60–'63; Tchr., Upper Arlington (Oh.) HS, '58–'60; Asst. Ed., Good Living, PR Pubns., '54–'58; Auth., "The Co-ed Decorating Book" (Scholastic, '68); WNBA, Theta Sigma Phi, Jnlsm. Educ. Assn., Chi Delta Phi; Nat. Scholastic Press Assn. aw., '69; Oh. State Univ., BA, BS (Educ.), '58 (cum laude), MA, '63; b. Mt. Vernon, Oh.; p. Robert and Madge Cassady Fry; h. F. Eugene Smith; c. Kyla Iolene Smith; res: P.O. Box 97, Fanwood, N.J. 07023.

SMITH, RUTH HALL, Ed., Partner, Craft Patterns

Newspaper Service, North Ave. and Rte. 83, Elmhurst, Ill., '59–; Asst. Ed., '41–'59; Ed., Secy., Treas., Craft Products Corp., '59–; Co-owner, Craft Clock and Gift Shop, '59–; Co-auth., "Home Handicraft for Girls" (Jr. Lit. "Bk. of the Month"); Theta Sigma Phi, Alpha Xi Delta; active in civic groups; Univ. of Ill., '37–'40; Northwestern Univ.; b. Chgo., Ill., 1918; p. Albert N. and Bertha E. Cassidy Hall,; h. Robert J. Smith; c. Gregory H., Gerald E., Marilyn E., Brian W.; res: 313 N. Rte. 83, Elmhurst, Ill. 60126.

SMITH, SANDRA JEAN, Copywtr., Yeck & Yeck Advertising, 349 W. First St., Dayton, Oh. 45402, '67–; Asst. to AEs, '67–; Staff Wtr., Asst. PR Dir., NCR Employees Credit Un., '64–'67; Contrb. Ed., Dayton USA Magazine; Free-lance Wtr., mag., nwsp; Dayton Adv. Club (ten aws., adv. copy, '68; 1st Pl. Aw., best annual rept., '67); Oh. Univ., BS (Jnlsm.), '64; b. Moultrie, Ga., 1943; p. Howard D. and Jean Warden Smith; res: 4341 Springcreek Dr., Apt. B, Dayton, Oh. 45405.

SMITH, SHARON LEWIS, Copywtr., Time Byr., Goodwin, Dannenbaum, Littman & Wingfield, Inc., 80 Interstate 10 N., Beaumont, Tex. 77706, '68–; Copywtr., Sls., KTRM, '64–'68; AWRT; McNeese State Col., '60–'62; b. La., 1942; p. Guthra and Glory Lacy Lewis; h. Kenneth H. Smith Jr.; c. Kisha Lynette; res: 525 24th St., Beaumont, Tex. 77706.

SMITH, SHIRLEY MARIE, Nat. Sls. Asst., KCMO-TV, 125 E. 31st St., Kan. City, Mo. 64108, '69–; Traf. Mgr., '68; Traf. Mgr., KCMO Radio, '65–'68; Traf. and Cont. Mgr., WDAF-TV, '62–'68; Traf. and Cont. Mgr., WDAF Radio (Topeka, Kan.), '57–'58; Traf. and Cont. Mgr., KAKE-TV (Wichita), '54–'57; Cont. Ed., KMBC-TV (Kan. City), '53–'54; Teaching Staff, Radio-TV Dept., Univ. of Mo. at Kan. City, '64–'65; AWRT (Nat. Bd. Dir.-at-large, '68–'69; W. Central Area Conf. Chmn., '63; Kan. City Chptr. Pres., '64), Kan. City Radio-TV Cncl. (Offcr., '69); Candidate for Nat. Wm. of the Yr., Am. Bus. Wms. Assn., '64; Washburn Univ., AB (Eng.), '51 (Tau Delta Pi); b. Kan. City, Mo., 1928; p. Virgil and Margaret Egan Smith; res: 103 N.E. 67th St., Kan. City, Mo. 64118.

SMITH, SUSY, Auth: "Ghosts Around the House" (World Publ. Co.), "Prominent American Ghosts" (World Publ. Co.), "Today's Witches" (Prentice-Hall); NLAPW, Auths. League of Am., Intl. Platform Assn., Am. Soc. for Psychical Rsch.; Univ. of Tex.; Univ. of Ariz.; b. Wash., D.C.; p. Merton and Elizabeth Hardegen Smith; h. (div.); res: 6580 Satona St., Coral Gables, Fla. 33146.

SMITH, THELMA SHIPLEY, Co-publr., Ed., The Taylor Clarion, Taylor, Neb. 68879, '42–; 27 yrs. nwsp. work: Colmst., Edtl. Wtr., News, Features; Neb. Press Assn., Neb. Press Wm., Neb. Wtrs. Guild; b. Custer County, Neb., 1915; p. Charley and LaVerne Richardson Shipley; h. Hazen E. Smith; c. Leland, Danny, David, Mrs. Elaine Harris, Mrs. Jeanette Lewis, Mrs. Carole Conner; res: Taylor, Neb. 68879.

SMITH, VICTORIA DAVIS, Asst. Adv. Mgr.-Ed., Alabama Power Company, 600 N. 18th St., Birmingham, Ala. 35202, '62–; Asst. to Adv. Mgr., Ala. Power Co., '45–'62; Tchr., '30–'37; Southern Cncl. Indsl. Eds. (Pres., '52–'53); Birmingham Cncl. Indsl. Eds. (Founder; Pres., '49, '52, '55); Theta Sigma Phi (Birmingham Chptr. Pres., '54–'55), Kappa Delta Pi; Mortar Bd.; Algernon Sidney Sullivan aw., '30; Univ. of Ala., '30; Grad. Work, '31–'33; b. Birmingham, Ala. 1908; p. Henry and LouElla Harton Davis; h. Robert W. Smith (div.); c. Robert W. Jr., William Ashley; res: 2109-22nd Ave. S., Birmingham, Ala. 35223.

SMITH, VIRGINIA ANDREWS, Wms. Ed., Palm Desert Post, Palm Desert, Cal. 92260, '68–; Contrb. Ed., Bay Window Magazine (Newport Beach); Ed., Sun Spots mag., '67; b. L.A., Cal., 1913; p. Willedd Andrews and Helen Stocker Andrews Carpenter; h. Edward Lester Smith; c. Joyce (Mrs. William Martin); res: 72835 Homestead Rd., Palm Desert, Cal. 92660.

SMITH, VIRGINIA WARGO, Adv. Media Specialist, General Electric Co., 570 Lexington Ave., N.Y., N.Y. 10022, '60–; Contracts and Schedules, '52–'60; Consumer Inquiries, '49–'52; Adv. Accounting and Statis., '44–'49; Assn. of Indsl. Advs., Adv. and Mktng. Assn.; Merrills Bus. Col., '38–'40; b. Canastota, N.Y., 1920; p. John and Rose Moltz Wargo; h. Edward W. Smith; res: Five Old Stone Rd., Darien, Conn. 06820.

SMITH, WINONA M., Secy.-Treas., The Pittsburg Publishing Company, 701 N. Locust, Pittsburg, Kan. 66762, '40–; Stenographer, adm., circ., edtl., depts.; Kan. State Col.; b. W. Mineral, Kan., 1908; p. Samuel C. and Margaret Steele Smith; res: 705 N. Pine, Pittsburg, Kan. 66762.

SMITHWICK, BARBARA BERNHARD, AE, David Olen Advertising, 6430 Sunset Blvd., L.A. Cal. 90028, '68–; Publicist, Cal. Mart Dir. of Cal. Apparel Industry, '68–'69; Dir., John Robert Powers Sch. of Self Improvement (Beverly Hills), '58; Byr., Hale's & Lockes Drug Chain (Reno, Nev.), '45–'53; Nat. TV Comml. Spokeswm., 15 yrs; Univ. of Nev. '45; b. Sacramento, Cal., 1923; p. Frederick and Hazel Johnson Bernhard; c. Michael Vincent, Daniel Patrick; res: 620 Westmont Dr., L.A., Cal. 90069.

SMITMAN, SUSAN ELLEN, TV Comml. Prodr., Young & Rubicam, Inc., 285 Madison Ave., N.Y., N.Y. '66–; Fac., Sch. of Visual Arts, '69–; Grey Adv., '65–'66; Compton Adv., '59–'65; aws: Venice Festival, N.Y. Art Dirs. Show, Am. TV Commls. Festival; Syracuse Univ., BS (Speech), '59; b. Jersey City, N.J., 1938; p. Ralph and Molly Cooper Smitman; res: 1 Bank St., N.Y., N.Y. 10014.

SMOLENS, ALICE HOLMES, Dir., Wms. Div., Licensed Beverage Industries, Inc., 155 E. 44th St., N.Y., N.Y. 10017, '70–; Dir. of Commty. Rels., Camp Fire Girls, Inc., '64–'70; Dir. of PR, Fairleigh Dickinson

Univ. (Madison, N.J.), '60–'63, '64; Cnslt. in PR, Grad. Sch. Bus. Adm. (Rutherford Campers), '64–; Case Worker, Morris County Welfare Bd., '63–'64; Reptr.-Colmst., Eagle-Courier nwsps. (Madison/Chatham, N.J.), '58–'60; Pubcty. Club of N.Y., AWNY, LWV (Phila. and Chatham Twp. Dir.), active in many civic groups; Randolph-Macon Wms. Col., '31–'33; Univ. of Pa., BA, '35 (Bd. of Dirs., Alumnae, '53–'54); b. Phila., Pa., 1913; p. Dr. John W. and Alice Ake Holmes; h. Stanley Smolens (dec.); c. John H., Sheila J.; res: 46 Green Village Rd., Madison, N.J. 17940.

SMOLENS, GLICKSE SUTLAND, Cnslt. for Adv., PR, West Philadelphia Federal Savings & Loan Assn., 5225 Chestnut St., Phila., Pa. 19139, '67–; Dir., Adv., PR, '54–'67; Ed., "Friend to Friend" (Am. Friends of Hebrew Univ., '64–'69); Theta Sigma Phi (Treas., '67); Univ. of Pa., Columbia Univ.; b. Phila., Pa.; p. Samuel and Anna Deitz Sutland; h. Charles H. Smodens; c. Marilyn Smolens Taub; Margot Smolens Blum; res: 517 Haverford Rd., Wynnewood, Pa. 19096.

SNIDERMAN, GLORIA MELE-DARDARIAN, Ext. Librn., Rm. 438, General Library, Detroit, Mich. 48202, '69–; Lib. Sci. Instr., Wayne State Univ., '66–'67; Rsch. Asst., '64–'66; Sch. Librn., Detroit Public Schs., '61–'64; R. and D. Librn., Bower Div., Fed.-Mogul, '59–'61; Co-compiler, "Culturally Disadvantaged," Detroit (Wayne State Univ. Press, '66), "Sources in Educational Research" ('69); SLA, ASIS, WNBA; Wayne State Univ., BA, '55; Tchrs. Cert., '62; MS (Lib. Sci.), '66; b. Detroit, Mich.; p. Spiridhonos and Vrisidha Kondakci Mele; h. David Sniderman; res: 1127 W. McNichols, Apt. 302, Highland Park, Mich. 48203.

SNOW, HELEN FOSTER (pseud: Nym Wales), Auth., Histrn.; seven bks. on China and Korea, incl. "Inside Red China" (Doubleday-Doran, '37), "Women in Modern China" (Mouton & Co., '67); Contrbr., 10 bks.; Reviewer, Saturday Review, '41–'49; Intl. Platform Assn., Assn. for Asian Studies, Conn. Soc. of Genealogists; 2,000 Wm. of Achiev., Who's Who of Am. Wm., Dic. of Intl. Biog., other ref. listings; Univ. of Ut., Yenching Univ.; b. Ut., 1907; p. John and Hannah Davis Foster; h. Edgar Snow (div.); res: 148 Mungertown Rd., Madison, Conn. 06443.

SNOW, MARY, Artist; many group exhbns., incl.: U.S. Dept. of State, L.A. County Art Museum, Nat. Acad. of Design, Nat. Acad. of Arts and Ltrs.; numerous one-man shows, incl. Panoras Gallery, '65 and Wash. Gallery of Art, '65–'66; Soc. of Wash. Artists (1st wm. Pres., '52–'53; 1st prize Smithsonian Inst., Nat. Collection Fine Arts; 3rd prize, Arts Club of Wash.; Hon. Mention, Arts Club of Wash.), Artists Guild of Wash. (Pres.), Wash. Watercolor Assn., Nat. Assn. of Wm. Artists, Artists Equity Assn. (selected for reproduction in "Washington Artists Today", '67; Massillon, Oh., Show, '69; Corcoran Gallery, '68), Chi Delta Phi, Chi Omega, Adviser to Arlington Va. Bd. of Educ., numerous ch., civic, and pfsnl. groups; Grumbacher

Watercolor aw., '66; Univ. of Ut., AB, '29; Art Students League; Grand Central Sch. of Art; Corcoran Sch. of Art; L.A. County Sch. of Art; Phillips Gallery Sch. of Art; also studied in Berlin, Germany, with Karl Hofer and Max Pechstein; studied in France; b. Logan, Ut., 1908; p. Melvin and Martha Jones Ballard; h. 1. Col. Ralph Dale Snow (dec.); 2. Philip Joseph Corr; c. Dr. Peter Ballard Snow; res: 4856 Loughboro Rd., Wash., D.C. 20016., and 204 River Dr., Tequesta, Fla.

SNOW, VERA BALDAUF, Adv. Prod. Mgr., Geo. A. Pflaum, Publisher/Div. of Standard International Corp., 38 W. Fifth St., Dayton, Oh. 45402, '66–; Secy., revenue adv., Edtl., '65–'66; '64–'65; part-time entry cl., '57–'64; b. Acme, Pa., 1926; p. Benedict and Mary Skovira Baldauf; h. Lewis Snow; c. Lewis M., Jr., Rebecca; res: 242 Braun, New Carlisle, Oh. 45344.

SNYDER, ADELAIDE R., Dir. of Univ. Rels., Florida Atlantic University, Boca Ration, Fla. 33432, '62–; educ: Kent State Univ., BA; MA, '50; b. Rochester, N.Y.; h. Joseph G. Snyder; c. Richard, Florence; res: 2360 N.W. 182 Terr., Miami, Fla. 33054.

SNYDER, BERLE CHRISTIANSON, Asst. to Publr., Ruidoso News, Ruidoso, N.M. 88345, '69–; Interim Publr., Seminole (Tex.) Sentinel, '68–'69; Jnlsm. Lectr., Col. of Artesia (Artesia, N.M.), '67–'68; Dir. of Public Info., '66–'68; Secy.-Aide to State Rep. Jesse T. George (Austin, Tex.), '66; Nwsp. work, 25 yrs., Ia., Cal., Tex., incl. 11 yrs. as publr.; Tex. Press Assn. (Best Colm., '60), W. Tex. Press Assn., N.M. Press Assn., N.M. PR Assn., Col. & Univ. Pers. Assn.; Outstanding Personalities of the South, '67; Denver City (Tex.) C. of C. Bd. of Dirs., Yoakum County (Tex.) Legislative Cncl. Secy.; Ia. State Tchrs. Col.; b. Ruthven, Ia., 1920; p. Frank and Lela Powers Christianson; h. Cal Snyder (dec.); c. Lt. David M. Synder; res: ℅ Ruidoso News, Rudoso, N.M. 88345.

SNYDER, IDA SLOAN, Assoc., News Dir., Bureau of Communications, National Board, Young Women's Christian Association, 600 Lexington Ave., N.Y., N.Y. 10022, '61–; Staff Wtr., '53–'61; Reptr., The Norman (Okla.) Transcript, '35–'53; Theta Sigma Phi (N.Y.C. Chptr. Pres., '60–'62), Commty. Agcy. PR Assn.; Univ. of Okla., BA, '35; N.Y.U.; b. Wichita, Kan., 1913; p. Alfred and Caroline Dohl Sloan; h. Leonard M. Snyder; res: 221 E. 116th St., N.Y., N.Y. 10029.

SNYDER, JEAN MACLEAN, Supvsr., Home Safety Information, Department of Public Information, National Safety Council, 425 N. Michigan, Chgo., Ill. 60611, '68–; Rsch. Assoc., Comm. on Cutaneous Health and Cosmetics, Am. Med. Assn., '66–'68; Rsch. Asst., Drug Dept., '63–'66; Info. Cncl. on Fabric Flammability, Soc. of Cosmetic Chemists, Am. Med. Wtrs. Assn., AWRT; Univ. of Chgo., BA (Literature), '63; b. Chgo., Ill., 1942; p. Norman and Jessie Burns Maclean; h. Joel Snyder; res: 5627 S. Dorchester, Chgo., Ill. 60637.

SNYDER, LOUISE ANN, AE, WTAK, 32500 Parklane, Garden City, Mich. 48135, '66–; AE, other area radio stations; Wtr., local nwsp.; AWRT; Hillsdale Col.; h. Roy Snyder; c. Amy, Shelly; res.: 35700 Schoolcraft, Livonia, Mich. 48150.

SNYDER, RACHEL F., Ed.-in-Chief, Flower and Garden Magazine, 4521 Pennsylvania, Kan. City, Mo. 64111, '60–; Ed., '57–'60; Assoc. Ed., The Workbasket, '52–'57; Ed., "The Complete Book for Gardeners ('64); Garden Wtrs. of Amer. (VP, '65–'67; Reg. Dir., '69); Amer. Seed Trade Assn. (Pfsnl. Wtrs. Aw., '67); Washburn Univ., BA, '45 (cum laude).

SNYDER, SARA MITTEN, Teaching Assoc., Indiana University School of Dentistry, 1121 W. Michigan St., Indpls., Ind. 46202, '63–; Free-lance PR, '62–'63; Assoc. Ed., Jnl. of the Ind. State Med. Assn., '59–'62; Theta Sigma Phi, Gamma Alpha Chi; Ind. Univ., AB, '59; b. Indpls., Ind., 1937; p. George W. and Josephine Harstine Mitten; h. William F. Snyder, Jr.; c. Jayne L., Elizabeth L., Catherine J.; res: 7849 S. Belmont, Indpls., Ind. 46217.

SOBEL, JOANNE WOLFE, Owner, Sobel Avertising, 678 Barberry Lane, San Rafael, Cal. 94903, '64–; AE, Vernor Advertising, '55–'63; R. L. Sines & Assoc., '52–'54; Adv. Prod., Koret of Cal., '50–'52; Alpha Epsilon Phi, Pi Alpha Sigma, Congregation Rodef Shalom (Bd. of Dirs.), Wms. Ort, S.F. Wms. Variety Club, Marin Humane Soc.; Univ. of Wash., '46–'49; b. Seattle, Wash., 1929; p. George and Gertrude Pearl Wolfe; h. Earl L. C. Sobel; c. David Samuel, Daniel George; res: 678 Barberry Lane, San Rafael, Cal. 94903.

SODERBERG, JULIETTE MEADE, PR Dir. and Pubns. Ed., Quality Bakers of America Cooperative, Inc., 120 W. 42nd St., N.Y., N.Y. 10036, '64–; Wtr., Product Prom., Parents' Magazine, '61–'64; Radio Cont. Wtr., WCAX (Burlington, Vt.), '55–'61; Nwsp. Feature Wtr., Greenwich Time, '51–'55; created and wrote human rights pamphlet for UN affiliated orgs., '68; founded Image/Commtns., '69; AWNY, BPW, Baha'i Faith (Natl. OBS Un., '67; N.Y.C. Assembly, '66–); Lawrence Univ.; b. N.Y.C.; p. Otto and Julia Meyer Muller; h. William Soderberg; c. Lance P. Meade; res: 110 Bank St., N.Y., N.Y. 10014.

SOHL, MARJORIE ANN, Head of Adult Svcs., Hammond Public Lib., 564 State St., Hammond, Ind. 46320, '46–; Lib. Asst., '37–'42; ALA, Ind. Lib. Assn., Beta Phi Mu; Ind. Univ., BA, '44; Univ. of Ill., BS (Lib. Sci.), '46; b. Hammond, Ind., 1919; p. Claude Clifford and Anna Marie Doehring Sohl; res: 5615 Sohl Ave., Hammond, Ind. 46320.

SOLIMENA, ANTOINETTE, Free-lance Artist; Asst. to Art Designer, Avon Pubns., '53–'55; Asst. to Prom. Art Designer, Charm mag., '51–'53; Cooper Un., '51–'55; b. Bklyn, N.Y., 1932; p. Gerardo and Jennie Sciré Solimena; h. Stanley R. Cohen; c. David Gerard; res: 193-01 F 73rd Ave., Fresh Meadows, N.Y. 11366.

SOLIMENA, MARY, Chief Copy Ed., Art Ref. Bks., Frederick A. Praeger, Inc., 111 Fourth Ave., N.Y., N.Y. 10003, '67–; Queens Col., Instr., Art Hist., '66–'67; Harper & Row, '65; Grolier, Inc. '61–'64; Barnard Col., BA, '61; N.Y.U., MA, (Fine Arts), '67; b. N.Y.C., 1940; res: 216 East 19 Street, N.Y., N.Y. 10003.

SOLIT, ADELE PISKULICK, Secy./Treas., Dir., Clayton-Davis & Assoc., Inc., 408 Olive St., St. Louis, Mo. 63102, '61–; Design Corp. of Am., '62–; Clayton-Davis, Inc. '64–; Celebrities Unlimited, Inc. '66–; AWRT, Am. Mgt. Assn., AIM, Wms. Ad Club; Harris Tchrs. Col., BS, '45; b. St. Louis, Mo., 1925; p. William and Estelle Kamer Piskulick; h. Samuel Solit (dec.); c. Luann Estelle (Mrs. William M. Stover); res: 8650 Otto Westway, Sunset Hills, Mo. 63127.

SOLL, HARRIET PREMACK, Edtl. Cnslt., Systems Development Corp., Falls Church, Va.; Free-lance Mag., TV Wtr.; Theta Sigma Phi; Univ. of Minn.; b. Mpls., Minn.; p. J. D. and Ida Amdur Premack; h. Arthur Soll (dec.); c. Elinor (Mrs. Ira Priesman), Sherna; res: 1931 Pine St., Phila., Pa. 19103.

SOLMN, JEAN HUNNICUTT, Public Info. Offcr., University of Cincinnati, College-Conservatory of Music, Cinn., Oh. 45221, '67–; PR Dir., NuTone, Inc., '56–'67; PR Dir., Adv. Copy Dir., Gruen Watch Co., '46–'56; PRSA, Theta Sigma Phi, Sigma Alpha Iota, ZONTA; Univ. of Cinn., BS; b. Wilmington, Oh., 1918; p. Walter and Margaret D. Hunnicutt; res: 575 Evanswood Pl., Cinn., Oh. 45220.

SOLOMON, BARBARA PROBST, Free-lance Wtr.; Auth., "Beat of Life"; Eng. Prof., State Univ. of N.Y. (Buffalo), '67–'68; Columbia Univ., BS; b. N.Y.C., 1929; p. J. Anthony and Frances Probst; h. Harold Solomon (dec.); c. Carla Marianne, Maria Deborah; res: 271 Central Park W., N.Y., N.Y. 10024.

SOMAN, SHIRLEY CAMPER, Freelance Non-Fiction mag. Wtr.; VP, Associated Film Consultants, '66–; Ed., Highlights, and Family Life Cnslt., Cnslt. on Public Info., Family Svc. Assn. of Am., '57–'64; PR Wtr., Bur. of Child Guidance of N.Y., '56–'57; Assoc. Ed., My Baby; Magazine and Shaw's Market News; Soc. of Mag. Wtrs., Auths. League of Am., Am. Assn. of Med. Wtrs.; Univ. of Wis., BA, '45; Smith Col., MSS, '46; b. Boston, Mass., 1922; h. Robert O. Soman; c. Fred D. Camper, Frances A. Camper. res: 40 W. 77th St., N.Y., N.Y. 10024.

SOMERS, SELMA, Adv. Dir., Vera Industries, 417 Fifth Ave., N.Y., N.Y. 10016, '67–; AE, Mervin & Jesse Levine Adv., '57–'67; Jr. AE, Friend-Reiss Adv., '55–'57; Fashion Group; Bklyn. Col., BA, '55; res: 123 E. 75th St., N.Y., N.Y. 10021.

SOMMARS, JULIE, TV Actress, Co-star, "The Governor and J.J.," Columbia Broadcasting System, Inc., 4024 Radford Ave., Studio City, Cal.; Free-lance TV Actress; SAG, AFTRA, AEA; San Bernardino Valley

Col.; b. Fremont, Neb., 1942; p. Louis and Helen Drummond Sommars; res: 11558 Canton Dr. Studio City, Cal. 91604.

SOMMERER, WILMA JEAN, Customer Rep., Xerox Corporation, 1425 Hampton Ave., St. Louis, Mo. 63139, '70–; Media Dir., Hall, Haerr, Peterson & Harney, Inc., (Jefferson City, Mo.) '67–'70; local nwsp. adv. b. Jefferson City, Mo., 1944; p. Paul and Frances Schubert Sommerer; res: 513 E. Capital Ave., Jefferson City, Mo. 65101.

SONGAILO, ALYCE H., Exec. Designer, Nugent Wenckus Studio Inc., 1100 Northwest Hwy., Des Plaines, Ill. 60018; Mdsng., Furniture Byr., Carson Pirie Scott & Co.; Int. Designer, Ill. Bell Telephone Co.; Int. Decorator, Marshall Field & Co.; Aldens Mail Order Decorating Svc. (pseud: Claudia Scott), '67–'68; Nat. Soc. of Int. Designers, Fashion Group, NHFL, AMC Steering Comm. ('57–'59), Jr. Achiev.; Art Inst.; Northwestern Univ.; h. R. Bruce Kopseker.

SONNE, ANN VIERHUS, Head, Ann Sonne Public Relations and Publicity, 1425 Laurel St., S. Pasadena, Cal. 91030, '68–; Theta Sigma Phi, Jr. League of L.A.; Univ. of Southern Cal., BA (Jnlsm.); b. San Diego, Cal., 1931; p. Albert and Elizabeth Blakeslee Vierhus; h. Roscoe Sonne; c. Elizabeth, Margaret, Christian, James Paul; res: 1425 Laurel St., S. Pasadena, Cal. 91030.

SONSINI, JENNIFER BYRNE, Free-lance Copy Ed., Fodor's Modern Travel Guides (Random House), '65–; b. London, England, 1932; p. Raymond and Doreen Crouch Byrne; h. Raymond Sonsini; c. Lizette, Juliet; res: 83–25 Vietor Ave., Elmhurst, N.Y. 11373.

SORGE, YVONNE McGEHEE, AE, Adv. & PR, Gordon Marks & Company, 4915 55 N., P.O. Box 1757, Jackson, Miss. 39205, '60–; Sls. Prom., Adv. Mgr., Kennington Co., '56–'60; Copywtr., John Gerver Co., '52–'56; Adv. Copywtr., Rosengarten & Steinke, '50–'52; Jackson Adv. Club (Secy., '63), Miss. Art Assn. (Pres., '68–'69), Jackson Symphony League (Mbr., Bd. of Dirs.); Adv. Club of Miss. Wm. of the Yr., '62; Wheaton Col., '44–'45; Memphis State Univ., '45–'46; h. Alfred F. Sorge.

SOULE, JEAN CONDER, Free-lance Wtr., children's bks., mag. articles, poems; Edtl. Asst., Jnl. of the NEA; Fiction Ed., Sr. Citizen Magazine; Tchr., Phila. Wtrs. Conf.; Pfsnl. Storyteller, schs. and libs.; Wtrs. Club of Delaware County (Pres., '56–'58), Pfsnl. Wtrs. Club (Phila.), Delaware County Fed. of Wms. Clubs (poetry aws.); Mt. Holyoke Col., BA, '42; b. Brookline, Mass., 1919; p. Ralph Edwin and Mabel Pierce Conder; h. George H. Soule; c. David Conder, Douglas Benton, Nancy Jean; res: 125 N. Norwinden Dr., Springfield, Pa. 19064.

SOUTHARD, HELEN FAIRBAIRN, Dir., Bureau of Research and Program Resources, National Board,

Young Women's Christian Association, 600 Lexington Ave., N.Y., N.Y. 10022, '67–; Colmst., Co-Ed Magazine; family life and sex educ. cnslt., '50–; Sch. Cnslt., Family Life programs, '68–; Cnslt., Plays for Living, '67; CBS series on family problems, '67; Panelist, NBC, '54–'58; teaching records and bks. on sex educ.; AFTRA; Am. Psychological Assn., N.Y. State Psychological Assn.; Univ. of Buffalo, BA, MA, '29–; (cum laude); Columbia Univ. Grad. Sch., '32–'35; b. Buffalo, N.Y., 1906; p. Robert and Rena Klock Fairbairn; h. Paul Southard; c. John Brelsford II, Robert Fairbairn; res: 100 E. Palisade Ave., Englewood, N.J. 07631.

SOWERS, MARY ALICE, retired; Dir., Family Life Institute, Univ. of Okla. (Norman), Specialist in parent educ., Nat. Congress of Parents and Tchrs.; Dir., Family Life Radio Forum wkly. bdcst., WNAD Univ. Sta. and 9 state radio stas.; Talent, "The Open Window," Tulsa and Okla. City Stas.; Auth., mag. articles; more than 300 pamplets; wkly. articles, "Families First," 90 state nwsps.; Collaborator, two pfsnl. comml. films; various orgs. and aws.; Miami Univ. (Oh.); Univ. of Cinn., BS (Home Econs.); MA (Educ.); Cornell Univ., PhD (Family Life; Scholarship, Laura Spellman Fund, Rockefeller Fndn.); b. Springfield, Oh., 1892; p. Samuel and Minnie Shuey Sowers; res: 613 Tulsa St., Norman, Okla. 73069.

SPAIN, FRANCES LANDER, Dir., Lib. Svcs., Central Florida Junior College, P.O. Box 1388, Ocala, Fla. 32670, '61–; Ed: "Reading Without Boundaries" (N.Y. Public Lib., '56), "The Contents of the Basket" (N.Y. Public Lib., '60); Coordr., Children's Svc., N.Y. Public Lib., '53–'61; Asst. Dir., Lib. Sci. Sch., Univ. of Southern Cal., '49–'53; Head Librn., Lib. Sci. Dept., Winthrop Col., '36–'48; Asst., Jacksonville (Fla.) Public Lib., '19–'21; Ed., "Books for Young People" in Saturday Review, '54–'59; Lectr., several univs.; ALA (Pres.), '60–'61), S.C. Lib. Assn. (Pres.), '47), AAUW, Who's Who of Am. Wm.; Winthrop Col., AB, '25; Emory Univ., AB (Lib. Sci.), '36; Univ. of Chgo., MA, '40; PhD, '44; b. Jacksonville, Fla., 1903; p. Malcolm and Rosa Dantzler Lander; h. Donald Grant Spain (dec.); c. Donald Jr. (dec.), Barbara (Mrs. Porter W. Dobbins Jr.); res: P.O. Box 128, Anthony, Fla. 32617.

SPALDING, MARTHA ELIZABETH, Pers. Dir., WDAF-TV-AM-FM, Signal Hill, Kansas City, Mo. 64108, '58–; Exec. Secy. to Gen. Mgr., '64–; Exec. Secy. to Gen. Mgr. WDAF-TV-AM, '31–'58; Radio Bdcstr.-Commentator, WDAF-AM, '31–'61; Off. Mgr., WDAF-TV-AM, '58–'64; AWRT (Kan. City "Wm. of the Yr.," '65); Aw. for Public/Svc. in Bdcst. from N. Am. Air Defense Command, Who's Who of Am. Wm.; Adv. and Sales Execs. Club. Wm. of Yr., '69; b. Kan. City, Mo.; p. Henry Matthew and Carrie Lawson Spalding; res: 1116 W. 77th St., Kan. City, Mo. 64114.

SPANDORF, LILY GABRIELLA, Artist: 1528 Connecticut Ave., N.W., Wash., D.C. 20036; Contrbr., Evening & Sunday Star, Washington Post, Christian Science

Monitor, others; WNPC, Artists Equity Assn., Wash. Water Color Soc., Intl. Platform Assn.; Designer, U.S. Christmas postage stamp, '63; numerous aws., group shows in several U.S. cities, Italy, Eng.; paintings presented to Pres. of Korea, Pres. of Iceland, Princess Margaret, Gt. Britain, by Pres. Johnson; Acad. of Arts (Vienna, Austria), diploma; b. Vienna, Austria; p. Leon and Regina Bronstein Spandorf; res: 1528 Connecticut Ave., N.W., Wash., D.C. 20036.

SPARKS, MARY GAMBILL, Ed., Big Sandy News, Big Sandy Publishing Company, Inc., 208 Main St., Louisa, Ky. 41230, '53–; Elementary Tchr., '12–'15; Ky. Press Assn., Nat. Edtl. Assn., Ky. Hist. Soc., Nat. Platform Assn.; Ky. Normal Col.; b. Martha, Ky., 1891; p. William O. and Mallie Hunter Gambill; h. Dr. Hugh Herbert Sparks (dec.); c. Hugh Homer (dec.), Mrs. Jack W. Strother; res: 315 Lady Washington St., Louisa, Ky. 41230.

SPARKS, NANCY CAYTON, Entertainment Ed., Wichita Beacon, 825 E. Douglas, Wichita, Kan. 67201, '66–; Eng., Jnlsm. Tchr., Wichita Southeast HS, '58–'66; Eng. Tchr., Augusta Jr. HS, '57–'58; Theta Sigma Phi (Wichita Chptr. Treas., '67–'68), NFPW, Kan. Press Wm., Wichita Press Wm.; Wall Street Journal Fndn. Aw., '66; Kan. State Univ., BS, '57; b. Abilene, Kan., 1935; p. Francis and Rema Vilander Cayton; h. Howard Sparks; res: 6102 E. Morris, Wichita, Kan. 67218.

SPARKS, PAT CROWELL, Exec. Asst. to Pres., Schindler, Howard & Raut Advertising, Inc., 530 Maxwell Ave., Cinn., Oh. 45219, '59–; Asst. to Pres., Ross Wilson Adv.; Sls. Prom. and Adv. Mgr., Royal Home Products; Prod. Mgr., S. C. Baer Adv.; Copywtr., Media Dir., Time Byr., Prod. Mgr., Julian Behr Adv.; articles on sales; Cinn. Adv. Club, Wtrs. Club of Cinn.; Wms. Col. of Ala.; b. Montgomery, Ala., 1924; p. William C. and Jessie Moore Crowell; h. Steven Sparks; c. Edward Michael, William Thomas, Shirley Rigdom, Sandy Jones; res: 1518 Brandon Ave., Cinn., Oh. 45230.

SPAULDING, IMOGENE (JEAN) KELLY, Media Dir., Jack M. Doyle Advertising Inc., 305 W. Broadway, Louisville, Ky. 40202, '59–; Adv. Club of Louisville, Ky. Indsl. Adv. Assn., Basset Hound Club of Am.; Univ. of Louisville; b. Burlington, Ky., 1930; p. Robert and Katherine Bates Kelly; h. William C. Spaulding; c. William C., Jr., Richard J.; res: 121 E. Francis Ave., Louisville, Ky. 40214.

SPEARE, ELIZABETH GEORGE, Auth., bks. for young people, incl: "Calico Captive," "The Bronze Bow"; novel, "The Prospering"; Tchr., Eng., Mass. high schs., '30–'36; Auths. Guild Cncl.; Newberry aw., '59, '62; Smith Col., '26–'27; Boston Univ., AB, '30; MA, '32; b. Melrose, Mass.; p. Harry A. and Demetria Simmons George; h. Alden Speare; c. Alden, Jr., Mrs. Elizabeth Speare Carey; res: Bibbins Rd., R.F.D. #1, Fairfield, Conn. 06430.

SPEARMAN, ANITA JONES, City Ed., The Palm Beach Post-Times, 2751 S. Dixie, West Palm Beach, Fla. 33405, '67–; Asst. City Ed., '66–'67; City Hall Reptr., '63–'66; Reptr., '62–'63; City Ed., The Evening Herald (Rock Hill, S.C.), '61–'62; Reptr., '60–'61; Jnlsm. Cnslr.-Instr., Nat. H.S. Inst., Northwestern Univ., summer '61; Pub. Inf. Offcr., Winthrop Col., Rock Hill, summer, '60; Advisor-Instr., S.C. Scholastic Press Assn. Summer Seminar for H.S. Eds., '56–'57; various organizations and aws.; Winthrop Col., BA (Jnlsm., Eng.), '60 (1st Hon. Grad., magna cum laude); Northwestern Univ., MS (Jnlsm.), '62; b. Gaffney, S.C., 1936; p. Louransey and Louise Pettit Jones; h. Robert Spearman; res: 2367 Bay Circle, Lake Park, Fla. 33403.

SPECHT, DORIS SMITH, Head Humanities Librn., California State College, 6101 N. 7th St., Long Beach, Cal. 90801, '60–; Sci. Librn., '58–'60; Opns. Librn., Jet Propulsion Lab., Cal. Inst. of Tech., '56–'58; Cataloger, Douglas Aircraft, '55–'56; Engineering Librn., Northrop Aircraft, '53–'55; AAUP, AAUW, Cal. State Employees Assn. (Chptr. Pres., '65–'66), Cal. Lib. Assn., ALA, Music Lib. Assn.; Univ. of Minn., BS, '34 (magna cum laude); Univ. of Southern Cal., MS (Lib. Sci.), '52; b. Aberdeen, S.D., 1913; p. Fred William and Lavinia Shaffer Smith; h. Walter Specht; c. Dr. Walter Albert Specht, Jr., Mrs. Patricia Sprouse; res: 124 Stanford Lane, Seal Beach, Cal. 90740.

SPECKHART, KATHRYN PERRINE, Wms. Ed., Courier-Post, 200 N. Third St., Hannibal, Mo. 63401, '52–; Music Librn., Radio Station KHMO, '48–'49; BPW (Hannibal Pres., '67–'68), NPWC, Mo. Press Wms. Assn. (1st aw., wms. pg.; 2nd, photog.; 3rd, pg. make-up, '69); Best wms. pg., Mo. Press Assn., '69; Best Club Reptr., Mo. Fedn. of Wms. Clubs, '62; b. Quincy, Ill., 1925; p. Ellis E. and Elizabeth Tammen Perrine; h. (div.); c. Sgt. John Wayne Bowen, Pvt. Terrill E. Bowen; res: 1522 Booker St., Hannibal, Mo. 63401.

SPECKMANN, MAYBELLE PILLAR, Music Ed., Critic, Independent Journal, 1040 B St., San Rafael, Cal. 94902, '59–; Wms. Wtr., '51–'59; Rels., Training Offcr., U.S. Govt. (S.F.), '42–'47; Jnlsm., Eng. Tchr., various schs.; Kappa Delta Pi; Colo. Col., BA (Music, Eng.), '30 (Phi Beta Kappa); Univ. of Denver, MA (Ed. Psych., Eng.), '31; Grad. Work, Univ. of Colo., Univ. of Chgo., Columbia Univ.; b. N.Y.C., 1912; p. Frederick and Olive Markle Pillar; h. Waybe R. P. Speckmann; res: 766 Lovell Ave., Mill Valley, Cal. 94941 (mail address: P.O. Box 65, Mill Valley, Cal. 94941).

SPECTOR, JOAN FREEDENBERG, Pres. and Owner, Joan Spector/Public Relations Inc., 12472 Keystone Rd., N. Miami, Fla. 33161, '57–; Edtl. Assoc., Universal Publ. & Distrb. Corp., '49–'57; Fla. PR Assn., Theta Sigma Phi; Certs. of Appreciation; N. Miami Soc. of the Arts, Educ. TV Ch. 2; Columbia Univ., '47–'48; Syracuse Univ., '47, '48; Tobe-Coburn Sch. of Fashion, '49; b. Mt. Vernon, N.Y., 1929; p. Ben and Helen

Freedenberg; h. Ralph Spector; c. Andrea Jean; res: 12472 Keystone Rd., N. Miami, Fla. 33161.

SPEECE, WINIFRED HUBLER, Wms. Dir., Bdcstr., WNAX, Third and Mulberry Sts., Yankton, S.D. 57078, '41–; Cont. Dept., '39–'41; Auth: "Your Neighbor Lady" (homemaking bk., annually, '41–); AWRT, Zeta Phi Eta (Chptr. Pres. '38–'39; Alumnae Chptr. Pres., '47); Drake Univ., BS (Speech), '39; b. Marshalltown, Ia., 1917; p. Walter and Florence Pepper Hubler; h. Harry Speece; c. Dorothy (Mrs. Howard Shields), Gretchen (Mrs. Larry Roberts), Peter Lawrence, Todd H.; res: 314 E. 15th St., Yankton, S.D. 57078.

SPEER, KATHLEEN ABBY, Ed.-in-Chief, Children's Book Clubs, The Literary Guild of America, 277 Park Ave., N.Y., N.Y. 10017, '69–; Dir., Lib. Svcs., Charles Scribner's Sons; Dir., Lib. Svcs., Dial Press/Delacorte Press; Mgr., Adv. and Prom., D. C. Heath Co.; Publrs. Lib. Prom. Group (Past Secy.), Exhibits Round Table; Northwestern Univ., BS (Jnlsm.), '60.

SPEICHER, HELEN ROSS, Co-auth. with Kathryn Kilby Borland, children's bks., fictional, biographical; bks. incl: "Southern Yankees" (Bobbs-Merrill), "Everybody Laughed" (E. C. Seale Co.), "Clocks-From Shadow to Atom" (Follett Publ. Co.), others; Ed., Photogr., plant mag., Intl. Harvester; revsd. apprentice printer texts, Intl. Typographical Un., '37–'41; Theta Sigma Phi; Butler Univ. (Indpls., Ind.), '37 (magna cum laude); b. Indpls., Ind., 1915; p. Orren and Nellie Schrock Smith; h. Kenneth Speicher; c. David R., Stephen L., John Allan, Susan Jane; res: 9620 Willow View Dr., Indpls., Ind. 46280.

SPELLER, MAXINE WATKINS, Secy., Treas., Robert Speller & Sons, Publishers, Inc., 10 E. 23rd St., N.Y., N.Y. 10010, '57–; VP, Fashion Form Mfg. Corp., '43–'56; Designer, '38–'56; Tchr., '32–'34; Dir., Hough's Ency. of Am. Woods Fndn.; Louisburg Col., '25–'27; Duke Univ., BA, '32; b. Roseboro, N.C.; p. Daniel and Louise Patterson Watkins; h. Robert Speller; c. Robert E. B. Jr., Jon P.; res: 39 Gramercy Park, N.Y., N.Y. 10010.

SPENCE, BARBARA ANN, Pres., Ed., Proceedings in Print, Inc., P.O. Box 247, Mattapan, Mass. 02126, '66–; Ed., '64–; Tech. Librn., Avco Everett Rsch. Lab. (Everett, Mass.), '55–'68; Children's Librn., '53–'55; Special Libs. Assn.; ACLU, Inner-City Lib. Commtns.; Emmanuel Col., BA, '52; Simmons Col., MS, '53; b. Boston, Mass., 1929; p. John L. and Mary Ormond Spence; res: 72 Milton St., Arlington, Mass. 02174.

SPENCE, HOLLY DEE, Entertainment, Youth Ed., Lincoln Evening Journal, Sunday Journal & Star, 926 P St., Lincoln, Neb. 68501, '66–; Wms. News Wtr., '65–'66; Corr., Variety, '67–'68; Pubn. Adviser, State Youth in Govt.; hist. article, Cent. Nebraskaland Magazine; Guest Lectr., youth forums, Univ. of Neb. (Project Adult Adviser); Nat. Screen Cncl., Gamma Alpha Chi; Univ. of Neb. Sch. of Jnlsm., BA, '65; b.

Pender, Neb., 1943; p. Harold L. and Stella Lucier Spence; h. Donald Ferguson; res: 7611 Englewood, Lincoln, Neb. 68510.

SPENCER, DEE, Wms. Ed. and Entertainment Ed., Review-Journal, 737 N. Main St., Las Vegas, Nev. 89101; Wms. Ed. '60–; Entertainment Ed., '64–; Soc. Ed., Daily Republican (Belvedere, Ill.); Gen Reptr., Feature Wtr., Rockford Morning Star; Stringer: Billboard Magazine, Women's Wear Daily; Entertainment and Fashion Pubcty.; TV, radio Interviewer; Lectr.; Las Vegas Press Club (past Secy.); b. Belvedere, Ill., 1925; p. Gerald and Mildred Renwick Swail; h. (div.); c. Valeria Spencer, Bradley Palmer; res: 1088 Sierra Vista Dr., Las Vegas, Nev. 89109.

SPENCER, ELIZABETH, Wtr.; Wtr.-in-Residence, Univ. of N.C., '69; Bryn Mawr '63 (Donnelly Fellowship, '62–'63); Tchr. writing, English, Univ. of Miss., '52–'53, '48–'51; Reptr., Nashville Tennessean, '45–'46; PEN, Auths. Guild; Guggenheim Fellowship, '53–'54; Rosenthal Aw., '57; Kenyon Rev. Fiction Fellowship, '57–'58; Hon. Doctorate, Southwestern Univ., '68; Bellaman Aw., '68; Belhaven Col., AB, '42 (cum laude); Vanderbilt Univ., MA, '43; b. Carrollton, Miss., 1921; p. James and Mary McCain Spencer; h. John Rusher; res: 507-44th Ave., Lachine, Quebec, Canada.

SPENCER, ELIZABETH SUPPLEE, Assoc. Prof. of Jnlsm., Memphis State Univ., Patterson St., Memphis, Tenn. 38111, '56–; Fac., Univ. of Mo., '44–'49; PR, Univ. of Kan., '43–'44; Trenton (Mo.) Republican Times, '42–'43; PR, St. Louis Health and TB Soc., '40–'42; Free-lance Wtr.; Theta Sigma Phi, Assn. for Educ. in Jnlsm.; Cornell Univ., AB, '37; Univ. of Mo., BJ, MA, '41; b. Ithaca, N.Y., 1916; p. George Supplee and Ruth Cook Supplee; c. John Henry Spencer, Elizabeth Anne Spencer; res: 1602 Vinton Ave., Memphis, Tenn. 38104.

SPENCER, FERN SEATON, Ed. of Pubns., Bankers Life Nebraska, Cotner and O Sts., Lincoln, Neb. 68501, '69–; Staff Wtr., Neb. Dept. of Rds., '69; Wms. News Reptr., Lincoln Journal, '68–'69; Theta Sigma Phi, Kappa Tau Alpha; Univ. of Neb., BA (Jnlsm.), '68; b. Lincoln, Neb., 1946; p. James and Blanche Stempel Seaton; h. Warren H. Spencer; res: 3250 Adams #27, Lincoln, Neb. 68504.

SPENCER, GLENNA HUNTER, Radio-TV Ed., Youth Pg. Ed., Woman's Club Ed. Ohio State Journal, '52–'59; Prodr., WBNS-TV, '57–'59; Theta Sigma Phi (Columbus Chptr. Past VP); b. Columbus, Oh., 1934; p. Charles and Cleo Heinz Hunter; h. William Spencer; c. William Wesley, Susan Elizabeth; res: 1955 Walnut Hill Park Dr., Columbus, Oh. 43227.

SPENCER, JEAN BALLARD, Ed., State of Ala. Department of Pensions & Security, 64 N. Union St., Montgomery, Ala. 36104, '39–; Secy. to Ed., '36–'39; Cnslt., State Comm. on Status of Wm.; Cnslt., Ala. League of Aging Citizens; numerous civic activities; Theta Sigma

Phi, Cncl. Indsl. Eds. (Montgomery Secy., '67); Intl. Cncl. Indsl. Eds.; Ala. Conf. of Child Care, Ala. Conf. Social Work (Secy.); State Univ. of Ia., B.A., '34 (Phi Beta Kappa); Univ. of Tex., Northwestern Univ., MS (Jnlsm.) '52; b. Natchez, Miss., 1912; p. Dr. James C. and Luda Bowman Ballard; h. James A. Spencer; c. Jimmie L., Patricia Ann; res: 1451 Marlowe Dr., Montgomery, Ala. 36111.

SPENCER, JEAN ELIZABETH, Special Asst. to the Vice President, United States Government, Office of the Vice President, Exec. Off. Bldg., Wash., D.C. 20503, '69–; Rsch. Dir., Exec. Reorg. Comm., State of Md., '68–'69; Asst. Dir., Governor's Task Force on Modern Mgt., '67–'69; Rsch. Dir., Constitutional Conv., '67–'68; Staff Dir., Governor's Modernization Commn., '66; Asst. Prof., Govt., Polits., Univ. of Md., '65; Rsch. Assoc., Bur. of Governmental Rsch., '63–; Auth., "Modernizing the Executive Branch of the Maryland Government (State of Md., '67); Univ. of Md., BA (Polit. Sci.), '55 (Phi Kappa Phi); MA, '61; PhD, '65 (Outstanding Wm. Doctoral Candidate); Univ. of Wash. (Seattle), '55, '58; b. Somerset, Pa., 1933; p. James D. and Mabel Sidell Spencer; res: 7702 Adelphi Rd., Apt. 34, W. Hyattsville, Md. 20783.

SPENCER, JEAN ROSEMARY, AE, Doyle Dane Bernbach, 20 W. 43rd St., N.Y., N.Y. 10036, '62–; Fashion Dir., J. M. Mathes; Asst. Byr., Lord & Taylor; Fashion Cnslt., Barbizon Corp.; Fashion Group, NHFL, Nat. Soc. of Interior Designers; N.J. Col. for Wm.; N.Y.U.; b. Providence, R.I., 1926; p. Anthony and Sophie Spencer; res: 8 Peter Cooper Rd., N.Y., N.Y. 10010.

SPENCER, LILA, PR Dir., Pet Incorporated, Pet Plaza, 400 S. Fourth St., St. Louis, Mo. 63166, '68–; Group Mgr., PR Dept., '67; Product Publicist, '63; Pubcty. Home Econst., '60; Field Home Econst., '53; Home Econs. Tchr., '49–'53; Auth., "Exciting Careers for Home Economists" (Julian Messner, '67); articles, Jr. Miss Magazine, others; PRSA, Am. Home Econs. Assn., Home Econsts. in Bus., AWRT; Southern Ill. Univ., '45–'47; Univ. of Ill., BS, '49; b. Murphysboro, Ill., 1928; p. M. K. and Villa Gates Spencer; res: 4400 Lindell Blvd., St. Louis, Mo. 63108.

SPENCER, MADELINE WHITE, Wms. Ed., Rogers Daily/Sunday News, Donrey Media Group, 104 W. Poplar St., Rogers, Ark. 72756, '60–; NLAPW, Ark. Press Conv. Aw., '68; Okla. Presbyterian Col.; b. Chickasha, Okla., 1907; p. James Edward and Myrtle Plato White, Jr.; h. John Spencer; c. Mrs. Patricia Webb; res: R.F.D. 2, Box 203, Rogers, Ark. 72756.

SPENCER, MADERA ADAMS, Wms. Dept. Ed., Advertiser-Journal, 107 S. Lawrence St., Montgomery, Ala. 36101, '55–; European Tour Conductor; Ala. Wtrs. Conclave (Pres., '54–'55), Judson Col. Advisory Bd. of Visitors, NLAPW (State Pres., '56), Bd. Mbr: Eng. Speaking Un., Ala. Wtrs. Conclave, Interfaith Cncl. of Wm., Montgomery Fedn. of Garden Clubs, Keep Montgomery Beautiful; Who's Who of Am. Wm.; Dic. of Intl. Biog; b. Aldalusia, Ala., 1920; p. J.

Festus and Alice Wall Adams; h. John Spencer; c. John Jr.; res: 2292 Country Club Dr., Montgomery, Ala. 36106.

SPENCER, MARY CROTHERS, Sunday Mag. Ed., The Blade, 541 Superior St., Toledo, Oh. 43604, '68–; Wms. News Ed., '63–'68; Fashion Ed., '58–'68; Asst. Wms. News Ed., '60–'63; Staff Wtr., '48–'58; ZONTA, Oh. Nwsp. Wms. Assn. (aws., '67–'68, '59–'65, '56), Alpha Phi Gamma; Toledo Cncl. of BPW Wm. of the Yr., '67; Univ. of Toledo, AB, '48; b. Garrett, Ind., 1926; p. Rollie and Fleta Schumaker Crothers; h. J. Robert Spencer; res: 4015 N. Lockwood Ave., Toledo, Oh. 43612.

SPENCER, MILDRED DOLORES, Sci. Wtr., The Buffalo Evening News, 218 Main St., Buffalo, N.Y. 14240, '41–; Reptr., The Rochester Dem. and Chronicle, '40–'41; Prodr., public svc. progs., WBEN; Free-lance Sci. Wtr.; Nat. Assn. of Sci. Wtrs. (Pres., '65–'66), Theta Sigma Phi; Blakeslee aw., Au. Ht. Assn., '61; Am. Med. Assn. Med. Jnlsm. aw., nwsp. writing; '65; Liberty Bell aw., Nat. Assn. of Mental Health, '63; state and area aws., med. writing; Univ. of Ill., BS (Jnlsm.), '40 (hons.); b. Rochester, N.Y., 1917; p. Earl C. and Edith Timerman Spencer; res: 214 Highland Ave., Buffalo, N.Y. 14222.

SPENCER, NANCY HESS, VP, Spencer-Claire Associates, Inc., 1845 Post Rd., Warwick, R.I. 02886, '67–; Mkt. Rsch., Wtr., '63–'67; Mkt. Rsch., Fram Corp., '62–'63; PR, The Mdsng. Group, '58–'61; Mkt. Rsch., Indsl. Nat. Bank, '50–'55; Pubcty., Pembroke Col., '46–'48; Reptr., Providence Jnl., '43–'45; Pembroke Col., BA, '43 (hons. in Eng.); b. Providence, R.I., 1923; p. John R., Jr., and Dorothy O'Leary Hess; h. Sheldon D. Spencer; c. Susan, Deborah; res: 72 Thomas Olney Common, Providence, R.I. 02904.

SPENCER, OLGA MARIE, Mng. Ed., Rawlins Daily Times, Sixth and Buffalo Sts., Rawlins, Wyo. 82301, '67–; Wms. Pg. Ed., '65–'66; Staff Wtr., Lusk (Wyo.) Herald, '61–'63; BPW (VP); Wyo. Press Assn. aws., '65–'68; Univ. of Wyo.; b. Globe, Ariz., 1944; p. Henry and Ruth Hughes Hytrek; h. Frederick L. Spencer; res: P.O. Box 851, Rawlins, Wyo. 82301.

SPENSLEY, NORRI BILLINGS, Free-lance Wtr.; Cont. Dir., KWWL-TV (Waterloo, Ia.), '63; PR, Univ. of Neb. (Lincoln, Neb.) '62; Theta Sigma Phi; Univ. of Neb. grad., '62; h. David R. Spensley; res: 3238 Waterloo Rd., Cedar Falls, Ia. 50613.

SPERBER, ANN MARGARET, Ed., Jr. Bks., McGraw-Hill Book Co., 330 W. 42nd St., N.Y., N.Y. 10036, '68–; Ed., Juv. Bks., G. P. Putnam's Sons, '62–'67; Asst. Ed., Juv. Dept., Collier Bks., '61–'62; Reviewer, American Record Guide, Library Journal; Wms. Nat. Bk. Assn. N.Y.C. Opera Guild (Exec. Comm.), Fulbright Fellowship, '56–'57; Barnard Col., BA, '56; b. Vienna, Austria, 1935; p. Dr. Fred and Liselotte Suss Sperber; res: 160 West End Ave., N.Y., N.Y. 10023.

SPICER, DOROTHY GLADYS, Free-lance Wtr., Folklorist and expert on folk arts and customs; Ed., The Grolier Soc., '47–'58; Dir., Fgn. Commtys. Dept., YWCA (Bklyn., N.Y.), '45–'47; Art Advisor, N.J. State Museum, '30–'41; Folk Arts Specialist, Nat. Bd. YWCA, '19–'29; Auth: "13 Goblins" (Coward-McCann, '69), "The Owl's Nest" (Coward-McCann, '68), 11 other folk tale bks. numerous other books on folk customs, festivals, feast-day foods; Vassar Col., AB, '16; Radcliffe Col., AM (Fine Arts), '18; Columbia Univ., N.Y.U.; p. J. Lindley and Phoebe Washburn Spicer; h. Malcolm Fraser; res: 16 Ralph Ave., White Plains, N.Y.

SPIVEY, MELBA DANIEL, Ed., Palomino Horses, Palomino Horse Breeders of America, Inc., P.O. Box 249, 204 S.E. Third Ave., Mineral Wells, Tex. 76067, '57–; Staff, '50–'57; Who's Who of Am. Wm., Nat. Register of Prominent Ams.; b. Mineral Wells, Tex., 1923; p. James and Lela Majors Daniel; h. Neal Spivey; c. Gail, Tami; res: 1402 S.E. 23rd Ave., Mineral Wells, Tex. 76067.

SPRADLING, JEAN JOHNSON, Free-lance Wtr., 817 W. Lakeside St., Madison, Wis. 53715, '69–; Coordr., Student Pubn., Univ. of Wis. Center System, '66–'69; Instr., Summer HS Jnlsm. Workshop, '67–'68; Theta Sigma Phi (Madison Chptr. Pres.-elect, '69); Univ. of Wis., BA (Jnlsm.), '66 (Outstanding Jr. Wm. in Jnlsm., '65); Univ. of Oslo, Norway, '65; b. Racine, Wis., 1944; p. John and Loretta Richards Johnson; h. David Spradling; c. Eric David.

SPRAGUE, JEAN NEAL, Prodr., Modr., "The Open Door," KETA (TV), 18th and N. Ellison, Okla. City, Okla. 73106, '68–; Prodr., Co-modr., "Project People," '68–'69; Prodr., Modr., "PTA Pointers," '65–'68; Co-prodr., Storyteller, "Children's TV Bible Hour" (Lawton, Okla.), '56, '57; AWRT; Bdcst. Ctr. aw., exemplary svc., commty. affairs bdcst., '68; Okla. Assn. for Mental Health (State Bd.); Abilene Christian Col., BS, '49; Okla. City Univ., '66, '67; b. Commerce, Tex., 1929; p. Argus D. and Ruby M. Barnett Neal; h. David Sprague; c. Anji, Bob; res: 5644 N. Barnes, Okla. City, Okla. 73112.

SPRAKER, NANCY GENE, Wtr., Ed., Woman's Day, 67 W. 44th St., N.Y., N.Y. 10036, '64–; Prom. Copywtr., House & Garden, Collier Bks., '63–'64; Sr. Copywtr., Macy's, '61–'63; Wtr., Good Housekeeping, '54–'60; Bennington Col., BA, '54; b. Johnstown, N.Y., 1933; p. Robert and Ruth Sponnoble Spraker; h. David L. Schraffenberger; res: 77 Seventh Ave., N.Y., N.Y. 10011.

SPRINGBORN, ROSEMARY KELLY, Supvsr. of Edtl. Prod., Harper & Row, Publishers, Inc., 2500 Crawford Ave., Evanston, Ill. 60201, '69–; Ed.-in-Chief, Bks. Div., Soc. of Mnfg. Engineers (Dearborn, Mich.), '65–'69; Tech. Copywtr., Gray & Kilgore Adv. (Detroit), '64–'65; Tech. Wtr., Adv. Mgr., Ex-Cell-O Corp. (Warren, Mich.), '63–'64; Sr. Tech. Wtr., Adv. Copywtr., Bendix Aerospace Div. (Ann Arbor, Mich.) '60–'63; Ed., Non-Traditional Machining Processes, '67; other bks.; Copyright Soc. of Am.; Soc. of Tech.

Wtrs. & Publrs. aw., '68; two Aviation Week Reader Feedback aws., '62; Purdue Univ., BS, '53; b. South Bend, Ind., 1932; p. Edward and Hazel Thompson Kelly; h. Bruce A. Springborn; res: 225 Francis Lane, Barrington, Ill. 60010.

SPROWLS, CAROLE JEANNE, Asst. Dir., News Service, Bowling Green State University, Adm. Bldg., Bowling Green, Oh. 43402, '68–; Reptr., Photogr., Norwalk Reflector, '65–'68; Oh. Univ., BS (Jnlsm.), '65; b. Canonsburg, Pa., 1943; p. Wilbert and Bella Douglass Sprowls; res: Apt. 102, Greenview Apts., Napoleon Rd., Bowling Green, Oh. 43402.

SPURR, ELIZABETH BOWLES, Free-lance Wtr., '59–; Ed., Under the Spire, Orthopaedic Hosp. (L.A., Cal.); Copywtr., Young & Rubicam (N.Y.; L.A., Cal.), '52–'57; Theta Sigma Phi; AAW aws., '58–'59; BA (Jnlsm.), '49; b. L.A., Cal., 1926; p. Theodore C. and Florence McGrath Bowles; h. Reginald Spurr (dec.); c. Matthew, Susan, Peter, Stephanie, Maureen; res: 785 S. El Molino Ave., Pasadena, Cal. 91106.

SQUAIRES, G. MARJORIE PRIOR, Coordr.-Admr., Continuing Education in Nursing, University of California at Los Angeles, 1000 Veteran Avenue, L.A. Cal. 90024, '64–; AWRT, Southern Cal. Nursing TV Advisory Bd. (Chmn., '66–'69); numerous nursing and educ. orgs. Long Beach State Col., BA, '57; MA, '61; b. Long Beach, Cal., 1912; p. Herman and Kate Thorne Prior; h. (div.); c. Mrs. Coy Swanson, Mrs. Fred Moore, R. Michael; res: 5416 Horizon Drive, Malibu, California 90265.

STABILE, TONI (ANTOINETTE D.), Auth., Freelance Wtr., Cnslt., former Colmst., Copywtr., Fashion Coordr., AE, Prom. Dir.; Contributor to nat. and intl. mags; Auth., "Cosmetics: Trick or Treat?" ('67); OPC, Theta Sigma Phi; Univ. of Ky., AB (Jnlsm.); Columbia Univ.; b. N.Y.C.; p. Nicola and Rosina Tramontano Stabile; Studio: 411 E. 53rd St., N.Y., N.Y. 10022.

STACK, BETTE, Mdse. Mgr., Family Circle, 488 Madison Ave., N.Y., N.Y. 10022, '64–; Mdse. Mgr., Ladies' Home Journal; Mgr., Strawbridge & Clothier Dept. Store; Macy's Bloomingdales; NHFL, Fashion Group, Electrical Wms. Round Table; Hood Col., BS (Home Econs.), '50; N.Y.U., MS (Retailing), '53; h. Earl Duchesne (div.); c. one daughter; res: 301 E. 49th St., N.Y., N.Y. 10017.

STACK, NICOLETE MEREDITH MC GUIRE, (pseuds: Eileen Hill, Kathryn Kenny), Free-lance Wtr., Auth. of 28 bks. for young people; Story County, Ia., Bd. of Social Welfare; Chmn., Old Age Asst. Commn., '35–'40; Auths. League of Am., NLAPW, St. Louis Wtrs. Guild (past Pres.); Mo. Wtrs. Guild bk. of the yr. Aw. ('57), Catholic Young People's bk. of the yr. Aw. ('54, '57); Univ. of Colo., Highland Park Col; b. Des Moines, Ia., 1899; p. Patrick Henry and Frances Lynch McGuire; h. 1. Edward Randolph Meredith (dec.), 2. Charles Monroe Stack (dec.); res: 8 Colonial

Village, Jamestown House, Webster Groves, St. Louis, Mo. 63119.

STAFFORD, I. ELIZABETH, Dir. of Sch. Libs. and Audio Visuals, Dist. 4 Offices, Bowman Ave., Port Chester, N.Y. 10573, '60–; Jr. High Sch. Librn., '35–; Tchr., Librn., Dolgeville HS, '30–'35; N.Y. Lib. Assn. (VP, '62), Westchester County Educ. Cmmtns. Assn. (Secy.); Syracuse Univ., AB, '30 (Phi Kappa Phi); Columbia Univ., BS (Lib. Sci.), '42; b. Clinton, N.Y.; p. Earl and Wilhelmina Simon Stafford; res: 237 Columbus Ave., Port Chester, N.Y. 10573.

STAHL, ANNE COUSER, Pres., The Stahl Associates, Inc., Advertising/Marketing, 1002 Buffalo Rd., Bryan, Oh. 43506, '54–; Ritchie-Safford Adv. (Houston, Tex.) '41; Copywtr., Prod. Mgr., Robert L. Wilson Co. (Tulsa, Okla.), '38–'41; Wms. Adv. Club of Toledo, BPW, Lit. Forum; Who's Who of Am. Wm.; Who's Who in the Midwest; b. Independence, Mo., 1921; p. William and Nellie Carey Couser; h. David W. Stahl; c. John M., Charlotte Anne (Mrs. Russell Ameter), Margaret A., Barbara L.; res: 504 Newdale Dr., Bryan, Oh. 43506.

STAHNKE, ETHEL CERNIK SMITH, Ed., Top Drawer, Bliss & Laughlin Industries, 122 W. 22nd St., Oak Brook, Ill., '67–; Exec. Secy., '57–'67; b. Chgo., Ill.; h. George Stahnke; c. Bonnie Jean (Mrs. Robert Small), Cindy (Mrs. Joseph H. Barber), Amy, Dixie.

STAMBUL, DIANA H., PR Assoc., Philadelphia National Bank, Broad and Chestnut Sts., Phila., Pa. 19101, '68–; Free-lance Wtr.; Ed., PR Assoc., Franklin Inst., '65–'67; Wtr., Smith, Kline & French Labs., '63–'65; Edtl. Asst., Holiday, '59–'63; Theta Sigma Phi; Univ. of Pa., BA, '58 (Phi Beta Kappa); b. Phila., Pa., 1937; p. Joseph and Rae Heller Stambul; res: Hopkinson House, Phila., Pa. 19106.

STANARD, CARALEE STROCK, Ed., The Adelphean, '62–; Instr. of Jnlsm, Webster Col., '64–'68, Dir. of PR, '62–'68; Fashion Wtr., St. Louis (Mo.) Post-Dispatch, '32–'60; Mng. Ed., Pubns. Dir., Southern Dry Goods Merchant, '24–'31; Wms. Ed., St. Louis (Mo.) Times, '19–'21; Reptr., St. Louis (Mo.) Star, Peoria (Ill.) Journal-Transcript; Theta Sigma Phi (St. Louis Chptr. Pres., '66–'67, '31–'32; Nat. Cncl. Mbr., '32–'36), Fashion Group (Reg. Dir., '60–'61), Alpha Delta Pi (Grand Pres., '38–'48); St. Louis Wms. C. of C. cit., '42; Univ. of Mo., BJ; h. Sidney R. Stanard (dec.); c. Caralee; res: 14 Colonial Village Ct., St. Louis, Mo. 63119.

STANDS, TALMADGE HORN, Adm. Asst., Oklahoma Arts and Humanities Council, 30 N. Hudson, Suite 412, Okla. City, Okla. 73102, '69–; radio shows: KOME (Tulsa, Okla.), KFDM (Beaumont, Tex.); Free-lance Talent: Nehaus Blumberg' (Houston, Tex.), Photo Lab., Shakespeare Soc., other groups, '64–'69; PR, Wms. Pavilion, San Antonio World's Fair, '68, Dir., Drama Workshop, Tchr., Country Playhouse, '56–'61; Wtr., sls.-training programs; Tchr., Bethany Col., '45–'47; Wtr., plays, pageants; AWRT (Nat. Chmn.,

'69), other orgs., aws.; Bethany Col., BA (Speech), '47; Rice Univ., Univ. of Okla., b. Beaumont, Tex., 1921; p. Carroll and Mary Withers Horn; h. Jacob Stands; c. Catherine Sue, Kahla Joy; res: 701 Mockingbird Lane, Norman, Okla. 73069.

STANFORD, ANN, Wtr.; Prof. of Eng., San Fernando Valley State College, 18111 Nordhoff St., Northridge, Cal. 91324, '68–; Asst. Prof., Assoc. Prof., '62–'68; Poetry Reviewer, L.A. Times, '57–'69; Co-ed., San Fernando Valley State Renaissance Editions; Ed., Uclan Review, '61–'64; several poetry bks., articles; Modern Lang. Assn., Am. Studies., Renaissance Soc. of Am., Col. Eng. Assn., Philological Assn. of the Pacific Coast; Silver Medal of Commonwealth Club of Cal. for "Magellan: A Poem to Be Read by Several Voices," '58; Shelley Memorial Aw. for Distg. Achiev. in Poetry, '68; Stanford Univ., BA, '38 (Phi Beta Kappa); U.C.L.A., MA, (Jnlsm.), '58; MA (Eng.), '61; PhD, '62; b. La Habra, Cal.; p. Bruce and Rose Corrigan Stanford; h. Ronald Arthur White; c. Patricia, Susan, Bruce, Rosanna Norton.

STANLEY, DOROTHY EVELYN, Asst. Prof. of Fgn. Lang., Old Dominion University, Hampton Blvd.- Bolling Ave., Norfolk, Va. 23508. '60–; Translator, Interpreter, First Nat. City Bank (N.Y.), '52–'59; Tchr. Acad. of Lang., '49–'52; Tchr., Acad. Sacred Heart, '46–'49; Tchr., Lycée Française, '45–'46; Asst., Head Monitoring Sec., Overseas Radio Div., U.S. State Dept., '42–'45; Head, Proof Room, George Grady Press, '39–'42; Exhibitor, art galleries: N.Y.C., '54–'59, and Va., '60; Lectr. on Creative Living, '59–; Auth: "They Call it Courage" ('68), two children's bks. in German; AAUW, Tidewater Artists Assn., Intl. Platform Assn., Alliance Française; listed in numerous dirs.; Maidenhead Col., London, BA, '28; Hunter Col., MA, '51; Post-Grad. work: Columbia Univ., '46–'47, and Paris, Munich, Univ. of Heidelberg; b. Nuremberg, Germany 1909; p. Dr. William Sellings and Lucie Danziger Peiser; c. Mrs. Peter A. Saunders, Frank Strauss; res: 1349 Buckingham Ave., Norfolk, Va. 23508.

STANWOOD, SUSAN, Sr. Ed., Book Div., McCall Publishing Co., 230 Park Ave., N.Y., N.Y. 10017, '69–; Sr. Ed., Saturday Evening Post, '63–'69; Copywtr./Asst. Ed., St. Martin's Press, '62–'63; Copywtr., Macmillan Publishing, '60–'62; free-lance adv. and writing; Vassar Col., BA, '58; b. Boston, Mass., 1937; res: 166 E. 75th St., N.Y., N.Y. 10021.

STAPLES, CHERYL WILLIAMS, Ed., The Fort Worth National Bank, P.O. Box 2050, Seventh and Main Sts., Ft. Worth, Tex. 76101, '67–; Am. Inst. of Banking, AAIE, Phi Chi Theta, Alpha Delta Pi; Tex. Christian Univ., '64–'66; b. El Paso, Tex., 1947; p. Vernon and Irene Moore Williams; h. Robert C. Staples; res: 1701 Rogers Rd., Ft. Worth, Tex. 76107.

STAPLES, LINNEA STADIG, Ed., Natural Resources & Wildlife; Union Leader Corp., Amherst St., Manchester, N.H. 03105, '59–; Rochester Courier, '58–'59;

Free-lance Lectr., nat. resources, wildlife, hist.; Outdoor Wtrs. Assn. of Am., N.H. Archeological Soc., Appalachian Mt. Club, Nat. Wildlife Fedn., Soc. for Protection of N.H. Forests, N.H. Granges; N.H. Arms Collectors; National Rifle Assn.; Governor's Aw., Best Outdoor Wtr. in Commtns., '65; b. New Sweden, Me., 1913; p. Albert N. and Jertrud Wiik Stadig; h. Robert Staples; c. Nathan L., Calvin L., Rolf R., Karl L., John A; res: Moose Trail Farm, Candia, N.H.

STARK, BEVERLY, TV Comml. Spokeswm., Shirley Hamilton Talent Agency, 360 N. Michigan Ave., Chgo., Ill., '60–; Nat. Spokeswm. for Electric Industry, '60–'66; TV Spokeswm., Sears, '68–'69; Wms. Dir., WMTV-Radio-TV (Madison, Wis.), '53–'60; nat. synd. radio show, '65–'67; synd. wms. nwsp. colm., '66; bklt., "Beverly Stark Talks to Teens"; Phi Beta Theta Sigma Phi, Madison Adv. Club; Madison's trade rep. abroad, '65–'66; Univ. of Wis., '47–'50; b. Milw., Wis., 1928; p. Clarence A. and Norma Reinhardt Muth; h. Richard Stark; c. Shelley, Randall; res: 6202 Old Sauk Rd., Madison, Wis. 53705.

STARKEY, MARION L., Auth., non-fiction bks., mag. articles; bk. revs., Boston Globe, N.Y. Times; Asst. Prof. of Eng., Univ. of Conn., '46–'61; Prof. of Eng., Hampton Institute, Va., '30–'43; Reprtr., Boston Sunday Advertiser, '28; Ed., Saugus Herald, '24–'27; Saugus League of Wm. Voters (secy., '66–'68); Hon. Phi Beta Kappa, Boston Univ., '50; Guggenheim Fellowship, '53, '58; Boston Univ., BS, '22; MA, '35; Harvard Sch. of Educ., '46; b. Worcester, Mass., 1901; p. Arthur E. and Alice Gray Starkey; res: 7 Stocker St., Saugus, Mass. 01906.

STASIO, MARILYN LOUISE, Theatre Critic, Cue Magazine, 20 W. 43rd St., N.Y., N.Y. 10036, '68; Feature Ed.; Ed.-in-Chief, Bklyn. Graphic; Tchr. Bertold Brecht, New Sch.; Drama Desk; Regis Col., BA, '60 (cum laude); Columbia Univ., MA, '61; b. Revere, Mass., 1941; p. Joseph and Margaret Crivello Stasio; res: 49 Jane St., N.Y., N.Y. 10014.

STASSEL, RUTH BACHMANN, Wms. Pg. Ed., LaPorte Herald Argus, 701 State St., LaPorte, Ind. 46350, '66–; County News Ed., '51–'54; Sigma Phi Gamma (Province Pres.); Northwestern Univ.; b. LaPorte, Ind., 1920; p. Albert and Margaret Peterson Bachmann; h. Alexander Stassel; c. Diane, Rita, Ramona, Darlene, Alex, Margaret, Douglas; res: 717 Waverly Rd., LaPorte, Ind. 46350.

STATMAN, JUDITH M., Media Dir., Bloom Advertising Agency, Inc., 512 S. Akard, Dallas, Tex. 75202; Asst. Prod. Mgr., Asst. to AE, Time Byr., Media Byr.; Assn. of Bdcst. Execs. of Tex. (Bd. of Dirs., '62–'63; Secy. '63–'64, '65–'67); Univ. of Tex., '55–'56; b. Dallas, Tex., 1938; p. Joe and Lillian Tolmich Statman; res: 5016 Les Chateaux, Dallas, Tex. 75235.

STATON, SUE KAREN, Dir., PR, Indianapolis Symphony Orchestra, 4600 Sunset Ave., Indpls., Ind. 46208, '65–; Sls. Svc. Dir., WFBM-TV, '60–'65; Lectr.,

Wms. Dir., Ind. Univ. Radio/TV Dept. (Bloomington, Ind.), '59; nat. sls. dept., WTTV; radio programming dept., WFBM (Indpls.); AWRT (Hoosier Chptr. Pres.), Adv. Club of Indpls. (Bd. of Dirs., '64–'69; Wm. of Yr., '63–'64), Theta Sigma Phi; Who's Who of Am. Wm.; Ind. Univ., BS, '54; b. Indpls., Ind., 1932; p. Fayne E. and Veronica Doyle Staton; res: 512 E. Washington St., Lebanon, Ind. 46052.

STAUBER, ANNA KLINE, Owner, Operator, Anndi Creative Advertising Company, 4330 Willys Pkwy., Toledo, Oh. 43612, '61–; Wtr. nwsps., trade jnls.; Ed., Toledo Calling; News Corr., Variety, Film Daily, Am. Banker, other pubns.; Wm.'s Adv. Club of Toledo; Theta Sigma Phi aw., '32; Sigma Delta Chi aw., '32; Oh. State Univ., BS (Jnlsm.), '32; h. F. I. Stauber (div.); c. Mrs. Jerome Phillips, Ronald J.; res: 4330 Willys Pkwy., Toledo, Oh. 43612.

STAUDACHER, ROSEMARIAN VALENTINER, Freelance Wtr., Juv. Bks., Lit. Cnslt., Lectr., Critic, 2023 E. Olive St., Shorewood, Wis. 53211, 'News Wtr., Marquette Univ. News Bur., '55–'56; Pubcty. Dir., Marygrove Col., '46–'48; Critic, Writer's Digest, '45–'46; Asst. to P.R. Dir., Xavier 4., Cin., O., '46; Assoc. Ed., Geo. A. Pflaum Publ., '41–'46; Fictioneers, Theta Sigma Phi; Edgecliff Col., BA, '40; Marquette Univ., MA (Jnlsm.), '47; Univ. of Wis.; b. Cinn., Oh., 1918; p. Richard and Marie Haegel Valentiner; h. Lucas G. Staudacher; c. Ann Marie, James Joseph; res: 2023 E. Olive St., Shorewood, Wis. 53211.

STAUNTON, HELEN M., Mng. Ed., Publishers-Hall Syndicate, 30 E. 42nd St., N.Y., N.Y. 10017, '48–; Reprtr., Feature Wtr., Editor & Publisher, '42–'48; Eng. Tchr., Harrisburg (Ill.) HS, '40–'42; News Ed., Town Topics (Chgo., Ill.), '38–'39; Pubcty. Dir., Universal Prod. Co. (Fairfield, Ia.), '37–'38; Reprtr., Feature Wtr., South Bend (Ind.) Tribune, '36–'37; Catholic Press Assn., Catholic Inst. of the Press (Past VP, Secy.); Univ. of Chgo., BA (Eng.), '35; Univ. of Southern Ill., '40; Univ. of Mich., MA (Jnlsm.), '40; b. Binghamton, N.Y., 1913; p. Henry and Florence Jameson Staunton; res: 30 Locust Hill Ave., Yonkers, N.Y. 10701.

STEARNS, BETTY JANE, Dir., Wms. Dept., Sr. VP, The Public Relations Board Inc., 75 E. Wacker Dr., Chicago, Ill. 60601, '63–; Dir., Wms. Dept., '53–; VP, '53–'63; '50–; Ed., Chgo. Stagebill; Copywtr., Chas. A. Stevens & Co.; "How American Women See Feminine Types" (monograph, '60), "Women & the Dollar" (monograph, '63); numerous articles, mktng. to wm., bus., mktng. pubns.; NHFL, Fashion Group (Chgo.; Reg. Dir., '67–'69; Secy. '65–'67), PRSA (Accredited Mbr.); first aws., Pubcty. Club of Chgo., '59, '64, '68; hon aws., '62, '64; The Univ. of Chgo., PhB, '45; MA, '48 (Alumni Assn. Exec. Comm.); Univ. of London, Cert. of Advanced Studies, '49; b. St. Paul, Minn.

STEBBINS, EMILY WITHROW, PR, Dir., Evanston Hospital, 2650 Ridge Ave., Evanston, Ill. 60201, '51–; Free-lance Wtr., '47–'51; Pubcty. Dir., Evanston

Commty. Chest, '38–'40; Sls. Prom. Dir., Bookhouse for Children, '25–'32; Edtl. Dept., Scott Foresman, '24–'25; Acad. of Hosp. PR (Fellow), Soc. for Hosp. PR, Chgo. Fund-raising Execs., Theta Sigma Phi, Chgo. Hosp. Cncl. of PR Dirs., North Shore PR Club, numerous Helen Cody Baker aws., Chgo. Welfare PR Forum; State Univ. of Ia., BA, '24 (cum laude; Phi Beta Kappa); b. Mt. Pleasant, Ia., 1903; p. Winfield Scott and Anna Webb Withrow; h. Frank L. Stebbins; c. Ann Fox, Scott Withrow; res: 925 Michigan Ave., Evanston, Ill. 60202.

STEBBINS, HAZEL STRUBLE, Wms. Dir., KFOR, Stuart Bldg., 13th and P St., Lincoln, Neb. 68510, '52–; AWRT (Corn Husker Chptr. Pres., '53, '69; Heart of Am. Chptrs. Pres., '55), Altrusa; Univ. of Neb., AB, '30, MA, '64; b. Hastings, Neb., 1909; p. Carl and Evelyn Gilbert Struble; h. Harold Stebbins; c. Ann Stebbins Sidles; res: 3634 S. 40th St., Lincoln, Neb. 68506.

STECKLER, PHYLLIS SCHWARTZBARD, Project Dir., CCM Information Corporation, 909 Third Ave., N.Y., N.Y. 10022, '69–; Dir. of Bibliography, R. R. Bowker Co., '65–'69; formerly Sr. Ed.; Auth: "How to Run a Paperback Bookshop," "Literary Market Place," "Bowker Annual of Library and Book Trade Information," many others; annual contrbr., Encyclopedia Britannica Yearbook; Wms. City Club of N.Y., WNBA; Hunter Col., BA, '54; N.Y.U., MA, '58; b. N.Y.C., 1933; p. Irwin and Bertha Fellner Schwartzbard; h. Stuart Steckler; c. Randall Ian, Sharon Royce; res: 172 Daytona St., Atlantic Beach, N.Y. 11509.

STEELE, LEE ZAPPULLA, Religion Ed., Toledo Blade, 541 Superior St., Toledo, Oh., '67–; Reptr., Music, Drama Critic, '50–'67; Instr. Jnlsm., Bowling Green State Univ., '47–'51; Reptr., Star Free Press (Ventura, Cal.), '45; Reptr., Newark (N.J.) Evening News, '43;' Oh. Nwsp. Wms. Assn. (Pres., '64–'66; VP, '62–'64; numerous writing aws.), Theta Sigma Phi, Kappa Tau Alpha, Toledo Hearing and Speech Ctr. (Pres., '56–'58); Syracuse Univ., MA, '45; Univ. of Toledo Law Sch., '67; Douglass Col., LittB; b. Newark, N.J., 1920; p. William and Beatrice LaFerrera Zappulla; h. Herman P. Steele; res: 2805 Emmick Dr., Toledo, Oh. 43606.

STEERS, CHRIS CHRISTENSEN, Assoc. Prof. of Commtns., Miami-Dade Junior College, 11380 N.W. 27th Ave., Miami, Fla. 33167, '61–; Instr., Coral Gables H.S.; various organizations and aws.; Univ of Ore., BA (Econs.), '25 (Honors); MA, '38 (honors); Columbia Univ., '40–'42; b. Seattle, Wash. 1901; p. Rev. M. A. and Regina Hilleboe Christensen; h. William Steers (dec.); c. Charles; res: 11770 W. Golf Dr., Apt. E. 411, Miami, Fla. 33167.

STEFANSSEN, STEPHANIE, Acc. Group Supvsr./PR, Batten, Barton, Durstine & Osborn, Inc., 383 Madison Ave., NY., N.Y. 10017, '67–; Owner, Stephanie Stefanssen PR, '64–'67; Assoc. Ed., Bonanza mag., San Fran-

cisco (Cal.) Chronicle; PR, Wilmarth/Stefanssen; Ed., "Great Restaurants Cookbook, U.S.A.;" PRSA, IRTS; Intl. TV & Film Festival aw., '69; Gov. of Spain jnlsm. aw., '63; b. N.Y.C.; h. (div.); c. Alison Anne Wilmarth; res: 300 E. 40th St., N.Y., N.Y. 10016.

STEGEMAN, EVELYN HAND, Pubns. Dir., Sundberg Printers, Inc., 1819 Ninth St., Rockford, Ill. 61108, '61–; Rockford Indsl. Eds. Assn. (Pres., '67; VP, '66), ZONTA; h. Richard Stegeman; res: 4303 Singleton Close, Rockford, Ill. 61111.

STEIGER, ALAYNE ROBERTS, Coordr., PR, Commty. Rels., Packard Bell Electronics Corp., Virginia & Summers Sts., Charleston, W. Va. 25301, '65–; Instr., Polit. Sci. Dept., Morris Harvey Col., '60–'61; PRSA, Theta Sigma Phi; Oh. State Univ., BA (Jnlsm.), '48; b. N.Y.C., 1925; h. Sherwin Steiger; c. Stephanie, James; res: 205 McKinley Ave., Charleston, W. Va. 25314.

STEIN, HANNAH, Exec. Dir., National Council of Jewish Women, Inc., 1 W. 47th St., N.Y., N.Y. 10036, '59–; Assoc. Dir., Zionist Org. of Am.; Bd. Dir., Am. Immigration Citizenship Conf.; Cncl. for Social Planning and Program Dev. of Nat. Assembly for Social Policy and Dev., Nat. Commty. Rels. Advisory Cncl., Nat. Fndn. for Jewish Culture, PRSA, Am. Jewish PR Soc., Nat. Conf. of Social Welfare, numerous other groups; St. Andrews Col., BA (Jnlsm.); Ravensfield Col.; Philathea College (Can.), LHD; Ecole Benedict; b. Germany.

STEIN, PATRICIA DAY, VP, Publr., Stein and Day, Inc., 7 E. 48th St., N.Y., N.Y. 10017, '62–; VP, Mid-Century Book Society, '59–'62; Barnard Col., '48; State Univ. of Ia., MA, '50; Univ. of Paris, Columbia Univ.; b. Villisca, Ia., 1926; p. Russell W. and Bernice King Day; h. Sol Stein; c. Robert, David, Elizabeth; res: Linden Circle, Scarborough, N.Y. 10510.

STEINBERG, BERNICE, Pres., Ani-Live Film Service, Inc., 45 W. 45th St., N.Y., N.Y. 10036, '54–; Academy Pictures, '53–'54; Tempo Prods., '52–'53; Paramount Pictures, '44–'52; NATAS; film ed. for numerous aw.-winning comml., '52–; Julliard Sch. of Music; h. Sidney Cooper.

STEINBERG, CAROL S., Art. Assoc., Scholastic Magazines, Inc., 50 W. 44th St., N.Y., N.Y. 10036, '68–; Mechanical Artists, '66–'68; aw., "Printing Promotes Progress," New Eng. Printers, '66; Boston Univ., BFA, '66; b. Newark, N.J. 1945; p. Joseph and Florence Kiell Steinberg; res: 55 W. 14th St., N.Y., N.Y. 10011.

STEINBERG, HATTIE MARIE, Jnlsm. Tchr., St. Louis Park Schools, 33rd & Dakota Sts., St. Louis Park, Minn. 55426, '63–; Neb. Schs. Tchr., '43–'62; Theta Sigma Phi, Am. Fedn. of Tchrs., BPW (Neb. State Pres., '50–'52, Nat. Secy., '54–'58), Freedom's Fndn. Tchr. medal, '53; Univ. of Neb. Tchr. aw., '62; Neb. State Tchrs. Col., BS, '37; Univ. of Minn., MA, '63; b. York, Neb., 1916; p. Paul and Effie Conway Steinberg; res: 2505 Nevada Ave., St. Louis Park, Minn. 55426.

STEINEM, GLORIA MARIE, Contrb. Ed., New York magazine, 207 E. 32nd St., N.Y., N.Y. 10016, '68–; Contrb. Ed., Glamour, '62–; Contrb. Ed., Curtis Publ., '64–'65; Contrb. Ed., McCall's; '66–'67; Wtr., "This is the Week that Was" (NBC-TV, '64–'65); Auth., "The Beach Book" (Viking Press, '63); AFTRA, Soc. of Mag. Wtrs., Wtrs. Guild of Am., Auths. Guild, NATAS; active in politics; Smith Col., BA, '56 (magna cum laude, Phi Beta Kappa); b. Toledo, Oh., 1936; p. Leo and Ruth Nuneviller Steinem; Agent: c/o Sterling Lord Agency, 660 Madison Ave., N.Y., N.Y.

STEINER, GLADYS FIST, Dir. of PR, Lester Harrison Advertising, Inc., 825 Third Ave., N.Y., N.Y. 10022, '46–; Fashion Group; Phi Kappa Phi, O'Henry aw.; Univ. of Wis., BA, '28; b. Pueblo, Colo., 1906; p. Adolph and Sophia Heilbronner Fist; h. Aaron B. Steiner; res: 340 E. 57th St., N.Y., N.Y. 10022.

STEINER, LEE R., Prodr., Modr., "Psychologically Speaking," WEVD, 1700 Broadway, N.Y., N.Y. 10019, '49–; "Make Up Your Mind," CBS, '53; "What Makes You Tick," ABC, '50; "How's Your Mental Health," WGN (Chgo., Ill.), '34; Lectr., Fordham Univ., Hunter Col., Rutgers Univ.; Assoc. Prof., Queens Col. Am. Psych. Assn., N.Y. State Psych. Assn., Acad. of Pysch. in Marital Counseling (founder); Oh. State aws. in radio, TV; Union. of Minn., BA, '24; Smith Col., MS, '29; b. Superior, Wis., 1901; p. Harry and Sarah Rabinowitz; h. Paul J. Gutenstein; Office: 45 W. 81st St., N.Y., N.Y. 10024.

STEINER, MONICA WILLIAMS, Wms. and Food Ed., Herald-Tribune and Sarasota Journal, 801 S. Tamiami Trail, Sarasota, Fla. 33578, '59–; Feature Wtr., Make-up Ed., Wms. Dept. Reptr., '55–'59; Fla. Wms. Press Club (Pres., '69–; Secy. 1st and 2nd VP, numerous awds.), Theta Sigma Phi, Cape Coral Press Club; Vest Aw., '64 (hon. mention, '65, '68); Oh. Northern Univ., Univ. of Fla., Fla. State Univ.; b. Venedocia, Oh., 1921; p. Edwin and Veronica Sever Williams; h. Franklin G. Steiner; c. Jane (Mrs. Wayne A. Boynton), Franklin William, William Henry; res: 1112 23rd St., Sarasota, Fla. 33580.

STEINER-PRAG, ELEANOR F., Free-lance Ed., Indexer; Ed., Directory, Special Libraries of Greater New York (12th ed., '70–'71); Ed., American Book Trade Directory, American Library Directory, R. R. Bowker Company, '56–'70; Rsch. Asst., Gen. William J. Donovan, '50–'56; Cataloger and Ref. Librn., Woodrow Wilson Meml. Lib., '45–'50; Cataloger and Ref. Librn., Off. of War Info. Lib., N.Y., '42–'44; Contributing Ed., '52–'53; Contributer, bibliographic and lib. work for Print. mag., New Haven and N.Y., '40–'51; Cataloger, Yale Univ., '40–'42; Exec. Secy., Intl. Collection of Modern Book Art, Prague, '34–'38; Bibliotheque Nationale, Paris, '33–'34; Am. Soc. of Indexers (Pres., '70–); Book Trade Sch., Grad., '23; Lib. Sch., Leipzig, '25; b. Bochum, Germany; p. Albert and Emmy Opdenhoff Fiesenberger; h. Hugo Steiner-Prag (dec.); res: 125 Christopher St., N.Y., N.Y. 10014.

STEINHEIMER, LEODA LOUISE, Owner, Crtv. Dir., Leoda Steinheimer Advertising, Suite 1106, Shell Bldg., 1221 Locus St., St. Louis, Mo. 63103, '51–; Exec. Asst., Copy Chief, Marjorie Wilten Adv., '48–'50; Adv. Dir., Rosenthal Ackerman Millinery Co., '45–'48; Adv. Dir., Mary Muffet, Inc., '44–'45; Prom. Mgr., Walk-Easy Foot Rest Mfg. Co., '43–'44; Prom. Mgr., Maritz Sales Builders, '37–'45; Wms. Adv. Club of St. Louis, AFA,; Who's Who of Am. Wm.; City Col., St. Louis; b. St. Louis, Mo.; p. Arthur Daniel and Della Hance Steinheimer; res: 4949; Wise Ave., St. Louis, Mo. 63110.

STEINKE, BETTINA, Artist; one-man shows, Okla. City, '68; Tulsa, Okla., '54; N.Y.C., '50; Curacao, N.W.I., '47; Wash., D.C., '43; Portraits for NBC (N.Y.C.), '38–'45; Illus. for Standard Oil Co. of N.J., Un. Fruit Co., Baldwin Piano Co.; Auth., N.B.C. Symphony Orchestra (bks. of portraits); Soc. of Illus.; Cooper Union Art, '30–'32; Phoenix Art Inst., '32–'35; b. Biddeford, Me., 1913; p. William and Alice Staples Steinke; h. Don Blair; res: Box 933, Taos, N.M. 87571.

STEINMAN, EDNA LOUISE, Dir. of Pubns., California State College, 5500 State College Pkwy., San Bernardino, Cal. 92407, '68–; Dir. of News, Pubns., Univ. of Redlands, '64–'68; Reptr., Albuquerque Journal, '60–'64; Reptr., American-News (Aberdeen, S.D.), '54–'60; Jnlsm. Instr., Univ. of Mo., '53–'54; Theta Sigma Phi (Albuquerque Chptr. Pres., '64), NFPW, N.M. Press Wm., Cal. Press Wm., ACPRA (Dist. Secy.); Who's Who Of Am. Wm.; Huron Col., '48–'50; Univ. of Mo., BJ, '53; res: 627 E. Cypress Ave., Redlands, Cal. 92373.

STEMMLER, HARRIET RAYMOND, Cnslt., Plastics and Packaging; Adv. Mgr., Plastics Div., Celanese Corp.; AWNY, Adv. Club of N.Y., Adv. Wm. of the Yr., '59; b. Bklyn., N.Y. 1900; p. Richard and Mary Herrmann Raymond; h. Arthur J. Stemmler; res: 568 Bird Key Dr., Sarasota, Fla. 33577.

STENHOLM, KATHERINE CORNE, Dir. of Unusual Films, Bob Jones University, Greenville, S.C. 29614, '50–; Chmn., Dept. of Cinema; Admr., Tchr., Stage Dir.; Keynote Speaker: Cannes Film Festival, Intl. Congress of Motion Picture and TV Schls. in Paris (U.S. Rep., '58); Dir. and Lead in numerous stage and opera prods.; articles in trade and pfsnl. periodicals; Soc. of Motion Picture and TV Engineers, Univ. Film Assn., Nat. Evangelical Film Fndn. (3 times Dir. of the Yr.); Personalities of the South; Who's Who of Am. Wm.; Bob Jones Univ., BA, '39; Northwestern Univ., MA, '49; Univ. of Southern Cal., '50; b. Hendersonville, N.C., p. George Few and Luvenia Heaton Corne; h. Dr. Gilbert Ralph Stenholm; c. Gilbert Ralph, Jr.; res: Bob Jones University, Greenville, S.C. 29614.

STENSON, BARABARA HISCOCK, TV News News Reptr., King Broadcasting Co., 320 Aurora Ave. N., Seattle, Wash. 98109, '65–; Reptr., Wenatchee Daily World, '64; Mng. Ed., Univ. of Wash. Daily, '64;

various organizations and aws.; Univ. of Wash., BA (Hist.), '64; b. Seattle, Wash. 1942; p. Frank and Barbara Burns Hiscock; h. George Alfred Stenson, Jr.; c. Eric Burns; res: 2033 34th Ave. S., Seattle, Wash. 98144.

STEPHAN, RUTH, Free-lance wtr.; Auth: "Various Poems ('63), "My Crown, My. Love" ('60), "The Flight" ('56), "Prelude to Poetry" (Peru, '46); Ed., "Spoken Anthology of American Literature, I & II (Univ. of Ariz., '62, '65), "The Singing Mountaineers" (Univ. of Tex., '57); Ed., Publr., The Tiger's Eye, '47-'50; Auths. League of Am., PEN; Founder, Ruth Stephan Poetry Ctrs., Univ. of Ariz., Univ. of Tex.; b. Chgo., Ill., 1910; p. Charles and Myrtle Norton Walgreen; h. John C. Franklin; c. Justin Dart, Jr., Peter Dart, John J. Stephan; res: Khakum Wood, Greenwich, Conn. 06830.

STEPHENSON, HELEN R., Supvsr., Consumer Printed Material, General Foods Corporation, 250 North St., White Plains, N.Y. 10602, '64-; PR Supvsr., Ketchum, MacLeod & Grove, Inc. (Pitt., Pa.), '51-'61; fiction, non-fiction articles in Esquire, Better Homes & Gardens, Editor & Publisher, others; Wtr., Ed., cookbks.; Wm's. Press Club of Pitt. (Aw. '58, '60, '61), NHFL; Sigma Delta Chi Golden Quill Aw., '60; Univ. of Pitt.; b. Pitt., Pa.; p. Charles E. and Ruth Bowers Gibson; h. George M. Stephenson; c. Rosalind Ruch, Karen (Mrs. Robert Burgess); res: 72 Honey Hill Rd., Wilton, Conn. 06829.

STEPHENSON, MARION, VP, Adm., Radio Div., National Broadcasting Company, 30 Rockefeller Plaza, N.Y., N.Y. 10020, '66-; VP, Adm., Radio Network, '62-'66; Dir., Bus. Affairs, Radio Network '59-'62; with NBC, '44-; Standard Oil Co. (N.J.), '43-'44; AWRT, Bdcst. Pioneers, IRTS; Marcus Nadler fin. aw.; Antioch Col., AB, '43; N.Y.U., MBA, '48; Bryant Col., DSc (Bus. Adm.), '63 (honoris causa); b. Green Bay, Wis., 1921; p. Marvin and Louise Ckyler Stephenson; res: 1352 Midland Ave., Bronxville, N.Y. 10708.

STEPHENSON, PATRICIA PETERS, Artist, Auth., Home Econst.; Co-auth., Illus., "Discovering Tucson" ('54); Auth., Illus., "Discovering Mexican Cooking" (Naylor, '58-); Tchr. (Tucson, Ariz.), '52-'55; Am. Home Econs. Assn., Cal. Home Econs. Assn.; 2,000 Wm. of Achiev.; Marquis Biog. Soc.; Univ. of Ariz., BS (Home Econs.), '51; b. Tucson, Ariz., 1928; p. Ivan and Wilma Croxen Peters; h. Roger E. Stephenson; c. Carol Ann, Roger, Jr., Brian; res: 19144 E. Puente, Covina, Cal. 91722.

STEPP, ANN WYANT, Ed., Employee Pubns., General Cable Corp., 730 Third Ave., N.Y., N.Y. 10017, '68-; N.Y. Assn. of Indsl. Communicators, ICIE, Soc. of Tech. Wtrs. & Publrs.; Tex. Christian Univ., BA (Jnlsm.), '66 (cum laude); b. Tulsa, Okla., 1944.

STERLING, DOROTHY, Auth. of 29 juv. bks. '50-; Edits bks. for Doubleday, Scholastic Bks., '68-; Rschr,

Life, Secy., The Architectural Forum, '36-'49; various orgs., aws.; Wellesley Col., '30-'32; Barnard Col., BA, '34; b. N.Y.C., 1913; p. Joseph and Elsie Darmstadter Dannenberg; h. Philip Sterling; c. Peter, Mrs. Anne Fausto; res: Kirby Lane North, Rye, N.Y. 10580.

STERLING, TISHA ANN, Actress, '63-; Social Work; Tchr. (N.Y.C.); Duchesne Sch. for Girls (N.Y.C.); b. L.A., Cal., 1945; p. Robert and Ann Sothern Lake Sterling; h. Lal Baum; res: 360 N. Camden Dr., Beverly Hills, Cal. 90210.

STERN, ARLENE, Free-lance Radio-TV Commentator and Jnslt.; Actress, film dubbing, '50-'60; Free-lance Corr. and Jnslt., Paris, '57-'62; Radio Commentator, Voice of Am., '65-, '55-'57; Radio Commentator, WOL, '54-'56; Mag. Ed., U.S.I.A., '52-'53; Feature Wtr., '50-'52; State Dept. Intern, '50; Free-lance Radio Actress, Cartoonist, Wtr., '48-'54; cartoons, colm., Christian Science Monitor; cartoon series for Treasury Savings Bond drive, '50; AWRT; Sears B. Condit Aw., '48, '49; Ford Aw., '48; Wm. of the Yr. Aw., '49; Northeastern Univ., BA, '49 (magna cum laude, alumni aw.); Leland Powers Sch. of Radio, TV and Theater; Stage Studio; b. Boston, Mass., 1928; p. Joseph and Gertrude Stern; h. Paul Bergman; c. Mark, Philip, Anne; res: 1805 Parkside Dr., N.W., Wash., D.C. 20012.

STERN, EDITH MENDEL, Free-lance Wtr., 301 G St. S.W., Wash., D.C. 20024, '27-; Special Cnslt., Nat. Inst. of Mental Health, '58-'61; Staff Wtr., Wms. Home Companion, '47-'51; Edtl., Knopf, '23, Liveright, '23-'27; Auth: "Mental Illness: A Guide for the Family" ('42; Fifth Edition, '68), "The Handicapped Child: A Guide for Parents" ('50); Co-auth., "You and Your Aging Parents" ('52; Second Edition, '65), many other bks., incl. fiction, pamphlets, more than 300 mag. articles, '28-; Lectr., '28-'39; Tchr., writing to mental health pfsnls.; various orgs. and aws.; Barnard Col., BA, '22; b. N.Y.C., 1901; p. Leon and Sadie Jacobs Mendel; h. William A. Stern, II; c. Monica Mary.

STERN, MADELEINE BETTINA, Partner, Leona Rostenberg—Rare Books, 152 E. 179th St., N.Y., N.Y. 10453, '45-; Auth: "Louisa May Alcott" ('50), "We the Women: Career Firsts of 19th Century America" ('63), "The Pantarch: A Biography of Stephen Pearl Andrews" ('68), other bks. and numerous articles on 19th-century biog. and Americana; Antiquarian Bksellers. Assn. of Am. (Gov., '66-'69); Guggenheim Fellowship, '43-'45; Barnard Col., BA, '32 (Phi Beta Kappa); Columbia Univ., MA, '33; b. N.Y.C., 1912; p. Moses and Lillie Mack Stern.

STERN, MIRIAM, Bus. Mgr., Composer Jimmy Van Heusen, '69-; Exec. Dir., Am. Guild of Auths. and Composers, '47-'49; Bus. Rd. Mgr., Sammy Kaye Orchestra, '41-'47; Copyright Circle Luncheon; Who's Who of Am. Wm.; b. Jersey City, N.J., 1912; p. Isador and Anna Van Doren Stern; res: 301 E. 69th St., N.Y., N.Y. 10021.

STEVENS, GEORGIANA GERLINGER, Polit. Corr., Atlantic Monthly and London Economist, 1641 Green St., S.F., Cal. 94123; Auth: "Jordan River Partition" (Hoover Inst., Stanford Univ., '65), "Egypt, Yesterday and Today" (Holt Rinehart, '63), "Jordan River Valley" (Carnegie Endowment, '58); Ed., "The United States and the Middle East" (Am. Assembly, '64); Exec. Secy., Middle East" (Am. Assembly, '64); Exec. Secy., Middle East Univ. Survey Commn., AID, '60; Rsch. Analyst, Dept. of State, '45–'46; Theta Sigma Phi, Middle East Inst. (Bd. of Govs., '60–'69); World Affairs Cncl. of Northern Cal. (Trustee); Berkeley (Univ. of Cal.) Fellow, '68; Univ. of Cal., AB, '26; b. Portland, Ore., 1909; p. George T. and Irene Hazard Gerlinger; h. Harley C. Stevens; res: 1641 Green St., S.F., Cal. 94123.

STEVENS, MURIEL GODOROV, Wms. Ed., The Muriel Stevens Show—Cookery and Conservation, KLAV Radio, 2634 State St., Las Vegas, Nev. 89109, '68–; Talent, Viewer's Digest, KSHO TV, '67–'68; Ed.-Wtr., Las Vegas Life, '65–'67; Prodr., Talent, Cookery Show, KLAS TV, '56; News Dept., KRAM Radio, '54–'56; AWRT (Nev. Chptr. VP, '69), Las Vegas Press Club, NLAPW; Univ. of Nev., Las Vegas, '60–'64; b. Phila., Pa. 1925; h. Maury Stevens; c. Robin Leslie, Bruce Allan; res: 3719 Central Park Circle, Las Vegas, Nev. 89109.

STEVENS, SARAH McNEAMER, Ed., The Mississippi Enterprise, 110 E. Monument St., Jackson, Miss. 39202, '34–; Typist, '33–; Owner, operated Ltr. Shop, '36–; Owner, Mgr., restaurant, '64–; Owner-Mgr., Stevens Enterprise, '64–'68; Staff Wtr., Daily Colm., Jackson Daily News, '66–; Notary Public, '53–; Iota Phi Lambda (Reg. Dir., '67–; Southwestern Reg., Outstanding Wm. of Yr., '58), active in hosp., Elks, ch., civic groups; cited, svc. to youth, Radio Sta. KOKJ, local Boy Scouts; cited, local Elks, svc. to public in commtn., '68; Henderson Bus. Col. (Memphis, Tenn.); b. Jackson, Miss.; p. John E. and Ida Bell King McNeamer; h. Willie Stevens; c. Dr. William McNeamer Harvey; res: 800 Woodrow Wilson Ave., Jackson, Miss. 39213.

STEVENSON, FLORENCE EZZELL, Artist, Lectr.; Exhibitor, numerous museums, one-man shows; former Head, Art Dept., Conservatory of Art and Music (Tuscaloosa, Ala.); NLSPW (aws., '45–'47); Am. Artists Pfsnl. League (N.Y.); Intl. Platform Assn., Am. Fedn. Wms. Clubs, Municipal Art League, All Ill. Soc. of Fine Arts (Gold Medal aw.); b. Russellville, Ala.; p. John and Laura Ezzell; h. Earle Dodds Stevenson; res: 9411 Longwood Dr., Chgo., Ill. 60620.

STEVENSON, GRACE THOMAS, Lib. Cnslt., Wtr.; Deputy Exec. Dir., Am. Lib. Assn. (Tucson, Ariz.), '52–'65; Dir., Am. Heritage Project (Ala.), '51–'52; Head, Adult Educ. Dept., Seattle (Wash.) Public Lib., '45–'51; Head, Pers. Dept., Hunter's Point Naval Shipyard (S.F., Cal.), '43–'45; Cnslt: U.C.L.A., Ariz. State Univ., San Diego Public Lib.; Auth.: "Arizona Library Survey" ('68), "A Proposed Reference Service for San Diego and Imperial Counties" ('69), numerous arti-

cles; Pacific N.W. Lib. Assn. (Chmn., Adult Educ. Sec., '41–'42), Adult Educ. Assn. (Nat. Pres., '57–'58), Pres. Comm. on White House Conf. on the Aging ('60–'61), Educ. Film Lib. Assn. (Distg. Service aw., '67); Mt. St. Joseph Col. (Ky.), '17–'19; Evansville Col. (Ind.), '19–'20; b. Morganfield, Ky., 1900; p. Lloyd P. and Martha Holbrook Thomas; c. Mary Ellen (Mrs. Harmon G. Harrison), Thomas C.; res: 2833 E. Malvern St., Tuscon, Ariz. 85716.

STEVENSON, JANET, Free-lance Wtr.; c/o Barthold Fles, 507 Fifth Ave., N.Y., N.Y. 10017; Auth: "Weep No More" (Viking Press), "The Ardent Years" (Viking); "Sisters and Brothers" (Crown); four biogs., one travel bk.; Auths. Guild of Am.; Nat. Arts of the Theatre aw., '51; John Golden Fellow, '38–'39; Bryn Mawr Col., BA, '33 (magna cum laude); Yale Univ., MFA, '37; h. Benson Rotstein.

STEVENSON, MARY PASCO CONRAD, retired; Librn., Clemson Univ., (Clemson, S.C.), '27–'68; Wtr., Illus., Rschr., non-profit orgs.; S.C. Lib. Assn., Southeastern Lib. Assn., S.C. Hist. Soc., Am. Assn. for State and Local Hist., Soc. of Am. Archivists, Un. Daughters of the Confederacy, Nat. Trust for Hist. Preservation, Nat. Genealogical Soc., Fndn. for Hist. Restoration (Pendleton, S.C., Bd. of Dirs.); Oberlin Col., '22–'23; Randolph Macon Wms. Col., BA, '24; Lib. Sch. of N.Y. Public Lib., Cert., '26; Am. Univ. of Nat. Archives Genealogical Rsch. Inst., Cert., '60; b. Harrisonburg, Va., 1902; p. George N. and Emily Pasco Conrad; h. James A. Stevenson; c. Emily, James C.; res: 103 Hillcrest Ave., Clemson, S.C. 29631.

STEVENSON, RACHEL WAPLES, Wtr., Prodr., International Film Bureau, 332 S. Michigan Blvd., Chgo., Ill.; Wtr., Prodr., Soc. for Visual Educ., '66–'69; TV Prodr., New Merritt Enterprises, '63–'64; TV Prodr., Dir., WTTW, '55–'64; Wtr., Prodr., ("Quiz Kids" program), Louis G. Cowan, '40–'55; Pioneer, TV for deaf children; Golden Mike aw., '61; Rice Univ., BA; b. Cody, Wyo.; p. Frank and Cora Riggs Waples; h. Allan Stevenson; c. Margaret Quinlan; res: 1018 N. State St., Chgo., Ill. 60610.

STEVES, GALE C., Home Econst., U.S. Dept. of Interior, Bureau of Commercial Fisheries, 110 E. 45th St., N.Y., N.Y. 10017, '69–; Edtl. Asst., Ladies' Home Journal, '66–'69; Instr., N.Y.U., '68; Am. Dietetic Assn., Am. Home Econs. Assn., Am. Public Health Assn., Omicron Nu (N.Y. Chptr. Pres., '69–'69); Cornell Univ., BS, '64; N.Y.U., MA, '66; b. Mineola, N.Y., 1942; p. W. Harry and Ruth May Steves; res: 345 E. 72nd St., N.Y., N.Y. 10021.

STEWART, BARBARA HOME, Prof., Lectr., Film Prodr., Nat. Audubon Soc., '69–'70; Lib. Rep., Ed., House Organ, J. B. Lippincott Co., E. Washington Sq., Phila., Pa. 19105, '66–; Dir., Pubcty., D. Van Nostrand Co. (Princeton, N.J), '63–'66; Assoc. Ed., Florida mag., '61–'63; PR, '60; Wtr., TV scripts, Sea Scope Prodns.,

'55–'56; Asst. Dir. PR, Miami Seaquarium, '54–'55; Assoc. Mgr., Fla. Building Journal, '53–'54; Owner, Ed., Publr., Newberry News, '48–'53; Sierra Club, Outdoor Wtrs. Assn. of Am., Phila. Bksellers Assn., Amer. Lib. Assn.; aw., '59; Univ. of Fla., BA, '52; b. St. Augustine, 1931; p. Peter and Lala Home Stewart; h. Orin Good Fogle (div.); res: 1517 Spruce St., Phila., Pa. 19102.

STEWART, CATHLEEN BRADY, Adv. & PR Mgr., American International Group, Inc., 102 Maiden Lane, N.Y., N.Y. 10005, '68–; Adv. Mgr., Nat. Union Ins. Cos., '65–'67; Ins. Adv. Conf. (numerous aws.); Muskingum Col., '64–'65; Univ. of Pitt., '65–'67; b. Pitt., Pa., 1946; p. Brady and Marjorie Stewart; res: 240 E. 35th St., N.Y., N.Y. 10016.

STEWART, EVELYN S., Info. Specialist, Berkeley Unified Sch. Dist., 1414 Walnut St., Berkeley, Cal. 94704, '64; Cal. Fair. Employment Practices Commn., '59–'60; Nwsp. PM (N.Y.C.), '43–'44; Wash., D.C., '42–'43; N.Y. World Telegram, '34–'35, '31–'32; Jnlsm. Tchr., N.Y.U., Sarah Lawrence Col. (Bronxville); Co-auth: "The Berkeley Story" (Anti-Defamation League, '69), "Now Is the Time" (Ind. Univ. Press, '69); Wtr., articles in nat. mags.; various orgs. and aws.; Mont. State Col., BS, '23; b. Maple Park, Ill., 1901; p. Thomas and Florence Whitney Seeley; h. Kenneth Stewart; c. Mrs. Gerald Ramsey, Stephen A.; res: 2124 Cedar Ave., Menlo Park, Cal. 94025.

STEWART, IDA CRAWFORD, VP, Mdsng., Estee Lauder, 767 Fifth Ave., N.Y., N.Y. 10022, '67–; Publicist, '61–'67; Coty, '59–'60; Ed. Dir., Bristol-Myers, '50–'59; Instr., Univ. of Md., '49–'50; Co-Auth., Illus., "Camp Counseling" ('50); AWNY (VP), AAUW, Fashion Group; Who's Who in Commerce and Industry; Who's Who in the East; Who's Who in Educ.; Winthrop Col., AB, '43; Univ. of Md., MA, '50; b. Clinton, S.C., 1922; p. J. Roy and Fannie Wade Crawford; h. Robert M. Stewart; res: 77 W. 55th St., N.Y., N.Y. 10019.

STEWART, JANICE LAND, Central Lib. Head, San Diego Public Library, 820 E St., San Diego, Cal. 92101, '63–; City Librn., Chula Vista, '51–'62; Gov. Ref. Lib., San Diego, '46–'47; Montgomery (Ala.) Public Lib., '46; Lieut., U.S. Navy Wms. Reserve, '42–'46; Bookmobile Librn. (Lorain County, Oh.), '41–'42; ALA, Cal. Lib. Assn. (Palomar Dist. Pres.), League of Wm. Voters, Altrusa Club (Pres.); Univ. of Akron, BA, '36; Western Reserve Univ., BS (Lib. Sci.), '40; b. Cuyahoga Falls, Oh., 1914; p. Arthur and Blanche Pryor Land; h. Frank Howard Stewart; c. Howard L., Janice (Mrs. John F. Genzale); res: 526 J St., Chula Vista, Cal. 92010.

STEWART, LINDA ASHTON, VP, Copywtr., Prodr., McCann Erickson, 485 Lexington Ave., N.Y., N.Y. 10017, '70–; Copywtr., Prodr., '67–; Copy Supvsr., Wtr., Grey Adv., '59–'64; Copywtr., BBDO; Auth., revue material for Julius Monk, off-Broadway; Andy aw., '65; Mademoiselle Mag. Col. Bd., '57; Brandeis

Univ., BA, '58 (cum laude); b. N.Y.C.; p. Hyman and Ruth Ryskind Ashton; h. (div.).

STEWART, LLOYD MAY, Wms. Ed., Fort Worth Star-Telegram, 400 W. 7th St., Ft. Worth, Tex. 76102, '63–; Reptr., Art Wtr., '49–'62; Reptr., Wichita Falls Record News; Marshall News-Messenger; Ed., Cleburne (Tex.) Times Review; Tex. AP Wms. News Writing Aw., '63; Theta Sigma Phi (Nat. Pres., '68–; VP, Pfsnl. Chptrs., '66–'68); Press Club of Ft. Worth; Univ. of Tex., BJ, '45; b. Port Arthur, Tex., 1924; p. Lloyd M. and May Cowart Stewart; res: 710 N. Main St., Cleburne, Tex. 76031.

STEWART, LOIS ANN, Mng. Ed., Management Services, American Institute of Certified Public Accountants, 666 Fifth Ave., N.Y., N.Y. 10019, '64–; Ed., Management Controls, '61–'63; Asst. Mgt. Ed., Business Week, '59–'61; Staff Wtr., PR, Am. Mgt. Assn., '51–'59; Asst. News Ed., Electrical World, '48–'51; Reptr., Lawton (Okla.) Morning Press, '47–'48; Edtl. Asst., Civil Engineering, '47; Reptr., Ames (Ia.) Daily Tribune, '44; Soc. Ed., Wadsworth (Oh.) News, '43; articles on bus., mgt.; OPC, Theta Sigma Phi (N.Y. Chptr. past Secy., Treas.); Ia. State Univ., BS (Hist.), '46 (Phi Kappa Phi, Sigma Delta Chi aw.); Columbia Univ. Grad. Sch. of Jnlsm., MS (Jnlsm.), '47; N.Y.U., MA (Econs.), '54; b. Albion, Mich., 1924; p. Lowell and Gladys Comfort Stewart; h. William Wolman; c. Ann; res: 508 Seventh St., Bklyn., N.Y. 11215.

STEWART, LUCILLE, Free-lance Wtr., Photogr.; Contrbr., nat. mags.; Nat. Press Photogrs. Assn., S. Cal. Press Photogrs. Assn., Gtr. L.A. Press Club, Pfsnl. Photogrs. of Am., Cal. Pfsnl. Photogrs., Professional Photogs. West, Soc. of Photo Optical Instrumentation Engineers; many aws., honors; b. L. A., Cal., 1913; p. John and Mattie Sowell Stewart; res: 4925 Edgerton Ave., Encino, Cal. 91316.

STEWART, LYNNE SALINAS, AE, Spade and Archer Inc., 320 Park Ave., N.Y., N.Y. 10022, '68–; AE, Chirug & Cairns, '66–'68; AE, Ashe & Englemore, '64–'66; Asst. Pubcty. Dir., Cone Mills Inc., '62–'64; Fashion Inst. of Tech., AAS, '62; N.Y.U., '63; French Inst., '66; b. Holbrook, N.Y., 1942; p. Adolfo and June Hall Salinas; h. Donald Stewart; res: 1160 Third Ave., N.Y., N.Y. 10021.

STEWART, MARIE McCAFFERTY, Exec. Dev. Dir., Edmundite Fathers and Brothers, 15 Allen St., Mystic, Conn. 06355, '63–; Tchr., 36 yrs.; Co-Auth., 10 Eng., Commtns. textbks.; Contrbr., pfsnl. journals; Nat. Bus. Educ. Assn., Eastern Bus. Educ. Assn., Conn. Bus. Educ. Assn. (Pres., '51); Who's Who of Am. Wm., Contemporary Auths.; Central Conn. Col., BA, '44; Univ. of Conn., MA, '48; PhD, '58; h. Samuel Stewart; c. Mrs. Eileen S. Bessette, Mrs. Maryann S. Bessette; res: Alpha Ave., Stonington, Conn. 06378.

STEWART, MARY LOVE, Crtv. Dir. and AE, Smith & Douglas Advertising, Inc., Suite 1102, 211 N. Ervay, Dallas, Tex. 75201, '67–; Copy Chief, AE, Rogers & Smith Adv. Agcy., '44–'67; Dallas Adv. League (Dir.,

'64–'66; Adv. Wm. of Yr., '63), Dallas Adv. Club (Secy.'Treas., '69–'71), Theta Sigma Phi (Dallas Chptr. Pres., '61–'62; Matrix Aw., '38, '64), AWRT, Gamma Alpha Chi, AAF; Who's Who of Am. Wm., Dic. of Intl. Biog.; Mary Stewart Adv. Aw. established at Tex. A & M Univ.; Tex. Wms. Univ., BS, '38; Grad. Sch., '41–'43; b. Graham, Tex.; p. Alonzo Douglass and Grace Haden Stewart; res: 3883 Turtle Creek Blvd., Dallas, Tex. 75219.

STEWART, ORA PATE, Lectr., National Artist and Lecture Service, 139 S. Beverly Dr., Beverly Hills, Cal., '53–; Auth., 22 bks., '34– (Several Bk. of Month, Bk. of Yr. Selections); Composer, 20 songs, incl. "To a Child," nat. Song of Am. Mothers of Yr., '69; World Poetry Soc., PSA, Ariz. State Poetry Soc., Ut. Poets, NLAPW (Hollywood Chptr. Pres., '68–'70), San Joaquin Wtrs. and Artists, ASCAP; Gold Medal, Intl. Poets' Shrine, '69; Cal. State Merit Mother of the Yr., '68; Nat. 1st Pl. aw., "Genealogy Book of Remembrance," '64; Philippine Chptr. Achiev. aw., Poets Laurate Intl., '69; numerous other writing aws.; Brigham Young Univ., '28–'30 (Alumni Aw., '67); Univ. of Ut., '43; b. Bates, Idaho, 1910; p. Ezra and Ada Sharp Pate; h. Col. Robert W. Stewart; c. Sharon (Mrs. Ray Nielson), Robert W., Jr., Janet (Mrs. Edward Geary), Allen Paul, David Grant, Glenda (dec.), Wendell Justin; res: 11282 Anabel Ave., Garden Grove, Cal. 92640.

STEWART, RAMONA, Auth: "The Surprise Party Complex" (William Morrow, '63), "Professor Descending" (Doubleday, '64), "A Confidence in Magic" (Doubleday, '65), "Casey" (Little, Brown, '68); Auths Guild; Univ. of Southern Cal., '38–'41; b. S.F., Cal., 1922; p. J. O. and Theresa Waugh Stewart; res: 535 Hudson St., N.Y., N.Y. 10014.

STEWART, VIRGINIA RUTH, VP, Robert E. Wilson Advertising Agency, 575 Lexington Ave., N.Y., N.Y. 10022, '59–; Dir. of Media, '52–'59; Dir. of Media and Prod. Mgr., '45–'52; Prod. Asst., Murray Breese Assocs., '44–'45; Clinic Mgr., Memorial Hosp., '42–'44; Asst. to the Ed., Jnl. of the Ia. State Med. Soc., '28–'42; AWNY, Pharmacuetical Adv. Club; Drake Univ., BA, b. Kan. City, Mo., 1908; p. Charles and Myrtle Anderson Stewart; res: 1700 York Ave., N.Y., N.Y. 10028.

STICHT, ELISE M., Assoc. Food Ed., Redbook, McCall Publishing Co., 230 Park Ave., N.Y., N.Y. 10017, '61–; Asst. Home Econst., Nat. Dairy Corp., '57–'61; Asst. Home Econst., Gertrude Lynn Home Econs. Cnslt., '52–'57; Asst. Home Econst., Penick and Ford, '50–'52; Am. Home Econs. Assoc., Home Econs. in Bus.; Pratt Inst., BS (Home Econs.), '48; b. Woodhaven, N.Y., 1926; p. Herman and Henrietta Lauterbach Stricht; res: 84-25 105th St., Richmond Hill, N.Y. 11418.

STICKLER, MYRA COLLIER, Area Ed., Sidney News, Sidney Printing and Publishing Co., 119 E. Court St., Sidney, Oh. 45365, '58–; Reptr., Piqua Daily Call,

'39–'57; Pubcty. Dir., Shelby County Am. Red Cross Oh. Nwsp. Wms. Assn.; Oh. Univ.; b. Sidney, Oh., 1911; p. William Parker and Martha Black Collier; c. David C., James D., Joseph C.; res: 306 N. West Ave., Sidney, Oh. 45365.

STIKA, ELAINE ANN, Adv. and Sls. Svc. Admr., Macwhyte Wire Rope Co., 2906 14th Ave., Kenosha, Wis. 53140, '66–; Asst. to Sls. Prom., Adv., PR. Mkt. Dir., '49–'65; Asst. to Mgr., Mkt. list Div., '43–'49; Mkt. Advisory Comm., Kenosha Tech. Inst., '67–; Assn. Indsl. Advs., Construction Equipment Advs., Kenosha Adv. Club (VP, '61–'62; Pres., '63–'64); active in civic orgs.; Kenosha Col. of Commerce, '43; Marquette Univ., '60; Univ. of Wisc., '63; De Paul Univ., '63; b. Kenosha, Wis., 1924; p. Alexander and Paulina Janota Stika, Jr.; res: 922 48th St., Kenosha, Wis. 53140.

STILLMAN, FRANCES JENNINGS, Free-lance Wtr., Ed., '45–; Assoc. Ed., Thomas Y. Crowell, '63–'64; Asst. Ed., '43–'45; Auth: "The Poet's Manual and Rhyming Dictionary" (Crowell, '66); "Oriental Love Poems" (Crowell, '50); Translator, "Flemish Tapestries" (Universe Bks., '66); Lectr., Hunter Col., '60–'66; Bklyn. Col., '64–'67; AAUW (N.Y.C. Br. VP, '61–'65); Univ. of Mich., AB, '31; AM, '32; b. Detroit, Mich., 1910; p. Harry and Esther Munger Jennings; h. E. Clark Stillman; res: 24 Gramercy Park, N.Y., N.Y. 10003.

STILLMAN, MYRA STEPHENS, Wtr., children's non-fiction; Tchr.; Librn.; Social Worker; Co-Auth: "Understanding Food" ('62), "Understanding Light" ('60), three other bks.; State Univ. of N.Y., AB, MA, '37; b. Albany, N.Y., 1915; p. Frank and Myra de Rouville Stephens; h. Nathan Stillman; c. Robert, Michael; res: 245 Unquowa Rd., Fairfield, Conn. 06430.

STILZ, ELIZABETH WALDFOGLE, Dir. PR & Sls. Prom., Cincinnati Symphony Orchestra, 1313 Central Trust Tower, Cinn., Oh. 45202, '68–; Dir. Prom. & Pubcty., WLWT, Avco Bdcst. Co., '63–'68; Mktng., Sls. Prom., KDKA TV, '61–'63; Dir., Adv. & Pubcty., Decorator Industries, '58–'61; Art Dir., Boggs & Buhl, '56–'58, '49–'51; PRSA, Theta Sigma Phi, AAF; Univ. of Pitt., '58–'63; b. Pitt., Pa., 1925; p. Albert and Loretta Miller Waldfogle; h. William R. Stilz; c. Fay Elizabeth, Patricia Jane; res: 56 Creekwood St., Cinn., Oh. 45246.

STINCHCOMB, BERNICE CARAWAY, Soc. Ed., Griffin Daily News, 323 E. Solomon St., Griffin, Ga. 30223, '61–; BPW (Spalding Club Pres., '67); Gordon Military Col., '58; b. Thomaston, Ga., 1938; p. J. D. and Annie Crane Carway; h. Donald J. Stinchcomb; c. James Jr.; res: 1314 S. Cherokee Ave., Griffin, Ga. 30223.

STINETORF, LOUISE A. (Emily Allender Wilson), Auth., fiction (juvenile, adult), biog., short stories for church sch. pubns.; Prof., Baptist Missionary Training Sch.; Am. Friends Svc. Comm.; b. 1900; h. Henry Loel Wilson (dec.); res: 2305 Harbor Point Dr., Celina, Oh. 45822.

STIPP, MARY FOX, Wms. Ed., Bedford Daily Times-Mail, 813 16th St., Bedford, Ind. 47421, '68–; '48–'51; Sch. Pg. Ed., '65–; gen. news, '65–'68; Asst. Proofreader, '59–'65; part-time gen. news, '55–'59; Beta Sigma Phi; b. Bedford, Ind., 1930; p. John and Elizabeth Bueter Fox; h. Robert Stipp; c. Robert G. II, Claudia Anne, John Kevin; res: 1903 I St., Bedford, Ind. 47421.

STITZ, JANE MARYLIN, Fashion Ed., Chicago Today, 441 N. Michigan, Chgo., Ill. 60611, '67–; Sls. Mgr., Asst. Byr., L. S. Ayres and Co., (Indpls.), '64–'67; Phi Mu, Theta Sigma Phi, Fashion Group; Purdue Univ., AB; Tobe-Coburn; b. Lafayette, Ind.; p. Ervin O. and Charlotte Moeller Stitz; res: 260 E. Chestnut, Chgo., Ill. 60611.

STOCH, ESTER, Controller, Spade and Archer Inc., 320 Park Ave., N.Y., N.Y. 10022, '67–; Asst. Controller, Carl Ally Inc., '64–'67; Controller, Bridal Modes, '63–'64; Asst. Controller, Belgium Stores Ltd., '60–'63; Bkkeeper-Secy., House of Stars, '59–'60; Typist-Cl., RCA Victor (Montreal, Can.), '54–'59; McGill Univ., '61–'63; b. Memel, Lithuania, 1937; p. Moses and Mary Hosiosky Stoch; res: 233 W. 77th St., N.Y., N.Y. 10022.

STOCKERT, HELEN, Dir. of Libs., Assoc. Prof., West Virginia Wesleyan College, Annie Merner Pfeiffer Library, Buckhanon, W. Va. 26201, '46–; Tchr., Librn., '24–'46; W. Va. Lib. Assn., ALA, AAUW, Tri-State Lib. Assn., Delta Kappa Gamma; W. Va. Wesleyan Col., AB, '23; Columbia Univ., BS (Lib. Sci.), '37; b. Buckhannon, W. Va.; p. John and Mary Jane Rexroad Stockert; res: 91 Elm St., Buckhannon, W. Va. 26201.

STOIANOFF, ELLEN ARDERY, Fiction and Poetry Ed., Mademoiselle, Condé Nast Publications, Inc., 420 Lexington Ave., N.Y., N.Y. 10017, '66–; Asst. Fiction & Poetry Ed., '64–'66; Secy. to Mng. Ed., '63; Nat. Soc. of Arts and Letters scholarship; Newcomb Col.; Am. Acad. of Dramatic Arts; b. Wash., D.C., 1937; p. William B. and Georgiana Weedon Ardery; h. Carroll B. Stoianoff; res: 285 Riverside Dr., N.Y., N.Y. 10025.

STOKES, PEG EWING, Dir., Dorothy Carnegie Course, Indiana Institute of Leadership Training, Marott Hotel, Suite 203, Indpls., Ind. 46208, '68–; Lectr., Redpath Lectr. Bur. (Chgo., Ill.), '65–; Town and Country Dir., Wilkings Music Co., '62; CCA Dir., WFBM-TV (Indpls.), '57–'60; Dir. of Med. Svc., Wright Field (Dayton, Oh.), '43–'45; Auth: "Think and Grow Slim" ('63), "I Am Anthony" ('61), "Out of the Darkness" ('51) and many nwsp articles; NLAPW (1st VP, '67–'68), Lakeland Humane Soc. (Dir. Emeritus), Theta Sigma Phi, WPC of Ind., NFPW; Gold Charm aw. ('68), Sterling Silver aw. ('68), Who's Who of Am. Wm.; Dir. of British and Am. Wtrs.; Conservatory of Music, South Bend, Ind.; h. Lyall Stokes; res: 3240 E. Fall Creek Pkwy. N. Dr., Indpls., Ind. 46205.

STOLZ, MARY SLATTERY, Wtr.; Auths. League, active in peace movements; New Col., Columbia

Univ.; b. Boston, Mass., 1920; p. Thomas F. and Mary Burgey Slattery; h. Thos. C. Jaleski, M.D.; c. William Stolz; res: 46 Bird Song Lane, Stamford, Conn. 06903.

STONE, BARBARA M., PR Supvsr., Consumer Products Division, Uniroyal, Inc., 53 Maple St., Naugatuck, Conn. 06770, '60–; Clerical Supvsr., '56–'60; Ed., Nauganotes (plant pubn.), '50–'56; Asst. Ed., '48–'50; Expeditor, '37–'48; Social Svc. Worker, Lincoln House, '32–'36; Albertus Magnus Col., '27–'29; Mary Baldwin Col., BA, '32; b. Bridgeport, Conn., 1901; p. Robert C. and Clara A. McAlenney Stone, Sr.; res: 109 Sunset Dr., Naugatuck, Conn. 06770.

STONE, CHARLOTTE BRIGHTMAN, W. Coast Ed., Discovery, Allstate Enterprises, Allstate Plaza, Northbrook, Ill. 60062, '56–; Contrb. Ed., Home and Highway, '52–'56; Edtl. Staff, Coronet, '50; Household Finance Corp., '51; Ladies' Home Journal, '45–'47; Mademoiselle, '45; Rsch. Analyst, Opinion Rsch. Corp., '40–'45; Theta Sigma Phi, Cal. Wtrs. Club; Syracuse Univ., AB, '37 (Phi Beta Kappa, Phi Sigma Phi); Columbia Univ., '38–'39; b. Greencastle, Ind., 1915; p. Charles and Charlotte Clarkson Brightman; h. Joseph K. Stone; res: 761 Spruce St., Berkeley, Cal. 94707.

STONE, HELEN VIRGINIA, Free-lance Wtr., Illus.; Auth., "Pablo the Potter" (Lantern Press, '69); Phila. Junto Wtrs. aw., '57; Pa. Governor's cit., '56; Pa. Acad. of Fine Arts, '38–'45; b. Phila., Pa.; p. Raymond and Eliza Olivit Stone; res: 6621 Blakemore St., Phila., Pa. 19119.

STONE, LINDA WRAY, Prom. Mgr., WUSN-TV, P.O. Box 879, Charleston, S.C. 29401, '67–; Wms. Dir., Talent, Prodr., Wtr., '67–; Prod. Asst., Wtr., Bernstein Adv., '66–'67; Copywtr., Prom., (talent, WCIV-TV, '65–'66; Resident Actress, Pocket Theatre, Atlanta Ga., '63–'64; Dancer, "The Good Morning Show," WSB-TV, '63–'64; Mu Rho Sigma, AWRT; "Miss Emmy" for NATAS, '61; Phoenix Jr. Col., '59–'61; Ga. State Col., '64–'65; b. Atlanta, Ga., 1941; p. Russell Wray and Bernice Wray States; h. Edward Stone; res: 20 31st Ave., Isle of Palms, S.C. 29451.

STONE, MARILYN MOORE, Wms. Pg. Ed., Poughkeepsie Journal, Memorial Sq., Poughkeepsie, N.Y. 12602, '68–; Cornell Univ., BA, '57; b. Albany, N.Y., 1935; p. Donald and Virginia Hall Moore; h. (div.); c. Andrew Roy Stone; res: 96 S. Hamilton St., Poughkeepsie, N.Y. 12601.

STONE, MILDRED F., Ed., Contrbr., house pubns., Mutual Benefit Life Insurance Co., 520 Broad St., Newark, N.J. 07101, '29–'67; Auth: "A Calling and Its College ('63), "The Teacher Who Changed an Industry" ('60), three other non-fiction bks.; several citizen aws.; Vassar Col., AB, '24 (Phi Beta Kappa); b. Bloomfield, N.J., 1902; p. Franklin and Ida Sarabrant Stone; res: 23 Clarendon Pl., Bloomfield, N.J. 07003.

STONE, MURIEL JUNE OBERSON, Media Dir., Jerry Della Femina & Partners, Inc., 635 Madison Ave., N.Y.,

N.Y. 10020, '68–; VP, Delehanty, Kurnit & Geller, Inc., '62–'68; Media Dir., Macmillan-Crowell-Collier, '61–'62; Media Supvsr., Kastor Hilton Chesley Clifford & Atherton, '57–'61; Media Rsch. Analyst, S.S.C.&.B., '55–'57; AWNY; City Col. of N.Y.

STONE, PEGGY, Exec. Vice-chmn. of Bd., H-R Representatives, Inc., 277 Park Ave., N.Y., N.Y. 10017, '69–; Pres., Stone Representatives, '47–'69; Bdcst. Sls., '44–'47; Spot Sales, Inc., '39–'44; Hearst Radio, '38–'39; Columbia Bdcst. Co., '29–'38; IRTS, Bdcst. Pioneers (N.Y. Chptr. Pres.); b. N.Y.C.; p. Charles and Anne Ross Stone; h. Leon S. Gilbert; c. Greta Beckhardt, Thomas E. Stone, Stephen Gilbert; res: 35 E. 35th St., N.Y., N.Y. 10016.

STONE, RUTH ANDRESS, Artist, painting, sculpture, glass and fiberglass constructions, other art; exhbns. incl: Laguna Beach Art Assn., '67, '68, '69; San Diego Art Guild, '67; City Art Museum (St. Louis, Mo.), many others; one-wm. shows; special commns. incl. stained glass; articles, Sch. Arts Magazine, other pubns.; teaching incls: Art, Southfield Sch., private classes, lect. demonstrations; numerous organizations and aws.; All Saints Col., '32–'33; Univ. of Mo., BFA, '35; b. St. Louis, Mo.; 1914; p. Harry R. and Ethel R. Davis Andress; h. Dean B. Stone; c. Mrs. Don Kneeburg, Mrs. Charles Smith, Alan; res: 14611 Emerywood Rd., Tustin, Cal. 92680.

STONER, DOROTHY CURTIS, Soc. Ed., Charles City Press, 100 N. Main St., Charles City, Ia. 50616, '61–; b. Rowan, Ia. 1916; p. Leon L. and Mabel Henry Curtis; h. Ross A. Stoner (dec.); c. Sybil Jeanne (Mrs. Paul Carter); res: 1002-1/2 Hulin St., Charles City, Ia. 50616.

STONESTREET, MARTHA McKEE, Ed., Vick Manufacturing Div., P.O. Box 22086, 100 Swing Rd., Greensboro, N.C. 27420, '66–; Charlotte Observer; Carolina Bus. Communicators (Pres., VP), S. Atlantic Cncl. Indsl. Eds. (Secy.); Jr. Achiev. media aw., '66–'67; Guilford Col., E. Carolina Univ.; b. Gastonia, N.C., 1942; p. Wilbur and Ola Price McKee; h. John M. Stonestreet; res: 4201 Bramlet Pl., Greensboro, N.C. 27407.

STOPPLE, AVIS BRYSON, Chief, Main Lib., San Francisco Public Library, Larkin & McAllister Sts., S.F., Cal. 19102, '63–; Librn., '35–'36; Head Librn., Santa Rosa Jr. Col., '56–'63; Coordr., Ins. Manual, Cal. State Dept. of Ins., '43–'44; Head Librn., Fire Underwtrs. Assn. of the Pacific, '36–'43; Tchr., Librarianship, Univ. of S.F.; Bk. Club of Cal., Cal. Lib. Assn., Gleason Lib. Assocs. (Pres.); Univ. of Cal. (Berkeley), AB, '34 (Hons. with Jr. Cert., '32); Lib. Sch. Grad., '35; Sch. Lib. Credential, '56; b. Portland, Ore., 1913; p. Richard and Rachel Bynon Bryson; h. Lee Lawrence Stopple; c. Mrs. Suzanne Weakley, Lois Eleanor; res: 2850 Steiner St., S.F., Cal.

STORER, FERN HARRIS, Food Ed., The Cincinnati Post and Times Star, 800 Broadway, Cinn., Oh. 45202, '51–; Home Econ. Cnslt., Family Svc.; Head of Dietary Dept., William Booth Memorial Hosp. (Covington, Ky.); Dietary Internship, Univ. Hosp. of Cleve.; HS Home Econs. Tchr.; Am. Home Econs. Assn., Home Econsts. in Bus., Am. Dietetic Assn., Theta Sigma Phi; numerous aws. for work in Home Econs.; Kan. State Univ., BS (Home Econs.), '28; Univ. of Cinn. Evening Col.; b. Osborne County, Kan., 1906; p. Edward Arthur and Lydis Catherine McNeal Harris; h. Sheldon Batchelder Storer; res: 1402 Highland Pike, Covington, Ky. 41011.

STORM, DORIS F., Sr. VP, Prodr., Guidance Associates, Harcourt, Brace & World, 757 Third Ave., N.Y., N.Y. 10017, '61–; Free-lance Prodr., Dir., Wtr., indsl., educ., comml. films, '49–'61; Dir., Prodr., WATV, '48–'49; SAG, AFTRA, Past Dem. Comm. Wm.; Am. Film Festival aws.; Bklyn. Col., BA (magna cum laude; Phi Beta Kappa); Julliard; b. N.Y.C., 1926; p. Manheim and Fannie Shafsky Rosenzweig; h. Frank Jacoby; c. Douglas Evan, Bruce Hale, Jeffrey Mann; res: 8 W. Branch Rd., Westport, Conn. 06880.

STOUT, VELMA CRITZ, Prod. Mgr., Edtl., Art in America, Inc., 635 Madison Ave., N.Y., N.Y. 10022, '67–; Assoc. Ed., '59–'67; Photo. Ed., AP, '37–'41; Pic. Ed., Des Moines (Ia.) Tribune, '33–'37; Edtl. Asst., Tchrs. Col., Columbia Univ., '31–'33; Instr., Rept., Univ. of Ia., '27–'30; Reptr., Cedar Rapids (Ia.) Gazette, '26–'27; OPC, Theta Sigma Phi; Who's Who of Am. Wm.; Univ., BA, '26, MA, '30; b. Riverside, Ia.; p. Sylvester and Louise Mentzer Critz; h. Edwin Stout (dec.); c. John; res: 240 W. 98th St., N.Y., N.Y. 10025.

STOUTENBURG, ADRIEN PEARL, Auth., 38 juv. books, '51–'68; two adult poetry vols., '64, '69; PSA (Edwin Markham Aw., '61; Michael Sloan Fellowship, '61), Auths. Guild; Lamont Poetry Aw., '64; Borestone Poetry Aws., '57, '60, '62, '65–'67; b. Darfur, Minn. 1916; p. Lace and Madeline Christy Stoutenburg; res: P.O. 291, Lagunitas, Cal. 94938.

STOVER, RUTH MILLER, Ed., House Organ, Indiana Blue Cross and Blue Shield, 110 N. Illinois St., Indpls., Ind. 46204, '68–; Copywtr., Davidson & Hardy & Assoc., '68; Ed., Bloomington (Ind.) Courier Tribune, '66–'68; Reptr., Kokomo (Ind.) Morning Times, '65–'66; Ind. Indsl. Eds. Assn. (nwsltr. aw., '68); b. Sparta, Tenn., 1942; p. John and Ova Mayfield Miller; h. Larry Stover (div.); c. Bryan Leslie, Trent Alan, Malea Lenore; res: Lot 196, Wheel Estates, Rte. 2, Greenwood, Ind. 46234.

STRAHLER, CLYTIE EVELYN, Assoc. Dir., University Libraries, Wittenberg University, Springfield, Oh. 45501, '68–; Asst. Dir., Chief of Reader Svcs., '67; Chief of Reader Svcs., '64–'67; Asst. Head Librn., '62–'64; Assoc. Prof. Lib. Sci., '54–; Coordr., pers. svcs., Dayton, Montgomery County (Oh.) Public Lib., '56–'62; lib. work, '25–'56; Cncl., Sinclair Col., '69–; ALA, AAUP (Local Chptr. Secy.), various others; Beta Phi Mu; Whittenberg Univ., AB, '34 (cum laude); Univ. of

Ill. Lib. Sch., BS (Lib. Sci.), '38 (with high hons.); b. Dayton, Oh., 1907; p. Ezra F. and Bertha Daniels Strahler; res: 5340 Brendonwood Lane, Dayton, Oh. 45415.

STRAIGHT, BEATRICE WHITNEY, Actress, Prodr., Chekhov Theatre, 156 E. 62nd St., N.Y., N.Y. 10021, '38–; Antoinette Perry aw. for part in Arthur Miller's "The Crucible" b. Old Westbury, N.Y., 1918; p. Willard and Dorothy Whitney Straight; h. Peter Cookson; c. Gary, Tony, Peter Jr., Brooksie.

STRAIN, PAULA MARY, Head Librn., Booz, Allen Applied Research, Inc., 4733 Bethesda Ave., Bethesda, Md. 20014, '68–; Tech. Librn., IBM Corp., Owego, N.Y., '60–'68; Sr. Rsch. Analyst, Lib. of Congress, Wash., D.C. '57–'60; Liaison and Collections Offcr., '48–'57; Librn., U.S. Navy Photographic Interpretation Ctr., '46–'48; U.S. Naval Reserve, '44–'46; Librn., U.S. Steel Corp., Pitt., Pa., '40–'44; Asst. Librn., Westminster Col., New Wilmington, Pa., '38–'40; John Cotton Danna Lectr., '70; auth., articles in pfsnl. jnls., papers at pfsnl. meetings; Co-auth., "A Directory of Special Libraries and Research Resources in New York State," '66; Special Libs. Assn. (Chptr. Pres., '67–'68; Div. Chmn., '68–'69); Bethany Col., AB, '37; Carnegie Inst. of Tech., BS (Lib. Sci.), '38; b. Brooke County, W.Va.; p. Paul and Margaret Evans Strain; res: Apt. 1201, 8315 N. Brook Lane, Bethesda, Md. 20014.

STRAKER, EASTER I., Wms./Commty. Svc. Dir., Northwestern Ohio Broadcasting Co., 223 N. Main St., Lima, Oh. 45801, '59–; Prog. Dir., WIMA Radio-TV, '49–'59; Asst. Prog. Dir., WIND (Chgo., Ill.), '45–'48; Prog. Dir., WSOY (Decatur, Ill.), '43–'45; Wms. Dir., '41–'43; Intl. Platform Assn.; LaSertoma Intl. Wm. of the Yr., '67; Northwestern Oh. Ad Club Silver Mike aw.; Sertoma Club Wm. of the Yr., '58; Ind. State Univ., AB, '39; MA, '40; b. Lima, Oh., 1918.

STRANDHOLM, SHIRLEY BAKER, Comml. Mgr., AE, Cont., Talent, KWKY, 419 Locust, Des Moines, Ia. 50322; Wms. Adv. Club (Secy., '64), AWRT, (Secy., '66), Am. Bus. Wms. Assn., AFA; b. Cambridge, Ia 1918; p. M. H. and Vera Baker; h. Robert Strandholm; c. Mrs. Max Fogel, Mrs. Rex Walker; res: 8602 Urbandale Ave., De Moines, Ia. 50322.

STRASSER, ROBIN LOBLE, Prom. Copywtr., Cahners Publishing Co., 5 S. Wabash Ave., Chgo., Ill. 60603, '69–; Copy-wtr., Continental Assurance Co.; Edtl. Asst., Dartnell Publ. Co.; Copywtr., Continental Casualty Co.; Chgo. Soc. of Communicating Arts, Indsl. Eds. Assn. of Chgo. (Secy., '69–'70); Drake Univ., BA, '50; b. Chgo., Ill., 1929; p. Arthur and Elizabeth Van Gelder Loble; h. Edgar Strasser; c. Deborah, Barbara, Lawrence; res: 1529 W. Touhy Ave., Chgo., Ill. 60626.

STRASSMAN, TONI, Owner, Toni Strassman Agcy. (auths. rep.), 130 E. 18th St., N.Y., N.Y. 10003; N.Y.U.; Univ. of Ariz.; New Sch.; b. N.Y.C.; p. Joseph and Pauline Gottlieb Strassman; res: 130 E. 18th St., N.Y., N.Y. 10003.

STRASSMEYER, MARY, Soc. Ed., The Plain Dealer, 1801 Superior Ave., Cleve., Oh. 44114, '65–; Travel, Beauty Ed., '63–'65; Feature Wtr., '60–'65; Schs. Wtr., Cleve. News, '58–'60; Co-creator, "Sneakers" teenage panel (King Features Synd., '64–); Theta Sigma Phi, Kappa Gamma Pi, Soc. of Am. Social Scribes (Founder, '69); Notre Dame Col., AB, '51 (cum laude); Toledo Univ.; res: 2110 Broadview Rd., Cleve., Oh. 44109.

STRATEMEYER, HARRIET (pseuds: Carolyn Keene, Laura Lee Hope, Franklin Dixon, Helen Louise Thorndyke, Ann Sheldon) Stratemeyer Syndicate 519 Main St. East Orange, N.J. 07018; Auth., 120 juv. bks.; h. Russell V. Adams (dec).

STRAUSS, HELEN MARION, VP, Universal Pictures, Exec. Asst. to Jennings Lang, Universal City Studios, Inc., Universal City, Cal. 91608, '68–; VP, World Wide Story Operations, Warner-Bros.-Seven Arts, '67–'68; Lit. Dept., William Morris Off., '44–'67; Columbia Univ.; b. N.Y.C., 1914; p. Edward and Josephine Kahn Strauss; res: 1043 Maybrook Dr., Beverly Hills, Cal. 90210.

STRAUSS, LUCILLE JACKSON, Chemistry, Physics Librn., Pennsylvania State University, 303 Whitmore Laboratory, University Park, Pa. 16802, '48–; Tchr., '48–; Librn., Rsch. & Dev. Lab., Vanadium Corp. of Am. (Bridgeville); Co-auth., two textbks.; Am. Chemical Soc., Special Libs. Assn. (Achiev. aw., '64), AAUW, Am. Soc. for Info. Sci., Iota Sigma Pi (Palladium Chptr. Pres., '50–'51), Sigma Delta Epsilon; Chatham Col., BA, '30 (cum laude); Pa. State Univ., MS, '31; b. Pitt., Pa., 1908; p. Robert and M. Elizabeth Kreimendahl Jackson; h. Jerome Strauss; res: 520 W. Nittany Ave., State College, Pa. 16801.

STRAUSS, SALLY BANKS, Mng. Ed., The Counselor Magazine, Advertising Specialty Institute, N.B.S. Building, Second and Clearview Ave., Trevose, Pa. 19047, '68–; Assoc. Ed., '67–'68; Theta Sigma Phi; Syracuse Univ., BS (Jnlsm., Bus. Adm.) '67 (Vedder Fdn. Aw.); b. Bronx, N.Y., 1945; p. Norman and Betty Harris Banks; h. Melvin Strauss; res: 532 Harbour Dr., Salem Harbour, Andalusia, Pa. 19020.

STRECK, SR. HELEN, Head Librn., Sacred Heart College, 3100 McCormick St., Wichita, Kan. 67213, '66–; Tchr., '60–'66; Academic Dean, '56–'60; ALA, Beta Phi Mu; Friends Univ., BA; Wichita State Univ., MA; Rosary Col., MA (Lib. Sci.).

STREET, JULIA MONTGOMERY, Auth. of six hist. juvs., stories, poems, articles, '36–; Tchr., public schs., Univ. of N.C. at Greensboro, '18–'24; various orgs. aws.; Univ. of N.C., AB, '23; b. Concord, N.C. 1898; p. Samuel and Elizabeth Norris Montgomery; h. Claudius A. Street; c. Carol (Mrs. Archibald McMillan), Claudius A., Jr.; res: 545 Oaklawn Ave., Winston-Salem, N.C. 27104.

STREETER, MARJORIE MALCOLM, Free-lance

Wtr.; Ed., Designer, Crossbeat mag. (Australia), '65–'66; Ed., Univ. Pubns,, Columbia Univ. (N.Y.C.), '54–'64; Bard Col., Columbia Univ.; b. N.Y.C., 1934; p. MacKay and Louise Bailey Malcolm; h. Robert Streeter (div.); c. Wendy; res: 34 Huntting Dr., Dumont, N.J. 07628.

STREISAND, BARBRA JOAN, Actress, c/o Martin Erlichman Assocs., Inc., 677 Fifth Ave., N.Y., N.Y. 10022; Hollywood Fgn. Press Assn. Golden Globe aw., Best Actress, '69; Oscar, Best Actress, "Funny Girl," '68; Peabody aw., '66; Emmy, "My Name Is Barbra," '65; Grammy Aws: Best Solo Vocal Performance, '63, '64, '65; Album of the Yr., '63; N.Y. Critics Poll, Best Supporting Actress, '62; numerous other acting, singing aws.; b. Bklyn., N.Y., 1942; p. Emanuel and Diana Rosen Streisand; h. Elliott Gould; c. Jason Emanuel.

STRELSKY, KATHARINE ANDERSON, Auth.; Ed., Harvard Center for Intl. Affairs, '67–'68; Fellow, Radcliffe Inst., '63–'65; Asst. Ed., Daedalus, '58–'63; Asst. Ed., Isis, '54–'58; Translator, "The Notebooks for 'The Idiot' " ('68); Auth., poems, bk. revs., articles; Who's Who of Am Wm., Who's Who in the East; Who's Who in Commerce and Industry; Univ. of Rochester, AB, Columbia Univ., '35 Univ. of Florence, '49; b. Rochester, N.Y.; p. Willis and Maud Harrington Anderson; h. Nikander Strelsky (dec.); res: 19 Everett St., Apt. 5, Cambridge, Mass. 02138.

STRICKLAND, MILDRED GRISWOLD, Ed., Field Publications, The Columbus Mutual Life Insurance Company, 303 E. Broad St., Columbus, Oh. 43215, '64–; Asst. Ed., '62–'64; Ed., Ohio Architect, Architects Soc of Oh., '61–'62; Edtl. Asst., int. employee mag., Columbus and Southern Oh. Electric Co., '59–'61; Central Oh. Bus. and Indsl. Eds. (Pres., '66; VP, '65; Secy., '64); All-Ohio Indsl. Eds. Competition: 1st Pl., '64; 2nd Pl., '65; Bowling Green State Univ., '56–'58; Columbus Col. of Art and Design, '60–'62; b. Painesville, Oh., 1938; p. Gerald P. and Glenadore Brockway Griswold; h. William Strickland; c. Valerie Lynne; res: 2357 Joyce Ave., Columbus, Oh. 43211.

STRICKLER, JOAN MULHOLLAND, Wtr.; Dir. of Pubcty., PR, Federation for Handicapped Children, Riley County Assn. for Retarded Children; Kan. Assn. for Retarded Children (3rd VP; Ed., Tracks), Theta Sigma Phi, Cncl. for Exceptional Children; Outstanding Young Wm.; Who's Who of Am. Wm.; Univ. of Mo., BJ, '57; b. St. Louis, Mo., 1935; p. Edward and Constance Libby Mulholland; h. John Strickler; c. John Edward, Carole Jean; res: 1523 University Dr., Manhattan, Kan. 66502.

STRINE, N. LORRAINE SMITH, Controller, The Herald-Mail Company, 25–31 Summit Ave., Hagerstown, Md. 21740, '44–; Inst. of Nwsp. Controller and Finance Offcrs.; b. Hagerstown Md., 1925; p. Paul and Lillie Shry Smith; h. Charles Strine; c. Charles William, Jr.; res: 328 Devonshire Rd., Hagerstown, Md. 21740.

STROBEL, JUDY STRECKER, Publr., Protection Post, 458 N. Broadway, Protection, Kan. 67127, '49–; Kan. Press Assn., Bucklin BPW (Pres., '68–'69), Kan. Fed. of Press Wm.; b. Barada, Neb., 1927; p. Charles and Julia Schawang Strecker; h. Orin Strobel; c. Susan (Mrs. Myron Edmonston), Sally (Mrs. Michael Robinson), Nancy (Mrs. Richard Trease), Steven, JoAnn; res: Front St., Bucklin, Kan. 67834.

STROH, LINDA, Wms. Ed., The Daily Report, 212 E. B. St., Ontario, Cal. 91764, '62–; Asst. Wms. Ed., Soc. Ed., Food Ed., '60–'62; Delta Psi Omega; Chaffey Col.; b. Upland, Cal., 1939; p. Conrad H. and Naoma Keplinger Stroh; res: 541 W. Flora #19, Ontario, Cal. 91762.

STROM, INGRID MATHILDA, Assoc. Prof. of Eng. Educ., Indiana University, Bloomington, Ind. 47401, '44–; Tchr., '37–'42; Who's Who of Am. Wm.; Univ. of Minn., BE, '35, MA, '44, PhD, '55; b. Duluth, Minn., 1912; p. John and Mary Gragg Strom; res: 3801 E. Third St., Bloomington, Ind. 47401.

STROMBERG, MARJORIE THERESA, Exec. Asst.; Mbr., Plans and Opns. Bd., Pacific National Advertising Agency, 217 Sixth Ave. N., Seattle, Wash. 98109, '57–; Exec. Secy. to Bd. Chmn., '52–'57; Seattle Adv. and Sls. Club; Univ. of Wash., '41–'43; Seattle Univ. '44; b. Seattle, Wash., 1923; p. George and Agatha Gibbons Stromberg; res: 1912 N.E. 113th St., Seattle, Wash. 98125.

STRONG, HOPE JOHNS, Wms. Ed., The Lima News, 121 E. High St., Lima, Oh. 45802, '55–; former Reptr., Social Wtr.; AAUW, Allen County Hist. Soc., Lima Art Assn.; First Spadea Fashion Aw., '55; J. C. Penney-Univ. of Mo. aw., '63; Miami Univ., '48–; b. Lima, Oh., 1924; p. William and Mildred Rafay Johns; h. James W. Strong; res: 1509 Lakewood Ave., Lima, Oh. 45805.

STROUD, ELIZABETH MITCHAM, Asst. Secy.-Treas., Goldsboro News-Argus, Wayne Printing Co., Inc., 116 N. James St., Goldsboro, N.C. 27530, '63–; Inst. Nwsp. Controllers and Fin. Offcrs., Pilot Club Intl. (VP, Treas.); Louisburg Col., Atlantic Christian Col.; b. Goldsboro, N.C.; p. William and Irene Bowden Mitcham; h. Charles H. Stroud; c. C. Mitcham, James R; res: 1015 Evergreen Ave., Goldsboro, N.C. 27530.

STROUD, MYRA JAMES, Free-lance Wtr.-PR Cnslt., '58–; Staff Reptr., Boxoffice Weekly, '64–; Exec. Dir., Nat. Assn. of Theatre Owners, Mo., Ill., '49–'58; Adv., Pubcty., Prom., Fanchon and Marco Theatres, '39–'49; Wms. Adv. Club of St. Louis, AAF; St. Louis Univ.; b. Red River Parish, La., 1916; p. J.B. and M.E. Harris Stroud; res: 4209 Ellenwood Ave., St. Louis, Mo. 63116.

STROWBRIDGE, CYNTHIA COX, Free-lance Wtr., Ed.; Co-auth., "A Feast of Flowers" (Funk & Wagnall,

'69); Assoc. Ed., Bernard Geis Assocs.; Asst. Ed., Prentice Hall; News Ed., Wms. News Svc.; News Ed., Glenview Announcements; Miami Univ. (Oh.), BA, '54 (summa cum laude, Phi Beta Kappa); Columbia Univ., MS (Jnlsm.), '56; b. Cinn., Oh., 1932; p. Vincent and Frances Wakefield Cox; h. Clarence Strowbridge; c. Benjamin; res: 7 McBride Ave., White Plains, N.Y. 10603.

STRUPP, SYLVIA DEAN, News Ed., The Mt. Vernon Democrat, 430 Main St., Mt. Vernon, Ind. 47620, '67–; News Reptr., '66–'67; nwsp. adv. sls., '63–'64; retailing, '57–'65; Tchr., private art classes; Ind. Univ., '57–'58; Univ. of Evansville, '59–'62 (Kappa Pi, Secy., '61); b. Evansville, Ind., 1939; p. Harold E. and Ama Lee Hunt Strupp; res: RR 2, Box 274 Caborn Rd., Mt. Vernon, Ind. 47620.

STUART, CONSTANCE CORNELL, Staff Dir. to Mrs. Richard Nixon, White House, Wash., D.C., '69–; PR Supvsr., C & P Telephone Co., '69; Prod. Supvsr., Film-CCTV American Telephone & Telegraph (N.Y.C.), '67–'69; AE, Vic Maitland & Assoc., '64–'67; AE, Phil Dean Assoc., '62–'64; Asst. Instr. Speech Dept., Univ. of Md., '60–'62; Univ. of Md., BA, '60 (Hon. Grad.; Hale Aw. for dramatics; Sorority Wm. of the Yr., '59; W. Va. Forest Festival Queen, '59; Queen of Queens, '57; Univ. of Md. Gtr. N.Y. Alumni Assn. (Bd. of Dirs.), Kappa Kappa Gamma (N.Y. Alumnae Assn. past Pres.); b. Wheeling, W. Va., 1938; p. Vernon Everett and Ada Kathleen Bellis Cornell; h. Charles Edward Stuart; res: 9801 Mill Run Dr., Gt. Falls, Va. 22066.

STUART, DONNA, Bdcst. Dir., M. M. Fisher Associates, Inc., 180 N. Michigan Ave., Chgo., Ill. 60601, '57–; Wms. Adv. Club; Univ. of Ill.

STUART, JOAN SHULINDER, Actress; Pres., JS Enterprises, 210 E. 73rd St., N.Y., N.Y. 10021, '63–; Fashion Dir., Abraham & Straus, '53–'63; Prof., Lectr., Pratt Inst., '53–'67; AWNY, Fashion Group, AFTRA, SAG; Antioch Col.; h. Clement M. Stuart; res: 24 W. 55th St., N.Y., N.Y. 10019.

STUART, NEAL GILKYSON, Fiction Ed., Redbook, 230 Park Ave., N.Y., N.Y. 10017, '65–; Text Ed., Life Bks., '63–'65; Assoc. Ed., Ladies Home Journal, '55–'63; Ed., Wms. Pg., Portland (Ore.) Journal, '54–'55; Smith Col., AB, '42 (Phi Beta Kappa; summa cum laude); Columbia Univ.; b. Mont Clare, Pa., 1920; p. Hamilton and Phoebe Hunter Gilkyson; c. Alfred Jr., James G., Leila B.; res: 1133 Park Ave., N.Y., N.Y. 10028.

STUBER, IRENE M., Mng. Ed., Dania Press/Broward Newsday, P.O. Box 187, Dania, Fla. 33004, '69–; Staff Wtr., Ft. Lauderdale (Fla.) News, '67–'69; Staff Wtr., Hollywood (Fla.) Sun Tattler, '66–'67; Pubns. Dir., Miami-Dade C. of C., '63–'65; Ed., Par mag., '61–'63; Fla. Wms. Press Club, Theta Sigma Phi, Miami Adv. Club, BPW; Fla. AP public svc. aw., '68; Cleve. Col.; b. Cleve., Oh., 1928; h. (div.); c. three.

STUCKERT, BEATRICE STACKHOUSE, Dir., Haddonfield Public Library, Hadden and Tanner Sts., Haddonfield, N.J. 08033, '46–; Page, Asst. Lib. Dir., '30–'46; ALA, N.J. Lib. Assn., Lib. PR Assn. of Gtr. Phila., ZONTA (Gtr. Camden Pres., '60–'62), Intl. Platform Assn.; State Tchrs. Col., '30–'34; b. Camden, N.J.; p. LeRoy and Myrtle Warner Stackhouse; c. Susan (Mrs. Rodger J. Watson); res: 265 Hawthorne Ave., Haddonfield, N.J. 08033.

STUDER, LILLIAN ROSS, Pres., Irving Studer, Inc., 347 Madison Ave., N.Y., N.Y. 10017, '69–; Copy Supvsr., Robert A. Becker, Inc., '66–'69; Copy Chief, Mohr & Co., '63–'66; AWNY, Copy Club, Soc. of Photogrs. and Artists Reps.; Univ. of Pitt., BA, MA; b. Pitt., Pa.; p. Harry and Ida Barmen Rosenberg; h. Irving Studer; res: 305 E. 24th St., N.Y., N.Y. 10010.

STUDER, ROSEMARIE, Mgr. of Bdcst. Svcs., Ohio Education Association, 225 E. Broad St., Columbus, Oh. 43215, '66–; PR, Ohio Univ., '65–'66; Traf., Cont., and Prom. Mgr., Fla. Atlantic Univ., '64–'65; Secy. and Rschr., Broadcasting Magazine, '61–'63; Cont. Executor, WTTG TV, '60–'61; AWRT (Columbus Chptr. Secy., '69), NATAS; Univ. of Tenn., BA, '60; Oh. Univ., MS, '66; b. Evansville, Ind., 1938; p. Dr. S. N. and Gladys E. Studer; res: 626 Mohawk St., Columbus, Oh. 43206.

STUMBOUGH, VIRGINIA CARTER, Sr. Rep., Field Enterprises Educational Corp., Box 113, Cascade, Colo. 80809, '62–; Ed., Curriculum Units, Chgo. off., '51–'52; Free-lance Wtr., '30–; Columst., Feature Wtr., Gazette Telegraph (Colorado Springs, Colo.), '57–'59; Lang. Arts Ed., Soc. Visual Education (Chgo.), '53); Mgr., Evanston Book Store, '50; Music Dir., Owner, nursery schs., '31–'40; Auth: two books; textbook units, Scott Foresman, Wilcox and Follett; articles, stories, and poems in 50 pubns.; Theta Sigma Phi (Colo. Springs Club. Founder, '61; Nat. Cits., '60, '61), Children's Reading Round Table (Chgo. Pres., '52–'53; Colo. Springs Chptr. Founder, '64), Poetry Fellowship; Okla. City Univ., '26–'28; Univ. of Missouri, BJ, '30; Northwestern Univ., '32; Univ. of Okla., MA (Jnlsm.), '33; b. Shawnee, Okla. 1910; p. Charles and Cosette Keegan Carter; h. Harold D. Stumbough; c. John, Galen, Mrs. Gene Nora Jessen.

STURGES, JOANNA CARROLL, Space Salesman, New York magazine, 207 E. 32nd St., N.Y., N.Y. 10016, '67–; Corr. with Fgn. Students, Am. Field Svc., '63–'65; Moreland Commn. on Welfare, '61–'63; Bennett Col., '57–'59; Villa Mercede (Florence, Italy), '59–'60; Am. Theater Wing, '60–'61; b. N.Y.C., 1939; p. John and Alice Schumacher Sturges; res: 305 E. 72nd St., N.Y., N.Y. 10021.

STURGIS, GLADYS MARIE, Rschr., The Afro-American Bibliographic Researcher, 3344 Lucas Hunt Rd., St. Louis, Mo. 63121, '67–; Bibliographer, The Soc. of African Am. Studies, '67–'69; Librn. and Specialist in Negro works, Xavier Univ., New Orleans, '61–'67; Black Studies Cnslt., '68–; published bibliographies: "The Black Experience in Books" for The Soc. of Afro-American Studies, "School Desegregation: A Selected Bibliography" for La. Lib. Assn. Bulletin; "The Professional Guide to the Afro-American in Print: A Bibliography of Current Works by and About the Black Man in America" for The Afro-American Bibliographic Researcher; Chmn., The Soc. of Afro-Am. Studies, '67–'69; ALA, NAACP, Nat. Urban League, AAUW, NEA, Alpha Kappa Mu, Black Studies and Book Clubs; Dir. of Resources on Race, '70; Piney Woods Jr. Col, AA, '54 (salutatorian); Stillman Col., AB, '56 (magna cum laude); Univ. Sch. of Lib. Sci., MS (Lib. Sci.); b. Crystal Springs, Miss.; p. Ples and Annie B. Jenkins Sturgis; c. Josye Maria Sadler.

STURM, EVELYN CALVER, Licensed Pers. Cnslr., Plaza Personnel Service, Inc., 22 West Madison, Suite 226, Chgo., Ill. 60602, '69–; PR, Ill. Soc. Prevention Blindness, '62–'68; Interviewer and prog. prod., FM Radio, '61–'62; PR, own agcy., '56–'61; Welfare PR Forum (1st VP, '68; Secy. of Bd., '67), Indsl. Eds. Assn. of Chgo. (VP, '68–'69; Secy. of Bd., '66–'67), Ill. Council Vol. Health Agencies (Charter Mbr.; Bd. of Dirs., '66, '67, '68), Pubcty. Club of Chgo.; Helen Cody Baker aws: annual rept. brochure, '66; 28 min. color film, '67; Northwestern Univ.; b. Beverly, N.J., 1910; p. Curtis and Georgia Sundstrom Calver; h. Myron A. Sturm; c. Richard P., Mrs. Perry Smith; res: 277 South Grace, Elmhurst, Ill. 60126.

SUBA, SUSANNE, Free-lance Wtr., Illus.; Auth., Illus., "The Man With the Bushy Beard" ('69); Illus., 150 bks.; paintings in permanent collections of Met. Museum of Art (N.Y.C.), Art Inst. of Chgo., Bklyn. (N.Y.) Museum; Art Dirs. Club of N.Y.; Pratt Inst.; b. Budapest, Hungary; p. Miklos and May Edwards Suba; res: 1019 Third Ave., N.Y., N.Y. 10021.

SUBOTNIK, NADINE, Entertainment Ed., Cedar Rapids Gazette, 500 Third Ave., SE, Cedar Rapids, Ia. 52406, '41–; Proofreader, '40; Coe Col., BA, '38 (magna cum laude); b. Cedar Rapids, Ia., 1915; p. Abe and Anna Goldstein Subotnik; res: 907 Ninth St. SW., Cedar Rapids, Ia. 52404.

SUEDKAMP, HARRIET GRAVES, Dir of Pubcty., St. Paul Dispatch and Pioneer Press, 55 East Fourth St., St. Paul, Minn. 55101, '63–; Northwestern Indsl. Eds. Assn. (Employee Nwsp. aw., '67, '68), Theta Sigma Phi, Phi Upsilon Omicron; Ia. State Univ., BS, '40; b. Ames, Ia., 1917; p. George and Mattie Johnson Graves; h. (div.); c. Stephen, Stanley, Stuart, Stafford, Stacey, Sherwin, Susan, Sarah (Mrs. James Eral); res: 1445 Wilson Ave., St. Paul, Minn. 55106.

SUHRHEINRICH, JEANNE BEELER, Entertainment Ed., The Evansville Courier, 201 N.W. Second St., P.O. Box 268, Evansville, Ind. 47705, '55–; Univ. of Evansville; b. Evansville, Ind. 1919; p. Jerome and Helen Tucker Beeler; h. Robert Louis Suhrheinrich; c. Robert Jerome, Jerry William; res: 700 S. Norman Ave., Evansville, Ind. 47714.

SUITT, EUNA LOWE, Wtr., Arkansas Democrat, Little Rock, Ark.; BPW, Am. Pen Wm.; Who's Who of Am. Wm.; Henderson State Tchrs. Col., Arkadelphia, Ark.; b. Hot Springs, Ark. 1910; p. William and Jeannie Box Lowe; h. Cecil L. Suitt (div.); c. Billy, Bobby, Gloria Ann, Euna Janice (Mrs. Brent Cater); res: 184 Ramble, Hot Springs, Ark. 71901.

SULLIVAN, BARBARA STEWARD, Pres., Steward Associates, Inc., 210 E. 36th St. N.Y., N.Y. 10016, '68–; Dir. of Commtns., Filmex, '66–'68; AE, Cunningham & Walsh, Inc., '64–'66; Cnslt., Pelican Films, '68–; PRSA, Adv. Club of N.Y.; Nat. Arts Club, Gotham Young Republican Club; Univ. of Conn., BA, '61 (summa cum laude); N.Y.U., MA, '65; b. N.Y.C., 1939; p. Alvin and Helen Hanley Steward; h. Daniel J. Sullivan.

SULLIVAN, ELEANOR REGIS, Mng. Ed., Ellery Queen's Mystery Magazine, Davis Publications, Inc., 229 Park Ave. S., N.Y., N.Y. 10003, '70–; Ed., Charles Scribner's Sons, '62–'69; Edtl. Asst., Pocket Books, Inc., '61–'62; Tchr., White Plains, N.Y., '57–'60; Cambridge, Mass., '53–'57, Clinton, Conn., '50–'53; weekly TV colmn., Cambridge (Mass.) Chronicle; Salem State Col., BS; b. Cambridge, Mass., 1928; p. Timothy J. and Katherine Dowd Sullivan; res: 7 Stuyvesant Oval, N.Y., N.Y. 10009.

SULLIVAN, ELIZABETH BAXTER, Dir. of Home Econs., Hamilton Beach, Division of Scovill Manufacturing Co., 208 E. Wisconsin Ave., Milw., Wis. 53202, '55–; Asst. Dir. of Home Econs., John Oster Mfg. Co., '50–'55; De Pauw Univ., BA (Home Econs.); b. Springfield, Ill.; p. Albert and Ethel Mitchell Baxter; h. Thomas Sullivan; c. Tom Jr., Bruce E., Brian E., William A. Mudge III, James A., Mrs. Susan Gieler; res: 709 William St., Racine, Wis. 53402.

SULLIVAN, ELIZABETH LOUISE, Radio-TV Ed., Boston Globe, Boston, Mass. 02107, '36–; Boston Opera House, '24; Wtr., news svcs. incl., N. Am. Nwsp. Alliance; Newsweek Magazine; Advisor, numerous TV program sources; Operator, Amateur Radio Station, W1HRB; Boston Wms. Symphony (Secy.); numerous public svc. groups; Boston Col., Emmanuel Col., Univ. of Dublin; b. Cambridge, Mass.; p. Peter and Agnes Higgins Sullivan; res: 163 Wachusett St., Forest Hills, Mass. 02130.

SULLIVAN, MARGARET ANNE, Educ. Cnslt., Colonial Films, Inc., 752 Spring St., N.W., Atlanta, Ga. 30308, '63–; Ed., Soc. for Visual Educ., '62–'63; Wtr., Sears, Roebuck and Co., '52–'62; Asst. to Ed. of Edtl. Pg., Chgo. Sun-Times, '48–'49; Auth: "Decorating Made Easy"; Tchr., Chgo. Public Schs.; Nat. Cncl. of Tchrs. of Mathematics, Zonta Club of Atlanta, NHFL; Rosary Col., BA, '46; DePaul Univ., '46–'62; b. Sioux Falls, S.D., 1924; p. Jeremiah J. and Margaret Boyle Sullivan; res: 336 Herrington Dr., N.E., Atlanta, Ga. 30305.

SULLIVAN, MARTHA, AE, Byer & Bowman Advertising Agency, Inc., 66 S. Sixth St., Columbus, Oh. 43215, '58–; Asst. AE, '54–'58; Copywtr., '50–'54; Edtl. Wtr., Columbus Dispatch, '49; Tchr., Franklin County Schs., '45–'49; Adv. Club of Columbus (Wm. of Year Aw., '63), AAF, Theta Sigma Phi, Press Club of Oh.; Oh. Dominican Col., BA, '45; Oh. State Univ., '48; b. Columbus, Oh. 1925; p. Dr. Frank J. and Marie Driscoll Sullivan; res: 2873 Ashby Rd., Columbus, Oh. 43209.

SULLIVAN, MARY BARRETT, Free-lance Wtr.; China Weekly Review, '48–'50; U.S. Info. Svc. (China), '46–'48; Off. of War Info., '42–'46; Time mag., '42; Auth., "Careers in Government" (Henry Z. Walck, Inc., '64); Wash. State Univ., BA, '40; Columbia Univ., MS, '42; b. N.Y.C.; h. Walter Sullivan; c. Elizabeth Anne, Catherine Ellinwood, Theodore Loomis; res: 66 Indian Head Rd., Riverside, Conn. 06878.

SULLIVAN, MARY IDA, Ed., The Workbasket Magazine, Modern Handcraft, Inc., 4251 Pennsylvania Ave., Kan. City, Mo. 64111, '49–; Supvsr., Food Svc. Dept., Stephens Col., Columbia, Mo.; Instr.: Singer Sewing Machine Co., Kan. City, Mo., and Govt. Power Sewing Sch.; Christian Col., '34–'36; Univ. of Mo., '38–'40; b. Sibley, Mo., 1916; p. John P. and Aline Brown Sullivan; res: 124 East Linden Ave., Independence, Mo. 64050.

SULLIVAN, MAUREEN, Ed., New Book Review, Herder & Herder, 232 Madison Ave., N.Y., N.Y. 10016, '68–; Copywtr., Bk. Reviewer, '67–'68; Asst. Ed., Catholic News, '64–'66; Eng. Lectr., John Carroll Univ., '64; Outstanding Young Wm. in Am.; Wheeling Col., BA, '62; John Carroll Univ., MA, '64; b. Columbus, Oh.; p. James and Ammrita Sullivan Sullivan; res: 515 E. Fifth St., N.Y., N.Y. 10009.

SULLIVAN, PAULA E., Free-lance Publicist, U.S. Grant Hotel, 326 Broadway, San Diego, Cal. 92101, '64–; PR for supermarket chain, '62–'64; Pubcty. Chief, adv.-PR agcy., '59–'62, Press staff, Gov. Pat Brown, '58; Pubcty. Dir., desert resort, Borrego Springs, '55–'57; Wtr., Borrego Sun and San Diego Union, '55–'57; Partner, Sullivan & Sample, Adv. & PR, '50–'54; Pubcty. Wtr., adv. agcy., '47–'50; PR staff, WACs, World War II; PRSA, Adv. and Sales Club, Theta Sigma Phi, San Diego Soc. of Communicating Arts.

SULLIVAN, PEGGY WISELY, Exec. Asst. to VP in charge of adv., prom., PR, Metromedia Television, 5746 Sunset Blvd., Hollywood, Cal. 90028, '63–; Owner-Prodr., "Capitol Reptr.," radio-TV program, '61–'63; Ed., Western Ins. Inf. Svc. News, '52–'61; various organizations and aws.; U.C.L.A.; b. Marissa, Ill. 1915; p. James and Amanda Crain Wisely; h. Robert M. Sullivan (dec.); res: 631 N. La Jolla Ave., L.A., Cal. 90048.

SUMMERS, EILEEN VINCENT, Edtl. Wtr., WCBS, Columbia Broadcasting System, 51 W. 52nd St., N.Y.,

N.Y., '68–; Edtl. Wtr., Waterbury (Conn.) Republican, '67; Staff Wtr., Washington (D.C.) Post, '53–'59; Staff Wtr., Palo Alto (Cal.) Times, '46–'51; Co-Auth., "The Patient" (play, Universalist Theatre, N.Y.C.); AWRT; h. (div.).

SUMMERS, HOPE, Actress; Pres., New Theatre, Inc., Studio for Actors, 1945 Westwood Blvd., W. L.A., Cal., '65–; Tchr., Northwestern Univ.; Bradley Univ.; AWRT, Zeta Phi Eta (merit aw., '69); Univ. of Wash.; Goucher Col.; Northwestern Univ., BA, '23; b. Mattoon, Ill., 1902; p. John and Jennie Burks Summers; h. James Witherell (div.); c. Bambi Witherell Fernandez, James Summers Witherell; res: 9609 Olympic Blvd., Beverly Hills, Cal. 90212.

SUMMERS, RUTH BANNING, Ed., The Pierceton Press, 103 E. Market, Pierceton, Ind. 46562, '62; Repl. Wms. Club; b. Toledo, Oh., 1915; p. Frank and Marie Picard Banning; h. Kermit F. Summers; c. Robert L.; res: R #2, Covington, Va. 24426.

SUMMO, BEVERLY CROOKSTON, Music and Drama Ed., Inglewood Daily News/Citizen, 121 North La Brea Ave., Inglewood, Cal. 90307, '59–; Ed., Citizen Weekly, '66–; Copy Ed., '56–'66; L.A. Press Club; Sawyer's Business Col., '32–'33; b. Pocatello, Idaho; p. William and Doris Larsen Crookston; h. Dominic Summo; c. Mrs. Theresa Oehrli, Mrs. Linda Danforth; res: 5841 W. 85th Pl., L.A., Cal. 90045.

SUMRALL, VELMA EVERHART, Dir. of Pubns., Church of the Redeemer, 4411 Dallas St., Houston, Tex.; PR, Houston YWCA, '57–'60; Theta Sigma Phi (Houston Chptr. Pres., '58; VP, '57); John Tarleton Col., AS; Univ. of Tex.; BJ, '48; b. N.O., La.; p. James and Ursula Bettison Everhart; h. George Sumrall; c. Laura, Paula, Mary Ann; res: 6911 Kopman, Houston, Tex. 77017.

SUNDERLIN, SYLVIA SWEETMAN, Assoc. Ed., Association for Childhood Education International, 3615 Wisconsin Ave., N.W., Wash., D.C. 20016, '67–; Asst. Ed., '65–'67; Univ. of Mont., BA (Eng.), '33; Oxford Univ. (Eng.), '35–'36; b. Lakeside, Mont., 1911; p. Luke D. and Alice Waterman Sweetman; h. C. E. Sunderlin; c. Elizabeth, Mary, Katherine, William; res: 3036 P St., N.W., Wash., D.C. 20007.

SUPER, BEATRICE PERRON, VP, Bd. of Dirs., Distrib-u-mats, Inc., VP, Bd. of Dirs., Advertising Mats, Inc., Pres., Bea Perron Photography Rep., Inc., '70–; Adv. Mats, Inc., '68–; Bea Perron Photo. Rep., '66–; VP, Barclay-Perron Photog., '58; AWNY, Soc. of Photogrs. and Artists, Fashion Group; Bklyn. Col.; b. N.Y.C.; p. Michael and Rose Paley Perron; h. Seymour Super; c. Drew Robert, Glenn Alan; res: 7 Robin Hill Rd., Great Neck, N.Y. 11024.

SUSANN, JACQUELINE, Novelist, 112 Central Park S., N.Y., N.Y.; Auth: "Every Night Josephine" (nonfiction); "Valley of the Dolls," "The Love Machine"; b. Margate, N.J., 1927; p. Robert and Rose Susann; h.

Irving Mansfield; c. son; res: 112 Central Park S., N.Y., N.Y. 10019.

SUTHERLAND, LINDA BARRETT, Actress, c/o Walter Kohner, Paul Kohner Agency, 9169 Sunset Blvd., L.A., Cal. 90069; radio, TV, theater, films; AEA, SAG, AFTRA, Phi Beta (Pi Iota L.A. Alumni Chptr. Secy., '69); Northwestern Univ., BA (drama); b. Chgo., Ill.; p. John and Marie La Vicka Dubsky; h. Victor Sutherland (dec.); res: 916 N. Alfred St., L.A., Cal. 90069.

SUTHERLAND, MADGE FRENCH, Dir., Secy-Treas., Sutherland's Jewelry, 18 N. Fourth St., Great Falls, Mont. 59401, '67–; Strain Brothers, Stellar's Jewelry, Kellogg's Jewelry, Huntington, Cal.; AWRT (Great Falls Charter Mbr.), Comm. of 100, BPW, Retail Jewelers of Am. (Advisory Cncl., '68–'69), Mont. Retail Jewelers & Watchmakers Assn. (Pres., '68–'69); Sterling Silversmiths' Guild aw., '40; b. Bonner, Mont., 1905; p. Olin and Alice Moon French; h. Donald H. Sutherland; res: 416 N. Fourth Ave., Apt. 2, Great Falls, Mont. 59401.

SUTTER, PAT FREESTONE, Ed., Roy Sun Chroncile, 5388 S. 1900 W., Roy, Ut. 84067, '64–; Open Door Fndn. for Handicapped (Bd. of Dirs.); h. Neil B. Sutter.

SUTTON, AUDREY LATSHAW, Auth., Ed., nursing bks. and articles; Case Cnslt., Blue Cross of Philadelphia, 1333 Chestnut St., Phila., Pa., '68–; Dir. of Nursing, Edgewood Hosp., '62–'68; Instr., H. Fletcher Vocational Sch., '59–'62; Clinical Instr., Wilmington Gen. Hosp., '52–'59; Critique Lit. Aw., '55; Jefferson Med. Col., Sch. of Nursing, '50; Eastern Pilgrim Col., BS, '52; b. Herndon, Pa. 1933; p. Fred and Helena Updegrove Latshaw; res: Rt. 73, Berlin, N.J. 08009.

SUTTON, MARGARET BEEBE, Free-lance Auth.; bks. incl. Judy Bolton mystery series (38 titles, Grosset and Dunlap, '32–), "Jemima, Daughter of Daniel Boone (Scribners, '42), Palace Wagon Family (Knopf, '57), "The Weed Walk (Putnam's, '65); Adult Educ. Tchr., '50–; Tchr., Summer Workshops: Iona Col., Dixie Cncl. of Auths.; Auths. League of Am., Wms. Nat. Bk. Assn.; b. Odin, Pa., 1903; p. Victor and Estella Andrews Beebe; h. William Sutton; c. Mrs. Dorothy Wolfe, Mrs. Peggy Eckstein, Mrs. Eleanore Kratzat, Thomas, Mrs. Linda Stroh; res: 261 Rutland Rd., Freeport, N.Y. 11520.

SUTTON, NANCY LEA, VP-Crtv. Supvsr., Grey Advertising, Inc., 777 Third Ave., N.Y., N.Y. 10017, '62–; Adv. Dir., Neiman-Marcus, '60–'62; Wtr., Kal Erlich & Merrick, '59–'60; Adv. Mgr., Saks 34th St., '55–'59; Copywtr., '46–'50; Adv. Mgr. and Copy Chief, Jelleff's, '50–'55; TV Commls. Festival aws., '64, '66–'69; Adv. Wtrs. Assn. Silver Key, '63; Andy, '68; Allegheny Col., BA, '44; b. Indiana, Pa., 1922; p. J. Blair and Florence Downing Sutton; res: 110 Riverside Dr., N.Y., N.Y. 10024.

SWAEBLY, FRANCES MARGARET, Drama Ed., The Miami Herald, 1 Herald Plaza, Miami, Fla. 33101, '68–; Amusements Ed., Asst. to Radio-TV Ed., Reptr.; Prod. Asst., WTHS-TV; Univ. of Miami, BA, '57; b. Norwalk, Oh.; p. Louis and Loretta O'Mara Swaebly; h. Allan Webb; c. Ann Aileen, Allan Trusten, Daphne Sarah, Daniel Joseph.

SWAFFORD, PATRICIA DEVLIN, Treas., Swafford & Company, Advertising, 9896 Wilshire Blvd., Beverly Hills, Cal. 90210, '60–; Media Dir., Prod. Mgr.; Univ. of Southern Cal., BS, '47; Delta Gamma; b. Chgo., Ill., 1925; p. John and Margaret Beck Devlin; h. Murray Swafford; res: 610 Tuallitan Rd., L.A., Cal. 90049.

SWAIL, DOLORES SPENCER, Wms. Entertainment Ed., Review-Journal, 737 N. Main St., Las Vegas, Nev. 89101, '60–; Wms. Ed., Belvidere (Ill.) Daily Republican, Rockford (Ill.) Morning Star and Register Republic; Press Club, Art League of Las Vegas, Nev. Heart Assn., Am. Cancer Soc. (aw.), '67); Girl Scouts of Am. aw., '68; b. Belvidere, Ill., 1925; p. Gerald and Mildred McFarland Swail; c. Valerie Spencer, Bradley S. Palmer; res: 1088 Sierra Vista Dr., Las Vegas, Nev. 89109.

SWAIM, ALICE MACKENZIE, Poet, Critic, Reviewer; Poetry Corr., Carlisle (Pa.) Evening Sentinel, '65–; Auth: "Beneath a Dancing Star" ('67), "Here on the Threshold" ('66), seven other bks.; PSA, Acad. of Am. Poets, Am. Poetry League (VP, '64–'70), World Poetry Soc.; many prizes, honors for poetry; Chatham Col., '28–'30; Wilson Col., BA, '32; b. Scotland, 1911; p. Donald and Alice Murray MacKenzie; h. William T. Swaim; c. Elizabeth Anne, Kathleen; res: 26 N. Chestnut St., Dillsburg, Pa. 17019.

SWALLEN, MARGUERITE A., Wtr.; Adm. Asst., Legal Dept., Kellogg Company, 235 Porter St., Battle Creek, Mich. 49106, '61–; Staff Asst., Adv. Dept., '52–'61; Theta Sigma Phi, Jr. League, Chi Omega, AAUW; Syracuse Univ., BA (Jnlsm.), '48; Univ. of Lausanne, Switzerland, '50–'51; b. Cleve., Oh., 1927; p. Norwood and Gladys Spies Swallen.

SWANSON, BEVERLEY DRESSER, AE, KRLC, 8th and Stewart Sts., Lewiston, Idaho. 83501, '58–; Store Rep., '53–'58; numerous radio prod. aws.; b. Orofino, Idaho, 1925; p. Hugh and Emma Phillips Dresser; h. N. Arthur Swanson; c. Carol (Mrs. David Brunzell), Dawn; res: 1111 University St., Clarkston, Wash. 99403.

SWANTON, IRENE WRAY, Asst. Dir., Livingston and Wyoming County Library Systems, 303 E. Main St., Avon, N.Y. 14414, '62–; Dir., Avon Free Lib., '51–'57, '60–'62; Lib. Asst., Randolph Macon Col., Lynchburg, Va., '57–'58; Geologist, Museum of Natural Hist., Worcester, Mass., '37–'38; Asst., Dept. of Geology, Univ. of Rochester (N.Y.), '34–'36; ALA, N.Y. Lib. Assn.; Sigma Xi, Avon Central Sch. Bd. (two-term

Pres.), PTA (Pres., '58–'59), Univ. of Rochester, BS, '34, MS, '36; Clark Univ.; State Univ. at Geneseo, N.Y., MS (Lib. Sci.), '62; b. Rochester, N.Y., 1911; p. Delos and Irene Warner Wray; h. Walter Swanton; c. Susan, Carolyn; res: 86 E. Main St., Avon, N.Y. 14414.

SWARTZ, SUSAN FREY, Fashion Ed.-Feature Wtr., San Diego Evening Tribune, 912 Second Avenue., San Diego, Cal. 92112, '67–; Rptr., '66–'67; Rptr., Erie Times-News, Erie, Pa., '65–'66; Copley Ring of Truth Aw., '67; Oh. Univ., BS (Jnlsm.), '65; b. Meadville, Pa., 1943; p. V. Paul and Helen Arnold Frey; h. William Swartz; res: 4860 Coronado Ave., San Diego, Cal. 92107.

SWARTZLOW, RUBY JOHNSON, Tchr., Paradise Unified School District, 5972 Skyway, Paradise, Cal. 95969, '60–; Auth., "Lassen, His Life and Legacy" (Loomis Museum Assn., '64); Rsch., Paradise Fact & Folklore, '60–; NLAPW (Butte County Br. VP, '68–'70), Conf. of Cal. Hist. Socs. (Aw. of Merit, Tchr.-Histrn., '68) Butte County Hist. Soc. (Pres., '65; merit aw., '66); Delta Kappa Gamma (Hon. Mbr.) Lawrence Univ., BA, '24 (Phi Beta Kappa); Univ. of Mo., MA, '33; p. Uriah and Anna Butler Johnson; h. Carl Swartzlow; c. Mrs. John McDougal; res: 6346 Diamond Ave., Paradise, Cal. 95969.

SWARZMAN, SUE JEAN, Retail, Apparel Adv. Mgr., Life Magazine, Time, Inc., 1271 Ave. of Americas, N.Y., N.Y. 10020; Prom. Dir., McCall Corp., '60–'65; Fashion Coordr., Saks Fifth Ave. (Chgo., Ill.), and Mgr.-Byr. (S.F., Cal.), '58–'60; Br. Mdse. Distributor, Lord & Taylor, '56–'58; Fashion Group, Nat. Retail Merchants Assn. (Advisory Comm. Assoc. mbr.); Who's Who of Am. Wm.; Marquis Biog. Lib. Soc. Advisory Mbr.; Northwestern Univ., BS; b. Des Moines Ia.; p. Roy and Dorothy Pike Swarzman; res: 203 E. 72nd St., N.Y. N.Y. 10021.

SWEDBURG, WILMA ADELINE, Asst. Prof., Augsburg College, 731-21st Ave., Mpls., Minn., '69–; Tchr., Mpls. Public Schs., '54–'68; Auditor, Inv. Synd., '45–'54; Head Start materials (Cook Publ. Co., '66); Children's Auth: "World Around Johnny" ('68),"Jeannie Goes to Sunday School" ('62), "Just Like Me" ('62) (all Standard Publ.); Christmas Donkey (Augsburg Press, '62); AAUW, MEA, NEA; Who's Who of Am. Wm., ('68–'69), Who's Who in Midwest, ('69–'70); Adult Tchr., Mpls. Cncl. of Chs.; Univ. of Minn., BS, '54; MA, '56; Educ. Spec., '62; b. Nora Springs, Ia.; p. Lee H. and Laura Ellington Swedburg; res: 5720-27 Ave. S., Mpls., Minn. 55417.

SWEED, PHYLLIS, Ed., Gifts & Decorative Accessories, Gayer-McAllister Publications, 51 Madison Ave., N.Y., N.Y. 10010, '68–; Mng. Ed., '66–'68; Mng. Ed., Haire Pubns., '62–'66; Products and Materials Ed., McGraw-Hill, '57–'61; Assoc. Ed., Fox-Shulman Pubns., '51–'57; NHFL, China, Pottery & Glass Assn.; Dallas Mkt. Ctr. edtl. aw., '69; Indsl. Mktng. aw., '64;

Wash. Sq. Col., BA, '50; b. N.Y.C., 1929; p. Paul and Frances Spitzer Sweed; h. Leonard Bogdanoff; c. Patricia M., James Alan; res: 505 La Guardia Pl., N.Y., N.Y. 10012.

SWEENEY, LORRAINE THEBODEAU, Wms. Ed., Worcester Telegram and Evening Gazette, 20 Franklin St., Worcester, Mass. 01601, '64–; Wms. Staff, Evening Gazette, '43–'64; BPW, Worcester Wms. Club; b. Manchester, N.H., 1918; p. Wilfred and Beatrice Milne Thebodeau; h. Robert F. Sweeney; res: 7 Bay Edge Dr., Worcester, Mass. 01604.

SWEETSER, MARY CHISHOLM, Auth., "The Extra Gift" (Macrae-Smith Co., '69); Founder, Dir., Star Island Wtrs. Conf., '57–; Manuscript Club of Boston (Past Pres., aws.); Who's Who of Am. Wm.; b. Malden, Mass., 1894; p. Frank and Nellie Hopkins Chisholm; h. Sidney Sweetser (dec.); c. Jean (Mrs. Walter E. Kelley), Donald Arthur; res: 10 Kneeland St., Malden, Mass. 02148.

SWENSON, MARLETTE E., Assoc. Sci. Ed., University Industry Research Program, 7 Bascom Hall, University of Wisconsin, Madison, Wis. 53706, '66–; Adm. Wtr., Sci. Writing Program, '66–; Asst. Sci. Ed., '66–'69; Sci. Writing Rsch.; Theta Sigma Phi, Natl. Assn. of Sci. Wtrs., Madison Press Club; Augustana Col., Rock Island, Ill., BA (Bio., Chem.) '64; (Mortarboard, Who's Who Among Students, Beta Beta Beta); Grad. Work, Univ. of Wis. Sch. of Jnlsm.; b. Rockford, Ill., 1942; p. Bertil and Alice Rosell Swenson; h. James A. Larsen; res: 765 W. Washington Ave., Madison, Wis. 53715.

SWINFORD, BETTY WELLS, Wtr., 21 bks., children's, adult's, incl., "Beyond the Night" (published in Finland, Denmark, U.S.); approximately 2,000 short stories published; articles; publrs. incl: Moody Press, Zondervan, Gospel Publ. House; Speaker, Crtv. Writing, schs.; pulpit ministry; Active in ch. groups; Who's Who of Am. Wm., aw., '69, collection of writing, set up by Univ. of Southern Miss.; Bible Col., Ariz. Bible Inst., '47–'48; b. Cartersburg, Ind., 1927; p. John and Dora Price Wells; h. Robert Swinford; c. Stephen R., Carolyn Renee, Jennie Lynn; res: 9243 N. 18th Dr., Phoenix, Ariz. 85021.

SWING, MARY EUYANG, Chief, Asian Feed Service, Voice of America, 330 Independence Ave., S.W., Wash., D.C. 20547, '60–; Script Wtr., Special Events Offcr., Chinese Br. (N.Y.C. and Wash., D.C.), '51–'60; Info. Cl., Econ. Coop. Adm., '50–'51; Adm. Asst., ECA/JCRR (Shanghai, Canton and Taipei, China), '48–'50; AWRT; U.S.I.A. Meritorious Svc. aw., '62; Who's Who in Am. Cols. and Univs.; St. John's Univ., Shanghai, '42–'43; Chungking Post-Grad. Sch. of Jnlsm., Grad. Cert., '43–'44; Wesleyan Col., BA, '46; b. Chgo., Ill., 1924; p. Herbert and Pauline Chiang Euyang; h. Raymond Swing (dec.); c. Paul Loh; res: 3116 Rodman St., N.W., Wash., D.C. 20008.

SWISHER, VIOLA HEGYI, W. Coast Ed., Dance

Magazine, After Dark Magazine, 345 So. Curson Ave., L.A., Cal. 90036, '65–; Dance Critic and Special Reviewer, Los Angeles Mirror, '48–'62; Colmst., Daily Variety, '51–'52; Lectr. on dance; Ghost Wtr.

SYDENSTRICKER, MARGARET HOLDERBY, Adv. Dir., The C. H. Parsons Company and Parsons Furniture Store, Inc., 1620 Winchester Ave., Ashland, Ky. 41101, '63–; Adv. Sls. Prom. Mgr., Huntington Dept. Store, '48–'63; Adv. Club of Huntington, W. Va. (Pres. '61–'62; Secy.), Ashland Area C. of C., Adv. Wm. of the Year, '59, '62; Printers Ink Silver Medal, '63; Oh. State Univ., '57–'59; b. Proctorville, Oh., 1923; p. Jesse and Estella Simpson Holderby; h. Forrest Sydenstricker; c. Mrs. Marcella Voitik; res: Point of View Farm, Box 419, Rte. 2, S. Point, Oh. 45680.

SYDLOW, JOAN GRACE, Staff Photogr., Business Week, 330 W. 42nd St., N.Y., N.Y. '65–; Edtl. Asst., '55–'65; Edtl. Asst., Time, Inc., '50–'55; Barnard Col., AB, '49; b. Akron, Oh., 1923; p. Matthew and Mary McGuckin Sydlow; h. Ellis C. Newman (dec.); c. Mary Randolph Newman; res: 166 Clinton St., Bklyn. Heights, N.Y. 11201.

T

TABER, GLADYS BAGG, Auth., Brandt and Brandt, 101 Park Ave., N.Y., N.Y. 10017; Asst. Ed., Ladies Home Journal, '37–'58; Instr., Columbia Univ., '36–'40; Randolph-Macon Wms. Col., '26; Lawrence Col., '21–'22; Auth., 40 bks., short stories; Auths. League, PEN, Kappa Alpha Theta; Best Seller, "Especially Father" ('49), Best Dog Bk., Best Non-tech. Dog Bk., "Especially Dogs" ('68), from Dog Wtrs. Assn.; Wellesley Col., BA, '20; Lawrence Col., MA, '21; b. Colorado Springs, Colo.; p. Rufus and Grace Raybold Bagg; h. Frank Albion Taber; c. Constance Anne (Mrs. Curtis Colby); res: Stillmeadow, Southbury, Conn. 06488.

TABRAH, RUTH M., Fiction, Non-fiction Auth: "Pulaski Place" ('50), "Voices of Others" ('59), "Hawaiian Heart" ('64), "Hawaii Nei" ('67); AAUW, Auths. League, League of Wm. Voters, Natl. Assn. State Bds. of Educ. (Pacific Area VP, '68), Hawaii State Bd. of Educ., Hawaiian Island Sch. Advisory Cncl. (Chmn. '64–'66), U.S. Off. of Educ. (Cnslt. '69–'70); Univ. of Buffalo, N.Y., BA, '41 (Phi Beta Kappa); b. Buffalo, 1921; p. Henry Milander and B. A. Harwood Milander Flock; h. Frank Tabrah; c. Joseph Garner, Thomas Frank; res: Box 308, Kapaau, Hawaii 96755.

TAIT, LUCILLE BURGES, Owner and Publr., Milbank Herald Advance, Main Street, Milbank, S.D. 57252, '57; formerly Owner and Ed.; orgs.: S.D. Press Assn., S.D. Presswm., S.D. Educ. Assn.; numerous nat. and S.D. aws. for nwsp. achiev.; S.D. Gov.'s Comm.

on Children and Youth; N.E. Mo. State Tchrs. Col., BS (Educ.), '30; b. Downing, Mo., 1908; p. James and Mary Laws Whittom; h. Frank S. Tait (dec.); c. Joanne (Mrs. Lawrence Andersen), Mary Anne (Mrs. Donald J. McClure).

TALBOT, CAROL TERRY, Auth.; Western Rep., Ramabai Mukti Mission, India, GPO Box 354, N.Y., N.Y. 10001, '64–; Dir. of Pubcty.; Superintendent; Dir. of revision, reprinting of Bible in India's Marathi language; Woodbury Col., BS, '32 (Leo V. Youngworth Aw., '32); Bible Inst. of L.A., '40; L.A. Theological Seminary, BCE, '46; b. L.A., Cal., 1913; p. Vinal and Wilhelmina Reid Terry; h. Louis T. Talbot; res: 13560 St. Andrews Dr., Apt. 3C, Seal Beach, Cal. 90740.

TALBOT, CHARLENE JOY, Auth., juv. novel, "Thomas Takes Charge" (Lothrop, Lee & Shepard, '65); Kan. State Univ., BS.

TALBOT, NITA, Actress, TV, motion pics., Broadway, Michael Hartig Agent, 157 W. 57th St., N.Y., N.Y. 10019; SAG, AFTRA, Actors Equity, AMPAS; nominated for Emmy by NATAS, '67; b. N.Y.C., 1930; p. Anthony and Helen Lake Sokol; c. Nicole Andrea Geas; res: 3420 Merrimac Rd., L.A., Cal. 90049.

TALKINGTON, DOLLIE DUTTON, Program/Traf. Dir., KVSO Broadcasting Company, 115 W. Broadway, Ardmore, Okla. 73401, '37–; Pianist and Organist, theatres in Cal., Tex., Okla. and KVSO, '29–'37; Altrusa Intl. Club (Local Pres.), Philharmonic Music Club (Pres.), Okla. Federated Music Club, AWRT; Lion's Club (Hon. Mbr., '48–); St. Gregory Col., '26; McAlester Bus. Col.; b. Mammoth Springs, Ark., 1914; p. Albert and Annie Laurie Mauldin Dutton; h. Sam Talkington; c. Mrs. Richard Alkire; res: 520 Northwest Ave., Ardmore, Okla. 73401.

TALL, EUNICE ARMSTRONG, Coordr., H. F. Fibers Pubcty., Eastman Chemical Products, Inc., 260 Madison Ave., N.Y., N.Y. 10016, '59–; Home Furnishings Mkt. Rep., '53–'58; Fibers Publicist, '49–'53; Edtl. Asst., House & Garden, '47–'49; NHFL, Fashion Group, AWRT; N.Y.U., N.Y. Sch. of Interior Design; b. N.Y.C.; p. Leon and Muriel F. Armstrong; h. Donald G. Tall; res: 62 Pierrepont St., Bklyn., N.Y. 11201.

TALLEY, CAROL L., Polit. Ed., The Daily Advance, 87 E. Blackwell St., Dover, N.J. 07801, '66–; Reptr., Educ. Ed., N.J. Herald, Newton, '62–'66; Reptr., Easton (Pa.) Express, '60–'61; 3rd place, N.J. Press Assn. Best Colms. Contest, '66; Special Mention, '68; 2nd place for Best Series, 3rd place for Best News Story on Deadline, N.J. Daily Nwsp. Wm. Annual Contest, '69; Univ. of Ky.

TALLMAN, JOHANNA ALLERDING, Librn., Engineering and Mathematical Sciences Library, University of California at Los Angeles, 405 Hilgard Ave., L.A., Cal. 90024, '45–; Lectr., Sch. of Lib. Svc.,

U.C.L.A., '60–; Fulbright Lectr., Brazil, '66–'67; Lib., cnslt. work; numerous lib. assns.; Am. Soc. of Info. Sci., Soc. for the Hist. of Tech.; Univ. of Cal. at Berkeley, BA, '36; Sch. of Librarianship, Cert., '37; b. Lübeck, Germany, 1914; p. Friedrich and Johanna Voget Allerding; h. Lloyd Tallman; res: 2253 Linda Flora Dr., L.A., Cal. 90024.

TALLTREE, LUANA BARBARA, Owner, Interglobal Productions, '67– (aw. for special radio coverage of Robert Kennedy assassination, '68); Actress, U.S. Films and Screen Gems Studios, '65–'68; KTTV, '59; Auth., drama, "The Wishing Tree" ('68); Poetess, "Watts-65"; Song Wtr.; SAG; various aws.; Pasadena City Col.; L.A. State Col.; b. L.A., Cal.; p. Wallace and Louise Donahue Tollin; h. (div.); c. Lara Marshall; res: 597 Dolores, San Francisco Cal. 94110.

TAMBURINE, JEAN H., Free-lance Artist, Auth., Designer, Illus., Lectr., '50–; numerous bks. for children; Designer, Rust Craft (Dedham, Mass.), '55–'57; Norcross (N.Y.C.), '48–'50; Auths. Guild, Intl. Platform Assn., Wms. Nat. Bk. Assn., Allied Artists of Am., Conn. Commn. on the Arts; Who's Who in the East, Who's Who of Am. Wm.; Traphagen Sch. of Fashion, '48–'49; Art Students League, '48–'50; b. Meriden, Conn., 1930; p. Paul and Helen Marks Tamburine; h. Eugene E. Bertolli; c. E. Robert, Lisa Marie; res: 73 Reynolds Dr., Meriden, Conn. 06450.

TANKERSLEY, ANN COLLINS, Pubns. Ed., Community relations, Liberty Life Insurance Company, Box 789, Wade Hampton Blvd., Greenville, S.C. 29602, '64–; Reptr., The Greenville News, '55–'58; Reptr., The Hendersonville (N.C.) Times-News, '55; Reptr., Teenage Colmst., The Western Carolina Tribune, '53–'54; Coordr., S.C. teenage art exhbns.; Cnslt., S.C. Tricentennial Commn.; ICIE; Mars Hill Col., '54–'55; b. Hendersonville, N.C., 1936; p. Charles Creighton and Edna Hudson Collins, Sr.; h. L. C. Tankersley, Jr.; c. Rebecca Lea, Mark Brooks, David Cameron; res: Rte. 1, Locust Hill, Travelers Rest, S.C. 29690.

TANNENBAUM, BEULAH GOLDSTEIN, Auth., juv. sci. bks. incl: "Understanding Light," "Understanding Maps," "Understanding Sound;" Nat. Sci. Tchrs. Assn., ALA; Columbia Univ., MA, '38; State Univ. of N.Y., MS (Lib. Sci.), '65; b. N.Y.C., 1916; p. Sol and Clara Fleischman Goldstein; h. Harold E. Tannenbaum; c. Robert S., Carl R.; res: 170 West End Ave., N.Y., N.Y. 10023.

TANNENBAUM, ELAYNE MYRA, Bdcst. Byr., Doyle Dane Bernbach, 20 W. 43rd St., New York, N.Y. 10036, '66–; Bdcst. Byr., Campbell Ewald Co., '65–'66; Print Byr., Wunderman, Ricotta & Kline, '64–'65; NATAS; Syracuse Univ., Fairleigh Dickinson Univ., BS (Mktng.), '64; b. Newark, N.J., 1942; p. Charles and Ethel Sirkin Tannebaum; h. Alvin A. Davidson; res: 380 Mountain Rd., Union City, N.J. 07087.

TANNER, BARBARA R., VP, Doherty Associates, Inc., 551 Fifth Ave., N.Y., N.Y. 10017; formerly AE, Staff Wtr.; free-lance articles, home furnishings mags.; NHFL; Hunter Col., AB (Constitutional Law Prize; Hist., Social Studies Hon. Socs.); b. N.Y.C.

TANNER, CLARA LEE FRAPS, Wtr.; Prof., The University of Arizona, Department of Anthropology, Tucson, Ariz. 85721; Prof. '68–; Assoc. Prof., '57–'68; Asst. Prof., '35–'57; Instr., '28–'35; Auth. of numerous articles, two bks. on Southwest Indians and Indian art; Ariz. Press Wm., NFPW, Theta Sigma Phi, Delta Kappa Gamma, numerous anthropological and archaeological socs.; Univ. of Ariz., AB, '27; MA, '28; grad. studies in several univs.; b. Biscoe, N.C., 1905; p. Joseph and Clara Lee Fraps; h. John F. Tanner; c. Mrs. Sandra Lee Elers; res: P.O. Box 4606, Tucson, Ariz. 85717.

TANNER, MONA CLAIR, Ed., The Columbus Publishing Company, Inc., 215 S. Kansas, Columbus, Kan. 66725, '52–; Soc. Ed., '48–'52; Ed., Modern Light (Columbus Weekly), '57–; Corr., The Wichita Eagle-Beacon; Outdoor Wtrs. of Kan.; C. of C. (Columbus Dir. '68–'69); b. Columbus, Kan. 1930; p. Edgar and Eva Auman Tanner; res: R.R. 4, Columbus, Kan. 66725.

TAPERT, MARGARET ANNE, TV Bdcst. Mgr., Geer, DuBois & Company, Inc., 220 E. 42nd St., N.Y., N.Y. 10017, '69–; Assoc. Prodr., AC & R Adv.; Asst. Fashion Designer, Bergdorf Goodman; b. Grosse Pointe, Mich., 1947; p. Dr. Julius and Margaret Kornmeier Tapert.

TARBOX, RUTH W., Exec. Secy., Children's and Young Adult Svcs. Divs., American Library Association, 50 E. Huron St., Chgo., Ill. 60611, '66–; Dir., Sch. Lib. Svc., Field Enterprises, '46–'65; Dir., Work With Children, River Forest Public Lib., '43–'46; Head, Roxboro Jr. HS Lib., '42–'43; Elementary Sch. Librn., '35–'42; Cnslt., Sch. Lib. workshops; WNBA (Chgo. Br. Bd. of Dirs.), ALA, Beta Phi Mu (Bd. of Dirs., '63–'66); Northland Col., BA, '32; Univ. of Minn., BS (Lib. Sci.), '41; res: 1360 Lake Shore Dr., Chgo., Ill. 60610.

TARNAWSKY, PATRICIA WARREN, Assoc. Bk. Ed., Reader's Digest Association, Inc., Pleasantville, N.Y. 10570, '64–; Copy Ed., '59–'64; Ukrainian Wtrs. Assn. of Am.; Atlantic "First" story, '54; Stephens Col., AA, '55; Manhattanville Col. of the Sacred Heart, BA, '57; b. Helena, Mont., 1936; p. Conrad and Nellie Flinn Warren; h. George Orest Tarnawsky.

TARR, KATHLEEN ANN, News Ed., Coldwater Daily Reporter, 15 W. Pearl St., Coldwater, Mich. 49036, '65–; Theatre Ed., '63–; Wms. '63–'65; Mich. Wms. Press Club (aw., '65); b. Coldwater, Mich., 1944; p. William and Anita Volk Tarr; res: Rte 2, Box 4, Coldwater, Mich. 40036.

TARSON, RUTH, Asst. Copy Chief, Diener Hauser Greenthal Advertising Co., 25 W. 43rd St., N.Y., N.Y. 10036, '68–; Copy Trainee, Copywtr., '58–'68; Auth., "A Lute Song to Baseball" (World-Telegram), '56; Gold Key Aw., '62.

TARWATER, LEAH ROSS, Dir. of PR, Girl Scout Council of the Nation's Capital, 1815 N. Ft. Meyer Dr., P.O. Box 9155, Arlington, Va. 22209, '67–; Traf. Coordr., WRC-TV (NBC), '65–'67; Media Dir., R. M. Gamble, Jr., '59–'60; Traf. Mgr., WTOP, '56–'59; Instr., Eng. Dept., Univ. of Kan., '53–'56; Univ. of Kan., BA (Eng.), '53; MA (Eng.), '57; c. Kathryn Lynn.

TARZIAN, MARY MANGIGIAN, Corporate Exec., Sarkes Tarzian, Inc., E. Hillside Dr., Bloomington, Ind. 47401, '44–; Co-Owner, Lu-Mar Newspapers, Inc.; ANPA, NAB, Inland Nwsp. Assn.; Univ. of Pa., BS (Educ.), '27; MA (Polit. Sci.), '29; PhD (Intl. Law), '34; b. Phila., Pa., 1905; p. Peter and Natalie Kassabian Mangigian; h. Sarkes Tarzian; c. Thomas, Joyce Patricia; res: 515 Kessler Blvd., West Dr., Indpls., Ind. 46208.

TASHJIAN, VIRGINIA AGABABIAN, Asst. City Librn. and Storyteller, Newton Free Library, 414 Centre St., Newton, Mass. 02158, '67–; Storyteller and Bk. Reviewer, '43–; Br. Librn., '43–'67; Auth.; Lectr. and Tchr. of children's lit.; ALA, New Eng. Lib. Assn., Mass. Lib. Assn., NEA, Roundtable of Children's Librns. (Secy., Treas., Chmn., '63–'69), Charles River Lib. Club; Simmons Col. Sch. of Lib. Sci., BS, '43; MS, '69; b. Boston, Mass.; p. Vahan and Zvart Agababian; h. James H. Tashjian; c. Douglas S.; res: 278 Belmont St., Watertown, Mass. 02172.

TATTER, "STORMY," Ed., The Activist, Activist Publishing Company, 27-1/2 W. College, Oberlin, Oh. 60305, '69–.

TAYLOR, ALICE LOUISE, Ed., Focus, American Geographical Society, Broadway at 156th St., N.Y., N.Y. 10032, '50–; Auth., 11 bks., "Around the World" prog., Doubleday & Co., '59–'69; Am. Assn. for the Advancement of Sci., Assn. of Am. Geographers, Nat. Cncl. for the Social Studies; Soc. for Intl. Dev.; b. N.Y.C., 1911; p. Norman and Bertha Fanning Taylor; h. (div.); res: 120 E. 36th St., N.Y., N.Y. 10016.

TAYLOR, BETTY JO, Dir. of Media, Presbyterian United States Board of National Ministries, 341 Ponce de Leon Ave., N.E., Atlanta, Ga. 30308, '66–; Ed., "Church-in-Mission" bi-monthly mag., '67–; Auth., "Where The Clock Walks" (Friendship Press, '64); numerous religious articles, '55–; Dir. of Info., Bd. of World Missions of Presbyterian Ch., '59–'66; Ed. of co. mags., Republic Nat. Life Ins. Co. (Dallas, Tex.), '57–'59; Reptr., The Dallas Times Herald, '55–'56; PRSA, RPRC (Nat. aws. for writing, '66, '68), Theta Sigma Phi, Press Club of Atlanta; 1st pl. nat. aw. for black and white ad series in a consumer mag., Am. Adv. Fedn., '68; reg. aw. for same campaign, Time

Magazine; Univ. of Texas, BJ, '55 (cum laude); Vanderbilt Univ.

TAYLOR, DONNA DOWLING, Instr., Dept. of Lib. Sci., Wayne State University, 455 Gen. Lib., Detroit, Mich. 48202, '65–; Sch. Librn., '64–'65, '53–'55, '44–'49; Contrbr. to pfsnl. jnls.; WNBA (Chptr. VP, '68–), Pi Lambda Theta, ALA, Am. Assn. of Sch. Librns., Mich. Assn. of Sch. Librns., Assn. for Supervision and Curriculum Dev., Dept. of Audio-Visual Instr., Am. Educ. Rsch. Assn., Assn. for Student Teaching; Who's Who in Lib. Svc., Who's Who of Am. Wm.; Wayne State Univ., BA (Educ., Lib. Sci.), '44; MEd (Sch. Librnship.), '64; EdD Applicant (Curriculum Dev.), '65– (Ex Officio Mbr., Library Sci. Alumni Assn. Exec. Bd.); b. Detroit, Mich.; p. Frank and Melba Cavill Dowling; h. James Taylor; c. Brian, Kim; res: Detroit, Mich. 48239.

TAYLOR, DORIS MARJORIE, Town Librn., Lucius Beebe Memorial Lib., Main St., Wakefield, Mass. 01880, '57–, Head Librn. (Gloucester, Mass.), '52–'57; Librn. (Ilkley, Yorkshire, Eng.), '40–'52; Lib. Asst. (Cambridge, Eng.), '28–'40; ALA, Mass. Lib. Assn.; educ: FLA, London, Eng.; res: 19 Eaton St. Wakefield, Mass. 01880.

TAYLOR, FLORENCE FERGUSON, Head Librn., Guyton Library, Blue Mountain College, Blue Mountain, Miss. 38610, '54–; Lib. Sci. Instr., '47–; Librn., Clinton (Miss.) HS, '42–'47; Eng. Tchr., '23–'26; Eng. Tchr., D'Lo (Miss.) HS, '22; Elementary Tchr., '21; Miss. Educ. Assn., AAUW; William Carey Col., BA, '20; Miss. Col., BA, '46; Peabody Lib. Sch., MA (Lib. Sci.), '58; b. Learned, Miss., 1899; p. Roderick and Cora Ervin Ferguson; h. Walter Fuller Taylor; c. Walter Fuller, Jr., Donn Ervin; res: Box 216, Blue Mountain, Miss. 38610.

TAYLOR, JEANNE, Shop Wise Ed., Seventeen Magazine, 320 Park Ave., N.Y., N.Y. 10022, '67–; Asst. Shopping Ed., Mademoiselle, '65–'67; Co-auth., "Where the Boutiques Are" (Simon & Schuster, '67); Manhattanville Col., BA, '65; b. Bridgeport, Conn., 1943; p. Larison and Lucille Maestri Taylor; res: 220 E. 73rd St., N.Y., N.Y. 10021.

TAYLOR, JERELYN MERLE, Ed., Ranger/Pan American Insurance Co., P.O. Box 2807, Houston, Tex. 77001, '68–; Ed., Bur. of Bus. Rsch., Univ. of Tex. (Austin); Eng. Tchr.; S.E. Tex. Indsl. Eds. Assn.; Tchr. aw., '62; N. Tex. State Univ., BA (Eng.); Univ. of Tex., MA (Eng./Educ.); b. Athens, Tex.; p. A. B. and Paralee Taylor.

TAYLOR, MARGARET KIRKWOOD, Cnslt., Margaret K. Taylor Public Relations, 3636 16th St., N.W., Wash., D.C. 20010, '54–; Educ. Dir., Nat. Milk Prodrs. Fedn., '44–'54; Legislative Rep., '43–'44; PR and Field Rep., United Dairy Comm., '42–'43; Commty. Radio Program, WHCU, Cornell Univ., '41–'42; Cnslt., White House Conf. on Children and Youth, '58–'60;

Partner, Convention and Conf. Coordrs., '60–'62; Exec. Dir., Am. Parents Comm. and Bd. of Parents Magazine, '62–'64; BPW (D.C. Pres., '55; Bus. Wm. of Yr., '57); numerous commty. orgs., activities; Cornell Univ., '17–'21; b. Harding, Pa.; p. Thomas and Harriet Welter Kirkwood; h. J. Laning Taylor; c. John Laning, III, Jean Taylor Mize.

TAYLOR, MARIAN YOUNG (pseud: Martha Deane), Bdcstr., WOR, 1440 Broadway, N.Y., N.Y. 10018, '41–; Wms. Ed., NEA, Scripps-Howard Synd., '34–'41; Staff Corr., '30–'34; Foreign Corr., '36–'37; Jnlsm Instr., Centenary Jr. Col., '38–'40; The Fashion Group (Bd. of Govs.), Intl. Rescue Comm. (Bd. of Trustees); Newsp. Wms. Club prize "best column in specialized wms. field," '37; radio colmsts. prize "best radio program for wm.," '42; Oh. State Univ. aw. "best wm. commtr.," '44, '48, '49, '52; Bdcst. Pioneers Dist. Svc. aw., '68; Auth., "Cooking for Compliments," '54.

TAYLOR, Dr. MARY-JEANNETTE, Dean of Student Pers. Svcs., Miami-Dade Jr. Col., 11380 N.W. 27th Ave., Miami, Fla. 33167, '66–; Chmn. Dept. of Speech, Drama, and Jnlsm.; Tchr. of speech, drama, and radio, Mich. State Univ.; N.Y.U.; Univ. of Fla.; Tobe-Coburn Sch. for Mdsng. (N.Y.C.).

TAYLOR, MARY KATHLEEN, Ed., General Federation Clubwoman Magazine, 1734 N St., N.W., Wash., D.C. 20036, '54–; WNPC, EPAA; b. Napa, Cal.; p. Walter and Hulda Block McGinn; c. Robert (dec.).

TAYLOR, RHOBIA CAROLYN, Reg. Dir., Women's Bureau, U.S. Department of Labor, 411 N. Akard St., Dallas, Tex. 75201, '64–; several PR, cnslt. positions; Assoc. Dir., USO in Fla.; AAUW, PRSA, BPW, Theta Sigma Phi, Nat. League for Nursing, Zeta Phi Beta, various aws.; Mary Hardin-Baylor Col., BA; Tchrs. Col., Columbia Univ.; Am. Univ., Univ. of Buffalo; b. Navasota, Tex.; p. Lawrence and Nora Stephenson Taylor; res: 903 Kelley St., Houston, Tex. 77009.

TAYLOR, SUE, Actress; SAG, AFTRA; Syracuse Univ., N.Y.U., '56 (summa cum laude, Phi Beta Kappa); b. Bklyn., N.Y., 1934; p. Nathaniel and Hilda Senft Taylor; h. Bill Persky; c. Dana, Jamie, Liza; res: 1500 Sunset Plaza Dr., L.A., Cal. 90069.

TAYLOR, SYLVIA SIROTA, Radio-TV Prodr., Moderator, Sylvia Taylor Productions, 22 E. 36th St., N.Y., N.Y. 10016, '54–; Dir., Press and PR, N.Y.C. Dept. of Welfare, '46–'51; Prodr., "International Interview," WNYC; Prodr., Moderator, "Careers," WNYC; "Worlds Fair Today," '64–'65; "Who's News" (TV), '54–'56; "Welfare Stories," '46–'51; Ed., Marlboro Hosp. Newsletter, '53; N.Y. Juror, Am. Film Festival, '63–'65; Critic, Film News, '63–'64; Auth., "Handbook for Democratic Candidates"; OPC, AWRT, ANWC; Cert. of Appreciation for Contrb. to Intl. Understanding, Mayor Lindsay, '67; Offcl. Aw.-Cooperation Golden Anniversary, '50; N.Y.U.; b. Bklyn., N.Y.;

p. George and Jennie Talley Sirota; c. Lawrence H., II, Patricia H.

TAYLOR, THELMA VOGT, Coordr. of Lib. Svcs., Los Angeles Harbor College, '48–'68; Tchr., Librn., numerous schs., cols., '23–'48; Cnslt., organizer of new libs., '33–'67; Judge, Commty. Achievs. Projects for S.W. L.A., '68; NEA, Cal. Tchrs. Assn., ALA (Secy., '53–'54), AAUP (Emeritus), AAUW, Cal. Sch. Librns., L.A. Sch. Librns. (Pres., '51–'52); Western Mich. Univ., AB, '23; Univ. of Chgo., MA, '30; Columbia Univ., MLS, '41; b. Battle Creek, Mich., 1902; p. Herman and S. Lillian Balcom Vogt; h. Jean Landon Taylor; c. Mrs. Jane Ann Roy; res: 916 Via Nogales, Palo Verdes Estates, Cal. 90274.

TAYLOR, VIVIAN LALAH, Pres., Taylor Associates International, P.O. Box 2252, Ft. Lauderdale, Fla. 33303; Med. Ed., J. B. Lippincott, Phila., Pa., '56; Sci. Ed., Benjamin Franklin Inst., '55; Reprtr., Ed., New York (N.Y.) Times, Philadelphia (Pa.) Bulletin, Detroit (Mich.) Free Press, Dallas-Ft. Worth (Tex.) Construction Record, Texas Jewish Post, TV Guide, '53–'56; Sci. Ed., Puerto Rico Nuclear Ctr., Mayaguez, '65–'67; Coast Guard Aux., C. E. Insp., Civil Air Patrol P. I. Offcr., Cert. SCUBA Diver, Ft. Lauderdale Symphony Soc., Circuit Lectr. (Intl.) Bahai Faith; Who's Who in the South and Southwest, Who's Who of Am. Wm., Dic. of Intl. Biog., Royal Blue Bk; Fla. Bahai State Public Info. Rep., '67–; Centenary Col., AA (Eng., Psych.), '44; Tex. Christian Univ.; Wayne State Univ.; Handels Hochschule, Switzerland; Univ. of Puerto Rico; b. N.Y.C., 1924; p. Wallace and Lalah Garrett Taylor.

TAYLOR, ZONA DALE LYONS, Prof. of Home Econs., Mississippi State University, P.O. Drawer HE, State College, Miss., '69–; Equipment & Home Furnishings Ed., The Progressive Farmer and Southern Living, '64–'67; Home Econst., Miss. Power Co., '61–'64; Am. Home Econs. Assn., Miss. Home Econs. Assn., Meridian BPW (Pres., '63–'64, VP, '62), AAUW, Home Econsts. in Homemaking (Lake Charles Chptr. Pres., '69); Who's Who of Am. Wm.; Univ. of Miss., BS, '61; McNeese State Univ., MEd, '69; b. New Albany, Miss., 1939; p. V. T. and Mary Aldridge Lyons; h. Charles Douglas Taylor; res: Box 3904, State College, Miss. 39762.

TEAGUE, SARAH ANN CRUMBLEY, Fashion Ed., The Birmingham Post-Herald, 2200 Fourth Ave. N., Birmingham, Ala. 35205, '64–; PR Asst., Samford Univ., '59–'64; Fashion articles, Birmingham mag., '67–'68; Birmingham Press Club (Charter Mbr.), Birmingham's Fall Fashion Time Comm., Chi Omega, Samford Alumni Assn. (Nat. Secy., '63–'64); BPW Outstanding Career Wm. of Birmingham, '68; Who's Who of Am. Wm; Samford Univ., AB (Jnlsm.), '59 (Dean's List); b. Holly Pond, Ala., 1938; p. James and Alma Reid Crumbley; h. D. Wayne Teague; res: 1429 S. 28th St., Birmingham, Ala. 35205.

TEAM, VIRGINIA CLARKE, Assoc. Art Dir., Columbia Records, 6121 Sunset Blvd., Hollywood, Cal. 90028, '69–; Designer, Columbia Records (N.Y.C.), '66–'68; Designer, New Center Studios (Detroit, Mich.), '64–'66; Detroit Art Dirs. aw., '65; N.Y. Soc. of Illus. cert., '68; Va. Commonwealth Univ., BFA, '64 (cum laude); b. Camden, S.C., 1942; p. John and Helen Clarke Team; res: 500 N. Martel, Hollywood, Cal. 90036.

TEARS, RUTH McCULLEY, Artist; Commn. Portraits, '61–; Tchr., painting, drawing, '58–; Staff Mbr., Dallas Col., Dallas Museum of Fine Arts, Southern Methodist Univ.; exhibited Burr Gallery (N.Y.C.), Sarasota (Fla.) Museum, Delgado Museum (N.O., La.), many others; Designer, Muscular Dystrophy Assn. of Am. Christmas card, '65; Leukemia Assn. Christmas card, '64; many aws., honors; Who's Who of Am. Wm., Dic. of Intl. Biog.; b. Detroit, Mich., 1919; p. Henry and Emma Marquardt McCulley; h. Claude F. Tears Jr. (div.); c. Claude III, Lisa Michele; res: 5924 Burgundy Rd., Dallas, Tex. 75230.

TEDESCO, ANGELA, Info. Supvsr., American Telephone & Telegraph, 32 Avenue of the Americas, N.Y., N.Y. 10013, '69–; Info. Asst., '67–'69; AE, BBD&O, '64–'67; Theta Sigma Phi; Northwestern Univ., BS (Jnlsm.).

TEETERS, PEGGY LANG, Wtr.; Writing Tchr., Arlington Adult Education Association, 1212 N. Quincy, Arlington, Va. 22207, '68–; Radio Script Wtr., Educ. Radio in Scandanavia, '69; F&P Prods., Kan. City, Mo., '67–'68; Bdcstr., AFN, '59–'67; Bdcstr., network wms. show, Berlin, '58–'59; Auth., "This Is the Army, Mrs. Jones" ('63); AWRT, Intl. Bdcstrs. Soc., AAUW, NEA, Arlington Wms. Club; Montclair State Col., '36–'39; St. Norbert Col., BS, '53; b. Hoboken, N.J., 1918; p. William and Elsie Schiesel Lang; h. Bernard Teeters; c. Bonnie (Mrs. Anthony Jezior), Michael, Bernard, David, Alan; res: 3125 N. Inglewood St., Arlington, Va. 22207.

TEICHMAN, SABINA, Artist, 27 E. 22nd St., N.Y., N.Y. 10010; Represented at ACA Galleries (N.Y.C.), Whitney Museum of American Art, Balt. Museum of Art, Smithsonian Institution, others; Audubon Artists (Secy., '65–'69); Columbia Univ., MA, '33; b. N.Y.C.; p. Maurice and Esther Goldberg Goldman; h. David A. Teichman; c. Wendy Levine; res: 1120 Fifth Ave., N.Y., N.Y. 10028.

TELFORD, PAULINE LEDFERD, Wms. Ed., Colmst., Illinois State Journal and Register, 313 S. Sixth St., Springfield, Ill. 62701, '59–; Publicist, '51–'59; Ed., Assoc. Gen. Contractors mag., '47–'51; City Ed., Ill. State Register, '44–'46; News Reptr., '36; Wms. Club of Springfield (Past Pres.), Springfield Art Assn., DAR; Copley Press Aws., '61, '68; Ill. Col., BS; b. Springfield, Ill.; p. Harry and Estella Plain Ledferd; h. Wil-

liam Charles Telford; c. Constance (Mrs. Fred Platt); res: 1551 W. Cook St., Springfield, Ill. 62704.

TELKES, MARIA, Head of Solar Energy Applications Laboratory, Melpar Inc., Falls Church, Va., '65–; Wtr., numerous pfsnl. articles and chptrs in bks.; Dir. of Rsch. and Dev., Cyo-Therm Co. (Fogelsville, Pa.), '61–'65; Rsch. Dir., Solar Energy Lab., Curtiss-Wright Co., '58–'60; Project Dir., Engineering, N.Y.U., '53–'58; Rsch. Assoc., Mass. Inst. of Tech., '39–'53; Rsch. Engineer, Westinghouse Rsch. Labs., '37–'39; Biophysicist, Cleve. Clinic, '25–'37; Rsch. Asst., Univ. of Budapest, '23–'24; Univ. of Budapest, PhD, '24; DSc (hon.); St. Joseph Col., '57; b. Budapest, Hungary, 1900; p. Aladar and Maria Laban Telkes; res: 2301 E. St. N.W., Wash., D.C. 20037.

TELLEEN, CARLA REYNOLDS, Entertainment Sec. Ed., Moline Daily Dispatch, 1720 Fifth Ave., Moline, Ill. 61265, '66–; TV Ed., '55–; Church Ed., '55–'69; Fashion Ed., '53–'66; Gen. News Reptr., '55–'66; Soc. Reptr., '51–'55; AAUW; Augustana Col., (Rock Island, Ill.), BA; b. Moline, Ill., 1927; p. Wesley and Irma Cox Reynolds; h. Frank F. Telleen; c. Nancy (Mrs. John Califf), William F.; res: 1221 45th St., Rock Island, Ill. 61201.

TEMBY, MABEL KUEHL, Co-owner, Enterprise Printing Company, 206 Ellis St., Kewaunee, Wis. 54216, '43–; Ed., The Kewaunee Enterprise, '52–; Ed., Lectr. for bus. and press groups; Wis. Press Wm. (State Edtl. 1st place aws., '53–'68; Pres., '53–'55), NFPW (Nat. Pres., '57–'59; Ed., "The Press Woman" '61–'69; edtl. aws., '53, '57), Theta Sigma Phi, Wis. Press Assn. (aw. for excellence, '68), Nat. Nwsp. Assn., C. of C.; Who's Who in the Midwest, Who's Who of Am. Wm.; b. Kewaunee, Wis., 1912; p. Herman and Frances Wodsedalek Kuehl; h. Charles Temby; c. Sandra (Mrs. Edward Christenson), Linda (Mrs. E. Robert Classon); res: 208 Vliet St., Kewaunee, Wis. 54216.

TEMKIN, SARA SCHLOSSBERG, Auth.; Asst. Dir., Cranford Public Library, 224 Walnut Ave., Cranford, N.J., '56–; Head of Serials, Ref. Dept., Army Med. Lib. (Wash., D.C.), '44–'48; Hosp. Librn., Goldwater (N.Y.) Memorial Hosp., '44; Ref. Librn., Linden (N.J.) Public Lib., '30–'43; Ed., N.J. Bibliographer; N.J. Lib. Assn., Col. Club (Linden, N.J.); N.J. Tchrs. Col., '40–'43; George Washington Univ., '44–'48; b. Hoboken, N.J., 1914; p. Morris and Katherine Sherman Schlossberg; h. Edward A. Temkin; c. Suzanne Mara; res: 15 Lenox Ave., Cranford, N.J. 07016.

TEMPLEMAN, ELEANOR LEE, Secy., Society of the Lees of Virginia, '49–; Auth.-Publr: "Arlington Heritage," "Northern Virginia Heritage" ('66); Hist. Colmst., '57–'59; Sci. Illus., U.S. Geological Survey, '35–'44; Staff Artist, Nat. Hq. Am. Auto Assn., '29–'35; Lectr.; various orgs.; Univ. of Cal., '25–'26; Critcher Sch. of Art; b. Wash., D.C., 1906; p. Robert and Ellen

Clarkson Reading; h. (div.); c. Robert Lee; res: 3001 N. Pollard St., Arlington, Va. 22207.

TEN HOOR, ELVIE, Artist, 6740 Oglesby Ave., Chgo., Ill. 60649; 11 one-wm. shows; numerous exhbns., prizes, incl. Margaret R. Dingle Aw. for most original art work, '61; Hadassah 1st Prize Monoprint; Dunes Art Fndn. Outstanding Prize, '58; others, '59, '61, '63, '64, '67; Co-auth., "College and Found Art" (Reinhold); Wtr., art and tech. articles in numerous pubns.; Lectr. on collage; various orgs., aws.; Sch. of Art Inst. of Chgo., Famous Artist Schs. grad., '58; Inst. de Allende, San Miguel Agt., Mexico; b. Watseka, Ill., 1900; p. John and Emma Kemnitz Mortensen; h. Perry John Ten Hoor (dec.); c. Gloria (Mrs. George H. Scofield), Perry John, Jr.

TENNANT, PATRICIA, Mdse. Mgr., Henri Bendel, 10 W. 57th St., N.Y., N.Y. 10019; '66–; Byr., '61; Retail Adv. Mgr., Clairol, '60; Adv. Dir., DePinna, '55; Asst. Adv. Mgr., Abercrombie and Fitch.

TENSEN, RUTH MARJORIE, Auth: "Come to See the Clowns" ('63), "Come to the Pet Shop" ('54), "Come to the City" ('51; Catholic Children's Bk. Club selection, '52), "Come to the Farm" ('49), "Come to the Zoo" ('48; N.Y. Times Outstanding Picture Bk. listing, '49); Primary Grade Tchr. (Rochester, N.Y.) '26–'61; Auths. Guild, Delta Kappa Gamma, N.Y. State Tchrs. Assn., N.Y. Intl. House; Who's Who of Am. Wm.; Contemporary Auths.; Teachers Col., Columbia Univ., BS, '43; MA, '45; Grad. Work, '48–'49; b. Rochester, N.Y., 1905; p. John and Frances Rykenboer Tensen; h. John A. De Witte.

TEPPER, FLORENCE HOGENCAMP, Program Dir., WCAT, Brookside Rd., Orange, Mass. 01364; Bdcstr.; Asst. Mgr., J. A. Tepper Co., '44; Real Estate Agt., Robichaud Ins. and Real Estate Co.; Travel Lectr., Fashion Show Commentator, '58–'63; Quota Club of Athol (VP, '66; Pres., '67), AWRT (Pres., '68–'70) Intl. Ctr. of Worcester (Bd. of Dirs.); Real Estate Sch., '65; b. Boston, Mass., 1919; p. William and Mary Fitzpatrick Hogencamp; h. Stanley Edmund Tepper; c. Patricia Ann, Michael Leonard, Lawrence Edmund, John Charles; 52 Highland St., Orange, Mass. 91364.

TERRA-NOVA, ESTELLE ANN, Prod. Mgr., A. S. Barnes and Company, P.O. Box 421, Cranbury, N.J. 08512, '69–; Asst. Prod. Mgr., '65–'69; WNBA; Bradley Univ., BFA, '62; b. Jersey City, N.J.; p. George and Estelle Terra-Nova; res: 343 Walnut St., Dunellen, N.J. 08812.

TERRELL, MARGARET ANN, PR Dir., Corporate Secy., The WDXB Broadcasting Company, The Read House, Chattanooga, Tenn. 37402, '68–; Program Dir., '66–'68; Exec. Secy. to Gen. Mgr., '64–'66; AWRT (Chattanooga Chptr. VP, '68–), Chattanooga Art Assn., Symphony Guild; Univ. of Chattanooga, '58

(Alumni Assn.); Webster Col., '59; b. Chattanooga, Tenn., 1940; p. Emmett and Adeline Stewart Terrell; res: Normandy Apts., No. A-1, 3501 Dayton Blvd., Chattanooga, Tenn. 57415.

TERRILL, ESTEL LUAN, Fine Arts, Mag. Ed., Register Division, Freedom Newspapers, Box 11626 Santa Ana, Cal. 92711, '60–; Orange County Press Club, Freedoms Fdn. (Orange County Wms. Div. VP), Orange County Performing Arts Cncl., Orange County Reg. Arts Cncl.; b. L.A., Cal., 1925; p. Elmer and Stella Schellenger Terrill; h. Robert H. Signor (div.); c. Carol Ann, John Robert; res: 13011 Ponderosa St., Santa Ana, Cal. 92705.

TERWILLIGER, ARDELLE PROSEK, Co-publr., Vernon County Broadcaster-Censor, Viroqua Newspapers Inc., 122 W. Jefferson St., Viroqua, Wis. 54665, '64–; Viroqua C. of C.; Wis. Press Assn.; b. Hurley, Wis., 1915; p. Edward and Ottillie Schmolinski Prosek; h. Reginald Terwilliger (dec.); c. James Reed, Joan Rhea Everson, Jeanne Ann Zeman; res: 409 North Main St., Viroqua, Wis. 54665.

TERZIAN, HELEN, Planning Dir., Norcross, Inc., 244 Madison Ave., N.Y., N.Y. 10016, '64–; Edtl. Dept., '50–'63; Assoc. Ed., Armenian Mirror-Spectator, '45–'50; Edtl. Bd. Mbr., Contrb., Ararat mag., '61–; Hunter Col., '32–'34; N.Y. Phoenix Sch. of Design, '32–'36; b. N.Y.C., 1914; p. Bedros and Anna Avedissian Terzian; res: 68–38 Groton St., Forest Hills, N.Y. 11375.

TETA, LILLIAN MORAN, Hostess, "Town & Country," WTEN, Capital Cities Broadcasting Company, 341 Northern Blvd., Albany, N.Y. 12210, '59–; Fashion Commentator, area stores, orgs., '58–; Hostess, "Woman's World," WTEN, '64–'68; Voice Tchr., '56–'65; Wms. News, Weather, WROW-Radio, '59–'60; TV Traf. Mgr., Wms. Dir., WTEN, '58–; Fashion Coordr., Commentator, Lord and Tann (Troy, N.Y.), '54–'58; Wms. Social News, WRGB, Schenectady, '57; WAST, Albany, '56–'57; various orgs., aws.; b. Balt., Md.; p. Lee and Sara Kogler Moran; h. Nicholas R. Teta; c. William Buck Halbert, Jr.; res: 25 Phillip St., Troy, N.Y. 12180.

TETER, THELMA FAY, Ed., employee pubns., Scott, Foresman and Company, 1900 E. Lake Ave., Glenview, Ill. 60025, IEA of Chgo., AAIE; Silver Aw., Scott, Foresman and Co., '66; b. Chgo., Ill.; res: 1400 N. Lake Shore Dr., Chgo., Ill. 60610.

TETLOW, KARIN COCUZZI, Rsch. Assoc., Fortune Magazine, Time Inc., Time and Life Bldg., N.Y., N.Y. 10020, '64–; Econ. Asst., Bus. Roundup, '62–'64; Edtl. Asst., Leather Trades Review, Benn Brothers, London, '58–'59; Nwsp. Guild of N.Y. (Shop Steward); Keele Univ., (England), BA (Hons.), '58; b. London, England, 1936; p. Luigi and Rachel Pinney Cox; h. Timothy C. Tetlow; res: 101 W. 80th St., N.Y., N.Y.

10024, also: Peterskill Heights, Alligerville, N.Y. 12440.

TEUFERT, JUDITH ANN, Prod. Mgr., Johnson-Livingston Advertising, Inc., 600 Foshay Tower, Mpls., Minn. 53402, '66–; Asst. to Prod. Mgr., Erle Savage Co., '63–'66; Col. of St. Benedict, BA (Art), '63; b. Minn. Lake, Minn., 1941; p. Harold and Marjorie Migelis Teufert; res: 2936 45th Ave. S., Mpls., Minn. 55406.

TEWS, RUTH MARIE, Supvsr., Hospital Library, Mayo Clinic, 200 First Ave. S.W., Rochester, Minn. 55901, '46–; Chief, Hosp. Lib. Div., St. Paul (Minn.) Public Lib., '39–'46; Lectr., Cnslt., libs., hosps., nursing schs.; Wtr., articles on bibliotherapy; ALA, numerous hosp., lib. orgs.; Univ. of Minn., BS (Lib. Sci.), Hospital Lib. Cert. (cum laude); b. Lewiston, Minn., 1907; p. Paul and Whilhelmina Janzow Tews; res: 23 Seventh Ave. S.W., Apt. 21, Rochester, Minn. 55901.

TEZACK, ANN ELIZABETH FRY, Prod. Mgr., Edward Owen & Company, 195 W. Main St., Avon, Conn. 06001, '66–; DAR, VFW Aux.; Tulane Univ., '42; b. N.O., La., 1921; p. George and Vera Glozier Fry; h. Charles Tezack; res: 1 Little Brook Rd., RFD 2, Winsted, Conn. 06098.

THACKREY, JESSIE DEAN, Ed., Falls Church School Report Card, Falls Church School Board, Falls Church, Va. 22046, '67–; Ed., Radio Anncr., Kan. State Ext. Svc., '34–'35; Theta Sigma Phi, Am. Field Svc., N.Va. Educ. TV Assn. (Bd. Mbr.); Kan. State Univ., BS, '34 (Phi Kappa Phi); b. Princeton, Kan., 1913; p. John and Eva Bice Dean; h. Franklin Thackrey; c. Janet Daugherty, Kent Dean, Maureen, Sue, Keith Richards; res: 102 W. Rosemary Lane, Falls Church, Va. 22046.

THALHEIMER, FLORENCE WEISS, Prodr., Modr., Public Affairs Dir., KCOP-TV, 915 N. La Brea Ave., Hollywood, Cal. 90038, '51–; programs: "Intelligent Parent," "Essentially Sex," "Potentially Potent," "World Talk," 44 aws., incl. First wm. to receive Justicia Aw. of Wilshire Bar Assn. for "Law for the Layman," and Am. Legion and Consular Corps; AWRT, Crippled Children's Soc., L.A. Mayor's Youth Advisory and Anti-Drug Comms., Pasadena Mayor's Comm. for Employment of Handicapped, Regional Educ. TV Conslt., Gov. Earl Warren's Educ. TV Comm. ('51), Beverly Hills Bd. of Educ. (three-time Pres.); b. Chgo., Ill., 1904; p. Leo and Edith Pacyna Weiss; h. Byron A. Thalheimer; res: 511 N. Maple Dr., Beverly Hills, Cal. 90210.

THANE, ELSWYTH, Auth., fiction; biog: "The Williamsburg Series" ('43–'57), "Dolly Madison" ('70), others; Wtr., Hist: "Mount Vernon is Ours," "Mount Vernon, The Legacy" ('66–'67); h. William Beebe; res: Wilmington, Vt.

THARP, LOUISE HALL, Auth. of 15 bks., primarily biography; NEA (Outstanding Bk., '53), ALA (aw., '53), PEN, Boston Auths. Club, Theta Sigma Phi (Hon. Mbr.), Delta Kappa Gamma (Educators Aw., '50); Hon. degrees: R.I. Col., Northeastern Univ., Wheaton Col., Mount Holyoke Col.; Educ: Sch. of Fine Arts, '17–'19; b. Oneonta, N.Y., 1898; p. Newton and Louise Varney Hall; h. Carey Edwin Tharp; c. Carey E., Jr., Marshall Allen; res: 20 Arrowhead Way, Darien, Conn. 06820.

THAYER, JANICE LARSON, Wms. Dir., KRGI, Stuart Broadcasting, Box G, Grand Island, Neb. 68801, '65–; created own radio show, "Food For Thought," '64–; Nursing Instr., St. Francis Hosp., '60–'63; Chief Dietitian, '60–'63; Chief Dietitian, Bryan Memorial Hosp. (Lincoln, Neb.), '58–'60; Cnslt. Dietitian, Howard County Hosp., '67–; Talent, Multi-Vue TV, '68; AWRT, numerous dietitian, home econs. orgs.; Finalist in Mrs. Neb. pageant, '68; Outstanding Young Wm. of the Yr., '69; Personalities of the West and Midwest, '69–'70; Univ. of Neb., BS (Home Econs.), '58; b. Grand Island, Neb., 1937; p. Alfred and Evelyn Andrews Larson; h. Ernest Thayer; c. David, Danny, D.J.; res: 390 E. 21st St., Grand Island, Neb. 68801.

THAYER, LORNA, Actress, theater: "The Only Bathtub in Cassis," "After the Fall," "Carousel," others; film: "I Want to Live," others; TV: "It Takes a Thief," "Garrison's Gorillas," others; AFTRA, SAG; Loyola Univ. Best Character Actress Aw., '47; Immaculate Heart Col., AB, '41; b. Boston, Mass., 1919; p. George J. and Lillian G. Harrington Casey; h. George N. Neise (div.); c. Adrienne Leonetti and Nikke.

THEDFORD, JULIA WARD, Wtr., agricultural articles; Ed., Assoc. Credit Bur. of Am., '66; Free-lance Wtr., '65–'66; Part-time Instr. of Jnlsm., Central Tex. Col., '67; Theta Sigma Phi, Southeast Tex. IEA ('65–'66); Tex. Wms. Univ., BA (Jnlsm., Hist.), '64; b. Houston, Tex., 1942; p. Theodore and Mary Powers Ward; h. Marvin Thedford; res: 1504 San Antonio, Tyler, Tex. 75701.

THEODORE, Sr. MARY, O.S.F. (Hegeman), Superintendent, St. Coletta School (for exceptional children), Jefferson, Wis. 53549, '64–; Prin., '50–'64; Tchr., '40–'50; Tchr., St. Lawrence School, Jefferson, '26–'30; Grad. Comm., Cardinal Stritch Col. '56; Auth: "The Challenge of the Retarded Child" ('57; rev. '63), "The Retarded Child in Touch With God" ('66); Nat. Conf. of Catholic Charities (VP, '52), Am. Assn. on Mental Deficiency, Nat. Assn. for Retarded Children; Delegate, Intl. Congress for Scientific Study of Mental Deficiency, Copenhagen, Den., '64; Intl. Aws. Symposium, Kennedy Fndn., Boston, '66; signing of HR 6430 at White House, '67; Wms. Aux., Catholic War Veterans, Wm. of the Year Aw., '60; Univ. of Wis. Phi Mu Sigma Aw. '67; Catholic Univ., MA (Psych.), '40; b. Burlington, Wis., 1907; p. Theodore and Mary Harter Hegeman; res: St. Coletta School, Jefferson, Wis. 53549.

THERRIAULT, SELMA CROW, Bus. Mgr., Staff Wtr., Grant County Journal, Box 998, Ephrata, Wash. 99823, '44–; Wash. Press Wm. (Pres., '65–'67, VP, '63–'65; aw., '66), BPW (State Pres., '56–'57; Whitman Col., '25 (cum laude); Univ. of Minn., MA, '30; p. Clarence and Alice Fox Crow; h. Frank Therriault; res: Box 505, Ephrata, Wash. 98823.

THIBAULT, MARILOU ELAINE, Bdcstr., KSTP-TV, Hubbard Broadcasting, 3415 University Ave., St. Paul, Minn. 55114, '68–; Continuity Dir., Bdcstr., WOW-TV (Omaha, Neb.), Meredith Bdcst., '64–'68; various positions, KBON Radio, '62–'64; Guest Lectr., Univ. of Neb., '67–'68; AWRT (Omaha Chptr. Pres., '68); Outstanding Young Wm. of Am., Who's Who of Am. Wm.; Univ. of Neb., BS (Jnlsm.), '64; b. Omaha, Neb., 1942; p. Lorin and Mary Thompson Thibault; res: 2710 Florida Ave., N. Mpls., Minn. 55427.

THIEL, EVE, VP, Crtv. Group Head, William Esty Company, 100 E. 42nd St., N.Y., N.Y. 10017, '67–; VP, J. M. Mathes; Copy Supvsr., Kenyon & Eckhardt; Wtr., Young & Rubicam, '55–'67; Finch Col.; b. Bronxville, N.Y.; p. Charles and Eva Thiel; res: 2665 Windsor Ave., Rockville Centre, N.Y. 11572.

THOMA, PAULINE LEONHARD, Ed., West Life, 26915 Westwood Rd., Westlake, Oh. 44145, '65–; Wtr., '60–; Corr., Cleveland Plain Dealer, '57–; Secy.-Treas., W. Cleve. Insulating Co. and Malco Distributing Corp.; Reptr., Oklahoma City Times, '44–'45; Wtr., Cleveland Press, '36–'43; Oh. Nwsp. Wms. Assn., Press Club of Cleve.; Ed. of Week Aw., Publrs. Aux., '67; b. Irwin, Pa., 1918; p. Howard and Mary Hlava Leonhard; c. Deborah, Judy (Mrs. William Mengerink); h. Walter Thoma; res: 3829 W. 210 St., Fairview Park, Oh. 44126.

THOMAE, BETTY KENNEDY, Exec. Secy., Bessey & Bessey Attorneys at Law, 330 S. High St., Columbus, Oh. 43215, '60–; Wtr., non-fiction mag. articles, '60–; "Stand Still, Summer" (Centro Studi E Scambi Internazionali of Rome, '68), poems in many anthologies; Marquis Biog. Lib. Soc., ASCAP; Centro Studi E Scambi Internazionali Medal of Hon. in Lit. and Cert. of Merit, '68 (Bd. of Dirs.); Glover Collection of Verse Intl. Poetry Competition hon. mention, '68; Danae of Intl. Poetry Glover Assn., '69; Franklin Univ., '65; b. Columbus, Oh., 1920; p. Ralph and Pearle Bawden Kennedy; h. Edwin Leroy Thomae (div.); c. Bonnie Sue Horstman (Mrs. Jack Stephen), William Lee; res: 10008 Hardesty Pl. W., Columbus, Oh. 43204.

THOMAS, B. ANNE, Ed., Ginn Publishers, Statler Office Bdlg., Boston, Mass. 02117, '69–; Educ. Info. Offcr., Mass. Dept. Educ., '64–'68; prom., polit. writing in Mass., free-lance writing, '58–'69; PR Dir., Stonehill Col. (N. Easton, Mass.), '57–'58; Jnlst., Boston Post, '52–'57; Congressional Quarterly News Features (Wash., D.C.), '49–'52; Assoc. Pubcty. Dir., aviation exec. N.E. Cncl. (Boston) and News and

Prom. Dir., Newsome PR, '46–'49; UP, '42–'45; Taunton Daily Gazette, '41–'42; NWPA, ANWC, Am. Col. PR Assn., Nat. Sch. PR Assn., AAUW (Dir., Boston Br.), others; Boston Univ., BA, '41; MA, '69; Univ. of Chgo., '47–'48; Harvard, '52–'53; p. George and Tamena (John) Thomas; res: 271 Dartmouth St., Apt. 6E, Boston, Mass. 02116.

THOMAS, BERTHA COMBS, Adv. Mgr., The Duke Times, Box 189, Main St., Duke, Okla. 73532, '42– (Marshall Gregory Aw., '68); Feature Wtr.; Soc. Ed., Adv. Mgr., The Eldorado (Okla.) Courier, '42–'46; Okla. Press Assn., Am. Legion Aux. (Pres., '47–'48); Okla. Natural Gas Co. edtl. aws., '57, '61; Okla. Col. for Wm.; b. Eldorado, Okla., 1918; p. William and Bertha Simmons Combs; h. Eugene Preston Thomas; c. Linda (Mrs. Paul Sherman), David Mitchell.

THOMAS, CELESTE MORRIS, Ed.-Publr., The Ropes Plainsman, 108 Hockley, Ropesville, Tex. 79358, '64–; Linotype Operator; Composing Room Foreman; Music Tchr., '56–'64; Tex. Technological Col.; b. Hamblin, Tex., 1930; p. Troy and Irene Dean Morris; h. B. J. Thomas; c. Berrilyn Whitehead, James Artie, Melonee Irene; res: 608 Timmons, Ropesville, Tex. 79358.

THOMAS, DIANE COULTER, Entertainment Ed., Atlanta Constitution, 10 Forsyth St., Atlanta, Ga. 30303, '69–; '66–'67; Reptr., '65–'66; Atlanta Critics Aws. Comm.; Emory Univ.; Ga. State Col., BA, '64; Columbia Univ., MFA, '69; b. Oakland, Cal., 1942; p. Charles and Mildred Coulter Thomas; res: 294-A Peachtree Hills Ave. N.E., Atlanta, Ga. 30305.

THOMAS, KAY (di ZEREGA), Fashion Ed., Daily News, 220 E. 42nd St., N.Y., N.Y. 10017, '61–; Mng. Ed., Charm Magazine, '59; Assoc. Fashion Ed., '50–'59; Fashion Ed., New York Sun, '32–'42; Auth., "Secrets of Loveliness" (Scholastic Bks., '63); NWC (N.Y. Pres., '42; Best Wms. Feature in N.Y. Nwsp. Aw., '41); Oh. State Univ., BA, '26; Sorbonne, '26–'27; b. Newark, Oh., 1903; p. Gilbert and Elizabeth Flanigan Daugherty; h. Louis di Zerega; c. Victoria (Mrs. Donald Thoman), Diana (Mrs. Russell Rockman); res: 554 E. 82nd St., N.Y., N.Y. 10028.

THOMAS, MARGARET DUDLEY, Owner, Margaret Thomas Public Relations, 1336 E. Vermont Ave., Phoenix, Ariz. 85014; Pubns. and Social Dir., Phoenix C. of C., '63–; PR Coordr., Metropolitan YMCAs, '63–'69; Feature, Wms. Page Wtr., Arizona Republic, '61–'63; Asst. Soc. Ed., '42–'44; PR Dir., Camelback Inn, '55–'61; Phoenix Rep., Laurence Laurie and Assocs. and McCulloch Properties, '64–; PR Dir., Goodwill Industries of Ariz., '69–; Ariz. Press Wm. (State Secy., '66–'67), PRSA, Theta Sigma Phi (Phoenix Chptr. Pres., '68–'70); state aws. for writing, poetry, direct mail; Phoenix Col., '41; b. Kingman, Ariz., 1921; p. Brooks and Margaret Hay Dudley; c. J. Evans II, Brooks Dudley, Betty Brooks.

THOMAS, PAT NEWSOME, Media Byr., Long, Haymes & Carr, Inc., 2006 S. Hawthorne Rd., Winston-Salem, N.C. 27103, '59–; Secy.-Receptionist, '58–'59; Twin City BPW (VP, '66–'68); Univ. of N.C., '56–'58; b. Winston-Salem, N.C., 1938; p. Jay and Ila Crabbe Newsome; h. Noal Thomas; c. Shannon Elizabeth, Brad Edward, Jay Gilbert; res: 3315 Stockton St., Winston-Salem, N.C. 27103.

THOMAS, PATRICIA KRESHA, Co-Publr., Pleasant Hill Times, 126 First St., Pleasant Hill, Mo. 64080, '69–; Univ. of Colo. Ext. Div. (Boulder), '66–'69; Co-Publr., Fruita Times (Fruita, Colo.); Co-Publr., Huerfano World (Walsenburg, Colo.); Univ. of Neb. Lincoln Ext.; Mesa Jr. Col.; Midland Col.; Univ. of Colo. Boulder Ext.; b. Osceola, Neb., 1929; p. Adolf, Sr., and Eva Karges Kresha; h. H. Eugene Thomas; c. Joseph, Karen Marie, Teresa Rose, Gloria Jean; res: 118 S. McKissock, Pleasant Hill, Mo. 64080.

THOMAS, ROSE MARIE PESCHAN, Free-lance Feature Wtr.; PR, Marietta (Oh.) Memorial Hospital, '55–'59; Reptr., Ed., Columbus (Oh.) Dispatch, '51–'55; Ed., Oh. Univ., '50; Edtl. Asst., Eastman Kodak Co., '46–'48; Ed., '43–'46; Theta Sigma Phi (aw., '51), Nat. Soc. of Arts and Letters; Kappa Tau Alpha, Sigma Delta Chi aw., '51; Univ. of Rochester; Ohio Univ., AB, '51 (Phi Beta Kappa, magna cum laude); b. Rochester, N.Y., 1924; p. Otto and Emma Walter Peschan; h. Richard J. Thomas; c. Gregory, Stephanie, Johanna; res: 101 Merryhill Dr., Marietta, Oh. 45750.

THOMAS, SHIRLEY, Auth., non-fiction bks. on space; VP, Annis & Thomas, '52–; Sr. Cnslt., George Wash. Univ., '65–; Stanford Rsch. Inst., '67–; Corr., CBS, Voice of Am., '55–'57; NBC, '52–'55; Nat. Assn. of Sci. Wtrs., Intl. Platform Assn., Aviation and Space Wtrs. Assn., Intl. Soc. of Aviation Wtrs., numerous sci., aeronautics, astronautics socs.; Frances Holmes Best Program Aw., '50, '51, Airpower Arts and Letters Aw., '60–'61; Aviation Educ. Assn. special aw., '62; U.C.L.A., Univ. of Southern Cal.; b. Glendale, Cal.; p. Oscar M. and Ruby Thomas Annis; h. William C. Perkins; res: 8027 Hollywood Blvd., Hollywood, Cal. 90046.

THOMPSON, BETTY ANNE, Asst. Gen. Secy., United Methodist Board of Missions, 475 Riverside Dr., N.Y., N.Y. 10027, '65–; Dir. of Commtns., '65–; Auth: "Thomas Wolfe: Two Decades of Criticism" in "Enigma of Thomas Wolfe" (Harvard Univ. Press, '53), "Turning World" (Friendship Press, '60), many articles, film strips; Ed.-at-Large, The Christian Century, '64–; PR Dir., World Cncl. of Chs., '57–'64; Pubcty. Secy. (Geneva, Switzerland), '55–'56; PR Dir., Wesleyan Col. (Macon, Ga.), '47–'49; Spanish Refugee Aid (Bd. of Dirs.), RPRC; Who's Who in PR; Who's Who of Am. Wm.; Wesleyan Col., AB, '47 (cum laude); Kenyon Sch. of Eng., '48–'49; b. Atlanta, Ga., 1926; p. Joseph Rogers and Anna Mary Jamerson Thompson.

THOMPSON, CHARLOTTE ANNE, Librn., University of Tampa, 401 W. Kennedy Blvd., Tampa, Fla. 33606, '36–; Fla. Lib. Assn. (Secy., '36–'37), Southeastern Lib. Assn., ALA, Zeta Tau Alpha, Delta Kappa Gamma, AAUW; Hollins Col., '27–'30; Univ. of Mich., AB, '31; AB (Lib. Sci.), '32; Columbia Univ., MS (Lib. Sci.), '55; b. Lansing, Mich., 1909; p. James and Mary Ardis Thompson; res: 4015 Bayshore Blvd., Tampa, Fla. 33611.

THOMPSON, CHARLOTTE KELLY, Mgr. of Mag. Pubcty., National Broadcasting Company, 30 Rockefeller Pl., N.Y., N.Y. 10020, '68–; PR Dir., Fawcett Pubns., '64–'67; PR Mgr., Ladies' Home Journal, '61–'64; Prod. Supvsr. to David O. Selznick, '59–'61; Ed., house organ, Foote, Cone & Belding, '51–'59; AWNY, AWRT; U.C.L.A., '48–'49; b. L.A., Cal.; p. Charles Kinney and Anne Marie Ferrero Kelly; h. W. Page Thompson; res: 18 E. 84th St., N.Y., N.Y. 10028.

THOMPSON, CONSTANCE PURTELL, Fgn. Lang. Ed., Gambit, Inc. Publrs., 53 Beacon St., Boston, Mass. 02108, '69–; Adv. Mgr., Houghton Mifflin Co., '43–'69; Radcliffe Col., AB, '35 (cum laude); Univ. of Munich; b. Brookline, Mass.; p. Lawrence and Elizabeth Streamberg Purtell; h. Lovell Thompson; res: 142 Arqilla Rd., Ipswich, Mass. 01938.

THOMPSON, DORIS STROMBERG, Ed., Howard County Times, Columbia Times; VP, Stromberg Publications, Inc., Box 312, Ellicott City, Md. 21043, '66–; b. Ellicott City, Md., 1924; p. Paul and LaRue Radcliffe Stromberg; h. Phillip St. Clair Thompson; c. Ann T. (Mrs. Charles E. Hogg Jr.), Sally Harman Thompson, Mary Ellen, Susan Jane, Amy LaRue; res: Petticoat Hill, Ellicott City, Md. 21043.

THOMPSON, DOROTHY BROWN, Wtr., verse; 2,000 poems in mags., nwsps., textbks., anthologies; Hist. Rschr.; Staff, numerous wtrs. confs., '53–'66; Lectr., Univ. of Kan., '65; Diversifiers, Poetry Soc. of Am., Am. Hist. Assn., Theta Sigma Phi, Filson Club, MacDowell Assn., numerous other cultural orgs.; Browning Soc. Aw., '37; Univ. of Kan. City Wtrs. Conf. Poetry Aw., '49; La. Poetry Soc. Space Aw., '58; many other state, local aws.; Univ. of Kan., AB, '19; b. Springfield, Ill., 1896; p. William Joseph and Harriet Gardner Brown; h. Dale Thompson; c. William B.; res: 221 W. 48th St., Regency House, Kan. City, Mo. 64112.

THOMPSON, EILEEN, Auth., fiction: "The Dog Show Mystery" (Abelard-Schuman, '66), "The Apache Gold Mystery" (Abelard-Schuman, '65), others; Auths. League; AAUW Short Story Aw., '62; Mystery Wtrs. of Am. Scroll, '66; Miami Univ., BA, '41 (cum laude; Phi Beta Kappa); Famous Wtrs. Sch. Cert., '63; b. Lincoln, Neb., 1920; p. Hugh and Nelle Masters Thompson; h. John B. Panowski; c. Thomas Michael, Bruce Philip, Lynn Eileen, Daryl Anne; res: 1267 46th St., Los Alamos, N.M. 87544.

THOMPSON, ELAINE HENSON, Sls. Prom. Mgr., Fidelity Bankers Life Insurance Company, Ninth and Main Strs., Richmond, Va. 23219, '69–; Asst. Dir. of Sls. Prom., '66; PR Mgr., '64–'66; Ed., '63–'64; Asst. Ed., '62–'63; Free-lance PR Cnslt. and Tech. Copywtr.; Assoc. Bus. Eds. of Va. (former Secy.), Life Ins. Advs. Assn.; Co. aws. for dept. work, '62–; Mary Washington Col., BA, '46–'50; b. Lynchburg, Va., 1929; p. Edwin and Hilda Marsh Henson; h. (div.); c. Burn Claire, Grant Bradford; res: 1514 Brigham Rd., Richmond, Va. 23226.

THOMPSON, ERA BELL, Intl. Ed., Johnson Publishing Co., 1820 S. Michigan Ave., Chgo., Ill. 60616; Co-Mng. Ed., Ebony, '51–'64; Assoc. Ed., '47–'50; Mng. Ed., Negro Digest, '50–'51; Sr. Interviewer, Ill. State Employment Svc., '42–'47; Auth: "Africa, Land of My Fathers" (Doubleday, '54), "American Daughter" (Univ. of Chgo. Press, '46); Soc. of Midwest Auths. (Bd. of Dirs., '61–), ZONTA, various other organizations and aws.; Univ. of N.D., '29–'31 (LLD Hon. degree, '69); Morningside Col., BA, '33 (LLD Hon. degree, '65); b. Des Moines, Ia.; p. Stewart C. and Mary Logan Thompson; res: 2851 S. King Dr., Chgo., Ill. 60616.

THOMPSON, HELEN KELLY, Product Cnslr., Avon Products, Inc., 30 Rockefeller Plaza, N.Y., N.Y. 10020, '65–; Mng. Sls. Prom. Materials, Warner Lambert, Ind.; Wtr., Revlon, Inc.; AWNY, Fashion Group.

THOMPSON, HELEN SMITH, Pres., Helen and John Thompson Foundation, 190 N. Center, Orange, Cal. 92666, '64–; Dir., The Thompson Reading Clinic, '50–; Tchr., Reading Specialist, Long Beach (Cal.) Schs., '28–'58; Assoc. Prof., Chapman Col., Visiting Lectr., Univ. of Cal., '58–; Auth., "The Art of Being a Successful Student" ('64), other educ. pubns.; Cnslt. Ed., Jnl. of Experimental Eds., '65–; Am. Psych. Assn., Intl. Am. Psych. Assn., Am. Educ. Rsch. Assn., N.Y. Acad. of Sci., Cal. Psych. Assn.; Drake Univ. Alumnae of the Yr., '66; Who's Who in Orange County, Cal. ('64); Drake Univ., AB, '26; Claremont Grad. Sch., MA, '50; b. Rock Rapids, Ia., 1903; h. John Thompson; res: 335 W. Orangewood Ave., Anaheim, Cal. 92802.

THOMPSON, JEAN, Ed., The Southland Family, The Southland Corporation, 2828 N. Haskell, Dallas, Tex. 75204, '68–; Mng. Ed., Dallas Magazine, Dallas C. of C., '61–'68; Ed., Tex. Employers Ins., '56–'60; Ed., Fed. Reserve Bank, '54–'56; Radio Continuity Wtr., KRLD, '52–'54; Dallas Adv. League, Dallas IEA (Ed. of the Yr., '59), Press Club of Dallas, Altrusa Club of Dallas; Theta Sigma Phi Matrix Aw., '67; N. Tex. State Univ., BA (Jnlsm.), '52; b. Mangum, Okla., 1932; p. William and Grayce Richardson Thompson; res: 1042 N. Winnetka, Dallas, Tex. 75208.

THOMPSON, LAURA DESMOND, Tchr., Ocean County School District, N.J.; Dir., Pers. and PR, Commty. Mem. Hosp., '64–'67; Ocean County Col.,

AA (Phi Theta Kappa), '69; h. William Thompson; c. William, Drew, Lynne; res: 148 James St., Toms River, N.J. 08753.

THOMPSON, MARGUERITE GRAMLING, Dir., Florence County Library, 319 S. Irby St., Florence, S.C. 29501, '61–; Librn., Colleton County Lib., '48–'61; Librn., Randolph County Lib. (Asheboro, N.C.), '45–'48; Librn., Rockingham (N.C.) HS, '43–'45; Eng. Tchr., '32–'43; ALA, BPW (Walterboro, S.C. Pres., '49; Asheboro, N.C. Pres., '45–'48), S.C. Lib. Assn. (Pres., '60, VP, '59, Treas., '57–'58), Delta Kappa Gamma (Psi Chptr., Pres., '62–'64, Treas., '66–'70); Univ. of S.C., BA (Eng.), '32 (cum laude); Emory Univ., BA (Lib. Sci.), '43; b. Orangeburg, S.C., 1912; p. Thomas and Rosa Stroman Gramling; h. Ralph B. Thompson (dec.); res: 1012 Woodstone Dr., Florence, S.C. 29501.

THOMPSON, MARJORIE A., Media Byr., Meltzer, Aron & Lemen, 165 Post St., S.F., Cal. 94108, '69–; Media Byr., Dieterich & Brown, '66–'69; Media Asst., BBDO; Briarcliff Col., '61; b. Baldwinsville, N.Y. 1941; p. Walter and Kathryn Kost Thompson; res: 3555 Broderick St., S.F., Cal. 94123.

THOMPSON, MARY JO, Assoc. Ed., The Advertiser-Tribune, 52 E. Market, Tiffin, Oh. 44883; Stringer, Cleveland Plain Dealer; NFPW; Heidelberg Col., AB, '34; b. Tiffin, Oh., 1912; p. Emil and Mathilde Ehrenfried Wagner; h. John Harold Thompson (dec.); c. Dr. John H., Christopher, Jane L. Paige; res: 118 Mohawk, Tiffin, Oh. 44883.

THOMPSON, MARY LEE, Wms. Ed., National Association of Manufacturers, 277 Park Ave., N.Y., N.Y. 10017, '68–; Food Ed., Feature Wtr., Today (nwsp., Cocoa, Fla.); Wms. Ed., Newark Star Ledger; Fashion, Beauty Ed., Chicago Herald American; Colmst.; b. Meadville, Pa.; p. Henry and Bertha Hyatt Thompson; res: 211 E. 18th St., N.Y., N.Y. 10003.

THOMPSON, VIVIAN L., Auth: "Camp-in-the-Yard" (Jr. Lit. Guild selection, '61); "Sad Day, Glad Day" (N.J. Assn. of Tchrs. of Eng. cit., '63); eight other children's bks., numerous children's mag. articles; Tchr., '30–'51; Marine Corps Wms. Reserve (Educ. Offcr.), '43–'45; Lib. Advisory Commn., '60–'67; Delegate Govs. Lib. Commn., '66; Auths. Guild, Mark Twain Soc., ALA; Tchrs. Col.; Columbia Univ., BS (Educ.), '39; MA, '43; Elwood Sch. of Pfsnl. Writing, '48–'49; b. Jersey City, N.J., 1911; p. Harry and Letty Lendrum Laubach; h. Daniel Thompson; res: Box 297, Paauilo, Hi. 96776.

THOMSEN, MARY ANN GROSSMANN, Wms. Ed., St. Paul Dispatch-Pioneer Press, 55 E. 4th St., St. Paul, Minn. 55101, '65–; City Desk Reptr., Fashion Wtr; UPI, Mpls. Bur., '60–'61; Twin Cities Nwsp. Guild Page One Aw.; Macalester Col., '60 (Jnlsm./Social Sci.); b. St. Paul, Minn., 1938; h. Tom Thomsen Jr.; res: 214 W. Curtis St., West St. Paul, Minn. 55101.

THOMSON, ELIZABETH WILLCOX, Dir., Hewlett-Woodmere Public Library, 1125 Broadway, Hewlett, N.Y., 11557, '47–; Chief, Reference Dept., Cuyahoga County, Oh., '47; Young Adult Librn., Cleve. Public Lib., '45–'46; Librn. P-1, Regimental Lib., U.S. Navy, Sampson, N.Y., '42–'45; Sr. Librn., Rochester Public Lib., '41–'42; Lib. Asst., Hobart Col., '37–'41; Lib. Cnslt., Brandeis Sch., Cederhurst; Lawrence Sch., Hewlett; East Rockaway Pub. Lib.; Publr.-Ed., Children's Record Revs., '57–'65; Auth: articles in Pfsnl. jnls., "The Fourth Wiseman: A Chancel Drama"; LPRC, Adult Educ. Assn., N.Y. Lib. Assn.; Nassau County Lib. Assn. (Pres., '54–'56; 1st Vice Pres. '52–'54; Secy., '50–'52), Nassau Lib. System Exec. Bd.; Five Towns Commty. Cncl., Music & Arts Fndn., Econ. Opp. Cncl., Golden Age Club; William Smith Col., BA (Eng.), '36 (Phi Beta Kappa); Hobart Col., MA, '37; Columbia Univ., BS (Lib. Sci.) '41; b. Hendersonville, N.C.; p. Rev. Reginald and Nell Gray Willcox; h. Walter Thomson; c. Douglas; res: 1140 E. Broadway, Hewlett, N.Y. 11557.

THOMSON, JOAN SCHURCH, Visiting Lectr., University of Wisconsin, Dept. of Agricultural Journalism, Madison, Wis. 53706, '69–; Instr., '67–'68; Rsch. Fellow, '64–'65; Cnslt., Voice of Am., '66; Am. Home Econs. Assn., Assn. for Educ. in Jnlsm., Theta Sigma Phi; Univ. of Wis., BS (Home Econs. Jnlsm.), '64 (high hons.); MS (Agricultural Jnlsm.), '65; PhD (Mass Commtns.), '69; b. Madison, Wis., 1941; p. Alfred and Velma Reich Schurch; h. Dennis Thomson.

THORNBURG, SUSAN HICKS, Program Dir., Wms. Ed., WIPC, P.O. Box 712, Lake Wales, Fla. 33853, '68–; Prodr., "Woman's World" daily show; b. Cleve., Oh., 1946; p. James and Jeannie Sell Hicks; h. Thomas Thornburg; c. Jeffrey Allan, David Scott; res: 1332 Morningside Dr., Lake Wales, Fla. 33853.

THORNTON, BARBARA, Dir., Ann Pillsbury Consumer Service Kitchens, Pillsbury Company, 608 Second Ave., Mpls., Minn. 55402, '67–; Assoc. Dir., Grocery Mix Area, New Product Dev., '64–'67; Assoc. Dir., Grocery Mix Area, '62–'64; Product Head, '60–'62; Product Head, Specialty Grocery Products, '57–'60; Mgr., Consumer Corr., '55–'57; numerous home econs. orgs., AWRT, Mpls. Adv. Club; Delta Delta Delta; Univ. of Minn., BS, '53; b. Mpls., Minn., 1931; p. Mathew and Stella Lien Thornton; res: 8300 Cedar Ave. S., Mpls., Minn. 55420.

THORNTON, EILEEN, Librn., Oberlin College, Oberlin, Oh. 44074, '56–; Vassar Col., '45–'56; Univ. of Chgo., '43–'45; Bemidji State Col., '39–'42; Cnslt., Col. Ctr. of the Finger Lakes, '63–'64; N.Y. State Educ. Dept., '55; Visiting Lectr., Columbia Univ., '49; Western Reserve Univ., '53, '61; U.S. Delegate, First Bi-Nat. Conf. on Libs. and Info. Sci., Tokyo, '69; Examiner, Middle States ('45–'56) and North Central ('56–) Assns. of Cols. and Secondary Schs.; ALA (Life Mbr.; Exec. Bd., various offs.), Oh. Lib. Assn., AAUP; Univ.

of Minn., BS, '31 (cum laude; Outstanding Achiev. Aw., '69); Univ. of Chgo., MA, '45; b. Wexford, Ireland, 1909; p. George and Eileen Geoghegan; res: 164 S. Prospect St., Oberlin, Oh. 44074.

THORNTON, FLORENCE TOBIN, Colmst., Independent, Woodburn, Ore. 97071; Speaker (travel, art); Nwsp. Wtr. (Alaska), '21–'53; Violin Tchr., (Alaska), '21–'31; Crtv. Wtrs. Club, Woodburn, Ore. (Leader, '64–'69); Alaska Fedn. of Music Clubs (Pres., '30–'45); Emerson Col. of Oratory, '18–'20; b. Boston, Mass., 1897; p. August and Emma Ericson Tobin; h. Laurance C. Thornton (dec.); res: 1291 Princeton Rd., Woodburn, Ore. 97071.

THORNTON, KATHLEEN BAUER, Prodr.-Hostess, "Panorama," WDBJ-TV, P.O. Box 227, Roanoke, Va. 24002, '66–; Free-lance Lectr., '66–; Free-lance Photogr., '61–'66; PR, Nelson Bond Assocs., '59–'60; Soc. Ed., Colmst., Adv. Mgr., Times-Register, '52–'59; AWRT (Blue Ridge Chptr. Pres., Golden Mike Aw., '67), Salem C. of C., Commty. Theatre (Co-Founder); Roanoke Col., BA, '52; b. Bismark, N.D., 1930; p. Otto and Laura Pearson Bauer; h. David F. Thornton; res: 324 Hawthorn Rd., Salem, Va. 24153.

THORNTON, THELMA SIEGEL, Dir. of PR, North Hills Passavant Hospital, 9100 Babcock Blvd., Pitt., Pa. 15237, '57–; Adult Educ. Tchr., City of Pitt., '57–; Instr., Prin., Noble-Thompson Inst., '46–'53; Am. Soc. for Hosp. PR Dirs., Pa. Hosp. Assn. of PR Dirs., PR Soc. of Western Pa. Hosp. (Treas., '69; VP), Nat. Assn. for Public Sch. Adult Educ., BPW; Thiel Col., BA (Eng.), '40 (magna cum laude); Univ. of Pitt. Grad. Sch. of Bus., Teaching Cert.; b. Irwin, Pa., 1919; h. (div.); c. James R. Thornton II, Paul B.; res: 8202 Peebles Rd., Pitt., Pa. 15237.

THORSEN, RUTH GALE, Asst. to Adult Educ. Dir., Ohio University, Belmont County Branch, St. Clairsville, Oh. 43950, '67–; Free-lance Model; Modeling, I. Miller, Vanity Fair, Chanel, '48–'56; "Miss Marine Corps" (Wash., D.C.), '45; b. N.Y.C.; p. Archibald and Freda Hintze Gale; h. William Thorsen (dec.); c. Dianne Lynn; res: R.D. #4 Nat. Rd. E., St. Clairsville, Oh. 43950.

THORSON, MARILYN McCRUDDEN, Free-lance PR, '68–; PR Dir., James Dines and Co., '67–; Pubcty. Dir., Girl Scout Cncl. of Gtr. N.Y.; PR, Clark-Nelson, Ltd., '67–'69; Radio-TV Spokeswm., '60–'67; Wms. Architectural Aux., Am. Inst. of Architects (N.Y. Chptr. Pres., '65–'66); Univ. of Minn., '51 (cum laude); b. Rochester, Minn.; p. William and Beatrice Johnson McCrudden; h. Robert L. Thorson; c. Blake, Bret; res: 360 E. 65th St., N.Y., N.Y. 10021.

THUDIUM, LILLIAN MARIE, Co-owner, Thudium Mail Advertising, 3553 N. Milwaukee Ave., Chgo., Ill. 60641, '49–'69; Wms. Adv. Club, Mayor Daley's Comm. for Betterment of Chgo., YMCA (Bd. of

Dirs.); Univ. of Southern Cal.; b. Elkhorn, Wis., 1915; p. Joseph and Lillian Maly Kurik; h. Joseph Paul Thudium; c. Terrence, Mrs. Joan Pena.

THURSH, JUNE ROSEN, Sls. Prom. and Adv. Dir., J. C. Penney Company, 1301 Ave. of the Ams., N.Y., N.Y. 10019, '64–; Partner, William Barton Marsh Co.; Adv. Mgr., Lit. Bros. (Phila., Pa.); AE, WHKC (Columbus, Oh.); Wms. Program Dir.; Adv. Colmst., Minneapolis Tribune; Instr., Fashion Inst. of Tech.; Dir. of Sls. Prom. Div., Nat. Retail Merchants Assn.; AWNY; 12 Seklemian Aws.; 9 Addy Aws.; AFA Aw.; Carleton Col., '39; Univ. of Minn., BA, '40; b. Duluth, Minn., 1917; p. Joseph and Sarah Crystal Rosen; h. Joseph J. Thursh; c. Joan M., Donald R.; res: 415 E. 52nd St., N.Y., N.Y. 10022.

TIBBETTS, ALMA L., Off. Mgr., The Chelsea Record, 18 Fourth St., Chelsea, Mass. 02150, '51–; Am. Intl. Col., BS, '35–; b. Gloucester, Mass., 1914; p. Curtis and Agatha Cameron Tibbetts; res: Kent Rd., Gloucester, Mass. 01930.

TICHY, KATHRYN STINSON, Ed., Publr., Niobrara Tribune, Niobrara, Neb. 68760; h. Edward Tichy.

TIEDT, IRIS McCLELLAN, Co-auth., "Contemporary English in the Elementary School" (Prentice-Hall, '67); Ed., The Elementary Teacher's Ideas & Materials Workshop (Parker monthly pubn.); Dir. of Tchr. Educ., Univ. of Santa Clara (Cal.), '68–; San Jose State Col., '62–'68; Univ. of Ore., '60–'62; Nat. Cncl. of Tchrs. of Eng., Modern Lang. Assn., Intl. Reading Assn., Lambda Theta Pi, Sigma Delta Pi; AAUW doctoral study grant, '66; Northwestern Univ., BS, '50; Univ. of Ore., MA, '61; b. Dayton, Oh., 1928; p. Raymond and Ermalene Swartzel McClellan; h. Sidney Tiedt; c. Pamela Lynne, Ryan Sidney; res: 1654 Fairorchard Ave., San Jose, Cal. 95125.

TIERNEY, DONNA MIRARCHI, VP, Acc. Supvsr., Sullivan, Stauffer, Colwell & Bayles, Inc., 575 Lexington Ave., N.Y., N.Y. 10022, '65–; Compton Adv., '56–'65; Instr., Cornell Univ., '53–'56; Adjunct Assoc. Prof. of Mktng., Pace Col.; Am. Chemical Soc.; Am. TV and Radio Commls. Festival cert., '69; two Am. Mktng. Assn. aws., '69; Delta Tau Alpha, Alpha Epsilon Delta; Adelphi Univ., BA (Biology, Chemistry, Psychology; Phi Beta Kappa); Cornell Univ., MA; b. N.Y.C.; p. Giacinto and Adeline Zollo Mirarchi; h. Francis Tierney; res: 30 Langdon Terr., Bronxville, N.Y. 10708.

TIFFIN, PAMELA K., Actress; Films: "Harper," "One, Two, Three," "Summer and Smoke;" Hunter Col., '59–'61; Columbia Univ., '62–'65; b. Okla. City, Okla., 1942; res: Vicolo Borghetto 20, Rome, Italy.

TILGHMAN, MAZA C., Dir., PR, Church Women United, 475 Riverside Dr., N.Y., N.Y. 10027, '64–; AWRT, PRSA, Commty Agcys. PR Assn., Am. Jewish Congress, CWPR; N.Y.U., BS, '56; b. Atlantic City, N.J., 1926; p. Clarence and Catherine Coleman Tilghman; res: 191-12 Hollis Ave., Hollis, N.Y. 11423.

TILLEY, BETTY FLEETWOOD, Soc. Ed., Tribune Publishing Company, 249 S. Tennessee St., Cartersville, Ga. 30120, '67–; Program Dir., WGRA Radio (Rome, Ga.); Free-lance Feature Wtr., The Atlanta Journal; BPW (VP, '69; Secy., '68), Beta Sigma Phi (Alpha Mu Chptr. Pres.), Child Welfare Cncl., Wms. Soc. of Christian Svc.; Outstanding Young Wm. of Am., '68; Univ. of Ga., '62–'63; Ext., '65; Shorter Col.; b. Manhattan, Kan., 1944; p. John and Jane Ackert Fleetwood; h. Joe Tilley; c. Carrie Beth; res: Rte. 4, One Cherokee Heights, Cartersville, Ga. 30120.

TILLINGHAST, PHYLLIS VAN HORN, Mgr., Travel Dev., Saturday Review, Inc., 380 Madison Ave., N.Y., N.Y. 10027, '68–; Mgr., Special Adv. Secs., Holiday, '62–'68; Dir., Educ. Dept., Cosmopolitan, '58–'62; Info. Wtr., Ore. State System of Higher Educ., '56–'57; AWNY, Hotel Sls. Mgt. Assn., Am. Hotel and Motel Assn., Carribbean Hotel Assn.; Pembroke Col., AB, '51; b. Jamaica, N.Y., 1929; p. Henry and Elsie Frick Van Horn; h. David R. Tillinghast; res: 300 E. 74th St., N.Y., N.Y. 10021.

TIMCHICK, MARY ROBERTA, Reviewer, Jr. Bks., The Cleveland Press, 901 Lakeside Ave., Cleve., Oh. 44114, '66–; Dir., World Friends Club, '66–'68; Oh. Nwsp. Wms. Assn., WNBA (Cleve. Chptr. Secy., '67–'69); Oh. Univ., BS (Jnlsm.), '64; b. Cleve., Oh.; p. Michael and Bertha Timchick; res: 3319 Saratoga Ave., Cleve., Oh. 44109.

TIMMER, SHARON NIDORF, Owner, Timmerco, 11294 Graham Pl., L.A., Cal. 90064; AE; Free-lance Wtr., fiction; Special Asst. to Publr., Hollywood Reporter, '68; AE, L. J. Globus, '66–'67; Media VP, Nides Cini Adv., '63–'65; AE, Reeves, Andrews & Stern, '59–'62; Media Dir., Wexton Co., '56–'57; Asst. Media Dir., J. R. Pershall Co., '57–'58; Artist, mags. and several exhbns.; Adv. and Edtl. Art in the West aw. for copy, '67; Goodman Theater, BDA (Dramatic Arts, '56); b. Detroit, Mich., 1934; p. Manuel and Evelyn Goldis Nidorf; h. John J. Timmer; c. Stacy, Adrienne, Gayle.

TIMMERMANN, SANDRA, Dir. of Info. and Pubns., Educ. Commtns., State University of New York, 60 E. 42nd St., N.Y., N.Y. 10017, '67–; Asst. Dir. of Pubcty., '67; AE, Rowland Co., '65–'66; Dir., Youth for Keating, '64; AWRT, State Univ. PR Cncl., NAEB; Univ. of Colo., BA, '63; Columbia Univ., MA, '66; b. Orange, N.J., 1941; p. Bernhard and Matilda Schaaf Timmermann; res: 460 E. 79th St., N.Y., N.Y. 10021.

TINDALL, MARILYN ANN, Model, fashion and TV, 8743 Sunset Blvd., L.A., Cal. 90069, '66–; Actress, roles in 3 Dean Martin films; Miss. Cal. Beauty Assn. (Pres., '69–'70); SAG, AFTRA; Model of the Yr., '67; Miss Cal., '63; Miss Universe Pageant; b. L.A., Cal., 1940; p. George Ernest and Evelyn Tindall; res: 1422 Kelton Ave., Westwood, Cal. 90024.

TINSLEY, PAULA L., Off. Mgr./Accountant, Mark Schreiber Advertising, Inc., 1090 Fox St., Denver, Colo. 80204, '62–; Am. Soc. of Wm. Accountants (Denver Chptr. #26 Pres., '69–'70; VP, '68–'69; Secy., '67–'68); Univ. of Colo.; b. Fruita, Colo., 1924; p. Ted and Nellie Redding Reed; c. Duane L., Michael R.; res: 525 E. Fifth Ave., Denver, Colo. 80203.

TISDALE, MARIE NOFER, Ed., World of Pretzels, Exec. Secy., National Pretzel Bakers Institute, Cherry Lane Farm, Star Rte., Pottstown, Pa. 19464, '66–; Wms. Ed., Pottstown News.; Century Club (Pres., '36–'38), Am. Red Cross (Past Bd. Mbr.); h. Alex V. Tisdale (dec.).

TITCOMB, MARGARET, Librn., Bernice P. Bishop Museum, P.O. Box 6037, Honolulu, Hi. 96818, '31–; Lib. Asst., Am. Museum of Natural Hist., '24–'31; Auth: "Native Use of Fish in Hawaii," "Kava in Hawaii," "Dog and Man in the Pacific"; other rsch. on Hawaiian food customs; Hi. Audubon Soc. (Pres., '68–'69), Conservation Cncl. of Hi., Fauna Commn. (Chmn., '68–'69); Packer Collegiate Inst., Bklyn., N.Y., '06–'10; Columbia Univ.; Univ. of Hi.; b. Denver, Colo., 1891; p. Ernest and Mary Rowbotham (adopted father George W. Titcomb); res: 3653 Tantalus Dr., Honolulu, Hawaii, 96822.

TITELBAUM, OLGA ADLER, Asst. Geog. Ed., Encyclopaedia Britannica, Inc., 425 N. Michigan, Chgo., Ill. 60611, '67–; Rsch. Asst. on atlas, '41, revision, '55; translations from Russian; Cnslt. Ed., Russian-Eng. dic., Follett Publ. Co., '64–'65; Translator, Ed., Nat. Sci. Fndn. Suvey of E. European Mathematical Literature, Univ. of Chgo., '59–'61; Lectr., Geog. of the U.S.S.R., Downtown Col., '59, '60; Statis. Secy., Grad. Lib. Sch., '35–'41; compiled, "Glossary of Terms in Water Resources," Assn. of Am. Geographers; Univ. of Chgo., BA (Geog.), '37; PhD (Slavic Linguistics), '67; b. Petrograd, Russia, 1916; p. Michael and Sophie Gunther Adler; h. Sydney Titelbaum; c. Daniel E.; res: 2003 W. 102nd St., Chgo., Ill. 60643.

TJADER-HARRIS, MARGUERITE, Auth: "Theodore Dreiser, A New Dimension" ('65), "Borealis" ('30); Ed., Publr., Direction, '37–'45; Translator; Wms. Intl. League for Peace and Freedom; Bryn Mawr Col., BA; b. N.Y.C., 1907; p. Richard and Margaret Thorne Tjader; h. (div.); c. Hilary Harris; res: Vikingsborg, Darien, Conn. 06820.

TOBIN, CLARA WILLARD, Ed., Co-publr., The Alaska Sportsman, Alaska Magazine Publishing Company, Ketchikan, Alaska, 23 yrs.; Tchr., Wash. and Alaska public schls.; Ketchikan C. of C. Soroptimist Club (Past Pres.), Am. Legion Aux. (Ketchikan Unit Past Pres.), Tongass Hist. Soc., Ft. Vancouver Hist. Soc., Pioneers of Alaska Aux.; Western Wash. State Col.; Univ. of Wash.; b. Willard, Wash., 1900; p. Emile and Barbara Egger Willard; h. Emery Tobin; c. Doris (Mrs. Gordon Bordine); res: 4304 Willamette Ct., Vancouver, Wash. 98661.

TOBIN, FRANCES CECELIA, Actress; SAG; Univ. of Cal., '38–'39; b. Victoria, British Columbia, 1920; p. James and Elizabeth Mooney Tobin; h. Richard R. Hipp (dec.); c. Richard F.; res: 605 N. Rodeo Dr., Beverly Hills, Cal. 90210.

TOBIN, LOIS WAGNER, Media Byr., Liller Neal Battle & Lindsey, Inc., 1300 Life of Georgia Tower, Atlanta, Ga. 30308, '66–; Media Byr., Harris & Weinstein Assoc., '65–'66; Governor's Commn. for Efficiency & Improvement in Govt.; Carolina Nitrogen Corp.; Sears Roebuck; Union Carbide; Atlanta Media Planners Assn.; Univ. of Pa., '48; b. Chgo., Ill., 1931; p. Fred and Johanna Macas Wagner; h. (div.); c. James, Andrea, Kevin, David; res: 3519 Glensford Dr., Decatur, Ga. 30032.

TOBIN, PATRICIA ELIZABETH, Fashion Cnslt., Actress; Wms. Programming Dir., Lane Bryant, '68; Dir. of Admissions, Berkeley Sch., '66–'68; Dir., Charm Dept., '66; Free-lance Actress-Commentator, '51–'66; Sls. Prom., Time, '60–'65; "Pat and Johnny" TV Show, '49–'51; AWNY, Episcopal Actors Guild, SAG, AFTRA, AEA; Stephens Col., AA, '45; b. Detroit, Mich.; p. Richard and Emma Thomas Tobin; h. Lewis Wollman; c. Jodi and Eric; res: 139 E. 63rd St., N.Y., N.Y. 10021.

TOD, DOROTHY, Free-lance Film Ed. and Prodr., Children's TV Workshop, 1865 Broadway, N.Y., N.Y. 10023, '69–; Film Ed., PBL, '69; Captain Kangaroo, '68; Ed., numerous feature films, TV Documentaries; Vassar Col., BA, '64; b. Youngstown, Oh., 1942; p. Fred and Nancy Brockett Tod; res: 797 Madison Ave., N.Y., N.Y. 10021.

TODD, FRANCES ELEANOR, Supvsr., Health Educ., San Francisco Unified School District, 135 Van Ness Ave., S.F., Cal. 94102, '31–; Auth, tchrs. guides, textbks.; Contrbr., pfsnl. jnls.; Am. Red Cross, Nat. Educ. Assn., Cal. Tchrs. Assn., Cal. Assn. for Health, Physical Educ., Recreation (two svc. aws.), Delta Kappa Gamma, numerous other orgs.; Who's Who of Am. Wm.; Who's Who of Am. Wm. in the West; Contemporary Auths.; Dic. of Intl. Biog.; Univ. of Cal., AB, '30; MA, '33; Stanford Univ., EdD, '51; Grad. work: Columbia, Yale, Univ. of Cal., Stanford, Univ. of Vienna; b. S.F., Cal., 1910; p. Frank and Ella Mattingly Todd; res: 1001 Pine St., S.F., Cal. 94109.

TODESCA, EDITH SHARPLES, Free-lance Wtr.; 36 yrs. with CBS as Exec., Prod. Mgr., Program Mgr., Wtr., Pers. Head; Wms. Ad. Club, Robert Browning Soc., Radio and TV Wm. Nat. and Intl. (Cal. Distg. Wm. Aw.), NATAS, Zeta Phi Eta, Nat. and Pacific Coast Radio Pioneers, L.A. C. of C., L.A. Heart Assn. (Bd. Mbr.; Outstanding Aw.); Aw. for First Wm. Program and Prod. Mgr. on West Coast; Boston Univ., Emerson Col., Univ. of Southern Cal.; b. Lancashire, Eng., 1898; p. Edward and Ellen Ashworth Sharples; h. Harry Todesca; res: 1811 Grace Ave., Apt. C, Hollywood, Cal. 90028.

TOFFEL, NANNIE JORDAN, Librn., Demonstration School Media Ctr., Stafford Elementary Sch., 1614 15th Str., Tuscaloosa, Ala. 35401, '68–; Librn., many schs., univs., '30–'68; NEA, Ala. Lib. Assn., other educ. orgs., Delta Kappa Gamma, Kappa Delta Pi, Alpha Beta Alpha (past Pres.), PEO, Intl. Platform Assn.; Troy State Col., '28–'30; Univ. of Ala., BS, '33; MA, '56; b. Midway, Ala., 1911; p. William and Jennie Stallings Jordan; h. George Mathias Toffel; c. George Jordan (dec.), Randall Keith (dec.), Miriam Abigail (Mrs. E. F. Dusza), Jennifer Maria; res: 303 Queen City Ave., Tuscaloosa, Ala. 35401.

TOLCHIN, SUSAN POPPER, Free-lance Wtr., '69–; Feature Ed., Co-ed, Scholastic Magazines, Inc., 50 W. 44th St., N.Y., N.Y. 10036, '67–'69; Feature Wtr., '66–'67; Theta Sigma Phi; Syracuse Univ., BA (Polit. Sci., Jnlsm.), '66 (cum laude); b. Mt. Vernon, N.Y., 1944; p. Milton and Berenice Solomons Popper; h. Lawrence Tolchin; c. Josh Michael; res: 360 E. 65th St., N.Y., N.Y. 10021.

TOLHURST, JOAN GAULENE, PR Dir., United Fund For Greater New Orleans Area, 211 Camp St., N.O., La. 70130, '65–; PR Dir., Arthritis Fdn., '64–'65; PR Asst., United Fund, '61–'64; PR Asst., Loyola Univ., '57–'60; ICIE (Nat. VP, '68–'69; S. Cncl. VP, '67–'68; N.O. Chptr. Pres., '66–'67; writing aw., '68), Un. Commty. Funds & Cncls. of Am., PRSA, Press Club of N.O.; Loyola Univ., '58; b. N.O., La., 1934; p. Bayard and Marie Grivas Gaulene; h. James Tolhurst; c. Evann Marie; res: 6631 Ave. B., N.O., La. 70124.

TOLLES, MARIAN DONAHUE, Mng. Ed., Administrative Science Quarterly, '66–'68; Mng. Ed., Soc. for Applied Anthropology, '58–'66; Secy., '64–'66; Smith Col., BA, '25; MA, '32; b. Cleve., Oh., 1902; p. Charles and Mary Crowell Donahue; h. N. Arnold Tolles; c. Patricia Eckert, Harriet Clement; res: 115 Orchard Pl., Ithaca, N.Y. 14850.

TOLLEY, EMELIE, Acc. Supvsr., VP, Benton & Bowles, 909 Third Ave., N.Y., N.Y. 10022, '68–; AE, '62–'68; Fabric Ed., Seventeen, '58–'62; Fabric Coordr., Celanese Corp., '55–'58; Fashion Group (VP, '69–'71); Wellesley Col.; N.Y. Sch. of Interior Design; p. Albert and Myra Polley Tolley; res: 142 E. 37th St., N.Y., N.Y. 10016.

TOLLIVER, MELBA, Reptr., American Broadcasting Company, 77 W. 66th St., N.Y., N.Y. 10023, '68–; Bdcst. News Trainee, '67–'68; NATAS (Edtl. Bd., Television Journal; Full Opportunities Comm.), Nat. Urban League, Odyssey House (Adv. Bd.); Bellevue Sch. of Nursing, Diploma, '59; N.Y.U.; Columbia Univ.; b. Rome, Ga., 1938; p. Emory and Susan Turner Tolliver.

TOMARA, SONIA, Reptr. (Foreign and War Corr.), Edtl. Pg. Wtr. for N.Y. Herald Tribune, '28–'53; OPC (V.P., '46); NWC (N.Y. Pres., '42); Univ. of Moscow, Russia, '18; b. St. Petersbourg, Russia, 1897; p. Michael and Olga Mamontoff Tomara; h. William Clark; res: 74 Russell Rd., Princeton, N.J. 08540.

TOMBRAS, ELIZABETH COLLINS, AE, Tombras & Payne, Inc., CTA Bldg., Central at Main, Knoxville, Tenn. 37902, '66–; AAF (Ed., Seventh Dist. Newsletter, '69–'70), Greater Knoxville Adv. Club. (Secy., '67–'69; Second VP, '69–'70); Univ. of Tenn., BS, '65; b. Knoxville, Tenn., 1940; p. William and Helen Wilson Collins; h. Charles P. Tombras, Jr.; res: 7100 Sherwood Dr., Knoxville, Tenn. 37919.

TOMLIN, ANNE P., Media Byr., Lawler Ballard Little Advertising, Suite 308, 800 Peachtree, N.W., Atlanta, Ga. 30309, '69–; Secy.-Treas., Dawson Daniels, Sullivan & Dillon (Nashville, Tenn.), '60–'69; Traf. Mgr., Doyne and Assoc., '54–'59; WMAK Radio, '53; AWRT (Nashville Chptr. Past Scy., Treas.), Exec. Secys., Inc. (Nashville Chptr. Past Pres., VP, Treas.).

TOMPKINS, ANGEL, Actress, c/o Kumin-Olenik, 400 S. Beverly Dr., Beverly Hills, Cal.: "The Dating Game" (Universal TV, '69), "Here Come the Brides" (CBS Studio Ctr., '68), "John and the Angel" (WCIU-TV, Chgo., Ill., '67; Emmy nomination), others; Corp. Image and Spokeswm., Milway Inc. (Milw., Wis.), '66–'67; SAG, AFTRA; Univ. of Tex. (Speech, Drama); Univ. of Ill.; b. Albany, Cal., 1945; p. Martin and Helen Robertson Stromberg; c. Troy Douglas Stromberg; res: 1651 Haslam Terr., L.A., Cal. 90069.

TOMPKINS, BERTHA M. TODD, Program Analyst, Voice of America, 330 Independence Ave. S.W., Wash., D.C. 20547, '69–; Special Events Offcr., '60–'68; Prod. Asst., '57–'60; Special Projects; D.C. Assn. for Mental Health, D.C. Dem. Wms. Club, NAACP, AWRT, Capital Press Club; b. Phila., Pa., 1934; p. J. Maxwell and Nana Westbrooke Todd; h. Albert E. Tompkins; res: 4222 17th St. N.W., Wash., D.C. 20011.

TOMPKINS, DOROTHY CAMPBELL, Public Adm. Analyst IV, Institute of Governmental Studies, Univ. of Cal., Berkeley, Cal. 94720, '52–; Asst. Public Adm. Analyst; Sr. Rsch. Tech.; Rsch. Asst.; Ed., Cal. Public Survey bi-monthly digest, '49–; Bibliographer: "The Confession Issue: "A Bibliography" ('68), "Strikes by Public Employees and Professional Personnel" ('67), others; Contrb. Ed., Criminologica; Western Govt. Rsch. Assn., Am. Soc. of Criminology, Am. Soc. of Indexers; Univ. of Cal., AB, '29; MA, '37; b. St. Paul, Minn., 1908; p. Harry and Alta Hayes Campbell; h. John Barr Tompkins; res: 909 Regal Rd., Berkeley, Cal. 94708.

TONNING, HELEN McKINLEY, Traf. Supvsr., National Broadcasting Company, 30 Rockefeller Plaza, N.Y., N.Y. 10020, '68–; Standards & Practices, WNBC, '67–'68; Spot Sls. Svc. Supvsr., NBC, '67; Network Sls. Svc. Coordr., '57–'66; Traf. Asst., WNBC-TV, '55–'57; WNBC Billing Dept., '51–'55; b. N.Y.C., 1932; p. George and Stella Sinani Galanis; h. Merrill Tonning; c. Karen, Karla, Kerry; res: 99-15 66th Ave., Forest Hills, N.Y. 11374.

TOOMEY, ALICE F., Chief, Catalog Maintenance

and Publication Division, Library of Congress, 10 First St. S.E., Wash., D.C. 20540, '63–; Head, Manuscripts Sec., '62–'63; Ed., Catalog Pubns., '50–'62; Cataloger, '49–'50; various other cataloger positions, '31–'49; ALA, Potomac Tech. Processing Librns., D.C. Lib. Assn., Church and Synagogue Lib. Assn.; Converse Col., BA, '27; Columbia Univ., BS (Lib. Sci.), '32; MA, '45; b. Orangeburg, S.C. 1906; p. Karl and Minnie Rosenbaum Finkelstein; h. John Toomey (dec.); res: 2601 Woodley Pl. N.W., Wash., D.C. 20008.

TOOMEY, JEANNE ELIZABETH, Free-lance Wtr., 49 W. 44th St., N.Y., N.Y. 10036; PR Dir., Girls Clubs of Am., '67–'68; Wtr., AP, '63–'64; Reptr., Reno (Nev.) Evening Gazette, '61–'62; New York Journal-American, '55–'61; Brooklyn Eagle; King Features Synd.; N.Y. NWC (Past Treas.), OPC, Nwsp. Reptrs. Assn. of N.Y.C.; Wms. Press Club aw., '60; Nev. Press Assn. aw., '61; Hofstra Col.; p. Edward and Gene O'Grady Toomey; h. Charles Ward; c. Sheila Terranova, Peter Terranova; res: Gondola Gardens, N. Sea Rd., Southhampton, N.Y.

TOOMEY, RUTH CONFORTE, TV Casting Dir. of Commls., Norman, Craig, and Kummel Advertising, 488 Madison Ave., N.Y., N.Y. 10022, '67–; Casting Dir., "Hawk" TV series, Screen Gems, '66; "The Doctors," Easterly Prods., '64–'66; Asst. Casting Dir., "The Nurses," "The Defenders," Plautus Prods., '63; Asst. and Casting Dir., live dramatic shows and series, Talent Assocs.; h. Jack Toomey; res: 6 Maple Ave., Demarest, N.J. 07627.

TOOZE, RUTH ANDERSON, Free-lance Lectr., Wtr., '61–; Auth., juv. bks. incl. "Our Rice Village in Cambodia" publ. by Viking Press, John Day Co., Prentice-Hall; AID Educ. Tech., Cambodia, '58–'61; Dev., Children's Book Caravan, '35–'48; WNBA, ACEI, ASCD, NCTE, AAUW; Delta Kappa Gamma; Oberlin Col., AB, '14 (Phi Beta Kappa); Columbia Univ., MA, '17; Nat. YWCA Training Sch., '16–'17; grad. work, Stanford Univ., '28–'30; b. Chgo., Ill.; p. Ernest and Amanda Seidel Anderson; h. William C. Tooze; c. Nancy Tooze Hansen; res: 946A Avenida Carmel, Laguna Hills, Cal. 92653.

TOPKINS, KATHARINE THEDA, Auth: "Kotch" ('65), "All The Tea In China" ('62); Co-auth., "Passing Go," (68); Rockefeller grant, '66; Columbia Univ., BS, '49; Claremont Sch., MA, '51; b. Seattle, Wash., 1927; p. Paul and Katharine Crane Theda; h. Richard Topkins; c. Rick, Deborah, Joan; res: 635 Robin Dr., Corte Madera, Cal. 94925.

TORNQUIST, HELEN TRIPLETT, Adv. Make-up Mgr., Modern Handcraft, Inc., 4251 Pennsylvania Ave., Kan. City, Mo. 64111, '60–; Publr., Canyon Courier, Evergreen, Colo., '58–'60; Triplett Composition Svc., Wichita, Kan., '53–'58; Asst. Supvsr., Printing Dept., Kan. City Life Ins. Co., '41–'53; b. Riverton, Wyo., 1917; p. Guy and Roda Mitchell Triplett; h.

Jack Tornquist; c. Linda McNally, Jerry Manning; res: 4608 E. Red Bridge Rd., Kan. City, Mo. 64137.

TORREY, JEAN SANDERS, TV Fashion Coordr., Fashion Commtr.; Photog. Model, Nina Blanchard Agency, 1717 N. Highland Ave., Hollywood, Cal. 90028, '51–; Free-lance TV Commls.; Partner in photog. workshop for new models; Instr., numerous assistance leagues; Tour Chmn., Mayor Yorty's Celebrity Comm. (L.A.); Mannequins Assn. (Pres., '69–'70; Secy., '68–'69); cited as one of 14 outstanding U.S. models in "Modeling and Other Glamorous Careers"; Ky. Wesleyan Col., '55–'58; Northwestern Univ., '48–'60; b. Owensboro, Ky., 1937; p. Rex and Margaret Anna Goodaker; h. Roger Torrey; res: 5646 Noble Ave., Van Nuys, Cal. 91401.

TOTH, MARILOU HARR, Wms. Pg. Ed., Union-Sun and Journal, S. Transit and Summit Sts., Lockport, N.Y. 14094, '69–; Gen. Reptr., '63–'68; Assn. of Pfsnl. Wm. Wtrs.; Sigma Delta Chi; two N.Y. State Publrs. Assn. Distg. Commty. Svc. Aws., '66; b. Bronxville, N.Y., 1933; p. John and Margaret Morrissey Harr; h. Carl Toth; four children; res: 5657 W. Bluff Rd., Olcott, N.Y. 14126.

TOTTEN, BETTY DAVIS, Classified Adv. Mgr., Mitchell's Publications, 113 W. Harvey, Wellington, Kan. 67152, '66–; '44–'45; Southwestern Bell Telephone, '45–'46; Attica Independent, '42–'44; BPW; b. Oberlin, Kan., 1923; h. Melvin Totten; res: RR #1, Wellington, Kan. 67152.

TOW, HAZEL HARTZOG, Club Ed., Evening Tribune, Union Tribune Publishing Co., 919 Second Ave., San Diego, Cal. 92101, '69–; Corr. and Wms. Dept., San Diego Union, '56–'69; Imperial Valley Superintendent of Schs., '66; Imperial Valley Weekly, Imperial Valley Post Press, '48–'56; Instr., Ed., Ia. State Univ. (Ames, Ia.), '47–'48; Night Cable Ed., UP (S.F., Cal.), '46–'47; Warr Corr., '43–'46; Picture Ed., Caption Wtr., Acme Newspictures (L.A., Cal.), '43; Asst. to Ed., Cal. Taxpayers Digest, '42; Wms. Ed., Visalia (Cal.) Times Delta, '40; various orgs.; Univ. of Southern Cal., BA, '40; b. Plato, Mo., 1920; p. John and Nellie Sullins Hartzog; h. (div.); c. Kristin; res: 2256 Albatross St., San Diego, Cal. 92101.

TOWERS, JUDY ANNE, Assoc. Prodr., National Broadcasting Company, 30 Rockefeller Plaza, N.Y., N.Y. 10019, '69–; Rschr., CBS News, '61–'69; Prod. Asst., WETA-TV (Wash., D.C.), '59–'61; Nat. Assn. of Sci. Wtrs., Wtrs. Guild; Wellesley Col., BA, '58; b. Wash., D.C., 1936; p. Frederic and Dorothy Close Towers.

TOWNLEY, BETTY LOU NEEL, Exec. Dir., Oklahoma County Libraries, 131 N.W. Third, Okla. City, Okla. 73107, '66–; Ext. Librn., '65–'66; Belle Isle Br. Librn., '63–'65; Asst. Dir., Pioneer Multi-County Lib. (Norman, Okla.), '61–'63; Tech. Svcs. Librn., Ponce City (Okla.) Public Lib., '59–'60; Offcr., Naval Reserve; Okla. Lib. Assn., ALA, Southwest Lib. Assn.;

Univ. of Tulsa, BA, '57; Univ. of Okla., MLS, '61; b. Pampa, Tex., 1935; p. Walter Merle and Leona McMurtrey Neel; h. Sam A. Townley; res: 4416 N.W. 11th Terr., Okla. City, Okla. 73107.

TOWNSEND, DORIS McFERRAN, Ed.-in-Chief, Rutledge Books, Inc., 17 E. 45th St., N.Y., N.Y. 10017, '60–; Free-lance Wtr., '42–'60; Ed., Radio-TV Mirror Magazine, '42–'52; Free-lance Wtr., Actress, '37–'42; Prog. Dir., WDGY (Mpls., Minn.), '36–'37; Auth., "Consumers' Buying Guide" ('69), many others incl. children's bks. under pseuds. Ann McFerran and Hannah Rush; Delta Phi Lambda, Auths. Guild; Univ. of Minn., BA, '34; Univ. of Kan., MS, '40; b. Mpls., Minn., 1914; p. Robert and Edith Hoar McFerran; h. William Porter Turner Townsend; c. Karen Ann (Mrs. Thomas McLaughlin), Lynne Mary (Mrs. Frank Turley); res: 301 E. 48th St., N.Y., N.Y. 10017.

TOWNSEND, K. JILL, Actress, c/o Herb Tobias and Assoc., 1901 Ave. of the Stars, L.A., Cal.: "Inadmissable Evidence" (Broadway), "Cimarron Strip" (TV), Old Vic Theater (London, Eng.); USO Volunteer (voluntary svc. aw.; numerous other aws.); AEA, SAG; Royal Acad. of Dramatic Art, '63–'65; b. Santa Monica, Cal., 1945; p. Robert and Joan Tours Townsend; h. John Thomas Sutton; res: 24878 Long Valley Rd., Hidden Hills, Cal. 91302.

TOWSLEY, ALICE CATHERINE, PR Dir. of Info. Svcs., Ed., American Field Service International Scholarships, 313 E. 43rd St., N.Y., N.Y. 10017, '67–; Free-lance Wtr., mags.; Contrb. Ed., Medical World News, '64–'68; Ed., Asst. Publr., The Doctor's Wife, '59–'64; Publ. Ed., Assn. of Jr. Leagues of Am., '54–'59; Reptr., Colmst., Honolulu Advertiser; Adv. Mgr., Paterson (N.J.) Morning Call; Nat. Soc. for the Prevention of Blindness, New York Herald Tribune, Idaho Free Press; OPC, AWNY; Univ. of Hi.; Columbia Univ.; b. N.Y.C.; p. George and Alice Kunkeli Goldsmith; res: 5 Tudor City Pl., N.Y., N.Y. 10017.

TOY, NOÉL, Actress; Asst. VP, Castagna Realty, 6350 Homewood Ave., Hollywood, Cal. 90028; b. S.F., Cal.; p. Hom and Mar Shee Gin; h. Carleton Young; res: 5506 Tuxedo Terr., Hollywood, Cal. 90028.

TRACER, JANNIE LOUISE CROWE, Head Librn., Placentia District Library, 143 S. Bradford Ave., Placentia, Cal. 92670, '61–; Head Librn., Gardner-Webb Col. (Boiling Springs, N.C.), '57–'61; Librn., Burlington City Schs., '50–'57; Librn. and Tchr: Piedmont HS ('48–'50), Hollis HS ('46–'48); Cal. Lib. Assn., Orange County Lib. Assn, N.C. Lib. Assn; Appalachian Univ., BS, (Lib. Sci.); b. Rutherford County, N.C., 1922; p. Audley and Hattie McSwain Crowe; h. Orvel Tracer; res: 131 Alta St., P.O. Box 615, Placentia, Cal. 92670.

TRACEY, W. ANN SCHOENMAN, Wms. Ed., News Journal, 70 W. Fourth St., Mansfield, Oh. 44901, '65–; Reptr., '48–'49; Oh. Nwsp. Wms. Assn., Mansfield Altrusa Club; Bowling Green State Univ., '48–'49; b. Albany, Ga., 1930; p. Robert and Anna Aughinbaugh

Schoenman; h. Carl E. Tracey; c. Stephen Michael, Vikki Ann; res: 571 W. Hanley Rd., Mansfield, Oh. 44904.

TRACY, PAULINE ALOISE SOUERS, Auth., numerous bks. of poetry; Ill. Pen Wm., Ill. Wm's Press Assn., NFPW, NLAPW; Eastern Ill. Univ. B.Ed., '37; b. Bridgeport, Ill., 1914; p. William and Carrie Milhous Souers; h. James Tracy; res: 447 Chestnut, Bridgeport, Ill. 62417; winter: Gulf Shores, Ala. 36542.

TRACY, VIRGINIA CORRIGAN, Fashion, Beauty Ed., News American, Lombard and South Strs., Balt., Md. 21203, '59–; Wms. Wtr., Evening Sun; Soc., Feature Wtr.; Wms. News; Sch. Ed.; Free-lance Pubcty.; participated in numerous col. career confs.; Fashion Group of Balt. (Wm. of the Yr., '63), Nwsp. Guild (former mbr.), numerous collegiate orgs.; Montgomery Ward Fashion Ed. of the Yr. aw., '69; numerous nat. aws. for fashion and beauty; Mt. St. Agnes Col.; John Hopkins Univ. (Jnlsm.); b. Balt., Md., 1903; p. James and Mary Burch Corrigan; h. Daniel O'Connell Tracy; c. Daniel, Jr., George, Mary Burch, Virginia Randolph; res: 109 Woodlawn Rd., Roland Pk., Balt., Md. 21210.

TRACY, WANDA NORINE, Traf. Mgr., Gulf Television Corp., KHOU-TV, P.O. Box 11, Houston, Tex. 77001, '58–; Cl., '56–'58; Ia. State Tchrs. Col., '39–'42; b. Lake Mills, Ia., 1921; p. Clifford and Iva Christie Tracy; h. (div.); res: 4747 W. Alabama, Houston, Tex. 77027.

TRAEGER, MILDRED, PR Dir., The Salvation Army, Southern California Division, 832 W. Ninth St., L.A., Cal. 90015, '64–; Owner, PR agcy., '58–'64; PRSA, L.A. Adv. Wm. (aw.), '67; Pubcty. Club of L.A., Public Info. Radio, TV Educ. Soc.; h. Lawrence Traeger; c. Suzanne, Jamie; res: 6300 Jumilla Ave., Woodland Hills, Cal. 91364.

TRAGER, RUTH ESTES, Media Planner-Supvsr., Tucker Wayne & Company, 2700 Peachtree Center Bldg., Atlanta, Ga. 30303, '66–; Media Byr., '57–'66; Traf. Mgr., WAGA-TV '51–'54, '55–'57; WAGA Radio, '48–'51; Sls. Prom. Mgr., WLAC-TV (Nashville, Tenn.), '54–'55; AWRT (Pres. Atlanta Chptr., '61–'62), Theta Sigma Phi, Atlanta Media Planners Assn., Atlanta Bdcst. Execs. Club; Southern Reg. Opera Cncl.; Alpha Omicron Pi; Univ. of Ga., AB (Jnlsm.) '47; Grad. Sch., (Adv.), '47; Emory Univ., (TV), '50; b. Pitt., Pa., 1925; p. Ralph and Rosa Holland Estes; h. Albert Trager; res: 3660 Peachtree Rd. NE, Apt. E-6, Atlanta, Ga. 30319.

TRAHEY, JANE, Pres., Trahey/Wolf Advertising, Inc., 477 Madison Ave., N.Y., N.Y. 10021, '66–; Pres., Trahey Advertising, '60–'66; Adv. Dir., Kayser-Roth, '56–'60; Adv. Dir., Neiman-Marcus (Dallas), '47–'56; Auth: "Life With Mother Superior," "The 100 Years of Harper's Bazaar," "Taste of Texas," "Pecked to Death by Goslings"; Fashion Group, AWNY (Adv. Wm. of 1969), WGA; Erma Goetz Aw.; Dallas Adv.

Aw.; Mundelein Col., BA, '44; grad. study, Univ. of Wis.; '46; b. Chgo., Ill.; p. David and Margaret Hennessy Trahey; res: 121 E. 69th St., N.Y., N.Y. 10012.

TRAINOR, JULIETTE ALICE, Head Librn., Paterson State College, 300 Pompton Rd., Wayne, N.J. 07470, '50–; Assoc. Prof., '52–; Asst. Prof., '46–'52; Instr., '38–'46; Asst. Librn., '38–'50; adjutant staff, Rutgers Univ., '48–'53; N.J. Lib. Assn. (Secy., '56–'57), Col. and Univ. Librns. of N.J. (Secy., '55–'56), Cncl. of N.J. State Col. and Univ. Librns. (Secy., '68–'69); N.Y.U., BA, '31; Sorbonne, Paris, Diplomèe, '33 (summa cum laude); Trenton State Col., BS (Lib. Sci.), '53; b. Bklyn., N.Y., 1911; p. James Trainor and Gabrielle Morda-Lefevre Trainor Marten; res: 120 Ridge Rd., Rutherford, N.J. 07070.

TRATNIK, ISABEL, Adv. Assoc., The Louis Allis Company, Division of Litton Industries, 427 E. Stewart St., Milw., Wis. 53201, '61–; Ed., The Louis Allis Messenger, '52–'60; Adv. Mgr., '47–'52; Milw. Adv. Club (Pres., '44–'45); Marquette Univ.; Univ. of Wis.; b. Manistee, Mich., 1911; p. Cecil and Blanche Czarnecki Brace; h. Joseph Tratnik (dec.); res: 319 E. Wilbur Ave., Milw., Wis. 53207.

TRAVER, DOROTHY ALICE, County Librn., San Bernardino County Library, 104 W. Fourth St., San Bernardino, Cal. 92401, '57–; Head, Br. Dept., '50–'57; Sch. Dept., '36–'50; Librn., Elsinore Union HS, '33–'66; Co-Auth: "Growing Oranges" ('58), "History of San Bernardino County Free Library" ('65); ALA, Cal. Lib. Assn.; Pomona Col., BA, '31 (magna cum laude); Univ. of Cal. Sch. of Lib. Sci., Cert., '33; b. Highmore, S.D., 1909; p. Eugene and Mabel Miller Traver; res: 3052 Genevieve, San Bernardino, Cal. 92405.

TRAVIS, JEAN SECO, Graphic Arts Mgr., Professional Products Divisions, Warner-Lambert Pharmaceutical Company, 201 Tabor Rd., Morris Plains, N.J. 07590, '47–; Adv. Prod. Mgr., Display and Convs. Mgr.; Packaging and Labelling Supvsr.; AWNY, Pharmaceutical Adv. Club of N.Y.; numerous aws. in graphic arts; Newark State Tchrs. Col., '26; b. Newark, N.J., 1905; p. Peter and Antonia Staiano Seco; h. Carroll Jackson Travis; res: 7 Sparrow Dr., Livingston, N.J. 07039.

TREADWELL, EMMA, Partner, Treadwell and Paul, 132 W. 23rd St., N.Y., N.Y. 10011, '66–; VP, David Bates Assoc., '65–'66; Prom. Cnslt., Salesmakers, '62–'65; Retail Prom. Mgr., Dow Chemical, '58–'62; Fashion Advisor, Butterick Co., '56–'57; Educ. Cnslt., The Jam Handy Org., '54–'56; Nat. Visual Presentation Assn. (VP and Dir., '63–'64), AWNY (VP, Dir., '68–'69), Fashion Group NHFL (VP, Dir., '69–'70); Tchrs. Col., BS, '48 (Kappa Delta Pi); Stanford Univ., MA, '53; b. Norwalk, Conn.; p. John and Ruth Stone Treadwell; h. Paul Spyropoulos.

TREDWAY, BEVERLY JEAN, Soc. and Feature

Coordr., Lawrenceville Publishing Co., 1209 State St., Lawrenceville, Ill. 62439, '67–; Morisawa Photo Typesetter, Type Coordr., '67; Friden Typist, '66; Ill. Press Assn., Southern Ill. Edtl. Assn.; b. St. Francisville, Ill., 1947; p. John and Betty Payne Tredway; res: 1110 Cherry St., Lawrenceville, Ill. 62439.

TREIMAN, JOYCE WAHL, Artist, Visiting Prof. at several schs. and cols.; many shows and exhibits, over two dozen aws. and prizes; Stephens Col., AA, '41 (Deering Aw., '40); State Univ. of Ia., BFA, '43 (Grad. Fellowship); b. Evanston, Ill., 1922; p. Rene and Rose Doppelt Wahl; h. Kenneth Treiman; c. Donald; res: 712 Amalfi Dr., Pacific Palisades, Cal. 90272.

TRELEASE, JULIA, Assoc. Ed., Playboy Magazine, 919 N. Michigan Ave., Chgo., Ill. 60611, '69–; Asst. Ed., '68–'69; Edtl. Asst., '68; Edtl. Secy., '65–'68; Carnegie Inst. of Tech., '55–'57; b. N.Y.C., 1937; p. J. Woodrow and Blanche Wagner Mathews; h. David Justin Trelease; res: 1460 N. Sandburg Terr., Chgo., Ill. 60610.

TRENHOLM, VIRGINIA COLE, Free-lance Wtr., Auth., four bks., numerous articles on frontier hist.; Instr., Park Col., '28–'31; Pubcty. Dir., Instr., Stephens Col., '26–'28; Pubcty., Sch. of Jnlsm., Univ. of Mo., '25–'26; Wyo. Press Wm., Western Wtrs. of Am., Theta Sigma Phi, Kappa Tau Alpha, Delta Gamma, several hist. socs.; Who's Who of Am. Wm., '68; Univ. of Mo., BJ, '25; MA, '26; grad. work, Univ. of Wyo.; b. Columbia, Mo.; p. James and Virginia Bedford Cole; h. Robert S. Trenholm (dec.); c. James R., Mrs. Virginia Phillippi; res: 2524 Maple Way, Cheyenne, Wyo., 82001.

TRENT, HELEN GEORGIE, Soc. Ed., The Pueblo Star-Journal, The Pueblo Chieftain, 825 W. Sixth, Pueblo, Colo. 81005, '50–; Wtr., The Colo. Fuel and Iron Corp. house organ, '43–'45; Colo. Press Wm; numerous aws. in nwsp. pubcty., prom., page makeup, layout; Pueblo Col.; Univ. of Colo.; b. Pueblo, Colo.; res: 515 W. Routt, Pueblo, Colo. 81005.

TREUTER, FLORANCE OWEN, Publr.-Owner, Commercial Recorder, 414 Dolorosa, San Antonio, Tex. 78204, '62–; Food Ed., The San Antonio Light; Reptr.; Theta Sigma Phi, Intl. Quota Club; b. San Antonio, Tex., 1906; p. James and Mary Nickelson Owen; h. Charles D. Treuter Jr.; res: 114 Hermosa Dr. E., San Antonio, Tex. 78212.

TREVASKIS, JANE LOUISE, PR Specialist, Penn Federal Savings and Loan, 1627 Walnut St., Phila., Pa. 19103, '69–; Assoc. Ed., SK & F News, Smith Kline & French Labs., '67–'69; Ed., Weatherheadliners, Weatherhead Co., '65–'67; Ed., Blue Cross News, Blue Cross of W. Pa., '63–'65; Pubns. Asst., Univ. of Pitt., '62–'63; Theta Sigma Phi, ICIE, AAIE; Pa. State Univ., BA (Jnlsm.), '62; b. Pitt., Pa. 1941; p. John and Isabella Muir Trevaskis; res: 2135 Spruce St., Phila., Pa. 19103.

TRICHEL, MABURL STILES, Wms. Dept. Ed., The Shreveport Times, 222 Lake St., Shreveport, La. 71102, '68–; Soc. Wtr., '64–'68; Adv. Copywtr., Sears, '63–'64; Wtr., The Natchitoches Times, '61–'62; Shreveport Press Club (Bd. of Dirs., '67–'69), Outdoor Wtrs. Assn. of Am. (Assoc. Mbr.); Northwestern State Col. of La., BA (Jnlsm.), '62 (cum laude, Phi Kappa Phi); b. Texarkana, Ark., 1941; p. Arthur and Evelyn McMain Stiles; h. Harry Trichel; c. Weyman; res: 818 Willow Dr., Shreveport, La. 71108.

TRIEM, EVE, Auth: "Poems" (Swallow Press, '65), "Heliodora" (translated from the Greek anthology, Olivant Press, '68), "Parade of Doves" (E. P. Dutton, '46), others; Dir., poetry workshops; Lectr.; Guest Ed., Poetry Pilot, other poetry mags.; Bk. Reviewer; numerous civic orgs.; Nat. Endowment for the Arts grant, '68; Nat. Inst. of Arts and Lts. aw., '66; League to Support Poetry aw., '46; numerous other poetry prizes; b. S.F., Cal., 1902; h. Paul Ellsworth Triem; c. Mrs. Joseph Prete, Peter D.; res: 911 Alder St., Seattle, Wash. 98104.

TRILLING, DIANA, Free-lance Wtr., non-fiction; Critic, The Nation, '41–'49; Auth., "Claremont Essays" (Harcourt Brace, '64); Ed., "Viking Portable D. H. Lawrence," "Letters of D. H. Lawrence" (Farrar, Straus); Am. Comm. for Cultural Freedom (Chmn., Bd. of Dirs., '55–'57); Guggenheim Fellowship, '50–'51; Radcliffe Col., AB; b. N.Y.C.; h. Lionel Trilling; c. James Lionel; res: 35 Claremont Ave., N.Y., N.Y. 10027.

TRIMBLE, EVE PEASNER, Exec. VP, Design/Southwest, Inc., 4432 Dallas Trade Mart, Dallas, Tex. 75207, '68–; PR Dir., Flexsteel Industries, '62–'68; Mng. Ed., Southwest Furniture News, '60–'62; PR, Adv. Mgr., The Datics Corp., '58–'60; Lectr.; Wtr.; NHFL (Dallas Chptr. VP, '64–), NSID (Trade Mbr.); North Tex. State Univ., '47–'49; b. Dallas, Tex. 1930; p. Marvin and Neitha Oliver Lackey; h. James W. Trimble; c. Thomas R. Peasner III, Dana Caprice Peasner, Elena Catherine Peasner; res: 11451 Cromwell Ct., Dallas, Tex. 75229.

TRIMBLE, LORA GARRETSON, Free-lance Wtr., non-fiction, PR; Theta Sigma Phi; Southern Methodist Univ., BA, '61 ("M" Aw.); b. Wichita Falls, Tex., 1935; p. J. C. and Geneva Higgenbottom Garretson; h. James C. Trimble; c. Christiana, James C., Jr.; res: 9445 Hunters Creek, Dallas, Tex. 75231.

TRINER, ALMA, Asst. VP, Dir. of PR, Crowell Collier and Macmillan, Inc., 866 Third Ave., N.Y., N.Y. 10022, '68–; Corporate Dir. of PR, '64–'68; PR Dir., Gen. Publ. Div., '63–'64; VP, N.Y. Br. Mgr., Daniel J. Edelman, '57–'63; Acc. Supvsr. (Chgo. Off.), '55–'57; AE, '53–'55; PRSA; Bklyn. Col., BA, '44; b. N.Y.C., 1926; p. Abraham and Frances Tennenbaum Triner.

TRISTER, BARBARA LEIPSIC, Pres., B.L.T.'S Fashion Inc., 819 Santee, L.A., Cal. 90014, '57–; Publicity, P.R., Fashion Mdsng.; Fashion Ed., Cal. Fashion Pubns., '45–'57; Univ. of Southern Cal. Jnlsm. Alumni Assn. (Pres., '60–'61, '66–'68; Distg. Svc. Aw., '67) Theta Sigma Phi (L.A. Chptr. Exec. VP, '68–'69), Gamma Alpha Chi (Hon. Mbr., '58); PRSA, Fashion Circle West (Pres., '66–'68), Fashion Group (Treas., '62–'63), Fashion Auxiliary, The Colleagues; Univ. of Southern Calif., BA; b. Redlands, Cal.; p. Aaron and Sophia Koeningheim Leipsic; h. Harry Trister; res: 581 Lorna Lane, L.A., Cal. 90049.

TROBE, GERTRUDE BRAUDE, Dir. of Wms. Activities, Beaver Valley Broadcasting, Inc., WBVP, 1400 Seventh Ave., Beaver Falls, Pa. 15010, '48–; Tchr., '44–'47; Wtr., Prodr., children's operettas, Selma Prods., '30–'40; AWRT (Nat. Dir., Pa. State Pres., Pitt. Chptr. Pres.), Cncl. of Jewish Wm. (Pres.), BPW, Quota Club; AP Wms. News aw., '56–'60; Who's Who of Am. Wm., '59; b. Harmony, Pa.; p. Joseph and Rose Zeman Braude; h. Max Trobe; res: Old Oak Dr., Patterson Heights, Beaver Falls, Pa. 15010.

TROKE, MARGARET KLAUSNER, Admr., '49–'99 Cooperative Library System, Stockton, Cal., '67–; Dir./Lib. Svcs., Stockton-San Joaquin Co. Pub. Lib., '46–; Librn., Napa County Lib., '44–'46; Sacramento City Free Lib., '29–'44; ALA, Cal. Lib. Assn., Commty Youth and Welfare Cncl., AAUW, Am. Soc. for Public Adm., BPW (Pfsnl. wm. of Yr., Stockton, '63), League of Wm. Voters, Sierra Club of Cal.; Citizen of the Month Aw., Civitan Club, '57; b. Omaha, Neb., 1911; h. Frank Troke; res: 825 W. Euclid, Stockton, Cal. 95204.

TROLLER, DOROTHY JOHNSON, VP of Adv., Coolant Equipment Corporation, 102 S. Lincoln St., Verona, Wis. 53593, '66–; Adv. Wtr., '56–; Wtr., scripts, WHA Radio, '50–'52; Wtr., trade mag., Edward J. Mayland, '48–'50; Copywtr., '47–'48; Theta Sigma Phi; Univ. of Wis., BA, '49; b. Oshkosh, Wis., 1928; p. Irvin and Hedwig Hever Johnson; h. Robert Troller; c. Susan, Thomas, Robert; res: 5810 Barton Rd., Madison, Wis. 53711.

TROTMAN, ROSALIE MOORE, Wms. Ed., The Daily Reflector, 209 Cotanche St., Greenville, N.C. 27834, '63–; Darkroom Tech., '58–'63; N.C. Press Wm., Jr. Wms. Club of Greenville; Nat. Fedn. of Music Clubs aw., '59; E. Carolina Univ., '56–'58; b. Durham, N.C., 1938; p. David and Idell Moore; h. John Trotman; c. John Anthony; res: 204 N. Warren St., Greenville, N.C. 27834.

TROTT, ROSEMARY CLIFFORD, Staff Corr., Dealerscope, Northeast, 115 Second Ave., Waltham, Mass. 02154, '69–; Poet: "Sea Mist and Balsam" ('58), poems published in many periodicals; Ed., "From One Bright Spark" ('59); Hist. Rschr., "Maine Islands" (Lippincott); News Reptr., WLOB, '57; Feature Wtr., Lewiston Journal, '47–; Copywtr., WPOR, '49; Feature Wtr., Corr., Brunswick Record, Portland Press Herald, Evening Express, Sun Telegram, '42–'47; Colmst., Portland Evening Express, '32; numerous orgs., aws.; Bates Col., '42; Columbia Univ. (Jnlsm.), '47; b. Mt. Vernon, N.Y., 1914; p. Edward and Beatrice Wright Clifford; h. James Edwin Trott; c. Donald Victor, Rosemary Diane; res: Blueberry Hill, Freeport, Me. 04032.

TROTTA, GERALDINE (Geri), Auth.; Feature and Travel Ed., Harper's Bazaar, 717 Fifth Ave., N.Y., N.Y. 10022, '59–; bks: "Veronica Died Monday" (Dodd, Mead, '51), "Dead As Diamonds" (Bordman, London, '56), "Dune House" (Farrar, Straus, '60); Contrb. Ed., Mademoiselle, '48–'59; features in N.Y. Times, Playbill, Mademoiselle, Look, numerous other national magazines; Auths. Guild, N.Y. Travel Wtrs. (Pres., '69–'71), Am. Soc. of Travel Wtrs.; Barnard Col., BA (Fine Arts); b. N.Y.C.; p. Pasquale and Katherine Marconi Trotta.

TROUBETZKOY, ULRICH (Dorothy), Colmst.-Feature Wtr., Richmond News Leader, 333 E. Grace St., Richmond, Va. 23213, '59–; Ed., Virginia Cavalcade, '59–'63; Info. Offcr., City of Richmond, '56–'58; Asst. Ed., Virginia Wildlife, '51–'56; Assoc. Ed., Virginia and the Virginia County, '51–'53; Colmst., Richmond Times-Dispatch, '51–'56; Contrbr., Ed., Avocations, '37–'39; "Arts Alive," WRVA-Radio, '63–'64; "Shapes & Sounds of Poetry," WCVW-TV, '67–; Instr., Va. Commonwealth Univ., '61–; Pres., Writers Unlimited, '69–; Auth: "Bluebonnets and Blood," (68), "Where is Christmas?" ('60), "Richmond, City of Churches," ('58), "Out of the Wilderness" ('57), "Edwin Arlington Robinson" ('37); NFPW (Pres., '67–'69), ANWC, Poetry Soc. of Am., Va. Wtrs. Club, New Eng. Wtrs. Club, Poetry Soc. of Va., Acad. of Am. Poets, Va. Press Wm.; numerous aws. and hons.; Vassar Col., '32–'33; Univ. of Chgo., BA, '36; Columbia Univ. Grad. Sch., '36–'38; Cornell Univ., '45; b. Hartford, Conn., 1914; p. George and Alice Smith Ulrich; h. Serge Troubetzkoy; c. Daria (Mrs. Robert Lewis), Sergei, Vilna; res: 2223 Grove Ave., Richmond, Va. 23220.

TROWER, DOROTHY HARDING, Bdcstr.-Prodr., Feature Wtr., Fashion Ed., Brockton Enterprise and WBET, 60 Main St., Brockton, Mass. 02403, '47–; Feature Wtr., '40–; Fashion Ed., '56–; WCOP, '39–'40; WMEX, '38–'39; Lectr.; AWRT (Nat. Secy.), '50; Eastern VP), Boston Fashion Group, Little Theatre (Brockton Founder), Wms. Club (Brockton Pres., '58–'60), Brockton Art Ctr. (Bd. of Govs., '69), civic orgs.; Radcliffe, AB, '30; b. Quincy, Mass., 1907; p. Henry and Persis Thayer Harding; h. Ralph E. Trower; c. Mrs. Alvin S. Graves, Myron F. Fuller; res: 55 Rock Meadow Dr., Brockton, Mass. 02401.

TRYON, IOLA B., Dir. of Film Dept., Russell Library, 119 Broad St., Middletown, Conn. 96457, '48–; Asst. Librn., Buck Lib. (Portland, Conn.); Tchr., Univ. of Conn., '67–'68; Contrb. Auth., "Using Films," '67; Wtr., film reviews, Film News; Educ. Film Lib. Assn., ALA, Am. Film Festival, New Eng. Lib. Assn., Conn. Lib. Assn., AAUW, Soroptimist Club, numerous cultural orgs.; Univ. of Conn., BS, '32; S.

Conn. State Col., MS, (Lib. Sci.), '62; b. Ansonia, Conn., 1908; p. Elmer and Ethel Buck Tryon; res: 54 Gleason Rd., Middletown, Conn. 06457.

TRZOS, CAROLE A., Prod. Mgr., E. W. Baker, Inc., 1750 Buhl Bldg., Detroit, Mich. 48226, '67–; Media, J. Walter Thompson, '63–'64; Pers. Staff, Gen. Motors, '64–'67; Prod. Men's Club of Detroit; Mich. State Univ., BA (Adv.), '63; b. Pontiac, Mich., 1941; p. Otto and Muriel Chatfield Trzos; res: 611 Orleans, Detroit, Mich. 48207.

TUCHMAN, FRAN HARRIS, VP, Crtv. Dir., Harris-Tuchman Productions, Inc., 751 N. Highland Ave., L.A., Cal. 90038, '50–; Founder, Head of TV-Motion Pic. Dept., Ruthrauff and Ryan (Chgo., Ill.), '45–'50; Wtr., WBKB-TV, '42–'45; Dir., Tech., Actress, radio and theater, '42–'43; Guest Lectr.; Contrbr., Delphian Quarterly; L.A. Adv. Wm. (Pres., '61–'62; VP, '60–'61; Treas., '57–'59; 16 Golden Lulu Achiev. Aws., '53–), Intl. Platform Assn., numerous civic orgs.; Radio-TV Wm. of Southern Cal. Merit Aw., many other pfsnl. aws.; Faust Sch. of Theatre Arts; b. N.Y.C., 1915; p. David and Tillie Rosen Yampolsky; h. Ralph G. Tuchman.

TUCKER, AVIS GREEN, Ed.-Publr., The Daily Star-Journal, Pres., The Star-Journal Publishing Company, Inc., Johnson County Broadcasters, Inc., 135 E. Market, Warrensburg, Mo. 64093, '66–; VP, Johnson County Bdcstrs., '60–'66; VP, Star-Jnl. Publ. Co., '47–'66; Children's Mercy Hosp. Central Governing Bd., '62–, Green Securities (Kan. City Dir., VP, '62–), C. of C., Kappa Alpha Theta (Nat. Dir., Secy., '68–; Kan. City Alumnae Chptr. Theta of the Yr., '62); Outstanding Boss Aw. by Warrensburg and U.S. Jaycees, '68; Univ. of Mo., AB, '37; b. Concordia, Kan., 1915; p. Ralph and Nelle Schroer Green; h. William C. Tucker (dec.); res: Sunrise Farm, Centerview, Mo. 64019.

TUCKER, CAROLE ANN, Mng. Ed. and Former Adv. Svc. Dir., 'Teen Magazine, Petersen Publishing Company, 8490 Sunset Blvd., L.A., Cal. 90069, '66–; Opns. Asst., Pacific Tel. & Tel., '64–'66; New Eng. Tel. & Tel. (Boston, Mass.), '62–'64; Ed., Triangle Topics, Telephone Pioneers of Am.; Programmer, PR Central Area Speakers' Bur. and Script Dev.; Shakespeare Soc. of Am., Paulist Players, Southern Cal. Eds. Assn.; Pacific Telephone Speakers' Contest Wm. Champion Oratorical Winner, '56; Boston Univ., '62–'64; U.C.L.A. (Adv. Mgt.); b. Newton, Mass., 1943; p. Markham and Ursula Foley Lyons; h. Jack Tucker; res: 1360 S. Kelton, W. L.A., Cal. 90034.

TUCKER, CAROLYN COSTIN, Dir. of Public Educ., Bd. of Dirs., Crossroads Rehabilitation Center, 3242 Sutherland Ave., Indpls., Ind. 46205, '61–; Dir. of Special Events, '60–'61; PRSA (Hoosier Chptr. Secy.), PR Soc. of the Am. Hosp. Assn., AWRT, Wms. Press Club of Ind. (Golden Quill Aw., '68), Jr. League, Govs. Commn. on the Handicapped; De Pauw Univ., BA, '49; b. Indpls., Ind. 1927; p. James and Mildred

Chandler Costin; h. John D. Tucker; c. John David, Jr., Tracy Lee; res: 6160 Afton Crest, Indpls., Ind. 46220.

TUCKER, MAE S., Head of Main Lib. Public Svcs., Public Library of Charlotte and Mecklenburg County, 310 N. Tryon St., Charlotte, N.C. 28202, '56–; Ref. Asst., '45–'56; compiled "Textiles, A Bibliography" ('52); ALA, Special Libs. Assn., Southeastern Lib. Assn., N.C. Lib. Assn. (Corr. Secy., '55–'57; Rec. Secy., '63–'65), Mecklenburg Lib. Assn. (Pres., '62–'63), AAUW, BPW, Beta Phi Mu; Appalachian State Tchrs. Col., BS, '43; Univ. of N.C., BS (Lib. Sci.), '45; b. Mount Holly, N.C., 1922; p. Walter Lee and Mamie Lantz Shuford Tucker; res: 108 W. Catawba Ave., Mount Holly, N.C. 28120.

TUCKER, PATRICIA, Free-lance Jnlst.-PR Cnslt.; Info. Offcr., E. Central Fla. Reg. Planning Cncl., '65–'68; PR-Offcr.-Dir., Eastern Forestry, '56–'60; PR-Sls. Dir.-Offcr., Dwight Corp., '56–'57; PR-Legal Cnslr., Johnson-Crooks Alaska, '54–'55; Mng. Ed., Sci. Illustrated, '44–'45; Reptr.-Rschr., Time, Inc., '41–'44; Comm. for the Effective Use of Intl. Court, '63, Texas Bar, '40–; OPC, World Peace Through Law (Exec. Comm., '68), Missile, Space & Range Pioneers; Tulane Univ.; b. Red Lodge, Mont.; p. Royal and Juliet Luttrell Tucker; c. Lael Hollister Jackson; res: 2917 Timberlake Dr., Orlando, Fla. 32806.

TUFTY, ESTHER VAN WAGONER, Pres., Tufty News Service, 997 National Press Building, Wash., D.C. 20004, '36–; News Commentator, NBC, '52–; Lectr.; Fgn. Corr.; Mng. Ed., Evanston (Ill.) News Index: Reptr., Pontiac (Mich.) Daily Press; WNPC (Pres., '42), Theta Sigma Phi Headliner Aw., '66), ANWC, AWRT (Nat. Pres., '60–'61); Aw. for Dist. Svc. from President Lyndon Johnson, '63, Nat. Achiev. Aw., Nat. Assn. of Colored Wms. Clubs, '62, Cert. of Appreciation, Radio Free Europe; Univ. of Wis., BA (Jnlsm.), '21; Mich. State Univ.; b. Kingston, Mich.; p. James and Florence Loomis Van Wagoner; h. Harold Tufty (dec.); c. Harold G., Jr., James Van Wagoner; res: 820 Arcturus-on-Potomac, Alexandria, Va. 22308.

TUGGLE, MABEL ALICE, Staff Wtr., Communications Bureau, National Board, YWCA of the U.S.A., 600 Lexington Ave., N.Y., N.Y. 10022, '45–; Edtl. Staff, New York Daily News; Edtl. Staff, New York Herald Tribune; Ed., Danville (Va.) Commercial Appeal; Colmst., Lynchburg (Va.) Daily Advance; Pubcty. Club of N.Y. (Past VP), Theta Sigma Phi, Nat. Religious PR Soc. Wayne State Univ., BA, '31; Northwestern Univ., MS (Jnlsm.), '45; b. Stonewall, Va., 1912; p. Thomas and Rose Ingram Tuggle; res: 150 E. 52nd St., Apt. 304, N.Y., N.Y. 10022.

TURKEVICH, LUDMILLA BUKETOFF, Prof., Chmn. of Russian, Douglass College of Rutgers University, Arts Bldg., New Brunswick, N.J. 08903, '60–; Lectr. in Russian, Princeton Univ., '46–'61; Lectr. in Modern Langs., '42–'44; Visiting Lectr. in Spanish and Russian,

N.J. Col. for Wm., '45–'46; Instr. in Spanish, Wash. Sq. Col. of N.Y.U., '42–'44; Ed., Auth. of numerous bks. on lang., literature; Modern Lang. Assn., Eng. Speaking Un. many lang. assns.; Aw. for Distinguished Svc. (U.S.I.A., '60); Wash. Sq. Col., BA, '31; Univ. of Kan., MA, '32; Columbia Univ., Ph.D., '35; b. New Britain, Conn., 1909; p. Constantine and Militza Lebedeff Buketoff; h. John Turkevich; c. Marina (Mrs. Robert Naumann), Tamara (Mrs. Daniel Skvir); res: 109 Rollingmead, Princeton, N.J. 08540.

TURMELL, KITTE, Synd. Nwsp. Colmst., "Teenager," '69–; Wtr., articles in over 50 mags.; Guest Speaker, radio and TV shows; Social Case Worker; Future Jnlsts. of Am. (Hon. Mbr.), Theta Sigma Phi, Phi Kappa Phi, Cal. Press Wm.; Sigma Delta Chi aw.; Univ. of Wis., AB (Jnlsm.); Mt. St. Joseph Col.; Univ. of Southern Cal., grad. work; b. Bay City, Mich., 1909; p. Charles and Katherine Thompson Mitchell; h. Jerome Wilfred Turmell; c. Charles, Susan; res: 4345 Talofa Ave., N. Hollywood, Cal. 91602.

TURNBO, SHARON LEE, Wms. Ed., Daily Democrat, Southeastern Publishers, Inc., 106 E. Cherokee, McAlester, Okla. 74501, '66–; Food Ed., '67–; Kiamichi Magazine Ed., '69; Okla. Baptist Univ. (Jnlsm.); b. McAlester, Okla., 1942; p. Frohman and Bernice Meador Turnbo; res: 303 E. Peoria, McAlester, Okla. 74501.

TURNBULL, MILDRED BROWN, Librn., Venice (Fla.) Area Public Library, '66–'69; Librn., Warder Public Lib. (Springfield, Oh.), '48–'65; Librn., Carnegie Public Lib. (Steubenville, Oh.), '46–'47; Librn., Harbor Public Lib. (Ashtabula, Oh.), '24–'45; ALA, Fla. Lib. Assn., Oh. Lib. Assn., League of Wm. Voters, Humane Soc. of the U.S.; Western Reserve Univ., BA, '44; Grad. Sch. of Lib. Sci., '44–'45; b. Ashtabula Oh., 1900; p. H. Merton and Edith Rotheram Brown; h. Alex Turnbull (dec.); res: 329 Sunrise Dr., Nokomis, Fla. 33555.

TURNER, DOROTHY BANKER, Owner-Publr., The Creative Press, '55–; Crtv. Writing Instr.: Univ. of Southern Cal., '59–'61; Univ. of Redlands, '49, '55; Edtl. Positions: Claremont Courier, '43–'45; Tustin News, '46; Pomona Progress-Bulletin, '30–'41; Ontario (Cal.) Daily Report, '29; Free-lance Ed., Cnslt., Wtr.; Auths. League, Auths. Guild, Cal. Wtrs. Guild, AAUW (hon. mbr.), Theta Sigma Phi; cultural orgs.; Pomona Jr. Col., '26–'28; Univ. of Southern Cal, AB (Jnlsm.), '30; b. Anaheim, Cal, 1909; p. James and Thora Ingjaborg Banker; h. Welford Burgess Turner (dec.); res: 891 South K St., San Bernadino, Cal. 92410.

TURNER, JANET ELIZABETH, Prof. of Art, Chico State College, Chico, Cal., 95926, '59–; Asst. Prof., Stephan F. Austin State Col. (Nacagdoches, Tex.), '47–'56; Tchr., Girl's Collegiate Sch. (Claremont, Cal.), '42–'47; Artist: paintings and prints in over 400 reg., nat., intl. exhibitions; numerous aws.; works in many museums, galleries, incl. Benzalei Nat. Museum, Jerusalem; Biblioteque Nationale, Paris; Victoria and

Albert Museum, London; Metropolitan Museum of Art, N.Y.C.; numerous art orgs., incl. Nat. Acad. of Design (Assoc. Mbr.), NAEA, Who's Who in Am., Who's Who in Am. Art, Who's Who of Am. Wm., Intl. Dir. of Arts, 2,000 Wm. of Achiev. ('69), Dic. of Intl. Biog., others; Stanford Univ., AB (Far Eastern Hist.), '36; Claremont Col., MFA, '47; Columbia Univ., EdD, '60; b. Kan. City, Mo.; p. James and Hortense Taylor Turner; res: 317 Ivy St., Chico, Cal. 95926.

TURNER, MOLLY, Public Affairs Dir., WLBW-TV, 3900 Biscayne Blvd., Miami, Fla. 33137, '61–; WPST-TV, '56–'61; Talent, Dir., Wtr., Prodr., WTVJ-TV, '51–'56; Copywtr., '48; Theta Sigma Phi, AWRT (Gold Coast Chptr. Pres.), Cncl. of Un. Fund Wm. (VP); Freedom Fndn. aw., '68; Fla. State Col., Univ. of Ala.; b. Anniston, Ala.; p. Mahan and Meeks Theora Hopkins; h. Philip Ruppenthal; c. Lyle Cameron, John Christian; res: Coral Gables, Fla.

TURNER, RUTH NEWHALL, Coordr., Informational Programs, Contra Costa County Library, 1750 Oak Park Blvd., Pleasant Hill, Cal. 94523, '64–; Head, Readers Svcs., '58–'64; Supervising Branch Librn., '44–'58; Ref. Librn., '34–'44; Asst., '31–'34; San Francisco Chronicle, '27–'29; ALA, Cal. Lib. Assn., Theta Sigma Phi; Univ. of Cal., BA, '26; Grad. Sch. of Librarianship, Cert., '27; b. Dayton, Ohio; p. Herbert and Mary Burroughs Turner; res: 162 Hemme Ave., Alamo, Cal. 94507.

TURNER, SUE LONG, Cont. Wtr., Sls. Svc. Dir., KAWZ-TV, Wichita Falls, Tex., '69–; Wtr., Hallmark Communications (Abilene), '66–'69; AE; Off. Mgr., KRAM, Nevada Bdcst., '69–; Cont. Dir., KRBC TV, '54–'55, '56–'61; Free-lance Wtr., fiction, non-fiction in mags. and nwsps., '50–'54; '56–'57; Adv. Fedn., AAUW (Abilene, Tex. Crtv. Writing Div. Pres., '58); short story aws.; adv. aws.; Hardin-Simmons Univ. (Jnlsm.), '37–'40; b. Albany, Tex., 1922; p. Henry and Mary Burke Long; h. Russell K. Turner (div.); c. Mrs. Jerry Leonard, Russ, Ronald E.; res: 1674 Dayton, Wichita Falls, Tex.

TURNEY, ESTHER NUERNBERGER, Ed.-Publr., Wakefield Republican, 224 Main St., Wakefield, Neb. 68784, '44–'69; Home Econst., General Electric Co., '38, !a.-Neb. Light and Power Co., '28; Neb. Press Assn. (Ak Sar Ben Aw., '61), NPA, Wakefield Commty. Club, Lions Club (Hon. Mbr.); Univ. of Neb., Home Econs. Deg. ('28); b. Wakefield, Neb. 1905; p. Henry and Anna Roost Nuernberger; h. Frank Turney (dec.); c. Thomas, Charles; res: 611 Oak St., Wakefield, Neb. 68784.

TUSA, ROSA, Food Ed., Milwaukee Sentinel, 918 N. Fourth St., Milwaukee, Wis. 53201, '63–; Feature Wtr., '52–; Educ. and Pubcty. Dir., Am. Cancer Soc., Milwaukee County, '49–'52; Nat. Press Photogrs. Assn., Wis. Press Photogrs. Assn.; Ala. Col., '41; h. Kyril Vassilev; res: 5570 N. Lake Dr., Whitefish Bay, Wis. 53217.

TUTEN, SIMONA MORINI, Wtr., Vogue, Conde Nast Publications, 420 Lexington Ave., N.Y., N.Y. 10017, '69–; Feature Rschr., '66–'69; Rights Asst., New Am. Lib., '65–'66; Reader, Farrar, Straus and Giroux, '64–'65; Translator, UN Italian Mission, '61–'64; Univ. of Rome, '57 (Doctore in Lettere); b. Naples, Italy, 1932; p. Bruno and Eleonora Aidinyan Morini; h. Frederic Tuten; res: 319 E. 10th St., N.Y., N.Y. 10009.

TUTTLE, DOROTHY EDITH, Public Info. Offcr., Ed., Navy Department Headquarters, Pentagon 5E789, Wash., D.C. 20350, '66–; Public Affairs Offcr., '65–'66; Nat. Dir. of PR, Wms. Div., Repl. Nat. Comm., '62–'64; Nat. Public Affairs Offcr., Off. of Secy., Housing and Urban Dev., '60–'62; Public Info. Specialist, Voice of Am., '49–'60; Offcr., U.S. Navy, '42–'46; Theta Sigma Phi, WNPC, ANWC (VP), OPC, AAUW, Intl. Soc. of Tech. Wtrs. and Publrs.; U.S. Fed. Svc. aw., '69; Am. Univ., BA, '55; Mich. State Univ.; b. Seattle, Wash., 1916; p. William and Maude Fuller Tuttle; res: 3315 Wisconsin Ave. N.W., Wash., D.C. 20016.

TUTTLE, HELEN WELCH, Prof., Asst. Univ. Librn. for Preparations, Princeton University Library, Princeton, N.J. 08540, '68–; Prof. of Lib. Admin., Univ. of Ill., '62–'68; Acquisition Librn., '52–'68; Asst. Acquisition Librn., '47–'52; Bibliographer, '42–'47; Asst. Ed. for Acquisitions, "Library Resources and Technical Services," '57–'60; Contrbr., pfsnl. pubns., ency.; ALA (Pres., Resources and Tech. Svcs. Div., '61–'62), Ill Lib. Assn. (Treas., '48–'52), Phi Kappa Phi, Pi Mu Epsilon, Beta Phi Mu, Pi Lambda Theta; Univ. of Kan., AB, '35 (Phi Beta Kappa); MA, '36; Univ. of Ill., BS (Lib. Sci.), '42; b. Larned, Kan., 1914; p. George and Gertrude Jones Welch; h. Preston Tuttle; c. Laurence H., David L.; res: 75 S. Stanworth Dr., Princeton, N.J. 08540.

TUTTLE, LURENE, Actress; "Hannah Yarby" in "Julia" TV series, 20th Century-Fox Studios, Hollywood, Cal., '68–; stock cos., eight yrs.; radio, 20 yrs.; movies, live TV, three TV series; Radio, TV Tchr., Univ. of Southern Cal., '45–'51; Altrusa Club, AFTRA (Nat. and Local Bd. Mbr., '39–); four times winner, Best Actress in Radio, West Coast, '40–'50; Pasadena Jr. Col., Univ. of Southern Cal.; b. Pleasant Lake, Ind., 1907; p. Clair and Verna Long Tuttle; c. Barbara Ruick (Mrs. John Williams); res: 940 Hancock Ave., W. Hollywood, Cal. 90069.

TWEEDY, MARY JOHNSON, Edtl. Dir., The Brownington Foundation, 860 First Ave., N.Y., N.Y. 10017, '69–; Dir. of Educ., The Starr Fndn., '65–'69; Dir. of Educ., Time, Inc., '51–'65; Gen. Mgr., Time (China), '46–'48; War Corr., '44–'46; Exec. Asst. to VP, WNSH, '42–'44; Corr., Time-Life, '37–'40; N.Y. Edtl. Staff, Time, '36–'37; Auth., "Bermuda Holiday;" OPC, WNPC; Nat. Assn. of Col. Stores aw.; Southeast Mo. State Col., AB, '35; b. Cape Girardeau, Mo.; p. Benjamin and Caroline Woodburn Johnson; h. Gordon

Tweedy; c. Clare Bradford, Ann Sellett, Margot Martin; res: 860 United Nations Plaza, N.Y., N.Y. 10017.

TWIGGS, MARGARET SINKLER, Govt., Political Reptr., Augusta Herald, News Bldg., Broad St., Augusta, Ga. 30903, '56; Wms. Ed., '51–'56; Soc. Ed., Ft. Lauderdale (Fla.) Daily News, '49–'50; Am. Red Cross European Theatre, '44–'45; Soc. Ed., Augusta Chronicle, '41–'44; '46–'49; Founder, Ga. Fedn. of Repl. Wm., '57, numerous political, hist., civic orgs.; Ga.-Carolina Press Assn. feature writing aw., '48, Ga. Press Assn. Svc. Aw., '64; Univ. of Ga., BA (Jnlsm.), '40; b. Augusta, Ga. 1919; p. John and Meta Sinkler Twiggs; res: 2804 Bellevue Ave., Augusta, Ga. 30904.

TWISS, MAURINE CHRISTMAN, Dir. of Public Info., University of Mississippi Medical Center, 2500 N. State St., Jackson, Miss. 39216, '55–; Feature Ed., Jackson Daily News, '54–'55; Wms. Ed., '50–'54; Edtl. Copy Desk, Chicago Tribune, '48–'49; Copywtr., Montgomery Ward, '41–'42; PR Cnslt., Miss. Heart Assn., '53–; Commtns. Specialist, Miss. Reg. Med. Program, '67–; PR Cnslt., Southwestern Med. Sch., Dallas, '66–; Assn. of Am. Med. Cols. (Chmn., '67–'68), Miss. Press Wm. (Pres., '58–'60) NFPW (Reg. 8 Dir., '61–'65), PR Assn. of Miss. VP, '60), ACPRA; Who's Who of Am. Wm., Who's Who in Am. PR; numerous writing aws.; Miss. Wms. Cabinet of Pub. Affairs (Pres., '63–'64); Ill. Wesleyan Univ. (Theta Alpha Phi, Phi Sigma Iota); b. Westervelt, Ill., 1919; p. Paul and Leota Jenkins Christman; h. Armin Twiss (div.); c. Belinda; res: 1738 Douglass Dr., Jackson, Miss. 39211.

TYLER, ANN GLENN, Rsch. Assoc., Fortune Magazine, Time Inc., Rockefeller Ctr., N.Y., N.Y. 10020, '61–; Rsch. Dept., Merrill Lynch Pierce, Fenner & Smith, '54–'60; Hollins Col., BA (Econ.) '53 (cum laude); b. Winston-Salem, N.C., 1932; p. Robert and Lucille Glenn Tyler.

TYLER, BETTY SESSLER, Asst. to Sun. Ed., Teenage, Arts Ed., Feature, news Wtr., Post Publishing Company, 410 State St., Bridgeport, Conn., 06602; Asst. to Sun. Ed., Richmond (Va.) Times Dispatch, '50–'54; Educ., Med. Wtr., '44–'50; Feature Wtr.; Asst. Wms. Ed., '43–'44; Monroe (Conn.) Lib. Bd. (Chmn.), Monroe Friends of the Lib. (Past Pres), Commty. Development Action Plan; New Eng. Nwsp. Wm. of the Yr. Aw., '60, '61; Richmond, Va.; p. Grover and Hannah Engelberg Sessler; h. George B. Tyler Jr.; res: 233 Old Newtown Rd., Monroe, Conn. 06468.

TYLER, CAROLINE, Mgr., Edtl. Staff, State Street Bank and Trust Company, 225 Franklin St., Boston, Mass. 02110, '70–; Visual Info. Specialist, U.S. Information Agency, '67–'68; Pub. Info. Asst., Appalachian Regional Commission, '65–'67; Ed., Rhode Island Telco News, New England Telephone Company, '62–'64; Mass. Indsl. Eds. Assn., ICIE (aw. for R. I. Telco News, '63); Univ. of Vt., BA (Eng.), '61 (Mortar

Board); b. Hot Springs, Ark., 1940; p. Nathaniel and Elizabeth Williams Tyler; res: 57 Longwood Ave., Brookline, Mass. 02146.

TYLER, JANE ABBOT, Staff Wtr., Press Bureau, Colonial Williamsburg, Goodwin Building, Williamsburg, Va. 23185, '68–; Dir. of Ark., Ky., and Tenn. Offs., Care, '64–'67; Va. Rep., '62–'64; Dir. of Volunteers, Am. Red Cross (Norfolk, Va.), '60–'62; Radio Traf., WAVY Radio (Portsmouth), '60; Latin Tchr., Granby Hs, '59–'60; AWRT, PRSA (Assoc. Mbr.); Mary Washington Col. of Univ. of Va., BA (Latin), '53; b. Lynchburg, Va., 1933; p. John Lewis and Elizabeth Palmer Lee Abbot; h. J. Allen Tyler; res: Rte. 1, Box 58B, Williamsburg, Va. 23185.

TYLER, LEONA ELIZABETH, Dean, Graduate School, University of Oregon, Eugene, Ore. 97403, '65–; Prof. of Psych., '40–'65; Auth: "The Work of the Counselor" (3rd ed., '69), "The Psychology of Human Differences" (3rd ed., '65), "Tests and Measurements" ('63), Co-auth., several others; Am. Psychological Assn. (Dir., '65–'68), Western Psychological Assn. (Pres., '57–'58); Univ. of Minn., BS, '25; MS, '39; PhD, '41 (Outstanding Achiev. Aw., '63); b. Chetek, Wis., 1906; p. Leon and Bessie Carver Tyler; res: 3565 Glen Oak Dr., Eugene, Ore. 97405.

TYLER, RUTH VINE, Lib. Dir., Salt Lake County Library, 80 E. Center St., Midvale, Ut. 84047, '39–; Staff, Salt Lake City Pub. Lib., '22–'38; Tchr., Ut. Elementary Schs., '20–'21; ALA, Ut. Lib. Assn. (Pres.), Bk. of Month Club Dorothy C. Fisher Aw., '63; Ut. PTA (State Secy.); Univ. of Ut., '19; Brigham Young Univ. '23; U.C.L.A. '54–'55; b. Salt Lake City, Ut., 1899; p. George and Annie Galde Vine; h. Wilfrid Tyler; c. Jack, Mrs. Vine Holladay; res: 4900 Atwood Blvd., Murray, Ut. 84107.

TYMIENIECKA, ANNA-TERESA, Visiting Prof., Univ. of Waterloo, Dept. of Philosophy, Waterloo, Ontario, Canada; Auth: "Eros et Logos" (Editions Universitaires, Fribourg, '69), "Why is There Something Rather Nothing" ('67), "Leibniz Cosmological Synthesis" (Humanities Press, '65), "Phenomenology and Science in Contemporary European Thought" (Noonday, '61), "Essence and Existence" (Aubier, '55); Asst. Prof., Pa. State Univ.; Lectr., Bryn Mawr Col.; Assoc. Scholar, Radcliffe Inst.; Visiting Prof., Duquesne Univ.; Am. Philosophical Assn., Metaphysical Soc. of Am., Société Européenne de Culture; Educ: Univ. of Paris, Univ. of Cracaw, Univ. of Fribourg; b. Marianowo, Poland; p. Wladyslaw and Maria-Ludwika de Lanval Zaremba-Tymieniecki; h. Hendrik Houthakker; c. Louis, Isabel, Jan-Nicolas; res: 4330 Yuma St., N.W., Wash., D.C. 20016.

TYROLER, JAN, Special Project Dir., New York City Human Resources Administration, 220 Church St., N.Y., N.Y. 10013, '69–; PR Dir., Addiction Svcs. Agcy., '68–'69; Free-lance Special Events Coordr., political

'66–'68; PR Dir., Mount Sinai Hosp., '58–'66; PRSA; Ind. Univ., BA, '49; res: 165 W. 20th St., N.Y., N.Y. 10011.

U

UDELL, BARBARA ANNE, Wms. Ed., Janesville Gazette, One S. Parker Dr., Janesville, Wis., 53545, '68–; Asst. Wms. Ed., Beloit Daily News, '56–'68; Entertainment Ed., '61–'68; Ch. Ed., '60–'67; Lectr. on Jnlsm., '60–'68; Dale Carnegie Grad. Asst.; Self Defense Grad. Asst.; Univ. of Ala.; Univ. of Wis.; b. Beloit, Wis., 1934; p. Roy and Irene Schulter Udell; res: 1417 Portland Ave., Beloit, Wis. 53511.

UNDERWOOD, AGNESS WILSON, Asst. Mng. Ed., Los Angeles Herald-Examiner, 1111 S. Broadway, L.A., Cal. 90015, '64–'68; Exec. City Ed., '62–'64; Exec. City Ed., Los Angeles Herald-Express, '47–'62; Reptr., '33–'47; Reptr., Los Angeles Record, '26–'35; Auth., "Newspaperwoman" (Harper, '49); top stories; numerous orgs., aws.; Woodbury Col., MA (Bus. Adm.), '51; Cal. Col. of Med., Univ. of Cal., Dr. of Laws (hon.), '58; b. S.F., Cal., 1902; p. Cliff and Mamie Sullivan Wilson; h. (div.); c. Mary E. (Mrs. William A. Weed), George; res: 26403 Dunwood Rd., Rolling Hills Estates, Cal. 90274.

UNLAND, MAXINE GATES, Actress, c/o Mr. Herman Zimmerman, 12077 Ventura Pl., Studio City, Cal.; Off. Mgr., Secy.-Treas., Sea-Land Electric Co., '64–; films: "Nobody Loves Flapping Eagle," "Giant," others; TV: Red Skelton, Bob Hope, Lucille Ball, Danny Thomas Shows, "Rawhide," "Lost in Space," many others; appearances in leading West Coast theaters, night clubs and hotels; AGVA, SAG, AFTRA, many commty. orgs.; b. Hebron, Neb., 1917; p. Fred and Gladys Turner Gates; h. Frank William Unland; c. LaVina Jean Smith; res: 13122 Hart St., N. Hollywood, Cal. 91605.

UNTERMANN, ESTHER KAWOLSKY, Newark (N.J.) Civil Defense-Disaster Control, '53–'62; Judge of Municipal Courts, '44–'48; Tch., '20–'44; BPW (Newark Chptr. Charter Mbr.; Wm. of Yr., '60; Pres., '28–'31), Intl. Col. Wms. Club, AAUW, Wms. Forum, Nat. Travel Club; Welfare Commn. of Newark Central Planning Bd., '44–'52; AWRT (N.J. Charter Mbr.; Secy. '54–'60; Treas.; N.Y. Chptr. Mbr.); Panzer Col. Alumni Assn. Aw., '61; Nat. B'Nai B'rith Cit. for Youth Svc., '44, '62; Who's Who of Am. Wm., Who's Who of World Jewry; Columbia Univ. Tchs. Col., BS, '42; b. Pitt., Pa. 1896; p. Joseph and Charlotte Felser Kawolsky; h. William M. Untermann (dec.); res: Hotel Suburban, 141 S. Harrison St., E. Orange, N.J. 07018.

UNTERMEYER, JEAN STARR, Auth: "Private Collection" (Alfred A. Knopf, '65), "Job's Daughter" (W.

W. Norton, '67), others; Translations incl: "Re-Creations" (W. W. Norton, '70), "The Death of Virgil" (Pantheon, '45); PEN; Dr. of Ltrs. (Hon.), Universite Libre (Asia), Karachi, Pakistan; b. Zanesville, Oh.; p. Abram and Johanna Schoenfeld Starr; h. Louis Untermeyer (div.); c. Richard S. (dec.); res: 235 E. 73rd St., N.Y., N.Y. 10021.

UPTON, LENORE RIPLEY, Press, Radio and TV Relations Dir., Goodwill Industries of Greater Detroit, 6522 Brush St., Detroit, Mich. 48202, '67–; PR Dir., Fred Yaffe and Co., '60–'66; Copywtr., Davis Daniels Co. and MP Patten Co., '54–'59; Free-lance Wtr., fiction (Dell Pubns. Story of the Yr. 2nd Prize, '49); Theta Sigma Phi (Detroit Pfsnl. Chptr. Pres., '66; VP, '65), Wms. Ad Club of Detroit (VP, '63–'65; Secy., '62–'63; Treas., '59–'60; Gold Heart Volunteer Aw., '65), Detroit Press Club, PRSA; Detroit Adv. Wm. of the Yr., '67; Graphic Arts Aw., '66; Wayne Univ.; b. St. Paul, Minn.; p. Raymond and Amelia Cable Ripley; h. (div.); c. Dorothy (Mrs. Ervin Esch), Donald Robert; res: 1915 N. Washington, #6, Royal Oaks, Mich. 48073.

UPTON, LUCILLE MORRIS, Sunday Colmst., Springfield Newspapers, Inc., 651 Boonville, Springfield, Mo. 65801, '64–; Feature Wtr., '64–; Colmst., '42–; Reptr., '26–'64; Auth: "Bald Knobbers" (Caxton Printers, '39), "Battle of Wilson's Creek" ('50), short stories, mag. articles; Reptr., Denver Express, El Paso Times, '23–'25; Crtv. Writing Tchr., Drury Col. Div. of Continuing Educ., '47–'52, '66–'67; Mo. Wtrs. Guild (Pres., '42), Mo. Wms. Press Assn., Nat. Wms. Press Assn., numerous hist. orgs.; Springfield C. of C. Wm. of Achiev., '67; Drury Col., '19–'20; S.W. Mo. State Col., '20–'22; b. Dadeville, Mo., 1898; p. Albert G. and Veda Wilson Morris; h. Eugene V. Upton (dec.); res: 1305 Kimbrough, Springfield, Mo. 65804.

URBAITIS, DOROTHY STRIMPLE, Pres. and Mgr., Adeco Advertising Agency, 109 S. Taylor, Oak Park, Ill. 60302, '69–; Adv. and Prod. Mgr., Intl. Film Bur. (Chgo.), '64–'69; Artist, Cnslt., educ. audio-visuals, '68–; Recording for the Blind; Northern Ill. Univ. '58–'59; b. Omaha, Neb., 1941; p. Austin and Louise Hylen Strimple; h. Richard Urbaitis.

URBANEK, MAE BOBB, Auth: "Memoirs of Andrew McMaster" ('69), "Know Wyoming" ('69), "Almost Up Devils Tower" ('68), "Wyoming Place Names" ('67), other western bks.; Rancher, 38 yrs.; Ed., Paintbrush; Western Wtrs. of Am., Wyo. Press Wm. (Pres., '64–'65; First VP, '61–'63; Treas., '59–'61), Delta Kappa Gamma (Hon. Mbr.); Northwestern Univ., BS (Jnlsm.), '27; b. Denver, Colo., 1903; p. Boyd and Matilda Hotze Bobb; h. Jerry Urbanek; res: Lusk, Wyo. 82225.

URE, VIRGINIA PAGELS, Rsch. Asst., Field Enterprises Educational Corp., Merchandise Mart Plaza, Chgo., Ill. 60654, '65–; VP, Geo. Pagels Co.; Theta

Sigma Phi, Young Repls. (Secy.); Univ. of Ill., BA, '62 (cum laude); Univ. of Cinn., MA, '65; b. Evergreen Park, Ill., 1941; p. George and Sarah Patterson Pagels; h. J. Allen Ure; res: 9117 S. Oakley St., Chgo., Ill. 60620.

URNER, DAISY JOHNSON, Art Gallery Dir.; Color Coordr., Urner's Home Furnishing Center, 212 21st St., Bakersfield, Cal. 93303, '44–; Gallery Dir., Cunningham Memorial Art Gallery, '52–'60, '54–'65, '69–'70; helped establish Annual Sidewalk Art Festival, '37–; TV Hostess, '53–'54; Bakersfield Art Assn. (Pres., '44–'50, '62–'63; Co-founder); Cancer Rsch. Cit., '68; Cal. Tchrs. Assn. Cit., '66; numerous art aws; honored by portrait by famous artist for permanent collection in Cunningham Gallery, '69; Who's Who of Am. Wm., Wm. of West, Dic. of Intl. Biog.; b. Muskogee, Okla.; p. Thomas and Carrie Ross Johnson; h. Philip Urner; c. James P., Peggyrose, Donald R., Gerald E., Phyllis Urner Herrick; res: Bakersfield, Cal. 93306.

USHER, LENORE H., Radio-TV Dir., Herbert S. Benjamin Assoc. Inc., 2736 Florida St., Baton Rouge, La. 70821, '65–; Home Econst., Public Svc. Co. (Lawton, Okla.), '62; Press Club of Baton Rouge (VP, '69); Carnegie Inst. of Tech., '57–'58; La. State Univ., '58–'60; b. Port Arthur, Tex., 1940; p. John and Juliette G. Hickey; h. (div.); c. Scott, Lance, Aaron; res: 440 West Dr., Baton Rouge, La. 70806.

USOSKIN, JOAN, VP-Assoc. Crtv. Dir., Norman, Craig & Kummel, Inc., 488 Madison Ave., N.Y., N.Y. 10022, '67–; Copy Group Head, '66–'67; Copy Supvsr., Foote, Cone & Belding, '64–'66; Sr. Copywtr., Ogilvy & Mather, '59–'64; Copywtr., Calkins & Holden, '55–'59; Cnslt. on retail TV adv.; Prodr.-Wtr., TV commls., program material; Wtr., poetry, song lyrics; Copywtrs. Club Aw. in Print., '65; Cit. 10 Best Print Ads, '59; N.Y.U., BA; b. N.Y.C.; p. Joseph and Syd Mendelson Usoskin; res: 405 E. 54 St., N.Y., N.Y. 10022.

UTZMAN, ELSIE VAN SLYKE, Free-lance Wtr.; Special Educ. Tchr. of Blind, Okla., La., Ariz., '18 to Retirement; Theta Sigma Phi (Treas., '66); Who's Who in Am. Educ.; Univ. of Okla., AB, '18 (Mortar Bd., Hon. Alumni); Grad. Work, Univ. of Okla., Univ. of Ariz.; b. Hamilton, Mo., 1898; p. Everett and Elizabeth Keys Van Slyke; h. Clarence E. Utzman; c. Elizabeth (Mrs. Wallace Wiley), Patricia (Mrs. Willis B. Tolley); res: 2322 E. Helen, Tucson, Ariz. 85719.

V

VALENCIK, MAY VIRGINIA KUNZ, Lib. Dir., White Plains Public Library, 115 Grand St., White Plains, N.Y. 10601, '63–; Head Librn., Allentown (Pa.) Free Lib., '42–'63; State Supvsr., Ky. Statewide Lib. Project, '41–'42; Sr. Ref. Asst., Public Lib. (Utica, N.Y.), '36–'41; Lib. Asst., Public Lib. (Passaic, N.J.), '31–'36; ALA, Public Lib. Assn., Pa. Library Assn. (Pres., '50–'51), Westchester Lib. Assn., Middle Atlantic States Lib. Conf., (Pres., '53–'57), Quota Intl. (Pres., 1955–'57) Delta Kappa Gamma (Local Pres., '47–'49); Who's Who of Am. Wm.; Who's Who in the East; Who's Who in Lib. Svc.; Who's Who in Educ.; Douglass Col., Rutgers Univ., BA, '31, Cedar Crest Col., Hon. Doctor of Laws, '52; b. Newark, N.J., 1909; p. Charles and Helen Riley Kunz; h. Gus Valencik; res: 10 Nosband Ave., White Plains, N.Y. 10605.

VALENTINE, MARY PERRY, Adv. Mgr., The New Jersey Afro-American Newspaper, 190 Clinton Ave., Newark, N.J. 07108, '68–; Staff Wtr. and Social Colmst., '67–'70; Pubcty. Dir., "Queen of Angel Players," '65; Wtr., Prodr., play "Hawaiian Musical," '41; Guest Soloist for Cecil B. DeMille, '41; Soc. Colmst., Albany (Ga.) Star, '41; Singer-Dancer, Silas Green Show, '40–'41; Dixie Theatre (W. Palm Beach, Fla.), '35–'37; NAACP (N.J. Exec. Bd.), Negro Cncl. of Wm. (N.J. Corr. Secy.), BPW, N.J. Adv. Club, N.J. Assn. of Communicators, hons.; Albany (Ga.) State Col., one yr.; training in music, nursing, drama, currently Famous Wtrs. Sch.; b. Americus, Ga., 1922; p. Edgar and Mary Cottle Perry; c. Susan P. Simmons, Maria A. Johnson A'Nese Valentine; res: 25 Kipp, Newark, N.J. 07108.

VAN BRIGGLE, MARGARET JESSUP, Auth: "The High Place" (Zondervan Publ. Co., '64), "Eternal Heritage" (Beacon Hill Press, '55), "Wild Olive" (Western Publ. Co., '50); Frankfort Pilgrim Col., '51–'54 (Music; Alumni Aw. for Distg. Svc. as Christian Layman); b. Decatur County, Ind., 1917; p. Frank and Myrtle Patrick Jessup; h. Vard Van Briggle; c. Nancy J. (Mrs. Donald Shook); res: 903 E. Washington, Greensburg, Ind. 47240.

VAN BUREN, ABIGAIL (Abigail Phillips), Pres., Phillips-Van Buren, 9000 Sunset Blvd., L.A., Cal., 90069; Advice Colmst., "Dear Abby," Chicago Tribune-New York Daily News Syndicate (1,000 nwsps., U.S. and abroad), '56–; Auth: "Dear Abby," "Dear Abby on Marriage," "Dear Teenager;" Synd. Daily Program, CBS Radio; Contrbr. to McCall's, Ladies' Home Journal, Family Circle, Reader's Digest, Pageant; Franz Alexander Fndn. (Dir.), Guthrie Theatre Fndn. (Dir., '69–), S.F. Helping Hand, Nat. Soc. for Crippled Children and Adults (Nat. Campaign Chmn. '61); Cal. Univ. Wm. of the Yr.; Los Angeles Times Mother of the Yr., '60; b. Sioux City, Ia., 1918; h. Morton Phillips; c. Jeanne, Edward Jay; res: 740 River Dr., St. Paul, Minn. 55116.

VAN BUREN, ANNA-LOU DAVIS, Dir. of PR, National Kidney Foundation; Dir. of PR, Am. Bon Voyage; Dir. of Conv. Travel, Benedetti Travel; Dir. of Public Info., Commty. Rels., Camp Fire Girls; Copy Group Head, Pedlar & Ryan Adv.; TV-Radio Wtr., Prodr., Compton Adv., N. W. Ayer & Son; Asst. Prod. Mgr., Hart & Downey; Synd. Colmst., "Sew It

Seams;" AWNY, AWRT, Educ. Film Lib. Assn.; PRSA aw., '62; Hunter Col., New Sch. for Social Rsch., N.Y.U.; b. Watervliet, N.Y. 1928; p. George and Isabelle Guy Davis; h. Frederick S. Van Buren; c. Frederick Jr., David S.; res: 506 Wolfs Lane, Pelham Manor, N.Y. 10803.

VANCE, ELEANOR GRAHAM, Free-lance Wtr., Lectr.; Auth: "Jonathan" ('66), "Tweets, The Story of a Cat" ('56), other juv. bks.; Poetry: "It Happens Every Day" ('62), "Store in Your Heart" ('50), "For These Moments" ('39); Delta Kappa Gamma, Poetry Soc. of Tex.; Freedoms Fnd. aw., '58; Westminster Col., AB, '30 (alumni aw., '56, Litt. D., '52); Northwestern Univ., MA, '31 (Alumni aw.); b. Pitt., Pa., 1908; p. J. Paul and Margaret Hargrave Graham; h. W. Silas Vance; c. Eleanor (Mrs. John Raders), Dale Lines; res: 109 Austin Blvd., Edinburg, Tex. 78539.

VANCE, MAE HOWARD, Artist: marine murals, watercolors, ceramic designer; Auth.; Independent Wash. Artists, NLAPW, Intl. Platform Assn., Marquis Biog. Lib. Soc. (Advisory Mbr.); Who's Who of Am. Wm.; Cleve. Inst. Art, '19-'21; Corcoran Art Sch., '23-'25; b. Rushsylvania, Oh.; p. William and Minnie Slater Vance; res: 3702 Northampton St. N.W., Wash., D.C. 20015.

VANCE, MARGARET A., Religion Ed., Evening News, 215 Market St., Newark, N.J. 07102, '45-; Gen. Assgt., '40-'45; Staff, '27-'40; News Bureau of Am. Bible Soc., Religion Newswtrs. Assn. (Founder, Past VP); Nat. Religious Pubcty. Cncl. aw., '50; N.J. Assn. of Daily Nwsp. Wm., '62; other aws.; b. Newark, N.J., 1906; p. Wilson and Florence Johnson Vance; res: 754 Scotland Rd., Apt. D-2, Orange, N.J. 07050.

VANDEBERG, SHIRLEY McDONALD, Soc. Ed., Mount Vernon News, 1820 E. Vine St., Mt. Vernon, Oh. 43050, '69-; Reptr., Feature Wtr., '68-'69; Teletype Setter Operator, '66-'68; b. Mt. Vernon, Oh., 1949; p. William and Martha Michael McDonald; h. Michael D. Vandeburg; res: 104 Maplewood Ave., Mt. Vernon, Oh. 43050.

VANDERBILT, GLORIA, Artist, one woman shows N.Y., Washington D.C., Dallas, Houston, Southampton. Dir. of Design Riegel Textiles; "Love Poems" (World, '54) "Gloria Vanderbilt Book of Collage" (Van-Nustrand Reinhold, '70) m. Wyatt Emory Cooper; c. Stan S., Christopher S., Carter V., Anderson H.

VAN der HEUVEL, GERRY BURCH, Am. Embassy, Via Veneto, Rome, Italy, '69-; Press Secy. to Mrs. Nixon (Wash., D.C.), '68-'69; Newhouse Nwsps., N.Y. Daily News, Editor & Publisher Magazine, Pat Munroe News Bur.; UPI (Phila., Pa.); WNPC (Pres.), '67-'68); h. Kenneth Van der Heuvel (dec.).

VAN DER SMISSEN, BETTY, Prof. of Recreation, Pennsylvania State Univ., 260 Recreation Bldg. 1 University Park, Pa. 16802, '68-; Auth., "Legal Liability of Cities and Schools Relating to Recreation and Parks" (W. H. Anderson, '68); Assoc. Prof., '65-'68; Dir. of Rsch., Nat. Recreation Assn., '64-'65; Assoc. Prof., Univ. of Ia., '56-'64; Soc. of Pk. and Recreation Educs. (Bd. of Dirs., '68-'70); Am. Camping Assn. (Bd. of Dirs., '59-'64); Garret Eppley Distg. Alumni Aw., '69; Univ. of Kan., AB, '49, JD, '52; Ind. Univ., MS, '54, ReD, '55.

VAN DER VEEN, LUCY ELLEN, Educ. Ed., Wtr., The Kokomo Tribune, 300 N. Union St., Kokomo, Ind. 64901, '69-; Fashion Ed., '67-'69; Food Ed., '67; Elementary Tchr., St. John Catholic Sch. (Hartford City, Ind.), '66-'67; Guest Lectr., Ball State Univ. Jnlsm. Day, '66-'69; Gamma Delta, Theta Sigma Phi; Hope Col., '62-'63; Ball State Univ., BS, '66; b. Lafayette, Ind., 1944; p. Herbert and Dorothy Wierenga Van der Veen; res: 1015 W. Jackson St., Kokomo, Ind. 46901.

VANDER VELDE, WINIFRED BOUMA, Edtl. Asst., Baker Book House Company, 1019 Wealthy St., Grand Rapids, Mich. 49506, '59-; b. Grand Rapids, Mich., 1915; p. Peter and Bessie Bosscher Bouma; h. Maurice C. VanderVelde; c. Michael Curtis, William Peter; res: 1429 Hazen St., Grand Rapids, Mich. 49507.

VAN DOREN, DOROTHY GRAFFE, Colmst., numerous nwsps.; Auth., three bks. of essays ('50; '53; '59), five novels ('26-'42); Assoc. Ed., The Nation, '19-'37; Admr., Off. of War Info., '42-'45; Dept. of State, '46; Cornwall, Conn. Sch. Bd., '65; Barnard Col. Bd. of Trustees ('59-'64); Barnard Col., AB, '18; b. S.F., Cal., 1896; p. George and Frances Lane Graffe; h. Mark Van Doren; c. Charles, John; res: Falls Village, Conn. 06031.

VAN DUSEN, ELLEN WILKINSON, Dir., PR, Syracuse and Onondaga County Chapter, The American Red Cross, 700 E. Water St., Syracuse, N.Y. 13210, '68-; Mgr., Commtns., Pers., Crouse-Hinds, '42-'68; Placement Dir., Central City Bus. Inst., '42; E. C. Stearns, '39-'42; H. W. MacBean, '29-'38; Visiting Lectr., Syracuse Univ., Cornell Univ., Columbia Univ.; Theta Sigma Phi, AAIE (Past Pres.), Upstate N.Y. Cncl. of Indsl. Eds. (Past Pres.), PRSA, Indsl. Commtns. Cncl., N.Y. State Dept. of Commerce Wms. Cncl. ('64-'67, '68-'71); extensive civic, educ. activities; Syracuse Univ., '28-'29; b. Baldwinsville, N.Y., 1911; p. Stanworth and Flora Smith Wilkinson; h. Curtis Van Dusen; res: 408 Buckingham Ave., Syracuse, N.Y. 13210.

VAN GELDER, JEANNE PATRICIA, Mgr., Radio-TV Pubcty., Metropolitan Life Insurance Company, 1 Madison Ave., N.Y., N.Y. 10010, '69-; Radio-TV Publicist, Young & Rubicam, '55-'69; Publicist, Continental Can Co., '49-'52; Walt Framer, '46-'49; AWRT, Fashion Group; Queens Col., BA, '41; b. N.Y.C., 1920; p. George and Mollie Tisch Van Gelder; res: 166 E. 96th St., N.Y., N.Y. 10028.

VAN GELDER, LINDSY EVANS, Reptr., New York Post, 75 West St., N.Y., N.Y. 10006, '68–; Reptr., UPI, '67–'68; Contrbr., "The Hand That Cradles the Rock" (Ed., Robin Morgan; Random House, '70); Media Wm. (Co-founder); Medill Sch. of Jnlsm., '62–'64; Sarah Lawrence, BA, '66; b. Plainfield, N.J., 1944; p. Lester and Marilynn Chamberlain Evans; h. Lawrence Van Gelder; res: 817 West End Ave., N.Y., N.Y. 10025.

VAN HORN, VIRGINIA HOLLIMAN, Auth., "Wishing Star" (Naylor, '46); Dir., Brazoria County Library System, Old Courthouse, Angleton, Tex. 77515, '65–; Head Librn., Allan Shivers Lib. and Rare Bk. Rm., Woodville, '63–'65; Genealogy and Southwest Dept., Ft. Worth Public Lib., '59; Base Librn., Andersen Air Force Base, Guam, '52–'53; Contrbr., pfsnl. pubns.; Southwest Wtrs. Conf. Lyric Verse Aw., '48; Humorous Verse Aw., '49; Tex. Intercollegiate Press Assn. Poetry Aw., '46; Columbia Univ. Pfsnl. Workshop for Poets, '45; Sam Houston State Tchrs. Col., BS (Lib. Sci.), '46; Short Story, Poetry Studies under Robert P. Tristam Coffin, '48; Univ. of Tex. Grad. Sch. of Lib. Sci., '48–'49; b. Pt. Arthur, Tex., 1923; p. E. J. and Irene Stuckey Holliman; h. John Rogers Van Horn; c. James, Peter; res: P.O. Box 147, Angleton, Tex. 77515.

VAN KEUREN, DIANE LEE, Exec. Coordr., Clorox, Honig-Cooper & Harrington, 1275 Columbus Ave., S.F., Cal. 94133, '68–; Bdcst. Media Byr., '64–'68; b. S.F., Cal., 1940; p. John and Clementine Patrizi Lee; h. Ronald E. Van Keuren; c. Jeffrey; res: 435 Miller Creek Rd., San Rafael, Cal. 94903.

VANNIER, MARYHELEN, Auth., physical educ. textbks.; Dir., Wms. Physical Educ. Dept., Southern Methodist University, Box 353, Dallas, Tex. 75222, '50– (Resident Fellow of Grad. Cncl. of the Humanities, '62–'63); formerly Wms. Physical Educ. Dir., Drake Univ., St. Lawrence Univ., Wellesley HS; 11 bks., numerous articles in pfsnl. pubns.; Delegate, Intl. Congress for Physical Educ. Tchrs. of Girls and Wm., Copenhagen ('49), London ('58); Nat. Conf. on Rsch. in Therapeutic Recreation; AAHPR (numerous offs.; Nat. Hon. Aw.); Who's Who in Am. Educ., Contemporary Auths., many other dirs.; James Millikin Univ., BA (Distg. Alumni Aw.); Columbia Univ. Tchrs. Col., MA; N.Y.U., Ed.D.; res: 7006 Stefani, Dallas, Tex. 75225.

VANNOY, JOELLENE, Home Econst., Western Wheat Associates, U.S.A., Inc., 1030 15th St. N.W., Suite 1008, Wash., D.C. 20005, '64–; Nutritionist, Millers' Nat. Fedn., '58–'64; Reg. Home Econst., Wheat Flour Inst., '46–'56; Ark., Tex., Ext. Svcs., '34–'45; AWRT, Intl. Platform Assn., Am. Home Econs. Assn., Home Econsts. in Bus., Intl. Bdcst. Assn.; Who's Who of Am. Wm., '57–; Dic. of Intl. Biog., '66–; Tex. Tech., BS, '31; Columbia Univ., MA, '44; EdD, '63; b. McLean, Tex., 1910; p. John and Cora Mills Vannoy.

VAN OMMEN, IRMA GRANDIA, Order Librn.-Secy., Wilcox Library, William Penn College, Trueblood Ave., Oskaloosa, Ia. 52577, '64–; Head of Food Svc., '54–'63; BPW; William Penn Col. and Corr. Courses; b. Oskaloosa, Ia., 1919; p. A. Clarence and Alice Brummel Grandia; h. Garry Van Ommen; c. Jerry C., Mrs. Janna Karen Van Roekel; res: R. #1, Oskaloosa, Ia. 52577.

VAN ORDEN, PHYLLIS JEANNE, Instr., Dept. of Lib. Sci., Wayne State University, Detroit, Mich. 48202, '66–'70; Lectr., Mich. State Univ. Ext., '66; Head, Instr. Materials Ctr., Oakland Univ., '64–'66; Instr. Materials Cnslt., Royal Oak, Mich. Public Schs., '60–'64; Bkmobile. and Children's Librn., San Diego, Cal. Public Lib., '58–'60; Librn., E. Detroit Public Schs., '54–'57; Contrbr., pfsnl. jnls.; WNBA (Chptr. Treas.), various state educ. and lib. orgs. (numerous offs.); Pi Lambda Theta; Eastern Mich. Univ., BS; Univ. of Mich., AM (Lib. Sci.), '58; Wayne State Univ., EdD Applicant; res: 630 Merrick, Apt. 407, Detroit, Mich. 48202.

VAN SICKLE, CAROL SHELLEY, Ed., Continental Insurance Companies, 80 Maiden Lane, N.Y., N.Y. 10038, '65–; Assoc. Ed., '63–'65; PR Wtr., Nat. Bd. Fire Underwriters, '52–'63; PR Dir., Sch. of Radio Technique, '49–'52; Edtl. Asst., Assn. of Casualty & Surety Cos., '45–'49; Nat. Safety Cncl., ZONTA; Univ. of N.C., AB, '45 (Phi Beta Kappa); b. Paterson, N.J., 1923; p. Howard and Winifred Shelley Van Sickle; res: 84 Valley View Ave., Ridgewood, N.J. 07450.

VAN STRATEN, FLORENCE W., Cnslt. in Atmospheric Physics, '62–; Head of Tech. Requirements Sec., U.S. Naval Weather Svc. Command, '46–'62; Commander, U.S. Navy, '42–'46; Instr., Chemistry Dept., N.Y.U., '33–'42; Auth., "Weather or Not" (Dodd, Mead & Co., '66), U.S. Govt Printing Off. pubns., "Radar as a Meteorological Tool" ('57), others; Am. Meterological Soc., Am. Geophysical Un., Aero-Space Med. Soc. Wm. of the Yr., '59; U.S. Navy Civilian Svc. Aw., '58; N.Y.U., BS, '33 (Phi Beta Kappa); MA, '37; PhD, '39; b. Darien, Conn., 1913; p. Jacques and Rosette Roozeboom van Straten; res: 5306 Veutnor Rd., Wash., D.C. 20016.

VAN VELTZER, VERNA JEAN, Head Librn., Electromagnetic Systems Laboratories, Inc., 495 Java Dr., Sunnyvale, Cal. 94086, '66–; Librn., '51–'66; Univ. of Ill., BS (Lib. Sci.), '50; Syracuse Univ., MLS (Pi Lambda Sigma; Beta Phi Mu), '57; b. State College, Pa., 1929; p. Harry and Golda Cline Van Velzer; res: 4048 Laguna Way, Palo Alto, Cal. 94306.

VAN VELZER, VIRGINIA CLAIRE, Sr. Tech. Wtr. (Ed.), Sylvania Electronic Systems—Western Div., P.O. Box 595, Mountain View, Cal. 94040, '64–; Head of Tech. Pubns. and Sr. Tech. Wtr., Microwave Electronics Corp., '61–'64; Sr. Tech. Wtr.-Ed., General Electric Co., Palo Alto, Cal. and Syracuse, N.Y., '56–'61; Librn., Syracuse, '55–'56; Asst. Statistician, Syracuse Bd. of Educ., '54–'55; Asst. Librn., Batelle Mem. Inst., '53–'54; Pers. Tech., Wright-Patterson Air Force Base, '52–'53; Auth., "Sylvania Publications Index and Style Guide," '66 (Merit Aw.); Ed., "Physics and Chemistry of Electronic Technology" (McGraw-Hill, '62); auth. of numerous articles in the field of electronics; numerous pfsnl. offcrships., chmnships. and aws.; Who's Who; Scholarship and Grad. Fellowship awarded; Univ. of Ill., BS, '50 (magna cum laude, Bronze Plaque, Phi Beta Kappa, Phi Kappa Phi, Alpha Lambda Delta, Psi Chi); grad. work, Syracuse Univ., '56; b. State College, Pa., 1927; p. Harry and Golda Cline Van Velzer; res: 4048 Laguna Way, Palo Alto, Cal. 94306.

VAN WAGENEN, PAMELA PRIVETTE, Beauty Ed., Met. Ed., Parents Magazine, 52 Vanderbilt Ave., N.Y., N.Y. 10017; Youth Activities Dir., Best & Co.; AEA, AGVA, SAG; Hunter Col., '65–'69; b. Richmond, Va., 1946; p. Millard and Dorothy Daneman Privette; h. H. William Van Wagenen Jr.; res: 121 Elderwood Ave. Pelham, N.Y. 10803.

VAN WANING, MURIEL BIEBER, Lectr., Interior Designer, John M. Smyth Company, 1537 Western Ave., Chgo. Heights, Ill. 60411, '59–; Pakan Furniture Manufacturers, '58; C. A. vander Pol (Sumatra, Java), '49–'58; Paris Decorators (N.Y.C.), '42–'43; Guest Lectr., Northwestern Univ., Ill. Inst. of Tech.; NHFL, Wms. Intl. Club of Indonesia (Secy., '52–'58); Columbia Univ. Tchrs. Col., '37–'41; b. N.Y.C., 1917; p. Jacob and Frances Koon Bieber; h. Carl von Waning; c. Nancy Elizabeth; res: 2051 Marston Lane, Flossmoor, Ill. 60422.

VAN WILGEN, MARIA, Head Librn., The James Blackstone Memorial Library, 758 Main St., Branford, Conn. 06405, '59–.

VAN WINKLE, BONNIE DODSON, Exec. VP, Wm. D. Murdock Advertising Agency, Inc., 300 N. Lee St., Alexandria, Va. 22314, '62–; Time Byr., AE; '50–'62; Sls. Dept., WWDC Radio, '45–'50; Program Dept., WTOP Radio, '42–'45; AWRT, BPW, Soroptimist Club; Strayer Bus. Col.; b. Kenosha, Wis., 1920; p. Clarence and Violet Shell Dodson; h. LeRoy Van Winkle; c. Mrs. Nancy Hoover; res: 5421 Powhatan Rd., Riverdale, Md. 20840.

VARNER, JEANNETTE JOHNSON, Head of Ref., Austin Public Library, P.O. Box 2287, Austin, Tex. 78767, '48–; numerous teaching positions; Co-Ed., Co-Translator, "The Florida of the Inca" (Univ. of Tex. Press, '51); Am., Tex., Southwest Lib. Assns., several Spanish socs., Alpha Delta Pi; Univ. of Ala., AB, '30; MA, '31; Univ. of Va., PhD, '38; b. Selma, Ala.; p. Chester and Ruby West Johnson; h. John Grier Varner; res: 2510 Jarratt Ave., Austin, Tex. 78703.

VARNER, VELMA V., Dir., Ed., Viking Junior Books, The Viking Press, Inc., 625 Madison Ave., N.Y., N.Y. 10022, '64–; VP, World Publ. Co., '56–'64; Ed., Children's Bks., William Morrow, '55–'56; Ed., Children's Bks., G. P. Putnam, '53–'55; Asst. Ed., Children's Bks., Harcourt, Brace & World, '46–'53; Children's Bk. Cncl. (Secy.; Pres., '60–'61), PEN, WNBA, ALA; West-

ern Mich. Col., BA, '37; Western Univ., BS (Lib. Sci.), '41.

VARRO, BARBARA JOAN, Fashion Ed., Chicago Sun-Times, 401 N. Wabash Ave., Chgo., Ill. 60611, '64–; Asst. to Fashion Ed., Feature Wtr.; Fashion Group of Chgo., Chgo. Cncl. of Fgn. Rel., Chgo. Press Club; Duquesne Univ., BA, '59; b. E. Chgo., Ind. 1938; p. Alexander and Lottie Bess Varro; res: 260 E. Chestnut St., Chgo., Ill. 60611.

VAUGHAN, Dr. DOROTHY MANSFIELD, Librn., Histrn., Portsmouth Public Library, 8 Islington St., Portsmouth, N.H. 03801, '45–; Asst. Librn., '22–'45; A Founder of "Strawberry Banke" Restoration (Pres., '59–'65; Second VP, Exec. Bd. Mbr.); rsch. for numerous auths.; DAR (Chptr. Charter Mbr.), Colonial Dames (Past N.H. VP), N.E. Hist. and Genealogical Soc., N.H. and Portsmouth Hist. Socs., Soc. of Architectural Histrns., Thomas Bailey Aldrich Soc. (Dir.), N.H. Lib. Assn. (Past Pres.); BPW Career Wm. Leader, '68; Alpha Delta Kappa Wm. of Distinction Aw., '69; Univ. of N.H., courses in Lib. Sci.; Dr. of Humane Ltrs. (Hon.), '66; Univ. of Chgo. Grad. Lib. Sch.; b. Penacook, N.H., 1904; p. Raymon and Mary Smith Vaughan; res: 202 Summer St., Portsmouth, N.H. 03801.

VAUGHAN-JACKSON, GENEVIEVE, Auth: "Animals and Men in Armor" ('58), "Mountain of Fire" ('62), "Carramore" ('68); illus. of numerous children's bks.; Artist, A. A. Johnson, Inc. (Marine Engineers), '45–'48; Atelier Armand-Delille, '32–'35; London County Cncl. Sch. of Arts and Crafts, '35–'37; b. London, Eng., 1913; p. Percy and Genevieve Winter Vaughan-Jackson; h. John Shimer; res: 411 W. 21st St., N.Y., N.Y. 10011.

VAUGHN, BETTY, PR, Sls. Prom. Cnslt., 52 Park Ave., N.Y., N.Y. 10016, '66–; PR Dir., Sandgren and Murtha, Inc.; PR, Lippincott & Margulies; Prom. Wtr., Time; Ed., Conover-Mast Pubns.; AWNY, PRSA; Dir. Mail Leadership aw., '65; Oh. Univ., BS (Jnlsm.); b. El Paso, Tex., 1926; p. Edward and Mable Bowden Vaughn; res: 33 East End Ave., N.Y., N.Y. 10028.

VAUGHT, BARBARA LEE, Comptroller, Off. Mgr., Harmon Smith, Inc., 800 W. 47th St., Kan. City, Mo. 64112, '66–; Media, '62–'66; General Mills, '56–'62; Wms. C. of C., Kan. City Ballet Co., '63–'65; Kan. City Jr. Col., '57–'58; Univ. of Mo., '66–'67; b. Kan. City, Mo., 1938; p. Harold and Helen Cook Vaught; res: 4611 Summit, Kan. City, Mo. 64112.

VECCHIO, DORIS VAN PATTEN, Fashion Dir., Hystron Fibers, Inc., 485 Lexington Ave., N.Y., N.Y. 10017, '66–; Deering Milliken, '59–'66; Byr., Lord and Taylor, '54–'59; Henri Bendel, '52–'54; Rike-Kumler, '50–'52; John Shillito, '47–'50; Photo-jnlst.; Cnslt., long range color, fabric and fashion trend dev., '59–; Fashion Group; Nat. Hon. Sociological Soc., '39;

Miami Univ., BA, '40 (summa cum laude); b. Litchfield, Mich.; p. Dewitt and Maud Powers Van Patten; h. Walter Vecchio.

VEDDER, MARION HELENE, Assoc. in Inst. Lib. Svcs., New York State Education Department-State Library, Division of Library Development, Albany, N.Y. 12224, '50–; Public Lib. Cnslt., '45–'50; Br. Librn., Head of Ext., Rochester Public Lib., '35–'45, '30–'32; Sch. Librn., Eng. Tchr., Fayetteville HS, '32–'35; Am. Correctional Assn. (Auth., "Library Services" chptr., "Manual of Correctional Standards," '66; Bd. of Dirs., '57–'59; E. R. Cass Achiev. Aw., '66), ALA (Cncl. Mbr., '60–'67), Assn. of Hosp. and Inst. Libs. (Pres., '66–'67); Exceptional Svc. Aw., '66); State Univ. of N.Y. at Albany, AB, '27; Syracuse Univ. Sch. of Lib. Sci., BS, '30; res: 1075 Park Ave., Schenectady, N.Y. 12308.

VERCINI, EDNA LINDHOLM, Publicist, General Electric, S.E. 42nd St., N.Y., N.Y. 10017, '64–; Press Rel., '50–; Reptr., Asst. County Ed., Post Publ. Co. (Bridgeport, Conn.), '43–'45; Electrical Wms. Round Table (Past N.Y.C. Chptr. Secy.) NHFL, AWRT; Who's Who Among Students in Am. Cols. and Univs.; Adelphi Univ., BA, '42; b. Bklyn., N.Y., 1923; p. F. Edward and Mary Dean Lindholm; h. Fred Vercini; c. Melinda M.; res: 32 Linley Rd., Trumbull, Conn. 06611.

VERHINE, PATRICIA ANNE, VP, Dir. of Research, Ted Bates & Co., 666 Fifth Ave., N.Y., N.Y. 10019, '68–; Rsch., '57–'68; Rsch. Dir., Mumm, Mullay & Nichols, '54–'57; Rsch. Analyst, Tatham-Laird, '52–'54; Rsch. Analyst, Monsanto, '51–'52; Rsch. Field Supvsr., Procter & Gamble, '49–'51; Am. Mktng. Assn.; Oh. State Univ., BS (Bus. Adm.), '49; b. Columbus, Oh.; p. Carl and Mary Fitzpatrick Verhine; res: 145 E. 15th St., N.Y., N.Y. 10003.

VERNAZZA, MARCELLE WYNN, Prof. of Music, San Francisco State College, 1600 Holloway Ave., S.F., Cal. 94132, '45–; Wtr., non-fiction; Whitman Conservatory of Music, Diploma; S.F. State Col., AB; Mills Col., MA; h. Jerome Vernazza.

VERNON, ROBERTA F., Free-lance Fashion Pubcty. Cnslt., 1408 S. Bayshore Dr., Miami, Fla. 33131; Press Rels. Mgr., Burdine's Dept. Stores, '60–'67; Fashion Pubcty. Dir., Nat. Assn. Hosiery Manufacturers (N.Y.C.), '54–'58; Fashion Pubcty. Dir., Ruth Lundgren Co., '51–'53; Pubcty., Hattie Carnegie, '47–'50; Pubcty. Club of N.Y., Fashion Group of N.Y., Theta Sigma Phi; Carnegie Inst. of Tech. (Fine Arts); Art Inst. of Pitt. (Comml. Art); b. Covington, Ky.; p. Emil and Nettie Crockett Forbriger; h. John O'Brien.

VERPLANK, CHARLOTTE WHEELER, Ed., Lake County Star, 21 N. Court St., Crown Point, Ind. 46307, '49–; Newswtr., '33–'47; Adv. Copywtr., Mgr. Bk. Dept., Tribe of K Stationery Store; Tchr., Crown Point HS, '20–'27; Theta Sigma Phi, Delta Zeta; Who's Who of Am. Wm.; Ind. Univ., BA, '20; b. Crown

Point, Ind., 1898; p. Fred and Jeanette Hughes Wheeler; h. Adelbert Verplank; res: 135 N. Court St., Crown Point, Ind. 46307.

VERY, ALICE N., Auth.; Ed. and Clerk, Branden Press, 221 Columbus Ave., Boston, Mass. 02116, '62–; bks: "The Human Abstract," "Round the Year Plays for Children," "Write on the Water;" Wellesley Col., AB, '16; b. Allegheny, Pa., 1894; p. Frank and Portia Vickers Very; h. Edmund R. Brown; c. Rosalys, Edmund H., Charlotte Jackson, Cynthia, Martha Bragg; res: 10 Edge Hill Rd., Sharon, Mass. 02067.

VESPA, MARY CATHERINE, Mng. Ed., 1,001 Decorating Ideas, Conso Publishing Company, 27 W. 23rd St., N.Y., N.Y. 10010, '69–; Assoc. Ed., '68–'69; Gift and Tableware Reporter, Billboard Pubns., '67–'68; Edtl. Asst., Ency. of Sci. and Tech., McGraw-Hill; City Col. of N.Y., BA (Eng.), '67; N.Y. Sch. of Interior Design, '69; b. Arlington, Va., 1945; p. Paul and Molly Gordon Vespa; res: 51 W. 87th St., N.Y., N.Y. 10024.

VETRI, CECILIA VICTORIA, Actress, Singer, Dancer, Arthur Kennard Agent, 8776 Sunset Blvd., L.A., Cal. 90069; Co-star, "Rosemary's Baby"; Star, "When Dinosaurs Ruled the Earth"; lead in 26 TV shows; b. L.A., Cal. 1944; p. William and Cesarina Liberatore Vetri; res: 2049 N. Curson Ave., L.A., Cal. 90046.

VIDGERHOUSE, MILDRED A., PR Dir., Paul Venze Associates, Inc., 295 Madison Ave., N.Y., N.Y. 10017; Vigderhouse, Cotton & Bass; Dir., TV Dept., Ruder & Finn; Prodr., TV Programs, Dumont; NATAS, PRSA, NHFL; George Washington Univ., BA; b. Wash., D.C., 1927; p. Samuel and Mary Vigderhouse; res: 401 E. 89th St., N.Y., N.Y. 10028.

VILAR, CAROLE MARIE, Mdsng. Mgr., Family Weekly, Inc., 641 Lexington Ave., N.Y., N.Y. 10022, '69–; Adv. Svs. Mgr., Woman's Day, '67–'69; Asst. to Crtv. Mdse. Mgr., Look, '66–'67; Marjorie Webster Jr. Col., AA (Mdsng.), '59; b. E. Orange, N.J., 1939; p. Albert Vilar and Mrs. Roger T. McLean (Walsh); res: 235 E. 46th St., N.Y., N.Y. 10017.

VILS, URSULA, Feature Wtr., Los Angeles Times, Times Mirror Sq., L.A., Cal. 90053, '64–; PR, '62–'64; Feature Wtr., Los Angeles Mirror, '60–'62; Valley Ed., Citizen News, '55–'57; Wms. Ed., '54–'57; Theta Sigma Phi; Univ. of Southern Cal. (Phi Beta Kappa, Phi Kappa Phi); h. Kenneth Vils.

VINCENT, KATHLEEN JOHNSON, Tape Ed. and Copywtr., Capitol Records, 1750 N. Vine St., Hollywood, Cal. 90028, '67–; Wtr., Capitol Record Club, '67; Copywtr., Walter F. Bennett Adv., '66–'67; Haston Assocs., '66–'67; Dialog Wtr., feature film, "Without Getting," Desert Film Prods. (Phoenix, Ariz.), '66; NARAS; Ithaca Col., BS (Radio & TV), '67; b. Buffalo, N.Y., 1945; p. Alfred and Marjorie Hoyt Johnson; res: 496 Crane Blvd., L.A., Cal. 90065.

VINCENT, NORMA, PR Asst., Hillcrest Medical

Center, Utica on the Park, Tulsa, Okla. 74104, '68–; Prom. Dept., KOTV, '62–'68 (News prom. prize); News Ed., Oil and Gas Journal, '62; PR Dept., Blue Cross-Blue Shield, '60–'62; KTUL-TV, '58–'59; AWRT, PR Soc. of Okla. Hosp. Assn., Indsl. Eds. of Tulsa; Univ. of Tulsa, BA (Jnlsm., Home Econs.), '59; b. Tulsa, Okla., 1937; p. George and Willie Jordan Vincent; res: 2540 E. Seventh, Tulsa, Okla. 74120.

VINTON, IRIS, Free-lance Auth., Ed., Cnslt. on children's bks.; Dir., Pubns. Dept., Boys' Clubs of Am., '44–'64 (Hon. Life Mbr., Boys' Club Pfsnl. Assn., '63); Assoc. Ed., Breskin Publ. Co., '40–'44; Ed.-in-Chief, You and Your Child, '36–'40; Asst. to Dir., Educ. Dept., Nat. Recreation Assn., '29–'36; bks: "The Folkways Omnibus of Children's Games" (Stackpole, '70), "Missy and the Mountain Lion" (Singer-Random, '67), 33 others; WNBA (Past Mbr., Bd. of Mgrs.; Ed., The Bookwoman; Pen and Brush (many offs.); Elected to Scholarship Socs. of the South, '27; Cert. of Aw., Navy Training Sch. (Salvage), '45; Univ. of Tex., Permanent State Tchrs. Cert., '23; Incarnate Word Col., AB, '28; special courses, Columbia Univ., N.Y.U., Univ. of Mex.; b. West Point, Miss.; p. William and Maud Best Vinton; res: 23 Bethune St., N.Y., N.Y. 10014.

VOELKER, CHARLOTTE VELMA, Copy Dir., Assoc. Crtv. Dir., Franznick-Charny, Inc., 215 E. 49th St., N.Y., N.Y. 10017, '66–; Sr. Copywtr., Campbell-Ewald (Detroit, Mich.), '57–'65; Copywtr., Wrigley Stores, '56–'57; Detroit Copy Club; Bravo aw., '63; Andy aw., '68; Univ. of Mich., BA.

VOGEL, FAYE HENLE, Free-lance Wtr., Bdcstr.; Auth., "350 Ways to Make Your Money Grow" (Universal Publ. Co., '69); Colmst., NEA; "The Faye Henle Show," WOR Radio, '61–'67; OPC, N.Y. Soc. Security Analysts; Barnard Col., BA, '40; N.Y.U.; b. N.Y.C.; p. Frederick and Mary Henle; h. Ray Vogel; c. Frederick R., Carol Mary; res: 49 E. 96th St., N.Y., N.Y. 10028.

VOGEL, HELEN WOLFF, Auth., "Ocean Harvest" ('62); Columbia Univ., New Col., BS, '38; Tchrs. Col., MA, '39; b. N.Y.C., 1918; p. Herbert and Daisy K. Wolff; h. John H. Vogel; c. Virginia, John, Jr., Thomas H.; res: 18 Wynmor Rd., Scarsdale, N.Y. 10583.

VOGL, LYNN M., Staff Asst., General Mills, Inc., 9200 Wayzata Blvd., Mpls., Minn. 55440, '68–; Travel Wtr., Minn. State AAA, '65–'68; Minn. Press Club; Clarke Col., BA, '63; b. Dubuque, Ia.; p. A. L. and Mary Hanson Vogl; res: 1216 Douglas Ave., Mpls., Minn. 55403.

VOGT, ESTHER LOEWEN, Auth: "Cry to the Wind" (Zondervans, '65); "The Sky Is Falling" (Herald Press, '68); "High Ground" ('70); Kan. Auths. Club (Fourth Dist. Pres., '64–'65; State Fiction aws., '68), Mentor Study Club, YWCA; Native Sons and Daughters short story contest, '65; Tabor Col., AA, '39 (Poet Laureate); b. Collinsville, Okla., 1915; p. Henry and Agnes Penner Loewen; h. Curt Vogt; c. Shirley (Mrs. Danny Williams), Ranney Lee, Naomi Ruth; res: 502 E. First, Hillsboro, Kan. 67063.

VOISIN, ELLEN S., Pres., Voisin, Marshall and Ross Advertising, Inc., 509 Madison Ave., N.Y., N.Y. 10022, '64–; Copy Chief, Crtv. Planner, J. C. Penney Co., '52–'64; Copy Head, Home Fashions, Furniture, Loeser's Dept. Store, '50–'52; Copywtr., D'Arcy Adv., '44–'48; Pubcty. Wtr., 20th Century Fox Film Corp., '42–'44; AWNY, AAF, NHFL, Sigma Tau Delta; Addy aws., '69, '68; Hunter Col., BA, '41; b. Magna, Ut.; h. C. V. Voisin; c. Elizabeth; res: 100-10 Ascan Ave., Forest Hills, N.Y. 11375.

VOIT, HELEN LEETE-SPAULDING, Lectr.; Investment Cnslt., The International Securities Corporation, Box 3, Palm Beach, Fla. 33480, '68–; Investment Co. Off. Mgr., '59–'60, '67–'68; Univ. of Mo., Hunter Col.; b. Longmeadow, Mass., 1913; p. Theodore and George O. M. Ames Leete; h. Eugene F. Voit (div.); c. Lucie Leete (Mrs. William D. Cavanaugh, Jr.), Karl Spaulding; res: 408 Chilian Ave., Palm Beach, Fla. 33480.

VOLTOS, DANAE VIRGINIA, Asst. Ed., Venture, 488 Madison Ave., N.Y., N.Y. 10022, '66–; Edtl. Asst., '64–'66; Rschr., Show, '62–'64; b. London, England, 1938; p. Constantine and Elizabeth Balfour Voltos; res: 1374 Third Ave., N.Y., N.Y. 10021.

VOLTZ, JEANNE APPLETON, Food Ed., The Los Angeles Times, Times Mirror Sq., L.A., Cal. 90053, '60–; Miami Herald, '52–'60; Reptr.; '47–'52; Mobile (Ala.) Press Register, '42–'45; Theta Sigma Phi, Food Eds. Advisory Comm., '58, Porcelain Enamel Inst. Advisory Cncl.; Fla. Wms. Press Club aws., '55–'57; Vesta aws. for excellence in food rept., '63, '65–'68; Ala. Col., AB, '42; b. Collinsville, Ala. 1920; p. J. Lamar and Marie Sewell Appleton; h. Luther Voltz; c. Luther, Jr., Jeanne M.; res: 5266 White Oak Ave., Encino, Cal. 91316.

VON EKENBERGER, JEANNIE PETERSON, Adv. Wtr., McCann Erickson, Inc., 44 Montgomery St., S.F., Cal. 94104, '67–; Travel Wtr., '65; Adv. Wtr., Benton & Bowles (N.Y.C.), '63–'64; Wtr., Childcraft, Field Enterprises (Chgo., Ill.), '61; Soc. of Am. Travel Wtrs., Theta Sigma Phi; AAF aw., '69; S.F. Art Dirs. and Artists Club aws., '69; L.A. Art Dirs. aws., '68; Northwestern Univ., BS (Jnlsm.), MS (Jnlsm.); b. Traverse City, Mich., 1940; p. Paulus and Ellen Glommen Peterson; h. Kurt Von Ekenberger.

VON LOSS, ADELE CLAIRE, TV, Motion Pic., Stage Actress; Wtr.; Acad. of TV Arts and Scis., Masquerettes (VP), Pet Assistance Fndn.; Stars in Your Eyes Aw., Publicists Guild for Blind Children; U.C.L.A.; b. Koln, Germany, 1937; p. Frank and Ella Von Loss Blasberg; res: 2261 Alcyona Dr., L.A., Cal. 90028.

VON OESEN, (ANNA) ELAINE, Asst. State Librn.,

North Carolina State Library, P.O. Box 2889, Raleigh, N.C. 27602, '65–; Ext. Svcs. Librn., '56–'65; Field Librn., N.C. Lib. Commn., '52–'56; Army Librn., '43–'44; Dir. of Libs., LaFayette, Ga., '42–'43; Asst. Librn., Rockingham County Lib., '40–'42; Instr., Asst. Prof., Univ. of N.C., '47–'52; Ed., North Carolina Libraries, '53–'57; ALA, Southeastern Lib. Assn., Am. Assn. of State Libs.; Who's Who Among Col. and Univ. Students, '38; Lenoir Rhyne Col., AB, '38; Univ. of N.C., BA (Lib. Sci.), '40; MA (Hist.), '51; b. Wilmington, N.C.; p. Martin and Adeline Behrens von Oesen; res: 100 Snow Ave., Raleigh, N.C. 27603.

VON RICHTER, ZOYA KLEMENTINOVSKI, Asst. Librn., specialist on Slavic Material, Processing Dept., Library of Congress, Wash., D.C. 20540, '51–; Tolstoy Fndn. (Treas., '46–'50); Inst. of J. J. Rousseau, Lausanne, Switzerland (Langs.), '22; b. Moscow, Russia, 1905; p. Paul and Sole Mareche Klementinovski; h. 1. Randolph Dickins (dec.) 2. Lothrop Stoddard (dec.) 3. Nicholas A. von Richter; c. Randolph Dickins, Zoya Dickins (Mrs. Hilliard E. Miller, Jr.), Mary Alice Stoddard (Mrs. Arthur J. Smith); res: 2500 Q St. N.W., Wash., D.C. 20007.

VOORHEES, MARIELLA PAVLOVICH, AE, Carson/Roberts Inc., 8322 Beverly Blvd., L.A., Cal. 90048, '64–; Asst. Adv. and Prom. Dir., Rose Marie Reid; Adm. Asst. Mktng. Dir., Hycon Mfg. Co.; Fashion Group; L.A. Adv. Wm. Lulu Aws., '68, '69; U.C.L.A.; b. L.A., Cal. 1933; p. Marin and Lucille Bupich Pavlovich; h. (div.); c. Michael, Viktoria; res: 2427 Nalin Dr., Bel Air, Cal. 90024.

VORDENBERG, ROSEMARY RAVET, Dir. of Media and Rsch., Ralph H. Jones Co., 3100 Carew Tower, Cinn., Oh. 45202, '61–; Media Dept. Mgr., Stockton West Borkhart, '53–'61; Cinn. Indsl. Advs., Am. Mktng. Assn., Altrusa; Univ. of Cinn., BA, '43; Western Reserve, BS (Lib. Sci.), '44; b. Cinn., Oh.; p. Elmer and Florence J. Vordenberg; res: 3132 Portsmouth Ave., Cinn., Oh. 45208.

VOSS, CARROLL SCHELL, Auth: "Come Before Winter" (Muhlenberg, '53), "Never the White Rose" ('57), "White Cap for Rechinda" (Ives Washburn, '66); Tchr., '56–'62; Sioux Wtrs., Boston Auths. Club, NLAPW, Intl. Platform Assn.; BPW Sioux City Wm. of the Yr., '47; Drury Col., '16–'17; Western Col. for Wm., AB, '21; Columbia Univ., '23; Gettysburg Col., LLD (hon.), '54; b. Marysville, Kan., 1899; p. Ulysses and Hattie Orr Schell; h. Walter Andrew Voss; c. Walter Andrew Jr., Wendell Grant, Mariel Anne (Mrs. Roger William Haugen); res: 3255 Grandview Blvd., Sioux City, Ia. 51104.

VOSS, JANE HOPE, Prodr., Bdcstr., "Modern Woman," WMT-TV, Broadcast Park, Cedar Rapids, Ia. 52406, '65–; Free-lance Scout, Better Homes & Gardens, '69–; numerous bdcst. positions, '52–'65; AWRT (Hawkeye, Ia. Chptr. Pres., '65–'66; West Central Area VP, '67–'68), Theta Sigma Phi, Intl. Platform Assn., numerous civic, charitable orgs.; Who's Who of Am. Wm., Who's Who in the Midwest, 2,000 Wm. of Achiev., Personalities of the West and Midwest, '68; Hunter Col., '42; b. Exira, Ia., 1922; p. George and Evelyn Rendleman Voss; h. Conrad Johnson; c. Mrs. Dawn Neathery, Lisa, Scott, Harry, Mrs. Joyce Arbuckle, Paul, David; res: 2247 Meadowbrook Dr. S.E., Cedar Rapids, Ia. 52403.

VOSS, RUTH HEMMERT, Ed., The Cincinnati Enquirer's Teen-age Tabloid, 617 Vine St., Cinn., Oh. 45201, '65–; Sch. Ed., Cincinnati Times-Star, '50–'58; Sch. Colmst., '46–'58; Theta Sigma Phi, Cinn. Teens for Decency (Adult Advisor); Univ. of Cinn., BA, '50; b. Cinn., Oh., 1928; p. Michael and Catherine Reichardt Hemmert; h. Robert Voss; c. Michael, Richard, Peter, Mary Ann, Daniel, Catherine, Andrew, Joseph; res: 1570 Elizabeth Pl., Cinn., Oh. 45237.

VREELAND, DIANA DALZIEL, Ed.-in-Chief, Vogue, 420 Lexington Ave., N.Y., N.Y. 10017, '62–; Fashion Ed., Harper's Bazaar, '37–'62; b. Paris, France; h. Thomas Reed Vreeland; c. Thomas R., Frederick D; res: 550 Park Ave., N.Y., N.Y. 10021.

VUILLEUMIER, MARION RAWSON, Auth., nonfiction bks.; Dir., Craigville Conference Center, Craigville, Mass. 02636, '65–; Feature Wtr., Sun. Cape Cod Standard Times, Barnstable Patriot; various educ. positions, '51–'62; Cape Cod Wtrs. Conf. (Secy., '64), NEA, numerous hist. socs.; Gordon Col., AB, '40; b. Worcester, Mass.; p. Walter and Mary White Rawson; h. Pierre DuPont Vuilleumier; c. Virginia Marion (Mrs. Louis R. Lobo), Prince DuPont II, Louis Edward; res: Box 111, Green Dunes Dr., W. Hyannisport, Mass. 02672.

VUJICA, NADA KESTERCANEK, Auth. of Yugoslavian bks.; Head Librn., Eugene Shedden Farley Library of Wilkes College, Wilkes-Barre, Pa. 18703, '52–; Asst. Librn., '47–'51; Croatian Acad. of Am., AAUP, ALA, Pa. Lib. Assn.; Univ. of Zagreb, MA, '40; Marywood Col., MA (Lib. Sci.), '52; b. Sarajevo, Yugoslavia; p. Vladimir and Maria Brajenovic Kestercanek; h. Stanko Vujica; res: 95 Miner St., Wilkes-Barre, Pa. 18702.

W

WADDELL, PATRICIA COLBOURNE, Free-lance Adv. and Prom. Wtr., Home Furnishings and Fashion Cnslt.; AE, Retail Marketers Adv., '64–'67; Fashion Dir., Couture Adv., '63–'64; Asst. Mdsng. Dir., Ingenue, '61–'62; Asst. Retail Prom. Mgr., Dow Badische Co., '58–'60; Asst. Byr., Lord and Taylor, '57–'58; Exec. Trainee, Bonwit Teller, '56–'57; AWNY, NHFL;

b. London, Eng.; p. George and Kathleen Duffy Colbourne; h. C. Eugene Waddell; res: 903 Park Ave., N.Y., N.Y. 10021.

WADDLE, MARY STEIDLEY, Owner/Publr., DeRidder Enterprise, 125 N. Washington Ave., DeRidder, La. 70634, '60–; La. Press Assn., Nat. Edtl. Assn., Nat. Nwsp. Assn., BPW (Citizen of the Yr. Aw., '60; Pres.); Mansfield Col.; b. DeRidder, La., 1907; p. James and Ethel Burge Steidley; h. Claude B. Waddle (dec.); c. Everett, Claude, Ethel Carrier; res: S. Texas, DeRidder, La. 70634.

WADE, ELIZABETH CAROL, Copywtr., LaRoche, McCaffrey and McCall, Inc., 575 Lexington Ave., N.Y., N.Y. 10022, '67–; Wilson Col., BA, '64; b. Cleve., Oh., 1942.

WADE, JANE ST. CLAIR, Free-lance Wtr., non-fiction; Reptr., Kansas City (Mo.) Star, '42–'46; Pubcty. Dir., YWCA, '33–'36; Theta Sigma Phi (Kan. City Chptr. Pres., '33–'35); Univ. of Kan., AB, '32; b. Kan. City, Mo., 1910; p. Arthur and Anna Ryan St. Clair; h. Frederick Wade; c. Frederick E. Jr.; res: 413 W. 62nd St., Kan. City, Mo. 64113.

WAGES, ELEANOR VANDER PLOEG, TV Specialist, Bdcstr., New York State Cooperative Extension, 207 Federal Bldg., 441 Broadway, Albany, N.Y. 12207, '67–; Home Econst., Albany County, '63–'67; Am. Home Econs. Assn., AWRT, Ext. Home Econsts., Cncl. on Consumer Info.; Ia State Univ., BS (Home Econs. Educ.), '62; b. Sioux Center, Ia., 1941; p. Lawrence and Anna Vander Burg Vander Ploeg; h. Sherrie Wages; res: 1101 Millington Rd., Schenectady, N.Y. 12309.

WAGNER, G. P., Media Dir., Corp. Dir. and Offcr., Doe-Anderson Advertising Agency, Inc., 315 Commonwealth Bldg., Louisville, Ky. 40202, '68–; Media Byr., '50–'68; Prod. Mgr., '43–'50; Off. Mgr., '40–'43; Secy., '36–'40; Outstanding Bus. Wm. of '59, Bluegrass Chptr. Am. Bus. Wms. Assn.; res: 3301 Stratford Ave., Louisville, Ky. 40218.

WAGNER, JEANETTE SARKISIAN, Dir., Special Projects Div., Cosmopolitan, Hearst Corporation, 224 W. 57th, N.Y., N.Y. 10019, '69–; Ed.-in-Chief, Eye, '68–'69; Sr. Ed., Saturday Evening Post, '62–'68; Ed., Chicago Life mag., '58–'62; Film, TV Prodr., '56–'58; Film Dir., WTTW-TV (Chgo., Ill.); Dir. of Pubns. and PR, Film Cncl. of Am.; Fashion Group; Northwestern Univ., BS, '51 (cum laude); b. Chgo., Ill., 1929; p. Souren and Nazeny Norsigian Sarkisian; h. Paul A. Wagner; c. Paul III, Paula Ann; res: 333 E. 30th St., N.Y., N.Y. 10016.

WAGNER, JOAN, Copywtr., Ogilvy & Mather, 2 E. 48th St., N.Y., N.Y. 10017, '68–; Copywtr., Keynon & Eckhardt, '66–'68; Copywtr., R. H. Macy & Co., '64–'66; League of Wm. Voters; Conn. Col. for Wm., BA, '59; b. N.Y.C.; res: 343 E. 30th St., N.Y., N.Y. 10016.

WAGNER, JOYCE AILEEN, TV Ed., Colmst., Critic, Kansas City Star, 1729 Grand Ave., Kan. City, Mo. 64108, '65–; TV Ed., Kansas City Kansan, '63–'65; Reptr., Bailey Pubns., '62–'63; Ed., Warrenville (Ill.) News, '60; Mo. Press Wm.; Univ. of Mo., '59–'61; Am. Acad. of Music, '61–'62; b. Aurora, Ill., 1941; p. Julius and Laura Timmerman Wagner.

WAGNER, JULIA COPPA, Mng. Ed., Dell Publishing Company, Inc., 750 Third Ave., N.Y., N.Y. 10017, '59–; Edtl. Asst., '56–'59; Pubns. Ed., Dept. of Defense (Wash., D.C.), '51–'55; U.S. Govt., '41–'51; Gen. Alumni Assn., Am. Fedn. of Astrologers; George Washington Univ., BA, '48; MA, '50; b. Alexandria, Va., 1924; p. Luigi and Domenica di Giammarino Coppa; h. Edward Wagner; res: 211 E. 51st St., N.Y., N.Y. 10022.

WAGNER, LINDA WELSHIMER, Assoc. Prof. of Eng., Michigan State University, E. Lansing, Mich. 48823, '68–; Auth: "Phyllis McGinley" (Twayne, '70), "Denise Levertov" (Twayne, '67); "The Poems of William Carlos Williams" (Wesleyan U. Press, 1964); Modern Lang. Assn., Intl. Platform Assn., Oh. Eng. Assn. (Pres., '65–'66); Bowling Green Univ., '57 (magna cum laude); PhD, '63; b. St. Marys, Oh., 1936; p. Sam and Esther Scheffler Welshimer; h. Paul Wagner; c. Douglas, Thomas; res: 1620 Anderson Way, East Lansing, Mich. 48823.

WAGNER, MARGARET DALE (Peggy Wagner), Auth, "Hurrah for Hats" (Childrens Press, '64); Col. Bd., Mademoiselle Magazine, Contemporary Auths.; Jackson Col., Tufts Univ.; b. Chgo., Ill., 1949; p. Vernon and Marcia Nierman Wagner; res: 477 Monroe Ave., Glencoe, Ill. 60022.

WAGNER, SUSAN, AE, Jacobson/Wallace/Westphal, 60 E. 42nd St., N.Y., N.Y., 10017, '69–; formerly PR Mgr., Avianca Airlines; Asst. to PR Dir., Varig Airlines; Travel Cnslt., KLM; PR Dir., United Cerebral Palsy of Greater Boston; numerous travel articles; Soc. of Am. Travel Wtrs.; Pan Am. Union Essay Contest Prize; Harvard-Radcliffe Program in Bus. Adm.; Instituto Tecnologico y De Estudios Superiores, Monterrey, Mexico; Simmons Col.; b. N.Y.C.; p. George and Clara Wagner.

WAGSTAFF, BARBARA JANE, AE, Sonderling Broadcasting Corporation, KFOX-AM/FM, 666 E. Ocean Blvd., Long Beach, Cal. 90802, '69–; AE, KSOM-AM/FM (Ontario, Cal.), '68; Dir. of Adv. and Prom., J. Jessop & Sons, (San Diego), '66–'67; Nat. Prom. Dir., Wilbur Clark's Crest Hotels/Inns (La Jolla), '64–'66; Self-employed (Adv., PR, Photo., Graphic Design, Crtv. Arts, L.A.), '62–'64; Prom. Advisor, Home of Guiding Hands; San Diego Adv. & Sales Club (Dir. '67–'68); L.A. Adv. Wm., Dallas Adv. Club; U.C.L.A., '58–'59; Southern Methodist Univ., '57; Sam Houston State Col., '52–'54; b. Beaumont, Tex., 1934; p. Martin and Elberta Parker Wagstaff; res: 1749 E.

Yale, Ontario, Cal. 91762; 5587 La Jolla Mesa Dr., La Jolla, Cal. 92037.

WAHOSKI, HELEN I., Dir. of Libs., Assoc. Prof. of Lib. Sci., Forrest R. Polk Library, Wisconsin State University, 800 Algoma Blvd., Oshkosh, Wis. 54901, '50–; Asst. Cataloger, '46–'50; Ref. Librn., Wis. Hist. Soc., '37–'46; Intl. Platform Assn., ALA, Wis. Lib. Assn. (Librn. of the Yr., '58), Beta Phi Mu, Delta Kappa Gamma, numerous civic, bus. orgs.; Ripon Col., BA, '32; Univ. of Wis., BS (Lib. Sci.), '46; Univ. of Mich., MA (Lib. Sci.), '52; b. Ripon, Wis., 1910; p. Frank and Clara Wochnitz Wahoski; res: 1005 E. New York Ave., Oshkosh, Wis. 54901.

WAITZMANN, DOROTHEA MILDRED, Colmst., Green Bay Register, P.O. Box 909, Green Bay, Wis. 54302, '64–, and Walworth Times, Walworth, Wis. 53184, '69–; Auth., "A Special Way of Victory" (John Knox Press, '64'); AAUW, Wis. Press Wm.; St. Norbert Col., BS, '63; b. Chgo., Ill., 1915; p. Otto and Clara Frerck Waitzmann; res: Box 98, Walworth, Wis. 53184.

WALDEN, AMELIA ELIZABETH, Auth: 41 novels, incl. "What Happened to Candy Carmichael?" (Westminster, '70), "Basketball Girl of the Year" (McGraw-Hill, '70), "The Case of the Diamond Eye" (Westminster Press, '69), "Same Scene, Different Place" (J. B. Lippincott, '69), "The Spy Who Talked Too Much" (Westminster Press, '68); Western Conn. Col.; Columbia Univ., BS; Am. Acad. of Dramatic Arts; b. N.Y.C.; p. William and Elizabeth Wanner Walden, Sr.; h. John William Harmon (dec.); res: 89 N. Compo Rd., Westport, Conn. 06880.

WALDEN, CAROL MARGARET, Ref. Librn., Wellesley Free Library, Washington St., Wellesley, Mass. 02181, '68–; Head Librn., New England Conservatory of Music, '49–'68; Music Librn., Radcliffe Col., '47–'48; Head Cataloguer, Brookline Public Lib., '31–'47; Musician: Marimba concerts in New England; entertained for Am. Red Cross, Am. Theatre Wing I; The Cecilia Soc. (Music Librn.), Music Lib. Assn., Mass. Lib. Assn.; Radcliffe Col., BA, '28; Simmons Col., BS (Lib. Sci.), '44; b. Montville, Conn., 1907; p. Clarence and Jennie Browning Walden; res: 146 Great Plain Ave., Needham, Mass. 02192.

WALDEN, MAY DAY LO, Info. Specialist, Office of the Mayor, City and County of Honolulu, 530 S. King St., Honolulu, Hi. 96813, '61–; PR Specialist, Dept. of Parks and Recreation, '53–'61; PR Asst., Honolulu C. of C., '52–'53; PR Dir., Mental Health Assn. '49–'51; Ed., Chronicle Publ., '47–'49; Colmst., Star-Bulletin, '44–'65; Reptr., '36–'42; Theta Sigma Phi (Honolulu Chptr. Pres., '49), PR Wm. of Honolulu (Pres., '55), Honolulu Press Club, Recreation Assn. of Honolulu; Univ. of Hi., '32–'34; Univ. of Mo., BJ, '36; b. Hilo, Hi.; p. Yuet Fu and Ngan You Tse Lo; h. David Walden (div.); c. David Jun Wai; res: 3340 Mooheau, Honolulu, Hi., 96816.

WALDO, DOROTHY BRACHER, Adv. Mgr., Glass Block Department Store, 128 W. Superior St., Duluth, Minn. 55802, '61–; Freimuth's, '55–'61; Free-lance Adv., '48–'55; Radio Show, WDSM, '53–'54; Nat. Retail Merchants Assn. Silver Aw., '67; Duluth Playhouse Encore Aw., '63, '65; Northern State Col., BA; b. Marquette, Mich.; p. Edward and Margaret Wellman Bracher; h. Neil Waldo; c. Neil, Jr., Edward B., James R.; res: 224 W. St. Andrews, Duluth, Minn., 55803.

WALDO, MYRA, Food, Travel Ed., WCBS, 51 W. 52nd St., N.Y., N.Y. 10019, '68–; Special Projects Dir., Macmillan and Co.; Food, Travel Ed., This Week; Auth: 43 books on food, travel, incl: "Myra Waldo's Travel and Motoring Guide to Europe," "Myra Waldo's Travel Guide to South America," "Round the World Cookbook"; OPC (Gov.), AWRT, Soc. of Mag. Wtrs., Soc. of Am. Travel Wtrs., N.Y. Soc. of Travel Wtrs.; Columbia Univ.; h. Robert J. Schwartz; res: 900 Fifth Ave., N.Y., N.Y. 10021.

WALDON, MARY CLERKIN, Home Furnishings Ed., Indianapolis Star, 307 N. Penn St., Indpls., Ind., '63–; Tchr., Music, Art and Eng.; Social Secy. for Gov. Harold W. Handley; Theta Sigma Phi; Wms. Press Club of Ind.; Am. Inst. of Interior Designers; NPWC Aw., Aws. from Mens' and Wms.' press clubs of Ind. for features, series and home furnishings stories; Butler Univ., Arthur Jordan Sch. of Music; h. Scott Waldon; res: 3625 Alexandria Ct., Indpls., Ind. 46205.

WALDRON-SHAH, D'LYNN, Auth. of bks., articles on Asia, Africa, Arab World; Dir. of Rsch., Board of Supervisors, County of Los Angeles, County Hall of Administration, L.A., Cal. 90012, '68–; Auth., Artist, Photogr., Fgn. Corr., Harper & Row, Scripps-Howard, the B.B.C., Asia, Africa, Arab World, '56–'64; Wash. Univ., BA, '65 (summa cum laude, Phi Beta Kappa, Ford Fndn. SMDP Rsch. Fellow, '64); MA, '65; Claremont Grad. Sch. and Univ. Ctr., PhD, '67 (All Univ. Fellow, '65–'66; Hoskins Prize, '66; Haynes Interdisciplinary Fellow, '66–'67); b. Bergen County, N.J. 1936; p. George E. and Hazel G. Waldron; res: Santa Monica, Cal. 90402.

WALKER, ALEXANDRA EAMES, Assoc. Decorating Ed., American Home Magazine, 641 Lexington Ave., N.Y., N.Y. 10022; Asst. Decorating Ed., American Home, '66–'69; Asst. to Paul Krauss, AID, '64–'66; Parsons School of Design, '64; b. N.Y.C.; p. J. Owen and Olive Dean Eames.

WALKER, ALYCE BILLINGS, Assoc. Ed., The Birmingham News, 2200 Fourth Ave. N., Birmingham, Ala. 35202, '60–; Feature Wtr., Dir., Wms. Dept., '44–'60; Wms. Ed., Birmingham Post, '30–'43; Jnlsm. Instr., Samford Univ., '61–'62; Theta Sigma Phi,

WNPC, numerous civic orgs.; Who's Who of Am. Wm., Delta Kappa Gamma (hon. mbr.), U.S. Steel Jnlst. of the Year, '65, numerous cits.; Birmingham Southern Col., Judson Col., AB (alumnae aw., '58); b. Birmingham, Ala.; h. Erskine Walker (div.); res: 1100 27th St., S., Birmingham, Ala. 35205.

WALKER, ANN BOSTON, Asst. Dir., Commty. Svcs., WLWC-TV, 3165 Olentangy, Columbus, Oh. 43202, '68–; Wms. Ed., Asst. News Dir., WVKO Radio, '61–'68; Wms. Ed., Edtl. Wtr., Columbus Sentinel, '49–'61; Reptr., Chicago Defender, '51; AWRT (Columbus Chptr. Secy., Treas.), Theta Sigma Phi, numerous civic orgs.; Am. Legion Aux. Golden Mike Aw., '67; Mayor's Cit., '65; b. Columbus, Oh.; p. Samuel and Iola Benson Boston; h. Linwood Walker; c. Phillip, Julialyn, Amelia, Keith; res: 1819 Franklin Park So., Columbus, Oh. 43205.

WALKER, BETTY, Free-lance Artist, Painter, Decorator, '46–; Exhbns.: Nat. Acad. Galleries, Nat. Soc. of Painters in Casein, Contemporary Arts Gallery, many others; one-man shows in Dallas, Tex., N.Y.C., Pa., Bklyn; Tchr., Art Haven Guild, '46–'57; represented in numerous private collections; Met. Motion Pic. Club (Bd. of Dirs.; Ed., Close-Up, '65–'70), Three Eyes Art Group (Charter Mbr.; Tchr., Three Eyes Art Sch.), AWNY; George Swetnick Memorial Aw., '68; W. Orange, N.J. C. of C. Art Aw., '66; David Friend Art Group Highest Aw. of Merit, '65; Nat. Painters in Casein Patrons Prize, '67; Nat. Acad. of Design (Scholarship; Sch. Prize, '34); Pratt Inst.; Bklyn. Museum Art Sch.; Joseph Wyckoff; b. Dallas, Tex.; p. Robert and Loretta Lane Walker; h. (div.); c. Loretta Anne Mills, Susan Doherty; res: 4076 Bedford Ave., Bklyn., N.Y. 11229.

WALKER, CHARLOTTE McGILLIVRAY, Food Ed., Charleston Evening Post, News and Courier Publishing Co., 134 Columbus St., Charleston, S.C. 29402, '57–; Wms. Ed., '51–'62; Edtl. Staff, '50–'51; Ed., Feature Wtr., The Western Star (Corner Brook, Newfoundland), '42–'45; Auth., "The Post Courier Cookbook" ('66), "Loved and Lost" ('69); S.C. Press Assn. (Wms. Div. Pres., '57); S.C. Nwspwm. of the Yr., '56; Vesta Aw., Am. Meat Inst., G.E. plaque for edtl. excellence ('65); b. Montreal, Canada, 1909; p. John and Charlotte Renshaw McGillivray; h. Henry F. P. Walker; c. Mary Ann (Mrs. A. L. Wardlaw); res: 30 Savage St., Charleston, S.C. 29401.

WALKER, ESTELLE HARRIS, Ed.-Publr., Walker Publishing Co., 2016 W. Main St., Sedalia, Mo. 65301, '44–; Am. Coon Hound Assn., Mo. Coon Hunters, Outdoor Wtrs. of Am., Mo. Outdoor Wtrs. Assn., Dog Wtrs. Assn. of Am., Great Rivers Outdoor Wtrs., BPW, Altrusa Intl., Nat., state, local C. of C.; Key to City (Anderson, S.C.); b. Duluth, Ga.; p. Jenner and Florence Smith Harris; h. Muriss Walker; c. Ralph, Mary F. Heyven, Barbara A. Deady; res: 1217 W. 4th, Sedalia, Mo. 65301.

WALKER, ESTELLENE PAXTON, Librn., South Carolina State Library, 1500 Senate St., Columbia, S.C. 29201, '46–; Materials Supply Librn., Army Special Svc. (European Theater of Operations), '45–'46; Post Librn., Ft. Jackson (S.C.), '41–'45; Head, County Dept., Lawson McGhee Lib. (Knoxville, Tenn.), '35–'41; Contrbr. to pfsnl. jnls.; Advisory Comm. to Off. of Educ. on Lib. Svcs. Act ('56–'57); Am. Assn. of State Libs. (Pres., '67–'68), ALA, Southeastern Lib. Assn., S.C. Lib. Assn.; Progressive Farmer Wm. of the Yr., '68; Univ. of Tenn., BA, '30; Emory Univ., BS (Lib. Sci.), '35; b. Wash. County, Va., 1911; p. John Camp and Willie Ropp Walker; res: 3208 Amherst Ave., Columbia, S.C. 29205.

WALKER, ESTHER SUMNER, Wms. Ed., San Jose Mercury-News, 750 Ridder Park Dr., San Jose, Cal. 95131, '49–; Police Reptr., '42–'45; Soc. Ed., Police Reptr., San Luis Obispo Telegram-Tribune, '37–'42; Reptr., Lynwood Tribune, '29–'37; Nat. Footwear Inst. top aw. for rept., '69; Am. Inst. of Men's and Boy's Wear aw., '69; various fashion aws.; U.C.L.A., BA, '34 (hons.); b. Boulder, Mont.; p. Ernest and Viola Southworth Sumner; h. Edwin Walker; c. Lynn; res: 3973 Golf Dr., San Jose, Cal. 95127.

WALKER, JESSIE LOUISE, Pres., Jessie Walker Associates, 241 Fairview Rd., Glencoe, Ill. 60022, '55–; Midwest Ed., The American Home, '67–'68; Auth., three bks., many articles on interior design; Theta Sigma Phi (N. Shore Chptr. Headliner of the Yr.), NHFL; Northwestern Univ., BS (Jnlsm.), MS (Jnlsm.); b. Milw., Wis.; p. Stuart and Loraine Walker.

WALKER, JOYCE HULL, Adm. VP, Mbr., Bd. of Dirs., Meltzer, Aron & Lemen, Inc., 165 Post St., S.F., Cal. 94108, '64–; Adm. Dir., '61–'64; Asst. Secy.-Treas., '58–'61; AE, '64; Off. Mgr., Edlo, Inc., '65; W. M. Gillies & Co., '55; Sullivan-Mears Co., '54; Alpha Gamma Delta; Univ. of Ill., BA, '48 (summa cum laude; Phi Beta Kappa, Phi Kappa Phi); b. E. St. Louis, Ill.; p. Dean and Stella Sullivan Hull; h. William Walker; c. William Dean; res: 5 Barrie Way, Mill Valley, Cal. 94941.

WALKER, LORRAINE WILBER, Exec. VP, Gen. Mgr., KCBN, BBC, Inc., 674 N. Arlington, Reno, Nev. 89503, '67–; AE, Sls. Mgr., Gen. Sls. Mgr., KFBB (Great Falls, Mont.); Nev. Bdcstrs. Assn. (Secy. Treas., '68–), Ad Club, Press Club; The Sorbonne; George Wash. Univ.; b. Lewistown, Mont., 1922; p. Irving and Georgia Pense Wilber; c. William W.; res: 1975 Lakeside Dr., Reno, Nev. 89502.

WALKER, MARY IONE, Owner, Publr., Buyers Directory, 11014 26th Ave. S., Seattle, Wash. 96168, '60–; Ed., Pacific Marketer, '59–'62.

WALKER, MARY T., Prodr., Fashion Shows, Radio-TV PR, Carl Byoir & Associates, 800 Second Ave., N.Y., N.Y. 10017, '69–; Taylor Walker Assoc., '57–'69; Hill & Knowlton, '53–'57; Steve Hannagan, '51–'53; NBC, '49–'51; AWRT (Pres., '60–'61); Nat. Thespian Soc. aw.; Chestnut Hill Col., AB, '45; b. Phila., Pa., 1923; p. William and Julia Teti Walker; h. William E. Hawley; res: 345 E. 56th St., N.Y., N.Y. 10022.

WALKER, PATRICIA CHAPMEN, Mgr., Employe Commtns., Parke, Davis & Company, GPO Box 118, Detroit, Mich. 48232, '53–; Asst. Ed., Ed., '49–'51; free-lance articles in Detroit News, Detroit Free Press, trade jnls.; ICIE (Area Secy., '66–'67), Indsl. Eds. Assn. of Detroit (Pres., '61–'62; VP, '60–'61; aws., '64–'66); Detroit Wm. Wtrs., Detroit Press Club, ZONTA; AAIE aw., '65; Univ. of Detroit, BS (Jnlsm.), '47; b. Detroit, Mich., 1925; p. Harry and Margaret Henigan Chapman; h. William J. Walker; c. Patricia, William Jr.; res: 14036 Artesian, Detroit, Mich. 48223.

WALKINSHAW, JEAN STRONG, Prodr., Commty. Svc. Dept., KING Broadcasting Company, 320 Aurura North, Seattle, Wash. 98109, '66–; Prodr., "Face to Face," KING-TV, '66–'69; Prodr., "Face to Face," KCTS-TV, '65–'66; Talent, Prodr., "Seattle Profile," KING-TV, '63–'65; AWRT, NATAS, NPWC; Wash. Press Wm. Sugar Plum Aw., '65; Stanford Univ., BA, '48; b. Tacoma, Wash., 1926; p. Arthur and Margaret Henderson Strong; h. Walter Walkinshaw; c. Charles, Robert, Margaret; res: 1303 E. Lynn, Seattle, Wash. 98102.

WALL, MAXINE KELLOGG, Reg. Media Byr., Communication Counselors Network, Div. of McCann-Erickson, 615 Peachtree St. N.E., Atlanta, Ga. 30308, '67–; Estimator-Media Byr., Marschalk, '62–'67; AWRT, Media Planners Group; h. Hardy Wall.

WALLACE, ANNE PARKS, Asst. Ed., Agricultural Information Service, University of Idaho, '69–; Artist, Ed., '61–; Ed., Pammel News, '59–'61; Wtr.-Ed., Ia. State Info. Svc., '57–'58; Wtr., USDA, Agricultural Rsch. Svc., '56; Theta Sigma Phi (Ia. Chptr. Pres., '59; Houston Chptr. Treas., '66–'68); Ia. State Tchrs. Col., '53–'55; Ia. State Univ., BS (Tech. Jnlsm.), '57; b. Lincoln, Neb., 1935; p. F. B. and Avis Olson Parks; h. Richard W. Wallace; c. Matthew Bruce, Laura Kathleen, Elsbeth Ellen; res: 410 S. Blaine, Moscow, Idaho 83843.

WALLACE, LILA ACHESON, Co-chmn., Reader's Digest Association, Inc., Pleasantville, N.Y. 10570, '65–; Co-founder, Co-ed., '21–; VP, Dir., Boscobel Restoration, '55–; Dir., Juilliard Sch. of Music, '68–; aws: Theodore Roosevelt Distg. Svc., '54; Syracuse Univ. Sch. of Jnlsm. Distg. Svc., '55; George Wash. Freedoms Fndn., '65; George McAneny Hist. Preservation, '67; Order of Civil Merit Dongbaeg Medal, Govt. of the Republic of Korea, '68; Ward Belmont Col., Univ. of Ore., BA, '17; b. Virden, Manitboa, Can.; p. Thomas and Mary Huston Acheson; h. DeWitt Wallace; res: High Winds, Mt. Kisco, N.Y. 10549.

WALLACE, MARCIA VICKERY, Travel Ed., The Bride's Magazine, Conde Nast Publications, 420 Lexington Ave., N.Y., N.Y. 10017, '59–; Travel Ed., Glamour, '55–'58, '49–'54; Edtl. Asst., '47–'49; Pubcty. AE, Victor A. Bennett Co., '54–'55; N.Y. Travel Wtrs. Assn.

(VP, '53–'54; Secy., '51–'53), Soc. of Am. Travel Wtrs. (Bd. of Dirs.); Wellesley Col., BA, '47; b. Evansville, Ind., 1926; p. James and Jeanie Sonntag Vickery; h. William S. Wallace; c. James D., David C., Kate Anne; res: 554 E. 87th St., N.Y., N.Y. 10028.

WALLE, PAULINE, Family Fare Ed., Rochester Post-Bulletin, 18 S.E. First Ave., Rochester, Minn. 55901, '63–; Area Ed., '62–'63; Info. Rep., Univ. of Minn. (Duluth), '59–'62; Wms. Ed., Hibbing (Minn.) Daily Tribune, '58–'59; Minn. Press Wm. (Treas., '63–'64; numerous aws.), Am. Inst. Interior Designers Press Assoc.; Who's Who of Am. Wm., Outstanding Young Wm. of Am., '68; Univ. of Minn., BA, '58; b. Duluth, Minn., 1936; p. Michael and Josephine Lewkiewicz Walle; res: 104 16th Ave. S.W., Rochester, Minn. 55901.

WALLER, JUDITH CARY, Public Affairs, Educ. Dir., National Broadcasting Co., Chgo., Ill., '31–'57; Mgr., WMAQ, '22–'31; Auth., "Radio, The Fifth Estate"; many civic, educ., indsl. orgs.; Sch. Bdcst. Conf. Aw. of Merit, '40; Judith Waller Aw., Wash. State Col., established '47; Northwestern Univ. Centennial Aw., '51; Chgo. Cncl. on Fgn. Rels. World Understanding Aw., '55; Hon. Dr. of Humane Ltrs., Northwestern Univ., McMurray Col.; many other hons., aws.; b. Oak Park, Ill.; res: Evanston, Ill.

WALLEY, DEBORAH E., Actress, TV, motion pics., c/o Jerry Levy, 243 Lasky Dr., Beverly Hills, Cal.; starring role: TV series, "The Mothers-in-Law"; Photoplay mag. Most Promising Actress Aw., '61; Am. Acad. of Dramatic Arts, N.Y.C.; b. Bridgeport, Conn.; p. Nate and Edith Dustman Walley; h. Chet McCracken; c. Anthony Brooks Ashley; res: 11631 Laurelcrest Dr., Studio City, Cal. 91604.

WALLS, ESTHER JEAN, Dir., Bk. and Lib. Svcs., Franklin Book Programs, 432 Park Ave. S., N.Y., N.Y. 10016, '68–; Asst. Dir. for Africa, '66–'68; Dir., Adult New Literates Project, '65–'66; Dir., N. Manhattan Lib. Project, N.Y. Public Lib., '64–'65; Supvsr., Countee Cullen Lib., '61–'64; ALA, N.Y. Lib. Club, African Studies Assn., Phi Sigma Iota; Who's Who of Am. Wm.; State Univ. of Ia., BA, '49 (summa cum laude, Phi Beta Kappa); Columbia Univ., MS (Lib. Svc.), '51; b. Mason City, Ia., 1926; p. Eldist and Jewette Lewis Walls; res: 160 West End Ave., N.Y., N.Y. 10023.

WALLS, MARTHA WILLIAMS, Chmn. of Bd., Pres., Walls Newspapers, Inc., 134 S. Panama St., Montgomery, Ala. 36107, '67–; Secy.-Treas., Dir., Southern Nwsps., '54–'67; b. Gadsden, Ala. 1927; p. Aubrey and Inez Cooper Williams; h. B. Carmage Walls; c. Byrd Cooper, Lissa W.; res: Walhaven, Rte. 7, 148 Bell Rd., Montgomery, Ala. 36109.

WALLS, SARA LOUISE, Ed., The Green Tree nwsp., The News Bag mag., The Gulf States Paper Corporation, P.O. Box 3199, 615 Queen City Ave., Tuscaloosa, Ala. 35401, '66–, '63–; Asst. Ed., '61–'63; PR Asst.,

'54–'61; Chief Cl., Div. Secy. to Forestry Mgr., '48–'54; BPWC, Zonta Club, Phi Chi Theta, Birmingham Assn. of Indsl. Eds. (Best External Nwsp., '68; Aw. of Excellence, '68, '66; Best Mag. Aw., '67; Best Int. Mag. Aw., '63), Southern Cncl. of Indsl. Eds. (Aw. of Achiev., '67, '66), mag. articles; Univ. of Ala., '40; b. Bessemer, Ala., 1917; p. Odie and Stella Taylor Walls; res: Rte. 2, Box 149 A, Lake Wildwood, Cottondale, Ala. 35453.

WALRATH, ELIZABETH ELSOM, Ed., Clinton Topper nwsp., 241 Allen St., Clinton, Wis. 53525; Freedom's Fdn. aw., '69; Wis. Press Assn. aw., '69, '68; Beloit Col., BA, '41; b. Oak Park, Ill., 1919; p. Wright and Edna Potter Elsom Jr.; h. Donald C. Walrath; c. Donald E., Robert A.; res: 1525 S. Ridge Rd., Beloit, Wis. 53511.

WALSH, ANN WATSON, Dir. of PR and Retail Prom., Germaine Monteil Cosmetiques Corp., 730 Fifth Ave., N.Y., N.Y. 10019, '69–; Dir. of PR, Lentheric, '68–'69; Dir. of PR, Helena Rubinstein, '61–'68; Ed., Publicist, '53–; Fashion Group, AWRT, Committee on Wm. in PR, PRSA; Smith Col., BA, '53; b. Cambridge, Mass., 1932; p. Wallace and Marie Dunn Watson; h. Thomas deWitt Walsh; c. Gloria Ewing, Brooke Marie, Thomas deWitt Jr., Hughes deWitt; res: 1356 Madison Ave., N.Y., N.Y. 10028.

WALSH, CARMEN WILSON, Supvsr., Information Center, International Minerals & Chemical Corp., Growth Sciences Center, Libertyville, Ill. 60048, '66–; Librn., '56–; Chief, Tech. Dept., John Crerar Lib., '49–'56; Ref. Asst., '47–'49; Circ. Librn., Univ. of Ill., '47; Librn., Northwestern Univ., '43–'46; Circ. Asst., '41–'43; Clerical Asst., '39–'40; Special Libs. Assn., Am. Mgt. Assn., Am. Chemical Soc., ALA; Northwestern Univ., BS, '39 (magna cum laude, Phi Beta Kappa); Univ. of Illinois, BS (Lib. Sci.), '41; b. Detroit, Mich., 1916; p. Harold and Geraldine Wheelock Wilson; h. Daniel J. Walsh; res: 890 W. Deerpath, Lake Forest, Ill. 60045.

WALSH, MARY E. HILLSETH, VP, Secy.-Treas., The Company, Inc., Advertising/Public Relations, 4621 S.W. Kelly Ave., Portland, Ore. 97201, '69–; Media Dir., Prodn. Mgr., Coit & Assoc., '65–'69; Traf., Young & Rubicam (L.A. Cal.). '63–'65, Oregon Ad Club, AAF, AOI, Cal. State Polytechnic; b. L.A., Cal., 1944; p. Kermit and Isabell O'Brien Hillseth, h. Michael D. Walsh; res: Rte. 2, Box 332, Molalla, Ore. 97308.

WALSH, MYRNA CHAISON, Edtl. Asst., New England Telephone, 185 Franklin St., Boston, Mass., '64–; AWRT (Chptr. Secy., '67–'69); Simmons Col., BS (Jnlsm.), '64 (Hons.); h. Robert Walsh.

WALSH, ROSE A., Soc. Ed., Record American-Sunday Advertiser, 5 Winthrop Sq., Boston, Mass. 02106, '56–; Boston Post, '45–'56; Beauty and Charm Ed., '40–'45; Contrbr., Town and Country, Diplomat; Boston Veteran Jnlsts. (Pres., '52–'53), Wms. City

Club, N.E. Wms. Press Club, Boston Press Club (Secy.); St. Charles Notre Dame, '17; Emanuel Col.; b. Woburn, Mass.; p. Richard and Delia Murphy Walsh; res: 28 Newbury, Woburn, Mass. 01801.

WALTER, BERYL, Dir., Consumer Svcs., Tea Council of the U.S.A., Inc., 10 E. 56th St., N.Y., N.Y. 10022, '61–; Product Publicist, General Foods Corp., '54–'61; Food Ed., Seventeen, '48–'54; Staff Asst., Am. Red Cross, '44–'47; Prod. Mgr., Glamour, '40–'43; AWRT; Wells Col., BA, '36 (Phi Beta Kappa); b. Leigh-on-Sea, Essex, Eng., 1915; p. Theodore and Christine Parry Walter; res: 10 W. 15th St., N.Y., N.Y. 10011.

WALTER, DOROTHY BLAKE, Free-lance Wtr., Ed., '68–; Eng. Instr., Adm. Asst. to Grad. Study Dir., Pacific Union Col. (Angwin, Cal.), '65–'68; Adm. Asst. to Dir. of Admissions and Records, Dir., Grad. Study, '63–'65; Adm. Asst., '50–'53; Recorder, '46–'48; Auth., "Worship Time" ('61; Pacific Press aw. bk.); St. Helena Hosp. Sch. of Nursing, R.N., '34; Pacific Union Col., BS, '59; b. Stroud, Okla., 1908; p. T. J. and Beulah Henry Blake; h. Edwin C. Walter; c. Linda Katherine; res: 922 Kenbrook Dr., Wheaton, Md. 20902.

WALTER, MARILYN C., TV Prodr., J. Walter Thompson Company, 420 Lexington Ave., N.Y., N.Y. 10017, '67–; Secy., Asst. Prodr., '65–'67; Hollywood Radio and TV Soc. Intl. Bdcst. Aw., '67; Recognition, Am. Radio and TV Commls. Festival, '68; Columbia Univ., BS, '64; h. Peter M. Grounds; res: 55 East End Ave., N.Y., N.Y. 10028.

WALTER, MARY MINAHAN, Assoc. Ed., Post Crescent, Appleton, Wis. 54911, '64–; Edtl. Wtr., Commtr., WLUK-TV, '69–; Staff Wtr., Green Bay Press-Gazette, '54–; Vassar Col., '37–'39; Lawrence Univ., '50–'51; St. Norbert Col., '52–'60; b. Battle Creek, Mich., 1919; p. Victor and Bertha Bush Minahan; h. John Walter; c. Wendy (Mrs. Edward L. Williams), Dinah, Anthony Minahan, Michael Cowan, Heidi, Tara, Rory; res: Box 155, Baileys Harbor, Wis. 54202.

WALTER, NINA WILLIS, Auth., six bks., over 3,300 stories, articles, poems; Lectr.; Prof. Emeritus, L.A. City Col., '46–'65; Tchr., L.A. City Schs., '23–'46; Prin., Slusner HS (Lexington, Mo.), '19–'22; Intl. Platform Assn., Am. Poetry League, Wtrs. Club of Whittier, Cal. Fedn. of Chaparral Poets, Cal. Tchrs. Assn., Nat. Ret. Tchrs. Assn., Mensa; U.C.L.A., AB, '30 (Phi Beta Kappa); Univ. of Southern Cal., MA, '35 (Phi Kappa Phi); b. Palmyra, Mo., 1900; p. Silas and Mary Stickletts Willis; h. Leslie H. Walter (div.); c. Leslie H., Jr.; res: 9331 Cosgrove St., Pico Rivera, Cal. 90660.

WALTER, RUTH, Public Info. Offcr., Voice of America, U.S. Information Agency, 330 Independence Ave. S.W., Wash., D.C. 20547, '66–; various staff positions, '53–'66; Fgn. Press Rep., Dept. of State, '45–'47, '48–'53; Intl. Div., PR Dept., Girl Scouts of the U.S.A., '47–'48; Outpost Rep., Off. of War Info., '41–'45; AWRT (Wash., D.C. Chptr: Dir., various offs.), PRSA; Barnard Col. of Columbia Univ., BA; Tchrs. Col. of Columbia, MA; b. Yonkers, N.Y.; p. Oliver and Meta Ehlenberger Walter; res: 6200 29th St. N.W., Wash., D.C. 20015.

WALTER, SUSAN D., Dir. Transportation Sales and Special Projects, Joseph E. Seagram and Sons Inc., 375 Park Ave., N.Y., N.Y. 10022, '63–; Special Sls., '60–'63; Plans Mgr., New York Journal American, '59–'60; Asst. to V.P. and Adv. Dir., New York Post, '54–'59; Asst. to Henry J. Taylor, '46–'54; AWNY; Am. Acad. Dramatic Arts; N.Y.U.; b. Ridgewood, N.J.

WALTERS, BARBARA, Hostess, "Today," NBC Television Network; Newswoman, "Monitor," "Emphasis," NBC Radio Network, 30 Rockefeller Plaza, N.Y., N.Y. 10020; with "Today" show since '61, starting as behind-the-scenes writer and reporter; formerly with CBS-TV's "Good Morning"; Harper's Bazaar selection as one of the two outstanding women in the field of television; Fieldston Academy, Sarah Lawrence Col.; b. Boston, Mass.; p. Lou and Dena Walters; h. Lee Guber; c. Jacqueline.

WALTERS, DOROTHY WELLS, Auth., "Selling Power of a Woman" ('62); Owner, Double HH Press; Owner, Hospitality Hostess Service, 600 W. Foothill Blvd., Glendora, Cal. 91740, '49–; Tchr., sls. course; Wtr., articles on sls. methods; Sls. and Mktng. Execs., Intl. Platform Assn.; L.A. Bd. of Supvsrs. cit., '61; b. L.A., Cal., 1924; p. Harold and Lillian Burke Wells; h. Robert Walters; c. Lillet, Jeanine, Robert; res: 18825 Sierra Madre, Glendora, Cal. 91740.

WALTERS, TOMASINA MARY, Art Dir., Needham, Harper & Steers, Inc., 909 Third Ave., N.Y., N.Y. 10021, '68–; Group Art Dir., S. H. Benson Ltd. (Nigeria, Eastern Africa), '65–'68; Hausman, Langford & Partners (London), '64–'65; Group Art Dir., Crane Adv., '62–'64; Visualiser, Foote, Cone & Belding, '60–'62; Asst. to Art Dir., W. H. Gollings, '59–'60; Masius & Fergusson, '56–'59; Cheltenham Ladies' Col., Cert. of Educ., '54; b. Walton-on-Thames, England, 1936; p. John and Alison Cunningham Walters; res: 415 E. 80th St., Apt. 5-E, N.Y., N.Y. 10021.

WALTHER, SUSAN ELIZABETH (Gloria Upson), Singer-Actress, Mame, Fryer, Carr and Bowab, 445 Park Ave., N.Y., N.Y. 10016, '68–; theater, opera, concert work, '64–'68; TV, motion pic. work for MGM, Disney Studios, Gen. Svc. Studios, ABC, NBC; AEA, SAG, AFTRA, AGMA (aw. of special recognition), Sigma Alpha Iota (Beta Nu Chptr. VP, '63–'64); Immaculate Heart Col., BA, '64; Music Acad. of the West; U.C.L.A. Opera Workshop; Univ. of Southern Cal. Musical Theatre Workshop; b. N.Y.C.; p. Herbert and Mary Mayer Walther; h. Dallas Johann; res: 25 W. 89th St., N.Y., N.Y. 10024.

WALTNER, ELMA, Free-lance Wtr.; Co-auth: "Hobbycraft Around the World," "Hobbycraft for

Juniors," others; Yankton Col., BA, '35 (cum laude); b. Yankton, S.D., 1912; p. Emil and Mary Goering Waltner; res: Box 190, Freeman, S.D. 57029.

WALTON, ELIZABETH CHEATHAM, Free-lance Wtr., children's bks., incl: "Voices in the Fog," "Treasure in the Sand," others; Goucher Col., Boston Univ. (Phi Beta Kappa); b. Wash., D.C.; p. David and Katharine Cheatham Walton; res: 3131 38th, Wash., D.C. 20016.

WALTRIP, LELA KINGSTON, Auth. of juv. bks.; Tchr., Artesia Public Schools, 1105 W. Quay St., Artesia, N.M. 88210, '31–; Auths. Guild, Delta Kappa Gamma, local, state, nat. educ. assns., AAUW, BPW; Corpus Christi, Tex. Wtrs. Conf., juv. bk. aw., '58; Highlands Univ., AB, '36; Eastern N.M. Univ., MA, '55; b. Coleman, Tex.; p. Ollie and Elon Johnson Kingston; h. Rufus Charles Waltrip; c. Rufus Charles, Jr.; res: 811 S. Fourth St., Artesia, N.M. 88210.

WALZ, INEZ WITTMAN, AE, Sykes Advertising, Inc., 411 Seventh Ave., Pitt., Pa. 15219, '63–; Copywtr., Pittsburgh Press; Prom. Mgr., Bulletin Index; Sr. Copywtr., Sun-Telegraph; TV-Radio Copywtr., Cavanaugh-Morris Adv.; AAAA, Nat. Adv. Assn. Network (aw., '68); Duquesne Univ., Carnegie Tech.; b. Pitt., Pa.; p. Robert and Melva Hunt Wittmann; c. Gregory Joseph, Robert C.; res: 3327 Allendorf St., Pitt., Pa. 15204.

WANG, JULIANA, Free-lance Cinematographer; TV: "Way Back Home" (ABC-TV special; Emmy plaque); "Take It Off" (ABC-TV special, '67; Emmy aw.); "Bell Telephone Hour"; many TV commls., indsl. films; b. The Hague, Holland, 1929; p. Nietsou and Krystyna Kawecka Wang; res: 234 E. 5th St., N.Y., N.Y. 10003.

WANNER, SUSAN HIRTH, Edtl. Rschr., Reader's Digest, 200 Park Ave., N.Y., N.Y. 10017, '61–; Conn. Col. for Wm., BA, '58; b. New Haven, Conn. 1937; p. Karl and Bernice Chittenden Hirth; h. Charles Wanner; res: 14 Christopher St., N.Y., N.Y. 10014.

WARBURG, SANDOL STODDARD, Auth., eight juv. fiction bks., incl. "Saint George and the Dragon" (Houghton-Mifflin, '63, ALA Notable Bk. Aw.); Bryn Mawr Col., '59 (magna cum laude); b. Birmingham, Ala. 1927; p. Carlos and Caroline Harris Stoddard; h. Frank Drew Dollard; c. Anthony, Peter, Gerald, Jason, Katherine, Suzanne; res: P.O. Box 704, Ross, Cal. 94957.

WARD, EVELYN, Actress, TV and motion pics., roles in many TV shows, motion pics., plays; Equity, AFTRA, SAG, AGUA; Juilliard Sch. of Music; U.C.L.A.; b. Orange, N.J.; p. Fred and Ethel Wheeler Ward; h. 1. Jack Cassidy (div.), 2. Elliot Silverstein (div.); c. David Cassidy.

WARD, HELEN RENNIE, Free-lance Wtr.; Colmst.,

Kansas Outdoors; Colmst., Outdoor Times, '61–'64; Outdoor Wtrs. of Kan. (Secy.-Treas.), Great Rivers Outdoor Wtrs.

WARD, MAY WILLIAMS, Auth., six non-fiction bks.; Bk. Ed., Ret., Daily News, Kansas; Edtl. Bd., The Harp; Penwomen (Kan. State Pres., '63), Kan. Auths. Club (Pres., '40), Poetry Soc. of Kan. (Pres., '48; two aws.); inclusion in more than 20 anthologies; Univ. of Kan., '05 (Phi Beta Kappa); b. Holden, Mo., 1882; p. George and Sara Smith Williams; h. Merle C. Ward; res: 519 North B Street., Wellington, Kan. 67152.

WARE, CELLESTINE CAROLINE, Reptr., Rschr., Life, Time-Life Bldg., 50th St. at Ave. of the Americas, N.Y., N.Y. 10020, '69–; Caseworker, Dept. of Social Svcs., '67–'68; Assoc. Ed., Arab World, '66–'67; Copy Ed., Columbia Records, '64–'65; Rsch. Asst., Crowell-Collier, '64; Librn., Cambridge (Mass.) Public Lib., '62–'63; Radcliffe Col., BA (Hist.), '62; b. Cleve., Oh., 1940; p. Henry Ware and Minnie Collins Ware Zellner; res: 70 E. Seventh St., N.Y., N.Y. 10003.

WARE, WILLI FRETTE, Pres., Willi Ware & Associates, Inc., 222 United Federal Bldg., Des Moines, Ia. 50309, '67–; Free-lance PR Cnslt., '57–'60; '63–'67; Adv., PR Dir., Un. Fed. Savings, '60–'63; Exec. Asst., PR and Radio-TV Dir., Wesley Day & Co. Adv., '55–'57; Wms. Adv. Club of Des Moines (Secy., '55–'56), AAF (Ninth Dist: 1st Lt. Gov., '69–'70; 2nd Lt. Gov., '68–'69; Adv. Wm. of Yr., '66), AWRT (Hawkeye-Iowa Chptr. Pres., '64; Secy., '62); Drake Univ. Commty. Col., '54–'56; b. Buffalo Ctr., Ia., 1927; p. Ole and Martha Miner Frette; h. Gerald Ware; c. Marty Lou, Janis Marie; res: 1600 Porter Ave., Des Moines, Ia. 50315.

WARNER, ANNE RATHBUN, Dir. of PR, American Nurses' Association, 10 Columbus Circle, N.Y., N.Y. 10019, '66–; Asst. Dir., '62–'66; Asst. Dir. of Info., Area Dev. Comm. (Akron, Oh.), '56–'62; Ed., Monarch Life Insurance Co. (Springfield, Mass.), '53–'55; Asst. Librn., N. Canton (Oh.) Public Lib., '51–'53; PRSA, Akron Adv. Club, AAU; Heidelberg Col., BA (Eng.), '50; Kent State Univ., Akron Univ., Pace Col.; b. Detroit, Mich., 1928; p. Irvin and Estelle Kuhlman Rathbun; h. Richard Warner; res: 124 Heather Hill Rd., Cresskill, N.J. 07626.

WARNER, GERTRUDE CHANDLER, Free-lance Wtr.; Tchr., 32 yrs.; Auth: Boxcar Children series for slow readers (Scott Forsman & Co., textbk.; Albert Whitman Co., trade edition); articles, essays; Am. Red Cross 50-yr. aw. for pubcty.; b. Putnam, Conn., 1890; p. Edgar and Jane Carpenter Warner; res: 22 Ring St., Putnam, Conn. 06260.

WARNKE, LANGLEY TOLBERT, Free-lance Wtr., '69–; Edtl. Asst., Cooperative Ext. Svc., Auburn (Ala.) Univ., '68–'69; Copywtr., Radio-TV Prodr., Frank M.

Taylor Adv. (Birmingham), '66–'68; AWRT; Univ. of Ala., Univ. of N.C., AB (Eng.), '66; b. Parkersburg, W.Va., 1945; p. Bruce and Carolyn Tolbert; h. Charles Warnke; res: 701 Middle St., Montevallo, Ala. 35115.

WARRAN, BEVERLY REISER, Info. Specialist, National Institute of Health, Division of Educational and Research Facilities, Bldg. 31, Bethesda, Md. 20014, '69–; Bdcstr., WTIP (Charleston, W.Va.); Radio Wtr., Dept. of Defense; Radio-TV Script Wtr., Fed. Civil Defense Adm.; Info. Offcr., Civil Air Patrol; Asst. Info. Offcr., News Dept., Fed. Aviation Agcy.; AWRT (Treas., '59), WNPC, ANWC; Hunter Col., BA, '40; b. N.Y.C., 1921; p. Alexander and Rhoda Levy Reiser; h. Irving I. Warran; c. Jason, Gary, Anne; res: 4220 Dresden St., Kensington, Md. 20795.

WARREN, BETSY AVERY, Free-lance Artist-Wtr., '50–; Furniture Illus., Chgo. Studio of Mary Webb, '40–'42; Organist, Tchr.; Auth: "Indians Who Lived in Texas," "Make A Joyful Noise"; several bk. aws; Austin Am.-Statesman Outstanding Wm., '66; Miami Univ., '37; b. St. Louis, Mo. 1916; p. Albert and Ethel Mitchell Avery; h. William Warren; c. Bill Jr., Stephen, Mark, Melissa; res: 2409 Dormarion, Austin, Tex. 78703.

WARREN, DAISY DOZIER, Ed., Mature Years, Methodist Publishing House, 201 Eighth Ave. S., Nashville, Tenn. 37204, '55–; Asst. Ed., International Lesson A Manual, '55–'69; Ed., Wesley Quarterly, '55–'59; Social Case Worker, Tchr.; AAUW, UN Assn., Intl. Assn. of Gerontology; Univ. of Ala., AB, '44 (Phi Beta Kappa); Scarritt Col., MA, '49; p. Slater and Stella Gibson Dozier; h. James Warren; res: 1106 Woodvale Dr., Nashville, Tenn. 37204.

WARREN, ELIZABETH ANNE, Ed./Photogr., The Bank of New York, 48 Wall St., N.Y., N.Y. 10015, '68–; Free-lance Europe and N. Africa, '66–'68; Edtl. Asst., Holt, Rinehart and Winston, '65–'66; Ed., PR Asst., Tamblyn and Brown, '63–'65; Asst. Ed., Babcock and Wilcox Co., '61–'63; Reptr., The Record, N.J., '58–'61; ICIE, N.Y. Assn. of Indsl. Communicators, Photographic Soc. of Am.; Washington Col. of Md., BA, '58; Famous Photogrs. Sch., '68–; b. N.J., 1936; p. Albert and Dorothy Morris Warren; res: 250 Circle Ave., Ridgewood, N.J. 07450.

WARREN, JUNE ETTA, Ed., Wtr., Wagner-Allen Company, 626 S. Federal St., Chgo., Ill. 60605, '47–; Free-lance Wtr.; Astro-Guide synd. nwsp. feature, Publishers-Hall Synd., '52–; Millikin Univ.; b. Decatur, Ill. 1914; p. John and Grace Vogel Warren; h. (div.); res: 6401 Sheridan Rd., Chgo., Ill. 60626.

WARREN, PAMELA S., Reg. Librn., Rolling Hills Regional Library, 413 N. Belt, St. Joseph, Mo. 64506, '66–; Admn. Asst., Trails Reg. Lib., Warrensburg, Mo., '63–'66; ALA, Mo. Lib. Assn. (Secy., '69–'70), AAUW, Beta Sigma Phi, Altrusa, BPW; Neb. Wesleyan Univ.,

BA, '62; Univ. of Ill., MA (Lib. Sci.), '63; b. Maryville, Mo. 1940; p. Clyde and Elizabeth Scamman Warren; res: 1211 Carol Dr., St. Joseph, Mo. 64506.

WARRICK, GERALDINE EVERETT, TV Bdcst. Standards Supvsr., Assoc. Prodr., "It's Academic," National Broadcasting Company, Merchandise Mart, Chgo., Ill. 60654, '65–; Tchr., Cnslr., '52–'65; Phi Lambda Theta, AWRT, Alpha Kappa Alpha; 2,000 Wm. of Achiev., '69, Outstanding Young Wm. of Am., '65; Hampton Inst., AB, '52; Univ. of Chgo., MA, '56; b. Gary, Ind. 1930; p. John and Marguerite Glapion Everett; h. John Warrick; c. Alan Everett, Ingrid-Joy; res: 6811 S. Crandon Ave., Chgo., Ill. 60649.

WARWICK, BETSEY LARRIMORE, Asst. Ed., Audio-Digest Foundation, 619 S. Westlake Ave., L.A., Cal. 90057, '59–; Grad. Rschr. Asst., Anatomy Dept., Univ. of Cal. Sch. of Med., '56–'58; Reptr.-Colmst., Beverly Hills Citizen News, '50–'51; Theta Sigma Phi, Am. Med. Wtrs. Assn.; U.C.L.A., BA, '56; MS (Jnlsm.), '58; b. Hollywood, Cal. 1933; p. Robert and Stella Larrimore Warwick.

WARWICK, ROSAMOND ANN, Wms. Ed., Ridgewood Newspapers, Inc., 30 Oak St., Ridgewood, N.J. 07451, '69–; Asst. Wms. Ed., '69; Col. of St. Elizabeth, AB (Eng.), '68 (Second Place, Nat. Poetry Contest); Fairleigh Dickinson Univ., work toward MA (Eng. Lit.); b. N.Y.C., 1946; p. Andrew and Rosamond McHale Warwick; res: 368 Longbow Dr., Franklin Lakes, N.J. 07417.

WASEY, SHEILA STEWART, Dir. of Special Progs., WQXM(FM), P.O. Box 4809, Clearwater, Fla. 33518; Prog. Dir., WTCX-FM (St. Petersburg), '59–'62; (station Blue Ribbon Aw. for music, '61); Prodr. of Wms. Prog., WDCL (Clearwater), '55–'57; BBC, 20 yrs., (first Wm. Announcer); Fashion Cnslt., BBC's World Svcs., '42–'52; Teenage Finishing Sch. of Poise, Drama, Poetry and Speech, '55–'60; Auth., poetry published in Eng., '30–'50; Pinellas Wms. Press Club (first Pres., '55); AWRT; Asolo Theatre Festival Assn., Sarasota (Dir.); Fine Arts Soc. of Fla. Gulf Coast Art Ctr.; Rosina Filippi Sch. of Drama; b. Harrow-on-the-Hill, Eng., 1906; p. Edward and Mary Stewart Graham; h. Gager Wasey; c. Jeremy Armit Borrett; res: 1365 Pinebrook Dr., Clearwater, Fla. 33515.

WASH, MELBA WILSON, Reg. Dir., Reelfoot Regional Library, 408 Jackson St., Martin, Tenn. 38237, '50–; Librn., '42–'50; Tchr., '39–'42; ALA, Tenn. Lib. Assn. (Treas., '54), Southeastern Lib. Assn., AAUW; Berea Col., AB, '39; George Peabody Col., BS (Lib. Sci.), '42; b. Benton, Tenn., 1918; p. John and Marchia Cook Wilson; h. George Wash (dec.); res: 126 Fonville, Martin, Tenn. 38237.

WASHBURN, SANDRA GAIL, Ed., Pillar, Northwestern Mutual Life Insurance Co., 720 E. Wisconsin Ave., Milw., Wis. 53202, '68–; PR Wtr., '67–'68; Asst.

News Ed., Modern Beauty Shop, Vance Publ. Co. (Chgo., Ill.), '67; Wis. Indsl. Eds. Assn.; Valparaiso Univ., Wis. State Univ., BS (Eng.), '67; b. Carthage, Mo., 1944.

WASHBURN, SUSANNE SCHUPPEL, Edtl. Rschr., Time, Inc., Rockefeller Center, N.Y., N.Y. 10020, '60–; Edtl. Cl., '58–'60; Albertus Magnus Col., AB, '58; N.Y.U., MA, '62; b. N.Y.C., 1936; p. George and Katharine Brooks Schuppel; h. A. Lawrence Washburn Jr.; c. Arthur L. 3rd, Niall Quin; res: 924 West End Ave., N.Y., N.Y. 10025.

WASSER, GLADYS ELVA, Supvsr., TV copy, traffic, Triangle Publications, Radio-TV Division, WNBF-TV, 50 Front St., Binghamton, N.Y. 13902, '66–; Supvsr., radio-TV copy, traffic, '62–'66; Radio Continuity Dir., '60–'61; Radio Copywtr., WKOP-AM, '57–'60; Wtr., Prodr., numerous scripts; AWRT, ZONTA (Bd. of Dirs., '68–'70); Ithaca Col., BS (Radio and TV), '57 (cum laude).

WASSERMAN, ANITA, Exec. Asst. to Pres., Media Dir., Cooper Square Advertising Agency, Inc., 50 Cooper Square, N.Y., N.Y. 10003, '69–; Media Planner, Sr. Buyer, Gumbinner-North Co., '48–'68; Free-lance radio, TV scripts, commls.; numerous articles on media for trade pubns.; NATAS; Hunter Col., BA, '48; b. N.Y.C., 1919; p. Frank and Beatrice Mirchin Wasserman; res: 98-05 67th Ave., Forest Hills, N.Y. 11374.

WASSERMAN, RUTH RUSSELL, Rsch. Staff, Adv. Dept., Trailer Life Publishing, 10148 Riverside Dr., Toluca Lake, Cal. 91602, '68–; Media Byr., Asst. Adv. Mgr., Pubcty., Magna Adv.; Asst. to Ed., Screenwriter Magazine; Asst. Dir., several radio-TV commls. as performer; Radio Wms. War Svc. (Hon. Life Mbr.), AFTRA; Hunter Col., BA; h. Jess Wasserman; c. Robert Z.; res: 4509 Vista Del Monte, Sherman Oaks, Cal. 91403.

WASTJER, NATALIE CHURCH (Cissy), Wms. Ed., The Courier, Second and Vine Sts., Evansville, Ind. 47705, '67–; Asst. Wms. Ed., '61–'67; Sunday Courier and Press, '53–'58; Evansville Press Club (Bd. Mbr.); Bramwell's Bus. Col.; b. Evansville, Ind. 1920; p. Alvin and Lola Crilley Church; h. Thomas F. Wastjer; res: 7133 E. Blackford, Evansville, Ind. 47705.

WATANABE, RUTH T., Auth: "Five Books of Italian Madrigals" ('53), "Introduction to Music Research" ('67), articles in pfsnl. pubns.; Librn., Sibley Music Library, Eastman School of Music, University of Rochester, 26 Gibbs St., Rochester, N.Y. 14604, '48–; Assoc. Prof. of Musicology, '59–; Instr., Music Hist., '46–'59; Circ. Librn., '44–'47; Cnslr., Wms. Residence, '44–'46; active in local music groups, orgs.; Lib. Cnslt.; Ed., music and music lib. pubns.; Music Lib. Assn. (VP, '67–'68), Am. Musicological Soc., Mu Phi Epsilon (Nat. Librn., '56–'68; Musicological Rsch. Aw., '44), Pi Kappa Lambda, Intl. Assn. of Music Libs.,

AAUW (Br. Pres., '69–; Fellowship, '49–'50); Univ. of Southern Cal., B. Mus., '37 (summa cum laude); AB, '39 (summa cum laude); MA, '41; M.Mus., '42; Univ. of Rochester, PhD, '52; b. L.A., Cal.; p. K. H. and Iwa Watanabe Watanabe.

WATERFALL, BETH LIEN, Ed.-in-Chief, Mothers' Manual, Inc., 420 Lexington Ave., N.Y., N.Y. 10017, '66–; Ed.-in-Chief, Lady-Fare, '64–'66; Feature Ed., Glamour, '60–'63; Assoc. Ed., Mademoiselle, '59–'60; Reptr., Indianapolis Times, '56–'59; Soc. of Mag. Eds.; Luther Col., BA, '51; Columbia Col., MA, '52; b. Johnson County, Ia., 1929; p. J. A. and Cornelia Wahl Lien Sr.; h. Wallace K. Waterfall; c. Ann, Clark, Eve; res: 176 Cleveland St., Croton-on-Hudson, N.Y. 10520.

WATERMAN, HARRIETTE, Treas., Waterman, Getz, Niedelman Advertising, Inc., 3 W. 57th St., N.Y., N.Y. 10019, '68–; Pres., '58–'68; AE, Huber Hoge, Inc., '52–'58; Jr. AE, Wexton Assoc., '50–'52; Publrs. Adv. Club, Publrs. Pubcty. Club, Wms. Nat. Bk. Comm., Am. Bksellers. Assn.; New Sch. for Social Rsch.; h. Alden Getz; c. Deren Seth; res: 1000 Park Ave., N.Y., N.Y. 10028.

WATERS, ELEANOR CONNORS, VP, The Seamen's Bank for Savings, 30 Wall St., N.Y., N.Y. 10005, '67–; Asst. VP, '58–'67; PR, 1st wm. offcr.; '54–'58; '39–'54; Savings Bank Wm. of N.Y. (Pres., '53–'54; VP, '52–'53), APRA (N.Y. Chptr: Treas., Dir., '58–'59; Secy., Dir., '55–'57), Nat. Assn. of Bank Wm. (Met. N.Y. Group Chmn., '59–'60; V. Chmn., '58–'59); ICIE, N.Y. Fin. Advs. (Dir., '60–'63), PRSA, numerous other bank, PR, commty. orgs.; Pratt Inst., Am. Inst. of Banking; p. Michael and Mary Wachter Connors; h. Robert H. Waters; res: 227 E. 57th St., N.Y., N.Y. 10022.

WATKINS, LINDA MATHEWS, Artist; Theatre Guild Sch.; b. Boston, Mass., 1908; p. Gardiner and Elizabeth Mathews Watkins; h. Gabriel Hess (dec.); c. Adam Hess; res: 303 Garden St., Wethersfield, Conn. 06109.

WATKINS, MARILYN, Prom. Asst., WSM-TV, 5700 Knob Rd., Nashville, Tenn. 37202, '67–; Sch. Tchr. (Sarasota, Fla.); Jnlsm. Tchr., David Lipscomb Col.; Pi Delta Epsilon, Sigma Tau Delta, AWRT (Histrn., '68–'69); Nashville BPW Outstanding Young Career Wm., '69; David Lipscomb Col., BA (Eng. and Psych.), '66 (cum laude; Who's Who in Am. Univs. and Cols.; Ed., "Backlog"; jnlsm. medal); b. Margarita, Panama Canal Zone, 1945; p. Lee J. and Marian McElrath Watkins; res: 5000 Hillsboro, Nashville, Tenn. 37203.

WATROBSKI, CHARLOTTE M., Ed., Pubns., Pfizer Laboratories, 235 E. 42nd St., N.Y., N.Y. 10017, '66–; Ed., Wtr., Spectrum; sls. pubns., programmed instr. courses, adv. copy, sls. prom., '51–; Am. Med. Wtrs. Assn., ICIE, N.Y. Assn. of Indsl. Commtns.; Bklyn. Col., BA (Eng.), '59; City Col. of N.Y.

WATSON, BETTY SNYDER, Adv. Exec., Betty Zane

Watson Adv. Agcy., 3409 Paris Blvd., Westerville, Oh. 43081; F & R Lazarus Co.; Radow Adv. Agcy.; Adv. Dir., Ontario Stores; Oh. Univ., '38; Darvas Sch. of Design and Art, '39; Muskingum Col., '40; b. Uhrichsville, Oh., '21; p. Ralph S. and Clara E. Suepply Snyder; h. Lee A. Watson; c. Lee A., III, Kristen Anne, David Kelly; res: 3409 Paris Blvd., Westerville, Oh. 43081.

WATSON, CAROLYN HOPE, Asst. Ed., Scholastic Magazines, Inc., 50 W. 44th St., N.Y., N.Y. 10036, '67–; Free-lance Photogr., Fine Arts Photog., Dun's Review, '67–'69; Free-lance Wtr.; City of London Col., '65; Beaver Col., BA, '66; Syracuse Univ. Grad. Sch. of Jnlsm., '66–'67; b. Syracuse, N.Y. 1944; p. Kenneth and Hope Upton Watson; One Univ. Pl., Apt. 22D, N.Y., N.Y. 10003.

WATSON, CATHERINE ELAINE, Reptr., Minneapolis Tribune, 425 Portland Ave., Mpls., Minn. 55415, '66–; Univ. of Minn., BA, '66 (Phi Beta Kappa); b. Mpls., Minn., 1944; p. Richard and LaVonne Slater Watson.

WATSON, DOROTHY MARGARET, City Ed., Daily News, 45-140 Towne Ave., Indio, Cal. 92201, '60–; Valley Ed., Los Angeles Mirror, '56–'59; City Ed., Hollywood Citizen-News, '42–'56; Reptr., Baton Rouge (La.) Morning-Advocate, '40–'42; Free-lance mag. articles, photographs; Theta Sigma Phi; Gtr. L.A. Press Club (Bd. of Dirs., '52–'56); Desert Press Club; La. State Univ., B.A., '40; Univ. of Cal., MA, '58; b. Little Rock, Ark., 1912; p. Edward and Pearl Jarnagin Watson; res: 81373 Palmyra Ave., Indio, Cal. 92201.

WATSON, HELEN ORR, Auth: "Top Kick" and "Beano, Circus Dog" (Jr. Lit. Guild), "Shavetail Sam," "High Stepper" (Houghton-Mifflin), five other juv. bks.; numerous short stories, articles; Mbr., Mrs. Eleanor Roosevelt's Press Conf.; Crtv. Writing Tchr., Wash., D.C., Kan., Philippine Is.; NLAPW (Nat. Pres., '54–'56), Children's Bk. Guild of D.C. (Founder, Pres.); Carleton Col., BA (Alumnae Achiev. Aw., '54); Grad. Work, Boston Univ., '26–'27; Northwestern Univ., '25–'26; b. Pipestone, Minn.; p. Charles and Lillian Simpson Orr; h. Col. James T. Watson, Jr. (dec.); c. Margaret Jean (Mrs. E. E. Hebditch), Donald S.; res: 217 Hunt Rd., Pitt., Pa. 15215; Watson Ranch, Lathrop Wells, Nev. 89020.

WATSON, MARGARET G., Free-lance Wtr.; Tchr., Cnslr., El Monte Union High School District, 9063 E. Mission Dr., Rosemead, Cal. 91770, '50–; Schs. in Cal., Tex., Nev., Minn., '33–'50; Lectr., Hist. Cnslt.; Auth., "Silver Theatre" (Arthur H. Clark Publ. Co., '64), numerous articles, hist. features, poems, juv. stories, scripts; numerous hist. socs., tchr. assns.; Contemporary Auths., '66, Phi Alpha Theta, Kappa Delta Pi (Southern Cal. Alumni Chptr: Pres., '67–'68; VP, '66–'67; Secy., '57–'59), Sigma Phi Lambda, Col. Poetry Soc. of Am. (Beta Chptr. Secy., '38); Colo.

State Col., BA (Soc. Sci.), '39; Univ. of Nev., MA (Hist.), '40; b. Minot, N.D., 1913; res: 3357 Villa Grove Dr., Altadena, Cal. 91001.

WATT, FRANCES DAVIS, Owner, Publr., Stroud American, 406 W. Third St., Stroud, Okla. 74079, '52–; Owner, Glenwood (Ark.) Herald, '46–'47; C. of C. (Secy.-Treas., '53–'54), Okla. Press Assn., NEA, Selected Weeklies of Okla. (Pres., '58), BPW, AAUW; Theta Sigma Phi State Wm. of the Yr., '66; Stroud Citizen of the Yr., '60; Okla. State Univ., BS, '35; b. Konawa, Okla., 1915; p. Charles and Elizabeth Burkhart Davis; h. Billy Watt (dec.); c. W. Wesley; res: 904 N. Second St., Stroud, Okla. 74079.

WATTERS, BARBARA HUNT, Free-lance Wtr., novels and short stories; bks: "A Little Night Music" ('47); "The Villa and the Horde" (MacDonald of London, '57); "Cotton Web" (Dutton, '60); Auths. Guild of Am., Am. Fedn. of Astrologers; Univ. of Chgo., Brown Univ.; b. Chgo., Ill.; h. James Watters (dec.); res: 1331 21st St., N.W., Wash., D.C. 20036.

WATTS, CLAUDIALEA LEDGER, Ed., Record-Courier, Inc., Box 205, Johnson City, Tex. 78636, '66–; Free-lance Wtr., Ed., PR, '24–'66; Tchr., '29–'36; Tex. Press Assn., Houston Pen Wms. Club, Tex. Fedn. Wms. Club; Tex. Tech. Univ., BA, '28; b. Aspermont, Tex., 1910; p. Claude and Bessie Ramsey Ledger; h. William Ray Watts; c. Gene Ledger Watts; res: Rte. 2, Johnson City, Tex. 78636.

WATTS, MABEL PIZZEY, Auth: 25 juv. bks. incl. "The King and the Whirlybird" (Parents' Mag. Press, '69), "Yin Sun and the Lucky Dragon" (Westminster Press, '69), "I'm For You . . . and You're For Me" (Abelard-Schuman, '67); Burlingame Wtrs. Club (Pres., '62), Cal. Wtrs. Club (Treas., '68), Auths. Guild of Am.; b. London, England, 1906; p. Ernest and Edith Elias Pizzey; h. William Watts; c. Patricia Linda Babcock, Stanley David McEtchin, Robert Lloyd McEtchin; res: 1520 Ralston Ave., Burlingame, Cal. 94010.

WAY, ESTHER MARGARET, Wms. Ed., Colmst., Saginaw News, 203 S. Washington Ave., Saginaw, Mich. 48603, '45–; Colmst., '55–; edtl. positions, '40–; Mich. Wms. Press Club, Saginaw Valley Press Club, Saginaw News Quarter Century Club, Jr. League, Saginaw Wms. Cncl.; Marygrove Col.; Univ. of Mich.; p. Elmer and Margaret Farrell Way; res: 1556 Sullivan Dr., Saginaw, Mich. 48603.

WAYBURN, PEGGY ELLIOTT, Auth: "The Last Redwoods," other Sierra Club pubns.; Copywtr., J. Walter Thompson, '45–'48; Writing Staff, Conde Nast, '44–'45; Assoc. Ed., Country Book Magazine, '43–'45; Contrbr., various pubns.; numerous conservation orgs.; Cal. Conservation Cncl. Aw., '64; Sierra Club Special Aw., '67; Barnard Col., BA, '42; b. N.Y.C.; p. Thomas and Cornelia Ligon Elliott; h. Edgar Wayburn; c. Cynthia, William, Diana, Laurie; res: 30 Sea View Terr., S.F., Cal. 94121.

WAYNE, JUNE, Artist., Founder and Dir., Tamarind Lithography Workshop, 1112 No. Tamarind Avenue, L.A., Cal. 90038, '60–; workshop funded through the program for Arts & Humanities on a Ford Foundation grant; Stone Circle Fndn. (Pres.), Intl. Platform Assn., Nat. Citizens Comm. for Bdcst.; L.A. Times Wm. of the Yr., '52; numerous painting, printmaking aws.; The Art of June Wayne, by Mary Baskett, (Harry N. Abrams, '68), h. Henry Plone.

WAYNE, SUSAN, Pres., Gotham Film Productions, 11 E. 44th St., N.Y., N.Y. 10017, '66–; Exec. positions; AWRT (N.Y.C. Chptr.: Treas., VP); four 1st prizes, several 2nd prizes from Am. Film Festival, Intl. Film & TV Festival, Nat. Visual Presentation Assn.; Conservatory of Music, Vienna; b. Vienna, Austria 1926; p. Alfred and Marcella Rand Weiss; h. (div.); res: 420 E. 55th St., N.Y., N.Y. 10022.

WEAVER, ANNIE BELLE, Dir. of Libs., West Georgia College, Carrollton, Ga. 30117, '68–; Librn., '33–'68; Cataloger, Southwestern (Memphis, Tenn.), '31–'33; Librn., Emory Jr. Col., '28–'31; Eng. Tchr., '26–'27; ALA, Southeastern Lib. Assn., Ga. Lib. Assn. (Secy., '28–'30); W. Ga. Col. aw., '52; Miss. State Col. for Wm., AB, '26; Emory Univ., BA (Lib. Sci.), '28; b. Tupelo, Miss., 1904; p. Robert and Georgia Allen Weaver; res: 705 Rome St., Carrollton, Ga. 30117.

WEAVER, AUDREY TURNER, City Ed., Chicago Daily Defender, 2400 S. Michigan Ave., Chgo., Ill. 60616, '59–; Reptr., Copy Ed., '55–'59; Assoc. Ed., Jet Magazine, '53–'54; Copy Ed., Afro-American Newspapers (Balt., Md.), '43–'53; Reptr.; Media Wm., Inc. (Treas.), NAACP; Univ. of Wis., '43; b. Racine, Wis.; p. Thaddeus and Esker Trabue Turner; h. Albert L. Weaver (dec.); res: 534 E. 89th Pl., Chgo., Ill. 60619.

WEAVER, BEVERLY ANNE DENT, Copy Chief, Media Dir., McCrary-Powell Advertising, Inc., 12th and Bishop, Suite 209, Dallas, Tex. 75208, '67–; Free-lance PR, Pubcty., Prom., Copy, and Feature Wtr.; Media-Mktng. Cnslt., local, reg., and nat. bus. and consumer pubns.; Theta Sigma Phi, theatre (incl. summer stock); talent (voice) for radio commercials; Pianist; seven state and nat. poetry aws.; b. Houston, Tex., 1940; p. DeWitt Talmadge and Geraldine Givens Dent; h. Frank Weaver; res: 4107 Cole, #103, Dallas, Tex. 75204.

WEAVER, DE LORES, Reptr., News Wtr., Film Ed., WREC-TV, Sheraton-Peabody Hotel, Memphis, Tenn. 38103, '69–; Prod., WHBQ, Anncr., WTGR; Chi Delta Sigma, Alpha Epsilon Rho; Memphis State Univ.; b. Memphis, Tenn., 1947; p. George and Margaret Weaver; res: 4608 Verne Rd., Memphis, Tenn. 38117.

WEAVER, JENNIE COX, Yrbk. Advisor, South Madison County Community Schools, 301 S.E., Pendleton, Ind. 46064, '58–; Eng. Tchr., Pendleton HS, '53–'69; Eng. Tchr., Nwspr. Adviser, Marion (Ind.) HS, '50–'53;

Theta Sigma Phi (Muncie, Ind., Chptr. Secy. '65–'67), Nat. Cncl. of Tchrs. of Eng., Ind. Cncl. of Tchrs. of Eng., Ind. State Tchrs. Assn.; Indiana Univ., BA, '23; MS, '55; b. Gaston, Ind., 1901; p. William and Fannie Johnson Cox; c. Linda Lee (Mrs. Jack Hays), Susan Jane (Mrs. Randy Pleasant); res: 406 W. State, Pendleton, Ind. 46064.

WEAVER, MARGARET DUNLOP, Soc. Ed., Colmst., The Cincinnati Post Times-Star, 800 Broadway, Cinn., Oh. 45202, '32–; Oh. Nwsp. Wms. Assn., Kappa Alpha Theta, The Cinn. Club; Univ. of Cinn., '28–'31; Cinn. Art Acad., '31–'32; b. Springfield, Ill., 1909; p. George and Pearl Rodgers Dunlop; h. Robert George Weaver; c. Andrew, Randall, Michael; res: 1215 Halpin Ave., Cinn. Oh. 45208.

WEAVER, MARSHA JEAN, Asst. Dir., PR, Welfare Federation of Cleveland, 1001 Huron Rd., Cleve., Oh. 44115; Dir., PR, St. Thomas Hosp. (Akron); Coordr., Seminars on PR; Tchr., Courses on PR for workshop supvsrs.; Northern Ohio IEA; Kent State University, BA (Jnlsm.), '60.

WEBB, NANCY BUKELEY, AE, Batten, Barton, Durstine & Osborn, 383 Madison Ave., N.Y., N.Y. 10017, '68–; '56–'59; Ketchum, MacLeod & Grove, '61–'68; T. N. Palmer, '59–'61; Bernard L. Lewis, '49–'56; Auth., six bks., over 500 radio scripts, 500 colms. for nat. mags.; AWRT; Herald-Tribune Hon. Bk. for "Kaiulani" (Viking, '62); Univ. of Hi.; b. Honolulu, Hi.; p. Rudolph and Lucinda Butler Bukeley; h. Jean Francis Webb III; c. Jean Francis IV, Rodman Bukeley, Morrison DeSoto, Alexander H.; res: Sabrina Rock, Benedict Rd., S. Salem, N.Y. 10590.

WEBB, TESSA SWEAZY, Poet, Auth., three poetry bks.; Financial Asst. (ret.), Agricultural Extension Service, Oh. State University, Columbus, Oh., '18–'54; Asst. Supvsr., Oh. Dept. of Educ., preparing five state poetry anthologies, '41–'50; Colmst., Poetry Ed., Columbus Sun. Dispatch, '28–'41; Reviewer, '27–'42; numerous orgs., aws., Who's Who in Am., '42–; Columbus Bus. Col., '12; Hartsough Col., '16; Free Univ., Karachi, Pakistan, H.L.D. (hon.), '68; b. Logan, Oh., 1886; p. John and Elizabeth Lanning Sweazy; h. Reuben Webb (dec.); res: 815 N. High St., Apt. 39, Columbus, Oh. 43215.

WEBBER, CAROL-ANN, VP-AE, di Russo Advertising, Inc., 866 Third Ave., N.Y., N.Y. 10022, '69–; Exec. positions, '63–'69; AWNY; City Col. of N.Y.; b. N.Y.C., 1942; p. Raymond and Jen Amato Webber; res: 632–75 St., Bklyn., N.Y. 11209.

WEBBER, ELIZABETH JEAN, Asst. Mng. Ed., College Department, Rand McNally and Company, P.O. Box 7600, Chgo., Ill. 60680, '69–; Ed., '68–'69; Ed. Dir., World Publ. Co., Cleve., '67–'68; Trade Map Ed., Rand McNally, '62–'66; Assoc. Ed., Non-fiction, '55–'62; Wms. Nat. Bk. Assn. (Nat. Treas., '57–'60), ZONTA (N.W. Chgo. Chptr. Pres.), '61–'63); Law-

rence Univ., BA, '42 (Phi Beta Kappa, magna cum laude); Univ. of Wis., MA, '43.

WEBBER, MELVA, Bdcstr., two daily programs; Wms. Program Dir., James Broadcasting Company, Hotel Jamestown Bldg., Jamestown, N.Y. 14701, '55–; Copywtr., '54; Am. Nat. Red Cross (Chautauqua County Chptr. Bd. of Dirs., '65–'67); Comm. of 100, AWRT, BPW (Jamestown Chptr. VP, '62–'63); Thomas A. Edison Vocal Music Scholarship, '44; Mozart Club Music Scholarship, '46; Central Acad. of Comml. Art, '44–'45; Albright Art Sch., '45–'47; Fredonia State Tchrs. Col., '47–'48; b. Jamestown, N.Y., 1926; p. Truman and Florice Laird Webber; c. Laird MacCubbin, Jeffrey MacCubbin, Deborah MacCubbin; res: 50 W. Terrace Ave., Lakewood, N.Y. 14750.

WEBER, CHARDELLE ANN, Wms. Ed., Middletown News Journal, S. Broad-First Ave., Middletown, Oh. 45042, '58–; Soc. Wtr., '53–'58; four aws., Oh. Nwsp. Wms. Assn.; aws. from civic orgs.; b. Middletown, Oh., 1924; p. Walter and Marie Holland Weber; res: 3307 Wildwood Rd., Middletown, Oh. 45042.

WEBER, GRETCHEN ALICE, Fashion Colmst., Denver Post, 650 15th St., Denver, Colo. 80201, '70–; Fashion Ed., '50–'70; Edtl. Artist, '31–'50; Fashion and Jnlsm. Instr., Denver Univ. night sch., '56; Lectr., '59; portraits exhibited in Western Artists Show, Chappell House Gallery; represented in permanent collection, Central City, Colo.; Conductor, Eur. Fashion Tour, '68; Denver Art Museum, Nat. Wms. Wtrs. Assn., Fashion Group (Denver Organizer, '57), WNPC; Nat. Red Cross Cit. from Pres. Truman, '46; March of Dimes Aw., '53; Fur Info. and Fashion Cncl. Annual Eds. Aw., '62; Fur Fashions Excellence Aw., '69; AIMBW-MRA Press Aw., '64; Univ. of Colo., '27–'29; Mpls. Sch. of Fine and Applied Arts, '30; Parsons Sch.; Univ. of Colo. Ext., summer '30; b. Boulder, Colo.; p. Adam and Alice Lytle Weber; res: 60 Adams St., Denver, Colo. 80206.

WEBER, JOSEPHINE (JOSIE) CANTU, Feature Wtr., Houston Chronicle, 512 Travis, Houston, Tex. 77002, '67–; PR, South Park Independent Sch. Dist., '65–'66; PR and HS Jnlsm. Tchr., '64–'65; Reptr., The Beaumont Jnl., '63–'64; Theta Sigma Phi (Pres. '62–'63, Histrn. '61–'62); N. Tex. State Univ., BA, '63; b. San Antonio, Tex. 1941; p. Jesse Joe and Mary Gallardo Cantu; h. John Warren Weber; res: 3300 Yorktown, #18, Houston, Tex. 77027.

WEBER, JUDITH R., Pubcty. Dir., Avon Books, 959 Eighth Ave., N.Y., N.Y. 10019, '69–; Assoc. Dir. of Pubcty., Bantam Bks., '68–'69; Pubcty. Asst., New Am. Lib., '64–'68; Publrs. Pubcty. Assn.; Bklyn. Col., BA (Eng.), '64; N.Y.U., MA (Eng.), '68; b. Queens, N.Y., 1942; p. Irving and Miriam Cohen Weber; res: 424 W. 46th St., N.Y., N.Y. 10036.

WEBER, RENNIE CIVETTE, Mdsng. Mgr., Look

Magazine, 488 Madison Ave., N.Y., N.Y. 10022, '69–; Asst. Mdsng. Mgr., '65–'69; Asst. Mgr., '62–'65; Copywtr., '54–'62; AWNY, AAF (five aws.), '68); Pace Col., Sch. of Int. Design; Columbia Univ.; b. N.Y.C., 1927; p. Rinaldo and Teresa Civette; h. Dennis E. Weber (div.); res: 971 First Ave., N.Y., N.Y. 10022.

WECKSLER, SALLY, Mng. Dir., Intl. Opns., Parents Magazine Enterprises, 52 Vanderbilt Ave., N.Y., N.Y. 10017, '69–; Dir., Intl. Projects, R. R. Bowker Co.; Assoc. Ed., Publrs. Weekly; Am. Bk. Publrs. Cncl., OPC; City Col., BBA; b. Chgo., Ill.; p. Max and Tessie Isaacson Wecksler; res: 170 West End Ave., N.Y., N.Y. 10023.

WEDDLE, ETHEL HARSHBARGER, Chief Librn., Girard Township Library, 147 S. Second St., Girard, Ill. 62640, '47–; Auth., five bks.; Who's Who of Am. Wm.; LaVerne Col., '12–'13; b. Girard, Ill., 1897; p. Isaac and Martha Brubaker Harshbarger; h. Lemon Talmadge Weddle; c. Edgar L. (dec.), Mrs. Oscar Rutherford, Jr., Mrs. Henry L. Tipton, Leroy; res: Rte. 1, Girard, Ill. 62640.

WEDEMEYER, DEE, Reptr., The Associated Press, 50 Rockefeller Plaza, N.Y., N.Y. 10020, '68–; Legislative Corr., Knickerbocker News; Wms. Dept., Washington Post; Wms. Press Club of N.Y. State (Secy.), '67), Legislative Corrs. Assn., Am. Polit. Sci. Assn. Hon. Mention, '66; George Wash. Univ., BA, '65; French Inst., '67–'68; b. Pinehurst, N.C.; p. Frederick Wedemeyer and Carra Maultsby Glass; res: 12 Gramercy Pk., N.Y., N.Y. 10003.

WEEKS, CAROL TYLER, Hardware Ed., Horn Computer Research Corp., 233 Broadway, N.Y., N.Y. 10007, '68–; Chgo. Films, '65–'68; Robert Golden Studio, '63–'65; Colmst., Computer, Equipment and Forms Bulletin; Friends World Col., BA (Liberal Arts), '62; Univ. of Prague, MA (Polit. Econ.), '63; b. Rochester, N.Y. 1940; p. Ben and Rita Homanos Korenstein; h. Charter Weeks.

WEEKS, MARILYN ARVIDSON, Free-lance Wtr.; Reptr., The Suffolk Sun, 303 Marcus Blvd., Deer Park, L.I., N.Y. 11729, '68–'69; Wms. Dept., The Miami (Fla.) Herald, '63–'68; Waterloo (Iowa) Daily Courier, '59–'63; Theta Sigma Phi 3rd pl., Catherine L. O'Brien Aw. for outstanding achiev. in wms. int. nwsp. rept., '66; numerous Fla. Wms. Press Club aws.; Distg. Svc. Aw., Jackson Mem. Hosp., '68; Univ. of Neb. at Lincoln, BS (Jnlsm.), '59; b. Hastings, Neb., 1937; p. Otto and Marjorie Stunkard Arvidson; h. J. Stephen Weeks; res: 130 Glenoak Rd., Wilmington, Del. 19805.

WEEKS, RAMONA MAHER, Poet, Auth., juv. bks.; Ed., Arizona Historical Foundation, Charles Trumbull Hayden Memorial Library, Arizona State University, Tempe, Ariz. 85281, '68–'69; Free-lance Ed., Wtr., '67–'68; Mng. Ed., Univ. of Wash. Press, '63–'67; Tech.

Ed., U.S.A.F. Shock Tube Facility (N.M.), '62; Ed., Univ. of N.M. Press (Albuquerque), '56–'61; 1st Prize, Seventeen short story contest, '54, Samuel French and Dallas Little Theatre play aws., '54, Western Wtrs. of Am. Spur Aw., '60, Nat. Endowment for the Arts poetry grant, '68; numerous other aws.; b. Phoenix, Ariz., 1934; p. Raymond and Josephine Allen Maher; h. Tim Weeks; c. Ramon E.; res: 326 W. Dobbins Rd., Phoenix, Ariz. 85041.

WEES, FRANCES SHELLEY, Free-lance Wtr.; formerly PR co. AE; UNRRA (WW II); Tchr., Chautauqua Dir., Art Gallery of Toronto PR; Genealogy Cnslt.; Nat. Genealogical Assn., Canadian Auths. Assn., Canadian Wms. Press Club, DAR, others; Nutana Collegiate, Normal Sch., Saskatoon, Sask.; b. Gresham, Ore., 1902; p. Ralph and Rose Shelley Johnson; h. Wilfred Rusk Wees; c. Margarita Josephine (Mrs. R. W. Belfry), Timothy John; res: R.R. #3, Stouffville, Ont., Can.

WEESNER, BETTY JEAN, Pres.-Treas., Hendricks County Republican, Inc., Six Main St., Danville, Ind. 46122, '65–; Secy.-Treas., '51–'65; Theta Sigma Phi, Wms. Press Club of Ind., NFPW, Ind. Rep. Edtl. Assn.; Ind. Univ., AB, '51; b. Danville, Ind., 1926; p. Edward and Ruth Daugherty Weesner; res: 48 Maple Row, Danville, Ind. 46122.

WEICHEL, DAISY MARTHA, Dir. Pubcty., PR, The Statler Hilton, Park Square, Boston, Mass. 02117, '57–; Sales Prom., Pubcty. and Group Sales, MGM, Cinerama, Paramount, J. Arthur Rank, Columbia and Buena Vista Films, '54–'55; TV interviews, WBZ, Boston, New England Reg. Network, '55–'57; Pubcty., Prom. Adv., Hotel Touraine, '44–'51; Ed., The Breezy Corner, '44–'51; Pubcty. Club of Boston (Co-founder), New England Wms. Press Assn., AWRT, Boston Press Club, AWRT, Fashion Group, Pubcty. Club; civic orgs.; USO Cit.; Goodwill Ambassadress; b. Boston, Mass.; res: Tremont on the Common, 151 Tremont St., Boston, Mass. 02111.

WEINBERG, LILA SHAFFER, Free-lance Wtr., Manuscript Ed., University of Chicago Press, 5750 S. Ellis, Chgo., Ill. 60637, '66–; Edtl. positions, Ziff-Davis Publ. Co., '43–'52; bks: "The Muckrackers" (Co-auth. with husband, '61), "Verdicts Out of Court" ('63), "Instead of Violence" ('63), "Passport to Utopia" ('68); Soc. of Midland Auths.; b. Chgo., Ill.; p. Sam and Blanche Hyman Shaffer; h. Arthur Weinberg; c. Hedy, Anita, Wendy; res: 5421 S. Cornell, Chgo., Ill. 60615.

WEINBERG, MARY HOLSINGER, Ed., The Catalyst, Griffith Public Schools, 132 Broad St., Griffith, Ind. 46319, '68–; Reptr., Indianapolis Daily News, '48–'49; Fashion Copywtr., Charm (N.Y.C.), '46–'48; Soc. Ed., Milwaukee (Wis.) Jnl., '44–'46; Feature Wtr., Chicago Tribune, '42–'44; Police Reptr., Chicago City News Bur., '42; Reptr., Gary (Ind.) Post Tribune, '40–'42; Theta Sigma Phi, Classroom Tchrs. Assn. (Pres., '65),

Ind. State Tchrs. Assn.; Freedoms Fndn. Aw., patriotic sch. program, '68; Ind. Univ., BA (Jnlsm.), '46; MS (Educ.), '58; b. Wolcottville, Ind. 1918; p. Ellis and Marie Eshelman Holsinger; c. Daniel Jay Ellis; res: 343 Wright St., Griffith, Ind. 46319.

WEINBRECHT, RUBY YORK, Chief, Technical Information Division, Equal Employment Opportunity Commission, 1800 G. St. N.W., Wash., D.C. 20506, '67–; Ed., Mktng. Info. Guide, Dept. of Commerce, '65–'67; Librn. positions, '50–'65; Wash., D.C. Lib. Assn., Editor, D.C. Libraries, '67–, Am. Mktng. Assn., Educ. Press Assn. of Am., various state, local lib. orgs.; cert. of achiev., Dept. of the Army, '54; Pi Gamma Mu, '48; Alpha Phi Sigma, '45; Mary Wash. Col. of the Univ. of Va., BA, '48: George Peabody Col., MA, '49–'50; Grad. Lib. Sch., Univ. of Chgo.; b. Spartanburg, S.C., 1927; p. Tyre and Mae Rollins York; h. Standau E. Weinbrecht; res: 8107 Touchstone Terr., McLean, Va. 22101.

WEINER, ELIZABETH HIRZLER, Edtl. Dir., Youth Enterprises Syndicate, 866 U.N. Plaza, N.Y., N.Y. 10017, '69–; Ed., Scholastic Roto, '65–'69; Mng. Ed., '63–'65; Oberlin Col., BA, '58; b. N.Y.C., 1936; p. William and Frieda Durieux Hirzler; h. Saul D. Weiner; res: 220 E. 73rd St., N.Y., N.Y. 10021.

WEINER, FLORENCE CHAIKEN, Auth: "How to Survive in New York with Children" (Corinthian-Scribner's), "Westchester Guidebook" (Umbrella Press); former PR AE, Richard Weiner, Inc. and Ruder and Finn, Inc.; Univ. of Del., BA, '53; b. N.Y.C., 1931; p. Edward and Gussie Longwell Chaiken; h. Richard Weiner; c. Jessica, Stephanie; res: 277 West End Ave., N.Y., N.Y. 10023.

WEINER, SHARON R., AE, J. Walter Thompson, One Maritime Plaza, S.F., Cal., '69–; AE, The PR Bd. (Chgo., Ill.), '67–'69; Adv., Sls. Prom. Asst., CBS, '65–'67; Pubcty. Club of Chgo. Golden Trumpet Aw., '69; Northwestern Univ., BA, '65; b. Rochester, N.Y., 1944; p. M. M. and Elaine Feinberg Weiner; res: 1611 Vallejo St., S.F., Cal. 94123.

WEINGARTEN, VIOLET BROWN, Free-lance Wtr.; Auth: "A Loving Wife" (Alfred Knopf, '69), "Mrs. Beneker" (Simon and Schuster, '67), others; documentary film scripts; VP, Victor Weingarten PR; Reptr., Ed., The Brooklyn Eagle; Am. film aws., Venice, Edinburgh Film Festival aws.; Cornell Univ., BA, '35 (Phi Beta Kappa, Phi Sigma Phi); b. S.F., Cal. 1915; p. William and Elvira Fleischman Brown; h. Victor Weingarten; c. Jan (Mrs. Lester Greenberg), Kathy (Mrs. Hilary Worthen); res: Croton Lake Rd., Mount Kisco, N.Y. 10549; 45 Sutton Pl. S., N.Y., N.Y. 10022.

WEINSTEIN, GRACE WOHLNER, Edtl. Assoc., Party Line, PR/Aids, 305 E. 45th St., N.Y., N.Y. 10017, '61–; Free-lance Wtr., articles in Parents' Magazine, Family Weekly, Science Digest, others; League of Wm. Voters (Dir., '68–'70); Cornell Univ., BA, '57; b.

N.Y.C., 1935; p. David and Esther Lobel Wohlner; h. Stephen Weinstein; c. Lawrence, Janet; res: 283 Maitland Ave., Teaneck, N.J. 07666.

WEIR, JANET DOUTHIT, Crtv. Dir., Wolff & & Weir, Inc., 3216 Arapahoe Ave., Boulder, Colo. 80302, '68–; Copy Chief, Dacey, Wolff & Weit, '64–'68; Free-lance Wtr.; AWRT, Adv. Club of Denver (Copywtr. of the Yr., '66, '68, '69); L.A. Assoc. of Adv. Wm. Golden Lulu Aw., '67; three times Colo. Assn. of Indsl. Advs. Golden Key Aws., numerous cits. for copy; Univ. of Neb., '41–'46; Univ. of Colo., BA, '64 (with distinction); b. Lincoln, Neb., 1923; p. Harold and Edith Benjamin Douthit; h. Dr. Walter Weir; c. Charles H., II, Ellen Tiffany; res: "Ty Cerrig Bryn Cwm" Rte. 1, Boulder, Colo. 80302.

WEIS, BETTY COLETTE SAPHIER, PR Advisor, Olin Corporation, 460 Park Ave., N.Y., N.Y. 10022, '64–; Staff Wtr., '56–; Adv. Copywtr., Squibb; Asst. to Dir. of Pfsnl. Svcs.; PR, U.S. Army Air Force; Tchr., Eng., Citizenship; Free-lance Wtr.; Guest Lectr., Queensborough Col.; PRSA, City Col. Alumni Assn.; City Col. of N.Y., BBA, '39; b. N.Y.C.; p. Joseph and Julie Pollard Saphier; h. Richard Weis; res: 690 Ft. Washington Ave., N.Y., N.Y. 10040.

WEISBERG, MARIAN COLER, Sculptor, 30 E. 20th St., N.Y., N.Y.; many exhbns. incl. Nat. Sculpture Soc., Nat. Arts Club ('64; Bronze Medal, '68), Allied Artists of Am. (aw., '68); Catherine Lorillard Wolfe Art Club (aw., '69); Who's Who of Am. Wm.; Westchester Art Soc. Aw. for Sculpture, '66; Parsons Sch. of Design, '50; Bklyn. Museum Art Sch., '51; Bklyn. Col., '51–'60; N.Y.U., '60–'69; Art Students League, '68; h. Alan Weisberg; c. David; res: 35 W. 9th St., N.Y., N.Y. 10011.

WEISENBORN, CLARA NIES, Garden Ed., Dayton Journal Herald, 11 S. Ludlow, Dayton, Oh. 45402, '42–; Oh. Senate, '67–; House of Reps., '53–'67; VP, Imperial State Bank; Lectr.; Travel Tour Conductor; various orgs., aws.; b. Dayton, Oh., 1907; p. William and Edna Hartung Nies; h. Herbert Edison Weisenborn; c. Donald Harold, Howard Ellwood; res: 4940 Chambersburg Rd., Dayton, Oh. 45424.

WEISER, JANET ANN, Adv. Mgr., The Springdale News, 132 W. Emma, Springdale, Ark. 72764, '59–; Adv. Mgr., Benton Co. Democrat, '54–'59; classified adv., '51–'54; Speaker, Ar. Press Assn. Adv. Clinic, '67; Univ. of Ark. Jnlsm. Day, '68; Ark. Press Wm. (First Place Aw., Nat. Writing Contest, '69), Intl. Nwsp. Adv. Execs., BPW, Beta Sigma Phi (Pres., '57–'58); First Place adv. aws., state contests, '63, '64, '65, '66, '67; b. Wheatland, Wyo., 1930; p. Judge James and Florence Winter Shope; c. Christopher G.; res: 1002 N. Pleasant, Springdale, Ark. 72764.

WEISS, DORA CHARLOTTE, Owner, Pres., Dora C. Weiss Associates, 320 North American Rockwell Bldg., Pitt., Pa. 15222, '58–; AE, VP, Dubin Adv., 14 yrs.; Adv. Mgr., Milo Harding Co. (L.A., Cal.), six yrs.; Arlac Dry Stencil Corp. (Pitt.), five yrs.; Asst. to VP, Old Town Ribbon and Carbon Co. (N.Y.C.); AWRT (Chptr. Pres., '52), Assn. of Pitt. Bus. Wms. Clubs (Pres., '51); Pitt. Adv. Club. Wm. of Yr., '55; Univ. of Pitt., Evening Sch. Div., '20–'25; b. McKeesport, Pa.; p. Emanuel and Rose Linder Weiss; res: 621 Madison Ave., McKeesport, Pa. 15132.

WEISS, GERALDINE M., TV/Radio Bus. Affairs Mgr., Needham, Harper and Steers, Inc., 909 Third Ave., N.Y., N.Y. 10022, '68–; Compton, '47–'67; Asst. Bus. Affairs Mgr., '47–'62; Mgr., '63–'67.

WEISS, MARGARET R., Photog. Ed., Saturday Review, 380 Madison Ave., N.Y., N.Y. 10017, '61–; Assoc. Ed., The American Mercury; Mng. Ed., Living For Young Homemakers; Entertainment Ed., American Magazine; Camera Ed., Scholastic Magazines; Instr., N.Y.U.; Lectr., Fordham Univ.; Auth., "The Television Writer's Guide;" Wtrs. Guild of Am., Puerto Rico Gov. aw.; Fla. Southern Univ. cit.; Barnard Col., Columbia Univ. (Phi Beta Kappa, magna cum laude); b. N.Y.C.; p. J. J. and Isabel E. Weiss; res: 360 W. 55th St., N.Y., N.Y. 10019.

WEISS, MARGUERITA, Free-lance Copywtr./Cnslt., '61–; Reliance Standard Life Insurance, Co., Campbell Soup Co., The Green Frog (Kaleidoscope), Sherry Wine & Spirits, Columbia Record Club, '58–'61; Newsweek, '56–'58; Copy Club of N.Y., Hundred Million Club, Direct Mail Adv. Assn., Nat. Assn. of Direct Mail Wtrs. (VP, Treas., '69); Henry Hoke aw., '62; Direct Mail Adv. Leader aw., '66; The Gold Mailbox Award '68; N.Y.U., BS (Educ., Sci.) Art Students League, New Sch. for Social Rsch.; b. Bronx., N.Y., 1932; c. David Weiss; res: 2599 Davidson Ave., Bronx, N.Y. 10468.

WEISS, ROCHELLE, Rsch., Project Dir., Batten, Barton, Durstine and Osborn, Inc., 383 Madison Ave., N.Y., N.Y. 10017, '69–; Asst. Project Dir., '67; Project Dir., Needham, Harper and Steers, '67–'69; Rsch. Asst., Kenyon and Eckhardt, '66; Am. Mktng. Assn.; Farleigh Dickinson Univ., BA, '66; New Sch. for Social Rsch., MA, '68; b. Jersey City, N.J., '46; p. Murray and Ruth Cohen Weiss; res: 100 Glenwood Ave., Jersey City, N.J. 07306.

WEISSLEDER, ROBERTA LEWIS, Assoc. Art Dir., Ladies Home Journal, Downe Publishing, Inc., 641 Lexington Ave., N.Y., N.Y. 10022, '68–; Art Asst., '65–'68; Art Dir., MacFadden-Bartell, '61–'65; State Univ. of N.Y., Columbia Univ., New Sch. for Social Rsch.; b. Bklyn., N.Y., 1942; p. Mel and Dorothy Piven Lewis; h. Michael Weissleder; res: 41–11 Parsons Blvd., Flushing, N.Y. 11355.

WELBORN, ELIZABETH CHARLES, Librn., Lander College Library, Lander Col., Greenwood, S.C. 29646, '48–'49, '52–'68; Wtr., poetry and travel; Lib. Asst., Univ. of Fla., '49–'52; Head of Tech. Processes Dept.,

Charlotte and Mecklenburg County Lib., '47–'48; Chief Cataloguer, Jacksonville (Fla.) Public Lib., '42–'45; various organizations; Furman Univ., AB, '23; Univ. of Fla., MAE, '34; Columbia Univ., BS (Lib. Sci.), '48; Peabody Lib. Sch., MS (Lib. Sci.), '56; b. Williamston, S.C., 1903; p. Frank Thompson and Carrye Acker Welborn; res: 303 Willson St., Greenwood, S.C. 29646.

WELCH, ELIZABETH MADDEN, VP, Copy Chief, Media Dir., Yancy and McGee Advertising, Inc., 1118 McCullough, San Antonio, Tex. 78212, '62–; 12 yrs. with three adv. agcys.; formerly tchr.; Theta Sigma Phi, AWRT (Pres., '66; Bd. Mbr., '69), Gamma Phi Beta; Univ. of Tex., BA, '53; b. San Antonio, Tex., 1932; p. J. W. and Pauline Zanderson Madden; h. Thomas Peter Welch; res: 102 W. Rampart, K-13, San Antonio, Tex. 78216.

WELCH, JEAN NETTLETON, Co-owner, KERB Broadcasting Inc., Box 760, Kermit, Tex. 79745, '68–; Off. Mgr., Kermit Bdcst., '68–; KAVE (Carlsbad, N.M.), '66–'67; KVKM-AM-TV (Monahans, Tex.), '57–'66; KHEM (Big Spring), '56–'57; Prog. Dir., KTXC '52–'56; KGKL (San Angelo), '43–'52; Beta Sigma Phi; Angelo State Col., '42–'43; Southern Methodist Univ., '43–'44; b. San Angelo, Tex., 1926; p. John and Marguerite Hardin Nettleton; h. M. F. Welch; c. Doug, Mrs. Jerry Adams; res: 907 E. Austin, Kermit, Tex. 79745.

WELCH, NANCY TURNER, Wms. Dir., Hostess, "Nancy Welch Show," WSPA-TV, 123 N. Converse St., Spartanburg, S.C. 29301, '67–; "Lila McLeod Show with Nancy Welch," '66; Tchr., Interior Decorating, Spartanburg Tech. Educ. Ctr.; Auth., "Nancy Welch Cookbook," '67; AWRT, Zeta Tau Alpha Alumni Assn.; Outstanding Young Wm. of Am.; 2,000 Wm. of Achiev.; Fla. State Univ., BS (Home Econs.), '63; b. Nashville, Tenn., 1941; p. Fred and Alice Archambeau Turner; h. Charles Welch; res: 813 N. Main St., Greer, S.C. 29651.

WELCH, VIRGINIA BROWN, Bdcst. Media Dir., Rives Dyke & Company Advertising, 2503 Robinhood, Houston, Tex. 77035, '64–; Berkley Adv., '63–'64; KXYZ, '62–'63; KWBB, Wichita, Kan., '51–'62; KLUF, Galveston, Tex., '49–'51; Grand Prix Adv. Aws. for Best Radio Campaign, Best TV Campaign, '67–'68; Univ. of Houston, '44–'46; Univ. of Wichita, '54–'56; b. Eagle Lake, Tex.; p. Philip and Maude Ryan Brown; h. Donald Welch (dec.); c. Donni, Sharon; res: 5563 Beechnut, Houston, Tex. 77035.

WELCHER, ROSALIND MAXINE, Art Dir., Panda Prints, Inc., 220 Fifth Ave., N.Y., N.Y. 10001, '46–; Art Dir., Ed., Jean and Ginger's Magazine; Auth., Illus. juv. bks., incl: "Do You Believe in Magic?" ('69), "Wouldn't You Like to Run Away?" ('69), "There is Nothing Like a Cat" ('68), 12 others; Hunter Col., BA, '42 (magna cum laude, Phi Beta Kappa); b. N.Y.C., 1922; p. Peter and Ida Rubenstein Welcher; h. Fred Slavic; res: 69 Fifth Ave., N.Y., N.Y. 10003.

WELD, CAROL, Free-lance Wtr., Publicist, 115 Southwest Eighth St., Miami, Fla. 33130; Southeastern Dir., Adv. and Pubcty., RKO-Radio Pictures, '43–'49; Pubcty. Dir., British-Am. Volunteer Ambulance Corps, Hollywood, '40–'42; Am. Volunteer Ambulance Corps, France, '40; Publicist, Frank Buck's Jungleland, '39; Wtr., N.Y.C., '38–'39; Paris, '30–'38; Co-Auth. (with Frank Buck), "Animals Are like That"; news, mag. features; prom. campaigns, hotels and tourism; OPC; L'Alliance Francais, '30–'32; Art Students League; b. N.Y.C.

WELDON, HYLDA LONG, Wms. Pg. Ed., Soc. Ed., The Messenger, S. Main St., Madisonville, Ky. 42431, '35–; BPW, Hopkins County Wms. Repl. Club (Secy.), Wms. Club of Madisonville, b. Providence, Ky., 1913; p. Thomas and Elizabeth Gill Long; h. Freeman Weldon; c. Mrs. Joe B. Adams; res: 36 Waddill Ave., Madisonville, Ky. 42431.

WELLER, ETHELYN TOWNSEND, Auth., hist. non-fiction; formerly Tchr., Librn.; bk., "North Collins Remembers"; published hist. of towns of Erie County, '40–'50; hists. of Buffalo and Rochester indsl. plants; N. Collins Town Histrn., '41–'68; N. Collins Hist. Soc. (Pres.), '45–; Who's Who of Am. Wm.; Who's Who in the East; Hamilton, Ontario, Normal Sch.; Toronto Univ., BS, '25; b. Buffalo, N.Y., 1901; p. William and Carrie Thomas Townsend; h. William Weller; c. George Robert; res: 383 Sanders Rd., Buffalo, N.Y. 14216.

WELLINGTON, JEAN WILLETT, Asst. Prof. of Educ., Tufts University, Lincoln Filene Ctr., Medford, Mass. 02155, '52; Psychologist, Eastern Middlesex Guidance Ctr., '60–; Auth., four bks. on educ., articles in pfsnl. jnls.; Am. Psychological Assn., Am. Personnel & Guidance Assn., Mass. Psychological Assn., NEA, Mass. Educ. Assn., Pi Lambda Theta; Boston Univ., AB, '45; Tufts Univ., MA, '47; Columbia Univ., EdD, '51; b. Lynn, Mass.; p. Harold and Jeanette Shrum Willett; h. C. Burleigh Wellington; c. Leigh, Beth; res: 50 Gleason Rd., Reading, Mass. 01867.

WELLMAN, ELIZABETH PIERSE, Negotiator, Bus. Affairs, Sls., Columbia Broadcasting System, Inc., 51 W. 52nd St., N.Y., N.Y. 10019, '67–; Mgr., Synd., '62–'67; Synd. Adm. Asst., '57–'61; Atty., RKO Teleradio, '53–'57; N.Y. State Bar Assn., Catholic Apostolate of Radio-TV-Adv.; St. John's Univ. Sch. of Law, LLB; N.Y.U. Sch. of Law, LLM; h. Arthur Wellman; c. Maryann, Patricia Ann Bova; res: Peekskill Towers, Lakeview Dr., Peekskill, N.Y. 10566.

WELLS, DOROTHY VIOLA, Librn., Government and Public Affairs Reading Room, University of California, Los Angeles, 405 Hilgard Ave., L.A., Cal. 90024, '62–; John Randolph Haynes and Dora Haynes Fndn. Collection, '62–; Bur. of Governmental Rsch., '42–'62; Guest Lectr., U.C.L.A. Sch. of Lib. Svc.; Special Libs. Assn. (Southern Cal. Chptr. VP, '48–'49), Cncl. of Planning Librns., Pi Gamma Mu; Univ. of Wyo., BA, '38; Univ. of Ill. Grad. Sch. of Lib. Sci., BS, '39; b. Boulder, Colo., 1916; p. Harold and Laura McCardie Wells.

WELLS, FAY GILLIS, Bdcstr., Wtr.; White House Corr., Storer Broadcasting Co., 1725 K St., N.W., Wash., D.C. 20006, '64–; formerly Fgn., Hollywood Corr., N.Y. Herald Tribune; Colmst., Herald Tribune Synd.; Free-lance Wtr., NANA, AP; extensive radio, TV appearances; bk. revs., mag. articles; AWRT (D.C. Chptr. Pres., '68–'69), ANWC, WNPC, OPC; Lady Hay Drummond Hay aw., '64; Sherman Fairchild Intl. Air Safety Writing aw., '65; Caterpillar Club; Mich. State Col. 99's; b. Mpls., Minn., 1908; p. Julius and Minnie Shafer Gillis; h. Linton Wells; c. Linton II; res: 2601 Woodley Pl. N.W., Wash., D.C. 20008.

WELLS, GLORIA DELLI-BOVI, Sr. Art Dir., Ogilvy and Mather, 2 E. 48th St., N.Y., N.Y., '68–; Art Dir., Grey Adv., '67–'68; Art Dir., Warnick & Legler, '60–'67; Art Dirs. aw., '65; Pratt Inst., '54–'56; Am. Univ., '56–'57; N.Y.U., '60; b. N.Y.C., 1937; p. Lawrence and Vincenza Infante Delli-Bovi; h. Alfred B. Wells Jr.; c. Gregory Ercolano; res: 815 Park Ave., N.Y., N.Y. 10021.

WELLS, HELEN, Auth., juv. fiction; bks: Cherry Ames, Vicki Barr stories (Grosset and Dunlap), "Escape by Night" (Winston), "Barnum" (McKay), "Dr. Betty" (Messner-Simon & Schuster), numerous others; Auths. Guild, WNBA, MWA (N.Y. Regional Bd.); N.Y.U., BS (Philosophy), '34; courses at Columbia Univ., Art Students League, New Sch. for Social Rsch., N.Y.U.; Programming and Systems Inst. diploma, '69; b. Danville, Ill., 1915; p. Henry and Henrietta Basch Weinstock; res: 345 E. 57th St., N.Y., N.Y. 10022.

WELSCHMEYER, MARY LOU, Supvsr., Product Info. Dept., Corning Glass Works, Corning, N.Y. 14830, '66–; Asst. to Adv. Mgr., '65–'66; Supvsr., Field Home Econsts., '63–'65; Corning Ware Mktng. Team, '58–'60; Field Home Econst., '55–'58; formerly refrigerator, freezer sls. Prom., Intl. Harvester; Home Econs. Tchr., St. Genevieve, Mo.; Home Demonstration Agt., Univ. of Mo. Agricultural Ext. Svc.; Am. Home Econs. Assn., N.Y. State Home Econs. Assn. (Bd. Mbr.), Home Econsts. in Bus. (Chptr. Chmn.-Elect), Intl. Fedn. of Home Econs., AWRT, BPW, Electrical Wms. Round Table, NHFL, AAUW; Who's Who of Am. Wm., Dic. of Intl. Biog.; Univ. of Mo., BS (Home Econs.; Cit. of Merit).

WELSH, LORRAINE THOMAS, Dir. of Pubns., Ed.-in-Chief, Museum of Science, Science Park, Boston, Mass. 02114, '69–; Ed.-in-Chief, '58–; Asst. Dir. of PR, News Assoc., '58–'69; Press Dir., United Commty. Svcs., '58; Met. Press Rep., '52–'54; Soc. Ed., Corr., The Needham Chronicle, '47–'52; Mass. IEA (Treas.), '65; Pubcty. Chmn., '61–'64), ICIE (Dir. of Nat. Affairs, '66–'67); Boston Univ. Sch. of PR, BS (Jnlsm.), '50; b. Bklyn., N.Y., 1928; p. Joseph and Marie Stengle Thomas; h. Laurence T. Welsh; res: 42 Gayland Rd., Needham, Mass. 02192.

WENDLER, ALICE COLE, Asst. Ed., Secy.-Treas., Miami Beach Times Publishing Corp., 1428 Alton Rd., Miami Beach, Fla. 33139, '62–; Asst. Ed., '63–; Asst. to Comptroller, Danny's Hide-Away (Surfside), '57–'58; Asst. PR Dir., L'Aiglon, La Bastille Clubs, '55–'57; aws: Dade Co. Chptr., Am. Red Cross, '62, '64, '65; Pres. Truman, '48; Brenau Col., '26; p. Howard and Janet Pope Cole; h. James P. Wendler; res: 8841 Froude Ave., Surfside, Fla. 33154.

WENDT, INGRID D., Wtr., poems, short stories; Asst. Prof. of English, Fresno State College, Fresno, Cal. 93726, '68–; Instr., Univ. of Ore.; Mng. Ed., Northwest Review, '67–'68; Teaching Asst., '66–'67; Modern Language Assn.; Carnegie Sr. Humanities Fellowship, '65–'66; Cornell Col., BA, '66 (magna cum laude; Phi Beta Kappa); Univ. of Ore., MFA, '68 (Neuberger Annual Poetry Prize); b. Aurora, Ill., 1944; p. Edward and Matilda Petzke Wendt; h. Ralph Salisbury; res: Fesno, Cal. 93704.

WENK, JENNY, Adv. Sls. Prom. Wtr., Dow Jones & Company, Inc., 30 Broad St., N.Y., N.Y. 10004, '68–; Prom. Asst., Owens Publication, '65–'67; Adv. Sls., Menlo Park Recorder, '65; Prod. Asst., Meltzer, Aaron & Lemen, '64–'65; AWNY; Univ. of Cal. at Berkeley, BA, '64 (Commtns.); b. Pitt., Pa., 1942; p. Samuel and Jean Barnes Wenk.

WENTZ, EVELYN SHULTZ, Painter, Enamelist, '49–; ten one-man shows; represented in many permanent U.S., fgn. collections; Am. Craftsmen's Cncl., World Crafts Cncl., Nat. Assn. of Wm. Artists, numerous other art socs.; Who's Who of Am. Wm., Who's Who of Midwest, Intl. Dir. of Arts, Dic. of Intl. Biog., Royal Blue Bk.; scholarship grants, Art Interests, Inc., '51, '52, '54; Toledo Museum of Art Sch. of Design, '49–'54; b. Sandusky County, Oh., 1915; p. Alfred and Edna Roush Shultz; h. Paul L. Wentz; c. Mrs. John F. Haley, Mrs. Jerry J. Leeson, Mrs. Charles D. Wilson, Craig V., Paul E.; res: 1733 N. Countyline St., Fostoria, Oh. 44830.

WERESCH, GAY STARRAK, Assoc. Dir., Home Econs. Dept., National Live Stock and Meat Board, 36 S. Wabash Ave., Chgo., Ill. 60603; Dir., "Mary Blaine Time" daily radio program, '59–'69; Wkly. Nwsp. Colmst., "Calling All Cooks," '49–'59; Food Ed., Chgo. Daily News, '39–'41; AWRT, Theta Sigma Phi, Am. Home Econs. Assn., Home Econsts. in Bus.; Ia. State Univ., BS, '39 (Mortar Bd., Omicron Nu, Phi Upsilon Omicron); b. MacDonald Col., Quebec, Can.; p. James and M. Hazel Hudson Starrak; c. Michael J., William H., Joseph M.; res: 11 Elizabeth Ct., Lombard, Ill. 60148.

WERKMEISTER, LUCYLE THOMAS, Wtr., Rschr., specialty: Coleridge, late 18th century London; Instr., Univ. of Neb., '45–'47; bks., articles in scholarly jnls.; Modern Lang. Assn., Conf. on British Studies; Grants from Am. Philosophical Soc., '59, '63; Phi Kappa Lambda, Mu Phi Alpha; Univ. of Kan., BM, '30; Univ. of Neb., BA, '39 (Phi Beta Kappa); PhD, '56; Univ. of Southern Cal., '54–'55; b. Okla. City, Okla., 1908; p. Reuben and Blanche Stumbo Thomas; h. William Henry Werkmeister; res: 3354 E. Lake Shore Dr., Tallahassee, Fla. 32303.

WERLIN, ROSELLA HARWOOD, Wtr., Lectr.; Pres., Werlin International Cultural Tours, 2340 Underwood Blvd., Houston, Tex. 77025, '40–; Pubcty., Badget Quads, '41–'47; Pubcty. Dir., Galveston C. of C., '37–'42 (1st wm. in U.S. to hold such post); Jnlsm. Instr., Sam Houston Sch., '35–'38; Pubcty. Wtr., '34, '29–'30; Nwsp. Reptr., '24–'32; Who's Who in Am.; Univ. of Houston, BS, '35; MS, '50; b. N.Y.C., 1904; p. Henry and Cecilia Feinberg Horowitz; h. Joseph Werlin (dec.); c. Dr. Herbert H., Ernest P., Joella B. (Mrs. Lawrence Zivin).

WERNER, ELEANOR DONOHUE, Wtr., Batz, Hodgson, Neuwoehner Advertising and Marketing, 411 N. Tenth St., St. Louis, Mo. 63101, '66–; Crtv. Dir., Rutledge Adv., '64–'66; Prog.-Prod. Dir., KPLR-TV, '60–'64; Radio-TV Dir., Ridgeway-Hirsch Adv., '57–'60; Prodr.-Dir., KWK-TV, '54–'57; KACY-TV, '53–'54; NATAS (St. Louis Chptr. Bd. of Governors, '68–'69), AWRT (St. Louis Chptr. Pres., '59–'60), Wms. Adv. Club of St. Louis, St. Louis Wtrs. Club; Adv. Agcy. Group aw., '58; Who's Who of Am. Wm.; Who's Who in the Midwest; World Who's Who of Commerce and Industry; Harris Tchrs. Col., '41–'43; Wash. Univ., '47; Kroeger Sch. of Music, '47–'50; b. St. Louis, Mo.; p. Raymond and Emily LeRoy Donohue; h. Andrew T. Werner; res: 15 Orchard Dr., Florissant, Mo. 63033.

WERSHBA, SHIRLEY LUBOWITZ, News Wtr., American Broadcasting Co., 7 W. 66th St., N.Y., N.Y. 10023, '65–; News Wtr., CBS News, '63–'65; CBS Radio Wtr., '62–'63; NATAS, Wtrs. Guild; Bklyn. Col., BA, '43; b. N.Y.C., 1922; p. William and Ada Stein Lubowitz; h. Joseph Wershba; c. Randi, Donald; res: 70 Country Village Lane, New Hyde Park, N.Y. 11040.

WERTENBAKER, LAEL TUCKER, Free-lance Wtr., '47–; former Rschr., Reptr., Fgn., War Corres. for Time, Inc.; TV scripts for Orson Wells series, Rediffusion (Great Britain); "20th Century," CBS; Contrbr., Harper's, Reporter, Life, others; Auth: five novels, five non-fiction bks., three juv. bks.; OPC, PEN, Nat. Repertory Theatre, Monadnock Music, MacDowell Colony Assn.; Univ. of Louisville; b. Bradford, Pa., 1909; p. Royal and Juliet Luttrell Tucker; h. Charles Christian Wertenbaker (dec.); c. Christian T., Timberlake; res: R.F.D., Marlborough, N.H. 03455.

WERTZ, VIRGINIA LORYMA, Cir. Desk Supvsr., District of Columbia Public Library, Connecticut Ave. and McKinley St., N.W., Wash., D.C. 20015, '63–; Cir. Desk Supvsr., '65–; C&P Telephone Co., '51–'62; Theta Sigma Phi; Night Sch., American Univ., AA, BA, '51–'61; b. Wash., D.C., 1933; p. Melvin and Ruth Johnson Wertz; res: 5332 41st St. N.W., Wash., D.C. 20015.

WESLEY, JOEL, TV Comml. Spokeswm.; VP, J/J Productions, 11633 Gorham Ave., Suite 18, L.A., Cal. 90049; Pres., Continental Girl Cosmetics; Exec. VP, Royal Viking, Inc.; Asst. to Pres., Denise Richards Cosmetics, '68; West Coast Dir. of Franchising, Lilly Dache Cosmetics, '65–'68; TV and Radio Dir., Am. West Commtns., '64; TV/Speech Tchr., Mary Webb Davis Schs., '64; first closed circuit TV comml. training sch., "Kids on Kamera," '61–'63; AFTRA, SAG, AEA; Linfield Col., BA, '44 (Pi Kappa Delta, Alpha Psi Omega); b. Dayton, Ore., 1922; p. Joseph and Ella Leckband Fulham.

WESSEL, HELEN STRAIN, Auth., Lectr.; Cnslt., Royal Scroll Book Reviewers, 14429 E. Leffingwell, Whittier, Cal. 90604, '69–; bk., "Natural Childbirth and the Christian Family" (Harper and Row, '63); Intl. Childbirth Educ. Assn. (Pres., '64–'66), Childbirth Assn. of Greater Mpls./St. Paul, active in ch., commty., civil rights orgs.; Equipo Medico de Estudios Psicofisicos de Analgesia Obstetrica, Bogota, Colombia (Hon.); Sioux Falls Col., BA, '60 (cum laude); Univ. of Minn., grad. studies; b. San Anselmo, Cal., 1924; p. John and Laura Hammerli Strain; h. Walter Wessel; c. Margaret, Sharyl, Deborah, Dorothy, Daniel, Donald; res: 3905 Rolling Hills Rd., St. Paul, Minn. 55112.

WESSMANN, LUCILE TOMLINSON, VP, Nuveen Corporation, 61 Broadway, N.Y., N.Y. 10006, '67–; Partner, Arthur Wissenberger & Co., '65–'67; Ed., '50–'65; Edtl. Staff, Barron's, '33–'43; Auth., "Practical Formulas for Successful Investing" ('53); Wms. Bond Club of N.Y. (Pres., '46–'48); Mt. Holyoke Col., BA, '33 (magna cum laude, Phi Beta Kappa); b. N.Y.C., 1912; p. William and Beatrice Westover Tomlinson; h. Alfred Wessmann; c. Frances (Mrs. James E. Foley); res: 30 Ivy Way, Port Washington, N.Y. 11050.

WEST, CAROLYN V., Commtns. Mgr., Crouse-Hinds Co., Syracuse, N.Y. 13201, '68–; Staff, incl. Adv. Copywtr., '53–; Free-lance Wtr.; Theta Sigma Phi; active in civic, religious orgs.; Syracuse Univ., BS, '50; b. Syracuse, N.Y., 1928; p. Peter and Mabel Feigel West; res: 1365 Oak St., Syracuse, N.Y. 13203.

WEST, JACKIE AGNEW, VP, Crtv. Supvsr., Cunningham & Walsh, Inc., 260 Madison Ave., N.Y., N.Y. 10016, '59–; Copy Group Head, '58; Compton, '55–'58; D-F-S, '52–'55; Copywtr., Y&R, '43–'52; AWNY, Adv. Club of N.Y., Adv. Wtrs. of N.Y., Fashion Group, Gamma Alpha Chi; Who's Who in Adv.; 100 Top Copywtrs. and Their Favorite Ads; Univ. of Mo., BJ, '37; Univ. of Wis., '38; b. Bonham, Tex., 1915; p. William and Dora Sowell Agnew; h. Robert West; res: 200 E. 66th St., N.Y., N.Y. 10021.

WEST, JUDITH FREEMAN, Media Dir., Wyse Advertising, 777 Third Ave., N.Y., N.Y. 10017, '67–; Media Dir., Sudler & Hennessey, '58–'67; Gen. Prom. Mgr., Imprints, '56–'58; AWNY; N.Y.U., '38–'41; b. N.Y.C., 1923; p. Julius and Dorothy Baum Freeman;

h. Daniel A. West (div.); c. Paul Smirnoff, Joel Philip Smirnoff; res: 845 West End Ave., N.Y., N.Y. 10025.

WEST, KITTY MAYER, Auth.; Pres., National Retouchers Guild, 615 Alameda Padre Serra, P.O. Box 535, Santa Barbara, Cal. 93103, '66–; Instr., Fred Archer Sch. of Photog., '48–'57; Owner, art gallery, '60–'64; three bks. on retouching (Amphoto Publ. Co., '55, '62, '67); Publr., The Retoucher; Painter; Charles Univ., Prague, Czechoslovakia, BA (German, English); b. Munich, Germany, 1908; p. August and Katharina Maier Mayer; h. John J. West; c. Richard Vincent, Robert Henry.

WESTLAKE, RUTH LUCILE, Ed., The Times-Leader, 200 S. Fourth St., Martins Ferry, Oh. 43935, '56–; Reptr., News Ed.; Oh. Nwsp. Wms. Assn., Theta Sigma Phi; Kent State Univ., BS (Jnlsm.), '56; grad. work, Oh. Univ.; b. Colerain, Oh., 1934; p. Merle and Virginia Fox Westlake; res: Joella Dr., St. Clairsville, Oh. 43950.

WESTLING, JEANINE NELSON, Public Info. Dir., Metropolitan Area Safety Council of Minnesota, 625 Second Ave. S., Mpls., Minn. 55402, '65–; Staff Wtr., Ed., Mpls. C. of C., '61–'65; Pubcty. Asst., N. Central Airlines, '58–'60; PR Dir., Minn. Farm Bur., '57–'58; Copywtr., Montgomery Ward, '57; PRSA, ICIE, Northwestern Indsl. Eds. Assn. (Ed. of the Yr., '63); Who's Who of Am. Wm.; Univ. of Minn., '52–'56; b. Mpls., Minn.; p. Stanley and Evelyn Nelson; h. Oren Westling.

WETMORE, SUSAN, Sub-Reg. Ed., TV Guide Magazine, 2020 University Club Bldg., 136 E. S. Temple, Salt Lake City, Ut. 84101, '65–; Free-lance Artist (Salt Lake) County Fair oil painting aw., '63); AWRT (Treas., '67–'68); Univ. of Ut., '64–'67; b. Salt Lake City, Ut., 1946; p. Carl and Hanna Ivory Wetmore; res: 1675 Roosevelt Ave., Salt Lake City, Ut. 84105.

WETTENSTEIN, BEVERLY A., PR Dir., U.S. National Student Travel Association, Inc., 70 Fifth Ave., N.Y., N.Y. 10011, '68–; Prom. Mgr., N.Y. Convention & Visitors Bur., '67–'68; Prom. Copywtr., Good Housekeeping, '66–'67; Edtl. Asst., '65–'66; Venture, '64–'65; AWRT, Theta Sigma Phi, AWNY, Pubcty. Club of N.Y.; Temple Univ., BS (Jnlsm.), '64; p. Milton and Sylvia Gordon Wettenstein; res: 121 E. 82nd St., N.Y., N.Y. 10028.

WHALEN, JULIA MARY, Prod. Mgr., Kim & Gifford Productions, 342 Madison Ave., N.Y., N.Y. 10017, '58–; several positions, J. Walter Thompson, '55–'58; Col. of New Rochelle, BA, '55 (Ursula Laurus Cit.; Alumnae Assn.); Columbia Univ., MA (Hist.), '60; b. N.Y.C., 1933; p. Myles and Julia Quinn Whalen; res: 525 W. 238 St., N.Y., N.Y. 10463.

WHALEY, CAROL JEAN SUTTON, Wms. Ed., The Courier-Journal, 525 W. Broadway, Louisville, Ky. 40202, '63–; News Reptr., Feature Wtr., '55–'63; Univ.

of Missouri, BA, '55; b. St. Louis, Mo., 1933; p. Dallas and Marie Marler Sutton; h. Charles E. Whaley; c. Carrie Elizabeth, Kate Wallace; res: 2531 Cherokee Pkwy., Louisville, Ky. 40204.

WHALEY, MARY GILBERT, Edtl. Asst., Churchman Magazine, 1074 23rd Ave. N., St. Petersburg, Fla. 33704; Auth., "Sailor's Handbook" ('58); Univ. of Tenn.; b. Orlinda, Tenn., 1908; p. Harold and Minnie Shannon Gilbert; h. Fred E. Whaley (dec.); c. Fred E. Jr., Charles W., Robert W.; res: 166 18th Ave. N., St. Petersburg, Fla. 33704.

WHEATLEY, DORCAS LOUISE, Wms. Ed., WOI-AM-TV, Ames, Ia. 50010, '67–; Ia. State Univ. Coop. Ext. Svc., '64–'67; Ia. Div. Vocational Rehabilitation, '61–'63; various orgs., aws.; Purdue Univ., BS (Home Econs.), '48; b. Spencer, W.Va., 1927; p. L. L. and Lelah Keith Ball; c. David, Katherine, Christine; res: 1536 Maxwell Ave., Ames, Ia. 50010.

WHEATLEY, MARY ESTHER, Dir., "Child's Play," WGSM Radio, 900 Walt Whitman Rd., Huntington Sta., N.Y. 11746, '68; Tchr., '58–'68; fine arts, '52–'53; AWRT; Buffalo State Univ., BA (Fine Arts), '52; Columbia Univ., MA, '57; b. Buffalo, N.Y., 1930; p. William and Esther Leary Wheatley; h. Martin Schneider; c. Elizabeth; res: 50 Colonial Dr., Huntington, N.Y. 11743.

WHEDON, PEGGY BRUNSSEN, Prodr. "Issues and Answers," American Broadcasting Company, 1124 Connecticut Ave. N.W., Wash., D.C. 20036, '60–; Asst. Prodr. "College News Conference," '54–'60; wtr. of feature spots for radio network; White House Corr.; numerous orgs. aws.; Univ. of Rochester; Hunter Col.; Rochester Bus. Inst.; b. N.Y.C., 1926; p. Henry and Anna Nichol Brunssen; h. G. Donald Whedon; c. Karen Anne, David Marshall; res: 5605 Sonoma Rd., Bethesda, Md. 20034.

WHEELER, CHRISTINE GILLISPIE, Wms. Ed., Reptr., Hamilton Journal-News, Court St. and Journal Sq., Hamilton, Oh. 45012; b. Sadieville, Ky., 1923; p. Luther and Ura Wilson Gillispie; h. John Wheeler; c. Michael Lee; res: 685 Franklin St., Hamilton, Oh. 45013.

WHEELER, EVANNE, County Librn., County of Humboldt, 825 Fifth St., Eureka, Cal. 95501, '64–; Librn., '51–'64; ALA, Cal. Lib. Assn. (Golden Empire Dist. Pres.; '62; Redwood Dist. Pres.; '67); Friends of the Redwood Libs.; John Cotton Dana Pubcty. Aw.; '67; Long Beach State Col., BA (cum laude), '51; Univ. of Cal., BLS, '52; b. Chgo., Ill., 1916; p. Claude and Eva Toresen Wheeler; res: 2260 Crest Dr., Fortuna, Cal. 95540.

WHEELER, LORA JEANNE, Librn., Thunderbird Graduate School of International Management, P.O. Box 191, Phoenix, Ariz. 85001, '58–; Univ. of Ut. Lib., '48–'53; Univ. of Ut. Lib., '45–'48; Auth., "Interna-

tional Commerce and Foreign Business: A Management Guide" (Gale Rsch. Co., '69); ALA, Ariz. State Lib. Assn. (Secy., '60–'61), Alpha Delta Kappa; Univ. of Ut., BA, '44; Columbia Univ. Sch. of Lib. Svc., BS, '45; grad. work, Univ. of Cal., Univ. of Ill.; b. Rockland, Idaho, 1923; p. Jesse and Mary Miller Wheeler.

WHEELER, MARY COGSWELL, Dir. of Educ. TV, East Texas State University, Audio-Visual Center, Commerce, Tex. 75428, '69–; Tchr.-Admr.; Wms. Ed., Program Dir., KTAR (Frederick, Okla.), '49–'62; various organizations, aws. and hons.; Tex. Christian Univ., BS, '38; E. Tex. State Univ., MA, '63; PhD, '69; b. Bloomington, Ind., 1919; p. Claude E. and Dordelia F. Jones Cogswell; h. Ronald W. Wheeler; c. Wendelyn (Mrs. Don White), Marilyn (Mrs. Jon Kindred), Gregg, Carol, Scott; res: 2810 Tanglewood Dr., Commerce, Tex. 75428.

WHEELER, RUTH CARR, Ed., health-sci. textbks., General Conference of Seventh-day Adventists, 6840 Eastern Ave., N.W., Takoma Park, Wash., D.C. 20012, '65–; Tchr., Pacific Un. Col., '55–'65; Auth., "California Heritage of Riches" (Graphic Arts Aw., '65); Co-Auth., "My Father's World" (Pacific Press Publ. Assn., '65); Pacific Un. Col., BA, '38; MA, '60; b. Artesia, Cal., 1899; p. Charles and Mary McCulloch Carr; h. Herschel Wheeler; c. Donald, Gordon; res: 22 Manor Circle, Takoma Park, Md. 20012.

WHEELING, MARY ELLEN RYAN, Media Dir., The Bowes Company, 1010 S. Flower St., L.A., Cal. 90015, '66–; Media Dir., Anderson McConnell Adv. Agcy., '59–'66; Media Dir., M. B. Scott, Inc., '56–'59; Chief Time Byr., Mottel and Siteman, '55–'56; VP, James C. Wheeling, '51–'55; Sls. Prom., PR, Raymond R. Morgan Co., '49–'51; Chief Time Byr., '47–'49; Copywtr., H. J. Wendland Adv., '46–'47; Asst. Pubcty. Dir., Don Lee Bdcst. System, '45–'46; Traf. Mgr., '42–'45; Hollywood Radio TV Soc., BPW (Hollywood Chptr. Pres., '49–'50; Cal. Fedn. Bd. Mbr., '48–'49), Sierra Club (Auth., Angeleus Chptr. training films), Repl. Assoc., L.A. County Museum of Art (Patron), U.C.L.A. Friends of Archaeology, U.C.L.A. Art Cncl.; educ: U.C.L.A.; Univ. of Southern Cal.; b. Rawlins, Wyo., 1921; p. Thomas and Elizabeth Eddy Ryan; h. J. C. Wheeling (dec.).

WHIPPLE, JOE ANN FEELEY, Owner, Pres., Whipple House-Public Relations, Gipsy Trail Rd., Carmel, N.Y. 10512, '61–; Copywtr., BBDO, '51–'55; Publicist, Casita Maria Settlement House, '58–'61; Vice Chmn., Putnam Commty. Hosp. Aux., '60–; Dir., Putnam County Children's Welfare Comm., '63–; active in numerous commty., charitable orgs.; PRSA; Endicott Col., '51; b. Syracuse, N.Y., 1930; p. Robert and Marie Willy Feeley; h. George C. Whipple, Jr.; c. George C., III, Meredith Ann, Allison H.; res: Pine View Farm, Carmel, N.Y. 10512.

WHIPPLE, MAURINE, Auth., Lectr.; Contrbr., Saturday Evening Post, Look, Life; Auth: "This is the

Place, Utah" (Knopf, '45); "The Giant Joshua"; Intl. Platform Assn., Desert Protective Assn., Chi Delta Phi; Univ. of Ut., AB (cum laude); b. St. George, Ut., 1909; p. Charles and Annie McAllister Whipple; res: 410 W., 600 North St., George, Ut. 84770.

WHITAKER, MARY REASONOVER, Owner, The Kemp News, Kemp, Tex. 75143; Trinity Univ., '27–'29; b. Kemp, Tex., 1910; p. Ossie and Carrie French Reasonover; h. Aaron D. Whitaker; c. Aaron David, Jr., James V., Virginia; res: Kemp, Tex. 75143.

WHITCOMB, HELEN HAFEMANN, Wtr.; Mng. Ed., Today's Secretary, McGraw-Hill Book Co., '51–'55; Asst. Ed., Chain Store Age, '47–'51; Co-auth: "Charm for Miss Teen" (McGraw-Hill, '69), "Charm— The Career Girl's Guide to Business and Personal Success" (McGraw-Hill, '64), others; AAUW; Ursinus Col., AB, '46; b. Oradell, N.J., 1925; p. Frank and Elizabeth Buedinger Hafemann; h. John Whitcomb; c. Claire, Jonathan; res: 111 Timber Dr., Berkeley Heights, N.J. 07922.

WHITE, ANN LITTLE, Prod. Coordr., Traffic Exec., WAPI-TV, Newhouse Broadcasting, Box 1310, Birmingham, Ala. 35201, '69–; Traf. Exec., '67–'69; AWRT, Birmingham Press Club; Stephens Col., BA, '67; b. Denver, Colo., 1945; p. Richard and Evelyn Little White; res: 102 Hollywood Blvd., Birmingham, Ala. 35209.

WHITE, ANNE BEINETTI, Media Dir., Woodard, Voss & Hevenor, Inc., 15 Elk St., Albany, N.Y. 12207, '56–; Asst. Treas., Hevenor Adv., '38–'56; De Rouville Adv., '22–'38; Albany Altrusa Club (Past Pres.), Americanization Cncl. (Corr. Secy.); b. Albany, N.Y., 1905; p. Salvini and Louise Mittelberger Beinetti; res: 203 Jay St., Albany, N.Y. 12210.

WHITE, ANNE CANTRELL, Colmst., Greensboro Daily News, Davie St., Greensboro, N.C. 27402, '65–; Wms. Ed., '28–'65; Theta Sigma Phi, N.C. Press Wm., many times aw. winner; Greensboro Wm. of the Yr., '67; N.C. Governor's Comm. on Beautification; Univ. of N.C., AB, '22; Univ. of Wis., MA (Jnlsm.) '23; b. Monroe County, Miss., 1902; p. Eugene and Katherine Smith Cantrell; h. Benajah White (dec.); res: 129 Oak Ct., Greensboro, N.C. 27401.

WHITE, BERTHA ROTHE, Asst. Head Ref. Librn., Los Angeles County Law Library, 301 W. First St., L.A., Cal. 90012, '64–; Asst. Ref. Librn., '62–'64; Law Librn., Social Security Admin. (Balt., Md.), '60–'62; George Washington Univ. (Wash., D.C.), '53–'60; Housing and Home Fin. Agcy., '50–'53; Ref. Librn., U.S. Dept. of Justice, '48–'50; Cataloger, Lib. of Congress, '45–'48; Dept. of State, '43–'45; Auth., Ed., Lectr.; Law Librns. Soc. of Wash., D.C. (Pres., '56–'58); Southern Cal. Assn. of Law Librns. (Pres., '65–'67); Am. Assn. of Law Libs.; Phi Kappa Phi, Pi Lambda Theta; Syracuse Univ., AB (Phi Beta Kappa), AM, '35; BS (Lib. Sci.), '40; George Washington Univ., JD, '48; LLM, '56; b.

Syracuse, N.Y., 1915; p. Oscar and Cora Fahrenwald Rothe; h. Kermit Derwent White; res: 7125 Sunnybrae Ave., Canoga Park, Cal. 91306.

WHITE, DARLEENE BRUNDELL, AE, Southern Region OpenRoad International, Inc., 407 N. Eighth St., St. Louis, Mo. 63101, '67–; Free-lance Wtr., '64–'67; Mgr., Corporate Int. Commtns., Tex. Instruments Inc., '57–'64; Assoc. Ed., Dallas Athletic Club, '55–'57; European Corr., Dallas Morning News, '54; Reptr., Dallas Times Herald, '50–'54; Soc. of Am. Travel Wtrs., Fashion Group, Who's Who of Am. Wm.; Southern Methodist Univ., BA (Theta Sigma Phi); grad. work, Sorbonne Inst.; b. Dallas, Tex., 1932; p. George and Gertrude Bush White; res: 8333 Inwood Rd., Dallas, Tex. 75209.

WHITE, ETHYLE HERMAN, Artist, Illus., Sculptress, Poet; represented in private collections in Switzerland, Germany, Sweden; numerous one-man art, sculpture shows; poetry bks.; NLAPW, Nat. Wtrs. Club, Federated Fine Arts Club, Tex. Fine Arts Assn., Tex. Poetry Soc.; numerous aws., hons.; Who's Who of Am. Wm., Who's Who in the South and Southwest, Dic. of Intl. Biog., other dirs.; art educ. in Germany and Switzerland; h. S. Roy White; res: P.O. Box 176, Anahuac, Tex. 77514.

WHITE, EVA ANDERSON, Make-up Ed., Co-publr., The Naperville Sun; Secy., The Naperville Sun, Inc., 9 W. Jackson Ave., Naperville, Ill. 60540; former Assoc. Ed., Adv. Mgr.; Tchr., Batavia and Aurora, Ill.; 52 state and nat. contest aws. for nwsp., '47–; Stephens Col., '30–'31; Chgo. Acad. of Fine Arts, '31–'32; North Central Col., '32–'33; b. Aurora, Ill., 1913; p. Claus and Anna Nelson Anderson; h. Harold E. White; res: 9S 281 Aero Dr., Naperville, Ill. 60540.

WHITE, HEDY KELLER, Sr. Ed., Pet Digest, Penthouse Periodicals, Inc. 312 W. 73rd St., N.Y., N.Y. 10023, '58–; VP, Penthouse Periodicals, '57–; Ed., Our Pet World, '50–'58; Free-lance Wtr., '41–'50; various orgs., aws.; First Nat. Univ., BS (Educ.), '36 (summa cum laude); b. N.Y.C., 1920; p. Maurice and Molly Sloane Keller; h. Dean Casey White; res: 312 W. 73rd St., N.Y., N.Y. 10023.

WHITE, HELYN HILL, Mgr., Adv. Dev., Saturday Review, 380 Madison Ave., N.Y., N.Y. 10017, '60–; Nat. Adv. Mgr.; Adv. Dir., United Nations World; Dir., Bk. Adv., New York Post; Colmst., Feature Wtr., San Francisco Chronicle; Talent, KQW (S.F., Cal.); Wtr., Houston (Tex.) Post, Dallas (Tex.) News; Bdcstr., Wtr., KPRC, KTRH, KXYZ (Houston); AAF, AWNY, Tex. Club of N.Y.C. (Pres., '68–'70); Univ. of Tex.; b. Marquez, Tex.; p. Arthur and Mary Rankin Hill; h. (div.); res: 155 E. 52nd St., N.Y., N.Y. 10022.

WHITE, HILDA CRYSTAL, Auth: "Song Without End" (E. P. Dutton, '59), "Wild Decembers" (E. P. Dutton, '57); Assn. For Performing Arts; b. Okla. City, Okla., 1917; p. Sam and Rose Kaplan Crystal; h.

Arthur White; c. Mrs. Catherine Kahn, Julie Anne White; res: Northridge Rd., Box 62, Shrub Oak, N.Y. 10578.

WHITE, JEAN MARIE, Nat. Staff Rptr., Washington Post, 1515 L St., N.W., Wash., D.C. 20005, '53–; WNPC; several Pg. One aws., Wash. nwsp. clubs; Catherine O'Brien Aw., '68; Buchnell, BA (summa cum laude), '50; Columbia Grad. Sch. of Jnlsm., MS, '53 (Phi Beta Kappa); res: 3800 Reno Rd., N.W., Wash., D.C. 20008.

WHITE, JOAN, Contemporary Ed., The Denver Post, 15th & California Sts., Denver, Colo. 80201, '65–; Wms. Dept., '63–'64; Colo. Silver Bell Aw., '67; State Mental Health Aw., '68; Mount Mercy Col., '58–'60; Regis Col.; b. Chgo., Ill., 1940; p. Leo and Helen Blake White; res: 115 Clarkson St., Denver, Colo. 80218.

WHITE, JOAN MARGARET, Adm. Asst. to the Pres., Market Sense, Inc., 920 Winton Rd. S., Rochester, N.Y. 14618, '69–; Dir., Bdcst. Prod., Hutchins Adv., '64–'68; Prom. and Sls. Asst., WHEC, '60–'64; AWRT; Intl. Film & TV Festival of N.Y. Bronze Medal, '67; various aws., Rochester Art Dirs. Club; Lasell Jr. Col., '60; b. Rochester, N.Y., 1941; p. John and Doris Burton White; res: 3110 Elmwood Ave., Rochester, N.Y. 14618.

WHITE, JOAN STOUT, VP, AE, Jay Scott Associates, 1420 Union Ave., P.O. Box 4065, Memphis, Tenn. 38104, '63–; AE, Rosengarten and Steinke, '59–'63; Fashion Coordr., B. Lowenstein's, '56–'59; Soc. Ed., Independence (Kan.) Daily Reporter, '54–'56; Talent, Copy, Traffic, KSEK (Pittsburg, Kan.) '52–'53; Fashion Coordr., Special Events Dir., Wieboldt's, (Chgo., Ill.), '47–'52; Memphis Ad Club (Dir., '64–'68; Wm. of Yr., '65), AWRT; Knox Col., BA, '47; b. Chgo., Ill., 1926; p. William and Mary Sternshein Stout; c. Peter B.; res: 1347 Harbert, Memphis, Tenn. 38104.

WHITE, LAURA, Feature Wtr., Herald Traveler, Boston, Mass. 02106, '65–; Auth., "How to Enjoy Yourself in Boston and Cambridge" guidebk., '68; New Eng. Wms. Press Assn. (Pres., '69–'70), Boston Press Club; Cit. from Army for articles recruiting med. pers. for Vietnam; Northeastern Univ.; res: 236 Newbury St., Boston, Mass. 02116.

WHITE, MARGOT TRAYLOR, Asst. Dir., PR, American Red Cross, Houston-Harris County Chapter, 2006 Smith, Houston, Tex. 77002, '68–; Edtl. Asst., PR, '67–'68; Free-lance Scriptwtr., films; Houston Adv. Club, River Oaks BPW, Theta Sigma Phi, Southeast Tex. Indsl. Eds.; Univ. of Houston, BA (Jnlsm.), '66; b. Tyler, Tex., 1944; p. John and Margot Fitzgerald Traylor; h. Gordie L. White II; res: 1714 Wroxton Ct., Houston, Tex. 77005.

WHITE, MARJORIE POHL, Colmst., Los Angeles Herald Examiner, 1111 S. Broadway, L.A., Cal. 90015,

'39–; Contrbr., articles on sports, entertainment, to various nwsps., mags.; Desert Press Club; Mills Col., BA, '32; b. Redlands, Cal.; p. Egmont and Kate Grant Pohl; h. T. Robert White; res: 245 W. El Portal, Palm Springs, Cal. 92262.

WHITE, MARY JANUARY, Off. Mgr., Bdcst. Rep., The Tacher Company, 1730 S.W. Skyline Blvd., Portland, Ore. 97221, '68–; Media Byr. Geyer, Oswald, Inc., '64–'68; AWRT; Brigham Young Univ., '56–'57; b. Coos Bay, Ore., 1939; p. George and Lillie Butler January; h. Larry White; c. Susan Janis, Max Kevin; res: 7215 S.W. 195th St., Beaverton, Ore. 97005.

WHITE, NANCY, Ed.-in-Chief, Harper's Bazaar, Hearst Corp., 717 Fifth Ave., N.Y., N.Y. 10022, '57–; Fashion Ed., Good Housekeeping, '47–'57; Pictorial Review; Fashion Group (Advisory Comm., past Pres.), President's Cncl., Anti-Defamation League; Lighthouse Wm. of the Yr., '68; Italian govt. aw.; Spanish govt. aw.; h. Ralph D. Paine Jr.

WHITE, NANCY BEAN, Auth., children's bk., "Meet John F. Kennedy" (Random House, '64); Asst. Ed., New York Times Sunday Magazine, '58–'60; Free-lance Wtr., '48–'53; Rschr., Life Magazine, '45–'48; Off. of War Info., '43–'45; Sweet Briar Col., BA, '43; b. Hartford, Conn., 1922; p. George and Adelaide Bostelmann Bean; h. Theodore H. White; c. Ariana van der Heyden, David Fairbank; res: 168 E. 64th St., N.Y., N.Y. 10021.

WHITE, PHYLLIS RUTH, Pubcty. Dir., Fawcett World Library, 67 W. 44th St., N.Y., N.Y. 10036, '69–; Asst. Pubcty. Dir., '66–'69; Secy., Asst. to Pubcty. Dir., New Am. Lib., '65–'66; Publrs. Pubcty. Assn.; Am. Univ., BA (PR, Jnlsm.), '65; b. Bklyn., N.Y., 1943; p. Albert and Betty Becker White.

WHITE, ROSEMARY BRANDENBURG, Bdcst. Byr., Cole & Weber, Inc., 220 S.W. Morrison St., Portland, Ore. 97204, '69–; Asst. AE, Exec. Secy., Acc. Secy., '67–'69; Partner, McMurphey & White Adv.; Ore. Food Merchants Assn.; Ore. Adv. Club, Wms. Adv. Club, AWRT; b. N.O., La., 1940; p. Barney and Ina Case Brandenburg; h. Richard Hedrick White; res: 2615 N.E. 40th Ave., Portland, Ore. 97212.

WHITE, RUTH BEELER, PR Dir., Leake and Watts, Inc., 463 Hawthorne Ave., Yonkers, N.Y. 10705, '67–; PR Cnslt., '64–'67; Dir., Wms. Program Div., Am. Petroleum Inst., '58–'64; PR Cnslt., CCI, '57–'58; Commty. Cnslt., Health Ins. Plan of Greater N.Y., '54–'56; Copy Ed., House and Garden, '53; Staff Exec., Nat. Fedn. BPW Clubs, '49–'53; Exec. Comm., Cncl. of Nat. Orgs. on Adult Educ.; Cncl. of Cnslts., Pres. Comm. on Highway Safety, '62–'64; Am. Mgt. Assn., Modern Lang. Assn., PRSA, Eng. Grad. Union, Gamma Alpha Chi; Univ. of Mo., BJ, '37; Washington Univ., MA, '47; Columbia Univ., PhD, '66; b. Cabool, Mo.; p. James Walter and Myrtle Forrester Beeler; c. Buel; res: 258 Riverside Dr., N.Y., N.Y. 10025.

WHITE, RUTH MARGARET, Exec. Secy., Adult Svcs. Div. and Ref. Svcs. Div., American Library Association, 50 E. Huron St., Chgo., Ill. 60611, '68–; Hq. Librn., '63–'67; Asst. to Exec. Secy., '58–'62; Librn., '41–'58; ALA, Special Libs. Assn., Ill. Lib. Assn., Pi Lambda Theta, Beta Phi Mu; Oh. State Univ., BS (Educ.), '35; Case-Western Reserve Univ., BS (Lib. Sci.), '38; Univ. of Chgo., AM, '63; b. Ludlow, Ky., 1914; p. Carl and Mary Irvin White; res: 5518 S. Cornell Ave., Chgo., Ill. 60637.

WHITE, SALLY FOX, Textile Fiber Cnslt., The Merchandising Group, Inc., 477 Madison Ave., N.Y., N.Y. 10022, '67–; Retail Prom. Acc. Mgr., '50–'67; Adv. Mgr., Meacham's (Ft. Worth, Tex.), '48–'49; Wms. Ed., KGKL Radio (San Angelo, Tex.), '47; Fashion Copy Chief, Joske's (San Antonio, Tex.), '46; Adv. Mgr., Daily Texan (Austin), '44–'46; Fashion Group (Reg. Dir., '57 and '67), Theta Sigma Phi (Chptr. Pres., '49–'50), AAUW, BPW, Atlanta Press Club; Sigma Delta Chi wms. press aw., '46; Univ. of Tex., BJ, '46; b. Waxahachie, Tex.; p. J. Gilbert and Nelia Carter Fox; h. Joseph A. White; c. Clair F.; res: 224 Franklin Rd. N.E., Atlanta, Ga. 30305.

WHITE, VIRGINIA BETTS, Asst. to the Pres., AE, Hausman Publications, Inc., 11901 Olive Blvd., Creve Coeur, Mo. 63141, '68–; Dir. PR, St. Louis Public Lib., '63–'68; Wms. Club News Ed., St. Louis Post-Dispatch, '62–'65; Dir. special PR, St. Louis Univ., '59–'62; Dir. News Bur., Ed., Alumni Magazine, Washington Univ., '41–'58; Ed., South Side Journal, '40–'41; various orgs., aws.; Washington Univ., AB (Phi Beta Kappa), '40; b. St. Louis, Mo., 1918; p. Benjamin and Hazel Deffry Betts; h. Buel White; res: 7736 Blackberry Lane, University City, Mo. 63130.

WHITEHEAD, IDELLE ROBERSON, Librn., Arkansas A & M College, Box 1119, Col. Heights Br., Monticello, Ark. 71655, '64–; Asst. Librn., E. Tex. Baptist Col., '57–'64; Tchr., '31–'57; Ark. Educ. Assn., AAUW, Ark. Lib. Assn.; active in commty. health groups; E. Tex. Baptist Col., BS, '60; E. Tex. Univ., MS (Lib. Sci.), '63; b. Elk City, Okla., 1912; p. John and Anna Campbell Roberson. h. Shelby A. Whitehead; c. Victor Shelby, John Martin, Rodney Lee; res: P.O. Box 563, College Heights, Ark. 71655.

WHITEHEAD, LEATRICE JOY, PR Dir., Goodwin, Dannenbaum, Littman and Wingfield, Inc., 2400 West Loop S., Houston, Tex. 77027, '60–; Pubcty. Coordr., Foley's, '58–'60; Pubcty. Dir., Asst. to Fashion Coordr., Battelstein's, '56–'58; Adv. Prod. Mgr., Sakowitz, '52–'54; Brown Radio Prods., Nashville, Tenn., '51–'52; Copywtr., John Gerber Co., '50–'51; Wms. Pg. Ed., Big Spring (Tex.) Daily Herald, '48–'50; PRSA, Press Club of Houston (Dir., '68); Howard Country Jr. Col., '46–'48; Univ. of Tex. (Jnlsm.), '48–'50; b. Big Spring, Tex., 1927; p. Leonard and Beatrice McNew Carlton; h. Robert George Whitehead; c. Ryne P. Lilly; res: 6427 Buffalo Speedway, Houston, Tex. 77005.

WHITEHEAD, MARY INGRAHAM, Free-lance Prod. Coordr., Stylist, Designer; '68–; Stylist, Melvin Sokolsky, '68; Stylist, Doyle, Dane, Bernbach, '67; Stylist, J. Walter Thompson, '65–'66; Graphics Design, Glen of Mich., '64; Sportswear Designer, Sacony, '63; Apparel Designer, Alex Colman, '62; Costume Designer, Blue Hill Troupe, '66–; R.I. Sch. of Design, BFA, '62; b. Princeton, N.J., 1940; p. Robert and Jane Willis Whitehead; res: 27 E. 92nd St., N.Y., N.Y. 10028.

WHITELAW, ELEANOR BOYD, News Dir., Columbus Broadcasting Company, 1350 13th St., Columbus, Ga. 31902, '69–; Prodr., Dir., Wtr., numerous half-hr. shows (two Inst. Aws., '68, '69), Auburn Univ. ETV, '66–'69; Talent, Sister Alice, Capote's "The Thanksgiving Visitor," ABC, '69; Copy Wtr., Talent, Bdcstr., Program Dir., Sls., Prom., Photogr., News Ed., WRBL, '54–'66; Sls. Exec., Bdcstr., WAUD, '53–'54; Sls. Mgr., Bdcstr., WJHO, '50–'52; Copy Wtr., Bdcstr., '38–'39; Program Dir., Sls. Rep. Bdcstr., WPCF, '48–'50; Copy Dir., Bdcstr., WABB, '46–'48; free-lance copy wtr., bdcstr., '44–'46; tchr., '36–'40; AWRT (Chattahoochee Valley Chptr. Pres.), Radio-TV News Dirs. Assn., NAEB, AAUW, Who's Who of Am. Wm., numerous orgs., many commty. and writing cits. and aws.; Auburn Univ., BS (Educ.), '36; b. Elba, Ala., 1914; p. Ja Penn and AnnaRosa McGee Boyd; h. G. Mills Whitelaw (div.); c. A. Boyd (Mrs. Ernest Brown, Jr.), E. Drake; res: 1106 Henry Ave., Columbus, Ga. 31906.

WHITESIDE, RUTH KINYON, Mng. Dir., Founder, Overseas Features Ltd., 32 Lexington St., London, W1, Eng., '60–; J. Walter Thompson (N.Y.C.), Charles W. Hoyt Co.; Wms. Press Club of London, Intl. Wm. in Radio & TV (Past Dir., Treas.), Wms. Adv. Club of N.Y. (Past Dir., Treas.), AFA, Gamma Alpha Chi (Nat. Pres., '45–'47); Univ. of Mo., BJ, '38; b. Kan. City, Mo., 1914; p. Henry and Mabel Browne Kinyon; h. Robert Fisher; res: Paddocks Green, Picketts Lane, Salfords, Surrey, Eng.

WHITFORD, MARIE DEADY, Social Ed., The Saratogian, 20 Lake Ave., Saratoga Springs, N.Y. 12866, '63–; Wms. Press Club of N.Y., Catholic Daughters of Am.; active in commty. affairs; b. Phila., Pa.; p. Hughie and Marion Ricklie Deady; h. Arthur Whitford; c. Robert Renn, James Dennis; res: 54 Webster St., Saratoga Springs, N.Y. 12866.

WHITING, BEATRICE BLYTH, Ed., Six Culture Series (studies of child rearing in non-Western world); Lectr. on Educ., Harvard Graduate School of Education; Rsch. Assoc., Center for the Behavioral Sciences, 458 William James Hall, Harvard University, Cambridge, Mass. 02138, '69–; Rsch. Assoc. in Social Rels., Lectr. in Social Anthropology, '63–'69; Rsch. Assoc., Lab. of Human Dev.; Human Rels. Svc. of Wellesley Rsch. Staff, '51–'53; Lectr. in Social Rels., Brandeis Univ., '49–'52; Rsch. Assoc., Child Dev. Rsch. Unit, Univ. Col., Nairobi, Kenya; numerous pfsnl. orgs.; Bryn Mawr, AB, '35; Yale Univ., PhD (Anthropology), '43; b. S.I., N.Y., 1914; p. Bertram and Bertha Read Blyth; h. John W. M. Whiting; c. Susan B.; res: 15 Robinson St., Cambridge, Mass. 02138.

WHITLOCK, BETTY, Pres., Carlocke/Langden, Inc., 505 N. Ervay Bldg., Dallas, Tex. 75201, '64–; Exec. VP, '62–'64; VP, '60–'62; Asst. Adv. Dir., Southern Union Gas Co., '53–'59; Adv. Dir., Ashley-Mexican Foods, '52–'53; Adv. Dir., Billy the Kid Boyswear, '50–'52; AE, White & Shuford Adv., '47–'50; Asst. AE, Mithoff & White Adv., '44–'47; BPW ('43–'47), Dallas Adv. League (Dir., '60–'63), Adv. Club of Dallas (Dir., '60–'63), AWRT, Press Club of Dallas, ZONTA Intl.; Dallas Adv. Wm. of the Yr., '65; Theta Sigma Phi Matrix Aw., '66; W. Tex. State Univ., BS, '43; b. Wichita Falls, Tex., 1921; p. Robert and Minnie Prince Whitlock; res: 6912 Arboreal Dr., Dallas, Tex. 75231.

WHITMAN, VIRGINIA BRUNER, Outdoor Colmst., News-Leader, Springfield, Mo., 65801, '55–; Auth: "Devotionals for All Occasions" (Moody Press, '59), "Ozark Obie" (Broadman, '61), "Illustrations from Nature" (Baker Bk. House, '65), "Vengeance Afoot" (Zondervan, '66), other bks.; various aws.; Univ. of Kan. City, BA, MA (distinction); b. Colo. Springs, Colo.; p. Charles and Mary Palmer Bruner; h. Edwin W. Whitman; c. B. L.; res: Eden Acres, Climax Springs, Mo. 65324.

WHITMIRE, ANN, Prod. Mgr., Midland Advertising, 1100 First Nat. Bank Bldg., Cinn., Oh. 45202, '67–; Rowe & Wymar Adv., '66–'67; Fashion Frocks, '41–'66; Miami Univ., BFA, '50; grad. work, Cinn. Art Acad.; b. Cinn., Oh., 1929; p. Julius and Charlotte Froerdhoff Whitmire; res: 3526 Pembroke, Cinn., Oh. 45208.

WHITNEY, CE CE, Actress, Armstrong-Deuser Agency, 425 S. Beverly Dr., Beverly Hills, Cal.; TV: 187 shows; Theatre: "Rainmaker," "The Odd Couple," "Born Yesterday," "Miracle Worker"; SAG, AFTRA, AEA, Actors Studio West, Theatre East, Theatre Guild; Univ. of Cal., Pasadena Playhouse; b. Shawnee, Okla., 1933; p. Cecil and Myrtle Powers Shipman; h. Jimmy Zito (div.); res: 840 N. Ogden Dr., L.A., Cal. 90046.

WHITNEY, ELMA AURELIA, Asst. Librn., Capital University, 2199 E. Main St., Columbus, Oh. 43209, '67–; Librn., '32–'67; ALA, Oh. Lib. Assn. (Pres., '58–'59), Ohioana Lib. Assn., Columbus Altrusa Club, Delta Sigma Rho; active in numerous civic groups; Oh. State Univ., BS (Educ.), '30; Western Reserve Univ., '32; b. Columbus, Oh.; p. James and Daisy Ball Whitney; res: 3105 Oakridge Rd., Columbus, Oh. 43221.

WHITNEY, EUNICE ENGLEKE, Mktng. Engineer, Lockheed Aircraft Corp., 2555 Hollywood Way, Burbank, Cal. 91503, '69–; Ed., Lockheed-Cal. Co., '60–'69; Pubns. Engineer, Lockheed Missiles and Space Co., '57–'60; Mng. Ed., Palos Verdes News,

'51–'52; Dir., Educ. Bur., Los Angeles Times, '50–'51; Am. Astronautical Soc., Soc. of Tech. Wtrs. and Publrs., Phi Delta Delta; CNPA Special Editions aw., '51; Stanford Univ., BA, '36; Stanford Univ. Sch. of Law, '36–'38; Stanford Univ. Grad. Sch. of Bus., '38–'39; b. Taft, Cal., 1914; p. Walter and Eunice Causey Engelke; h. George Whitney; c. George Anne; res: 12648 Darla Ave., Granada Hills, Cal. 91344.

WHITNEY, PHYLLIS AYAME, Auth: "Mystery of the Crimson Ghost" ('70), "The Winter People" ('69), 44 other juv.; adult bks.; Children's Bk. Ed., Chicago Sun; Philadelphia Inquirer; Instr., Juv. Writing, N.Y.U., '47–'58; WNBA, MWA, Midland Auths, Children's Reading Round Table; numerous aws. for bks.; b. Yokohama, Japan; p. Charles and Lilian Mandeville Whitney; h. L. F. Jahnke; c. Mrs. Georgia Pearson; res: N.J.

WHITNEY, RUTH REINKE, Ed.-in-Chief, Glamour, Conde Nast Publications, Inc., 420 Lexington Ave., N.Y., N.Y. 10017, '67–; formerly Exec. Ed., Assoc. Ed., Seventeen; Ed.-in-Chief, Better Living; Copywtr., Time, Inc.; Fashion Group, ASME (Exec. Comm.), Alpha Chi Omega; Northwestern Univ., BA (Eng.), '49 (Dept. Hons.); b. Oshkosh, Wis., 1928; p. Leonard and Helen Diestler Reinke; h. Daniel Whitney; c. Philip; res: Riverview Rd., Irvington, N.Y. 10533.

WHITTAKER, ALMA TEELE, Wtr.; Dir.-Ed., Monthly Newsletter, Springfield Gardens Community Center, 121–65 Farmers Blvd., Springfield Gardens, N.Y. 11413, '67–; Guest Colmst., Queens Voice, '69; Feature Wtr., Elegant Teen, '66; Colmst., New York Courier; Lectr.; various orgs., aws.; Va. Union Univ., '31–'35; Temple Univ., '43; N.Y.U., '54; b. Richmond, Va., 1916; p. Joseph and Bessie Scott Teele; h. Virgil Whittaker; c. Sylvester E. Dance, Jr.; res: 111–31 144th St., Jamaica, N.Y. 11435.

WHITTINGHILL, LIZABETH (Ann) WILSON, Wms. Ed., Messenger and Inquirer, 1401 Frederica St., Owensboro, Ky. 42301, '61–; formerly Classified Cl., Proof Reader, Librn., Reptr., Soc. Asst.; Nat. Soc. of Interior Designers (Press Mbr.); Va. Polytechnic Inst., '49–'51 (Pi Delta Epsilon); Brescia Col., BS (Eng.), '59 (Jnlsm., Eng. Aws.); b. Frankfort, Ky., 1931; p. Charles Russell and Elizabeth Marshall Wilson; h. T. D. Whittinghill; res: 2121 Bittel Rd., Owensboro, Ky. 42301.

WHITTINGTON, EDNA, Asst. Supvsr., TV Opns., WCAU-TV, City Line and Monument Aves., Phila., Pa. 19131; WRCV; WVCH (Chester, Pa.); AWRT, Bdcst. Pioneers; Sch. of Design for Wm., '31; b. N.Y.C.; p. Arthur and Mary Jordan Whittington; c. Karl, Judith Ann (Mrs. O. J. Kralovec); res: 61 Sayers Ave., Lansdowne, Pa. 19050.

WICKENDEN, ELIZABETH, Prof. of Urban Studies, City University of New York, Graduate Center, 33 W. 42nd St., N.Y., N.Y. 10036, '68–; Social Policy Cnslt.,

Nat. Assembly for Social Policy and Dev., '53–; Cnslt. to numerous agcys., '51–'59; Wash. Rep., Am. Public Welfare Assn., '40–'51; various exec. positions in the fed. govt., '32–'40; Auth., articles on urban studies; numerous orgs., aws.; Vassar Col., grad., '31; b. Wis.; p. William and Marion Lamb Wickenden; h. Arthur Goldschmidt; c. Arthur, Jr., Mrs. Raymond Richardson, Mrs. J. M. Kempton, Jr.; res: 544 E. 86th St., N.Y., N.Y. 10028.

WICKER, IREENE, Wtr., Singer, Radio and TV Talent, 667 Madison Ave., N.Y., N.Y. 10021; wkly. radio program, WNYC-AM and FM, '59–; with Shakespearian group, Am. Theatre Wing, and with Stella Adler and Joseph Kramm, '55–'56; Co-dir., "Merry-Go-Round Children's Theatre," ABC-TV, '51–'54; Originator, Wtr., Talent, "Singing Lady," radio program; "Ireene Wicker Music Plays," NBC and Mutual; others; dramatic staff, CBS, '32–'36; at Goodman Theatre (Chgo., Ill.), '30–'32; child actress in stock; Talent, 12 Golden Bk. Records, recordings by Regal, Deluxe, Decca, Victor, Mercury, others; Auth., bks., plays, songs for children; numerous high hons. for children's radio programs; Bdcst. Pioneers, AWRT, NATAS, IRTS, Auths. Guild, Auths. League, Intl. Platform Assn.; Univ. of Ill., one yr.; Goodman Theatre Sch. and Chgo. Art Inst., '27–'30; b. Quincy, Ill., p. Kenner and Margaret Hunsaker Seaton; h. 1. Walter C. Wicker 2. Victor J. Hammer; c. Walter Charles, Nancy; res: 781 Fifth Ave., N.Y., N.Y. 10022.

WICKHAM, MYRTICE MORRIS, Supvsr. and Coordr. of Libs., Mount Pleasant School District, Washington St. Ext. and Marsh Rd., Wilmington, Del. 19809, '58–; Librn., '52–'58; Librn., N.Y. State Jr. Col. (Middletown, N.Y.), '50–'51; Ext. Librn., Univ. of Tenn., '30–'31; Ref. Librn. (Boise, Idaho), '27–'29; Librn. (Sherman, Tex.), '23–'26; ALA, Del. Lib. Assn. (Pres.), Del. State Educ. Assn. (Pres., Sch. Lib.), NEA, Del. Hist. Soc., Del. Archaeology Soc., Delta Kappa Gamma; Baylor Univ., AB, '23; Columbia Sch. of Lib. Sci., BS, '27; Grad Work: Rutgers, Drexel, Univ. of Del., Univ. of Ill.; b. Denison, Tex., 1901; p. Herman and Lucy Haskell Morris; h. G. Dorrance Wickham; c. Robert D, Francis C.; res: 1100 Brandywine Blvd., Wilmington, Del. 19809.

WICKS, MARIETT ROLLESTON, Copy Chief, WCSC-TV, 485 E. Bay St., Charleston, S.C., '65–; Copy Dir., Harry Gianaris & Assoc., '60–'65; Copy Chief, WCSC-TV, '59–'60; Copywtr., '58–'59; Free-lance Wtr., documentary films; AWRT; Univ. of Mich., AB, '43; b. Detroit, Mich., 1922; p. Elias and Nancy Bird Rolleston; h. Rev. Earl Stuart Wicks; c. Deborah (Mrs. Arthur Lenwood Williams III), Raynor Kirby; res: 147-A Church St., Charleston, S.C. 29401.

WICKWIRE, NANCY, Actress, Stage, Broadway, Off-Broadway, Bahamas, N.Y. Shakespeare Festival, Am. Shakespeare Festival, Boston, Bucks County; Tyrone Guthrie Theatre (Mpls.), TV, Records; Obie Aws: "Cherry Orchard" ('55), "Clearing in the Woods" ('59); Lola D'Annuzio Aw., '62; Carnegie Inst. of Tech., Sch. of Drama, BA, '48; Old Vic. Sch., London, '49–'51; b. Harrisburg, Pa.; p. Alva and Ruth Larson Wickwire; res: 39 W. 56th St., N.Y, N.Y. 10019.

WIDENER, MARY McNUTT, Assoc. Ed., Changing Times Magazine, Kiplinger Washington Editors, Inc., 1729 H St. N.W., Wash., D.C. 20006, '64–; Pubcty. Dir., '59–'64; Rsch. Dir., Nat. Repl. Congressional Campaign Comm., '55–'59; Digest Ed., Citizens Comm. for the Hoover Repts., '54–'55; Fashion Ed., Richmond News Leader (Va.), '51–'53; Fashion Ed., Reptr., Bristol Va.-Tennessean, '49–'51; Herald Courier, '46–'47; ANWC; Boston Col. Ctr. for the study of franchise distrb. aw., '68; Sullins Col., '44; Univ. of N.C., BA (Jnlsm.), '46; b. Abingdon, Va., 1925; p. H. Emory and Douglas Peck Widener; res: 1600 S. Eads St., Arlington, Va. 22202.

WIDIGER, JAN STRASZHEIM, Owner, Promotive Arts, 701 Coolidge Dr., Midland, Mich. 48640, '58–; Publicist, Dow Chemical Co., '53–'58; AWRT, Am. Mktng. Assn. (Saginaw Valley Chptr. Secy., '68–'69); ZONTA (Midland Club Pres., '65–'67, VP, '63–'65, Treas., '69–'70, '62–'63); Purdue Univ., BS, '49; Ind. Univ., MBA (Mktng.), '53; b. Columbus, Oh., 1929; p. Robert and Clara Shepherd Straszheim; h. A. T. Widiger.

WIDMANN, NANCY CLIFFORD, Sr. Bdcst. Byr., Needham, Harper & Steers, Inc., 909 Third Ave., N.Y., N.Y. 10022, '67–; Sales Asst., Metro Radio Sales, '65–'67; Regis Col., BA (Eng.); b. Boston, Mass., 1942; p. Arthur and Eileen McCabe Clifford; h. Anthony Widmann; res: 1148 Fifth Ave., N.Y., N.Y. 10028.

WIEBE, PHYLLIS KUSMAUL, Lib. Dir., Englewood Public Library, 3400 E. Elati St., Englewood, Colo. 80110, '66–; Adult Svcs. Librn., '63–'66; Instr., Lib. Sci., Northwest Mo. State Col., '60–'62; Bibliographer, Univ. of Denver Libs., '58–'60; AAUP, AAUW, ALA, Colo. Lib. Assn., Univ. of Denver, BA, '59; MA, '61; b. Emporia, Kan., 1929; p. Carl and Esther McDaniel Kusmaul; c. Cynthia Renee, Greta Christine; res: 2730 S. Lafayette, Denver, Colo. 80210.

WIEMAN, JEAN, Supvsr. of Learning Resources Svcs., Superintendent of Public Instruction, P.O. Box 528, Olympia, Wash. 98501; Alpha Delta Kappa, ALA, Wash. Lib. Assn., Wash. State Assn. of Sch. Librns., Wash. Educ. Assn., Fed. Way Educ. Assn., NEA; Seattle Pacific, BA (Educ.), '54 (cum laude); Pacific Lutheran; Univ. of Wash., MS (Lib. Sci.), '62; grad. work at several cols. and univs.

WIESNER, MALINDA HAWKINS, Fashion Ed., The Des Moines Register and Tribune, 715 Locust St., Des Moines, Ia. 50304, '63–; Ia. State Univ., '63 (Outstanding Young Alumnus Aw., '68); b. Ames, Ia., 1941; p. Lewis and Harriet Olsen Hawkins; h. Douglas Wiesner; res: 1904 75th St., Des Moines, Ia. 50322.

WIGHT, KAY JEANNETTE, Coordr. Commty. Rels.,

WCBS-TV, Columbia Broadcasting System, 51 W. 52nd St., N.Y., N.Y. 10019, '67–; TV Opns. Dept., '65–'66; Prod. Asst., CBS News, '64–'65; Secy. to Chmn. of the Bd., '63–'64; AWRT, Theta Sigma Phi (Treas., '64–'65), Pi Beta Phi; Wash. State Univ., BA (Speech), '63; b. Tacoma, Wash., 1941; p. Thomas and Faye Nelson Wight; res: 301 E. 64th St., N.Y., N.Y. 10021.

WILBUR, JUDYTHE E., Dir. of Commtns., Boston Mutual Life Insurance Co., 156 Stuart St., Boston, Mass. 02116, '67–; Pubns. Asst., '66–'67; Mng. Ed., Cape Cod Illustrated, '66; Assoc. Ed., Poor Howard's Wednesday Afternoon Post, '66; Adv. Club of Greater Boston, Mass. IEA, ICIE, Life Advs. Assn.; Syracuse Univ., BA (Jnlsm., Sociol.), '66; b. Rutland, Vt., 1944; p. Roscoe and Bernecia Doty Wilbur; res: 163 Beacon St., Boston, Mass. 02116.

WILBUR, RUTH JORDAN, Advisory Mbr., Marquis Biographical Library Society; Theta Sigma Phi, Who's Who of Am. Wm.; Stanford Univ., BA, '27; (with distinction); S.F., Cal., 1907; p. Benjamin and Laura Ireland Jordan; h. Dwight L. Wilbur, M.D.; c. Dwight Locke, III, Jordan Rockwood, Gregory Fiske; res: 140 Sea Cliff Ave., S.F., Cal. 94121.

WILCOX, ELEANOR REINDOLLAR, Free-lance Artist and Wtr.; Partner, Wilcox and Wilcox (indsl. illus.), '46–; Auth: "Cornhusk Doll" (Dodd, Mead, '56; Libs. Aw.), "Mr. Sims' Argosy" (Dodd, Mead, '58); Tchr., Balt. City Public Schs., '63–'67; PR, Park Sch. of Balt., '56–'59; Librn., '41–'46; Exhibits Asst., Enoch Pratt Free Lib., '36–'41; Johns Hopkins Univ. (crtv. writing; hon.), '34; Md. Inst., Fine and Applied Arts, '35; b. Balt., Md., 1915; p. William and Marcella Atkinson Reindollar; h. George C. Wilcox, Jr.; c. David William; res: 4006 Liberty Heights Ave., Balt., Md. 21207.

WILCOX, MELISSE, Traffic Supvsr., KIRO Television, Broadcast House, Third and Broad, Seattle, Wash. 98121, '63–; Dir. of Continuity Acceptance and Public Svc., KPIX-TV (S.F., Cal.), '61–'62; Program Asst., KING (Seattle), '60–'61; AWRT (Chptr. Pres., '69, VP, '68; Secy., '67), NATAS, Theta Sigma Phi; Wash. State Univ., BA (Radio-TV, Speech), '60; Univ. of Wash., '63–'64; b. Seattle, Wash., 1939; p. Milo and Gertrude Janson Wilcox; res: 2616 58th Ave. S.W., Seattle, Wash. 98121.

WILCOX, VIRGINIA LEE, Head Librn., Colorado School of Mines, Arthur Lakes Library, Golden, Colo. 80401, '56–; Acting Librn., '55–'56, Asst. Librn., '46–'55; Army Librn., '43–'46; Tech. Librn., '37–'40; Auth., "Colorado: A Selected Bibliography of its Literature, 1858–1952" (Sage Bks.), '54; others; Special Libs. Assn., Am. Soc. for Engineering Educ., Colo. State Hist. Soc.; Univ. of Denver, AB, '37; MA, '53; b. Portsmouth, Oh., 1911; p. Lloyd and Sallye Foley Wilcox; res: 792 S. Youngfield Ct., Denver, Colo. 80228.

WILDER, ULAH, Head Librn., Oakland City College, Oakland City, Ind. 47560, '62–; Asst. Librn., '56–'62; Tchr., Lib. Sci., '66–; ALA, Ind. Lib. Assn., Alpha Beta Alpha; Oakland City Col., BA (cum laude), '56; Ind. State Univ., MA, '59; b. Winslow, Ind., 1916; res: 218 N. Clay, Oakland City, Ind. 47560.

WILDS, NANCY ALEXANDER, Pres., Rose Hill Studio, 245 Greenville St. N.W., Aiken, S.C. 29801, '68–; Designer, stained glass windows, Binswanger Studio, '48–'49; Designer, church furnishings; Auth., "Church Grounds and Gardens" (Seabury Press), '64); Univ. of Chgo., PhB, '45; b. Little Rock, Ark., 1926; p. George and Gladys McCollough Alexander; h. Preston L. Wilds (div.); c. Ellen S., Alexander, Stephanie.

WILEY, MARCIA DELIER, Mng. Ed., Yachting Publishing Corp., 50 W. 44th St., N.Y., N.Y. 10036, '64–; Assoc. Ed., '46–'64; Sweet Briar Col., '37–'39; Conn. Col., BA, '41; b. Bellrose, N.Y., 1918; p. Harry and Nona Regnier Wiley; res: 201 E. 79th St., N.Y., N.Y. 10021.

WILEY, MARGARET LENORE, Auth; Prof. of Eng., Brooklyn College of the City University of New York, Bklyn., N.Y. 11210, '67–; bks: "The Subtle Knot" (Allen and Unwin, London, '52), "Creative Sceptics" ('66); Lectr., Asst. and Assoc. Prof., '46–'67; Student Advisor, New Sch. for Social Rsch., '44–'46; Head of Eng. Dept., Emerson Col., Boston, '38–'43; High Sch. Tchr., Ore., '33–'36; Grad. Asst., Univ. of Ore., '32–'33; Reed Col., '29–'31; Modern Lang. Assn.; AAUW Fellowship, '37; Fulbright Grant to India, '57–'58, '58–'59; Reed Col., AB, '29; MA, '31; Univ. of Chgo., summer sch., '31; Univ. of Ore., '32–'33; Radcliffe Col., PhD, '40 (Phi Beta Kappa); b. Portland, Ore., 1908; p. John and Minnie Burnett Wiley; h. Roderick Marshall; c. Janet, Mrs. Barry Sales; res: 420 Riverside Dr., N.Y., N.Y. 10025.

WILKENS, EMILY, Synd. Colmst., "A New You," King Features, 235 E. 45th St., N.Y., N.Y. 10017, '67–; Auth: "A New You" (G. P. Putnam, '67), "Here's Looking at You" (G. P. Putnam, '59); Lectr.; Fashion Inst. of Tech. (Trustee, Dir.); Costume Inst. (Founder); Coty fashion critics aw., '45; Neiman Marcus aw., '46; Mademoiselle aw., '44; Pratt Inst., '38; b. Hartford, Conn., 1918; p. Morris and Rose Drey Wilkens; h. Irving L. Levey; c. Jane W., Hugh W.; res: 200 East End Ave., N.Y., N.Y. 10028.

WILKERSON, JOY (Joy Wright Cardoza), Actress, Model, Lectr., Glenn Shaw Agency, 8440 Sunset Blvd., L.A., Cal. 90069, '63–; Miss South Vietnam, '66–; Several trips to South Vietnam, aw. from Gen. William Westmoreland, '67; Lockheed Missiles and Space Div. (Van Nuys), '60–'63, '56–'57; U.C.L.A. Med. Ctr., '54–'56; Security 1st Nat. Bank, '52–'54; numerous benefit shows for U.S. charities; U.C.L.A., '49–'51; John Robert Powers Modeling Sch., '64; b. Detroit, Mich., 1930; p. Charles and Vera Hahn Wright; h. Anthony Cardoza; c. Craig D., Candice C., Kimberly C.; res: 4705 Whitsett, N. Hollywood, Cal. 91604.

WILKERSON, MARIE, Owner, Park Avenue Literary Agency, 230 Park Ave., N.Y., N.Y. 10017, '62–; Pres., Dir., '61; Mng. Dir., '60–'61; Secy., Dir., Day-Putnam Corp., '43–'59; WNBA; Who's Who of Am. Wm.; Who's Who in the East; World Who's Who in Commerce and Industry; World Who's Who in Finance and Industry; Hunter Col., BA, '34; b. N.Y.C.; p. Albert and Elizabeth McKendry Wilkerson; res: 321 W. 24th St., N.Y., N.Y. 10011.

WILKES, BONNIE WRIGHT, Radio and TV Prod. Mgr., PR Dir., Beals Advertising Agency, Inc., 4040 N. Lincoln, Okla. City, Okla. 73105, '65–; Wtr./Prodr., Humphrey, Williamson and Gibson, '65; McCord Assocs., '64; Feature Wtr., Gadabout, '64–'65; Newsfilm Ed., KWTV, '54–'56, '58–'60; Contrbr., Les Femmes, '65–; Okla. State Univ., '49–'50 (Hon. Roll); N.Y.U., '50–'52; Univ. of Okla., BA (Spanish, French), '55 (Dean's Hon. Roll, Sigma Delta Pi); b. Sayre, Okla., 1931; p. James and May Hunt Wright; h. Thomas E. Wilkes; c. Thomas A.; res: 2268 N.W. 54th, Okla. City, Okla. 73112.

WILKIE, KATHARINE ELLIOTT, Wtr.; Former Tchr.; Theta Sigma Phi, Mortar Board, Kappa Delta Pi, Chi Delta Phi; Ky. Colonel, '69; Univ. of Ky., BA '24; MA, '39; b. Lexington, Ky., 1904; p. J. Milward and Kate Crockett Elliott; h. Raymond Abell Wilkie; c. Raymond Abell, Jr., Milward Eliott; res: 312 Irvine Rd., Lexington, Ky. 40502.

WILKINSON, FRAULINE WINEGAR, Nat. Adv. Mgr., Glasgow Publishing Corp., 301 S. Green St., Glasgow, Ky. 42141, '57–; Asst. Treas., '66–; b. Glasgow, Ky., 1918; p. John and Alice Polson Winegar; h. James W. Wilkinson; c. Leland (dec.), Jimmy C.; res: 123 St. Mary's Ct., Glasgow, Ky. 42141.

WILL, CHARLOTTE ELMORE, Moving Cnslt., United Van Lines, Inc., One United Dr., Fenton, Mo. 63026, '56–; Home Econst., Philco Distributor, '44–'56; AWRT, Wms. Adv. Club of St. Louis, Am. Home Econs. Assn. (Bd. of Dirs., '67–'68), Nat. Home Econsts. in Bus. (Chmn., '67–'68); Southern Ill. Univ., BA (Educ.); Kappa Delta Pi; b. Murphysboro, Ill., 1918; p. William and Lynn Bonham Elmore; h. Everett C. Will; res: 12026 Conway Rd., St. Louis, Mo. 63131.

WILLENS, DORIS, Dir. PR, Doyle Dane Bernbach Inc., 20 W. 43rd St., N.Y., N.Y. 10036, '69–; PR AE, '66–'69; Copy Ed., Washington Post, '64–'66; Corporate PR, Grey Adv., '61–'63; Colmst., New York Journal-American, '57–'61; Free-lance Wtr., '50–'57; Reptr., Minneapolis Tribune, '47–'48; Ed., Publr. (mag.), '48–'50; singer-songwtr., four children's albums (Vanguard Rec. Soc., '58, '57, '64, '68); Bdcst. Music Inc., PR Roundtable; U.C.L.A., BA, '45; Columbia Grad. Sch. of Jnlsm., MS, '47; b. N.Y.C., 1924; p. Sam and Bertha Heskin Willens; h. Milton Kaplan;

c. Jeffrey, Peter, Dan; res: 64 Edgecliff Terr., Yonkers, N.Y. 10705.

WILLETT, ROSLYN STERNBERG, Pres., Roslyn Willett Associates, 441 West End Ave., N.Y., N.Y. 10024, '59–; Head, Bus. and Indsl. Dept., Farley Manning Assoc., '54–'58; Ed., McGraw-Hill, other publrs., '49–'54; Tchr., Lectr. on PR; Contrbr., numerous articles to mags.; Intl. Soc. of Food Svc. Cnslts., Inst. of Food Tech., Pubcty. Club, Am. Mktg. Assn., Am. Acad. of Polit. and Social Sci., various pfsnl. groups; Hunter Col., BA, '44; b. N.Y.C., 1924; p. Edward and Celia Stickler Sternberg; h. Edward Willett; c. Jonathan.

WILLETTE, MARGARET PIERCE, Adm. Asst., Mission Broadcasting Co., P.O. Box 2338, 317 Arden Grove, San Antonio, Tex. 78206, '66–; Asst. Secy.-Treas., '67–; Mission Central Co. (KONO/KITY-FM; Asst. Secy.-Treas., '67–), Mission East Co. (WWOK, Miami; Dir., Asst. Secy.-Treas.; '68–), Mission Adv. Co. (San Antonio; Dir., Secy.-Treas., '68), Fononews, Inc. Asst. Secy., '67–; AWRT, BPW, Epsilon Sigma Alpha; b. Wichita Falls, Tex., 1931; p. Lee and Lula Cowan Pierce; h. Kenneth Willette; res: 102 Seashell Pl., San Antonio. Tex. 78242.

WILLEY, EDITH MARING, Artist; paintings exhibited in N.Y.C., Wash. D.C., Chgo., Cinn., Dallas, S.F.; one-man show, Frederick & Nelson, '37–'44; works in private collections; Wtr., articles, juv. and fiction; NLAPW, Wm. Painters of Wash., Pacific Coast Painters, Sculptors and Writers, Am. Fedn. of Arts, Altrusa Intl., PEO, DAR; Wash. Penny Art Fund Aw., '52; Who's Who of Am. Wm., Who's Who in Am. Art, Who's Who in The West, Who's Who on Pacific Coast, Dic. of Intl. Biog.; b. Seattle, Wash., 1891; p. C. C. and Francette Plummer Maring; h. Nahum C. Willey; c. Herbert M., Clark P.; res: 1715 S. Marine Dr., Bremerton, Wash. 98310.

WILLIAMS, ALICE JANE, Wms. Ed., News-Herald, Box 351, Mentor Ave., Willoughby, Ohio 44094, '64–; pubcty. workshops, '64–'69; Bus. Rep., Ohio Bell Telephone, '59–'62; various orgs., aws.; Flora Stone Mather, Western Reserve Col., '49–'50; Lake Erie Col. for Wm., '63–'64; b. Cleve., Ohio, 1930; p. Philip and Helen Lachner Jelco; c. Wayne; res: 95 E. Shore Blvd., Timberlake, Ohio 44094.

WILLIAMS, BARBARA JEAN, Head Librn., South Carolina State College, College Ave., Orangeburg, S.C. 29115, '62–; Ref., Docs. Librn., '58–'62; Reserve, Circ. Librn., '56–'58; S.C. Lib. Assn., NAACP; Who's Who of Am. Wm., Who's Who in Am., Who's Who in Lib. Svc.; Bennett Col., BA, '55; Univ. of Ill., MS (Lib. Sci.), '56; b. Union, S.C., 1934; p. Ernest and Johncie Sartor Williams; res: Box 1565, S.C. State College, Orangeburg, S.C. 29115.

WILLIAMS, CARLA SHRINER, Free-lance Consumer Cnslt., Rm. 887, Nat. Press Bldg., Wash., D.C.;

formerly Press Secy. to Vice Chmn. of Dem. Nat. Comm.; Dir. of Consumer Programming, Food and Drug Adm. (Annual Aw. of Merit); Specialist for Consumer Programs, Adm. on Aging; Dir., Speakers Comm., People to People Program; Legislative Asst. to U.S. Congressman; Red Cross, Chgo., Philippines, Okinawa, Japan; Pers. Testing Rsch., Western Electric; Auth., numerous papers; Consumer Educ. Chmn., Fairfax County, Va., Commty. Action Program; Legislative Advisor, Va. Citizens Consumer Cncl.; Fairfax County Dem. Comm., PRSA, AWRT, Wms. Adv. Club, ANWC, Capital Speakers Club, Va. League of Wm. Voters (Past State Bd. Mbr.); Stephens Col. (Annual Alumnae Aw.); Beloit Col. (Distg. Svc. Cit.), Univ. of Wis. Grad. Sch.; h. Carrington Williams; c. Barclay; res: 3543 Half Moon Circle, Falls Church, Va. 22044.

WILLIAMS, CAROLINE, Free-lance Artist, Non-fiction Auth.; Staff Artist, Cinn. Enquirer, '32-'41; bks: "The City on Seven Hills" (Reuter Press, '38), "Cincinnati Scenes" (Doubleday, '68); NLAPW, McDowell Soc., Cinn. Wms. Art Club, Theta Sigma Phi, Wms. Press Club of Cinn., Cinn. Hist. Soc.; Sachs aw., Cinn. Inst. of Fine Art, '62; Ohioana Cit., Martha Kinney Cooper Ohioana Assn., '63; Univ. of Cinn., '27-'28; Art Acad. of Cinn., '28; Art Students League of N.Y., '29-'30; res: 620 Belleview Rd., Burlington, Ky. 41005.

WILLIAMS, CARRIE DAVIS, Wms. Ed., Sun Reporter News, 1366 Turk St., S.F., Cal. 94115, '67-; Soc. Ed., Reptr., '60-'67; Averback & Norton PR, '63-'66; NAACP, Nat. Cncl. of Negro Wm., Las Amigas Civic & Social Club (Pres., '59-'63); Red Cross, TB cits.; S.F. City Col.; b. San Antonio, Tex. 1926; p. Floyd and Nellie Watson Gardner; h. Joe Williams; c. Markieth Wilson, Clint C. Wilson II; res: 765 Broderick St., S.F., Cal. 94117.

WILLIAMS, DOROTHY BAUM, Bus. Mgr., Pioneer Printing Co., Box 79, Ketchikan, Alaska, 99901, '68-; Petersburg Press; State Tchrs. Col.; b. Mitchell, Neb., 1930; p. Henry and Christena Maul Baum; h. Llewellyn M. Williams Jr.; c. Christena, Kathryn, Llewellyn; res: 755 Grant St., Ketchikan, Alaska. 99901.

WILLIAMS, DOROTHY EILEEN, Media Dir., Cooper, Strock, Scannell, 208 E. Wisconsin Ave., Milw., Wis. 53201, '64-; Prod., Hoffman-York, '63-'64; Media-Prod., Lawler, Kenney & Reichert, '62-'63; Langer Adv., '57-'62; Flight and Ground Sch., Instr., '40-'48; Wayne County Airport Flight Sch., '38-'40; b. Mitchell, S.D., 1920; p. Chester and Myrtle Peregrine Williams; res: 4321 N. Murray Ave., Milw., Wis. 53211.

WILLIAMS, DOROTHY FRANCES, Prof. of Publ., Mng. Ed, Simmons Review, Simmons College, 300 The Fenway, Boston, Mass., 02115, '48-; Ed., Your Home mag., '47-'52; Ed., Hammett Herald, '46-'47; News Ed., Raytheon News, '43-'45; Commtns. Cnslt., Rschr. for labor, mgt., alumni pubns.; Auth. of mag.

articles; Grants for Research, Shell Fndn., Cox and Cook Funds, '63-; Mass. IEA (Hon. Mbr., Past Treas.), Am. Alumni Cncl. (Annual Edtl. Achiev. Aws., '48-'68), AAF, numerous others; Lasell Jr. Col.; Simmons Col., BS, '41; Boston Univ., MS (Public Commtns.), '67; b. Brookline, Mass., 1918; p. John and Gertrude Riley Williams; res: 84 Davis Ave., Brookline, Mass. 02146.

WILLIAMS, ELIZABETH EVENSON, Asst. Ed., Journalism Quarterly, University of Minnesota School of Journalism, Minneapolis, Minn., '69-; Jnlsm. Instr., South Dakota State University (Brookings), '68-'69; Dir. of Student Pubns., Asst. Prof., Northern State Col. (Aberdeen, S.D.) '65-'68; Project Asst., Univ. of Wis. Ext. Public Info., '63-'65; various orgs.; S.D. State Univ., BS, '62 (with high hons.); Univ. of Wis., MA, '64; b. Sioux Falls, S.D., 1940; p. A. Duane and Eleanor Kelton Evenson; h. Louis Williams; res: #302, 212 Walnut St. S.E., Minneapolis, Minn. 55414.

WILLIAMS, ELIZABETH RAGLAND, VP, Radio/TV Dir., Adm. Mgr., Lennen & Newell, Inc., 9255 Sunset Blvd., L.A., Cal. 90067, '54-; Radio-TV Dir., '54-'58; Off. Mgr., '44-'54; Sam Jaffe Agcy., '42-'44; Hollywood Radio-TV Soc. (Secy., '66-'69), NATAS, Film Industry Workshop, L.A. Orphanage Guild (Bd. of Dirs.) Braille Inst. Auxiliary; Achiev. Aws. Col. Scis.; St. Anne's Acad.; b. Kan. City, Mo., 1920; p. Asher and Mary Mahoney Ragland; h. Rodney F. Williams; c. Jeffrey Fargo; res: 9255 Doheny Rd., L.A., Cal. 90069.

WILLIAMS, FRANCES ROYSTER, Auth., Illus., juv. stories; Creator, "Cuddles and Tuckie" wkly. children's feature, K.C. Sunday Star, 40 other nwsps., '32-'60; "Cuddles and Tuckie" bk. (Whitman Publ., '34); Wtr., Dir., "Cuddles and Tuckie Strange Adventures" radio series, '41-'58 (First Aw., 13th Am. Exhbn. of Educ. Radio Programs); Bcstr., Cont. Wtr., WDAF, '27-'33; NLAPW, Friends of Art, Jr. League (First Prize for Pen and Ink Drawing, Arts and Interests Exhbn., '35; Second Prize for Nwsp. Features, Reg. Art Conf., '37), numerous other civic, social orgs.; Art Exhbns., Armstrong Browning Lib., Baylor Univ.; Jackson County Hist. Soc.; Who's Who of Am. Wm., Royal Blue Bk., Dic. of Intl. Biog.; Pine Manor; K.C. Art Inst.; h. Winthrop Williams; two children; res: 4917 Glendale Rd., Shawnee Mission, Kan. 66205.

WILLIAMS, GLORIA JOHNSTON, PR Specialist, Asst. AE, The Tolle Company, 3590 Kettner Blvd., San Diego, Cal. 92101, '66-; Prod. Asst., '56-'66; Copywtr., '48-'50; PR Dir., San Diego Figure Skating Club, '65-; Theta Sigma Phi; Univ. of Mich., BA (Jnlsm.), '48; b. Detroit, Mich., 1926; p. Daniel and Esther Sanders Johnston; h. J. Keith Williams; c. Denise Gail, Janis Marie, Timothy Drake; res: 2015 Ainsley Rd., San Diego, Cal. 92123.

WILLIAMS, HELEN LUCILLE, Owner, H. L. Williams Associates, 820 Riedy Rd., Lisle, Ill. 60532, '65-;

Copywtr., MacManus, John and Adams, Chgo., '64-'65; Copy Chief, Burton G. Feldman, '63-'64; Copywtr., Cunningham and Walsh, '60-'62; Copy Chief, AE, PR Dir., M. L. Samson Co., '52-'57; Copywtr., LeVally, Inc., '49-'51; PR AE, Retail Copy and Fashion Prom., '47-'49; Photogr.; Owner-Packager, TV show format; Gamma Alpha Chi (Past Nat. VP), Theta Sigma Phi, AFA; St. Joseph's Col., '43-'44; Univ. of Okla., BA (Jnlsm.), '47; Writing and Art Classes, Univ. of Chgo., Art Inst. of Chgo., Northwestern Univ., Chgo. City Col., Oxbow Summer Sch. of Painting, Workshops; b. Arlington, Mass.; p. Capt. Milo Ryan and Mary Mooney Williams; h. Clifford John Tarr; c. Mary Beth; res: 820 Riedy Rd., Lisle, Ill. 60532.

WILLIAMS, HELENE KRAVADZE, Dir., The School of Protocol, 1295 National Press Bldg., Wash., D.C. 20004, '60-; Feature Wtr., Promenade, '47-'62; Dir., The Finishing Sch., Southeastern Univ., '47-'60; Dir., Sch. of Protocol, '48-'60; Colmst., Washington Evening Star, '39-'54; WNPC, Am. Nwsp. Wms. Club; Peabody Inst., '29; Md. Inst., '33; Johns Hopkins Univ., '31-'33; b. England; p. David and Blanche Livingston Kavadze; h. Gladstone Williams; res: 2132 R St. N.W., Wash., D.C. 20008.

WILLIAMS, JOAN, Auth: "The Morning and the Evening" ('61), "Old Powder Man" ('66); Contr., short stories, leading mags.; Auths. League of Am.; John P. Marquand 1st Novel Aw., '62; Nat. Inst. of Arts and Ltrs. Grant in Lit., '61; Bard Col., BA, '50; b. Memphis, Tenn., 1928; p. Priestly and Maude Moore Williams; h. Ezra Bowen; c. Ezra Drinker, Matthew Williams; res: 5 Stony Brook Rd., Westport, Conn. 06880.

WILLIAMS, JUDITH, Owner, Judith Williams Public Relations, 561 N. Fourth Ave., Tucson, Ariz. 85705, '63-; Dir., PR, Kalt and Lauver Adv., '62-'63; Dir., employee pubns., Tucson Missile Div., Hughes Aircraft Co., '57-'62; Prom. Head, Ed. of Special Secs., Tucson Nwsps., '52-'57; Reptr., Arizona Daily Star, '49-'52; Guest Lectr., Univ. of Ariz.; PRSA, AAF, Tucson Adv. Club (Secy., '65), NFPW (four aws., '61-'66), Ariz. Press Wm. (Dist. VP, '60; 17 aws., '61-'66), Tucson Press Club; Ariz. Adv. Aws. Craft Competition (four aws., '64-'65); Univ. of Ariz. '47-'50; b. Chgo., Ill., 1929; h. William C. Scott; c. Kirk, Kevin, Gillian; res: 2141 E. Third St., Tucson, Ariz. 85719.

WILLIAMS, KATHRYN VINSON, Auth., juv. novels: "The Luck of the Golden Cross" (J. B. Lippincott, '60), "Run with the Ring" (Harcourt, Brace and World, '65); Asst. Prof. of Eng., Col. of Orlando, '69-; Instr., '66-'69; AAUW, Southeastern Modern Language Assn., Nat. Cncl. of Tchrs. of Eng.; Delta Kappa Gamma; Contemporary Auths.; Ga. Col., BA, '32; Rollins Col., MA (Teaching), '66; b. Cordele, Ga., 1911; p. Edward and Cordelia Scott Vinson; h. Blenus Williams; c. Mrs. Arthur Sanford Kirkindall, Edward V.; res: 844 Kenilworth Terr., Orlando, Fla. 32803.

WILLIAMS, MARGARET URICH, Co-Publr., The Scotia Register, Scotia, Neb. 68875, '48-; Reptr., '36-'48; Neb. Press Wm. (writing aw., '58; Pres., '68-'70; VP, '66-'68; Secy., '64-'66; Treas., '62-'64); Ak-Sar-Ben Good Neighbor Aw., '57; various aws. for Scotia Register; b. Elkhorn, Neb., 1913; p. George and Anna Hoff Urich; h. Meredith Williams; c. Thomas G., Linda (Mrs. Jerry R. Woods); res: Scotia, Neb. 68875.

WILLIAMS, MARY DUANE, Ed., Hilltop News, Cincinnati Suburban Newspapers, Inc., 4415 Montgomery Rd., Norwood, Oh. 45212, '69-; Commtns. Ed., Supery Drug, '68-'69; Ed., Norwood Enterprise, CSNI, Inc., '67-'68; Reptr.-Mng. Ed., Jefferson (Ky.) Reporter, '63-'67; Tchr., Archdiocese of Louisville, four yrs.; Ky. Press Assn. (Best News Feature Aw., '65); Catherine Spalding Col.; b. Louisville, Ky., 1930; p. William and Gladys Reigel Duane; h. Hal Williams; c. Valerie, Mary Clare, Joe, Mike, Ken, Jim; res: 125 Forest Ave., Wyoming, Oh. 45215.

WILLIAMS, PARKER, Head Librn., San Jacinto College, 8060 Spencer Highway, Pasadena, Tex. 77505, '61-; Pasadena Public Lib., '55-'61; Grand Saline Public Schs., '49-'55; numerous orgs.; N. Tex. State Univ., BA, '49; ME, '53; E. Tex. State Univ., PhD, '69; b. Fruitvale, Tex., 1929; p. James and Bonnie Parker Williams; res: 1603 Ave. M., S. Houston, Tex. 77587.

WILLIAMS, PATRICIA PARKER, Owner, Pres., Radio WNNT AM-FM, Northern Neck & Tidewater Broadcasting Co., Inc., Warsaw, Va. 22572, '61-; Owner, Gen. Mgr., '60-'64; Commentator, "Chat With Pat," '52-'60; AWRT, Va. Assn. of Bdcstrs., Nat. Assn. of Arts and Letters, Nat. Assn. for Am. Composers and Conductors, Intl. Platform Assn.; Who's Who of Am. Wm., Who's Who in the South and Southwest, 2000 Wm. of Achiev.; Sullins, '39-'41; Univ. of Miss., '41-'43; p. George and Mildred Johnston Parker; h. M. Lee Williams; c. Phillip Lee; res: 203 Westway, Balt., Md. 21212.

WILLIAMS, PRIM CARTER, Music Dir., KPRS Broadcasting Corp., 2301 Grand Ave., K.C., Mo. 64108, '69-; FM Jazz Show, '67-'68; Wms. Dir., '67-'69; h. Robert Williams.

WILLIAMS, SALLY SCRIMGEOUR, Adv. Mgr., American Motorist, American Automobile Association, 1712 G St., N.W., Wash., D.C. 20006, '65-; Media Dir., Ketchum, MacLeod & Grove, '63; Asst. Dir. PR, Shoreham Hotel, '62; Asst. Bus. and Prod. Mgr., AOPA Pilot (mag.), '61; Sales, WTTG-TV, '60; media cnslt., rschr.; free-lance artist; various aws. and orgs.; Marjorie Webster Jr. Col., AA, '58; Am. Univ., BS (Commtns.), '60; b. Wash., D.C., 1938; p. Carter Maxwell and Letty Brown Scrimgeour; h. John Williams; res: 2102 Paul Edwin Terr., Falls Church, Va. 22043.

WILLIAMS, VERA KACKLEY, Free-lance Wtr.; Reptr., Art, Bk. Ed., Long Beach Independent, Press-Telegram, '27–'67; Reptr., Sheridan (Wyo.) nwsps., '19–'26; NLAPW, Cal. Wtrs. Guild; b. Hyannis, Neb. 1901; p. Charley and Clara Stump Kackley; h. Harold C. Williams (dec.); res: 1886 Litchfield Ave., Long Beach, Cal. 90815.

WILLIAMSON, JOANNE SMALL, Wtr., fiction, radio-TV scripts; Auth: "Jacobin's Daughter" (New York Herald Tribune Spring Bk. Festival Hon. Cit., '56), "The Eagles Have Flown" ('57), "The Glorious Conspiracy" (William Allen White Children's Bk. Aw. nominee, '63), "And Forever Free" ('66), "To Dream Upon a Crown" ('67); Prod. Mgr., Fairfield County Pubns., '55–'56; Ed., Retail Apparel Outlook, '51–'55; PR, Columbia-Presbyterian Med. Ctr., '50–'51; Fashion Ed., Feature Wtr., Bridgeport (Conn.) Herald, '48–'50; Auths. Guild, Intl. Platform Assn.; Barnard Col., '42–'44; Diller Quaile Sch. of Music, '44–'45; b. Arlington, Mass., 1926; p. Floyd and Gertrude Small Williamson; res: Box 491, Kennebunkport Me. 04046.

WILLINS, STELLA, Mgr., Sch. Dept., Royal Typewriter Co., Div. of Litton Industries, 150 New Park Ave., Hartford, Conn. 06106, '46–; Lectr.-Demonstrator, Bus. Educ., '37–'45; Contrbr., numerous articles, pfsnl. educ. jnls.; Lectr., grad. tchr. groups; numerous orgs., aws.; N.Y.U., '44–'45; b. Phila., Pa., 1906; p. Samuel and Sadie Talsky Willins; c. Mrs. Thelma O'Brien, Herbert E. Adelman; res: 31 Woodland St., Hartford, Conn. 06105.

WILLIS, KATHRYN SETZER, Wms. Dir., Hostess, Wms. Interest Show, WJHL-TV, 137 W. Main St., Johnson City, Tenn. 37601, '65–; Hostess, cooking show, '53–'56; Staff Anncr., Copywtr., WKPT (Kingsport, Tenn.), '44–'45; Actress, summer stock, '41–'43; Bdcstr., NBC shortwave radio, '41; various orgs., aws.; b. Johnson City, Tenn., 1922; p. Glenn and Kate Ross Setzer; h. John Willis; c. John Kelver, Katy Glenn; res: 1807 Hillsboro Ave., Johnson City, Tenn. 37601.

WILLIS, MARGARET, State Librn., Kentucky Department of Libraries, Box 537, Frankfort, Ky. 40601, '57–; Coordr., '55–'57.

WILLIX, DOROTHA RICKERS, Free-lance PR, 1614 Gaslight Tower Bldg., Atlanta, Ga. 30303; PR Acc. Mgr., Lando, Inc., '68; AE, PR, Ketchum, MacLeod & Grove, '65–'68; AE, Sls. Prom., '61–'65; Feature Wtr., Reptr., Colmst., various nwsps.; AWRT, PRSA, Pitt. Adv. Club (VP; Wm. of the Yr., '68), Assn. of Pitt. Bus. Wmns. Clubs, Pitt. Press Club, St. Lawrence Univ., '57–'58; b. Corry, Pa.; p. John and Jennie Rhebergen Rickers; h. Gilbert Willix; c. Nancy (Mrs. Gary B. Neyman), Susan K.; res: 435 Robin Court, Roswell, Ga. 30075.

WILLOUGHBY, MABEL ELIZABETH, Librn., Enterprise State Jr. Col., Enterprise, Ala. 36330, '69–; Dir. of Libs., Pahlavi Univ., Iran, '67–'68; (Fulbright Lectr.); Dir. of Lib., Hardin-Simmons Univ. (Abilene, Tex.), '56–'67; Librn., Samford Univ. (Birmingham), '31–'56; Ref. and Circ. Asst., Birmingham Public Lib., '29–'30; Tchr., Fla., '26–'29; Lectr., Bk. Reviewer; ALA, Ala. Lib. Assn. (Treas., '37–'40; VP, '49–'51; Pres., '51–'52); Altrusa Intl. (Chptr. Pres., '49–'50, '59–'60), AAUW (Chptr. Secy., '61–'62), NLAPW (Br. Histrn., '66–'67; Pres., '69); Who's Who of Am. Wm.; Samford Univ., AB, '25; Emory Univ., AB (Lib. Sci.), '31; Columbia Univ., MS, '42; b. Gordon, Ala.; p. Sidney and Sally Jessup Willoughby; res: 110 Mockingbird Lane, Enterprise, Ala. 36330.

WILLS, CAROLYN LEE, Rep., Wms. Activities, Eastern Airlines, 1422 W. Peachtree St. N.W., Atlanta, Ga. 30309; Nat. Rep., Delta Zeta Sorority, '60–'64; AWRT, Fashion Group, Atlanta Dogwood Festival Bd. of Dirs., Miss Atlanta Pageant; Bd. of Dirs.; Ga. State Univ., BA, '59; b. Henry County, Ga., 1936; p. Richard and Rosezena Cox Lee; h. Charles H. Wills; res: 165 The Prado N.E., Atlanta, Ga. 30309.

WILLSON, ELLA CONLEY, Supvsr. of Sch. Libs., Detroit Board of Education, 5057 Woodward, Detroit, Mich. 48202, '63–; High Sch. Librn., '62–'63; Jr. High Sch. Librn., '60–'62; Elem. Sch. Librn., '40–'59; Librn., Wayne State Univ., '38–'40; Lib. Sci. Instr., Univ. of Mich., '68–; Wayne State Univ., '65–; ALA, Mich. Lib. Assn., Mich. Assn. of Sch. Librns., WNBA; Wayne State Univ., BA, '34; BS (Lib. Sci.), '40; MA, '47; EdD, '65; b. Owen Sound, Ontario, Can.; p. Harold and Jean Conley; c. Sherman; res: 11611 Morang, Apt. 32, Detroit, Mich. 48224.

WILNER, MARIE SPRING, Free-lance Painter, fine arts; Secy.-Treas., Rosemarie Holding Inc.; Ojom Realty Corp.; Nat. Assn. of Wm. Artists, Artists Equity, Nat. Art League, Am. Artists Pfsnl. League (Gold Medal of Hon., '64), Intl. Arts Guild of Monaco, Centro Studi e Scambi Intl., Leonardo da Vinci Assn. of Italy, various art groups; Societe d'Encouragement au Progres (Bronze Medal of Hon., '68); Academie Internationale de Lutece Aw., '68; and many other art aws.; Hunter Col., BA; Art Students League; b. Paris, France, 1910; p. Joseph and Helene Spring; h. Joseph W. Wilner; c. Helene V. Cornell, Ira Harvey, George D.; res: 1248 White Plains Rd., N.Y., N.Y. 10473.

WILSON, CATHERINE JANE McBRIDE, Publr., Millard County Progress, Progress Printing Company, 41 S. Main St., Fillmore, Ut. 84361, '40–; Wtr., Reptr., Compositor, Co-Ed., Publr., '25–; Cl., Millard County Sch. Dist., '18–'22; Ut. State Press Assn., Nat. Nwsp. Assn.; Dir., Fillmore Indsl. Fndn., '67–'69; active in civic affairs, prom. of local orgs., clubs, chs.; Ut. State Master Ed.-Publr. Aw., '65; Univ. of Ut., '18, '24; San Diego Bus. Col., '23; b. Fillmore, Ut., 1898; p. William and Erma Kelly McBride; h. Vance Wilson; c. Vera D. (Mrs. Cleon B. Feight), William V., Samuel H.; res: 33 W. 300th S., Fillmore, Ut. 84631.

WILSON, CHARLOTTE LEHON, Bus. Mgr., The

North American Review, University of Northern Iowa, Cedar Falls, Ia. 50613, '69–; Instr. of Speech, '66–'68; Syracuse Univ., BS, '55; b. Syracuse, N.Y., 1932; p. Harold and Anna Thompson Lehon; h. Robley Wilson, Jr.; c. Stephen Eastman, Philip Beardsley; res: 4123 Clearview Dr., Cedar Falls, Ia. 50613.

WILSON, CORINNE GREEN, Librn., New College, Inc., Box 1898, Sarasota, Fla. 33578, '63–; Librn., Assoc. Prof. of Classics, '62–'63; Programmer, Ctr. for Programmed Instruction (N.Y.C.), '60–'62; Acting Prof., Hollins Col., '60; Ref. Librn., La. State Univ., '51–'52; Am. Philosophy Assn., ALA, Fla. Lib. Assn., AAUW, other orgs.; Rockford Col., AB, '43; Univ. of N.C., PhD, '47; BS (Lib. Sci.), '51; b. Muskogee, Okla., 1924; p. Benjamin and Julia Allen Green; h. Robert M. Wilson (dec.); c. Robert J.; res: 2300 Mietaw Dr., McClellan Park, Sarasota, Fla. 33579.

WILSON, DOROTHY CLARKE, Auth: "The Brother" ('44); "The Gifts" ('57); "Ten Fingers for God" ('65); "Lone Woman" ('70), numerous others bks., religious plays; Westminster Religious Fiction Aw. ("Prince of Egypt" '49); Bates Col., AB, '25; Litt. D., '47 (Phi Beta Kappa); b. Gardiner, Me., 1904; p. Lewis and Flora Cross Clarke; h. Elwin L. Wilson; c. Joan (Mrs. George Wilson), Harold E.; res: 114 Forest Ave., Orono, Me. 04473.

WILSON, ELIZABETH, Dir., Growers' Peanut Food Promotions, P.O. Box 409, Rocky Mount, N.C. 27801, '67–; Supvsr., Sch. Food Suc., N.C. Bd. of Educ., '66–'67; Food Econst., Jesse Jones Sausage Co., '64–'66; Dietitian, Hosp. Food Mgt., '62–'64; Asst. Home Agt., N.C. Agricultural Ext. Svcs., '61–'62; Am. Home Econs. Assn., Home Econsts. in Bus., AWRT, N.C. Cncl. on Food and Nutrition, N.C. Food Dealers Assn., N.C. Consumers' Cncl.; E. Carolina Univ., BS (Home Econs.), '61.

WILSON, GLORIA SCOTT, Audience Prom. Dir., WCSC (AM-FM), 485 E. Bay St., Charleston, S.C. 29402, '69–; Copy Dir., '59–'69; Prom. Mgr. and Talent, WUSN-TV, '57–'59; Copy Wtr., '51–'53; AAUW, AWRT (Palmetto Chptr. VP, '68); Northwestern Univ., BS, '49; b. St. Petersburg, Fla., 1929; p. Fred and Florence Cook Scott; h. Edwin R. Wilson; res: 59 S. Concord, Charleston, S.C. 29401.

WILSON, HELEN VAN PELT, Home & Garden Ed., Hawthorn Books, Inc., 70 Fifth Ave., N.Y., N.Y. 10011, '69–; Garden Cnslt., Simon & Schuster, '69–; Garden Ed., M. Barrows & Co., '65–'68, '47–'56; Garden Ed., D. Van Nostrand Co., '56–'65; Auth: "The Joy of Geraniums" (Barrows, '65), "The Gardener's Book of Verse" (Barrows, '66), 15 other flower, gardening bks.; Garden Wtrs. of Am., Am. Horticultural Soc., African Violet Soc. of Am. (Bronze Medal); Bryn Mawr Col., AB, '23 (cum laude); c. Mrs. Cynthia E. C. Luden; res: 65 Center St., Westport, Conn. 06880.

WILSON, IRENE MICHAILENKO, Ed.; Commtns., Employee Svcs. Specialist, Philadelphia Quartz Co., Sixth and Chestnut Sts., Phila., Pa. 19106, '68–; AAIE; Pa. State Univ., BA (Speech, Russian), '68; b. Munich, Germany, 1947; p. George and Sinaida Lugowoj Michailenko; h. Stuart N. Wilson; res: 640 S. Ave., Apt. C-9, Secane, Pa. 19018.

WILSON, JEANI GADDY, Dir., Off. of Public Info., Christian College, Eighth and Rogers, Columbia, Mo. 65201, '68–; News Wtr., '67–'68; Asst. Wms. Ed., The Missourian, '66–'67; News Lab. Instr., Univ. of Mo., '65–'66; Free-lance PR, Feature Wtr., Commtns. Rschr.; ACPRA, Mid-Mo. Press Club, C. of C., Kappa Tau Alpha, Theta Sigma Phi, Ci Omicron Mu; Bessie Marks Jnlsm. Scholarship, '65; Am. Bus. Wms. Assn. Founders Scholarship, '65; Univ. of Mo., BJ, '66.

WILSON, JUDITH VARNEY, Ed., Deerfeild Beach Observer, 316 E. Hillsboro Blvd., Deerfield Beach, Fla. 33441, '67–; Soc. Colmst., Broward edition of Miami Herald, '64–'67; Theta Sigma Phi (Broward County Chptr. VP, '64; Univ. of Fla. Chptr. Secy., '58), Fla. Wms. Press Club, Beta Sigma Phi, Deerfield Beach Jr. Wms. Club, Soroptimist Club; Univ. of Fla., BS, '59; b. Hartford, Conn., 1937; p. Kenneth and Lucille Burgess Varney; h. Richard L. Wilson; c. Timothy, Jeffrey; res: 124 N.E. Ninth Ave., Deerfield Beach, Fla. 33441.

WILSON, KATE SUPPLEE, Dir., Pubcty. and Lib. Svcs., Hammond Incorporated, 515 Valley St., Maplewood, N.J. 07040, '66–; Adv. Mgr., '62–'67; Mail Order Mgr., '60–'63; Publrs. Ad Club (Secy., '65–'67), Publrs. Lib. Prom. Group (VP, '67–'69), Publrs. Pubcty. Assn., Wms. Nat. Bk. Assn. (Bd., '65–'68); Wellesley Col., BA; b. Balt., Md.; p. Albert and Claudia Rutledge Supplee; h. John MacMillan Wilson; c. Susan Supplee, John MacMillan; res: 48 Euclid Ave., Maplewood, N.J. 07040.

WILSON, LUCY WOOD, Ref. Librn., Laney Junior College, 125-10th St., Oakland, Cal. 94606, '70–; Fed. Proj. Librn., Richmond Public Lib., '68–'70; Ref. Librn., Contra Costa County Lib., '64–'68; various libs., '39–'60; Cal. Lib. Assn.; Va. Union Univ., AB, '39; Columbia Univ., BS (Lib. Sci.), '44; b. Norfolk, Va.; p. Arthur and Rolande Wood; h. Charles Wilson; c. Margaret Ann, Patricia, Deborah, Charles, Wilhelmina; res: 1159 King Ct., El Cerrito, Cal. 94530.

WILSON, LYDIA ELLIOTT, Wms. Ed., Orange County Evening News, 13261 Century Blvd., Garden Grove, Cal. 92640, '59–; Social Worker, '54–'59; Edtl. Rschr., Clark Air Force Base, Philippines, '52; Reptr., Orange County Daily News, '49–'52, '43–'46; Soc. Ed., Richmond (Cal.) Record-Herald, '46–'47; Orange County Press Club (Secy., '66, '68), Cal. Press Wm. (Orange County VP, '67; Best Photo Layout, '66, '67; Best Wms. Pg., '66; several other aws.), Quill Pen Wtrs. Club (Secy., '59; Pres., '66); Santa Ana Col., AA, '41; Univ. of Philippines; Cal-State Fullerton; b. Kan.;

p. Charles and Eunice Hughes Elliott; h. Arthur B. Wilson; c. Frederick E.; res: 5772 Garden Grove Blvd., Space 275, Westminster, Cal. 92683.

WILSON, MARTHA LANGHELDT, Educ. Dir., KOMO-TV and Radio, Fisher Blend Station, 100 Fourth Ave. N., Seattle, Wash. 98109; Prodr., Moderator, Programming, '57–; AWRT (Evergreen Chptr. Pres., '64), NATAS (Bd., '64); Theta Sigma Phi Wm. of Achiev., '63; McCall's Golden Mike, '63; Wash. State Press Wm. Sugar Plum, '64; NEA Sch. Bell aw., '60; Wash. Educ. Better Understanding of Educ.: State Aw. '60, '69; Reg. Aw. '64, '65; Delta Kappa Gamma State aw., '66; S.F. State Col., '35 (Alumni Bd., '68–'69); b. Pocatella, Idaho, 1913; p. Harry and Mary Bess Ankrom Langheldt; h. James L. Wilson; c. Marliss Edwards, Stephen Camp, Rosemary Muse, Robert Camp; res: 4715 139th Ave. S.E., Belleview, Wash. 98004.

WILSON, MARY VALERIO, Stringer, The Miami Herald, 1 Herald Plaza, Miami, Fla., 33101, '69–; Asst. Wms. Ed., Herald & News (Livermore, Cal.), '67–'68; Col. of St. Rose, '45–'48; b. Syracuse, N.Y., 1927; p. Joseph and Teresa Fratianni Valerio; h. Harlan Wilson; res: Box 1509, Nassau, The Bahamas.

WILSON, PATRICIA TIERNEY, Prod. Coordr., Animatic Productions, Ltd., 2 W. 45th St., N.Y., N.Y. 10036, '67–; h. Henry Wilson.

WILSON, PENELOPE WAGNER, Prod. Dir., Radio-TV studios, Univ. of Mont., Missoula, Mont. 59801, '68–; Soc. Ed., Missoulian, '66–'68; Reptr., Ed., Valley Publ. Co., '64–'65; Court Reptr., Billings Gazette, '61–'64; Ed.-Wtr., AP, '60–'61; Theta Sigma Phi (Kappa Chptr. VP, '60–'61; Missoula Chptr. Pres., '67–'68), Kappa Tau Alpha, '65; Sigma Delta Chi Aw., '64; Univ. of Mont., BA (Jnlsm.), '61; MA, '67; b. Billings, Mont., 1939; p. Claire and Pauline Quarles Wagner; h. Wayne L. Wilson; res: 3102 Lester, Missoula, Mont. 59801.

WILSON, ROSALIE F., Supvsr., Public Info., County of Westchester, Dept. of Parks, Recreation & Conservation, County Off. Bldg., White Plains, N.Y. 10601, '61–; PR Staff Mbr., Standard-Vacuum Oil Co., '57–'61; Tchr., adult educ., '61–'69; crtv. writing, Iona Col., '68; Contrbr., mag. articles in U.S., Can., Europe, Australia, S. Africa; PRSA (Westchester Chptr. Secy.-Treas., '69); Barnard Col., BA; Columbia Grad. Sch. of Jnlsm., MS.

WILSON, THELMA BUCHANAN, Asst. Dir. of Public Affairs, Univ. of Oregon Medical School, 3181 S.W. Sam Jackson Park Rd., Portland, Ore. 97201, '68–; Asst. to Dir. of Public Affairs, '64–'68; Info. Rep., Ed., '61–'64; Free-lance Wtr., Oregonian, Oregon Journal, '48–'61; PR Dir., KGW, '46–'48; Columbia Aircraft, '42–'46; Contrbr., articles to nwsps., mags., med. jnls.; AWRT, ACPRA (Excellence Aw., '63), Theta Sigma Phi; Pacific Indsl. Communicators Pica

Aw., '62; Univ. of Ore., '30–'32; b. Spokane, Wash.; h. D. H. Wilson (dec.); c. Donald H., David P.; res: 5101 S.W. Richardson Dr., Portland, Ore. 97201.

WILSON, THEODORA NADELSTEIN, Special Reptr., The New York Daily News, 220 E. 42nd St., N.Y., N.Y. 10017, '52–; reptr. positions, Evansville (Ind.) Press, Indianapolis Times, Richmond (Va.) News Leader, Philadelphia Bulletin, AP; Theta Sigma Phi, numerous orgs., aws.; Univ. of Ky. (Phi Beta Kappa); b. Bklyn., N.Y.; p. Adolph and Rebecca Nadelstein; c. Delph Robert; res: 21 Chittenden Ave., N.Y., N.Y. 10033.

WILSON, YVONNE JOSSERAND, Civic Worker; Ed., Jackson County Historical Society editions of Journal, '63–'66; Jr. Svc. League (Treas., '57–'58), Kan. City Art Inst., Intl. Rels. Cncl. of Kan. City, Jr. Wms. Philharmonic Assn., DAR, Independence Symphony Guild, Kappa Kappa Gamma, Theta Sigma Phi, Gamma Alpha Chi, Phi Theta Kappa; Stephens Col., AA, '48; Kan. Univ., BS (Adv.), '50 (Most Outstanding Sr. Wm. Majoring in Adv.); b. Garden City, Kan., 1930; p. Guy and Gertrude Cleghorn Josserand; h. Keith Wilson, Jr.; c. Leslie Yvonne; res: 1215 W. 63rd Terr., Kan. City, Mo. 64113.

WILTON, VIRGINIA WEAVER, Prom. Mgr., Travel Forum Dir., Courier-Post, Camden, N.J. 08101, '47–; Asst. to Prom. Mgr., Phila. (Pa.) Record, '40–'46; Asst. to Prom. Mgr., Intl. Dept., Sterling Products, Newark, N.J., '38–'40; Jnlsm. and Commtns. Merit Badge Cnslr., Boy Scouts of Am.; Intl. Nwsp. Prom. Assn. (Eastern Reg. Pres., '60), N.J. Press Assn.; Editor and Publisher Aw. for Prom. Achiev., '54; Temple Univ., Grand Central Art Sch., Dale Carnegie; b. Phila., Pa., 1906; p. John and Virginia Sells Weaver; h. Edward Wilton; res: 45 Runnemede Ave., Lansdowne, Pa. 19050.

WIMBROW, DOROTHY LIVEZEY, Free-lance Wtr.; Assoc. Ed., New Vista, Sebastian Highlands, Fla., '64–'68; Ed., Pelican Post, '58–'64; Owner, Ed., Publr., Indian River News, '54–'66; Assoc. Ed., '48–'54; Free-lance Wtr., '36–'48; Radio Wtr., Vocalist, Actress, N.Y.C., Chgo., '25–'36; BPW (Hon.; Fla.° Wm. of Yr., '61; Hortense K. Wells Fla. State Legislative Trophy), Delta Kappa Gamma Oustanding Civic Leader, '63; Fla. Press Assn., Jaycee Aws.; Veterans Adm. Aw. for Outstanding Nwsp. Svc., '63; Nat. Wildlife Fedn. Recognition Cert. for Outstanding Svc., '58; Fla. Safety Cncl. Second Place Edtl. Aw., '56; Who's Who of Am. Wm., many other dirs.; Pearces' Bus. Col., '19–'21; b. Phila., Pa., 1901; p. Frank and Nellie McGloughnan Livezey; h. Peter Dale Wimbrow (dec.); c. Sallydale, Peter Dale, Jr.; res: P.O. Box #307, Sebastian, Fla. 32958.

WINCHESTER, ALICE, Ed., Antiques Magazine, Straight Enterprises, Inc., 551 Fifth Ave., N.Y., N.Y. 10017, '38–; Assoc. Ed., '34–'38; Auth., "How to Know American Antiques" ('51); Co-auth., "Living with

Antiques"; Lectr., decorative arts; Cnslt., hist. preservation; Dir., Old Sturbridge Village, N.Y. State Hist. Assn., Nat. Trust for Hist. Preservation; Am. Inst. of Int. Designers Hon., '60; Russell Sage Col., LHD Hon., '66; Smith Col., AB (Phi Beta Kappa), '29; b. Chgo., Ill., 1907; p. Benjamin and Pearl Gunn Winchester; res: 249 E. 48th St., N.Y., N.Y. 10017.

WINCHESTER, LILLIAN B., PR Dir., National Association of Furniture Manufacturers, 666 Lake Shore Dr., Chgo., Ill. 60611, '59–; Bus. Ed., Market Daily and Marketing, '57–'59; '40–'46; Ed., Chicago Market News, '54–'57; Assoc. Fashion and Furniture Ed., Chicago Daily News, '38–'39; PR Dir., L.A. Furniture Mart, '36–'38; PR, Nat. Assn. Furniture Manufacturers Intl. Fairs; Theta Sigma Phi, NHFL, Bruce Weirick Aw., '30; Univ. of Ill., BS (Jnlsm.), '31.

WINCHESTER, MARGOT, Assoc. Prodr., J. H. Secondari Productions Ltd., 212 W. 48th St., N.Y., N.Y. 10036, '68–; Assoc. Prodr., ABC-TV, '64–'68; Assoc. in Prod., '63–'64; Rschr., '61–'63; '70: "The Draft: Who Shall Serve"; "Cosmopolis" (Architects Critics Aw., Christopher's Aw., '69); "The Road to Gettysburg" (cited for Peabody Aw.); "Beethoven—Ordeal and Triumph," Landers Assocs., '67 (Aw. of Merit); Sch. Bell Aw., Thomas Alva Edison Aw. for "Saga of Western Man," '63, '64; Syracuse Univ., '55–57; Boston Univ., BA, '59; b. N.Y.C., 1938; p. Louis and Emma Stein Winchester; h. S. Arthur Schimmel; res: 301 E. 62nd St., N.Y., N.Y. 10021.

WINDERS, GERTRUDE HECKER, Auth., Illus., Lectr., Cnslt.; bks.: 11 fictionalized biogs. for juvs. (Illus., two) incl: "Sam Colt and His Gun" ('59 Jr. Lit. Guild selection), "Jeb Stuart: Boy in the Saddle" (reprinted in My Weekly Reader and two anthologies); Auth., numerous short stories, features for adults; Cnslt., Ind. Univ. Wtrs. Conf., '59–; Tchr.: 10 yrs. creative writing; AAUW; Indpls. Story-A-Month Club (Pres. '38–'39, '48–'49); Butler Univ., BA (Phi Kappa Phi); b. Indpls., Ind.; p. Edward and Harriet Humann Hecker; h. Garrison Winders; c. Mrs. Richard H. Wich; res: 2242 N. Alabama St., Indpls., Ind. 46205.

WINDHAM, EULA HEARD, Librn., Roberts Memorial Library, Middle Georgia College, Cochran, Ga. 31014, '61–; Asst. Librn., Hardin Simmons Univ., '56–'61; Tchr., Tifton Public Schs., '40–'44; Ga. Educ. Assn., NEA, Ga. Lib. Assn., ALA, Southeastern Lib. Assn.; Who's Who of Am. Wm., other selective dirs.; Ga. Col., AB, '40; Southern Baptist Theological Seminary, MRE, '50; Emory Univ., MLS '56; b. Tifton, Ga.; p. Guy and Eula Wilson Windham; res: 1003 Eighth St., Cochran, Ga. 31014.

WINDSOR, MARIE (Emily Bertelsen Hupp), Actress, 64 motion pics., 400 TV shows; Contract Player, Metro-Goldwyn-Mayer '46–'47; '40–; TV-Movie Colmst., L.A. Club and Sports mag., '62–'66; AMPAS, NATAS, SAG (Exec. Bd., Secy.); Look aw., best supporting actress, "The Killing," '57; Miss D&RG Railroad, '40; Queen of Ut. 49er Days, '39; Brigham Young Univ.; Maria Ouspenskia's Drama Sch.; Kahn Inst. of Art; b. Marysvale, Ut., 1919; p. Lane and Etta Long Bertelsen; h. Jack Rodney Hupp; c. Richard Rodney; res: 9510 Cherokee Lane, Beverly Hills, Cal. 90210.

WING, GERALDINE EADS, Off. Mgr., KODY Radio, Inc., 308 W. Fourth St., N. Platte, Neb. 69101, '44–; Radio Personality; AWRT (Cornhusker Chptr. Pres., '60–'61; Treas., '67–'69), BPW (Wm. of Achiev., '64), Altrusa Intl. (local Pres.); Civic Leader; Peru State Tchrs. Col., '37–'39; b. Peru, Neb., 1920; p. Harold and Gladys Ward Eads; h. Robert Wing; res: 2201 W. C. St., North Platte, Neb. 69101.

WINGERT, DOROTHEA HELEN, Reprtr., The Daily Journal, 295 N. Broad St., Elizabeth, N.J. 07207, '37–; Pubcty., Holland Am. Line, '36; Reprtr., Newark Evening News, '28–'34; Reprtr., Food and Travel Ed., Newark Sunday Call, '26–'28; N.J. Daily Nwsp. Wm. (Treas., '56–'59; Pres., '66–'68; 1st Prize, col. category, '66), NFPW (Reg. Dir., '68–); Patriotic Movement for Free Cuba Aw., '65; Georgian Court Col., '26; N.Y.U., Rutgers, Fordham; b. Elizabeth, N.J.; p. Charles and Annie Keeler Wingert; res: 18 Bayside Dr., Atlantic Highlands, N.J. 07716.

WINKELHORN, KARIN-MARIA, Fashion Ed., Vogue Magazine, 420 Lexington Ave., N.Y., N.Y. 10017, '65–; Asst. to Art Dir., '63–'65; Bryn Mawr Col., '61–'63; Oxford Univ., BA, '63; b. N.Y.C.; p. Kai and Sophie Kutuzov Winkelhorn.

WINKLER, LINDA GREEN, Free-lance Wtr.; Ed., Calendar, U.S. Navy Electronics Lab., '58–'60; Reprtr., North Shores Sentinel, '58; Tech. Wtr., Convair Astronautics, '57–'58; Prom. Wtr., KOMU-TV, '56; Cont. Dir., KSVP, '55; Theta Sigma Phi (Chptr. Secy.-Treas., '65–'67; Pres., '67–'69); Univ. of Mo. Sch. of Jnlsm., BJ, '55 (Hons.); b. Miami, Fla., 1934; p. John and Clara Morgan Green; h. Lutz Winkler; c. Lon K., Lana L.; res: 3955 Atascadero Dr., San Diego, Cal. 92107.

WINN, LAURA ROCKE, Auth., "Margie Asks Why" ('63); Press Secy., Keene (Tex.) Seventh-Day Adventist Church (PR Secy. Aw., '69); Nat. Guild of Piano Tchrs.; b. Hickman, Neb., 1902; p. John and Mary Steinke Rocke; h. Joseph Winn; res: P.O. Box 26, Keene, Tex. 76059.

WINNER, KARIN ELSA, Fashion Reprtr., Women's Wear Daily, 617 S. Olive St., L.A., Cal. 90014, '69–; Asst. Ed., Deli-News, '68–'69; PR, Pubcty. Asst., San Diego Convention and Visitors Bur., '66; Pers., San Diego Union-Evening Tribune, '63; Theta Sigma Phi (Achiev. Aw., '67); Univ. of Wis. Sch. of Jnlsm., '62–'64; Univ. of Southern Cal., BA (Jnlsm.), '67; b. White Plains, N.Y., 1944; p. George and Marie Smith

Winner; res: 9952 Robbins Dr., Beverly Hills, Cal. 90212.

WINSLOW, ANNE, Ed.-in-Chief, Prog. Offcr. (Intl. Org.), Liaison Offcr. with UN, Carnegie Endowment for International Peace, 345 E. 46th St., N.Y., N.Y., 10017, '47–; Comm. to Study the Org. of Peace, '46–'47; U.S. Army, Signal Intelligence, '43–'46; Auth., various monographs; Tech. Asst., Intl. Dev. Rev.; Offcr., Conf. of Consultive Non-governmental Orgs., '52–'60; Chmn., Convenor, Intl. NGO Conf. on Human Rights, '67–'68; Public Affairs Comm. (Bd. of Dirs.), Am. Political Sci. Assn., Intl. Studies Assn.; Vassar Col., AB, '30; b. Brookline, Mass., 1908; res: 70 E. 96th St., N.Y., N.Y. 10025.

WINSTON, GERTRUDE ELIZABETH, Head Librn., Delaware State College, Dover, Del., '67–; ALA, Del. Lib. Assn.; Savannah State Col., BA, '66, Atlanta Univ., MS (Lib. Sci.); b. Savannah, Ga., 1945; p. Daniel and Pearl Williams Winston; res: 108 Delaware State College, Dover, Del. 19901.

WINTER, ALICE GREER, Auth: "The Velvet Bubble" (Wm. Morrow, '65; Friends of Am. Wtrs. Distg. Recognition Aw.); "Only People Cry" (Wms. Day, '63); Auths. Guild; Univ. of Kan., BA, '42; b. Osage City, Kan., 1919; p. William and Gladys Guthrie Greer; h. Calvert Winter; c. Calvert, William, Michael; res: 2601 Wood, Kan. City, Kan. 66104.

WINTER, CHARLOTTE SAPHIER, Art Dir., Architectural Forum, 111 W. 57th St., N.Y., N.Y. 10019, '67–; Assoc. Dir., '53–'64; Assoc. Art Dir., House Beautiful, '65–'67; Pratt Inst., '40; b. N.Y.C.; h. Carter Winter; res: 62 Horatio St., N.Y., N.Y. 10014.

WINTER, CHRISTINE CANNON, Wms. Ed., Jacksonville Daily News, Bell Fork Rd., Jacksonville, N.C. 28540, '61–; Off. Mgr., U.S. Govt., '46–'51, '38–'40; N.C. Press Wms. Assn.; Univ. of Fla.; b. Pelham, Ga., 1916; p. Edward and Annie Newell Cannon; h. Carlton Winter; c. Mrs. John H. Sitton; res: 3938 Belshire Lane, Charlotte, N.C. 28205.

WINTER, GINNY LINVILLE, Free-lance Artist and Auth., '60–; Artist, Stevens Gross Studio, '55–'60; J. Walter Thompson, '43–'45; Auth.-Illus.: "The Ballet Book," '62; "What's In My Tree," '62; "The Riding Book," '63; "The Swimming Book," '64; poems and illus. for children's mags.; various orgs. and aws.; Art Inst. of Chgo., '43–'45; Am. Acad. of Arts, '45; Ill. Inst. of Design, '47–'49; b. W. Lafayette, Ind., 1925; p. James and Nellie Kendall Linville; h. Munroe Winter; c. Mary Adams, Kendall Linville; res: 333 Crescent Dr., Lake Bluff, Ill. 60044.

WINTER, RUTH GROSMAN, Sci. Ed., Star-Ledger, Newark, N.J., '58–; Gen. Assigt., '56–'58; '51–'55; Houston (Tex.) Press, '55–'56; Colmst., N. Am. Nwsp. Alliance; Contrbr. to consumer mags.; Auth., "Poisons in Your Food" (Crown, '69); various orgs., aws.; Upsala Col., BA, '51; b. Newark, N.J., 1930; p. Robert and Rose Rich Grosman; h. Arthur Winter; c. Robin, Craig, Grant; res: 44 Holly Dr., Short Hills, N.J. 07078.

WINTERS, JANET HAMILTON, Wms. Ed., Xenia Daily Gazette, Chew Publishing Co., 37 S. Detroit St., Xenia, Oh. 45385, '61–; Gen. Reptr., '60–'61; Oh. Nwsp. Wms. Assn. (for wms. news, cols., headlines, three aws.); b. Xenia, Oh., 1920; p. Charles and Margaret Barwise Hamilton; h. Ralph Winters; c. Michael, Sue; res: 860 Dayton-Xenia Rd., Xenia, Oh. 45385.

WINTHROP, MARIE MARGARET, Pres., Tech ADgency, Inc., 1004 E. Jefferson Ave., Detroit, Mich. 48207, '44–; Fashion Dir., J. L. Hudson, '42–'44; Fashion Reptr., WXYX, '41–'44; PR Dir., Oppenheim-Collins (N.Y.C.), '34–'40; Reptr., New York Herald Tribune, '32–'34; numerous orgs.; Univ. of Detroit; Oh. State Univ., BS; b. Detroit, Mich., 1908; p. Adam and Eugenie Burlen Winthrop; res: 1004 E. Jefferson, Detroit, Mich. 48207.

WIRSIG, JANE DEALY, Dir. of Pubns., Educational Testing Service, Princeton, N.J. 08540, '60–; Edtl. Cnslt., '57–'60; Ed.-Rewtr., Companion in Paris, Woman's Home Companion, '53–'56; Free-lance Mag. Wtr., '42–'50; News Wtr., CBS Radio Network, '42–'43; Vassar Col., BA, '41 (honors; Phi Beta Kappa); Columbia Univ., MS (Jnlsm.), '42; b. Boston, Mass., 1919; p. James and Anna McQuillen Dealy; h. Woodrow Wirsig; c. Alan R., Guy R., Paul H.; res: 777 W. State St., Trenton, N.J. 08618.

WISE, WINIFRED E., Auth: "Rebel in Petticoats" (Chilton, '60; New York Times 100 best bks. for young people, '60); "Harriet Beecher Stowe" (Putnam, '65); "Fanny Kemble, Actress, Author, Abolitionist" (Putnam, '66; Univ. of Cal. Friends of the Lib. Aw., '67); "Fray Junípero Serra and the California Conquest" (Scribner, '67), several other biog. bks.; Adv. Exec., Marshall Field (Chgo., Ill.), '39–'52; Staff Ed., Compton's Pictured Encyclopedia, '30–'33; Theta Sigma Phi (Silver Cup Aw., '65), active in commty. affairs; Univ. of Wis., BA (cum laude); b. Fond du Lac, Wis.; p. William and Jennie Jones Wise; c. Jenifer Ann Graham, Mrs. Penelope Gilde, Philip Palmer; res: Box 294, Laguna Beach, Cal. 92652.

WISEMAN, ANNE MURRAY, Auth., non-fiction, c/o Houghton Mifflin Company, 2 Park St., Boston, Mass.; Remedial Reading Tchr., N. Andover Public Schs., '68–; Librn., (Balt., Md.) '62–'65; Tchr., '54–'59; ALA, numerous educ. orgs.; Mass. State Col., BS (Educ.), '54; MS (Educ.), '69; b. Salem, Mass., 1932; p. James and Genevieve McNally Murray; h. Charles Wiseman; c. Anne, Charles, James; res: 83 Elm St., Andover, Mass. 01810.

WITHROW, BETTY ANN, Librn., California College of Medicine, University of California, Irvine, Cal. 92664, '67–; Librn., Bowman Gray Sch. of Med., Wake

Forrest Univ., '63–'67; Librn., Health Sci. Lib., State Univ. of N.Y. (Buffalo), '61–'63; Librn., Univ. of Vt. Col. of Med., '57–'61; Ref. Librn., Univ. of Miami Sch. of Med. '55–'57; Ref. Librn., Univ. of Ala., Med. Ctr., '52–'55; Asst. Librn., Cinn. Gen. Hosp. Med. Lib., '49–'52; Intern, Vanderbilt Univ. Sch. of Med. Lib., '48–'49; articles, pfsnl. jnls.; Med. Lib. Assn. (Secy., '64–'66).

WITT, JEANNE St. ONGE, Sch. Ed., Corr. Ed., TV Ed., Svc. Ed., News Reptr., Faribault Daily News, 514 Central Ave., Faribault, Minn. 55021, '67–; Univ. of Minn., BA (Eng., Jnlsm.), '49; b. St. Paul, Minn., 1926; p. William and Alvina Young St. Onge; h. Charles Witt; c. Charles, III, Steven; res: 1027 Westwood Dr., Faribault, Minn. 55021.

WITTEN, MERRILL SAPHRO, Exec. Dir., Mental Health Assoc. of Mecklenburg City, Charlotte, N.C. 28202, '69–; Prom. Dir., Central Charlotte Assn., '66–'68; Exec. Secry., Gaston Med. Soc., '64; Radio Bdcstr., WGNC, '57–'63; ABC, '48; CBS, '47; Mutual, '46; Free-lance TV and Stage Actress; AWRT, Mint Museum Drama Guild; Northwestern Univ., BS, '44; b. Bklyn., N.Y., 1922; p. Benjamin and Etta Morris Saphro; h. (div.); c. Eric, Daniel; res: 1030 Edgehill Rd., Charlotte, N.C. 28202.

WITTNER, MIRIAM HALPERIN, Treas., Fred Wittner Company, Inc., 850 Third Ave., N.Y., N.Y. 10022, '59–; Partner, '43–'59; Tchr. (Israel), '33–'34; Univ. of Wis., BA, '31; p. Simon and Minnie Rosenberg Halperin; h. Fred Wittner; c. Simon David, Deborah Ellen; res: 22 Cornell St., Scarsdale, N.Y. 10583.

WOFFORD, DOROTHY FERGUSON, Children's Dir., Third Baptist Church, 620 N. Grand Ave., St. Louis, Mo. 63103, '62–; Tchr., 15 yrs.; Wtr. of articles for children's tchrs., stories and articles for religious pubns.; Ch. Fedn. Ecumenical Aw., '62; active in commty. affairs; Who's Who of Am. Wm.; Wash. Univ., '25; Brookes Bible Inst., '31; b. St. Louis, Mo., 1903; p. Theodore and Annie Mae Ferguson; h. George H. Wofford; c. Theodore John; res: 4940 Magnolia Ave., St. Louis, Mo. 63139.

WOHLBERG, HELEN, Pres., Helen Wohlberg, Inc., 331 E. 50th St., N.Y., N.Y. 10022, '63–; WNBA, Soc. of Photogrs. and Artists Reps. (Exec. Bd.).

WOLCOTT, BETTY DALE, Ed., Corp. Info., Eastman Kodak Company, 343 State St., Rochester, N.Y. 14650, '69–; Publicist, Edtl. Svc. Bur., '49–'69; Applied Physics Lab., Johns Hopkins Univ., '46–'47; Offcr., U.S. Navy, '44–'47; Ed., Galva (Ill.) News, '43–'44; Asst. Ed., Collinsville (Ill.) Herald, '40–'43; AWRT, Theta Sigma Phi; Univ. of Ill., BS (Jnlsm.), '40; b. Fillmore, Ill., 1918; p. Earl and Ruby Wright Wolcott; res: 730 Lake Shore Blvd., Rochester, N.Y. 14617.

WOLF, ELLIE EPARD, Cont. Dir., Wms. Program Dir., Dir. of Public Svc., Golden Plains, Inc., Radio

Station KXXX, P.O. Box 127, Colby, Kan. 67701, '68–; Shopworth Talent for Symns-Shafer Mercantile Co., '58–'59; Mo. Valley Assn., Amateur Athletics Un.; Brown Mackie Sch. of Bus., '51–'52; b. Colby, Kan., 1932; p. Arthur and Mable Strait Epard; h. Neil D. Wolf; c. Gregory Lynn, Judy Kay, Rod Allen; res: 740 E. Eighth, Colby, Kan. 67701.

WOLF, MIRIAM BREDOW, Free-lance Med.-Tech. Wtr.; Dir., Eastern Sch. for Physicians' Aides, '59–'60; Dean of Wm., Asst. Dir., '41–'59; Med. Secy., '29–'41; Am. Embassy (Paris), '21–'22; U.S. Consulate, Buenos Aires, '19–'21; various orgs.; b. Bklyn., N.Y., 1895; p. Alfred and Anita Adkins Bredow; h. Heinrich F. Wolf (dec.); res: 227 E. 57th St., N.Y., N.Y. 10022.

WOLF, SUSAN ANDERSON, Assoc. Ed., American Photographic Book Publishing Co., Inc., 915 Broadway, N.Y., N.Y. 10010, '69–; Asst. Ed., '67–'69; Am. Veterinary Med. Assn., '64–'65; Free-lance ed.; active in conservation and population control vol. orgs.; Bryn Mawr Col., AB, '66 (cum laude); b. Chgo., Ill., 1942; p. Raymond and Ardys Belisch Breinin; h. John Wolf; res: 60 Park Terrace West, N.Y., N.Y. 10034.

WOLF, W. MAXINE, State Ed., The Lincoln Star, 926 P St., Lincoln, Neb. 68501, '42–; Theta Sigma Phi; Univ. of Neb., BA (Jnlsm.), '42; b. Omaha, Neb.; p. Otto and Dora Petersen Wolf; res: 2021 S. Cotner, Lincoln, Neb. 68506.

WOLFE, ANITA MIRONOV, Fashion Coordr., Needham, Harper & Steers, 909 Third Ave., N.Y., N.Y., '66–; Fashion Stylist, Lord and Taylor, '66; Asst. to Beauty Ed., Glamour mag., '65–'66; Roving Secy., Condé Nast; Drexel Inst. of Tech., BS, '65 (with hons.); b. New Brunswick, N.J., 1943; p. Jack and Blanche Balaban Mironov; h. Benjamin Wolfe; res: 10 S. Station Lane, Huntington, N.Y. 11743.

WOLFE, RUTH HASLAM, Free-lance Edtl. Cnslt., 736 West End Ave., N.Y., N.Y. 10025, '68–; Art in America, '66–'68; American Heritage Publ. Co., '60–'66; Smith Col., BA, '58 (magna cum laude); b. Milledgeville, Ga., 1936; p. George and Maye Stanley Haslam; h. Leonard Wolfe; res: 186 Sturges Ridge Rd., Wilton, Conn. 06897.

WOLFF, ALICE ECKSTEIN, Ed., Bk. Reviewer, The Kirkus Reviews, The Kirkus Service, 60 W. 13th St., N.Y., N.Y. 10011, '62–; various exec. positions, '36–; Smith Col. (Sophia Smith Fellowship); b. N.Y.C., 1914; p. Henry and Alice Raphael Eckstein; h. Werner Wolff; c. Steven, Mark; res: 397 Bleecker St., N.Y., N.Y. 10014.

WOLFF, JANET L., Exec. VP-Crtv. Svcs., Crtv. Dir., William Esty Co., 100 E. 42nd St., N.Y., N.Y. 10017; Sr. Copy Group Head, VP, J. Walter Thompson, '51–'61; Auth., "What Makes Women Buy" (McGraw-Hill, '58); Fashion Group; Adv. Wm. of the Yr., '58; Finch Col., Tobe Coburn Sch. of Fashion Careers, Columbia Gen. Studies; b. S.F., Cal., 1924; p. Albert and Aurene Goddard Loeb; h. James Alexander Wolff; c. James A., Jr., John K., Barbara A., Timothy G.; res: 4139 Waldo Ave., N.Y., N.Y.

WOLFF, MARY L., Pres., Wolff & Weir, Inc., 3216 Arapahoe Ave., Boulder, Colo. 80302, '66–; VP, '65–'66; Asst. to Dir., Nat. Ctr. for Atmospheric Rsch., '60–'64; Asst. to Dir., High Altitude Observatory, '56–'60; Assn. of Indsl. Advs., Adv. Club of Denver, Am. Mktng. Assn. (Colo. Chptr. Secy., '69–); Univ. of Mich., Univ. of Minn.; Univ. of Denver, AB, '55; b. St. Paul, Minn., 1923; p. Charles and Linda Baker Ames; h. Edwin L. Wolff; c. Linda Andrews Freilich, William Kent Andrews, Lesley Andrews; res: 1228 17th St., Boulder, Colo. 80302.

WOLFF, MILLIE BENDER, Pubcty. Dir., Arts and Education Council Greater St. Louis, 607 N. Grand, St. Louis, Mo. 63103, '67–; Gateway Theatre, '63–'67; Dir. Special Events, Gem Intl., '62; Colmst., Globe Democrat; Coordr., KETC-TV, '64; Prodr., "Critic on the Go," KSD; St. Louis Wtrs. Guild, Auths. Guild of Am., League of Wm. Voters, Who's Who of Am. Wm.; Oh. State Univ.; Univ. of Miami; Akron Univ.; b. Mt. Pleasant, Pa.; p. Ben and Ruth Murstein Bender; h. (dec.; div.); c. Mack B. Shaw, Henry S. Shaw, Alvin Wolff, Jr.; res: 6 Blaytonn Lane, St. Louis, Mo. 63124.

WOLFF, SELMA STRAUSS, Assoc. Ed., Fortune, Time-Life Building, Rockefeller Center, N.Y., N.Y. 10020, '57–; Rsch. Assoc., '43–'57; Edtl., Rsch. Cnslt.

WOLFRAM, BONNIE REDMOND, M.D., Pres., Educational Media Inc., 620 New Center Bldg., Detroit, Mich. 48202, '67–; Cnslt., Dept. of Health, Educ. and Welfare; Nat. Chmn., Nat. Kidney Fndn.; Med.-Coordr., "Lifeline to Tomorrow" (motion pic.; Gold Medal Aw., '68–'69); active in prod. of multimedia prods. in the health and med. fields for pfsnl. and public audiences; various orgs.; Mich. State Univ., BS, '47; MS, '51; Univ. of Mich., MD, '57; b. Franklin, Pa., 1925; p. Raymond and Lyda M. Redmond; h. Lawrence H. Regan; c. Jill Rae; res: 65 N. Deeplands, Grosse Point Shores, Mich. 48236.

WOLFSON, SUZANNE OST, Media Dir., Hegelmann & Bartolone, Inc., 500 Fifth Ave., N.Y., N.Y. 10036, '68–; Lambert & Feasley; Pharmaceutical Adv. Club; Fashion Inst. of Tech., AAS, '65; Hunter Col., New Sch. for Social Rsch.; b. N.Y.C., 1944; p. Harold and Beatrice Hirsch Ost; h. Jeffrey Wolfson; res: 65–09 99th St., Forest Hills, N.Y. 11375.

WOLLAN, LOIS GUTZKE, VP, Wollan & Wollan, Inc., 4600 W. 77th St., Mpls., Minn. 55435, '63–; Freelance Wtr., '52–'63; Reprt., UP, '51–'52; Univ. of Wis. News Svc., '50–'51; La Crosse (Wis.) Tribune, '45–'50; various orgs., aws.; La Crosse State Tchrs. Col., BS; Univ. of Wis., '50–'51; b. Marshfield, Wis., 1928; p.

Walter and Doris Ott Gutzke; h. Gerald C. Wollan; c. Eric Conrad, Christine Rae, Lisa Margaret.

WOLLE, MURIEL SIBELL, Artist, Auth., Lectr.; Art Prof., Univ. of Colo., '26–'66; N.Y. Sch. of Fine and Applied Art, '23–'26; State Col. for Wm. (Denton, Tex.), '20–'23; Auth.-Illus.: "Ghost Cities of Colorado" ('33), "Stampede to Timberline" ('49), "The Bonanza Trail" ('53), "Montana Pay Dirt" ('63); various orgs., aws.; N.Y. Sch. of Fine and Applied Art, '17–'20; N.Y.U., BS (art educ.), '28; Univ. of Colo., MA, '30; b. Bklyn., N.Y. 1898; p. Harry and Florence Underwood Sibell; h. Francis Wolle; res: 500 Mohawk Dr., Apt. 204, Boulder, Colo. 80303.

WOOD, BERTHA EMMA, Chmn. Commtns. Div., New York State Federation of Women's Clubs, S. New Berlin, N.Y. 13843, '66–; Free-lance Publicist; Bernhard Ulmann Co. (N.Y.C.), '30–'67; Fleisher Yarns (Phila., Pa.), '28–'30; Tchr. of Design, City Col., '40–'46; Wms. Press Club of N.Y.C. (Pres., '62–'66); Navy Cit. for voluntary work, '46; b. Phila., Pa.; p. Elmer and Clementine Allen Wood; res: 45–14 43rd St., L.I. City, N.Y. 11104.

WOOD, BEVERLY PRIEST, Assoc. Dir. of Info., University of Arkansas Medical Center, Markham at Hooper Dr., Little Rock, Ark. 72201, '68–; Asst. Dir., '65–'68; News Asst., Div. of Info., '62–'65; Free-lance Wtr., '60–'61; News Ed., Little Rock Bur., AP, '52–'55; Wms. Page Ed., Arkansas Farmer, '49–'50; Reprtr., Adv. Sls., Boone County Headlight, '46–'47; Asst. State Ed., Arkansas Gazette, '45–'46; Co-auth., "Impact and Promise" (Univ. of Ark. Med. Ctr., '64); various orgs.; Univ. of Ill. Sch. of Jnlsm., '44–'45; b. Little Rock, Ark., 1925; p. Glynn and Rubye Deahl Priest; h. Farris W. Wood; res: 29 Ardmore Dr., Little Rock, Ark. 72204.

WOOD, DORIS M., Pres., Patricia Stevens Finishing School, Inc., 107 Clifford St., Detroit, Mich. 48226, '59–; Prodr.-Narrator, WXYZ-TV, '59–'67; PR Dept., Jam Handy Org., '49–'54; AWRT, Fashion Group; Wayne State Univ., '50; b. Hamilton, Ontario, Can.; p. John and Ella Reid Wood; h. (div.); res: 21726 Olmstead, Dearborn, Mich. 48124.

WOOD, ELEANOR NORTON, Info. Offcr., Press Info. Dept., Div. of Highways, State of California, 120 S. Spring, L.A., Cal. 90012, '65–; Colmst., Feature Wtr., Sierra Madre News, '51–'64; Owner, Norton Wood/Edtl. Svc., '60–'65; Wtr., consumer and tech. articles; Theta Sigma Phi, various orgs.; Syracuse Univ., BA (Jnlsm.), '46 (cum laude); b. Cambridge, Mass., 1925; h. Nathaniel Wood; c. Gary Nathaniel, Janet Anne; res: 1430 Tropical Ave., Pasadena, Cal. 91107.

WOOD, EMMA S., Adv. Staff, The Philadelphia Bulletin, Market St., Phila., Pa. 19101, '26–'69; Dir., World Poetry Day Assn., '61–; Ed.-Publr., World Poetry Day Magazine, '61–; Co-auth., "Eleven" (Penn

Laurel Poets, '57); Pa. Poetry Soc. (Mary O'Connor Chptr. Founder, '62); Mary O'Connor Memorial Lib. of Poetry, Founder, '63; numerous orgs., aws.; Univ. of Pa.; N.Y.U.; Charles Morris Price Sch. of Adv.; b. Goshen, N.Y. 1904; p. Burr and Jerusha Wright Sheeley; h. (dec.); c. Mrs. James Gowdy; res: 27 W. Mt. Pleasant Ave., Phila., Pa. 19119.

WOOD, JEANNE WIEGAND, City Ed., Ludington Daily News, 202 N. Rath Ave., Ludington, Mich. 49431, '66–; Gen. Reptr., Mason County Press; Coor., Feature Wtr., Grand Rapids Herald, Detroit Free Press; Mich. Wms. Press Club; b. Conrad, Mont., 1921; p. William and Louise Hapke Wiegand; h. William J. Wood; c. Mrs. Michael W. Laufer.

WOOD, JOAN HERROLD, AE, J. Walter Thompson Company, 420 Lexington Ave., N.Y., N.Y. 10017, '59–; Reptr., Pittsburgh (Pa.) Press, '52–'59; Pitt. Wms. Press Club (Pres., '58–'59); Oh. Univ., BS (Jnlsm.), '52; h. David C. Wood; res: 201 E. 62nd St., N.Y., N.Y. 10021.

WOOD, LELA WALTERS, Dir. of Pers., American National Bank and Trust Company, 101 N. Michigan St., S. Bend, Ind. 46601, '69–; Pers. Mgr., Studebaker Corp., '68–'69; Admr. Pers., '66–'68; Ed., Studebaker Spotlight, '62–'68; Asst. Ed., '60–'62; Understudy, Dir. Indsl. Rels., '59–'60; Ind. Communicators Cncl. (Past VP), Am. Mgt. Assn. (Past Secy.); Univ. of Ind., Univ. of Mich.; b. Cassville, Ark., 1921; p. Lawrence and Victoria Cox Walters; h. Alfred Wood (dec.); c. Gregory L.; res: 310 Rue Flambeau, South Bend, Ind. 46615.

WOOD, MARCIA TEMPEL, Wms. Ed., The Ann Arbor News, 340 E. Huron St., Ann Arbor, Mich. 48106, '67–; Theta Sigma Phi; Mich. Wms. Press Club Story Aw., '69; Univ. of Colo., BS (Jnlsm.), '67 (cum laude); Univ. of Hi., '64; b. Lamar, Colo., 1945; p. Ernest and Dorothy Gist Tempel, Jr.; h. Guy H. Wood; res: 2211 Dexter Ave., Ann Arbor, Mich. 48103.

WOOD, MARYESTHER, Actress, TV and Motion Pics.; Adult Educ. Tchr.; Acad. of TV Arts and Scis.; Delta Psi Omega (Pres.), 1st Place, N.Y. Festival of TV and Radio for Radio Comml.; Univ. of Cal. at Berkeley; b. Dell Rapids, S.D., 1918; p. Vaughn and Anna M. Wood; h. (div.); c. John Vaughn Denver, Lisa Denver; res: 1581 Manning Ave., Apt. 3, L.A., Cal. 90024.

WOOD, MARYLAIRD (Larry), Colmst., Oakland Tribune, Journalist and Free-lance Wtr. for nwsp. and nat. mags. in the fields of home, garden, travel, sports, parks and recreation; Free-lance Publicist, civic orgs. and social agencies; Co-auth., "English for Social Living" (McGraw-Hill); Phi Beta Kappa, Theta Sigma Phi, Cal. Wtrs. Club, Eastbay Women's Press Club, Pi Lambda Theta; Univ. of Wash., BA (magna cum laude), '41; MA (with highest honors) '42; Stanford Univ., '42–'45 (West Coast communications fel-

lowship); Univ. of Cal., '46–'47; b. Sandpoint, Idaho; p. Edward and Alice Small; h. Byron Wood; c. Barry, Mary, Marcia. Res: 6161 Castle Drive, Oakland, Cal. 94611.

WOOD, NATALIE, Actress, Rona Corporation, 9465 Wilshire Blvd., Beverly Hills, Cal. 90212, '43–; Films: "Bob & Carol & Ted & Alice" ('69), "Love With the Proper Stranger" ('64, Acad. Aw. nomination), "Splendour in the Grass" ('61, Acad. Aw. nomination), "West Side Story" ('61), "Rebel Without a Cause" ('55, Acad. Aw. nomination); b. S.F., Cal., 1938; p. Nicholas and Maria Zudiloff Gurdin; h. Richard Gregson; res: 191 N. Bentley Ave., L.A., Cal. 90049.

WOOD, PAULA LeCLER, Free-lance Wtr.; Lectr. on Fgn. Affairs, Colston Leigh Bureau, Harold Peet, N.Y.C., '36–; Fgn. Corr., INS, UPI, AP, NANA, NEA Overseas News Agcy., Transradio Press Svc., London Daily Telegraph, Opera Mundi, others, '32–'58; Contrbr., New Yorker, McCall's, other mags.; OPC (Contrbr., "As We See Russia," "How I Got That Story"), AAUW, Brevard Poetry Club (Pres.); Columbia Univ., AB, AM; St. Lawrence Univ. (Bklyn. Law Sch.), LLB, '35; b. N.Y.C.; h. Walter D. Wood; res: 185 Westover Dr., P.O. Box 1393, Melbourne, Fla. 32901.

WOOD, SHIRLEY MARIE, Talent Coordr., "Tonight Show," National Broadcasting Company, 30 Rockefeller Plaza, N.Y., N.Y., '67–, '62–'63; Jerry Lewis Show, ABC-TV, '63; "Les Crane Show," ABC, '65; "Girl Talk," '63; PR Dir., Oleg Cassini, '61; PR, Pubcty., Lanvin, '55–'60; S.F. Jr. Col.; Univ. of Cal. at Berkeley, BA; b. San Jose, Cal.; p. Carl and Mary Kinder Wood; res: 40 E. 72nd St., N.Y., N.Y. 20021.

WOOD, TONI WARD, Soc. Ed., Reptr., San Clemente Daily Sun Post; Ed., Dana Point Lamplighter, Coastline Publishers, 1542 N. El Camino Real, San Clemente, Cal. 92672, '69–; Colmst., South Coast News, '64–'69; Sch. Cnslt.; Auth., Illus., Publr., pubcty. chmns. handbk.; Jr. Wm. of Yr., '67; San Diego State Col.; Ore. State Univ. (Hons.); b. L.A., Cal., 1935; p. Mueller and Gwendolyn Thompson Ward; h. Leonard Wood; c. Jeffrey, Matthew, Robert; res: 33126 Sea Bright, Dana Point, Cal. 92629.

WOODARD, HEATHER R., Asst. Dir. PR for Special Events, University of Miami, P.O. Box 8105, Coral Gables, Fla. 33124, '68–; Prom., Cont. Dir., Weather Girl, WINZ (Miami, Fla.), '67–'68; Dir. of Info. Svcs., WTHS-TV, '66–'67; Asst. to Program Dir., WSAI Radio (Cinn., Oh.), '65–'66; Traffic Mgr.-Public Svc. Dir., WQAM (Miami, Fla.), '56–'65; various orgs. and aws.; Univ. of Miami, BA (Mortar Bd.; Who's Who in Am. Cols. and Univs.), '56; b. Miami, Fla., 1933; h. William D. Bischoff; res: 7801 S.W. 66th St., Miami, Fla. 33143.

WOODMAN, BETZI DEKEMA, Alaska Corr., Reuters Ltd., 1212 Ave. of the Ams., N.Y., N.Y. 10036, '63–; Assoc. Ed., "Today in Alaska" ('69–); Anchorage Corr., Fairbanks News-Miner, '63–'66; Free-lance Jnlst., Photogr.; Stringer, UPI, '63–'66; Wms. Ed., Anchorage Daily News, '61–'63; Gen. Assigt., Anchorage Daily Times, '59–'60; Colmst., '54–'56; Staff Wtr., Independent Journal (San Rafael, Cal.), '59; numerous orgs.; Univ. of Chgo.; Univ. of Md.; George Wash. Univ.; b. Kalamazoo, Mich., 1913; p. Bert and Wilhelmina Bradley Dekema, Sr.; h. Lyman L. Woodman; c. Kent Lee, Ross Littlefield, Karen Leslie Lew; res: 117 E. Cook Ave., Anchorage, Alaska 99501.

WOODMANSEE, MIGNON RITTENHOUSE, Auth: "Seven Women Explorers" (Lippincott, '64; Cadmus Edition, '67), "The Amazing Nellie Bly" (Dutton, '56; condensation in Good Housekeeping, movie sold to MGM); Edtl. work, Fawcett Pubns., '38–'48; Reptr., Brooklyn Daily Eagle, '24–'36; stories for New York World, Morning Telegraph, Auths. League of Am.; Wheaton Col.; b. N.Y.C.; p. George and Catherine Meisier Rittenhouse; h. Horace Albro Woodmansee; c. George Horace, Lois Kathleen (Mrs. Harold Kellerman); res: 3925 202nd St., Bayside, N.Y. 11361.

WOODRING, MIRIAM LANDIS, Wms. Ed., North Augusta Star, P.O. Box 6095, N. Augusta, S.C. 29841, '54–; E. I duPont Co., '51–'54; Pa. Power & Light Co., '50–'51; Contrbr., Sandlapper Magazine (Columbia, S.C.); S.C. Press Assn. (Tad Quattlebaum Aw., '59; Nwsp. Wm. of the Yr., '66), Nat. Fedn. of Press Wm.; Juniata Col., BS; b. New Castle, Pa., 1928; p. George and Nora Walsh Landis; h. Samuel Woodring; res: 800 Dunbarton Dr., N. Augusta, S.C. 29841.

WOODS, BRENDA AILEEN, Ed. of Doris Blake Column, The New York Daily News, 220 E. 42nd St., N.Y., N.Y. 10017, '58; Edtl., Rsch., Adm. positions, '46–'58; N.Y. Nwsp. Wms. Club; Elmira Col., BA, '46 (Phi Beta Kappa); b. Flushing, N.Y.; p. Frederick and Florence Kuell; h. George G. D'Amato; c. David Paul.

WOODS, ERIKA DOERRWAECHTER, Ed., The Crew's News, Chrysler Marine Products, P.O. Box 27, Hartford, Wis. 53027; Wis. Indsl. Eds. Assn.; Commerce Inst. (Heilbronn, Germany); Univ. of Wis.; b. Karlsruhe, Germany, 1929; h. Richard Woods (div.); c. Thomas, Gregory; res: RFD 1, Box 55, Slinger, Wis. 53086.

WOODS, JOAN LeSUEUR, Tchr., piano; Auth., "Maudie's Mushpots" (Abingdon Press, '63); Contrbr., musical mags.; Lectr. on music teaching methodology; Am. Music Tchrs. Assn., Phoenix Piano Tchrs. Guild (Secy., '69), Music Tchrs. Nat. Assn.; Who's Who of Am. Wm., Dic. of Intl. Biog., 2,000 Wm. of Achiev.; Brigham Young Univ., '50–'52; Ariz. State Univ., '67–'69; b. Phoenix, Ariz., 1932; p. LeRoy and Ruby Kinsey LeSueur; h. Kenneth R. Woods (div.); c. Gregory, Victori, Monica, Cynthia; res: 1401 W. Pepper Pl., Mesa, Ariz. 85201.

WOODSIDE, CHARLOTTE ATWELL, Dir. of Commty. Rels., WQED-WQEX, Metropolitan Pittsburgh Educational Television, 4337 Fifth Ave., Pitt., Pa. 15213, '62–; Ed., Asst. PR Dir., Plymouth Oil Co., '46–'61; Mgr., J. W. Henry Ins. Co., '40–'43; NAEB, Nat. Soc. of Fund Raisers; Univ. of Pitt., BA, '37; b. Pitt., Pa., 1915; p. Ralph and Laura Price Atwell; h. Samuel P. Woodside (dec.); c. Carol W. (Mrs. Mervin C. Stover III); res: 426 Orchard Ave., Pitt., Pa. 15202.

WOODSON, HORTENSE CAROLINE, Auth., biographical and genealogical; Secy. to U.S. Senator Strom Thurmond, Aiken, S.C., '60–'68; Corr., Edgefield Advertiser, '25–'60; Bd. of Trustees, Anderson (S.C.) Col., '58–'62; S.C. Press Assn. Wms. Auxiliary Trophy; Winthrop Col., '17; b. Edgefield, S.C., 1896; p. Tucker and Agatha Abney Woodson; res: 225 Church St., Edgefield, S.C. 29824.

WOODWARD, HILDEGARD, Auth., Illus., Children's Bks. for Scribners, Doubleday, Lippincott; Illus., Sch. Bks. for Ginn & Co., Houghton Mifflin, Macmillan; Art and Stage Dir., Spence Sch. (N.Y.C.), '41–'62; Sch. of Museum of Fine Arts (Boston, Mass.); Sch. of Fine Arts; art works in collections of Univ. of Southern Miss., Smithsonian, Hartford Atheneum, Univ. of Minn.; Sch. of Museum of Fine Arts (Boston), grad., '20 (design); b. Worcester, Mass., 1898; p. Rufus and Stella Brooks Woodward; res: Old Middle Rd., Brookfield, Conn. 06804.

WOODWARD, VIRGINIA BEALL, Reptr., Hattiesburg American, W. Front St., Hattiesburg, Miss. 39401, '61–; Ed., Ft. Lauderdale News, '54–'61; Reptr., '50–'54; Wms. Ed. and Industry Reptr., Zanesville (Oh.) Publ. Co., '30–'50; Educ. article for Southern Educ. Rept.; AP Features, free-lance nwsp. articles; Miss. Press Wm. ('65–'68; aws. '65, '66, '67); active various civic orgs.; Western Col. for Wm., '27–'29; Oh. Wesleyan Univ., '29–'30; Oh. State Univ., '30–'31; b. Barnesville, Oh., 1909; p. Dr. Isaac and Georgia Okey Beall; c. Gregg, Mrs. Robert Bowling; res: 607 Magnolia, Hattiesburg, Miss. 39401.

WOODY, REGINA JONES, Auth., juv. bks.: "A Time to Dance," "TV Dancer 1967," "One Day at a Time," '68; "The Young Medics," '68, others; Ballerina; Auths. Guild, ALA, Wms. Bk. Assn.; b. Boston, Mass., 1894; p. Lewis and Regina Lichtenstein Jones; h. McIver Woody; c. McIver Wallace, Regina (Mrs. John Butler), Emma (Mrs. James M. Sowa); res: 552 Westminster Ave., Elizabeth, N.J. 07208.

WOOLCOCK, OZEIL FRYER, Wms. Interest Ed., Atlanta Daily World, 210 Auburn Ave. N.E., Atlanta, Ga. 30303, '60–; Colmst., Soc. Ed., Food Page Ed., '44–'67; Auth: "A Visit to Havana" ('54), "Traveling U.S.A., Canada and Mexico" ('67), "Events of the Inaugural" ('69); Tchr., lang. arts, Atlanta Public Schs., '52–; numerous orgs., aws.; Clark Col., AB, '32; b. Atlanta, Ga.; p. John and Carrie Moreland Fryer; h. Harold Woolcock (div.); res: 175 Florida Ave. S.W., Atlanta, Ga. 30310.

WOOLFE, MARIANNE STANDING, Dir., Danbury Public Library, 254 Main St., Danbury, Conn. 06810, '68–; Deer Park Public Lib., '65–'68; Lindenhurst Memorial Lib., '62–'65; Librn., Queens Borough Public Lib. System, '61–'62; ALA, Conn. Lib. Assn., Educ. Film Lib. Assn., Suffolk County Lib. Assn.; N.Y. State Univ., BA (cum laude), '49; Pratt Inst. of Lib. Sci., MLS (cum laude), '61; b. Berea, Ky., 1928; h. George Woolfe.

WOOLLEY, CATHERINE (pseud: Jane Thayer), Auth., juv. bks.; Adv., PR (N.Y.C.), '27–'47; Auths. Guild of Am.; Univ. of Cal., BA; b. Chgo., Ill., 1904; p. Edward and Anna L. Woolley; res: 43 High St., Passaic, N.J. 07055.

WOOLSEY, JANETTE, Co-auth., juv. bks.: "It's Time for Thanksgiving" ('57), "It's Time for Christmas" ('59), "It's Time for Brotherhood" ('62), "Terribly Strange Tales" ('67) (all Macrae Smith), many others; Librn., '26–'69; ALA, Pa. Lib. Assn., Pa. State Ret. Tchrs. Assn., York League of Wm. Voters; Middlebury Col., AB, '25; Pratt Inst., BS (Lib. Sci.), '26; Columbia Univ., MS, '31; b. Livingston Manor, N.Y., 1904; p. George and Nellie Dodge Woolsey; res: 450 Madison Ave., York, Pa. 17404.

WOOTTON, THELMA McCARTY, Dir., Albert A. Wells Memorial Library, 638 North St., Lafayette, Ind. 47901, '55–; Asst., '45–'55, '38–'43, '22–'23; Ind. Lib. Assn., Delta Kappa Gamma, Altrusa; Ind. Univ., BA, '27; MA (Lib. Sci.), '59; b. Bringhurst, Ind., 1905; p. Vinson and Mabel Cleaver McCarty; h. Ralph Wootton; c. Alice (Mrs. William Humphrey), Mack E.; res: 2605 S. 9th St., Lafayette, Ind. 47905.

WORCESTER, DOROTHY F., VP, Dir. of Consumer Rsch. and Crtv. Guidance, Harvey and Carlson, Inc., 477 Madison Ave., N.Y., N.Y. 10022, '66–; VP, '69–; Dir. of Crtv. Guidance, J. Walter Thompson, '64–'66; Free-lance Rsch. Cnslt., '57–'64; Special Projects Dir., Grey Adv., '56–'57; Rsch. Dir., Everywoman's Magazine, '54–'56; Asst. to Rsch. Dir., Esquire, '53–'54; Youth and Career Guidance Cnslt.; TV Ghost Wtr.; BA (Social Rels.), MA (Bus. Adm., Social Psych.), PhD (Clinical Psych.); Radcliffe Col., Harvard Univ., City Col. of N.Y., Columbia Univ.; res: Whippoorwill Valley Rd., M. R. Atlantic Highlands, N.J. 07716.

WORLEY, C. JOAN, Ed., Famous-Barr Company, 601 Locust St., St. Louis, Mo. 63101, '68–; Prod. Mgrs. Club, Indsl. Press Assn.; Bradley Univ., AB (Speech, Radio, Theatre), '64; MA (Eng.), '66; b. Houston, Tex., 1941; p. Don and Dorothy McGowan Worley; res: 12132 Valencia, St. Louis, Mo. 63138.

WORLEY, ELEANOR DAVIDSON, Pres., Atlas Foreign Press Service, 30 Sutton Pl., N.Y., N.Y. 10022, '63–; Publr., Ed., Atlas mag., '60–'65; Assoc. Ed., "Best Articles & Stories," '57–'59; Co-owner, Copley Press, '49–'56; Bk. Reviewer, The New Republic, '44–'45; Colmst., Junior League Mag., '36–'39; Reptr., Pasa-dena Post, '29–'31; Bdcst. Fndn. of Am. (Trustee, '64–); Univ. of Cal., '28–'30; b. Chgo., Ill., 1912; p. John Worley and Delia Davidson Worley Copley; h. James H. Jenkins; c. William W. Wilbourne, III; res: Jericho Hill, Mountain Rd., W. Redding, Conn. 06896.

WORTHINGTON, CAROL, Actress, c/o Creative Management Assoc., L.A. and N.Y., and Abrams-Rubaloff & Assoc., L.A. and N.Y.; Commls., Stage, TV, Motion Pics.

WORTHINGTON, DIANE MOFFATT, Film-Talent Coordr., Benton & Bowles, Inc., 909 Third Ave., N.Y., N.Y. 10022, '66–; Free-lance Film Wtr., Rschr., Cnslt., '68–'69; Prod. Asst., Europix Consolidated Corp., '66; Asst. Prodr., Cahill, Kacine & Heimann, '65–'66; Prod. Secy., Young & Rubicam, '63–'65; Encorp; Phi Theta Kappa, Delta Psi Omega, Am. Film Festival Judge, '67, '68; Endicott Jr. Col., '59–'61; Univ. of Wis., BS, '63; b. New Milford, Conn., 1942; p. Elmer and Mildred Knight Worthington; res: 214 E. 51st St., N.Y., N.Y. 10022.

WORTHINGTON, LEE SIMS, Free-lance PR Cnslt., '65–; Part Owner, Tranter Mfg., Inc., Lansing, Mich., '35–'65; Adv. Wtr., The Jaqua Co., Grand Rapids, '27–'35; Webber Adv. Assocs., '25–'27; Contrbr., numerous trade mags.; Adv. Roundtable of Mich. (many offs.); Wms. Adv. Club of Detroit, AIA (Bd. Mbr., '52–'53); numerous commty., polit., ch. orgs.; Dir. Mail Adv. Assn. Aw.; AFA and Printers Ink Silver Aw., '63; Lansing Altrusa Club Wm. of Yr., '43; b. Bancroft, Mich.; p. William and Carol Fleming Sims; h. Robert J. Worthington; c. Mrs. J. J. Metroka; res: 525 Northlawn, E. Lansing, Mich. 48823.

WORTHINGTON, MARJORIE M., Auth., c/o Harold Matson, 22 E. 40th St., N.Y., N.Y. 10016; Auth: 11 bks., incl. novels and biogs.; one children's bk.; numerous short stories in Harper's, McCalls, Harper's Bazaar, others; Lectr.; Dir., wtrs. workshops; Auths. League; stories selected for O'Brien, O'Henry anthologies; b. N.Y.C.; h. (1) Carlton Beecher Stetson (dec); (2) Lyman Worthington (div.); (3) William B. Seabrook (dec.); res: 1708 N.E. 24th St., Ft. Lauderdale, Fla. 33305.

WORTHYLAKE, MARY MOORE, Tchr., Vancouver (Wash.) Schools; Auth: "Nika Illahee," "Moolack—Young Salmon Fisherman," "Children of the Seed Gatherers" (all publ. by Melmont Press); Ashland Tchrs. Org. (Pres., '49–'50), Orinda Tchrs. Org., Delta Kappa Gamma; Bellingham Wtrs. aw., '61–'62; Western Wash. Col. of Educ., BA, '41; MEd, '54; b. Wakonda, S.D., 1904; p. Harry and Abigail Noyes Moore; h. Harry V. Worthylake; c. Mary Jo Paxton, Frank Bernard Barrows, Patricia Huntington, Barbara Jean Wyatt, Ralph D. Worthylake, Margaret Louise Franz (dec.); res: 1881 Country Club Rd., Woodburn, Ore. 97071.

WOTRING, MARY ALICE, Mgr., CBS/Columbia Group Archives, 51 W. 52nd St., N.Y., N.Y. 10019, '67–; Masterworks Coordr., CBS Records, '64–'67; Lake Erie Col., BA, '58; Univ. of Mich., MM, '62; b. West Reading, Pa., 1938; p. John and Laura Britton Wotring; res: 304 E. 73rd St., N.Y., N.Y. 10021.

WREN, SUZANNE E., Commtns. Specialist, Sr. Staff Wtr., Fensholt Public Relations, Inc., 22 E. Huron St., Chgo., Ill. 60611, '68–; Asst. AE, PR Wtr., Gerson Howe & Johason, '67–'68; Acc. Coordr., Robert Vogele, Inc., '67; R. R. Donnelley & Sons, '61–'66; Adm. Staff, U.S. Olympic Comm., '57–'61; Free-lance PR; Miami (Oh.) Univ., '54–'57; Northwestern Univ., '56; b. Chgo., Ill.; p. Thomas and Esther Stroh Wren; res: Chgo., Ill.

WRIGHT, ALICE EDWARDS, Head Librn., Morley Library, 184 Phelps St., Painesville, Oh. 44077, '64–; Burbank (Cal.) Public Lib., '59–'64; Akron (Oh.) Lib., '51–'59, '28–'37; Oh. Univ. Lib., '24–'27; Dayton (Oh.) Public Lib., '20–'23; ALA, Oh. Lib. Assn., Oh. Univ. Alumni Assn. (Southern Cal. Pres., '64), Daughters of the Am. Colonists; Oh. Univ., BA, '27; Kent State Univ., MA (Lib. Sci.), '52; b. New Lebanon, Oh., 1905; p. John and Maud Vaniman Edwards; h. Earl O. Wright (dec.); c. Robert B., Richard J., David (dec.), Jane (dec.); res: 7 N. Park Pl., Apt. 31, Painesville, Oh. 44077.

WRIGHT, ALMA McINTYRE, Pres., Indoor Gardener Publishing Company, Inc., P.O. Box 549, 1800–1802 Grand Ave., Knoxville, Tenn. 37901, '63–; Ed., African Violet mag., '47–'63; Exec. Dir., African Violet Soc. of Am., '60–'63; Ed., "The Master List of African Violets"; Contrb. Ed., numerous horticulture bks.; Garden Wtrs. of Am., Am. Horticulture Soc.; Saintpaulia Intl. aw., '66; Univ. of Tenn., BS (Educ.), '32; b. Knoxville, Tenn., 1909; p. William and Theresa Biagiotti McIntyre; h. Robert Oliver Wright; c. Robert Oliver Jr.; res: 4752 Calumet Dr. S.W., Knoxville, Tenn. 37919.

WRIGHT, BETTY RHOADS, Dir. of Mbrship., The National Historical Society, '68–; Prom. Dir., Historical Times, Inc., 302 York St., Gettysburg, Pa., '62–; formerly Prom. Mgr., Bus. Exec. Pubns.; Asst. Prom. Mgr., U.S. News and World Report; Free-lance Publicist, Wtr., Adv. Cnslt.; b. Asheville, N.C.; p. Edward and Gladys Buckner Rhoads; h. Frank L. Wright; res: 212 S. Fairfax St., Alexandria, Va. 22314.

WRIGHT, ELEANOR AMANDA, Nat. Adv. Mgr., Secy. to Publr., The Republican Publishing Company, 18-20 E. Vine St., Mount Vernon, Oh. 43050, '67–; Secy., Intl. Div., Cooper-Bessemer, '64–'67; Secy. to Chief Execs., Flexible Packaging Div., Continental Can Co., '40–'64; b. Mount Vernon, Oh., 1921; p. Carl and Izora Belt Wright; res: 601 Gambier Ave., Mount Vernon, Oh. 43050.

WRIGHT, ELEANOR STRAUB, Assoc. Ed., Electrical

Apparatus Service-Volt/Age, Barks Publications, Inc., 360 N. Michigan Ave., Chgo., Ill. 60601, '65–; Colmst., Webster Advertiser, Mo., '60–'65; Pubcty., Trenton, N.J. Commty. Chest, '47–'49; Soc. Reptr., St. Louis Post-Dispatch, '45–'47; Free-lance Edtl. Wtr.; Theta Sigma Phi (Past Chptr. Pres.; Nat. PR Dir., '56–'60); Monticello Col., AA, '43; Northwestern Univ., BS, MSJ, '45; b. Webster Groves, Mo., 1923; p. Charles and Edna Schulz Straub; h. James A. Wright; c. Carolyn, Betsy; res: 550 Lee Ave., Webster Groves, Mo. 63119.

WRIGHT, IONE STUESSY, Ed., Journal of Inter-American Studies, University of Miami, P.O. Box 8134, Coral Gables, Fla. 33124; '66–; Advisor, Hispanic-Am. Studies, '64–; Faculty Mbr., Summer Workshop, Oaxaca, Mex., '53–'57; Rsch., '41–'46; Prof. of Hist.; articles, bks.; AAUW, Southeastern Conf. on Latin Am. Studies (Pres., '67), Southern Hist. Assn., Conf. of Latin Am. Hist.; Am. Hist. Assn. Aw., Phi Alpha Theta; Westhampton Col., BA, '26; Univ. of Richmond (Va.), MA, '37; Univ. of Cal. (Berkeley), Ph.D, '40; b. La Grange, Ill., 1905; p. Samuel and Augusta Ek Stuessy; h. Victor A. Wright (dec.); c. Mrs. Robert P. Hunter, Clyde Lee, Keith Albert, Mrs. William G. Lacey; res: 485 N.E. 94th St., Miami, Fla. 33138.

WRIGHT, KATHRYN HUTCHINSON, Sunday Ed., The Billings Gazette, Fourth Ave. N., Billings, Mont. 59101, '61–; Reptr., Feature Wtr., Photogr., '42–'50; Special Sections Ed., '42–; Auth: "Billings—The Magic City," "Montana—Territory of Treasures."

WRIGHT, MARGUERITE WITTWER, Commty. Rels. Specialist, Oregon Board of Education, 942 Lancaster Dr. N.E., Salem, Ore. 97310, '69–; Pubns. Ed., '69; Commty. Organizer, Mid-Willamette Valley Commty. Action Prog., '66–'68; Health Educ., Marion County Health Dept., '65–'66; Wms. Ed., Capital Press, '63–'65; Theta Sigma Phi (Achiev. aw.), Ore. Civil Rights Adv. Comm., Marion County Dem. Club (Pres., '64), Salem Art Assn. (Bd. of Dirs., '63–'66); City of Salem svc. aw., '66; U.S. OEO aw., '68; Univ. of Ore., BA (Jnlsm.), '47; b. Scharnachthal, Switzerland, 1926; p. Jacob and Madeleine Hari Wittwer; h. Thomas G. Wright; c. Suzanne Katherine, Patricia Madeleine, Sarah Elizabeth, Jeanne Marguerite; res: 7315 S.W. 13th Dr., Portland, Ore. 97219.

WRIGHT, PHYLLIS MANN, Free-lance Wtr.; Med. Ed., Ladies' Home Journal, 641 Lexington Ave., N.Y., N.Y. 10022, '66–; Co-Dir., Cystic Fibrosis Clinic, U.C.L.A. Ctr. for Health Scis., '64–; Pediatrician, U.C.L.A., '53–'69; Dir., Birth Defects Ctr. (Honolulu, Hi.), '67–'68; Tech. Advisor, "Dr. Kildare," '61–'63; Pediatrician, Atomic Bomb Casualty Commn. (Nagasaki, Japan), '50–'52; various pediatric socs.; L.A. Commty. Chest Wm. of Tomorrow, '54; Phi Beta Kappa, Alpha Omega Alpha; Barnard Col., BA, '41; Cornell Univ., MD, '45; b. Saratoga Springs, N.Y., 1921; p. Horace and Hazel Becker Mann; h. Stanley

Wright; c. Carol Lynn, Brian; res: 16065 Jeanne Lane, Encino, Cal. 91316.

WRIGHT, SARAH M. (Sally), Religion Ed., Feature Wtr., The Concord Transcript, P.O. Box 308, 1741 Clayton Rd., Concord, Cal. 94520, '69–; Gen. Assignment Reptr., Feature Wtr., The Cinn. (Oh.) Enquirer, '66–'69; Tucson (Ariz.) Daily Citizen, '63–'65; Omaha (Neb.) World Herald, '60–'62; Peru (Ind.) Daily Tribune, '56–'60; Theta Sigma Phi (Col. Chptr. Pres., '59–'60; Cinn. Chptr. Treas., '67–'69); Best Feature Story, Nat. Softball Wtrs. and Sportscasters Assn., '68; two Oh. Nwsp. Wms. Assn. Contest aws., '68; Franklin Col., BA (Jnlsm.; Who's Who in Am. Cols. and Univs.); Univ. of Ariz.; Grad. Work toward MA (Govt.; Phi Sigma Alpha); b. Peru, Ind., 1938; p. Woodkirk and Eulee Croft Wright; res: 161 Ellis St., Apt. 218, Concord, Cal. 94520.

WUNSCH, JOSEPHINE McLEAN, Wtr., fiction, non-fiction; Wms. Dept., Detroit Free Press, '38–'40; Auth: "Summer of Decision" (David McKay, '68), "Passport to Russia" (David McKay, '65), "Flying Skis" (David McKay, '62); Detroit Wm. Wtrs., Theta Sigma Phi, Jr. League; Univ. of Mich., '36; b. Detroit, Mich., 1914; p. John and Georgiana Grant McLean; h. Edward Wunsch; c. Katherine G., Elizabeth (Mrs. Ralph Gordon), Edward Seward, Jr.; res: 31 McKinley Pl., Grosse Pointe Farms, Mich. 48236.

WURSTER, MARGUERITE SMITH, Asst. Librn., The Extension Library, University of South Florida, 845 First St. S., St. Petersburg, Fla. 33701, '65–; Asst. Dir. of Lib., Fla. Inst. for Continuing Univ. Studies, '63–'65; Head Librn., Div. of Plant Industry, Fla. State Dept. of Agriculture, '58–'63; Lib. Asst., Univ. of Fla. Libs., '52–'58; Special Lib. Assn. (Fla. Chptr. Pres.), Southeastern Lib. Assn., Fla. Lib. Assn.; Who's Who in Lib. Svc., Intl. Dic. Biog., Who's Who of Am. Wm., Royal Blue Bk., Who's Who in the South and Southeast; Univ. of Fla., BA, '63; b. Ocala, Fla., 1916; p. William and Inez Ray Smith; h. Robert Wurster; c. Hal Smith Batey, Marilyn Batey (Mrs. James Holeman), Diana Batey (Mrs. David Pettengill); res: 6514 27th Ave. N., St. Petersburg, Fla. 33710.

WURTENBURG, GLADYS V., Dir. of Col. Rels., Queens College of the City University of New York, Kissena Blvd., Flushing, N.Y. 11367, '66–; Assoc. in PR, '60–'66; Asst. Pubcty. Dir., Intl. Comm. of YMCAs, '57–'60; Field Exec., Girl Scouts U.S.A., '51–'55; Dir. Customer Svcs., A. B. Dick, '47–'51; Lectr., PR, Queens Col.; Bk. Reviewer, Artist, Park East; Cnslt.; USO mag., Port Wash. Commty. Action Cncl., C.U.N.Y. Program of Study Abroad, "University of the Air"; PRSA, ACPRA, Met. PR Assn., Long Island PR Assn.; Queens Col., BA, '47; b. N.Y.C.; res: Port Wash., N.Y. 11050.

WYATT, MELAINE MILDRED, Wyatt Communications, 401 N. Michigan Ave., Chgo., Ill. 60611, '69–; VP, PR, K & A, Inc., '68–'69; AE, Griswold-Eshleman,

'65–'68; AE, Fulton, Morrissey, '64–'65; AE, Donald Young & Assoc., '62–'64; Mng. Ed., Industrial Research, '61–'62; Assoc. Ed., Purchasing News, '58–'60; Supvsr., Press Rel., IIT Rsch. Inst., '53–'58; Reptr., Feature Wtr., Logansport (Ind.) Pharos-Tribune, '46–'52; Contrbr., World Book Encyclopedia Annual Year-Book, '54–'58; Wms. Adv. Club of Chgo., Pubcty. Club of Chgo., PRSA, Theta Sigma Phi, Ind. Univ., AB (Jnlsm., Polit. Sci.), '46; b. Gary, Ind.; res: 5905 Forest Ave., Gary, Ind. 46403.

WYCKOFF, EDITH HAY, Ed.-Publr., Founder, The Leader, Locust Valley, N.Y. 11560, '46–; Specialties Inc., '43–'45; Newsday, '40–'43; Nassau Daily Journal, '39; Long Island Star Journal, '36; North Shore Daily Journal, '35; Auth., "Editing and Producing the Small Publication" (Van Nostrand '56); N.Y. Press Assn. (numerous photog., edtl. aws.); b. Pitt., Pa., 1916; p. Thomas and Helen Goldsmith Hay; h. William Wyckoff (div.); res: Box 468, Locust Valley, N.Y. 11560.

WYGANT, ALICE FINCH, Info. Offcr., California Department of Public Works, Division of Highways, 703 B St., Marysville, Cal. 95901, '66–; Asst. Info. Offcr., '65–'66, '63–'64; Ed., Publr., Western Confectioner, Western Tobacconist, '64–'65; Edtl. Rept. Svc., '54–'63; Colmst., The Piedmonter (Oakland), '57–'63; Ed., Colmst., The Montclarion, '50–'54; Cal. Wtrs. Club, State Info. Offcrs. Cncl., Sierra Club; Who's Who of Am. Wm., Dic. of Intl. Biog.; grad., Columbia Hosp. School of Nursing; b. Joliet, Ill., 1921; p. Winfield and Berd DeViney Finch; h. Willis Wygant Jr.; c. Willis Edward III; Scott; res: 716 Mayfair Ave., Yuba City, Cal. 95991.

WYLER, GRETCHEN, Talent; Broadway Theatre: "Guys and Dolls," "Damn Yankees," "Where's Charley," "Bye Bye Birdie," "Silk Stockings;" West End (London, Eng.): "Sweet Charity"; Film: featured role, "Devil's Brigade"; TV: synd. series, "Step This Way"; Co-Host, "Perry Como Replacement Show"; Outer Circle Critics aw., best supporting actress, "Silk Stockings," '55; active in animal welfare legislation; b. Okla. City, Okla.; p. Louis and Peggy Highley Wienecke; res: 44 E. 64th St., N.Y., N.Y. 10990.

WYNDHAM, LEE, Auth., "Writing for Children and Teenagers," 48 juv. bks.; Free-lance Ed., Critic, Cnslt. on writing for young people; Lectr., N.Y.U., '63–; Instr., '58–'62; Lectr. and Workshop Leader, many wtrs. confs. and seminars; WNBA, Auths. League; many bk. club selections; numerous bks. on "best," "distg." lists; Contemporary Auths., Who's Who, More Jr. Auths.; educ. U.S. and abroad; private instruction in music, art; N.Y.U.; h. Robert Wyndham; c. William L., Jane E.; res: Blackwell Ave., Rte. 12, Morristown, N.J. 07960.

WYNN, JOAN LEVENTHAL, Ed.-in-Chief, Ingenue Magazine, 750 Third Ave., N.Y., N.Y. 10017, '67–; Edtl. positions, Seventeen, '63–'67; Commty. Progress,

New Haven, Conn., '63; New Haven Redevelopment, '62–'63; Conn. Col. for Wm., '62 (cum laude, hons. in French lit., Nassau-Suffolk Alumni Club); b. N.Y.C., 1941; p. Jack and Rose Binder Leventhal; h. Richard Wynn; c. Andrew Michael; res: 25 Chapel Pl., Great Neck, N.Y. 11021.

WYNNE, MARIAN FEIT, Reptr., Staff Wtr., Miami News, One Herald Plaza, Miami, Fla. 33101, '69–; Reptr., Entertainment Ed., Coral Gables Times, '63–'69; Wtr., Hollywood (Fla.) Sun-Tattler; Eng. Tchr.; Theta Sigma Phi, Fla. Wms. Press Club, B'nai B'rith (Secy., '63); Fla. Press Assn. commty. svc. aw., '66; Univ. of Fla., AA, '56; Univ. of Miami, BA (Jnlsm.), '58; b. N.Y.C., 1936; p. Louis and Sara Ingber Feit; h. Sheldon Wynne (dec.); c. Susan Kay, Robert W.; res: 9240 S.W. 58th Terr., Miami, Fla. 33143.

WYRICK, MARY CATHERINE WILLIAMSON (pseud: Mary K), Bdcstr., "Mary K's News and Views," KVMA, N. Jefferson, Magnolia, Ark. 71753, '49–; Free-lance PR, adv., '47–; Magnolia Greeting Svc., '47–; formerly tchr., nwsp. corr.; Offcl. City Hostess, '49–; Intl. Platform Assn.; nominated for McCalls 'Golden Mike' Aw., '60; Cited by Look, '56; Who's Who in Ark.; Who's Who in South; Dic. of Intl. Biog.; Top Ten Ark. Wm., '66; Ark. Mother, '66; Who's Who of Am. Wm.; Life Mbr., Nat. PTA; Souther State Col., '34 (special courses, '34–'60) b. Magnolia, Ark.; p. Walter and Willie Merritt Williamson; h. Tullie M. Wyrick; c. Mary Tullie (Mrs. Leonard Critcher), Walter Kelvin; res: 226 Oakland, Magnolia, Ark. 71753.

WYSE, LOIS WOHLGEMUTH, Exec. VP, Wyse Advertising, 2800 Euclid Ave., Cleve., Oh. 44115, '65–; Edtl. Prom. Dir., Cleveland News; Reptr., Cleveland Press; Auth: "Love Poems for the Very Married" (World, '67), "Are You Sure You Love Me?" (World, '69), "Two Turtles, A Guppy, and Aunt Edna" (World, '66), other adult and children's bks., poetry; AWNY, Flora Stone Mather Col., '48; h. Marc Wyse; c. Katherine, Robert.

Y

YAGER, ROSEMARY, Organizer of TV programs, St. Peters Parish, Church and Water Sts., Chillicothe, Oh. 45601, '66–; Auth: "James Buchanan Eads, Master of the Great River" ('68), other bks, numerous religious articles; Telcom, '66–; Crtv. Writing Tchr., St. Peters Sch., '68–; Elementary Tchr., '32–'65; Authors Guild, educ. orgs., numerous hist., restoration orgs.; Oh. State Univ., BS, '33; b. Chillicothe, Oh., 1909; p. Edward and Anna Ritter Yager; res: 199 Church St., Chillicothe, Oh. 45601.

YAMASHITA, ELIZABETH SWAYNE, Assoc. Prof., Northwestern University School of Journalism, Evanston, Ill. 60201, '63–; Cnslt.-Rsch.; Northwestern Univ., PhD, '69; h. Donald Yamashita.

YAP, VIOLET YEE, Dir., Contemporay Arts Center of Hawaii, 605 Kapiolani Blvd., Honolulu, Hi. 96815, '60–; Univ. of Hi., BA; Columbia Univ., MA; h. Peter Yap.

YARBOURGH, BETTY JANE HATHAWAY, Dir. of Lang. Arts, Chesapeake Public Schools, P.O. Box 15204, Chesapeake, Va. 23320, '66–; Dir. of Dev. Reading Prog., Norfolk County Schs., '57–'66; Supvsr. of Lang. Arts, '56–'57; Tchr., Cradock HS (Portsmouth), '51–'56; Visiting Instr., numerous univs.; Auth: "Teaching English to Slow Learners" (Harcourt, Brace and World, '62), "Sound and Sense in Spelling" (Harcourt, Brace and World, '64), others; Nat. Cncl. of Tchrs. of Eng., Modern Lang. Assn., Intl. Reading Assn. (Chmn., Nat. Comm.), Va. State Reading Assn. (Pres., '68–'69), Nat. Conf. on Rsch. and Eng., Am. Psychological Assn., Va. Assn. of Tchrs. of Eng. (Secy.-Treas., '60–'62); Who's Who of Am. Wm., Dic. of Am. Scholars, Chesapeake C. of C. aw., '65; Duke Univ., AB, '48; Col. of William and Mary, MA, '55; Univ. of Va., EdD, '64; b. Portsmouth, Va., 1927; p. Joseph and Isabelle Rountree Hathaway; h. (div.); res: 3008 Ferguson Dr., Portsmouth, Va. 23703.

YARCHO, YVONNE V., Media Supvsr., Smock/Waddell, Inc., 900 Wilshire Blvd., L.A., Cal. 90017, '68–; Media Byr., '65–'68; Media Byr., Young & Rubicam, '63–'65; Bdcst. Asst. Byr., BBDO, '59–'62; Chi Omega, Phi Beta (Pasadena-Glendale Secy., '65–'67), PEO; Univ. of N.M., BFA, '55; Stanford Univ., MA, '59 (KNBR radio aw.); p. Raymond and Mary Yarcho.

YARDENA (Yardena Shapira Huckman), Free-lance Wtr. and Actress, Chmn., Bat Eilat Charity Org., '67–'68; Anncr., Disc. Jockey, Actress, Prodr., Kol Yisrael Radio Station, '53–'57; bks. and plays published, '55–'57; translator for Israeli publ. cos.; sketches and TV appearances for charity orgs.; past ten yrs.; Actors Fund of Am. (Aw. of Merit, '69), Jewish Nat. Fund (Aw. of Merit, '68), Help the Children Fndn.; Hebrew Univ.; Am. Theatre Wing, '60; b. Jerusalem, Israel; p. Moshe and Elisheva Shimshoni Shapira; h. Frederick Huckman; c. Opher; res: 220 S. Williman Dr., Beverly Hills, Cal. 90211.

YARDUMIAN, MURIEL LINEY, PR Asst., Holy Redeemer Hospital, 1648 Huntingdon Pike, Meadowbrook, Pa. 19046, '70–; Ed., PR Assoc., Phila. Nat. Bank, '67–'69; Retail Mktng. Staff Asst., '64–'66; Asst. Field Dir., A. J. Wood Research Co., '62–'64; Un. Fund Communicators, '67–'69; Pa. State Univ., BA, '62; b. Phila., Pa., 1941; p. John, Jr., and Rosa Acquesta Liney; h. Vartan Yardumian; res: 2543 Huntingdon Pike #2, Huntingdon Valley, Pa. 19006.

YARMON, BETTY GROSS, Dir. of PR, Abe Schrader Corp., 530 Seventh Ave., N.Y., N.Y. 10018, '52–;

Founder, Betty Yarmon Associates, '63–; Founder, Mng. Ed., Party Line nwsltr. for PR trade, '60–; Auth., wkly. colm., "Your Family Finance," synd. by Wms. News Svc., '63–; "Getting the Most for Your Money When You Buy a Home," Assn. Press, '66; Fashion Group; L.A. City Col.; b. Plainfield, N.J.; p. Dr. Samuel and Ruth Livingston Gross; h. Morton Yarmon; res: 35 Sutton Place, N.Y., N.Y. 10022.

YARNALL, CELESTE, Actress, P.O. Box 75951, L.A., Cal., 90005; Movies incl. "Eve" (Commonwealth United), "Live a Little Love a Little" (MGM), "Generation" (Warner Bros.), "Phynx" (Warner Bros.); TV guest roles incl. "Bonanza," "Star Trek," "Hogan's Heroes"; Nat. Assn. of Theatre Owners Most Promising New Star of 1968; Deb star, '67; Miss Rheingold, '64; b. Long Beach, Cal; p. Forest and Helene C. Yarnall; h. Sheldon Silverstein; res: P.O. Box 75951, L.A., Cal. 90005.

YATES, MARIE ZWEEGMAN, Founder, Zweegman School for Medical Secretaries, S.F., Cal., '34–'68; Dir., '34–'61; VP, '61–'68; Auth., Gregg Medical Dictation Series, '39–'42, Orthopedics (Gregg Med. Dictation Series, Rev., Book I), '69; Tchrs. Manual, '69; numerous others; Cnslt., Adv. Comm. on Med. Secys., Miller Commty Col., L.A.; Who's Who of Am. Wm., Dic. of Intl. Biog., 2,000 Wm. of Achiev.; b. Lynden, Wash., 1902; p. Leonard and Margretha Schuyleman Zweegman; h. Claude Yates; res: 900 Judson, Lynden, Wash. 98264.

YATES, MAYA, Sr. Articles Ed., Venture, Cowles Communications, 488 Madison Ave., N.Y., N.Y. 10022, '68–; Travel Svc. Ed., '67–'68; Assoc. Ed., '66–'67; Asst. Ed., '64–'66; Edtl. Asst., '63–'64; PR, Reader Mail, Look Magazine, '61–'63; Eng. Tchr., Acton-Boxborough Reg. HS (W. Acton, Mass.), '59–'61; Smith Col., BA, '53; Univ. of Cape Town (S. Africa), MA, '54; b. Hamburg, Germany, 1932; p. Lloyd and Catherine Condict Yates; res: 300 E. 33rd St., N.Y., N.Y. 10016.

YAVORSKE, CAROL BLANCHE, Cont. Dir., WLOF Radio, P.O. Box 15746, Orlando, Fla. 32808, '68–; Colmst., weekly paper, '66–; AWRT; Col. of Orlando, AA, '68; b. Bklyn., N.Y. 1947; p. Albert and Carrie Yander Yavorske; res: 226 Coleus Dr., Orlando, Fla. 32807.

YEAGER, CAROLINE J., Ed., Employee Pubns., Strawbridge and Clothier, 801 Market St., Phila, Pa. 19105, '55–; Tour Bus. Mgr. and Escort, World Wide Travel, '60–; Former Reptr., Delaware Valley Advance; Free-lance Corr., Reptr., Chgo. trade pubns. '55–; Ed., Employee Pubns., Philco Corp.; Theta Sigma Phi; Del. Valley Assn. of Communicators (VP, Treas., Secy.; Commtns. Aw., '68), AAIE (Secy., Bd. of Dirs.); Temple Univ., BS, '49; b. Phila., Pa.; res: 3432 Temple Ave., Trevose, Pa., 19047.

YEATON, BARBARA NILES, Corr., Colmst., Free-

lance Photogr., Lewiston Daily Sun, Lewiston Franklin Journal, Farmington, Me. 04938, 20 yrs.; also UPI, WCSH-TV News, Portland; b. Wilton, Me., 1914; p. Harvey and Effie Russell Niles; h. Stanton Yeaton; c. Virginia (Mrs. David Abell), Marolyn (Mrs. Charles Reed), Stanton N.; res: R.F.D. #2, Farmington, Me. 04938.

YEGLIN, DOROTHY MILLER, Food Ed., Des Moines Register, 715 Locust St., Des Moines, Ia. 50309, '65–; Staff Wtr., '58–'63; Staff Wtr., Minneapolis (Minn.) Star & Tribune, '56–'58; Edtl. Asst., Better Homes & Gardens, '53–'54; Promotion Copywtr., Meredith, '51–'53; Iowa State Univ., BS, '50; b. Des Moines, Ia.; p. Oliver and Ruby Norman Miller; h. Harold Yeglin; c. Kent, Sara; res: 5508 Westwood Dr., Des Moines, Ia. 50312.

YELLIN, CAROL GILMER, Ed., Reader's Digest Condensed Book Club, Pleasantville, N.Y. 10570, '65–; Co-auth., "Bound for Freedom" (Little, Brown & Co., '65); articles for mags. incl. Harper's, Vogue, Coronet, Collier's; Assoc. Ed., Reader's Digest mag., '49–'64; Theta Sigma Phi; Northwestern Univ., BS, '41 (with honors); MSJ (cum laude); b. Clinton, Okla., 1920; p. Thomas and Eulala Rogers Gilmer; h. David Yellin; c. Charles F., Thomas G., Douglas S., Emily A.; res: 4241 Park Ave., Memphis, Tenn. 38117.

YEUELL, EUGENIA O., Head, Tech. Processing, Portsmouth Public Library, 601 Court St., Portsmouth, Va., '62–; Instr., Bk. Selection, Univ. of Va. Ext. (Norfolk), '62; Asst. Cataloger, Amherst Col. Lib., '58–'60; Army Librn., European Command, '56–'57; Asst. Librn., Westover Sch. (Middlebury, Conn.), '54–'56; ALA, Southeastern Lib. Assn., Alpha Beta Alpha, Va. Lib. Assoc., Who's Who of Am. Wm., Who's Who in Lib. Svc.; Averett Jr. Col., Lit. Diploma '51; Univ. of Ala., BS (Lib. Sci.), '54; MA (Lib. Sci.), '58; b. Tuscaloosa, Ala., 1932; p. Gladstone and Eugenia Osburn Yeuell; res: 1 Crawford Pkway., Apt. 703, Portsmouth, Va. 23704.

YIONOULIS, MARY NACKOS, Ed., Tech. Pubns., North Carolina State University, 243 Riddick Bldg., Raleigh, N.C. 27607, '57–; Continuity Dir., radio personality, WGTM, '54–'57; faculty, Atlantic Christian Col., '43–'52; Evening Col., '54–'57; Soc. of Tech. Wtrs. and Publrs. (Sr. Mbr.; Chptr. Secy., '69–'70), AAUW, Engineering Public Info. Cncl. of Am. Soc. for Engineering Educ.; Who's Who of Am. Wm., Who's Who in South and Southwest; Univ. of N.C., AB, '42; b. Wilson, N.C.; p. John and Evanthia Mischou Nackos; h. George Yionoulis; c. Evan Dena, Emmanuel John; res: Creedmoor Rd., Raleigh, N.C. 27607.

YODER, MARIE ANGELINE, Auth., "The Nurse's Victory" ('62); Head Nurse, Beatitudes Retirement Homes, 1616 W. Glendale Ave., Phoenix, Ariz., '67–; Missionary Nurse (Puerto Rico), '47; Off. Nurse, '41; Nursing Sch. grad. '37; Goshen Col., BA, '47; b.

Wakarusa, Ind.; p. Ray and Clara Smeltzer Yoder; c. Kaylene Maria; res: 2641 W. Columbine Rd., Phoenix, Ariz. 85029.

YOLEN, JANE H., Auth., children's bks.: "The Emperor and the Kite" (World, '67; Caldecott Medal runner-up, '68; Lewis Carroll Shelf Aw., '68); "The Minstrel and the Mountain" (World, '67; Boys Club of Am. Jr. Bk. Aw., '68); others; bk. and lyrics, "Robin Hood, A Musical for Children" (Prod., Boston, Mass., '67; Northampton, '68); Asst. Juv. Ed., Alfred A. Knopf, '65; Rutledge Bks., '62–'63; Edtl. Staff: Saturday Rev., This Week, Bridgeport Sunday Herald; Boston Auths. Club, Acad. of Am. Poets, Auths. Guild, PEN, Poetry Soc. of Am.; Smith Col., BA, '60; b. N.Y.C., 1939; p. Will and Isabelle Berlin Yolen; h. David W. Stemple; c. Heidi Elisabet, Adam Douglas; res: Four Chimneys, Still River Rd., Bolton, Mass. 01740.

YORK, CAROL BEACH, Auth., juv. and teenage bks: "Sparrow Lake" (Coward-McCann), "Doll in the Bakeshop" (Franklin Watts), many others; short stories; b. Chgo., Ill. 1928; p. Harold and Mary Cantwell Beach; h. Richard York; c. Diana Carol; res: 14839 Main St., Harvey, Ill. 60426.

YORK, MARY LEWIS, Dir., Radio/TV, Peace Corps, 806 Connecticut Ave., Wash., D.C. 20525, '68–; Special Asst. to the Dir., Nat. Collection of Fine Arts, '67–'68; Dir. of PR, Time-Life Intl., London, Eng., '65–'66; Reptr., Life, Beverly Hills, Cal., '61–'64; Western Pubcty. Dir., '56–'61; Hollywood Wms. Press Club; Mich. State Univ. (Jnlsm.); Univ. of London, Degree Course (Eng. Lit.), '66; b. Lansing, Mich.; p. LeRoy and Helen Peez Lewis; h. (1) Eugene F. Sherman (dec.), (2) Dr. Carl York; c. Diane Sherman; res: 10478 Hollman Ave., W. Los Angeles 90024.

YOUNG, CHURCHILL BUCK, Media Dir., Noble-Dury & Associates, Inc., Life and Casualty Tower, Nashville, Tenn. 37219, '69–; Cargill, Wilson and Acree (Atlanta, Ga.), '67–'69; (Charlotte, N.C.), '62–'67; (Richmond, Va.), '58–'62; Atlanta Media Planners, Atlanta Bdcst. Exec. Club.

YOUNG, ERMA L., Ed. of Wms. News, Kansas City Star, 1729 Grand Ave., Kan. City, Mo. 64108, '54–; Ed., "The Star Cookbook" ('70); Asst. Wms. Ed., '50–'54; City Desk Reptr., '44–'50; St. Joseph News-Press, '36–'44; Sun. Ed., '35–'36; Bk. Reviewer, '31–'35; Univ. of Missourian Assn.; Mo. Commn. on Status of Wm., '64–'67; Kan. City Commn. for Intl. Rels. and Trade, '59–'61; Alliance Francaise of Kan. City (Charter Mbr., Bd. Mbr.), Bus. Wms. Assn., Fashion Group, Alpha Chi Omega, Kan. City Wms. C. of C. (Hon.); Wm. of Yr., Adv. and Sls. Execs. Club, '64; Theta Sigma Phi Matrix Table Aw., '67; Univ. of Mo. Sch. of Jnlsm., '29 (Wm. of Achiev. Centennial Aw., '68); b. McFall, Mo.; p. James and Bettie Abbott Young; res: 4966 Westwood Rd., Kan. City, Mo. 64112.

YOUNG, ETHELYN E., Dir. of Wms. News, Valley Daily News and Daily Dispatch, 210 Fourth Ave., Tarentum, Pa. 15084, '58–; Wms. Ed., The Leader-Times (Kittanning); Pa. Wms. Press Assoc. (Dist. Dir., '65–'67; Keystone Press Aws. with Pa. Nwsp. Publrs. Assoc.), BPW (Kittanning Past Pres.), Soroptimist Club (Armstrong County Past Pres.); b. Clarion County, Pa., 1908; p. Delo and Cora Berg Young.

YOUNG, GENEVIEVE, Mng. Ed., Trade Dept., Harper & Row, 49 E. 33rd St., N.Y., N.Y. 10016, '68–; Asst. Mng. Ed., '66–'68; Ed., '64–'66; Asst. Ed., '60–'64; Story Cnslt., Warner Bros.-7 Arts, '68; Wellesley Col., BA, '52; h. Cedric Sun.

YOUNG, GEORGIA VOSS, Assoc. Ed., Wtr., Better Homes and Gardens, Meredith Corporation, Des Moines, Ia. 50303, '62–; Ia. Licensed Agt.-Securities and Stocks; Nat. PR Mgr., St. Charles Mfg. Co. (St. Charles, Ill.); Nat. Design Cnslt., Lectr., Kitchen Rsch., Curtis Cos. (Clinton, Ia.); Cnslt., Instr., Nat. Inst. of Wood Cabinet Manufacturers (Chgo., Ill.); V.P., Voss Mfg. (Atlantic, Ia.); Art Inst. of Chgo., Vogue Sch. of Art, Grinnell Col.; b. Atlantic, Ia., 1928; p. George and Evelyn Rendleman Voss; h. Edgar M. Young; c. Siria Elaine, Mrs. Melinda Tully, Norris; res: 2922 Terrace Dr., Des Moines, Ia. 50312.

YOUNG, JANET RANDALL, Auth., juv. bks., '50–; Co-ed., several wkly. nwsps., '40–'50; bks. (Janet Randall): "Brave Young Warriors" ('69), "Buffalo Box" ('69), 10 others; (Bob and Jan Young) "The Story of the Rocky Mountains" ('69), "Seven Faces West" ('69), 16 others; Western Wtrs. of Am., Whittier Wtrs. Club; UCLA, AA; b. Lancaster, Cal., 1919; p. Jay and Blanche Barrett Randall; h. (dec.); c. Michael, Timothy, Gary, Randi; res: 8638 S. Greenleaf Ave., Whittier, Cal. 90602.

YOUNG, JEANE RIDGE, Dir. of Commty. Rels., WKNO-TV, Memphis, Tenn. 38111; Instr., Jnlsm., Memphis State Univ., '67–; Head, Jnlsm. Program, Univ. of Evansville (Ind.), '65–'67; PR, Univ. of Wis. Ext. Div., '62–'65; Mng. Ed., Furniture and Woodworking, '59–'61; Adv., Memphis Publ. Co., '50–'52; Assoc. for Educ. in Jnlsm., Wis. Acad. of Sci., Arts and Ltrs., Am. Assn. for the Advancement of Sci., Theta Sigma Phi; Mid-South PR Soc. Aw., '61; Memphis State Univ., BS, '62; Univ. of Wis., '62–'65; b. Memphis, Tenn., 1930; p. Alfred and Bernice Aycock Ridge; h. (div.); c. Cynthia A., Alfred H.; res: 190 Waynoka Lane, Memphis, Tenn. 38111.

YOUNG, KATHERINE ANN, City Govt. News Reptr., The Lawton Constitution and Morning Press, Third and A, Lawton, Okla. 73501, '69–; Gen. News Reptr., Teen Ed., The Duncan (Okla.) Banner, 73533, '65–'69; Wms. Ed.; Farm Ed.; Ch. Ed.; Cnslt., 4-H Reptrs. Workshops; Who's Who of Am. Wm.; Central State Col.; E. Central State Col.; b. Comanche, Okla., 1943; p. Woodrow and Marie Stephens Young; res: 108 Eastland, Duncan, Okla. 73533.

YOUNG, LEONTINE R., Exec. Dir., Child Service Association, 284 Broadway, Newark, N.J. 07104, '60–; Auth., non-fiction: "Life Among the Giants" ('66), "Wednesday's Children" ('64), "Out of Wedlock" ('54); Visiting Prof., Rutgers Univ. Sch. of Social Work, '61–'64; Prof. in Casework, Oh. State Univ. Sch. of Social Adm., '52–'60; Asst. Prof., Columbia Univ., N.Y. Sch. of Social Work, '45–'52; Assoc. Prof.; Wtr. of pfsnl. and popular articles; Am. Humane Soc., Child Welfare League of Am. (Bd. Mbr.), SIE-CUS (Bd. Mbr.), Essex County Planned Parenthood (Bd. Mbr.); Social Worker of the Yr., '68; Univ. of Denver, BA, '33; N.Y. Sch. of Soc. Work, MS, '44; Columbia Univ. Sch. of Social Work, DSW, '63; b. Palmyra, N.Y., 1910; p. Sanford and Genevieve Belty Young; res: 381 Broad St., Newark, N.J. 07104.

YOUNG, LINDA E., Edtl. Rschr., Time Magazine, Time-Life Bldg., Rockefeller Center, N.Y., N.Y. 10020, '64–; Mkt. Rsch. Investigator, Procter & Gamble, '60–'62; Nat. Wildlife Fdn., Sierra Club, Antique Bottle Collectors Assn.; Syracuse Univ., AB (Rho Delta Phi), '60; Columbia Univ.; b. Paterson, N.J., 1938; p. William and Elizabeth Hyslop Young; res: 38 Pomona Ave., Fair Lawn, N.J. 07410.

YOUNG, LOUISE KERN, Ed., Nazareth Item, 46–48 S. Main St., Nazareth, Pa. 18064; '66–; Corr., Call-Chronicle Nwsps. (Allentown), '68–; Tchr., Nazareth Area Sch. Dist., '42–'45; Nazareth Sr. Wms. Club; Ursinus Col., BA, '41; Univ. of Pa.; Westchester State Col.; b. Nazareth, Pa., 1920; p. Andrew and Alma Hoch Kern; h. Glenn Young; c. Andrew R., Linda L., Glennys J.; res: 342 S. Broad St., Nazareth, Pa. 18064.

YOUNG, LYNN POVICH, Wtr., Reptr., Newsweek, 444 Madison Ave., N.Y., N.Y. 10022, '69–; Sr. Edtl. Asst., '67–'69; Edtl. Asst., '66–'67; Girl Friday (Paris Bur.), '65–'66; Vassar Col., BA, '65; h. Jeffrey Young.

YOUNG, MARGUERITE, Lectr., New School for Social Research, 66 W. 12th St., N.Y., N.Y. 10014; Fordham Univ., Columbia Univ., Univ. of Ia.; Auth: "Angel in the Forest," "Miss MacIntosh, My Darling"; AAUW, Am. Acad. of Arts and Ltrs. Aw.; Univ. of Chgo., MA, '36; b. Indpls., Ind.; p. C. E. and Faye Knight Young; res: 375 Bleecker St., N.Y., N.Y. 10014.

YOUNG, MARIAN C., Coordr., Children's Svcs., Detroit Public Library, 5201 Woodward Ave., Detroit, Mich. 48202, '46–; Supvsr., Children's Work, Des Moines Public Lib., '38–'46; Children's Librn., Cinn. Public Lib., '30–'38; Instr., Univ. of Mich. Sch. of Lib. Sci., '60–; Mich. Lib. Assn. (Pres., '50–'51), ALA (Children & Young People Libs. Div. Pres., '53–'54), WNBA (Detroit Chptr. Pres., '66–'69), Detroit Children's Bk. Fair Cncl. (Chmn., '70); Univ. of Cinn., AB, '29, BE, '30; Columbia Univ., BS (Lib. Sci.), '37; b. Cinn., Oh.; p. Guy and Eleanor Young; res: 1057 Yorkshire Rd., Grosse Pointe Park, Mich. 48230.

YOUNG, MARJORIE WILLIS, Travel Ed., The Daily

Mail and Independent Tribune, P.O. Box 19, Anderson, S.C. 29621, '49–; Prom. Dir., David McKay Publ., '45–'48; Lectr., Nat. Concert and Artists Corp., '42–'43; Feature Wtr., Saturday Pictorial Review, N.Y.C., '41–'45; King Features Synd., '39; Far Eastern Colmst., INS, Tokyo, Japan, '38–'41; Ed., The Safety Journal, '53–; Fodor's Tour Guide, S.C., '66–'68; Asst. Tech. Dir., "Behind the Rising Sun," RKO, '43; Am. Soc. Safety Engineers (Assoc.), Nat. Press Photogrs. Assn., Soc. of Am. Travel Wtrs., WNPC, ANWC, OPC; Who's Who of Am. Wm.; Cornell Univ., '24; Art Students League, Cooper Union, '25–'27; Columbia Univ., '27; Sorbonne, '30; Japanese Lang. Sch., '34–'35; b. Mansfield, Oh.; p. John and Mary Reiter Willis; h. James Russell Young; c. Willis P.; res: 2003 Laurel Dr., Anderson, S.C. 29621.

YOUNG, MARY MARINO, Bus. Mgr., Prindle, Weber and Schmidt, Inc., 53 State St., Boston, Mass. 02109, '65–; D.C. Heath, '63–'65; Bowen Corp., Cambridge, '57–'62; Bookbuilders of Boston (Secy., '63–'64); Temple Univ., '36, '47; b. Bristol, Pa., 1918; p. Nicholas and Rose Diodati Marino; h. Harold Young; c. William F., Sharon Marlene, Mrs. Nicholas W. Johns.; res: 14 Dudley St., Arlington, Mass. 02174.

YOUNG, MILDRED CHESTNUT, Asst. to Publr., New York Amsterdam News, 2340 Eighth Ave., N.Y., N.Y. 10027, '65–; Secy., '49–'65; Delta Sigma Theta, NAMW (N.Y.C. Chptr. Fin. Secy., '66–'67); active in neighborhood, civil rights orgs.; S.C. State Col., BS (Bus. Adm.), '47; b. Spartanburg, S.C., 1925; p. Lewis and Connie Miller Chestnut; c. Robert Donald; res: 1603 President St., Bklyn., N.Y. 11213.

YOUNG, OLIVIA KNOWLES, Reg. Dir., Watauga Regional Library, P.O. Box 3250 CRB, Johnson City, Tenn. 37601, '63–; Chief Librn., U.S. Army Spec. Serv. (Ft. Stewart, Ga.), '60–'63; Bkmobile Librn., Caney Fork Reg. Lib. (Sparta, Tenn.), '58–'59; Asst. Librn., Cairo (Ga.) Public Lib., '55–'58; Area Librn., U.S. Army Spec. Serv. (Linz, Austria), '49–'51; Per. and Doc. Librn., George Peabody Col., '46–'49; ALA, Southeastern Lib. Assn., Tenn. Lib. Assn. (Treas., '69), BPW (Secy., '57–'58), Altrusa Club (Secy. '65–'66); Tenn. Polytec. Inst., BS, '42; George Peabody Col., BS (Lib. Sci.), '46; b. Benton, Ark., 1922; p. Wesley and Med Crawford Knowles; h. Calvin B. Young; c. Taylor B.; res: 1206 Welbourne, Johnson City, Tenn. 37601.

YOUNG, PRISCILLA HALL, Free-lance TV-Radio Cnslt., Bdcstr. (Reynolds Metals Co., Polaroid Corp., WDBJ), '66–; Art Colmst., Roanoke (Va.) Times, '58–; Prodr. "Profile," WSLS-TV, '61–'66 (McCall's Golden Mike Aw., '60, '65; AP Aw., Best Wms. Program in Va., '61–'66); Prodr., Bdcstr., "A Start in Art," WDBJ-TV, '57–'58; AWRT (Blue Ridge Chptr. VP, '68–), Va. Press Wm.; NFPW 1st pl. Aw. for TV, '67; Wheaton Col., AB; Art Students League; Hollins Col.; b. Boston, Mass.; p. Malcolm and Rita Buisiere Hall; h. Charles A. Young, Jr.; c. Charles

Augustus, III, Kendall Y.; res: 3001 Maywood Rd. S.W., Roanoke, Va. 24014.

YOUNG, SHIRLEY, VP, Dir. of Mktg. Rsch., Grey Advertising, Inc., 777 Third Ave., N.Y., N.Y. 10017, '69–; VP, '68–; Assoc. Dir., '65–'68; Group Head, '61–'64; Project Dir., '59–'61; Hudson Pulp and Paper Corp., '58–'59; Benton and Bowles, '57–'58; Alfred Politz, '55–'57; Wellesley Col., BA, '55 (Phi Beta Kappa); N.Y.U., Grad. Econs., '56–'57; b. Shanghai, China, 1935; p. Clarence and Juliana Yen Young; h. George Hsieh; c. David W., William C., Douglas H. L.; res: 177 E. 75th St., N.Y., N.Y. 10021.

YOUNG, VIRGINIA GARTON, Auth. and Lectr.; bks: "The Library Trustee: A Practical Guidebook" (R. R. Bowker Company, '64), "The Trustee of a Small Public Library" (ALA, '62); numerous articles in lib. mags.; speaker at numerous Governor's, state, Can. lib. confs.; dedication of Southeast Mo. State Col., '68; Guest Lectr., Sch. of Lib. Svc., Columbia Univ., '66; Visiting Comm., Sch. of Lib. Svc., Case Western Reserve Univ., '68–; Trustee, Am. Lib. in Paris, '68–; Nat. Bk. Comm., '66–; Nat. Lib. Week Steering Comm., '61–'63; Advisory Comm. to U.S. Commissioner of Educ., Lib. Svcs. Br., '60–'63; various organizations; Southwest Mo. State Col., BA, '39 (Outstanding Alumnus Aw., '65); Univ. of Okla., MS (Lib. Sci.), '40; b. Mountain View, Mo., 1919; p. Charles and Matibel Cartwright Garton; h. Raymond A. Young; c. David B.; res: 10 E. Parkway Dr., Columbia, Mo. 65201.

YOUNTS, ELIZABETH MENDENHALL, VP, WUSM, Comml. Shopping Ctr., Havelock, N.C. 28532, '62–; Secy.-Treas., WEEB (Southern Pines, N.C.), '47–; Music and Program Dir., '47–; Free-lance Organist, CBS and NBC (N.Y.C.), '45–'46; Staff Organist and Pianist, ABC, '43–'44; numerous fund raising activities, '65–'67; NAB, N.C. Assn. of Bdcstrs., AWRT, numerous cultural and civic orgs.; Greensboro Col., '36–'39; Univ. of Rochester Eastman Sch. of Music, BM, '41 (Georga Eastman Fellowship, '41); Julliard Sch. of Music, '41–'42 (Fellowship); b. Winston-Salem, N.C., 1919; p. Robah K. and Erma M. Teague Mendenhall; h. Jack S. Younts; c. Sandra Louise, Millard Stephen, Gerlind Elizabeth; res: Bethesda Rd., Southern Pines, N.C. 28387.

YOURCENAR, MARGUERITE, Wtr., many novels, essays, poems, plays, in French; incl: "L'Oeuvre au Noir" ('68), "Fleuve Profond, Sombre Riviere" (translation of Negro Spirituals with critical preface, '64); Prix Femina, '68; Prix Combat, '63; Page One Aw., Nwsp. Guild of N.Y., '55; Prix Femina Vacaresco, '52; Prix de l'Academie Francaise, '52; Bowdoin Col. (Hon. D. Litt., '68); Smith Col. (Hon. D. Litt., '61); b. Brussels, Belgium, 1903; p. Michel de Crayencour and Fernande de Cartier de Marchienne; res: Northeast Harbor, Me. 04662.

YUNCKER, BARBARA, Med., Sci. Wtr., The New York Post, 75 West St., N.Y., N.Y. 10006, '59–; Med.

Colmst., Good Housekeeping, '63–; Copy Ed., N.Y. Post, '58–'59; Asst. Deputy Commissioner of Commerce, N.Y. State, '56–'57; Lasker Aw., '69, '67; various orgs., aws.; DePauw Univ., AB (summa cum laude), '63; b. Greencastle, Ind.; p. Truman and Ethel Claflin Yuncker; res: 361 W. 22nd St., N.Y., N.Y. 10011.

YUNDT, CECILIA LYONS, Librn., Plaquemines Parish Commission Council, 203 Highway 23 South, Buras, La. 70041, '62–; Librn. and Asst. Principal, Port Sulphur HS, '42–'62; Tchr., Buras HS, '35–'42; NEA, La. Tchrs. Assn., Plaquemines Parish Tchrs. Assn. (3 times Pres.), Delta Kappa Gamma (Upsilon Chptr. Pres., 2 terms); La. N.W. State Col., BA, '35; Loyola Univ., La. State Univ.; b. Homeplace, La.; p. Martin and Fanny Ballay Lyons; h. John Yundt (dec.); c. Janet; res: Rt. 2, Box 281-A, Port Sulphur, La. 70083.

YURCHENCO, HENRIETTA WEISS, Asst. Prof., City College of New York, 133rd St. and Convent Ave., N.Y., N.Y. 10031, '62; Ethnomusicologist, Tchr.; Bklyn. Col., '66–'69; New Sch., '61–'68; Bdcstr., folk music, WNYC, '60–'69; WBAI, '59–'60; WNYC, '39–'41; Folk Music Ed., Am. Record Guide, '59–; Contrbr. to musical pubns.; Auth: "Russian Song Book (Simon & Shuster), "A Fiesta of Folk Songs from Spain and Latin America" (Putnam, '67); Intl. Folk Music Cncl., Soc. of Asian Music, Folk Music Panel for Cultural Presentations of U.S. State Dept.; Lib. of Congress funded work in Mexico and Guatemala; State Dept. grant for Guatemala; five grants from Am. Philosophical Soc.; Yale School of Music; David Mannes; b. New Haven, Conn., 1916; p. Edward and Rebecca Bernblum Weiss; h. Irving Levine; c. Peter; res: 118 W. 87th St., N.Y., N.Y. 10024.

YUSPEH, SONIA NEJAME, Exec. Rsch. Dir., Grey Advertising, 777 Third Ave., N.Y., N.Y., '69–; Mkt. Rsch. Dir., D'Arcy Adv., '68–'69; Assoc. Rsch. Dir., Grey Adv.; Sr. Project Dir., Marplan Div. of Interpublic; Project Dir., Audits and Surveys; Syracuse Univ., BA (Phi Beta Kappa); Cornell Univ., MA, '53; b. Syracuse, N.Y., 1928; p. Fareed and Nancy Mandour NeJame; h. Michel Yuspeh; c. Leo, Denise; res: 390 West End Ave., N.Y., N.Y. 10024.

YUSS, IRENE ANNE, Prod. Mgr., Paperback Div., Dell Publishing Company, 750 Third Ave., N.Y., N.Y. 10003, '62–; Hayden Publ., '58–'62; Ogden Publ., '56–'58; Bklyn. Col., BA, '56.

Z

ZACHARY, JANE, Actress, c/o International Famous Agency, 1301 Ave. of the Americas, N.Y., N.Y. 10009; Stage roles incl: "Cactus Flower," "Sound of Music" (nat. co.), "Mary, Mary," "You Can't Take It with You"; TV roles incl: "Wonderful

World of Color," "Bonanza," "My Three Sons," "Death Valley Days," "Felony Squad"; Indsl. Shows; SAG, Actors Equity Assn., AFTRA; Hunter Col.; b. N.Y.C.; p. Sol and Evelyn Back Zuckerman; res: 305 E. 72nd St., N.Y., N.Y. 10021.

ZACK, DONNA F., Ed., Today's Secretary, McGraw-Hill Book Company, 330 W. 42nd St., N.Y., N.Y. 10036, '69–; Assoc. Ed., Junior Secy., '67–'69; Tchr., Duval County Public Schs. (Jacksonville, Fla.), '60–'67; Am. Soc. of Bus. Press Eds. (Secy., '69–'70), Delta Pi Epsilon; Univ. of Fla., BS (Educ.), '60; MA, '66; b. Uniontown, Pa.; p. Charles and Ella Broderick Zack.

ZAGAT, CORNELIA ERNST, Reviewer, Child Study Association of America, 9 E. 89th St., N.Y., N.Y. 10028, '37–; New Republic, '31; h. Eugene H. Zagat (div.).

ZAGOREN, RUBY, Auth., numerous children's stories, bks., poetry, articles; Lectr. in Continuing Educ., Univ. of Conn., '68–; Lectr. in Eng., '67–'68; Reptr., Hartford Courant, '43–'45; Country Corr., Hartford Times, '36–'40; Litchfield Hills Audubon Soc.; Conn. Col., B.A., '43; b. New Britain, Conn., 1922; p. Louis and Marie Klaz Zagoren; h. Samuel Silverstein; c. Zona Finley and Grant Merlin; res: Felicity Lane, Torrington, Conn. 06790.

ZAHRT, PAT LEONARD, Pubns. Mgr., Braniff International, Exchange Park, Dallas, Tex. 75235, '45–; Adv. Dept., Carson Pirie Scott (Chgo., Ill.); Asst. to AE, N. W. Ayer; Free-lance Colmst; Theta Sigma Phi (Dallas Chptr. Past Pres; Matrix Aw., '66) DIEA (Dallas Chptr. Past Pres.; Ed. of Yr. '53), ICIE (Past Area Dir.); Press Club of Dallas (Charter Mbr., Past Treas.; Bronze Medallion Aw., '56), Airline Eds. Assn.; b. Dallas, Tex.; p. Ernest and Lily Bell Leonard; h. Walter S. Zahrt (div.); c. Kathleen; res: 8516 Midway Rd., Dallas, Tex. 75209.

ZANG, MARIANNE GUGLIELMO, Media Byr., Lewis and Gilman, 1700 Market St., Phila., Pa. 19103, '69–; Rumrill-Hoyt, '68–'69; N.W. Ayer, '66–'67; Sls. Pres. Wtr., Phila. Bulletin, '67–'68; TV, Radio Adv. Club; Charles Morris Price Sch. of Adv., Univ. of Pa. Evening Sch.; b. Phila., Pa., 1938; p. Thomas and Jean Ercolani Guglielmo; h. Robert Zang; res: 220 Locust St., Phila, Pa. 19106.

ZAPOLEON, MARGUERITE WYKOFF, Wtr., Lectr., Cnslt.; Auth: "The College Girl Looks Ahead" (Harper), "Occupational Planning for Women" (Harper); Auth., numerous govt. pubns., pfsnl. articles; Edtl. Advisory Bd., Occupations mag.; Lectr., Visiting Fac. Mbr., various univs.; Labor Econ., U.S. Dept. of Labor; Special Asst: Wms. Bur., '55–'59; Bur. of Labor Statis., '51–'55; Chief, Employment Opportunities Bur., Wms. Bur., '45–'51; Manual Wtr.-Training Specialist, U.S. Army Svc. Forces, '44–'45; NLAPW, Nat. Vocational Guidance Assn. (Trustee, '45–'51), Alliance for Guidance of Rural Youth (2nd VP, '51–'58), Am. Econs. Assn., numerous others;

Aws: War Dept. Svcs., '44; Labor Dept. Performance, '56; Kappa Kappa Gamma Alumnae Achiev., '68; Univ. of Cinn., BA, Comml. Engineer deg., '28; Am. Univ., MA, '38; b. Cinn., Oh., 1907; p. Fred and Elizabeth Voth Wykoff; h. Louis Zapoleon; res: 816 S.E. Riviera Isle, Ft. Lauderdale, Fla. 33301.

ZATURENSKA, MARYA, Auth., poetry: "Threshold and Hearth" ('34; Shelley Aw. Poetry Soc. of New Eng., '35); "Cold Morning Sky" ('37; Pulitzer Prize, '38), "The Listening Landscape" ('41; Guarantors Aw. Poetry mag.), "The Golden Mirror" ('44), "Selected Poems" ('54), "Terraces of Light" ('60), "Collected Poems" (Viking Press, '66); other aws.; Co-auth., with husband, "History of American Poetry Since 1900" ('46), a biog. of Christina Rosetti ('49), three others; two anthologies, "The Crystal Cabinet" and "The Silver Swan," in collaboration with Horace Gregory; intros. to poetry vols.; Valparaiso Univ., '21–'23; Univ. of Wis. Lib. Sch., '25; b. Kiev, Russia, 1902; p. Abram and Johanna Lubovska Zaturensky; U.S.A., '10; naturalized, '14; h. Horace V. Gregory; c. Joanna (Mrs. S. H. Zeigler), Patrick B.

ZAVIN, THEODORA STUART, Sr. VP, Broadcast Music, Inc., 589 Fifth Ave., N.Y., N.Y. 10017, '68–; Asst. VP, '64–'68; Resident Cnsl., '52–'57; Atty., Greenbaum, Wolff & Ernst, '44–'50; George Z. Medalie, '43–'44; Co-auth: "Your Marriage and the Law" (Rinehart, '52), "Rights and Writers" (Dutton, '60); "The Working Wives' Cookbook" (Chilton, '63); AWRT, (Past Dir.), Am. Bar Assn., Assn. of the Bar of the City of N.Y., Copyright Soc. of U.S. Trustee; Hunter Col., AB, '41; Columbia Law Sch., LLB, '43; b. N.Y.C., 1922; h. Benjamin B. Zavin; c. Jonathan, Daniel; res: 79 W. 12th St., N.Y., N.Y. 10011.

ZAX, CORINNA TSOPEI, Actress, 20th Century Fox Motion Pictures Inc., P.O. Box 900, Beverly Hills, Cal. 90213, '66–: "Caprice," "Sweet Ride," "A Man Called Horse" (CBS Film); Fashion Advisor, Gulf Pacific Industries ('68–'69); Art Cnslt.; Assoc. Prodr., "Maternity," Ampex Corp.; SAG, AFTRA; Miss Greece, '64; Miss Universe, '64–'65; Daphne Sch. for Wm. (Athens, Greece), '57–'63; U.C.L.A., '67–'68; b. Athens, Greece, 1944; p. George and Maria Amalia Tsopei; h. Steven Zax; res: 10385 La Grange Ave., Beverly Hills, Cal. 90025.

ZEBAL, PATRICIA THURBER, Asst. Dir., PR and Dev., Hoag Memorial Hospital, 301 Newport Blvd., Newport Beach, Cal. 92660, '67–; Asst. VP of PR/Adv., Mariners Savings and Loan, '63–'67; Asst. Dir., PR, Bowl Am. Inc. (Arlington, Va.), '61–'63; ZONTA (Pres., '67), Newport Harbor C. of C. (Wm. Div. VP, '69), Am. Soc. for Hosp. PR Dirs.; PR Sec., Hosp. Cncl. of Southern Cal., PRSA; Who's Who of Am. Wm.; Henry Ford Citizen of the Yr. Aw., '66; Commty. Svc. Aw., '65; Un. Fund Angel Aw., '65; Costa Mesa C. of C. Wm. of the Yr., '64; Pasadena City Col., '39–'40; Univ. of Southern Cal., '68; Univ. of Cal., '69; b. Springfield, Ill., 1919; p. Walter Dennison and Ruth Agnew Thurber; h. George P. Zebal; c. Bradley H., Ronald T.; res: 2110 E. Ocean Blvd., Balboa, Cal. 92661.

ZEEK, EVELYN R., Ed., Spartan Stores, Inc., 1111 44th St. S.E., Grand Rapids, Mich. 49508, '64–; Freelance Photogr., Feature Wtr., '46–; Lectr. in Photog., Univ. of Mich. Ext. Svc., '45–'60; ICIE, Mich. Communicators Assn., Photographic Soc. of Am., Southwestern Mich. Cncl. of Camera Clubs, Grand Rapids Color Camera Club Lectr. on Photog.; 25 aws. in intl. photog. competitions; Royal Photographic Soc. of Great Britain, Assoc., '39 (hon. deg.); b. Indpls., Ind., 1913; p. Charles and Helan Wisehart Fuson; h. Lou Zeek; c. Barbara Lynn; res: 1053 Ottilia St. S.E., Grand Rapids, Mich. 49507.

ZEHNPFENNIG, GLADYS BURANDT, Auth., Men of Achiev. Biogs., T. S. Denison, Inc., Publishers, 5100 W. 82nd St., Mpls., Minn. 55432, '62–; Biogs. incl: "Henry R. Luce" ('69), "Hubert H. Humphrey" ('66), "Carl Sandburg" ('63), others; Novels incl: "Son of Nazareth" ('57), "Search for Eden" ('55); NLAPW, Intl. Platform Assn., Delta Phi Lambda, Marquis Biographical Lib. Soc. (Advisory Mbr.); Daughter of Mark Twain, '68; Dic. of Intl. Biog. Cert. of Merit, '68; S.D. State Col. (Jnlsm); b. Watertown, S.D., 1910; p. Adolph and Ida Baumann Burandt; h. Frank Zehnpfennig; c. Ted F., Gary H.; res: 75 Battle Creek Rd., St. Paul, Minn. 55106.

ZEIDERS, BARBARA, Pres., Science Bookcrafters, Inc., 5 Boulanger Plaza, Hastings-on-Hudson, N.Y. 10706, '63–; Mng. Ed., W. A. Benjamin, Inc., '61–'63; Head, Ed. Sec., Interscience Publrs., '59–'61; Ed., Col. Dept., McGraw-Hill, '56–'59; Head, Edtl. Dept., State Geological Survey (Urbana, Ill.), '54–'56; Univ. of Ill., BS, BLS, '50 (high honors, Phi Kappa Phi,); b. Paterson, N.J., 1930; p. E. P. and Cornelia Van Der Vliet Zeiders; res: RD 1, Box 228A, Winfield, Pa. 17889.

ZEILINGER, IRENE CLARA, Ed., The Frankenmuth News, 613 S. Main, Frankenmuth, Mich. 48734, '52–; Reptr., '48–'52; WAVES, '44–'48; Civic Events Cncl., City Planning Commn.; b. Bach, Mich., 1921; p. Gottlieb and Augusta Matzke Zeilinger; res: 352-1/2 S. Franklin, Frankenmuth, Mich. 48734.

ZEITZ, EDNA SCHWAGER, Pubcty. Dir., College Division, Prentice-Hall, Inc., Englewood Cliffs, N.J. 07632, '67–; Pubcty., PR Coordr., '61–'67; Sls. Corr. Supvsr., '58–'61; PRSA; Who's Who of Am. Wm.; Fairleigh Dickinson Univ., '58; b. Jersey City, N.J.; p. William and Mamie Schwartz Schwager; h. Elliot Zeitz; c. David S., Marc F.; res: 20 E. 67th St., N.Y., N.Y. 10021.

ZELKOWITZ, HELEN WEINER, Pres., Mount Vernon Broadcasting Company (WMVO), '58–; Mount Vernon Cablevision Company, '68–; Box 348, Mount Vernon, Oh. 43050; AWRT (Educ. Fndn. Exec. Bd.), J. C. Outstanding Citizen Aw., '70; Oh. Sch. Bell Aw., '68; Oh. State Univ., '29–'32; b. Columbus, Oh., 1911;

p. Samuel and Sarah London Weiner; h. Charles Zelkowitz; c. Stephen W.; res: 5 W. Hamtramck, Mount Vernon, Oh. 43050.

ZEMLANSKY, NAOMI, Mng. Ed., Vogue Pattern Book, 161 Sixth Ave., N.Y., N.Y. 10022, '64–; Fabric Ed., Advance Pattern Co., '63–'64; Asst. to Ed., Simplicity Magazine, '58–'62; Fashion Group, Am. Home Econs. Assn.; Russell Sage Col., BS, '58 (cum laude); b. Paterson, N.J., 1936; p. Peter and Adeline Kahman Zemlansky; res: 250 E. 51st St., N.Y., N.Y. 10022.

ZENS, PATRICIA MARTIN, Auth., juv. bks. incl. "The Thank You Book" (Golden Press '67); verse, features; Lectr.; Eng. Instr., Mount Mary Col. (Milw.); '64–'65; Instr., Alverno Col., '69–'70; Eng. Tch., Marquette Univ., '48–'50; Wis. Cncl. of Wtrs., AAUW; Rosary Col., BA '48; Marquette Univ., MA, '50; b. Chicago, Ill., 1926; p. Andrew and Anne Smith Martin; h. Robert D. Zens; c. Michael, Julie, Martin, Jeanie; res: 340 Westmoor Blvd., Brookfield, Wis. 53005.

ZERBE, NANCY CASON, Prom. Asst., WAPI Television, P.O. Box 1310, Birmingham, Ala. 35201, '60–; Prom. Dept., '56–'60; Copywtr., WQSN (Charleston, S.C.), '55–'56; AWRT (Heart of Dixie Chptr. Pres., VP, Treas.); Birmingham Ad Club aw., '67; Univ. of Miss.; b. Birmingham, Ala., 1936; p. John and Sally Love Cason; h. Richard T. Zerbe; res: 4972 Scenic View Dr., Birmingham, Ala. 35210.

ZIBURIS, EDNA LAZDAUSKAS, Ed.-Sls. Prom. Coordr., MITE Corporation, 446 Blake St., New Haven, Conn., 06515, '67–; Indls. Ed., Stromberg Div., General Time Corp., '59–'67; Indls. Ed., G. Fox & Co., '46–'50; PR Asst., Warner Bros., '45–'46; Indsl. Ed., Intl. Mutoscope Corp., '44–'45; Advisor, Catholic Youth Org. publn., '59–; various organizations; N.Y.U., BS (Jnlsm; Achiev. in Adv. Aw.); b. Waterbury, Conn.; h. Joseph Ziburis; c. Mark A.; res: 220 Middlebury Rd., Watertown, Conn.

ZIEGLER, ELSIE REIF, Auth: "The Blowing Wand" (Holt, Rinehart and Winston, '55; Jr. Lit. Guild selection), "The Face in the Stone" (David McKay, '59; Jr. Lit. Guild selection), "Light a Little Lamp" (John Day, '61); Soc. of Midland Auths.; Univ. of Ill., Northwestern Univ.; b. Chgo., Ill., 1918; p. Peter and Emma Simon Reif; h. Norman Ziegler; c. Peter, Gail, Karen.

ZIFF, RUTH BARON, VP, Assoc. Rsch. Dir., Benton & Bowles, Inc., 909 Third Ave., N.Y., N.Y. 10022, '67–; Dir. of Mkt. Rsch., '58–'67; Supvsr. of Consumer Rsch., '52–'58; Consumer Rsch. Analyst, '50–'52; Dir. of Psychological Barometer, Psychological Corp.; numerous published articles; Am. Mktng. Assn.; AAPOR; AWNY (Treas., '68–'70); Who's Who of Am. Wm.; Hunter Col., BA, '44 (cum laude, Phi Beta Kappa, Alpha Chi Alpha); Columbia Univ., MA, '48; b. N.Y.C., 1924; p. Herman and Lena Medoff Baron; h. Solomon Ziff; c. Charles, Ellen; res: 3 Valley Lane, Chappaqua, N.Y. 10514.

ZIGNER, GLORIA EGGER, Commtns. Cnslt., Gloria Zigner Public Relations; Project Coordr., "Smoke Out," U.S. Public Health Svc., '68–'69; Met. Area Cnslt., City of Bakersfield, '65–'68; PRSA, Orange County Adv. Club, Orange County Press Club, L.A. Press Club, L.A. Pubcty. Club; AAF multi-media aw., '69; L.A. Adv. Wm. aw., '69; Who's Who of Am. Wm.; U.C.L.A.; b. Bakersfield, Cal.; p. Henry and Ida Hoffman Egger; h. Melvin Zigner; c. Mark Alan, Jeffrey Laurence; res: 1146 Polaris Dr., Newport Beach, Cal. 92660.

ZIMMERMAN, JOAN DUNHAM, Acc. Supvsr., Papert, Koenig, Lois, Inc., 777 Third Ave., N.Y., N.Y. 10017, '63–; Free-lance Copywtr., '61–'63; Prom. Copywtr., Time, '58–'61; Copywtr., J. Walter Thompson, '56–'58; Fashion Group; Conn. Col. for Wm.; Tobe-Coburn Sch. for Fashion Careers; b. N.Y.C., 1937; p. Charles and LaVerta McCormick Goudiss; h. Theodore Zimmerman; c. Christopher Dunham; res: 63 E. 82nd St., N.Y., N.Y. 10028.

ZIMMERMAN, NAOMA GIBSTINE, Auth., Caseworker-Therapist, Cnslt., Family Service of South Lake County, 1725 McGovern St., Highland Park, Ill.; bks. incl. "Farm Animals" (Rand McNally, '66), "Corky in Orbit" (Reilly & Lee, '62), "Little Deer" (Rand McNally, '56), "Sleepy Forest" (Ziff-Davis '43), other juv. bks.; Tchr., Univ. of Chgo.; Caseworker, Jewish Children's Bur. of Chgo., '37–'41; Camp. Dir. '37; Nat. Assn. of Social Work; Contemporary Auths.; Who's Who of Am. Wm.; Washington Univ., Univ. of Chgo., BA, '35; MA (Social Service), '40; b. St. Louis, Mo., 1914; p. Samuel and Sadie Cohen Gibstine; h. Alvin Zimmerman; c. Ann, Frank; res: 465 Drexel Ave., Glencoe, Ill. 60022.

ZIMMERMANN, CAROLINE A., VP/Client Svcs., William Steiner Associates, Inc., 527 Madison Ave., N.Y., N.Y. 10022, '68–; Asst. to VP, Gen. Mgr., Christian Herald Assn.; AE, Rsch. Librn., Coolidge Co.; Mkt. Rsch., Young & Rubicam; Mkt. Rsch., C. E. Hooper; Nat. Assn. of Direct Mail Wtrs., Subscription Fulfillment Mgrs. Assn. (Secy., Bd. Mbr.); Albright Col.; Ga. State Col., BA (Eng., Educ.), '66; b. Amityville, N.Y., 1944; p. H. Paul and Frances Short Zimmermann; h. Paul R. Tully; res: 46 W. 88th St., N.Y., N.Y. 10024.

ZINER, FEENIE KATZ, Auth.; Tchr. of Contemporary Literature, McQuill University, W. Sherbrooke, Montreal, Canada, '69–; Tchr., Sir George Williams Univ. (Quebec), '67–'69; Bks: "A Full House" (Simon & Schuster, '67), "Dark Pilgrim" (Chilton Bks., '65; World Bk. outstanding cit.), "Pilgrims and Plymouth Colony" (Am. Heritage Jr. Lib., '61), others; Social Worker for six yrs.; Brooklyn Col., BA, '41; N.Y. Sch. of Social Wk., MSS, '44 (Conn. Children's Aid Soc. Fellowship); b. Bklyn., N.Y., 1921; p. Morris and Sophie Guttman Katz; h. Zeke Ziner; c. Marc, Joe, Amie, Eric, Ted; res: 31 Chesterfield Ave., Montreal 217, Canada.

ZOBLE, ADRIENNE KAPLAN, Media Dir., Keyes, Martin & Company, 841 Mountain Ave., Springfield, N.J. 07081, '66–; Media Dir., Bruce Friedlich & Co., N.Y.C., '65–'66; Timebyr., Maxon, Inc., '64; Asst. Timebyr. Estimator, '64; Bdcst. Estimator, J. Walter Thompson, '63–'64; Secy.-Asst. to Head Timebyr., '61–'63; Secy. to Head Space Byr. –'61; Douglass Col.; Univ. Col.-Rutgers Univ., BA, '63; b. Newark, N.J., 1940; p. Herman and Mary Miron Kaplan; h. Jacob Zoble; c. Allison L.; res: 1735 Merriam Dr., Martinsville, N.J. 08836.

ZOEGER, SHIRLEY STUCKERT, Free-lance Wtr.; Secondary Eng.-Jnlsm. Tchr., Los Angeles Public Schools, 450 N. Grand Ave., L.A., Cal., '61–; Colmst., Woodland Hills Times; Eng. Tchr.-Yrbk. Advisor, Santa Monica HS, '50–'51; Ed., Wauwatosa (Wis.) News-Times, '47–'48; Photogr., Reptr., Feature Wtr., Mexico Hoy mag. (Mexico City, Mexico), '46; News Ed., Texas City Sun, '46; Theta Sigma Phi, ACLU, Friends of Operation Bootstrap; Univ. of Wis., '42–'44; Northwestern Univ., BS, '46; U.C.L.A. Grad. Sch., '48–'50; b. Milw., Wis., 1924; p. Felix and Katherine Hirsch Stuckert; c. Katherine Jon, Kristine Edith; res: 21421 Villena Ave., Woodland Hills, Cal. 91364.

ZOELLER, CAROLE KLEMM, Adv. Prod. Mgr., Air Force/Space Digest Magazine and Aerospace International Magazine, Air Force Association, 1750 Pennsylvania Ave. N.W., Wash., D.C. 20006, '67–; Edtl. Asst., '66–'67; Adv. Prod. Asst., '65–'66; PR Asst. Warnaco, Inc. (Bridgeport, Conn.), '64; Simmons Col., BS, '64; b. Bridgeport, Conn., 1942; p. Curt and Helen Zimmer Klemm; h. Laurence Zoeller; res: 4000 Tunlaw Rd. N.W., Wash., D.C. 20007.

ZOLOTOW, CHARLOTTE SHAPIRO, Sr. Ed. of Jr. Bks., Harper Row Publishers, Inc., 49 E. 33rd St., N.Y., N.Y. 10016; Auth. of 48 bks. for children; Lectr. on children's bks. and writing at various schs., univs., and summer writing confs.; PEN, Auths. Guild; Univ. of Wis., '33–'36; b. Norfolk, Va., 1915; p. Louis and Ella Bernstein Shapiro; h. Maurice Zolotow; c. Stephen, Ellen; res: 29 Elm Pl., Hastings-on-Hudson, N.Y. 10706.

ZORNOW, EDITH, Film Cnslt., Children's Television Workshop, 1865 Broadway, N.Y., N.Y. 10019, '70–; Dir., Film Div. Grove Press, '66–'67; Prodr., TV Special, "Standwells at Home" (Emmy nomination, '66); Prodr., "Art of Film" program, WNDT-TV, '61–'66 (Emmy, '64; NET Aw. for Excellence in Educ. Programming, '66); VP, Dir., Go Pictures-George K. Arthur, '59–'61; Mgr., Film Librn., Brandon Films, '52–'59; Asst. to program dir., WLIB-radio, '41–'51; selection comm., N.Y. Film Festival, '67; Trustee, Flaherty Film Seminars; active in programming seminars; N.Y. Film Cncl. (Bd. Mbr., '64–'65), EFLA; St. John's Univ., BBA, '40; b. N.Y.C., 1920; p. Morris and Sophie Polakoff Zornow; res: 20 Fifth Ave., N.Y., N.Y. 10011.

ZUCKER, DOLORES BOLTON (pseuds: Dee Hill; Devera), Free-lance Wtr.; 714 N. Crescent Dr., Beverly Hills, Cal. 90210; Auth: "My Name is Leona Gage," "Three to Make Merry," "You Better Believe It"; Hollywood Wms. Press Club (Secy., '64); Univ. of Cal., S.F. State Col.; b. Berkeley, Cal.; p. James and Giovanna Muzio Bolton; h. Irwin Zucker; c. Lori B., Judi M., Shari L.; res: 714 N. Crescent Dr., Beverly Hills, Cal. 90210.

ZUCKERKANDEL, DOROTHY ELLEN KAHN, PR Dir., Philadelphia State Hospital at Byberry, 14000 Roosevelt Blvd., Phila., Pa. 19114, '67–; PR Dir., YWCA of Phila., '52–'67; AE, Adelphia Assocs., '51–'52; Radio-TV Wtr., United Fund of Phila., '50–'51; Publicist, Phila. Fellowship Comm., '49–'50; Cnslt., Phila. Home & Sch. Cncl., '67; Cnslt., Citizens Comm. on Public Educ. in Phila., '64–'66; Cnslt., Child Growth & Maternal Health Program, Nat. Insts. of Health, '62–'63; various organizations; Temple Univ., BS, '49 (with hons., merit scholarship); Univ. of Pa. (Sociol.), '51–'52; b. N.Y.C., 1927; p. Edward and Eva Lubin Kahn; h. David Zuckerkandel; c. Eva, Abbe, Mia; res: 1077 Wellington Rd., Jenkintown, Pa. 19046.

ZUELKE, RUTH EVELYN, Art. Coord., Birmingham Public Schools, Birmingham, Mich., 48012; Auth: "The Horse in Art" ('65), "The Art Museum and the Secondary School" (Random House, '68); Ed., "Art Appreciation", ('66); Instr., Univ. of Minn.; Command Dir., Army Artists' and Photo program, U.S. Army Spce. Svcs., (W. Germany); Delta Phi Delta, NAEA, Art Educ. Dirs. of Mich., Nat. Art Educ. Dirs. and Supvsrs. Comm (Acting Secy.), Mich. Art Educ. Assn., Met. Detroit Bur. of Sch. Studies Art Comm.; Univ. of Minn., BS, '52, MA, '62.

ZWECKER, MARGARET BUSHEE, Fashion, Beauty Ed., The Chicago Daily News, 401 N. Wabash Ave., Chgo., Ill. 60611, '50–; Fashion Ed., The Sun-Times, '45–'49; Fashion, Beauty Ed., The Times, '41–'45; Food, Home Furnishings Ed., '37–'41; Fashion Group, WNPC, Eds. Exec. Comm. of Am. Designers; active in commty. affairs; FRANY Aws., '66, '69; Chgo. Nwsp. Guild Aw., '65; p. Dr. Grant and Mabel Hamilton Bushee; h. William Zwecker; c. Janet (Mrs. Richard D. Stannard), William R., Jr.; res: 305 North East Ave., Oak Park, Ill. 60302.

ZWIRN, LILLIAN, Media Byr., AE, Barbet & Weigert Assoc., Inc., 477 Madison Ave., N.Y., N.Y. 10022, '65–; Feature Wtr., Central Feature News, '52–'65; OPC, AWNY, Sls. Prom. Execs. Assn.; N.Y.U., BA, '41; b. N.Y.C.; c. Laurence, Mel; res: 2095 Creston Ave., Bronx, N.Y. 10453.

Geographical and Subject Cross-index

This index is designed to make the names of **Foremost Women in Communications** accessible by geographical location (see States), then by industry or work category (see Arabic Numerals), then by the individual's profession (see Letters), and then by the individual's specialty (see Italics).

Geographical Location The listing of states is in alphabetical order, with Washington, D.C. under District of Columbia. Because this is a professional directory, individuals with addresses in different states for home and business are listed in the states of their businesses. Foreign countries follow the states.

Industry or Work Category These are divided into fifteen groups in the Master Plan. I to 6, 9, 10, and 11 are recognized categories in communications. 7, Other Firms in Communications, includes companies with functions considered "subsidiary" or "complementary" to the major industries. Included here are media buying firms, media representatives, design shops, production houses, photography firms, and research companies. To identify the company function, the position usually reserved for the individual's specialty (Italics) is used in 7 category to refer back to the specialty of the company.

Professions These are broken into fourteen groups in the Master Plan. The groups were altered in some industries to include professions distinctive to those industries. For categories 1 and 2, Group B (Production) includes Programming; for category 3, group C (Sales and Marketing) includes Rights and Permissions, and Group E (Writers) refers to Authors; for category 6, group G (Advertising) refers to Account Executives; for category 10, group H (Public Relations) refers to Account Executives. Group A (Management) includes both staff and line management, usually beginning with the title of Manager; Group F (Creative) includes Artists, Photographers, and Illustrators; group J (Talent) includes Actresses, Broadcasters, Commentators, and Lecturers; Group N (Special Consultants) includes Translators and frequently Home Economists in communications. Women classified under K, L, M, and N are found in category 14, Allied Professionals. Many women are classified two or three times, in different industries and professions. For example, women who are Authors (under 3 E) are frequently Free-lance Writers (under 13 E) or Educators (under 14 L).

Specialties These notations have been supplied by the biographees and indicate their particular interests or areas of concentration. They include media and/or subjects. Thus, a user may find magazines, journals, or articles separately or possibly joined with subjects such as foods or architecture. Because categories 8 and 12 cover a wide range of companies and organizations, no attempt was made to include specialties of individuals (or companies as in 7). It should be understood that women in management and women who are department heads may not have specialties, as their areas of responsibility may be very broad. This accounts for the many people who do not have designations in italics.

Master Plan

Industry or Work Category
1. Television
2. Radio
3. Book Publishing
4. Newspapers
5. Magazines
6. Advertising and Marketing
7. Other Firms in Communications
8. Financial Institutions and Industry Firms
9. News Services and Syndicates
10. Public Relations
11. Library Science
12. Government Agencies, Organizations, Councils, Associations
13. Free-lance
14. Allied Professionals
15. Services

Professions
A. Management
B. Production
C. Sales and Marketing
D. Editors
E. Writers
F. Creative
G. Advertising
H. Public Relations, Publicity, and Promotion
I. Research
J. Talent
K. Personnel
L. Education
M. Representatives and Agents
N. Special Consultants

ALABAMA

1-A

GAUT, B. S.
women's, promotion
HANSON, B. L.
women's programs

1-B

FICHTNER, M. C.

1-H

FINCHER, B. C.
GAUT, B. S.
ZERBE, N. C.
promotion

1-I

LUCAS, R. D.
hostess

2-A

BENNS, I. W.
GIBSON, E. G.
women's programs
HANSON, B. L.
women's programs

3-E

CHITWOOD, I. D.
fiction, non-fiction
GREER, V. B.
non-fiction
HUTCHENS, E. N.
writing
JOHNSTONE, K. Y.
non-fiction
ROBERTS, F.
non-fiction
SANGUINETTI, E. A.
SIZEMORE, M. D.

4-A

AYERS, E. Y.
BOWERS, V. V.
advertizing
PARISH, B. G.
WALLS, M. W.

4-D

BAKER, S. L.
women's
CALDWELL, L. M.
fine arts

CANNON, V.
FALKENBERRY, E. R.
women's
HOFFMAN, M. C.
editorial page
PARISH, B. G.
SIDEBOTHAM, P. J.
women's
SPENCER, M. A.
women's
TEAGUE, S. A. C.
fashion
WALKER, A. B.

4-E

BIGBEE, N. M.
correspondent
CANNON, V.
PRINCE, L. C.
staff

4-F

CANNON, V.

6-A

BOGLE, P. S.
research, development
CLISBY, A. D.
print media
CULVERHOUSE, R. J.
radio, TV
PERRY, J. P.
SMITH, J. R.
media

6-C

PONDER, L. C.
broadcast

7-A

HUTCHENS, E. N.

8-D

ALDRIDGE, A. L.
CRUSE, I. R.
SMITH, V. D.
WALLS, S. L.

8-E

MEADOWS, J. C.

8-G

SMITH, V. D.

8-H

CRUSE, I. R.

10-A

FLIRT, J. A.

11

AGNEW, N. R.
CARR, A. B. M.
DURKIN, M. L.
HAYES, A. G.
KING, A. G.
MARTIN, N. N.
consultant
PEERSON, E.
TOFFEL, N. J.
media
WILLOUGHBY, M. E.

12-A

SIEGELMAN, M. K.

12-D

LEONARD, N. T.
SPENCER, J. B.

12-H

BERGIN, M. W.
FINCHER, B. C.
GORMAN, E. M.
MURPHREE, J. T.

13-E

GREER, V. B.
articles
HILL, M. G.
articles
WARNKE, L. T.

13-J

JOHNSTONE, K. Y.
lecturer

14-L

HILL, M. G.
HUTCHENS, E. N.
English
ROBERTS, F.
history
SIZEMORE, M. D.

ALASKA

3-D

MIELKE, M. G.
poetry

3-E

MACHETANZ, S. B.
juvenile
PEDERSEN, E. K.
juvenile
WOODMAN, B. D.
non-fiction

3-F

MACHETANZ, S. B.
photographer

4-A

CHARLES, M. P. F.

4-D

BAKER, M. A. H.
city
CHARLES, M. P. F.
women's
SHROYER, M. S.
women's

4-E

ATWOOD, E. R.
feature, promotion

9-E

WOODMAN, B. D.
correspondent

11

SAMSON, I. G.

12-I

MIELKE, M. G.

13-E

MIELKE, M. G.
poetry

13-J

HARRISON, L. C.
broadcasting

15

WILLIAMS, D. B.
printing

ARIZONA

1-J

PAQUETTE, L. L.
singer

2-A

GILBERT, A. M.

3-A

BUCHANAN, G. D.
FRANCIS, M. A.

3-D

SCHEIFELE, K. S.

3-E

BAKER, B.
novels
CLARK, L. H.
Indians
COTHERN, F. H.
non-fiction
EVANS, E. H.
FRANCIS, M. A.
poetry
GILLMOR, F.
biographies, novels
HARTER, H. O.
HENDERSON, Z. C.
JONES, D. M.
reading
LAUGHLIN, F.
juvenile
LOVELL, E. K.
non-fiction
MATTINGLY, A. S.
non-fiction
PULLIAM, N. M.
ROBINSON, H. M.
music textbook
SHAFFER, P. S.
historical novels
SHANK, M. E.
fiction

SHAY, M. Q.
juvenile
STEVENSON, G. T.
non-fiction
SWINFORD, B. W.
children's, adults
TANNER, C. L. F.
Indians, Indian art
WEEKS, R. M.
juvenile
WOODS, J. LeS.
YODER, M. A.

3-F

HARTER, H. O'C.
illustrator

4-A

PULLIAM, N. M.

4-D

BACH, M. C.
women's
BAGLEY, G.
women's
BAKER, V. M. D.
women's
ENGLISH, S. D.
food
HODGE, V. L. F.
women's
HOPKINS, W. K.
city
MACKLEY, E. H.
society, fashion
PEDEN, C. L.
teen
POLSON, D. S.
food
SABO, P. P.
women's
SCHULTZ, E. N.
club

4-E

COBB, C. C. M.
reporter
KEATING, M.
feature, movie, drama
KUEHLTHAU, M. W.
reporter, feature
SCHULTZ, E. N.
feature

4-F

SCHULTZ, E. N.
photographer

5-D

FENTON, E.

6-A

BLESCH, R. G.
production, media
COWEN, S. B.
media
HARWOOD, S. H.
KLINE, C. T.
ORSBORN, N. N.

6-B

GATES, C. C.
HARWOOD, S. H.

6-D

GATES, C. C.

6-E

GATES, C. C.

8-F

EITZMAN, A. McG.

9-E

ENGLISH, S. D.
columnist

10-A

GARLAND, A. P.
consultant
KLINE, C. T.
ORSBORN, N. N.
PATTON, J. S.
SARLAT, G.
SIMUNICH, M. H.
THOMAS, M. D.
WILLIAMS, J.

11

DOWNUM, E. B.
FIELDING, J. P.
school
KRAKAUER, E. G.
PHELPS, W. A.
STEVENSON, G. T.
consultant
WHEELER, L. J.

12-A

BENNETT, H. T.
JOHNSTON, B. J.
SMITH, K. S.
THOMAS, M. D.

12-B

McQUOWN, P. T.

12-D

HARRIS, P. A.
HEALD, P. W.
KLINE, C. T.
SHAW, E. L.
WEEKS, R. M.

12-H

DAUGHERTY, J. S.
HINSHAW, H. E.
ORSBORN, N. N.
PINE, B. R.
SEARS, B. P.
STEVES, G. C.

13-E

BROWN, C. O.
BUCHANAN, G. D.
COTHERN, F. H.
CROWE, R. R.
history
FRANCIS, M. A.
poetry
GILLMOR, F.
reviews, articles
HEALD, P. W.
plays
HULL, E. H.
HYDE, H. P.
LAUGHLIN, F.
fiction, non-fiction
LOVELL, E. K.
MATTINGLY, A. S.
reviews
SHAY, M. Q.
fiction, poetry, articles
STEVENSON, G. T.
libraries
SWINFORD, B. W.
short stories, articles
TANNER, C. L. F.
Indians, Indian art
UTZMAN, E. VanS.
WEEKS, R. M.
poetry
WOODS, J. LeS.
music

13-F

BROWN, C. O.

photographer
CLARK, LaV. H.
photographer
SCHIFFELER, M. W.
artist

13-I

CLARKE, LaV. H.
Indians
CROWE, R. R.
historical

13-J

PAQUETTE, L. L.
singer

14-L

COTHERN, F. H.
journalism
EVANS, E. H.
English
JONES, D. M.
education
KRAKAUER, E. G.
research methods
MATTINGLY, A. S.
speech
ROBINSON, H. M.
music
SCHIFFELER, M. W.
art
SHANK, M. E.
English
TANNER, C. L. F.
anthropology

14-N

HARTER, H. O'C.
translator

ARKANSAS

2-J

HARRIS, E. C.
poetry program
WYRICK, M. C. W.
broadcaster

3-E

ALLEN, R. E.
non-fiction
COMPTON, S. LaN.
poetry
HARRIS, E. C.
poetry

HEAGNEY, A.
juvenile history
MALONE, R. M.
cook books
PETER, L.
poetry

4-A

BEERSTECHER, F. A.
CARNAHAN, A. W.
HALLEY, L. S.
advertising
SCHEXNAYDER, C. T.
WEISER, J. A.
advertising

4-D

ALDRIDGE, H. K.
food, home
BEERSTECHER, F. A.
CORDELL, F. W.
women's
DOUGLAS, M. L.
TV
DOZIER, K. C.
women's
FULKERSON, B. F.
women's
NEWMAN, C. G.
city
NEWTON, L. S.
society
SCHEXNAYDER, C. T.
SPENCER, M. W.
women's

4-E

DOUGLAS, M. L.
TV columnist
DRESBACH, B. G.
literary critic
HANDFORD, C. C.
columnist
SUITT, E. L.

5-D

SAYLOR, N. S.
poetry

6-A

KENNEDY, S. R.
research

8-D

MALONE, R. M.

10-A

HOBBS, D. J.

11

BIRDSALL, S. A.
BISHOP, I. S.
BROTHERS, C. C.
school
COMPTON, S. LaN.
catalogue
DORSETT, C. M.
GRIFFITH, M. B. T.
GRIFFITHS, E. P.
KRONE, G. L.
LEVECK, R. A.
medical
NEAL, F. P.
SHARP, A. C.
technology
SHINN, E. A.
consultant
WHITEHEAD, I. R.

12-A

CALDWELL, B. McD.
NEAL, F. P.

12-D

CALDWELL, B. McD.
FENTON, E.

12-E

HEAGNEY, A.

12-H

WOOD, B. P.

13-E

ALLEN, R. E.
DAVIS, A. K.
KENNAN, C. B.
articles, poetry
LETZIG, M. H.
PETER, L.
articles, poetry
SAYLOR, N. S.
poetry

13-G

WYRICK, M. C. W.

13-H

WYRICK, M. C. W.

14-L

BERRY, R. A.
education
KENNAN, C. B.
English, writing

14-N

HARRIS, E. C.
poetry

CALIFORNIA

1-A

BROWN, D. L.
standards, practices
OLSEN, N. T.
operations
SCOFIELD, S. C.
women's
THALHEIMER, F. W.
public affairs

1-B

CAMPBELL, J. B.
DUNCAN, V. B.
ELLIS, J. W.
MOCK, J. McK.
MURPHY, C. M.
MURPHY, W. S.
PENNELL, R. H.
SCOFIELD, S. C.
THALHEIMER, F. W.

1-D

BROUGH, J. W.
west coast, story

1-E

CAMERON, S.
reporter
DAY, G.
scripts
EDWARDS, J. C.
educational series
EDWARDS, J. C.
religious
ELLIS, J. W.
GARFF, G.
reporter
HITE, K.
fiction
MURPHY, C. M.
PENNELL, R. H.
PETERSEN, N. K. W.

1-G

SULLIVAN, P. W.

1-H

CARRIKER, W. G.
promotion
SULLIVAN, P. W.

1-I

PETERSEN, N. K. W.

1-J

DE VIVIER, J. F.
coordinator
ELLIS, J. W.
narrator
McCURDY, M. B.
TV teacher
RAMEY, W.
newscaster
REID, V. M.
SCOFIELD, S. C.
hostess
THALHEIMER, F. W.
moderator
TORREY, J. S.
commentator
WESLEY, J.
commercials

2-A

BANOCZI, J.
BROWN, D. L.
standards, practices
BUCHANAN, J. De J.
DUFFY, F. H.
office
SHIRCLIFF, J. S.
operations

2-B

JOHNSON, E. B.

2-C

McELROY, R. F.
WAGSTAFF, B. J.

2-D

RIEGLE, B. R.

2-E

EBERLY, C. P.

2-J

MILLER, M. F.
hostess
NOEL, C.
personality
RIEGLE, B. R.
broadcaster
VAN BUREN, A.
advice show

2-H

ENGELMYER, R. L.
awards

3-A

ARDOUREL, J.
production
ARMSTRONG, A. C.
directories
BASTIEN, F.
BUCHANAN, C. D.
DURAN, J. C.
GROSSO, E. G.
HENDERSON, S. V.
MILLER, G.
NORTH, F. d'I.
ORDONEZ, B. W.
PARKER, P. K.
advertising, promotion
TURNER, D. B.

3-B

BUTTERFIELD, C. W.

3-D

BOAZ, M.
DOUGLAS, A. M.
DUNNING, V. T.
ENFIELD, G. D.
biography
HASKIN, D. C.
LOCKHART, A. S.
consulting
MASTERSON, I. J.
PENNIMAN, G. B.
poetry
PONLEITHNER, R. R.

3-E

ALBERT, D.
non-fiction
ANNIXTER, J.
juvenile, adult
ARDMORE, J. K.
ARMER, A. R.
children's
ARMSTRONG, A. C.
juvenile
ARVEY, V.
music, dance

BAKER, L. N.
children's
BARTLETT, E.
BAUER, H.
non-fiction
BEATTY, P. R.
children's
BEHRENS, J. Y.
children's
BENZ, M. O.
BERNSTEIN, B. C.
BOAZ, M.
BOGGESS, L. B.
writing techniques
BOGUE, L. M.
BOYD, M. W.
non-fiction
BOYLE, K.
fiction
BRAY, D.
folklore, law
BRECKENFELD, V. G.
young adult
BRISTOW, G.
fiction
BRODIE, F. McK.
biography
BROWN, M. B.
children's
BRYANT, K. P.
business
BUCHANAN, C. D.
reading textbooks
BUCHANAN, P.
BUCK, M. A.
economics
BURDEN, J.
poetry, essays
BURNS, C. W.
children's
CAMPBELL, B. F.
food
CANNON, C. M.
CLAIRMONTE, G.
biography
CLEMONS, E.
non-fiction, juvenile
COATES, B.
juvenile fiction
COGGINS, C.
food, entertaining
COLSON, E. F.
anthropology
DAY, G.
novels
DINERMAN, B.
public administration
DONNELLY, Sr. D.
religion
DORCY, Sr. M. J.
children's
DOWDELL, D. K.
juvenile non-fiction
EDWARDS, J. C.
teen mysteries
ENFIELD, G. D.
non-fiction
FITCH, G. T.
FREDERICK, C.
housekeeping

FREEDMAN, N. M.
novels
FRESCHET, B. S.
children's
GIBERSON, D. D.
GLASSCOCK, A. B.
novels
GRAVES, P. B.
interiors
GREENE, C.
children's non-fiction
HABER, J. B.
children's
HANNA, L. A.
textbooks
HARKNESS, G. E.
religion
HARMER, R. M.
HASKIN, D. C.
HELMING, A.
novels
HENDERSON, S. V.
cookbooks
HOFFMAN, G. K.
textbook
HOOS, I. R.
automation, manpower
HORN, J. D.
non-fiction
HUGHES, J. K.
computor programming
HURD, E. T.
children's
JACKSON, C. C.
children's
JAFFA, A. R.
poetry
JOHNSON, W. MacN.
junior novels
KENOYER, N. P.
horses, animals
KNIGHT, R. A.
novels
KROEBER, T. K.
KURSH, C. O.
LAMBERT, H. M.
textbooks
LANE, M. B.
human relations
LAWLESS, D. K.
handicraft
LeCOCQ, R. P.
Asia
LEE, V. Y.
fiction, non-fiction
LEONARD, E. M.
non-fiction
LESLIE, A.
novels, plays
LEWIS, J.
novels
LININGTON, B. E.
*mysteries, detective
stories*
LOCKHART, A. S.
anthology, music
LYONS, D. M.
teen fiction
LYTLE, R. C.
non-fiction

MANDLER, J. M.
psychology
MARTIN, P. M.
children's
MAY, E.
music
McCALL, V. N.
mysteries, novels
McWILLIAMS, M. E.
food
MENDENHALL, R. D.
out-of-doors
MILES, J.
poetry, style
MILLER, M. F.
non-fiction: spies
MOYER, C. I.
non-fiction
MUIR, J.
mysteries, juvenile
MULLEN, M.
guide
NELSON, E. Deu P.
NICHOLS, C. F.
science fiction, psychic
NEILSEN, H. B.
mysteries
NORELL, I. P.
non-fiction
OFFORD, L. G.
novels, mysteries
OLENDER, T. T.
crime, law
OSBORN, B. M.
*textbook: community
health*
OTCHIS, E. H.
juvenile
PAYNE, A. S.
non-fiction
PECK, H. E.
children's
PENNIMAN, G. B.
poetry, plays
PHILLIPS, B. H.
biography
PHLEGER, M. T.
juvenile fiction
PIERRE, D. B.
POHLMANN, L. G.
*children, young adult
fiction*
PONLEITHNER, R. R.
REID, V. M.
TV education
RICHARD, J. McB.
novels, poetry
ST. JOHNS, A. R.
SARVIS, S. J.
cookbook
SASNETT, M. T.
*systems, planning
financial education*
SCHELLENBERG, H. C.
SCOBEY, M.-M.
education
SCOTT, L. B.
*children's textbooks,
filmstrips*
SEAGOE, M. W.

non-fiction
SELLERS, N. W.
SHANNON, A. A.
craft
SHURA, M. F.
SIEGEL, D. T.
novels
SINGER, J. S.
biography, mystery
SMITH, O. S.
history
STEPHENSON, P. P.
cookbook
STEVENS, G. G.
Near East
STEWART, E. S.
non-fiction
STOUTENBERG, A. P.
juvenile, adult poetry
SWARTZLOW, R. J.
biography
THOMAS, S.
space
THOMPSON, H. S.
education
TIEDT, I. McC.
education
TODD, F. E.
textbooks
TOOZE, R. A.
juvenile
TOPKINS, K. T.
WALDRON-SHAH, D'L.
Asia, Africa
WALTER, N. W.
WALTERS, D. W.
sales
WARBURG, S. S.
juvenile fiction
WATSON, M. G.
WATTS, M. P.
juvenile
WAYBURN, P. E.
conservation
WISE, W. E.
young adult, biography
YOUNG, J. R.
juvenile
ZUCKER, D. B.

3-F

LYTLE, R. C.
pen and ink illustrator
STEPHENSON, P. P.
illustrator

3-G

BUTTERFIELD, C. W.

3-H

DOUGLAS, A. M.

3-I

DURAN, J. C.
BURNS, C. W.
historical

4-A

ASH, M. S.
legislative newsletter
BRAY, D.
BROWN, N. C.
CAMPBELL, M. D.
CARLTON, M. E.
special sections
CROWE, M. B.
DEAN, R. A.
ENSIGN, A. T.
art
FUNK, E. McC.
GERMAIN, A. M.
HANCHETT, B. H.
LITTLE, M. C.
office
McHUGH, R. J.
MILES, T. W.
SMITH, J. H.
*promotion, community
services*

4-D

ALLEN, V. P.
education
ANDERSON, B. P.
society
ANDERSON, V. D.
ARTERBURN, H. C.
BAKER, N.
art
BARKLEY, S. J.
women's
BAXTER, M.
women's
BEAVERS, J. B.
women's
BELLOWS, M. C.
society
BELYEA, D. C.
women's
BILLHEIMER, R. M.
society, fashion
BLACKWOOD, J. O.
news
BLADEN, B. C.
drama
BOGERT, Z. S.
travel
BOQUIST, F. M.
women's
BRANIN, J. W.
club
BROWN, N. C.
CAMPBELL, M. D.
CLINTON, M. J.
society
COUPE, I. D.
COWING, J. L.

women's
CRANDALL, O. M.
food
CROWE, M. B.
DANFIELD, B. E.
women's
DELANEY, M. A.
women's
EVERY, M. P.
women's
FLANARY, M. K.
home economics
FORTIS, G. S.
FRIEDRICH, D. T.
women's
GERGELY, S. S.
women's
GERICH, C. K.
arts, teen
GREEN, C. C.
GROVES, S. M.
society
HAGBERG, M. H.
art
HALL, N. G.
society
HALPERN, F. I.
political
HAMMOND, F. C.
fashion
HANCHETT, B. H.
HERD, B. W.
real estate
HILL, F. E.
HOSMER, B. J.
women's
HOXIE, J. S.
TV, radio
HUTMACHER, B. P.
living
IMPERATO, M. L.
fashion
JACKSON, C. C.
children's book
JARVIS, K. H.
food
JENSEN, H. J. A.
city
KAISER, J.
fashion, beauty
KRATZMIER, P. T.
women's
LANE, M. T.
women's
LERNER, S. G.
women's
MacLEAN, J. T.
family
MacMINN, A. B.
entertainment
MASTERSON, I. J.
society
McCUNE, P.
food
McHUGH, R. J.
McKNIGHT, E. E.
city
MITCHELL, L. V.
MOFFAT, F. A.
society

OILER, B. P.
women's
PARDIECK, E. L.
women's
PASSINI, M. W.
society
PENDERGAST, M. B. LeM.
women's
REMILLARD, M. G.
women's
ROBERTS, J. P.
women's
SAMUELSON, M. B.
women's
SARGENT, S.
SIMPSON, J. U.
women's
SLINGSBY, P. C.
women's
SMITH, V. A.
women's
SPECKMANN, M. P.
music
STROH, L.
women's
SUMMO, B. C.
music, drama
SWARTZ, S. F.
fashion
TERRILL, E. L.
fine arts, magazine
TOW, H. H.
clubs
UNDERWOOD, A. W.
VOLTZ, J. A.
food
WALKER, E. S.
women's
WATSON, D. M.
city
WILLIAMS, C. D.
women's
WILSON, L. E.
women's
WOOD, T. W.
society
WRIGHT, S. M.
religion

4-E

BEFAME, J.
reporter, feature
BERNSTEIN, B. C.
reporter
BRAY, D.
staff
BRENT, C. S.
articles
BROWN, B. R.
courthouse
BROWN, N. C.
correspondent
CARLIN, E. O.
building
COWING, J. L.
columnist
DAVIS, N. A. C.
columnist

DAVIS, N. A. C.
women's
EDWARDS, B. S.
staff
FOX, C.
columnist
FRIEDRICH, D. T.
columnist
GOTT, G. S.
women's
HAGBERG, M. H.
art, architecture
HALPERN, F. I.
staff
HARFORD, M.
staff, critic
HARRIS, B. N.
columnist, book reviewer
HOLLINS, V. Van D.
reporter, deskwoman
JACKSON, E. D.
social columnist
KAY, V.
columnist
LOPER, M. L. B.
LUDWIG, J. M.
MASTERSON, I. J.
columnist
McCLOSKEY, K.
reporter, staff
McKNIGHT, E. E.
columnist
McMAHAN, V. E.
police
MOFFAT, F. A.
columnist
MORGENTHALER, A. K.
reporter
OFFORD, L. G.
mystery reviewer
OLTEN, C. M.
staff
PELUSO, P. S.
columnist
PENNIMAN, G. B.
columnist
RIEGLE, B. R.
political
ROBBINS, M. B.
columnist
ROBERTS, J. P.
feature
SARGENT, S.
columnist
SCHULTZ, J. L.
education
SEAGOE, M. V.
book reviewer
SPECKMANN, M. P.
critic
SWARTZ, S. F.
feature
VILS, U.
feature
WHITE, M. P.
columnist
WINNER, K. E.
fashion
WOOD, M.
columnist

WOOD, T. W.
reporter
WRIGHT, S. M.
feature
ZOEGER, S. S.
columnist

4-F

HALL, N. G.
photographer

4-G

DEERE, G. R. C.
classified
MILLS, A. E.
classified

5-A

ARNETT, V. L.
JONES, R. R.
production
LANGDON, P. M.
advertising
McCUNE, S. M.
PATAKY, J. R.
TURNER, D. B.

5-B

FOGLE, C. M.
editor

5-C

LEIBELL, M. L.
advertising
  representative
LEIMER, M.
circulation
REINHARDT, D. P.
advertising analyst

5-D

ARNETT, V. L.
BURDEN, J.
poetry
CHAMBERLAIN, B.
picture
CLARKE, M. M.
COUPE, I. D.
DINSMORE, N. R.
west coast
DI VECCHIO, J. R.
home economics
DOUGLAS, A. M.
DRIGGS, L. R.
home economics,
  consulting
FREESE, W. A.
GRAY, N. C.
west coast

HILLYARD, K. A.
cooking
LOTT, L. A.
PATAKY, J. R.
PHILLIPS, E. R.
west coast
POST, A. D.
home economics
PRATT, V. M.
contributing
SIMPSON, J. K.
SWISHER, V. H.
west coast
TIEDT, I. McC.
education
TUCKER, C. A.
WRIGHT, P. M.
medical

5-E

GAUREAU, W. R.
book reviewer
HILLYARD, K. A.
columnist
HOFFMAN, G. K.
contributor
STEVENS, G. G.
political correspondent

5-F

CHAMBERLAIN, B.
picture

5-G

GOTTLIEB, C. M.
production

5-H

DOUGLAS, A. M.

5-I

WASSERMAN, R. R.
trailer living

6-A

ALEXANDER, B. B.
production
BRETON, L. R.
production
COATES, G. B.
client services
CRAWFORD, I. S.
DUNNE, F. R.
ELFWING, M. R.
research
FOSSCECO, R. A.
FULTZ, M. M.
media

HAGEN, P. M.
HALL, A. K.
HARPER, J.
media
JOHNSON, M. L.
media
LAGER, T.
MALLICOAT, L. E.
production
McCLELLAND, J. S.
MENNELL, C. J.
media
MONTGOMERY, J. J.
art
NICCUM, G. P.
OSTRANDER, K. A.
media
PATTON, E. J.
PUCKETT, M. S.
media
ROBERTS, J.
media
RYDEN, S. H.
media
SELSNIK, A. B.
media
SHERF, T.
SOBEL, J. W.
SWAFFORD, P. D.
VAN KEUREN, D. L.
coordinator
WALKER, J. H.
WHEELING, M. E. R.
media
WILLIAMS, E. R.
radio, TV

6-B

KRAUSHAAR, D. A.
radio, TV

6-C

CAIN, M. K.
CLYMER, C.
boradcast
DAVID, T.
traffic
DEAN, S.
DE HAVEN, K.
HANRAHAN, L. S.
KILEY, N. J.
LOEBER, M.
buying
PAGAN, R.
broadcast
THOMPSON, M. A.
media buyer
YARCHO, Y. V.

6-D

O'GORMAN, M. W.

6-E

LAFRANO, C. R.
MEYER, J.
VON EKENBERGER, J. P.

6-F

LANCASTER, P. W.
LAWRENCE, C.

6-G

DIXON, S. S.
FULCHER, N. J.
JACOBS, C. J.
JOHNSON, M. L.
MONAHAN, M.
SHORT, M. K.
SMITHWICK, B. B.
VOORHEES, M. P.
WEINER, S. R.
WILLIAMS, G. J.

6-H

JOHNSON, M. L.
WILLIAMS, G. J.

7-A

ANDERSON, M. L.
*commercials production
company*
ANGEL, B. W.
TV production company
BALL, L.
TV production company
BARHAM, P. A.
customs clearing
BERGEN, P.
TV productions company
BURLEY, T. T.
photographers
CAMERON, S.
CARLSON, K.
*music publishing
company*
CORNSWEET, S. D.
production company
COX, B. J.
film company
DEMING, A. H.
photographers
DODD, E. C.
production company
FOWLER, F. H.
production company
HENDERSON, W. R.
*environmental
consultants*
HIMES, K. E.
film company
JORDAN, H.
production company
JORDAN, H.
production company

LADD, S. C.
production company
MANSON, P.
*music production
company*
McDERMOTT, B. F.
designers
McINTIRE, V. A.
photographers
NELSON, K. H.
studio, gallery
PERRY, B.
theatre studios
ROSENQUEST, B. U.
film company
RYDEN, S. H.
*communications
company*
SHAW, B.
production company
STRAUSS, H. M.
motion pictures
SUMMERS, H.
studio
TALLTREE, L. B.
production company
TIMMER, S. N.
writing company
WESLEY, J.
production company

7-B

DODD, E. C.
production company
FETTO, E. P.
production company
JORDAN, H.
production company
MASSEY, J. L.
production company
McCONNELL, D. Du B.
production company

7-D

VINCENT, K. J.
record company

7-E

VINCENT, K. J.
record company
MATCHINGA, C. T.
film production company

7-F

DE VIVIER, J. F.
production company
LEE, V. A.
production company
LAWSON, K. D.
production company
McCONNEL, D. Du B.
production company

TEAM, V. C.
record company
TUCHMAN, F. H.
production company

8-A

DEAN, R. A.
HENSLEY, A. O.
PINTER, E. L.
RIGLER, R. L.
TOY, NOËL

8-B

HUTTON, R.

8-C

HEILY, K. A.
ROYAL, J.
WHITNEY, E. E.

8-D

BENZ, M. O.
CHRISTOFF, M. M.
CLINTON, M. J.
COLSON, G. A. A.
DANFORTH, M. A.
DIEGEL, J. M.
HARRIS, E. T.
PARKS, M. S.
SALTER, P. H.
SHULER, L. W.
STONE, C. B.
VAN VELZER, V. C.

8-E

MOSER, R. C.
ROGERS, K.
SALTER, P. H.
VAN VELZER, V. C.

8-F

RUSKEY, N. W.

8-G

PUSTARFI, B. A.

11

ALLEN, C. Van B.
ARMSTRONG, E. P.
BECKER, C. D.
BISHOP, E. P.
CANNON, C. M.
CARLSON, M. C.
CASEY, N.

CHADWICK, C. S.
CONKLIN, G. P.
  children's work
CHAMBERLIN, V. S.
CLIFTON, J. A. C.
  technical
DALTON, P. B.
DONAHUE, K. I.
DORAN, M. C.
DREBERT, E. C.
DRAKE, D. M.
FLEMING, J. D.
POLLY, J. L.
  technical education
FOSTER, P. B.
  reference
GRAMS, R. P.
JOHNSON, T. L.
KOOLWYK, L. L.
LEIGH, C. R.
LYONS, H. P.
  engineering
McCOLM, C. L.
  reader service
MAGEE, L. C.

8-H

CHIVERS, J. C.
DIEGEL, J. M.
DIXON, R. H.
FLORIANI, E. W.
HENSLEY, A. O.
KENDALL, D. J.
KERR, J. B.
KRONENBITTER, A. W.
MARKS, R. McL.
McLOUD, M.
PUSTARFI, B. A.
ROACH, S.
SAMMONS, M. B.
SAUNDERS, C. H.
SMALL, J. M.

8-I

NORTH, J. B.
  artificial intelligence

8-L

HUGHES, J. K.

9-A

DROSSEL, M. R.
LANDAU, I. B.
  west coast
SINGER, J. S.
VAN BUREN, A.

9-D

CRANDALL, O. M.
  food

9-E

BARHAM, P. A.
  columnist
BECK, M. M.
  Hollywood columnist
BOTTEL, H. B.
  columnist
BRANDVIG, M. B.
  California correspondent
DORCY, Sr. M. J.
GRAVES, P. B.
  feature
HABER, J. B.
  columnist
KENNEDY, E. K.
  cooking, columnist
TURMELL, K.
  teen columnist
VAN BUREN, A.
  advice columnist

10-A

BAKER, E. S.
  consultant
BEST, B.
  publicity
BRASS, C. K.
  promotion
BURDEN, J.
CARROLL, S.
  publicity
CHRISTIANSEN, V.
  publicity
DOERING, P. F.
FAIRFIELD, V. A.
FINLAY, D. M.
GILROY, G. A.
HERNANDEZ, A. C.
HUNZIKER, P. S.
KAUFFMAN, H. R.
LUBAR, R.
  publicity
MARTIN, N. L.
McCLELLAND, J. S.
MIDDIONE, E. D.
MORTIMER, C. P.
  publicity
NIELSEN, H. R.
PERSONS, M.
PETAL, B. D.
  fashion publicity
SHERF, T.
SONNE, A. V.
ZIGNER, G. E.
  consultant

10-H

BERGER, K. S.
GRATTAN, S. M.
HOWIE, M. C.
McRAE, S. W.
  food service
MILLER, K. J.

11

ALLEN, C. VAN B.
ARMSTRONG, E. P.
BISHOP, E. P.
BYRNES, H. S. W.
CANNON, C. M.
CARLSON, M. C.
CASEY, N.
CHADWICK, C. S.
DALTON, P. B.
DONAHUE, K. I.
DREBERST, E. C.
DRAKE, D. M.
FLEMING, J. D.
FERRING, G.
GRAMS, R. P.
JOHNSON, T. L.
KOOLWYK, L. L.
LEIGH, C. R.
MAGEE, L. C.
McNABB, K. C.
MINUDRI, R. U.
  young adult
MORRIS, E. L.
  children's services
NESBIN, E. W.
NURNEY, G. L.
PROCTOR, V.
  medical
REYNOLDS, C. C.
ROSS, V. L.
SHERWOOD, J. S.
  children's
SILBERBERG, E.
  bibliographer
SIMPSON, V. S.
  *books for blind and
    handicapped*
SMITH, M. McG.
  business
SPECHT, D. S.
  humanities
STEWART, J. L.
STOPPLE, A. B.
TALLMAN, J. A.
  engineering, math
TAYLOR, T. V.
  coordination
TRACER, J. L. C.
TRAVER, D. A.
TROKE, M. K.
TURNER, R. N.
  information coordinator
VAN VELZER, V. J.
  technical
WELLS, D. V.
  government
WHEELER, E.
WHITE, B. R.
  reference
WILSON, L. W.
  reference
WITHROW, B. A.
  medical

12-A

ARMSTRONG, A. C.

BUCHANAN, P.
CALLAN, M. A.
DEARMIN, J. T.
DONNELLY, Sr. D.
DORR, M. W.
EDWARDS, J. C.
GEORGE, V. L.
HEISE, A.
HERNANDEZ, A. C.
HOFFMAN, G. K.
HOOS, I. R.
JOHNSON, E. B.
LOFTUS, M. T.
MADAFFER, R. M.
MAHOOD, R. L.
O'NEIL, C.
PEARCE, K.
REINHART, M. B.
SQUAIRES, G. M. P.
THOMPSON, H. S.
TOMPKINS, D. C.
WAYNE, J.
WILBUR, R. J.

12-B

DUNCAN, V. B.
KEMP, R. B.
HEISE, A.
LAMBERT, H. W.
MOCK, J. McK.
MURPHY, W. S.

12-C

ROBINSON, D. J.

12-D

BAACK, B. M.
BARTLETT, E.
BLAKE, S. M.
CLARK, D. J.
CURRIER, B. Y.
FREESE, W. A.
HELLER, J. S.
LOFTUS, M. T.
LUGLIANI, C. S.
MERO, A. H.
SCOBEY, M.-M.
STEINMAN, E. L.
WARWICK, B. L.
WINKLER, L. G.

12-E

BROWN, V.
FORSYTH, R.
RAPPAPORT, C.
TALBOT, C. T.

12-F

ENSIGN, A. T.

12-H

BAACK, B. M.

BANKS, A. L.
CALLAN, M. A.
CASSIDY, G. R.
CLARK, D. J.
COLLINS, M. B.
CRAWFORD, G. J.
DE ARMOND, C. S.
DORSEY, D.
ERICSSON, M. K.
FORTIER, L. S.
FREED, N. W.
HALL, C. H.
HEISE, A.
HICKS, H. S.
HORNBAKER, A. G.
HUBIK, D. H.
HUNT, B. E. H.
JELM, H.
JOHNSON, P. J.
KRETZER, C. L.
LEAPER, R. A.
LeCOCQ, R. P.
LeSIEUR, H. E.
MARTIN, N. L.
MULANEY, K. E.
MURPHY, C. M.
PAPPAS, I.
PETKOVSEK, M. L.
POLAKOWSKI, P. K.
    military
PRIEST, M. McQ.
RIZNIK, C. B.
RUEHLIN, P. R.
STEWART, E. S.
TRAEGER, M.
WOOD, E. N.
WYGANT, A. F.
ZEBAL, P. T.

12-I

DINERMAN, B.
HOOS, I. R.
KURSCH, C. O.
MANDLER, J. M.
RAPPAPORT, C.
TOMPKINS, D. C.
WALDRON-SHAH, D'L.

12-J

RAMEY, W.

12-N

SCHMID, L. McC.

13-B

BEYER, B.
    TV
GAYLORD, J.
    producer, director
HUDSON, E. J.
    operettas
KINGSTON, L.
    producer

LUDWIG, J. M.
    TV programs, director
MAINA, J. D.
    radio
McDONALD, J. G.
    travel films
SCHROEDER, M. D.
SIDNEY, S.

13-D

BALFOUR, B. B.
    copy
DAY, G.
    radio, TV, film
LOCKHART, A. S.
    physical education

13-E

ALBERT, D.
ALEXANDER, L.
ALLEN, H. G.
    non-fiction
ANDERSON, E. B.
    fiction, TV, screen
ANDREEVA, T.
ARMER, A. R.
    juvenile stories
ARDMORE, J. K.
    magazine
ARVEY, V.
    music, dance
BAKER, L. N.
    children's
BALFOUR, B. B.
BARBER, M. K.
BAXTER, M.
    poetry, stories
BENZ, M. O.
BEYER, B.
    food
BIGELOW, M. G.
BOYD, M. W.
    non-fiction
BRANDVIG, M. B.
BRECKENFELD, V. G.
    reviewer: books, plays
BRODIE, F. McK.
BURDEN, J.
BURNS, C. W.
CAMPBELL, B. F.
    food, homemaking
CLAIRMONTE, G.
CLARKE, D. C.
    scholarly articles
COATES, B.
    short stories
DANFORTH, M. A.
DAY, G.
    radio, TV, film
DELANEY, M. A.
    magazine, anthology
de RIVER, J. R.
    plays
DORCY, Sr. M. J.
DUNNING, V. T.
    TV, motion pictures

FITCH, G. T.
    stories, Far East
FREDERICK, C.
FREEDMAN, N. M.
    articles
FREEMAN, C. M.
GARCIA, S. L.
GAYLORD, J.
GEORGE, V. L.
GIBERSON, D. D.
    articles, reviews, short
        stories
GRAVES, P. B.
    feature
GREENE, C.
    radio, magazine,
        advertising
HABER, J. B.
    articles
HARMER, R. M.
HASKIN, D. C.
HAYES, Sr. M. A.
    professional journals
HILLYARD, K. A.
HITE, K.
    TV fiction
HORN, J. D.
HOWARD, H. A.
HUNT, M. M.
IKERMAN, R. C.
    non-fiction
JEWETT, A. W.
    non-fiction
JOHNSON, W. MacN.
    articles, poetry
KELLEY, H. H.
KENOYER, N. P.
    horses, animals
KING, L. G.
KINGSTON, L.
    non-fiction
KIRK, P.
    TV scripts
LANE, M. B.
    professional journals
LASCOLA, E. W.
    articles: mental health
LAWLESS, D. K.
    articles: handicraft
LeCOCQ, R. P.
    short stories
LESLIE, A.
    radio, screen, TV comedy
LOCKHART, A. S.
    physical education
LOWE, B. W.
LUBAR, R.
    poetry, articles
LUXFORD, N.
    foreign correspondent
LYTLE, R. C.
    articles, poetry, short
        stories
MacMILLAN, N. K.
    films, TV
MAHOOD, R. L.
    history
MAINA, J. D.
MANDLER, J. M.
    research articles:
        psychology

MASON, N.
MATCHINGA, C. T.
    screen writer
MATHEWSON, E. L.
MENDENHALL, R. D.
    out-of-doors
MILLER, K. J.
    articles
MUIR, J.
    magazine
MULLEN, M.
    non-fiction
NELSON, E. Deu P.
    magazine
NICHOLAS, C. F.
    articles, plays, short
        stories
NIELSEN, H. B.
    magazine fiction, TV
PETKOVSEK, M. L.
    articles
PHILLIPS, B. H.
PULLING, H. A.
    library science
REHMEYER, S. S.
RICHARD, J. McB.
    songs, short stories,
        poetry
ROBINETTE, V. B.
    poetry
ROGERS, K.
SARTAIN, G.
SARVIS, S. J.
    food
SELLERS, N. W.
    short stories
SHANNON, A. A.
    articles, fiction, poetry
SHURA, M. F.
SIDNEY, S.
SMITH, O. S.
    history
SPURR, E. B.
STANFORD, A.
    poetry
STEWART, E. S.
    articles
STEWART, L.
    articles
STEWART, O. P.
    songs, poetry
STONE, R. A.
    art
TALLTREE, L. B.
    plays, poetry, song writer
TIMMER, S. N.
    copy
TODD, F. E.
    education
TODESCA, E. S.
TOOZE, R. A.
TURMELL, K.
    magazine
VAN BUREN, A.
    advice
VERNAZZA, M. W.
    non-fiction
VON LOSS, A.
WALDRON-SHAH, D'L.
    Asia, Africa

WALTER, N. W.
  poetry, articles, stories
WALTERS, D. W.
  sales
WATSON, M. G.
  articles, poetry, stories, scripts
WAYBORN, P. E.
  conservation
WENDT, I. D.
  poetry, stories
WHITE, M. P.
  entertainment, sports
WILLIAMS, V. K.
WINKLER, L. G.
WOOD, E. N.
  technical, consumer articles
WOOD, L.
  homes, gardens, travel
YARDENA
ZOEGER, S. S.
ZUCKER, D. B.

13-F

BIGELOW, M. G.
  composer
CLAIRMONTE, G.
DANFORTH, M. A.
  photographer
ENSIGN, A. T.
  artist
GAYLORD, J.
  artist
GEORGE, V. L.
  photographer
HUNT, M. M.
  illustrator
KELLEY, H. H.
  photographer
ROBERTS, J.
  photographer
STEWART, L.
  photographer
STONE, R. A.
  artist, sculptor
TIMMER, S. N.
  artist
TURNER, J. E.
  artist

13-G

KENT, P.
  marketing consultant
LAVERY, B. C.
  consultant

13-H

BENZ, M. O.
  consultant
COLLINS, M. B.
  publicity
CROWDER, C. A.
FRANKLIN, M. H.

HELLMAN, D. R.
  publicity
HERNANDEZ, A. C.
KENT, P.
  promotion, marketing consultant
LAVERY, B. C.
  consultant
McKELVY, T.
MOORE, C. F.
  special events
NIELSEN, H. R.
  consultant
PIERRE, D. B.
  theatre advance agent
ROMNEY, B.
  publicity
SULLIVAN, P. E.
  publicity
TRISTER, B. L.
  fashion

13-I

HORN, J. D.
SMITH, O. S.
  history

13-J

ABERG, S. M.
  actress
ACKERMAN, B. L.
  actress
ADAMS, E.
  actress, singer
ALBERGHETTI, C.
  actress
ANDERSON, B. J.
  actress
ANN-MARGRET
  actress
BADHAM, M. H.
  actress
BAIRD, J.
  actress
BALL, L.
  actress
BALLARD, S.
  actress
BARRY, P. W.
  actress
BASS, F. G.
  lecturer
BEAIRD, B.
  actress
BERGEN, P.
  actress
BERGER, E.
  actress, disease simulator
BEYER, B.
  TV hostess
BIGELOW, M. G.
  broadcaster
BLAKE, J. B.
  actress
BLONDELL, J.
  actress

BOUCHER, P. E.
  actress, singer
BRONSON, L. R.
  actress
BROWN, V.
  actress
BURNETT, C.
  comedienne, singer
BURRELL, J.
  actress
CAMERON, S.
  TV reporter
CANOVA, J.
  actress, comedienne
CAPERS, E. V.
  actress, singer
CARLSON, K.
  actress
CARROLL, V.
  actress
CARTER, J.
  actress
CARTWRIGHT, A. M.
  actress
CASEY, S.
  actress
CHANDLER, L.
  actress
CHAUVIN, L.
  actress
CHEATHAM, M.
  actress
CHRISTIE, A.
  actress
CHRISTOPHERSON, S.
  actress, singer
COFFIN, W. DeF.
  actress
COLLIER, S. P.
  actress
CONWELL, C. M.
  actress
COON, J. M.
  TV model
COOPER, J.
  actress
CROSBY, C. L.
  actress, singer, model
DARC, K.
  actress
DEBORD, S. L.
  actress
DAY, L. L.
  actress
DEININGER, D.
  actress
DELAMATER, G. G.
  actress
DEL REY, P.
  actress
DEVRY, E.
  actress, model
DE WINTER, J.
  actress
DREW, D. G.
  spokeswoman
DORR, M. W.
  lecturer
DUNCAN, P. R.
  actress

DUSAY, M. M.
  actress
EATON, M. M.
  actress
FARRELL, B.
  actress
FARRELL, S.
  actress
FERGUSON, A. C.
  actress
FERRAR, C. A.
  actress
FONG, F. C.
  actress
FRIEBUS, F.
  actress
FROST, A.
  actress
FULLER, C. L.
  actress
GAMMILL, N.
  actress
GARCIA, S. E.
  actress
GARNER, P. A.
  actress
GAYLORD, J.
  actress
GEFFERT, E. R.
  actress, singer
GERSON, J.
  actress
GILBERT, P.
  actress
GILGREEN, M. M.
  actress
GOLD, S. L.
  actress
HACKETT, J.
  actress
HALE, C.
  actress
HANNA, L.
  actress, announcer
HARRIS, V. S.
  actress
HAY, A. L.
  actress
HOBART, R.
  actress
HOLLAND, K.
  actress
HOWARD, C. C.
  actress
HOWERTON, C.
  actress
HYLAND, D.
  actress
JACKSON, M.
  actress
JACOBS, N. T.
  actress
JAFFA, A. R.
  artist
JAFFE, N. S.
  actress
JUSTICE, K.
  actress
KAYA, O.
  actress

KENNEDY, M. J.
actress
KING, A.
actress
KINGSTON, L.
TV hostess, actress
KIRK, P.
actress, commentator,
lecturer
KIRSHNER, D. C.
actress
KULP, N. J.
actress
LANDGARD, J. A.
actress
LANG, D.
actress
LANGDON, S. A.
actress
LARKEN, S. A.
actress
LEARNED, M.
actress
LEE, R.
actress
LEMANI, T.
actress, singer, dancer
LEWIS, N.
actress
LOCKE, S.
actress
LOWE, B. W.
interviewer
LUND, D. P.
actress
MacLACHLAN, J.
actress
MacLAINE, S.
actress
MacMILLAN, N. K.
recording artist,
actress
MAINA, J. D.
actress, announcer
MARGETTS, M.
actress
MATCHINGA, C. T.
actress
McANDREW, M. C.
actress
McBAIN, D. J.
actress
McCARTHY, N.
actress
McDONALD, J. G.
broadcaster
McKELVY, T.
TV, radio
MEDFORD, K.
actress
MENZIES, H. M.
actress
MERIWETHER, L. A.
actress
MILES, V.
actress
MILLER, M. F.
lecturer
MOCK, L. C.
actress

MOOREHEAD, A.
actress
MORRISON, B.
actress
MORROW, P.
actress
NUNN, A. E.
actress
O'NEILL, E.
actress
PERRY, B.
actress
PETERSON, M. D.
actress
REDDING, T. G.
actress, model
REINHART, A. J.
actress
RHODES, V. N.
actress
RICH, S. W.
actress
ROBERTSON-RIEHL, K.
actress
RODMAN, N. C.
actress
ROGERS, K.
actress
ROMNEY, B.
spokeswoman
RYAN, F.
actress
SALE, V.
actress
SCHROEDER, M. D.
actress
SCHUBER, M. A.
actress, model
SELSMAN, M. S.
actress
SEURAT, P. H.
actress
SHAW, R.
actress
SHIBE, H. B.
artist, designer
SHINN, M. A.
actress
SIMS, F. A.
actress
SKANTZ, P. B.
actress, interviewer,
fashion commentator
SOMMARS, J.
actress
STERLING, T. A.
actress
STEWART, O. P.
lecturer
SUMMERS, H.
actress
SUTHERLAND, L. B.
actress
TALBOT, N.
actress
TAYLOR, S.
actress
THAYER, L.
actress

TINDALL, M. A.
model, actress
TOBIN, F. C.
actress
TOMPKINS, A.
actress
TOOZE, R. A.
lecturer
TORREY, J. S.
model
TOWNSEND, K. J.
actress
TOY, N.
actress
TREIMAN, J. W.
artist
TURMELL, K.
TV, radio guest
TUTTLE, L.
actress
UNLAND, M. G.
actress
VICTORIA, C. V.
actress
VON LOSS, A. C.
actress
WALLEY, D. E.
actress
WARD, E.
actress
WAYNE, J.
artist
WHITNEY, C. C.
actress
WILKERSON, J.
actress, model
WINDSOR, M.
actress
WOOD, M.
actress
WOOD, N.
actress
WORTHINGTON, C.
actress
YARDENA
actress
YARNALL, C.
actress
ZAX, C. T.
actress

14-K

ALLENDER, C. H.
AVERY, R. L.

14-L

BEHRENS, J. Y.
reading specialist
BERNSTEIN, B. C.
BOAZ, M.
library science
BOGGESS, L. B.
BOGUE, L. M.
BOYLE, K.
BRENT, C. S.
adult education

BRODIE, F. McK.
history
BRYANT, K. P.
government
BUCK, M. A.
economics
BRYNES, H. W.
CLARKE, D. C.
Spanish
COGGINS, C.
COLSON, E. F.
anthropology
CYR, H. W.
instructional media
EDWARDS, J. C.
history, Spanish
FERRING, G.
FORSYTH, R.
FREDERICK, C.
HANNA, L. A.
HARKNESS, G. E.
applied theology
HARMER, R. M.
HAYES, Sr. M. A.
library science
JEWETT, A. W.
agriculture, economics
JOHNSON, E. B.
KELLEY, H. H.
photojournalism
KENNEDY, E. K.
LAMBERT, H. M.
education
LANE, M. B.
education
LEONARD, E. M.
LEWIS, J.
creative writing
MATHEWSON, E. L.
adult education
McCURDY, M. B.
TV teacher
McWILLIAMS, M. E.
home economics
MILES, J.
NORELL, I. P.
librarianship
OBERLE, M.
OSBORN, B. M.
OTCHIS, E. H.
REID, V. M.
English
SANDERS, T. G.
drama
REHMEYER, S. S.
English
SASNETT, M. T.
international education
SCHELLENBERG, H. C.
creative writing
SEAGOE, M. V.
education
SELLERS, N. W.
SQUAIRES, G. M. P.
nursing
STANFORD, A.
English
SWARTELOW, R. J.
TIEDT, I. McC.

TREIMAN, J. W.
  art
TURNER, J. E.
  art
VERNAZZA, M. W.
  music
WENDT, I. D.
  English
ZOEGER, S. S.
  English, journalism

14-M

ALLEN, H. G.
  English textbooks
COLLIER, S. P.
  authors: motion picture
  rights
CUMBER, L. J.
SHIBE, H. B.
  sculptor's

14-N

ANDREEVA, T.
  translator
CRANDALL, E. J.
  nursing
CROWE, M. B.
  anti-poverty
EDWARDS, J. C.
  education
HERNANDEZ, A. C.
  industrial consultant
HUDSON, E. J.
  theatre director
MAY, E.
  music specialist
MILLER, G.
  interior design
MOORE, C. F.
  special events
OSBORN, B. M.
  health
SARVIS, S. J.
SCHMID, L. Mc.
  art education
STEPHENSON, P. P.
  home economics
THOMAS, S.
  science, writing
THOMPSON, H. S.
  reading
TRISTER, B. L.
  fashion
YARDENA
  translator

15

AICHOLTZ, V. L. Z.
  TV/recorders
ALLEN, A. G.
  education consultants
CLAIRMONTE, G.
  manuscript analyst

COLLIER, S. P.
  motion picture rights
CRANDALL, E. J.
  nursing
KNIGHT, G. P.
  circulation auditors
McDERMOTT, B. F.
  kitchens
SCHWARTZ, M. S.
  creative services
URNER, D. J.
  home furnishings center
WALTERS, D. W.
  hostess service, press
WEST, K. M.
  retouching

COLORADO

1-A

SEGELKE, E. R.

1-B

WHITE, A. L.
  traffic

1-J

DELUISE, E. S.
  children's teacher
HILTON, D. S.
  personality
JETER, L. K.
  personality

2-A

BLAIR, K. R.
  music
EAST, S. R.
JETER, L. K.
  women's
MOSIER, S.
  women's
ROWE, J. A. O.
  women's
SCHULTHEIS, E. E.
SEARS, V. LaC.
  sales
SEGELKE, E. R.
SHAFFER, A. M.
  women's

2-C

BOYES, A. D.
  representative

2-J

HILTON, D. S.
  personality

JETER, L. K.
  personality
ROWE, J. A. O.
  hostess

3-C

STUMBOUGH, V. C.
  field representative

3-E

BEVLIN, M. E.
  art textbook
BLAIR, K. R.
  non-fiction
BLOCH, M. H.
  children's
CALHOUN, M.
  children's
CLIFFORD, M. C.
DEGERING, E. F.
  children's biographies
ELLIS, A. M.
  historical novels
EVANS, N. W.
FISHER, A. L.
  children's
FORSEE, F. A.
  children's
HAMMERSLEY, E. B.
  cookbooks, other
HUNT, S. I. W.
  poetry, other
KOSTKA, D. P.
LENNON, F. T.
  poetry, non-fiction
MALLON, P.
  poetry, non-fiction
MARSH, S. R.
  maps
MEANS, F. C.
PETTEYS, A. F.
RECK, A. K.
  juvenile
ROWE, J. A. O.
  cookbook
SMITH, B. J.
STUMBOUGH, V. C.
WOLLE, M. S.
  non-fiction

3-F

DEGERING, E. F.
  picture books
WOLLE, M. S.
  illustrator

4-A

DEMPSEY, M. J.
  advertising
PETTEYS, A. F.

4-D

BARRETT, M. C.
  women's
BEATTY, S. L.
  society
BEAIRD, H. L.
  society
BIRKHEAD, E. McM.
  food, family
BROWN, E. L.
CARTER, P. P.
  society
DOLLAGHAN, H. F.
  food
FLANDERS, L. H.
  living
LAHMAN, R. G.
  editorial page
MALLON, P.
  women's
MORRISSEY, S. T.
  women's
MULBERY, E. L. D.
  social, church
NEILL, A. M.
  feature
SHAW, M. H.
  book
TRENT, H. G.
  society
WHITE, J.
  contemporary

4-E

BEAIRD, H. L.
  feature
CASSIDY, M. F.
  feature, columnist
CLIFFORD, M. C.
  columnist
CURTIS, O.
  feature
HADDAD, B. A.
  editorial
HILTON, D. S.
  columnist
KOSTKA, D. P.
  magazine section
  columnist
NEILL, A. M.
  reporter
SHAW, M. H.
  editorial
WEBER, G. A.
  fashion columnist

5-D

LINDER, J. J.
  regional
SCHOEN, E. F.

6-A

DENTON, G. P.
 media, research
LUSKY, L. F.
TINSLEY, P. L.
 business
WEIR, J. D.
 creative
WOLFF, M. L.

6-E

McCAIG, N. P.

6-G

BROCK, K. C.
LUSKY, L. F.

6-H

McCAIG, N. P.
 publicity

7-A

BARBRE, A. T.
 production company
LAMBKA, M. L.
 communications
MAGGARD, C. C.
 publishing company

7-C

BABCOCK, L. H.
 promotion company

7-H

BABCOCK, L. H.
 promotion company
McKECHNIE, M. A.
 computer company

8-E

BROWN, B. L.
RECK, A. K.

8-H

GREBE, Z. G.
McGRATH, P. K.
NEWTON, H. T.

10-A

MILLER, M. A.

11

AHERN, A. F.
 acquisitions, archives
ALEXIS, I. C. C.
CAMPBELL, F. F.
 law
COTELLESSA, H. D.
 trustee
DUNHAM, P. L.
FOLTZ, E. P.
HASTINGS, M. L.
HEMPHILL, J. F.
REID, M. G.
ROGERS, R. J.
 military history
RULE, B. B.
 public information
WIEBE, P. K.
WILCOX, V. L.
 mining

12-A

SMITH, B. J.

12-D

MALSAM, M. H.
SCHOEN, E. F.

12-E

DUHON, H. B.

12-H

CHAPMAN, M. L. S.
DANBOM, R. B.
GALLAHER, M. M.
HAMMERSLEY, E. B.
LEECH, C. S.
NEWTON, H. T.
RULE, B. B.

13-D

DeGERING, E. F.
 braille transcriber

13-E

BEATTY, S. L.
EVANS, N. W.
 articles, columnist
FASEL, I.
 professional articles,
 poetry
FISHER, A. L.
 children's
FLANDERS, L. H.
FORSEE, F. A.

HAMMERSLEY, E. B.
 radio
HATCH, L.
 reviews, articles
HUNT, S. I. W.
 feature
KEESHAN, M. P.
 columnist
KOSTKA, D. P.
MALSAM, M. H.
MARSH, S. R.
 articles
MEANS, F. C.
RECK, A. K.
 articles
STUMBOUGH, V. C.
 articles, stories, poetry

13-F

EVANS, N. W.
 artist
MARSH, S. R.
 photographer
WOLLE, M. S.
 artist

13-H

FLANDERS, L. H.

13-J

HAMMERSLEY, E. B.
 broadcaster
HATCH, L.
 lecturer
MEANS, F. C.
 lecturer
WOLLE, M. S.
 lecturer

14-L

BEVLIN, M. E.
 art
CRAWFORD, C.
 librarianship
ELLIS, A. M.
FASEL, I.
 English
FOLTZ, F. P.
 library science
HATCH, L.
 librarianship
HEMPHILL, J. F.
 bibliography
LENNON, F. T.
 poetry

14-N

DUNHAM, P. L.
 translator

15

CLARK, R. C.
 book center

CONNECTICUT

2-A

MONTOOTH, M. B.
 women's

2-D

McCARTY, M. K.
 women's

2-E

MONTOOTH, M. B.

2-J

MONTOOTH, M. B.
 interviewer

3-A

BASINGER, J. D.
 consultant
OTTEMILLER, F. T.

3-D

ANTELL, J. B.
 history
ASH, M. N.
 university
DUBOSE, D.
 education
JOHNSON, E. M.
 education
KENNEDY, M. L.
 education
WILSON, H. VanP.
 home, garden

3-E

AMES, L. B.
 science
BALDWIN, F.
 novels, non-fiction
BORLAND, B. D.
 fiction, poetry
BRADBURY, B. R.
 teen-age novels
BUTTERS, D. G.
 fiction, juvenile

COLMAN, H. C.
DRURY, M. C.
  children's
FOX, P. C.
  children's
FUTH, S. M. B.
  dog training
HOLDEN, S. McC.
  education
HUBBELL, P. A.
  children's
HYMAN, F. C.
  Judaism
KANE, D. N.
KINNEY, J. B.
  children's, non-fiction
KRAUSS, R.
  children's, poetry
LANDIS, J. R.
  autobiography
L'ENGLE, M. C.
  fiction
LIFTON, B. K.
  children's
LOESER, K.
LUND, D. H.
  children's
MERCIER, J. D.
  novels
NYE, S. L.
  poetry
PARKER, C. T.
PARTINGTON, S. T.
  modeling
PURDY, S. G.
  juvenile
RANDALL-MILLS, E. W.
  poetry
ROBBINS, J. S.
  biography
RUGH, B. D.
SCHULTZ, S.
  non-fiction
SNOW, H. F.
  history
SPEARE, E. G.
  juvenile, novels
STEPHAN, R.
  poetry
STILLMAN, M. S.
  children's non-fiction
SULLIVAN, M. B.
  non-fiction
TAMBURINE, J. H.
  children's
THARP, L. H.
  biography
TJADER-HARRIS, M.
  non-fiction
VAN DOREN, D. G.
  essays, novels
WALDEN, A. E.
  juvenile
WARNER, G. C.
  children's
WILLIAMS, J.
WOODWARD, H.
  children's
ZAGOREN, R.
  poetry, children's

3-F

FOX, P. C.
  illustrator: children's
LUND, D. H.
  illustrator
PURDY, S. G.
  illustrator: juvenile
WOODWARD, H.
  illustrator: children's

3-G

FOLLMER, M.

4-D

BATES, A. E.
  women's
MASTERS, A. V.
  copy
McSHERRY, E. A.
  book
PROWSE-PARSONS, B.
  women's
QUINT, R. J.
  women's
TYLER, B. S.
  arts, teenage

4-E

BAER, A. D.
  drama critic
BARRETT, M. E.
  women's
CAVANAUGH, J. F.
  society
CLOUSE, R. G.
  society
EASTLAND, D. P.
  editorial
HAMEL, M. Q.
  society
HEMENWAY, P. O'D.
  feature
LENGYEL, E. A.
  women's
MASTERS, A. V.
  feature
PARSONS, R. D.
  education
TYLER, B. S.
  feature, news
VAN DOREN, D. G.
  columnist

4-H

CLARK, P.
  promotion

5-A

FISHER, E. A.
GRAY, F. duP.
KESTEN, D. K.

5-D

ANTELL, J. B.
BURCH, D. R.
FISHER, E. A.
KESTEN, D. K.
RUNGE, A.

5-E

GRAY, F. duP.
  essays, fiction
HEMINGWAY, M. M.
  columnist

6-A

BALCIUS, H
  production
OLER, M. M.
  media
OMOHUNDRO, D. D.

6-D

PLANTS, M. S.

6-G

O'BRIEN, E. B.

7-A

FOSTER, J.
  film company
TEZACK, A. E. F.
  production company

8-D

BRAYCHAK, S. J.
DANIELL, E. F.
KERERIAN, L. N.
KINGSFORD, J. E.

8-F

BRAYCHAK, S. J.

8-G

HALL, B. I.

8-H

KING, V. E.
STONE, B. M.

10-A

BYRUM, S. S.
LUND, E. W.
  publicity

11

ANDERSON, P. H.
BELAIR, M. P.
GIBSON, E. B.
  catalogue
HURLEY, M. V.
LECHNER, M. G.
  insurance company
McCAULEY, E. B.
  coordinator
O'NEIL, D. C.
  picture
TRYON, I. B.
  film
VAN WILGEN, M.
WOOLFE, M. S.

12-A

AMES, L. B.
ARNOLD, M. L.
CHASE, A. E.
CLARK, R. A.
FAST, E. T.
KAUNITZ, R. D.
McGEE, P. S.
STEWART, M. McC.

12-D

DOUCETTE, G. I.
OLSON, J. V.

12-H

HAYNES, D. F.
MORRA, M. E.
OTWAY, R.

13-A

KEMBLE, D. A.
  radio consultant

13-B

KEMBLE, D. A.
  radio, TV

13-D

FUTH, S. M. B.

13-E

ANTELL, J. B.
magazine
AYER, M.
BALDWIN, F.
short stories, screen plays
BORLAND, B. D.
fiction, poetry
BUTTERS, D. G.
short stories
COLMAN, H. C.
stories, articles
FOSTER, J.
FUTH, S. M. B.
columnist
GRAY, F. duP.
fiction, critic
HAYNES, D. F.
HEMINGWAY, M. M.
HOGAN, A. H.
stories
HYMAN, F. C.
stories, poetry
KAUNITZ, R. D.
urban affairs
KEMBLE, D. A.
radio, TV
LIFTON, B. J. K.
plays, articles
LOESER, K.
LUND, D. H.
MERCIER, J. D.
short stories
NOYES-KANE, D.
articles
STOLZ, M. S.
PARKER, C. T.
PARTINGTON, S. T.
ROBBINS, J. S.
SCHULTZ, S.
STEPHEN, R.
STOLZ, M. S.
SULLIVAN, M. B.
TAMBURINE, J. H.
WARNER, G. C.
articles, essays
WILLIAMS, J.
short stories
WILLINS, S.
professional journals

13-F

AYER, M.
artist, illustrator
FOSTER, J.
HAYNES, D. F.
artist
LUMPKIN, T. S.
graphic designer
LUND, D. H.
artist

13-D

MULDOON, N. D.
book designer
PURDY, S. G.
designer, illustrator
TAMBURINE, J. H.
designer, illustrator
WATKINS, L. M.
artist

13-G

KINNEY, J. B.
consultant

13-J

JOBERT, E. C.
TV broadcaster
LANDIS, J. R.
actress
PARTINGTON, S. T.
commentator

14-L

BASINGER, J. D.
film history
HEMINGWAY, M. M.
HOGAN, A. H.
English
KRAUSS, R.
poetry
NOYES-KANE, D.
education
NYE, S. L.
writing
ZAGOREN, R.
adult education

14-M

GIESEN, E. J.
artists, lecturers

14-N

AMES, L. B.
psychology

15

WILLINS, S.
typewriter company

DELAWARE

2-A

EVANS, E. G.

4-D

ESPEDAHL, M. E.
fashion
McNEAR, B. H.
women's

5-D

PONSELL, M. L.

11

HENDERSON, J. T.
MESSICK, V. F.
WICKHAM, M. M.
WINSTON, G. E.

12-A

LAWS, R. M.

12-H

HASTINGS, J. A.

13-D

PONSELL, M. L.

13-E

PONSELL, M. L.
WEEKS, M. A.

DISTRICT OF COLUMBIA

1-A

BROWN, L. B.
CAMPBELL. E. P.
educational TV
CAVIN, P. B.
CORCORAN, K. S.
LOWE, F. S.
special projects
SCHAEFER, R. C.
women's
SIOUSSAT, H. J.
consultant

1-B

COX, M. W.
DUKERT, B. C.
MICHAELIS, D. T.
MILLER, H. R.
consultant
RITACCO, J. M.
WHEDON, P. B.

1-E

DICKERSON, N. H.
correspondent
JOHNSON, R. S.
correspondent
MACKIN, C. P.
correspondent
SMITH, J. F.
reporter

1-H

NEWMAN, M. W.
information services

1-I

FARFEL, L.
documentary films

1-J

CLARK, D. S.
broadcaster
DICKERSON, N. H.
newscaster
DORESE, E. B.
broadcaster, MC
GATES, P. L.
appearances
GILLIAM, D. B.
broadcaster
GROEBLI, B. G. P.
commentator

2-A

BROWN, L. B.
CAVIN, P. B.
LANDRETH, L. K.
educational
LOWE, F. S.
special projects
PIERCE, T. S.
advertising, promotion
SCHAEFER, R. C.
women's
SIOUSSAT, H. J.
consultant

2-B

GATES, P. L.
HILSINGER, J. L.
LANG, N.
music
TOMPKINS, B. M. T.
program analyst

2-D

HOLMES, M. F.
JURMA, M. K.

ROSS, W. S.

2-E

BLAIR, A. D.
  correspondent
DAY, K. M.
  correspondent
DORESE, E. B.
  correspondent
HOLMES, M. F.
JURMA, M. K.
MACKIN, C. P.
  correspondent
ROSS, W. S.
WELLS, F. G.
  correspondent

2-H

NEWMAN, M. W.
  information services
WALTER, R.

2-J

BLAIR, A. D.
  commentator
CLARK, D. S.
  broadcaster
DORESE, E. B.
  broadcaster
GATES, P. L.
  broadcaster
GROEBLI, B. C. P.
  commentator
HOLMES, M. F.
  broadcaster
TUFTY, E. VanW.
  commentator
WELLS, F. G.
  broadcaster

3-D

APPEL, M. C.
  TV directory
BRIGGS, S. A.
  natural history
FORD, A. E.
WHEELER, R. C.
  health textbooks

3-E

ARMSTRONG, P. C.
  non-fiction
BROWN, L. B.
  non-fiction
BURROS, M. F.
  cookbooks
CARPENTER, F.
  children's
CAVANAH, F.
  young people's

CHENNAULT, A. C.
CLINARD, D. L.
  children's
CLINE, C. A.
  history
CLOSE, A. K.
DAVIS, M. M.
  non-fiction
DULLES, E. L.
  world affairs
DUNNE, E. K.
  copyrights
EDWARDS, J. S.
FENNER, M. L. S.
  education
FORD, A. E.
  non-fiction, biography
FULLING, K. P.
GREEN, C. McL.
  non-fiction
HETZELL, M. C.
  public relations, religion
HOLMES, M. R.
  non-fiction
INNIS, P. L.
JACOBS, F. G.
  dolls, other
JONES, F. G.
  churches
JORDAN, G. E.
KEMPER, I.
KING, M.
  juvenile, adult
LANDON, M. M.
  fiction
LARSON, J. P.
LEIGHTON, F. S.
MEANS, M.
MEGGERS, B. J.
  anthropology,
  archeology
MILLER, H. R.
  non-fiction
MURRAY, I.
OSBORN, S.
PALCIC, J. A.
PAUL, C.
PENNEY, A. C.
  biographies
PRICE, W. A.
  biographies
PRUITT, E.
  geography
PUNDT, H. M.
  juvenile
RINGER, B. A.
  copyrights
ROBINSON, A. G.
  textbook
SANDOR, V. I. K.
SAVAGE, P.
  senior citizens
SCOTT, T. S.
  textbooks
SIOUSSAT, H. J.
  broadcasting
SMITH, M. D.
  biography
STERN, E. M.
  health, mental illness

TYMIENIECKA, A.
  philosophy
van STRATEN, F. W.
  weather
WALTON, E. C.
  children's
WATTERS, B. H.
  novels
WHEELER, R. C.
  non-fiction

3-F

BRIGGS, S. A.
  illustrator: natural history

3-H

BARBER, V. F.
  promotion

4-A

GRAHAM, K. M.
MERCHANT, M. A.

4-D

DOBSON, G. A.
  women's
EPSTEIN, E. S.
  fashion, beauty
FORBES, M. L. W.
HYDE, N. S.
  fashion, beauty
MERCHANT, M. A.
OHLIGER, G. A.
  women's

4-E

BEALE, B.
  columnist
BURROS, M. F.
  food
EDSTROM, E. M.
  reporter
HOLMES, M. R.
  columnist
HUNTER, M. R.
  correspondent
JOHNSON, A. F.
  correspondent
JORDAN, G. E.
  columnist
KENDALL, E. A.
  reporter
MARTIN, J. S.
  reporter
MELZER, H. L.
  reporter
NOVER, N. G.
  columnist, reporter
OTTENBERG, M.
  reporter

SECREST, M. D.
  cultural reporter
SMITH, M. D.
  staff
WHITE, J. M.
  reporter

4-F

SPANDORF, L. G.
  artist

5-A

GRAHAM, K. M.
HIESTAND, E. W.
  advertising
REPPERT, B. H. S.
  advertising
ROBINSON, A. G.
  advertising
WILLIAMS, S. S.
  advertising

5-B

ZOELLER, C. K.
  advertising

5-D

AVERY, P. A.
  newsdesk
CAHN, P. L.
CONNALLY, E. H.
CRANE, M. H.
DREW, E. B.
  Washington
EBERHART, S. R.
  science book review
EDWARDS, V. L.
ELDRIDGE, H. L.
ERICKSON, J. L.
  feature
FELDMAN, J. M.
FENNER, M. L. S.
FOX, P. M.
HENDERSON, D. K.
HOWE, M. R.
KELLER, E.
LARSON, W. C.
MOLONY, M. M.
MURRAY, I.
PHELPS, F. L.
PRICE, W. A.
TAYLOR, M. K.
WIDENER, M. McN.

5-E

FURLOW, B. B.
  correspondent
HALL, A. J.
  legends
KENDALL, E. A.
SENTNER, M. S.
  Washington

5-I

RONHOVDE, A. R.

6-A

MANES, N. C.
SELBY, J. McN.
  media

6-C

LAUER, E. A.
  time buyer

6-E

LAUER, E. A.

7-A

KOESTER, D. A.
  media planning,
    production company
SEABOLT, B. R.
  film company

7-B

MARCHBANK, F. A.
  communications
    company
RITACCO, J. M.
  TV productions

8-A

CHENNAULT, A. C.
LEE, J. McE.
MARILLEY, J. E.

8-D

BENGTSON, C. L.
MANDES, C.

8-E

BENGTSON, C. L.

8-H

MANDES, C.
MESSENGER, R. S.
PENNEY, A. C.
ROSS, B.

9-A

TUFTY, E. Van W.

9-D

DAY, K. M.
  radio editors report
REICHMANN, J. Van V.

9-E

ALLEN, M. P.
  columnist
ALLEN, R. F.
  staff
CHENNAULT, A. C.
  correspondent
COLLIER, V. R.
  correspondent
GLASER, V. R.
  columnist,
    correspondent
HATCH, R. S.
  science news
KILGORE, M. A.
  reporter
La HAY, W.
  staff
LEIGHTON, F. S.
  correspondent
MEANS, M.
  columnist
PAYNE, E. L.
  correspondent
ROOSEVELT, E. K.

10-A

COLCLOUGH, E. S.
PHILLIPS, M. C.
RAINEY, J. O.
ROSEN, D. L.
  research
TAYLOR, M. K.

10-H

BYRNES, S. H.

11

BESS, S. Q.
BRANSTETTER, E. H.
COBB, J.
  iconography specialist
DUNNE, E. K.
  cataloger
FREEMAN, E.
GRIMES, B. C.
GROARK, D. K.
  cataloger, indexer
HAMER, E. E.
HILKER, H.
HILLS, V. C.
JENNINGS, A. R.
JOHNSON, L. C. T.
LOSEE, H. M. W.
RINGER, B. A.

TOOMEY, A. F.
  cataloger
VON RICHTER, Z. K.
  Slavic specialist
WERTZ, V. L.
  circulation

12-A

ANDREWS, M. G.
BAPTISTA, M. G.
BARKER, M. J.
BATES, M. J.
BEEMAN, A. L.
BROWN, B. L.
BROWN, L. B.
CAMPBELL, E. P.
COOKE, E. D.
FIELDING, E. M.
FREYMAN, E. G.
GILBERT, E. P.
GILCHREST, M. S.
HARMAN, M. B.
HUBBARD, C. M.
HYER, A. L.
LANDRETH, L. K.
MARTIN, N. D.
MICHAELIS, D. T.
OSBORN, S.
PALMOUR, C. T.
PRUITT, E.
STUART, C. C.
SWING, M. E.
WILLIAMS, H. K.
YORK, M. L.

12-B

GATES, P. L.
LANG, N.
SAYRE, C. C.
TOMPKINS, B. M. T.
ZOELLER, C. K.

12-D

BAGGETT, L. R.
BORAKS, J. M.
BRIGGS, S. A.
BROWN, B. L.
BROWN, P. S.
CAHN, P. L.
CLOSE, A. K.
CONNALLY, E. H.
DAVIS, M. M.
DUNNIGAN, A. A.
EBERHART, S. R.
EDWARDS, V. L.
ELDRIDGE, H. L.
FENNER, M. L. S.
FIORA, C. O.
FOX, P. M.
GABLE, M. A.
HALL, M. R.
HOLMES, M. F.
JOHNSON, W. M.
JURMA, M. K.

KELLER, E.
KERR, F. W.
LARSON, W. C.
MOLONY, M. M.
PALCIC, J. A.
PHELPS, F. L.
PRICE, W. A.
PUNDT, H. M.
ROSS, W. S.
SUNDERLIN, S. S.
TAYLOR, M. K.

12-E

DAVIS, M. M.
HOLMES, M. F.
JOHNSON, W. M.
JURMA, M. K.
KERR, F. W.
MARTIN, N. D.
MONTGOMERY, G. T.
ROSS, W. S.
WHEELER, R. C.

12-F

ATKISS, R. A.
LARSON, J. P.

12-G

KELLY, V. M.
WILLIAMS, S. S.

12-H

AHLGREN, M. C.
ARMSTRONG, P. C.
BARB, M. L.
BARBER, V. F.
BEAGLE, G. J.
BECK, S. A.
BOE, S.
BROOKOVER, S. S.
COAKLEY, E. M.
EASTHAM, G. R.
EVERETT, F. W.
FULLING, K. P.
HENNINGS, J. S.
HETZELL, M. C.
HOLLOWAY, I. N.
KELLY, K.
MOWER, P. G.
NOWAK, J. McD.
OLSON, L. M.
PETERSON, E. E.
RUCKER, J. M.
SHANAHAN, S.
TARWATER, L. R.
TUTTLE, D. E.
WALTER, R.

12-I

MEGGERS, B. J.
WEINBRECHT, R. Y.

12-J

HOLMES, M. F.
SANDOR, V. I. K.

12-N

VANNOY, J.

13-B

JEROME, B.
radio, TV producer
MICHAELIS, D. T.
TV producer
RITACCO, J. M.
TV

13-D

EDWARDS, J. S.
FORD, A. E.
LING, M.
*communications
consultant*
PUNDT, H. M.
ROBB, I. W.

13-E

ALLEN, M. P.
articles
BECK, S. A.
articles
CLARK, D. S.
CLINE, C. A.
professional journals
EDWARDS, J. S.
FENNER, M. L. S.
education
FORD, A. E.
GREEN, C. McL.
history
HOLMES, M. R.
articles
HYDE, N. S.
college life, fashion
INNIS, P. L.
JACOBS, F. G.
non-fiction
JOHNSON, L. C. T.
*bibliographies, book
reviews*
JOHNSON, W. M.
professional journals
JONES, O. A.
non-fiction
JORDAN, G. E.
fiction, non-fiction
KING, M.
fiction, non-fiction

LARSON, J. P.
articles
LARSON, W. C.
McLENDON, W. P.
articles
MEANS, M.
articles
MILLER, H. H.
magazine
MONTGOMERY, G. T.
science
PALCIC, J. A.
children's stories
PAUL, C.
stories, articles
PHILLIPS, M. G.
PUNDT, H. M.
RINGER, B. A.
copyrights
RUETHER, R. R.
non-fiction
SANDOR, V. I. K.
articles, essays, stories
STERN, A.
radio-TV journalist
STERN, E. M.
articles: health
TELKES, M.
professional journals
WATTERS, B. H.
short stories
WELLS, F. G.
articles: book reviews

13-F

BAGGETT, L. R.
artist
BRIGGS, S. A.
illustrator
SNOW, M.
artist
SPANDORF, L. G.
artist
VANCE, M. H.
artist: murals, ceramics

13-H

MARQUIS, E. T.
consultant

13-J

BARKER, M. J.
lecturer
GLASER, V. R.
lecturer
INNIS, P. L.
lecturer
JEROME, B.
moderator
KING, M.
lecturer
MEANS, M.
speaker
STERN, A.
commentator

14-L

BATES, M. J.
Spanish literature
CLINARD, D. L.
wriring
CLINE, C. A.
history
DULLES, E. L.
GILMORE, J. O.
graphic design
JOHNSON, L. C. T.
MURRAY, I.
writing
RINGER, B. A.
law
RUETHER, R. R.
theology
SANDOR, V. I. K.
Russian
TYMIENIECKA, A.

14-N

EDWARDS, V. L.
translator
LING, M.
communications
MADDEN, B. S.
home economics
MARQUIS, E. T.
education
NALLEY, L. M.
communications law
PENNEY, A. C.
interior design
SIEGEL, L. P.
communications law
TELKES, M.
solar energy
van STRATEN, F. W.
atmospheric physics
WILLIAMS, C. S.
consumers

FLORIDA

1-A

GOLD, S. F.
press information
PURINGTON, A. M.
continuity
TURNER, M.
public affairs

1-B

HOLLETT, R. D.
HOOK, P. A.
continuity
SAVELL, T. I.
producer
SCHWARTZ, M. R.
producer, director

1-H

ALTER, P. U.
publicity

1-J

BELL, L. P.
hostess
FINKELSTEIN, A. R.
hostess

2-A

SANDERS, D. J.
SAVELL, T. I.
special events
THORNBURG, S. H.
WASEY, S. S.
special programs
YAVORSKE, C. B.

2-B

SMITH, M. E. S.
THORNBURG, S. H.

2-C

PARKER, V. S.

2-D

THORNBURG, S. H.
women's

2-E

LEWIS, L.
travel, women's news

2-J

LEWIS, L.
broadcaster
MORRIS, J. A.
broadcaster
SAVELL, T. I.
commentator

3-A

HAROLD, M. P.

3-D

HAROLD, M. P.
compiler: art
IRVING, M. B.
consultant

MACBEAN, D. W.
  literary guild
SARETT, A. J.
  poetry

3-E

ALBRECHT, R. E.
  science, professional
ALLEN, E. B.
  religion
BACH, M. B.
  church history
BAUM, H. S.
  publicity
BEER, L.
CARR, H. H.
  young adult, biographies
CHAMBERLAIN, E. L.
  mysteries, fiction
CLEARY, F. D.
  non-fiction
CLEAVEN, C. L.
  young people's
CONNER, B. G.
  teaching handbooks
CRUICKSHANK, H. G.
  wild life
DEAL, B. H.
  novels
DANIEL, E. W.
  career guides
DOUGLAS, M. S.
  adult, junior
DUVALL, E. M.
  sex, family life
EDELL, C. L.
EHLERS, S. B.
  Hawaii
FISHER, M. B.
  non-fiction
FLOETHE, L. L.
  children's
FOGEL, R.
  poetry
FRAZER, W. D.
  non-fiction
GARRARD, J. S.
  horticulture
GORMAN, K. B.
  poetry
HAROLD, M. P.
  non-fiction
HAYS, W. P.
  children's
HEFFINGTON, V. K.
  cookbooks
HELLER, D. F.
  non-fiction
HOLLETT, R. D.
  textbook
HOLLOWAY, T. B.
  young adult
IRVING, M. B.
  non-fiction
KAHN, H.
  poetry

LARABEE, L. B.
  university administration
LAWRENCE, M. E.
  *children's, young
    people's*
LEE, M.
  *young adult fiction,
    novels*
LEEK, S.
LUNNON, B. S.
MacBEAN, D. W.
  children's
MUIR, H.
  non-fiction
ODOM, M. M.
  math texts
PHILLIPS, R. H.
  Cuba
PRIETO, M. B.
  juvenile
PRITCHARD, S. E.
  poetry
REID, E. C.
  children's fiction
RIEKER, J. L.
SARETT, A. J.
  non-fiction
SEGAL, M. M.
SHOEMAKER, V. B. K.
SMITH, M. E. S.
SMITH, S.
  ghosts, witches
SPAIN, F. L.
  non-fiction
WHALEY, M. G.
  sailing
WILLIAMS, K. V.
  juvenile novels
WORTHINGTON, M. M.
  novels, biographies
WRIGHT, I. S.
  non-fiction
ZAPOLEON, M. W.
  employment, women

4-A

DELANEY, M. C. M.
DUCKWORTH, S. A.
HALL, S. B.
OERTEL, A. G.
WENDLER, A. C.

4-B

CORAM, H. F.

4-D

ALBERT, I. H.
  feature
ANDERSON, M. W.
  women's
BARBER, J. Mc E.
  women's
BRITT, L. S.
BROOKS, F. J.
  women's

BROWN, P. S.
  restaurant, nightclub
BACH, M. B.
  women's
BARBER, J. McE.
  women's
COOLIDGE, M. R.
  entertainment, radio, TV
ELLIS, B. B.
  women's
HEFFINGTON, V. K.
  homemaking
INGALLS, C. E.
  women's
JONES, B. W.
  book
KAHN, H.
  poetry
KAHN, L. H.
  city
LAUBER, P. D.
LLOYD, P. A.
  fashion
LITTLES, C. R.
  society
LOOG, V. A.
  women's
McDUFFIE, A. G.
  food
McHALE, J. N.
  society, fashion
McKEE, A.
  fashion, society
McMURRIA, M. G.
  magazine section
McWHORTER, J. S.
  women's
MILLER, R. C.
  women's
MURPHY, K.
  home furnishing
PAXSON, M. B.
  news features
RAVESON, B. R.
RENO, D. S.
  music, dance
ROBINSON, H. G.
  women's
RUBIN, M. A.
  women's
SCHREIBER, N.
  music, art
SHRIVER, M. W.
  teen
SPEARMAN, A. J.
  city
STEINER, M. W.
  women's, food
STUBER, I. M.
SWAEBLY, F. M.
  drama
WENDLER, A. C.
WILSON, J. V.

4-E

ALBERT, I. H.
  columnist, critic

BELLAMY, J.
  editorial
CLAYDON, D. S.
  columnist
COBLE, H. B.
  reporter, columnist
KELLY, B. S.
  special feature
LAPHAM, G. M.
  columnist
LLOYD, P. A.
  columnist
NAUNTON, E. A.
  medical
ROBINSON, H. G.
  columnist
WYNNE, M. F.
  staff

5-A

de la SALLE, C. M.
  fashion
GARRARD, J. S.

5-C

SCHIELD, M. S.

5-D

EDWARDS, J. Du W.
GARRARD, J. S.
  scout
GREENBERG, R. P.
JOHNSON, E. R.
PAXON, M. B.
REIS-EL BARA, M. A.
  TV
WHALEY, M. G.
WRIGHT, I. S.

5-E

LEEK, S.
  columnist
REIS-EL BARA, M. A.
  columnist, feature
WIMBROW, D. L.

6-A

BORN, P. T.
  creative
CONTE, E. S.
  art
DUNLEVY, P. C.
GRAHAM, B.
LOVELACE, E. O'C.
  media
MOREHEAD, J. B.
OERTEL, A. G.
POWDERLY, B. K.
  media

6-B

RENAULT, B. P.
producer

6-C

NOLAN, M. C.
media buyer

6-H

LYNN, S. G.

7-A

LASSWELL, S. B.
*comic strips, related
products*
PERSSON, E. E.
editorial consultants
ROSS, C. J.
research institute

7-H

CURRIE, H. S.
promoters

8-D

BAGBY, M. G.
DOLAN, J. W.
JOYNER, L. Y.

8-E

LEBOWITZ, S.

8-G

EINIK, E.
EMBREE, M. L.
GOTTLIEB, A.
HART, M. T.

8-H

BAGBY, M. G.
DOLAN, J. W.
EINIK, E.
HARTMAN, M. C.
HENRY, A. G. W.
KASSEWITZ, R. B.
MACKIE, J. R.
MYRICK, I. M.
NEUMAN, S. C.
PEARON, A. T.

9-D

ASH, A. McC.
BIGGS, G. N.
women's
HOLLETT, R. D.
column

10-A

EHLERS, S. B.
KEUSCH, B.
MATHIS, B.
MOREHEAD, J. B.
SHAW, I.
SPECTOR, J. F.
TAYLOR, V. L.

10-H

ALBION, E.
BAUM, H. S.

11

BERHEL, M. M.
BUTTS, B. K.
CALHOUN, W. J.
DARROW, D.
DIXON, E. J.
GROOVER, E. T.
educational media
HARKNESS, M. L. B.
HUNTER, L. N.
LANGNER, M. C.
medicine
LUNNON, B. S.
medicine
PATTON, J. VanD.
PEELER, E. H.
technical services
SAVOYA, E. H.
reference
SMITH, C. A.
SPAIN, F. L.
THOMPSON, C. A.
TURNBULL, M. B.
WILSON, C. G.
WURSTER, M. S.
extension

12-A

GROOVER, E. T.
LARABEE, L. B.

12-D

JOHNSON, E. R.
WHALEY, M. G.
WRIGHT, I. S.

12-H

ERSOFF, M. F.
MYER, J. A.
OLSON, G. A. S.
SHAW, J. R.
SNYDER, A. R.
WOODARD, H. R.

13-B

GROSS, P. R.
fashion show coordinator
HARRISON, B. S.

13-D

ALBRECHT, R. E.
aging
HAHN, B. C.
food, home economics
IRVING, M. B.
consultant
NEAL, H. S.
SIMMONS, M. A.

13-E

ALBERT, I. H.
stories, lyrics, poetry
ALLEN, E. B.
magazine
ALTER, P. U.
articles, features
ASH, A. McC.
BAUM, H. S.
magazines
BRADLEY, J. S.
CONNER, B. G.
teaching handbooks
CULVER, K. B.
educational journals
CRUICKSHANK, H. G.
wild life
DANIEL, E. W.
articles, fiction
DEAL, B. H.
short stories
DOUGLAS, M. S.
short stories
DUVALL, E. M.
sex, family life
FOGEL, R.
poetry
GARRARD, J. S.
magazine
GETTEMY, G. H.
GORMAN, K. B.
GROSS, P. R.
fashion shows
HARRISON, B. S.
HOLLETT, R. D.
antiques
HOLLOWAY, T. B.
HUNT, M. A.
library science

KAHN, H.
poetry
KIRCHHOFF, V. S. S.
copy
LAWRENCE, M. E.
LUDLOW, J. H.
LUNNON, B. S.
articles, short stories
MUIR, H.
magazine
NEAL, H. S.
magazine
PATTERSON, O. W.
savings and loan
PHILLIPS, R. H.
columnist
PRIETO, M. B.
magazine
PRITCHARD, S. E.
poetry
PURINGTON, A. M.
SHOEMAKER, V. B. K.
articles, feature
SIMMONS, M. A.
reporter
SMITH, M. E. S.
Florida
TUCKER, P.
journalist
WELD, C.
WERKMEISTER, L. T.
18th century London
WIMBROW, D. L.
WOOD, P. LeC.
non-fiction
WORTHINGTON, M. M.
short stories
ZAPOLEON, M. W.
professional, government

13-F

BEER, L.
painter
CRUICKSHANK, H. G.
photographer

13-G

KIRCHHOFF, V. S. S.
copy

13-H

KORDSMEIER, B. B.
consultant
LANE, M. C.
McSTEA, E. M.
consultant
PATTERSON, O. W.
consultant
SHOEMAKER, V. B. K.
TUCKER, P.
consultant
VERNON, R. F.
fashion publicity

WELD, C.
publicist

13-I

WERKMEISTER, L. T.
18th century London

13-J

HAHN, B. C.
broadcaster
HOLLETT, R. D.
lecturer: antiques
MORRIS, J. A.
lecturer
VOIT, H. L.
lecturer: investments
WOOD, P. LeC.
lecturer: foreign affairs

14-K

TAYLOR, M. J.

14-L

ALBRECHT, R. E.
sociology, gerontology
BRADLEY, J. S.
counselor
CLEARY, F. D.
CONNER, B. G.
English
CULVER, K. B.
DALEY, N. O.
guidance
FISHER, M. B.
behavioral sciences
FRAZER, W. D.
English
GARFUNKEL, B.
journalism
GROOVER, E. T.
educational media
HUNT, M. A.
library science
JINKS, J. M.
journalism
LARABEE, L. B.
academic affairs
MILLER, D. M.
TV studio teacher
NEAL, H. S.
psychology
ODOM, M. M.
TV studio teacher: math
ORMSBY, V. H.
language arts
PREECE, B. P.
graphic science
PRIETO, M. B.
Spanish, English
SARETT, A. J.
speech

STEERS, C. C.
communications

14-N

CULVER, K. B.
educational media
DUVALL, E. M.
sex, family life
KORDSMEIER, B. B.
public relations
McSTEA, E. A.
public relations
PATTERSON, O. W.
public relations
STEMMLER, H. R.
plastics, packaging
VERNON, R. F.
fashion publicity
VOIT, H. L.
investments

GEORGIA

1-A

LETOWSKY, R.
publicity, public relations
SMITH, J.
traffic
SMITH, J. B.
WHITELAW, E. B.
news

1-E

FAYE, L.
reporter
FORD, L. W.
reporter

1-J

AVERY, P. H.
hostess
FAYE, L.
weather girl
FORD, L. W.
interviewer

2-A

HANEVOLD, C. L.
continuity
JORDAN, J. C.
NICHOLSON, E. C.
SCOTT, S. C.
SHROPSHIRE, R. M.
women's
SMALL, A. L. S.
SMITH, J. B.

WHITELAW, E. B.
news

2-B

HANEVOLD, C. L.

2-C

SHROPSHIRE, R. M.

2-D

ANDERSON, P. L.
women's

2-J

SHROPSHIRE, R. M.
hostess

3-A

ODDO, G. G.

3-E

BUGG, M. C.
FOSTER, E. L.
HOOD, F. M.
juvenile fiction
LaHATTE, P. N.
non-fiction
MATHEWS, M. M.
fiction, non-fiction
McKENZIE, B.
non-fiction
RADFORD, R. L.
children's, young adult
ST. JOHN, W. F.
mysteries
SULLIVAN, M. A.
decorating
WOOLCOCK, O. F.
non-fiction

4-A

BUFFINGTON, H. T.
JONES, B.
business
LaHATTE, P. N.
promotion

4-C

SCOTT, L. McA.
circulation

4-D

BROWN, M. F.
BUFFINGTON, H. T.
CARTER, A. C.
women's
CARTER, L. M.
farm
ESCHMANN, C. H.
food
HACKNEY, L. B.
women's
MAYES, R. L.
PERMAR, E. J.
women's
RANKIN, L. T.
SCOTT, L. McA.
society
SHEFFIELD, A. W.
society
SHURLING, S. C.
women's
SMITH, D. M.
telegraph
STINCHCOMB, B. C.
society
THOMAS, D. C.
entertainment
TILLEY, B. F.
society
WOOLCOCK, O. F.
women's

4-E

CARTER, L. M.
feature
HAYDEN, E. L.
feature
NADLER, F. K.
features: Sunday magazine
RANKIN, L. T.
feature, editorial
SMITH, R. B.
ST. JOHN, W. F.
staff
TILLEY, B. F.
feature
TWIGGS, M. S.
political reporter

5-A

LEWIS, A. E.
PORTER, M. McF.

5-D

TAYLOR, B. J.

6-A

ANDREWS, V. G.

HARRIS, C. H.
creative
KELLEY, F. E.
creative
McRAE, M. C.
NELMS, D. L.
media
SARTAIN, S. C.
public relations

6-C

COCHRAN, J.
media buyer
TOBIN, L. W.
media buyer
TOMLIN, A. P.
media buyer
TRAGER, R. E.
media planner
WALL, M. K.
media buyer

6-G

BUGG, M. C.
CAIN, M. W.

7-A

PRICE, J. C.
*radio-TV sales
representative*
SULLIVAN, M. A.
film

8-A

BOUNDS, S. M.

8-D

COBB, A. DeL.
HAMMONS, S. M.

8-G

CASE, V. E.

8-H

MOORE, R. D.
SENIOR, K. A.
WILLS, C. L.

9-A

DYAR, J. T.

9-D

DYAR, J. T.
RIDGWAY, F. S.

11

BAKER, M. V.
BRIGHTWELL, J. S.
services
BYERS, E. H.
CAVENDER, E. P.
services
CROSLAND, D. M.
DURHAM, M. J.
acquisitions
EVERETT, S. J.
FOSTER, E. L.
HAMBRICK, T. O.
MOORE, E. DuP.
OLSON, E. H.
PAYNE, E. C.
RHEAY, M. L.
RICE, L.
consultant
ROUNTREE, E. C.
SMITH, N. T.
WEAVER, A. B.
WINDHAM, E. H.

12-A

BAILES, E. S.
BYRON, D. L.
KILIAN, M. A.
RAKESTRAW, C. L.
TAYLOR, B. J.

12-D

NADLER, F. K.

12-H

BILL, D. C.
BRIDGES, D. M.
CRAVEN, K. M.
ELLIS, R. J.
KILIAN, M. A.
LEE, L. F.
MISCALLY, M. L.
SCHAUER, C. G.

12-I

SMITH, M. R.

13-E

BROWN, M. F.
trade magazine
BUELL, E. L.
reviews

BYRON, D. L.
articles
FOSTER, E. L.
articles, poetry
HOOD, F. M.
juvenile fiction
LEWIS, A. E.
history, travel
MATHEWS, M. M.
articles
MAYES, R. L.
poetry
PARKER, M. J.
*scripts, non-fiction,
poetry*
PERMAR, E. J.
fiction, non-fiction
RADFORD, R. L.
fiction, biography
SMITH, M. R.
education
TAYLOR, B. J.
religion
TILLEY, B. F.
feature
WHITELAW, E. B.

13-F

LaHATTE, P. N.
artist
McKENZIE, B.
photographer

13-H

BARRETT, G. A.
consultant
WILLIX, D. R.

13-J

BUELL, E. L.
lecturer

14-L

BRYAN, M. M.
JOHNSTON, M. M.
journalism
McKENZIE, B.
radio, TV, film

14-M

ANDERSON, B. S.
models, talents
BAUGHMAN, B. A.
models

14-N

BARRETT, G. A.
public relations
FOSTER, E. L.
library science
RICE, L.
library science
SMITH, M. R.
education
SULLIVAN, M. A.
education
WHITE, S. F.
textile fibers

15

BAUGHMAN, B. A.
fashion
BRAMBLETT, L. G.
theatre supplies

HAWAII

2-A

MONROE, J. C.

3-A

HEAVENRIDGE, J. H.
production

3-E

BANNICK, N. M.
non-fiction
McCARTHY, J. V.
MELLEN, K. D.
poetry, Hawaii
TABRAH, R. M.
fiction, non-fiction
THOMPSON, V. L.
children's
TITCOMB, M.
non-fiction

4-D

CASEY, T. O.
Sunday magazine section
CROWELL, N. L.

4-E

CASEY, T. O.
Sunday magazine section

5-D

BANNICK, N. M.

CASEY, T. O.

5-E

CASEY, T. O.
CLAIRMONT, I. H.

6-A

SMITH, N. G.
public relations

6-G

GILLILAND, M. B.
counselor
KRUEGER, C. W.

8-G

BOSTWICK, J.

8-H

BOSTWICK, J.

9-E

CLAIRMONT, I. H.
foreign correspondent

10-A

BEECH, L. M.

11

KAPST, M. I.
adult services
TITCOMB, M.

12-A

DARROW, E. L. S.
DAWSON, S. S.
McCANDLES, S. L.
YAP, V. Y.

12-H

KU, A. J. L.
WALDEN, M. D. L.

13-E

ALLEN, G. E.
GILLILAND, M. B.
articles

KRUEGER, C. W.
non-fiction articles
THOMPSON, V. L.
children's

13-I

TITCOMB, M.
Hawaiian food customs

14-N

McCARTHY, J. V.
home economist

IDAHO

2-A

BAUER, I. R.

2-G

SWANSON, B. D.

3-E

GOERTZEN, D. D.
Idaho
MOFFITT, H. R.
REID, F. P.
poetry, short stories

4-A

BYFORD, E. M.
business

4-D

BESSEY, C. H.
DeTHOMAS, R. N.
HERZINGER, N. M.
women's
MAREZ, J. C.
women's
MORRISON, J. S.
women's
PENSON, B. B.
travel, women's

5-A

MOFFITT, H. R.

5-D

MOFFITT, H. R.

11

LANCASTER, E. E.

12-A

HUNT, E. H.

12-D

WALLACE, A. P.

12-H

GOERTZEN, D. D.

13-E

HUNT, E. H.
REID, F. P.
poetry, short stories,
articles

13-F

HUNT, E. H.
artist
WALLACE, A. P.
artist

13-J

MALONE, N.
actress

14-L

REID, F. P.
English

ILLINOIS

1-A

AYLWARD, J. B.
women's
HOPPER, M. B.
educational
NEALIN, P. L.
film
NECKER, A. F.
film
REYNOLDS, D. M.
sales service
WALLER, J. C.
public affairs, education

1-B

BERGEN, Sr. M. J.
BROOKS, L.
MIGALA, L. J.
news
PRINDLE, K.
WARRICK, G. E.

1-D

BERRY, E. F.
desk
WARRICK, G. E.
standards

1-E

BERRY, E. F.
news
BROOKS, L.
LUELOFF, J. A. P.
reporter
MIGALA, L. J.
reporter

1-J

BELL, L. P.
hostess
BROOKS, L.
broadcaster
HORWICH, F. R.
children's programs
LUELOFF, J. A. P.
newscaster

2-A

ALYWARD, J. B.
women's
DAVIS, Z. B.
news
MONTGOMERY, L.
women's
ROHATS, H. M.
traffic, continuity
WALLER, J. C.
public affairs, education

2-B

BROOKS, L.
MIGALA, L. J.
news
OLAR, L. L.
SAUNDERS, D. E.

2-E

BROOKS, L.
LUELOFF, J. A. P.
reporter

MIGALA, L. J.
  reporter
SAUNDERS, D. E.

2-J

BROOKS, L.
  broadcaster
KEHM, F. S.
  personality
LENGELSEW, R. E.
  broadcaster
LUELOFF, J. A. P.
  newscaster
OLAR, L. L.
  hostess

3-A

BJORCK, M. W.
  audio-visual
BUERGER, J. T.
FAWCETT, E.
FITZGERALD, M. L.
FORD, V. H.
NEALE, J. R.
  publicity

3-B

KELLEY, M. R.
  editor
SPRINGBORN, R. K.
  editorial

3-D

BENSON, M. W.
  consultant
BERGMAN, R. J.
BJORCK, M. W.
  audio-visual
BROSAMER, V. M.
  employee publications
COLE, R. M.
  geography
COMER, B. L.
  textbook
DOWD, G. H.
  science
FAWCETT, E.
FRAKES, F. M.
FRISKEY, M. R.
GARTON, M. D.
HAAS, D. F.
HOLAHAN, J. B.
NEIGOFF, A.
  juvenile
TITELBAUM, O. A.
  geography
WEBBER, E. J.
WEINBERG, L. S.

3-E

ARKHURST, J. C.
  West African folklore
BAILEY, B. F.
  young people's
BAUER, F. M.
BIALK, E.
  children's
BRAUN, E. R.
  Baha'i religion
BROCKWAY, E. S.
  juvenile
BROOKMAN, D. C.
  love
BUERGER, J. T.
  religion
CASSELL, S. E.
  game, puppet
CAUDILL, R.
  juvenile
DOWD, G. H.
  science
DUBOIS, I. C.
  cookbook
FARISH, M. K.
  music
FISHER, H. S.
  party games
FORD, V. H.
  children's
FRAKES, F. M.
FRIEDERICHSEN, K. H.
  religion
FRISKEY, M. R.
  children's
GARTON, M. D.
  non-fiction
GRAFF, M.
  children's
GRIDLEY, M. E.
  American Indians
GRIFFIN, C. F.
  novels
HAAS, D. F.
  children's
HOGAN, B. H.
  non-fiction, juvenile
HOLSINGER, J. L.
  juvenile
JURGENSEN, B. B.
  non-fiction
KEHM, F. S.
  non-fiction
KELLY, R. Z.
  juvenile
KWEDER, A. N.
  cookbook
LAIRD, J. R.
LAVIN, P.
  graphology
LAWRENCE, I.
  junior historical fiction
LeBAR, L. E.
  religion
LeBAR, M. E.
  religion
LLOYD, N.
  novels, children's

MARQUARDT, D. A.
  juvenile non-fiction
MAYER, J. R.
MEILACH, D. Z.
  art, medicine, juvenile
MOORE, R. E.
  evolution, natural
    science
MOSS, R.
  education
PARIS, M. J.
  home economics, careers
PARKER, B. M.
  non-fiction
PODENDORF, I. E.
  children's science
PORTER, E. W.
RATZEBERGER, A.
  juvenile
RODGERS, E. S.
  non-fiction
ROLLINS, C. H.
ROM, M. E.
  travel
ROMMEL, M. D.
  novels
ROSS, C. M.
  children's
SAMACHSON, D. M.
  non-fiction
SIMON, R. M.
  non-fiction
THOMPSON, E. B.
TRACY, P. A. S.
  poetry
WAGNER, M. D.
WALKER, J. L.
  interior design
WALLER, J. C.
  radio
WEDDLE, E. H.
WEINBERG, L. S.
WINTER, G. L.
  children's
YORK, C. B.
  juvenile, teen
ZIEGLER, E. R.
ZIMMERMAN, N. G.
  juvenile

3-F

GRAFF, M.
  illustrator
WINTER, G. L.
  illustrator

3-H

BOUB, M. H.

3-I

URE, V. P.

4-A

BAILEY, M. P.
BERLIN, L. T.
  advertising
CRAIG, E. B.
ROM, M. E.
WHITE, E. A.

4-D

BARLOW, A. T.
  travel
BART, C. DeG.
  make-up
BASSIMER, V. M. C.
  society
BLEWETT, N. V.
  women's
BROCKWAY, E. S.
BUTCHER, F.
  society
CAYER, S. K.
CHURCH, H. S.
COCKING, G. N.
COPELAND, H. J.
  women's
CRAIG, E. B.
DeMUTH, A. H.
Du BOIS, I. C.
  home economics
GREGORY, J. L.
  society
HAUGH, D. G.
  women's
HILLYER, E.
  home furnishings
LEE, K. W.
LOUCKS, O. M.
  women's
MORELAND, G. W.
  society
NAHAS, A. N.
  women's
NOVAK, G. H.
  religion
PARKER, A. E.
PHELPS, J. K.
  feature
POTTKER, O. S.
  women's
RAMSEY, D. G.
  weekend life
ROM, M. E.
SERBUS, P. D.
STITZ, J. M.
  fashion
TELFORD, P. L.
  women's
TELLEEN, C. R.
  entertainment
TREDWAY, B. J.
  society, feature
VARRO, B. J.
  fashion
WEAVER, A. T.
  city
WHITE, E. A.
  make-up

ZWECKER, M. B.
fashion, beauty

4-E

BARZEL, A.
dance critic
BUTCHER, F.
reporter, music critic,
columnist
ERICKSON, A. G.
reporter
GEYER, G. A.
foreign correspondent
KWEDER, A. N.
historical feature
LEE, K. W.
staff
LENGELSEN, R. E.
columnist
LEONARD, S. P.
reporter
LOUCKS, O. M.
reporter, columnist
MOORE, R. E.
reporter
MORLAND, G. W.
news, columnist
MOSS, R.
feature
ODMARK, M. J.
columnist
O'HARA, J. A.
women's
OPPENHEIM, C.
reporter
PESMEN, S. Z.
reporter
RATNY, R. L.
marketing columnist
ROOT, S. P.
reporter
TELFORD, P. L.
columnist

4-F

KREHBIEL, B. F.
cartoonist
MORELAND, G. W.
photographer

4-I

MILKS, M. G.
market

5-A

ABRAMSON, M. F.
production
BECHNER, M. C.
PAPANGELIS, P. C.
administrative assistant

5-A

KESSEL, M. L.

5-D

ALTMAN, M. K.
cartoon
BARZEL, A.
BOURAS, A. A.
copy
BROOKMAN, D. C.
copy
CHAMBERLAIN, B.
picture
COSTANTINO, J. M.
EDWARDS, J.
FRAKES, F. M.
FRANZEN, J. G.
women's
FULLER, M. S.
GRABOWSKI, M.
picture
GREGORY, J. L.
HECHT, L. E.
KESSEL, M. L.
KRESICH, H. M.
LARSON, M. L.
MATTHEWS, M. H.
regional
McNEESE, G. G.
RAHM, V. M.
RATLIFF, S. L.
RATZESBERGER, A.
RUSKAMP, J. S.
THOMPSON, E. B.
international
TRELEASE, J.

5-E

STRASSER, R. L.
promotion

5-H

SIMPSON, P. L.

6-A

ALWIN, S. F.
broadcast traffic
ANDRUSKEVITCH, B. A.
BEAUDRY, M. P.
BECKNER, M. C.
COLBERT, J.
CORBETT, D. O.
traffic
DANIELS, M. J.
DOOLEN, D. H.
research
FLEMING, M. C.
broadcast production
GRAFF, M.
HEINZE, B. N.

HOLT, S. K.
media
McCAFFERTY, L.
public relations
McRAE, V. M.
METCALF, D.
media
MURRAY, J. E.
NEUMANN, R. V.
SHATTUCK, C. J.
media
SHIRLEY, V. L.
media
SIEMEK, S. L.
media
STUART, D.
broadcast
THUDIUM, L. M.
URBAITIS, D. S.

6-B

CONNELL, M. A. L.
TV
ESHELMAN, M. J.
FLEMING, M. C.
broadcast
PROCTOR, N. N.
client services
ROTH, J. S.
print

6-C

ANDERSEN, E. N.
BARTELSON, M.
CONNELL, M. A. L.
TV traffic
CRISAFULLI, M. A.
EGAN, M. M.
broadcast time buyer
FLOTRON, M. M.
FOERTSCH, K. A.
buyer planner
GUNTER, B. N.
media buyer
KRYL, S. F.

6-D

MURRAY, J. E.
PETERSEN, G. M.

6-E

COHEN, N. O.
MURRAY, J. E.
ROMMEL, D.

6-F

COLBERT, J.

6-G

CATES, A. K.

6-H

GILBERT, A. W.
GRANGER, D. A.

7-A

ALTSCHUL, E. S.
educational films
BARTH, B. J.
productions
BECKNER, M. C.
design research
DOWNE, L.
productions
GOLDSHOLL, M. M.
film production
MILLER, N. C.
productions
MURSET, S. J.
productions
RATNY, R. L.
motion picture company
RODGERS, E. S.
photographic studio
SAGER, S. L.
TV film

7-B

DE LAY, M. B.
film editor

7-D

HANRAHAN, J. H.
publications
STEGEMAN, E. H.
printers

7-G

HANRAHAN, J. H.
publications

8-C

BRAUN, M. C.
GIBSON, R. A.
JOHNSTON, J. E.
LITTIKEN, B. L.
MARTIN, K. K.
OLSHANSKY, R. H.
PARIS, M. J.
ROSS, L. I.
SHURPIT, J. J.

8-D

COTTRELL, G. G.
FOX, J. S.
GRACE, T. E.
GUTHAT, M. O.
HARPER, F. R.
JOHNSON, D. L.
KOLBA, B. M.
PESKIN, S. P.
SANNER, A. M.
SMITH, J. L.
STAHNKE, E. C. S.
TETER, T. F.

8-E

DOLIN, E. F.
KOLBA, B. M.

8-F

SONGAILO, A. H.
VAN WANING, M. B.

8-G

DANIELSON, D. A.
HOPKINS, M. R.
KAMINKOWITZ, G.
PACIGA, A. W.
PATRICH, L. M.
RINGEL, H. C.
SANNER, A. M.

8-H

ALEXANDER, A. L.
BUNKER, N. L.
DANIELSON, D. A.
EDGREN, M. L.
FOLEY, P. M.
HOPKINS, M. R.
KOBER, B. O.
LONGMEYER, J. S.
MCLANE, H. J.
NOEL, M. R.
RANCE, J. P.
RINGEL, H. C.
ROTMAN, S. L.
SIMPSON, P. L.

8-J

VAN WANING, M. B.

9-A

SMITH, R. H.
  patterns

9-D

SMITH, R. H.
  patterns

9-E

CONNERS, D.
  columnist
WARREN, J. E.

9-J

HORWICH, F. R.
  children's programs

10-A

ALLEN, B.
CAYLOR, M. L.
COHEN, B. L.
DRING, R. J. S.
FRIEDEL, M. L.
  *communications
  consultant*
GOYAK, E. F.
HAEGER, P. M.
HANDY, D.
HEINZE, B. N.
HOOBLER, M. J.
  consumer services
HUMPHREY, B.
  writing
LEINHAUSER, J.
RICCA, A. C.
SINDORF, G.
SCHUBERT, H. C.
STEARNS, B. J.
WILLIAMS, H. L.
WYATT, M. M.

10-D

ANDROS, E. A.
  employee publications

10-E

WREN, S. E.

10-G

ELLIS, H. W.

10-H

BLUM, R. M.
DAVID, M. L.
SAGER, S. L.
SHARPE, E.

11

ARKHURST, J. C.
BIGGS, M. L.
BLANKSTEN, D. S.
BOOK, I. C.
BOONE, L. S.

DAVIS, S. M.
  *research and
  development*
DUMBAULD, B. E.
FIELD, Sr. M.
FONSTEIN, E.
GILBORNE, J. E.
GOAN, F. E.
GRABB, M. S.
HARGRAVE, V. E.
HARRINGTON, P. A.
HOLLAND, E. W.
JOHNSON, E. R.
JOHNSON, M. R.
KAPLAN, S. K.
LENGELSEN, R. E.
LINCOLN, M. F.
MARQUARDT, D. A.
McKINLEY, A. E.
MISHKIN, L. Y.
MORRIS, M. S.
MUELLER, E. A.
ORFANOS, M. A.
PETERSON, M. E.
PETERSON, M. O.
PLAIN, E.
RADMACHER, C. J.
RADMACHER, M.
ROLLINS, C. H.
  children's
TARBOX, R. W.
  *children's and young
  adult*
WALSH, C. W.
WEDDLE, E. H.

12-A

BERGER, M. S.
BRAUN, E. R.
DOSCHER, V. B.
HOFFMAN, H. E.
MAXWELL, J. D.
MILLS, A. C.
MURRAY, D. R.
SCHWARTZ, L. S.
WERESCH, G. S.
WHITE, R. M.

12-B

STEVENSON, R. W.

12-C

SIME, S. E.

12-D

COREA, G. VAN P.
GIBBS, I. M.
GRANT, E. H.
GRODZINS, R. M.
HANSEN, K. G.
HARMAN, H. B.
KRESICH, H. M.

LARSON, M. L.
LUNEY, L. G.
McKENZIE, E. A.
RAHM, V. M.
RATZESBERGER, A.

12-E

DIBELKA, S. S.
FRIEDERICHSEN, K. H.
MORELAND, G. W.
STEVENSON, R. W.

12-G

KENT, M. K.

12-H

ABBOTT, K. N.
BADENOCH, N. W.
BROWN, P. S.
BROWN, V. K.
COHEN, S. B.
COREA, G. VAN P.
EERDE, E. E.
FISHER, H. S.
KRESICH, H. M.
KURTZMAN, B. L.
LANDEN, F. P.
LEONARD, S.
LEVY, M. M.
McLUCAS, G. B.
NEWMAN, N. B.
RAY, A. K.
SCHWARTZ, D. D.
SEMROW, E. H.
SIME, S. E.
SNYDER, J. M.
STEBBINS, E. W.
WINCHESTER, L. B.

12-I

FARISH, M. K.
HAYES, B. S.

13-B

KENT, M. K.

13-D

CARTER, G. M.
  political science

13-E

ALBERT, M.
BADENOCH, N. W.
  articles, cookbooks
BAILEY, B. F.

BARZEL, A.
 dance
BERGER, M. S.
 non-fiction
BIALK, E.
 short stories, poems
BLUM, R. M.
 copy
BRADY, B. R.
 articles
BROCKWAY, E. S.
 articles
BROOKMAN, D. C.
 short stories
BROWN, V. K.
 hospital communications
BUERGER, J. T.
 religion
BURTSCHI, M. P.
 American history
CARTER, G. M.
 political science
CASSELL, S. E.
 articles: games, puppets,
 activities
CLAFFORD, P.
 literary criticism
DANIELS, M. J.
 articles: marketing,
 advertising
DEMING, E. J.
 reviews
ERICKSON, A. G.
 articles, reviews
FISHER, H. S.
 articles
FULLER, M. S.
GEYER, G. A.
 articles
GRIDLEY, M. E.
GRIFFITH, M. B.
 articles
GROVES, R. C.
 articles, poetry
HORWICH, F. R.
JENNER, N. N.
 non-fiction
JURGENSEN, B. B.
 articles
KEAGY, I. S.
 short stories
KEHM, F. S.
 articles
KENT, M. K.
KRESICH, H. M.
 speeches
KWEDER, A. N.
 medical articles
LADD, N. L.
LAIRD, J. R.
 fiction, non-fiction
LAVIN, P.
 articles: graphology
LAWRENCE, I.
LEONARD, S.
MEILACH, D. Z.
 articles
MISHKIN, L. Y.
 bibliographies

NEUMANN, R. V.
 music, cooking
ORFANOS, M. A.
 articles: dental, library
PARKER, B. M.
 non-fiction
PETERSON, M. O.
POLLARD, F. M.
 articles: library science
POWELL, E. L.
 fiction, essays
ROMMEL, M. D.
 fiction, non-fiction
ROSS, C. M.
SAMACHSON, D. M.
SEMROW, E. H.
 articles: nutrition
STEARNES, B. J.
 articles: marketing
TEN HOOR, E.
 articles: art, technical
WALKER, J. L.
 interior design
WARREN, J. E.
WINIER, G. L.
 children's poems
YORK, C. B.
 short stories

13-F

BROCKWAY, E. S.
 illustrator
HILLYER, E.
 interior design
MEILACH, D. Z.
 photographer
PETERSON, M. O.
 photographer
RODGERS, E. S.
 photographer
ROONEY, R.
 graphic designer
RUBIN, H. H.
 artist
STEVENSON, F. E.
 artist
TEN HOOR, E.
 artist
WILLIAMS, H. L.
 photographer
WINTER, G. L.
 artist

13-G

BLUM, R. M.
 copywriter
JENNER, N. N.

13-H

ALBERT, M.
BADENOCH, N. W.
DEMING, E. J.
DUNLAP, M.

FISHER, H. S.
GRIFFITH, M. B.
JENNER, N. N.
KENT, M. K.
LADD, N. L.

13-J

CLAFFORD, P.
 lecturer
ESHELMAN, M. J.
 singer
FAWCETT, E.
 lecturer: book
 publishing
GRAFF, M.
 lecturer
HARRINGTON, P. A.
 lecturer
HORWICH, F. R.
 lecturer
INDORF, E.
 actress, pantomine
KWEDER, A. N.
 lecturer: medical
 superstition
LAVIN, P.
 entertainer, lecturer
LAWRENCE, I.
 lecturer
LEONARD, S.
 lecturer, actress
MEILACH, D. Z.
 lecturer
PETERSON, M. O.
 lecturer
SEMROW, E. H.
 speaker: nutrition
SIME, S. E.
SIMPSON, P. L.
 model
SINCLAIR, E. R.
 dramatist, lecturer
STEVENSON, F. E.
 lecturer
TEN HOOR, E.
 lecturer: college

14-K

COX, V. B.
FREDERICK, T. J.
RUSSELL, M. E.
STURM, E. C.

14-L

BERGEN, Sr. M. J.
 drama
BLUM, E.
 communications
BRADY, B. R.
 journalism
BURTSCHI, M. P.
 English

CARTER, G. M.
 African studies, political
 science
FLETCHER, K.
GROSSMAN, E. N.
 journalism
GRYSKA, G. M.
HOGAN, B. H.
 remedial reading
LAIRD, J. R.
 writing
LeBAR L. E.
 Christian education
LeBAR, M. E.
 Christian education
LOHRER, M. A.
MERRITT, H. H.
PODENDORF, I. E.
 science
POLLARD, F. M.
 library science
RINGEL, H. C.
 interior decoration
ROMMEL, M. D.
 creative writing
RUBIN, H. H.
 art
SIMON, R. M.
 communications,
 sociology
YAMASHITA, E. S.
 journalism

14-N

BARLOW, A. T.
 educational
BENSON, M. W.
 editorial
BERGER, M. S.
 city planning, education,
 careers
BLUM, R. M.
 advertising
DUNLAP, M.
 public relations
KRESICH, H. M.
 business
LARSON, M. L.
 Latin American affairs
MAYER, M. A.
 communications
OLSHANSKY, R. H.
 home economist
PARKER, B. M.
 translator
ROSS, L. I.
 home economist

15

PARSONS, V. J.
 mailings

INDIANA

1-A

COLONE, A. L. M.
women's
GEISLER, M.
LEVITT, F. M.
women's news

1-F

SCHROEDER, M. S.
art

2-B

REED, D.
program

2-F

SCHROEDER, M. S.
art

3-A

McLAUGHLIN, M. A.
advertising, promotion

3-D

FRANKLIN, L. M.
RUMPLE, C. A. S.

3-E

AMATORA, Sr. M.
ARBUCKLE, D. F.
fiction, non-fiction
BOWMAN, S. E.
biography
FITZSIMMONS, C.
home economics
FORD, M. F.
murder mysteries
HAMMONTREE, M. G.
juvenile
HASLEY, L. H.
IMMEL, M. B.
LEHNUS, O. H.
crafts
MYERS, E. P.
young people
MYERS, H.
juvenile
NASH, J. G.
NOLAN, J. C.
history, novels, juvenile
PEARSON, H. R.
mathematics textbooks

PIERCY, J. K.
literary history
RUSSELL, B. J.
SMITH, E. Y.
juvenile
SPEICHER, H. R.
children's
STOKES, P. E.
VAN BRIGGLE, M. J.
VAN DER SMISSEN, B.
recreation
WINDERS, G. H.
juvenile: biographies

3-F

SMITH, E. Y.
illustrator
WINDERS, G. H.
illustrator

4-A

FRANCIS, J. O'B.
HARRIS, O. E.
business
HAY, M. L.
business
HONEYWELL, E. H.
JAMISON, E. P.
NEAL, G. D.
PEELLE, V. C.
SCOTT, J. T.
TARZIAN, M. M.
WEESNER, B. J.

4-D

AYRES, J. M.
women's
BEARDSLEY, D. S.
BECK, R.
BERRY, M. M.
society
CHANEY, R. C.
women's
CHAVIS, V. S. M.
society
CROCKETT, O.
fashion
DURHAM, D. M.
women's
EMERSON, L. G.
FORD, B. S.
society
FRUECHTENICHT, B. G.
women's
GIBONEY, B. O'N.
farm
GREICUS, A. G.
music, education
HAMMAN, A. L.
food
HAPPER, A. E.
women's
HARRIS, O. E.

HATFIELD, E. B.
family living
HAYES, D. H.
food
INMAN, J. D.
radio-TV
JENSEN, J. R.
fashion
KELLER, L. J.
society
LIEBELER, D. O.
youth
McCANCE, J. D.
women's
McFADDEN, R. M.
women's
MOSS, M.
copy
RANES, R. V.
society
REED, J. J.
news
REHME, J. C.
family
RICHARDSON, S. K.
news
SEELY, J. B.
SHEETZ, A. K.
STASSEL, R. B.
women's
STIPP, M. F.
women's
STRUPP, D. S.
news
SUHRHEINRICH, J. B.
entertainment
SUMMERS, R. B.
VAN DER VEEN, L. E.
education
VERPLANK, C. W.
WALDON, M. C.
home furnishings
WASTJER, N. C.
women's

4-E

BAKER, N. B.
reporter
BARKER, M.
columnist
BEARDSLEY, D. S.
columnist
BOYCE, D. MACA.
feature
CHAVIS, V. S. M.
feature
CHIN, R.
columnist
EMERSON, L. G.
columnist
FRUITS, B. A. S.
feature
GREESON, R. A.
reporter
GREICUS, A. G.
reporter

HOLMES, L. B.
science columnist
JANOWSKI, B. E.
camera columnist
JONES, R. A.
columnist
LIEBELER, D. O.
MENTZER, A. B.
city hall, society, feature
MOORE, M. S.
politics, features
RIZZO, A. R.
reporter, education
SCOTT, J. T.
columnist
SMITH, M.
columnist
VAN DER VEEN, L. E.

4-F

GREESON, R. A.
photographer

5-A

COOPER, R. K.

5-D

COOPER, R. K.
GREEN, J. C.
HACKNEY, E. E.
copy

5-E

LIEBELER, D. O.

6-A

ACKLEY, B. F.
public relations
NESTER, K. A.
office
PLUMMER, A. D.

7-A

ANDRE, R. A.
audit services
DROST, E. H.
audit services
TARZIAN, M. M.
broadcast equipment

8-A

FRAKES, M. H.

8-D

HENDRICKS, S. C.
STOVER, R. M.

8-F

DABBS, E. O.

8-G

BOSWELL, S.
NASH, J. G.

8-H

BOSWELL, S.
BUNTIN, M. M. S.
DABBS, E. O.
DAMRON, R. J.
MATHIAS, C. S.
QUIRK, J. W.

9-E

HARRELL, K. S.
    reporter
MYERS, H.
    politics

11

BRACKWINKLE, H. L.
JOHNSON, M. J.
MATTHEW, J. M.
McMASTER, F. R.
    law
PARKS, A.
SHRADER, G. L.
SHREVE, I. M.
    consultant
SOHL, M. A.
WILDER, U.
WOOTTON, T. McC.

12-A

BURNETT, H. R.
IMMEL, M. B.
MEREDITH, S. V.
STOKES, P. E.

12-D

KLEINHENZ, L. E. R.
WEAVER, J. C.
WEINBERG, M. H.

12-H

FICKERT, P. S.

FRASER, V. M.
HITZ, M. C.
HOFHERR, W. R.
LEE, M. L.
STATON, S. K.
TUCKER, C. C.

13-D

WEAVER, J. C.
WEINBERG, M. H.

13-E

AMATORA, Sr. M.
    psychology
BRACKWINKLE, H. L.
CHURCH, M.
    literature
DROST, E. H.
    poetry
EMERSON, L. S.
    storytelling
FRANKLIN, L. M.
    curriculum
GREEN, J. C.
    non-fiction
IMMEL, M. B.
JONES, R. A.
    poetry
KLEINHENZ, L. E.
    non-fiction
McGAUGHEY, F. H.
    poetry, essays
McMASTER, F. R.
    law
MEEHAN, K. M.
    children's stories, articles
MILLER, F. F.
    TV programs
MOORE, M. S.
    politics
MYERS, E. P.
    travel, child care
PERKINS, N. J. S.
    religious curriculum
SARE, M. L.
    poetry
SELTZER, G. M.
SHEETZ, A. K.
    short stories, articles
SHREVE, I. M.
    library science
SMITH, M. R.

13-F

ARBUCKLE, D. F.
    composer
CHIN, R.
    photographer
DABBS, E. O.
    children's films
JUNAS, L. M.
    photographer

SMITH, E. Y.
    painter
SMITH, M. R.
    photographer

13-H

HILLMAN, C. H.
    counsel
SELTZER, G. M.

13-I

MILLER, F. F.

13-J

HASLEY, L. H.
    lecturer
STOKES, P. E.
    lecturer
WINDERS, G. H.
    lecturer

14-K

WOOD, L. W.

14-L

AMATORA, Sr. M.
    psychology
BACH, S. J.
    public relations
BLEWETT, M. S.
    journalism
BOWMAN, S. E.
    English
CHURCH, M.
    English
CLIFTON, M. A.
    physical education
EMERSON, L. S.
    speech
FITZSIMMONS, C.
    home economics
JONES, R. A.
    English, journalism
JUNAS, L. M.
    photojournalism
LEHNUS, O. H.
    art
McGAUGHEY, F. H.
    English
McMASTER, F. R.
    law
MEEHAN, K. M.
    English
PIERCY, J. K.
SNYDER, S. M.
STROM, I. M.
    English education
VAN DER SMISSEN, B.
    recreation

14-M

RUSSELL, B. J.
    literary

14-N

SHREVE, I. M.
    library science

IOWA

1-A

BRITZ, A. M.
BRUBAKER, M. C.
    women's
MONTZ, W. J.
    continuity
RUBENSTEIN, E. S.

1-B

MARVIN, J. E.
    traffic
VOSS, J. H.
    producer

1-D

WHEATLEY, D. L.
    women's

1-J

BRUBAKER, M. C.
    broadcaster
VOSS, J. H.
    broadcaster

2-A

BARNHART, L. S.
    continuity
BRITZ, A. M.
FABER, J. A.
    operations
FUHRMAN, L. K.
    women's program
HEATHMAN, A. F.
    women's program
RUBENSTEIN, E. S.
STRANDHOLM, S. B.

2-B

FABER, J. A.
MARVIN, J. E.
    traffic

2-D

WHEATLEY, D. L.
  women's

3-D

BURRELL, G. C.
GIFFORD, E. R.
JAMES, R. G.

3-E

BOHLMAN, E. McG.
  textbooks
CARTER, M. A.
CRARY, M. C.
  young people's fiction
EAKIN, M. K.
  bibliographies
EYERLY, J. H.
FREEMAN, M. N.
  religion
HUTTON, E. R.
IRWIN, C. F.
ISELY, H. P.
  verse
JOHNSTON, M. M.
  cookbooks
LAWLER, L. B.
  classics
MUEHL, L. B.
  juvenile
PEET, L. J.
  home economics
PHELAN, M. K.
  juvenile
VOSS, C. S.

3-H

GIFFORD, E. R.

4-A

BROKAW, E. G.

4-D

BLEDSOE, R. S.
  news
BOWERS, J. V.
BROKAW, E. G.
BROTHERS, B. S.
BURNSIDE, R. R.
  women's
DAVIS, J. W.
DUFFY, B. H.
  religion
FISCHER, L. O'C.
  women's news
HOSKINSON, M. P.
  women's

JAIMES, R. M.
  women's
KOERSELMAN, G. R.
KRIEGER, J. G.
  AP telegraph
LITZEL, G. D.
SINGER, P. W.
  women's
SINKEY, B. F.
  society
SKELLEY, G.
  women's
STONER, D. C.
  society
SUBOTNIK, N.
  entertainment
WIESNER, M. H.
  fashion
YEGLIN, D. M.
  food

4-E

BURNSIDE, R. R.
  feature
DUFFY, B. H.
  staff
HOLCOMB, C. J.
  reporter
LARSEN, B. N.
  columnist
MILLER, E. L.
  news correspondent
MILNER, S. A.
  reporter
SMITH, E. S.
  feature

4-F

MILNER, S. A.
  photographer

5-A

ATHERTON, E. M. A.
  production
WILSON, C. L.
  business

5-D

BRUNK, C. D.
  travel, book
CORDTS, N. F.
EDWARDS, J. DeW.
GARNER, C. J.
  home furnishings
JOHNSTON, M. M.
  food consultant
McCRACKEN, B. M.
  contributing
VOSS, J. H.
  scout
YOUNG, G. V.

5-E

YOUNG, G. V.

6-A

LAWRENCE, G. M.
  creative

8-D

SCHUMACHER, B. L.

10-A

DYAR, J. J.
REESE, F. C.
WARE, W. F.

11

BUCKINGHAM, B. J.
  consultant
BUTLER, F. W.
FAORO, M. MacF.
  adult services
KEELER, J. A.
SCHRITT, K. S.
SENG, M. A.
  cataloger
SMITH, H. S.
VAN OMMEN, I. G.
  order

12-A

PETERSON, J. J.

12-D

BROWN, S. A.
BULLARD, M. K.
DAILY, L. C.
FERGUSON, E. S.
HUTTON, E. R.
SCHACHT, J. C.

12-E

SCHACHT, J. C.

12-H

PRESCOTT, R. V.
SCHACHT, J. C.

13-D

BIGGS, M. McC.

13-E

BIGGS, M. McC.
BROWN, M. E.
BULLARD, M. K.
CRARY, M. C.
EYERLY, J. H.
FERGUSON, E. S.
FREEMAN, M. N.
FUHRMAN, L. K.
  farm
ISELY, H. P.
  poetry
LAWLER, L. B.
  book reviewer
MILLER, E. L.
  poetry
PHELAN, M. K.
SPENSLEY, M. B.

13-J

EYERLY, J. H.
  lecturer

14-L

BOHLMAN, E. McG.
  business, marketing
BROWN, M. E.
  guidance
CARTER, M. A.
  creative writing
EAKIN, M. K.
  education
FERGUSON, E. S.
  journalism
LAWLER, L. B.
  classics
PEET, L. J.
  family environment

14-N

BUCKINGHAM, B. J.
  library science
DAWSON, H. A.
  kitchens, equipment
JOHNSTON, M. M.
  food
SMITH, M. A.
  communications

15

SIEMON, M. W.
  children's bookstore

KANSAS

1-A

LIVINGSTON, J. S.
women's

1-C

BAIN, R. A.

1-F

SCHREIRMAN, M. T.
poet

1-J

LIVINGSTON, J. S.
broadcaster

2-A

WOLF, E. E.
*continuity, women's
program, public
service*

3-E

BOARDMAN, E. L.
music
CUNNINGHAM, R. A.
ENGLISH, E. L.
poetry
FRANCIS, H. D.
teenage, young adult
GROSS, S. M.
poetry
HALL, H. L.
genealogy
McLEAN, B. M.
non-fiction, poetry
VOGT, E. L.
WARD, M. W.
non-fiction
WINTER, A. G.

4-A

BOYD, M.
CONARD, V. P.
DEMARS, A. B.
HAMMOND, M. J.
KOHLENBERG, H. E.
SCHERLING, M. B.
SMITH, W. M.
STROBEL, J. S.

4-B

ERICKSON, L. D.

4-D

BEINEKE, V. A.
BOYD, M.
BRICKELL, B. G.
garden
CONARD, V. P.
DAVID, I. R.
society
DEANE, B. A.
women's
DeLONG, T. G.
society
HAMMOND, M. J.
HEENEY, M. E. B.
local
HILLIARD, G. J.
garden
KELLY, K.
modern living
KOHLENBERG, H. E.
LEE, R. M.
women's
LEWIS, D. C.
women's news
LISTER, R.
city
MAGRUDER, B. L.
women's
McCALLUM, M. H.
women's
MORICONI, J.McK.
women's
SPARKS, N. C.
entertainment
TANNER, M. C.

4-E

BRICKELL, B. G.
rural reporter
ERICKSON, L. D.
reporter
LAMBERT, K. A.
reporter
LISTER, R.
reporter
MISCH, N. S.
*special assignments
reporter*

4-F

LISTER, R.
photographer

4-G

LOGAN, S. T.
classified
TOTTEN, B. D.
classified

5-E

GUINAN, MILT.
field reporter
WARD, H. R.
columnist

6-A

PAIGE, D.

8-A

CORY, J. C.
office
ENGLISH, E. L.
RATCLIFF, O. M. M.

8-D

AUSTIN, N. K.
COREY, J. C.

8-H

LUTZ, L. A.

10-A

NORMAN, B.

11

CALDERWOOD, B. B.
CARSON, D. M.
HOLMES, B. J.
STRECK, Sr. H.

12-A

DODD, D. L.
McLEAN, B. M.

12-D

GALYARDT, C. C.
MENNINGER, J. L.
MUILENBERG, G. M.

12-E

SCHEIRMAN, M. T.

12-H

COOPER, C. L.
CUNNINGHAM, R. A.
LEWIS, R. A.
STRICKLER, J. M.

13-E

DOCKING, V. B.
columnist
FRANCIS, H. D.
RATCLIFF, O. M. M.
non-fiction, poetry
WARD, H. R.
WILLIAMS, F. R.
juvenile stories

13-F

WILLIAMS, F. R.
illustrator: juvenile stories

13-J

DOCKING, V. B.
lecturer
LIVINGSTON, J. S.
broadcaster

14-L

BOARDMAN, E. L.
music education
CARSON, D. M.
LUKENS, C. L.
library science
MUILENBURG, G. M.
technical journalism
SMITH, K. M.
writing

KENTUCKY

2-A

POTTER, C.
program

3-D

HARGREAVES, M. M.
history

3-E

CHAFFIN, L. D.
*juvenile, poetry, short
stories*
GENTRY, D. F.
HARGREAVES, M. M.
KASDAN, S. M.
LEE, R. S.
non-fiction
MOSELEY, E. R.
QUINN, M. B.
poetry

WILLIAMS, C.
non-fiction

4-A

DeSPAIN, D. S.
GORIN, E. C.
HENRY, H. K.
RAWLS, C. J.
SIZEMORE, P. A.

4-C

WILKINSON, F. W.
national advertising

4-D

ASHURST, B. B.
city
BAILEY, J. B.
women's
CECIL, B. K.
COLLINS, M. L.
sports, society
COOTS, O. B.
society
GALLAGHER, D. H.
society
GASSER, B. B.
telegraph
GENTRY, D. F.
HUTTON, J. B.
RAWLS, C. J.
SPARKS, M. G.
WELDON, H. L.
women's, society
WHALEY, C. J. S.
women's
WHITTINGHILL, L. A. W.
women's

4-E

FORTUNE, B. P.
staff
SCOTT, B. W.
reporter

4-I

DeSPAIN, D. S.
historian

6-A

BEAUCHAMP, C. D.
KAUFFMANN, K. A.
production
SMITH, D. K.
media
SPAULDING, I. K.
media

WAGNER, G. P.
media

8-D

REOTT, E. M.

8-E

REOTT, E. M.

8-F

REOTT, E. M.

8-G

SYDENSTRICKER, M. H.

10-A

BEAUCHAMP, C. D.

11

CHAFFIN, L. D.
DAWKINS, M. S.
ESTES, T. J.
library services
HELM, M. M.
HUFF, Sr. J. E.
LEWIS, A. G. S.
MUDD, Sr. J. E.
PHELPS, M. E.
ROADEN, J. T.
SCHULTZ, S. A.
WILLIS, M.

12-D

JENSEN, J. S.

12-H

HENRY, H. G.
MEYER, J. P.

12-I

JENSEN, J. S.

13-E

CECIL, B. K.
short stories, features
HARTER, M. B.
*book reviews, program
papers*
HELM, M. M.
library science

MARTIN, L. K.
library science
McDOWELL, A. A.
MEYER, J. P.
QUINN, M. B.
poetry
WILKIE, K. E.

13-F

WILLIAMS, C.
artist

13-G

McDOWELL, A. A.
copwriter

14-L

HARGREAVES, M. M.
history
JENSEN, J. S.
political science
MARTIN, L. K.
library science
MOSELEY, E. R.
counselor

LOUISIANA

1-J

SCHWAGER, G. DeV.
weather broadcaster

2-A

GIFFORD, M. B.
PELUSO, C. A.
office

3-D

BIENVENU, I. M.
ROBERSON, P. F.

3-E

BELL, S. L. R.
novels
FONTENOT, M. A.
juvenile
JOINER, V. J.
non-fiction

3-I

FONTENOT, M. A.

4-A

CART, L. J.
WADDLE, M. S.

4-D

BALL, M. P.
young people's
BIGNER, B. P.
women's
BOURDIER, L. J.
city women's
CAVIN, J. K.
LOUVIERE, D.
LYNE, L.
amusements
SCHOENBERGER, P.
science
TRICHEL, M. S.
women's

4-E

BURROWS, C. A.
*special assignment
reporter*
FONTENOT, M. A.
columnist
GOUREAU, L. R.
columnist
LYNE, L.
critic
MARTIN, M. A.
education, medical

4-G

LOUVIERE, D.
classified

5-A

ROBERSON, P. F.
business

5-D

GAUDET, C. K.
contributing

5-E

JOINER, V. J.

6-A

BROWN, H. D.
creative
USHER, L. H.
radio-TV

6-G

MOTE, A. C. I.

6-H

MOORE, E. P.

7-A

GREENBAUM, M. R.
films

8-A

JOHNSTON, E. E.

8-D

SCHINDLER, C. H.

8-G

HOFFMAN, E. E.

8-H

HOFFMAN, E. E.

10-A

BRUECK, V. L.

11

CASELLAS, E. B.
FLANDERS, F. V.
GREESON, G. W.
HAYWARD, O. H.
reference
HYMON, M. W.
SCHENKER, T. A.
YUNDT, C. L.

12-D

MAMALAKIS, M. J.

12-H

HUGH, S. E.
NORWOOD, L. S.
TOLHURST, J. G.

13-B

BROOKS, M. A.
producer

13-E

BIENVENU, I. M.
BROOKS, M. A.
CAVIN, J. K.
GAUDET, C. K.
Indians
LYNE, L.
opera librettist
MAMALAKIS, M. J.
ROBERSON, P. F.

13-F

EBERLE, A. R.
artist
MICHEL, M. G.
artist
SHELBY, L. N.
artist

13-G

BROOKS, M. A.
media buyer

13-H

BROOKS, M. A.

13-J

MOORE, D. F.

14-K

MICHEL, M. G.

14-L

EBERLE, A. R.
crafts
MAMALAKIS, M. J.

15

JOHNSTON, E. E.
bookstore

MAINE

3-E

CARROLL, G. H.
DORIAN, E. McE.
juvenile
FRENCH, M. F.
children's

GESNER, E. M.
GIESECKE, M. W.
JANE, M. C.
juvenile mysteries
SHUTE, A. VAN H.
SMALL, M. R.
biography, English education
WILLIAMSON, J. S.
fiction
WILSON, D. C.
religion
YOURCENAR, M.

4-D

FRENCH, M. F.
LOVEITT, H. S.
women's
MAGNUSON, D. S.
teen
MITCHELL, E. H.

4-E

FEARON, D.
feature
KIDNEY, D. B.
SMITH, B. F.
columnist
YEATON, B. N.
correspondent, columnist

8-D

NICKERSON, G. S.

11

LIBBEY, F. E.

12-D

SHUTE, A. VAN H.

13-E

CARROLL, G. H.
FRENCH, M. F.
GESNER, E. M.
KIDNEY, D. B.
articles, stories, poetry
SMITH, B. F.
poetry, short stories
WILLIAMSON, J. S.
fiction, radio-TV scripts
YOURCENAR, M.
novels, plays, essays, poetry

13-F

YEATON, B. N.
photographer

13-J

SMITH, B. F.
lecturer

14-L

LIBBEY, F. E.
library science
SMALL, M. R.
English

MARYLAND

1-A

McDERMOTT, A.
instructional TV
REEVES, J. A. W.
instructional TV

1-B

EPSTEIN, B.
news producer
KEMPER, E. W.
producer

1-J

KEMPER, E. W.
moderator

2-A

ALLEN, R. S.
women's
HAWKINS, S. M.
women's
PATE, V. E.

2-J

ALLEN, R. S.
broadcaster

3-E

ANDREWS, M. E.
juvenile
BRAND, J. L.
medical
COOLIDGE, M. E.
children's

730

COPLAN, K. M.
  exhibit techniques
FULLING, K. P.
GARDNER, M. H.
  chemistry
LEVIN, A. L.
  biography
LINCOLN, V.
  fiction, non-fiction
LLOYD, D. D.
MEIGS, C. L.
  children's
MERRELL, K. D.
  children's
SPENCER, J. E.
  government
STRAIN, P. M.
  special libraries
WILCOX, E. R.

4-A

ROSENBAUM, M. V.
STRINE, N. L. S.
  controller
THOMPSON, D. S.

4-C

FLINCHUM, M. D.
  credit

4-D

CHILDRESS, A. M.
  motion picture
DAHLHAMER, G. M.
  family
LEWIS, J. B.
  school
ROSENBAUM, M. V.
THOMPSON, D. S.
TRACY, V. C.
  fashion, beauty

4-E

LoCASCIO, S. P. M.
  reporter
SAVAGE, K.
  columnist

5-D

BLUHM, E. V.

6-A

BEARDMORE, J. F. S.
McINTOSH, S. H.
SHEA, R. S.
  production

7-A

RUSSELL, P. G.
  TV cable service

8-C

BLEES, M. C.
HEAPS, J. F.
MANDIGO, H. J.
MURRAY, M. P.

8-D

LILLARD, M. B.

8-H

DEGENHARD, H. N.
LOIZEAUX, F. H.
MURRAY, M. P.
SCHAEFER, D. M.

10-A

BROTMAN, P. B.
PARRY, B. W.

11

CASGRAIN, M. D.
CUNNINGHAM, V. M.
  music
DOUGHERTY, A. E.
HAGE, E. B.
SLOCUM, G. P.
STRAIN, P. M.

12-A

BENTLEY, H. D.

12-D

BRAND, J. L.
DOUGHERTY, C. A.
LLOYD, D. D.

12-E

SCOTT, R. B.

12-H

BROCARD, T. S.
DICKENSON, J. M.
EPSTEIN, K.
FULLING, K. P.
NTI, S. D.
PIE, V. H.

POPLIS, N. T.
SMITH, D. H.
SPENCER, J. E.
WARREN, B. R.

13-B

HOOK, I. R.
  producer

13-C

CONGDON, J. LeB.
  media planner

13-D

BENTLEY, H. D.
  maritime
DOUGHERTY, A. E.
  library science
DOWNS, R. G.
KITCHEN, H. A.
WALTER, D. B.

13-E

BENTLEY, H. D.
  maritime
BUCHMAN, M. F.
  poetry
COPLAN, K. M.
CULLIGAN, G.
DOWNS, R. G.
GRAMBS, J. D.
  education
KITCHEN, H. A.
  African affairs
LEVIN, A. L.
  articles
LINCOLN, V.
  articles, short stories
LoCASCIO, S. P. M.
  political speeches
SAVAGE, K.
STRAIN, P. M.
  library science
WALTERS, D. B.
WILCOX, E. R.

13-F

LoCASCIO, S. P. M.
  photographer
WILCOX, E. R.
  artist

13-H

COPLAN, K. M.
LoCASCIO, S. P. M.

13-I

DOWNS, R. G.

14-L

BUCHMAN, M. F.
  poetry
CLAUDEL, A. M.
  English
CULLIGAN, G.
  English
FEHL, A. E.
  radio–TV specialist
GARDNER, M. H.
  science education
GRAMBS, J. D.
  education
McDERMOTT, A.
  instructional TV
MEIGS, C. L.
REEVES, J. A. W.
  instructional TV

15

RONSAVILLE, P. H.

MASSACHUSETTS

1-A

BROMAN, K. F.
KEANE, B. G.
MORGAN, L.
  women's

1-B

KEANE, B. G.
  producer

1-E

SCOTT, S. A.
  reporter

1-H

DOHERTY, P. R.
  audience promotion
LOEWE, J. B.

1-J

BROMAN, K. F.
  hostess
CHILD, J. McW.
  personality

SCOTT, S. A.
newscaster

2-A

MORGAN, L.
women's
TEPPER, F. H.
program

2-B

TROWER, D. H.

2-D

TROWER, D. H.
fashion

2-E

TROWER, D. H.
fashion

2-G

COTREAU, J. E.

3-A

CUSACK, B. B.
HALBROOKS, E. S.
business
LAWRENCE, M. L.
MANTHORNE, M. A.
YOUNG, M. M.
business

3-B

HARDIN, E. E.
PRIDE, J.

3-C

BRIGGS, G. A
copyright

3-D

BURACK, S. K.
play anthologies
COLBY, J. P.
sports
DE SANTILLANA, D. T.
KINGMAN, L.
children's
LAWRENCE, M. L.
THOMAS, B. A.
THOMPSON, C. P.
foreign language

VERY, A. N.
WHITING, B. B.
education

3-E

ADAMS, P.L.
non-fiction
BAILEY, A. C.
juvenile
BERNAYS, A. F.
BERNAYS, D. F.
careers
BEYER, A. W.
juvenile historical fiction
CHILD, J. McW.
French cookbooks
COLBY, J. P.
non-fiction
COOPER, M. L.
children's
COSGRAVE, M. S.
biography
CUSACK, B. B.
history
DICKENS, M. E.
novels
DRESSER, H. McC.
fiction, non-fiction
FLETCHER, G. N.
FORBES, D. S.
mysteries
GILLESPIE, J. W.
non-fiction
HALL, E.
non-fiction
HARRIS, B.
sailing
HARRISON, E. C.
young adult's
HODGES, E. J.
HOLLANDER, S. S.
non-fiction
KEHOE, C. De M.
travel
KINGMAN, L.
children's
KUMIN, M. W.
novels, poetry, children's
LAMPORT, F.
LANGTON, J. G.
fiction
LAWRENCE, M. L.
translations
MacLEOD, M. McL.
adoption
MADLEE, D.
NEHRLING, I. D.
gardening
NEWMAN, S. P.
juvenile
PAGE, H. M.
PITCHER, E. G.
child study
PORTER, K. A.
fiction
PRIDE, J.
American folk songs

QUINTAL, C.
French biography
ROTHCHILD, S. R.
novels
RUGGLES, E.
non-fiction
SETON, C. P.
SEXTON, A. H.
poetry
SIMON, N. F.
children's
STARKEY, M. L.
non-fiction
STRELSKY, K. A.
SWEETSER, M. C.
TROTT, R. C.
poetry
VERY, A. N.
VUILLEUMIER, M. R.
non-fiction
WELLINGTON, J. W.
education
WHITE, L.
guidebook
WISEMAN, A. M.
non-fiction
YOLEN, J. H.
children's

3-F

COOPER, M. L.
*children's book
illustrator*

4-A

GIFFIN, F. M. R.
KLEIN, S. E.
consultant
SPENCE, B. A.
TIBETTS, A. L.
office

4-D

ANDERSON, H. A.
women's
BEAVER, M. DeB.
women's
CHAPMAN, M. C. L.
women's
CHRISTY, M.
fashion
COFFIN, B. J.
CRANDALL, D.
food
FORBES, D. S.
HILLERY, M. J. L.
KYPER, B. B.
society
LUCIER, V. M.
women's
McCAIN, N. J.
education

McCARTHY, M. B.
TV-radio
NEWELL, D. J.
religion
PERRIN, G.
women's
RICHMOND, S. B.
literary
SHEA, E. B.
women's, art
SHERMAN, M. W.
society
SPENCE, B. A.
SULLIVAN, E. L.
radio-TV
SWEENEY, L. T.
women's
WALSH, R. A.
society

4-E

BEAVER, M. deB.
*music, dance, theatre
critic*
BONO, L.
columnist
CANNELL, K. E.
dance critic
MADLEE, D.
feature
MAGIERA, M. A.
education
NEWELL, D. J.
*general assignment
reporter*
ROTHCHILD, S. R.
columnist
SETON, C. P.
columnist
SHEA, E. B.
book reviewer
WHITE, L.
feature

5-A

LUND, G. H. L.
business
MADFIS, M. G.
advertising, promotion

5-D

ADAMS, P. L.
BECKER, A. S.
BOONE, J. E.
BURACK, S. K.
COSGRAVE, M. S.
COTÉ, C. K.
CUMMING, P. A.
FLINT, E. P.
HALL, M. L.
travel
KANE, E. M.
copy

LANGDALE, S. H.
LINDEN, P.
LOVETT, L. L.
LUND, G. H. L.
ROME, A. P.
  manuscript
WILLIAMS, D. F.

5-E

HEINS, E. Y.
  book reviewer
TROTT, R. C.
  staff correspondent

6-A

CROWLEY, J. A.
  traffic
DANIELS, R.
DENNIS, M. B.
  media
DONDI, D. A.
  client services
FEGANS, E. W.
  copy
GURRIE, B. P.
  production
HAEBERLY, J. L.
  radio-TV
LIDDELL, A. M.
  media
LINDEN, P.
  consultant
SCHUR, S. E.
SLATER, M. T.
  media

6-C

CAMPBELL, M. K.
  media buyer
SHAFTER, A. E.
  print buyer

6-E

LYNCH, D. P.

6-G

LYNCH, D. P.

6-I

SIMON, N. F.
  consultant

7-A

KEANE, B. G.

7-B

KEANE, B. G.

8-A

BUELL, B. H.

8-C

KOPEL, E. A.
RATHMANN, D. M.

8-D

DAVIAU, I.
EISNOR, A. L.
JACQUES, S. J.
LUCKE, G.
LYNCH, M. C.
MANION, M. H.
McCULLOUGH-
  THOMPSON, J. F.
MYERS, S. F.
TYLER, C.
WALSH, M. C.

8-E

CORCORAN, J. K.

8-F

COOPER, M. L.

8-G

LYNCH, M. C.

LOW, J.
LYNCH, M. C.
McGOWAN, B. K.
MYERS, S. F.

8-H

BROWN, C. M.
KAPLOVITZ, S. E.
LOW, J.
LUCKE, G.
LYNCH, M. C.
MULHERN, S. F.
PORTER, P.
POWERS, M. M.
SMITH, E. J.
WEICHEL, D. M.
WILBUR, J. E.

9-A

ROBERTS, L. J. S.
  book reviews

9-D

CORSON, G.
  fashion

9-F

CORSON, G.
  illustrator

10-A

BERNAYS, D. F.
BROWN, A.
BONO, L.
MILLER, H. C.
NEWSOME, R. T.
POTTER, D. M.

10-H

CORCORAN, J. K.

11

ARNOLD, M. J.
CAMPBELL, A. T.
  cataloger
CHURCH, C. B.
  regional
CLARKE, J. D.
d'ASSISI, Sr. C.
DIKEMAN, H. G.
  research department
GALICK, V. G. B.
HABERLAND, J.
  consultant: adult services
HALL, E.
  services
HODGES, E. J.
  adult services
JORDAN, B. A.
KUSEK, R. B.
McDONALD, J. K.
  school libraries
McIVER, V. D.
MITCHELL, H. L.
MITCHELL, M. M
  services
MULLANEY, F. L.
  media specialist
NICOT, S. L.
PAGE, H. M.
RICHWAGEN, E. E.
ROBERTS, L. J. S.
SEVAGIAN, H. H.
TASHJIAN, V. A.
TAYLOR, D. M.

WALDEN, C. M.
  reference

12-A

ANDERSON, E.
RUTHERFORD, M. C.
VUILLEUMIER, M. R.

12-D

BATE, L. N.
BOONE, J. E.
CUMMING, P. A.
FOX, M. T.
OSGOOD, E. E.
ROME, A. P.
WELSH, L. T.

12-E

DARCY, M. D.

12-H

BROADCORENS, Y. R.
FIELDING, V. V.
HOUGHTON, R. A.
JACKSON, G. F.
KORNETZ, M.
RUSSELL, J. F.

13-B

ANDERSON, E.
  director, cameraman
CHAPMAN, M. C. L.
  producer, director
POTTER, D. M.
  *program creator-
  producer*

13-D

BURNS, J. S.
KINGMAN, L.
  children's
KUFTINEC, J. G.

13-E

ANDERSON, E.
BAILEY, A. C.
  stories, articles
BATE, L. N.
  plays
BERNAYS, A. F.
  reviews, poetry
BERNAYS, D. F.
  articles
BONO, L.

BURNS, J. S.
 non-fiction
CANNELL, K. E.
 scripts, book reviews,
 fashions
FEDOSIUK, P. C.
 children's fiction, non-
 fiction
FLETCHER, G. N.
 articles, stories
HALL, M. L.
 fiction: teenage girls
HARRIS, B.
HARRISON, E. C.
KEEFE, M. J.
 poetry
LAMPORT, F.
 articles, verse, book
 reviews
LINDEN, P.
 articles, speeches
MacLEOD, M. McL.
 poetry, articles
MADLEE, D.
McCULLOUGH-
 THOMPSON, J. F.
 design
McGOWAN, B. K.
 advertising copy
McLAREN, L.
 travel
NEHRLING, I. D.
 gardening
PRIDE, J.
 folksongs, articles, scripts
RATHMANN, D. M.
 nutrition
ROTHCHILD, S. R.
 stories, articles, reviews
SLOSBERG, M. D.
 travel
STARKEY, M. L.
 book reviews, articles
STRELSKY, K. A.
 poetry, reviews, articles
TASHJIAN, V. A.
 book reviews
TROTT, R. C.
 poetry
YOLEN, J. H.

13-F

COONEY, B. S.
 illustrator
COOPER, M. L.
 children's book
 illustrator
McGOWEN, B. K.
 artist, photographer
McLAREN, L.
 photographer
ROTHCHILD, S. R.
 cellist, artist
SLOSBERG, M. D.
 painter, sculptor
YOLEN, J. H.
 lyricist

13-G

DANIELS, R.

13-H

HARRIS, B.
JACKSON, G. F.

13-I

TROTT, R. C.
 historical

13-J

BAILEY, A. C.
 lecturer
BONO, L.
 lecturer, astrologer
CANNELL, K. E.
 lecturer
CHILD, J. McW.
 TV personality
COTREAU, J. E.
 actress
DICKENS, M. E.
 lecturer
FEDOSIUK, P. C.
 reader for radio
MacLEOD, M. Mcl.
 lecturer
TASHJIAN, V. A.
 story teller, lecturer
WALDEN, C. M.
 musician
WHITING, B. B.
 lecturer

14-L

BEYER, A. W.
CUMMING, P. A.
 English
GROSSHOLTZ, J.
 political science
HILLS, C. L.
 public communication
HOLLANDER, S. S.
KEEFE, M. J.
 dramatic art
KEHOE, C. De M.
 English
MURPHY, L. E.
 instructional materials,
 media personnel
PITCHER, E. G.
 child study
QUINTAL, C.
 French
VOGEL, K. L.
WELLINGTON, J. W.
 psychology, education
WHITING, B. B.
 education

WILLIAMS, D. F.
 publishing
WISEMAN, A. M.
 remedial reading

14-N

CANNELL, K. E.
 fashion
DOHERTY, P. R.
 public relations
HABERLAND, J.
 library science
JACKSON, G. F.
 public relations
KLEIN, S. E.
 newspaper
KORNETZ, M.
 executive training, media
 communications
LAWRENCE, M. L.
 translator
PAGE, H. M.
 library science
SIMON, N. F.
 childhood education

MICHIGAN

1-A

DIXON, M.
 women's
McWILLIAMS, E. M.
 public service

1-B

HARRIS, F. A.
 special features

1-E

BANCROFT, A. W.
 plays
DUVALL, C. R.

1-J

DIXON, M.
DUVALL, C. R.
 hostess
SHONTZ, P. O'D.
 economics commentator

2-A

DAITCH, P. F.
 continuity, public affairs
DAY, H.
 women's, public service

DIXON, M.
 women's
GAUSS, C. S.
HARRIS, J. D.
 special events
McWILLIAMS, E. M.
 public service

2-B

DAITCH, P. F.
HARRIS, F. A.
 special features
KEANE, L. R.

2-D

JACKSON, T.
 women's

2-G

SNYDER, L. A.

2-J

DIXON, M.
KEANE, L. R.
 hostess, moderator
MURRAY, L. L.

3-D

FISK, M. DeV.
SNIDERMAN, G. M.
VANDER VELDE, W. B.

3-E

BRAND, W.
 poetry
BROWN, B. T.
 American history
CLINE, N. J.
 juvenile
DONER, M. F.
 novels
DONNELLY, D. B.
 poetry
DUVALL, C. R.
 craft projects
ERICKSON, M. I.
 education
HAAS, R. E.
 poetry
HARTWIG, M. D.
 children's
HOOGASIAN-VILLA, S.
 folklore
HORVATH, B.
 children's
JENNISON, F. T.
 economics

KING, P. C.
KONKLE, J. E.
  juvenile's
LaSALLE, D. M.
  physical education,
  health
LEITHAUSER, G. G.
  children's fiction
McCONNELL, B. K.
  poetry
PITRONE, J. M.
  teenage biography
ROSE, E. K.
  light verse
SAVAGE, K.
  food
WAGNER, L. W.
  non-fiction
WUNSCH, J. McL.
  fiction, non-fiction
ZUELKE, R. E.
  art

3-F

COLMAN, J. E.
  graphic designer

4-A

BENENATI, V. H.
  business
BRADLEY, M. N.
CAMP. C. C.
CARSTENS, E. S.
CHAPELLE, E. H.
MINSKY, B. J. T.
  bureau chief

4-D

BADER, E. S.
  women's
BATDORFF, N. S.
  photography
BLACKMER, K. C.
  women's
BOUGHTON, A. P.
BRADLEY, M. N.
BREITMEYER, E. A.
  society
CHAPELLE, E. H.
CLEMENCE, J. A.
  women's
DANIELS, M. S.
  women's
D'ARCY, R. C.
  women's
DERRICK, A. A.
  women's
FIELDS, H. B.
  women's
FRIEDERICHS, M. A.
  family living
GASKILL, M. E.
  women's

GATES, G. A.
  women's
GONDECK, E. S.
  society
HARRIS, J. B.
  women's, church
HILLIER, H. R.
  home furnishings
JURNEY, D. M.
  women's
LaMARRE, L. A.
  home furnishings
MANCEWICZ, B. W.
  art
MARTIN, J. R.
  women's
NOTEWARE, B. H.
  city
ODELL, J. O.
  women's, food
PERPICH, M. J.
  youth
PETRIE, Y. E.
  fashion
SAVAGE, K.
  food
TARR, K. A.
  news
WAY, E. M.
  women's
WOOD, J. W.
  city
WOOD, M. T.
  women's
ZEILINGER, I. C.

4-E

BADER, E. S.
  columnist
BARNES, D. M.
  education
GATES, G. A.
  columnist
JENNISON, F. T.
  correspondent
MANCEWICZ, B. W.
  feature
SHONTZ, P. O'D.
  editorial, economics
SNYDER, L. A.
WAY, E. M.
  columnist

4-G

PROCTOR, V. R.

4-I

CARSTENS, E. S.

5-A

CARSTENS, F. E. G.
  advertising production

5-D

BASEMORE, J. M.
FEINSTEIN, N. C.
PITRONE, J. M.

6-A

BANCROFT, A. W.
COLON, C. R.
  public relations
DRYER, E. H.
  media
FLOOD, J. A.
  production, traffic
FRANKMAN, B. S.
  women's advertising and
  marketing
GAGLEARD, A. W.
GLAETTLI, H.
KIYAK, A. J.
  media
LesSTRANG, J. M.
TRZOS, C. A.
  production
REID, R. J.
  business
ROY, L. T.
  public relations
WINTHROP, M. M.

6-B

MILLS, A. F.
  radio-TV

6-C

BROSE, P. L.
  media estimator

6-G

GALEN, H.
REID, R. J.
ROY, L. T.

7-A

SHONTZ, P. O'D.
  economic research
  company

7-B

DeJONG, L. C.
  production company
MURRAY, L. L.
  production company

8-C

FRISBIE, R. G.

8-D

BEARD, A. M.
CARR, S. T.
EMMONS, F. M.
HUGHES, G. H.
RYAN, M. E.
ZEEK, E. R.

8-E

CLINE, N. J.

8-G

SHECTER, L. H.

8-H

ASLPAUGH, L. M.
JONES, J. C. B.
JONES, J. P.
MOODREY, D. L.
SHECTER, L. H.
SHERTZER, M. P.
WALKER, P. C.

9-E

ROSE, E. K.
  light verse

10-A

DEBRODT, B. J. R.
WIDIGER, S.
WOLFRAM, B. R.

11

BAXTER, E. H.
BURGESS, E. S.
  children's
CHARLESTON, G. H.
  schools division
DAUME, M. R.
EBLE, J. S.
  media specialist
FRESE, A. H.
HANNA, M. A. J.
  school consultant
HOLMES, M. H.
HUGHES, M. B.
JONES, C. S.
KENISTON, R. C.
KREMER, H. E.
  consultant
LEWIS, E. C.

MITCHELL, M. F.
MURDOCH, F. T.
  school
NAUGHTON, L. H.
NOTT, G. T.
PLEUNE, B. J.
REESE, V. J.
RIPS, R. E.
  history, travel
SHIPMAN, D. M.
SNIDERMAN, G.
WILLSON, E. C.
  school
YOUNG, M. C.
  children's

12-A

HAZZARD, G. C.

12-D

BAIRD, V. W.
JOHNSON, L. J.

12-E

HAAS, R. E.

12-H

CARTER, V. U.
CURTIS, A. P.
CUSHMAN, K. M.
DALKA, S. S.
DERDARIAN, M. M.
FORNERO, J. E.
JOHNSON, L. J.
KEANE, L. R.
NOLAN, B. P.
UPTON, L. R.

13-D

BANCROFT, A. W.

13-E

ALSPAUGH, L. M.
  articles
BANCROFT, A. W.
  plays, non-fiction
BRAND, W.
  publicity, house organs
BROMAGE, M. C.
  editorial
BROWN, B. T.
  American history
CASEY, G. M.
  book reviews
CURTIS, A. P.
  non-fiction
DONER, M. F.
  articles, reviews

EDMAN, M. L.
FRISBIE, R. G.
  *education, home
  economics*
GOLDEN, R. I.
  language usage
HARRIS, J. D.
HOUTZ, S. J.
  medical
KING, P. C.
  articles
KREMER, H. E.
  articles: library science
LaSALLE, D. M.
  *physical education,
  health*
LOWRIE, J. E.
  library science
MANCEWICZ, B. W.
  non-fiction
MAYHEW, J. B.
  speech
McCONNELL, B. K.
  book reviews, poetry
MINSKY, B. J. T.
  articles
MOODREY, D. L.
  advertising
NOBLE, V.
  *articles: libraries,
  advertising*
PITRONE, J. M.
  articles, stories
ROSE, E. K.
  light verse
SHECTER, L. H.
SWALLEN, M. A.
UPTON, L. R.
  fiction
WALKER, P. C.
  articles
ZEEK, E. R.
  feature

13-F

COLMAN, J. E.
  graphic designer
CURTIS, A. P.
  photographer
HAAS, R. E.
  artist
MANCEWIC, B. W.
  photographer
NOBLE, V.
  designer
ZEEK, E. R.
  photographer

13-H

GIBBS, M. G.
WORTHINGTON, L. S.

13-I

BROWN, B. T.

NOBLE, V.
  business analyst

13-J

GOLDEN, R. I.
  speaker: language usage
KREMER, H. E.
  speaker
ROSE, E. K.
  speaker

14-L

ALSPAUGH, L. M.
  *marketing,
  communications*
BATDORFF, N. S.
BROMAGE, M. C.
CASEY, G. M.
  library science
EDMAN, M. L.
  education
ERICKSON, M. I.
  special education
GOLDEN, R. I.
  English
HARTWIG, M. D.
  physical education
HOOGASIAN-VILLA, S.
  English
KONKLE, J. E.
  kindergarten
LEITHAUSER, G. G.
  English
LOWRIE, J. E.
  library science
LYNCH, M. E.
  journalism
MAYHEW, J. B.
  speech
PHILLIPS, E. C.
  library science
TAYLOR, D. D.
  library science
VAN ORDEN, P. J.
  library science
WAGNER, L. W.
  English
ZUELKE, R. E.
  art

14-N

BROMAGE, M. C.
  business
ERICKSON, M. I.
  special education
HANNA, M. A. J.
  school libraries
HOUTZ, S. J.
  *medical research and
  education*
KREMER, H. E.
  public libraries

LINDSAY, J. McK.
  *inter-group ethnic
  relations, Black history*
McCONNELL, B. K.
  poetry
MOODREY, D. L.
  communications
MURDOCH, F. T.
  library workshops
PLACE, D. McL.
  consumer specialist
SHONTZ, P. O. D.
  economics
WOLFIAM, B. R.
  medical

15

WOOD, D. M.

MINNESOTA

1-A

JOHNSON, N. G.
  women's, promotion
JOHNSTON, J.
  women's
KEWLEY, LaD. H.
  continuity

1-J

KYLE, M. J.
  commentator
THIBAULT, M. E.
  broadcaster

2-A

JOHNSTON, J.
  women's

2-J

KYLE, M. J.
  communicaster
NELSON, J. B.
  broadcaster

3-A

LERNER, S. G.

3-D

LERNER, S. G.
  art
LINDAHL, L. G.
SINNEN, J.

3-E

BERGEY, A. M.
juvenile
COEN, R. N.
children's
ELLIS, M. J.
teachers aids, children's
GRACZA, M. Y.
GRUHN, C. M.
novels
GYLDENVAND, L. M.
HOFF, M. G.
HUCK, A. V.
JENSEN, P. L.
juvenile
LERNER, S. G.
children's
LIND, M.
French poetry
QUINN, Sr. M. B.
poetry, history, religious biography
SCANLON, M. S.
children's
SIEGEL, M. A.
careers
SWEDBURG, W. A.
children's
WESSEL, H. S.
childbirth
ZEHNPFENNING, G. B.
novels, biographies

3-F

LERNER, S. G.
children's illustrator

4-A

JOHNSEN, J. A.
KYLE, M. J.
SUEDKAMP, H. G.
publicity

4-D

FLAHAVE, P. A.
women's
HAYENGA, L. W.
JOHNSEN, J. A.
KYLE, M. J.
MOHRENWEISER, R. B.
news
OLSON, R. M.
OSTMAN, E.
food, home furnishings
SIEMS, B. C.
THOMSEN, M. A. G.
women's
WALLE, P.
family fare
WITT, J. St. O.
school, TV, service, correspondence

4-E

FLANAGAN, B.
columnist
WATSON, C. E.
reporter
WITT, J. St. O.
news reporter

5-A

JOHNSEN, J. A.

5-D

COVET, S. S.
GIBBONS, C. T.
GYLDENVAND, L. M.
JOHNSEN, J. A.
SIEBERT, M. A.

6-A

BARR, G. D.
broadcast, business
DAVIDSON, D. G.
media
HOLLAND, P. H.
LUND, E. C.
MUNRO, B. J.
broadcast production
TEUFERT, J. A.
production

6-G

BARR, G. D.

7-A

BERGENE, R. A.
creative services
GIBBONS, C. T.
picture company

7-D

BLUMBERG, A. M.
premium corporation

8-A

GORHAM, T. T.
VOGL, L. M.

8-C

JENKS, M. E.
THORNTON, B.

8-D

GENETT, A. G.
JOHNSON, V. L.
KAUFMANN, A. E.
LOCKEN, L. D.

8-G

WALDO, D. B.

8-H

GIFFORD, D. S.
HULIN, B. S.
KAUFMANN, A. E.
PALAIA, C. T.

10-A

HOLLAND, P. H.
WOLLAN, G. L.

11

BLATZ, Sr. I.
BUSH, N. S.
school
CHEN, L. C. L.
cataloger
ESALA, L. D.
HANLEY, M. D.
biomedical
KLEIN, A. L.
RUSSELL, A. A.
TEWS, R. M.

12-A

JORGENSON, M. L.

12-D

GYLDENVAND, L. M.

12-H

DYBIEC, M. C.
FREY, H. LeB.
NELSON, J. B.
RANDALL, P. R.
WESTLING, J. N.

13-D

PRACHT, G. M.

13-E

COEN, R. N.
art history

CRONE, R. B.
articles, short stories, reviews
GYLDENVAND, L. M.
articles
HUCK, A. V.
JENSEN, P. L.
critic, articles, stories
LEE, C. B.
LIND, M.
articles
McKINNIE, P. T.
NELSON, J. B.
PRACHT, G. M.
SIEGEL, M. A.
non-fiction
TEWS, R. M.
bibliotherapy
WESSEL, H. S.

13-F

LEE, C. B.
artist
SIEMS, B. C.
artist

13-H

CHAR, S. R.

13-J

TEWS, R. M.
lecturer: bibliotherapy
WESSEL, H. S.
lecturer

14-K

BADE, A. W.

14-L

COEN, R. N.
art history
CRONE, R. B.
English
ELLIS, M. J.
GRACZA, M. Y.
GUINEY, E. M.
LIND, M.
French
MOHRENWEISER
NELSON, J. B.
QUINN, Sr. M. B.
English
SCANLON, M. S.
health education
STEINBERG, H. M.
journalism
SWEDBERG, W.

14-N

GRACZA, M. Y.
translator
TEWS, R. M.
bibliotherapy

14-O

VOGL, L. M.

15

NORTHRUP, S. M.
personality course

MISSISSIPPI

1-A

DEES, B. J.
women's

1-J

DEES, B. J.
hostess

2-A

DEES, B. J.
women's
CLARK, M. M.
local news

2-J

DEES, B. J.
hostess

3-D

McDUFF, M. McL.

3-E

CAIN, M. D.
GRAHAM, A. W.
novels
MEYER, E. L.
cook books
ORR, E.

4-A

ARRINGTON, A. R.
BIGGERS, J. R.
CAIN, M. D.

SMITH, H. B.

4-D

ARRINGTON, A. R.
BIGGERS, J. R.
women's
BOOKHART, M. A. W.
women's
BRUMFIELD, B. D.
women's
CAIN, M. D.
KELLY, C. T.
news
LEE, E. H.
news
NASH, V. L. W.
society
SANDERS, A. M.
city
SIMPSON, L. G.
women's
SMITH, H. B.
STEVENS, S McN.

4-E

BOOKHART, M. A. W.
ORR, E.
PERRY, J. W.
reporter, education
SALLIS, U. W.
reporter
SHERARD, M. M.
*library reporter, book
columnist*
STEVENS, S. McN.
columnist, staff
WOODWARD, V. B.
reporter

4-F

SALLIS, U. W.
photographer

6-A

McGINNIS, J. M.
media

6-G

SORGE, Y. McG.

6-H

SORGE, Y. McG.

8-D

HORTON, M. B.
ROBERTS, A. H.

8-H

DIAL, A. B.

11

BROACH, J. DuV.
HOLCOMB, E. C.
SHERARD, M. M.
TAYLOR, F. F.

12-D

HARRELL, L. D. S

12-H

SCOTT, A. L.
TWISS, M. C.

12-I

HARRELL, L. D. S.
KENNEY, B. S

14-L

HAAS, M. O.
Mississippi history
SCOTT, A. L.
journalism
TAYLOR, Z. D. L.
home economics

MISSOURI

1-A

CRAWFORD, G. C.
women's
GRISWOLD, E. D.
women's
NANCE, M. DeV
women's
OBERMIRE, N. A.
*sales promotion,
research*
SPALDING, M. E.
personnel

1-B

GRISWOLD, E. D.

1-C

SMITH, S. M.

1-J

CRAWFORD, G. C.
broadcaster
GRISWOLD, E. D.
hostess

2-A

BOYER, M. M.
KOCH, A. M.
program
NANCE, M. DeV.
women's, continuity
PATE, P. L.
SHEPHERD, E. L.
women's, fashion
SPALDING, M. E.
personnel
WILLIAMS, P. C.
music

2-J

MUELLER, L.
broadcaster

3-A

BROWN, V. S.
childhood education

3-D

McKINNEY, M. M.

3-E

ADAMS, B.
ALEXANDER, L. L.
children's
BELL, G. W.
juvenile
BROWN, V. S.
education
GASPAROTTI, E. S.
novels
GRUMME, M. F.
parliamentary procedure
HANSBROUGH, V. M.
history
HEIDERSTADT, D.
juvenile non-fiction
HUUS, H.
education
LEWIS, D. R.
women's
LONG, H. H.
social studies
LORBERG, A. D.
MAPLES, E. P.
religion
MARKSBERRY, M. L.
MOSLEY, J. B.

PENNINGTON, E. R.
ROGERS, K. E.
  interior design
SEIFERT, E.
  novels
SEIFERT, S. L.
  historical fiction
SPENCER, L.
  home economics
STACK, N. M.
  young people's
UPTON, L. M.
WHITMAN, V. B.
YOUNG, V. G.
  library

4-A

THOMAS, P. K.
TUCKER, A. G.
WHITE, V. B.

4-A

THOMAS, P. K.
TUCKER, A. G.
WHITE, V. B.

4-D

ALLISON, E. W.
  society
BLAKELEY, N. W.
  society
BRAINERD, D. M.
  food
DOYLE, P. J.
  education
ELDRIDGE, V. H.
  modern theatre
HUBBARD, C. R.
  entertainment
MUELLER, L.
  society
PHILLIPS, E. M.
SPECKHART, K. P.
  women's
TUCKER, A. G.
WAGNER, J. A.
  TV
YOUNG, E. L.
  women's

4-E

DEFTY, S. B.
  reporter
HUBBARD, C. R.
  reporter
LORBERG, A. D.
  columnist
STROUD, M. J.
  reporter
UPTON, L. M.
  feature, columnist

WAGNER, J. A.
  columnist, critic
WHITMAN, V. B.
  outdoor columnist

4-G

PHILLIPS, E. M.

4-H

PHILLIPS, E. M.

5-A

LIBERMAN, D. G.
WALKER, E. H.

5-B

TORNQUIST, H. T.
  advertising make-up

5-D

CHAISSON, D. K.
  art
FARRAR, S. G.
  area TV programs
LIBERMAN, D. G.
MAPLES, E. P.
McCLURE, E. B.
SNYDER, R. F.
SULLIVAN, M. I.
WALKER, E. H.
WRIGHT, E. S.

5-E

SKINNER, O. L.
  feature

5-I

STURGIS, G. M.
  Black studies

6-A

ADAMS, B.
ARNOLD, V. S.
  media
BLOCK, B. A.
  radio-TV
BLOSSOM, D. A.
DATCHÉ, R.
HELZBERG, S. B.
LOTKO, A. L.
  media
MANBECK, A. L.
POTTER, J. R.

RAYN, L. S.
  consultant
SHEAR, M. M.
SOLIT, A. P.
STEINHEIMER, L. L.
VAUGHT, B. L.
  comptroller, office

6-C

RODEKOHR, S. K.
  media supervisor

6-E

OHRN, E. H.
SMART, M. F.
WERNER, E. D.

6-G

MANSFIELD, P. L.

7-A

BUNCHEZ, G.
  broadcast representative
LONG, H. H.
  wholesale book company
STURGIS, G. M.
  Black studies research

8-C

SOMMERER, W. J.
WHITE, D. B.

8-D

BROOKS, G. L.
ELLINGTON, B.
ELLIS, L. A.
HOFFERT, J. R.
JAFFE, Y. U.
McKIM, R. S.
NOLAND, B. L.
SADLER, L. E.
WORLEY, C. J.

8-G

BLOSSOM, D. A.
CYHEL, F. V.
DODD, J. C.
LONGO, M. H.

8-H

BROOKS, G. L.
CRANK, N. M.
DODD, J. C.

ELLISON, J. D.
GUTHRIE, J. E.
LONGO, M. H.
SPENCER, L.

10-A

JACOBSON, R. K.
  special events
KAISER, I. Y.
MANBECK, A. L.
SCHACHT, B. M.

11

ALEXANDER, S. L.
BAER, E. A.
BENNETT, H. B.
  reference
DOERING, D. D.
GEARIN, L. A.
  school
HANSBROUGH, V. M.
  school
HEIDERSTADT, D.
LAUN, S.
LEUBBERT, K. M.
MAXWELL, M. A.
MILLAR, L. F.
OLIVER, S. B.
PENNINGTON, E. R.
SMITH, L. S.
  reader's service
WARREN, P. S.

12-A

MILLER, H. S.
MINNEY, M. A.

12-C

DAVIS, H. R.

12-D

ADAMS, P. S.
CALDWELL, D. J.
ELDRIDGE, V. H.
ENGLUND, S. S.
FREELAND, M. M.
HAVERFIELD, B. L.
MOTTIN, L. B.
NORMAN, E. K.
RUTZ, K. B.
STANARD, C. S.
WILSON, Y. D.

12-G

BROOKER, J. L.

12-H

BARTON, C. C.
CALVERT, N. A.
HAMILTON, S. W.
JANES, B. B.
MARTIN, M. D.
NORMAN, E. K.
ROTTMANN, B. C.
WILSON, J. G.
WILSON, Y. J.
WOLFF, M. B.

13-D

MOHIN, L. B.
NORMAN, E. M.

13-E

ADAMS, P. S.
articles
BELL, G. W.
juvenile
BROWN, V. S.
education
CALDWELL, D. J.
Missouri history
ELDRIDGE, V. H.
historical articles
ELLINGTON, B.
ELLIS, L. A.
poetry, stories
GASPAROTTI, E. S.
GRUMME, M. E.
parliamentary procedure
HANSBROUGH, V. M.
poems, articles
JAFFE, Y. U.
book reviews
KAISER, I. Y.
LORBERG, A. D.
short stories, articles
MAPLES, E. P.
poet
McCLURE, E. B.
horticulture
McKIM, R. S.
articles: crafts, decorating
McKINNEY, M. M.
short stories, articles
MOSLEY, J. B.
short stories, articles
NORMAN, E. K.
short stories, articles
NORMAN, E. M.
juvenile stories, features
PLANTHOOD, M. A.
commercials, scripts
SPENCER, L.
articles: home economics
STACK, N. M.
young people's
STROUD, M. J.
STURGIS, G. M.
*Afro-American book
reviews*

13-F

McCLURE, E. B.
*photographer, landscape
designer*

13-H

STROUD, M. J.
WILSON, J. G.

13-I

THOMPSON, D. B.
history
WILSON, J. G.
communications

13-J

CAMERON, J.
fashion commentator
GRUMME, M. E.
parliamentarian, lecturer
MUELLER, L.
broadcaster
PLANTHOLD, M. A.
*TV, food, flower
demonstration*
YOUNG, V. G.
lecturer: libraries

14-L

ALLEN, S. A.
journalism
BRATEK, R. B.
journalism
CAMERON, J.
feature writing
HUUS, H.
education
LEWIS, D. R.
journalism
MALTBY, F. G.
library science
MARKSBERRY, M. L.
*education, educational
psychology*
ROGERS, K. E.
interior design

14-N

BRIDE, E. L.
*TV, home economics,
photography,
advertising*
BROWN, V. S.
education
RAYN, L. S.
advertising
STURGIS, G. M.
Black studies

MONTANA

1-B

ASHBY, N. B.
CREECY, A. B.
MORASKO, R. B.
WILSON, P. W.

1-J

ASHBY, N. B.
CREECY, A. B.
hostess
MORASKO, R. B.
broadcaster

2-B

MORASKO, R. B.
WILSON, P. W.
university radio

2-C

SCHMIDT, M. H

2-J

BERTINO, B. W.
broadcaster
CLARKE, U.
commentator
MORASKO, R. B.
broadcaster

3-E

DAVIS, J. J. W.
Montana ghost towns
JOHNSON, D. M.
*ancient Greece, western
frontier*

4-A

BERTINO, B. W.

14-N

THOMPSON, D. B.
poetry
UPTON, L. M.
short stories, articles
WADE, J. St. C.
non-fiction
WILSON, J. G.
WOFFORD, D. F.
articles, stories

FINNICUM, B. J.
advertising

4-D

BERTINO, B. W.
DONOVAN, R. M.
news
DOWNING, M. H.
HILL, E. P.
poetry
REESE, E.
society
WRIGHT, K. H.
Sunday, special sections

4-E

DOWNING, M. H.
HILL, E. P.
reporter

4-F

DOWNING, M. H.
photographer

6-A

COX, J. T.
SHROEDER, Z. H.

8-A

COX, J. T.
*special communications
services*

8-H

OTIS, M. W.

10-A

COX, J. T.

12-B

WILSON, P. W.

13-E

BERTINO, B. W.
children's
CLARKE, U.
JOHNSON, D. M.
WILSON, P. W.
non-fiction

13-F

BERTINO, B. W.
photographer

14-M

BROOME, M. A. DeB.
literary

14-N

LARSON, L. H.
journalism

NEBRASKA

1-A

GRASZ, L. M.
promotion

2-A

BROWN, D. D.
women's
GUSTASON, M. C.
mailing services
STEBBINS, H. S.
women's
THAYER, J. L.
women's
WING, G. E.
office

3-A

BROWN, E. B.

3-D

FAULKNER, V. L.

3-E

ALBERTS, F. J.
BROWN, E. B.
teacher's aids
FAULKNER, V. L.
novels
FURNESS, E. L.
English language

4-A

COX, J. H.
HARSTICK, A. H.
NEU, J. B.
SMITH, T. S.

TICHY, K. S.
TURNEY, E. N.
WILLIAMS, M. U.

4-D

HAGGIE, H. M.
women's
HEMPHILL, H. A.
city
JUSTIS, N. R.
LARSEN, P. L.
women's
SMITH, T. S.
SPENCE, H. D.
youth, entertainment
TICHY, K. S.
TURNEY, E. N.
WOLF, W. M.

4-E

HAGGIE, H. M.
art critic

5-D

FAULKNER, V. L.

6-A

ALLEN, B. R.
media
KIESER, H. F.
creative

6-B

RUDOLPH, J. B.

6-G

BRINKER, J. S.

7-A

GOLDBERG, M. A.
*market research
company*
SMITH, M. K.
production company

8-D

SCHLEIGER, G. S.
SPENCER, F. S

8-G

CARPENTER, N. L.

CHISHOLM, G. H.

8-H

CARPENTER, N. L.

11

BUCK, K. L.
COLLINGS, L. W.
HETZNER, B. M.
HUNT, M. C.
KING, R. E.
PETERSON, V. A.
RENFRO, K. R.

12-A

GOLDBERG, M. A.

12-D

AKIN, L. Q.

12-E

SHEETS, P. Van M.

12-H

HAYS, J. M.

13-E

ALBERTS, F. J.
short stories, articles
CLAPPISON, K. G.
FAULKNER, V. L.
short stories, articles
FURNESS, E. L.
book reviews, articles
JOHNSON, S. K.
fiction, non-fiction

14-L

HETZNER, B. M.
library science
SHEETS, P. Van M.
science

NEVADA

1-A

BONTEMPI, F. M.
public affairs

1-J

SPENCER, D. L.
interviewer

2-A

WALKER, L. W.

2-D

STEVENS, M. G.
women's

2-J

BONTEMPI, F. M.
SPENCER, D. L.
interviewer
STEVENS, M. G.

3-E

HOHN, H. S.
children's fiction

4-A

DESKIN, R. G.

4-D

SPENCER, D. L.
entertainment, women's
SWAIL, D. S.
entertainment, women's

4-E

ALLEN, D. J.
columnist
MANNING, M. F.
SPENCER, D. L.
columnist

5-E

BONTEMPI, F. M.
food columnist
GAUREAU, W. R.
book review columnist

7-A

BELL, R. L.
ASCAP publishing

8-E

CRAFT, E. R.

12-D

CRAFT, E. R.

12-I

SIDLER, H. A.

13-J

BELL, R. L.
singer, actress

14-L

SIDLER, A.

NEW HAMPSHIRE

2-A

De LUDE, M. B.
women's

3-E

CURTIS, E. R.
fiction, non-fiction
HAUBRICH, A. C.
HUNTER, B. T.
natural foods, gardening
KELIHER, A. V.
non-fiction
MacDOUGALL, R. D.
MILNE, M. G.
nature, zoology
MOLLOY, A. B.
juvenile
REID, M. I.
writer's textbooks, novels
WERTENBAKER, L. T.
novels, non-fiction,
juvenile

4-D

KERSHAW, H. S.
women's
MORRISON, N. N.
women's
STAPLES, L. S.
natural resources,
wildlife

4-E

MORRISON, N. N.
reporter

5-D

GEORGES, J. F.

11

ADAMS, H. A.
CHANDLER, M. C.
VAUGHAN, D. M.

12-A

KNIGHT, A. T.

12-D

PETERS, J. A.

13-E

CURTIS, E. R.
poetry
GEORGES, J. F.
New England history
KELIHER, A. V.
non-fiction
MILNE, M. G.
articles, book reviews
MOLLOY, A. B.
magazine articles
MORRISON, N. N.
poetry
WERTENBAKER, L. T.
fiction, non-fiction

13-I

VAUGHAN, D. M.
history

13-J

HUNTER, B. T.
lecturer, ecology
KELIHER, A. V.
lecturer
REID, M. I.
lecturer: writing
STAPLES, L. S.
lecturer

14-L

MILNE, M. G.
PETERS, J. A.
home economics

REID, M. I.
creative writing

14-N

ADAMS, H. A.
library services
KELIHER, A. V.
Indian Affairs

NEW JERSEY

3-A

BROKAW, R. M.
BROWN, E. G.
office
FITZGERALD, K. S.
children's
ORR, C. W.
ROBICHAUD, B.

3-B

TERRA-NOVA, E. A.

3-D

BROKAW, R. M.
DeVRIES, M. A.
LOIZEAUX, M. D.
RIEDMAN, S. R.
medicine
SUTTON, A. L.
nursing

3-E

ARESTY, E. B.
CARLSON, B. W.
children's
COIT, M. L.
history
De LEEUW, C. W.
ELTING, M. L.
children's
GILLIES, M. D.
interior design
GREY, V. H.
non-fiction
GROHSKOPF, B.
HEALY, J. D.
fiction, non-fiction
JAUSS, A. M.
KATZ, C. K.
education
LAMB, M.
MARTINI, T.
juvenile
MIRSKY, J. R.
geography

NEWMAN, T. R.
art
NOGUCHI, S.
nature
PATTERSON, E. R.
cookbooks
RIEDMAN, S. R.
science, medicine
ROBICHAUD, B.
business
ROGEIS, M. D.
art
ROMANO, C. C.
art, art textbooks
ROTH, C. J.
careers
ROTH, J. S.
cookbooks
SCOTT, J. U.
teenage non-fiction
SHUTTLESWORTH, D. E.
nature
SMITH, F. C.
non-fiction
STONE, M. F.
non-fiction
STRATEMEYER, H.
juvenile
SUTTON, A. L.
nursing
TURKEVICH, L. B.
language, literature
WHITCOMB, H. H.
charm
WHITNEY, P. A. *fiction,*
non-fiction
WINTER, R. G.
ecology
WOODY, R. J.
juvenile
WOOLLEY, C.
juvenile
WYNDHAM, L.
juvenile
YOUNG, L. R.
non-fiction

3-F

JAUSS, A. M.
illustrator
NOGUCHI, S.
illustrator
PRESTOPINO, E. D.
illustrator

3-G

HITCHCOCK, J. G.
REDDING, A. R.

3-H

REDDING, A. R.
WILSON, K. S.
ZEITZ, E. S.

4-A

BARRETT, J. L.
DENNIS, K. S.
SERAFIN, D. K.
VALENTINE, M. P.
advertising
WILTON, V. W.
promotion

4-D

ADAMO, P. P.
women's
BABBAGE, J. D.
food
BILINKAS, M. L.
BOLTE, C. J.
fashion, women's
BUSH, M. R
COPES, J. McE.
society
DOWNIE, J. B.
women's
FARRELL, L. F.
women's, travel
FERRARA, P. D.
women's
HAINFELD, A.
religion
LAMBERT, V. Van H.
women's
LAZAR, E. L.
TV, radio
LOFFT, V. M.
women's
LONGO, R. F.
women's
MARKO, E.
women's, art
OLIS, R.
fashion
PHILBRICK, E. C.
SMITH, G. B.
women's
SMITH, M. H.
food
TALLEY, C. L.
politics
VANCE, M. A.
religion
WARWICK, R. A.
women's
WINTER, R. G.
science

4-E

CORBETT, L. S.
reporter, feature
COUCH, H. J.
women's reporter
DENNIS, K. S.
book reviewer
NEWELL, D. F.
reporter

OLICK, A. W.
education
PELLATON, J.
feature
PHILLIPS, J. T.
staff
ROSENHAUSE, S.
urban affairs
SAVAGE, M. A.
rewrite reporter
SERVIS, S. De L.
reporter
TOMARA, S.
reporter
WINGERT, D. H.
reporter

4-F

KATO, K.
cartoonist

5-A

MALKIN, M. A. O.

5-D

DeLONG, A.
HEMPEL, D. P.
HANNIGAN, M. M.
REINERT, B. J.

6-A

AIKEN, J. L.
POPICK, F. G.
finance
SCHMIDT, V. D.
ZOBLE, A. K.
media

6-C

JANOW, D. A.

7-A

BINDER, M. G.
creative services
DeVRIES, M. A.
editorial services

7-D

DeVRIES, M. A.
editorial services

7-H

JORDAN, A. S.
photography laboratory

8-A

HALPERN, E. D.
HINEK, E. A.
ROEBLING, M. G.
RUBIN, S. I.

8-C

BERGER, E. E.
BILAS, B. A.

8-D

BARBER, J. E.
BLASKA, W. M.
CARR, L. H.
CLEMENTE, E. H.
HINEK, E. A.
JONES, J. W.
LAUBENHEIMER, B. D.
LUKAS, E. S.
STONE, M. F.
WIRSIG, J. D.

8-E

SMITH, M. P.
STONE, M. F.

8-F

BLASKA, W. M.
TRAVIS, J. S.

8-G

AUCELLO, M. D.
BAUER, R. R.

8-H

AUCELLO, M. D.
BACKSTER, N. Van A.
MARTIN, P. J.
RIKER, E. M.

8-I

MAYER, M. A.

10-A

AIKEN, J. L.
KING, L. P.
SCHMIDT, V. D.

11

BEEBE, I. A.
school

BRAMBLE, A. F.
BUDELL, E. E.

11

BUFF, D. D.
CARY, V. F.
COACHMAN, D. L.
ELKS, H. H.
FISHLER, E. B.
GRADY, D. McC.
HENSEL, J. W.
cataloger
HERRMANN, E. M.
JAMES, B. B.
KLINGERMAN, E.
MARTIN, E. C.
POGANY, H. L.
cataloger
SCHNURMANN, E.
STUCKERT, B. S.
TEMKIN, S. S.
TRAINOR, J. A.
TUTTLE, H. W.
WILSON, K. S.

12-A

UNTERMANN, E. K.
YOUNG, L. R.

12-C

LARSEN, D. M.

12-D

BENJAMIN, A. S.
DeLONG, A.
DeVRIES, M. A.
HEMPEL, D. P.
ROGERS, G. McM.

12-F

NOGUCHI, S.

12-H

BERNHARDT, T. C.
CALDWELL, K. M.
EBERT, I. C.
FOSTER, O. O.
GEIGER, J. R.
MILLANE, J. E.
PERRY, P.
ROGERS, M. D.

13-B

SCHREPEL, C. T. M.
TV commercials

13-D

DeVRIES, M. A.
SAVAGE, M. A.
SUTTON, A. L.
nursing
WYNDHAM, L.

13-E

BERRIEN, E. H.
BINDER, M. G.
comedy scripts
CAMPBELL, P. C.
religious poetry, essays
CLARK, R. T.
poetry, articles
DeVRIES, M. A.
fiction, non-fiction
FISHLER, M. S.
GILLIES, M. D.
interior design
HARRIS, N. VerS.
poetry, non-fiction
HRUSKA, M. H.
columnist
KATZ, C. K.
educational systems
LAMB, M.
plays
LARSEN, D. M.
food service
LEE, F. H.
articles: education
LOFFT, V. M.
ecology
LONGO, R. F.
articles
MARTIN, E. S.
MARTINI, T.
stories, articles
MATHEWS, E. M.
*juvenile fiction,
curriculars*
MENZIES, E. G. C.
NEWMAN, T. R.
*articles: art, education,
travel*
SCHREPEL, C. T. M.
poetry, features
SCOTT, J. U.
non-fiction
SMITH, F. C.
SMITH, R. F.
STREETER, M. M.
SUTTON, A. L.
nursing
TEMKIN, S. S.
TUTTLE, H. W.
library science
VALENTINE, M. P.
WINTER, R. G.
articles
WYNDHAM, L.
critic
YOUNG, L. R.
articles

13-F

De LEEUW, C. W.
artist
JAUSS, A. M.
artist
JORDAN, A. S.
photographer
LEVINSON, M. P.
artist
MENZIES, E. G. C.
artist, photographer
NEWMAN, T. R.
photographer, artist
NOGUCHI, S.
illustrator
PRESTOPINO, E. D.
artist, illustrator
ROMANO, C. C.
artist

13-G

SCHREPEL, C. T. M.
copywriter

13-H

LOIZEAUX, M. D.
PELLATON, J.
SCHREPEL, C. T. M.

13-I

NEWMAN, T. R.

13-J

CLARK, R. T.
lecturer
COPES, J. McE.
lecturer: public relations
LARSEN, D. M.
cooking demonstration
MARTIN, E. S.
lecturer: food
NEWMAN, T. R.
lecturer
OSTERWALD, B.
actress
PATTERSON, E. R.
*lecturer, food
demonstrator*
SERVIS, S. D. L.
speaker

14-L

ARONFREED, E.
political science
BENJAMIN, A. S.
classics
BERRIEN, E. H.
English

COIT, M. L.
GAVER, M. V.
library science
GREY, V. H.
LEE, F. H.
teacher education
LOFFT, V. M.
creative writing
POGANY, H. L.
ROMANO, C. C.
art
THOMPSON, L. D.
TURKEVICH, L. B.
Russian
TUTTLE, H. W.
library science
WYNDHAM, L.
writing

14-N

BEEBE, I. A
library services
GILLIES, M. D.
interior design
HASERODT, E. M.
KATZ, C. K.
education
LARSEN, D. M.
food merchandising
LEVINSON, M. P.
advertising
LOFFT, V. M.
public relations
LUKAS, E. S.
editorial training
MARTIN, E. S.
home economics
McCULLOUGH, M. M.
fashion
PATTERSON, E. R.
food
RIEDMAN, S. R.
science, medicine
ROTH, C. J.
library, guidance
SAUL, M.
publishing
SCHREPEL, C. T. M.
WYNDHAM, L.
writing: young people's

15

McCULLOUGH, M. M.
modeling services
PATTERSON, E. R.
cooking school

NEW MEXICO

3-D

REDMAN, H. F.
weapons, reports

3-E

BAKER, P. B.
BEEBE, B. F.
children's wildlife
BENNETT, K. C.
non-fiction: Indians
CRANE, F. K.
mystery novels
EMBRY, M. J.
ESTERGREEN, M. M.
biography
HEAD, A. K.
MULCAHY, L. B.
PRIESTLEY, O. S.
*fiction, non-fiction,
picture*
REDMAN, H. F.
weapons data
ROBERTSON, L.
non-fiction
THOMPSON, E.
mysteries
WALTRIP, L. K.
juvenile

4-A

BRININSTOOL, J. A. M.
ENSLEY, B. E.
HEAD, A. K.
PRIESTLEY, O. S.
SNYDER, B. C.

4-D

ATTMORE, M. S.
home living
BRININSTOOL, J. A. M.
BUCKINGHAM, L. A.
arts
BULLOCK, A. L.
book review
COOPER, G. R.
women's
ENSLEY, B. E.
MORRIS, W. K. K.
Sunday, feature

4-E

BURKS, S. M.
reporter
ROBERTSON, L.
reporter

5-D

BULLOCK, A. L.
book

5-E

POWERS, M.

6-G

PRIGMORE, J. C.

7-A

BENNETT, K. C.
  Navajo song publisher

10-A

GREGORY, D. P.

11

ALTEPETER, Sr. M. P.
MULCAHY, L. B.
REDMAN, H. F.

12-A

BENNETT, K. C.

12-D

GREGORY, D. P.

13-D

BULLOCK, A. L.

13-E

BULLOCK, A. L.
  articles
CRANE, F. K.
  articles, novels
ELSTON, L. H.
ENSLEY, B. E.
  poetry, humorous fiction
POWERS, M.

13-F

STEINKE, B.
  artist, illustrator

13-H

POWERS, M.

14-L

EMBRY, M. J.
WALTRIP, L. K.

NEW YORK

1-A

ANDREWS, N. F.
  advertising operations
ANN, D.
  religious programs
BROWN, H. M.
BUTLER, K. R.
CHRISTIAN, C. J.
  media research, sales
COONEY, J. G.
  child education
COUCH, S. K.
  advertising
FOX, B. D.
  research
FRIEL, C.
  research administration
GIBSON, A. W.
  public communications
GRALNICK, B. B.
  research
HOFFMAN, B. K.
  corporate information
HOFFMEIR, M. F.
  program analysis
JOHNSEN, G. M.
  broadcast standards
MICHAUD, M. M.
  treasury affairs
MONROE, F. M.
O'REILLY, R. M.
  ratings
PARSON, M. J.
  program controllers
ROSS, J. F.
  awards
SCHELL, C. E.
  promotion, publicity

1-B

ADAMS, E. C.
ANN, D.
CALDER, E. S.
EDEN, D. F.
FAYE, D. R.
FINELL, A. S.
  producer
FRENZ, F.
  programs
GORDON, D.
GRALNICK, B. B.
HARRINGTON, D. K.
  traffic
HILL, P.
  news
HILL, R. K.
HOHMES, S. G.
  film
HINDLIN, P. L.
  casting
HUBER, E. S.
  music
ILOTT, P. C.

JARVIS, L. H.
KALISON, A.
KENNEDY, J. M.
KENT, J. A.
  commercial coordinator
KONNER, J. W.
KOPELMAN, J. R.
LYNCH, P. K.
MARTIN, M. A.
  film
MASON, L. S.
NICHOLL, J.
  news
O'BRIEN, M. E.
ORR, L. B.
OTT, N. G.
  clearance
POPERNIK, C. H.
POSNER, I. G.
  news
REARDON, M. B.
RICH, L. C.
  traffic
SCHANZER, B. M.
SHIRLEY, B. E.
  casting
TAYLOR, S. S.
  producer
TONNING, H. McK.
TOWERS, J. A.
  producer
WOOD, S. M.
  talent coordinator
ZORNOW, E.
  film consultant

1-C

BERGER, I. E.
  contracts
CHRISTIAN, C. J.
  media research
DRUCKER, T.
  development
REARDON, M. B.
  sales traffic
ROMAN, G. S.
WELLMAN, E. P.
  negotiator

1-D

ADAMS, E. C.
BLANKENSHIP, C.
  story
GRACE, J. H.
  broadcast standards
HOLMES, S. G.
  film
JACKER, C. L.
  story
MARTIN, M. A.
  film
RICH, L. C.
  assignment
WASSER, G. E.
  copy

1-E

BOSWORTH, P. R.
  news
CHU, D. C.
COUSIN, M.
EDEN, D. F.
FREDERICK, P.
  correspondent
HILL, R. K.
ILOTT, P. C.
KONNER, J. W.
LEVI, S. B.
LYNCH, P. K.
MASON, L. S.
MURRAY, J. E.
  correspondent
PAOLUCCI, B. R.
  correspondent
PIERCE, P.
  correspondent
RICH, L. C.
  reporter
SAARINEN, A.
  news correspondent
SANDERS, M.
  correspondent
SCHANZER, B. M.
TOLLIVAR, M.
  reporter
WERSHBA, S. L.
  news
WICKER, I.

1-F

COSTA, J. K.
DEMARAY, B. L.
HUBER, E. S.
  music
NORMAN, J.
  composer

1-G

COSTA, J. K.
  designer
COUCH, S. K.

1-H

CHIOTES, H. K.
  program information
COSTA, J. K.
  designer
DIETZ, M. J.
  community relations
FINELL, A. S.
  promotion
HOFFMANN, B. K.
  corporate information
PLAUTZ, G.
  press representative
POTTER, C. L.
SAVITCH, J. B.
THOMPSON, C. K.
WRIGHT, K. J.

1-I

BOSWORTH, P. R.
news
BUCHANAN, B. F.
CARTUN, S. H.
market analyst
DRUCKER, T.
EAST, C. S.
news, political unit
FOSTER, E.
political
GONZALEZ, M.
ratings
KAST, C. S.
news political unit
MANSFIELD, C. C.
rating services
MITCHELL, C. C.
news, elections
WOTRING, M. A.
archives

1-J

BALFOUR, K.
interviewer
BROOKS, M.
broadcaster
EDEN, D. F.
hostess
FRANCIS, A.
GALEN, H.
voice-over
HALL, H.
HEER, M. H.
performer
HILL, C.
HUBER, E. S.
music
LAWRENCE, V.
interviewer, moderator
LEVI, S. B.
NORMAN, J.
ORR, L. B.
broadcaster actress
SAVITCH, J. B.
STEINER, L. R.
TAYLOR, S. S.
moderator
TETA, L. M.
hostess
WALTERS, B.
hostess
WICKER, I.
singer, entertainer

1-N

BITENSKY, L. S.
network attorney

2-A

ANDREWS, N. F.
advertising operations

ANN, D.
religious programs
AUGBURN, M. K.
publicity, advertising
BARTLETT, E. W.
women's
BRADY, T. Z.
DE FRANCO, R. D.
women's
FRIEL, C.
research, administration
GENTHNER, A. D.
GRALNICK, B. B.
research
HOFFMAN, B. K.
corporate information
JOHN, A. V.
women's activities
JOHNSEN, G. M.
broadcast standards
LANG, L. A.
program
LARSON, M. K.
women's service
LENARD, K. P.
research
LESSER, J. L.
public relations
LEWIS, B. J.
MICHAUD, M. M.
treasury affairs
MONROE, F. M.
PARSON, M. J.
program controller
RANDALL, E.
advertising, promotion
ROSS, J. F.
awards
SHANK, D. R.
women's
STEPHENSON, M.
WEBBER, M.
women's

2-B

ANSCOMBE, D. I.
BACH, J. E.
BROWN, M. C.
BROWNLOW, D. M.
continuity
GLASER, R.
GORDON, D.
GRALNICK, B. B.
HILL, P.
news
KENT, J. A.
commercial coordinator
LEWIS, B. J.
NICHOL, J.
news
ORR, L. B.
OTT, N. G.
clearance
POSNER, I. G.
news
RAINONE, N.
Feminist series

STEINER, L. R.
TAYLOR, S. S.
producer
TONNING, H. McK.
traffic
TOWERS, J. A.
producer

2-C

WELLMAN, E. P.
negotiator

2-D

FRADIN, E. H.
standards
HALL, B. M.
women's
LESSER, J. L.
program guide
SHEPARD, J.
women's
WALDO, M.
food, travel
WASSER, G. E.
copy
WHEATLEY, M. E.

2-E

DIMOS, H. A.
continuity writer
ERICKSON, C. L.
copywriter
HEARD, A. LA R.
reporter
ORR, L. B.
RAINONE, N.
reporter
SAARINEN, A.
news correspondent
SANDERS, M.
correspondent
SHEPARD, E. E.
correspondent
SUMMERS, E. V.
editorial writer
WICKER, I.

2-H

LEIDERMAN, A. L.
press representative
PLAUTZ, G.
press representative
POTTER, C. L.
SAVITCH, J. B.
THOMPSON, C. K.
WERSHBA, S. L.
news

2-I

BUCHANAN, B. F.
news
WOTRING, M. A.
archives

2-J

BROOKS, M.
broadcaster
DE FRANCO, R. D.
broadcaster
FRANCIS, A.
hostess
GALEN, H.
voice-over
HALL, H.
broadcaster
HAYES, M. H.
hostess
KENNEDY, M. M.
hostess
McPHILLIPS, M.
broadcaster
NAREL, D. M.
commentator
ORR, L. B.
broadcaster
RAINONE, N.
interviewer
ROSS, B.
SCHULTZ, E. M.
broadcaster
SHANK, D. R.
broadcaster
STEINER, L. R.
moderator
TAYLOR, M. Y.
broadcaster
WEBBER, M.
broadcaster
WICKER, I.
singer, narrator

3-A

ADAMS, B. E.
subsidiary rights
ALPERT, S.
publicity, rights
ANDERS, N. C.
ANTHONY, C. T.
publicity, promotion
ARDEN, S. W.
public relations
ARMSTRONG, B. R.
publicity
ARTHUR, H. R.
AUERBACH, I.
education
BALLANTINE, B. J.
BANCROFT, C. J.
art
BARDACKE, B.
merchandising

BARONE, J. A.
  production
BARRY, J. W.
  art
BATES, N.
  subsidiary rights
BAUSSAN, N.
  advertising, promotion
BEILENSON, E. R.
BENNETTS, C. H.
  children's
BERGER, M.
  rights, permissions
BERNSTEIN, S.
  education services
BERTOLI, B. K.
  art
BLOOMBERG, S.
  trade sales promotion
BLUMENTAHL, G.
BOND, B.
  advertising, promotion
BOYD, A. L.
  publicity
BRAXTON, M. E.
BRIGGS, K. H.
BUSH, J. R.
  art
BUSHNELL, M. M.
BRYAN, D. M.
CAMERON, P.
  graphic arts
CARTER, H. H.
CERF, P. F.
  beginner books
CHEVALIER, J. G.
  publicity
DAY, P. J.
DE MARIO, J. J.
  production, design
DUFFY, C. C.
  publicity
DYER, M. C.
EBBE, D. W.
EICHELBERGER, R. K.
  consultant, representative
ESSIG, N. C.
  publicity
FABER, N. J.
  advertising, promotion
FELDMAN, E. G.
  publicity
FRASER, G. C.
FREEMAN, R. S.
GEISER, E. A.
  marketing
GINIGER, C. W.
GOULD, L. S.
  publicity
GRAVELLE, M. E.
  *trade promotion,
    advertising*
GRAY, M.
  publicity
GREVE, D.
  school library programs
HANSON, B. G.
  advertising, promotion
HART, M. W.
  promotion

HEATLEY, M. R.
  book club
HEIDEN, S.
HENDRA, B. J.
  publicity
HIMELSTEIN, M. N.
HOLMES, L. M.
  promotion
HOLSCHUH, J. H.
HUGHES, B. J.
  advertising
ISAACS, F. S.
  promotion
JOHNSON, D. S.
  development
KARL, J. E.
  children's books
KAUFMANN, M. M.
KISTER, H. S.
KRAMER, N.
  consultant
LEVY, R.
LEWIS, C. S.
  rights, permissions
LI, L. M. J.
  art
LIVINGSTON, C. R.
  publicity, production
LOO, B. J.
  subsidiary rights
LoPRETE, T.
  art
LORCH, E. B. P.
  permissions, royalties
LOVE, B. J.
LUEG, L. F.
  art
MARGOLIS, E. M.
  publicity
MARKS, B.
  marketing services
MARMYR, M. S.
  subsidiary rights
MARTONE, B. A.
  promotion
McMANUS, M. E.
  publicity
McNEILLY, E. J.
  production
MESROBIAN, A. S.
MEYER, H. H.
MURRAY, N. D.
MYLLER, L. W.
  school, library
NICHOLSON, M. K.
  subsidiary rights
NORDSTROM, U.
  junior books
PASANEN, J. S.
  publicity
PASCHALL, J.
  marketing research
PATTERSON, V. H.
  publicity, advertising
POGREBIN, L. C.
  *promotion, subsidiary
    rights*
PORTUGAL, R. P.
REID, W. K.
  promotion

SCHNEIDER, C. E.
  publicity
SCHULTHEIS, B. E.
  publicity
SCHWARTZ, F. B.
  juvenile
SPELLER, M. W.
STEIN, P. D.
STORM, D. F.
  producer
TRINER, A.
VARNER, V. V.
WEBER, J. R.
  publicity
WHITE, P. R.
  publicity
YUSS, I. A.
  production

3-B

ABBOTT, S. A.
  editor
BASS, B. R.
CHARNES, R.
FAIRHURST, M.
GIMPLE, J. H.
REPALONE, A. L.
ROSE, M. J.
  advertising traffic

3-C

BOCKMAN, P.
  subsidiary rights
FINNEGAN, H. M.
  Eastern representative

3-D

ADAMS, M. W.
ALLISON, M. L.
ANDERS, N. C.
AUERBACH, S. S.
AZARIAN, I.
BACH, A. H.
  young readers
BARTH, D.
BARTH, E. S.
BARTON, M. D.
  consultant
BECHTOLD, G.
BENEDUCE, A. K.
  children's
BERGIDA, H.
BERNKOPF, J. F.
BIRMINGHAM, M. B
  young readers
BIRNBAUM, A. B.
BLAKEMORE, C.
BLAU, M. T.
  education materials
BLEDSOE, R. L.
  art
BLUMENTHAL, G.
BOLTON, C. R.

BOND, A. M.
BOYKA, L. J.
BRAND, E. S.
BROOKS, P. J.
BRYAN, D. M.
BRYSAC, S. B.
  photo
BURAKOFF, S. W.
CARTER, H. H.
CASEY, R. C.
CERF, P. F.
  beginner books
CHAIKIN, M.
  young readers
CHAPMAN, P. A.
  home furnishings
CHARDIET, B. K.
CHENERY, J. D.
  children's books
CLAASEN, C.
  consultant
COFFEY, N. L.
COLLINS, C. P.
COSTELLO, J. M.
COURTNEY, W. F.
COUSINS, M.
DILWORTH, C. L.
  audio-visual
DOLINAR, J. M.
DUKES, E. A.
  food science
ENGELSON, J.
FARSACE, D. K.
  advance reader
FIRESTONE, S.
  Feminism
FITZGERALD, C. M.
FOGELMAN, P. G.
FORENBACH, R.
  juvenile
GILCHRIST, E. B.
  art
GRANN, P. E.
HARTMAN, J. F.
  regional
HEIDEN, S.
HOLL, A. H.
  school, library
HOPKINS, J. E.
  urban affairs, trade
HUFF, B. A.
  junior literary guild
ISAACS, F. S.
  newsletters
JACOBSON, S. R.
JOHNSON, D. S.
  reading
JOHNSON, J. G.
JONES, M. A.
KRIPKE, M. F.
  children's
LAWNER, L.
LEIPER, M.
LORANGER, J. A.
  young readers
LOVE, B. J.
MADIGAN, M. M.
  copy
MAJTHENYI, K.
MAYERSON, C. L.

McCULLOUGH, F. M.
McELDERRY, M. K.
  children's
MESROBIAN, A. S.
MESSING, D.
MILLSPAUGH, D. R.
MOSESSON, G. R.
  junior
NELSON, A. R.
O'HARA, R. E.
  children's
OUSTECKY, M. S.
OWEN, B. M.
  teenage
PORTUGAL, R. P.
RAFFERTY, K. K.
  puzzle publications
RAWSON, E. S.
REYNOLDS, J. E.
RICHTER, A. J.
ROBOTTI, F. VonS.
SACHS, A.
  educational media
SANDOW, L. A.
  educational media
SCHERMAN, B. K.
  book of the month
SCHMIDT, A. M.
SCHWARTZ, F. B.
  juvenile
SHAPP, M. S.
SHAW, G. G.
SMITH, B. E.
SOLIMENA, M.
  copy
SONSINI, J. B.
SPEER, K. A.
  literary guild
SPERBER, A. M.
  junior
STANWOOD, S.
TOWNSEND, D. McF.
TRILLING, D.
VARNER, V. V.
  junior
WAGNER, J. C.
WILSON, H. Van P.
  house, garden
WOLF, S. A.
YOUNG, G.
ZOLOTOW, C. S.
  junior books

3-E

ABEL, J. A.
AIMEE, Sr. M.
AINSWORTH, N. R.
ALDAN, D.
ALLISON, M. L.
  non-fiction
ANASTASI, A.
  psychology
ARTHUR, H. R.
  travel guides
AVERILL, E. H.
  juvenile
BACMEISTER, R. W.
  children's, adults

BAER, J. L.
BAKER, E. F.
  economic text
BAKWIN, R. M.
  child behavior
BARRY, J. P.
  novelist
BARRY, L. B.
  novelist
BARTH, E. S.
  children's
BARTON, M. D.
  French texts, workbooks
BEATY, J. J.
  non-fiction, children's
BEGNER, E. F.
  fiction
BENDICK, J. G.
BENJAMIN, A. F.
  non-fiction
BENKOVITZ, M. J.
BERK, P. L.
  juvenile
BESSER, M.
BIEMILLER, R. C.
BIRD, C.
  Feminism
Birstein, A.
  novelist
BOLTON, C. R.
BONIME, F. L.
BORTEN, H. J.
  children's
BOWERS, M. K.
BOYKA, L. J.
BRENNER, B. J.
  children's
BRILLER, S. W.
  non-fiction
BRINE, M. M.
  travel
BROWN, M. L.
BRUCE, J. M.
BRUFF, N.
BUCKLEY, H. E.
  juvenile
BYFIELD, B. N.
CALDWELL, F. M.
  non-fiction
CALDWELL, T.
  novels
CALLAHAN, S. DeS.
CASPARY, V.
  fiction, screenplays
CHAMPAGNE, M. M.
CLARK, M.
  medical
CLARK, M. G.
  mysteries
CLEMENT, J. T.
CORBETT, E.
  fiction
CORBIN, C. R.
  marketing
COUDERT, J.
  cooking, advice
CRANE, C.
CRAWFORD, J.
  autobiography
CRUSE, H.

CULLMAN, M. W.
  non-fiction
CURTIS, C. M.
  non-fiction
DAHL, A.
DANA, B.
DANIEL, A.
DANIELS, A. K.
  non-fiction
DAVIS, M. K.
  music
DAWKINS, C.
  fiction, drama
DEAN, V. M.
  world affairs
DeLAURENTIX, L. B.
DEVINE, J.
DICKSON, S.
  financial
di VALENTIN, M. A. M.
  fiction, non-fiction
DOLSON, H.
DONNA, N.
DORWORTH, A. G.
  economics
DRALLE, E. M.
ELSON, R. M.
  education
ETS, M. H.
  children's
FABER, D. G.
  children's
FEAGLES, A.
  children's, mystery novels
FIEDLER, J. F.
FIRESTONE, S.
  Feminism
FIRESTONE, L.
  decorating, beauty
FITZGERALD, C. M.
FLANNERY, N. F.
  homemaking
FLEISCHBEIN, Sr. M. C. F.
FLEMING, A. M.
  young people
FLETCHER, A. W.
  women's
FLETCHER, H. J.
FOX, R.
  alcoholic studies
FREEMAN, A. H.
FREEMAN, L.
  psychoanalysis
FREEMAN, R. S.
  children's, dolls
FRIEDAN, B.
  Feminism
FRIEDMAN, E. E.
FRIERMOOD, E. H.
  juvenile fiction
FRITZ, J. G.
  children's
GAM, R. F.
GARDNER, J. LeM.
GARRETT, A. J.
  non-fiction
GELLIS, R. J.
  fiction
GLUBOK, S.

GOLDFARB, L. B.
  children's
GOLDFRANK, H. C.
  juvenile fiction, non-fiction
GOLDIN, A.
GOLDSON, R. L.
  flower arranging
GOTTLIEB, R. G.
  juvenile
GRAU, S. A.
  fiction
GRAHAM, V.
GREEN, S. G.
GREER, R. E.
  non-fiction
GROCH, J.
  young people's
GRUBER, R.
GRUMBACH, D. I.
  non-fiction
HALL-QUEST, O. W.
  juvenile non-fiction
HANSL, E. VomB.
  music
HARRIETT
  juvenile
HATCH, C.
HAWES, E. J.
  fiction
HAYS, E. R.
  biographies, novels
HEIN, L. E.
HELFMAN, E. S.
  juvenile non-fiction
HELLMAN, L.
  playwright
HEMINGWAY, M. W.
  non-fiction
HENNE, F.
  library science
HILL, E. S.
  fiction, non-fiction
HIMMELFARB, G.
  history
HOLL, A. H.
  children's
HOOVER, H. B.
  nature
HOOVER, K. O'D.
  opera
HOPE, E. S.
HOPF, A. L.
  juvenile science fiction
HOPKINS, J. E.
HULL, E. M.
  fiction, non-fiction
HULL, H. R.
  mystery
JACKER, C. L.
  non-fiction, juvenile
JAHODA, G.
  novels
JEFFREY, M. M.
  novel
JOBES, G. B.
  fiction, non-fiction
JONES, B.
  non-fiction

JORDEN, E. H.
language textbooks
KAMINS, J.
KARL, J. E.
KAUFMAN, B.
KAUFMAN, S. E.
KAY, H.
juvenile
KAY, M. V.
young adults
KEATS, S.
non-fiction, music
KELSEY, A. G.
children's, religious
materials
KENNEDY, F. R.
abortion
KENNETH, C.
novels
KERMAN, G. L.
KIRSHNER, G. I.
KLAGSBRUN, F. L.
KLEIN, L. G.
juvenile picture
KONRAD, E.
KRANIDAS, K. C.
fiction
KRANTZ, H. N.
children's
KRAUS, B.
code, books
KREIG, M.
medicine
KUSKIN, K. S.
juvenile
LAKLAN, C.
sports
LANG, M. M.
LAUBER, P. G.
children's fiction, non-
fiction
LEMBO, D. MacD.
books
LENCI, M. Z.
LeSHAN, E. G.
psychology
LEVIN, M. O.
juvenile, teen
LEWIN, M. E.
non-fiction, women
LEWIS, C. L.
children's
LIEBERS, R. L.
non-fiction, children's
fiction
LINK, M. C.
sea diving
LIST, I. K.
juvenile non-fiction
LOBSENZ, A. F.
juvenile fiction
LONERGAN, P. J.
children's
LOWELL, J.
humor
LUCKHARDT, M. C.
LUDLAM, Y. deJ.
LYNCH, P. K.
LYND, Dr. H. M.
sociology, psychology

MACDONALD, Z. K.
juvenile
MacINNES, H.
novels, plays
MARGARET, H.
MANNES, M.
MARK, P. D.
fiction
MARKS, E. B.
careers
MASON, M.
fiction, poetry
MAXWELL, N. H.
fiction, non-fiction
MAXWELL, Sr. M. H.
non-fiction
McCLINTON, K. M.
antiques
MEAD, M.
anthropology
MEESE, M. F.
novels
MERRILL, J. F.
children's
MILES, B. B.
juvenile
MILLETT, K.
Feminism
MILLER, A. McC.
MILTON, S. F.
advertising, copy writing
MOERS, E.
MOORE, A. C.
MOORE, M. C.
poetry
MOSESSON, G. R.
non-fiction
MORHAIM-KELRICH, V.
NARELL, I. P.
NATCHEZ, G.
reading
NATHAN, A. G.
juvenile non-fiction
NEVILLE, E. C.
fiction
NIN, A.
novels, non-fiction
OLDS, H. D.
juvenile
O'NEILL, M. L.
junior, educational
screen plays
ORR, M. C.
OWENS, R. B.
poetry, plays
OZICK, C.
PALEN, J. M.
fiction, non-fiction
PARISH, P.
children's
PAULI, H. E.
non-fiction, children's
PEREIRA, I. R.
poetry, light, form
PICKEN, M. B.
sewing
POGREBIN, L. C.
POPHAM, E. L.
business education
PREMINGER, M. M.

RAEBECK, L. R.
children's, educational
RAMMEL, H. C.
RAND, A.
novels
RAND, A.
guides
RASKIN, E. L.
non-fiction
RAYWID, M. A.
READ, G.
REICE, S. S.
REY, Sr. M. D. R.
juvenile
RIVLIN, H. A. B.
ROBERTS, S. F.
witches, cookbooks
ROBOTTI, F. VonS.
cooking, non-fiction
RODMAN, M. W.
children's
ROGERS, D.
psychology
ROLLIN, B.
ROSENBERG, N. S.
children's
ROSMOND, B.
ROSS, I.
fiction, non-fiction
ROSSE, A.
ROSTENBERG, L.
printing
RUKEYSER, M.
poetry, prose, films,
juvenile
SACHS, H. G.
non-fiction
SAKOL, J.
SAMUELS, G.
SAURO, R. C.
juvenile
SAVARESE, J. A.
fiction, poetry, non-fictio
SCHERMAN, B. K.
non-fiction
SCHOR, R. K.
non-fiction, poetry
SCHREIBER, F. R.
SCHREIBER, J. L.
SCHROEDER, E. S.
religious
SCHULDER, D. B.
law
SCHULTZ, E. M.
non-fiction
SCHWABACHER, E. K.
SCOTT, L.
non-fiction
SCOTT, N. A.
novels
SCOVEL, M. S.
poetry
SEAMAN, B. R.
non-fiction
SHAPP, M. S.
series
SHAW, R.
SHORE, W.
SIMON, M. L.
juvenile fiction

SIMPSON, J. I.
cookbooks
SLOANE, P.
art instruction
SLOBODKINA, E.
children's
SMITH, J.
Russia, women
SOLOMON, B. F.
STABILE, T.
STECKLER, P. S.
trade books
STEINEM, G. M.
STERLING, D.
juvenile
STERN, M. B.
STEVENSON, J.
biography, travel, fiction
STEWART, R.
novels, historical novel
STILLMAN, F. J.
poetry, manual
STROWBRIDGE, C. C.
SUBA, S.
SUSANN, J.
novels
SUTTON, M. B.
juvenile mystery
TABER, G. B.
non-fiction
TALBOT, C. J.
juvenile
TANNENBAUM, B. G.
juvenile science
TAYLOR, A. L.
TENSEN, R. M.
children's
THOMPSON, B. A.
TOWNSEND, D. McF.
TRAHEY, J.
TRILLING, D.
TROTTA, G.
UNTERMEYER, J. S.
VANDERBILT, G.
VAUGHN-JACKSON, G.
VOGEL, F. H.
VOGEL, H. W.
WALDO, M.
food, travel
WATANABE, R. T.
WEINGARTEN, V. B.
WELCHER, R. M.
juvenile
WEINER, F. C.
"how to," guide
WELLER, E. T.
history
WELLS, H.
juvenile
WHITE, H. C.
WHITE, N. B.
children's
WILEY, M. L.
WILKENS, E.
WILSON, H. Van P.
home, gardening
WINCHESTER, A.
antiques
WOLF, J. L.
WOODMANSEE, M. R.

YOUNG, M.
ZATURENSKA, M.
poetry
ZAVIN, T. S.

3-F

AVERILL, E. H.
illustrator
BENDICK, J. G
illustrator
BERNSTEIN, L. B.
BORTEN, H. J.
illustrator
BRYSAC, S. B.
photos
BYFIELD, B. N.
illustrator
GOLDFARB, L. B.
illustrator
GRICALCONI, A.
illustrator
KUSKIN, K. S.
illustrator
MOSELEY, A. S.
book designer
O'HARA, R. E.
compiler, multi-media
SLOBODKINA, E.
illustrator
SUBA, S.
illustrator
VAUGHAN-JACKSON, G.
illustrator, children's
WELCHER, R. M.
art, illustrator

3-G

COLLETT, N. J.
PATTERSON, V. H.

3-H

BLACKER, H.
BOYKA, L. J.
COLLETT, N. J.
PATTERSON, V. H.
TRINER, A.

3-I

JENNINGS, G. F.
bibliography
MILLSPAUGH, D. R.

4-A

BERNSTEIN, A.
BUTLER, K. R.
CALLAWAY, R. H.
DAVIS, G. S.
DAVIS, J. L.
audio-visual
FELDMAN, G. S.

FOX, F. P.
FROOKS, D.
GRISWOLD, D.
public relations newsletter
HILL, M. E.
REID, B. G.
REID, H. R.
SCHIFF, D.
SEIDMAN, J. K.
WYCKOFF, E. H.
YOUNG, M. C.

4-B

MOREAU, L. M.

4-D

ADAMS, J. W.
good living
ADDIS, M. L.
ALDRIDGE, C. L.
women's
ALEXANDER, S.
AMES, E.
etiquette
BALAKIAN, N. H.
book reviews
BARROW, E. Q.
family living
BERNSTEIN, A.
BISSELL, E. McM.
women's
BOWMAN, L.
newsletter
CAIN, R. K.
society
CHASE, M. B.
CLAIR, V. F.
school
COLBY, E.
drama
CREASY, K. S.
women's
CURTIS, C. M.
women's
DOHERTY, A. M.
food
DOTY, J. G.
women's
DREIFUS, C.
news
ELVIN, E. I.
food
FISCH, J. J.
city
FORGANG, I. F.
shopping
FRASER, J. L.
family news
GANZ, I.
GARDELLA, K.
radio, TV
HARRINGTON, K. S.
women's
HERRIDGE, F.
drama, movie
JACOBS, M. J.

JONES, B.
garden, home
KANTOR, K. P.
fashion
KARNS, F. H.
drama, movie
KLASS, B. M.
women's
KRASNER, J. D.
women's
KRAVITZ, G.
KRUUSE, E.
KUSHNER, T. D.
marketing
LaRUE, A. C.
women's
LePINE, I. R.
society
LOPEZ, M. G.
women's
MASSOW, R.
women's, magazine
McELDOWNEY, P. E.
McHARRY, E. P.
MIKKANEN, M. I. E.
family
MILLER, N.
women's
MOGAVERO, J. N.
NASON, N. C.
education
NEWMAN, L. J. T.
NEY, E. M.
women's
OMMERMAN, B.
fashion
PATTERSON, A. S.
society
PRESTON, R.
fashion, beauty
PUSCZC, A. V.
fashion
QUA, E. H.
REID, B. G.
ROGERS, S.
home furnishings
SADTLER, B. K.
fashion
SCHIFF, D.
SCHURMACHER, S. J.
women's, society
SLACK, S. L.
women's
SMITH, R. I.
women's
STONE, M. M.
women's
THOMAS, K.
fashion
TOTH, M. H.
women's
WHITFORD, M. D.
social
WOODS, B. A.
WYCKOFF, E. H.

4-E

AMON, R. S.
reporter

BELL, B. S.
staff
BERNSTEIN, A.
feature
BLAHA, M. S.
editorial
BOYKA, L. J.
theatre reviewer
BROWN, M. M.
columnist
CARROLL, K. L.
movie critic, writer
COLBY, E.
drama film critic
CONNER, S. R.
reporter
CRAM, M. C.
columnist, horses
DELATINER, B. A.
TV critic
DOREN, M. N.
reporter
FLYNN, B. K.
correspondent
FRANZBLAU, R. N.
columnist
GOLDSTEIN, M. S.
reporter
GREENHOUSE, L. J.
reporter
GUARINO, A.
movie critic
HEARST, A. M.
columnist
HERZIG, D.
reporter
JOHNSON, H.
music critic
KENNEDY, F. R.
columnist
KETTEMAN, K.
columnist
KIRK, C.
feature
KLEMESRUD, J. L.
reporter
KRUMEICH, D. M.
reporter
KUSHNER, T. D.
reporter
LICHTENSTEIN, G. R.
reporter
MacLEOD, B. B.
drama critic
MATTHEWS, A. McI.
columnist
McMULLAN, P. E.
reporter
MOORE, C. S.
columnist
NEMY, E.
reporter
RECKERT, C. M.
financial reporter
REIF, R. M.
reporter
REINER, C. E.
reporter
SAMUELS, G.
staff

SCARBROUGH, L. C.
science
SCHETTERER, J. T.
reporter
SIMMONS, J. H.
music critic
SMITH, R. I.
travel columnist
SPENCER, M. D.
science
VAN GELDER, L. E.
reporter
WILSON, T. N.
reporter
YUNCKER, B.
medical, science

4-F

BOTTINI, I. G.
designer, illustrator

5-A

AYRES, P. M.
AUERBACH, V.
retail promotion
BAER, J. L.
public relations
BLACK, C. P.
special advertising
BOLSTER, J. N.
merchandising,
promotion
BOWER, R. A.
promotion, public
relations
BRADLEY, D. H.
BRIAN, D.
creative
BUHAGIAR, M.
story development
CALDERON, E. G.
art
CELLI, A.
reader relations
CHAPMAN, L. M.
COTTON, D. W.
de la SALLE, C. M.
fashion
DE MARIO, J. J.
production
DEMING, B.
FEDDER, F. R.
FRIES, M. L.
GASSERT, S. A.
public relations
GILMORE, A. A.
promotion
GRANT, J. C.
GUINAN, P. D.
GUTMAN, J. F.
editorial
HARDY, M.
production
HOLLAND, H.
advertising, exhibits

HUSTED-ANDERSON, A.
editorial board
JAMES, M. V.
research, sales
JOHANSEN, J. M.
research
JOHNSON, E. S.
advertising
KLESH, C. B.
KNAPIK, D. M.
production
KRAFT, M.
homes, decorating
LEE, F. H.
LEVINTHAL, S.
public relations
LOCKWOOD, L.
editorial section
LOCKWOOD, M.
advertising
LOOMIS, C. J.
board of editors
MACDONALD, N. M.
radio-TV publicity
MANNING, E. R.
institutional sales
McKIBBIN, B. C.
marketing
NEBEN, J.
merchandising,
promotion
PARKER, J. B.
editorial promotion
PRICE, J. M.
RICE, T. H.
press information
REED, J. H.
business, advertising
SANEHOLTZ, B. J.
consumer services
SAUNDERS, R. A.
editorial
SCHMIDT, A. G.
research
SCHULTZ, E. H.
art
SEEBACHER, S. S.
SEIDMAN, J. K.
SEVERN, S.
production
SHANNON, S. McN.
promotion
SHOUSE, L.
sales service
SILLS, L. G.
promotion
SMILEY, J. T.
consultant
SMITH, M. A.
STACK, B.
merchandising
SWARZMAN, S. J.
apparel advertising
VILAR, C. M.
merchandising
VREELAND, D.
WAGNER, J. S.
special projects
WALLACE, L. A.
WECKSLER, S.
international

WHITE, H. H.
advertising
WINTER, C. S.
art

5-B

HEINZE, L. H.
MOREAU, L. M.
PHIPPS, S. W.
editor
STOUT, V. C.

5-C

CALABRO, Dr. N.
marketing consultant
DUKE, J. S.
market development
BREENBERG, B. E.
representative
MOORE, E. M.
merchandising
MOSHER, M. E.
circulation
ROSS, P.
STURGES, J. C.
WEBER, R. C.

5-D

ABRAMOWITZ, S. I.
feature
ADAMS, E. F.
home economics
ADAMS, R. H.
decorating
ADAMS, S. P.
home equipment
AINSWORTH, N. R.
manuscript
ALEXANDER, S.
ANDERSON, J.
contributing
ARNOTT, A.
home equipment
BADGER, P. B.
letters
BAER, B. L.
BAER, J. L.
BANNON, B. A.
BARKER, J. M.
fashion
BAYER, A.
BECHTOS, R.
international
BENFORD, J.
fashion
BENSON, L. J.
merchandising
BERKELEY, E. P.
architecture
BERTIN, N. M.
beauty
BIRK, E. P.
copy
BISCHOFF, C. L.

BISHOP, C. B.
decorating
BLACKWELL, B. T.
BLAKEMORE, B.
BOND, B. J.
BRADLEY, D. H.
BROCK, C. L.
food
BROWER, B. M.
copy, travel
BROWN, H. G.
BROWN, R. M.
photo
BROWNE, R. B.
BUCKLEY, P. L.
BURKET, H. W.
BURNLEY, R. B.
home equipment
BUTLER, M.
beauty
BUTLER, R. B.
CADDEN, V. L.
CAMACHO, M.
CANNON, P.
roving gourmet
CANTWELL, M.
CARBINE, P. T.
CARROLL, A. Z.
movie
CHANEY, S.
CHARNEE, N. O'C.
CHENEY, R. H.
CHRISTOPHER, M. B.
broadcast
CLARK, E. M.
decorating
COFFIN, A. G.
COFFIN, P.
modern living
COHEN, S. J.
COMSTOCK, N. E.
COTTON, D. W.
CRANDALL, N.
book reviews
CRANE, C. L.
contributing
CRANE, L. G.
CUMMINS, L. L.
DALY, M. V.
shopping
DANDIGNAC, P.
DAVERN, J. M.
DAVIDSON, M. E.
home management
DAVIDSON, M. E.
home management
DAVIDSON, R. B.
contributing
DAVIS, E. L.
book review
De JONG, M.
DEVLIN, P.
contributing
DeWITT, C. K.
DINWIDDIE, A.
contributing
DOBELL, M.
DONOVAN, B. S. M.
DORAN, P. A.
fashion
DuBROFF, P. C.

ELKON, D. McK.
  fashion
FAGERSTROM, D. I.
  research
FALES, J. L.
FENN, D.
FERRANTE, C. F.
FEUERSTEIN, B.
  fashion
FISCHL, I. P.
  youth
FORD, B. O'C.
FRANCES, E. B.
  special projects
FRANCIS, A.
FRANK, E. P.
  articles
FRIEDMAN, G. G.
  fashion, china, glass
GAINES, E. Q.
GALLAGHER, R.
GARDINER, N. T.
  beauty
GELLER, E. C.
GERHARDT, L. N.
GIBSON, M. B.
GILBERT, M. T.
  international
GILBERT, R. H.
  section
GIRSON, R.
  book review
GITTELSON, N.
  special projects
GLASER, A. C.
GLENN, R. D.
GOLDEN, S. S.
  contributing
GOLDIN, A. M.
GOLDSMITH, B.
  contributing
GOLDSMITH, J. I.
GOUGH, M.
GRAVES, E. McK.
GRIEST, E. P.
GROSS, A.
GUINNESS, G.
  contributing
GUTMANN, J. F.
GUTSTEIN, L. A.
HAHN, V. D.
  decorating
HALM, M. J.
HAPPEL, M. M.
  food
HARVEY, M. K.
HATCH, C.
  guidance book
HAUPT, E. A.
HAVENS, S. E.
HENKEL, M. N.
  beauty
HENRY, M. R.
  feature
HERSHEY, L. O.
HICKEY, M.
  public affairs
HIGGINS, D. L.
HOVEY, K. K.
  fashion

HUDSON, P. D.
  radio-TV
HUSTED-ANDERSEN, A.
JACKSON, K. G.
  contributing, book review
JACOBSON, S. L.
JASOUS, J. M.
  fashion
JOHNSON, B. P.
JOHNSON, M. L.
  contributing
KANISHER, M.
  beauty
KAPSTEIN, D. M.
  fashion
KASTBERG, A. W.
  decorating
KAUFMAN, E. D.
  copy
KELLOGG, C.
KEMPNER, N. S.
  contributing
KINS, G. S.
  society, diplomatic
KLESH, C. B.
KOLTUN, F. L.
  travel
KONER, S. T.
  articles
KOPMAN, E. H.
KRAFT, V.
KUH, J. D.
KUH, K.
  art
LANDAU, G. H.
LAUDA, F. S.
  food
LEATHERBEE, M. L.
  travel
LEVINE, S. B.
LEVY, B. W.
  women's fashion
LEVY, P. S.
  fiction
LEWIN, S. G.
  design
LEWIS, M. W.
  health, beauty
LIBMAN, M.
LIPMAN, J.
LIVINGSTON, K. Z.
  feature
LOCKWOOD, L. P.
LOOMIS, C. J.
LURIE, D. M.
LUTER, Y.
  bureau chief
MAGER, J. A.
  fashion credits
MAJOR, G. H.
MALAMUD, P. C.
MARIAUX, H. L.
  home furnishings
MARKEL, H.
  articles
MARKEL, S. R.
MARKS, M. B.
MATTHEOS, E. R.
MAYES, A.
  marketing

McCARTHY, R. C.
McEVOY, M. S.
McMURRER, M. C.
MELLEN, H. A.
  fashion
MERCER, M.
  feature, consultant
MEYER, C.
MICHEL, J. H.
  contributing
MILES, L.
  sewing
MILO, M.
  health, beauty
MINTZ, J. M.
MOLTER, R. J.
  food
MORRIS, G. A. G.
  fashion
MUECKE, M. M.
MYERS, J. F.
NAISMITH, S.
NELSON, J. W.
NEUWIRTH, P. T.
NEWMARK, S. E.
  feature
NOLTE, J. A.
OBREN, S. M.
  beauty
O'BRIEN, M. E.
OWETT, T. H.
  fashion
PAINE, A. W.
PEACOCK, M. W.
PELLEGRINO, V. Y.
  articles
PENNEY, A. D.
  beauty
PLAUT, G. A.
  fashion
POMEROY, R. F.
  women's, service
PONTIUS, E. H.
PORTRAIT, E.
  fashion, beauty
POWELL, M. L.
  home
REDFORD, R.
REICE, S. S.
  youth
RHOADS, G. E.
RIPP, J. E.
  movie
ROCHE, M. McD.
ROGERS, C.
ROLLIN, B.
ROOT, L. S.
  science, medicine
ROSMOND, B.
  fiction
ROSS, R. N.
RUSH, A. F.
  household equipment
RUSSELL, B. A.
  copy, features
RUSSELL, M. E.
SAFRAN, C.
SALZBERG, E. M.
  copy
SANDERS, M. K.

SAUNDERS, R. A.
SCHORR, T. M.
SEEBACHER, S. S.
SEGAL, J. A.
  fashion
SEWELL, S. W.
SHEEHY, G. H.
  contributing
SHEMANSKI, F.
SHERRILL, S. B.
SIEGEL, M.
SIGRIST, H. Q.
SINGER, M. R.
SMITH, J.
SMITH, M. A.
SMITH, M. C.
SMITH, N. O'L.
  patterns
SPRAKER, N. G.
STEINEM, G. M.
  contributing
STICHT, E. M.
  food
STOIANOFF, E. A.
  fiction, poetry
STUART, N. G.
  fiction
SULLIVAN, E. R.
SULLIVAN, M.
SWEED, P.
TARNAWSKY, P. W.
  book
TAYLOR, J.
  shopping
TOLLES, M. D.
TROTTA, G.
  feature, travel
VAN WAGENEN, P. P.
  beauty, metropolitan
VESPA, M. C.
VOLTOS, D. V.
WALKER, A. E.
  decorating
WALLACE, M. V.
  travel
WATERFALL, B. L.
WATSON, C. H.
WEISS, M. R.
  photography
WHITE, H. K.
WHITE, N.
WHITNEY, R. R.
WILEY, M. D.
WINCHESTER, A.
WINKELHORN, K. M.
  fashion
WOLFF, S. S.
WYNN, J. L.
YATES, M.
  articles
ZACK, D.
ZEMLANSKY, N.

5-E

BROTHERS, J. B.
  columnist
BROWNE, R. B.
  art critic

CADDEN, V. L.
CALVERT, P. C.
  correspondent
CANNON, P.
  columnist
CRANDALL, N.
  book reviews
CRIST, J.
  film critic
EFRON, E. C.
  staff writer
FURNESS, B.
  columnist
HAMBLIN, D. J.
  staff writer
HARDY, H. N.
  staff writer
HOBSON, S. S.
  columnist
JOHNSON, B. P.
  staff writer
KAEL, P.
  movie critic
LEVIN, K.
MALAMUD, P. C.
  feature reporter
MARKS, M. B.
MEYER, C. H.
  staff writer
MONTGOMERY, C. N.
  columnist
PAVIA, N. E.
  art writer, critic
PFEIFFER, S. S.
  correspondent
ROBINSON, P.
  copywriter
SAVARESE, J. R.
SPRAKER, N. G.
STASIO, M. L.
  theatre critic
TUTEN, S. M.
WARE, C. C.
  reporter
YOUNG, L. P.
  writer, reporter

5-F

BILA, B. C.
  artist
CALIENDO, N. A.
  artist
DeSZEKELY, E. B.
  graphic artist
LEVIN, K.
  artist, photographer
RATHGEB, M. M.
ROSSE, A.
  illustrator
STEINBERG, C. S.
  artist
SYDLOW, J. G.
  photographer
WEISSLEDER, R. L.
  artist

5-G

SCHUSTER, I.

5-H

JAMES, M. V.
  sales
RATHGEB, M. M.
  promotion
REARICK, K. M.
  fashion, home
    furnishings
ROBINSON, P.
  promotion, copywriter
TILLINGHAST, P. Van H.

5-I

BECKERMAN, M. R.
  editorial
BRODY, L. G.
  market research
CALABRO, Dr. N.
  operations research
CALIENDO, N. A.
  art
CAPRIONI, J. S.
  market
CARSON, L.
  editorial
CLARKSON, J. N.
  editorial
FISCHER, J. H.
  editorial
FURNISS, M. Y.
  editorial
GORDON, L. S.
  editorial
GORDON, P. N.
  editorial, TV
JAMES, M. V.
McCALMONT, L. A.
  editorial
MICHAELIS, I. K.
  editorial
MULL, J. A.
  art
MUMBAUER, R. K.
  test kitchens
RABBIA, A. M.
  editorial
SANCHEZ, E. K.
  education
SCHACHNE, M.
  picture
SCOTT, A. C.
  editorial
TETLOW, K. C.
TYLER, A. G.
WANNER, S. H.
  editorial
WARE, C. C.
  editorial
WASHBURN, S. S.
  editorial
YOUNG, L. E.
  editorial

6-A

ALLOGGIAMENTO, N. T.
  media
ANDRY, D. B.
  public relations
AYRES, M. A.
AZORIN, E. S.
BARRY, A. M.
  media
BARTOS, R. R.
  creative research
BASCH, F. S.
BEAUCHAMP, B. G. E.
BERCKMANN, E. J.
  home economics
BERGANE, V.
  media
BERKOER, H.
  production, media
BERMAN, M.
BERNSTEIN, L. C.
  creative
BORLAND, J. S.
  radio-TV
BRANDWYNNE, J.
BUTLER, N. W.
  media
CADWELL, F. M.
COHEN, M. C.
  media
CONNELL, E. B.
CULLEN, B. M.
  broadcast
DaCOSTA, J.
  media, information,
    analysis
DUBE, M.
DULEY, P.
  office operations
EDDY, E. S.
  creative
EGGER, E.
  marketing research
FAGAN, B.
  fashion
FLINN, N. M.
  media
FOXWORTH, J.
FREEDMAN, B. L.
  creative
FRIEDMAN, M. M.
  public relations
GARRETT, P. E.
GARTNER, D.
  market research
GERACI, L. R.
  creative
GERNGROSS, F. B.
GERRY, R.
  publicity
GIMBEL, E. S.
GOLDBERG, B. F.
  research
GORDON, R.
  media
GOULD, N. M.
GRAF, D. E.
  media
GREENE, I. B.

GREENE, J. M.
  media
GREENE, P.
  publicity
GREENFELD, I.
  copy
GRIFALCONI, A.
HALL, M. F.
HANIFORD, B. G.
  TV
HANNON, M. G.
  research
HARRINGTON, G.
HARRIS, S. S.
  research, TV
HECTOR, S.
HELLER, G.
  fashion, women's
    services
HOLTZMAN, E. F.
  marketing services
HYMAN, B.
JACKSON, B.
  research
JAFFE, J. P.
  research, marketing
KENT, L. J.
KENT, P.
  copy
KNUDSON, R.
  media
KOMINIK, E. N.
KORDA, R. F.
  creative
KOREY, L. B.
  creative
LAMBERT, J.
LAUSTED, E. M.
LAWRENCE, M. B. W.
LIPPMAN, A. T.
LUEDERS, H. H.
LYONS, J.
  creative
MAHONEY, H. M.
MARCORDES, H. I.
  TV-radio production
MARENUS, F. N.
  media
MARJOLLET, J. E.
  broadcast operations
MARTENS, G. E.
  public relations
MASLOW, P. F.
  art
MASSING, H. H.
McGOVERN, M. J. F.
McGUINN, M. P.
McNAMARA, R. A.
MEAD, P. E.
  media
MEINHARDT, M. E.
  print media
MILES, V. G.
MORRIS, A. Z.
  art
MORRISON, N. R.
  publicity
MOSELEY, A. L.
  creative

NELSON, C. S.
art
NEWMAN, H. W.
radio-TV
NOVACK, E.
NUCCIO, S. K.
ORTIZ, S. M.
creative
OVESEY, R. H.
PALADINO, J. E.
public relations
PARKER, L. L.
copy
PLUNKETT, O. M.
consultant
POLLACK, B. J.
POLYKOFF, S.
PRESNICK, L. C.
research
PROTAS, J. C.
copy
REX, H.
copy
RICHARDSON, F. M.
production
RINDLAUB, J. W.
consultant
ROBIN, T.
RYAN, S.
SANTI, T. A.
radio-TV
SCHIFMAN, Y. S.
SCHILLER, S. A.
art
SCHULZE, L. E.
SCHULTZ, N. J.
SEELE, H. M.
media services
SEIDENBERG, B. E.
media
SELCER, J. R.
media
SHEARIN, R. A.
creative
SHEPPARD, J. H.
research
SHERMAN, M.
SHIRLEY, B. E.
casting
SIMMONS, S. H.
SKELLY, F. R.
STEBLER, M. S.
broadcast business
STEINER, G. F.
public relations
STEWART, L. A.
copywriter, producer
STEWART, V. R.
STOCH, E.
STONE, M. J. O.
media
SUTTON, N. L.
creative
TIERNEY, D. M.
TOLLEY, E.
TRAHEY, J.
USOSKIN, J.
creative
VOISIN, E. S.
WALTERS, T. M.
art

WASSERMAN, A.
media
WATERMAN, H.
WEBBER, C. A.
WEISS, G. M.
TV-radio business
WELLS, G. D. B.
art
WEST, J. A.
WEST, J. F.
media
WHITE, A. B.
media
WITTNER, M. H.
WOLFF, J. L.
creative services
WOLFSON, S. O.
media
WORCESTER, D. F.
research, creative
YOUNG, S.
marketing research
ZIFF, R. B.
research
ZIMMERMANN, C. A.
client services

6-B

CHARIF, J.
TV
COHAN, C. K.
TV
DURR, J.
FRUMKIN, F.
TV producer
GOLDFARB, L. B.
GUTCH, G. H.
estimator, TV
HEPP, S. H.
TV
HEWITT, P. P.
TV
JONAS, M.
casting
KATES, J. B.
TV
KEOWN, K. D.
KUNZELMANN, L. A.
clearance
LAYMAN, P. F.
McCARDLE, D. M.
broadcast
PASHKIN, R. L.
PHOENIX, A. L.
business coordinator
QUINLAN, K. A.
ROSS, E. D.
casting
SMITMAN, S. E.
TV
TAPERT, M. A.
TV broadcast
TOOMEY, R. C.
TV casting
WORTHINGTON, D. M.
film-talent coordinator

6-C

ALLES, S. M.
media buyer, planner
BELMAN, I. G.
media buyer
BINKOVITZ, F.
media planning
BLAKE, E.
media buyer
BRUNNER, J.
radio buyer
COLE, S.
media buyer
DEMY, C. S.
DINEEN, T. E.
media negotiator
DOWLING, S.
women's services
ELIAS, M.
media planner
GAINEY, L. H.
media buyer
GROTE, P. M.
broadcast coordinator
HALLIWELL, P. C.
media planner, buyer
HITTER, T.
media buyer
LANGBORT, P.
MELHADO, P. E.
media buyer
OLMSTEAD, B. C.
media buyer
SCHUR, E. K.
media
TANNENBAUM, E. M.
broadcast buyer
WIDMANN, N. C.
broadcast buyer
ZWIRN, L.
media buyer

6-D

JOHNSON, B. P.
SCHNEIDER, R. M.
THIEL, E.
WEST, J. A.

6-E

ABRAHAMS, S. C.
BAER, M. V.
BENEDICT, S.
BOREL, H. D.
BUCK, S. B.
BURR, B.
COLLINS, J. M.
DANIELS, A.
DAUM, R.
DeLAN, S. L.
DICKES, M. J.
DOORLEY, L. M.
EICHELSDOERFER, M.
ENID, H.
ESTIN, L. S.
medical
FREDE, M. S.

FUTTERMAN, E. S.
GRIFFIN, J. E.
HARRIS, M. E.
HAYES, M.
ITO, D. E.
JOSTEDT, M.
KEOWN, K. D.
LACHER, F. R.
LANGDON, A.
LAWRENCE, N. J.
LEHMAN, L. M.
LEVENSTEIN, R.
LEWIS, A.
LITT, J. S.
MELHADO, P. A.
MERSEY, E. H.
MEZEI-DELBOL, V.
MILLER, P. S.
MOHLMAN, M. A.
MORSICATO, Y. M. L.
OSTROM, D. A.
PATTERSON, S. H.
PEABODY, B. K.
ROBERTSHAW, S. J.
SACHS, P. S.
SAMEK, S.
SIMONS, E. A.
TARSON, R.
WADE, E. C.
WAGNER, J.
WILLENS, D.
songwriter
VOELKER, C. V.

6-F

BODINE, P. R.
BRANCHOR, R.
BREAKSTONE, E. P.
HAMM, M. N.
JOLOWICZ, K. A.
home furnishings
ORTIZ, S. M.
WOLFE, A. M.
fashion

6-G

ABRAHAMS, S. C.
ALTOMARI, G. M.
BAER, M. V.
BROWN, B.
BROWN, B. B.
BUTLER, N. W.
CUSTIN, J. V.
public relations
DAULTON, S. M.
ECKERT, M.
FORMAN, P. P.
FREDE, H. S.
GLANTZ, G. S.
GRAF, D. E.
media
GRIFFIN, E.
HELLER, G.
HILL, J. D.
HOPKINS, D. F.
HYMAN, B.
INERFELD, J. B.

JAFFE, J. P.
LAWSON, C. S.
LeVAN, S. K.
LEWIS, J. W.
LICHT, J. F.
LINN, A. E.
LUCAS, H.
MAHONEY, H. M.
MANSFIELD, R. E.
MATEER, S. A.
MATICKA, M. C.
MORCH, S. T.
MORSICATO, Y. M. L.
NORMAN, J.
ROSDAL, G. S.
SCHOENTHAL, H. G.
SMITH, F. M.
SPENCER, J. R.
STEFANSSEN, S.
STEWART, L. S.
TIERNEY, D. M.
TOLLEY, E.
WAGNER, S.
sales promotion
WEBB, N. B.
WEBBER, C. A.
WOOD, J. H.
ZIMMERMAN, J. D.
ZWIRN, L.

6-H

COLE, J.
GOLDSTEIN, D.
HAMILTON, I.
publicity
HARRAGAN, B. L.
publicity
HENDRY, G.
promotion
KEATING, M. B.
corporate
KRAKOWSKI, L. H.
book promotion
KUHN, R. R.
PEAKE, M.
RYAN, G. J.
STEFANSSEN, S.
WILLENS, D.

6-I

BLACK, A. E.
CARACCIOLI
market
CHENOWETH, P. G.
RICHARDS, E. A.
ROTHMAN, R. G.
VERHINE, P. A.
WEISS, R.
YUSPEH, S. NeJ.

6-J

WILLENS, D.
singer

7-A

ADAM, K.
design counsel
ANDERSON, K.
pictoral productions
BACHNER, A.
film, TV productions
BAIN, E. E.
broadcast representatives
BALDY, M. J.
TV-radio producers
BAZZINI, R.
motion pictures
BEETON, D. LaF.
casting service
BENDER, M. K.
industrial design
BERGMAN, S. B.
motion pictures
BROWNE, F.
book design, production
COOPER, B. S.
film service
COTTONE, M.
CRISPO, D. H.
surveys, writing assignments
DARER, S. S.
film producers
DEEMS, B.
film productions
DINERMAN, H. S.
research company
DUFFY, H. K.
book consulting
FULLERTON, G.
market research
GILBERT, P. S.
media representatives
GILL, H. G.
media representatives
GREENBERG, D. S.
music company
GRIFF, B. D.
production company, TV
HARTLEY, E. V.
film producer
HESSEL, E. B.
films
HILL, C.
training, radio-TV
KAHN, F. G.
sales, marketing
KASS, B.
research company
KENNEDY, B. C.
marketing
KONRAD, E.
KOSSOFF, R.
consultant, film company
KEISER, J. L.
photography
KRETZMER, B. F.
marketing
LEVY, R.
film company
LYDON, P.
publisher, graphic company
MARTINEZ, H. G.
media services

MELFORD, D. A.
producers
MISKE, F. R.
motion pictures
MUNHALL, D. S.
productions
NARELL, I. P.
production
OPATOW, L.
marketing research
ORR, L. B.
production services
OSBORN, I. C.
design
PENTLAND, M. E.
marketing, selling
RADIN, H. K.
films
RIZZO, F. J.
market research
ROGERS, H. J.
TV productions
RONTOWSKY, D. H.
art studios
ROTCHSTEIN, J. A.
media promotions
SCOTT, L.
art associates
SLOBODKINA, E.
art development company
SOMAN, S. C.
film consultants
STEINBERG, B.
film service
STERN, M.
music composing
WALLS, E. J.
book-library programs
WAYNE, S.
film productions
ZAVIN, T. S.
broadcast music
ZEIDERS, B.
science book services

7-B

BROWN, K. L.
TV systems
CAMELLI, I. W.
CLARKE, L. J.
book production
COHEN, B. K.
marketing
DURHAM, M. C.
management firm
FAYE, D. R.
production company
GALLIN, M. S.
film company
HALL, H.
production company
HOLETON, S.
film consultant
HUBLEY, F.
film studios
KENNEDY, J. M.
production company
KOPELMAN, J. R.
TV production company

MARCUS, H.
TV production company
NISSENSON, M. C.
educational materials
O'BRIEN, M. E.
TV production company
O'MEARA, S.
productions
ORR, L. B.
production company
POPERNIK, C. H.
production company
RABITCHEFF, J. G.
film
SALOMON, A. L.
productions
SIDES, P. A.
productions
WALEN, J. M.
production company
WILSON, P. T.
animated productions
WINCHESTER, M.
production company

7-C

BROWER, S.
management consultants
HEMLOCK, A. C.
design firm
PEARSON, S. N.
market research
SCHWARTZ, H. G.
film broker

7-E

HOBSON, S. S.
film strips, records

7-F

CUNNINGHAM, J. A.
record company

7-G

KOLLER, A. H.
photo products company

7-H

BOLAND, I. O.
contest promotions
CORMAN, J. L.
record company
FERRANTE, G. S.
consultants
MAMPE, M. S.
record productions
PETERSEN, E. W.
research firm
SHEEHAN, B. A.
producers

VIGDERHOUSE, M. A.
specialized marketing

7-I

CONFORTI, L. R.
DELMAN, A.
picture
PEARSON, S. N.
marketing
SARMENTO, A. M. DeM.
international research company

8-A

BASSIN, A. K.
CRAWFORD, J.
De LUISE, H. M.
EHRLICH, R. G.
FRIEDMAN, F. Z.
GRUBER, L. J.
GUIDO, S. A.
HIGUERA, C.
HOOD, C.
LESLIE, K. D.
LONGO, P. G.
MANTIUS, M. E.
MULLER, M. H.
NELSON, E. A.
OLSEN, F. J.
SLOVER, B.
STEWART, I. C.
WATERS, E. C.
WESSMAN, L. T.

8-B

FOURTON, R. M. DeM.
TENNANT, P.
WALTER, M.
TV producer

8-C

BISHOP, R.
COWAN, G. C.
CREEL, J. F.
CURTIS, L.
DAVITT, J.
ENNIS, L.
FLYNN, S. K.
GIBSON, M. S.
HALL, D. J.
HUGHES, P. DeM.
KELLY, H. E.
LANE, M.
LYNCH, E. M.
MALE, M. H.
MARTINEZ, E. R.
McGRIFF, V. B.
MELVIN, S. G.
MOHLER, J. F.
O'BRIEN, M. H. L.
OLIVER, T. F.
STECKLER, P. S.
TERZIAN, H.

THOMPSON, H. K.
TOBIN, P. E.
VECCHIO, D. Van P.
WALTER, S. D.

8-D

BLANCHFIELD, N. M.
BYRNE, B. B.
FOLEY, H. M.
FRARY, G. L.
FUJARSKI, S. W.
GODDARD, M. E.
HOPE, B.
HUGGARD, M. E.
KINGHAM, E. S.
KROFSKY, J.
LINDEMANN, R.
MADDOX, Y. T.
MALONE, M. K.
MURRAY, C. O.
SAMPOGNA, A. DuF.
SCHILLING, R. A.
SHERMAN, J. B.
SMITH, P. S.
SODERBERG, J. M.
STEPP, A. W.
THOMPSON, M. L.
Van SICKLE, C. S.
WARREN, A. E.
WATROBSKI, C. M.
WEEKS, C. T.

8-E

ABERNATHY, J. K.
BURNHAM, L. E.
COLLER, L.
DAVIS, E. S.
KRAL, M. A.
McKEE, M. J.
SCHILDT, S.
SCOTT, A. T.
WENK, J.

8-F

BLANCH, R. D.
DAVIS, A. C.
FLYNN, S. K.
GABRIEL, E. N.
HASTINGS, S. B.
LEVINE, B.
SCHULTZ, I. B.
LINDEMANN, R.
STEPHENSON, H. R.
WARREN, A. E.
WELCHER, R. M.

8-G

ABRUZZO, M. L.
BATTISTINE, R.
BROWN, R. S.
BUDDE, J. F.
CHRISTIE, I.

DAHLHAUS, E. Van B.
GOLDBERG, P.
GOLDFARB, M. B.
GURWITT, H. B.
HARRIS, L.
HAYNES, V. E.
HILLPOT, M. T.
KEAVENY, J. D. K.
KENT, G. T.
LEAMAN, J. T.
MELVIN, S. G.
MONAGHAN, L. M.
MORELLI, A. B.
PARK, N. L. B.
PIRK, H.
SCHARF, F. C.
SCHWARTZ, R. R.
SMITH, V. W.
SOMERS, S.
STEWART, C. B.
THURSH, J. R.

8-H

ABRUZZO, M. L.
ALLEN, A.
BALDRIGE, L. K.
BALDWIN, M. K.
BARNETT, P. S.
BATTISTINE, R.
BISHOP, A. J.
BOMBA, L. P.
BORDEN, F.
BROWN, E.
BROWN, R. S.
BRUCE, E. H.
BUDDE, J. F.
BUHR, D. F.
publicity
CHRISTIE, I.
CLARK, M.
COCHRANE, P. B.
CURTIS, L.
DREWELOW, G. K.
FRARY, G. L.
GAUTHIER, L.
GEARY, M. L.
GOEDECKE, S. A.
GOLDBERG, P.
GREGG, Dr. D.
HALL, D. J.
HARRIS, J. L.
HARWOOD, S. D.
HAYES, M.
HAYNES, V. E.
HOPKINS, J. M.
HORN, L.
JOHNSTON, P.
KEAVENY, J. D. K.
KERMEEN, D. C.
KING, E. L.
KLARK, P. J.
KUNIAN, M.
LAMBERT, C. F.
LARSEN, C. S.
LEE, N. A.
LEVIN, F. M.
LINK, M. C.
LUDORF, P. J.

MALMGREN, L. C.
MARTIN, J. M.
McKEE, M. J.
MELVIN, S. G.
MERRILL, M.
MILLER, J.
MITCHELL, J. A.
MOHLER, J. F.
MONTGOMERY, P. H. H.
MORELLI, A. B.
MORRIS, H. I.
MURPHY, M. E.
ODOM, R. B.
OLIVER, T. F.
ORTNER, R. R.
PITTS, E. H.
REICHENBACH, A.
SACHS, H. G.
St. MARIE, S. S.
SALISBURY, A. T.
SCHARDING, G. S.
SCHARF, F. C.
SCHILDT, S.
SCHWARTZ, R. R.
SMITH, N. R.
SODERBERG, J. M.
STEWART, C. B.
TALL, E. A.
TEDESCO, A.
THORSON, M.
THURSH, J. R.
Van GELDER, J. P.
VERCINI, E. L.
WALSH, A. W.
WEIS, B. C. S.
WELSCHMEYER, M. L.
WEST, C. V.
WETTENSTEIN, B. A.
WHITE, R. B.
WOLCOTT, B. D.
YARMON, B. G.

8-I

GELB, C. P.
IZAKSON, E.
MAYER, E. A.
ODOM, R.

9-A

BLOCK, L. R.
religious
BRANDT, D. M.
reviews
BRENT, L.
overseas
CRISPO, D. H.
KORD, J. M.
KRAUS, H. L.
home furnishings
LEWIS, B. B.
reviews
MARLOWE, J.
reviews
WORLEY, E. D.

9-D

BLOCK, L. R.
  religious
BRADFORD, B. T.
  home decorating
BURKE, R. M.
  women's
CONNOLLY, M. J.
CROSBY, J. C.
  entertainment
DeSANTIS, F. S.
  beauty, fashion
GOLDBERG, L. C.
  women's news
HANAUER, J.
  book reviews
HUMPHREY, S. W.
  food
LAWRENCE, K.
  women's, broadcast
LEWIS, B. B.
  reviews
MARLOWE, J.
  reviews
McGURN, B. A.
MEYER, G. F.
  interior decorating
MICHELS, M. A.
MOHR, B.
MOORE, A. C.
O'SULLIVAN, J.
  women's
PAULEY, G.
  women's
PETERSEN, A. L.
  food
ROSE, D. B.
  parents, children
SCHREIBER, J. L.
  sewing
STAUNTON, H. M.
WEINER, E. H.
WOLFF, A. E.
  book reviews

9-E

BASSETT, E. E.
  news
BATTELLE, P. M.
  columnist
BOLTON, V. B.
  news features
BRADFORD, B. T.
  columnist
BROTHERS, J. B.
  psychology
CANARY, B. J.
  columnist
CRUSE, H.
  columnist
DAHL, A.
  columnist
FLOOD, E. G.
  correspondent
HANAUER, J.
  feature writer

HARNETT, L. M.
  columnist
HUMPHREY, S. W.
  correspondent
KAZICKAS, J. C.
  feature writer
KENNEDY, J.
  reporter, news features
KERR, A.
KISH, H.
  *columnist,
    correspondent*
KUHN, L. C.
  columnist
LANDERS, A.
  *columnist, human
    relations*
LEWIS, F.
  columnist
LOWRY, C. C.
  columnist-TV
LUNDGREN, R.
  columnist
LYON, B. A.
  columnist
McCORMACK, P. S.
  columnist
MICHELS, M. A.
  columnist
MOORE, A. C.
MORAN, S. K.
  sports
MYRENE, M. E.
  features
PAYETTE, V. E.
  columnist
PORTER, S. F.
  financial columnist
PRICE, M. B.
  radio news
REISS, S. S.
  columnist
SHAW, T.
  reporter
SHERR, L. B.
  writer
WEDEMEYER, D.
  reporter
WILKENS, E.
  columnist
YARMON, B. G.
  columnist

9-J

CRUSE, H.
  broadcaster

10-A

ALDRICH, G.
  publicity
ALTMAN, R. U.
  radio-TV
ANSBERRY, L. S.
ARMSTRONG, C. V.
  publicity
ARONSON, M. F.
BAKER, P.

BAMBERGER, G. G.
BARKAN, K. K.
  publicity
BARNES, G. O'D.
  radio-TV
BASS, D. B.
BEAUMONT, L.
BERLOWE, P. H.
BERMAN, M.
BERMAN, S. R.
BLAISDELL, A.
BOYD, S. W.
BROOKS, A. H.
BROWDE, H.
  editorial
BROWN, M. L.
BURDICK, V.
  publicity
CALVERT, P. C.
CARR, A. E.
  advertising
CEBALLOS, J.
  Feminist talent collective
CHESROWN, M. A.
CHURCHILL, J. R.
COLLINS, D.
  home, fashion
COOPER, E. A.
  radio-TV
COTT, B.
COX, C.
COX, P.
CREE, D. A.
  consultant
CRUMPACKER, B.
de HELLERMAN, M. C.
  financial
De NAVE, C. M.
DICKSON, S.
DUTOIT, A. L.
  creative services
FIRESTONE, L.
FITZSIMONS, E.
FLANNERY, N. F.
GALT, A. S.
GREENE, A. S.
GRISWOLD, D.
  newsletter publisher
GUERIN, J. K.
GUERIN, P.
GURA, J. J.
HACKER, N. G.
HALLOWELL, J. I.
HAMMER, R.
  publicity
HAMRA, R. M.
HARRIMAN, J. F.
  consumer information
HENSELL, H. E.
  education
HERBST, M. M.
ISAAC, M.
  radio-TV publicity
IWAMOTO, R.
JACOBSEN, E. M.
JAYMES, G. E.
JOBSON, M.
JONES, F. K.
KAIDEN, N.
  fine arts

KASMAN, A. J.
KATZANDER, S. S.
KLEIN, C. C.
KONRAD, E.
LaCAILLE, J. B.
LAIB, J.
LARSON, M. A.
LERNER, C. S.
  fine arts
LIVINGSTON, L. E.
LOACH, J.
LOBSENZ, A. F.
LOVE, N.
LUNDGREN, R.
MAILMAN, V. S.
MANNING, R.
MARSHALL, B.
  magazines
MARSHALL, G.
  home economics
McGOVERN, M. J. F.
MILLING, E.
MOORE, C. G.
  women's services
MORRISON, L. E.
NATHAN, E. S.
NEWMAN, J.
NOVINA, T.
  *home furnishings,
    publicity*
NUCCIO, S. K.
OLSON, M. A.
ORENTE, R. J.
OSBORNE, M. C.
  publicity
PENTLAND, M. E.
  publicity
PERL, E. F.
PHILLIPS, J. B.
PINKERTON, J. D.
PINSKER, E. L.
POLL, C.
READ, G.
REAGAN, C. A.
REGENSBURG, A. B.
REILLY, M. H.
  fashion
REU, S. H.
RICH, E. M.
RIEDINGER, R. W.
RILEY, F.
  women's
RILEY, N.
  women's news
RIXON, B. S.
SALB, J. H.
  promotions
SCHLOSS, S. S.
SCHOONOVER, J. W.
SHAPIRO, H.
SHEPHARD, G.
SIEGEL, E.
SINGER, N. S.
SLATER, H. S.
SMARGON, A.
  publicity
SMITH, R. W.
STUART, J. S.
SULLIVAN, B. S.
TANNER, B. R.

TREADWELL, E.
  sales promotion
WHIPPLE, J. F.
WILLET, R. S.

10-B

WALKER, M. T.
  producer, fashion shows

10-D

AUGELLO, D. A.
BROWDE, H.
CHRISTENSEN, S. M.
GRISWOLD, D.
WEINSTEIN, G. W.

10-E

COOPER, E. A.
DEVINE, J.
FREUDEMANN, T. DeC.
  women's news
SAVARESE, J. R.

10-H

ANGLUND, S. P.
COHLER, J. S.
DAVIS, G. S.
DORFMAN, C. K.
DRISCOLL, L. V.
  account supervisor
DUVALL, M. G.
FAGG, E.
FENNEL, M. T.
FLANNERY, N. F.
FRANCIS, J.
FREUDEMANN, T. DeC.
GALT, A. S.
GORDON, E. T.
JASON, A. L.
MAY, M.
MODELL, J.
O'CONNOR, J. K.
PATRICOF, P. E.
PITT, H. P.
PROTHRO, L. G.
  consumer products
RILEY, F.
ROSSI, S. McK.

10-I

CARACCIOLI, K. F.
  market analyst
GALANOPLOS, R.
  magazines

11

ANTOINETTE, Sr. M.
  audio-visual

BAHRINGER, E. S.
  consultant
BANNIGAN, B. G.
  music, art, religion,
  philosophy
BARRY, L. B.
  film company
BATTS, N. C.
  cataloger
BAYNE, E. C.
  publishing company
BERG, F. R.
  heraldic research
BIDA, O. S.
BURSTINER, E. L.
  magazine publishing
CESARIO, V. N.
  public service
CLEMONS, C. F.
  music
COWELL, R. F.
CURLEY, D. N.
  adult services
DEARCOPP, J.
  publishing company
DOBLER, L. G.
  magazine publishing
EDSALL, S. A.
EVANS, M. E.
  religious
FANCHER, P. N.
FIEDLER, J. F.
FITZ, C. M.
FLEISCHBEIN, Sr. M. C. F.
GETMAN, L. W.
  technical
GIDNEY, M. D.
GLAZER, S. M.
  publishing company
GODFREY, J. O.
GRIFFITH, J. G.
GRUEN, S. S.
  medicine
HALFON, A.
  education
HARSHE, F. E.
HAVILAND, L.
  historical reference
HEINZ, C. F.
  TV trade
HEITMAN, E. A.
  history
HUTCHINS, E. M.
  advertising agency
JENNINGS, G. F.
  publishing company
JENNINGS, J. S.
  technical services
KIRSCHNER, M.
  foreign language
KISLING, F. R.
KLEIN, L. G.
KRAMER, E. C.
LATANIOTIS, D. A.
  magazine publishing
McGOVERN, Sr. A. M.
McGRAW, M. H.
MOELLER, P. L.
  art-special collections
MOTZ, M. R.
  school libraries

MUNGER, N. T.
  advertising
NEMEYER, C. A.
NEWCOMB, D. D.
OKUN, L.
  radio-TV specialist
PARCHE, M. C.
  special library
PARKER, M. L. G.
PELTZ, M. O.
  opera archivist
PORTER, J. H.
POUNDSTONE, S. H.
PRZYWARA, Sr. M. B.
  religious
RICHARD, S. C. S.
ROLLINS, O. H.
ROSBOROUGH, J. L.
  reference, interloan
ROUNDS, G. W.
SALVATO, J. D.
SMITH, E. T.
  education
SMITH, H. E.
STAFFORD, I. E.
  school, audio-visual
SWANTON, I. W.
THOMSON, E. W.
VALENCIK, M. V. K.
VEDDER, M. H.
WATANABE, R. T.

12-A

ALEXANDER, D. A.
AMOURY, G.
BEARN, M. S.
BRANSTON, V.
BROD, R. H.
BROWNE-MAYERS, C. B.
CARROLL, V. J.
CAVALLARO, J. F.
COONEY, J. G.
CORREA, C. T.
CUNNINGHAM, E.
DonDERO, G.
FISHER, W. H.
FOX, R.
FREED, L. E.
GIBSON, M. C.
GILDER, R.
GOLDSTEIN, N.
GORNEY, S. K.
GRANT, B. M.
HALL, G. B.
HERMANN, M. M.
HIGGINSON, M. V.
HOOVER, K. O'D.
KENNEDY, F. R.
KRAUS, B.
KRAWITZ, R. L.
LAYLAND, K. J.
LEWIS, D. M.
LIST, C.
LOBSENZ, D. H.
MARA, T.
MARKHAM, M.
MARTIN, B. S.
MATHEWS, V. H.
McCORMACK, M. W.

McMILLEN, E. E.
MODELL, J.
MONAGHAN, C. I.
NYDELE, A.
PEARLMAN, E. B.
PREMINGER, M. M.
PRINCE, J. L. E.
READ, G.
RENNER, J. R.
REVILLON, L.
RIVERS, P. W.
ROBBINS, M. E.
ROBERTS, S. F.
ROSEN, J. A.
SCHAFRAN, L. H.
SKILLMAN, H. C.
SMITH, R. W.
STEIN, H.
THOMPSON, B. A.

12-B

BARTON, J.
COLTON, S. B.
LINDEN, K. B.
SHEARER, S.
SHEPARD, M. J.
STRAIGHT, B. W.
ZORNOW, E.

12-C

ROGGERS, J.

12-D

ALEXANDER, L. K.
AMBROSE, L. G.
ANASTASI, A.
ANSBRO, M. C.
BAILEY, M. E.
BAUER, E. M.
BERKELEY, E. P.
CREAGH, A. E.
CUNNINGHAM, S. M.
DIETZ, M. J.
di SERNIA, P. R.
DOUGLASS, P.
ELLER, G. C.
ERLICH, L.
EVERHART, J. M.
FAIN, H. McC.
FINK, J. E.
GREENE, V. O.
HAYNES, G. W.
KEATING, A. S.
KLIJN, T. S.
LANE, N.
LEONARD, J.
LEUBNER, S. E.
LOMAX, B. F.
LUDLAM, Y de J.
LYON, B. A.
MASSEY, R. L.
MELLEN, J.
MYERS, J. F.
O'BRIEN, M. E.
PEARCE, J. C.

POOL, T. H.
PREUSS, A. MacD.
QUINLAN, L. W.
RAMBACH, P. S.
SEWELL, S. W.
STEWART, L. A.
TAYLOR, A. L.
TWEEDY, M. J.
WHITTAKER, A. T.
WINSLOW, A.

12-E

CARROLL, V. J.
FINKE, B. F.
HERMAN, H. J.
MELLEN, J.
TUGGLE, M. A.
ZAGAT, C. E.

12-F

ABBE, E. M.
DEMARAY, B. L.
FRANKEL, C. S.
MARA, T.
WINTER, C. S.

12-H

AMES, D. D.
ANDERSON, L. J.
ANSBRO, M. C.
BENDEL, P. R.
BOORSCH, S. R.
BRADY, A. E.
BRIGHT, S. E.
CEBALLOS, J.
CHILD, L. A.
CHOO, E. C.
CONNOLLY, V. M.
DAWES, N. R.
DOBRUSHIN, S.
DONALDSON, M. F.
DUCAS, D.
EICHELBERGER, R. K.
FARRAR, M. M.
FENMORE, S. T.
FINN, J. L.
FOONER, H. G.
FOSTER, P. C.
FOWLER, E. M.
GILBERT, M. J.
HABICHT, E. J.
HAGER, L. W.
HENRY, M. C.
HERMAN, H. J.
HUGHES, M. E.
IANNIELLO, L. Y.
ILACQUA, A. A.
KEENE, R. R.
KELLEY, S. W.
LAMPMAN, N. E.
LANGEVIN, D. S.
LOMAX, B. F.
LuTOUR, L.
MASON, L. G.
MICHELFELDER, P. R. D.

MICHELSON, D.
MORAN, I. E.
MORRIS, E. L.
MURPHY, J. F.
NEW, A. L.
POMPONIO, F.
PUDNEY, B. A.
REY, Sr. M. D. R.
RICHARD, St. C. S.
ROMANOW, B. E.
ROSEN, J. A.
SHAW, E. R.
SHELLEY, S. S.
SILVERMAN, J. A.
SMOLENS, A. H.
SNYDER, I. S.
TILGHMAN, M. C.
TIMMERMANN, S.
TOWSLEY, A. C.
TYROLER, J.
Van BUREN, A. L. D.
Van DUSEN, E. W.
WAGES, E. V. P.
WALTER, B.
WARNER, A. R.
WILSON, R. F.
WOOD, B. E.
WURTENBURG, G. V.

12-I

COHEN, D. B.
SOUTHARD, H. F.

12-J

KORLE, E. S.
WAGES, E. V. P.

13-B

COOKSON, B. S.
KERMAN, G. L.
  director
RABITCHEFF, J. G.
SHEPARD, M. J.
  director, producer
STIFF, N. K.
  TV producer
TOD, D.
  producer
WHITEHEAD, M. I.
WINCHESTER, M.
  producer

13-D

ABBOTT, S. A.
ANDERSON, M.
AUERBACH, S. S.
BANDLER, R.
  copy
BARTH, D.
BERNKOPF, J. F.
BORNE, R. Z.
  medical

BRIFFAULT, H. H.
BRILLER, S. W.
CLAASEN, C.
  editorial consultant
CONLEY, S. E.
  drama
COUNIHAN, M. C.
  TV public service
DALY, Sr. E. J.
  religious
DANIELS, P. H.
  copy
DIETZ, M. J.
  garden
DUFFY, D. B.
GARRETT, A. J.
GROSS, S. C.
HACK, K. P.
HARRIS, J. L.
KIRK, L. D.
  consultant
KLAGSBRUN, F. L.
  consultant
KOESTLER, F. A.
MADOW, P. R.
  non-fiction
MAGID, N. L.
MERCER, M.
  consultant
MOORE, A. C.
NEAL, M. F.
O'MEARA, M. E.
  consultant
RUTHERFORD, K.
RYAN, E. M.
SANGER, J. O.
SCHERR, B. J.
SEYBOLD, G.
SHEMANSKI, F.
SLAUSON, M.
SONSINI, J. B.
  copy
STEINER-PRAG, E. F.
  indexer
STILLMAN, F. J.
TOD, D.
  film
WATANABE, R. T.
WOLF, S. A.
WOLFE, R. H.
  consultant

13-E

ABBOTT, S. A.
  *urban problems,
  Feminism*
AIMEE, Sr. M.
ALEXANDER, D. A.
  magazine
AMOURY, G.
  short stories
ANDERSON, A. S.
ANDREN, C.
AUERBACH, S. S.
BACMEISTER, R. W.
BAKER, E. F.
  economics

BAKWIN, R. M.
BARKER, R. J.
BARRY, A. M.
  magazine
BARTH, D.
  *theatre, art, medicine,
  travel*
BEATY, J. J.
BEAUDRY, Y. A.
  *magazine, education,
  religion, literature*
BEEBE, K.
  non-fiction
BEGNER, E. F.
  fiction
BELL, J. D.
BENEDICT, S.
  film, radio, printer
BENJAMIN, A. F. L.
  non-fiction
BERK, P. L.
BERNAY, B.
  correspondent
BESSER, M.
  magazine
BIEMILLER, R. C.
  fiction, non-fiction
BINGHAM, J. R.
  non-fiction
BIRD, C.
  non-fiction
BIRSTEIN, A.
  magazine
BORNE, R. Z.
  medical
BRAUDY, S. O.
  magazine
BRENNER, B. J.
BRIFFAULT, H. H.
BRILLER, S. W.
  magazine
BRINE, M. M.
  travel, adventure
BROWN, R. M.
  Feminism, poetry, other
BROWNMILLER, S.
  *magazine, Feminism,
  other*
BRUCE, J. M.
  articles, short stories
BRUNO, A. T.
  magazine
BRYANT, B. S.
  travel
BRYSAC, S. B.
CALLAHAN, S. deS.
CARLIN, K. S.
  professional
CARTWRIGHT, M. D.
  correspondent
CHAPMAN, P. A.
CLARK, M.
  science, medical
CLARK, M. G.
  stories, plays, poetry
CLEMENT, J. T.
  short stories, lyrics
CONLEY, S. E.
  drama
CONNELL, E. B.
  articles

CONNELL, L. F.
  *articles: health, human
    relations*
COUNIHAN, M. C.
  TV public service
CROSBY, J. C.
CRANE, C.
CRISPO, D. H.
  gags, scripts
CULLMAN, M. W.
CURRO, E. M.
  art
CURTIS, C. M.
  magazine
DANIEL, A.
  correspondent
DAVIDSON, L. A. D.
  poetry, travel features
DAVIS, G. S.
DAY, B.
  *non-fiction, articles,
    books*
DeLAURENTIS, L. B.
  poetry
de LEON, S. F.
  articles: education, other
DELMAN, A.
DEMING, B.
  Peace Movement, other
DIETZ, M. J.
  garden
DOBIE, W.
DOLSON, H.
  magazine
DRALLE, E. M.
DUFFY, D. B.
  reviews
DUKES, E. A.
EICHELBERGER, R. K.
FAGG, E.
FARSAGE, D. K.
  poetry, short stories
FEAGLES, A. McR.
  book reviews
FIELD, B.
  TV advertising, fashion
FLEMING, A. M.
FLETCHER, A. W.
  magazine
FLETCHER, H. J.
FOX, R.
  alcoholic studies
FRANZBLAU, R. N.
  articles, human relations
FREEMAN, L.
  psychoanalysis, other
FRIEDAN, B.
  *Feminism, psychology,
    education*
GAMORAN, M. G.
  stories, poems, articles
GENN, L. G.
  articles
GIBSON, G.
GIBSON, M. S.
GOTH, T.
  art, music, travel
GOTTLIEB, R. G.
GRANT, J. C.
  articles
GRAU, S. A.

GREER, R. E.
  articles
GROSS, S. C.
  reviews
HACK, K. P.
HANSL, E. vom B.
HASSO, S.
  composer, lyricist
HAUTZIG, E. R.
HAYS, E. R.
  fiction, magazines
HEATLY, M. R.
HEIN, L. E.
HEMINGWAY, M. W.
  articles
HENNE, F.
  library science
HERMANN, M. M.
  articles
HOBSON, S. S.
  Black history
HOOVER, H. B.
  non-fiction
HOPE, E. S.
HOPE, M. C.
  *social revolution, war,
    peace*
HORNADAY, M.
  journalist
IWAMOTO, R.
  *Japanese magazine,
    articles*
JAHODA, G.
  articles, poetry
KAMINS, J.
  radio, TV, stage
KAUFMAN, S. E.
  short stories, articles
KERR, A.
KIRK, L. D.
KISH, F.
KOESTLER, F. A.
  community relations
KOMISAR, L.
  Feminism, other
KORLE, E. S.
  correspondent
KRANIDAS, K. C.
  poetry, fiction
KREIG, M.
  science, medicine
KUHN, I. C.
LAKLAN, C.
  sports
LAM, G. L.
  education
LAMBERT, C. F.
LAMBERT, E.
  columnist
LAMBERT, J.
  film critic, features
LeSHAN, E. G.
  *psychology: sex,
    parenthood*
LAWNER, L.
  poet
LENCI, M. Z.
  travel
LEWIS, C. L.
  *social anthropology,
    children, families*

LINK, M. C.
LINK, M. C.
LINN, J. M.
LITT, I.
  advertising, publicity
LOVE, N.
LUDLAM, Y. de J.
  ghostwriter
LUDORF, P. J.
LUNDGREN, R.
MAGID, N. L.
MANNES, M.
MARKHAM, M.
MAXWELL, Sr. M. H.
  articles, poetry
MAYO, M. B.
  folklore
McBRIDE, E. S.
McCLINTON, K. M.
  antiques, art, other
McGURN, B.
  travel, fiction
MERRIAM, E.
  non-fiction, poetry
MEYER, G. F.
  decorating
MIEL, A.
MILLER, A. McM.
  publishing, TV
MILLER, J. M.
MOORE, A. C.
  articles
MORHAIM-KELRICH, V.
  film, stories, ghostwriter
MUFFOLETTO, A.
  home economics
NELSON, J. W.
OAKLEY, H. McK.
O'HARA, H.
  non-fiction
OLDS, H. D.
O'MEARA, M. E.
  city planning, other
ORENTE, R. J.
  poetry
OWENS, R. B.
  critic
OZICK, C.
  reviews, poetry, essays
PARK, N. L. B.
PASCHALL, J.
  marketing
PHILLIPS, F. McA.
PICKEN, M. B.
PITT, M. P.
  *history of girl scouts,
    other*
PRICE, J. E.
  reporter
RABITCHEFF, J. G.
RAMMEL, H. C.
  correspondent
RAND, A.
  skiing
REICE, S. S.
  articles, short stories
RITTER, N. S.
  TV
RIVLIN, H. A. B.
  Middle East history
ROBERTS, S. F.

ROOT, L. S.
  articles, play, filmstrips
ROSENBERG, N. S.
ROSS, M. D.
  journalist
ROSTENBERG, L.
  printing, publishing
RUTHERFORD, K.
RYAN, E. M.
  magazine, TV
RYDEN, H. E.
SANGER, J. O.
  non-fiction
SARA, D.
  graphology
SAUNDERS, B. H.
  articles, poetry, plays
SAURO, R. C.
  juvenile stories, poems
SAYERS, E.
SCHAFRAN, L. H.
  art critic
SCHERR, B. J.
SCHULTZ, E. M.
  poetry
SCOTT, A. T.
  sales promotion
SCOTT, N. A.
  articles, stories
SCOVEL, M. S.
SEAMAN, B. R.
  medicine, psychology
SEYBOLD, G.
  business
SHAPIRO, L. L.
  reviewer
SHEARER, S.
  non-fiction
SHAW, R.
SHEMANSKI, F.
SHORE, W.
  short stories
SIEGEL, D. S.
  home, teens
SILVIAN, L.
SLAUSON, M.
SMITH, L.
  non-fiction
SMITH, N. R.
SOLOMON, B. P.
SOMAN, S. C.
  non-fiction
SPICER, D. G.
  folklore, art
STABILE, T.
STEINEM, G. M.
  politics, other
STEVENSON, J. T.
STILLMAN, F. J.
STROWBRIDGE, C. C.
SUMNER, M. B.
TABER, G. B.
  short stories
TANNER, B. R.
  home furnishing
THOMPSON, B. A.
THOMSON, E. W.
TOLCHIN, S. P.
TOOMEY, J. E.
TOWSLEY, A. C.

TRILLING, D.
  non-fiction
USOSKIN, J.
  poetry, lyrics
VOGEL, F. H.
WADDELL, P. C.
  advertising, promotion
WARNER, A. R.
WASSER, G. E.
  scripts
WASSERMAN, A.
  radio, TV scripts
WATSON, C. H.
WEINGARTEN, V. B.
  film scripts
WEINSTEIN, G. W.
  articles
WEISS, M.
  copywriter
WHITE, H. K.
WHITE, N. B.
WHITTAKER, A. T.
WICKENDEN, E.
  urban studies
WICKER, I.
  plays, songs
WILSON, R. F.
WOLF, M. B.
  medical, technical

13-F

ADLER, S.
  book designer
ARNDT, U. M.
  illustrator, magazines,
  books
BARRY, J. W.
  book designer
BECKWITH, E. S.
  graphic art designer
BERNAY, B.
  photographer
BINNS, B.
  graphic design
CONNOLLY, M. J.
  photographer
COOK, G. E.
  animal artist
CURRO, E. M.
  artist, illustrator
DABNEY, K. J.
  composer
DAVIS, M. K.
  composer
DONNA, N.
  game designer
DUNWIDDIE, C.
  sculptor
FALCON, E. D.
  art consultant
FRANK, H. S.
  costume designer,
  illustrator
FREEMAN, A. H.
  artist
GAYNES, C.
  artist, designer
GERARDIA, H.
  artist

GREEN, S. G.
  illustrator
HOPE, E. S.
  cartoonist
IWAMOTO, R.
  photographer, painter
KNOWLES, A.
  artist
LIST, I. K.
  sculptor
LYNCH, S.
  book designer
MARA, T.
  choreographer
MARCUS, H.
  photographer
McNEILLY, E. J.
  photographer
MILLETT, K.
  sculptor
MUFFOLETTO, A.
  photographer
NEAL, M. F.
PEREIRA, I. R.
  artist
PRICE, J. E.
  photographer
ROSENBLATT, A. A.
  artist
ROSENWASSER, D. E.
  artist
ROSSE, A.
  artist, illustrator
RUELLAN, A.
  painter, graphic artist,
  muralist
SCHAEFFER, H.
  painter, artist
SCHOR, R. K.
  sculptor
SCHUMAN, J. W.
  book designer
SCHWABACHER, E. K.
  artist
SCOTT, L.
  artist
SHAW, R.
  photo-journalist,
  portraitist
SHUMSKY, E.
  photographer: women's
  movement,
  international, other
SKILLMAN, H. C.
  textile designer
SLOANE, P.
  artist
SOLIMENA, A.
  artist
SUBA, S.
  illustrator
TEICHMAN, S.
  artist
VANDERBILT, G.
  artist
WALKER, B.
  artist, decorator
WANG, J.
  cinematographer
WEISBERG, M. C.
  sculptor

WHITEHEAD, M. I.
  stylist
WILNER, M. S.
  painter

13-G

McBRIDE, E. S.
  consultant

13-H

ARONSON, M. F.
  consultant
BARKER, R. J.
  promotion,
  merchandising
BEEBE, K.
BLOCK, F. B.
  consultant
CEBALLOS, J.
  Feminist activities
CHAPMAN, P. A.
  publicity
DALE, G. R.
  publicity
DOBIE, W.
DOBRUSHIN, S.
  publicity
EVERS, J. G.
  consultant, writer
FLACON, E. D.
FONTAINE, E. L.
  consultant
GRIMES, T.
HACK, K. P.
HARROP, N.
  publicity
HAUTZIG, E. R.
  children's books,
  consultant
HERMAN, M. J.
ILACQUA, A. A.
KOESTLER, F. A.
  consultant
LOVE, N.
MAYER, T.
  fashion, home furnishing
PHILLIPS, F. McA.
  consultant
PITT, H. P.
  non-profit
RABBITT, W. T.
RYAN, E. M.
SAYERS, E.
  publicity, consultant
SCHERR, B. J.
SLAUSON, M.
THORSON, M. McC.
VAUGHN, B.
  sales promotion

13-I

BIONDI, M. H.
  historian
BORNE, R. Z.
  medical

WHITEHEAD, M. I.
  stylist
DOBIE, W.
FALCO, J. A.
  statistician
KILEY, M. E.

13-J

BARRIE, B. A.
  actress
BERNAY, B.
  TV hostess
BERRY, L.
  actress, singer
BISHOP, R.
  fashion, home furnishing
BLOCK, F. B.
  broadcaster
BOLLING, T. R.
  actress
BRITTON, B.
  actress
BROOKS, G.
  actress
CALLAHAN, S. deS.
  lecturer
CARROLL, V. J.
  actress
CHOLAKIS, S. D.
  actress
COOKSON, B. S.
  actress
COSTELLO, M. C.
  actress
CRANE, T. L.
  actress
CRAWFORD, J.
  actress
CULLMAN, M. W.
  commentator
DABEY, K. J.
  actress, singer
DAVIED, C.
  lecturer: writing
DAHL, A.
  actress
DANA, B.
  actress
DIERKING, S. L.
  actress, singer
DURR, J.
  actress, singer, dancer
FEAGLES, A. McR.
  lecturer
FITZGERALD, P. S.
  artist-performer
FLAGG, F.
  actress, comedienne
FONTAINE, J.
  actress, lecturer, panelist
FRANCIS, A.
  actress, hostess
FRIEDAN, B.
  lecturer
FURNESS, B.
  lecturer
GABRIEL, E. N.
  trombonist
GALEN, H.
  voice-over

GAM, R. E.
actress
GLUBOK, S.
lecturer
GRAHAM, V.
actress, hostess
GRUBER, R.
lecturer
HASSO, S.
actress
HAILEY, M. W.
actress
HAMILTON, M.
actress
HAWKINS, V. F.
spokeswoman
HAYES, M.
actress
HAYNES, V. E.
actress
HILL, C.
KENNEDY, F. R.
actress, commentator, guest
KERMAN, G. L.
actress
KOCIN, I. G.
artist, designer
LAMPERT, Z.
actress
LANDAU, L. U.
actress
LEE, F.
actress
LEE, N. A.
lecturer
LIST, I. K.
sculptor
LUCKHARDT, M. C.
lecturer
LYON, S.
actress
MACRAE, E.
actress
MANNES, M.
commentator
McCALL, J. C.
actress
MILLETT, K.
lecturer
MURPHY, R.
actress
MURPHY, M. E.
actress
ORR, M. C.
actress
PARK, N. L. B.
fashion commentator
PETERS, L.
actress
PETERSEN, A. L.
PFEIFFER, S. S.
PITTS, E. H.
lecturer
RAINIER, P. A.
actress, model
RAND, A.
lecturer
SAVITCH, J. B.
radio, TV
SCOTT, R. F.
actress

SHAPIRO, L. L.
panelist
SHEPARD, E. E.
actress
SKILLMAN, H. C.
textile designer
STUART, J. S.
actress
STRAIGHT, B. W.
actress, producer
STREISAND, B. J.
actress
TOBIN, P. E.
actress, commentator
VOGEL, F. H.
broadcaster
WALTHER, S. E.
singer, actress
WICKWIRE, N.
actress
WYLER, G.
actress
YOUNG, M.
lecturer
YURCHENCO, H. W.
broadcaster
ZACHARY, J.
actress

14-K

AKULLIAN, H. D.
editorial
BROADLEY, H. L.
broadcasting
CLARK, T. T.
advertising, editorial
CURRY, J.
advertising
DEUVALL, J. A.
broadcasting, compensation
DOUGHERTY, M. B. W.
broadcasting
Du JEAN, R.
Black executives
KESSELMAN, A. G.
KESSLER, G. R.
broadcasting
MARKS, E. B.
editorial, advertising
MORRIS, M.
art and copy
PENMAN, R. H.
employee development
POWELL, A. M.
advertising
RATHER, S. B.
secretarial
REID, C.
REID, D.
SLADE, L. A.
SMITH, B. J.

14-L

AGNEW, N. L.
English

AIMEE, Sr. M.
adult education
ALDAN, D.
creative writing
ANASTASI, A.
psychology
BEARN, M. S.
merchandising
BENKOVITZ, M. J.
BERRY, O. C.
fashion
BONIME, F. L.
BOWERS, M. K.
psychology
BROTHERS, J. B.
psychologist
BROTMAN, M. G.
English, drama
BUCKLEY, H. E.
English
CARLIN, K. S.
CELENZA, R. G.
CLOUGH, R. T.
Italian
CORBIN, C. R.
marketing, management
DEAN, V. M.
intl. administration
DORWORTH, A. G.
ELSON, R. M.
history
FRANZBLAU, R. N.
psychology
GOLDIN, A.
GRUMBACH, D. I.
English
HENNE, F.
library science
HILL, C.
training, radio-TV
HIMMELFARB, G.
history
JEFFREY, M. M.
English
JORDEN, E. H.
modern languages
KAUFMAN, B.
English
KOCIN, I. G.
art
LANG, M. M.
English
LaROCQUE, G. E.
English
LEMBO, D. MacD.
library science
LuTOUR, L.
administration
MADOW, P. R.
history
MARGARET, H.
English
MASON, M.
writing
MAYO, M. B.
music, folklore
McENTEE, H. S.
library science
MEAD, M.
anthropology

MEESE, M. F.
creative writing
MILLETT, K.
sociology
MILTON, S. F.
fashion
MOERS, E.
NATCHEZ, G.
remedial reading
NELSON, I. N.
consultant, European schools
PARR, M. Y.
library science
PONSOT, M. B.
English
POPHAM, Dr. E. L.
business education
QUINN, E. C.
RAYWID, M. A.
education
RIVLIN, H. A. B.
history
ROACH, H. P.
speech
ROGERS, D.
psychology
ROSE, C. D.
SCHREIBER, F. R.
speech, radio, TV
SCHULDER, D. B.
law
SHAPIRO, L. L.
library science
SIFF, N. K.
SIMPSON, J. I.
foods
WICKENDEN, E.
urban studies
WILEY, M. L.
English
YURCHENCO, H. W.
ethnomusicology

14-M

ABELS, C.
literary
ANDERSON, B.
talent
BERKE, A. D.
literary
BRACKMAN, H.
photographer
BURKE, S.
literary
BROOKS, E. P.
models
CLEMMEY, M.
literary
DAPPER, G.
D'ESSEN, L. DeR.
animals
FOLEY, J. C.
literary
JOHNSON, M.
authors
MAROSSI, R.
literary

OTIS, E. R.
literary
SINGER, E.
literary
STRASSMAN, T.
authors
STUDER, L. R.
artists
WILKERSON, M.
literary
WOHLBERG, H.
photographers

14-N

ABILEAH, M. M.
translator, multi-lingual
ANDREN, C.
translator
BRIFFAULT, H. H.
translator
ABBOTT, E.
BARTON, M. D.
books
BOYD, S. W.
public relations
BRENT, L.
fashion: domestic, foreign
markets
BURNLEY, R. B.
home economics
CALABRO, N.
marketing consultant
CLAASEN, C.
editorial
DALY, Sr. E. J.
translator
EICHELBERGER, R. K.
book industry
FALCON, E. D.
arts
GILCHRIST, E. B.
translator
GOLDINA, M.
translator
GROSS, S. C.
translator
HENNE, F.
library programs
HUNTINGTON, D. P.
short story writing
KIRSHNER, G. I.
education
LAM, G. L.
education
LAMBERT, E.
fashion
LAWNER, L.
translator
MANSFIELD, S. S.
media
MIEL, A.
curriculum programs
MOERS, E.
MUFFOLEHO, A.
home economist
O'HARA, H.
footwear, color

OZICK, C.
translator
RINDLAUB, J. W.
RUKEYSER, M.
translator
STABILE, T.

15

ASSATOURIAN, A. H.
editing, typing
BEAURET, M. R.
BRODSKY, A.
mailing lists
CARY, Z. E.
TV talent, food
COLLINS, M. O'C.
publishing
COSGROVE, G. R.
book store
COSGROVE, V. S.
patterns
FRIEDMAN, L.
book store
GREEN, A. L.
printer
HANAU, S. B.
manuscript
KUPPER, L. H.
list rental
LAUB, G. J.
book store
MORROW, J. K.
typesetting
POPPER, H.
magazine services
PRAGER, A. H.
music licensing
PRESBERG, M. G.
author's, publisher's
ROSENBERG, L.
printing
SCOMA, S. N.
lithographers
SEGRE, A. W.
audio-visual school
SMITH, C. P.
book store: sports
STERN, M. B.
rare books
SUPER, E. P.
advertising mats

NORTH CAROLINA

1-A

DAVENPORT, D. L.
educational
FRANK, J. A.
women's
JENKINS-VAITEKUNAS,
K. T.
sales development

MANN, P. L.
women's
NEWSON, N. S.
program, sales, traffic
RAYBORN, P. MacK.
women's

1-B

MANN, P. L.
women's
MUSGROVE, V. D.
RAYBORN, P. MacK.

1-C

NORRIS, F. C.

1-E

JOHNSON, M. K.
newswoman
PUZAK, G. S.
reporter
RAYBORN, P. MacK.

1-J

FEEZOR, B. D.
home economics
demonstrator
HAWKINS, E. D.
storyteller
MANN, P. L.
women's broadcaster
MUSGROVE, V. D.
PUZAK, G. S.
hostess

2-A

JOHNSON, N. B.
continuity
KAPLAN, H. A.
RAYBORN, P. MacK.
women's
YOUNTS, E. M.
music, program

2-B

MUSGROVE, V. D.
RAYBORN, P. MacK.

2-D

BOONE, G. B.

2-E

PRESSLY, H. B.
reporter

PUZAK, G. S.
reporter
RAYBORN, P. MacK.

2-J

BOONE, G. B.
broadcaster
PUZAK, G. S.
hostess

3-D

FRANCIS, J.
advisor

3-E

ATHAS, D.
BEVINGTON, H.
non-fiction, poetry
BURGESS, M. E.
non-fiction
FORBUS, I. B.
juvenile, young adult
FRANCIS, J.
non-fiction
FEEZOR, B. D.
cook books
GALLOWAY, L. B.
GREEN, A. M.
HARRIS, B. K.
fiction, plays
HOFFMANN, P.
KOCH, D. C.
fiction
MANN, P. L.
non-fiction
MILLER, H. R.
novels, poetry
MITCHELL, M. F.
history
ROBERTS, N. C.
SHAMBURGER, A. P.
non-fiction
SIMENDINGER, M. R.
STREET, J. M.
juvenile history

4-A

EASTERLING, S. W.
JOHNSON, M. E.
business
STROUD, E. M.

4-D

ASCHMANN, R. E.
fashion
AUSTIN, L. P.
teenage, youth
BROYLES, M. G.
CABLE, D. A.
education

CHENEY, H. B.
women's
COULBOURN, L. C.
women's
EASTERLING, S. W.
society
GOODE, C. B.
women's
GUMMERSON, D. de W.
food
HAMILTON, E. L.
church
HARRELL, L. F.
news
JOHNSON, M. E.
LINDER, H. McD.
women's
MAYNARD, M. C.
city
SATTERFIELD, C. H.
women's
TROTMAN, R. M.
women's
WINTER, C. C.
women's

4-E

CABLE, D. A.
reporter
HAMMOND, T. D.
staff
WHITE, A. C.
columnist

5-A

PERRY, M. J. H.

5-D

SHAMBURGER, A. P.
contributing

6-A

McKNEELY, S. C.

6-C

THOMAS, P. N.
media buyer

7-A

BOST, C. R.
production company
BRICKWELL, M. A. W.
production agency

8-A

HILL, S. S.

8-C

HANEY, M. A.
MOYER, M. A.
WITTEN, M. S.

8-D

BLANCO, S. H.
CATON, H. R.
MOYER, M. A.
STONESTREET, M. McK.

8-F

DARDEN, N. W.

8-G

HANEY, M. A.

8-H

CATON, H. R.
GRIFFIN, F. B.

10-A

SHORT, B. W.
WILSON, E.

11

ALDRICH, W. L. B.
BOONE, W. G.
school
CARNES, F. C.
CAUDLE, V. K.
ELLIS, R. J.
GALLOWAY, L. B.
GREEN, A. M.
school
HAWKINS, E. D.
HODGIN, A. A.
reference
HOOKS, E. W.
IRVIN, A. R.
MATHIS, T. W.
McLARTY, M. A.
MELTON, V. B.
PERRY, P. E.
SHAMBURGER, P. G.
SHERRILL, J. P.
TUCKER, M. S.
public services
VON OESEN, E.

12-A

DAVENPORT, D. L.
PLEASANT, J. R.

12-C

BOYD, J.

12-D

MITCHELL, M. F.
MOORE, B. E.
YIONOULIS, M. N.

12-E

ROBERTSON, S. V.

12-H

CLARK, J. C.

13-B

BOST, C. R.
programs, commercials
BRICKELL, M. A. W.

13-D

FRANCIS, J.

13-E

ATHAS, D.
books, plays
BENSON, T. A.
romance stories
BETTS, D. W.
short stories
BEVINGTON, H.
magazines
BOST, C. R.
radio-TV commercials,
scripts, feature articles
BUCKNER, S. B.
plays
BURGESS, M. E.
articles
CLAYTON, M. McC.
FRANCIS, J.
non-fiction
GALLOWAY, L. B.
articles, stories
GLAZENER, M. U.
religious plays
GRIFFIN, F. B.
non-fiction
GROUT, R. E.
GUMMERSON, D. deW.
MILLER, H. R.
fiction, articles, poetry
MOORE, B. E.
articles
PRESSLY, H. B.
reporter
ROBERTS, N. C.
books, articles

SHAMBURGER, A. P.
non-fiction articles
SIMENDINGER, M. R.
stories
STREET, J. M.
stories, poems, articles

13-F

CLAYTON, M. McC.
photographer
SHAW, M. T.
artist

13-H

BOST, C. R.

13-J

BOST, C. R.
radio-TV scripts,
commercials
BRICKELL, M. A. W.
radio-TV broadcaster,
narrator
MOORE, B. E.
lecturer
PRESSLY, H. B.
lecturer
WITTEN, M. S.
actress

14-L

ATHAS, D.
creative writing
BETTS, D. W.
creative writing
BEVINGTON, H.
English
BUCHAN, E. L.
English, journalism
BUCKNER, S. B.
BURGESS, M. E.
GLAZENER, M. U.
GROUT, R. E.
HARRIS, B. K.
creative writing
JOHNSON, M. E.
mathematics
KOCH, D. C.
MILLER, H. R.
English
SHAW, M. T.
art

14-N

BURGESS, M. E.
DARDEN, N. W.
fashion design
FRANCIS, J.
editorial
GROUT, R. E.
health education

MOORE, B. E.
insurance

NORTH DAKOTA

1-A

HADLEY, C.
women's

1-B

NEWELL, V. B.

1-G

HADLEY, C.

1-J

NEWELL, V. B.
hostess

2-A

COOLEY, E. H.
DETROI, J. B.
women's

3-E

HANSEN, C. H.
*cookbook, laboratory
manual*
HILGER, Sr. M. I.
HOFFINE, L.
juvenile, young adult
HUDSON, L. P.
MILLS, B. L.
MOORE, C. W.
travel

4-A

MOORE, C. W.

4-D

HANSEN, C. H.
food
MIDDAUGH, G. L.
women's
MOORE, C. W.

8-D

PETERSON, M. A. C.

11

LASSEY, A. F.

12-A

BYRNES, H. W.

13-B

HADLEY, C.
fashion shows

13-E

BYRNES, H. W.
articles
HILGER, Sr. M. I.
poetry, articles, features
HUDSON, L. P.
*short stories, poetry,
articles*
MIDDAUGH, G. L.
MILLS, B. L.

13-I

HILGER, Sr. M. I.
historical

14-L

HUDSON, L. P.
English

OHIO

1-A

BLOOM, E. D.
promotion
DAVIS, H. F.
educational
PALMER, P.
women's
STUDER, R.
educational
YAGER, R.
church programs

1-B

BROWN, S. R.

1-E

BROWN, S. R.

1-H

BATES, M. R.
CAMPBELL, M. B.
WALKER, A. B.

1-J

BROWN, S. R.
broadcaster
PALMER, P.
hostess

2-A

BAUER, E. H.
program
BLOOM, E. D.
promotion
CRIDLAND, N. A.
office manager
DAEHLER, P. N.
women's
EWOLSKI, D. S.
traffic
GUTHERY, M. C.
women's
HEMINGER, G. McC.
HOLT, M. B.
women's
KESEG, E. F.
community services
OTT, B. S.
women's
PAGE, B. A.
promotion, publicity
STRAKER, E. I.
*women's, community
service*
STUDER, R.
educational
ZELKOWITZ, H. W.

2-B

BAUER, E. H.
German programs
BROWN, S. R.
HOUSE, H. G.

2-D

LANE, D. G.
fashion

2-E

BROWN, S. R.

2-H

BATES, M. R.
CAMPBELL, M. B.
GAFFNEY, B. J.

2-J

BAUER, E. H.
German announcer
BROWN, S. R.
broadcaster
DAEHLER, P. N.
broadcaster
EDWARDS, F.
*commentator, books,
events*
HENDRIX, M. W.
interviewer
HOLT, M. B.
broadcaster
JOHNSON, R. V.
broadcaster
OTT, B. S.
broadcaster

3-A

SNOW, V. B.
advertising production

3-D

ENGINTUNCA, L. H.
HOUSE, L. M.
copy
ROMERO, P. W.
Black history

3-E

ANTES, E. D.
history textbooks
BEERY, M.
young teenagers
BENEZRA, B. B.
BIESTERVELD, S. P.
children's
BOMBECK, E. F.
BOWER, T. G.
non-fiction
BRACHER, M. S.
religious
BRACKETT, L. D.
novels
CRAMER, P.
homemaking
EVANS, V. B.
language, literature
EVATT, H. T.
juvenile
FEIL, N. E.
cookbooks
GOULDER, G.
non-fiction
HARRIS, E. A.
obesity
HENDRIX, M. W.
writing textbooks
HEUSINKVELD, H. G.
non-fiction: retirement
JOHN, E. B.
science

JOHNSON, J. W.
fiction, non-fiction
KAEHELE, E. D.
fiction, non-fiction
KAUFFMAN, D. S.
novels, poetry
KENDALL, C. S.
fiction
KOVEL, T. H.
antiques
MARGOLIS, E.
folklore for children
MARTIN, E. T.
science fiction novels
McADAM, E. W.
non-fiction
McWHIRTER, M.
MILLER, G.
medicine
MULAC, M. E.
recreation
MULHAUSER, R. E.
French language, history
PALMER, P.
health
PHILLIPS, J. F.
children's
POLKING, K.
children's
RICKETTS, V. L.
animal
ROMERO, P. W.
Black history
SANDBURG, H.
novels
SHAFFER, W. L. H.
religion
SHEPHERD, E. S.
writing
SIMON, S. S.
juvenile
STINETORF, L. A.
fiction, biographies
WEBB, T. S.
poetry
WYSE, L. W.
YAGER, R.

3-F

EVALT, H. T.
illustrator

3-G

SNOW, V. B.

4-A

ANTES, E. D.
DALLAS, D. C.
business
DODDS, L. W.
DONOVAN, M. C.
budget
HEMINGER, G. McC.
MENTZ, LaR.

PARHAM, M. B.
RAUSCH, H. E.
WRIGHT, E. A.
advertising

4-D

ABEL, J. H.
women's
ADAMS, E.
society
ALBERS, J. H.
women's
ANTHONY, D. S.
religion
BARTH, P. L.
women's
BEIGHLE, J. A.
home, economics
BRATEL, B. R.
home economics, food
BRUNER, L. E.
art
DALLAS, D. C.
FARLEY, L. B.
FOSTER, E. S.
women's
FREED, L. W.
women's
FRANCE, M. B.
FRUTH, Z. F.
society
FRY, H. G.
religion
GIBSON, T. R.
home magazine section
GORDON, J. H.
county radio-TV
HAWK, D. W.
news
HEYDUCK, M.
HIVELY, S. L.
women's
INSKEEP, L. K.
women's
ISELE, E. W.
women's
JAYCOX, B. L.
JEVAS, R. J.
society
JONES, D.
garden
KELLY, V. M.
fashion
KERN, C. C.
KREBS, B. D.
fine arts
McCULLOUGH, M. P.
food
McGAREY, M.
women's
McVEIGH, B. W.
women's
MEEKER, H. F.
society
MENTZ, LaR.
PARKER, E. J.
Sunday women's section
PEMBERTON, M. M.
women's

PENDLETON, N. G.
RAINIE, D. E.
society, women's
REED, R. K.
women's
RYCKMAN, M. M.
food
SATTERTHWAITE, T. N.
home furnishings
SCOTT, J. M.
youth
SPENCER, G. H.
radio-TV, youth, women's club
SPENCER, M. C.
Sunday magazine section
STEELE, L. Z.
religion
STICKLER, M. C.
area
STORER, F. H.
food
STRASSMEYER, M.
society
STRONG, H. J.
women's
THOMA, P. L.
THOMPSON, M. J.
TRACEY, W. A. S.
women's
VANDEBERG, S. McD.
society
VOSS, R. H.
teenage
WEAVER, M. D.
society
WEBER, C. A.
women's
WEISENBORN, C. N.
garden
WESTLAKE, R. L.
WHEELER, C. G.
women's
WILLIAMS, A. J.
women's
WILLIAMS, M. D.
WINTERS, J. H.
women's

4-E

ANTES, E. D.
CARMAN, C. M.
reporter
CRAM, E. McK.
staff
CRAMER, P.
decorating
CRISS, C.
staff
ELLIOTT, K. D.
reporter
EVANS, V. B.
book reviewer
FOLEY, B. W.
book reviewer
FRANKE, D. McC.
FRUTH, Z. F.
columnist

FRY, H. G.
correspondent, reporter, feature
GOLDMAN, D. W.
urban affairs reporter
GOULDER, G.
magazine staff
HEYDUCK, M.
columnist
HOY, M. A. C.
business
JORDAN, J. A. K.
women's
JOSTEN, M. M.
community relations
KELLY, M. B.
columnist
KIBBEE, K. K.
reporter
KNAGGS, B. L.
correspondent
KOVEL, T. H.
columnist
LEE, V. H.
reporter
PEMBERTON, M. M.
feature
PENDLETON, N. G.
reporter
RICE, J. A.
teen
RYCKMAN, M. M.
feature
SHEEHAN, M. L. Mcl.
book reviewer
THOMA, P. L.
correspondent
THOMPSON, M. J.
stringer
TIMCHICK, M. R.
book reviewer
WEAVER, M. D.
columnist
WHEELER, C. G.
reporter

5-A

MEADOWS, L. H.

5-D

BUCHER, M. A.
FARLEY, J.
poetry
FOLEY, B. W.
HENDRIX, M. W.
KING, E. M. G.
POLASKY, C.
POLKING, K.
ROMERO, P. W.
Black history
SHAFFER, W. L. H.
TATTER, S.

6-A

BARON, S. A.

BING, B. C.
DROTAR, E. B.
  production
FITZPATRICK, A. F.
GAYNOR, H. I.
  production
HALL, N.
  broadcast services
HARRIS, E. A.
  copy
HOUSE, H. G.
KOBALLA, L. H.
  production
LAMB, G. J.
LOTT, H. J.
  media
MARTIN, E. T.
  radio-TV
MODE, R. R.
  public relations
NORTON, E. G.
  production
POJEFKO, J. T.
  collateral: production
ROSSNAGEL, N. L.
  radio-TV
SCOFIELD, N. W.
  radio-TV
SPARKS, P. C.
STAHL, A. C.
STAUBER, A. K.
VORDENBERG, R. R.
  media, research
WATSON, B. S.
WHITMIRE, A.
  production
WYSE, L. W.

6-C

HARTRICK, D. B.
SHAPIRO, E. B.
  radio-TV

6-D

CROOKSTON, M. E.
  house organ

6-E

POWELL, M. S.
SMITH, S. J.

6-G

GREER, P. J.
ORMSBY, J. L.
SHAPIRO, E. B.
SULLIVAN, M.

6-H

KENNEDY, D. D.

7-A

DALLAS, D. C.
  printing company
ZELKOWITZ, H. W.
  cable TV company

7-E

FEIL, N. W.
  *production company:
  scripts*

8-A

BASSETT, A. K.
BING, B. C.
BLAKE, B.
WEISENBORN, C. N.

8-C

ADAMS, D. A.
BING, B. C.
DONOVAN, M. C.
REMKE, M. H.

8-D

DONOVAN, M. C.
FORREST, J. E.
GRAEFF, L. E.
HAWLEY, M. D.
KAYE, L.
KIPLINGER, J. R.
MALUSO, C. S.
McGUCKIN, P. G.
MILLER, A.
NELSON, S. H.
POWELL, D. B.
REMKE, M. H.
STRICKLAND, M. G.

8-E

SIMON, S. S.

8-F

ROGERS, R. F.

8-G

REMKE, M. H.

8-H

ANDERSON, N. L.
BLOCK, J. L.
BRACKEN, H. O.
DONOVAN, M. C.
McCAFFERTY, A. J.
MURTHA, J. M.

NELSON, S. H.
REMKE, M. H.
ROGERS, R. F.
ROGERS, V. E.

9-A

MOONEY, J. M.
  women's
SPROWLS, C. J.
STRASSMEYER, M.
  teenage panel

9-E

BOMBECK, E. F.
  columnist
CRAMER, P.
  decorating columnist
GOULD, S. L.
  staff
JOHN, E. B.
  science columnist
KOVEL, T. H.

10-A

CONYERS, M. M.
FISHMAN, S. G.
HUNT, B.
MITCHEL, C. F.
REMKE, M. H.

10-C

SHAPIRO, E. B.
  radio-TV

10-H

SHAPIRO, E. B.

11

AIELLO, A. B.
  research
ANDERSON, H. J.
BENEZRA, B. B.
  school
BOWER, T. G.
  school
BREINING, E. T.
BUSHNELL, P. S.
  children's
CLINTON, E. K.
  technical services
CODY, S. I.
CRENSHAW, W. L.
  university
CROOKSTON, M. E.
  research
DARCY, K. M.
  young adult
EDWARDS, F.
  personnel

EMCH, L. B.
FARMER, V. G.
FOLEY, B. W.
FOLEY, H. E.
  school
GILLHAM, M. M.
  university
HELMER, C. A.
  newspaper
HENNINGE, R. E.
KING, M. M.
KRIEG, L. L.
MAUNU, H. J.
  book order
MUNTZ, M. M.
PETERS, M. E.
RANDLE, A. S.
  school
RYAN, L. D.
  university
SAVKKONEN, M. A.
  school consultant
SHEEHAN, M. L. McI.
SKIFF, M. S.
  children's
SCHROEDER, E. I. A.
  university
STRAHLER, C. E.
  university
THORNTON, E.
  university
WHITNEY, E. A.
  university
WRIGHT, A. E.

12-A

DAVIS, H. F.
JOHNSON, M. G.
KEATING, G. G. T.
MILLER, G.
O'NEIL, M. K.
PORTTEUS, E. M.

12-C

STILZ, E. W.

12-D

GRIFFITH, C. McE.
KING, E. M. G.
KIRKENDALL, N. A.
MARDIS, J. C.
NIXON, M. M.
POLASKY, C.
SCHNEIDER, J. E.
SPROWLS, C. J.

12-H

BALSOM, M. P.
BUERHAUS, K. W.
CORCELLI, D. M.
CUDDY, C. V.
DUNN, H. E.
GINSBERG, B. H.

HAMILTON, D. H.
HOUSSELL, J. S.
KELLY, M. B.
KIRKENDALL, N. A.
KNIGHT, M. E.
MITCHEL, C. F.
MUSTRIC, F.
NIXON, M. M.
PARKER, E. H.
SHEPHERD, B. B.
SOLMN, J. H.
STILZ, E. W.
WEAVER, M. J.
YAGER, R.

13-B

BROWN, S. R.
EVARTS, D. R.
HARBAGE, M.
HOUSE, L. M.

13-E

BALSOM, M. P.
  non-fiction
BEERY, M.
  young teenager's articles
BIESTERVELD, S. P.
  children's books, articles,
  poems
BRACHER, M. S.
BRACKETT, L. D.
  short stories, screen plays
BROWN, S. R.
  radio-TV
BRUNER, L. E.
  art
COOK, M. H.
  textbooks
CORBEN, B. B.
  non-fiction, poetry

CUDDY, C. V.
  booklets, magazine
  articles
DROTAR, E. B.
  advertising
DUNN, H. E.
  short stories, features
EVARTS, D. R.
  non-fiction
EVATT, H. T.
  juvenile fiction
FARLEY, J.
  poetry, reviews
FEIL, N. E.
  articles: food
FEIL, N. W.
  non-fiction, scripts
FRANKE, D. McC.
GOLDMAN, C. S.
  articles
GOULDER, G.
  non-fiction, history
GRAEFF, L. E.
  poetry
HARBAGE, M.
HOY, M. A. C.

HUNT, B.
  non-fiction
JOHN, E. B.
  natural history, science
JOHNSON, J. W.
  articles, short stories
KAEHELE, E. D.
  poetry, fiction, non-
  fiction
KAUFFMAN, D. S.
  poetry, songs, articles,
  fiction
KIRKENDALL, N. A.
  articles: religious
  education
KOVEL, T. H.
  articles: antiques
LATHAM, E. M.
  radio scripts
MARGOLIS, E.
  fiction, non-fiction
MARTIN, E. T.
  science fiction drama
McADAM, E. W.
  non-fiction
McWHIRTER, M.
MITCHEL, C. F.
  magazines, newspapers
O'NEIL, M. K.
  technical
PARKER, E. J.
PHILLIPS, J. F.
  articles, children's stories
POLKING, K.
  articles
RICKETTS, V. L.
  articles, fiction
SANDBURG, H.
  fiction, non-fiction
SHEPHERD, E. S.
  articles
SIMON, S. S.
  juvenile
SMITH, S. J.
  articles
SPARKS, P. C.
  articles: sales
STAUBER, A. K.
  non-fiction
STINETORF, L. A.
  religious stories,
  biographies
THOMAE, B. K.
  non-fiction, poems
THOMAS, R. M. P.
  feature
YAGER, R.
  articles: religion

13-F

CORBEN, B. B.
  artist
DROTAR, E. B.
  commercial artist
EVATT, H. T.
  illustrator
FRUTH, Z. F.
  photographer

WENTZ, E. S.
  painter, enamelist

13-H

HOY, M. A. C.

13-I

HARBAGE, M.

13-J

BROWN, S. R.
  broadcaster
FEIL, N. W.
  actress
KELLY, V. M.
  lecturer, fashion show
  commentator
KEMP, V. J. H.
  lecturer: publicity
  workshops
LOTT, H. J.
  musician
MOONEY, J. M.
  lecturer
SANDBURG, H.
  lecturer
THORSEN, R. G.
  model
WEISENBORN, C. N.
  lecturer

14-L

BEERY, M.
  French
COOK, M. H.
  English
COX, M. McC.
  learning aids
EMCH, L. B.
EVANS, V. B.
  English
FOLEY, B. W.
  creative writing
GUENTERT, M. A.
  English
HAMILTON, D. H.
  guidance
HARBAGE, M.
  education
JACKSON, C. O.
  library
MILLER, G.
  medical history
MULHAUSER, R. E.
  romance languages
PORTTEUS, E. M.
ROBINSON, W. S.
ROSE, T. M.
  foreign literature
STUDER, R.
  broadcast services
THORSEN, R. G.
  adult education

YAGER, R.
  creative writing

14-M

GOLDMAN, C. S.
  art

14-N

BING, B. C.
  cosmetics
BOWER, T. G.
  book
DONOVAN, M. C.
  budget
EDWARDS, F.
  library
MONTI, M. S.
  technical translator
MULAC, M. E.
  recreation
OLSEN, M. H.
  home economics
PHILLIPS, J. F.
  American history
PORTTEUS, E. M.
  educational planning
SAUKKONEN, M. A.
  library science
SCHROEDER, E. I. A.
  translator
SHEEHAN, M. L. McI.
STORER, F. H.
  home economics

OKALHOMA

1-A

ALLEN, P. G.
  public service
BOYD, B. C.
  public service
FELLOWS, A. R.
  public relations

1-B

BLACKBURN, I. T.
SPRAGUE, J. N.

1-D

JONES, G. L.
  women's

1-G

ADWON, S.

1-J

BLACKBURN, I. T.
BOYD, B. C.
broadcaster
SPRAGUE, J. N.
moderator

2-A

BAILEY, V. R.
TALKINGTON, D. D.
program/traffic

3-A

JOHNSTON, W.

3-D

JOHNSTON, W.

3-E

CARTER, O. B.
library science
FRENCH, D. K.
fiction
GRAVLEY, E.
HART, C. G.
juvenile fiction
HECK, B. H.
children's
HOLDING, V. Z.
poetry, teenage novels

4-A

BICKNELL, M. P.
business
MAYES, V. L.
PERKINS, L. H.
advertising
SCHOONMAKER, E. F.
THOMAS, B. C.
advertising
WATT, F. D.

4-D

ANDERSON, R. W.
women's
BACON, U. K.
news, society
BLAKELY, J. B.
women's
BRYANT, F. J.
BUSH, L. M.
women's
DECKER, M. R.
ENGLES, M. L.
news
FISHER, G. McC.
women's

GIBSON, F. M.
education, church, aviation
KEAHBONE, C. S.
women's
MORGAN, S. C.
women's
RUSSELL, V. H.
women's
SCHOONMAKER, E. F.
TURNBO, S. L.
women's, food, magazine sections

4-E

NELSON, M. J.
courthouse reporter
YOUNG, K. A.
city government news reporter

5-D

DEMPSEY, I. L.
poetry
HOLDING, V. Z.
RINGOLD, F. L.

5-E

WILKES, B. W.

6-A

BALES, C. G.
BREMKAMP, G. H.
public relations
BROWN, M. H.
media
GABBARD, R. J.
media, traffic
HALL, R. L. R.
production
LUCAS, K. E.
media
NECK, G. Y. B.
media
OWENS, N.
PATE, M. F.
ROBNETT, A. L.
production, art
WILKES, B. W.
radio-TV production, public relations

6-E

JONES, B. A.
McCARTY, J. A.

6-G

PATE, M. F.

6-H

PATE, M. F.

8-D

BRENZ, E. A.
COLLETT, L. B.
FENNER, T. H.
MICHAELS, M. B.
PRICKETT, R. E.

11

CARTER, O. B.
consultant service
COLLIER, V. S.
consultant
CRAMER, A.
university
DAY, B. M.
HENKE, E. M.
MARTIN, A. D.
TOWNLEY, B. L. N.

12-A

STANDS, T. H.

12-D

HENKE, E. M.

12-H

MATHESON, P. D.
RYAN, L. L.
VINCENT, N.

13-E

DEMPSEY, I. L.
poetry, critical essays
FENNER, T. H.
articles, poetry
FRENCH, D. K.
juvenile stories, articles
GRAVLEY, E.
short stories, articles
HOLDING, V. Z.
poetry, historical articles
JOHNSTON, W.
KEAHBONE, C. S.
articles
RINGOLD, F. L.
TV dramas, short stories
SOWERS, M. A.
articles, pamphlets

13-F

FISHER, G. McC.
composer

13-I

BLACKBURN, I. T.
market research

13-J

BLACKBURN, I. T.
speaker
GRAVLEY, E.
lecturer: writing

14-L

DUGAN, G. C.

14-N

BLACKBURN, I. T.
public relations
CARTER, O. B.
library service
COLLIER, V. S.
library
JOHNSTON, W.
media, education, entertainment

OREGON

1-A

HEISEL, J. M.
women's

1-B

BURNEY, V. P.
HESIEL, J. M.

1-D

GERVAIS, P. J. J.
film
SCOTT, R. P.

1-J

BURNEY, V. P.
broadcaster
HEISEL, J. M.
SCOTT, R. P.
anchorman

3-A

COLE, G.

3-E

ADRIAN, M.
juvenile, science
BLOCKLINGER, P. O'M.
medical, politics, crime,
teenager's
GILBERTSON, M. G.
fiction
MAYBERRY, G.
non-fiction
ROBINSON, M. C.
psychology
SHARPE, R. C.
poetry
TYLER, L. E.
psychology
WORTHYLAKE, M. M.
children's

4-A

BEDFORD, A. A.
printing

4-D

ALBRETHSEN, L. G.
ANDERSON, M. V.
FAGAN, B. V.
fashion, art
HENNIGER, J. F.
women's

4-E

HAMILTON, E. N.
staff, correspondent
LUDWIG, J. M.
news-editorial staff
THORNTON, F. T.
columnist

6-A

ANDRÉ, M. C.
media
BEBOUT, S. R.
copy, public relations
GREEN, B. B.
LITTLEFIELD, K.
media
WALSH, M. E. H.

6-B

SIMONTON, C. G.
radio-TV

6-C

WHITE, R. B.
broadcast buyer

6-E

SIMONTON, C. G.
broadcast copy

6-G

ANDRÉ, M. C.

7-A

DeLON, F. G.
photography studio

7-C

WHITE, M. J.
broadcast representative
company

8-C

BURNEY, V. P.

8-D

CONLEY, N. H.
HOENSHELL, M. Y.
JONES, S. T.

8-H

MAHAR, D. A. M.

10-A

MITCHELL, B. S.
PEEPLES, B. C.
WALSH, M. E. H.

11

FRANCIS, H. A.
school
MILLER, C. M.
reference
PHILLIPS, M. E.

12-A

GRIFFIN, R. S.

12-C

RODENWOLD, Z. F.

12-D

LANG, J. B.

LOCKWOOD, M. A.
McCLENDON, I. A.
MORGAN, C. G.
SEYMOUR, B. J.

12-H

JAMES, C. H.
McCLENDON, I. A.
MORGAN, C. G.
SEYMOUR, B. J.
WILSON, T. B.
WRIGHT, M. W.

13-B

GREEN, B. B.
documentaries
LUDWIG, J. M.

13-D

GRIFFIN, R. S.
art

13-E

CONLEY, N. H.
articles
GILBERTSON, M. G.
short stories
GRIFFIN, R. S.
art
MAYBERRY, G.
history
MITCHELL, B. S.
MORGAN, C. G.
articles: farm
PEEPLES, B. C.
specialized articles
SHARPE, R. C.
poetry
WILSON, T. B.
articles

13-F

MITCHELL, B. S.
design

13-H

HEISEL, J. M.

13-I

LUDWIG, J. M.
TV documentary
techniques
McCLENDON, I. A.
Black history

13-J

THORNTON, F. T.
speaker: travel, art

14-L

LOCKWOOD, M. A.
ROBINSON, M. C.
psychology,
communications
SHEETZ, A. R.
journalism, publications
advisor
SKINNER, E. A.
English, journalism
TYLER, L. E.
WORTHYLAKE, M. M.

14-N

ROBINSON, M. C.
psychological
RODENWOLD, Z. F.
home economics

PENNSYLVANIA

1-A

ADAMS, L. M.
copy
BOVAIRD, K. F.
CAMPBELL, A. J.
community relations
COHEN, J. E.
program
DURKIN, M. R.
community involvement
ELKUS, L. R.
GIRARD, J. A.
retail advertising
GOTTLIEB, I. B.
community programs
HOSTETLER, J.
JOHNSON, M. H.
community relations
SCHIMELFENIG, G. O'M.
WHITTINGTON, E.
WOODSIDE, C. A.
community relations

1-B

BARTLETT, V. K.
public affairs
BOVAIRD, K. F.
CAMPBELL, A. J.
DEVINE, L. A.
news
DRAKE, S. E.
school services

ELKUS, L. R.
  public affairs
FARLEY, M. M.
GUILD, C. W.

1-E

BOVAIRD, K. F.
OWENS, A. B.
  reporter

1-J

BOVAIRD, K. F.
FARLEY, M. M.
  hostess
GUILD, C. W.
  telecaster
HODGES, M. M.
  storyteller
JOHNSON, M.
  hostess
OWENS, A. B.
  newscaster
PARKER, F. M.
  interviewer
ROEDER, G. B.
  exercise instructor

2-A

ADAMS, L. M.
  copy
BANKS, D.
COLLANDER, R. R.
FIORANI, R. F.
  public relations
GRAY, A. L.
  sales
HOSTETLER, J.
KAUFMAN, Y. H.
  program
NAGY, H. W.
  sales
RAY, R. G.
  women's
TROBE, G. B.
  women's

2-B

COLLANDER, R. R.
  special features
KOPELAND, E. G.
  news

2-D

GOTWALT, H. M.
  research

2-E

KOPELAND, E. G.

2-J

DUNCAN, A. B.
DWPRCZAK, H. R.
  broadcaster
GRAY, A. L.
  commentator
HODGES, M. M.
  storyteller
NAGY, H. W.
  broadcaster
POISKER, D. M.
  broadcaster

3-A

BANTA, T. D.
  customer service
BLOCKI, P. C.
  promotion
DUFOUR, J. H.
OGLE, L. E.
  consultant
SHEPPARD, S. L.
  promotion, advertising
SMITH, D. A.
  art

3-D

BACHARACH, F.
BAKER, J. H.
BATES, B. S.
  juvenile
COGSWELL, C. N. H.
  poetry
GUNN, Sr. A. G.
  drama
NOBLE, R. V.
  non-fiction
SMOLENS, G. S.
WOOD, E. S.
  poetry

3-E

BATES, B. S.
  children's
BAYS, G. McK.
BELL, N. K.
BERG, J. L.
  juvenile
BIRMINGHAM, R. A.
BONNELL, D. H.
  teenage
BRAYMER, M.D.
  homemaking
BREARLEY, J. McD.
BREIG, J. M.
CAVALLO, D.
  fiction
CLARK, M. G.
  juvenile
COAKLEY, M. L.
COGSWELL, C. N. H.

CONNOR, M. J.
  historical novel
CRAWFORD, B.
  fiction, plays
DALE, M. L.
  French textbooks
DRUMMOND, E. L.
DUNCAN, A. B.
  children's
EINSELEN, A. F.
  novels
ERIKSSON, M. A.
  elementary foreign
    languages
EVERNDEN, M. E.
  children's, plays
FULLER, I.
  fiction
GERSTNER, E. S.
  fiction
GOTWALT, H. M.
  juvenile plays
HANFORD, F. P.
  cookbooks
HARBESON, G. B.
  needlework
HAY, S. H.
  poetry
HAYWOOD, C.
  children's
HEYA, M. E.
  literature
HINDMAN, J. F.
  non-fiction
HIRSCH, R. B.
  non-fiction
HODGES, M. M.
  children's
HUNTER, K.
  children's
KEITH, J.
KIRK, C. M.
  non-fiction
KLEIN, E. M.
  non-fiction
LIPPINCOTT, S. L.
  non-fiction
LOWRY, M. R.
  floral art
MACK, S. R.
McCLOSKEY, E. L.
  poetry, art
MELVIN, Sr. M. C.
  library science
MICHAEL, P. C.
  poetry
MOLAN, D. L.
  religious education
MUDD, E. H.
  psychiatry, sociology
MUTO, S. A.
  non-fiction
NOBLE, R. V.
  non-fiction
RICHTER, H.
SHAFFER, E. K.
SILVA, R. C.
  politics
SOULE, J. C.
  children's

STONE, H. V.
STRAUSS, L. J.
  science textbooks
SWAIM, A. M.
  poetry
VUJICA, N. K.
  Yugoslavia
WATSON, H. O.
  juvenile
WOOLSEY, J.
  juvenile

3-F

HAYWOOD, C.
  children's illustrator
McCLOSKEY, E. L.
  illustrator

4-A

BARNETT, H. C.
BERGER, F. S.
BLEAKLEY, H. R.
DURBIN, M. VAN H.
KLEIN, E. M.
KUTZ, M. L.
MACK, C. T.
MARTZ, J. Z.
MILLER, H. P.
POISKER, D. M.

4-D

BAILEY, M. G.
BERGER, F. S.
BLEAKLEY, H. R.
CLOUD, B. L.
  fashion
COWAN, F. G.
  city
DEVINE, L. A.
  news
DISSINGER, J. A.
  women's, copy
DURBIN, M. VAN H.
FLEDKAMP, O.
  fashion
GIDDENS, N. B.
  women's
GROSS, R. F.
HESTER, G. C.

4-D

HULL, D. H.
KUTZ, M. L.
LANGE, D. J.
  entertainment
LUDLUM, J. P.
  fashion
MADLEY, G. M.
  home furnishings
MILLER, N. R.
  city
READE, P. H.

ROHALY, R. K.
  women's club
SCHNEIDER, M. J. W.
YOUNG, E. E.
  women's
YOUNG, L. K.

4-E

BAILEY, M. G.
  reporter
COAKLEY, M. L.
  feature
CONNOR, M. J.
  columnist, news, feature
DISSINGER, J. A.
  reporter
ELKUS, L. R.
  columnist
GROVER, P. H.
  columnist, feature
JOHNSON, T. S.
  columnist, feature
McCALL, E. B.
  society correspondent
PATTERSON, M. J.
  feature
RODINI, E. L. B.
  correspondent
RUSSELL, R. R.
SWAIM, A. M.
  poetry correspondent
YOUNG, L. K.
  correspondent

5-A

BREARLEY, J. McD.
DIEKEN, G.
  creative
FOSTER, B. A.
  advertising
HEMENWAY, J. E.
  sales, advertising,
    promotion
WOOD, E. S.

5-C

LANGENFELD, E. G.

5-D

ADKINS, G.
BEARD, M. O.
  publicity
BELL, N. K.
BONNELL, D. H.
BREARLEY, J. McD.
CORBETT, J. M.
DIEKEN, G.
EAGER, B. T.
GILLIES, J. E.
  home management,
    equipment

GOULD, R. J.
  TV area
HEPPINSTALL, C. O.
  contributing
HINDMAN, J. F.
JOHNSON, P. P.
LANE, L.
  women's
LAUX, J. A.
LONG, L.
  fashion
MUTO, S. A.
POMPIZZI, C. T.
STRAUSS, S. B.
WOOD, E. S.

5-E

DORMAN, R. G.
  book reviewer

5-H

HEPPINSTALL, C. O.
LANGENFELD, E. G.

6-A

ALFONSI, M. R.
  traffic, radio-TV
BAUMANN, C. L.
  media
BRAYMER, M. D.
BREIG, J. M.
CALLOMON, J. L.
  creative
DICKERMAN, M. P.
  production
EITEL, C. H.
  production
GEORGE, E. W.
  art
GIEHLL, J. C.
  traffic
GRADY, R. G.
  production
GROBER, J. F.
  media
HARRIS, M. B.
  research
HIRSCH, R. B.
JONES, L. F.
  media
McMULLEN, C. D.
  public relations
PREISSER, B. G.
WEISS, D. C.

6-C

DOLAN, M. I.
  marketing
    communications
KEENAN, M. E.
  radio-TV

LOCKETT, M. W.
  media buyer
RUDOV, F. H.
  media buyer
SIMMONDS, G. B.
  media buyer
ZANG, M. G.
  media buyer

6-E

HEBENSTREIT, J. B.
MORTELL, P. S.
  fashion

6-F

BINKOFF, K. B.

6-G

ESCH, K. E.
MANDELL, B. D.
RUBIN, J.
SLOSBURG, B. L.
WALZ, I. W.

6-H

SLOSBURG, B. L.

7-A

COLWIN, E. W.
  art consultant
FOLEY, L. K.
  industrial designers,
    marketing consultants
PORTER, S. P.
  media consultant

7-D

PAGANO, E. B.
  graphic arts company

7-F

McCOLLUM-BLUNT, M. C.
  TV-movie studio

7-H

FOLEY, L. K.
  industrial designs,
    marketing consultants

8-A

PATTERSON, P. R.
RICE, A. W.

8-C

FUNDIS, D. L.
HANFORD, F. P.
HATCH, M. A.
STEWART, B. H.

8-D

BARAN, E. T.
CALLAHAN, E. B.
KUTLER, J. S.
MEYER, D. C.
NAUMANN, D. S. C.
SOLL, H. P.
STEWART, B. H.
WILSON, I. M.
YEAGER, C. J.

8-G

BAREN, E. T.
DORKEN, D. B.
HANFORD, F. P.
HATCH, M. A.
SMOLENS, G. S.

8-H

BUCKS, H. M.
HARVILL, E. K.
KUTLER, J. S.
LOCKHART, P. K.
MORASCO, L. M.
MORRISON, V. S.
PARTRIDGE, D. G.
SITLEY, D. W.
SMOLENS, G. S.
STAMBUL, D. H.
TREVASKIS, J. L.
WILSON, I. M.

8-I

HARVILL, E. K.

9-D

HEPPINSTALL, C. O.
  magazine

9-E

DANA, M.
  columnist

9-H

HEPPINSTALL, C. O.
  magazine

9-J

ROEDER, G. B.
  exercise instructor

10-A

GROSECK, J. B.
HEPPINSTALL, C. O.
HIRSCH, R. B.
LESKO, R. G.
RAMSEY, M. A.

10-H

MAZEFSKY, G. M.

11

ANDREWS, H. R.
ARCHIBALD, E. B.
ATWOOD, M. S.
BARTZ, A. P.
CATHON, L. E.
  children's
CHEESEMAN, E. M.
COLTMAN, N. W.
DAUTRICH, E. C.
DAVIS, M. F.
DONEGAN, Sr. M. D.
  acquisitions
DRAKE, V. L.
  film
FIELD, C. W.
  children's
FRANKENFIELD, P. D.
HEYA, M. E.
  serials
HOAG, M.
  cataloger
HOPPER, J. G.
  *business, science,
  industry*
KEMP, N. M.
LUCKHARDT, V. E.
MAXTON, L. P.
MAZEFSKY, G. M.
  reference, acquisitions
MOORE, H. J.
  university
PERKINSON, G. E.
  public relations
PETROSKY, G. K.
  public relations
PRESTON, A. E.
RAEPPEL, J. E.
  university
SEVY, B. S.
  art museum
SHAFFER, E. K.
  rare book
SHOREY, K. A.
STEWART, B. H.
STRAUSS, L. J.
  chemistry, physics
VUJICA, N. K.

12-A

COPELAND, A. S.
HOAG, M.
MELVIN, Sr. M. C.
MUTO, S. A.

12-B

DRAKE, S. E.
PARKER, F. M.

12-D

CARMOSIN, M. R.
DEVINE, L. A.
HERZEL, C. W.
HINDMAN, J. F.
MOLAN, D. L.
MUTO, S. A.
TISDALE, M. N.

12-F

CRAWFORD, B.

12-G

BERN, P. R.
HEMENWAY, J. E.

12-H

ABRAVANEL, D. R.
ARMSTRONG, M. M.
BERN, P. R.
BOOKER, J. L.
CARMOSIN, M. R.
DANENHOWER, E. G.
DORAN, C. E.
FLYNN, T.
GIPPLE, J. E.
GUNNING, V. F.
HAAS, B. Y.
HARVEY, A. E.
HEMENWAY, J. E.
JAMES, S. K.
LANDO, E. J.
LeJEUNE, D. T.
LEWIS, F. H.
MICHAELS, L. A.
MICHEL, M. L.
MILLER, C. R.
MILLIGAN, D. B.
PAYE, Sr. M. P.
REDENIUS, J. L.
SCHNEIDER, S. J.
SCHUDA, J. M.
THORNTON, T. S.
YARDUMIAN, M. L.
ZUCKERKANDEL, D. E. K.

12-I

CARUSO, E. F.
CLARK, M. G.
LIPPINCOTT, S. L.

13-B

COLLANDER, R. R.
  *feature radio-TV
  programs*
GUILD, C. W.
  documentaries

13-D

ALBERT, M. C.
BAKER, J. H.
CATHON, L. E.
EINSELEN, A. F.
FEINSILVER, L. M.
  copy
MORTON, E.
SHALLEY, D. P.

13-E

ALBERT, M. C.
  copy
BACHARACH, F.
BAYS, G. McK.
  articles
BERN, P. R.
  articles
BIRMINGHAM, R. A.
  TV scripts, plays
BOLTON, B. W.
BOOKER, J. L.
BOVAIRD, K. F.
CALLOMON, J. L.
  musical revue
CONNOR, M. J.
  short stories
CORBETT, J. M.
  religious articles
CRAWFORD, B.
  fiction, plays
DANA, M.
  consumer affairs
DANENHOWER, E. G.
  children's songs, stories
DAVIS, M. B.
DUNCAN, A. B.
  book reviews
EAGER, B. T.
  columnist
EINSELEN, A. F.
FEINSILVER, L. M.
  articles, features
FELDKAMP, P.
  magazine articles
GUNN, Sr. A. D.
  articles
HAY, S. H.
  poetry, literary criticism
HEMENWAY, J. E.
  articles: religion

HERSHEY, A. A.
HERZEL, C. W.
HIRSCH, R. B.
  articles
HIRSCHL, B. P.
  non-fiction
HUNTER, K.
JOHNSON, P. P.
  articles, poetry
JONES, N. C.
  articles
KEITH, J.
KIRK, C. M.
  articles, reviews
LIPPINCOTT, S. L.
  non-fiction
McCLOSKEY, E. L.
  art, poetry
McMULLEN, C. D.
  *speeches, articles, scripts,
  columns*
MICHAEL, P. C.
  *poetry, hymns, songs,
  articles*
MOLAN, D. L.
  religion
MUDD, E. H.
  psychiatry, sociology
NAUMANN, D. S. C.
  articles: industry
PARKER, F. M.
  articles
PARTRIDGE, D. G.
  articles: industry
RICE, A. W.
  *non-fiction scripts,
  publicity*
RICHTER, H.
  poetry, short stories
SILVA, R. C.
  articles
SOULE, J. C.
  *children's, poems,
  articles*
STAMBUL, D. H.
STONE, H. V.
SWAIM, A. M.
  poetry, criticism, reviews
WATSON, H. O.
  short stories, articles
YEAGER, C. J.
  *trade reporter,
  correspondent*

13-F

BACHARACH, F.
  photographer
CRAWFORD, B.
  artist, designer
HARBESON, G. B.
  designer
McCLOSKEY, E. L.
  artist
SMITH, D. A.
  illustrator, designer
STONE, H. V.
  illustrator

13-G

ABRAVANEL, D. R.

13-H

ABRAVANEL, D. R.
CLARKE, L. V.
HAAS, B. Y.
HERSHEY, A. A.
KINTER, O. L.

13-J

BOVAIRD, K. F.
  lecturer
CARMOSIN, M. R.
  lecturer
CATHON, L. E.
  lecturer, storyteller
DUNCAN, A. B.
  lecturer
GUILD, C. W.
  lecturer, fashion
    commentator
HAY, S. H.
  lecturer
KEITH, J.
LOWRY, M. R.
  floral art
RAY, R. G.
  fashion, travel
SOULE, J. C.
  storyteller

14-K

KAPUSTA, B. N.

14-L

BAYS, G. McK.
  French literature
CARUSO, E. F.
  library and information
    science
COGSWELL, C. N. H.
  English, humanities
DORMAN, R. G.
EBKIN, R. M.
  art
ERIKSSON, M. A.
  elementary French
EVERNDEN, M. E.
  English
FARLEY, M. M.
  radio-TV
FULLER, I.
  library science
GUNN, Sr. A. D.
  English
HODGES, M. M.
  library and information
    science
JONES, N. C.
  journalism

KIRK, C. M.
  Englisy
LIPPINCOTT, S. L.
  astronomy
LYTEL, J. W.
  English
MACK, S. R.
MEISTER, A. B.
MELVIN, Sr. M. C.
MEYERS, M. B.
MICHAEL, P. C.
MOORE, H. J.
  English
MUDD, E. H.
  psychiatry
MUTO, S. A.
PAYE, Sr. M. P.
  journalism
RICHTER, H.
  English
SILVA, R. C.
  political science
STRAUSS, L. J.

14-M

FEINSILVER, L. M.
  literary

14-N

BARTZ, A. P.
  library development
BOVAIRD, K. F.
  radio-TV
COLWIN, E. W.
  art
DANA, M.
  consumer affairs
DORMAN, R. G.
  school library organizing
    and administration
EINSELEN, A. F.
  publishing
FEINSILVER, L. M.
  editorial
FRANKENFIELD, P. D.
  library
HEPPINSTALL, C. O.
  cosmetics marketing
RAMSEY, M. A.
  medical public relations
SMOLENS, G. S.
  advertising, public
    relations
SOLL, H. P.
  editorial

RHODE ISLAND

2-G

SEWARD, B. S.

3-E

BROWN, A. K.
  military, history
CARLSON, N. S.
  children's fiction
CERJANEC, R. W.
  library science,
    education
HALL, R. H.
  children's
HARRIS, L.
  biography, history
SIMISTER, F. P.
  fiction, non-fiction

4-E

ALTMAN, J. A.
  reporter, columnist

6-A

SPENCER, N. H.

6-G

ROBSON, M. R.

11

MYER, E. G.

13-D

HALL, R. H.

13-E

CERJANEC, R. W.
  articles: library,
    education
SIMISTER, F. P.
  fiction, non-fiction

13-I

HARRIS, L.

13-J

BROWN, A. K.
  lecturer: military, history

14-L

BLOOM, L. B.
  English
CERJANEC, R. W.
  curricular services

14-N

CERJANEC, R. W.
  educational curriculum
    services

SOUTH CAROLINA

1-A

COPE, S. B.
  sales service
KALMBACH, M. H.
SEAMAN, E. L.
STONE, L. W.
  women's
WELCH, N. T.
  women's

1-B

QUATTLEBAUM, L. F.
STONE, L. W.

1-D

QUATTLEBAUM, L. F.
  social

1-E

HUNT, A. G.
  special assignments
LEE-BENNER, L. F.
  copy
STONE, L. W.
WICKS, M. R.
  copy

1-J

LEE-BENNER, L. F.
McCOY, A. W.
  hostess
QUATTLEBAUM, L. F.
  broadcaster
STONE, L. W.
WELCH, N. T.
  hostess

2-A

SAEMAN, E. L.

2-E

HUNT, A. G.
  copy

2-H

WILSON, G. S.

2-J

HUNT, A. G.
broadcaster

3-A

HALL, S. G.

3-D

HALL, S. G.
non-fiction

3-E

FREEMAN, G. B.
McMILLAN, P. J.
non-fiction
WALKER, C. McG.
WELCH, N. T.
cookbook
WILDS, N. A.
non-fiction
WOODSON, H. C.
biography, genealogy

4-D

ANDERSON, E. D.
religion
CLINE, D. H.
women's
GREEN, L. B.
religion
PEDEN, M. McK.
women's
WALKER, C. McG.
food
WOODRING, M. L.
women's
YOUNG, M. W.
travel

4-E

BARTON, E. K.
columnist, feature
BROWN, B.
staff reporter
GREEN, L. B.
education, fine arts critic

5-D

FREEMAN, G. B.

6-A

BERNSTEIN, A. K.
HAMBY, L. D.
LUCAS, D. K.

6-C

HILL, M. D.

7-A

WILDS, N. A.
art studio

8-A

DUCHEIN, A. O.

8-D

TANKERSLEY, A. C.

8-H

DUCHEIN, A. O.
TANKERSLEY, A. C.

11

BALD, M.
BETHEA, M. B. M.
CUTHBERT, E. R.
DIXON, E. C.
MARCUM, L. L.
MARTIN, R. S.
reference, serials
MILLER, L.
PORCHER, E. L.
SANDERS, E. C.
STEVENSON, M. P. C.
THOMPSON, M. G.
WALKER, E. P.
WELBORN, E. C.
WILLIAMS, B. J.

12-D

FREEMAN, G. B.

13-E

BALD, M.
religion
BARTON, E. K.
club histories
BOBULA, I.
history
CALDWELL, R. B.
articles: education
FREEMAN, G. B.

GREEN, L. B.
articles, features
- HAMBY, L. D.
publicity, lyrics, scripts
McCOY, A. W.
non-fiction articles
McMILLAN, P. J.
non-fiction articles
STENHOLM, K. C.
articles: film
STEVENSON, M. P. C.
WALKER, E. P.
library science
WELBORN, E. C.
poetry, travel
WICKS, M. R.
documentary films

13-F

STEVENSON, M. P. C.
illustrator

13-I

STEVENSON, M. P. C.

13-J

BOBULA, I.
lecturer

14-K

FOSTER, C. B. K.

14-L

ADAMS, J. P. McG.
BOBULA, I.
sociology, anthropology
CALDWELL, R. B.
library science
STENHOLM, K. C.
films

14-N

McCOY, A. W.
dietary
McMILLAN, P. J.
translator

SOUTH DAKOTA

2-A

DUHAMEL, H. S.
SPENCE, W. H.
women's

2-J

SPENCE, W. H.
broadcaster

3-E

FIELDLER, M. C.
history
SPENCE, W. H.
homemaking annual
WALTNER, E.
crafts

4-A

ADAMS, G. W.
BOORMAN, A. S.
TAIT, L. B.

4-D

FARRAR, S. H.
Sunday

5-D

WILLIAMS, E. E.

7-I

KNORR, L. H.
graphics company

8-A

DUHAMEL, H. S.

13-E

EDGINGTON, D. B.
articles: education
FIELDLER, M. C.
*history, juvenile stories,
poetry*
WALTNER, E.
non-fiction

14-L

WILLIAMS, E. E.
journalism

TENNESSEE

1-A

BARRY, J.
merchandising

WILLIS, K. S.
  women's
YOUNG, J. R.
  community relations

1-D

WEAVER, D.
  film

1-E

WEAVER, D.
  reporter, news

1-G

BARRY, J.

1-H

WATKINS, M.

1-J

BARKER, E. L.
  broadcaster
BARRY, J.
  broadcaster
BURNS, E. L.
  studio teacher
FREEMAN, D. B.
  broadcaster
HARRIS, C. T.
  hostess
ROACH, M. M.
  studio teacher
WILLIS, K. S.
  hostess

2-A

TERRELL, M. A.
  public relations

2-G

FREEMAN, D. B.

2-J

BARKER, E. L.
  broadcaster
MORTON, J.
  panelist

3-A

BECKER, P. L.
  public relations

3-C

HITE, C. H.
  rights and permissions

3-D

BARR, G. H.
JONES, M. A.
  consultant
WRIGHT, A. McI.
  horticulture
YELLIN, C. G.

3-E

BARR, G. H.
  novels, juvenile
BOOKER, H. A.
  food
BRANDON, F. S.
  juvenile
BROWN, I. C.
  anthropology, social
    studies
BULLARD, H.
  non-fiction
DYKEMAN, W.
  novels
GOVAN, C. N.
  adult, juvenile
HAMER, M. B.
  history
JONES, M. A.
  religion
JUSTUS, M.
  juvenile
MADDUX, R.
  fiction
MERCHANT, J. H.
  poetry
YELLIN, C. G.

3-G

FORDYCE, J. L.

4-A

EASTERLY, L. W.

4-D

ABAZORIS, N. H.
  women's
ADAMSON, J. N.
  women's, church
ARNOLD, B. W.
  food
CLEMENS, I.
  fashion, beauty
CLIPPARD, J. F.
  women's
DOUGLAS, M. S.
  book

HULBERT, J. G.
  social
MURRAY, J. A. G.
RIDINGS, N. S.

4-E

ADAMSON, J. N.
  reporter
CLEMENS, I.
  medical science
DYKEMAN, W.
  columnist
KISS, M. C.
  staff

5-A

BECKER, P. L.
  public relations
WRIGHT, A. McI.

5-D

BARNHART, M. L.
BRANHAM, S. C.
CROWE, L. R.
NOLAN, S. S.
WARREN, D. D.

5-E

COOK, E. R.

6-A

ABBOTT, D.
  radio-TV
COOK, E. R.
COX, R. C.
  traffic
HILLEY, D. W.
SANDUSKY, M. Q.
  media
WHITE, J. S.
YOUNG, C. B.
  media

6-C

MAYNARD, I. C.
  media

6-D

KLEIN, M. B.
  publications

6-H

TOMBRAS, E. C.
WHITE, J. S.

7-A

LYNCH, M. B.
  record company
MAXSON, H. W.
  broadcast music

7-B

LYNCH, M. B.
  record company

7-E

LYNCH, M. B.
  record company

8-D

CROWE, L. R.
HOFFERBERT, E. M.
PORTER, J. W.

8-G

ABBOTT, D.

8-H

FREEMAN, D. B.
SHERMAN, S. J. B.

8-I

BOOKER, H. A.

10-A

MORAN, R. R.

10-D

KLEIN, M. B.
  publications

11

BROWN, M. F.
  acquisitions
CLARK, L. N.
COLE, M. E.
COOKE, A. L.
  university
GLADISH, M. L.
  medical research
HARLAN, I. R.
KITTRELL, H. H.
LITTLE, M. E.
LOCKHART, H. DeL.
  community relations
MIDDLETON, M. D.

MITCHELL, M. J.
  school
PARKER, J. G.
  school
POSTELL, P. L.
RUSSELL, A. L.
  reference
SCOTT, W. A.
SMITH, J.
WASH, M. W.
YOUNG, O. K.

12-A

FARISS, H. B.
JONES, J. P.
MORTON, J.

12-C

BARKER, E. L.

12-D

BRANHAM, S. C.
LILLARD, P. L.
NOLAN, S. S.

12-H

BARKER, E. L.
DAVIDSON, M. B.
FORD, A. G.
KOSKOS, C.

12-I

NESTLER, A. T.
NICKS, I. C.

13-E

BOOKER, H. A.
  articles: non-fiction
BROWN, I. C.
  anthropology, social
    studies
BULLARD, H.
  non-fiction
DYKEMAN, W.
  articles, fiction, book
    reviews
GOVAN, C. N.
  book reviews, short
    stories
HAMER, M. B.
  historical articles
LITTLE, M. E.
  magazine and newspaper
    articles
MADDUX, R.
  fiction, short stories
MERCHANT, J. H.
  poetry

MORAN, R. R.
NOLAN, S. S.
  music, poetry, articles,
    children's stories
ROACH, M. M.
  films
SHERMAN, S. J. B.
YELLIN, C. G.
  articles

13-F

ABBOTT, D.
  composer
BULLARD, R.
  artist
NOLAN, S. S.
  artist

13-H

SHERMAN, S. J. B.

13-J

ABBOT, D.
  singer, lecturer
BARRY, J.
  actress
BROWN, I. C.
  lectures
CANNON, S. C.
  comedienne
DYKEMAN, W.
  lecturer
GOVAN, C. N.
  lecturer
NICKS, I. C.
  lecturer: safety
SHERMAN, S. J. B.
  broadcaster

14-L

BRANDON, F. S.
BURNS, E. L.
  science on TV
CHENEY, F. N.
  library science
GILLHAM, O. W.
HAMER, M. B.
  history
HARMAN, V. O.
  library science
HULBERT, J. G.
  history
ROACH, M. M.
  social science on TV
SPENCER, E. S.
  journalism
YOUNG, J. R.
  journalism

14-N

BROWN, I. C.
  anthropology, social
    studies
MORAN, R. R.
  politics
MORTON, J.
  public relations
NICKS, I. C.
  safety
ROACH, M. M.
  educational television

15

McMILLAN, B. M.
  reading system

TEXAS

1-A

BOYCE, M. B.
COLBURN, D. P.
  women's
KING, J. J.
  women's
LIPSCOMB, A. L.
  continuity
MULDER, F. J.
PETERSON, M. B.
  public service
ROWLEY, K. W.
  sales service, traffic
SALTER, A.
  program
SINCLAIR, D. T.
  educational
TRACY, W. N.
  traffic
TURNER, S. L.
  sales service
WHEELER, M. C.
  educational

1-B

BENJAMIN, M. D.
  special programs
BROWN, E. H.
DENMAN, M. W.
HODGE, B. W.
LANGE, J. R.
LEWIS, M. G.

1-C

JAMESON, F. B.

1-E

KELLER, J. P.
  copy

LANGE, J. R.
SALAUN, M. M.
  reporter
TURNER, S. L.
  continuity

1-H

RIGBY, B.

1-J

DENMAN, M. W.
HODGE, B. W.
LEWIS, M. G.
  moderator
RICHEY, D. H.
  broadcaster

2-A

ABOOD, F. B.
  sales
CALLAWAY, E.
  women's
FERRY, N. L.
  program
FINCHER, M.
JONES, J. E.
  traffic
ROWLEY, K. W.
  sales service, traffic
SINCLAIR, D. T.
  educational
WELCH, J. N.
WILLETTE, M. P.

2-B

BENJAMIN, M. D.
  special programs
HUNT, E. M.
  children's

2-D

RUSSELL, M. B.
  women's

2-E

KELLER, J. P.
  copy

2-J

BOSCH, P. C.
  broadcaster
CALLAWAY, E.
  hostess
FERRY, N. L.
  broadcaster

FINCHER, M.
 announcer
HEALY, M.
 commentator
JONES, J. E.
PARKS, J. F.
 announcer
RICHEY, D. H.
 broadcaster
RUSSELL, M. B.
 broadcaster

3-D

BOWDEN, A.
KAMENITSA, M. E.
 childhood education
 handbooks
McQUEEN, M. W.
 schools

3-E

ANDERSON, R. I.
 business textbooks
BONNER, J. W.
 homocide investigation
BOWDEN, A.
 non-fiction
BOYCE, M. B.
BRENNER, L.
CLARKE, M. W.
 westerns
CORBITT, H. L.
 cookbooks
CROFFORD, L. H.
DEEN, E. A.
 Christianity
DUNNAM, I. McC.
 children's
ELY, V. S.
ERDMAN, L. G.
 fiction, non-fiction
FAGG, D. P.
 non-fiction
FRANK, G.
GIBSON, J. H.
 fiction
HAAG, J. H.
 health textbooks
HERBST, D. F.
 teenage suspense novel
HUNT, G. M.
 educational and
 mathematics textbooks
IVAN, M. P.
 juvenile
KERR, L. F.
KREITZ, H. M.
 children's
LEVIN, B. S.
LIPSCOMB, A. L.
 continuity writing
LUCAS, G. B.
MacDOUGALL, M. K. S.
McGAW, J. B.
 juvenile

MAYHALL, M. M. P.
 Texas history
MORTON, L. B.
 non-fiction
MUELLER, E. L.
 history, folklore
O'BRIEN, E. F.
 juvenile non-fiction
OPPENHEIMER, E.
PAGE, T.
PAPPAS, G. B.
PASCHAL, N.
 junior novels
PONDER, C.
 non-fiction
QUILLIN, E. S.
 nature study
REUTHER, R. E.
RICE, E.
 children's
ROBERTS, M. D.
 fiction
SCHULTZ, J. R.
 non-fiction
SMITH, M. K. D.
VAN HORN, V. H.
VANCE, E. G.
 poetry, juvenile
VANNIER, M.
 physical education
 textbooks
WARREN, B. A.
WINN, L. R.

3-F

DOWNS, J. A.
 designer
RICE, E.
 illustrator

4-A

AUGUR, M. H.
BEIRPONCH, D. K.
BOSL, F. B.
EDWARDS, K. B.
ERNSTES, M. A.
FAIN, L. H.
GLIDDON, S. K.
HOBBY, O. C.
MOBLEY, P. H.
PAGE, T.
PAPE, G. H.
SALTER, C. A.
SCHOTT, B. J. W.
THOMAS, C. M.
TREUTER, F. O.
WHITAKER, M. R.

4-D

BARNES, J. J.
 home

BEIRPONCH, D. K.
BENELL, J.
 food
BENGTSON, C. S.
 fashion, beauty
BENNETT, W. M. S.
 society
BOYD, A. F.
 women's
BROWN, E. H.
 women's
BRYCE, M. D.
 women's
BURLESON, K. S.
BURNS, R. V.
 women's
BYRNE, R. S.
 fashion, home
 furnishings
CAPREOL, E. R.
 book
CARPENTER, M. C.
 news
CASTLEBERRY, V. A.
 women's
CHRISTIAN, S. S.
 women's
CORNWELL, B. T.
CRUTCHER, M. E.
 city
CUMMINGS, D. C.
 women's
DAVIS, L. R.
 amusements
DENKO, G. S.
 amusements
DILLARD, K. R.
 women's
EDWARDS, K. B.
ERNSTES, M. A.
FAGG, D. P.
 home furnishings
GLIDDEN, S. K.
HOBBY, O. C.
MOBLEY, P. H.
HOLMES, A. H.
 fine arts
HOLMQUIST, K.
 women's
HOPKINS, P. L.
 women's
LARREMORE, L. E.
 news
LEIBSON, P. P.
 book
OEFINGER, M. H.
 women's
PAGE, T.
PFENNIG, G. R.
 women's
SALTER, C. A.
SINZ, D. C.
 food
SLOAN, F. A.
STEWART, L. M.
 women's
THOMAS, C. M.
WATTS, C. L.

4-E

BODDY, E. N.
 reporter, columnist
CAPREOL, E. R.
 city hall reporter, feature
COCHRAN, K. R.
CRUMBAKER, M.
 magazine section
DAVIS, L. R.
 columnist
GLIDDON, S. K.
 columnist
HINCKLEY, J. B.
 columnist
JOHNSTON, M.
MANNING, D. F.
 golf columnist
MOBLEY, P. H.
 correspondent
ORTON, W. J.
 reporter, correspondent
RIMMER, M. K.
 columnist
WEBER, J. C.
 feature

4-H

HICKS, L. M.

5-A

CAMPBELL, D. G.
CHAPMAN, L. M.
 business

5-C

SHERWOOD, A. P.
 circulation

5-D

BELKNAP. O. S.
CAMPBELL. D. G.
GRAHAM, J. E.
HAAG, J. H.
MILLER, C.
PARTON, V.
SPIVEY, M. D.

5-E

BOSL, F. B.
CLARKE, M. W.
 feature
GRAHAM, J. E.
GUINAN, M. H.
 field reporter

5-G

MILLER, C.

6-A

ACHOR, J. B.
creative
ASHBURN, M. L.
media
BENGE, C. E.
BLOCK, M.
BOUNDS, M. J.
production
CERRATO, A. J. E.
CHESNAR, L. I.
production
ESTES, R. Z.
public relations
FEY, T. K.
radio-TV
FRANK, G.
GRAHAM, J. E.
HARRIS, L. B.
production
HARWELL, B. A.
creative
HERNANDEZ, P. O.
media
HOLZAUSER, K. C.
HARRIS, N. H.
KAY, G.
MANNING, M. A.
MATHERS, C.
media, traffic
MAY, A. B.
MAY, J. S.
research
McDONALD, C. A.
media
MITCHELL, M. B.
traffic
MOORE, G. S.
MORRISON, M. C.
radio-TV
PARKS, J. F.
radio-TV
PARR, S. C.
radio-TV
PAXSON, C. G.
radio-TV
PELKEY, C. C.
media
RIBNICK, G. R.
office
RIEGER, B. J.
print production
SMITH, H. M.
STATMAN, J. M.
media
WELCH, E. M.
copy media
WELCH, V. B.
broadcast media
WHITEHEAD, L. J.
public relations

6-C

LUND, W. S.
print media analyst
SMITH, S. L.
time buyer
WEAVER, B. A. D.
consultant

6-D

STEWART, M. L.

6-E

ANDERSON, L. W.
DUTCHER, V. B.
ROBINSON, A. D.
SCHLANSKER, J. T.
SMITH, S. L.
copy
WEAVER, B. A. D.

6-G

ANDERSON, L. W.
HUGHES, S. M.
SAGINAW, R. B.
STEWART, M. L.

6-I

McNAMEE, N. D.

6-H

SCOTT, B. W.

7-A

GRAHAM, J. E.
production company
MORGAN, E. G.
*business, market
research, analysis*
MORLEY, F. P.
media services
MURRELL, M. F.
*motion picture
producers*
ORNISH, N. G.
record company
WHITLOCK, B.
*motion picture
producers*

8-A

CORBITT, H. L.
DUNNAM, I. McC.
HARRIS, N. H.

McQUEEN, M. W.
MUTH, D.
PAPPAS, G. B.
RIMMER, M. K.

8-C

KUHLMAN, M. E.
MORRIS, N.
PACE, C. J.

8-D

ABSHIER, M. A.
ALLEN, V. R.
BETTERTON, S. B.
CALLAWAY, M. W.
COVINGTON, G.
DUNNAM, I. McC.
ELAM, B. A.
EVANS, J. L.
EVETT, A. C.
FLEMING, S. G.
HALBARDIER, L. I.
HESTER, L. H.
HOUP, D. D.
LINER, R. W.
McNAMARA, D. La C.
SCHAFER, P. G.
STAPLES, C. W.
TAYLOR, J. M.
THOMPSON, J.
ZAHRT, P. L.

8-E

FREDERICK, J. D.

8-F

HESTER, L. H.

8-G

BLOXOM, S. McQ.
GILBERT, V. B.
LETTS, L. M.
REDDICK, N. C.

8-H

ATHANASIOU, B.
BLOXOM, S. McQ.
DAVID, M. B.
PAPPAS, G. B.
RICHARDSON, S. H.
SCHAFER, P. G.

9-E

BOSL, F. B.
reporter

10-A

BELL, M. H.
BONNER, J. W.
BOSCH, P. C.
CHESNAR, L. I.
HOLZHAUSER, K. C.
RICHEY, D. H.
SCHULTZ, J. R.
TRIMBLE, E. P.

11

BOWDEN, A.
DUFFIELD, P.
medical
DYKE, J. S.
EAVES, C. V.
ELLIS, P. M.
GRAY, E. M.
GREEN, E. A.
LANEY, N. I.
OWENSBY, M. P.
SIVELLS, W. K.
VAN HORN, V. H.
VARNER, J. J.
reference
WILLIAMS, P.

12-A

CARTER, S. T.
HERBST, D. F.
SIMON, V. W.
QUILLIN, E. S.
TAYLOR, R. C.

12-B

BROWN, E. H.

12-C

HUTCHESON, D. F.

12-D

BEASLEY, M. S.
GAMEL, P. M.
NEAL, B. D.
SUMRALL, V. E.

12-E

MANNING, D. F.

12-H

AL-DOORY, S. R.
BEASLEY, M. S.
BOURGEOIS, M. K.

BRANDENBURGER, J. H.
CARMICHAEL, E. B.
DYKEMAN, A. J.
FOSTER, B. K.
HAMILTON, M. M.
HILL, L.
IVAN, M. P.
JONES, B. H.
KEAY, L. C.
MUGNO, M. J.
SAUNDERS, M. I.
WHITE, M. T.
WINN, L. R.

13-B

ACHOR, J. B.
BENJAMIN, M. D.
BRANDENBERGER, J. H.
   documentary films
GRAHAM, J. E.
HUNT, E. M.
   children's operettas

13-D

DENSON, M. G.
LEE, M. H.
MIKES, F. R.

13-E

ACHOR, J. B.
ALLEN, V. R.
   trade articles
BENJAMIN, M. D.
   advertising, film
BERNABEI, O. DeP.
BLOCK, M.
   advertising and business
   correspondent
BONNER, J. W.
   articles
BOSCH, P. C.
   non-fiction, newspaper
   columnist
BRANDENBERGER, J. H.
   documentary films
BRENNER, L.
   fiction, non-fiction
CAPREOL, E. R.
   magazine articles
CARTER, S. T.
   music
CORBITT, H. L.
   lecturer: cooking
CROFFORD, L. H.
   poetry
DYKEMAN, A. J.
   training programs,
   playlets, articles
ERDMAN, L. G.
   short stories, articles,
   novels
FAGG, D. P.
   poetry, short stories
FAY, M. S.

FRAME, H. D.
GOMEZ, R. P.
   reporter
GRAHAM, J. E.
GRAY, E. M.
   non-fiction
HARTMAN, J. S.
HOBBY, O. C.
HOLMES, A. H.
   articles: fine arts
KASHUBA, J. A.
   fiction, non-fiction
KREITZ, H. M.
   children's
LAWRENCE, J. M.
LEE, M. H.
   articles
LEVIN, B. S.
   fiction, short stories,
   articles
LUCAS, G. B.
MacDOUGALL, M. K. S.
   stories, articles
MAYHALL, M. M. P.
   ethno-history
McGIFFIN, L. S.
   short stories, juvenile
   fiction, non-fiction
McGUIRE, A. B.
   articles
McQUEEN, M. W.
   social science research
   studies
MOORE, B. M.
MORGAN, E. G.
   marketing articles

13-E

MORTON, L. B.
   non-fiction
MUELLER, E. L.
   history, folklore
O'BRIEN, E. F.
   reviews
ORNISH, N. G.
   plays, non-fiction
ORTON, W. J.
   articles
PAGE, T.
   magazine features
PASCHAL, N.
   book reviews
PFENNIG, G. R.
   articles
RICHEY, D. H.
   articles, newspaper
   columnist
RIMMER, M. K.
   columns: commercials,
   fashion commentary
ROBINSON, A. D.
   light verse
SANDERS, C. D.
   non-fiction
SAUNDERS, M. I.
SINCLAIR, D. T.
   textbooks

SMITH, M. K. D.
   reviews
THEDFORD, J. W.
   articles: agriculture
TRIMBLE, E. P.
   non-fiction
TRIMBLE, L. G.
   non-fiction
VAN HORN, V. H.
   articles: library science,
   poetry
VANCE, E. G.
   poetry, juvenile
VANNIER, M.
   physical education
WARREN, B. A.
WERLIN, R. H.
WHITE, E. H.
   poetry
ZAHRT, P. L.
   columnist

13-F

BENJAMIN, M. D.
   film designer
DUNNAM, I. McC.
   artist, children's dress
   designer
MAY, J. S.
   portrait photographer
ORNISH, N. G.
   composer
PAGE, F. E.
   composer
PAPPAS, G. B.
   portrait artist
RICE, E.
   illustrator
TEARS, R. McC.
   portraits
WARREN, B. A.
   artist
WHITE, E. H.
   artist, illustrator, sculptor

13-G

BENJAMIN, M. D.
   writer
HARTMAN, J. S.

13-H

FAOUR, A. R.
HARRIS, N. H.
MIKES, F. W.
MILLER, C.
SANDERS, C. D.
TRIMBLE, L. G.
WEAVER, B. A. D.

13-I

MAYHALL, M. M. P.
   ethno-history

13-J

BENELL, J.
   TV commercials
BENJAMIN, M. D.
   lecturer
COLBURN, D. P.
   TV guest: home
   economics
DEEN, E. A.
   lecturer: women and the
   Bible
FAY, J.
   broadcaster: radio, TV
FINCHER, M.
   voice talent
GRAHAM, J. E.
   broadcaster
HARTMEN, J. S.
JOHNSON, L. B.
   speaker: travel,
   conservation
MAYHALL, M. M. P.
   lecturer: ethno-history
O'BRIEN, E. F.
   lecturer: religion, travel,
   writing
ORNISH, N. G.
   lecturer
PAGE, F. E.
   conductor
PASCHAL, N.
   speaker: creative writing
RICHEY, D. H.
   lecturer: motivation
RIMMER, M. K.
   radio TV commercials,
   fashion commentator
ROBINSON, A. D.
SAUNDERS, M. I.
   lecturer
SMITH, M. K. D.
   lecturer
TRIMBLE, E. P.
   lecturer
VANCE, E. G.
   lecturer
WEAVER, B. A. D.
   actress, pianist
WERLIN, R. H.
   lecturer

14-L

ANDERSON, R. I.
   business administration
BENJAMIN, M. D.
   radio, TV producer
BLAKELEY, N. R.
   journalism, graphic arts
BOYVEY, M. O'N.
   media program
BROWN, D. L.
   radio, TV
BROWN, E. H.
CROFFORD, L. H.
DANIELS, M. G.
   journalism
DOLEZAL, W. H.

ERDMAN, L. G.
  *English, writer-in-
    residence*
FAOUR, A. R.
  English
GIBSON, J. H.
GILLEY, E. C.
  placement
GOMEZ, R. P.
HAAG, J. H.
  health education
HENTHORN, M. W.
  journalism
HUNT, G. M.
KREITZ, H. M.
LEVIN, B. S.
MacDOUGALL, M. K. S.
McGAW, J. B.
  English, Latin
McGUIRE, A. B.
MEYER, J. C.
  communication
MORTON, L. B.
  English, humanities
MURRAY, L. S.
  English
NEWTON, B. W.
PAGE, F. E.
  music
PRITCHETT, E. H.
  journalism
REUTHER, R. E.
  language arts
SINCLAIR, D. T.
  radio, TV film center
TEARS, R. McC.
  painting, drawing
WHEELER, M. C.
  TV

14-N

BENELL, J.
  food
BENJAMIN, M. D.
  broadcaster
BOSL, F. B.
  oceanography
CHESNAR, L. I.
  personnel administration
CORBITT, H. L.
  cooking school
DOLEZAL, W. H.
  educational curriculum
GILBERT, V. B.
  advertising
HAAG, J. H.
  health education
HAMILTON, N. M.
  communications
HICKS, L. M.
  youth freedom speaker
KAMENITSA, M. E.
  *early childhood
    curriculum specialist*
MOORE, E. M.
  *health, social
    development*

MORTON, L. B.
  education
MURRAY, L. S.
  human relations
SANDERS, C. D.
VARNER, J. J.
  translator

15

BLOCK, M.
  editorial services
ROSENGREN, F. K.
  book store

UTAH

1-A

NOKES, J. W.
  women's

1-B

DOUGAN, D. L.

1-J

DOUGAN, D. L.
  hostess
NOKES, J. W.
  hostess

3-E

BURT, O. W.
  *folklore, children's,
    poetry, plays*
FABIAN, J. C.
  fiction, non-fiction
GIBBONS, H. B.
HAIR, M. J.
  *library indexes,
    bibliographies*
LAURITZEN, E. M.
MINER, C. E.
  *fiction, non-fiction,
    poetry*
SANDERS, J. A.
  novels, biographies
WHIPPLE, M.

4-A

WILSON, C. J. McB.

4-D

SUTTER, P. F.
WILSON, C. J. McB.

4-E

WILSON, C. J. McB.

5-D

MIKE, G. M.
WETMORE, S.

6-A

COOK, E. H.
  media
FELT, L. C.
  radio, TV

6-C

COOK, E. H.
  space buyer

6-E

FELT, L. C.

6-F

KENNY, B. G.
  artist

6-G

FELT, L. C.

8-C

DOUGAN, D. L.

11

HAIR, M. J.
  behavioral science
JENSEN, I. C.
  reference
TYLER, R. V.

12-A

HARRISON, B. D.

13-E

BURT, O. W.
  *poetry, plays, articles,
    stories*
FABIAN, J. C.
  *fiction, non-fiction,
    plays, songs*
GIBBONS, H. B.

HARRISON, B. D.
  articles: psychology
LARSEN, M. J.
  non-fiction
SANDERS, J. A.
  stories
WHIPPLE, M.

13-F

WETMORE, S.
  artist

13-J

WHIPPLE, M.
  lecturer

14-L

ADAMS, E. D.
  media specialist
HAIR, M. J.
  library science
HARRISON, B. D.
JENSEN, I. C.
LAURITZEN, E. M.
  secondary literature
MINER, C. E.
  English
SANDERS, J. A.
  English

14-N

DOUGAN, D. L.
  marketing
HARRISON, B. D.
  *special education,
    learning disabilities*

VERMONT

2-A

FAHL, C. S.
  sales

2-J

FAHL, C. S.
  broadcaster

3-D

FENNER, P. R.
  anthology
SMITH, B. H.
  English literature

3-E

GOLDSTEIN, R. B.
poetry
HOWES, B.
poetry, short stories
PARSONS, C.
education
SMITH, B. H.
English literature
THANE, E.
fiction, biography,
history

4-A

DUDLEY, T. C.
promotion

4-D

PAGE, R. W.
SAK, E. J.
entertainment, education

4-E

CHASE, L. S.
COLLINS, K. J.
correspondent,
columnist, reporter
SCHWARTZ, L. C.
feature

4-F

COLLINS, K. J.
photographer
SAK, E. J.
photographer

4-G

DUDLEY, T. C.

6-A

BURCK, M. B.
KENNEDY, F. M.
creative

8-D

della CHIESA, A.
ERIKSEN, V. L.
MORGAN, I. F.

8-H

ERIKSEN, V. L.

11

GEARY, K. A.

12-H

NEIDLINGER, N.

13-E

BURCK, M. B.
plays
COLLINS, K. J.
FENNER, P. R.
HOWES, B.
poetry, short stories
KENNEDY, F. M.
articles
NEIDLINGER, N.
documentary
PAGE, R. W.
articles, book reviews
PARSONS, C.
educational subjects
SCHWARTZ, L. C.
newspaper features
THANE, E.
fiction, biography,
history

13-J

GOLDSTEIN, R. B.
lecturer: poetry, speech,
Jewish history

14-L

GOLDSTEIN, R. B.
speech therapist
SMITH, B. H.
English

14-N

NEIDLINGER, N.
special promotion

VIRGINIA

1-A

ALEXANDER, M. J.
women's, public affairs

1-B

THONTON, K. B.

1-E

BOWSER, B. A.
correspondent

1-J

BOECKER, B. B.
FANNING, M. H.
news features
GREEN, R. L.
THORNTON, K. B.
hostess
YOUNG, P. H.
broadcaster

2-A

ALEXANDER, M. J.
women's, public affairs
WILLIAMS, P. P.

2-B

HOWARD, A.

2-E

BOWSER, B. A.
correspondent

2-J

FANNING, M. H.
hostess, news features
GREEN, R. L.
broadcaster
HOWARD, A.
broadcaster
McDANIEL, A.
broadcaster
YOUNG, P. H.
broadcaster

3-A

TEMPLEMAN, E. L.

3-D

BAKER, P. M.
CARPENTER, M. H.

3-E

CARPENTER, M. H.
ENGLE, E. K.
FAULKNER, N. I.
fiction
FORMAN, B.
teenage educational

GREEN, M. M.
history
HEBSON, A. H.
fiction
JONES, D. H.
fiction
McCLARY, J. S.
non-fiction, juvenile
McDANIEL, A.
religion
MILLER, J. C.
MONTGOMERY, R. S.
non-fiction
ROBERTS, M.
English literature
SCHEIBLA, S. H.
non-fiction
SEE, R. D.
religion
STANLEY, D. E.
children's books in
German
TEETERS, P. L.
TEMPLEMAN, E. L.
Virginia history
TROUBETZKOY, U.
YARBOROUGH, B. J. H.
language arts

4-A

CARLIN, S. S.

4-D

AGNOR, E. B.
religion, art
ALFRIEND, R. K.
food
BAXT, S. Z.
copy
BLACK, H. L.
society, women's
BRINKLEY, M. B.
women's
CARLIN, S. S.
HOPKINS, M. L.
entertainment
SCHEIBLA, S. H.

4-E

AGNOR, E. B.
columnist
ATKIN, J.
horse columnist, feature
BRINKLEY, M. B.
feature
GOETZ, M. A.
reporter
KENNEDY, R. O'K.
ROBERTS, R. A.
poetry columnist
TROUBETZKOY, U.
columnist, feature

YOUNG, P. H.
  art columnist

4-F

GOETZ, M. A.
  photographer

5-A

WRIGHT, B. R.
  promotion

5-D

MONTGOMERY, S.
ROBERTS, R. A.
SCHEIBLA, S. H.

6-A

HICKEY, M. A.
  media
LINDMANN, M. R.
VAN WINKLE, B. D.

6-F

McDOWELL, J. L.
  artist, designer

7-J

McDANIEL, A.
  broadcaster

8-A

De LANEY, M. B.

8-C

THOMPSON, E. H.

8-D

BOWLING, N. P.
HOGG, J. K.
MADDENS, J. L.

8-G

De LANEY, M. B.

8-I

FORMAN, B.

9-A

BODEAU, V. F.
  military news bureau

9-D

BODEAU, V. F.
  military news bureau

10-E

BODEAU, V. F.

11

BEDA, M. G.
BELK, R. K.
BRADLEY, V. V.
  audio-visual
BURKE, E. C.
CLARK, L. L.
CROCKETT, F. W.
McCULLOCH, M. H.
NIDA, J. B.
PROPST, M. T.
RAMEY, M. R.
YEUELL, E. O.
  technical processing

12-A

BRADFORD, A. V.
REYNOLDS, W. J. McG.
TEMPLEMAN, E. L.
WRIGHT, B. R.

12-D

HARDEE, M. H.
THACKREY, J. D.

12-E

TYLER, J. A.

12-H

CANN, A. S.
HEBSON, A. H.
TYLER, J. A.

12-I

MILLER, J. C.

13-B

BRADFORD, A. V.
  film

FANNING, M. H.
GREEN, R. L.
  fashion shows

13-D

CARPENTER, M. H.
CRITTENDEN, L.
  juvenile non-fiction

13-E

ATKIN, J.
  articles
BODEAU, V. F.
  military news, scripts
BOECKER, B. B.
BRADFORD, A. V.
  booklets
CARPENTER, M. H.
CRITTENDEN, L.
  juvenile non-fiction
De LANEY, M. B.
  non-fiction
ENGLE, E. K.
FANNING, M. H.
FAULKNER, N. I.
  fiction
JONES, D. H.
  stories, articles
KENNEDY, R. O'K.
  *articles: sports, horses
    and horse racing*
McCLARY, J. S.
  non-fiction, juvenile
McDANIEL, A.
  religious books, music
MILLER, J. C.
ROBERTS, R. A.
  poetry
SCHEIBLA, S. H.
  articles
TEETERS, P. L.
THOMPSON, E. H.
  technical copy
TROUBETZKOY, U.
WRIGHT, B. R.
  non-fiction

13-G

WRIGHT, B. R.

13-H

THOMPSON, E. H.
WRIGHT, B. R.

13-J

AGNOR, E. B.
  *lecturer, workship
    conductor*

BODEAU, V. F.
  lecturer
BOECKER, B. B.
  *singer, lecturer,
    broadcaster*
FANNING, M. H.
GREEN, R. L.
  *broadcaster, fashion
    commentator*
McDANIEL, A.
  broadcaster
SCHEIBLA, S. H.
  lecturer
STANLEY, D. E.
  lecturer: creative living
TEMPLEMAN, E. L.
  lecturer
THORNTON, K. B.
  lecturer
YOUNG, P. H.
  broadcaster

14-L

GRAYBILL, M.
GREEN, M. M.
  English
MASON, Z. H.
  *teaching materials,
    library science*
ROBERTS, M.
  English
SEE, R. D.
  history
STANLEY, D. E.
  foreign language
TEETERS, P. L.
  writing
YARBOROUGH, B. J. H.
  language arts

14-N

GREEN, R. L.
  beauty pageants
McCULLOCH, M. H.
  library construction
WRIGHT, B. R.
  advertising
YOUNG, P. H.
  radio-TV

WASHINGTON

1-A

CHANDLER, G.
  *consultant: children's
    and community service
    programs*
EVANS, E. W.
  education
HAGERTY, M. F.
  advertising, promotion

HANNA, E. K.
promotion
WILSON, M. L.
education

1-B

PRINS, R. B.
WALKINSHAW, J. S.
community service
WILCOX, M.
traffic
WILSON, M. L.

1-E

STENSON, B. H.
news reporter

1-G

BRUMETT, R. E.

1-J

BYRD, R.
moderator
BORDEN, M. F.
hostess
WILSON, M. L.
moderator

2-A

KIMBALL, H. S.
women's
KOCHA, J. H.
office
WILSON, M. L.
education

2-B

WALKINSHAW, J. S.
community service
WILSON, M. L.

2-E

SAVOLA, J. B.
reporter

2-J

BYRD, R.
moderator
WILSON, M. L.
moderator

3-D

OLSEN, W. C.
history
PASCAL, N. B.
SMITH, P. L.

3-E

ANDERSON, S. F.
non-fiction
BIERMAN, M. T.
BOND, G. B.
young reader's
CAMPBELL, P. P.
novels
CONE, M. L.
children's
EMERY, A. McG.
young people
EMMONS, D. G.
fiction
FINLEY, G.
fiction
FINNEY, G. B.
young people's
KIRK, R. K.
non-fiction
McCARTY, R. L.
fiction
McDONALD, L. S.
teenage, adult
MONTGOMERY, E. R.
*juvenile fiction and non-
fiction*
MYRICK, J. L.
*chilren's poetry and
fiction*
OLSEN, W. C.
history
SHERBURNE, Z. M.
young adults
SLONIM, R.
TRIEM, E.
poetry
YATES, M. Z.
*medical secretary's
textbooks*

4-A

THERRIAULT, S. C.
business

4-D

BAZAR, J. W.
women's
BELL, E.
entertainment
RALEIGH, S. S.
women's
RUSSELL, N. H.
women's
SIBONGA, D. E.

4-E

BATIE, J. M.
art reviews
BELL, E.
reporter
BIERMAN, M. T.
reporter, feature
BRAZIER, D. B.
columnist
DUNKELBURG, B. R.
education
EVANS, E. W.
columnist
KEEL, M. A. C.
women's
LARSON, M. H.
feature
McCARTY, R. L.
columnist
THERRIAULT, S. C.
staff
POWERS, D. R.
feature, editorial

5-A

HARPER, E. C.
TOBIN, C. W.
WALKER, M. I.

5-D

FELT, M. E.
TOBIN, C. W.
TRIEM, E.
poetry

5-E

HARPER, E. C.

6-A

BRATTAIN, M.
media
DUNPHY, L. H.
MARSHALL, V. B.
ROWLEY, B. W.
media
SIGISMUND, R. St. J.
STROMBERG, M. T.

8-D

LAURANCE, M. D.
MURRAY, A. C.

8-H

DENNIS, S. R.
LAURANCE, M. D.
MATIN, D. H.

10-A

EVANS, E. W.
SIGISMUND, R. St. J.

11

BARCKLAY, S. S.
BORDEN, M. F.
public relations
ELSE, C. W.
EVANS, E. W.
public relations
HARLAMERT, R. E.
medical
MOORE, M. J.
MORRISON, L. B.
POUNDS, J. L.
WIEMAN, J.

12-A

PIKE, R. S.

12-D

MURPHY, E. M.

12-H

COX, J. V.
FELT, M. E.
FIELD, C.
HANNA, E. K.
HANSON, M. H.
KARABAICH, M. L.
LEONARD, M. B.
MILLER, B. J.
SCHRAM, J. I.
SMITH, P. McQ.

13-D

FILLEY, B. R.

13-E

BATIE, J. M.
poetry, plays
BIERMAN, M. T.
articles
BOND, G. B.
*short stories, novels,
picture books*
BRAZIER, D. B.
columns
DUNPHY, L. H.
scripts, articles
DUTHIE, H. J.
plays
EMMONS, D. G.
*historical novels, plays,
pageants, scripts*

FELT, M. E.
  articles
FILLEY, B. R.
FINLEY, G.
  fiction
FINNEY, G. B.
FRAZIER, N. L.
  young people's
HARPER, E. C.
  poetry, fiction
KIRK, R. K.
  non-fiction
MANN, J. J.
  articles
McCARTY, R. L.
  plays, fiction, poetry
McDONALD, L. S.
MILLER, B. J.
  plays, TV shows
MONTGOMERY, E. R.
  juvenile fiction and non-
    fiction, plays
MYRICK, J. L.
  children's poetry and
    fiction
SHERBURNE, Z. M.
  poetry, short stories,
    young adult
SIBONGA, D. E.
  TV documentaries
TRIEM, E.
  poetry, book reviews
WILLEY, E. M.
  fiction, juvenile articles

13-F

BOND, G. B.
  artist
KIRK, R. K.
  photographer
WILLEY, E. M.
  artist

13-H

FARMER, H. M.
NARODICK, B. G.

13-J

BOND, G. B.
  lecturer
FINNEY, G. B.
  speaker
NARODICK, B. G.
  speaker: publicity clinics
SHERBURNE, Z. M.
  lecturer: writing
TRIEM, E.
  lecturer

14-L

ABBEE, C. W.
  speech

ANDERSON, S. F.
  English
BATIE, J. M.
  English
BYRD, R.
DUTHIE, H. J.
  drama, speech
KIRK, R. K.
  photography
McCARTY, R. L.
MOORE, R. J.
  journalism
NARODICK, B. G.
  journalism
NORIN, G. B.
  drama, speech
OLSEN, W. C.
  Northwest history
POUNDS, J. L.
SLONIM, R.
  English
WIEMAN, J.
  learning resources
YATES, M. Z.
  medical secretary's

14-N

CHANDLER, G.
  children's and
    community service TV
    programs
NARODICK, B. G.
  editorial

WEST VIRGINIA

1-J

McKINNEY, J. L.
  broadcaster

4-A

HADDOCK, V. A.
ROSE, L. M.
SHARP, J. P.

4-D

AEIKER, C. S.
  society
COMER, E. F.
  food
DOEPKEN, K. J.
  women's
EVERSON, M. W.
HADDOCK, V. A.
ROSE, L. M.
SHARP. J. P.

4-E

COMER, E. F.
DOEPKEN, K. J.
  reporter, feature,
    columnist
FURROW, J. D.
  columnist

4-F

DOEPKEN, K. J.
  photographer

6-G

FINNEY, M. C.

6-H

BAILEY, S. M.

8-H

STEIGER, A. R.

11

ELLIOTT, J. A.
RITTENHOUSE, H. H.
STOCKERT, H.

13-E

CHAPMAN, J. R.
  Christian publications
HUNTER, D. S.
NASH, R. C.
OAKLEY, M. R.
  articles

13-J

DOEPKIN, K. J.
  lecturer
OAKLEY, M. R.
  lecturer

14-L

ELLIOTT, J. A.
  library science
STOCKERT, H.
OAKLEY, M. R.
  counseling, foods,
    nutrition
SIMPSON, D. S.
  journalism

WISCONSIN

1-A

ADES, K. E.
  promotion
EVANS, R. B.
  consultant
FOWLER, F. W.
  women's
GREEN, C.
  continuity
MACKEN, M. C.
  coordinator

1-B

FOWLER, F. W.

1-E

FOWLER, F. W.
GREEN, C.
WALTER, M. M.
  editorials

1-J

FOWLER, F. W.
  broadcaster
GREEN, C.
  hostess
RAASCH, H.
STARK, B.
  commercial
    spokeswoman
WALTER, M. M.
  commentator

2-A

EVANS, R. B.
  consultant
GREEN, C.
  continuity
HEGEMANN, D. A.
  educational consultant
HEROLD, F. N.
  women's
KENTZLER, C. P.
  educational coordinator
MACKEN, M. C.
  coordinator
MURPHY, V. L.
  traffic
RYAN, P. J.
  women's

2-B

ELPERN, B. S.

2-E

ELPERN, B. S.

2-J

GREEN, C.
  hostess
SIMPSON, N. L.
  moderator

3-D

ENTRINGER, R.
  railroad
JEFFERS, L. S.
  cookbook

3-E

ARCHER, M. F.
BUTLER, B. K.
  children's
De BORHEGYI, S. S.
  fiction, non-fiction
ECKBLAD, E. B.
  children's
ERVIN, J. H.
  cookbook
INGS, M. Y.
  children's
JEFFERS, L. S.
  medical writing
LAKRITZ, E. H.
  *children's fiction and
    non-fiction*
LEVI, Sr. M. C.
  non-fiction
MEUDT, E. K.
  poetry
POWERS, A. L.
  novels
RIOS, T.
  fiction
SMITH, H. M.
  poetry, juvenile
STAUDACHER, R. V.
  juvenile
THEODORE, Sr. M.
  *mentally retarded
    children*
WAITZMANN, D. M.
ZENS, P. M.
  juvenile

4-A

ANDERSON, P. L.
BICKING, D. S.
BUR, J. S.
ENERSEN, G. B.
MARTIN, L. S.
MORGENSTERN, L. C.
SCHOVILLE, E. P.
TEMBY, M. K.
TERWILLIGER, A. P.

4-D

ATTERBURY, A. L.
BERG, D. F.
BLACK, A. B.
  men's fashion
DANIELL, C.
  society
ENERSON, G. B.
FREIBURGER, R. McD.
GARDNER, M. J.
  women's
GAYLOR, A. N.
HAGEN, L. B.
  women's
HOPKINS, M. B.
  women's
KAWATZKY, V. T.
  fashion
MACKESY, L. S.
  food
MARQUARDT, E. M.
MARSTON, L. C.
  society
MORGENSTERN, L. C.
PULVERMACHER, M. B.
  feature section
RADKE, K. W.
  news
SCHOVILLE, E. P.
TUSA, R.
  food
UDELL, B. A.
  women's
WALRATH, E.
WALTER, M. M.

4-E

ABEL, B.
  reporter
BITKER, M. M.
  reviewer
BLACK, A. B.
  women's news reporter
BOCK, S. P. P.
  columnist
ERLANDSON, C. R.
JENSEN, A. K.
  staff
KENDRICK, R.
  reporter
LESLIE, G. G.
  staff
MACKESY, L. S.
  feature
MARQUARDT, E. M.
  *columnist,
    correspondent*
McBRIDE, M. D.
  staff
TEMBY, M. K.
TUSA, R.
  feature
WAITZMANN, D. M.
  columnist
WALTER, M. M.
  staff

4-F

FREIBURGER, R. McD.
  photographer

5-D

DIEZ, S. H.
ENTRINGER, R.
McMULLEN, C. E.

6-A

ANDERSON, L. M.
  media, production
DEANE, R.
  copy
MILLS, M. L.
  public relations
RADTKE, D. E.
  media
ROHN, M. J. T.
  creative
WILLIAMS, D. E.
  media

6-G

LINDLOFF, J. S.
MILLS, M. L.
PHELPS, N. A. W.
RADTKE, D. E.

7-J

STARK, B.
  *TV commercial
    spokeswoman*

8-C

HANSEN, C. L.
LENNON, M. L.
LOVRIEN, P. A.
SULLIVAN, E.
SITKA, E. A.

8-D

BAER, I. R.
INGS, M. Y.
WASHBURN, S. G.
WOODS, E. D.

8-G

STIKA, E. A.
TRATNIK, I.
TROLLER, D. J.

8-H

FOWLE, M. S.

HANSEN, C. L.
LENNON, M. L.
LOVRIEN, P. A.
MEDGYESY, L. J.

10-A

BEIJER, L. J.
  office assistant
JEFFERSON, D. C.
SKEEN, E. D.
  women's department

11

ARCHER, M. F.
GILLESPIE, Sr. M. J.
HOGUE, H. M.
KNIGHT, C. W.
  university
LEVI, Sr. M. C.
MADDOX, V.
WAHOSKI, H. I.
  university

12-A

KENTZLER, C. P.
MACKEN, M. C.
MANHART, S. R.

12-D

ARGALL, G. E.
DENNIS, B. D.
NOHLQUIST, B. G.
SWENSON, M. E.

12-E

SWENSON, M. E.

12-H

ABICHT, Sr. M. R. J.
MARINE, S. J.
MURPHY, G. W.
NOHLQUIST, B. G.
PARKER, E. M.
RADTKE, L. M.
RICE, L. M.

13-D

LAMBRECHT, E. G.

13-E

BERG, D. F.
  *historical articles,
    columnist*
BITKER, M. M.

BOCK, S. P. P.
  fiction, non-fiction
De BORHEGYI, S. S.
  fiction, non-fiction
DIEZ, S. H.
  non-fiction, light verse
DOOLEY, M. L.
  legal
ECKBLAD, E. B.
  poetry, children's
ERVIN, J. H.
FOWLE, M. S.
  articles
FOWLER, F. W.
  craft articles
FRANK, E. S.
HINDERSTEIN, J. C.
INGS, M. Y.
  plays, non-fiction
LAKRITZ, E. H.
  children's fiction, non-
    fiction
LEVI, Sr. M. C.
  articles
McCARTHY, D. G.
  non-fiction
MEUDT, E. K.
  poetry, plays, short
    stories
NAFZIGER, C. H.
  journalist
RIOS, T.
  articles, stories
SCHLATTER, J. McN.
SMITH, H. M.
  poetry, articles, juvenile
SPRADLING, J. J.
STAUDACHER, R. V.
  critic, juvenile
WAITZMANN, D. M.
ZENS, P. M.
  poetry, features, juvenile

13-F

BOCK, S. P. P.
  artist
ENGELS, L. G.
  artist, muralist

13-G

HACK, P. S.

13-H

ERDMANN, V. M.
HINDERSTEIN, J. C.
NAFZIGER, C. M.

13-I

De BORHEGYI, S. S.
  historical,
    anthropological,
    archeological

13-J

DEANE, R.
  actress: summer stock,
    repertory
FOWLER, F. W.
  lecturer: arts, crafts
MARSTON, L. C.
  speaker
MARTIN, B. R.
  interviewer,
    demonstrator, speaker
STAUDACHER, R. V.
  lecturer
TEMBY, M. K.
  lecturer
ZENS, P. M.
  lecturer

14-L

ARCHER, M. F.
  library science
BUTLER, B. K.
  creative writing
CROOK, C. B.
  student-industry
    relations
De BORHEGYI, S. S.
  world history,
    anthropology
DOYLE, I. M.
ENGELS, L. G.
  art
HOCKER, M. L.
  library education
KANE, B. C.
  English
LUNZ, L. M.
McCARTHY, D. G.
MEUDT, E. K.
  poetry
POWERS, A. L.
  creative writing
RIOS, T.
  creative writing
RUE, E.
  library and information
    science
THEODORE, Sr. M.
  exceptional children
THOMSON, J. S.
  agricultural journalism
WAHOSKI, H. I.
  library science

14-N

CROOK, C. B.
  student-industry
    relations
DEWEY, M. W.
  education
DOOLEY, M. L.
  business
EVANS, R. B.
  broadcasting

FOWLER, F. W.
  arts, crafts
HACK, P. S.
  advertising, fashion
HEGEMANN, D. A.
  educational radio
JEFFERS, L. S.
  medical writing,
    occupational therapy
MARTIN, B. R.
  consumer marketing
PARKER, E. M.
  public information
STAUDACHER, R. V.
  literary

WYOMING

2-A

BARTLETT, B. B.
  program

2-B

HILL, B. H.

3-E

BROWN, M. E.
  non-fiction
FISHER, L. H.
  novels
GARST, D. S.
  juvenile
TRENHOLM, V. C.
  frontier history
URBANEK, M. B.
  western

4-A

BROWN, M. E.
HUNTINGTON, L. B.
REYNOLDS, H. L.

4-D

BOOTH, A. P.
  society
LEE, D. S.
MEALEY, C. C.
SPENCER, O. M.

4-E

BOOTH, A. P.
  features
BROWN, M. E.
  correspondent
FIELD, E. W.

11

McCLAIN, I. W.
  reference, humanities
McFADDEN, W. C.

12-H

HILL, B. H.

13-E

FISHER, L. H.
  short stories, novels
McCLAIN, I. W.
  book reviews
TRENHOLM, V. C.
  articles: frontier history

13-I

GARST, D. S.

14-L

GARST, D. S.

14-N

BROWN, M. E.
  history

ARGENTINA

9-A

LERNOUX, P. M.
  news service

BAHAMAS

4-E

WILSON, M. V.
  stringer

CANADA

3-A

CLARKE, I. I.

3-E

DE GRÉ, M. H.
  cookbook
LOGAN, L. S.
  education

OATES, J. C.
 novels, poetry
ZINER, F. K.

4-E

BRYDON, J. A.
 columnist

8-G

McGILLIVRAY, K. F.

8-H

McGILLIVRAY, K. F.

11

McKILLOP, A.
 children's
PARKER, V.
 health sciences

12-H

BRYDON, J. A.
DE GRÉ, M. H.

13-E

BRYDON, J. A.
 columnist
McKILLOP, A.
 library science journals
OATES, J. C.
 fiction, poetry
PARKER, V.
 articles: medical history
SPENCER, E.
WEES, F. S.

14-L

LOGAN, L. S.
 education
ZINER, F. K.
 contemporary literature

14-N

WEES, F. S.
 genealogy

ENGLAND

4-E

MORGAN, G.
 foreign correspondent

9-A

ROSS-SKINNER, J.
 news bureau

10-A

WHITESIDE, R. K.

12-H

BENNETT, K. N.

13-E

LAHRMER, P.

13-J

LAHRMER, P.
 broadcaster
NEAL, P. L.
 actress

FRANCE

3-I

PANITZA, Y. F.

4-E

CUTLER, C. R.
 art critic
LEWIS, V. O.
 correspondent
PATTERSON, S. F.
 columnist

5-A

LAVAGNO, D. L.
 layout

5-D

PANITZA, Y. F.
ROCHAMBEAU, S. M.

5-E

CUTLER, C. R.
 art correspondent
PATTERSON, S. F.

5-F

LAVAGNO, D. L.
 layout designer

5-I

PANITZA, Y. F.

13-E

MONTAGUE, R. DuB.
PATTERSON, S. F.
 articles

13-F

LAVAGNO, D. L.
 designer
MONTAGUE, R. DuB.
 artist

13-J

MONTAGUE, R. DuB.
 lecturer

14-L

MONTAGUE, R. DuB.
 art

ITALY

10-A

NELSON, C. B.

12-E

VAN DER HEUVEL, G. B.

12-H

VAN DER HEUVEL, G. B.

13-J

KOSCINA, S.
 actress
LOLLOBRIGIDA, G.
 actress
TIFFIN, P. K.
 actress

LIBYA

13-E

LORY, B. B.

13-H

LORY, B. B.

14-L

LORY, B. B.
 English

MEXICO

3-E

HOBART, L. E.
 fiction

5-E

de TREVINO, E. B.

9-E

de TREVINO, E. B.
 correspondent

12-H

HOBART, L. E.

13-E

de TREVINO, E. B.
 fiction, non-fiction
HOBART, L. E.
 fiction, non-fiction

SWITZERLAND

13-E

LEIPMAN, R.

14-M

LEIPMAN, R.
 literary

VIETNAM

12-H

HERFURTH, H. J.

VIRGIN ISLANDS

3-A

HARMAN, J. P.
 guidebook

5-A	5-E	12-A	13-E
AUBLE, H. L.	HARMAN, J. P. *correspondent*	AUBLE, H. L.	BROWN, J. W. *short stories, articles:* *humor, travel* HARMAN, J. P. *articles*